THEODORE OF MOPSUESTIA:
COMMENTARY ON PSALMS 1–81

Society of Biblical Literature

Writings from the Greco-Roman World

John T. Fitzgerald, General Editor

Editorial Board

David Armstrong
Elizabeth Asmis
Brian E. Daley, S.J.
David G. Hunter
David Konstan
Margaret M. Mitchell
Michael J. Roberts
Johan C. Thom
James C. VanderKam

Number 5

Theodore of Mopsuestia
Commentary on Psalms 1–81

Volume Editor
Rowan A. Greer

THEODORE OF MOPSUESTIA:
COMMENTARY ON PSALMS 1–81

Translated with an Introduction and Notes

by

Robert C. Hill

Society of Biblical Literature
Atlanta

BS
1430.53
.T4813
2006

THEODORE OF MOPSUESTIA:
COMMENTARY ON PSALMS 1–81

Copyright © 2006 by the Society of Biblical Literature

All rights reserved. No part of this work may be reproduced or transmitted in any form
or by any means, electronic or mechanical, including photocopying and recording, or by
means of any information storage or retrieval system, except as may be expressly permitted by the 1976 Copyright Act or in writing from the publisher. Requests for permission
should be addressed in writing to the Rights and Permissions Office, Society of Biblical
Literature, 825 Houston Mill Road, Atlanta, GA 30329 USA.

Library of Congress Cataloging-in-Publication Data

Theodore, Bishop of Mopsuestia, ca. 350–428 or 9.
    [Commentary on the Psalms. English, Latin & Greek. Selections].
    Commentary on Psalms 1–81 / Theodore of Mopsuestia ; translated with an Intro-
duction and notes by Robert. C. Hill.
       p. cm. — (Writings from the Greco-Roman world ; v. 5)
    Text in original Greek with translations in Latin and English; notes and commentary
in English.
    Includes bibliographical references and indexes.
    ISBN-13: 978-1-58983-060-8 (paper binding : alk. paper)
    ISBN-10: 1-58983-060-1 (paper binding : alk. paper)
    1. Bible. O.T. Psalms—Commentaries. I. Hill, Robert C. (Robert Charles), 1931– .
II. Title. III. Series: Writings from the Greco-Roman world ; v. 5.
    BS1430.53.T4813 2006
    223'.207—dc22
                                                    2006007926

14 13 12 11 10 09 08 07 06   5 4 3 2 1
Printed in the United States of America on acid-free, recycled paper
conforming to ANSI/NISO Z39.48-1992 (R1997) and ISO 9706:1994
standards for paper permanence.

For George and Irene,
for Apostolos, Joy, and Polly

CONTENTS

ACKNOWLEDGMENTS

This volume on Theodore of Mopsuestia in the series Writings from the Greco-Roman World, and others on Diodore of Tarsus and Theodoret of Cyrus, will, I trust, contribute to a greater appreciation of the way the Old Testament was read in Antioch. That, at least, is my intention and hope.

I am grateful to the General Editor of the series, John T. Fitzgerald, and to the Editorial Director of the Society of Biblical Literature, Bob Buller, for acceptance of this work. For untiring attention to the text from his close acquaintance with Theodore, I am indebted to Rowan A. Greer, who kindly edited the volume.

Robert C. Hill

PREFACE

The first volume in the Writings from the Greco-Roman World (WGRW) series was published in 2001. From the beginning, the WGRW Editorial Board and the Society of Biblical Literature have endeavored to include the original text whenever possible. For the most part, we have been successful in achieving this goal. In some instances, however, we have found it necessary for various reasons to publish the volume with only the modern English translation.

The present volume presented extraordinary challenges. The critical edition of Theodore of Mopsuestia's *Commentary on the Psalms* was prepared by Robert Devreesse and published as *Le commentaire de Théodore de Mopsueste sur les Psaumes* (Studi e testi 93; Vatican City: Biblioteca apostolica vaticana, 1939). Given the situation in Europe in 1939 and in the years that immediately followed, it is not surprising that the book had a limited circulation. According to WorldCat, only one hundred or so libraries worldwide own the volume, making it difficult for many potential readers to obtain. Viewing the inclusion of Devreesse's critical edition as highly desirable, we used the good offices of Stanis A. McGuire, C.F.C., to approach the Vatican, which magnanimously granted the SBL permission to print the text and critical apparatus completely without charge. Unfortunately, however, the cost of having someone rekey the Greek and Latin text proved prohibitive. Doing so not only would have increased the cost of this volume dramatically but also would have delayed its publication for several years.

At the same time, we did not want to publish Professor Robert Charles Hill's translation without including the text on which it is based. After much debate, we decided to publish a reproduction of Devreesse's edition, which aesthetically was less than ideal in its original form. This decision was made in the conviction that most users of the volume would want the text included, even if the aesthetic quality should inevitably not be the same as that of other WGRW volumes.

Devreesse used the catenae to reconstruct Theodore's commentary on the Psalter. Sometimes Theodore's comments were preserved in Greek,

sometimes in Latin, and at other times in both Greek and Latin. The Greek text occasionally differs significantly from the Latin, but given the already large size of the volume, it was not feasible to translate both versions. Therefore, Professor Hill's translation renders the Greek text where it is available.

In closing, I wish to thank Professor Hill for his patience as we attempted to deal with all the problems surrounding the inclusion of Devreesse's text, and I join him in expressing deep appreciation to Professor Rowan A. Greer for his yeoman's service as volume editor.

John T. Fitzgerald

ABBREVIATIONS

AB	Anchor Bible
AG	Analecta gregoriana
Aug	*Augustinianum*
Bib	*Biblica*
CCSG	Corpus Christianorum: Series graeca. Turnhout, 1977–
CSCO	Corpus scriptorum christianorum orientalium. Edited by I. B. Chabot et al. Paris, 1903–
DBSup	*Dictionnaire de la Bible: Supplément.* Edited by L. Pirot and A. Robert. Paris, 1928–
EnchSym	*Enchiridion symbolorum, definitionum et declarationum de rebus fide et morum*
EstBib	*Estudios bíblicos*
ETL	*Ephemerides theologicae lovanienses*
FC	Fathers of the Church. Washington, D.C., 1947–
GO	Göttinger Orientforschungen
HeyJ	*Heythrop Journal*
ITQ	*Irish Theological Quarterly*
JECS	*Journal of Early Christian Studies*
LCL	Loeb Classicial Library
LEC	Library of Early Christianity
LXX	Septuagint
MSU	Mitteilungen des Septuaginta-Unternehmens
NJBC	*The New Jerome Biblical Commentary.* Edited by R. E. Brown et al. Englewood Cliffs, N.J.: Prentice-Hall, 1990.
OrChrAn	Orientalia christiana analecta
OTL	Old Testament Library
PG	Patrologia graeca [= Patrologiae cursus completus: Series graeca]. Edited by J.-P. Migne. 162 vols. Paris, 1857–1886
PL	Patrologia latina [= Patrologiae cursus completus: Series latina]. Edited by J.-P. Migne. 217 vols. Paris, 1844–1864
RB	*Revue biblique*

SC	Sources chrétiennes. Paris: Cerf, 1943–
ST	Studi e testi
StPatr	*Studia patristica*
TBRKA	Theophaneia: Beiträge zur Religions- und Kirchengeschichte des Altertums
TRE	*Theologische Realenzyklopädie.* Edited by G. Krause and G. Müller. Berlin, 1977–
TRu	*Theologische Rundschau*
VTSup	Supplements to Vetus Testamentum

INTRODUCTION

THEODORE: HIS LIFE AND WORKS

Born about 350, brother of Polychronius (later bishop of Apamea), Theodore received a rhetorical education in Antioch, along with Maximus (later bishop of Seleucia in Isauria), at the hands of the pagan sophist Libanius, as had his friend John.[1] It was John's exceptional talents, however, that were to win him his teacher's nomination as his successor and the later bestowal of his sobriquet Chrysostom ("Golden Mouth"). John persuaded his two friends to abandon secular life and join him in the asketerion of Diodore (later bishop of Tarsus in Cilicia), where he learned the method of Antiochene biblical exegesis from one who has been styled, if not its "initiateur" (a distinction belonging to Lucian), at least its "véritable fondateur."[2] Still a young man of twenty, Theodore tired of the simple life and returned to the world with marriage on his mind; again John intervened, writing him a letter (known now as *ad Theodorum lapsum*)[3] that moved him to return to the asketerion. Never again looking back, Theodore began his exegetical career with commentaries on Psalms and the Twelve (Minor) Prophets, and he gained a reputation throughout the whole church as a hammer of heretics. He was appointed bishop of Mopsuestia in Cilicia in 392, and before his death, around 428, he had completed, in addition to liturgical, christological, and ascetical works, commentaries on the bulk of the Old and New Testaments.

Though Theodore's reputation for orthodoxy and vigorous defense of the faith continued into the next generation—Theodoret, in his church his-

---

1. For background on Theodore's life and works, see Peter Bruns, "Theodor von Mopsuestia," *TRE* 33:240–46; Robert Devreesse, *Essai sur Théodore de Mopsueste* (ST 141; Vatican City: Biblioteca Apostolica Vaticana, 1948), 1–53. The early church historians who give an account of Theodore's life and work include Socrates, *Church History* 6.3 (PG 67:665–68); Sozomen, *Church History* 8.2 (PG 67:1516); Theodoret of Cyrus, *Church History* 5.39 (PG 82:1277).

2. The distinction is that of Jean-Marie Olivier, ed., *Diodori Tarsensis commentarii in Psalmos* (CCSG 6; Turnhout: Brepols, 1980), ciii.

3. PG 47:277–316. Sozomen identifies Theodore as the recipient of the letter.

tory, credited him in particular with protecting his flock against the errors of Arius, Eunomius, and Apollinaris—he fell foul of the controversy over the teachings of Nestorius, who became bishop of Constantinople in the year of Theodore's death. A campaign was mounted against him and Diodore, such as we find in the *Contra Diodorum et Theodorum* of Cyril of Alexandria,[4] on the grounds of their fathering Nestorian theology. Theodore's writings were condemned at the fifth ecumenical council at Constantinople in 553,[5] and the ensuing flames of prejudice consumed most of his exegetical compositions; the work on the Twelve Prophets alone survived completely in Greek[6] along with a substantial portion of the Psalms commentary, though we also have remnants of his work on Paul's letters, mainly in Latin,[7] and in Syriac the commentary on the Gospel of John.[8] In fact, it was the Nestorian Syriac church, by which Theodore was already known in the late sixth century as *Mephasqana,* "The Interpreter,"[9] that preserved a catalog of his exegetical and other works.

COMPOSITION OF THEODORE'S PSALMS COMMENTARY; ITS READERSHIP

Given the place and esteem held by the Psalter as a spiritual classic in Christian tradition, yielding pride of place only to the Gospels, it is not surprising

---

4. PG 57:1437–52.

5. See *EnchSym* 425–26, 433–37.

6. See Hans N. Sprenger, ed., *Theodori Mopsuesteni commentarius in XII Prophetas* (GO, Biblica et Patristica 1; Wiesbaden: Harrassowitz, 1977).

7. See Henry B. Swete, ed., *Theodori episcopi Mopsuesteni in epistolas B. Pauli commentarii* (2 vols.; Cambridge: Cambridge University Press, 1880, 1882).

8. A critical edition of the Syriac with a Latin translation was produced by Jacques M. Vosté, *Theodore Mopsuesteni commentarius in evangelium Iohannis apostoli* (CSCO 115–116, Scriptores syri 4.3; Louvain: Peeters, 1940). Vosté himself, however, admits that the Syriac has considerably embroidered the original Greek ("Le commentaire de Théodore de Mopsueste sur S. Jean d'après la version syriaque," *RB* 32 [1923]: 523). All the Greek fragments have been collected in Devreesse, *Essai,* 305–419, of which an English translation is now available; see George Kalantzis, trans., *Theodore of Mopsuestia: Commentary on the Gospel of John* (Early Christian Studies 7; Strathfield, NSW, Australia: St. Pauls, 2004).

9. The title appears in a text of a synod of the Eastern Syriac churches in 596 cited from J. B. Chabot, *Synodicon Orientale,* by Alphonse Mingana, ed. and trans., *Commentary of Theodore of Mopsuestia on the Nicene Creed* (Woodbrooke Studies 5; Cambridge: Heffer & Sons, 1932), 459. For the Syriac catalogs, see Ebedjesus, *Catalogue des livres ecclésiastiques syriens,* in vol. 3 of *Bibliotheca orientalis Clementino-Vaticana* (ed. G. S. Assemani; Rome: Sacrae Congregationis de Propaganda Fide, 1926), 30–35; J. M. Vosté, "Le commentaire," 522–51. A Syriac translation of Theodore's commentary on Pss 119; 139–147 is extant along with ninth-century exegesis by a disciple, Ishodad of Merw, in a study by Clemens Leonhard, *Ishodad of Merw's Exegesis of the Psalms 119 and 139–147: A Study of His Interpretation in the Light of the Syriac Translation of Theodore of Mopsuestia's Commentary* (CSCO 585; Louvain: Peeters, 2001).

that from the early church we have extant well over a score of commentaries on these songs of "blessed David," especially by the fathers from the East.[10] From the school of Antioch—if we may use that term[11]—we are in the fortunate and unique position of being able to read almost in their entirety such works in the language of composition by its dominant figures: Diodore, leader of the school in its heyday; his pupils in the Antioch asketerion John Chrysostom and Theodore; and in the next generation Theodoret (bishop of Cyrus from 423).[12] Celebrated and prolific biblical commentators though they were, nothing else of Holy Writ has been left us by all four members of this distinguished group in the form of ἑρμηνεῖαι from their hands or, in John's case, their pulpit or διδασκαλεῖον.[13]

In the case of Theodore, we saw, it is not simply the passage of time that accounts for the paucity of his literary remains; the flames of prejudice and condemnation consumed almost all of his texts. Fortunately, it has been possible to piece together Theodore's commentary on Psalms 1–81, found largely in Greek in the catenae and partly in Latin versions—sufficient to illustrate amply The Interpreter's approach to this spiritual classic after having benefited from the tutelage of his master Diodore on the same sacred text while a member of the asketerion. We are told that it was his first exegetical work (using that term loosely)—a traditional priority, it seems, to judge also from Chrysostom and Theodoret. Leontius of Byzanium, perhaps Theodore's most virulent traducer, informs us that Theodore "was no more

10. See Marie-Josèphe Rondeau, *Les commentaires patristiques du Psautier (IIIe–Ve siècles)* (2 vols.; OrChrAn 219–220; Rome: Pontificium Institutum Orientalium Studium, 1982–1985).

11. Though ambiguous, the term helpfully suggests a fellowship of like-minded scholars joined by birth, geography, and scholarly principles, with some exercising a magisterial role in regard to others. Johannes Quasten (*Patrology* [3 vols.; Westminster, Md.: Newman, 1950–1960], 2:121–23) adds to this sense "a local habitation and a name," in the poet's words, by speaking of "the school of Antioch founded by Lucian of Samosata" in opposition to the "school of Caesarea," Origen's refuge after his exile from Egypt.

12. Diodore of Tarsus, *Diodori Tarsensis commentarii in Psalmos;* John Chrysostom, *Expositio in Psalmos* (PG 55:39–498); ibid., *St. John Chrysostom: Commentary on the Psalms* (trans. Robert C. Hill; 2 vols.; Brookline, Mass.: Holy Cross Orthodox Press, 1998); Theodore of Mopsuestia, *Le commentaire de Théodore de Mopsueste sur les Psaumes (I–LXXX)* (ed. Robert Devreesse; ST 93; Vatican City: Biblioteca Apostolica Vaticana, 1939); Theodoret of Cyrus, *Expositio in Psalmos* (PG 80:857–1998); ibid., *Theodoret of Cyrus: Commentary on the Psalms* (trans. Robert C. Hill; 2 vols.; FC 101–102; Catholic University of America Press, 2000–2001).

13. Diodore, Theodore, and Theodoret composed their Psalms commentaries at their desks, but Chrysostom seems to have delivered his as homilies to congregation(s) assembled in a classroom setting, or διδασκαλεῖον, that were transcribed by stenographers. For evidence, see my introduction to John Chrysostom, *Commentary on the Psalms,* 1:9–17.

than eighteen years of age when he took to subjecting the divine Scriptures to drunken abuse."[14] Certainly, even if this remark is to be discounted, the text of the Psalms commentary as we have it suggests that at that stage Theodore felt no pastoral responsibility for his readers beyond explicating "the divine Scriptures" for them—application of the psalms to their lives not being part of his brief—and features of the work betray a youthful immaturity.

Right from Psalm 2, for instance, Theodore adopts a disparaging attitude toward alternative views of his predecessors (apart from master Diodore, of course, who himself could be withering in his criticisms), with whom he sees himself "doing battle." Like many another young scholar, such as Chrysostom, Theodore can make an unnecessary display of (false) erudition, as by a claim to support from Hebrew and Syriac (e.g., on Ps 16:3) when the commentary confirms his ignorance of these languages, and by a reference to the alternative Greek translations that is otiose, as in a citation of Symmachus on Ps 49:11.[15] His frequently infelicitous christological expressions (fueling the fire of adversaries, of course, rightly or wrongly) may also be due to his youth and inexperience. Those upholding Leontius's dating might claim that Theodore's status as a novice in the asketerion explains, in commentary on the picture of the princess entering the palace of the king in Ps 45, his gushing tributes to virginity ("the greatest and most special achievement of the church") and to priesthood ("the greatest of all the spiritual gifts")—the latter perhaps accounting for Bishop Theodoret's later qualification of the clergy's monopoly of spiritual gifts.

Is it thus for his own small religious community that Theodore is cutting his teeth on the Scriptures? If so, he does not credit some of them with much previous formation, if, for example, we take as typical his explanation to them of the meaning of "the watches of the night" in Ps 77:4, in which he takes nothing for granted. Other members, by contrast, are presented in a more flattering light as "any of our brethren who are of a more scholarly bent" in the introduction to Ps 2. The quaint practice he refers to in comment on "burning

---

14. Facundus of Hermianae tells us that the Psalms commentary was Theodore's first exegetical work (*Pro defensione trium capitulorum* 3.6 [PG 67:602]). Leontius mentions his age in his *Contra Nestorianos et Eutychianos* 8 (PG 86:1364)—though Rondeau finds this "a malicious exaggeration" (*Les commentaires,* 1.103–4). On the inapplicability of the term "exegetical" John N. D. Kelly says, "Neither John, nor any Christian teacher for centuries to come, was properly equipped to carry out exegesis as we have come to understand it. He could not be expected to understand the nature of Old Testament writings" (*Golden Mouth: The Story of John Chrysostom, Ascetic, Preacher, Bishop* [Ithaca, N.Y.: Cornell University Press, 1995], 94).

15. It probably is more helpful to cite the psalms in the numbering of the Hebrew and modern versions than in that of the Septuagint and Vulgate (the latter employed, of course, by Theodore and editor Devreesse).

loins" in Ps 38:7 may also refer to his celibate community: "Many people ... who want to render those organs unmoved bring immobility to them ... by administration of drugs." There is, on the other hand, one clue (on Ps 16:3) suggesting Theodore's more public involvement in homiletics (typically of a polemical nature) when he speaks of "our debating in the churches" and using the Bible to clinch a point. The Psalms commentary contains no reference to life in the secular world of the time except for a comment (by one who would turn to the law on quitting the asketerion) on bribery in Ps 15:2: "an abuse that has become common in our time in particular: a fair sentence is delivered only when palms have been greased." Otherwise, we gain little internal evidence that the work was not composed in a cloister for such a limited readership.

Text of the Commentary; Theodore's Biblical Text

Regrettably, we do not have Theodore's Psalms commentary as it left his hand. Thanks to the critical edition by Robert Devreesse, however, we have a text on eighty-one psalms derived from the catenae, of which those from Pss 33 to 61 come to us in "a precious volume," the fourteenth-century Codex Coislinianus 12, containing (at least in the editor's view) "une série d'extraits équivalents à une tradition directe, ou même [Pss 44–50] une exégèse continue."[16] Commentary on the first thirty-two psalms is extant in two eighth-century manuscripts containing a fifth-century Latin version, whereas on the final twenty psalms, beginning with Ps 62, commentary is extant in Greek from other catenae. Beyond Ps 81 editor Devreesse admits no guarantee of identifying any further authentic commentary of Theodore.[17] Comment on some of those first thirty-two psalms is quite fragmentary, and it can be observed from extant Greek fragments that the Latin translator felt at liberty to elaborate. The preface that Theodore wrote to the work, probably reflecting his master Diodore's own, is missing; in beginning comment on the opening psalm he commits himself to conciseness (a commitment often honored more in the breach than the observance) as "we promised in the preface,"

---

16. Devreesse, *Le commentaire,* xv. Olivier, who finds Devreesse's resistance to Diodore's authorship of the text generally attributed to him "mysterious," believes that this text of Theodore enjoys less credit: "It is a matter, not of a continuous text coming by way of direct tradition, but of a reconstituted text developed from extracts of an anonymous Latin version and of fragments from the catenae" (*Diodori Tarsensis,* lxxviii).

17. "Beyond this point, I found nothing extant that could be attributed with any certainty to Theodore of Mopsuestia" (Devreesse, *Le commentaire,* xxx). Alberto Vaccari (*Bib* 21 [1941]: 208), in reviewing the work, wonders whether Devreesse, in rigorously excluding any spurious elements of the text, has not also excluded some valuable authentic elements.

he says, and he refers to textual features of Ps 16:3–4 that "we highlighted in the preface in assembling particular features." To judge from the preface to Diodore's work (clearly, open before Theodore), the "particular features" probably included his position on the authorship of the psalms, and also on the provenance and reliability of the psalm titles, which he consistently ignores as a guide to a psalm's ὑπόθεσις (as Diodore also had challenged them), only in comment on Ps 51 admitting to "not being dictated to by the titles" as he had stated in his preface. Within these limitations, then, we have a corpus of material from Theodore's hand sufficient to allow us to identify his exegetical and hermeneutical approach.

Unable to access a Hebrew text (despite his occasional claims to Semitic lore), Theodore is reading the Psalter in his local Antiochene form of the LXX, one of the three current forms of which Jerome speaks, being that "which Origen and Eusebius of Caesarea and all the Greek commentators call the popular text, and which by most is now called the Lucianic text."[18] Although modern scholars debate whether the contribution of Lucian of Antioch a century earlier was to make a fresh translation or (more likely) to revise a local version of the Hebrew Bible,[19] Theodore reads it as a textus receptus, accepting it as a privileged work according to the legendary Letter of Aristeas (as he formally states in his next work, on the Twelve Prophets), though here he is not above citing its real or imagined shortcomings. Our knowledge of that Antiochene text of the LXX derives partly from its citation by the Antioch fathers; its divergences from other forms of the LXX ("Septuagint" not being a univocal term, *pace* many modern commentators on the biblical text)[20] emerge in publications from the Göttingen project. Distinctive

---

18. *Praefatio in Paralipomena* (PL 28:1324–25); *Epistulae* 106.2 (PL 22:838).

19. Paul Kahle (*The Cairo Genizah* [2nd ed.; Oxford: Blackwell, 1959], 257) posits a Greek translation made in Antioch, later revised by Lucian, that was "probably written before the text came into existence which we normally call the 'Septuagint,'" and was fixed toward the end of the second century B.C.E. in Alexandria. Sidney Jellicoe (*The Septuagint and Modern Study* [Oxford: Clarendon, 1968], 160–61) sees no grounds for believing that Lucian had enough Hebrew to produce an independent translation. The term "Lucianic" is acceptable to moderns such as Benjamin Drewery ("Antiochien," *TRE* 3:106) and Sebastian P. Brock ("Bibelübersetzungen I,2," *TRE* 6:166–67). Dominic Barthélemy (*Les Devanciers d'Aquila* [VTSup 10; Leiden: Brill, 1963], 126–27) prefers "texte Antiochien." Natalio Fernández Marcos (*The Septuagint in Context: Introduction to the Greek Version of the Bible* [trans. Wilfred G. E. Watson; Leiden: Brill, 2000], 54), who speaks interchangeably of Lucian, Lucianic recension, Antiochian recension, is not in favor of Kahle's idea of a number of translations like the many Aramaic Targumim, preferring instead to speak of "a stylistic revision" made in the first century C.E.

20. See Robert C. Hill, "Orientale Lumen: Western Biblical Scholarship's Unacknowledged Debt," in *Orientale Lumen Australasia—Oceania 2000: Proceedings* (ed. Lawrence Cross; Melbourne: Australian Catholic University, 2000), 157–72.

features of Theodore's own text of the Psalter are noted by Devreesse and by Alberto Vaccari,[21] but since the biblical text occurring in the Psalms commentary (even in its Greek form) is to some extent a matter of conjecture unless the commentator himself cites it verbatim, one should be cautious in identifying these cases. I have noted half a dozen in footnotes, as well as an equal number of instances where the editor seems astray in citing Theodore's biblical text.

Being ignorant of Hebrew and Syriac (though with youthful brashness unwilling to admit it), Theodore is not in a strong position to evaluate his LXX text.[22] Unlike his next work, however, where he evinces a decided animus against commentators who quote the Syriac (probably from the Peshitta, available by then), he is not defensive in upholding the value of his second-hand text.[23] Obviously, he has access to a copy of that great resource from Origen, the Hexapla, which offers him the ancient alternative Greek versions of the Hebrew text associated with the names of Aquila, Symmachus (proverbially conceded to be "clearer" than the LXX), and Theodotion, citing them frequently if haphazardly (Diodore not having encouraged such citation) to improve on or at least compare with his LXX text.[24] At one point, in comment on Ps 56, he finally summarizes his position on the respective value of *textus receptus* and variants: the former strives for effect, the latter for precision.

If you have an eye to sequence and composition of the sense of the text, you would never prefer another version to that of the Seventy. Not that

---

21. Devreesse, *Le commentaire*, xxx–xxxi; Alberto Vaccari, "Il testo dei salmi nel commento di Teodoro Mopsuesteno," *Bib* 23 (1942): 1–17. In the earlier review of Devreesse's work, Vaccari had noted in his text what he calls "original and genuine readings that are preserved in the present commentary but lost in the rest of the tradition" (*Bib* 21 [1941]: 212).

22. See evidence in the text and footnotes below. Devreesse seems to have been taken in by Theodore's show of (false) erudition—as Theodore hoped his readers would be—commenting, "He shows in his commentary an uncommon knowledge of the Bible; Hebrew, Syriac ... are checked, compared with the Septuagint, discussed, sometimes given precedence" (*Le commentaire*, vi). Devreesse, however, in his later work (*Essai*, 56 n. 3), concludes that Theodore's use of Hebrew shows that he did not understand it and accessed it only through intermediaries. L. Pirot (*L'oeuvre exégétique de Théodore de Mopsueste, 350–428 après J.-C.* [Rome: Sumptibus Pontificii Instituti Biblici, 1913], 96–100) painstakingly assembles evidence for this latter conclusion, with which a reader of the works on the Psalter and the Twelve Prophets would have to concur.

23. According to M. P. Weitzman (*The Syriac Version of the Old Testament* [Cambridge: Cambridge University Press, 1999], 253), the Peshitta of the Psalter and the Latter Prophets was available and had attained authoritative status by about 170. Theodore generally will cite the Syriac in conjunction with the Hebrew, as on Pss 16:3; 29:6, 8; 60:8.

24. Olivier (*Diodori Tarsensis,* c) doubts that Diodore, who so infrequently cites the alternative versions on the psalms, had access to a copy of the Hexapla for that work.

everything is translated better by them: there are places, in fact, where they offer the weaker interpretation, and sometimes they fall short of the others, who said things more clearly and logically. But in general by comparison with the others they are found far superior, even if saying a good many things in a rather unfamiliar way. For the student there are many signs of the greater attention to effect by the Seventy and the care for greater clarity by Symmachus.

Such a gratuitously magisterial summation may have been encouraged in a neophyte lacking familiarity with the original text by master Diodore.

THEODORE'S APPROACH TO SCRIPTURE

Lack of such an exegetical tool, of course, was not exclusive to Theodore or the Antioch fathers generally;[25] but in this work as well it proves to be a real handicap, on which only a youngster could dissimulate. In disputing an alternative interpretation of Ps 36:1, the youthful commentator will dismiss it loftily with this claim: "This form of interpretation happens to be at variance with the Hebrew, and interpreting from that is more authoritative than all." He has difficulties establishing the unity of Ps 34, unaware that it is in fact an alphabetic psalm in Hebrew—a datum he could have invoked to strengthen his case and a key factor also in commenting on the combination by the LXX of Pss 9 and 10 into a single psalm (if he had been aware of it). Time and time again he feels encouraged by Diodore's equal freedom to declare a change in tense or mood of a verb, using only logic, ἀκολουθία, as the criterion, being unable to refer to the form in the "original"[26] but vaguely attributing such a change to Hebrew morphology in general or the psalmist in particular, as in Ps 9:3, "They will lose their strength and vanish from their sight," where he observes, on the basis of logic, "There is a change of tenses here: he used the future tense for the past, as in fact is found frequently in the psalms." He speaks freely of "Hebrew idioms" to account for obscurities

---

25. Jerome is the celebrated exception. John N. D. Kelly (*Jerome: His Life, Writings, and Controversies* [London: Duckworth, 1975], 50) attributes Jerome's knowledge of Hebrew to time spent with a Jew in Chalcis. Origen had less familiarity with it, concedes Henri Crouzel, "but he must have had enough to direct the compilation of the Hexapla, even if the actual work was done by some assistant" (*Origen* [trans. A. S. Worrall; San Francisco: Harper & Row, 1989], 12). Fernández Marcos (*The Septuagint in Context,* 205) cites Origen's own admission of his shortcomings.

26. We concede, of course, that the (later) Masoretic Hebrew text we read in our Bibles does not correspond precisely in every detail to that read by the early translators or to the column in the Hexapla.

in the text (see comment on Pss 17:14; 33:6, 7; 36:6). Only at a late stage in the Psalms commentary (on Ps 35:8) will he come to see that the discrepancy in verb forms comes from the inadequacies of the translators, though he is prepared elsewhere to claim that his LXX translation does not measure up the Hebrew, as with Pss 10:14; 17:14; 29:3.

For all the rationalism for which his traducers criticized him, encouraged in him by master Diodore and made inevitable by this inadequate exegetical equipment, Theodore comes to the task of commenting on the sacred text with an unshakeable conviction of the inspiration of the biblical authors. Like many other church fathers, it is the opening verse of Ps 45 that prompts him to develop most fully his belief in it. Succeeding to a volume of previous teaching on the subject, he makes a contribution of his own.

> He goes on, *My tongue the pen of a rapid scribe.* The pen, you see, requires ink, and requires also the writer to put ink on it and move it to inscribe the letters. So he used his tongue in the role of a pen, and by scribe he refers to the Holy Spirit, so that what is inscribed by the Holy Spirit takes the place of ink. The Spirit, you see, like some excellent writer (he calls him *a scribe*), fills the heart with insights of revelation like ink, and thereby enables the tongue then to express and to form letters, as it were, in words and endue them with articulate speech for those wishing to receive benefit from them. So it means, What the tongue utters is not its own ideas, but comes from the revelation of the Spirit.

Though the notion of the Spirit as scribe making use of the author's tongue as pen (or stylus) harks back to Eusebius, and though Diodore had found the model too mechanical in not allowing adequately for the human author's role, Theodore adds the idea of ink as "the insights of revelation"—a thoughtful nuance by a neophyte.[27]

Thus enjoying the Spirit's communication, "blessed David" is seen by the Antiochene commentator not as mystic or guru, but as teacher, moralist, and (considering that Diodore had lent so many of the psalms a prospective viewpoint) prophet. "It behooved in particular the biblical authors who received the privilege of teaching from the grace of the Spirit to do what he had commanded them all to do," Theodore says in introducing Ps 78; and of the psalmist in Ps 33 he says, "This is what we should consider most of all in the psalms, that he moves from development of a theme to catechetical exhortation, conducting this in particular also for the benefit of the listeners"—this from the author also of a distinguished series of catechetical

---

27. See Robert C. Hill, "Psalm 45: A *locus classicus* for Patristic Thinking on Biblical Inspiration," *StPatr* 25 (1993): 95–100.

homilies.[28] The psalms can be thought of as oral compositions recited/sung to these "listeners," or meant also for reading; Theodore says at the opening of Ps 36, "For readers it was most necessary that the psalms composed by blessed David containing what he personally suffered be transmitted in writing." Yet for one who sat at the feet of the celebrated rhetorician Libanius, as well as studied under Diodore,[29] Theodore is not much interested in identifying the various genres of psalms (unless the missing preface had more to say on the subject). It is only with the encouragement of the latter mentor, who had addressed the matter in his preface,[30] that Theodore opens commentary on Ps 37 with the following useful distinctions.

> While all the psalms by blessed David have regard to people's benefit, he did not employ in them the one genre. Sometimes, in fact, he develops doctrinal treatises, sometimes he composes hymns of praise to the Lord from creation. On the other hand, there are other times as well when he also suggests future events, others when he prophesies them and develops the benefit coming from them to recommend what he considers adapted to the theme he is treating. There are times when he also instructs the listeners from his own situation, teaching what each person's attitude should be to what happens, what is the due response when living in a state of sin, what to say when under pressure from disaster. There are times when he also delivers an exhortation independently of the theme, forbidding what must be avoided and advising what should be done, as with this psalm.

The psalms' original and contemporary liturgical setting is likewise of little interest to Theodore. David did intend them to be functional, he concedes of Ps 65, presumably in a community, if not liturgical, context: "In composing all the inspired works, of course, he utters most things or in fact nearly all from the viewpoint of those about whom he is composing, not without purpose but to instruct them either in the case of good times to use such words in giving thanks to God, or in time of misfortune to confess their failings in such words and ask for good things from God the giver." Once the historical situation has passed, however, the psalms are not of continuing validity for later ages, such as in the worship of the Christian church.

---

28. The homilies (extant in Syriac) take pride of place in the Syriac catalogs after Theodore's exegetical works; they have been edited by Alphonse Mingana, *Commentary of Theodore of Mopsuestia on the Nicene Creed* (Woodbrooke Studies 5; Cambridge: Heffer & Sons, 1932); *Commentary of Theodore of Mopsuestia on the Lord's Prayer and on the Sacraments of Baptism and the Eucharist* (Woodbrooke Studies 6; Heffer & Sons, 1933).

29. So says the historian Socrates, *Historia Ecclesiastica* 6.3 (PG 67:665).

30. *Commentarii in Psalmos,* Prologus, 4–5.

Still less in the text as we have it do we find Theodore exploring the psalms for their general spiritual appeal, such as for personal prayer by the individual. Time and again, on poems and verses that are redolent of spiritual thought and emotion and are relevant for people in a range of situations, today's reader is given hardly a comment. We regret, for instance, that only two verses survive in Latin of any commentary on Ps 23 to give us a sense of Theodore's response to this "gem," which Artur Weiser has declared to have "gained immortality by virtue of the sweet charm of its train of thought and its imagery, and by the intimate character of the religious sentiments expressed therein."[31] The opening to Ps 27, "The Lord is my light and my salvation," and its fourth verse, "One thing I asked of the Lord...," also receive no extant comment, though Diodore's dry remarks on the psalm's historical setting give us no grounds for presuming an appropriate response to the psalmist's sentiments. We suspect, however, that the state of the text is not the excuse for the uninspiring commentary on Ps 42, opening with the words "As a deer longs for flowing streams, so my soul longs for you, O God," Diodore again having set the tone by assigning it an exilic context in Babylon and keeping comment to a minimum, and Theodore showing more interest in the datum (due to Origen) of the deer's thirst resulting from a diet of snakes. Chrysostom, by contrast, will go to great lengths in responding to the psalm's opening verses alone,[32] even the typically concise Theodoret also being affected by the pathos. The extant commentary of The Interpreter repeatedly disappoints readers in this regard, it has to be admitted; the psalms deserve better.[33]

The young commentator, if not yet spiritually attuned to the depths of this liturgical hymnody, has at least learned the elements of Antiochene literary appreciation, including his school's accent on ἀκρίβεια, "precision," both in the text and in the commentator. When he finds an apparently pointless particle, γάρ, in his text of Ps 71:22, "And I shall, in fact, confess to you among peoples, Lord," instead of passing on he observes, "The particle *in fact* is not completely in place here, instead being inserted as often by idiom, as in the verse, 'Earth shook and in fact the heavens' " (Ps 68:8), unaware that in the latter case (only) the LXX is rendering the Hebrew *aph-,*

---

31. Artur Weiser, *The Psalms: A Commentary* (trans. Herbert Hartwell; OTL; London: SCM, 1962), 227.

32. Chrysostom's commentary on Ps 42:1–2 (PG 55:155–67), although acknowledged as authentic, is not included in his series of fifty-eight homilies. Cf. Robert Charles Hill, "Psalm 41(42): A Classic Text for Antiochene Spirituality," *ITQ* 68 (2003): 25–33.

33. One recalls Louis Bouyer's summation of Antioch's reaction to the spirituality promoted by followers of Origen: an "asceticism without mysticism" (*The Spirituality of the New Testament and the Fathers* [trans. Mary P. Ryan; London: Burns & Oates, 1963], 446).

which modern grammarians would class as a stylistic particle, rhetorical and
poetic in particular. His exegetical instincts and formation tell him to omit
no detail from comment, even if it has to be rationalized. The principle is
formulated when he meets the repetition of a clause in Ps 56:1–2 for which
an Antiochene must find an explanation: "Some of the manuscripts do not
have *Because many of those warring against me from the height of the days,*
some scribes perhaps thinking the repetition superfluous and hence removing
the phrase—and they deserve our pity for thinking anything of the Scripture
is superfluous. Both phrases, however, occur in the inspired author of particular necessity...," and he proceeds to rationalize again. He can, rarely, at
least give the appearance of subjecting his text to criticism beyond consultation of the alternative versions; when his atypical text of Ps 50:9 reads, "I
shall not accept young bulls from your house, or goats [τράγους] from your
flock," his less-than-transparent comment is, "In some manuscripts 'he-goats'
[χιμάρους] appears in place of *goats* in the sense of winter ones, yearlings
that have experienced a single winter"—the latter term actually occurring in
Diodore's text before him, which he rationalizes with an exercise in popular
etymology by reference to χεῖμα, "winter," thereby embarrassing both his
mentors Diodore and Libanius. Many a neophyte doubtless has had recourse
to such stratagems when trying to impress superiors. In fact, it can only be
an unwillingness to see Theodore repeatedly singing treble to Diodore's bass
that leads Devreesse to give the former's work on the psalms such a high
rating in this respect: "Theodore, the first and arguably the only ancient commentator to do so, at this point invokes literary criticism."[34] When reading
Theodore's work in the light of Diodore's, one is tempted to apply the phrase
"His Master's Voice."[35]

THEODORE'S STYLE OF COMMENTARY ON THE PSALMS

With this general approach to Scripture, then, Theodore comes to the task
of commenting on the psalms for his readers. The copy of the Psalter he

---

34. Devreesse (*Essai,* 58) bases this judgment on Theodore's attention to literary features
of the text such as hyperbata, changes of tense, use of point of view, ἀκολουθία—all of which
he gains from Diodore's tutelage. Olivier (*Diodori Tarsensis,* viii) notes the reluctance ("pour
des raisons somme toute mystérieuses") of Devreesse to accept the authenticity of the text of
the Diodore commentary—a fact that may account for his failing to note the close dependence
of pupil on master. Vaccari also seems unfamiliar with Diodore's work in estimating Theodore's
significance.

35. What Theodore also gains from Diodore is a commendable reluctance to credit the
psalmist with an eschatology more appropriate to New Testament authors, unlike Theodoret
(and, more notoriously, a modern commentator such as Mitchell Dahood).

is reading is not divided into five books as in our modern Bibles; he does not take the final doxologies in Pss 41 and 72 as closing such a book. Thus, after the (missing) preface he proceeds from psalm to psalm, never citing psalm titles, and is thereby willy-nilly saved from the false clues contained in their LXX form that ensnared Chrysostom and Theodoret.[36] On Ps 51 he remarks, "At no stage have we given the impression of being dictated to by the titles, accepting only those we found to be true; and we said as much about this as was necessary in the preface before commentary on the text." Instead of the titles, he dutifully accepts from Diodore a cue as to a psalm's content, theme, and narrative setting, ὑπόθεσις, and the meaning as a whole, διάνοια (though for the benefit of his readers he develops these more fully, as in introducing Pss 46; 47). It is reference to the latter rather than close textual analysis, he claims, that will obviate misunderstanding. He chides those who want to apply Ps 72 to both Solomon and Christ for failing to grasp this principle (which, of course, supplies for his own linguistic limitations): "The cause of this problem is the fact of some people's commenting on the words by slavishly keeping to the text [λέξις] of the psalm and not having an overall view of the meaning [διάνοια]"—an interpretative stance we would class rather as eisegesis. Already on rather shaky ground, he can nonetheless adopt an attitude to predecessors other than master Diodore that is youthfully intolerant and disparaging, and that will continue unabated into his next work on the Twelve Prophets, to the extent that one glimpses at least one reason why critics such as Leontius will be so virulent. The alternative (Jewish) interpretation of Ps 45 is "deserving of mockery ... to be ridiculed as a fable" by comparison with his view adopted "on the basis of the movement of thought [ἀκολουθία]." It is this basis that encourages him also to rearrange the psalmist's text, as he frequently does without consulting the Hebrew, as in Pss 73:11; 74:12.

Psalm texts, of course, are notoriously obscure and even corrupt in places, putting a commentator on a mere version in a challenging position. Youthful commentators in particular are loath to admit ignorance. Theodore too has recourse in such situations to what might be styled "creative commentary." Mitchell Dahood classes verses 4–5 of Ps 74 as "among the most difficult of the entire Psalter."[37] Theodore simply blames the LXX—"the verse involves

---

36. For the solecisms committed by the LXX in rendering obscure Hebrew terms in the psalm titles, and the efforts of Chrysostom and Theodoret to deal with them, see the introductions to my translations of their commentaries. Diodore had declared the titles to be "in most cases faulty," and in this also Theodore heeds "His Master's Voice."

37. Mitchell Dahood, *Psalms* (3 vols.; AB 16–17a; Garden City, N.Y.: Doubleday; 1965–1970), 2:202.

great difficulty resulting from the translation"—and abandoning his choice of a theme related to the Maccabees, he clutches at the straw that Symmachus's version offers to develop an ingenious paraphrase. With his disparagement of commentators "who slavishly keep to the text," he is likewise not prepared to background his text to the extent we admire in Theodoret, who will ferret out the likely reference in a place name, for example. When Ps 48:7 mentions "ships of Tarshish," Theodore is content to presume, "Tarshish was a coastal city involved in much trade; hence Solomon's ships sailed for Tarshish for trading purposes," not inclined to join Theodoret in identifying this city, as in later commentary on Jonah 1:3 he will likewise deplore "this entire chase after detail," an exercise in ἀκριβολογία, "no matter which city you think it to be." Though once or twice he will in vague terms claim the support of Flavius Josephus for a position he reaches, it must be admitted that he is either youthfully impatient of detail or simply a lazy commentator. Hence we miss the richness of scriptural documentation that marks the commentary on the psalms by Chrysostom and Theodoret. Diodore likewise had been frugal in documenting his work more liberally from the Bible, and it will be noticeable also in Theodore's next work that the psalms alone spring to his mind.

The reader of Theodore's commentary (at least where the Greek text is extant) is often irked by the repetitiveness and prolixity that caught the notice also of Photius in the ninth century[38]—a trait he did not inherit from Diodore—and this despite the commitment he gave in the preface to conciseness, συντομία (he tells us in introducing the first psalm). He often seems unwilling to say a thing once clearly and move on. He comes, for instance, to a clause in Ps 11:2, "to shoot in the dark at the upright of heart," taken to refer simply to an ambush of David by Saul; he begins, "Now, he said *in the dark,* which in Greek is σκοτομήνη—that is to say, when the absence of the moon makes the dark of night even denser, since the Greeks speak of the moon as μήνη, and are therefore right to call months μήνης," which launches him into a lengthy disquisition on derivation and on lunar and solar calendars, the historical reference dropping from sight. Diodore, by contrast, who had raised the point, disposes of it in a dozen words. Likewise on the phrase in Ps 12:2 condemning duplicity Theodore makes the one point over and over.

---

38. Photius, *Bibliotheca* 38 (René Henry, ed. and trans., *Photius: Bibliothéque* [9 vols.; Paris: Belles Lettres, 1959–91], 1:23). Manlio Simonetti, by contrast, maintains that in Theodore "the tendency to conciseness is such that, on occasion, parts of his commentaries are nothing more than paraphrases of the scriptural text itself" (*Biblical Interpretation in the Early Church: An Historical Introduction to Patristic Exegesis* [trans. John A. Hughes; Edinburgh: Clark, 1994], 71). One wonders if Simonetti is taking into account the fragmentary nature of the extant remains of Theodore's work.

He took trouble to express the evil effects of the vice of which he is complaining when he said *in the heart and in the heart,* that is, two people talking to each other have exactly the same intention of deceiving the other. In fact, both strive to get the better of the other by smooth and duplicitous speech; it is not that one tells lies and the other speaks in a trustworthy and honest manner, nor that one party only is involved in deception—rather, the business of deceit is found equally in both. He suggests this, note, by saying *in the heart and in the heart,* that is, this person to that and that to this use words full of deceit, so that when they meet they are both deceived and deceive. Now, in this he wants to bring out that all are held in the grip of the same love of vice.

No wonder that Theodoret later will pledge himself, and keep the pledge, to avoid such circumlocution.[39]

THEODORE AS INTERPRETER OF THE PSALMS

It was, however, as interpreter and not generally as exegete/commentator that Theodore later won his sobriquet. Again the psalms offer a particular challenge in their figurative language. Like Theodoret, though not so gifted or so inclined, he can respond to the psalmist's imagery, showing some fruits of literary formation by Libanius and even Diodore, who, like him, had a fondness for lighting upon instances of synecdoche. In detecting a case of hendiadys in Ps 79:2, he reminds the readers that "we find this idiom repeatedly in blessed David," recalling Ps 56:6. He responds to what Dahood styles the "mythopoeic language and mythological motifs" of Ps 68,[40] remarking that "the whole psalm, in fact, is thus composed, brimful of figures and comparisons." Occasionally he feels that he should remind his readers to avoid taking anthropomorphisms in the text in a way that may impugn divine transcendence, as he does on Ps 13:1, "How long do you turn your face from me?" by commenting, "This is expressed by a bodily metaphor in our fashion, since when we are angry with people, we turn our face from them to another object or direction." But in the text as we have it we do not find him proceeding to discourse on divine considerateness, συγκατάβασις,

---

39. Note this remark in his preface: "We shall make every possible effort to avoid a superfluity of words, while offering to those ready for it some benefit in concentrated form" (PG 80:861).

40. Dahood, *Psalms,* 2:133. See n. 34 above for comment on the degree of originality in Theodore's attention to literary criticism.

thus manifested in the language of Scripture in the way Chrysostom mov-
ingly does.

It is when he addresses the overall διάνοια of a psalm, however, that
Theodore betrays his commitment to the Antiochene hermeneutical principles imbibed from Diodore—or, in the view of Christoph Schäublin, from
classical rhetoricians communicated by Libanius and Diodore.[41] He rarely
will allow himself the development of a hermeneutical perspective stretching forward to the New Testament and beyond it that Theodoret will enjoy
under the influence of Alexandrian commentators, and thus he qualifies as
one of those found wanting by Theodoret in his Psalms preface for "making
the inspired composition resemble historical narratives of a certain type with
the result that the commentary represents a case rather for Jews than for the
household of the faith."[42] He seems to have been drilled in the maxim of
Aristarchus, "Clarify Homer from Homer,"[43] so as to look for the realization of Old Testament prophecy within the bounds of the Old Testament. The
psalms are to be interpreted "in faithful accord with history," he says in introducing the first of them (his Greek text unfortunately missing):

> The task set us, you see, is not to follow up every matter in detail but suc-
> cinctly to touch on the sense of each statement so as to make possible some
> illumination of the obvious sense of the text, leaving those of greater intel-
> ligence to add other things if they wish, though not departing from the
> interpretation already given. A true understanding, in fact, results in such an
> insight that we should maintain a sequence of explanation in faithful accord
> with history, and accordingly should propose what ought be said.

The opening disclaimer, as we have noted, acquits him of the need to work
from λέξις to διάνοια; instead, begin with the interpretation already decided,
and bring the text into line with that—not a sound norm for winning the
accolade "The Interpreter."

The precise meaning of Diodore's hermeneutical dictum, "We far prefer
τὸ ἱστορικόν to τὸ ἀλληγορικόν," is not clear; as Frances Young observes, "It
was not exactly 'historical' in the modern critical sense."[44] One implication

---

41. Christoph Schäublin's basic position about Theodore's preparation for his exegetical
career is that "Theodore owed his formation as interpreter to pagan rhetoric" (*Untersuchungen
zu Methode und Herkunft der antiochenischen Exegese* [TBRKA 23; Cologne: Hanstein], 158).
He has little to say about the influence on him of Libanius.

42. PG 80:860.

43. See Schäublin, *Untersuchungen,* 159.

44. Diodore's maxim comes from a fragment of his work on the Octateuch. See Schäublin,
"Diodor von Tarsus," *TRE* 8:765; note his further remark on the ambivalence of the maxim:

of the cryptic principle was that Old Testament material rested not primarily on mere words (ονόματα) but on reality (ἀλήθεια), events (πράγματα), outcome (ἔκβασις)—in short, what Young styles "narrative coherence";[45] if the psalms are not immediately narrative, they can be made so if read correctly. Such a hermeneutical approach, of course, in being more text- and author-centered, represents a reaction against a more reader-centered approach, which in Origen's case earned the pejorative description of "biblical alchemy."[46] In Theodore's view, it is the facts, πράγματα, that establish, for instance, that Ps 72 can refer at least in part to Solomon but not at all to Jesus: "No comment is required to prove the truth of this; it was demonstrated by the facts," he smugly claims at the close of his comment on it. As a result of this conviction, the psalmist is turned (by Diodore and thence by Theodore) from simply an inspired author, προφήτης,[47] into a seer, and the psalms are given a prospective viewpoint to bring into focus figures and events from the historical foreground, such as Saul and Absalom, and from the remote background, such as exile, restoration, and Maccabean wars. While that leaves a few psalms without a historical substrate, fewer still need to be conceded a messianic character with an ἔκβασις in the New Testament. Hence, even a psalm such as Ps 22, five of whose verses are cited by the New Testament in reference to Jesus, is disallowed as messianic, Theodore maintaining (in a defective Latin text), "Those who wish ... this psalm to be spoken in the person of the Lord are led especially by this verse [22:1] to become guilty of no little rashness." Evangelist and apostle might find Ps 69:9, "Zeal for your house consumed me," applicable to Jesus, but Theodore brackets him out of consideration, ignoring the echoes familiar to a Christian ear.[48] We

---

"What in fact did the Antiochenes' 'historical' mean in real terms?" (*Untersuchungen,* 156). See also Frances M. Young, *Biblical Exegesis and the Formation of Christian Culture* (Cambridge: Cambridge University Press, 1997), 168. She traces this accent back to Eustathius as a reaction against Origen's "lexical approach" (162–63).

45. Young, *Biblical Exegesis,* 182; or, more accurate in the case of the psalms, "textual coherence" (184). An accent on ὀνόματα rather than πράγματα was, of course, the principal flaw in Origen's style of interpretation, in the view of Eustathius (E. Klostermann, ed., *Origenes, Eustathius von Antiochien, und Gregor von Nyssa über die Hexe von Endor* [KlT 83; Bonn: Marcus & Weber, 1912], 16).

46. Adolf Harnack's phrase of Origen's allegorization of Gospel parables, quoted by Anthony C. Thiselton, *New Horizons in Hermeneutics: The Theory and Practice of Transforming Biblical Reading* (London: HarperCollins, 1992), 170.

47. All Old Testament authors, in being inspired, are προφῆται, not simply the Latter Prophets. See Robert C. Hill, "Chrysostom's Terminology for the Inspired Word," *EstBib* 41 (1983): 367–73.

48. Rowan Greer puts (unduly?) positive interpretation on this: "The Bible is allowed to speak in his commentaries (and in his theology) as it is in those of few, if any, of the patristic

do not find Theodore in this commentary speaking of typology as a hermeneutical principle in the way it features prominently in his next work, on the
Twelve Prophets.

The upside of this reduced hermeneutical perspective, of course, is that
we gain from Theodore what we lack in Diodore, as also in Theodoret and
his Alexandrian sources, by way of responsible use of accommodation of
the Old Testament to the New. All the Antiochenes agree that Ps 44 is composed by David with the desperate situation of the Maccabees in mind. Paul,
in Rom 8:36, applies verse 11, "We are accounted as sheep for the slaughter," to the tribulations of ministers of the gospel. Theodore concedes only an
instance of accommodation: "The apostle cited this text, not as though there
were reference to them [the Maccabees] by David, but as no less suited for
citation in their case as well, insofar as they fell foul of numerous troubles
for Christ's sake." Again, in all four Evangelists there is an implicit citation
of Ps 69:21, "They gave me bile for food, and offered me vinegar to drink,"
but again Theodore properly warns against seeing reference to such details
of the crucifixion as anything more than accommodation, appropriate though
it is as such.

> It is not as though the psalm were referring to these things, in one case to
> one and in another case to another; instead, since they generally refer to
> the Jews' abandonment of God and the law and involve an accusation of
> their ingratitude, the use of the citations was inevitable, arising from the
> circumstances, such as *They gave me bile for food, and offered me vinegar
> to drink,* and at the same time involving an accusation of Jewish ingrati-
> tude as not originating just now but announced by the divine Scripture
> from of old.

Alexandria, if not always Antioch, could do with the reminder. Theodoret,
for his part, as though making a necessary rejoinder on these same verses,
insists that Antioch would see the evangelists licitly recognizing "two levels
of meaning"—a process of θεωρία on which master Diodore himself had
written approvingly.[49] The term θεωρία does not occur in Theodore's text

---

exegetes" (*Theodore of Mopsuestia, Exegete and Theologian* [London: Faith Press, 1961], 111).
Greer likewise points out that in being unwilling to bring Jesus into focus in such psalms, Theo-
dore "cut across opinions almost universally held in the ancient church" (James L. Kugel and
Rowan A. Greer, *Early Biblical Interpretation* [LEC 3; Philadelphia: Westminster, 1986], 182).
For such unwillingness, see also Theodore's comment on Pss 31; 68.

49. For Theodoret's words, see PG 80:1409. Diodore's work on θεωρία is discussed by
Schäublin, "Diodor von Tarsus"; Alberto Vaccari, "La θεωρία nella scuola esegetica di Antio-
chia," *Bib* 1 (1920): 3–36; and Paul Ternant, "La θεωρία d'Antioche dans le cadre de l'Ecriture,"
Bib 34 (1953): 135–38, 354–83, 456–86; their work is evaluated by Bradley Nassif, " 'Spiritual

as we have it; in fact, on Ps 33:6, "By the word of the Lord the heavens were made, and all their host by the breath of his mouth," he refutes those commentators who apply that process to see a reference to the Son and the Spirit. "Allegory," too, is a term not found on his lips, though he adopts an allegorical approach to Ps 45 in seeing Christ in focus (with encouragement from Diodore). A sacramental dimension to the meaning of verses, especially those found in the liturgy, such as Ps 35:8, "Taste and see that the Lord is good," is not developed in the way Theodoret will find so fruitful.

THE CHRISTOLOGY OF THE COMMENTARY; MORAL ACCENTS

If it is true that Theodore's commentary on the Twelve Prophets owes its complete survival in Greek to its possessing (in the oft-repeated, even hackneyed, and somewhat erroneous phrase) "almost nothing of Christological import,"[50] the more fragmentary condition of the Psalms commentary may be due in part to the imprecise and infelicitous christological expressions to be found there, as well as the inherited resistance to adopting a messianic interpretation to the psalms generally.[51] It was, of course, for his supposed christological errors in particular that Theodore fell foul of his critics' successful efforts at the third council of Constantinople in 553 to have him condemned—a condemnation that not all Eastern theologians today would endorse.[52] In fact,

---

Exegesis' in the School of Antioch," in *New Perspectives in Historical Theology* (ed. Bradley Nassif; Grand Rapids: Eeerdmans, 1996), 342–77. The fact that Theodore continued to resist a spiritual sense to biblical texts emerges from a fragment on Gal 4:24 in a Latin fragment (in Swete, *Theodori,* 1:74–75): "When they turn to expounding divine Scripture 'spiritually'—spiritual interpretation is the name they would like their folly to be given—they claim Adam is not Adam, paradise is not paradise, the serpent is not the serpent. To these people I should say that if they distort *historia,* they will have no *historia* left."

50. The phrase seems to appear first in Francis A. Sullivan, *The Christology of Theodore of Mopsuestia* (AG 82; Rome: Universitas Gregoriana, 1956), 1; then in Quasten, *Patrology,* 3:405; and later in Dimitri Z. Zaharopoulos, *Theodore of Mopsuestia on the Bible: A Study of His Old Testament Exegesis* (New York: Paulist, 1989), 32.

51. Rondeau speaks of the "effacement du Christ locuteur chez Diodore et Théodore" (*Les commentaires,* 2:303).

52. The text of his condemnation at that council appears in *EnchSym* 425–26, 433–37. A statement of conclusions was agreed upon by the Roman Catholic Church, the Syrian Orthodox Church of Antioch, and the Assyrian Church to the effect that Theodore's Christology is one of the legitimate expressions of orthodox belief, that the condemnation of Theodore in 553 had been planned beforehand and programmed by the emperor Justinian, and that Theodore should be recognized as a true father of the church (Alfred Stirnemann and Gerhard Wilflinger, eds., *Third Non-official Consultation of Dialogue within the Syriac Tradition* [Syriac Dialogue 3; Vienna: Pro Oriente, 1998], 51). Other Orthodox churches, on the other hand, want the anathemas to stand.

taking all his christological statements together from this work, one gets the overall impression of a young if unschooled theologian trying, in the face of Arian and Apollinarian opponents and an Alexandrian response that imperiled the reality of Jesus' humanity, to express the hypostatic union (not a term he employs, of course) in way that clearly distinguishes between the two natures as defined by Nicea and (later) by Constantinople I without giving the appearance of a "two sons" Christology. Figures occurring in the text of the psalms, of course, are not always susceptible of precise application to this mystery. Psalm 45:8, for example, which was accorded messianic reference by Diodore, reads, "Myrrh, resin, and cassia from your garments." Theodore used the following unhappy phrasing to interpret this verse: "By his *garments* he nicely referred to the body, in being something put on from outside, while inside there was the divinity on the basis of indwelling." In comment on Pss 2 and 8, for which we do not have an extant Greek text (unless quoted against him by adversaries or councils), there occur several well-meaning if infelicitous expressions by this dyophysite Antiochene trying to uphold both the ὁμοούσιον of the Word, against subordinationists, and the reality of the human nature. On Ps 2:6, which the LXX renders "I have been established as king by him," he claims the support of its citation in Heb 2:6–9 to uphold these necessary positions—again unhappily.

> That human being, therefore, on whom is conferred such great honor and who received rule over all things, blessed Paul confirms is Jesus, since while some of what is said refers to God, other things apply to the assumed man. After all, how can someone who is one and the same with respect to nature both be mindful and thought worthy of being called to mind, watch over and be watched over, crown with glory and honor and be crowned, bestow rule over all things and receive it? How likewise can the statement "You have made him somewhat less than the angels" be understood of God the Word? In all that was said, therefore, it is proven that the statement *I have been established as king by him* refers to the assumed man, who with God the Word conferring it received it so as to be Lord of all. If, on the other hand, you were to claim it was conferred on the human being by the Father, not by the Word, there is no difference whether the assumed man was given such great honor by God the Word or by the Father. My sole concern was to demonstrate that there is consequently no truth in the claim of those who take occasion of the divine plan for taking flesh to deceive simple and unlearned people and presume to understand the only-begotten Son as inferior in respect of divinity because authority was given him.

His good intentions are insufficient to avoid the impression of an adoptionist Christology—a risk that Antioch's two-nature Christology always ran; as John N. D. Kelly remarks, "It is characteristic of [Theodore] to describe

the humanity as 'the man assumed', and occasionally his language seems almost to suggest that the Word adopted a human being who was already in existence."[53] One can understand how unsympathetic adversaries such as Cyril of Alexandria could label him the father of Nestorianism.

Theodore, of course, has been accused of having additional chinks in his theological armor, especially in the area of morality and spirituality. Photius cites his label as an Eastern Pelagius, which Kelly finds unsubstantiated "unless the Eastern attitude generally is to be dismissed as Pelagian," though allowing that to typically Eastern optimism Antioch adds "an intensified emphasis on individualism."[54] The latter emphasis appears in this work (as in many Antiochene writings)[55] in the way the accents fall on the relationship between divine grace and human effort. Not that Theodore disputes the reality of the fall; though the issue is not debated here, even in the context of Ps 51, there seems in comment on Ps 35:5, "Lo, you made my days handbreadths," an implicit acceptance of its truth: "God, of course, manages affairs by a certain plan, making our nature subject to a sentence of death once and for all and rendering us capable of lasting for an acknowledged number of years, with the result that we do not undergo a speedy dissolution of our being nor have an immeasurable life span extended unconditionally." As we find frequently in Chrysostom and Theodoret, however, many of Theodore's statements are at least ambiguous on the balance between divine grace and human effort, Antioch ever reluctant to be seen to be undermining the role the latter plays in salvation. When the psalmist prays in Ps 33:21, "Let your mercy be shown to us, Lord, as we have hoped in you," Theodore thinks it only right that grace should follow human initiative: "After all, we thus hoped in you, and it is right for us to be accorded your gift given in consequence of our hope." The balance should not be tilted only one way, he maintains in comment on Ps 46:11: "*The Lord of hosts is with us, the God of*

---

53. John N. D. Kelly, *Early Christian Doctrines* (5th ed.; New York: Harper & Row, 1978), 305. Theodore could not claim that he was but following the lead of master Diodore in getting himself into hot water, theologically speaking. Almost perversely, he departs from the script of Diodore's commentary on Ps 8:5, "You have brought him a little lower than the angels; with glory and honor your crowned him," which saw in focus the incarnation and its effect of elevating humankind, as a chance to document his own dyophysite thinking: "The psalm brings out for us such a great distinction between God the Word and the man assumed." This further infelicitous expression merited inclusion in the condemnation of Nestorianism (if not of Theodore personally) in the Constitution of Pope Vigilius and the decrees of the council in 553.

54. Photius, *Bibliotheca* 177 (Henry, *Bibliothéque* 2:182); Kelly, *Early Christian Doctrines,* 372–73.

55. See Robert Charles Hill, "The Spirituality of Chrysostom's Commentary on the Psalms," *JECS* 5 (1997): 569–79; idem, "A Pelagian Commentator on the Psalms?" *ITQ* 63 (1998): 263–71.

Jacob is our supporter, indicating all the help and salvation coming to them through what happened before on account of the gift of God's favor and the attention shown by them to the temple and to the Lord." On the other hand, as usual with these Antiochene theologians, there is no denying the role, if not the priority, of the Spirit, as he admits in comment on the phrase "in golden tassels, clad in many colors" in Ps 45:13:

> Lest you believe, then, that the virtue of the faithful is completely their own achievement and they require nothing else for it, it was well that he proceeded to make mention of spiritual adornment to bring out that those choosing to live a life of virtue need it, since all those practicing virtue are easily able to be imbued with the cooperation of the Spirit.

Theodore and his Antioch peers also share with the East generally the truth of human nature's being unimpaired, fall or no fall—such is the message of Ps 51, he insists (with characteristic dogmatism), which Diodore would not allow to be taken to refer to David's sin, despite the psalm title. Our own individual mind-set (γνώμη) and free will (προαίρεσις) are to blame, not "original sin" (a term not found in his vocabulary, of course).

> *For, lo, I was conceived in iniquities, and in sins my mother carried me* (v. 5). He finds no fault with offspring on the basis of nature—perish the thought—nor is there any reference to nature in their case; rather, he comments adversely on the mind-set of the parents. That is to say, from *conceiving in iniquities* and *being carried in sin* by the mother it is clear that he refers to the fault of the parents, not the offspring, criticizing the mind-set of the former, not the nature of the children, as some foolish people would like to hold. David, in fact, is not referring to himself: how could he say this of his own nature, when God had said of him, "I found a man after my own heart" (1 Sam 13:14), far from finding fault with his nature but even admiring his use of free will? So David is not saying this of himself, and even if someone mistakenly put a title on the psalm to this effect, it does not bring the drift of the psalm into question.

Theodore and Antioch generally would vigorously resist Dahood's paraphrase of that verse, "All men have a congenital tendency towards evil";[56] it undercuts their whole attitude to soteriology, morality, and spirituality, not to mention their approach to the Scriptures and the person of Jesus.[57]

---

56. Dahood, *Psalms,* 2:4.

57. The interconnection of Theodore's hermeneutical method and theological positions (as also Origen's) is conceded by Greer, *Early Biblical Interpretation,* 181.

THEODORE'S ACHIEVEMENT IN THE COMMENTARY ON THE PSALMS

We are fortunate that the flames of prejudice and hostility that claimed the bulk of The Interpreter's works did not deprive us of this incomplete yet adequate sample of his treatment of a classic biblical text, albeit a work of his early years; and it is high time for its appearance in an English translation. Admittedly, it was produced in the shadow of Theodore's influential teacher Diodore, adopting his positions on authorship of the psalms, their titles, and their interpretation even in details of the text; and even if we did not have the critical edition of (partly extant) commentary on eighty-one psalms painstakingly assembled by Devreesse, we should still be aware of the Antiochene form of the LXX Psalter through the school's other figures. While conceding this, however, the reader of Theodore's Psalms commentary, in assessing his achievement, also has to bring into focus the fulsome accolades paid the author by modern commentators as "the most typical representative of the Antiochene school of exegesis," "the foremost exponent of Antiochene exegesis" (implying that he, not Theodoret, is, in Bardy's words, "le noyau ou le terme de comparaison indispensable"), and similar claims to preeminence as an exegete in Antioch or the East as whole.[58]

Theodore's achievement in this work as we have it, though real, is less considerable than that.[59] His youth explains his dependence on his mentor and his intolerance and disparagement of other predecessors. If by comparison with modern commentators on the Psalter we find his exegetical equipment limited, and are irritated by his falsely claiming a Semitic science in rationalizing the many obscure texts with which these poems teem, we have to concede that such limitation was shared by all his peers. If it was his Christology that earned him ire and condemnation by later ages, his adversaries should have conceded him the benefit of the doubt in his many imprecise theological expressions, his virulent critic Leontius himself admitting Theodore's youthfulness at the time. On the other hand, for his prolix style, his lazy approach to backgrounding his text, and his lack of interest

---

58. The views, respectively, of Quasten, *Patrology,* 3:402; Sullivan, *Christology,* iv; Gustave Bardy, "Interprétation chez les pères," *DBSup* 4:582. Schäublin cannot be considering Theodore's immaturity in this work in promoting him above his Antiochene fellows: "Unquestionably, with the commentary of the bishop of Mopsuestia the school had reached its zenith" (*Untersuchungen,* 171). Zaharopoulos likewise could be thought to give Origen grounds for taking umbrage in declaring of Theodore, "For the first time in the history of the church a book of the Bible was expounded from the perspective of a critical method by a scholar" (*Theodore,* 47). Devreesse's claim of Theodore being the first literary critic also we have assessed above.

59. Rondeau (*Les commentaires,* 1:104 n. 285) suggests that the Psalms commentary shows Theodore in a less flattering light than some of his later works, such as his New Testament commentaries accessible in fragments in the catenae.

in the psalms' liturgical setting and their spiritual depths, he must—to the extent that our present text represents this thinking—bear responsibility himself. Though we find his hermeneutical perspective limited, we can at least be grateful to him for reminding his fellows, and even master Diodore, of the danger of being too ready to interpret New Testament citation of the psalms as more than simple accommodation, though Theodoret will return the compliment by demonstrating the correlative hazard of closing one's mind to levels of meaning in a text. If the modest goal that this neophyte set for himself in commenting on the first of the psalms was that of "making possible some illumination of the obvious sense of the text,"[60] who could call into question his real achievement?

---

60. Theodore thus abjures the role of a preacher, as the commentary's lack of moralizing confirms. When he gets to his commentary on the Gospel of John, also an early work, he will repeat the disclaimer: "I judge the exegete's task to be to explain words that most people find difficult; it is the preacher's task to reflect also on words that are perfectly clear and to speak about them" (Vosté, *Iohannis apostoli,* 1:2).

COMMENTARY ON PSALMS 1–81:
TEXT AND TRANSLATION

<PSALMVS I>

Primum psalmum quidam in Ioam regem dictum esse uoluerunt, qui a Ioada principe sacerdotum et nutritus est et interfecta
Athalia in imperium subrogatus est, eo quod per omne tempus
5 in quo a pontifice eruditus est in lege Dei meditatus sit noctibus
ac diebus; sed non audiendi sunt hi, qui ad excludendam psalmorum ueram expossitionem falsas similitudines ab historia peti-
tas conantur inducere. Quomodo enim beatum istum pronuntiare
potuisset et ab omni errore amore uirtutis alienum, cui in Re-
10 gum libris nullum testimonium de perfectione perhibetur, in quibus ita dicitur: *Et fecit Ioas rectum ante Dominum omnibus diebus*
quibus inluminabat eum Ioada pontifex, uerumtamen ab excelsis non
recesit, adhuc populus sacrificabat in excelsis? Dicendo itaque *om-*
nibus diebus, quibus inluminabat eum Ioada princeps sacerdotum,
15 *fecit rectum ante Dominum*, indicat quod reliquis diebus, cessante
Ioadae magisterio, fecerit id quod primis institutionibus minime
conueniret. Refertur etiam in hisdem Regum libris, quod Azahelem
regem Siriae ab inpugnatione Hirusalem Ioas munerum oblatione
submouerit; quae quidem dona de templo sublata misit, quae prius
20 utique Deo tam ipse quam reges Iuda, id est maiores eius, obtu-
lerant; quod actum indicatur his uerbis (bonum est enim nos ad
agnitionem rei gestae testimonio lectionis accedere): *Et accipit*
Ioas rex Iuda omnia sancta, quae sanctificauit Iosaphath et Ioram
et Ochozias patres eius reges Iuda, et sancta sua et omne aurum
25 *quod inuentum est in tesauris domus Domini et in domu regis, et*
misit Azaheli regi Siriae. Huic ergo, qui templum Dei spoliauit et

3 cf. IV Reg. XII, 3 ss.   11-15 IV Reg. XII, 2-3   22-26 IV Reg. XII, 18.

2 primum] .i. beatus uir r(e)l(iqua) *supra scriptum*   ψalmum *ms et ita*
saepissime, litt. ψ *pro* ps. *usurpata*   ioas *ms*   6 audiendi sunt hi] *litt.* di
sunt hi *in rasura*   7 expossitionem] .i. narrationem *add. supra*   8 quo-
modo] qm̄d *ms*   istum] .i. ioam *add. supra*   pronutiare *ms*   9 cui] .i.
ioae *add. supra*   9-10 reg∗um *ms*   11 rectum] .i. opus *add. supra*   12 eum]
.i. io∗am *add. supra*   13 populus] pls *ms*   14 io∗da∗ *ms*   16 magisterio]
litt. erio *in rasura, ex* magistro (?)   18 mumerum *ms*   20 eius] .i. iodae *ms*
21 actum *in rasura*   testimonii *1ª m.*   24 sancta] .i. uasa *add. supra*   26 aza-
heli] .i. dati(uum) *add. supra*.

2

PSALM 1

Some commentators took this first psalm to refer to King Joash, who was brought up by the chief priest Jehoiada and, once Athalia was killed, was installed in office,[1] their argument being that all the time he was educated by the priest *he meditated on the law of God night and day* (v. 2). No credence is to be given, however, to these commentators, who try to derive false comparisons drawn from history with a view to eliminating the true interpretation of the psalms. After all, how could he have declared *blessed* (v. 1) and free from every error through love of virtue the man of whom no evidence of perfection is adduced in the books of Kings, "Joash did what was right before the Lord all the time the priest Jehoiada gave him enlightened guidance; but he did not withdraw from the high places, the people still sacrificing on the high places"?[2] Therefore, by saying, "All the time the chief priest Jehoiada gave him enlightened guidance he did right before the Lord," it suggests that the rest of the time, when Jehoiada's instruction came to an end, he did what was out of keeping with his earlier education.

There is also mention in the same books of Kings that Joash deterred King Hazael of Syria from besieging Jerusalem with the offer of gifts; actually, he sent as these presents what had been taken from the temple, offerings that both he and the kings of Judah—that is, his ancestors—had in fact made to God. This action is conveyed in these words (it is good for us to come to a knowledge of the event on the evidence of the text): "King Joash of Judah took all the things that his ancestors Jehoshaphat, Jehoram, and Ahaziah, kings of Judah, had dedicated, as well as his own offerings and all the gold to be found in the treasuries of the house of the Lord and in the house of the king, and sent them to King Hazael of Syria."[3] | How, then, could the prophet

---

1. Cf. 2 Kgs 11.
2. 2 Kgs 12:2–3.
3. 2 Kgs 12:18.

omnia intus possita dona conrapsit ac misit ea uiro alienigenae
impio atque sacrilego, quomodo profeta Dauid beatitudinis apicem
contulisset?

Talis ergo historiae usurpatio inconueniens adprobatur et quae
praesenti psalmo non possit abtari, in quo beatus Dauid pronun- 5
tiatur uir de quo sermo est atque omnis uirtutis perfectione conspicuus; in fine enim psalmi dicitur: *Ideo non resurgunt impii in
iudicio neque peccatores* usque *peribit.* Hoc dictum his conuenit
qui possunt et morum perfectione et pro bono conuersationis suae
apud Deum confidentiam habere non minimam; Ioas uero rex non 10
talis ostenditur historiae lectione, ut dignus beatitudine conpro-
betur.

Est ergo moralis psalmus; quod ex his quae sequuntur appa-
ret, in quibus et de uirtutum appetitu et de errorum abstinentia
disputatur, quod in Ioam proprie non potest conuenire. Paruulus 15
enim per illud tempus, in quo Ioada pontifice nutritus est, neque
auersari mala iudicio suo poterat, neque in meditatione legis curam sedulam admouere, qui ad omne studium pro nutrientis ducebatur arbitrio; septimum itaque aetatis agenti annum [honor]
insigne regiae dignitatis inpossitum est. 20

Duo itaque, quae faciunt hominem | ad beatitudinem peruenire:
dogmatis recta sententia, id est ut pie de Deo et intigre sentiatur,
et morum emendata formatio, per quam honeste saneque uiuatur;
neutrum ad perfectionem ualet sine altero, alterum uero altero aut
subpletur aut comitur; sed fides inter haec duo primum obtinet 25
locum, sicuti in corpore honorabilius caput inter reliqua membra
censetur. Ad perfectionem tamen hominis necessaria sunt etiam
reliquorum accesio et conpago membrorum; similiter et ad con-
summationem uitae haec oportet utraque concurrere, fidem scilicet et uitam: et fidei quidem ad perfectum compraehensio, res 30
ardua atque dificilis, custodia uero facilis; uitae autem ratio, ad

---

7-8 Ps. I, 5-6   19 IV Reg. XI, 21.

1 intus] .i. in templo *add. supra* __ conrassit *ms*   2 impio] imp(er)io *ms*
quomodo] q(uod) *ms*   4 ergo] fut xp (futurus christus?) *add. in margine*
6-7 conpicūs *ms*   8 peribit].i. quoniam nouit dominus uiam iustorum r(e)l(iqua)
add. in margine   13 quae] qui *ms*   15 ioas *ms*   paruulus] fuit *add. supra*
16 ioada] iada *1ª m.*   18 sedulus *1ª m.*   qui] .i. ioas *add. supra*   nutrien-
tis] .i. iodae *add. supra*   19 honor *reieci*   20 ad *scriptum supra* insigne
21 duo] sunt *add. supra*   22 dogmatis] l(uel?) adit neutrum ualet *add. supra*
recta] id est *add. supra*   23 morum] .i. perfectorum *add. supra*   saneque]
sanetque *1ª m.*   24 alterum] *litt.* m *in rasura* (alterum si?)   25 duo] ii *ms*
26 sicuti in] adit oportet *add. supra*   27 cense*tur *ms*   sunt *add. supra.*

David have conferred the height of beatitude on this man who plundered God's temple, stole all the gifts deposited inside it, and sent them to an impious and sacrilegious foreigner?

This, then, is the kind of inappropriate distortion of history that is given respectability, the sort that cannot be reconciled with the present psalm, where the man of whom David speaks is declared blessed and conspicuous for the perfection of every virtue. In fact, the statement is made at the end that *the godless or sinners will not rise up in judgment* down to *will perish* (vv. 5–6); this statement applies to those who can have no little trust in God through the perfection of their behavior and the soundness of their way of life. King Joash, by contrast, does not emerge from our reading of history as a person of the kind to be thought worthy of being pronounced blessed.

It is thus a moral psalm, as emerges from what follows, where there is question both of desire for virtues and abstinence from faults—something not properly applicable to Joash. In fact, as a child for that period of time, when he was raised by the priest Jehoiada, he was incapable of resisting vicious habits voluntarily or devoting earnest attention to meditation on the law, guided as he was to every occupation on the basis of his guardian's judgment; the trappings of royalty were bestowed on him in the course of his seventh year.[4]

There are therefore two things that contribute to a person's attaining beatitude: correct views on doctrine, for the purpose of having a dutiful and upright attitude toward God, and a disciplined moral upbringing, for living in an honorable and sound manner. Neither suffices for perfection without the other, each being supplemented or accompanied by the other; faith takes pride of place among them, just as in the body the head is given greater esteem than the other members. Still, for a person's perfection, relationship with the other members and conjunction of the limbs also are required; likewise, for the full development of life, both these things must come together—namely, faith and life. To the perfect, a grasp of faith is no easy or simple thing, but its retention is easy. The pattern of life, on the other hand, | which shows

---

4. Cf. 2 Kgs 11:4.

intellegendum prona et quae omnium intellectui tam in bonorum adpetitu quam in malorum fuga uideatur exposita, exhibitio uero non operis
parui ac laboris; sed non numquam uitae merito ad fidem aditus aperitur et, e diuerso, ad perfectam cognitionem eius peccatis obstruitur:
5 nam, uelut quibusdam tenebris, conuersationis sincerum eius inter-
cluditur et puritas inpeditur. Vnde hanc partem maxime scripturae
diuinae est moris excolere, et ideo, etiam in praesenti psalmo, ante
docomenta fidei, disciplina moralis indicitur: nam obesse perfectae
fidei morum uitia Apostolo teste discamus, qui ait ad Chorinthios:
10 *Non potui uobis loqui quasi spiritalibus, sed quasi carnalibus, quasi*
paruulis in Christo; et subiungit: *Cum enim sit inter uos zelus et*
contensio, nonne carnales estis et secundum hominem ambulatis? cum
e contrario Cornilius ad fidem sit sufragio conuersationis | admisus.

Hoc itaque argumentum est praesentis psalmi. Debemus iam,
15 adiuuante Domino, per partes ad reserandum intellectum eius accedere; et si necesse fuerit pro consideratione rerum occurentium
aliqua latius explicare, non obliuiscemur tamen eius, quam pro-
misimus in praefatione, breuitatis. Hoc autem maxime seruabimus
et in praesenti psalmo et in reliquis omnibus, ut, omnem intellec-
20 tum in summam redigentes, strictim quicquid dicendum est expli-
cemus; quoniam non est nobis propossitum latius cuncta persequi,
sed summatim dictorum omnium sensus adtingere, ut possit lecturis expossitionis prima facie relucere, illis relinquentes occasiones maioris intellegentiae si uoluerint aliqua addere, quae tamen
25 a praemissa interpretatione non discrepent: ista enim ueri est intel-
lectus perceptio, ut secundum historiae fidem tenorem expossitionis
aptemus et concinnenter ea, quae dicenda sunt, proferamus.

1. *Beatus uir qui non abiit in consilio* usque *sedit.* Interdum scriptura diuina inter impium et peccatorem facit differentiam, impium
30 uocans Dei ueri notitiam non habentem, peccatorem uero honesti

10-13 I Cor. III, 1, 3   13 cf. Act. X.

2 uedeatur *ms ex* uediatur   3 merito] ab(lativum) *add. supra*   5 sin-
cerum] *litt.* cerum *in rasura*   eius] .i. fidei *add. supra*; *fortasse legendum* et
fidei puritas inpeditur   8 docomenta] .i. fidei *add. supra*   abesse *1ᵃ m.*
9 chorin *ms*   12 nonne] uel non *add. supra*   ambulastis *1ᵃ m.*   13 su-
pragio *1ᵃ m.*   conuersationis] .i. perfectae *add. supra*   14 argumentum]
supra litt. um *scribitur* l(uel) o   15 adiuante *ms*   *per *in rasura*   18 hoc
autem] .i. praedictum *add. supra*   20 in sumã *ms*, .i. ad numerum *add. supra*
strictim] .i. breuiter *add. supra*   quicquid] *litt.* q(ui)c *in rasura*   22 docto-
rum *1ᵃ m.*   23 expossitionis] narrationis *add. supra*   25 praemisa *ms*   28 in-
terdum] *litt.* dũ *in rasura*   30 honesti] uiri *add. supra*.

readiness to understand and emerges both in a desire for good things and in a flight from bad things in understanding everything, is a quality involving no little effort and exertion. Sometimes, however, an approach by life to faith deservedly opens up, and on the other hand its way to perfect knowledge is blocked by sin, for by sin, as though by a kind of darkness, the genuineness and purity of its lifestyle are interfered with and obscured.

Hence, attention to this particular part of the divine Scripture is relevant to morality, and so in the present psalm, in advance of the proofs of faith, moral instruction is laid out. We learn, remember, from the witness of the apostle that vicious behavior is an obstacle to perfect faith, when he said to the Corinthians, "I could not speak to you as spiritual people but as people of the flesh, as infants in Christ," and went on, "For since there is jealousy and quarreling among you, are you not of the flesh and behave in human fashion?" whereas Cornelius, by contrast, was admitted to faith on the basis of his lifestyle.[5]

This, then, is the theme of the present psalm. Our task now is, with God's help, to proceed to plumb its meaning. If it should prove necessary to explain some things at greater length in the light of matters that arise, we shall nevertheless not be unmindful of the conciseness we promised in the preface.[6] Now, this practice we shall particularly observe both in the present psalm and in all the others, to make a summary of the overall meaning and thus unfold precisely what has to be said. The task set for us, you see, is not to follow up every matter in detail, but succinctly to touch on the sense of each statement so as to make possible some illumination of the obvious sense of the text, leaving those of greater intelligence to add other things if they wish, though not departing from the interpretation already given. A true understanding, in fact, results in such an insight that we should maintain a sequence of explanation in faithful accord with history, and accordingly should propose what ought be said.

Blessed is the man who did not go off in the counsel down to *sat* (v. 1). Sometimes the divine Scripture differentiates between the godless and the sinner, defining the godless as someone lacking knowledge of the true God, and the sinner | as someone not keeping to the straight and narrow, whereas

---

5. 1 Cor 3:1, 3; Acts 10:1–2.

6. As we noted in the introduction, the preface that Theodore composed dealing with matters pertaining generally to the psalms has been lost.

iustique tramitem non tenentem, tamen est ubi commoni uoca-
bulo utrumque significatur; in praesenti tamen uidetur facere distinctionem, quoniam uult qui sit status perfectionis exprimere,
cui etiam beatitudinem credit rite competere uel propter perfectam
de deitate notitiam uel propter studia uitae melioris. Quod uero 5
ait *non abi|it, non stetit, non sedit* animae motus corporalibus si-
gnàt indiciis, quoniam cum aliquid molimur efficere, primum ad
arripiendum opus mouemur ingresu, deinde subsistimus, ubi res
coepit esse in manibus; ad sedendum uero conuertimur, negotio
iam parato.   10

Hoc ergo sanctus Dauid ait, quoniam ille uere beatus sit qui
neque primis quidem uestigiis impietatum cogitationem adiit uel ingresus est, neque ad effectum praui operis gradum depressit, neque
ulla ita inretitus est malae dilectationis inlicebra, — quod nomine
cathedrae et sesionis ostenditur, — ut eorum consortio iungeretur 15
qui aliorum simplicitatem uenino suae prauitatis inficiunt: hos
enim pestilentes uocat, quorum est plane morbosa coniunctio; nam
et pestilentiae proprium est ab uno in alterum transeundo inficere
multorum corpora atque uitiare. *Non abiit* ergo dicendo adsensus
cogitationum notauit, quibus ad prauas suggestiones rapimur et 20
id, quod libuerit, implere properamus. Quod uero ait *Non stetit* in
opus, exiisse indicat id quod cogitatio ante suggeserat, quam tunc
inplemus cum dilectat in aliis operibus gradum figere ac sepius
restitare.

Per cathedrae autem sesionem ille signatur, qui ita delectatur 25
et requiescit in mala consuetudine, ut reliquis eiusdem studii hominibus sine ullo uerecondiae misceatur adpensu. Quod uero *impiorum* consilia possuit, peccatorum uero opera satis ad utrumque
respexit: impietas enim ad agitationem mentis pertinet et motus
non recte animae sentientis, | peccatum uero in rem actio iam 30
deducta.

2 significatur] sig *1ᵃ m.* nificatur *add. supra*   praesenti] salmo *add. supra*
3 exp(rae)mere *ms, et ita saepissime*   5 de•tate *ms*   uel propter] .i. p(ro). et
add. supra   6 motūs *ms*   7 indicīs *ms*   11 hoc ergo] non abiit *add. supra*
12 uestigis *ms*   uel] qui neque *add. supra*   13 effectum] fectum *1ᵃ m.*   praui]
litt. ra *in rasura*   depressit *conieci,* rep(rae)sit *ms*   14 dilectationis] dileqt.
uidetur prius scriptum   16 prauitatis] *litt.* ra *in rasura, ut supra l. 13*   18 tran-
seundo] pestilentia *add. supra*   19 adsensūs *ms*   21 non stetit] .i. iustus *add.*
supra   22 opus] malum *add. supra*   exiisse] .i. peccator *add. supra*   23 im-
plemus *1ᵃ m.*   figire *ms*   sepius] repius *uidetur prius scriptum*   24 resi-
stitare *2ᵃ m.*   26 studii] pestellentiae *add. supra*   29 agationem *1ᵃ m.*   30 pec-
catum] .i(d). (est) *add. supra.*

there are places where both ideas are conveyed by the one word. In the present instance, nonetheless, it seems to make the distinction, since it intends to describe the state of perfection to which it believes beatitude also belongs, either on account of perfect knowledge of the deity or on account of the occupations of a higher way of life. The phrases *he did not go off, did not stand, did not sit* suggest by bodily posture movements of the soul, since when we prepare to do something, we first make a movement to achieve it, then we stop when the object comes within our grasp, and we change to a sitting position when the task is completed.

This is what blessed David is saying, then, that that person is truly blessed who did not make the first movement or enter upon the thought of godless actions, did not take steps to achieve an evil action, and was not so caught up in any enjoyment of a wicked pleasure (implied by mention of a *seat* and *sitting*) as to enter into association with those who infect the guilelessness of other people with the poison of their own depravity (calling them *pestilential* because association with them clearly is contagious, the effect of pestilence being to infect and damage the bodies of a great number by passing from one to another). By saying *he did not go off,* therefore, he indicated the acquiescence in thinking by which we are caught up in evil suggestions and hasten to consummate our desire. By *he did not stand,* on the other hand, he indicated the fulfillment of what the thought originally had suggested, which we consummate at the time when it is our pleasure to initiate other actions and frequently persist in them.

By *sitting in the chair,* that person is indicated who so enjoys and adheres to an evil habit as to mingle, without any sense of shame, with other people of the same inclination. In speaking of *counsels of the godless,* he referred likewise to the deeds of sinners: whereas impiety has reference to disturbance of mind and movements of a spirit with disordered sentiments, sin refers to an action already put into effect. | To these two categories he listed a third

Tertium, quod addidit, utrisque subiecit, quoniam non solum hi pestilentes uocantur qui male sentiendo corrumpunt reliquos et societate sua perimunt, uerum etiam illi qui tabe consortii bonum conuersationis suae rectae infringunt, quibus in totum non admis-
5 ceri est sibi optime consulentis; et ideo hunc, qui per omnia declinat a talibus, beatum praesentis psalmi lectio difiniuit, qui ita actus suos circumspicit ut etiam aliena mala sollicitatione declinet et ueretur ne alienis maculis candor suus puritasque fuscetur hinc. Quoniam tendenti ad beatitudinem non sufficit recedere tantum a
10 malis, sed etiam bona facere necesse est, inferius ait:

2. *Sed in lege Domini fuit uoluntas eius* usque *die ac nocte.* Non solum, inquit, studet malorum consortia declinare, uerum adsidua et iugi meditatione legis discit qualem se formare conueniat; et, ut fructuosum huius modi, quod commendare nititur, probet studium,
15 inducit similitudinem per quam possit bonum eius, quem beatum dicit, hominibus relucere.

3. *Et erit sicut lignum quod plantatum est secus decursus* usque *prosperabuntur.* Sicut arbos, inquit, cui uirere iugiter natura est, etiam loci, in quo plantata fuerit, uiuificatur beneficio, ut ab ari-
20 ditate aquis defendatur inriguis atque ab hoc multis fit fructibus plena, quia neque aeris, neque loci, neque temporis iniurias sentit, — id enim indicat quod sequitur, dicens: *Et omnia quaecumque faciet prosperabuntur*; est omnibus, tam perpetuo uirore quam pomo|rum numerositate, conspicua, — ita etiam ille erit clarus, qui se
25 et a malis abstinuerit et bonorum studiorum amore diuinxerit, quem nec ulla peccatorum opera deturpant et meditatio continua legis exornat.

4. *Non sic impii non sic, sed tamquam* usque *a facie terrae.* Superioribus dictis omnes ad uirtutis studium prouocauit; praesen-
30 tibus deterret a uitiis, et per conparationem pulueris ostendit quanta sit uilitas impiorum, et qui indigni aliquo aestimantur

2 setiendo *ms ex* r(?)etiendo   4 infringunt] .i. peccatores *add. supra*
6 talibus] malis *add. supra*   7 declinaet *1ª m.*   8 hinc *suppl. in margine*
10 bona] opera *add. supra*   ait *om. 1ª m.*   13 iungi *1ª m.*   qualem] *litt.* al
in rasura   18 inquit] *litt.* a *inter litt.* n *et* q *inferius add., cui respondet* b
l. 24 supra erit *inscripta*   20 fit] .i. arbos *add. supra*   21 aeris] eris *ms*
22-23 faciet prosperabuntur] .i. arbos et beatus uir *add. supra*   25 et** *ms*
29 omnes] sanctos *add. supra*   praesentibus] dictis *add. supra*   30 uitis *ms*
31 aestimamantur *ms.*

point in addition, that *pestilential* is a term used not only of those who corrupt others with their evil views and destroy them with their association, but also of those who through coming in contact with disease impair the quality of their upright way of life; it is advisable not to get involved with them at all. Hence the text of the present psalm classes as *blessed* the person who avoids such people in everything and who is so attentive to his actions as to avoid any evil entreaty from outside and to be on the watch lest from that quarter his sincerity and purity be defiled by contamination from without.

Since for the person aspiring to that blessed state it is not sufficient only to avoid evil, but there is also a requirement to do good, he went on to say *Instead, his will was for the law of the Lord* down to *day and night* (v. 2): he not only takes pains to avoid the company of bad people, but also, by industrious study of the yoke of the law, he learns into what sort of person he should develop.[7] To encourage fruitful attention to the task he is taking pains to recommend, he introduces a comparison by which he may be able to illustrate to people the good qualities of the person he calls *blessed. He will be like a tree that is planted near streams* down to *will prosper* (v. 3): like a tree, which by nature flourishes constantly, and is enlivened by the advantage of the place in which it has been planted so as to be protected from aridity by flowing water and become loaded with fruit, experiencing no harm from climate, location, or season (as is clear from what follows, *everything he does will prosper*), and obvious to everyone, both by its evergreen condition and the abundance of its crop, so too will that person be illustrious who has abstained from evil and given himself to the love of noble exploits, who is unstained by any works of sinners and is distinguished by constant meditation on the law.[8]

Not so are the godless, not so; rather, like down to *from the face of the earth* (v. 4). With what was said above he prompted everyone to the practice of virtue; with his present words he discourages them from vice, and by the comparison with dust he brings out the complete worthlessness of the godless, regarded as they are as undeserving of any | esteem and so easily

---

7. It is not the psalmist who refers to the law as a yoke; the rabbis will come to speak in these terms.

8. Unlike Theodoret, Theodore has no problem with the psalmist's reference here to a "man," ἀνήρ, being declared blessed, with no mention of women.

adpensu et ita malis superuenientibus inpellantur facile ac stare
non possint ut puluis, qui pro tenuitate sua ac leuitate uentorum
flatibus huc illucque dispergitur.

5. *Ideo non resurgunt impii* usque *iustorum*. Haec dicens non
resurrectionem impiis denegauit, qui utique, si non resurgerent, 5
lucrificarent futura suplicia, quae quidem non aliter nisi restituti
in corpore sustinebunt. Nam ita erit commone animae corpo-
risque suplicium sicut fuit peccatorum commonis admisio. Quod
ergo dicit tale est: quia consueuimus in apertis creminibus
moras ad inquirendum nullas adhibere, sed statim condemna- 10
tionis ferre sententiam, ita et impii ad poenam resurgentes non
illam dilationem habebunt, quae solet iudiciariis inquesitionibus
admoueri; quos grauius manere supplicium per hoc indicatur,
quod statim et uelut adcelarata sententia in locum meritis suis
debitum et in ultimum contrudentur | exitium. Et ideo non dixit 15
absolute *Non resurgent* sed addidit *in iudicio*, hoc est non resurgent ad examinationem, sed resurgent ut statim sententiam
damnationis excipiant. Et ne forte ex commoni resurrectionis
nomine commonem aestimantes etiam expulsionem futuram esse
cunctorum, ostendit quoniam in eodem momento resurrectionis 20
magna futura sit diuersitas, ut alius per illam ad honorem per-
ducatur, alius mittatur in poenam: erit ergo pretiosa aliis et
remunerabilis, aliis grauis atque terribilis. Bene ergo inter impium et peccatorem fecit differentiam: et impios quidem ait in
iudicium non resurgere, id est, ut superius diximus, non in exami- 25
nationem uenire.

Peccatores autem *in consilio iustorum*, hoc est ut nulla illis sit
in iustorum remuneratione commonio; tradentur ergo etiam ipsi
suppliciis. Nam qui per peccata excluduntur a praemiis, ea sine
dubio, quae sunt praemiis diuersa, patientur. In hoc ergo erit dif- 30
ferentia, ut impii quidem resurgant non discutiendi sed statim lo-

1 malis] peccatis *add. supra*   4 impi *ms*   haec] praedicta *add. supra*
7 sustenebunt *1ᵃ m.*   8 admiso *1ᵃ m.*   10-11 contemnationis *ms*   11 impi
ms ut l. 4   12 delationem *ms*   13 suplicium *1ᵃ m.*   15 et in] in *add. supra* et
17 statim] *litt.* i *in rasura*   sententiam] uindictam *add. supra*   18-22 *verba*
et ne forte — in poenam *litteris* a-o *supra positis instruuntur, quibus syntaxeos
ordo scriptione diuersus indicatur*   19 aestimantes] pro estimamus *add. supr a*
21 illum *1ᵃ m.*   22 pretiosa] resurrectio *add. supra*   23 grauis atque] resurrectio *add. supra*   24 fecit] d(aui)d *add. supra*   deferentiam *ms et ita l. 30-31*
impios] *litt.* io *in rasura*   25 diximus] d̄x̄s *ms*, diximus *add. supra*   26 ue-
nire] .i. impii *add. supra*   29 supplicis *ms*   praemis *ms et ita infra*.

affected by troubles befalling them as to be unable to hold fast, like dust, which is scattered hither and thither by blasts of wind on account of its light and insubstantial character.

Accordingly, the godless do not rise down to *of the righteous* (v. 5). In saying this he does not deny resurrection to the godless, who, if they did not rise, would not pay due penalties, which in fact they will not suffer unless brought back in the body. There will, you see, be a common punishment of body and soul, just as there was a common committing of sins. What he means, then, is something like this: When a case is open-and-shut, we are in the habit, not of allowing any delay in investigating it, but rather of delivering a verdict of condemnation on the spot. Likewise the godless, too, on rising again, will enjoy no postponement, which is allowed for when judicial investigations are under way; that they await a heavier punishment is indicated by the fact that at once and as if by an accelerated verdict they will be consigned to a place corresponding to their deserts and to utter ruin. Hence, instead of saying simply *They will not rise,* he added *to judgment*—that is, they will not rise for examination, but will rise to receive the verdict of condemnation on the spot. And lest on the basis of the general name for rising we conclude that there will even be a general rejection of all people, he brings out that in the same moment of resurrection there will be great diversity, such that while one person as a result of it is conducted to a position of honor, another is consigned to punishment, and so while for some it will be a moment that is desirable and brings reward, for others it will be dire and frightening.

He was right, therefore, to make a distinction between the godless and the sinner. He said, in fact, that *the godless will not rise to judgment*—that is, as we said above, they will not enter into examination; *nor sinners in the council of the righteous*—that is, for them there will be no share in the reward of the righteous: those excluded by sin from remuneration will endure what is doubtless the opposite of remuneration. This, then, constitutes the difference, that while the godless will rise not for purposes of deliberation but for immediate | dispatch to places of grief, sinners will rise for no participation in any

cis tristibus deputandi, peccatores uero ut nulla iustis commonione
iungantur. Hoc autem manifestius ex his, quae sequuntur, ostenditur.

6. *Quoniam nouit Dominus uiam iustorum,* id est placitam sibi
5 et acceptam esse remunerationis testimonio perdocebit.

Et iter impiorum peribit. Ideo igitur non resurgunt ad examinationem impii, quia omnium uiae perfecta Dei notitia continentur,
atque ab hoc sine ulla dilatione resurrectionem eorum condicio et
sors digna suscipiet.

10   PSALMVS II

In secundo psalmo beatus Dauid profetans narrat omnia quae
a Iudeis passio|nis dominicae impleta sunt tempore, quorum sa-
crilegos contra Dominum motus rationis uacuos inanesque commemorat, et conatus noxios inanesque describit. Indicat etiam ius
15 imperii et potentiam dominationis insinuat, quam super omnia,
post resurrectionem, homo a Deo susceptus accipit. Exortatur quoque ad adpetitam beatitudinem, quam dicit per susceptionem fidei
conferendam; fugiendam infidelitatem monet, cuius fructus dam-
natio sit futura.

20   Haec autem in Christum praedicta si quis christianorum ambi-
git, utemur ad probationem beati apostoli Petri testimonio, in quo
ait: *Quare fremuerunt gentes et populi* usque *aduersus Christum
eius? Vere enim conuenerunt Herodes et Pontius Pilatus* cum principibus populi et senioribus *aduersus sanctum puerum Iesum.* Ad-
25 sumamus etiam beati apostoli Pauli dicta, in quibus ait: *Ad quem
autem angelorum dixit aliquando Filius meus es tu, ego hodie
genui te?*

Aduersum Iudeos uero, qui profetiae huius tenorem a persona
Domini detorquere conantur, quorum alii in Zorobabel, alii in Da-
30 uid uolunt dicta psalmi praesentis accipere, congrediendum est;

22-24 Act. IV. 25-27   25-27 Hebr. I, 5.

1 peccatores] erunt *add. supra*   2 hoc autem] .i. praedictum *add. supra*
6-7 examnationem *ms*   7 quia] quod *1ª m.*   perfecta] ab(lativum) *add. supra*
8 delatione *ms*   10 explicit psalmus .i. incipit s(ecund)us *ms*   14 discribit *ms*
15 super omnia] elimenta *add. supra*   17 adpetitum *1ª m.*   24 renioribus *1ª m.*
ihm *ms*   24-25 adsumamus] adsumus *ms*   29 quorum] pro quibus *add. supra*
30 acipere *ms.*

sharing with the righteous. In what follows he brings this out more clearly: *Because the Lord knows the way of the righteous* (v. 6)—that is, on the evidence of reward he will let it be clearly understood that their way is pleasing and acceptable to him—*and the way of the godless will perish:* the godless therefore will not rise to examination, because the ways of them all will come under the perfect knowledge of God, and for this reason without any delay their situation and fitting plight will undergo resurrection.

PSALM 2

In Psalm 2, David in his inspired composition narrates everything carried out by the Jews at the time of the Lord's passion; he recalls their sacrilegious plotting against the Lord, vain and futile as they were, and recounts their vicious and futile efforts. He suggests also his right to command and hints at the power of control that after the resurrection as a human being taken up by God he received for exercise over all. He also gives an exhortation to the beatitude that is desirable, and speaks of it being bestowed through adoption of faith, urging avoidance of infidelity, the fruit of which is future damnation.

Now, if any Christian has doubts as to what is foretold of Christ, let us cite as proof the quotation by the blessed apostle Peter, in which it is said, "*Why did the nations and peoples* down to *against his Christ?* For in fact Herod and Pontius Pilate joined forces with the leaders and elders of the people against his holy servant Jesus."[1] Let us cite also the words of the blessed apostle Paul, where he says, "Now, to which of the angels did he ever say, 'You are my Son, today I have begotten you'?"[2] Now, issue is to be taken with the Jews, who endeavor to deflect the reference in this prophecy away from the person of the Lord, some wanting to take the words of the present psalm in reference to Zerubbabel, some to David. | Leaving aside those who

---

1. Acts 4:25–27. In fact, it is the community to whom Peter and John report after their arraignment before the Jewish authorities who are speaking.

2. Heb 1:5.

sed omisis illis, qui dicta ista ad Zorobabel rapiunt, cum his manus
conserenda est qui eum in Dauid dictum conantur adstruere.· Relinquamus sane unicuique lecturo, si uelit hisdem uti argumentis etiam
contra eos qui ad Zorobabel hunc psalmum dixerint pertinere. Vtilius autem est cum fortioribus inire certamen; quibus uictis, necesse　5
erit etiam infirmiores quosque conruere: aequalis namque et par ab
utris|que contra nos pugnat intentio, etsi uerisimiliora dicant qui ad
Dauid quam qui ad Zorobabel psalmum conantur inflectire; unde
maius certamen elegimus, quia, deiecto ualentiore, eadem ruina etiam
inbicellus inuoluitur; hisdem sane obiectionibus, si qui studiosi sunt　10
fratrum, contra utrumque poterint armari sufficienter.

　　　1. *Quare fremuerunt gentes* usque *inania*. Fremitus proprie dicitur ille equorum sonus, quem naribus uicisim in lite positi indicem fororis emitunt, quando animos suos in iurgia flatibus ardere significant. Inrationabiles ergo beatus Dauid contra Dominum　15
Iudeorum motus indicans, non est dignatus eis illam, quae potest
in homines cadere, perturbationem mentis adscribere. In hoc autem
loco, si a Iudeis quaeritur quae gentes congregatae sint aduersus
Dominum, respondemus: Hirodis et Pontius Pylatus ac milites reliquique, qui eorum imperiis tunc parebant, quos consequenter uo　20
cat populos siue gentes, non ab uniuersitate eos, qui adfuturi erant,
sed a parte significans. Neque enim ita dicit *gentes*, ut omnes undique uelit intellegi, sed partionale uniuersali appellatione signauit;
diuisit uero inter populos et gentes, quoniam Iudei compraehendentes Dominum tradiderunt Pylato et non solum Pylato, sed etiam　25
Hirodi, quos utrosque gentiles fuisse non dubium est. Hoc est ergo
quod dicit *Quare fremuerunt gentes*. Quae fuit, inquit, tanta causa
quae illis motus furiales ingessit, aut quibus dementiae facibus accensi sunt populi, ut armari contra Dominum non timerent | et non
solum eum suis temerare manibus, uerum etiam gentibus tradendo　30
piaculi crimen augerent?

　　　1 omisis] *litt.* mi *in rasura*　　　cum his] aduersum eos *add. supra*　　　2 eum]
psalmum *add. supra*　　2-3 relinquamus] impr̄ (imperatiuum?) *add. supra*　　4 hunc
om. 1ᵃ m.　　7 utrisque] uiris *add. supra*　　etsi uerisimiliora] adit intellectiri (?,
intellectionem?) *add. supra*　　similliora *1ᵃ m.*, .i. iura *add. supra*　　9 qui adiecto
1ᵃ m.　　ualentiore] .i. fortiore *add. supra*　　10 obieconibus *ms*, interrogationibus *add. supra*　　11 arm *1ᵃ m.*　　12 fremū (fremunt?) *ms*　　18 quaeritur] qr̄
ms　　20 imperis *ms*　　21 ab *add. supra*　　21-22 *verba* non — significans *litteris*
a-g *supra aut infra exaratis distinguuntur ad ordinem syntaxeos insinuandum*
27 quae fuit] inrō (interrogatio?) *add. supra*　　29 timerent] merent *1ᵃ m.*
31 cremen *ms*　　augerent] ut *add. supra*.

maliciously refer these words to Zerubbabel, battle is to be joined with those who endeavor to apply the text to David. At any rate, let us leave it up to each reader whether or not to choose to employ these arguments also against those who claimed that this psalm refers to Zerubbabel.[3] It is, however, more useful to do battle with the stronger, and when they are vanquished, all the weaker ones consequently will be ruined, as the same thrust of equal force is directed at us by both groups, even if those who endeavor to refer the psalm to David are more plausible than those who refer it to Zerubbabel. Hence our option for the tougher struggle on the grounds that, with the more powerful foe overcome, the same fate will equally befall the weaker. At all events, any of our brethren who are of a scholarly bent will be able to equip themselves adequately with the same defense against both parties.[4]

Why did nations snort down to *futile?* (v. 1). *Snort* is a term properly applied to that sound of horses which they emit from their nostrils repeatedly as a sign of fury when arrayed in battle, indicating by their neighing that their spirits are aroused for the fray. To convey the Jews' irrational feelings against the Lord, blessed David was not prepared to attribute to them the mental disturbance that can occur in people. In this case, on the contrary, if the question is raised by the Jews as to which nations were gathered against the Lord, we reply, Herod, Pontius Pilate, soldiers, and the rest who at that time obeyed their orders,[5] whom he consequently calls *peoples* or *nations,* suggesting those who were present not in general terms but from individuals: he does not use *nations* from a desire that everyone on all sides be understood; instead, he conveyed partial attendance by use of a general term. He distinguished between *peoples* and *nations* because the Jews apprehended the Lord and handed him over to Pilate, and not just to Pilate but also to Herod, both of whom unquestionably were Gentiles—hence his saying *Why did the nations snort?* What was the extraordinary cause, he asks, that prompted in them emotions of fury, and with what torches of derangement were the peoples so ignited as to have no qualms about taking up arms against the Lord, and not only to lay hands on him, but even to aggravate the crime of sacrilege by handing him over to the nations? |

---

3. Theodore here regards an option for Zerubbabel as less convincing, whereas in his next work, on the Twelve Prophets, this figure is seen as replacing Jesus as the prophets' referent.

4. To this point (the preface not being extant), Theodore's intended readership is not defined. He allows for some better-informed readers among them.

5. Cf. Acts 4:27.

2. *Adstcterunt reges terrae et principes conuenerunt in unum.*
Eadem quae superius interrogationis figura magnitudo, cui non
subesset causa, furoris exprimitur: ausus enim tam nefarii multorum in se ora conuerlerant, et facti temeritas ad spectaculum
5 omnes excitauerat. Conuenerunt multi etiam longe possiti, maxime
uisione illa permoti quae de obscuratione solis facta est; qui quidem
illa hora, quando medium tenens caelum solet esse clarior, uirtute
Dei obscuratus omnem terram tenebrarum densitate uelauit. Similis
autem signi nouitas in diebus Ezechiae regis apparuit, quando sol
10 reuocatus est per ea spatia quae fuerat emensus: quod quidem et in
Regum libris et in Isaiae uolumine contenetur; quo facto motus Asi-
riorum rex misit dona Ezechiae attonitus miraculis signique nouitate.

Et principes conuenerunt in unum. Scribas Fariseosque significat, qui dum sententiarum impietate non discrepant mortem Domini
15 crimen commone fecerunt.

Aduersus Dominum et uersus christum eius. Aduersus Patrem, inquit, et Filium, quoniam ad contumiliam Patris et Filii spectat iniuria
et in utrumque committit, qui in alterutrum profanus exsteterit.

3. *Disrumpamus uincula eorum et proieciamus a nobis iugum*
20 *ipsorum.* Per id, quod superius dixit *Quare fremuerunt gentes,* in-
rationabilis furor et stultitiae plenus notatur, qui cum nullas habuerint offensionum causas, aduersus Dominum tamen facibus animi
dementis exarserint. | Per hoc autem, quod ait *Disrumpamus uin-
cula eorum,* aperitur quod uelut rationis intuitu ad ausus sacrilegos
25 uenerint, et quae fuerit intentio impii conatus ostenditur. A commoni ergo intellegentia intellegendum est quod dictum est tam ex
persona populi quam principum *Conuenerunt in unum aduersus
Dominum et aduersus christum eius.* Quid *Disrumpamus uincula
eorum, et proieciamus a nobis iugum ipsorum?* Hoc est remoueamus
30 a nobis Patris Filiique dominatum nec eorum ultra subdamur imperio. Sic enim agebant omnia, quasi qui nolint sub Dei legibus

9-12 IV Reg. XX, 9-11; Is. XXXVIII, 8.

2 superius] .i. quare frem(uer)unt *add. supra* figura] ab(latiuum) *add.
supra* 3 exp(rae)mitur *ms* 5 exciuerat *ms* maxime *ex* maximi 7 hora]
ab(latiuum) *add. supra* tenens] medio die *add. supra* solet] .i. sol *add. supra*
uittute *ms* 11 regnum *1ª m.* factus *in textu,* facto *in marg.* mo**tus (monitus?) *ms* 12 ezechiae attonitus] dati(vum?) rege p(rae)dicto *add. supra* 13 si-
gnificat] sig *ms* 14 sententiarum] crucifige *add. supra* 15 cremen *ms,* contra
gentes *add. supra* 17 et filii] et *om. 1ª m.* 18 alterutum] .i. in filium *add.
supra* 21 notatur] *supple e. g.* istorum 24 ausos *ms* 25 impi *ms* 26 intellegentia *suppl. in marg.* dictum] .dc. *ms* 30 nec] .n. *ms, ita inferius.*

The kings of the earth took their position and the leaders assembled together (v. 2). The same extent of their fury, for which there was no underlying cause, is expressed as was conveyed above in question form; such illicit exploits of a great many people led them to direct their words to one another, and the audacity of their behavior attracted everyone's attention. Although situated at a distance, great numbers of people assembled, especially perturbed by the phenomenon of the eclipse of the sun happening at the time when it is in the middle of the heavens and is usually clearer, but was obscured by God's power and covered the whole earth in thick darkness. Now, a similar strange sign occurred in the time of King Hezekiah, when the sun was brought back across the intervals it had covered, as is actually mentioned in the books of Kings and the book of Isaiah. Struck by this, the king of the Assyrians sent presents to Hezekiah, impressed by the remarkable wonders and signs.[6]

And leaders assembled together. It refers to the scribes and Pharisees, who in not dissenting from the impiety of the others' attitudes rendered the Lord's death a universal offense. *Against the Lord and against his Christ:* against the Father and the Son, since the crime involves an insult to Father and to Son and is directed to both, and both were treated sacrilegiously.

Let us break their bonds and thrust away from us their yoke (v. 3). In what is said above in *Why did the nations rage?* there is reference to the irrational frenzy that was full of stupidity on the part of those who without any cause by way of insult were nonetheless incensed with the brands of a deranged mind against the Lord. Here, on the contrary, in the words *Let us break their bonds* it emerges that as though by a glimpse of reason they proceeded to their sacrilegious exploits, and there is a revelation of the purpose of their godless endeavor. We therefore should realize by common sense that the words *They assembled together against the Lord and against his Christ* were spoken on the part both of the people and of the leaders. What of the words *Let us break their bonds and thrust away from us their yoke?* In other words, Let us remove from us the control of Father and Son and no longer be subject to their rule. In fact, they did everything in this spirit, as if they were not prepared to live under God's laws, | or be recalled

---

6. The incident of the sun's retreat is narrated in 2 Kgs 20:11 and Isa 38:8, whereas without recounting it, 2 Chr 32:31 mentions its notoriety, which leads Theodore to presume the reason for presents to Hezekiah from foreign royalty in 2 Kgs 20:12 (where, however, it is a Babylonian king who is the giver).

uiuere, nec ab impietate ulla diuini timoris consideratione reuocari. Dicit autem non quia talia locuti sunt Scribae atque Farisei,
sed quia talia fecerint, ut ex qualitate operis sermo talis proces-
sisse uideatur: consuetudo namque est diuinae scripturae, et maxime beato Dauid, ex operis merito formare uocem, ut cum dicit 5
de osoribus suis: *Narrauerunt ut absconderent laqueos, dixerunt
Quis uidebit eos?* non quia illi ista dixerint, sed quia talia egerint
ut putarent neminem futurum qui opera eorum possit inspicere et
eos contemplatione sui a prauis conatibus amouere.

Vincula eorum et iuga ius dominationis appellat, quoniam, sicut 10
uinculis abstricti et sub iugo possiti libertate carent neque possunt uel
in agendo uel in eundo copiam uoluntatis suae obsequi, ita et quem
condicio subdit inferior iugo seruitutis pressus praeceptis domini sui
parere conpellitur. Hoc itaque etiam beatus profeta Heremias ex per-
sona Domini exprobrat Iudeis, quod, abiecto eius famulatu, ido|la 15
colendo susciperint: *Non est placitum mihi in te inquit Dominus, quoniam a saeculo contriuisti iugum tuum, disrupisti uincula tua et di-
xisti Non seruio tibi*; hoc dicens remouisti a te dominationem meam.

4. *Qui habitat in caelis inredebit eos et Dominus subsannabit eos.*
Inefficaces casosque contra Dominum uult Iudeorum conatus osten- 20
dere, sicut et superius fecit dicendo *et populi meditati sunt inania.*
Etsi desideria, inquit, eorum atque opera uideantur impleta, uana
tamen eorum est omnis intentio, Domino actus eorum subsanna-
tione dignos risuque iudicante; per quod utique non solum inrita,
quae egerunt, sed et inutilia illis et noxia conprobantur. 25

5. *Tunc loquetur ad eos in ira sua et in furore suo conturbabit
eos.* Cum ea, quae audent atque moliuntur, perficerint, cum opus
uoluntatis suae impleuerint, crucifigentes et interficientes Dominum,
tunc motus ultoris pertinent, tunc iram uindicis sustenebunt, tunc
in omni conturbatione ac malis innumeris possiti operis sui me- 30
ritum cogentur agnoscere.

6-7 Ps. LXIII, 6^b   16-18 Ierem. II, 19-20   21 v. 1.

2 dicit] dauid *add. supra*   talia] uerba *add. supra*   3 talia] opera *add.
supra*   3-4 procesise *1ᵃ m.*   4-5 maximae *1ᵃ m.*   6 osoribus] *litt.* os *in rasura*
dixerunt] fecerunt *add. supra*   9 paruis *ms*   11 possunt] sicut *add. supra*
13 iugo] dati(uum) *add. supra*   pressus] p(rae)sus *ms*   14 parare *ms*   profeta]
pf *ms*   15 eius] filii *add. supra*   16-17 quoniam] *litt.* uo *in rasura*   18 non
seruio tibi *in rasura*   hoc] *siglum* est *add. supra*   23 intentio] *litt.* ti *in
rasura*   25 probantur *1ᵃ m.*   29-31 *verba* tunc-cogentur *litteris* a-h *infra aut
supra scriptis instructa sunt ad syntaxeos ordinem diuersum insinuandum.*

from godlessness by any thought of divine fear. Now, he means not that such things were said by the scribes and Pharisees, but that their behavior was such that language of that kind seems to have proceeded from the nature of their actions. It is, in fact, the custom of the divine Scripture, especially in the case of blessed David, to form a word on the basis of an action, as when he said of his calumniators, "They spoke of laying snares, they claimed, 'Who will see us?' "[7]—not that they said this, but that they acted in such a way that they thought no one would possibly detect their actions and deter them from their evil endeavors by observing them.

He calls the right of control *bonds and yokes* since, just as people constrained in bonds and put under the yoke are deprived of liberty and cannot follow their own will to the full either in behavior or in destination, so too the person whose lowly state subjects him to the yoke of slavery is forced to obey the orders of his master. The blessed prophet Jeremiah, speaking in the person of the Lord, also delivers this rebuke in similar terms to the Jews for rejecting his service and taking on the worship of idols: "I am not pleased with you," says the Lord, "because long ago you broke your yoke, you burst your bonds and said to me, 'I shall not serve you' "[8]—in other words, You removed yourself from my control.

He who dwells in the heavens will ridicule them, and the Lord will mock them (v. 4). He means to bring out the ineffectiveness of the Jews' efforts and endeavors against the Lord, as he did also above in saying *peoples made futile plans.* Even if their desires and actions seem to be put into effect, every purpose of theirs nonetheless is useless, the Lord judging their actions deserving of mockery and ridicule. For this reason, at any rate, what they did was not only pointless, but also shown to be both of no value to them and harmful. *At that time he will speak to them in his anger and confound them in his wrath* (v. 5): when they finish what they are attempting and striving for, when they carry out the deed they intend, crucifying the Lord and putting him to death, then they will feel the effect of the avenger's response, then they will bear the brunt of the judge's anger, then they will be reduced to complete confusion and innumerable troubles and be obliged to acknowledge what their exploits deserve. |

---

7. Ps 64:5.
8. Cf. Jer 2:20.

6. *Ego constitutus sum rex ab eo.* Hoc ex persona suscepti hominis, qui est crucifixus, inseritur, de quo et alibi ait: *Quid est*
homo quod memor es eius, aut filius hominis quoniam uisitas eum
usque *sub pedibus eius* ac reliqua, quae manifeste de suscepto ho-
5 mine dicta esse beatus Paulus ostendit dicens: *Contestatur autem*
quodam loco quis, dicens Quid est homo quod memor es eius, aut
filius hominis usque *coronasti eum.* Et subiungit: *Eum autem, qui*
modico quam angelus minoratus est, uidemus Iesum propter passio-
nem mortis gloria et honore coronatum. Deus enim Verbum non
10 est rex constitutus ex tempore, cuius utique non coepit ali|quando
sed fuit et est semper imperium; qui, ut in natura habuit creare
quae uoluit, ita in natura habet dominari omnium ut a se profecto iure factorum. Non ergo nuper additam et uelut nouellam
habet possesionem, quia inconueniens erat ut nihil iuris haberet
15 in his quae ipse condiderat. Susceptus itaque homo ius super
omnia dominationis accipit ab inhabitatore suo, Verbo suo, et hoc
manifeste indicat scriptura diuina, beato Dauid dicente: *Quid est*
homo quod memor es eius et reliqua; et apostolus Paulus hominem
adserit Iesum, cuius memor fuerit Deus et qui dignus tanto ho-
20 nore sit habitus. De hoc ergo et in praesenti profeta Dauid loquitur, id est suscepto homine a Deo Verbo, quod quidem etiam
ipse Dominus dictum esse testatur: *Domine dominus noster, quam*
admirabile est nomen tuum in uniuersa terra, quoniam eliuata est
magnificentia tua super caelos usque *sub pedibus eius* et reliqua.
25 Cum ingrederetur enim Hirusolimam occurrerunt ei pueri portantes
ramos palmarum et laudantes ac dicentes: *Osanna in excelsis, be-*
nedictus qui uenturus est in nomine Domini. Scribae uero inui-
dentes dixerunt ad eum: *Non uides quae isti dicunt?* Respondens
ait eis: *Etiam non legistis Ex ore infantium et lactantium perfi-*
30 *cisti laudem?* Si ergo ista dicta personae eius proprie conuenerunt,

---

2-4 Ps. VIII, 5-7   5-9 Hebr. II, 6-9   22-24 Ps. VIII, 1 ss.   25 Matth. XXI ss.
26 Matth. XXI, 9   27-30 Matth. XXI, 15-16; Ps. VIII, 3.

1 constitus *ms*   3 aut] .i. quid est *add. supra*   5 contestatur] .i. dauid
add. supra   6 dicens] d͞c͞s *ms ex* d͞r͞s   8 menoratus *ms ex* memoratus
9 hono͞ *1ᵃ m.*   12 omnium] elimentorum *add. supra*   13 nouellam] *litt.* u
in rasura   15 condiderat] considerat *ms*   17 dina *1ᵃ m.*   20 habetus *ms*
praesenti] .i. psalmo *add. supra*   profeta *conieci ut p. 10, l. 14*   22 dictum
conieci, d͞ic *ms*   destatur *videtur prius scriptum*   23 nomen] .i. iesus *add.*
supra   25 ei] .i. d(omin)o iesu *add. supra*   27 uenturus *in rasura,* uenit (?)
1ᵃ m.   nomine] .i. filius *add. supra*   28 eum] iesum *add. supra*   29 lac-
tantium] lact͞ *ms*   29-30 perficis *ms*   30 eius] christi *add. supra.*

I have been established as king by him (v. 6). This statement is made in the person of the assumed man who was crucified, of whom he also says elsewhere, "What is a man that you are mindful of him, or the son of a man that you watch over him … under his feet?" and so on. Blessed Paul shows that this refers clearly to the assumed man by saying, "But someone has testified somewhere in the words, 'What is a man that you are mindful of him, or the son of a man … crowned him,' " adding, "But him, who for a little while was made lower than the angels, we see to be Jesus, crowned with glory and honor on account of the suffering of death."[9] In other words, God the Word was not established as king when time began, since his rule did not begin at some point in time but has existed forever; just as by nature he had the power to create what he wanted, so by nature he has the power to rule over all things, duly made by him as they are. So he does not hold this as a recent and novel acquisition, since it would be inconceivable that he had no control over what he personally had created. It is therefore the assumed man that received the right of control over all things from his indweller, the Word; the divine Scripture clearly conveys this, blessed David saying, "What is a man that you are mindful of him?" and so on, and the apostle Paul identifies the man as Jesus, of whom God was mindful and who was considered worthy of such great honor.

It is of him, therefore, that David in prophetic mode speaks in the present psalm—namely, of the man assumed by God the Word—the Lord himself also confirming that this actually was said, "Lord, our Lord, how marvelous is your name in all the world, since your magnificence is raised up above the heavens … under his feet" and so on. When he entered Jerusalem, remember, those children met him carrying palm branches and praising him in the words "Hosanna in the highest, blessed is he who will come in the name of the Lord," whereas the scribes took exception and said to him, "Do you not see what they are saying?" In reply he said to them, "Have you not also read, 'From the mouths of infants and babes you have perfected praise'?"[10] If those words, then, were properly applicable to his person, | what follows is also

---

9. Cf. Ps 8:4–6; Heb 2:6–9.
10. Cf. Pss 8:1; 118:26; Matt 21:9, 15–16.

et reliqua conueniunt quae sequuntur, id est *Quid est homo quod memor es eius?* et *Minuisti eum paulum ab angelis* usque *sub pedibus eius.* Illum itaque hominem, cui tantus honor delatus sit et qui dominationem super omnia acciperit, beatus apostolus Iesum·esse confirmat, quoniam ex his quae dicta sunt alia constant 5 Deo, alia suscepto homini conuenire. Quomodo enim unus atque idem iuxta unam naturam et *memor* est et dignus memoria ducitur, uisitat atque uisitatur,| gloria uel honore coronat atque coronatur, dominationem super omnia confert et suscipit? Quomodo eti m possit intellegi de Deo Verbo quod dictum est *Minuisti eum* 10 *paulo minus ab angelis?* Per omnia igitur, quae dicta sunt, conprobatur hoc, quod dictum est *Ego autem constitutus sum rex ab eo,* ad adsumptum hominem pertinere, qui, ut omnium esset dominus, Deo Verbo conferente, hoc suscipit. Si quis uero dicat a Patre collatum esse homini, non a Verbo, non est ulla diuersitas 15 utrum a Deo Verbo an a Patre homo adsumtus sit tanto honore donatus.

Hoc solum mihi curae fuit ostendere nihil consequenter dicere eos, qui, ex dispensatione carnis adsumtae occasionem accipientes, semplices imperitosque decipiunt atque audent, cui datum sit 20 imperium et per hoc, minorem Vnigenitum Filium a parte deitatis accipere.

6b-7a. *Super Sion montem sanctum eius, praedicans praeceptum Domini.* Ita legendum atque intellegendum est: *Ego autem constitutus sum rex ab eo,* ut sit plena distinctio, et sequatur *super Sion* 25 *montem sanctum eius, praedicans praeceptum Domini.* Siquidem in Iudea maiore conuersatus tempore et studio dicendi instetit et insignorum curationumque opere atque admiratione uirtutis innotuit, unde dicit in euangelio: *Vae tibi Chorizain, uae tibi Bethsaida, quoniam si in Tyro et Sidone factae fuissent uirtutes olim in ci-* 30 *licio et cinere poenitentiam egissent.* Consequenter ergo superioribus iunguntur ista quae subdidit, id est: illi quidem operibus suis

---

1-3 Ps. VIII, 5-6, 7; vide infra, p. 43   11-17 cf. infra, p. 47-48   29-31 Matth. XI, 21.

3 dilatus *ms*   6 homine *ms*   7 memoria] ab(latiuum) *add. supra*   8 uitatur *1ᵃ m.*   honore] hōn *in textu,* re *add. supra*   coronat] .i. q(uo)mo(do) *add. supra*   11 sunt] ita *add. supra*   13 ad dsumptum *1ᵃ m.*   21 dietatis *ms*   27 conuersatis *ms*   27 _dicendi] .i. praedicationis *add. supra*   29 chorizai *1ᵃ m.*   31 poeniten *1ᵃ m.*   32 quidem] .i. iudei *add. supra.*

applicable, namely, "What is a man that you are mindful of him?" and "You have made him somewhat less than the angels … under his feet."

That man, therefore, on whom is conferred such great honor and who received rule over all things, blessed Paul confirms is Jesus, since while some of what is said refers to God, other things apply to the assumed man. After all, how can someone who is one and the same with respect to nature both be mindful and be thought worthy of being called to mind, watch over and be watched over, crown with glory and honor and be crowned, bestow rule over all things and receive it? How, likewise, can the statement "You have made him somewhat less the angels" be understood of God the Word? In all that was said, therefore, it is proven that the statement *I have been established as king by him* refers to the assumed man, who with God the Word conferring it received it so as to be Lord of all. If, on the other hand, you were to claim that it was conferred on the man by the Father, not by the Word, then there is no difference whether the assumed man was given such great honor by God the Word or by the Father. My sole concern was to demonstrate that there is consequently no truth in the claim of those who take occasion of the divine plan for taking flesh to deceive simple and unlearned people and presume to understand the only-begotten Son as inferior in respect of divinity because authority was given him.

On Sion his holy mountain, announcing the Lord's decree (vv. 6–7). The verse *But I have been established as king by him* should be read and understood as making a full distinction,[11] the logical sequel being *on Sion his holy mountain, announcing the Lord's decree.* In fact, he lived most of the time in Judah, devoted his attention to speaking, and gained a reputation for his work of signs and healing and by astonishment at his power—hence his saying in the Gospel, "Woe to you, Chorazin! Woe to you, Bethsaida! If the deeds of power had been worked in Tyre and Sidon, they would long ago have repented in dust and ashes."[12] So what follows should be related in theme to the above—that is to say, While they | are thought worthy of derision for

---

11. The distinction, that is, between the Word and the assumed man.
12. Matt 11:21.

digni inrisione sunt habiti, *ego autem* a Deo super omnia ius do-
minationis accipi, commoratusque in Iudea auditores | salutaribus
doctrinis institui; ex hoc autem ipso suplicio maiore sunt digni,
quia, cum in medio eorum uersarer, ad salutem tamen duci ne-
5 que perfectione magisterii mei, neque signorum multitudine atque
nouitate uoluerunt.

7ᵇ⁻ᶜ. *Dominus dixit ad me Filius meus es tu, ego hodie genui te.*
Ad eum sine dubio Filium dictum hoc referendum est, cui potest
praesentis temporis generatio conuenire et cuius natiuitatis diem
10 totus profecto orbis agnouit; illam autem generationem, quae ante
omnia tempora ex Patre est, Dei Verbi, non potuit fini, id est tempori, subiecere, quod praesentis diei appellatione signatur. Nam et
illud, quod dictum est *Hodie si uocem eius audieritis* et reliqua,
ita intellegendum est, ut non ad infinitum tempus, sicut quidam
15 putant, sed ad finitum praesensque referatur: finitum namque tempus in numero dierum est; hoc enim ipsum *hodie* indicat de praesenti tempore se dicere. Nam et nos tali appellatione, id est *hodie*,
praesens tempus consueuimus indicare; et, quoniam non infinitum
tempus tali signetur indicio, ostendit beatus apostolus dicens: *Ite-*
20 *rum determinat diem quendam, in Dauid dicendo Hodie si uocem*
eius audieritis. Hodie itaque ad finiti temporis spectat indicium,
quia infinitum non potest tali appellatione signari; unde et in praesenti lectione *hodie*, quod dictum est, ad illam aetatem refferendum quae erat in manibus, cui conpetebat Domini generatio cor-
25 poralis.

8. *Postola a me, et dabo tibi gentes hereditatem, et possessionem*
tuam terminos terrae. Aduersum heriticos quidem, ut haec non de
Deo Verbo sed de homine accipiantur, sufficienter in superioribus
actum uidetur; eadem sine dubio consequentia etiam haec, qua su-
30 periora, dicta sunt a profeta. Nunc iam contra Iudeos nobis sermo

---

13 Ps. XCIV, 8   19-21 Hebr. IV, 7.

1 habeti *ms*   4 mdio *ms*   eorum] iudeorum *add. supra*   5 magistri
uidetur scripsisse 1ᵃ m. magist(e)rii *corr.*   8 dubuio *ms*   filium *conieci,*
filii *ms*   10 profecto] adu(erbium) *add. supra*   11 fini∗ *ms*   14 intelle-
gendum] .i. hodie *add. supra*   quidem *ms*   15 sed ad infinitum *1ᵃ m.*   finitum namque] infinitum namque *ms*   16 hodie] die *1ᵃ m.*   20 uocem] uo-
uem *ms*   22 appellatione] .i. hodie *add. supra*   23 aetatem] filii *add. supra*
23-24 reffendum *1ᵃ m.,* est *add. supra*   24 in manibus] in praesenti *add. supra*
30 iudeos] ideos *ms*

their actions, I on the contrary received the right of control over all things, and dwelling in Judah I taught the listeners salutary doctrines. They deserve greater punishment for the reason that, though I lived in their midst, they refused to be led to salvation either by the perfection of my teaching or by the great number and novelty of the signs.

The Lord said to me, *You are my son, today I have begotten you.* Doubtless this statement should be referred to that son to whom generation in the present time can apply, and the day of whose birth the whole world surely acknowledges. The generation of God the Word, on the other hand, which is from the Father before all time, could not be subjected to limitation—namely, of time—as is suggested by mention of the present day. That statement, "If today you hear his voice" and so on,[13] you remember, is also to be understood in such a way that there is reference not to unlimited time, as some commentators think, but to the finite and present time. Time, of course, is determined by number of days, the very term *today* suggesting that there is reference to the present time. We are, after all, in the habit of indicating the present time by such a term, namely, *today;* the fact that unlimited time is not conveyed by such a term the blessed apostle shows in saying, "Again he sets a particular day by saying through David, 'If today you hear his voice.' "[14] "Today" therefore implies a limited time, because unlimited time cannot be conveyed by such a term; hence also in the reading *today* before us, what is said is to be referred to the time current when the bodily generation of the Lord was due.

Ask it of me, and I shall give you the nations for an inheritance and the ends of the earth for your possession (v. 8). It seems that enough was done above in opposition to heretics to offset this being taken in reference not to God the Word but to the human being; doubtless this too is said, like the above, by the inspired author to the same effect. At this point let some words be addressed by us in opposition to the Jews. | Let us ask them, therefore,

13. Ps 95:7.
14. Heb 4:7.

moueatur. | Interrogemus igitur illos quas gentes in hereditatem
et quos in possesionem terminos terrae Dauid beatus acciperit,
quando ita regnauerit ut ei totus subiceretur orbis, quando imperio eius ultimi terrarum fines accesserint. Si responderint: Quando
accipit hereditatem gentium et quarum sibi armis regna subiecit, — 5
id est uicinarum proximarumque nationum, — terminos autem
terrae dici fines Iudeae regionis multis locis scripturae diuinae
testimonio comprobari, interrogemus illos: Hoc, quod ait *Postola et
dabo tibi gentes* usque *terrae*, ac subiungitur:

9. *Reges eos in uirga ferrea* usque *fringes eos*, in commoni pu- 10
tent, — id est ad utrumque refferendum, ut sit et de gentibus et
de terminis Iudae terrae dictum, — aut de solis Iudeae terminis?
Dicens enim *et possessionem tuam terminos terrae*, statim iunxit:
Reges eos in uirga ferrea usque *eos*. Sub hac ergo condicione, o
Iudei, beatus Dauid in uos ius accipit imperii, ut uos comminueret 15
atque contereret, non ut prouidentia sua regeret atque defenderet?
Quid? Quod non legitur uobis ita praefuisse? Nam alio in loco ita
de ipso dicitur: *Elegit Dauid seruum suum*, ac motus imperii eius
dictis talibus explicatur: *Et pauit eos in innocentia cordis sui*; al-
ligatur mansuetudo cordis eius, ut non uideatur dure uobis et cru- 20
diliter imperasse. Quomodo igitur audebitis dicere ab hoc illum a
Deo percepisse imperium in uos et ita uos Deo fuisse uechimenter
exosos, ut constitueret uobis regem, qui uos non aleret et foueret,
sed ad similitudinem uasis fictilis suo rigore contereret? Sed neque
eritis tam amentes, ut uos saltim pudor ab hac profesione non re- 25
trahat!

Non ergo conueniunt | beato Dauid ista quae dicta sunt, Do-
mino uero iunguntur aptissime, cuius regnum porregitur ad ultimas terrae extrimasque regiones atque ad totius mundi partes
extenditur; qui, tam gentium quam Iudeorum statum percussum 30
uirga deiecit atque comminuit, non ut eos perdiret, sed ut in me-
·lius reformaret cogeretque, depossito uetere homine, in nouum per

---

18 Ps. LXXVII. 70   19 Ps. LXXVII. 72.

1 moueatur, interrogemus] imper(atiuum) *add. supra*   4 si] adit interrogemus *add. supra*   6 uiciniarum *ms*   6-7 autem terrae] si responderint
add. supra   8 hoc quod ait] adit putant *add. supra*   10-11 putent] .i. interrogemus *add. in margine*   11 sit] r(e)l(iqua) *add. supra*   20 uedeatur *1ᵃ m.*
21 illum] Dauid *add. supra*   22 praecipisse *uidetur prius scriptum*   24 con-
teret *ms*, uos *add. supra*   neque] nequaquam *add. supra*   25 hac] haec *1ᵃ m.*
27 conuenierunt *ms*.

Which *nations* did blessed David receive *as an inheritance* and which *ends of the earth as a possession,* when did he so reign as to have the whole world in subjection to him, when did the furthest limits of the earth come under his command? If they were to reply, When he received an inheritance of nations and by force of arms brought their kingdoms under subjection to himself— namely, nations near and close by (in many places in the divine Scripture it is confirmed that the territory of the region of Judah is called *the ends of the earth*)—let us ask them, Do they think that this verse, *Ask and I shall give you nations* down to *of the earth,* and the following verse, *You will rule them with a rod of iron* down to *smash them* (v. 9), are to be referred in general to both, so that it is directed both to the nations and to the boundaries of the land of Judah, or only to the boundaries of Judah? After saying *and the ends of the earth for your possession,* note, he immediately went on with *You will rule them with a rod of iron down to them.*

This being so, Jews, did blessed David receive the right of command so as to threaten and belabor you, not to rule and defend you with his providence? What? Do we not read that he ruled in this fashion? In another place, in fact, it is likewise said of him, "He chose his servant David," and the administration of his reign is recounted in such words, "He pastured them in the innocence of his heart,"[15] adducing his gentleness of heart, so that he does not seem to have ruled you harshly and cruelly. How, then, do you presume to claim from this that he received authority over you from God and you were so extremely hateful to God that he set a king over you, not to nourish and foster you, but to smash you in severity like a potter's vase? You will, however, not be so deranged that shame at least will fail to deter you from this claim.

Far from what was said being in reference to David, then, it most appropriately applies to the Lord, whose reign reaches the furthest and most remote regions of the earth and extends to the parts of the whole world. With a rod he struck, dislodged, and threatened the condition of both Gentiles and Jews, not to destroy them, but to reform them and force them to lay aside the old self and advance to the new through the | sacraments of baptism.[16] With the

---

15. Ps 78:70, 72.

16. Cf. Rom 6:4–6. The Latin text speaks of *sacramenta,* perhaps referring to several stages of initiation.

babtismi sacramenta migrare. Hoc namque indicare uolens beatus
Dauid profecto ait: *sicut uas figuli confringes eos*, ostendens per
similitudinem quoniam

contritione eorum non esset per-
5 ditio, sed innouatio secutura;
haec est etiam figuli omnis intentio, ut uasa, si non sunt facientis
manum ac uoluntatem secuta,
dum adhuc uiridia sunt et non-
10 dum fornace durata, comminuat
ac formanda rursus rotae inpo-
nat; huic namque sensui etiam
beatus Heremias perhibet testimonium, loquens ex persona Dei:
15 *Aut sicut figulus iste non potero
uos facere, domus Israel? dicit
Dominus*, hoc est lapsos e manibus meis reparare rursus nequeo,
et in meliorem statum formam-
20 que conuertere?

Οὐχ ὥστε ἀπολέσαι καὶ ἀναλῶ-
σαι συντρίβει, ἀλλ᾽ ὥστε ἀναπλάσαι·
πρὸς τοῦτο γὰρ σκοπὸς τῷ κεραμεῖ
συντρίβειν τὰ οἰκεῖα σκεύη ὅταν μὴ
ὑγιῆ καὶ ἀκέραιον σώζῃ τοῦ κεραμέως
τὴν διάπλασιν, οὐδέπω πυρὶ προσω-
μιληκότα· τούτοις δὲ μαρτυρεῖ καὶ ὁ
μακάριος Ἰερεμίας ὁ προφήτης λέγων
ὡς ἐκ Θεοῦ·ʼʼΗ καθὼς ὁ κεραμεὺς οὗτος
οὐ δυνήσομαι τοῦτο ποιῆσαι ὑμῖν, οἶκος
Ἰσραήλ; λέγει Κύριος, τουτέστι οὕτως
καὶ διαπεσόντας ἀναπλάσαι, καὶ πάλιν εἰς τὸ ἀρχαῖον ἀποκαταστῆσαι;

10. *Et nunc, reges, intellegite; erudemini, qui iudicatis terram.*
Iam utilitas exortationis inducitur et prouocantur omnes, ut ad
credendum Domino properantes accedant; necesarie autem ad reges
sermo diregitur, quoniam ipsi Christo dificilius crediderunt et non
25 parua inpedimenta etiam aliis credere uolentibus adtulerunt, dum
ad accesum fidei terrorem persecutionis opponunt; unde consequenter ipsos exortationis istius sermo conpellat.

11. *Seruite Domino in timore* usque *tremore.* Non coactum, ad
quem prouocat, sed deuotum uult esse famulatum; et ob hoc, quia
30 dixerat: *Seruite Domino in timore*, ne quis existimaret degenerem
illam, | quae extremae condicionis est, imperare formidinem, intulit

15-16 Ierem. XVIII, 6.

4 contritione] contritionem *videtur prius scriptum* 5 innouatio] *litt.* ou
in rasura 6 haec] *sequuntur litt.* n con (?), nam *interpretatus est Ascoli* fin-
guli *1ᵃ m.* 18 nequeo] *litt.* eo et *in rasura* 22 iam] hinc *add. supra* 23 ne-
cesariae *ms* 25 adtulerunt] .i. reges *add. supra* 26-27 sequenter *1ᵃ m.*

Οὐχ — ἀποκαταστῆσαι: (Θεοδώ. Αντιοχ) Vat. gr. 754, fol. 39 (Maius, p. 390, unde
P. G., 649 A 10-B 4); Paris. 166, fol. 4ᵛ-5; *inter Eusebiana* (P. G., XXIII, 89 D 9-92
A 7) *eadem irrepserunt.*

intention of conveying this, in fact, blessed David immediately said, *You will smash them like a potter's vase,* bringing out through a comparison that he smashes them not to ruin and waste them, but to reshape them. Such is the potter's purpose in breaking his own vessels, you see, when they are not sound and flawless and do not keep to the potter's molding, and when they are not yet fired. The blessed prophet Jeremiah confirms this when speaking on God's part, "'Or am I not able like this potter to do this to you, house of Israel?' says the Lord"[17]—namely, to reshape you in this fashion when you have fallen and to make you as good as new again.

And now, kings, understand; be instructed, you who judge the earth (v. 10). At this point the usefulness of exhortation is applied, and all are summoned to make their approach in haste to believe in the Lord. Now, the address is of necessity made to *kings,* since they were the ones who had more difficulty in believing in Christ and even raised no small problems for others prepared to believe, while setting the frightening prospect of persecution against the approach of faith. Hence the thrust of that exhortation logically brought pressure to bear on them. *Serve the Lord in fear* down to *trembling* (v. 11). He wishes the service to which he calls them to be not obligatory but voluntary; and on account of his saying *Serve the Lord in fear,* he added *Rejoice in him with trembling* in case he should think that he was requiring that unseemly dread which is characteristic of one's desperate plight. | By

---

17. Jer 18:6. For a few lines at this stage we have a fragment of a Greek manuscript extant, to which the Latin corresponds quite closely. The translation will be of the Greek where it is available, significant differences in the Latin being noted.

Exultate ei cum tremore. Per primum uersiculum, dum sollicitum seruitium imperat, uoluit honorem eius, cui seruiendum esset, ostendere, quia quanto sublimior est cui parendum est, tanto sollicitius ad officia eius acceditur; per sequentem uero laeti, non tristis animi subiectionem uerbo exultationis expraesit, et quae non 5 meroris causa futura esset seruientibus sed saluationis: nam, dum talis domini obedimus imperiis, et uitae nostrae consulimus et bono conscientiae purgatioris implemur.

12. *Adpraehendite disciplinam, ne quando irascatur Dominus.*

Volens nos tenacius diuinis magisteriis inherere, conuenienti uoce, ut disciplinam compraehenderemus, admonuit.

'Απρὶξ ἡμᾶς ἔχεσθαι τῆς τοῦ 10 Κυρίου διδασκαλίας βουλόμενος, εἰκότως τῇ τοῦ δράξασθε φωνῇ κέχρηται.

Et pereatis de uia iusta usque *eius.* Sciens profeta uirtutes pro praemiis, uitia numerare pro poenis, id pro maximo supplicio comminatur, ad quod illos neglecto Domini magisterio studia sua erant 15 uoluntasque raptura: scilicet, quod si nolint doctrinis caelestibus erudiri, per iram ulciscentis Domini a uiis iustitiae efficerentur alieni. His igitur dictis timorem inieciens auditori debuit, per quod inuitaretur subiecere, et ideo necesarie addidit: *Beati omnes qui* 20 *confidunt in eo.*

PSALMVS III

Psalmus hic proprium et specialem habet titulum et quidem ** uel inscriptione eum super alia praenotare. Dictus est autem a beato Dauid id temporis, quo Abisalon inuasso imperio aduersum eum 25 parricidalia arma arripuit.

25 II Reg. XV.

3 sublior *1ª m.*   parandum *ms*   4 per sequentem] .i. uersiculum *add. supra*   6 salautis *ms*   7 imperis *ms*   9 israscatur *ms*   11 magistris *1ª m.*, doctrinis *add. supra*   conueniente *1ª m.*   12 ut] aut *1ª m.*   14 et] .i. ne *add. supra*   15 praenis *ms*   17-19 *verba* scilicet-alieni *litteris* a-f *supra aut infra exaratis distinguuntur ad ordinem syntaxeos diuersum insinuandum* 19 per quod] subauditur .id. *add. supra*   22 expli(cit) psalmus ii. incipit iii *ms* 23 proprium] propri*um *ms*   ** *lacunam statui; cf. anonyma paraphasis* (CORD., p 40): 'Ακόλουθον ἔχει τὴν ἐπιγραφὴν τῇ ὑποθέσει   23-24 quidem uel in *supra rasuram*   24 inscriptione] ab(latiuum), tituli *add. supra*   eum] psalmum *add. supra*   26 parridalia *1ª m.*

'Απρὶξ — κέχρηται: (Θεο^δ αυ⁻) Vat. gr. 754, fol. 39ᵛ (Maius, p. 390, unde P. G., 649 A 12-14).

the first clause, where he required devoted service, he wishes to bring out the dignity of the one who is to be served, because the higher the personage to be obeyed, the greater devotion one brings to his service, whereas in the following clause he brought out by the word *rejoicing* the subjection of a soul that is not sad but joyful, and a subjection that would be the cause not of grief but of salvation to those who serve. When we obey the commands of such a master, you see, we serve the interests of our life and are filled with the benefit of a clearer conscience.

Embrace instruction lest the Lord be angry (v. 12). In his wish that we cling more closely to the divine teachings, he was right to apply the word *embrace. And lest you stray from the straight and narrow* down to *his wrath.* Being in the habit of counting virtues as rewards and vices as punishments, the inspired author makes a threat of the severest penalty for those who would neglect the Lord's teaching and whose own pursuits and pleasures would distract them—namely, for refusing to be instructed in heavenly doctrines, they would become strangers to the ways of righteousness through the wrath of the avenging Lord. Having thus instilled fear by these words, he was obliged to add a positive recommendation, and so of necessity he went on to say *Blessed are those who trust in him.*

PSALM 3

This psalm has its own special title and actually gives a premonition of its contents with the dedication.[1] It was composed by blessed David at the time when Absalom usurped power and took arms against him as a parricide.[2] |

---

1. Devreesse supposes that a lacuna has developed in the text at this point, the sense nevertheless being clear.
2. Cf. 2 Sam 13–17.

2. *Domine, quid multiplicati sunt qui tribulant me?* Manifesta
dictorum intellegentia; unde breuiter contra eos aliqua dicenda
sunt, qui uolunt eum non in persona Dauid, sed in populi esse
conscriptum. Animad|uertendum est igitur, quod uelut deflens et
5 conquerens beatus Dauid inducitur, eo quod ad augendam tribulationem eius multiplicatus sit numerus persequentium, et ad bellum ei inferendum conuenerint etiam hii qui prius non fuerant
inimici. Quorum quidem auxerit numerum partis aduersae contra
populum uero Israel hostis nulla uelut nouella seditio aut recens
10 tumultus exciuerat, quia gentes finitimae antiquo odio bellum gerebant aduersum Iudeos nullo foedere componendum.

3. *Multi insurgunt aduersum me.*

Aperte hoc ostenditur in per- | *Τοῦτο φανερώτερον δείκνυσιν ἐπὶ*
sona Dauid oportere nos huius | *τοῦ Δαυὶδ δεῖν λέγεσθαι τὸν ψαλ-*
15 psalmi intellegentiam uindicare: | *μόν· τὸ γὰρ « ἐπανίστασθαι » κυρίως*
insurgere enim proprie dicuntur | *λέγεται ἐπὶ τῶν πρότερον μὲν ἐν*
hii qui fuerunt antea subiecti, | *ὑπηκόων τάξει καθεστότων, μετὰ δὲ*
quique nuper subduxisse colla a | *ταῦτα πόλεμον ἀραμένων.*
iugo obidientiae conprobantur.

20 4. *Multi dicunt animae meae* usque in *Deo eius.* Consequenter
memoria dicti huius inseritur, per quod plurimum meroris acciperat: nam inter reliqua tribulationum mala grauius animam contumilia insultationis exasperat. Haec autem aduersum beatum Dauid
inimicorum obpropria erant religiosae mentis eius insignia. Nam
25 cum dicunt: *Non est salus ipsi in Deo eius*, ob hoc quod aliquid
in eum aduersis licuerit, satis ostendunt illum Dei adiutorio
semper innisum numquam fuisse inter discrimina successu pro-
spero distitutum; ideoque in praesenti ad exprobrationem inimicorum agitur, quare salus eius, quae erat in Deo possita, nutare
3) credatur.

---

3 eum] psalmum *add. supra*   8 quorum] .i. inimicorum *add. supra*
9 hostis] gen (gens, gentes?) *add. supra*   8-10 quorum — exciuerat] *sensus
non adeo clarus, ut nulla suspicatur lacuna*   10 finitiuae *ms*   19 iugo] ab(latiuum) *add. supra*   20 maeae *1ª m.*   22 grauis *ms*   24 erant *sequuntur
litt. quattuor omnino erasae*   25 ali*quid   26 aduersis] inimicis *add. supra*
27 sucessu *ms*   28 praesenti] psalmo *add. supra.*

Τοῦτο — ἀραμένων: (Θεο^δ ἀντιο^χ) Vat. 754, fol. 40; 1422, fol. 28ᵛ; Paris. 139,
fol. 13ᵛ (Mai, p. 390 ex Vat. 1682, fol. 11; P. G., 649 C); Agellius, p. 26.

2

Lord, why have those who oppress me become so numerous? (v. 1). The sense of the words is clear; hence something should be briefly said against those who take it as composed in the person not of David but of the people. Note should therefore be taken of the fact that blessed David is introduced as lamenting and perplexed for the reason that adding to his tribulation, the number of his persecutors is increased, and even those who previously were not hostile to him have joined forces to make war on him. No enemy increased their number as a hostile group as though an unexpected plot or recent uprising had developed against the people of Israel, because the neighboring peoples waged war against the Jews on the basis of a long-standing hatred without being combined in any new alliance.

Many people rise up against me. This brings out more clearly that the psalm should be read in reference to David, the verb *rise up* being properly applied to those who formerly were placed in the position of subjects but later declared war. *Many people say to my soul down to his God* (v. 2). Mention of this remark, which caused him most grief, occurs in keeping with the theme: amidst the other tribulations the great insult in the criticism upset him more severely. This reproach of his enemies to blessed David, however, was testimony to his pious frame of mind: when they claim, *There is no help for him in his God,* from the fact that his enemies took some satisfaction from this they clearly show that he always relied on God's help and never was bereft of a favorable outcome amidst his changing fortunes. Hence, in the present case the intention is to upbraid his enemies for believing that his security, which had rested upon God, was faltering. |

5. *Tu autem, Domine, susceptor* usque *caput meum*. Consideranda constantis animi firmitas, quae inter aduersa maxime conprobatur, quia de spei suae propossito, etiam inter angores maximos, nihil remisit. Illi, inquam, inludentes mihi talia loquuntur in doloris augmentum, ego uero id semel, | quod credidi, sperare non disinam 5 quoniam tu, Domine, laborantem adiuues et a malo periculi instantis ereptum in gradum dignitatis restituas et honoris.

6. *Voce mea ad Dominum clamaui*. Maximae fidei est, et quae de ferendo Dei sibi adiutorio nihil hessitationis admisserit, ad confidentiam postulationis accedere; statim enim sequitur: 10
Et exaudiuit me de monte sancto suo. Sufficit illi ad omnium, quae postulauerat, inpetrationem ad Dominum cum fidei suffragio proclamare. Montem uero sanctum dicit montem Sion, in quo et templum aedificari Deo placuit et hostias immolari, in quo etiam, secundum opinionem Iudeorum, Deus specialiter habitare credeba- 15 tur, sicut in viiii psalmo legitur: *Psalite Domino qui habitat in Sion*.

7. *Ego dormiui et soporatus sum*. Post tribulationem, quae praeceserat, liberatio secura promititur; dicendo autem: *Ego dormiui et soporatus sum*, humiliatum se tribulationum nimietate ac fuisse anxium confitetur, et subiungit: 20
Exsurrexi, quoniam Dominus suscipit me. Ostendit merore se magis quam somno fuisse resolutum dicendo *Dominus suscipit me*. Nam post commonem soporem, quo membra marcescunt, non magno molimine ac labore consurgetur.

8. *Non timebo milia populi circumdantis me*. Qui in tribulatio- 25 nibus suis non est loco motus, ut de Dei adiutorio disperaret, neque est uerbis exprobrantium de fidei statione depulsus, multo magis post Dei in se beneficia, quibus omnis desolutus est nexus angorum, confidenter clamat: *Non timebo milia populi circumdantis me*, experimento praecedentis adiutorii satis eruditus. 30

16 Ps. IX, 12.

5 id] .i. *ms* sperare] *litt.* per *in rasura* (superare?) 6 domine] d̄n̄ *1ᵃ m.* a malo] amabo *1ᵃ m.* 9 de ferendo] e ferendo *1ᵃ m., litt.* d *supra addita* 11 sufficit *sequuntur litt. tres erasae* illi] dauid *add. supra* 13 montentem *ms* 16 sicut in] in *add. supra* 25 circumdantis *conieci,* circūm *ms et ita infra* qui in trib.] adit clamat *add. supra* 26 loco] ab(latiuum) *add. supra* 30 adiutori *1ᵃ m.*

On the contrary, Lord, you are protector down to *my head* (v. 3). The stability that is demonstrated in particular against opposition is to be regarded as that of an unflinching mind in that, even amidst intense trials, it in no way withdraws the commitment of its hopes. They say such things, he means, to mock me and add to my suffering, whereas once I have placed my trust, I shall not cease hoping, since you, Lord, help me in my hardships, snatch me from the evil of impending danger, and restore me to the position of esteem and honor. *I cried aloud to the Lord* (v. 4). It is a mark of complete trust, one that unfailingly wins a person God's help, to achieve confidence in petition; in fact, the text immediately proceeds *He hearkened to me from his holy mountain.* It is sufficient for him to proclaim to the Lord with a vote of confidence the gaining of his petitions. Now, it is Mount Sion he calls *holy mountain,* for on it, according to the Jews' thinking, God was believed to dwell in a special manner, as it says in Psalm 9, "Sing praise to the Lord, who dwells in Sion."[3]

I slept and lost consciousness (v. 5). After the preceding tribulation a secure release is promised; by saying *I slept and lost consciousness* he admits that he was humbled by the extremity of tribulations and was at a loss, and he goes on, *I rose up because the Lord uplifts me.* He brings out that it was more from grief than from sleep that he was relieved when he says *the Lord uplifts me:* after ordinary sleep, in which limbs are relaxed, getting up involves no great effort and exertion. *I shall not be afraid of thousands of people surrounding me* (v. 6). The person who in his times of tribulation is not brought to the point of despairing of God's help, and is not dislodged from his steady faith by words of reproach, much more confidently declares, after God's favors to him by which the entire tangle of anxiety is loosed, *I shall not be afraid of thousands of people surrounding me,* quite convinced as he is by the experience of previous assistance. |

---

3. Ps 9:11.

9. *Exsurge, Domine, saluum me fac* usque *sine causa*. Iterum
tutionem a Deo suae salutis implorat. Quaeritur sane a | quibus-
dam, quare frequenter in psalmis inueniatur ista diuersitas, ut in
uno atque eodem loco nunc pro absolutione malorum refert gra-
5 tias, nunc iterum quasi nondum liberatus et adhuc in malis possitus se postulat liberari. Hoc, siue in sua siue in aliorum persona
faciat, spiritu profecto profetali implente se loquitur; quod aliquando
quidem sint in aduersis, aliquando quidem agant soluta tribulatione
securos animos, et nunc in requie laeti sint ac paulo post in an-
10 gore suspirentur, uarie igitur status et condicionis eorum diuersitas
indicatur. Huius autem rei causa utraque praelocutus est ut ea, quae
eis euentura erant, longe ante praenoscerent, et in malis possiti
absolutionis secuturae solacio non carerent; atque ex hoc ipso quod
praedicta mala uidebant rebus impleri et fidem sermonis profetici
15 exitu conprobari, de bonis quoque, quae similiter adnuntiata fuerant, disperare non possint. Curae igitur fuit profeticae non uaticinia sua per sequentiam dictionis ornare, sed inpendentia populis
sermone digerere, siue essent illa tristia siue laetiora. Quae quidem
ideo, ut diximus, praedicit omnia, ut cum in praedictorum malo-
20 rum, quae illis Deus peccantibus inferebat, experimenta uenissent
et facti essent correptione meliores, minime de promisione prosperitatis ambigerent. Exemplo utique tristium, quae exitu suo inesse
ueritatem dictis profeticis adprobant, siue uero de aliis siue de se
ipso profetet, has alternationes, quarum utilitatem praecedens sermo
25 patefecit, curat sollicite suis dictis inserere. Et ipse quidem inter
aduersa possitus nouerat per Spiritus sancti gratiam quod esset a
tribulatione liberandus; tamen ideo interdum angores suos deflet,
interdum uelut a malis omnibus absolutus agit gratias, ut exemplum eius apud alios utilitatem eruditionis operaretur et eos
30 emendationi per conuersionem studere non pigeat, quandoquidem
uident et istum multam habentem fiduciam in Domino nunc hu-
miliari et deieci, nunc a malis mirabiliter erui et honore facta rerum conuersione restitui. Signanter autem possuit *aduersantes mihi*

2-3 q(ui)b(us)d. *ms*, am uiris *add. supra*   7 implete *1ᵃ m.*   9 animos
suppl. supra   paulo *in rasura*   10 supirentur *1ᵃ m.*   13 carent *ms*   atque]
aq *ms*, atq(ue) *add. supra*   16 possit *1ᵃ m.*   18 digere *1ᵃ m.* re *add. supra*
21 et] cum *add. supra*   correptione] corrupt. *ms*, in tormentis *add. supra*
22 exemplo] adit curat *add. supra*   23-25 *verba* ueritatem — inserere *litteris*
a-d *supra scriptis ad syntaxeos ordinem insinuandum instructa sunt*   23 alis *ms*
24 sermo *suppl. in margine*   28 uel *1ᵃ m.*   29 eius] dauid *add. supra*   alios
om. 1ᵃ m.   32 et honore] et ** (in?) *ms*   33 conuersatione *ms*.

Arise, Lord, make me safe down to *without cause* (v. 7). Once more he begs a guarantee of his safety from God. The question is raised, at least by certain commentators, why it is that frequently in the psalms a diversity is found of such a nature that in one and the same place he gives thanks for relief from troubles in one breath, whereas in another breath he begs to be delivered as though not yet freed and still caught up in troubles. Doubtless he is filled with the prophetic spirit in saying this, whether doing so on his own account or in the person of others, be they sometimes in difficulties, be they at other times acting free from tribulation, now rejoicing in respite and shortly after sighing in agony, with the result that difference in their situation is suggested in various ways. For this reason he foretold both situations so that they might know well ahead of time what would happen to them, and when they found themselves in trouble, they would not be deprived of the comfort of the relief that would follow; and from the fact that they saw the predicted troubles coming into effect and their faith in the inspired word confirmed by the outcome, they would not be able to despair also of the good things that likewise had been forecast. It therefore was the role of prophetic responsibility not to dress up its oracles in sequence of expression, but to convey in speech what was about to befall the people, depressing or pleasant.

He foretells all this, therefore, as we said, so that when they came to experience the troubles prophesied that God inflicted on them for their sins, and they were reformed through chastisement, they would have no doubts about the promise of prosperity. By the example of depressing events, for instance, which by their occurrence prove the presence of truth in a prophet's statements, whether he prophesied about others or about himself, he takes great pains to insert in his statements these alternations, whose usefulness the preceding remarks exposed. Finding himself actually caught up in difficulties, he came to realize though the grace of the Holy Spirit that he was due to be freed from tribulation; yet on occasion he deplores his grief, on occasion he gives thanks as though rid of all troubles, so that his example may bring others the benefit of understanding, and they may not tire of attending to their reform through conversion, especially when they see the man with great trust in the Lord at one time humiliated and brought low, and at another time marvelously rescued from troubles and restored to respectability through the change in circumstance.

Now, it was significant of him to express it thus, *opposing me | without*

sine causa, ostendens quoniam iuste in illos a Deo uindicatum sit, qui ledere eum in nullo lesi et nocere uoluissent.

Dentes peccatorum contriuisti. Ita in uindictam mei seueritatis tuae manus motata est, ita inimicorum ora pulsauit, ut *dentes eorum*, quos in me acuebant, intigros esse non sineret; per quod no- 5 xios conatus eorum non solum ostendit uotiuo exitu destitutos, sed etiam iusta ultione conpraesos.

9. *Domini est salus, super* usque *tua*. Quoniam ex eodem tempore ab eo pars populi maxima dissidebat et quidam sequebantur Abesalon, quidam uero pro eius defensione certabant, hoc ait 10 quoniam cum a te [inquit] nobis salus facta fuerit, id est depulso periculo uitae securitas restituta, erit etiam super populum tuum benedictio tua. Quae est ista Dei benedictio? Sine dubio pax, sicut et in multis locis ait: *Pax super Israel*, in quibus uult ostendere benedictionis loco pacem populo conferendam, quam post 15 captiuitatis solutionem, inter se depossita simultate, quae prius dissederant, tribus habuerunt.

PSALMVS IIII

In praesenti psalmo beatus Dauid conuincit eos, qui ultro mundum adserunt ex se stetisse et audent dicere nulla prouidentia gu- 20 bernacula humanis rebus adhiberi, probatione uel a se petita uel a commoni omnium uiuentium cura, quibus dispensatrix Dei liberalitas bona cuncta largitur.

2. *Cum inuocarem exaudisti me, Deus iustitiae meae*. | Quoniam moris est dicere his qui uolunt a praesenti rerum statu dispensa- 25 tionem rationis amouere: Nulla Deo rerum homanarum cura est;

---

14 Ps. CXXIV, 5.

---

4 mota *1ᵃ m.*   5 in me] in memo(res?) *prius scriptum*   per quod] .i. p(rae)dīc (praedicti?) *add. supra*   6 uotiuo *** *ms*   9 desedebat *ms*   10 quidam] *litt.* am *add. supra*   eius] dauid *add. supra*   11 inquit *reieci*   13 quae est] .i. interro(gatio) *add. supra*   15 confer*endam *ms*   16 simultate] *litt.* tate *in rasura*   17 desiderant *ms*   18 explicit psalmus iii, incipit iiii *ms* 19 salmo *1ᵃ m.*   ultra *ms*   20 ex se stetisse *conieci*, exstetisse *ms*   [21 a se] .i. dauid *add. supra*   22-23 libertas *1ᵃ m.*   24 exaudīs *ms*   24-25 qnouiam moris est] adit consurgit *add. supra*.

cause, showing that it was right for vengeance to be taken on them by God, since they wanted to injure and harm him without injury dealt on his part. *You broke the teeth of sinners:* in such a way was the hand of your severity lifted in avenging me, in such a way did it strike the mouths of the enemy, as not to leave in one piece their *teeth,* which they sharpened to attack me. In this he shows their vicious endeavors not only failing to achieve their goal, but also meeting their just deserts.

Salvation belongs to the Lord down to *your blessing* (v. 7). Since from that time most of the people deserted him, and some followed Absalom, while some fought on his side, he says, When salvation comes to us from you—that is, when life is made secure with the removal of the danger—your blessing will also fall on your people. What is that *blessing* of God? Peace, doubtless, as he says in many other places, "Peace upon Israel,"[4] where he wants to show that peace is to be bestowed on the people in the place of blessing—something the tribes enjoyed after the close of the captivity, when the rivalry previously affecting them was to all appearances laid aside.

PSALM 4

In the present psalm blessed David gets the better of those who go so far as to claim that the world depends on them and presume to say that no control is exercised over human affairs by providence. Proof is looked for from his own experience or from the attention generally given to all living things, for whom God's generosity is the source of all good things and bestows them.

You hearkened to me when I called upon you, God of my righteousness (v. 1). Those who want to withdraw the present state of things from a plan characterized by reason are in the habit of saying, God has no interest in human affairs: | there is no one who applies the judgment of righteousness and res-

---

4. Cf. Pss 125:5; 128:6.

non est qui adhibita censura iustitiae bonos a malis eruat uel
ulciscatur iustos sub iniqua obpraesione laborantes; non est qui
periculorum casus uarios incertosque submoueat; omnia, ut fors
tulerit, aguntur incerta, et more uiuitur bestiarum, — nam ualentior
5 quis inbicillum opprimit, tenuior potentiori parere conpellitur et
punctrix peccatorum cessat aequitas, nec aliquid inter probos in-
probosque discretionis adhibetur, — contra hunc ergo errorem, qui
male hominum quorundam mentes insederat, totus profecto sermo
consurgit; cui mediri testimoniis a se petitis adgreditur atque ait:
10 *Cum inuocarem exaudisti me, Deus iustitiae meae.* Quare, inquit,
audetis in haec uerba prorumpere, ut dicatis non esse qui rerum
inspector insistat, apud quem cura uigeat ultionis, cum mihi inuocanti Deus ultor adsteterit? *Iustitiae* autem suae dicit, quam utique
sit circa illum Deus operatus dum illum inique oppraesum et exau-
15 dire et liberare curauit; optime contra opinionem dogmatis praui
probationem de experimentis oposuit, ut ostenderet et rebus Dei
iudicium non deesse, nec tamen omnes inter diuersa positos dignos eius adiutorio repperiri, sed eos qui ad tutionem eius sufragio uitae melioris accesserint. Hoc igitur responsionis genere
20 intigre occurritur errantium questioni, ut doceatur et rerum homanarum curam habere et inspectatores singulis negotiis oculos
admouere, sed frequenter permitere ut hi, qui se ab eius difen-
sione subtraxerint, pro meriti qualitate | aerumnis grauibus inpli-
centur.
25 *In tribulatione dilatas mihi.* Tam cito mihi, inquit, inuocanti
auditum suae auris admouit, ut adhuc in tribulationibus constitutus requiem amplam largamque praesteterit, quae me obliuisci
faceret omnium, quibus praemebar, angorum; per quod plane eui-
dens documentum est diuinum bonis adiutorium, exemplo Dauid,
30 semper adsistere.
Misserere mei et exaudi orationem meam. Illud, quod dixit superius Dauid, *Deus iustitiae meae,* hic ostendit non suam, in qua
confideret, se iactasse iustitiam neque quod sibi inesset aequitatis

---

1-2 uel ulciscatur] .i. non est qui *add. supra*   5 opprimit] opp(rae)mit *ms*
potentiori] *litt.* ri *in rasura*   6 nec] n̄ (non) *ms*   7-9 *verba* contra — consurgit *litteris a-c infra aut supra positis instruuntur ad alium syntaxeos ordinem
insinuandum*   10 exaudī *ms*   11 decatis *ms*   15 opinionem * *ms*   17 de
esse *ms*   inter *ex* hn̄t *corr.*   18 repperi *ms*   19 accesserit *1ᵃ m.*   20 intigrae
1ᵃ m.   21 curam *suppl. in margine*   inspectatores] in peccatores *1ᵃ m.*   22 eius]
dei *add. supra*   26 admonuit *ms*, .i. deus *add. supra*   26-27 constitutus] ad-
constitutos *ms*   31 exaudis *1ᵃ m.*   .i. dixit *add. supra* quod.

cues good people from trouble or avenges righteous people suffering under unfair oppression; there is no one to deflect changing and unexpected accidents; everything happens unpredictably, as chance determines, and our life is like that of the wild animals. In fact, stronger people oppress the weaker; the disadvantaged are forced to obey the more powerful; fairness is no longer a motive for sinners, nor is any distinction applied between lawful and lawless. It is against this error, then, which unfortunately occupies some people's minds, that the whole of his treatment is definitely addressed; he proceeds to remedy it with evidence gathered by himself, saying, *When I called upon you, you hearkened to me, God of my righteousness:* how dare you give vent to these words and claim there is no overseer of things in place who exercises a lively interest in vengeance, when God came to my side as an avenger when I called upon him?

Now, he says that his is the righteousness, which actually God brought into existence in his regard in taking pains to heed and free him in his unjust oppression. It was very commendable of him to contradict the conclusion of vicious teaching with proof from experience, and thus show that God's justice is not absent from events, and that not all people regardless of their situation are found worthy of his assistance but only those who make an effort to seek his assistance with the recommendation of a better life. The complaint of those in error therefore is completely dealt with by this kind of response, so that the lesson is given that God takes an interest in human affairs and directs his supervision to take an account of individual dealings even if he often permits those who withdraw themselves from his protection to be caught up in serious problems as they deserve.

In tribulation you give me space: he gave me a hearing so quickly when I called so as to provide me with deep and lasting repose even when I was held fast in tribulations, and it made me forget all the distress burdening me. From this the proof is clear from the example of David that divine help always comes to the good. *Have mercy on me and hearken to my prayer.* Like his phrase above, *God of my righteousness,* here David brings out that he was not boasting of the righteousness as his own in which he placed his trust, nor that he wanted irresponsibly to give the impression that attention to justice lay with him; | rather, that it was necessary to assert this because he was in

studium leuiter ostentare uoluisse, sed quia certamen sibi esset aduersum negatores prouidentiae ista necesario subdidisse; atque ideo adiecit: *Misserere mei et exaudi orationem meam.* Qui enim a Deo opem misserationis inquirit satis ostendit non se meriti sui fructum ac studii debitum postulare, sed indulgenti se uelle uti 5 Domino uel benigno: utrumque tamen necessarium in tribulationibus constituto, ut et Deo iugiter supplicet et probitatem, per quam inpetret, conversationis admoueat. Sic autem orans ad ipsos contradictores prouidentiae apostrofam facit.

3. *Filii*, inquit, *hominum usque quo graui corde?* Quid uocare 10 consueuimus, quod uel mole sui uel natura multi ponderis inuenitur adpensum, dicimus etiam illud g r a u e, quod est grandis praetii ab aestimationis suae utique quantitate; sed hic graues appellat distenti cordis et satis adipati. Ita ergo ait: *Vsque quo graui corde,* ac si diceret obesi cordis ac tardi et a cognitione ueritatis nimis 15 alieni.

Vt quid dilegitis uanitatem et queritis mendacium? Vanitatem errorem, qui eis insederat, opinionis appellat: nam dicere nulla mundum regi prouidentia, ut falsum, ita est hebetis mentis indicium. Re|linquite ergo cordis studia crassioris et experimento meo, 20 ut sciatis mundo praeesse rationem, ad cognitionem ueritatis accidite.

4. *Et scitote quoniam mirificauit Dominus sanctum suum.* Iterum, propter susceptae adsertionis causam, *sanctum* se appellare non timuit, quoniam omnis illi erat sermonis intentio contra eos qui pro 25 uidentiam summouebant. Volens ergo ostendere quoniam non gratificatione aliqua, sed dispensante iustitia in admirationem omnium Deo sit adiuuante perductus, ait quod non solum exaudiat clamantes ad se, sed etiam multo honore sublimet. Post quae adiunxit iterum:

Dominus exaudiet me cum clamauero ad eum. Ita illi iugis cura 30 est, ut me, quoties inuocauero eum, non detractet audire; constat ergo exemplo meo etiam alios ad eius prouidentiam pertinere. Et quoniam consuetudo est his qui sunt in miseriis constituti, quos

---

5 debetum *ms*   se *in rasura*   7 constituto] dati(uum) *add. supra*   suplicet *1ª m.*   8 inpeteret *ms*   13 hiic *ms*   14 adipati] *litt.* adip *in rasura* 19 ut] dicitis *add. supra*   falsum] adū (adiectiuum ?) *add. supra*   he∗be∗tis] *ms* 20 reliquite *1ª m.*   28 clamantes] clantes *1ª m.*   29 post quae] iura praedicta *add. supra*   30 me *om. 1ª m.*   clamauero] clamā *ms.*   31 ut — inuocauero *om. 1ª m.*   33 miseris *ms.*

dispute with those who denied providence—hence his addition *Have mercy on me and hearken to my prayer.* In other words, those who seek the offer of mercy from God bring out clearly enough that they are not demanding their just deserts and recompense for their efforts, but mean to profit from the indulgent and kindly Lord. Still, both are required of those caught up in tribulations, to ceaselessly make petition to God and to prompt themselves to uprightness of life, this being a means of obtaining their petition.

By praying in this fashion he achieves the rebuttal of those denying providence. *Mortals that you are, how long will you be heavy-hearted?* (v. 2). As we normally describe what is found to weigh heavily either by its mass or by its naturally great weight, we also call what is of great value *heavy* from an estimate of its amount. Here, on the other hand, he calls *heavy* those whose heart is bloated and quite fat—hence his saying *how long will you be heavy-hearted?* as if to say that they were far from a knowledge of the truth by being flabby in heart and slow to move. *Why do you love futility and search for deceit?* He calls the wrong ideas possessing them *futility:* to claim that the world is not governed by any providence is the mark of a feeble mind, false claim that it is. So abandon the efforts of a very dull heart, and through my experience come to the knowledge of the truth so as to understand the plan that controls the world.

Know that the Lord has made his holy one an object of wonder (v. 3). Once again, on account of the case he was building, he had no qualms about calling himself *holy one,* since the whole purpose of his treatment was in opposition to those who undermined providence. In his wish, then, to bring out that his motivation was not self-satisfaction but justice operating through God's assistance to the admiration of everyone, he says that not only does he hearken to those who cry to him, but even exalts them with great honor. After this he goes on further, The Lord will hearken to me when I cry to him: his interest is so constant that he does not cease listening to me, no matter how many times I call on him; it therefore follows that, on the basis of my experience, others also fall under his providence.

And since those in a condition of hardship, | whom bitterness drives to

in amentiam amaritudo conpellit, conquaeri de Deo ac dicere quod
nihil curae dignetur mortalium rebus adhibere nec gubernacula
humanae uitae tenere rationem, — proprium enim est talia dicere
his quos a sano sensu aduersa deducunt, — consequenter ergo
5 monet eos dicens:

5. *Irascemini et nolite peccare.* Quod quidem non ita legendum,
ut totum uideatur pronuntiantis esse. Nam posteaquam dixit *Iras-*
scemini subiunxit *Et nolite peccare*, scemate interrogationis admiso
ac si diceret *Irascemini? Et nolite peccare*: quamuis uos in offen-
10 sam animi inaequalis praesentium negotiorum status et confusus
inpellat, quamuis multa sint quae causas uideantur indignationis
ingerere, tamen nolite putare uerum esse quod uobis non ratio,
non disciplina tradidit, sed animus ira perturbatus ingesit; quod
quidem maximum testimonium est opinionem uestram carere ue-
15 ritate, quia ista quae sentitis, quae dicitis non a ratione, sed a
merore uenerunt. Et quasi interrogetur: Quomodo, inquit, potest | ab
hoc errore discedi?

Quae dicitis in cordibus uestris, et in cubilibus uestris conpunge-
mini. Ea, quae per diem occurentia oculis uestris occasiones uobis non
20 bene sentiendi uidentur ingerere, in stratis uestris possiti cogitationibus rectis adpendite, et ad sanum redeuntes intellectum errasse
uos prius testimonio poenitentiae et conpunctionis ostendite.

6. *Sacrificate sacrificium et sperate in Domino.* Ad hanc potius
partem studia uestra conuertite, ut, tam opinionum quam uerbo-
25 rum errore depossito, per curam per iustitiamque non inmerito
possitis diuinam sperare opem quotiens aduersa uobis prouenerint.
Post haec ad exortationem uerba infert ea, quae ab errantibus
contra ueritatem sepe dicuntur.

7. *Multi dicunt: Quis ostendit nobis bona?* Indicat quoniam non
30 pauci sint qui ad mouendam prouidentiam audent dicere: Si est
ratio quae mundum regat atque moderetur, quae ad nos dispen-
sationis eius documenta perueniunt, quae munera suae bonitatis
inpertit? Aduersum hanc errantium inquisitionem intulit, tenebras
stultitiae eis et caecitatem mentis exprobrans.

1 amritudo *ms*   3 tenere] .i. non *add. supra*   8 pecare *ms*   9 quamui suos]
adit nolite *add. supra*   15 quae] *litt.* ae *in rasura*   19 ea — diem] adit inpendite
add. supra   21 redeuntaes *ms*   25 curam iust. *1ª m.*   31 quae ad] .i. interro(gati-
vum) *add. supra*   32 eius] dei *add. supra*   praeueniunt *ms*   33 inquisionem *1ª m.*

distraction, normally make complaints about God and claim that he does not deign to take an interest in mortal things or plan the government of human life—typical remarks from those whom adversity deprives of their good sense—he therefore exhorts them, in the same vein, *Be angry and be unwilling to sin* (v. 4). This is not to be read as though it all seemed to come from the speaker:[1] after saying *Be angry* he went on to add *and be unwilling to sin,* with the interrogative form introduced as if he were saying *Be angry? Be unwilling to sin.* In other words, although the unfair and disturbed condition of your present affairs drives you to a resentful frame of mind, although there are many things that seem to provide reason for indignation, nonetheless do not think justified what is the effect in you not of reason or self-control; rather, your mind is upset with anger and is influencing you. In fact, the overwhelming evidence is that your train of thought lacks justification, because what you are feeling, what you are saying, stems not from reason but from grief. And as if he were asked, How is it possible to be rid of this mistake? *For what you say in your heart be repentant on your beds:* the events that happen by day and do not seem to provide you with the basis for sound thinking weigh up with sober meditation when in bed, recover a proper attitude, and with evidence of repentance and regret admit you previously made a mistake. *Offer a sacrifice and hope in the Lord* (v. 6): direct your attention rather in this direction, to set aside your error in both thought and word, and not without good reason to hope in divine assistance through assiduity and through righteousness as often as troubles beset you.[2]

After these words by way of exhortation, he adduces those often spoken against the truth by people in error. *Many people say, Who shows us good things?* (v. 6). He indicates that there are not a few who for the purpose of denying providence presume to say, If there is a plan to rule and guide the world, what proofs of his design come to our attention, conveying gifts of his goodness? He inveighs against this inquiry of those in error, upbraiding their opaque stupidity and blind thinking. | *The light of your countenance has left*

---

1. It is perhaps the LXX version that has given rise to this conundrum for its commentators, our Hebrew text not suggesting anger. While Chrysostom takes the simpler way to rationalize a perceived problem by citing several biblical instances of righteous indignation, Theodoret stays with Theodore (and Diodore before him) to divide the verse, though also seeing some excuse for irritation at life's inequities.

2. Where both the Hebrew and the LXX permit either "legitimate sacrifice" or "sacrifice of righteousness" as a translation, Devreesse's text of the verse omits the noun "righteousness," although Theodore's commentary and his fellow Antiochenes' text suggest that he is reading it.

Signatum est super nos lumen uultus tui, Domine. Tanta, inquit,
bonorum copia, quae de fonte tuae liberalitatis egreditur, ad nos
peruenit, ut non dubiis sed certis et expraesis documentis tua in
nos cura signetur; hoc est quod dicit *lumen uultus tui, Domine*.
In his enim profecto, quae largitur Deus, circa nos clemens dispen- 5
satio conprobatur. Dispensationem ergo Dei, quae nobis bona omnia
subministret, *lumen* diuini *uultus* appellat; uultum uero pro praesentia, qua adest rebus omnibus, ponit. Hoc est ergo quod dicit: ita
sunt circa nos prouidentiae tuae clara documenta, ut effectibus
expraesa et signata uideantur. Sed quae sit ista bonorum inper- 10
titio, per quam inpraesum | nobis *lumen uultus* esse Dei adserit, in
sequentibus curat aperire.

8. *Dedisti laetitiam in corde meo* usque *multiplicati sunt*. Dum
habunde ea, quae sunt esui necesaria, subministras, per cibum ac
potum sensum hominibus iucunditatis infundis. Bene ergo dixit: 15
Signatum est super nos lumen uultus tui, Domine. Cum enim his
muneribus continue utimur, largitoris gratia sensibus nostris inprae-
mitur; atque ideo fecit horum maxime mentionem, — id est *fru-*
menti et uini et olei, quae inter reliqua uictui necesaria primum
obtinent locum, — sine quibus in totum posse subsistere uita homi. 20
num non uidetur. Ideo haec tria ad documentum diuinae prouidentiae inserta sunt, quia a creatore ad conseruationem naturae
nostrae instituta sunt et parata, quorum utique institutio curam
erga nos nostri indicat conditoris. Hoc ergo exprobrat infitien-
tibus ueritati dicens quoniam, cum ita clara sint diuinae bonita- 25
tis testimonia, ut uice luminis resplendentia, ignorari non sinant
largitorem, cur uos ad agnitionem eius caecos oculos admouetis
ac dicitis: Quae autem ab eo bonorum documenta suscipimus?
cum tanta sint quae singulis temporibus usibus nostris inpertiat, sine quibus utique subsistere ac uitam ducere non ualemus. 30
Per quod plane manifesta rebus ipsis Dei prouidentia animum
sanum sapientibus adprobatur; post quae consequenter infert, dicens:

2 bonum *1ª m*.   libertatis *ms*   3 dubis *ms*   8 rebus] opibus *add. supra*
8-9 quod-sunt] .i. lumen uultus r(e)l(iqua) *add. supra*   10 expraesa] exsa *1ª m*.
quae] interroga(tiuum) *add. supra*   inpertio] .i. diuisio *add. supra*   17 lar-
gitores *1ª m*.   19 et uini] et *om. 1ª m*. necesaria] sunt *add. supra*   21 tria]
iii *ms*, .i. fru(mentum) et uinum et oleum *add. supra*   25 quoniam-clara] adit
cur admouetis *add. supra*   26 resplendentia-sinant] *litt.* dentia-sinant *in ra-*
sura   27 ad *in rasura*.

its mark on us, Lord: such an abundance of good things reaches us, coming from the fount of your generosity, that your care for us is marked by proofs that, far from being ambiguous, are certain and explicit (the meaning of *light of your countenance*). By what God bestows on us, to be sure, his kindly designs for us are established. Thus, by *light of* the divine *countenance* he refers to God's plan, which provides us with every good, while he uses *countenance* for his presence, by which he is in touch with all things. This, then, is his meaning: So clear are the proofs of your providence for us as to appear imprinted and made explicit in their effects.

The ways of imparting good things, through which the light of God's countenance is imprinted on us, he is at pains to bring out in what follows. *You have put gladness into my heart* down to *they grew prosperous* (v. 7): by making available what is necessary for life, you instill in human beings through food and drink a feeling of satisfaction. He was therefore right to say *The light of your countenance has left its mark on us:* when we constantly use these gifts, the grace of the giver is impressed on our senses. Hence his making particular mention of them—*grain, wine, and oil,* which have pride of place among the necessities of life—for without them human life seems completely impossible; for this reason these three are mentioned as proof of divine providence, determined and prepared as they are by the creator for conserving our nature, their determination thus suggesting our maker's care for us. He therefore censures those denying the truth, when he asks, Since the evidence of divine goodness is so clear as to shine like light and permit of no ignorance of the giver, why do you blind your eyes to acknowledgment of him and ask, What proof do we have of good things from him? Especially since what he imparts time after time for our needs is so abundant, and without it we cannot even exist and prolong life.

Through this God's providence is clearly manifest in reality and in wise people confirms a sound attitude. He continues in the same theme, saying, | *In*

9. *In pace in id ipsum dormiam et requiescam.* Quoniam superius contra praui dogmatis adsertores dixerat: *Quae dicitis in cor-*
dibus uestris et *in cubilibus uestris conpungemini,* consequenter ait:
In pace in id ipsum dormiam et requiescam. Vos, ait, qui malis dis-
putationibus et opinionibus pessimis totum diei tempus impen-
ditis, in stratis uestris, cum somno membra commititis, reuocate
in memoriam quae inepte praueque sentitis et repraehendentes
uosmet ipsos aculeum uobis reatus adfi|gite. Ego uero talis recor-
dationis emendatione non egeo, quia neque huius modi cogitationibus lucis tempus inpendi, sed ordinatis sensibus meis nihil perturbationis incurri. Hoc est enim quod dicit *in id ipsum,* ac si
diceret: mecum ipse non dissideo neque aliquas disentionum suggestiones experior; dormiens ergo non necesse habeo propter diur-
nas agitationes, in strato possitus, stimulis reatus urgeri. Sed hoc,
ne uideatur de se ipse gloriari, Dei beneficiis maluit inputare dicendo:

Quoniam tu, Domine, singulariter in spe constituisti me. Tu, inquit, singulariter me instituisti, separans ab illorum consortio qui
ita praue atque impie sentire non metuunt, ut credant nullam rebus
praeesse rationem. *Constituisti me,* ut ab spei meae propossito non
mouerer, sed confiterem numquam mihi tuum adiutorium defutu-
rum. Inpossibile est autem aliquem sperare de Deo, cuius nutat de
prouidentiae ratione sententia; propterea ergo illos uerbo exortationis instituit, dicens *Sperate in Domino,* hoc est dicere: Credite
quoniam est illi cura de omnibus. De se quoque, quasi certa
scientia conpraehenderit id quod suadet aliis, ait *Quoniam tu, Do-*
mine, singulariter in spe constituisti me, ac si diceret: *Constituisti*
me ut de tua prouidentia numquam in animum aliquid dubitatio-
nis admiterem.

2-3 v. 5ᵇ   24 v. 6.

1 quoniam] adit ait *add. supra*   2 praui] *litt.* ui *in rasura*   3 uestris
et *in rasura*   12 ipse] ipsum *ms,* .i. secundum id ipsum *add. supra*   desi-
deo *ms, cf. p. 20, ll. 9, 17*   13 abeo *1ᵃ m.*   14 possitus *om. 1ᵃ m.*   15 beneficis *ms*   19 non *om. 1ᵃ m.*   20 ut *in rasura*   21 numquam] nq *in textu,*
numquam *add. supra*   defuturam *ms*   22 cuis *ms*   24 instituit] docuit
add. supra.

peace I shall go to sleep and in the same instant find rest (v. 8). Since he had
said above, in refutation of those asserting wrong teaching, *For what you say
in your hearts* and *be repentant on your beds,* he proceeds to say *In peace I
shall go to sleep and in the same instant find rest.* You who spend the whole
day in vicious wrangling and worthless ideas, he is saying, when on your
beds you commit your limbs to sleep, call to mind your foolish and depraved
thoughts, upbraid yourselves, and feel the sting of your guilt. For my part,
on the other hand, I do not require correction through recollection, because
instead of devoting daytime to thoughts of this kind, I have not run the risk
of restlessness, my senses being in proper order—the meaning of *in the same
instant,* as if to say, I am not at odds with myself, and I feel no other pangs of
discord, so when I go to sleep, I consequently do not need to feel the goad of
guilt when I lie in bed as a result of the day's upsets.

Lest he seem to be boasting, however, he preferred to attribute this to
God's goodness, saying *Because you, Lord, have in a special way established
me in hope:* you specially instructed me, setting me apart from association
with those have no qualms about such vile and godless thoughts as to believe
that no plan governs events. *You established me* so that I should not be discouraged from my commitment to hope, maintaining instead that your help
would never desert me. Now, it is impossible for someone to hope in God
whose views on God's providential plan waver; hence he gives such people
this piece of advice: *Hope in the Lord*—that is, believe that he has care for
everyone. In his own case likewise, as if unwavering realization embraced
what he advised others, he says *Because you, Lord, have in a special way
established me,* as if to say, You have established me in such a way as never
to allow into my mind a doubt as to your providence. |

PSALMVS V

Profetat ex persona populi,
qui in Babillonem ductus est a
Naboconodosor rege captiuus.

Ἐκ προσώπου τοῦ λαοῦ φησι
τοῦ ὑπὸ Ναβουχοδονοσὸρ αἰχμαλισθέντος.

2. *Verba mea auribus percipe, Domine.* *Auribus* percipere proprie 5
dicimur quando adcommodata aure sollicite uerba loquentis audimus. Rogans ergo populus Deum, ut audiat petitionem eius, adten-
tius uerbis utitur de nostri usus familiaritate nascentibus; alioquin
quomodo possunt dicta haec Deo incorporeo conuenire, cui neque
aures insunt neque p|ars ulla membrorum, cuius natura semplex 10
est sine ulla partium deuersitate atque conpage? Similiter igitur
etiam in sequentibus per uerba corporalia Deo admouet preces
more utique nostro, quia non nos aliter Deo nouimus supplicare
nisi his in petendo utamur uerbis, ad quae nos loquendi consuetudo formauit propter naturae nostrae et sermonis angustias, et 15
quia alia uerba nisi quae habet usus inuenire non possimus. Vnde
multo magis sub persona iudaici populi aliter sanctus Dauid Deum
orare non poterat, cum praesertim esset ille populus, pro quo ora-
bat, carnalibus studiis tardus et crasior. Ob hanc igitur causam,
quam dicimus, frequenter inuenitur profeta haec uerba precibus 20
admouere.

Intellege clamorem meum. Etiam hoc similiter pro more hominum dicitur: nam a Dei natura extranea sunt ista uocabula satisque
perigrina. Secundum consuetudinem igitur nostram supplicationes
admouet Deo; quomodo et nos, — cum aliquem rogamus, et ille 25
dicta nostra disimulat, admonemus ut intentius quae dicuntur
accipiat et sollicitas petitioni aures accommodet, — hunc ad
Deum ubique morem transferens praestari sibi adtentionem auditus implorat.

1 expli(cit) psal(mus) iiii. incipi(t) .u. *ms*   10 neque] .i. est *add. supra*
12 sequentibus] dictis *add. supra*   13 more] *litt.* re *in rasura*   14 nisi] non
videtur prius scriptum   17 iudaci *ms*   18 populus *suppl. supra*   20 uerba
precibus] i. praedicta in psalmo *add. supra*   25 quomodo *conieci* quoniam
ms, adit implorat *add. supra*   et nos] et *in rasura*.

Ἐκ προσώπου — αἰχμαλισθέντος: Vat. 1789, fol. 31 (Διώδωρος καὶ Θεόδωρος).

PSALM 5

He is speaking in the person of the people taken captive by Nebuchadnez-
zar. *Give ear to my words, Lord* (v. 1). We rightly claim to grasp "with our
ears" when we listen to the words of the speaker by carefully adjusting our
hearing. Asking God to hear their petition, then, the people deliberately
employ words arising from our colloquial usage; otherwise, how could they
apply these terms to God, who is incorporeal, who has neither ears nor any
other bodily parts, who is simple by nature, without any diversity or combination of parts? In similar fashion, therefore, also in what follows they
direct prayers to God in corporeal language in our fashion, because we have
no idea how to beseech God except by using these expressions in asking.
Habitual patterns of speech accustomed us to this on account of the limitations of our nature and way of communicating, and because we cannot find
words other than those that usage offers. Hence, much more was holy David,
speaking in the person of the Jewish people, unable to beg God in any other
way, especially since that people in particular whose prayers he was representing was slow and rather obtuse by reason of its carnal occupations.
For this reason, therefore, the inspired author frequently is found addressing
these words in prayer.

Understand my cry. This, too, is likewise spoken in human fashion: the
words are out of keeping with God's nature and rather inappropriate. It is
therefore from our customary usage that he addresses supplications to God;
as with us, when we ask someone, and they ignore our words, and we urge
them more insistently to accept what we say and lend their ears to our petition, in every case he adapts the custom to God and implores him to pay
attention by listening. |

3. *Intende uoci orationis meae.* Et hoc, ut superiora, a similitudine corporis est petitum.

Rex meus et Deus meus. Vult ostendere populum captiuitatis Babiloniae castigationibus eruditum, relictis idolis, ad Deum esse
5 conuersum et, quasi qui prius errauerit, in gaudium cognitione ueritatis erumpere ac dicere *Rex meus et Deus,* hoc est: Tu mihi audenti praebe, tu suscipe quae alligare conpellor, qui es uerus *rex meus et Deus;* idola enim dei non erant, errabam ego cum illa deos esse credebam. Consequenter igitur infert:
10 *Quoniam ad te orabo, Domine.* Ideo me conuenit non desimulanter audire, quoniam tibi iam in reliquum iugiter | supplicabo, simulacra non rogaturus ulterius. Indicat autem per haec, quoniam ante tempus captiuitatis suae neglegentes circa offerendas Deo supplicationes exsteterint.

15 **4.** *Mane et exaudies uocem meam. Mane* in scripturis diuinis dici tripliciter inuenimus: aut enim ad uelocitatis indicium ponitur, aut ad laetitiam reffertur, aut ad tempus certe matutinum. Indicatur autem laetitia hoc nomine ob hoc, quia, cum diei tempus, in quo curarum fluctus et solicitudines experimur, noctis uicisitudo
20 exciperit, relaxatis otio corporibus et obliuione in locum angoris admisa, ita mane securi laetique consurgimus quasi omnis praeterita sollicitudo fuerit cum nocte finita; sed in hoc loco pro tempore accipiendum est. Ideo etiam sequitur:
Mane adstabo tibi et uidebo. Hoc est ad offerendas praeces de
25 strato meo matutinus adsurgam, et cum deuote tibi antelucanus adstitero, tu quoque uocem meam sollicita benignitate suscipito.

5. *Quoniam non Deus uolens iniquitatem tu es.* Quod signanter Deus nolle iniquitatem dicitur, non ad hoc ualet ut alium aliquem deum iniustitiae amatorem esse credamus, sed ad distinctionem
30 demonum, quibus familiare est iniquitate gaudere. Notandum autem hoc contra hereticos: si enim in hoc loco ait *quoniam non Deus uolens iniquitatem tu es,* non solum Deum Patrem indicat qui iniquitatem nolit, — neque enim hoc uult ostendere quoniam

---

1 superiora] iura *add. supra*   6-7 audienti *1ᵃ m.*   7 uerrus *1ᵃ m.*   9 credabam *ms*   11 relinquum *1ᵃ m.*   17 matinum *1ᵃ m.*   20 exciperit] uel sus(ciperit) *add. supra*   25 matinus *ms*   26 solita *1ᵃ m.,* ł (= uel) *et litt.* ci *add. supra* benignitaitate *ms*   28 ualet] *litt.* l *in rasura*   30 notandum *scripsi ex gloss. hib.,* non tantum *ms*   30 — p. 28, 2 *verba* non tantum — iniquitatem *litteris* a-g *supra additis instruuntur ad syntaxeos ordinem insinuandum*   31 non *om. 1ᵃ m.*

Attend to the sound of my prayer (v. 2). This request, too, like the one above, is expressed in a corporeal manner. *My king and my God.* He wants to portray the people as corrected by the chastisements of the captivity of Babylon, abandoning the idols and turning back to God, like someone who first erred and then bursting out in joy at the knowledge of the truth and saying *My king and God*—that is, Respond to me as I listen, accept what I am obliged to mention, you who are truly *my king and God;* the idols were not gods, I was wrong when I believed they were gods. He therefore goes on, in the same vein, *Because I shall pray to you, Lord:* hence, It behooves me to listen without pretense, since it is you I shall always in the future implore, no longer addressing requests to images. Now, in this he suggests that before the time of their captivity they were negligent in offering supplications to God.

In the morning you will hearken to my voice. In the divine Scriptures we find *in the morning* used in three ways: it is used as an indication of speed, it refers to joy, and of course to morning time. Now, joy is suggested by this term for the reason that whereas the troubles of night succeed the period of the day, when we experience a flood of worries and anxieties, and our bodies relax and oblivion takes the place of anxiety, so in the morning we rise settled and joyful as if all the previous worry was over with the night. In this verse, on the other hand, the word is to be taken as a time index. Hence, he goes on, *In the morning I shall make my approach to you and see*—that is, in the morning I shall rise from my bed to offer prayers, and when I am devoutly in attendance on you before dawn, in your turn accept my prayer with attentive kindness.

Because you are not a God who wills iniquity (v. 4). The fact that God is said characteristically to have no wish for iniquity implies not that we should believe that some other god is a lover of injustice, but that this distinguishes him from the demons, whose habit is to rejoice in iniquity. Now, this point is made against the heretics: if at this point he says *Because you are not a God who wills iniquity,* he is not suggesting that it is only God the Father who does not love iniquity, nor does it imply that | it is God's Son who loves

Filius Dei sit qui uelit iniquitatem, — sed ad discritionem malorum, qui dii putantur, dicitur *Deus iniquitatem non uolens*, quibus est error familiaris et amica peruersitas; unde et quod solus uerus Deus Pater, ac si inuenitur aliquid simile quod honorem Patris indicet, non tamen id aufertur a Filio. In hoc ergo loco, ut diximus, ad 5 idulorum differentiam soli Deo iniquitatis odium inesse perhibetur.

Non habitauit iuxta te malignus. Quia haec erat opinio Iudeorum quod in Hirusolimis et monte Sion Dei esset habitatio, — commorantem in terra repromisionis in uicinia Dei habitare credebant, — non patieris, inquit, loca tibi dicata ab his incoli, quorum uita est 10 ab studio bonitatis aliena; ob hoc etiam nos pro morum nequitia atque foeditate longius expullisti, ne nominis tui posesio de consortio nostro iniuriam sustineret.

6. *Neque permanebunt iniusti ante oculos tuos.* Solicite prursus et caute *Neque permanebunt* dixit, quoniam ad tempus aliquos manere 15 constabat, quibus diuturnitatem manendi concedi negat et spatia longiora.

Odisti, Domine, omnes operantes iniquitatem. Operarios iniquitatis uocat Babilonios, qui eos in captiuitate retinebant; ac si diceret: Non solum a tuae habitationis uicinia summouisti, sed etiam istos 20 auersaris et dignos odio iudicas, qui nos tenent uictorum iure captiuos, pro operum plane suorum iniustitia, per quam tibi iuste exosi esse meruerunt.

7. *Perdes omnes qui loquuntur mendacium.* De his ipsis Babiloniis etiam ista dicuntur. 25

Virum sanguinum et dolosum habominabitur Dominus. Viros *sanguinum* uocat adsidua sanguinis effusione gaudentes.

8. *Ego autem in multitudine misericordiae tuae introibo in domum tuam.* Bene ait *in multitudine misericordiae tuae ego introibo in domum tuam*, quia superius dixerat *non Deus uolens iniquitatem* 30 *tu es* et malignum iuxta te habitare non patieris, neque iniquos ante oculos tuos manere permitis. Ego autem, quia non sum ab

29 v. 5.

2 deus *om. 1ᵃ m.*   non uolens *om. 1ᵃ m.*   3 quod] .i. dicitur *add. supra*   uerus] uersus *1ᵃ m.*   6 deferentiam *ms*   inesse] *litt.* esse *in rasura*   7 quia haec erat] adit credebant *add. supra*   10 pateris *1ᵃ m.*   14 solite *1ᵃ m.*   15 ad *om. 1ᵃ m.*   16 diuternitatem *ms*   23 exosi] *litt.* o *in rasura*   meruerueruerunt *ms*   21-25 babilonis *ms*   27 sangnium *ms*   sanginis *ms*   31 pateris *ms.*

iniquity. Rather, the phrase *not a God who wills iniquity* is used to distinguish him from the evil beings thought to be gods, because to them error is beloved and perversity a friend. It follows that only the Father is true God, and if any other similar attribute is found suggesting the status of the Father, it is still not taken from the Son. In this verse, therefore, as we said, by way of differentiating him from the idols a hatred of iniquity is predicated of God alone. *A malicious person has not dwelt in your presence.* This was the belief of the Jews, that God's dwelling was in Jerusalem and Mount Sion; they believed that living in the promised land was to dwell in proximity with God. So he says, You will not allow places dedicated to you to be inhabited by those whose life is removed from the pursuit of goodness; you even drove us out for wicked and abhorrent behavior to avoid possession of your name being impaired by association with us.

The wicked will not remain before your eyes (v. 5). Deliberately, to be sure, and not idly did he say *they will not remain,* since evidently some last for a time, and it is to them he denies length of dwelling for a longer period. *You hate, Lord, all who do wrong.* By *those who do wrong* he refers to the Babylonians, who kept them in captivity, as if to say, You not only removed us from closeness to your dwelling, but also turn away from them and judge those who hold us as prisoners by right of conquest worthy of hatred for reason of the outright injustice of their actions, on account of which they fairly deserved to be hateful to you. *You will destroy all who speak falsehood* (v. 6). This also is said of those same Babylonians. *The Lord abhors a man of blood and deceit,* by men *of blood* referring to those rejoicing in avid bloodshed.

I, on the other hand, by the abundance of your mercy shall enter your house (v. 7). He is right to say *by the abundance of your mercy I shall enter your house,* since above he had said *You are not a God who wills iniquity* and do not allow the malicious person to dwell in your presence, nor do you permit the wicked to remain before your eyes. I, on the other hand, not being |

istis, quos detestaris, alienus sed innumeris peccatis obnoxius, quae
me in captiuitatis huius miserias conpullerunt, *in multitudine mi-
sericordiae tuae in|troibo in domum tuam*. Aditum, inquit, quem mihi
peccata obstruxerunt, ut abductus ab solo patrio domum tuam in-
5 trare non possem, nunc reducto tua misericordia reseruabit.

Adorabo ad templum sanctum tuum in timore tuo. Ostendit quod
prius absque timore, quem solet reuerentia sacri loci et diuini
cultus incutere, templum intrauerint orationum officia reddituri.
Hoc ergo emendaturos se post reditum pollicentur.

10   9. *Domine, deduc me in tua iustitia, propter inimicos meos, direge in conspectu tuo uiam meam.*

Vnum atque idem est ac si
diceret: Reuoca me, ut tibi possim templum ingresus adsistere.

15   *Direge* autem id est: omnia
uiae meae inpedimenta submoue
et sine deflexionum moris fac
iter in directum agere, ut rediun-
tis ad te gresus nullus impediat.

20 Hoc autem dicit secundum opinionem illam, qua Deum in monte
Sion credit habitare. Quod autem possuit *propter inimicos meos*
interpossitum est et ad utrumque
25 respicit, ut sit ita: *Deduc me in
tua iustitia propter inimicos meos,*
et iterum *propter inimicos meos
direge in conspectu tuo uiam
meam*, id est: Reuoca me, ut de
30 inimicorum, qui me tenent, potestate et uinculis captiuitatis ab-
soluas. Et quoniam addidit *in
iustitia tua*, id est sicut tibi mo-

Τὸ ὁδήγησόν με καὶ τὸ κατεύθυνον ἐνώπιόν σου τὴν ὁδόν μου τὸ
αὐτὸ λέγει, ἀντὶ τοῦ Ἐπανάγαγε.

Τὸ γὰρ ἐνώπιόν σου, ἀντὶ τοῦ
Πρός σέ μου κατεύθυνον τὴν ὁδόν,
ἵνα ἐπανέλθω πρός σε,

κατὰ τὴν ἰουδαϊκὴν ὑπόληψιν ὡς ἐν
τῷ Σιὼν ὄρει τοῦ Θεοῦ διάγοντος.
Τὸ οὖν ἕνεκα τῶν ἐχθρῶν μου διὰ
μέσου πρὸς ἀμφότερα ἔχον τὴν ἀνταπόδοσιν.

Ἐπανάγαγε γάρ μέ φησιν, ὥστε
ἀπαλλάξαι τῶν κατεχόντων ἐχθρῶν.

Καὶ ἐπειδὴ εἶπεν ἐν τῇ δικαιοσύνῃ
σου, τουτέστιν καθὼς ἔθος σοί ἐστιν

---

1 detestaris *in rasura*   alienos *ms*
supra   patrio] uel proprio *in margine*
seruauit *ms*   7 timore *suppl. in marg.*

4 ut abductus] adit reseruauit *add.*
5 reducto] dati(uum) *add. supra*   re-
locii *1ª m.*   27 et] ait *add. supra.*

Τὸ ὁδήγησόν με — ποιούμενον: Paris. 139, fol. 19ᵛ; Vat. 754, fol. 43; Vat. 1682,
fol. 21ʳˑᵛ *sub lemm.* Θεοδώρου Ἀντιοχείας (Mai, p. 390; P. G., 649 C 9-D 6); Barbaro, p. 57.   12 καὶ τὸ] τὸ *om.* P   16 τὴν *om.* P   17 ὑπανελθὼν P.

different from those you detest, but abhorrent on account of my sins beyond number, which drove me into the hardships of this captivity, *by the abundance of your mercy shall enter your house.* The entrance, he is saying, which my sins prevented, in that I was removed from my ancestral land and unable to enter your house, your mercy now restores to me on my return. *I shall bow down toward your holy temple in awe of you.* He brings out that previously, without the awe that reverence for the holy place and the divine worship normally instills, they entered the temple to perform the duty of prayer. So they promise to change their ways after return.

Lord, *guide me in your righteousness, on account of my enemies, direct my path in your sight* (v. 8). Both expressions mean the same, *guide me* and *direct my path in your sight*—namely, Lead me on: *direct my path in your sight* means "toward you so that I may return to you," since in Jewish belief God dwells on Mount Sion. So the phrase *on account of my foes* occurs in between both and has reference to both; he means, Lead me so that I may be freed from the foes besetting me. And since he said *in your righteousness*—that is, as it is your custom | to judge righteously—he brings out at

ris iudicare, ostendit in sequentibus quomodo aequum sit illum
ab inimicis erui, dum mores eorum et uitia producit in medium.

κρίνειν δικαίως, δείκνυσιν εὐθὺς ὅπως
αὐτὸν ἀπαλλαγῆναι δίκαιον τῶν ἐχθρῶν, ἀπὸ τοῦ ἐκείνων τρόπου τὴν
ἀπόδειξιν ποιούμενος.

10. *Quoniam non est in ore eorum ueritas, cor eorum uanum* 5
est. Accussantur Babilonii, et tam mentis eis uanitas quam men-
dacii familiaritas inputatur, quique ob hoc non sint digni qui pro
populo Iudeorum imperent atque dominentur.

Sepulcrum patens est gutor eorum. | Amore et asiduitate bello-
rum occisorum strage laetantur, et quia rem mortis operantur se- 10
pulcrorum uice longe horrorem foetoris eructant.

Linguis suis dolose agebant. Ad crudilitatis horrorem malumque
fraudis adiungitur.

11. *Iudica illos, Deus. Iudica* hic pro « condemna » possitum est.
Quoniam, inquit, omnia in illis sunt quae merentur horrorem, ius- 15
tum est illos sententiam damnationis excipere, quia conuenienter
pro uitae merito sustinebunt. Nos igitur libertati, illos trade supliciis.

Decedent a cogitationibus suis. Ea quae moliuntur contra nos
non sortiantur effectum.   20

Secundum multitudinem impietatum eorum expelle eos, reliqua.
Et si nos, inquit, digni tua defensione minime iudicemur, in illos
tamen, propter ausus graues et impietatis nimietatem, conuenit
iudicari.

12. *Et laetentur omnes qui sperant.* Consequenter hic possuit 25
qui sperant, quod facere didicerunt captiuitatis tribulationibus
eruditi.

In aeternum exultabunt et inhabitabis in eis. Aeternum hic uitae
eorum tempus indicat qui de captiuitate redierunt. Quod autem
ait *laetentur* rerum exigit consequentia, ut succedentibus prosperis 30
tristitiae amaritudo pellatur, – et perditio siue cessatio malorum laetitia consueuit esse iustorum. *Inhabitabis* uero *in eis,* hoc est: Com-
memoraberis in templo quod est Hirusolimis exstructum, ac si

10 laetentur *ms,* ut *add. supra*   14 hiic *ms, et ita inferius*   17 nos] *litt.* s
in rasura, nobis *uidetur prius scriptum*   libertatis *I*ᵃ *m.*   tradi *I*ᵃ *m.*   26 de-
decerunt *ms*   32 inhabitabis — est] *litt.* bis — est *in rasura*   33 si *in rasura.*

1 *εὐθὺς*] *ἑξῆς* P.

once how it is right for him to be freed from the foes by giving an example of their behavior. *There is no truth in their mouths, their heart is frivolous* (v. 9). It is the Babylonians who are being criticized, accused of both frivolity of mind and a habit of falsehood, and for this reason they do not deserve to rule and control in place of the people of the Jews. *Their throat is an open grave:* in their love and devotion to war they rejoice in the slaughter of the slain, and because they are engaged in a labor of death, they emit a dreadful stench from afar like graves. *They act deceitfully with their tongues:* to the horror of their cruelty the vice of deception is added.

Judge them, Lord (v. 10). Here, *judge* is used in the sense of "condemn": since everything about them provokes horror, it is just that they receive a verdict of condemnation, because it is appropriate for them to suffer in keeping with their life. Now that we are freed, therefore, consign them to punishment. *They will fall victim to their own schemes:* may what they devise against us be to no purpose. *To the measure of the vast number of their godless deeds drive them out* and so on: if we were to be found hardly worthy of your support, it is still fitting for them to be judged on account of awful exploits and extreme godlessness.

Let all who hope rejoice (v. 11). He logically said here *who hope* because they learned to do it when schooled by the tribulations of captivity. *They will exult forever, and you will dwell in them.* Here, by *forever* he suggests the lifetime of those who returned from captivity.[1] Now, the sequence of events requires that he say *Let them rejoice,* so that the bitterness of sorrow would be expelled by the prosperity that followed, it being normal for the end or cessation of troubles to mean the joy of the righteous. *You will dwell in them has this meaning:* You will abide in the temple built in Jerusalem—as if | to say, Once we return, you will once more be the occu-

---

1. Most forms of the LXX and the text of his fellow Antiochenes include "in you" after "who hope."

diceret: Reuersis nobis, iterum loci illius eris habitator testimonio
eorum quae inter nos mira frequenter operaris.

Et gloriabuntur in te qui dilegunt nomen tuum. Consequenter
omnia, quae secutura erant, enumerat. Deletis enim Babiloniis et
5 soluta captiuitate, populo erunt gaudia conferenda.

13. *Quoniam tu, Domine, benedicis iusto.* Iustum appellat popu-
lum non uirtutis studio, sed | in conparationem Babiloniorum ha-
bentem sui notitiam conditoris.

Domine, ut scuto bonae uoluntatis tuae coronasti nos. Dicendo *ut*
10 *scuto* admouit similitudinem per quam augmentum diuinae protec-
tionis exprimeret; bona uero uoluntas clemens Dei circa populum
liberalisque sentedia. Ita autem ait

ut scuto bonae uoluntatis tuae
coronasti nos, ac si diceret: Valde
15 nos decreti auxilio communisti,
ut et honorabiles apud te simus
et nullo hostium ledamur incursu.
Apte autem cum de Dei loqueretur adiutorio scutum uocauit,
20 similitudine a uiris petita stre-
nuis, qui inermes alios solent a
telorum ictibus scuti sui oppos-
sitione defendere.

Ὡς πανοπλίᾳ τῇ εὐαρεστήσει στε-
φανώσεις ἡμᾶς, τουτέστιν τῇ σφόδρα
ἀσφαλεστάτῃ βοηθείᾳ τῆς εὐαρεσ-
τήσεώς σου, ἵνα εἴπῃ· Ἣν παρασχεῖν ἡμῖν ἤρεσέν σοι καὶ ἧς ἐδοκίμασας μεταδοῦναι ἡμῖν ἀσφαλείας,
ταύτῃ ἐπιδόξους καὶ ἐντίμους κατέστησας ἀβλαβεῖς ἡμᾶς ὑπὸ τῶν πολεμίων πάντη διατηρήσας, — καλῶς
ὅπλον καλέσας τὴν τοῦ Θεοῦ βοήθειαν.

PSALMVS VI

25 De peccato beatus Dauid proprio confitetur, quod Bersabae
mixtus admisit. Vtimur autem
his uerbis in tribulationibus constituti, in quas specialiter merito
30 facti deformis incederat.

Ἐξομολογεῖται τῷ Θεῷ ὁ μακάριος Δαυὶδ περὶ τῆς ἰδίας ἁμαρτίας,
ἣν εἰργάσατο συγκαθευδήσας τῇ
Βερσαβεέ· λέγει δὲ ταῦτα ἐν συμφοραῖς ὤν, ἐν αἷς καὶ ἐξητάζετο διὰ
τὴν ἁμαρτίαν.

2 operairis *ms*   3 dilegunt *in rasura*   4 enumerant *ms, litt.* nt *in rasura*
babilonis *ms*   7-8 habentem].i. populum *add. supra*   10 scuto *add. supra*   admonuit *ms*   15 decretui *ms*   auxilio] ab(latiuum) *add. supra*   commonisti *ms*
17 ostium *1ᵃ m.*   24 expli(cit) .u. incipit .ui. *ms*   26 confitetur] *litt.* tetur
in rasura   28 constituti * *ms*   30 facti deformis] fornicationis *add. supra*

Ὡς πανοπλίᾳ — βοήθειαν: (Θεοδώρου) Paris. 139, fol. 19ᵛ; Vat. 1682, fol. 22.
Ἐξομολογεῖται — ἁμαρτίαν: (Θεοδ Ἀντιόχ) Paris. 139, fol. 20ᵛ; Vat. 1682, fol. 23
(Mai, p. 390; P. G., 649 D 8-11); Barbaro, p. 61.

pant of that place on the evidence of the marvels you frequently perform in our midst. *And those who love your name will boast of you.* He logically lists everything due to follow: with Babylon destroyed and the captivity over, joys will be due to be bestowed on the people.

Because you, Lord, bless the righteous (v. 12). He calls the people *righteous* not by virtue of their pursuit of virtue, but through their having a knowledge of their creator in comparison with the Babylonians. *Lord, you crowned us as with a shield of your good will.* By saying *as with a shield,* he adopted a comparison to express an increase in divine protection; it is God's good and merciful will for the people and his generous attitude. The phrase *as with a shield you crowned us with your good will* means "with the very secure help of your good will," as if to say, With the security that it was your pleasure to accord us and with your decision to communicate to us, you made us glorious and honorable and kept us completely unharmed by the enemy (nicely referring to God's help as a shield).[2]

PSALM 6

Blessed David confesses to God his own sin, committed when he slept with Bathsheba.[1] He recites it when in difficulties, by which he was also tested on account of his sin. |

---

2. The occurrence of the final sentence in Greek reveals the occasional expansiveness of the Latin translator's rendition, which is as follows: "The phrase *as with a shield you crowned us with your good will* means, You have powerfully fortified us with the help of your decree so that we may be both honorable in your sight and unharmed by any attack of enemies. Moreover, when he speaks of God's help, he appropriately calls it a shield, the comparison being drawn from vigorous men who customarily defend others, keeping them unharmed from the blows of weapons by the barrier of their shields."

1. Cf. 2 Sam 11. This historical reference Theodore would have derived from Diodore, possibly also by noting the church's use of this psalm as the first of the seven penitential psalms (the Latin text here, where the Greek is also extant, saying, "*We* recite it …").

2. *Domine, ne in furore tuo arguas me, neque in ira tua corripias me.* Vt seruus, apud quem est domini magna reuerentia, cum conscius sibi fuerit peccati grandis admisu, non audet quidem in totum facti sui ueniam postulare, rogat tamen ut ita in se uindicetur ne castigatio modum accensa indignatione non teneat, ita et 5
Dauid argui quidem non refugit neque in totum declinat correptionis seueritatem, sed supplicat non cum furore et ira, quae est mensurae nescia, in se uindicari. Hoc autem dicit humanae consuetudinis morem secutus, quoniam nos, cum ira in ultionem delicti accendimur, iustitiae non tenemus mensuram. 10

3ᵃ. *Miserere mei, Domine, quoniam infirmus sum.* In tantum grauiora uerbera ferre non possum, ut sim miserationi magis pro ipsa mei adten|uatione uicinior: mala namque tribulationum, quibus propter peccatum meum traditus sum, omne robur meae ualitudinis adtriuerunt et possunt mihi ad emendationem uel sola sufficere. 15

3ᵇ⁻⁴ᵃ. *Sana me, Domine, quoniam conturbata sunt* usque *ualde·*

Ad augmentum dicti superioris uim mali, quo tabefactae carnes eius fuerunt, dicit etiam ossa sentire, quae conturbata reddunt grauis adflictionis indicium. Quod autem addit *et anima mea turbata est ualde*, ita possuit ac si diceret: Tribulatio ista, quam patior, excesso corpore usque ad animae interiora peruenit.

Τὸ αὐτὸ μειζόνως εἶπεν· τὸ μὲν γὰρ ἐταράχθη τὰ ὀστᾶ μου τὸ ἰσχυρὸν τοῦ συντριμμοῦ καὶ τῆς ταραχῆς παρίστησιν, τὸ δὲ καὶ ἡ ψυχή μου 20 ἐταράχθη σφόδρα, τουτέστι συντρίψασά μου τὸ σῶμα διέδυ μέχρις αὐτῆς τῆς ψυχῆς ἡ ταραχή.

25

4ᵇ. *Et tu, Domine, usque quo?* Quasi in longum castigatione protracta ait: *Et tu, Domine, usque quo?* Interrogantis specie quaerit quando Dominus malorum eius terminum ponet, timens ne, si ultra eius protrahatur offensa, pondus uerberum fere non possit. 30

2 ut seruus] adit non refugit *add. supra* 5 teneat] ut *add. supra* 7-8 ira in se — uindicari *ms* mesurae *ms* 9 cum] c⃰ *ms* dilicti *ms* 10 acendimur *1ᵃ m.* 12 posum *ms* 13 aditenuatione *1ᵃ m.* 15 adtriuerunt] *litt.* triu *in rasura* 16 sane *prius scriptum* conturbata] *litt.* b *in rasura* 17 dicti sup.] .i. quoniam infirmus sum *add. supra* 22 addit] uel ait *add. supra* 25 excesso] uel cesso sit in aliis (?) *2ᵃ m. in margine* 28 usque quo] .i. pones *add. supra.*

Τὸ αὐτὸ — ταραχή: (Θεοδώρου Ἀντιοχείας) Paris. 139, fol. 21; Vat. 1682, fol. 23ᵛ (Mai, p. 391; P. G., 649 D 12-652 A 2); Barbaro, p. 63.

Lord, do not censure me in your anger, nor correct me in your wrath (v. 1). A servant with great respect for his master, when he is aware of the commission of a great sin, does not even dare to ask for complete pardon of his sin, and instead begs that action be taken against him in such a way as to avoid chastisement exceeding limits once anger is aroused. So too David does not avoid censure or completely avoid the severity of correction, but asks that he not be punished with wrath and anger, which respect no limit. He says this in accordance with what is customary in human behavior, since when we are roused angrily to avenge a crime, we do not respect the limit of justice. *Have mercy on me, Lord, because I am weak* (v. 2): such is my inability to bear more severe scourging that I am closer to suffering by my very infirmity. In fact, the hardship of tribulation to which I was reduced by my sin eroded all the strength in my condition, and even of itself can be sufficient for my correction.

Heal me, Lord, for my bones are quivering down to *severely* (vv. 2–3). He said the same thing with greater stress: while *my bones are quivering* suggests the force of the impact and alarm, so too does *my soul is disturbed severely,* meaning, The alarm affected my body and penetrated to my very soul. *And you, Lord, how long?* as if he said in a long, drawn-out correction, *And you, Lord, how long?* In question form he asks when the Lord will bring his troubles to an end, afraid lest he not be able to bear the effect of the blows if his assault is prolonged further. |

5. *Conuertire, Domine, et eripe animam meam.* Bene, ut irato et
qui auerterit ab eo faciem supplicat, quo conuersis in eum oculis
exoratus aspiciat; quod uero ait *eripe animam meam,* quoniam
ipsi specialiter adflictionis et meroris pondus incubuit.

5   *Saluum me fac propter missericordiam tuam.* Medicinam sibi
fieri, id est a malis se erui inpertitu diuinae misserationis, inplorat,
cum possit in sufragium ueniae multa a se prius bene acta numerare, quae utique sunt diuino testimonio conprobata; sed ut seruus
offensam timens domini atque ad promerendam benignitatem eius
10 adtentior se ipse condemnat, nihil eorum in memoriam, quae bene
egit, reuocare confidit, deleta aestimans omnia tanti admisione peccati; quasi nullius ergo iustitiae sibi conscius solam Dei misericordiam ad restitutionem salutis inplorat.

6. *Quoniam non est in morte* usque *tui.* Id non dixit absolute *in*
15 *inferno* | possitos mortis lege Dei obliuia sustinere, sed ita nemi-
nem esse Dei memorem ut peccatis satisfactionem possit adhibere
et per penitentiam — quia non est penetentia de peccatis ⟨in⟩ inferno — errata corregere: finem enim uitae huius sequitur expunctio
futura meritorum. Hoc est ergo, quod uult dicere: Quoniam tempus
20 confitendi, id est penitendi, uitae nostrae finibus terminatur, hic
ergo satis agendum ut reatus honera deponantur, ut remisionis sententia seueritatem ultionis anticipet: ubi enim est tempus poeni-
tendi, ibi est tempus et ueniae; hic ergo, inquit, ubi est satisfactionis locus, pro errore supplico, quia uolo fieri de accepta remisione
25 securus. Ostendit autem in sequentibus quam sollicite satisfecerit,
id est quod poenitentiam non usque ad uerba susciperit, ut iuste
uideatur indulgentiam postulare.

7. *Laboraui in gemitu meo* usque *rigabo.* Pro praeterito futurum
tempus admouit: nam pro eo quod est *laui* et *rigaui,* ut sequenter
30 dicto superiori possit adiungi, *lauabo* possuit et *rigabo,* uarie

1-3 *verba* bene — aspiciat *litteris instruuntur ad syntaxeos ordinem insinuandum*   4 ipsi] dauid *add. supra*   7 cum possit] adit inplorat *add.
supra*   7-13 *verba* cum possit — inplorat *litteris* a-n *instruuntur*   11 ro-
uocare *ms*   omnia] opera bona *add. supra*   12 nullius] *litt.* ius *in rasura*
sibi] *litt.* bi *in rasura*   14 id *om. 1ª m.*   16 peccatis] *litt.* cati *in rasura*
17 quia — inferno *suppl. in marg.* in *supplevi*   18 errata] erra *1ª m.*   19 .i.
tempus *suppl. supra*   21 agendum *conieci,* augendum *ms*   doponantur *ms*
22 anticipiet *2ª m.*   23 uiniae *ms*   19-20 quoniam-penitendi] *cf. glossa apud*
Ascoli, *p. 48*   23 hiic *ms*   24 supplicio *1ª m.*   30 labauo *ms*   uariae
1ª m.

Turn, Lord, and rescue my soul (v. 4). He does well to implore him as though angry, with face averted from him, so that when asked, he may turn his eyes to him and look at him. He said *rescue my soul,* since the weight of affliction and grief lay on him in a special way. *Save me for your mercy's sake.* He begs that a cure be effected in him—that is, that he be rescued from trouble by a share in divine mercy—since as a claim on pardon he is in a position to list many previous good deeds of his, which in fact were confirmed by divine testimony. But as a servant fearful of offending his master condemns himself to prompt his benevolence more readily, he places no trust in recalling anything of good he had done, believing that all had been canceled by the commission of such a grave sin. As if aware of no righteousness of his own, therefore, he implores only the mercy of God with a view to restoration of his health.

For in death there is no down to *you* (v. 5). Instead of saying without qualification that in hell those overtaken by death suffer forgetfulness of the divine law, he says that so unmindful is anyone of God as to be unable to apply satisfaction of sins or through repentance (there being no repentance of sin in hell) to correct mistakes, since future cancellation of merits follows the end of this life. His meaning, then, is this: since the time for confession—that is, repentance—is finished at the end of our life, it is therefore here that we must take action to have the weight of guilt disposed of so that the verdict of forgiveness may anticipate the severity of vengeance. After all, where there is time for repentance, there is time also for pardon; here, therefore, he is saying, Where it is the place of satisfaction, I make supplication for mistakes, because I wish to be sure of the receipt of forgiveness.

Now, in what follows he brings out how carefully he made satisfaction—that is, that he undertook penance not just in words, so that he might properly be seen to seek forgiveness. *I grew weary with my groaning* down to *I shall drench* (v. 6). He used the future tense for the past: instead of "I flooded" and "I drenched," which could be added in keeping with what was said above, he put *I shall flood* and *I shall drench,* | changing the tense freely and in

tempora, ac licenter, inmotans. Dicuntur autem ista cum enfasi, ut etsi non tantos quantos sonant, tamen ad poenitentis fletus uberes indicandos.

8. *Turbatus est prae ira oculus meus.* Prae ira utique Dei, quam meritum peccantis accenderat, id est: irato te ita consternatus sum ac mente confusus, ut etiam corporis mei sensus officia sua explicare non ualeant.

Inueteraui inter omnes inimicos meos. Id est ab usu uestium; sic hi qui me oderant uiliter tractarunt: uestimentum enim, quod inueterescit, ipsa sui atritione testatur friquentis usus se iniuriam pertulisse. Indicat uero quod in tribulationibus possitus ossoribus suis dispectui fuerit atque contemtui, | quas quidem tribulationes Deo permittente sustenuit, ut afflictus et sollicitus curaret quod otiosus et remisus incurrerat; et ob hoc poenitentiae suae modum non tacuit, atque enumerauit in quibus malis propter iram Dei fuerit; dicit iam in sequentibus quoniam confundentur inimici eius cum ipse de aduersariis fuerit, Deo miserante, liberatus. Propterea ergo ait:

9-10. *Discedite a me omnes qui operamini iniquitatem* usque *suscipit.* Et in hoc loco sunt tempora commotata: nam pro « exaudiet » et « suscipiet » dixit *exaudiuit Dominus uocem fletus mei* et *Dominus orationem meam suscipit.* Hoc ⟨est⟩ igitur: semper non ero ergo in angoribus, quoniam exaudiet me Dominus et peccatis meis uiniam largietur; unde conuenit uobis, o inimici, obsidendi malignitate discedere, quoniam id etiam inuiti, cum coeperit me Deus adiuuare, facietis.

11. *Erubescant et conturbentur omnes* usque *uelochiter.* Et hic praesens possuit pro futuro: nam pro « erubescent » et « conturbabuntur » *erubescant* et *conturbentur* dixit. Consequens est enim inritis conatibus deformis misericordiae pondus incumbere.

1 enfasi *suppl. in marg.*   1-3 dicuntur — indicandos] *cf. glossa apud* Ascoli, *p. 49*   2 poenitentis] *litt.* is *in rasura*   4 turbata *ms*   ira] .i. uindicta *add. supra*   5 meretum *ms*   6 sensus] .i. auditus gus(tus) r(e)l(iqua) *add. supra*   8 abussu *ms*   10 iniriam *ms*   11 pertulisse] et *add. supra*   14 remisus] .i. lux (?) *add. supra*   modum] *litt.* odum *in rasura*   17 aduersaris *1ᵃ m.*   20 commota *1ᵃ m.*   21 suscipiet et *ms*   22 .i. est *add. supra*   23 .i. ero *add. supra*   24 obsidendi *conieci*, absidiendi *ms*   27 erubescant, conturbentur] impera(tiuum) *add. supra*   28 pro *om. 1ᵃ m.*   30 deformis] *aliquid deesse uidetur.*

different ways. Now, this is said with emphasis to suggest abundant tears of repentance, even if the expression is not precise. *My eye was affected by anger* (v. 7)—by God's anger, which the sinner deservedly aroused. In other words, When you became angry, I was so alarmed and confused in mind that even my bodily senses could not manage to discharge their functions. *I grew old in the midst of all my foes:* a metaphor from the way clothes are treated, those hating me likewise treating me abominably; clothing that grows old, you see, testifies by its very worn-out appearance that it has suffered the damage of frequent use. He implies that when he was in a condition of tribulation, he suffered the scorn and contempt of those who hated him, and it was with God's permission that he sustained these tribulations, so that in his affliction and anxiety he might ponder what he had incurred when a man of leisure and inactivity. For this reason he did not keep silence about the manner of his repentance, enumerating the troubles he encountered owing to God's anger.

In what follows he says that his enemies will be confounded when with God's mercy he is rid of his adversaries. Hence he goes on, *Depart from me, all you who are guilty of iniquity* down to *accepts* (vv. 8–9). In this place as well the tenses are changed: instead of "He will hearken" and "He will accept," he said *The Lord hearkened to the sound of my weeping* and *The Lord accepts my prayer.* The meaning is, therefore, I shall therefore not always be in distress, since the Lord will hearken to me and grant pardon for my sins. Hence it behooves you, O enemies, to desist from your malicious assault, since willy-nilly you will do so when God begins to help me. *Let them all be ashamed and confused down to rapidly* (v. 10). Here, too, he used the present for the future: instead of "They will be ashamed and confused," he said *Let them be ashamed and confused:* it follows that the weight of mercy will overwhelm their futile efforts. |

PSALMVS VII

Psalmus hic conuenienti titulo praenotatur. Cum enim a Chussi
Achitofel fuisset sententia dissoluta, reuersus Achitofel in domum
suam dolorem repudiati consilii sui suspendio publicauit. Quo au-
5 dito beatus Dauid id, quod factum fuerat, adscribens Deo psalmum
istum pro gratiarum cecinit actione.

2. *Domine, Deus meus, in te speraui, saluum me fac.* Quamuis
ipse Dauid Chussi consilio instructum ad ciuitatem remisserit, ut
id quod suadebat Achitofel suus sermo cassaret, tamen, ne uidea-
10 tur id quod acciderat suae sapientiae reputare, ait: *In te speraui,
saluum me fac.* Etsi | aliquid, inquit, ipse utiliter mentis intentione
prospexi, tamen quicquid animo concoepi a te id credidi prosperari. Docet autem nos per haec, ut cum operis aliquid arripimus,
etsi proprium quidem ad effectum rei studium requiratur, non nos
15 errare tamen si, in Domino spe possita, ea quae agenda sunt nihilo
minus intente faciemus.

Ex omnibus persequentibus me libera me. Quoniam a pessimis
Achitofel consiliis et omni eius nequitia praeter spem fuerat ereptus,
a Domino petit ut a caeteris aeque persequentibus eruatur. Nam
20 Achitofel, cum in repulsionem consilii sui uidisset Chussi sententiam fuisse susceptam, reuersus ad ciuitatem suam uelut in doloris
solacium uitam laqueo terminauit.

3. *Ne quando rapiat ut leo animam meam* usque *faciat.* Et infirmitatem suam et aduersarii potentiam alligat, ut per haec libe-
25 rantis Dei adiutorium manifestius adprobetur.

II Reg. XVI-XVII, 23.

1 expli(cit) ui. incipit uii *ms*   2 titulo] tulo *ms*   chussi] ab(latiuum)
add. supra   3 achitofel] geni(tiuum) *add. supra*   desoluta *ms*   4 suspendio
publ. *conieci*, supendio pauplicauit *ms*   quo] facto *add. supra*   6 cicinit *ms*
7 saluum] psalmum *ms*   quamuis] adit ait *add. supra*   7-11 *verba* quamuis —
me fac *litt.* a-i *supra scriptis instruuntur ad syntaxeos ordinem insinuandum*
11 mentis] perfectae *add. supra*   13 per haec] praedicta *add. supra*   14 nos]
.i. docet *add. supra*   19 ae*que *ms*   20 repulsionem *scripsi*, repulsam *ms*, .i.
pro in repulsionem *in margine*   24 potentiam] *litt.* po *in rasura, praecedunt
duae litterae erasae.*

To this psalm is prefixed an appropriate title: when Ahithophel's opinion was annulled by Hushai, Ahithophel went home and bruited abroad his disappointment at the rejection of his advice by hanging himself.[1] On hearing this, blessed David attributed to God what had happened and sang this psalm in thanksgiving.

Lord my God, in you I hoped; save me (v. 1). Although it was David himself who gave Hushai instructions and sent him back to the city so that his words might undermine what Ahithophel was advising,[2] nevertheless in case he should attribute to his own sagacity what had happened, he said *In you I hoped; save me.* He is saying, Even though I foresaw something of advantage with my mind's eye, I still believed that whatever I had in mind would succeed with your help. Now, he teaches us in this that when we undertake some exploit, even if for a successful outcome careful implementation is required, we will not go wrong if after placing hope in God we do what has to be done no less deliberately. *From all my pursuers deliver me.* Since he was rescued unexpectedly from the baleful advice of Ahithophel and all his malice, he asks of the Lord to be saved likewise from the other pursuers. Ahithophel, remember, on seeing Hushai's opinion accepted to the rejection of his own advice, returned to his own city and put an end to his life with a rope as though some solace for his disappointment.

Lest like a lion they should seize my soul down to *make me* (v. 2). He adduces his own weakness and the power of the adversary so as by this to highlight more clearly God's power. | *O Lord my God, if I have done this*

---

1. Cf. 2 Sam 16–17.
2. Cf. 2 Sam 15:33–37.

4. *Domine Deus meus, si feci istud.*

Id est: si feci quod nunc patior, si in aliquem quippiam iniquitatis admisi; quod manifestius in sequentibus dicit:
Si iniquitas in manibus meis.
Si iniustitiam a me commissam actuum meorum testimonio perdocetur.

Εἰ ἐποίησα τοῦτο, ὃ νῦν πάσχω, τουτέστιν εἰ ἠδίκησα.
Ὅθεν φανερώτερον ἐπάγει λέγων· 5
Εἰ ἔστιν ἀδικία ἐν χερσί μου, ἀντὶ τοῦ Εἰ εὕρημαί τι ἀδικὸν ἐργασάμενος.

5. *Si reddidi retribuentibus mihi mala.* 10

Ea quae merito prima sunt in relationis ordine secunda ponuntur: amplioris enim uirtutis testimonium est iniuste in se agentem alterum sustinere patienter quam ipsum non agere aliquid inique.

Εἰ ἀνταπέδωκα τοῖς ἀνταποδιδοῦσίν μοι κακά. Ἀεὶ τὸ μεῖζον δεύτερον τάττει τοῦ ἐλάττονος·
μεῖζον τοίνυν ὂν τοῦ ἀδικοῦντας ὑποφέρειν, τὸ μὴ ἄρξαι ἀδικίας δεύ- 15 τερον λέγει.

Decidam merito ab inimicis meis inanis.

Id est: Conatus mei nullum sortiantur effectum, nec ualeam aliquid in aduersarios meos ultionis exercere.

Ἀναχωρῆσαί μέ φησιν ἀπὸ τῶν ἐχθρῶν μου ἄπρακτος, μὴ δυνηθεὶς 20 φησιν μηδὲ τὸ τυχὸν αὐτοὺς ἀντιδικῆσαι.

6. *Persequatur inimicus animam meam et conpraehendat.*

Et illi quidem, qui me oderunt, nihil a me patiantur aduersi, sed e contrario impleant quicquid nituntur aduersum me efficere.

Αὐτοί τέ φησιν μηδὲν πάθοιεν δεινὸν παρ' ἐμοῦ, καὶ ἐμὲ διαθεῖεν 25 ἅπερ ἂν ἐθέλοιεν κακά.

Hoc est grauis deiec|tionis testimonium, si expossitus inimicis, se adserere et defensare non possit.

---

3 in] .i. contra *add. supra*   8 actuum meorum] *litt.* uum m(eorum) *in rasura*   10 reddi *ms*   11 prima] .i. si est iniquitas r(e)l(iqua) *add. supra* 12-13 ponuntur] si reddi r(e)l(iqua) *add. supra*   20 sortiuntur *ms*   ualeam] .i. ut *add. supra*   22 exserere *ms*   26 implent] ut *add. supra*   27 deictionis *ms.*

Εἰ ἐποίησα — δεύτερον λέγει: (Θεο⸌ ἀντιο⸍) Paris. 139, fol. 22ᵛ; Vat. 1682, fol. 26 (Mai, p. 391; PG., 652 A 4-10); Barbaro, p. 71.   15 ἀκηδίας P.
Ἀναχωρῆσαι — ἐθέλοιεν κακά: (Θεο⸌) Paris. 139, fol. 22ᵛ; Vat. 1682, fol. 26; Barbaro, p. 71 (Ἀναχωρῆσαι — ἀντιδικῆσαι).

(v. 3)—that is, If I caused what I now suffer; in other words, If I did wrong. Hence, to make it clearer he says *If there is wrong on my hands,* meaning, If I am found to have done anything wrong. *If I repaid evil for evil* (v. 4). He always places greater things second in order to the lesser; accordingly, since putting up with wrongdoers is greater, he means that not becoming involved in wrongdoing is of secondary importance. *May I duly yield to my foes empty-handed:* may I be unsuccessful and yield to my foes, unable to repay them any kind of evil.

    Let the foe hunt down my soul and lay hold of it (v. 5): may they suffer no harm from me, and cause me whatever trouble they wish. (This is evidence of deep depression, his being vulnerable to the enemy and unable to resist and defend himself.) *Let them trample my life into the ground*—that is, | Wipe

Et conculcet in terra uitam meam.

Ita me aterat, ut nihil memoriae meae superesse patiatur.

Τουτέστιν Ἐξαλεῖψαι μού φησιν
τὸ μνημόσυνον· τοῦτο γάρ ἐστιν
τὸ καταπατῆσαι εἰς γῆν τὴν ζωήν
μου.

5

Et gloriam meam in puluerem deducat.

Ita, inquit, aduersum me confortentur inimici, ut cum interficerint atque in inferna depulerint,
10 etiam posteritatis meae indicia
non relinquant. Id enim temporis Israhelitae pro felicitate maxima conputabant si relinquerent
filios qui eos ab iniuria obliuio
15 nis adsererent; nam, e contrario,
mori sine superstite uel herede,
id est sine eo in quo pignus nominis sui uel seminis resideret,
reputabatur dedecoris et pudoris:
20 ob hoc itaque erat etiam lege
praeceptum, ut morientis filii sine
filiis uxorem frater acciperet ac
semen in defuncti memoriam suscitaret.

Τουτέστιν οὕτως μοι περιγένοιτο,
ὡς ἀνελεῖν με καὶ ἐγκαταχῶσαι τῇ
γῇ καὶ μὴ περιλιπεῖν μου τῆς ζωῆς
μνημόσυνον. Διά τοι τοῦτο; Ἐπειδὴ
δόξα τοῖς Ἰσραηλίταις ἦν τὸ μνημό
συνον τελευτῶντας καταλιπεῖν,

ἀδοξία δὲ τὸ
ἐναντίον· τούτων γὰρ ἕνεκεν καὶ ὁ
νόμος προσέταττεν τοῦ τελευτῶντος
ἄπαιδος τὸν ἀδελφὸν λαμβάνοντα
τὴν γυναῖκα ἀνιστᾶν σπέρμα τῷ ἀδελ
φῷ, ὡς ἂν μὴ τὸ μνημόσυνον τοῦ
τελευτῶντος ἀφανίζοιτο.

25 7. *Exsurge, Domine, in ira tua.* Non quod aliquando Deus sedeat
nunc rogatur ut exsurgat, sed quoniam nos, cum in ultionem accingimur, promtos nos ad uindicandum esse tali motu corporis
indicamus. Verba ergo nostrae consuetudinis ad exorandum admouet Deo, ac si diceret: sollicite in uindictam mei ac proprie com
30 mouere; atque ideo intulit *in ira tua*, id est: commotior ad ulciscendum uelut aspectu indignantis accede.

11-24 Deut. XXV, 5; cf. infra in ps. XXXIV, 12.

1 uitam m.] .i. si feci r(e)l(iqua) *add. supra*   2 a me *ms*   8 ut cum *om.*
1ᵃ m.   14 iuria *ms*   16 here *1ᵃ m.*   23 semen] sem *1ᵃ m.*   23-24 suscitaret] ut *add. supra.*

Τουτέστιν — ἀφανίζοιτο: (Θεοδώρου) Paris. 139, fol. 22ᵛ; Vat. 1682, fol. 26ʳ·ᵛ; Barbaro, p. 71.

out memory of me (the meaning of *trample my life into the ground*). *And bring my glory down into the dust*—that is, Let them so prevail over me as to destroy me; bring me down to the dust and leave no memory of my life. Why on earth? Since for the Israelites the leaving of a memorial for the dead was their glory, whereas the opposite fate was inglorious. This, in fact, was the reason why the law also commanded that the brother of a man who died without children should take his wife and have children for his brother lest the memory of the dead man perish.[3]

Rise up, Lord, in your anger (v. 6). It is not that God is sometimes seated that he asks him to *rise up;* rather, it is because we, when bent on vengeance, suggest by such a bodily movement that we are ready to take punitive action. Thus, we apply words from our normal procedure to present petitions to God, as if to say, Take action to avenge me really and truly. Hence he adds as well *in your anger*—that is, Come to take vengeance more resolutely as though with an angry aspect. | *Be exalted in the boundaries of your enemies,* not that

---

3. Cf. Deut 25:5–6.

Exaltare in finibus inimicorum tuorum.

Non quod aliquo loci supe-   Οὐχ ὅτι αὐτὸς ὑψοῦται· οὐ γὰρ
rioris erectio faciat altiorem, ne-
que enim secundum naturam   προσδεῖται ὑψώ-
suam indiget eliuari, sed cum   σεως, — ἀλλ' ὅτι ἐν ταῖς διανοίαις   5
quid miri operis facit, uelut cres-   ἡμῶν τοιαύτη ἐγγίνεται ἔννοια περὶ
cat in agnitione nostra atque   αὐτοῦ ἐπειδάν τι ποιήσῃ φοβερὸν
intellectibus nostris ostenditur.   σημεῖον, διὰ τοῦτο λέγει ἐν τοῖς
Quod autem ait *in finibus inimi-*   πέρασι τῶν ἐχθρῶν μου, τουτέστι
corum tuorum id est: in uniuersos   πάντας περιλαβὼν τῇ τιμωρίᾳ τοὺς   10
aduersarios tuos seuerus exsiste;   ἐχθροὺς γνώρισον ἅπασι τὸ ὑψηλόν
per hoc enim agnoscetur uirtutis   σου καὶ τὸ ἰσχυρόν· τοῦτο γὰρ μά-
tuae potentia, si omnes inimici   λιστα ἐγνωρίζετο ἐκ τοῦ πάντας τι-
tui tuam sentiant ultionem.   μωρηθῆναι.

Exsurge, Domine Deus meus, in praecepto quod mandasti. Quo-   15
niam inter reliqua legis mandata praeciperat Dominus, | ut iniqui-
tatis ausus uigor iudicii frenaret et praemeret, hoc ait: Censura,
quam nobis mandas, contra partes improbas per te ipse exsequere, ut mandatorum tuorum ueritas rerum testimoniis adprobetur.   20

8. *Et sinagoga populorum circumdabit te.* Erat iste mos apud
filios Israel, ut ad psallendum Deo concurrerent bi ad quorum
spectabat officium. Hoc est ergo quod ait: Facientes choros, psalmos tibi consona uoce cantabimus et altare tuum in modum co-
ronae circumpossiti ex omni parte cingemus.   25

Et propter hanc in altum regredere, Domine. Propter hanc, id est
sinagogam, quoniam a bellorum sollicitudine liberis licebit tuis laudibus occupari. *In altum regredere*, id est: prostratis, inquit, inimicis nostris, nihil de te humile sinas ab omnibus aestimari, ut conueniens operibus tuis laudum nostrarum reddatur officium.   30

2 quod om. *1ª m.*   aliquo] .i loco *add. supra*   6 quid *suppl. in marg.*
9-11 *verba* quod — exsiste *litteris* a-e *instruuntur ad syntaxeos ordinem insi-*
nuandum   11 seuerus] *litt.* eu *in rasura*   existe *1ª m.*   14 sentiat *1ª m.*
17-18 *verba* hoc — exsequere *litteris* a-i *instruuntur ad syntaxeos ordinem in-*
sinuandum   18 improbos per te ipse partes *ms*   exsequere] imper(ativum)
add. supra   19 rerum] .i. operum *add. supra*   22 israel *in rasura*   sallendum *ms*   23 hoc *in rasura*   choros psalmos] chorus psalmus *prius scriptum*
27 a om. *1ª m.*   29 aestimari] *litt. fin.* i *in rasura.*

Οὐχ ὅτι — τιμωρηθῆσαι: (Θεοδ Αντιχ) Paris. 139, fol. 23; Vat. 1682, fol. 27
(Mai, p. 391; P. G. 652 A 12-B 4); Barbaro, p. 73.

he personally is lifted up, not needing to be lifted up, but because in our ways of thinking such an understanding arises in his regard when he works some fearsome sign. For this reason he says *in the boundaries of my foes*[4]—that is, Enveloping all the enemy in punishment, make known to them all your elevation and strength (this being made known to them all especially by the punishment of them all). *Arise, Lord, in the commandment you have delivered.* Since among the other precepts of the law the Lord commanded that the full force of judgment should rein in and keep in check the temerity of evildoing, he says, The censure you require of us carry out yourself against lawless groups so that the authenticity of your precepts may be confirmed by evidence.

The assembly of peoples will surround you (v. 7). The custom with the people of Israel was for those whose responsibility it was to assemble to sing praise to God. His meaning here is, then, Forming a choir, we shall sing psalms to you in harmony, gather around your altar in the shape of a crown, and assemble from every quarter. *And on account of it return on high, Lord:* on account of it—the assembly, that is—since people free from the concerns of war will be able to be engaged in praising you. *Return on high*—that is, With our enemies laid low, you allow no lowly attitude to be held of you by anyone, with the result that our duty of praise will be performed in keeping with your deeds. |

---

4. The manuscripts generally do not include the biblical text on which Theodore is commenting; Devreesse supplies it. In this case an extant Greek manuscript reads "my foes," as does Theodoret's but not Diodore's or Chrysostom's or the Latin (Vulgate) text supplied by Devreesse, who admits that inevitably there can be discrepancies (*Le commentaire,* xxx). In the word "arrogance" of the Hebrew text, the LXX sees a similar form meaning "boundaries."

9. *Dominus iudicat populos.* Id est, quam iustas inter se mutuo bellorum causas diuersi habeant, iudicii sui adpendit examine.

Iudica mihi, Domine, secundum iustitiam meam. Dignum me, in-
5 quit, auxilii tui inpertitione decerne, sciens profecto quoniam equissime opem tuae defensionis inploro: nam cum nihil ipse in quempiam inique fecerim iniquitate praemor aliena. Quod autem dicit *iustitiam meam,* siue ex sua siue ex persona loquatur aliena, hoc indicat quod iuste aduersum inimicos Dei poscat auxilium, a quibus
10 ledatur iniuria; nusquam hoc ita iustitiae suae meminit, ut ad studium uitae suae eam referre uideatur. Docet etiam nos quod tunc possimus inter aduersa possiti diuinas aures aspectumque conuertere si sub aliena iniquitate laborantes ipsi tamen iustitiae seruiamus, atque ideo consequenter intulit:

15 *Et secundum innocentiam meam super me.*

Hic *innocentiam* non pro sem-   Ἀκακίαν δὲ οὐ τὴν ἁπλότητα,
plicitate possuit, quae mali expers
uicina uidetur infantiae, sed eam
quae nihil in eum, a quo iniu-   ἀλλὰ τὸ μηδὲν ἐρ-
20 riam accipit, sit iniquitatis ope-   γάσασθαι κακῶν λέγει.
rata. Sicut ergo, inquit, cum ab   Ὥσπερ τοίνυν φησὶν ἐγὼ
inimicis affligor | uicem malitiae   κακῶς μὲν αὐτοὺς οὐ διέθηκα, πάσχω
refferre non studeo, ita me opor-   δὲ νῦν ὑπ᾽ ἐκείνων κακῶς, οὕτω μοι
tet absolui et in illos seueris-   κρῖνον ἀδικουμένῳ μάτην καὶ μὴ δι-
25 sime uindicari.   καίως πάσχοντι.

10. *Consumetur nequitia peccatorum.* Finem nocendi ei faciat modus a te correptionis inlatae.

Et direges iustum. Proficit ad iustitiae commendationem aduersum iniquos prolata sententia. Nam tanto magis a bonis studio
30 aequitatis insistitur, quanto in malos uiderint uindicari; et quoniam se diregi *nequitia peccatorum* poposcerat terminata, iustas alligationes suas nititur adprobare.

1-2 motuo *ms*   1-3 *verba* quam — examine *litt.* a-e *instruuntur ad syntaxeos ordinem insinuandum*   2 diuersi habeant] *litt.* uersi ha *in rasura* èxanime *ms*   4 mihi] mi *ms*   5 inpertione *1ª m.*   10 ledatur *in rasura* 11 docet] *.i.* dauid *add. supra*   12 aspectumque] *.i.* dei *add. supra* 16 hiic *ms*   23 studio *ms*   24-25 seuerssime *1ª m.*   26 faciat] imper(atiuum) *add. supra.*

Ἀκακίαν — πάσχοντι: (Θεοῦ ἀντιοχίας) Paris. 139, fol. 23ᵛ; Vat. 1682, fol. 28 (Mai, p 391; P. G., 652 B 13-C 2).

The Lord judges peoples (v. 8)—that is, he determines by his weighing of the evidence how just are the declarations of war among the various peoples. *Judge me, Lord, according to my righteousness:* recognize my worthiness of a share in your help, clearly aware that it is most fair that I should beg the assistance of your defense; after all, though I personally did nothing wrong to anyone, I am oppressed by others' wrongdoing. Now, the fact that he says *my righteousness,* whether speaking in his own person or in someone else's, suggests that he is right to demand God's help against his enemies, having been harmed by them; nowhere does he make reference to his own righteousness in such a way as to appear to attribute it to the zeal of his own life. It teaches us as well that at the time we are placed in a hostile situation we can attract the attention of the divine hearing and regard if when suffering from others' wrongdoing we still serve the cause of justice. Hence, he goes on in the same vein *And according to my innocence over me.* By *innocence* it is not simplicity he is referring to, but not doing any wrong. So his meaning is, Just as I am not badly disposed to them, and yet am ill-treated by them, so judge me as someone wronged without cause and suffering unjustly.

The wickedness of sinners will come to an end (v. 9): may the manner of the chastisement imposed by you put an end to the harm it causes. *And you will guide the righteous.* The sentiment expressed is of value in praising righteousness in the face of wrongdoers: the greater the accent that falls on the pursuit of justice by good people, the more they appear to be vindicated against evil people; and since he requested that he himself be guided once *the wickedness of sinners* is brought to an end, he makes the effort to confirm his affirmations as justified. | *You who test hearts and entrails* down to *of heart*

10c-11. *Scrutans corda et renes Deus* usque *corde.* Cum profunda cogitationis inspicias et mentium secreta rimeris, profecto nosti quia iure tuum adiutorium postolamus; quia etiam consuescas saluos facere eos, quos nulla familiaritas tortuosae prauitatis inplicuit et a recti calle detorsit, et cum istud familiare sit tibi, conpetenter 5 petimus ut aduersariis tuis adminiculis eruamur. Sed quoniam dixerat de Deo quod *saluos* faceret *rectos corde,* occurrebat aliquid quaestionis, — id est, quod inuenerentur frequenter iusti qui de uitae periculo non nihil trepidationis incurrerent, cum e diuerso peccatores dies suos non solum in securitate, uerum etiam in lae- 10 titia terminarent, — subdidit:

12. *Deus iudex iustus et fortis et patiens* usque *dies.* Etsi eueniat, inquit, ista meritorum confusio, ut bonis malorum dominetur inprobitas, tamen apud examen Dei iustitiae monimenta non pereunt, qui, quamuis per patientiam peccata disimulet, et tamen uehimen- 15 ter uindicat cum ultionis tempus insteterit. Et quoniam iustum et patientem Deum dixerat, patientiae testimonium ostendit per hoc quod ait: *Num quid irascitur per singulos dies.* Iustitiae uero in sequentibus documenta subiecit dicendo:

13. *Nisi conuersi fueritis gladium suum uibrabit.* Id est: Non 20 usque in finem per bonum patientiae inpunita uitia sustinebit, sed exspectat conuersionem; quae si non sequatur nec fecerit dilatio meliores, non morabitur ultio, partes iudicii exsequente iustitia.

13b-14b. *Arcum suum tendit* usque *efficit.* Vt terribilem peccatoribus ac minacem ostenderet Deum, uerba nostri moris inseruit et, 25 ut diceret quia ultionis eius seueritatem noxiorum nullus effugeret, ait: *Arcum suum tendit,* — quo solent utique etiam longe stantes laetale uulnus accipere, — *sagitas suas ardentes effecit.* Duo quae reos terreant in uno ictu amara iunguntur, ignis et ferrum, ut per aliud urantur, per aliud inquietentur.   30

15. *Ecce parturit iniustitiam.* Ad pessima Achitofel consilia et funestum eius finem transitum fecit; personam tamen indulgentio-

---

3-6 *verba* quia — eruamur *litteris* a-e *instruuntur ad syntaxeos ordinem insi-nuandum*   4 eos om. *1ᵃ m.*   prauita ** *ms*   et] quos non *add. supra*   5 arrecti calli *ms,* .i. iteneris *add. infra,* uel callide *2ᵃ m. in margine*   16 et om. *1ᵃ m.*   17 dixerat et *1ᵃ m.*   26 eius] dei *add. supra*   27 longe stantes] .i. in peccatis *add. supra*   29 iuctu *ms*   30 inquitantur *ms*   31 Accitofel *ms*   et] .i. ad *add. supra.*

(vv. 9–10): since you scrutinize deepest thoughts and examine the secrets of minds, surely you know that it is right for us to ask your help. You are accustomed to save those not caught up in a habit of twisted depravity or deviating from the straight and narrow, and since that is known to you, we properly ask to be rescued from our adversaries with your support.

Since, however, he said of God that he saves *the right of heart,* a question arose: that righteous people often are found entertaining no little anxiety about the risk to life, while on the contrary sinners end their days not only serenely but even joyfully. So he went on to say *God is a just judge, strong and long-suffering* down to *day* (v. 11): even if a reversal of fortunes takes place such that the lawlessness of evil people oppresses the good, yet the records of righteousness will not go unnoticed by the examination of God, who, although passing over sin in his long-suffering, will yet come to justice in a severe manner when the time of vengeance arrives. And since he said that God is *just* and *long-suffering,* he provides evidence of his long-suffering through his further remark *Surely he is not angry every day?*

In what follows he provides proofs of righteousness when he says *If you are not converted, he will wield his sword* (v. 12)—that is, far from leaving vicious deeds unpunished without limit for the sake of long-suffering, he awaits conversion; if it does not follow and delay does not lead to reform, vengeance will not be postponed, righteousness taking the role of a court. *He draws his bow* down to *makes* (vv. 12–13). To present God as terrifying and threatening to sinners, he employs terms describing our behavior, and to convey that no harmful action will escape the severity of his vengeance, he says *he draws his bow* (from which even people standing at a distance normally receive a lethal wound) and *he made his arrows fiery:* two harsh effects that frighten the guilty are combined in one blow—fire and steel—with the result that through one they are burnt and through the other tormented.

Lo, he gave birth to iniquity (v. 14). He moved on to Ahithophel's baleful counsels and his dire end; yet he maintained the role of a rather indulgent |

ris patris seruauit sollicite ubique, ne uel inpraecaretur filio uel
amarius quaeri de iniquo tamen pignore uideretur. Signanter uero
ait: *Ecce*, ut uelut digito extento Achitofel indicare uideatur, illud
etiam tali ostentione contingens quod superius dixerat: quoniam
5 etsi non quotidie in peccantes ulciscatur Deus, tamen in contemp-
tores emendationis uindicare non differat. Ecce, inquit, Achitofel,
cum aduersum nos consilia maligna concoeperit, qualiter est in
illum pro cogitatione uel suasione noxia uindicatum.

Concoepit dolorem et peperit iniquitatem. Dolorem uocat rem de
10 qua doloris causa nascatur. Quoniam ergo consilium, quod dederat
Achitofel, erat plenum periculi uel doloris, bene illud uocauit non
consilium sed *dolorem*, uocabulum operi de effectu et actioni de
fine suo nomen inponens.

16. *Lacum aperuit et effodit eum.* Non tenui, inquit, nequitia et
15 quaesiuit ut superficie proderetur, sed dolis in altum dimisis ad
nostrum est armatus interitum.

Per similitudinem ergo lacus *Βαθυτέραν φησὶν εἰργάσατο τὴν*
in profundum defossi, grauia eius *ἐπιβουλήν, ἐκ μεταφορᾶς τὸ δολερὸν*
et noxia consilia uoluit indicare. *καὶ βαθὺ τῆς βουλῆς παραστήσας.*

20 16ᵇ-17ᵇ. *Et incidit in foueam* usque *discendet.* In ipsum, inquit,
consiliorum eius est uersa malitia: nam ipse mortem, quam alii
parabat, incurrit; quod quidem ita factum est. Nam cum non potuisset id, quod suasserat, obtinere et, Deo faciente, consilium
Chussi fuisset melius | adprobatum, egresus laqueo sibi guttur ad-
25 strinxit.

18. *Confitebor Domino secundum iustitiam* usque *altissimi.* Pro
his ergo agam gratias Domino, qui in Achitofel iustissime uindicauit.

1 inpraecaretur] .i. uindictam *add. supra* 2 quaeri] *litt.* ri *in rasura*
3 degito *ms* uideatur] dauid *add. supra* 4 ostentione *in rasura* (*ex* osten-
tatione?) continguens *ms* 6 emedationis *ms* inquit] dauid *add. supra*
7 maligna] magna *1ᵃ m.* 8 illum] .i. in Achitofel *add. supra* 12 uocabu-
lum] .i. dolor *add. supra* actione *ms* 13 nomen] dolor *add. supra* 13 ape-
riut *ms* 16 nostrum *in rasura* 20 ipsum] .i. achitofel *add. supra* 21 eius]
achitofel *add. supra* ipse] achitofel *add. supra* alii] dauid *add. supra*
24 fuisset] cum *add. supra* gutor *ms* 27 iustissime] *litt.* iu *in rasura.*

Βαθυτέραν — παράστησας: Paris. 139, fol. 25 (Θεοˢ αντιοˣ); Coisl. 10, fol. 1
(Θεοˢ); Vat. 1422, fol. 35 (an.); Vat. 1682, fol. 29ᵛ (Mai, p. 391; P. G., 652 D
4-6).

father, always on the lookout lest he either be berated by his son or appear to be questioned more bitterly about the wicked pledge. It was not without purpose that he said *Lo,* as if to give the impression of pointing his finger at Ahithophel, achieving the same effect as he had with what he said above— namely, that even if God does not take vengeance on sinners every single day, yet he does not postpone punishing those who scorn reform. See Ahitho- phel, he is saying, when he devised his malicious plans against us: how he is punished for his harmful scheming and advice. *He conceived distress and brought forth lawlessness.* By *distress* he refers to that from which the cause of distress springs. Since, then, what Ahithophel offered was full of peril and distress, he was right to call it not advice but *distress,* naming the deed after its effect and describing the action by its outcome.

He dug a pit and excavated it (v. 15): it was with no slight malice that he took steps to gain a superficial advantage; rather, he went to great heights in devising his plots and was ready to achieve our downfall. He hatched a profound scheme, he is saying, using a metaphor to compare the perfidy and depth of the plot. *He fell into the hole* down to *will descend* (vv. 15–16): the malice of his counsels has been turned onto himself, meeting the death he had prepared for others. This actually happened: when he could not achieve what he recommended, and with God's intervention Hushai's advice was taken as preferable, he went out and hanged himself with a noose. *I shall confess to the Lord in keeping with his righteousness* (v. 17): For this I therefore shall give thanks to the Lord, who most justly punished Ahithophel. |

PSALMVS VIII

In hoc psalmo beatus Dauid
profetali repletus spiritu de Domini incarnatione praeloquitur
et ea dicit de Christo quae sunt
postea rebus inpleta, per quod
sane confutatur omnis iudaicae
contradictionis inprobitas. Nam
hoc, quod dictum est *ex ore infantium et lactantium perfecisti laudem*, constat in Domino ipsis esse
rebus impletum quando profetiae
ac profetato testimonium opera
reddiderunt.

Visum sane est quibusdam
quod in Tabernaculorum con-
fixione a beato Dauid sit psalmus iste conpossitus, quo tempore etiam frugum, quae per
decimas offerebantur, fieri solebat inlatio, et ideo superscriptum
esse illum « pro torcularibus ».

Καὶ ἐν τούτῳ τὰ κατὰ τὸν Χρι-
στὸν ἡμῖν προφητεύει ὁ μακάριος
Δαυίδ· προαναφωνεῖ γὰρ τῇ τοῦ
Πνεύματος ἐνεργείᾳ   5

ὡς ἂν ὑμνήσωσιν αὐτὸν
ἐν τῷ ἱερῷ οἱ παῖδες, οἵ τε οἱ ὑπομά-
ζιοι καὶ οἱ ἕτεροι νήπιοι.

Φασὶ δέ τινες καὶ εἰς τὸν κοινὸν 15
εἰρῆσθαι ἄνθρωπον, ἐν τῇ τῶν Σκη-
νοπηγίων ἑορτῇ τοῦτον λελέχθαι τὸν
ψαλμὸν ὑπὸ τοῦ μακαρίου Δαυὶδ καθὸ
ἡ τῶν καρπῶν συγκομιδὴ γίνεται,
καὶ διὰ τοῦτο ἐπιγέγραπται « παρὰ 20
τῶν ληνῶν ».

Sed, siue hoc uerum sit siue falsum, non uidetur magnopere
requirendum, quia ad psalmi magis intellectum nitimur peruenire.
Nam si sciatur tempus in quo psalmus decantatus est, potest qui- 25
dem superscriptioni, quod uera sit, perhibere testimonium, tamen
non potest etiam dictorum notitiam tradere intellectumque rese-
rare, sicut, e contrario, etiam si ignoretur tempus et falsa sit in-
scriptio, nihil intellectui commutat nec per hoc dictorum erit di-
ficilior et tarda cognitio.   30

9-11 v. 3; cf. Matth. XXI, 15-16 et supra, p. 11.

1 expli(cit) uii psal(mus). incipi(t) uiii *ms*   3 spiritu] .i. sancto *add. supra*
12 rebus] .i. operibus *add. supra*   20 decimas] deci∗mas *ms, litt.* mas *in
rasura*   21 et ideo] .i. uisum est uel constat *add. supra*   22 illum] psalmum *add. supra*   28 sicut] si *ms*   e *in rasura*   29 commutat] commo-
dat *ms*.

Καὶ ἐν τούτῳ — παρὰ τῶν ληνῶν: (Θεο᷍ ἀντ.) Paris. 139, fol. 25ᵛ; Vat. 1682,
fol. 30ᵛ (Mai, p. 391; P. G., 652 D 11-653 A 5); Barbaro, p. 84.

Psalm 8

In this psalm blessed David delivers a prophecy about Christ; under the influence of the Spirit he predicts that the children will sing his praises in the temple, both children at the breast and other infants.[1] Now, some commentators claim that this psalm was composed by blessed David even for people in general on the Feast of Tabernacles, when the harvest of crops happens, and hence is given the title "on the winepresses."[2] Be this true or false, however, there seems no particular need for us to settle this, because we are interested rather in arriving at the psalm's meaning: if the time when the psalm was sung were known, it could provide confirmation of the truth of the title, but it could not also suggest knowledge of the contents and convey understanding; just as, on the other hand, even if the time were unknown and the title were false, it does not in any way change the sense, nor will knowledge of the contents thus be more difficult and slow in coming. |

---

1. Both opening sentences are extant also in Latin, the former reading, "In this psalm blessed David, filled with a prophetic spirit, predicts the Lord's incarnation and speaks of events concerning Christ later fulfilled, thus soundly refuting the dishonesty of all the Jewish opposition."

2. Theodore—like Diodore, but unlike Theodoret, who will be less rationalistic about the titles—sees no value in following up the significance of the phrase in the psalm title rendered "on the winepresses" by the LXX translator, who erroneously saw *gat* in the Hebrew *gittith,* a term that also puzzles modern commentators. Unaware, like them, of this solecism, he argues that the (false) clue, even if of relevance to *Sitz im Leben* (not a usual concern for him and his Antiochene contemporaries), does little to help one grasp the meaning, διάνοια, the true object of a commentator's search.

Notandum est sane illud contra heriticos, — qui quidem, ita ut nos, tam uetus quam nouum testamentum recipiunt, — quoniam grandem differentiam inter Deum Verbum et susceptum hominem profetiae ipsius carmen ostendit, et tantam distinctionem inter
5 susceptum et suscipientem facit quanta discritio inter Deum et reliquos omnes inuenitur. A Iudeis quoque psalmus iste in Deum et hominem, cui conueniant illa quae inferius dicuntur, indubitanter accipitur. Inter susceptum uero hominem et Deum Verbum, quod diximus, tantam esse diuersitatem quanta est
10 omnis hominis ad Deum, ad naturae distinctionem uolumus accipi, non ad honoris diuersitatem: nam honoris titulus in suscepto homine | omnem creaturam longe transgreditur, quam quidem honoris eminentiam per coniunctionem personae homo Deo unitus accipit.
15 Sed iam strictim carpentes singula, non patiemur expossitionem nostram longius euagari, quoniam hoc nobis in omnibus facere psalmis propossitum est ut, relinquentes quae extrinsecus incurrere poterant, ea quae ad expossitionem pertinent sola dicamus.

2. *Domine Dominus noster, quam admirabile est* usque *terra.*
20 sancti Spiritus gratia reuelante in contemplationem futurorum adductus, ingenti stupore conpletur et inter ipsa psalmi initia uocem admirationis emittit. *Domine,* inquit, *Dominus noster, quam admirabile est nomen tuum in uniuersa terra.* Hac autem uoce, quam magnitudo admirationis elicuit, spicialiter indicatur quoniam omnem
25 terram praedicatio euangelii completura sit et gentes Christo post adnuntiationem fidei, relictis idolis, crediturae: per doctrinam enim euangelii in uniuersa terra factum esse *admirabile nomen* Domini conprobatur. Quod ergo ait *Quam admirabile est nomen tuum ⟨in⟩ uniuersa terra,* uelut stupens ad rerum magnitudinem pronuntiat,
30 et quod uidebat per consequentiam esse secuturum; recipietur, inquit, praedicatio euangelii in omni terra et nomen tuum erit

1-2 ut nos] .i. recipimus *add. supra* 3 deferentiam *1ᵃ m.,* deff. *corr.* 4 ostendat *1ᵃ m.* 5 faciat *ms* deum] .i. patrem *add. supra* 6 omnes] homines *add. supra* 7 cui] .i. homini *add. supra* 8 et *om. 1ᵃ m.* 8-10 *verba* hominem — uolumus *litteris* a-k *supra aut infra additis instruuntur ad syntaxeos ordinem insinuandum* 9 quanta] diuersitas *add. supra* 15 strictim] breuiter *add. supra* 17 relinquentes] .i. ea *add. supra* 19 domine — noster] hic est sensus .i. nolinfed *etc.* (Ascoli, p. 59⁸) *add. supra* 20 reualante *ms,* litt. an *in rasura* 21 initia *in rasura* 26 crediturae] sint *add. supra* 28 in *om. 1ᵃ m.* 29 in *suppleui* 30 securturum] *supple* e. g. proclamat recipietur] fu(turum) *add. supra.*

It should at least be noted in opposition to the heretics—who, like us, in fact, accept both Old and New Testament—that the song of this prophecy brings out a great difference between God the Word and the man assumed, and draws as great a distinction between the one assumed and the one assuming as there is between God and all others. By Jews as well this psalm is accepted unhesitatingly as referring to God and to the man to whom applies what is said below. Between the man assumed and God the Word, as we said, we want such a diversity to be accepted in regard to distinction of nature as there is between every human being and God, but not in regard to a diversity of status; in fact, the claim on status in the man assumed far surpasses every creature, since the man received this eminence of status by his union with God through a joining of person.

Let us now, however, take up details in regular order, and not allow our commentary to be further sidetracked, since it is our purpose in all the psalms to ensure that we leave aside what can be irrelevant and mention only what pertains to the commentary.

O Lord our Lord, how wonderful down to *earth!* (v. 1). Brought to a contemplation of future events by the revealing grace of the Holy Spirit, he is filled with great astonishment and utters a cry of wonder at the very beginning of the psalm. *O Lord our Lord, how wonderful is your name in all the earth!* Now, by this cry, which the extent of his wonder drew forth, he suggests in particular that the preaching of the gospel would fill the whole earth, and the nations would abandon the idols and believe in Christ after the preaching of the faith; he confirms that through the teaching of the gospel the Lord's name is made wonderful in all the earth. This, then, is the meaning of *how wonderful is your name in all the earth,* as though in uttering it he is astonished at the extent of the event and what seemed to follow as a consequence. The preaching of the gospel, he is saying, will be accepted in the whole earth, and your name will be | famous wherever word of your teaching penetrates.

celebre quaqua doctrinae tuae sermo peruenerit; quod quidem per
ea quae sequuntur fecit esse manifestum.

Quoniam eliuata est magnificentia tua super caelos. Ita, inquit,
omnes mundi partes honor tui nominis occupauit, ut amplitudo
gloriae tuae, emensa terrarum breuitate, ad caelorum altiora 5
peruenerit; hanc enim de te notitiam cuncta mortalium pec-
tora reciperunt, quam haberi de Deo conuenit et opifice caelorum.

Ex ore infantium et lactantium perfecisti laudem. Hoc in Domino
opere est et rebus impletum: ingredienti enim Hirusolimam occu- 10
rentes paruuli | cum palmarum ramis et olearum frondibus clama-
uerunt dicentes *Osanna in excelsis, benedictus qui uenit in nomine
Domini.* Quae quidem dicta de Christo adplicat psalmi praesentis
oraculum; conuincit etiam Iudeos, qui rebelli animo manifestas
profetias inpugnare non metuunt; atque ideo etiam beatus Dauid, 15
immo sancti Spiritus gratia, ita dispensauit, ut hic profetia, quae
in Christo dicta est, alia quae euidenter facta sunt miscerentur,
per quae etiam illa, quae superius in honorem eius relata sunt,
ad ipsum pertinere nullus ambigeat.

Propter inimicos tuos, ut distruas inimicum et defensorem. Lau- 20
dem, quae *ex infantium ore* procesit, ob hanc causam dicit Deum
perficisse, ut inimicorum suorum, id est Iudeorum, uel infidilitatem
conuinceret uel inpudentiam confutaret: ideo enim paruuli Dei sunt
uirtute et gratia congregati, ut rebus ipsis ea quae de Christo praedicta sunt implerentur et honoris dominici magnitudo aperte psalmi 25
testimonio diceretur. *Inimicum* uero et *defensorem* uocat populum
Iudeorum, quoniam non suscipiendo, immo persequendo Filium
Dei, manifestas in Deum professi .sunt inimicitias, legis ut a Deo
datae defensores se esse simulantes.

4. *Quoniam uidebo caelos* usque *fundasti.* Cognoscam, inquit, et 30
credam omnium esse factorem; pro « intellegam » atque « cognoscam » possuit *uidebo.* Haec ⟨de⟩ Deo Verbo ita manifeste dicuntur,

---

9 Cf. Matth. XXI, 8ss. et supra p. 11-12.

2 sequuntur] sqñr *ms, litt.* qnr *in rasura*   6 mortalium] .i. hominum *add.*
supra   12 in nomine] .i. filius *add. supra*   16 profetia] ab(latiuum) *add. su-*
pra   17 alia quae] testimonia *add. supra*   19 ipsum] christum *add. supra*
ambigeat] ut *add. supra*   24 rebus] operibus *add. supra*   26 uero *suppl. in*
marg.   30 cognoscam] *supple e. g.* te, Deum   31 omnium] creaturarum *add.*
supra   32 de *suppleui.*

This, in fact, he makes manifest in what follows. *Because your magnificence is exalted above the heavens,* esteem for your name so possessed all parts of the world that the extent of your glory spanned the limitations of lands and reached to the heights of heaven; every human breast accepted this news, as was appropriate in regard to God, maker of the heavens.

Out of the mouths of infants and babes at the breast you have prepared praise (v. 2). This was fulfilled in actual fact in the case of the Lord: when he was entering Jerusalem, children came running with palm branches and olive leaves and cried aloud in the words, "Hosanna in the highest! Blessed is he who comes in the name of the Lord."[3] The oracle of the present psalm is in fact a reference to what was said of Christ, overcoming the objections of Jews, who in their obstinacy have no qualms about calling into question prophecies that are crystal clear. Blessed David—or, rather, the grace of the Holy Spirit—so disposed that here with a prophecy that is in reference to Christ other things that clearly happened were combined, and through them as well no one should be in any doubt that what was conveyed above in his honor refers to him. *On account of your enemies, so as to destroy enemy and defender.* He says that God prepared the praise that proceeded *out of the mouths of infants* with the purpose either of overcoming the infidelity or of refuting the audacity of his enemies, that is, the Jews. Hence, children were assembled by the power and grace of God so that what was foretold of Christ should be fulfilled in actual fact, and the greatness of the Lord's dignity should be confirmed by the psalm. By *enemy and defender,* on the other hand, he refers to the people of the Jews, since by not accepting—and, in fact, persecuting—the Son of God, they manifested open hostility to God while pretending to be defenders of the law given by God.

Because I shall see the heavens down to *you have put in place* (v. 3): I shall come to know and believe that he is maker of everything (using see for understand and learn). Now, this so clearly refers to God the Word | that

---

3. Cf. Matt 21:9, 15–16.

ut nemo possit uocem contradictionis opponere: siquidem et ipse
Dominus in euangelio, cum Scribae ac Farisei dicerent: *Non uides*
quae isti dicunt? et agerent ut sua Dominus correptione paruulos
a laudandi studio summoueret, respondens ait: *Etiam, Non legistis*
5 *Ex ore infantium et lactantium perfecisti laudem,* ostendens ideo
illa a beato Dauid esse praedicta quoniam erant operibus ac rebus
implenda. Quae quidem de ipso esse profetata constat atque ipsi
manifestissime conuenire, quoniam addidit in sequentibus dicens:

5. *Quid est homo quod memor es eius* usque *sub pedibus eius.*
10 Vnus atque idem et Deus Verbum, cui principia psalmi constant,
et homo his, quae inseruimus, dictis esse signatur, cuius memor
est et quem uisitat et quem minuit *paulo minus ab angelis,* quem
honore coronat et gloria et quem constituit *super opera manuum*
suarum. In quo quanta sit naturarum diuersitas hinc ostenditur,
15 quod eius, cuius Deus meminisse dignatus est, ita humilis est condicio atque mediocris, ut collecta haec in illam, quam diximus,
beatus Dauid stupeat ac miretur. Nam cum dicit: *Quid est homo*
quod memor es? et reliqua, naturae nostrae aperte indicat uilitatem
et quae non sit tanti meriti, cuius debeat Deus ita meminisse, ut
20 unitam sibi etiam titulo honoris exaequet: ob hoc enim profeta Dei
bonitatem cum stupore miratur, quoniam ita humilem uilemque
naturam in consortium suae dignitatis adsciuerit. Deum ergo esse
Verbum qui memor fuerit, qui uisitauerit, qui imminuerit hominem
paulo minus ab angelis, qui *gloria et honore* coronauerit, ostensum
25 est sufficienter. Qui uero sit iste homo, in quem tanta beneficia
conlata sunt, ab apostolo Paulo discamus dicente: *Testatus est au-*
tem quodam loco quis dicens Quid est homo quod memor es eius
usque *sub pedibus eius,* et adiungens dicit: *Eum, qui paulo minus*
ab angelis minoratus est, uidimus Iesum propter passionem mortis
30 *gloria et honore coronatum.*

2-5 Matth. XXI, 16; cf. supra p. 11, atque Cosmas Indiscopleustes, *Christ. Top.,*
252 AB   12-13 v. 6.   26-30 Hebr., II, 6-7. 9; cf. supra, p. 11-12.

1-4 *verba* siquidem — legistis *litt.* a-d *supra positis instruuntur ad synta-*
xeos ordinem proponendum   3 isti] .i. paruuli illi *add. supra*   7 ipso ... ipsi]
christo *add. supra*   9 est *om. 1ª m.*   15 miminisse *ms*   16 quam] quae
ms   19 memisse *ms*   25 sufficenter *ms*   qui uero] interro(gatiuum) *add.*
supra   26 testatus] distatus *ms*   28-30 *verba* et adiungens — coronatum
litt. a-i *instruuntur ad syntaxeos ordinem insinuandum; in margine legitur:*
hic ordo, qui minoratus est paulo minus ab angelis propter passionem mortis
28 adiungens] .i. paulus *add. supra*   29 Iesum *om. 1ª m.*

no one can possibly raise a voice in objection. The Lord himself, actually, in the Gospel, when the scribes and Pharisees asked, "Do you not see what they are saying?" and tried to get the Lord to discourage the children from their actions in praise of him by rebuking them, replied, "In fact, have you not read, 'Out of the mouth of infants and children at the breast you have prepared praise'?"[4] thus showing that this had been forecast by blessed David because it had to be fulfilled in actual fact. Now, it is clear that this had been prophesied of him and manifestly is applicable to him, because he goes on to say in what follows, *What is the human being for you to be mindful of him* down to *under his feet?* (v. 4). By these words that we have quoted is indicated both God the Word, to whom the beginning of the psalm applies, and the man of whom he is mindful, whom he visits, whom he has made *a little less than the angels* (v. 5), whom he *crowns with honor and glory,* and whom he placed *over the works of his hands* (v. 6).

How great is the diversity of natures in him emerges here in that so lowly and insignificant is the condition of him whom God deigned to call to mind that blessed David was struck with astonishment and wonder at their combination in it, as we said. I mean, when he says *What is the human being for you to be mindful* and so on, he openly implies the lowliness of our nature and the absence of merit of the one of whom God is supposed to be so mindful as even to give it equal claim to honor in being united to him. This is, in fact, the reason for the prophet in his astonishment to marvel at God's goodness, that he combined in association with his dignity such a lowly and insignificant nature. It therefore is clear enough that it is God the Word who was *mindful,* who paid the visit, who made the human being *a little less than the angels,* and who *crowned him with glory and honor.* Let us learn from the apostle Paul who is that human being on whom such great benefits have been bestowed, when he says, "Someone has testified somewhere, 'What is the human being that you are mindful of him … his feet," and going on, "We see Jesus as the one who was made a little less than the angels, now crowned with glory and honor on account of the suffering of death."[5]|

---

4. Matt 21:16
5. Heb 2:6–9.

Διὰ τοῦτο τοίνυν τὴν μὲν διαφορὰν τοῦ τε Θεοῦ Λόγου καὶ τοῦ ἀναληφθέντος ἀνθρώπου τοσαύτην ἡμῖν δείκνυσιν ὁ ψαλμός· διῃρημένα δὲ ταῦτα ἐν τῇ καινῇ διαθήκῃ εὑρίσκεται, τοῦ μὲν Κυρίου ἐφ᾿ ἑαυτὸν λαμβάνοντος τὰ πρότερα τοῦ ψαλμοῦ, ἐν οἷς ποιητήν τε αὐτὸν ⟨λέγει⟩ εἶναι τῆς κτίσεως καὶ ἐπῃρμένην ἔχειν ὑπεράνω τῶν οὐρανῶν τὴν μεγαλοπρέπειαν καὶ τεθαυμαστῶσθαι ἐν πάσῃ τῇ γῇ, τοῦ δὲ ἀποστόλου τὰ δεύτερα περὶ τοῦ ἀνθρώπου τοῦ τῆς τοσαύτης εὐεργεσίας ἀξιωθέντος τοῦ Ἰησοῦ λαμβάνοντος. Πῶς οὐ πρόδηλον ὅτι ἕτερον μὲν ἡμᾶς ἡ θεία γραφὴ διδάσκει σαφῶς εἶναι τὸν Θεὸν Λόγον, ἕτερον δὲ τὸν ἄνθρωπον, πολλήν τε αὐτῶν οὖσαν δείκνυσιν ἡμῖν τὴν διαφοράν; Ὁ μὲν γὰρ μνημονεύει, ὁ δὲ τῆς μνήμης ἀξιοῦται, καὶ ὁ μὲν ἐπισκέπτεται, ὁ δὲ καὶ ταύτης

Grandis igitur differentia inter Deum Verbum et susceptum hominem lectione psalmi praesentis ostenditur; quae etiam nouo quoque testamento similiter indicatur: nam Dominus in euangelio quae inter principia psalmi dicta sunt praesentis sibi conpetere demonstrat, in quibus plane totius creaturae factor ostenditur; cuius magnificentia impleta omni terra transcendisse caeli spatia perhibetur, apostoli sequentia de homine Iesu, qui tantis beneficiis ostensus sit, dicta esse confirmat. Mani|festum ergo est quod aliam diuinae scripturae nos doceant Dei Verbi esse substantiam et aliam hominis suscepti naturam, multamque inter utrasque esse distinctionem: nam alia *memor* est, alia me-

Ideo ergo differentiam quidem Dei Verbi et recepti hominis tantam nobis ostendit psalmus. Diuisa uero 5 haec in nouo testamento inueniuntur: Domino quidem in se accipiente primordia psalmi, in quibus factorem eum dicit esse 10 creaturae et eleuatam habere super caelos magnificentiam et mirificari in omni terra; 15 apostolo autem secunda, quae de homine sunt, qui tantum beneficium meruit, in Iesu accipiente. Quo- 20 modo non manifestum, quod alterum quidem nos diuina scriptura docet euidenter esse Deum 25 Verbum, alterum uero hominem et multam eorum esse ostendit nobis differentiam? Nam iste qui- 30 dem memorat, ille autem memoriam meretur; et iste quidem uisitat, alter autem,

8 similiter] .i. ut fuit in uetere lege *add. supra*   12 λέγει *supplevi*   20-21 sequentia] testimonia *add. supra*.

Διὰ τοῦτο — τὴν ἐξουσίαν affert Leo Byzantius (Vat. gr. 2195, fol. 156ᵛ: τοῦ αὐτοῦ ἐκ τῆς ἑρμηνείας τοῦ η΄ ψαλμοῦ). — Ideo ergo — potestatem, ex Vigilii *Constituto*, c. xx (GUENTHER, *Collectio Avellana*, I, p. 255); conc. Constant. II, apud MANSI IX, 211. — Cf. MANSI, 234 ss.; SWETE, *Theodori... in epistolas B. Pauli commentarii*, t. II, p. 301-302.

Hence, therefore, while it is the psalm that brings out for us such a great distinction between God the Word and the man assumed, they are found distinguished in the New Testament. The Lord takes upon himself the beginning of the psalm, where it says that he is the maker of created thing and his magnificence is exalted above the heavens and marveled at in all the earth, whereas the apostle applies the second part to the human being Jesus, who was the object of such favor. How could it fail to be obvious that the divine Scripture clearly teaches us that God the Word is one thing and the human being another, and shows us the great difference between them?[6] After all, one calls to mind, the other is the beneficiary of the calling to mind; one visits, the other | is blessed in being accorded the visit; one as a favor assigns

6. For obvious theological reasons, this paragraph is extant also in two Latin versions, one occurring in the Constitution of Pope Vigilius in 553 condemning views of Theodore and in the decrees of the Council of Constantinople of that year, and one in the Ambrosian manuscript representing a fifth-century version. The former preserves verbatim the critical distinction made in this particular sentence, whereas the latter expresses it differently: "It is clear that the divine Scriptures teach us that the *substantia* of God the Word is one thing, the *natura* of the man assumed another, and the distinction between the two is great."

ἀξιούμενος μακαρίζεται,
καὶ ὁ μὲν εὐεργετῶν
ἐλαττοῖ βραχύ τι παρ'
ἀγγέλους, ὁ δὲ εὐεργε-
5 τεῖται καὶ ἐπὶ τῇ τοιαύτῃ ἐλαττώσει, καὶ ὁ μὲν
δόξῃ καὶ τιμῇ στεφανοῖ,
ὁ δὲ στεφανοῦται καὶ
ἐπὶ τούτοις μακαρίζεται,
10 καὶ ὁ μὲν κατέστησεν
αὐτὸν ἐπὶ πάντα τὰ
ἔργα τῶν χειρῶν αὐτοῦ
καὶ πάντα ὑπέταξεν
ὑποκάτω τῶν ποδῶν αὐ-
15 τοῦ, ὁ δὲ ἠξιώθη τοῦ
δεσπόζειν τούτων ὧν
πρότερον οὐκ εἶχεν τὴν
ἐξουσίαν.

20

moria digna censetur;
et alia quidem uisitat,
alia beata dignatione
uisitationis efficitur;
alia etiam in hoc be-
nefica est si *ab ange-
lis paulo* faciat mino-
rem, alia uero etiam
beneficium accipit si
angelorum fastigio
non aequetur; et haec
quidem coronat *glo-
ria* uel *honore*, haec
autem insigni *** de-
coratur; haec con-
stituit *super omnia
opera manuum* sua-
rum *pedibus* adsum-
tae cuncta subieciens,
ista uero adsumitur,
ut dominetur his quae
prius subiecta non
habuit.

cum uisitationem me-
retur, beatus dicitur;
et iste quidem benefi-
cium dando minuit
*paulo minus ab ange-
lis,* ille autem et per talem minutionem be-
neficium accepit; et
iste quidem *gloria et
honore* coronat, alter
autem coronatur et
pro his beatus dici-
tur; et iste quidem
constituit ipsum *su-
pra omnia opera ma-
nuum* eius et omnia
subiecit *sub pedibus
eius,* alter autem me-
ritus est dominari eis,
quorum antea non
habebat potestatem.

Cum ergo audimus scripturam dicentem aut honoratum esse
25 Iesum, aut clarificatum, aut collatum illi esse aliquid, aut accipisse
super omnia dominationem, non Deum Verbum intellegamus, sed
hominem susceptum et, siue a Patre haec in eum collata siue a
Deo Verbo dixerimus non errabimus, quia id dicere scripturae
diuinae sumus magisteriis eruditi. Nam et beatus Apostolus, postea-
30 quam testimonio psalmi huius, quod de homine dictum fuerat,
usus est, intulit: *In eo enim quod ei omnia subiecit, nihil dimisit
non subiectum ei* — cum in hoc psalmo Deus Verbum intellegatur
omnia subiecisse — et paulo post sequitur: *Nunc autem necdum
uidemus omnia subiecta ei,* sine dubio homini, — nam Deus Verbum

---

24-29, cf. supra, p. 12   31-32 Hebr. II, 8   33-34 ib.

5-6 benefica] *litt.* ca *in rasura*   14 insigni] *supple e. g.* corona, beatitudine, captiptis *ms*   16 omnia] .i. elimenta *add. supra*   17 opera mea *ms*
18-19 adsumtae] .i. substantiae *add. supra*   subiecens] .i. diuinitatis *add. supra*   29 magistris *ms*   30 salmi *ms*   31 omnia] .i. elimenta *add. supra*
subiecit *suppl. in margine*   32 non subiectum ei *in rasura*.

a rank a little less than the angels, the other is done a favor even in such less-ening; one crowns with glory and honor, the other is crowned and blessed in this; one set him over all the works of his hands and put everything under his feet, the other was accorded lordship over the things of which he did not previously have authority.

Since, then, we hear Scripture saying that Jesus is both honored and celebrated, something is conferred on him and he has received rule over all, let us not take it to mean God the Word but the man assumed, and whether we say this has been conferred on him by the Father or by God the Word, we shall not be in error, because we have been instructed by the teachings of the divine Scripture to say so. The blessed apostle also, in fact, after invok-ing the testimony of this psalm referring to the human being, argued, "In subjecting all things to him, he left nothing outside his control" (since in this psalm God the Word is understood to have subjected everything), and shortly after goes on, "As it is, we do not yet see everything in subjection to him"[7] (to the human being, doubtless, for God the Word was and always is Lord of all). Likewise, | when he says in the letter to the Corinthians, "When he has

---

7. Heb 2:8.

omnium et fuit et semper est Dominus, — ita et cum dicit in epistola
ad Chorinthios: *Cum euacuerit omnem principatum, et potestatem, et*
omnem dominationem, oportet illum regnare donec ponet omnes ini-
micos sub pedibus eius, de homine intellegendum est. Statim enim
id, quod dixerat, psalmi lectione firmauit. Nam *omnia subiecit sub* 5
pedibus eius de psalmo translatum esse manifestum est ex his quae
addidit: *Cum autem dicat Omnia subiecta sunt ei, sine dubio praeter*
eum, | *qui subiecit* ⟨*ei*⟩ *omnia*; si proprium Apostoli fuisset hoc
dictum *subiecit sub pedibus eius*, superflue adderet *cum autem di-*
cat; sed quia psalmi utebatur testimonio consequenter intulit *cum* 10
autem dicat. Quis dicat? Sine dubio beatus Dauid: nam ipsa simi-
litudo dictorum ostendit et in hoc loco et ad Ebreos psalmi insertum esse testimonium. Nam quod dicit ad Ebreos: *Nunc autem*
necdum uidemus omnia subiecta ei — simile est dicto quo ait: *Oportet*
eum regnare donec ponat omnes inimicos sub pedibus. Nouissima 15
inimica distruetur mors — et post pauca infert: *Cum autem subiecta*
fuerint illi omnia, — sine dubio quae nunc subiecta non sunt ei, —
cum enim dicat Omnia subiecta sunt, tunc et ipse Filius subiectus erit
hominem debemus accipere; et *qui sibi subiecit omnia*, siue hoc de
Patre siue de Deo Verbo senserimus, non patemus errori. Osten- 20
dit autem scriptura diuina omnia a Deo Verbo homini esse subiecta; indicatur etiam in alio loco de quo sit sermo Apostoli iste,
utrum de Deo Verbo an de homine; et sicut ad Ebreos testimonio
psalmi usus est dicendo: *Quid est homo quod memor es eius*, ita ad
Chorinthios ait: *Quoniam per hominem mors, et per hominem resur-* 25
rectio mortuorum. Et sicut in Adam omnes moriuntur ita et in Christo
omnes uiuificabuntur et reliqua, quae sequuntur. Quod si dictum
fuerit a quibusdam, quoniam haec a beato Dauid de commoni homine dicta sunt, apostoli quidem Pauli, qui haec oppossuerit, dictis
uidebitur esse contrarius. Sed confirmabit quae a nobis sunt su- 30
perius disputata: si enim his uerbis — quae beatus Dauid de commoni homine dixerat, quod dignus habeassit tanti beneficii —

2-6 I Cor. XV, 24-26   7-8 I Cor. XV, 26-27   13-14 Hebr. II, 8   14-19 I Cor. XV, 25.
26. 28. 27   24 Hebr. II, 6   24-27 I Cor. XV, 21-22   27 v. 10.

2 euacuerit] *litt.* er *in rasura*   5 dixerat] *litt.* at *in rasura*   6-10 *verba*
his — dicat *litteris* a-i *instruuntur*   7 dicat] *litt.* at *in rasura*   8 ei *supplevi*
9 adderet] .i. apostolus *add. supra*   10 intulit] .i. apostolus *add. supra*   14 si-
mile] *litt.* ile *in rasura*   16 infert] .i. apostolus *add. supra*   22 de quo] in-
terro(gatiuum) *add. supra*   25 quoniam] .i. data est *add. in margine*   27 ui-
ficabuntur *ms*   30 confirmabit] .i. apostulus *add. supra*   quae a nobis] .i.
omnia subiecisti, r(e)l(iqua) *add. supra*   31 disputa *1ª m.*

destroyed every rule, power, and every control, he must reign until he has
put all his enemies under his feet," it is to be understood of the human being.
Immediately, in fact, he confirmed what he had said by citing the psalm: the
fact that he quoted *He put everything under his feet* from the psalm is clear
from what he went on to say, "But when it says, 'All things are subjected to
him,' it doubtless excepts the one who subjected everything to him."[8] If the
saying *He put them under his feet* had been the apostle's own, it would have
been unnecessary for him to add "But when he says"; since he was using
the psalm verse, however, he consequently added "But when he says." Who
says? Blessed David, doubtless: the very resemblance of the words shows
that the verse of the psalm has been cited both in this place and in the letter
to the Hebrews, what is said to the Hebrews, "Now, we do not yet see everything in subjection to him," being similar to the statement here, "He must
reign until he has put all his enemies under his feet. The last enemy to be
destroyed is death." Shortly after he adds, "Now, when everything has been
subjected to him"—doubtless, what is not now subject to him—when it says,
"All things are subjected, then the Son himself will be subjected," we ought
to see the human being referred to; and whether we take "He who subjected
everything to him" to refer to the Father or to God the Word, we shall not be
in error.

Now, the divine Scripture brings out that everything has been subjected
by God the Word to the human being. It suggests also in another place
to whom those words of the apostle refer, whether to God the Word or to
the human being: just as he cited a verse from the psalm in saying to the
Hebrews, "What is a human being that you are mindful of him?" so he says to
the Corinthians, "Since death came through a human being, through a human
being came the resurrection of the dead likewise; and as in Adam all die,
all likewise will be brought to life in Christ" and so on in the following.[9] If
this claim were made by certain commentators that this was said by blessed
David of people in general, he would be seen to contradict the words of the
apostle Paul, who said the opposite of this. But he will confirm the argument
mounted by us above: if by these words, by which blessed David referred to
people in general as being thought worthy of such a great favor, | blessed Paul

8. 1 Cor 15:24–27.
9. 1 Cor 15:21–22.

beatus Paulus suscepti hominis honorem a Deo inpertitum uoluit
adprobare, sine dubio probauit, quantum ad naturae proprietatem
pertinet, magnam esse inter | Verbum et hominem diuersitatem
illam, apud nos fide absque dubio permanente quoniam post
5 ascensionem tantum honoris accipit, ut omnem creaturam longe
transcenderet et unitus cum Deo Verbo sit ab omnibus adorandus;
quod uero beatus Dauid ait: *Omnia subiecisti sub pedibus eius*, et
intulit:

8. *Oues et boues, uniuersa peccora* usque *maris*. Dicendo quidem:
10 *Omnia subiecisti sub pedibus eius*, ostendit quod sermo illi sit de
praestantiore persona quam est nostra mensura; sed quod addidit,
Oves et boues ac reliqua, ad commonem respicit hominem propter
infirmitatem id temporis auditorum, quorum capacitate dictorum
suorum modum uoluit exaequaere; atque ita de Christo profetans
15 et in nos Dei beneficia enumerans psalmum stupentis uoce conclusit dicendo: *Domine Dominus noster*, usque *terra*.

PSALMVS VIIII

Omnes circumpossitae Israheli populo uicinaeque nationes inimicitias aduersus eum atque odia inpaccata geserunt; praecipue
20 uero Arabes, — quos Moabitas et Ammonitas atque Idumeos diuinae scripturae moris est nuncupare, diuersis uocans eos nominibus pro maiorum de quibus oriundi fuerant distinctione, — plurimi
quoque potentium ac diuitum de eodem Israheli populo tenuiores
quosque praedam sibi rapinamque faciebant. Vnde beatus Dauid
25 de utrisque, id est tam externis quam domesticis malis, in hoc loco
uel supplicationes populi inserit uel querellas: et in primis quidem
psalmi partibus sermo est de hostibus agunturque Deo gratiae,
quod eos sit ultione iustissima persecutus ac praeter spem Israhelitas liberauerit sub eorum dominatu atque honere laborantes; in
30 posterioribus uero mala domestica describuntur, id est quod gemere
pauperes populi diuitum iniquitas et rapina conpelleret.
Hic autem nonus psalmus, cum apud Ebre|os et Siros diuisus
sit in duos, nescio quare apud nos sit in unum redactus: neque

3 magnam] *litt.* am *in rasura*   7 quod uero] adit ostendit *add. supra*   10 omnia *in rasura*   17 explicit psalmus uiii. incipit uiiii *ms*   20 moabditas *ms*
22 pluri *1ª m.*   27 est *conieci*, sit *ms*   28-29 israhelit *1ª m.*   30 domistica
disc. *ms*   33 nos] .i. lati(nos) *add. supra*   unum] psalmum *add. supra*.

wanted to establish the dignity of the man assumed that had been conferred by God, doubtless he proved, as far as what is proper to nature goes, that there is that great diversity between the Word and the human being; our faith remains unquestioning that after the ascension he received so much honor as to transcend by far every creature and be adored by everyone as being united with God the Word.

This is what blessed David said: *He put all things under his feet,* and went on, *sheep and oxen, all cattle* down to *the sea* (vv. 7–8). In fact, by saying *he put all things under his feet,* he brings out that his remarks refer to a person more illustrious than we can estimate, whereas what he goes on to say, *sheep and oxen* and the rest, refers to an ordinary human being on account of the limitations of the listeners at the time, to whose capacity he wishes to adapt his manner of speaking. And so in prophesying of Christ and listing God's benefits to us, he closed the psalm in an expression of astonishment by saying, *Lord our Lord* down to *earth* (v. 9).

PSALM 9

All the nations surrounding the people of Israel and close by felt enmity and implacable hatred for them, and the Arabs in particular, whom the divine Scripture normally calls Moabites, Ammonites, and Idumeans, giving them various names in accordance with the different ancestors from whom they took their origin. As well, most of the powerful and rich members of the people of Israel pillaged and sacked all the more defenseless ones. Hence, blessed David in this place adduced the people's petitions and laments on both scores, namely, both foreign and domestic problems. In the first part of the psalm, in fact, his words are about the enemies, and thanks are given to God for pursuing them with righteous vengeance and freeing the Israelites unexpectedly from their control and hard labor. In the latter part, on the other hand, domestic problems are described—that is, the fact that injustice and robbery by the rich members of the people force the poor to lament.

Now, this ninth psalm, which is divided into two in the Hebrew and Syriac, has been combined into one with us for reasons I am unaware of.[1] In fact, it is not only the | break in the middle that demonstrates that consequently

1. "The Seventy" (the translators who produced the LXX) were guided by the psalm's alphabetic structure in Hebrew to keep it as one—a fact ignored by our (Masoretic) Hebrew text. Theodore's knowledge of that language does not allow him to detect that, and so he falls back on more superficial features.

enim sola, quae est in medio possita, incisio ostendit illum apud
Ebreos consequenter esse distinctum, sed etiam ipsae quae continentur causarum diuersitates.

2. *Confitebor tibi, Domine, in toto corde meo.* Confessio pro gratiarum ponitur actione; quod in hoc loco non solum, sed in multis   5
aliis inuenitur.

Narrabo omnia mirabilia tua. Relatione eorum, quae a te nobis
praestita sunt, beneficiorum multos ad reddendas tibi gratias congregabo: ostenditur enim uere gratus cum beneficiorum sibi a Deo
praestitorum memoriam non amittit.   10

3. *Letabor et exultabo in te.*

Posteaquam operum tuorum mirabilia sermone digessero, ut beneficiorum tuorum memor in laetitiam mentis adducar.

Μετὰ γὰρ τὴν διήγησιν τῶν σῶν
θαυμασίων πρόσεσταί μοι καὶ τὸ
εὐφραίνεσθαι ἐπί σοι, ἀναμιμνησκο-
μένῳ τῆς σῆς εὐεργεσίας.   15

3^b-4^a. *Psalam nomini tuo, altissime,* usque *retrorsum.* Quoniam
repullisti a me hostes meos et in terga uertisti, debitum tibi meae
laudis exsoluam.

4^b. *Infirmabuntur et peribunt a facie tua.* Temporum est hic
commotatio: nam pro praeterito possuit futurum, quod quidem in   20
psalmis frequentissime repperitur. *Infirmabuntur,* ait, *et peribunt*
pro « infirmati sunt atque perierunt ».

5. *Quoniam fecisti iudicium meum et causam meam.* Id est: Iuste
inter me et meos aduersarios iudicasti, ut me ab iniquitate dominationis eorum atque oppraesionis erueris.   25

Sedisti super thronum usque *iustitiam.* Iudiciali suggestu eme-
nentior atque districtior egisti quae cognitori aequissimo conuenirent, id est ea, quae ab aliis fiebant, in examen uocasti, ut recte in

---

2 sed etiam] .i. ostendunt *add. supra*   2-3 continentur] contentur *ms,*
.i. in hoc psalmo *add. supra*   5 non *om.* 1^a m.   8 reddas 1^a m.   gratias]
add. animus accipientis *postea expunct.*   11 exultabo] exaltā *ms*   16 altis-
sime] uoca(tiuum) *add. supra*   19 et peribunt *om.* 1^a m.   hiic *ms*   26-27 emen-
tior 1^a m.   28 ab *om.* 1^a m.   aliis] hominibus *add. supra*

Μετὰ γὰρ — εὐεργεσίας: (Θεοδώρου ἀντιο΄.) Paris. 139, fol. 28; Vat. 1682, fol. 34^v
(Mai, p. 391; P. G., 653 A 7-9).

it was divided in Hebrew, but as well the actual differences in content.

I shall confess to you, Lord, with all my heart (v. 1). *Confession* is used to mean thanksgiving, as occurs not only here but also in many other places. *I shall recount all your marvels:* by recounting what has been vouchsafed us by you I shall assemble many to give thanks to you for your benefits. He is shown to be truly grateful, note, when he does not fail to remember benefits vouchsafed him by God. *I shall rejoice and exult in you* (v. 2): after the account of your marvels, rejoicing in you will also affect me as I remember your kindness.

I shall sing to your name, Most High down to *backwards* (vv. 2–3): since you repelled my enemies from me and routed them, I shall discharge the debt of my praise to you. *They will lose their strength and vanish from their sight.* There is a change of tenses here: he used the future tense for the past, as in fact is found frequently in the psalms; he says *they will lose their strength and vanish* to mean, They lost their strength and vanished. *Because you upheld my justice and my cause* (v. 4)—that is, You judged justly between me and my adversaries, with the result that you delivered me from the injustice of their control and oppression.

You sat on your throne down to *justice:* in your capacity as judge you were quite rigid and demanding in doing what was appropriate to the fairest of observers—that is to say, You subjected what was done by them to examination so that the | verdict of your severity should be delivered against

illos sententia, pro his quae in nos peccauerunt, tuae seueritatis
exiret. A similitudine igitur iudicum terrenorum ista dicuntur,
qui residentes pro tribunali in reos consuerunt gladium ultionis
exserere.
5 Sicut autem, cum exurgere dicitur, uindicta eius ex adiutorio
signatur, et sicut, cum dormire dicitur, | patientia et dilatio osten-
ditur, ita et cum *super thronum* sedere dicitur iudicantis seueritas
indicatur.

6. *Increpasti gentes et periit impius.* Ad profanorum, inquit, inte-
10 ritum comminationis tuae seueritas sola sufficit. Signanter uero
possuit *periit impius*, ut ostenderet ultionem procesisse iustissi-
mam, quae sit uiuentes impie persecuta.
Nomen eorum delesti usque *saeculi.* Ita eos omnes mors inlata consumpsit, ut nihil ex eis ad posteritatis memoriam ser-
15 uaretur.

7. *Inimici defecerunt frameae* usque *distruxisti.* Aduersarii quidem nostri omnes contra nos bellorum machinas admouerunt et
omnia in nos tela uibrauerunt ita ut deficeral eis quod in nos tor-
quere possint atque iaculari; sed cum illi multis in nos modis ac
20 uariis armarentur, uacuos conatus eorum casusque fecisti ita ut
ciuitates eorum munitionesque distrueres.
Perit memoria eorum cum sonitu. Ita extincti sunt ac deleti, ut
interitus eorum ad omnium notitiam perueniret. Haec autem dicit
de his hostibus qui ab ipso Dauid ad internicionem caesi sunt:
25 multos enim uicinarum gentium armis belloque superatos in
totum deleuit, quorum opera in Regum historia apertissime continentur.

8. *Et Dominus in aeternum permanet.* Horum, inquit, ita gesto-
rum non erit ulla commotatio, siquidem qui ea operatus est Domi-
30 nus nullo regni sui utatur fine.
Parauit in iudicio suo usque *suum.*

---

5 autem cum] adit indicatur *add. supra*   6 si(cut) *add. supra*   10 com-
minutionis *ms*   13 delisti *ms*   19 modis] uindictae *add. supra*   20 uaris
1ª m.   21 monitionesque *ms*   26 opera *supplevi ex glossula marg.*   regum historia] in libris regnum *add. supra*   26-27 continentur] .i. bella uel
opera *add. supra*   28-29 gestorum] .i. operum *add. supra.*

them for the sins they committed against us. This is expressed, therefore, as a metaphor from earthly judges, who preside over a tribunal and normally wield the sword of vengeance on the guilty. Now, just as from mention of his rising there is a suggestion of his vindication by way of assistance, and just as from mention of his sleeping there is an indication of his patience and long-suffering, likewise when he is said to *sit on his throne,* the judge's severity is implied.

You rebuked the nations and the godless perished (v. 5): the severity of your threat suffices by itself for the destruction of the profane. Now, he was right to put *the godless perished* so as to bring out that it was most just for vengeance to proceed and fall upon those living godlessly. *You canceled their name* down to *ages:* thus death overtook and consumed them all, so that nothing of them survives for posterity's remembrance. *The enemy's spears failed* down to *you destroyed* (v. 6): our adversaries employed weapons of war against us and brandished all their weapons in our faces to such an extent that they lost what they needed to discharge and hurl them against us. Instead, although they were equipped in many ways against us, you made their efforts and attempts so futile as to destroy their cities and fortifications. *Memory of them has disappeared resoundingly:* they were so wiped out and destroyed that their destruction came to the notice of everyone. Now, he says this of the enemy who were cut down and killed by David himself: he overcame by force of arms and utterly destroyed many of the neighboring nations, the account of it clearly recorded in the narrative found in the book of Kings.

The Lord abides forever (v. 7): there will be no change in these deeds, since the Lord who performs them is subject to no end to his reign. *He prepared his throne in judgment.* | Symmachus: "He established his throne in

⟨Symmachus⟩: *Firmauit in iudicio sedem suam*, id est stabilis erit huius decreti examinisque sententia, nec ulla rerum commotatione soluetur.

Σύμμαχος· ἔδρασε κρίσει τὸν θρόνον αὐτοῦ, τουτέστι βεβαίαν τὴν κρίσιν ταύτην ἐποιήσατο καὶ μεταβολὴν τὰ ὑπ᾽ αὐτοῦ κριθέντα οὐκ ἐπιδέχεται.

Et ipse iudicabit orbem terrae usque *in iustitia. Orbem terrae* hic dicit terram repromisionis, *populos* uero filios Israel, igiturque pro nobis iudicat cum inique ab aliquo fuerimus | oppraesi. Quotiescumque autem iudiciorum Dei mentionem facit iustitiam his semper adiungit, aequum illum iudicem uolens per omnia conprobare, qui aequitate motus auxilietur sub iniquitatis honere constitutis.

10. *Et factus est Dominus refugium pauperi.*
Factus est dixit pro «faciat»; hoc enim exigit consequentia, et more ergo suo tempora commotauit.

Ἀντὶ τοῦ καὶ γενήσεται καταφυγή· τοῦτο γὰρ ἡ ἀκολουθία βούλεται, ἐνήλλακται δὲ ὁ χρόνος.

Pauperem uocat populum Israhel propter adsiduos hostilis uastationis incursus: nam humiliati fuerunt in diebus Iudicum et multa mala a uicinis gentibus passi.

Adiutor in oportunitatibus, in tribulatione.

Numquam ita gratum et probabile est adiutorium nobis cum laborantibus adhibetur: commendatio namque eius adiutorii artis rebus augetur et spebus in angustum redactis amplum eius munus efficitur.

Εὔκαιρος γὰρ ἡ βοήθεια κατὰ τὸν τῆς θλίψεως γενομένη καιρόν.

11. *Et sperant in te qui nouerunt nomen tuum* usque *Domine. Sperant* pro «sperabunt» beneficio acceptae defensionis edocti; hic iam sermo exortationis inducitur, ut discat populus experimento rerum praeterita Dei beneficia uelut idoneum pignus retinens, nihil de diuino praesidio in animum suum disperationis admittere.

1 Symmachus *supplevi*　7 hiic *ms*　igiturque *in rasura*　8 iudicat] .i. uindicat *add. supra*　11 auxiletur *ms*　honore *1ᵃ m.*　13 faciat] *litt.* at *in rasura*　14 consequentia] ab(latium) *add. supra, perperam vero*　17 iudicium *1ᵃ m.*　18 passi] .i. sunt *add. supra*　22 commendatio] *litt.* dat *in rasura*　adiutorii *suppl. in margine*　23 eius] dei *add. supra* monus *ms*　26 edocti] *litt.* edo *in rasura*　27 experimento] perimento *ms, litt.* ex *erasis*　28 rerum] .i. operum dei *add. supra*　idonium *ms*　29 disperationis] .i. aliquid *add. supra.*

Σύμμαχος — καιρόν: (Θεο˙ ἀντιο˙) Paris. 139, fol. 29; Vat. 1682, fol. 35ᵛ-36 (Mai, p. 391; P. G., 653 A 10-B 2); Barbaro, p. 95.

judgment"—that is, He made this judgment firm, and what was judged by him gives no evidence of change.[2] *He will judge the world* down to *in righteousness* (v. 8). By *the world* he means "the promised land," and by *peoples,* "the children of Israel." In other words, he judges in our favor since we were unjustly oppressed by some. As often as he makes mention of God's judgments, he always adds *justice* in his wish to demonstrate in everything that judge to be fair who is motivated by fairness and helps those falling under the burden of injustice.

The Lord became a refuge for the poor (v. 9), meaning, He will become a refuge; while the sense requires this, the tense has changed. By *poor* he refers to the people of Israel on account of unceasing inroads of enemy destruction: in the days of the judges they were humbled and suffered many troubles from neighboring nations. *A helper at the right time, in tribulation:* assistance is timely at the time when it comes at a period of tribulation; appreciation of his assistance is heightened in difficult times, and when hope dwindles under pressure, his role is amplified. *Those who know your name hope in you* down to *Lord* (v. 10): instructed by the favor of receiving defense, they *hope*—that is, they will hope. At this point exhortation is introduced for the people to learn from experience, by recalling God's favors in the past like a suitable pledge, not to admit into their soul any despair of divine support. |

---

2. This is the first appearance in our Latin text of a citation of one of the alternative Greek versions (retained in Greek along with its explication), perhaps to explain an awkward usage.

12. *Psalite Domino qui habitat in Sion.* Haec erat apud Iudeos opinio, quoniam etiam ante templi aedificationem in monte Sion Deus habitaret et, postea quam templum aedificatum est, in interiorioribus edis sacratae consisteret.

Adnuntiate inter gentes studia eius. Haec, inquit, quae circa subditos sibi populos est illi moris operari, facite in omnium notitiam peruenire, ut in gloriam eius proficiat quod nobis mira ac magna largitur.

13. *Quoniam requirens sanguinem eorum recordatus.* Est enim illi cura nostri, ideo etiam caedis in nos admisae ultor esse non destetit.

Non est oblitus clamorem pauperum. Iterum gentis suae populum pauperem uocat.

14. *Miserere mei, Domine,* usque *inimicis meis.*

Ex more etiam hic tempora commutantur: | nam pro « misertus est » *miserere* possuit; sic etiam et Aquila dicit: *Donauit mihi Dominus ut uiderem laborem meum.* Hoc enim etiam consequentia dictorum uidetur expetere.

Qui exaltas me de portis mortis.

Portas *mortis* uocat periculum quod ducit ad mortem, per quod aditus quidem ad inferna reseratur.

Κἀνταῦθα πάλιν ἐναλλαγὴ χρόνου· ἀντὶ τοῦ «ἠλέησεν» γὰρ ἐλέησόν φησιν. Οὕτως καὶ Ἀκύλας φησίν· Ἐδωρήσατό μοι Κύριος, εἶδεν κακουγίαν μου. Τοῦτο δὲ καὶ ἡ ἀκολουθία βούλεται.

Πύλας θανάτου τὸν κίνδυνον καλεῖ τὸν ἄγοντα ἐπὶ τὸν θάνατον.

15. *Vt adnuntiem omnes* usque *Sion.* Propterea, inquit, exaltasti *me de portis mortis,* id est saluti meae — qui eram morti proximus — reddidisti, ut ab omni hostili metu liber atque Hierusolimis habitans in dicendis tibi laudibus occuparer. Filiam uero *Sion* uocat Hirusalem.

---

1 ideos *1ᵃ m.*   2 Sion] *litt.* o *in rasura*   3 est *om. 1ᵃ m.*   5-7 *verba* haec — peruenire *litteris* a-k *instruuntur ad syntaxeos ordinem insinuandum* 6 omnium] hominum *add. supra*   7 gloram *1ᵃ m.*   8 magna] *supple e. g.* bonitate   14 hiic *ms*   15 commotantor *ms*   29 reddidisti] .i. me *add. supra.*

Κἀνταῦθα — θάνατον: (Θεο˙ ἀνᵗ) Paris. 139, fol. 29ᵛ; Vat. 1682, fol. 36ᵛ (Mai, p. 191-2; P. G., 653 B 3-11); Vat. 1422, fol. 37ᵛ (Θεοδ˙); Barbaro, p. 98.

Sing to the Lord, who dwells in Sion (v. 11). This was the view among the Jews, that even before the building of the temple God dwelt on Mount Sion, and after the temple was built, he was to be found inside the consecrated building. *Announce his exploits among the nations:* ensure that what he customarily does regarding peoples subject to him comes to the attention of everyone so that his wonderful generosity to us redounds to his glory. *Because he who insists on blood is mindful of them:* he has such care of us that he does not withdraw from being the avenger of bloodshed against us. *He has not forgotten the cry of the poor.* Again by *poor* he refers to the people of his nation.

Have mercy on me, Lord down to *my enemies* (v. 13). Here, too, there is again a change in tense: for "He had mercy" he put *Have mercy.* Aquila put it likewise: "The Lord gave me a gift, he saw my maltreatment." This is also what the sequence requires. *You who lift me up from the gates of death.* By *gates of death* he refers to the danger bringing him to death. *So that I may proclaim all* down to *Sion* (v. 14): this was the reason *you lifted me up from the gates of death*—that is, You restored me to salvation, near to death as I was, so that I might be free from all fear of enemies, dwell in Jerusalem, and be occupied in reciting praises to you (by *Sion* referring to Jerusalem). *I shall* |

108 THEODORVS MOPSVESTENVS

Exultabo in salutari. Aquila: *dilectatus in salute tua.* Ordo rerum exigit ut ab omnibus periculis eruti et laetitiam de praestita a te nobis salute capientes, canamus iugiter, id est quod possit tuis laudibus conuenire.

16. *Infixae sunt gentes in interitu* usque *pes eorum.* 5

Hostes, inquit, nostri traditi sunt malis quae nobis conabantur inferre et incederunt ea quae facere uolebant.

Οἷς ἐμηχανήσαντό φησιν καθ᾽ ἡ-μῶν οἱ πολέμιοι, τούτοις ἑάλωσαν αὐτοί, ἀντὶ τοῦ Ἅπερ ἐσπούδαζον καθ᾽ ἡμῶν τοῦτο ἔπαθον αὐτοί.

17. *Cognoscitur Dominus iudicia faciens.* Quoniam commonis 10 Domini, ut commonis quippe factoris, nationes idolis seruientes beneficia non intellegunt, et quae bona usui eorum ministraret ignorant nec student referre gratias largitori, cognoscent illum cladibus suis cum iuste in se uiderint uindicari, et ultionis magisterio ad potentiae eius documenta peruenient. 15

In operibus manuum suarum conpraehensus est peccator. In ipso, inquit, actu ac studio prauitatis aut eum poena aut uitae ultimus finis inueniet.

18. *Conuertentur peccatores in infernum.* Familiare est sacris literis indiscrete et peccatores uocare impios et impios peccatores 20 dicere, sed in hoc loco uidetur quod pro impiis *peccatores* possuerit; infert enim:

18ᵇ-19ᵃ. *Omnes gentes quae obliuiscuntur Dominum* usque *pauperis.* Etsi aliqua, quae motum eius desiderant, dilatione suspendat, nihil tamen memoriae eius elabitur. Videtur autem per omnia 25 in hoc loco impios alienigenas | dicere et ab hoc maxime perditione dignos, quia neque scire Deum curent neque ut iudicem formidare.

---

1 aquila] .i. dicit *add. supra* 10-15 *verba* quoniam — peruenient *litteris* a-n *instruuntur ad syntaxeos ordinem insinuandum* 14 magistrio *ms* 19-20 sacris litteris] scripturae diuinae *add. supra* 23 obliuiscuntur] .i. impii *add. supra* 25-26 *verba* uidetur — impios *litteris* a-d *instruuntur ad syntaxeos ordinem insinuandum* 25 omnia] .i. uerba *add. supra* 26 et] uidetur *add. supra.*

Οἷς ἐμηχανήσαντο — ἔπαθον αὐτοί: (Θεο᾽ αὐ⁻) Paris. 139, fol. 29ᵛ; Vat. 1682, fol. 37 (Cord., p. 195; P. G., 653 D 2-4); Barbaro, p. 98.

exult in salvation. Aquila: "Delighted in your salvation." The order of events requires that, since we are rescued from all dangers and experiencing joy from the salvation accorded us by you, we should sing at all times, namely, whatever can contribute to your praises.

Nations are stuck fast in the ruin down to *their foot* (v. 15): what our enemies plotted for us they were caught up in themselves—that is to say, The fate they had in mind for us they suffered themselves. *By making judgments the Lord is known* (v. 16): since the nations that serve idols do not acknowledge the kindnesses of the Lord of all in being the creator of all, are ignorant of the goods he imparts for their use, and take no pains to return thanks to the giver, they will come to know him in their disasters when they see punishment rightfully befalling them, and by the lessons of vengeance they will arrive at the proofs of his power. *The sinner has been caught by the works of his hands:* caught in the act and pursuit of wickedness, he will meet with punishment or the final end of life.

Sinners will be sent off into Hades (v. 17). While it is common in the sacred writings to call the godless "sinners" and to speak of sinners as "the godless" indiscriminately, in this place he put *sinners* for the godless. In fact, he goes on, *All the nations that are unmindful of the Lord* down to *the poor* (vv. 17–18): even if he is tardy in doing some things that require action on his part, nevertheless nothing will escape his memory. Now, he seems to be referring in everything here to foreigners who are godless and on this score particularly deserving of perdition on the grounds that they neither take steps to know God nor are afraid of him as judge. | *The endurance of the poor will*

19ᵇ. *Patientia pauperum non peribit in finem.* Pauperes more suo uocat Israhelitas; et expectationem, inquit, eorum, quam de conferendo diuino adiutorio susciperunt, inritam esse non patietur. Patientiam hic pro expectatioue dixit; ita namque et Symma-
5 chus interpraetatus est: *Expectatio quietorum non peribit in finem*; etiamsi tempus pati illos aduersa permitat, non tamen in longum eius ultio protrahetur.

20. *Exsurge, Domine, non confortetur homo.* Acingere in ultionem, ne insolescant qui nos tribulant successu prosperitatis
10 elati.

Iudicentur gentes in conspectu tuo. Id ⟨est⟩ supliciis subdantur et morti. Nam *iudicentur* beatus Dauid pro « confundentur » ponit, ut est illud: *Iudica illos, Deus,* id est Condemna. Cum autem non condemnationem sed ultionem postolat non dicit: *Iudica illos,* sed
15 *Iudica illis.* Per omnes prope psalmos tali distinctione uerbi, hu. ius soluit ambiguum, ut inimicos dicat *Iudica* — id est Condemna, nobis uero *Iudica* — id est Vltor adsiste.

21. *Constitue, Domine, legislatorem super eos* Cum uelut soluta libertate nullum se habere Dominum suspicantur neque censura
20 legis aliqua conteneri, et ab hoc etiam peccare non metuunt nec ipsi pro male actis aestimant uindicari; cum igitur pro iniquitate in nos admisa senserint ultionem, scient et agnoscent quoniam sit illis et nobis commonis iudex et Dominus, — is profecto, quem nos confitemur et nouimus, — qui in uindictam nostri seuerus ex-
25 steterit, ut inlato suplicio meritum operis exerciti in nos cogerentur agnoscere; hoc enim ipsum apud eos uicem legis implebit, id est: inlata supplicia docebunt eos, ut seruos et subditos Domino esse se nouerint qui in peccantes soleat seuerissime uindicare. Consequenter intulit:

13 Ps. V, 11   15 cf. Ps. IX, 39; XXXVI, 33; CIX, 6.

1 peribit] ibit *1ᵃ m.*   2 uocat] dauid *add. supra*   israhelitas] *litt.* rahe *in rasura*   expectationem] spectationem *1ᵃ m.*   4 hiic *ms*   5 quetorum *ms*
6 illos] sanctos *add. supra*   8 fortetur *1ᵃ m.*   9 sucesu *ms*   11 iudicentur]
.i. confundentur *add. supra*   conspectu] spec̄ *ms*   est *supplevi*   suplicis
1ᵃ m.   sudantur *1ᵃ m.*   14 contemnationem *ms*   15 uerbi huius] iudico *add.
supra*   17 iudica *om. 1ᵃ m.*   18 cum uelut] adit non est i(am?) *add. supra*
19 liberate *ms*   26 implebit] uel u *add. supra, hoc est* impleuit   27 doce̜-
bant *ms*.

not perish forever. In his usual fashion he refers by *poor* to the Israelites. He
will not allow to go unrealized their expectation, he is saying, which they
adopted regarding the gift of divine help. By *endurance* he meant expectation, which is the way Symmachus rendered it, "The expectation of the
peaceful will not perish forever": even if he allows them for a time to suffer
adversity, yet their revenge will not be long in coming.

 Rise up, Lord, let human beings not grow strong (v. 19): address yourself
to punishment lest those puffed up with the arrival of prosperity and causing
us distress grow too confident. *Let nations be judged in your presence*—that
is, let them fall victim to punishment and death. Blessed David, in fact, used
judged for confounded, like the verse "Judge them, Lord" to mean "condemn"; but since he demands not condemnation but vengeance, he does not
say, Judge them, but, Be a judge for them. In almost all the psalms he generally employs this word in a twofold sense: judge enemies in the sense of
"condemn," but, judge us in the sense of "be our avenger." *Appoint a lawgiver
over them, Lord* (v. 20): they form the opinion that as though in complete liberty they have no Lord over them and are not restrained by any legal control,
and for this reason are not afraid even to commit sin and believe that they
will not be punished for evil behavior. Since, then, they have experienced
punishment for injustice committed against us, they will know and acknowledge that they and we have a judge and Lord in common—namely, he whom
we confess and know—who appeared in all severity to avenge us, with the
result that they are obliged to acknowledge by the imposition of punishment
what their behavior toward us deserves. This very fate will take the place of
a law among them; in other words, the imposition of punishment will teach
them to know that they are slaves and subjects of a Lord who is in the habit
of punishing sinners most severely. Hence, he goes on, | *And let the nations*

Et sciant gentes quoniam homines sunt. Id est castigationibus suis se ipsos cogantur agnoscere et condicionem propriam confiteri quia non ab alio facti sunt, sed te Dominum, etiamsi nolint, patientur inuiti.

22. *Vt quid, Domine, recissisti longe?* Vsque ad hunc locum de 5 uicinis gentibus sermo fuit, quae adsiduo filios Israhel incursu belloque quatiebant; hinc uero contra ipsius populi potentes, qui tenuiores quosque uexabant, omnis querella consurgit. Nam tam apud Syros quam apud Ebreos alter psalmus hinc incipit. Quod autem dicit *Vt quid, Domine*, uox percunctationis est, non que- 10 rellae. Ostendit autem quod sit rationis aliquid, propter quam patiatur Dominus sub diuitum iniquitate laborare pauperem, quam quidem rationem ignorantibus taceret, ut ius sit quam temerarium quippiam contra Deum ore proferre: credere namque oportet quo niam factor omnium curam proprii operis non omittat. Vnde, si est 15 illi rerum suarum sollicitudo, non in totum disimulat id quod operatus est aliorum iniquitate uexari. Affectionaliter autem, non localiter, Deus uel recedere uel accedere dicitur — nam qui ubique per naturam est omnibus semper praesens.

Dispicis in oportunitatibus in tribulatione. Id est pateris nos 20 tribulationibus atteri, quarum oportunitas adiutoria tua potest apud nos gratiae maioris efficere.

23-24ᵇ. *Dum superbit impius incenditur pauper* usque *benedicitur.*

Consequentia dictorum hunc habet ordinem: *Dum superbit impius incenditur pauper, quoniam laudatur peccator in desideriis animae suae. Compraehenduntur in consiliis* autem *quibus cogitant*

Ἡ ἀκολουθία τῆς διανοίας ἐστὶν 25 αὕτη· Ἐν τῷ ὑπερηφανεύεσθαι τὸν ἀσεβῆ ἐμπυρίζεται ὁ πτωχός, ὅτι ἐπαινεῖται ὁ ἁμαρτωλὸς ἐν ταῖς ἐπιθυμίαις τῆς ψυχῆς αὐτοῦ· τὸ δὲ συλλαμβά νονται ἐν διαβουλίοις οἷς διαλογίζον- 30

2 ipsos] ipso *1ᵃ m.* cogantur] imp(eratiuum) *add. supra* 3 ab alio] ab-
lio *ms* sunt *in rasura* 6 ihl *ms*, israhel *add. supra* 10 percunctionis *ms*
13 quid *1ᵃ m.*, quidem *add. supra* temerarium] *litt.* u *in rasura* 18 re-
cecedere *1ᵃm.* accedere] .i. ille *add. supra* 21 alteri *1ᵃ m.* 21-22 *verba*
quarum — efficere *litteris* a-h *instruuntur ad syntaxeos ordinem insinuandum*
22 gratiae] .i. esse subaudit *add. in margine* 27 incenditur] inditur *ms.*

Ἡ ἀκολουθία — ἀπόφασιν: (anon.) Paris. 139, fol. 30ᵛ; Vat. 1422, fol. 38ᵛ
(anon.); Vat. 1682, fol. 38ʳ·ᵛ; Barbaro, p. 103 (Theodori Antiochensis).

know that they are human—that is, by their chastisements let them be forced to acknowledge and confess their proper status, that they were not made by anyone else, and instead will accept you as Lord, albeit unwillingly.

PSALM 10

Why, Lord, did you stand far off? (v. 1). While to this point the theme concerned the neighboring nations that terrified the children of Israel by constant invasion and warfare, from here onwards, by contrast, all the complaint is directed against the mighty ones of the people itself who thus far were harassing the less fortunate, a different psalm beginning at this point in both Syriac and Hebrew.[1] Now, the remark *Why, Lord?* expresses a question, not a complaint. He brings out what the reason is why the Lord allows the poor person to experience difficulties from the injustice of the rich, a reason he is silent about to the ignorant with the result that there are grounds for some rash person to make complaints against God. After all, we must believe that the creator of all does not neglect his own work. Hence, if he has care for what is his own, he does not completely turn a blind eye to the effect of being harassed by others' injustice. Now, God is said to move away or come close in terms of disposition, not place, he by nature being everywhere and present to everyone. *Why do you look down on us in good times and in bad?* That is to say, You allow us to be affected by bad times, and they can be good times for your help to bring us greater grace.

While the godless acts disdainfully, the poor person is inflamed down to *is blessed* (vv. 2–3). The sequence of meaning is as follows: The poor person is inflamed by the disdainful behavior of the godless because the sinner is commended for the desires of his soul. The statement *They will be caught up in the schemes they have devised* | occurs in the middle, being placed in the

---

1. Theodore already has conceded the propriety of the division of the single LXX psalm into two, as occurring in the Hebrew and confirmed (in his view, i.e., Diodore's) by the change in content. It is also convenient for us to adhere to this numbering, which is that of modern versions, based as they are on the Masoretic Text. Consequently, the numbering of the psalms used for the English translation will subsequently be different from what appears in Devreesse's edition.

interpossitum est propter metri
necessitatem. Non enim soluta
oratione psalmi conscripti sunt,
sed mensuris certis et numeris;
5 ad custodiam ergo disciplinae
aliquid frequenter inseritur, ut
est hoc quod possuimus et alia
similia, quae sepe inueniuntur
huius modi. Vult autem hoc | di-
10 cere, quoniam elatio profani hominis atque prosperitas et hoc,
quod a multis pro opum conge-
stione laudatur atque suscipitur,
— quem nequitia pro morum de-
15 formilate facere deberet exosum,
— ignem in osibus pauperis offensionis ac meroris accendat; qui
quidem contristatur primo loco
de iniquitate quam sustenet; cre-
20 scit autem amaritudo eius quoniam is qui iniquus in illum fuit
non solum nulli uindictae subiacet, sed etiam rebus bene sibi
cedentibus eleuatur atque adu-
25 latorum laudibus insolescit. Ita
est ergo conexio recta uerborum.
Quod autem interpossitum est,
id est *Conpraehendentur in consiliis quibus cogitant*, de ipsis di-
30 uitibus dicitur, quo non in locum
sint iniquitatum suarum inpunitate potituri; nam dum mala opera
pessimis consiliis ordinant et id,
quod nequiter facturi sunt, deli-
35 beratione commoniant, continuatione peccatorum usque ad exci-
piendae ultionis tempora perdu-
cuntur.

ται διὰ μέσου εἴρηται, τὰ δὲ διὰ
μέσου παρεμβέβληται διὰ τὸ μέτρον.
Ἐπειδὴ γὰρ οὐ λογάδην εἴρηται τὰ
τῶν ψαλμῶν, ἀλλὰ μέτρῳ τινί, ὑπὲρ
τοῦ σῴζεσθαι τὸ μέτρον, πολλάκις
τινὰ ἐντίθεται διὰ τοῦ μέσου, οἷόν
ἐστιν μὲν αὐτὸ τοῦτο — εὑρήσομεν δὲ
καὶ ἕτερα. Βούλεται δὲ εἰπεῖν ὅτι
ἡ τοῦ ἀσεβοῦς ὑπερηφανία καὶ ἡ
εὐπραγία, καὶ τὸ ἐπαινεῖσθαι παρὰ
πάντων αὐτὸν ἐφ᾽ οἷς ἀδικῶν ἑτέρους πλουτεῖ, καὶ ἐπὶ τούτοις θαυμάζεσθαι παρὰ τῶν πολλῶν δι᾽ ὧν
ἐγκαλεῖσθαι καὶ μισεῖσθαι διὰ τὸν
τρόπον προσῆκεν, μειζόνως ἐκτήκει
τὸν πένητα· λυπεῖ μὲν γὰρ προη-
γουμένως ἡ ἀδικία τοὺς πένητας,
λυπεῖ δὲ αὐτοὺς μειζόνως τὸ τοὺς
ἀδικοῦντας αὐτοὺς μὴ διδόναι δίκας
παραχρῆμα, ἀλλ᾽ ἔτι ἐξετάζεσθαι ἐν
εὐπραγίᾳ παρὰ πάντων θαυμαζομέ-
νους διὰ τὸν περιόντα πλοῦτον ἐξ
ἀδικίας. Ἡ οὖν ἀκολουθία τῆς διανοίας αὕτη, τὸ δὲ διὰ μέσου — τὸ
συλλαμβάνονται ἐν διαβουλίοις οἷς
διαλογίζονται — περὶ τῶν πλουσίων
λέγει· ἐν αὐτοῖς φησιν οἷς διαλογίζονται συλλαμβάνονται, τουτέστιν ὑπ᾽
αὐτῶν τῶν ἰδίων ἐνθυμημάτων κατα-
κρίνονται καὶ συνάγονται καὶ συνω-
θοῦνται εἰς τὴν τοῦ Θεοῦ ἀπόφασιν.

---

1 metri] *litt.* etri *in rasura*   5 disciplinae].i. metri *add. supra*   23 rebus]
opibus *add. supra*   26 conexio] ut praediximus *add. supra*.

middle for the sake of the meter. You see, since the body of the psalms was composed on the basis not simply of content but also of some kind of meter, frequently to preserve the meter something is inserted in the middle, as in this case, and we find other cases as well. Now, the meaning is, The arrogance and the prosperity of the godless, their being commended by everyone for their ill-gotten gains, and admired by the general run of people for what should on moral grounds bring them censure and hate, distresses the poor person greatly. While it is particularly the injustice that grieves the needy, what affects them more keenly is the fact that the wrongdoers are not immediately called to account, and instead are admired by all for still appearing to enjoy prosperity on account of the proceeds of injustice. The sequence of meaning, then, of the part in the middle, *They will be caught up in the schemes they have devised* is in reference to the rich: they will be caught up in what they have devised—that is, they will be condemned by their own desires, assembled together, and led off for God's sentencing. |

25. *Exacerbauit Dominum peccator.* *Exacerbauit*, dum est et uita inprobus et iniquus in pauperem. Hinc iam quae sint diuitum ad peccandum studia expraemitur, et quas frequentent delictorum species indicatur.

Secundum multitudinem irae suae non quaerit.   5

Dum diripiendi auidus est et pauperi, quem nudat, infensus, ad Deum oculos non retorquet,neque intellegit quod possint conditori suo quae fecit opera displicaere.

> Διὰ τὴν ὑπερβολήν φησι τῆς ὑπ-
> ερηφανίας αὐτοῦ καὶ τοῦ θυμοῦ τοῦ
> κατὰ τῶν πενήτων, οὐκ ἐκζητεῖ τὸν
> δεσπότην οὐδὲ νοεῖ ὅτι ἀπαρέσκον
> αὐτῷ τὸ γινόμενον.   10

Non est Deus in conspectu eius. Iniquitatum, inquit, cumulo et superbiae tumore lumen in eo rationis extinguitur, nec aliquando mentis eius oculos reuerentia creatoris ingreditur.

26. *Inquinatae sunt uiae illius in omni tempore.* Ideo omni tempore sordidi operis squallore turpatur, quoniam ab ea, quae purifi- 15 care solet oculos suos, Dei contemplatione, detorsit; necesse est enim eum, qui iudicem non timet, delicta et cremina semper augere.

Auferentur iudicia tua a facie eius. Nullum, inquit, malorum operum formidat, aut futurum arbitratur examen; et ideo bene possuit *a facie eius,* illi scilicet futura non uidentur esse iudicia, non quia non 20 sint futura, sed quia ille hoc in animum malae persuasionis induxit.

Omnium inimicorum suorum dominabitur.

Motauit tempus; nam pro « dominatur » *dominabitur* dixit, ut id quod inique faciebat ostenderet, id est: quoniam nihil de iudiciis Dei cogitat, ideo dominationi suae subicere omnes nititur, et inique cunctos oppraemere non ueretur. Manifestius hoc Simmachus possuit: *Omnes inimicos suos exsufflat,* id est aut contumaciter tractat aut uiliter.

> Ἐναλλαγὴ κἀνταῦθα χρόνου, ἀντὶ
> τοῦ « κατακυριεύει » · τὸ γὰρ γινόμε-
> νον ὑπὸ τοῦ ἀδικοῦντος διηγεῖται, 25
> ἀντὶ τοῦ διὰ τοῦτο πάντων κρατεῖ
> καὶ πάντας ἀφειδῶς ἀδικεῖ. Σαφέστε-
> ρον δὲ Σύμμαχος εἶπεν · Πάντας τοὺς
> ἐχθροὺς αὐτοῦ ἐκφυσᾷ.
>   30

1 uita] ab(latium) *add. supra*   12 n(on) *ms*   13 creatoris] .i. dei *add. supra* 18 nullum] .i. examen *add. supra*   19 futurum] non *add. supra*   20 illi] malo homini *add. supra*   21 illi *ms*   28 subicere *ms*   31 omnes *add. supra.*

Διὰ τὴν ὑπερβολὴν — γινόμενον: (Θεοˢ αντιοˣ) Paris. 139, fol. 30ᵛ; Vat. 1682, fol. 39 (Mai, p. 392; P. G., 653 C 4-7).

Ἐναλλαγὴ — ἐκφυσᾷ: (Θεοδώρου) Paris. 139, fol. 30ᵛ; Vat. 1682, fol. 39 (Mai, p. 392; P. G., 653 C 7-12); Barbaro, p. 104 (Theod. Antiochensis).

The sinner provoked the Lord (v. 4). He provoked him by being of dissolute life and unjust to the poor. Here there is reference to the involvement of the rich in sin and mention of the sorts of crimes they repeatedly commit. *In the intensity of his wrath he will not conduct a search:* on account of the excess of his arrogance and his anger against the poor he will not seek out the Lord or understand that what is done is unpleasing to him. *God is not before his eyes:* by the vast number of injustices and the flush of arrogance the light of reason is extinguished in him, and at no time does reverence of the creator enter his mind's eye.

His ways are profaned at every moment (v. 5): he therefore is stained at every moment with the squalor of his sordid enterprise because he has turned his eyes away from what normally purifies them, the contemplation of God. It is inevitable, you see, that the one who does not fear the judge augments his crimes and misdeeds. *Your judgments will be removed from his view:* he shrinks from none of his evil exploits nor does he have a thought of a future interrogation. Hence the appropriate mention of *from his view*—that is to say, to him there seem to be no judgments in the future, not because there are none in the future, but because he convinced himself of this by evil persuasion. *He will gain control of all his foes.* There is a change of tense here, too, to mean "He gains control." He is, in fact, describing what is done by the wrongdoer—namely, for this reason he is in control of everyone and mercilessly wrongs them. Symmachus put it more clearly: "He snorts at all his foes." |

27. *Dixit enim in corde suo* usque *malo.* Hoc sibi, inquit, cogitatione persuassit quoniam a prosperitate praesenti nullis aduersitatibus deducatur, neque commotationem aliquam ita sustineat ut in locum felicitatis eius aduersa succedant. Dicendo autem *a*
5 *generatione in generationem* continuationem uoluit temporis indicare; quod uero possuit *Dixit enim,* non quia in talem diues uocem erumperit, sed quia ita agat atque ita pauperes oppraemat ut merito secum ita loqui uideatur, quasi nihil mali sit ipse pasurus atque, oblitus naturalis infirmitatis, nesciat quod sit post omnia,
10 quae fecerit, mala moriturus.

28. *Cuius maledictione os plenum* usque *dolo.* Non solum iniquus iniquitatibus occupatur, sed etiam cuncta linguae uitia familiaritaritate facta concelebrat, ut neque maledictum a uerbis eius aliquando, neque calliditas et circumuentio deesse uideatur; per haec autem
15 omnia tota uitia eius | prauitas arguitur.
Sub lingua eius labor et dolor. Laborem et dolorem dicit quae malis studet frequenter incutire; ad facienda, inquit, mala promtus ac paratus.

29. *Sedet in insidiis cum diuitibus* usque *innocentem.* Non unus, sed multi talis studii in populo esse signantur, qui sibi in opprae-
20 sionem pauperum operas multas et adiutoria soleant alterna praebere: non, inquit, — quod habet in se notam iniquitatis publicae, — aperte tenuiores quosque deripiunt, sed callide excogitant quo ad nuditatem eorum colore perueniant, ut id, quod faciunt inique, specie honestatis inuoluant. Insidias ergo appellat occulta consilia
25 quibus disponunt, ut id, quod agunt, rationis non malitiae esse uideatur; quod quidem studium est familiare eis qui patrimonia sua uolunt semper augeri.
Oculi eius in pauperem respiciunt. Semper, inquit, ante oculos eius, quem circumscribere conatur, pauper occurrit. Ostendit per
30 hoc, quoniam iugis rapinarum meditatio in eius corde uersetur.

30. *Insidiatur in abscondito* usque *sua.* Non leui, inquit, sed infinito cupiditatis igne succenditur.
Insidiatur ut rapiat pauperem usque *eum.* In totum mentis callidae uersatur ingenium qualiter inlaqueari pauper possit et dissipari.

---

3 susteniat *ms*   6 possuit] dauid *add. supra*   7 agat] diues *add. supra* 9 quod]
quid *ms*   12 lingae *ms, l. 16* linga   14 uidetur *1ª m.*   15 uita *1ª m.*   16 quae] mala
.i. labo(rem) et dolo(rem) *add. supra*   18 insedis *ms*   21 puplicae *ms*   22 quo]
quod *ms*   32 insidiatur] indicator *ms*   34 ingenio *ms*   poss*it *ms*   dissipi *ms.*

He said in his heart, in fact down to *evil* (v. 6): he convinced himself that he would not be diverted from his present prosperity by any adversaries or so be affected by any disturbance that adversity would take the place of his enjoyment. Now, by saying *from generation to generation* he meant to suggest continuity, and he put *He said, in fact* not that the rich person said as much, but because he so behaves as to oppress the poor to such an extent that it is just as if he were talking this way to himself, as if he for his part would suffer no trouble, unmindful of his natural infirmity and unaware that after all the evil he committed he would die. *His mouth is full of cursing* down to *deceit* (v. 7): far from being involved only in injustices, the unjust man also conducts all his vicious deeds with a smooth tongue so that no curse ever seems to issue from his mouth nor does he seem to be short of sweet-talking and half-truths. By all these vicious actions his utter depravity is established. *Trouble and deceit are under his tongue.* By *trouble and deceit* he refers to the evil that he is ever striving to cause; he is ready and willing to practice them, he is saying.

He lies in hiding with the rich down to *the innocent* (v. 8): not simply an individual, but many are notorious for this intrigue among the people, being in the business of practicing many acts of oppression against the poor and assisting others to do so. Not that they openly rob all the less affluent, this being too obviously a sign of flagrant injustice, but that they cunningly plan how to dress up their barefaced actions so as to wrap their unjust behavior in an appearance of respectability. By *in hiding,* therefore, he refers to hidden schemes by which they arrange that what they do seems to be the result not of malice but of reason—a practice common among those always on the watch to add to their fortune. *His eyes are on the poor:* the poor person is always the center of his attention, and he tries to get the better of him. By this he brings out that he is ever pondering robbery in his heart.

He lies in wait under cover down to *his den* (v. 9): he is aflame with no feeble flame, but with an infinite fire of avarice.[2] *He lies in wait to snatch the poor* down to *him:* he is totally absorbed in the scheme of his clever mind as to the ways in which the poor may be ensnared and despoiled. | *He will*

---

2. We have no comment from Theodore on the phrase "like a lion in its den."

31. *In laqueo suo humiliabit eum.* Laqueum uocat fraudem quae est ad capiendum diuitis arte conpossita.

Inclinauit se et cadet usque *pauperum.* Posteaquam enumerauit quibus studiis uita rapacium diuitum esset intenta, quam in se no- xio opere manciparent seueritatem ultionis adiungit — quae omnia   5 ueluti uestigio male facta consequitur: cum, inquit, se crediderint oppraesisse pauperes, tunc eos ruina exitialis inuoluet et tunc la- psus uitae | censura uindice sustinebunt.

32. *Dixit enim in corde suo* usque *in finem. Enim* in hoc loco non est conuenienter possitum, quia non causa id aliqua postula-   10 uit; etiam locis ⟨aliis⟩ inproprie coniunctiones possitas inuenimus. Hoc ergo uult dicere : Quando diues conputauerit sibi iam se pau- perem subiecisse, tunc in eum ultio iusta consurgit; ita enim sibi persuasserat atque ita omnia in afflictionem pauperum sine timore faciebat, quasi Deus curam rerum talium non haberet nec aliquid   15 horum in memoriam suae cognitionis admiteret; non quod talia diuites cum oppraemerent pauperes sint locuti, sed quia ita illos sentire factorum suorum ipsa opera testarentur.

33. *Exsurge, Domine Deus meus,* usque *tua.* Ne haec, inquit, apud diuitem opinio conualescat, quod inpunita sint mala quae   20 fecerit, et securitatis persuasione in pauperem afflictione sit gra- uior, accingere in ultionem et uindica in illos qui iniquitatem sine timore committunt; cum enim ultus fueris, ipsa animaduersio, quam excoeperit cupiditas, te esse altissimum conprobabit.

Ne obliuiscaris pauperum in finem. Quoniam superius perso-   25 nam diuitis talia loquentis induxerat, — *dixit enim in corde suo Oblitus est Deus,* — bene hic ait: *Ne obliuiscaris pauperum tuorum in finem,* id est persuasionem hanc eorum, qua credunt tuae memo- riae pauperes excidisse, falsam esse conuince et opere ostende

26 v. 32.

3-5 *verba* posteaquam — adiungit *litteris* a-g *instruuntur ad syntaxeos ordi- nem instituendum*   11 aliis *suppleui*   12 hoc ergo] ait *add. supra*   uult] uelut *1ᵃ m.*   dicere] .i. diceret *add. supra*   quando diues *conieci,* q(uonia)m dies *ms*   13 eum] diuitem *add. supra*   14 timore] .i. dei *add. supra* 16 cognitionis] uel cogitationis *add. supra*   quod] quo *ms*   talia] alia *ms* 19 inquit] adit accingere *add. supra*   20 opinio] *litt.* in *in rasura*   21 et] uel ne *add. supra*   23 timore] .i. dei *add. supra*   enim *add. supra*   ani- maduersio] *litt.* io *in rasura*   25 quoniam superius] adit bene ait *add. supra* 27 obliuitus *ms*   ait *suppl. in margine*   29 falsam] .i. causam *add. supra.*

humiliate him in his trap: by *trap* he refers to the deceit designed to seize him in the rich man's wiles.

He stooped and will fall down to *of the poor* (v. 10). After listing the schemes to which the greedy rich devote their lives, he goes on to mention the severity of the vengeance that they bring on themselves by their harmful activity, being the result of all their evil deeds like a footprint. Since they committed themselves to oppressing the poor, he is saying, the resulting ruin will then befall them and they will suffer loss of life as judgment goes against them. *In fact, he said in his heart* down to *in the end* (v. 11). *In fact* does not in this case rightly suggest consequence, there being no cause requiring it; likewise in other places we find linkages improperly occurring. His meaning, therefore, is, When the rich man calculated that he would bring the poor into subjection, then it was that he met with just punishment, for he had convinced himself and had thus without qualms taken every step to afflict the poor as if God had no concern for such events and kept none of them in his memory (not that the rich said as much when oppressing the poor, but because the very implementing of their deeds confirmed that this was the way they felt).

Rise up, Lord my God down to *your hand* (v. 12): lest this view gain force with the rich person, that the evil he is guilty of goes unpunished, and through belief in his security he become worse in afflicting the poor, set about taking vengeance and punish those who commit injustice heedlessly. When you take vengeance, in fact, the very punishment that greed attracts will prove that you are the Most High. *Do not forget the poor forever.* Since above he had taken on the part of the rich person saying such things, *In fact, he said in his heart, God has forgotten,* here he was right to say *Do not forget your poor forever*—that is, Convince them that this impression of theirs that the poor have escaped your attention is false, and show in reality | that those

quoniam curae tibi sint hi qui per tenuitatem suam exponuntur iniuriae. Et quoniam talis diuitum cogitatio non solum de errore, sed
etiam de profanitate nascatur meritoque in uindictam pauperum
Deum ualeat commouere, addidit hoc per interrogationis spe-
5 ciem:

34. *Propter quid inritauit impius Deum?* et post hoc sequitur
Dixit enim in | corde suo: Non requirit.

In hoc ergo maxime impius
Deum ad iracondiam prouocauit,
10 quia ausus est talem cogitationem mente concipere: nulla Deum
ea, quae inique fiunt, iudicii seueritate conpraemere.

Ἐν τούτῳ γὰρ μάλιστά φησιν
παρώξυνε τὸν δεσπότην ὁ ἀσεβὴς
ἐν τῷ τολμῆσαι ἐννοῆσαι περὶ αὐτοῦ
ὅτι ἐκδίκησιν τῶν ἀδικουμένων οὐ
ποιεῖται.

Vocem secundum consequentiàm ex operum qualitate formauit,
15 ut diceret: Hoc est quod maxime Deum iusta indignatione com-
mouit, quoniam sine ullo diuini timore iudicii pauperes opprime-
bant, quia ita diripiebant ac si nulla apud Deum esset cura iustitiae. Hoc enim, quod ait *Dixit enim*, per omnia susceptum semel
scema seruauit, ut qualia agebant talia loqui uiderentur, quo maior
20 per profanam sententiam uitae eorum prauitas appareret.

35. *Vides quoniam tu laborem et furorem consideras* usque *tuas.*

Dictorum est ordo conuersus.
Nam haec est consequentia: *Quoniam uides tu laborem;* quod prae-
25 posterans posuit: *Vides quoniam.*
Quae quidem uerborum conuersio per interpraetationis, quae de
ebreo in graecum facta est, necessitatem sepe continguit. Quo-
30 niam ergo de male potentibus
querela praecesserat, uidilicet

Πρωθύστερόν ἐστι τὰ ῥήματα·
ἀντὶ γὰρ τοῦ Ὅτι βλέπεις κεῖται Βλέπεις ὅτι. Τοῦτο δὲ ἀπὸ τῆς ἑρμηνείας γεγένηται τοῦ ἑβραϊκοῦ.

---

1 expon*untur *ms*   1-2 iniuriae].i. dati(uum) *add. supra*   6 quid] quod *m.*
17 diribiebant *ms*   19 loqui] dicitur hic dicta pro opera *add. in margine*
21 uque *1ª m.*

Ἐν τούτῳ — οὐ ποιεῖται: (Θεοδώρου ἀντιοχ) Paris. 139, fol. 31; Vat. 1682, fol. 40
(Mai, p. 392; P. G., 653 D 6-9); Barbaro, p. 107.

Πρωθύστερον — μακροθυμίαν: (Θεοδ αντ) Paris. 139, fol. 31ᵛ; Vat. 1682, fol. 40ᵛ
(Mai, p. 392; P. G., 656 A 1-B 3); Barbaro, p. 110.

whose neediness makes them vulnerable are your responsibility.

Since such an impression in the rich springs not only from error but also from irreligion, and is sufficient to prompt God deservedly to vindication of the poor, he goes on in a kind of questioning, *Why did the godless provoke God?* and then follows with *He said in his heart, in fact, He does not require an account* (v. 13): by this in particular the godless provoked God, by presuming to form the idea of him that he does not avenge the wronged. He developed this expression by reasoning from the nature of the actions, as if to say, This is what particularly prompted God to righteous indignation, that with no qualms about divine judgment they oppressed the poor in despoiling them in such a way as if God had no interest in justice. The statement *He said, in fact* maintained in every instance the intention once formed, so that they seemed to speak in the manner suggested by their actions, and thus through their irreligious sentiments the depravity of their life took on a worse character.

You do see, because you give thought to hardship and anger down to *your hands* (v. 14). The order of the words is back to front: *You do see, because* means "Because you see." Now, this results from translation from the Hebrew:[3] | since in regard to the wrongdoers he said *He said in his heart,*

---

3. Comment on this verse is extant in Greek and Latin, the latter adding that translation from Hebrew necessarily results in such inversion of word order—mere supposition on Theodore's part, of course.

quod apud semet ipsos ita loquerentur, — *dixit enim in corde suo
Non requirit*, — intulit *Vides quoniam tu laborem et furorem consideras*, quasi ad Deum profetae
sermo deregatur. Quia, inquit, in
tantum proficit iniquitas, ut tali
in dies fiet genere cogitationis
audentior, dicendo quoniam non
sit tibi curae oculos ad opera
humana conuertere neque inter
opprimentes et oppraesos aliquod
examen adhibere aut procesus
malitiae ultione conpraemere; tu
autem haec uidens desimulas et
exspectas ut manibus tuis ad ex-
cipiendam poenam peccatorum
suorum cumulis ingerantur, et
ultricem in se iram iniquitatis
congestione succendant. | Hoc au-
tem dicit de his qui peccatis non
sunt paucis exiguisque contenti,
sed ad multa scelera, usu inui-
tante, procurrunt; et fit eis congestio creminum et numerus le-
sorum, quaerentium ac deploran-
tium calamitates suas maior
causa poenarum. Per haec tamen
omnia Dei patientiam uoluit indicare.

Ἐπειδὴ γὰρ περὶ τῶν ἀδικούντων εἶπεν τὸ Εἶπεν γὰρ ἐν καρδίᾳ αὐτοῦ Οὐκ
ἐκζητήσει, ἐπήγαγεν τὸ Βλέπεις; ὅτι
σὺ πόνον καὶ θυμὸν κατανοεῖς, τοῦτο
βουλόμενος ὡς πρὸς τὸν Θεὸν εἰ- 5
πεῖν ὅτι προήχθη δὲ ἐκεῖνος ὁ ἄδικος ταῦτα λογίσασθαι, ὅτι μὴ μέλει
σοι περὶ τῶν ἀδικουμένων μηδὲ ἐκζητεῖς τὰ γινόμενα, ἐπειδὴ ὁρῶν αὐτῶν τὴν ὀργὴν καὶ τὴν πονηρίαν οὐκ 10
εὐθὺς ἐξέρχῃ τοῖς γινομένοις, ἀλλὰ
κατανοεῖς, τουτέστι μένεις ἕως ἂν
ἐκ τοῦ πλήθους τῶν ἰδίων κακῶν
ἑαυτοὺς ἐκεῖνοι ταῖς σαῖς παραδῶσιν χερσίν, τὸ πλῆθος τῆς οἰκείας 15
ἀδικίας ἐπισπασάμενοι καθ᾽ ἑαυτῶν
τὴν τιμωρίαν.

Τοῦτο δὲ λέγει ἐκ μεταφορᾶς τῶν 20
μέχρις μὲν ἑνὸς καὶ δευτέρου κακοῦ
μὴ ἱσταμένων, τὸ δὲ πλῆθος τῶν
γινομένων ἑαυτοὺς ἀγόντων εἰς τὰ
δικαστήρια, τὸ τῶν ἀδικουμένων πλῆ-
θος· βούλεται δὲ δεῖξαι τοῦ Θεοῦ 25
τὴν μακροθυμίαν.

30

Tibi derilictus est pauper usque *adiutor*. Quoniam, inquit, et illi
in nocendi studio perseuerant et pauperes atque orfani sunt humano
praesidio destituti, tua tantum superest utriusque defensio.

36. *Contere brachium* usque *maligni*. *Brachium* uocat, ut non
tenue indicet sed grande opus iniquitatis; id quod fit, ab ea quae 35

9 dicendo] peccator *add. supra*   10 tibi] .i. deus *add. supra*   13 adhibere]
deus *add. supra*   aut] neque *add. supra*   16 expectas *1ᵃ m.*   manibus] .i. potestatibus *add. supra*   20 congestione] co(n)gregatione, *l.* 24-25 congregatio *add.*
supra   succendant] ut *add. supra*   24 procurr *1ᵃ m.*   33 destituti] .i. sunt *add.*
supra   utriusque] .i. pauperis et orfani *add. supra*   35 indicet *suppl. in margine.*

He does not require an account, he went on to say *You do see, because you give thought to hardship and anger,* intending by this to direct the accusation against God, namely, That unjust person was encouraged to form the idea that you have no interest in the wronged and will not follow up what is done, since on seeing their wrath and wickedness you do not immediately deal with what happens. Instead, *you give thought*—that is, you wait until from the great number of their own vices they deliver themselves into your hands, bringing the mass of their own injustice down on themselves in punishment. Now, he says this metaphorically of those who do not stop at one or two vices, but bring themselves to the tribunal by the multitude of their deeds, the multitude of the wronged. His intention is to bring out God's long-suffering. *The poor person is left to your care* down to *helper:* since they went on with the business of doing injury, and the poor and orphaned are bereft of human support, the defense of each is left to you alone.

Break the arm down to *evildoer* (v. 15). He uses *arm* to suggest that the process of injustice is not slight but extreme, indicating what happens from the member that | caused it. He is saying, What they are in the pro-

facit parte signauit; id, inquit, quod in pauperum moliuntur, attritu cessare fac, operis ministeria ipsa soluendo.

Quoniam quaeretur peccatum illius et ⟨non⟩ inuenietur.

Propter eum tanta est, ait,
5 quam in pauperes excercet iniquitas, ut si peccati sui ab eo
ratio postuletur, nullam inuenire
possit nec ualeat uel paululum
in sui adsertionem defensionem-
10 que consistere aut aliquo peccatorum suorum multitudinem co
lore uelare.

Τοσαύτη γάρ φησίν ἐστιν ἡ κατὰ
τῶν πενήτων ἀδικία, ὅτι ἐὰν ζητήσῃς
καὶ ἐξετάσῃς ⟨ὅθεν⟩ γίγνηται τῆς
ἁμαρτίας αὐτοῦ ⟨αἰτία⟩, οὐδὲ ὑποστῆναι δυνήσεται δι᾽ αὐτὴν τὴν ἁμαρτίαν αὐτοῦ ζητουμένην — τουτέστιν
τῆς ἁμαρτίας αὐτοῦ, διὰ τὸ μεγάλην
εἶναι, οὐδὲ τὴν ἐξέτασιν ὑπενεγκεῖν
δύναται.

37. *Dominus regnauit in aeternum* usque *saeculi.* Qui est iniquitatis ultor et iniuriae consulator. Bene regni Dei aeternitas
15 indicatur ad utriusque partis, id est tam patientis quam facientis
iniquitatem, uel solacium uel timorem.

Peribitis, gentes, de terra illius. *Gentes* hic uocat filios Israhel,
pro conuersionis suae malo, non alio quam alienigenas dignos titulo nuncupari. *Peribitis* ergo *de terra eius*, id est: Haec Dei in uos
20 ultio proferetur, ut de terrae suae uos habitatione perturbet. Frequenter terra Dei dicitur terra repromisionis, ideo quod eam uelut
praestantiorem elegerit atque ipse filiis Israhel in hereditatem pos-
sesionemque diuiserit.

Quoniam ergo electione sui uelut melior iudicata est et ab hoc
25 populo | sortita, id est diuisa, ut separatus a gentibus caeteris in
adseruatione iustitiae et pietatis studio uersaretur, bene illis comminatur expulsionem, quoniam nihil dignum ea habitatione facerent,
quae a Deo non solum in requiem eorum, sed etiam propter bonum
fuerat conuersationis electa. *Peribitis* ergo, ait, *gentes, de terra eius*,
30 ne eam scelerum uestrorum opere polluatis.

---

1 parte] .i. brachio *add. supra*   3 non *suppleui*   4-6 *verba* propter —
iniquitas *litt.* a-e *instruuntur ad syntaxeos ordinem insinuandum*   7 nullam]
.i. causam *add. supra*   8 ualeat] ut *add. supra*   13-14 iniquitas 1ª *m.*
14-16 *verba* regni — timorem *litt.* a-i *instruuntur*   20 suae] .i. dei *add. supra*
21-23 terra dic. Dei *ms*   24 ergo electione] adit comminatur *add. supra*
25 sortita] terra *add. supra*   diuisa] id est *add. supra*   seperatus *ms*   27 uer-
saretur] populus *add. supra*   30 pulluatis *ms.*

Τοσαύτη — δύναται: (Θεοδ αντ) Paris. 139, fol. 32; Vat. 1682, fol. 41; Barbaro, p. 111.   6-7 ὅθεν... αἰτία *supplevi.*

cess of doing against the poor, put an end to with your assault, impairing the actual instruments of action. *Because his sin will be looked for and will not be found:* so grave is the injustice against the poor that if you look for it and examine whence comes the cause of his sin, he will be unable to bear it on account of the search for his sin; in other words, he will be unable to bear the examination of his sin on account of its gravity.

The Lord reigned forever down to *forever* (v. 16), being avenger of injustice and consoler of injury. It is good that God's eternity is suggested to both groups, namely, both to those suffering injustice and to those causing it, as both solace and fear. *You will perish, nations, from his earth.* Here by *nations* he refers to the children of Israel, who were worthy of being called by no other name than foreigners on account of the wickedness of their relapse. So *you will perish from his earth*—that is, This is the punishment of God that will be inflicted on you, your being driven from occupancy of his land. Often the promised land is called God's land because he chose it as special and divided it among the children of Israel as an inheritance and possession. Since, then, by his choice the better part was decided on and inherited by this people—that is, divided up—so that they might live apart from the other nations in adherence to righteousness and the pursuit of piety, he was right to threaten them with expulsion, since they had done nothing worthy of occupancy, which had been decided on by God not only for their rest, but also on account of their good life. So he says *You will perish, nations, from his earth* lest you defile it with the practice of your crimes. |

38. *Desiderium pauperum exaudiuit Dominus.*

Desiderium hic pro oratione posuit, quoniam ea quae desideramus adsidua oratione deposcimus; id autem *pauperum desiderium*, quo cupiunt ab oppraesione sua iniqua diuitum onera summoueri.

Ἐπιθυμίαν ἐνταῦθα ἀντὶ τοῦ τὴν προσευχὴν λέγει, ἐπειδὴ ἅπερ ποθοῦμεν γίγνεσθαι ταῦτα καὶ εὔχεσθαι φιλοῦμεν.   5

Praeparationem cordis usque *auris tua.* Quoniam superius dixerat: *Desiderium pauperum exaudiuit Dominus*, ut ostenderet non 10 iniusta pauperum uota Deo esse suscepta, addidit: *Praeparationem cordis eorum audiuit auris tua.* Probabilem et rectam petitionem *praeparationem cordis* appellat: aequissime enim cupiebant in eos, qui se oppraeserant, uindicari; et, quo amplius hoc ostenderet, intulit:

39. *Iudicare pupillo et humili.* Patefecit quod in desideriis pau- 15 perum et pupilli uigor aeterni iudicis appareret.

Vt non adponat usque *terram.* Dixit quod erat consequentia operis inlatura, sine dubio quia sub animaduersione positi sapere de se magna non possint.

PSALMVS X   20

Cum beatum Dauid persecutio Saulis urgeret, hi, quos fugae eius aut calamitas aut necessitudo coniunxerat, suadebant quae uel timor uel periculum suggerebat, ut de hoc monte ad alium transeundo atque ab illo rursus ad alium migrando periculum conpraehensionis et mortis effugeret; tunc igitur hunc psalmum cicinit.

Ὅτε ὑπὸ τοῦ Σαοὺλ ἐδιώκετο, τινὲς τῶν συνόντων οἷα εἰκὸς ἐν τοσούτῳ καὶ τηλικούτῳ φόβῳ καὶ κινδύνῳ συνεβούλευον αὐτῷ, φεύγειν τε καὶ μεθίστασθαι τούτου τοῦ ὄρους 25 εἰς ἐκεῖνο καὶ ἀπ᾽ ἐκείνου πάλιν εἰς τὸ ἕτερον, ὡς ἂν μὴ καταληφθεὶς ὑπὸ τοῦ Σαοὺλ ἀναιρεθῇ. Τότε τοίνυν τοῦτόν φησιν τὸν ψαλμόν.

30

9 superius] adit addidit *add. supra* rasura   15 quid *ms*   19 posint *ms* psalmus *ms*   21 cum beatum] adit suadebant *add. supra* subauditur *add. supra*   28 alium] montem *add. supra*.

11 praeparationem] *litt.* praepar *in* 20 expli(cit) psalmus .uiiii. incipit .x. 24 quae uel] .i. ea

Ἐπιθυμίαν – φιλοῦμεν: (Θεο⸱ αντ) Paris. 139, fol. 32; Vat. 1682, fol. 41ᵛ (Mai, p. 392; P. G., 656 B 4-6); Barbaro, p. 111.

Ὅτε ὑπὸ τοῦ Σαοὺλ — τὸν ψαλμόν: (anon.) Paris. 139, fol. 32ᵛ; Vat. 1682, fol. 41ᵛ.

The Lord hearkened to the desire of the poor (v. 17). Here he puts *desire* to mean prayer, since what we long to happen we also like to pray for. Now, the *desire of the poor* is their longing for the removal of the unjust burdens of the rich imposed by their oppression. *The readiness of their heart* down to *your ear.* Since he had said above *The Lord hearkened to the desire of the poor* to bring out that wishes of the poor that are not unjust are accepted by God, he went on to say *Your ear listened to the readiness of their heart.* By *readiness of their heart* he refers to a commendable and proper petition: it is most reasonable for them to want to have punishment imposed on those who oppressed them. To bring this out more adequately, he proceeded with *To judge in favor of the orphaned and lowly* (v. 18). He made clear that the eternal judge is seen actively concerned to meet the desires of the poor and orphaned. *So that he may not go further* down to *the earth.* He said that the result of this act would doubtless be that when falling under notice, they would not be in a position to entertain an exalted idea of themselves.

PSALM 11[1]

When he was being pursued by Saul, some of those who accompanied him predictably advised him in the midst of the awful fear and danger to flee and move from this mountain to that, and from that to another, so as to avoid being taken by Saul and put to death.[2] It was at that point, then, that he recites this psalm. |

---

1. On the difference henceforth between Devreesse's numbers for the psalms and those used for the translation, see note 1 to Psalm 10.

2. Cf. 1 Sam 23–26.

1-2ᵃ. *In Domino confido.* | *Quomodo dicitis animae* usque *arcum?*
Quare, inquit, suadetis debere me effugientem montes uice passeris
commotare? Quia peccatores, id est Saul, ad capiendum me intenti
sunt? Sed ego *in Domino confido* et ab hoc declinandas eius insidias
5 cum magna cura sollicitor. *Peccatores* uero uocat Saulem et eos qui
cum eo erant, ex opere eis nomen inponens, ideo quod sine causa
odientes Dauid eius persecutione peccarent. Hoc ergo, quod ait
Transmigra in montem sicut passer quoniam ecce peccatores inten-
derunt arcum, a comitibus Dauid dicitur, ut loca fugiens diuersa
10 commotet.

2ᵇ⁻ᶜ. *Parauerunt sagitas suas* usque *corde.* Sermo ex persona
ipsius Dauid de Saulis opere et de conatibus conquirentis inducitur.
Ita, inquit, paratus est nos interficere quasi tenebris densitate sui
cuncta inuoluentibus testem operis non sit habiturus.
15 *In obscuro* autem dixit, quod est in graeco CKOTOMHNH, id est
cum noctis tenebras facit etiam lunae absentia densiores. Mene
enim lunam Greci uocant, unde etiam m e n e s, quod est m e n s e s,
rectissime nuncupauerunt: m e n namque proprie apud eos certus
dierum numerus dicitur, ac finitius, ut puta qui prima die crescen-
20 tis lunae usque ad ultimum dificientis impletur, post quem iterum
ipsius lunae incipiunt incrementa reparari; qui numerus est semper
aequalis, neque augmenta aliqua respiciens neque ulla sentiens de-
trimenta: nam lunae cursus sub uno semper eodemque dierum numero terminantur; quae quidem, ut post impletionem sui uacuatur,
25 ita iterum uacuata conpletur. Vnde, siue xxx lunae dies quidam
uelint interesse, siue medium diem — id est vi horas diei — subdu-
cant hi qui sibi uidentur diligentius supputare, ut sint xxviiii et
medium diei, secundum unam tamen summam circulus lunaris im-
pleretur. Nam hi qui uulgo dicuntur menses, | per quos anni orbis
30 uelint in xii partes caeditur, nomen hoc non proprie reciperunt;
neque enim ideo menses uocantur quod eorum spatia astrorum
certis cursibus includantur, neque hoc exaequantur omnes dierum
numero: nam aliis mensibus post xxx dies unus additur; alii

---

3 com***motare *ms*   3-4 int. sunt] int. est *ms,* .i. intenti sunt *corr. in mar-*
gine 2ᵃ m.   4 eius] .i. saulis *add. in margine 2ᵃ m.*   6 nomen] .i. peccatores *add. supra*   7 persecutio *1ᵃ m.*   ergo] est *add. 2ᵃ m.*   8 transmigra]
imper(atiuum) *add. supra*   paser *ms*   9 fugens *1ᵃ m.*   12 et de] de *om.*
1ᵃ m.   13 quasi tenebris] quando dixit in obscuro *add. supra*   14 cuncta]
.i. opera et consilia *add. supra*   15 CKOTOMENH *ms*   22 augmenta *ex* augmentum   sensiens *ms*   26 uelint] uel *ms*   27 xx*viiii *ms*   31 neque]
nam *ms*   hoc] autem *fortasse legendum.*

In the Lord I trust. How do you say to my soul down to *bow* (vv. 1–2): why do you recommend that I should leave the mountains and be on my way like a sparrow? Is it because *sinners*—namely, Saul—are bent on capturing me? But as for me, *I trust in the Lord,* and hence take great care to avoid his ambush. Now, by *sinners* he refers to Saul and those in his company, naming them from their behavior, for the reason that they hated David without cause and sinned by persecuting him. So the statement *Move to the mountain like a sparrow since, lo, sinners have bent the bow* is made to David by his companions so that he should leave the place and go somewhere else.

They prepared their arrows down to *heart.* The verse is introduced in the person of David himself when analyzing Saul's action and his designs. He is ready to kill us, he is saying, just as if dense darkness enveloped all his doings and he was not likely to have any witness of his behavior. Now, he said *in the dark,* which in Greek is σκοτομήνη—that is to say, when the absence of the moon makes the dark of night even denser, since the Greeks speak of the moon as μήνη, and are therefore right to call months μήνης. You see, with them μήν has the precise meaning of a definite number of days, and more precisely from the first day of the waxing moon to the last day of the waning moon, after which in turn the stages of the moon begin to be repeated. This number is always the same, no account being taken of an increase or allowance made for any decrease, the moon's course being completed in an unvarying number of days; it is completed when the number expires, just as it expires after its completion.

Hence, whether some would like a moon to have thirty days, or those who flatter themselves on more accurate calculations reduce it by half a day—that is, six hours of the day—with the result that there are twenty-nine and a half days, the lunar cycle is completed in one and the same period. In fact, what are commonly called "months," by which they mean the span of the year is divided into twelve parts, did not get this name properly: they are not given this name because their extent is determined by the definite course of stars, nor are they all equal as to number of days. I mean, some months have one extra day added to thirty, one | has two days subtracted so as to

uero duo, ut ad **xxx** perueniat, subducuntur; et hoc non semper:
nam post anno ɪɪɪɪ unum recipit, ut ˈuno tantum a **xxx** minua-
tur. Vnde, cum sit illis diuersus numerus, inproprie menses uocantur; lunae autem, sub hisdem semper spatiis crescentis ac sene-
scentis, merito hoc conuenit; cuius uocabuli ignorantes uim atque 5
rationem, statutum dierum numerum **m e n s e m** uocarunt, quem
cursus proprie efficit lunae impleto dierum orbe ad initia reuersus.
Nam sicut annum itenera solis explicant certo temporis fine in
orbitas suas recurrentia, — quibus, uelut a ianuis ueris egresus
decursis spatiis, ut annum impleat, aduersus iterum initia, reuoca- 10
tur, — ita et luna per tramites suos ascendens discendensque implet
menstruum tempus; unde et proprie **m e n s i s** uocatur praefinitus
dierum numerus ab ea, quae hoc efficit, **m e n e**, id est luna.

Quod ergo ait *in obscuro*, id est in scotomene, ita possuit ac
si diceret: In tenebrarum et caliginis densitate ita nos alienos a 15
culpa interficere nituntur, quasi noctem patiantur inlunem, quae
nullius ad uidendum quod faciunt oculos testes admitat. Frequenter uero inueniuntur in psalmis ita quaedam posita, ut eis non
addatur particula « quasi », quam reposcit causae consequentia, ut
possit facilius id, quod dicitur, relucere, sicut et in hoc | loco 20
oportuit dici, *ut sagitent in obscuro rectos corde. Rectos* autem *corde*
appellat, quantum ad praesentem causam pertinet, qui non sint sibi
culpae ullius conscii, per quam digne odia Saulis incurrerint, neque aliquid iniquitatis admiserint ut persecutionem illam uideantur merito sustinere; quasi *peccatores* pro rerum uocat merito illos 25
qui iungebantur Sauli, ita et *rectos*, ad causam respiciens eos qui
recti erant, appellare non dubitat.

3. *Quoniam quae tu perficisti distruxerunt.* Statuta, inquit, ac
decreta tua inrita moliuntur efficere. Nam conantur occidere quem
tu in regem infusione signasti. 30
Iustus autem quid fecit?

Scema interrogantis et uelut   Ἐρωτιματικῶς Τί οὖν φησιν πρὸς
quaerentis inducitur. Quid ad   ταῦτα ὁ δίκαιος, τουτέστιν ἐγώ, δί-

---

1 ut *conieci*, n(on) *ms*   7 cursus om. *1ᵃ m.*   10 aduersis *ms*   14 obscuro]
.i. consilio *add. supra*   15 tenebrarum] .i. cogitationum *add. supra*   16 in-
terficere] .i. insidiis *add. supra*   patientur *ms*   17 nullius] operis *add. su-*
pra   18 quaedam] .i. nomina *add. supra*   21 obscuro] .i. consilio *add. su-*
pra   25 quasi] adit non dubitat *add. supra*   28 di∗struxerunt *ms.*

Ἐρωτιματικῶς — συνήθως: Paris. 139, fol. 33 (Θεοˢ Ἀντιοχ); Vat. 1682, fol. 42ᵛ (Θεοˢ).

arrive at thirty—but not consistently: after the fourth year it gets one, with the result that it falls short of thirty by one only. Hence, with their number being diverse, they are improperly called "months," whereas the term rightly applies to the moon, which always waxes and wanes in the same period. It was in ignorance of the force and basis of this term that they called a set number of days a "month," which the cycle of the moon properly establishes when the period of days is completed and it returns to the beginning. You see, just as the progress of the sun unfolds the year in a definite period of time by rotating on its orbits (on which it goes out, as if by actual doors, on its passage into space and is summoned back again so as to complete the year), so too the moon by climbing up its path and descending completes its monthly time frame, and hence "month" is the name properly given to a number of days determined by what establishes it, μήνη—in other words, the moon.

In saying *in the dark*, then, that is, ἐν σκοτομήνῃ, he expressed it like that to give the meaning, In the thick darkness and gloom they make such an effort to kill us, guiltless though we are, as if putting up with a moonless night that allowed for no witnesses to see what they were doing. Frequently you find things in the psalms so expressed that a particle "as if" is not added, though the sense requires it for making what is said more obvious, as should be said also in this place, *to shoot in the dark at the upright of heart*. Now, he calls them *upright of heart* in terms of the present theme because they are not guilty of any fault of deservedly incurring Saul's hatred, nor did they commit any crime so as rightly to undergo that persecution; as he deservedly calls those supporting Saul *sinners* in the circumstances, so too he has no qualms about using the term *upright* with an eye to those who were upright in the situation.

Because what you completed they destroyed (v. 3): they endeavor to render futile your statutes and decrees by trying to kill the one you anointed as king. *But what did the righteous one do?* He is saying in question form, What was the righteous man's response—mine, that is? | In customary fash-

haec, inquit, iustus faciet, id est
ego? Iustum se appellat, respiciens ad causam in qua est alienus a culpa.

καιον ἑαυτὸν ἀπὸ τοῦ πράγματος
καλῶν συνήθως.

5 **4. Dominus in templo sancto eius.** Subicitur cum multa osten-
sione responsio. Dominus, inquit, eius in templo sancto est, ac si
diceret: adiutor eius est Dominus. Frequenter enim pro indicio adiutorii solum Domini nomen inseritur. Vult autem indicare quod eo,
qui in templo habitet, defensore utatur et uindice, in quo spe pos-
10 sita securus contra omnium consistere possit insidias. Templum
dicit autem tabernaculum in quo erat arca Dei possita: nam templum nondum fuerat extructum; et quoniam tabernaculum templum uocatum sit, manifesto Regum testimonio perducitur, — *et*
dormiebat, inquit, *Samuel in templo Dei in quo erat Dei arca*, —
15 cum templi aedificatio id temporis non coepisset.

Dominus in caelo sedes eius. Iterum hic uelut magna promitens
ait: *Dominus* eius, cuius habitatio est ac sedes *in caelo*; sub ipsius
agit patrocinio ac tutione securus: aestimatio namque ac dignitas
Domini adtollit animos nec patitur iacere famulorum. Ita enim ait:
20 *Dominus in caelo sedes eius*, ac si diceret: potens est et | uinci
nescius cuius iste securus est. Sicut etiam nobis moris est dicere:
iste Illius est, iste ad Illum pertinet, id est domini est potentis et
magni, ita ergo praesenti psalmo: Iustus, inquit, habet dominum,
cuius testatur sedes in caelo possita dignitatem; cum sit igitur illi
25 talis defensor, quippe ut proprius possessor ac dominus, confidens
in illum insidias aduersarii non ueretur. Et ne aestimes quoniam
hic *Dominus in caelo* possitus ab his qui in terra sunt ipsa sit re-
gionum diuersitate sepossitus, intulit:

Oculi eius in orbem terrae aspiciunt usque *hominum.* In caelo,
30 inquit, est, sed oculis eius subiacet quicquid extremus terrae finis

13-14 I Reg. III, 3.

6 inquit] .i. dauid *add. supra*   eius] dauid *add. supra*   8 nomen] .i.
dominus *add. supra*   uult] dauid *add. supra*   9 defensiore *ms*   14 dor-
miebat] .i. in libris regum dicitur *add. supra*   16 sedis *ms et ita infra*
hiic *ms*   17 ipsius] domini *add. supra*   18 agit] .i. se *add. supra*   securus]
securum *1ᵃ m.*, uel (securu)s *corr.*, .i. dauid *add. supra*   19 patitur] deus
add. supra   21 cuius] .i. dei *add. supra*   iste] .i. seruus *add. supra*   se-
curus] .i. dauid *add. supra*   23 psalmo *add. supra*   25 posesor *ms*   26 il-
lum] .i. dominum *add. supra*   aestimes] *litt.* aesti *in rasura*   30 eius] dei
add. supra.

ion, on the basis of what transpired he called himself *righteous.*

The Lord is in his holy temple (v. 4). The reply comes in demonstrative fashion. The Lord, he is saying, is in his holy temple, as if to say, his helper is the Lord, simple mention of the name of the Lord occurring in many cases as an indication of assistance. Now, he means to suggest that he finds in him who dwells in the temple a defender and vindicator, and that hope in him can stand firm against the schemes of all. By *temple* he refers to the tabernacle in which was placed the ark of God, the temple not yet having been built; and since the tabernacle was called *temple,* he is making a clear reference to Kings—"Samuel was sleeping in the temple of God where the ark of God was"[3]—since the building of the temple had not begun by that time. *The Lord, his throne is in heaven.* Again here, as though promising great things, he says, His Lord, whose habitation and throne are in heaven; he acts securely under his protection and guardianship, the Lord's esteem and honor raising the spirits of his servants and not allowing them to fall.

Hence, in fact, his saying *The Lord, his throne is in heaven,* as if to say, the man who depends on him is strong and a stranger to defeat. Just as it is also our habit to say, He belongs to him, he is one of his—in other words, he belongs to a strong and mighty lord—so in the present psalm likewise: The righteous man has a lord whose throne in heaven testifies to his dignity; since he has such a defender as his own lord and master, therefore, he will not fear schemes of an adversary when he trusts in him. And in case you should think that the title *Lord in heaven* expressed here means that he is cut off from those on earth by the very diversity of regions, he goes on to say *His eyes behold the world* down to *human beings:* he is in heaven, but with his eyes he surveys whatever lies within the ends of the earth. | Now, the expression *his*

---

3. 1 Sam 3:3.

includit. Quod autem dixit: *Palpebrae eius interrogant filios hominum* — id est: ita sollicita examinatione omnium facta diiudicat, ut cognitione eius nihil possit elabi — ex more nostro dicitur, quoniam et nos palpebras intendimus cum aliquid uolumus diligenter inspicere.

5. *Dominus interrogat iustum et impium.* Nullus, inquit, ab eius   5 iudicio subtrahetur, sed tam iustus quam peccator meritorum suorum fructus, ipso discernente, percipiet.

Qui autem dilegit iniquitatem usque *suam.* Quoniam praemiserat sub interrogatione, id est examine Dei, tam iusti probanda esse merita quam profani, consequenter intulit quoniam *qui dilegit ini-* 10 *quitatem odit animam suam*: nam cum singulorum opera appendat libra iustitiae, proprii, sine dubio, fructus praemisa semina consequentur. *Odit* ergo *animam suam*, quia illam iniquis actibus mergit ad poenam.

6. *Pluit super peccatores laqueos* usque *procellarum.* Varia per- 15 ditionis genera dicuntur a Deo peccatoribus inferenda.

Pars calicis eorum. Poenarum enumerata diuersitas erit, inquit, *pars calicis*, ut totus calix, profecto ac plenus, intellegatur contenere grauiora; *calicis eorum*, ac si diceret: hoc potabunt, hoc eorum | austibus ingeretur.   20

7. *Quoniam iustus Dominus et iustitias* usque *eius.* Haec iniqui et talia sustinebunt *quoniam iustus Dominus.* Iustitiae autem reposcit officium, sequi merita et reddere quod debetur singulis, non motare.

PSALMVS XI

Deplorat in hoc psalmo atque conquiretur, quod relicta simpli- 25 cate certatim multi se ad studia fallendi simulandique contullerint, et quod amicitiarum fidem atque puritatem doli admixtione corrumperint; generali autem sermone in commone consulit, ut hi, qui se tali uitae generi dederant, uel emendentur dictis eius uel certe caueantur.   30

---

3 eius] dei *add. supra*   ex more — quoniam] .i. dicitur .i. palpebrae eius r(e)l(iqua) *add. supra*   7 ipso] domino *add. supra*   8 quoniam] adit intulit *add. supra*   promiserat *ms*, .i. pro prae *corr. in margine*   14 ad *om. 1ª m.* 18 calix *om. 1ª m.*   19 grauiora] .i. tormenta *add. supra*   calicis] calis *1ª m.* 24 expli(cit) psal(mus) .x. incipit xi *ms*   26 fallandi *ms.*

gaze examines human beings—that is, he deliberates by such a careful scrutiny of the deeds of everyone that nothing can escape his knowledge—comes from our customs, since we too concentrate our gaze when we want to study something closely.

The Lord examines the righteous and the godless (v. 5): far from anyone being withdrawn from his judgment, both the righteous and the sinner will reap their rewards when he discerns them. *Those who love iniquity* down to *their own soul.* Since previously he had stated that the deserts of both the righteous and the irreligious have to be submitted to God's examination—that is, his scrutiny—he necessarily went on to say *those who love iniquity hate their own soul:* since the scales of justice weigh up each one's deeds, doubtless the seeds sown return a yield of their particular crop. Hence, *they hate their own soul* because it is by their own deeds that they fall foul of that punishment.

He rains snares on sinners down to *storms* (v. 6). Various kinds of ruin are mentioned as due to be inflicted on sinners by God. *The portion of their drinking cup.* A range of penalties will be listed, he is saying: *the portion of a drinking cup* so that the whole cup, filled to overflowing, will be understood to contain heavier penalties, and *their drinking cup,* as if to say, They will drink it; it will be swallowed by their sipping it. *Because the Lord is righteous* down to *his eyes* (v. 7): the unjust will endure these and other such things *because the Lord is righteous.* Now, he requires the administration of justice, being guided by deserts and rendering to all individuals what is their due, not depriving them.

PSALM 12

In this psalm he laments and ponders the fact that many people abandon honest dealings and aggressively give themselves to the process of dishonesty and deception, and that they undermine the trust and purity of friendship by introducing deceit. With remarks of a general nature he urges all in common that those who have given themselves to such a lifestyle should learn from his words and definitely be on the watch. |

2. *Saluum me fac, Deus, quoniam deficit sanctus.* Publicae labis
periculum in morum corruptione uersatur: nam cum relicta fide ab
omnibus in cola simulationis studiumque concurritur, nusquam
intigra amicitiae iura seruantur. Vt autem magnum et singulare
5 bonum amicus uerus, cuius societas quietis quidem rebus iucunditatem, aduersis uero exhibet consolationem, ita graue et intolle-
rabile malum est cum sub amicitiarum specie dolus tegitur et uirus
fraudis absconditur. Nam si desit is in cuius quispiam confidat affectu et quem securus uel consilii uel negotii sui faciat esse parti-
10 cipem et cum quo ita ac secum loquatur, grauis illi uita tristisque
ducetur: timet enim omnia et quasi infida circumspicit, cum non
sit qui commonicatione sui, dum patitur, aduersa onera meroris
inminuat. Atque ideo beatus Dauid talis uitae, quae sit plena insidiis, cupiens miserias explicare, rogat, uelut in medio discrimi-
15 num constitutus, ut ei salus a Deo specialiter conferatur quasi in
defectu profecto amicorum et abundantia perfidorum. Hoc enim eius
uerba indicant cum dicit: | *Saluum me ⟨fac⟩, Domine,* usque *sanctus.*
Quoniam, inquit, tales amicitiae sunt periculis plenae, Dei adiutorium
necesarium est, ut de tantorum laqueorum medio possit euadi.

20   Sanctos autem in hoc loco   Ὁσίους ἐνταῦθα καλεῖ τοὺς ἀλη-
uocat qui haec prius familiarita-   θινῇ τῇ διανοίᾳ σῴζοντας τὴν φιλίαν,
tis officia nulla doli admixtione   ὡς ὅσιόν τι καὶ μάλα θαυμαστὸν δια-
temerabant, apud quos relegio   πραττομένους.
erat amicitiae intemerata iura ser-
25 uare; unde manifestius id, quod
dixerat, ut aperiret, addidit:

Quoniam inminutae sunt usque *hominum.*

    Inminutionem possuit pro de-   Τὸ ὠλιγώθησαν ἀντὶ τοῦ ἐξέλι-
fectu. Ita Symmachus ait: *quo-*   πον εἶπεν· οὕτω γὰρ καὶ Σύμμαχός
30 *niam fides est exacta de medio,*   φησιν· Ὅτι ἐκποδὼν ἡ πίστις, ἀντὶ

---

1 puplicae *ms*   3 omnibus] homi(nibus) *add. supra*   4 ut] .i. est *add.*
supra   6 consulationem *ms*   8-10 *verba* nam — tristisque *litt.* a-r *instruuntur*
ad syntaxeos ordinem insinuandum   8 desit] .i. is *add. supra*   9 et quem]
si desit .is. *add. supra, ita l. sequenti supra vv.* et cum, *et supra vv.* ac secum
11 omnia] .i. consilia *add. supra*   12 partitur *ms*   15 constitus *ms*   17 sa-
lum *ms*   fac *suppleui*   26 .i. ut *supra* aperiret *scriptum.*   27 inminutae]
uel d(iminutae?) *add. supra.*

Ὁσίους ἐνταῦθα — διαπραττομένους: (Θεο˝ αντο˝) Paris. 139, fol. 33ᵛ; Vat. 1422,
fol. 41ᵛ; Vat. 1682, fol, 43ᵛ; Barbaro, p. 118.

Τὸ ὠλιγώθησαν — ἀλήθεια; (τοῦ αὐτοῦ) Paris. 139, fol. 33ᵛ; Vat. 1682, fol. 42ᵛ;
Barbaro, p. 118.

Save me, Lord, because there is no holy person left (v. 1): there is a risk of widespread infection from the corruption in morals; with the general loss of trust there follows an adoption of duplicity, the bonds of friendship nowhere being preserved intact. As a true friend is a great good, since association with such a one brings enjoyment of untroubled affairs, on the one hand, and on the other hand it provides comfort in time of trial, so it is a serious and intolerable hardship when under the guise of friendship deceit is concealed and the malady of duplicity is hidden. I mean, if you have no one in whose friendship you trust, whom you are safe in making a sharer in your advice and business affairs, and with whom you converse as with yourself, life proves for you dull and depressing: you are afraid of everything and look on everything as untrustworthy, since there is no one to relieve by sharing the heavy burden of grief when you are suffering it. Blessed David, too, was anxious to unfold the hardships of a life full of snares, and as though finding himself embroiled in challenges, he asks for salvation to be conferred on him by God in a special way as if he were suffering complete loss of friends and a plethora of traitors. His words suggest as much, in fact, when he says *Save me, Lord* down to *holy person:* since such friendships are full of peril, God's help is necessary for avoidance of so many pitfalls. Now, by *holy ones* here he refers to those maintaining true friendship of mind, which is something holy and really remarkable to achieve.

Since they are of little esteem down to *people.* He used *of little esteem* to mean absent, Symmachus likewise saying, "Fidelity is missing"—that | is,

ac si diceret: Apud nullum re-
mansit studium curaque ueritatis,
apud nullum fidelis uel sermo
uel familiaritas inuenitur, omnes
sese ad simulationis ac fallendi
studia contullerunt.

τοῦ οὐκ ἔστι παρ᾽ οὐδενὶ ἡ ἀλήθεια.

Qualiter uero ista fiant sequenti sermone patefecit.

3. *Vana locuti sunt unusquisque ad proximum suum.*

Vana appellat pro fictis ac
subdolis; et generaliter *uana* dicere consueuit ea quae sunt plena
errore et distituta ueritate, eo
quod nullus ex his fructus oria-
tur nihilque commodi talium constet operum capere sectatores.

Μάταια ἀντὶ τοῦ δολερά. Κοινῶς
δὲ μάταια οἶδεν ἅπαντα καλεῖν τὰ
ἄτοπα ὡς εἰκῇ παρὰ τῶν πραττόντων γινόμενα.

Vanam ergo appellat nequam hominum uel intentionem uel consuetudinem mentiendi, quippe ut totius boni et utilitatis expertem,
quae frustretur mentes eorum quos in sui inquisitionem meditatio-
nemque conuerterit; quam tamen in hoc ostendit esse grauiorem,
dum dicit: *Vnusquisque ad proximum suum.* Non enim subdola
atque fallacia ad quoscumque loquuntur ignotos, sed neque cum his
fidelia conserunt uerba cum quibus necessitudinis iure iunguntur.

Labia dolosa usque *locuti sunt.* Mala uitii, de quo queritur, argu-
menta curauit expraemere, cum dicit *in corde et corde,* id est: duo-
rum mutuo sibi loquentium par ad dicipiendum alterum est uoluntas et similis; ambo enim sibi uicisim nituntur inponere sermone
callido atque simulato, non est | ut uno mentiente alter fidiliter lo-
quatur et pure, nec una tantum pars captioni studet, sed aequaliter
in alterutroque fallendi studium repperitur. Hoc enim indicat, quod
dixit *in corde et corde,* quoniam tam hic ad illum quam ille ad istum
plena fraudis conserunt uerba, ut occurentes mutuo fallantur et
fallant. Vult autem per hoc ostendere, quod omnes uitiorum uno
amore teneantur. Quid autem his pro talibus studiis inpraecatur?

9-10 ac subdolis et *suppl. in margine*   15 capere] .i. ni(hil) *add. supra*
16 appellat] .i. e(st) *add. supra*   18 inquitionem *1ª m.*   meditatiomque *1ª m.*
20 subdola] uerba *add. supra*   22 necessitunis *ms*   23 queritur *in marg.,* q̄r̄
1ª m.   25-31 motuo *ms*   31 fallantur] .i. ambo *add. supra.*

Μάταια — γινόμενα: (Θεοῦ αὐτοῦ) Paris. 139, fol. 33ᵛ; Vat. 1682, fol. 44 (Mai,
p. 392; P. G., 656 B 8-10).

no one practices truth.[1] What the situation is he made clear in the following words. *Everyone spoke vain things to their neighbor* (v. 2), *vain things* meaning lies; he is in the habit of using *vain things* of all the wrong things done rashly by those guilty of them. So he uses *vain* of people's malicious intention or habit of lying as being devoid of all value and usefulness because it misleads the minds of those involved in inquiry and analysis. He presents it as more serious by saying *everyone to their neighbor:* they say deceptive and erroneous things to every passing stranger, nor is their speech trustworthy, even to those with whom they are linked by the bonds of necessity.

Lying lips down to *they spoke.* He took trouble to express the evil effects of the vice of which he is complaining when he said *in the heart and in the heart*—that is, two people talking to each other have exactly the same intention of deceiving the other. In fact, both strive to get the better of the other by smooth and duplicitous speech; it is not that one tells lies and the other speaks in a trustworthy and honest manner, nor that one party only is involved in deception—rather, the business of deceit is found equally in both. He suggests this, note, by saying *in the heart and in the heart*—that is, this person to that and that to this use words full of deceit, so that when they meet, they are both deceived and deceive. Now, in this he wants to bring out that all are held in the grip of the same of love of vice.

What does he pray for by way of response to such behavior? | *May the*

---

1. Comment in Greek briefly extant at this point, and translated here, contrasts with the more expansive Latin accent on duplicity, infidelity, and simulation.

4. *Disperdat Dominus uniuersa labia dolosa* usque *magniloquam*.
Rectissime talia interitus et perditio ora concludit, quae numquam
ueritati sed mendacio iugiter studioseque patuerunt; quod uero
addidit, *et linguam magniloquam*, continuum est uitium et satis
5 uicinum: necesse est enim, ut de se magna loquantur quibus est
familiare mendacium; iungunt autem ad fallendi studium etiam
malum iactantiae, ut digni perditione merito censeantur; est igitur
ista oris petulans et immoderata iactatio.

5. *Qui dixerunt Linguam nostram magnificabimus* usque *Quis*
10 *noster dominus est?*

Libertatem, inquiunt, quae
inest nobis, uolumus linguae li-
centia conprobare; nullius dominationis timore compraemimur,
15 ut non, quae libuerint, uerba proferamus; nostro iuri in loquendo,
non alieno seruimus imperio. Non
quia omnimodo talia dicerent,
sed quia ita se posse loqui rebus
20 ostenderent: nam cum sine timore ullo in uitia libere pro-
curritur iudicis seueritas non
timetur.

Λέγουσι γάρ φησιν ὅτι ἐπ᾽ ἐξουσίας ἡμῶν ἐστιν ἃ βουλόμεθα φθέγ-
γεσθαι· τίνα γὰρ ἔχομεν δεσπότην,
ὃν καὶ δεῖσαι δεῖ;

Τοῦτο δὲ ⟨οὐχ⟩ ὡς πάντως λεγόντων
ἐκείνων φησίν, ἀλλ᾽ ὡς τῷ πράγματι
δεικνύντων τὸ οὕτως ἀδεῶς ἅπαντα
πράττειν, ὡς οὐκ ὄντος κριτοῦ.

Consuetudo autem est sancto Dauid uocem ex operum qualitate
25 formare ut id, quod agit, clarius faciat relucere; sicut in psalmo VIIII,
Dixit enim in corde suo Non requiret, ita hoc loco ab his, quae fiebant, insolentia sermonis inducitur. Consequenter ergo ait: *linguam*
magnificabimus, ut uideantur meritum operis uerba signare; et quia
linguae spectat officium omne quod loquimur, seruat ubique solli-
30 cite consequentiam a rerum tenore susceptam.

26 Ps. IX, 34ᵇ; cf. supra p. 60.

1 magniloquam] loquam *1ᵃ m.* 4 continum *ms* 5 quibus est *suppl.*
in margine 12 lingae *ms* 16 iuri] dati(uum) *add. supra* 18 talia]
uerba *add. supra* 25 sicut] adit inducitur *add. supra* 26 ab his] .i. operibus *add. infra.*

Λέγουσι — κριτοῦ: (Θεοῦ ἀντιοχ) Paris. 139, fol. 33ᵛ; Vat. 1682, fol. 44 (Mai,
p. 392; P. G., 656 C 2-7); Barbaro, p. 118. 18 οὐχ *supplevi.*

Lord destroy all deceitful lips down to *boasting* (v. 3). It is quite just for ruin and destruction to be the fate of such mouths, which opened only for the set purpose of lying, never for telling the truth. His further remark *and a boasting tongue* suggests a vice that is of the same order and related to it; it is inevitable that people who boast are accustomed to tell lies, the vice of boasting being connected to the practice of telling lies, so they rightly deserve ruination. Rash and intemperate boasting, therefore, comes from such a mouth. *Those who say, We shall give free rein to our tongue* down to *Who is our master?* (v. 4). They claim, he is saying, What we wish to utter is our own business: what master do we have of whom we need to be afraid? Not that they say as much, he is saying, but that they betray by their behavior that they do everything with such brashness as if there were no judge. Now, it is the habit of blessed David to match his language to the quality of behavior so that what happens appears more clearly; as in Psalm 10, *He said in his heart, He does not require,*[2] so here the insolent way of speaking comes from what is done. Hence he says *We shall give free rein to our tongue* so that the words should give the impression of the value of the action; and because everything we say is the responsibility of the tongue, he is consistent in carefully maintaining the theme drawn from the drift of the actions. |

---

2. Ps 10:13 (in the numbering of modern versions).

6. *Propter miseriam inopum et gemitum pauperum* usque *dicit Dominus*. | Inopes uocat et pauperes qui, propter morum modestiam atque probitatem, sine ulla malorum cautione his, de quibus supra quaestus est, miscebantur et ob hoc patebant inproborum homi- num captioni. *Propter* tribulationem ergo *et gemitum pauperum* in 5 opus ultionis accingar et eorum, qui circumueniuntur, uel simpli- citatem uel iniuriam uindicabo. Bene autem praemittens *miseriam* adiunxit *et gemitum*, ut causam non tenuis sed grauis doloris osten- deret, per quem usque ad suspiria ueneretur: consuerunt enim homines onera angorum suorum amaris gemitibus indicare.   10

Ponam in salutari usque *in eo*. Cum exurgente me iniquitatis ausus ultio iusta conpraeserit, saluti pauperum poena proficiet in- proborum; praestabo, inquit, illis salutem et praestabo non remisse ad uindicandum, sed exserto uigore consurgens ita, ut id, quod passi fuerint, nequeat ignorari. Ostendit autem per haec in eos, 15 quibus familiare erat circumuenire simpliciores quosque atque de- cipere, non esse liuiter uindicandum; et, sicut scemate petito, ut iniquitatem expraemeret, ab operibus ad uerba transitum fecit, ut illos etiam superba loquentes induceret, ita quoque ut ostendat sup- plicii grauioris horrorem, quod fallentum nequitiae praeparatur, 20 uocem Dei minantis induxit, quae promiteret, dicens: *Propter mi- seriam inopum et gemitum pauperum nunc exsurgam dicit Dominus* et eorum, qui circumueniuntur, *fiducialiter*, id est cum multa auc- toritate, iniurias uindicabo.

7. *Eloquia Domini casta, argentum* usque *septuplum*. Verba, 25 inquit, autem, quae comminationem sonuerunt Domini, non sunt mendacii admixtione corrupta, sed casta sunt, id est a uitio uarie- tatis aliena; quod, ut manifestius faceret, addidit: *argentum igni examinatum, probatum terrae*, | *purgatum septuplum*. Decretum, in- quit, quod animaduerti iustitia promulgauit, ita probum et colatum 30

3 malorum] .i. operum uel uirorum *add. supra*   4 quaestus est] .i. dauid *add. supra*   patebant] pauperes *add. supra*   7 promitens *ms*, .i. pro. prae *add. supra*   9 superia *1ᵃ m*.   11 exsurgente] adit praestabo *add. supra* 12 proficiet] cum *add. supra*   15 pasi *ms*   fuerint] pauperes *add. supra* ignorari] .i. ab omnibus hominibus *add. supra*   16 simpliores *1ᵃ m*.   17 et] adit induxit *add. supra*   18 expraemeret] .i. ut narraret *add. supra*   20 ne- quitiae] dati(uum) *add. supra*   26 comminutionem *ms*   28 aliena] sunt *add. supra*   ut *om. 1ᵃ m*.   addidit] .i. eloquia domini casta *add. supra*   30 ani- maduerti *cautissime conieci*, anima aduersarii *ms*, .i. persecutoris *add. su- pra*   iustitia] .i. abla(tiuum) dei *add. supra*   promulgauit] .i. uocauit *add. supra*,

On account of the hardship of the needy and the groaning of the poor down to *says the Lord* (v. 5). By *needy and poor* he refers to those who on account of temperate and upright behavior are caught up in the troubles forming the basis of complaint by not being alert to evil people and thus are vulnerable to dishonest people. Hence, *On account of the groaning of the poor* and their distress I shall address myself to the task of their vindication and champion the honesty and the injury done to those who are involved. He was right to put *hardship* first and proceed with *and groaning* to show that it is the cause of a distress that is serious, not insignificant, because it can bring people to their last gasp, as they normally betray the pressure of their pain with bitter groans. *I shall place them in safety* down to *them:* when I rise up, and just punishment curtails the inroads of injustice, the punishment of the wicked will result in the rescue of the poor. I shall provide them with rescue, and I shall not be remiss about moving to their vindication; instead, I shall arise with such a display of determination that what they suffer will not be able to be ignored. Now, in this he brings out that no light punishment is to be inflicted on those who are in the habit of getting the better of every more ingenuous person and deceiving them; and just as, to give the impression he intends, he moves from actions to words so as to portray injustice and thus presents also those speaking haughtily, so too in order to emphasize the horror of the graver punishment prepared for the wickedness of the deceivers, he presents the voice of God threatening and promising, *On account of the hardship of the needy and the groaning of the poor I shall now arise, says the Lord,* and shall faithfully—that is, with full authority—vindicate those who have been outwitted.

The Lord's sayings are pure, silver down to *seven times* (v. 6): words that betray the Lord's threats, by contrast, are not flawed by being mixed with lies, but are pure—that is, untarnished with the flaw of inconsistency—hence his adding to make this clearer *silver tested by fire, proven in the ground, purified seven times.* The decree that he announced to be taken note of in the interests of justice is as proven and tested | as silver, which is purged of

est ut argentum, quod admixtione uilioris materiae ignis admuni-
tione purgatur, et ita sincerum redditur ut etiam probum uocetur,
quo uilitatis contumilia ab eius estimatione pellatur. Ita ergo a
Deo prolata sententia, cum uelut de iustitiae fornace processerit,
5 non potest inprobari, sed, ita ut egresa est, in opus effectumque
ducetur.

8. *Tu, Domine, seruabis nos* usque *in aeternum.* Quoniam in
principio psalmi *saluum* se a Deo fieri postul·uerat — difficienti-
bus his, quibus moris erat sanctum opus, id est officium amicitiae,
10 absque doli admixtione seruare — et sufficienter studia iniquae simulationis expraeserat sententiamque Dei uindictam promitentis
ostenderat, consequenter addidit: *Tu, Domine, seruabis nos* usque
in aeternum. Cum sit multa iniquitas inproborum et amicitiarum
nulla sinceritas, recta consilia a Deo, ut contra haec mala custo-
15 diatur, inplorat, quia urgentibus periculis aliunde spem salutis sperare non poterat.

Quod autem ait *a generatione*
hac, subauditur « mala »: ita enim
et cum dictis superioribus con-
20 sequentiae ordo seruatur, ac si
diceret: a uiris nocentibus uitae
praesentis et temporis. Sicut et Iohannes Babtista in euangelio ait:

Τῷ δὲ ἀπὸ τῆς γενεᾶς ταύτης
προσυπακούεται τὸ « τῆς πονηρᾶς »·
οὕτω γὰρ καὶ ἡ ἀκολουθία σῴζεται
πρὸς τὰ ἀνώτερα, τουτέστιν ἀπὸ
τῶν ἀνδρῶν τῆς γενεᾶς ταύτης τῆς
πονηρᾶς.

Generatio mala et adultera, quis demonstrauit uobis fugere ab ira
25 *uentura?* — generationem malam uocat homines praesentis aetatis — ita et in hoc loco ait: *a generatione hac,* id est mala, ac si di-
ce|ret hominum pessimis studiis deditorum. *In aeternum* autem,
quod possuit, secundum consuetudinem suam, aeternum uocat

8 supra v. 2   24-25 Matth. III, 7, *progenies uiperarum.*

1 ut] .i. est *add. supra*   uilioris] .i. terrae *add. supra*   matiriae *ms*
3 quo] .i. pro eo quod *add. supra*   eius] .i. argenti *add. supra*   4 sen-
tentia] .i. uindictae *add. supra*   processerit] .i. a deo *add. supra*   7 quo-
niam] adit add:dit *add. supra*   10 et] quoniam *add. supra*   12 ostenderat]
quoniam *add. supra*   14 recta] consilia *add. supra*   15 aliunde] .i. nisi a
deo *add. supra*   19 superioribus] superiribus *1ª m.*   23 iohannis *ms*   24 generatio, adultera] uoca(tiuum) *add supra*   uobis uobis *prius scriptum*   25 uen-
tura] uel su(a) *add. supra*   26 gneratione *ms.*

Τὸ δὲ — πονηρᾶς: (Θεοˢ αντοˣ) Paris. 139, fol. 34; Vat. 1682, fol. 44ᵛ-5; Barbaro, p. 121.

contamination with base matter by the application of fire and is rendered so flawless as even to be called *proven,* and so the contamination of base metals is missing when its value is measured. In like manner, therefore, when a verdict delivered by God is emitted as though from the furnace of justice, it cannot be faulted, and instead takes effect just as it is delivered.

You, Lord, will protect us down to *forever* (v. 7). Since in the beginning of the psalm he had asked to be made safe by God—there being a lack of people who felt that custom obliged them to preserve a sacred responsibility, the duty of friendship, without admixture of guile—and had adequately expressed instances of unjust duplicity and had brought God's verdict promising punishment, he logically proceeded with *You, O Lord, will protect us* down to *forever.* Since the iniquity of the wicked is immense and there is no genuine friendship, he implores from God right counsel so as to be protected against these evils, because he could not elsewhere hope for rescue from the dangers besetting him. Now, an additional term, "wicked," is implied in the phrase *from this generation,* in this way preserving the sense from the above—in other words, from the men of this wicked generation. John the Baptist spoke in similar terms in the Gospel, "Wicked and adulterous generation, who has shown you the way to flee from the wrath to come?"[3] He calls the people of that age "wicked generation," and likewise here it says *from this generation*—that is, a wicked generation, as if to imply people given up to the worst kind of activities. Now, in his usual fashion he used *forever* to refer to an everlasting | time of our life that goes on without any

---

3. Matt 3:7.

tempus uitae nostrae sine ulla interreptione continuum. Per omne, inquit, uitae nostrae spatium, tu nobis custodias admoueto, ne dolis hominum ac fraude capiamur; neque enim per nosmet ipsos uel praehendere eas possimus uel cauere. Quare, inquit, hoc tam sollicite postolas ?

5

9. *In circuitu impii ambulabunt.* Quoniam et grandis est, quo circumdamur, numerus profanorum et sunt ad dicipiendum semper intenti.

Secundum altitudinem tuam eleuasti filios hominum. Etsi impiorum nos agmen includat, etsi illi ideo ambulent ut aliquem inno- 10 centum ualeant inretire, tu autem sublimior es et praestantior, qui nos de impiorum medio, uelut in edito possitos, possis eripere et in superioris loci munitione erutos conlocare. Nam quod ait, *exaltasti filios hominum*, id est: *Eleuasti* nos super eos qui nos sua numerositate cingebant. *Filios* autem *hominum* possuit, ac si dice- 15 ret: Nos, quos secundum altitudinem tuam defensionis tuae fecisti adminiculis eminere.

PSALMVS XII

A peccato, quod Bersabae forma captus admisit, nititur beatus Dauid confessionis satisfactione, uelut hostiae intercessione, purgari. 20 Nemo uero miretur si dicta quae poenitentiam continent, ut per gratiam sancti Spiritus prolata, inter psalmos possita repperiamus. Statim namque conuictus a Nathan profeta foeditatem peccati sui, ut reuerens Domini famulus, non disimulatione texit, sed confesione notauit dicens: *Peccaui, Domine* — et continuo uocem poenitentiae 25 est indulgentia subsecuta, ita ut Nathan, qui haec uerba confitentis audiret, statim diceret: *Et Dominus abstulit peccatum tuum.* Post

27 II Reg. XII, 13.

4 eas *suppl. in margine   fortasse legendum est* possumus   cauere] .i. scire *add. supra*   9 altitudinem *corr. ex* multitudinem   etsi] uel adit sublimior es *add. in margine*   11 inretiere *ms*   13 monitione *ms*   nam] .i. est *add. suprá*   16 nos] .i. eliuasti *add. supra*   ficisti *ms*   17 adminiculis] ab(latiuum) *add. supra*   18 expli(cit) psal(mus) xi. incipit xii *ms*   19 quo *ms*   21 meretur *ms*   poenetiam *ms*   25 poenitiae *ms*   26 confitentis *ms*.

In v. 9. - (Θεο⁵ αντο⁷) Paris. 139, fol. 34; Vat. 1632, fol. 45 (Mai, p. 392; P. G., 656 C 7-9); Barbaro, p. 121: Ἐπειδὴ τοὺς ὑπὸ τῶν ἀσεβῶν κυκλωθέντας οὐκ ἔνεστιν ἑτέρως τὴν τούτων ἀπαλλαγὴν εὑρᾶσθαι μὴ τῷ Θεῷ βοηθῷ χρωμένους.   χρώμενος *ms*.

interruption: he is saying, For the whole period of our life, supply us with your protection lest we fall foul of people's guile and deceit, being unable of ourselves to detect them or avoid them.

Why, he asks, do you make this request so earnestly? *The godless roam around* (v. 8): because there is a great number of godless people ever ready for deception, and we are surrounded by them. *In your loftiness you elevated human beings:* even if the mass of the godless includes us, even if they so behave as to succeed in involving some innocent person, yet you are too lofty and eminent, and are in a position to rescue us from the midst of the godless as though in confinement, and to place us in the protection of a higher position once rescued. The phrase *you elevated human beings* means, You elevated us beyond those who surrounded us in their vast numbers. Now, he said *human beings,* as if to say, Us whom in the loftiness of your defense you caused to take a high position.

PSALM 13

From the sin that he committed when captivated by Bathsheba's charm blessed David strives to be purified by making satisfaction in confession as though by the intercession of an offering. Let no one be surprised at finding occurring in the psalms words that contain repentance, conveyed as they are by the grace of the Holy Spirit. As soon as he was persuaded of the vileness of his sin by the prophet Nathan, being a devout servant of the Lord he did not hide it under any pretext, but admitted it in confessing, "I have sinned, Lord"; and at once pardon followed the expression of repentance, so that Nathan, who heard the words of the penitent, said straightway, "The Lord has removed your sin."[1] After | the forgiveness of his offense, therefore, he

---

1. Cf. 2 Sam 12:13. Theodore anticipates some query as to why a lament and admission of sin should appear in the Psalter, as though sin were an impediment to the inspiration of the Spirit.

indulgentiam igitur creminis recipit etiam Spiritus sancti gratiam,
qua prius solebat repleri. Sed quia erat *uir iustus et timens Deum*,
si quando aliqua incurrisset aduersa, statim ad peccati sui memoriam recurrebat ac propter illud pati se ea, quae illum conpraehen-
5 derant tristia, iudicabat, sicut scriptum est: *Iustus sui accusator est
in primordio sermonis*; et hoc non solum in tribulationibus possitus
agebat, sed etiam quietis rebus et a curis liber externis sibi omnem
inpendebat operam, ut peccatum suum iugibus deploraret lacrimis
et uelut recenti semper tristitia compleretur, atque ita continuam
10 ageret poenitentiam quasi nuper et non multo ante peccasset. Merito
ergo psalmorum numero oratio confesionis eius inseritur, quia et
confesionem uenia secuta est et conlatae ueniae testimonium gratia
recepta post praebuit. Quod uero post remisionem peccati agit poenitentiam, grandis in illo diuini timoris cura signatur: nam et ma-
15 gni peccati sibi conscius, idoneam satisfactionem Deo et tantam
quae eius peccata dissolueret non aestimat obtulisse, et ideo con-
fugit ad continua remedia lacrimarum. Dicta sunt autem haec illo-
rum maxime tempore | quo aduersum eum Abessalon surrexit in-
probitas; qui quidem ideo est aduersum patrem insolenter elatus,
20 quia Dauid ob meritum facti sui, permitente Deo, fuerat tribulationibus illis expossitus. Nam dedit quidem Deus statim ueniam
confitenti, flagillari uero eum tribulatione permisit, ut castigatione
sua melior factus sollicitior esset in reliquum.

Consequenter ergo ista — et si qua sunt alia huiusmodi beati
25 Dauid dicta — psalmis probantur inserta, quia poterant plurimum
utilitatis conferre lecturis: docent enim quod debeat modus confessionis adhiberi; id est, quod non solum in ipso peccati tempore
operam gemitibus dare conueniat, sed continuis fletibus ora perfun-
dere, etiam si multus dierum numerus elabatur, et per recordatio-
30 nem deformis facti semper inuocare tristitiam; neque enim oportet
ad momentum sensum meroris admittere et postea per obliuionem
aculeum doloris excludere. Si enim beatus Dauid post spem acceptae
ueniae — de qua quidem, profeta spondente, dubitare non poterat —

---

2 cf. Iob 1, 1.   5-6 Prov. XVIII, 17.

1 ingentiam *1ª m.*   3 incurrisset] uel (incurre)ret *add. supra.*   4 illud]
.i. peccatum *add. supra*   6 et *conieci*, ut *ms*   10 ageret] ut *add. supra*
11 numero] da(tiuum) *add. supra*   17-18 illorum] .i. operum uel uirorum
add. supra   18 eum] dauid *add. supra*   22 eum] dauid *add. supra*   24-25 *verba*
consequenter -- inserta *litt.* a-k *instruuntur ad syntaxeos ordinem insinuandum*
24 *fortasse legendum* si aliqua sunt   29 elebatur *ms*   32-76, 4 *verba* si —
effundere *litt.* a-r *instruuntur ad syntaxeos ordinem insinuandum.*

also received the grace of the Holy Spirit, with which he used to be filled before. But because he was "a righteous man who feared the Lord,"[2] if ever he met any problem, at once he called to mind his sin and judged that it was on that account he suffered the hardships that overtook him—as it is written, "A righteous person takes the initiative in accusing himself."[3] This he did not only when in distress, but also when affairs were peaceful and he was free of external concerns; he weighed up all his activity, with the result that he deplored his sin with constant tears and always was filled with sadness as though it were fresh, and did continual penance as if he had sinned lately and not in the distant past.

It is appropriate, then, that a prayer of confession appears within the collection of psalms, because pardon was dependent on confession, and the reception of grace provided a confirmation of pardon conferred. The fact that he does penance after the forgiveness of sin suggests his great concern for divine reverence: conscious of his grave sin, he does not think that he has offered suitable satisfaction to God of a kind sufficient to cancel his sins, and therefore he has recourse to the constant remedy of tears. Now, these words were said at the particular time when Absalom's lawlessness broke out against him; he behaved, in fact, with such exorbitant insolence to his father because as a result of his crime, David was, with God's permission, vulnerable to those troubles. That is to say, while God immediately granted pardon to him on his confession, he still allowed him to be tortured by tribulation so that he might be the better for the chastisement and be more careful in the future.[4]

Consequently, those words (and any other such of blessed David) have come to be inserted into the psalms because they could bring a great deal of benefit to the reader, teaching what style of confession should be adopted, namely, that it is not only suitable to give oneself to groaning at the time of the sin, but also to shed continuous tears, even if a great number of days has elapsed, and ever to maintain a sad disposition in recalling the disordered deed. In other words, one should not allow a sense of grief for a time, and afterwards exclude the pangs of sorrow by forgetfulness: if blessed David, after the hope of receiving pardon—which in fact he could not doubt once the prophet replied— | was still not content with making satisfaction but so

---

2. Cf. Job 1:1.

3. Prov 18:17.

4. In fact, the account in 2 Samuel does not associate this lament with Absalom's revolt. A shedding of tears comes when David hears of Absalom's death (2 Sam 18:33).

tamen non quiescit satisfacere et ita gemitibus insistit quasi recenti peccati memoria peruratur, quanto magis nos, quibus pro
uenia accepta nullus sponsor accessit, continua recordatione reatus
nostri poenitentiae lacrimas debemus effundere!

2. *Vsquequo, Domine, obliuisceris me in finem?* Sexto psalmo   5
praesens ut causae unitate, ita etiam supplicationum similitudine
multa, coniungitur. Nam sicut in illo non refugit in totum argui
neque poenitus a correptionis asperitate se subtrahit, sed rogat ut
sine fu|rore, id est ne commotius in se quam modus patitur et se-
ueritas, uindicetur, ita et in praesenti non absolute possuit: *Vsque*   10
quo Domine, obliuisceris me? sed *Vsque quo obliuisceris mei in finem?*
Sicut igitur deuotus famulus, timens offensam Domini longiorem
propter peccatum quidem suum iuste se excedisse, zeli memoriae
confitetur, rogat tamen ne protractione obliuionis, uelut oculis Domini, diutius emendetur — in quo quidem multa cura sancti ti-   15
moris ostenditur. Neque enim beatus Dauid his, quae illum prae-
mebant, angitur malis, sed ad hoc solum tota est animi intentione
sollicitus quando possit in Domini gratiam, depossita memoria offensionis, admiti. Omnia ergo sustinere dura, omnia aspera ferre
non refugit, tantum ut sit de reconciliatione securus.   20

Vsquequo auertis faciem tuam a me? A corporis similitudine
et a nostro more ista dicuntur, quoniam cum aliquibus irascimur,
facies nostras ab his in aliam partem aspectumque conuertimus.

3. *Quandiu ponam consilia* usque *et noctem?*

De diuina profecto propitia-   Εἰκὸς ἦν αὐτὸν τούτου μόνον   25
tione sollicitum necesse erat ta-   φροντίζοντα τοῦ τὸν Θεὸν ἔχειν καὶ
lia cogitatione uoluere ac mente   κατηλλαγμένον, ἑκάστοτε διαλογί-
tractare: putasne reconciliatus   ζεσθαι φοβούμενον ἐν τῇ ψυχῇ·
est mihi? putasne suscepta ad-   Ἄρα κατήλλακταί μοι ὁ Θεός; ἆρα
uersum me eius indignatio con-   πέπαυται τῆς κατ᾿ ἐμοῦ ὀργῆς, ἢ   30
quieuit? an adhuc irascitur? an   ὀργίζεται ἔτι; καὶ ὅσα τοιαῦτα.

1 ita] .i. si it(a) *add. supra*   2 peccati] pecti *1ᵃ m.*   3 recodatione *ms*
5 psalmo] .i. Domine, ne in furore r(e)l(iqua) *add. supra*   6 praesens ut causae]
psalmus .i. usquequo r(e)l(iqua) *add. supra*   7 nam sicut] adit possuit *add. supra*
illo].i. psalmo *add. supra*   refugit].i.dauid *add. supra*   10 obsolute *ms*   26 sol-
licitum] adū (adiectum?) *add. supra*   28 putas] .i. interro(gatiuum) *add. supra*,
item inferius, ne om. *1ᵃ m.*   30 eius] .i. dei *add. supra*   30-31 conquesiuit *ms*.

Εἰκὸς ἦν — λογίζεσθαι: (Θεοˢ αντιοˣ) Paris. 139, fol. 34ᵛ; Vat. 1682, fol. 45ʳ·ᵛ
(Mai, p. 392; P. G., 656 C 13-D 10); Barbaro, p. 123.   25 αὐτοῦ V   26 ἔχει P.

maintained his groaning as if singed by the recent memory of sin, how much more should we, to whom no guarantor of the receipt of pardon has come, shed tears of penance by constantly recalling our guilt.

How long, Lord? Will you forget me forever? (v. 1). The present psalm is linked to the sixth on the basis of similar content, as also by way of great resemblance in supplication: as in that psalm he does not at all resist accusations being made or withdraw himself completely from the harshness of correction, and instead asks that he be punished without rage—that is, no more harshly than a moderate severity allows—so also in the present psalm he did not say absolutely *How long, Lord? Will you forget me?* but *How long? Will you forget me forever?* It is, then, like a devoted servant who fears he has rightly incurred a longer chastisement from his master, admits to remembering his anger, and yet begs that he be corrected no longer by a protracted forgetfulness as if banished from the lord's sight, which actually reveals great attention to holy fear. Blessed David, you see, was affected by the troubles that oppressed him, but was totally concerned in his soul's disposition as to when he could be admitted to the Lord's grace once the memory of the offense lapsed. He therefore does not resist putting up with harsh penalties and bearing bitter sanctions, provided that he be sure of reconciliation. *How long do you turn your face from me?* This is expressed by a bodily metaphor in our fashion, since when we are angry with people, we turn our face from them to another object or direction.

How long shall I hold counsels down to *and night?* (v. 2). It is probable that his only concern was for God to be reconciled, fearfully going over the thought in his soul repeatedly, Is God reconciled with me? Has his anger with me come to an end, or is he still angry? and so on. | So he says, How

offensionis meae adhuc apud eum
memoria perseuerat? et quae-
cunque in hunc modum sollicita
mente dicuntur. Hoc est ergo
5 quod ait: Quandiu me ista cogitatio adficiet? quandiu discrucians
me haec in animo sollici|tudo uer-
sabitur? Donec, inquit, tu *auertis
faciem tuam a me*, id est non me
10 rectis oculis intueris, necesse est
me haec suspicionum et cogita_
tionum onera sustinere.

Τοῦτο οὖν φησιν· Ἕως
πότε τὰ τοιαῦτα ἐνθυμηθήσωμαι καὶ
βουλεύσωμαι;

Μέχρι ἀποστρέφῃς τὸ
πρόσωπόν φησι, τουτέστιν ὀργίζῃ
κατ᾽ ἐμοῦ, ἀνάγκη με τὰ αὐτὰ ὑποπτεύειν καὶ ταῦτα λογίζεσθαι.

Bene autem dolores cordis tales cogitationes uocauit quae sine
dubio animae eius dolores incuterent.

15 *Vsque quo exaltabitur inimicus meus super me?*

Quia propter peccatum suum
diuino fuerat auxilio distitutus
confortabantur aduersarii eius et
malis eum sine inpedimento ali-
20 quograuissimis adterebant; erant
autem id temporis hi quos in
inpugnationem eius Abesalon
factio congregaret. Hoc est quod
ait: Quem ad finem exaltabun-
25 tur hi qui me inpugnare coeperunt?

Τοῦ Θεοῦ πάσχειν συγκεχωρη-
κότος διὰ τὴν ἁμαρτίαν, ἰσχυροὶ μὲν
ἦσαν οἱ πολέμιοι κατ᾽ αὐτοῦ, πάντες
δὲ μετὰ πολλῆς τῆς ἀδείας τὰ δοκοῦντα διετίθεσαν. Ἦσαν δὲ τότε οἱ
περὶ τὸν Ἀβεσσαλὼμ πολεμοῦντες
αὐτόν. Τοῦτο οὖν φησι· Μέχρι
πότε οἱ ἐχθροὶ ὑψηλοὶ κατ᾽ ἐμοῦ
ἔσονται;

4. *Respice et exaudi me, Domine Deus meus*. Hinc iam oblatione
praecum a seueritatis rigore Dominum, ut reconcilietur sibi, nititur
inclinare.
30 *Inlumina oculos meos* usque *mortem*. Reconciliationis tuae gratia,
uelut claro lucis radio, tenebras meae disperge tristitiae, ne meroris
onere et continuatione consumar; et quoniam in angore possitis
tenebrae, uelut erepta laetitiae luce, nascuntur, bene ait: *Inlumina oculos meos*. Reuerso enim Domino in gratiam eius, is qui

---

4 dicuntur] dūr *ms, litt.* nr *in rasura*   9 non me] .i. quandiu *add. supra*
17 distutus *ms*   22 eius] dauid *add. supra*   32 possitis] .i. dati(uum) *add. supra*

Τοῦ Θεοῦ – ἔσονται: (Θεο⁵ αντοˣ) Paris. 139, fol. 35ᵛ; Vat. 1682, fol. 45ᵛ (Mai,
p. 393; P. G., 656 D 11-657 A 4); Barbaro, p. 123.

long am I to ponder and reflect on such things? As long as *you turn your face away*—that is, are angry with me—I must presume and take this for granted. Now, he was right to call such thoughts *pangs in my heart,* for doubtless pangs of soul affected him. *How long will my foe be exalted over me?* With God's permission on account of my sin, the enemy gained the upper hand over me, and all felt completely secure in doing as they pleased. Now, at that time those of Absalom's party were hostile to him—hence his asking, *How long will my foes be exalted over me?*

Look at me and hearken to me, Lord my God (v. 3). At this point he makes an effort with an offering of prayers to divert the Lord from the rigor of his severity and be reconciled to him. *Give light to my eyes* down to *death:* with the grace of your reconciliation, as though with a bright ray of light, disperse the gloom of my sadness lest I be consumed with the burden of protracted grief. And since darkness falls on those in anguish as though the light of joy had been withdrawn, he was right to say *Give light to my eyes:* once the Lord returns to bestowing grace, the one who | was sorrowful is liberated

moerebat omni tristitia liberatur et sereno lumine gaudii reddito
rarescunt tenebrae, quas offensa densauerat; quod quidem tunc
plene fit cum minime de spe reconciliationis ambigitur.

5. *Ne quando dicat inimicus meus* usque *eum*. Ne forte, te diutius irascente, inimicus meus factus fortior insolescat et glorietur 5
quod in me placita sui cordis impleuerit.

Qui tribulant me exultabunt si | motus fuero. Si protractae
longius erumnae me ostenderint a tua protectione summotum,
inimicis meis, ut rebus ex uoto caedentibus, nasceretur materia
gratiarum. 10

6. *Ego autem in tua misericordia speraui*. In tua misericordia,
id est uenia atque clementia. Bene misericordiam possuit: siquidem pro peccato confidens nihil sibi de suis uirtutibus ad spem
salutis, nisi Dei scit misericordiam suffragari.

Exultauit cor meum in salutari tuo. Laetabor, inquit, cum a te 15
mihi salus fuerit restituta.

Cantabo Domino qui bona tribuit mihi usque *altissimi*. Non
solum gaudio accepta salute conplebor, sed etiam ad cantandum
et psallendum tibi ut benefico et excelso, et qui me ab inimicis
meis liberaueris, omni studio praeparabor. 20

PSALMVS XIII

Sub Ezehia rege Iudae Sennacerib Assyriorum rex, multis Iudeae ciuitatibus bello armisque superatis, x tribus captiuas iure
uictoris abduxit; conpraehendit etiam plurimos sub Ezehiae imperio constitutos. Nam et Hirusalem uolens obpugnare misit Rabsa- 25
cen ut populum, qui erat in ciuitate, uel promisionibus inliceret
uel comminatione terreret. Qui ueniens, inter uerba iactantiae,

21 ss. Cf. Is. XXXVI.

1 merebat *ms*   omnis *prius scriptum*   sereno] .i. lumine *add. supra*
3 fit] sit *ms*.   7 si protractae] adit nasceretur *add. supra*   9 nasceretur] .i.
ut *add. supra*   matiria *ms*   11 misericordia] miserum *ms*   12 uinia *ms*
uinia, clementia] .i. in tua a*dd. supra*   15 exultaui *ms*   18 cantandum est
1ª *m.*   19 sallendum *ms*   21 expli(cit) psal(mus) xii. incipit xiii. *ms*   22 Eze-
hia] adit abduxit *add. supra*   22-23 Iudeae] .i. regionis *add. supra*   27 com-
minuatione *ms*   terreret] ut *add. supra*.

from all sadness, and with the return of the bright light of joy the darkness that the offenses had accumulated is dissipated, as happens completely when there is no uncertain hope of reconciliation.

In case my foe should ever say down to *him* (v. 4): in case, when you are angry for a long period, my foe becomes stronger, grows insolent and boasts of putting into effect the desires of his heart against me. *Those distressing me will exult if I falter:* if long sustained troubles show me to be removed from your protection, my enemies will find grounds for gratification in a turn of events acceptable to them. *For my part, on the contrary, I hoped in your mercy* (v. 5): in your mercy—that is, in pardon and clemency. It was right for him to speak of *mercy* for the reason that, if on account of his sin he has no grounds for confidence in his own virtues to hope for salvation, he is aware of nothing to appeal to except God's mercy. *My heart rejoiced in your salvation:* I am glad that salvation has been restored to me by you. *I shall sing to the Lord my benefactor* down to *Most High:* not only am I filled with joy in receiving salvation, but also I am ready with all zeal to sing and praise you as my lofty benefactor who delivered me from my enemies.

PSALM 14

In the time of Hezekiah, king of Judah, Sennacherib, king of the Assyrians, took captive the ten tribes by a conqueror's right after the defeat of many cities of Judah by force of arms, including also a great number of people under Hezekiah's jurisdiction.[1] Intending to besiege Jerusalem as well, in fact, he sent Rabshakeh to terrify the people in the city or win them over with promises or threats. On arrival, amidst the boastful words | that he delivered

---

1. The fall of the northern kingdom in 722 should be credited to Shalmaneser V and Sargon II (the latter's name not occurring in the Bible), whereas Sennacherib came to power only in 704 and launched this campaign against Jerusalem in 701.

quae minando ⟨ex parte⟩ regis pertulerat, non a Dei blasfemia
temperauit, ad terrorem populi tali personans uoce: *Non uos seducat
Ezehias dicens quoniam Deus uos liberabit. Numquid liberauerunt
dii gentium unus quisque regionem suam de manu regis Asyriorum?*
5 *Vbi est deus Emath et Arfath?* atque iterum: *Quis eruit terram
suam de manu mea?* Haec atque alia his similia uanitatis et superbiae plena iactabat, per quae credi uolebat quod potentiae eius
neque Deus possit obsistere; quae quidem | uerba stultitiae eius
erant certa documenta. Haec ergo beatus Dauid in praesenti psalmo
10 longe ante futura praeloquitur.

1. *Dixit insipiens in corde suo: Non est Deus.* In hebitudinis
profunda palude demersum uocat Asyrium, qui nullum profecto
Deum credit dum se praeferre non metuit. Insipientis igitur est et
boni luce et rationis extranei dicere: *Non est Deus*, cuius notitia
15 cunctis naturaliter uidetur inserta.

Corrupti sunt et abominabiles usque *suis.* Consequens est, ut
qui uacuus a cognitione sui fuerit conditoris, omnibus uitiorum
sordibus impleatur: non enim dubitabit ad probra uitae omnia pro-
silire, quem nulla diuinorum cura conpraeserit. *In studiis* uero pos-
20 suit, ac si diceret: in operibus suis; uult autem ostendere quod et
morum feritate et ignorantia diuini cultus longe ab omni humani-
tate discesserint.

Non est enim *qui faciat bonum.* Ita, ait, apud illos uitiorum
familiaritas inoleuit, ita peccandi consuetudo omnes inplicuit, ut
25 nemo apud eos possit boni operis inueniri. Consequenter uero de
Asyriis ista dicuntur, qui uictoria insolenter usi in omnes uictos
crudeles exstiterant.

1-3 Is. XXXVI, 18-20.

1 ex parte *suppleui*   regis] .i. Sennacherib *add. supra*   3 numquid] .i.
rabsacen d(ixi)t *add. supra*   4 quisque] .i. non deus *add. supra*   5 ubi] in-
terro(gatiuum) *add. supra*   deus *om. 1ª m.*   atque iterum] .i. rabsacen d(i-
xi)t *add. supra*   quis] .i. deus *add. supra*   6 his] uerbis *add. supra*   7 quae]
uerba *add. supra*   uolebat] .i. rabsacen *add. supra*   quod] quo *ms*   po-
tentiae] dati(uum) *add. supra*   eius] .i. sennacherib *add. supra*   12 uocat]
.i. insepientem *add. supra*   13 inpientis *1ª m.*   13-14 *verba* et — non est
litt. a-f *instruuntur ad syntaxeos ordinem insinuandum*   14 boni] .i. dei operis, uel (bon)ae *add. supra*   et *om. 1ª m.*   18-19 prosilere *ms*   19 diuino-
rum] operum *add. supra*   22 discesserint] .i. Asyrii *add. supra*   23 ait *in
rasura*   26 Asyris *ms*   uictoria] ab(latiuum) *add. uspra*   27 crudiles *ms*,
crud. uictos *ms*   exterant *ms*.

as a threat on the king's part, he did not stop short of blaspheming God, shouting in tones meant to terrify the people, "Do not let Hezekiah deceive you with the claim that God will deliver you. Did any of the gods of the nations deliver their own region from the hand of the king of the Assyrians? Where is the god of Hamath and Arpad?" and again, "Which of them delivered his land from my hand?"[2] He uttered this and similar boasts full of vanity and arrogance, through which he wanted it to be believed that not even God could resist his power, his words being unequivocal proof of his stupidity.

Blessed David, then, forecasts this a long time beforehand. *The fool has said in his heart, There is no God* (v. 1). He is referring to the Assyrian, sunk in the deep mire of stupidity, who without belief in any God had no qualms about giving himself pride of place. It is therefore the mark of a foolish person, devoid of the light of goodness and reason, to say *There is no God,* despite awareness of him seeming to be naturally inherent in all people. *They were corrupt and loathsome in their pursuits:* it follows that anyone bereft of the knowledge of their creator would be filled with every vicious defilement, having no qualms about rushing headlong into every wicked lifestyle because unconstrained by attention to the divinity. He said *in their pursuits,* meaning "in their works"; he intends to bring out that they had abandoned any vestige of humanity by the ferocity of their behavior and the ignorance of divine worship. *There is no one who does good,* in fact: vicious habits so embroiled them, the habit of sinning so involved them, that no one of good behavior could be found in their midst. Logically, then, this was said of the Assyrians, who exploited their victory to behave with cruelty to all the vanquished. |

---

2. Cf. 2 Kgs 18:32–35.

2. *Dominus de caelo respexit super* usque *requirens Deum.* Quoniam non erat ⟨in⟩ profetia tantum pondus examinis, ut possit de
omnibus talem ferre sententiam ac pronuntiare quod non esset in
his qui possit facere bonum, Dei intuentis dicit oculis esse per-
spectum et considerationis eius acie conpraehensum, quod nemo 5
in eis uel a malo uacaret opere uel ad cognitionem Dei curae
aliquid ac sollicitudinis admoueret. Quales ergo Dei apparuerint
oculis, sequenti sermone producuntur.

3. *Omnes declinauerunt* usque *ad unum.* Grandis his uerbis —
dum dicit: *Omnes declinauerunt usque ad unum* — errantium consen- 10
sus ostenditur, cum in tanta profanorum multitudine nullus iustus
excipitur. Vitia autem, quae in eis generali sermone conpraehen-
derat, per species latius pergit aperire.

Sepulcrum patens guttur eorum. Qui mentis indicium in sermonis
prolatione uersatur fetor, de ore eorum malae uoluntatis egreditur. 15
Nam id, quod loquntur, desideria eorum ac uota manifestat, quae
ita et ad cedem hominum auida sunt et interfectorum gaudent multitudine, ut sepulcra, quae condendis cadaueribus parata sunt, uideantur imitari.

Linguis suis dolose agebant. Necesse est ut quorum studia ad 20
efundendum sanguinem sunt semper intenta, ut eorum lingua sit
ad dicipiendum parata.

Veninum aspidum sub labiis eorum. Vt qualitatem doli expraemeret, quem dixerat in eorum ore uersari, ne de rebus forte leui-
bus crederetur, per exsecutionem uenini ostendit noxium esse at- 25
que mortiferum.

Quorum os maledictione usque *plenum est.* Varietate sermonum
feritatis eorum et truculentiae crimen exagitat: quod non manus
eorum a cede hominum, non a dicipiendo lingua cessaret, quod
laqueos mortis his, quos dicipire parabant, fallendo praetenderet. 30
Nam Rapsaces populum, qui sedebat in muro, hac uerborum

de v. 2 et 3 vide infra, p. 85-86.

1-2 quoniam] adit d(ici)t *add. supra* 2 profetia] ab(latiuum) *add. supra*
in *suppleui* 4-7 *verba* dei — admoueret *litt.* a-g *instruuntur ad ordinem syntaxeos insinuandum* 5 conpraehensum] .i. esse *add. supra* 6 uacuaret *ms,
litt.* uar *in rasura* 10 dum *in rasura* 11 iustus *om. 1ª m.* 12 sermone]
.i. quando dixit declinauerunt *add. supra* 13 spicies *ms,* .i. peccatorum *add.
supra* latius] .i. ut infra dicet *add. supra* 14 patiens gutor *ms* qui]
fetor *add. supra* 17 abida *ms* 19 emitari *ms* 23 ut] adit ostendit *add.
supra* 28 cremen *ms* 29 adicipiendum *ms* 31 muro hac] muru(m) ac *uidetur prius scriptum.*

The Lord looked down from heaven on down to *seeking after God* (v. 2). Since in the inspired composition there was not such a claim to authoritative judgment that he could deliver such a sentence about everyone and affirm that none of them were capable of doing good, he says that it falls under God's gaze and comes to his attention that none of them desists from evil behavior or takes any steps or shows any interest in the knowledge of God. What they seem in God's eyes emerges from the following verse. *All went astray* down to *not even one* (v. 3). By these words—his saying *All went astray ... not even one*—a great consensus of those going off the track is demonstrated, since no righteous person is excepted in the vast numbers of irreligious people.

Now, he proceeds to reveal in greater detail the vices found among them that he had included in general terms. *Their throat is an open grave:*[3] a stench issues from the mouth of those of evil intent as an indication in the speech they utter of their frame of mind; in other words, what they say declares their desires and wishes, which are so avid for people's death and which take such satisfaction in the numbers of the slain as to resemble graves dug for concealing corpses. *With their tongues they acted deceitfully.* It follows that as their exploits are always aimed at shedding blood, their tongues are ready to deceive. *The venom of asps is under their lips.*[4] To bring out the kind of deceit he said was present in their mouth, lest it be thought possibly of little consequence, he shows that it is harmful and lethal through the administration of poison.

Their mouth is full of cursing.[5] He elaborates on the ferocity and savagery of their crime by the variety of his expressions, that their hands did not stop killing people, their tongue did not stop deceiving them, by their guile they set the snares of death for those whom they were ready to deceive. Rabshakeh, in fact, was bent on deceiving with the promises he made the people seated on the wall: | "If you want blessing, come out to us, and each

---

3. At this point some forms of the LXX (Diodore's text but not Theodoret's) include a lengthy coda to verse 3 drawn from Paul's catena of psalm verses and Isaiah at Rom 3:14–18 following his citation of this psalm's opening. Does Theodore realize that some verses, beginning with Ps 5:10, have been inserted? Like Diodore, he proceeds to comment on them, if briefly.

4. Ps 140:3.

5. Ps 10:7.

uolebat pollicitatione decipere: *Si uultis benedici, | exite ad nos, et manducabitis unus quisque de uinea sua et de ficu sua, et bibetis singuli aquam de lacu uestro, donec ueniam et accipiam uos in terram meam, terram quae est sicut uestram terram, terram frumenti et uini.* Haec
5 autem dicebat ut, populo tali ipsa misione decepto, uolentibus ciui-tatem capire manum nullus opponeret; cuius semel facti domini uterentur captiuo populo prout ira uictorum aut libido uoluisset. Merito ergo fallacie suae conuenientibus uerbis et quodam nequi-tiae caractere signantur qui humanitatem quidem uerbis praeten-
10 derent, re enim ipsa exitium urbi molirentur inferre.

Veloces pedes eorum ad effundendum sanguinem. Subiectio uer-suum singulorum accussationis continet incrementum. Nam dicendo superius: *Sepulcrum patens est guttur eorum*, indicauit quod nimia hominum morte gauderent; per hoc uero, quod ait: *Veloces pedes*
15 *eorum ad effundendum sanguinem*, ostendit eos ad strages facien-das non praelii necessitate inpelli sed solo furore raptari.

Contritio et miseria in uiis eorum. Ei in memores eorum uitu-peratio dirigitur, et tota generali accussatione uita damnatur. Aliena, inquit, sunt a salute et morti uicina quae faciunt: nam id, quod
20 contritum est amisa soliditate, ad nihilum ipsa sui uel tenuitate uel infirmitate perducitur. Volens ergo omnia opera eorum opera mortis ostendere, contritionem *in uiis eorum* ait infelicitatemque uersari.

Et uiam pacis non cognouerunt. Ferro atque armis adsueti sunt,
25 a consiliis quietis et pacis alieni.

Non est timor Dei ante oculos eorum. Subiecit causam unde eis mala, quae enumerauerat, cuncta processerunt. Vbi enim non est timor Dei, ibi uniuersis parantur regna criminibus.

1-4 Is. XXXVI, 16-17.

1 uolebat] *litt.* uo *in rasura*　2 unus] .i. manducauit *add. supra*　uinia *ms*　4 frumenti] .i. in terram *add. supra*　haec] .i. uerba *add. supra*　5 di-cebat] .i. rabsaces *add. supra*　populo] .i. hierusalem *add. supra*　ipso *ms* uolentibus] assyris *add. supra*　5-6 ciuitatem] .i. hieru(salem) *ms*　6 ma-num] .i. potestatem *add. supra*　7 uterentur] .i. ut assirii *add. supra*　po-pulo] .i. filiorum israel *add. supra*　8 uerbis] .i. rabsaces *add. supra*　9 ca-rectere *ms*　signantur] .i. rabsaces et assirii *add. supra*　10 urbi] .i. hieru(salem) *add. supra*　11 ad effund.] affund. *ms*　subiectio] .i. infra *add. supra*　13 guttur] gutor *ms*　17 miseria] conclusori (?) *add. ms*　eorum] .i. assiri(o)rum *add. supra*　19 quae] .i. opera *add. supra*　21 uolens] .i. da-uid *add. supra*　eorum] .i. assiriorum *add. supra*　22 ostendire *ms*　28 cre-minibus *ms*, .i. peccatis *add. supra*.

of you will eat of your own vine and your own fig tree, and you all will drink water from your own cistern until I come and take you to my country, a country like your own, a country of grain and wine."[6] Now, he said this so that the people would be deceived by such a reprieve and no one would raise a hand against those aiming to take the city; once they were in control, they would treat the captive population exactly as the conquerors' anger and lusts dictated. Rightly, then, were their lies conveyed by appropriate words and a particular mark of malice, since those who made a verbal show of humanity were in fact intent on bringing ruin to the city.

Their feet swift to shed blood.[7] The occurrence of successive verses results in an increase in the accusation: by saying above *Their throat is an open grave,* he suggested that their joy at people's death was excessive, whereas here in saying *Their feet swift to shed blood,* he brings out that in causing slaughter they were not under the pressure of the necessity of battle but were only caught up in rage. *Destruction and hardship in their paths:* he incurs obloquy by recalling them, and their life meets with condemnation in an overwhelming accusation. What they do, he is saying, is divorced from salvation and bordering on death: what is destroyed with the loss of its solidity is reduced to nothingness even by its insubstantial condition. In his wish to emphasize that all their deeds are the works of death, he says that destruction and unhappiness are *in their ways. The way of peace they have not known:* accustomed as they are to steel and weapons, they are strangers to counsels of repose and peace. *There is no fear of God before their eyes.*[8] He supplied the reason whence all their evils he had listed issued forth: where there is no fear of God, there kingdoms rise on utter lawlessness. |

---

6. Cf. 2 Kgs 18:31–32; Isa 36:16–17.
7. Cf. Isa 59:7–8.
8. Ps 36:1.

4-5. *Nonne scient omnes qui operantur iniquitatem* usque *iusta est.* Propter metri custodiam yperbaton fecit. Nam consequentia dictorum hunc ordinem poscit: *Nonne scient qui operantur iniquitatem, qui deuorant plebem meam sicut cibum panis, quoniam Deus in generatione iusta est?* et tunc inserendum quod dictum est: *Deum* 5 *non inuocauerunt, illic tripidauerunt ubi non erat timor.* Quorum dictorum hoc modo sensus absoluitur:

Isti, inquit, qui familiaritatem cum iniquitate fecerunt ad sumendum populum meum ita auidi sunt, ut uideantur esuriem sustinere; et ita ad interfectionem eorum festinant, ut quasi longam famem 10 passi uice panis eos cupiant deuorare. Nonne rerum magisterio perdocentur *quoniam Deus in generatione iusta est,* id est in genere populi Israhel? Iustos autem uocat non uirtutis studio, sed ad conparationem Asyriorum, quos Deum dixerat ignorare. Quomodo scient Asyri quod *Deus in generatione iusta* sit? Plaga, sine dubio 15 illa qua caesi sunt, qua magnitudine sui Deum esse in medio iustorum euidentissime conprobauit. Siquidem ira, qua extincti sunt, omnia quae Dei uirtute retro acta fuerant nouitate sui et admiratione superauit: nam in uno temporis puncto CLXXXV ⟨millia⟩ angelo caedente deleta sunt. Bene ergo dixit: *Nonne scient,* quem 20 dixerat Asyrius: *Quis eruit terram suam de manu mea, quoniam liberabit Deus Hirusalem de manu mea?* et multa his similia per quae esse Deum negabant. | Quod autem in medio positum est, *Deum non inuocauerunt,* de ipsis Asyris dicitur, id ⟨est⟩: non cognouerunt, quoniam quem cognoscit inuocat. Constabat ergo illos 25 Deum, quia non *inuocauerunt,* ignorasse.

Quid ergo illis euenit, quia *Deum non inuocauerunt? Illic timuerunt timore ubi non erat timor.*

Id est: Vnde non sperauerunt se aliquid pasuros aduersi, inde illos periculum mortis oppraesit.

Τουτέστιν ὅθεν οὐ προσεδόκησάν τι κακὸν πείσεσθαι, ἐκεῖθεν αὐτοὺς 30 μέγας κίνδυνος περιέστη.

---

19 Is. XXXVII, 36   21-22 XXXVI, 20

1 sciant *ms,* scient *conieci;* cf. *infra ll. 3, 15*   2 fecit] .i. dauid *add. supra* 6 trip.] tripā *ms*   8 familiariatem *ms*   9 sustinere] sustire *Iᵃ m.*   11 pasi *ms* rerum] .i. operum *add. supra*   14 deum *om. Iᵃ m.*   dixerat] dauid *add. supra* 15 geratione *ms*   plaga] ab(latiuum) *add. supra*   17 conprobauit] .i. plaga *add. supra.*   18 sui] .i. irae *add. supra*   19 millia *suppleui*   20 sciaent] *ms,* .i. eum *add. supra*   quem] .i. interro(gatiuum) *add. supra*   24 est *suppleui* 26 inuocant *uidetur prius scriptum,* .i. deum *add. supra*   30 aduersis *ms.*

Τουτέστιν — 83, 11 νεκρῶν: (Θεοˢ αυ⁻) Paris. 139, fol. 35ᵛ; Vat. 1682, fol. 47ᵛ.

Have they no knowledge, all those who commit lawlessness down to *accompanies the righteous* (vv. 4–6). To maintain the meter he had recourse to hyperbaton:[9] the sequence of thought requires this order, *Have they no knowledge, all those who commit lawlessness, who eat up my people like a meal of bread, since God accompanies the generation of the righteous?* and then should be inserted the words *They did not invoke the Lord. There they were gripped with fear where there was no fear.* The sense of these words emerges thus: Those who developed a habit of iniquity were so desirous of consuming my people as to give the impression of hunger, and they are in such a hurry to slay them that they long to devour them like bread as though suffering from hunger. Have they not been taught the lesson of experience that *God accompanies the generation of the righteous?*—that is, the people of Israel. Now, he calls them *righteous* not from their pursuit of virtue, but by comparison with the Assyrians, who, he said, had no knowledge of God. How will the Assyrians come to know that *God accompanies the generation of the righteous?* Doubtless from that disaster by which they were slain, in which he proved that God in his greatness was most obviously in the midst of the righteous. In fact, the anger with which they were wiped out surpassed by its novelty and marvelous character everything that previously had been done by the power of God: in a flash one hundred eighty-five thousand were destroyed by the angel's blow.[10] He therefore was right to say *Will they have no knowledge* of him of whom the Assyrians had said, "Which of them delivered his country from my hand to make you think that God would deliver Jerusalem from my hand?" and his many similar statements in denying God's existence. What occurs in the middle, *They did not invoke God,* applies to the Assyrians themselves to mean, They did not know, since one invokes whom one knows. It is obvious, therefore, that they did not know God, because they did not invoke him.

So, because *they did not invoke God,* what happened to them? *They were gripped with fear where there was no fear*—that is, from the quarter whence they expected to come to no harm a great disaster befell them: | they went

---

9. Having assigned Assyrians and the population of Jerusalem parts to play in a dialogue (as he will do also in commenting on the almost identical Ps 53), Theodore has to continue dividing up the verses, creating a problem that does not otherwise exist.

10. 2 Kgs 19:35.

Ascenderunt enim ad Hirusalem elati multis succesionibus prae-
liorum; et freti tam uirtute quam numero nihil de se humile sentie-
bant, dispicientes quoque hostium paucitatem credebant eos impetu
primo se esse capturos. Ita namque et ad Iudeos dixerat Rapsaces
5 misus a rege Asyriorum: *Dabimus uobis II milia equorum si po-
teritis uos dare ascensores eorum.*

Contra ergo omnem spem non   Παρὰ πᾶσαν γὰρ προσδοκίαν,
acie certatum est, non uel pri-   οὔτε παρατάξεως, οὔτε πολέμου γε-
mis telis belli temtatus euentus,   γενημένου, οὔτε πεπτωκότος τινὸς
10 nullo Iudeorum loetali uulnere   τῶν Ἰσραηλιτῶν, ἄπειρον πλῆθος αὐ-
conruente, sub unius noctis spa-   τῶν διὰ τῆς νυκτὸς εὑρέθη νεκρῶν.
tio tantae multitudines armato-
rum sub manu angeli conruerunt.

5. *Consilium inopis confudistis.*

15 Inopem uocat Ezechiam, quip-   Πτωχοῦ τοῦ Ἐζεκίου ἐνταῦθα
pe humanis copiis et subsidiis   λέγει διὰ τὸ ὀλίγους ἔχειν τοὺς ὑπ'
distitutum, qui paucis ad conpa-   αὐτόν.
rationem Asyriorum in armis possitis, non modo a uictoriae spe
20 aberat, sed nec ad resistendum
putabatur idoneus. Quod autem
consilium Ezechiae, quod ab illis   Βουλὴν δὲ ἦν συνεβούλευεν τοῖς Ἰου-
dicit esse dirisum? Sine dubio   δαίοις, λέγων καταφρονεῖν μὲν ἐκεῖ-
illud quo suadebat Iudeis, ut con-   νον, πεποιθέναι δὲ ἐπὶ τὸν δεσπό-
25 fitentes in Deo Asyrios minime   την.
formidarent, cum, e contrario,
Asyrii loquerentur ad populum:
*Nos uos seducat Ezechias uerbis quibus non poterit uos eruere, et
non dicat uobis Ezechias quoniam liberabit uos Dominus, et non
30 tradetur ciuitas haec in manu regis Asyriorum; nolite audire Ezechiam.* Haec ergo dicentes Asyrii beati Ezechiae consilia diridebant,

---

5-6 Is. XXXVI, 8   28-31 Is. XXXVI, 14-16.

---

4 rapaces *ms*   5 aequorum *ms*   5-6 potetis *ms*   8 certatum] certum *1ᵃ m.*
8-9 uel primis] adit conruerunt *add. supra*   12 multitunes *ms*   16 copis *ms*
22 illis] .i. assiriis *add. supra*   23 dicit] .i. ezechias uel dauid *add. supra*   24 il-
lud] .i. consilium *add. supra*   26 e *om. 1ᵃ m.*   29 ezchias *ms.*

Πτωχοῦ — 84, 5 ἐλπὶς αὐτοῦ ἐστιν: (Θεὸς ἀντοχ) Paris. 139, fol. 35ᵛ; Vat. 1422,
fol. 43ᵛ; Vat. 1682, fol. 47ᵛ-48 (Mai, p. 393; P. G., 657 A 6-11); Barbaro, p. 129.

up to Jerusalem elated at their many successes in war; and relying on both their power and their numbers, they had no lowly thoughts of themselves, despising the small numbers of the enemy and believing that they would take them at the first assault. In fact, Rabshakeh, on being sent by the king of the Assyrians, spoke in these terms to the Jews, "We shall give you two thousand horses if you can provide riders for them."[11] It thus was against all expectation, you see, that without any deployment of troops or outbreak of battle or any of the Israelites being cut down, their countless host was found to have died during the night.

You confounded the purpose of the poor (v. 6). By the *poor* here he refers to Hezekiah on account of his having few men under him. The *purpose* is the advice he gave to the Jews, to despise the Assyrian and trust in the Lord, whereas the Assyrians were saying to the people, "Do not let Hezekiah deceive you in words with which he will not succeed in rescuing you, and do not let Hezekiah tell you the Lord will deliver you, and not let this city be delivered into the hand of the king of the Assyrians; do not listen to Hezekiah."[12] In saying this, therefore, the Assyrians kept mocking the advice of blessed Hezekiah | in the desire to undermine his encouraging words by

---

11. 2 Kgs 18:23, the Latin version of the comment that follows making mention of the destroying angel.
12. 2 Kgs 18:29–31.

exortationum eius dicta, quibus confortabat populum, eneruare cupientes.

Vos, inquit, inridetis *consilium* illius; *Deus* autem *spes eius*, id est qui ea, quae loquitur Ezechias ad populum, irrita esse non patiatur: nam id, quod ille uerbis pollicebatur, est postea rebus impletum.

Ὑμεῖς μέν φησιν ἐγελᾶτε τὴν βουλὴν αὐτοῦ, ὁ δὲ Κύριος ἐλπὶς αὐτοῦ ἐστιν. 5

7. Quis dabit ex Sion salutare Israhel?

Quoniam et sacrificia et oblationes atque omne diuini cultus ministerium, ut in monte Sion offerrent, erat lege praeceptum, habebant hanc opinionem apud semet ipsos quod in monte Sion Deus habitaret; atque ideo ait: *Quis dabit ex Sion salutare Israel?* id est: Quis de monte Sion praestabit nobis salutem et adiutorium largietur? ut subaudiatur Deus, manifeste indicans neminem esse alium nisi Deum montis Sion, qui a periculis instantibus possit eruere.

Ἐπειδὴ καὶ τὰς θυσίας ἐν τῷ ὄρει 10 Σιὼν ἀναφέρειν προστεταγμένοι ἦσαν καὶ τὰς προσφορὰς καὶ πᾶσαν αὐτῶν τὴν λατρείαν ἐκεῖ ἐπιτελεῖν ἦσαν νενομοθετημένοι, εἶχόν τε δόξαν ὡς ἐκεῖ καὶ τοῦ Θεοῦ τυγχάνοντος, διὰ 15 τοῦτό φησιν· Τίς δώσει ἐκ Σιὼν τὸ σωτήριον τοῦ Ἰσραήλ, τουτέστι Τίς ἀπὸ τοῦ Σιὼν ὄρους παρέξει τὴν σωτηρίαν καὶ τὴν βοήθειαν ἡμῖν; ἵν' εἴπῃ Ὁ Θεὸς κατὰ ἀποσιώπησιν, ὡς 20 ὁμολογούμενον σημήνας τὸ μηδὲν ἕτερον εἶναι ἐν τῷ Σιὼν τὸ σώζειν ἀπὸ κινδύνων ἢ Θεὸν μόνον.

Cum auertit Dominus captiuitatem populi sui exsultabit Iacob 25 *et laetabitur Israel*. Tunc, inquit, plena laetitia perfruemur cum populus, solutis captiuitatis uinculis, fuerit reuersus ad propria (x tribus dicit, quae nuper captae ab Assiris in regiones illorum de proprii soli habitatione grauarentur). Consequenter ergo ait tunc perfectam illis laetitiam conferendam, cum etiam reliquos generis 30 eorum ita Deus de captiuitate reuocauerit, sicut istos in Iudea positos contra omnem spem a malis eximit instantibus.

1 exorationum *ms*   enerauare *ms*   2 cupientes] assirii *add. supra*   3 inquit] .i. dauid *add. supra*   inritis *1ª m.*   irrita non esse pat. *ms*   7 id *om.* *1ª m.*   7-8 polliciebatur *ms*   8 rebus] operibus *add. supra*   9 salū *ms, ita l. 17* 13 offerent *ms*   14 abiebant *1ª m.*, hab. *corr.*   18. 20 praestabit, largietur] .i. deus *add. supra*   23 qui a] q(uia) *ms*   27 populos *prius scriptum* propria] .i. loca *add. supra*   29 grauarent *ms*   30 reliquos] requos *1ª m.*   31 de] di *ms*.

Ἐπειδὴ — Θεὸν μόνον: (Θεοδώρου ἀντοχ) Paris. 139, fol. 36; Vat. 1682, fol. 48ᵛ (Mai, p. 393; P. G., 657 A 12-B 7); Barbaro, p. 131.

which he consoled the people. While you derided his advice, he is saying, the Lord is his hope.

Who will give from Sion the salvation of Israel? (v. 7). Since they had been commanded to offer sacrifices on Mount Sion and were required by the law to perform the offerings and all their worship there, and held the view that God also was there, hence he says *Who will give from Sion the salvation of Israel?*—in other words, Who will provide us from Mount Sion with salvation and assistance? As if to imply by use of aposiopesis, God—thus implying the belief that there was nothing else on Mount Sion to save them from danger except God alone. *When the Lord averts the captivity of his people, Jacob will rejoice and Israel will be glad:* we shall be filled with joy at the time when the bonds of captivity are undone and the people has returned to its own country (he means the ten tribes, which recently had been captured by the Assyrians and imprisoned in their country away from their own home). Hence, he is saying that perfect joy is to be conferred on them at the time when God also recalls from captivity the rest of their race, just as against all hope he rescued those situated in Judah from the impending troubles. | Blessed David added this further remark in this psalm to bring out

Hoc autem addidit in hoc psalmo beatus Dauid, ostendens quoniam et reditum illorum praecipere animo conueniret, sicut et impletum est tunc, cum omnes a Cyro rege Persarum dimisi sunt, cunc-
tisque data libertas, si uel|lint, in Iudeam redire.

5 Notandum autem quod, cum psalmus hic in Asyrios specialiter
dictus est, beatus apostolus Paulus disputans ad Romanos testimonio eius usus est, ut dictis eius uellit generaliter adprobare
omnes homines peccati ferre dominatum. Ita enim ait: *Quid ergo?*
Tenemus amplius? Causati enim sumus Iudeos et Graecos omnes sub
10 *peccato esse, sicut scriptum est: Quoniam non est iustus quisquam,*
intellegens et reliqua. Quid nos ad haec adferemus? A beato quidem
Dauid, propter praemisam causam, quae hoc psalmo non continetur, dicta esse non dubium est; et hoc aperte ipsa consequentia
lectionis ostenditur, quoniam non poterit generaliter de omnibus
15 hominibus talem ferre sententiam; | quoniam si sine exceptione a
profeta uita omnium culparetur, quasi a recti calle deuia, de quibus
adderet id, quod sequitur: *qui deuorant plebem meam?* — quo dicto
ostendit esse plebem ad Deum proprie pertinentem, quam oppri-
mere aduersariorum labor et intentio, et cuius se curam Deus pro-
20 mittit habere. Talis ergo uerborum interpositio non conueniebat ei
cuius in omnes superius querella processerat, uidilicet quod se im-
pietati iniquitatique tradidissent; sed ut uerbis profeticis Assyriorum dedita peccatis uita damnatur, ita etiam post illam aetatem
omnibus peccandi amore peruasis ac uitiorum adsiduitate corruptis
25 eadem ratione praesentia dicta conueniunt. Vsus est ergo testimonio
hoc beatus apostolus, non quia ob id a profeta dictum sit, sed quia
non falleret etiam si illius temporis hominibus aptaretur, per quod
quidem Iudeorum grandia peccata signantur, quorum moribus con-
ueniunt quae a profeta in solos | diriguntur Assyrios. Hoc autem
30 adsumpsit apostolus ut nos facere solemus, non solum cum scribimus

8-11 Rom. III, 9-11   29-86, 5: cf. comm. Theodori in epist. ad Romanos (ed. K. STAAB,
Pauluskommentare, p. 117).

4 si uellint in iudeam] si in iudeam uellit *ms*   5 notandum] est *add. supra*
7 eius] .i. psalmi *add. supra*   9 iudeo *1ª m.*   11 ad haec] dauid uerba *add.*
supra   13 dicta] .i. uerba   esse] .i. a dauid *add. supra*   14 lectionis] .i.
psalmi *add. supra*   16 recti] operis *add. supra* A   callide uia A   18-19 oppraec-
mire A   19 cuius] plebis *add. supra* A   20 hab. prom. B   interpossitio A
conueniat A   ei] apos(tolo) *add. supra* A   21 querella] querelba B¹   22-23 asyriorum A   23 ita* B   24 peruassis B   adsiduetate A   25 usus] .i. est
add. supra A   26 dictuum B¹   27 falleret] .i. apostolum *add. supra* A   28 si-
gnentur A   29 asyrios A   hoc] .i. testimonium *add. supra* A   autem] ita A
30 adsumsit A   nos *om.* A   soleamus A.

that it was suitable for him to give instructions in spirit for their return, just as it was fulfilled at the time when they were all released by Cyrus, the king of the Persians, and liberty was granted to them to return to Judah if they wanted.

Now, it should be noted that while this psalm was composed specifically with the Assyrians in mind, the blessed apostle Paul, in the course of argument to the Romans, used it as a text to be able to prove from its verses in general terms that all people are under the control of sin. He speaks in these terms, in fact, "What, then? Are we any better off? For we have already charged that all, Jews and Greeks, are under the power of sin, as it is written, 'There is no one who is righteous, intelligent'" and so on.[13] What is to be our attitude toward this? There is no doubt that the words were spoken by blessed David on account of an earlier question that is not contained in this psalm. It clearly emerges from the actual sequence of the text that it could not sustain the view in general terms about all human beings, since if without exception the life of everyone was held to be blameworthy by the prophet, as if straying from the straight and narrow, of whom did he add what follows *who eat up my people*? By this phrase he brings out that the people properly belongs to God, and it is the effort and aim of adversaries to oppress it, while God promises to take care of it. Insertion of such verses, then, did not suit someone whose complaint was directed against all those above, namely, that they had given themselves to godlessness and injustice; but as it is the life of the Assyrians that was condemned in the inspired words as given over to sin, so also after that age the present words for the same reason apply to everyone in the grip of a love of sinning and corrupted by vicious practices.

The blessed apostle, therefore, cited that verse, not because it was spoken by the prophet to that effect, but because it would not be wrong for it to be applied also to people of that time so as to convey the grave sins of the Jews, since what was directed by the prophet against the Assyrians alone suits their behavior also. Now, the apostle adopted it as we are in the habit of doing, not only when we are writing | something, but also when we are debating in

---

13. Rom 3:9–11. Some commentators on Rom 3, such as Martin Dibelius ("Zur Formgeschichte des Neuen Testaments [außerhalb der Evangelien]," *TRu* NS 3 (1931): 228), believed that Paul came across a catena of texts already in existence, a view that Joseph Fitzmyer finds plausible ("The Letter to the Romans," *NJBC,* 839). Theodore (perhaps unaware of their origin [see n. 3]) has a scruple about the apposite nature of the texts and in particular the opening verses of this psalm, which he rightly observes is directed at a different group on a different theme. But, he concludes, with the passage of time the text arguably can be adduced to support the more general message.

aliqua sed et cum in ecclesiis disputamus ac dicta nostra uolumus scripturarum testimoniis adprobare, quae sermoni nostro similitudine magna iungantur, — ut puta aliquod adferamus exemplum
quo possit clarius id, quod dicimus, relucere, si quis uideat multos
hominum relicta probitate morum uitia passim cuncta sectari nec 5
ullam honestatis habere rationem causeturque de tali inproborum
studio atque addat illud, quod a profeta dictum est, quoniam *periit
reuerens de terra.* Hoc autem dicit, non quia de illo sit tempore
profetatum, sed quod causis, quibus motus est, possit plurimum
conuenire. Sic ergo et beatus apostolus ait: *Causati enim sumus* 10
Iudaeos et Grecos omnes sub peccato esse, et intulit: *sicut scriptum*
est Non est iustus quisquam et reliqua. Vsus est ergo conuenienti
testimonio et quod dicta eius adstrueret. Sic itaque accipiendum
est apostolum uerba profetae ideo ad suam epistolam necessitate
transtulisse, quia causae de qua agebat constabat plurimum conue- 15
nire; quod quidem, ut dixi, et nobis moris est facere.

Haec autem consuetudo a plurimis ignorata maximi fuit erro-
ris occassio, his uidelicet qui scripturarum consuetudinem nescien-
tes, omnia quae Novo Testamento inserta sunt, per profetiam | dicta
esse crediderunt, et ob hoc non ueritatem rerum, sed fabulas in 20
suis expossitionibus adtulerunt.

PSALMVS XIIII

Hic psalmus praecedenti, non solum ordine quo subiectus est,
sed etiam causae uicinitate coniungitur. Beatus namque Dauid, ut
omnem filiis Israhel spem noxiae securitatis | incideret, quae per 25
hoc, quod recenti Dei auxilio extra periculum omne constiterant ac
de metu fuerant captiuitatis erepti, poterat eorum sensus adtollere,

7-8 Mich. 7, 2.

1 aeclesis A ecclesis B   disputamus] .i. praedicamus *add. supra* A   2 test.
script. A   3 iniungantur A   4 reluere A¹   si] adit causetur *add. supra* A
5 nec] non A   8 de terra *om.* A¹   dicit] dico A   9 causis] dati(uum) *add.*
supra A   12 usus est] est *om.* A¹   13 eius] .i. pauli *add. supra* A   itaque]
igitur A   14 est *om.* A¹ B   necessitate *om.* B   15 plurimum] plumum A¹
17 consuetuetudo A   18 hiis B   uidilicet A   19 nouo] dati(uum) *add. supra* A
20 ob] ab A   21 adtullerunt A   22 expli(cit) psal(mus) xiii. incipit xiiii A,
incipit xiiii B   24 beatus namque] nam et A   dauid] adit cicinit *add. supra* A
25 israel B   26 constiterant] constituerant A, .i. se *add. supra*   27 attol-
lere B,

the churches and want to confirm our words with testimonies of the Scriptures that bear a close relationship to our argument. For instance, we cite an example to shed clearer light on what we are saying if someone sees many people abandoning an upright life, adopting every vice indiscriminately and retaining no shred of honor, and we discourse on such an involvement in improper behavior and add what was said by the prophet, "Those fearing God have disappeared from the earth"[14]—something he said not because the prophecy had reference to that time, but because it could apply particularly to the questions preoccupying him. Likewise, the blessed apostle also says, "For we have already charged that Jews and Greeks are all under the power of sin," and he adduces in support, "As it is written, 'There is no one who is righteous'" and so on. So he employed a suitable text to support his statement. Accordingly, it likewise should be accepted that the apostle transferred the words of the prophet to his epistle because it obviously was very suitable to the case he was mounting—which is, as I remarked, what we normally do. Now, the general ignorance of this custom was the basis of a serious error on the part of those unaware of the habit of the Scriptures and convinced that everything incorporated in the New Testament has been spoken through divine inspiration, and for this reason they introduced into their commentaries not actual truth but fairy tales.

PSALM 15

This psalm is joined to the preceding one not only by the order in which it occurs, but also by similarity in theme. So as to eliminate from the children of Israel all trust in a harmful security, which on account of the fact that they were free of every danger through God's recent help and relieved of fear of captivity could raise their spirits | to the extent of having great confidence in

---

14. Mic 7:2.

ut uidelicet de se magna sentirent ac non parui apud Deum
meriti esse se crederent; ne ergo abiecta omni sollicitudine uitae
melioris in otium se desidiamque laxarent, hunc psalmum cecinit,
qui uicem magisterii et exhortationis impleret, quatenus placere
5 Deo morum probitate contenderent et in adpetitu se grandi cura
omnis uirtutis extenderent nec crederent aliter se posse esse de
urbis illius habitatione securos, nisi ea quae uellet Deus agere cu-
rassent atque omne studium suum depellendis uitiis admouerent:
qui si hoc non facerent, de habitationis suae securitate nutarent,
10 etiamsi uiderentur contra omnem spem de malis circumstantibus
nuper erepti.

1. *Domine, quis habitabit in tabernaculo tuo aut quis requiescet
in monte sancto tuo?* Non ab hominibus quaerit (ne minus ponderis adferat secutura responsio) ac uelut otiosus interrogat dicens:
15 *Quis* est qui *habitabit in tabernaculo* Dei, *aut quis requiescet in
monte sancto* eius? sed uelut sollicitam consultationem admouet
Deo, dicens: *Domine, quis habitabit in tabernaculo* ⟨*tuo*⟩? *aut quis
requiescet in monte sancto tuo*, ut, post attentam inquissitionis curam, sententiam Dei respondentis inducat, per quam maiore aucto-
20 ritate Iudaeos ad appetitum uirtutis et custodiam probitatis accin-
gat. Specie ergo interrogantis adsumpta ait: O Domine, doce nos
qualem patiaris hominem secure in hac ciuitate consistere, ut co-
gnoscamus pariter quibus nos rebus studere conueniat | uel que-
madmodum sit possibile mala tribulationis effugere atque aduersa-
25 riorum insidias declinare ac, sub tua tutione positos, incursus
hostium non timere.

2. *Qui ingreditur sine macula et operatur iustitiam.* Quasi Dei
magisteriis eruditus incipit docere quae didicit. Iste, inquit, in hac
ciuitate positus poterit longa habitatione consistere, cuius actus

1 uidilicet A 2 se *om.* A crederent] ut *add. supra* A 3 cicinit AB
4 uicem] uocem AB, psalmi *add. supra* A magistri et exortationis inpleret A
6 extenderent] ut *add. supra* A nec] non A crederent] ut *add. supra* A
7 urbis illius] .i. hierusalem *add. supra* A 8 admouerent] ut *add. supra* A
12 in — requiescet] usque A 14 secutura *conieci*, secuta AB ac] .i. ne
add. supra A hotiosus A 15 requescet A 16 consulationem A 17-18 in —
monte] usque A 17 tuo *suppleui* 18 atentam inquitionis A 20 iudeos A
20-21 accingat] *fortasse legendum* accendat 22 ciuitate] .i. herusalem *add. supra* A 23-24 quemadmodum] q(uam) A 25 sub tua] subita A possitos A
27 et operatur] usque A 28 magisteriis] magistrio A[1], uel magistri A[2] *in marg.*
magisteris B didicit] dedicit B dicit] .i. documenta *add. supra* A 29 possitus A.

themselves and not giving great credit to God, blessed David sang this psalm
to prevent their abandoning all interest in a better life and giving themselves
up to leisure and sloth. It was meant to have the function of teaching and
exhortation so that they might strive to please God by upright behavior and
develop a desire for it by constant attention to every virtue, not believing
that they could be secure in their occupancy of that city unless they took
pains to do what God wanted and made every effort to ward off vice. If
they did not do this, they would forfeit the security of occupancy despite
seeming recently to have been snatched against all hope from the troubles
besetting them.

*Lord, who will abide in your tent or who will rest on your holy moun-
tain?* (v. 1). He does not direct the inquiry to human beings (lest the reply
that followed carry less weight) or pose the question casually, as it were,
Who is he who will abide in God's tent *or who will rest on your holy mountain?* Rather, it is as though addressing an earnest inquiry to God that he says
Lord, who will abide in your tent or who will rest on your holy mountain? so
that after the deliberate effort at inquiring, he may elicit a verdict from God
in reply, and with its great authority he may prompt the Jews to a desire for
virtue and maintenance of upright living. Adopting the manner of a question,
then, he says, O Lord, teach us what kind of person you allow to remain
securely in this city, so that we may learn both what things it behooves us to
be engaged in and how it is possible to escape the hardships of tribulation, to
avoid the schemes of adversaries and by enjoying your protection to have no
fear of assaults of the enemy.

The one who walks blamelessly and performs righteousness (v. 2). As
if schooled in God's instruction, he begins to teach what he learns. That
person living in this city, he is saying, will be able to enjoy lengthy habita-
tion whose behavior | and life are not contaminated with any element of sin,

ac uita nulla peccati admixtione fuscatur; cuius opera, ne quid prauum tortumque habeant, ad normam iustitiae diriguntur. Iste, inquam, securus *habitabit* Dei munitus semper auxilio.

Quod autem ait *Qui ingreditur sine macula et operatur iustitiam* tale est ac si diceret: Qui et ab omni malo se abstinet et bona facere non omittit — neque enim perfecta uirtus est tantum uitiis non foedari et nullis uitae insignibus cumulatius * * *. Sane hoc exhortationis genus aperit in sequenti, ut sciamus et quae facere et quae uitare conueniat.

Qui loquitur ueritatem in corde suo. A quo abest studium fallendi, non prout fors tulerit, sed ex decreto mentis atque proposito.

3. *Qui non egit dolum in lingua sua, nec fecit proximo suo malum.* Hoc est, qui non aliud corde retinet, aliud ore promittit. Et quoniam superius dixerat: *Qui ingreditur sine macula et operatur iustitiam,* uidelicet qui utrumque pari cura obseruationis exsequitur, ut et uacuus a uitiis possit et plenus uirtutibus inueniri, pro operatione ergo iustitiae posuit: *Qui loquitur ueritatem in corde suo.* Ambulantem autem *sine macula* eum uult intellegi, qui etiam linguae lapsus effugiat nec faciat umquam quod ad incommodum proximi spectare uideatur: per haec enim omnis pec|cati species submouetur.

Et opprobrium non accipit aduersus proximum suum. Qui non ita usus est consanguineis suis (istos enim uocat proximos qui generis adfinitate iunguntur), ut malae tractationis opprobrio uel ab ipsis uel ab extraneis inuratur.

4. *Ad nihilum deductus est in conspectu eius malignus.* Apud quem tantum est probitatis studium, ut discedentes ab ea, etiamsi sint diuitiis et honore conspicui, auersetur atque dispiciat.

---

1 nulla *om.* A¹   1-2 ne quid prauum tortumque] paruum mal(um) tormentumque A, nequit parauum B¹   5 qui et] et *om.* A   6 uirtu**s B (*ex* uirtutis) 7 fedari A   nulli*s B (*ex* nullus)   cumulatius A comilatius *bis* B; *lacunam statui; fortasse legendum* cumulari *ut notauit* A²   8 exortationis A sequenti] iure *add. supra* A   9 quae *om.* A   12 nec — suo] usque A   suo suo B   13 hoc] id A   retinet corde A   promittit] qui non *add. supra* A 13-14 et quoniam] adit possuit *add. supra* A   14 incleditur A   15 uidilicet A 16 uirtutibus] .i. bonorum operum *add. supra* A   17 operatione] oratione A possuit A   19 linguae *om.* A¹   nec faciat] non facit A   20 per haec] .i. praedicta *add. supra* A   enim *om.* A   21 summouetur B   22 obproprium A 23 consanguneis A   proiximos A   26 est *om.* B   27 discedentes] discidentes A discendentes B   28 atque] ut *add. supra* A.

whose deeds are aligned with righteousness so as not to contain anything base or dishonest. That person, I say, will dwell secure, being ever fortified with God's help. Now, the meaning of *The one who walks blamelessly and performs righteousness* is something like this: The one who both abstains from every evil and does not omit doing good, perfect virtue consisting not merely in not being stained with vices and loaded down with any of life's honors....In fact, in what follows he develops this form of exhortation for us to realize both what we should do and what we should avoid.

The one who speaks truth in his heart: the one free of the practice of deceit, not by chance but from a decision and purpose of mind. *The one who committed no guile with his tongue or did no harm to his neighbor* (v. 3)— that is, the one who does not keep one thing in his heart while promising something else in word. And since he had said above *The one who walks blamelessly and performs righteousness*—namely, the one who gives equal care in both respects so as to be able to be found free from vices and full of virtues—he therefore interpreted the performance of righteousness by saying *The one who speaks truth in his heart.* Now, by the one walking *blamelessly* is meant the one who even avoids lapses of the tongue and never does anything that might seem to be aimed at the neighbor's disadvantage, every kind of sin stemming from these. *And does not level a reproach against his neighbor:* the one who does not so treat his kith and kin (by *neighbors* referring to those related by race) as to be scorched by the reproach of evil treatment from them or from foreigners.

The one in whose eyes an evildoer is despised (v. 4): with this person there is such a concern for upright behavior that those who abandon it, even if distinguished by riches or status, are avoided and scorned. | *But who*

Timentes autem Dominum glorificat. Ista mentis affectio de praemissa uirtute generatur: sequitur enim ut, in cuius conspectu ui-
lis | et detestanda fuerit iniquitas, illa quae ex timore Dei nascitur
probitas digna honore ducatur. Qui ergo *glorificat timentes Domi-*
5 *num,* non paupertatem eorum auersatur, non proposito humilitatis
offenditur.

Qui iurat proximo suo et non decipit eum. Quoniam sub lege
positis loquebatur, non remouet iusiurandum, sed periurii imperat
cautionem.

10 5. *Qui pecuniam suam non dedit ad usuram.* Notandum quoniam et sub lege usurae prohibebatur exactio, et quasi unum, inter
reliqua quae castigabantur uitia, ducebatur; usura enim unum iniquum, miserum alterum facit: dum et ille ma^{i}orem, quam dederat,
summam exigit; et iste, qui ideo accepit quia non habebat, dum
15 reddit amplius quam accepit, incipit plus egere.

Et munera super innocentes non accipit. Duplex in hoc uersi-
culo sensus inducitur, id est quod neque condemnauerit, acceptis
muneribus, innocentem neque id quod innocenti iure conpetebat,
muneribus acceptis, addixerit. Vult itaque iustitiam non esse uena-
20 lem et merito eam suo, non pecuniae quantitate, taxari. Notat uitium quod nostris praecipue diebus increbuit: nam tunc a mul-
tis, | cum manus aere plena fuerit, sententia iusta profertur.

Qui facit haec non mouebitur in aeternum. Quoniam in principio psalmi admota percunctatione quaesiuit: *Domine, quis habita-*
25 *bit in tabernaculo tuo aut quis requiescet in monte sancto tuo?* atque
intulit: *Qui ingreditur sine macula et operatur iustitiam, qui loqui-*
tur ueritatem in corde suo et quae sequuntur, conuenienter ergo
subiecit: *Qui facit haec non mouebitur in aeternum*; id est: Qui se
harum uirtutum, quas superior sermo digessit, studio et amore de-
30 uinxerit, nullam praesentis securitatis mutationem poterit formidare

1 ista] ita A   1-2 praemisa A   2 gneratur A   3 iniquitas].i. maligni
add. supra A   5 propossito, .i. dati(uum) *add. supra* A   7 iurat iurat A¹
et *om.* A   dicipit A   eum].i. proximum *add. supra* A   8 possitis loquie-
batur A   remouet].i. dauid *add. supra* A   periurii *suppl. in marg.* A   9 ca-
uitionem A   11 prohibeatur A   unum] uitium *add. supra* A   12 unum].i. ui-
rum *add. supra* A   13 ille].i. diues *add. supra* A   derat A   14 iste] pauper
add. supra A   14-15 accipit AB   15 reddidit A²   16 innō ñ a͞c. B   18 neque]
nec B   19 uult] dauid *add. supra* A   itaque] igitur A   20 peccuniae A   no-
tat] *fortasse legendum* nota, σημείωσαι   22 manus aere] manu sapere A   23 quo-
niam] adit subiecit *add. supra* A   24 quaessiuit B   26-27 et — ueritatem] usque A
27 secuntur B   29 digessit] egesit A¹ degesit A²   30 motationem AB.

honors those who fear the Lord. That attitude of mind springs from preexist-ing virtue: it follows that by the person in whose eyes injustice is horrid and detestable the uprightness born of the fear of God is considered worthy of honor. So the person *who honors those who fear the Lord* does not turn away from their poverty, is not upset by their humble attitude. *The one who makes an oath to his neighbor without breaking it.* Since he was speaking to those under the law, instead of abolishing oaths he delivered a warning against perjury.

Who did not lend his money at interest (v. 5). We should realize that usury was prohibited under the law and was regarded as special among the vices that were condemned.[1] Usury, you see, makes one party unjust and the other wretched, the former demanding a return greater than he lent, and the latter, in borrowing what he did not have and repaying more than he bor-rowed, becoming even more needy. *And does not take bribes against the innocent.* There is a double sense contained in this verse: the person did not condemn someone innocent after accepting bribes and did not take what rightfully belonged to someone innocent after accepting bribes. So he wants justice not to be for sale and to be decided on merit, not on the amount of money available. He takes note of an abuse that has become common in our time in particular: a fair sentence is delivered by many only when palms have been greased.

The one who does this will never be moved. Since at the beginning of the psalm he asked *Lord, who will abide in your tent or who will rest on your holy mountain?* and went on *The one who walks blamelessly and performs righteousness, who speaks the truth in his heart* and so on, it is appropriate that he proceeded with *The one who does this will never be moved.* In other words, The one who devotes himself to the practice and love of these virtues that the above discourse described will have no reason to be afraid of any alteration in his present security | and through God's help will be sure of

---

1. Cf. Exod 22:25; Lev 25:36–37.

et erit per Dei adiutorium de habitationis suae perpetuitate securus. Ostendit autem per hoc, quoniam is qui fuerit a proposito
praedictae uirtutis alienus, etiam si uideatur in locis illis ad tempus habitare, tamen firmam in ciuitate mansionem habere non
possit — nam aut malis illum patere sequentibus, aut insperata   5
morte subduci, aut captiuitatis uincula non uitare; qui autem ita
uiuere decreuerit, et habitaturum in ciuitate Dei et non mouen-
dum in aeternum. *Aeternum* autem more suo praesens et unius
cuiusque uiuentis indicat tempus

PSALMVS XV   10

Psalmus praesens pro causae
similitudine sub eodem quo no-
nus argumento conscribitur: nam
pro caesis finitimis gentibus aguntur gratiae — quas quidem Dauid
omnes pene, Deo adiuuante, prostrauerat.

Canitur ergo ex persona populi totus psalmus, in cuius commodum fuerat omnis manus
hostium caesa. Docentur etiam
qualiter in reliquum et quibus
utantur uerbis, cum Deo pro in-
terfectione aduersariorum necesse fuerit supplicare.

⟨Ὁ παρὼν ψαλμὸς⟩ ὅμοιός ἐστι
τῷ ἐννάτῳ κατὰ τὴν ὑπόθεσιν. Κἀνταῦθα γὰρ ⟨ὁ Δαυὶδ⟩ εὐχαριστεῖ
ὑπὲρ τῆς τῶν περιοίκων ἀναιρέσεως
τιμωρηθέντων ὑπὸ Θεοῦ, ὃ δὴ καὶ   15
γέγονεν ἐπ᾽ αὐτοῦ· πολλοὺς γὰρ καὶ
μικροῦ πάντας τοὺς περιοίκους ἐτιμωρήσατο διὰ τῆς τοῦ Θεοῦ συμμαχίας.

Ἅπαντα μέντοι τὰ τοῦ ψαλμοῦ   20
ὡς ἐκ προσώπου τοῦ λαοῦ φησιν·
ἐπειδὴ γὰρ ἐκείνων ἦν κέρδος ἡ τῶν
ἐχθρῶν ἀναίρεσις, ἐκείνους διδάσκει
ὅπως αὐτοὺς προσήκει καὶ τίσιν
κεχρημένους τοῖς ῥήμασιν εὐχαρισ-   25
τεῖν τῷ Θεῷ ὑπὲρ τῆς τῶν πολεμίων
ἀναιρέσεως.

---

3 uidetur A   4 ciuitate] .i. heru(salem) *add. supra* A   5 nam] .i. ostendit *add. supra* A   insperat*a B   6 autem] ostendit *add. supra* A   7 decreuerit *conieci*, decerneret AB; *supple* ostendit   10 expli(cit) psalmus xiiii A
incipit xu AB   12-13 nonus] uiiii A, .i. psalmus *add. supra*   14 cessis B
14-15 augentur A   15-16 omnes dauid B   16 adiuante A   22 fuerat *om.* A¹
fuerit A²   24 reliquum] .i. tempus *add. supra* A.

Ὁ παρὼν ψαλμὸς — ἀναιρέσεως: (Θεοˢ ἀντιοχ̄) Paris. 139, f. 37ᵛ; Vat. 1682,
fol. 51; Cord. I, 272 (P. G., 657 B 10-C 5); Barbaro, p. 139.   11 ὁ π. ψαλμὸς,
13 ὁ Δαυὶδ *supplevi*.

perpetuity in his occupancy. Now, in this he brings out that the person who is a stranger to the aforementioned virtue, even if seeming to dwell in those places for a time, nevertheless can have no firm tenure in the city, being vulnerable to successive troubles, taken by untimely death or failing to escape the bonds of captivity. But the person who decided to live in that fashion would live in the city of God and not be moved forever (by *forever* meaning, in his usual fashion, each person's present existence).

PSALM 16

The present psalm resembles the ninth in its theme. Here too, in fact, David gives thanks for the destruction of the neighboring peoples punished by God, which actually happened also in his time: he punished almost all the neighboring peoples with God's assistance. He recites all the psalm, however, from the point of view of the people: since the destruction of the foe was of advantage to them, he teaches them what words they should employ in thanking God for the destruction of the enemy. |

1. *Conserua me, Domine, quoniam in te speraui.* Quia uicinarum undique gentium premebatur incursibus, consequenter se a Deo postulat custodiri.

2. *Dixi Domino: Deus meus es tu.* Id est: Omnia abiciens ac sper-
5 nens idola et eos qui dii a gentibus aestimantur, in te spei meae praesidium collocaui ac te sum Dominum me habere professus.

Quoniam bonorum meorum non eges. In graeco quidem huius-modi sensus est: Quoniam bonis, quae apud me sunt, ipse non indiges; apud Syros autem: *Quoniam bona mea a te sunt*, et tu
10 mihi haec, quibus fruor, cuncta largiris; — quae quidem, id est bona mea, non habes necessaria. Ista intellectus consequentia concurrit ad reliqua — *Dixi Domino: Deus meus es tu, quoniam bona mea a te sunt*.

Id est: Dominum te meum sum, dicata tibi seruitute, pro- 15 fessus et bonorum, quae apud me sunt omnium, largitorem ac nullius rei, quae apud me est, inopem uel egentem. Haec autem loquitur, ut ostendat longe sibi 20 aliam causam esse quam genti-bus. Ego profecto iuste te Do-minum uoco, quoniam bona quae habeo, te conferente possedeo, et tu nihil a me in usum tuum 25 uelut egens reposcis; gentium uero dii neque praestant bona aliqua cultoribus suis, et ipsi ue-lut inopes spectant quid eis ma-nus | hominis largiatur emendi- 30 cantque honorem, quia sibi eum per se praestare non possunt.	Τουτέστιν Δεσπότην σε εἶναι ἔφην ἐμὸν καὶ χορηγὸν τῶν ὑπαρ-χόντων μοι ἀγαθῶν καὶ μηδενὸς τῶν παρ᾽ ἐμοὶ χρήζοντα. Ἐπειδὴ γὰρ πρὸς ἀντιδιαστολὴν τῶν ἐχθρῶν ταῦτα διαλέγεται, εἰκότως τοῦτό φησιν· Ὅτι σὺ μὲν κἀμοὶ πλῆθος πα-ρέχεις ἀγαθῶν καὶ τῶν παρ᾽ ἐμοὶ οὐ χρήζεις, διὰ τοῦτό σε δικαίως Κύριον ἔφην ἐμόν. Οἱ δέ γε τῶν ἐθνῶν ⟨θεοὶ⟩ οὔτε ἀγαθόν τι παρέχειν δύνανται, καὶ χρήζουσι τῆς παρ᾽ ἐκείνων τιμῆς, ἐπειδὴ ταύτην οἴκοθεν ⟨οὐκ⟩ ἔχουσιν.

1 ui∗cinarum B   2 praemebatur AB¹   4 abieciens A   4-5 spernens]
sernens A¹   5 idula B   et eos] *om.* A¹ et deos A²   qui] et qui A   6 profesus AB   7 greco B   9 tu *om.* A   12 reliqua] .i. testimonia psalmi *add.*
supra A   14 dicatam t. seruitutem profesus A   16 largitor∗em B   19 longe
sibi *om.* A¹, longue sibi A² *in marg.*   21 te *om.* A   26 dii] dī A   28 spec-
ta∗nt A   29 hominis] uel (homi)num *add. supra* A.

Τουτέστιν δεσπότην — οὐκ ἔχουσιν: (Θεο˙ αντιοχ) Paris. 139, fol. 38; Vat. 1682,
fol. 51ᵛ; Barbaro, p. 140.   22 ἐμοῦ ms   25 θεοὶ *supplevi*   28 οὐκ *supplevi.*

Protect me, Lord, for in you I have hoped (v. 1). Because he was under pressure on all sides from invasions of neighboring nations, he naturally asks to be protected by God. *I said to the Lord, You are my God* (v. 2)—that is, Rejecting everything and scorning the idols and those that are considered gods by the nations, I put my hope for protection in you and professed that I have you as my Lord. *Because you have no need of my goods.* In Greek the sense is actually something like this: Because you have no need of the goods in my possession. In Syriac, on the other hand, it is, Because my goods are from you, and you provide me with all these things I enjoy; you have no need of them—that is, my goods. The movement of thought is in keeping with what follows, I said to the Lord, You are my God, because my goods are from you—that is, I said, You are my master and the source of the good things belonging to me, needing nothing from me. You see, since he is saying this to differentiate himself from the foe, he is right to remark, You provide me with a multitude of good things and need nothing from me; hence, I was right to call you my Lord. The gods of the nations, by contrast, are powerless to provide any good thing, and they are in need of honor from them, not possessing it of themselves. |

3. *Sanctis qui in terra sunt mirificasti, quoniam omnes uoluntates meae in eis.* Secundum intellectum, qui de graeca lectione uelut in promptu positus uidetur occurrere, facile potest aliquis suspicari de Israhelitis dictum esse *Sanctis qui in terra sunt*; ita namque quidam istum sensum tamquam ad manum positum sequentes multum deuia- 5 runt a ueritate et uirtute dictorum. Apud Syros autem siue Hebraeos non ita habetur, apud quos hoc modo positum est: Superbis ac magnis, potentibus ac robustis | — id est gentibus, quae in circuitu nostro sunt et nobis molestae esse non desinunt — admirabilis ostensus es ita, ut *omnes uoluntates meae* fierent *in illis*, dum te perse- 10 quente pereunt atque exitio deputantur et gladio. Haec namque erat populi Israhel uoluntas, ut inpugnatores eius ultio diuina disperderet.

Iuxta hunc sensum grandi consequentia omnia sibi dicta iunguntur. Nam cum dixerit superius *Dixi Domino: Deus meus es tu, quoniam bona mea sunt a te*, ad probationem bonorum a Deo prae- 15 stitorum intulit: Finitimis gentibus admirabilis ostensus es, caede illos maxima persecutus; uere enim inter reliqua Dei beneficia etiam hoc populo praestitum esse constabat, ut inimici eius gladio caedente conruerent; unde hoc, quod ait: *Quoniam bona mea a te sunt*, consequenter etiam per id uoluit adprobare, quod Deo dicit 20 persequente suos aduersarios interisse. Ita et Symmachus pro *sanctis « valde magnos »* posuit. Secundum hunc igitur intellectum et ea, quae sequuntur, inueniuntur esse conexa; intulit namque:

4. *Multiplicatae sunt* enim *infirmitates eorum, postea adcaelerauerunt.* 25

Symmachus: *Multiplicata*   Σύμμαχος λέγει 'Επληθύνθησαν
sunt idola eorum, retrorsum fes-   τὰ εἴδωλα αὐτῶν, εἰ; τὰ ὀπίσω ἐτά-
tinauerunt. Quod uult dicere   χυνχν. Τί οὖν βούλεται λέγειν; Ὅτι

1 mirificā A   1-2 quoniam — meae] usque A   2 secundum] adit potest *add. supra* A   greca B   uel A[1]   3 promtu possitus A prumptu positus B   4 hisrahelitis B   5 possitum A   6 ebreos A   7 possitum A   8 robostis A, *cf. glossa hibernica apud* Ascoli, *p. 119,10*   superbis] adit ostensus est *add. supra* A   circumcitu A   9 moleste A   10 es] est A, i. deus *add. supra* ita *om.* A   12 disperdet A   13 gradi A[1]   15 ad *om.* A[1]   15-16 praeteritorum A   16 es] est B   17 illos] illorum m. persequtus A   18-20 hoc populo — consequenter etiam *in* B *prius omissa suppleuit alia ut uidetur manus*   19 cedente AB   conruerant A   22 possuit A   igitur] itaque B   23 sequntur A secuntur B   26 simmachus A, .i. dicit *add. supra*   multiplicat A[1]   27 idula B   retrorsum retrorsum B[1]   28 uul B[1].

Σύμμαχος — συνετρίβετο: (Θεο͂ͅ ἀντ᾽) Paris. 139, fol. 38; Vat. 1682, fol. 52; Vat. 1422, fol. 45 (Θεοδ͂ͅ ἀντιο᾽); Barbaro, p. 141.

You have shown your wonders to the holy ones who are in the land, because all my wishes are in them (v. 3). By the meaning that at first glimpse seems to arise from the Greek text, you could easily get the impression that the phrase *the holy ones who are in the land* was said of the Israelites; in fact, some commentators have taken that sense as being readily accessible, and thus have missed the truth and the force of the words. That is not the meaning in Syriac and Hebrew, however, where it reads this way: To the proud and mighty, to the powerful and strong—that is, the nations, who do not cease to surround us and cause us trouble—you have made yourself so much an object of wonder that *all my wishes were in them* when they perish under your attack and are consigned to ruin and the sword. This, in fact, was the wish of the people of Israel, for divine vengeance to scatter their assailants. According to this meaning, everything said by him comes together with complete consistency:[1] after saying above *I said to the Lord, You are my God, because my goods are from you,* he went on by way of confirming the goods supplied by God, You showed yourself an object of wonder to the nearby nations, pursuing them with great loss of life. It truly is clear, after all, that among the other benefits conferred on the people there is also this, that his enemies fell before the sword—hence his saying *because my goods are from you;* so he intended to prove it as well by the fact that his enemies perished under his attack. Symmachus, likewise, for *holy ones* put "the high and mighty."

By this meaning, then, what follows is also seen to have a connection; he goes on with *Their weaknesses were multiplied, later they accelerated* (v. 4). Symmachus says, "Their idols were multiplied, they went speedily backwards." So what does he mean? | Their idols prospered to the extent of

---

1. The adequacy of the LXX version of vv. 2–3 Theodore disputes, perhaps at the prompting of unnamed "commentators" (not including Diodore) from whom he may have derived data from the Hebrew and Syriac, in which he is not fluent. Though an alternative version is also adduced, as usual it is "consistency," ἀκολουθία, that is the clinching factor.

tale est, quoniam idola, quae fecerat gentium error innumera,
quorumque apud profanos erat
frequens celebrisque cultura, fe
5 stinato et uelociter perierint. Deo
enim alienigenas persequente,
cum ciuitates hostium in solum
Israhelitarum manu aries actus
effunderet, ruinis urbium tem
10 plorum quoque euersio et idolorum contritio iungebatur.

ἤνθησεν τὰ εἴδωλα αὐτῶν, ὡς καὶ
πληθυσμὸν ἐπιδέξασθαι καὶ πολλὴν
γενέσθαι τὴν περὶ αὐτὰ θρησκείαν
τε καὶ τιμήν, καὶ εἰς τάχος συνετε
λέσθη. Τοῦ γὰρ Θεοῦ τιμωρησαμένου
τοὺς ἀλλοφύλους, δῆλον ὅτι καὶ οἱ
ναοὶ ὑπὸ τῶν Ἰσραηλιτῶν καθαιρού
μενοι κατελαμβάνοντο καὶ τὰ εἴδωλα
τὰ ἐν αὐτοῖς συνετρίβετο.

Nam sanctus Dauid pro zelo religionis et deuoto in Deo animo
persequebatur simulacra quotiens fuisset uictoria prosperatus:
unde conuenienter adiunctum est, quia caesis hostibus sint eorum
15 etiam idola comminuta.

Si ergo hoc, quod dictum est *Sanctis qui in terra sunt mirificasti, quoniam omnes uoluntates meae in eis*, secundum Syros intellegatur (id est quod fortes nationes, quae in circuitu fuerant,
uindicta sit diuinitus persecuta) et hic sensus qui occurrit de syro
20 hebraeoque teneatur, iungentur sibi aptissime omnia quae sequuntur. *Multiplicatae sunt*, inquit, *infirmitates eorum*, utique gentium
uicinarum, quae populo Ishrael uincente conruerunt. Si uero quis
ea aliter uoluerit accipere secundum eum sensum qui facile occurrit e graeco, — quoniam *Sanctis in terra*, id est Iudaeis, admi
25 rabilis ostensus sit, — secundum quam consequentiam iungetur
quod intulit: *Multiplicatae sunt infirmitates eorum?* Dicendo enim
eorum, aperte ostendit de his se dicere, de quibus sermo praecesserat. Qui, si Israhelitae intellegantur, quis audebit dicere de populo Iudaeorum accipiendum *Multiplicatae sunt infirmitates eorum?*
30 Vnde ille magis sensus, qui de syro siue hebraeo nascitur, est sequendus; unde et reliquorum dictorum consequentia repperitur.

1-2 fecerit A   2 innumera] sunt *add. supra* A   3 quorum A[1]   4 cultura]
ut *add.* A   5 perirent A   10-11 idulorum B   12 relegionis B   de*uoto B
deo AB, *fortasse legendum* deum   14 cessis B   16 sunt in terra A   mirifificasti B[1]   17 quoniam] sunt *add. supra* A   18 est *om.* A   circuitu] filiorum
israel *add. supra* A   19 syro] .i. sermone *add. supra* A   hebraeoque] hebreoq. A,
haebreoq. B   20 iugentur A[1]   aptisme A[1]   seq(u)n(tu)r A secuntur B   21 infirmitates] iniquitates A   22 conruerant A   23 ea] uerba *add. supra* A   24 e
graeco] a graeco A, e greco B, .i. sermone *add. supra* A   sanctis] qui sunt
add. in marg. A   iudeis A   25 iungetur] coniungentur A   26 multiplicati A
27 eorum] .i. sanctorum *add. supra* A   hiis B   dicere *om.* A   28 si] se A
29 iudeorum A   multiplicati A   30 ebreo A haebreo B   31 relicorum A.

enjoying an increase in numbers and attracting much worship and honor to themselves, and quickly met their end; with God punishing the foreigners, it is clear that the shrines destroyed by the Israelites were taken over and the idols in them were smashed. Blessed David, remember, from his zeal for religion and with a spirit devoted to God, made an assault on shrines whenever he was blessed with victory—hence the logical addition that when the enemies were slain, their idols also were reduced in numbers.

If, then, the verse *You have shown your wonders to the holy ones who are in the land because all my wishes are in them* is understood according to the Syriac—namely, that vengeance from heaven was taken on the strong nations that were nearby—and this meaning found in the Syriac and Hebrew is maintained, everything that follows will be suitably connected to it. *Their weaknesses were multiplied,* namely, of the neighboring nations, which collapsed before the victorious people of Israel. If, on the other hand, you wanted to take it differently according to the sense that at first glimpse emerges from the Greek—that he showed himself an object of wonder to *the holy ones in the land,* that is, the Jews—what connection will be made with what follows, *Their weaknesses were multiplied*? You see, by saying *their,* he makes it perfectly clear that he is referring to those with whom the previous verse dealt; if these are taken to be the Israelites, who will dare to claim that *Their weaknesses were multiplied* is to be taken in reference to the people of the Jews? Hence, that meaning is to be preferred that comes from the Syriac or Hebrew; and thus a connection with the rest of the verses is also discovered. |

Difficultas uero siue ambiguitas intellegentiae istius de interpraetationis necessitate prouenit: multa namque apud Hebraeos
inueniuntur, quae ex rebus sibi insitis nomen accipiunt (quod quidem inter proprietatum collectiones in praefatione signauimus), ut
est hoc de quo sermo uersatur. Omne « sanctum » singulare 5
etiam et praecipuum uocauerunt, eo quod in communionem uel
in exaequationem reliquorum per meriti eminentiam non ueniret:
hinc etiam uasa | templi sancta dixerunt a promiscuo usu in Dei
ministerium separata; nam et homines uocamus sanctos, utique
quos uitae meritum a uulgari conuersatione distinxerit. Praeci- 10
puum ergo generaliter dicimus quid per id quod aliqua sui praestantia distat a reliquis: hinc praecipuos forma aliquos dicimus
uel decore, eo quod sint elegantiae singularis; praecipuos etiam
uocamus quos multa peritia facit ab eiusdem artis consortibus
eminere; sic et robore praecipuum aliquem appellare consueui- 15
mus, quem inter reliquos corporis uirtus adtollit; sed non huiusmodi etiam sanctos uocamus. Hebraeus uero, ab eo quod sancto
etiam praecipuum inest, praecipuum sanctum appellare consueuit;
unde in hoc loco sanctos pro fortibus posuit, finitimos utique
populi habitatores quasi uirtute praestantes, ut cresceret in lau- 20
dem Dei quod ualentes uiribus prostrauerat atque deiecerat.

Simile est et quod idola eorum *infirmitates* uocauit, ab eo quod
cultores suos iuuare non possint nec adminiculo suo facere fortio-
res, de re, quae illis inerat, conueniens nomen inponens. Ob hoc
etiam Deum uirtutem populi appellare consueuit, quoniam, qui- 25
bus auxiliatur, posse eos plurimum faciat ac ualere, ut cum dicit:
Dominus uirtus mea et *Deus meus fortitudo mea.*

Non congregabo conuenticula eorum de sanguinibus. Ex persona
igitur populi consequenter ista dicuntur. Nam cum superius, caesis

---

27 Ps. XVII, 2-3.

1 dificultas A   2 multa] .i. elimenta *add. supra* A   hebraeos] eobreos
A ebreos B   3 accip. nomen A   5 hoc] .i. no(men) *add. supra* A   6 prae-
cipium A   uocauerunt] .i. ebrei *add. supra* A   commonionem A   7 exaequa-
tionem] exsecutio A¹ exsecutionem A²   per *om.* B¹   emenentiam B   8 uassa B
ussu B   9 uoacamus A   10 distinxerit] distinx A¹   11 quidem A   12 a
reliquis *suppl. in marg.* A¹   15 emire A   16 attollit B   17 hebreus A
haebreus B   19 posuit] possuit, .i. dauid *add. supra* A   21 deicerat B
22 idula B   23 facere] face A¹   24 illis] idulis *add. supra* A   ob] ab A
25 consueuit] dauid *add. supra* A   26 posse] .i. uirtus *add. supra* A   faciat]
uel (fa)cit *add. supra* A   ut] .i. est *add. supra* A   dicit] dauid *add. supra* A
27 deus] dominus A   29 decuntur A, dñr B   cum *om.* B¹, dauid *add. supra* A
caessis AB.

The difficulty or ambiguity of that meaning, however, results from the need for interpretation: many things are found in the Hebrew that take their name from innate qualities (as, in fact, we highlighted in the preface in assembling particular features), like the one we are dealing with. By *holy* they referred to everything special or extraordinary in the sense of not being shared or paralleled with other things on the basis of its particular value— hence their also calling temple vessels holy in being kept apart from ordinary use for the service of God, and we also call people holy to distinguish the value of their life from ordinary existence. So we generally call something special on the basis of its distance from other things on account of some excellence it has; hence, we say some people are special in shapeliness or adornment for having a particular elegance, and we call those people special whom great learning makes excel their peers in the subject. Likewise, we are in the habit of speaking of someone as being special for strength when bodily powers elevate that person above the others. But we do not call such people holy. A Hebrew, on the other hand, was in the habit of calling a special thing *holy* from that innate quality which is special to the holy thing. Hence, in this place he used *holy* of the strong—that is, the people's neighboring residents who excelled in strength—so that the fact that he laid low and dislodged warriors of great strength redounded to the glory of God.

A similar instance is his calling their idols *weaknesses* from the fact that they were unable to help their worshipers or make them stronger with any support of theirs; so he gives the name suiting their innate condition. For this same reason he normally referred to God as the people's strength since he makes those he helps particularly capable and strong, as when he says, "God my strength," and, "My God, my courage."[2] *I shall not assemble their assemblies of blood.* He thus is speaking in the same vein in the person of the people: after he had said above | that the enemy had been slain by God, and

---

2. Cf. Pss 46:1; 140:7.

a Deo hostibus, etiam idula, quibus famulabantur alienigenae,
dixisset esse contrita, bene intullit dicens: *Non congregabo con-*
uenticula eorum de sanguinibus, | id est: Nulla in operum cru-
delium imitationem aemulatione transibo, ut congregem turbas
5 ad opera cruenta populosque in effusionem humani sanguinis co-
gam, sicut illis moris est facere. *Conuenticula* itaque sanguinis
dicit coitiones inter se gentium, quibus ad belli praeparabantur
accinctum, in quo necesse erat multum occisorum sanguinem
fundi.

10   *Nec memor ero nominum illorum per labia mea.* In tantum quae
alienigenae faciunt auersabor, ut etiam uocabula eorum obliuioni
tradam et in memoriam meam uenire non patiar.

Si hoc, inquit, promittis, ut te a bellorum usu uel ab hostium
caede suspendas, quomodo terram possessionis tuae uel defen-
15 surus es uel certe tenturus? Occurrit huic quaestioni, optime accidit:

    5. *Dominus pars hereditatis meae* usque *meam mihi*. Neque ar-
morum praesidio indigeo neque inferendi praelii cura sollicitor:
quoniam *hereditatis meae*, quae mihi in terra repromissionis data
20 est, *et calicis mei*, id est omnis iucunditatis meae atque laetitiae,
Dominum habeo portionem, qui mihi haec omnia praestitit et re-
stituit *mihi hereditatem meam*, id est firma me eius possessione
donauit. Sub tali ergo adiutore non utar in defensionem meam
telis et gladio, neque caede hominum meae quieti securitatique
25 prospiciam.

Quod uero ait *Tu es qui restituisti hereditatem meam mihi*, id
est: Firmam me | ac stabilem ab his, qui incursabant fines meos
et nitebantur inuadere, possessionem habere fecisti.

---

1 famulantur A   aliene A¹, enig *add. supra* A²   2 intullit A   congrebo A¹
3 est om. A¹   3-4 crudilium emitationem emul. AB   5 effussionem B   sain-
guinis A   6 est moris A   itaque] igitur A   sangui*nis B   7 praepa-
rantur A   8 occisiorum A occissorum B   11 alieniginae A alienig*enae B
13 a *om.* A   14 cede A   possesionis A   15 es *om.* A¹   quaest.] questioni et A   15-16 accedit A; *fortasse legendum* et optime accinit *uel* addidit
17 heriditatis A herē B   18 neque] nec B   sollitor B   19 heriditatis A
repromisionis A repromīs B   19 qualicis A   iuconditatis B   21 praestetit A
22 heriditatem A herē B   possesione A   23 defentionem A   24 telis]
talis A   quieti securitatique] cietis securitatique A¹, securitatisque A²   25 pro-
spiccam A   26 restitues A   mihi herid. m. A   27 incursabant] incurre-
bant A   28 possesionem A.

the idols whom the foreigners served had been smashed, he was right to proceed with *I shall not assemble their assemblies of blood*—that is, I shall not
emulate them and move to imitate their cruel works so as to assemble mobs
for cruel actions and force peoples to shed human blood, as is their custom.
By *assemblies* he therefore refers to bloodthirsty leagues among the nations
in which they girded themselves for war, the shedding of much blood being
a necessary element. *Nor shall I make mention of their names on my lips:* I
shall so far turn away from what the foreigners do as even to consign their
names to oblivion and not allow them to lodge in my memory.

If you make this promise to abstain from recourse to war and slaughter
of the enemy, he asks, how will you defend the land you possess or even
retain it? In response to this question he does well to proceed with *The Lord
is part of my inheritance* down to *mine to me* (v. 5): I have no need of protection from weapons, nor am I interested in engaging in battle, since I have the
Lord as the portion of *my inheritance,* which is given to me in the land of
promise, *and my cup,* that is, my complete enjoyment and happiness. He is
the one who provided me with all this and restored to me my inheritance—in
other words, He gave me secure possession of it. With such an ally, therefore,
I shall not call on javelins and sword to my defense, nor have an eye to the
slaughter of men for my peace and quiet. The meaning of *You are the one
who has restored my inheritance to me* is this: You made me enjoy secure
and lasting possession in the face of those who attacked and strove to invade
my territory. |

6. *Funes ceciderunt mihi in praeclaris.*

Quoniam moris est terram in portiones funis extensione et limitis inpraessione signari (nec tantum haec inter unius | familiae contribules consuetudo seruatur, nam et singulae quaeque gentes a commixtione aliarum suis finibus separantur) ita et populo Ishrael terram repromissionis uelut circumducto fune in hereditatem dicit possessionemque cessisse. Hoc itaque uult dicere quod, sicut admota dimensione, ita in portionem meam mihi terrae optima pars, id est uberior gleba, prouenit. Nam quod posuit *ceciderunt*, similitudem qua sortes iaciuntur expraessit, sicut in Actibus Apostolorum refertur: *Cecidit sors super Mathiam.*

Etenim hereditas mea praeclara est mihi. Haec, inquit, *hereditas* — id est possessio terrae repromissionis — *praeclara est mihi*, ac si diceret: inmobilis et de cuius periculum amissione non uerear; quae mihi uelut sortito, ita te adiuuante prouenit.

'Επειδὴ σχονίοις ἀεὶ μετρεῖσθαι πέφυκεν ἡ γῆ,

ὥσπερ δὲ ἕκαστον ἔθνος ἰδίαν εἶχε   5
γῆν ἣν κατώκει,

οὕτω καὶ τῷ λαῷ τῶν 'Ισραηλιτῶν,
ὥσπερ ἰδίαν τινὰ γῆν ἀπεκλήρωσεν,   10
τὴν τῆς ἐπαγγελίας.

Τοῦτο βούλεται λέγειν ὅτι ὥσπερ κατὰ διαμέτρησιν ἐκληρώθη μοι τὸ ἄριστον μέρος τῆς γῆς.   15

Τὸ γὰρ ἔπεσεν ἀντὶ τοῦ « ἐκληρώθη » ἐκ μεταφορᾶς τῶν κλήρων, ὡς καὶ ἐν ταῖς Πράξεσί φησιν· καὶ ἔπεσεν ὁ κλῆρος ἐπὶ Ματθίαν.   20

---

22 Act. I, 26.

---

1 ciciderunt A, *ita l. 18*   3 extentione A   4 inpraessione] in praecisione A nec] non A   7 quoque AB¹   8 gentes *om.* A   10-11 repromisioris A reprō B 11 uelud B   12 heriditatem A   possesionem A   13 cessise A caessisse B itaque] igitur A   17 uberior] superior A   18 possuit A   19-20 ieciuntur expraesit A   21 cicidit fors A   22 mathiam] maden A   24 possesio A repromisionis A   25 et] est A   ammisione A   26 quae] quoniam A   mihi *om.* A¹ mihi**B   adiuante A.

Έπειδὴ σχοινίοις — Ματθίαν: (Θεο⁵ αντο^χ) Paris. 139, fol. 39; Vat. 1682, fol. 53 (Mai, p. 393; P. G., 657 C 6-15); Barbaro, p. 141.

Cords fell out for me among the finest (v. 6). Since it is natural for the land always to be measured by cords, so that each nation owned the land it occupied, likewise also for the Israelite people, so that it chose its own land by lot, the land of promise. This means, The best part of the land was allotted to me as if by measure (*fell out* meaning "was allotted," from a metaphor from lots, as it says also in the Acts, "The lot fell on Matthias").[3] *My inheritance, after all, is the finest for me:* this inheritance—namely, possession of the land of promise—is the finest for me, as if to say, I am secure and am not afraid of running the risk of losing it; it came to me with your help, as though by lot. |

---

3. Acts 1:26.

7. Benedicam Domino qui mihi tribuit intellectum.

Ad confitenda eius beneficia
agendasque gratias mea iugiter
ora reserabo, quoniam non so-
5 lum mihi opimam terram in possessionem dedit, sed quoniam in·
tellectu me ac sa|pientiae magi-
steriis erudiuit, legis sanctionibus
praescribens quae me facere,
10 quae uitare conueniat.

Οὐκοῦν εὐχαριστήσω σοι ὑπὲρ
ἁπάντων, ὅτι

οὐ μόνον γῆν μοι δέδωκας ἐξαίρετον
εἰς κτῆσιν, ἀλλ᾽ ὅτι τὴν σύνεσιν παρέσχες καὶ σοφίαν τοῦ πράττειν ἃ
δὴ νομοθετήσας περὶ τὴν τῶν πρακτέων καὶ τῶν μὴ τοιούτων.

Insuper et usque ad noctem erudierunt me renes mei. Noctem uocat tribulationem, quia in tristitia positi uelut quodam meroris nu-
bilo continentur. *Renes* autem cogitationes dicit, quia de renibus
concupiscentiales motus oriuntur, qui naturae insiti frequentes con-
15 suerunt animae suggestiones ingerere. Agam, inquit, gratias, quia
neque ipsas tribulationes infructuosas mihi esse permittit, sed ita
me earum exercet angoribus, ut sensus uel cogitationes, quae mihi
de ipsis nascuntur, sint mihi utiles et uice me magisterii efficacis
erudiant. Quomodo, inquit, sub tribulationum proficisti onere?

20 **8. Prouidebam Dominum in conspectu meo semper.** Cum utique
amaritudine earum urgerer, ad Deum oculos dirigebam.

Quoniam a dextris est mihi ne commouear.

Illum intuens opem solitam
praestolabar, quoniam adiutor
25 meus est et non permittit me inter
aduersa concidere. Quod autem
ait *a dextris est mihi ne commo-*
uear, id est: adiutorio suo inter aduersa mihi constantiam praebet;
30 adiutorium autem Dei *a dextris,*
a melioribus partibus indicauit.

Προσδεχόμενος ὅτι βοηθεῖ μοι

καὶ οὐκ ἐᾷ περιτραπῆναι.

Τὸ γὰρ ἐκ δεξιῶν μού ἐστιν, ἵνα μὴ
σαλευθῶ, ἀντὶ τοῦ βοηθεῖ μοι, ἀπὸ
τοῦ δεξιοῦ καὶ τοῦ κρείττονος τὴν
βοήθειαν καλέσας.

2 confitienda A   3 mea] labia *add. supra* A   4 ora *om.* A   5-6 possesionem A   6 quoniam *om.* A   7-8 magistris A   11 et *om.* A   eruderunt A
renis A   uocat**** B   12 possiti A   uelud B   12-13 nibulo A   13 (con)-
tinenter B¹   renib*** B   15 sugestiones A   17 me] mihi A   quae] qui A
18 magistri A   19 onere proficisti B¹   22 dexteris A, *ita l.* 27   23 illam A
24 praestulabar A   26 concedere A.

Οὐκοῦν — τοιούτων: (Θεοδώρου Ἀντιοχείας) Paris. 139, fol. 39; Vat. 1682, fol. 53ᵛ
(Mai, p. 393; P. G., 657 D 1-5); Barbaro, p. 144.

Προσδεχόμενος — καλέσας: (Θεοδˢ⁰ αντοˣ) Paris. 139, fol. 39ᵛ; Vat. 1682, fol. 54;
Cord. I, 276; Barbaro, p. 146.

I shall bless the Lord, who gave me wisdom (v. 7): I shall therefore give thanks to you for everything, because you not only have given me a choice land for my possession, but also have provided me with understanding and wisdom to carry out what you laid down about what should be done and its opposite. *Even until night my entrails brought me to my senses.* By *night* he refers to tribulation, because they find themselves in sadness as though enveloped in a kind of cloud of grief. By *entrails* he means "thoughts," because unruly desires originate in the entrails, and being rooted in our nature, they normally give rise to frequent inclinations of the spirit. I shall give thanks, he is saying, because instead of allowing the very tribulations to be of no avail, he so stimulates me with their pangs that the feelings and thoughts that come to me from them are of value to me and instruct me in the manner of useful teaching. How did you benefit, he asks, from the weight of tribulations? *I kept the Lord ever in my sight* (v. 8): although I was under pressure from their bitterness, I kept my eyes on God. *Because he is on my right hand lest I be moved:* expecting him to help me and not let me be overwhelmed (the phrase *on my right hand lest I be moved* means "He helps me"—referring to help by *right hand,* being the stronger one).

Hence my heart rejoiced and my tongue was glad (v. 9). Why so? | Because

9. *Propter hoc laetatum est cor meum et exultauit lingua mea.*

Propter hoc? Quoniam *proui-debam Dominum in conspectu meo semper* et in illum tendens oculos spei meae non sum frustratione deceptus. Quoniam, inquit, a te adiuuandum esse me credidi, inpleta sunt quae quaerebam collataque est mihi magna laetitia.

Insuper et caro mea requiescit in spe.

Id est ego: a parte totum uocauit. Consuetudo est diuinae scripturae integrum hominem et a parte animae et a parte carnis uocare: a parte carnis, ut cum dicit: *Corrupit omnis caro uiam suam*; a parte animae, cum ait: *In* LXXV *animabus discendit Iacob in Aegyptum.* In praesenti igitur hoc ait, quoniam Longa habitatione et cum multa fidu-, cia in solo proprio commorabor, nihil aduersi metuens, nihil quo offendar aspiciens, propter spem quae mihi in te posita est. Nam *insuper* ita posuit ac si diceret d i u .

Διὰ τοῦτο ποῖον; Ἐπειδὴ προο-ρώμην τὸν Κύριον ἐνώπιόν μου διὰ παντός, καὶ οὐκ ἀπεσφάλην φησὶ τῶν ἐλπίδων.   5

Ἀλλ' ἐπειδὴ ἀεὶ τὴν παρά σου προσεδεχόμην βοήθειαν, ἔτυχον ὧν ἐζήτουν καὶ ἐν εὐφροσύνῃ κατέστην πολλῇ.

                                    10

Ἡ σάρξ μου ἀντὶ τοῦ ἐγώ, ἐκ τοῦ μέρους τὸ ὅλον καλέσας. Ἔθος γὰρ τῇ θείᾳ γραφῇ καὶ ἀπὸ τῆς σαρ-κὸς τὸ ὅλον καλεῖν, καὶ ἀπὸ τῆς 15 ψυχῆς ὁμοίως· ἀπὸ μὲν τῆς σαρκός, ὡς ὅταν λέγῃ ὅτι Κατέφθειρεν πᾶσα σὰρξ τὴν ὁδὸν αὐτῆς, ἀπὸ δὲ τῆς ψυ-χῆς ὡς ὅταν λέγῃ Ἐν σε' ψυχαῖς κατέβη Ἰακὼβ εἰς Αἴγυπτον. Λέγει 20 δὲ ἐνταῦθα ὅτι καὶ ἐπὶ πλεῖστον μὲν ὁ ἐν τοῖς ἐμοῖς μετὰ πολλῆς τῆς πεποιθήσεως οὐδὲν δεινὸν δεδιὼς ἢ ὑφορώμενος διὰ τὴν εἴς σε ἐλπίδα. Τὸ γὰρ ἔτι ἀντὶ τοῦ ἐπὶ πλεῖστον. 25

2-4 v. 8   17-18 Gen. VI, 12   19-20 Gen. XLVI, 27.

1 et exult.] usque A   mea *om.* B   2 hoc *om.* A¹   quoniam *om.* B   2-3 prae-uidi A¹ praeuidiebam A² prouidi B   4 oculos *om.* B   8 querebam B   12 id est] requiescam *add. supra* A   parte] carne *add. supra* A   14 intigrum AB *et ita inferius, p. 99, 2*   17 corrumpit A   18 part A¹   19-20 Iacob in] in *om.* A   20 in Aeg.] hegiptum A in aeḡ B   21 igitur] itaque B   21-22 longua habi-tione A   25 aspicens A   26 mihi** B   in te posita] (inter)possita A   27 possuit A.

Διὰ τοῦτο — πολλῇ: (Θεοδ ἀντο⁖) Paris. 139, fol. 39ᵛ; Vat. 1682, fol. 54 (Mai, p. 393, P. G., 657 D 7-11); Barbaro, p. 146 (Cyrilli).   4. 9 ἀπεσφάλη, κατέστη *ms.*
Ἡ σάρξ μου — ἐπὶ πλεῖστον: (Θεο⁵ αντιο⁖) Paris. 139, fol. 39ᵛ; Vat. 1682, fol. 54; Barbaro, p. 146 (Cyrilli).

I kept the Lord ever in my sight and my hopes were not disappointed; rather, in always expecting help from you, I attained what I looked for and was brought to great joy. *Further, my flesh will rest in hope.* By *my flesh* he means "I myself," naming the whole from the part, the divine Scripture normally referring to the whole person by flesh and likewise by soul —by flesh in saying, "All flesh had corrupted its way," and by soul in saying, "Jacob went down into Egypt with seventy-five souls."[4] He means here, Though for a long time on my own, in great trust I feared or suspected nothing on account of hope in you (*further* meaning "for a long time"). *Because you will not abandon my soul in Hades* (v. 10). Here again | he names the whole person

---

4. Gen 6:12; 46:27 (the numbers in Hebrew and LXX differing).

10. *Quoniam non derelinques animam meam in infernum.*
Iterum hic ab anima integrum uocat hominem. Fruar, inquit, omni securitate, quoniam sub tui-
5 tione tua positum non patieris aerumnis ac periculis deperire.

Κἀνταῦθα πάλιν ἀπὸ τῆς ψυχῆς τὸ ὅλον καλεῖ. Ἀπολαύσω δὲ τούτων φησίν, ἐπειδή με αὐτὸς φυλάττων οὐκ ἐᾷς ἐναπολέσθαι τοῖς κινδύνοις,

Neque dabis sanctum tuum uidere corruptionem.
Non trades me, inquit, id est: non sines ut aduersariorum ini-
10 quitate corrumpar. *Sanctum* autem uocat populum in conparationem gentium, quae Dei notitiam non habebant.

οὐδὲ παραδώσεις με διαφθαρῆναι ὑπ' αὐτῶν, ὅσιον κἀνταῦθα τὸν λαὸν καλῶν πρὸς ἀντιδιαστολὴν ἐκείνων, ὡς ἔχοντα τοῦ Θεοῦ τὴν γνῶσιν.

11. *Notas mihi fecisti uias uitae.* Sicut uia ciuitatis dicitur | quae
15 ducit ad ciuitatem, ita et *uias uitae* uocat eas per quas itur ad uitam. Hoc ergo in praesenti dicit: Eripiens me de periculis per itinera uitae salutisque duxisti. Statuisti me, inquit, in uiis uitae, id est uiuere me fecisti.

Adimplebis me laetitia cum uultu tuo.
20 Proueniet mihi, inquit, laetitia a facie tua, id est: Cum apparueris mihi, cum me adiutorio tuo dignum iudicaueris, laetitiae iucunditate conplebor.

Ἀντὶ τοῦ ἐκ προσώπου σου, τουτέστιν ἐκ τῆς ἐπιφανείας σου καὶ τῆς παρά σου βοηθείας, πληροῦμαι εὐφροσύνης.

25 *Dilectatio in dextera tua usque in finem.* Adiutorii tui est proprium ab aduersariis liberatos etiam magna gaudii uoluptate conplere.

Tale est et, quod non derelicta est anima eius in inferno

Notandum autem quoniam ultima parte psalmi beatus Petrus

Ἐπισημαντέον δὲ κἀνταῦθα ὅτι τοῖς τελευταίοις τοῦ ψαλμοῦ ὁ μα-

29 Act. II, 31.

1 non *om.* A¹   2 hiic A   intigrum AB   4-5 tutione A   5 possitum A
6 erumnis A   8 tradis A   10 conrumpar A   17 itenera AB   19 tuo *om.* B
20 proueniat A   21 facie] facia A   21-22 apparuerit A   25 dilectationes A
26 libera**tos B   uoluptate] uoluntate AB.

Κἀνταῦθα — Θεοῦ τὴν γνῶσιν: (Θεοδ⁰ ἀντιοχ) Paris. 139, fol. 39ᵛ; Vat. 1682, fol. 54ʳ·ᵛ (Mai, p. 393; P. G., 657 D 12-660 A 4).

Ἀντὶ τοῦ — εὐφροσύνης: (Θεο᷆ ἀντιοχ) Paris. 139, fol. 39ᵛ; Vat. 1682, fol. 54ᵛ (Mai, p. 393; P. G., 660 A 5-7).

Ἐπισημαντέον — ἀποφαινούσης: (Θεο᷆ ἀντιοχ) Paris. 139, fol. 39ᵛ; Vat. 1682, fol. 54ᵛ (Mai, p. 393; P. G., 660 A 7-B 2). — Tale est — Domino Christo, ex Vigilii *Constituto*, cap. xx (GUENTHER, p. 256); cf. conc. CP. xxi (MANSI, IX, 212).

from the soul. I shall enjoy this, he is saying, since you personally protect me and will not allow me to succumb to the dangers. *Nor will you allow your holy one to see corruption:* nor will you hand me over to be destroyed by them (by *holy one* here referring to the people by way of differentiating them, since they had the knowledge of God).

You made known to me paths of life (v. 11). As we speak of a city's way as what leads to a city, so also he calls *paths of life* the means by which one travels to life. So he means here, Rescuing me from dangers, you led me by the journeys of life and salvation; you set me on the paths of life—that is, you made me live. *With your presence you will fill me with joy:* I shall be filled with happiness *with your presence*—that is, with your appearance and with help from you. *With delight at your right hand forever:* it is characteristic of your help to fill with complete enjoyment of happiness those also freed from adversaries.

Now, it should be noted here that the blessed apostle Peter in the Acts quoted the end of the psalm | as referring to the Lord.[5] So we should under-

---

5. Acts 2:31, where Peter cites verse 10 as David's prophecy of the resurrection of Jesus; Theodore might have recalled also Paul's similar application of the verse in Acts 13:35. In his initial comment on verse 10 he saw the people in focus, but he has to admit (as had Diodore in similar terms) that the New Testament applies it differently, and he has no quarrel with its christological application. Devreesse cites the comment also in Greek (as above), and in addition a second Latin paraphrase from the Constitution of Vigilius.

nec caro eius uidit corruptionem; nam propheta quidem supra modum ipsum ponit circa populum, prouidentiam dicens, uolens dicere, quoniam inextemptabiles eos ab omnibus conseruauit malis. Quoniam autem hoc uerum et ex ipsis rebus euentum accepit in Domino Christo, sequentissime de eo loquens beatus Petrus utitur uoce ostendens, quoniam quod de populo supra modum scriptum est ex quadam ratione utente uoce propheta, hoc uerum euentum in ipsis rebus accepit nunc in Domino Christo.

in Actibus Apostolorum | ita usus est, ut proprie dicta de Domino. Non ergo ab apostolo testimonium hoc usurpatum est, sed causae suae redditum: nam fuerat uidilicet a profeta praedictum, et ideo conuenienter est personae Domini uindicatum; nam prius in similitudine dictum fuerat et figura. Proprie ergo et secundum uerum intellectum, qui ipsis rebus impletus est, Domino conuenit, ad quem eum pertinere impletae sine dubio res loquuntur.

κάριος ἀπόστολος Πέτρος ἐν ταῖς Πράξεσιν ὡς περὶ τοῦ Κυρίου εἰρημένοις ἐχρήσατο. Ἰστέον τοίνυν ὅτι κἀνταῦθα κατὰ τὴν αὐτὴν ἔννοιαν ἐξείληπται τῷ μακαρίῳ ἀποστόλῳ, ἐπειδὴ ἐνταῦθα μὲν προτρεπτικώτερον εἴρηται, κυρίως δὲ καὶ κατὰ τὴν ἀληθῆ ἔννοιαν, τὴν πρὸς τὰ ῥητὰ λέγω τὴν ἔκβασιν ἔχει ἐπὶ τοῦ Κυρίου, ἐφ' οὗ καὶ τῇ μαρτυρίᾳ ἐχρήσατο ὡς τῆς τῶν πραγμάτων ἐκβάσεως ἐπ' αὐτοῦ κυριωτέραν τὴν μαρτυρίαν ἀποφαινούσης.

PSALMVS XVI

Cum Saulis persecutione beatus Dauid in periculum fuisset salutis adductus, hunc psalmum cecinit qui uicem orationis impleret.

1. *Exaudi, Domine, iustitiam meam, intende depraecationi meae.* Non ob meritum iustitiae suae audiri se a Deo postulat neque insolenter de aequitatis suae uirtute gloriatur, sed absolutionem

3 dicta] dicatur A   5 apōs̄ A apostulo B   7-8 reditum A[1]   11 est *om.* A 12-13 uendicatum A   21 eum] cum A   22 sine dubio] sint A   27 expli(cit) psal(mus) xu. incipit xui. AB   28 persequtione A   29 cicinit A   31 Domine] deus A   intende depraecationi (— nem B[1])] usque A   meae *om.* B   32 meritum *sequuntur litterae septem erasae in* B   postolat A   33 equitatis A, suae *sequuntur litterae octo erasae in* B.

stand that here, too, it was taken in the same sense as by the blessed apostle, since while here it is expressed by way of parenesis, in a true and proper sense the words reach their fulfillment in the case of the Lord, to whom he also applied the text, since the factual outcome revealed the meaning of the text more properly in his case.

PSALM 17

With Saul's persecution David's life was put in danger, and he sang this psalm in place of a prayer. *Hearken, Lord, to my righteousness, attend to my pleading* (v. 1). Far from asking to be heard by God on the grounds of his righteousness or boldly glorying in the virtue of his fairness, | he says he has

⟨a⟩ malis suis, quippe qui iniqua Saulis persecutione laboraret, dicit se iustissime postulare.

Auribus percipe orationem meam non in labiis dolosis. Proprium est cum dolo loquentium aliud corde tegere atque aliud ore pro-
5 ferre. | Quod itaque superius dixerat *Exaudi iustitiam meam,* — id est iuste me postulantem non uelut surda aure praetereas, — hoc iterata petitione geminauit. *Auribus percipe orationem meam non in labiis dolosis* id est: *Exaudi orationem meam,* quoniam nosti non me simulatis labiis supplicare neque sola uoce iustitiam prae-
10 tendere et re atque opere a uicissitudine malorum, dum me de aduersariis uindico, minime temperare; ipse enim nosti quam iusta postulem, quoniam nullas offensionis Sauli praebens causas odia eius iniqua sustineo.

2. *De uultu tuo iudicium meum prodeat.* Sub conspectu tuo, id
15 est adstante ac praesente te, in-
ter me et inimicos meos aequitas tuae examinationis agitetur.
Vultum posuit pro praesentia
siue ostensione manifesta: | mul-
20 tam uero serui de operibus suis
habentis fiduciam est Domini
ad iudicandum praesentiam postulare.

'Επιφάνηθί μοι καὶ ποίησαι τὴν κρίσιν τῶν κατ' ἐμέ. Τὸ γὰρ ἐκ προ- σώπου ἐκ τῆς ἐπιφανείας λέγει.

Oculi mei uideant aequitatem. Quoniam Saul et hi, qui eius
25 amentiae iungebantur, iniquo mentis proposito persequebantur Dauid et socios eius nec ullam rationem inimicitiarum iustique odii proferebant, — hoc autem recti regula non probabat eratque peruersum, ut bonos mali, iustos persequerentur iniusti, — ideo ait: *Oculi mei uideant aequitatem.* Vindicante enim Deo et ausus
30 iniquitatis seueritate debita conpraemente, partes suas inplebat aequitas; quod quidem uidere Dauid beatus optabat.

---

1 a *suppleui* ＊ labo＊＊raret B 3 labis A 4 aliut ... aliut A 5 itaque] igitur A 6 uelud B surda] sord＊a B[1] praeterias A 9 labis supli- care A 12 postolem A Saulis B[1] praebiens A 14 prodiat A 15 prae- sente] praestante A te] de (?) B 18 possuit A 19 hostensione A 25 pro- possito A sequebantur A[1] 27 probat A 30 impleat A.

'Επιφάνηθι — λέγει: (Θεο⁵) Paris. 139, fol. 40; Vat. 1682, fol. 55. 16 κατ' ἐμοῦ *fortasse legendum.*

good right to ask for relief from his troubles in struggling under Saul's unjust persecution. *Give ear to my prayer from lips that are not deceitful.* It is characteristic of those who speak deceitfully to cloak what is in their heart by telling something different by mouth. What he said above, therefore, *hearken to my righteousness*—that is, do not turn a deaf ear to my just request—he repeated with a double request. *Give ear to my prayer from lips that are not deceitful* means *hearken to my righteousness*—that is, You know that I do not make an appeal with deceitful lips or make a pretense by voice alone, while under pressure of troubles I show no restraint in taking action in resisting the adversary. I give Saul no grounds for taking offense, whereas I have to put up with his unjustified hatred.

Let my judgment proceed from your countenance (v. 2): declare to me and execute the judgment against me (*from your countenance* referring to the declaration). A servant with great confidence in his own actions typically requests the master's presence for judgment. *Let my eyes see fairness.* Saul and those associated with his folly had an unfair attitude in pursuing David and his supporters and offered no reason for their hostility and unjust hatred; the norm of what is right did not apply in this case, which was distorted, so that the evil persecuted the good, and the unjust the just. Hence his saying *Let my eyes see fairness:* when God comes to judgment and suppresses with due severity the exploits of iniquity, fairness plays its part, as blessed David in fact wanted to witness. |

3. *Probasti cor meum et uisitasti nocte.* Dixerat superius: *Oculi mei uideant aequitatem,* id est conpraessam malitiam et innocentiam subleuatam, ut ostenderet inmerito se Saulis odia sustinere. Ad fidem ergo rerum faciendam testem aduocat Deum. Tu, inquit, nosti quoniam nulla exstante causa inferuntur mihi aduersa quae 5 patior, | qui cordis et cogitationum mearum probationem etiam inter aduersa fecisti. Hoc est enim, quod ait, *Visitasti nocte*: indicat namque quod inter aerumnas et tribulationum mala affectum et motus cordis eius inspexerit. *Noctem* autem more suo periculi indicat tempus, cum uice tenebrarum patitur quis tristitiae densitatem. 10 Quibus consequenter intulit:

Igne me examinasti et non est inuenta in me iniquitas. Sicut ignis, inquit, admotione, ita me ussisti periculis uel aerumnis, probumque in temptationibus inuenisti et quem nulla tribulatio a iusti proposito summoueret atque ad iniquitatem malorum praessura 15 deduceret, — quod profecto loquitur consequenter. Nam cum eum persecutio Saulis urgeret | et esset illi de uita ac salute certamen, traditum manibus suis inimicum dimisit inlaesum, elegens cum metu in periculis uiuere quam mercari peccato securitatem.

4. *Vt non loquatur os meum opera hominum.* Cum me inter 20 adustiones tribulationum et maximi angoris inspiceres, ita inuenisti ab omni operatione iniquitatis alienum et longe positum a mali uicissitudine, quam recipere merentur inimici, ut ea quae ab illis fiunt neque tenui relatione contingerem aut in familiarem usum sermonis admitterem; in tantum a malorum operum imitatione 25 discessi.

Propter uerba labiorum tuorum ego custodiui uias duras. Magna superius de se et laudis plena protulerat, id est ⟨quod⟩ laesus ab inimicis in tantum se a mali uicissitudine suspenderit, ut caueret etiam ea quae ab illis fiebant sermone contingere. Consequenter 30 ergo causam tantae custodiae uirtutisque reserauit dicens: | *Propter uerba labiorum tuorum ego custodiui uias duras.* Omnia, inquit, egi atque sustenui, ut praeceptis tuis atque imperiis oboedirem,

---

2 aequitates B   conpraesam A   3 ut ostenderet] ostenderat A   7 ficisti A   8 erumnas A   9 inspexirit A   10 quis] qui A   13 inquit ignis A   ussisti periculis] usis periculi A erumnis A   14 inuinisti A   15 proposito] praepossito AB   ad *om.* A[1]   presura A   16 profecto] perfecto (?) A   18 inlesum A eligens B *et ita p. 103, l. 1*   19 in *om.* A   uiuire A   21 inspiceris A   22 possitum A   23 uicisitudine A *et ita l.* 29   25 imitatione] intentione A   27 duras] das A[1]   28 'quod *suppleui*   lesus A   31 reserauit A   33 obcderem A.

You tested my heart and came to me in vision by night (v. 3). He had said above *Let my eyes see fairness*—that is, malice suppressed and innocence uplifted, so as to bring out that he was undeservedly enduring Saul's hatred. To lend substance to his words, therefore, he appeals to God as witness: You know that there is no outstanding reason for the adversity I suffer to be inflicted on me, since even in the midst of adversity you conducted a test of my heart and thoughts. *You came to me in vision by night* suggests, in fact, that amidst the troubles and tribulations he had scrutinized his feelings and the movements of his heart. Now, by *night* he implies in usual fashion the time of danger, when a person suffers deepest sadness in place of darkness. Hence his proceeding with *You examined me by fire, and no wrong was found in me:* as if by application of fire, you scorched me with dangers and hardships, and found me unaffected by temptations and someone whom no tribulation would seduce from upright purpose and no pressure of evils would bring down to a level of iniquity. He proceeds to say as much: when the pursuit by Saul was pressing and his life and safety were at risk, he let his enemy go unharmed, though delivered into his hands, preferring to live in fear and danger than to trade safety for sin.

There was no way my mouth spoke of people's doings (v. 4): when you tested me with the fires of tribulation and intense pain, you found me to such an extent unacquainted with every involvement in iniquity and removed from the experience of evil that enemies deserve to undergo as to have not the slightest connection with what is done by them or introduce it into my normal patterns of speech—such being the distance I kept from imitation of wicked deeds. *On account of the words of your lips I have kept to the straight and narrow.* He had above had much to say to his own credit for so far removing himself from the experience of evil, despite being harmed by the enemy, as to take precautions not to let his speech be affected by what was done by them. Hence, in reference to such virtuous precautions, he repeats the statement *On account of the words of your lips I have kept to the straight and narrow:* I have even put up with everything so as to obey your precepts and commands, | opting to put up with every harsh and dif-

elegens aspera quaeque et grauia sustinere quam iniuriam man-
dati tui praeuaricatione committere. Erat enim res non parui operis
et laboris adsidua inimicorum iniquitate pulsari et nihil laedenti-
bus iniuriae reponere uel doloris. Sed ne uideatur gloriosa de se
5 magnaque iactare sibi opus tantae uirtutis adscribens, petit ut a
Domino talis sibi operis perfectio conferatur, et ait:

5. *Perfice gressus meos in semitis tuis, ut non moueantur uestigia mea.* Haec, inquit, opera mea ita ad finem ducantur, ut a tua
uoluntate non discrepent, ne quando ab his, quae mihi bene acta
10 sunt, sinistra uoluntate commuter.

6. *Ego clamaui, quoniam exaudisti me, Deus.*
Mutauit tempus: nam pro   Ἐναλλαγὴ χρόνου γεγένηται,
clamabo et exaudies *clamaui*   ἀντὶ τοῦ ἄρον τοῦ ὅτι ἐπακούεις μοι,
et *exaudisti me* dixit. Recurrit   ὅτι ἐπήκουσά; μου εἶπεν.
15 hinc ad principia atque iterum
incipit supplicare. Media autem,
quae dicta sunt, interposita uidentur ad iustae petitionis probationem, id est quod ipse quidem multa aduersa pertulerit et nihil mali
inimicis referre curauerit, — quae quidem ideo fecerit, ut Dei man-
20 data seruaret. Laesus igitur ab inimicis et nullius mihi facti similis
conscius magna petitionis meae uoce proclamo, pro certo sciens
quoniam exaudias iustis allegationibus perorantem.

Inclina aurem tuam et exaudi uerba mea. Hic ostendit quod
sit tempus superius commutatum. Nam si ibi fuisset *exaudisti* de
25 praeterito utique dictum, superflue hic diceret *Inclina aurem tuam
et exaudi uerba mea*: haec enim uox adhuc rogantis est et adhuc
adiutorium postulantis.

7. *Mirifica misericordias tuas, qui saluos facis sperantes in te
a resistentibus dexterae tuae.* Ostendit quod non ideo tantum Dei
30 inplorat auxilium, ut ipse a malis circumstantibus eruatur, sed ut

---

1 quam in A   7 gresus A greš B   ut — uestigia] usque A   9 discri-
pent B̄   hiis B   10 commuter] commotes A   12 mutauit] motauit A m•u-
tauit B   13 clamabo et *om.* B   17 interpossita A   ad] et B¹   20 Iesus
A **laesus B (*ex* inlaesus ?)   igitur] itaque B   22 alligationibus AB   per-
orantem] periurantem A   23 hic] hiic A *et ita l.* 25   24 sit] fit A   com-
motatum A   fuisset ibi A   28-29 qui — resistentibus] usque A, tū qui saĪ.
fā. spē. B   29 risistentibus B¹   dex B.

Ἐναλλαγὴ — εἶπεν: (Θεοˢ αντοχ) Paris. 139, fol. 40ᵛ; Vat. 1682, fol. 56 (Mai,
p. 393; P. G., 660 B 4-6); Barbaro, p. 150.

ficult thing in preference to undermining your commission by half-hearted effort. It required, in fact, no slight effort and commitment to be the butt of the enemies' constant injustice and repay with no harm or grief those injuring me. Lest he seem, however, to be boasting by giving himself the credit for a work of such great virtue, he requests that such perfect behavior be permitted him by the Lord, saying *Train my steps to follow your paths lest my footsteps fail* (v. 5): let my conduct be brought to completion in such a way as not to stray from your will, in case it should ever deviate by a contrary decision from what has been properly done by me.

I cried aloud because you hearkened to me, God (v. 6). He changed the tense, putting *cried* and *hearkened to me* for "will cry" and "will hear me." At this point he goes back to the beginning and recommences making supplication, whereas what was said in between seems to have been inserted as proof of a justified appeal, namely, that he actually put up with many adversities and took care not to repay the enemy with any malicious behavior, which he really did for the purpose of keeping God's commands. So he means here, Abused by the enemy and conscious of no such action on my part, I shall utter a loud cry of petition, being convinced that you will hear my presentation of righteous accusations. *Incline your ear and hearken to my words.* This shows that the tense was changed above: if *hearkened* had been used to suggest past time, it would have been superfluous for him to say *Incline your ear and hearken to my words,* since this is a cry of someone still asking and still begging help.

Make a display of your mercies, you who render those hoping in you safe from those resisting your right hand (v. 7). He brings out that he implores God's help not so much to be rescued personally from the troubles besetting him as | in the hope that glory should redound to the giver through the assis-

per adiutorium sibi praestitum gloria in largitorem recurrat. Ita,
inquit, fac mecum misericordiam, ut mirentur omnes liberatio-
nemque meam in occasionem tuae laudis accipiant. Conuenienter
ergo addidit: *Qui saluos facis sperantes in te a resistentibus
dexterae tuae.* Quoniam moris, inquit, tibi est speranles in te 5
saluos facere, haec etiam circa me tua consuetudo seruata docebit
omnes per adiutorii mihi praestiti documenta quod fidere in te
debeant, mirarique faciet quoniam non sinas eos, qui tuo innituntur praesidio, opprimi ab his qui dexterae tuae obsistere non
uerentur.   10

Resistunt autem *dexterae*   Τουτέστι τῶν ἀνθεσ-
tuae, id est adiutorio | tuo, hi qui   τηκότων τῇ βοηθείᾳ σου · ἐπειδὴ
inpugnant quos tu protegis ac   γὰρ εἶπεν Ὁ σῴζων τοὺς ἐλπί-
tueris. Et quoniam dixerat: *Qui*   ζοντας ἐπὶ σοί — τοῖς δὲ ἐλπίζουσιν
saluos facis sperantes in te, id est   ἐπ᾽ αὐτῷ αὐτὸς ἐπαμύνει καὶ βοηθεῖ, 15
continuam eis inter aduersa opem   τοὺς ἀνθεστηκότας τοῖς ἐλπίζουσιν
salutis impertis, bene ait: ἐπ᾽ αὐτὸν τῇ αὐτοῦ βοηθείᾳ — κα-
                                    λῶς ἔφησεν.

8. *Custodi me, Domine, ut pupillam oculi.* Vt contra omnes periculorum casus munimen sibi a Domino sufficiens inpetraret, bene 20
a pupilla aduocauit exemplum, cui a factore mire ipsa operis qualitate et ingenti cautione prospectum est, ut non facile aliquo
extrinsecus laederetur incursu. Nam primo tunicis est multis et fortibus inuoluta; post etiam ad tuitionem eius palpebrarum tegmen
expansum est oppositique orbes quos superciliorum et genarum 25
uicinitas fabricatur, ut primi exciperent si quos fors ictus inferret:
quis rebus munita raro pateret ad noxam.

Sub umbra alarum tuarum protege me. Post pupillam a similitudine auium sedulae auxilium tuitionis implorat, quae pennis suis
conplexae fetus non solum fouent, sed etiam ab insidiantium pro- 30
tegunt raptu.

---

2 misericordiam] tuam *add.* A²   2-3 liberationem A¹   3 occassionem B
5 tibi *om.* A, B *in rasura*   9 hiis B   12 hi qui] iniqui A   13 impugnant A
16 continuam eis] continua in eis A   20 cassus A   impetraret B   22 in-
geti A   23 est tunicis A   24 tutionem A   25 oppossitique A   26 excipe-
rant A   28 umra A *et ita p. 105, l. 1*   29 sedule A   tutionis A   pinnis A
30 foetus B   insidientum A.

Τουτέστιν — ἔφησεν: (Θεο̂ αντιο̂̔) Paris. 139, fol. 40ᵛ; Vat. 1682, fol. 56 (Mai,
p. 393; P. G., 660 B 7-11).   17 καλοὺς *ms, aliquid deesse videtur.*

tance accorded him. Accord me your mercy to such an extent, he is saying, that all will marvel and take my deliverance as a basis for praising you. It therefore was appropriate for him to go on with *you who render those hoping in you safe from those resisting your right hand:* since it is your custom to render those hoping in you safe, observing this habit in my regard will teach everyone by the proof of the help accorded me that they ought trust in you, and will cause them to marvel that you do not allow those who rely on your support to be overwhelmed by those who do not fear to resist your right hand—in other words, those who resist your help. You see, since he had said *you render those hoping in you safe,* and he helps and assists those hoping in him, he was right to say "those resisting ... those hoping in him with his help."[1]

Guard me, Lord, as the pupil of your eye (v. 8). So as to beg sufficient protection for himself from God against every onset of danger, he does well to adduce the figure of the pupil of the eye, to which by the very quality of the work and extreme carefulness sight is marvelously communicated by the maker, with the result that it is not easily damaged from outside by any assault. For a start, you see, it is wrapped in many strong dressings; then a covering of its eyelids is spread out for its protection, as well as the place-ment of orbs achieved by the closeness of eyebrows and cheeks, with the result that it is fortified against any chance blow and rarely exposed to harm. *Protect me under the shadow of your wings.* After the pupil he begs the help of careful protection through a comparison with birds, which by enclosing the chicks in their wings not only nourish them, but also protect them from being snatched by poachers. | *Under the shadow of your wings protect me*

---

1. Something is missing here from the Greek, which is extant, and also from the Latin.

8ᵇ-9ᵃ. *Sub umbra alarum tuarum protege me a facie impiorum qui me adflixerunt.* Id est: Adiutorio tuo defensum me ab omnibus impiorum malefactis adserua, qui me aerumnis multis adficiunt, dum cogunt persequentes de hoc loco ad alium atque inde rursus
5 ad alium saepe transfugere.

9ᵇ. *Inimici mei animam meam circumdederunt.* Admotis undique tribulationibus coartarunt me atque in omnes uitae angustias conpulerunt.

10. *Adipem suum concluserunt.*

10 Ita, inquit, eorum prosperitas tuta est, ut ad nullum patere uideantur incommodum; ita obesa ac distenta nequitia, ut inminui macie non putetur: id enim | quod
15 conclusum est, uelut custodiae traditum perire non sinitur. Hoc indicat dicendo *concluserunt*, uidelicet quod ita secundis rebus afluant, ut omnes aerumnis adi-
20 tus obstruxisse credantur.

Οὕτω φησίν εἰσιν εὐπαθεῖς

ὡς μὴ διαδύναι αὐτῶν τὸν λιπασμόν, ἐπειδὴ γὰρ τὸ συγκεκλεισμένον ἐν ἀσφαλείᾳ πλείστῃ καθέστηκεν. Τοῦτο λέγει τὸ συνέκλεισαν, ἀντὶ τοῦ Τὴν εὐθηνίαν αὐτῶν ἐν πλείστῃ ἔχουσιν ἀσφαλείᾳ, ὡς μηδὲ προσδοκᾶν αὐτῶν διαπεσεῖν — ἵν᾿ εἴπῃ ὅτι οὐκ ἀπέβαλον τοῦ βίου τὴν εὐπραγίαν.

Os eorum locutum est superbiam. A prosperitate uitae rerumque afluentia in superbiae et blasfemiae uerba procurrunt, et quia nullo aduersae rei feriuntur incommodo, neque facere quicquam norunt neque dicere modeste.

25 **11.** *Eicientes me nunc circumdederunt me.*

Qui aliquando me inquit, laudibus efferentes beatum dicebant, nunc persecuntur et in inferendo

Οἱ ποτέ φησιν μακαρίζοντες νῦν καταδιώκουσι καὶ περικυκλοῦσιν ὥστε ἀνελεῖν.

1-2 a facie — qui me] usque A   3 erumnis A   adfaciunt B   5 sepe A   transfugere *sequitur in* B *rasura lineae fere dimidiae*   10 properitas A   11 ad *om*, A   12 obesa] obsessa AB   15 custodia A   16 perirere A   17 dicando AB   17-18 uidilicet A   19 erumnis A   19-20 abditus B¹   21 est] in *add.* A   rerum A¹   22 plasfemiae A   praecurrunt A   25 iecientes A, *et ita p. 106 l. 3-4*   circ̅. B   me *om.* A   26 qui] quia A   28 persequntur A.

Οὕτω — εὐπραγίαν: (Θεοδ⁰ ἀντιοχ) Paris. 139, fol. 41; Vat. 1422, fol. 46ᵛ; Vat. 1682, fol. 56ᵛ (Mai, p. 393; P. G., 660 C 3-9).   12 διαδοῦναι 1422.

Οἱ ποτέ φησιν — 106, 9 ἐκέχρηντο: (Θεοˢ αντιοχ) Paris. 139, fol. 41; Vat. 1682, fol. 57; Cord. I, 296 (P. G., 661 D 1-9).

from the presence of the godless, who afflicted me (vv. 8–9): by your help keep me safe from all the evil doings of the godless, who heap much tribulation on me, while forcing pursuers often to flee from one place to another and back again.

My enemies surrounded my soul: by plying me with tribulations from all sides they invested me and drove me into all life's hardships. *They hemmed in their fatness* (v. 10): they are so prosperous that their affluence is invulnerable, since it is enclosed and placed in the tightest security. By *hemmed in* he means, They have their opulence in a very secure condition so as to expect that it would not deteriorate—in other words, they did not forfeit life's prosperity. *Their mouth uttered arrogance:* from life's prosperity and their affluence they proceed to words of pride and blasphemy because they are struck by no blows of adversity and do not know how to do or say anything with restraint.

Having cast me out, they have now surrounded me (v. 11): those who once declared me blessed now pursue and encircle me so as to do away with me. | Symmachus, in fact, likewise says, "Declaring me blessed, they imme-

mihi interitu congregantur. Ita
et Symmachus: *Beatificantes me
statim circumdederunt me. Eicientes* autem in hoc loco maluit pro beatificantibus dicere,
quia non erant illae laudes
puri affectus officia sed captio-
num retia, ut adulationibus inretitus et fomentis inmodicae
laudis abstractus eiceretur de
uia modestiae suae atque cor-
rueret.

Οὕτως γὰρ λέγει καὶ Σύμμαχος·
Μακαρίζοντες παραχρῆμα περιεκύ-
κλωσάν με. Ἐκβάλλοντας δὲ τοὺς μα-
καρίζοντας ἐνταῦθα ἐκάλεσεν, ἐπειδὴ
μὴ γνησίᾳ τῇ διανοίᾳ τὸν μακαρισμὸν 5
ἐποιοῦντο τὸ πρότερον, ὥστε δὲ ἐκβαλεῖν καὶ ἐκτρέψαι τῆς προσηκούσης ὁδοῦ, ἀπάτης ἕνεκεν τοῖς τοῦ
μακαρισμοῦ ῥήμασιν ἐκέχρηντο.

10

11b. *Oculos suos statuerunt declinare in terram.*

Haec, inquit, eorum sententia
est, ad hoc eorum omnis tendit
intentio, ut me de solo hereditatis meae, id est de terra repromissionis, eiciant.

Πρὸς τοῦτο ἀφορῶσι καὶ πρὸς
τοῦτο ἔχουσι πᾶσαν τὴν σπουδήν, 15
ὥστε ἐμὲ τῆς γῆς ἐκβαλεῖν τῆς κληρονομίας, τουτέστιν τῆς γῆς τῆς
ἐπαγγελίας.

12a. *Susciperunt me sicut leo paratus ad praedam.*

Vice, inquit, leonis, quem
famis armat in praedam, insi-
diantes uitae meae oportunum
inferendae mihi mortis tempus
exspectant. Nam pro « expec-

Περιμένουσί με ὥστε ἀνελεῖν, δί- 20
κην λέοντος θήραν προσδοκῶντος.

Ἀντὶ δὲ τοῦ « περιμένουσιν » εἶπεν

---

2 sim A sym̄ B   3 circumdederunt A   4-5 malluit A   8 adolationibus B
8-9 inrettitus A   10 abstrachtus A   iecieretur A   11-12 conrueret A
13-18 *affert* A, f. 4a   13 ter̄ B   16-17 heriditatis A   17-18 repromisionis A   19 ieciant A   19-107, 3 *affert* Ae (Ascoli, p. 133, 24-134, 1)   19 par.
ad praed. *om.* Ae   23 mortis mihi Ae   nam pro exp. *om. 1a m.* Ac.

Πρὸς — ἐπαγγελίας: (Θεοˢ αντιοχ) Paris. 139, fol. 41; Vat. 1682, fol. 57 (Maius,
p. 393; P. G., 660 C 10-13.
Περιμένουσι — 107, 10 φιλανθρωπίαν: (Θεοˢ αντιοχ) Paris. 139 fol. 41; Vat. 1682,
fol. 57; Cord., p. 296 (P. G., 660 D 10-661 A 7); Barbaro, p. 152.

13-18 *Incipit hoc loco in codice Ambrosiano nulla facta distinctione epitomatoris* (Ae) *opus* (Ascoli, p. 133, 20-24): Oculos suos statuerunt.. merito in terram declinant oculi a caelo euersi hoc student contenduntque ut me de heriditatis meae ieciant.

diately encircled me." Now, by *cast out* here he meant "declared blessed," since it was not with sincerity that they initially uttered the blessing; rather, with the intention of expelling and diverting me from the proper direction they used the words of blessing by way of deceit.[2] *They set their eyes to bring me to the ground:* they concentrate on this goal and display complete zeal for it, to expel me from the land of inheritance—that is, the land of promise.

They came upon me like a lion ready for the prey (v. 12): they lie in wait so as to do away with me, like a lion awaiting its prey. Instead of "lie in wait" | he used *came upon,* since those who suspect something is going to

---

2. The Hebrew term (to which, of course, Theodore cannot turn) is obscure, giving rise to quite different versions, which nonetheless the commentator tries to reconcile.

tant » posuit *susciperunt*, quoniam qui opinantur aliquid futurum, rerum opperiuntur euentus.
Hanc, inquit, persuasionem de
5 me animo conceperunt, quoniam
sicut uenatio possim in eorum
captiones incidere. Ita et in XLVII
psalmo positum est: *Suscipimus,
Deus, misericordiam tuam in me-*
10 *dio populi tui,* id est Sustinui-
mus atque exspectauimus ut in
nos opus tuae benignitatis in-
pleres.

τὸ Ὑπέλαβον, ἐπειδὴ οἱ ὑπολαμβά-
νοντες ἔσεσθαί τι προσδοκῶσι, —
τουτέστι ταύτην ἔχουσι περὶ ἐμοῦ τὴν
ὑπόληψιν ὅτι λήψονται ὥσπερ τινὰ
θῆρα.

Οὕτω καὶ τὸ Ὑπελάβομεν, ὁ Θεός,
τὸ ἔλεός σου, τουτέστι Περιεμείναμεν
καὶ προσεδοκήσαμεν ἔσεσθαί σου ἐν
ἡμῖν τὴν φιλανθρωπίαν.

12ᵇ. *Et sicut catulus leonis habitans in abditis.*
15 Et in hoc loco CKYMNOC positus est in graeco, de cuius nominis
proprietate aliquanta disserui. Superiora itaque dicta repetitione
geminauit. Quod uero ait *habitans in abditis,* latentes eorum dolos
et subitos uoluit impetus indicare. Quoniam ita, inquit, in me saeuis
atque inplacatis animis opus crudelitatis extremae moliuntur atque
20 in captionem meam dolos machinantur innumeros, tuum circa me,
Domine, adiutorium non moretur. Propter quod consequenter
intulit:

13ª. *Exurge, Domine, praeueni eos et supplanta eos,* id est: Consilia quae aduersum me concipiunt, et machinas quas meae
25 praeparant captioni festinum defensionis tuae munimen excludat,
ut praeuenti id quod intenderant inplere non possint. Quod autem
ait, *et supplanta eos,* id est: Quod aduersum me statuerunt, prorue
et deice tuae uirtutis inpulsu.

8-10 Ps. XLVII, 10.

2-3 futurarum Aᵉ   3 operiuntur Aᵉ   aduentus Aᵉ; *quae sequuntur usque
ad finem psalmi solus* B *exhibet; epitomatoris* (Aᵉ) *uarietates notaui*   4 per-
suassionem B   5 concoeperunt B   6 in *om.* B   7 incedere B   15 CKΥΝΗC B
16 disseruit B¹   23-25 exurge — excludat *affert* Aᵉ (Ascoli, p. 134, 2-6)
23 supplanta] subuerte Aᵉ   24 concipiuntur Aᵉ   et — meae *om.* Aᵉ   25 prac-
parantque Aᵉ   captionis B¹   difensionis Aᵉ   munimem] numen Aᵉ.

13-15: Aᵉ (p. 134, 1-2) Sicut catulus leonis... geminauit priorem sententiam.

happen wait for it—that is, they have this suspicion about me that they will take me like some animal of prey. Likewise the verse "We suspected, O God, your mercy"—that is, We lay in wait and expected that your lovingkindness would come to us.[3] *And like a lion cub lurking in hiding.* In this place, too, *skymnos* occurs in Greek, and I have discussed the suitability of this term to some extent.[4] Therefore, he duplicated his previous words. By saying *lurking in hiding,* on the other hand, he wanted to suggest their hidden stratagems and furtive attacks. Since, he is saying, they are thus conducting an exploit of extreme cruelty against me with a savage and implacable spirit and hatch innumerable plots to entrap me, let your help for me not be delayed, Lord.

Hence, he logically proceeded with *Rise up, Lord, anticipate them and trip them up* (v. 13)—that is, The plans they form against me and the schemes they hatch for my capture, let the protection of your defense obstruct, so that they may be anticipated and unable to carry out what they intend. He said as much in *trip them up*—that is, steal a march on what they planned against me and undo it by the impact of your power. | *Rescue my soul from the god-*

---

3. Ps 48:9.

4. Another manuscript reads "he has discussed," which makes more sense—although, in fact, neither Theodore nor the psalmist has discoursed on cubs to this point (cf. Ps 57:4).

13ᵇ-14ᵃ. *Eripe animam meam ab impio, a framea inimicorum manus tuae.*

Quidam *frameam* legunt per accussatiuum casum, sed non recte: per septimum potius est legendum. Ita namque et Aquila posuit *a framea*, non « frameam »... | *Eripe animam meam, id est me, ab impio et a framea inimicorum manus tuae.*

Τινὲς ῥομφαίᾳ σου ἀναγινώσκουσιν, ἐπὶ τῆς δοτικῆς πτώσεως λέγοντες· ἔστι δὲ οὐχ οὕτως, ἀλλὰ 5 *ῥομφαίας σου τῇ γενικῇ πτώσει λεγόμενον. Οὕτως γὰρ καὶ Ἀκύλας εἶπε μαχαίρας σου. Ὁ δὲ βούλεται εἰπεῖν τοιοῦτόν ἐστιν· Ῥῦσαι τὴν ψυχήν μου, τουτέστιν ἐμέ, ἀπὸ τού-* 10 *των τῶν ἀσεβῶν καὶ ἀπὸ τῆς ῥομφαίας τῶν ἐχθρῶν τῆς χειρός σου.*

Frameam autem uocat captionem fraude dispositam, quae conpraehensum uice acuti gladii uel teli possit occidere; *inimicos* uero *manus* Dei eos qui conabantur eum regno uitaque priuare, cum utique ipse a Deo esset unctus in regem: unde manifestum erat quod essent inimici Dei qui statutis eius conabantur obsistere.

Ῥομφαίαν γὰρ καλεῖ τὴν κατ᾽ αὐτοῦ γινομένην ὑπ᾽ αὐτῶν μηχανὴν πά- 15 *σης μαχαίρας κατ᾽ αὐτοῦ τμητικωτέραν τὴν ἐπιβουλὴν ἐργαζομένην, ἐχθροὺς δὲ τῆς χειρὸς τοῦ Θεοῦ καλεῖ τοὺς ἐχθροὺς τοὺς αὐτοῦ, ἐπειδὴ τὸν ὑπ᾽ αὐτοῦ χρισθέντα εἰς βασιλέα* 20 *ἑλεῖν ἐσπουδακότες, αὐτῷ δῆλοι ἦσαν ἐχθραίνοντες τῷ Θεῷ καὶ τοῖς ὑπ᾽ αὐτοῦ γενομένοις ἀνθίστασθαι ἐσπουδακότες.*

14ᵇ-ᶠ. *Domine, disperdens disperti eos in uita: de absconditis tuis* 25 *inpleatur uenter eorum. Saturati sunt filiis et dimiserunt reliquias suas paruulis suis.* Difficultas in hoc loco et obscuritas ex interpraetatione greca prouenit, quam adiuuante Deo adhibita expositione soluemus. Fecerunt autem nobis hunc locum difficilem maxime proprietates hebraicae, quae per translationem grecam explicari 30 minime potuerunt.

7 framea **** B   8 *post* frameam *deciderunt ex codice* [*initium fol.* 5ᶜ] *litterae fere* 15   9 ab impio et *evanuerunt in cod.*   17-24 inimicos — obsistere *affert* Aᵉ (p. 134, 7-12)   18 manus suae Aᵉ   eos dicit Aᵉ   19 a regno Aᵉ   20 esset a Deo Aᵉ   22 erat quod] est qui Aᵉ   25 Domine a paucis a terra dispertire eos in uita eorum Aᵉ   26 inpleatur] adinpletus * (est?) B¹   30 haebreicae B.

Τινὲς — ἐσπουδακότες: (Θεοδώρου ἀντιοχ᾽) Paris. 139, fol. 41ᵛ; Vat. 1682, fol. 57ᵛ (Mai, p. 393-394 (P. G., 661 A 9-B 7); Barbaro, p. 153.

less, from your sword of the foes of your hand (vv. 13–14). Some read "by your sword," taking it as the dative case, but it is not correct; rather, it is to be taken in the genitive case, "from your sword," Aquila also having "from your sword." The meaning is something like this: Rescue my soul—that is, me—from these ungodly people and from the sword of the foes of your hand.[5] By *sword* he referred to the scheme plotted by them against him that created a plan sharper than any sword against him, and by *foes of God's hand* he refers to his foes, since they were anxious to seize the one anointed by him as king; and it suggests that they were hostile to God and anxious to oppose what was done by him.

Sow confusion in the ranks of those who live this way so as to destroy them from the face of the earth; let their belly be filled with what is hidden. Their sons were sated, they left their remnants to their sons. The difficulty and obscurity in this place arise from the Greek translation, which we shall resolve by proceeding with God's help to the interpretation. Now, it is Hebrew idioms in particular that made this place difficult for us, since they can hardly be explained through the Greek translation.[6] | The phrase *Destroy*

---

5. Although the Greek text of the commentary is also extant here (as above), we suffer from not having Theodore's biblical text. The LXX generally and Theodoret's text read "sword" in the accusative. Theodore seems to know also a reading in the dative but takes a lead from Diodore and Aquila to opt for a genitive reading. Theodoret, on the other hand, gets support from Symmachus for his accusative form.

6. The verse is indeed obscure, modern commentators having recourse to linguistic data to resolve the obscurity. The text that Theodore is reading, we surmise from his comment (extant also in Greek), is that read by Diodore, which differs from the Vulgate cited by Devreesse.

Disperdens ergo *a terra* ad
Deum dicit, id est quod omnes
homines prima statuti eius sententia ac lege moriantur, ac si
5 diceret: Tu qui mori omnes homines prima constituti tui sanctione iussisti, *Disperti illos*, id est
disperge, quoniam id quod dispergitur huc atque illuc sua di-
10 uisione iactatur. *De absconditis*
uero *tuis*, ac si diceret: De animaduersionibus tuis atque suppliciis, quae uelut reposita apud
te continentur et clausa, quae
15 in uindictam hominum subito et
cum uolueris proferes ac produces. *Saturati sunt* autem *filiis* pro
saturentur filii eorum posuit: mutauit tempus. *Et reliquerunt* pro
20 relinquant, similiter per commutationem temporis, dixit. Hoc est
itaque quod ait, breuiter: O Domine, qui omnes homines generali mortis sententia uitae huic
25 perire conpellis ac de terrae huius
habitatione disperdis, ipse et istos
etiam in hac praesenti uita ab hac
quam inter se habent societate
partire, id est disperge illos adhuc
30 uiuentes, ut pro actibus suis luant

Τὸ μὲν οὖν ἀπολλύων ἀπὸ τῆς
γῆς εἶπε πρὸς τὸν Θεόν, ὡς ἂν αὐτοῦ τὴν τοῦ θανάτου ἀπόφασιν κατὰ
τῶν ἀνθρώπων ἐξενέγκαντος, ἵν᾽ εἴπῃ
ὅτι Σὺ ὁ πάντας ἀποθνήσκειν ποιῶν.

Τὸ δὲ διαμέρισον, ἀντὶ τοῦ διασκόρπισον, ἀπὸ τοῦ τὸ σκορπιζόμενον
πάντως τῇδε κακεῖσε μερίζεσθαι. Τὸ
δὲ τῶν κεκρυμμένων, ἀντὶ τοῦ τῶν
τιμωριῶν σου ὧν ἔχεις ἐν ἀποκρύφῳ,
ἃς ὅτε θέλεις ἐκφέρεις τιμωρούμενος
ἀπροσδοκήτως τοὺς ἀνθρώπους καὶ
ὡς οὐκ ἴσασιν.

Τὸ δὲ ἐχορτάσθησαν
υἱῶν, ἀντὶ τοῦ χορτασθήτωσαν δὲ
καὶ οἱ υἱοί· ἐνήλλακται γὰρ συνήθως
ὁ χρόνος Καὶ τὸ ἀφῆκαν, ὁμοίως ἀντὶ
τοῦ ἀφέτωσαν. Τοῦτο οὖν βούλεται
συντόμως εἰπεῖν ὅτι Σύ, ὦ δέσποτα,
ὡς πάντας ἀνθρώπους τῇ κοινῇ ἀποφάσει τοῦ θανάτου ἀπολύεις ἐκ τῆς
γῆς, αὐτὸς καὶ τούτους ἐν τῇ ζωῇ
αὐτῶν διαμέρισον, τουτέστι διασκόρπισον αὐτοὺς ἔτι ζῶντας, ἵνα
πρὸ τοῦ κοινοῦ θανάτου ἐφ᾽ οἷς
διαπράττονται ὑπομείνωσί τινα τιμωρίαν, καὶ τῶν τιμωριῶν δὲ τῶν

10-17 de absconditis — produces *affert* A^e (p. 134, 17-22) 11 uero *om.* A^e
13 quae* B 14 retinentur A^e clusa A^e et quae A^e 16 proferis A^e
18-19 motauit B^1 30 ut] et B^1.

Τὸ μὲν — ἴσασιν: (Θεοῦ αντιοχ) Paris. 139, fol. 41^v; Vat. 1682, fol. 57^v-58 (Mai,
p. 394; P. G., 661 B 8-C 1; Barbaro, p. 154. 12 ἐκφέρης ms. – ρης Mai.

Τὸ δὲ — 110, 31 κεκτημένους: (Θεοῦ αντιοχ) Paris. 139, fol. 41^v; Vat. 1682,
jol. 58; Barbaro, p. 154 ut] et B^1.

A^e 17-18 (p. 134, 22-24): Saturati sunt filiis et relinquerunt quae superfuerint
(tormenta) paruulis suis. 22-110, 2 (p. 134, 13-17): Tu, qui homines mori
prima constitui sanctione iusisti, dispertire illos, hoc est disperge eos de terrae
huius habitatione, ut dispersi luant poenas ante commonis mortis incursum.

them from the face of the earth, then, he addressed to God, as though death itself were delivering a verdict against human beings, as if to say, You who cause everyone to die. He said *sow confusion* in the sense of scatter, since what is scattered is totally sent in various directions. He said *what is hidden* in the sense, The punishments you are keeping under cover, which at will you deliver unexpectedly to punish human beings when they are unaware. He said *their sons were sated* in the sense, Let their sons be sated (with the customary change in tense); and *they left* in the sense, Let them leave. In short, then, he means, As you, Lord, destroy all human beings from the face of the earth by the general sentence of death, sow confusion in them also in their life—that is, scatter them while still alive, so that before the death to which they are all liable they will suffer some punishment for what they do. | Discharge your punishments upon them to such an extent that their off-

poenas ante communis mortis aduentum; | atque ita illos reple miseriis, ut usque ad filios eorum seueritas tuae transeat ultionis atque a filiis in nepotum decurrat aetatem. Hoc itaque uult dicere: Ita illos puni, ut neque ipsis neque filiis eorum neque nepotibus parcas.

σῶν οὕτω πλήρωσον αὐτῶν καὶ τὰ ἐνδότατα ὡς πληρωθῆναι μὲν τῆς παρά σου τιμωρίας μετὰ αὐτῶν, καὶ τοὺς υἱοὺς τοὺς αὐτῶν ἐνεχθῆναι δὲ μέχρι καὶ τῶν ἐγγόνων τῆς τιμωρίας 5 τὰ λείψανα. Βούλεται δὲ εἰπεῖν ὅτι Τιμώρησαι αὐτούς, μήτε αὐτῶν μήτε τῶν υἱῶν μήτε τῶν ἐγγόνων φεισάμενος.

Filios autem posuit, non (ut quidam aestimant) carnes: qui 10 quidem error natus est una littera addita uel praelata, ut per Y͞W͞N — quod est filiorum, — C͞Y͞W͞N scriberet, quod est porcorum; sed in hoc loco filios euidenter posuit. Pro eo ergo ut diceret: Poenis a te impleatur uenter eorum, dixit *de absconditis tuis adinpleatur uenter eorum.* Siquidem diuinae scripturae consuetudo est quasi de rege 15 quodam ita de Deo facere sermonem, in cuius thessauris atque horreis uentorum, niuium, suppliciorum atque poenarum aliarumque huius modi rerum uelud congestio facta seruetur, sicut idem beatus Dauid in alio psalmo ait: *Qui producit uentos de thessauris suis*, et Moyses in cantico Deuteronomii: *Ecce haec omnia congregata sunt* 20 *apud me et signata sunt in thessauris meis*, cum de plagis utique populi et animaduersionibus disputaret. Ita ergo in hoc loco *de absconditis tuis*, id est de cruciatibus tuis dixit; absconditas autem uocauit plagas quae inferuntur a Deo, quoniam non semper illis nec passim utatur, sed cum merita fuerint castiganda peccantium, ex similitudine eorum quae in thessaurorum abdito reponuntur proferenda cum usus possidentis exegerit.

κεκρυμμένας καλέσας τὰς τιμωρίας διὰ τὸ μὴ παντότε, ἀλλ᾽ ἐν καιρῷ τῷ 25 δέοντι αὐταῖς κατακεχρῆσθαι, ἐκ μεταφορᾶς τῶν ἐν θησαυροῖς ὄντων, ἅπερ κέκρυπται μὲν ἐν ταῖς ἀποθήκαις ὄντα, ἐκφέρεται δὲ καὶ εἰς φανερὸν ἄγεται ὅταν ἡ χρεία συνελαύ- 30 νει τοὺς κεκτημένους.

Hoc etiam de bonitate Dei dicitur, quod uelut abscondita sit et uelut certo in loco custodiae mancipata, quia uidelicet per honoris sui meritum non semper pateat, sed oportuno a Deo tempore proferatur, sicut et in xxx psalmo ait: *Quam magna multitudo boni-* 35 *tatis tuae, Domine, quam abscondisti timentibus te.*

---

19 Ps. CXXXIV, 7   20-21 Deuter. XXXII, 34   35-36 Ps. XXX, 20

2-9 ita — parcas *affert* A^e (p. 134, 25-29)   3 misseriis A^e   ut] et B^l
4 saeueritas B   8 punias A^e   9 eorum *om.* A^e   14-15 dixit — uenter eorum *om.* B^l   26 * utatur B.

spring also will be sated with your punishments along with them, and the remnants of the punishment will be inflicted on their sons and their offspring. He means, Punish them, showing no mercy to them, their sons or their offspring.

Now, he said *sons,* not (as some commentators believe) "flesh"—an error coming from addition or supplement of a letter to produce *suōn,* "swine," for *huiōn,* "sons." In this place he clearly put *sons,* his sense therefore being, Let their belly be filled by you with punishments—hence his saying *Let their belly be filled with what is hidden.* It is, in fact, the habit of the divine Scripture to speak of God as though he were some king in whose storehouses is kept a collection of winds, snow, sanctions, and other punishments of this kind, as blessed David likewise says in another psalm, "He brings winds from his storehouses," and Moses in the canticle of Deuteronomy, "Lo, is not all this laid up with me and sealed in my storehouses?"[7] when there was question of sanctions and chastisement of the people. Likewise, at this point he said *what is hidden* in reference to their sufferings, using *what is hidden* of the punishments on account of their being inflicted on them not at all times but when needed, from the metaphor of the contents of storehouses, which are kept hidden in the barns and then brought out and displayed when need obliges the owners. This applies also to God's goodness in its being hidden and as it were kept under guard in a certain place, not always being obvious as it deserves, and displayed by God at the opportune moment, as he says also in Psalm 31, "How great the abundance of your goodness, Lord, which you hide for those who fear you."[8] |

---

7. Ps 135:7; Deut 32:34.
8. Ps 31:19.

15. *Ego autem in iustitia apparebo conspectui tuo: satiabor cum apparuerit gloria tua puero tuo.* Superius omnia in se aduersariorum mala sermone digesserat dicens: *Os eorum locutum est superbiam, iecientes me | nunc circumdederunt me, oculos suos statue-*
5 *runt declinare in terram, susciperunt me sicut leo ꝑ aratus et sicut catulus leonis habitans in abditis* et reliqua. Post quorum relationem intulit rogans ne inulta essent quae in illum sine causa iniquitas frequenter admiserat: *Domine, disperdens de terra partire illos in uita eorum, et de absconditis tuis inpleatur uenter eorum*
10 et quae secuntur. Quia ergo et mala in se ab inimicis admissa narrauerat et pro ultione sua Deo supplicationes admouerat, bene addidit: *Ego autem cum iustitia apparebo conspectui tuo, satiabor cum apparuerit gloria tua puero tuo,*

id est: Illi quidem tradantur
15 suppliciis et recipiant digna pro merito; *ego autem cum iustitia apparebo conspectui tuo,* id est nihil in uindictam mei reponens iniuriae uel doloris, sed e con-
20 trario iniquitates eorum sustinens ac patientiae uirtute supportans plene tuo adiutus auxilio gloriae

Τουτέστιν ἐκεῖνοι μέντοι τοιαῦτα διαπραξάμενοι ταύτης δίκαιοι τιμωρίας ἀπολαῦσαι, ἐγὼ δὲ μετὰ δικαιοσύνης σοὶ φανείς, τουτέστιν οὐδὲν ἄδικον εἰς αὐτοὺς διαπραξάμενος, πληρωθήσομαι τῆς σῆς βοηθείας καὶ ἀπολαύσω τῆς δόξης σου παρὰ σοῦ.

tuae largitate donabor. Gloriam vocauit praesidium diuinum, quo est ab insidiis Saulis erutus ac defensus: nam in uindictam eius
25 exsurgens Deus primo eum periculo depulso fecit esse conspicuum, secundo maiore gloria reddidit clarum, regnum depulso Saule Israhelitici populi conferendo. Finis itaque psalmi respondet initio in quo ait: *Exaudi, Domine, iustitiam meam;* quoniam ea quae postulauerat ostendit esse iustissima.

3-6, vv. 10-12.

1 in conspectu B¹   10 admisa B   12 **conspeċ (in conspectu?) B¹
cf. supra l. 1 et infra l. 17 satiabor] saī B   17 in conspeċ tu * B¹   22 a*u-
xilio B   27 respondit B¹ Aᵉ.

Τουτέστιν — σοῦ: Paris. fol. 42; Vat., fol. 58ᵛ (Mai, p. 394; P. G., 661 C 2-7).

Aᵉ 16-29 (p. 134, 30, 135, 3-9): Ego autem cum iustitia apparebo.. quod ait in conspectu tuo semper illi quod (quidem?) tradantur suppliciis. Ego autem innocentiam meam seruabo, ne quando reddam uicem iniuriae.. satiabor dum manifestabitur gloria tua.. explebor bonis omnibus si adiutorii tui gloriossa deffensione fuero ereptus Saulis insidiis.. (p. 135, 1-3) Pulchre fine suo psalmi respondit initio quo precum suarum commendauerat aequitatem.

As for me, in righteousness I shall appear in your sight, I shall be satisfied when your glory will have appeared to your servant (v. 15). He had outlined above all the adversaries' abuse of him in the words *Their mouth uttered arrogance: Having cast me out, they have now surrounded me. They set their eyes to bring me to the ground: They came upon me like a lion ready for the prey, and like a lion cub lurking in hiding* and so on. After saying that, he proceeded to ask that what iniquity often had been committed against him should not go unpunished: *Lord, sow confusion in the ranks of those who live this way; let their belly be filled with what is hidden* and what follows. Because he had both recounted the troubles caused him by the enemy, therefore, and had directed to God requests for his revenge, he was right to proceed with *As for me, in righteousness I shall appear in your sight, I shall be satisfied when your glory will have appeared to your servant.* In other words, While those guilty of such crimes deserve to receive this punishment, *in righteousness I shall appear in your sight*—that is, Guilty of no wrong against them, I shall be abundantly rewarded with your help and shall enjoy from you your glory. By *glory* he referred to the divine protection by which he was rescued and defended against Saul's schemes: by rising up to vindicate him and repelling the danger he first made him famous, and then rendered him conspicuous with greater glory by deposing Saul and conferring on him the kingship of the Israelite people. The end of the psalm thus corresponds to its beginning, where it said *Hearken, Lord, to my righteousness,* since he shows what he requested do be very fair. |

PSALMVS XVII

Hunc septimum decimum psalmum uidemus secundi Regum libri, et si commutatis quibusdam uerbis, historia contineri. Dictus autem est a beato Dauid prope uitae ultimum finem, cum Deo pro omnibus in se beneficiis grates deuotus exsolueret, quia eripuisset 5 eum primo ab insidiis Saulis atque ab omni discrimine quod frequenter incurrerat eruisset, et ad extremum pro cunctis quae per omne uitae suae tempus inter aduersa positus miserationum Dei fuisset expertus, liberatus quippe ab inimicis est et nihil aduersi sustinere permissus. Vnde manifestum est quod conuenienti titulo 10 praenotetur; nam ut canticum quoddam pro gratiarum actione psalmus iste cantatur.

v. 6ᵇ. Τὸ δὲ προέφθασάν με τοιοῦτόν τι λέγειν βούλεται· Τοσαῦται φησιν καὶ τοιαῦται κατ᾽ ἐμοῦ τῶν ἐχθρῶν ἐπιβουλαὶ γεγόνασι, ὡς προφθάσαι μου καὶ τὸν λογισμὸν καὶ μηδὲ καιρὸν ἐνδοῦναί μοι καὶ κατανόησιν καὶ 15 πρὸς τὸ ἀφιδεῖν τίνι δὲ τρόπῳ τὴν φυγὴν τὴν ἐξ αὐτῶν πορίσασθαι.

v. 7ᶜ. *Et exaudiuit de templo sancto suo uocem meam.* Templum sanctum hic tabernaculum uocat in quo arca Dei | erat posita. Tabernaculum ergo templum populus appellare consueuerat, etiam antequam templi structura consurgeret.
20

1 expl(icit) xui B, incipit xuii psal(mus) A, xuii B *in marg.*　2 sepdeci-
mum A　3 commotatis A　4 c̄** A　5 erupuisset A　7 incurreret A
extrimum A　8 possitus misserationum A　9 inmicis A　aduersi] persi Aˡ
peruersi A²　10 permisus AB　conueniente Aˡ　11 quodam A　17 exaudiuit me Bˡ　18 possita A　19 consuerat A.

Τὸ δὲ — πορίσασθαι: Paris. 139, fol. 42ᵛ; Vat. 1682, fol. 59ᵛ (Mai, p. 394;
P. G., 661 C 10-15); Barbaro, p. 158.

Argumentum psalmi habet Aᵉ (p. 135, 13-17) *his verbis*: Etsi quibusdam
uerbis commotatur, hic psalmus regum historia contenetur prope ultimum
uitae suae tempus a sancto Dauid pro gratiarum actione cantatus, titulo suo
contenens argumentum. Cf. PSEVDO-BEDA (P. L., XCIII, 566): Hunc psalmum
Dauid prope ultimum uitae suae tempus pro gratiarum actione cantauit.
　　Aᵉ 13-17 (p. 136, 7-9): Tam insperatis plerumque insidiis circumuentus sum
ut locus deesset efugionis.

PSALM 18

This eighteenth psalm we see contained in the narrative of the second book of Kings,[1] if with some word change. It was composed by blessed David near the end of his life when he devoutly gave thanks to God for all his favors to him in snatching him first from Saul's schemes and rescuing him from every peril that frequently beset him, and finally for experiencing God's mercy in every adversity he found himself in throughout his life, namely, in being freed from his enemies and allowed to suffer no hardship. Hence, it is clear that the title it bears is appropriate: this psalm is sung as a kind of canticle of thanksgiving.

Now, the phrase *caught me unawares* (v. 5)[2] means something like this: The enemies' schemes against me were so many and so great as to catch me unawares and allow me neither thought nor opportunity nor reasoning to determine how to achieve a way out of them.

He heard my voice from his holy temple (v. 6). By *holy temple* here he refers to the tabernacle in which the ark of God was placed. So the people were accustomed to call the tabernacle temple even before the building of the temple arose. |

---

1. Cf. 2 Sam 22. The lengthy title to the psalm gives this digest of its content.
2. The Greek text of the commentary is not extant to this point, nor the Latin to verse 6b.

v. 8ᵇ. *Et fundamenta montium conturbata*, reliqua.

Audiente, inquit, Deo uocem   *Ἵν' εἴπῃ ὅτι τοῦ Θεοῦ ἀκούσαν-*
meam commota est omnis terra   *τος καὶ συγκινηθέντος εἰς ὀργήν, πρῶ-*
ab irae magnitudine, quam contra   *τον μὲν ἅπαντα ἐσαλεύετο, γῆ τε καὶ*
5 inimicos accenderat.   *ὄρη, εἶτα ἐδείχθη καπνὸς τῆς ὀργῆς*
αὐτοῦ τὸ προοίμιον, καὶ μετὰ τοῦτο πῦρ ἀνήφθη, τουτέστι φανερῶς ὀργι-
ζόμενος ἐδείχθη διὰ τῆς κατὰ τῶν ἐχθρῶν τιμωρίας. Εἶτα βουλόμενος καὶ
τῆς τιμωρίας τὴν ἐπίτασιν εἰπεῖν, τῇ ἀκολουθίᾳ τῆς οἰκείας χρησάμενος σωμα-
τοποιήσεως ἐπήγαγεν·

10   9ᵃ. Ἀνέβη καπνὸς ἐν ὀργῇ αὐτοῦ. Ἐπειδὴ γὰρ πῦρ ἀεὶ καλεῖ τοῦ
Θεοῦ τὸ τιμωρητικόν, καὶ ἔθος αὐτῷ τοῦτο σχηματίζειν ὡσανεὶ πυρὸς προ-
τρέχοντος καὶ προσδεικνύντος αὐτοῦ τοῦ Θεοῦ τὴν κατὰ τῶν ἐχθρῶν ὀργήν,
ὡς ὅταν λέγῃ πῦρ ἐνώπιον αὐτοῦ προπορεύεται, τῇ αὐτῇ συνηθείᾳ κἀνταῦθα
κεχρημένος εἰσάγει ὡσανεὶ πυρὸς δειχθέντος πρὸ τοῦ Θεοῦ καὶ σημαίνον-
15 τος τὴν ὀργὴν αὐτοῦ τὴν κατὰ τῶν ἐχθρῶν. Ἀκόλουθον οὖν ἑαυτῷ κατὰ
τὴν σωματοποίησιν εἶπεν τὸ Ἀνέβη καπνὸς ἐν ὀργῇ αὐτοῦ, ἐπειδὴ καπνὸς
ἀεὶ προτρέχων σημαίνει τοῦ πυρὸς τὴν ἔκκαυσιν. Διὸ μνημονεύσας τοῦ
καπνοῦ ἀκολούθως ἐπήγαγεν·

  9ᶜ. Ἄνθρακες ἀνήφθησαν ἀπ' αὐτοῦ. Πυρὸς γὰρ ἐπὶ πολὺ γενομένου,
20 ἄνθρακας ἐπὶ πολὺ γενέσθαι συμβαίνει, δι' ὅλων βουληθεὶς εἰπεῖν ὅτι ἅμα
τε ἤκουσεν εὐξαμένου, καὶ ἐκινήθη κατὰ τῶν ἐχθρῶν καὶ εὐθὺς μὲν πάντα
ἐσαλεύετο. Ὑπεφαίνετο δὲ αὐτοῦ κατὰ μέρος καὶ διὰ τῶν πραγμάτων ἡ
ὀργή, νῦν μὲν ἀρχομένου τιμωρεῖσθαι τοὺς πολεμίους, προϊόντος δὲ καὶ
σφοδρότερον αὐτοὺς κολάζοντος, εἶτα τῆς παραμονῆς καὶ παντελῶς
25 αὐτοὺς ἀφανίζοντος· τότε γὰρ ἔθος ἐστὶν ἀποτελεῖσθαι τοὺς ἄνθρακας,
ἐπειδὰν τὸ πῦρ ἐπὶ πλεῖον γινόμενον τὰς ὑποκειμένας ὕλας καταφλέξῃ
τῶν ξύλων.

13 Ps. XCVI, 3.

1 contur(bantur?) A   reliqua *om*. A   2 Deo inquit A   4 magnitudinae A¹.

8ᵇ. *Ἵν' εἴπῃ — ἐπήγαγεν*: (Θεοˢ ἀντιοχ) Paris. 139, fol. 43; Vat. 1682, fol. 60ᵛ;
Cord. p. 328 (P. G., 661 D 1-9); Barbaro, p. 162.   6 *ἐνήφθη* P.
   9ᵃ. *Ἐπειδὴ — ἐπήγαγεν*: (Θεοδ°ᵘ) Paris. 139, fol. 43; Vat. 1682, fol. 60ᵛ; Barbaro, p. 161-162.
   9ᶜ. *Πυρὸς γὰρ — ξύλων*: (Θεοˢ ἀντιδοχείας) Paris. 139, fol. 43; Vat. 1682, fol. 60ᵛ
(Mai, p. 394; P. G., 661 D 11-664 A 10); Barbaro, p. 162.

Aᵉ 16-18 (p. 136, 24-25): Proprium siquidem fumi est ut ignem nun-
tiat secuturum atque ideo post intulit.   25 (p. 137, 1): Quod igni est
familiare.

The foundations of the hills were shaken (v. 7) and so on, as if to say, When God listened and was moved to anger, first everything shook, both land and mountains, then the smoke of his anger appeared as a premonition, and after this fire burst out—in other words, he was shown to be clearly wrathful in the punishment against the foes. Then in his wish to express also the intensity of the punishment, he continued the theme of his own image to say *In his anger smoke arose* (v. 8). In other words, since he always refers to God's punishing as fire, and it is his custom to present it as fire going before and depicting God's wrath against the foe, as when it says, "Fire goes forth before him,"[3] here too he follows the same custom and introduces it as though fire were shown as God and suggesting his wrath against the foe. So it is logical for him in terms of his image to say *In his anger smoke arose,* since smoke always goes ahead and suggests the burning of a fire. Hence, having made mention of the smoke, he logically went on with *Coals were kindled by him:* when fire breaks out fiercely, it happens that coals burn fiercely; so in all this he means that as soon as he heard his prayer, he moved against the enemy, and immediately everything shook. Now, his anger is suggested in stages through what happens: at one time he begins to punish the enemy, but goes further and chastises them more severely, then continues and completely wipes them out; at another time it is normal for coals to be consumed, since the fire burns more fiercely and consumes the material of the logs laid on it. |

---

3. Ps 97:3.

vv. 10-12ᵇ. Ἀλλ' ὅταν ἀπὸ τοῦ σχηματισμοῦ ἴδῃ τινὰ ἀπρέπειαν ὑπερφαινομένην ἢ ταπεινότητα, τῇ παρενθέσει τῶν ἐν μέσῳ πάλιν αὔξει τὸν λόγον, οἷον εἶπεν ὅτι Κατέβη ἐκ τῶν οὐρανῶν καὶ εἶχεν γνόφον ὑπὸ τοὺς πόδας αὐτοῦ· ἐπειδὴ τοίνυν ταπεινή τις ἐντεῦθεν ὑπεφαίνετο ἡ παρουσία, παρενέθηκε τὸ 5

Et posuit tenebras latibulum suum. Hoc, quod posuit Ascendit super Hirubim et reliqua, interpositum est ut honoratior aduentus Dei et honestior fingeretur. Iterum recurrit ad consequentiam superioris dicti, in quo ait: Caligo sub pedibus eius; conuenienter igitur iungit: Et posuit tenebras latibulum suum, ut sit secundum conexionem intellegentiae et caligo sub pedibus eius et posuit tenebras latibulum suum.

Ἐπέβη ἐπὶ Χερουβίμ, δεικνὺς αὐτὸν ὡς βασιλέα ἐφ' ἅρματος ὀχούμενον καὶ οὕτω παραγινόμενον. Εἶτα τῆς ἀκολουθίας λαβόμενος, πάλιν εἶπεν τὸ 10

Καὶ ἔθετο σκότος ἀποκρυφὴν αὐτοῦ, ἀκόλουθον ὂν τὸ καὶ γνόφος ὑπὸ τοὺς 15 πόδας αὐτοῦ.

Ἀλλ' ἐπειδὴ πολὺν περὶ τοῦ σκότους ἐποιήσατο τὸν λόγον, ὡς ὄντος ὑπὸ τοὺς πόδας αὐτοῦ καὶ ἀποκρύπτοντος αὐτούς, 20

Sic cum de scemate adsumpto aliquid uidetur indecens nasci, studet id interpositionibus recurare.

ἐδόκει δέ τις ἀπρέπεια ἐγγίνεσθαι τῷ σχηματισμῷ,

ἀσφαλιζόμενος τὸ ὑποπῖπτον, κύκλῳ αὐτοῦ φησιν ἡ σκηνὴ

αὐτοῦ. Ἀλλὰ τὸ μὲν σκότος φησὶν κατὰ τῶν ἐχθρῶν προὐβέβλητο, ἀπο- 25 κρύπτων αὐτὸν καὶ οὐδὲ ὁρᾶσθαι τοῖς ἐναντίοις ποιοῦν. Περὶ αὐτὸν δὲ ἡ σκηνὴ αὐτοῦ ἦν, ἵν' εἴπῃ τὸ φῶς, ὡς καὶ ὁ μακάριος Παῦλος περὶ αὐτοῦ φησιν φῶς οἰκῶν ἀπρόσιτον. Τῆς δὲ αὐτῆς ἐννοίας ἔχεται ἀμφότερα· ὥσπερ

28 Timoth. VI, 16.

6 possuit A et ita ll. 7, 14   8 **uper, s ex f B   hiř A, hirū B   8-9 interpossitum A   10 et] uel et A supra lin., ad in text.   fringeretur A   13 eius add. supra A, om. B¹   14 igitur] itaque B   18 suum reliqua B   22 indicens B   23 interpossitionibus A.

Ἀλλ' ὅταν — 115, 11 συστροφῇ: (Θεοδώρου ἀντιοχείας) Paris. 139, fol. 43ᵛ; Vat. 1682, fol. 61ʳ·ᵛ (Mai, p. 394; P. G., 664 A 11-D 1); Cord., p. 330; Barbaro, p. 163.   8 παραγινόμενον des. Cord.   25 προβέβλητο PV.

Aᵉ 8-10 (p. 138, 3-4): Vt non uilis esse crederetur discensio (Dei ad terras), currum Hirubin et uentorum pennas admouit.

When, however, he observes some inappropriate or unbecoming aspect developing from the image, he once more elevates his discourse with an insertion. For example, he said *He descended from the heavens and had thick gloom under his feet* (v. 9); so since his presence in this manner seemed somewhat unbecoming, he inserted *He mounted cherubim* (v. 10) to present him as a king riding on a chariot and arriving in that fashion. Then, continuing his theme, he said again *He set darkness as his concealment* (v. 11), which is in keeping with *thick gloom under his feet.* But since he had laid great emphasis on darkness as being under his feet and hiding them, and a certain inappropriateness seemed to emerge from the image, in an effort to improve the inclusion he says *his tent around him.* While the darkness enveloped the enemy, making him invisible and unable to be seen by the adversaries, around him was his tent—in other words, light: Paul says of him, "dwelling in unapproachable light."[4] Now, both expressions have the same meaning: as | he is

---

4. 1 Tim 6:16.

γὰρ φῶς οἰκεῖν λέγεται, οὕτω καὶ ἡ σκηνὴ τοῦ Θεοῦ λέγοιτο ἂν κυρίως
τὸ φῶς.

12ᶜ. Σκοτεινὸν ὕδωρ ἐν νεφέλαις ἀέρων. Παρεντεθεικὼς τὸ κύκλῳ αὐτοῦ ἡ
σκηνὴ αὐτοῦ, πάλιν ἀκολούθως τοῖς προηγουμένοις (τὸ καὶ ἔθετο σκότος
5 ἀποκρυφὴν αὐτοῦ) ἐπήγαγεν Σκοτεινὸν ὕδωρ ἐν νεφέλαις ἀέρων· ἀκόλουθον
γὰρ ἦν τὸ γνόφος καὶ σκότος· συνέχεεν γάρ φησιν ἅπαντα τὸν ἀέρα καὶ
ἐζόφωσεν καὶ ἦν τὰ πάντα σκότος καὶ γνόφος, ἀπὸ τοῦ περὶ τὸν ἀέρα
γιγνομένου σχηματίσας τοῦ Θεοῦ τὴν ὀργήν· ἡ γὰρ τοῦ ἀέρος συστροφὴ
πάντως ζόφον ἐργάζεται, γνόφος τε καὶ σκότος. Διὸ καλῶς εἶπεν σκοτει-
10 νὸν ὕδωρ ἐν νεφέλαις· ἀνάγκη γὰρ τὸ τοιοῦτον εἶναι καὶ τὸ ὕδωρ ἐν ταῖς
νεφέλαις μελανθείσαις τῇ τοῦ ἀέρος συστροφῇ.

13. *Prae fulgore in conspectu eius nubes transierunt.* Facta sunt
ergo haec de fulgore Dei, — ac si diceret de praesentia eius, qui cum
multa gloria et claritate in necem armatus aduenit.

15 21ᶜ. *Et retribuit mihi Dominus secundum iustitiam meam.* | *Iusti-
tiam* in hoc loco more suo dicit, quod ipse non laeserit eos qui
eum laedere sint parati, non illam iustitiam quae libra iudicii inter
merita discernit.

22. *Quoniam custodiui uias Domini,* reliqua. Suscepto insistit sen-
20 sui: illas se uias Domini adserit custodisse, ut caueret ne nocendo
alteri innocentiae suae corrumperet dignitatem. Illi igitur impie
egerunt in Deum, qui inimicos se sine causa et ratione profitentes
me interficere sunt conati, in quos ipse nihil quod merito culpa | ri
possit admisi.

13 ergo] uero B   15-16 iustitiam] et puritatem A   16 lesserit A laesse-
rit B   17 lidere A¹ ledere A²   libera A¹   19 reliqua *om.* A   20 custo-
diisse A²   20-21 ut–dignitatem *affert* Aᵉ (p. 140, 8-10)   21 igitur] itaque B
21-22 impii egerunt A impiegerunt B   24 admissi A.

Exegesis v. 12ᶜ mendis scatet in editione Mai, e. g. 3 παρενθεντικῶς   4 ἔθετο]
ἔκειτο   6-7 τὸν ἀέρα — τὸν ἀέρα *om.*   8 γινομένου   9 εἰργάσατο   9-10 γνόφος —
ἀνάγκη γὰρ τὸ *om.*

Aᵉ 12ᶜ (p. 138, 7-11): Ad superiora reuertitur [in] quibus ait *possuit tenebras latibulum suum* et subdendo *in nubibus tenebrosa aqua aeris* (sic).. per
hanc turbati aeris faciem mire Dei fingitur apparatus.   13 (p. 138, 12-13):
Pro praesentia Dei fulgida.   22 (p. 140, 10-12): *Nec impie* usque *meo.* Quod
fecerunt emuli qui inimicos se sine causa profitentes me interficere sunt
conati.

said to dwell in light, so too God's tent is properly called light.

Waters of darkness in clouds of air. Having inserted *his tent around him,* once more following on what went before (*He set darkness as his conceal-ment*), he went on to say *Waters of darkness in clouds of air.* Gloom and darkness are in keeping: he says he confused and darkened the sky, and everything was gloom and darkness, presenting the anger of God from the viewpoint of what was happening to the sky, the confusion of the sky causing complete darkness. Hence, he was right to say *Waters of darkness in clouds of air:* of necessity the water was like that in the clouds darkened by the con-fusion of the sky. *In the distant splendor before him clouds pass by* (v. 12). This happened, then, in respect of God's splendor—that is, his presence—since he came armed for slaughter with much glory and brightness.

The Lord will repay me for my righteousness (v. 20). By *righteousness* here, in his usual fashion, he means that he did no harm to those who were ready to harm him, not the righteousness that distinguishes between just des-erts by the scales of justice. *Because I kept the ways of the Lord* and so on (v. 21). He keeps on in the sense adopted, insisting that he has kept those ways of the Lord so as to avoid impairing the dignity of his innocence by harming another. They therefore acted in godless fashion against God who without cause or reason declared themselves my enemies and tried to kill me, though I committed nothing against them that could rightfully be faulted. |

36ᶜ. *Et disciplina tua correxit me in finem.* Disciplinam in hoc loco uocat instituta legis atque praecepta, non, sicut quidam putant, insidias ab inimicis et discrimina frequenter admota.

46ᵇ. *Et claudicauerunt a semitis suis.* Quoniam non uoluntate ad cerimonias iudaicas sed necessitate uenerunt, et paternum ergo 5 morem reliquerant et ritum alienae obseruationis non pura ac deuota mente susciperunt.

PSALMVS XVIII

In praesenti psalmo beatus Dauid institutae a Deo creaturae ordinem narrat, ipsius etiam creatoris prouidentiam operum adserit 10 testimonio atque ab elementorum ordinatione opificem nititur adprobare, qui ex hoc ipso multam curam hominum se habere signauit, dum ita elementa conponit, ut per ipsa possit agnosci. Manifestum namque est quod multa procurauerit ac uelut studio quodam egerit qualiter in hominum notitiam perueniret: qui dum humanae scien- 15 tiae prouidentiam commendat, errorem contrarii dogmatis amolitur eorum scilicet qui aut infectum mundum aut ultro ex se stetisse dicunt aut nulla aestimant prouidentia gubernari.

9 ss. cf. supra in ps. IV, p. 20-21.

1 mē A   2 institu A¹   sicut] *litt.* ic *in rasura* A   3 et] ex A   8 incipit xuiii AB   11 elimentorum AB   12-13 qui — agnosci *affert* Aᵉ (p. 145,4-6) 12 ex hoc ohoc B¹   signauit] monstrauit Aᵉ   13 elimenta A Aᵉ, a se creata *add.* Aᵉ   cognosci Aᵉ   14 uelud B   quod• • • B   15 honum A 17 exstetisse A *cf. p. 20, l. 20* extitisse B   18 estimant A.

Aᵉ **46ᵇ** (p. 144, 1-6): *Et claudicauerunt* usque *suis.* Claudicare dicuntur, dum et sacra paterna diuturna subiectione deserunt uel in gratiam dominorum [suorum] se deserere mentiuntur et in ueritatem religionis nostrae utpute inuiti non transeunt, licet affectare uideantur.

Argumentum psalmi XVIII in Aᵉ (p. 144, 27-148, 3): Hunc quoque psalmum ad euangelium transferre apostolus abusus in oportunitate sententiae dixit: *In omnem terram exiit sonus eorum* (v. 5) ..caeterum proprium argumentum eius est institutae a Deo creaturae ordinem pandere, aperire causam, per haec adprobare prouidentiam Dei qui — cognosci (v. *supra l. 12-13*). Cf. Pseudo-Beda (P. L., XCIII, 579 B): Approbatur in hoc psalmo providentia Dei, qui ex hoc ipso multam hominum curam se habere monstrauit, cum ita elementa a se creata componit, ut per (post ed.) ipsa possit cognosci.

Your instruction guided me to the end (v. 35). By *instruction* here he refers to the commandments and precepts of the law, not (as some commentators think) to the schemes and charges often adduced by the enemy.

They went limping from their paths (v. 45). Since they came to the Jewish rituals not by choice but of necessity, they therefore abandoned the paternal ways and adopted a rite of foreign observance with an attitude that was not sincere or devout.[5]

PSALM 19

In the present psalm blessed David describes the order in creation instituted by God, endorses the providence of the creator himself from the evidence of his artifacts, and strives to give proof of the artificer from the arrangement of the elements. From this very fact he indicated that he has great care for human beings, and so arranged the elements that he could be recognized through them. It is, in fact, obvious that he took great care and made a special study, as it were, of the ways he might come to be known by human beings: while he recommends providence to human knowledge, he rebuts the error of their contrary teaching, namely, of those who claim the world is not created or it exists of itself, or think it is not governed by any providence. |

---

5. Theodore's biblical text of verses 45–46 speaks of foreign sons being false to God— hence the mention here of "abandoning paternal ways."

2. *Caeli enarrant*, reliqua. Quoniam de duobus caelis illud quod est superius non uidetur, inferius uero oculis nostris ingeritur, proprie intulit: *Opera manuum eius annuntiat firmamentum. Firmamentum* utique hoc caelum uisibile | quod intuemur, manu se
5 propemodum formatum ipsa sui facie confitetur.

6. *In sole posuit tabernaculum ei.* Post caelos, dies ac noctes ad narrationem solis accessit, | discribens primo positionem eius, deinde matutinum ortum, cursum quo diem peragit, iteneris causas ac spatia. Et positionem quidem ita indicat dicendo: *In sole posuit*
10 *tabernaculum ei.* Hoc obscurius LXX dixerunt, manifestius uero interpretatus est Symmachus dicens: *Soli posuit tabernaculum in eis*, id est in caelis. Vnde manifestum est apud LXX *In* syllaba adiecta sensum esse corruptum, cuius intellectus euidenter appa-reat *Soli posuit tabernaculum in eo*, id est in caelo; quod Sym-
15 machus manifestius et plurali numero dixit: nam pro « in eo » *in eis* posuit, id est in caelis. Quidam uero non intellegentes *In* syllabae adiectionem et quod per hyperbaton dictum est *In sole po-suit tabernaculum ei*, quasi emendantes tulerunt *ei* et posuerunt *suum*, opinati quod in sole dixisset Dauid positum tabernaculum,
20 non in caelo, secundum *In* syllabae adiectionem, ita ut responderet *ei*, id est ut in eo appareret. Huic, inquit, soli tabernaculum posuit in caelo, atque hoc modo possitionem eius explicuit. Matutinum uero ortum ita indicat dicens:

Et ipse tamquam sponsus procedens de thalamo suo. Sponso con-
25 paratur sol propter splendorem nimium uel decorem: id enim

---

1 enar̄. B   reliqua] gloriam A   1-5 quoniam — confitetur *affert* Aᵉ (p. 145, 11-16)   illud efficeret Aᵉ   2 nostris oculis A   3 annuntiat *om.* A¹, adnūn A²   3-4 firmamentum *om.* A Aᵉ   4 uissibile B   quod intue-mur *om.* A¹   manus se A¹ opera manuum eius Aᵉ   6 possuit A   ei] suum A   7 solis] polis B¹   acessit A¹   7.9 possitionem A   9 quidam A possuit *in rasura* A   10 ei hoc ob *in rasura* A   11 interp̄ B interp̄datus A possuit A   12 sillaba A *et ita infra*   14-15 sim AB   16 possuit A   17 hiber-baton A   dictum] dic̄ *in rasura* A   18 emendentes tullerunt A   possuerunt A 19 tabernaculum possitum A   21 possuit A   22-118, 4 atque hoc modo — cursum *om.* B   22 matinum A   24-25 sponso — decorem *affert* Aᵉ (p. 146, 20-21).

Aᵉ 6-9 (p. 146, 13-17): Post discriptionem possitionis eius et egresus dicit et cursum sine aliquo impedimento confectum, ut alicuius potentis currendi spatia et causas simul amplectitur.   11 ss. (p. 146, 17-19): Simmachus dicit *soli possuit tabernaculum in eis*, id est in caelis habitationem mobilem soli constituit.

The heavens tell (v. 1) and so on. Since the upper of the two heavens is not seen, whereas the lower is taken in by our eyes, he was right to proceed with *the firmament announces work of his hands*. In fact, *the firmament* is this visible heaven, which we see, and by its very appearance it confesses it has been made by hand, as it were. *In the sun he set his tent* (v. 4). After the heavens, days, and nights, he went on to describe the sun, mentioning first its position, then its rising in the morning, its course by which it traverses the day, the sources and span of its journey. Its position, for example, he indicates in these terms: *In the sun he set his tent.* Though the Seventy said this rather obscurely, Symmachus rendered it more clearly: "He set a tent for the sun in them," that is, in the heavens. Hence, it is clear that in the Seventy the meaning has been spoiled by the addition of the preposition *In,* which obviously would give the meaning "He set a tent for the sun in it," that is, in heaven; Symmachus put it more clearly and in the plural, saying "in them"—that is, in the heavens—for "in it." Some commentators, however, did not recognize the addition of the preposition *In* and the fact that *In the sun he set a tent for it* was said by way of transposition; so, as if to emend it, they removed *for it* and put *his,* thinking that David had said, according to the addition of the preposition *In,* that the tent was placed in the sun, not in heaven, in such a way as to correspond to *for it,* that is, so as to appear in it. He placed a tent for this sun in heaven, he is saying, and he thus explained its position.

Its morning rising he conveys in these terms: *And he emerges like a bridegroom from his chamber* (v. 5). The sun is compared with a bridegroom on account of its exceeding splendor or charm: at that | time in particular,

temporis maxime, cum coeperit matutinus adsurgere, pulcrior oculis occurrit et gratior, commendantibus illum etiam noctis tenebris et in spectaculum eius desideriis ipsa dilatione crescentibus. Post igitur possitionem eius et egresum dicit et cursum.

7ᶜ. *Non est qui se abscondat a calore eius.* Lucem in calore 5 conpraehendit, sed in calore communis omnium utilitas est: si enim aut in uno loco tantum maneret aut per eadem semper itenera graderetur, non omnes possent eius calore contingi sed luce.

9. *Iustitiae Domini rectae.* Sicut his qui nolunt credere factori, 10 lex ista contestatio est *testimonium Domini* denuntians ultionem, ita cognoscentibus | per haec factorem optima iustificationis est causa.

10. *Timor Domini sanctus.* Haec enim non solum factorem indicant, sed etiam magnum contestantur atque terribilem. *Sanctus* 15 ergo *timor* est qui conuerti nos ad sanctum iubet, iustus qui uerum facit Dominum formidari — non hii qui idula colunt formidant.

Iudicia Dei uera, iustificata in semetipsa. Vera, quia non fallunt adnuntiatione sua; *iustificata,* id est optime statuta atque firmata.
20

14. *Et ab alienis parce seruo tuo.* Eripe me, inquit, ne sim sub hostium potestate. Alienos ergo in hoc loco hostes uocat.

Si mei non fuerint dominati usque *maximo.* Noui enim quoniam si me non praeserit hostium metus, si ab incursione eorum liber fuero, potero in requie et otio constitutus sollicitius peccata uitare. 25

---

1 caeperit matinus A   2 tebris A   3 speculum A   delatione A
post Aᵉ (p. 146, 14) cum A   3-4 igitur *in rasura* A   5 a caelore A¹
6 commonis A   8 possint B   contingui A   11 testimonium Domini
(v. 8) B *affert in margine iuxta uerbum* contestatio   denuntias A   12 iustificatiotionis A   16 qui uerum] quia uerum B   16-17 qui facit uerum
facit A   17 idula *om.* A   25 sollicitus A.

Aᵉ 3-4 (p. 146, 21-147, 1): Pulcrior et gratior procedit tenebris praecedentibus
commendatis (!) in expec⟨ta⟩tionem desideriis ipsa delatione crescentibus.
18-20 (p. 148, 6-9): Haec, inquit, iudicia uera sunt, id est non fallunt adnuntiatione sua relucere in ;factura Dei iudicium atque prudentiam; *iustificata*
uero, id est optime statuta atque firmata.

when it begins in the morning to rise, it is more beautiful and pleasing to the eyes, since the darkness of night is in its favor, and the desire for a view of it increases as it expands. So after its position he mentions also its emergence and circuit. *There is nothing concealed from its warmth* (v. 6). Although he includes light in mentioning *warmth,* it is in warmth that there is general benefit for everyone: if it were to stay in only one place or always climb through the same degrees, not everyone would be able to be affected by its heat, only its light.

The judgments of the Lord are right (v. 8): just as for those who refuse to believe in the creator that the law is an affirmation, *the Lord's testimony,* declaring vengeance, so for those who through these things recognize the creator it is an excellent cause of vindication. *The fear of the Lord is holy* (v. 9): these things not only suggest the creator, but also provide powerful and terrible witness. *Holy fear,* therefore, is that which bids us be converted to the holy, *upright* in making us dread the true Lord, which is not the dread of those who worship idols. *The judgments of God are true, justified in themselves* (v. 9), *true* because they are not deceptive in their proclamation, *justified* in the sense of being well established and secured.

And spare your servant from foreigners (v. 13): rescue me from being under the power of the enemy. By *foreigners,* therefore, he is here referring to the enemy. *If they do not gain dominion* down to *serious:* I knew that if fear of the enemy did not control me, if I were free of their assault, I would be able to be settled in rest and leisure and avoid sin more earnestly. | Yet he

Optime uero et ualde sollicite a Deo postulat dicens: *Ab ocultis meis munda me et ab alienis parce seruo tuo*. Tuo ergo adiutorio tam necessitatis quam ignorantiae lapsus effugiam: nullus quippe hominum per se idoneus est huius modi peccata uitare.

5   **15.** *Et erunt ut conplaceant*, reliqua. Pro his hymnos me tibi psalmosque dicente.

Et meditatio cordis. Ac si diceret: Cum uacauero ab omnibus occupationibus hoc meditabor, hoc agam, quae tibi placere non ambigo.

10   PSALMVS XX

5. *Longitudinem dierum in saeculum et in saeculum saeculi*. Saeculum indifferenter etiam breue tempus appellat.

10. *In tempore uultus tui*, id est: cum apparueris. Similiter etiam uultum Dei uocat apparitionem eius atque praesentiam, siue cum 15 adiuuat, siue cum uindicat.

13. *In reliquiis tuis praeparabis uultum eorum*. Multa in hoc loco commutatio est ordinis atque uerborum: nam per conuersionem dictum est (quam nisi quis aduerterit, sensum dictorum non poterit explicare; est autem difficile ad intellegendum ob hoc, quia 20 longa interpositio facta est, | per quam hiatu longo uidetur consequentia separata) | pro *in reliquiis eorum praeparabis uultum tuum*, ut sit *eorum*, quod est in fine uersus positum, adiunctum *reliquiis*, illud uero, quod ait *tuum*, *uultui* postponendum: quae quidem

1 uero] ergo AB[1]   2 me *om.* B   3 labsus B   nullus ** B   quipe A
4 uitarē A[1]   5 imnos AB   7-9 ac si diceret — ambigo *affert* A[e] (p. 149, 18-21)
7 uocauero A uacuero A[e]   8 occupantibus A   metabor A   agam] quomodo
ea faciam *add.* A[e]   10 psalmus xx *suppleui*   11 saeculi *om.* A saeē B   12 indi-
ferenter A indeferenter B   14 apparationem A   16 reliquis AB   17 commotatio A   uersionem A   18 sensum] senum A   19 autem est dificile A
20 longua interpossitio A   est facta A   21.22 reliquis A   22 possitum A.

A[e] 5-6 (p. 149, 15-18): In hoc meae uitae statu possito cum multo affectu etiam ipse respicies et efficeris iucunditate plurima ymnos me tibi psalmosque dicente.   **10** (p. 153, 14-17): Pones eos usque tui.. pro «cum apparueris» in utraque parte ussurpat hoc uel in aduersam partem uel in prosperam, siue cum adiuuat siue cum uendicat.

makes an excellent and very anxious appeal to God in the words *Purify me of my hidden faults and spare your servant from foreigners:* with your help, then, I shall avoid faults both of necessity and of ignorance, no one being able of themselves to avoid sins of this kind.

My mouth's utterances will meet with your favor (v. 14) and the rest: for this I sing hymns and psalms. *And my heart's attention:* as if to say, When I am rid of all concerns, this I shall ponder, this I shall do, being unwavering in what pleases you.

PSALM 21[1]

Length of days for age upon age (v. 4). He refers indiscriminately even to a brief time as an age.

At the time of your appearance (v. 9)—that is, when you come. He likewise refers to God's coming and presence as his *appearance,* both when he helps and when he punishes.

In your remnants you will prepare their countenance (v. 12). At this point there is considerable change in the order and the words, the statement being made with transposition; if you did not notice it, you would not be able to explain the meaning of the words.[2] It is difficult to understand because a lengthy insertion has been made, as a result of which the thought seems to be interrupted by a lengthy gap. It has been altered from *In their remnants you will prepare your countenance,* with the result that *their* at the end of the verse should be joined to *remnants,* while *your* has to be moved down to *countenance.* This | change in words, in fact, often is found also in profane

---

1. No comment by Theodore is available on Ps 20, on which Diodore had been brief and Theodoret also is more concise than usual.

2. Modern commentators admit the obscurity in the clause arising out of *hapax legomena* in the Hebrew text, Dahood (*Psalms,* 1:134) referring to Ugaritic for enlightenment. Theodore's tactic is to recast the text, as Diodore had done.

conuersio uerborum etiam apud scriptores foris positos inuenitur. Haec autem, ut diximus, consequentia dictorum est: *in reliquiis eorum praeparabis uultum tuum*, id est: Punies etiam eos qui remanserint.

14. *Exaltare* pro exaltaberis per commutationem temporum dixit.

PSALMVS XXI

Hunc psalmum beatus Dauid orationis uice cecinit, in tribulationibus quae illi ab Abisalon inlatae fuerant constitutus, in quas maxime propter peccatum adulterii perpetrati Deo fuerat permittente conlapsus.

2[b]. *Longe a salute mea uerba delictorum meorum.* Causam relictionis suae subdidit, ne ⟨per⟩ id, quod superius dixerat *Quare me*, uelut conqueri de Deo uideretur: sibi ergo ipsi adscribit. Qui uolunt hunc psalmum in Domini persona * * *, ex hoc loco praecipue conuincuntur non paruum temeritatis incurrere. Quomodo enim potest accipi quia hoc de se Dominus dixerit: *Longe a salute mea* et reliqua? Constat quidem tempore passionis suae dixisse in cruce positum: *Deus, Deus meus, respice in me*; hoc

12-13 v. 2ª   19 cf. Matth. XXVII, 46.

1 possitus A positus B   2 reliquis A   3-4 remanserunt B[1] remansēt A
5 altaberis B[1]   commotat. temporis A   7 xxi *in marg. man. rec. add.* A
8 Dauid *om.* A[1]   ortationis A   cicinit AB   9 ab *om.* A[1]   abisolon A   constitus A   10 aduulterii A adulte*rii B   11 conlabsus B   12 uerba del.] usque A
13 per *suppleui*   14 me *om.* B   conquiri A   ipsi *om.* B[1]   discripsit A[1],
uel ad(scripsit) *add. supra*   15 * * * *lacunam statui, supple e. g.* dictum esse
16 incurre A[1]   18 mea r(eliqua) A   19 possitum A   in me] r(eliqua) B.

A[e] 8-11 (p. 154, 19-155, 1) ... historiae quae narrat Dauid coniuratione Abisolon in erumnas coactum, in quibus possitus hoc carmen uice orationis cecinit. Cf. PSEUDO-BEDA (P. L., XCIII, 589): Rogat Dominum Dauid factione Absalom laborans.

In XXI, 2, 17-19 haec ostendunt Vigilius atque conc. Constantinopolitanum II. Constit., XXIII (GUENTHER, p. 257); conc. CP., XXII (MANSI, IX, 212): Eundem intellectum habet et illud: *diuiserunt sibi uestimenta mea et super uestimentum meum miserunt sortem.* Quod enim psalmus nullatenus conuenit Domino, certum est. Neque enim erat Domini Christi, *qui peccatum non fecit nec inuentus est dolus in ore eius*, dicere: *Longe a salute mea uerba delictorum*

writers. Now, as we said, this is the sequence of the words: *In their remnants you will prepare your countenance*—that is to say, You will also punish those who remain.

Be exalted is his way of saying, through change of tense, You will be exalted.

PSALM 22

Blessed David sang this psalm as a prayer when he found himself in troubles brought on him by Absalom, being caught up in them with God's permission particularly on account of the sin of adultery.

The words of my failings are far from saving me (v. 1). He includes the cause of his abandonment lest through what he said above, *Why me?* he should seem to be complaining of God; so he attributes it to himself. Those who wish ... this psalm to be spoken in the person of the Lord are led especially by this verse to become guilty of no little rashness.[1] After all, how could it be accepted that the Lord said this of himself, *far from saving me* and the rest? It is agreed, of course, that when on the cross at the time of his passion he recited this: *O God, my God, attend to me;*[2] | but these words do

---

1. Citation in footnotes by Devreesse of passages from the Constitution of Vigilius shows that our Latin text provides only fragments of Theodore's commentary on this psalm.
2. Cf. Matt 27:46.

autem dictum non omni modo ad eum psalmum hunc indicat pertinere. Neque enim quasi prius per profetiam dicto et tunc rebus
inpleto, ita hoc usus est testimonio; sed cum passionem, flagilla,
uerbera, clauos et patibulum suscipisset, consequenter hac uoce
5 usus est, quam conuenit omnes pios, cum aliquid huius modi
patiuntur, emittere. Aperte autem per haec uerba Saluator propriam
indicat | passionem, ‖ ne secundum quosdam fantasma totum pie-
tatis eius opus et misterium crederetur. Ostendit autem in his
numquam se paternae uoluntati fuisse contrarium; nam Iudei
10 ideo illum crucifigebant quasi legem solueret. Propter hanc igitur
causam hoc testimonio usus est, non quod de ipso per profetiae
uaticinium sit praedictum, aut certe de ipso psalmus iste con-
positus.

11. *In te proiectus sum ex utero.* Per hoc religiosae uitae testi-
15 monium parentibus datur: neque enim poterat ipse statim natus
se Deo deuotione oblationis offerre, sed parentes eius hoc facere
curarunt.

1 omni ∗∗ B   hunc psalmum hunc A   3 hoc *om.* A   ussus A *et
ita l.* 5   fallagilla A   4 suscipisset et A   7-8 pietas A   8 credetur A[1]
9 numquam] n̄q (neque) A   10 solueret] distrueret B[1]   igitur] itaque B
11 quod] quo B   per] prius A proprius B[1], *legendum fortasse* prius per
12 uaticinia B   salmus A[1]   12-13 conpossitus A   14 regiosae A[1]
relegiosae B.

meorum. Sed et ipse Dominus secundum communem hominum legem, dum in passione opprimeretur, *Deus, Deus meus, quare me reliquisti?* emisit uocem et apostoli *diuiserunt sibi uestimenta mea et super uestimentum meum miserunt sortem*
ad eum traxerunt manifeste, quoniam quod supra modum dictum fuerat prius
a Dauid propter inlata ei mala, hoc ex operibus euenit in Domino Christo, cuius
et uestimenta diuiserunt et sorti tunicam subiecerunt.   Constitut., xxiv
(Guenther, p. 258); conc. CP., xxiii (Mansi, 212-213). *Foderunt manus meas
et pedes*: et omnia perscrutabantur, et quae agebam et quae conabar; nam
'foderunt' ex translatione dixit eorum, qui per fossionem scrutari quae in
profundo sunt, temptant. *Dinumerauerunt omnia ossa mea*: totius meae forti-
tudinis et totius meae substantiae detentores facti sunt, ut etiam numero mea
subicerent. Istud autem ex consuetudine, quam habent hostes, dixit, qui
quando optinuerint, numero et talis subtilem notitiam inuentorum faciunt.
Propterea et sequenter dicens: *ipsi considerauerunt et conspexerunt me*, intulit:
diuiserunt sibi uestimenta mea et super uestimentum meum miserunt sortem.
'Considerantes' enim 'me', ait, 'et conspicientes' quod omnia eis euenerunt
in me desiderata ('conspicere' enim ita ut apud nos dicitur pro eo, quod est
'uidit in eum, quae uolebat pati eum'), iam tamquam me omnino malis dedito

A⁶ 16-17 (p. 157, 8-9): Tuae tutellae a parentibus commissus.

not imply that this psalm applies to him in every way. You see, he did not quote this verse as though it were said first in prophecy and then fulfilled in events; rather, when he had endured the passion, scourging, beating, nails, and gibbet, he naturally used this verse, which it behooves all pious people to recite when they suffer something of this kind. On the other hand, through these words the Savior openly conveys his own passion lest the whole work and mystery of his piety in the view of some people be believed to be imaginary. In them he shows that he was never opposed to the paternal will; thus the Jews crucified him on the grounds that he was undermining the law. This was the reason, then, that he quoted this verse, not that an oracle was given about him in prophecy, and certainly not that this psalm was composed in reference to him.

On you I was cast from the womb (v. 10). In this, witness is given to his parents for their religious way of life: he himself from his very birth could not offer himself to God as a votive offering; rather, his parents took care of this. |

17^c. *Foderunt manus meas*, reliqua. Omnia scrutati sunt opera mea, et quibus rebus confiderem uel inniterer sollicite quaesiuerunt. *Foderunt* autem dixit a similitudine eorum, qui fodiendo ea quae sunt in abdito uel depresso terrae loco conantur eruere. 5

23. *Narrabo nomen tuum fratribus meis*. Videlicet Iudeis.

26. *Apud te laus mea*. A te, inquit, mihi confertur hoc ipsum, quod exsultans laudare te possum.

28. *Omnis finis terrae*. Videlicet repromissionis.

31^b. *Adnuntiabitur Domino generatio uentura*. Filios suos dicit. 10 Nuntiabuntur tibi, id est cognoscentur a te ac maxima tibi familiaritate iungentur. *Cognouit*, inquit, *Dominus, qui sunt eius*.

PSALMVS XXII

3^b. *Deduxit me super semitas iustitiae*. Captiuitatis nos tribulationibus erudiuit, ut in callem disciplinae reuocaret ac doceret nos 15 uiis iustitiae ac ueritatis insistere.

4^c. *Virga tua et baculus tuus*, reliqua. Virgam et baculum uocauit Dei auxilium. Virgam qua infirmorum uestigia diriguntur:

12 **2** Tim. II, 19.

1-3 omnia — quaesiuerunt *affert* A^e (p. 159, 3-4) **2** mea *om.* A^e et] ex A^e ininiterer A 2-3 quaesiuerunt] q̄si ergo A quesierunt A^e quessiuerunt B 4 dipraehenso A depraesso B 6 uidelicet] ueluti A *et ita l.* 9 uidilicet B 7-8 a · te — possum *affert* A^e (p. 160, 3-5) inquit non alio A^e 8 te *om.* A^e 9 fines B repromisionis A 12 iugentur A 13 psalmus xxii *supplevi* 14 duxit B 16 uis A insistire A 17 reliqua *om.* A 17-18 uirgam — diriguntur *affert* A^e (p. 162, 6-8) uocat A^e 18 auxilium] adiutorium A^e uirga A uestiga A^1 deriguntur A^2.

sicut hostes mea post uastationem et captiuitatem diuiserunt sorte diuisionem eorum facientes '. Et euangelista quidem in Domino uerba ex rebus adsumens eis usus est, sicut et in aliis diximus: nam quod non pertineat ad Dominum psalmus, in superioribus euidenter ostendimus. At uero beatus Dauid supra modum ista magis ex his, quae ad Abessalom facta sunt, dixit, quoniam, dum recessisset Dauid, iure belli metropolim ingressus omnes quidem optinuit res regales, non piguit autem etiam patris cubile inquinare.

They dug my hands (v. 16) and the rest: they examined all my doings and closely inquired into what I trusted and relied on. Now, he said *dug* as a figure from those who by digging try to come up with what is in hiding or in a sunken part of the land.

I shall tell of your name to my brothers (v. 22), namely, the Jews.

From you comes my praise (v. 25): by you this is bestowed upon me, that in my exultation I can praise you.

All the ends of the earth (v. 25): that is, the land of promise.

The generation to come will be reported to the Lord (v. 30). He refers to his sons: They will be reported to you, he is saying—that is, they will be known to you and related to you in close familiarity. "The Lord knows those who are his," Scripture says.[3]

PSALM 23

He guided me in the paths of righteousness (v. 3): he corrected us with the troubles of the captivity so as to call us back to narrow ways of discipline and teach us to adhere to the paths of righteousness and truth.

Your rod and your staff (v. 4) and so on. By *rod and staff* he refers to God's help, a rod being the way by which infirm people's steps are guided. |

---

3. 2 Tim 2:19; cf. Num 16:5.

siquidem moris est his, qui capti | sunt oculis, duce uirga ac praeuia
qualitatem agendi iteneris explorare: baculum uero, qui suppleret
sustentatione sua quod captiuitatis fuerat miseriis inminutum; nam
homines infirmi et senes innituntur baculis.

5

PSALMVS XXIII

Sollicite beatus Dauid atque admota in hanc rem opera profetat in praesenti psalmo, uolens quidem omnes homines ad studium
uirtutis accendere, sed praecipue Iudaeos ac populum in Babilone
ducendum. Praedicit ergo longe antea | non debere eos de diuino
10 adiutorio disperare, sed studium omne ad correctionem uitae emen-
dationemque conuertere, per quod utique possint etiam de captiuitate reuocari.

1. *Domini est terra et plenitudo eius.* Quia haec opinio apud
Iudeos erat, quod in Iudea tantum Deus habitaret, — nam et ob
15 hoc putabant non oportere in extraneis locis sollempnitatem ei
debiti cultus adhiberi, sicut et in centesimo tricesimo sexto psalmo
ait: *Quomodo cantabimus canticum Domini in terra aliena?* — hoc
ergo nunc dicit beatus Dauid quoniam Non debetis, uelut in extraneis locis, longe uos a Deo positos aestimare nec putare illum
20 non posse aliquid uobis opis adhibere. *Ipsius,* inquit, *est omnis
terra,* reliqua.

7. 9. *Adtollite portas, principes, uestras. Principes* uocat sacerdotes ac duces populi. Imperat ergo illis profeta: Heia, inquit, o
principes, portas quae prius fuerant clausae patefacite.

17 Ps. CXXXVI, 4.

2-3 baculum — inminutum *affert* A⁰ (p. 162, 9-11)   baculum A⁰ baculus AB
3 miseris •A   4 homines] omnes A¹B, uel homines *add. supra* A²   5 psalmus *supplevi*   6 admota * * A   8 iudeos A   9 longue A   debere] de••r A¹
10 disp. adiut. A, auiutorio B¹   correptionem A   11 conuertire A¹   13 plenitudo eius] plinitudo est A, plenitudo reliqua B   14 ob *om.* A   16 debeti B
centissimo AB   tricesimo *om.* AB   17 canticum — aliena] reliqua B
18 ergo *om.* A¹   quoniam] quomodo A   19 possitos A   estimare non A.

A⁰ 6-8 (162, 26-163, 1): Praedicitur de populo, immo praecipitur (!) in praesenti psalmo quibus uitae sufragiis ualeat de captiuitate Babilona liberari.
Cf. Pseudo-beda (P. L., XCIII, 604): Ex persona populi in Babylone degentis
oratio formatur. 1 (163, 2-3): Ne in Iudea tantum crederent seruiendum Deo,
ubi uideretur tanquam propria habitatio.

At least it is normal in the case of those with weak eyes to explore the way of conducting their journey with a rod guiding them and going ahead. A staff, on the other hand, was to make up with its support for what had failed through the hardships of captivity, infirm and elderly people leaning on staffs.

PSALM 24

In the present psalm blessed David carefully prophesies also works performed to this purpose, wishing to stimulate all people to the pursuit of virtue, but in particular Jews and the people being conducted to Babylon. He therefore predicts long before that they should not despair of divine help, but rather direct every effort to correction and reform of their life with a view to being able also to be recalled from captivity.

The earth is the Lord's, and its fullness (v. 1). This opinion prevailed among the Jews, that God dwelt only in Judah—hence their thinking it was not proper to honor the observance of due worship to him in foreign places, as it is said also in Psalm 137, "How shall we sing a song of the Lord in a foreign land?"[1] So here blessed David says, Though in foreign parts, you should not believe that you are far removed from God, nor think that he cannot bring you any support. All the earth is his, and so on.

Lift up your gates, rulers (v. 7). By *rulers* he refers to the priests and leaders of the people. So the prophet orders them, Ah, rulers, open the gates that previously were closed. |

---

1. Ps 137:4.

PSALMVS XXIV

3ᵇ. *Confundantur iniqua agentes superuacue.* Illos conatibus suis uotiuo exitu distitutis confundi oportet, qui nobis sine causa tanta inferunt mala.

4. *Vias tuas, Domine, notas fac mihi et semitas tuas edoce me.* 5
Sicut uiam hominum uocat actus atque studia (ut est illud *Viam mandatorum tuorum cucurri,* ac si diceret: Facere mandata tua atque obseruare decreui) ita et uiam Dei appellat quicquid Deus aut creando aut dispensando dignatur operari. *Doce* ergo *me uias tuas,* dicit, id est: Fac me in opere tuo atque dispensatione laetari; sicut 10
et in xv psalmo | ait: *Notas mihi fecisti uias uitae,* ⟨hoc est⟩ In uitae me securitate certissima collocasti. Quas autem dispensationes Dei uidere desiderat?

5. *Direge me in ueritate tua et doce me, quoniam tu es Deus saluator meus.* Vt cum de diuina misericordia loquitur, ueritatem ei 15
frequenter adiungit, hoc indicans quod misericordia eius sit uera nec aliquo umquam fallat incerto; ita et in praesenti loco, | quia petiuerat salutem sibi a Deo debere conferri, ueritatis ei merito nomen adsciuit, ac si diceret: Praesta mihi ueram atque indubitatam salutem. *Doce* autem *me, quia tu Deus saluator meus;* prout 20
diceret: Saluum me fac, ait *Doce me,* id est: Ipsis rerum effectibus fac me ad deitatis tuae notitiam peruenire. *Direge* ergo *me et doce me,* salutem quam postulo conferendo. *Deduc* autem *me* posuit pro In ipsa me rei, quam postulo, possessione constitue, ex similitudine eorum qui ducatum uiae ignorantibus 25
praebent.

6-7 Ps. CXVIII, 32   11 Ps. XV, 11.

1 psalmus xxiu *supplevi*   3 distitutos A   4 infer∗ A¹   5 et — edoce]
usque A   6 atque] ac B   9 dispensando] dissipando A   tuas tuas A
10 fac — laetari *affert* Aᵉ (p. 166, 3-4)   opere — atque] tua Aᵉ   11 salmo A
hoc est *supplevi*   12 disideras A, uel — t *add. supra* desideras B   14-15 quoniam — saluator] usque A   15 de *om.* A¹   17 nec] non A   aliquor A¹
18 a] ad A   19-20 praesta — salutem *affert* Aᵒ (p. 166, 5-6)   19 atque] et A
indubitam A¹   20 autem *om.* A¹   21 me *om.* A¹   22 dietatis A   dirige B
23 conferendo ei A   24 possuit A   in *om.* A   postolo B.

PSALM 25

Let those who break the law for no reason be confounded (v. 3): those who inflict such troubles on us without cause should be confounded, and their exploits deprived of the outcome they desire.

Make your ways known to me, Lord, and teach me your paths (v. 4). As he refers by *way* to people's actions and exploits (as in that verse, "I have run in the way of your commands,"[1] as if to say, I determined to do and observe your commands), so he calls God's *way* whatever God deigns to do by creating or arranging. So *teach me your paths* means, Make me rejoice in your acting and planning, as he says in Psalm 16, "You made known to me the paths of life"[2]—that is, You guaranteed me security in life. Now, which arrangements of God does he desire to see?

Guide me in your truth and teach me that you are the God who is my savior (v. 5). Just as in cases when he is speaking of divine mercy he often associates him with truth, indicating that his mercy is true and never fails through any uncertainty, so too in the present case, because he begged that salvation should be conferred on him by God, he properly applies to him the term truth, as if to say, Grant me true and unquestioned salvation. Now, *teach me that you are the God who is my savior:* as if to say, Save me, he says *Teach me*—that is, Cause me to arrive at the knowledge of your divinity by the actual outcome of events. *Guide me and teach me,* therefore, by according the salvation that I beg. Now, he put "Lead me" in the sense, Grant me possession of what I beg, by comparison with those who provide the ignorant with leadership along the way. |

---

1. Ps 119:32.
2. Ps 16:11.

8. *Dulcis et rectus Dominus.* Est illi, inquit, familiaris misericordia; est etiam cura iustitiae. Dissimulat quidem bonitatis suae
studio saepe peccata, nec singulorum actus seuera examinatione
deiudicat; sed cum uiderit quosdam in erroribus sine emendatione
5 persistere, admouet iustitiae rigorem et flagillat ut corrigat, atque
amaritudine uerberum in disciplinam reducit errantes. Hoc ergo
ut manifestius faceret beatus Dauid ait: *Propter hoc legem dabit
delinquentibus in uia.* Quoniam, inquit, ita bonus est, ut rectus esse
non desinat, ob hoc ad recti callem auios castigando conpellit.
10 Quod ergo ait *legem statuit,* hoc est: Sicut legis magisterio, ita
peccatores tribulationibus inlatis facit aduersisque meliores, sicut
et in nono psalmo dictum est *Constitue, Domine, legislatorem super eos,* ⟨ubi⟩ conuersionem de correptione uenientem | legislationem uocauit, quae in se utrumque et recti curam et bonitatis stu
15 dia contineret. Nam peccatores castigare atque corripere ad officium
pertinet ueri, mala autem facientes non in totum punire | sed meliores tribulationibus uelle facere, opus misericordiae atque bonitatis.

9. *Direget mansuetos in iudicio, docebit mites uias suas.* Iterum
in praesenti loco *Direget* ac *docebit,* ita ut in superioribus, ad ef
20 fectus retulit rerum. Ita enim superius dixerat *doce* et *direge,* id
est: Praesta mihi ipsam rem quam postulo, atque in eius me possessione constitue, — hoc est dicere: In uias suas nos cum iudicio
et examinatione reuocabit, cum prius castigationibus suis emendauerit atque correxerit. Quae sunt istae Dei uiae, ad quas cum *iu
25 dicio* conuertit emendatos ac reuocat?

10. *Vniuersae uiae Domini misericordia et ueritas.* Istae sunt,
inquit, uiae Domini. Ex more uero suo ueritatem et misericordiam
copulauit ac si diceret: Hoc est opus Dei, haec uia eius, haec operatio
eius, ut firmam ac ueram quibus decreuerit praestet salutem.

12-13 Ps. IX, 21   20 v. 5.

1-2 est — iustitiae *affert* Aᵉ (p. 166, 23-24)   inquit *om.* Aᵉ   2 disimulat A
3 sepe A   nec] non A   seuera] seruare A   5 corregat A   6 uerborum A
8 ita inquit A   esse *om.* A¹   10 ergo *om.* A¹   magistro A¹   11 aduersariisque melioris A   13 ubi *suppleui*   14 uocauit *om.* A¹   curam et] et *om.* A
16 punire] peruenire A¹   17 misserico∗rdiae B¹   18 diregit B   docebit — uias] usque A   21-22] possesione A   22-23 in uias — examinatione
affert Aᵉ (p. 167, 2-3)   23 et] atque B   examin∗∗∗ A¹   reuocauit A¹   26 istae]
iustae B   27 inquit *om.* B¹   27-29 ex — salutem *affert* Aᵉ (p. 167, 4-7)
uero *om.* Aᵉ   misericordiam et ueritatem A   28-29 hoc est — operatio eius]
haec est operatio A, haec est uia id est opus Dei Aᵉ   29 praestat Aᵉ.

Good and upright is the Lord (v. 8): mercy is customary with him; righteousness is his constant concern. Often, in fact, he obscures sin with a show of his goodness, and he does not submit individuals' behavior to harsh scrutiny; rather, when he sees some people persisting in their errors without amendment, he applies the rigor of justice and chastises them for the purpose of correcting them, and by the bitterness of the blows he brings the errant ones back to a life of discipline. Hence, to make this clearer, blessed David said *Hence he will legislate for sinners in the way:* since he is so good as not to cease to be upright, he therefore drives the recalcitrant to the straight and narrow by chastising them. Hence his saying *He will legislate*—that is, As by the teaching of the law, so by the imposition of tribulations and adversities he makes sinners better, as is said also in Psalm 9, "Appoint them a lawgiver, Lord,"[3] where by *lawgiver* he refers to conversion coming from correction, which involves both things, attention to righteousness and works of goodness. To the exercise of truth, you see, it belongs to chastise and correct sinners, whereas it is the work of mercy and goodness not to punish evildoers totally but by tribulations to make them want to be better.

He will guide the gentle in judgment, he will teach the gentle his ways (v. 9). Likewise in the present case, *He will guide and teach,* as above, he referred to the outcome of events: above he said *guide and teach*—that is, Grant me the very thing I ask and allow me to possess it, as if to say, He will recall me to his ways by judgment and scrutiny when he has first corrected me by chastisement and reform. What are these *ways* of God to which he converts and recalls those reformed by *judgment*? *All the ways of the Lord are mercy and truth* (v. 10): these are the ways of the Lord. Now, he habitually links truth and mercy, as if to say, This is God's work, this his way, this his action, to accord secure and true salvation to those he has chosen. | He

---

3. Ps 9:20.

Has uias etiam nos docebit, id est cum nos conuerterit et correptione sua meliores effecerit. Quod erit, inquit, huius conuersionis
lucrum uel quales erunt in reliquum qui fuerint hanc misericordiam consecuti?

10[b]. *Requirentibus testamentum eius et testimonia eius propter*   5
nomen tuum, Domine. Hi, inquit, quos reddiderint aduersa meliores, quibus fixam et inmobilem misericordiam largietur, hoc lucri
de correptione et correctione sua capient, | ut per legis obseruatio-
nem et mandatorum Dei custodiam digni fiant quibus misericordia
conferatur.   10

11. *Propter nomen tuum, Domine.* Ac si diceret: Praestabis his
misericordiam, qui, ut tibi placerent, omne studium curamque posuerunt et qui legem tuam tota mente perquirunt.

12. *Quis est homo qui timeat Dominum?* Ad ea quae praemisit
consequenter intulit. Dixerat de Deo quod esset *suauis et rectus*   15
et quod correptionibus peccatores conuerteret ⟨et⟩ faceret meliores. Nos, inquit, sua animaduersione correctos miseratus est atque
efficaciter docuit ut mandata eius seruare curemus. | Bene ergo
intulit: *Quis est homo qui timeat Dominum?* Quicumque, inquit,
timuerit Dominum...   20

Legem statuit ei in uia quam elegit. Etiam hoc superioribus con-
nexum est, sed per commutationem temporis dictum: nam *statuit*
dixit de praesenti. Non ergo hoc indicat, quoniam timenti se Deus
legem ponat, sed qui timere Dominum et in uia eius, quam sibi
ipse elegit, ambulare decreuerit, — ut ambulare *in uia quam elegit*   25
et *timere Dominum* unum atque idem esse uideatur et a communi

15 v. 8.

1 uias eius A   1-2 correctione A   2 efficerit B   4 secuti A   5-6 et testimonia — tuum] usque A   testimonia] testī B   6 hii A   6-7 melioris A[1]
7 misericordiam A   8 correctione] correption AB   capient uel A   8-9 obser-
uationem] obseruantiam A   13 possuerunt A   perquirunt tuta mente A
16 correptiobus A[1]   et *suppleui*   faciret A   18 curremus A   19 timeat] timī A
tī B   quicumq(ue *in rasura*) A   inquit] *litt.* it *in rasura* B   20 timueruit A[1]
post Dominum *plura desiderantur, cf. infra* A[e]   21 eglegit A   21-22 conexus A[1]
connexus A[2]B[1]   22 commot. A   24-25 ipse sibi A   26 timemere A[1]   ā commoni A.

A[e] **10**[b] (p. 167, 8-11): Qui fructus eorum erunt quos reddiderunt aduersa
meleores? Testamentum eius et testimonia deligenter exquirent ut digni fiant
diuina clementia atque misericordia.   **20** *Haec uidentur supplenda ex* A[e] (p. 167,
15-18): Sub scemate inquirentis uel putius (potius?) dubitantis indicat solum
illum posse consequi quae superior sermo discripserit.

will also teach us these ways, that is, when he converts and makes us better by correction.

What, he asks, will be the benefit of this conversion, and in what condition will they be in future who are granted this mercy? *Those who seek out his covenant and his testimonies for your name's sake, O Lord* (vv. 10–11): those whom adversity made better, whom he will regale with unchanging and continuing mercy, will gain this benefit from chastisement and correction, namely, becoming worthy through observance of the law and keeping God's commandments to have mercy conferred on them. *For your name's sake, Lord:* as if to say, You will grant mercy to those who devoted every attention and care to pleasing you, and who devote themselves to your law with all their mind.

Who is the person who fears the Lord? (v. 12). He logically proceeded with what he had already said. He had said of God that he is *good and upright* and that he converts sinners through correction and makes them better; he had mercy on us when corrected by his attention, he said, and taught us efficaciously to be careful to observe his commands. So he was right to go on with *Who is the person who fears the Lord?* Whoever fears the Lord, he is saying, … *He will legislate for him in the way he has chosen.* This too is related to the above, but expressed with a change in tense, taking *will legislate* in a present sense: he implies that God imposes his law not on the one fearing him but on the one who has chosen to *fear the Lord* and *walk in his way,* which he had personally chosen for himself (*walking in the way he has chosen* and *fearing the Lord* seeming to be the same thing and understood alike). *He will legislate* | —that is, He will regale him with all the good

intellegi. *Legem statuit,* id est: Omnia quidem ei bona quae praesens uita postulat largietur, praecipue tamen ea quibus animae
uirtus augeatur.

13. *Anima eius in bonis demorabitur.* Vult dicere quoniam prae-
5 stabuntur nobis bona, si timuerimus Deum et ad manda|torum eius
custodiam fuerimus intenti.

14c. *Et testamentum eius ut manifestetur eis.* Graeca lectio hoc
uidetur dicere, quoniam testamentum Dei rerum utilium conferat
disciplinam; in ebreis uero uoluminibus ita est positum: *Sed et*
10 *testamentum suum manifestabit eis*; ita namque et Symmachus
ait: *Et pactum suum notum faciet illis,* id est: Ipse eis et ultor
adstabit et uoluntatem propriam, per quam discant quae his
agenda sint, faciet esse manifestam.

21. *Innocentes et recti adheserunt mihi, quoniam sustinui* ⟨*te*⟩.
15 Spe in te posita talis esse studui ut innocentes mihi iungerentur
ac mea familiaritate gauderent.

PSALMVS XXV

In populo Israhel, quem captiuum Nabocodonosor rex Babilonem adduxit, fuerunt, etsi perpauci numero, Deo moribus et studio
20 uirtutis accepti, qualis fuit Ezechiel, Danihel ac tres pueri aliique,
quos in simili uitae proposito legis magisteria continebant. Et quoniam consequens erat huiusmodi uiros pro conscientiae bono habere non paruam apud Deum confidentiam ac postulare ab eo captiuitatis solutionem, profetat ⟨Dauid⟩ in multis psalmis ex persona
25 eorum ac loquitur quae illis uideantur merito conuenire; e quibus
psalmis iste unus est, quem conamur exponere.

4 quoniam] quomodo A   4-5 praestabunt A   5 ad *om.* A   9 possitum A
10 suum] eius A   manifestabit] manifes A   et *om.* A   sim A simm B   12 ad-
stauit A¹   per] si (secundum?) A   13 manifestam] *reliqua fortasse praebet* Aᵉ
(p. 168, 6-8): Inter caetera bona notitiam suae uoluntatis dignis aperit.
14 te *suppleui*   15 in te posita] interpossita A   studui ut] studiuit A   16 fami-
liariatate A   17 xxu A *in marg.* xxu∗∗ B   18-19 babī A bab̄ B   19 pauci A¹
20 daniel A   tres] iii A   aliique] aliqui A   21 propossito A   22 consc.]
continentiae A   23 postolare A   24 dauid *suppleui*   25 merito uideantur A.

18-26 cf. Aᵉ (p. 169, 20-26): Psalmus Dauid ex persona captiuorum apud
Babilonem uerum sanctorum componitur carmen profetiae.. qui pro bono
conscientiae captiuitatis resolutionem confidentius postularent (= P. L., XCIII,
608-609), idcirco meritis eorum conuiniens aptatur oratio.

things that the present life requires, especially those by which virtue of soul is promoted. *His soul will repose in good things* (v. 13). He means that good things will be provided to us if we fear God and are bent on observance of his commandments.

And his covenant to make revelations to them (v. 14). The Greek text seems to say that God's covenant will confer training in useful things, whereas in the Hebrew volumes it is expressed this way: "But he will also manifest his covenant to them." Symmachus also puts it this way: "And he will reveal his treaty to them"—that is, He will both take his stand as their avenger and make known his will, through which they may learn what has to be done.[5]

Innocent and upright people stayed close to me, because I waited for you (v. 21): placing my hope in you, I took pains to be such a person that innocent people might associate with me and take pleasure in my company.

PSALM 26

Among the people of Israel whom Nebuchadnezzar, king of Babylon, took captive there were those, even if very few in number, who were acceptable to God for their behavior and pursuit of virtue. Such were Ezekiel, Daniel and the three boys, and others who observed the law's teachings in a similar pattern of life. Since it followed that men of this kind had no little influence with God for the sound state of their conscience and begged him for the end of the captivity, blessed David in many psalms prophesies on their part and says what seems very appropriate to them. This is one of those psalms, and we do our best to interpret it. |

---

5. Although it is the first half of the verse that has considerable textual problems, Theodore passes over that part to find a lesser difficulty in the second half, where in fact the LXX is ambiguous. Symmachus is closer to the Hebrew and may have been Theodore's way to access "the Hebrew volumes": To which textual resource is he referring?

1. *Iudica mihi, Domine, quoniam ego in innocentia mea ingressus* ⟨*sum*⟩. Non est legendum, sicut quidam legunt, *Iudica me, Domine.* Si enim ita legatur *Iudica me*, intellectum facit longe contrarium, ut uideatur dicere: Condemna me, sicut et in quinto psalmo quibusdam inpraecatur ac dicit: *Iudica illos, Deus*; hoc autem oranti 5 pro se non conuenit postulare. Legendum ergo *Iudica mihi*, id est Iudica pro me et in ultionem meae oppressionis accingere. *In innocentia mea*: hoc uocat innocentiam suam, nihil quod alicui incommodet atque obsit operari.

Et in Domino sperans | *non infirmabor*, pro Non sum infirma- 10 tus in fide; mutauit tempus ex more. *Iudica*, inquit, *mihi quoniam* ab innocentiae proposito non recessi neque, ex quo spem in te posui, aliquid dubitationis incurri. Et quoniam dixerat se a proposita sibi spe non esse deductum, probari hoc a Deo postulat, quem operum suorum scit idoneum testem futurum, atque ait: 15

2. *Proba me, Domine*, reliqua. Vt scias uera esse quae dico.

Vre renes meos et cor meum. A similitudine auri sumpsit hanc uocem, cuius qualitatem prodere solet ignis; *renes* uero cogitationes uocat, ex quibus motus et concupiscentialis generatur affectio; nam concupiscentia naturae insita cogitationes nouit inportunas et 20 adsiduas suscitare.

3. *Quoniam misericordia tua ante oculos meos est.* Ad illud, quod dixerat *Et in Domino sperans non infirmabor* *** *quoniam misericordia tua*, reliqua. Vnum namque atque idem est sperare in Domino et ad misericordiam eius uelut oculis intentis aspicere. Ad 25 id uero, quod ait *In innocentia mea ingressus sum*, subdidit *et*

---

5 Ps. V, 11; cf. supra in IX, 20   23 v. 1ᵇ.

1 mihi] me A   mea *om.* B   2 sum *suppleui*   3 longe facit A   4 contemna A   4-5 .u. psalmo quibus A   6 dicere postulare AB¹   7 oppraesionis A   8 suam] sīm A   10-11 pro — fide *affert* Aᵉ (p. 169, 28-29)   pro non] non *om.* A¹   infirmus Aᵉ   11 in fide *om.* B¹   motauit A   12 proppossito A   recesi A   ex quo ex quo B   13 possui A   aliquit B   14 esse] ne A   15 ideneum A¹   17 ure] uere A¹   sumpsit auri A   19 * * uocat, dx̄ (dixit) *eras.* B   20 inportunitas AB   23 *** *lacunam statui, supple e. g.* consequenter intulit   23-24 misericordia] missecor A mīs B   24-25 in domino *om.* A   26 in *om.* A.

Aᵉ 18-19 (p. 170, 3-5): Pro cogitationibus quae sunt motus mentis a quibus concupiscensialis generatur affectio.   22-23 (p. 170, 7): Hoc est quod supra *et in Domino sperans.*

Give me a just verdict, O Lord, because in my innocence I have kept to the straight and narrow (v. 1). It is not to be read, as some commentators claim, *Judge me, Lord:* if it is read *Judge me,* it gives quite a different sense, as though to say, Condemn me, as also in Psalm 5 he appealed in the words "Condemn them, Lord,"[1] which is not appropriate for a suppliant to ask for in his own case. So it is to be read as *Give me a just verdict*—that is, Judge in my favor and take action to avenge my oppression. *In my innocence.* By *my innocence* he claims that no one could find anything out of order as an obstacle to this being done.

And by hoping in the Lord I shall not fail: I am not weak in faith (he changed the tense, as usual). *Give me a just verdict,* he is saying, because I did not swerve from my innocent purpose, nor did I have any doubts about the hope I placed in you. And since he said that he had not been led astray from the hope placed in him, he asks this to be confirmed by God, who he knows is a suitable witness of his actions. He goes on with *Test me, Lord* (v. 2) and so on, so that you may know what I say is true. *Use fire to test my entrails and my heart.* He made a comparison with gold, whose quality fire usually reveals. By *entrails* he refers to thoughts, from which arise movements and feelings of concupiscence; he knows that nature's innate concupiscence stirs up inappropriate and recurring thoughts.

Because your mercy is ever before my eyes (v. 3). To what he had said *And by hoping in the Lord I shall not fail ... because your mercy* and so on: it is one and the same thing to hope in the Lord and to look to his mercy as though with fixed gaze. To what he said, *In my innocence I have kept to the straight and narrow,* he added | *and I took delight in your truth.*

---

1. Diodore had made the distinction at this point.

conplacui in ueritate tua. Hinc iam prolixius narrat quomodo, ut placeret Deo, ab omni studuerit iniquitate seiungi, dicens: *Non sedi,* reliqua.

6. *Lauabo inter innocentes manus meas.* Illos, inquit, refugiens
5 studebam istis iungi, quibus studium est peccata uitare. Consuetudo erat antiquis, cum se uoluissent | a quorumcumque societate suspendere, lauare manus suas.

7. *Vt audiam uocem laudis*, reliqua. Id est: ut me narrante mirabilia tua alii erumpant in uocem actionis gratiarum.

10 **9. *Ne perdas cum impiis animam meam.*** Ne longo tempore in eorum societate positus a propositi sui disciplina atque honestate mutetur.

12. *Pes meus stetit in directo.* Nosti, inquit, quemadmodum a recti tramite numquam in praua | detorserim. *Benedicam te, Do-*
15 *mine.* Post reditum ...

PSALMVS XXVI

1b. *A quo trepidabo.* Plus est non trepidare quam non timere: semper enim quasi minoribus maiora subduntur.

2a. Ἐν τῷ ἐγγίζειν ἐπ' ἐμὲ κακοῦντας τοῦ φαγεῖν τὰς σάρκας μου.
20 Ἡνίκα οὖν πλησίον οὗτοι γεγόνασιν, ὡς καὶ ἀπογευσάμενοί μου τῶν σαρκῶν· τοῦτο γὰρ βούλεται εἰπεῖν τὸ τοῦ φαγεῖν τὰς σάρκας μου, ὥστε δεῖξαι αὐτῶν τὴν ὠμότητα καὶ τὴν ὀργὴν μεθ' ἧς ὥρμων ἐπ' αὐτούς. Τὸ

1-2 placeret] procederet A proceret B¹   2 studierit A   sé iungi A   4 nocentes A
in* noc̄ B   meas om. B   5 studiebam A, studiui innocentibus coniungi —
uitare *affert* Aᵉ (p. 170, 20-22)   est studium Aᵉ   5-6 seutudo A¹ conseutudo A²
10 an. meam om. B   11 societate *bis scriptum* A¹   possitus A   praepossiti A
12 motetur A   13 dreō A   dir̄ B   quemadmodum] quam A   15 reditum]
cetera fortasse seruauit Aᵉ (p. 171, 20-22): (Post reditum), inquit, meum in
conuenticulis nostris non quiescam tibi gratiarum actiones ymnosque cantare   16 psalmus xxui *suppleui*   17 tripidabo tripidare AB   non om. A.

2a. Ἡνίκα — κακοῖς: (Θεοˢ 'Αντιοχ) Vat. gr. 754, fol. 82ᵛ (Mai, p. 394-395; P. G., 665 A 2-10); Coisl. 10, fol. 45.   22 ὥρμουν V.

Aᵉ 1-2 (p. 170, 8-11): Enumeratio est latior, quemadmodum uel quibus Deo placuerit dum ab omni iniquitate studierit seiungi.   9-14 (p. 171, 9-10)... uerentur ne uicti scilicet prauorum cohabitatione moterentur.

From this point he outlines at greater length how, to please God, he made it his concern to be separated from all iniquity, saying *I did not sit* and the rest. *I shall wash my hands among innocent people* (v. 6): shunning the others, I took care to associate with those who have a concern to avoid sin. It was a custom with the ancients, when they wanted to remove themselves from association with people of some type or other, to wash their hands.[2] *So as to hear the voice of your praise* (v. 7) and so on—that is, So that when I recount your marvels, they may burst out in a sound of thanksgiving.

Do not destroy my soul along with ungodly people (v. 9), lest he spend much time in their company and be diverted from the discipline and integrity of his purpose.

My foot stood on level ground (v. 12): you know how I never strayed from the path of righteousness into evil ways. *I shall bless you, Lord.* After the return ...

PSALM 27

Of whom shall I be in dread? (v. 1).[1] Having no dread is more than not fearing: greater things always take second place to lesser ones. *When evildoers pressed upon me to devour my flesh* (v. 2): when these people were nearby, then, as though even tasting my flesh (the meaning of *to devour my flesh,* bringing out their savagery and the rage with which they advanced upon them). The term | *pressed upon* means "when they were so near as not to

---

2. Cf. Deut 21:1–9; Ps 73:13 (a doublet of this verse); Matt 27:24.

1. Theodoret informs us that in other forms of the LXX (not in the Hexapla, he adds) he found attached to the psalm title, "A psalm of David," a further phrase, "before he was anointed" (PG 80:1048). Before proceeding to justify it, he dismisses those who "reject all the titles as lacking authenticity"—Diodore's explicit position, and effectively Theodore's.

δὲ ἐγγίζειν, ἀντὶ τοῦ ἡνίκα οὕτω πλησίον γεγόνασιν, ὡς μηδὲν ἐλλείπειν πρὸς τὴν ἐκπλήρωσιν τῆς προθέσεως αὐτῶν. Καλῶς δὲ αὐτοὺς κακοῦντας ἐκάλεσεν, ὡς διὰ τὴν προσοῦσαν αὐτοῖς ἰσχὺν ἅπαντας μυρίοις περιβαλόντας κακοῖς.

2ᵇ. Οἱ θλίβοντές με καὶ οἱ ἐχθροί μου αὐτοὶ ἠσθένησαν καὶ ἔπεσαν. 5 Καλῶς τὸ αὐτοί, ὅτι ἡμᾶς μὲν ἠδίκησαν οὐδέν· ἔπαθον δὲ ταῦτα αὐτοὶ ἅπερ ἡμᾶς διαθεῖναι προσεδόκων. Ἐμφαντικώτερον δὲ τὸ ἠσθένησαν καὶ ἔπεσον **, ἀντὶ τοῦ οὐχ ὑπὸ πολεμίων ἀνῃρέθησαν, οὐδὲ ὑπὸ ἀνθρώπων ἔπαθόν τι δεινόν, ἀλλὰ παραδόξως ἄνευ πάσης ἀνθρωπείας χειρὸς ἐξαίφνης εἰς ἀσθένειαν τῇ τοῦ Θεοῦ κατηνέχθησαν τιμωρίᾳ. 10

3ᵇ. Ἐὰν ἐπαναστῇ ἐπ᾽ ἐμὲ πόλεμος, ἐν ταύτῃ ἐγὼ ἐλπίζω. Ὅτι ἀπόδειξιν ἔχων αὐτάρκη τὰ γεγονότα τῆς τοῦ Θεοῦ βοηθείας, παρεμβολῆς ὅλης κινηθείσης καὶ πολέμου, δέδοικα οὐδένα, ταύτῃ πεποιθὼς τῇ τοῦ Θεοῦ συμμαχίᾳ. Τὸ δὲ ἐν ταύτῃ, τουτέστι τῇ βοηθείᾳ καὶ τῇ συμμαχίᾳ τοῦ δεσπότου.

5ᵃ. Ὅτι ἔκρυψέν με ἐν σκηνῇ ἐν ἡμέρᾳ κακῶν μου. Ὥσπερ τινὶ σκηνῇ 15 τῇ οἰκείᾳ σκεπάσας βοηθείᾳ, μετὰ πολλῆς με τῆς ἀσφαλείας ἐφύλαξεν. Σκηνὴν γὰρ τοῦ Θεοῦ καλεῖ τὴν βοήθειαν ὡς σκεπάσασαν αὐτὸν ἀπὸ τῶν κακῶν, τὸ δὲ ἔκρυψεν ἀντὶ τοῦ ἐφύλαξεν, ἀπὸ τοῦ κατακρύπτειν ἀεὶ τοὺς βουλομένους τι φυλάττειν. Ἐν ἡμέρᾳ δὲ τῶν κακῶν μου, ἐν τῷ καιρῷ τῆς συμφορᾶς, ὅτε πολλῶν προσεδόκησα πειραθήσεσθαι κακῶν. 20

5ᵇ. Ἐσκέπασέν με ἐν ἀποκρύφῳ τῆς σκηνῆς αὐτοῦ. [Σκηνὴν καλεῖ τοῦ Θεοῦ τὴν βοήθειαν]. Καὶ εἰπὼν ὅτι ὡς ἐν σκηνῇ με κρύψας ἐφύλαξας, ἐπήγαγε τὸ ἐν ἀποκρύφῳ τῆς σκηνῆς αὐτοῦ, τὸ ἀσφαλέστατον τῆς βουλῆς τοῦ Θεοῦ σημάναι βουλόμενος.

5ᶜ. Ἐν πέτρᾳ ὕψωσέν με τῆς αὐτῆς ἔχεται ἀκολουθείας. 25

2ᵇ. Καλῶς — τιμωρίᾳ: (Θεοϛ Ἀντιοχ) Vat. 754, fol. 82ᵛ (Mai, p. 395; P. G., 665 A 10 — B 3; cf. P. G., LXXX, 1049 n. 64); Coisl. 10, fol. 45ᵛ (anonym.); Paris. 166, fol. 67ᵛ (αντιοχ). 6 τὸ αὐτὸ Paris. 166 ἔπαθον δὲ καὶ Coisl. et Paris. 166 7 προσεδόκουν Paris. 166 8 ** lacunam statui, supple e. g. ἐπήγαγεν.

3ᵇ. Ὅτι ἀπόδειξιν — δεσπότου: Vat. 754, fol. 82ᵛ, τοῦ αὐτοῦ (Mai, p. 395; P. G., 665 B 4-8); Coisl. 10, fol. 45ᵛ (Θεοϛ).

5ᵃ. Ὥσπερ τινὶ — κακῶν: (Θεοϛ Ἀντιοχ) Vat. 754, fol. 83 (Mai, p. 395; P. G., 665 B 9 — C 1); Coisl. 10, fol. 46-46ᵛ.

5ᵇ. Σκηνήν — βουλόμενος: Coisl. 10, fol. 46ᵛ (Θεοϛ αν̄); Paris. 166, fol. 68 (Θεοδρ) 21-22 σκηνὴν — βοήθειαν reieci (cf. supra l. 17).

5ᶜ-6ᵃ. Τῆς αὐτῆς ἔχεται ἀκολουθείας — 131, 4 ὑψώσεται: Borgianus gr. 2, fol. 140ʳ·ᵛ: Ὁ Μοψυ(εστίας).

be short of fulfilling their purpose." Now, he was right to refer to them as evildoers, since on account of the strength they possessed they enveloped everyone in countless troubles. *Those who distressed me and my foes themselves fainted and fell.* He was right to say *themselves* to give the sense, Though doing us no harm, they themselves suffered the fate they expected ours to be. The phrase *fainted and fell* is more emphatic in the sense, They were not wiped out by the enemy nor did they suffer abuse from people; instead, strangely, without any human hand, they suddenly were reduced to impotence by God's punishment.

If war broke out against me, I would still hope in it (v. 3): because I have in what has happened sufficient proof of God's assistance, I fear nothing, even if the enemies' complete array should be assembled, trusting as I do in support from God (*in it* meaning "in the assistance and support of the Lord"). *Because he hid me in his tabernacle in the days of my troubles* (v. 5): by sheltering me with his characteristic help as though by some tabernacle, he guarded me with tight security (by God's *tabernacle* referring to his help as sheltering him from troubles, and *hid* meaning "guarded," from the invariable practice of concealment by those wishing to guard something). *In the day of my troubles:* at the moment of disaster, when I expected to be subjected to many troubles. *He kept me in hiding in his tabernacle.* After saying, He guarded me by hiding me in a tabernacle, he added *in hiding in his tabernacle,* wanting to underline the tight security of God's plan. *He set me high on a rock* maintains the same sense. |

6ᵃ. Καὶ νῦν ἰδοὺ ὕψωσεν τὴν κεφαλήν μου ἐπ' ἐχθρούς μου. Τὸ δὲ καὶ νῦν ἰδοὺ ἐκ τοῦ ἑβραϊκοῦ ἐπισέσυρται. Βούλεται γὰρ εἰπεῖν Καὶ νῦν ἀνώτερόν με πεποίηκε τῶν ἐχθρῶν· τοῦτο γὰρ λέγει τὴν κεφαλήν μου. Τὸ ὕψωσας ἀντὶ τοῦ ὑψωθήσεται.

5   6ᵇ. Circuiui et immolaui in tabernaculo eius, reliqua. Tabernaculum templum dicit. Commutauit etiam tempora, ut praeteritum diceret pro futuro.

8ᵇ. Exquesiuit facies mea, id est Quaeret, tempore commutato.

10ᵇ. Ὁ δὲ Κύριος προσελάβετό με. Ὑπὸ δέ σοῦ φησι προσελήφθην 10 καὶ ἐπαιδεύθην τὴν εὐσέβειαν, — ἵνα μὴ δόξῃ τὴν γνῶσιν τῆς εὐσεβείας τῇ ἑαυτοῦ ἐπιγράφειν προθέσει, ἀλλὰ τῇ τοῦ Θεοῦ χάριτι. Ταῦτα μέντοι ὅλα φησὶν ἀκολούθως ὅτι Ἐρῶ ἐν τῷ τὸ θυσιαστήριον κυκλοῦν, τοῦτο βουλόμενος εἰπεῖν ὅτι καὶ ὑπὲρ τῶν παρελθόντων εὐχαριστήσω καὶ περὶ τῆς ἑξῆς βοηθείας σου δεηθήσομαι, πρὸς ἕτερον δὲ οὐ βλέψω οὔτε μὴν παρ' 15 ἑτέρων τῶν καλῶν ἐκδέξομαι.

12ᵃ. Μὴ παραδῷς με εἰς ψυχὰς θλιβόντων με. Κἂν ἐγώ φησι μὴ ἄξιος ὦ τοῦ τυχεῖν τῆς παρά σου βοηθείας, ἀλλὰ διὰ τοὺς ἐχθροὺς μὴ ἐάσῃς με αὐτοῖς παραδοθῆναι, μὴ δὲ παθεῖν τὰ ἐκείνοις περισπούδαστα. Τοῦτο γάρ ἐστι τὸ εἰς ψυχάς, τούτοις τοῖς βουλήμασιν αὐτῶν μὴ παραδῷς με 20 καὶ ταῖς ἐπιθυμίαις.

12ᶜ. Et mentita est iniquitas sibi. Aquila manifestius dixit Et apparuit iniquitas. Tuo adiutorio claruit quod mendaciter loquerentur et uane, et se ipsam iniquitas seduxit, non alios.

12 Ps. XXV, 6.

6 commotauit A   praeteri|teritum B   8 exquessiuit B   queret B   commotato A; in eodem loco A plures uoces affert, in margine alia manu longe posteriore additas, quae ad textum minime spectare uidentur: ego seg coi et et ego (?) 21 dicit A   22-23 adiutorio tuo — uane affert Aᵉ (p. 173, 31-174, 1)   22 loquentur Aᵉ.

10ᵇ. 12ᵃ. Ὑπὸ δὲ σοῦ — ἐπιθυμίαις: (Θεοˢ Ἀντιο⸴) Vat. 754, fol. 84; Coisl. 10, fol. 47ᵛ-48.

Aᵉ 6ᵇ (p. 173, 4): In hoc loco tabernaculum templum dicit.   10-11 (p. 173, 19-20): Religiose Deo adscribit inbumenta legis.   12 (p. 173, 23-28): Et si non merita mea meruerint, saltim inimicorum meorum feritas te ad opem ferendam commoueat.. animas uocauit hostium uota atque consilia.

Now see, he lifted my head above my foes (v. 6). The phrase *Now see* is also a slovenly translation of the Hebrew: he means, He now caused me to be superior to my foes (the meaning of *my head,* and *lifted* meaning "will be lifted"). *I circled about and sacrificed in his tabernacle, tabernacle* meaning "temple." He also changed the tense, using past for future. *My face sought you out* (v. 8)—that is, "will seek," the tense being changed.

But the Lord accepted me (v. 10): I was accepted by you and schooled in piety (lest he seem to attribute the knowledge of piety to his own initiative, and not to God's grace). He says all this, of course, in keeping with the statement "I love to move around the altar,"[2] meaning, I shall give thanks on behalf of all comers and beg your help in future, and shall have no eyes for anyone else or expect anything even from other good people.

Do not hand me over to the souls of those harassing me (v. 12): even if I am not worthy to receive help from you, on account of the enemy do not allow me to be handed over to them or suffer what they have in mind. This, in fact, is the meaning of *to the souls:* Do not surrender me to their schemes and desires. *Injustice gave false testimony against itself.* Aquila said this more clearly: "And injustice was unmasked"—it became clear with your help that they spoke falsely and wrongly, and injustice deceived itself, not others.[3] |

---

2. Ps 26:6 loosely cited.
3. No comment is extant on vv. 13–14.

PSALMVS XXVII

1ᶜ. *Et adsimilabor discendentibus in lacum.* Discendentes *in la-cum* appellat mortuos siue morientes, quoniam apud multos id temporis haec erat opinio, quod deorsum nescio quo sub terram abirent mortui; neque enim resurrectionis aut paradisiacae habi- 5
tationis uel certe ascensionis in caelum notitiam tunc habe-bant.

PSALMVS XXVIII

Post inlatam a Deo iram quae consumpsit Assyrios (nam cae sis CLXXXV milibus reliqui timore conpulsi soluta obsidione fuge- 10
runt) oportebat beatum Ezechiam pro diuini cultus studio et reli-gionis cura oblatis Deo uictimis gratiarum uota persoluere, quia fuerant praeter spem per Deum aduersa omnia dissoluta. Ob hoc igitur hunc psalmum | beatus Dauid sub eiusdem Ezechiae persona cecinit, eumque post caedem Assyriorum introducit Deo triumpha- 15
les hostias immolare. Nemo autem miretur si, quosdam psalmos exponentes praetermisisse Ezechiam diximus post collatam sibi de Assyriis uictoriam | uota gratiarum et ob hoc fuisse graui infirmi-tate correptum; postea tamen poenituisse eum de neglecto officio in aliis psalmis ostendimus, ex quibus est hic praesens in quo 20
gratiae Deo pro collata aguntur uictoria et de offerendis aperte hos-tiis imperatur. Beatus enim Dauid futura praedicens loquitur ex persona eorum qui interfuturi erant rebus ac negotiis post futuris, et ea loquitur non quae ab illis sine dubio erant dicenda, sed quae

9-11 cf. Is. XXXVII, 36   11-13 cf. II Paralip. XXXII, 22-23.

1 psalmus xxuii *supplevi*   2 adsimulabor AB   3 siue] pro A   moren-tes A¹   id est A   4 opio A¹   paradisi|cae A   7 xxuii A xxuiii *man. rec.*
9 Assirios A *et infra* Assiriorum. Assiriis   9-10 cessis AB   10 obseditione A
10-11 fugerunt] fuerunt A¹   11 ezechiel A   11-12 religionis B   13 fuerā A
per Deum] domini A   desoluta A   ob] ab A   14 igitur] itaque B   15 cicinit A
cem A¹ cedem A²B   17 praetermisse A   de] ab A   18 uta A *ota B¹   ob]
ab A   19 penetuisse A   21 uitoria A   offendis A¹   21-22 hos***tiis B
22 Dauid *om.* B   futur A¹   24 illis] liis (his?) A   sed quae] sed A.

Aᶜ *Argumentum ps. XXVIII* (p. 175, 28-176, 3): Profetatur qua exor-tatione Ezechias ab Assiris et a periculo mortis abductus ussurus sit ad Iudeos ut gratiarum actiones agantur Deo et uota reddantur pro tantis beneficiis. *Eadem fere leguntur in* PSEUDO-BEDA (P. L., XCIII, 622).

PSALM 28

I shall become like those going down into the pit (v. 1). By *those going down into the pit* he refers to the dead or dying, since many at that time had the idea that the dead went somewhere or other under the earth. At that time they had no knowledge of resurrection or living in paradise, and certainly not of ascension into heaven.

PSALM 29

After the effect of God's anger that consumed the Assyrians (one hundred eighty-five thousand fell, and the rest fled, thus ending the siege),[1] it behooved blessed Hezekiah as part of his attention to the divine cult and his devotion to piety to perform rites of thanksgiving with victims offered to God because against hope all troubles had ceased, thanks to God. For this reason, therefore, blessed David sings this psalm in the person of the same Hezekiah, and presents him as sacrificing victims to God in celebration of the slaughter of the Assyrians. Now, let no one be surprised if in commenting on certain psalms we said that, despite the victory over the Assyrians granted him, Hezekiah neglected rites of thanksgiving and hence was struck with a serious illness.[2] We showed him in other psalms nonetheless later repenting of his neglect of duty; this present psalm is one of them, and here thanksgiving is made to God for the granting of victory, and the command is given for public offering of victims.

Blessed David, note, in foretelling the future, speaks in the person of those destined to be involved in events and affairs happening later; he mentions not things that doubtless would have been said by them, but those | that

---

1. Cf. 2 Kgs 19:35–36.
2. Cf. 2 Kgs 20.

conueniebat illis dicere et quae pro successu rerum ipsa consequentia suggerebat. Simul etiam docet posteros, ut prosperatis
negotiis suis studeant circa Deum deuoti esse semper et grati. Et
quid dico posteros? Omnes etiam homines, quibus praestante Deo
5 res ex uoto proueniunt, instituit quae illos dicere de Deo et sentire par sit. Non ergo quasi omni modo dicenda, sed quasi conuenientia ac rebus apta praeloquitur; ideoque ergo hunc psalmum
ita conposuit, eo quod uerba congruant rebus, ac docet huius
modi sermonibus uti Ezechiam siue post collatam uictoriam siue
10 de periculo infirmitatis ereptum. Ob hoc namque et sub populi in
Babilone positi persona talia frequenter loquitur, quae transcen-
dant quidem mensuram eorum, tamen necessaria sint ad continen-
das in timore diuino animas et pietatis magisteria conferenda;
qualis est maxime xli psalmus et si qui sunt eius similes,
15 in quibus religiosae et deuotae in Deum mentis affectus ostenditur.

6. *Et comminuit eas tamquam uitulum Libani.* Quidam *uitulum
Libani* in hoc loco putauerunt | dici eum ‖ quem uulgus appellat,
id est foetum bouis, hoc modo conantes exponere: *Tamquam* uitu-
20 lus, inquit, est ferus et indomitus qui inter siluarum lustra nutri-
tur, ita etiam istos ualidos et potentes infirmos fecit ac debiles. Sed
particula *tamquam*, quae posita est, hoc sic non permittit intellegi.
Neque enim ita dixit *et confringit uitulum Libani*, sicut dixerat
Confringet Dominus cedros Libani, sed *Confringet eos tamquam ui-
25 tulum Libani.* Vnde, si secundum istum intellectum accipiatur, erit
contrarium: si enim ferus est et potens Libani uitulus, — dicit autem
quod ita eos confringat ut uitulum Libani, — manifestum est quod
eos pro similitudine inducta ualidos faciat ac robustos. Non ergo
hoc dicit, sed *uitulum* in hoc loco uoluit dicere pro uitulamine:
30 ita namque et Hebraeus habet *sicut uitulamina Libani; uitulamina*
uero *Libani* dicuntur parua uirgulta, quae sunt pro ipsa sui tenuitate

24 v. 5ᵇ.

1 illis] eis A   sucessu A   2 suggerabat A   8 conpossuit A   11 possiti A   tali A   11-12 transcendunt A   13 diuino] personas A   15 religo-
sae A   17 uitulum Libani] uituleuani A   18 leuani A   19 tamquam] quam A
quoniam B   20-21 nutritus A   21 facit A   dibiles A   22 possita A   est
om. A   intell. non permittit A   24 2° *loco* confring A confrīn. B   25 si *om.* A
26 libā A, *litt.* a *in rasura et ita l.* 27   uitulū A   27 ita *om.* A   confrin-
guat A   28 pro *om.* A   rubustos A   29 in hoc — 134,8 surgentia *edidit*
MURATORI, *Antiq. Ital.,* III, 858 A   30 hebreus A.

it was appropriate for them to say and would also give hints of the outcome. At the same time he also teaches later ages to be sure to be always devout and grateful to God when things turn out well for them. Why mention later ages? He also instructs all people for whom, with God's help, things turn out as desired in what it is right for them to say and feel about God. It is not, therefore, as though he were foretelling what absolutely would have been said, but what was appropriate and suited to the occasion. Hence, he composed this psalm so that the words would match the events, and he teaches us that Hezekiah used words of this kind whether on the granting of the victory or on his recovery from the perils of illness. It is, in fact, for this reason that also on the part of the people located in Babylon he often mentions such things as transcend their limited reference and yet are required for keeping souls in the fear of God and conveying teachings of piety—for example, Psalm 42 in particular and any others like it, in which is revealed the condition of a mind that is pious and devoted to God.

He beat them to powder like the calf of Lebanon (v. 6).[3] Some commentators thought that by *calf of Lebanon* here reference is made to a common term, the offspring of an ox, and they try to explain it this way: As a calf is wild and indomitable and feeds itself in the forest glades, so too he made those strong and powerful people ailing and weak.[4] But the particle *like* occurring here does not permit such an interpretation: he did not say, "And he shatters the calf of Lebanon," as he had said *He will shatter the cedars of Lebanon* (v. 5), but *He will beat them to powder like the calf of Lebanon*. Hence, if it were taken in the other sense, there would be a contradiction: if the calf of Lebanon is wild and strong (he says that he would beat them to powder like the calf of Lebanon), it is clear from the figure involved that he would make them sturdy and robust. This is not what he means here, then; rather, here by moschos he meant "sucker," the Hebrew also likewise having *like the suckers of Lebanon*. By *suckers of Lebanon* reference is made to small plants that by their very slenderness are | fragile. And since he had

---

3. Devreesse does not accept from Angelo Mai (PG 66:665) a comment on v. 3: "Of this abyss of murmuring waters David says, *The voice of the Lord over the waters*." After the lengthy statement on the psalm's point of view, comment is extant on only two verses.

4. Theodore could not know that the psalm has pagan origins and that, as Dahood says, "virtually every word can now be duplicated in older Canaanite texts" (*Psalms,* 1:175), which accounts for the unusual animal imagery. He takes a lead from Diodore to disqualify (wrongly) the meaning "calf" for the form in his text, μόσχος, and choose the other available meaning, "young plant." He is in error in faulting the LXX's version of the Hebrew, and his appeal to Syriac, also a language with which he is unfamiliar, is not seconded by the Syriac-speaking Theodoret, who thinks instead of the golden calf in the wilderness.

fragilia. Et quoniam *cedros Libani* Assyrios uocauerat propter ingentes corporum formas, intulit *et comminuit eos tamquam uitulamen Libani.* Ita, inquit, illos sublimes et grandes breui tempore comminuit atque contriuit sicut uitulamina, quae exilitate sui facile conteruntur. Syrus namque quod hic positum est, *et comminuit eos tamquam uitulum Libani,* ita ait: *Inimicos sicut germina cedrorum. Germina* autem *cedrorum* optime uirgulta uocauit ab arborum radice surgentia.

6[b]. *Et dilectus,* reliqua. Id est Israhel; ita Syrus *Israhel. Sicut filius unicornium,* id est Saluabitur.

8. *Vox Domini concutientis desertum.* Sicut superius ait quia *intonuerit,* ita etiam hoc loco quod commouerit desertum, quod etiam terrae motus fuerit et locus ille tremore concussus sit in quo erant Assyrii, quem ante *desertum* fecerant.

Et commouebit Dominus desertum Caddis. Eadem repetit | *desertum* indicans, quod desertum Caddis non est, ut quidam putauerunt scriptum *Cadis,* sed *Caddis.* Caddis uero non est nomen loci atque regionis, sed *caddis* dicitur a Syro uel Hebreo sanctum. Sanctum ergo dixit locum qui erat ante ciuitatem, in quo Assyrii castra posuerunt. Et remansit hic sermo secundum linguam syram uel hebraeam etiam in uoluminibus graecis, ut Adonai atque Sabaoth et alia similia.

---

1 assirios A   2-3 uitū. A uīt. B   4 exsilitate A   5 sirus A *et ita infra* possitum A   commī AB   6 gremina A   9 israhel ... israhel (pro σαριών?) 10 saluabitur] roborabitur A   11 disertum A *1º loco*   12 comminuerit A   13 concusit A   15 cadis AB   15-22 eadem — similia *ed.* MURATORI, *loc. cit.* 15 repetit] sepe A saepius *Mur.*   16 cadis A[1]   18 cadis B   19 dicit *Mur.* assirii A asyrii B   20 possuerunt A   21 in] hoc A.

A[e] 1-5 (p. 177, 1-3, 9-12): Assirios (appellat) per metaforam a superba altitudine a firmitatis successu et ualentia corporum.. Pro uitulaminibus.. uitulatamina (*sic*) enim dicuntur parua uirgulta, quae se subieciunt sub ingenti huius modi arboris umbra.   17-20 (p. 178, 3-8): Ebreus uel Sirus Cadis legit non Cades, quod interpretatur sanctum.. cum ergo locum indicat (Cades) qui in prospectu ciuitatis sanctae uel templi situs in exitium Assiriorum motus et sanctus abussiue dictus est.

called the Assyrians *cedars of Lebanon* on account of their huge frame, he went on to say *He beat them to powder like the sucker of Lebanon.* So he is saying, Those who are lofty and mighty he beat to powder in a short time and crushed like suckers, which are easily crushed by reason of their fragility. For what is said here, in fact, *He beat them to powder like the shoot of Lebanon,* the Syriac has "enemies like the seeds of cedars," by "seeds of cedars" expressing in excellent manner stems rising from the trees' roots.

And the beloved and the rest—that is, Israel, the Syriac also having "Israel." *Like a son of unicorns*—that is, he will be saved.[5]

The voice of the Lord, who shakes the wilderness (v. 8). As he said above that *he thundered* (v. 3), so here too he says that he shook the wilderness, there being an earthquake, and that place was shaken where the Assyrians were, which they had previously made a wilderness. *The Lord will shake the wilderness of Kadess.* He repeats the same words to suggest the wilderness, which is not the wilderness of Kadesh, as some thought from a form Kades, but Kadess. Kadess, however, is not the name of a place or district; rather, it means "holy" in Syriac and Hebrew. So he calls holy the place that previously was a city where the Assyrians pitched camp. This term retained its form in Syriac and Hebrew even in the Greek volumes, like "Adonai," "Sabaoth," and other similar terms. |

---

5. Theodore would have done better to leave well enough alone in a clause where the LXX seems to have missed the sense of the Heb. completely, coming up with "unicorns." He will make an unnecessary and equally unsuccessful appeal to Hebrew and Syriac in the next verse.

PSALMVS XXVIIII

Interfectis Assyriis et bello, quod instabat ciuitati contra omnem spem Dei adiutorio dissoluto, multum beato Ezechiae gloriae atque elationis accessit, cunctis illum iure stupentibus cunctisque laudan-
5 tibus quod ita in gratiam eius res mirae ac plenae terrore conti-gerant. Elatus est ergo animo | ipsa rerum magnitudine ac laude multorum, sicut in Paralipomenis scriptum est, *et corruit Ezechias ab exaltatione cordis sui.* Ob hunc ergo mentis tumorem, ut cu-raret eum Deus atque ad sanitatem redire conpelleret, graui illum
10 malo corporeae infirmitatis implicuit et passus est usque ad uici-niam mortis accedere, quo ipsa disperatione uitae suae nihil de se superbum sentire doceretur ac disceret non sibi magnum aliquid sed Deo adscribere, per quem ita gloriosus exstiterat. Tali igitur curatione medicatus sanitati eum reddidit et a periculo quoque,
15 quod metuebat, mortis eripuit. Haec nunc beatus Dauid profetat sub persona eiusdem Ezechiae agentis gratias quod fuerit ab errore correctus et de infirmitate liberatus et [quod] ab hostibus erutus, ac pro omnibus studet grates referre.

2. *Quoniam suscipisti me.* Videlicet de morte in uitam redire
20 fecisti.

Nec dilectasti inimicos meos. Vel finitimas gentes uel quosdam de populo suo qui gaudebant de | morte illius.

.   7 II Paral. XXXII, 24 ss.   7-8 v. 26.

---

   1 explicit xxuiii B, incipit xxuiiii A, xxuiiii B   2 assiriis A   3 disoluto *ex* disolato A   multo A   4 stupientibus AB   5 ac] atque A   7 paraliponis A conruit A   8 exaltitune A   8-9 curat A[1]   10 inplicuit A   13 igitur] itaque B   14 reddit A   16 agentis gentis A[1] gratis A[1]   17 de *om.* A[1] quod *deleui*   18 studeat AB   gratias A   19 uli A[1] ueluti A[2] uidilicet B 21 infinitimas A.

   A[e] 6-18 (p. 179, 2-13): Elatus Ezechias uictoriae et tam gloriose pro euentu, ut historia Paralipiminon testis est, qua ait *Conruit Ezechias ab exaltatione cordis sui,* egrotatione correptus est ut humanae fragillitatis admonitione didiceret adrogantiam.. sub eius deinde persona ab errore correcti ab infir-mitate salua[l]ti el ab hostibus eruti gratiarum actio hoc carmen profetatur. Cf. PSEUDO-BEDA (P. L., XCIII, 625).   *In ll. 21-22 (p. 179, 20-180, 7) fusiora leguntur.*

PSALM 30

The slaughter of the Assyrians and, with God's help in defiance of all expectation, the end of the war that pressed upon the city brought great glory and elation to blessed Hezekiah. Everyone was rightly astonished at him, and everyone was full of praise for his successful emergence from the remarkable and terrifying events. He was, as a result, carried away by the very magnitude of events and the plaudits of everyone, as is written in the Chronicles, "Hezekiah was carried away by the exultation of his heart."[1] As a result of this conceit, therefore, God afflicted him with a grave attack of bodily infirmity to cure him and force him to return to sound thinking, and he was ill to the point of dying. By actually despairing of his life he was taught to claim no credit for himself, and he learned to attribute any great achievement not to himself but to God, through whom he emerged with such glory. By this treatment, then, he cured him, restored him to good health, and also snatched him from the danger of death that he was fearing.

Blessed David now prophesies this in the person of the same Hezekiah when giving thanks for being saved from error, released from illness, and rescued from the enemy, and he makes the effort to give thanks on behalf of everyone.

Because you have supported me (v. 1)—that is, You caused me to return from death to life. *You have not let my foes rejoice:* either the neighboring peoples or some of his own people who were pleased about his dying. | *Lord*

---

1. Cf. 2 Chr 32:23.

3. Κύριε ὁ Θεός μου, ἐκέκραξα πρός σε καὶ ἰάσω με. Ἀντὶ τοῦ ἐκέκραξα καὶ ἐδεήθην· ἐνήλλακται γὰρ κἀνταῦθα ὁ χρόνος. Ἐν τούτοις οὖν φησιν ὑπὸ τῆς ἀρρωστίας καταστὰς καὶ γνοὺς ἐκ τῶν συμβεβηκότων τὴν τῆς φύσεως ἀσθένειαν, ἔγνων ὅτι πρός σε δεῖ βοῆσαι καί σου δεηθῆναι καὶ παρά σου τὴν βοήθειαν ἐκλέξασθαι. 5

5. *Psallite Domino sancti eius.* Consequenter, velud ad emendationem culpae suae, ingerit memoriam praestitorum ⟨beneficiorum⟩.

6. *Quoniam ira in indignatione eius,* reliqua. Iram uocat poenam atque supplicium; siquidem iram diuina scriptura esse uult non primum motum tantum sed permanentem indignationem. Iram 10 ergo malum ultionis appellat, indignationem uero commotionem quae in peccatores merito suscitatur, nominibus ex consuetudine nostra mutuatis. Quoniam, inquit, et ulciscitur iratus et proposito est ac uoluntate beneficus.

6ᶜ. *Ad uesperum demorabitur fletus,* reliqua. Id est demoratus 15 est; tempus est ex more mutatum.

9. *Ad te, Domine, clamabo,* reliqua. Id est clamaui.

10. Τίς ὠφέλεια ἐν τῷ αἵματί μου; Ἀντὶ τοῦ ταῦτα ἔλεγον· Ἐὰν ἀποθάνω τί τὸ ὄφελος; Ἀποθανὼν γὰρ διαφθείρομαι, τέφρα γινόμενος καὶ σποδός. 20

7 beneficiorum *suppleui* (*cf. infra* Aᵉ)   8 reliqua *om.* A   9 siquidem] quidem A   12 nominibus] noḇ (nobis) A   13 mutuatis] commotatis A commutatis B *in textu* mutuatis *in margine*   propossito A   15 flēt B   reliqua *om.* AB¹   16 tempus est] est *om.* A   16 motatus A.

3. Ἀντὶ τοῦ — ἐκλέξασθαι: (Θεοˢ ἀντιοˣ) Vat. 754, fol. 88ᵛ; Coisl. gr. 10, fol. 54; Paris. gr. 166, f. 77 (anon.)   2 χρόνος] des. Paris.
10. Ἀντὶ τοῦ — σποδός: (Θεοˢ ἀντοˣ) Vat. gr. 754, fol. 89 (Mai, p. 395; P. G., 665 C 10-12); Coisl. 10, fol. 54.

Aᵉ 5 (p. 180,14-16): ... quam graue fuerit quod mutus priora beneficia Dei transierit conualescens..   6ᶜ Aᵉ (p. 181, 6-7): Demorabitur autem pro demoratus est possuit.   10 Aᵉ (p. 181, 25-27): Quae erit utilitas si mortuus fuero et extinctus corrum par atque in cinerem redegar et fabillas.

my God, I cried to you and you healed me (v. 2)—that is, I cried and begged (a change of tense occurring here, too). So he is saying, Reduced to this condition by illness and aware of the weakness of nature from what befell me, I realized that I needed to appeal to you and beg you and receive help from you.

Sing to the Lord, you his holy ones (v. 4). Logically, as though to atone for his fault, he recalls to mind benefits supplied. *Because there is wrath in his anger* (v. 5) and so on. By *wrath* he refers to punishment and retribution, by *wrath* the divine Scripture meaning not only the initial response but also lasting anger. So by *wrath* he refers to the awful process of vengeance, and by *anger* the effect it rightly has on sinners, the terms being interchanged as usual. He means, Because he takes vengeance when angered and is beneficent by purpose and intention. *Weeping will last until evening* (v. 5) and the rest—that is, it lasted (with the usual change in tense).

I shall cry to you, O Lord (v. 8) and the rest—that is, I cried. *What good is there in my blood?* (v. 9)—that is, I said this: If I die, what is the good of that? In dying I decay and become dust and ashes. |

13. Καὶ οὐ μὴ κατανυγῶ. Εἰπὼν οὐ μὴ κατανυγῶ, ἀντὶ τοῦ οὐ μετα-
γνώσομαι ἐπὶ τῇ ψαλμωδίᾳ, ἐπήγαγεν
Εἰς τὸν αἰῶνα ἐξομολογήσομαί σοι,　In aeternum confitebor tibi.
τουτέστι διατελέσω σοι ἀπαύστως　　　Aeternum uitae suae tempus
5 εὐχαριστῶν, αἰῶνα καλῶν τὸν τῆς　　appellat.
οἰκείας ζωῆς χρόνον.

PSALMVS XXX

3ᶜ. Γενοῦ μοι εἰς Θεὸν ὑπερασπιστήν. Ὑπεράσπισον καὶ ἐπάμυνον ἐν
τοῖς κακοῖς. Ἰδίωμα δὲ τοῦτο ἑβραϊκόν, ἀντὶ τοῦ ὑ π ε ρ ά σ π ι σ ο ν λέγειν
10 γενοῦ μοι εἰς Θεὸν ὑπερασπιστήν, ὡς καὶ ἀλλαχοῦ Καὶ ἐγένετό μοι Κύριος
εἰς καταφυγήν, ἀντὶ τοῦ κατέφυγον ἐπ᾽ αὐτόν.

5. Ἐξάξεις με ἐκ παγίδος ταύτης ἧς ἔκρυψάν μοι. Παγίδα ἐκάλεσε τὴν
αἰχμαλωσίαν ἐφ᾽ ᾗ συνείληπτο, ὥσπερ εἴς τινα κίνδυνον προφανῆ. Τὸ δὲ
ἧς ἔκρυψάν μοι ἀκολούθως εἶπεν τῷ παραδείγματι, ἐπειδὴ παγίδα τὴν αἰχ-
15 μαλωσίαν ἐκάλεσεν. Ἴδιον δὲ τῆς παγίδος τὸ λανθανόντως τίθεσθαι κρυπ-
τομένην, οὕτω τε ἀπροόπτως λαμβάνειν τοὺς θηρωμένους.

6. *In manus tuas commendo spiritum meum.* Tuae tuitioni animam meam committo atque custodiae: tu eam saluam fac atque
defende. Notandum uero quoniam hac uoce usus est Dominus in
20 patibulo constitutus, non quod profetice de ipso dicta sit, sicut
opinantur quidam, sed quod ei inter mortis ac passionis pericula

---

Argumentum psalmi XXX fortasse seruatum est a Pseudo-Theodoro Heracleensi (cf. Vat.
gr. 627, ff. 41-42; latine sine auctoris nomine apud Barbaro, p. 271).　　10-11 Ps. XCIII, 22
19 Luc. XXIII, 40; ct. supra p. 120-121.

4 tempus uitae suae A　　7 explicit xxuiiii A　explicit B　　17 tutioni A
18 aeam A¹　　20 quo A　　21 quo AB　ac] et A.

13. Εἰπὼν — χρόνον: (Θεοᵟ αντοˣ) Vat. gr. 754, fol. 89ᵛ (Mai, p. 395; P. G., 665 D
2-6); Coisl. 10, fol. 54ᵛ; Paris. 166, ff. 78ᵛ-79　3 εἰς τὸν αἰῶνα] αἰωνίως Paris. 166.
3ᶜ. Ὑπεράσπισον—ἐπ᾽αὐτόν: (Θεοᵟ αντοˣ) Paris. 166, fol. 79ᵛ; Coisl. 10, fol. 55ᵛ;
Vat. 754, fol. 90; cf. P. G., LXXX, 1077 n. 99.　　ὑπεράσπισον — κακοῖς *affert*
Petrus Laod. (Cord. I, 526).　　9 ἑβραϊκῇ 754.
5. Παγίδα — θηρωμένους: (Θεοᵟ᾽ αντοˣ) Vat. 754, f. 90ᵛ (Mai, p. 395; P. G., 668 A
6-12); Coisl. 10, fol. 55ᵛ-56.　　14-15 αἰχμαλωσίαν] ἐκκλησίαν Coisl.

Aᵉ 4-5 (p. 182, 21-23): Pro omni tempore uitae suae consequenter iuge
pollicetur officium.　　19 ss. *vide pag, sequenti.*

So that I might feel no compunction (v. 12). After saying *so that I might feel no compunction,* meaning, I shall not desist from hymn-singing, he went on to say *I shall confess to you forever*—that is, I shall continue giving thanks to you unceasingly (by *forever* referring to the span of his own life).

PSALM 31

Become a protector God for me (v. 2): protect and assist in my troubles. Now, this is a Hebrew idiom, saying *Become a protector God for me* to mean "Protect," as happens elsewhere as well, "The Lord became a refuge for me,"[1] meaning "I took refuge in him."

You will draw me out of this snare that they have hidden for me (v. 4). By *snare* he referred to the captivity in which he was held, as though in some obvious danger. Similarly, he said *that they have hidden for me* in a figurative manner, since he had spoken of captivity as a snare: it is normal for a snare to be hidden out of sight, and thus to catch the prey unawares.

Into your hands I entrust my spirit (v. 5): I commit my spirit to your protection and guard; save and defend it. Now, it is to be noted that the Lord cited this verse when on the gibbet,[2] not that it was said of him in prophetic manner, as some commentators think, but because these words suited him when exposed to the risk of death and passion. | So he cited this verse at the

---

1. Ps 18:2. Although the expression is indeed unusual, it is not so much from Hebrew usage as from the LXX version, into which "God" has intruded.
2. Luke 23:46.

posito haec uerba conuenerint. Vsus ⟨est⟩ ergo hac uoce id temporis, cum anima eius separabatur a corpore, quam iuste commendabat Patri, ut eam corpori conpetenti resurrectionis tempore redderet.

Redimisti me, Domine, reliqua. Diuerse et frequenter in huius 5 modi psalmis nunc mala captiuitatis enumerat, nunc felicitatem reuersionis adnuntiat.

Ἐντεῦθεν προφητεύει τὴν ἀπαλλαγὴν τῆς αἰχμαλωσίας. Καλῶς δὲ ἐν αἰχμαλωσίᾳ καὶ δουλείᾳ κατεχόμενος, ἀντὶ τοῦ Ἀπήλλαξάς με εἶπεν ἐλυτρώσω με, ἐκ μεταφορᾶς τῶν δῶρα διδόντων καὶ οὕτως ἐξαιρουμένων τοὺς 10 ἐν ταῖς δουλείαις κατεχομένους· λύτρα γὰρ λέγεται τὰ τοιαῦτα δῶρα. Τὸ δὲ ὁ Θεὸς τῆς ἀληθείας, ἀντὶ τοῦ Ὁ πάντα ἀληθῶς καὶ δικαίως διαπραττόμενος.

7. Ἐμίσησας τοὺς διαφυλάσσοντας ματαιότητας διὰ κενῆς. Διὰ τοῦτο γάρ φησιν ἡμᾶς δικαίως ἀπήλλαξας, ἐπειδὴ ἐκείνους ἐμίσησας καὶ ἀπέ- 15 στράφης τοὺς μετὰ πολλῆς ἐπιμελείας τὰ ἄτοπα διαπραττομένους· οὐ γὰρ ἀπὸ συναρπαγῆς διαπράττονται τὸ κακόν, ἀλλ᾿ ὥσπερ τι ἀναγκαῖον τοῦ κακοῦ φυλάττουσι τὴν πρᾶξιν (τοῦτο γὰρ σημαίνει τὸ διαφυλάσσοντας). Ματαιότητα δὲ λέγει τὰς ἀτόπους πράξεις. Τὸ δὲ διὰ κενῆς, ὅτι οὐδὲν ὠφελοῦνται ἐκ τῆς περὶ τὸ κακὸν πράττειν ἐπιμελείας, διὰ τὸ μισεῖν αὐ- 20 τοὺς καὶ τιμωρεῖσθαι καὶ μὴ ἐᾶν εἴς τι πέρας ἄγειν αὐτοῖς τὸ σπουδαζόμενον.

10ᵇ. *Conturbati sunt in ira oculi mei. In ira,* id est tua. Irascente, inquit, te ita sum | turbatus aduersis, ut etiam oculi mei incursu uarii tumultus uim amitterent intuendi. 25

1 possito A   est *suppleui*   2 cum a B¹ seperabatur A   7 denuntiat A   23 mei *om.* A   25 induendi A.

Ἐντεῦθεν — διαπραττόμενος: (Θεοˢ αντοˣ) Coisl. 10, fol. 56; Vat. 754, fol. 90ᵛ; 9-11 cf. Petrus Laod. (Cord. I, 527, 4-7) Πρὸς τὴν αἰχμαλωσίαν δὲ καὶ τὸ ἐλυτρώσω, ἐκ μεταφορᾶς τῶν δῶρα διδόντων, καὶ οὕτως ἐξαιρουμένων· ἃ λύτρα λέγεται.   10 ἐξαιρουμένους 754.

7. Διὰ τοῦτο — σπουδαζόμενον: (Θεοˢ αντοˣ) Vat. 754, fol. 90ᵛ (Mai, p. 395; P. G., 668 A 13 — B 8); Coisl. 10, fol. 56-56ᵛ (anon.)   18-19 τοῦτο γὰρ — πράξεις *om.* Mai   21-22 τῶν σπουδαζομένων Coisl.

Aᵉ 1-2 (p. 183, 29-31): Vtitur hac uoce Dominus in patibulo tamquam apta, non tanquam propria; quia concinebat causam, non quia praedixerat passionem.   24-25 (p. 184, 25-26): Aut lacrimis Aut incurrentium rerum tumultu.

time when his soul was separated from his body, and rightly entrusted it to the Father so that he might restore it to his body when it was in need of it at the time of the resurrection. *You redeemed me, Lord* and the rest. Often and in various ways in psalms of this kind he at one time enumerates the troubles of the captivity, and at another he proclaims the joy of return; at this point he prophesies the release from captivity. Held in captivity and slavery, he was right to say, instead of "You freed me," *You redeemed me,* using the metaphor of those giving gifts and thus ransoming those held in slavery, such gifts being called ransom. The address *O God of truth* means "O you who do everything truly and righteously."

You hated all those who paid constant attention to futile things in vain (v. 6): it was right for you to free us for this reason, that you hated them and rebuffed those paying constant attention to doing wrong; far from doing evil in the heat of passion, they involve themselves in the practice of evil as though an obligation (the sense of *paid constant attention*). By *futile things* he refers to the wrongdoing. By *in vain* he means that they got no benefit from their involvement in evildoing because of his hating and punishing them and not allowing them to bring to completion the object of their efforts.

Anger has upset my eye (v. 9). By *Anger* he means "Your anger": Since you were angry, he is saying, I was so upset by adversity that even my eyes lost the power of sight through the effect of various disturbances. |

14ᵇ. *In eo dum conuenirent simul*, reliqua. Quoniam hi qui me in captiuitate retinebant, congregati in unum de adflictione mea ac morte cogitabant. Manifestius autem Symmachus posuit: *Cum in uno conuenientes cogitassent accipere animam meam*, infremebant.

5 **19.** *Muta fiant labia dolosa.* Id est effectibus distituta non habeant in quo gloriari possint quasi uoti sui conpotes facti.

24ᵇ. *Quoniam ueritates requiret Dominus.* Aquila *quoniam fideles custodit Dominus*, LXX *ueritates* dixerunt, id est ueros qui fidem suam adprobarent.

10 ## PSALMVS XXXI

Etiam in tricesimo primo psalmo beatus Dauid profetans de Ezechia commemorat qualiter sit eius infirmitas dissoluta, indicans specialiter quod, ut propter peccatum malum infirmitatis incurrerit, ita accepta peccatorum uenia sit ei etiam sanitas, quam amiserat, 15 restituta. Sub hoc igitur argumento docet omnes, etiam si iusti sint, non debere eos in operum suorum merito confidere nec sibi aliquid boni operis adrogare, sed totum quicquid boni operis egerint diuinae reputare gratiae et semper sibi Dei misericordiam necessariam confiteri ac tunc se beatos credere, si clementem circa 20 se Deum habere mereantur. In communi ergo cunctos hortatur homines ut deuoto animo officiis insistant diuinis nec exspectent ut ad notitiam et cultum Dei signis et correptionibus cogantur accedere.

1 simul et B   2 congrati A   3 simm. B   possuit A   5 non] nec B
6 in quo] quo A   gloari *ex* glo ∗∗ A   quasi] ∗ ssi *in rasura* A¹   7 ueritā
A ueritatem B¹   9 suam] s. A¹ *litt.* uam *add. supra*   10 xxx B *om.* A
11 xxx A triccissimo B salmo A   12 dissola A   13 infirmitatis *om.* A¹
14 uinia A   etiam ei A   15 igitur] itaque B   16 nec] non A   17 boni
operis *1° loco inter puncta* B   18-19 necesariam A   20 commoni A   cuntos A¹
ortatur A   21 nec] non A   22 correptiobus A.

Aᵉ 1-3 (p. 185, 11-13): Haec autem non absque oportunitate faciebant quando Caldei super captiuitatis mala de nostro exitio cogitabant.   11 ss. (p. 187, 20-188, 1): Etiam praesentis argumentum carminis super Ezechiae sanatione est, cum langorem ipsum ob superbiam incederit.. Instituitur ergo sermo qui Ezechiae et personae et causae conueniat ac per illum cunctis in simili statu degentibus iustis instructio et admonitio comprobatur. Cf. PSEUDO-BEDA (641): Oratio Ezechiae, quia in languorem ob superbiam inciderit; conuenit et caeteris sanctis simili statu degentibus.

As they assembled together against me (v. 13) and so on: when those who held me in captivity came together and planned my tribulation and death. Symmachus put it more clearly: "As they came together and planned to take my life," they raged.

Let the lying lips become mute (v. 18)—that is, let them be deprived of their effect and have nothing to boast of by attaining their goal.

Because the Lord looks for truths (v. 23). Aquila said, "Because the Lord guards his faithful ones," whereas the Seventy said *truths*—that is, true souls who kept faith.

PSALM 32

Also in Psalm 32 blessed David prophesies about Hezekiah, and recounts how his illness came to an end, suggesting in particular that as he had incurred the affliction of illness on account of sin, so after he had received pardon for sin, the health that he had lost was also restored. Adopting this line of thought, therefore, he teaches everyone, even if they are righteous, that they ought not trust in the merit of their actions nor attribute to themselves any good work. Rather, whatever good work they perform they should ascribe to divine grace and confess that God's mercy is necessary for them, and should believe themselves blessed if they deserve to have God well disposed toward them. In general, then, he exhorts all people to persevere in divine duties with a devout mind and not wait to be forced by signs and chastisements to come to the knowledge and worship of God. |

2ᵇ. *Neque est in ore eius dolus.* Quia beatum per omnia superius dixerat cui indulgentia peccatorum ueniam contulisset, ne uideretur auditoribus suis otii occasionem ac remissionis ingerere,
intulit: *Neque est in ore eius dolus.* Beatus, inquit, qui ad delictorum ueniam, quam de diuina bonitate promeruit, studium sempli- 5
citatis accommodat et sollicite dolum omnem fraudemque deuitat,
ut post gratiae liberalitatem uirtuti et moribus colendis inuigilet·
In ore uero *eius* melius Aquila et Theodotion dixerunt *in spiritu
eius,* id est in anima eius. *Dolum* autem in hoc loco nequitiam ait
atque malitiam. 10

3-4. *Dum clamarem tota die, quoniam die ac nocte,* usque *dum
infigitur mihi spina.* Consequentia dictorum huius modi est: *Dum
clamarem tota die, quoniam die ac nocte grauata est super me manus tua, dum infigitur mihi spina, conuersus sum in erumnam. Conuersus sum in aerumnam* interpositum est propter metri necessita- 15
tem, sicut et alia multa frequenter ostendimus.

Dum infigitur mihi spina. Spinam uocauit egrotationem propter
subitum doloris incursum.

Conuersus sum in aerumnam. Vult dicere Quoniam clamaui iugiter, accessio mihi facta est egritudinis et doloris: clamaui autem 20
ob hoc iugiter, quia continue mihi uis langoris incubuit. Egrotatio
ergo mihi necessitatem uociferationis inposuit, uociferatio malum
infirmitatis adiecit. *Conuersus sum in erumnam,* id est: de infirmitate ad aliam infirmitatem transitum feci.

5. *Peccatum meum cognitum tibi feci,* reliqua. Id est: Conuertar 25
ad confessionem peccati. Nam *cognitum tibi feci* Aquila *cognitum
tibi faciam.*

Et non abscondi. Symmachus *Non abscondam.*

16 cf. supra p. 57, 61-62.

1 uel neque *add. supra lineam* A nec *in textu*　　2 ueniam] niam A¹
3 ocassionem A　　remisionis B　　5 uiniam A　　6 accomod∗t B¹　　omnem
om. A¹　　diuitat A　　7 collendis A　　8 theō AB　　9-10 dolum — malitiam
affert Aᵉ (p. 188, 9-11)　　10 atque] aut A　　11-12 quoniam — infigitur] usque A
13-14 quoniam — conuersus sum in] usque A　　13 est *om.* B　　14 tua *om.* B
15 sum *om.* A¹　　erum. interpossitum A　　16 frequenter] consequenter A
19 erumnam A　　20 accesio A　　21 egrota|tatio A　　22 inpossuit A　　24 ad]
in A　　firmitatem A　　fecit B¹　　25 reliqua *om.* A　　28 ab|abscondi B, Aᵉ
(p. 188, 30) pro non abscondam.

In whose mouth there is no deceit (v. 2). Because in everything above he had declared blessed the one on whom mercy bestowed pardon for sin, to avoid his listeners gaining the impression that he had taken occasion for easygoing ways, he went on to say *In whose mouth there is no deceit.* Blessed is the person, he is saying, who directs the pursuit of honesty to pardon for sins, which he would attain from divine goodness, and carefully avoids all deceit and deception so as to stay on the alert after the generous gift of grace by cultivating virtue and good behavior. *In whose mouth* Aquila and Theodotion expressed better: "In whose spirit"—that is, in whose soul. By *deceit* here he refers to wickedness and malice.

From crying aloud all day, because day and night down to with a thorn being fixed in me (vv. 3–4). The meaning is something like this: From crying aloud all day, because day and night your hand was heavy upon me, I was reduced to distress with a thorn being fixed in me. The phrase *I was reduced to distress* was inserted on account of the need of the meter, as we have often shown in many other cases. *With a thorn being fixed in me,* by *thorn* referring to the illness because of the sudden onset of pain. *I was reduced to distress.* He means, Since I cried out incessantly, grief and pain came upon me, and I constantly suffered the effect of exhaustion through crying out incessantly. So illness forced me to shout aloud, and the shouting increased the feeling of weakness. *I was reduced to distress*—that is, I passed from one infirmity to another.

I made the sin known (v. 5) and so on—that is, I shall be brought to confession of sin (Aquila putting "I shall make known to you" for *I made known,* and for *And I did not hide* Symmachus putting "I shall not hide"). |

6. *In tempore oportuno.* Id est in tempore conpetenti, ac si diceret: Cum fuerit ab aliis curis atque occupationibus liber, tunc erit ad confitendum intentus ac sollicitus.

Verumtamen in diluuio aquarum, reliqua. Quod Symmachus ita
5 ait: *Ne ut fluctuantes aquae multae illi obuient. Fluctuantes* aquas uocauit | uehementia discrimina. Omnia haec sub Ezechiae exemplo de omni iusto dicuntur.

7. *Tu mihi es refugium meum* usque *quae circumdedit me.* Quam illi Assyrius nuper intulerat.
10 *Exultatio mea, erue me a circumdantibus me.* Optime exultationem suam uocat Deum, qui eum et a grandi merore liberauerit et laetitia atque exultatione conpleuerit. *A circumdantibus* dicit, siue a malis, quae ei per infirmitatem acciderant, siue ab his qui de ipsa eius infirmitate gaudebant.

15 **8.** *Intellectum tibi dabo,* reliqua. Quia cum esset Ezechias iustus, cogitationem recepit animo quae proposito eius minime conueniret.

9. *Nolite fieri,* reliqua. Quia Ezechias illa infirmitate quasi quodam camo reuocatus est. *Frenum* ergo et *camum* uocauit correptiones breues et ad tempus inductas, *flagilla* uero castigationem
20 diu longeque protractam. *Nolite,* inquit, ad praesentes tantum correptiones aspicere et Dominum pro castigationum lenitate dispicere: nouit in peccatis permanentes suppliciis longis adficere.

11ᵇ. *Et gloriamini omnes recti.* Melius Aquila: *Et laudate eum omnes recti corde.*

---

2 ocupationibus A¹   3 fitendum AB   4 diluio A d͞i͞l B   reliqua] mul-
(tarum) A   5 f*luctantes B   aquae] aq(ue) A   6 uechimentia A uehimen-
tia B   haec] has uero A¹   8 quae *om.* A   quam] *subintellige e. g.* tribulationem   9 assirius A   intullerat A   12 exultat. atque laet. A   13 qui]
q(uae) A   15 *ad v.* intellectum B *praefert inter coll.* ex persona Dei   16 recipit AB   propossito A   17 quasi quasi B   18 camo *om.* B   20-21 ad — aspi-
cere] ad correptiones aspicere tantum correptiones A, *v.* aspicere *inter virgulas*
duplices includitur   22 permantes A.

Aᵉ 18-19 (p. 190, 9-10): Pro breui correptione et temporali.

At the right time (v. 6)—that is, at an appropriate time, as if to say, When he is free of other concerns and occupations, then he will be earnest and careful to confess. *Even in the rush of mighty waters* and so on. Symmachus put it this way: "Lest mighty waters become a flood and approach him," by "mighty waters become a flood" referring to severe difficulties. All this is applicable to every righteous person on the example of Hezekiah. *You are my refuge* down to *surrounding me* (v. 7), which the Assyrian lately inflicted on him. *My joy, rescue me from those surrounding me.* He did very well to call God his *joy,* since he rid him of extreme grief and filled him with joy and exultation. He said *from those surrounding,* either from troubles that happened to him through illness or from those people who rejoiced in his illness.

I shall give you understanding (v. 8) and so on. Though Hezekiah was righteous, he entertained thoughts in his mind that were by no means appropriate to his purpose. *Do not be* (v. 9) and so on. Hezekiah was held in check by that illness as if by a kind of rein. By *muzzle* and *rein,* therefore, he referred to brief periods of correction inflicted for a time, and by *whips,* to chastisement long and drawn out. *Do not,* he is saying, have regard only for the present correction and despise God for the lightness of the chastisement: he can inflict extended punishment on those persisting in sin.

Boast, all you are upright (v. 11). Aquila put it better: "Praise him, all you who are upright of heart." |

PSALMVS XXXII

Τὴν ἐπὶ τοῦ μακαρίου Ἐζεκίου παρασχεθεῖσαν νίκην τοῖς Ἰσραηλίταις ὑπὸ τοῦ Θεοῦ, διὰ τῆς παραδόξου τῶν Ἀσσυρίων ἀναιρέσεως, προφητεύων ἐν τούτῳ τῷ ψαλμῷ ὁ μακάριος Δαυίδ, ὥσπερ τινὰ ἐπινίκιον ὕμνον
ἐπὶ τοῖς γεγενημένοις αὐτῷ ἀνεβόησε, τὸ σύνηθες αὐτῷ κἀντεῦθεν δια- 5
πραττόμενος, καὶ ἀπὸ τῆς κατὰ τοὺς Ἀσσυρίους ὑποθέσεως τρεπόμενος μὲν
εἰς καθολικὴν ὑμνῳδίαν τοῦ δεσπότου καὶ ἐξήγησιν τῶν ὑπ᾽ αὐτοῦ γεγονότων, παιδεύων δὲ πάντας μὴ ἐπὶ τοῖς παροῦσι μεγάλοις πεποιθέναι, ἀλλὰ
πάντων ἡγεῖσθαι δυνατωτέραν τὴν τοῦ Θεοῦ βοήθειαν. Τοῦτο γὰρ μάλιστα
ἀφορᾶν ἐν τοῖς ψαλμοῖς προσήκει, ὅτι ἐκ τῶν ὑποθέσεων ἐπὶ κατηχητικὴν 10
τρέπεται παραίνεσιν, διαφόρως ταύτην ποιούμενος καὶ τοῖς ἀκροαταῖς ὠφε-
λίμως, ὥστε ἀναγκαῖον μὲν ἡμῖν εἰδέ|ναι τὰς ὑποθέσεις πρὸς γνῶσιν τῆς
τῶν ψαλμῶν δυνάμεως, προσεκτέον δὲ καὶ τοῖς λοιποῖς, οἷς ἐκ τῶν ὑποθέσεων κέχρηται πρὸς τὴν τῶν ἐντυγχανόντων ὠφέλειαν.

1ᵃ. Ἀγαλλιᾶσθε, δίκαιοι, ἐν τῷ Κυρίῳ. Δικαίους ἐνταῦθα καλεῖ τοὺς 15
Ἰουδαίους, οὐκ ἀπὸ τῆς τοῦ βίου ἀρετῆς, ἀλλ᾽ ἀπὸ τῆς τοῦ Θεοῦ γνώσεως. Εἰκότως δὲ εἰπὼν τὸ Ἀγαλλιᾶσθε προσέθηκε τὸ ἐν Κυρίῳ. Ἐπειδὴ γὰρ
ἐν τοῖς ἀνθρωπίνοις εὐτελεῖς ἦσαν καὶ ταπεινοὶ καὶ πρόχειροι τοῖς Ἀσσυρίοις πρὸς ἅλωσιν, πολλοῖς τε οὖσι καὶ ἰσχυροῖς καὶ ἐμπειρίᾳ πολεμικῇ
κεκοσμημένοις, ἐν τῷ Κυρίῳ τὴν ἀγαλλίασιν αὐτοῖς προευαγγελίζεται, οὗ 20
τῇ βοηθείᾳ παραδόξως τετυχήκασι τῆς σωτηρίας, οὐκ ἐν πολέμῳ καὶ
παρατάξει ἀλλὰ μόνῃ τῇ τοῦ Θεοῦ πληγῇ τῶν Ἀσσυρίων ἀναιρεθέντων.

*Ab hoc loco Coisliniani gr. 12 textum, nisi aliter signetur, uno tenore perscripsi.
Commentarium uniuscuiusque fere versiculi praecedit, in codice, nomen aut siglum
Theodori. — Excerpta anonyma (anon.) notavi, fragmenta ex aliis codicibus deprompta
suo loco indicavi.*

Τὴν — ὠφέλειαν: (Θεο? αντοχ) Paris. 139, fol. 67; Vat. 1682, fol. 96ᵛ; Cord. I,
574 (P. G., 668 C 11-669 A 3); Barbaro, p. 286 (παιδεύων — ὠφέλειαν). 5 κάν-
ταῦθα C 6 μὲν om. C 8 παιδεύων] παιδάσων P παῖδας ὢν V 13 ἐκ] ἐπὶ PV Cord.
1ᵃ. Δικαίους — ἀναιρεθέντων: (Θεο? αντιοχ) Paris. 139, fol. 67; Vat. 1682, fol. 97;
Cord., p. 575 (P. G., 669 A 4-15); Barbaro, p. 287; cf. Petrus Laodicenus [L]
(Cord., p. 562, 5-16). 17 ἐπ(ε)ὶ PV Cord. 18 ἀνθρώποις C 19 πρὸς] εἰς PV
Cord. 20 αὐτῶν PV Cord. 22 τῇ τοῦ om. C.

Aᵉ 2-14 (p. 190, 21-26): Post uictoriam de Assiris profetice carmen hoc uelut
triumphale componitur, doceturque sub occassione huius argumenti inritae
spei esse uel rei omnia quibus praeter Dominum mortales exultant. Cf. PSEUDO-
BEDA (615). 1ᵃ (p. 190, 27-29): Iudaei ob notitiam conditoris, non in equis
et prosperorum successu (sucensu *ms*), gauisi sunt ut Assirii.

PSALM 33[1]

In this psalm blessed David prophesied the victory granted the Israelites by God in the time of Hezekiah through the unexpected slaughter of the Assyrians. He burst forth, as it were, into a triumphal hymn on what had happened to him, making his point here in his customary fashion: he moves from treatment of the Assyrians to general praise of the Lord and an explanation of what had been done by him; and he instructs everyone not to trust in the mighty ones of this world, but to consider God's help more powerful than all. In fact, this is what we should consider most of all in the psalms, that he moves from development of a theme to catechetical exhortation, conducting this in various ways also for the benefit of the listeners. The result is that it is necessary for us to recognize the themes with a view to knowledge of the psalms' drift, on the one hand, while on the other hand it behooves us to attend also to the other aspects that arose from the themes and that he employed with the readers' benefit in mind.

Rejoice in the Lord, you righteous ones (v. 1). By *righteous* here he refers to the Jews on the basis not of their virtuous living but of their knowledge of God. Now, he was right to add *in the Lord* after saying *Rejoice:* since in human terms they were insignificant, lowly, and vulnerable to capture by the Assyrians, who were numerous, strong, and equipped with military experience, he brought them ahead of time the good news of rejoicing *in the Lord,* by whose help they unexpectedly attained salvation with the slaughter of the Assyrians, not by fighting and battle array, but solely by God's intervention. | *Praise becomes the upright.* An excellent extension of

---

1. It is from this point on that editor Devreesse finds Theodore's Greek text in the Codex Coislinianus to be so complete as to be "équivalent à une tradition directe" (*Le commentaire,* xv).

1ᵇ. Τοῖς εὐθέσι πρέπει αἴνεσις. *Καλὴ ἡ ἐπαγωγὴ τοῦ ῥητοῦ καὶ μάλιστα τῶν ἑξῆς ἔνεκεν.* Ἐπειδὴ γὰρ τὴν εὐφροσύνην αὐτοῖς εὐηγγελίσατο, ἤμελλε δὲ ἐπὶ τὴν ὑμνῳδίαν καὶ τὴν ὑπὲρ τῶν γεγονότων εὐχαριστίαν προτρέπειν, ἑξῆς βουλόμενος αὐτοὺς ἐμφόβους πρὸς τὸ πρᾶγμα καταστῆσαι, ὥστε
5 μετὰ τῆς προσηκούσης γνησιότητος ἀναπέμπειν τὴν ὑμνῳδίαν καὶ τὴν εὐχαριστίαν τῷ Θεῷ τελεῖν, προλαβὼν τοῖς εὐθέσι φησὶν τὴν αἴνεσιν πρέπειν, ἵνα ἀκούσαντες ὅτι μὴ πάντων ἐστὶν ὑμνεῖν τὸν Θεόν, ἀλλὰ μόνων τῶν μεθ᾽ εὐθύτητος λογισμῶν τοῦτο ποιουμένων, οἷς καὶ πρέπον ἐστὶ τὸ ὑμνεῖν ἐπὶ τοῖς παροῦσιν ἀγαθοῖς, ἐπείπερ καὶ τοῦ τυχεῖν αὐτῶν ἄξιοι καθεσ-
10 τήκασι μετὰ πολλῆς εὐλαβείας προσέλθωσι τῇ τοῦ Θεοῦ ὑμνῳδίᾳ.

2ᵃ. Ἐξομολογεῖσθε τῷ Κυρίῳ ἐν κιθάρᾳ. *Ὥσπερ προοιμιασάμενος τὰ ἀνώτερα καὶ πρότερον μὲν εὐαγγελισάμενος τὴν εὐφροσύνην, μετὰ δὲ ταῦτα καταρτίσας πρὸς τὴν ὑμνῳδίαν τῇ ἐπαγωγῇ τοῦ ἑξῆς ῥητοῦ, ἐντεῦθεν λοιπὸν ἐπ᾽ αὐτὴν προτρέπεται τὴν ὑμνῳδίαν καί φησιν* Ἐξομολογεῖσθε τῷ
15 Κυρίῳ ἐν κιθάρᾳ. Ἐξομολογεῖσθε *δὲ* Εὐχαριστεῖτε *λέγει· τὸ δὲ ἐν κιθάρᾳ κατὰ τὴν τότε συνήθειαν, ἐπειδὴ τοιούτοις ὀργάνοις ἐκέχρηντο πρὸς τὴν τοῦ Θεοῦ ὑμνῳδίαν.*

2ᵇ. Ἐν ψαλτηρίῳ δεκαχόρδῳ ψάλατε αὐτῷ. *Ἑτέρου πάλιν ὀργάνου μνημονεύει, ᾧπερ ἐκέχρηντο πρὸς τοῦτο, τῷ διαφόρῳ τῶν ὀργάνων σεμνοπρε-*
20 *πεστέραν τὴν ὑμνῳδίαν ἐργαζόμενος.*

3ᵃ. Ἄσατε αὐτῷ ᾆσμα καινόν. *Ἐπειδὴ σύμφωνον ἀνάγκη τῷ πράγματι εἶναι τὸ ᾆσμα, καινὸν παρακελεύει ᾆσμα ᾀσθῆναι τῷ Θεῷ ὡς ἐπὶ καινῷ καὶ παραδόξῳ πράγματι καὶ παρὰ τὴν κοινὴν τῶν ἀνθρώπων συνήθειαν γεγενημένῳ.*

1ᵇ. Καλὴ — ὑμνῳδίᾳ: (Θεοδώρου αντοχ) Paris. 139, fol. 67; Vat. 1682, fol. 97 (Mai, p. 395; P. G., 668 B 10-C 9); Barbaro, p. 288.   1 καλὴ — ῥητοῦ, 2-6 ἐπει(δὴ) — τὴν εὐχαριστίαν ἀναπέμψαι affert L (Cord. 562, 45-50).   πρὸς] περὶ PVL   5 ἀναπέμψαι PVL   6 τῷ Θεῷ om. C   τελεῖν om. PV   τὴν om. C.
2ᵃ. Ὥσπερ — ὑμνῳδίαν: (Θεοδώρου) Paris. 139, fol. 67; Vat. 1682, fol. 97. 15 ἐξομολογεῖσθε — κιθάρᾳ om. C   16 ἐπειδὴ] ἐπὶ PV   ἐκέχρητο C.
2ᵇ. Ἑτέρου — ἐργαζόμενος: (Θεοδώρου) Paris. 139, fol. 67ᵛ; Vat. 1682, fol. 97ᵛ. 19 ὅπερ C ὥσπερ PV.
3ᵃ. Ἐπειδὴ — γεγενημένῳ: (Θεοδώρου) Paris. 139, fol. 67ᵛ; Vat. 1682, fol. 97ᵛ; Barbaro, p. 290; ἐπει(δὴ) — πράγματι affert L (p. 564, 11-14).   21 ἐπισύμφωνον V.

Aᵉ 1ᵇ (p. 190, 29-191, 2): (Laus) deferenda Deo auctori operis.   2ᵃ (p. 191, 2-4): Generali praefatu ad laudes diuinas coartatus nunc ipsas species, quibus laudetur, enumerat.   2ᵇ (p. 191, 5-6): Alterius namque musici meminit instrumenti.   3ᵃ (p. 191, 7-8): Nimirum qui magna et noua contulit.

the verse, particularly in the light of what follows: since he brought them the good news of happiness, and intended proceeding to a hymn of praise and to thanksgiving for what had happened, he meant to go on and render them apprehensive about the action so that with due sincerity they could offer up a hymn of praise and perform thanksgiving to God. He begins by saying that praise becomes the upright, so that when they hear that it is not for everyone to praise God but only for those doing so with the highest motives—to whom it is also appropriate to sing praise for the current prosperity, especially since they were made worthy of attaining it—they may proceed with deep piety to hymn-singing to God.

Confess to the Lord with a lyre (v. 2). As he had begun with the above remarks, first of all bringing good news of rejoicing and later completing the introduction to the hymn-singing by addition of the following phrase, at this point he now introduces the hymn-singing itself with the words *Confess to the Lord with a lyre.* Now, by *Confess* he means "Give thanks," and *with a lyre* according to the custom of the time, since they used such instruments for singing hymns to God. *Sing to him with a ten-stringed harp.* He mentions in turn another instrument that they used for this purpose, making the hymn-singing more solemn with a range of instruments.

Sing to him a new song (v. 3). Since the song needed to be in harmony with the occasion, he gives instructions for a new song to be sung to God as in the case of a new and extraordinary development surpassing people's general practice. | *Sing a beautiful song to him with full voice.* Symmachus

3ᵇ. Καλῶς ψάλατε ἐν ἀλαλαγμῷ. Σύμμαχος ἐπιμελῶς ψάλατε, σαφέστερον αὐτὸ λέγων. Τοῦτο γὰρ βούλεται εἰπεῖν· Καλῶς, μετὰ προσηκούσης
ἐπιμελείας ἐπιτελεῖσθε τὸ πρᾶγμα. Εὐκαίρως δὲ εἶπεν ἐν ἀλαλαγμῷ·
ἀλαλαγμὸς γὰρ λέγεται κυρίως ἡ βοὴ ἣν ἐν τοῖς πολέμοις εἴωθεν ἀφιέναι ὁ στρατὸς ὁπόταν ἢ πολεμίους διώκη τρέψας εἰς φυγὴν ἢ πόλεως 5
τείχη κρατήσας, ἢ καί τινα νίκην ἐργάζηται, — καὶ ὅλως ἀλαλαγμὸς κυ-
ρίως ἡ τοιαύτη λέγεται φωνὴ ἣν ἀφιᾶσιν | ὥσπερ τι σύμβολον νίκης
γεγενημένης.

4ᵃ. Ὅτι εὐθὴς ὁ λόγος τοῦ Κυρίου. Προτρεψάμενος ἐπὶ τὴν ὑμνῳδίαν
καὶ τὴν ἐπὶ τῇ νίκῃ εὐχαριστίαν, ἀσφαλίζεται πρότερον τοῦ παρασχομένου 10
τὴν νίκην τὸν ὗμνον, ὡς ἂν μὴ δόξῃ κεχαρισμένη τις εἶναι καὶ ἀδιάκριτος ἡ
παρασχεθεῖσα αὐτοῖς παρὰ τοῦ Θεοῦ βοήθεια. Τοῦτο δὲ ποιεῖ ἐπειδὴ
μὴ μόνον προφητεύειν προῄρηται τὸ πρᾶγμα, ἀλλὰ καὶ ἑτέρους παιδεύειν
τῇ τῶν ἐσομένων προφητείᾳ, καί φησιν ὅτι εὐθὴς ὁ λόγος τοῦ Κυρίου, τουτέστιν ὅτι δίκαιον αὐτοῦ τὸ πρόσταγμα, δικαία ἡ ἀπόφασις εὐθύτητος 15
πεπληρωμένη, τοῦτο λέγων ὅτι δικαίως ἡμῖν ἐπήμυνεν. Ἔθος δὲ αὐτῷ τοῦτο
ποιεῖν ὁσάκις ἂν μνημονεύσῃ βοηθείας παρασχεθείσης αὐτοῖς παρὰ τοῦ
δεσπότου κατὰ τῶν πολεμίων, τοῦτο σπουδάζοντι δεικνύναι ὅτι οὔτε τούτους χάριτι εὐεργετεῖ ματαίᾳ, οὔτε τοὺς ἐναντίους ὀργῇ τιμωρεῖται, δικαίᾳ
δὲ ψήφῳ τὴν κατὰ τῶν ἐναντίων ἀπόφασιν ἐκφέρει. 20

4ᵇ. Καὶ πάντα τὰ ἔργα αὐτοῦ ἐν πίστει. Καὶ πάντα τὰ ὑπ᾽ αὐτοῦ πραττόμενα βέβαια καὶ ἀμετάθετα· ἀμφοτέρων δὲ τούτων ἡ ἐπαγωγὴ τῶν ῥητῶν
ἀναγκαία πρὸς τὰ προηγούμενα. Ἔδει γὰρ ἐπὶ τὴν εὐχαριστίαν προτρεψά-
μενον καὶ τὸ δίκαιον δεῖξαι τῆς νίκης καὶ τὸ ἀμετάθετον τῆς δωρεᾶς, ἵνα
ἐξ ἀμφοτέρων ὀφειλομένη δειχθῇ ἡ εὐχαριστία καὶ ὑμνῳδία ἡ εἰς αὐτόν, 25

3ᵇ. Σύμμαχος — γεγενημένης: (Θεοδωρήτου) Paris. 139, fol. 67ᵛ; Vat. 1682,
fol. 97ᵛ-98. 1-3 Συμμ. — ἐπιμελείας affert L (p. 564, 23-25) 4 πολεμίοις PV
6 τύχη C 7 τινα σύμβολον PV.
4ᵃ. Προτρεψάμενος — ἐκφέρει: (Θεοδωρήτου) Paris. 139, fol. 67ᵛ; Vat. 1682,
fol. 98. 9 τῇ ὑμνῳδίᾳ C 11 ὗμνον] τρόπον PV εἶναι om. C ἄκριτος PV
12 τοῦ om. C ἐπεὶ PV 17 παρασχεθείσης αὐτοῖς om. C.
4ᵇ. Καὶ πάντα — ἐπάγει: (Θεοδωρήτου) Paris. 139, fol. 68; Vat. 1682,
fol. 98ʳ·ᵛ.

3ᵇ (p. 191, 8-13): Pro diligenter, intente ac modolate.. uociferatio hic uel
iubilatio clamor ille militum dicitur in praelium aut hostibus fugatis insistunt..
oportune ergo hic tali uociferatione hortatur ut psallant. 4ᵇ (p. 194, 14-18):
More suo per alias quoque oportunitates dispensationes diuinas commendat
simul[que] discribit dignitatem eius, quem laudari meruerat quia [uel inspexit]
utrorumque merita inspiciens Iudeos.

puts it more clearly: "Sing with care," meaning "Perform the task beautifully, with due care." Now, it was fitting for him to say *with full voice:* by *full voice* is properly described the cry that the army normally raises in war when pursuing the enemy after routing them, mounting the city walls, or achieving any other victory—and in general *full voice* properly describes the cry they utter as a kind of sign of a victory won.

Because the word of the Lord is upright (v. 4). Having recommended their hymn-singing and thanksgiving for the victory, he first ensures the hymn to the one responsible for the victory lest someone seem not to be grateful and the help provided them by God go unacknowledged. Now, he does this since he chooses not only to prophesy the event, but also to instruct others with the prophecy of the future, saying *Because the word of the Lord is upright*—that is, his command is just, his just verdict is full of uprightness, meaning that he was right to come to our aid. Now, it is customary for him to do this whenever he mentions help provided us by the Lord against the enemy, anxious as he is to bring out that it is not by an idle favor that he benefits them nor in rage that he punishes the adversaries; instead, it is by a just verdict that he delivers the sentence against the adversaries.

And all his works in faithfulness: everything done by him is firm and permanent. The insertion of both these phrases was necessary in the light of the foregoing: he had to recommend thanksgiving and show the justice of the victory and the permanence of the gift so that the thanksgiving and hymn-singing to him would emerge as a response to both, | the provision of just

ἀπό τε τοῦ δικαίαν παρεσχηκέναι
τὴν βοήθειαν καὶ ἀπὸ τοῦ βεβαίαν
δεδωρῆσθαι τὴν εὐεργεσίαν. Ταῦτα
οὖν ἀμφότερα προσεῖναί φησι τοῖς
5 ἀπὸ τοῦ Θεοῦ γεγενημένοις, ὧν ὅπερ
ἂν μὴ προσῇ ἐλαττοῦν τὸ τῆς εὐχαριστίας ἠδύνατο. Εἴτε γὰρ ἄδικος ἦν
ἡ βοήθεια, οὐκ ἄξιον ἦν ὑπὲρ τού-

Merito laudabilis, quia aequissime auxiliatus est et quia firmum esse fecit quod contulit.
Haec autem utraque dicit inesse
operibus Dei; quorum si unum
deesset, gratiarum inminueret
dignitatem, id est si iniuste defenderet eos

των εὐχαριστεῖν, εἰ καὶ ὀφειλόμενον παρὰ τῶν εἰληφότων τὴν χάριν, εἴτε
10 ὀξεῖαν ἐπεδέχετο τὴν μεταβολήν, καὶ οὕτως περιττὸν ἦν εὐχαριστεῖν ἐπὶ
τοῖς οὐ παραμένουσιν ἀγαθοῖς. Καὶ   uel praestita permanere non pos-
ἐπειδὴ εἶπε δικαίαν τὴν ἀπόφασιν,   sent.
ἵνα μὴ δόξῃ πάλιν ἀμελεστέρους περὶ τὴν εὐχαριστίαν ἀπεργάζεσθαι ὡς
οὐδὲν τοῦ Θεοῦ δωρησαμένου, ἀλλ' ὠφελῆ προσνείμαντος τὴν βοήθειαν,
15 ἐπάγει·

5ª. Ἀγαπᾷ ἐλεημοσύνην καὶ κρίσιν. Πρόσεστί φησι τοῖς ὑπ' αὐτοῦ γινομένοις καὶ χάρις καὶ τὸ δίκαιον· ἀντὶ δὲ τοῦ προσεῖναι τὸ ἀγαπᾶν
εἶπεν, ἐκ πολλοῦ τοῦ περιόντος ἴσως λέγων ὅτι οὐ μόνον τοῖς νυνὶ γεγενημένοις πρόσεστιν ἀμφότερα ταῦτα, ἀλλὰ γὰρ καὶ μετὰ πολλῆς τῆς δια-
20 θέσεως φίλον αὐτῷ τοιαῦτα διαπράττεσθαι οἷς ἀμφότερα ταῦτα προσεῖναι συμβαίνει. Πῶς οὖν πρόσεστι καὶ ἡ χάρις καὶ τὸ δίκαιον; Τὸ μὲν
δίκαιον ὅτι μὴ ἀδίκως ἐπήμυνε δικαιότατα τοὺς ἀδικοῦντας τιμωρησάμενος,
ἡ δὲ χάρις ὅτι οὐκ ἀπὸ τῆς οἰκείας ἀρετῆς ἀξίων ὄντων τοσοῦτον τῶν εὐερ-
γετηθέντων παρέσχε τὴν ἐκδίκησιν ὁ Θεός, τῇ δὲ αὐτοῦ φιλανθρωπίᾳ τὸ
25 πρέπον διαπραττόμενος δίκας παρὰ τῶν ἀδικούντων ἐλάμβανεν. Εἶτα βουλόμενος ὁμοῦ μὲν δεῖξαι μεγάλην τοῦ Θεοῦ τὴν φιλανθρωπίαν καὶ μείζονα
ταύτην καὶ πολὺ πλεονάζουσαν τοῦ δικαίου, — συνεβάλετο γὰρ εἰς μείζονα
προτροπὴν ἐκείνων, οὓς ἐπὶ τὸν ὕμνον ἐκάλει καὶ τὴν εὐχαριστίαν τοῦ
Θεοῦ, — ὁμοῦ δὲ καὶ τὸ σύνηθες αὐτῷ διαπραττόμενος, καὶ ἐπὶ μείζονα
30 ἐκτρέχων ὑμνῳδίαν, τρέπεται ἐπὶ τὴν τῶν καθολικω|τέρων ἐξήγησιν καί
φησιν·

2 βεβαίαν] δικαίαν C   8 ὑπὲρ] ἐκ V   12 ἐπεὶ PV   13 ἐργάζεσθαι PV
14 ὀφειλῆ codd.
Merito — non possent: A, fol. 9ª; B, fol. 11ᵇ. — Praemittitur textus
sacer: Quia rectum est uerbum Domini et omnia opera.   1-2 equissime A
7 iuste AB.
5ª. Πρόσεστι — φησιν: (Θεοδώρου) Paris. 139, fol. 68; Vat. 1682, fol. 98ᵛ.
16-17 ἀπ' αὐτοῦ γιγνομένοις PV   18 ἴσως om. PV   20 οἷς om. C   21 πῶς οὖν] οἷς
νῦν C   22 δίκαιον καὶ PV   τιμωρούμενος PV   23 τοσοῦτον om. PV   29 αὐτῶν C
30 ἐξήγησιν] προφητείαν C.

assistance and the gift of abiding beneficence. He is saying, then, that both these features characterize what is done by God, and if either is missing, the level of thanksgiving could be diminished. That is to say, if the assistance were unjust, it would not be appropriate to offer thanks on their behalf, even though thanks are due for what is received, or if it underwent rapid change, it thus would be unnecessary to give thanks for good things that do not last.

Since he had said that the verdict was just, lest he seem to make them careless about thanksgiving as though God had given nothing instead of supplying further useful assistance, he goes on to say *The Lord loves mercy and justice* (v. 5): grace and righteousness are characteristic of what is done by him. In other words, he said that loving is characteristic of him, speaking perhaps excessively and meaning that not only does what has been done in the past have these two characteristics, but also he is very fond of doing such things as happen to have these two characteristics. So how is it that grace and righteousness are characteristic? While it is right that God is not unjust in promoting righteousness by punishing the wrongdoers, and there is grace in his securing vengeance for those who benefited so much yet did not deserve it of their own virtue, he was acting out of his lovingkindness when he took the appropriate action in calling the wrongdoers to account.

Then, he wished to show God's great lovingkindness to be more comprehensive and abundant than justice required, since he was delivering further exhortation to those whom he summoned to hymn-singing and thanksgiving to God. Also, in his customary fashion he made a digression to hymn-singing as a whole, turning to more general comment. | *The earth is full of the Lord's*

5ᵇ. Τοῦ ἐλέους Κυρίου πλήρης ἡ γῆ. Πολλή τίς φησίν ἐστιν ἡ τοῦ Θεοῦ φιλανθρωπία καὶ τοσαύτη ὡς οὐχ ἡμᾶς μόνον αὐτῆς ἀπολαύειν, ἀλλὰ γὰρ καὶ κατὰ πάσης ἐκκεχύσθαι τῆς γῆς. Καλῶς δὲ εἶπε Τοῦ ἐλέους Κυρίου πλή-

ρης ἡ γῆ, ἐπειδὴ ἐκ ταύτης ἅπαντα	Misericordia Domini plena est
ἀναδίδοται τὰ πρὸς διατροφὴν καὶ	terra. Quia in ipsa cuncta na- 5
χρείαν καὶ σύστασιν τῶν ἀνθρώπων·	scuntur quae sunt necessaria
ὧν ἅπαντες ἀπολαύοντες οἱ κατὰ τὴν	nutrimentis hominum uitaeque
οἰκουμένην ζῶσί τε καὶ συνεστᾶσι	mortalium.

καὶ διαμένουσι, πλουσίως τοῦ δεσπότου κατὰ πᾶσαν ἁπλώσαντος τὴν γῆν
τὴν οἰκείαν δωρεάν.   10

6ᵃ. Τῷ λόγῳ τοῦ Κυρίου οἱ οὐρανοὶ ἐστερεώθησαν. Καὶ οὐ μόνον φησὶ τὰ ἑκάστοτε γινόμενα τῇ αὐτοῦ ἀναδίδοται φιλανθρωπίᾳ, ἀλλὰ καὶ τὰ πάντα τῷ αὐτοῦ προστάγματι συνέστη, ἀπὸ τοῦ μείζονος καὶ κυριωτέρου τῶν ὁρατῶν τὰ πάντα περιλαβών.

6ᵇ. Καὶ τῷ πνεύματι τοῦ στόμα-	Et spiritu oris eius omnis vir- 15
τος αὐτοῦ πᾶσα ἡ δύναμις αὐτῶν. Οὔτε	tus eorum. Neque uerbo Domini,
τῷ λόγῳ Κυρίου, ὥς τινες ἐνόμισαν,	sicut quidam putauerunt, de Fi-
τῷ Υἱῷ λέγει, οὔτε τῷ πνεύματι τοῦ	lio dicit, neque spiritu oris eius
στόματος αὐτοῦ τῷ Πνεύματι τῷ ἁγίῳ·	de Spiritu sancto; siquidem Fi-
οὔτε γὰρ ὁ Υἱὸς λόγος Κυρίου λέ-	lius non dicitur uerbum Dei, sed 20
γεται, ἀλλὰ Λόγος ἁπλῶς, ἀπολύτως.	Verbum	absolute atque sim-
Τίς δὲ ἡ διαφορὰ τοῦ οὕτως λέγε-	pliciter. Quae vero sit differentia,
σθαι ἢ ἐκείνως, οὐ νῦν λέγειν καιρός·	ut aliquando quidem ita dicatur,
ἀρκεῖ δὲ τοῦτο πρὸς τὰ παρόντα	aliquando uero ita, non est nunc
ἐπισημήνασθαι ὅπως ἔθος τῇ γραφῇ	temporis dicere, et ad praesentem 25
τῇ θείᾳ λέγειν, ὅταν τοιαῦτα λέγειν	causam sufficit adnotasse quae

5ᵇ. Πολλὴ — δωρεάν: (Θεοδώρου) Paris. 139, fol. 68; Vat. 1682, fol. 99.
1 ἐστιν om. PV   τοῦ Θεοῦ ἡ PV   3 κυρίου om. C   4-5 πάντα ἀναδίδονται C
7 ὧν om. V   9 πάσης ἀπλ. τῆς γῆς PV.
4-8 Misericordia — mortalium: A, fol. 9ᵃ; B, fol. 11ᶜ.   4 misericordi A
5-6 nascuntur in rasura A   6 necesaria A.
6ᵃ. Καὶ οὐ μόνον — περιλαβών: (Θεοδώρου) Paris. 139, fol. 68ᵛ; Vat. 1682, fol. 99.
12 γιγνόμενα PV   ἀναδίδονται C.
6ᵇ Et spiritu — 149, 8 seruatur: A, fol. 9ᵃ⁻ᶜ; B, fol. 11ᶜ⁻ᵈ.   19 sancto in
rasura A   22 diferentia A defferentia B   26 suffecit A.

Aᵉ 5ᵇ (p. 191, 26-192, 3): Ab speciale laude misericordiae Dei conuertitur
ad uniuersalem eius bonitatis praedicationem, quae in omnium rerum crea-
tione clara est, omnibus experta mortalibus; habunde bonitatem Dei loquitur
terrae creatio.

mercy: God's abundant lovingkindness is so great that not only do we enjoy it, but also it is poured out on the whole earth. Now, he was right to say *The earth is full of the Lord's mercy,* since from it springs everything needed for people's nourishment and sustenance; it is by enjoying it that everyone living throughout the world is kept in existence and abides, the Lord richly supplying his gift throughout the earth.

    By the word of the Lord the heavens were established (v. 6): not only did what was created at each time come into being through his lovingkindness, but also everything came into existence at his command. He includes all visible things by mentioning the greater and more important. *And by the breath of his mouth all their power.* He neither refers to the Son, as some commentators believed, by *the word of the Lord,* nor to the Holy Spirit by *the breath of his mouth:* the Son is not called *word of the Lord,* but simply and absolutely Word. Now, this is not the time to discuss the difference between one statement and the other; it is sufficient for the present to indicate what the divine Scripture normally says when it wants to express such things. | Nor is the

βούληται, οὔτε τὸ Πνεῦμα τὸ ἅγιον
πνεῦμα στόματος αὐτοῦ, ἀλλὰ πνεῦμα
Θεοῦ καὶ πνεῦμα Κυρίου καὶ Πνεῦμα
ἅγιον.

5

Οὐδὲ γὰρ πρέπουσα ἡ τοιαύτη
φωνὴ τῇ τοῦ ἁγίου Πνεύματος ἀξίᾳ.
Στόμα γὰρ ἐπὶ τούτοις ὅταν εἴπῃ,
ἐνέργειάν τινα παρασημαίνειν βούλε-
10 ται τὴν ἐπὶ τῆς ὁρωμένης πληρουμέ-
νην κτίσεως, ὡς καὶ χεῖρας ὅταν
λέγῃ καὶ πόδας καὶ εἴ τι τοιοῦτο
οὕτως.

Καὶ ἀλλαχοῦ ἡ γραφή· τὸ γὰρ
15 στόμα Κυρίου ἐλάλησε ταῦτα, ἵνα εἴπῃ
Ταῦτα ὁ Θεὸς ἀπεφήνατο τὰ περὶ
ἡμῶν ὁρισθέντα· οὐδαμοῦ γὰρ σωματικῇ τοιαύτῃ φωνῇ τὴν φύσιν ἐξηγεῖται ἡ θεία γραφὴ τοῦ δεσπότου

20

ἢ ἀοράτου
25 φύσεως δημιουργίαν, οἷον ἀγγέλων
καὶ τῶν τοιούτων, ὡς ἐφ᾽ ἡμῶν οἶδε
λέγειν τὸ αἱ χεῖρές σου ἐποίησαν
με.

30

Πνεύματι οὖν στόματος αὐτοῦ
λέγει τῇ ἀποφάσει.

scripturae diuinae consuetudo
sit, cum uult dicere Filium. Neque *spiritum* ergo *oris eius* appellat, sed spiritum Dei, spiritum
Domini, Spiritum sanctum: indecens namque esset Spiritui
sancto huiusmodi uocabulum.
Cum uero os Domini in scripturis sanctis dicitur, diuinae operationis species indicatur, quae
huic uisibili interuenit creaturae,
sicut et cum manus dicit ac
pedes et quicquid huiusmodi
est. Nam et alibi scriptura ait *Os
Domini locutum est ista*, ac si
diceret: Haec, quae statuta sunt,
Dei sententia uoluntasque decre-
uit. Nusquam uero diuina scriptura naturam quae est in Deo
corporali indicat uoce; si quando
uero his utitur nominibus, quae
uidentur Filio aut sancto Spiritui conuenire, operationem magis significat aut inuisibilis naturae, ut angelorum ac similium
potestatum, aut certe nostram,
de quibus dicit: *Manus tuae fecerunt me*. Quis ergo ita erit obsti-
pus et saxeus ut, cum audit
et Spiritu oris eius, Spiritum
sanctum audeat dicere? *Spiritu*
ergo *oris eius*, ac si diceret Pro-
mulgatione eius atque sententia.

8-10 cf. in Oseam I, 1 (P. G., LXVI, 125 C); in Aggaeum II, 5 (484 C-485 C)   14-15 Is. I,
20; XL, 5   27-28 Iob X, 8; Ps. CXVIII, 73.

3 ergo sanctum A   5-6 indicens AB¹   7. 13 huiusmodi] hm A¹ hominum A²
11 inuisibili B¹   creturae A   15 locum A   17 sententia] sentia A¹   19 na-
turam] nat** B   deo] diuina A   20 corpurali A¹   21 nominibus] nobis A
23-24 magis] mg A *in textu*, magnam *add. supra*   25 simi A¹   26 aut * A
28 quis] qsi (quasi) A¹   31 sanctum *om* A¹   spiritui A¹   32 oris eius *subin-
tellege e. g.* idem est.

Holy Spirit called *breath of his mouth,* but Spirit of God, Spirit of the Lord, Holy Spirit, such an expression not befitting the dignity of the Holy Spirit. You see, when it says *mouth* in these cases, it intends to indicate an operation affecting visible creation, as when it also says "hand" and "feet" and the like. Elsewhere, too, Scripture says, "The mouth of the Lord said this,"[2] in the sense, God revealed what had been determined in our regard; nowhere does the divine Scripture by such corporeal expression describe the Lord's nature or the creation of invisible nature, such as angels and the like, as in our case it is in the habit of saying, "Your hands made me."[3] So by *breath of his mouth* he means "by his decision." | Now, he expressed it this way in keeping with

2. Cf. Isa 1:20; 40:5.
3. Job 10:8.

Οὕτω δὲ αὐτὸ ἔφρασεν ἀκολουθῶν ἑαυτῷ. Ἐπειδὴ γὰρ λόγον Κυρίου σωματικώτερον ἀνωτέρω εἶπεν τὸ βούλημα τὸ τοῦ Θεοῦ καθ᾽ ὃ συνέστησαν οἱ οὐρανοί, — εἰώθαμεν δὲ τὸ πνεῦμα τοῦτο, λέγω δὴ τὸν ἀέρα, πλήττοντες τῷ τῆς γλώττης ὀργάνῳ οὕτως ἀποτελεῖν διὰ τοῦ στόματος τὴν ἔναρθρον φωνὴν τὸν λόγον προφέροντες, — ἀκολουθῶν ἑαυτῷ πλατυτέρῃ τῇ ἐξηγήσει καὶ σωματικωτέρᾳ τὴν ἀπόφασιν οὕτως ἐκάλεσεν.

Τὸ δὲ ἡ δύναμις αὐτῶν, τουτέστι τῶν οὐρανῶν, καλῶς εἶπε Σύμμαχος ἡ διακόσμησις αὐτῶν. ἵνα ᾖ ἥλιος καὶ σελήνη καὶ ἀστέρες· ταῦτα γάρ ἐστιν οὐρανοῦ διακόσμησις εἰς τὸ εὐπρεπέστερον τῇ τούτων δημιουργίᾳ καταστάντος. Δυνάμεις μέντοι τῶν οὐρανῶν ταῦτα καὶ ὁ Κύριος ἐν τοῖς εὐαγγελίοις ἐκάλεσεν εἰπών· Αἱ δυνάμεις τῶν οὐρανῶν σαλευθήσονται, δυνάμεις αὐτὰ εἰπὼν ὡς πάντων μάλιστα τῶν ὑπὲρ γῆς ὁρατῶν μείζονα τῆς δυνάμεως τὴν ἀπόδειξιν παρεχόμενα. Εἰ δὲ πληθυντικῶς λέγει οὐρανοὺς οὐ θαυμαστόν· ἔθος γὰρ τῷ ἑβραίῳ πληθυντικῶς καλεῖν τὸ ἑνικόν. Τούτου δὴ πρόσεστί τι καὶ ἡμῖν τοῦ ἔθους, ὃ καὶ μάλιστα ἐν

Sic autem locutus est, ut consequentiam praemissam per cuncta seruaret. Nam quia uoluntatem Domini, corporali usus uocabulo, superius *uerbum Domini* dixerat 5 per quod caelorum sit magnitudo conpacta, — consueuimus autem, cum uerba proferimus, spiritum hunc, id est aerem, lingua percutientes articulatam uocem red- 10 dere, — insistens ergo consequentiae latiore et corpo|rali expositione sententiam Dei | *spiritum oris eius* appellat.

Omnis uero *uirtus eorum*, id 15 est caelorum, optime Symmachus posuit *ornatus eorum*, id est sol, luna, stellae; inde Dominus in euangelio ait: *Et uirtutes caelorum commouebuntur. Uirtu-* 20 *tes* autem *caelorum* haec eadem ornamenta ideo uocantur, quod prae omnibus uisilibus creaturis praestent operationis ac potentiae suae maiora documenta. 25

Quod autem pluraliter caelos dicit, non est nouum; quia consuetudinis hebreae est pro 30 singulari numero ponere pluralem, sicut et nobis moris est

-20 Matth. XXIV, 29.

    raemisam AB   3 quia] que A¹   10 articulatad A¹   12 latiore] u(el) n [= latione] add. supra A   15 uero] ergo A   17 possuit A   25 suae om. A 30 consuitudinis B   31-32 pluralem et A.

    Aᵉ   29 ss. (p. 192, 4-9): ldioma Ebriorum est plurali numero pro singulari uti; ideo hic « eorum », non « eius », possuit. Virtus autem caelorum uel ipsa firmitas elimenti uel ornatus astrorum; nam et Simmachus ita possuit: *Omnis ornatus eorum.*

his own thought: since above he referred in a rather corporeal fashion to the will of God by which the heavens were established (we normally manipulate this breath—I mean air—with the instrument of the tongue and produce through the mouth the articulated sound and thus utter the word), in keeping with his own thought he referred to the decision in this way by a more expansive and corporeal explanation.

Now, for *all their power*—that is, the heavens'—Symmachus well said "their adornment," meaning the sun, moon, and stars, these being the adornment of heaven, which is lent greater charm by their creation. By "powers of heaven" the Lord also referred to them in the Gospels, "The powers of the heavens will be moved,"[4] calling them "powers" particularly for being greater than all the things visible above earth in providing proof of power. Now, if he says "heavens" in the plural, it is not surprising: Hebrew normally refers to the singular in the plural. This resembles our custom, too, | which

---

4. Matt 24:29.

ταῖς ἐπιστολαῖς ποιεῖν εἰώθαμεν καὶ
ἐν ταῖς πρὸς τοὺς πολλοὺς διαλέ-
ξεσιν, ὧν γὰρ εἷς ὁ γράφων « γρά-
φομεν » καὶ « προσαγορεύομεν »
5 πληθυντικῇ τῇ ἐκδόσει κεχρημένος.
Ἔστι τοίνυν τοιοῦτο καὶ παρὰ τοῖς
Ἑβραίοις ἔθος, ᾧ κεχρῆσθαι φιλοῦσιν ἐπὶ τῶν μειζόνων.

facere cum scribimus aut certe
cum loquimur.

Haec ergo apud Ebreos, etiam
cum de maioribus rebus sermo
fit, forma seruatur.

7ᵃ. Συνάγων ὡσεὶ ἀσκὸν ὕδατα θαλάσσης. Ἐμνημόνευσε γῆς, οὐρανῶν,
10 τῆς τούτων διακοσμήσεως, μνημονεύει καὶ τῶν ὑδάτων μηδὲν τῶν καθολικῶν
παραλιμπάνων. Τὸ δὲ ὡσεὶ ἀσκὸν εἶπε τὸ εὐχερὲς καὶ δυνατὸν τοῦ Θεοῦ
τῆς ἐνεργείας παρασημαίνων, ὅτι οὕτως εὐχερῶς καὶ δυνατῶς εἰς ἓν τὰ
τοσαῦτα τῆς θαλάσσης ὕδατα συγχέει ὡς εἴ τις ἐν ἀσκῷ ὕδωρ συνέχοι,
τῆς ἔξωθεν περιβολῆς | ἐξ ἀνάγκης αὐτὸ κατεχούσης.

15 7ᵇ. Τιθεὶς ἐν θησαυροῖς ἀβύσσους. Ἵνα εἴπῃ ὡς ἐν θησαυροῖς. Ἰδίωμα
δὲ καὶ τοῦτο ἑβραϊκὸν ἄνευ τοῦ « ὡς » τῇ παραβολῇ κεχρῆσθαι, ὡς τὸ Καὶ
ἔθετο τόξον χαλκοῦν τοὺς βραχίονάς μου, ἀντὶ τοῦ ὡς τόξον. Καλῶς δὲ
εἶπεν ὡς ἐν θησαυροῖς ἀβύσσους· ἐπειδὴ γὰρ τὸ ἐν θησαυροῖς ἀποκείμενον
εἴωθεν ἀμετάθετον ἔν τινι τόπῳ καθεστάναι, τοῦτο βούλεται εἰπεῖν περὶ
20 τοῦ Θεοῦ ὅτι Τὰς τοσαύτας ἀβύσσους οὕτως ἐν ἑνὶ τόπῳ συναγαγὼν ἀκι-
νήτους φυλάττεις καὶ ἀμεταθέτους, οὐκ ἐῶν κατὰ τὸν νόμον τῶν ὑδάτων
χωρεῖν τε προσωτέρω καὶ ἐπιπολάζειν τῇ γῇ, ὡς ἂν εἴ τις τῶν βαρυτάτων
τε | ὑλῶν τι θησαυρίζειν βουλόμενος ἀποθοῖτο, συναγαγὼν ἐν τόποις ἰδίοις.

17 Ps. XVII, 35ᵇ.

7 de *om.* A¹.

7ᵃ. Ἐμνημόνευσεν — κατεχούσης: (Θεοδώρου) Paris. 139, fol. 68ᵛ; Vat. 1682,
fol. 99ᵛ; Barbaro, p. 294.   11-14 τὸ εὐχερὲς — κατεχούσης *affert* L (p. 567, 10-14)
13 συνέχει C.
7ᵇ Ἵνα εἴπῃ — 23 ἰδίοις: (Θεοᵈ) Paris. 139, fol. 69; Vat. 1682, fol. 100; Barbaro, p. 295.   16 καὶ τὸ PV   18 ἀβύσσους *om.* C   ἐπεὶ PV   20 τὰς *om.* PV
21 νόμον ὑδάτων PV   22 βραχυτάτων C   23 τι *om.* PV   ἀπέθοιτο PV   ἰδία C.

7ᵇ Aᵉ (p. 192, 9-21): Vt facilitate omnipotentiae maria cohibentis exprimeret.
Ponens in tesauris abisos. Obdendo concludens; quasi Ebrorum ussu qui com-
parationibus copolationibusque non praeponunt aduerbia, ut sit sensus: tanquam
solidas quasque materias, quae semel conditae non mouentur, sic fluentes
natura abysos eadem potentia, qua condit, terminauit litoribus, conclusit ualli-
bus, ad instar tesauri abditi et per hoc immoti, ut non progrederentur, efficit;
totum autem dicit augenter.

we normally follow particularly in letters and in conversation with the general run of people, the single writer using the plural expression "we write" and "we greet." Such, then, is normal practice with the Hebrews, and they are fond of adopting it in a great many cases.

Collecting all the waters of the sea like a flask (v. 7). Having mentioned earth, and heavens and their adornment, he mentions also *the waters,* leaving nothing of the whole array untouched. By the phrase *like a flask* he suggested the facility and power of God's operation, that he easily and powerfully pours together into one mass such great waters of the sea as if someone poured water into a flask, the outside container holding it under pressure. *Putting the deeps in storehouses,* as if to say, as in storehouses. Now, it is also a Hebrew idiom to make a comparison without "as," as in the verse, "He made my arms a bronze bow"—that is, as a bow.[5] It was well put, *the deeps as in storehouses:* since we usually put permanently in some place what is deposited in storehouses, he wants to say this about God: You thus collect such great deeps in one place and keep them unmoved and unchanged, not allowing them by the norm for waters to advance further and flood the earth, like someone wanting to store something of the heaviest materials and deposit them, collecting them in their own places. | For *collecting* and *putting* Aquila

---

5. Ps 18:34.

Ακύλας τὸ συνάγων καὶ τὸ τιθεὶς ὡς ἐπὶ παρεληλυθότος λέγει συνήγαγε καὶ ἀπέθετο. Ἀκολουθότερον μὲν οὖν ἐκεῖνο εἶναι δοκεῖ — τὸ συνήγαγε καὶ ἀπέθετο — ὡς ἐπὶ παρεληλυθότος τὸ γεγονὸς ἐξηγουμένου, ἀξιοπρεπέστερον δὲ τοῦτο καὶ συμφωνοῦν μᾶλλον τῇ λοιπῇ διανοίᾳ τῆς θείας γραφῆς· ἧ κέχρηται πολλαχοῦ περὶ τοῦ γεγονότος, ὡς ἑκάστοτε γινομένου λέγουσα 5 κυριώτερον, νῦν ἐπὶ τῶν ὑδάτων ἐχρήσατο. Τῶν μὲν γὰρ ἄλλων ὅπερ ἄν τις συναγάγοι ἢ ἀποθοῖτο ἐξ ἀρχῆς μένει κατὰ τὴν τοῦ συναγαγόντος συναγωγήν, τὰ δὲ ὕδατα, κἂν πλεονάκις τις συναγάγοι μὴ ἐμβαλὼν ἀγγείῳ ἢ ἐργασάμενός τι τὸ κωλῦον τὴν ἐπὶ τὰ πρόσω πρόοδον, πάλιν διολισθαίνοντα κατὰ τὴν οἰκείαν φύσιν προσωτέρω χωρεῖ. Ἐπειδὴ τοίνυν ταῦτα, 10 λέγω δὴ τὰ ὕδατα, οὐδὲν ἔχοντα τὸ ἐπέχον τῇ τοῦ Θεοῦ ἀποφάσει κωλύεται, καλῶς εἶπε τὸ συνάγων καὶ τὸ τιθείς, ὡς ἀεὶ αὐτοῦ τῷ βουλήματι τοῦτο ἐνεργοῦντος παρὰ τὴν τῶν ὑδάτων φύσιν.

8ª. Φοβηθήτω τὸν Κύριον πᾶσα ἡ γῆ. Μετὰ τὴν καθολικὴν ἐξήγησιν καὶ τὴν ἐπὶ τῇ τῶν ὅλων δημιουργίᾳ ὑμνῳδίαν, καθολικὴν ποιεῖται καὶ τὴν 15 παραίνεσιν, πᾶσι φοβεῖσθαι παραγγέλλων εἰκότως τὸν τοσαῦτα καὶ τηλικαῦτα ἐργασάμενον.

8ᵇ. Ἀπ᾽ αὐτοῦ δὲ σαλευθήτωσαν πάντες οἱ κατοικοῦντες τὴν οἰκουμένην. Τὸ σαλευθήτωσαν, ἀντὶ τοῦ σφόδρα φοβηθήτωσαν, ἐπειδὴ ἔθος τὸν ὑπερβαλλόντως φοβούμενον καὶ σαλεύεσθαι τρόμῳ κατεχόμενον. 20

9. Ὅτι αὐτὸς εἶπεν, καὶ ἐγενήθησαν. Σύντομον καὶ ἀναγκαίαν εἶπε τοῦ φόβου καὶ τοῦ τρόμου τὴν αἰτίαν· τοὺς γὰρ ὑπ᾽ αὐτοῦ γινομένους προσῆκόν ἐστι φοβεῖσθαι τὸν ποιητήν. Εἶτα εἰρηκὼς αἰτίαν πασῶν μὲν ἀναγκαιοτέραν, ἅπαξ δὲ γενομένην τῶν ὄντων τὴν δημιουργίαν λέγει καὶ τὰ ἑκάστοτε γινόμενα παρ᾽ αὐτοῦ ἢ ἃ ποιεῖν δύναται, ἀναγκαίως αὐτὸν δεῖν φοβεῖσθαι 25 διὰ πάντων δεικνύς, ὁμοῦ δὲ καὶ τὰ ἁρμόττοντα τῇ παρούσῃ ὑποθέσει τοῦ ψαλμοῦ λέγων, ἵνα καὶ τὴν ἀλήθειαν ἔχῃ τὰ λεγόμενα ἀπὸ τῶν γεγονότων μὴ ῥήματα εἶναι δοκοῦντα, ἀλλὰ καὶ τοῖς πράγμασιν οὕτω δεικνύμενα. Καὶ τί φησιν;

4 λυπῇ C.
8ª·ᵇ. Μετὰ — κατεχόμενον: (Θεοδώρου) Paris. 139, fol. 69; Vat. 1682, fol. 100ᵛ.
15 τὴν ἐπὶ] τῇ ἐπὶ PV   δημιουργίαν PV.
9. Σύντομον — τί φησιν: (Θεοδώρου) Paris. 139, fol. 69ᵛ; Vat. 1682, fol. 101;
Barbaro, p. 296.   26 τὰ om. C   ὑποθέσει om. PV   28 μὴ] εἰ καὶ C   καὶ om. PV
δεικνύμενα] διακείμενα C.

Aᵉ 24-26 (p. 193, 8-9): Causas obtexiuit quibus merito timeatur Deus.

says "collected" and "deposited," as though in the past. While it seems more logical, then, to take "collected" and "deposited" as an event in the past, the other version is more seemly and more consistent with the rest of the sense of the divine Scripture; in many places it treats of a past event by speaking of it more accurately as continuing to happen each time. This convention is here applied to the waters: while whatever else one collects or deposits originally remains in the collection of the collector, even if one frequently collects water without putting it into a jar or creating some obstacle to its flow, it seeps out according to its nature and moves on. Since, then, this—I mean *the waters*—met with no obstacle but was prevented by God's decree, he was right to say *collecting* and *putting,* as he constantly causes this to happen by his will in defiance of the nature of water.

Let all the earth fear the Lord (v. 8). After the general explanation and the hymn-singing on the creation of all things, he also makes a general exhortation, rightly giving instructions for the maker of so many wonderful things to be feared by everyone. *Let all the inhabitants of the world tremble before him,* the word *tremble* meaning "fear deeply," since it is normal for the one with extreme fear to be seized with shaking and to tremble. *Because he spoke, and they were made* (v. 9). He mentioned a concise and basic reason for the fear and trembling: it behooved those made by him to fear the maker. Then, after mentioning the most basic reason of all, he cites the creation of existing things that happened once as well as the things being done by him that he is able to do, bringing out that consequently he must be feared in everything. At the same time, he mentions also the matters relevant to the present theme of the psalm, so that the claims arising from what was made may contain the truth, not seeming to be mere words but thus proved also by facts.

What does he say? | *The Lord frustrates nations' plans* (v. 10): he wreaks

10ᵃ. Κύριος διασκεδάζει βουλὰς ἐθνῶν. Διασκορπίζει αὐτῶν τὰ βουλεύματα, οὐκ ἐῶν εἰς πέρας ἐλθεῖν.

10ᵇ·ᶜ. Ἀθετεῖ δὲ λογισμοὺς λαῶν. Ἀπράκτους αὐτοὺς καθίστησιν, ἀκύρους καὶ ματαίους. Καὶ ἀθετεῖ βουλὰς ⟨ἀρχόντων⟩. Τὸ αὐτὸ διαφόρως ἐξη-
5 γήσατο ἐθνῶν εἰπὼν καὶ λαῶν καὶ ἀρχόντων, τοῦτο βουλόμενος εἰπεῖν ὅτι κἂν πλῆθος ᾖ τὸ βουλευόμενον, τοῦ Θεοῦ τὸ ἐναντίον βουλομένου, ἀνωφελὲς τὸ πλῆθος ἐν τοῖς βουλευομένοις, κἂν ἄρχοντές τι λογίζωνται, ἄπρακτον αὐτοῖς τὸ σπουδαζόμενον γίνεται, οὐδὲν ὠφελουμένοις ἐκ τῆς ἀρχῆς ἢ τοῦ πλήθους τῶν ὑπηκόων. Εἶτα τὸ μεῖζον.

10   11. Ἡ δὲ βουλὴ τοῦ Κυρίου εἰς τὸν αἰῶνα μένει, λογισμοὶ τῆς καρδίας αὐτοῦ ἀπὸ γενεῶν εἰς γενεάς. Οὐ γὰρ μόνον φησὶ τὰ τῶν ἄλλων ἄκυρα ἀποφαίνειν δύναται, ἀλλὰ καὶ τοῖς οἰκείοις πολλὴν προστιθέναι τὴν βεβαίωσιν. Λογισμοὺς δὲ τῆς καρδίας εἶπε σωματικῶς, τὸν κεκριμένον ὅρον καὶ τὴν κυρίαν ἀπόφασιν οὕτω καλῶν τοῦ Θεοῦ, ἵνα εἴπῃ ὅτι ἀμετάθετος ἡ τοιαύτη
15 γνώμη τοῦ δεσπότου. Ὥσπερ δὲ ἐκεῖνα διαφόρως εἶπε βουλὰς ἐθνῶν καὶ λογισμοὺς λαῶν καὶ λογισμοὺς ἀρχόντων, οὕτω πάλιν καὶ τὰ τοῦ Κυρίου διαφόρως ἐξηγήσατο βουλὴν Κυρίου εἰπὼν καὶ λογισμοὺς καρδίας αὐτοῦ, μεγαλοπρεπέστερον αὐτὰ ἐξηγήσασθαι βουλόμενος τῇ διαφορᾷ τῶν λεγομένων. Ταῦτα δὲ οὕτω γενέσθαι παρὰ τοῦ Θεοῦ ὡς ἀπὸ τῶν παρόντων φησίν·
20 διὸ μετὰ τὴν καθολικὴν ἐξήγησιν καὶ μετὰ τὴν καθολικὴν ὑμνῳδίαν τρέπει καὶ ἐπὶ τὴν ὑπόθεσιν αὐτὴν τὸν λόγον ἀπὸ τῆς ἐξηγήσεως καί φησιν· Λογισμοὶ τῆς καρδίας ⟨αὐτοῦ ἀπὸ γενεῶν εἰς γενεάς⟩.

    12. Μακάριον τὸ ἔθνος οὗ ἐστιν Κύριος ὁ θεὸς αὐτοῦ, λαός ὃν ἐξελέξατο εἰς κληρονομίαν ἑαυτῷ. Ἐπειδὴ τοίνυν οὕτω φησί τά τε τῶν ἄλλων
25 ἄπρακτα δείκνυσι καὶ τοῖς οἰκείοις πολλὴν παρέχει τὴν βεβαίωσιν, μακάριοι

---

10. Διασκορπίζει — μεῖζον: (Θεοδώρου) Paris. 139, fol. 69ᵛ; Vat. 1582, fol. 101ʳ·ᵛ; Barbaro, p. 297; cf. L (p. 569, 19-23).   1 διασκορπίζει] διασκεδάζει C   2 ἐᾷ PV   4 καὶ — βουλὰς om. PV   ἀρχόντων supplevi   9 ἦ om. PV.

11. Οὐ γὰρ — γενεᾶς: (Θεοδώρου) Paris. 139, fol. 69ᵛ; Vat. 1682, fol. 101ᵛ; Barbaro, p. 297.   11 γὰρ om. PV   15-18 ὥσπερ — λεγομένων affert L (p. 570, 13-18)   18 αὐτὸ PV   19 γίγνεσθαι PV   22 λογισμοὶ τῆς καρδίας om. PV   αὐτοῦ — γενεάς supplevi.

12. Ἐπειδὴ — καί φησιν: (Θεοδώρου) Paris. 139, fol. 70; Vat. 1682, fol. 101ᵛ-102; Barbaro, p. 298.   24 φησὶν οὕτω C   ἄλλων φησὶν C   25 βεβαίωσιν] βελτίωσιν C.

Aᵉ 11 (p. 193, 17-20): Ad superiora retulit cogitationes et consilia; dixerat enim Dominus dissipat consilia gentium, reprobat autem cogitationes cordis.

confusion on their plans, not allowing them to take effect. *He sets aside people's thoughts:* he renders them futile, ineffectual, and pointless. *He sets aside rulers' plans.* He made the same comment in different ways in reference to nations, peoples, and rulers, meaning that even if a vast number were scheming, while God wanted the opposite, the vast number would be of no significance to the schemes. Even if rulers planned something, the object of their concern would come to nothing, and they would get no benefit from the government or the vast number of the subjects. Then the more important consideration. *But the plan of the Lord abides forever, thoughts of his heart from age to age* (v. 11): not only can he render the schemes of others ineffectual, but also he can bring great reliability to his own. Now, *thoughts of his heart* is a bodily expression by which he refers to God's determined limit and authoritative decree, as if to say, Such a decision of the Lord is irrevocable. As he expressed his idea in different ways as *nations' plans, peoples' thoughts,* and *rulers' plans,* so in turn in different ways he also explained *the plan of the Lord and thoughts of his heart,* wanting to explain them in more fitting fashion with different forms of expression. He says that these things were thus done by God as though from the present; hence, after the general explanation and the general hymn-singing he directs consideration also to the theme itself from the explanation in the words *thoughts of his heart from generation to generation.*

Happy the nation whose God is the Lord, the people he chose as his own inheritance (v. 12): since, then, he thus shows that the plans of the others are futile and provides his own with stability, | you who are dedicated to

ὑμεῖς οἱ τῷ δεσπότῃ ἀνακείμενοι, καὶ μακάριοι ὑμεῖς οἱ παρ' αὐτοῦ λαὸς ἐκλεχθείς, ἐπείπερ ἀμετάθετος ἡ εἰς ὑμᾶς εὐεργεσία τοῦ δεσπότου γίγνεται. Ἰδοὺ γὰρ καὶ τοιούτων τετυχήκατε, τοῦ Θεοῦ τὰ μηχανήματα τῶν πολεμίων περιτρέψαντος εἰς τὸ ἐναντίον. Τὸ δὲ εἰς κληρονομίαν ἑαυτῷ ἀντὶ τοῦ εἰς ἐξαίρετον | ἀφόρισμα, εἰς ἰδιάζουσαν δεσποτείαν, ἐπεὶ ἡ κληρονομία 5 ἰδιαζόντως ὑπὸ τὴν τῶν κληρονομούντων κεῖται δεσποτείαν. Εἶτα ὡς πρὸς ἀπόδειξιν τῶν λεχθέντων καὶ σύστασιν ἐξηγεῖται τὰ γεγονότα καί φησιν·

13ᵃ. Ἐξ οὐρανοῦ ἐπέβλεψεν ὁ Κύριος. Ἐπειδὴ τὸν ὀφθαλμὸν ἐπὶ τοῦ Θεοῦ καλεῖ τὸ διορατικὸν καὶ διαγνωστικὸν εἴτε ἐπὶ τῶν δικαίων ἐπ' εὐεργεσίᾳ γιγνόμενον, εἴτε ἐπὶ τῶν ἁμαρτωλῶν ἐπὶ τιμωρίᾳ, τὸ ἐξ οὐρανοῦ ἐπέβλε- 10 ψεν ὁ Κύριος ἀκολούθως φησὶ τοῖς ἄνω ὡς πρὸς ἀπόδειξιν τῶν λεχθέντων, ὅτι οὕτω φησὶν μακάριοι ὑμεῖς οἱ ἐκλεγέντες παρ' αὐτοῦ, ὅτι ἰδοὺ οὐ κατέλιπεν ἀνεξέταστα τὰ γεγενημένα.

13ᵇ. Εἶδεν πάντας τοὺς υἱοὺς τῶν ἀνθρώπων. Τὸ αὐτὸ πάλιν λέγει· ὅμοιον γάρ ἐστι τῷ εἶδε τὸ ἐπέβλεψεν, ἀντὶ τοῦ προσέσχε, διέγνω τὰ γεγενημένα. 15

14. Ἐξ ἑτοίμου κατοικητηρίου αὐτοῦ ἐπέβλεψεν ἐπὶ πάντας τοὺς κατοικοῦντας τὴν γῆν. Τὸ δὲ ἐξ ἑτοίμου κατοικητηρίου αὐτοῦ Σύμμαχος λέγει φανερώτερον ἀπὸ τῆς ἑδραίας κατοικίας αὐτοῦ, ἵνα δείξῃ φοβερωτέραν τὴν ἐξέτασιν τὴν παρὰ τοῦ Θεοῦ γινομένην τῷ ἑδραίαν ἔχειν καὶ βεβαίαν τὸν ἐξετάζοντα τὴν ἐξουσίαν. Τοῦτο γὰρ βούλεται ἐνταῦθα εἰπεῖν τὸ κατοι- 20 κητήριον αὐτοῦ, ἀπὸ τῆς κατοικίας αὐτοῦ τὸ τῆς φύσεως αὐτοῦ καὶ τῆς ἐξουσίας βέβαιον παριστάς, ὡς καὶ ἐν τῷ Ἰὼβ φησιν ἐᾷ δὲ τοὺς κατοικοῦντας οἰκίας πηλίνας, ἐξ οὗ καὶ αὐτοί ἐσμεν ἐκ τοῦ αὐτοῦ πηλοῦ, ἀπὸ | τῆς οἰκήσεως τὸ εὐδιάλυτον καὶ ἀσθενὲς τῆς φύσεως τῶν ἀνθρώπων παραδεικνύς. Τὸ δὲ ἑδραῖον ἕτοιμον ἐκάλεσεν, ἐπεὶ τὸ μὲν ἑδραῖον πάντως ὂν καὶ 25 διαμένον ἕτοιμόν ἐστιν καὶ εὐπρεπές, οὐ δεόμενόν τινος παρασκευῆς, τὸ δὲ ἑτοιμασίας δεόμενον οὐδὲ εἶναι δύναται καθό τινος ἑτοιμασίας καὶ παρασκευῆς προσδεῖται.

22-23 Iob IV, 19.

151, 25 μακάριοι — 152, 6 δεσποτείαν *affert pluribus omissis* L (p. 570, 26-31) 1-2 ἡμεῖς ... ἡμᾶς V² 2 ἐκλεγεῖς PV 5-6 ἐπεὶ — δεσποτείαν *om.* C. **13ᵃ⁻ᵇ.** Ἐπειδὴ — γεγενημένα: (Θεοδώρου) Paris. 139, fol. 70; Vat. 1682; fol. 102; Barbaro, p. 299; cf. L (571, 10-12). 10 γενόμενον C 11 φησι *om.* PV. **14.** Τὸ δὲ — προσδεῖται: (Θεοδώρου) Paris. 139, fol. 70; Vat. 1682, fol. 102ᵛ; Barbaro, p. 300; cf. L (p. 571, 1-7, 19-23). 23 καὶ ἡμεῖς τοῦ αὐτοῦ ἐσμὲν πηλοῦ PV 25 ἐπειδὴ C πάντως] πᾶν καὶ C 26 ἐστιν] ἐστῶς C.

Aᵉ 4-6 (p. 193, 23-25): Id est tanquam tam proprie esset plebs eius et peculialiter, ut sunt heriditates heredum.

the Lord are fortunate, and you the people chosen by him are fortunate for the reason that the Lord's kindness to you is unchanging. After all, see the kind of favors you have received when God turned the enemies' schemes to opposite effect. Now, *his own inheritance* refers to exclusive choice, special lordship, since the inheritance falls exclusively under the control of those inheriting.

Then, by way of proof of the reality of what had been said, he comments also on what had been made, saying *From heaven the Lord looked down* (v. 13). Since he uses the eye in God's case to refer to differentiating and distinguishing what happens either to the righteous by way of kindness or to sinners by way of punishment, he logically said *From heaven the Lord looked down* on those below as a proof of what was said, meaning, You are fortunate in being chosen by him because, lo, what had been made he did not leave without surveillance. *He saw all human beings.* He says the same thing again: *He looked down* is similar to *He saw*—that is, he paid attention; he exactly discerned what had been made.

From his ready abode he looked on all the inhabitants of the earth (v. 14). For *From his ready abode* Symmachus said more clearly "from his established dwelling," so as to present the examination by God as more fearsome for the reason of the examiner's having an established and unchanging authority. This, you see, is the meaning here of *his abode,* presenting under the notion of his dwelling the stability of his nature and authority, as he also says in Job, "He allows those who dwell in houses of clay, since we ourselves are also of the same clay,"[6] by the idea of a dwelling highlighting the instability and weakness of human nature. By *ready* he meant "established," since what is completely established is also in a ready and seemly condition, needing no equipment, since what is in need of readying cannot even exist insofar as it requires readying and equipping. | *He looked on all the inhab-*

---

6. Cf. Job 4:19 LXX.

14ᵇ. Ἐπέβλεψεν ἐπὶ πάντας τοὺς κατοικοῦντας τὴν γῆν. Πάλιν προστίθησι τὴν τῆς ἐξετάσεως ἐξήγησιν ἵνα εἴπῃ ὅτι οὐδενὸς καταμελεῖ, μακαριστοὺς ἐκ τούτου τοὺς ὑπὸ τὴν αὐτοῦ πρόνοιαν δεῖξαι βουλόμενος τῷ μὴ δύνασθαι ῥαθυμηθῆναι ὑπ' αὐτοῦ.

15. Ὁ πλάσας κατὰ μόνας τὰς καρδίας αὐτῶν, ὁ συνιεὶς πάντα τὰ ἔργα αὐτῶν. | Τινὲς ᾠήθησαν τὸν μακάριον Δαυὶδ ἐνταῦθα λέγειν ὅτι κατὰ μόνας ἔπλασε τὰς ψυχὰς τῶν ἀνθρώπων κεχωρισμένως τοῦ σώματος, ὡς καρδίας τὰς ψυχὰς λέγοντος. Εἴτε δὲ οὕτως ἔχει, εἴτε καὶ μὴ — μακροτέρων γὰρ ἐκεῖνο δεῖται τῶν λόγων — οὐ τοῦτο ἐνταῦθα εἰπεῖν βούλεται, ἀλλὰ τὰς καρδίας αὐτῶν, ἵνα εἴπῃ αὐτούς, ἀπὸ τοῦ μερικοῦ λέγων τὸ ὅλον.

Ὁ πλάσας οὖν αὐτοὺς κατὰ μόνας, ἀντὶ τοῦ οὐδενὸς παρόντος ἀνθρώπων,

ἵνα εἴπῃ Οὐκ ὄντας παρήγαγε, τοῦτο ἀπὸ τοῦ πρωτοπλάστου ἐξηγούμενος, ἐν ᾧ πρῶτον τὴν φύσιν κατεβάλετο τῶν ἀνθρώπων· ἀνάγκη γὰρ ἦν τὸν ἄνθρωπον, οὐδενὸς ὁμοίου παρόντος, γεγενημένον οὐκ ὄντα παρῆχθαι.

Corda hominum pro ipsis hominibus posuit, a parte totum hominem more suo indicans. Qui fingit igitur eos *singulatim*, operi suo nullo adstante hominum uel praesente, ac si diceret: Cum necdum essent, ipse eos, ut subsisterent, fecit. Hoc autem de primo plasto dicitur, in quo natura hominum sumpsit exordium. Hic ergo necessario, cum nullus adhuc esset mortalium qui operi diuino adsisteret, formam hominis primus accepit.

Οὕτω γὰρ καὶ ἀλλαχοῦ φησιν Ἡ καρδία μου ἐταράχθη ἐν ἐμοί, ἵνα εἴπῃ ἐγώ, — ἐπάγει γὰρ φόβος καὶ τρόμος ἦλθεν ἐπ' ἐμέ, — ἀλλ' οὐδὲ ἐγχωρεῖ τὴν καρδίαν ταράσσεσθαι κεχωρισμένως τοῦ λοιποῦ σώματος. Ἔθος δὲ αὐτῷ ἀπὸ τῶν μερικῶν τὰ ὅλα οὐ γὰρ ἁπλῶς σημαίνειν, ἀλλ' ὡς ἐπὶ πολὺ κυριωτέρου τινὸς πρὸς τὴν τῶν λεγομένων σημασίαν μνημονεύοντι, οἷον τὸ ἡ καρδία μου ἐταράχθη ἐν ἐμοὶ εἶπεν, ἐπειδὴ τῆς ταραχῆς τὸ κυριώτερον καὶ ἡ αἴσθησις ἐγγίνεται τῇ καρδίᾳ, καὶ τὸ τὰ χείλη μου ἐπαινέσουσί σε λέγει,

---

24-25 Ps. LIV, 5, 6   30 Ps. LXII, 4ᵇ.

14ᵇ. Πάλιν — ὑπ' αὐτοῦ: (Θεοδώρου) Paris. 139, fol. 70ᵛ; Vat. 1682, fol. 102ᵛ.
15. Corda — accepit: A fol. 9ᶜ; B, fol. 11ᵈ. — *Praecedit textus sacer*: Qui finxit singulatim corda eorum.   11 possuit A   13 igitur A *in rasura* itaque B singillatim B *et ita supra*   13-15 operi — praesente *affert* Aᵉ (p. 195, 12-13) 14 adsistante A   16 necdum] ñ đ A, dum *add. supra lin.*   16-17 ut subs.] ait subsistirent A   18 psalto B   19 sumsit A   exordi··· B   20 necesario A 23 accipit AB.

Aᵉ 10-12 (p. 195, 3-4): Vel animas uel ipsum hominem: a parte totum.

itants of the earth. Again he provides a comment on his scrutiny, as if to say, He excludes no one from his care, wanting to show that those under his providence are to be regarded as fortunate by the impossibility of their being neglected by him.

He forms their hearts individually, he understands all their deeds (v. 15). Some commentators thought that here blessed David means that he individually formed people's souls apart from their body, as though *hearts* meant "souls." Whether this be so or not (it is a topic requiring fuller treatment), here it does not have that sense—rather, *their hearts* means "them," referring to the whole from the part. So *He forms them individually* means that none of humankind was in existence, as if to say, When they did not exist, he produced them—drawing this explanation from the first-formed, from whom human nature took its beginning. It was necessary, after all, for the human being to be brought into being from nonbeing when no one similar existed. He expresses himself likewise elsewhere as well, remember, "My heart was disturbed within me,"[7] as if to say, I (was disturbed), "for fear and trembling came upon me"; he does not allow the heart to be disturbed separately from the rest of the body. Now, it is customary with him not simply to suggest the whole from the parts, but in most cases to mention something more closely related to the meaning of the words—for example, "My heart was disturbed within me," because the essence of disturbance and its sensation occur in the heart. He also says, "My lips will praise you,"[8] | not that the lips by them-

---

7. Ps 55:4–5.
8. Ps 63:3.

οὐχ' ὅτι τὰ χειλη κεχωρισμένως εἶχεν ἐπαινεῖν τὸν Θεόν, ἀλλ' ὅτι δι' ἐκείνων ὁ ἔπαινος ἐγγίνεται. Κἀνταῦθα τοίνυν ἀπὸ τῆς καρδίας τὸ ὅλον ὠνόμασε, διὸ τὸ ἑξῆς ὁ συνιεὶς εἰς πάντα τὰ ἔργα αὐτῶν· βούλεται γὰρ εἰπεῖν διὰ τούτου ὅτι ἁπάντων ἔχω τῶν ὑφ' ὑμῶν γιγνομένων τὴν γνῶσιν. Ἐπειδὴ τοίνυν τὸ κυριώτερον πρὸς ἐξέτασιν τῶν γιγνομένων ἐστὶν ἡ τῶν λογισμῶν 5 γνῶσις, — οἳ καὶ πάσης εἰσὶν αἴτιοι πράξεως τῆς διὰ τοῦ ἀνθρώπου γιγνομένης καὶ ἐν τῷ βάθει κειμένης, οἷα γνωστότεροι καθεστήκασι τῆς καρδίας ἐκπορευόμενοι κατὰ τὴν Κυρίου φωνήν, — ὁ πλάσας τὰς καρδίας αὐτῶν εἶπε, δεικνὺς ἐντεῦθεν ὅτι οὐ δυνατὸν αὐτόν τι λαθεῖν τῶν γιγνομένων παρὰ τῶν ἀνθρώπων, ἐπεὶ καὶ τοῦ ταμείου τῶν λογισμῶν, τουτέστι τῆς καρδίας, αὐτός 10 ἐστιν ὁ δημιουργός. Τοῦτο γὰρ ἠβουλήθη εἰπεῖν, διόλου ἀκολούθως τοῖς προκειμένοις, ὅτι Μακάριοί ἐστε οἱ αὐτῷ ἀνακείμενοι, ὃς πάντων μὲν ποιεῖται τὴν ἐξέτασιν τῶν πραττομένων, λανθάνει δὲ αὐτὸν οὐδὲν ἀλλ' ἔχει πάντων ἀκριβῆ τὴν γνῶσιν. Οὗτος γάρ φησι καὶ τὰ καθ' ὑμᾶς ἐξετάσας καὶ τὰ γινόμενα περισκοπήσας, θεασάμενος τὴν ἄδικον ἔφοδον τῶν πολε- 15 μίων ἀπήλασε καὶ ταῦτα ἰσχυροὺς ὄντας τιμωρησάμενος. Διό φησιν·

16ᵃ. Οὐ σώζεται βασιλεὺς διὰ πολλὴν δύναμιν, τὸ παρ' αὐτοῖς γεγονὸς καθολικῶς ἐξηγούμενος, διόλου ταύτῃ τῇ ἀκολουθίᾳ χρησάμενος. Καὶ γὰρ ἀνωτέρω τὸ Κύριος διασκεδάζει βουλὰς ἐθνῶν καὶ τὸ ἑξῆς καθολικῶς ὡς τοῦ Θεοῦ ἐνεργοῦντος ἀεί φησιν ἀπὸ τοῦ γεγονότος παρ' αὐτοῖς ἐξη- 20 γησάμενος, καὶ ἐνταῦθα ὁμοίως κατὰ τὴν αὐτὴν ἀκολουθίαν λέγει τὸ οὐ σώζεται βασιλεὺς διὰ πολλὴν δύναμιν. Τοῦτο δὲ μετὰ καὶ τῶν ἑξῆς ἐπὶ τῆς παρούσης ὑποθέσεως ἁρμόττει λέγεσθαι ἐπὶ τοῦ τῶν Ἀσσυρίων βασιλέως, ὅτι οὐδὲν ὤνησεν αὐτὸν ἡ πολλὴ ἰσχὺς τοῦ στρατοπέδου, τῆς τοῦ Θεοῦ ὀργῆς ἀπροσδοκήτως αὐτὸν τιμωρησαμένης. 25

16ᵇ. Καὶ γίγας οὐ σωθήσεται ἐν πλήθει ἰσχύος αὐτοῦ. Γίγαντα καλεῖ τὸν δυνατόν· οὕτω γὰρ καὶ Σύμμα-

Et gigans, reliqua. Gigantes uocat uiros proceros ac ualidos. Ita namque et Symmachus: *Ne-*

7-8 Matth. XV, 19   19 v. 10

3 εἰπεῖν ὅτι *ms.*
16ᵃ. (l. 21) Τοῦτο δὲ — τιμωρησαμένης: (Θεοδώρου) Paris. 139, fol. 70ᵛ; Vat. 1682, fol. 103; Barbaro, p. 301.   20 Θεοῦ τὸ *ms.*   22 ἐπὶ] εἰ PV   24 αὐτὸν *om.* V.
16ᵇ. Γίγαντα — γεγόνασιν: (Θεοˢ) Paris. 139, fol. 70ᵛ; Vat. 1682, fol. 103; Barbaro, p. 301.   27 καλεῖ] λέγει C.
Et gigans — 155, 2 suae: A, fol. 9ᶜ; B, fol. 11ᵈ.   28 namque] neque A¹.

Aᵉ 24-25 (p. 195, 16-18): Nullus... uindictam iudicantis effugiet.

selves could praise God, but that the praise is given through them. So here, too, he referred to the whole by mentioning the heart; hence the following clause *He understands all their deeds,* meaning by it, I have knowledge of everything done by you.

Thus, the knowledge of thoughts is more relevant to the scrutiny of what happens, since these are responsible for every action done by the human being and lie within, becoming better known by issuing forth from the heart, according to the Lord's statement.[9] Hence it said *He forms their hearts,* emphasizing by this that nothing done by human beings can escape his attention, since he is the creator of the thoughts' inner chamber, namely, the heart. In fact, this was the meaning, completely consistent with what went before: Blessed are you who are devoted to him who conducts an examination of everything that is done; instead of anything escaping his notice, he has a precise knowledge of everything. He is the one, you see, who scrutinized our situation and surveyed what happened, who was alert to the enemies' unlawful incursion and repelled it, punishing them despite their being strong.

Hence, he says *A king is not saved by great power* (v. 16), making a general comment on what happens to them, following his overall theme: above he had said *The Lord frustrates nations' plans* and so on in general terms, explaining this on the basis of what happened in their case since God is ever in action; here, similarly, along the same lines he says *A king is not saved by great power.* Now, together with what follows on the present theme this is applicable to the king of the Assyrians, for the great might of the army was of no good to him since God's wrath unexpectedly punished him. *Nor will a giant be saved by his excessive strength.* By *giant* he refers to the mighty one; thus Symmachus | put it, "Nor will a warrior escape with his excessive

---

9. Cf. Matt 15:19.

χός φησιν Οὐδὲ ἀνδρεῖος διαφεύξε-   que fortis effugiet propter multi-
ται διὰ πλῆθος ἰσχύος αὐτοῦ. Δῆλον   tudinem uirtutis suae.
οὖν ὡς ὅταν λέγῃ ἡ γραφὴ τοὺς γίγαντας τοὺς ἀπ' αἰῶνος, οὐ ταῖς
μυθοποιΐαις ἀκολουθοῦσα λέγει ταῖς περὶ τῶν γιγάντων, ἀλλὰ τούς
5 ποτε ἰσχυροὺς εἰπεῖν βουλομένη. Ἐπισημαντέον δὲ ἐκεῖνο, ὅτι οὐδαμοῦ
δικαίους ἀνδρείους καλεῖ γίγαντας, ἀλλ' ὅσοι ἀνδρεῖοι καὶ ἀσεβεῖς γεγόνασιν.

17ᵃ. Ψευδὴς ἵππος εἰς σωτηρίαν. Καλῶς τὸ ψευδής. ἐπειδὴ ἵππος πολλὴ
προσοῦσα τοῖς πολεμίοις δύναται τῷ σχήματι τὴν σωτηρίαν ὑπισχνεῖ-
10 σθαι, ἀλλὰ ψεύδεται τὴν τοῦ προσχήματος ἐπαγγελίαν, τῆς τοῦ Θεοῦ ὀργῆς
δυνατωτέρας τυγχανούσης. Εὐκαίρως δὲ εἶπε τὸ ἵππος, ἐπειδὴ μάλιστα ἐπὶ
τῷ πλήθει τῶν ἵππων ηὔχουν οἱ Ἀσσύριοι.

17ᵇ. Ἐν δὲ πλήθει δυνάμεως αὐτοῦ οὐ σωθήσεται. Τουτέστι, κἂν πολλὴ
ᾖ ἵππος ἢ καὶ ἰσχυρά, τὴν σωτηρίαν οὐ παρέξει. Διὰ τί ἑξῆς φησιν.

15 18ᵃ. Ἰδοὺ οἱ ὀφθαλμοὶ Κυρίου ἐπὶ τοὺς φοβουμένους αὐτόν. Ἐπειδὴ ὁ
δεσπότης ἐπιβλέπει τοῖς ἐπιμελουμένοις αὐτοῦ τῆς εὐαρεστήσεως καὶ τῶν
προσταγμάτων. Τοῦτο γάρ ἐστι τὸ τοὺς φοβουμένους αὐτόν, ἐπειδήπερ οἱ
οἰκέται φόβῳ κατεχόμενοι πληροῦν τῶν δεσποτῶν ἐσπουδάκασι τὰ προ-
στάγματα, τοῦ φόβου | συνελαύνοντος πρὸς τὴν ἐκπλήρωσιν καὶ καταρρᾳ-
20 θυμεῖν οὐκ ἐῶντος.

18ᵇ-19. Τοὺς ἐλπίζοντας ἐπὶ τὸ ἔλεος αὐτοῦ. ῥύσασθαι ἐκ θανάτου τὰς
ψυχὰς αὐτῶν, καὶ διαθρέψαι αὐτοὺς ἐν λιμῷ. Τοὺς ἀναμένοντας τὴν τοῦ
Θεοῦ φιλανθρωπίαν ὥστε ἀπαλλαγῆναι μὲν αὐτοὺς θανάτου, ἐν δὲ τῷ καιρῷ

---

3 Gen. VI, 4.

17ᵃ. Καλῶς — Ἀσσύριοι: (Θεοδώρου) Paris. 139, fol. 71; Vat. 1682, fol. 103ʳ·ᵛ;
Barbaro, p. 302; cf. L (p. 572, 39-45).
17ᵇ. Τουτέστι — φησιν: (Θεοῦ) Paris. 139, fol. 71; Vat. 1682, fol. 103ᵛ; Barbaro, p. 302; cf. L (p. 572, 45-47).   13-14 πολλὴ ἵππος PV.
18ᵃ. Ἐπειδὴ — ἐῶντος: (Θεοδώρου) Paris. 139, fol, 71; Vat. 1682, fol. 103ᵛ;
Barbaro, p. 302; cf. L (p. 573, 5-7).   15 ἐπειδὴ] ἐπεὶ PV   16 τοὺς ἐπιμελουμένους C.
18ᵇ-19. Τοὺς ἀναμένοντας — παρ' αὐτοῦ: (Θεοδώρου) Paris. 139, fol. 71; Vat. 1682,
f. 103ᵛ; Barbaro, p. 302.   22 τὴν om. PV.

Aᵉ 11-12 (p. 195, 22-23): Oportune de Assiris equorum numero gloriantibus
dicit.

strength." So it is clear that when Scripture mentions the giants of old, it is not speaking in acceptance of the fairy tales of the giants, but with the intention of referring to the strong ones of former times. Now, it should be noted that it nowhere refers by *giants* to righteous people who were virile, but only to people who were virile and irreligious.

Deceptive a horse for salvation (v. 17). The term *deceptive* was well put, since the enemies' possession of many horses can on appearance promise them salvation, but it belies the promise of the appearance, God's wrath proving more potent. It was appropriate to mention the *horse* because the Assyrians boasted particularly of the vast number of their horses. *It will not be saved by its excessive power*—that is, even if their horses are numerous and strong, they will not provide salvation.

Hence his proceeding to say *Lo, the eyes of the Lord are on those who fear him* (v. 18), since the Lord looks on those responsive to his good pleasure and his commands (this being the meaning of *those who fear him,* since servants seized with fear are anxious to fulfill their masters' commands, fear leading them to performance and not allowing them to be lethargic). *Those who hope in his mercy, to rescue their souls from death, to sustain them in famine:* those awaiting God's lovingkindness so as to be freed from death, and in the time | of calamity to attain relief. By *famine* he refers to tribulation

τῆς συμφορᾶς ἀνέσεως τυχεῖν. Λιμὸν μὲν γὰρ καλεῖ τὴν θλίψιν ὡς ἀγαθῶν στέρησιν ἐργαζομένην, διάθρεψιν δὲ τὴν ἄνεσιν καὶ τὴν τῶν κακῶν ἀπαλλαγὴν ὡς μετουσίαν παντὸς ἀγαθοῦ χορηγοῦσαν. Τούτοις οὖν προσέχει ὁ δεσπότης καὶ παρέχει ταῦτα ἃ κἀκεῖνοι λαβεῖν ἐλπίζουσι παρ' αὐτοῦ.   5

20ᵃ. Ἡ ψυχὴ ἡμῶν ὑπομένει τῷ Κυρίῳ. Ἐξηγησάμενος τοῦ Θεοῦ τὴν εἰς αὐτοὺς εὐεργεσίαν, ἑξῆς ἐπάγει ταῦτα. Τί βουλόμενος εἰπεῖν; Ὅτι τούτων ἕνεκεν δικαίως | ἀναμένομεν καὶ ἐκδεχόμεθα τοῦ Θεοῦ τὴν βοήθειαν. Τὸ δὲ ἐκδέχεσθαι καὶ προσδοκᾶν τοῦ Θεοῦ τὴν βοήθειαν ὑπομένειν ἐκά-λεσεν, ἐπειδὴ οἱ θλιβόμενοι, ὅταν ὑπομένωσι πάντως, ἐπί τινος προσδοκίᾳ   10
ὑπομένουσι γενναίως, ἢ ἐπὶ προσδοκίᾳ τῶν ἐσομένων ἀγαθῶν, ἢ δόξης ἐλπίδι, ἤ τινος τοιούτου διὰ ποίαν οὖν ἐκδέχεσθαι τὴν παρὰ τοῦ Θεοῦ βοήθειαν.

20ᵇ. Ὅτι βοηθὸς καὶ ὑπερασπιστὴς ἡμῶν ἐστιν. Ὅτι αὐτὸς ἀεὶ βοηθῶν ἡμῖν παρέχει τὴν σωτηρίαν. Τὸ γὰρ ὑπερασπιστὴς ἐκ μεταφορᾶς λέγει τῶν   15
ἐν τοῖς πολέμοις προτιθέντων τὰς οἰκείας ἀσπίδας καὶ ὑπὸ ταύταις πολ-λάκις σκεπόντων ἑτέρους καὶ ἀπαλλαττόντων πάσης συμφορᾶς.

21ᵃ. Ὅτι ἐν αὐτῷ εὐφρανθήσεται ἡ καρδία ἡμῶν. Καὶ ὅτι βοηθήσας παρέξει τὴν εὐφροσύνην.

21ᵇ. Καὶ ἐν τῷ ὀνόματι τῷ ἁγίῳ αὐτοῦ ἠλπίσαμεν. Εἰρηκὼς τὰς αἰτίας   20
δι' ἃς ἀναμένει τοῦ Θεοῦ τὴν βοήθειαν, πάλιν τὸ αὐτὸ ἐπήγαγε συμπλέξας καὶ φησιν Διὰ ταῦτα ἠλπίσαμεν ἐπ' αὐτόν, ταῖς αἰτίαις δι' ἃς ἠλπικέναι φησὶν ἐπισυνάπτων τὸ ἠλπίσαμεν. Τοῦτο δὲ ποιεῖ πρὸς παράστασιν τοῦ τῆς ἐλπίδος εὐλόγου. Οὕτω γὰρ ἔθος ἡμῖν ἐστι ποιεῖν ἐπὶ τῶν τοιούτων·
ὅταν γὰρ αἰτίας μνημονεύσωμεν ὑφ' ἧς τι διαπράξασθαι παρεσκευάσθημεν,   25
ὥσπερ ἀνάγκῃ τινὶ τῷ εὐλόγῳ τῆς αἰτίας ἐπὶ τὴν ἐκπλήρωσιν ἀχθέντες τῆς πράξεως, ἀναγκαίως μετὰ τὴν τῆς αἰτίας μνήμην πολλάκις ἐπισυνάπτομεν

1-2 λίμον — ἄνεσιν affert L (p. 573, 14-16).
20ᵃ. Ἐξηγησάμενος — βοήθειαν: (Θεοδώρου) Paris. 139, fol. 71; Vat. 1682, fol. 104; Barbaro, p. 303.   8-9 τὸ δὲ ἐκδέχεσθαι — βοήθειαν om. PV   10 ἐπί τινι PV.
20ᵇ. Ὅτι αὐτὸς — συμφορᾶς: (Θεοδ ω) Paris. 139, fol. 71ᵛ; Vat. 1682, fol. 104; Barbaro, p. 304.   15-17 Τὸ γὰρ — ἑτέρους affert L (p. 573, 33-36).   17 σκεπ-τόντων PV.
21ᵃ. Καὶ ὅτι — εὐφροσύνην: (Θεοδώρου) Paris. 139, fol. 71ᵛ; Vat. 1682, fol. 104ᵛ.
21ᵇ. Εἰρηκὼς — ἐπάγει: (Θεοδώρου) Paris. 139, fol. 71ᵛ; Vat. 1682, fol. 104ᵛ; Barbaro, p. 304.   23 τὸ καὶ PV   παράτασιν PV.

for causing loss of good things, and by *sustaining,* to relief and freedom from troubles for providing a share in every good. So the Lord attends to these people and provides them with what they hope to receive from him.

Our soul waits for the Lord (v. 20). He adds this by way of explaining God's kindness to them. What does he mean? For the sake of these things we are right to await and expect God's help. He referred to expecting and looking forward to God's help by *wait for,* since the distressed, when they wait, nobly wait in expectation of something, either in expectation of future goods or in hope of glory or something similar as a result of looking forward to some help from God. *He is our help and our protector:* he is always helping and providing us with salvation. The term *protector,* you see, is a metaphor from those thrusting their own shields among the enemy and by protection from these often sheltering others and freeing them from every disaster.[10]

Because our heart rejoices in him (v. 21): and because by helping us he provides us with joy. *And we hoped in his holy name.* After mentioning the reason why he waits for help from God, once more he proceeds to interweave the same theme, saying, For these reasons we hoped in him—giving the reason for which they hoped and attaching the verb *we hoped.* Now, he does this as a presentation of the reasonableness of hope, which is likewise customary with us in such matters: when we mention the reasons why we were prepared to do something, brought to the performance of the action by its reasonableness as though by some necessity, we necessarily often associate with the mention of the reason | the phrase "I did it for these reasons,"

---

10. Theodore traces the term ὑπερασπιστής to ἀσπίς, "shield."

τὸ Διὰ ταῦτα τόδε ἐποίησα, διὰ ταῦτα τόδε διεπραξάμην, ἀντὶ τοῦ ἀναγκαίως διὰ ταῦτα τόδε ἐποίησα. Εἶτα δείξας τῆς ἐλπίδος τὸ εὔλογον τῆς ἐπὶ τὸν Θεὸν ἐπάγει·

21ᵇ. Γένοιτο τὸ ἔλεός σου, Κύριε, ἐφ' ἡμᾶς, καθάπερ ἠλπίσαμεν ἐπὶ σοί.
5 Οὐκοῦν φησιν οὕτως εἰς ἡμᾶς ἡ φιλανθρωπία σου γενέσθω, ὥσπερ καὶ ἡμεῖς ἠλπίσαμεν. Τί δέ ἐστιν τὸ καθάπερ ἠλπίσαμεν; Ἐπειδὴ εἶπεν ἀνωτέρω ὅτι τὴν σὴν περιεμείναμεν ἀντίληψιν ὡς βοηθοῦ, ὡς ὑπερασπιστοῦ, ὡς εὐφροσύνην παρέχειν δυναμένου, ἐπήγαγε τὸ Παράσχου τὸ ἔλεός σου καθάπερ ἠλπίσαμεν, τουτέστιν ὡς βοηθός, ὡς ὑπερασπιστής, ὡς εὐφραίνων ἡμῶν τὰς
10 καρδίας, ὡς πάντα ἡμῶν ὢν καὶ πάντα ἡμῖν παρέχων, οὕτως ἡμᾶς καὶ νῦν εὐεργέτησον· οὕτω γὰρ ἡμεῖς τε | ἠλπίσαμεν ἐπί σοι καὶ τὴν σὴν δωρεὰν δίκαιον ἡμῖν παρασχεθῆναι ἀκόλουθον τῇ ἡμετέρᾳ δοθησομένην ἐλπίδι.

PSALMVS XXXIII

Σύμφωνα τῷ πρὸ αὐτοῦ ψαλμῷ
15 καὶ ἐνταῦθα προφητεύει, ὥσπερ τινὰς εὐχαριστηρίους φωνὰς τὸν ψαλμὸν τοῦτον ὑπὲρ τῶν γεγενημένων ἀναπέμπων εἰς τὸν δεσπότην ἐκ προσώπου τοῦ Ἐζεκίου, παιδεύων τε ἐκ
20 τῆς παρούσης ὑποθέσεως ἅπαντας, κἂν ἐν μέσοις ὦσι τοῖς κακοῖς, παρὰ τοῦ Θεοῦ τὴν βοήθειαν ἐκδέχεσθαι ὡς πάντως τευξομένους διὰ τούτου τῶν ἀγαθῶν, μακαρίζων τε ἐντεῦθεν
25 τοὺς ἐπὶ τὸν Θεὸν ἐλπίζοντας ὡς πλεῖστα προξενεῖν αὐτοῖς ἀγαθὰ

Μετὰ τὴν ὡς ἐκ τοῦ Ἐζεκίου προτροπήν, πρὸς ἀπόδειξιν τῆς παραινέσεως μνημονεύσας τῶν κατ' αὐτὸν λέγει, καὶ ὅπως αὐτοῖς ἐπαμύνει ὁ Θεὸς ἐὰν ἐλπίζειν ἐπ' αὐτὸν σπουδάζωσιν, ἀπὸ τῆς παρούσης ὑποθέσεως καὶ ἀπὸ τῶν κατὰ τὸν Ἐζεκίαν γεγενημένων καὶ τὸν τρόπον ἐξηγούμενος τῆς βοηθείας ὃν παρέξει αὐτοῖς πάντως ὁ Θεὸς ἐλπίσασιν ἐπ' αὐτόν. Διό φησι παρεμβαλεῖ ἄγγελος Κυρίου κύκλῳ τῶν φοβουμένων αὐτὸν καὶ ῥύσεται αὐτούς.

21ᵇ. Οὐκοῦν — ἐλπίδι: (anonym.) Paris. 139, fol. 71ᵛ; Vat. 1682, fol. 104ᵛ; 5-6 οὕτως — ἠλπίσαμεν affert L (p. 574, 4-6)   5 ἡ φιλ. σου εἰς ἡμᾶς PVL   6 τί δέ — ἠλπίσαμεν om. C   8 σου om. PV   10 καὶ νῦν ἡμᾶς PV.

Μετὰ τὴν — αὐτούς: (Θεοδώρου) Paris. 139, fol. 73ᵛ; Vat. 1682, fol. 107ᵛ; Barbaro, p. 313. Hanc exegesim v. 8 catenis adscriptam cum argumento melius convenire censui.

Aᵉ 11-12 (p. 196, 8-9): Vt uotis sperantium clementia tua plene respondeat.
14 ss. (p. 194): Hic psalmus cantatur sub persona Ezechiae, qui superato Assirio semper se benedicturum Dominum promittit et angelum Dei adiutorem inmitti sibi precatur; posteriori quoque parte psalmi ad exemplum sui cunctos in laudem Dei provocat. Cf. Pseudo-Beda (651 B).

"I acted this way for these reasons," meaning, "I necessarily did it for these reasons."

Then, to bring out the reasonableness of hope in God, he goes on to say *Let your mercy be shown to us, Lord, as we have hoped in you* (v. 22): let your lovingkindness therefore be upon us, as we too have hoped. Now, what is the meaning of *as we have hoped*? Since he said above, We waited for assistance from you as a helper, as a protector, as one able to provide joy, he went on, Provide us with your mercy as we have hoped—that is, As helper, as protector, as one giving joy to our hearts, as one being our all and supplying us with all, so now, too, be favorable to us. After all, we thus hoped in you, and it is right for us to be accorded your gift given in consequence of our hope.

PSALM 34

Here, too, he prophesies things in accord with the psalm before this, taking the part of Hezekiah in offering up this psalm as some sentiments of thanksgiving to the Lord.[1] On the basis of the present theme he instructs everyone, even if surrounded by troubles, to look to God for help, through whom they will always attain good things. He also at this point declares blessed those hoping in God, since hope in God is capable of providing them with many good things. | He offers also a catechetical exhortation, teaching all those to

---

1. In addition to this introduction from Codex Coislinianus, Devreesse offers also one from other Greek MSS that he considers "better adapted to the theme" (*Le commentaire,* 157), as follows: "After the exhortation from Hezekiah, as it were, he cites his own story in support of the exhortation and states how God will assist them if they are careful to hope in him, using the present theme and the events affecting Hezekiah to explain the manner of assistance that God doubtless will supply to those hoping in him. Hence, he says that the angel of the Lord will encircle those who fear him and will rescue them."

τῆς ἐπὶ τὸν Θεὸν ἐλπίδος δυναμένης. Ἐκτίθεται δὲ καὶ κατηχητικὴν παραίνεσιν, διδάσκων εὐλαβείας ἅπαντας ἐπιμελεῖσθαι | τοὺς ἐντεῦθεν ὑπὸ τὴν τοῦ Θεοῦ κεισομένους πρόνοιαν, καὶ ῥυσθησομένους παρ᾽ αὐτοῦ τῶν κακῶν κἂν ἐν μέσοις πολλάκις τοῖς κινδύνοις ἐξετασθῶσιν.

2ᵃ. Εὐλογήσω τὸν Κύριον ἐν παντὶ καιρῷ. Τὸ εὐλογήσω ἀντὶ τοῦ εὐφη-   5
μήσω, ὑμνήσω, — τὸ δὲ ἐν παντὶ καιρῷ, τουτέστι καὶ ἐν ἀνέσεως καιρῷ καὶ ἐν
θλίψεως. Καλῶς δὲ τοῦτο μάλιστα ἐπὶ τοῦ Ἐζεκίου· καὶ γὰρ καὶ ἐν τοῖς
κακοῖς ὤν, τῶν Ἀσσυρίων κεκυκλωκότων αὐτούς, ἐπὶ τὴν προσευχὴν ἐτρέ-
πετο τοῦ Θεοῦ. Εἰκότως οὖν ἐπ᾽ αὐτοῦ καὶ μετὰ τὴν νίκην φησὶν ἐν παντὶ
καιρῷ, ὃς καὶ ἐν τῷ καιρῷ τῶν συμφορῶν οὐκ ἐπελάθετο τῆς τοῦ Θεοῦ   10
ὑμνῳδίας.

2ᵇ. Διὰ παντὸς ἡ αἴνεσις αὐτοῦ ἐν τῷ στόματί μου. Διὰ παντὸς αὐτὸν
ὑμνῶν διατελέσω, οὐ διδοὺς σχολὴν πρὸς τοῦτο τῷ στόματί μου. Διὰ τί
οὖν οὕτω σύντονον ποιεῖ τὴν ὑμνῳδίαν ἑξῆς φησιν.

3ᵃ. Ἐν τῷ Κυρίῳ ἐπαινεθήσεται   In Domino laudabitur anima   15
ἡ ψυχή μου. Ἐπαινεθήσεται ἀντὶ τοῦ   mea, pro Glorificabitur atque erit
δοξασθήσεται, θαυμασθήσεται. Ἡ   in admiratione omnium uel stu-
ψυχή μου ἀντὶ τοῦ ἐγώ, τὸν ὅλον   pore. Anima uero, id est ego, to-
ἄνθρωπον ἀπὸ τῆς ψυχῆς καλῶν, ὡς   tum ab anima uocans hominem.
τὸ ἐν ἑβδομήκοντα πέντε ψυχαῖς κατέβη Ἰακὼβ εἰς Αἴγυπτον. Διὰ τοῦτο   20
οὖν φησιν ἀδιαλείπτως αὐτὸν ὑμνήσω, ἐπειδὴ τῇ αὐτοῦ βοηθείᾳ θαυμαστὸς
παρὰ πᾶσι καὶ ἐπίδοξος καθέστηκα. Ἀκολούθως δὲ τοῦτό φησιν· ἀνάγκη
γὰρ ἦν, τοῦ Θεοῦ διὰ τὴν περὶ αὐτὸν πρόνοιαν τοσούτους ἀνῃρηκότος,
ἁπανταχοῦ περιαγγελλομένου τοῦ γεγονότος, ἐπαινεῖσθαι παρὰ πᾶσιν
αὐτὸν δι᾽ ὃν τοσούτους ὁ δεσπότης οὕτω συντόμως ἐτιμωρήσατο. Εἶτα τὴν   25
αἰτίαν τῆς ἀδιαλείπτου εὐχαριστίας εἰπών, ἑξῆς δεικνὺς τὸ μέγεθος τοῦ
γεγονότος, ἐπάγει·

---

8 Is. XXXVIII, 10-20   20 Gen. XLVI. 27; cf. in ps. XV, 9.

2ᵃ. Τὸ εὐλογήσω — ὑμνῳδίας: (Θεοδώρου) Paris. 139, fol 72ᵛ; Vat. 1682, fol. 105ᵛ;
Barbaro, p. 308.   5 τὸ om PV   6 καὶ om. PV   6-7 ἐν θλίψεως καιρῷ καὶ ἐν
ἀνέσεως L (p. 592, 3-4).
    2ᵇ. Διὰ παντὸς — φησίν: (Θεοδώρου): Paris. 139, fol. 72ᵛ; Vat. 1682, fol. 106;
Barbaro, p. 309.   14 οὕτω σύντονον] οὕτως αὐτόν V.
    3ᵃ. Ἐπαινεθήσεται — ἐπάγει: (Θεοδώρου) Paris. 139, fol 72ᵛ; Vat. 1682, fol. 106;
Barbaro, p. 309.   21 θαυμαστῶς PV.
    In Domino — hominem: A, fol. 9ᶜ; B, fol. 11ᵈ.   17 uel pro A.

practice reverence who would feel the influence of God's providence as a result of it and be rescued by him from troubles, even if often tested in the midst of perils.

I shall bless the Lord at every moment (v. 1). By *I shall bless* he means "I shall praise, sing praise," and by *at every moment,* "in times both of relaxation and of tribulation." Now, this is particularly applicable to Hezekiah: even when in trouble, with the Assyrians surrounding him, he turned to prayer to God. So it was right to apply *at every moment to him,* even after the victory, since even at the time of calamity he did not forget hymn-singing to God.[2] *Praise of him always in my mouth:* I shall continue singing his praises always, giving my mouth no respite from this. The sequel explains why he is so earnest in hymn-singing.

In the Lord my soul will be commended (v. 2), by *commended* meaning "glorified, admired," and *my soul* meaning "I," referring to the whole person by soul as in the verse "Jacob went down into Egypt with seventy-five souls."[3] Hence, he is saying, I shall sing his praises incessantly, since with his help I have emerged as the cynosure of all eyes. It made sense for him to say this: it was inevitable that, after God had slain so many on account of his care for him and the deed had been bruited abroad, he would be the object of everyone's commendation for the Lord's taking retribution on so many in one fell swoop. Then, after giving the reason for the unceasing thanksgiving, he proceeds to bring out the greatness of the deed. | *Let the gentle hear and*

2. Cf. Isa 38:10–20.
3. Cf. Gen 46:27 LXX.

3ᵇ. Ἀκουσάτωσαν πραεῖς καὶ εὐ-
φρανθήτωσαν. | Περιαγγελθήτω δέ φη-
σιν τὸ γεγονὸς ἅπασι τοῖς ταπεινοῖς.

5 Πραεῖς γὰρ ἐνταῦθα τοὺς ταπεινοὺς λέγει, ὥστε αὐτοῖς εὐφροσύνην
ἐκ τῆς γνώσεως ἐκγενέσθαι. Οὕτω
γάρ φησίν ἐστι μέγιστον καὶ παράδοξον τὸ γεγονὸς καὶ παρὰ πᾶσαν
προσδοκίαν ἐκβάν, ὡς δεῖν μὲν αὐτὸ πᾶσι πανταχοῦ περιαγγελθῆναι τοῖς
πραέσι, δυνατὸν δὲ εἶναι περιαγγελθὲν ἅπασι μεγίστην ἐμποιῆσαι τὴν
10 εὐφροσύνην. Διὰ τί δὲ εἶπεν Ἀκουσάτωσαν πραεῖς καὶ εὐφρανθήτωσαν,
πραεῖς λέγων τοὺς ταπεινούς; Ἐπειδὴ
μάλιστα τούτους ηὔφρανεν ἡ τοιαύτη
ἀκοὴ γνωρίζουσα θάνατον μὲν τῶν
δυνατῶν, ἀπαλλαγὴν δὲ κινδύνων πα-
15 ραδόξως παρασχεθεῖσαν τοῖς ἀσθε-
νέσιν. Εἶτα καὶ τρέπει τὸν λόγον
πρὸς αὐτούς.

Audiant mansueti et | laeten-
tur.

Mansuetos in hoc loco uocat
quos res artae docuerunt de se
non magna sentire.

Humiles namque, audita morte
potentium et liberatione tenuiorum, uelut pro ipsa conditionis
suae similitudine erant tali nun-
tio laetaturi: ad quos sermonem
conuertit.

4ᵃ. Μεγαλύνατε τὸν Κύριον σὺν
ἐμοί | Μεγάλα φθέγξασθε περὶ αὐ-
20 τοῦ, εἴπατε οἷα πρέπει τῷ μεγαλείῳ τοῦ Θεοῦ. Ἀναγκαίως δὲ καὶ κοινω-
νοὺς καλεῖ τῆς ὑμνῳδίας αὐτοῦ, ὡς πάντως καὶ αὐτῶν ἀπολαυσάντων τῆς
τοιαύτης εὐεργεσίας τοῦ Θεοῦ ὀφείλοντος τιμωρεῖσθαι μὲν τοὺς δυνατοὺς
ἐπὰν ἀδικεῖν ἐθέλωσιν, ἐπαμύνειν δὲ τοῖς ταπεινοῖς ἀδικουμένοις.

Magnificate Dominum, reliqua.

4ᵇ. Καὶ ὑψώσωμεν τὸ ὄνομα αὐτοῦ ἐπὶ τὸ αὐτό. Μετὰ μεγίστου ὕψους
25 μνήμην αὐτοῦ ποιησώμεθα τοῦ ὀνόματος, ἀντὶ τοῦ μνημονεύσωμεν αὐτοῦ
ὑψοῦντες αὐτὸν καὶ θαυμάζοντες. Τὸ δὲ ἐπὶ τὸ αὐτό, τουτέστι συμφώνως.
Διὰ τί οὖν φησι καλεῖς τοὺς πραεῖς πρὸς τὸ συμφώνως καὶ ἅμα σοι τὴν
ὑμνῳδίαν ἀναπέμψαι;

3ᵇ. Περιαγγελθήτω — πρὸς αὐτούς: (Θεοδώρου) Paris. 139, fol. 72ᵛ; Vat. 1682,
fol. 106; Barbaro, p. 309.　　6 ἐγγενέσθαι C　　7 ἐστι om. PV　　8 ὡσθεῖν PV
9 πᾶσιν PV　　11 ἐπεὶ PV　　12 ηὔφραινεν P ἦν φραῖνεν V.

Audiant mansueti — 19, reliqua: A, fol. 9ᶜ⁻ᵈ; B, fol. 11ᵈ.　　4-6 mansuetos — sentire *affert* Aᵉ (p. 196, 16-18)　　5 artae] ante Aᵉ　　docuerant Aᵉ
11 humilis A　　12 *** tenuiorum B　　13 uelud B　　13-14 consue***tionis A¹
suae conditionis A².

4ᵃ. Μεγάλα — ἀδικουμένοις: (Θεοˢ) Paris. 139, fol. 73; Vat. 1682, fol. 106ᵛ;
Barbaro, p. 310.　　20 δὲ om. PV　　20-21 κοινωνῶς PV　　22 ὀφείλοντος] φιλοῦν-
τος PV　　τιμωρήσασθαι C　　23 ἐπὰν ἀδ. ἐθέλ. om. C.

4ᵇ. Μετὰ μεγίστου — ἀναπέμψαι: (Θεοδώρου) Paris. 139, fol. 73; Vat. 1682,
fol. 106ᵛ; Barbaro, p. 310.　　27 καλεῖ PV.

be glad: let the deed be reported to all the lowly (by *gentle* here referring to the lowly) so that joy may spring up in them from knowledge of it. The deed is so awesome and incredible, he is saying, and surpassing all expectation that it ought to be reported to all the gentle, and once reported, it has the power to instill great joy. Now, why did he say *Let the gentle hear and be glad,* calling the lowly *gentle?* Because such a report, bringing news of the death of the mighty and the unexpected rescue from perils procured for the weak, brought joy to them in particular.

He then also directs his attention to them. *Magnify the Lord with me* (v. 3): utter great things about him; tell what befits the greatness of God. It was necessary also to summon people to share in his hymn-singing, since absolutely everyone enjoyed such a great favor from God, who is obliged to punish the mighty when they are bent on doing wrong and to assist the lowly when they are wronged. *And let us exalt his name together:* along with a mighty hymn of praise let us make mention of his name—in other words, Let us recall him to mind by exalting and marveling at him (*together* meaning "in concert"). Why, he asks, does he summon the gentle to offer you hymn-singing in concert and as one? | *I sought out the Lord, and he heeded me* (v.

5ᵃ. Ἐξεζήτησα τὸν Κύριον, καὶ ἐπήκουσέν μου. Ἐπειδὴ ἤτησα παρ' αὐτοῦ φησι τὴν βοήθειαν καὶ ἔτυχον ὧνπερ ἤτησα.

5ᵇ. Καὶ ἐκ πασῶν τῶν παροικιῶν μου ἐρύσατό με. Καὶ πάντων με τῶν περιεχόντων κακῶν ἀπήλλαξε. Τί οὖν φησι τοῦτο πρὸς τοὺς πραεῖς; Ὅτι σὺ αἰτήσας ἔτυχες τῆς παρ' αὐτοῦ βοηθείας, ὥστε ἐκείνους ὑμνεῖν ἅμα σοι. 5

6ᵃ. Προσέλθατε πρὸς αὐτὸν καὶ φωτίσθητε. Ἐξέσται γάρ φησι καὶ ὑμῖν ὁμοίως προσελ|θοῦσιν αὐτῷ καὶ αἰτησαμένοις τὴν παρ' αὐτοῦ βοήθειαν τυχεῖν τῆς τε βοηθείας καὶ ἀντιλήψεως. Τὸ γὰρ φωτίσθητε ἀντὶ τοῦ ἀπολαύσατε αὐτοῦ τῆς βοηθείας, φωτισμὸν ἐνταῦθα καλῶν τὴν ἀντίληψιν ὡς ἀπαλλάττουσαν θλίψεως, ἥτις ὥσπερ σκότῳ τῇ ἀθυμίᾳ περιβάλλειν δύναται. 10

6ᵇ. Καὶ τὰ πρόσωπα ὑμῶν οὐ μὴ καταισχυνθῇ. Οὐδὲ γάρ ἐστιν ὑμᾶς προσδοκῶντας καὶ ἀπεκδεχομένους τὴν παρ' αὐτοῦ βοήθειαν αἰσχυνθῆναι ἐπὶ τῇ ἐλπίδι τῇ εἰς αὐτόν. Τὰ δὲ πρόσωπα ὑμῶν εἶπεν, ἐπειδὴ ὅταν τινὰ προσδοκῶμεν τὰ πρόσωπα ἀνατείνειν εἰώθαμεν περιμένοντες αὐτοῦ τὴν παρουσίαν. 15

7. Οὗτος ὁ πτωχὸς ἐκέκραξεν, καὶ ὁ Κύριος εἰσήκουσεν αὐτοῦ, καὶ ἐκ πασῶν τῶν θλίψεων αὐτοῦ ἔσωσεν αὐτόν. Πάλιν εἰς ἑαυτὸν ἀνατρέχει, δι' ὅλων ἐν τῇ προτροπῇ τὴν ἀπόδειξιν τῶν λεγομένων ἐκ τῶν καθ' ἑαυτὸν παρεχόμενος. Δῆλον γάρ φησιν ὅτι πάντως ἐπαμυνεῖ τοῖς ἐπ' αὐτὸν ἐλπίζουσιν, ἐξ' ὧν οὗτος ὁ εὐτελὴς καὶ ταπεινός, ἵνα εἴπῃ· Ἐγὼ κεκραγὼς πρὸς 20 τὸν δεσπότην καὶ εἰσηκούσθην καὶ ἐκ πάσης ἐρρύσθην θλίψεως. Πτωχὸν δὲ αὐτὸν καλεῖ τῇ τε οἰκείᾳ δυνάμει καὶ τῇ τῶν ὑπηκόων εὐτελείᾳ πτωχότατόν τε ὄντα πρὸς παράθεσιν τῆς τῶν Ἀσσυρίων δυνάμεως, οἳ πλήθει τῶν

5ᵃ. Ἐπειδὴ — ἤτησα: (Θεοδώρου) Paris. 139, fol. 73; Vat. 1682, fol. 106ᵛ; Barbaro, p. 311.   1-2 φησι παρ' αὐτοῦ PV   2 ὥσπερ C.
6ᵃ. Ἐξέσται — δύναται: (Θεοδώρου) Paris. 139, fol. 73; Vat. 1632, fol. 107; Barbaro, p. 312; cf. L (p. 594, 21-24).   8 καὶ τῆς V   10 περιβαλεῖν C.
6ᵇ. Οὐδὲ — παρουσίαν: (Θεοδώρου) Paris. 139, fol. 73; Vat. 1682, fol. 107. 11 ἔνεστιν PV   12 καὶ ἀπεκδεχομένους om. PV.

Aᵉ 6-8 (p. 196, 24-197, 2): Vos quoque si conueneritis ad precandum Dominum pro nostris commodis contingetur.   13-15 (p. 197, 6-8): Pro expectatione, quae ad aliquam rem uultum facit intentum.   20-23 (p. 197, 8-16): Ac si diceret: Ego, uel quilibet dispectus; iterum ad suam personam recurrit et per omnia, probatione a se petita, utilitatem exortationis inculcat; pauperem uocat se propter tenuitatem uirium suarum et paruum atque exiguum numerum subditorum, quia uere erat pauper Assiriorum multitudini potentiaeque comparatus.

4): because I sought help from him, and I received what I sought. *And from the midst of all my tribulations he rescued me:* and he freed me from all the troubles besetting me.[4] So why does he say this to the gentle? Because on asking, you received help from him, and so they sing with you.

Approach him and be enlightened (v. 5): it is possible also for you likewise, when you approach him and ask help from him, to attain help and support. By *be enlightened* he means "enjoy his help," and by *enlightenment* he refers here to support in being released from tribulation, which can envelop one in depression like darkness. *And your faces will not blush:* nor is it possible for you when expecting and looking forward to help from him to be disappointed in your hope in him. He said *your faces,* since whenever we expect someone, we normally lift up our faces in expectation of that person's arrival. *This poor man cried out, and the Lord hearkened to him, and saved him from all his tribulations* (v. 6). Once again he reverts to himself, right throughout the exhortation providing a proof of what was said from his own situation. It is clear, he is saying, that there is no doubt that he assists those hoping in him, among whom is this insignificant and lowly person. What he means is, I cried to the Lord, and was heard and rescued from all my tribulation. Now, he refers to himself as *poor* for the reason of his being most poor in his own power and the insignificance of his subjects when compared with the power of the Assyrians, who | were notorious for the size of their army

---

4. Theodore clearly is reading the verse in the Antioch form of the LXX (*pace* Devreesse), as do Diodore and Theodoret, in which "tribulations" occurs.

στρατοπέδων ἦσαν λαμπροὶ καὶ τῷ πλήθει τῶν ἵππων περίβλεπτοι. Εἶτα
ἀκολούθως | ἐπάγει κα τὰ ἑξῆς.

8. Παρεμβαλεῖ ἄγγελος Κυρίου κύκλῳ τῶν φοβουμένων αὐτὸν καὶ ῥύσεται αὐτούς. Ὑπισχνεῖται γὰρ αὐτοῖς ἄγγελον τοῦ Θεοῦ σύμμαχον ἔσεσθαι
5 κυκλοῦντα αὐτοὺς καὶ ἐπαμύνοντα, οὕτω τε πάσης θλίψεως αὐτοὺς ῥυόμε-
νον. Τὸ γὰρ παρεμβαλεῖ ἀντὶ τοῦ συμμαχήσει λέγει, ἐπειδὴ παρεμβο-
λὰς ἔθος τὰ στρατόπεδα καλεῖν τῇ θείᾳ γραφῇ. Τοῦτο δὲ γέγονεν ἐπὶ
τοῦ Ἐζεκίου· ἄγγελος γὰρ Κυρίου πατάξας τοὺς Ἀσσυρίους, τούτους ἀπήλλαξε τῶν κακῶν. Τὸ δὲ κύκλῳ λέγει πολλὴν ἀσφάλειαν ἔσεσθαι αὐτοῖς ἐκ
10 τῆς τοῦ ἀγγέλου βοηθείας, φάσκων ἀπὸ τοῦ τοὺς ἐν μέσοις ὄντας καὶ
ἀσφαλείᾳ τινὶ κεκυκλωμένους ἢ τείχους ἢ ἀνθρώπων ἀνεπηρεάστους εἶναι
τοῖς ἐναντίοις. | Ἀνωτέρω δὲ τὸν λόγον ἁπλῶς πρὸς πραεῖς ποιούμενος,
ἐνταῦθά φησι κύκλῳ τῶν φοβουμένων αὐτόν, ὡς ἂν μὴ οἰηθῇς ὅτι πρὸς
πάντας ἁπλῶς αὐτῷ τοὺς εὐτελεῖς ὁ λόγος, ἀλλὰ ⟨πρὸς⟩ τοὺς ἐκ προαι-
15 ρέσεως ἐν τῇ καρδίᾳ τὴν ταπείνωσιν κεκτημένους καὶ στέργοντας μὲν τὴν
σωματικὴν εὐτέλειαν, κεκτημένους δὲ τὸν δεσποτικὸν φόβον. Εἶτα ὑποσχόμενος αὐτοῖς ἐλπίζουσιν ἐπὶ τὸν Θεόν, εἰ ἐπιβουλεύοιντο ὑπὸ τῶν ἐχθρῶν,
τὴν διὰ τοῦ ἀγγέλου παρασχεθήσεσθαι βοήθειαν, ἐπειδὴ τοιοῦτο καὶ ἐπὶ τῶν
κατὰ τὸν Ἐζεκίαν ἐγεγόνει, τῇ τε μνήμῃ τῶν κατ᾿ ἐκεῖνον διόλου τῶν λεχ-
20 θέντων παρέσχετο τὴν ἀπόδειξιν καὶ τῆς ὑποσχέσεως τὴν πίστιν φησί·

9ᵃ. Γεύσασθε καὶ ἴδετε ὅτι χρηστὸς ὁ Κύριος. Ὅτι γὰρ οὕτω ταῦτα
ἔχει φησί, καὶ ὅτι ἄγγελος συμμαχεῖ τοῖς φοβουμένοις αὐτὸν ἀπαλλάττων
αὐτοὺς πάσης θλίψεως, πεῖραν λάβετε ἀπὸ τῶν ἀρτίως γεγονότων. Τὸ
γὰρ γεύσασθε — ἀντὶ τοῦ, λάβετε τῶν ἔργων τὴν πεῖραν — ἀπὸ τῶν μέλιτος
25 καὶ οἴνου καὶ τῶν τοιούτων, ὁποῖόν ἐστι κάλλιστον ἢ τὸ ἐναντίον ἀπὸ
τῆς γεύσεως, τὴν πεῖραν λαμβανόντων· | πρὸς δὲ ἀπόδειξιν τῆς τοῦ ἀγγέ-
λου συμμαχίας εἰρηκὼς τὸ γεύσασθε καὶ ἴδετε, ἐπήγαγε τὸ ὅτι χρηστὸς ὁ
Κύριος, τοῦτο βουλόμενος εἰπεῖν ὅτι χρηστότητι καὶ ἀγαθότητι τῇ περὶ
τοὺς εὐεργετουμένους τὴν τοῦ ἀγγέλου συμμαχίαν παρέχεται.

7 cf. Gen. XXXII, 2   8 ss. Is. XXXVI.   *Post exegesim v. 7 plura praebent*
catenae PV et Barbaro quae superius ut argumentum psalmi reposui (Μετὰ τὴν —
διὸ φησιν); *prosequuntur* Ὑπισχνεῖται — πίστιν φησίν.

4 αὐτοὺς V   6 παρεμβαλεῖ — συμμαχήσει *affert* L (p. 595, 33-34)   8 γὰρ *om.* V
10 μέσῳ PV   12 πρὸς] ὡς PV   14 πρὸς *supplevi*   18 τοιοῦτος PV   τῶν *om.* PV
19 τὸν *om.* V   γεγόνει PV.

Aᵉ   8-9 (p. 197, 19-20): Qui (angelus) inuastauit Assirios, et unumquem-
que tuetur supplicem.   24-26 (p. 197, 21-22): A similitudine earum rerum quae
gustu intelleguntur.

and famous for the number of their horses.

Then he continues on the same theme in what follows. *An angel of the Lord will encamp round those who fear him, and will rescue them* (v. 7). He promises that an angel of God will be an ally surrounding and assisting them, and thus rescuing them from every tribulation (by *encamp* meaning "be an ally," since the divine Scripture normally calls armies "encampments"). Now, this happened in the case of Hezekiah: an angel of the Lord struck the Assyrians[5] and freed his people from their troubles. The term *round* means that great security would come to them from the angel's help—a claim made on the basis of those on the inside and surrounded by the security of a wall or people being invulnerable to the adversaries. After addressing himself above simply to the gentle, here he says *round those who fear him,* lest you should think that his remarks are addressed simply to all the insignificant rather than to all who adopt lowliness of heart by choice and are fond of physical insignificance while evincing fear of the Lord.

He then promises those hoping in God that if they are the object of the enemies' schemes, help will be provided by the angel, since such a thing happened also in the case of Hezekiah, and by mention of what was said strictly of him it provided a proof and guarantee of the promise. He says *Taste and see that the Lord is good* (v. 8): for proof that this is so and that an angel is an ally to those fearing him and freeing them from every tribulation, receive confirmation from recent events. The word *taste*—that is, receive confirmation from the facts—comes from honey and wine and such things as are sweet to taste or the opposite for those experiencing them. After saying *taste and see* by way of proof of the angel's assistance, he goes on to say *the Lord is good,* meaning that in his goodness and kindness he provides the angel's assistance to the recipients of his favor. | *Blessed is the man who*

---

5. Cf. 2 Kgs 19:35.

9ᵇ. Μακάριος ἀνήρ, ὃς ἐλπίζει ἐπ' αὐτόν. Καλῶς μετὰ τὴν τῶν λεχθέντων ἀπόδειξιν τὸν μακαρισμὸν ἐποιήσατο, ὅτε οὐκ ἀμφίβολος ἐδόκει τοῖς ἀκροαταῖς ὁ μακαρισμὸς εἶναι. Μετὰ γὰρ τὸ προτρέψασθαι ἐλπίζειν ἐπὶ τὸν Θεὸν καὶ εἰπεῖν ὅτι βοηθείας πάντως τεύξεσθαι, καὶ ὥσπερ ἀποδείξεσι βεβαιῶσαι τὴν τοῦ πράγματος ἀλήθειαν, ἑξῆς ἐπήγαγε τὸ Μακάριος ἀνήρ 5 ὃς ἐλπίζει ἐπ' αὐτόν, τοῦτο λέγων ὅτι τούτων οὕτως ἐχόντων μακαριστὸς ὁ ἐλπίζων ἐπὶ τὸν Θεὸν τοσαύτης βοηθείας καταξιούμενος.

10ᵃ. Φοβήθητε τὸν Κύριον πάντες οἱ ἅγιοι αὐτοῦ. Τοὺς αὐτοὺς καλεῖ καὶ πρᾳεῖς | καὶ φοβουμένους τὸν Κύριον καὶ ἁγίους· πραῢν γὰρ καλεῖ τὸν ἐπιεικείᾳ τρόπων τοιοῦτον καθεστῶτα, ὃν ἐπ' ἀνάγκης ἐστὶ φόβῳ τοιοῦτον 10 εἶναι τῷ περὶ τὸν δεσπότην. Δῆλον δὲ ὡς ὁ τὸν Θεὸν φοβούμενος ἀκριβὴς μέν ἐστι φύλαξ τῶν προσταγμάτων αὐτοῦ, μετέχει δὲ καὶ ἁγιωσύνης εἰκότως. Πολλὴ δέ ἐστι τῶν ῥημάτων ἡ τάξις. Πρότερον γὰρ αὐτοῖς προσέταξεν αἰνέσαι ἅμα αὐτῷ τὸν Θεὸν ὡς τοῦ μὲν Θεοῦ πάντως σῴζοντος τοὺς τοιούτους, αὐτῶν δὲ ἐξ ἀνάγκης ἀπολαυόντων τῆς χάριτος, τῇ δὲ ὁμοιότητι 15 τῶν τρόπων ὁμοίας καὶ τῆς δωρεᾶς καταξιωθησομένων. Εἶτα προτρέπει βεβαιῶν ἐπὶ τὴν τοῦ Θεοῦ ἐλπίδα. Χρεία γὰρ καὶ ἐλπίδος ἦν τοῖς μέλλουσιν ἅμα αὐτῷ ἐπὶ τοῖς τοιούτοις δοξάζειν τὸν Θεόν, ἵνα βεβαίως ἐλπίζοντες οὕτως ὑπὲρ τῶν γεγενημένων εὐχαριστῶσι, πιστεύοντες ὡς καὶ αὐτοὶ τεύξονται τῶν ὁμοίων ἐν καιρῷ. Διὸ καὶ βεβαιοτέραν αὐτοῖς τὴν ἐλπίδα κατασκευάζων, 20 ὑποδείγμασί τε τοῖς τῶν γεγενημένων πείθει πρὸς τοῦτο καὶ μακαρισμοῖς τοῖς προσήκουσι. Μετὰ δὲ τὴν τῆς ἐλπίδος βεβαίωσιν καὶ τὴν τῆς ὑμνῳδίας παραίνεσιν, καὶ φοβεῖσθαι αὐτοῖς τὸν δεσπότην παρακελεύεται λέγων· φοβήθητε τὸν Κύριον πάντες οἱ ἅγιοι αὐτοῦ, δεικνὺς ὡς χρεία καὶ ὕμνων καὶ ἐλπίδος καὶ φόβου, — ὕμνων μὲν ὥστε εὐχαρίστους καὶ ἐπὶ τοῖς 25 ἤδη γεγενημένοις δείκνυσθαι, | ἐλπίδος δὲ ὥστε τῶν μελλόντων ἑαυτοὺς ἀξίους ἀποδείκνυσθαι, φόβου δὲ ὥστε ἐπιμελεῖς εἶναι περὶ τὴν ἀρετήν.

10ᵇ. Ὅτι οὐκ ἔστιν ὑστέρημα τοῖς φοβουμένοις αὐτόν. Τουτέστιν οὐδὲ γὰρ ἀκερδὴς ὁ φόβος τοῦ Θεοῦ τοῖς κεκτημένοις αὐτόν, ἀλλὰ καὶ μάλα ἐπωφελής· ἐνδεῖ γὰρ αὐτοῖς οὐδὲν τῶν καλῶν.
30

9ᵇ. Καλῶς — καταξιούμενος: (Θεοδώρου) Paris. 139, fol. 74; Vat. 1682, fol. 108ʳ·ᵛ; L (p. 596, 46-597, 4); Barbaro, p. 315.   1 λεχθέντων] εἰρημένων L   3 εἶναι om. L 3-4 ἐπὶ τῷ θεῷ C   4 πάντως τεύξεται βοηθ. L   4-5 καὶ ὥσπερ — ἑξῆς om. L 6-7 ὡσεὶ λέγων, οὕτως ἐχόντων τούτων, μακάριος ὁ διὰ τὸ εἰς αὐτὸν ἐλπίζειν, τοσαύτης ἀξιούμενος βοηθείας L.

10ᵃ. Τοὺς αὐτοὺς — ἀρετήν: (anonym.) Paris. 139, fol. 74; Vat. 1682, fol. 103ᵛ; Barbaro, p. 315-316 (Cyrilli).   9 ἁγίους] υἱοὺς PV   10 ἐπάναγκες PV   10-11 τοιοῦτον εἶναι] τοιούτῳ PV   11 ὁ om. C   13 ῥητῶν PV   18 ἐπὶ τοῖς τ. ἅμα αὐτῷ C 21 τοῖς om. C   25 εὐχαρίστως V   καὶ om. C   27 ἀποδεικνύναι C.

10ᵇ. Τουτέστιν — καλῶν: (Θεοδώρου) Paris 139, fol. 74ᵛ; Vat. 1682, fol. 109; Barbaro, p. 316.

hopes in him. After the proof of what was said he did well to deliver the beatitude when to the listeners the beatitude did not seem to be ambiguous: after recommending hope in God, saying that they doubtless would gain help, and confirming the truth of the matter as if by proof, he went on to say *Blessed is the man who hopes in him,* meaning that, with things as they were, the one hoping in God was considered blessed in being the recipient of such great help.

Fear the Lord, all you his holy ones (v. 9). He refers to the same people as *gentle, fearing the Lord* and *holy,* by *gentle* referring to the person who becomes such by simplicity of behavior and is necessarily like this from fear of the Lord. It is clear that the one who fears the Lord is a careful observer of his commandments and naturally shares also in his holiness. Now, there is a definite order in his statements: he first bid them praise God with him, since God doubtless saves such people, and they necessarily enjoy his grace while being vouchsafed the gift that is in keeping with their behavior. Next, he exhorts them and strengthens their hope in God, hope being needed for those due to glorify God with him for such things so as with a strong hope thus to give thanks for what occurred, believing that they also would be granted similar things at the right time. Hence, by also making their hope stronger, he convinces them of it with proofs from past events and with appropriate beatitudes. After the strengthening of their hope and the exhortation to hymn-singing he bids them also fear the Lord in the words *Fear the Lord, all you his holy ones* to bring out the need for hymns, hope, and fear—hymns to show themselves thankful also for what has already occurred, hope to prove themselves worthy of what is to come, and fear so as to be attentive to virtue. Because those who fear him *want for nothing*—that is, the fear of God is not without benefit to those who possess it, but is very advantageous, since they lack no good thing. |

11. Πλούσιοι ἐπτώχευσαν καὶ ἐπείνασαν, οἱ δὲ ἐκζητοῦντες τὸν Κύριον οὐκ ἐλαττωθήσονται παντὸς ἀγαθοῦ. Εἰπὼν ὅτι οὐκ ἔστιν ὑστέρημα τοῖς φοβουμένοις αὐτόν, τὸ μεῖζον ἐπήγαγεν ἑξῆς· Πλούσιοι ἐπτώχευσαν καὶ ἐπείνασαν, οἱ δὲ ἐκζητοῦντες τὸν Κύριον οὐκ ἐλαττωθήσονται παντὸς ἀγαθοῦ.
5 Οὕτως γὰρ αὐτούς φησιν οὐδενὸς ἐνδεεῖς ἐγχωρεῖ γενέσθαι, ὅτι πολλῷ δυνατώτερόν ἐστι καὶ εὐχερέστερον πλούσιον ἐν πενίᾳ καὶ πείνῃ ἐξετασθῆναι ἢ τὸν ἐκδεχόμενον τὴν παρὰ τοῦ Θεοῦ βοήθειαν καὶ αἰτοῦντα τὴν παρ' αὐτοῦ σωτηρίαν ἐνδεῆ γενέσθαι τινὸς ἀγαθοῦ. Μέχρι τούτου τὸν πρὸς τοὺς δικαίους στήσας λόγον καὶ βεβαιώσας μὲν αὐτοὺς ἐν τῇ τοῦ Θεοῦ ἐλπίδι, συναινέσαι
10 δὲ ἐπὶ τοῖς γεγενημένοις τῷ μακαρίῳ Ἐζεκίᾳ παρακελευσάμενος, ἔχειν δὲ καὶ τὸν φόβον τοῦ Θεοῦ παρεγγυή|σας, — ἅπαντα μέντοι ὡς ἐκ προσώ- που τοῦ Ἐζεκίου εἰπὼν ὡς ἂν ἁρμοττόντων αὐτῷ κατ' ἐκεῖνο καιροῦ τῶν τοιούτων λόγων, — ἐντεῦθεν λοιπὸν καὶ τῇ οἰκείᾳ κεχρημένος ἀκολουθίᾳ, ὡς ἂν ἐξ αὐτοῦ λέγων καὶ ταῦτα, κοινὴν πρὸς ἅπαντας ἐκφέρει παραίνεσιν
15 ἁρμόττουσαν μὲν καὶ τοῖς ἐπ' αὐτοῦ, ἁρμόττουσαν δὲ καὶ τοῖς ἐπὶ τοῦ μακαρίου Ἐζεκίου, οὐδὲν δὲ ἔλαττον παιδεύειν καὶ τοὺς ἑξῆς ἅπαντας δυνα- μένην. Ἔν τε τῇ παραινέσει τοῖς τε εὐαρεστεῖν ἐσπουδακόσι Θεῷ τὰ αὐτὰ ὑπισχνεῖται ἔσεσθαι τοῖς ὑπὸ τοῦ μακαρίου Ἐζεκίου γεγονόσι πρὸς εὐερ- γεσίαν τῶν Ἰσραηλιτῶν, καὶ πάλιν τοῖς πολλὴν ἔχουσι τῶν κακῶν τὴν
20 μελέτην τὰ ὅμοια ἔσεσθαι φάσκειν τοῖς ὑπ' αὐτοῦ κατὰ τῶν Ἀσσυρίων γεγονόσι, εἰ τοῖς κακοῖς ἐπιμένοιεν, — ἀκόλουθά τε τῇ ὑποθέσει φθεγγόμενος τοῦ ψαλμοῦ καὶ τὴν ἀλήθειαν τοῖς λεγομένοις ἀπὸ τῶν πραγμάτων εἰκότως μαρτυρῶν. Τούτου γὰρ ἕνεκεν πολλαχοῦ μὲν ἑτέρωθι καὶ ἐν τούτῳ δὲ τῷ ψαλμῷ διόλου ἔνθα ἑτέρους προτρέπεται τῶν ὁμοίων τῇ ὑποθέσει μνημο-
25 νεύει καί φησι·

12. Δεῦτε, τέκνα, ἀκούσατέ μου, φόβον Κυρίου διδάξω ὑμᾶς. Τὸ δεῦτέ φησι συγκαλῶν ἅπαντας ἐσπουδασμένως ἐπὶ τὴν τῶν λεγομένων ἀκρόασιν ὡς ἀναγκαίων. Τέκνα δὲ αὐτοὺς καλεῖ, τὴν ἑαυτοῦ διάθεσιν καὶ τὸ τῆς παραι- νέσεως γνήσιον ἀπὸ τῆς φωνῆς δεικνύς.

11. Εἰπὼν — καί φησι: (Θεοδώρου) Paris. 139, f. 74ᵛ; Vat. 1682, fol. 109; Bar- baro, p. 317. 8 ἐνδεᾶ PV 11 μέντοι] μὲν PV ἐκ om. C 12 ἐκείνου PV 13 καὶ om. PV 14 ἅπασαν PV 16-17 δυναμένων PV 17 τε 1° loco om. PV 20 φάσκει V ὑπ' αὐτοῦ] ἐπ' αὐτῷ PV.
12. Τὸ δεῦτε — εἶναι: (Θεοδώρου) Paris. 139, fol. 74ᵛ; Vat. 1682, f. 109ᵛ; Bar- baro, p. 317. 28 αὐτοὺς] αὐτοῦ C καὶ τὴν C αὐτοῦ PV.

Aᶜ 5-7 (p. 198, 3-4): Ac si diceret Citius diuites egebunt quam timentes Deum; cf. L (p. 597, 30-32: ἐγχωρεῖ — χρηστοῦ). 8 ss. (p. 198, 5-11): Huc usque tam sua quam sub Ezechiae persona iustos, quos commonuit ad ferendas Deo gratias, hortatus est. Nunc uelut propriam orationem format, qua inbuit audien- tes et diuino aptat seruitio: qui tamen sermo in omnia tempora futura a stu- diosis quibusque ualeat usurpari.

Wealthy people felt poverty and hunger, whereas those who seek out the Lord will not suffer lessening of any good (v. 10). Having said *Those who fear him want for nothing,* he goes on with a more weighty statement: *Wealthy people felt poverty and hunger, whereas those who seek out the Lord will not suffer lessening of any good.* This is the way he says that they incur no need, that it is far more likely and easier for a rich person to be tested by poverty and hunger than for the one who looks for help from God and begs salvation from him to be in need of any good.

To this point he had directed his words to the righteous, strengthening their hope in God, bidding them praise God in his company for what happened to blessed Hezekiah, and exhorting them to have the fear of God. Moreover, he says everything from the viewpoint of Hezekiah, since such words suited him at that time. From here on he adopts his own theme, as if speaking on his own account, and delivers a general exhortation applicable to everyone, including those of his own time, and applicable also to those of the time of blessed Hezekiah, and no less capable of instructing everyone in later times as well. By the exhortation he promises those anxious to please God that the same things would happen to them as were done by blessed Hezekiah for the benefit of the Israelites. To those in turn much concerned by troubles he says that the same things would occur as were done by him to the Assyrians if they should suffer problems.

What he says is in keeping with the theme of the psalm, and he naturally confirms the truth of the words from the events; for this reason in many other places as well as in this psalm, where he exhorts different people, he mentions similar things to the theme, and says *Come, children, listen to me, I shall teach you fear of the Lord* (v. 11). By *Come* he invites everyone zealously to attention to the words as important, and he calls them *children* to show his affection and the sincerity of the exhortation from the term. | *I shall*

Καλῶς δὲ τὸ Φόβον Κυρίου διδάξω ὑμᾶς.

Ἐπειδὴ γὰρ ἀνωτέρω εἶπε Φοβήθητε τὸν Κύριον πάντες οἱ ἅγιοι
αὐτοῦ, ἵνα μὴ δόξῃ τὸν φόβον τὸν
δεσποτικὸν εἰς τοὺς ἁγίους μόνον
ἱστᾶν, συγκαλέσας ἅπαντας πρὸς
τὴν ἀκρόασιν, Δεῦτέ φησι, διδάχθητε
ἐπωφελὴς ἅπασιν ἡ γνῶσις τοῦ φόβου.

Siquidem superius dixerat:
Timete Dominum omnes sancti
eius, ne uideretur ad sanctos tantum timoris diuini magisterium 5
pertinere.

τὸν φόβον· ἀναγκαῖα γάρ ἐστι καὶ

Διὰ τοῦτο, ὅπου μὲν ἁγίων μνημονεύει, οὐ λέγει διδάξω ὑμᾶς, ἀλ-
λ᾽ ἁπλῶς φοβήθητε, — ὑπομνήσεως
γὰρ μόνης ἦν χρεία τοῖς τοιούτοις, —
ὅπου δὲ κοινὴν πρὸς ἅπαντας ποιεῖται τὴν παραίνεσιν, ἐκεῖ τὸ διδάξω
προστίθησιν, ὡς διδαχῆς προσδεο-
μένων· ἀνάγκη γὰρ τοιοῦτο τὸ πλῆθος εἶναι.

Vbi sanctos tantum sermone
conpellat, non dicit docebo vos, 10
sed sempliciter timete Dominum,
quia sola eis commonitio uidetur posse sufficere; ubi uero in
commune hortatur omnes, adiungit docebo vos, quoniam doctrina 15
et institutione uulgaris et promiscua indiget multitudo. Tali au-

tem uerborum genere utitur, quod conueniat et his qui sub eius
imperio tunc erant, conueniat etiam illis qui erant sub Ezechia
futuri, ac reliquis per ordinem post futuris. 20

13ª. Τίς ἐστιν ἄνθρωπος ὁ θέλων ζωήν, ἀγαπῶν ἰδεῖν ἡμέρας ἀγαθάς;
Μετὰ τὸ συγκαλέσαι καὶ διδάσκειν, ἐπαγγείλασθαι ἀναγκαίως προτέθεικε
τοῦτο τῆς διδασκαλίας, τῆς ἑκάστου προθέσεως ἐξάπτων τὸ πρᾶγμα. Εἴ
τις οὖν ἐστί φησιν ἐν ἀνθρώποις ζωῆς ἐφιέμενος καὶ ἐπιθυμῶν ἡμέρας ἀγαθάς, τουτέστιν ἀνέσεώς τε καὶ τοῦ ἀπολαῦσαι τῶν παρὰ τοῦ Θεοῦ καλῶν, 25
οὗτος παιδευθήτω τὰ λεγόμενα, — δεικνὺς ὅτι χρεία μετὰ τῆς αὐτοῦ διδαχῆς
καὶ τῆς ἑκάστου προθυμίας, ἐξ᾽ ἧς τὸ ὑπακούειν τῷ βουλομένῳ προσγίνεται. Ἐξῆς δὲ λοιπὸν καὶ αὐτὴν ἐπάγων τὴν διδασκαλίαν φησί·

2 — 4 v. 10.

2 ἐπεὶ PV   5 μόνον om. PV   11-17 ὑπομνήσεως — εἶναι affert L (p. 598, 19-24)
12 ἦν — τοιούτοις] ἐχρῆζον L   15 διδαχῆς] διαδοχῆς L   15-16 δεομένων L   16 τοιοῦτον γὰρ ἀνάγκη L.
    Siquidem — futuris: A, fol. 9ᵈ; B, fol. 12ª. — Praecedit textus psalmi: Venite,
filii, audite me, reliqua.   3 timite A   4 uedeatur A   sanctorum A¹   9 tan-
tum] litt. tan in rasura A   12 eius eis A   comminutio A communitio B
14 commone A   ortatur ex oratur A   15 docebuos A   16-17 ** promiscua A
indiget] litt. in eras. A   18 conuenat A.

Aᵉ 23 ss. (p. 198, 14-16): Id est qui uellit in multa requie bonis a Deo praestitis habunde perfrui, hic percipiet ista quae dico.

teach you the fear of the Lord was well put: since he had said above *Fear the Lord, all you his holy ones,* lest he seem to confine the fear of the Lord to the holy ones, he invites all to attention in the words *Come, learn fear*—in other words, acquaintance with fear is necessary and useful for everyone. Hence, when he mentions holy ones, he says not *I shall teach you,* but simply *Fear,* such people requiring only a reminder, whereas when he gives his exhortation to everyone, then he adds *I shall teach,* since they are in need of teaching, this being required by the general run of people.

Who is the person who chooses life, who loves to see good days? (v. 12). After the invitation and promise to teach, he necessarily proposes this before the teaching, relating the outcome to each one's purpose. If there is someone, he therefore is saying, who is longing for life and desirous of *good days*—that is, relaxation and enjoyment of good things from God—let them be instructed in what is said. He shows that along with his teaching there is need also of each person's enthusiasm, and from this the response comes to the one who is willing. He then goes on to supply the teaching itself. |

14. Πρῶτον τὴν γλῶσσάν σου ἀπὸ κακοῦ, καὶ χείλη τοῦ μὴ λαλῆσαι δόλον. Ἐπειδὴ δὲ ἔμελλεν ἀπὸ τῶν κατὰ τὸν Ἑζεκίαν καὶ τῆς εὐεργεσίας τοῦ Θεοῦ καὶ τῆς τιμωρίας μνημονεύειν, εἰκότως καὶ ἐν τῇ ἀπαγορεύσει τῶν κακῶν ταῦτα μάλιστα αὐτοῖς ἀπαγορεύει ἃ πραχθέντα τοῖς Ἀσσυρίοις
5 μεγίστην ἤνεγκεν αὐτοῖς τῆς τιμωρίας τὴν ἀπόφασιν. Ἀπόσχου τοίνυν φησὶ παντὸς ῥήματος ἀτόπου, ἀλλὰ καὶ παντὸς δόλου καθαρεύειν σπούδαζε. Ταῦτα γὰρ μάλιστα πέπρακτο τῷ Ῥαψάκει κακὰ μὲν καὶ σφόδρα κάκιστα φθεγξαμένῳ, ἡνίκα ὑπερηφάνῳ γλώσσῃ τήν τε πόλιν αἱρήσειν ἠπείλει καὶ τὸν Θεὸν μηδὲν ἔφασκεν ἰσχύειν, ἀλλὰ καὶ κρατήσειν ἀπάντων ἀπεφήνατο
10 ⟨τὸν βασιλέα⟩ τῶν Ἀσσυρίων οὐδὲν αὐτῶν τοῦ Θεοῦ προστῆναι δυναμένου, ὡς οὐδὲ τὰ λοιπὰ ἔθνη ὤνησέ τι τῶν παρ' αὐτοῖς θεῶν ἡ ἰσχύς. Δολερὰ δὲ ἐφθέγγετο, ἡνίκα αὐτοῖς προσδεδωκόσι τὴν πόλιν καὶ δεξαμένοις τὸν βασιλέα ὑπισχνεῖτο γῆς πλουσίας παρέξειν ἀπόλαυσιν καὶ πολλῶν ἀγαθῶν μετουσίαν.

15 15ᵃ. Ἔκκλινον ἀπὸ κακοῦ καὶ ποίησον ἀγαθόν. Ἀλλὰ μὴ μόνον φησὶν ἀπέχου τοῦ κακοῦ, — οὐ γὰρ ἀρκεῖ, — σπούδαζε δὲ καὶ τὸ καλὸν διαπράττεσθαι.

15ᵇ. Ζήτησον εἰρήνην καὶ δίωξον αὐτήν. Πανταχοῦ ὡς φιλοπολέμους αἰτιᾶται τοὺς Ἀσσυρίους ὁ προφήτης· ἀκολούθως οὖν καὶ τοῦτο αὐτοῖς
20 ἀπαγορεύει τὸ πάθος, ὅπερ μάλιστα νοσοῦντες ἐκεῖνοι μεγίστην ὑπέστησαν τὴν τιμωρίαν, πείθων αὐτοὺς τὴν πρὸς πάντας εἰρήνην ἀσπάζεσθαι καὶ φιλίαν, μισεῖν δὲ πόλεμον καὶ ἔριδας καὶ ὅσα τοιαῦτα. Διὰ τί δὲ προσήκει μετὰ πολλῆς τῆς σπουδῆς ἀπέχεσθαι μὲν τῶν κακῶν, μεταδιώκειν δὲ ὅσα χρηστὰ ἑξῆς φησι, τὸ ἐπὶ τῶν Ἀσσυρίων καὶ τῶν Ἰσραηλιτῶν γεγο-
25 νὸς ἐξηγούμενος ὡς ἐπὶ παντὸς τοιούτου παρὰ Θεοῦ γινόμενον.

7-14 Is. XXXVI, 13-21.

14. Ἐπειδὴ — μετουσίαν : (Θεοῦˢ) Paris. 139, fol. 75; Vat. 1682, fol. 110; Barbaro, p. 319.   2 ἐπεὶ PV   5 μεσίτην PV   8 χλώσσῃ PV   αἱρήσειν] ἐρημώσιν PV   9 ἐπισχύειν PV   10 τὸν βασιλέα supplevi   τῶν Ἀσσ.] τὰς σύριον PV αὐτῶν] αὐτοῦ V   12 ἡνίκα — τὴν] ἡνικὴ αὐτῶν προσδεδωκὼς ἦν PV.

15ᵃ. Ἀλλὰ μὴ — διαπράττεσθαι : (Θεοδώρου) Paris. 139, fol. 75; Vat. 1682, fol. 110ᵛ; Barbaro, p. 320.

15ᵇ. Πανταχοῦ — γινόμενον : (Θεοδώρου) Paris. 139, fol. 75; Vat. 1682, fol. 110ᵛ; Barbaro, p. 320.   21 ἅπαντας V   24 ὡς ἄχρηστα PV   25 παρὰ τοῦ θεοῦ γιγνομένου PV.

Aᵉ 14 (p. 198, 22-299, 5): Per exemplum rerum sub Ezechia gestarum uirtutem commendat... ut Rabsacis, qui parans exitium ciuitatis terras obtimas promittebat.   15ᵇ (p. 199, 8-12): Quia multis locis profeta quasi amatores belli et feritatis accussat Assirios, quae res illis exitio fuit, consequenter auditores suos ad studia pacis hortatur.

Keep your tongue from evil, and your lips from speaking guile (v. 13). Since he intended on the basis of what happened to Hezekiah to mention both God's beneficence and his punishment, naturally in forbidding evil he particularly forbade them that which was committed by the Assyrians and brought them the heavy sentence of punishment. So renounce every inopportune word, he is saying, and be careful to rid yourself of all guile. This vice in particular, in fact, was committed by Rabshakeh, who was saying vile things when with arrogant tongue he threatened to destroy the city and claimed that God was powerless, and even stated that the king of the Assyrians controlled everything and God was incapable of protecting them, as the power of their gods had been of no benefit to the other nations.[6] He spoke falsehood when he promised to give them enjoyment of a wealthy land and a taste of many good things if they surrendered the city and accepted the king.

Turn away from evil and do good (v. 14): not only desist from evil, this not being enough, but take care also about doing good. *Seek peace and go after it.* Everywhere the inspired author blames the Assyrians for being bellicose; so he is consistent in also forbidding this passion to them, as it was for being addicted to it in particular that the former suffered the heaviest punishment. So he urges them to be peaceable and friendly toward all, and to hate war, disputes, and the like. Why it is necessary to desist from evil with great earnestness and in the future pursue whatever is good he explains by commenting on what happened in the case of the Assyrians and the Israelites as something done by God in every such case. |

---

6. Cf. 2 Kgs 18:28–35.

16ᵃ. Ὅτι ὀφθαλμοὶ Κυρίου ἐπὶ δικαίους. Προνοεῖ γάρ φησι τῶν δικαίων ὁ Θεός· ὀφθαλμοὺς γὰρ ἐνταῦθα οὐχ ἁπλῶς καλεῖ τὸ ἐποπτικόν, ἀλλὰ τὸ ἐπὶ εὐεργεσίᾳ καὶ προνοίᾳ παρὰ τοῦ Θεοῦ γινόμενον.

16ᵇ. Καὶ ὦτα αὐτοῦ εἰς δέησιν αὐτῶν. Καὶ προσίεται αὐτῶν φησι τὰς αἰτήσεις.

17ᵃ. Πρόσωπον δὲ Κυρίου ἐπὶ ποιοῦντας κακά. Ἐποπτεύει δέ φησι καὶ 5 τοὺς κακούς, οὐχ ὁμοίως δὲ τοῖς ἀγαθοῖς, ἀλλ᾽ ὥστε τί;

17ᵇ. Τοῦ ἐξολοθρεῦσαι ἐκ γῆς τὸ μνημόσυνον αὐτῶν. Διὰ ταῦτα οὖν φησι περισπούδαστον ὑμῖν εἶναι προσήκει τὴν δικαιοσύνην, ἐπειδήπερ ὁ Θεὸς πολλὴν μὲν ἐπιδείκνυται περὶ τοὺς δικαίους τὴν πρόνοιαν, προσδεχόμενος αὐτῶν καὶ τὰς ἱκεσίας, ἀποβλέπων δὲ καὶ πρὸς τοὺς τὰ ἄτοπα διαπραττομένους 10 παντελῆ τὸν ἀφανισμὸν αὐτοῖς ἐπάγει. Καὶ τίς τούτου ἡ ἀπόδειξις, τὸ γεγονὸς ἐξηγεῖται, διὰ τοῦτο ταῦτα εἰρηκὼς γίγνεσθαι παρὰ τοῦ Θεοῦ ἵνα τῇ ὁμοιότητι τοῦ γεγονότος διὰ τῆς μνήμης βεβαιώσῃ τῶν λεγομένων τὴν ἀλήθειαν.

18. Ἐκέκραξαν οἱ δίκαιοι, καὶ ὁ Κύριος εἰσήκουσεν αὐτῶν, καὶ ἐκ πασῶν τῶν θλίψεων αὐτῶν ἐρύσατο αὐτούς. Δικαίους ἐνταῦθα καλεῖ τοὺς Ἰσραηλίτας, συνη- 15 θῶς ἀπὸ τῆς γνώσεως οὕτω καλῶν πρὸς ἀντιπαράθεσιν τῶν Ἀσσυρίων. Ἰδοὺ γάρ φησι τούτων βοησάντων εἰσήκουσε, πάσης αὐτοὺς ἀπαλλάξας θλίψεως.

19ᵃ. Ἐγγὺς Κύριος τοῖς συντετριμμένοις τὴν καρδίαν. Ἀλλὰ καὶ σφόδρα φησὶν ἐπιμελεῖται πάντων τῶν ταπεινῶν ὁ Θεός, οἰκειοῦσθαι αὐτοὺς σπουδάζων· τὸ γὰρ ἐγγὺς τὴν διάθεσιν λέγει καὶ τὴν σχέσιν. Συντετριμμένους 20 δὲ τὴν καρδίαν ἐκάλεσε τοὺς ταπεινούς, τοὺς μηδένα ὑπέρογκον λογισμὸν κεκτημένους, ἀλλὰ σφόδρα ἑαυτοὺς εὐτελεῖς ὑποπτεύοντας εἶναι καὶ ἀσθενεῖς καὶ μηδεμίαν μεγίστην ὑπόληψιν περὶ ἑαυτῶν κεκτημένους, — ἐπειδὴ συντετριμμένον τὸ ἀσθενὲς καλεῖν εἰώθαμεν.

15-16 cf. supra in XXXII, 1ᵃ (p 142, 15-17).

16ᵃ. Προνοεῖ — γινόμενον: (Διδύμου) Paris. 139, fol. 75ᵛ; Vat. 1682, fol. 110ᵛ (= P. G., XXXIX, 1329 C); Barbaro, p. 321. 1 προνοεῖται PV 2-3 ὀφθαλμοὺς προνοίᾳ affert L (p. 599, 32-34). 17ᵇ. Διὰ ταῦτα — ἀλήθειαν: (Βασιλείου) Paris. 139, fol. 75ᵛ; Vat. 1682, fol. 111; Διὰ ταῦτα — 12 ἐξηγεῖται affert pluribus mutatis L (p. 600, 1-7). 18. Δικαίους — θλίψεως: (Θεοδ⁸) Paris. 139, fol. 75ᵛ; Vat. 1682, fol. 111; Barbaro, p. 322. 19ᵃ. Ἀλλὰ καὶ — εἰώθαμεν: (Θεοδώρου) Paris. 139, fol. 76; Vat. 1682, fol. 111ᵛ; Barbaro, p. 322. 19 πάντων ἐπιμ. PV 20-22 ἐγγὺς — κεκτημένους affert L (p. 600, 34-36) 20 τῇ διαθέσει... τῇ σχέσει C 20-21 συντετριμμένους — ἐκάλεσε τοὺς om. L 22 εὐτελεῖς ἑαυτοὺς PV 23 ὑπόληψιν μεγίστην PV 24 καλεῖν om. PV.

Aᵉ 17ᵃ (p. 199, 16): Id est, considerat etiam malos. 18 (p. 199, 20-23): Iustos hoc loco propter cognitionem Dei more suo Israelitas uocat, ut eos profanitate Assiriorum distinguat. 21-22 (p. 199, 24): Qui nihil de se magnum senserunt.

The eyes of the Lord are on the righteous (v. 15): God takes care of the righteous (by *eyes* referring not simply to sight but also to what is done by God in beneficence and providence). *And his ears open to their appeal:* he also accepts their requests. *But the face of the Lord is on evildoers* (v. 16): but he has an eye also for the wicked, though not in the same way as for the good. To what effect? *To destroy remembrance of them from the land:* so this is the reason for you to be devoted to righteousness, because God gives evidence of great care for the righteous, accepting their supplication while completely disregarding those guilty of wrong actions and inflicting destruction on them. The facts explain what is the proof of this; the reason for his saying that this was done by God was to confirm the reality of the words by mention of it.

The righteous cried aloud, and the Lord hearkened to them; he rescued them from all their tribulations (v. 17). By *the righteous* here he refers to the Israelites, in customary manner referring to them in this way by contrast with the Assyrians on the basis of their knowledge. Lo, he hearkened to those who cried out, he is saying, freeing them from every tribulation. *The Lord is near to the contrite of heart* (v. 18): God will also take extraordinary care of all the lowly, being anxious to make them his own (by *near* referring to his disposition and attitude, and calling the lowly *contrite of heart,* since they entertain no overweening thoughts, having instead an estimation of themselves as insignificant and feeble, and forming no exalted notion of themselves, since it is our habit to refer to weakness as contrition). |

19ᵇ. Καὶ τοὺς ταπεινοὺς τῷ πνεύματι σώσει. Φανερώτερον αὐτὸ ἐνταῦθα εἶπεν. Ἔδειξε γὰρ ὅτι ταπεινοὺς καὶ συντετριμμένους τὴν καρδίαν οὐχ ἁπλῶς τοὺς ἀπὸ συμφορῶν τοῦτο πάσχοντας καλεῖ, ἀλλὰ τοὺς τῷ λογισμῷ καὶ τῇ προθέσει τοιούτους, — οἳ κἂν ἐν συμφοραῖς ἐξετασθῶσιν, ἀπὸ τῆς
5 κατὰ τοὺς λογισμοὺς ταπεινώσεως ἄξια πάσχειν νομίζοντες, μετὰ τῆς προσηκούσης εὐλαβείας αἰτοῦντες τοῦ Θεοῦ τὴν βοήθειαν, λαμβάνουσι ταύτης τὴν ἀπόλαυσιν. Δῆλον οὖν ἐντεῦθεν ὅτι καὶ ἀνωτέρω λέγων Ἀκουσάτωσαν πραεῖς καὶ εὐφρανθήτωσαν, οὔτε τοὺς ἀπὸ συμφορῶν ἀνάγκης ταπεινοὺς καλεῖ, οὔτε τοὺς ἀπὸ φύσεως τοιούτους καθεστῶτας, — οὓς ἐν τῇ συνη-
10 θείᾳ πραεῖς οἱ πολλοὶ καλοὶ φιλοῦσιν, — ἀλλὰ τοὺς τῇ καρδίᾳ καὶ τῇ προθέσει τοιούτους, οἳ δείκνυνται ὅταν γενναίως τὰς εἰς αὐτοὺς ἀδικίας φέρειν σπουδάζωσιν, ἐκδεχόμενοι τὴν παρὰ τοῦ Θεοῦ βοήθειαν. Τοῦτο γάρ ἐστι πραότης, οὐχὶ τὸ ἀκίνητον, οὐδὲ τὸ πάντη παρασιωπᾶν παραλιμπάνοντα τὴν κίνησιν καὶ ἐφ᾽ ὧν πολλάκις ἀναγκαῖα καθέστηκεν, ὅταν μέγιστον ἀγαθὸν
15 ἐργάζεσθαι δύναται. Εἶτα ἐπειδὴ διόλου ἐπηγγείλατο τοῖς δικαίοις τοῦ Θεοῦ τὴν χορηγουμένην βοήθειαν, — πολλάκις δὲ ἐν μεγίστοις κακοῖς καὶ ἐν πολλαῖς θλίψεσι τοὺς δικαίους | ἐξετάζεσθαι συμβαίνει, — ἀκολούθως ἐπήγαγε·

20. Πολλαὶ αἱ θλίψεις τῶν δικαίων, καὶ ἐκ πασῶν αὐτῶν ῥύσεται αὐτούς. Κἂν ἐν πολλοῖς δέ φησιν ἐξετασθῶσί ποτε τοῖς κακοῖς καὶ ἐν πολλαῖς
20 θλίψεσιν, — τοῦτο τοῦ Θεοῦ συγχωροῦντος διὰ τὸ συμφέρον, — ἀλλὰ πάντως αὐτοὺς ἀπαλλάττει τῶν κακῶν, οὐκ εἰς τέλος ἐῶν ταῖς συμφοραῖς περικεῖσθαι. Καὶ ἐπειδὴ εἶπεν ὅτι κἂν ἐν πολλαῖς ἐξετασθῶσιν οἱ δίκαιοι ταῖς θλίψεσιν, ἀλλ᾽ οὖν γε πάντως αὐτοὺς ὁ Θεὸς ἀπαλλάττει, ἐγχωρεῖ δὲ τὸν ἐν πολλαῖς θλίψεσιν ἐξεταζόμενον ἐν ὅσῳ τῆς τοῦ Θεοῦ τυγχάνῃ βοηθείας
25 καί τι καὶ παθεῖν ὑπὸ τοῦ πλήθους τῶν θλίψεων, ἐπήγαγεν·

21. Κύριος φυλάσσει πάντα τὰ ὀστᾶ αὐτῶν, ἓν ἐξ αὐτῶν οὐ συντριβήσεται. Καὶ οὐδὲ ἐν ταῖς θλίψεσιν ὄντας φησὶν ἁπλῶς ἐᾷ πάσχειν ὑπὸ τῶν θλιβόντων, ἀλλὰ συγχωρεῖ μὲν τὰς θλίψεις τέως διὰ τὸ συμφέρον, μετὰ ταῦτα ῥυόμενος, καὶ ἐν μέσαις δὲ ταῖς θλίψεσιν ὄντας ἀνεπηρεάστους πρὸς
30 βλάβην καθίστησι, πᾶσαν αὐτῶν διαφυλάττων τὴν ἰσχύν. Τοῦτο γὰρ λέγει πάντα τὰ ὀστᾶ αὐτῶν, τουτέστιν ὡς μηδένα κίνδυνον αὐτοὺς ὑποστῆναι βαρύν. Διὰ τοῦτο καλῶς εἶπεν οὐ συντριβήσεται, τουτέστιν οὐδένα κίνδυνον ὑποστήσεται, ἐπειδὴ τὸ συντριβόμενον εἰς παντελῆ πέφυκε χωρεῖν ἀφανισμόν.

7-8 v. 3ᵇ.

21. Καὶ οὐδὲ — ἀφανισμόν: (Θεοδώρου) Paris. 139, fol. 76; Vat. 1682, fol. 111ᵛ-112; Barbaro, p. 323 (Καὶ ἐν μέσαις [l. 29] κ. τ. λ.).   27-28 ἐ]ᾷ πάσχειν — θλίψεις om. PV.

Aᵉ 21 (p. 200, 12-14): Etiam pro uirtutis experimento pulsentur, moueri tamen conterique non poterunt.

And he will save the lowly in spirit (v. 18). Here he said the same thing more clearly, showing that he did not apply the terms *lowly* and *contrite of heart* simply to those reduced to this condition from the disasters, but to those in this condition by intent and resolve. Even if tested by disasters, on the basis of their lowliness of intent they thought that they received their just deserts, asked God with due reverence for help, and received it by gift. So it clear from this that even by saying above *Let the gentle hear and be glad* he refers neither to those humbled of necessity by disasters nor to those in this condition by nature, whom the general run of good people like to think gentle, but to those in this condition in heart and purpose, who emerge by their zeal in bearing nobly the wrongs done them since they look to God for help. This, in fact, is gentleness, not being insensitive nor keeping complete silence while ignoring sensation even in situations that are often unavoidable, when it is possible to effect a greater good.

Next, since he had made an unconditional promise of God's help supplied to the righteous, whereas it often happens that the righteous are put to the test in extreme troubles and severe tribulations, he logically proceeded to say *Many are the tribulations of the righteous, and from them all he will rescue them* (v. 19): even if they are tested by many troubles and many tribulations, God allowing this to their advantage, he nevertheless definitely frees them from the troubles, not allowing them to be overcome by the disasters in the end. And since he said that even if the righteous are tested by the tribulations, God definitely will deliver them, though he allows the person tested by many tribulations, insofar as he gains help from God, also to suffer something else from the great number of tribulations. So he went on to say *The Lord protects all their bones, not one of them will be broken* (v. 20): far from simply allowing even those in tribulations to suffer under those distressing them, he rescues them after allowing the tribulations for a while to their advantage, keeps those in the midst of tribulations free from harm, and preserves their strength completely. This is the meaning of *all their bones*—that is, so that they incur no severe risk. Hence, *will not be broken* was well put, meaning "they will incur no risk," since what is broken naturally meets with complete destruction. |

22ᵃ. Θάνατος ἁμαρτωλῶν πονηρός. Καλῶς ἐνταῦθα προσέθηκε τὸ πονη-
ρός, ἵνα εἴπῃ ὅτι καὶ ὁ θάνατος τῶν | τοιούτων πονηρός. Ὥσπερ γὰρ ἐπὶ
τῶν δικαίων φησὶν ὅτι φυλάξει αὐτοὺς καὶ ἐν ταῖς θλίψεσιν, ὥστε μηδὲν
ἐπικίνδυνον ἢ ἀδιόρθωτον παθεῖν κακόν, τῆς περὶ αὐτοὺς προνοίας τὸ μέγεθος ἐξηγούμενος διὰ τούτου, οὕτως καὶ ἐπὶ τῶν ἁμαρτωλῶν τὸ ἐναντίον 5
φησίν, ὅτι καὶ ὁ θάνατος αὐτῶν οὐ κοινός ἐστι τοῖς λοιποῖς ἀνθρώποις
καὶ ὅμοιος, ἀλλ᾽ ἔχει τι πλέον καὶ βαρύτερον, ἀπὸ τῶν παρόντων καὶ
τοῦτο ἐξηγούμενος τοῦτον γεγενημένον τὸν τρόπον. Οἱ μὲν γὰρ περὶ τὸν
μακάριον Ἐζεκίαν ἐξητάσθησαν μὲν ἐν θλίψεσι καὶ λύπαις, περιεστηκότων
τὴν πόλιν τῶν Ἀσσυρίων, ἔπαθον δὲ δεινὸν ἢ ἀνήκεστον οὐδέν, οἱ δέ γε 10
Ἀσσύριοι καὶ τὸν θάνατον ὑπέμειναν φοβερόν, οὕτως αἰφνίδιον τῇ πληγῇ
τοῦ ἀγγέλου ἀναιρεθέντες.

22ᵇ. Καὶ οἱ μισοῦντες τὸν δίκαιον πλημμελήσουσιν. Καὶ οὐ μόνον φησὶν
οἱ ἁμαρτωλοὶ τοιαῦτα πάσχουσιν, ἀλλὰ καὶ οἱ ἀπεχθῶς πρὸς τὸν δίκαιον
ἔχοντες περιπεσοῦνται κακοῖς. | Τοῦτο δέ φησι δεικνὺς ὅσην ποιεῖται ὁ 15
Θεὸς τοῦ δικαίου τὴν πρόνοιαν. Τὸ δὲ πλημμελήσουσί φησιν ἀντὶ τοῦ
πταίσουσι, σφαλήσονται, ἁμαρτήσονται τοῦ σκοποῦ τῆς κατὰ τοῦ δικαίου
ἔχθρας ὑπὸ τοῦ Θεοῦ τιμωρηθέντες· πλημμελῆσαι γὰρ λέγεται τὸ
ἁμαρτεῖν, ἁμαρτεῖν δὲ τὸ ἀποτυχεῖν τῆς προθέσεως καὶ τοῦ σκοποῦ ἐκτὸς
καταστῆναι — ὅθεν καὶ ἁμαρτίαν τὴν ἄτοπον πρᾶξιν καλοῦμεν ὡς ἐκτὸς τοῦ 20
πρέποντος καθισταμένου τοῦ πράττοντος. Τοῦτο δέ φησι γίγνεται διὰ τί;

23ᵃ. Λυτρώσεται Κύριος ψυχὰς δούλων αὐτοῦ. Ἐπειδὴ γὰρ ὁ Κύριος
ἀπαλλάττει τοὺς οἰκείους δούλους πάσης συμφορᾶς, ἀνάγκη τοὺς ἀπεχθῶς
καὶ πολεμίως πρὸς αὐτοὺς διακειμένους τιμωρίαις περιπίπτειν. Τὸ δὲ λυτρώσεται ἀντὶ τοῦ ἀπαλλάξει, ἀπὸ τῶν τοὺς ἐν αἰχμαλωσίᾳ ληφθέντας καὶ 25
παρ᾽ ἀξίαν δουλεύοντας δώροις τῆς δουλείας ἐξαιρουμένων· λύτρα γὰρ λέγεται τὰ τοιαῦτα δῶρα.

22ᵃ. Καλῶς — ἀναιρεθέντες: (Θεοδώρου) Paris. 139, fol. 76ᵛ; Vat. 1682, fol. 112;
Barbaro, p. 324; eadem fere ad verbum apud L (p. 601, 9-20). 5 καὶ om. PV
9 περιεσχηκότων V.
22ᵇ. Καὶ οὐ μόνον — διὰ τί: (Θεοδώρου) Paris. 139, fol. 76ᵛ; Vat. 1682, fol. 112ʳ·ᵛ;
Barbaro, p. 324-325. 13-21 οὐ μόνον — τοῦ πράττοντος pluribus omissis affert L
(p. 601, 27-36). 15 κακῶν PV 17 πταίσωσι PV 19 ἐκτὸς τοῦ σκοποῦ PV.
23. Ἐπειδὴ — δῶρα: (Θεοδώρου) Paris. 139, fol. 76ᵛ; Vat. 1682, fol. 112ᵛ; Barbaro, p. 325. 23 ἀπεχθῶς] ἐπαχθῶς V 24-27 τὸ λυτρώσεται — δῶρα quibusdam
mutatis aut omissis affert L (p. 602, 11-14) 25 ἐν om. PV.

Aᵉ 22ᵃ (p. 200, 15-18) Bene addidit pessima ut diceret: Nullum est malis
uel in morte solacium, non commonis (mors) ut ceterorum, sicut Assiriorum.
16-21 (p. 201, 1-4): Id est ab spe sua decedent, fallentur, peccabunt; peccare
etiam dicuntur, cum intentione frustrentur euentus. 26-27 (p. 201, 7-8): Redem-
tiones namque huiusmodi Dei dicuntur dona.

Sinners come to a bad end (v. 21). He was right to introduce the word *bad* at this point, as if to say that such people have a bad death: as he says in the case of the righteous that he will guard them even in tribulations lest they suffer any dangerous or irremediable trouble (thus explaining the extent of the providence shown them), so also in the case of sinners he says the opposite, that their death is not that of the rest of humankind or similar to theirs, but involves some further and more severe element. He explains this by reference to the way it took place in the present circumstances: whereas those in the company of blessed Hezekiah were tested by tribulation and distress when the Assyrians besieged the city yet suffered no dire or unbearable fate, the Assyrians for their part even met with a fearful death, being struck down so suddenly by the angel's assault. *Those who hate the righteous will come to grief:* not only do sinners meet such a fate, but also those hostile to the righteous will fall foul of troubles. Now, he says this to bring out the extent of the providence that God shows for the righteous. *Will come to grief* means that they will stumble, will trip up, will fail in their hostile intent against the righteous by being punished by God, *come to grief* meaning "missing the mark," which means failing to achieve a purpose and intent at odds with that prescribed—hence our calling a wrong action a sin as being at odds with the proper intention.

He asks for what purpose does this happen. *The Lord will ransom the souls of his servants* (v. 22): since the Lord frees his own servants from every calamity, it follows that those with hostile and aggressive attitudes toward them will meet with punishment. *Will ransom* means "will set free"—an expression taken from people rescuing from slavery with payment those held in captivity and enslaved undeservedly, such payments being called ransoms. | *And all who hope in him will not come to grief:* hence, those who

23ᵇ. Καὶ οὐ μὴ πλημμελήσουσιν πάντες οἱ ἐλπίζοντες ἐπ᾽ αὐτόν. Διὰ τοῦτό φησιν οἱ μὲν τοῖς δικαίοις πολεμοῦντες ἀποτεύξονται τοῦ σκοποῦ συμφοραῖς περιπεσόντες, οἱ δὲ ἐπὶ τὸν δεσπότην ἐλπίζοντες, παντὸς ἐλεύθεροι κακοῦ διατηρούμενοι, οὐκ ἀποτεύξονται οὐδὲ σφαλήσονται τῶν ἐλπίδων.

5

PSALMVS XXXIV

Ἐν τούτῳ τῷ ψαλμῷ τὰ κατὰ τὸν Ἱερεμίαν ὁ μακάριος προφητεύει Δαυίδ, τό τε ἐκείνου πρόσωπον ἀναλαβὼν ἐν τῇ προφητείᾳ ταῦτα φθέγ-
10 γεται ἅπερ εἰκὸς ἦν ἐκεῖνον εἰπεῖν ἐν τῷ πράγματι καθεστῶτα, ταύτῃ μάλιστα κεχρημένος ἐν τοῖς πλείοσι τῇ συνηθείᾳ, λέγων τε ἅπερ ἐκείνοις εἰπεῖν ἁρμόττει περὶ ὧν ποιεῖται τὴν
15 προφητείαν.

Διαλλάττει δὲ οὐδὲν ὁ ψαλμὸς ὅδε πλὴν τοῦ προσώπου τῶν

20

περὶ τοῦ λαοῦ τοῦ ἐν Βαβυλῶνι. Κατὰ γὰρ τὸν αὐτὸν γενομένου καιρὸν τοῦ προφήτου, κἀκεῖνα προλέγοντος ἐγ-

Profetat in hoc psalmo beatus Dauid ea quae in Heremiam, tam a populo quam a principibus Iudeorum constat admisa; ac persona illius adsumpta loquitur quae illum dicere res ipsae in tempore conpulerunt: hanc namque in multis locis beatus Dauid seruat consuetudinem, ut conuenientia eis aptet uerba, quibus uaticinandi impendit officium. Differt autem hic psalmus ab ipso Heremiae uolumine personis tantum: nam eadem nunc dicuntur a Dauid quae postea ab Heremia dicta sunt. Qui eo profetauit tempore quo erat populus in Babilonem ducendus, ac uicina eis adnuntiauit mala quae

---

23ᵇ. Διὰ τοῦτο — ἐλπίδων: (Θεοᵈ) Paris. 139, fol. 76ᵛ; Vat. 1682, fol. 112ᵛ; Barbaro, p. 325.   4 οὐδὲ τῶν ἐλπίδων σφαλήσονται L (p. 602. 21).

xxxiv. arg. Ἐν τούτῳ — 170, 17 προαγορεύει: (Θεοδώρου) Paris. 159, fol. 77; Vat. 1682. fol. 112ᵛ-113 (Mai, Nova Patrum Bibliotheca III, p. 455-456; P. G., LXVI, 669 BC); Barbaro, p. 325-326.   14 πεποίηται PV   17 οὐδ᾽ PV 18 ὧδε PV.

Profetat — 175, 23 apparebit: A, fol. 9ᵈ-10ᵈ; B, fol. 12ᵃ-12ᶜ.   5 psalmus xxxiiii A *in textu*, xxxiiii B *in marg*.   11 illum illum A¹   12 conpullerunt A   16 inpedit A   17 difert A deffert B   23 babiloniam A.

Aᵉ **23ᵇ** (p. 201, 9): Qui erunt compotes uotorum.   *Argumentum ps. XXXIV hoc modo refertur* (p. 201, 11-14): Occassionem erumnarum suarum hoc carmine Dauid in tempore Heremiae profetae componit, quaeque in eum principes commesserunt persequitur. Cf. Pseudo-beda (658).

are hostile toward the righteous will fail in their purpose and fall foul of disasters, whereas those hoping in the Lord, kept free of every trouble, will not fail or be disappointed in their hope.

PSALM 35

In this psalm blessed David prophesies the events concerning Jeremiah. Adopting his point of view in the inspired composition, he gives voice to what he probably would have said in the situation. He employed this usage in particular in many cases, saying what was appropriate for the people to say with whom the composition deals.[1] Except for the viewpoint adopted, this psalm is no different from those dealing with the people in Babylon: the prophet lived at the same time and foretold from close at hand | the future

---

1. The introduction to this psalm at great length makes the point that Jeremiah is in focus; the syntax is also irregular, as comparison with the extant Latin version discloses. Diodore likewise had seen Jeremiah in focus; Theodoret, by contrast, will ignore the supposed resemblance to Jeremiah, instead relating the psalm briefly to troubles in David's own life.

γύθεν ἐσόμενα ἄπερ καὶ οἱ λοιποὶ
πόρρωθεν ἔλεγον προφῆται, καὶ διὰ
τοῦτο ἄπαντα πάσχοντος ὑπὸ τοῦ
λαοῦ ὅσα δὴ καὶ πέπονθε, τὸ τὰ
περὶ ἐκεῖνον εἰπεῖν σαφῶς ἐστιν
ἐκεῖνα εἰπεῖν πρὸς τὸ δεῖξαι ὅτι καὶ
δικαίως ἔπασχον, οὐδὲ τῷ πλησίον
τῶν καιρῶν προφήτῃ πειθόμενοι ὅτε
καὶ ἡ ἔκβασις ἐγγύθεν ἐπιστοῦτο τὴν
πρόρρησιν τῶν λεγομένων.

Ποιεῖται
δὲ τὴν περὶ τοῦ μακαρίου Ἰερεμίου
προφητείαν ὁ μακάριος Δαυίδ, οὐ γὰρ
ἁπλῶς, ἀλλ᾽ ἐπειδὴ διόλου ἐν τοῖς
πλείοσι | τῶν ψαλμῶν τὰ τοῖς λαοῖς
συμβησόμενα προαγορεύει. Ὁμοῦ μὲν
τοὺς ἐν συμφοραῖς ἐξεταζομένους ὠ-
φελῶν, ἐξομολογεῖσθαί τε γὰρ ἐπαί-
δευεν αὐτοὺς ἐν ταῖς συμφοραῖς ὑπὲρ
τῆς ἁμαρτίας καὶ εὐέλπιδας καθίστη
διὰ τῆς τῶν καλῶν ὑποσχέσεως, ὁμοῦ
δὲ καὶ πᾶσι κατάδηλον τοῦ Θεοῦ τὴν
φιλανθρωπίαν ἐργαζόμενος, ὅτι διὰ
πάντων τῶν προφητῶν οὕτω συνεχῆ
τὴν προαγόρευσιν ἐποιήσατο τῶν
συμβησομένων αὐτοῖς κακῶν, βουλόμενος ἐπιστρέψαντας φυγεῖν τῶν
κακῶν τὴν πεῖραν.

Τοῦτο καὶ ἐν-
ταῦθα ποιεῖ ἐπὶ τοῦ προφήτου Ἰερεμίου, ὃς παρ᾽ αὐτὸν γεγόνει τῆς
αἰχμαλωσίας τὸν καιρόν, — δεικνὺς
ὅση μὲν τοῦ Θεοῦ ἡ φιλανθρωπία, ὅτι
καὶ παρ᾽ αὐτοῖς ὄντας τοῖς κακοῖς

reliqui profetae multo ante prae-
dixerant; atque ideo uehementio-
res in se populi accendit iras ac
multa a furentibus aduersa su-
stinuit, quia aperte ea quae pas- 5
suri erant instare dicebat. Vnde
constat eos | iuste pertulisse om-
nia, qui ne tunc quidem profetae
uoluerunt credere cum iam malorum tempus urgeret, cum rebus 10
praedictis fidem facerent ipsi exitus rerum. Profetiam ergo hanc
sub persona Heremiae beatus
Dauid non otiose et absque ulla
consideratione utilitatis induxit, 15
sed, ut in multis psalmis, ea quae
erant populo uentura dicebat. Ita
et hic, ⟨ut⟩ prodesset his qui
erant aduersa passuri, docet eos
confiteri peccata sua atque offen- 20
sam satisfactione depellere, quo
bonae spei facti possent exspec-
tare meliora; Dei quoque bonitatem omnibus facit esse manifestam, qui idcirco a cunctis 25
profetis uolebat eis quae passuri
erant aduersa praedici, ut con-
uerterentur atque effugerent ea
quae fre|quens comminatio nun-
tiabat. Hoc ergo et in praesenti 30
agit sub persona Heremiae qui
in ipso captiuitatis profetauit
tempore, uolens ostendere quanta
esset Dei bonitas, qui iam uicinis atque urgentibus malis mit- 35

14-15 οὐχ ἁπλῶς PV   21 καθίστα ms.
2-3 uechimentioris A¹ — iores A² uehimentiores B   4-5 sustenuit A
5-6 pasuri A   9 iam om. B   10 urgueret B   11 fecerent A¹   17 ita ** A
18 ut supplevi   prodisset A   22 bona A   29 comminutio A   30 hoc —
171, 14 permiserit om. B.

that the other prophets also spoke of from a distance. Hence, he suffers at the hands of the people all that they too had suffered; describing their fate was tantamount to showing that they had even suffered with good reason, and they were not convinced by the prophet even closer to the time when the outcome at close quarters lent substance to the prophecy in his words.

Now, blessed David delivers the inspired discourse about blessed Jeremiah not without reason but because in most of the psalms he foretells what will happen to the peoples. By way of benefiting those being tested by calamities he instructed them to confess their sins in the calamities, and he made them hopeful with a promise of good times. He likewise brought God's lovingkindness to the attention of everyone in that through all the prophets he delivered such a constant prediction of the troubles that would befall them, wishing as he did that they would be converted and avoid experiencing the troubles. This he also does here in the case of the prophet Jeremiah, who lived at the time of the captivity. He shows, on the one hand, the extent of God's lovingkindness | in sending the prophet to summon them to repentance

ἀπέστειλε τὸν προφήτην, ἔτι καλῶν
αὐτοὺς εἰς μετάνοιαν ὥστε τῶν ἐσομένων λυπηρῶν ἀνάκλησιν ἐργάσασθαι διὰ τῆς ἐκείνων μετανοίας, ὅπου
5 δὲ ἐπέμενον ἐκεῖνοι ἔτι μὲν ἀπειθῶς
ἔχοντες περὶ τὰς τοῦ Θεοῦ προαγορεύσεις, ἐπαχθῶς δὲ διακείμενοι
καὶ πρὸς τὸν ἀποστελλόμενον· δι᾿
ὧν ἁπάντων ἐδείκνυτο μὲν μάλιστα
10 ἡ τοῦ Θεοῦ φιλανθρωπία καὶ τὸ δίκαιον, οὐκ ὠμότητι τῇ αἰχμαλωσίᾳ
παραδεδωκότος αὐτοὺς καὶ τοῖς τότε
κακοῖς, ἐδείκνυντο δὲ δικαίως τε καὶ
ἀξίως τοῦ οἰκείου τρόπου τὴν τιμω-
15 ρίαν δεχόμενοι. Τούτου δὴ ἔνεκεν εἰκότως ἐξηγεῖται τὰς τοῦ μακαρίου
Ἰερεμίου ἀποδυσπετήσεις, ἃς ἐπὶ τῷ
πλήθει τῶν ἐπαγομένων αὐτῷ παρὰ
τῶν Ἰουδαίων κακῶν ἐποι|εῖτο.
20

tebat profetas ut eos ad poenitentiam prouocaret et seueritatem
seuerioris correptionis instantis
auerteret; indicat etiam qualiter
populus in infidelitate permanens
erit, non credens his quae man-
dante Deo a profeta dicebantur,
offensus in ipsum quoque profetam ac uechimenter infestus: per
quae omnia Dei bonitas praecipue et iustitia adseritur, quod
eos in captiuitatem, non crude-
litate aliqua, pro meritorum suorum qualitate ire permiserit. In-
ducuntur etiam beati Heremiae
querellae, in quas conpellebatur
iniuriarum onere, quas a Iudaeis
eo praesertim tempore, quo pro
salute eorum sollicitus erat, in-
latas dissi|mulare non poterat.

Τὸ μὲν γὰρ μέγεθος τῶν συμφορῶν καὶ τὰς τιμωρίας, ὅσας ἐπέτριβον
τῷ προφήτῃ καὶ ταῦτα αὐτοῖς τὰ μέλλοντα προαγορεύοντι ὑπὲρ τῆς ἐκείνων
σωτηρίας, ἐδείκνυ διὰ τῶν τοῦ δικαίου ἀποδυσπετήσεων. Ἐποίει δὲ τοῦτο
τὴν τοῦ Θεοῦ φιλανθρωπίαν κατάδηλον, ὅση τίς ἐστι περὶ τοὺς ἀπειθοῦν-
25 τας μὲν τοῖς αὐτοῦ ῥήμασιν, ἐνυβρίζοντας δὲ καὶ τοὺς ἀποστελλομένους παρ᾿
αὐτοῦ πάντας, καὶ οὕτω πληροῦντος ὅσα περὶ τῆς ἐκείνων σωτηρίας [ἔνεκεν]
γενέσθαι προσῆκον ἦν, — καὶ ὅτι δικαίως τοιούτους ὄντας τιμωρίαις καὶ τοῖς
τῆς αἰχμαλωσίας περιέβαλε κακοῖς.

Ἰστέον δὲ πρὸς τῇ αἰτίᾳ ταύτῃ
30 καὶ ἑτέραν εἶναι τῆς τούτων προαγορεύσεως. Ἐπειδὴ γὰρ πλεῖστα μὲν
αὐτὸς ἐν τοῖς ψαλμοῖς προφητεύων
διετέλεσε τὰς ἐπαχθησομένας αὐτοῖς
προλέγων συμφοράς, — πλεῖσται δὲ
35 ὅσαι γεγόνασι περὶ τούτων καὶ παρὰ

Sciendum autem, praeter hanc
quam praediximus, etiam aliam
esse causam praedicationis. Siquidem aperte atque sollicite in
psalmis discrimina, quae eis sunt
postea inlata, praedicit — de quibus ne reliqui quidem profetae

---

26 ἔνεκεν delevi.
1-2 poenitiam A   4 aduerteret A¹   5 infidilitate A   12-13 creduli-
tate A   13 meritorum] mortuorum A   14 praemiserit A   17 iniuriarum
uel A   iudeis A   18 quod A¹   20 disimulare A   29 sciendum — 172, 10 inplenda om. B   30 diximus A¹   35 reliqui neque quidem A

when in the midst of the troubles so as to cause a cancellation of the coming woes through their repentance, and on the other hand how they persisted in a lack of response to God's prophecies, and were also ill-disposed toward the one who sent them.

In all this God's lovingkindness and righteousness were most of all revealed in surrendering them to captivity and the troubles of the time without cruelty, while they were shown to be the object of punishment both justly and as their conduct deserved. For this reason he is right to comment on the complaints that blessed Jeremiah made about the great number of troubles inflicted on him by the Jews: the magnitude of all the hardships and punishments that they inflicted on the prophet despite his forecasting the future to them for the sake of their salvation he revealed through the righteous man's complaints. Now, this brought out the degree of God's lovingkindness regarding those who did not believe in his words and abused all those sent by him, despite his performing everything that had to be done for the sake of their salvation. It also brought out that he was within his rights to invest such people with punishments and the troubles of the captivity.

Now, it should be realized that in addition to this reason for the prediction of these things there was also another. You see, in the psalms he continued prophesying the disasters due to be inflicted on them, and most of the prophecies of these things were also delivered by the other prophets. |

τῶν λοιπῶν προφητῶν αἱ προαγορεύσεις, ὑφ᾽ ὧν οὐδαμῶς ἐντραπεὶς
ὁ λαὸς ἠνέσχετο τῶν οἰκείων ἀποστῆναι πλημμελημάτων, —

εἰκότως
κατὰ τὸν προφήτην τοῦτον προλέγει ἐν αὐτοῖς μὲν τοῖς κακοῖς προα-
γορεύοντα, ὅτι καὶ σύντομον καὶ ἀκόλουθον τὴν ἔκβασιν ἐλάμβανεν, — οὐ
μόνον δὲ οὐκ ἐπιστρέψαντα τοὺς
ἁμαρτάνοντας, ἀλλὰ γὰρ καὶ προ-
παθόντα ὑπ᾽ αὐτῶν καὶ ὑποστάντα
μυρία ὅσα κακά, — δεικνὺς ὡς ἐπί-
στατο μὲν ὁ Θεὸς οὐ μεταβληθησο-
μένους αὐτούς. Οὐκ ἀγνοίᾳ | τε τού-
του τὴν προαγόρευσιν ἐποιεῖτο,
ἔλεγε δὲ ὅμως διὰ τῶν προφητῶν,
ὁμοῦ μὲν τοὺς καθ᾽ ἑκάστην γενεὰν
ὄντας καλοὺς ἐπιστηρίζων, —

ἀνάγκη
γὰρ εἶναι τοιούτους, εἰ καὶ εὐαρίθμη-
τοί τινες ὄντες ἐτύγχανον, — ὁμοῦ δὲ
καὶ τοὺς κατ᾽ αὐτὴν αἰχμαλωσίαν
τοιούτους ἀμεταθέτους τῆς ἀρετῆς
ἐργαζόμενος, οἳ τὴν τῶν κακῶν ἔκκαυσιν θεασάμενοι πρὸ πολλῶν
προαγορευθεῖσαν γενεῶν, εἰκότως
εὐλαβείᾳ καὶ φόβῳ τοῦ Θεοῦ τὴν
ὀργὴν ἐκκλίνειν ἐσπουδακότες, ἐπι-
μένειν ἔσπευδον τῇ ἀρετῇ, αὐτῇ τῇ
πείρᾳ διὰ τῆς ἐκβάσεως γνόντες ὅση

tacuerunt; sed quamuis nunquam admonitionis sermo ces-
sauerit, populus tamen neque
melior factus est, neque a conuersationis suae prauitate dis- 5
cessit. Tunc et consequenter
etiam hoc profeta inducit in ipso
stantis captiuitatis tempore, ad-
nuntians ea quae cito erant rebus inplenda, — qui non solum 10
non conuertit peccatores, sed in
suas eos afflictiones atque iniurias
concitauit. Ostendit ergo per haec
quoniam sciebat quidem Deus
illos ad conuersionem non esse 15
uenturos; unde non ignorantia
obstinationis eorum, sed reliquorum cura, praedici eis faciebat
omnia ac sepissime nuntiari, ut
et per singulas quasque genera- 20
tiones eos, qui futuri erant, studii melioris instrueret. Constat
autem quamuis exiguos numero
tamen fuisse per diuersa tempora, qui bonis moribus eluce- 25
rent, simul ut etiam eos qui sub
ipso captiuitatis tempore emen-
datioris erant uitae, adtentiores
circa studium uirtutis efficeret;
qui praedictorum olim malorum 30
considerantes exitum, studebant
iram imminentem timore Dei et
sanctitatis proposito declinare
atque in uirtutis studio permanere, experimento rerum satis 35

11 ἐπιστρέψαντας ms.

1-2 nq̄ A¹ nequam add. supra   5 paruitate A   7 inducitur A   10 quique A   12 adflictiones A   13 haec] hoc A   15 conuersione A   23 quamuis
exiguos] q̄ (in rasura)* exiguo* A   25 m**oribus (maioribus?) A   27-28 emen-
tatiores A   32 inminentem timori A   33 propossito A   34 atque] quodque A
35 experimento — 173, 12 ad meliora conari om. B.

But the people were in no way converted by them or brought themselves to desist from their failings. So naturally he prophesies through this prophet's predictions in the midst of the troubles, and the prophecy had a swift and due outcome; he not only failed to convert the sinners, but also was subjected by them to countless hardships. He shows that God knew that they would not change; he did not deliver the prediction in ignorance. Rather, his purpose in speaking through the prophets was both to encourage good people in every generation (there were inevitably some such, few though they happened to be) and to encourage such people in the same captivity to remained steadfast in virtue. They had pondered the conflagration of the disasters foretold many generations earlier, and they were properly anxious in piety and fear to divert God's wrath and to persevere in their zeal for virtue, knowing from actual experience through the outcome what was the extent of | the punish-

τοῖς ἁμαρτάνουσι παρὰ τοῦ Θεοῦ
προσγίνεται ἡ τιμωρία.

Εἰκὸς δὲ ἦν καὶ τῶν τὰ φαῦλα
διαπραττομένων πολλοὺς μὲν καὶ τῶν
5 πρὸ τῆς αἰχμαλωσίας, τῷ φόβῳ τῆς
τῶν κακῶν προαγορεύσεως, ἐγκόπ-
τεσθαι τῆς ἐπὶ τὰ χείρω προόδου.

῝Ην δὲ καὶ τοῦτο οὐ βραχὺ τοῖς
10 παντελῆ τὴν ἐπὶ τὰ κρείττω μεταβολὴν οὐ δεχομένοις,
πολλοὺς δὲ καὶ
τῶν παρ᾽ αὐτὸν τὸν τῆς αἰχμαλωσίας
καιρόν, ἀπὸ τῆς ἐκβάσεως λοιπὸν τῶν
15 προαγορευθέντων κακῶν, φόβῳ τὴν
ἐπὶ τὰ κρείττω δέξασθαι μεταβολήν.
Καὶ ταῦτα μὲν εἴρηται ὥστε τὴν αἰτίαν ἡμῖν εἶναι κατάδηλον, δι᾽ ἣν
πολλῶν προφητῶν ταῦτα προαγο-
20 ρευσάντων, πλεῖστά τε ὑπὸ ᾽Ιου-
δαίων διὰ τὴν περὶ τούτων προαγόρευσιν πεπονθότων, μόνων τῶν κατὰ
τὸν ᾽Ιερεμίαν ὁ μακάριος Δαυὶδ ἐποιήσατο τὴν ἐξήγησιν,

25

δῆλον πρὸ πάντων
ἐκείνου καθεστῶτος, ὡς ἔθος αὐτῷ
30 ποιεῖσθαι τῶν ἐσομένων τὴν προαγόρευσιν ἀπὸ προσώπου λέγοντι τῶν
κατ᾽ ἐκεῖνο καιροῦ γενησομένων τὰ
ἁρμόττοντα, ὡς ὅταν τὰ τῶν Ἀσσυρίων προαγορεύῃ ἐκ προσώπου τοῦ
35 Ἐζεκίου, λέγων τὰ τοῖς τε πράγμασι καὶ τῷ προσώπῳ κατάλληλα.
Οὕτω γὰρ κἀνταῦθα τὰ ἐν Βαβυ-

eruditi qualiter in peccatores Dei
seueritas uindicaret.

Euenire uero poterat ut etiam
ex his multi, | quos uitiorum con-
suetudo retinebat, ipso captiuitatis tempore ac praedicatione
malorum, a prauitatis suae studio reuocari non pati, in peiora
prodisse. Pertinet autem non ad
paruum profectum, si praepe-
diantur hii, ne proficiant in peius,
qui nolunt ad meliora conari.
Credendum est etiam multos in
ipso captiuitatis tempore, cum
uiderent ea impleri quae praedicta fuerant, ipso fuisse timore
correctos. Haec autem a nobis
dicta sunt ut fieret argumentum
psalmi causaque manifesta, quare
cum multi profetae eadem prae-
dixissent ac passi fuissent grauia mala propter praedicationis
officium, tantum de solo Heremia
beatus Dauid narrare curauerit. Ob hoc utique tantum Heremiae memor est, quod inter illius
temporis profetas uidetur solus
eminere. Consuetudo namque est
beato Dauid, cum futura praedicit, sub alicuius clarioris persona
profetare, atque ea dicere quae
eius personae conueniant, sicut
et cum de Assyriorum caede
praeloquitur, ex persona Ezechiae ea inserit quae possint rebus aptissime conuenire. Ita ergo
et in praesenti, ituro in Babilo-

10-11 ** praedicantur A¹ uel pe *add. supra*   14 temporis B   18 dicta *om*. B
21 ac si B   fuerint A   23 hiremia A   28 eminiere A   est *om*. A   30 ali-
cuis A   persona ** B   33 assiriorum A   cede AB.

ment coming from God to sinners.

Now, it was likely that many of those guilty of vicious behavior even before the captivity were diverted from the downward path by fear of the prediction of the disasters, and this was no slight gain for those completely unreceptive of a change for the better. It was also likely that many of those at the very time of the captivity, moved by the outcome of the disasters foretold, underwent a change for the better through fear. These things have been said so that the reason might be clear to us why, though many prophets foretold it and the Jews suffered greatly as a result of the prophecies about them, it was only what concerned Jeremiah on which blessed David commented, he being the most conspicuous of all. It was customary with David to compose a prediction of the future from the viewpoint of someone saying what was applicable to what would take place at that time; for example, when he forecasts the events concerning the Assyrians from the viewpoint of Hezekiah, he mentions what was appropriate to both the events and the person. This is the way, in fact, he foretells also in this case the events in | Babylon—namely,

λῶνι ἤτοι τὴν ἐκεῖ αἰχμαλωσίαν τοῦ λαοῦ προαγορεύει ἐκ προσώπου τοῦ Ἰερεμίου, λέγων τὰ ἀρμόττοντα τῷ προφήτῃ ἀπό τε τῶν καιρῶν καὶ τῶν γιγνομένων.

Πρὸς τὸ καὶ τῶν εἰρημένων ἡμῖν ἀρτίως ἑκοῦσαν παρέχεσθαι τὴν ἀπόδειξιν, ἔστι δὲ καὶ αὐτῇ τοῦ μακαρίου Ἰερεμίου ἐντετυχηκότα τῇ βίβλῳ εὑρεῖν ἐν πολλοῖς τὴν συμφωνίαν τῶν τε παρ᾽ ἐκείνου λεγομένων ἢ καὶ εἰς αὐτὸν γεγονότων καὶ τῶν ὑπὸ τοῦ μακαρίου Δαυὶδ ἐν τούτῳ τῷ ψαλμῷ προαγορευομένων, ὥστε καὶ ἐνεῖναι μαθεῖν ἐντεῦθεν ὅση τις τοῦ προφήτου ἡ ἀλήθεια ὡς πολλάκις καὶ τὰ πράγματα καὶ τὰ ῥήματα μετὰ πολλῆς φθέγξασθαι τῆς ἀκριβείας.

Ἐντεῦθεν μὲν γάρ φησι Γενηθήτω ἡ ὁδὸς αὐτῶν σκότος καὶ ὀλίσθημα, παρὰ δὲ τῷ προφήτῃ Ἰερεμίᾳ Διὰ τοῦτο γενέσθω ἡ ὁδὸς αὐτῶν αὐτοῖς ὀλίσθημα ἐν γνόφῳ. Καὶ ἐνταῦθα μέν φησιν Ὅτι δωρεὰν ἔκρυψάν μοι διαφθορὰν παγίδος αὐτῶν, ἐκεῖ δὲ ἐξηγεῖται ὁ προφήτης ὡς τῶν τοῦ λαοῦ εἰρηκότων Τηρήσατε τὴν ἐπίνοιαν αὐτοῦ εἰ ἀπατηθήσεται, καὶ δυνησόμεθα αὐτῷ. Πάλιν ἐνταῦθα ὁ μακάριος Δαυὶδ φησιν Ἀναστάντες μοι μάρτυρες ἄδικοι ἃ οὐκ ἐγίνωσκον

nem aut certe in Babilone posito populo, personam Heremiae induit | et ea in profetia loquitur quae uel rebus possint uel tempori conuenire. 5

Ad probationem autem horum, quae diximus, ipsum uolumen Heremiae sumentes in manibus, multam dictorum similitudinem inter Heremiam et psal- 10 mum hunc possumus inuenire, ut ex hoc discamus quantum profetae studium | fuerit adnuntiandae ueritatis, ut se ipsa ac uerba quae tunc ab Heremia 15 dicta sunt uaticiniis suis diligenter insereret.

Nam in hoc psalmo ait: *Fiat uia illorum tenebrae et lubricum;* 20 in uolumine uero Heremiae: *propterea fiat uia eorum ipsis lubricum in caligine.* Hic: *Quoniam absconderunt gratis mihi in interitum laquei sui;* ibi loquitur 25 sub populi persona dicens: *Obseruate ab inuentione eius si seducitur et poterimus ad eum.* Iterum in praesenti beatus Dauid dicit: *Surgentes testes iniqui quae* 30 *ignorabam interrogabant me;* ibi

---

19-21 v. 6   22-23 Ierem. XXIII, 12   23-25 vv. 7-8   26-29 Ier. XX, 10   30-31 v. 11.

1 possito A   2 hiremiae A   3 in om. A   p*rofetia B   4 ** quae B posst (possunt?) A   8 hieremiae A   9 multa A   10 hieremiam A   11 possimus A   12 ut om. A   dicamus A   13 fuerit om. A   13-14 adnuntiatae A¹   14 ipsas AB   15 tunc] litt. t reprob. B (pro nunc?)   17 inseret A 20 tebrae A   21 hieremiae A   22 propter B   uia om. A¹   23 quoniam — 30 dicit om. B   30-31 quae — me] reliqua B.

the people's captivity there—from the viewpoint of Jeremiah, citing aspects of the time and the events appropriate to the prophet.

By way of supplying proof of what has just been said by us, it is possible for someone reading the actual book of blessed Jeremiah to find in many places agreement between what is said by him or done to him and what is forecast by blessed David in this psalm. The result is that it is also possible to learn from there that the prophet's accuracy is such that he often states with great precision both the events and the words. In the text, for example, he says *Let their way be darkness and sliding* (v. 6), while in the prophet Jeremiah it says, "Hence let their way be for them sliding in gloom."[2] In our text he says *Because they hid their destructive snare for me without cause* (v. 7), whereas there the prophet says on behalf of the people, "Observe his intentions to see if he will be led astray and we shall prevail over him."[3] Again, in our text blessed David says *Unjust witnesses rose up against me and | asked*

---

2. Jer 23:12.
3. Jer 20:10 LXX.

ἠρώτων με, ἐκεῖ δὲ ἐξηγεῖται ὡς ὅτι
καθ' ὃν καιρὸν ἡ τῶν Χαλδαίων δύναμις ἀνέβη ἐπὶ τὴν Ἰερουσαλήμ,
ἐξελθόντος τοῦ προφήτου Ἰερεμίου
5 πορευθῆναι εἰς γῆν Βενιαμεὶν ὥστε
ἄρτον ἐκεῖθεν ὠνήσασθαι, συνέλαβεν
αὐτόν τις Σαρουΐα συκοφαντῶν καὶ
λέγων ὡς ὅτι πρὸς τοὺς Χαλδαίους
φεύγειν πειρᾶται. Ἀλλὰ καὶ τοῦ Ἀν-
10 ταπεδιδοσάν μοι πονηρὰ ἀντὶ ἀγαθῶν,
ὅπερ φησὶν ὁ μακάριος Δαυίδ, ὅμοιον
εὑρήσεις καὶ παρὰ τῷ προφήτῃ κείμενον Ἰερεμίᾳ· εὐχόμενος γάρ φησι
τῷ Θεῷ κατ αὐτῶν Εἰ ἀνταποδιδο-
15 ται κακὰ ἀντὶ ἀγαθῶν. Καὶ ὅλως ἀκριβέστερον ἐντυγχάνοντα τῇ βίβλῳ
πολλήν ἐστιν εὑρεῖν πρὸς τὸν ψαλμὸν ὁμοιότητα τῶν ἢ γεγονότων εἰς
αὐτὸν ἢ λεχθέντων παρ' αὐτοῦ. Οὕτω
20 γὰρ καὶ τὸ ἀληθὲς τῆς προφητείας
καὶ τὸ ἀκριβὲς δειχθήσεται ἔκ τε τῆς
τῶν ῥημάτων συμφωνίας καὶ ἐκ τῆς
τῶν πραγμάτων ὁμοιότητος.

refertur quod illo tempore quo
Caldeorum exercitus ad obseden-
dam ciuitatem Hierusalem ascen-
derat, exisse Hieremiam ut iret in
terram Beneamin ad comedendos
panes et conpraehensum a Saruia
et calumniam passum atque
obiectum illi fuisse quod ad Caldeos transfugeret. Sed et hoc,
quod ait beatus Dauid *Retribuebant mihi mala pro bonis*, inuenies etiam apud ipsum profetam
possitum Hieremiam, — orans
namque contra eos ait ad Deum:
Si retribuantur mala pro bonis. Si
quis uero sollicitus ipsum librum
legat multam similitudinem in
hoc psalmo aut factorum aut dictorum ab Heremia poterit inuenire; ita namque et ueritas profetiae et dilegentia ex uerborum
consonantia, ex rerum similitudine manifestius apparebit.

1ᵃ. Δίκασον, Κύριε, τοὺς ἀδικοῦντάς με. Πρέπουσα ἀρχὴ τῷ μέλλοντι
25 δικαίως αἰτεῖν παρὰ τοῦ Θεοῦ τὴν κατὰ τῶν ἀδικούντων αὐτὸν τιμωρίαν.
Ἐπειδὴ γὰρ ἡ δίκη καὶ ἡ ἀκρόασις τῶν πραγμάτων φανερὰν καθίστησι τὴν
ἀλήθειαν, ἔμελλε δὲ ἀξιοῦν τὸν δικαίως κολάσαι τοὺς εἰς αὐτὸν ἁμαρτάνοντας δυνάμενον, δικάσαι αὐτὸν πρὸ τῶν ἄλλων ἁπάντων ἀξιοῖ τοὺς ἀδικοῦντας, ὅπερ ἦν πεποιθότος ὡς δικασθέντες καὶ ἐξετασθέντες τιμωρίαν
30 ὑποστήσονται. Διὸ ἑξῆς ἐπάγει·

1-9 cf. Ier. XXXVII, 12-14   9-11 v. 12   14-15 Ier. X. III, 20.

1 refertur quod] *quae sequuntur in epitome sic constringit* B: refertur
quod obiecerent ei quod fugeret ad Caldeos; hic *Retribuebant mihi mala pro
bonis*, ibi orans contra eos ait ad Dominum *Si retribuantur mala pro bonis* et
caetera repperiuntur ibi similia   3 ciuitatem *om.* A¹   3 4 ascenderant A¹
exisse asc. A   5 comi*endos A¹ comidendos A²   6 conpraechensum A   sar-
rauia A¹   8 abiectum A¹   13 or*ans (ornans?) A   17 multum A.

Aᵉ 1ᵃ (p. 201, 18-21): Confisus de causae suae iustitia iudicalem aduersus
inimicos suos postulationem poscit.

me of matters of which I had no knowledge (v. 11), whereas there it explains that at the time when the Chaldean force went up to Jerusalem the prophet Jeremiah left and traveled to the land of Benjamin to buy bread there, but a certain Irijah detained him, misrepresenting him and claiming that he was trying to flee to the Chaldeans.[4] And the words said by blessed David *They repaid me evil for good* you will find in similar terms also in the prophet Jeremiah, such as when he prays to God against them, "Is evil a recompense for good?"[5] And one who reads closely can find in the book much, both of what happened to him and of what was said by him, that resembles the psalm. In this way, in fact, both the truth and the precision of inspired composition is proven from the harmony of the words and from the similarity of the events.

Judge, Lord, those who wrong me (v. 1). This is a fitting beginning for one intending to make a just request of God for punishment of those wronging him. You see, since justice and attention to events make the truth obvious, and since he intended to make a request of the one capable of justly punishing those sinning against him, he requests him to judge the wrongdoers before all others, as was right for one believing that they would be judged, examined, and would suffer punishment. Hence, he goes on to say | *War against those*

---

4. Cf. Jer 37:11–14.
5. Jer 18:20.

1ᵇ. Πολέμησον τοὺς πολεμοῦντάς με. Τοῦτο αἰτῶν ὅπερ ἔδει τῇ ἐξετάσει τῶν πραγμάτων πάντως ἑψόμενον. Ἔδειξε δὲ ὁμοῦ καὶ τῆς κατ᾽ αὐτῶν αἰτήσεως τὸ δίκαιον, ἐκεῖνα παθεῖν αὐτοὺς ἀξιώσας ἅπερ αὐτοὶ μάτην αὐτὸν διετίθεσαν.

2. Ἐπιλαβοῦ ὅπλου καὶ θυρεοῦ, καὶ ἀνάστηθι εἰς βοήθειάν μου. Ὅπλα 5 λέγεται πάντα τὰ σκεύη τὰ πολεμικά, θυρεὸς δὲ ἡ τετράγωνος ἀσπίς, — ὅθεν καὶ τὴν προσηγορίαν τοῦ θυρεοῦ ἀπὸ τοῦ σχήματος ἔχει τῷ ἔχειν τι τῆς παρ᾽ ἡμῖν λεγομένης θύρας ἀπομίμημα, — ἵνα οὖν εἴπῃ Μεταχείρισαι τὰ ὅπλα, ὁπλίσθητι κατ᾽ αὐτῶν ὑπὲρ τῆς εἰς ἐμὲ βοηθείας· τὸ δὲ ὅλον λέγει σωματικῶς, ἐπειδὴ παρ᾽ ἡμῖν οἱ κατά τινων ὁπλιζόμενοι πάντως τιμω- 10 ρίαν λαβεῖν τινα παρ᾽ αὐτῶν καὶ ἀνελεῖν αὐτοὺς σπουδάζονται.

3ᵃ. Ἔκχεον ῥομφαίαν καὶ σύγκλεισον ἐξ ἐναντίας τῶν καταδιωκόντων με. Φανερώτερον αὐτὸ λέγει Σύμμαχος· φησὶ γὰρ Γύμνωσον λόγχην καὶ περίφραξον ἐξ ἐναντίας τῶν καταδιωκόντων με. Τὸ δὲ γύμνωσον εἶπεν ἔκχεον, ἐπειδὴ καὶ τὸ ἐκχεόμενον ἀπό τινος ἀγγείου ὕδωρ ὥσπερ ἀποκεκρυμμένον ἔνδον πρὸ τούτου προβάλλεται καὶ δῆλον τοῖς ὁρῶσι καθίσταται, καὶ ἡ λόγχη σπωμένη ἐκ τῆς θήκης προβάλλεται καὶ γυμνοῦται. Οὐκ εἶπεν δὲ Σπάσον ἢ Ἕλκυσον ἐπειδὴ καμάτου χρείαν ἔχει καὶ

Effunde frameam et conclude, reliqua. Manifestius autem Symmachus dixit: *Nuda lanceam et obstrue ante eos qui persequuntur* 15 *me.* Siquidem et cum aqua de uase effunditur, quasi de aliquo in quo tegebatur loco, profertur in medium et fit uidentibus conspicua, ita et lancea cum de 20 theca sua educitur, nudatur atque detegitur. Non dixit Educ aut Extrahe, ne labor aut mora uideatur.

χρόνου τὰ τοιαῦτα, ἀλλ᾽ Ἔκχεον, ἀπὸ 25 τοῦ μετὰ πολλῆς εὐχερείας ἐκχεῖν τὸ ὕδωρ τὸν βουλόμενον, ἵνα δείξῃ τὴν προσοῦσαν τῷ Θεῷ εὐχέρειαν ἐν τῇ κατὰ τῶν ἁμαρτανόντων τιμωρίᾳ. Καὶ σωματοποιήσας τὸ πρᾶγμα κέχρηται τῇ ἀκολουθίᾳ συνηθῶς· ἐπειδὴ γὰρ τοῦ ἀριστέως γυμνοῦντος τὴν λόγχην ἔθος ἐστὶν φυγῇ κεχρῆσθαι τοῖς πολε-

---

1 ἔδει conieci, ἤδει ms. (al. man.?).
3ᵃˑᵇ om. C, praebent Paris. 139, fol. 77ᵛ atque Vat. 1682, fol. 113ᵛ sub lemmate Θεοδώρου; Barbaro, p. 328.	24 uerba οὐκ εἶπεν κ. τ. λ. affert nonnullis mutatis aut abbreviatis L (p. 623, 39-46)	24-25 ἢ ἕλκυσον om. V	26 τὸ βουλ. PV.
Effunde — uidetur: A, fol. 10ᵈ; B, fol. 12ᶜ.	12 framiam A fraᵐ B	14 lanciam A	16 et] ut (?) A¹	17 uasse AB.

Aᵉ 1ᵇ (p. 201, 21-23): Talionem ex lege poscit eorum quae ipsi ante in eum commiserunt.	24-26 (p. 201, 27-29): Pro Duc tanta facilitate gladium ut effundantur aquae.

who war against me. He asks for what he needed as one following everything by examination of events. At the same time, he brought out also the justice of the petition against them in requesting that they suffer what they had unsuccessfully intended for him.

Take up weapon and shield and arise to help me (2). By *weapon* is meant all the instruments of war, and by *shield,* the square one; he takes the term for *shield* from its shape in having a resemblance to what is called a door by us, the meaning being, Take up the weapons; arm yourself against them for the sake of helping me.[6] Now, his whole expression is physical, since in our experience those armed against some people are totally bent on wreaking vengeance on them and destroying them. *Pour forth a sword and hem in those pursuing me.* Symmachus says the same thing more clearly: "Lay bare your spear and obstruct those pursuing me." Now, "lay bare" means "release," since water released from a jar is cast forth as though hidden within and becomes apparent to onlookers, and the spear drawn from its sheath is thrown and laid bare. He did not say "Draw" or "Brandish," since that requires effort and time, but rather *Pour forth,* from the ease of pouring the required amount of water, to bring out God's ease in the punishment of sinners. Expressing the matter in physical terms is, as usual, in accord with the movement of thought: since the warrior stripped for battle customarily has a spear to use on the enemy in flight, | *Pour forth a sword and hem in*

---

6. Theodore goes to considerable trouble to unpack the anthropomorphic figure, explaining that the θυρεός is an oblong shield, as the word for "door," θύρα, suggests. Diodore also had taken pains to explain the terms involved, although defining them differently.

μίοις, καὶ ἔκχεόν φησι ῥομφαίαν καὶ σύγκλεισον ἐξ ἐναντίας τῶν καταδιωκόντων με, τουτέστι κώλυσον αὐτοὺς φυγῇ χρήσασθαι ἐπὶ τὰ πρόσωπα χωρῆ-
σαι βουλομένους· οὕτω γὰρ πάντες ὑποπεσοῦνται τῇ κολάσει τοῦ ξίφους.
Σύμμαχος γὰρ τὸ σύγκλεισον φανερώτερον λέγει καὶ περίφραξον.

5   3ᵇ. Εἰπὸν τῇ ψυχῇ μου Σωτηρία σου ἐγώ εἰμι. Τὸ εἰπὸν ὁ προφήτης
ὡς πρὸς τὸν Θεὸν λέγει παρακλητικῶς, οὐχ ὡς περὶ αὐτοῦ. Οὐ γὰρ τοῦτο
βούλεται εἰπεῖν ὅτι ἐγὼ εἶπον, ἀλλ᾽ ὅτι σὺ εἰπὸν τῇ ψυχῇ μου καὶ ἐπάγ-
γειλαι σῴζειν αὐτήν, ἀντὶ τοῦ Γενοῦ αὐτῇ σωτηρία. Τιμωρησάμενός φησιν
ἐκείνους σῶσόν με καὶ ἀπάλλαξον τῶν κινδύνων. Πολλαχοῦ γὰρ ἀντὶ τοῦ
10   ἔργου τῷ εἰπεῖν κέχρηται, ὡς καὶ τὸ εἶπαν Τίς ὄψεται αὐτούς; τοῦτο δὲ
ἡμῖν ἐπισεσήμανται πολλαχοῦ· ἐκείνους οὖν φησι τιμωρησάμενος ἐμοὶ παράσχου τὴν σωτηρίαν.

7ᵃ. Ὅτι δωρεὰν ἔκρυψάν μοι διαφθορὰν παγίδος αὐτῶν. Σύμμαχος τὸ
ὅτι δωρεὰν ὅτι ἀναιτίως λέγει. Ταῦτα δέ φησιν αὐτοὺς ἀξιῶ παθεῖν,
15   ἐπειδὴ ἄνευ λόγου καὶ αἰτίας ἐπιβουλεύειν μοι σπουδάζουσι, δόλους ῥάπτοντες κατ᾽ ἐμοῦ. Τὸ γὰρ ἔκρυψάν μοι διαφθορὰν παγίδος αὐτῶν, ἀντὶ τοῦ
ἔκρυψάν μοι παγίδα διαφθεῖραι καὶ ἀνελεῖν δυναμένην. Τοῦτο δὲ εἶπεν ἐκ
μεταφορᾶς τῶν ταῖς παγίσι λαθραίως συλλαμβανομένων εἰς θάνατον τοὺς
στρουθοὺς καὶ διαφθειρόντων· τοιοῦτο γάρ τι διαπράττονται καὶ οἱ μετὰ
20   δόλου τὰ πρὸς θάνατον ἑτέρου βουλευόμενοι, ὥσπερ τινὰ παγίδα τοὺς
οἰκείους δόλους ἀρτύοντες καὶ τὰς οἰκείας μηχανάς.

7ᵇ. Μάτην ὠνείδισαν τὴν ψυχήν μου. Εἰκῇ μοι ἐλοιδορήσαντο. Τὸ γὰρ
ὠνείδισαν ἀντὶ τοῦ ἐλοιδορήσαντο, ἐπειδὴ καὶ ὁ ὀνειδίζων ἐπὶ πάθει λοι-
δορεῖται πάντως τῷ ὀνειδιζομένῳ, οἷον εἴ τις τὸν τὰς ὄψεις ἐστερημένον
25   βούλοιτο καλεῖν πηρόν· τούτῳ γὰρ καὶ ὀνειδίσαι τὸ πάθος ἐστὶ καὶ λοι-
δορήσασθαι. Διὰ τοῦτο ἐνταῦθα ἀντὶ τοῦ ἐλοιδορήσαντο τὸ ὠνείδισαν
εἶπεν.

10 Ps. LXIII, 6ᵉ; cf. supra in ps. II, 3 (p. 10, 4-9).

3ᵇ. PV, cf. in 3ᵃ; Barbaro, p. 329.   6-9 πρὸς τὸν Θεὸν — ἐκείνους pluribus
mutatis apud L (p. 624, 3-7).   5.7 εἶπον ms. (cf. p. 179, nota in l. 14)   10 τὸ
εἶπεν ... εἶπεν ms.
7ᵃ. Σύμμαχος — μηχανάς: (anonym.) Paris. 139, fol. 78; Vat. 1682, fol. 114ᵛ;
cf. L (p. 625, 11-17).   14 παθεῖν αὐτοὺς ἀξιῶ PV   15 ἐπεὶ C.

Aᵉ 7ᵃ (p. 202, 21-22): Tectis me captionibus, ut interficerent, laqueare
uoluerunt me.

those pursuing me means, Stop them opting for flight when they want to take to their heels; they will thus come up against the punishment of the sword. Symmachus's "obstruct" also expresses *hem in* more clearly.

Say to my soul, I am your salvation. The prophet says *Say* as an appeal to God, not as a statement about himself: he did not mean, I said, but rather, You say to my soul and promise to save it—in other words, Prove to be its salvation; in punishing thèm, save me and free me from danger. In many places, in fact, he uses *Say* to mean action, as in the verse "They said, 'Who will see them?' "[7] They have indicated this to us in many places. So his meaning is, By punishing them, provide me with salvation.

Because they hid their destructive snare for me without cause (v. 7). For *without cause* Symmachus says "gratuitously." I ask that they suffer this, he is saying, because for no rhyme or reason they were bent on plotting against me, hatching schemes against me (the sense of *they hid their destructive snare*—that is, they hid a snare capable of destroying and annihilating me). He said this as a metaphor from those catching swallows furtively with snares as game and destroying them: they are guilty of a similar thing who plot the death of another by hatching their own schemes and designs like a snare. *Rashly they reproached my soul:* they abused me pointlessly (*reproached* meaning "abused," since the one who reproaches abuses the reproached because of a weakness, like someone intent on calling the person with no eyesight maimed; to reproach the person for a weakness is to abuse that person). So here *reproached* meant "abused." |

---

7. Ps 64:5.

8ᵃ. Ἐλθέτω αὐτῷ παγὶς ἣν οὐ γινώσκει. Μνημονεύσας τῆς αἰτίας πάλιν
ἐπαρᾶται (Σύμμαχος Ἀαβέτω αὐτὸν αἰφνίδιον ὃ μὴ εἶδεν, ἀντὶ τοῦ Λαβέτω
αὐτὸν συμφορὰ ἀπροσδόκητος), διόλου δὲ κατάλληλον τὴν τιμωρίαν αἰτεῖ
τοῖς παρ᾽ ἐκείνων γινομένοις. Ὥσπερ γὰρ ἄνω εὐθὺς ἐν ἀρχῇ τοῦ ψαλμοῦ φησι Πολέμησον τοὺς πολεμοῦντάς με, ἀντὶ τοῦ Τοῦτο αὐτοὺς διάθες   5
ὅπερ ἐμὲ διατεθείκασιν, οὕτως κἀνταῦθα, ἐπειδὴ τὴν ἐκείνων ἐπιβουλὴν
ἐξηγούμενός φησιν Ἔκρυψάν μοι διαφθορὰν παγίδος αὐτῶν, ἐπαρώμενος
αὐτῷ φησιν Ἐλθέτω αὐτῷ παγὶς ἣν οὐ γινώσκει. τοῦτο αὐτοῖς ἀντὶ τιμωρίας ἐπαρώμενος ὅπερ αὐτὸς ἔπασχεν ὑπ᾽ ἐκείνων. Παγίδα γάρ φησιν
αὐτοὶ ἔκρυψαν κατ᾽ ἐμοῦ, ἀντὶ τοῦ ἐπιβουλήν· παγίδι καὶ αὐτοὶ περι-   10
πέσοιεν. Καὶ τὸ ἣν οὐ γινώσκει ὅμοιόν ἐστι τῷ ἔκρυψάν μοι· καὶ γὰρ καὶ
ὁ τῇ κεκρυμμένῃ παγίδι περιπεσὼν ὑπ᾽ ἀγνοίας ὑπομένει τὸν ἐκ τῆς παγίδος θάνατον. Τὸ δὲ ἐλθέτω αὐτῷ ἀντὶ τοῦ αὐτοῖς, ἀπὸ τοῦ ἑνικοῦ τοὺς
πάντας περιλαμβάνων. Οὕτω γὰρ πολλάκις οἱ παρὰ πολλῶν ἐπιβουλευό-
μενοι λέγουσι « Κύριε, τιμώρησαι τὸν ἐπιβουλεύοντά μοι», οὐχ ὡς ἑνὸς ὄντος   15
τοῦ ἐπιβουλεύοντος ἀλλ᾽ ἵνα εἴπῃ πάντα ἐπιβουλεύοντα.

8ᵇ⁻ᶜ. Καὶ ἡ θήρα ἣν ἔκρυψε συλλαβέτω αὐτόν, καὶ ἐν τῇ παγίδι πεσεῖ-
ται ἐν αὐτῇ. Παγίδα καλεῖ καὶ θήραν τὴν ἐπιβουλήν, ἀπὸ τοῦ εἰς θάνατον
συλλαμβάνειν τὸν ἐπιβουλευόμενον. Τοῦτο γὰρ καὶ ἡ παγὶς ἐργάζεται,
ὁμοίως καὶ ἡ θήρα τὸ θηρώμενον συλλαμβάνουσα καὶ ὑπὸ τὴν ἐξουσίαν   20
ἐργαζομένη τῶν θηρευόντων. Τὸ γὰρ καὶ ἡ θήρα ἣν ἔκρυψε φανερώτερον
λέγει Σύμμαχος καὶ δίκτυον αὐτοῦ ὃ ἔκρυψεν. Τοῦτο δὲ λέγει, ὅτι τῇ ἐπι-
βουλῇ ἣν ἐμηχανήσατο κατ᾽ ἐμοῦ περιπέσοι ταύτῃ ἐκεῖνος, οὐχ ὅτι ταύτῃ
τῇ ἐπιβουλῇ περιπίπτειν ἐκεῖνος ἔμελλε (πῶς γὰρ ἐνῆν τὸν ἐ|πιβουλεύ-
οντα τῷ προφήτῃ αὐτὸν δέξασθαι ταύτην ἐκ τῆς ἐπιβουλῆς τὴν βλάβην   25
ἧς ἐμηχανᾶτο κατὰ τοῦ προφήτου;) ἀλλὰ ἀντὶ τοιαύτῃ αὐτὸς περιπέσοι,
οἷα ἐμοὶ ἐμηχανήσαντο τοιαῦτα πάθοιεν ἐκεῖνοι, — ὡς καὶ τὸ ἐπὶ τοῦ Ἀχι-
τόφελ ἐν τῷ ἑβδόμῳ ψαλμῷ, ὅταν λέγῃ· καὶ ἐμπεσεῖται εἰς βόθρον ὃν εἰργάσατο. Οὐχ ὅτι τοῦτο αὐτὸς ἔπαθεν ὅπερ διαθεῖναι τὸν Δαυὶδ ἠβούλετο, —
οὐ γὰρ ἀντὶ τοῦ Δαυὶδ ἐπεδίωξεν αὐτὸν ὁ Ἀβεσσαλὼμ καὶ ἀνεῖλεν, — ἀλλ᾽   30
ὅτι ἀπὸ τῆς ἐπιβουλῆς πρὸς οἷς οὐδὲν ἤνυσε, κακὸν αὐτὸς ἐδέξατο τὸ τέλος
ἑαυτὸν ἀνελὼν διὰ τὴν τῆς ἀποτυχίας ἀγανάκτησιν. Ὅμοιον οὖν καὶ τοῦτο

5 v. 1ᵇ   7 v. 7ᵃ   28-29 Ps. VII, 16ᵇ   27-32 II Reg. XVII.

13-16 Σημειωτέον ὅτι καὶ Ἐλθέτω αὐτῷ — ἐπιβουλεύοντα: (Θεοδώρου) Paris. 139,
fol. 78ᵛ; Vat. 1682, fol. 115; Barbaro, p. 331.

8ᵃ Aᵉ (p. 202, 23-24): Hoc illis pro ultione inprecatur quod supra ab illis
se passum esse conquestus est.   18-19 (p. 203, 1-3): Laqueum et captionem
inimicorum appellat insidias quibus eum molliebantur disperdere.

Let a trap fall on him of which he ignorant (v. 8). Recalling the cause once again, he gets carried away; Symmachus said, "Let what he did not see take him by surprise"—that is, Let disaster catch him unawares. He asks for punishment completely appropriate to what was done by them. You see, as he says right at the beginning of the psalm, *War against those who war against me,* in the sense, Take the attitude toward them that they take toward me, so here too, since in commenting on their wiles he says *They hid their destructive snare for me,* he is carried away with it and says *Let a trap fall on him of which he is ignorant,* proposing for them (punishment, that is) what he suffered from them. In other words, *They hid a snare for me*—that is, their scheme—and they also fell into a snare. The phrase *of which he is ignorant* is similar to *They hid it for me:* by falling into the hidden snare from ignorance, he suffers death from the snare. *Let it fall on him*—that is, on them, including everyone in the singular. Likewise, those plotted against by many say, Lord, punish the one scheming against me—not that there is only one schemer, but as if to say, everything scheming.[8]

Let the ruse he hid take him; in that trap he will fall. By *trap* and *ruse* he refers to the scheme, from the fatal capture of the one schemed against, this being the result of the trap, as the ruse also snares the one hunted and takes effect under the direction of the hunters. Symmachus, in fact, put *the ruse he hid* more clearly: "his net he hid." He means, Let him fall foul of the scheme that they engineered against me—not that he was likely to fall foul of that scheme; after all, how was it possible for the one scheming against the prophet to receive this harm himself from the scheme that he devised against the prophet? Rather, instead of falling foul of it, let him suffer the kinds of things that they devised for me—as, for example, in the case of Ahithophel in Psalm 7, when he says, "He will fall into the pit he had made."[9] Not that he personally suffered what he intended for David (Absalom did not in place of David pursue and kill him), but that from the scheme that proved fruitless he finally came to grief by taking his life in disappointment at his misfortune.[10] So it was a similar case to | *Let the ruse he hid take him:* not that he fell foul

---

8. The number of the pronouns in this verse varies from singular to plural in different forms of the LXX.

9. Ps 7:15.

10. Cf. 2 Sam 17:1–23.

ἐκείνῳ τὸ ἡ θήρα ἣν ἔκρυψε συλλαβέτω αὐτόν, οὐχ ἵνα αὐτῇ τῇ αὐτοῦ ἐπι
βουλῇ περιπέσοι, ἀλλ᾽ ἀντὶ τοῦ Ὑπὸ τοιαύτης ληφθείη παγίδος, ὑπὸ τοιού
του δικτύου, ὑπὸ τοιαύτης ἐπιβουλῆς· οὕτως καὶ ὅταν ἐν τῷ λα΄ ψαλμῷ λέγει
Ὑπὲρ ταύτης προσεύξεται πρός σε πᾶς ὅσιος ἐν καιρῷ εὐθέτῳ, οὐχ ὑπὲρ
5 αὑτῆς λέγει τῆς ἐκείνου ἁμαρτίας, ἀλλ᾽ ὑπὸ αὐτοῦ τοῦ εἴδους τῆς ἁμαρτίας,
ἵνα εἴπῃ Ὑπὸ τοιαύτης.

Πεσεῖται, ἀντὶ τοῦ πέσοιεν, — ἐπαρώμενος γὰρ ἀκολούθως λέγει | τοῖς
ἄνω· οὕτω γὰρ ἀκόλουθον, ἡ δὲ ἐναλλαγὴ τοῦ χρόνου καθὼς πολλαχοῦ
ἀπὸ τῆς ἑρμηνείας γίγνεται. Βούλεται δὲ εἰπεῖν ὅτι Καὶ περιπέσοι αὐτῇ τῇ
10 ἐπιβουλῇ· δῆλον ὡς οὐ τῇ αὐτῇ, ἀλλ᾽ ἀντὶ τοῦ τοιαύτῃ. Τοῦτο δὲ ἐπήγαγε
βουλόμενος δεῖξαι τὸ εὔλογον τῆς αἰτήσεως, ὅτι οὐδὲν αἰτεῖ βαρὺ κατ᾽
αὐτῶν, ἀλλ᾽ ὅπερ αὐτὸν ἐκεῖνοι διατεθείκασιν· ἀκόλουθα αἰτῶ τῷ νόμῳ
ἴσην ὁρίζοντι τοῖς ἀδικοῦσι τὴν τιμωρίαν.

9. Ἡ δὲ ψυχή μου ἀγαλλιάσεται ἐπὶ τῷ Κυρίῳ, τερφθήσεται ἐπὶ τῷ
15 σωτηρίῳ αὐτοῦ. Ἵνα δείξῃ διόλου ὅτι τοσοῦτον ἦν τῶν κακῶν τὸ μέγεθος,
ὡς αὐτῆς ἅψασθαι τῆς ψυχῆς. Πῶς οὖν ἀγαλλιάσεται ἐπὶ τῷ Κυρίῳ, ἑξῆς
ἐπάγει. Τερφθήσεται ἐπὶ τῷ τῆς σωτηρίας φησὶ τῆς παρὰ τοῦ Θεοῦ ἀπολαύ
σας, ἐν τέρψει καὶ εὐφροσύνῃ καταστήσομαι. Τὸ δὲ τερφθήσεται εἶπεν ἀντὶ
τοῦ χαρίσεται, ἐπειδήπερ ὁ τερπόμενος καὶ χαίρει πάντως ἐπὶ τῷ τέρποντι.

20 10ᵃ. Πάντα τὰ ὀστᾶ μου ἐροῦσι· Κύριε, τίς ὅμοιός σοι; Ἀνωτέρω δείξας
ὅτι δικαίως αὐτοὺς ἀξιοῖ τιμωρηθῆναι ὡς μάτην ἐπιβουλεύοντας, εἶτα εἰπὼν
ὅτι προσγενήσεται αὐτῷ εὐφροσύνη ἀπὸ τῆς ἐκείνων τιμωρίας σωθέντι
παρὰ τοῦ Θεοῦ, ἑξῆς πάλιν δείκνυσιν ὅτι δικαίως τεύξεται τῆς σωτηρίας
καὶ τῆς εὐφροσύνης, ἀπὸ τοῦ εἰπεῖν Πάντα τὰ ὀστᾶ μου ἐροῦσι· Κύριε, Κύριε,
25 τίς ὅμοιός σοι; Τυχὼν γάρ φησι τούτων οὐκ ἀρκεσθήσομαι ἁπλῶς τῇ εὐ
φροσύνῃ, ἀλλ᾽ εὐχαριστήσω καὶ δοξάσω ἐπὶ τοῖς γεγενημένοις, ὁμολογῶν
σε μέγαν καὶ πάντων μείζονα. Τὸ δὲ πάντα τὰ ὀστᾶ μου, ἵνα εἴπῃ ὅτι ἐκ
πάσης ἰσχύος εὐχαριστήσω· τὰ γὰρ ὀστᾶ ἐπὶ τῆς ἰσχύος λαμβάνει, ὡς καὶ
ἀλλαχοῦ Ἴασαί με, Κύριε, ὅτι ἐταράχθη τὰ ὀστᾶ μου, ἀντὶ τοῦ Ὅτι ἐτα
30 ράχθην ἰσχυρῶς.

4 Ps. XXXI, 6	29 VI, 2.

9 γίγνεται] γένηται ms.

14. *Post prima versiculi verba* (Ἡ δὲ ψυχή μου) *Coislinianus noster plura addit
quae Theodoro videntur absona*: Συνεχῶς τὸ εἶπον τῇ ψυχῇ μου [v. 3ᵇ] ἀντὶ τοῦ ἐγώ·
καὶ γὰρ τὴν βοήθειαν αἰτῶ τοῦ Θεοῦ (Εἶπόν φησι τῇ ψυχῇ Σωτηρία σού εἰμι ἐγώ), καὶ
τοὺς πολεμοῦντας αἰτιώμενος (Οἱ ζητοῦντες τὴν ψυχήν μου [v. 4], καὶ ὠνείδισαν τὴν ψυχήν
μου [v. 7ᵇ]), καὶ τὴν ἐκ τῆς ἀπαλλαγῆς εὐφροσύνην ἐξηγούμενος (Ἡ δὲ ψυχή μου ἀγαλ
λιάσεται ἐπὶ τῷ Κυρίῳ), ἵνα δείξῃ κ. τ. λ. *Interpretatio v. 3ᵇ exegesi superius datae
aperte repugnat; cetera epitomen vel paraphrasin satis redolent.*

of the scheme itself, but that he was taken by such a ruse, by such a net, by such a scheme. Likewise, when in Psalm 32 he says, "For this every holy one will pray at the right time,"[11] he is speaking not of this very sin but of the very kind of sin, as if to say "of such a sin." *He will fall*—that is, Let them fall: in his agitated condition he speaks in keeping with the aforementioned; while it is thus in keeping, there is a change in tense, as often happens from the translation. His meaning is, Let him fall foul of the scheme itself—by "itself" referring to the kind, not the actual sin. Now, he added this in his wish to bring out the reasonableness of the request, that he requests nothing severe against them, but only what they had in mind for him. I request, he is saying, what is in keeping with the law's provision for equal punishment for the wrongdoers.

My soul[12] *will rejoice in the Lord; it will delight in his salvation* (v. 9): to convey fully that so great was the extent of the troubles as to seize upon his very soul. How he *will rejoice in the Lord,* then, the sequel goes on to explain: *It will delight in salvation* enjoyed from the Lord; I shall be brought to a condition of delight and joy (*will delight* meaning "will rejoice," since the one who is delighted also rejoices completely in the one giving delight). *All my bones will say, Lord, Lord, who is like you?* (v. 10). Having brought out above that he was within his rights to request that they be punished for scheming against him without cause, and then saying that joy will come to him from their punishment when he is saved by God, he goes on to show that he rightly received salvation and joy in the verse *All my bones will say, Lord, Lord, who is like you?* In other words, Having attained this, I shall not be content simply with joy, but shall give thanks and glory for what has been done, confessing that you are great and greater than all—as if to say, I shall give thanks with all my strength. He uses *bones* in the sense of strength, as elsewhere also, "Heal me, Lord, because my bones are disturbed"[13]—that is, I am strongly disturbed. |

---

11. Ps 32:6.

12. Devreesse notes that at this point in the text of Codex Coislinianus appears a comment "apparently not consistent with Theodore," giving "an interpretation clearly opposed to that given to v. 3 above" (*Le commentaire,* 179). It reads, "The term 'my soul' generally means 'I': I ask help from God ('I said to my soul,' he is saying, 'I am your salvation'), and blaming those who are hostile ('Those who seek my life' [v. 4] and 'reproached my soul' [v. 7]), and commenting on the joy coming from freedom ('My soul will rejoice in the Lord'), in order to show [etc.]."

13. Ps 6:2.

10ᵇ. Ῥυόμενος πτωχὸν ἐκ χειρὸς στερεωτέρων αὐτοῦ. Σύμμαχος τὸ ῥυόμενος ἐξαιρεῖ λέγει. Ἐρῶ φησιν οὐδένα σοι ὅμοιον εἶναι, καὶ πάντων
ὁμολογήσω δυνατώτερον καὶ μόνον πάντων τῶν νομιζομένων ἰσχυρῶν καὶ
δυνατῶν, τοὺς πτωχοὺς καὶ εὐτελεῖς ῥύεσθαι δυνάμενον, παραδόξως τε
ἀπαλλάττοντα τῆς ἐκείνων ἐπιβουλῆς. Ἐπισημαντέον δὲ κἀνταῦθα ὅτι ὅταν   5
λέγῃ πρὸς τὸν Θεὸν Τίς ὅμοιός σοι, οὐ πρὸς ἀντιδιαστολὴν Υἱοῦ λέγει,
ἀλλὰ πρὸς τὴν τῶν λεγομένων ἀκολουθίαν. Ἐπειδὴ γὰρ δυνατοὶ μὲν ἦσαν
οἱ τὸν προφήτην διαφόροις τοῖς κακοῖς περιβάλλοντες, τῶν δὲ τοιούτων
ῥύεσθαι τοῦ παντὸς ἦν δυνατωτέρου, ὡς πρὸς ἐκείνους φησὶν ὅτι Πάντων
ὁμολογήσω σε δυνατώτερον ὡς καὶ τῶν μεγάλων τοὺς εὐτελεῖς ἀπαλλάτ-   10
τειν δυνάμενον. Τοῦτο οὖν φησιν Ἐρῶ τυχὼν τῆς παρά σου σωτηρίας, καὶ
ἐξηγούμε|νος αὐτὸ καθολικῶς ἀπὸ τῶν κατ᾽ ἐμὲ αὐτός τε προσεῖναι πιστεύω
τῷ λεγομένῳ τὴν ἀλήθειαν, καὶ ἑτέροις παρέχων τὴν ἀπόδειξιν.

10ᶜ. Καὶ πτωχὸν καὶ πένητα ἀπὸ τῶν διαρπαζόντων αὐτόν. Καὶ πτωχὸν
καὶ πένητα τὸ αὐτὸ λέγει διαφόρως, ἵνα τὴν ὑπερβάλλουσαν εὐτέλειαν   15
παρασημάνῃ· διὰ τοῦτο ἐπὶ τῶν ἐπιβουλευόντων οὐκ εἶπεν ἁπλῶς, ἀλλ᾽
ἀπὸ τῶν διαρπαζόντων αὐτόν, δεικνὺς καὶ τὸ πλῆθος τῶν ἐπιβουλευόντων
καὶ τῆς ἐπιβουλῆς τὸ μέγεθος· διηρπάχθαι γάρ τινά φαμεν κυρίως, ὅταν
ὑπὸ πολλῶν τοῦτο παθὼν πάντα ζημιωθῇ. Ταῦτα δὲ λέγει πρὸς παράστασιν τοῦ μεγέθους τοῦ Θεοῦ, ὅπερ ἐξηγεῖσθαι ἐπαγγέλλεται ὅταν ἀπο-   20
λαύσῃ τῆς παρ᾽ αὐτοῦ εὐεργεσίας· ἐδείκνυ γὰρ αὐτοῦ τὸ μέγεθος ἥτε τοῦ
πάσχοντος καὶ ῥυσθέντος εὐτέλεια παρ᾽ αὐτῷ καὶ τὸ τῶν ἐπιβουλευόντων
μέγεθος· ὅσον γὰρ δυνατὸν τὸ τῆς ἀπαλλαγῆς τῶν ἐπιβουλευόντων κατε-
φαίνετο, τοσοῦτον δυνατώτερος ὁ τοῦτο ἐργαζόμενος ἐδείκνυτο. Εἶτα ἐπα-
ρασάμενος αὐτοῖς καὶ εἰπὼν ὅτι τιμωρητῶν ἐκείνων γενομένων προσέσται μὲν   25
εὐφροσύνη ἐμοί, ἀναπέμψω δὲ καὶ τῷ εὐεργέτῃ τὴν εὐχαριστίαν, πάλιν ἐξηγεῖται τὰ παρ᾽ ἐκείνων γινόμενα, καί φησιν·

11. Ἀναστάντες μοι μάρτυρες ἄδικοι ἃ οὐκ ἐγίνωσκον ἠρώτων με.
Ἐνταῦθα αὐτὸ τὸ γεγονὸς ἐξηγεῖται. Πολλοὶ γὰρ πολλὰ τοῦ προφήτου
κατεμαρτύρουν ὡς | χαριζομένου τοῖς ἐναντίοις κατ᾽ αὐτῶν καὶ διὰ τοῦτο   30
τὴν ἅλωσιν τῆς πόλεως αὐτοῖς προσαγορεύοντος, ὥστε καταβαλεῖν τὰ

6 Ps. VI, 3ᵇ   29-181, 17 cf. Ier. XXXVII, 12 ss. et argumentum psalmi.

23 ὅσῳ ms.
10ᶜ. Τὸ αὐτὸ — 19 ζημιωθῇ: (Θεοδώρου) Paris. 139, fol. 78ᵛ-79; Vat. 1682,
fol. 115ᵛ; Barbaro, p. 332; L (p. 626, 43-49) pluribus mutatis.

Aᵉ 21-24 (p. 203, 11-13): Auxit erumnam suam, cum se diripi dicit post latentes insidias et probrosa conuicia, ut potentiam saluantis faciat clariorem.

Rescuing the poor from the hand of those stronger than he. For *rescuing* Symmachus put "He delivers." I shall say no one is like you, he means, and shall confess you to be more powerful than everyone, even those considered strong and powerful; you are capable of rescuing the poor and insignificant and delivering them from their scheming against the odds. Now, it should be noted here, too, that when he says to God *Who is like you?* he is not speaking by way of distinguishing the Son, but to maintain sequence in thought: since those involving the prophet in various troubles were powerful, and rescuing him from such people was the work of someone more powerful than all, he says as if to them, I shall confess you to be more powerful than all in being able to deliver the lowly from the mighty. So he means, This I say in receiving salvation from you, and in accounting for it in general terms from what happened to me, I personally believe that truth is present in what is said and offer proof of it to others. *And the poor and needy from those despoiling him.* By *And the poor and needy* he says the same things in different ways so as to suggest the extreme degree of lowliness. This was the reason that in the case of the schemers he did not simply say as much, but *those despoiling him,* bringing out both the great number of the schemers and the extent of the scheme; after all, we properly claim that someone is despoiled when that person loses everything at the hands of many people. Now, he says this by contrast with God's greatness, which he promises to explain when he enjoys a favor from him. You see, both the insignificance by comparison with him of the one who suffers and is rescued and also the might of the schemers brought out his greatness: the more effective the release from the schemers was shown to be, the more powerful did the one who effected it appear.

He then exults over them in saying, Once they have been punished, joy will come to me, and I shall also offer thanks to the benefactor. And he comments on what they have done in the words *Unjust witnesses rose up against me, questioning me on matters of which I had no knowledge* (v. 11). Many people testified at length against the prophet with the claim that he was favorable to their adversaries and hence predicted to them the capture of the city, their purpose being to reject | the idea of the troubles circulating in rumor.

φρονήματα τῶν ἔσω τῇ φήμῃ τῶν κακῶν. Ποτὲ δὲ καὶ ἐξιόντα τῆς πόλεως
ἄρτον ὠνήσασθαι εἰσήγαγέ τις εἰς τὴν πόλιν συκοφαντῶν ὡς αὐτομολεῖν
ἐθέλοντα πρὸς τοὺς Χαλδαίους, ὡς ἀπὸ ταύτης τῆς αἰτίας τραυματισθέντα
καὶ φυλακῇ παραδοθῆναι, καὶ ἐφ᾽ ἑτέροις δὲ πολλοῖς συκοφαντηθεὶς μυρίων
5 ἔλαβε πεῖραν κακῶν. Πρὸς οὖν τούτους καὶ τοὺς τοιούτους φησὶ τὸ Ἀν-
στάντες μοι μάρτυρες ἄδικοι ἃ οὐκ ἐγίνωσκον ἠρώτων με, ἀδίκους μάρτυρας
καλῶν τοὺς συκοφαντεῖν ἐσπουδακότας. Ἐπειδὴ γὰρ ὁ εἰς πράγματος
μαρτυρίαν καλούμενος συνίστησι δι᾽ ὧν λέγει τὴν τοῦ πράγματος ἀλήθειαν,
μάρτυρα ἄδικον καλεῖ τὸν τὰ ἐναντία τῇ ἀληθείᾳ συνιστᾶν ἐσπουδακότα.
10 Καὶ τὸ ἠρώτων με ἀντὶ τοῦ ἐσυκοφάντουν οὐχ ἁπλῶς εἶπεν, ἀλλ᾽ ἐπειδὴ
εἰς κρίσιν αὐτὸν ἄγοντες, ἐπειρῶντο μὲν ἐν προσχήματι κρίσεως ἐξετάζειν
ὡς δὴ μαθεῖν βουλόμενοι διὰ τῆς ἐρωτήσεως τὸ γεγονός, συκοφαντοῦντες
δὲ ὡς ἐβούλοντο κατέκρινον ἀναιτίως. Τὸ ἠρώτων εἶπεν ἀντὶ τοῦ ἐσυκοφάντουν, ἀπὸ τοῦ γινομένου παρ᾽ αὐτῶν τὸ ἀποτέλεσμα καλέσας, ἤτοι
15 τὸν σκοπὸν καθ᾽ ὃν ἐποιοῦντο τὴν ἐρώτησιν. Ἐξηγησάμενος δὲ διὰ τούτων
τὴν παράνομον αὐτῶν πρᾶξιν, δείκνυσι τῆς παρανομίας καὶ τῆς ἀδικίας τοῦ
γινομένου τὸ μέγεθος, τῇ ἐπαγωγῇ, τοῦ ἑξῆς | ῥητοῦ εἰπών.

12ᵃ. Ἀνταπεδίδουν μοι πονηρὰ ἀντὶ ἀγαθῶν. Συκοφαντεῖν γὰρ καὶ ἀδικεῖν ἔσπευδον, καίτοι πολλῶν ἀγαθῶν ἀπολαύσαντες παρ᾽ ἐμοῦ. Ἐγὼ μὲν
20 γὰρ αὐτοῖς τὰ κάλλιστα βουλόμενος, τὰ ἐσόμενα προηγόρευον διὰ τὴν
αὐτῶν ὠφέλειαν, ἐκεῖνοι δὲ ἀπιστοῦντες τοῖς λεγομένοις κάκιστα μὲν διετίθεσαν, διαφόροις περιβάλλοντες τοῖς κακοῖς. Ὁ μὲν γὰρ μακάριος Ἱερε-
μίας ἔλεγεν· Οὕτως εἶπε Κύριος· Ὁ καθήμενος ἐν τῇ πόλει ταύτῃ ἀποθανεῖται ἐν ῥομφαίαις καὶ ἐν λιμῷ καὶ ἐν θανάτῳ, καὶ ὁ ἐκπορευόμενος πρὸς τοὺς
25 Χαλδαίους ζήσεται, καὶ ἔσται ἡ ψυχὴ αὐτοῦ εἰς εὕρεμα καὶ ζήσεται. Ὅτι
τάδε λέγει Κύριος Παραδόσει παραδοθήσεται ἡ πόλις αὕτη εἰς χεῖρας δυνάμεως βασιλέως Βαβυλῶνος, καὶ λήψεται αὐτήν, ταῦτα λέγων οὐχ ἁπλῶς,
ἀλλὰ βουλόμενος αὐτοὺς πεῖσαι παραδόντας ἑαυτοὺς τοῖς Χαλδαίοις εὑρέ-
σθαι διὰ τούτου τὴν σωτηρίαν καὶ τῶν κακῶν τὴν ἀπαλλαγήν, ἅπαξ τοῦ
30 Θεοῦ καταψηφισαμένου τῆς πόλεως ἀφανισμόν. Οἱ δὲ κατὰ τὴν πόλιν
ἄρχοντες, — δέον πειθομένους τοῖς λεγομένοις κερδαίνειν τῶν κακῶν τὴν
πεῖραν, — οἱ δὲ καὶ προσοργισθέντες τοῖς λεγομένοις | ἐνέβαλον αὐτὸν τῷ
λάκκῳ τοῦ βορβόρου· εἰρηκότος γὰρ τοῦ μακαρίου Ἱερεμίου τὰ προειρη-

23-27 Ierem. XXXVIII, 2-3   32-33 Ierem. XXXVIII, 6.

13 εἶπον ms.

Aᵉ   1-5 (p. 203, 18-21): Et quoniam Siris placeret Heremias quoque, cum
diceretur, obsessa ciuitate, ad Caldeos transfugere, qui ad mercandos cibos
pergebat.   12ᵃ (p. 203, 21-204, 3): Vel cum praediceret pro utilitate audentium
capiendam urbem, uaticinari in favorem hostium putabatur... id est, cum ego
illis bona suadendo consularem, illi me iniuriae subdere festinabant.

At one time, when he was leaving the city to buy bread, one of his critics took him into the city on the charge of leaving to go over to the Chaldeans, with the result that he suffered for this charge and was put in custody;[14] he was misrepresented by many others and had experience of countless hardships. So it was in regard to these people and many like them that he says *Unjust witnesses rose up against me, questioning me on matters of which I had no knowledge,* by *unjust witnesses* referring to the fanatical critics. You see, since the one called to give witness to the matter came up with things that he claimed to be the facts of the matter, he refers to him as an "unjust witness" for his determination to come up with the opposite to the truth. And it was not without point that he called their misrepresentation *questioning;* rather, since in bringing him to trial they tried to examine him under the guise of a trial with no wish to learn by examination what really happened, they misrepresented him and willfully condemned him without cause. The term *questioning* means "misrepresenting," referring to their exploit from what was done by them or to the purpose they had in doing their questioning.

Commenting in this way on their unlawful behavior, he brings out the extent of their lawlessness and injustice, and he goes on to say in what follows *They repaid me evil for good* (v. 12): they were bent on misrepresentation and perverting justice, despite enjoying many favors from me. Whereas I had the best of intentions toward them and foretold the future for their good, they did not believe my words and were most ill-disposed toward me, involving me in a range of troubles. Blessed Jeremiah said, in fact, "Thus says the Lord, 'Those who stay in this city will die by the sword, by famine, and by death, whereas those who go out to the Chaldeans will live; their life will be a godsend, and they will live.' Thus says the Lord, 'This city surely will be handed over to the powerful king of Babylon, and he will take it.' "[15] He did not say this without a point, but in his wish to persuade them to give themselves up to the Chaldeans and thus find salvation and release from the troubles, once God had decided on the destruction of the city. By contrast, though they should have believed the words so as to save themselves from the experience of the troubles, the rulers of the city and those irritated by the words threw him into the depths of the pit.

In fact, when blessed Jeremiah uttered the prophecies, | as his book

---

14. Cf. Jer 37:12–16.
15. Jer 38:2–3.

μένα, ὡς ἡ βίβλος ἡ αὐτοῦ περιέχει, εἶπον οἱ ἄρχοντές φησι τῷ βασιλεῖ
Ἀρθήτω δὴ ὁ ἄνθρωπος ἐκεῖνος, ὅτι αὐτὸς ἐκλύει τὰς χεῖρας τῶν ἀνθρώπων
τῶν πολεμούντων τῶν καταλελειμμένων. Καλῶς οὖν πρὸς ταῦτά φησιν
Ἀνταπεδίδουν μοι πονηρὰ ἀντὶ ἀγαθῶν· ἀναγκαίων γὰρ ὄντων καὶ πρὸς
σωτηρίαν αὐτοῖς συμβαλέσθαι δυναμένων τῶν παρ' αὐτοῦ λεγομένων, μέγιστα   5
αὐτῷ κακὰ ἀπεδίδοσαν διαφόροις αὐτὸν ὑπὲρ τούτων τιμωρίαις περιβάλλοντες.
Ἄνω μὲν οὖν φησιν Ὅτι δωρεὰν ἔκρυψάν μοι διαφθορὰν παγίδος αὐτῶν,
αἰτιώμενος ὡς ὅτι μηδὲν ἠδικημένοι ἀναιτίως ἐπεβούλευον, ἐνταῦθα δὲ μεῖζόν
φησιν ὅτι ὑπὲρ τῶν παρ' ἐμοῦ καλῶν εἰς ἑαυτοὺς γινομένων ἐκεῖνοι κακοῖς
ἠμείβοντό με. Τοῦτο δὲ μεῖζόν ἐστι τοῦ προτέρου· οὐ γὰρ ὅμοιόν ἐστι   10
μηδὲν ἠδικημένους ἀδικῆσαι καὶ εὐεργετηθέντας κακὰ διαθεῖναι.

12ᵇ. Καὶ ἀτεκνίαν τῇ ψυχῇ μου.
Ἐν τῷ νόμῳ τῶν τετελευτηκότων ἡ
μνήμη τῇ διαδοχῇ τῶν τικτομένων ἐν
ταῖς βίβλοις ἐφυλάττετο, ἔνθα γε-
γράφθαι συνέβαινε τὰς διαδοχὰς τῶν
Ἰουδαίων. Διὰ γὰρ τοῦτο καὶ ὁ Θεὸς
προσέταξε τοῦ τελευτῶντος ἀτέκνου
τὸν ἀδελφὸν λαμβάνοντα τὴν γυναῖκα
ἀνιστᾶν αὐτῷ σπέρμα, ὥστε τὸ
μνημόσυνον αὐτοῦ μὴ ἐξαλείφεσθαι.

Τοῦτο δὲ ἐγίνετο διὰ τὸ μὴ τῆς ἀναστάσεως ἀκριβῆ τὴν ἐπαγγελίαν ἔχειν,
ὡς ἂν μὴ τῆς εὐσεβείας καταμελοῖεν,
οὐδὲν ἔτι εἶναι πλείονα τοῖς μετὰ
θάνατον προσδοκῶντες.

Διὰ γὰρ τοῦτο
καὶ ὁ Ἀβεσσαλώμ, ὡς ἡ τῶν Βασιλειῶν
βίβλος φησίν, ἄτεκνος ὢν στήλην

Et sterilitatem animae meae.
In lege uetere per successionem
filiorum mortuorum memoria
seruabatur; mandabantur etiam   15
libris nomina | singulorum, in
quibus moris erat generationes
Iudeorum omnes per ordinem
scribi; atque ob hoc Deus praeciperat, ut morientis uiri sine filiis   20
uxorem frater acciperet ac semen
in defuncti ⟨memoriam⟩, ne obliuione deleretur eius uocabulum,
suscitaret. Hoc autem fiebat propterea, quia resurrectionis manifes-   25
tam notitiam non habebant, ne
dum nihil superesse spei mor-
tuis uident, | neglegentiores circa
cultum honestatis et circa religionem fierent segniores. Ob hanc   30
causam, propter resurrectionis
incertum, etiam Abisalon, cum

1-3 Ierem. XXXVIII, 4   13 Deuteron. XXV, 5 ss.; cf. supra in ps. VII, 6 (p. 37)
30 ss. II Reg. XVIII, 18.

Et sterilitatem — uindicaret: A, fol. 10ᵈ-11ᵃ; B, fol. 12ᶜ-ᵈ.   18 ideorum A
20 morientis *** B   21-23 semen in in difunctione (uel difuncti *add. supra*) obliuione deletur A   22 memoriam *supplevi (cf. p. 37, l. 23)*   28 negligentiores B
circa] erga A   29-30 religionem B   30 signiores AB   hanc*** A   31-32 resurrectionem incertam A.

describes, the rulers said to the king, "Let this fellow be done away with, because he is taking the heart out of the fighters who are left."[16] So he was right to say *They repaid me evil for good:* despite his words being what was required and capable of contributing to their salvation, they repaid him with extreme evil by investing him in a range of punishments for his words. Whereas above he said *They hid their destructive snare for me,* alleging that because they had in no way been wronged, their schemes were without cause, here he alleges a worse fault: They rewarded me with troubles for the good deeds done by me for them. The latter was worse than the former: nothing matches the wrong done by those never wronged and the ungrateful response of those in receipt of good.

And sterility for my soul. By the law the memory of the dead was preserved by the succession of the offspring in the books where the succession of the Jews was recorded; this was also God's purpose in commanding the brother of the man who died childless to marry his wife and have offspring to him so that memory of him might be retained.[17] Now, this was done on account of their not having a precise promise of resurrection, to prevent their failing in piety through the belief that they had nothing further to look forward to after death—hence Absalom's erecting a pillar to himself (as the book of Kings says),[18] childless as he was, | so that thus he

---

16. Jer 38:4.
17. Deut 25:5–6.
18. Cf. 2 Sam 18:18.

ἀνέστησεν ἑαυτῷ, ὡς ἂν δι' ἐκείνης   esset sine filiis, titulum sibi ere-
μνημονεύοιτο μετὰ τὸν θάνατον.   xit qui eum ab obliuione, dum
praetereuntium occurrit oculis, uindicaret.

Ἐπειδὴ τοίνυν οἱ μὲν τέκνα καταλιμπάνοντες ἐξ ἀνάγκης δι' ἐκείνων
5 ἐμνημονεύοντο διὰ τῶν διαδοχῶν, τῶν δὲ ἀτέκνων ἠφανίζετο τὸ μνημόσυνον,
οὐκ ὄντων διαδόχων δι' ὧν ὁ τελευτῶν μνημονεύεσθαι ἠδύνατο, τοῦτο βούλεται εἰπεῖν, τὴν ἐπίτασιν τῶν ἐπαγομένων αὐτῷ κακῶν δεικνύς, ὅτι κακοῖς
μέ φησιν ἠμείβοντο τὰ καλὰ αὐτοῖς βουλευόμενον, οὐ τοῖς τυχοῦσι κακοῖς,
ἀλλὰ καὶ αὐτό μου τὸ μνημόσυνον   Meam, inquit, memoriam au-
10 ἐξαλεῖψαι βουλόμενοι· τοῦτο δὲ   ferre moliuntur. Hoc autem fece-
ἐποίησαν ἡνίκα ἐν τῷ λάκκῳ τοῦ βορ-   runt eo tempore quo eum in la-
βόρου ⟨αὐτὸν⟩ ἔρριψαν. Ἐπειδὴ   cum miserunt; in quo etiam si
γὰρ ὁ θαπτόμενος διὰ τοῦ τάφου   fuisset mortuus signa sui posteris
τοῦ ἐπ' αὐτῷ γινομένου καὶ διὰ τοῦ   nulla reliquisset: nam eos qui ex
15 μνήματος μνημονεύεται παρὰ τῶν   more sepulturae mandantur ipsa
ὁρώντων, — ὅθεν καὶ μνῆμα λέγε-   sepulcri constructio in obliuio-
ται τὸ τοιοῦτον ἀπὸ τοῦ εἰς μνήμην   nem uenire non patitur. Missus
ἄγειν τοὺς ἐν αὐτῷ κειμένους τοὺς   ergo in lacum, si ibi fuisset mor-
ὁρῶντας, — βληθεὶς δὲ ἐν τῷ βορ-   tuus, sine tumulo absque dubio
20 βόρῳ, ἐκεῖ τελευτήσας ἄταφος ἔμενεν   ac sepultura iacuisset, nihil ha-
ἐξ ἀνάγκης οὐδὲν ἔχων | εἰς τὸ ἑξῆς   bens in reliquum quod eius me-
μνημόσυνον.   moriam possit suscitare.

Τοῦτο προφητεύων ὁ μακάριος Δαυὶδ φησιν ὅτι Καὶ αὐτό μου τὸ μνημόσυνον ἐξαλεῖψαι ἠβούλοντο, ὅπερ φησὶν ἀτεχνίαν τῇ ψυχῇ μου ἀκολού-
25 θως τῷ ἄνω, τουτέστιν ἀνταπεδίδοσάν μοι κακὰ ἀντὶ ἀγαθῶν. Ποῖα κακά;
Ἀτεχνίαν τῇ ψυχῇ μου· ταῦτά μοι ἀνταπεδίδοσαν τὴν ἀτεχνίαν, τὸ σπουδάζειν ἐξαλεῖψαί μου τὸ μνημόσυνον. Εἶτα εἰρηκὼς ὅτι κακὰ διετίθεσαν
αὐτὸν εὐεργετούμενοι παρ' αὐτοῦ, ὡς καὶ τὸ μνημόσυνον αὐτοῦ ἐθέλειν ἀφανίσαι, ἑξῆς λέγει τίνα μὲν τὰ παρ' αὐτοῦ ἀγαθὰ εἰς ἐκείνους γιγνόμενα,
30 τίνα δὲ πάλιν τὰ ἀντὶ τούτων εἰς αὐτὸν παρ' ἐκείνων φησίν.

13ᵃ. Ἐγὼ δὲ ἐν τῷ αὐτοὺς παρενοχλεῖν μοι ἐνεδυόμην σάκκον. Οἱ μέν
φησι τοιαῦτα προηροῦντο, ἐγὼ δὲ καὶ ἐν αὐτῷ τῷ πάσχειν παρ' αὐτῶν
κακῶς σάκκον ἠμφιεννύμην ὑπὲρ αὐτῶν.

13ᵇ. Καὶ ἐταπείνουν ἐν νηστείᾳ τὴν ψυχήν μου. Καὶ ἐνήστευον ὑπὲρ
35 αὐτῶν. Τὸ δὲ ἐταπείνουν ἐν νηστείᾳ τὴν ψυχήν μού φησιν, ἐπειδὴ ἡ νηστεία

12 αὐτὸν supplevi.
3 praeteriuntium A.
Meam — suscitare: A, fol. 11ᵃ; B, fol. 12ᵈ.   11 eo* A   13. 19 mortus A
16 sepulchri A¹   16-17 oblionem A   17 misus AB   18 fuisse A   21-22 possit memoriam B.

might be remembered after death. Since, then, those leaving children behind were of necessity remembered through their successors whereas the remembrance of the childless was lost, there being no successors through whom the dead could be recalled, here he means, to bring out the extent of the troubles inflicted on him, Despite my wishing them well, they repaid me with evil—and not any chance evil, but in the wish to cancel my very memory. This they did in casting him into the depths of the pit: whereas the person buried in the tomb built over him is remembered by the onlookers also by the memorial (hence its being called a memorial since such a thing recalls him to the memory of those seeing it placed over him), the one cast into a pit and dying there remained unburied and necessarily had no future memory. This is what blessed David is prophesying in saying, Even my very memory they wanted to obliterate—which he called *sterility for my soul* in line with the verse above, *They repaid me evil for good.* What kind of evil? *Sterility for my soul:* this is the sterility they repaid me, their determination to obliterate my memory.

Next, after saying that his beneficiaries treated him badly to the extent of wanting to obliterate his memory, he goes on to say what the good things were that were done to them by him, and in turn what was done by them to him in return. *On my part, by contrast, I wore sackcloth when they troubled me* (v. 13): whereas they were responsible for their own fate, for their sake I clad myself in sackcloth despite being treated badly by them. *And I humbled my soul with fasting:* I even fasted for them (the meaning of *I humbled my soul with fasting,* since by ill-treating the body, fasting | normally makes the

εἴωθε κακοῦσα τὸ σῶμα ταπεινότεραν καὶ τὴν ψυχὴν τοῖς λογισμοῖς διὰ
τῆς τοῦ σώματος κακώσεως ἐργάζεσθαι. Ἐγὼ οὖν φησιν ὑπὲρ ἐκείνων προ-
σέπιπτον τῷ Θεῷ καὶ νηστείαις | ἐκεχρήμην, συγχώρησιν αἰτῶν ἐκείνοις τῶν
πλημμελημάτων· τοῦτο γάρ ἐστιν εὑρεῖν συνεχῶς παρ' αὐτοῦ γεγονός,
ἐξ' ὧν πού φησι πρὸς αὐτὸν ὁ Θεὸς διὰ τὸ συνεχὲς τῆς προσευχῆς· Καὶ   5
σὺ μὴ προσεύχου περὶ τοῦ λαοῦ τούτου. Τὸ δὲ ἐνεδυόμην σάκκον εἶπεν,
ἐπειδὴ ἔθος ἦν παρὰ Ἰουδαίοις, ἡνίκα ἂν συμφοραῖς περιπίπτοντες αἴσθησιν
ἐλάμβανον ἀπὸ τῆς περιπτώσεως τῶν συμφορῶν ὅτι δι' ἁμαρτίας πάσχουσι,
σάκκους περιβαλλομένους προσπίπτειν τῷ Θεῷ καὶ οὕτω γε αἰτεῖν παρ' αὐτοῦ τῶν πλημμελημάτων τὴν συγχώρησιν. Τοῦτο ἔθος αὐτοῖς εἶναι φανε-   10
ρώτερον Ἰώσηπος ἐν ταῖς τῆς Ἀρχαιολογίας βίβλοις φησιν.

13ᶜ. Καὶ ἡ προσευχή μου εἰς κόλπον μου ἀποστραφήσεται. Ἔθος ἐστὶ
τῇ θείᾳ γραφῇ τοῦ κόλπου μεμνῆσθαι, ὅταν μὴ αὐτὸν καλῇ τὸν παρ' ἡμῖν
ὀνομαζόμενον κόλπον, τὸ ἀχώριστον καὶ ἡνωμένον σημαίνειν βουλομένη, ὡς
ὅταν λέγῃ Ἀπόδος τοῖς γείτοσιν ἡμῶν ἑπταπλασίονα εἰς τὸν κόλπον αὐτῶν   15
τὸν ὀνειδισμὸν αὐτῶν, ὃν ὠνείδισάν σε, Κύριε, — ἵνα εἴπῃ ὅτι Ἀπόδος
αὐτοῖς τὸν ὀνειδισμόν, ἑνώσας αὐτοῖς καὶ ἀχώριστον αὐτὸν ἐργασάμενος
ὥστε μηδέποτε αὐτῶν ἐξαλειφθῆναι τὸν ὀνειδισμὸν ὑπὲρ ὧν ὠνεί|δισάν σε, —
καὶ ὅταν πάλιν λέγῃ Μνήσθητι τοῦ ὀνειδισμοῦ τῶν δούλων σου, οὗ ὑπέσχον
ἐν τῷ κόλπῳ μου πολλῶν ἐθνῶν, — ἵνα εἴπῃ Μνήσθητι ὡς πολύν τινα καὶ   20
ἀχώριστον καὶ ἄπαυστον τὸν ὀνειδισμὸν ⟨ὃν⟩ ὑπομένομεν. Οὕτως καὶ ὅταν
λέγῃ Ὁ μονογενὴς Υἱὸς ὁ ὢν εἰς τὸν κόλπον τοῦ Πατρὸς ἐκεῖνος ἐξηγήσατο,
τοῦτο βούλεται εἰπεῖν ὅτι σὺν αὐτῷ ὁ ἀχώριστος αὐτοῦ ὢν ἐκεῖνος ἐποιήσατο τὴν ἐξήγησιν — διὸ καὶ πιστεύεσθαι ἄξιον τὰ λεγόμενα· εἰπὼν γὰρ
ὅτι Θεὸν οὐδεὶς ἑώρακε πώποτε πρὸς πίστωσιν τοῦ ὅτι τοῦτο ἀληθές, —   25
ἐπειδὴ πολὺ ἐν τῇ θείᾳ γραφῇ τῆς παλαιᾶς διαθήκης τὸ ὑπεμφαῖνον, ὡς
ὅτι δὴ ὤφθη προφήταις καὶ πολλοῖς τῶν δικαίων, — ἐπήγαγε ὅτι Ὁ μονογενὴς Υἱὸς ὁ ὢν ἐν τοῖς κόλποις τοῦ Πατρὸς ἐκεῖνος ἐξηγήσατο, τουτέστιν
ἀξιόπιστον τοῦτο ἐπειδὴ ἐξηγήσατο ὁ πάντοτε συνὼν τῷ Πατρί, ἀχώρι-
στός τε αὐτοῦ διὰ παντὸς ὢν καὶ ἱκανῶς τὴν φύσιν αὐτοῦ γνωρίζειν   30

5-6 Ierem. VII, 16   11 cf. Iosephi Ant. V, 37; VII, 154, 327   15-16 Ps. LXXVIII, 12
19-20 Ps. LXXXVIII, 51   22. 25 Ioh. I, 18.

21 ὃν supplevi   21-23 cf. L (p. 628, 24-26).

Aᶜ 13ᶜ (p. 204, 17-26): Sinum sanctus Dauid pro indiuisa adhessione sepe
ponit; si tamen non de uestimento loquatur sinum dicit, ut est illud *Redde
uicinis nostris septuplum in sinu eorum*, ac si diceret: inseparabile opprobrium
adfige merentibus; et iterum *Memor esto obprobrii seruorum tuorum*. Hoc
uult indicare: numquam a me promouit, oratio mea adhesit mihi.

soul also more humble in thinking through the abuse of the body). So he is saying, I had recourse to God and took to fasting, begging forgiveness of sins for them. In fact, you can constantly find this happening with him, as a result of which God somewhere says to him on account of the constancy of prayer, "Do not pray for this people."[19] He said *I wore sackcloth* because it was the custom with the Jews, when they fell foul of disasters and came to appreciate through the experience of disasters that it was because of sin that they were suffering, to wear sackcloth and have recourse to God and thus beg from him forgiveness for their sins. Josephus, in his *Antiquities,* explains more clearly that this was their custom.

My prayer will be directed at my lap. It is customary with the divine Scripture to mention the *lap* not when referring to the actual thing called "lap" by us, but when wanting to suggest something inseparable and indivisible—as when it says, "Return sevenfold into the lap of our neighbors the taunting with which they taunted you, O Lord," as if to say, Repay them the taunting, attaching it to them and making it inseparable so that taunting of them may never be abolished in return for their taunting of you; and again as when it says, "Remember the taunting of your servants, which from many nations I bore in my lap,"[20] as if to say, Remember the great taunting, inseparable and unceasing, that I bore. Likewise when it says, "The only-begotten Son, who is in the lap of the Father, is the one who made him known,"[21] it means that the one who is inseparable from him is the one who gave the explanation, and hence his words are worthy of belief; after saying, "No one has ever seen God," as confirmation that this is true (there being much in the divine Scripture of the Old Testament calling it in question, like the fact that he was actually seen by prophets and many righteous people), he added, "The only-begotten Son, who is in the bosom of the Father, is the one who made him known." In other words, it is worthy of belief because he made him known who is always with the Father, ever inseparable from him and quite capable of revealing his nature | insofar as he exists together with

19. Jer 7:16.
20. Pss 79:12; 89:50.
21. John 1:18.

δυνάμενος, ὡς ἅτε δὴ συνυπάρχων αὐτῷ καὶ πολλῷ πάντων διὰ τοῦτο ἀξιο-
πιστότερος. Καὶ ἐνταῦθα τὸ καὶ ἡ προσευχή μου εἰς κόλπον μου ἀποστραφήσεται τοῦτο βούλεται εἰπεῖν ὅτι οὐκ ἐχωρίσθη μου ἡ δέησις, οὐ προῆλθεν
ἀπ' ἐμοῦ, ἀλλ' ἔμενεν ἐν ἐμοὶ μὴ χωρισθεῖσά μου, μὴ προελθοῦσα, μὴ προσ-
5 δεχθεῖσα. Ἐπειδὴ γὰρ ἀλλαχοῦ λέγει Εἰσελθέτω ἐνώπιόν σου ἡ προσευχή
μου, ἀντὶ τοῦ προσδεχθείη, καλῶς ἐνταῦθά φησι τὸ εἰς κόλπον μου ἀπο-
στραφήσεται, ἀντὶ τοῦ | οὐ προῆλθεν, οὐκ εἰσῆλθε πρὸς τὸν Θεόν — ἵνα εἴπῃ
οὐ προσεδέχθη· ἀκολουθεῖ γὰρ ἑαυτῷ ἐν ταῖς σωματοποιήσεσιν.

14ᵃ. Ὡς πλησίον, ὡς ἀδελφόν ἡμέτερον, οὕτως εὐηρέστουν. Ἐπειδὴ
10 ἀνωτέρω εἶπεν ὅτι χλευαζόμενος παρ' αὐτῶν σάκκου τε ἐνδύματι ἐκεχρήμην
καὶ ταπεινώσει νηστείας, — οὐδὲν δέ φησιν ὠφέλησα, τῆς δεήσεώς μου διὰ τὴν
ἐκείνων μοχθηρίαν ἀπροσδέκτου γιγνομένης, — ἵνα μή τις οἰηθῇ τὴν εὐχὴν
παρ' αὐτοῦ ἁπλῶς γεγενῆσθαι, οὐ μετὰ διαθέσεως, ἐπήγαγε τὸ ὡς ἀδελφὸν
ἡμέτερον, οὕτως εὐηρέστουν, ἀντὶ τοῦ Οὐ μόνον δὲ ηὐχόμην ὑπὲρ αὐτῶν,
15 ἀλλὰ καὶ ὡς περὶ ἑταίρων καὶ ἀδελφῶν διεκείμην. Τὸ δὲ εὐηρέστησα, ἵνα
εἴπῃ τὴν ἐπίτασιν τῆς διαθέσεως, ἀντὶ τοῦ σφόδρα ἠρεσκόμην εἶναι πρὸς
αὐτὸν ὡς πρὸς ἀδελφόν· Σύμμαχος ὡς πρὸς ἑταῖρον ἢ πρὸς ἀδελφὸν ἀνε-
στρεφόμην· τὸ γὰρ ἀνεστρεφόμην τὴν πολλὴν συνήθειαν καὶ τὴν ἐν τοῖς
πράγμασι δείκνυσιν ὁμιλίαν ὥς που καὶ λέγειν εἰώθαμεν Ἀνεστρέφει ὅδε
ἐν τοῖς πράγμασι, τουτέστιν ἐν αὐτοῖς ἐξεταζόμενος διατελεῖ.
20

14ᵇ. Ὡς πενθῶν καὶ σκυθρωπάζων οὕτως ἐταπεινούμην. Καὶ ηὐχόμην φησὶν
ὑπὲρ αὐτῶν, καὶ διεκείμην | ὡς πρὸς ἀδελφούς, καὶ πενθῶν ἐπὶ τοῖς συμ-
βαίνουσιν αὐτοῖς λυπηροῖς διετέλουν, — Σύμμαχός φησιν Ὡς πενθῶν ὁμομή-
τριον σκυθρωπὸς ἔκυφον, — τοσαύτην εἶχόν φησιν ἐφ' οἷς ἔπασχον τὴν ἀθυ-
25 μίαν. Ἔδειξε δὲ διὰ τούτων τίνα εἶχε γνώμην περὶ αὐτοὺς καὶ οἷα αὐτοῖς
ἤθελεν ἀγαθά, — ὅτι ηὐχόμην φησὶν ὑπὲρ αὐτῶν, ὅτι διεκείμην ὡς πρὸς ἀδελφούς, ὅτι πενθῶν διετέλουν ἐφ' οἷς ἔπασχον ὡς ἐπ' ἀδελφῷ. Εἶτα ἐξηγεῖται ἀντὶ τούτων τῶν ἀγαθῶν τίνα αὐτῷ κακὰ ἐκεῖνοι ἀπέδωκαν.

15ᵃ. Καὶ κατ' ἐμοῦ ηὐφράνθησαν καὶ συνήχθησαν. Καὶ οὕτω φησὶν ἐμοῦ
30 περὶ αὐτοὺς διακειμένου καὶ οὕτως ἔχοντος γνώμης περὶ αὐτούς, ἀντὶ τούτων
ἐκεῖνοι κατ' ἐμοῦ εὐφραίνοντο καὶ συνήγοντο, — ἵνα εἴπῃ ὅτι συνέδρια ἐποιοῦντο κατ' ἐμοῦ, καὶ εὐφροσύνην ἐτίθεντο τὰ ἐμὰ κακά. Ἔδειξε δὲ συντόμως τὴν ἐναντίωσιν ὅτι αὐτὸς μὲν ἐπένθει ἐφ' οἷς ἔπασχον, καὶ ταῦτα τοῦ

5-6 Ps. LXXXVII, 3　　10. 11. 15 cf. L (p. 626, 16-18).

Aᵉ 14-18 (p. 205, 3-9): Pro dilegebam. Non solum, inquit, oraui non prome-
rentibus, sed affectu proximorum dilexi. Simmachus ait: *Sicut lugens germanum
tristis eram.*

him and is therefore much more worthy of belief than anyone. Here, too, the verse *My prayer will be directed at my lap* means, My petition was not kept apart; it did not go ahead of me, but remained within me unseparated from me, not going ahead, not accepted. You see, since elsewhere he says, "Let my prayer come into your presence"[22] (that is, let it be accepted), here he well says that it *will be directed at my lap*—that is, it did not go forward, it did not approach God, as if to say, It was not accepted (in keeping with his bodily expressions).

I *was pleased as though for a neighbor, for our brother* (v. 14). Since he had said above, Mocked by them, I put on vesture of sackcloth and lowliness of fasting (it did me no good, my prayer not being acceptable owing to their depravity)—in case anyone should think the prayer from him was aimless and lacked feeling—he added the clause *I was pleased as though for our brother*—that is, Not only did I pray for them, but I even treated them like companions and brothers. The phrase *I was pleased* implies the depth of feeling in the sense, I was very delighted to be in the same relation to him as to a brother. Symmachus said, "I related to him as to a companion or a brother"—that is, I displayed deep kinship and gave evidence of association in affairs; as we also normally say, This person is involved in affairs—that is, he continues to be found among them. *I was humbled as though sorrowful and downcast:* I prayed for them, I felt for them like brothers, and kept grieving for the misfortunes befalling them; Symmachus puts it, "I was bowed low and downcast as though bewailing a blood brother," I felt such depression for what they suffered. Now, in this he revealed the attitude he had toward them and the good things he wished them: I prayed for them, I felt for them like brothers, I kept grieving for what they suffered as though for a brother.

Then he explains the evil recompense that they gave him for these good things. *They gloated over me and gathered together* (v. 15): despite my being so well-disposed toward them and having such an attitude toward them, in response to this they gloated over me and got together, as if to say, They formed a clique against me and made my troubles a source of joy. In a concise manner he brought out the contrast, that whereas he grieved for what they suffered, despite | God's rejecting them, they, by contrast, gloated over

---

22. Ps 88:2.

Θεοῦ αὐτοὺς ἀποστρεφομένου, οὗτοι δὲ ἐκ τῶν ἐναντίων ηὐφραίνοντο ἐπὶ
τοῖς ἐκείνου κακοῖς. Τὸ οὖν κατ' ἐμοῦ ἐπὶ κοινοῦ καὶ ἐπὶ τοῦ ηὐφράνθησαν
καὶ ἐπὶ τοῦ συνήχθησαν· τὸ μὲν γὰρ κατ' ἐμοῦ ηὐφράνθησαν ἀντὶ τοῦ τὰ
ἐμὰ κακὰ ἐκείνοις εὐφροσύνην ἐποίει, τὸ δὲ κατ' ἐμοῦ συνήχθησαν ἀντὶ τοῦ
κατ' ἐμοῦ συνέ|δρια ἐποιοῦντο βουλευόμενοι ὅτι με διαθῶσι κακόν.   5

15ᵇ. Συνήχθησαν ἐπ' ἐμὲ μάστιγες καὶ οὐκ ἔγνων. Συνέδρια ποιησάμε-
νοι ἦγον εἰς μέσον, καὶ ἐμαστίγουν, — τοῦτο γὰρ αὐτὸν καὶ διέθηκαν, —
καὶ ἐμαστίγουν δὲ ἐφ' οἷς οὐκ ἠπιστάμην, ἵνα εἴπῃ ἀναιτίως.

15ᶜ. Διεσχίσθησαν καὶ οὐ κατενύγησαν. Σύμμαχος φανωτέρως φησὶν
'Απορήσαντες οὐκ ἠρέμουν· πολλάκις δέ φησι καὶ ἀπορήσαντες ἐπὶ τοῖς   10
γιγνομένοις ὑπ' αὐτῶν, ἄγειν τε αὐτὰ εἰς πέρας οὐ δυνάμενοι, οὐδαμῶς
μετετίθεντο τῆς κατ' ἐμοῦ ἐπιβουλῆς. Τὸ γὰρ διεσχίσθησαν ἀντὶ τοῦ ἠπό-
ρησαν λέγει, ἐπειδὴ τὸ διασχιζόμενον ἱμάτιον γυμνὸν ἐργάζεται τὸν ἐνδε-
δυμένον. Καὶ ἡ τούτων βουλὴ εἰς πέρας οὐκ ἐρχομένη μόνον ἐγύμνου καὶ
ἤλεγχε τὴν προαίρεσιν αὐτῶν καὶ τὰς ἐπιβουλάς, — ὅπερ καλῶς εἶπε Σύμ-   15
μαχος ἀπορήσαντε:, — ἀντὶ τοῦ εἰς ἔργον αὐτὰς ἐκβαλεῖν οὐ δυνηθέντες, πό-
ρον αὐτοῖς ἐπιθεῖναι καὶ διέξοδον καὶ τέλος οὐκ ἴσχυσαν, ὅμως οὐδὲ μετε-
νόουν· τοῦτο | γάρ ἐστι τὸ οὐ κατενύγησαν. Τοῦτο δὲ μάλιστα γέγονεν
ὁπηνίκα τῷ λάκκῳ μὲν ἐνέβαλον τοῦ βορβόρου ὡς ἀναιρήσοντες, παραδόξως δὲ Θεοῦ βουλήσει ἀνεσπάσθην διὰ τοῦ εὐνούχου, καὶ ὅμως ἐπέμενον   20
ἀδικεῖν τολμῶντες.

16ᵃ. Ἐπείρασάν με, ἐξεμυκτήρι-
σάν με μυκτηρισμόν. Μεθ' ὑποκρίσεως
φησιν ἐφθέγγοντό μοι, πολλάκις πεῖ-
ράν μου λαμβάνοντες, εἶτα ἐχλεύαζον
μετὰ τὴν ἀπόκρισιν· μυκτηρισμὸν γὰρ
καλεῖ τὴν ἐπίτασιν τῆς χλεύης. Εἰκὸς
γὰρ ἦν τινὰς μετὰ χλεύης αὐτῷ προ-
σιόντας ἐρωτᾶν Τί ἄρα ἔσται; εἶτα,
μετὰ τὴν ἀπόκρισιν τοῦ προφήτου

Temptauerunt et subsannaue-
runt me. Simulantes, inquit, se
id quod mandabat Deus uelle
cognoscere, loquebantur mihi ac 25
fictis me, ut caperent uerba mea,
interrogationibus consulebant; id
uero quod respondissem inrisio-
nibus suis contemptibile ac uile
faciebant.   30

τὴν τῶν ἐσομένων λυπηρῶν προαγόρευσιν ποιουμένου, χλευάζειν ὡς οὐδὲν
ὄντων τῶν λεχθέντων οὐδὲ ἐσομένων.

18 20 ler. XXXVIII, 6-13.

Temptauerunt — faciebant: A. fol. 11ᵃ; B, fol. 12ᵈ.   23 similantes A¹ inquit se om. A   26 fictissime A   27 consulabant A   28 respondessem A¹
28-29 inrisionis A¹.

Aᵉ   8 (p. 205, 16-17): Ac si diceret Sine causa uerberabar.   16ᵃ (p. 205,
19-21): Simulantes se quod mandabat Deus uelle cognoscere, agnitas praedica-
tiones aut deridebant aut ulciscebantur.

his troubles. So the phrase *over me* applies to both *gloated* and *gathered: they gloated over me* means, They took pleasure in my troubles; whereas they gathered together against me means, They formed a clique against me with the intention of bringing trouble upon me. *Scourges were piled on me, and I did not understand:* they formed a clique, brought me out and scourged me (this being their treatment of him), and they scourged for reasons I did not understand—that is, without cause. *They were rent asunder and had no regrets.* Symmachus said more clearly, "They were at a loss but did not cease": though often unsure of what was being done by them, he is saying, and incapable of bringing it to completion, in no way did they desist from their scheming. *They were rent asunder* means "they were at a loss," since a rent garment leaves the wearer naked: their plan did not come to fulfillment, but only laid bare and exposed to censure their intentions and schemes (well said by Symmachus in "at a loss"), meaning, Unable to carry out them out, they did not succeed in bringing them to a result, outcome, and fulfillment, yet they did not change their mind (the meaning of *had no regrets*). Now, this happened in particular when they threw him into the depths of the pit as though doing away with him, but by God's will he was, against the odds, drawn out by the eunuch,[23] and yet they continued in their efforts to do him wrong.

They made attempts on me; they sneered at me with sneers (v. 16): they spoke to me with dissimulation, often putting me to the test; then they mocked me when I replied (by *sneers* referring to the extent of the mockery). In fact, some probably came up to him in mockery and asked, What is going to happen? Then, following the reply from the prophet, who delivered a prophecy of the misfortunes to come, they would mock him as though nothing of what was said would come to pass. | *They gnashed their teeth at me:*

---

23. Cf. Jer 38:6–13. The LXX rather than Symmachus, in fact, is right about the verb "rend asunder," if opting wrongly for the passive voice (as reference to the Hebrew would have shown).

16ᵇ. Ἔβρυξαν ἐπ' ἐμὲ τοὺς ὀδόντας αὐτῶν. Καὶ μεγάλην φησὶν ἐπεδείκνυντο τὴν κατ' ἐμοῦ ὀργήν· ἔθος γὰρ τοῖς σφόδρα ὀργιζομένοις τοὺς
ὀδόντας συνθήγειν καὶ κινεῖν. Διόλου δὲ πάντα ἐξηγεῖται, πολλά τε ὄντα
καὶ διάφορα τὰ παρ' αὐτῶν εἰς τὸν προφήτην γεγονότα. Εἰρηκὼς καὶ τὰ
5 παρ' αὐτοῦ εἰς ἐκείνους ἀγαθὰ καὶ τὰ ἀντὶ τῶν ἀγαθῶν γινόμενα παρ' ἐκείνων εἰς αὐτόν κακά, λοιπὸν ἀκολούθως μετὰ παρρησίας αἰτεῖ τοῦ Θεοῦ
τὴν βοήθειαν καί φησι·

17ᵃ. Κύριε, πότε ἐπόψει; Μέχρι πότε ἀνέξῃ | τοιαῦτα τούτων διαπρατ-
τομένων ὁρᾶν κατ' ἐμοῦ, καίτοι πολλῆς τῆς παρ' ἐμοῦ πειραθέντων διαθέ-
10 σεως; Τὸ δὲ Κύριε, πότε ἐπόψει φησὶν δεικνὺς μὲν καὶ τὸ πλῆθος τῶν
παρ' ἐκείνων κακῶν καὶ τὴν ἐπὶ τούτοις τοῦ Θεοῦ μακροθυμίαν. Ὅμοιον δὲ
τούτῳ καὶ ἐν τῷ προφητικῷ εὑρήσεις λέγοντα τὸν Ἱερεμίαν· φησὶ γάρ
Κύριε, μὴ εἰς μακροθυμίαν σου λάβῃς με. Τί οὖν βούλει φησὶ γενέσθαι;

17ᵇ. Ἀποκατάστησον τὴν ψυχήν μου ἀπὸ τῆς κακουργίας αὐτῶν. Ἐξη-
15 γησάμενος τῶν κακῶν τῶν εἰς αὐτὸν τὸ μέγεθος καὶ εἰρηκὼς πρὸς τὸν Θεὸν
Μέχρι πότε τούτων ἀνέξῃ, ἀκολούθως ἐπήγαγε τὸ Ἀποκατάστησον τὴν
ψυχήν μου ἀπὸ τῆς κακουργίας αὐτῶν. Τοῦτό φησιν μόνον αἰτῶ τῶν κακῶν,
ὧν ἐπάγουσί μοι, τὴν ἀπαλλαγήν. Τὸ δὲ ἀποκατάστησον εἶπεν ἀντὶ τοῦ
ἀπάλλαξον, ἵνα εἴπῃ Ἀπάλλαξόν με τούτων, εἰς τὸ πρότερόν με ἀποκα-
20 θιστῶν ὁπηνίκα τῆς τούτων ἐκτὸς καθειστήκειν θλίψεως. Ἀντὶ τοῦ ἀπὸ
τῶν κακῶν ἢ ἀπὸ τῆς θλίψεως εἶπεν ἀπὸ τῆς κακουργίας αὐτῶν, δεικνὺς
ὅτι πονηρίᾳ καὶ κακίᾳ πάντα διεπράττοντο κατ' αὐτοῦ, μελέτην τιθέμενοι
τὴν κατ' αὐτοῦ ἀδικίαν.

17ᶜ. Ἀπὸ λεόντων τὴν μονογενῆ μου. Μονογε|νῆ συνηθῶς τὴν ψυχὴν
25 λέγει τὴν ἰδίαν· ἀνωτέρω γὰρ εἰπὼν Ἀποκατάστησον τὴν ψυχήν μου,
ἐνταῦθα ἐπήγαγε τὴν μονογενῆ μου, ἀντὶ τοῦ ἣν μόνην κέκτημαι, ἵνα
συμπαθεστέραν δείξῃ τὴν αἴτησιν. Ἀπάλλαξον αὐτήν φησιν ἀπὸ τῶν
ἀρχόντων τούτων τῶν θρασέων· πλεῖστα γὰρ ἐκίνουν κατ' αὐτοῦ οἱ τοῦ
λαοῦ ἄρχοντες, πολλὴν ἐπιδεικνύμενοι κατ' αὐτοῦ τὴν ὀργήν, — οὓς λέοντας
30 καλεῖ. Οὐδὲ γὰρ ἁπλῶς ἔθος τῇ γραφῇ ταύτῃ τῇ προσηγορίᾳ καλεῖν τοὺς
θρασεῖς, ἀλλὰ τοὺς ἐν ἀρχῇ καθεστῶτας καὶ θρασύτητος πεπληρωμένους
ἀπὸ τοῦ τοὺς λέοντας τὴν ἀρχήν τε λέγεσθαι ἔχειν τὴν κατὰ πάντων τῶν
θηρίων καὶ θρασύτητος γέμειν ὑπερβαλλούσης.

18ᵃ. Ἐξομολογήσομαί σοι, Κύριε, ἐν ἐκκλησίᾳ πολλῇ. Καὶ ἀνωτέρω τὴν
35 παρὰ τοῦ Θεοῦ αἰτήσας βοήθειαν ἐπήγαγεν ὅτι Εὐχαριστήσω σοι τούτου
τυχών (πάντα γὰρ τὰ ὀστᾶ μου ἐροῦσί φησιν Κύριε, Κύριε, τίς ὅμοιός σοι;)

13 Ierem. XV, 15   36 v. 10.

they displayed great anger against me (the custom being for those exceedingly enraged to grind and gnash their teeth).

Now, he goes into all this in great detail, their actions against the prophet being many and varied. Having mentioned both the good things done by him to them and in return for these good things the troubles brought on him by them, he then logically asks God's help with confidence in the words *Lord, when will you take note?* (v. 17). How long, he asks, will you put up with seeing them committing such crimes against me, despite my great affection for those testing me? The words *Lord, when will you take note?* bring out both the vast number of the troubles from them and God's long-suffering in their regard. You will also find Jeremiah saying similar things to this in the prophetic text: "Lord, in your long-suffering do not take me away."[24] So what does he want to happen? *Restore my soul from their evildoing.* Having remarked on the great number of the troubles affecting him and having said to God, How long will you allow this? he proceeds to say *Restore my soul from their evildoing:* this alone is my request, a release from the troubles that afflict me. *Restore* means "release," as if to say, Release me from them, return me to my former state, when I was rid of these tribulations. Instead of "from the troubles" or "from the tribulations," he said *from their evildoing* to bring out that they did all this against him in wickedness or malice, painstaking in their injustice against him. *Rescue my solitary life from the lions.* He frequently refers to his own soul as *solitary:* above he said *Restore my soul,* and here he went on to say *my solitary life,* meaning "the only life I have," to make the request more appealing. Free it from these rash rulers, he is saying; after all, the rulers of the people moved might and main against him, giving evidence of intense rage against him, so he refers to them as *lions.* It is not the habit of Scripture, remember, to use this name simply of rash people; rather, those appointed to power are said to be filled with audacity because lions are said to have control over all the wild beasts and be characterized by surpassing boldness.

I shall confess to you, Lord, in the great assembly (v. 18). After asking above for help from God, he went on to say, I shall give thanks to you for being granted this (he said, remember, *All my bones will say, Lord, Lord, who is like you?*); and after | asking for release from the troubles, he went

---

24. Jer 15:15.

καὶ ἐνταῦθα αἰτήσας τῶν κακῶν τὴν ἀπαλλαγὴν ἐπήγαγεν ὅτι ' Ἐξομολογήσομαί σοι, Κύριε, ἐν ἐκκλησίᾳ πολλῇ. δεικνὺς ὅσον τῆς εὐχαριστίας τὸ
μέγεθος καὶ ὅτι ἀναγκαῖον ὄφλημα δικαιότατα πληρούμενον παρὰ τῶν ἀπο-
λαυόντων τῆς τοῦ Θεοῦ δωρεᾶς. Τυχὼν γὰρ τούτου καὶ τὴν ἀπαλλαγὴν
εὑράμενος τῶν συμφορῶν, εὐχαριστήσω σοί φησιν ἐπὶ συνόδου πολλῶν, 5
διηγούμενός σου τὰς εἰς ἐμὲ χάριτας.

18ᵇ. ' Ἐν λαῷ βαρεῖ αἰνέσω σε. Φανερώτερον Σύμμαχος εἶπεν ' Ἐν λαῷ
παμπληθεῖ αἰνέσω σε. Οὐ μόνον δέ φησιν ἐπὶ πλήθους ἔξω σοι χάριτας,
ἀλλὰ καὶ ὑμνήσω σε τούτων ἕνεκεν.

Ἕτερον γάρ ἐστιν ἐξομολογήσομαι
καὶ ἕτερόν ἐστιν αἰνέσω. Τὸ μὲν γὰρ
ἐξομολογήσομαι ἀντὶ τοῦ εὐχαρι-
στήσω· εὐχαριστία δέ ἐστι τῶν τοῦ
Θεοῦ δωρεῶν ἡ ἐξήγησις. Τὸ δὲ
αἰνέσω ἀντὶ τοῦ ὑμνήσω· ὕμνος δέ
ἐστιν ἡ διήγησις τοῦ μεγέθους τοῦ
Θεοῦ, ἥτις πληροῦται ἢ τὸ μεγα-
λεῖον τῆς φύσεως ἐξηγουμένων ἡμῶν
ἢ τὴν δημιουργίαν τῆς κτίσεως.

Confitebor tibi Domine, in ecclesia magna, in populo grani 10
laudabo te. Aliud est confiteri,
aliud est laudare; confiteri est
praestita sibi a Deo beneficia
narrare, laudare uero est ymnos
dicere, cum laus in Deum de 15
operum et creaturarum disposi-
tione concipitur, aut cum de naturae eius eminentia sermo formatur. 20

19ᵃ. Μὴ ἐπιχαρείησάν μοι οἱ ἐχθραίνοντές μοι ματαίως. Ἐπειδὴ τοίνυν
φησὶ τυχὼν τῶν παρά σου δωρεῶν τὴν δικαίαν εὐχαριστίαν καὶ ὑμνῳδίαν
ἀποδίδωμι, μὴ τύχοιεν ὧν ἐπιθυμοῦσιν οἱ μάτην μοι ἐχθραίνοντες. Τοῦτο
γάρ ἐστι τὸ μὴ ἐπιχαρείησαν, ἐπειδὴ ὁ θεασάμενος τὰ ἐπιθυμήματα αὑτῷ
ἐπὶ τοὺς ἐχθροὺς πληρωθέντα πάντως ἐπιχαίρει τῷ ἐχθρῷ. Καλῶς δὲ προ- 25
σέθηκε τὸ οἱ ἐχθραίνοντές μοι ἀδίκως, δεικνὺς ὅτι δικαίως αὐτοὺς μὴ τυχεῖν
ὧν ἐπιθυμοῦσιν ἀξιοῖ, ἐπειδὴ μάτην καὶ ἀδίκως τὴν ἔχθραν ἔχουσι τὴν
κατ' αὐτοῦ· διὸ δὴ καὶ δεύτερον αὐτὸ ἐπάγει·

19ᵇ. Οἱ μισοῦντές με δωρεὰν καὶ διανεύοντες ὀφθαλμοῖς. Προσέθηκε δὲ
τὸ διανεύοντες ὀφθαλμοῖς, τὸ γινόμενον παρὰ τῶν μισούντων καὶ ἀποστρε- 30
φομένων ἐξηγούμενος, οἳ πολλάκις, ἐπειδὰν καθεζόμενοι | ἢ παριόντας που

8 παμπληθεῖ] πάμπαν θεῖα ms.
Confitebor — formatur: A, fol. 11ᵃ; B, fol. 12ᵈ.   9-10 in ecclesia — graui]
usque A   11 te om. B   12 est 1° loco om. B   confeteri A   14-15 ymn.
dicere in rasura A   16 creturarum A   16-17 dispossione A¹ dispossitione A²B
17 cum om. A   18 ementiae *** A.

Aᵉ 31,-189, 2 (p. 207, 12-13): Oblica significatione oculorum oblocuntur in visu.

on to say *I shall confess to you, Lord, in the great assembly* to bring out the magnitude of the thanksgiving and the fact that it was a necessary and most just repayment by those enjoying God's gift. In receipt of this, he is saying, and experiencing release from the calamities, I shall thank you in the large gathering by recounting your kindnesses to me. *I shall praise you in a mighty people.* Symmachus puts it more clearly: "I shall praise you in a multitudinous people." Not only shall I enjoy your favors in great numbers, he is saying, but also I shall sing your praises for them. *I shall confess* is one thing, you see, *I shall praise,* another: *I shall confess* means "I shall give thanks," and thanksgiving involves an outline of God's gifts, whereas *I shall praise* means "I shall sing your praises," and singing involves an account of God's greatness, which occurs when we describe the magnificence of his nature or the formation of created things.

Let those opposed to me without cause not rejoice over me (v. 19): since, then, I am in receipt of gifts from you and make a return of due thanksgiving and hymn-singing, let those opposed to me without cause not attain their wishes (the sense of *not rejoice,* since the one who sees his desires fulfilled against his enemies rejoices greatly over his enemy). He was right to include *those opposed to me unjustly* to bring out that he is within his rights to ask that they not attain what they desire, since they bear him hostility without cause and unjustly.[25] Hence, he proceeds to say the same thing a second time: *Those hating me without reason and winking their eyes.* He included *winking their eyes* to comment on what is done by those hating and avoiding people, who frequently, when they are seated and see those they hate | present or

---

25. Forms of the LXX differ in reading "without cause" or "unjustly," perhaps influenced by similar phrasing in Ps 3:7. Theodore seems to know both readings.

ἢ πλησιάζοντας θεάσονται τοὺς μισουμένους, εὐθὺς διαστρέφειν τοὺς ὀφθαλμοὺς εἰώθασι καὶ διανεύειν, ἢ βαρύ τι τὴν θεάν τιθέμενοι τοῦ μισουμένου, — καὶ τοῦτο δεικνύντες ὅση τίς ἐστιν αὐτοῖς ἡ κατ᾽ ἐκείνων ἀπέχθεια, — ἢ καὶ χλευάζοντες αὐτοὺς πολλάκις. Δεικνὺς δὲ αὐτὸ τῆς κακίας τὸ μέγεθος ἐπάγει·

5 20. Ὅτι ἐμοὶ μὲν εἰρηνικὰ ἐλά- λουν, καὶ ἐπ᾽ ὀργὴν γῆς ἐλάλουν. Προσποιοῦνται μὲν γὰρ ῥήματα εἰρή- νης ἔχοντα πρόσχημα φθέγγεσθαι, τὸ δ᾽ ἀληθὲς πάσης ὀργῆς τε καὶ 10 κακίας ἔγεμεν αὐτῶν τὰ ῥήματα. Οὐ γὰρ ἦν εἰρήνης οἷα δὴ ἀπὸ τοῦ σχή- ματος εἶναι ἐδόκει, ἀλλ᾽ ἦν ἀπὸ πολλῆς κακίας μεθ᾽ ὑποκρίσεως λεγόμενα· δόλους γὰρ ῥάπτοντες καὶ ἐπιβουλὰς κατ᾽ ἐμοῦ διετέλουν, τοιαῦτα λογι- ζόμενοί τε καὶ στρέφοντες ἐπὶ τῆς οἰκείας ψυχῆς.

15 Ἔστιν οὖν καθ᾽ ὑπερβατὸν τὸ καὶ ἐπ᾽ ὀργὴν γῆς ἐλάλουν, ἵνα ᾖ τὸ ὀργὴν διὰ μέσου, καθὰ πολλὰ καὶ ἕτερα εὑρήκαμεν.

20

Λέγει δὲ αὐτὸ συνηθῶς, ὅτι ἐπὶ τῆς γῆς τοιαῦτα λαλοῦσιν ἢ τοιάδε πράττουσι, καὶ μάλιστα ἐπὶ πονη- ρίας τῆς κατὰ ψυχὴν αὐτὸ συνηθῶς 25 κεχρημένος,

οἷόν ἐστι τὸ καὶ γὰρ ἐν καρδίᾳ ἀνομίαν ἐρ|γάζεσθε ἐν τῇ γῇ 30 ἐν τῷ νζ΄ κείμενον·

Quoniam mihi quidem paci- fice loquebantur usque cogitabant. Simulabant quidem uerbis paci- ficis se mecum inire conloquia, re autem uera omnis sermo eo- rum felle et ueneno odii non ca- rebat.

Est igitur cum yperbato dic- tum et in iracundia terrae lo- quentes, pro eo ut diceret: Super terram positi iram loquebantur, ut sit interpositum terrae, sicut et multa alia interposita saepius inuenimus. Dicit autem hoc ex more suo, quoniam in terra mala loquuntur uel certe in terra talia faciunt; utitur autem hac elocu- tione maxime cum de malitia at- que iniquitate conqueritur, ut est illud in quinquagessimo sep- timo psalmo positum: Etenim in corde iniquitates operamini in terra.

---

21 cf. supra e. g. in ps. IX, 23-24; XX, 13; XXXI, 3-4   28 Ps. LVII, 3.

15 καθ] μεθ᾽ ms.

20. Quoniam — carebat: A, fol. 11ᵇ; B, fol. 12ᵈ.   6 loquebantur om. A 9 ** re, litt. ue in rasura B   10 uenino A.
Est igitur — 190, 13 naturae: A, fol. 11ᵇ: B, fol. 12ᵈ-13ᵃ.   15 igitur] itaque B cum om. A¹   yberbato A   16 in om. A   iracondia A   17 eo om. A 18 possiti A¹   19 interpossitum A¹   20 interpossita A¹   sepius A   22 terra mala om. A¹   23 locuntur B   in] uel A¹   terra om. A¹   26 iniquitate om. A¹ 27-28 luii A   28 possitum est A   29 iniquitatis A   30 tera A.

approaching, generally divert their eyes and turn their head, either becoming upset at the sight of those they hate (thus revealing the degree of hostility they have for them) or even often mocking them.

To bring out the actual magnitude of the vice, he goes on to say *Because they spoke words of peace to me, but spoke in anger of the earth* (v. 20): they make a pretense by uttering words under the guise of peace, but in reality their words are completely full of anger and evil. All the words, in fact, were not of peace, though they seemed to give that impression; rather, they were spoken with complete viciousness under pretense, for they continued hatching plots and schemes against me, planning such things and turning them over in their soul. So the phrase *but spoke in anger of the earth* is therefore a case of transposition to have *anger* in the middle, as we found in many other cases. Now, as usual he says the same thing, that they say such things or do them *on the earth,* employing it constantly of evil against the soul in particular, such as "In your heart you commit lawlessness on the earth" in Psalm 58, |

καὶ τὸ πονηρία ἐν
ταῖς παροικίαις αὐτῶν ἐν τῷ νδ΄, ὡς
καὶ ἡμῖν ἔθος λέγειν πολλάκις οἷα
ἐν τῷδε γίνεται τῷ βίῳ. Οὐχ ἀπλῶς
δὲ κέχρηται τῷ ἔθει τούτῳ ὁ μακάριος Δαυίδ, ἀλλὰ πρὸς ἔμφασιν
τοιοῦτό τι λέγειν βουλόμενος, ὅτι καὶ
ἐπὶ τῆς γῆς ὄντες ὅμως κέχρηνται τῇ
πονηρίᾳ, τουτέστιν εὐτελεῖς ὄντες, καὶ
τὸ μηδὲν ἀπὸ τοῦ οἰκητηρίου τὸ εὐτελὲς τῆς φύσεως αὐτῶν σημάναι
βουλόμενος. Καὶ φθέγγονταί φησι καὶ
ποιοῦσι πονηρίας μεστά, οὐδὲ πρὸς

Vtitur autem hac con-
suetudine beatus Dauid ad exag- 5
gerationis schema faciendum,
tale aliquid uolens dicere | quo-
niam et super terram positi, id
est cum uiles sint ac nihilum, ni-
hilominus nequitiam non relin- 10
quunt, a positione terrenae habitationis uilitatem uolens indicare
naturae.

τὸ θνητὸν τῆς φύσεως αὐτῶν ἀποβλέποντες, — καὶ κἂν διὰ τοῦτο αἰδούμενοι
καὶ ἀφιστάμενοι τοῦ δολεροῖς καὶ πονηρίας μεστοῖς κεχρῆσθαι λογισμοῖς. 15

21ª. Καὶ ἐπλάτυναν ἐπ' ἐμὲ τὸ στόμα αὐτῶν Ἀλλὰ καὶ ἐπὶ ταῖς συμφοραῖς αἷς περιεβαλόμην εὐφραίνοντο, καὶ τοιαῦτα ἐφθέγγοντο ἐπικερτο-
μοῦντές μου τοῖς κακοῖς. Τὸ δὲ ἐπλάτυναν τὸ στόμα αὐτῶν εἶπεν οὐχ
ἀπλῶς, ἀλλ' ἐπειδὴ ἡ μὲν θλῖψις οἶδε λυπεῖν, ἡ δέ γε ἄνεσις καὶ ὁ πλα-
τυσμὸς εὐφραίνειν. Ἐπλάτυναν, εἶπεν, ἐπ' ἐμὲ τὸ στόμα αὐτῶν, ἀντὶ τοῦ 20
εὐφραινόμενοι τοιαῦτα ἐφθέγγοντο κατ' ἐμοῦ οἷα εἰκὸς εὐφραινομένους καὶ
τοῖς κακοῖς ἐπιχαίροντας τοῖς ἐμοῖς φθέγγεσθαι.

21ᵇ. Εἶπαν Εὖγε Εὖγε, εἶδαν οἱ ὀφθαλμοὶ ἡμῶν. Τὸ εὖγε φωνή ἐστιν
ἀποδεκτική. Τοῦτο οὖν βούλεται εἰπεῖν, ὅτι ὁρῶντες τὰς ἐπαγομένας μοι
θλίψεις ἀπεδέχοντο, καὶ ἠρέσκοντο τοῖς γινομένοις, ὡς τὰ ἐπιθυμήματα 25
αὐτῶν ὁρῶντες. Τοῦ δὲ εὖγε εὖγε τῷ διπλασιασμῷ ἐχρήσατο, τὴν ὑπερβάλλουσαν αὐτῶν εὐφροσύνην ἐπὶ τούτοις δεικνύς.

22ª. Εἶδες, Κύριε, μὴ παρασιωπήσῃς. Ἐκ μεταφορᾶς τῶν δεσποτῶν, οἳ
πολλάκις ὁρῶντες ἄτοπα παρὰ τῶν οἰκετῶν γινόμενα σιωπῶσιν, οὐδὲ γὰρ
ἐπιπλήττοντες αὐτοῖς. 30

1-2 Ps. LIV, 16ᵇ.

6 scema A   7-8 quoniam] *inc. cod.* B *fol. 13ª supra columellam haec prae-*
bens: iudica mihi s(ecundum) iustitiam tuam (?)   8 possiti A¹   11 possitione A¹B.

Aᵉ 21ª (p. 206, 16-18): Laeti malis meis toto, ut dicitur, ore insultantes
loquebantur. 26-27 (p. 206, 18-21): Repetitione uero *Euge Euge* usus est, ut
effusos illos in gaudium et se non contenentes expraemeret.

and "Evil is in their dwellings" in Psalm 55,[26] as it is also our custom to say when such things happen in this life. Far from this usage being without purpose for blessed David, he uses it in his wish to say something of the kind with emphasis, that though on this earth—that is, insignificant—they commit wickedness, his intention being to suggest the lowliness of their nature from their lowly dwelling. What they say and do, he means, is full of wickedness, and they have no regard to the mortality of their nature, even if on this account ashamed and reluctant to implement thoughts that are full of guile and wickedness.

They opened wide their mouths toward me (v. 21): even in the calamities in which I was enveloped they rejoiced, and said such things to mock me for my troubles. It was not without point that he said *They opened wide their mouths,* but because tribulation is in the habit of grieving, but relaxation and mockery, of rejoicing; so *They opened wide their mouths toward me* means, They uttered such things in rejoicing over me as you would expect people rejoicing and exulting in my troubles to utter. They said, *Aha, aha, our eyes saw it.* The term *aha* is one of approbation; so he means, On seeing the tribulations befalling me, they approved and were pleased with what was happening, as though witnessing the object of their desires. In *Aha, aha* they used repetition to indicate their surpassing contentment with them.

You have seen, Lord; do not be silent (v. 22): a metaphor from masters, who often keep silent on seeing inappropriate behavior by their servants, and do not beat them. | *Lord, do not keep your distance from me:* do not stay far

---

26. Pss 58:2; 55:15. The obscure v. 20b contains a *hapax legomenon* in the Hebrew, rendered "the oppressed in the land" by Dahood (*Psalms,* 1:215), reflected also in the version of Symmachus but not in the LXX. Theodore seems to be working from the LXX, while also aware of the version of Symmachus.

22ᵇ. Κύριε, μὴ ἀποστῇς ἀπ᾽ ἐμοῦ. Μὴ μακρύνῃς φησὶ σεαυτὸν ἀπ᾽ ἐμοῦ, ἀντὶ τοῦ μὴ ἄποθέν μου τὴν βοήθειάν σου καταστήσῃς· τὸ γὰρ μὴ ἀποστῇς οὐ τόπῳ λέγει, ἀλλὰ τῇ τῆς διαθέσεως ἐγγύτητι.

23. Ἐξεγέρθητι, Κύριε, καὶ πρόσχες τῇ κρίσει μου, ὁ Θεός μου καὶ ὁ
5 Κύριός μου, εἰς τὴν δίκην μου. Ἀνάστηθί φησι καὶ φρόντισον τοῦ ποιήσασθαι ἐξέτασιν τῶν κατ᾽ ἐμὲ ἀπὸ τῶν πρότερον καθεζομένων, εἶτα δια-
νισταμένων καὶ ἐναρχομένων τοῦ ὅ τί ποτ᾽ ἂν βούλοιντο διαπράττεσθαι.
Ὁ Θεός μου καὶ ὁ Κύριος κατὰ κοινοῦ ✳✳ τὸ πρόσχες ἀντὶ τοῦ πρόσχες τῇ
κρίσει μου, καὶ εἰς τὴν δίκην μου μελησάτω σοι τῆς ἐξετάσεως τῶν κατ᾽
10 ἐμέ. Τὸ δὲ ὁ Θεός μου καὶ ὁ Κύριός μου, ἀντὶ τοῦ Σὺ ὁ ποιητής μου καὶ ὁ
δεσπότης μου — καὶ πᾶν ὅτι δήποτε, σὺ φρόντισόν μου· δικαίως γὰρ τοῦτο
ποιήσεις.

24ᵃ. Κρῖνόν μοι, Κύριε, κατὰ τὴν δικαιοσύνην σου, Κύριε ὁ Θεός μου.
Ἐπειδὴ ἠξίωσεν ἀνωτέρω δικάσαι αὐτῷ τὸν Θεόν, ἐνταῦθα ἐπήγαγε τὸ
15 Κρῖνόν μοι, Κύριε, κατὰ τὴν δικαιοσύνην σου, ἀντὶ τοῦ Ἀξιῶ δὴ τὴν ἐξέ-
τασίν μου μετὰ τοῦ δικαίου τοῦ σοι πρέποντος γενέσθαι. Εἶτα δεικνὺς τῆς
αἰτήσεως τὸ εὔλογον ἐπάγει·

24ᵇ. Καὶ μὴ ἐπιχαρείησάν μοι. Τοῦτό φησιν αἰτῶ τὸ τὴν ἐπιθυμίαν
αὐτῶν τὴν κατ᾽ ἐμοῦ εἰς πέρας μὴ ἐλθεῖν, μοχθηράν τε οὖσαν καὶ ἄγαν
20 ἀδικωτάτην.

25ᵃ. Μὴ εἴποιεν ἐν καρδίαις αὐτῶν Εὖγε Εὖγε τῇ ψυχῇ ἡμῶν. Μὴ
τυχόντες φησὶν ὧν ἐπιθυμοῦσιν εὐφρανθῶσι τῇ ψυχῇ ἐπὶ τοῖς κακοῖς τοῖς
ἐμοῖς· τὸ γὰρ μὴ εἴποιεν ἀντὶ τοῦ μὴ εὐφρανθεῖεν, τὸν λόγον ἀπὸ τοῦ
ἔργου λέγων ὡς πολλαχοῦ ἀποδέδεικται, — καὶ ἐν αὐτῷ δὲ τῷ ψαλμῷ τούτῳ
25 ἐν ἀρχῇ, ἀντὶ τοῦ Γενοῦ τῇ ψυχῇ μου σωτηρία φησιν Εἰπὸν τῇ ψυχῇ μου
Σωτηρία σου ἐγώ εἰμι.

25ᵇ. Μηδὲ εἴποιεν Καταπίωμεν αὐτόν. Μηδὲ εὐφρανθεῖεν ὡς καταπε-
πωκότες με, ἀντὶ τοῦ Μὴ ἀνελόντες με καὶ ἀφανίσαντες εὐ|φρανθεῖεν, ὥστε
τετυχηκότες τοῦ οἰκείου σκοποῦ.

25-26 v. 3ᵇ; cf. p. 177, 7-8.

1 φησὶν ἑαυτὸν ms   2 καταστήσεις ms   8 ✳✳ lacunam statui   15 δὴ] δὲ ms
25 εἶπον ms.

Aᵉ 1-3 (p. 206, 21-25) Id est: Adiutorium tuum mora ac dilatione ne suspendas ... non localiter de Deo, sed effectionaliter dicitur.   23 (p. 206, 29-207, 2):
Haec est meae petitionis intentio, ne desidiria inimicorum meorum, quae sunt
iniqua, obtatis succesionibus inplicantur.   21-23 (p, 207, 3-4): Super mala mea
tamquam in uotis propriis non laetentur.

from me—that is, Do not keep your help far from me (the phrase *Do not keep your distance* referring not to space but to closeness of disposition). *Awake, Lord, and attend to my judgment, my God and my Lord, for the sake of my just cause* (v. 23): rise up and give a thought to examination of those who were on my side originally but then kept a distance and began to do whatever they wanted. *My God and my Lord* in general ... the word *attend* in the sense *attend to my judgment for the sake of my just cause:* take an interest in examining my situation. The phrase *my God and my Lord* means, You, my maker and my Lord; whatever it is, have me in mind, for you do it justly.

Judge me, Lord, according to your righteousness, Lord my God (v. 24). Since he asked above for God to judge him, here he went on to say *Judge me, Lord, according to your righteousness*—that is, For myself I ask examination with the justice that becomes you. Then to bring out the reasonableness of the request, he goes on to say *And let my foes not gloat over me:* I ask that their desires against me not take effect, being wrong and very unjust. *Let them not say in their hearts, Aha, aha, in our soul* (v. 25): let them not attain what they desire and rejoice in spirit in my troubles. The phrase *Let them not say* means "Let them not rejoice," using the term from the action, as has often been demonstrated; also in the very beginning of this psalm he says, instead of "Be the salvation of my soul," *Say to my soul, I am your salvation.*[27] *Nor let them say, Let us swallow him up:* nor let them rejoice as though having swallowed me, meaning, Let them not rejoice at having destroyed and eliminated me, and so attained their purpose. |

---

27. Ps 35:3.

26ᵃ. Αἰσχυνθείησαν καὶ ἐντραπείησαν ἅμα οἱ ἐπιχαίροντες τοῖς κακοῖς μου. Αἰσχύνης δὲ καὶ ἐντροπῆς πληρωθεῖεν μᾶλλον οἱ εὐφροσύνην τὰ ἐμὰ τιθέμενοι κακά· τοῦτο γὰρ δίκαιον. Καὶ τὸ αὐτὸ δὲ πάλιν ἑτέρως φησίν.

26ᵇ. Ἐνδυσάσθωσαν αἰσχύνην καὶ ἐντροπὴν οἱ μεγαλορρημονοῦντες ἐπ'
ἐμέ. Ὅλοι φησὶ περιβληθεῖεν αἰσχύνην οἱ εὐφραινόμενοι ἐπὶ τοῖς ἐμοῖς 5
κακοῖς· τοῦτο γάρ ἐστι τὸ οἱ μεγαλορημονοῦντες ἐπ' ἐμέ. Ἀκολούθως δὲ
καὶ ταῦτα εἶπεν οἷς ἀνωτέρω παρεκάλεσεν, ἀξιώσας αὐτοὺς μὴ εὐφρανθῆ-
ναι ἐπ' αὐτῷ τοῖς κακοῖς περιπεπτωκότι. Ἀνάγκη γὰρ ἦν αὐτοὺς ἐπὶ τούτοις μὴ εὐφραινομένους, πάντη τῶν κακῶν ἀπαλλαγέντος τοῦ προφήτου
διὰ τὴν παρὰ τοῦ Θεοῦ βοήθειαν, αἰσχύνης πληροῦσθαι ὡς οὐδενὸς ὢν 10
ἐσπούδαζον κατ' αὐτοῦ εἰς ἔργον ἐκβῆναι δυνηθέντος.

27ᵃ. Ἀγαλλιάσαιντο καὶ εὐφρανθείησαν οἱ θέλοντες τὴν δικαιοσύνην μου.
Ἐκεῖνοι μὲν οὖν τοιαῦτα πάθοιεν, εὐφροσύνης δὲ πληρωθεῖεν οἱ ἐπιθυμοῦντες ἰδεῖν τῶν ἐμῶν κακῶν τὴν ἀπαλλαγήν. Οὐχ ἁπλῶς δὲ ἐκάλεσε τὴν
δικαιοσύνην, ἀλλὰ δεικνὺς ὅτι δικαίως εὔξεται τούτοις. 15

27ᵇ. Καὶ εἰπάτωσαν διὰ παντός Μεγαλυνθείη ὁ Κύριος. Σύμμαχός φησι
μέγας Κύριος. Ἐκεῖνοι τοίνυν φησὶν οἱ ἐπιθυμοῦντες τὴν εὐεργεσίαν ἰδεῖν
τὴν ἐμήν, εὐφροσύνης δικαίας ἐπ' ἐμοὶ τυχόντες, εἴποιεν ὅτι Μέγας ὁ Κύριος,
ὁμοίως κἀνταῦθα τὸ εἰπάτωσαν ἀντὶ τοῦ ἔργου λαβών, τουτέστιν | ἔργῳ τὴν
πεῖραν λάβοιεν ὅτι μέγας εἶ, ὁ Θεός, ῥυόμενος τοὺς ἐν θλίψεσι καθεστῶτας. 20

27ᶜ. Οἱ θέλοντες τὴν εἰρήνην τῷ δούλῳ σου. Οὗτοί φησιν οἱ τὴν εἰρήνην
ἐπιθυμοῦντες ἰδεῖν τὴν ἐμὴν ταῦτα εἴποιεν, ἀντὶ τοῦ ἐπιτύχοιεν ὧν ἐπιθυμοῦσιν. Εἰρήνην δὲ τῷ δούλῳ σού φησι τῶν κακῶν τὴν ἀπαλλαγήν, ὡς
ἐν εἰρήνῃ καταστησομένου.

28ᵃ. Καὶ ἡ γλῶσσά μου μελετήσει τὴν δικαιοσύνην σου. Καὶ μελέτην 25
φησὶ ποιήσομαι τὴν διήγησιν τῆς εὐεργεσίας σου τῆς εἰς ἐμέ, ἀντὶ τοῦ
συνεχῶς εὐχαριστῶν σοι ταῦτα ἐξηγήσομαι· τοῦτο γάρ ἐστι τὸ μελετήσει,
ἐπειδὴ γὰρ τὸ ἐν μελέτῃ καθεστὼς συνεχῶς τις ἐπέρχεται. Κἀνταῦθα δὲ
δικαιοσύνην ἐκάλεσε τοῦ Θεοῦ τὴν βοήθειαν, ὡς δικαίως αὐτῷ παρασχε-
σθησομένην. Τὸ δὲ ἡ γλῶσσά μου ἀντὶ τοῦ ἐγώ, ἀπὸ τοῦ μερικοῦ τὸ ὅλον 30
δηλῶν, οὐχ ἁπλῶς ἀπὸ τῆς γλώσσης τὸ ὅλον εἰρηκώς, ἀλλ' ἐπειδὴ αὕτη
ἐν ταῖς ἐξηγήσεσι τὸ ἔργον πληροῖ.

19 cf. p. 177, 10; 191, 23-24.

15 τούτους ms.   22 εἴποιαν... ἐπιτύχοιαν ms.

Aᵉ   23 (p. 207, 14): Id est malorum cessatione.

Let those who rejoice in my troubles feel shame and reproach at the same time (v. 26): let those taking satisfaction in my troubles rather be filled with shame and reproach, as is just. He says the same thing again in a different form, *Let those who exalt themselves over me wear shame and reproach:* let those rejoicing in my troubles be all covered in shame (the sense of *those exalting themselves over me*). Now, logically he also says this to those he exhorted above, asking them not to rejoice over him as a victim of the troubles: far from rejoicing in them, since the prophet was completely freed from the troubles through help from God, they should be filled with shame, no one being able to put into effect what they were anxious to do to him.

Let those who wish justice for me rejoice and be glad (v. 27): on the one hand, let those suffer this fate, while on the other hand, let those wanting to see relief from my troubles be filled with joy. Now, it was not without point that he referred to *justice:* it was to show that he will justly pray for them. *Let them always say, The Lord be magnified.* Symmachus said "mighty Lord." So his meaning is, Let those desirous of seeing a kindness to me, enjoying a justified joy in my case, say, The Lord is mighty; here in similar fashion he takes the phrase *Let them say* from the action—that is, Let them experience in reality that you are great, O God, since you rescue those reduced to tribulation. *Those who wish your servant's peace:* let those wanting to see my peace say this—that is, let them attain what they desire. *Your servant's peace* refers to relief from the troubles in bringing him to peace.

My tongue will ponder your righteousness (v. 28): I shall ponder the account of your kindness to me—that is, I shall constantly give thanks to you in recounting them (the meaning of *will ponder,* since anyone pondering something constantly goes over it). Here, too, he referred by *righteousness* to help from God, since it was right for it to be provided. *My tongue* means "I," suggesting the whole by mention of the part, choosing to refer to the whole from the tongue not by chance, but because it is the member that takes the part of narration. | *Your praise all day long*—that is, forever—reference

28ᵇ. Ὅλην τὴν ἡμέραν τὸν ἔπαινόν σου. Ἀντὶ τοῦ ἀεί· πολλαχοῦ γὰρ λέγει τὸ ὅλην τὴν ἡμέραν ἀντὶ τοῦ διὰ παντός. Ἀεὶ οὖν φησιν ἐξηγήσομαί σου τὴν εἰς ἐμὲ εὐεργεσίαν, τούς τε ὕμνους ἀναπέμψω τοὺς εἰς σε διὰ παντός. Τὸν γὰρ ἔπαινόν σου βούλεται εἰπεῖν τοὺς ὕμνους· ἐπαίνου γὰρ 5 καὶ ἐγκωμίων ὁ ὕμνος τόπον ἐπέχει, ἐξήγησιν ἔχων τοῦ μεγέθους τῆς φύσεως τοῦ δεσπότου.

PSALMVS XXXV

Ἐν τοῖς κατὰ τὸν Σαοὺλ ἐξεταζόμενος ὁ μακάριος Δαυὶδ τοῦτον
10 ἐξεφώνησε τὸν ψαλμόν, ἡνίκα ὁ μὲν
Σαοὺλ ἐδίωκεν αὐτὸν σπεύδων ἀνελεῖν.
Ὁ δὲ μακάριος Δαυίδ, καὶ ὑπὸ χεῖρα
λαβών, ὅμως οὐ διεχρήσατο οὐδὲ ἀνελεῖν ἐβουλήθη, ἀλλὰ καὶ τοὺς ἰδίους
15 ἐπέσχε τοῦτο ποιῆσαι βουληθέντας,
— ἐφ᾽ οἷς ἤδη, καὶ τὸν φακὸν τοῦ

Cum bealus Dauid Saulis insidiis et persecutione praemere-
tur, hunc psalmum cecinit, id
praecipue temporis quo egresus
est Saul, ut in heremo in quo
eum audierat latere perquireret,
quando Dauid scifum et hastam
eius furatus, noluit eum interficere.

ὕδατος λαβὼν παρ᾽ αὐτῷ κείμενον καὶ τὸ δόρυ πλησίον πεπηγός, πόρρωθεν ἐπὶ τοῦ ὄρους γενόμενος ἐξεβόησε καλῶν καὶ τὰ ληφθέντα δεικνύς, γνωρίζων τε ὅτι δυνατὸν μὲν ἦν αὐτῷ ἀνελεῖν βουλομένῳ, ὅπερ καὶ εὐχερέστερον ἦν 20 ἐκείνῳ διαπράξασθαι ἢ τὰ πλησίον κείμενα ἀπονητὶ καὶ ἀκινδύνως λαβόντα παρελθεῖν. Ὁ δέ γε Σαοὺλ οὐδὲ ἐπὶ τούτοις ἐντραπείς, τέκνον μὲν ἀπεκάλει, καὶ διάθεσιν ἐσχηματίζετο, καὶ ἕλκειν ἐπειρᾶτο πρὸς ἑαυτὸν καὶ βούλεσθαι ἐπὶ τὰ οἰκεῖα ἀνάγειν προσεποιεῖτο, τόδ᾽ ἀληθὲς ἐσχηματίζετο τὴν διάθεσιν ἵν᾽ ὑποχείριον λαβὼν ἀνέλῃ· οὐδὲ γὰρ | μετ᾽ ἐκεῖνο τοῦ διώκειν ἀπέ-
25 σχετο, ἔμενε δὲ πλείστῃ χρώμενος ἔτι σπουδῇ πρὸς τὴν τοῦ μακαρίου Δαυὶδ ἀναίρεσιν. Ἀναγκαιότατον δὲ ἦν
σφόδρα τοῖς ἐντυγχάνουσι καὶ τοὺς

Necessarium autem fuit et
ualde utile etiam huiusmodi psal-

8-26 I Reg. XXVI, 5 ss.

Cum – prouocentur: A, fol. 11ᵇ; B, fol. 13ᵃ. 8 beatus] beatus add. A¹ litt. eat primo reprobalis, deinde erasis 9 persequutione A 10 cicinit A 12 herimo AB 27 huiusmodi] ̄hm A¹, hominum add. supra A².

Aᵉ 1-2 (p. 207, 16): Toto die, pro omni tempore. Argumentum ps. XXXV (p. 207, 20-208, 1): Cum Sauelis insidiis urgeretur, hunc psalmum cicinit, eo praecipue tempore cum in suam potestatem insidiator (Saul) uenisset, ab eiusque internecione temperasset, sublato tamen scipho et hasta pro manifestatione negotii; more suo opus ad uerba retulit. Cf. PSEUDO-BEDA (666 B).

frequently being made to the whole day in the sense of always. So he means, I shall always recount your kindness to me, and sing hymns to you forever (*praise* meaning "hymns," the hymn taking the place of praise and commendation in giving an account of the greatness of the nature of the Lord).

PSALM 36

Under pressure from Saul's doings, blessed David gave voice to this psalm at the time when Saul was pursuing him in his anxiety to do away with him. Blessed David, by contrast, though having him in his power, nevertheless did not take advantage of him or wish to do away with him; instead, he even checked his own men, who wanted to do so. At this time he took possession of the water jar lying near him and the spear fixed in the ground nearby, and when at some distance on the mountain he called out to summon them and show what he had taken, making it known that it would have been possible for him to do away with him had he wished. This would have been easier for him to accomplish than to skip away unnoticed and without risk after taking what lay nearby. Saul, on the contrary, not brought around even by this, called him "child" and made a show of affection, trying to attract him to himself and pretending to want to bring him back to his own home; but in fact he was making a show of affection so as to get him in his power and do away with him.[1] In fact, even after this he did not stop the pursuit, still continuing to show the most intense zeal in doing away with blessed David.

Now, for readers it was most necessary both that | the psalms composed

---

1. Cf. 1 Sam 26.

ἐφ' οἷς αὐτὸς ἔπασχεν ὁ μακάριος | mos, in quibus de passionibus
Δαυὶδ ῥηθέντας ψαλμοὺς ἐγγράφως | suis beatus Dauid loquitur, mo-
φέρεσθαι καὶ συντετάχθαι τοῖς ἄλ- | nimentis tradere propter eos qui-
λοις. Τοῦτο γὰρ καὶ ἐν ταῖς βίβλοις | bus erat talis lectio profutura,
τῶν λοιπῶν εὑρίσκεται προφητῶν· | ut ad imitationis studium prouo- 5
ἐγκείμενά ἐστιν ἰδεῖν καὶ τὰ πάθη | centur.

τῶν προφητῶν καὶ τὰς ἐπὶ τούτοις αὐτῶν φωνὰς γεγενημένας, — οἱάπερ ἐστὶν
ἡ τοῦ μακαρίου Δανιὴλ καὶ ἡ τοῦ μακαρίου Ἰερεμίου μάλιστα, περιέχουσα
καὶ τὰς αὐτοῦ φωνὰς ἃς ἐπί τε τοῖς οἰκείοις ἐποιήσατο παθήμασι καὶ τῇ
τῶν Ἰουδαίων ἀπιστίᾳ, οὐχ ἁπλῶς τοῦτο τῆς χάριτος οἰκονομησάσης ὥστε 10
πάντα φέρεσθαι ἐγγράφως, ἀλλ' ἵνα μὴ μόνον διὰ τῶν παραινέσεων τῶν
προφητικῶν παιδευώμεθα, ἀλλὰ καὶ τὰς πράξεις αὐτῶν ἀκούσαντες μείζονα
τὴν ὠφέλειαν λαμβάνωμεν πρὸς μίμησιν ἐντεῦθεν ἐξελκόμενοι. Εἰ γὰρ καὶ οἱ
τοιοῦτοι τοῦ μακαρίου Δαυὶδ ψαλμοὶ ἱστορικὴν ὧν ἔπαθεν ἐξήγησιν οὐκ
ἔχουσιν, ἀλλ' οὖν γε διὰ τῶν αὐτοῦ φωνῶν ἐστι γνῶναι ὁποῖός τις ἦν ἐφ' 15
οἷς ἔπασχεν, οὐ περὶ ἀποδυσπετήσεις ἀτόπους ἀσχολούμενος ἀλλὰ περὶ
τὴν εὐχαριστίαν τοῦ δεσπότου τρεπόμενος. Τοιοῦτος γάρ ἐστι μάλιστα
οὗτος ὁ ψαλμός, ἐξηγουμένου μὲν τὸν ἐκείνου τρόπον μόνον, τὸ δὲ ὅλον
εὐχαριστοῦντος τῷ Θεῷ καὶ δοξάζοντος τῇ δι|ηγήσει τῶν περὶ αὐτοῦ
θαυμάτων.   20

2ᵃ. Φησὶν ὁ παράνομος τοῦ ἁμαρ- | Dixit iniustus ut delinquat in
τάνειν ἐν ἑαυτῷ. Οἴεταί φησιν ὁ πα- | semet ipso. Opinatur, inquit, is qui
ράνομος ἐν ἑαυτῷ ἁμαρτάνειν, ἀντὶ | inique agit in semet ipso delin-
τοῦ ἁμαρτάνων λανθάνειν νομίζει, — | quere, id est putat se latere cum
τοιοῦτο γάρ τι λέγει τὸ τοῦ ἁμαρ- | peccat, — hoc est quod ait ut de- 25
τάνειν ἐν ἑαυτῷ, — οἱονεὶ νομίζει ἐν | linquat in semet ipso, — aestimat
ἑαυτῷ ἁμαρτάνειν καὶ οὐκ εἶναι κα- | quod in se peccet nec putat ea
τάδηλον αὐτὸν ἡμῖν ἐφ' οἷς βεβού- | quae facit ad aliorum notitiam
λευταί τε καὶ προῄρηται, ἀλλ' ἐν | peruenire, sed in se ita peccatum
ἑαυτῷ κρύπτεσθαι τῆς ἁμαρτίας τὴν | suum abscondi credit ut a reli- 30
πρόθεσιν, ἄγνωστον οὖσαν ἑτέροις. | quis ignoretur. Siquidem Saul,
Τοῦτο δὲ εἶπεν εἰκότως ἐπειδὴ σχη- | simulata dilectione, fallere se

9 τῆς ms.
    3 tradire A   5 ut om. A¹   emendàtionis A emitationis B   5-6 pro-
uocetur A.
    Dixit — 195, 3 blanditiis: A, fol. 11ᶜ; B, fol. 13ᵛ.   21 ut delinquat]
usque A   22 opinator AB¹   inquietis AB   24-25 putat — peccat affert Aᵉ
(p. 208, 2-3)   26 aestimet A   27 nec] non A   30 suum in rasura A
32 fallere ex psallere A.

by blessed David containing what he personally suffered be transmitted in writing and that they be combined with the others. This, in fact, is found also in the books of the other prophets; you can see contained there the sufferings of the prophets and the oracles on them, especially those of blessed Daniel and of blessed Jeremiah, including also his oracles that he uttered on his own sufferings and the Jews' unbelief, not simply because grace arranged that everything be transmitted in writing,[2] but for us not only to be instructed through the prophetic exhortations, but also to hear of their doings and gain greater benefit from being drawn thereby to imitation. After all, even if such psalms of blessed David do not actually contain a historical account of what he suffered, nevertheless it is thus possible at least to find out from his words the kind of person he was through what he suffered, since he was not engaged in some pointless problems but was devoted to giving thanks to the Lord. This, in fact, is what this psalm in particular is like: whereas he comments only on that man's behavior, he is totally caught up in thanking and glorifying God by outlining the marvels in his own regard.

The lawbreaker speaks within himself with a view to sinning (v. 1): the lawbreaker thinks his sinning is within—that is, he believes that he is escaping notice in sinning (the meaning of *within himself with a view to sinning*), as if he believes that his sinning is within himself and he is not transparent to us in what he has planned and decided, his choice instead being hidden *within himself,* unknown to others. Now, he was within his rights in saying this since | Saul meant to make a pretense of affection, thinking that what he

---

2. Theodore is usefully distinguishing between the oral composition of psalms and prophetic oracles and their transmission in written form. He sees divine providence in the latter process with later readers' benefit in view.

ματίζεσθαι διάθεσιν ὁ Σαοὺλ ἐβού-   Dauid posse credebat ac spera-
λετο, λανθάνειν οἰόμενος τὸν Δαυὶδ   bat se eum uerborum circumue-
ἐφ' οἷς προήρητο, καὶ δὴ καὶ ἀπα-   nire blanditiis.
τᾶν αὐτὸν τῇ κολακείᾳ τῶν ῥημάτων ἐλπίσας. Παράνομον δὲ ἐκάλεσεν, ὡς
5 ἀδικεῖν καὶ φονεύειν εἰκῇ καὶ μάτην παρὰ τὸ βούλημα τοῦ νόμου προῃρημένον. Τὸ δὲ φησὶν ἀπὸ τοῦ πράγματος λαβὼν εἶπεν ὃ διεπράττετο, ὡς
καὶ ἐν τῷ θ' ψαλμῷ Εἶπε γὰρ ἐν καρδίᾳ αὐτοῦ Ἐπιλέλησται ὁ Θεός (οὐ
γὰρ ὅτι τοῦτο πάντως εἶπεν, ἀλλ' ἀπὸ τοῦ πράγματος, ὅτι ὥσπερ οὐκ
ἐφορῶντος τοῦ Θεοῦ τοῖς γινομένοις, οὐδὲ προνοουμένου τῶν πενήτων ἠδί-
10 κουν ἀδεῶς τὸν προστυχόντα) οὕτως κἀνταῦθα· οὐχ ὅτι τοῦτο εἶπεν ὁ
Σαοὺλ ἀλλ' ὅτι ὡς οὐκ ἂν γνώριμος ἐχθρὸς τῷ Δαυίδ, ἔτι δὲ ἀγνοούμενος,
οὕτως ὑποκρίνεσθαι ἐπειρᾶτο τὴν πρὸς αὐτὸν σχηματιζόμενος διάθεσιν. Τοῦ|το
δὲ ἄχρι τῆς δεῦρο τὸ ἔθος καὶ παρὰ τοῖς πολλοῖς κρατοῦν ἐστιν εὑρεῖν,
καὶ μάλιστα παρὰ τοῖς ἰδιώταις, οἷον ὅταν τις λέγῃ περὶ τῶν ὑπερόγχον
15 ἐχόντων τὸ φρόνημα· λέγουσί σοι ὅτι Ἡμεῖς ἐσμεν καὶ ἕτερος οὐκ ἔστι, —
καίτοι οὐ πάντως λέγουσιν, ἀλλ' ἀντὶ τοῦ «οἴονται» τὸ «λέγουσι» φάσκων, — οὕτως κἀνταῦθα τὸ φησὶν ἀντὶ τοῦ «οἴεται» εἶπεν.

Τινὲς δὲ τὸ φησὶν ὁ παράνομος τοῦ ἁμαρτάνειν ἐν ἑαυτῷ οὕτως ἐνόησαν, ἀντὶ
τοῦ Ἅπαξ ἔκρινε τοῦ ἁμαρτάνειν. Τοῦτο δέ, εἰ καί τισιν ἀκολουθότερον εἶναι
20 νομίζεται, πρὸς τὸ ῥητόν, διὰ τὴν ἀπὸ τῆς ἑρμηνείας αὐτῷ προσοῦσαν δυσχέ-
ρειαν, ἀλλ' οὖν γε καὶ τῇ ἀκολουθίᾳ πάσῃ τῆς ἑρμηνείας ἐναντίον· οὐδὲ γὰρ
σύμφωνα ταύτῃ τῇ ἑρμηνείᾳ τὰ ἑπόμενα, ὡς τῇ παρ' ἡμῶν ἐκτεθείσῃ καθὼς ἀκριβέστερον ἐντυχόντα ἑξῆς ἐστιν εὑρεῖν. Καὶ τῷ ἑβραϊκῷ δέ, ὅπερ ἐστὶ πάντων
κυριώτερον τὸ ἐκεῖθεν ἑρμηνεύεσθαι, ἐναντίον τοῦτο τὸ εἶδος τῆς ἑρμηνείας εἶναι
25 συμβαίνει· διόλου γὰρ αὐτὸν ὡς δόλῳ καὶ θωπείᾳ κεχρημένον αἰτιᾶται. Ἴδιον δέ
ἐστι τῶν τῷ δόλῳ κεχρημένων τὸ νομίζειν λανθάνειν τοὺς ἐπιβουλευομένους,
ὅτι ποτὲ κατὰ διάνοιαν ἔχοντες τῇ τῶν ῥημάτων κέχρηνται θωπείᾳ· μὴ γὰρ
λανθάνειν ἐλπίσαντες οὐδ' ἂν ἔμειναν ἐπὶ τοῦ σχήματος τῆς ἀπάτης.

2ᵇ. Οὐκ ἔστι φόβος Θεοῦ ἀπέναντι τῶν ὀφθαλμῶν αὐτοῦ. Ἀκολούθως
30 τοῦτο καὶ μάλα ἐντρεπτικῶς. Ἔστω γάρ φησιν ἐμὲ λανθάνειν νομίζεις, οὕτω
σε ἀποβαλεῖν τῆς διανοίας τοῦ Θεοῦ τὸν φόβον ἐχρῆν, ὡς μὴ ἐννοεῖν ὅτι
κἂν μυριάκις δόξῃς λανθάνειν ἡμᾶς, τὸν Θεὸν οὐ λήσῃ ἐφ' οἷς βουλεύῃ καὶ
μηχανᾶς καθ' ἡμῶν, ἀλλ' ἕξεις αὐτὸν τιμωρὸν τῶν οἰκείων βουλευμάτων. Πόθεν
οὖν τοῦτο; Ὅτι τοῦ Θεοῦ τὸν φόβον οὐκ ἔχει πρὸ τῶν ὀφθαλμῶν.

7 Ps. IX, 32.

20 post νομίζεται aliquid videtur deesse   33 μηχανᾶ ms.

Aᵉ 2ᵇ (p. 208, 5-10) ... Increpatorie legendum est, ac si diceret: Fallat licet
uniuersos homines, demens est tamen qui nec timore Dei frenatur a scelere, quem
nulla potest latere quamuis secreta molitio (molestio ms).

had decided escaped David's notice, and even hoping to deceive him by his
flattering speech. He called him *lawbreaker* for having decided to commit the
crime of killing him idly and to no purpose, against the provisions of the law.
He used *speaks* to imply the deed he had committed, as also in Psalm 10,
"He said in his heart, God has forgotten"[3]—not that he actually said as much,
but to imply the deed, namely, that just as if God did not observe what happens or make provision for the poor, they would have no qualms in harming
any person at all, so too here. Not that Saul said as much, but that in being no
notorious foe of David's, and still not recognized as such, he tried to give a
false impression by pretending affection for him. Now, this is the custom to
our own day, and you can find it operating in the general run of people, and
especially the ignorant, when someone says of those with an inflated sense of
their own importance, They tell you, Here we are without peer—not actually
saying as much, but meaning "thinking" for "saying," just as here, too, *He
says* means "He thinks."

Now, some commentators took the verse *The lawbreaker speaks within
himself with a view to sinning* in the sense, On one occasion he made the
judgment to sin. But even if it is thought by some to be more in keeping with
the verse on account of the difficulty of the interpretation attaching to it, nevertheless it is in fact actually opposed to the sequence of the interpretation as
a whole, what follows not being in accord with such an interpretation, as one
who reads more precisely what follows can find from our explanation. This
form of interpretation happens to be at variance with the Hebrew, and interpreting from that is more authoritative than all; in fact, it absolutely blames
him for using deceit and flattery. Now, it is typical of the person employing
deceit to think that schemers escape notice, because they are always under
that impression when they use flattering language; after all, unless they
expected to escape notice, they would not have persisted in their deceitful
pretense.

There is no fear of God before his eyes. It is consistent for him to say
this in a very scolding manner: If you believe that you escape my notice, he
is saying, you should so put the fear of God from your mind as to give no
thought to the fact that, even if you seem countless times to have escaped our
notice, your schemes and wiles against us will not escape God; instead, you
will have him as punisher of your evil designs. What grounds are there for
that? Because he does not have the *fear of God before his eyes.* | *He was not*

---

3. Ps 10:11.

3ª. Ὅτι ἐδόλωσεν ἐνώπιον αὐτοῦ. Ἐξ ὧν φησιν ἐπ᾽ ὄψεσι ταῖς αὐτοῦ τὸν δόλον ἐργάζεται· δῆλον γὰρ ὡς ὁρᾷ Θεὸς οὐ τὰ γινόμενα μόνον παρ᾽ αὐτοῦ, ἀλλὰ γὰρ καὶ τῆς ψυχῆς τὰ βουλεύματα. Ὥστε εἴπερ εἶχε τοῦ Θεοῦ τὸν φόβον πρὸ τῶν ὀφθαλμῶν οὐκ ἂν ἐκέχρητο τῷ δόλῳ λανθάνειν ἡμᾶς νομίζων (ᾔδει γὰρ ὅτι οὐχ οἷόν τε ἦν λανθάνειν τὸν Θεόν, ἁπάντων 5 αὐτῷ γνωρίμων ὄντων, εἰδότος δὲ ἅπαντα καὶ σαφῶς ἐπισταμένου), εἴπερ ἐδεδίει τὸν δεσπότην μετὰ πολλῆς ἂν τῆς σπουδῆς τὸ ἁμαρτάνειν ἐφυλάξατο.

3ᵇ. Ὥστε εὑρεῖν τὴν ἀνομίαν αὐτοῦ καὶ μισῆσαι. Ἐνταῦθα τοῦ δόλου τὴν αἰτίαν ἐξηγεῖται. Διὰ τοῦτο δέ φησι πολλοῖς καὶ ποικίλοις κέχρηται τοῖς | δόλοις ὥστε εὑρεῖν τὴν ἀνομίαν   *Vt inueniatur iniquitas eius* 10 αὐτοῦ, ἵνα εἴπῃ ὥστε εὑρεῖν τὴν ἑαυτοῦ   *et odium.* Ac si diceret: Vt desi- ἐπιθυμίαν καὶ πληρῶσαι τὸ σπουδαζό-   deria sua, quae de interfectione μενον αὐτῷ, τὸν κατ᾽ ἐμοῦ φόνον.   mea concoepit, impleat.

Ἀνομίαν δὲ καλεῖ τὴν πρόθεσιν τοῦ Σαοὺλ ἀνελεῖν αὐτὸν ἐσπουδακότος, ὡς σφόδρα ἀνόμως καὶ ἀσεβῶς τοιαῦτα βουλευομένου, ὡς καὶ ἐν τῷ νς᾽ φησὶν 15 Ἕως οὗ παρέλθῃ ἡ ἀνομία, ἀντὶ τοῦ Μέχρις ἂν τῆς συμφορᾶς αὐτῆς ἀπαλλαγῶ καὶ τῆς ἐφόδου τῶν πολεμίων, ἀνομίαν αὐτὸ καλέσας ὡς σφόδρα ἀδίκως ἐπιχει- ρούντων. Καλῶς δὲ τὸ εὑρεῖν ἀντὶ τοῦ ἐπιτελέσαι, ἵνα δείξῃ τὴν περὶ τὸ πρᾶγμα σπουδὴν ἀπὸ τοῦ τοὺς εὑρίσκειν τι βουλομένους σφόδρα ζητεῖν καὶ μετὰ σπου- δῆς, ὅπερ καὶ ὁ Σαοὺλ ἐποίει πάντα πράττων εἰς τὸ δυνηθῆναι ἀνελεῖν τὸν Δαυίδ, 20 οὕτως καὶ ὁ Ἡσαΐας Ἐν γὰρ ταῖς νηστείαις ὑμῶν εὑρίσκετε τὰ θελήματα ὑμῶν, ἀντὶ τοῦ ἐπιτελεῖτε, πρὸς τὸ δεῖξαι καὶ τὴν περὶ τὸ ἁμαρτάνειν σπουδήν.

Τὸ δὲ καὶ μισῆσαι περὶ τοῦ Θεοῦ   Quod uero adiecit *et odium,* λέγει, ὡς τοῦ Θεοῦ μισήσαντος τὸν   Dei sine dubio dicit, quod pro Σαοὺλ ὑπὲρ τοῦ δόλου καὶ τῆς τοῦ   dolo suo atque occidendi studio 25 φονεῦσαι σπουδῆς. Οὕτω γὰρ λέγει   Deo esset exosus. Ita namque et καὶ Σύμμαχος εἰς τὸ μισηθῆναι,   Symmachus posuit *ut odibilis* αὐτὸ τὸ γινόμενον ἀκολούθως εἰπών·   *fiat.* Ambiguum profecto non τούτου γὰρ καὶ δόλοις κεχρημένου   erat circa hunc, qui proximo ten- καὶ πᾶσαν πρὸς τὸ ἀνελεῖν αὐτὸν   debat insidias et mortem eius 30 τιθεμένου σπουδὴν αὐξάνεσθαι αὐτῷ   animo ac mente uoluebat, Dei τὸ παρὰ τοῦ Θεοῦ μῖσος ἦν ἀνάγκη.   odia in dies crescere.

16 Ps. LVI, 2ᵈ   21 Is. LVIII, 3.

15 βουλευομένω *ms.*

Vt inueniatur — crescere: A, fol. 11ᶜ; B, fol. 13ª   11 odium] hō B 11-13 *affert* Aᵉ (p. 208, 11-12): pro Vt desideria sua de me interficiendo impleat 30 et *in rasura*   31 uolebat A.

Aᵉ 21 (p. 208, 12-15): Sic ait Esaias *In ieiuniis uestris inueniuntur uolun- tates uestrae,* id est complentur.

honest with him (v. 2): he commits deceit with eyes closed, for it is clear that God sees not only what is done by him, but also the plans in his heart. So if he had *the fear of God before his eyes,* he would not have employed deceit in the belief that he was escaping our notice (realizing that it was not possible to escape God, everything being known to him, who knows and understands everything clearly). If he really had dread of the Lord, he would have shown much zeal in guarding against sin.

So as to discover and hate his lawlessness. At this point he explains the reason for the deceit. The reason why he uses many and varied forms of deceit, he is saying, is to "discover his lawlessness," as if to say, So as to realize his desire and achieve the object of his efforts, namely, my death. By *lawlessness* he refers to the decision of Saul in his obsession with killing him, planning this as he did in a very lawless and godless manner, as he says also in Psalm 57, "Until lawlessness pass by"—that is, Until I am rid of calamity itself and the assault of the enemy, by "lawlessness" referring to it as the work of extremely lawless adversaries.[4] Now, he did well to speak of *discovery* in the sense of carrying out, to bring out his relish for the task, from people intent on discovering something by seeking with great zeal, as Saul also demonstrated in doing everything possible to dispose of David. Isaiah likewise says, "In your fasting you discover your own desires"[5]—that is, You carry out, to bring out also the relish for sinning. The *hatred* refers to God, God hating Saul for his deceit and his eagerness for murder. Symmachus likewise says "in order to be hated" in logical reference to the deed itself: since he employed deceit and displayed complete eagerness for doing away with him, God's hatred of him necessarily increased. |

---

4. The "lawlessness" in the LXX of Ps 57:1 in fact renders "scourge" in the Hebrew.
5. Isa 58:3.

4ᵃ. Τὰ ῥήματα τοῦ στόματος αὐτοῦ ἀνομία καὶ δόλος. Πάντα τὰ ἄτοπα ἀνομίαν καλεῖ. Ὡς γὰρ ἄνω τὴν ἐπιθυμίαν αὐτοῦ ἀνομίαν ἐκάλεσεν ὡς ἄτοπον οὖσαν, οὕτω καὶ ἐνταῦθα τὰ ῥήματα ἀνομίαν ἐκάλεσεν ὡς ἄτοπα, τὰ δὲ ῥήματα αὐτοῦ ἀνομίαν καλεῖ καὶ δόλον, οἷς ἐκέχρητο τέκνον καλῶν καὶ
5 διάθεσιν σχηματιζόμενος. Ταῦτα γὰρ δόλος μὲν ἦν ὑποκρινομένου διάθεσιν, ἀνομία δὲ ἐπεὶ ἄτοπα λεγόμενα καὶ κατασκευὴν ἔχοντα τοῦ φόνου τοῦ κατ᾽ αὐτοῦ.

4ᵇ. Οὐκ ἐβουλήθη συνιέναι τοῦ ἀγαθῦναι. Σύνεσιν ἀγαθοσύνης ὅλως οὐκ ἔλαβεν, οὐδὲ ἐδέξατό τινα λογισμὸν ἐπὶ τῆς διανοίας τοῦ τι περὶ ἐμὲ δια-
10 πράξασθαι καλόν. Καλῶς οὖν ἐκάλεσε δόλον τὰ ῥήματα· εἰ γὰρ οὐδ᾽ ὅλως ἀγαθόν τι περὶ αὐτοῦ ποτε ἐβουλεύσατο, δόλος ἦν ἀληθὴς καὶ πρόσχημα τὰ λεγόμενα.

5ᵃ. Ἀνομίαν ἐλογίσατο ἐπὶ τῆς κοίτης αὐτοῦ. Τὸ γὰρ ἐναντίον φησὶν οὐ μόνον οὐκ ἀνεδέξατο ἀγαθὸν λογισμὸν περὶ ἐμοῦ, ἀλλὰ καὶ ἐπὶ τῆς
15 κοίτης, καθ᾽ ὃν δ᾽ ἂν ἀναπαύεσθαι καὶ ἡσυχάζειν ἔδει καιρόν, πᾶν εἴ τι ἄτοπον ἐλογίζετο κατ᾽ ἐμοῦ, τῆς ἡσυχίας τὸν καιρὸν ἐν τοῖς κατ᾽ ἐμοῦ λογισμοῖς ἀσχολῶν, — ὁμοίως κἀνταῦθα ἀνομίαν | τοὺς περὶ αὐτοῦ λογισμοὺς ὡς ἀτόπους καλῶν. Ἀκολούθως δὲ ταῦτα ἐπήγαγε τῷ τὰ ῥήματα τοῦ στόματος αὐτοῦ ἀνομία καὶ δόλος· τὸ γὰρ μήτε συνιέναι τι περὶ αὐτοῦ
20 χρηστὸν καὶ πάντα περὶ αὐτοῦ λογίζεσθαι τὰ ἄτοπα, δόλον ἐδείκνυ σαφῶς τὰ τῆς διαθέσεως ῥήματα, ἐπειδὴ τοίνυν ἄπιστος εἶναι ἐδόκει λέγων καὶ ἀποφαινόμενος περὶ τῶν κατὰ διάνοιαν ὅτι οὐδὲν ἐλογίζετο χρηστὸν καὶ ὅτι πᾶν εἴ τι ἄτοπον ἐνενόει κατ᾽ αὐτοῦ. Καὶ διὰ τοῦτο δόλον ἀποκαλῶν αὐτοῦ τὰ ῥήματα ἐπάγει·

25 5ᵇ. Παρέστη πάσῃ ὁδῷ οὐκ ἀγαθῇ. Δεῖγμα δὲ τοῦτό φησι τὸ πάσαις αὐτὸν ταῖς ἀτόποις πράξεσι κατεγχειρεῖν· ὁδὸν γὰρ οὐκ ἀγαθὴν τὴν ἄτοπον πρᾶξιν καλεῖ. Εἰκότως οὖν ἀφ᾽ ὧν ἔπραττεν, ἀτόπων ὄντων, κατεμάνθανε τοὺς τῆς καρδίας λογισμοὺς καὶ ἠπίστει τοῖς ῥήμασιν.

5ᶜ. Κακίᾳ δὲ οὐ προσώχθισεν. Ἐπίτασίς ἐστι τοῦ ἀνωτέρω τοῦ πα-
30 ρέστη πάσῃ ὁδῷ οὐκ ἀγαθῇ. Ὅλως γάρ φησι τὸ κακὸν οὐκ ἀπεστράφη, — ἵνα εἴπῃ ὅτι καὶ πᾶν εἴ τι ἄτοπον διεπράξατο, καὶ μῖσος αὐτῷ τῆς ἀτόπου πράξεως οὐκ εἰσῆλθεν, — ἀλλ᾽ ἐπέμενε τῇ πράξει σπουδαίως, οὐδὲ τῷ

4 1 Reg. XXVI, 17.

Aᵉ 4 (p. 208, 15): cum filium uocaret.   15-17 (p. 208, 22-24): Augenter, etiam tempus quieti datum pravis et noxiis cogitationibus occupabat.

The words of his mouth were lawlessness and deceit (v. 3). By *lawlessness* he refers to every wrong thing: just as above he referred to his desire as lawlessness for the reason of its being wrong, so too here he referred by *lawlessness* to the words as being wrong; and his words he calls *lawlessness and deceit* because he employed them to use the word "child" and make a pretense of affection. In other words, while it was *deceit* for him to feign affection, it was *lawlessness* since what was said by him was wrong and involved preparations for his murder. *He had no wish to understand and do good:* he had no understanding of goodness whatsoever, and he gave no thought to performing any good to me. So it was good for him to refer to the words as *deceit:* if he never intended any good to him, it was deceit for his words to pretend to be true.

In bed he plotted lawlessness (v. 4): on the contrary, he not only had no good thought about me, but also, even in bed, a time when he should have rested and been at peace, he was plotting every possible wrong against me, spending the time for rest in thoughts against me. Likewise here, too, he used *lawlessness* to refer to thoughts about him as being wrong. Now, it was logical for him to add this to the verse *The words of his mouth were lawlessness and deceit:* his not entertaining any good thoughts about him and planning every wrong for him showed clearly his words of affection to be deceit, since he seemed to be false in claiming and giving an impression of his thinking, because he planned no good and because he meditated on every possible wrong against him. Hence, after calling his words deceit, he went on to say *He took every path that is not good:* his involvement in all these wrong deeds is proof of this (by *path that is not good* referring to the wrong behavior). So it was right that from what he did, wrong as it was, he should learn the thoughts of his heart and not trust his words. *He did not abhor evil.* This is an implication of the above statement *He took every path that is not good:* in no way did he abjure evil—in other words, he even committed every possible wrong deed and gave no entry to hatred of his wrong behavior. Instead, he persisted enthusiastically in his behavior, not | being content

ἐπιτελέσαι πολλάκις αὐτὴν ἀρκεσθεὶς καὶ εἰς μῖσος ἐλθὼν τῆς | ἀτόπου
πράξεως. Οὕτως γὰρ λέγει καὶ Ἀκύλας τὸ κακίᾳ δὲ οὐ προσώχθισε κακὸν
οὐ κατέλιπεν, — ἀντὶ τοῦ Οὐκ ἀπέλαβε τοῦ κακοῦ τὴν πρᾶξιν, ἀλλ᾽ ἐπέ-
μενεν ἐν αὐτῇ.

6ᵃ. Κύριε, ἐν τῷ οὐρανῷ τὸ ἔλεός
σου. Ἐξηγησάμενος τοῦ Σαοὺλ τὸν
τρόπον, τρέπεται λοιπὸν ἐπὶ δοξολογίαν τοῦ Θεοῦ, ἀκολούθως τοῖς
ἄνω τὴν δοξολογίαν ἐπάγων οἰονεὶ λέγων ὅτι
τῇ κακίᾳ προστετηκὼς καὶ ἀεὶ τούτου
Μέγας δὲ σύ, ὡς ἀληθῶς, καὶ μεγάλη σου ἡ φιλανθρωπία, ὃς ἐκείνου
τε τοιαῦτα ποιοῦντος ἀνέχῃ καὶ ἡμᾶς
τῶν τοσούτων ῥύῃ κακῶν ἐν μέσαις
ταῖς ἐπιβουλαῖς καὶ τοῖς κινδύνοις
στρεφομένους. Τοῦτο γάρ ἐστι καὶ περὶ ἐκείνους ἀνεξικάκως διακειμένου καὶ
ἡμῶν πολλὴν ποιουμένου τὴν ἐπιμέλειαν.

Domine, in caelo misericordia
tua. Expositis Saul moribus, ad
laudes Dei conuertit sermonis
officium.
Τοιοῦτος μὲν ἐκεῖνος οὕτως
τὴν μελέτην ποιούμενος,
Magna, inquit, est et ingens
tua bonitas, qui et illius pro patientia dissimulas iniquitatem et
nos de medio insidiarum eius pe-
culiari tuitione subducis.

6ᵇ. Καὶ ἡ ἀλήθειά σου καὶ ἕως
τῶν νεφελῶν. Συνήθως τῷ ἐλέῳ τὴν
ἀλήθειαν ἐπισυνῆψεν, | τὴν ἀληθῆ
λέγων καὶ βεβαίαν τοῦ Θεοῦ φιλανθρωπίαν. Τὸ δὲ ἐν τῷ οὐρανῷ καὶ
ἕως τῶν νεφελῶν μεγαλύνων τοῦ
Θεοῦ τὴν φιλανθρωπίαν τοῖς ἐπαίνοις ἔφη, ἵνα εἴπῃ ὅτι Μεγάλη τις
καὶ ὑπὲρ ἡμᾶς ἡ φιλανθρωπία σου
καὶ ἡ χρηστότης, ἀπὸ τοῦ πλεῖστον
καὶ τὰς νεφέλας.

Et ueritas tua usque ad nubes
Vera est, inquit, et non est incerta
et dubia misericordia tua, | ac si
diceret: Grandis est in nos tua
bonitas, grandis clementia cuius
mensura astra contingat. Caelum
autem ac nubes posuit, eo quod
nihil his uidetur apud nos esse
sublimius.
ὅσον εἶναι ὑπὲρ ἡμᾶς τὸν οὐρανὸν

7ᵃ. Καὶ ἡ δικαιοσύνη σου ὡσεὶ ὄρη Θεοῦ. Οὐ μόνον δέ φησιν ἡ φιλανθρωπία σου μεγάλη, ἀλλὰ καὶ ἡ δικαιοσύνη· φιλανθρωπεύεται γὰρ ὑπερβαλλόντως τοὺς ἀξίους καὶ τὸ δίκαιον νέμει ἑκάστῳ. Κἀνταῦθα δὲ πάλιν
τῆς δικαιοσύνης τὸ μέγεθος παραστῆσαι βουλόμενος ὄρεσιν αὐτὴν παρα-

---

6ᵃ. Domine — subducis: A, fol. 11ᶜ; B, fol. 13ᵃ.　　6 expossitis AB　　13 di-
simulas A　　15 tutione A

6ᵇ. Et ueritas — sublimius: A, fol. 11ᶜ; B, fol. 13ᵃ⁻ᵇ.　　19 uera est est A
non est] est om. A　　23 conting·at A　　24 posuit] possunt A.

Aᵉ 2-3 (p. 209, 2-3): Quia scilicet non fuerat auersatus malitiam, id est non
oderat.　　19-22 (p. 209, 9-12): More suo misericordiae sociauit ueritatem, ut
certam circa se indu'gentiam Dei et mansuram adserat.

with performing it often or coming to hate his wrongdoing. Aquila, in fact, likewise says, "He did not repudiate evil," for *He took every path that is not good*—that is, Far from giving up the practice of evil, he persisted in it.

Lord, your mercy is in heaven (v. 5). After commenting on Saul's behavior, he now turns to praise of God, logically appending to the above a hymn of praise, as if to say, That man is of such a kind as to hold fast to evil and ever meditate on it, whereas you are mighty, to be sure, and great is your lovingkindness, because despite his doing such things, you show patience, and you rescue us from such troubles when we are caught up in the schemes and perils. It is, in fact, characteristic of you to be patient with them and show us close attention. *Your truth extends as far as the clouds.* He frequently associated truth with mercy, saying that God's lovingkindness is true and unwavering. He said *in heaven* and *as far as the clouds* to magnify God's lovingkindness with praises, as if to say, Your lovingkindness and goodness are great and beyond us to the extent that heaven and the clouds are beyond us.

Your righteousness like God's mountains (v. 6): not only is it your lovingkindness that is great, but also your righteousness. He shows lovingkindness in surpassing fashion to the worthy and distributes justice to each. Here, too, in turn in his wish to present the magnitude of his righteousness he compares it to mountains, | not for us to think that God's righteousness is of that kind,

βάλλει, οὐχ ἵνα τοιαῦτα εἶναι μόνον οἰηθῶμεν τὴν τοῦ Θεοῦ δικαιοσύνην, ἀλλὰ τὸ μέγεθος τῶν ἐπαίνων ἀπὸ τῶν παρ' ἡμῖν νομιζομένων μεγάλων ποιούμενος. Τὸ δὲ ἡ δικαιοσύνη σου ὡς ὄρη Θεοῦ φησιν, οὐχὶ τὴν τοῦ Θεοῦ δικαιοσύνην ὁμοίαν εἶναι ὄρεσιν ἑτέρου θεοῦ βουλόμενος, ἀλλ' ἀντὶ
5 τοῦ σοῦ. Ἰδίωμα γάρ ἐστι τοῦτο ἑβραϊκόν, τὸ περὶ τοῦ αὐτοῦ διαλεγόμενον ὥσπερ ἐναλλαγὴν προσώπων ποιεῖσθαι· ὅθεν καὶ ἐν τοῖς τῆς καινῆς διαθήκης πολλάκις εὑρίσκεται ἐκ τοῦ ἑβραϊκοῦ ἰδιώματος διὰ τῶν μακαρίων ἀποστόλων μετακομισθέν, ὡς ἐν τῇ πρὸς Ῥωμαίους τὸ τοῦ ὁρισθέντος υἱοῦ Θεοῦ ἐν δυνάμει κα|τὰ πνεῦμα ἁγιωσύνης ἐξ ἀναστάσεως νεκρῶν, Ἰησοῦ
10 Χριστοῦ τοῦ κυρίου ἡμῶν, ἀντὶ τοῦ εἰπεῖν ἐκ τῆς ἀναστάσεως αὐτοῦ τῆς ἐκ νεκρῶν. Εἰ καὶ νῦν σφόδρα αὐτῷ μέλει τοῦ νέμειν ἑκάστῳ τὸ δίκαιον, τίνος ἕνεκεν πολλοὶ μὲν καὶ ἕτεροι πλείστων ἀδίκως πειρῶνται κακῶν, καὶ σὺ δὲ αὐτὸς μάτην ἐν πολλαῖς ἐξετάξῃ συμφοραῖς, ἑξῆς ἐπάγει.

7ᵇ. Τὰ κρίματά σου ὡσεὶ ἄβυσσος πολλή. Τὰ βουλεύματα αὐτοῦ φησι
15 καὶ τὰ δόγματα, οἷς κεχρημένος κρίνει καὶ ἐξετάζει τοὺς ἀνθρώπους, ἀμέτρητά ἐστι δίκην ἀβύσσου· διὰ τοῦτο οὐ δυνατὸν ἐξευρεῖν τίνος ἕνεκεν συγχωρεῖ πολλάκις δικαίους πάσχειν ὑπὸ ἀδίκων, εὑρίσκω δὲ ταῦτα οὕτως ἔχοντα ἐκ τῶν κατ' ἐμέ. Ὅτι μὲν γὰρ πολλή τις αὐτοῦ ἡ κηδεμονία καὶ ἡ περὶ ἡμᾶς πρόνοια δῆλον ἐξ ὧν οὐδέποτέ τι ἀνήκεστον παθεῖν ἡμᾶς συνε-
20 χώρησεν, τίνος δὲ ἕνεκεν οὐκ ἐν παντελεῖ καθίστησιν ἀνέσει, ἀλλ' ἐᾷ τέως ὑπ' ἐκείνων ἀδίκως διώκεσθαι, ἀκριβῶς εὑρίσκειν οὐ δύναμαι. Διὰ τοῦτο τὰ κρίματά σου ἀβύσσου μοι πάσης ἀνεφικτότερα εἶναι δοκεῖ. Ἐκπλαγεὶς τοίνυν πρότερον μὲν τὴν φιλανθρωπίαν τοῦ Θεοῦ καὶ τὴν χρηστότητα, ἔπειτα τὴν δικαιοσύνην, εἶτα καὶ πρὸς τὸ ἀντιπῖπτον ἀποκρινόμενος καὶ δεδωκὼς τούτου
25 τὸν λόγον, τίνος ἕνεκεν τοῦ δικαίου φροντίζων πολλάκις συγχωρεῖ δικαίους ὑπὸ ἀδίκων διώκεσθαι, ἐντεῦθεν λοιπὸν πλείονα ποιε|ῖται τὸν λόγον περὶ τῆς τοῦ Θεοῦ προνοίας, βουλόμενος δεῖξαι ὅτι κήδεται πάντων καὶ σφόδρα αὐτῷ μέλει. Ἐφαίνετο γὰρ διὰ τούτων οὐ περιορῶν τοὺς ἀνθρώπους ἀλλ' ἀρρήτῳ τινὶ λόγῳ τὰ καθ' ἡμᾶς οἰκονομούμενος καὶ διὰ τοῦτο μὴ παρέχων ὀξεῖαν πολλάκις
30 τοῖς πάσχουσι τῶν λυπηρῶν τὴν ἀπαλλαγήν. Διὰ τοῦτο ἑξῆς φησιν·

7ᶜ. Ἀνθρώπους καὶ κτήνη σώσεις, Κύριε. Δῆλον γάρ φησιν ὅτι αὐτὸς οἰκονομῶν τι κάλλιστον ταῦτα συγχωρεῖς, ἀκατάληπτα δὲ καὶ ἀνέφικτά σου τὰ κρίματα, ἐξ ὧν τοσαύτη τίς ἐστιν ἡ πρόνοιά σου καὶ ἡ κηδεμονία ὡς μὴ μόνον τοὺς ἀνθρώπους αὐτῆς ἀπολαύειν, ἀλλὰ γὰρ ἤδη καὶ μέχρι τῶν
35 κτηνῶν αὐτὴν κεχύσθαι. Εἶτα ἀκολούθως ἐπήγαγεν·

8-10 Rom. I, 4   18-30 cf. in Habacuc 1, 1-2 (P. G., LXVI, 428 B).

11. 27 μέλλει ms.

Aᵉ 28-33 (p. 210, 2-5)... homanorum actuum concertationes et immeritas erumnas dispensas, licet tamen haec te facere prouidenter.

but to achieve magnitude in praise from things thought great by us. By the statement *Your righteousness like God's mountains* he does not mean that God's righteousness is like the mountains of another god, meaning instead yours; it is a Hebrew idiom for the one speaking about himself to make a change of person—hence, even in the New Testament it is found imported from the Hebrew idiom by the blessed apostles, as in the statement in the letter to the Romans, "who was appointed Son of God in power according to the spirit of holiness by resurrection from the dead, Jesus Christ our Lord," as if to say, By his resurrection from the dead.[6] If in this case, too, it is very much within his care to distribute justice to each, why it is that many others unfairly experience a great number of troubles while you yourself idly test them with numerous calamities, the sequel goes on to explain. *Your judgments are like the great deep:* his decisions and decrees, which he applies in judging and examining human beings, are immeasurable, like the deep. Hence, it is impossible to find out why he allows righteous people often to suffer at the hands of the unrighteous, as I find happening in my own case: while the fact that his care and providence for us is wonderful is clear from his never allowing our sufferings to be unbearable, I am unable to discover precisely why he does not leave us in perfect peace but permits us for a time to be pursued unjustly by them. Hence, *your judgments* strike me as more inaccessible than any *deep.*

So, astonished first by God's lovingkindness and goodness, then by his righteousness, then also responding to the objection and offering an explanation as to why in his care for justice he often allows the just to be persecuted by the unjust, he finally at this point treats of God's providence in his wish to prove that he cares for all things and they are very much his concern. It emerges from this, you see, that far from overlooking human beings, he manages our situation with ineffable consideration, and for this reason in many cases he does not provide relief from hardships to those suffering. Hence, he goes on to say *You will save human beings and livestock, Lord:* it is clear that in your excellent conduct of affairs you personally allow this to happen, and that your judgments are beyond our grasp and understanding, as a result of which your providence and care are so wonderful that not only do human beings benefit from them, but also they are even bestowed upon livestock. He then, in the same vein, continues with | *How you extended your mercy, O*

---

6. Rom 1:4. The idiomatic Hebrew usage here that Theodore claims to find is not the change in person (the polite indefinite), but the use of *el* (which LXX takes to be "God") as a superlative to give us "the towering mountains."

8ᵃ. Ὡς ἐπλήθυνας τὸ ἔλεός σου, ὁ Θεός. Οὐκοῦν φησι μεγά|λη μέν σου
ἀληθῶς ἡ χρηστότης καὶ ἡ πρόνοια, εἰ καὶ μέχρι τῶν κτηνῶν ταύτην **
οὐκ ἐνῆν δὲ τὸν οὕτω πάντων τῆς συστάσεως κηδόμενον, ὡς ἑκάστοτε τὰ
πρὸς διατροφὴν αὐτῶν δαψιλῶς διδόναι, διὰ τῶν καθόλου σαφῆ τῆς οἰκείας
προνοίας παρεχόμενον τὴν ἀπόδειξιν, ἐν τοῖς κατὰ μέρος τοὺς ἀνθρώπους   5
περιορᾶν μάτην ἀπολλυμένους, — ὥστε δῆλον ὅτι ἔστι τις ἄρρητος καὶ ἀνέ-
φικτος λόγος δι᾽ ὃν ταῦτα γίνεσθαι συγχωρεῖς. Εἰρηκὼς δὲ ὅτι πολλὴ ἡ
τοῦ Θεοῦ φιλανθρωπία φθάνουσα καὶ μέχρι τῶν κτηνῶν, ἵνα μὴ δόξῃ ἰσό-
τητος μεταδιδόναι παρὰ τῷ Θεῷ τοῖς κτήνεσι πρὸς τοὺς ἀνθρώπους, λέγει
καὶ τὸ τῶν ἀνθρώπων ἐξαίρετον καί φησιν·   10

8ᵇ. Οἱ δὲ υἱοὶ τῶν ἀνθρώπων ἐν σκέπῃ τῶν πτερύγων σου ἐλπίζουσιν.
Καὶ κοινῶς μέν φησιν ἀπολαύει τά τε κτήνη καὶ οἱ ἄνθρωποι τῆς σῆς κηδεμονίας καθὰ κἀκεῖνα δημιουργῆσαί τε ἠξίωσας καὶ ζωῆς αὐτοῖς μεταδοῦναι
ἠβουλήθης, καὶ τῆς προνοίας αὐτὰ καταξιοῖς τῆς σῆς, τὸ διαμένειν αὐτοῖς
χαριζόμενος δι᾽ ἐκείνων ἅπερ ἀπὸ τῆς γῆς ἀναδίδοσθαι πρὸς τὴν σύστα-   15
σιν αὐτῶν πεποίηκας. Οἱ δέ γε τῶν ἀνθρώπων υἱοί, τουτέστιν οἱ ἄνθρωποι,
ἔχουσί τι πλέον καὶ ἐξαίρετον παρ᾽ ἐκεῖνα, τὸ ἐπὶ τῇ βοηθείᾳ ἐλπίζειν
τῇ σῇ. Σκέπην γὰρ τῶν πτερύγων καλεῖ τὴν βοήθειαν ἐκ μεταφορᾶς τῶν
ὀρνίθων, ἃ τῇ σκέπῃ τῶν πτερύγων ἔνδον σκέπει τοὺς νεοσ|σοὺς ** Βού-
λεται δὲ εἰπεῖν ὅτι τοῖς ** ος τι δέδωκας, τὴν γνῶσιν τὴν σὴν καὶ τὰ   20
ἐντεῦθεν καλά· ἐκεῖνα μὲν γὰρ ἄλογα γενόμενα ἐστέρηται τούτου, Θεὸν
γνωρίζειν οὐκ ἔχοντα δύναμιν, — τουτουσὶ δὲ λογικοὺς πεποιηκώς, φύσιν
αὐτοῖς καὶ δύναμιν δέδωκας τοῦ δύνασθαι τῆς σῆς ἐφικνεῖσθαι γνώσεως.
Καλῶς οὖν τὸ ἐλπίζουσιν ἀντὶ τοῦ γινώσκουσιν εἶπε, τοῦτο βουληθεὶς παραστῆσαι ὅτι τὰ μὲν κτήνη τῶν κοινῶν ἀπολαύει μόνον καὶ τῶν ἐν τῇ φύσει   25
δοθέντων αὐτοῖς τὴν ἀρχήν, οἱ δὲ ἄνθρωποι καὶ γινώσκειν σε ὡς Θεὸν καὶ
κηδεμόνα λαβόντες παρά σου καὶ τὸ ἐλπίζειν ἐπί σοι ὡς εὐεργέτῃ διὰ
τούτου κτησάμενοι, ἀπολαύουσι καὶ ἰδικῶν πολλῶν τῶν κατὰ μέρος, ὅσαπερ
αὐτοῖς τὸ βέβαιον τῆς εἰς σε ἐλπίδος παρέχειν ἐπίσταται.

---

2 vox una effluxit humore et blattis fere deleta, supple e. g. ἐκτείνεις
19-20 litterae plures ceciderunt codice corrupto; post τοῖς supple e. g. ἀνθρώποις
μεῖζον(os).

Aᵉ   3-4 (p. 210, 7-9): Non ergo uerisimile ut tu homines neglegas, qui
mutis animalibus consules.   17 ss. (p. 210, 10-14): Sub generali prouidentiae
tuae bono, quo creaturas cunctas susteneas, hominem rationis ussu et tui notitia
praestare fecisti... alarum tuarum sperabunt, pro Intellegent te et cognoscent te.

God! (v. 7). While your goodness and providence are therefore really wonderful if you extend them even to livestock, it would not be possible for the
one showing so much care for the welfare of all as in each instance to make
generous provision for their nourishment, in every case giving clear proof of
his providence, yet to overlook in some instances the unnecessary death of
some people. So it is clear that there is a certain ineffable and incomprehen-
sible plan by which you allow this to happen.

After saying that God's wonderful lovingkindness anticipates our needs
and reaches even to livestock, lest the impression be given that it be conferred by God equally on livestock as on human beings, he mentions also
human beings' pride of place in the words *Human beings will hope in the
shelter of your wings:* both the livestock and the people benefit together from
your care, just as you deigned to create both and wished to share life with
them, and vouchsafed them your providence, granting them survival through
the things that you caused to spring from the earth for their sustenance. Now,
human beings—that is, people—have a further and special place among
them, hoping in your help (by *shelter of your wings* referring to that help as a
metaphor from birds, which shield their chicks in the shelter of their wings).
He means, You gave human beings something more, knowledge of you and
the good things stemming from that, depriving brute beasts of that, so that
they do not have the power to know God; in making them rational you also
gave them a nature and capacity to be able to achieve knowledge of you. So
he was right to say *they will hope* in the sense "they know," meaning this to
convey that while the livestock enjoy only what is common to both and what
was given to them by nature in the beginning, human beings also receive
from you knowledge of you as God and carer and acquire hope in you as
benefactor through this, and for their part enjoy also many particular advan-
tages calculated to promote in them firmness of hope in you. |

9ᵃ. Μεθυσθήσονται ἀπὸ πιότητος τοῦ οἴκου σου. Ἔχουσι δέ φησιν ἐν-τεῦθεν καὶ τὸ ἀπολαύειν τῶν ἐν τῷ οἴκῳ σου λειτουργικῶν τε καὶ θυ-5 σιῶν· πιότητα γὰρ τοῦ οἴκου τοῦ Θεοῦ καλεῖ τῶν λειτουργιῶν τὴν ἐκ-πλήρωσιν, ἐπειδὴ δόξα καὶ εὐθηνία ἦν τοῦ οἴκου τὸ τὰς προσηκούσας ἐν αὐτῷ λειτουργίας ἀποπληροῦ-10 σθαι. Ἔστι δὲ καὶ τοῦτο ἐξαίρετον τῶν ἀνθρώπων· γνῶσιν γὰρ οὐκ ἔχοντα τοῦ Θεοῦ τὰ κτήνη, οὔτε οἶκον οἶδεν ἀφωρισμένον Θεῷ, οὔτε ἱερέας ἔχει Θεοῦ, οὔτε λειτουργίαν 15 ἐπίσταται, οὔτε τόπον | τῆς τοιαύτης συνελεύσεως.

Inebriabuntur ab ubertate domus tuae. De agnitione, inquit, tua hoc illis praecipuum munus accedit, ut colant te ac ministeriis quae in domo tua sunt intersint, sacrificiorumque apparatu ac uictimarum oblationibus perfruantur. *Vbertatem* namque *domus Dei* uocat perfectam ministeriorum atque ordinum disciplinam, *iumenta* autem quae a notitia Dei longe sunt neque domum Dei norunt neque sacerdotes neque sacrificia.

9ᵇ. Καὶ τὸν χείμαρρουν τῶν τρυφῶν ποτιεῖς αὐτούς. Ἔχουσι δὲ καὶ τοῦτο ἐξαίρετον τὸ ἀθρόως πολλῶν τῶν παρά σου τρυφῶν ἀπολαύειν. Καὶ οὐκ εἶπε «τρυφῆς» ἀλλὰ τρυ-φῶν πληθυντικῶς, ἐπειδὴ πολλὰ καὶ 20 διάφορα τὰ ἀπὸ τῆς γῆς ἀναδιδόμενα πρὸς τὴν τῶν ἀνθρώπων μετάληψιν· ποτά τε καὶ ἐδέσματα σπερμάτων διάφορα καὶ καρπῶν ποικιλίαι, καὶ ὅλως πολλή τίς ἐστι καὶ διάφορος καὶ πολυειδὴς ἡ τῶν ἀγαθῶν μετάληψις, ὧνπερ ἀπολαύειν συμβαίνει τοὺς ἀνθρώπους πολλὴν κεκτημένους ἐντεῦθεν τὴν τρυφήν, καὶ οὐχ ὥσπερ ἐπὶ 25 τῶν κτηνῶν μονοειδής τίς ἐστι τῶν ἐκ τῆς γῆς ἀναδιδομένων ἡ τροφή. Χεί-μαρρουν δὲ τῶν τρυφῶν εἶπε τὸ ἀθρόον τῆς παρουσίας σημαίνων, ὅτι μὴ πολλὰ ὄντα καὶ διάφορα ἐν διαφόροις χορηγεῖται τοῖς καιροῖς, νῦν μὲν τούτων ἀναδιδομένων, νῦν δὲ ἄλλων, μετ᾽ ὀλίγον δὲ αὖθις ἑτέρων, ἀλλ᾽ ὑπὸ τοὺς αὐτοὺς καιροὺς ἡ πάντων ἀνάδοσις γίνεται ταῖς αὐταῖς τροπαῖς πάν-30 των συμπληρουμένων τῶν καρπῶν, καίτοι πολλῶν καὶ διαφόρων. Καὶ οὐκ εἶπεν «ψωμιεῖς» ἀλλὰ ποτιεῖς, ἵνα δείξῃ τὸ ἄφθονον καὶ εὐμαρὲς τῆς

Torrentem uero *uoluptatis* dixit habundantiam fructuum quibus homines nutriuntur.

Inebriabuntur — nutriuntur: A, fol. 11ᵈ; B, fol. 13ᵇ.   3 illis *om.* A monus A   4 accidit A   colant] tollat A *fortasse pro* colat   5 domu A 6 sacrificiorumquae A¹   apparatum A   7 ablationibus A   8 ubertatem — 10 disciplinam *affert* Aᵉ (p. 210, 18-19)   9-10 minister.] miniteriorum A sacrorum Aᵉ   11 disc.] perfectam *add.* Aᵉ   iu**menta B   12-13 domus A 18 dexit A *ex* dixe*.

Aᵉ 26-202, 4 (p. 210, 22-26): Pro Summa felicitate reficis, ut affluentiam et facilitatem largitionis diuinae pariter indicaret potus nomine, quo nihil est in ussu nostro facilius.

They will be intoxicated with the rich fare of your house (v. 8): they thus will be able also to enjoy the rites of worship and sacrifice in your house (by *rich fare of the house* referring to the performance of worship of God, since the glory and prosperity of the house was the performance of due rites in it). Now, this also is a privilege of human beings; livestock, not having knowledge of God, have no experience of a house dedicated to God, have no priests of God, nor are they familiar with worship or a place of assembly like that. *And you will give them to drink of the flood of your delicacies:* they also have this privilege of enjoying in abundance many delicacies from you. He said not "delicacy," but *delicacies,* in the plural, since many and varied are the things that spring from the earth for people's consumption—food and drink, many and varied kinds of seeds and crops: the consumption of good things is manifold, diverse, and varied, and it belongs to people to enjoy them by finding great delicacy therein; and it is not a case of a single kind of nourishment springing from the earth, as with livestock. He spoke of a *flood of delicacies* to suggest the abundance of the offering, that the supply was not many and varied at different times, at one time springing up from these crops, at another time from others, and shortly after from still others; instead, in the same seasons the yield of them all came at the same times with all the crops maturing, though many and varied. He said not "You will feed them crumbs," but *You will give them to drink* to bring out the abundance and ease of | partaking, especially as drinking is a simple matter for the one wishing to

μεταδόσεως, ἐπείπερ εὐχερές ἐστι μετα|λαμβάνειν ποτοῦ τὸν βουλόμενον
καὶ οὐχ ὥσπερ * * ἐδεσμάτων ἐγχρονίζοντα καὶ πόνων δεόμενον εἴς τε τὴν
τῶν ὄψων σκευασίαν, καὶ μετὰ τοῦτο τὴν μάσησιν, τὴν πέψιν, τὴν ἔκκρι-
σιν. Εἶτα ἀκολούθως ἐπάγει·

10ᵃ. ῞Οτι παρά σοι πηγὴ ζωῆς. Παρέχεις οὖν φησι τούτων ἀθρόον τοῖς 5
ἀνθρώποις τὴν μετάληψιν, ἐπείπερ ἀφθόνως αὐτοῖς παρέχεις τὴν ζωὴν καὶ
μονονουχὶ πηγάζειν αὐτὴν ἐδοκίμασας, οὕτω διὰ πάντων αὐτὴν συρρεῖν ἐπ᾽
αὐτὴν παρασκευάζων· πηγὴν γὰρ ζωῆς ἐκάλεσε τὸ ἄφθονον τῆς χορηγίας,
ἀπὸ τοῦ ἄφθονον ἀεὶ ἀπὸ τῶν πηγῶν προχεῖσθαι τὸ νᾶμα. Τοῦτο οὖν
εἶπεν ὅτι Πηγάζεις ἡμῖν τὴν ζωήν, ἀφθόνως αὐτὴν παρέχων διὰ τοῦ πλή- 10
θους καὶ τῆς ποικιλίας τῶν διδομένων ἡμῖν παρά σου πρὸς σύστασίν τε
καὶ ζωήν, — οὐχ, ὥς τινες ᾠήθησαν, ὅτι πηγὴν ζωῆς καλεῖ τὸν Υἱόν. Τοῦτο
γὰρ ἔθος τῇ γραφῇ, καὶ μάλιστα τῷ μακαρίῳ Δαυίδ, τὸ λέγειν καὶ θησαυροὺς εἶναι τῶν δημιουργημάτων — ὡς ὅταν λέγῃ Ὁ ἐξάγων ἀνέμους ἐκ θησαυρῶν αὐτοῦ — καὶ θησαυροὺς τιμωριῶν — ὡς ὅταν λέγῃ Καὶ τῶν κεκρυμμένων 15
σου ἐπλήσθη ἡ γαστὴρ αὐτῶν, — ἵνα δείξῃ ἀφθόνως ἅπαντα αὐτῷ παρόντα
ὥσπερ ἀπό τινων θησαυρῶν ἀνελλειπῶς προφέροντος ὅσα βούλεται. Οὕτω
καὶ πηγὴν ζωῆς τὸ τῆς ζωῆς ἄφθονον καλεῖ· ὥσπερ γὰρ χειμάρρουν τρυφῶν οὐχ ὑπόστασίν τινά φησιν ἀλλὰ τὸ ἀθρόον καὶ δαψιλὲς τῶν διδομένων, οὕτω καὶ πηγὴν ζωῆς οὐχ ὑπόστασίν τινα, ἀλλὰ τὸ ἄφθονον τῆς ζωῆς. 20

10ᵇ. ᾿Εν τῷ φωτί σου ὀψόμεθα φῶς. Καὶ τοῦτο πάλιν τινὲς οὕτως ἐξέ-
λαβον· ἐν τῷ φωτί σού φησιν, ἐν τῷ Υἱῷ, ὀψόμεθα φῶς, τὸ Πνεῦμα τὸ
ἅγιον. ῎Εχει γὰρ οὐ ταύτην τὴν ἔννοιαν· ἄτοπον γὰρ σοφίσμασι κεχρημένους τὰ οἰκεῖα κατασκευάζειν δόγματα, κἂν τὴν ἀλήθειαν τοῖς δόγμασι
προσεῖναι συμβαίνῃ — δυνατὸν γὰρ μετὰ ἀληθείας τῆς προσηκούσης ποιεῖσ- 25
θαι μάλιστα τῶν τῆς ἀληθείας δογμάτων τὴν σύστασιν.
῝Ο δὲ βούλεται εἰπεῖν τοιοῦτόν ἐστιν. Οὐδὲν τῶν ὄντων ὁρᾶν ἄνευ φωτὸς δυνάμεθα· ὅταν γὰρ ἔρημοι τυγχάνωμεν φωτὸς ἐν σκότῳ καθεστῶτες
οὐδενὸς ἔχομεν τῶν παρόντων διάκρισιν, φωτὸς δὲ παρόντος ἅπαντα ὁρῶμέν τε καὶ διακρίσει ὑποβάλλομεν. Πρὸς οὖν τὸ θεωρεῖν τὰ ἄλλα χρήζομεν 30
τοῦ φωτός, αὐτὸ δὲ τὸ φῶς οὐκέτι ἑτέρου τινὸς χρήζει πρὸς τὸ ὁρᾶσθαι
ὑφ᾽ ἡμῶν, ἀλλ᾽ αὐτῷ τῷ φωτὶ συνεργῷ χρώμενοι οὕτω τε τὸ ὁρᾶν προσ-
λαμβάνοντες διὰ τοῦ φωτὸς ἅπαντά τε θεωροῦμεν τὰ λοιπὰ καὶ δὴ

14-15 Ps. CXXXIV, 7ᶜ   15-16 XVI, 14ᶜ.

2 * * litterae plures perierunt.

Aᵉ 10ᵃ (p. 210, 27-211, 4): In morem aquarum sine cessatione manantium
ea quae sunt uel ussui nostro uel uoluntati necessaria subministras, liberalitate (-tatis ms) inriguam uitam sustentans.

do so, unlike the time taken in eating and the effort required for preparation of the ingredients, then chewing, digesting, and passing.

He then proceeds, in the same vein, to say *Because with you is a fountain of life* (v. 9): you provide human beings with an abundant share of these things, since you abundantly provide them with life and see fit for it to gush up, as it were, thus in every way causing it to be in flood (by *fountain* referring to the abundance of the supply—a metaphor from an abundant flood constantly issuing from fountains). His meaning is, therefore, You flood us with life, abundantly supplying us with it from the great number and variety of what is given us by you for sustenance and life. By *fountain of life* he does not mean the Son, as some commentators thought; it is the custom of Scripture, and especially blessed David, to use this expression of the storehouses of created things, as when he says, "Who brings forth the winds from his storehouses," and of the storehouses of punishments, as when he says, "And their belly is filled with what is hidden,"[7] so as to present everything as abundantly present to him as though he unfailingly offers from storehouses of some kind whatever he wishes. Similarly, by *a fountain of life* he refers to the abundance of life: just as the *flood of delicacies* is not a person but the abundant and generous supply of what is given, so too *a fountain of life* is not a person but the abundance of life.

In your light we shall see light. This, likewise, some commentators took in the same fashion: *in your light,* in the Son, *we shall see light,* the Holy Spirit. In fact, it does not have this sense: it would be wrong for those having recourse to wordplay to devise their own doctrines, even if there happens to be truth in their doctrines; it is possible to come up with the basis of the doctrines of truth, especially with truth available. What he means is something like this: Without light we can see nothing that exists, for when we are deprived of light and plunged into darkness, we have no recognition of what is at hand; whereas when light is available, we see and discern by recognition. So for discerning other things we need light, whereas light itself requires nothing else any longer for our being able to see; instead, with the aid of light itself we succeed in seeing everything through light and discern everything, including even | light itself. The verse *In your light we shall*

---

7. Pss 135:7; 17:14.

καὶ αὐτὸ τὸ φῶς. Τὸ οὖν ʾΕν τῷ φωτί σου ὀψόμεθα φῶς τοῦτο βούλεται εἰπεῖν ὅτι ἐν αὐτῷ τῷ φωτὶ ἀπολαύομέν σου τοῦ φωτός, τουτέστι
τὸ φῶς τὸ δοθὲν ἡμῖν παρά σου παρέχει ἡμῖν καὶ τὸ ὁρᾶν καὶ τὸ ὁρῶν-
τας αὐτοῦ πρό|τερον ἀπολαύειν — ὡς εἶναι διπλῆν ἡμῖν ἐκ τοῦ φωτὸς τὴν
5 χάριν, τήν τε τῶν ἄλλων θέαν καὶ τὴν αὐτοῦ τοῦ φωτὸς ἀπόλαυσιν. Τοῦτο
οὖν ἠβουλήθη εἰπεῖν ὅτι καὶ τὴν ζωὴν ἄφθονον ἡμῖν παρέχεις καὶ δέδωκας
ἡμῖν σύντομον τοῦ φωτὸς τὴν ἀπόλαυσιν, ἐν αὐτῷ τῷ φωτὶ τὸ ἀπολαύειν
σου τοῦ φωτὸς χαρισάμενος, ἵνα μὴ ἑτέρου τινὸς χρήζωμεν πάλιν πρὸς
τὴν τοῦ φωτὸς θέαν ὥσπερ ἐπὶ τῶν ἑτέρων, ἀλλʾ αὐτὸ τὸ φῶς ἔχοντες
10 ἀρκοῦν καὶ πρὸς τὴν οἰκείαν θέαν, εὐθὺς ἐν τῇ τοῦ φωτὸς ἀνατολῇ τό τε
ὁρᾶν προσλαμβάνομεν καὶ τὸ αὐτοῦ ἀπολαύειν — διόλου τῆς δωρεᾶς τοῦ
Θεοῦ τὸ δαψιλὲς καὶ ἄφθονον παραστῆσαι βουληθείς. Διὸ τούτων μάλιστα
ἐμνημόνευσε τῶν δύο, τῆς τε ζωῆς — ἐξ ἧς ὅτι τὸ εἶναί τε ἡμῖν αὐτὸ καὶ
συνεστάναι παρέσχεν ἐδήλου — καὶ τῆς τοῦ φωτὸς ἀπολαύσεως, διʾ ἧς ἐγνώ-
15 ριξε τὸ τερπνὸν τῆς ζωῆς. Τοῦτο δὲ μέγιστον ἐν τῇ ζωῇ μάλιστα καὶ
χρησιμώτατον ἡμῖν ἡ τοῦ φωτὸς ἀπόλαυσις, ὡς καὶ αὐτὸ περιττὸν ἡμῖν
τὸ ζῆν ἄνευ τῆς χρείας του φωτός· ἐν γὰρ τῷ φωτὶ πρόσεστιν ἡμῖν καὶ
τὸ βαδίζειν, καὶ τὸ μεταχειρίζεσθαι τὰ πρακτέα, καὶ τὸ διακρίνειν τὰ
παρόντα, καὶ τὸ ταῖς τέχναις κεχρῆσθαι, — καὶ ὅλως ἐν φωτὶ πάντα δια-
20 πραττόμεθα ὅσαπερ ἂν βουλώμεθα, ἐν αὐτῷ δὲ καὶ τῶν τερπνῶν καὶ
τοιούτων ἔχομεν τὴν διάγνωσιν, καὶ τῶν ὡραίων καὶ μὴ τοιούτων ποιούμεθα
τὴν διάκρισιν. Τοῦτό τε ἡμῖν συντόμως εἰπεῖν πρὸς ἅπαντα χρησιμώτατον
ἐν τῇ ζωῇ καθέστηκεν, δύο τοίνυν τῶν κορυφαίων τῇ μνήμῃ τὴν παντελῆ
τοῦ Θεοῦ περὶ ἡμᾶς ἐξηγήσατο δωρεάν, διὰ πάντων οὐ δημιουργὸν μόνον,
25 ἀλλὰ καὶ προνοητὴν ἐπιδείξας σαφῶς, ἐξ ὧν οὐχ ἡμᾶς πεποίηκε μόνον
ἀλλὰ καὶ ἕτερα πολλὰ ὧν τοῖς μὲν τὸ διαμένειν ἡμῖν καὶ συνεστάναι ἐδω-
ρήσατο, τοῖς δὲ τὸ τερπνὴν καὶ ὠφελιμωτάτην ἔχειν τῆς ζωῆς τὴν ἀπόλαυσιν. Μέχρι δὲ τούτων ἐξηγησάμενος τίνα ἰδιαζόντως ὑπὸ τοῦ Θεοῦ τοῖς
ἀνθρώποις δεδώρηται ὑπὲρ τὰ κτήνη, ἐξηγεῖται καὶ ἐν τοῖς ἀνθρώποις
30 πάλιν τίνα προσήκει ὑπερβολὴν ἔχειν τοὺς δικαίους ὑπὲρ τοὺς λοιποὺς τῶν
ἀνθρώπων. Καὶ τί φησιν;

11ᵃ. Παράτεινον τὸ ἔλεός σου τοῖς γινώσκουσίν σε. ʾΩσπερ δέ φησιν
οἱ ἄνθρωποι ἔχουσί τι πλέον παρὰ τὰ κτήνη, οὕτως ἐχέτωσάν τι πλέον
καὶ ἐν τοῖς ἀνθρώποις οἱ δίκαιοι τοῦ ἐλέους τὴν παράτασιν, ἵνα μὴ δόξῃ
35 ἴση περὶ πάντας εἶναι ἡ φιλανθρωπία, ἀλλὰ γὰρ μετὰ τοῦ δικαίου κατʾ ἀξίαν

Aᵉ 1-2 (p. 211, 5-12): Et uitae nobis amplas opes et uidendi luminis facul-
tatem in ipso lumine contulisti.　　4-6 (p. 211, 14-15): Duo quae sunt maxima
in hominibus conlata memorauit, uitam cum instrumentis suis et ussuram lucis,
sine qua uita esset odibilis.　　32-34 (p. 211, 14-16): Obtat ut iustissimi hominum indulgentius caeteris mortalibus habeantur.

see light means, therefore, By light itself we enjoy your light—that is, The light given us by you provides us with both sight and enjoyment of it once we have seen, as the gift of light to us is twofold, the sight of other things and the enjoyment of light itself. So his meaning is, You provide us with life in abundance and have given us a brief enjoyment of light so that we need nothing else for seeing the light as in the case of the other things, being content with light itself even for our own sight, and thus immediately gaining sight once light dawns and enjoying it.

His meaning was to present the utter generosity and abundance of God's gift—hence his mention of these two things in particular: the light (he made clear that from it he provided us both with existence itself and with sustenance) and enjoyment of the light, through which he conveyed the pleasure of life. Now, this is the greatest and most useful thing for us in life, the enjoyment of light, as living without the help of light would be futile for us: by means of light we are in a position to move about, get involved in what has to be done, discern what befalls us, employ skills—in short, by means of light we do whatever we want; by it we can also discern pleasurable things and the like, and can distinguish between beautiful things and those that are not. In short, he has assigned this as the most useful thing for us in life in every respect, and hence by mention of two principal things he has commented on the totality of God's generosity to us, giving clear evidence in every case not only of a creator but also of a provider, for from them he made not only us but also many other things that he has given, some for our continuance and sustenance, some for us to have a pleasurable and beneficial enjoyment of life.

Having to this point explained what has been given by God to human beings exclusively in preference to livestock, he explains also in turn the superiority that righteous people among human beings enjoy by comparison with the rest of humankind. What does he say? *Extend your mercy to those who know you* (v. 10): just as human beings possess something more than livestock, so too let righteous people among human beings have something more by way of the extent of mercy, lest lovingkindness seem to be equal for all, whereas | the extent seems to be accorded in the case of the righteous in

ἑκάστῳ νεμομένη φαίνηται ἔχουσα ἐπὶ τῶν δικαίων τὴν παράτασιν, διαρκῶς αὐτῆς ἀπολαυόντων ἐκείνων διὰ τὴν ἀξίαν τῆς οἰκείας δικαιοπραγίας. Ἄνω μὲν οὖν τὴν διαφορὰν λέγων τῶν ἀνθρώπων | τὴν πρὸς τὰ κτήνη φησὶν Οἱ δὲ υἱοὶ τῶν ἀνθρώπων ἐν σκέπῃ τῶν πτερύγων σου ἐλπιοῦσι, τουτέστιν Οὕτω κατεσκευάσθησαν παρά σου ὥστε δύνασθαι, εἰ βούλοιντο, 5 καὶ γινώσκειν σε καὶ ἐλπίζειν ἐπί σοι καὶ τῶν ἐνταῦθα ἀπολαύειν καλῶν· ἐνταῦθα δὲ περὶ τῶν ἐπιμελομένων τοῦ πράγματος λέγων καλῶς εἶπε τοῖς γινώσκουσί σε, τουτέστι Τοῖς ἐπιμελομένοις τοῦ πρέποντος κατὰ τὴν ἐναποτεθεῖσαν αὐτοῖς τῇ φύσει δύναμιν παρά σου, τούτοις ἐπέκτεινόν σου τὴν κηδεμονίαν. Διὸ καὶ ὡς προσευχόμενος εἶπε Παράτεινον τοῖς γινώσκουσιν, 10 ἐπειδὴ τοῖς μὲν ἀνθρώποις τὸ πλέον παρὰ τὰ κτήνη καὶ τὸ δύνασθαι γνωρίζειν τὸν Θεὸν ἐν τῇ τῆς φύσεώς ἐστι κατασκευῇ καὶ τῇ τοῦ Θεοῦ δημιουργίᾳ, ἡ δέ γε ὑπεροχὴ τῶν δικαίων ἡ πρὸς τοὺς λοιποὺς τῶν ἀνθρώπων οὐκ ἀπό τινός ἐστιν ἀκολουθίας φυσικῆς, ἀλλὰ προσευχῇ κατορθοῦται καὶ ἀρετῆς ἐκπληρώσει. 15

11ᵇ. Καὶ τὴν δικαιοσύνην σου τοῖς εὐθέσι τῇ καρδίᾳ. Καλῶς ἐπὶ τούτων τὸ ἔλεος καὶ δικαιοσύνην ἐκάλεσεν, ἐπειδὴ καὶ δικαίως ἀπὸ τοῦ τρόπου τῶν παρὰ τοῦ Θεοῦ καλῶν ἀπολαύειν ἤμελλον.

12ᵃ. Μὴ ἐλθέτω μοι ποὺς ὑπερηφανίας. Πόδα ἡ ἑβραῒς καλεῖ τὴν ἐπίβασιν· οὕτω γὰρ καὶ ἀλλαχοῦ Ἐπὶ τὴν Ἰδουμαίαν ἐκτενῶ τὸ ὑπόδημά 20 μου, ἀντὶ τοῦ Ἐπιβήσομαι αὐτῶν καὶ καταπατήσω αὐτούς. Τοῦτο οὖν φησι μὴ ἐλ|θέτω μοι ποὺς ὑπερηφανίας, τουτέστι μὴ ἐπιβαῖέν μου οἱ πολέμιοι.

12ᵇ. Καὶ χεὶρ ἁμαρτωλῶν μὴ σαλεύσαι με. Χεῖρα πάλιν καλεῖ τὴν κράτησιν τῶν πολεμίων, ἀπὸ τῶν μελῶν τὰ προσόντα λέγων καὶ τὰς τῶν μελῶν ἐνεργείας. Μὴ δὲ κρατήσαντές μού φησι σαλεύσαιέν με, περιτρέψαντες 25 ἐπὶ τὰ κακά. Ἀπὸ δὲ τῶν κατὰ τὸν Σαοὺλ εὔχεται καὶ πάσης ἐφόδου πολεμίων ἀπαλλαγῆναι καὶ πάσης κρατήσεως.

13ᵃ. Ἐκεῖ ἔπεσον πάντες οἱ ἐργαζόμενοι τὴν ἀνομίαν. Ἀντὶ τοῦ ἐπὶ τούτου τοῦ πράγματος τῆς ὑπερηφανίας δὲ λέγει * * * ἐκεῖ εἰς τὸν πόδα τῶν ὑπερηφάνων καὶ τὴν χεῖρα τῶν ἁμαρτωλῶν, ἵνα εἴπῃ Ὅτι τοὺς ἁμαρτω- 30 λοὺς ἔθος καὶ ἐν ταῖς τῶν ἐθνῶν ἐπιβάσεσιν ἡττᾶσθαι καὶ κρατεῖσθαι

20-21 LIX, 10ᵇ.

Marg. ext. f. 136ʳ·ᵛ exciso perierunt lemmata atque litterae nonnullae. 24 προσόντα conieci προσ⟨ ⟩τα ms 29 post λέγει spatium uacuum sex aut septem litt.

Aᵉ 12ᵃ (p. 211, 19-212, 1): Pedem pro incursu; sic alibi ait: Super Edumeam extendam calciamentum meum, id est Ascendam super Edumeam. 12ᵇ (p. 212, 2-4): Pro conprehensione; a membris opera officiaque membrorum. Petit ut subito Sauelis incursu liberetur. 13ᵃ (p. 212, 5-8): Hoc est In cursu et comprehensione hostium suorum peccator quique conruit, qui tuo non meretur auxilio liberari.

keeping with their righteousness, since they continue to receive it in accord with their righteous behavior. Above, then, he mentioned the difference between human beings and livestock by saying *Human beings will hope in the shelter of your wings*—that is, They were formed by you so as to be able, if they wished, both to know you and to hope in you, and to enjoy the good things stemming from this. Here, on the other hand, in reference to those attentive to the matter, he put it well in saying *those who know you*—that is, To those attentive to their duty, according to the power you implanted in them by nature, extend your care. Hence, in his prayer he said *Extend to those who know you,* since while to human beings belongs something more than cattle from the formation of their nature and by God's creative act—namely, the ability to know God—the superiority of the righteous compared with the rest of humankind comes not from some natural effect, but is achieved by prayer and the performance of virtue. *And your righteousness to the upright of heart.* In their case he did well to speak of *mercy* and *righteousness,* since it was also right that they should be due to enjoy good things from God on the basis of their behavior.

May the foot of arrogance not come my way (v. 11). By *foot* Hebrew means "stepping on"; elsewhere, likewise, he says, "I shall stretch out my shoe upon Edom"[8]—that is, I shall step on them and trample them down. So he is saying *May the foot of arrogance not come my way*—that is, May the enemies not step on me. *And a sinner's hand not move me.* By *hand,* likewise, he refers to the control of the enemy, speaking of what is proper to the limbs and the operation of the limbs. Let those with power over me, he is saying, not move me, diverting me to evil. He prays to be released from the plotting of Saul and from every attack and all control of the enemy.

All evildoers fell there (v. 12)—that is, in this instance of arrogance … there to the foot of the arrogant and the hand of sinners, as if to say, It is normal for sinners to be vanquished by the stepping of the nations and always fall under the control | of the enemy, since as a result of the deprav-

8. Ps 60:8.

πάντοτε ὑπὸ τῶν πολεμίων, ἐπειδὴ διὰ τὴν τοῦ τρόπου μοχθηρίαν ἔρημοι
τῆς σῆς εἰκότως καθεστήκασι βοηθείας (οὕτω γὰρ λέγει καὶ Σύμμαχος "Ὅπου
πίπτουσι πάντες οἱ ἐργαζόμενοι τὴν ἀνομίαν), μὴ τὰ αὐτὰ ο⟨ῦν⟩ πάθοιμι
ἐκείνοις τοῖς ἁμαρτωλοῖς ὑπὸ τοῖς πολεμίοις γενόμενος.

5   13ᵇ. Ἐξώσθησαν καὶ οὐ μὴ δύνωνται στῆναι. Οἱ γὰρ τοιοῦτοί φησιν,
οἱ τὴν ἀνομίαν ἐργαζόμενοι, οὐχ ἡττῶνται μόνον ὑπὸ τῶν πολεμίων, ἀλλὰ
καὶ ἐξωθοῦνται εἰς τὸ παντελές, ὡς μηκέτι ἀντισχεῖν δυνηθῆναι τοῖς κακοῖς.
Καὶ τοῦτο | τῶν συμβάντων τῷ Σαοὺλ ἐξηγεῖται· καὶ γὰρ κἀκεῖνος ἅμα
τοῖς σὺν αὐτῷ ἐν τῇ τῶν πολεμίων ἐπιβάσει θανάτῳ τε ὑπέπεσε καὶ ἀντι-
10 σχεῖν τοῖς κακοῖς οὐκ ἠδυνήθη.

PSALMVS XXXVI

Πάντες μὲν οἱ ψαλμοὶ τῷ μακαρίῳ Δαυὶδ πρὸς τὴν ὠφέλειαν βλέ-
πουσι τῶν ἀνθρώπων, οὐχ ἑνὶ δὲ
15 τρόπῳ κέχρηται αὐτοῖς· ὅπου μὲν
γὰρ δογματικοὺς ἐκτίθεται λόγους,
ὅπου δὲ ὑμνῳδίας ἀπὸ τῆς δημιουρ-
γίας πλέκει τῷ δεσπότῃ. Ἔστι δὲ
καὶ ὅπου καὶ πράγματα ἐσόμενα
20 ὑποτίθεται, ὁμοῦ τε ἐκεῖνα προφητεύων καὶ τὴν ἀπ' αὐτῶν ὠφέλειαν
ἐργαζόμενος ταῦτα παραινῶν ἃ συμβουλεύειν ἀπὸ τῆς ὑποθέσεως περὶ
ἧς ποιεῖται τὸν λόγον ἡγεῖται κατάλ-
25 ληλον. Ἔστι δὲ ὅπου καὶ ἐκ τῶν
καθ' ἑαυτὸν παιδεύει τοὺς ἀκούοντας,

Omnes quidem psalmos beatus
Dauid ad profectum hominum uti-
litatemque conscripsit, non tamen
omnes ad unum docendi genus
formamque conposuit. Nam in
quibusdam de dogmatibus dispu-
tat, in quibusdam uero ipsam
diuinorum operum dispositionem
ad laudandum Deum materiam
sibi proponit et causam. In aliis
autem, dum praedicit futura pro
rerum ipsarum, quas adnuntiat,
qualitate, quid faciendum, quid
cauendum sit, diligenter inculcat; non numquam etiam sub

8·I Reg. XXXI.

3 οὖν conieci ο⟨ ⟩ ms   7 ἐξωθοῦνται ms.
Omnes — inducitur: A, f. 11ᵈ-12ᵃ; B, fol. 13ᵇ.   11 xxxui in marg. A
12 psamos A¹   13 hominem A   14 * sciripsit A   15 docendumī A   16 conpossuit A   in] hoc A   19 dispossitionem B   24 facendum A¹   26 non
nequam A, litt. equam in rasura.

Aᵉ 8-10 (p. 212, 9-10): Quod Saueli inruentibus Allofilis euenisse manifestum
est.   12 ss. (p. 212, 11-16): Quoniam plerique mortalium afflictione proborum
et impiorum prosperitate turbantur, ut inremuneratas in hac uita uirtutes dese-
rant et uitia consectentur felicia, ad huiusmodi depellendum errorem iste
psalmus conponitur. Cf. Pseudo-Beda (671).

ity of their behavior they are naturally deprived of your help (Symmachus also says, in similar terms, "Where all the evildoers fall"); may I therefore not suffer the same fate as those sinners by becoming subject to the enemy. *They were thrust out; may they be unable to stand:* may such people who are evildoers not only be vanquished by the enemy, but also be completely thrust out, as no longer capable of resisting disaster. This is his comment on what happened to Saul: he, too, together with those of his company, met their death, trampled by the enemy, unable to resist disaster.[9]

PSALM 37

While all the psalms by blessed David have regard to people's benefit, he did not employ in them the one genre. Sometimes, in fact, he develops doctrinal treatises, and sometimes he composes hymns of praise to the Lord from creation. On the other hand, there are other times as well when he also suggests future events, at one and the same time prophesying them and developing the benefit coming from them by recommending what he considers adapted to the theme he is treating. There are times when he also instructs the listeners from his own situation, | teaching what each person's attitude should be

---

9. Cf. 1 Sam 31, where in fact Saul falls on his sword.

διδάσκων ὅπως περὶ τῶν συμβαινόντων ἕκαστον διατίθεσθαι προσήκει
καὶ τί μὲν προσήκει λέγειν ἐν ἁμαρτίαις ἐξεταζόμενον, τί δὲ προσήκει
φθέγγεσθαι ἐν συμφοραῖς καθεστῶτα. Ἔστι δὲ ὅπου καὶ παραινέ-
σεις ἐκτὸς ὑποθέσεως ποιεῖται, ἀπα-
γορεύων ὅσον τε καὶ ἀπέχεσθαι
χρή, συμβουλεύων ἃ πράττειν προ-
σήκει· | οἷος δὴ καὶ οὗτος ὁ ψαλμός.

Οἱ γὰρ πολλοὶ τῶν ἀνθρώπων
πεφύκαμεν, μάλιστα τοὺς πονηροὺς
ὁρῶντες ἐν εὐθηνίᾳ, δάκνεσθαι καὶ
λέγειν ὡς οὐδὲν ὄφελος τῆς δικαιοσύνης. Πλεῖστοι γὰρ τῶν δικαίων ἐν
συμφοραῖς καθεστήκασι, καὶ ταῦτα
ὑπὸ φαύλων ἀνθρώπων πάσχοντες·
τοῦτο δὲ ὃ μάλιστα βαρυτέραν ἐργάζεται τῆς συμφορᾶς τὴν αἴσθησιν,
ἀλλ᾽ οὐδὲ ἐπιβλαβὲς ἡ πονηρία τῷ
διαπραττομένῳ, ἐξ ὧν πολλοὶ φαῦλοι
τὸν τρόπον ἐν πλούτῳ καὶ εὐθηνίᾳ
ἐξετάζονται οὐδὲν ὑφιστάμενοι δεινόν.

Τοῦτο τὸ νόσημα ἐξησόμενος,
τὸν πλεῖστον ἐν τῷ ψαλμῷ περὶ
τούτου κατατείνει λόγον.

exemplo suo docet auditores
qualiter ea quae euenerint portare conueniat et quid, si in peccatum lapsi fuerint agere, quid
dicere debeant in tribulationibus 5
constituti. Sunt etiam alii psalmi
in quibus sine aliquo huiusmodi
argumento magisterium exhortationis inducit, interdicens omnibus uitiis et omnia uirtutum 10
studia sollicite ac diligenter in-
sinuens: qualis est etiam praesens psalmus. In quo, quoniam
non nulli consueuimus malorum
ac nequam hominum prosperi- 15
tate morderi ac dicere quod non
prosit probitati dare operam atque honestis studiis occupari,
quandoquidem multi iustorum in
necessitates ultimas et, quod est 20
grauius, agentibus malis hominibus, conruunt; — quod quidem
amplius sensum doloris exagge-
rat, dum prauitas operis nihil eis
qui | ea utuntur officit: multi 25
namque nequam homines in diuitiis sunt et rerum omnium habundantia perfruuntur neque
aliud interim patiuntur aduersi;
— ad huiusmodi ergo depellen- 30
dum errorem sermo psalmi huius
et oratio inducitur.

---

13 ss. cf. in ps. IX, 23 (supra, p. 57).

19 καθεστήκα ms   30 ἐξιώμενος ms.
4 labsi B   5 debeant dicere A   7 quibusdam A   huiusmodi] hominum A, ita l. 30 et saepissime   8-9 exortatis A¹   9 induci A   10 uirtutem A
14 non om. A¹   15 omnium A¹   16 moderi A   17 probati A   21-22 omnibus A   30 ad — 32 inducitur affert Aᵉ (p. 212, 16-17)   30 ergo om. Aᵉ
31 sermo — oratio] iste psalmus Aᵉ.

toward what happens, what is the due response when living in a state of sin, what to say when under pressure from disaster. There are times when he also delivers an exhortation independently of the theme, forbidding what must be avoided and advising what should be done. This psalm is of that kind.

The general run of people, you see, especially when observing the wicked prospering, grind their teeth and claim that there is no benefit in being righteous: most righteous people are under pressure from disaster, even suffering this at the hands of villains. This it is that particularly renders the experience of calamity more depressing, whereas vice brings no harm to those guilty of crimes from which many villains are found to be living a life of wealth and prosperity without succumbing to any disaster. To dispel this ailment, he devotes most of this psalm to treating of it at length. |

1ᵃ. Μὴ παραζήλου ἐν πονηρευομένοις. Ζηλοῦν λέγεται κυρίως τὸ ὁρῶντα ἕτερον ἔν τινι ἀγαθῷ, ἢ ἀληθῶς ὄντι ἢ νομιζομένῳ, θαυμάζειν καὶ ἐκπλήττεσθαι ἐπὶ τῷ προσόντι ἀγαθῷ, — ὅθεν καὶ ζηλωτὸς ἄνθρωπος λέγεται ὁ περίβλεπτος καὶ μακαριστὸς τοῖς πολλοῖς καθεστώς· ἐνταῦθα οὖν τὸ μὴ παραζήλου ἐν
5 πονηρευομένοις ἀντὶ τοῦ Μὴ θαύμαζε τοὺς τοιούτους τοῦ πλούτου ἕνεκεν καὶ τῆς εὐθηνίας. Οὐδὲ γὰρ ἁπλῶς περὶ πονηρευομένων ποιεῖται τὸν λόγον, ἀλλὰ τῶν πονηρῶν καὶ ἐν εὐθηνίᾳ καθεστώτων. Τοῦτο δὲ δηλοῖ διὰ τοῦ μὴ παραζήλου (οὐδεὶς γὰρ πονηρίας μόνης ἕνεκεν θαυμάζει τινά) καὶ τοῦτο ἐν τοῖς ἑξῆς φανερώτερον λέγει Μὴ παραζήλου ἐν τῷ κατευοδουμένῳ ἐν
10 τῇ ὁδῷ | αὐτοῦ, ἀντὶ τοῦ Μὴ μακάριζε τὸν ὅσα βούλεται διαπράττεσθαι δυνάμενον ὡς ἰσχυρόν.

1ᵇ. Μηδὲ ζήλου τοὺς ποιοῦντας τὴν ἀνομίαν. Ἔστι μὲν συμπλοκὴ τοῦ προτέρου, ἔχει δέ τι πλέον. Μὴ παραζήλου μὲν γὰρ ἐν τοῖς πονηρευομέ-νοις εἰπών, ἑνὸς εἴδους ἐμνήσθη κακίας, τοῦ πονηρεύεσθαι. Προστεθεικὼς
15 δὲ μὴ ζηλοῦν τοὺς ποιοῦντας τὴν ἀνομίαν περιληπτικῶς τῷ τῆς ἀνομίας ὀνόματι τὸν πᾶσαν ἔκτοπον πρᾶξιν ἐργαζόμενον ἀπεφήνατο, μηδένα μακαρίζειν ὑπὲρ τῆς ἐν τῷ βίῳ εὐθηνίας, ἐλεεινὸν δὲ ὑπὲρ τῆς ἁμαρτίας ἡγεῖσθαι.

2ᵃ. Ὅτι ὡσεὶ χόρτος ταχὺ ἀποξηρανθήσονται. Κᾂν γὰρ ἐν εὐθηνίαις
20 φησὶν ἐξετάζεσθαι νομίζωσιν, ἀλλ᾽ ἀπόβλεψον πρὸς τὸ πρόσκαιρον τῆς εὐθηνίας, ὅτι δίκην χόρτου μαραίνεται αὐτοῖς τὰ τῆς εὐπραγίας. Ἔδειξε δὲ ἐνταῦθα φανερώτερον ὅτι περὶ πονηρῶν ὁ λόγος αὐτῷ τῶν ἐν τῷ βίῳ εὐθηνουμένων, ἀπὸ τοῦ Ὅτι ὡσεὶ χόρτος ταχὺ ἀποξηρανθήσονται.

2ᵇ. Καὶ ὡσεὶ λάχανα χλόης ταχὺ ἀποπεσοῦνται. Φανερώτερον εἶπεν
25 Ἀκύλας Καὶ ὡς χλωρὸν χλόης· ὥσπερ ἐκείνου τὸ χλωρὸν εὐθέως μετα-βάλλεται εἰς λευκότητα τῆς τοῦ ἡλίου θερμότητος ἐπιπεσούσης, οὕτως εὐχερῶς καὶ τούτοις ἡ εὐθηνία διαλύεται.

9-10 v. 7ᵇ.

16 μηδεὶς ms.

Aᵉ **1ᵃ** (p. 213, 3-7): Zelotiphia est si alter tecum fruatur quod concuperis. Ipse ergo *Noli emulari* siue mirari eos qui, cum sint mali, tamen in diuitiis sunt et rerum omnium habundantia constituti. **1ᵇ** (p. 213, 8-12): Generaliter nomine iniquitatis imperauit, ne quem improbi hominem operis diceremus beatum etiam in habundantia cons.itutum, quem uerius miserabilem pro peccato con-ueniat dici prouidendo.

Do not vie with evildoers (v. 1). Emulation is properly applied to the person who sees another involved in some good, real or imagined, who admires or is struck by the good in question—hence, a person is said to be emulated who has become the object of attention or blessing by the general run of people. Here, therefore, *Do not vie with evildoers* means, Do not admire such people for their wealth and affluence. He does not make his remarks about evildoers in general, note, but about the wicked and those enjoying affluence; he makes this clear in the word *vie* (nobody admires a person for wickedness alone, after all), and says it more clearly in a later clause, *Do not vie with that one who prospers in his way*[1]—that is, Do not count as blessed the one in a position from his strength to do everything he wishes. *Nor rival those committing iniquity.* While this is connected with the preceding, it contains something more. You see, in saying *Do not vie with evildoers,* he mentioned one vice, evildoing, whereas in proceeding to say *Nor rival those committing iniquity,* he embraced in the word *iniquity* everyone responsible for any deviant act, leaving no one to be blessed for an affluent lifestyle but to be pitied for their sin.

Because they will quickly dry up like grass (v. 2): even if they think that they are enjoying affluence, yet have an eye to the impermanence of affluence, that their prosperity fades like grass. Now, he brought out more clearly here that his thinking is directed to the wicked who prosper in their life, from the statement *Because they will quickly dry up like grass. And quickly fall like green foliage.* Aquila put this more clearly: "Like pale foliage"; as its pale shade changes to white once the heat of the sun declines, so too their affluence easily disappears. |

---

1. Ps 37:7.

3ᵃ. Ἔλπισον ἐπὶ Κύριον καὶ ποίει χρηστότητα. Ἐκείνους οὖν φησι παῦσαι μακαρίζων διὰ τὸ εὐμετάπτωτον, | περίμενε δὲ παντὸς ἀγαθοῦ μετουσίαν ἐκ τοῦ Θεοῦ καὶ διαπράττου τὰ πρέποντα. Χρηστότητα γὰρ εἶπεν ἀντὶ τοῦ πᾶν εἴ τι χρηστὸν καὶ ἀγαθόν. Πρῶτον οὖν εἶπεν

Ἔλπισον ἐπὶ Κύριον, εἶτα Καὶ   Spera in Domino et fac bo- 5
ποίει χρηστότητα, ἵνα μὴ ἁπλῶς   num. Vt non infructuose, sed
πράττῃς τὸ ἀγαθόν, ἀλλὰ διὰ τὴν   propter spem in Deum positam
εἰς τὸν Θεὸν ἐλπίδα.   boni operis uoluntatem intentio-
     nemque succenderet.

3ᵇ·ᶜ. Καὶ κατασκήνου τὴν γῆν καὶ ποιμανθήσῃ ἐπὶ τῷ πλούτῳ αὐτῆς. 10
Τὸ κατασκηνοῦν οὐκ ἀντὶ προστάγματος ἢ παραινέσεως τίθησιν, ἀλλὰ τὸ
ἑπόμενον τῇ ἐπὶ τὸν Θεὸν ἐλπίδι καὶ τῇ τῆς χρηστότητος πράξει λέγων,
ἀντὶ τοῦ Κατασκηνώσεις ἐπὶ τῆς γῆς,   Et inhabita terram, pro inha-
καὶ ποιμανθήσῃ ἐπὶ τῷ πλούτῳ αὐ-   bitabis.
τῆς, ἵνα εἴπῃ ὅτι ἔσῃ ἐπὶ τῆς γῆς ἀπολαύων πάντων αὐτῆς τῶν ἀγαθῶν· 15
πλοῦτον γὰρ τῆς γῆς καλεῖ τὰ ἐξ αὐτῆς ἀγαθά. Τὸ οὖν ποιμανθήσῃ, τουτέστιν ὑπὸ τοῦ Θεοῦ· αὐτός σού φησιν ἐπιμελήσεται καὶ κατασκηνώσει
σε ἐν τῇ ἀπολαύσει τῶν ἐκ τῆς γῆς ἀγαθῶν, — γῆς λέγων τῆς ἐπαγγελίας,
ἐπειδὴ τοῖς ἐν νόμῳ διαλέγεται, καὶ τοῦτο ἐν μέρει τιθεμένοις μακαρισμοῦ
τὸ κατοικεῖν ἐν αὐτῇ.   20

4. Κατατρύφησον τοῦ Κυρίου, καὶ δώσει σοι τὰ αἰτήματα τῆς καρδίας
σου. Μετὰ πολλῆς φησι τῆς σπου-   Cum multa, inquit, alacritate
δῆς διαπράττου τὰ τοῦ δεσπότου,   mentis Domini suscipe seruitu-
εὐφροσύνην καὶ τρυφὴν τιθέμενος τῶν   tem.
ἐντολῶν αὐτοῦ τὴν ἐκπλήρωσιν, καὶ λήψῃ μισθὸν τὸν ἴσον. Τὰ αἰτήματα 25
τῆς καρδίας σου· τὰ βουλεύματά φησιν | τὰ αὐτοῦ πληρῶν μετὰ πολλῆς
τῆς εὐφροσύνης λήψῃ καὶ αὐτὸς παρὰ τοῦ Θεοῦ τῶν σῶν βουλευμάτων
τὴν ἀπόλαυσιν.

5. Ἀποκάλυψον πρὸς Κύριον τὴν ὁδόν σου καὶ ἔλπισον ἐπ' αὐτόν, καὶ
αὐτὸς ποιήσει. Ἐὰν δέ φησι καὶ ἐν συμφοραῖς ἐξετασθῇς, αὐτῷ γνώρισον 30
πᾶσάν σου τὴν πρᾶξιν, αὐτῷ ἀνάθου πάντα τὰ κατά σε καὶ παρ' αὐτοῦ
ἔκδεξαι τὴν ἀντίληψιν καὶ τεύξῃ πάντως.

Spera — inhabitabis: A, fol. 12ᵃ; B, fol. 13ᶜ.   5-6 bonum] bō B   7 possitam A.

Cum — seruitutem: A, fol. 12ᵃ; B, fol. 13ᶜ. — Praecedit textus sacer: Dilectare in Domino, reliqua.

Aᵉ 5-7 (p. 214, 3-4): Quia finis est bonis spes in Deum.   18 (p. 214, 6-7)
... repromisionis scilicet.

Hope in the Lord and do good (v. 3): stop thinking those people blessed for their good fortune; wait for a share in every good from God and do what becomes you. By good he means "everything useful and honorable"—hence his saying first *Hope in the Lord,* then *and do good,* so that you may do good, not idly but as a result of hope in God. *Inhabit the earth and you will be fed on its riches.* He puts *Inhabit* not as a command or recommendation, but to express the consequence of hope in God and practice of good, meaning, You will inhabit the earth and be fed on its riches—as if to say, You will be on the earth enjoying all its good things (by *riches of the earth* referring to the good things from it). So *you will be fed,* that is, by God: he is the one who will care for you and settle you in the enjoyment of the good things of the land (meaning "land of promise," since he is speaking to those under the Law, and inhabiting it is for them part of the blessing). *Delight in the Lord, and he will grant you your heart's desire* (v. 4): carry out with great zeal the Lord's wishes, finding happiness and enjoyment in the performance of his commandments, and you will gain an equivalent reward. By *your heart's desire* he means, By carrying out his wishes with great joy, you in turn will receive from God the granting of your wishes.

Disclose your way to the Lord, hope in him, and he will act (v. 5): even if you experience misfortunes, make known to him all your doings, commit to him all that affects you, and you will receive repayment from him and complete recompense. | *He will highlight your righteousness like a light* (v.

6ᵃ. Καὶ ἐξοίσει ὡς φῶς τὴν δικαιοσύνην σου. Καὶ παρέξει σοί φησι τὴν
βοήθειαν. Δικαιοσύνην δὲ εἶπεν ἀντὶ   Iustitiam uocauit quod iuste
τοῦ δικαίως· ἀρετῆς γὰρ ἐπιμελομέ-   uirtutum sectatoribus tuitionem
νοις δῆλον ὅτι δικαίως παρέξει τὴν   suae defensionis inpertiat.
5 βοήθειαν. Τὸ δὲ ἐξοίσει ὡς ἐπὶ κριτοῦ ἔνδοθέν ποθεν ἐξάγοντος τὴν
ἀπόφασιν. Ὡς φῶς; δὲ εἶπεν ἀντὶ τοῦ Προφανῶς σοι βοηθήσει, ὥστε πᾶσι
καταφανῆ γενέσθαι τὴν εἴς σε τοῦ Θεοῦ βοήθειαν.

6ᵇ. Καὶ τὸ κρίμα σου ὡς μεσημβρίαν. Ἀκολούθως τῷ ἄνω ἐπήγαγε
Καὶ τὸ κρίμα σου ὡς μεσημβρίαν, τουτέστιν οὐδὲν ἀνεξετάστως ἐάσει τῶν
10 κατά σε, ἀλλὰ κρίνας καὶ δικάσας μετὰ τοῦ δικαίου παρέξει σοι τὴν βοήθειαν. Τὸ δὲ ὡς μεσημβρίαν εἶπε, τὴν ἐπίτασιν τῆς φανερώσεως σημαίνων, ἐπειδὴ μάλιστα ἐν ἐκείνῳ τῷ καιρῷ ἐπιτεταμένον τοῦ ἡλίου τὸ φῶς
δείκνυται τοῖς ἀνθρώποις. Τὴν δὲ δικαιοσύνην εἶπε καὶ τὸ κρίμα, τοῦτο
βουλόμενος | εἰπεῖν ὅτι ἀναγκαίως σοι παρέξει τὴν βοήθειαν, δικαίως ἐπα-
15 μύνων ἂν οὕτως ἔχῃ τὰ κατά σε, ὡς ἄξιόν σε εἶναι τῆς βοηθείας τῆς παρὰ
τοῦ Θεοῦ, — ὥστε φησὶ ταῦτα διαπραττόμενος κἂν ἐν συμφοραῖς ᾖς, μὴ
ἀμφίβαλε περὶ τῆς τοῦ Θεοῦ σωτηρίας.

7ᵃ. Ὑποτάγηθι τῷ Κυρίῳ καὶ ἱκέτευσον αὐτόν. Αὐτῷ φησιν ὑποτετάχθαι
σπούδαζε, τὰ αὐτοῦ προστάγματα πληροῦν καὶ παρ᾽ αὐτοῦ αἰτεῖν τῶν
ἀγαθῶν τὴν μετάληψιν, μὴ ἀπὸ πονηρίας ταύτην ἐκζητῶν.

7ᵇ·ᶜ. Μὴ παραζήλου ἐν τῷ κατευοδουμένῳ ἐν τῇ ζωῇ αὐτοῦ, ἐν ἀνθρώπῳ
ποιοῦντι παρανομίαν. Εἰ καί τινά φησιν ὁρᾷς τὰ μὲν φαῦλα διαπράττεσθαι ἐσπουδακότα, κατευοδούμενον δὲ ἐν τῇ οἰκείᾳ προθέσει καὶ ἄπαντα
ῥᾳδίως ἄγειν εἰς πέρας δυνάμενον ὅσαπερ ἄτοπα διαπράττεσθαι ἐσπού-
25 δακε, μὴ τοῦτον θαύμαζε καὶ μακαριστὸν νόμιζε ὡς οὐδεμίαν τιμωρίαν ἐφ᾽
οἷς διαπράττεται ἀτόποις ὑπομένοντα.

8ᵃ. Παῦσαι ἀπὸ ὀργῆς καὶ ἐγκατάλιπε θυμόν. Ἐπειδὴ εἶπε Μὴ παραζήλου ἐν τῷ κατευοδουμένῳ, ἐν ἀνθρώπῳ ποιοῦντι παρανομίαν, ἐπήγαγε τὸ

19 L (p. 674, 3): φυλάττων αὐτοῦ τὰ προστάγματα.
Iustitiam uocauit — inpertiat: A, fol. 12ᵃ; B, fol. 13ᶜ. *Praecedit textus
psalmi*: Et producet quasi lumen iustitiam tuam.   tuam] suam A   3 tutionem A   4 difensionis A.

Aᵉ 9-12 (p. 214, 20-26): Id est, nihil indiscusum circa te esse patietur, sed
examinans cuncta atque deiudicans iuste tibi adiutor adstabit; *meridiem* ergo
dicit ut augmentum manifestationis expraemeret.   7ᵃ (p. 214, 26-29): Stude,
inquit, ut mimineris te sub Dei imperio agere et quod necesse tibi sit praecepta eius inplere.

6): he will provide you with help (by *righteousness* meaning "rightly": it is clear that he will rightly provide help to those attentive to virtue). The verb *He will highlight* describes a judge publishing his verdict kept within; and *like a light* means, He will publicly help you so that help for you from God will be obvious to everyone. *And your judgment like midday.* He went on in the same vein as above to say *And your judgment like midday*—that is, He will not allow any of the charges against you to go unexamined, instead judging and ruling with justice and providing you with help. By *midday* he suggests the degree of clarity, since it is at that time in particular that the sun's rays shine most intensely on people. By *judgment* he meant "righteousness," intending to convey that he has no choice but to provide you with help by justly defending you if there are charges against you, since you deserve help from God; and so if you act this way even in misfortune, have no doubt of God's salvation.

Be subject to the Lord and beseech him (v. 7): be zealous in submitting to him by carrying out his commands, and in asking from him a share in good things, not looking to wickedness for this. *Do not vie with the one who prospers in his way, with the human being who commits lawlessness:* if you see someone who is bent on committing villainy, and yet who prospers in his own purposes and is in a position easily to put into effect whatever wrongs he is bent on committing, do not admire him and consider him blessed as though not liable to any punishment for the wrongs he commits.

Refrain from rage and desist from anger (v. 8). Since he said *Do not vie with the one who prospers, with the person guilty of lawlessness,* he went on to say | *Refrain from anger and desist from lawlessness*—that is, Do not

Παῦσαι ἀπὸ ὀργῆς καὶ ἐγκατάλιπε   *Desine ab ira et derelinque*
θυμόν, τουτέστι *Μηδὲ ὀργίζου ὅτι μὴ*   *furorem.* Quidam ob hoc indigna-
διδῶσι δίκας ἐφ᾽ οἷς διαπράττεται   tionis felle commouentur, quia in
ἀτόποις· οἱ γὰρ πολλοὶ οὐ μακαρί-   impios non uident uindicari.
ζουσι μόνον τοὺς πονηροὺς | ἐν εὐθηνίᾳ καθεστῶτας, ἀλλὰ καὶ δάκνονται 5
τὸ πλέον ὅτι μὴ διδόασι δίκας ἐφ᾽ οἷς διαπράττονται.

8ᵇ. Μὴ παραζήλου ὥστε πονηρεύεσθαι. *Μηδὲ μακαρίζων ἐκεῖνον ὡς δυνα-*
τὸν καὶ ὅσα βούλεται διαπραττόμενον, καὶ ἀποβλέψας ὅτι μηδὲν πάσχει
δεινὸν ἐγχειρῆσαί ποτε καὶ αὐτὸς τί πρᾶξαι τῶν ἀτόπων βουληθῇς.

9ᵃ. Ὅτι οἱ πονηρευόμενοι ἐξολοθρευθήσονται. *Οἱ γὰρ τὰ πονηρὰ δια-* 10
πραττόμενοι δώσουσί ποτε δίκας πάντως καὶ ἀπολοῦνται.

9ᵇ. Οἱ δὲ ὑπομένοντες τὸν Κύριον αὐτοὶ κληρονομήσουσιν τὴν γῆν. *Οἱ*
μέντοι φησὶν ἐπὶ τὸν Θεὸν πεποιθότες, οὗτοι βεβαίαν ἕξουσιν ἐπὶ τῆς γῆς
τὴν οἴκησιν, τουτέστιν οὐκ ἀπαναστήσουσιν αὐτοὺς τῆς οἰκείας γῆς πολέ-
μιοι. Τὸ γὰρ κληρονομήσουσιν ἀντὶ τοῦ βεβαίαν ἕξουσιν εἶπεν, ἀπὸ τοῦ 15
τοῖς κληρονομοῦσι βεβαίαν ἐγγίνεσθαι τῶν κληρονομουμένων τὴν δεσποτείαν.

10ᵃ. Καὶ ἔτι ὀλίγον καὶ οὐ μὴ ὑπάρξῃ ἁμαρτωλός. *Ὁ δὲ κακὸς καὶ εἰ*
εὐθηνεῖταί φησιν, ἀλλὰ βραχύ τι ἀνάμεινον καὶ ὄψει πάντως αὐτοῦ τὴν
ἀπώλειαν.

10ᵇ. Καὶ ζητήσεις τὸν τόπον αὐτοῦ καὶ οὐ μὴ εὕρῃς. *Εὑρήσεις γὰρ μετὰ* 20
τοῦ θανάτου καὶ τὸ μνημόσυνον αὐτοῦ πᾶν ἐξαλειφόμενον.

11ᵃ. Οἱ δὲ πραεῖς κληρονομήσουσιν γῆν. *Τοὺς δὲ ἐν πραότητι καὶ χρη-*
στότητι διάγοντας, τούτους ὄψει βεβαίαν κεκτημένους τὴν ἐπὶ γῆς οἴκησιν.

11ᵇ. Καὶ κατατρυφήσουσιν ἐπὶ πλήθει εἰρήνης. *Καὶ ἀπολαύσουσι πλου-*
σίως τῶν ἀγαθῶν μετὰ πολλῆς τῆς εἰρήνης, οὐδενὸς αὐτοῖς διακόπτοντος 25
τὴν ἀπόλαυσιν τῆς εὐθηνίας. Καλῶς δὲ εἶπε τὸ κατατρυφήσουσιν· ἐπειδὴ

5-6 L (p. 674, 14-15): μὴ δάκνου, μηδὲ δυσφόρει ὅτι μὴ διδόασι δίκην οἱ πονηροί.
Desine — uindicari: A, fol. 12ᵃ; B, fol. 13ᶜ.   1 disine A dissine B   diri-
(linque) A derilinq(ue) B   2 ob] ab A   3 in] hic A.

Aᵉ   14-15 (p. 215, 9-11): Id est, non eos poterunt hostes de terra habitationis suae abducere uel mouere.   10ᵇ (p. 215, 14-16): Ita, inquit, delebitur, ut
memoriae eius nulla signa remanere uideas.   24-25 (p. 215, 17-18): Fruentur,
inquit, bonis terrae cumulata pace.

be angry because they do not pay the penalty for the wrongful actions. Most people, you see, do not only consider blessed the wicked enjoying affluence; they also grind their teeth further for their not paying the penalty for their actions. *Do not vie to the extent of doing evil:* do not consider blessed those people for being in a position even to do whatever they wish, nor with your eyes on their suffering no harsh fate decide to attempt at any time in your own case to do some wrong. *Because the evildoers will be wiped out* (v. 9): those guilty of wickedness will some day pay the full penalty and perish. *Those who wait on the Lord will inherit the land:* those who believe in the Lord, to be sure, will be the ones to enjoy secure occupancy of the land—that is, enemies of their land will not challenge them (*will inherit* meaning that they will have secure occupancy, from the secure control of the inheritance coming to the heirs).

Yet *a little while and the sinner will not be around* (v. 10): even if the evil person is prospering, wait only a little while, and you will see his total ruin. *You will look for his trace and not find it:* after his death you will not find even any memory of him left. *The gentle, on the other hand, will inherit the land* (v. 11): you will see those living a life of gentleness and goodness enjoying occupancy of the land. *And will find delight in the abundance of peace:* they will richly enjoy good things with much peace, with no one to interrupt their enjoyment of affluence. *Will find delight* was well put: since |

γὰρ ἄνω συμβουλεύων εἶπε Κατατρύφησον τοῦ Κυρίου, καὶ ἐπὶ τῆς ἀπο
λαύσεως καὶ τοῦ μισθοῦ τῆς ἀρετῆς κατατρυφήσουσιν εἶπεν, ἀντίρροπον
τῇ ὑπακοῇ τὸν μισθὸν ὁριζόμενος.

12ᵃ. Παρατηρήσεται ὁ ἁμαρτωλὸς τὸν δίκαιον. Ἀλλὰ μηδὲ τοῦτό σέ
5 φησι ταραττέτω εἰ τὸν ἄδικον ὁρᾷς ἐπιβουλεύοντα τῷ δικαίῳ.

12ᵇ. Καὶ βρύξει ἐπ᾽ αὐτὸν τοὺς ὁδόντας αὐτοῦ. Καὶ κἂν τοσοῦτον ὀργί
ζηται κατ᾽ αὐτοῦ ὥστε τῇ ὑπερβολῇ τοῦ θυμοῦ βρύξαι κατ᾽ αὐτοῦ τοὺς
ὁδόντας διαπριόμενος, μηδὲ ἐπὶ τούτῳ δυσχέραινε.

13ᵃ. Ὁ δὲ Κύριος ἐκγελάσεται αὐτόν. Τὴν γὰρ ὀργὴν αὐτοῦ φησι τὴν
10 τοιαύτην ὁ Θεὸς ὡς περιττὴν καὶ ματαίαν ἐξουδενώσει.

13ᵇ. Ὅτι προβλέψει ὅτι ἥξει ἡμέρα αὐτοῦ. Οἶδε γὰρ τὸ τέλος, ὅπερ
ὑποστὰς ἀνόνητον δείξει καὶ ματαίαν τὴν κατὰ τοῦ δικαίου ὀργήν. Κατὰ ταύτην
γοῦν τὴν ἀκολουθίαν ἑρμηνεύει καὶ Σύμμαχος τὰ ῥήματα, ὡς δῆλον εἶναι ὅτι
ἀπὸ τῆς ἑρμηνείας ἡ τῶν χρόνων ἐναλ-   Ab interpraetibus tem-
15 λαγὴ γεγένηται, τῷ μέλλοντι ἀντὶ τοῦ   pora commotata sunt.
ἐνεστῶτος χρησαμένων διόλου τῶν ἑρ-
μηνευτῶν.

Σύμμαχος οὕτω φησὶν Ἐννοεῖ ὁ   Symmachus namque ait: Cogitat
ἀσεβὴς περὶ τοῦ δικαίου καὶ πρίει   impius de iusto et dissicatur ad-
20 κατ᾽ αὐτοῦ τοὺς ὁδόντας αὐτοῦ. Κύριος   uersus eum.
καταγελάσει αὐτοῦ προβλέπων ὅτι ἥξει ἡ ἡμέρα αὐτοῦ.

14. Ῥομφαίαν ἐσπάσαντο οἱ ἁμαρτωλοί, ἐνέτειναν τόξον αὐτῶν τοῦ κατα
βαλεῖν πτωχὸν καὶ πένητα, τοῦ σφάξαι τοὺς εὐθεῖς τῇ καρδίᾳ. Εἰ καὶ μάχαι
ράν φησιν ἀπὸ τῆς ὑπερβαλλούσης ὀργῆς μεταχειρίζονται οἱ ἁμαρτωλοί
25 [ἐνέτειναν τόξον] καὶ τὰ τόξα ἐντείνουσι τὰ ἴδια, — ἵνα εἴπῃ ὅτι ἐὰν δὲ

1 v. 4.

25 ἐνέτειναν τόξον delevi.
Ab interpraetibus — eum: A, fol. 12ᵃ; B, fol. 13ᶜ. Praecedit textus sacer:
Obseruabit peccator iustum et stridebit.   iustum om. B   15 commota A
commota *** B   18 cogit A   19 desiccatur A (cf. Act. VII, 54: διεπρίοντο ...
ἔβρυχον, dissecabantur ... stridebant).

Aᵉ   12ᵃ (p. 215, 19-21): Non, inquit, terreat si insidiari iusto peccatorem
uideas.   12ᵇ (p. 215, 22-26): Et si in tantum fuerit aduersus eum stimulis
furoris accensus, ut attritu dentium in eum uideatur armari, neque ex hoc
aliquid tibi timoris accedat.   9-10 (p. 215, 27-29): Illam, inquit, uechimentem
iram eius inritam Dominus faciet (feciat ms) effectumque distituet.

above he had given the advice *Delight in the Lord,*[2] he also said *they will find delight* in the case of the enjoyment and reward of virtue, determining the reward in accordance with the response.

The sinner will scrutinize the righteous one (v. 12): do not let it disturb you if you see the unrighteous scheming against the righteous. *And gnashes his teeth against him:* even if he is so enraged with him as in an excess of anger to gnash his teeth against him in frustration, do not be upset by it. *But the Lord will mock him* (v. 13): his wrath, great as it is, God will render idle and futile. *Because he foresees that his day will come:* he knows the end that he will come to and prove the wrath against the righteous to be pointless and in vain. Symmachus, at any rate, also interprets the words in this sense, so that it is clear that in the course of translation a change in tense has occurred, the translators definitely using the future for the present. Symmachus put it this way: "The godless considers the righteous and gnashes his teeth against him. The Lord will mock him, foreseeing that his day will come."

The wicked drew a sword and bent the bow to overthrow the poor and needy, to slaughter the upright of heart (v. 14): even if the sinners in their excessive wrath take sword in hand and bend their bow—as if to say, even | if

---

2. Ps 37:4.

καὶ ἐπιβουλεύοντες πλησίον γένωνται τοῦ ἀνελεῖν, — ὥστε ἀνελεῖν τοὺς δικαίους διὰ τὴν ἀσθένειαν τὴν σωματικὴν καὶ τὸ εὐτελὲς καταφρονοῦντες αὐτῶν (τοῦτο γὰρ λέγει πτωχὸν καὶ πένητα) μηδὲ τότε φησὶ φοβηθῇς. Διὰ τί;

15. Ἡ ῥομφαία αὐτῶν εἰσέλθοι εἰς τὴν καρδίαν αὐτῶν, καὶ τὰ τόξα 5 αὐτῶν συντριβείησαν. Οὐκ ἐπαρώμενος λέγει ἀλλ᾽ ἐξηγούμενος, ἀντὶ τοῦ Ταῦτα γὰρ τὰ κακὰ ἃ μηχανῶνται κατὰ τῶν δικαίων εἰς αὐτοὺς περιτραπήσεται ὑπὸ τοῦ Θεοῦ.

Ἡ δὲ ἐναλλαγὴ τῶν χρόνων ἀπὸ τῆς ἑρμηνείας, καθὼς πολλαχοῦ ἡμῖν ἐπισεσήμανται. Οὕτω γὰρ λέγει καὶ Σύμμαχος· Ῥομφαίαν σπῶσιν οἱ ἁμαρτωλοί, καὶ τείνουσι τόξον αὐτῶν καταβαλεῖν πτωχὸν καὶ πένητα, μαγειρεῦσαι ἁπλοῦς τῇ ὁδῷ· ἡ μάχαιρα αὐτῶν εἰσελεύσεται εἰς καρδίαν αὐτῶν	Immotatio temporum facta est, sicut in multis locis ostendimus. Ita namque Symmachus dicit: Gladium euaginant peccatores et intendunt arcum; gladius eorum intrabit in corda ipsorum et arcus eorum confringentur. καὶ τὰ τόξα αὐτῶν συντριβήσεται.

Διόλου γὰρ τοῦτο βούλεται εἰπεῖν· Μὴ θαύμαζε, μηδὲ μακάριζε τοὺς τὰ ἄτοπα ποι|οῦντας καὶ εὐθηνουμένους, μηδὲ δάκνου ἐπ᾽ αὐτοῖς ὅτι μὴ δίκας διδόασιν ὑπὲρ ὧν διαπράττονται· ἐκεῖνοι γὰρ ἀπολοῦνται καὶ ἀφανισθήσεται αὐτῶν τὸ μνημόσυνον. Οἱ δὲ δικαιοσύνης ἐπιμελόμενοι μετὰ πολλῆς 20 τῆς εἰρήνης ἀπολαύσουσι τῶν ἐκ τῆς γῆς ἀγαθῶν. Εἰ δὲ καὶ ἐπιβουλεύειν ὁ ἁμαρτωλὸς πειρᾶται τῷ δικαίῳ καὶ τοῦτο παντὶ τρόπῳ ποιεῖν ἐσπούδακε, μηδὲ τότε δάκνου ὡς ἀτιμωρήτου διαμένοντος αὐτοῦ· διαπτύει γὰρ αὐτοῦ τὴν ἐπιβουλὴν ὁ Θεός, εἰδὼς ὅτι ποτὲ ὑπομενεῖ καὶ ὅτι τῆς κατὰ τοῦ δικαίου ἐπιβουλῆς καὶ αὐτὸς δέξεται τὴν βλάβην. 25

16. Κρεῖσσον ὀλίγον τῷ δικαίῳ ὑπὲρ πλοῦτον ἁμαρτωλῶν πολύν. Τούτων τοίνυν φησιν οὕτως ἐχόντων, αἱρετωτέρα ἐστὶν ἡ λογικὴ κτῆσις τοῦ δικαίου παντὸς τοῦ πλούτου τῶν ἁμαρτωλῶν, κἂν πολὺς ᾖ.

17. Ὅτι βραχίονες ἁμαρτωλῶν συντριβήσονται, ὑποστηρίζει δὲ τοὺς δικαίους Κύριος. Διὰ τοῦτό φησιν αἱρετώτερον τοῦ δικαίου τὸ ὀλίγον ὑπὲρ τὸν 30

12-15 v. 14.

Immotatio — confringentur: A, fol. 12ᵃ; B fol. 13ᶜ. *Praemittitur textus scripturae*: Gladius eorum intret in corda ipsorum. 9 inmotatio A 13 arcum] a͞r A 14 corda] co͞r A 15 confringetur A.

Aᵉ 1-3 (p. 216, 7-9): ... deinde quod facile eos obpraemere pro ipsa census sui tenuitate se credunt. 24-25 (p. 216, 17-20): Id est mala, quae aduersus iustum molliuntur, ipsi ea inferente Domino sustenebunt.

they conspire to commit murder—and so murder the just on account of their physical weakness and with scorn for their insignificance (the meaning of *poor and needy*), never fear. Why? *Their swords will enter their own hearts, and their bows will be broken* (v. 15). He speaks not with a sense of exultation, but by way of comment, meaning, All the troubles they devise against righteous people will be turned back on them by God. Now, there has been a change in tense in translation, as often mentioned by us, Symmachus also putting it this way: "Sinners draw the sword and bend their bow to overthrow the poor and needy, to butcher simple people in the way; their sword will enter their own heart, and their bows will be broken." His overall meaning, in fact, is, Do not admire, do not declare blessed wrongdoers who are prospering, do not grind your teeth at them for not paying the penalty of their deeds: they will perish and their memory will disappear. Those devoted to righteousness, by contrast, will enjoy the good things of the earth in deep peace. Even if the sinner tries to plot against the righteous person and is bent on carrying it through in every way, do not then grind your teeth at his going unpunished: God will spit upon his plot, knowing that he will suffer sometime and that it is he who will sustain harm from his plot against the righteous.

Better a little for the righteous than much wealth for sinners (v. 16): this being the case, then, the reasonable possessions of the righteous are preferable to all the wealth of sinners, abundant though it be. *Because sinners' arms will be broken, but the Lord upholds the righteous* (v. 17): hence, the little of the righteous is preferable to the | wealth of the unrighteous, because once

πλοῦτον τῶν ἀδίκων, ὅτι ἐκείνων μὲν τῆς δυναστείας ἀφανισθείσης εἰς τὸ παντελὲς ὁ πλοῦτος αὐτῶν διαρρεῖ καὶ ἀπόλλυται, τῶν δὲ δικαίων καὶ τὸ ὀλίγον ἀνορθοῦται καὶ βεβαιοῦται ὑπὸ τοῦ Θεοῦ καὶ τὴν προσθήκην λαμβάνει.

18ᵃ. Γινώσκει Κύριος τὰς ὁδοὺς τῶν ἀμώμων. Οἶδε γάρ φησιν ὁ Θεὸς
5 τῶν δικαίων τὰς πράξεις καὶ οὐ λέληθεν αὐτῷ ἡ δικαιοσύνη τῶν ἀρετῶν, ὥστε παραλιπεῖν τὰ εἰς αὐτοὺς γενέσθαι ὀφείλοντα | παρ᾽ αὐτοῦ.

18ᵇ. Καὶ ἡ κληρονομία αὐτῶν εἰς τὸν αἰῶνα ἔσται. Καὶ τὸ βέβαιον τῆς ἀπο-λαύσεως διὰ παντὸς ἕξουσι παρὰ τοῦ Θεοῦ εἰδότος μὲν τὰ κατ᾽ αὐτούς, βεβαι-οῦντος δὲ αὐτοῖς τῆς ἀρετῆς τὴν ἀντιμισθίαν ἐν τῇ τῶν ἀγαθῶν ἀπολαύσει.

10 19ᵃ. Οὐ καταισχυνθήσονται ἐν καιρῷ πονηρῷ. Εἰ δὲ καί ποτέ φησιν ἐν συμφοραῖς ἐξετασθεῖεν, οὐκ εἰς τὸ παντελὲς ἐγκαταλειφθήσονται ὑπὸ τοῦ Θεοῦ, ὥστε αἰσχυνθῆναι ἐπὶ τῇ εἰς αὐτὸν ἐλπίδι.

19ᵇ. Καὶ ἐν ἡμέραις λιμοῦ χορτασθήσονται. Λιμὸν ἐνταῦθα καλεῖ τῶν ἀγαθῶν τὴν ἔνδειαν. Κἂν γὰρ ἐν τοιούτοις ἐξετασθῶσί φησι καιροῖς, ἡνίκα
15 πολλὴ μὲν ἡ θλίψις αὐτοῖς περιγίνεται, ἔνδεια δὲ ἔχει αὐτοὺς παντὸς ἀγα-θοῦ, καὶ τότε πλουσίαν ἕξουσι τὴν ἀπόλαυσιν τῶν ἀγαθῶν παρὰ τοῦ Θεοῦ ὡς εἰς κόρον αὐτοὺς ἁπάντων λαβεῖν τὴν μετουσίαν.

20ᵃ. Ὅτι οἱ ἁμαρτωλοὶ ἀπολοῦνται. Τὴν γὰρ παντελῆ φησιν ἀπώλειαν ἔθος ὑπομένειν τοῖς ἁμαρτωλοῖς.

20 20ᵇ. Οἱ δὲ ἐχθροὶ τοῦ Κυρίου ἅμα τῷ δοξασθῆναι αὐτοὺς καὶ ὑψωθῆναι ἐκλιπόντες ὡσεὶ καπνὸς ἐξέλιπον. Καὶ τοῖς ἐχθροῖς τοῦ Θεοῦ τοῦτο προσ-γίνεται τὸ ὅταν ἐν πολλῇ τινι δόξῃ καὶ τιμῇ ἐξετασθῶσι δίκην καπνοῦ ἐκλιμπάνειν, διαλυομένης αὐτοῖς τῆς εὐθηνίας· οὕτω λέγει καὶ Σύμμαχος Φαῦλοι ἀπολοῦνται.

24 *Siglo Theodori praefixo, versiculi initio denuo scripto* (Οἱ δὲ ἐχθροὶ τοῦ), *codex addit:* Ὡς μονοκέρωτες ἀναλωθήσονται, ὡς καπνὸς ἀπολοῦνται, *quae mihi pror-sus dubia videntur.*

Aᵉ 1-3 (p. 216, 21-26): Exigua iusti posessio praestat ingentibus opibus pec-catorum, quoniam illorum causae dilabuntur, cum fuerit eorum potentia deso-luta; iustorum uero exigua substantia semper augebitur.   18ᵃ (p. 216, 27-30): Pro gratias habebit; grata est, inquit, et accepta Deo iustorum conuersatio et propossitum uirtutis eorum.   18ᵇ (p. 216, 31-33): Firmum ac stabile iugiter erit quicquid a Deo pro meritorum uirtute acciperint.   19ᵃ (p. 217, 1-7): Etsi aliquando pro ipsa uiuendi commonione artiores rerum praesentium necessitates incurrent, non deserentur penitus a Deo ita [non] ut necesse sit eis destitutionis (distutionis *ms*) suae merorem et uerecondiam sustinere.   20ᵇ (p. 217, 9-13): Eo, inquit, temporis quo multo, ut putant, fuerint honore sublimes, uice fumi omnis eorum elatio euanescit et deperit.

their influence fades, their wealth runs away and is lost, whereas the little of the righteous is restored and confirmed by God and undergoes increase.

The Lord knows the ways of the blameless (v. 18): God knows the doings of the righteous, and the righteousness of their virtues has not escaped his notice, and so he does not omit what is due to be done to them by him. *And their inheritance will last forever:* they will ever have confirmation of enjoyment from God, who, on the one hand, knows their situation, and on the other hand confirms them in the reward of virtue by the enjoyment of good things. *They will not be put to shame in bad times* (v. 19): if they were to find themselves in misfortune, they would not be totally abandoned by God so as to be disappointed in their hope in him. *And will have their fill in times of famine.* By *famine* here he refers to the scarcity of good things: even if they find themselves in such times, when great distress will envelop them and they are affected by scarcity of every good, even then they will have abundant enjoyment of good things from God so as to partake of them all to their satisfaction.

Because sinners will perish (v. 20): sinners generally meet with complete ruin. *And the enemies of the Lord at the time of being glorified and exalted failed like smoke:* this is the fate that befalls God's enemies, that when they enjoy great glory and respect, they fail like smoke, their prosperity evaporating. Symmachus likewise says, "Villains will perish." | *The sinner borrows*

21ᵃ. Δανείζεται ὁ ἁμαρτωλὸς καὶ οὐκ ἀποτίσει. Ὁ μὲν οὖν ἁμαρτωλός φησιν ἐν τοιαύταις ἐξετάζεται συμφοραῖς, ὥστε καὶ χρήζειν τῶν δανειζόντων καὶ δανειζόμενος μὴ δύνασθαι ἀποδιδόναι.

21ᵇ. Ὁ δὲ δίκαιος οἰκτείρει καὶ δίδωσι. Ὁ δὲ δίκαιος ἐκ πολλῆς τῆς περιουσίας καὶ ἑτέροις δωρεῖται.					5

22. Ὅτι οἱ εὐλογοῦντες αὐτὸν κληρονομήσουσι γῆν, οἱ δὲ καταρώμενοι αὐτὸν ἐξολοθρευθήσονται. Οἱ εὐλογοῦντες αὐτὸν καὶ οἱ καταρώμενοι, τουτέστι τὸν Θεόν. Ἐπειδὴ γὰρ εἶπεν ἀνωτέρω Οἱ δὲ ἐχθροὶ τοῦ Κυρίου ἅμα τῷ δοξασθῆναι αὐτοὺς καὶ ὑψωθῆναι ἐκλιπόντες ὡσεὶ καπνὸς ἐξέλιπον, εἶτα ἐπήγαγε Δανείζεται ὁ ἁμαρτωλὸς καὶ οὐκ ἀποτίσει, ὁ δὲ δίκαιος οἰκτείρει καὶ 10 δίδωσι, πρὸς ἐκεῖνα ἀπέδωκε τὸ Ὅτι οἱ εὐλογοῦντες αὐτὸν κληρονομήσουσι γῆν, οἱ δὲ καταρώμενοι αὐτὸν ἐξολοθρευθήσονται. Ταῦτά φησιν ἔσται ἐπειδὴ οἱ μὲν τὸν Θεὸν εὐλογοῦντες ἀπολαύουσι τῶν παρ᾽ αὐτοῦ ἀγαθῶν, οἱ δέ γε τὰς εἰς αὐτὸν τείνοντες βλασφημίας παντελῆ ὑπομένουσιν ἀπώλειαν.

Σύμμαχος οὕτως λέγει Ὅτι οἱ εὐ-λογημένοι ὑπ᾽ αὐτοῦ κληρονομήσουσι γῆν, οἱ δὲ καταρώμενοι ὑπ᾽ αὐτοῦ ἐκ-κοπήσονται. Καὶ Ἀκύλας καὶ Θεοδο-τίων οὕτω λέγουσιν ὅ τι οἱ ἠὐλογη-μένοι αὐτοῦ κληρονομήσουσι γῆν. Εἴτε δὲ οὕτως, εἴτε δὲ ἐκείνως, φανερὰ ἡ διάνοια· δῆλον μέντοι ὅτι τὸ αὐτὸ περὶ τοῦ Θεοῦ λέγει οὐχ, ὥς τινες ᾠήθησαν, περὶ τοῦ δικαίου.

Symmachus ita dicit: *Quo-* 15 *niam qui benedicentur ab eo he-reditabunt terram, qui uero ma-ledicentur ab eo excidentur.* Aquila etiam et Theodotion concinenter: *Benedicti ab eo hereditabunt ter-* 20 *ram.* Sed siue ita sit positum, ut alii interpraetantur, siue ut LXX dixerunt, manifestus intel-lectus est quoniam id, quod dixit *Benedicentes ei,* de Deo accipien- 25 dum sit, non, sicut quidam opi-nati sunt, de iusto.

23ᵃ. Παρὰ Κυρίου τὰ διαβήματα ἀνθρώπου κατευθύνεται. Διὰ τοῦτο δέ φησιν οἱ μὲν εὐλογοῦντες καθέξουσι βεβαίως τὰ ἀγαθά, οἱ δέ γε βλασφη-

---

4 δίδωσι *scripsi, cf. infra l. 11*	8 ἅμα τοῦ *ms.*
Symmachus — de iusto: A, fol. 12ᵃ; B, fol. 13ᶜ; *ed.* MURATORI, *Antiq. Ital.,* III, p. 858-859 *haud diligenter. Praemittitur textus scripturae:* Quoniam bene-dicentes ei hereditabunt terram.	15 dicit *om.* A¹B	18 excidentur] *litt.* cid *in rasura* A	19 theod.] theotō A theō B	21 possitum A	22 interpnr A¹ praetantur *add. supra lin.* ut *om.* B¹	25 accipendum A	27 iusto] deo A Dauid *Mur.*

Aᵉ 21ᵇ (p. 217, 17-21): Non solum nihil, inquit, angustiae sentiat, sed ita habundabit ut etiam ad alios manum possit suae liberalitatis extendere.

and will not pay back (v. 21): whereas the sinner is caught up in such awful disasters as to have recourse to borrowing without being able to pay back what he borrows, *the righteous person has pity and gives:* from his abundant resources the righteous person also makes gifts to others. *Because those who bless him will inherit the land, whereas those who curse him will be wiped out* (v. 22). *Those blessing and those cursing him* (that is, God): since he said above *The enemies of the Lord at the time of being glorified and exalted failed like smoke,* then added *The sinner borrows and will not pay back, whereas the righteous person has pity and gives,* to that he made the response *Because those who bless him will inherit the land, whereas those who curse him will be wiped out.* This will happen, he is saying, because while those blessing God will enjoy good things from him, those directing blasphemies to him will meet with utter ruin. Symmachus put it this way: "Because those blessed by him will inherit the land, whereas those cursed by him will be cut down"; and Aquila and Theodotion put it this way: "Because his blessed ones will inherit the land." One way or other, the meaning is clear; in any event, it is a statement about God, not (as some commentators believed) about the righteous.[3]

A person's steps are guided by the Lord (v. 23): for this reason those blessing will have firm possession of good things, whereas those | blas-

---

3. Theodore has noticed that the alternative versions differ from the LXX in taking the verb "bless" as passive, not active; after paraphrasing the LXX rendering, he does the same for Symmachus, Aquila, and Theodotion, peremptorily deciding for the latter (probably on the basis of numbers) without checking the Hexapla also for the Hebrew (where, in fact, the verb form is indeed Pual and not Piel, as those three commentators realized).

μοῦντες τὸ ἐναντίον ἐκκοπήσονται, ἐπειδὴ ἐν τῷ Θεῷ ἐστιν οὗπερ ἂν ἐθέλῃ
κατευθῦναι τὰ διαβήματα, τουτέστι τὴν πρόθεσιν αὐτοῦ καὶ τὰς ἐνθυμήσεις
καὶ τοὺς λογισμοὺς εἰς τὸ πέρας ἀγαγεῖν.

23ᵇ. Καὶ τὴν ὁδὸν αὐτοῦ θελήσει τῷ ἄνω ἐπισυνῆπται, ἀντὶ τοῦ Τοιού-
5 του δὲ ἀνθρώπου κατευθύνει τὰ διαβήματα, οὗπερ ἂν σφόδρα ἀρεσθῇ τῇ
βουλῇ καὶ τῇ πράξει· ἐὰν γὰρ ἴδῃ φησὶ τὰ κάλλιστα προῃρημένον καὶ
ἀρεσθῇ αὐτῷ τῷ βίῳ καὶ τῇ προθέσει, ἅπαντα αὐτῷ κατευθύνει, καὶ περαιοῖ
τὰ σπουδαζόμενα διὰ τῆς οἰκείας βοηθείας.

24ᵃ. Ὅταν πέσῃ οὐ καταρραχθήσεται. Κἂν περιπτώματι δέ τινί φησιν ὁ
10 τοιοῦτος περιπέσῃ ποτέ, ἀλλ᾽ οὐκ εἰς τὸ παντελὲς δέξεται τὴν πτῶσιν.

24ᵇ. Ὅτι Κύριος ἀντιστηρίζει χεῖρα αὐτοῦ. Ὁ γὰρ Θεός φησιν ἀνίστη-
σιν αὐτὸν καὶ ἀπαλλάττει τῶν προσπιπτόντων λυπηρῶν. Τὸ δὲ ἀντιστηρίζει χεῖρα αὐτοῦ ἀκολούθως τῷ Ὅταν πέσῃ οὐ καταρραχθήσεται, ἐπείπερ
οἱ πίπτον|τες δέονται τοῦ τὴν χεῖρα ἐρείδειν πρὸς τὸ ἔδαφος πρὸς τὸ
15 μὴ παντελῶς καταπεσεῖν.

25ᵃ. Νεώτερος ἐγενόμην, καὶ γὰρ ἐγήρασα. Τὸ γὰρ περισσὸν ὅσον πρὸς
τὴν διάνοιαν· οὕτω γὰρ λέγει καὶ Σύμμαχος Νέος ἐγενόμην καὶ γὰρ ἐγήρασα.

25ᵇ. Καὶ οὐκ εἶδον δίκαιον ἐγκαταλελειμμένον. Καὶ νέος φησὶν ἐγενόμην
20 καὶ εἰς γῆρας ἤλασα λοιπόν, καὶ ἐν τοσούτῳ χρόνῳ οὔτε δίκαιον ἐθεασάμην
ἐναφεθέντα τοῖς κακοῖς ὑπὸ τοῦ Θεοῦ, οὔτε τοὺς τούτου ἐκγόνους ἐν θλίψεσιν ἐξετασθέντας.

25ᶜ-26. Οὐδὲ τὸ σπέρμα αὐτοῦ ζητοῦν ἄρτους. Ὅλην τὴν ἡμέραν ἐλεᾷ
καὶ δανείζει, καὶ τὸ σπέρμα αὐτοῦ εἰς εὐλογίαν ἔσται. Τὸ δὲ ἐναντίον φησὶν
25 ὁρῶ ὅτι οἱ δίκαιοι καὶ ἑτέροις χαρίζονται, καὶ τὸ σπέρμα καὶ τοὺς ἐγγό-
νους αὐτοῦ παρὰ πᾶσι μακαριζομένους ἐφ᾽ οἷς ἐδέξαντο παρὰ τοῦ πατρὸς
ἀγαθοῖς.

Aᵉ 23ᵇ (p. 217, 24-30): Pro Conatus iusti prosperabuntur, id est: huius
hominis gresus deregit, qui eos probaliter et ordinate ad opera facienda commouerit; bona enim cogitantem et bona uolentem facere adiuuat, nec placitum
sibi opus patitur prosperitate distitui. 24ᵇ (p. 217, 32-218, 1): Is, cuius gresus
dereguntur sancte, numquam ita labi poterit ut aliquit debilitatis incurrat.
25ᶜ-26 (p. 218, 4-9): Non solum ipse nihil in rerum difectu sentit angustiae, sed
etiam egentes sua liberalitate sustentat ... etiam filii eius ab hominibus dicantur (decantur ms) beati.

pheming will, by contrast, be cut down, since it is with God's help that it is possible to guide one's steps (that is, one's purpose) where one wishes, and to bring one's desires and thoughts to fulfillment. *And he will take great delight in his way*—that is, He guides the steps of such a person whose intentions and actions are to his great satisfaction: if he sees the person opting for the highest values and meeting with his satisfaction in life and purpose, he guides everything for him, and fulfills his goals with his characteristic help. *Whenever he falls, he will not be broken in pieces* (v. 24): even if such a person ever suffers a fall, he will nonetheless not completely come to grief. Because the Lord strengthens his hand: God lifts him up and relieves him of the hardships besetting him. The phrase strengthens his hand is consistent with the verse Whenever he falls, he will not be broken in pieces, since those who fall need a hand up from the ground so as not to collapse completely.

I have been younger and am now grown up (v. 25). The verse has some superfluity as far as the meaning is concerned. Symmachus expresses it this way: "I was young and have grown up." *I have not seen a righteous person abandoned:* I was young, and then I came to old age, and in all that time I did not see righteous people embroiled in troubles by God or their offspring caught up in tribulations. *Nor his offspring looking for bread. All day long the righteous person shows mercy and lends money, and his offspring will bring a blessing* (vv. 25–26): on the contrary, I observe that the righteous also give freely to others, and their offspring and descendants are declared blessed by everyone for the good things that they received from their forebear. |

27ᵃ. Ἔκκλινον ἀπὸ κακοῦ καὶ ποίησον ἀγαθόν. Οὐκοῦν φησι τούτων οὕτως ἐχόντων, ἀπόστηθι μὲν τῆς τῶν ἀτόπων πράξεως, ἐπιμελοῦ δὲ τῶν εὐαρέστων Θεῷ.

27ᵇ. Καὶ κατασκήνου εἰς αἰῶνα αἰῶνος. Πάλιν ἐνταῦθα τὸ κατασκήνου οὐχ ὡς παραίνεσιν λέγει, ἀλλ᾽ ἀντὶ τοῦ κατασκηνώσεις. Οὕτω γοῦν 5 λέγει καὶ ὁ Σύμμαχος Καὶ ἠρεμήσεις εἰς αἰῶνα αἰῶνος, ἀντὶ τοῦ Ἐν ἡσυχίᾳ διατελέσεις τῇ ἀπὸ τῶν κακῶν.

28ᵃ·ᵇ. Ὅτι Κύριος ἀγαπᾷ κρίσιν, καὶ οὐκ ἐγκαταλείψει τοὺς ὁσίους αὐτοῦ, εἰς τὸν αἰῶνα φυλαχθήσονται. Τὴν δικαιοκρισίαν φησιν. | Ἐπιμελεῖται γάρ φησι τοῦ δικαίου ὁ Θεός· τοῦτο γὰρ λέγει τὸ ἀγαπᾷ, τὸ ἐπιμελεῖται, 10 ἐπείπερ εἰώθαμεν ἐπιμελεῖσθαι πάντως ὃν ἀγαπῶμεν, ὡς καὶ ἐν τῷ λβ΄ τὸ Ἀγαπᾷ ἐλεημοσύνην καὶ κρίσιν ὁ Κύριος. Ἐπιμελόμενος δέ φησι τοῦ δικαίου οὐ καταλείψει τῆς αὐτοῦ βοηθείας τοὺς δικαίους ἐρήμους, ὅτι εἰς τὸν αἰῶνα φυλαχθήσονται. Διατηρήσεις δὲ αὐτούς φησιν εἰς τὸ παντελές.

28ᶜ·ᵇ. Ἄνομοι δὲ ἐκδικηθήσονται, καὶ σπέρμα ἀσεβῶν ἐξολοθρευθήσεται. 15 Καὶ οἱ μὲν ἄνομοί φησιν ἐν διωγμοῖς καὶ κακοῖς διατελέσουσι καὶ τὸ σπέρμα τῶν τοιούτων ἀφανισθήσεται.

29. Δίκαιοι δὲ κληρονομήσουσι γῆν, καὶ κατασκηνώσουσιν εἰς αἰῶνα αἰῶνος ἐπ᾽ αὐτῆς. Οἱ δὲ δίκαιοί φησι βεβαίως ἔσονται ἐπὶ τῆς γῆς καὶ διηνεκῶς μενοῦσιν ἐπ᾽ αὐτῆς. Ἐπὶ δὲ τῆς γῆς φησιν τῆς ἐπαγγελίας, ὡς πρὸς Ἰου- 20 δαίους διαλεγόμενος, ἐπειδὴ τοῦτο ἀντὶ εὐεργεσίας ὁ Θεὸς τοῖς Ἰουδαίοις ἐπηγγείλατο καὶ πάλιν ἀντὶ τιμωρίας ἠπείλει τὴν ἐκεῖθεν μετάστασιν.

30ᵃ. Στόμα δικαίου μελετήσει σο-   Os iusti meditabitur sapien-
φίαν. Ὁ δὲ δίκαιός φησι μελετήσει   tiam. Sapientiam uocat id quod
πᾶν εἴ τι σοφόν· σοφὸν δὲ καλεῖ   Deo placere potest atque eius 25
τὸ τῷ Θεῷ εὐάρεστον.   iudicio conprobatur.

4-5 cf. supra in v. 3ᵇ·ᶜ   12 Ps. XXXII, 5.

13 καταλήψει ms.
Os iusti — conprobatur: A, fol. 12ᵃ; B, fol. 13ᶜ.   23 ** sap̄ in rasura B
25 a Deo A.

Aᵉ 29 (p. 218, 16-22: Promisionis dicit siquidem cum de Iudeorum genere loquitur, quibus et pro beneficio terrae illius habitationem promissit Deus, et e contrario etiam expulsionem de ea peccantibus comminatur.   30ᵃ (p. 218, 23-25): Pro uoluntatis diuinae scientia, inquit, Deo placere potest atque eius iudicio conprobari.

Turn away from evil and do good (v. 27): since this is the way things are, then, desist from wrongful behavior and attend to what pleases God. *And dwell forever.* In this case, too, instead of giving an exhortation he means, You will dwell—Symmachus, at any rate, putting it in those terms, "You will be at rest forever"—that is, You will continue to enjoy relief from trouble. *Because the Lord loves judgment, and does not abandon his holy ones, because they will be protected forever* (v. 28). He is speaking of right judgment: God takes care of the righteous (by *loves* meaning "takes care of," since we normally take care of what we love, as it says in Psalm 33, "The Lord loves mercy and judgment").[4] Taking care of the righteous, he is saying, he will not leave righteous people bereft of his help, because *they will be protected forever* (meaning "he will watch over them completely"). *Whereas lawless people will be banished, and offspring of ungodly people will be destroyed:* while the lawless will live their days in harassment and trouble and their offspring will be destroyed, *righteous people, on the other hand, will inherit the earth and dwell in it forever* (v. 29): the righteous will live securely in the land and abide in it unceasingly. Now, he means the land of promise, speaking as he is to Jews, since God promised this to the Jews as a gift, and likewise threatened removal from it as a punishment.

The mouth of the righteous one will utter wisdom (v. 30): the righteous person will pay attention to everything wise (by *wise* meaning "what is pleasing to God"). *And his tongue | will give judgment:* everything he utters will

---

4. Ps 33:5.

30ᵇ. Καὶ ἡ γλῶσσα αὐτοῦ λαλήσει κρίσιν. Καὶ φθέγξεται πᾶν εἴ τι δίκαιον.

31ᵃ. Ὁ νόμος τοῦ Θεοῦ αὐτοῦ ἐν καρδίᾳ αὐτοῦ. Ταῦτα δέ φησι μελετήσει καὶ φθέγξεται ἐπὶ τῆς διανοίας, ἔχων τὴν περὶ τὸν νόμον τοῦ Θεοῦ διάθεσιν.

5 **31ᵇ.** Καὶ οὐχ ὑποσκελισθήσεται τὰ διαβήματα αὐτοῦ. Διὰ τοῦτο οὐδὲ περι|τραπήσεται ἀπὸ τῶν προσπιπτόντων αὐτῷ λυπηρῶν.

32. 33ᵃ. Κατανοεῖ ὁ ἁμαρτωλὸς τὸν δίκαιον, καὶ ζητεῖ τοῦ θανατῶσαι αὐτόν. Πάλιν ἀκολούθως τῷ ἀνωτέρω. Εἰ δὲ καὶ ὁ φαῦλός φησι καὶ πονηρὸς ἀποβλέπει πρὸς αὐτὸν ἀνελεῖν αὐτὸν ἐσπουδακότες, — ὁ δὲ Κύριος οὐ μὴ
10 ἐγκαταλίπῃ αὐτὸν εἰς τὰς χεῖρας αὐτοῦ διόλου τὸ ἀνώτερον δευτεροῖ, — ἀλλ᾽ οὐ συγχωρήσει φησὶν αὐτὸν ὁ Θεὸς ὑπὸ τὴν ἐκείνου πεσεῖν ἐξουσίαν.

33ᵇ. Οὐδὲ μὴ καταδικάσηται αὐτὸν ὅταν κρίνηται αὐτῷ. Τουτέστιν ὅταν αὐτὸς ἐξετάζηται. Ὡς πολλάκις καὶ παρ᾽ ἡμῖν λέγειν εἰώθασί τινες Ἀπῆλθεν αὐτὸς ἀντὶ τοῦ Ἀπῆλθεν οὗτος, καὶ τὸ ὅταν κρίνηται αὐτῷ ἀντὶ τοῦ
15 Ὅταν κρίνηται, ἵνα εἴπῃ· Καὶ οὐ καταδικάσει αὐτὸν ἐν τῷ κρίνεσθαι αὐτῷ.
Οὕτω καὶ Σύμμαχος Οὐδὲ κατα-   Symmachus: *Non condemna-*
δικάσει κρινόμ̣ενον αὐτόν.   *bit iudicatum eum.*

Τὸ οὖν οὐδὲ μὴ καταδικάσηται, ἀντὶ τοῦ Ὁ Θεός. Τὸ δὲ ὅλον ἀκολούθως τέθεικε τῷ ἀνωτέρω, τῷ ὁ δὲ Κύριος οὐ μὴ ἐγκαταλίπῃ αὐτὸν εἰς
20 τὰ̣ς χεῖρα̣ς. Βούλεται γὰρ εἰπεῖν ὅτι ὁ Κύριος οὐκ ἐναφήσει αὐτὸν εἰς τὰς χεῖρας τῶν ἁμαρτωλῶν· εἰ δὲ καὶ ὑποπέσοι τῷ ἁμαρτωλῷ ὁ δίκαιός ποτε ὡς καὶ ὑπὸ τὴν κρισιν αὐτοῦ πεσεῖν καὶ τὴν ἐξέτασιν, ἀλλ᾽ ὁ Θεὸς οὐ καταψηφιεῖται αὐτοῦ, τουτέστιν οὐκ ἐάσει αὐτὸν εἰς τὸ παντελὲς ὑπὸ τὴν ἐκείνου πεσεῖν ἀπόφασιν — ἵνα εἴπῃ ὅτι καὶ κρινόμενον αὐτὸν ὑπ᾽ αὐτῶν
25 ἀπαλλάξει παραδόξως τῆς ἐκείνων ἀποφάσεως.

34ᵃ. Ὑπόμεινον τὸν Κύριον καὶ φύλαξον τὴν ὁδόν αὐτοῦ. Οὐκοῦν | ἐπειδὴ τοὺς δικαίους, κἂν ὑποχείριοι γένωνται τοῖς ἁμαρτωλοῖς, οὐκ ἐᾷ ὁ Θεὸς

18-19 ἀνακολούθως *prius scriptum, litt.* ἀν *punctis reprobatae.*
Symmachus — eum: A, fol. 12ᵃ⁻ᵇ; B, fol. 13ᶜ. *Praemittitur textus sacer:* Nec damnabit eum cum iudicabitur illi.   nec] non A   16 contempnabit A.

Aᵉ **31ᵇ** (p. 218, 29-30): ... stabit etiam si inpellatur aduersis.   **33ᵃ** (p. 218, 31-34): Per omnia, id quod superius dixerat, repetit: in potestatem, inquit, eius eum uenire non patitur.   20-25 (p. 218, 34-219, 5): Id est Deus. A peccatorum inpotentiumque sententia iustum condempnatum separauit (seperauit *ms*) Deus; ac si diceret: Et non damnauit eum cum iudicium eius agitari coeperit.

be just. *The law of God is in his heart* (v. 31): he will attend to it and utter it in his mind, having affection for the law of God. *And his steps will not be upset:* hence, he will not be upset by the misfortunes befalling him.

The sinner scrutinizes the righteous one and seeks to kill him (v. 32). Again consistent with the above: even if the villain and the rogue set eyes on him in their anxiety to do away with him, *the Lord will not abandon him into his hands* (v. 33), which completely duplicates what came before, meaning, God will, however, not allow him to fall into his hands. *Nor condemn him when it is his turn for judgment*—that is, when he is subjected to interrogation (following the custom even with us for some to say, Himself took his leave, meaning, He left); so here *When it is his turn for judgment* means, When he is being judged—as if to say, He will not condemn him when it is his turn for judgment. Symmachus employs similar terms: "Nor will he condemn him when being judged." So the phrase *nor condemn* refers to God. It is completely consistent with the above, *The Lord will not abandon him into their hands,* his meaning being, The Lord will not give him into the hands of sinners; and even if the righteous person ever has the misfortune to fall under the judgment and interrogation of a sinner, God still will not abandon him—that is, will not allow him completely to be subject to his verdict, as if to say, He will against all odds release him from their verdict when being judged by them.

Wait upon the Lord and keep his way (v. 34): since, then, God does not allow the righteous, even if vulnerable to sinners, | to be subject com-

εἰς τὸ παντελὲς τῇ ἐκείνων ἀποφάσει ὑποπεσεῖν, μὴ ἀθύμει κἄν ποτε ἐν
συμφορᾷ περιπέσῃς, ἀλλ᾽ ἐκδέχου τοῦ Θεοῦ τὴν βοήθειαν, φυλάττων αὐτοῦ
τὰ βουλεύματα καὶ τὰ προστάγματα, καὶ τῆς εὐαρεστήσεως ἐπιμελόμενος,
καὶ μὴ διὰ τὰ περιέχοντα λυπηρὰ ἀφιστάμενος τῆς ἀρετῆς.

34ᵇ. Καὶ ὑψώσει σε τοῦ κατακληρονομῆσαι τὴν γῆν. Ταῦτα γὰρ 5
ποιοῦντα, κἄν ᾖς ὑποχείριος τῷ ἁμαρτωλῷ, σκεπάσει καὶ ὑψηλότερον ἀπο-
φανῇ, παρέχων σοι βεβαίαν τὴν ἐν τῇ γῇ οἴκησιν.

34ᶜ. Ἐν τῷ ἐξολοθρεύεσθαι ἁμαρτωλοὺς ὄψῃ. Καὶ οὐ μόνον φησὶν ἀπαλ-
λαγήσῃ τῆς ἐκείνων ἐπιβουλῆς, ἀλλὰ γὰρ καὶ ἀπολλυμένους αὐτοὺς θεάσῃ.
Καὶ πόθεν τοῦτό φησιν;   10

35. Εἶδον ἀσεβῆ ὑπερυψούμενον καὶ ἐπαιρόμενον ὡς τὰς κέδρους τοῦ
Λιβάνου. Ταῦτά φησι λέγω ἐξ᾽ ὧν τὴν πεῖραν παρέλαβον· ἐθεασάμην γὰρ
πολλοὺς κατὰ τὴν εὐπραγίαν μεγαλυνθέντας καὶ ἐπαρθέντας μέγα.

36. Καὶ παρῆλθον, καὶ ἰδοὺ οὐκ ἦν. Καὶ βραχύ τι διαγεγονὼς οὐδὲ λείψανον αὐτοῦ τῆς μεγαλωσύνης περιλειφθὲν ἐθεασάμην· τοῦτο γάρ ἐστι τὸ 15
Καὶ ἰδοὺ οὐκ ἦν, ὡς ἐπὶ δένδρου εἰρηκώς, ἐπειδὴ καὶ κέδρῳ παρέβαλεν αὐτοῦ
τὸ μέγεθος εἰρηκὼς Καὶ ἐπαιρόμενον ὡς τὰς κέδρους τοῦ Λιβάνου. Τοῦτο οὖν
ἠβουλήθη εἰπεῖν ὅτι ἐξεσπάσθη ἐκ ῥιζῶν ὡς μηδὲν τοῦ μεγέθους αὐτοῦ
περιλειφθῆναι μνημόσυνον.

PSALMVS XXXVII   20

Ἔστι μὲν ὁ λζ΄ ψαλμὸς ἐξομο-
λόγησις τοῦ μακαρίου Δαυὶδ τῆς κατὰ
τὴν Βερσαβεὲ ἁμαρτίας ἕνεκεν. Τινὲς
δὲ ἠβουλήθησαν μηδένα δεῖν ἐκλαμ-
βάνεσθαι τῶν ψαλμῶν κατὰ ταύτην

Est xxxvii psalmus confessio
beati Dauid pro peccato, quod
in Bersabe uxorem Vri legitur
admisisse. Quamuis quidam nolint sub tali argumento aliquem 25

19 *cetera desunt, uno folio post 144ᵛ perdito.*
Est xxx psalmus — 222, 15 pudoris occurrere: B, fol. 6ᵇ.

Aᵉ 1-3 (p. 219, 5-8): Expecta Dei adiutorium; ad faciendam uoluntatem ac
mandata eius esto semper intentus.   35 (p. 219, 12-15): Haec, inquit, dico
quae experimentis accipi: uidi namque multos in sublime aura prosperitatis
elatos.   36 (p. 219, 15-20): Intento oculo ad curam inquisitionis accesi, si forte
aliquas magnitudinis eius reliquias inuenirem, sed nulla potentiae eius uestigia, nulla signa residerunt.

pletely to their verdict, do not be despondent if ever you fall foul of disaster; instead, expect help from God by observing his decrees and commands, being attentive to his good pleasure, and not withdrawing from virtue on account of the hardships besetting you. *And he will exalt you to inherit the land* (v. 34): if you do this, he will shelter you, even if vulnerable to the sinner, and make you exalted by ensuring you secure occupancy of the land. *In the destruction of sinners you will see:* not only will you be freed from their scheming, but also you will see them destroyed. What is his reasoning for saying this?

I have seen the godless exalted and lifted up like the cedars of Lebanon (v. 35): I say this from experience; I observed many people carried away with prosperity and greatly conceited. *I passed by and, lo, he was no more* (v. 36): I observed that he did not long survive, nor was a vestige of his greatness left (the meaning of *lo, he was no more,* making reference to a tree, and comparing his proportions to a cedar in saying *lifted up like the cedars of Lebanon*). His meaning was, then, He was rooted up, with the result that no memory of his greatness survived.[5]

PSALM 38

Psalm 38 is a confession by blessed David of the sin involving Bathsheba. Some commentators, however, were unwilling to accept that any of the psalms should be taken in this | sense, claiming that it was most inappropri-

---

5. Comment on the final four verses is missing with the loss of a page from the codex.

τὴν ὑπόθεσιν, ἀτοπώτατον εἶναι φή-
σαντες τὸ τοῖς ψαλμοῖς ἐγκεῖσθαι
τοῦ μακαρίου Δαυὶδ τὴν ἐξαγόρευσιν,
ἀλλ᾽ ἐμοί γε δοκοῦσιν οἱ τοιοῦτοι
5 πάντη τῆς ἐκθέσεως τῶν θείων γρα-
φῶν τὴν δύναμιν ἀγνοεῖν, καὶ μάλιστα τῶν ψαλμῶν.

Εἰ γὰρ ἠπίσταντο ὡς δι᾽ οὐδὲν
ἕτερον ἐγγράφως τοὺς ψαλμοὺς τοῦ
10 μακαρίου Δαυὶδ παρειλήφαμεν ἀλλ᾽
ἢ ὥστε παιδεύεσθαι τὸ ἦθος παρ
αὐτῶν, ἐπέγνωσαν ἂν ὅτι πρὸ τῶν
ἄλλων ἁπάντων τούτους ἔδει κεῖσθαι
τοὺς ψαλμοὺς τοὺς ἐξαγορευτικούς,
15 ἐπειπερ οὐχὶ ἔλαττον πάντες ἄνθρωποι δεόμεθα παιδεύεσθαι τὴν ἐξομολόγησιν τὴν τῶν ἠθῶν παραίνεσιν.

Ἐν μὲν γὰρ τοῖς ἤθεσιν εὑρήσει τις
20 πολλάκις καὶ πρῶτον καὶ δεύτερον
πολλοῖς τῶν ἀνθρώπων κατορθωθέν,
ἁμαρτίας δὲ οὐχ οἷόν τε οὕτω καθα-
ρεύσαι εἰς τὸ παντελὲς ὡς πάντη μὴ
δεῖσθαι ἐξομολογήσεως.

25

Καιρὸς δὲ ἤδη τοὺς τοιούτους καὶ
ἐκ τῆς βίβλου τοῦ μακαρίου Ἡσαΐου
τοῦ προφήτου περιελεῖν Οἴμοι τάλας
30 ἐγώ, ὅτι κατανένυγμαι, ὅτι ἄνθρωπος
ὢν | καὶ ἀκάθαρτα χείλη ἔχων ἐν
μέσῳ λαοῦ ἀκάθαρτα χείλη ἔχοντος
ἐγὼ οἰκῶ. Εἰ δὲ τῶν προφητῶν,
πολλῷ μᾶλλον τῶν ἀποστόλων πε-
35 ριελεῖν προσήκει τὰς τοιαύτας φωνάς, ἐν αἷς ἁμαρτωλοὺς ἑαυτοὺς καλεῖν οὐ παραιτοῦνται.

29-33 Is. VI, 5.

8 ἠπίστατο ms.
10 accipimus ms.

accipi debere psalmorum, incon
ueniens esse dicentes ut confessionem peccati sui Dauid psalmis insereret, sed mihi uidentur
huiusmodi homines Scripturae
diuinae utilitatem, et praecipue
psalmorum, penitus ignorare.

Si enim nossent quoniam non
ob aliud litteris mandatos beati
Dauid psalmos accepimus nisi ut
erudiremur per eos atque doce-
remur, aduerterent sine dubio
quoniam prae omnibus aliis hos
oportuit scribi in quibus peccatorum satisfactio continetur. Siquidem non minus omnes homines ad confitenda peccata quam
ad moralem institui conuenit disciplinam: multos namque hominum inuenies, qui studio uitae
melioris non uno tantum bono
gaudeant; nullus autem in tantum
a culpa alienus est, ut credat se
satisfactionis remediis non egere.

Quod si de psalmis talia dicta tollenda sunt, etiam de libris
profetarum, et praecipue beati
Issaiae, huiusmodi uerba conuenit amoueri, qui ait: *Heu me mi-*
serum, quoniam conpunctus sum,
quia cum sim homo et inmunda
labia habeam, in medio populi in-
munda labia habentis ego habito.
Quod si et de profetis remouenda
sunt, multo magis de apostolorum dictis, in quibus se non eru-
bescunt dicere peccatores.

ate for an admission by blessed David to be contained in the psalms. Such people strike me as completely ignorant of the force of the exposition of the divine Scriptures, especially the psalms. After all, if they understood that we have received the psalms of blessed David in writing for no other purpose than our moral instruction by them, they would acknowledge that these penitential psalms ought to have been composed before all the others,[1] especially since all we human beings are in no less need of instruction in confession than in moral exhortation. I mean, while you will often find one or two virtuous actions in the general run of people in matters of morals, it is impossible to be so completely free from sin as to have no need of confession at all. It would actually be appropriate to do away with such pieces also from the book of blessed Isaiah the prophet: "Alas, wretch that I am! I am filled with compunction, human being that I am, with unclean lips, living in the midst of a people with unclean lips."[2] Now, if it is necessary to remove such words from the prophets, then much more so from the apostles, for in their works they have no qualms about calling themselves sinners. | And so

---

1. Theodore is referring to the seven penitential psalms (Pss 6; 32; 38; 51; 102; 130; 143), nominated as such by the early church. For him, the psalms' moral value is exceeded by their usefulness in the (then novel) rite of confession, or penance—especially in the case of these seven, which deserve their place, *pace* some commentators.

2. Isa 6:5, which, as another penitential pericope, would also be at risk (as the Latin version emphasizes).

Ὥστε ἀναγκαιότατα μὲν καὶ τούτους κειμένους εὑρήσομεν τοὺς ψαλμούς, τοῖς δὲ εὖ φρονοῦσι τῶν δικαίων καὶ Θεῷ ἀνακειμένων ἀνθρώπων
καὶ αἱ κοιναὶ λέξεις πλείστην δύναν-
ται φέρειν τὴν ὠφέλειαν ἔγγραφοι
φερόμεναι.

Ἡμεῖς μέντοι οὐδὲ πρὸ τῆς ἀφέ-
σεώς φαμεν τῆς ἁμαρτίας ταῦτα εἰρῆσθαι παρὰ τοῦ μακαρίου Δαυίδ, ὥστ'
ἂν οἴεσθαί τινα οὐκ ἀξίους τῆς τοιαύτης ἐκθέσεως εἶναι τοὺς τοιούτους
ψαλμούς, ὡς οὐ πνευματικῆς κατα-
ξιουμένου χάριτος καθ' ὃν ταῦτα ἐ-
φθέγγετο καιρόν, ἐπειδὴ τῆς μὲν ἀφέσεως ἔτυχεν οὐ μετὰ πολύ. Εὐθὺς
γὰρ ἀποσταλέντος πρὸς αὐτὸν τοῦ
Νάθαν καὶ ἐλέγξαντος ἐπὶ τῇ ἁμαρτίᾳ καὶ μετὰ τὴν τῆς πλημμελείας
ὁμολογίαν ἀποφηναμένου περὶ τῆς
συγχωρήσεως τῆς ὑπὸ τοῦ Θεοῦ
δωρηθείσης αὐτῷ, αὐτὸς ἀνάλογα κἂν
τούτῳ τῆς οἰκείας ἀρετῆς διαπραττόμενος οὐ παρελόγισατο τὴν πλημμε-
λείαν μετὰ τὴν συγχώρησιν, ἀλλὰ
γὰρ ἑκάστοτε εἰς ὑπόμνησιν ἐρχό-
μενος τοῦ πταίσματος τὴν οἰκείαν
στενάζων ἐξηγόρευεν ἁμαρτίαν, τὴν
μὲν συγχώρησιν τῆς ἁμαρτίας τῇ τοῦ
Θεοῦ λογιζόμενος φιλανθρωπίᾳ, ἑαυ-
τῷ | δὲ προσήκειν ἡγούμενος τὸ πάν-
τοτε ἐξομολογεῖσθαι ὑπὲρ αὐτῆς.

Καὶ τοῦτο διεπράττετο μάλιστα
ἡνίκα ταῖς τοῦ Ἀβεσσαλὼμ περι-
πεπτώκει συμφοραῖς· καὶ δι' αὐτὸ

Vnde utiliter et ad profectum
eorum, qui recte sapiunt ac Deo
tota mente iunguntur, huiusmodi
psalmos et conscriptos et poste-
ritati traditos inuenimus: com- 5
munia namque uerba, id est quae
possunt omnibus conuenire in
scripturis, multum solent singulis
utilitatis adferre.

Nos tamen non dicimus bea- 10
tum Dauid ante remisionem peccati ista dixisse, ut uideantur non
esse idonea atque auctoritate digna, quippe ut eo dicta tempore
quo beato Dauid nulla spiritalis 15
inerat gratia: non enim post multum temporis est peccati sui ueniam consecutus. Nam missus ad
eum Natham profeta et de peccato eum conuicit, et post confes- 20
sionem datae illi ueniae sponsor
accessit. Et beatus Dauid remis-
sione illa non est factus negli-
gentior: eodem namque tempore,
quo erat uirtuti semper intentus, 25
in memoriam delicti sui reduce-
batur iugiter et ingemescens peccatum suum confessione prode-
bat, - remissionem quidem, quam
acceperat, Dei misericordiae re- 30
putans, sibi uero necessarium
credens ut semper memor esset
nec aliquando a satisfactione de-
sisteret.

Et hoc maxime agebat eo 35
tempore quo eum Abisalon, per-
uasso regno, in periculum uitae

19 ss. II Reg. XII, 1 ss.

22 beatus] b *ms, ceteris perditis*
fectis 30 acciperat *ms.*
24 tempore *supplevi, litteris madore con-*

we shall find it indispensable that these psalms as well were composed. On the other hand, the recital in community of texts transmitted in writing can impart great benefit to right-minded members of the good people who are dedicated to God.

We do not claim, of course, that this was recited by blessed David before forgiveness of the sin, in which case you might think such psalms not deserving of such explication, since spiritual grace had not been accorded at the time he uttered them. Actually, he attained forgiveness not long after: Nathan was immediately dispatched to David; he accused him of the sin, and after confession of the sin, he revealed the pardon granted him by God. Even in this matter David displayed his characteristic virtue, and far from minimizing the sin after the pardon, confessed his sin with groaning each time he called to mind the fall, attributing the pardon to God's lovingkindness and convinced that it behooved him always to confess it. He did this in particular when he fell foul of the calamities brought on by Absalom; and | God

τοῦτο ἐπαχθῆναι συνεχώρησεν ὁ
Θεός, παιδεύων αὐτὸν ὑπὲρ τῆς ἁμαρτίας καὶ εἰς τὸ ἑξῆς ἀσφαλέστερον
ἐργαζόμενος. Ἡνίκα γοῦν διωκόμενος
5 ὑπὸ τοῦ Ἀβεσσαλώμ, καὶ φεύγοντα
ὕβριζέ τε ῥήμασι ἐκτόποις ὁ Σεμεεὶ
καὶ λίθοις βάλλων διετέλει, εἶτα ἀγανακτήσας ἐπὶ τοῦτο ὁ Ἀβεσσὰ ὁ
τοῦ Δαυὶδ στρατηγὸς ἀνελεῖν αὐτὸν
10 ἠβούλετο, ἀγανακτήσας πρὸς τὸν
Αβεσσὰ ὁ μακάριος Δαυίδ, ἐπι-
στραφεὶς δὲ πρός τε τὸν Ἰωὰβ
καὶ τοὺς λοιποὺς ἅπαντας τοὺς ἑπο-
μένους φησίν· Ἰδοὺ ὁ υἱός μου ὁ
15 ἐξελθὼν ἐκ τῆς κοιλίας μου ζητεῖ τὴν
ψυχήν μου, ἔτι καὶ νῦν ὁ υἱὸς τοῦ
Ἰεμενεὶ· ἄφες αὐτὸν καταρᾶσθαι, ὅτι
Κύριος εἴρηκεν αὐτῷ ὅπως ἴδῃ τὴν
ταπείνωσίν μου, καὶ ἀνταποδώσει μοι
20 Κύριος ἀγαθὰ ἀντὶ τῆς κατάρας αὐτοῦ τῆς ἐν τῇ ἡμέρᾳ ταύτῃ.

Καὶ ὅτι τοῦτο ἅπασιν ἔθος τοῖς
δικαίοις, μεγίστη ἀπόδειξις ὁ μακάριος ἀπόστολος Παῦλος λέγων· Ἐγὼ
25 γάρ εἰμι ὁ ἐλάχιστος τῶν ἀποστόλων,
ὃς οὐκ εἰμὶ ἱκανὸς καλεῖσθαι ἀπόστο-
λος, διότι ἐδίωξα τὴν ἐκκλησίαν τοῦ Θεοῦ, μετὰ τοσούτους πόνους, οὓς ὑπέμεινεν ὑπὲρ Χριστοῦ, οὕτως τὰ πρὸ τῆς κλήσεως ὀδυρόμενος καὶ οὐκ ἄξιον
ἑαυτὸν λογιζόμενος τῆς τοῦ ἀποστόλου προσηγορίας διὰ τὴν τότε τῆς ἐκκλη-
30 σίας δίωξιν. Καὶ ἀλλα|χοῦ δέ φησιν· Πιστὸς ὁ λόγος καὶ πάσης ἀποδοχῆς
ἄξιος, ὅτι Χριστὸς Ἰησοῦς ἦλθεν εἰς τὸν κόσμον ἁμαρτωλοὺς σῶσαι, ὧν πρῶτός
εἰμι ἐγώ· ἀλλὰ διὰ τοῦτο ἠλεήθην, ἵνα ἐν ἐμοὶ πρώτῳ ἐνδείξηται Ἰησοῦς
Χριστὸς τὴν πᾶσαν μακροθυμίαν.

Ὥστε οὐκ ἀπεικὸς καὶ τὸν μα-
35 κάριον Δαυὶδ μετὰ τὴν συγχώρησιν
τοῦ Θεοῦ ἐξαγορευτικοὺς φθέγξα-

ac salutis adduxerat; quam quidem tribulationem propter hoc
ipsum ei Deus permisit inferri
ut, castigatus pro peccato suo, in
reliquum cautior redderetur. Nam
cum persequente Abisalon fugeret, et Semei eum conuiciis ac
maledictis urgeret mittens in illum lapides, indignatus Abisai,
qui erat unus ex ducibus Dauid,
uoluit maledici linguam capite
eius amputato compraemere,
quod moleste ferens beatus Dauid conuersus ad Ioab et ad reliquos omnes, qui sequebantur,
dixit: *Ecce filius meus, qui egre-*
sus est de utero meo, quaerit ani-
mam meam usque *pro maledi-*
ctione eius in hoc die.

Et quoniam haec sit omnium
consuetudo iustorum, magnam
adfert probationem apostolus
Paulus dicens: *Qui sum minimus*
omnium apostolorum, et reliqua.

Vnde non est inconueniens
si etiam beatus Dauid post acceptam a Deo ueniam confessio-

4-7 cf. II Reg. XVI, 7, 13   8 XVI, 9   14-21 XVI, 11-12   24-27 I Cor. XV,
9 30-33 I Tim. I, 15-16.

6 ῥήμα *ms*   16 ἔτι] εἰ δὲ *ms.*
17 querit *ms*   18-19 maledic̄ *ms.*

allowed him to be caught up for the same reason, to teach him about his sin and make him stronger in future. He was pursued by Absalom, and in his flight Shimei verbally abused him and kept pelting him with stones. Then when David's general Abishai was annoyed by this and wanted to do away with him, David got angry with Abishai and turned to Joab and all the rest of his followers with the words "Lo, my son, the fruit of my loins, seeks my life, and even now the Benjaminite as well; let him curse me, for the Lord has told him that he saw my lowliness, and the Lord will reward me for his cursing today."[3] And the greatest proof that this is the way with all righteous people is the blessed apostle Paul's saying, "I am the least of the apostles, and am not worthy to be called an apostle, because I persecuted the church of God."[4] Despite so many hardships suffered for Christ, he was so sorry for what happened before his calling that he thought himself unworthy of the title of apostle on account of his persecution of the church at that time. Elsewhere also he says, "The saying is sure and worthy of full acceptance, that Christ Jesus came into the world to save sinners, of whom I am the foremost; but I was shown mercy for the reason that in me, as the foremost, Jesus Christ might give evidence of complete long-suffering."[5]

And so, far from it being unlikely that blessed David even after God's pardon gave utterance to penitential | psalms, it was very fitting for him with

---

3. Cf. 2 Sam 16 (Joab not figuring in this incident).
4. 1 Cor 15:9.
5. 1 Tim 1:15–16.

σθαι ψαλμούς, ἀλλὰ γὰρ καὶ σφόδρα γε ἁρμόττον αὐτῷ πρὸς τὴν ἑτέρων ὠφέλειαν.

Εἰ γὰρ ὁ μακάριος Δαυὶδ ὀδύρεται ἡμαρτηκὼς καίτοι τετυχηκὼς τῆς παρὰ τοῦ Θεοῦ συγχωρήσεως, βαρὺ τὸ ἁμαρτεῖν αὐτῷ τιθέμενος, πόσῳ μᾶλλον ἅπαντας συγκινεῖσθαι εἰκός, ὅσοιπερ εὖ φρονοῦσιν, εἰς σύντονον ἐξομολόγησιν ὑπὲρ ὧν ἑαυτοῖς συνίσασιν ἡμαρτηκόσιν.

nis psalmos cecinit, sed aptum illi ac familiare plurimum, qui uolebat exemplo suo alios erudire. Nam si beatus Dauid etiam post acceptam a Deo ueniam in- 5 gemuit uehimenter ac doluit, ipsum peccasse se deflens, et confessionum psalmos in suffragium indulgentiae et conscripsit et cecinit, quanto magis omnes 10 qui sanum sapiunt pro conscientia reatus ac delicti sui ad confessionem peccatorum debent absque impedimento uericondiae et pudoris occurrere. 15

Ταῦτα δὲ ἐπισεσήμανται ἡμῖν καὶ ἐν ἑτέρῳ ψαλμῷ. Οὐκ ἄκαιρον δὲ ἐνομίσαμεν καὶ τῇ δευτερώσει χρήσασθαι νῦν, ὥστε ἅπαντας γνῶναι τοὺς ἐντυγχάνοντας τῷ τοιούτῳ ψαλμῷ τῆς παρενθέσεως τό τε εὔκαιρον καὶ τὸ ἀναγκαῖον· οὕτω γὰρ καὶ μεμαθηκότες τὴν αἰτίαν προσεχέστερον δυνήσονται τῆς ἐξ αὐτῶν ὠφελείας ἀπολαύειν. 20

2. **Domine, ne in furore tuo arguas me**, reliqua. Vnum atque idem argumentum est sexti psalmi et praesentis.

3a. Ὅτι τὰ βέλη σου ἐνεπάγησάν μοι. Σύμμαχος· καθίκοντό μου. Διὰ δὴ τοῦτό φησιν ἀξιῶ μὴ μετὰ θυμοῦ γενέσθαι τὸν ἔλεγχον, μηδὲ μετὰ ὀργῆς τὴν παιδείαν, ἐπειδὴ αἱ τιμωρίαι σου ἐμπεπήγασί μοι· βέλη γὰρ καλεῖ τὰς 25 τιμωρίας, ἀπὸ τοῦ πλήττειν καὶ θανατοῦν. Καλῶς δὲ εἶπε τὸ ἐνεπάγησαν, ἀκολούθως τοῖς ἀνωτέροις, ἐπειδὴ γὰρ τὸ βέλος, μέχρις ἂν ἐμπεπηγὸς ᾖ, ἴασιν οὐ συγχωρεῖ προσαχθῆναι τῷ τραύματι, — τοῦτο λέγει ὅτι αἱ τιμω-

16-17 cf. argum. ps. VI (p. 31) et infra in v. 2.

23 καθίκεται ms, cf. Ps.-Basilius in loc. (P. G., XXX, 89 A 11)   24-25 ἀξιῶ — παιδείαν cf. L (p. 699, 50-700, 1)   25-26 βέλη — τιμωρίας (p. 699, 44-45)   27-28 (ib. 46-47).
1 cicinit ms   5-6 ingemit 1ª m.   12 dilecti ms   14 abque ms   15 occurre 1ª m.
Domine — praesentis: A, fol. 12b; B, fol. 13c; cf. Ae (p. 220, 9-12).

Ae 3ª (p. 220, 13-14): Cum furore uero corripi et cum ira argui dicit... (p. 220, 18-20) pro uechimenti et herenti castigatione, ac si diceret: quoniam ultionum tuarum uerbera mihi grauiter insidentur... (p. 220, 22-24) pro inmobili castigatione, pro opere ultorio... quia sagitae in uulnere sunt.

a view to the benefit of others. After all, if blessed David was sorry for sinning despite having received pardon from God, depressed by his sin, so much the more does it behoove all right-minded people to be moved in concert to a brief confession of the sins that they are aware of in their own case. Now, this was suggested to us by another psalm as well,[6] but we thought it not out of place for us to duplicate it here, too, for all the readers of such a psalm to recognize the timeliness and necessity of its inclusion. In this way, you see, by learning the more immediate occasion, we shall be in a position to enjoy the benefit from them.

Lord, do not accuse me in your anger and so on (v. 1). Psalm 6 and this one have the same theme.[7] *Because your arrows have sunk into me* (v. 2). Symmachus: "They cleaved to me." I ask that your accusation not be made in anger, he is saying, nor your chastisement in rage, for the reason that your punishments have sunk into me (by *arrows* referring to the punishments, from the action of striking and killing). *Sunk into* was well put, consistent with what was said above, since the arrow, as long as it is sunken, does not allow treatment to be applied to the wound; he means, | Your punishments

6. Theodore is referring to his opening words on Ps 6, as he says in comment on v. 1 below.

7. This comment is from the Latin version and perhaps corresponds to the Greek above.

ρίαι σου ἐναπέμειναν μοι, λύσιν οὐ λαμβάνουσαι. Οὐ τὸν ἔλεγχον τοίνυν
φεύγω οὐδὲ τὴν παιδείαν ἀποστρέφομαι, ἀλλὰ μὴ διηνεκῶς ἐναφανισθῆναι
ταῖς συμφοραῖς παρακαλῶ, τοῦτο λοιπὸν θυμοῦ καὶ ὀργῆς εἶναι τιθέμενος.

3ᵇ-4ᵃ. Καὶ ἐπεστήριξας ἐπ' ἐμὲ τὴν χεῖρά σου, καὶ οὐκ ἔστιν ἴασις ἐν
5 τῇ σαρκί μου ἀπὸ προσώπου τῆς ὀργῆς σου. Χεῖρα καλεῖ τοῦ Θεοῦ τὴν
ἐνέργειαν εἴτε ἐπὶ τιμωρίᾳ, εἴτε ἐπὶ εὐεργεσίᾳ γιγνομένην· ἐνταῦθα τοίνυν
τὴν ἐπὶ τιμωρίᾳ | γεγενημένην λέγει, — δῆλον γὰρ ἐκ τῆς ἀκολουθίας πάσης
τοῦ ψαλμοῦ. Ἐπεστήριξάς μοι τοίνυν φησὶ τὴν χεῖρά σου, τουτέστι τὴν
τιμωρίαν σου ἐπέθηκάς μοι ἑδραίως — ἀκολούθως τῷ ἐνεπάγησαν καὶ τὸ ἐπε_
10 στήριξας εἰπών, ἵνα εἴπῃ ὅτι ἐμπεπηγμένοι τὰ κακὰ λύσιν οὐ προσδοκώ-
μενα λαβεῖν. Ἀκολουθεῖ ἑαυτῷ δὲ διόλου. Ἐπειδὴ γὰρ εἶπεν Ὅτι τὰ βέλη
σου ἐνεπάγησάν μοι καὶ ἐπεστήριξας ἐπ' ἐμὲ τὴν χεῖρά σου, πρὸς τὸ τὰ
βέλη σου ἐνεπάγησάν μοι ἐπήγαγε τὸ οὐκ ἔστιν ἴασις ἐν τῇ σαρκί μου·
οὐδὲ γὰρ δυνατὸν ἐμπεπηγμένου τοῦ βέλους τὸν δεξάμενον τὴν πληγὴν
15 ἰάσεως τυχεῖν ποτε. Οὕτως τοίνυν φησὶ τυχεῖν οὐ προσδοκῶ θεραπείας
καὶ ἀπαλλαγῆς τῶν κακῶν, λύσιν οὐδεμίαν εὑρίσκων τῶν συμφορῶν διὰ τὸ
τὴν ὀργήν σου μὴ συγχωρεῖν. Τὸ δὲ ἀπὸ προσώπου σωματοποιήσας περὶ
τῆς ὀργῆς ἔφησεν, ἵνα εἴπῃ ὅτι Ἡ ὀργὴ ὥσπερ παροῦσα τοῖς γιγνομένοις
καὶ ἐπιβλέπουσα οὕτως διατίθησι τὰς κατ' ἐμοῦ συμφοράς.

20 4ᵇ. Οὐκ ἔστιν εἰρήνη τοῖς ὀστέοις μου ἀπὸ προσώπου τῶν ἁμαρτιῶν μου.
Ὥσπερ πρὸς τὸ τὰ βέλη σου ἐνεπάγησάν μοι ἀκολούθως ἐπήγαγε τὸ οὐκ
ἔστιν ἴασις ἐν τῇ σαρκί μου, οὕτως πρὸς τὸ καὶ ἐπεστήριξας ἐπ' ἐμὲ τὴν χεῖρά
σου τοῦτο τὸ οὐκ ἔστιν εἰρήνη τοῖς ὀστέοις μου ἀπὸ προσώπου τῶν ἁμαρτιῶν μου, τουτέστιν Ἡ χείρ σου βαρεῖά τις οὖσα καὶ δυνατὴ ἐπιτεθεῖσα
25 πάντα μου διέλυσε καὶ διεσάλευσε τὰ ὀστᾶ. Σωματικῶς γὰρ τῆς τοῦ Θεοῦ
τιμωρίας ἐπιμνησθεὶς ἀ|κολουθεῖ διόλου ἑαυτῷ κατὰ τὴν τῆς σωματοποιή-
σεως ἀρχήν· ταύτῃ γὰρ ἁπανταχοῦ κέχρηται τῇ συνηθείᾳ. Ἐμνημόνευσε
δὲ τῶν ὀστέων πρὸς παράστασιν τῆς ἰσχυρᾶς συντριβῆς, ὡς καὶ ἀλλαχοῦ Καὶ τὰ ὀστᾶ μου ἐταράχθη σφόδρα, ἵνα εἴπῃ ὅτι ἰσχυρῶς ἐταρά-
30 χθην. Καλῶς δὲ ἐπήγαγε τὸ ἀπὸ προσώπου τῶν ἁμαρτιῶν μου, ἐπειδὴ

29 Ps. VI, 3ᵇ (cf. p. 179, 27-30).

26 ἀκοθεῖ ms.

Aᵉ 25-27 (p. 220, 25-28): Quia semel sub corporali habitu iram formauerat uindicantis, tenet per omnia consequentiam ut a corporea specie non recedat.
27-28 (p. 221, 1-3): Pro ualida attritione ossa posuit, singulis praemisis singula
retulit. 30-224, 3 (p. 221, 6-10): Superius furoris et irae et grauissimae
ultionis mentionem fecerat, ut ostenderet quod non inrationabiliter fuisset ira
commota sed iuste in peccata eius accensa.

stayed with me, allowing no relief; so instead of shunning your accusation or turning away from your correction, I am asking not to be completely wiped out by the calamities, citing this as a final mark of anger and rage.

And you have fastened your hand upon me, and there is no healing in my flesh in the face of your wrath (vv. 2–3). By *hand* he refers to God's action exercised at times in punishment, at times in kindness; so in this case he means its exercise in punishment, as emerges from the sequence of the whole psalm. So, *you have fastened your hand upon me* means, You inflicted punishment firmly upon me (using *sunk in* and *fastened* consistently to mean "with the troubles sunken in and unlikely to experience relief"). You see, since he had said *Because your arrows have sunk into me, and you have fastened your hand upon me,* to *your arrows have sunk into me* he added *there is no healing in my flesh,* since with the arrows sunk in, it was not possible for the wound that had been inflicted ever to find healing. Likewise, he is saying, I therefore do not expect to find healing and freedom from the troubles, gaining no relief from the calamities because your wrath does not permit it. He used *in the face* in reference to wrath by use of a bodily comparison, as if to say, It is wrath that is thus the cause of my calamities as though present to what happens and watching it.

There is no peace in my bones in the face of my sins. Just as to *your arrows have sunk into me* he proceeded to add *there is no healing in my flesh,* so to *and you have fastened your hand upon me* he added *there is no peace in my bones in the face of my sins*—in other words, Your hand, heavy and powerful as it is, is completely placed upon me, and has loosened and shaken my bones. He mentions God's punishment in bodily fashion consistently with his principle of using bodily comparisons, this being the convention he adopts everywhere. Now, he made mention of the bones to highlight the severe impact, as elsewhere as well he said, "My bones were severely shaken,"[8] as if to say, I was severely shaken. He did well to proceed to say *in the face of my sins,* since | above he had made mention of wrath, anger, and severe

---

8. Cf. Ps 6:2–3, loosely recalled.

ἄνω θυμοῦ καὶ ὀργῆς ἐμνημόνευσε καὶ τιμωρίας βαρυτάτης, ὥστε δεῖξαι ὅτι
οὐκ ἄλογός τις ἦν ἡ τοῦ Θεοῦ ὀργὴ ἀλλὰ δικαίως ἀπὸ τῶν αὐτοῦ ἁμαρτιῶν κινουμένη. Διὰ τοῦτο ὥσπερ ἐπὶ τῆς ὀργῆς εἶπεν ἀπὸ προσώπου,
οὕτως καὶ ἐπὶ τῶν ἁμαρτιῶν — τουτέστιν ὅτι αὐταὶ αἱ ἁμαρτίαι ὥσπερ ὁρώ-
μεναι διὰ τὸ μέγεθος τούτων μοι πρόξενοι τῶν κακῶν γεγόνασιν. Εἶτα καὶ 5
βαρύτερον αὐτὸ δεικνὺς καὶ εὐγνωμόνως τοῦ μεγέθους τῶν συμφορῶν ἑαυτῷ
περιάψαι τὴν αἰτίαν βουληθείς, ἐπάγει·

5ª. Ὅτι αἱ ἀνομίαι μου ὑπερῆραν τὴν κεφαλήν μου. Τοιαῦται γάρ εἰσι
τῷ μεγέθει ὡς ὑπεραίρουσαι καθέλκειν, καὶ ταπεινοῦν, καὶ καθιστᾶν ἐν τῷ
πλήθει τῶν συμφορῶν· τὸ γὰρ ὑπὲρ κεφαλῆς ὂν εὐχερῶς συνωθεῖ καὶ 10
καθέλκει.

5ᵇ. Ὡσεὶ φορτίον βαρὺ ἐβαρύνθησαν ἐπ᾽ ἐμέ. Πολλαὶ τοίνυν οὖσαί φησι
καὶ μέγισται, ὥσπερ τι φορτίον βαρὺ καὶ ἀνύποιστον ἐπικείμεναι, συνώθησαν εἰς τὰς συμφοράς.

6ª. Προσώζεσαν καὶ ἐσάπησαν οἱ μώλωπές μου. Διὰ τοῦτό φησι γέγονε 15
μεγάλα τὰ τραύματά μου οὐκέτι ἴασιν ἐπιδεχόμενα· τὰ γὰρ ἕλκη προσώζεσαν τὰ ἀνέλπιστον ἔχοντα λοιπὸν τὴν ὑγείαν.

6ᵇ. Ἀπὸ προσώπου τῆς ἀφροσύνης μου. Ταῦτα δὲ πάσχω φησὶν ὑπὲρ
ὧν ἀφρόνως ἔπραξα, πάλιν κἀνταῦθα τῆς οἰκείας ἁμαρτίας ἐξάπτων τῶν
συμφορῶν τὴν αἰτίαν.   20

7ª. Ἐταλαιπώρησα καὶ κατεκάμφθην ἕως τέλους. Διὰ ταῦτα ἐξητάσθην
ἐν ταλαιπωρίαις καὶ πολλῶν ἐπειράθην κακῶν. Τὸ δὲ κατεκάμφθην, ἀντὶ τοῦ
σφόδρα ἐταπεινώθην ὑπὸ τῶν κακῶν, ἐπειδὴ ὁ κατακαμπτόμενος τοῦ οἰκείου
τῆς ἡλικίας ὕψους πλεῖστον ὅσον ταπεινότερος γίνεται.

7ᵇ. Ὅλην τὴν ἡμέραν σκυθρωπάζων ἐπορευόμην. Διετέλουν τοίνυν φησὶν 25
ἐν σκυθρωπότητι.

8ª. Ὅτι αἱ ψύαι μου ἐπλήσθησαν ἐμπαιγμάτων. Ἐπειδὴ ἀποβλέπων
φησὶ πρὸς τὸ πλῆθος τῶν ἁμαρτιῶν τῶν ἐμῶν, οὐδεμίαν ἴασιν προσεδόκων
ἐπὶ ταῖς συμφοραῖς.

Aᵉ 6ˡ (p. 221, 18-21): Ideo malum eorum inmidicabile factum est, nec tabo
ocubante omnia potui recipere sanitatem.   7ᵇ (p. 222, 1-3): Continuus me
possedebat meror iugisque tristitia.

punishment, so as to bring out that God's wrath was not without reason but rightly aroused by his sins. Hence, just as he said in the case of wrath *in the face of,* so too in the case of the sins—that is, These sins proved to be the cause of my troubles, as though visible for their magnitude.

Next, both to bring out its severity and in his wish candidly to attach the blame for the magnitude of the calamities to himself, he goes on to say *Because my iniquities reached beyond my head* (v. 4): they were so great in magnitude as to rear up and drag me down, abase me and plunge me into a plethora of calamities (what is beyond one's head easily crushing and dragging one down). *They weighed me down like a mighty burden:* being many and mighty, therefore, resting on me like a heavy and insupportable burden, they crushed me to a calamitous state. *My scars became putrid and rotten* (v. 5): hence, my gaping wounds were no longer receptive of healing, since the sores turned putrid when they no longer had any hope of healing. *From the face of my stupidity:* I suffer this for acting foolishly (here again ascribing to his sin the blame for the calamities). *I became miserable and downcast forever* (v. 6): hence, I was reduced to misery and experienced deep trouble. *I was downcast* means "I was severely humbled by the troubles," since the greater the heights reached by the person who is downcast, the lower he falls. *I went about with sad countenance all day long:* so I continued to be sad.

Because my loins are filled with mockery (v. 7): since, considering the vast number of my sins, I expected no healing in my troubles. | The phrase

Τὸ γὰρ αἱ ψύαι μου ἐπλήσθησαν
ἐμπαιγμάτων σεμνότερον τὴν ἁμαρ-
τίαν αἰνίττεται· αἱ | γὰρ ψύχι παρά-
κεινται τοῖς νεφροῖς, οἱ δὲ νεφροὶ
5 γεννητικοὶ τῆς κινήσεώς εἰσι.

Quoniam lumbi mei impleti sunt
inlusionibus. Peccati sui speciem
uericondius indicauit: nam lumbi
adherent renibus, in renibus uero
concupiscentialis motus nascitur.

Ἀμέλει πολλοὶ τῶν ἀκίνητα ἐκεῖνα τὰ μόρια ἐργάζεσθαι βουλομένων,
φαρμάκων ἐπιθέσει τοὺς νεφροὺς νεκροῦντες, οὕτως ἀκινησίαν αὐτοῖς ἐργά-
ζονται· διὰ τοῦτό φησιν ὅτι αἱ ψύχι μου ἐπλήσθησαν ἐμπαιγμάτων, ἀπὸ
τοῦ μέρους τοῦ περὶ τοὺς τόπους εἰρηκώς, καὶ ἐμπαιγμάτων καλέσας τὴν
10 ἐπιθυμίαν ὡς κατακρατήσασαν καὶ παίγνιον αὐτὸν καὶ χλεύην ἐργασαμένην.

Ἔθος δὲ τοῦτο τῇ γραφῇ ἀπὸ
μέρους τοῦ περὶ τοὺς τόπους ἐκείνους
πολλάκις τὴν γέννησιν λέγειν — ὡς
παρὰ τῷ ἀποστόλῳ· ἔτι γὰρ ἐν τῇ
15 ὀσφύι τοῦ πατρὸς ἦν. Ἀκύλας καὶ Θεοδοτίων τὸ ἐπλήσθησαν ἐμπαιγμάτων
φανερώτερον εἶπον ἐπλήσθησαν ἀτι-
μίας.

Consuetudo uero est Scripturae a parte locorum illorum effectum generationis ostendere, sicut
in apostolo possitum est: adhuc
in lumbis patris erat. Aquila et
Theodotion manifestius dixerunt: Impleti sunt ignominia.

9ᵃ. Ἐκακώθην καὶ ἐταπεινώθην ἕως σφόδρα. Καὶ διὰ ταῦτά φησι πολ-
20 λῶν ἔλαβον πεῖραν κακῶν.

9ᵇ. Ὠρυόμην ἀπὸ στεναγμοῦ τῆς καρδίας μου. Ἀπό τε τοῦ πλήθους
τῶν κακῶν, οὐ φέρων τῆς καρδίας τὸν στεναγμόν, ἐκβοᾶν ἠναγκαζόμην. Ὠρυόμην δὲ εἶπεν ἀντὶ τοῦ ἐξεβόων, ἐπειδὴ ἔθος τοῖς κυσίν, ἐπειδὰν καιριαν
λάβωσι τὴν πληγήν, πενθικήν τινα καὶ θρηνητικὴν ἀποτελεῖν φωνήν — ὅπερ
25 ὠρύεσθαι λέγεται κυρίως. Τὴν οὖν ἐπίτασιν βουλόμενος εἰπεῖν, ἐχρήσατο
τῇ ἐπὶ τῶν ἀλόγων λεγομένῃ φωνῇ· διὰ τὸ μέγεθος τῆς συμφορᾶς οὐδὲ
ἀνθρωπίνως ἐβόων, ἀλλὰ δίκην κυνὸς ὠρυόμενος διετέλουν.

10ᵃ. Κύριε, ἐναντίον σου πᾶσα ἡ ἐπιθυμία μου. Τοῦτο μάλιστα τῆς εὐλαβείας τοῦ μακαρίου Δαυὶδ τὸ γνώρισμα. Εἰρηκὼς γὰρ διὰ πολλῶν τῶν ἁμαρ-
30 τιῶν τὸ πλῆθός τε καὶ τὸ μέγεθος, καὶ μνημονεύσας τῆς ἐπὶ τούτοις κινη-

14-15 Hebr. VII, 10.

Quoniam lumbi — ignominia: A, fol. 12ᵇ; B, fol. 13ᶜ. 1. 17 inpleti A
1 sunt om. A   2-3 peccati — indicauit affert Aᵉ (p. 222, 4-5)   2 speciem
om. AB   3 uerecondius A   16 theotō A theō B   manifeš A.

Aᵉ 3-5. 9-10 (p. 222,5-8): ...apte enim locorum genitalium comixtionis ostendens inlusiones uocauit ipsam concupiscentiam quae ei a se capto uechimen-
tius inluserit.   26 (p. 222, 13-14): Augenter pro doloris cumulo.

my loins are filled with mockery, in fact, hints more gravely at the sin: the *loins* lie close to the kidneys, and the kidneys are responsible for emotion. Many people, of course, who want to render those organs unmoved bring immobility to them by mortifying the kidneys by administration of drugs— hence his saying *my loins are filled with mockery,* referring to the part near the places, and by *mockery* referring to lust as being in control and bringing him mockery and jesting. Now, it is the frequent custom of Scripture to refer to begetting by mention of the part near those places, as with the apostle, "He was still in the loins of his ancestor."[9] For *they were filled with mockery* Aquila and Theodotion said more clearly, "They were filled with ignominy." *I was afflicted and humbled to the breaking point* (v. 8): for this reason I experienced many troubles. *I howled from the sighing of my heart:* from the great number of the troubles, and unable to bear the sighing of my heart, I was forced to cry aloud (*howled* meaning "cried aloud," since when dogs get a blow in a vital part, they normally utter a cry of pain and lament, which is properly called howling). In his wish to express the intensity, therefore, he used the word applicable to irrational animals, meaning, From the magnitude of the calamity I cried aloud, not in human fashion, instead continuing to howl like a dog.

Lord, all my desire is before you (v. 9). This most of all is the talisman of blessed David's piety: speaking as a result of the great number and magnitude of sins, and mentioning | God's anger prompted against him by them,

---

9. Heb 7:10, in reference to Levi. Theodoret, with typical conciseness, does not beat about the bush in this way to say that the psalmist is hinting at a sexual sin. On the other hand, he does not mention the odd practice of using drugs to mortify the sexual organs. Was this practice in force in Theodore's monastery?

θείσης ὀργῆς τοῦ Θεοῦ κατ᾽ αὐτοῦ, οὐκ εἶπεν ὅτι Κύριε, ἀπάλλαξόν με.
Ἀλλὰ τί φησιν; Κύριε, ἐναντίον σου πᾶσα ἡ ἐπιθυμία μου. Οὐ τολμῶ φησιν
ἀπαλλαγὴν αἰτῆσαι τῶν συμφορῶν, — οὐ γὰρ ἐᾷ τῶν ἁμαρτιῶν τὸ πλῆθος
μετὰ παρρησίας ποιήσασθαι τὴν αἴτησιν, — ἐναντίον σου οὖν | φησι πᾶσα
ἡ ἐπιθυμία μου, τουτέστιν Αὐτὸς οἶδας τί ἐπιθυμῶ, τὴν ἀπαλλαγὴν τῶν   5
κακῶν τῶν περιεχόντων με. Ἐπειδὴ οὖν ἐγὼ μὲν αἰτῆσαι οὐ τολμῶ, αὐτὸς
δὲ οἶδας ὅπερ ἐπιθυμῶ, τοῦτο πλήρωσον ὅπερ αὐτὸς οἶδας χρήσιμον.

10ᵇ. Καὶ ὁ στεναγμός μου ἀπό σου οὐκ ἀπεκρύβη. Κατάδηλός σοί ἐστί
φησι καὶ ὁ στεναγμὸς ὁ ἐμός, τουτέστιν αἱ θλίψεις καὶ αἱ ὀδύναι, καὶ οἶδάς
φησιν ὃ ἐπιθυμῶ, καὶ τῶν συμφορῶν ὧν ὑπέστην τὸ πλῆθος οὐκ ἀγνοεῖς.   10
Ἑξῆς δὲ καταλέγει καὶ τὰς ἐπιγεγενημένας αὐτῷ συμφοράς.

11ᵃ. Ἡ καρδία μου ἐταράχθη. Τοῦτο καὶ τὰ ἑξῆς πρὸς τὸ οὐκ ἀπεκρύβη
ἐπάγει, ἵνα εἴπῃ ὅτι Οἶδας ὅπως τόδε ὑπέστην καὶ ὅπως τόδε. Οἶδας οὖν
φησιν ἐν ὅσῃ κατέστην ταραχῇ τὴν καρδίαν ὑπὸ τοῦ πλήθους τῶν κακῶν
ἐν ἀπορίᾳ πολλῇ καταστάς, καὶ ὅπως ἐξησθένησα πάσης ἐκτὸς κατασταθεὶς   15
τῆς οἰκείας ἰσχύος.

11ᵇ·ᶜ. Ἐγκατέλιπέν με ἡ ἰσχύς μου, καὶ τὸ φῶς τῶν ὀφθαλμῶν μου οὐκ
ἔστιν μετ᾽ ἐμοῦ. Καὶ ὅτι φησὶν ἀπὸ τῆς ὑπερβαλλούσης ἀθυμίας ὥστε ἐν
σκοτώσει καταστάς, οὐκέτι οὐδὲ διορᾶν δύναμαι.

12. Οἱ φίλοι μου καὶ οἱ πλησίον μου ἐξ ἐναντίας μου ἤγγισαν καὶ ἔστησαν.   20
Ἀλλὰ καὶ τοῦτό φησιν ἐπίστασαι ὅτι οἱ φίλοι καὶ οἱ σφόδρα γνήσιοι ἀεὶ
μετ᾽ ἐμοῦ ἀναστρεφόμενοι καὶ πλησιάζοντές μοι, καὶ οὗτοι μετὰ τῶν ἐχθρῶν
κατέστησαν εἰς τὸν κατ᾽ ἐμοῦ πόλεμον. Τὸ οὖν ἐξ ἐναντίας μου ἤγγισαν, ἵνα
εἴπῃ ὅτι Τοῖς ἐξ ἐναντίας μου ἤγγισαν καὶ μετ᾽ αὐτῶν ἔστησαν κατ᾽ ἐμοῦ.

12ᵇ. Καὶ οἱ ἔγγιστά μοι ἀπὸ μακρόθεν ἔστησαν. Καὶ οἱ ποτέ μοι ἐγγί-   25
ζοντες ἤγγιζον μὲν ἑτέροις, ἐμηκύνοντο δὲ ἐμοῦ | — ἵνα εἴπῃ ὅτι Οἱ πρότε-
ρόν μου φίλοι εἰς ἐχθροὺς κατέστησαν.

5-6 οἶδας — τολμῶ cf. L (701, 50-702, 2)   8 ἀπό σου οὐκ ἀπεκρύβη restitui ex
comment. versiculi 15 (p. 228, 12).   25 ἀπό addidi, cf. infra p. 227, 9   27-28 cf. L
(p. 702, 26-27).

Aᵉ 3-4 (p. 222, 14-16): Quia ego illud male mihi conscius uerbis supplicare
non audeo.   9-11 (p. 222, 18-20): Et uota nosti et necessitates obtandi, quas
consequenter enumerat.   13-16 (p. 222, 21-24): Nosti in quanta cor meum
conturbatione consteterit, in quantum sit difectum propriae uirtutis addictus.
12ᵃ (p. 222, 27-31): Etiam hoc, inquit, nosti quoniam hos, quos mihi uel necessitudo
uel familiaritas longua coniunxerat, et ipsi in partem meorum hostium transerunt.

he did not say, Lord, grant me relief. Instead, what did he say? *Lord, all my desire is before you:* I do not presume to request relief from the calamities (the multitude of his sins not allowing him to make the request with any confidence), so *all my desire is before you*—that is, You know what I desire, relief from the troubles surrounding me; since I do not presume to ask it on my own behalf, then, whereas you know what I desire, grant what you know is useful. *And my sighing was not hidden from you:* my sighing is obvious to you—that is, the tribulations and pangs—and you know what I desire, and you are not unaware of the great number of calamities I suffered.

He went on also to list the calamities befalling him. *My heart was disturbed* (v. 10). This and the following he adds to *was not hidden,* as if to say, You know how I endured this and that; so you know to what kind of disturbance my heart was reduced by the large number of troubles I was subjected to in great bewilderment, and how I was weakened by being left without my usual strength. *My strength left me, and the light of my eyes is not with me:* as a result of excessive depression I am plunged into darkness, and no longer can I see clearly. *My friends and my neighbors took up a position against me* (v. 11): you also know that my friends and close neighbors, who constantly accompanied and stayed close to me, also conspired with the enemy in warring against me. So *took up a position against me* means, They approached those opposed to me and sided with them against me. *And those close to me kept their distance:* those once close to me got close to the others and distanced themselves from me, as if to say, Those formerly friendly to me became hostile. |

13ᵃ. Καὶ ἐξεβιάζοντο οἱ ζητοῦντες τὴν ψυχήν μου. Περὶ τῶν αὐτῶν
λέγει. Καὶ οὐ μόνον φησὶν ἐχθροί μου κατέστησαν, ἀλλὰ γὰρ καὶ σφόδρα
ἠγωνίσαντο εἰς τὸ τὴν ψυχήν μου λαβεῖν, τουτέστιν εἰς τὸ ἀνελεῖν με.

5 Τὸ οὖν Οἱ ἀπὸ τοῦ ἰδιώματος παράκειται τοῦ ἐβραϊκοῦ· τὸ γὰρ ῥητὸν ἀκολούθως τῷ ἄνω κεῖται. Πρὸς
οὖν τὴν τῆς διανοίας ἀκολουθίαν οὕτως
ἀναγνωστέον· Καὶ οἱ ἔγγιστά μοι ἀπὸ
10 μακρόθεν ἔστησαν καὶ ἐξεβιάζοντο
ζητοῦντες τὴν ψυχήν μου. Οὕτως εἶπε
καὶ Ἀκύλας· Ζητοῦντες τὴν ψυχήν
μου, τὸ Οἱ μὴ τεθεικώς.

Et uim faciebant qui quaerebant animam meam.

Interposuit Qui de familiaritate sermonis ebreici: nam dictorum consequentia cum praecedentibus connexa est. Ad facilio-
rem uerum intellectum ita legendum est: Et qui iuxta me erant
de longe steterunt et uim faciebant, quaerebant animam meam,
praetermissa syllaba Qui.

13ᵇ. Καὶ οἱ ζητοῦντες τὰ κακά μοι
15 ἐλάλησαν ματαιότητας. Ὁμοίως κάν-
ταῦθα πάλιν τὸ Οἱ παράκειται. Ἡ
γὰρ ἀκολουθία αὕτη· Ζητοῦντες τὰ
κακὰ ἐλάλησαν ματαιότητας, βουλόμενος εἰπεῖν ὅτι Καὶ ἀνελεῖν με

Et qui quaerebant mala mihi
loquebantur uanitates. Similiter
et in praesenti loco Qui additum
est. Nam ordo huiusmodi est:
Quaerentes mihi mala locuti sunt
mihi mala.

20 ἐσπούδαζον οἱ ποτέ μου φίλοι, καὶ ἐπάγειν μοι σπουδάζοντες πᾶν εἴ τι
κακὸν ἄτοπα ἐφθέγγοντο κατ' ἐμοῦ καὶ ψευδῆ.

13ᶜ. Καὶ δολιότητας ὅλην τὴν ἡμέραν ἐμελέτησαν. Καὶ μετὰ πολλῆς τῆς
πανουργίας ἐβουλεύοντο κατ' ἐμοῦ.

14. Ἐγὼ δὲ ὡσεὶ κωφὸς οὐκ ἤκουον, καὶ ὡσεὶ ἄλαλος οὐκ ἀνοίγων τὸ
25 στόμα αὐτοῦ. Καὶ τοσούτων γενομένων διεκείμην ὡς οὐδεμίαν αἴσθησιν ἔχων
τῶν λεγομένων, καὶ διετέλουν σιωπῶν καὶ μὴ ἀποκρινόμενος πρὸς τὰ παρ'
ἐκείνων λεγόμενα, ὡσπερεὶ ἄλαλος τυγχάνων καὶ ἀνοίγειν τὸ στόμα οὐ δυνά-

10 ἐξεβιάζοντο] add. oi deinde erasum.
Et uim — mala: A, fol. 12ᵇ; B, fol. 13ᶜ.   1-2 qui quaerebant] usque A
querebant B et ita l. 14   2 anī meae A anī mē B   5 interpossuit A
8 conexa B   9-10 intellegendum A²   11-12 et uim — quaerebant] usque A
13 praemisa A   sillaba A   15 loqū A loq̄ B   17 huiusmodi] hm̄ A¹
hominum add. supra de more   18 querentes B   19 mala AB (pro uanitates ?).

Aᵉ 14 (p. 223, 6-10): Fictas falsasque iactantes, ut Semei, qui, ut lapides
in eum, ita etiam mala dicta iaculatus est; quo quidem tempore ita selentium
tenuit, ut etiam comiti suo irasceretur uindicare cupienti.

Those seeking my life pressed hard (v. 12). He is referring to the same people: Not only did they become hostile to me, he is saying, but they also strove hard to take my life—that is, to do away with me. *Those* has been inserted in keeping with Hebrew idiom: the verse follows on from above, so it should be taken in keeping with the overall meaning: *Those close to me kept their distance and pressed me hard in seeking my life.* Aquila also put it this way, "Seeking my life," not introducing *those. Those seeking my harm spoke empty words.* Here, too, likewise *Those* has been inserted; the sequence is as follows: "In seeking harm they spoke empty words," meaning, Those who were once my friends were anxious to do away with me, and in their anxiety to inflict any harm at all on me they uttered wrong and false things against me. *And plotted treacherous schemes all day long:* they plotted against me with great villainy.

For my part, however, like a deaf person I did not hear, and like a mute not opening his mouth (v. 13): when this happened, I felt like someone with no sense of what was said, and I kept silence, not replying to what was said by them, like a dumb person unable to open my mouth. | Now, though he

μενος. Τοῦτο δὲ εἰκὸς μὲν αὐτὸν ἐπὶ πολλῶν πεποιημένον, δείκνυται δὲ καὶ ἐπὶ τοῦ Σεμεεὶ γεγονός, ἡνίκα καταρωμένου ἐκείνου καὶ λίθοις βάλλοντος τοσοῦτον ἀπέσχε τοῦ τι ἀποκρίνασθαι πρὸς τὰ παρ᾽ ἐκείνου λεγόμενα, ὅτι καὶ τῷ στρατηγῷ προσηγανάκτησεν ἀμῦναι αὐτῷ βουληθέντι.

15. Καὶ ἐγενόμην ὡσεὶ ἄνθρωπος οὐκ ἀκούων καὶ οὐκ ἔχων ἐν στόματι 5
αὐτοῦ ἐλεγμούς. Πάλιν δευτεροῖ μειζόνως αὐτὸ ἐξηγούμενος. Διετέθην γάρ
φησιν ὡς οὐκ ἀκούων τῶν γινομένων καὶ ὑπέμενον ἅπαντα· ὥσπερ ἂν εἴ
τις ἐν κρίσει ἐξεταζόμενος καὶ ἐλέγχειν τὰ κατ᾽ αὐτοῦ μὴ δυνάμενος ὡς
ψευδῆ πρὸς μηδὲν ἀποκρίνοιτο τῶν ἐπαγομένων, ἀλλὰ καταδέχοιτο μετὰ
σιωπῆς ἅπαντα, κἀγώ φησι διὰ τὴν ἁμαρτίαν ἠνειχόμην τῶν ἐπαγομένων 10
μοι κακῶν, εἰδὼς ὅτι δικαίως ἅπαντα πάσχω. Ταῦτα δὲ ὅλα ἀπέδωκε πρὸς
τὸ Καὶ ὁ στεναγμός μου ἀπό σου οὐκ ἀπεκρύβη, τὸν στεναγμὸν εἰπὼν ἀντὶ
τοῦ τὰς συμφοράς, ἐπειδὴ πᾶσα θλίψις στεναγμὸν εἴωθε ποιεῖν τῷ πάσχοντι. Ἑξῆς οὖν τῶν συμφορῶν ἐποιήσατο κατάλογον, ἵνα εἴπῃ ὅτι Οὐ
λέληθέ σε τὸ μέγεθος τῶν κακῶν μου, οὐχ ὅσα ὑπέστην ὑπὸ τοῦ μεγέ- 15
θους τῶν συμφορῶν, οὐχ ὅσα οἱ φίλοι διατεθείκασιν, οὐχ ὅπως διετέθην
πρὸς τὰ ἐπαγόμενα.

16. Ὅτι ἐπί σε ἤλπισα, Κύριε·
σὺ εἰσακούσῃ, Κύριε ὁ Θεός μου. Οἶδας δέ φησιν ὅτι, τούτων ἁπάντων
γιγνομένων, εἴς σε ἤλπισα ὡς ἔχοντα
εἰσακοῦσαι τῶν ῥημάτων μου.

Ποίων
δὴ ῥημάτων ἑξῆς φησιν.

Quoniam in te, Domine, speraui; exaudies, Domine Deus
meus. Ob hoc, | inquit, uniuersa 20
quae fiebant mihi patienter excipi,
quia in te sperare non desteti,
sciens me habere qui quaerel-
las ac uerba mea possit audire.
Quae sint autem ista uerba dicit 25
in sequentibus.

1-4 II Reg. XVI, 12 cf. supra p. 221   12 v. 10ᵇ.

1-4 cf. L (p. 702, 48-50) atque THEODORETVS (1141 C5-10).
    Quoniam — 229, 14 aduersum me: A, fol. 12ᵇ⁻ᶜ; B, fol. 13ᶜ⁻ᵈ.   19 exaudies
domine] usque A   20 ob] ab A¹   22 quia in te sperare *bis script. deinde
punctis reprob.* A   24 pos•sit B   habere audire AB   25 sint *in rasura* A

Aᵉ 6-11 (p. 223, 13-21): Cum ita aduersum me inimici mei amicique con-
surgerent, ad tantam animum praeparaui patientiam, quasi ad sensum meum
ea quae fiebant uel dicebantur minime peruinerent... Causa autem tam grandis
patientiae erat peccatorum conscientia: sciebam namque quod iuste omnia
sustenerem.   16 (p. 223, 22-23): Tot modis adflictus a tua exspectatione non
deficiam.

probably was left in this condition with many people, he was also this way in the case of Shimei, when at his cursing and pelting stones he so far refrained from making any reply to what was said by the fellow that he was even angered by his general's wish to take action on his behalf.[10] *I became like a person who does not hear and has no accusations in his mouth* (v. 14). He repeats himself in giving further comment on it: I was left like someone not hearing what happens, he is saying, and he suffered everything like a person brought to judgment and unable to refute charges against him so as to make no reply to false accusations against him, instead accepting everything in silence; I bore the troubles inflicted on me on account of the sin, conscious that I was suffering everything justly. Now, all this corresponded to the verse *My sighing was not hidden from you,*[11] using *sighing* to refer to the calamities, since every tribulation normally causes sighing in the sufferer. He went on to list the calamities, therefore, as if to say, The magnitude of my troubles did not escape your notice—not all I suffered from the magnitude of the calamities, not all my friends' treatment, not the way I felt toward what befell me.

Because it is in you, Lord, that I hoped; you will hearken to me, Lord my God (v. 15): you know that when all this happened, I hoped in you as one able to hearken to my words. In what follows he tells what words he used. | *Because I said, Let my enemies never rejoice over me* (v. 16): this

10. Cf. 2 Sam 16:10–12.
11. Ps 38:9.

17ᵃ. *Quoniam dixi :| Ne quando supergaudeant mihi inimici mei.* Haec fuit mea postulatio, ne inimicorum meorum conatus uotiuis successibus implerentur.

17ᵇ. Καὶ ἐν τῷ σαλευθῆναι πόδας
5 μου ἐπ᾽ ἐμὲ ἐμεγαλορρημόνησαν. Καὶ μὴ περιτραπέντος μου ὑπὸ τοῦ μεγέθους τῶν κακῶν ὑπερήφανα φθέγξονται, καυχώμενοι ἐπὶ τοῖς ἐμοῖς κακοῖς. Οὕτω λέγει καὶ Σύμμαχος·
10 Ἔλεγον γὰρ Μή ποτε ἐπιχαρῶσί με οἱ ἐχθροί μου, κἂν περιτραπῶσιν οἱ πόδες μου καταμεγαλύνοντές μου.

Et dum commouentur pedes mei super me magna locuti sunt. Et ne, dum ego magnitudine malorum a propossito meo moueor ac deducor, illi possint aduersum me | extolli atque gloriari. Ita et Simmachus dicit: *Dixi enim Ne quando supergaudeant mihi inimici mei, cum moti fuerint pedes mei, ne magnificentur aduersum me.*

15 18ᵃ. Ὅτι ἐγὼ εἰς μάστιγας ἕτοιμος. Ὅτι πρόκειμαι πάσχειν τῷ βουλομένῳ.

Quoniam ego in flagilla paratus sum. Expossitus sum enim ad sustinendum quicquid fuerit mihi ab inimicis inpossitum.

18ᵇ. Καὶ ἡ ἀλγηδών μου ἐνώπιόν μου διὰ παντός;. Καὶ ὁ πόνος καὶ ἡ
20 θλίψις τῶν κακῶν πρὸ τῶν ὀφθαλμῶν εἰσι τῶν ἐμῶν, τουτέστιν ἀχώριστοί μου καθεστήκασιν.

19. Ὅτι τὴν ἀνομίαν μου ἀναγγελῶ, καὶ μεριμνήσω ὑπὲρ τῆς ἁμαρτίας μου. Ταῦτα δὲ ὅλα ἀπέδωκε πρὸς τὸ Κύριε, ἐναντίον σου πᾶσα ἡ ἐπιθυμία μου καὶ ὁ στεναγμός μου | ἀπό σου οὐκ ἐκρύβη, τουτέστι Ταῦτα πάντα
25 ἐπίστασαι καὶ ὅτι ἑκάστοτε ἐξαγορεύω τὴν ἀνομίαν μου, καὶ ἐξαγορεύω οὐχ ἁπλῶς, ἀλλὰ μεριμνῶν ταύτης ἕνεκεν πότε ἄρα τυχεῖν τῆς ἀφέσεως δυνηθῶ.

23-24 v. 10.

2-3 succ. uot. A   3 successionibus A²   5 super me magna] usque A
10 dicit *om.* B   11 supergaudiunt A   12 mei *om.* B   commoti A
13 ne *om.* A.
Quoniam — impossitum: A, fol. 12ᶜ; B, fol. 13ᵈ.   15-16 paratus sum *om.* A
17 sustendum A   18 inimicis] meis *add. supra* A.

Aᵉ 17 (p. 223, 30-224, 2): Et ne, dum ego magnitudine malorum a propposito meo moueor ac deducor, illi possint aduersum me extolli atque gloriari.
18ᵃ (p. 224, 3-4): Prumtus ad ferendum quicquid ab inimicis ingeritur.

was my request, that my enemies' efforts not have the outcome they wish. *When my feet slipped, they gloated over me:* when I am overwhelmed by the magnitude of the troubles, they may not boast and take satisfaction in my troubles. Symmachus also puts it this way, "For I said, May my enemies never rejoice over me and be conceited, even should my feet trip." *Because I am ready for the whips* (v. 17): I am exposed to suffering at the hands of anyone who wishes. *My distress is ever in my sight:* the hardship and tribulation from my troubles are ever before my eyes—that is, they never leave me. *Because I shall declare my lawlessness and ponder my sin* (v. 18). All this corresponded to *Lord, all my desire is before you, and my sighing was not hidden from you*—in other words, You know all this and the fact that each time I confess my lawlessness, and not simply confess but also have concern as a result of it, I may succeed in gaining forgiveness. |

20ᵃ. Οἱ δὲ ἐχθροί μου ζῶσιν καὶ κεκραταίωνται ὑπὲρ ἐμέ. Καὶ οἱ ἐχθροί μου διαμένουσι καὶ ἰσχυροποι|οῦνται ἑκάστοτε.

20ᵇ. Καὶ ἐπληθύνθησαν οἱ μισοῦντές με ἀδίκως. Καὶ οὐ τοῦτο μόνον, ἀλλὰ καὶ ἑκάστοτε πληθύνονται καὶ προστίθενται οἱ ἐχθροί μου, καὶ ταῦτα ἀδίκως, οὐδεμίαν ἔχοντες αἰτίαν εὔλογον τῆς ἔχθρας τῆς κατ᾽ ἐμοῦ. Πόθεν 5 δὲ τοῦτο ὅτι μισοῦσιν ἀδίκως, ἐξῆς ἐπάγει.

21ᵃ. Οἱ ἀνταποδιδόντες κακὰ ἀντὶ ἀγαθῶν. Ποίαν γὰρ εἶχον αἰτίαν εὔλογον τῆς ἔχθρας τῆς κατ᾽ ἐμοῦ, εὐεργετηθέντες ὑπ᾽ ἐμοῦ καὶ ἀντὶ τῶν ἀγαθῶν ὧν ἔλαβον παρ᾽ ἐμοῦ κακά μοι ἀποδιδόντες;

21ᵇ. Ἐνδιέβαλλόν με, ἐπεὶ κατεδίωκον δικαιοσύνην. Καὶ ἐμοῦ φησι δικαιοσύνης ἐπιμελουμένου διαβάλλοντες ἐκεῖνοι καὶ κατηγοροῦντες διετέλουν· ὅπερ ἐγένετο μὲν παρὰ πολλῶν καὶ πρὸς τὸν λαὸν καὶ πρὸς τὸν Ἀβεσσαλὼμ διαβαλλόντων, ἐγένετο καὶ παρ᾽ αὐτοῦ τοῦ Ἀβεσσαλὼμ ἡνίκα ἕκαστον τῶν κρίσιν ἐχόντων παρὰ τῷ βασιλεῖ ἐφείλκετο πρὸς ἑαυτὸν ἀπατῶν καὶ λέγων· Οἱ λόγοι σου ἀγαθοὶ καὶ καλοί, εἰ δὲ καὶ ἀκούων γένοιτο ἐν Ἰσραήλ.

Detrahebant mihi quoniam se- 10 quebar iustitiam. Me in studio adseruandae iustitiae constituto obloquebantur illi, et criminationibus suis ac maledictis studebant facere uiliorem; quod et a 15 multis et praecipue ab Abisalom factum est,

cum diceret: Verba 20 tua bona sunt ac recta, sed qui iudicet non est.

Καὶ ἀπέρριψάν με τὸν ἀγαπητὸν ὡσεὶ νεκρὸν ἐβδελυγμένον. Καὶ τοῦτό φησιν ἐποίουν ἐπ᾽ ἐμὲ τόν ποτε ἀγαπώμενον αὐτοῖς, ἀπορρίψαντες ὥσπερ τινὰ νεκρὸν ἐβδελυγμένον. Τὸ δὲ ἐβδελυγμένον παρατέθεικεν, ἐπειδὴ ἐγχω- 25 ρεῖ καὶ νεκρὸν ἐν τιμῇ καθεστάναι γονεῦσιν, ἢ ὅλως τοῖς διάθεσιν περὶ αὐτὸν ἔτι ζῶντα κεκτημένοις, — ταῦτα δὲ πρὸς τὸ Κύριε, ἐναντίον σου πᾶσα ἡ ἐπιθυμία μου ἀκολούθως ἐπαγαγών, ἀντὶ τοῦ Οἶδας ἃ ἐπιθυμῶ, οἶδας

20-22 II Reg. XV, 3   23 vv. καὶ ἀπέρριψαν — ἐβδελυγμένον non praebent LXX nec hebraïcum; leguntur uero et interpretantur apud THEODORETUM (P. G., LXXX, 1144 B) 27-28 v. 10.

Detrahebant — non est: A, fol. 12ᶜ; B, fol. 13ᵈ.   10-11 consequebar A 11-15 me in — uiliorem affert Aᵉ (p. 224, 29-225, 1)   11 stadio A¹   12 aduersandae A   13-14 cremenationibus AAᵉ   16 abisolon A.

Aᵉ 20ᵃ (p. 224, 15-17)... inimicorum meorum aduersum me non solum studia perseuerant, sed augentur in dies singulos.   5-9 (p. 224, 21-25): Quasi (uel quas add. supra) iustas odiorum suorum causas possuit ostendere, quia meis beneficiis sunt praeuenti (praebet — ms), apud quos, priusquam mihi essent usui, dilectationis pignera collocaui.

My foes, however, are alive and prevail over me (v. 19): my foes persist and make a brave showing each time. *Those who hate me unjustly are multiplied:* and not only this, but also the fact that my foes are multiplied each time and augmented, despite the injustice of it, since they have no grounds for their hostility against me. The proof that their hatred is unjust he proceeds to supply. *They repay me evil for good* (v. 20): what grounds did they have for their hostility to me, being the object of my kindness? But for the good they received from me, they repaid me with evil. *They calumniated me since I followed after goodness:* though I was attentive to righteousness, they kept calumniating and accusing me. While this was done by many who misrepresented him to the people and to Absalom, it was done also by Absalom himself when he drew to himself everyone with a case for the king's judgment and won them over in the words "Your claims are good and right, if only there were someone in Israel to hear them."[12] *Though I was beloved, they rejected me, loathed like a corpse:*[13] they did this to me, though I was once loved by them, rejecting me like some loathsome corpse. He included *loathed* because to hold even a dead person in honor is possible for parents or those who were totally fond of them when alive. This is relevant to *Lord, all my desire is before you*—that is, You know what I desire, you know |

---

12. 2 Sam 15:3.

13. This clause, which has some similarity in wording to Isa 14:19, does not occur in the Hebrew or most forms of the LXX. Theodoret's comment on it also shows that it appears in the Lucianic text.

ἃ ἔπαθον, οἶδας ὅτι ἐπί σοι ἤλπισα, οἶδας ὅτι ἐξηγόρευσα τὴν ἁμαρτίαν, οἶδας ὅτι μὴ διέλιπον πάσχων τὰ κακά, οἶδας τὰ ἐπαχθέντα μοι παρὰ τῶν φίλων. Εἶτα ἑξῆς φησιν·

22ᵃ. Μὴ ἐγκαταλίπῃς με, Κύριε. Τουτέστι ταῦτα πάντα ἐπιστάμενος, 5 μὴ ἐναφῇς με τοῖς κακοῖς· ἀρκεῖ γὰρ ταῦτα ἐκκαλέσασθαί μοι τὴν παρά σοι βοήθειαν, τὸ μέγεθος τῶν θλίψεων ἀρκούντως ὑπὲρ ὧν ἥμαρτον πεπονθότος, ἡ ἐμὴ διάθεσις πολλάκις τὴν ἁμαρτίαν ἐξαγορεύοντος.

22ᵇ. Ὁ Θεός μου, μὴ ἀποστῇς ἀπ᾽ ἐμοῦ. Μὴ μακρύνῃς σού φησιν τὴν βοήθειαν ἀπ᾽ ἐμοῦ.

10 23. Πρόσχες· εἰς τὴν βοήθειάν μου, Κύριε τῆς σωτηρίας μου. Ἀλλ᾽ αὐτός φησιν ὁ καὶ τῆς σωτηρίας μου δεσπότης, ὁ ταύτην μοι χαρίζεσθαι ἐξουσιαν ἔχων, αὐτὸς πρόσχες εἰς τὸ βοηθῆσαί μοι, τουτέστι Φρόντισον τοῦτο διαπράξασθαι.

PSALMVS XXXVIII

15 Ἐν μὲν ταῖς κατὰ τὸν Σαοὺλ ἐξεταζόμενος συμφοραῖς ὁ μακάριος Δαυὶδ καὶ ἐν ἀθυμίᾳ μεγίστῃ καθεστὼς τοῦτον ἀπεφθέγξατο τὸν ψαλμόν. Ἔστι δὲ παιδευτικὸς ἤπέρ τις 20 ἔτερος, ἱκανώτατα διδάσκειν δυνάμενος τὸ καρτερικὸν ἐν ταῖς συμφοραῖς ἐπιδείκνυσθαι. Λέγει γὰρ ἐν αὐτῷ καὶ περὶ τῶν κατὰ τὸν βίον τοῦτον ἐν εὐθηνίαις καὶ πλούτῳ κα- 25 θεστώτων καὶ πολὺν ὑπὲρ τοῦ πλου-

Inter discrimina quae ei Saulis persecutio frequenter intulerat, sub grandi tristitia constitutus beatus Dauid hunc psalmum cecinit qui, prae omnibus sub hoc argumento scriptis, esset utilis auditori. Sufficienter namque docet qua uirtute animi oportet tristia atque aduersa portare; repraehendit etiam studia eorum, qui pro praesentis uitae bonis,

Inter discrimina — implicari: A, fol. 12ᶜ; B, fol. 13ᵈ.   14 xxxuiii A *in marg.*   16 persequtio A   16-17 intulleret A   19 cicinit A   20 scriptis] uel u (scriptus) *add. supra* A   21 auditori] adiutorio A   22 qua] quia A 23 tristitia AB¹.

Aᵉ 5-6 (p. 225, 2-4): Saltim ob ista ad ueniam commouere.   15 ss. (p. 225, 9-14): ...anguentibus sub Saule meroribus atque periculis hunc psalmum cecenit, qui plurimam speciem doctrinae non tantum depraecationis de se praeferet quantum in profectum audientium. Cf. PSEUDO-BEDA (686).

what I suffered, you know that I hoped in you, you know that I confessed my sin, you know that I never stopped suffering troubles, you know what was inflicted on me by my friends.

He then continues to say *Do not abandon me, Lord* (v. 21)—that is, Knowing all this, do not embroil me in troubles: what suffices to attract help for me from you is my suffering the magnitude of calamities as adequate repayment for my sins, with my attitude ever being that of one confessing sin. *O my God, do not keep far from me:* do not keep your help far from me. *Come to my help, Lord of my salvation* (v. 22): it is you who are the Lord of my salvation, the one with power to grant me this favor; it is you who are concerned to help me—that is, Give thought to doing this.

PSALM 39

Although blessed David uttered this psalm when under pressure from the hardships involving Saul and reduced to deep depression, it is instructive beyond any other, capable of giving more than adequate instruction in how to give evidence of endurance in the midst of hardships. You see, in it he treats also of people whose position in this life is one of prosperity and wealth and who exert much effort in getting rich, | efforts that are futile and useless.

τεῖν πόνον ἐπιδεικνυμένων, ὡς μάταια
καὶ ἀνωφελῆ πονούντων,

ἀπὸ τῆς
ὑποθέσεως συνηθῶς τῶν τοιούτων λόγων τὴν ἀφορμὴν δεξάμενος, δι᾽ ὧν
παιδεύει πάντας ἀνθρώπους μὴ πολλὴν εἰς μάτην ἐπιδείκνυσθαι τὴν περὶ
ταῦτα σπουδήν.

id est ut diuites sint, multum
sollicitudinis sustinent ac laboris,
dicens quod inutiliter rebus minime profuturis inuigilent. Ac
more suo ab argumento psalmi 5
occasione exhortationis accepta,
monet omnes homines non debere eos pro rebus fluentibus ac
praetereuntibus curis grauissi-
mis implicari.   10

2. Εἶπα Φυλάξω τὰς ὁδούς μου τοῦ μὴ ἁμαρτάνειν με ἐν γλώσσῃ μου·
ἐθέμην τῷ στόματί μου φυλακὴν ἐν τῷ συστῆναι τὸν ἁμαρτωλὸν ἐναντίον
μου. Ἔθος ἐστὶ τοῖς ἀνθρώποις ἅπασι δυσχεραίνειν μὲν ὁπόταν ἴδωσι
τοῖς ἁμαρτωλοῖς κατευθυνομένας τὰς προθέσεις, δυσχεραίνειν δὲ καὶ ἐπὶ
ταῖς οἰκείαις συμφοραῖς, μάλιστα ὅταν ὑπὸ ἀδίκων πάσχοντες ἑαυτοῖς ὦσιν 15
ἀρετῆς τρόπον συνειδότες· ἐκτρέπονταί τε οἱ πολλοὶ ἀπὸ τῶν τοιούτων
ἐπὶ δυσφημίας καὶ ἀποδυσπετήσεις τὰς εἰς τὸν Θεὸν τῶν ὅλων. Διό φησιν ὁ
μακάριος Δαυίδ· εἶπα Φυλάξω τὰς ὁδούς μου τοῦ μὴ ἁμαρτάνειν με ἐν γλώσσῃ
μου. Εἶπόν φησι κατ᾽ ἐμαυτόν, τουτέστιν ἐδοκίμασα καὶ ἔκρινα, φυλά-
ξαι | ἐμαυτὸν ἀπὸ πάσης ἁμαρτίας. Τὸ δὲ ἐν τῷ συστῆναι οὐκ εἶπε τὸν 20
ἐχθρόν, ἀλλὰ τὸν ἁμαρτωλόν, ἀπὸ τῆς αἰτίας δι᾽ ἣν ἤχθραινεν ἀδίκως ἁμαρτωλὸν καλέσας εἰκότως, ἵνα δείξῃ ὅτι τοῦτο ἦν ὅπερ αὐτὸν ἐλύπει ὅτι
ἀδίκως ἔπασχεν.

3ᵃ. Ἐκωφώθην καὶ ἐταπεινώθην καὶ ἐσίγησα ἐξ ἀγαθῶν. Ὡς δὲ μετὰ
τὴν δοκιμασίαν ταύτην ἐν μεγίσταις συμφοραῖς ἐξετασθείς, παντὸς ἀγαθοῦ 25
κατέστην ἀλλότριος. Τὸ γὰρ ἐκωφώθην καὶ ἐσίγησα ἐξ ἀγαθῶν εἶπε, τουτέστιν ἄμοιρος καὶ ἀλλότριος ἐγενόμην παντὸς ἀγαθοῦ, οὐδενὸς ἀπολαύσας
ἢ μετεσχηκὼς χρησίμου, ἀπὸ τοῦ τῶν τοιούτων μήτε ἀκούειν τι τῶν λαλου-
μένων ὑπὸ κωφότητος ἐμποδιζομένων, μήτε ἀποκρίνασθαι πρὸς τὰ λεχθέντα
δύνασθαι· πῶς γὰρ ὧν οὐκ ἤκουσε σιγῇ δὲ κατεχόμενον, ὥσπερ ἀλλότριόν 30
τινα δοκεῖν εἶναι καὶ ἀμέτοχον τῶν λεχθέντων.

20 ἐμαυτὸν] ἑαυτὸν ms   22 ἐλύπη prius scriptum.
5 suo om. A¹   6 occassione B exortationis A; — in v. 2 (ib.): Custodiam
uias meas, uitae meae actus ac studia.

Aᵉ 13-19 (p. 225, 19-23): Cum uideam ⟨et⟩ experiar inimicos innocentum
afflictione prosperari, rerum homanarum Deum quasi negligentem offensus
non arguam.

As usual, he takes his theme as the basis for such a treatment, and in it he instructs everyone not to display great zeal for these things to no purpose.

I said, I shall guard my ways so as not to sin with my tongue. I placed a guard on my mouth when the sinner took up a position against me (v. 1). It is a universal custom to be upset when you see your plans at the mercy of sinners, and to be upset also at the your own misfortunes, especially when you are badly treated by wrongdoers while conscious of your own virtuous behavior. The general run of people react to such developments by turning to criticism and displeasure with the God of all. Hence, blessed David says *I shall guard my ways so as not to sin with my tongue:* I kept my words to myself—that is, I made a decision and judgment to guard myself against any sin. The phrase *took up a position* refers not to the foe but to the sinner, rightly making mention of *sinner* for the reason of his unjust hostility, so as to show that what he lamented was the unjust treatment.

I kept mute and was humiliated; I made no mention of good things (v. 2): finding myself after this decision in the worst of calamities, I was deprived of every good. This is the meaning of *I kept mute and made no mention of good things*—that is, I was bereft and deprived of every good, not enjoying or sharing any advantage, because of not hearing anything spoken to this effect on account of the impediment of deafness,[1] and not being able to respond to what was said. After all, a person is somehow reduced to silence on what he did not hear, giving the impression of being deprived and estranged from what is said. | *And my grief was renewed:* after that decision, then, I was

---

1. Is the psalmist referring to a speech or a hearing impediment? Theodoret, who immediately applies the verse to David's keeping silent in the face of Shimei's abuse, takes the verb κωφοῦν (appearing in the Greek Bible only in this psalm) to mean the former, as the adjective κωφός (with one exception, Hab 2:18) also refers to being mute. Theodore, however, seems to think of deafness, using κωφότες, which generally (not appearing in the Bible) has this sense. The Hebrew has no such ambiguity.

3ᵇ. Καὶ τὸ ἄλγημά μου ἀνεκαινίσθη. Μετὰ τοίνυν τὴν δοκιμασίαν ἐκείνην ταπεινωθεὶς μὲν ὑπὸ τῶν συμφορῶν, μηδενὸς δὲ ἀπολαύσας ἀγαθοῦ ἀλλὰ πάντη τῶν τοιούτων ἀκοινώνητος καταστάς, ἔσχον πάλιν ἀνακαινισθεῖσαν ἐπὶ τῆς καρδίας τὴν ἐπὶ τούτοις ὀδύνην. Διὰ τοῦτο οὖν καλῶς εἶπε τὸ
5 ἀνεκαινίσθη, ἐπειδὴ δοκιμάσας τούτων ὑπερφρονεῖν καὶ μηδὲν ἐπὶ τούτοις φθέγγεσθαι ἄτοπον, καὶ καταπαύσας τῷ λογισμῷ τὴν ἐπὶ τούτοις ὀδύνην, ὥσπερ παλαιωθεῖσαν πάλιν εἶχεν ἀνακαινιζομένην ἐν ἑαυτῷ τὴν ἀθυμίαν, τῶν γινομένων τοῦτο ἐξ ἀνάγκης ἐργαζομένων.

4ᵃ. Ἐθερμάνθη ἡ καρδία μου ἐντός μου. Πάλιν ἐπὶ τούτοις φησὶν ὀργι-
10 ζόμενος ἐκινήθην τὸν λογισμόν. | Τὸ δὲ ἐθερμάνθη εἶπεν ἡ καρδία μου, ἐπειδὴ μάλιστα ὅταν ἐπί τισιν ὀργιζώμεθα, κινουμένης τῆς ψυχῆς, εἰώθαμεν ἀναζεῖν τὸ περὶ τὴν καρδίαν αἷμα. Διὰ τοῦτο εἶπε τὸ ἐθερμάνθην, ἀντὶ τοῦ ὠργίσθην· ἐπὶ γὰρ τοῖς τοιούτοις μετά τινος ὀργῆς ἡ ἀθυμία γίνεται.

4ᵇ. Καὶ ἐν τῇ μελέτῃ μου ἐκκαυθήσεται πῦρ. Καὶ ἐφ' ὅσον φησὶν ἐθεώ-
15 ρων ταῦτα γινόμενα, ἀναλαμβάνων αὐτῶν τὴν μνήμην ἐπὶ τῆς καρδίας, μει-ζόνως ἐξεκαιόμην τὸν λογισμόν· μελέτην γὰρ καλεῖ τὴν μνήμην, ἀπὸ τοῦ τὸ μελετώμενον πάντως ἐν μνήμῃ καθεστάναι τοῦ μελετῶντος, — οὕτω λέγει καὶ Σύμμαχος· Καὶ ἐν τῷ ἀναπολεῖν με ἀνεκαιόμην πυρί. Διὸ καλῶς εἶπεν ἀνωτέρω ἐθερμάνθη, εἶτα ἐνταῦθα ἐκκαυθήσεται πῦρ, τὴν ἐνθύμησιν καὶ
20 τὴν ἐπὶ τούτοις αὔξησιν τῆς ὀργῆς παρασημαίνων, ἐπείπερ τὸ πῦρ ἀρχό-μενον μὲν ἔτι διαθερμαίνει μόνον, περιδραξάμενον δὲ τῶν ὑλῶν ἐξαφθὲν ἐπὶ πολὺ κατακαίειν δύναται.

5ᵃ. Ἐλάλησα ἐν γλώσσῃ μου· Γνώρισόν μοι, Κύριε, τὸ πέρας μου. Ἐπειδὴ τοίνυν ἐδοκίμαζον μὲν ἐπὶ τῶν τοιούτων μηδὲν ἄτοπον φθέγγεσθαι ἀλλὰ
25 πάντων ὑπερορᾶν καὶ καταφρονεῖν, τὰ δὲ γινόμενα εἰς ὀργὴν καὶ ἀθυμίαν κινοῦντα παρεσκεύαζε καὶ ἄκοντά με πολλάκις τοῖς τοιούτοις χρῆσθαι ῥήμασι, δεδιὼς μὲν τὸ ἁμαρτάνειν, τὰ γινόμενα δὲ ὁρῶν ἱκανὰ πρὸς τοῦτο

---

10 ἐκινήθη ms   10-12 cf. L (p. 720, 15-16): Ἐπειδὴ ἔθος τοῖς ὀργιζομένοις ἀνάπ-τεσθαι τοῦ περικαρδίου αὐτοῖς αἵματος περιζέοντος   18 ἀναπολᾶν ms.

Aᵉ 4ᵃ (p. 226, 9-12): Cum indignationis motus, quos consilio praeseram, perseuerans flammaret adflictio.   5ᵃ (p. 226, 12-23): Pro recordatione (rcor-tione ms) et intenta consideratione noxiarum. Quando discretam tacendi patien-tiam, offensionum adsiduetate uictus, tenere non potui, inter metum peccandi de prouidentia et acerbitatem (aceruitate ms) experientiae uel perseuerantiae, statui finem obtare uiuendi; cuius agnito tempore aliquid consulationis, si non malorum a tenuitate, saltim terminus afferret afflictionis.

humbled by the calamities, instead of enjoying good things I was completely prevented from sharing in such things, and once again I felt afresh in my heart the pain from them. For this reason, then, *was renewed* was well put, since having decided to rise above these things and say nothing untoward in response to them, and after putting an end to his pain from them in his thinking, once again he felt in himself the former depression, recent events naturally giving rise to it.

My heart became hot within me (v. 3): once again I was moved to rage in my thinking at these events (the meaning of *my heart became hot,* since it is particularly when we become angry with someone, our spirit being stirred, that we normally feel the blood around the heart seething). Hence his saying *My heart became hot*—that is, My depression was mingled with rage at this. *And in my meditation fire burned:* the more I perceived this happening, recalling the memory of it in my heart, the more I was inflamed in my thinking (by *meditation* referring to memory, from the effect of what is the object of constant meditation on the memory of the one meditating). Symmachus also puts it in similar terms: "In my reflection I was burnt up with fire." Hence, *became hot* was well put above, then here *fire burned,* combining the pondering and the increase in anger at these events, since fire begins simply by giving warmth, but by taking hold it has the power to burn up materials that are set alight.

I spoke with my tongue, Make known my end to me, Lord (vv. 3–4): since I saw fit, then, to utter nothing untoward at these events and instead to overlook and scorn everything, and yet what happened caused me anger and depression and against my will to have frequent recourse to such words, in dread of sinning and yet seeing that the events sufficed to draw me to that condition, | I gave voice and begged to know the end of my life. For

κατασπᾶν, ἐφθεγξάμην καὶ ἤτησα γνῶναι τὸ τέλος τῆς ζωῆς τῆς ἐμῆς·
τότε γάρ ᾔδειν ὅτι παύσεταί μοι τὰ τῶν συμφορῶν καὶ ἡ τῶν γινομένων
αἴσθησις ἐξ ἀνάγκης, οὐ τότε ὀργή με ἐπὶ τοῖς γινομένοις οὐδεμία καθέξει

5ᵇ·ᶜ. Καὶ τὸν ἀριθμὸν τῶν ἡμερῶν μου τίς ἐστιν, ἵνα γνῶ τί ὑστερῶ
ἐγώ. Ἡίτησά φησι γνῶναι τὸ τέλος καὶ πόσος ἐστὶν ὁ τῶν ἡμερῶν ἀριθμὸς   5
τῆς ζωῆς τῆς ἐμῆς, ἵνα δυνηθῶ μαθεῖν πόσος μοι χρόνος ἔτι εἰς ζωὴν κατα-
λέλειπται, οὕτω τε παραμυθίαν λάβω τῶν κακῶν, ἐκτείνων εἰς τὸ πέρας τῆς
ζωῆς τὸν λογισμόν, ἔνθα τὴν ἀπαλλαγὴν πάντως ἔξω τῶν κακῶν. Ἀνάγκη
γὰρ ἦν μαθόντα πάσης αὐτοῦ τῆς ζωῆς τὸν χρόνον καὶ εἰδότα τὸν ἀριθμόν,
ὃν ἤδη ἐν τῇ ζωῇ διατετελέκει, γνωρίσαι τὸ ὑπολιμπανόμενον.   10

Τοῦτο δὲ λέγει, οὐχ ὡς πάντως | Hoc dicit, non quo omni
ἑκάστῳ τοῦ Θεοῦ μετροῦντος τῆς | modo Deus tempora uiuendi sin-
ζωῆς τὸν χρόνον, ἀλλ᾽ ὡς εἰδότος τῇ | gulis sit dimensus, sed quia uir-
προγνωστικῇ δυνάμει ὅσον ἕκαστος | tute | praescientiae suae nouit
ζήσεται τῶν ἀνθρώπων. | quantum sit hominum quisque   15
                                     | uicturus.

6ᵃ. Ἰδοὺ παλαιστὰς ἔθου τὰς ἡμέ- | *Ecce mensurabiles posuisti dies*
ρας μου. Ταῦτα δέ φησιν αἰτῶ μαθεῖν | *meos.* Scire desidero, inquit, quan-
εἰκότως· ἐπίσταμαι γὰρ ὅτι οὐκ εἰς | tum mihi temporis deest: siqui-
ἀΐδιόν με ζωὴν κατεσκεύασας, ἀλλ᾽ | dem noui quoniam non me in-   20
ὥσπερ μέτροις τισὶν ὑπέβαλές μου | mortalem feceris, sed uitam meam
τὴν ζωήν, τουτέστιν ἐκτείνεσθαι ἡμῶν | quasi quibusdam mensuris inclu-
τὴν ζωὴν ἁπλῶς οὐκ ἔταξας. | seris, id est: non mihi dedisti
                                     | hanc condicionem, ut in inmen-
                                     | sum uitae meae spatia tenderen-   25
Εἰ γὰρ ἑκάστῳ τῶν ἀνθρώπων | tur. Nam etsi singulis uiuentibus
οὐκ ἐμέτρησε τὴν ζωήν, ἀλλ᾽ οὖν γε | non sit uelut ad mensuram prae-
κοινῶς ἐμέτρησε τοῖς ἀνθρώποις, οἷον | finitum uitae spatium, tamen in
εἰπεῖν οὐκ ἐπιτρέπων ἀνθρώπῳ ὑπερ- | commune omnibus certum est
βαίνειν ἑκατὸν πεντήκοντα ἐτῶν ἀριθ- | uiuendi tempus impositum — ut   30

1-8 cf. L (p. 720, 39-45) atque *Paraphrasis anonyma* (p. 717).   11-15 *sub
nomine* Θεοδώρου Ἡρακλεώτου, *paucis mutatis, in cod.* Ambros. H 257 inf., f. 4
(ed. Ioh. MERCATI, *Varia sacra*, 1903, p. 100).   17-235, 4 ταῦτα — συμβαίνῃ
affert codex Ambros. (MERCATI, *loc. cit.*) *pluribus omissis aut mutatis; cf.* L
(p. 720, 46-48): Οὕτω μαθεῖν ἀξιῶ, τί τὸ πέρας ἔσται μετὰ τὰ συμβεβηκότα μοι, ποίου
τέλους τεύξομαι.

Hoc dicit — uicturus: A, fol. 12ᶜ-12ᵈ; B, fol. 14ᵃ. *Praecedit textus sacer*:
Notum fac mihi, Domine, finem meum et numerum dierum meorum quis est,
reliqua.   finem — meorum] usque A   14 norit.

Ecce mensurabiles — 238, 22 reuertendum est: A, fol. 12ᵈ-13ᵇ; B, fol. 14ᵃ-14ᵇ.
26 etsi] si A¹ et A²   27 uelud A   29 commone A   30 impossitum A   * ut A.

I then realized that my misfortunes and the sense of what was happening would necessarily cease, then no anger at the events would hold me in its grip. *What is the number of my days, so that I may know what is left to me?* I begged to know my end and the number of days of my life so as to be able to learn how much time was left to my life, and thus gain consolation in the troubles by projecting my thinking to life's end, when I would have complete relief from the troubles. After all, it is necessary for one to learn the complete span of life, and by being aware of the amount of life already spent to know how much is left. Now, he says this not that God altogether measures each person's lifetime, but that he is aware by his power to know in advance how long each human being will live.

Lo, you made my days handbreadths (v. 5): I am within my rights in asking to learn this, aware as I am that far from making me for everlasting life, you subjected my life to certain limits—in other words, You did not ordain that our life should be extended indefinitely. After all, even if he did not set the same limits to each person's life, he did set limits to people in general, as, for instance, in not allowing a person to exceed the number of a hundred and fifty years | in the generation in which blessed David uttered

μὸν ἐν τῇ παρούσῃ γενεᾷ καθ᾽ ἣν
ταῦτα ἐφθέγγετο ὁ μακάριος Δαυίδ,
κἂν τὸν μὲν ἐπὶ πλεῖον τοῦ ἑτέρου,
τὸν δὲ ἐπ᾽ ἔλαττον ζῆν συμβαίνῃ.

Καὶ γὰρ ταῦτα περὶ τῆς φύσεως τῶν
ἀνθρώπων ὡς ὀλιγοχρονίου ὑπὸ τοῦ
Θεοῦ κατασκευασθείσης λέγει, καὶ
10 οὐχ οἷον εἰπεῖν ἀδιαλύτου ὡς ἡ
τῶν ἀγγέλων ἢ ἑτέρου τινὸς τῶν νοητῶν. Ὁ γάρ τοι Θεὸς λόγῳ τινὶ
κρατίστης οἰκονομίας, θανάτου μὲν ἅπαξ ἀποφάσει τὴν ἡμετέραν φύσιν
ὑποβαλών, κατεσκεύασεν εἰς φανερὸν ἐτῶν ἀριθμὸν διαρκεῖν δυναμένους, ὡς
μήτε ταχεῖαν ἅμα τῇ πλάσει τὴν διάλυσιν ὑπομένειν, μήτε ἁπλῶς ἡμῖν εἰς
15 ἄπειρον ἐκτείνεσθαι τὴν ζωήν, ὅπερ ἀδύνατον ἦν ἅπαξ τῆς ἀποφάσεως τοῦ
θανάτου κρατούσης ἐν ἡμῖν συμφερόντως, — ὥσπερ καὶ οἱ τὰς οἰκίας κατα-
σκευάζοντες | ἀπὸ τῆς περὶ τὴν οἰκοδομὴν σπουδῆς τε καὶ ἐπιμελείας τὴν
ποσότητα τῆς τοῦ χρόνου διαμονῆς ταῖς οἰκίαις χαρίζονται, πλείονα μὲν
εἰ μᾶλλον σπουδάσαιεν, ἐλάττονα δὲ εἰ τούτῳ χρήσαιντο ἐπὶ τῆς οἰκοδομῆς
20 τῷ τρόπῳ.

Τὸν δέ γε τῶν ἐτῶν ἀριθμόν, εἰς ὃν διαρκεῖν ἡμῶν ἠβουλήθη τὴν ζωήν,
περιγράψας, οἷον εἰπεῖν ὡς ἐφ᾽ ἡμῶν
ὡς ρ᾽ ἢ βραχύ τι πλέον ἢ ἔλασσον,
ἕκαστον ὡς ἂν ἔχοι κράσεως ἀπο-
25 πληροῦν τὸν τῆς οἰκείας ζωῆς ἀριθμὸν
συγχωρήσας καὶ τὰ πάθη κρατεῖν ἐν
ἡμῖν ἅτε δὴ ὡς ἐν φύσει θνητῇ καὶ
τὰς ἀπὸ τῶν συμπτωμάτων ἀρρωστίας τε καὶ θανάτους,

ἀφ᾽ ὧν ἐπ
ἔλαττόν τινας ἑτέρων ζῆν συμβαίνει.
35 Αὐτὸν γὰρ ὁρίζειν τῷ καθενὶ τὸν
χρόνον τῆς ζωῆς ἄγαν ἀπρεπέστα-
τον ἦν. Εἴτε γὰρ τῷ μὲν ὥριζε πλέον,

puta quantum ad illam generationem pertinebat in qua haec
beatus Dauid loquebatur, non
permisit ulli CL annos uiuendo
transcendere, etiamsi eueniret ut
alius ab alio plus minusue uiue-
ret. Nam haec generaliter de natura hominum dicit, quae est a
Deo parui temporis facta, quae
utique non potest esse continua:
uerbi gratia, ut nostro tempore
usque ad C annos aut paulo amplius uiueretur pro tempera-
mento corporis, quod ex diuersis
qualitatibus constat atque con-
trariis, permisit etiam nos diuersis infirmitatibus et exposuit ca-
sibus; quippe ut naturae passibilis
conpassiones, etiam ut aliud mem-
brum alterius membri sentiret
uel incommodum uel dolorem,
sensus iniecit: hinc fit ut minus
alii ab alteris uiuant. Nam si
ipse singulis uiuendi praefinisset
tempora, esset quod moueret merito quaestionem. Nam si uni plus

19 χρήσαιτο ms.
4 permissit A   CL ex graeco restitui, C A   centum B   5 euiniret A
8 est om. A   22 nostro] nō A   26 con**stat B   26-27 contrarius A   27 permissit B   23 expossuit A   28-29 cas*ibus B   33 hi*nc B   35 praefiniisset.

this sentiment, even if one person happens to live longer and another less. You see, he says this in regard to human nature as made short-lived by God, and not imperishable, as it were, like the nature of angels or any other of the spiritual beings. God, of course, manages affairs by a certain plan, making our nature subject to a sentence of death once and for all and rendering us capable of lasting for an acknowledged number of years, with the result that we do not undergo a speedy dissolution as soon as we are fashioned, nor do we have an immeasurable life span extended indefinitely. This was impossible once the sentence of death came into effect appropriately in our case, just as people building houses determine the extent of their duration by the zeal and care in building, longer if they are more zealous, shorter if they adopt this attitude in building. He limited the number of years he wanted our life to last—for example, in our case a hundred years more or less—by allowing all persons to run the course of their own lives as their makeup permits, and the ailments natural to our mortal condition and the sickness and decease arising from circumstance to run their course in us, the result being that some have shorter lives than others.

After all, it would have been most inappropriate for him to determine the length of each one's life: had he personally set a longer time for one | and

τῷ δὲ ἔλαττον, ἀδικίας ἦν οὐ κατ'
ἰσότητα νέμοντος τὴν ζωὴν τοῖς ἀνθρώποις.

Εἴτε καὶ τὴν ἰσότητα ἐφύ-
λαττεν, ἔδει τὴν φύσιν ἐν τῷ μέσῳ
χρόνῳ μένειν ἀπαθῆ ὡς ἂν διαρκῇ
μέχρι τοῦ τῆς ζωῆς ὅρου, μὴ διακοπ-
τομένη ὑπὸ τῶν ἐν τοῖς σώμασι παθῶν, καὶ πάλιν ἀνῃρεῖτο ὁ τοῦ θανάτου ὅρος συμφερόντως κείμενος ἐν
τῇ φύσει. Ἀπαθῆ γὰρ οὖσαν, ἀνάγκη
πᾶσα καὶ ἀθάνατον εἶναι, ἀνῃρεῖτο
δὲ καὶ τὸ ὑπὲρ Χριστοῦ παθεῖν τῷ
σώματι εἴτε ἐν τοῖς μαρτυρίοις, εἴτε
καὶ τῷ τῆς ἐγκρατείας λόγῳ,

ἀνῃρεῖτο δὲ καὶ τῶν κατὰ τὴν
ἀρετὴν πόνων ὁ μισθός. Ἀπαθοῦς
μὲν γὰρ οὔσης τῆς φύσεως, πόνον
ἀκολουθεῖν οὐκ ἐνεδέχετο· πόνων δὲ
οὐκ ὄντων, οὐδὲ μισθὸν ἐκδέχεσθαι
ἐνῆν. Ὅλως δὲ τῆς φύσεως ἡμῖν θνη-
τῆς κατασκευασθείσης διὰ τὸ μὴ τῷ
φρονήματι ἐπαιρομένους μείζονα φαν-
τάζεσθαι περὶ ἑαυτῶν, καὶ ὥστε μὴ
σφόδρα ἀμετραίνειν εἰς τὴν ἁμαρτίαν,
τῶν λογισμῶν ἡμῖν ὑπὸ τῆς θνητό-
τητος ταπεινουμένων, ἀναγκαῖον ἦν
καὶ τὰ πάθη κρατεῖν, οὐ μόνον καθὸ
ἕπεσθαι τοῦ|το ἀνάγκη τῇ φύσει
θνητῇ κατασκευασθείσῃ, ἀλλὰ καὶ
καθὸ ὑπόμνησις ὄντα τοῦ θανάτου

statuisset temporis, alii uero minus, querella iniustitiae nascere-
tus quia non aequa omnibus hominibus essent uiuendi tempora
constituta. E diuerso uero, si 5
unum omnibus modum posuisset
annorum, necesse erat ut inpassibilis natura medio fieret tempore, quo possit ad statuta sibi
tempora peruenire nec ullis in- 10
firmitatibus | frangeretur. Nam
facta inpassibilis natura, necesse
erat ut inmortalis quoque fieret,
et occasionem exercendae uir-
tutis amitteret, | id est ut non 15
possit pro Xpisto aliquid marti-
rii tempore sustinere aut absti-
nentiae et districtioris propossiti
agone sudare; tolleretur postremo
omnis spes praemii. Nam inpass- 20
sibilis facta natura laboris onera
non subiret; cessante uero labore,
merces utique nulla sequeretur.
Ideo autem nobis est facta natura mortalis, ne elati superbia 25
maiora de nobis quam mensurae
nostrae conuenit sentiremus et
ne praecipites laberemur in uitia, appetitus noxios mortis memoria conpraemente. Vtile uero 30
fuit ut etiam infirmitatibus sub-
deremur, quae naturam mortalem
factam necessario consequuntur,
ut commemoratio ipsa mortis

7 χρόνον ms.
1 ali B   6 potuisset A   10 nec] non A   11 nam] n *ex* f A   14 occass-
sionem B   14-15 uirtutem A¹   15 ut *add. supra* A   16-17 materii A
17-18 abstinere A¹   18 districtiori A¹   19 sudare] *litt.* dare *in rasura* A
19-20 postremo omnis] prae sermones A¹ post sermo omnes A²   22 censante A
24 est nobis A   25 supibia A¹   26 maira A¹   27 et *om.* A   28 labore-
mur A   33 consecuntur B.

less for another, it would have been unfair for him not to allot people length of life equally; and if he had maintained equality, it would have been necessary for human nature to remain proof against illness in the meantime for the period of their life span, not falling victim to bodily complaints. As well, the onset of death befitting our nature would have been abolished: being impassible, we necessarily would have to be also immortal, and the possibility of suffering bodily for Christ's sake would be abolished in the case both of martyrdom and of self-control, and along with it the reward for virtuous effort. You see, if we were naturally impassible, it would follow that we would not feel effort; but if there were no effort, we could not earn a reward, either. Our nature, however, has been made quite mortal with a view to our not being carried away with exalted ideas of ourselves and to prevent our being led astray into sin. Once our thinking was humbled by our mortality, it followed that ailments also took effect, not only as a consequence of our natural mortality, but also as a reminder of death | capable of producing a greater benefit.

τὴν ὠφέλειαν μείζονα ἐνεργάζεσθαι
ἠδύνατο. Εἰ γὰρ νῦν, τῶν παθῶν
διοχλούντων, πολλοὶ τῶν ἀνθρώπων
οὕτω τὰ ἄτοπα διαπράττονται ὡς
5 οὐδεμίαν ἔχοντες ἐνθύμησιν τοῦ θανάτου, πολλῷ δήπουθεν τούτων ἀπηλ-
λαγμένοι οὐδέποτ' ἂν εἰς νοῦν ἐβά-
λοντο τοῦ θανάτου τὴν μνήμην.

10   Τὸ
δέ γε διαφόρως ζῆν τοὺς ἀνθρώπους
κατὰ τὰς γενεὰς ̀𝔟´, γενεῶν εἰ τύχοι
τῶν πρὸ τοῦ κατακλυσμοῦ γεγονότων, ρ´ δὲ ο´ τῶν ἐπὶ τοῦ Ἀβραάμ,
15 καὶ τῶν μετ' αὐτὸν ρ´ καὶ ι´ καὶ εἰ
βραχύ τι πλέον, οὐδὲν τῷ νοήματι
λυμαίνεται. Πανταχόθεν γὰρ δῆλον
ὅτι οὐδὲ οἱ κατὰ τὴν αὐτὴν γενεὰν
ἴσον ἔζων τὸν ἀριθμόν,

20
                    ὅπερ οὐκ ἂν
ἦν εἰ ὁ Θεὸς ἑκάστῳ τὴν ζωὴν ἐμέ-
τρει· πάντως γὰρ ἂν τοῖς κατὰ τὴν
αὐτὴν γενεὰν ἐφύλαξε τὴν ἰσότητα.
25
Κατὰ γὰρ τὰς γενεὰς διάφορον ἔθηκε
τῆς ζωῆς τὸν ἀριθμόν, τοῖς μὲν ἐν
ἀρχῇ προσθήκην παρέσχεν ἐτῶν
ὥστε πλεονάσαι τῇ πολυτεκνίᾳ, ἐπὶ
30 μακρὸν βιούντων τῶν ἀνθρώπων·
προστιθεμένοις δὲ ἠλάττωσεν εἰκότως
τὰ ἔτη, ἢ τάχα καὶ αὐτὴ ἡ φύσις

attentiores nos circa studium uirtutis efficeret. Si enim nunc sub
egritudinum adsiduitate multi
hominum positi ita se uitiis et
erroribus manciparunt, ut nihil
de morte cogitare uideantur,
multo magis, si essent ab his ne-
cessitatibus liberi, neque cogitationem aliquando eorum memoria
mortis intraret. Nam quod diuersae aetates singulis sunt gene-
rationibus attributae — ut DCCCC
annis ante diluuium, C et LXX
tempore Abrahae, et post eum C
uel parum quid amplius — nihil
hoc superioribus dictis incommo-
dat: per cunctas namque aetates
probatur quoniam numquam omnes aequalem annorum numerum
habuerint sub una generatione
uiuentes, — quod utique euenire
minime potuisset si Deus singulis
uiuendi tempora praefinisset:
nam sine dubio omnibus in eadem aetate positis aequa uitae
spatia contulisset. Per singulas
autem generationes diuersum posuit uiuendi modum prout hominum utilitas postulauit; et ob hoc
inter initia protractus est anno-
rum numerus, ut rari|tas homi-
num, dum diu uiuunt, frequentia

---

12 cf. Gen. V, 5, 8 ss.   14 cf. Gen. XXV, 8.

---

1 adtentiores A   3 egritudinem B¹   adsiduetate A   4 uitis A
5 mancipauerunt A   7 magis] mḡ *in textu,* magis *in marg.* A   hiis B
8 neque] ñq A   10-11 diuesae aetatis A   13 diluium A   15 paruum B
16 superius A   18 nq(uam) A¹, *litt.* um *add. supra*   20 habuert A   23 praefiniisset A   25 possitis A   27-28 possuit A   30 est *om.* A   32 fre-
quenti B.

After all, if in the present situation despite the annoyance of ailments many people are guilty of such wrongdoing as to give no thought to death, much more likely is it that once rid of them they would never admit the remembrance of death into their minds.

Now, the fact that people lived different ages in different periods—such as nine hundred before the flood, a hundred and seventy in the case of Abraham,[2] and after him a hundred and ten a little more—does not undermine our argument: in every case it is clear that those in the same period did not have equal life spans, which would not have been the case if God had allotted each one a life span, since in the same period he definitely would have maintained equal life spans. In fact, he assigned different life spans in different periods, giving advanced age in the beginning for an increase in the size of families through people's living longer, and rightly reducing the number of years in succeeding ages, perhaps because human nature | has become weaker as time

---

2. Cf. Gen 5:8; 25:7 (which speaks of 175 years).

ἀσθενεστέρα ἑαυτῆς τῷ χρόνῳ γι-   suppleretur; accessu uero tem-
γνομένη ἐπ᾽ ἔλαττον διαρκεῖν ἰσχύει.   poris inminuta est illa aeui pro-
lixitas, quia et mundus erat
habitatore plenus et grandis
facta fuerat iniquitatis accessio,   5
quod quidem aperte Scriptura dicit: *Videns autem Dominus Deus
quia habundauerunt malitiae hominum super terram et omnes cogitant in corde suo studiose ad malitiam*; et ob hoc ait: *Erunt anni
eorum cxx.*

Καὶ ταῦτα μέν, ἐπειδήπερ ζητεῖ-   Haec autem ideo a nobis 10
ται παρὰ τοῖς πολλοῖς πῶς ἔχειν   dicta sunt, — siquidem a multis
προσήκει περὶ τούτου, — πρὸς ἀπό-   quaeritur quid de his credi con-
δειξιν τοῦ μὴ ὑπὸ Θεοῦ ἑκάστῳ   ueniat ac teneri, — sed ad pro-
τῶν ἀνθρώπων μετρεῖσθαι τὸν τῆς   bationem, quia non a Deo sin-
ζωῆς χρόνον πλειόνων ὄντων τῶν δυ-   gulorum hominum uita dimensa 15
ναμένων ἄτοπον δεῖξαι τὸ πρᾶγμα, —   sit, congeri multa potuerant; a
συντόμως εἰρήσθω, οὐκ ἀκαίρως πα-   nobis tamen breuiter dictum est
ρεντεθέντα ἢ ἐκτὸς εἶναι δοκεῖ τῆς   et non inoportune, quamuis ex-
ἑρμηνείας τῶν ῥητῶν τοῦ ψαλμοῦ.   tra explanationis necessitatem
Προσεκτέον δὲ λοιπὸν καὶ τῇ τῆς ἑρ-   uideatur adiectum. Nunc.uero ad 20
μηνείας ἀκολουθίᾳ.   expositionis ordinem reuerten-
dum est.

Παλαιστὰς δὲ οὐχ, ὥς τινες ᾠήθησαν, λέγει ὅτι εἰς τὸ παλαιειν μετε-
σκεύασας, — οὕτω γοῦν τινες οἰηθέντες εἰς μέγεθος μυθολογίας | ἐξηνέχθησαν,
ἀλλ᾽ ἐπειδὴ π α λ α ι σ τ ὴ λέγεται μέτρον τι διὰ τῆς χειρὸς γινόμενον ἐν ταῖς 25
τῶν ἱματίων ὑφαῖς παρὰ τῶν γυναικῶν, τοῦτο ἠβουλήθη εἰπεῖν ὅτι τὴν
ζωήν μου ὥσπερ μέτρῳ τινὶ ὑφήνας, οὐχ ἁπλῶς ἀόριστον αὐτὴν πεποίηκας, ἀλλ᾽ ὅροις χρόνων αὐτὴν ὑπέβαλες.

6ᵇ. Καὶ ἡ ὑπόστασίς μου ὡσεὶ οὐ-   *Et substantia mea*, reliqua.
δὲν ἐνώπιόν σου. Οὕτως οὖν φησιν   Manifestum est per hoc, quod 30
ἐμέτρησάς μου τὴν ζωήν, ὥστε τὴν   ait *Et substantia mea tanquam*

6-9 Gen. VI, 5 et 3.

26-28 cf. L (p. 721, 7-9): οὐδὲ γὰρ ἀμέτρητόν μοι τὸν χρόνον τῆς ζωῆς ὥρισας,
ἀλλὰ περιέγραψας αὐτὸν μέτρῳ. Eadem in *Paraphrasi* (p. 717).

1 supplerentur AB   accesu A   5 fuerit A   accesio A   7 habunda-
uer̄t A   8 ob om. A¹ ab add. supra   12 queritur B q̄r A   15 demensa A
16 potuer̄t A potuer̄ B   18 non om. A   quamuis] qq̄ (quoque, quamquam?) A
19 necessitate A   20 uidiatur A   21 expossitionis A.

Et substantia — inposita: A, fol. 13ᵇ; B, fol. 14ᵇ.   30 est om. A.

Aᵉ 27-28 (p. 227, 2-3): Ac si diceret Terminalis non aeternos.

passed and can last a shorter time.[3]

I have said this concisely because people in general are anxious to find out what should be said on this topic and also to prove that each person's life span is not determined by God, even though there are many considerations that are not untimely, however much they seem irrelevant to interpreting the words of the psalm. At this point, however, there is need to resume the theme of the commentary. By handbreadths he means not, as many commentators believed, that he made us for fighting,[4] certain commentators of this mind being swept away to the extremes of fairy tales. Instead, since handbreadth refers to the hand measurements made by women in weaving garments, he meant here, You wove my life as with a kind of measurement, not making it indeterminate and without conditions, but subjecting it to time limits.

And my being is as nothing before you: you measured my life in such a way that | my existence and constitution are counted as nothing in com-

---

3. The Latin version elaborates on the reduction in life spans to introduce a moralizing interpretation about proclivity to evil, even citing Gen 6:5.

4. The suggested interpretation, although allowed no grounds by Theodore, arises from the resemblance of παλαιστής to the verb παλαίειν, "to fight." His own explication is helpful and plausible.

ἐμὴν ὕπαρξιν καὶ σύστασιν μηδὲν λε-
λογίσθαι ἀντικρύ σου, τουτέστι Πρὸς
τὸ ἄπειρον τῆς σῆς ζωῆς ἡ ἐμὴ ὑπόστασις οὐδὲν ἐν τοῖς οὖσι λελόγισται.
5 Δῆλον δὲ ἐκ τούτου ὅτι καὶ τὸ Ἰδοὺ
παλαιστὰς ἔθου τὰς ἡμέρας μου κατὰ
τὸ ὀλιγοχρόνιον εἶπεν, οὐχ ὡς τοῦ
Θεοῦ μετρήσαντος ἑκάστῳ ἀνθρώπῳ

nihilum — id est ad inmensitatem
tuam — ante te, etiam per illud dictum Mensurabiles posuisti dies
meos uoluisse eum breuitatem
uitae mortalis ostendere, non singulis certa spatia ac mensuras
inposita.
τὸν τῆς ζωῆς χρόνον.

6ᶜ. Πλὴν τὰ ἄπαντα ματαιότης,
10 πᾶς ἄνθρωπος ζῶν. Τὸ πλὴν οὐδαμοῦ κατὰ ἀκολουθίαν διανοίας κεῖται ἐν τοῖς ψαλμοῖς, ἀλλὰ πανταχοῦ
πρόσκειται περιττόν, ἀπὸ τοῦ ἑβραϊκοῦ ἰδιώματος ἴσως προσριφέν, ὡς
15 καὶ τὸ σὺν ἐν τῷ ἑβραϊκῷ ἀπό τινος ἰδιώματος πρόσκειται, οὐκ εἰς
διάνοιαν συντελοῦν. Τοῦτο γοῦν βούλεται εἰπεῖν, ἀκολούθως τῷ Καὶ ἡ
ὑπόστασίς μου ὡσεὶ οὐδὲν ἐνώπιόν σου,
20 ὅτι Οὐ μόνον φησὶν ἐν συγκρίσει σῇ
τὸ μηδὲν ἐγώ, ἀλλὰ καὶ ἄπαντα τὰ
ἐν τῷ βίῳ τούτῳ ματαιότης καὶ πᾶς
ἄνθρωπος ζῶν.

Verumtamen uniuersa uani-
tas, omnis homo uiuens. Verumtamen nusquam propter intellectus necessitatem positum est,
sed, cum sit otiosum, tantum
propter proprietatem hebreici
sermonis inseritur.

Hoc ergo dictis superioribus
consequenter adiecit Et substantia mea, reliqua. Non solum, inquit, in conparationem tui nihil
sum ego, sed omnia praesentis
uitae negotia grandis uanitas.

Πάντα φησὶν εἰκαῖα τὰ ἐν τῷ βίῳ πράγματα καὶ αὐτὸς ὁ ἄνθρωπος,
25 ὅμοιον δὲ ἐστὶ τῷ τοῦ Ἐκκλησιαστοῦ Ματαιό|της ματαιοτήτων, τὰ πάντα
ματαιότης. Τίς περισσεία τῷ ἀνθρώπῳ ἐν παντὶ μόχθῳ αὐτοῦ ᾧ μοχθεῖ
ὑπὸ τὸν ἥλιον;

25-27 Eccl. I, 2-3

20-22 cf. L (p. 721, 9-10): Οἷον δ' ἂν ᾖ τοῦτο τῆς ζωῆς μου μέτρον, οὐδέν ἐστιν
ἐν συγκρίσει τοῦ ἀεὶ ὄντος σου. Eadem in Paraphrasi (p. 717) et in cod. Ambros. H. 257 inf. sub lemmate Θεοδώρου Ἡρακλειώτου   24 εἰκαῖα τὰ conieci,
ἠκαίατα ms.
1-2 id est — tuam suppl. inter column. B   3 possuisti A   6 mensurae
7 inpossita A¹.
Verumtamen — uanitas: A, fol. 13ᵇ; B, fol. 14ᶜ.   11-12 intellectum AB
12 necessitatem om. A   possitum A   17 superioribus] sermonibus A.

Aᵉ 20-24 (p. 227, 5-11): Immensitatis tuae conparatione substantiae mea
uita tamquam numquam fuerit estimatur. Non tantum mea uita sed omnis
praesentium status inanitas est uanitas.

parison with you—in other words, In the light of the infinity of your life my existence does not count among living things. Now, it is clear from this that the verse *Lo, you made my days handbreadths* also referred to brevity of time, not to God's determining each person's life span. *Yet everything is futility, every living person.* The word *Yet* does not occur in the psalms from sequence of thought; rather, its occurrence is everywhere superfluous, proba- bly inserted by Hebrew idiom,[5] as "with" also occurs in the Hebrew by some idiom, not required by the thought. At any rate, the meaning here, following on from *And my being is as nothing before you* is, Not only am I nothing in comparison with you, *but everything in this life is futility, every living person:* all affairs of this life and humankind itself are without purpose, like the saying in Ecclesiastes, "Vanity of vanities, all is vanity. What do people gain from all the toil at which they toil under the sun?"[6] |

---

5. Theodore (taking a lead from Diodore) is right to sense the inappropriateness of an adversative adverb at this point but is unable to be definite that the Hebrew does not contain such a particle (as it does). His mention of an interpolated "with" possibly refers to the quirk of Akiba, in the second century, in taking the particle *eth* (direct object marker) in the Hebrew of "heaven and earth" in Gen 1:1 to mean "with," his pupil Aquila rendering it σύν in Greek.

6. Eccl 1:2–3.

7ᵃ. Μέντοι γε ἐν εἰκόνι καὶ γραφῇ διαπορεύεται ἄνθρωπος. Ἀμέλει φησὶν οἱ ἄνθρωποι ὡς ἐν εἰκόνι τινὶ καὶ γραφῇ οὕτω καθεστήκασιν. Ὥσπερ γὰρ ἐν τῇ γραφῇ φησι δοκεῖ μὲν τὸ σχῆμα τοῦ στρατιώτου ἢ τοῦ βασιλέως ἐκπλήττειν τῇ θέᾳ, βραχεῖα δὲ ἀλοιφὴ πάντα διαλύει, οὕτω καὶ οἱ ἄνθρω- ποι τῷ σχήματι δοκοῦμεν καταπλήττειν ὥσπερ ἐν τῇ εἰκόνι, ὁ δὲ θάνατος 5 ἐλθὼν καὶ διαλύσας τὸ ἐπικείμενον σχῆμα ἐλέγχει μάταια πάντα καὶ περιττά. Τὸ γὰρ ἐν εἰκόνι οὐχ, ὥς τινες ἐνόμισαν, τῇ τοῦ Θεοῦ λέγει· ἐπεὶ εἰ ἐν εἰκόνι Θεοῦ ἔλεγε, πῶς ἐπήγαγε Πλὴν μάτην ταράσσεται, πῶς δὲ καὶ προέ- λεγε ματαιότης πᾶς ἄνθρωπος ζῶν;

7ᵇ. Πλὴν μάτην ταράσσεται. Ὁμοίως κἀνταῦθα τὸ πλὴν περιττὸν ὡς εἰς διάνοιαν.

Verumtamen uane conturba- 10 *tur.* Similiter hic, ut superius, superfluum est *uerumtamen*, nec intellectui aliquid conferens.

Ἐπειδὴ τοίνυν φησὶν ὡς ἐν γραφῇ καὶ σχήματι ψιλῷ τῷ βίῳ τούτῳ καθεστήκαμεν, δῆλον ὅτι περιττὸν καὶ ἀνωφελῆ πόνον ὑφιστάμεθα τῶν ἐν 15 τῷ βίῳ πραγμάτων ἕνεκεν πονοῦντες. Τὸ δὲ ταράσσεται εἶπεν ἐμφαντικώ- τερον, τὸ μάταιον τῶν πόνων δεικνὺς ἐκ μεταφορᾶς τῶν ὀρνίθων, ἅπερ σφαγέντα ταράσσει τοὺς πόδας εἰς οὐδὲν ὄφελος. Διὰ τί οὖν μάτην ταράσσεται;

7ᶜ. Θησαυρίζει, καὶ οὐ γινώσκει τίνι συνάξει αὐτά. Ἐπειδὴ κἂν πλεῖ- 20 στα συναγάγωσιν ἀπὸ τῶν πόνων ἑτέροις κοπιῶσι πολλάκις, οἷς οὐκ ἴσασι, μετὰ τὸν ἐκείνου θά|νατον ἑκάστου διαρπάζοντος τὰ κτηθέντα κατὰ δύναμιν καὶ μετὰ πολλῶν αὐτῷ συναθροισθέντα τῶν πόνων. Δεικνὺς ὃν ὑφί- στανται πάντες ἄνθρωποι ὑπὲρ τῶν ἐν τῷ βίῳ πραγμάτων, ταύτῃ τῇ ἀκο- λουθίᾳ τῆς διανοίας χρησάμενος ἐν ὅλῳ τῷ ψαλμῷ, ἐσπούδασά φησι φυλά- 25 ξασθαι τοῦ φθέγξασθαί τι ἄτοπον, ἀλλὰ νικώμενος πάλιν ἀπὸ τῶν γινομένων εἰς ἀγανάκτησιν ἐκινούμην· δεδιὼς οὖν τὸ ἁμαρτάνειν καὶ τὰς περιστάσεις τῶν πραγμάτων ὑφορώμενος, ηὐξάμην γνῶναι τὸ τέλος τῆς ζωῆς, εἰδὼς ὅτι καὶ ὁ χρόνος τῆς ζωῆς ἡμῶν ὀλίγος σφόδρα καθέστηκε, καὶ ἅπαντα τὰ ἐν τῷ βίῳ νομιζόμενα μεγάλα καὶ περιττά, καὶ μάταιος ὁ ὑπὲρ τούτων πόνος. 30 Καὶ οὐδέν φησιν ὄφελός μοι κἂν ζήσας ἐν βασιλείᾳ ἐξετασθῆναι δυνηθῶ,

25-30 vv. 1-7.

7 λέγειν ms   23 ὃν subintellige e. g. πόνον (cf. supra l. 15).
Verumtamen — conferens: A, fol. 13ᵇ; B, fol. 14ᶜ.   12 superflum A   nec]
non A.

Aᵉ 20-23 (p. 227, 24-28): Cum multa, inquit, laborans parauerit atque con-
gesserit, aliis interdum et ignotis reliquit proprio sudori quesita.

At any rate, a human being goes about in an image and a picture (v. 6): to be sure, human beings are constituted as though *in an image and a picture;* just as by his picture the likeness of the soldier or the king seems to instill terror at the sight, but a little paint wipes it all out, so too we human beings give the impression of causing terror in appearance as though by an image, whereas death comes and wipes out the appearance adopted, proving everything to be futile and purposeless. The phrase *in an image,* you see, does not, as some commentators thought, refer to that of God: if *in an image* referred to God, why did he go on to say *But he is worried to no purpose,* and why did he also foretell that *every living person is futility? But he is worried to no purpose.* Similarly here, too, the word *But* is not required by the thought. So since, he is saying, we are in this life reduced to a picture and a flimsy likeness, it is clear that we subject ourselves to idle and useless labor in laboring for the things of this life. *He is worried* made the point more forcefully, bringing out the futility of the labor in a metaphor from birds, which, when killed, shake their feet to no advantage. So why is he *worried to no purpose?*

He stores up treasures and does not know for whom he is collecting them, since even if they collect a great amount, they in many cases labor at the task for others unknown to them, everyone as far as possible after his death stealing his possessions and what he amassed with great effort. To bring out what all people commit themselves to for the things of this life, and adopting this theme consistently in the whole psalm, he says, I was anxious to keep myself from saying anything wrong, but I eventually was overcome by what was happening and was moved to anger; fearful of sinning, therefore, and suspecting a turn for the worse, I begged to know the end of my life, aware that our life span is very short, and that everything considered great in life is futile, and effort for it is in vain. It is of no advantage to me, he is saying, even if I manage to live in a palace in my lifetime, | whereas sinning is

βαρὺ δὲ τὸ ἁμαρτεῖν, ὃ δέδοικα μὲν μὴ ὑπὸ τῆς τῶν γιγνομένων ἀνάγκης περιπέσω καὶ μὴ βουλόμενος, τὴν δὲ ἀπαλλαγὴν ἁπάντων κρίνω μακαριστοτέραν.

8ᵃ. Καὶ νῦν τίς ἡ ὑπομονή μου· οὐχὶ ὁ Κύριος. Ἐπειδή φησιν οὕτως
5 οὐδαμινὰ τὰ ἐν τῷ βίῳ καὶ εὐτελῆ, ἐδοκίμασα εἴς σε πᾶσαν ἔχειν τὴν προσδοκίαν. Καλῶς δὲ τοῦτο εἶπεν ὁ μακάριος Δαυὶδ ἐπειδὴ ὁ Σαοὺλ δῆλος ἦν μηδεμίαν ἔχων εἰς Θεὸν προσδοκίαν, ὅπου γε ἐδίωκε τὸν Δαυὶδ βασκαίνων καὶ δεδιὼς μὴ τὴν βασιλείαν αὐτοῦ ἀφέληται, — καὶ ταῦτα παρὰ τοῦ Θεοῦ αὐτὴν εἰληφώς, — δέον πιστεύειν ὅτι πάντως ὁ δεδωκὼς καὶ φυλάξει ἀξίῳ
10 καθεστῶτι τοῦ ταύτης ἀπολαύειν, ὥσπερ καὶ τὸ ἐναντίον ἄξιον οὐκ ὄντα πάντως αὐτὴν ἀφαιρήσεται.

8ᵇ. Καὶ ἡ ὑπόστασίς μου παρὰ σού ἐστιν. Παρ᾽ οὗ γὰρ ἔχω τὸ ὑφεστάναι, εἰκότως καὶ τὴν βοήθειαν προσδοκῶ παρ᾽ αὐτοῦ. Αἰτῶ δέ φησιν οὐ πλοῦτον καὶ βασιλείαν· περιττὰ | γάρ μοι ταῦτα ἅπαξ ἅπαντα κατα-
15 φαίνεται καὶ οἶδα τῆς τούτων περιουσίας τὸ ἀνωφελές. Ἀλλὰ τί;

9ᵃ. Ἀπὸ πασῶν τῶν ἀνομιῶν μου   *Ab omnibus iniquitatibus meis*
ῥῦσαί με.   *erue me.* Non audebat quaeri de
Deo quod iniuste erumnis tradi-
tus est, sed sibi magis adscribit.
20   Τῶν ἁμαρτιῶν φησι παράσχου μοι τὴν συγχώρησιν, ἵνα ἔχω τὴν πρός σε παρρησίαν· τούτου γὰρ οὐδὲν κρίνω μακαριώτερον.

9ᵇ. Ὄνειδος ἄφρονι ἔδωκάς με. Διὰ γὰρ ταύτας φησὶ τὰς ἁμαρτίας οἶδα πάσχων ἃ πέπονθα καὶ ὄνειδος ἐκ τούτου τοῖς ἄφροσι γεγονώς. Ὥσπερ δὲ ἄνω ἁμαρτωλὸν τὸν ἐπιβουλεύοντα ἐκάλεσεν ἀδίκως τοῦτο διαπραττό-
25 μενον, οὕτως καὶ ἐνταῦθα τοὺς ὄνειδον καὶ γέλωτα τιθεμένους αὐτὸν ἐφ᾽ οἷς ἔπασχεν ἀδίκως, δέον συναλγεῖν καὶ ἀθυμεῖν, ἄφρονας εἰκότως ἐκάλεσεν, οὐκ ἀπὸ τοῦ εὐλόγου συνέσει κρίνοντας τὰ γινόμενα, ἀλλὰ ἀφρόνως χλευάζοντας διὰ τὰ συμβαίνοντα.

6 cf. I Reg. XVIII, 8   24 v. 2ᶜ.

Ab omnibus — adscribit: A, fol. 13ᵇ; B, fol. 14ᶜ.   18-19 tratitus A   19 sed om. A¹   magis A² *supra lin.* mg̅ A¹ *in textu.*

Aᵉ 8ᵃ (p. 227, 29-33): Et his malis possito sub praesentis uitae uanitate degenti, quam Saul studio iniquitatis ammisserat.   20 (p. 228, 10-11)... idcirco remisionem prius postulat peccatorum.

grave, and on the one hand I dread falling into it under the pressure of events, albeit unwillingly, and on the other hand I judge freedom from everything to be most blessed.

And now what is my expectation? Is it not the Lord? (v. 7). Since things of this life are of no value and so vile, he is saying, I saw fit to place all my expectations in you. Blessed David was right to say this, since Saul clearly placed no expectations in God when he pursued David out of envy and fear of losing his kingship, despite receiving it from God. He ought to have trusted that the one who gave it to him would also definitely preserve it for the one in a worthy state to enjoy it, just as, on the contrary, he would definitely wrest it from the unworthy. *My being is from you:* from you I have support, and with good reason I look for help from you. I do not ask for wealth and kingship: all this once and for all strikes me as superfluous, and I realize the uselessness of possessions. Why so?

From all my iniquities rescue me (v. 8): grant me pardon of my sins so that I may have confidence in your presence, nothing in my estimation being more blessed. *You gave me as an object of scorn to the fool:* I realize that it was on account of my sins that I suffered what I suffered and became an object of scorn to fools for it. As he had referred above to the one guilty of this as a scheming sinner, so here, too, those leveling scorn and mockery at him for what he was unjustly suffering, when they should have been sympathetic and disconsolate, he rightly referred to as fools, since far from judging events with an insight into what was reasonable, they foolishly scoffed at developments. |

10. Ἐκωρώθην καὶ οὐκ ἤνοιξα τὸ στόμα μου, ὅτι αὐτὸς ἐπήγαγες. Ἐγὼ μέντοι ὀνειδιζόμενός φησιν καὶ χλευαζόμενος οὐδὲ ἀπεκρινάμην τοῖς χλευάζουσιν, ἀλλ᾿ ὡς οὐδὲ ἀκούων τῶν λεγόντων οὕτω σιγῶν διετέλουν, δικαίως πάσχειν ἡγούμενος, ἐπειδὴ αὐτός μοι ταῦτα ἐπήγαγες, οὐκ ἂν οἰηθείς ποτε ἀδίκως τι ἐπάγεσθαι παρά σου. Τὸ δὲ ὅτι αὐτὸς ἐπήγαγες, τουτέστι 5 παθεῖν συνεχώρησας· τοῦτο γὰρ ἰδίωμα τῆς γραφῆς τὸ τῷ Θεῷ τὴν πρᾶξιν ἐπιγράφειν ὧν συνεχώρησε, δυνάμενος ἐπισχεῖν. Διὰ τοῦτο οὖν φησιν ἀξιῶ τῶν ἀνομιῶν ῥυσθῆναι, ἐπειδὴ ταῦτα ἃ πέπονθα οἶδα διὰ τὰς ἁμαρτίας πεπονθώς. Καὶ μηδεὶς θαυμαζέτω εἰ ἁμαρτιῶν ἀξιοῖ ῥυσθῆναι ὁ μακάριος Δαυίδ· οὐ γὰρ ὡς εἶχεν ἐν τῷ βίῳ τὰ κατ᾿ αὐτὸν οὕτως καὶ αὐτὸν 10 ἔδει οἴεσθαι περὶ αὐτοῦ. Ἡ δὲ τοῦ δικαίου ἀπόδειξις, ὅτι οὐκ ἐκ τοῦ πάσχειν ἀγεννῶς διατιθέμενος | ἐπὶ ἐκφωνήσεις ἀπρεπεῖς ἐξεφέρετο, καίτοι δίκαιος ὤν, ἀλλ᾿ ἑαυτῷ τῶν γινομένων ἐπέγραφε τὴν αἰτίαν ὡς ἐκ τῶν οἰκείων πράξεων ταῦτα πάσχων δικαίως, οὐκ ἂν τοῖς κακοῖς ἀδίκως ἡγούμενος ἐναφεθῆναι παρὰ τοῦ Θεοῦ, ὡς καὶ ἡ γραφή φησι· Δίκαιος ἑαυτοῦ 15 κατήγορος ἐν πρωτολογίᾳ.

11ᵃ. Ἀπόστησον ἀπ᾿ ἐμοῦ τὰς μάστιγάς σου. Παῦσον δή φησι καὶ τὴν τιμωρίαν τὴν κατ᾿ ἐμοῦ, μάστιγας τοῦ Θεοῦ καλῶν τὰ κατὰ συγχώρησιν αὐτοῦ γινόμενα εἰς αὐτόν. Ὅταν γάρ με τούτων ἀπαλλάξῃς, τότε οἶδα καὶ τῶν ἁμαρτιῶν ἐσχηκὼς τὴν ἄφεσιν. 20

11ᵇ. Ἀπὸ τῆς ἰσχύος τῆς χειρός σου ἐγὼ ἐξέλιπον. Διὰ γὰρ τὸ βαρὺ τῆς τιμωρίας ἀνηλώθην ἐγώ, ὥστε δικαίως αἰτῶ τὴν συγχώρησιν καὶ τὴν ἀπαλλαγὴν τῶν κακῶν, ἐπειδὴ ἱκανὰ ἅπερ ὑπέστην.

12ᵃ. Ἐν ἐλεγμοῖς ὑπὲρ ἀνομίας   Propter iniquitatem corripui ἐπαίδευσας ἄνθρωπον. Καὶ γὰρ οὐκ   sti hominem. Non solum me. 25 ἐμὲ μόνον φησίν, ἀλλὰ καὶ πάντα ἄνθρωπον παιδεύεις, ἐλέγχων ὑπὲρ τῆς ἁμαρτίας. Τὸ γὰρ ὑπὲρ ἀνομίας, ἀντὶ τοῦ διὰ τὰς ἀνομίας, — οὐχ, ὥς τινες ἐνόμισαν, ὑπὲρ τὰς ἀνομίας, ὅτι πλέον τῶν ἁμαρτιῶν παιδεύει· τοῦτο γὰρ οὐ πρέπον ἐπὶ Θεοῦ νοεῖσθαι. Καὶ τὸ ἐπαίδευσας, ἀντὶ τοῦ παιδεύσεις, ἐναλλαγὴ χρόνου ἐκ τῆς ἑρμηνείας ἐγγενομένη. Οὕτω γοῦν λέγει Σύμμαχος 30 Ἐν ἐλεγμοῖς διὰ κακίαν παιδεύεις ἄνθρωπον.

15-16 Prov. XVIII, 17; cf. supra, p. 75.

Propter ueritatem — solum me: A, fol. 13ᵇ; B, fol. 14ᶜ.

Aᵉ 14-15 (p. 228, 12-13): Vt insultaret tamquam merito sustinenti. 19-20 (p. 228, 16-19): …cum, inquit, me ab istis liberaueris, tunc sciam quod etiam a uinculo reatus absolueris (obs — ms). 25-26 (p. 228, 25-26): Non solum me, sed multos plerumque castigas.

I kept mute; I did not open my mouth, because you did it (v. 9): though mocked and scoffed at, I made no reply to the scoffers; instead, not even listening to the speakers, I continued to keep silence in the belief that I suffered justly *because you did it,* and I would not believe that anything was unjustly done by you. The phrase *you did it* means "you allowed me to suffer," it being customary with Scripture to attribute to God the deed he permitted when he could have prevented it. For this reason, then, he is saying, I deserve to be rescued from the lawless because I know that I suffer what I suffer on account of sin. Let no one be surprised if blessed David asks to be rescued from sins: it was not that he was guilty of them in his life and needed to think this way of himself. The proof of his righteousness is that he was not ill-disposed toward suffering or gave vent to inappropriate outbursts; even though he was righteous, he instead ascribed to himself the cause of what happened as grounds for rightly suffering this way for his own deeds, not convinced he was unjustly involved in the troubles by God, as Scripture also says, "A righteous person is the first to turn accuser against himself."[7] *Remove the scourge from me* (v. 10): put an end to punishment of me (by God's *scourge* referring to what happened to him with God's permission); when you rid me of it, then I know I also have forgiveness of sins. *I have fainted with the strength of your hand:* I am wasted by the severity of the punishment, and so rightly beg pardon and relief from the troubles, since what I have endured is enough.

You chastised the human being with accusations of transgression (v. 11): you chastise not only me, but also every human being, accusing them of sin. By *of transgression* he means "on account of transgression," not, as some commentators believed, "in excess of the transgressions," to mean that his chastisement exceeds the sins, this being an interpretation not befitting God. The form *You chastised* stands for "You will chastise," a change of tense occurring in translation; Symmachus, at any rate, puts it in similar terms: "You chastise the human being with accusations of evil." | *And you wasted*

---

7. Prov 18:17 LXX.

12ᵇ. Καὶ ἐξέτηξας ὡσεὶ ἀράχνην τὴν ψυχὴν αὐτοῦ. Καὶ οἶδάς φησι τοὺς ἡμαρτηκότας τιμωρίᾳ περιβάλλων οὕτως αὐτῶν διαλύειν τὴν ζωὴν ὡσεὶ ἀράχνην, ἧς οὐδὲν μνημόσυνον λυθείσης περιλιμπάνεται. Ταῦτα δὲ ἀπέδωκε πρὸς τὸ ἀπὸ πασῶν τῶν ἀνομιῶν μου ῥῦσαί με. Τοῦτο γάρ φησιν αἰτῶ
5 παρά σου, — ἐπειδὴ καὶ ἃ πέπονθα διὰ τοῦτο οἶδα πεπονθώς, καὶ πάντως ὁ ἡμαρτηκὼς δίδω|σι δίκας ὑπὲρ τῆς ἁμαρτίας, — διὰ τοῦτο τῶν ἁμαρτιῶν ἀξιῶ ῥυσθῆναι· οἶδα γὰρ ὅτι τότε μοι παυθήσεται τὰ κακά.

12ᶜ. Πλὴν μάτην ταράσσεται πᾶς ἄνθρωπος. Ἔδει τοίνυν φησὶ περὶ ταῦτα ἔχειν καὶ περὶ ταῦτα ἀσχολεῖσθαι — περὶ τὸ τῶν ἁμαρτιῶν ῥυσθῆ-
10 ναι καὶ περὶ τὸ τῆς σῆς τυχεῖν καταλλαγῆς, ἀφ᾽ ἧς πάντως καὶ τὰ λυπηρὰ λύεσθαι πέφυκε — καὶ μὴ περὶ ἕτερα πονεῖν, ἅπερ μάταια καὶ ἀνωφελῆ τῷ πονοῦντι καθέστηκεν, οὐδαμῶς τέλος αὐτῷ τῶν πόνων παρεχόμενα, οὔτε μὴν ὠφέλειαν μόνιμον αὐτῷ διὰ τῶν πόνων χαριζόμενα. Καὶ τοῦτο εἰρηκὼς πάλιν ἀναλαμβάνει τὸν οἰκεῖον λόγον καί φησιν·

15 13ᵃ. Εἰσάκουσον τῆς προσευχῆς μου καὶ τῆς δεήσεώς μου. Ἐγὼ τοίνυν τοῦτο αἰτῶ παρά σου, τὸ εἰσακουσθῆναί μου τὴν προσευχήν.

13ᵇ·ᶜ. Ἐνώτισαι τῶν δακρύων μου, μὴ παρασιωπήσῃς. Καὶ τὸ τὰ δάκρυά μου μὴ παροφθῆναι. Διὰ τί;

13ᶜ·ᵈ. Ὅτι πάροικος ἐγώ εἰμι ἐν τῇ γῇ καὶ παρεπίδημος, καθὼς πάντες
20 οἱ πατέρες μου. Ἐπειδή φησι βραχύς ἐστιν ὁ βίος καὶ ὥσπερ ἐν ἀλλοτρίοις ἐσμὲν παροικοῦντες πρὸς βραχύ, εἶτα μεθιστάμενοι καὶ ὡς ἐπιδεδημηκότες πρὸς βραχύ, εἶτα ἐκδημοῦντες· οὕτως γὰρ καὶ οἱ πρὸ ἐμοῦ πάντες πρὸς βραχὺ ζήσαντες μετῆλθον ἐντεῦθεν.

14. Ἄνες μοι ἵνα ἀναψύξω πρὸ τοῦ με ἀπελθεῖν καὶ οὐκέτι οὐ μὴ ὑπάρξω.
25 Ἀξιῶ τοίνυν φησὶν ἐν τῇ βραχείᾳ ταύτῃ ζωῇ ἄνεσίν μοι γενέσθαι καὶ ἀνά-
παυσιν τῶν κακῶν, ἵνα δυνηθῶ ἐν βραχείᾳ ἀνέσει καταστῆναι καὶ ἐν τῷ βίῳ τούτῳ πρὶν ἀπελθεῖν· τότε γάρ, οὐκέτι κατὰ τὴν ζωὴν ταύτην ὤν, οὐδὲ χρῄζω λοιπὸν τῆς ἐνταῦθα ἀνέσεως.

4 v. 9.

Aᵉ 2-3 (p. 228, 28-229, 1)... et uitam eorum sic merore consumes, ut instar aranearum telae discisae (discire *ms*) dispereant. 20-22 (p. 229, 10-13): Siqui-dem exigui temporis uita nostra est, sicut in alienis locis habitantes cito trans-ferimur atque migramus. 25-28 (p. 229, 17-22): Commemoratio breuis uitae ob celiritatem adiutorii conferendi inlata est, quia exiguitas uelocitasque tem-poris in delationem consulationis non patitur.

his soul like a spider's web: you know those who are sinners, investing them with punishment in such a way as to destroy their life *like a spider's web,* so that once it is destroyed, no memory of them survives. Now, this was his response to *From all my iniquities rescue me:*[8] I beg this of you, he is saying, since what I suffer I know I suffer for this reason, and the sinner definitely pays the penalty for sin; so for this reason I beg to be rescued from sin, aware as I am that my troubles will come to an end. *Every human being is worried about a nothing:* so this is what should concern us, being rescued from sins and attaining reconciliation with you, which results in complete resolution of problems, and not taking pains over other things, which are futile and useless for the painstaker, never bringing one an outcome for the pains, nor providing one with lasting benefit from the pains.

After speaking in these terms, he resumes his particular theme as follows. *Hearken to my prayer, Lord, and to my request* (v. 12): I therefore beg this of you, that you hearken to my prayer. *Give your ear to my weeping; do not keep silent:* do not ignore my tears. Why? *Because I am a stranger on earth and a pilgrim like all my ancestors:* since life is brief, and we are like those sojourning briefly in foreign parts, at one time shifting and settling down briefly, at another moving on, this being the case also with all those who lived a while before me and moved on from here. *Give me relief so that I may catch my breath before departing and be no more* (v. 13): I therefore beg to be given in this brief life forgiveness and cessation of troubles so as to be able to enjoy some brief respite even in this life before departing; for at that time, when I am no longer in this life, I shall have no further need of relief here. | The phrase *I shall be no more* means not "completely," but "as

---

8. Ps. 39:8.

Τὸ γὰρ οὐκέτι οὐ μὴ ὑπάρξω οὐκ εἰς τὸ παντελὲς λέγει, ἀλλ᾽ ὡς πρὸς τὴν ζωὴν ταύτην, ἐν ᾗ τυχεῖν ἀνέσεως προσεύχεται.

Et amplius non ero. Nam cum dicessero de hac uita, illam, quae nunc | in praesenti necessaria est, requiem non requiro.

PSALMVS XXXIX

Ἐνταῦθα προφητεύει τὰ κατὰ τὸν λαὸν αἰχμαλωτισθέντα ὑπὸ τῶν Βαβυλωνίων βασιλέων, ἐκ προσώπου μὲν τοῦ ἐκείνων φθεγγόμενος ὡς εὐχαριστούντων ἐπὶ τῇ ἀπαλλαγῇ τῆς αἰχμαλωσίας, ἐν δὲ τῷ φθέγγεσθαι τὰ ἐκείνοις ἁρμόττοντα δεικνὺς ὅτι ἐν συμφοραῖς καθεστὼς καὶ τὴν παρὰ τοῦ Θεοῦ προσδοκίαν ἀναμένων πάντως τυγχάνει τῆς παρ᾽ αὐτοῦ βοηθείας. Μακαρίζει τε ἐντεῦθεν ἅπαντας τοὺς πάσης μὲν ἐκτόπου πράξεως καθαρεύειν ἐσπουδακότας, ἐλπίζοντας δὲ ἐπὶ τὸν Θεὸν ὡς πάντως τυγχάνοντας τῶν παρ᾽ αὐτοῦ ἀγαθῶν.

Καὶ ἐν τούτῳ προφητεύει τὰ κατὰ τὸν λαὸν ὡσανεὶ αἰχμαλωτισθέντα ὑπὸ τοῦ Βαβυλωνίου βασιλέως, καὶ ἐκ τοῦ ἐκείνων προσώπου φθέγγεται εὐχαριστῶν τῷ Θεῷ, ὡς μελλόντων 10 αὐτῶν ἀπαλλαγήσεσθαι τῆς αἰχμαλωσίας· διδάσκων ὡς ἐὰν ἐν ταῖς συμφοραῖς ἐπὶ τὸν Θεὸν θῶνται τὴν ἐλπίδα, δυνήσονται ῥυσθῆναι τῶν κατεχόντων αὐτοὺς ἀνιαρῶν. Ἔπειτα 15 καὶ μακαρίζει τοὺς ἐν ταῖς συμφοραῖς ἐξετασθέντας, πάσης δ᾽ ἐκτὸς γεγονότας ἐκτόπου πράξεως, καὶ τοῦ Θεοῦ ἠρτημένους ὥσπερ αὐτοῦ τευξομένους μόνου βοηθείας. 20

2ᵃ. Ὑπομένων ὑπέμεινα τὸν Κύριον, καὶ προσέσχε μοι. Ἰδίωμα καὶ τοῦτο τῆς θείας γραφῆς ὅταν τὴν ἐπίτασιν δεικνύναι θέλει τοῦ γινομένου, ὡς ὅταν λέγῃ παιδεύων ἐπαίδευσεν ἀντὶ τοῦ σφόδρα ἀληθῶς ἐπαίδευσεν, οὕτως καὶ τὸ ὑπομένων ὑπέμεινα ἀντὶ τοῦ σφόδρα ὑπέμεινα τὸν Κύριον· τῇ δὲ ἐπι-

Et amplius — requiro: A, fol. 13ᵇ⁻ᶜ; B, fol. 14ᶜ.   2 discesero A   3 necesaria A.

Καὶ ἐν τούτῳ — βοηθείας: Paris. 139, fol. 100ᵛ; Vat. 1682, fol. 143ᵛ (Mai, N.P.B. III, 290; P. G., 669 CD); *quam ἑρμηνείαν reiecit Cyrillus Alexandrinus* (Mai, *loc. cit.*)   22 cf. L (p. 738, 7-8) Ὁ διπλασιασμὸς σημεῖόν ἐστιν ἐπιτάσεως   23 παιδεύων ἐπαίδευσεν (Ps. CXVIII, 18)... ἐπαίδευσεν *conieci*, ποιῶν ἐποίησεν ... ἐποίησεν *ms*.

Aᵉ 6-8 (p. 229, 27-30): In persona populi gratias agentis ob reditum de Babilone hoc carmen formatur. Cf. PSEUDO-BEDA (p. 692): Populus de Babylone reuersus Domino gratias agit.   2ᵃ (p. 229, 31-230, 5): Mos Scripturae est in augmentum significationis geminare uerba; perseuerantiam longanimitatis usum esse dicit se, ut tractae in longum moras captiuitatis ostenderet, quibus tamen a proposito (praepossito *ms*) exspectandi minime si deductus.

far as this life is concerned," for it is in it that he prays for relief.

PSALM 40

Here he prophesies the events affecting the people taken captive by the Babylonian kings. While speaking in their person as giving thanks for their freedom from captivity, in saying things applicable to them he brings out that he found himself in a calamitous situation, had set his expectations on God, and definitely attains help from him. He then declares blessed all those who, on the one hand, are zealous to be rid of every unseemly act, and on the other hand hope in God as recipients of good things from him in every case.

Waiting, I waited on the Lord, and he attended to me (v. 1). This is characteristic of the divine Scripture when it wishes to bring out the intensity of an event. For example, when it says, "Correcting he corrected,"[1] it means, He really and truly corrected; likewise also, *Waiting, I waited* means, I really waited on the Lord. He | used the intensification of the waiting to bring out

---

1. Ps 118:18.

τάσει τῆς ὑπομονῆς ἐχρήσατο πρὸς τὸ δεῖξαι τῆς αἰχμαλωσίας τὴν ἐπίτασιν, ὑφ᾽ ἧς οὐ παρεσαλεύθη τῆς ἐπὶ τὸν Κύριον ὑπομονῆς. Εἰ καὶ ἐπὶ
πολὺ τοίνυν φησὶν ὑπέμεινα, ὅμως οὐκ ἀπέτυχα, ἀλλὰ καὶ προσέσχε μοι,
τουτέστι ἐφρόντισέ μου.

5   2ᵇ. Καὶ εἰσήκουσεν τῆς δεήσεώς μου. Καὶ φροντίσας προσεδέξατό μου
τὰς αἰτήσεις. Εἶτα τί πεποίηκεν;

3ᵃ. Καὶ ἀνήγαγέ με ἐκ λάκκου ταλαιπωρίας. Καὶ ὥσπερ ἐν λάκκῳ βαθυ-
τάτῳ, τῷ πλήθει καὶ τῷ μεγέθει τῶν κακῶν ἐξ ὧν ἐταλαιπώρουν, καθεστῶτα
ἐξέσπασε τῇ ἑαυτοῦ βοηθείᾳ· λάκκον γὰρ ταλαιπωρίας ἐκάλεσε τὰ κατὰ
10 τὴν αἰχμαλωσίαν κακά, διὰ τὸ δυσανάγωγον καὶ δυσαπάλλακτον τὸ ἐξ᾽
αὐτῶν.

3ᵇ. Καὶ ἀπὸ πηλοῦ ἰλύος. Πηλὸν ἰλύος τὸ αὐτὸ καλεῖ διὰ τὸ δυσέκ-
σπαστον καὶ καθεκτικόν, τῇ διαφορᾷ τῶν προσηγοριῶν τὸ διάφορον τῶν
κακῶν σημαίνων τῶν κατὰ τὴν αἰχμαλωσίαν· διὰ τοῦτο εἶπε πηλοῦ ἰλύος.
15 ἐπειδὴ μάλιστα δυσαπόσπαστός ἐστιν ὁ τοιοῦτος πηλός, ὁ ἀπὸ ἐπιφορᾶς
ποταμῶν ἀποτελούμενος. Ταῦτα οὖν μοί φησι παρέσχεν εἰσακούσας μου
τῆς δεήσεως· δῆλον γὰρ ὅτι τοῦτο ηὔχετο τῆς αἰχμαλωσίας τὴν ἀπαλλαγὴν καὶ τὴν ἐπὶ τὰ κρείττω μεταβολήν.

3ᶜ. Καὶ ἔστησεν ἐπὶ πέτραν τοὺς πόδας μου. Καὶ ἀπαλλάξας φησὶ τῶν
20 τοσούτων κακῶν, ἐν ἀσφαλείᾳ με κατέστησε βεβαίᾳ· ἀσάλευτον γὰρ καὶ
ἀμετάθετον ἡ πέτρα.

3ᵈ. Καὶ κατηύθυνεν τὰ διαβήματά μου. Ἀκύλας· Καὶ ἥδρασε τὰ βήματά
μου, ἀντὶ τοῦ ἐν βεβαιότητί με κατέστησεν, ὥστε μὴ δεδοικέναι πάλιν μετα-
νάστασιν.

25 4ᵃ. Καὶ ἐνέβαλεν εἰς τὸ στόμα μου ᾆσμα καινόν. Τὸ ἐπὶ τῇ ἐπανόδῳ, ὅπερ
οὐκ ἦσαν πρότερον ᾄσαντες διὰ τὸ ἐν αἰχμαλωσίαις τὸν οἰκεῖον διατετελεκέναι
βίον. Ἐνέβαλεν οὖν εἰς τὸ στόμα τὸ ᾆσμα, ἐν τοιούτοις αὐτοὺς καταστήσας
ἀφ᾽ ὧν ἔμελλον ᾄδειν ᾄσματα εὐφροσύνης γέμοντα. Οἷον δὲ τὸ ᾆσμα;

13-15 cf. L (p. 738, 33-35): ἢ λάκκον τῆς αἰχμαλωσίας ὕλην ἔχοντος πολλήν, ἀφ᾽ οὗ
δυσανασπάστως ηυρίσκετο ὁ ἐμπεσών.

Aᵉ 12-14 (p. 230, 9-10): Pro imo ceno; per haec uero scalorem captiuitatis
ostendit.   3ᵈ (p. 230, 14-17): Id est, tantam mihi reditus securitatem dedit
ut necessitatem transmigrationis minime formidarem.   26-27 (p. 230, 18-20):
Reducto mihi libuit cantare quod in captiuitate non licuit.

the intensity of the captivity, which failed to divert them from waiting on the Lord. So he is saying, Even though I waited on the Lord for a long time, I still did not fail: rather, *he attended to me*—that is, He gave heed to me. *He hearkened to my prayer:* he gave heed to me and accepted my petition. Then what did he do?

He drew me out of a pit of wretchedness (v. 2): held fast though I was in the mass and magnitude of the troubles I was suffering, as though in a very deep pit, he drew me out with his help (referring to the troubles in captivity by *pit of wretchedness* on account of the difficulty of extrication and relief from them). *And from a miry bog.* He refers to them as *a miry bog* on account of the difficulty of escaping their grip, suggesting by the different names the difference in the troubles in captivity. Hence his saying *a miry bog,* since it is particularly difficult to escape from mire of this kind, which is the result of a river's flood. So he is saying, He granted me this on hearing my request (it being clear that he made this request for freedom from captivity and a change for the better). *He set my feet on a rock:* after freeing me from such troubles, he established me in continuing security (a rock being immobile and irremovable). *And he guided my steps.* Aquila: "He set my footsteps in place"—that is, He established me in stability so that I should have no fear of further change.

He put into my mouth a new song (v. 3): the song on their return, which they were not singing before on account of living their life in captivity. *He put the song in their mouth,* therefore, by bringing them into such conditions as made them likely to sing songs full of joy. What kind of song? | *A hymn*

4ᵇ. Ὕμνον τῷ Θεῷ ἡμῶν. Περιέχοντα ἐγκώμια τοῦ εὐηργετηκότος ἡμᾶς Θεοῦ.

4ᶜ. Ὄψονται πολλοὶ καὶ φοβηθήσονται, καὶ ἐλπιοῦσιν ἐπὶ Κύριον. Ἐντεῦθέν φησιν ἐπὶ τῷ παραδόξῳ τῶν | γεγονότων εἰς ἡμᾶς πολλοὶ τῶν ἐκτὸς τὴν σὴν καταμαθόντες δύναμιν ἐπιγνώσονταί σε καὶ σπεύσουσι τὸ πρὸ 5 τῶν ἄλλων ἀπάντων ἐλπίζειν εἴς σε — ὅπερ καὶ γέγονεν ἐν τῇ ἐπανόδῳ. Διὰ γὰρ τὸ μέγεθος τῶν περὶ αὐτοὺς γεγενημένων θαυμάτων, ἱκανὴν λαβόντες τοῦ Θεοῦ τῆς δυνάμεως τὴν ἀπόδειξιν, πολλοὶ μὲν ἐπίστευσαν τῷ Θεῷ· τινὲς δὲ διὰ τὸ μέγεθος τῆς περὶ αὐτοὺς τιμῆς καὶ ὑπεκρίνοντο τὸν ἰουδαϊσμὸν μέχρι περιτομῆς.					10

5. Μακάριος ἀνὴρ οὗ ἐστιν τὸ ὄνομα Κυρίου ἐλπὶς αὐτοῦ, καὶ οὐκ ἐνέβλεψεν εἰς ματαιότητας καὶ μανίας ψευδεῖς. Καὶ ἤλπισαν δέ φησι δικαίως· ἀληθῶς γὰρ μακαριστὸς ὁ εἴς σε ἐλπίζειν καταξιούμενος καὶ μὴ ἀποβλέπων εἰς εἴδωλα, μηδὲ ἀσχολῶν τὸν ἑαυτοῦ λογισμὸν περὶ τὴν τούτων θρησκείαν. Τοῦτο δὲ εἶπεν ὡς αὐτῶν, ὅτε ἐκείνοις μὲν προσεῖχον πρότερον, 15 οὐ μόνον οὐδὲν ὠφεληθέντων ἀλλὰ καὶ παραδοθέντων εἰς αἰχμαλωσιαν· ὅτε δὲ ἐκείνων ἀποστάντες ἐπέγνωσαν Θεόν, τότε καὶ τῆς κατεχούσης ἀπαλλαγέντων αἰχμαλωσίας καὶ ἐν εὐθηνίᾳ πλείστων ἀγαθῶν καταστῆναι δυνηθέντων. Τὴν δέ γε περὶ τὰ εἴδωλα θρησκείαν ματαιότητα μὲν ἐκάλεσεν ὡς οὐδὲν ὄφελος τῷ πονοῦντι παρέχειν δυναμένων, μανίαν δὲ ὡς οὐ καθεστῶτι 20 λογισμῷ παρὰ τῶν πραττομένων ἐπιτελουμένην, καὶ ψεῦδος δὲ ὡς οὐδὲν ἀληθὲς ἢ βέβαιον κεκτημένου τοῦ περὶ αὐτῶν λόγου.

6ᵃ. Πολλὰ ἐποίησας σύ, Κύριε ὁ Θεός μου, τὰ θαυμάσιά σου. Ὅτι γὰρ μακαριστόν φησιν ἡ εἴς σε ἐλπὶς καὶ τὸ ἀπηλλάχθαι τῆς | τῶν εἰδώλων θεραπείας, ἐξ αὐτῶν ἐστιν ἰδεῖν πραγμάτων ἀφ᾽ ὧν τὰ θαύματά σου καὶ 25 αἱ εὐεργεσίαι αἱ εἰς ἡμᾶς πλεῖσταί τινές εἰσι καὶ ὡς ἀληθῶς ἀνεκδιήγητοι.

6ᵇ. Καὶ τοῖς διαλογισμοῖς σου οὐκ ἔστιν τις ὁμοιωθήσεται. Ἀλλ᾽ οὐδὲ δυνατόν φησι τοῖς βουλεύμασί σου τοῖς περὶ ἡμῶν ἰσωθῆναί τινα, τουτέστιν οἷς ἐβουλεύσω περὶ ἡμῶν εἰς εὐεργεσίαν.

13-14 L (p. 739, 28-30): Μακάριστός φησι τῷ ὄντι, ὃς τὸν Θεὸν μόνον ἔσχεν ἐλπίδα, καὶ οὐκ ἐπέστρεψεν ἐπὶ τὰ εἴδωλα.

Aᵉ 4ᵇ (p. 230, 21-22): Pro carmine laudes Dei continente.   3-5 (p. 230, 23-27): *Videbunt multi et timebunt*, et admiratione rerum circa nos gestarum in tuum cultum migrabunt alienigenae.   13 (p. 230, 28-29): Beatitudo est namque sperare in Domino.   6ᵇ (p. 231, 7-10): Contemplatio operum tuorum et dispensationum uarietas, quibus utiletates nostras exsequiris, nullum tibi patitur adaequari.

to our God containing praises of the God who bestowed kindnesses on us. *Many will see and will fear, and hope in the Lord:* at this surprising development in our favor, many foreigners will come to know your power, will acknowledge you and be quick to hope in you beyond everything else. This actually happened at the return: on account of the magnitude of the marvels worked in their regard, many people had sufficient proof of God's power and came to faith in God, while as a result of the honor shown them some even pretended to adopt Judaism to the point of accepting circumcision.

Blessed is the man whose hope is in the name of the Lord, whose eyes were not on futilities and deceitful frenzies (v. 4): they were right to have hope, truly blessed being the one who is deemed worthy to hope in you and does not look to idols or devote his thoughts to their worship. This means that whereas in the past they gave their attention to them, and far from gaining anything they were even consigned to captivity, on withdrawing from them and acknowledging God they were freed from the grip of captivity and in a position to be established in the enjoyment of many good things. By *futilities* he referred to the cult of idols as capable of providing no benefit to the devotee, by *frenzies* as to their being performed by worshipers out of their mind, and by *deceitful* as to the basis for them being bereft of any real or lasting quality.

Many are the marvels you have performed, Lord my God (v. 5): because hope in you and deliverance from the worship of the idols is a blessed thing, it is possible to see from the facts themselves the nature of your wonders and numerous kindnesses toward us and how truly ineffable they are. *And in your thoughts there is no one to compare with you:* nor is it possible to make any comparison with your plans for us—that is, what you had in mind for our benefit. | *I proclaimed and spoke of them; they were multiplied beyond*

6ᶜ. Ἀπήγγειλα καὶ ἐλάλησα, ἐπληθύνθησαν ὑπὲρ ἀριθμόν. Τοσαῦτα γάρ
φησι τὰ θαυμάσιά σου τὰ εἰς ἡμᾶς γεγονότα, ὅτι καὶ πολλάκις αὐτὰ διη-
γησάμην καὶ πάλιν διηγήσομαι, καὶ ὅμως ὑπερεπλεόνασε τὴν διήγησιν ἀναρίθμητα ὄντα καὶ ἀνεκδιήγητα διὰ τὸ πλῆθος. Φανερώτερον δὲ ⟨Σύμμαχος⟩
5 λέγει· ἃ καὶ ἂν ἀπαγγέλλων καταγγέλλω, πλείω ἐστὶ τοῦ διηγηθῆναι.

7ᵃ. Θυσίαν καὶ προσφορὰν οὐκ ἠθέλησας. Διάφοροι ἦσαν ἐν νόμῳ αἱ
θυσίαι· αἱ μὲν ὁλοκαυτούμεναι, αἱ δὲ ὑπὲρ εὐχαριστίας, αἱ δὲ ὑπὲρ ἁμαρτιῶν, αἱ δὲ συνηθῶς προσαγόμεναι καθ᾽ ἑκάστην ἡμέραν, καὶ ἄλλαι πάλιν
ἑτέρως· διὰ τοῦτο καὶ διαφόροις αὐτὰς ὀνομάζει ταῖς προσηγορίαις, θυσίαν
10 λέγων καὶ προσφορὰν καὶ ὁλοκαυτώματα καὶ περὶ ἁμαρτίας, διόλου τοῦτο
εἰπεῖν βουλόμενος ὅτι θύματα οὐκ ᾔτησας παρ᾽ ἐμοῦ, οὐδέ τι τοιοῦτον.

7ᵇ. Ὠτία δὲ κατηρτίσω μοι. Τῇ	**Aures autem perficisti mihi.**
δὲ ὑπακοῇ ἠρκέσθης τῇ ἐμῇ. Καλῶς	Siquidem hoc egerat Deus, ut
δὲ κατηρτίσω εἶπεν, ἐπειδὴ αὐτὸς ὁ	per captiuitatis correptionem sibi
15 Θεὸς διὰ τῆς κατὰ τὴν αἰχμαλωσίαν	eos doceret oboedire.
παιδείας εὐτρεπεῖς αὐτοὺς εἰργάσατο	
πρὸς τὴν ἰδίαν ὑπακοήν.	
Ὠτία δὲ καλεῖ τὴν ὑπακοήν, ὡς	**Aures** autem posuit pro oboe-
καὶ ὁ Κύριος ἐν τῷ εὐαγγελίῳ· ὁ	dientia.
20 ἔχων ὦτα ἀκούειν ἀκουέτω, ἀντὶ τοῦ Ὁ πρόθεσιν ἔχων τοῦ ἀκούειν ἀκουέτω	
τῶν λεγομένων.	

7ᶜ. Ὁλοκαυτώματα καὶ περὶ ἁμαρτίας οὐκ ᾔτησας. Ἀντὶ τοῦ οὐδὲν τοιοῦτον ᾔτησας παρ᾽ ἐμοῦ τὸ σύνολον.

8ᵃ. Τότε εἶπον Ἰδοὺ ἥκω. Ὅτε τοίνυν φησὶν ἐθεασάμην ὅτι τὴν συνεί-
25 δησιν ζητεῖς καὶ τὴν τῆς ὑπακοῆς πρόθεσιν μόνον, οὔτε θυσίαν αἰτῶν οὔτε

19-20 Matth. XI, 15.

4 Σύμμαχος supplevi ex Eusebio (P. G. XXIII, 356 C 1).   18-23 L (p. 740,
18-20): οὐκ ἠβουλήθης παρ᾽ ἐμοῦ θυσίας, ἀλλ᾽ ὑπακοήν με ἀπήτησας μόνην. Ὦτα γὰρ τὴν
ὑπακοὴν λέγει, ὡς καὶ ὁ Σωτήρ· Ὁ ἔχων — ἀκουέτω.
Aures — oboedientia: A, fol. 13ᶜ; B, fol. 14ᶜ.   18 possuit A   18-19 obi-
dientia A.

Aᵉ 3-4 (p. 231, 11-12): Plura sunt, quae contulisti, quam ut narrari queant
7ᵃ (p. 231, 26-232, 4): Species sunt diuersae rei diuinae: sacrificium diuina
accensio, oblatio specialis consecratio pro gratiarum actione, holochaustum,
actio pro peccato, causalis immutatio.   25 (p. 231, 25-26): Pro uictimis solam
obidentiam postulasti.

counting: so many are the marvels worked in our regard that I often have recounted and shall continue to recount them. Yet they exceeded my report, being innumerable and beyond all telling on account of their great number. Symmachus says it more clearly: "What I declare in my report surpasses all description."

Sacrifice and offering you did not desire (v. 6). Different sacrifices were required by the law, some being whole burnt offerings, some being for the purpose of thanksgiving, some for sins, some usually offered each day, and others again in a different manner. Hence, he also gives them different names, citing *sacrifice and offering and holocausts even for sin,* meaning in general, You did not ask for victims from me or anything of the kind. *But ears you fashioned for me:* you were content with my attention. Now, he was right to say *fashioned,* since God himself through the chastisement of the captivity made them ready to give him their exclusive attention. By *ears* he refers to obedience, the Lord himself saying in the Gospel, "Let anyone with ears listen"[2]—that is, Let anyone interested in listening listen to what is said. *Holocausts even for sin you did not look for*—that is, In no way did you look for such a thing from me.

Then I said, Behold, I am coming (v. 7): so when I perceived that you look only for a good conscience and an obedient attitude, requiring neither sacrifice nor | anything else to offer up, then I had hopes and expectations of

2. Matt 11:15. While most forms of the LXX in this verse, including, apparently, that read by Theodore's fellow Antiochene Theodoret, speak of "body" (possibly under the influence of Heb 10:5), both Diodore and Theodore read (as does our Hebrew) "ears." Theodore does not immediately acknowledge the citation in Hebrews.

ἕτερόν τι πρὸς τὸ ἀναγαγεῖν, τότε ἤλπισα καὶ προσεδόκησα ἐπανελεύσεσθαι, πρὸ τούτου οὐδεμίαν ἔχων προσδοκίαν ἐπειδὴ οὔτε εἶχον θυσίας πρὸς τὸ ἀναγαγεῖν. Πῶς γὰρ ἐν αἰχμαλωσίᾳ καὶ κινδύνοις καθεστώς, οὔτε δὲ ἔχων, ἠδυνάμην προσάγειν τοῦτό που, μακρὰν διάγων, ἐν ᾧ προσάγειν θεμιτὸν ἦν; Τοῦτο γὰρ ὁ νόμος ἠβούλετο, τὸ μὴ ἀπανταχοῦ προσάγεσθαι 5
τῷ Θεῷ τὰς θυσίας, ἀλλὰ μᾶλλον ἐν τῷ ὄρει τῷ Σιών.

8ᵇ. Ἐν κεφαλίδι βιβλίου γέγραπται περὶ ἐμοῦ. Εἶχον δέ φησιν ἀναμφίβολον τῆς ἐπανόδου τὴν προσδοκίαν, εἰς ἔννοιαν λαμβάνων καὶ τὰ ταῖς βίβλοις ἐγγεγραμμένα τῶν προφητῶν προαγορευσάντων τὴν ἐπάνοδον. Ἀποβλέπων οὖν εἰς τὰς προρρήσεις καὶ πάλιν εὐχερῆ τοῦ βίου τὴν ἀγω- 10
γὴν ὁρῶν ἢν ἀπῄτεις, ὥστε οὕτω βιοῦντάς τε καὶ πράττοντας ἐπαναγαγεῖν, πανταχόθεν βεβαίαν τῆς ἐπανόδου προσεκτώμην τὴν ἐλπίδα.

Τὸ δὲ ἐν κεφαλίδι βιβλίου Ἀκύλας ἐν εἰλήματι λέγει· καὶ γὰρ τοιαῦται ἦσαν τὸ παλαιὸν παρ' Ἰουδαίοις αἱ βίβλοι ἐν εἰλητοῖς γεγραμ|μέναι.

In capite libri Aquila in uolumine libri posuit. Nam apud Ebreos tam legis quam profeta- 15
rum libri singuli singulis erant uoluminibus conscripti.

Ταῦτα δὲ εἴρηται παρὰ τῷ μακαρίῳ ἀποστόλῳ ἐν τῇ πρὸς Ἑβραίους ἐπιστολῇ· ὧν τινες τὸν τρόπον ἀγνοοῦντες, καθ' ὃν ὁ μακάριος ἀπόστολος ἐχρήσατο τῇ μαρτυρίᾳ, οἴονται περὶ τοῦ Κυρίου εἰρῆσθαι τὸν ψαλμόν. 20
Ὅσος δὲ κίνδυνος ταῦτα ὡς ἐκ προσώπου τοῦ Κυρίου ἐκλαμβάνειν, οὐ χαλεπὸν συνιδεῖν. Τίς γὰρ ἂν εἴποι ἐκ προσώπου τοῦ Κυρίου λέγεσθαι τὸ ἀνήγαγέ με ἐκ λάκκου ταλαιπωρίας καὶ ἀπὸ πηλοῦ ἰλύος, καὶ τὸ ἐνέβαλεν εἰς τὸ στόμα μου ᾆσμα καινόν, ὕμνον τῷ Θεῷ ἡμῶν, ἢ τὸ ἀπήγγειλα καὶ ἐλάλησα, ἐπληθύνθησαν ὑπὲρ ἀριθμόν; Πῶς γὰρ οὐκ ἀτοπώτατον ὅλως τῆς 25
ὑπάρξεως τῆς πατρικῆς ἔχοντα τὴν γνῶσιν ἀκριβῆ εἰς τὴν τῶν θυμάτων διήγησιν ἀνεφίκτως ἔχειν; Ὥστε τοῦτο μὲν παρὰ τοῦ μακαρίου ἀποστόλου ἐκ προσώπου εἴρηται τοῦ Κυρίου, εἴρηται δὲ κατὰ ταύτην τὴν διάνοιαν.

5-6 cf. supra, p. 18, 13-16   18 Hebr. X, 4-7   23-25 vv. 3ᵃ·ᵇ. 4ᵃ·ᵇ. 6ᶜ.

26 θυμάτων conieci sequentibus melius cohaerens, θαυμάτων ms.
In capite — conscripti: A, fol. 13ᶜ; B, fol. 14ᶜ; ed. MURATORI, Antiq. Ital. III, 858 D.   14 possuit A.

Aᵉ 3-5 (p. 232, 4-8): Nihil ergo horum a captiuo quessisti... in captiuitate posito huiusque modi ritibus uacare neque libui neque licuit.   8-9 (p. 9-11): Pro uolumine cuiuslibet profetae, qui tam de captiuitate mea quam de reuersione praedixit.   18-249, 7 (p. 231, 13-19): Vtitur hoc testimonio Paulus apostolus ad Ebreos, uerum ad hoc ut, de simili exemplo contra sacrificia disputans, doceret ita post Christi aduentum inrita dibere esse holochausta, sicut non sunt quesita ad soluendam de Babilone captiuitatem.

returning, whereas before this I had no expectations since I had no sacrifices to make, either. After all, how on earth could I make this offering while kept in captivity and in a perilous situation, with nothing to offer that it was lawful to offer, living far away as I was? The law required, remember, that sacrifices be offered to God not anywhere at all, but rather on Mount Sion. *In the scroll of the book it is written of me:* I had an unwavering expectation of returning, taking to heart what was written in the books of the prophets foretelling the return. With an eye to the prophecies, therefore, and envisaging that the way of life you require is within my reach once again so as to lead back those living and behaving in this fashion, I developed a firm hope of return from all quarters. For *in the scroll of the book* Aquila has "in a roll," books being written this way on rolls by the Jews in ancient times.

Now, this is quoted by the blessed apostle in the letter to the Hebrews. Some commentators, ignorant of the way the blessed apostle cited the text, believe that the psalm refers to the Lord. But the extent of the risk of taking it as said in the person of the Lord is not difficult to imagine: who would claim that it is in the person of the Lord that the words are said *He drew me out of a pit of wretchedness and from a miry bog,* and *He put into my mouth a new song, a hymn to our God,* or *I proclaimed and spoke of them; they were multiplied beyond counting*? I mean, how would it not be quite out of the question for one with a precise knowledge of the Father's being to be unable to give an account of the sacrifices? And so while this is cited by the blessed apostle in the person of the Lord, it is cited in the following sense: | Speaking

Περὶ τῶν θυσιῶν τῶν ἐν νόμῳ διαλεγόμενος ἐκεῖ καὶ ὅτι μὴ δυνατὸν
ἄφεσιν ἁμαρτιῶν παρέχειν ἐκεῖνα τὰ θύματα, καὶ βουλόμενος δεῖξαι περιτ-
τὰς καὶ οὐκ ἀναγκαίας τὰς θυσίας τὰς ἐν νόμῳ, κέχρηται ταύτῃ τῇ μαρτυρίᾳ τοῦ λαοῦ ἱκανῇ πρὸς ἀπόδειξιν τοῦ ὅτι κρείττων θυσίας ὑπακοὴ καὶ
5 πολὺ τοῦτο διαπράττεσθαι ἀναγκαιότερον ἢ ἐκεῖνο, ἐξ ὧν οἱ ἐν αἰχμαλωσίᾳ καθεστῶτες οὔτε θυσίαν οὔτε ἕτερόν τι ἐπιδειξάμενοι, μόνον δὲ ἀκριβῆ
τὴν ὑπακοὴν τὴν εἰς Θεὸν φυλάττοντες, ἔτυχον τῆς ἐπανόδου.

Εἰπὼν οὖν ἀδύνατον αἷμα ταύρων καὶ τράγων ἀφελεῖν ἁμαρτίας, τότε
ἐπάγει· Διὸ εἰσερχόμενος εἰς τὸν κόσμον λέγει Θυσίαν καὶ προσφορὰν οὐκ
10 ἠθέλησας, σῶμα δὲ κατηρτίσω μοι, ὑπαλλάξας τὰ ὠτία εἰς σῶμα, — ὃ καὶ
ἡμῖν ἔθος ἐστὶ ποιεῖν, τὸ κεχρῆσθαι μὲν πολλάκις μαρτυρίαις πρὸς ἀπόδειξιν πραγμάτων, βραχὺ δέ τι ὑπαλλάττοντες διὰ τὴν χρείαν τοῦ λόγου.
Ἐποιήσατο δὲ τὴν ὑπαλλαγήν, τοῦτο σημάναι βουλόμενος | ὅτι, ὥσπερ
ἐκεῖ τῆς ὑπακοῆς πληρουμένης οὐ θυσιῶν γέγονε χρεία, οὐχ ἑτέρου τινὸς
15 τοιούτου, ἀλλ' εὐθὺς ἔτυχον τῆς ἐπανόδου τῆς αἰχμαλωσίας ἀπαλλαγέντες,
οὕτω φησὶ καὶ ὁ Κύριος ἐκεῖνα μὲν ἅπαντα ἀνελεῖν, ἐν δὲ τῷ σώματι τῷ
ἰδίῳ τὴν οἰκονομίαν τὴν περὶ ἡμῶν πληρώσας τῷ πάθει τοῦ οἰκείου σώματος, κοινήν φησι παρέσχετο τῆς ἁμαρτίας τὴν ἄφεσιν καὶ τῶν κακῶν τὴν
ἀπαλλαγήν. Καὶ τὰ ἀκόλουθα δὲ πάντα κατὰ ταύτην λέγει τὴν ἔννοιαν,
20 ὥστε ὁ μὲν μακάριος ἀπόστολος Παῦλος κάλλιστα ἐχρήσατο μαρτυρίᾳ πρὸς
ἀπόδειξιν οὗπερ ἐχρήσατο. Οἱ δὲ μὴ μεμαθηκότες τοῦ ἀποστόλου τὸν
σκοπὸν καὶ τὴν διάνοιαν, τὸν μὲν ψαλμὸν ἠβουλήθησαν περιάψαι τῷ Χριστῷ, τὸ δὲ ὠτία κατηρτίσω μοι — οὕτω γὰρ καὶ τὸ ἑβραϊκὸν — ἀλλάξαν-
τες τεθείκασι σῶμα δὲ κατηρτίσω μοι, οὐ προσεσχηκότες τῇ αἰτίᾳ τῆς ὑπαλ-
25 λαγῆς τοῦ ἀποστόλου.

9ᵃ. Τοῦ ποιῆσαι τὸ θέλημά σου, ὁ Θεός μου, ἐβουλήθην. Θεασάμενος
τοίνυν φησὶν ὅτι τοῦτο ζητεῖς παρ' ἐμοῦ, τὴν ὑπακοήν, ἐδοκίμασα τοῦ λοιποῦ πᾶσαν θέσθαι σπουδὴν ὥστε τῆς σῆς ἐπιμελεῖσθαι εὐαρεστήσεως.

9ᵇ. Καὶ τὸν νόμον σου ἐν μέσῳ τῆς καρδίας μου. Καὶ ὥστε τὰ σὰ προσ-
30 τάγματα ἔνδοθεν κατέχειν.

10ᵃ. Εὐηγγελισάμην δικαιοσύνην ἐν ἐκκλησίᾳ μεγάλῃ. Καὶ ὥστε τῆς ἐπανόδου τυχὼν ἀεί σου τὴν εὐεργεσίαν ταύτην εἰς ἡμᾶς γενομένην ἐπὶ πάσης

8-10 Hebr. X, 4-5   10-12 cf. supra, p. 85, 29-86, 5   23 cf. Field, Origenis Hexa-
plorum, t. II, p. 151.   Totam hanc expositionem prae oculis habuisse videtur L (p. 740,
29-45).

Aᵉ 9ᵇ (p. 232, 14-15): Decreui etiam ut memor essem tuorum iugiter mandatorum.   31-250, 2 (p. 232, 17-21): Pro Non silebo gratias agere sic reductus
(- tis ms); cum nos in terra nostra possitos sollemnitas congregauerit, nota ea
facere et auribus omnium insinuare curabo.

of the sacrifices mentioned in the law and the fact that it was impossible for those sacrifices to ensure forgiveness of sins, and wishing to bring out that sacrifices under the law were pointless and unnecessary, he cites this text confined to the people as proof that obedience is superior to sacrifices and that practicing it is much more necessary than the alternative. Hence, those kept in captivity, though giving evidence neither of sacrifice nor of anything else, but simply maintaining obedience to God, were granted return.

Having mentioned the impossibility of the blood of bulls and goats removing sin, therefore, he goes on, "Hence, on coming into the world he says, 'Sacrifice and offering you did not desire, but a body you fashioned for me,' " changing *ears* to "body"—something we also customarily do, often using a text as a proof of facts but making a slight change as the argument requires.[3] Now, he made the change in his wish to indicate that, in that case, when obedience was fulfilled, there was no need of sacrifices and that there was nothing else required for them to be freed from captivity and granted return. So also, he says, when the Lord did away with all those things, in his own body he implemented the plan for us by the passion of his own body and made available general forgiveness of sins and freedom from evil.

All the rest, too, he says in this sense, and so for his part the blessed apostle Paul very appositely cited a text in proof of what he was saying. For their part, on the contrary, those who did not appreciate the apostle's purpose and sense, preferring not to apply the psalm to Christ, changed *ears you fashioned for me* (this being the Hebrew as well) and put "a body you fashioned for me," not attending to the apostle's argument.

My wish was to do your will, my God (v. 8): perceiving that this is what you require of me—obedience—I therefore saw fit in future to make every effort to give attention to pleasing you. *And your law in the depths of my heart:* and so to hold fast within me to your commandments.

I told the good news of righteousness in a great assembly (v. 9): and so, on being granted return, I kept reporting this favor conferred on us to the whole | congregation, at that time in particular when we were all assembled

---

3. So in his view the variant reading of Heb 10:5 comes, not (as we would guess from Theodoret) from a variant LXX form (based on a different Hebrew form), but from the New Testament author's tampering with the text (of the Hebrew, he insists) for the sake of his argument, as with all who did not appreciate the psalm verse.

ὁμοῦ τῆς συναγωγῆς ἐξαγγέλλειν, τότε μάλιστα ὅταν ἅπαντες ὦμεν κατὰ
ταὐτὸν ἐπὶ τῆς οἰκείας συναθροιζόμενοι γῆς. Βούλεται δὲ εἰπεῖν, ὡς ἐκ τοῦ
λαοῦ, ὅτι Θεασάμενος ὡς | ὑπακοή σοι καὶ συνείδησις ἀρίστη πάντων προ-
τιμοτέρα, καὶ ταῦτα παροφθέντα μὲν τὴν ἀρχὴν ἐν τούτοις με κατέστησε
τοῖς κακοῖς, πληρούμενα δὲ οἶδεν ἅπαντα ὁμοῦ παρασχεῖν τὰ καλά, ἐδο- 5
κίμασα ὥστε τοῦ λοιποῦ ἐπιτελεῖν μέν σου τὸ θέλημα, πολλὴν δὲ περὶ τὸν
νόμον σου τὴν διάθεσιν ἔχειν, διατελέσαι δὲ καὶ μετὰ τὴν ἐπάνοδον ἐν
ὕμνοις καὶ ᾠδαῖς τὴν ὑπὲρ τῶν δοθέντων εὐχαριστίαν ἀποπληρῶν.

Τὸ γὰρ εὐηγγελισάμην ἀντὶ τοῦ   Adnuntiaui iustitiam tuam,
Εὐαγγελίσομαι, συνηθῶς τὸν χρόνον   pro Adnuntiabo.   10
ἐναλλάξας. Ἐπάγει οὖν περὶ τοῦ αὐ-
τοῦ λέγων· Ἰδοὺ τὰ χείλη μου.
Δικαιοσύνην ἐκάλεσε τὴν εὐεργεσίαν,   Iustitiam dicit liberationis bene-
καθ᾽ ἣν ἐπανήγαγεν αὐτούς, ὡς δι-   ficium, quod eos iuste reuoca-
καίως νῦν μάλιστα τοιαῦτα προῃρη-   uerit.   15
μένους ἀνάγοντος τοῦ δεσπότου.

10ᵇ. Ἰδοὺ τὰ χείλη μου οὐ μὴ κωλύσω. Οὐ καθέξω τοίνυν τὰ χείλη
μου εἰς τὴν διήγησιν τῶν θαυμάτων, τουτέστι Παρασκευάσω αὐτὰ συνεχῆ
ποιεῖσθαι τὴν ἐξήγησιν. Εἰ δὲ ἦν τὸ εὐηγγελισάμην ἐπὶ παρεληλυθότος,
πῶς τὸ κωλύσω ἐξῆς ἐπήγαγε, μέλλοντος ὄντος; Ἡ ἐναλλαγὴ τοῦ χρόνου 20
ἐκ τῆς ἑρμηνείας γεγένηται.

11ᵃ. Κύριε, σὺ ἔγνως τὴν δικαιοσύνην μου. Οἶδας δέ φησιν αὐτὸς ὅτι
πάντων ἕνεκεν ὧντε ἐδοκίμασα ἐπιμελεῖσθαι, καὶ ὧν περὶ τὴν φυλακὴν ἔχειν
ἔκρινα μετὰ τὴν ἐπάνοδον, δίκαιόν με τῆς παρά σου εὐεργεσίας ἀπολαύ-
σαντα τυχεῖν τῆς ἐνανόδου, — δικαιοσύνην ἐνταῦθα συνηθῶς καλῶν τὸ δικαίως 25
μέλλειν τοῦ πράγματος ἀπολαύειν.

11ᵇ⁻ᶜ. Οὐκ ἔκρυψα ἐν τῇ καρδίᾳ μου. Ἀντὶ τοῦ οὐ κρύψω· ἀπολαύσας
γὰρ τῆς παρά σου δωρεᾶς, οὐ κρύψω παρ᾽ ἐμαυτῷ τὴν χάριν, — πάλιν
ὁμοίως δικαιοσύνην αὐτὴν καλῶν διὰ τὴν προειρημένην αἰτίαν. Οὐ κρύψεις
οὖν, ἀλλὰ τί ποιήσεις;   30
Τὴν ἀλήθειάν σου καὶ τὴν σωτηρίαν σου εἶπον. Ἐρῶ καὶ ἐξηγήσομαι
πολλάκις τὴν παρασχεθεῖσαν ἡμῖν παρά σου σωτηρίαν. Τὸ γὰρ εἶπον ἀντὶ

Adnuntiaui — reuocauerit: A, fol. 13ᶜ; B, fol. 14ᶜ; cf. L (p. 741, 31-32): Τὸ
γὰρ εὐηγγελισάμην ἀντὶ τοῦ εὐαγγελιοῦμαι.

Aᵉ 13-14 (p. 232, 22-23): Iustitiam uocauit reuersionis beneficium.   27 (p. 232,
25-26): id est Non occultabo.

together in our own country. He means to say, on the people's part, I perceived that obedience and a good conscience are most esteemed by you, and
that when these were neglected, you initially consigned me to these troubles,
whereas when they are attended to, you are in the habit of providing all good
things at once. So I decided to carry out your will in future and to have great
affection for your law, and on return to live a life offering thanks for the gifts
with praise and singing. *I told the good news,* note, means "I shall tell the
good news," with the usual change in tense. So he proceeds to say of him *Lo,
my lips.* By *righteousness* he referred to the favor by which he brought them
back since they now rightly opted for such things, once the Lord brought
them back. *Lo, my lips I shall not forbid:* I shall therefore not prevent *my lips*
recounting the marvels—that is, I shall cause them to give constant commentary. Now, if the verb *I told the good news* were past tense, how would he
proceed to say *I shall not forbid* in the future? The change of tense happened
in translation.

    You know my righteousness, Lord (v. 10): you yourself know that it was
right that, on the basis of what I opted to attend to and chose to observe
after the return, I should enjoy your kindness and be granted the return (by
righteousness here, as usual, referring to his rightly being due to enjoy the
experience).[4] *I did not conceal it in my heart*—that is, I shall not conceal:
having received the gift from you, I shall not conceal the grace within me
(again in similar fashion referring to it as *righteousness* on account of the
aforementioned argument). Far from concealing it, then, what will you do? *I
spoke of your truth and your salvation:* I shall tell and explain on many occa-
sions the salvation accorded us by you (by *spoke* meaning | "will speak").

---

4. Theodore seems to be reading the LXX verse (differing from the Hebrew) this way to
include "my righteousness," like Diodore but unlike Theodoret.

τοῦ Ἐρῶ. Συνηθῶς δὲ κἀνταῦθα τῇ   *Veritatem tuam dixi*, pro dicam,
σωτηρίᾳ τὴν ἀλήθειαν συνέζευξε,   tempore motato.
δεικνὺς τὸ ἀληθὲς καὶ βέβαιον τῆς εὐεργεσίας.

11ᵈ. Οὐκ ἔκρυψα τὸ ἔλεός σου καὶ τὴν ἀλήθειάν σου ἀπὸ συναγωγῆς
5 πολλῆς. Τὸ αὐτὸ πάλιν ἑτέρως λέγει. Πολλῶν δέ φησιν ἐπὶ τὸ αὐτὸ συνηγ-
μένων, ἐξηγήσομαι τῶν σῶν ἀγαθῶν. Τὸ γὰρ αὐτὸ δικκιοσύνην καλεῖ καὶ
ἔλεος καὶ σωτηρίαν, — δικαιοσύνη μέν, ὅτι κάλλιστα προελομένοις δικαίως
παρέξεις τὴν χάριν· ἔλεος δέ, ὅτι τοῦτο φιλανθρωπίᾳ μᾶλλον ἢ κατὰ τὴν
αὐτῶν ἀξίαν παρέχειν, ἀμνησικακῶν ἐπὶ τοῖς προλαβοῦσι· σωτηρίαν δὲ
10 ὡς ἐπικειμένων ἀπαλλάττοντος κινδύνων.

12ᵃ. Σὺ δέ, Κύριε, μὴ μακρύνῃς τοὺς οἰκτιρμούς σου ἀπ᾽ ἐμοῦ. Οὐκοῦν
φησιν ἐπειδὴ ταῦτα ποιεῖν ἑτοίμως ἔχω, μὴ ὑπέρθῃ τοῦ ταχεῖαν ποιήσασθαι τὴν εἰς ἡμᾶς φιλανθρωπίαν.

12ᵇ. Τὸ ἔλεός σου καὶ ἡ ἀλήθειά   *Misericordia tua et ueritas*
15 σου διὰ παντὸς ἀντελάβοντό μου.   *tua semper susciperunt me*. Opus,
Διηνεκῆ δέ μοι μᾶλλον τὴν φιλαν-   inquit, mihi tuae bonitatis, quod
θρωπίαν σου ἐκείνην τὴν ἀληθῆ καὶ   est uerum atque certissimum, iu-
βεβαίαν παράσχου. Τὸ γὰρ ἀντε-   giter conferatur: nam *susciperunt*
λάβετο ἀντὶ τοῦ ἀντιλάβοιτο,   *me* pro suscipiant per com-
20 ἐναλλαγὴ χρόνου ἀπὸ τῆς ἑρμηνείας   motationem temporis positum
ἐγγενομένη.   est.

13ᵃ. Ὅτι περιέσχον με κακὰ ὧν οὐκ ἔστιν ἀριθμός. Καὶ γὰρ ἀναρίθμη-
τον τῶν κακῶν τὸ περιεσχηκός με πλῆθος.

13ᵇ. Κατέλαβόν με αἱ ἀνομίαι μου, καὶ οὐκ ἠδυνάσθην τοῦ βλέπειν.
25 Τοσούτοις δέ φησιν οἶδα περισχεθεὶς κακοῖς ὑπὸ τοῦ πλήθους τῶν ἀνομιῶν, ὑφ᾽ ὧν καταληφθεὶς καὶ κυκλωθεὶς ἐν τοῖς παροῦσιν ἐξετάζομαι κακοῖς,
ὡς μικροῦ μηδὲ δύνασθαι διορᾶν.

Veritatem — motato: A, fol. 13ᶜ; B, fol. 14ᶜ.
Misericordia — positum est: A, fol. 13ᶜ; B, fol. 14ᶜ.   15 me *om*. AB
20 possitum A.

Aᵉ 1-3 (p. 232, 27-29): Et more suo salutari ueritatem iunxit ut beneficii
ueritas indicaretur et firmitas.   6-7 (p. 232, 31-33). Vnam eademque iustitiam et
salutem nominauit mise⟨r⟩icordiam.   13ᵇ (p. 233, 1-6)... Siquidem non sunt exigua nec pauca numero aduersa quae patior... et oculos eleuare nequiui pondere debiti pudoris obpraesus.

Here, as usual, he associated *truth* with *salvation* to bring out the reality and permanence of the favor. *I did not conceal your mercy and your truth from a numerous congregation.* He says the same thing again in a different way: When many people are assembled, I shall comment on your good things. He uses *righteousness, mercy,* and *salvation* interchangeably; note: *righteousness* in the sense, You will rightly provide the grace to those opting for the best things; *mercy* in the sense, You provide it out of lovingkindness rather than on the basis of their deserts, unmindful of their former sins; and *salvation* in the sense, You free them from impending dangers.

But as for you, Lord, do not keep your pity far from me (v. 11): since I am ready to do this, then, do not neglect to confer your lovingkindness quickly on us. *Your mercy and your truth always assisted me:* instead, provide me constantly with that true and steadfast lovingkindness of yours (*assisted* in the sense of "may it assist," a change in tense occurring in translation). *Because evils beyond counting encompassed me* (v. 12): the multitude of troubles gripping me were innumerable. *My transgressions laid hold of me, and I could not see:* I am beset with so many troubles at the hands of the vast number of evildoers, by whom I am caught up and surrounded when invested in the present troubles, that I can scarcely see my way ahead. | *They became*

13ᶜ. Ἐπληθύνθησαν ὑπὲρ τὰς τρίχας τῆς κεφαλῆς μου. Ἀντὶ τοῦ σφόδρα εἰσὶν ἀναρίθμητοι.

13ᵈ. Καὶ ἡ καρδία μου ἐγκατέλιπέν με. Διὰ τοῦτό φησιν ὑπὸ τοῦ πλήθους τῶν κακῶν ὥσπερ τις ἀκάρδιος ἤμην, οὐδεμίαν ἔχων σύνεσιν τῶν παρόντων.

14ᵃ. Εὐδόκησον, Κύριε, τοῦ ῥύσασθαί με. Θέλησον τοίνυν ἀπαλλάξαι με 5 τῶν κακῶν. Τὸ δὲ εὐδόκησον, ἀντὶ τοῦ σφόδρα θέλησον.

14ᵇ. Κύριε, εἰς τὸ βοηθῆσαί μοι πρόσχες. Ταχεῖάν σου καὶ ἐσπουδασμένην ποίησον τὴν βοήθειαν.

15ᵃ ᵇ. Κατασχυνθείησαν καὶ ἐντραπείησαν ἅμα οἱ ζητοῦντες τὴν ψυχήν 10 μου τοῦ ἐξᾶραι αὐτήν Περὶ τῶν Βαβυλωνίων λέγει. Οὗτοί φησιν οἱ ἀνελεῖν με ἐσπουδακότες αἰσχυνθεῖεν ἐπὶ τῇ οἰκείᾳ σπουδῇ, ἀπράκτων αὐτοῖς γενομένων τῶν κατ᾽ ἐμοῦ βουλευμάτων διὰ τὴν σὴν βοήθειαν.

15ᶜ. Ἀποστραφείησαν εἰς τὰ ὀπίσω καὶ ἐντραπείησαν οἱ θέλοντές μοι κακά. Οἱ ἐπιθυμοῦντές με διάγειν ἐν συμφοραῖς πολλὴν δέξαιντο τὴν ἐπὶ 15 τούτοις αἰσχύνην, εἰς μάταιον αὐτοῖς τῆς ἐπιθυμίας μετατραπείσης. Τὸ δὲ ἀποστραφείησαν εἰς τὰ ὀπίσω ἐκ μεταφορᾶς τοῦ τοὺς αἰσχυνομένους σφόδρα ἀποστρέφειν τὸ πρόσωπον ὑπὸ τῆς αἰδοῦς.

16. Κομισάσθωσαν παραχρῆμα αἰσχύνην αὐτῶν οἱ λέγοντές μοι Εὖγε Εὖγε. Ταχεῖαν δέξαιντο τὴν αἰσχύνην οἱ ἐπιχαίροντες ταῖς συμφοραῖς· τὸ 20 γὰρ εὖγε εὖγε ἐπιφώ|νησίς ἐστι εὐφραινομένων καὶ ἡδομένων ἐπὶ τοῖς γιγνομένοις.

17ᵃ. Ἀγαλλιάσαιντο καὶ εὐφρανθείησαν ἐπὶ σοὶ πάντες οἱ ζητοῦντές σε, Κύριε. Κἀκεῖνοι μέν φησι τοιαῦτα πάθοιεν. Οὗτοι δὲ οἱ ζητοῦντές σε λάβοιεν τὴν ἐπὶ σοὶ εὐφροσύνην, τουτέστι τὴν ἐπὶ τοῖς σοῖς ἀγαθοῖς, οἷς παρέ- 25 σχες αὐτοῖς· λέγει δὲ τοὺς Ἰουδαίους ζητοῦντας αὐτὸν ὡς κεκτημένους αὐτοῦ τὴν γνῶσιν καὶ ἐλπίζοντας τυχεῖν τῆς παρ᾽ αὐτοῦ βοηθείας.

3-4 cf. L (p. 742, 23-25): Διὰ τὸ πλῆθος τῶν περιστοιχισάντων με κακῶν, ἀκάρδιός τις ἔδοξα καὶ ἄνους εἶναι.　21-22 L (p. 743, 6-8): Οἱ λέγοντες Εὖγε εὖγε, ἀντὶ τοῦ Οἱ ἐφηδόμενοι αἰσχυνθήσονται.

Aᵉ 14ᵃ (p. 233, 13-15): Sit tibi uoluntas haec atque sententia, ut omnia quae me adstri⟨n⟩gunt aduersa desoluas.　15ᵃ·ᵇ (p. 233, 16-22): Isti, qui me molliuntur interficire, effectibus distituti ferant male uoluntates, reatum et confusionis tormenta patientur... Babiloniis impraecatur ᵃaduersa.　17-18 (p. 233, 23-24): Pro pudore occurrentes intuere non audeant (audient ms).　20-22 (p. 233, 28-29): Qui uocem letitiae meis aduersis erumpunt.

more numerous than the hairs of my head—that is, They were very numerous. *And my heart failed me:* hence, under the pressure of the multitude of the troubles I became like a person without a heart, with no understanding of what was occurring.

Be pleased, Lord, to rescue me (v. 13): so please rid me of the troubles (*Be pleased* meaning "Please, I beg you"). *Lord, attend to helping me:* make your help swift and attentive. *Let those be put to shame and overturned together who seek my life to do away with it* (v. 14). He is referring to the Babylonians. Let those who are anxious to do away with me be ashamed of their anxiety, he is saying, their plots against me failing them as a result of your help. *Let them be turned back and put to shame who wish me harm:* let those desiring me to live in misfortune incur deep shame for this, their desires being brought to nothing. The phrase *Let them be turned back* is a metaphor from people in shame who turn their face away in confusion. *Let them meet with shame from the outset who say to me, Aha, aha* (v. 15): let those rejoicing at my misfortune feel rapid shame (*Aha, aha* being an exclamation of people rejoicing and taking satisfaction in events).

Let all who seek you be glad and rejoice in you, Lord (v. 16): let those others suffer such fate, and on the other hand, let the people who seek you feel joy in you—that is, in your good things with which you provide them. He is referring to the Jews seeking him on the basis of gaining knowledge of him and hoping to gain help from him. | *And may they say always, The*

17^b. Καὶ εἰπάτωσαν διὰ παντὸς Μεγαλυνθήτω ὁ Κύριος. Ὥστε διηνεκῶς θαυμάζοντας λέγειν ὅτι μέγας εἶ ἀληθῶς καὶ τὴν δύναμιν ἐξαίσιος, τῆς εὐεργεσίας τοῦτο λέγειν αὐτοὺς προαγομένης.

17^c. Οἱ ἀγαπῶντες τὸ σωτήριόν σου διὰ παντός. Οἱ τὴν παρά σου
5 σωτηρίαν ἀεὶ ἀπεκδεχόμενοι — ἵνα εἴπῃ Οἱ εἴς σε ἐλπίζοντες — ἵνα οὗτοι ταῦτα λέγωσι· λέξουσι δὲ τῆς παρά σου τυχόντες βοηθείας.

18^a. Ἐγὼ δὲ πτωχὸς καὶ πένης εἰμί, Κύριος φροντιεῖ μου. Σύμμαχος· λόγισαι περὶ ἐμοῦ. Ἐπειδὴ γάρ φησιν εὐτελής εἰμι καὶ ἀσθενής, αὐτὸς φρόντισον προνοῆσαί μου.

10 18^b. Βοηθός μου καὶ ὑπερασπιστής μου σὺ εἶ, ὁ Θεός μου, μὴ χρονίσῃς. Ἀλλὰ καὶ αὐτὸς εἶ φησιν ὁ ἀεί μοι βοηθήσας, ὥστε καὶ διὰ τὴν ἀσθένειαν τὴν ἐμὴν καὶ διὰ τὸ αὐτόν σε εἶναι τὸν ἀεί μου προνοοῦντα, μὴ παρατείνῃς τῆς βοηθείας τὴν ὑπέρθεσιν.

PSALMVS XL

15 Προφητεύει ἐν τῷ παρόντι ψαλμῷ
τὰ κατὰ τὸν μακάριον Ἐζεκίαν, ὅπως
τε ἠρρώστησε καὶ τίνα τὰ παρὰ τῶν
φίλων αὐτῷ κατὰ τὴν ἀρρωστιαν γε-
γο|νότα, καὶ τὴν ἀπαλλαγὴν δὲ τῆς
20 ἀρρωστίας ὡς ἀπὸ τοῦ Θεοῦ παρα-

Praedicitur in praesenti psalmo qualiter beatus Ezechias ualitudine aduersa laborauerit et quales se hi, qui prius amici uidebantur, tempore eius infirmitatis ostenderint; quomodo etiam

Argumentum paulo breuius ex Vat. gr. 1682, f. 148^v edidit A. Mai (N. P. B. III, 297; P. G., LXVI, 670): Ἐν τούτῳ τὰ κατὰ τὸν μακάριον Ἐζεκίαν προφητεύει ὁ μακάριος Δαυίδ, ὅπως τε καὶ τίνος ἕνεκεν ἠρρώστησε, λέγω δὴ τῆς ἁμαρτίας, καὶ τί ἐν τῷ καιρῷ τῆς ἀρρωστίας ὑπὸ τῶν φίλων αὐτῷ γέγονεν. Ἔπειτα διδάσκει ὡς διὰ τὴν εἰς τοὺς πένητας ἐπιμέλειαν τῆς ὑγείας ἔτυχε, πάντας ἐξῆς προτρεπόμενος τοῦτο ποιεῖν. Eadem apud Paris. 139, f. 100^v; cf. L (p. 757, 14-19). — Huiusmodi exegesim reprehendit Cyrillus Alexandrinus (Mai, p. 296-297).
Praedicitur — liberari: A, fol. 13^c; fol. 14^c.   18 se hi] hii A   prius] primus A.

A^e 18^a (p. 233, 34-234, 1): Quoniam, inquit, contemptibilis atque infirmus captiuitatis condicione sum factus, o Domine, conuenit esse sollicitum. 11-13 (p. 234, 3-5): Adiutorium tuum, quia ipse mihi semper auxiliatus es, nulla delatione suspende.   15-254, 5 (p. 234, 6-9): Praedicitur hoc psalmo de infirmitate Ezechiae et curatione eius atque occassione langoris eius. Cf. PSEUDO-BEDA (698).

Lord be magnified: so as constantly to say in their admiration, You are truly great and extraordinary in your power, your favor prompting them to say this. *Those who love your salvation always:* those ever in receipt of your salvation (as if to say, "those hoping in you") so that they may say it, as they will say it on receiving help from you.

But I am poor and needy; the Lord will be concerned for me (v. 17). Symmachus: "Spare me a thought." Since I am lowly and weak, he is saying, think of showing me your providence. *You are my help and my protector, my God, do not delay:* but you are also the one who always helped me, and so on account of my weakness and on account of your ever showing me providence, do not prolong the delay in giving help.

PSALM 41

In the present psalm he prophesies the situation of blessed Hezekiah, his illness, what happened to him in his illness at the hands of his friends, and the improvement in his condition granted him by God, | because his illness was

σχεθεῖσαν αὐτῷ, ὅτι τε δι' ἁμαρτίαν αὐτῷ γένονεν ἡ ἀρρωστία, — ὃ καὶ ἑτέρωθι πολλαχοῦ ἐν τοῖς περὶ τῆς ὑποθέσεως ταύτης ψαλμοῖς ἐπισημηνάμενος φαίνεται.

Ἐν ἀρχῇ δὲ τοῦ ψαλμοῦ μακαρίζει τοὺς μεταδιδόντας προθύμως τοῖς πένησιν, ὡς τοῦ Ἐζεκίου διὰ ταύτην τὴν αἰτίαν μάλιστα ἐν τῇ ἀρρωστίᾳ τετυχηκότος τῆς παρὰ τοῦ Θεοῦ βοηθείας, παιδεύων καὶ τοὺς λοιποὺς προθύμως διακεῖσθαι περὶ τοῦτο, ὅπερ φαίνοιντο διαπραττόμενοι ἐν καιρῷ κακίστῳ τυγχάνειν τῆς ἀπαλλαγῆς.

ab infirmitate ipsa, Deo miserante, surrexerit, et quod ipsa quoque egritudo de peccati illi admissione prouenerit — quod quidem in aliis psalmis, qui sub hoc ar- 5 gumento scripti sunt, sollicite curat ostendere. Inter principia autem psalmi *beatos* dicit qui student manu liberali necessitates pauperum subleuare et imitari Eze- 10 chiam, qui ob hoc praecipue studium meruerit ut incommodo eius curatio diuina mederetur. Docet ergo reliquos, ut ad simile opus prumpti sint, quo possint 15 similiter inter aduersa liberari.

2ᵃ. Μακάριος ὁ συνιὼν ἐπὶ πτωχὸν καὶ πένητα. Ὁ συνιών, τουτέστιν ὁ ἐννοῶν ἃ προσῆκε περὶ τῶν πενήτων, ὁ τοῦτο ἔχων κατὰ διάνοιαν ὅτι προσῆκε τὰς χρείας αὐτῶν παραμυθεῖσθαι ἐπαρκοῦντας αὐτοῖς κατὰ τὸ δυνατόν. Πῶς δὲ μακάριος εἴη; Ἐπειδὴ μεγάλων τεύξεται τῶν μισθῶν. Τίνων 20 δὲ τούτων;

2ᵇ. Ἐν ἡμέρᾳ πονηρᾷ ῥύσεται αὐτὸν ὁ Κύριος. Ἐν γὰρ καιρῷ τῶν κινδύνων ἀπαλλάξει αὐτὸν τῶν κακῶν ὁ Θεός, κατάλληλον αὐτῷ τὸν μισθὸν χαριζόμενος· ὡς γὰρ ἐκεῖνος ἐπαρκεῖ δεομένῳ τῷ πένητι, ἐπαρκέσει πάντως καὶ αὐτῷ ὁ Θεὸς δεομένῳ τῆς αὐτοῦ βοηθείας. Ἡμέραν γὰρ πονη- 25 ρὰν οὐκ ἐκ τῆς φύσεως καλεῖ, ἐπεὶ καὶ ἀλλαχοῦ ἡμέραν οἶδε καλεῖν ἀγαθὴν (πῶς δὲ δυνατὸν τὸ αὐτὸ καὶ ἀγαθὸν καὶ πονηρὸν εἶναι τῇ φύσει;) ἀλλ' ἡμέραν πονηρὰν καλεῖ ἐκείνῳ τῷ ἐν κινδύνοις ἐξεταζομένῳ. Οὕτως γὰρ

4-5 cf. p. 135 (ps. XXIX), p. 139 (ps. XXXI)   26-27 Ps. XXXIII, 13ᵇ.

17-18 ὁ ἐννοῶν — πενήτων affert L (p. 760, 27-28).   25-255, 5 L (p. 760, 7-1 ab imo): Ἡμέραν πονηράν, οὐ τὴν φύσει οὖσαν πονηρὰν (οὐ γάρ ἐστι φύσει πονηρά ...) ἀλλὰ πονηρὰν καλεῖ, ἐν ᾗ πόνῳ τις περιβάλλεται ... ἑτέρῳ κινδύνῳ. Ἡ κατὰ Σύμμαχον ἐν ἡμέρᾳ κακώσεως.

3 illius A   3-4 admisione A   7 principalia A   9 necessitudines A 10 emitari A emittari B   12 meruerit] meruit A¹, et add. A   13 ederetur A 15 prumti A.

Aᵉ 28 (p. 234, 16-17): Pro tempore aduerso uel adflictione.

the result of sin, as emerges also in different ways elsewhere in the psalms on this theme.[1] In the beginning of the psalm he declares blessed those who give liberally to the poor, since Hezekiah on this score in particular gained help in illness from God. He also instructs others as well to be zealous in this matter, so that by practicing it in bad times they may be seen to gain relief.

Blessed is the one who understands the poor and needy (v. 1).[2] *The one who understands*—that is, the one considering his duty to the needy, who keeps in mind that there is an obligation to meet their needs sufficiently to the extent possible. In what way *blessed*? By receiving great rewards. Of what kind, specifically? *On an evil day the Lord will rescue him:* in time of danger God will free him from the troubles, granting him a commensurate reward; as he helps the needy on request, doubtless God will also help him when requesting his assistance. In calling the day *evil,* note, he does not refer to its nature, since elsewhere he is also in the habit of speaking of "a good day"[3] (how could the same thing be both good and evil by nature?). Rather, he calls it an evil day for the person exposed to dangers, as | it also says

1. Cf. Theodore's introduction to Pss 30; 32.

2. We cannot be sure that this is precisely the text before Theodore. Theodoret comments on his (also Antiochene) text, "The phrase 'and needy' I found in some manuscripts, but it is not in the Hebrew, or the Syriac, or the other translators." Diodore had noted that Symmachus did not include the phrase.

3. Cf. Ps 34:12 LXX.

καὶ ἀλλαχοῦ φησιν · "Ἱνα τί ὑμῖν ζητεῖν τὴν ἡμέραν Κυρίου; καὶ αὕτη ἐστὶ σκό|τος καὶ οὐ φῶς — καὶ μὴν ἀνάγκη τὴν ἡμέραν φῶς εἶναι, ἀλλὰ σκότος ἐκείνοις τοῖς ἐν συμφοραῖς ἐξετάζεσθαι μέλλουσι κατ' ἐκείνην τὴν ἡμέραν καὶ ὥσπερ ἐν σκότῳ τινὶ ὑπὸ τοῦ πλήθους τῶν κακῶν καθεστάναι. Σύμ-
5 μαχος οὕτω λέγει · ἐν ἡμέρᾳ κακώσεως Κύριος διαφυλάξαι αὐτὸν καὶ ζήσαι αὐτόν.

3ᵃ. Κύριος φυλάξαι αὐτὸν καὶ μακαρίσαι αὐτὸν ἐν τῇ γῇ Διαφόρως ἐξη-γεῖται τοῦ Θεοῦ τὰς εἰς αὐτὸν εὐεργεσίας. Καὶ γὰρ ἀπαλλάξει φησὶ τῶν κινδύνων, καὶ διαφυλάξει ὥστε μηδὲν παθεῖν, καὶ ζωὴν αὐτῷ παρέξει, καὶ τῷ
10 πλήθει τῶν εὐεργεσιῶν μακαριστὸν ἀποφανεῖ παρὰ πᾶσιν. Ἐν γὰρ τῇ γῇ λέγει, τουτέστι παρὰ πᾶσι τοῖς ἐπὶ τῆς γῆς.

3ᵇ. Καὶ μὴ παραδοῖ αὐτὸν εἰς χεῖ-ρας ἐχθροῦ αὐτοῦ. Ἀντὶ τοῦ Οὐ πα-ραδώσει. Σύμμαχος · Καὶ οὐκ ἐκδώσει
15 αὐτόν, τουτέστιν οὐκ ἐάσει τοῖς ἐχ-θροῖς ὑποχείριον γενέσθαι.

Et non tradat eum in animam inimicorum eius. Non tradat, id est Non tradet. Symmachus: *Non dabit eum.*

4ᵃ. Κύριος βοηθῆσαι αὐτῷ ἐπὶ κλίνης ὀδύνης αὐτοῦ. Καὶ ἀρρωστήσαντι δὲ αὐτῷ παρέξει τὴν βοήθειαν. Βούλεται δὲ εἰπεῖν ὅτι τῷ ἐπαρκοῦντι ταῖς χρείαις τῶν πενήτων, ἐν πάσῃ χρείᾳ τὴν οἰκείαν ἐπαρκέσει βοήθειαν ὁ
20 Θεός. Ταῦτα δὲ πάντα εἶπε κοινὴν ποιησάμενος τὴν παραίνεσιν ἀπὸ τῶν κατὰ τὸν Ἐζεκίαν, ὡς ἐκείνου διὰ τὴν περὶ τοὺς πένητας πρόνοιαν πάντων τούτων τετυχηκότος. Καὶ γὰρ καὶ ἐρρύσατο αὐτὸν ἐκ κινδύνου τῶν Ἀσσυ-ρίων κεκυκλωκότων τὴν πόλιν καὶ ἐφύλαξεν οὐδὲν παθεῖν ἐάσας, καὶ ἐν ζωῇ κατέστησεν ἀπαλλάξας τοῦ προσδοκωμένου θανάτου, καὶ μακαρίζεσ-
25 θαι παρὰ πάντων ἐποίησεν οὕτω παραδόξως ἀπαλλάξας αὐτὸν τῶν κιν-δύνων, καὶ ἀρρωστήσαντι δὲ αὐτῷ μετὰ ταῦτα πάλιν ἐβοήθησε. Διὰ τοῦτο τῇ παραινέσει χρησάμενος, ἑξῆς ἐπὶ τὰ περὶ αὐτοῦ μεθίσταται εἰς ἀπό-δειξιν ἕλκων | αὐτὰ τῶν λεχθέντων παρ' αὐτοῦ. Μέμνηται μέντοι τῶν κατὰ τὴν ἀρρωστίαν, ἅπαντα ἐάσας τὰ λοιπά, ἐπειδὴ καὶ τοῦτο προσαγορεύειν
30 αὐτῷ πρόκειται ἐν τῷ παρόντι ψαλμῷ.

1-2 Amos V, 18 (οὐαὶ οἱ ἐπιθυμοῦντες vulg.) 20 ss. cf. supra p. 254, 5 atque ar-gum. ps. XXVIII et XXXIII.

Et non — eum: A, fol. 13ᶜ; B, fol. 14ᶜ. 13 dradat A 14 sim A¹.

Aᵉ 13-14 (p. 234, 24): Id est pro Non tradet. 15-16 p. (235, 1-3): Non, inquit, patietur eum inimicis suis subieci. 20 ss. (p. 235, 4-6): Vt contiguit Ezechiae taliter operatio, et sub eius exemplo cunctis similiter meritis non dificulter eueniat.

elsewhere, "Why do you look for the day of the Lord? It is darkness and not light";[4] and while of necessity day is light, it is darkness for those destined to be exposed to calamities on that day as though plunged into darkness by the multitude of troubles. Symmachus puts it that way: "In the day of misfortune the Lord will closely guard him and give him life."[5]

The Lord will closely guard him and make him blessed in the land (v. 2). He comments on God's favors to him in different ways: He will give freedom from perils, he says, will closely guard him so that he will suffer nothing, provide him with life, and make him appear as blessed by the vast number of favors in the sight of everyone (saying *in the land*—that is, in the sight of everyone in the land). *And may he not give him into the hands of his foes*—that is, He will not give him up. Symmachus: "He will not hand him over"—that is, He will not allow him to fall into the foes' hands.

The Lord will help him on his bed of pain (v. 3), and provide him with help in his illness. He means, Since he meets the needs of the needy, God on his part will provide him with his characteristic help in his every need. Now, he said all this by way of a general exhortation on the basis of Hezekiah's situation, since he received it all as a result of his care for the needy: he rescued him from the danger of the Assyrians encircling the city and protected him by allowing him to suffer nothing; he established him in life by freeing him from the expectation of death, caused him to be blessed by everyone by freeing him in such an extraordinary manner from the dangers, and later in turn he helped him in his illness. Hence, in supplying this exhortation he proceeds to move from his situation to proof by making a quotation of what was said by him. He cites, of course, details of his illness, not to mention all the rest, since it is his purpose to foretell it also in the present psalm. | *He*

---

4. Amos 5:18.
5. Is this the text of Symmachus of v. 1 or, rather, of the following verse?

4ᵇ. Ὅλην τὴν κοίτην αὐτοῦ ἔστρεψεν, μετέβαλε τὴν ἀρρωστίαν αὐτοῦ. Ὅτι δέ φησι ταῦτα οὕτως ἔχει, δῆλον ἐκ τῶν γεγονότων. Ἀμέλει πᾶσαν αὐτοῦ τὴν ἀρρωστίαν μετέβαλε · κοίτην γὰρ ἐν-   *Stratum eius* ipsum malum ae-
ταῦθα τὴν ἀρρωστίαν ἐκάλεσεν, ὡς   grotationis appellat.
ἐπ᾽ αὐτῆς πάντως τοῦ ἀρρώστου κατακειμένου. Τὸ δὲ μετέβαλε τὴν   5
ἀρρωστίαν, ἀντὶ τοῦ ἀπὸ ἀρρωστίας εἰς ὑγείαν αὐτὸν μετέστησεν. Καλῶς
δὲ τὸ ἔστρεψεν ὥστε δεῖξαι τὸ αἰφνήδιον καὶ ὀξὺ τῆς ἰάσεως, καὶ τὸ
ὅλην ἵνα εἴπῃ Μηδὲ βραχὺ λείψανον   *Vniuersum* autem dixit, ut | nul-
τῆς ἀρρωστίας κατέλιπεν αὐτῷ · δι᾽   las reliquias langoris remansisse
ἀμφοτέρων γὰρ ἡ τοῦ Θεοῦ ἐδείκνυτο   indicaret.   10
δύναμις καὶ τῇ ὀξύτητι καὶ τῷ πᾶσαν ἀποβληθῆναι συντόμως τὴν κάκωσιν,
τῶν ἰατρῶν χρόνῳ τε καὶ τάξει τὰς ἰάσεις ἐπαγόντων καὶ ταῖς κατὰ μέρος
θεραπείαις. Λοιπὸν διηγεῖται καὶ τῆς ἰάσεως τὸν τρόπον καί φησιν·

5ᵃ. Ἐγὼ εἶπα· Κύριε, ἐλέησόν με. Γεγονὼς γάρ φησιν ἐν τῇ ἀρρωστίᾳ
ἐβόησε πρὸς τὸν Θεὸν καὶ ᾔτησε παρ᾽ αὐτοῦ τὸν ἔλεον. Ταῦτα γὰρ λοι-   15
πὸν ὡς ἂν τοῦ Ἐζεκίου εἰρηκότος φησί, διηγούμενος πάντα ὡς ἐκ τῆς ἀκολουθίας τὰ κατὰ τὴν ἀρρωστίαν ἐπὶ μηνύσει μὲν τῶν ἐσομένων, διδασκαλίαν
δὲ τῶν ἀκουόντων.

5ᵇ. Ἴασαι τὴν ψυχήν μου, ὅτι   *Sana animam meam quoniam*
ἥμαρτον σοι. Καὶ θεράπευσόν μου   *peccaui tibi.* Huic parti medicas   20
τὴν | ψυχήν· οἶδα γὰρ ἡμαρτηκὼς   manus admoue, ex qua ad cor-
εἴς σε καὶ διὰ τοῦτο ταῦτα ὑπομένω.   pus egritudo peruenit: nam, ad-
Καὶ καθὼς εἶπε τὴν ψυχήν μου·   miso peccato, manifesto patet
ἁμαρτίας γὰρ πραχθείσης, εὔδηλον   animam egere medicina.
ὅτι ψυχὴ δεῖται τῆς ἰατρείας.

  25

6ᵃ. Οἱ ἐχθροί μου εἶπαν κακά μοι. Ἰδοὺ γάρ φησιν εἰς οἷα ὑπὸ τῆς
ἀρρωστίας κατέστην, ὡς τοὺς ἐχθροὺς ἐφήδεσθαί τε καὶ ῥήματα φθέγγεσθαι πάσης γέμοντα κακίας. Ποῖα δὲ ταῦτα;

5-6 cf. L (p. 761, 16-18) ... ἀντὶ τοῦ Ὅλην τὴν ἀρρωστίαν ἔστρεψας, καὶ μετήμει-
ψας πρὸς ὑγείαν. *Eadem fere affert Paraphrasis* (p. 758).
Stratum — indicaret: A, fol. 13ᶜ⁻ᵈ; B, fol. 14ᶜ⁻ᵈ. — *Praemittitur textus Scrip-*
turae: Vniuersum stratum eius, reliqua.   3-4 egrotatationis A.
Sana — medicina: A, fol. 13ᵈ; B, fol. 14ᵈ.   23 patet *conieci*, peccato AB.

Aᵉ 8-10 (p. 235, 7-9): Vt nullas remansisse reliquias langoris ostenderet
uniuersum stratum possuit.   6ᵃ (p. 235, 20-236, 3): Sub infirmitatis, inquit,
uexatione discrimineque constitutus (constitus *ms*) inimicis meis fui gaudio,
qui loquebantur idquod eorum uota conceperant. Quae uero illa erant?

overthrew his bed completely; he transformed his illness: It is clear from events, he is saying, that this was the situation. Of course, he transformed his illness (referring to illness as *his bed,* since the ill generally lie on it). The phrase *transformed his illness* means, He brought him from sickness to health. *Overthrew* was well put, to bring out the unexpected and rapid cure, as was *completely,* as if to say, Not the slightest vestige of the illness remained with him; in both cases, in fact, God's power is revealed, both in the rapidity and in the speedy banishment of the complete ailment, since physicians apply remedies over time and in a certain order and by the use of individual treatments.

He then describes the manner of the healing as well. *I said, Lord, have mercy on me* (v. 4): being in this condition of illness, he cried aloud to God and begged mercy of him. It is now Hezekiah speaking, he is saying, on the one hand describing everything in sequence to do with the illness by mention of what would happen, and on the other hand giving instruction for the listeners. *Heal my soul because I sinned against you:* cure my soul; I am aware that I have sinned against you, and on this account I endure these sufferings. *My soul* was well put: it is clear that, after sin was committed, the soul needed healing. *My foes spoke evil against me* (v. 5): see to what dire straits I am reduced, with the enemy exulting and uttering words quite full of malice. What were they? | *When will he die and his name perish?* Ah, when may he

6ᵇ. Πότε ἀποθανεῖται καὶ ἀπολεῖται τὸ ὄνομα αὐτοῦ; Πότε ἄρα ἀποθάνοι καὶ ἀφανισθείη αὐτοῦ τὸ μνημόσυνον;

7ᵃ. Καὶ εἰσεπορεύετο τοῦ ἰδεῖν, μάτην ἐλάλει. Καὶ τὸ μεῖζόν φησι κακόν, ὅτι εἰσιὼν μὲν ἕκαστος αὐτῶν ὥστε ἐπισκέψασθαι ἐφθέγγετο ῥήματα
5 συμπαθείας μεστά. Καλῶς δὲ εἶπε μάτην, ὅτι οὐκ ἀπὸ συγκαταθέσεως ἐφθέγγετο καρδίας, ἀλλὰ ἁπλῶς ἀπάτης ἕνεκεν. Σύμμαχος· Εἰσπορευόμενος τοῦ ἐπισκοπῆσαι, μάτην ἐλάλει.

7ᵇ. Ἡ καρδία αὐτοῦ συνήγαγεν ἀνομίαν ἑαυτῷ. Ἐν δὲ τῇ καρδίᾳ εἶχε τὴν ἐπιθυμίαν τοῦ θανάτου τοῦ ἐμοῦ. Ἀνομίαν οὖν ἐκάλεσε τὴν ἐπιθυμίαν
10 τὴν τοιαύτην, ὡς ἀνοσίαν καὶ παράλογον, καὶ οὐκ ἀπὸ δικαίας αἰτίας γενομένην τῷ μηθὲν ἠδικῆσθαι παρ᾽ αὐτοῦ.

8ᵃ. Ἐξεπορεύετο ἔξω καὶ ἐλάλει ἐπὶ τὸ αὐτὸ κατ᾽ ἐμοῦ. Μετὰ γὰρ τὸ ἐξελθεῖν ἐφθέγγοντο ἄτοπα περὶ ἐμοῦ. Σύμμαχος· Ἐξερχόμενος κατελάλει.

15 8ᵇ. Ἐψιθύριζον πάντες οἱ ἐχθροί μου κατ᾽ ἐμοῦ. Καὶ οὐ μόνον φησὶν ἰδίᾳ | ἕκαστος ταῦτα διεπράττετο, ἀλλὰ καὶ συνερχόμενοι πάντες οἱ ἐχθραίνοντες κατὰ ταὐτὸν πλεῖστα ὅσα ἐφθέγγοντο κατ᾽ ἐμοῦ. Καλῶς δὲ εἶπε τὸ ἐψιθυρίζον· ἀνάγκη γὰρ ἦν ὡς βασιλέα δεδιότας μὴ εἰς τὸ προφανὲς φθέγγεσθαι.

20 8ᶜ. Ἐλογίζοντο κακά μοι. Κατ᾽ ἐμοῦ ἐλογίσαντο, ἐνενόουν ἄτοπα, καὶ ἐβουλεύοντο κατ᾽ ἐμοῦ.

9ᵃ. Λόγον παράνομον κατέθεντο κατ᾽ ἐμοῦ. Καὶ ῥήματα ἄτοπα καὶ παράνομα κατ᾽ ἐμοῦ ἐβεβαιοῦντο· κ α τ α θ έ σ θ α ι γὰρ κυρίως λέγεται ὅταν τις ἐπὶ ὑπομνημάτων καταθῆται φωνήν, ἥτις λοιπὸν μένει βεβαία, καὶ ὅλως ἡ
25 φωνὴ ἐπὶ τῶν μετά τινος βεβαιώσεως γιγνομένων λέγεται. Τοῦτο οὖν λέγει ὅτι οὐχ ἁπλῶς ἐφθέγγοντο, ἀλλὰ μετὰ βεβαιώσεως πολλῆς καὶ συγκαταθέσεως τῆς πρὸς τὰ λεγόμενα.

18-19 L (p. 761, 41-43): Ὁ γὰρ βασιλείας φόβος παρεσκεύαζεν αὐτοὺς μὴ ἐν φανερῷ τὴν ἔχθραν ἐνδείκυσθαι.

Aᵉ 6ᵇ (p. 236, 3-5): Quando, inquit, a luce priuabitur et in aeterna obliuia contrudetur?　　9-10 (p. 236, 12-13): ... *iniquitatem* uocat uota fictorum. 18-19 (p. 236, 19-22): Quia palam obloqui regi non poterant, inquerebant atque trachtabant qualiter mea infirmitas augeretur.

die and his memory be obliterated?

He came in to see; he spoke idly (v. 6): the worse evil was that each of them, on coming in to visit me, uttered words full of sympathy. *Idly* was well put, because they spoke not from a sincere heart but with the simple intention of deceiving. Symmachus: "Entering on a visit, he spoke idly." *His heart heaped up lawlessness for himself:* in his heart he had a desire for my death (by *lawlessness* referring to such a desire as noxious and unreasonable, with no basis in a just complaint of any wrong done to him). *He went out and spoke the same thing against me:* on going out, they uttered falsehoods about me. Symmachus: "Going out, he traduced me." *All my foes whispered together against me* (v. 7): not only did each one do this on his own, but also all the adversaries came together and uttered a great number of things against me at the same time. The verb *whispered* was well put: naturally, those fearing a king do not speak openly. *Against me they devised troubles:* they plotted against me; they devised wrongful plans and schemed against me. *They set up a lawless plan against me* (v. 8): they laid down false and criminal statements against me ("setting up" properly referring to when someone puts a statement on record, which then remains in place, and the statement is taken without question as confirmation of events). So he means that far from being open, they spoke so as to give confirmation and consensus to what was said. |

9ᵇ. Μὴ ὁ κοιμώμενος οὐχὶ προσθήσει τοῦ ἀναστῆσαι; Ἆρα τοίνυν
φησὶ διαναστήσομαι καὶ ἀπαλλαγή-
σομαι τῆς ἀρρωστίας, ἵν᾽ ὥσπερ ἀπὸ
ὕπνου τῆς κακώσεως διαναστὰς ποιήσω τούτους πεῖραν λαβεῖν τῆς ματαιότητος τῶν κατ᾽ ἐμοῦ ῥημάτων;

Numquid qui dormit non adi-
ciat ut resurgat? Quamuis, inquit, inimicorum talia uota sint
talisque conlatio, putas non re-   5
surgam atque ab ista infirmitate
liberabor et tamquam excitatus
quondam euigilem, faciamque
istos quam fuerint uana eorum
aduersum me uerba sentire?

Καὶ καλῶς εἶπε Μὴ ὁ κοιμώμενος· τοῦ γὰρ Θεοῦ βοηθήσαντος, ὥσπερ   10
ἀπὸ ὕπνου διανίστατο τῆς ἀρρωστίας μετὰ πολλῆς τῆς εὐχαριστίας.

10. Καὶ γὰρ ὁ ἄνθρωπος τῆς εἰρήνης μου, ἐφ᾽ ὃν ἤλπισα, ὁ ἐσθίων ἄρτους
μου, ἐμεγάλυνεν ἐπ᾽ ἐμὲ πτερνισμόν. Τὸ γάρ μοί φησι χεῖρον ἁπάντων, καὶ
ὃ μάλιστά μοι πολλὴν παρέχει τὴν ἀθυμίαν, ὅτι | καὶ οἱ φιλίαν προσποιού-
μενοι, οἷς καὶ ἐπήλπιζον ὡς φίλοις πάντα ἀνατιθέμενος, οἳ καὶ συνήσ-   15
θιόν μοι ἑκάστοτε ὤφθησαν μάλιστα ἀπατῶντές με, καὶ χλευάζοντες, καὶ
σχηματιζόμενοι μὲν τὴν φιλίαν, ἕτερα δὲ κατὰ διάνοιαν ἔχοντες ἐμεγάλυναν
οὖν πτερνισμόν, ἐπειδὴ μείζων ἦν ἡ ἀπάτη ὅσῳ καὶ μεῖζον τὴν φιλίαν ἐσχη-
ματίζοντο.

11. Σὺ δέ, Κύριε, ἐλέησόν με καὶ ἀνάστησόν με, καὶ ἀνταποδώσω αὐτοῖς.   20
Ἐπειδὴ τοίνυν τοιαῦτα μὲν τὰ παρὰ τῶν ἐχθρῶν, χείρονα δὲ καὶ παρὰ τῶν
φίλων, σύ φησιν ἐλεήσας ἀνάστησον καὶ ἀπάλλαξον τῆς κακώσεως· λήψομαι γὰρ δίκας παρὰ τούτων.

12. Ἐν τούτῳ ἔγνων ὅτι τεθέληκάς με, ὅτι οὐ μὴ ἐπιχαρῇ ὁ ἐχθρός μου
ἐπ᾽ ἐμέ. Ταύτην φησὶ λήψομαι ἀπόδειξιν μεγίστην τοῦ πεφροντικέναι σε   25
ἐμοῦ, τὸ μὴ συγχωρῆσαί με τοιαῦτα παθεῖν ἀφ᾽ ὧν ἐπιχαρῆναί μοι τοὺς
ἐχθροὺς συμβήσεται.

Numquid — sentire: A. fol. 13ᵈ; B, fol. 14ʲ.   1 dormiat B   1-2 adiec̄ ut
resur̄ A   2 quamuis] q̄q̄ (quamquam) A   6 tam excitus A¹   7 quodam AB
(*pro* quodam modo?)   8 istos] iustos A.

Aᵉ 10 (p. 237, 6-9): Hoc grauius mihi magis ad sensum doloris accessit,
quoniam et hii, qui amicitias ante praetenderent, non dissimiles ab inimicis meis
extiterunt. (p. 237, 11-22): Magis nocuit similatione amicitiae. Quos ad maiorem familiaritatem (faliaritatem *ms*) conuictus mihi ac mensa iungebat, ipsi ad
dicipiendum atque inridendum mei inuenti sunt prumtiores; simulantes quidem
amicitias, sed longe aliud retinentes corde, *amplicauerunt subplantationem*, quoniam grauior est fraus quae simulatione amicitiae et dilectionis absconditur.
22-23 (p. 237, 25-238, 3):... Tu, inquit, misserans me suscita atque ab hac infirmitate liberato ut persequar infideles animo ultione.

Surely if I lie down, shall I not succeed in rising? So he says, Shall I get up and be rid of the illness so as to rise from the bout as though from sleep and make them appreciate the futility of their words against me? *Surely if I lie down* was well said: with God's help, very thankfully he rose up from illness as if from sleep. *The person at peace with me, in whom I had hope, who eats bread with me, has behaved in dastardly manner to me* (v. 9): worst of all, and something that in particular imparts to me deep discouragement, is the fact that even those pretending friendship, whom I completely trusted as friends, and who dined with me, were on each occasion evidently deceiving me, mocking me, and making a pretense of friendship. But at heart they felt differently and *behaved in a dastardly manner,* since their deceit was greater the more they protested friendship.[6]

But you, Lord, have mercy on me, raise me up, and I shall repay them (v. 10): since such were the deeds of my foes, then, and worse those of my friends, have mercy on me, raise me up and rid me of the harsh experience, for I shall take vengeance on them. *By this I knew that you were pleased with me, that my foe did not rejoice over me* (v. 11): this I shall take as the greatest proof of your interest in me, that you did not allow me to suffer such things from which the foes will take occasion to exult over me. | *But you*

---

6. Cf. John 13:18.

13ᵃ. Ἐμοῦ δὲ διὰ τὴν ἀκακίαν ἀντελάβου. Ἐβοήθησας δέ μοί φησι δι-
καίως· ᾔδεις γὰρ ὅτι καὶ τοῖς φίλοις
ἐμαυτὸν ἐπίστευσα, λογισμὸν περὶ
5 αὐτῶν κακίας οὐδένα ποτὲ παρα-
δεξάμενος, οὔτε μὴν ὑποπτεύσας τι
περὶ αὐτῶν ἄτοπον, καὶ τοῖς ἐχθροῖς
οὐκ ἐσπούδασά τι διαθεῖναι κακόν.

10 Τοῦτο γὰρ λέγει ἀκακίαν τὸ μηδένα
μηδὲν εἰργάσθαι κακόν, καὶ τὸ ἄνευ
πάσης κακίας συνδιατεθεῖσθαι τοῖς
φίλοις.

*Me autem propter innocentiam
suscepisti.* Iuste mihi tuum praestabis auxilium. Nosti enim quoniam et amicis me fidelem ami-
cum et simplicem semper exhibui,
numquam de illis aliquid mali
nec in sensum meae suspicionis
admittens, et inimicis numquam
uicem malitiae refferre curaui.
Hoc est enim quod *innocentiam*
uocat, nullum in nullo ledere et
puras omnibus amicitias exhibere.

Ταῦτα δὲ ὁ μακάριος Δαυὶδ ὡς ἐκ τοῦ Ἐζεκίου — καί ποτε μὲν λέγων
15 Σὺ δέ, Κύριε, ἐλέησόν με, ποτὲ δὲ Ἐμοῦ δὲ διὰ τὴν ἀκακίαν ἀντελάβου —
παιδεύει πάντας ἀνθρώπους ὅτι καὶ προϋπάρχειν δεῖ τὰ παρ᾽ ἡμῶν, ὥστε
ἐν κινδύνοις δύνασθαι τυγχάνειν τῆς τοῦ Θεοῦ βοηθείας, καὶ γενομένους ἐν
ταῖς συμφοραῖς οὐχ ὑπτιοῦσθαι δεῖ πεποιθότας ἐφ᾽ ἑαυτοῖς, ἀλλ᾽ εἰδότας
ὡς χρεία τῆς τοῦ Θεοῦ φιλανθρωπίας σύντονον ποιεῖσθαι τὴν προσευχήν.

20 **13ᵇ.** Καὶ ἐβεβαίωσάς με ἐνώπιόν σου εἰς αἰῶνα. Ἐπειδὴ μετὰ τὴν κατὰ
τῶν Ἀσσυρίων νίκην ἐπαρθεὶς τῷ φρονήματι καὶ καταλιπὼν τὸ ὡς προσῆκον ἦν εὐχαριστῆσαι τῷ Θεῷ τῇ ἀρρωστίᾳ περιέπεσε, τοῦτο λέγει ὅτι
Λοιπὸν βεβαιώσεις με ἐν τοῖς προσήκουσιν, ὥστε μὴ ἡμαρτηκότα πάλιν
ἀρρωστίᾳ περιπεσεῖν, ὡς καὶ ἐν τῷ λα΄ λέγει ὡς ἐκ τοῦ Θεοῦ· Συνετιῶ
25 σε καὶ συνβιβῶ σε ἐν ὁδῷ ταύτῃ ᾗ πορεύσῃ, ἐπιστηριῶ ἐπί σε τοὺς ὀφθαλμούς μου.

14. Εὐλογητὸς Κύριος ὁ Θεὸς Ἰσραὴλ ἀπὸ τοῦ αἰῶνος καὶ εἰς τὸν αἰῶνα·
γένοιτο, γένοιτο. Ἐπειδὴ γάρ φησι τοιαῦται καὶ τοσαῦται αἱ παρά σου
εὐεργεσίαι, ἄξιος εἶ, ὁ τοῦ Ἰσραὴλ Θεός, διηνεκῶς ὑμνεῖσθαι οὐ παρ᾽ ἐμοῦ

---

15 v. 11.   24-26 Ps. XXXI, 8.   20 cf. argum. ps. XXVIII et XXIX.

Me autem — exhibere: A, fol. 13ᵈ; B, fol. 14ᵈ.   6 numquam] neque A¹
uel numquam *add. supra lin.* A²   7 nec] non A   9 ** ferre B   13 exhi-
bere] *in A manus posterior add.* In maithan dubsoamne.

Aᵉ 12 (p. 238, 4-8): Haec mihi erit maxima probatio quod sub tuae prouidentiae difensione consistam, si me non patiaris talia sustinere per quae gaudent atque letentur inimici.   21-24 (p. 238, 16-19): Dum indeuotionem infirmitate castigas, in omni tempore uitae meae ad agendas gratias hac eruditione
confirmas.

supported me for my innocence (v. 12): you were right to help me, aware that I even trusted myself to my friends, never entertaining any thought of their malice nor suspecting anything untoward from them, nor was I ready to attribute evil to the foe. This is what *innocence* means, in fact, doing no one any harm and relating to friends without any malice.

Now, blessed David says this on the part of Hezekiah, at one time saying *But you, Lord, have mercy on me,* and at another *But you supported me for my innocence,* instructing everyone to begin with their own affairs and so be in a position to gain help from God, and that it is necessary not to be upset when involved in misfortune by trusting in themselves; instead, aware of the need of God's lovingkindness, they should address an ardent prayer. *And you confirmed me in your presence forever.* Since he grew conceited after the victory over the Assyrians and neglected the duty of giving thanks to God, and so fell ill, he means here, Now you will confirm me in my duties so that I may not sin again and fall ill; as he also says in Psalm 32 on God's part, "I shall give you understanding and confirm you in the way you should travel; I shall fix my eyes upon you."[7]

Blessed be the Lord, the God of Israel, from everlasting to everlasting! May it be, may it be! (v. 13) Since so wonderful and numerous were the favors from you, worthy are you, truly worthy, God of Israel, to be praised in song constantly, not | only by me, but also by everyone (Aquila saying for

---

7. Ps 32:8.

μόνου, ἀλλὰ γὰρ καὶ παρὰ πάντων καὶ ἀληθῶς ἄξιος. Τὸ γὰρ γένοιτο
γένοιτο Ἀκύλας πεπιστωμένως λέγει, τουτέστιν ἀληθῶς εὐλογητός. Τὸ γὰρ
ὄντως, ἀληθῶς καὶ πίστεως ἄξιον τῷ διπλασιασμῷ χρησάμενος παρεδήλωσε.
Θεὸν δὲ Ἰσραὴλ εἶπεν, ἀντὶ τοῦ Σὺ πάντοτε τοῦ Ἰσραὴλ προνοησάμενος,
ὃν καὶ ἐπικέκληται ὁ Ἰσραήλ, ἀληθῶς ἄξιος ὕμνων ὅτι | καὶ πάντων προ- 5
νοεῖς καὶ τοῦ καθ' ἕκαστον φροντίζειν οὐκ ἀπαξιοῖς.

PSALMVS XLI

Τὰ κατὰ τὸν λαὸν τὸν ἐν Βαβυλῶνι προφητεύων ἐνταῦθα ὁ μακάριος
Δαυίδ, ἀναλαβὼν δὲ τοῦ λαοῦ τὸ πρόσωπον ὡς ἐν αἰχμαλωσίᾳ καθεστῶτος,
ταῦτα φθέγγεται ἅπερ ἐκείνοις εἰπεῖν ἥρμοττε κατ' ἐκεῖνον τὸν καιρόν. Εἰ 10
δὲ τὰ λεγόμενα μείζονος ἔχει πόθου τὴν ἀπόδειξιν ἢ κατὰ τὸν λαόν, οὐ
θαυμαστόν. Ὁ γὰρ μακάριος Δαυὶδ τῇ πνευματικῇ χάριτι λαβὼν τῶν ἐσομένων τὴν ἀποκάλυψιν εἰς ἔννοιάν τε αὐτῷ γιγνομένων, κεχωρισμένων τῆς
ἀποκληρωθείσης αὐτοῖς παρὰ τοῦ Θεοῦ γῆς καὶ τοῦ τόπου ἐν ᾧπέρ τε ὁ
ναὸς ᾠκοδόμητο καὶ αἱ θυσίαι ἐπετελοῦντο, καὶ οἰκειούμενος τῇ διαθέσει 15
τὸ πάθος, ἐκ προσώπου τοῦ ἐκείνων ταῦτα φθέγγεται ἅπερ ἂν αὐτὸς
ἐφθέγξατο, χωρισθεὶς τῶν προειρημένων, ἐκείνους παιδεύων τοσαύτην λαβεῖν τοῦ πάθους τὴν ἐπίτασιν. Τὴν γάρ τοι γνῶσιν τῶν ἐσομένων ἐκ τοῦ
Πνεύματος λαβών, τὴν τῶν λεγομένων διάθεσιν ἐκ τῆς οἰκείας περὶ τὸν
Θεὸν σχέσεως, τῷ ἐκείνων περιῆπτε προσώπῳ, ἐπεὶ καὶ ἄχρι τῆς δεῦρο 20
ὑπὲρ τῶν ἁμαρτανόντων μεῖζον ἄλγος ἐστὶν ἰδεῖν ἔχοντας τοὺς δικαίους,
καὶ ταῦτα πολλάκις ἐκείνων ἀναλγήτως ἐπὶ τοῖς πταίσμασι διακειμένων.
Ἄλλως δὲ καὶ ὁ μακάριος Δαυὶδ οὐ|χ ἅπερ ἐκεῖνοι λέγειν ἤμελλον φθέγγε-

Argumentum psalmi sub nomine Theodori paullo brevius praebent Paris. 139,
fol. 103; Vat. 1682, fol. 152; Barbaro, p. 418: Κἀνταῦθα τὰ κατὰ τὸν λαὸν τὸν
αἰχμαλωτισθέντα προφητεύει ὁ μακάριος Δαυίδ, καὶ ἀναλαβὼν τὸ ἐκείνων πρόσωπον φθέγγεται ἅπερ ἐκείνοις ἥρμοττεν ἐπιτυχοῦσι τῆς ἐπανόδου. Τῇ γὰρ πνευματικῇ χάριτι εἰς
ἔννοιάν τε αὐτῶν γενόμενος κεχωρισμένων τῆς — ἐπετελοῦντο, οἰκειοῦτο τὰ ἐκείνων καὶ
ἀπὸ πολλῆς τῆς περὶ Θεὸν διαθέσεως οὕτω περὶ πάθους φθέγγεται ὑπὲρ ἐκείνων αὐτῶν.
Εἰ δὲ μετὰ ταῦτα οὐ τοιαῦτα ἐφθέγξαντο τυχόντες τῆς ἐπανόδου, οὐδὲν παρὰ τὸν προφήτην ἃ ἥρμοττεν αὐτῶν εἰπεῖν προφητεύσαντα.   L (p. 773): Ἔστι δὲ ἐκ προσώπου τῶν
ἐν Βαβυλῶνι ἐπιθυμούντων ἰδεῖν τὰ οἰκεῖα, καὶ παρακαλούντων ἐπανελθεῖν ἐν Ἰερουσαλήμ,
ἧς ἡ μνήμη αὐτοὺς ἐξέκαιεν.

Aᵉ 2 (p. 238, 20-21): Pro fideliter uel uere benedictus Dominus Deus.
8-13 (p. 238, 25-31): Ea quae erat populus Iudeorum in Babilonia captiuitate passurus beatus David praevidens et praedicens, ex persona ipsius populi
praesens carmen instituit, talem orationem formans quae tempori illi captiuis-
que conueniat. Cf. Pseudo-Beda (701): Populus in Babylona captiuus patriae
memor erat.

May it be, may it be! "faithfully"—that is, "truly praised," the use of repetition suggesting really and truly and worthy of faith). He said *God of Israel* in the sense, You who always cared for Israel, whom Israel invokes, are really worthy of songs of praise because you care for all and do not think it beneath you to show an interest in each one.

PSALM 42

Here blessed David prophesies the fortunes of the people in Babylon. Adopting the point of view of the people languishing in captivity, he pronounces what was appropriate to them at that time. If what is said, however, gives evidence of a deeper longing than befits the people, it is not surprising: by spiritual grace blessed David received in his mind a revelation of the people's future situation, cut off from the land apportioned them by God and from the place in which the temple was built and the sacrifices performed. He makes his own their interior sufferings, and adopting their point of view, he expresses what they would have expressed, cut off from the aforementioned, and instructing them how to deal with the intensity of the suffering. On receipt of the knowledge of the future from the Spirit, you see, he associated with their point of view the feelings in the words arising from his characteristic attitude toward God, since up to our own day also you can see righteous people displaying greater grief for sinners while the latter in many cases are unmoved by their falls. Blessed David in particular expresses not what they were likely to say, | but what it would have been appropriate for

ται, ἀλλ' ἅπερ εἰπεῖν ἐκείνοις ἥρμοττεν, ἐντεῦθεν ἤδη παιδεύων ἐκείνους οὕτω διακεῖσθαι τότε ὅταν ἡ τῶν πραγμάτων ἔκβασις πληρωθῇ. Τὰ μὲν οὖν πάθη τοῖς παθοῦσι λογιστέον, τὴν δὲ πρόγνωσιν τῇ τοῦ Πνεύματος ἀκολουθίᾳ, τὴν δὲ τῶν λεγομένων εὐλάβειαν τῇ ἀρετῇ τοῦ φθεγγομένου.

5   2ᵃ. Ὃν τρόπον ἐπιποθεῖ ἡ ἔλαφος ἐπὶ τὰς πηγὰς τῶν ὑδάτων. Πολὺν δεῖξαι βουλόμενος τὸν πόθον, ἐχρήσατο τῷ τῶν ἐλάφων ὑποδείγματι – οὐχ εὑρηκὼς παρὰ ἀνθρώποις ἱκανὸν ὑπόδειγμα πρὸς τὴν τοῦ πόθου παράστασιν, ἀληθῶς τῇ οἰκείᾳ περὶ τὸν Θεὸν διαθέσει, ἐκ τοῦ ἐκείνων προσώπου ταῦτα φθεγγόμενος. Ἔστι γὰρ ταῖς ἐλάφοις ἡ ἐπιθυμία τοῦ πότου
10   τῶν ὑδάτων πολλή τις, ἀεὶ μὲν διὰ τὴν τῆς φύσεως ξηρότητα, μάλιστα ἐπειδὰν μεταλάβῃ τῶν ἑρπετῶν τῆς κατὰ φύσιν ξηρότητος αὐτοῖς ἀπὸ τοῦ ἐδέσματος ἐπιτεινομένης.

2ᵇ. Οὕτως ἐπιποθεῖ ἡ ψυχή μου πρός σε, ὁ Θεός. Οἷον ἔχει τοίνυν ἐκεῖνα περὶ τὰ ὕδατα πόθον ἀπὸ τῆς φύσεως πρὸς τοῦτο συνελαυνόμενα,
15   τοιαύτην ἐκ προαιρέσεως ἐγὼ κέκτημαι πρός σε τὴν διάθεσιν.

3ᵃ. Ἐδίψησεν ἡ ψυχή μου πρὸς τὸν Θεὸν τὸν ζῶντα. Καλῶς τὸ ἐδίψησεν ἡ ψυχή μου εἶπεν, ἀντὶ τοῦ ἐπόθησα, καὶ σύμφωνον τῷ ὑποδείγματι καὶ ὡς ἐνεργέστερον πρὸς παράστασιν τοῦ πόθου.

3ᵇ. Πότε ἥξω καὶ ὀφθήσομαι τῷ προσώπῳ τοῦ Θεοῦ. Τοῦτό φησιν
20   ἐπιθυμῶ, πότε δυνηθῶ ἐλθὼν παραστῆναί σοι καὶ ὀφθῆναί σου τῷ προσώπῳ. Σωματικώτερον δὲ αὐτὸ κατὰ τὴν ἰουδαϊκὴν ὑπόληψιν εἶπεν, ὡς ἐν τῷ ναῷ μόνον ὄντος τοῦ Θεοῦ καὶ οἰομένων οὐκ ἂν αὐτῷ ἑτέρωθι παραστῆναι εἰ μὴ ἐν ἐκείνῳ γένοιντο τῷ τόπῳ.

4ᵃ. Ἐγενήθη τὰ δάκρυά μου ἄρτος ἡμέρας καὶ νυκτός. Ἦν δέ μοί φη-
25   σιν ἀκόρεστα διόλου καὶ τὰ δάκρυα. Ἄρτον δὲ ἐκάλεσε τὰ δάκρυα διὰ τὸ ἀκόρεστον εἰκότος, ἐπειδὴ οἱ ἄνθρωποι ἀεὶ κατὰ τὸν τοῦ ἐσθίειν καιρὸν τοῦ ἄρτου μεταλαμβάνοντες οὐδέποτε τοῦ πράγματος κόρον ἔχουσι διὰ τὸ τῆς τροφῆς χρειῶδες καὶ ἀναγκαῖον, τῆς φύσεως αὐτοὺς οὕτω διακεῖσθαι παρασκευαζούσης.

Aᶜ 2ᵃ (p. 238, 32-239, 4): Ingens disiderium expraemere uolens, ceruorum est usus exemplo, quibus potandae aquae est fere semper permagna cupiditas propter naturalem suorum corporum siccitatem, praecipue tamen cum serpentium uescuntur carnalibus.   2ᵇ (p. 239, 5-7): Aqua illi naturali appetitu, ego te spontanea deuotione disidero.   3ᵃ (p. 239, 8-9): Pro sitiui et bene sitiui, ut comparationi seruiret.   20-21 (p. 239, 11-14): Ad expraemendam uim deuotionis corporali significatione secundum morem Iudeorum locutus est.   4ᵃ (p. 239, 15-19): Inexplebiter pascebar lacrimis in instar panis, qui, cum sit in ussu diurno, nunquam tamen fastiditur; quod in caeteris cibis non fere contingit.

them to say, in this instructing them to have such dispositions at the time the outcome of events should take effect. While the sufferings are attributable to the sufferers, then, the foreknowledge is due to the Spirit's theme, and the religious content due to the virtue of the speaker.

As the deer longs for the springs of water (v. 1). Wanting to bring out the deep longing, he employed the example of deer, not finding among human beings an adequate example for the desperation of the longing, and adducing his own feelings for God in giving vent to this on their part. With deer, you see, there is a constantly deep desire for a water source due to their natural thirst, especially since they eat serpents, and their natural thirst is heightened by eating them.[1] *So my soul longs for you, O God:* the longing that they have for water naturally attracting them to it is the kind of feeling that I have for you from my free will. *My soul thirsted for God, who is strong and living* (v. 3).[2] *My soul thirsted* was well put—that is, "I longed"—both in keeping with the example and to heighten the desperation of the longing. *When shall I come and see the face of God?* This I desire, he is saying, the time when I will be able to come and be present to you and appear in your presence. Now, the implication of the remark was more in keeping with the concept of Jews, who believed that God was present only in the temple and he would not be present to him in any other way than if he were in that place.

My tears have become my bread night and day (v. 3): even my tears were completely unceasing. He referred to his tears as bread probably because of an insatiable appetite, since generally speaking, people in their consumption of bread when dining never have enough of it on account of the need and demand for sustenance, nature making them feel that way. | *As they say to*

---

1. It seems that from the time of Origen the deer's longing has been interpreted in the light of this zoological "datum," a naturally intense thirst heightened by a diet of snakes. Chrysostom and Theodoret cite both factors, while Diodore cites only the former. See Hill, "Psalm 41 (42)," 25–33.

2. The Antiochene text incorporates both terms "living" and "strong," as Chrysostom and Theodoret indicate, although the former knows also a form of the LXX without the latter term (Dahood [*Psalms,* 1:256] maintains that the Hebrew is susceptible of both meanings). It is not clear whether Theodore's text includes both terms.

4ᵇ. Ἐν τῷ λέγεσθαί μοι καθ᾽ ἑκάστην ἡμέραν Ποῦ ἐστιν ὁ Θεός σου. Παρεσκεύασε γάρ με οὕτως διακεῖσθαι τὰ παρὰ τῶν ἐχθρῶν ῥήματα ὀνειδιζόντων τὴν παρά σου βοήθειαν καὶ λεγόντων Ποῦ ὁ Θεὸς ἐφ᾽ ᾧ καυχᾶσθε, καὶ ποῦ ἐφ᾽ ᾧ πεποίθατε;

5ᵃ. Ταῦτα ἐμνήσθην, καὶ ἐξέχεα ἐπ᾽ ἐμὲ τὴν ψυχήν μου. Ταῦτα ἃ 5 ἐξῆς μέλλει λέγειν. Ἀκούων γάρ φησι παρὰ τῶν ἐχθρῶν τοιαῦτα καὶ ὑπομιμνησκόμενος τῶν παλαιῶν, διεχεόμην ἅπας καὶ διελυόμην τὴν ψυχὴν ὑπὸ τοῦ μεγέθους τῆς ἀθυμίας. Οὕτω λέγει Σύμμαχος Ἀναπολῶν, διέχεα ἐπ᾽ ἐμαυτόν. Ποῖα δὲ ὧν ὑπομιμνησκόμενος ἠθύμεις;

5ᵇ⁻ᶜ. Ὅτι διελεύσομαι ἐν τόπῳ σκηνῆς θαυμαστῆς ἕως τοῦ οἴκου τοῦ 10 Θεοῦ, ἐν φωνῇ ἀγαλλιάσεως καὶ ἐξομολογήσεως, ἤχου ἑορτάζοντος. Σκηνὴν θαυμαστὴν καλεῖ τὸν τοῦ Θεοῦ ναόν, τόπον δὲ σκηνῆς τὰ Ἱεροσόλυμα ἤτοι τὸ ὄρος ἐν ᾧπερ ὁ ναὸς ᾠκοδόμητο. Ἠθύμουν οὖν φησιν ὑπομιμνησκόμενος τῶν παλαιῶν, διεχεόμην ὑπομιμνησκόμενος ὅπως πρὸ τούτου παραγινόμενοι ἐν τοῖς Ἱεροσολύμοις εἰσίῃ|μεν ἕως καὶ αὐτοῦ τοῦ οἴκου σου, μετὰ μεγάλης 15 φωνῆς εὐφραινόμενοι καὶ μετὰ εὐχαριστίας ἣν ἀνεπέμπομεν μετὰ πολλοῦ τοῦ ἤχου ἐν ταῖς ἑορταῖς· καὶ γὰρ ἐν ταῖς ἑορταῖς ὁ νόμος προσέταττε συνεῖναι ὁμοθυμαδὸν ἅπαντας. Τοῦ δὲ ἤχου εἶπεν, ἵνα δείξῃ τὸ πλῆθος τῶν ἐν ταῖς ἑορταῖς συνιόντων, ἀφ᾽ ὧν ἀπετελεῖτο δηλονότι μέγας ἦχος τῆς φωνῆς· τὸ γὰρ ἤχου ἑορτάζοντος Σύμμαχος λέγει πλῆθος πανηγυρι- 20 ζόντων. Βούλεται οὖν εἰπεῖν ὅτι δακρύων διετέλουν ἀκούων μὲν τῶν καθ᾽ ἑκάστην ἡμέραν λεγομένων ὑπὸ τῶν ἐχθρῶν διὰ τὰς κατεχούσας ἡμᾶς συμφοράς· ὑπομιμνησκόμενος δὲ ἐν οἵᾳ ἦμεν δόξῃ τὸ παλαιόν, — ὅτε συνιόντες ἐν Ἱεροσολύμοις ἅπαντες κατὰ ταὐτὸν ἐν ταῖς ἑορταῖς εἰσήμεν εἰς τὸν οἶκον τὸν σόν, μετὰ εὐφροσύνης καὶ μεγέθους φωνῆς καὶ μετὰ 25 ἤχου πολλοῦ ἀναπέμποντές σοι τὰς εὐχαριστίας ὑπὲρ τῶν εἰς ἡμᾶς ἀγαθῶν, καὶ οὕτω τὴν ἑορτὴν μετὰ πολλῆς ἐπιτελοῦντες τῆς φαιδρότητος, — ἀποβλέπων οὖν πρὸς τὴν ἀποβολὴν ἠθύμουν εἰκότως. Βούλεται δὲ

8-9 Σύμμαχος — ἠθύμεις affert L (p. 777, 34-36).   15-19 cf. L (p. 777, 36-42); eadem fere praebet Paraphrasis (p. 775).

Aᵉ 4ᵇ (p. 239, 23-25): Est uox exprobrantium mihi adiutorium tuum atque dicentium: Vbi est deus, in quo gloriari et confidire solebas? 6-7 (p. 239, 26-27): Cum ista scilicet audiens meminissem status prioris. 14-19 (p. 240, 1-8): Deficiebam (dificebam ms) igitur, inquit, riminiscens quemadmodum ante hoc tempus venientes Hirusolimam ingredebamur usque in domum tuam cum uoce magna laetantes et cum actionibus gratiarum, quas indisinenter in dierum sollemnitatibus tibi solebamus offerre.

me each day, Where is your God? I was made to feel this way by the words of the foe taunting me about help from you, and saying, Where is the God in whom you boast, and where is the one in whom you trust?

These things I remembered, and I poured out my soul upon me (v. 4). This is what he intends to go on and say: Listening to such things from the foe and recalling the things of yore, I went completely to pieces and was distraught in soul under the magnitude of my despair. Symmachus likewise says, "When I thought about it, I went to pieces in myself." What were the things you were distressed to recall? *Because I shall arrive at the place of the wonderful tabernacle as far as the house of God, with sounds of exultation and praise, a roar of celebration.* By *wonderful tabernacle* he refers to God's temple, and by *place of the tabernacle* to Jerusalem or the mountain on which the temple was built. So he is saying, I was distressed to recall the days of yore; I went to pieces remembering how before this, when we were in Jerusalem, we went right into your house, exulting in a loud voice and with thanksgiving that we offered with a loud cry on the festivals, the law requiring that everyone come together with one accord on the festivals. He mentioned the *roar* to bring out the vast number of those assembling on the festivals, from whom obviously arose the mighty sound of a roar, Symmachus speaking of *a roar of celebration* as "a vast number of celebrants." His meaning is, then, I began to weep when I heard what was said each day by the foe on account of the calamity gripping us; but on recalling the glory we enjoyed of old, when everyone assembled in Jerusalem at the same time on the festivals and entered your house, with joy and a loud cry and a great roar offering you thanksgiving for the good things done to us, and thus observing the feast with great splendor, I naturally was discouraged by considering the loss. His intention is | to emphasize the many reasons he has to ask to return:

δεῖξαι πολλὰς τὰς αἰτίας δι' ἃς ἐπανελθεῖν ἀξιοῖ· ὅτι τε ποθεῖ σφόδρα
παραστῆναι Θεῷ ἐν τοῖς Ἱεροσολύμοις γεγονώς, καὶ ὅτι ἐν πολλοῖς ἐξη-
τάσθη κακοῖς, καὶ ὅτι ὀνειδιζόμενος ὑπὸ τῶν ἐχθρῶν διετέλει, καὶ ὅτι πόθον
ἔχουσι τῆς ἐπανόδου ἵνα ἐν τοῖς οἰκείοις διάγοντες ἑορτάζωσι τῷ Θεῷ.

5   6ᵃ. Ἵνα τί περίλυπος εἶ, ἡ ψυχή, καὶ ἵνα τί συνταράσσεις με; Εἶτά
φησι μετὰ τὴν ἐπὶ τούτοις ἀθυμίαν ἔλεγον κατ' ἐμαυ|τὸν Τίνος ἕνεκεν
οὕτως ἀθυμεῖς, καὶ τίνος ἕνεκεν οὕτω συνταράττῃ;

6ᵇ. Ἤλπισον ἐπὶ τὸν Θεόν, ὅτι ἐξομολογήσομαι αὐτῷ. Ἐξομολογήσομαι,
τουτέστιν εὐχαριστήσω. Καταλιπὼν οὖν φησι τὴν ἀθυμίαν, μᾶλλον ἔλπισον
10 ἐπὶ τὸν Θεὸν ὅτι πάντως αὐτῷ εὐχαριστήσω, ἀντὶ τοῦ ὅτι τεύξομαι τῶν
ἀγαθῶν· τυχὼν γάρ τινος, τότε πάντως ἤμελλεν ὑπὲρ τῶν δοθέντων εὐχαριστεῖν. Ἐπειδὴ εἶπεν ἄνω ὅτι Εἰσῄειν εἰς τὸν ναὸν ἐν φωνῇ ἀγαλλιάσεως
καὶ ἐξομολογήσεως, ἐπήγαγεν ὅτι ἐξομολογήσομαι αὐτῷ, ἀντὶ τοῦ Ἤλπισον
ὅτι πάλιν σοι τοῦτο προσγενήσεται;

15 6ᶜ. Σωτήριον τοῦ προσώπου μου ὁ Θεός μου. Ἐλπίσεις γὰρ δικαίως,
ἐπειδὴ αὐτός ἐστιν ὁ δεσπότης μου καὶ ὁ τὴν σωτηρίαν μοι παρεχόμενος.

7ᵃ. Πρὸς ἐμαυτὸν ἡ ψυχή μου ἐταράχθη. Καὶ ὅμως φησὶν οὐδὲν ὠφέ-
λουν ἐμαυτὸν παρακαλεῖν ἐσπουδακὼς τοῖς ῥήμασι τούτοις· πάλιν γὰρ
πρὸς ἐμαυτὸν ἐταραττόμην, τουτέστιν αὐτὴ πάλιν ἐφ' ἑαυτῆς ἡ ψυχή μου
20 τοῖς οἰκείοις λογισμοῖς ἐταράττετο. Πῶς καὶ τίνα τρόπον;

7ᵇ. Μνησθήσομαί σου ἐκ γῆς Ἰορδάνου καὶ Ἑρμωνιείμ, ἀπὸ ὄρους μικροῦ.
Ὑπεμιμνησκόμην γὰρ πάλιν τοῦ Ἰορδάνου, καὶ τῆς γῆς, καὶ τοῦ ὄρους τοῦ
Ἀερμών — Ἑρμωνιείμ γὰρ καλεῖ τὸ Ἀερμών. Προσυπακούεται οὖν τὸ « διὰ

19-20 L (p. 778, 20): κατὰ λογισμὸν ἐταραττόμην; cf. Paraphrasis (p. 775): Ἀλλὰ
μετὰ τοὺς λογισμοὺς τούτους φησὶ πάλιν ἐταραττόμην.   22-264, 2 cf. THEODORETUS
(1172 C 10-13).

Aᵉ 1-4 (p. 240, 8-16): Ad inpetrandi autem facilitatem proficit enumeratio
tantarum causarum, quia et desideraret (dissideraret ms) adsistere Deo Hirusolimis, et quia mala iam multa perpessus sit, et quia inimicorum iniuria induratur
exprobrationibus, uel quia ideo desideraret (dissid — ms) reuersionem ut sol-
lemnitates sacras instauraret.   9 (p. 240, 17): Id est, iterum gratias agam.
12-14 (p. 240, 18-22): Qui supra dixerat *Quoniam ingrediebar templum in
uoce exultationis*, bene nunc subiecit *quia confitebor illi*, id est: *Spera*, anima,
quia rursus talia qualium reminiscemur consequantur.   6ᶜ (p. 240, 23-24):
Ac si diceret: Merito in eum *spera*, anima, quia ipse est qui largitur salutem.
7ᵃ (p. 240, 25-29): Et tamen, inquit, nihil ad consulationem meam in istis sermonibus promouebar, quando rursus anima mea... se ipsa turbabat.

that he deeply longs to be present to God in Jerusalem; that he is caught up in many troubles; that he is constantly taunted by the foe; and that he has a desire for return so that when living at home, they may celebrate a festival to God.

Why are you disconsolate, O soul, and why do you disturb me? (v. 5). He then says, After the discouragement at this I said to myself, Why are you so discouraged, and why so disturbed? *Hope in God, because I shall confess to him,* meaning by *I shall confess,* I shall give thanks. So he is saying, Setting aside discouragement, instead hope in God, because I shall definitely give thanks to him—that is, Because I shall be granted good things (since once he was granted something, he then definitely intended to give thanks for what was given). Since he had said above, I went into the temple *with sounds of exultation and praise,* he went on to say *I shall confess to him*—that is, Have hope, because this will once more be accorded you. *My personal savior is my God:* you will be justified in hoping, because he is the one who is my Lord and the one who provides me with salvation.

My soul is confused within itself (v. 6): yet it did me no good to console myself with my attention to these words; once again I began to be disturbed in myself—that is, My very soul was disturbed in itself by its own thoughts. How and in what fashion? *Hence,*[3] *I shall remember you from the land of Jordan and Hermonim, from a small mountain:* I began to remember Jordan again, the land, and Mount Hermon (by *Hermonim* referring to Hermon). So we should understand him to say that the reason was | that he remem-

---

3. Theodoret's text (and apparently Diodore's) begins v. 6b with the term "Hence," evidently not in Theodore's text, but (he says) to be supposed. Symmachus also includes it.

τοῦτο » ὅτι ὑπεμιμνήσκετο τοῦ Ἰορδάνου καὶ τῆς γῆς· – ἵνα εἴπῃ | τῆς γῆς τῆς
ἐπαγγελίας. Ἠθύμουν γὰρ ἐννοῶν ὅτι κεχώρισμαι τῶν οἰκείων ἀπὸ τοῦ ὄρους
καὶ ἀπὸ τοῦ ποταμοῦ τοῦ ἐν τοῖς τόποις, βουλόμενος εἰπεῖν τὴν πᾶσαν
γῆν. Ἔδειξε δὲ τοῦ πόθου τὴν ἐπίτασιν εἰπὼν ὄρους μικροῦ, ἐπειδὴ τὰ
μικρὰ μάλιστα ποθεινὰ ἡμῖν καθέστηκεν, — ὡς ἄν τις εἴποι « ἐκείνου τοῦ   5
μικροῦ ὡραίου ».

8ª. Ἄβυσσος ἄβυσσον ἐπικαλεῖται εἰς φωνὴν τῶν καταρρακτῶν σου.
Ἐταραττόμην οὖν ὑπομιμνησκόμενός τε ἐκείνων καὶ ἀποβλέπων εἰς τὰ περιέχοντα κακά· ἄβυσσον δὲ καλεῖ τὸ ἄπειρον πλῆθος τῶν στρατιωτῶν.
Τοῦτο οὖν λέγει, ὅτι πλήθη στρατιωτῶν ἀλλήλοις συμμαχοῦντα συναθροί-   10
ζονται κατ' ἐμοῦ διὰ τὸ μέγεθος τῆς ὀργῆς τῆς σῆς. Τὸ γὰρ ἐπικαλεῖται
εἶπεν, ἀντὶ τοῦ Στρατιὰ μεγίστη ἑτέραν ὁμοίαν ἐπικαλεσαμένη εἰς συμμαχίαν οὕτως ὥρμησε κατ' ἐμοῦ· τοῦτο δὲ ὑφίσταμαι διὰ τό σέ μοι ὀργί-
ζεσθαι. Καλῶς δὲ τοῦ Θεοῦ τὴν ὀργὴν ἐνταῦθα κ α τ α ρ ρ ά κ τ α ς ἐκάλεσεν,
ἐπειδὴ ἄβυσσον εἶπε τῶν στρατιωτῶν τὸ πλῆθος· οἱ γὰρ τοῦ οὐρανοῦ   15
καταρράκται ἀφεθέντες δηλονότι ἀβύσσους καὶ κατακλυσμὸν ἐργάζονται,
ὥσπερ καὶ ἐπὶ τοῦ Νῶε.

8ᵇ. Πάντες οἱ μετεωρισμοί σου καὶ τὰ κύματά σου ἐπ' ἐμὲ διῆλθον.
Ἠκολούθησε τῇ οἰκείᾳ σωματοποιήσει συνήθως. Ἐπειδὴ γὰρ ἀβύσσους
ὠνόμασε μεταφορικῶς, ὡς ἐπὶ θαλάσσης εἶπεν Οἱ μετεωρισμοί σου καὶ τὰ   20
κύματά σου, ἵνα εἴπῃ ὅτι Τοῦτο ὅλον τὸ πλῆθος καὶ ἡ τοῦ πλήθους ἐπ-
ανάστασις κατ' ἐμοῦ συνήχθη. Τοῦ Θεοῦ δὲ εἶπε τοὺς μετεωρισμοὺς καὶ
τὰ κύματα, ὡς τῇ αὐτοῦ ὀργῇ τῆς ἐπαναστάσεως τοῦ πλήθους γεγενημένης.

9ª. Ἡμέρας ἐντελεῖται Κύριος τὸ ἔλεος αὐτοῦ, καὶ νυκτὸς δηλώσει παρ'
ἐμοί. Ἀλλ' ἐνενόουν πάλιν ὅτι καὶ τοσούτων ὄντων τῶν περιεχόντων   25

4-6 cf. Paraphrasis (p. 775).   8ª cf. Paraphrasis (p. 775).   9ª cf. L (p. 779,
27. 29-33) atque Paraphrasis (p. 775).

Aᵉ 1-6 (p. 241, 1-8): Commemoratione montis et fluminis totam terram repromisionis ostendit. Et Hermonin a monte modico: Expresit autem hoc magnitudinem desiderii, dicens a monte modico, quia nobis ea quae parua sunt uidentur quodam modo dulciora, ut si quis dicat: Illius collis breuiculi atque
pulcherrimi disiderium ferre uix possum.   9-11 (p. 241, 9-12): Ac si diciret:
Turmae militum et magnus exercitus, aliis copiis in auxilium convocatis, inruit
super me.   14-17 (p. 241, 12-15): Bene enim iram Dei catarectas vocat, quia
hostium agmina abysos appellauerat; quae, cum dimittuntur, sollent diluuium
creare.   8ᵇ (p. 241, 21-242, 2): Secutus est eam, quam instituerat comparatio-
nem figurae ut, quia abyssos (abysossos ms) nominauerat hostiles exercitus, per
eadem trationem (sic) tanquam de mari loqueretur; excelsa et fluctus adiecit,
ut inimicorum copias in suum exitium conglobatas ostenderet.

bered Jordan and the land—that is, the land of promise. I was discouraged, he is saying, by the thought that I was cut off from my own country, from the mountain and the river in those places (meaning the whole land). Now, he highlighted the depth of longing by mention of *a small mountain,* since small things are particularly desirable to us, as if to say, "that charming little thing."[4]

Deep calls on deep to the sound of your cataracts (v. 7): so I was disturbed when I recalled them and caught sight of the impending troubles (*deep* referring to the unparalleled number of troops). So he means, Vast numbers of troops allied with one another assemble against me as a result of the intensity of your wrath (*calls on* meaning, A mighty army called on another of similar size to join forces and thus advanced against me, and I submit to it on account of your being angry with me). He was right to refer to God's wrath here as *cataracts,* since he called the vast number of the soldiers *deep:* the cataracts of heaven, when released, obviously cause depths and flooding, as in the case of Noah. *All your heights and your billows have passed over me.* As usual, he continued the figure: since he had used *abyss* metaphorically, he said, as if of the sea, *your heights and your billows*—in other words, This complete horde and the assault of the horde combined against me. He called them God's heights and billows, since the assault of the horde was launched by his wrath.

By day the Lord will show his mercy, and by night his song is with me (v. 8): I considered further that though the impending troubles are so numerous, |

---

4. An appealing argument (of Diodore's) for inclusion of the LXX's "small mountain." In fact, however, the LXX is thus reading a form similar to the *hapax legomenon* in the Hebrew, generally rendered "Mount Miszar," thought to be at the foot of Mount Hermon.

κακῶν, εὐχερές σοι σφόδρα τὴν λύσιν παρασχεῖν. Ἐὰν γὰρ ἐν ἡμέρᾳ προστάξῃς τὴν φιλανθρωπίαν τὴν εἰς ἡμᾶς, τουτέστι τῶν κακῶν τὴν λύσιν γενέσθαι, οὕτως συντόμως γίνεται ὡς εὐθὺς ἀγαθῶν ἀπολαύσαντας διὰ τῆς ἐπερχομένης νυκτὸς ᾄδοντάς σοι ὕμνους ὑπὲρ τῶν γεγενημένων ἀναπέμπον-
5 τας διατελεῖν. Τοῦ Θεοῦ οὖν τὸ ἔλεος ἐντειλαμένου ἐν ἡμέρᾳ, εὐθὺς ἐν τῇ νυκτὶ ᾠδὴ αὐτοῦ ἐστι παρ' ἐμοί, — ἵνα εἴπῃ ὅτι Οὕτω συντόμως ἔσται τοῦ προστάγματος αὐτοῦ ἡ ἐκπλήρωσις, ὥστε ἐν ἡμέρᾳ προστάξαντος ἐξεῖναί | μοι ᾄδειν ἐν νυκτὶ ὑπὲρ τῶν γεγενημένων ἀγαθῶν παρ' ἐμοί.

9ᵇ. Προσευχὴ τῷ Θεῷ τῆς ζωῆς μου. Τοῦτό φησι πεπεισμένως ἀεὶ
10 ἔσχον παρ' ἐμαυτῷ τὴν προσευχήν σου, τουτέστιν Οὐδὲ ἐν ταῖς συμφοραῖς ἀπέβαλον τὸ προσεύχεσθαί σοι προθυμίᾳ ἀσαλεύτῳ.

10ᵃ. Ἐρῶ τῷ Θεῷ· Ἀντιλήμπτωρ μου εἶ, διὰ τί μου ἐπελάθου; Διετέλουν δὲ ἑκάστοτε προσευχόμενος καὶ λέγων ὅτι βοηθός μου εἶ, καὶ μὴ
ποιήσῃς μου λήθην.

15 10ᵇ-11ᵃ. Ἵνα τί σκυθρωπάζων πορεύομαι ἐν τῷ ἐκθλίβειν τὸν ἐχθρόν
μου, ἐν τῷ καταθλάσαι τὰ ὀστᾶ μου; Μηδὲ καταλίπῃς με ἐν σκυθρωπότητι
διάγοντα καὶ θλιβόμενον ὑπὸ τοῦ ἐχθροῦ καὶ καταθλώμενον ὑπ' αὐτοῦ τὰ
ὀστᾶ, ἵνα εἴπῃ Καταδαπανηθέντα τὴν ἰσχὺν ὑπὸ τοῦ ἐχθροῦ ταῖς συμφοραῖς μὴ περιΐδῃς.

20 11ᵇ. Ἐν τῷ λέγειν αὐτούς μοι καθ' ἑκάστην ἡμέραν Ποῦ ἐστιν ὁ θεός
σου; Ἀλλὰ καὶ ἑκάστοτέ μοί φησιν ὀνειδίζοντες οἱ ἐχθροὶ διατελοῦσιν ἐπὶ
τῇ σῇ προστασίᾳ, λέγοντες Ποῦ ἐστιν ὁ θεός; Τὸ ἐν τῷ αὐτοὺς λέγειν μοι
Σύμμαχος λέγοντές μοι, τουτέστιν ὠνείδιζόν με τοῦτό μοι λέγοντες. Ὥστε
φησὶ καὶ ἐπειδὴ αὐτός μοι γέγονας προστάτης ἀεί, καὶ διὰ τὸ πλῆθος τῶν
25 κακῶν καὶ διὰ τὰς θλίψεις τὰς παρὰ τῶν ἐχθρῶν καὶ ὀνείδων τῶν ἐπί
σοι, ταχέως τῶν περιεχόντων ἀπαλλάξας κακῶν, μὴ περιΐδῃς ἐν τοσαύταις
καθεστῶτα συμφοραῖς. Ταῦτα δὲ ὅλα πρὸς τὸ Παρ' ἐμοὶ ἡ προσευχὴ τῷ
Θεῷ τῆς ζωῆς μου ἀπέδωκεν, ἵνα εἴπῃ Τά σοι ἀρεστὰ ἀεὶ προσευχόμενος
καὶ ἐν ταῖς συμφοραῖς διετέλουν.

27-28 v. 9ᵇ.

Aᵉ 3-5 (p. 242, 3-8): Declaruit uidilicet Tam uelox est diuinae iusionis in-
pletio ut, illo per diem de mea absolutione iubente, consecuta statim nox
me faciet pro reddenda libertate uel liberatione gratulari.   9ᵇ (p. 242,
9-11): Huic fidei semper innexus habui apud me studium supplicandi tibi.
16-18 (p. 242, 15-17): Vt diceret Ne sinas quicquid in me firmitatis est hostili
inmanitate consumi.   27-29 (p. 242, 17-21): Haec omnia ad illum uorsum
reddit, in quo dixerat *Apud me oratio Deo uitae meae*, ac si diceret: Haec
sunt, quae tibi semper suplicans in calamitatibus ingerebam.

it is very easy for you to provide a solution; if by day you bid lovingkindness to be shown us—in other words, relief from the troubles to occur—it happens so quickly that immediately those in receipt of good things set about singing through the night and offering hymns of praise to you for what has happened. When God enjoins mercy by day, then, immediately by night *his song is with me,*[5] as if to say, So prompt will be the discharge of his command that, with his command given by day, it is possible for me to sing by night of the good things done to me. *A prayer to the God of my life:* trusting in this, I always had your prayer with me—that is, Even in calamities I did not desist from praying to you with unshaken zeal.

I shall say to God, You are my support: why have you forgotten me? (v. 9). I continued, he says, each time praying and saying, You are my help; do not forget me. *Why do I go about with my face downcast while the foe afflicts me by trampling on my bones?* (vv. 9–10). Why do you leave me living in a downcast state, afflicted by the foe, my bones trampled on by him? That is to say, Do not ignore my strength expended by the foe in my misfortunes. *By their saying to me each day, Where is your God?* Instead, each day, he is saying, the foe continues taunting me about your support with the jibe *Where is God?* For *By their saying to me,* Symmachus has "Saying to me"—that is, They mocked me by saying this. And so, since you were always my support, and on account of the multitude of the troubles and the tribulations from the foe and the taunts about you, quickly rid me of the troubles besetting me and do not ignore me in such awful calamities. Now, all this is in response to the verse *A prayer from me to the God of my life,* as if to say, I continued constantly, even in calamities, to pray for what is pleasing to you. |

---

5. This is the reading of the Antiochene text, *pace* Devreesse, and of some other forms of the LXX.

12ᵃ·ᵇ. Ἵνα τί περίλυπος εἶ, ἡ ψυχή, καὶ ἵνα τί συνταράσσεις με; Ἔλπισον ἐπὶ τὸν Θεόν, ὅτι ἐξομολογήσομαι αὐτῷ. Αἰτῶν δὲ ταῦτα παρά σου
παρεκάλουν ἐμαυτὸν ὥστε μὴ λυπεῖσθαι ἐπὶ τοῖς περιέχουσι κακοῖς,
ἐλπίζειν δὲ μᾶλλον πιστεύοντα ὅτι πάντως εἰσακουσθήσομαι καὶ ἀπαλλα-
γήσομαι τῶν κακῶν, τεύξομαι δὲ τῶν ἀγαθῶν ὥστε καὶ εὐχαριστῆσαί σοι   5
ἐπὶ τοῖς παρά σου χορηγουμένοις ἀγαθοῖς.

12ᶜ. Σωτήριον τοῦ προσώπου μου ὁ Θεός μου. Ἐπίστευον δὲ ὅτι πάντως παρέξεις, ἐπειδὴ αὐτὸς εἶ ἡ σωτηρία μου καὶ ὁ δεσπότης μου. Τὸ δὲ
τοῦ προσώπου μου, ἵνα εἴπῃ τῆς ὑπολήψεώς μου, τῆς δόξης μου, ἀντὶ τοῦ
Αὐτὸς εἶ ὁ ταῦτά μοι παρέχων.   10

PSALMVS XLII

Τὰ κατὰ τὸν λαὸν τὸν ἐν Βαβυλῶνι κατεχόμενον καὶ ἐνταῦθα προφητεύει αἰτοῦντα τῶν κακῶν τὴν ἀπαλλαγήν.

1ᵃ. Κρῖνόν μοι, ὁ Θεός, καὶ δίκασον τὴν δίκην μου ἐξ ἔθνους οὐχ ὁσίου.
Θεασάμενός φησιν ὅσα ἠδίκημαι ὑπὸ τῶν κατεχόντων τούτων τῶν ἀνοσίων   15
καὶ βεβήλων, ἐξέτασιν ποιῆσαι τῶν κατ' ἐμὲ καὶ τὰ πρέποντα ἐφ' οἷς
ἠδίκημαι παρ' αὐτῶν διάπραξαι. Εἰ γὰρ καὶ δι' ἁμαρτίας παθεῖν αὐτοὺς
συνεχώρησεν ὁ Θεός, ἀλλ' οὖν γε οὐκ ἀνεύθυνοι οἱ Βαβυλώνιοι ἐφ' οἷς
αὐτοὺς διέθηκαν· οὐ γὰρ ἐκεῖνος πρᾶξαι ἠνάγκασεν ἅπερ εἰς τὸν λαὸν
διεπράξαντο κακά, ἀλλὰ τούτοις συνεχώρησεν οὐ βοηθήσας αὐτοῖς διὰ τὰς   20
ἁμαρτίας. Ἔδειξε δὲ τῷ εἰπεῖν ἀνοσίους, ὅτι ἄξιοι τιμωρίας καὶ διὰ τὸν
τρόπον καὶ διὰ τὴν εἰς αὐτοὺς ἀδικίαν.

1ᵇ. Ἀπὸ ἀνθρώπου ἀδίκου καὶ δολίου ῥῦσαί με. Ἀνθρώπου, τουτέστιν
ἀνθρώπων τούτων τῶν δολίων καὶ ἀδίκων, ἀπάλλαξόν με.

12-13 Τὰ κατὰ τὸν λαὸν — ἀπαλλαγήν praebent Paris. 139, f. 106ᵛ atque Vat. 1682
f. 156ᵛ, et addunt: ποικίλλει γὰρ τὰ σχήματα, μιᾶς οὔσης τῆς ὑποθέσεως τῆς κατὰ τὴν
αἰχμαλωσίαν, καί ποτε μὲν ὡς ἔτι ὄντων ἐν τοῖς κακοῖς, ποτὲ δὲ ὡς ἐλπιζόντων ἀπαλλαγήσεσθαι, καὶ πάλιν ὡς ἀπαλλαγέντων τελείως καὶ τὰ τοιαῦτα λέγει.

Aᵉ 12ᵃ·ᵇ (p. 242, 23-243, 3): Cum te prece sedula conuenirem, me tamen
tali oratione solabar (solebar ms), quoniam scilicet exaudires orantem et bonorum
mihi agenti successu copiam tibi gratias largieris.   17-22 (p. 243, 16-20): Nos
quippe reos soli tibi iniustissime Babilonii crudeliterque detenerunt, digni
supplicio etiam ob profanitatem.   1ᵇ (p. 243, 21-23): Pro hominibus uidilicet;
ab istis me libera, quos plenos esse doli iniquitatisque consideras.

Why are you disconsolate, O soul, and why do you disturb me? Hope in God, because I shall confess to him (v. 11): requesting this of you, I comforted myself so as not to grieve over the troubles enveloping me, trusting rather to have hope that I will doubtless be hearkened to and freed from the troubles, and will attain the good things so as to give thanks to you for the good things provided by you. *My personal savior is my God:* I trusted that you would doubtless meet my request, since you personally are my salvation and my Lord (the term *personal savior*[6] meaning "my support, my glory"—in other words, It is you yourself who provides me with this).

PSALM 43

He prophesies here, too, the situation of the people held in Babylon, who are asking for release from the troubles. *Give judgment for me, O God, and decide in my favor against a nation that is not holy* (v. 1): perceiving the extent to which I have been wronged by the unholy and profane captors, conduct a trial of those who are against me and do what befits the wrongs I suffered from them. After all, even if God allowed them to suffer for their sins, the Babylonians still were not guiltless of the way they treated them. In fact, he did not oblige them to do the evil things they perpetrated against the people: he permitted them by not helping them on account of their sins. By saying *unholy,* he brought out that they deserved punishment on account both of their behavior and of their injustice to them. *From an unjust and deceitful person rescue me: person*—that is to say, Free me from these deceitful and unjust people. |

---

6. Modern commentators also wrestle with the term in the Hebrew, found also in v. 5.

2ᵃ. Ὅτι σὺ εἶ ὁ Θεὸς κραταίωμά μου. Αἴτω δὲ ταῦτά φησι παρά σου εὐλόγως, ἐπειδὴ σὺ εἶ ὁ δεσπότης μου, ὁ ποιητής μου, ἡ ἰσχυροποίησίς μου — ἀντὶ τοῦ Τῇ σῇ βοηθείᾳ κρατύνομαι ἀεὶ καὶ ἰσχυρὸς δείκνυμαι.

2ᵇ. Ἵνα τί ἀπώσω με; Ὁπότε τοίνυν αὐτὸς εἶ ὁ τὰ πάντα μοι παρέ-
5 χων, μὴ καταλίπῃς οὐκ ἔχοντα παρ' ἑτέρου βοήθειαν.

2ᶜ. Καὶ ἵνα τί σκυθρωπάζων πορεύομαι ἐν τῷ ἐκθλίβειν τὸν ἐχθρόν μου; Μηδὲ ἐάσῃς με ἐν σκυθρωπότητι διατελεῖν ὑπὸ τῶν ἐχθρῶν ἐκθλιβόμενον καὶ τοιαῦτα πάσχοντα. Τὸ γὰρ ἵνα τί οὐχ ὡς αἰτιώμενος λέγει, ἀλλ' ἰδίωμά ἐστι τοῦτο τῆς γραφῆς καὶ μάλιστα τοῦ μακαρίου Δαυίδ· ἐπειδὴ γὰρ ἐν
10 τοῖς μεγάλοις αἰτιώμεθα κακοῖς, κέχρηται τῇ αἰτιατικῇ φωνῇ πρὸς παράσ-
τασιν τοῦ μεγέθους τῆς συμφορᾶς.

3ᵃ. Ἐξαπόστειλον τὸ φῶς σου καὶ τὴν ἀλήθειάν σου. Ἐπειδὴ σκότος καλεῖ τὰς συμφοράς, φῶς καλεῖ τοῦ Θεοῦ τὴν ἀντίληψιν ὡς τῶν συμφορῶν ἀπαλλάττουσαν, — παράσχου σου τοίνυν τὴν ἀντίληψιν. Τὸ δὲ καὶ τὴν
15 ἀλήθειάν σου συνήθως, τουτέστι τὴν βεβαίαν καὶ ἀληθῶς εὐεργετεῖν δυναμένην.

3ᵇ·ᶜ. Αὐτά με ὡδήγησε καὶ ἤγαγέν με εἰς ὄρος ἅγιόν σου καὶ εἰς τὰ σκηνώματά σου. Ὡδήγησε καὶ ἤγαγεν, ἀντὶ τοῦ ὁδηγήσει καὶ ἄξει (ἐπεὶ πῶς λέγει ἐξαπόστειλον. εἰ ὡδήγησε;) δῆλον οὖν ὅτι ἐναλλαγὴ χρόνου ἀπὸ τῆς ἑρμηνείας γεγένηται. Βούλεται οὖν εἰπεῖν ὅτι Τοῦτό μοι παράσχου τὴν
20 βεβαίαν σου ἀντίληψιν· τοῦτο γὰρ δύναταί με καὶ | τῶν κακῶν ἀπαλλάξαι τῶν περικειμένων καὶ ἀγαγεῖν εἰς τὰ Ἱεροσόλυμα. Ὄρος γὰρ ἅγιον καλεῖ τὸ Σιών, ἐφ' ᾧ ᾠκοδόμητο ἥ τε πόλις καὶ ὁ ναός, — καὶ σκηνώματα Θεοῦ τὴν πόλιν καὶ αὐτὸν τὸν ναὸν βούλεται εἰπεῖν, τὰ Ἱεροσόλυμα.

12-14 L (p. 792, 37-39): Ἡ τὰς συμφορὰς ὀνομάσας σκότος, φῶς καλεῖ τὴν τούτων
ἀπαλλαγήν.   18 L (p. 792, 30-31): Ἐνταῦθα τὸν χρόνον ἐνήλλαξαν οἱ Ἑβδομήκοντα.
21-22 (ib. 43): εἰς ὄρος ἅγιόν σου, τουτέστιν εἰς τὴν Σιών.

Aᵉ 2-3 (p. 243, 24-27): Tuo quippe adiutorio ego semper fortis efficior, cuius etiam bonitate creatus sum.   2ᵇ (p. 243, 27-30): Cum igitur tu sis qui haec mihi uniuersa contribuis, ne dirilinquas me nullo ab alio adiuuari praesto-
lantem.   8-11 (p. 244, 1-5): Idioma est Scripturae et eius propriae, ut quasi causatoria uoce, sub intentione tamen precandi, expraemat magnitudinem cala-
mitatis.   3ᵃ (p. 244, 6-9, 11-13): Quia calamitatem tenebras uocat, conse-
quenter libertatem auxiliumque diuinum appellat lucem... more autem suo, ob iudicium firmitatis, difensioni et luci copulat ueritatem.   21-23 (p. 244, 14-16): Sion, in quo templum est; solita hic temporum quoque in declinatione commotatio est.

Because you, O God, are my force (v. 2): it is reasonable for me to ask this of you, since you are my Lord, my maker, my champion—in other words, I am made strong by your help and am shown to be strong. *Why do you repulse me?* Since it is you, then, who provides me with all this, do not abandon the one with no help from anyone else. *And why do I go about downcast while the enemy afflicts me?* Do not allow me to continue in a downcast state because afflicted by the foe and suffering such things. The term *why* he does not use by way of complaint; rather, it is an idiom of Scripture and especially of blessed David: since we complain in times of deep trouble, he adopts a plaintive tone to highlight the magnitude of the calamity.

Send forth your light and your truth (v. 3). Since he refers to the calamities as "darkness" and refers to God's support as "light" in that it frees from calamities, therefore he means, Provide support. The phrase *and your truth,* as usual, refers to support that is firm and truly capable of doing good. *They guided me and led me to your holy mountain and your tabernacles.* By *guided and led* he means "will guide and will lead," because how can he say *Send* if he had led? So it is clear that the change in tense happened in translation. His meaning is, then, Provide me with your firm support: it can free me even from the impending troubles and lead me to Jerusalem (by *holy mountain* referring to Sion, on which both city and temple were built, and by God's *tabernacles* referring to the city and the temple itself, Jerusalem). |

4ᵃ. Καὶ εἰσελεύσομαι πρὸς τὸ θυσιαστήριον τοῦ Θεοῦ. Τότε φησὶ τούτων τυχὼν καὶ ὑπ' αὐτῶν ὁδηγηθεὶς εἰς τὸν τόπον σου τὸν ἅγιον δυνήσομαι εἰσελθεῖν, ἔνθα κεῖται τὸ σὸν θυσιαστήριον.

4ᵇ. Πρὸς τὸν Θεὸν τὸν εὐφραίνοντα τὴν νεότητά μου. Τότε εἰσελεύσομαι
φησι πρός σε, τὸν ἐξ ἀρχαίου πολλήν μοι τὴν εὐφροσύνην παρεσχηκότα. 5
Νεότητα γὰρ τοῦ λαοῦ καλεῖ τοὺς προτέρους αὐτῶν· οὕτω καὶ ἐν τῷ Ἰεζεκιὴλ ὀνειδίζει αὐτοῖς τὴν ἐν νεότητι ἁμαρτίαν, περὶ τῶν ἐν Αἰγύπτῳ ἁμαρ-
τησάντων λέγων.

4ᶜ. Ἐξομολογήσομαί σοι, Κύριε ὁ Θεός μου, ἐν κιθάρᾳ. Ἐπανελθὼν δέ
φησιν ἀναπέμψω σοι τὰς εὐχαριστίας μετὰ κιθάρας. 10

5ᵃ. Ἵνα τί περίλυπος εἶ, ψυχή, καὶ ἵνα τί συνταράσσεις με; Παῦσαι
τοίνυν, ὦ ψυχή, φησι τῆς λύπης καὶ ἀπαλλάγηθι πάσης ταραχῆς.

5ᵇ. Ἔλπισον ἐπὶ τὸν Θεόν, ὅτι ἐξομολογήσομαι αὐτῷ. Καὶ μᾶλλον ἔλ-
πιζε τῷ Θεῷ, ὅτι παρέξει σοι τὴν βοήθειαν.

5ᶜ. Σωτήριον τοῦ προσώπου μου, ὁ Θεός μου. Ὅτι αὐτός ἐστιν ὁ σωτήρ 15
μου καὶ ὁ δεσπότης μου.

PSALMVS XLIII

Μετὰ τὴν ἀπὸ Βαβυλῶνος ἐπάνοδον πάλιν ἐν τοῖς οἰκείοις οἱ Ἰσραηλῖται γεγονότες καὶ τῶν ἐκ τῆς γῆς ἀπολαύσαντες ἀγαθῶν ἐξώκειλαν ἐπὶ
τὸ χεῖρον, ἀποστάντες μὲν τῆς τῶν προσηκόντων | ἐπιμελείας καὶ τῶν τῆς 20
ἀρετῆς κατορθωμάτων, πᾶσαν δὲ μετιόντες ἀδεῶς ἀτοπίαν. Κρατεῖ τοίνυν

7 Ezech. XXIII, 3   18 ss. cf. I Macc. I-III.

Eadem fere, etsi paullo strictius, praebent Ambros. C 98 sup. atque Vat.
gr. 1422 (ed. G. MERCATI, Varia Sacra, p. 111-112); latine, ultima sententia omissa,
apud Barbaro (p. 430-431).

Aᵉ 4ᵃ (p. 244, 19-22): Tunc, inquit, lucis et ueritatis tuae donis potitus
(putius ms) et ab ipsis deductus, in consecratos locos introeam.   5ᶜ (p. 245,
6-7): lpse enim est meus saluator et dominus.   Argumentum psalmi XLIII
(p. 245, 8-22): Post reditum de Babilone filii Israhel inmemores beneficiorum
Dei ad peccandi demum studia sunt reuersi. Ob quae facta meruerunt a Domino
relinqui et in dicionem uenire regis Antiochi; quo deterrente subditos et profa-
nante (profante ms) consecratos locos, emersit tandem Mathathias ultor uiolate
(uinolate ms) legis, Machabeorum pater, in quorum tempora hoc carmen format,
adflictiones eorum enumerans supplicationesque connectens. Cf. PSEUDO-BEDA
(709): Machabeorum pressuras propheta supplicationesque commemorat.

I shall go into the altar of God (v. 4): then, after attaining this and being led by them to your holy place, I shall be able to go into where your altar is situated. *To God, who brings joy to my youth:* I shall then go into you, who have provided me with great joy from of old. By the people's *youth* he refers to their forebears; thus, in Ezekiel also he reproaches them for their sin "in their youth," meaning those who sinned in Egypt.[1] *I shall confess to you on a lyre, Lord my God:* on return I shall offer you thanksgiving with a lyre. *Why are you disconsolate, O soul, and why do you disturb me?* (v. 5): so put an end, O soul, to grieving and be rid of all disturbance. *Hope in God, because I shall confess to him:* rather, hope in God, because he will provide you with help. *My personal savior is my God* because it is he who is my savior and my Lord.

PSALM 44

After the return from Babylon, when the Israelites once again were settled in their own country and enjoyed the good things from the land, they took a turn for the worse, forsaking attention to their duty and the practice of virtue, and having no qualms about pursuing every excess. At this point, then, |

---

1. Ezek 23:3.

αὐτῶν ἐντεῦθεν Ἀντίοχος ὁ Ἐπιφανὴς προσαγορευόμενος, καὶ διαφόροις
αὐτοὺς περιβαλὼν κακοῖς τέλος θύειν ἠνάγκαζε τοῖς αὐτῷ νενομισμένοις
θεοῖς· βωμὸν δὲ ἐν τῷ ναῷ καθιδρύσας ἐπ᾽ ὀνόματι τῶν οἰκείων δαιμόνων,
καὶ ἑτέρους τε πλείστους καθ᾽ ἑκάστην τε πόλιν καὶ τόπον ἀναστήσας ἐν
5　τῇ χώρᾳ τῶν Ἰσραηλιτῶν παραβαίνειν ἅπαντας τὸν πάτριον παρεσκεύαζε
νόμον. Καὶ δήποτε καὶ ἐφειστήκει μὲν ὁ ὑπὸ Ἀντιόχου ἀπεσταλμένος, θύειν
ἕκαστον ἀναγκάζων κατὰ τὸ πρόσταγμα τὸ βασιλικόν. Καὶ προσῆλθε δέ
τις Ἰσραηλίτης ὡς θύσων καὶ τῷ νόμῳ πειθαρχῶν τοῦ βασιλέως. Ἐνταῦθα
ζηλώσας Ματταθίας τις οὕτω προσαγορευόμενος τῷ νόμῳ, τόν τε πειθαρχῆ-
10　σαι τῷ προστάγματι σπεύσαντα τοῦ βασιλέως Ἰσραηλίτην καὶ θῦσαι
βουληθέντα ἀνεῖλε καὶ τὸν ἐξανύειν τὸ πρόσταγμα τὸ βασιλικὸν ἐσπουδακότα. Καὶ ἀγωνισάμενος λαμπρῶς ὑπέρ τε τοῦ οἰκείου ἔθνους καὶ τῶν
πατρῴων νόμων, οὕτω τελευτήσας παρέδωκε τὴν ἀρχὴν τοῖς ἰδίοις υἱοῖς,
Ἰούδᾳ τῷ ἐπιλεγομένῳ Μακκαβαίῳ καὶ τῆς ἐξουσίας τὸ πλέον δεδωκώς,
15　καὶ τὸ κατάρχειν τῶν τε πολέμων καὶ τῶν κινδύνων ἐγχειρίσας αὐτῷ ὡς
ἀνδρείῳ καὶ περὶ ταῦτα ἐπιτηδείως ἔχειν δυναμένῳ. Οἳ καὶ πολεμεῖν ὑπὲρ
τοῦ ἔθνους ἑλόμενοι καὶ ὑπὲρ τῶν νόμων τῶν τοῦ Θεοῦ, ἐν πολλοῖς καὶ
διαφόροις ἐξητάσθησαν κακοῖς, καὶ μεγίστους διανύσαντες πολέμους πρός
τε τοὺς Ἀντιόχου στρατηγοὺς καὶ τοὺς ἑξῆς διαδεξαμένους τὴν βασιλείαν,
20　μόλις ποτὲ χρόνοις πολλοῖς τῇ τοῦ Θεοῦ βοηθείᾳ τροπώσασθαι παντελῶς
τοὺς ἐχθροὺς ἠδυνήθησαν, | ἐξάρχοντος καὶ στρατηγοῦντος αὐτῶν ἐν τοῖς
πολέμοις κατὰ τὰς ἐντολὰς τοῦ πατρὸς Ἰούδα τοῦ καὶ Μακκαβαίου. Ὅθεν
δὴ καὶ Μακκαβαῖοι ἀπὸ τοῦ ἄρξαντος τῶν ὑπὲρ τοῦ ἔθνους πόνων ἐπε-
κλήθησαν οἱ ἐκ τοῦ γένους, κατὰ διαδοχὴν παρειληφότες καὶ τὴν ἀρχὴν τοῦ
25　ἔθνους καὶ τοὺς ὑπὲρ αὐτῆς πολέμους, ἐπειδὴ καὶ ἔθος ἦν παρὰ Ἰουδαίοις
ἀπὸ τῶν παρ᾽ αὐτῆς ἐπισήμων τὰς πατρίδας καλεῖσθαι καὶ τὸ ἐξ αὐτῶν
ἔθνος, ὡς καὶ ἀπὸ τοῦ Δαυὶδ οἱ ἀπ᾽ ἐκείνου οἶκος Δαυὶδ χρηματίζων.
Ἐνταῦθα τοίνυν τὰ ἐπ᾽ ἐκείνων συμβάντα ὁ μακάριος Δαυὶδ προφητεύει τὸ
τῶν Μακκαβαίων πρόσωπον ἀνειληφὼς ἐξαγορευόντων τὸ ἐπενεχθὲν παντὶ
30　τῷ ἔθνει πλῆθος τῶν κακῶν ὑπὸ Ἀντιόχου, καὶ ἐκ τοῦ ἐκείνων προσώπου
τὰ τῶν ψαλμῶν φθεγγόμενος.

2a·b. Ὁ Θεός, ἐν τοῖς ὠσὶν ἡμῶν ἠκούσαμεν, οἱ πατέρες ἡμῶν ἀνήγγειλαν ἡμῖν. Ἴσμεν πολλάκις ἀκηκοότες, ὦ δέσποτα, τῶν πατέρων ἡμῖν ἐξη-
γησαμένων καὶ οὐχ ἑτέρου τινὸς ἀλλοτρίου ὥστε καὶ ἀπιστῆσαι τοῖς
35　λεχθεῖσι. Τί δὲ ἠκούσαμεν ἐξηγουμένων;

Aᵉ 33-34 (p. 245, 22-25): Non, inquit, externi testes aut praeceptores sub-
dolite (?) tuis nos mirabilibus inbuerunt, sed patres nostri.

Antiochus surnamed Epiphanes came to power over them, enveloped them in different troubles, and, to cap it off, obliged them to sacrifice to what were thought gods by him. He set up an altar in the temple under the name of his own evil demons, raised many others in every city and place in the land of the Israelites, and caused everyone to transgress the ancestral law.

At one time there came to power one sent by Antiochus, forcing every person to sacrifice by royal command. A certain Israelite came forward as if to sacrifice and obey the royal command. At this, a man named Mattathias, zealous for the law, slew the Israelite who was anxious to obey the command, intent on sacrifice and concerned to observe the royal command. After a conspicuous struggle for his own nation and the ancestral laws, he died and handed over control to his own sons, giving supreme authority to Judas surnamed Maccabeus and entrusting conduct of the wars and exploits to him as a warrior capable of their suitable management. Those chosen to fight for the nation and for the laws of God were exposed to many and varied troubles; they were involved in mighty wars against the generals of Antiochus and his successors in the monarchy, and scarcely on any occasion over a long period, thanks to divine help, were they able to be utterly worsted by the enemy, since Judas Maccabeus was in command and their general in the wars in keeping with his father's direction. Hence, those of this family were called Maccabees, from the one who directed the efforts for the nation, succeeding to command of the nation and the wars for its sake, since it was normal with the Jews for their clans to be called after the country's distinguished people, as, for instance, in the case of David, his successors being styled "house of David."

At this point, then, blessed David prophesies the events of their time from the viewpoint of the Maccabees, who state the multitude of troubles inflicted on the whole nation by Antiochus, and he utters the contents of the psalm from their viewpoint. *O God, we have heard with our ears, and our fathers have told us* (v. 1): we often heard, Lord, our fathers' account; it was no stranger's, such that we should not believe what was said. What did we hear them recount? | *The work you accomplished in their days, in the days*

2ᶜ. Ἔργον ὃ εἰργάσω ἐν ταῖς ἡμέραις αὐτῶν, ἐν ἡμέραις ἀρχαίαις. Τὰ θαυμάσια τὰ ἐπιτελεσθέντα ὑπό σου τὸ παλαιόν. Βούλεται δὲ εἰπεῖν τὰ ἐν Αἰγύπτῳ, καὶ τὰ κατὰ τὴν ἔρημον καὶ ἐν τῇ γῇ τῆς ἐπαγγελίας, ἀρχαίας ἡμέρας ἐκείνας καλῶν· πολλὰ γὰρ ἦν ὡς πρὸς τοὺς Μακκαβαίους ἀρχαῖα τὰ κατ᾽ Αἴγυπτον γεγονότα. Ποῖον ἔργον ἤκουσαν; 5

3ᵃ. Ἡ χείρ σου ἔθνη ἐξωλόθρευσεν, καὶ κατεφύτευσας αὐτούς. Ὅτι ἡ σή φησι δύναμις ἠφάνισεν ἔθνη, τούτους δὲ ἐγκατέστησεν. Τὸ γὰρ ἡ χείρ σου, ἵνα εἴπῃ Σὺ καὶ ἡ σὴ δύναμις, οὐκ ἐκεῖνοι τοῦτο ποιῆσαι ἴσχυσαν παρ᾽ ἑαυτῶν. Τὸ δὲ κατεφύτευσας οὐχ ἁπλῶς εἰσήγαγεν, ἀλλ᾽ ἑδραίως κατῴκησας. Ἔθνη δὲ ἐξωλόθρευσας περὶ τῶν Χαναναίων λέγει καὶ τῶν Ἀμορ- 10 ραίων καὶ τῶν λοιπῶν· τούτους γὰρ ἐξολοθρεύσας τὴν ὑπ᾽ αὐτῶν κατε- χομένην | γῆν παρέδωκας τοῖς Ἰσραηλίταις.

3ᵇ. Ἐκάκωσας λαοὺς καὶ ἐξέβαλες αὐτούς. Καὶ πλήθη δὲ ἀναρίθμητα πλείστοις κακοῖς περιέβαλες, ὥστε τούτους ἐκβαλεῖν καὶ ἀπαλλάξαι τῆς ὑπ᾽ ἐκείνους δουλείας. Τοῦτο δὲ λέγει περὶ τῶν Αἰγυπτίων· ἐκείνους γὰρ 15 ἐκάκωσεν, ὥστε τούτους ἐκβαλεῖν. Τὸ γὰρ ἐξέβαλες αὐτοὺς περὶ τῶν Ἰσραη- λιτῶν λέγει, ἀντὶ τοῦ ὥστε ἐκβαλεῖν αὐτοὺς ἐκάκωσας ἐκείνους.

4ᵃ·ᵇ. Οὐ γὰρ ἐν τῇ ῥομφαίᾳ αὐτῶν ἐκληρονόμησαν γῆν, καὶ ὁ βραχίων αὐτῶν οὐκ ἔσωσεν αὐτούς. Ἐπειδὴ εἶπεν ὅτι ἔθνη ἀφανίσας ἐκείνους κατῴ- κισας καὶ λαοὺς ἀπώλεσας δισσῶς, ἐπάγει πρὸς ἀμφότερα· Οὐ γὰρ ἐν τῇ 20 ῥομφαίᾳ αὐτῶν ἐκληρονόμησαν γῆν, καὶ ὁ βραχίων αὐτῶν οὐκ ἔσωσεν αὐτούς. Οὐδὲ γὰρ τῇ οἰκείᾳ μαχαίρᾳ ἔσχον τῆς γῆς τὴν κληρονομίαν, — ἵνα εἴπῃ ὅτι οὐ πολέμου νόμῳ νικήσαντες ἔλαβον τῆς γῆς τὴν κτῆσιν, — ἀλλ᾽ οὐδὲ τῇ οἰκείᾳ ἰσχύϊ ἔσχον τὴν ἀπὸ τῶν Αἰγυπτίων σωτηρίαν· βραχίονα γὰρ καλεῖ τὴν ἰσχύν. Βούλεται δὲ εἰπεῖν ὅτι οὐδενὸς ἀπήλαυσαν δι᾽ οἰκείαν σχύν· 25 οὕτω γὰρ καὶ Ἰησοῦς ὁ τοῦ Ναυὶ μετὰ τὴν τῆς γῆς κατάσχεσιν λέγει πρὸς αὐτούς· Καὶ ἐξέβαλεν αὐτὸς ἀπὸ προσώπου ἡμῶν, ιβ᾽ βασιλεῖς τῶν Ἀμορραίων, οὐκ ἐν τῇ ῥομφαίᾳ σου οὐδὲ ἐν τῷ τόξῳ σου.

27-28 Iosue XXIV, 12.

7-8 L (p. 803, l. 2 ab imo): Τὸ ἡ χείρ σου δὲ ἀντὶ τοῦ Ἡ δύναμις.

Aᵉ 2-3 (p. 245, 28-30): Scilicet quae uel in Egipto, uel in herimo, uel quae ingresu terrae repromisionis effecta erant.   22-24 (p. 246, 10-14): Nec terram repromisionis patres nostri coeperunt possederuntque iure bellorum, neque propriis uiribus sunt ab Egiptiorum seruitio liberati.

of old: the marvels performed by you in the past. He is referring to those in Egypt, those in the desert, and in the land of promise, calling them *days of old:* there were many things of old done in Egypt like those done to the Maccabees. Of what work did they hear?

Your hand utterly destroyed nations and you planted them (v. 2): your power wiped out nations while establishing them. *Your hand* means "You and your power," as they were powerless to do it of themselves; the term *planted* means not simply "introduced" but "settled securely"; and by *utterly destroyed nations* he is referring to the Canaanites, the Amorites, and the rest, giving the sense, You utterly destroyed them and gave the land occupied by them to the Israelites. *You afflicted peoples and drove them out:* you invested innumerable hordes with numerous troubles so that they expelled the Hebrews and released them from slavery to them. This refers to the Egyptians: he afflicted them so that they expelled the others (the clause *You drove them out* referring to the Israelites in the sense, You afflicted the former so as drive them out).

It was not by their own sword, in fact, that they inherited the land, nor their own arm that saved them (v. 3). Since he had said with double focus, You wiped out nations, settled these and destroyed peoples, he proceeds to say in reference to both: *It was not by their own sword, in fact, that they inherited the land, nor their own arm that saved them.* In other words, it was not by their own sword that they attained the inheritance of the land (as if to say, It was not by right of war that they prevailed and took possession of the land); it was not by their own might that they enjoyed rescue from the Egyptians (by *arm* meaning "strength"). He means, They enjoyed nothing on their own account; as Joshua son of Nun said to them after the occupation of the land, "It was he who drove them out before you, twelve kings of the Amorites, not with your sword or your bow."[1] | *Instead, it was your right hand,*

---

1. Josh 24:12 LXX (where our Hebrew has read "two kings" under the influence of the two kings Sihon and Og alluded to in 24:8).

4ᶜ. Ἀλλ' ἡ δεξιά σου καὶ ὁ βραχίων σου καὶ ὁ φωτισμὸς τοῦ προσώπου σου. Ἀλλὰ παρεσχέθη αὐτοῖς ταῦτα ὑπὸ τῆς σῆς βοηθείας, ὑπὸ τῆς σῆς ἰσχύος καὶ ὑπὸ τῆς σῆς ἀντιλήψεως, τῆς ἐπιφανείας σου· δεξιὰν γὰρ καλεῖ τὴν βοήθειαν, βραχίονα δὲ τὴν ἰσχύν, καὶ πρόσωπον τὴν ἐπι-
5 φάνειαν· φωτισμὸν οὖν προσώπου τὴν ἀντίληψιν τὴν ἀπὸ τῆς τοῦ Θεοῦ ἐπιφανείας αὐτοῖς παρασχεθεῖσαν.

4ᵈ. Ὅτι εὐδόκησας ἐν αὐτοῖς. Καὶ ταῦτα αὐτοῖς παρεσχέθη ἐπειδὴ ἀρεστόν σοι τὸ εὐεργετῆσαι αὐτοῖς κατεφάνη.

5. Σὺ εἶ αὐτὸς ὁ βασιλεύς μου καὶ ὁ Θεός μου, ὁ ἐντελλόμενος τὰς σωτη-
10 ρίας Ἰακώβ. Καὶ σῴζεσθαι τὸ ἔθνος τὸ ἡμέτερον προστάττων, ἀντὶ τοῦ ὁ βουλό|μενος ἡμᾶς μὴ διαφθαρῆναι καὶ ἀπολέσθαι, ἀλλὰ διαμένειν — καλῶς τοῦτο τοῖς προτέροις ἐπαγαγών. Δῆλον γάρ φησιν ἐξ ὧν τοὺς πατέρας δουλεύοντας οὐκ ἀφῆκας, ἀλλ' ἐρρύσω τῶν κακῶν, ἔδωκάς τε αὐτοῖς καὶ κατάσχεσιν γῆς, ὅτι διαμένειν καὶ σῴζεσθαι θέλεις τὸ ἡμέτερον ἔθνος.

15 6ᵃ. Ἐν σοὶ τοὺς ἐχθροὺς ἡμῶν κερατιοῦμεν. Δικαίως οὖν φησι καὶ νῦν τῆς σῆς τευξόμεθα βοηθείας, ὥστε ἀμύνασθαι τοὺς ἐχθροὺς τοὺς ἡμετέρους, ἐπείπερ αὐτὸς εἶ καὶ νῦν Θεὸς φροντίζων τῆς ἡμετέρας σωτηρίας. Τὸ δὲ κερατιοῦμεν, ἀντὶ τοῦ κερατίσομεν, τουτέστι Τοῦτο ποίησον, τοῦτο παράσχου· οὕτω γὰρ ἁρμόττει τυχεῖν ἡμᾶς τούτων τῆς σῆς βοηθείας. Ἐκ
20 μεταφορᾶς δὲ εἶπε τῶν ἀλόγων τῶν τοῖς κέρασιν ἀμυνομένων.

6ᵇ. Καὶ ἐν τῷ ὀνόματί σου ἐξουθενώσομεν τοὺς ἐπανισταναμένους ἡμῖν. Καὶ τῇ σῇ ἐπικλήσει δικαίως καταναλώσομεν καὶ εἰς τὸ μηδὲν τοὺς ἡμετέρους ἐχθρούς.

7. Οὐ γὰρ ἐπὶ τῷ τόξῳ μου ἐλπιῶ, καὶ ἡ ῥομφαία μου οὐ σώσει με.
25 Οὐδὲ γὰρ ἐγὼ προσδοκῶ τῇ οἰκείᾳ ἰσχύϊ καὶ πολέμου νόμῳ περιγενόμενος αὐτῶν κρατῆσαι καὶ τυχεῖν τῆς σωτηρίας· τόξον γὰρ καὶ ῥομφαίαν τοῦτο λέγει, ἀντὶ τοῦ ὅτι οὐ προσδοκῶμεν πείρᾳ πολεμικῇ κρατῆσαι τῶν ἐχθρῶν.

18-20 cf. L (p. 804, 40-44): Τὸ κερατιοῦμεν, ἀντὶ τοῦ ἀμυνούμεθα... ἀπὸ μεταφορᾶς τῶν κερασφόρων, ἃ τούτῳ κέχρηται ὅπλῳ κατὰ τῶν ἀδικούντων.

Aᵉ 5-6 (p. 246, 16-18): Inluminationem uultus Dei uocat ipsum adiutorium, quod a Deo apparente coeperint.   10-11 (p. 246, 23-25): Qui uis populum tuum non in totum consumi nec penitus interire.   19-20 (p. 246, 30-31):... quod comparatione animantium, quae se cornibus ulciscuntur, expraesit.

your arm, and the light of your countenance: this was accorded them with your help, with your strength and with your support, your appearance (by *right hand* referring to help, by *arm* to strength, by *countenance* to appearance, and by *light of your countenance* to the support provided by God's appearance to them). *Because you took delight in them:* this was accorded them because beneficence to them was deemed pleasing to you.

You are my king and my God, commanding the salvation of Jacob (v. 4): giving directions for our nation to be saved—that is, wanting us not to be destroyed and perish, but to survive. He applied this nicely to their predecessors: It is clear, he is saying, from your not allowing the ancestors to be enslaved and instead rescuing them from troubles, and from giving them also occupation of the land, that you wish our nation to survive and be saved. *Through you we prevail over our foes* (v. 5). So he is right to say also, We shall now receive your help so as to repel our foes, especially since it is you who as God even now give thought to our salvation. The verb *we prevail* means "we shall prevail"—that is, Do this, provide it, for it is appropriate for us to receive your help in this (using a metaphor from brute beasts defending themselves with their horns). *And through your name we bring to naught those who rise up against us:* by invoking you, we shall rightly wipe out our foes and reduce them to nothing.

Not in my bow shall I hope, after all, nor will my sword save me (v. 6): I do not look to my own strength and the norms of war to survive, get the better of them, and attain salvation (this being the meaning of *bow and sword*—that is, I do not expect to get the better of the enemy by warlike skills). | *In fact, you saved us from those oppressing us, and put to shame*

8. Ἔσωσας γὰρ ἡμᾶς ἐκ τῶν θλιβόντων ἡμᾶς, καὶ τοὺς μισοῦντας ἡμᾶς κατήσχυνας. Καὶ ἀεὶ τοὺς ἐχθροὺς τοὺς ἡμετέρους αἰσχύνῃ περιβάλλεις· οὐ γὰρ συνεχώρησας αὐτοῖς εἰς ἔργον ἐκβαλεῖν τὰ κατ᾿ ἐμοῦ σπουδαζόμενα.

9ᵃ. Ἐν τῷ Θεῷ ἐπαινεσθησόμεθα ὅλην τὴν ἡμέραν. Ὅθεν φησὶ καὶ πεποίθαμεν διηνεκῶς ἔχειν τὸ ἔν σοι καυχᾶσθαι, τουτέστιν ἐν τῇ σῇ βοη- 5 θείᾳ· τὸ γὰρ ἐπαινεσθησόμεθα, Καὶ καυχησόμεθα λέγει Ἀκύλας. Ὅλην τὴν ἡμέραν, ἀντὶ τοῦ Δοκῶμεν καὶ νῦν παρασχεθήσεσθαι ἡμῖν παρά σου τὴν βοήθειαν.

9ᵇ. Καὶ ἐν τῷ ὀνόματί σου ἐξομολογησόμεθα εἰς τὸν αἰῶνα. Καὶ τῇ σῇ ἐπικλήσει προσδοκῶμεν ἀεὶ τὰς εὐχαριστίας ἀναπέμψειν, ἵνα εἴπῃ τεύξεσ- 10 θαι τῶν ἀγαθῶν· τότε γάρ | τις εὐχαριστεῖ.

10ᵃ. Νυνὶ δὲ ἀπώσω καὶ κατήσχυνας ἡμᾶς. Τοιαῦτα δέ φησι πάλαι γεγενῆσθαι ἀκούσαντες καὶ νῦν προσδοκῶντες, εἰκότως ἐναντία ὁρῶμεν τὰ πράγματα· νυνὶ γὰρ ἐν αἰσχύνῃ κατέστησας.

10ᵇ. Καὶ οὐκ ἐξελεύσῃ ἐν ταῖς δυνάμεσιν ἡμῶν. Οὐ γὰρ στρατηγήσεις 15 ἡμῖν εἰς τοὺς πολέμους, τουτέστιν οὐκ ἐπαμυνεῖς ἡμῖν ἐν τοῖς πολέμοις. Τὸ γὰρ οὐκ ἐξελεύσῃ ἀνθρωπινώτερον εἶπεν ἀπὸ τῶν εἰς συμμαχίαν ἐξιόν- των. Τὸ δὲ ἐν ταῖς δυνάμεσιν ἡμῶν, ἀντὶ τοῦ σὺν ταῖς δυνάμεσιν, ἵνα εἴπῃ ἡμῖν, — δυνάμεις λέγων τὴν στρατιάν, ὡς καὶ ἄχρι τῆς δεῦρο δύναμιν βασι- λέως καλεῖν εἰώθαμεν τὸν στρατόν. 20

11ᵃ. Ἀπέστρεψας ἡμᾶς εἰς τὰ ὀπίσω παρὰ τοὺς ἐχθροὺς ἡμῶν. Ὑπο- χειρίους δὲ ἡμᾶς τοῖς ἐχθροῖς κατέστησας καὶ πάσης ἐπλήρωσας αἰσχύνης, ἡττηθῆναι παρασκευάσας.

4-6 cf. *Paraphrasis* (p. 799, l. 1-3 ab imo).   18-20 L (p. 805, 24-25. 28-29): ... καὶ οὐ προσέρχῃ ἐν τοῖς στρατεύμασιν ἡμῶν... ἐν δυνάμεσι δέ φησιν, ἀντὶ τοῦ ἐν στρα- τεύμασιν ἡμῶν οὐ παραγίνῃ.

Aᵉ 8 (P. 247, 5-7): Frustratione uotorum erub⟨u⟩erunt quae de me conceperant obpraemendo.   4-5 (p. 247, 8-9): Ac si diceret Inde est quod tuo in nomine cupimus gloriari.   10ᵃ (p. 247, 12-17): Quia magna a patribus de tuis factis audiuimus, et maiora aut similia praestulamur, contra⟨r⟩ietate accidentium rerum sumus omnino confussi, cum nos reiectos a te non sine pudore maximo cerneremus.   18-20 (p. 247, 18-23): *Nostris* enim ex ussu hominum possuit, secundum id uidilicet quod nostros uocamus qui in auxilium egredi consuerunt, pro copiis militaribus, sicut hodie uirtutem regis appellare solemus exercitum.   11ᵃ (p. 247, 27-30): Prae inimicis nostris graui nos pudore operuisti, quos toties passus es ab hostibus superari.

those hating us (v. 7): you always cover our foes in confusion, not allowing them to put into effect their intentions against me. *In God we shall take pleasure all day long* (v. 8): hence, we trusted constantly to be able to boast in you—that is, in your help (for *we shall take pleasure* Aquila putting "we shall boast"). *All day long* means, We seem even now to be provided with help from you. *And we shall confess in your name forever:* by invoking you, we look forward to offering thanksgiving forever—that is, to attaining good things; for that is when someone gives thanks.

As it is, however, you rejected and shamed us (v. 9): having heard of such things being done in the past and having present expectations, what we see is naturally the reverse; for you have reduced us to a shameful condition. *And you did not sally forth in our forces:* you will not be our leader in war—that is, You will not assist us in time of war (using the term *sally forth* in rather human fashion of those joining forces). The phrase *in our forces* means "with our forces"—that is, "with us," by *forces* referring to the army, as even to this day we normally refer to the army as the king's force. *You turned us back in battle with our foes* (v. 10): you made us vulnerable to the foe and covered us completely in shame, causing us to be vanquished. | *And those hating us*

11ᵇ. Καὶ οἱ μισοῦντες ἡμᾶς διήρπαζον ἑαυτοῖς. Οἱ γὰρ ἀπεχθῶς διακείμενοι περὶ ἡμᾶς διέσπων ἡμᾶς τῇδε κάκεῖσε, ὡς ἠβούλοντο γὰρ ἑαυτοῖς,
ἀντὶ τοῦ κατὰ τὴν οἰκείαν γνώμην καὶ κατὰ τὴν οἰκείαν βούλησιν, οὐδενὸς
ὄντος ἀνθισταμένου.

5   12ᵃ. Ἔδωκας ἡμᾶς ὡς πρόβατα βρώσεως. Παρεδόθημέν φησιν ὑπό
σου εἰς τὸ ἀναιρεῖσθαι ὑπὸ τῶν ἐχθρῶν ὡσεὶ πρόβατα ἄλογα τὰ εἰς
βρῶσιν προκείμενα τοῖς ἀνθρώποις, καὶ ἕτοιμα σφάττεσθαι ὑπὸ τῶν
βουλομένων.

12ᵇ. Καὶ ἐν τοῖς ἔθνεσι διέσπειρας ἡμᾶς. Καὶ τοσοῦτον περιέβαλες
10 κακοῖς, ὥστε φεύγοντας διασπαρῆναι τῇδε κάκεῖσε.

13ᵃ. Ἀπέδου τὸν λαόν σου ἄνευ τιμῆς. Συνεχώρησας ἡμᾶς ταῦτα πάσχειν, πάντως ὡς οὐδενὸς λόγου ἀξίους προδεδωκὼς τῷ θανάτῳ καὶ τοῖς
παθήμασιν, ἐκ μεταφορᾶς τῶν τοὺς ἀχρήστους οἰκέτας ἄνευ τιμῆς προϊε-
μένων. Καὶ ἐπειδὴ εἶπεν ἀπέδου τὸν λαόν σου ἄνευ τιμῆς, τῇ ἀκολουθίᾳ τῆς
15 μεταφορᾶς χρησάμενος ἐπήγαγεν·

13ᵇ. Καὶ οὐκ ἦν πλῆθος ἐν τοῖς ἀλαλάγμασιν αὐτῶν. Τουτέστιν ὡς οὐδε-
νὸς ἄξιοι οὕτως παρεδιδόμεθα τοῖς | ἐχθροῖς, καὶ οὕτως ἡμᾶς ἀνῄρουν ἀφει-
δῶς ὡς ἂν οὐδενὸς χρήματος ἀνταλλάξασθαι ἀξίους.

14ᵃ. Ἔθου ἡμᾶς ὄνειδος τοῖς γείτοσιν ἡμῶν. Ἐπὶ τούτοις παρεσκεύα-
20 σας ἡμᾶς ὀνειδίζεσθαι ὑπὸ τῶν ἐχθρῶν τῶν πλησιοχώρων.

14ᵇ. Μυκτηρισμὸν καὶ καταγέλωτα τοῖς κύκλῳ ἡμῶν. Καὶ ὑπὸ τῶν
περιοικούντων χλευάζεσθαι πεποίηκας.

13-14 προϊμένων ms.

13ᵃ Paraphrasis (p. 800): ... πέπρακας ἡμᾶς ἐν τοῖς ἔθνεσι τοῦ μηδενὸς (τοῦτο γὰρ
λέγει ἄνευ τιμῆς) ὡς ἀχρήστους δούλους, καὶ οὐδ᾽ ὡς ἀξίους.

Aᵉ 11ᵇ (p. 247, 30-248, 2): Apud hostes licentiam dipraedandi nullus
difensionis tuae frenabat occursus.   6-7 (p. 248, 4-5): Tamquam aptas ad
essum mutasque animantes.   11-12 (p. 248, 8-10): Et tamquam inutiles seruos ad mortem tra⟨di⟩disti gratis.   13ᵇ (p. 248, 11-15): Tamquam nullae esti-
mationi⟨s⟩ digni traditi sumus hostibus, a quibus ita trach⟨t⟩abamur ac si
nulla conpensatione commotandi.

took plunder for themselves: those hostile to us pulled us this way and that, as they wished to their own advantage—that is, by their own will and whim, with no one to oppose them.

You gave us like sheep for eating (v. 11): we were given up by you to be wasted by the foe like mindless sheep available to people for eating, and ready to be slaughtered by those who wanted. *And you scattered us among the nations:* to such an extent did you invest us in troubles that in flight we were scattered hither and thither. *You disposed of your people at no cost* (v. 12): you allowed us to suffer this, consigning us to death and suffering as of no account (using a metaphor from people valuing useless servants as of no worth). And since he had said *You disposed of your people at no cost,* he continued to employ the metaphor *There was no charge for their changing hands*—that is, We were handed over to the foe as of no value, and they disposed of us in such a pitiless way that we were not worth exchanging at any cost.

You set us as an object for taunting by our neighbors (v. 13): about this you caused us to be taunted by our nearby foes. *An object of derision and mockery to those round about us:* and made us mocked by the neighbors. |

15ᵃ. Ἔθου ἡμᾶς εἰς παραβολὴν ἐν τοῖς ἔθνεσιν. Τοιαῦτα δέ φησι γέγονε τὰ καθ᾽ ἡμᾶς καὶ οὕτω πᾶσιν ἐξάκουστα, ὥστε ἀεὶ ἐν παραβολαῖς ἡμῶν μνημονεύειν τοὺς ἀνθρώπους λέγοντας ὅτι Τοιαῦτα ἔπαθον οἵδε οἷα οὐδὲ οἱ Ἰσραηλῖται· ἀεὶ γὰρ τοὺς ἐν συμφοραῖς ἀνηκέστοις περιπίπτοντας ἐν παραβολαῖς εἰώθασιν ἔχειν οἱ ἄνθρωποι, λέγοντες Οἷα ὅδε ἢ ὅδε ὑπέστη κακά.　5

15ᵇ. Κίνησιν κεφαλῆς ἐν τοῖς λαοῖς. Ἐπειδὴ τοὺς ἐν συμφοραῖς καθεστῶτας εἰώθαμεν ὁρῶντες συναλγεῖν πολλάκις καὶ τὴν κεφαλὴν συνεχῶς ἐπινεύειν, τοῦτο λέγει ὅτι οἴκτου τοῖς ὁρῶσιν ἄξιοι κατεφαινόμεθα διὰ τὴν τῶν κακῶν ὑπερβολήν.

16ᵃ. Ὅλην τὴν ἡμέραν ἡ ἐντροπή μου κατεναντίον μού ἐστιν. Ἀεί　10
φησι πρὸ τῶν ὀφθαλμῶν ἔσχον τὴν ἐντροπήν, τουτέστιν ὑπὸ τοῦ πλήθους τῶν κακῶν ἀεὶ ἐνετρεπόμην τοὺς ἐντυχάνοντας.

16ᵇ. Καὶ ἡ αἰσχύνη τοῦ προσώπου μου ἐκάλυψέν με. Καὶ αἰσχύνης φησὶν ἐπληρώθην ἐπὶ τοῖς συμβεβηκόσι κακοῖς, ἐντροπῆς φησι καὶ αἰσχύνης ἐπληρούμην. Πῶς;　　　　　　　　　　　　　　　　　　　　15

17ᵃ. Ἀπὸ φωνῆς ὀνειδίζοντος καὶ καταλαλοῦντος. Ἀπὸ τῶν ὀνειδιζόντων μοι ἐπὶ τοῖς κακοῖς καὶ λοιδορουμένων· καταλαλεῖν γάρ φησι τὸ λοιδορεῖσθαι.

17ᵇ. Ἀπὸ προσώπου ἐχθροῦ καὶ ἐκδιώκοντος. Ἀπὸ τούτων φησὶν ἐνετρεπόμην τῶν ὀνειδιζόντων, τῶν λοιδορουμένων, τῶν ἐχθραινόντων, τῶν ἐπι-　20
βουλευόντων.

18ᵃ. Ταῦτα πάντα ἦλθεν ἐφ᾽ ἡμᾶς, καὶ οὐκ ἐπελαθόμεθά σου. Τοσούτων δὲ κακῶν ἐληλυθότων ἐφ᾽ ἡμᾶς λήθην σου οὐδαμῶς ἐποιησάμεθα. Πρέπει δὲ ταῦτα λέγειν τοῖς Μακκαβαίοις ἐν αὐτοῖς τοῖς κακοῖς τῷ νόμῳ ζήσασιν.　　　　　　　　　　　　　　　　　　　　　　　25

1-4 L (p. 806, 5-8): Τοιαῦτα δὲ ἐπάθομεν κακὰ καὶ οὕτως ἐξάκουστα, ὡς τοὺς ἐν συμφοραῖς ἀνηκέστοις περιπίπτοντας λέγειν· τοιαῦτα οὐδὲ οἱ Ἑβραῖοι πεπόνθασι. 7-8 L (p. 806, 14-15): ...κινεῖν τὴν κεφαλήν, συνεχῶς ἀλγοῦντας τοὺς ὁρῶντας ἡμᾶς.

Aᵉ 15ᵃ (p. 248, 17-21): Ac si diceretur In obprobrium parabulam uersi sumus ad omnem infelicitatis commemorationem, ut nostrum occurrat exemplum.　7-9 (p. 248, 22-24): Mos quippe iste est misserantium, ut commotu capitis dolentia ingemescentes...　16ᵃ (p. 248, 27-249, 1): Pro doloris pudorisque magnitudine, omni tempore oculis aliorum uerebar occurrere.　16ᵇ (p. 249, 3-4): Ignominia calamitatis inpletum se dicit.　23-25 (p. 249, 9-11): Apta est uox Machabeis, qui inter magna pericula possiti zelum tamen legis habuerunt.

You have set us as a proverb for the nations (v. 14): our fate proved to be of such a kind and so familiar to everyone that people always mentioned us in proverbs, saying, Such-and-such people suffered what the Israelites did (people normally citing in proverbs those who fall victim to intolerable misfortunes, saying, So-and-so suffered such a fate). *A shaking of the head among the peoples.* Since on seeing people in a calamitous state we normally sympathize and repeatedly wag our head, he means, To the onlookers we appeared deserving of pity on account of the extremity of the troubles.

All day long my humiliation is before me (v. 15): I had my humiliation ever before my eyes—that is, Under pressure from the multitude of troubles I was ashamed to meet people. *And I am covered in blushes:* and I am filled with shame at the troubles befalling me; I am filled with humiliation and shame. How so? *From the sound of the one taunting and slandering* (v. 16): from those taunting me with the troubles and abusing me (*slandering* meaning "abusing"). *From the face of foe and persecutor:* because of these people's taunts, abuse, hostility, scheming, I was ashamed.

All this came upon us, and we did not forget you (v. 17): though such great troubles befell us, we did not at all leave you forgotten. Now, it is appropriate to say this of the Maccabees, who in the midst of the troubles were zealous for the law. | *And we did not do wrong by your covenant.* Aquila:

18ᵇ. Καὶ οὐκ ἠδικήσαμεν ἐν διαθήκῃ σου. Ἀκύλας Καὶ οὐκ ἐψευσάμεθα ἐν διαθήκῃ σου, — ἵνα εἴπῃ ὅτι Τῶν νομίμων σου, ὧν διέθου πρὸς ἡμᾶς, οὐδὲν ἠδικήσαμεν, οὐδὲν παρελύσαμεν, οὐδὲν παρετρέψαμεν.

19ᵃ. Καὶ οὐκ ἀπέστη εἰς τὰ ὀπίσω ἡ καρδία ἡμῶν. Καὶ τοῖς λογισμοῖς
5 οὐκ ἀπεστράφημεν ἐπὶ τὸ χεῖρον, οὐδὲ παρετρέψαμέν τι τῆς τοῦ νόμου τηρήσεως.

19ᵇ. Καὶ ἐξέκλινας τὰς τρίβους ἡμῶν ἀπὸ τῆς ὁδοῦ σου. Καίτοι φησὶ τοσούτων ἡμῖν συμβεβηκότων κακῶν, ἅπερ ἱκανὰ καθειστήκει παρατρέψαι ἡμῶν τοὺς λογισμοὺς ἀπὸ τῆς σῆς εὐχαριστήσεως. Τὸ δὲ ἐξέκλινας, ἵνα
10 εἴπῃ ὅτι παθεῖν συνεχώρησας τοιαῦτα, ἀφ᾽ ὧν καὶ τοῦτο παθεῖν συνεχώ-
ρησας.

20ᵃ. Ὅτι ἐταπείνωσας ἡμᾶς ἐν τόπῳ κακώσεως. Ἐξέκλινας δὲ τὸ συγ-
χωρηθῆναι ἡμᾶς ταπεινωθῆναι ὑπὸ τοῦ πλήθους τῶν κακῶν. Τὸ δὲ ἐν τόπῳ κακώσεως, ἵνα εἴπῃ ἐν κακώσει.

15 20ᵇ. Καὶ ἐπεκάλυψεν ἡμᾶς σκιὰ θανάτου. Καὶ κατέλαβον ἡμᾶς φησι κίνδυνοι ἐγγίζοντα προδεικνύντες τὸν θάνατον, ἀπὸ τοῦ τὴν σκιὰν τοῦ σώματος προδεικνύναι παρουσίαν ἀφ᾽ οὗ πάντως ἀποτελεῖται.

21ᵃ. Εἰ ἐπελαθόμεθα τοῦ ὀνόματος τοῦ Θεοῦ ἡμῶν. Ἐπειδὴ εἶπεν ἀνωτέρω ὅτι Οὐκ ἐπελαθόμεθά σου, καίτοι μεγάλων ὄντων τῶν συμβεβηκότων
20 ἡμῖν κακῶν, ἐνταῦθά φησιν ὅτι Εἰ ἐπιλαθόμεθά σου, ὦ δέσποτα.

21ᵇ. Καὶ εἰ διεπετάσαμεν χεῖρας ἡμῶν πρὸς θεὸν ἀλλότριον. Καὶ εἰ ἑτέρῳ φησὶ θεῷ λατρεῦσαι προεθέμεθα.

19 v. 18ᵃ.

10-11 συνεχώ ms.
3-6 L (p. 806, 29-31): οὐδὲ περὶ τὰ προστάγματά σου ἐγενόμεθα ἄδικοι, οὐδὲ τῆς ἀπεναντίας ἤλθομεν λογισάμενοι ὅτι ἐγκατέλιπες ἡμᾶς.   8-9 L (p. 807, 2-3): ἃ ἱκανὰ ἦν ἐκτρέψαι ἡμᾶς ἀπὸ τῆς ὁδοῦ σου.   9-11 cf. in Oseam VI, 5 (P. G., LXVI, 161 C 1-3).   16 cf. Paraphrasis (p. 802, 3-4): Σκιὰ θανάτου. ἀντὶ τοῦ κίνδυνοι παραπλήσιοι θανάτῳ.

Aᶜ 2-3 (p. 249, 12-14): Legitima tua nec sub terrore nimio temerando.
19ᵃ (p. 249, 14-16): Neque offensi tantis malis aliquando de obseruanda lege contempsimus.   8-9 (p. 249, 17-20): Ea nos adflictione passus es uexari, quae etiam corruptionem posset nobis religionis operari.   20ᵇ (p. 249, 24-27): Vmbram mortis periculum uocat, quemadmodum corpora uicina esse et inmi-
nere umbra prius uisa testatur.   21ᵃ (p. 249, 28-31): Cum etiam talia patere-
mur, secundum quod supra diximus *Et obliti non sumus te.*

"And we were not false to your covenant," as if to say, Your laws, which you imposed on us, we did not break, did not infringe, did not transgress. *Our heart did not turn back* (v. 18): in our thinking we did not take a turn for the worse, nor did we transgress in any way the observance of the law. *You moved our steps from your way:* although such awful troubles befell us, which were sufficient to make our thoughts stray from giving thanks to you. The term *you moved* means, You allowed us to suffer such things, as a result of which you allowed us to suffer this as well. *Because you humiliated us in a place of affliction* (v. 19): you moved—that is, you permitted—us to be humiliated by the multitude of the troubles (*in the place of affliction* meaning "in affliction"). *And wrapped us in the darkness of death:* dangers betraying the approach of death laid hold of us (a figure from the shadow that betrays the presence of the body that, of course, produces it).

If we forget the name of our God (v. 20). Since he had said above *We did not forget you,* here he says, Although there are great troubles that have befallen us, *if we forget* you, O Lord. *And if we have spread out our hands to a foreign god:* and if we devoted ourselves to worshiping another god. |

22ª. Οὐχὶ ὁ Θεὸς ἐκζητήσει ταῦτα; Οὐκ αὐτός φησι ταῦτα ἐκζητεῖς;

22ᵇ. Αὐτὸς γὰρ γινώσκει τὰ κρύφια τῆς καρδίας. Σὺ γάρ φησι καὶ τοὺς ἐν τῷ βάθει λογισμοὺς ἐπίστασαι, ἵνα εἴπῃ ὅτι Σοὶ μάρτυρι κέχρημαι τοῦ μὴ παραβεβηκέναι.

23ª. Ὅτι ἕνεκά σου θανατούμεθα ὅλην τὴν ἡμέραν. Αὐτὸς οἶδάς φησιν 5 ὅτι δι᾽ οὐδὲν ἕτερον ἀλλ᾽ ἢ διὰ τὸ σὸν ὄνομα διηνεκῶς τοῖς θανάτοις περιβαλλόμεθα.

23ᵇ. Ἐλογίσθημεν ὡς πρόβατα σφαγῆς. Καὶ διά σε ὑπὸ τῶν ἐχθρῶν ὡς πρόβατα ἀναιρούμεθα. Ταύτῃ δὲ ἐχρήσατο τῇ μαρτυρίᾳ ὁ ἀπόστολος, οὐχ ὡς περὶ αὐτῶν | εἰρημένῃ ὑπὸ τοῦ Δαυίδ, ἀλλ᾽ ὡς ἁρμοττούσῃ καὶ ἐπ᾽ 10 αὐτῶν οὐκ ἔλαττον λέγεσθαι, ὅσῳ καὶ πλείοσιν ὑπὲρ τοῦ Χριστοῦ περιέπιπτον τοῖς κακοῖς.

24ª. Ἐξεγέρθητι· ἵνα τί ὑπνοῖς, Κύριε; Ἀνθρωπινώτερον λέγει· Κινήθητι εἰς βοήθειαν ἡμετέραν, μέχρι πότε μακροθυμεῖς; Τὸ δὲ ἵνα τί ὑπνοῖς, Κύριε, Σύμμαχος Ἵνα τί ὡς ὁ ὑπνῶν εἶ, δέσποτά. 15

24ᵇ. Ἀνάστηθι καὶ μὴ ἀπώσῃ εἰς τέλος. Κινήθητι πρὸς βοήθειαν ἡμετέραν, καὶ μὴ παντελῶς ἡμᾶς ἀπορρίψῃς.

25ª. Ἵνα τί τὸ πρόσωπόν σου ἀποστρέφεις; Παῦσαι τῆς καθ᾽ ἡμῶν ὀργῆς, ἀπὸ τῶν ὀργιζομένων καὶ τὰ πρόσωπα ἀποστρεφόντων.

25ᵇ. Ἐπιλανθάνῃ τῆς πτωχίας ἡμῶν καὶ τῆς θλίψεως ἡμῶν. Παῦσαι καὶ 20 τοῦ καταρρᾳθυμεῖν ἡμῶν ἐν συμφοραῖς καὶ θλίψεσιν ἐξεταζομένων.

26ª. Ὅτι ἐταπεινώθη εἰς χοῦν ἡ ψυχὴ ἡμῶν. Καὶ γὰρ μέχρι τῆς γῆς αὐτῆς κατηνέχθημεν.

26ᵇ. Ἐκολλήθη εἰς γῆν ἡ γαστὴρ ἡμῶν. Καὶ ὑπὸ τῶν ἐχθρῶν κατεπατήθημεν πρηνεῖς, ὡς αὐτὴν ἡμῶν τὴν γαστέρα τῷ ἐδάφει προσπαγῆναι. 25

9 Rom. VIII, 36.

11 αὐτῶν] litt. ων in rasura (ex ῶ?); aliquid fortasse deest.

Aᵉ 23ᵇ (p. 250, 9-15): Tamquam inermes pecodes sic tibi crediti trucidamur ab hostibus. Vsurpat hoc testimonio etiam beatus apostolus Paulus tamquam simile, non tamquam proprium, quod non minus Machabeis quam apostolis conueniret. 16-17 (p. 250, 23-24): Mouere ad iuuandum nos. 26ª (p. 250, 28-29): Vsque ad solum inclinati sumus. 26ᵇ (p. 250, 30-251, 1): Adeo ab inimicis nostris prostrati sumus, ut uenter noster humo uideatur adfixus.

Will not God find this out? (v. 21). Will you not, he asks, make a personal search for this? *After all, he knows the secrets of the heart:* you know our deep thoughts—as if to say, I call you to witness that I have not transgressed. *Because for your sake we are being put to death all day long* (v. 22): you yourself know that we are always exposed to death for no other reason than your name. *We are accounted as sheep for slaughter:* for your sake we are done away with like sheep by the foe. The apostle cited this text,[2] not as though there were reference to them by David, but as no less suited for citation in their case as well, insofar as they fell foul of numerous troubles for Christ's sake.

Wake up! Why do you sleep, Lord? (v. 23). Speaking in rather human fashion, he means, Be moved to help us; how long will you be patient? For *Why do you sleep?* Symmachus has "Why are you like one sleeping, Lord?" *Arise, and do not drive us off forever:* be moved to help us, and do not completely cast us off. *Why do you turn your face away?* (v. 24): bring your anger against us to an end (a metaphor from people in anger turning their faces away). *You have forgotten our poverty and our tribulations:* stop ignoring us in our misfortunes and tribulations. *Because our soul has been humbled to the dust* (v. 25): we are brought down to the very earth. *And our stomach is stuck fast to the ground:* we have been made by the enemy to fall on our faces, so that our very stomach is pinned to the floor. | *Rise up, Lord,*

---

2. Rom 8:36, in reference to the tribulations of the ministers of the gospel. Theodoret unaccountably omits mention of Paul's citation, as had Diodore (but not Chrysostom).

27ᵃ. Ἀνάστα, Κύριε, βοήθησον ἡμῖν. Διεγέρθητι τοίνυν πρὸς βοήθειαν ἡμετέραν.

27ᵇ. Καὶ λύτρωσαι ἡμᾶς ἔνεκεν τοῦ ὀνόματός σου. Καὶ ἀπάλλαξον ἡμᾶς τῶν κακῶν τούτων διὰ τὸ ὄνομά σου τὸ ἐπικεκλημένον ἐφ' ἡμᾶς — ὅπερ καὶ
5 νῦν ὑβρίζεται τοιαῦτα πασχόντων ἡμῶν — καὶ τότε δοξασθήσεται ἐπειδὰν ἀπαλλαγέντες τῶν συμφορῶν ἐν ἀνέσει διὰ τῆς σῆς καταστῶμεν βοηθείας.

PSALMVS XLIV

Ἐν τούτῳ προφητεύει τῷ ψαλμῷ τὰ κατὰ τὸν Χριστόν, προαγορεύων
ὅπως μὲν πολλοὺς προσάξεται τῷ λόγῳ τῆς διδασκαλίας, ὅσα δὲ καὶ
10 κατορθώσει παραγεγονώς, καὶ τῆς ἐκκλησίας τὴν σύστασιν, ἣν ἀπὸ τοῦ
συναθροίσματος ἐποιήσατο τῶν πιστῶν. Μνημονεύει δὲ καὶ τῶν πνευματικῶν χαρισμάτων, τῆς τε παρασχεθείσης ὑπ' αὐτοῦ δωρεᾶς τοῖς ἁγίοις,
καὶ τῆς ἀρετῆς ὡς πολλὴν ἐν τῇ ἐκκλησίᾳ δεξομένων τὴν ἐπίδοσιν. Ἕτερά
τε ὅσα τούτοις ἀκόλουθα λέγει, μάλα τὴν περὶ αὐτῶν προφη|τείαν ἀκρι-
15 βεστάτην ποιούμενος. Ἄρχεται δὲ ἀπὸ προοιμίων, καὶ τὴν πρόρρησιν μετὰ
πολλῆς ποιεῖται τῆς τάξεως. Προσεκτέον οὖν ἀκριβῶς τῇ ἑρμηνείᾳ, μάλιστα
ἐπειδὴ καὶ παρατρέπειν Ἰουδαῖοι τολμῶσι τὸν ψαλμόν. Μυθικώτερον, μᾶλλον
δὲ καταγελαστότερον αὐτὸν ἐξηγούμενοι — οἷς οὐδὲ προσέχειν ἐχρῆν — οὕτω
χλεύης ἀξίαν τὴν προφητείαν τό γε ἐπ' αὐτοῖς ἀποφαίνειν τολμῶσιν· εἰς
20 γὰρ τὸν Σολομῶντα καὶ τὴν τούτου γυναῖκα βούλονται εἰρῆσθαι τὸν ψαλμόν. Τί δ' ἂν εἴη τούτου χεῖρον πρὸς ἄνοιαν τὸ τοῦ πνευματοφόρου τὰς
ῥήσεις εἰς τὸ μηδὲν ἐκτρέπειν, καὶ εἰς ὕμνους καὶ ἐγκώμια γυναικῶν καὶ

---

4 *Paraphrasis* (p. 803, 19): διὰ τὸ σὸν ὄνομα τὸ ἐπικεκλημένον ἐφ' ἡμᾶς. 8-20
L (p. 831, 27-29): Ἀριδήλως οὖν εἰς τὸν Χριστὸν ὁ ψαλμὸς ἀναφέρεται, κἂν Ἑβραῖοι
βιάζωνται εἰς τὸν Σολομῶντα εἰρῆσθαι.

Aᵉ 27ᵇ (p. 251, 7-13): Quod et super nos inuocatum est et quod ab istis
nunc contumaciter profaneque dispicitur; quod solum gloriabitur, cum post
tantam disperationem per te fuerimus de calamitatibus liberati. 8-16 (p. 251,
16-31): In hoc psalmo profetat ea quae de Christo sunt, quemadmodum uidilicet
uerbo doctrinae suae plurimam multitudinem congregabit, quanta etiam perfi-
ciat miranda, constitutionem eclesiae decursu fidelium conparandam. Facit
etiam commemorationem donorum spiritalium, quae fidelibus quibusque lar-
gitus est, et quod moralis uirtus per institutionem euangelii creuerit. Horum
omnium praenuntialionem sedulo persequutus praefatur aperte multumque
ordinem in praefatione ipsa custodens. PSEUDO-BEDA (714): Propheta de Christo ad Ecclesiam dicit.

come to our aid (v. 26): arise, then, and come to our help. *And redeem us for your name's sake:* and free us from these troubles for the sake of your name, which has been invoked upon us, and which even now is being insulted by these sufferings of ours. It will be glorified at the time when we are freed from the troubles and given relief through your help.

PSALM 45

In this psalm he prophesies events concerning Christ, foretelling how he will attract many people on the basis of his teaching and, as well, all that he will accomplish by his coming, including the establishment of the church by achieving the assembly of the faithful. He mentions also the spiritual graces, the gift provided by him to the saints, and the virtue of those in the church who experience a great increase. He also mentions other related matters, giving a very precise prophecy of them, beginning with the introduction and delivering the prediction in a very orderly fashion. So we need to attend precisely to the commentary, especially since Jews presume to distort the psalm, turning it into fairy tales, or rather an object of derision, of which no heed should be taken. Thus, they presume to present the inspired writing, at least in their view, as deserving of mockery, taking the psalm as referring to Solomon and his wife. Yet what could be a worse example of folly than this, reducing the sayings of the inspired author to nonsense and to the praise and commendation of women and | what follows from that, by interpreting the

ὅσα τούτοις ἕπεται, κατὰ τὴν ἐκείνων γνώμην ἑρμηνευομένου τοῦ ψαλμοῦ·
Ταῦτα μὲν οὖν καὶ γελᾶν ὡς μυθώδη προσῆκε, προσέχειν δὲ δεῖ πάντων
ἕνεκεν τῇ τοῦ ψαλμοῦ ἑρμηνείᾳ ἀκριβέστερον.

2ᵃ. Ἐξηρεύξατο ἡ καρδία μου λόγον ἀγαθόν. Καταιδείτω πρὸ τῶν ἄλλων
ἁπάντων αὐτοὺς τὸ προοίμιον. Δῆλον γὰρ ἐντεῦθεν ὅτι τὴν τοῦ ψαλμοῦ 5
τούτου προφητείαν ἀναγκαιοτέραν τίθεται πασῶν τῶν ἐν τοῖς λοιποῖς ψαλμοῖς προσαγορεύσεων. Ἐξ ὧν βουλόμενος δεῖξαι τῶν λεγομένων τὴν ὑπερο-
χήν, ἤρξατο λέγειν Ἐξηρεύξατο ἡ καρδία μου λόγον ἀγαθόν· οὐ γὰρ εἴποιεν
ὅτι τὸ μὲν τοῦ Σολομῶντος καὶ τῆς τούτου γυναικὸς ἐγκώμιον λόγος ἦν
ἀγαθός, — οἱ δὲ κατὰ τὸν Ἐζεκίαν ἢ τὸν λαὸν προαγορεύοντες οὐ πολλῷ 10
τούτου κρείττους ἐτύγχανον, ὥστε αὐτοὺς ἀξιωθῆναι τούτου τοῦ προοι-
μίου, — ἀλλ' ὅμως δεικνὺς τὸ μέγεθος τῶν ἐν τῷ ψαλμῷ τούτῳ λέγεσθαι
μελλόντων ὁ μακάριος Δαυὶδ τούτῳ κέχρηται τῷ προοιμίῳ.

Τί δ' ἂν εἴη μεῖζον τῶν κατὰ τὸν | Quid itaque inuenietur maius
Χριστόν, δι' οὗπερ τοσαύτη μετα- | his quae a Christo facta sunt in 15
βολὴ τῆς οἰκουμένης γεγένηται, πάν- | tanta mundi commutatione om-
των ἐπεγνωκότων τὸν τῶν ὅλων Θεόν, | nibus agnoscentibus, Deum uni-
καὶ εὐσεβείας καὶ ἀρε|τῆς ἐπιμελεῖ- | uersorum et pietatis atque uirtu-
σθαι ἐσπουδακότων, καὶ δοξαζόντων | tis diligentiam habere festinan-
μὲν τὸν τοῦ Θεοῦ Μονογενῆ, ἀπο- | tium, et glorificantium quidem 20
διδόντων δὲ καὶ τὴν πρέπουσαν | Dei Vnigenitum, exhibentium
προσκύνησιν τῷ ἁγίῳ Πνεύματι· | vero sancto Spiritui condignam
ἐφ' οἷς ὁ μακάριος Δαυὶδ ἔφασκεν | adorationem; pro quibus beatus
Ἐξηρεύξατο ἡ καρδία μου λόγον | David ait: Eructauit cor meum
ἀγαθόν; | uerbum bonum? 25

Τὸ γὰρ ἐξηρεύξατο ἔθος αὐτῷ λέγειν ὅταν βούληται τὴν πρὸς τὰ λεγόμενα τῆς καρδίας συγκατάθεσιν δεικνύναι, ἐπειδήπερ κάτωθεν ἐκ τοῦ βάθους
ἡ ἐρυγὴ πέφυκε γίνεσθαι, καὶ ὅλως ὅταν τῶν λεγομένων τὸ ἀναγκαῖον παρίστησιν, ἐπειδὴ τὰ τοιαῦτα ἀπ' αὐτῆς ὡς εἰπεῖν τῆς καρδίας τις φθέγγεται
μᾶλλον συντιθέμενος τοῖς λεγομένοις διὰ τὸ οἰκεῖον αὐτῶν μέγεθος. Ἐνταῦθα 30
γοῦν, ὅσῳ καὶ μείζονα ἦν τὰ λεγόμενα, οὐδὲ εἶπεν ἐξηρεύξαντο τὰ χείλη

14-25 Quid itaque — bonum *affert* Facundus Hermianensis, *Pro defensione
trium Capitulorum* IX, 1 (P. L., LXVII, 739 C 2-9).   30-279, 2 *cf.* L (p. 831, 39-42):
Ἵνα γὰρ τὸ μεγαλοπρεπὲς καὶ ἐνδιάθετον παραστήσῃ τῶν λεχθησομένων ἐξηρεῦχθαί φησιν
οὐ τὰ χείλη, ἀλλὰ τὴν καρδίαν.

Aᵉ 26-28 (p. 252, 6-10): Eructationis uerbo utitur, cum intentum ad ea quae
dicenda (dec- *ms*) sunt monstrare uult cordis affectum, et non tenere labiis sed
de intimis praecordi⟨i⟩s.

psalm from that standpoint? So, while this approach is to be ridiculed as a fable, there is need to attend to the commentary on the psalm in every detail very precisely.

My heart belched a good word (v. 1). Let the introduction before all the rest give them pause: it is clear from it that he regards the inspired composition of this psalm as more significant than all the openings to the other psalms. Wishing to bring out its superiority with these words, he began by saying *My heart belched a good word.* After all, they would not claim that commendation of Solomon and his wife was *a good word,* while those foretelling the situation of Hezekiah or the people were not much better than that to the extent of being deemed worthy of this introduction. Instead, to bring out the importance of the contents about to be recited in this psalm, blessed David employs this introduction. Now, what could be more important than the events concerning Christ, through whom such a wonderful transformation of the world was achieved, with everyone acknowledging the God of all, zealous for attention to piety and virtue, and glorifying God's Only-begotten while rendering also due adoration to the Holy Spirit?

It was of these things that blessed David exclaimed *My heart belched a good word.* It is his custom to use *belched* whenever he wishes to bring out the endorsement by the heart of what is said, especially since a belch normally is produced from the very depths. He uses the expression most of all whenever he emphasizes the importance of what is said, since a person utters such things from the very heart, as it were, preferring to let the contents convey their own significance.[1] In this case, at any rate, when the contents are so much more important, instead of saying "My lips belched," | as else-

---

1. The verb in the LXX, ἐξερεύγομαι, although occurring elsewhere in the Psalms, as Theodore observes, is employed here to render a *hapax legomenon* in the Hebrew. While Diodore and Chrysostom take it to suggest the involuntary character of the utterance and hence the Spirit's involvement, Theodore sees it as an index of the significance of the contents in the view of the psalmist. See Hill, "Psalm 45," 95–100.

μου, ὡς ἀλλαχοῦ φαίνεται λέγων ἐξηρεύξαιντο τὰ χείλη μου ὕμνον, ἀλλ'
ἐξηρεύξατο ἡ καρδία μου, ἵνα δείξῃ μείζονα τὴν πρὸς τὰ λεγόμενα συγκατάθεσιν ἣν ἐκέκτητο ἐφηδόμενος τῷ μεγέθει τῶν λεγομένων. Καλὸν μὲν γὰρ
κρίνειν καὶ τὸ προφητεύειν τὰ κατὰ τὸν λαόν, κρείττονα δὲ κατὰ τὸν
5 Χριστόν, ὅσῳ καὶ μείζονα ἔχει τὰ κατορθώματα· διόπερ ἐνταῦθα μάλιστα
εἶπε τὸ λόγον ἀγαθόν, ἐπειδὴ καὶ πολλῶν ἀγαθῶν παρεκτικὰ ἔμελλεν ἐξηγεῖσθαι πράγματα.

2ᵇ. Λέγω ἐγὼ τὰ ἔργα μου τῷ βασιλεῖ. Αὐτῷ φησι τῷ βασιλεῖ λέγω
τὰ ἔργα μου, τουτέστι τῷ Χριστῷ, ἔργον ἑαυτοῦ καλῶν τὴν προφητείαν
10 δι' ἧς ἐπαίδευε τοὺς πειθομένους, — ὡς καὶ ὁ ἀπόστολός φησιν Οὐκ εἰμι
ἐλεύθερος; οὐκ εἰμι ἀπόστολος; οὐ τὸ ἔργον μου ὑμεῖς ἐστε ἐν Κυρίῳ; καὶ
ἀλλαχοῦ Εἴ τις ἐπισκοπῆς ὀρέγεται καλοῦ ἔργου ἐπιθυμεῖ, καὶ ἀλλαχοῦ
περὶ διδασκάλων Εἴ τινος τὸ ἔργον μενεῖ ὃ ἐπῳκοδόμησεν, μισθὸν λήψεται,
εἴ τινος τὸ ἔργον κατακαήσεται, ζημιωθήσεται καὶ τὰ ἑξῆς, — ἐπειδήπερ ἅπας
15 προχειρισμὸς χάριτι πνευματικῇ εἰς οἰκοδομὴν ἑτέρων γιγνόμενος ἔργον
καλεῖται. Ἔργον γάρ ἐστιν ὃ ἐρ|γάζεσθαι καὶ ἐπιτελεῖν τὸν προχειρι-
ζόμενον προσήκει πρὸς τὴν ἑτέρων ὠφέλειαν, ὅπερ ἀπὸ τῆς τοῦ ἀποστελ-
λομένου σπουδῆς τε καὶ ῥαθυμίας ἢ ἐπαινετὸν ἢ ψεκτὸν τὸν ἐγχειριζόμε-
νον καθίστησιν· οὕτω κἀνταῦθα ἔργα οἰκεῖα καλεῖ τὴν προφητείαν, ἣν
20 εἰργάζετο τῇ χάριτι τῇ πνευματικῇ πρὸς τὴν ἑτέρων ὠφέλειαν. Τὰς οὖν
νῦν προαγορεύσεις αὐτῶν φησιν ἀνατίθεμαι, οὐκ ἀσχολῶ περὶ ἑτέρους.
Πῶς; Ἐπειδὴ τὰ περὶ αὐτοῦ προαγορεύειν μέλλει, αὐτῷ οὖν λέγω, τοῦ-
τέστιν αὐτῷ ἀφορίζω τὸν νῦν λόγον, εἰς αὐτοῦ δόξαν ποιούμενος τὴν προαγόρευσιν τὰ περὶ αὐτοῦ προφητεύων. Οὐ γάρ, ὥς τινες ᾠήθησαν, ἑτέρου
25 ἐστὶ προσώπου τὸ Λέγω ἐγὼ τὰ ἔργα μου τῷ βασιλεῖ, ὡς τοῦ Θεοῦ
λέγοντος περὶ τοῦ Δαυὶδ ὅτι αὐτῷ μέλλει λέγειν τὰ ἔργα.

Βασιλέως γὰρ ἐνταῦθα ἐν πλείοσι μέμνηται τόποις — Ἔντεινον γάρ φησι,
καὶ κατευοδοῦ καὶ βασίλευε ἐν καρδίᾳ τῶν ἐχθρῶν τοῦ βασιλέως, καὶ ῥάβδος εὐθύτητος ἡ ῥάβδος τῆς βασιλείας, καὶ ἐπιθυμήσει ὁ βασιλεὺς τοῦ κάλ-
30 λους σου, καὶ ἀπενεχθήσονται τῷ βασιλεῖ παρθένοι ὀπίσω αὐτῆς — καὶ βασιλίσσης δὲ μέμνηται, βασιλέα μὲν καλῶν τὸν Χριστόν, βασίλισσαν δὲ τὴν
ἀπὸ τῶν πιστῶν συνεστῶσαν ἐκκλησίαν. Δῆλον δὲ ὅτι περὶ τοῦ αὐτοῦ
κἀνταῦθα λέγει βασιλέως· ὃν γὰρ ἂν δι' ὅλων νοήσωμεν λέγεσθαι βασιλέα,
τὸν αὐτὸν δηλονότι κἀνταῦθα εἶναι τὸν λεγόμενον παραδεξόμεθα.

1 Ps. CXVIII, 171   10-11 I Cor. IX, 1   12 I Tim. III, 1   13-14 I Cor. III, 14-15
27-28 v. 5ᵃ   28 v. 6ᶜ   28-29 v. 7ᵇ   29-30 v. 12ᵃ   30 v. 15ᵃ.

Aᵉ 2-6 (p. 252, 12-16) : Sicut refic⟨i⟩ens bonum quadam delectatione eructatio
fieri adsolet corporalis, pro obtima adnuntiatione ceteris profetalibus *uerbum*
posuit.   9-10 (p. 252, 17-19) : In Christi gloriam opus praedicationis exerceo;
opus autem suum profetiam uocat.

where he is found saying "May my lips belch praise,"[2] he says *My heart belched* so as to bring out more clearly the endorsement of the contents that he found in exulting over the import of the contents. In other words, while inspired composition about the people's situation is good to expound, that concerning Christ is of a higher order to the extent that the achievements are also greater—hence his saying here *a good word,* since he was also on the point of narrating things productive of much good.

I tell of my works to the king. He means, I tell of my works to the king in person—that is, to Christ, by his "work" referring to the inspired composition by which he instructed the believers. The apostle likewise says, "Am I not free? Am I not an apostle? Are you not my work in the Lord?" and elsewhere, "Anyone aspiring to the rank of bishop desires a noble work," and elsewhere about teachers, "If anyone's work built on the foundation survives, he will receive a reward; if the work is burnt up, he will sustain loss" and so on.[3] This is especially so since every commission from the grace of the Spirit for the upbuilding of others is called a "work": work is a commission that has to be performed and carried out for the benefit of others, earning the person commissioned either praise or blame depending on the zeal or the sloth displayed. So here he refers to inspired composition as his own works, since he produced it by the grace of the Spirit for the benefit of others. So he is saying, I am now imparting predictions of them; I am not concerned with others. In what sense? Since he is on the point of predicting matters affecting him, it is to him therefore that I *tell* them—that is, it is to him that I dedicate the composition, giving glory to him by prophesying matters affecting him.

It is not, you see, as some commentators believed, that the verse *I tell of my works to the king* comes from another person, as though God were saying of David that he is about to tell him his works. He mentions *king* here, in fact, at several points: *advance, proceed and reign ... in the heart of the king's foes... the rod of your kingship a rod of equity ... the king will long for your beauty... maidens will be brought to the king after her* (vv. 4, 5, 6, 11, 14). He also mentions a *queen* (v. 9), by *king* referring to Christ, and by *queen* to the church composed of the faithful. It is clear that here, too, he is speaking of the same king: the one whom we understand to be referred to as king throughout we take to be clearly the one mentioned here as well. | Now, this is our claim

---

2. Ps 119:171.

3. 1 Cor 9:1; 1 Tim 3:1; 1 Cor 3:14–15. As good Antiochenes, Chrysostom and Theodore both insist that inspired composition is the result both of the Spirit's grace and of the industry of the human author (Chrysostom comparing it to shipbuilding).

Τοῦτο δὲ ἡμῖν εἴρηται πρὸς τοὺς οὕτως νοοῦντας τῶν Χριστιανῶν, οἳ καὶ σφόδρα συνεργοῦσιν Ἰουδαίων τῇ κακοτεχνίᾳ, τὴν ἐναλλαγὴν τοῦ προσώπου παρεισάγοντες, — ὅπερ ἐὰν δοθῇ, πᾶσαν εὐχερῶς Ἰουδαῖοι παρατρέψουσι τὴν ἀληθῆ τοῦ ψαλμοῦ διάνοιαν, ὡς ἑξῆς ἐστιν ἐκ τῆς ἑρμηνείας ἰδεῖν, μάλιστα εἰ λάβοιεν καὶ βασιλέα ἐν τῷ ψαλμῷ ἕτερόν τινα νομίζεσ- 5 θαι παρὰ | τὸν Χριστόν.

Φαίνεται τοίνυν τοῦτο οὐ παρὰ τοῦ Θεοῦ πρὸς τὸν Δαυὶδ λεγόμενον, ἀλλὰ παρὰ τοῦ Δαυὶδ περὶ τοῦ Χριστοῦ, ὃν καὶ βασιλέα συμφώνως ἑαυτοῦ δι᾿ ὅλων τοῦ ψαλμοῦ τῶν ῥημάτων φαίνεται προσαγορεύων. Ἐναλλαγὴ δὲ προσώπων ἐστὶ μὲν κατὰ τὸ ἀληθὲς ἐν τοῖς ψαλμοῖς οὐδεμία· καλὸν γὰρ 10 μηδὲ τοῦτο παραλιπεῖν, μάλιστα μὲν διὰ Ἰουδαίους τοὺς τούτῳ κεχρημένους πρὸς παρατροπὴν τῆς ἀληθοῦς διανοίας καὶ πρὸς ἀπόδειξιν δὲ τῶν λεγομένων ἀκριβῆ, ὥστε μηδένα τῶν πιστῶν περιπίπτειν τῷ σφάλματι τῶν ἁπλῶς καὶ ὡς ἔτυχεν ἀπὸ στοχασμοῦ διανοίας τὰ πολλὰ ἑρμηνεύειν ἐθελόντων.

Ἡ δέ γε δοκοῦσα εἶναι, ἢ οὖσα κατ᾿ αὐτούς, εὑρίσκεται τότε ὅταν περὶ 15 ἑτέρων φθέγγεσθαι τὸν προφήτην συμβαίνῃ. Ἐναλλαγὴ δὲ προσώπου, ὡς ἐκεῖνοί φασιν, ἵνα καὶ τοῦτο δοίημεν οὕτως ἔχειν, οὐδαμοῦ κατὰ τοῦτον οὖσα τὸν τρόπον ἐν τοῖς ψαλμοῖς φαίνεται ὡς νῦν μὲν τοῦ προφήτου φθεγγομένου πρὸς τὸν Θεόν, αὖθις δὲ τοῦ Θεοῦ πρὸς τὸν προφήτην ἀντιφθεγγομένου· ἀλλ᾿ ἐπειδὰν περί τινων λογοποιεῖται — ἡγεμόνα ἐξηγούμενος, ἢ ἐσόμενα 20 προφητεύων — ἀπὸ τῆς τῶν λεγομένων ἀκολουθίας πάντως παρεντίθησι τὰ ὑπὸ τοῦ Θεοῦ λεγόμενα ἁρμοδίως ἐκείνοις περὶ ὧν καὶ ποιεῖται τὸν λόγον.

Ἐπειδὴ γὰρ ἔθος αὐτῷ ἀντὶ πράγματος λέγειν τὴν φωνήν, ὡς ἀποδέδεικται ἡμῖν πολλαχοῦ, ἐνίοτε μὲν ἐπὶ τῶν ἀνθρώπων, ἔστι δὲ ὅτε καὶ ἐπὶ τοῦ Θεοῦ· οἷόν ἐστιν ἐν τῷ δευτέρῳ τὸ Κύριος εἶπε πρός με Υἱός μου εἶ 25 σύ — ἀντὶ τοῦ Μετέδωκέ μοι τῆς υἱότητος — ἐκ προσώπου τοῦ ληφθέντος ἀνθρώπου λεγόμενον, τὸ Ὅτι λαλήσει εἰρήνην ἐπὶ τὸν λαὸν αὐτοῦ — τουτέστιν ὅτι παρέξει ἡμῖν τὴν εἰρήνην. Καὶ πολλάκις ἀπὸ τῆς τῶν πραγμάτων ἀκολουθίας, ὡς ὑπὸ τοῦ Θεοῦ γεγονός | τι σημάναι βουλόμενος, περιτίθησιν αὐτῷ φωνὴν ὡσανεὶ λέγοντος καὶ ἀποφαινομένου ἢ καὶ ἐπαγγελλομένου, οὐ 30 προστιθεὶς τὸ εἶπεν ἢ ἐλάλησεν. Ὥσπερ γὰρ ἐπὶ τῶν ἀνθρώπων τὸ εἶπεν ἀντὶ πράγματος λαβὼν (ὡς τὸ Εἶπεν γὰρ ἐν καρδίᾳ αὐτοῦ Ἐπιλέλησται ὁ Θεός, καὶ Εἶπεν ἐν καρδίᾳ αὐτοῦ Οὐκ ἐκζητήσει, ἀντὶ τοῦ Οὕτω πράττει ὡς οὐκ ἐκζητοῦντος τοῦ Θεοῦ τὰ ἠγνοημένα) ἐνίοτε ἀπὸ ἀκολουθίας τίθησιν αὐτὸ ὡσανεὶ λεγόντων τινῶν, οὐ τίθησι δὲ τὸ εἶπεν ἢ λέγων 35 (οἷόν ἐστιν τὸ ἐν τῷ β΄ Διαρρήξωμεν τοὺς δεσμοὺς αὐτῶν) εἴληπται δὲ ἀπὸ τοῦ πράγματος — ἀντὶ Τοῦτο ἐποίουν καὶ οὗτος ἦν αὐτοῖς τοῦ πράγματος

24 cf. p. 177, 10; 191, 23-24; 192, 19; 195, 6   25-26 Ps. 2, 7ᵇ   27 ps. 84, 9ᵇ   32-33 ps. 9, 32ᵃ   33 ps. 9, 34ᵇ   36 ps. 2, 3ᵃ.

15 αὐτοὺς conieci (cf. p. 281, 31), αὐτοῦ ms.

in response to those Christians who are of such a mind as vehemently to support the Jews' malpractice by introducing a change in person; if this were conceded, it would be easy for the Jews to distort the true sense of the psalm entirely, as is possible to see in the rest of the commentary, especially if they were to take the king in the psalm to refer to some person other than Christ.

It emerges, then, that this is said not by God to David but by David of Christ, whom in all the verses of the psalm he also consistently calls his king. A change of persons is not at all in keeping with the true sense of the psalms; it is not right to pass over this point, especially in view of Jews using it to distort the true meaning, and as it serves as a precise demonstration of the contents, the risk being that some of the faithful may be brought down by the wiles of those wishing to interpret most things simply and solely by guesswork. The apparent meaning—or, in their view, the real meaning—is found when it turns out that the author is speaking about different persons. There is a change in person, so they claim, intending us to concede that this is the case, whereas nowhere in the psalms does it occur in this way, that sometimes the author speaks to God, and sometimes God speaks to the author. Instead, when he is discoursing on certain things—presenting himself as a leader or prophesying the future—on the basis of the theme of the verses in every case he inserts what is said by God consistently with the matters on which he is discoursing.

You see, it is his custom to use the word to mean the action, as has frequently been demonstrated by us, sometimes in the case of human beings, sometimes in the case of God. For example, in the verse in Psalm 2, spoken on the part of the man assumed, "The Lord said to me, 'You are my son,' " he means, He gave me a share in sonship; and the verse "Because he will speak peace to his people"[4]—that is, He will provide us with peace. And often from the sequence of events, as in his wish to indicate something done by God, he ascribes to him a speech as though he were speaking or declaring or even ordering, without supplying the words "he said" or "he spoke." You see, in the case of human beings he uses the words "he said" to mean the deed (for example, "He said in his heart, 'God will forget,' " and "He said in his heart, 'He will not search,' " meaning, He behaves as if God were not searching for unknown things).[5] Sometimes, in accordance with the movement of thought he does the same thing, as if certain people were speaking, but without putting "he said" or "saying" (as, for example, in Psalm 2, "Let us break their bonds");[6] instead, it is taken from the action, as if to say, They did it, and this was the purpose of the action. |

4. Pss 2:7; 85:8.
5. Ps 10:11, 13.
6. Ps 2:3.

ὁ σκοπὸς — οὕτω καὶ ἐπὶ τοῦ Θεοῦ λέγει μέν τι τοιοῦτον ἐνίοτε ἀπὸ τοῦ πράγματος περιάπτων αὐτῷ φωνήν, οὐ τίθησι δὲ τὸ εἶπεν, ἀπὸ κοινοῦ νοεῖσθαι καταλιμπάνων αὐτὸ ἐν τῇ τοῦ λόγου ἀκολουθίᾳ τε καὶ τάξει, — οἷον ἐν τῷ λα΄ λέγει μέν τινα ἐκ τοῦ Ἐζεκίου ὡς ἂν ἐν τῷ καιρῷ
5 τῆς ἀρρωστίας ἐξομολογησαμένου περὶ τῆς ἁμαρτίας, ἀφ᾽ ἧς εἰς τὴν ἀρρωστίαν κατέπεσεν, ὑπὲρ τῆς κοινῆς ἁπάντων ὠφελείας τὰ κατ᾽ ἐκεῖνον ἐξηγούμενος. Βουλόμενος δὲ εἰπεῖν τίνα παρέχει Κύριος τοῖς ἐξομολογουμένοις ὑπὲρ ὧν ἥμαρτον, φωνὴν αὐτῷ περιτίθησιν, ὡς ἂν ταῦτα ποιήσειν ἐπαγγειλαμένῳ καί φησι Συνετιῶ σε καὶ συμβιβῶ σε ἐν ὁδῷ ταύτῃ ᾗ
10 πορεύσῃ καὶ τὰ ἑξῆς, ἀντὶ τοῦ Ταῦτα δὲ αὐτῷ ὑπέσχετο ὁ Θεὸς ὑπὲρ τῆς ἐξομολογήσεως, ἵνα εἴπῃ ὅτι ταῦτα ποιήσει, — καὶ οὐ προσέθηκε τὸ εἶπεν, ἀπὸ δὲ τῆς τῶν εἰρημένων ἀκολουθίας προσεπινοεῖται ὅτι πρὸς τὰ τοῦ Ἐζεκίου ῥήματα ταῦτα εἶπεν ὁ Θεός.

Οὕτω καὶ ἐν τῷ οδ΄ ψαλμῷ Ἐξομολογησόμεθά σοι, ὁ Θεός φησιν, ἐξο-
15 μολογησόμεθά σοι, διηγήσομαι πάντα τὰ θαυμάσιά σου ὅταν λάβω καιρόν, εἶτα ὡς ἐκ τοῦ Θεοῦ Ἐγὼ εὐθύτητας κρινῶ· τοῦτο γὰρ δηλονότι οὐ περὶ τοῦ προφήτου φησὶν ὁ Θεός, ἀλλὰ περὶ ἑτέρων — ὡς καὶ ἐπαγαγὼν Ἐτάκη ἡ γῆ καὶ πάντες οἱ κατοικοῦντες ἐν αὐτῇ, πάλιν ὡς ἐκ τοῦ Θεοῦ φησιν Ἐγὼ ἐστερέωσα τοὺς στύλους αὐτῆς. Καὶ ὅλως ἡ δοκοῦσα ἐναλλαγὴ τοῦ
20 προφήτου συμφωνίαν ἔχειν τινὰ πρὸς τὴν ἀκολουθίαν ὀφείλει τῶν λεγομένων, ὥσπερ οὖν κἀνταῦθα, ἐπειδὴ εἶπε Διηγήσομαι τὰ θαυμάσιά σου ὅταν λάβω καιρόν, ἑξῆς λέγει ποῖα θαυμάσια — ἐγὼ εὐθύτητας κρινῶ (τουτέστιν ὅτι τοῦτο εἶπας καὶ τοῦτο ποιεῖν ἐπηγγείλω, ἵνα εἴπῃ ὅτι ἐποίησας) εἶτα διὰ μέσου παρενθείς, ὥσπερ οὖν ἔθος αὐτῷ — τὸ ἐτάκη ἡ γῆ καὶ
25 πάντες οἱ κατοικοῦντες ἐν αὐτῇ, ἀκολούθως ἐπήγαγεν Ἐγὼ ἐστερέωσα τοὺς στύλους αὐτῆς.

Ἐνταῦθα μέντοι Λέγω ἐγὼ τὰ ἔργα μου τῷ βασιλεῖ οὐ περὶ ἑτέρου λέγει, ἀλλὰ περὶ αὐτοῦ τοῦ προφήτου, κατὰ τοὺς οὕτως ἑρμηνεύοντας — ὅπερ οὐδαμοῦ εὑρίσκομεν ἐν τοῖς ψαλμοῖς· οὐδαμοῦ γὰρ λέγοντός τι τοῦ
30 Δαυὶδ πρὸς τὸν Θεόν, ὁ Θεὸς πάλιν ἀποκρινόμενος λέγει πρὸς αὐτόν.

Ὅλως δὲ εἴ που ἡ κατ᾽ αὐτοὺς δοκοῦσα ἐναλλαγὴ τοῦ προσώπου εὑρίσκεται, κατὰ τοῦτον οὖσα φαίνεται τὸν τρόπον· τοῦ προφήτου, ἐν τῷ ἐξηγεῖσθαι τὰ περὶ ἑτέρων, παρεμβάλλοντος ἐκ τῆς τῶν λεγομένων ἀκολουθίας τὰ περὶ αὐτῶν ἐκείνων, περὶ ὧνπερ λέγει, ὡς ἐκ τοῦ Θεοῦ εἰρη-
35 μένα, ἀκόλουθα ὄντα καὶ τοῖς λοιποῖς πᾶσι τοῖς περὶ ἐκείνων λεγομένοις περὶ ὧν ποιεῖται τοῦ ψαλμοῦ τὴν ὑπόθεσιν — καὶ τοῦτο δὲ ποιοῦντος, ὥστε τι πραχθὲν ἢ γενησόμενον εἰπεῖν, διὰ τὸ ἀπὸ τοῦ οἰκείου ἰδιώματος συνεχῶς ἀπὸ τοῦ πράγματος φωνὴν ἀνατυποῦν, ἣν τῷ ποιοῦντι περιτίθησιν. Καὶ τοῦτο μὲν ὡς πρὸς Ἰουδαίους μάλιστα ἡμῖν ὠφελίμως ἐπιτετήρηται.

4 ss. cf. supra p. 139   9-10 Ps. 31, 8ᵃ   14-19 ps. 74, 2-7ᵇ.

So also in the case of God, while he says such a thing sometimes by associating the word with him from the action, he does not use "he said," leaving it to be generally understood from the sequence and order of the discourse. For instance, in Psalm 31 he tells some things from the viewpoint of Hezekiah in the time of illness confessing his sin, which was the cause of his falling ill, explaining his situation for the common good of all. But in his wish to say what the Lord provides to those who confess their sins, he attributes to him a speech as if he were promising to do it, and he says, "I shall instruct you and guide you on this way that you should travel" and so on,[7] meaning, God promised this in return for the confession; as if to say, He will do it—without adding "he said," yet from the sequence of thought it will be understood: In response to the words of Hezekiah God said this.

Likewise also in Psalm 75, "We shall confess to you, O God, we shall confess to you, we shall recount all your marvels when I seize the opportunity"; then, as if on God's part, "I shall judge uprightness," which God says obviously not with regard to the author but with regard to others, and so he goes on, "The earth is wasted and all its inhabitants"; and again on God's part it says, "I established its pillars."[8] In general, the author's apparent change ought bear some consistency with the movement of thought, as in the present case as well: after saying "I shall recount your marvels when I seize the opportunity," he goes on to say what sort of marvels, "I shall judge uprightness" (that is, You said this, and you promised to do it, as if to say, You did it), and then made his customary insertion, "The earth is wasted and all its inhabitants," and logically proceeded, "I established its pillars."

In this case, by contrast, he says *I tell my works to the king,* not of someone else but of the author himself in the view of those taking it this way—something we find nowhere in the psalms: nowhere does David say something to God, and in reply God speaks to him.[9] Generally, if what strikes them as a change of person occurs anywhere, it emerges in reality to be of the following kind. In commenting on matters affecting others, the author in the course of his treatment inserts matters affecting those same people, of whom he makes statements as if on God's part, which are in keeping with all the rest of the things about those of whom he develops the theme of the psalm. He does this so as to mention what has been done or will happen with a view to framing words on the basis of an action in his habitual manner and attributing it to the one delivering them. While for our own good we should be on the lookout for this in opposition to Jews, | it would suffice to prove

---

7. Ps 32:8.

8. Ps 75:1–3 LXX.

9. Cf. Pss 60; 82; 108 for an oracular response by the Lord to the psalmist—a feature of "prophetic psalms," in Sigmund Mowinckel's term.

Πρὸς δὲ τοὺς Χριστιανούς, εἰ καὶ τοῦτο γίνεσθαι ἐγχωρεῖ, αὔταρκες ἦν
ἐνταῦθα δεῖξαι μηδεμίαν ἐναλλαγὴν γεγενῆσθαι τῷ πολλαχοῦ τὴν τοῦ
βασιλέως προσηγορίαν ἐν τῷ ψαλμῷ κειμένην εὑρίσκειν. Ὃν γὰρ ἂν διόλου
γνωρίσωμεν βασιλέα, δῆλον ὅτι τὸν αὐτὸν καὶ ἐνταῦθα νοήσομεν, ἢ παρα-
φθεροῦμεν ὅλην τοῦ ψαλμοῦ τὴν διάνοιαν νῦν μὲν οὕτως νῦν δὲ ἑτέρως   5
νοοῦντες· ἔσται δὲ εἴπερ βασιλέα ἐνταῦθα ἑαυτὸν καλεῖ, κατὰ τοὺς οὕτως
ἑρμηνεύοντας, ἐν παντὶ τῷ ψαλμῷ περὶ βασιλέως ἑαυτοῦ λέγων, καὶ οὐκέτι
τοῦ δεσπότου Χριστοῦ, ᾧ δὴ καὶ μόνῳ τὸ ἑξῆς ἁρμόττειν δύναται. Ἓν
τοίνυν πρόσωπόν ἐστι διόλου· ἐπειδὴ οὖν εἶπεν ὅτι Λέγω ἐγὼ τὰ ἔργα
μου τῷ βασιλεῖ, — οὐκ ἦν δὲ ἐκεῖνος ἱκανὸς τὰ τοῦ βασιλέως ὑπαγο-   10
ρεύειν, — ἐπάγει·

2ᶜ. Ἡ γλῶσσά μου κάλαμος γραμματέως ὀξυγράφου. Ὁ γὰρ κάλαμος
δεῖται μέλανος, δεῖται δὲ καὶ τοῦ γραφέως ὡς καὶ τὸ μέλαν αὐτῷ ἐπιβάλ-
λειν καὶ κινεῖν πρὸς τὸ ἐκτυπῶσαι τὰ γράμματα. Τὴν μὲν οὖν γλῶσσαν
ἔθηκεν ἐν τάξει καλάμου· γραμματέα δὲ καλεῖ τὸ Πνεῦμα τὸ ἅγιον, ἵν᾽ ἐν   15
χώρᾳ μέλανος ᾖ τὰ ἐντυπούμενα ὑπὸ τοῦ Πνεύματος. Τὸ γὰρ Πνεῦμα, ὥς
τις γραφεὺς ἄριστος, — τοῦτο γὰρ λέγει γραμματέα, — δίκην μέλανος πλη-
ρῶσαν τὴν καρδίαν τῶν τῆς ἀποκαλύψεως νοημάτων, ἐκεῖθεν παρέχει τῇ
γλώσσῃ λοιπὸν τὸ φθέγγεσθαί τε καὶ ὥσπερ γράμματα διατυποῦν τοῖς
λόγοις καὶ διαρθροῦν τοῖς βουλομένοις δέχεσθαι τὴν ἐξ αὐτῶν ὠφέλειαν.   20
Τοῦτο οὖν βούλεται εἰπεῖν ὅτι οὐκ οἰκεῖα ἡ γλῶττα φθέγγεται νοήματα,
ἀλλὰ τῆς ἀποκαλύψεως τοῦ Πνεύματος· διόπερ ἀξιόπιστος ἡμῖν τὰ τοῦ
βασιλέως ἐξηγούμενος.

Εἰπὼν δὲ γραμματέως ὀξυγράφου, ἔδειξε καὶ τὸ δυνατὸν τῆς τοῦ Πνεύματος ἐνεργείας καὶ τὸ εὔθετον τῆς οἰκείας γλώττης. Καὶ γὰρ ὀξυγράφος   25
γραμματεὺς τοιοῦτος ἀπὸ τῆς ἐπιστήμης καθέστηκε τῆς οἰκείας, | καὶ ὁ
κάλαμος τοῦ τοιούτου ἐξ ἀνάγκης τοιοῦτός ἐστιν ὥστε δύνασθαι ἀναλέγειν
τῇ τέχνῃ τοῦ γραφέως. Ἦν δὲ τῆς γλώττης τοῦ προφήτου τὸ εὔθετον
οὐκ ἀπὸ τῆς οἰκείας στροφῆς, ἀλλ᾽ ἀπὸ τῆς εὐθύτητος τῆς διανοίας. Ταῦτα
προοιμιασάμενος καὶ ἐκπλαγεὶς μὲν πρότερον τὸ μέγεθος τῶν λέγεσθαι   30
μελλόντων, ποιησάμενος δὲ συντόμως τοῦ μεγέθους αὐτῶν τὴν ἀπόδειξιν
καὶ τὴν πρὸς τοὺς λοιποὺς τῶν ψαλμῶν διαφορὰν τῷ εἰπεῖν ὅτι περὶ
αὐτοῦ τοῦ βασιλέως φθέγγεσθαι μέλλει, τότε ἀξιόπιστον ἑαυτῷ κατασκευάσας τοῦ δύνασθαι φθέγγεσθαι περὶ τῶν τοιούτων ἀπὸ τοῦ μὴ τὰ ἴδια

1 αὐτάρκης *ms*
15 L (p. 832, 25): Γραμματεὺς οὖν τὸ Πνεῦμα, διότι σοφόν.

Aᵉ 24-28 (p. 252, 20-24): Ac si diceret Lingua mea impar est tantae adnun-
tiationis, sed ministerium praebet Spiritui sancto et tanquam cuidam scribae
docto calamus aptus obsequitur.

to Christians, even should this happen, that no change has occurred, the evidence being the appearance of the word *king* in many places in the psalm. In fact, if we identify this king throughout, it is clear that in this case also we shall take the view that it is the same king, or else distort the whole sense of the psalm by taking it one way now and another way at another time. If, on the other hand, it is to himself he refers by *king* in this case, as those commentators claim, he speaks of himself as king in all of the psalm, and no longer of Christ the Lord, to whom alone the sequel also can be applied. There is, therefore, one person throughout.

Since, then, he said *I tell my works to the king* (he would not have been up to dictating the king's affairs), he goes on to say *My tongue the pen of a rapid scribe.* The pen, you see, requires ink, and requires also the writer to put ink on it and move it to inscribe the letters. So he used his tongue in the role of a pen, and by *scribe* he refers to the Holy Spirit, so that what is inscribed by the Holy Spirit takes the place of ink. The Spirit, you see, like some excellent writer (he calls him a *scribe*), fills the heart with insights of revelation like ink, and thereby enables the tongue then to express and to form letters, as it were, in words and endue them with articulate speech for those wishing to receive benefit from them.[10] So it means, What the tongue utters is not its own ideas, but comes from the revelation of the Spirit. Hence, in commenting on the king's affairs he is trustworthy.

Now, by mentioning *a rapid scribe* he brought out both the force of the Spirit's operation and the promptness of his own tongue: a rapid scribe is made such by his own skill, and such a person's *pen* is necessarily of such a kind as to keep up with the writer's facility. The promptness of the author's tongue, however, arose not from his own nimbleness but from his uprightness of mind. After giving this introduction, he was first struck by the magnitude of what was due to be told, and concisely presented the proof of their magnitude and the difference from the rest of the psalms by saying that he was going to speak of the king himself. Then he won credit for himself as one in a position to speak of such matters, not by speaking on his own, | but by the

---

10. See the volume introduction for the degree of originality in Theodore's contribution to thinking on biblical inspiration.

φθέγγεσθαι, ἀλλ᾽ ἀπὸ τῆς τοῦ Θεοῦ δωρεᾶς, ἄρχεται λοιπὸν αὐτῶν τῶν λόγων καί φησιν·

3ª. Ὡραῖος κάλλει παρὰ τοὺς υἱοὺς τῶν ἀνθρώπων. Κάλλος οὐ πάντως τὸ ἀπὸ τῆς τοῦ σώματος λέγει κατασκευῆς ἢ ἀπὸ τῆς κατὰ τὴν μορφὴν
5 εὐπρεπείας, ἀλλὰ κάλλος οἶδε λέγειν τὸ ἐπίδοξον, ὡς ἐν ἑτέρῳ ψαλμῷ περὶ τοῦ Ἐζεκία λέγων Κύριε, ἐν τῷ θελήματί σου παρέσχου τῷ κάλλει μου δύναμιν — κάλλος αὐτοῦ καλῶν τὴν βασιλείαν ἀφ᾽ ἧς ἐπίδοξος ἐνενόμιστο. Ἐπειδὴ γὰρ ὅλως τὸ κάλλος περίδοξον ἐργάζεται, εἰκότως πᾶν ἀφ᾽ οὗ τις περίβλεπτος καθίσταται κ ά λ λ ο ς καλεῖ· οὕτως οὖν κἀνταῦθα τοῦτο
10 βούλεται εἰπεῖν ὅτι Θαυμαστὸς εἶ καὶ σφόδρα ἐπίδοξος παρὰ πάντας τοὺς ἀνθρώπους, — καὶ γὰρ ἐθαυμάζετο παρὰ πάντων διά τε τὸ πλῆθος τῶν σημείων καὶ τῶν ἐπιτελουμένων. Ὅταν δὲ λέγῃ ὁ προφήτης περὶ αὐτοῦ ὅτι Καὶ εἴδομεν αὐτόν, καὶ οὐκ εἶχεν εἶδος οὐδὲ κάλλος οὐκ ἐναντιοῦται τῷ λεγομένῳ· περὶ γὰρ τοῦ πάθους ἐκεῖ προφητεύων, εἰκότως φησὶ
15 μὴ ἔχειν εἶδο; μηδὲ κάλλος. Ὥσπερ γὰρ ἀπὸ τῶν γινομένων ἐπίδοξος ἦν, οὕτως πάλιν ἐκ τοῦ πάθους ἄτιμος ἐνομίσθη παρὰ τοῖς πᾶσι πρὸ τῆς ἀναστάσεως, ὅπου γε καὶ τῶν | μαθητῶν ἐστιν ἰδεῖν τὸν μὲν ἀρνησάμενον, τοὺς δὲ φεύγοντας, καθὼς καὶ ὁ Κύριός φησι πρὸς αὐτοὺς ὅτι Πάντες σκανδαλισθήσονται ἐν ἐμοί.

20 **3ᵇ.** Ἐξεχύθη χάρις ἐν χείλεσί σου. Θαυμαστὸς δὲ οὕτως εἶ παρὰ πᾶσιν, ἐπειδὴ χάριτός σου πεπλήρωται τὰ χείλη καὶ φθεγγόμενος πάντας ἐφέλκῃ πρὸς σεαυτόν, πάντων θαυμαζόντων τὰ λεγόμενα. Οὕτως γὰρ καὶ ὁ εὐαγγελιστὴς ἐπισημαίνεται ὅτι ποτὲ μὲν ἔλεγον ὅτι Πόθεν αὐτῷ ἡ σοφία
αὕτη καὶ Πόθεν οὗτος οἶδε γράμματα μὴ μεμαθηκώς; ποτὲ δὲ ἀποσταλέν-
25 τες ὑπηρέται ὑπὸ τῶν Φαρισαίων ὥστε αὐτὸν συλλαβεῖν, ἐκπληττόμενοι ὑπέστρεψαν ὅτι Οὐδέποτε οὕτως ἐλάλησεν ἄνθρωπος.

6-7 Ps. 29, 8   13 Is. LIII, 2   18-19 Matth. XXVI, 31   23-24 Matth. XIII, 55
24 Ioh. VII, 15   26 Ioh. VII, 46.

22 ἑαυτὸν ms.

21-22 L (p. 833, 28-30): Ἐπειδὴ τοσαύτης ἔγεμεν αὐτοῦ τὰ ῥήματα χάριτος, ὡς ἑλκεῖν πρὸς αὐτὸν ἅπαντας.

Λᵉ 3-8 (p. 252, 25-253, 7): Facit ita pulchritudo conspicu⟨u⟩m sicut praestantia dignitatis. Pro gloriosso *speciosum* uocat; sic est et in uicissimo uiiii psalmo: *In uoluntate tua praestitisti decori meo uirtutem*, pulchritudinem uidilicet eius appellans ipsum, quo putabatur inclitus, principatum.   12-14 (p. 253, 7-10): Vnde et e regione profetae passionem eius dedecorationem uocant: *Et uidimus*, inquit, *eum et non habebat speciem neque decorem*.   3ᵇ (p. 253, 14-19): Ideo cunctis mirabilis quia labia tua gratia diuina inpleuit, auditoribus stupore defixis modo dicentibus: *Vnde huic sapientia haec?* modo praenuntiantibus quia *Numquam homo sic locutus est.*

gift of God.

At that point he commences his actual words: *Graceful in your beauty beyond the children of human beings* (v. 2). By *beauty* he refers not at all to that which comes from bodily makeup or from comeliness of form; rather, by *beauty* he usually refers to what is glorious, as in another psalm about Hezekiah he says, "Lord, in your good pleasure give me power in my beauty,"[11] by his "beauty" referring to kingship, by which he was considered glorious. You see, since it is definitely beauty that makes one splendid, he was right to refer by beauty to everything by which a person becomes the cynosure of all eyes. So likewise here, too, he means, You are admirable and extremely glorious in the sight of all people—admired as he was by all for the great number of signs and accomplishments. When, however, the prophet says of him, "We have seen him, and he had no form or beauty,"[12] there is no contradiction of this statement: in that place he is prophesying about the passion, and it is right for him to say "he had no form or beauty"; just as he was glorious in what had been done, so in turn he was considered by everyone as of no esteem in the passion before the resurrection, when you can even see the disciples denying him and taking to flight, as the Lord also said to them that they would all become deserters "because of me."[13]

Grace was poured out on your lips: you are so admired by everyone since your lips are filled with grace and by speaking you draw everyone to yourself, everyone admiring what you say. The evangelist, in fact, indicated that at one time they asked, "Whence comes this wisdom of his?" and "How does he know this when he has never had an education?" and at another time underlings were sent by the Pharisees to trap him, but were astounded and forced to admit, "No human being has ever spoken like this."[14] | *Hence,*

---

11. Ps 30:7.
12. Isa 53:2.
13. Matt 26:31.
14. Matt 13:54; John 7:15, 46.

3ᶜ. Διὰ τοῦτο εὐλόγησέ ὁ Θεὸς εἰς τὸν αἰῶνα. Τουτέστιν εὐλογεῖσθαι
σε ἐποίησε, διὰ τοῦτο ὑμνεῖσθαί σε παρὰ πάντων παρεσκεύασεν, ἁπάντων
θαυμαζόντων τῶν λεγομένων τὸ μέγεθος.

4ᵃ. Περίζωσαι τὴν ῥομφαίαν σου ἐπὶ τὸν μηρόν σου, δυνατέ. Ἐξηγησάμενος αὐτὸ τὸ θαῦμα τὸ παρὰ πᾶσι, τρέπει λοιπὸν πρὸς αὐτὸν τὸν λόγον   5
καί φησιν Ὁπλίσθητι καὶ περίθου τῷ μηρῷ τὴν μάχαιραν, ἐκ μεταφορᾶς
τῶν πολεμιστῶν τῶν τὰς μαχαίρας ἐχόντων ἐπὶ τὸν μηρόν. Διαγράφει μέντοι τοὺς λόγους, ὡς ἐπὶ εἰκόνος τὰ περὶ αὐτοῦ· οὕτω τε ποιεῖται τὸν
πλείονα λόγον περὶ τῶν κατ᾽ αὐτόν.

4ᵇ. Τῇ ὡραιότητί σου καὶ τῷ κάλλει σου. Ἀντὶ τοῦ σ ὺ ν τ ῇ ὡραιότητί   10
σου καὶ σ ὺ ν τῷ κάλλει σου. Ἐπειδὴ γὰρ εἶπεν ἄνω Ὡραῖος κάλλει παρὰ
τοὺς υἱοὺς τῶν ἀνθρώπων, ἐνταῦθα ἐπήγαγε τὸ Περίζωσαι τὴν ῥομφαίαν σου
ἐπὶ τὸν μηρόν σου, δυνατέ, τῇ ὡραιότητί σου καὶ τῷ κάλλει σου· τουτέστι
μετὰ δὲ τὸ θαυμάζεσθαι ἐπὶ τοῖς λόγοις παρὰ τῶν πιστῶν, ὁπλίσθητι καὶ
κατὰ τῶν ἐναντίων ὥστε αὐτοὺς τιμωρήσασθαι.   15

5ᵃ. Καὶ ἔντεινον, καὶ κατευοδοῦ, καὶ βασίλευε. Τὸ ἔντεινον ὡς ἐπὶ τοῦ
τόξου· ἐκείνων γὰρ ἴδιον τὸ τείνειν τὰς νευράς. Τόξευε τοίνυν φησὶν ὑπ᾽
οὐδενὸς ἐναντίου | κωλυόμενος, καὶ μεταχείρισαι τὴν βασιλείαν. Διὰ τί;
Ὥστε τί κατορθῶσαι;

5ᵇ. Ἕνεκεν ἀληθείας καὶ πραότητος καὶ δικαιοσύνης. Διὰ ταῦτά φησι   20
χρῆσαι σου τῇ ἰσχύϊ, διὰ ταῦτα ἐπίδειξαί σου τὸ μέγεθος, διὰ ταῦτα
κράτησον πάντων καὶ βασίλευε, ὥστε ταῦτα ἐνσπεῖραι τῷ γένει τῶν
ἀνθρώπων, ἀλήθειαν καὶ πραότητα καὶ δικαιοσύνην. Ἀλήθειαν μὲν γὰρ ἐδίδασκε διὰ τῶν οἰκείων διδαγμάτων, τὴν ἀληθινὴν τοῦ Θεοῦ προσκύνησιν
παιδεύων τοὺς ἀνθρώπους, καθὼς αὐτός φησιν Ἔρχεται ὥρα καὶ νῦν ἐστιν,   25
ὅτε οὔτε ἐν τῷ ὄρει τούτῳ οὔτε ἐν Ἱεροσολύμοις προσκυνήσουσιν, ἀλλ᾽ οἱ
ἀληθινοὶ προσκυνηταὶ προσκυνήσουσι τῷ Πατρὶ ἐν πνεύματι καὶ ἀληθείᾳ·
πραότητα, λέγων Μάθετε ἀπ᾽ ἐμοῦ ὅτι πρᾷός εἰμι καὶ ταπεινὸς τῇ καρδίᾳ·

11-12 v. 3ᵃ   25-27 Ioh. IV, 21.23   28 Matth. XI, 29.

Aᵉ 2-3 (p. 253, 20-21): Fecit te cunctis esse laudabilem.   4-7 (p. 253, 22-27):
Absoluta (obs — ms) eius admiratione, quae omnium corda spectantium con-
pleuerat, ad ipsum iam conuertitur, ut et armetur... a bellicosis hominibus
petita similitudine corporali.   4ᵇ (p. 253, 28-254, 3): Ac si diceret Cum *specie
tua et pulchritudine tua* armare; et est sensus: sicut es credentibus admirabilis,
sic reluctantibus (resultantibus ms) debes esse terribilis.   17 (p. 254, 3-4): Monus
quippe proprium sagitarum.   23-28 (p. 254, 10-16): Veritatem, qua docuit *ueros
adoratores adorare Patrem spiritu et ueritate*; mansuetudinem, quam commendabat dicendo *Discite a me quia mitis sum et humilis corde.*

God blessed you forever—that is, He caused you to be blessed. Hence, he is saying, he made sure that your praises would be sung by everyone, since everyone admired the magnitude of what was said.

Gird your sword on your thigh, mighty one (v. 3). Having commented on the actual admiration of everyone, he then directs his attention to him in the words "Arm yourself, and strap a sword to your thigh," using a metaphor from the warriors with swords on their thigh. He uses words to paint a picture, giving an account of him in the form of an image, going into greater detail of his condition. *In your grace and your beauty*—that is, with your grace and your beauty. Since he had said above *graceful in your beauty beyond the children of human beings,* here he went on to say *Gird your sword on your thigh, mighty one, in your grace and your beauty.* In other words, After the admiration of the words by the faithful, arm yourself also against the adversaries so as to punish them.

Strain ahead, proceed and reign (v. 4). *Straining* has to do with the bow, tightening the strings being proper to archers. Shoot with the bow, then, he is saying, let no adversary hinder you, and administer the kingdom. Why? To achieve what goal? *For the sake of truth, gentleness, and righteousness:* use your power for these causes, give evidence of your greatness for these causes, and gain control and rule over all for these causes so as to disseminate them among the human race—*truth, gentleness, and righteousness. Truth* he taught through his own teachings, instructing people in the true adoration of God, as he himself says, "The hour is coming and is now here when neither on this mountain nor in Jerusalem will they adore; instead, the true adorers will adore the Father in spirit and in truth"; *gentleness* in saying, "Learn of me that I am gentle and humble of heart";[15] | *righteousness* in giving instruc-

---

15. John 4:21, 23; Matt 11:29.

δικαιοσύνην δὲ καθὸ πᾶσαν ἀρετὴν ἐκπαιδεύων, μάλιστα τῆς δικαιοσύνης
ἐπιμελεῖσθαι ἐδίδασκε — δικαιοσύνη γὰρ ἅπασα πρᾶξις ἐνάρετος καλεῖται, ὅθεν καὶ δικαίους τοὺς τοιούτους ἐν τῇ συνηθείᾳ καλεῖν εἰώθαμεν.
Δῆλον τοίνυν ἐντεῦθεν ὅτι μὴ περὶ ἀνθρώπου λέγει βασιλέως. Οὐδεὶς γὰρ
5 ἀνθρώπων πολλῇ κεχρημένος σπουδῇ πρὸς τὸ τὴν βασιλείαν ἑαυτῷ κατορθῶσαι ὅπλον μεταχειρίζεται καὶ ὅσα τοιαῦτα ὥστε πρᾳότητα διδάξαι τοὺς
οἰκείους, τοὐναντίον δὲ ὥστε κρατῆσαι καὶ ἀνελεῖν τοὺς ἐναντίους ἐσπού-
δακε καὶ παντὶ τρόπῳ τοὺς οἰκείους φοβεροὺς τοῖς πολεμίοις καταστῆσαι.
Ὥστε ληροῦσι μὲν ἄντικρυς Ἰουδαῖοι.
10 Δύναται δὲ ταῦτα λέγεσθαι προφανῶς ἐπὶ τοῦ Χριστοῦ, ὡς τιμωρησάμενος μὲν τοὺς ἐναντίους, ὑπηκόους δὲ αὐτῷ τοὺς πιστοὺς καταστήσας καὶ
διὰ πολλῶν καταστήσας τὴν εἰς αὐτοὺς βασιλείαν· οὐδενὸς ἕνεκεν αὐτοὺς
ἑτέρου προσηγάγετο ἢ ὥστε ταῦτα παιδεῦσαι, ὅθεν ὁ Κύριός φησι πρὸς
τοὺς ἑαυτοῦ μαθητὰς Ἰδοὺ ἀποστέλλω ὑμᾶς ὡς πρό|βατα ἐν μέσῳ λύκων,
15 δεικνὺς ὅτι οὐχ ὥστε διαθεῖναί τι φαῦλον τοὺς ἐχθροὺς ἀποστέλλονται,
ἀλλ᾽ ὥστε μετὰ πάσης ἐπιεικείας ἐν τῷ πάσχειν αὐτοὺς τὴν κατὰ τῶν
ἐχθρῶν νίκην τοῦ εὐαγγελίου διὰ τῆς τοῦ Πνεύματος ἄρασθαι χάριτος.

5ᶜ. Καὶ ὁδηγήσει σε θαυμαστῶς ἡ δεξιά σου. Τῇ οἰκείᾳ ἐχρήσατο ἀκολουθίᾳ. Ἐπειδὴ γὰρ ὡς ἐπὶ πολεμιστοῦ εἶπεν ὅτι Μεταχείρισαι μάχαιραν
20 καὶ ἔντεινον τόξον καὶ τὰ τοιαῦτα, — ἀνάγκη δὲ τὸν τοιοῦτον ἀναιροῦντα
τῇ δεξιᾷ τοὺς προστυγχάνοντας τῶν πολεμίων ἀκωλύτως ἐπιδιώκειν τοὺς
ἐχθρούς, τὴν ἐπὶ τὰ πρόσω πρόοδον ἐπέχοντα, καὶ τὸ ἀκώλυτον αὐτῷ
γίνεται ἀπὸ τῆς οἰκείας δεξιᾶς, — διὸ τοῦτο εἶπε Καὶ ὁδηγήσει σε θαυμαστῶς ἡ δεξιά σου, τουτέστι παρέξει σοι τὴν ὁδηγίαν ἡ σὴ δεξιά, ἵνα
25 εἴπῃ ὅτι Οὐ δεηθήσῃ τῆς ἑτέρου βοηθείας, ἀλλὰ τῇ ἰσχύϊ τῇ οἰκείᾳ πάντας τροπώσῃ τοὺς ἐναντίους, καὶ τῇ οἰκείᾳ δυνάμει ὁδηγῷ χρήσῃ πρὸς
τὴν τῶν σπουδαζομένων κατόρθωσιν, πάντων μὲν περιγενόμενος καὶ πάντων κρατῶν, οὐδενὸς δὲ ἐμποδὼν ἱσταμένου σου τοῖς βουλεύμασι. Πῶς οὖν
ὁδηγήσει; Πολλοὶ γὰρ καὶ μάλιστα τῶν Ἰουδαίων διετέλεσαν ἐχθραίνον-
30 τες, οἳ καὶ πλεῖστα μὲν αὐτὸν διατεθεικότες κακὰ ὕστερον καὶ σταυρῷ
παρέδοσαν, πλεῖστα δὲ καὶ πολλῷ χείρονα περὶ τοὺς μαθητὰς ἐπεδείξαντο.

6. Τὰ βέλη σου ἠκονημένα, δυνατέ, λαοὶ ὑποκάτω σου πεσοῦνται, ἐν
καρδίᾳ τῶν ἐχθρῶν τοῦ βασιλέως. Ἐπειδὴ εἶπεν ἄνω ἔντεινον — τοῦτο δὲ

14 Luc. X, 3.

Aᵉ 4-6 (p. 254, 18-20): Notandum sane quia nemo hominum propter ista
arma regnum suscipiet.   24-26 (p. 254, 30-32): Ac si diceret Nullius alterius
auxilio indegebis, ut fias uictor.   33-286, 8 (p. 255, 8-21): Quia supra dixerat
Intende — id autem erat sagitarii proprium — subdidit consequenter quia acu-
tae erunt (erant *ms*) sagitae tuae et herebunt in cordibus inimicorum tuorum,

tion in every virtue, teaching them especially to attend to righteousness, by *righteousness* referring to all virtuous behavior—hence our generally calling such people righteous.

It is therefore clear from this that he is not speaking of a human being as king: no human being exercises such zeal for bringing about the kingdom in himself and uses weapons and all such things so as to teach gentleness to his own; on the contrary, he is concerned to gain power, and wipe out the opposition, and in every way make his own people fearsome to the enemy. And so Jews are talking patent nonsense. On the other hand, it is possible for this to be said openly of Christ, since he punishes the adversaries, makes the faithful subject to him, and in many cases brings the kingdom to them. He drew them to himself for no other reason than to instruct them in this—hence the Lord's saying to his disciples, "Lo, I send you like sheep in the midst of wolves,"[16] bringing out that they were not being sent to impose anything worthless on the enemy, but to win the victory of the gospel against the foe through the grace of the Spirit with all forbearance in suffering.

Your right hand will guide you in marvelous fashion. He developed his train of thought. He had spoken as though of a warrior, Use your sword, stretch the bow, and the like; and of necessity such a person uses his right hand to destroy those of the enemy he encounters, and without hindrance pursues the foe and checks their advance, the lack of hindrance being due to his own right hand. For this reason he said *Your right hand will guide you in marvelous fashion*—that is, Your right hand will provide you with guidance, as if to say, You will not need the help of anyone else; instead, with your own strength you will utterly rout the adversaries, and you will use your own power as guide in achieving your goals, prevailing over all and gaining control of all, no one standing in the way of your intentions.

So how will it guide? After all, many continued to be hostile, especially of the Jews, later inflicting great abuse on him and giving him up to the cross, and giving evidence of much worse and more numerous crimes in regard to the disciples. *Your arms are sharpened, mighty one; peoples will fall under you in the heart of the king's foes* (v. 5). Since he had said above *Strain ahead,* the task of | an archer, he logically proceeds to say, In the hearts of

---

16. Luke 10:3.

ἦν τοξότου — ἐπάγει ἀκολούθως ὅτι ἔσται ἐν ταῖς καρδίαις τῶν ἐχθρῶν
σου ἠκονημένα τὰ βέλη, τὸ βαρὺ τῆς ἐπαχθησομένης αὐτοῖς τιμωρίας
παρὰ τοῦ Θεοῦ σημάναι βουληθεὶς διὰ τούτου · ἐπώδυνον γὰρ πολεμοῦντι
τὸ κατὰ καρδίας δέξασθαι βέλος ἠκονημένον. Καλῶς δὲ ἐπὶ τῶν ἐχθρῶν
εἶπε τὸ ἐν καρδίᾳ, ἐπειδὴ οἱ ἀνθιστάμενοι | ἐν τοῖς πολέμοις ἐπὶ τοῦ   5
ἐμπροσθίου μέρους δέχονται τὰς φορὰς τῶν βελῶν. Τὸ δὲ λαοὶ ὑποκάτω
σου πεσοῦνται διὰ μέσου τέθεικε διὰ τὸ μέτρον, ὃ καὶ ἀλλαχοῦ ἡμῖν ἐπισεσήμανται. Ἐβουλήθη δὲ εἰπεῖν ὅτι μηδὲν αὐτὸν λυπήσοιεν τῶν ἐχθρῶν αἱ
ἀντιστάσεις καὶ αἱ ἐπιβουλαί, — ἀναιρεθήσονται μὲν γὰρ ἐκεῖνοι, πολλοὶ
δὲ ὑποταγήσονται, καὶ γνωρίσαντες βασιλέα τὴν δεσποτίαν ὁμολογήσουσι.   10
Διόλου δέ, ὡς ἐπὶ γραφῆς εἰκόνος, τοὺς μὲν ἔδειξεν ἀνῃρημένους τῷ λόγῳ,
τοὺς δὲ ὑποκύπτοντας καὶ τὴν βασιλείαν ὁμολογοῦντας. Ἠκολούθησε μέντοι ἑαυτῷ · ὡς γὰρ πρὸς τὸ ὁδηγήσει σε θαυμαστῶ; ἡ δεξιά σου ταῦτα ἐπισυνῆψε, τοῦτο λέγων ὅτι πάντα οὕτως αὐτῷ διὰ τῆς οἰκείας κατορθώσει
δυνάμεως καὶ διὰ τῆς ἑαυτοῦ δεξιᾶς, τοὺς μὲν ἐχθροὺς βάλλων τοῖς βέλεσι,   15
τοὺς δὲ λοιποὺς καταπλήττων καὶ μετὰ πολλοῦ τοῦ δέους ὑποτάττων ἑαυτῷ.

Ἐπειδὴ τοίνυν πρότερον μὲν
εἶπε Βασίλευε, ὕστερον δὲ ἐμνημόνευσεν ἐχθρῶν ἀνῃρημένων καὶ τῶν
λοιπῶν ὑποτεταγμένων, ἵνα μή τις
οἰηθῇ πρόσφατον αὐτῷ γεγενῆσθαι
τὴν βασιλείαν ἢ καὶ δύνασθαι πάλιν
αὐτῆς ἀποπεσεῖν, ἐπάγει ·

7ᵃ. Ὁ θρόνος σου, ὁ Θεός, εἰς
αἰῶνα αἰῶνος. Τουτέστι καὶ εἰκότως ἀναιρεθήσονται μὲν οἱ ἐχθροί,
οἱ δὲ λοιποὶ πάντες ὑποταγήσονται, ἐπείπερ οὐκ ἐπείσακτον ἔχεις

Quoniam quidem prius ait Regna, postea autem memoratus est
inimicorum perditionem et reliquorum subiectionem, ne aliquis   20
existimet nuper ei accessisse regnum, uel certe posse eum denuo priuari eadem potestate, post
haec infert: Sedes tua, Deus, in
saeculum saeculi, hoc est: Con-   25
sequenter quidem interimentur
inimici, reliqui uero omnes su-
bicientur, quoniam quidem non
subintromissum habes regnum,

7 cf. supra p. 57.   8 λυπήσοιεν conieci, λυπήσειε ms   14 κατορθώσεις ms.

Quoniam — p. 290, 3, in unitatem personae affert FACUNDUS HERMIANENSIS
(740 A 13-741 A 4, 741 C 15-D 10).

uolens per hoc pondus illud inducendae a Deo ultionis expraemere: laetale quid-
dem demicantibus est sagittas in ipso corde suscipere. Bene autem dixit de inimicis in corde: semper quippe obnoxio animo confligentes aduersis corporibus
et pectoribus uulnerantur. Populi sub te cadent interpossitum est inter metrum,
ut frequenter ostendimus.   Aᵉ 10-16 (p. 255, 23-35): Regem te, cui seruire
debent, confitentes. Vniuersa autem narrandi contextione quasi in picturae
imagine quae efficienda essent degesit, ut uidilicet ostenderet alios uerbi potentia morientes, alios uero imperio eius colla subdantes et regnum ei deberi certissimum confitentes.

the foe *your arms are sharpened,* his intention being to indicate in this the severity of the punishment imposed on them by God, a sharp weapon in the heart being excruciating for a warrior. *In the heart* was well put in the case of the foe, since the vanguard in wars meets the onset of weapons head-on. The clause *peoples will fall under you* he inserted in the middle on account of the meter, as has been pointed out by us elsewhere as well. His meaning is that the foes' assaults and schemes would cause him no distress: they will be done away with, and many will be brought under subjection, will acknowledge him as king and confess his lordship. Overall, by word, as in the drawing of a picture, he depicted the slain, on the one hand, and on the other hand those bowing low and confessing his kingship. He followed his own train of thought, of course: he associated this with the verse *Your right hand will guide you in marvelous fashion,* meaning that he will achieve everything in this way for himself through his own power and his own right hand, striking the enemy with arrows, terrifying the others and subjecting them to himself in deep fear.

Since he had first said *reign,* therefore, and afterwards had mentioned enemies slain and the rest subjected, lest anyone think that kingship had only lately come to him or that he could in turn be deprived of it, he goes on to say *Your throne, O God, is forever and ever*—that is, The foe will rightly be done away with and all the rest brought under subjection, since it is not under false pretenses that you have | the kingship; instead, you reign over everyone

τὴν βασιλείαν, ἀλλ᾽ ἐξ ἀϊδίου πάντων
βασιλεύεις, καὶ εἰς ἀεὶ βασιλεύσεις,
καὶ ἡ βασιλεία σου μένει διηνεκής.
Μυθεύουσι δῆτα Ἰουδαῖοι τολ-
5 μῶντες ταῦτα νομίζειν εἰρῆσθαι περὶ
ἀνθρώπου. Τίνι γὰρ ἀνθρώπων ἁρμόσει τοῦτο κατόρθωμα ἢ τῶν λεγομένων τὸ μέγεθος;
 Τίνι δὲ καὶ ἁρμό-
10 σει τὸ Ὁδηγήσει σε θαυμαστῶς ἡ
δεξιά σου; τῆς θείας γραφῆς οὕτως
ἀεὶ περὶ πάντων λεγούσης τῶν
δικαίων ὡς τῇ τοῦ Θεοῦ βοηθείᾳ τὴν
σχὺν κεκτημένων. | Δῆλον γὰρ ἐν-
15 ταῦθα κἀκεῖνο, ὅτι οὐ περὶ ἀσεβοῦς
ποιεῖται τὸν λόγον καὶ τῇ οἰκείᾳ
πεποιθότος ἰσχύϊ. Πρὸς τίνα δὲ ἂν
καὶ λέγων τῶν ἀνθρώπων ἐπήγαγεν
Ὁ θρόνος σου, ὁ Θεός, εἰς τὸν αἰῶνα
20 τοῦ αἰῶνος;
 Εἰ δὲ περὶ βασιλέως λέγει τοῦ
Θεοῦ, δῆλον ὅτι καὶ περὶ βασιλίδος οὐ γυναικός, ἀλλὰ τῆς Ἐκκλησίας, ἣν ὁ Χριστὸς αὐτῷ διὰ τῆς
25 πίστεως ἡρμόσατο ἐπὶ τῇ κατὰ τὴν
διάθεσιν τῆς ψυχῆς συναφείᾳ. Καὶ
γὰρ καὶ ἔθος τῇ θείᾳ γραφῇ τῶν
οἰκειωμένων ἀεὶ τῷ Θεῷ διὰ τῆς γνώσεως τὴν συναγωγὴν γυναῖκα αὐτοῦ
30 καλεῖν, ὥστε δεῖξαι τὴν ἄκραν πρὸς
τὸν Θεὸν οἰκείωσίν τε καὶ ἕνωσιν,
ὡς ἐν τῷ Ἰεζεκιὴλ φησιν ὁ Θεὸς Δύο γυναῖκές εἰσι θυγατέρες μητρὸς μιᾶς, τοὺς
Ἰσραηλίτας καλῶν. Καὶ δύο μὲν εἰρηκὼς διὰ τὸ διηρῆσθαι τάς τε δέκα φυλὰς
καὶ τὰς δύο, ἑκατέρων εἰς ἰδίαν συντελούντων βασιλείαν, μιᾶς δὲ μητρὸς ἐπειδὴ
35 εἰς μίαν πρότερον συντελοῦντες διηρέθησαν, εἶτα μετ᾽ ὀλίγον Καὶ ἐγένετό
μοι, καὶ ἔτεκον υἱοὺς καὶ θυγατέρας, — τὴν ἐπίδοσιν αὐτῶν λέγων, — εἶτα τίνες

sed ex sempiterno omnium regnas, et in aeternum regnas, et
regnum tuum manet in aeternum.
 Haec Iudaei ut fabulas ina-
nes intelligunt, existimantes de
homine rege dicta. Cui enim
hominum tantum hoc insigne
uirtutum, aut talium magnitudo
dictorum? Cui uero conueniet *Et
deducet te mirabiliter dextera
tua?* diuina Scriptura de omnibus iustis semper ita loquente,
quia ex diuino adiutorio uirtutem possideant. Manifestum autem hic et illud est, quia non de
alio impio loquatur in propria
uirtute fidente. Ad quem itaque
hominum loquens infert *Sedes
tua, Deus, in saeculum saeculi?*

 Si autem de rege Deo dicit,
manifestum quoniam et de regina
non muliere, sed Ecclesia, quam
Christus sibi per fidem despon-
sauit, per affectum animae scilicet sibi iungendam. Etenim moris est Scripturae diuinae, eos qui
per scientiam adiunguntur Deo,
coniugem eius uocare, ad osten-
dendam eorum cum Deo plenis-
simam copulationem et unitatem,

32 Ezech. XXIII, 2   35–288, 1 v. 4

7 τοῦτον *ms.*

Aᵉ 22–24 (p. 257, 2–4): ... Vnde cum reginam nominauit Eclesiam, non
mulierem quampiam debemus accipere.

from eternity, you will reign always, and your kingship abides without end. Jews, to be sure, are in the realm of fairy tales in presuming to think that this refers to a human being. I mean, to what human being would he apply this achievement or the magnitude of what is described? To whom would he apply the verse *Your right hand will guide you in marvelous fashion* when the divine Scripture consistently says of all the righteous that it is with God's help that they acquire strength? That fact, too, is clear from this, that he is not treating of a godless person who trusts in his own strength. To which human being would he have said that, and gone on to say *Your throne, O God, is forever and ever*?

If, on the other hand, he is speaking of God as king, it is clear that it is no woman who is queen but the church, whom Christ betrothed to himself through faith in a union of the soul's affection. It is customary with the divine Scripture, remember, to refer to the assembly of those ever related to God through knowledge as his wife, so as to bring out their close relationship and union with God. In Ezekiel, for instance, God says, "There are two women, daughters of one mother," in reference to the Israelites. He spoke of "two" on account of the division of the tribes into ten and two, each group forming its own kingdom, but of "one mother" since they first formed one kingdom and were divided. Then a little later he says, "They became mine, and bore sons and daughters" (referring to their increasing numbers), and then who | they

αὗται· καὶ τὰ ὀνόματα αὐτῶν φησι Σαμάρεια ἡ Ὀλλὰ καὶ Ἰερουσαλὴμ ἡ Ὀλλιδά.

Καὶ ἐν τοῖς εὐαγγελίοις δὲ νυμφίος καλεῖται ὁ Χριστὸς καὶ νύμφη ἡ Ἐκκλησία, καθὼς Ἰωάννης ὁ Βαπτιστής φησιν Ὁ ἔχων τὴν νύμφην νυμφίος ἐστίν. Ἐπειδὴ τοίνυν ἀεὶ τοῦ Θεοῦ γυνὴ λέγεται ἡ οἰκειωμένη αὐτῷ συναγωγὴ κατὰ τὴν γνῶσιν, βασιλέα ἐκάλεσε τὸν Χριστὸν εἰκότως.

sicut et Iohannes Baptista dicit: *Qui habet sponsam sponsus est.* Quoniam igitur semper Dei 5 coniux dicitur congregatio hominum qui ei per scientiam copulantur, regem autem Christum conuenienter appellavit:

Ἀνάγκη δὲ τὴν τοῦ βασιλέως γυναῖκα βασίλισσαν εἶναι, οὐχ ἑτέρου προχειρισμοῦ γινομένου ἀπ᾿ ἐκείνης, ἀλλὰ κοινωνούσης τῷ ἀνδρὶ τῆς ἀξίας· εἰκότως βασίλισσαν καλεῖ τὴν Ἐκκλησίαν, δεικνὺς ὅσης ἔτυχεν ἀξίας ἀπὸ τῆς πρὸς τὸν Χριστὸν ἑνώσεως, ἥτις αὐτῇ προσγέγονε διὰ τῆς πίστεως. Ὅτι γὰρ οὔτε περὶ τοῦ Θεοῦ καὶ Πατρὸς λέγεσθαι τοῦτο δύναται, τὰ ἑξῆς σαφῶς παρίστησιν.

necessario ergo est regina, quae 10 regia uxor est, non alia promotione circa illa procedente, quam ea quam de uiri dignitate communicat. Consequenter ergo reginam uocat Ecclesiam, ostendens 15 quantam sortita sit ex Christi adunatione dignitatem, quae ei accessit ex fide. Quoniam aut de Deo et Patre haec dici non possunt, quae sequuntur astruunt 20 manifeste.

7ᵇ. Ῥάβδος εὐθύτητος ἡ ῥάβδος τῆς βασιλείας σου. Ἐπειδὴ κατεῖχον τὰ σκῆπτρα οἱ βασιλεῖς τὸ παλαιὸν ὥσπερ σύμβολον τῆς ἐξουσίας, τοῦτο λέγει ὅτι τὴν ἀρχὴν τῆς βασιλείας σου μετὰ πολλῆς διέπεις τῆς εὐθύτητος. Ἐνταῦθα Ἰουδαῖοι μάλιστα κακουργότατα ὑποκλέπτουσι τοῦ ψαλ- 25 μοῦ τὴν διάνοιαν, ἐναλλαγὴν φάσκοντες προσώπου γεγενῆσθαι καὶ τὸν Θεὸν ἀντιστρέψαντα λέγειν πρὸς τὸν Δαυὶδ Ῥάβδος εὐθύτητος ἡ ῥάβδος τῆς βασιλείας σου, ἵνα τὸ Διὰ τοῦτο ἔχρισέ σε ὁ Θεός, ὁ Θεός σου ἔχῃ χώραν ἐπὶ τοῦ Δαυὶδ λεγόμενον. Ἀλλὰ τούτων μὲν τί ἄν τις εὐηθέστερον εἴποι, εἰ μέλλοι τις ἐξηγεῖσθαι τὸν προφήτην καὶ τὸν Θεὸν κατ᾿ ἀντίδο- 30 σιν εἰς ἀλλήλους ποιεῖσθαι τὰ ἐγκώμια; Ἀρκούντως δὲ περὶ τῆς τοιαύτης τῶν πρωσώπων ἐναλλαγῆς ὡς ἀδυνάτου ἐν ἀρχῇ τοῦ ψαλμοῦ εἰρηκότες, πάντη καταλείπωμεν ἐκείνων μὲν τό τε μανικὸν καὶ εὔηθες, ἡμεῖς δὲ τῇ ἀκολουθίᾳ προσέχωμεν τῶν λεγομένων.

4-5 Ioh. III, 29   28 v 8ᵇ.

24 ὅτι] ὁ ms.

2-15 cf. Cosmas Indicopleustes, *Topographia christiana* (253 D): Ὅλον δὲ αὐτὸν τὸν ψαλμὸν περὶ τοῦ Χριστοῦ καὶ τῆς ἐκκλησίας, ὡς ἐπὶ βασιλέως νυμφίου καὶ νύμφης βασιλίδος ἐξειπών, διετέλεσεν.

were: "Oholah, a name for Samaria, and Oholibah, a name for Jerusalem."[17] And in the Gospels Christ is called a bridegroom, and the church a bride, as John the Baptist says, "He who has the bride is the bridegroom."[18] So since the congregation related to him in knowledge is always called God's wife, he was right to refer to Christ as king. Now, the king's wife is necessarily a queen; it is a case not of some other appointment made because of her, but of her sharing in her husband's dignity. He rightly calls the church queen to bring out the high dignity she attained from union with Christ, which came to her through faith. Proof that this could not refer to the God and Father the sequel clearly provides.

The rod of your kingship a rod of equity. Since in olden times kings held scepters as a symbol of authority, this means, You conduct the government of your kingdom with great equity. At this point in particular Jews most maliciously undermine the meaning of the psalm, claiming that a change in person has taken place and that God has turned to David and said, *The rod of your kingship a rod of equity,* so that the verse *Hence, God your God anointed you* (v. 7) occurs in reference to David. But what could be sillier for any of them to claim than this, the interpretation that the author and God were paying each other compliments? Since, however, we have said enough at the beginning of the psalm about the impossibility of such a change of person, let us leave aside their insanity and silliness altogether and proceed with the theme of the discourse. | After mentioning a throne, he logically went on to

17. Ezek 23:2, 4.
18. John 3:29.

Ὁ γὰρ θρόνου μνημονεύσας ἀκολούθως ἐπήγαγε Ῥάβδος εὐθύτητος ἡ ῥάβδος τῆς βασιλείας σου. Ἐπὶ γὰρ τοῦ βασιλεύειν καὶ δικάζειν κέχρηται τῇ τοῦ θρόνου φωνῇ, ὡς ὅταν ἀλλαχοῦ λέγῃ Ἐκάθισας ἐπὶ θρόνου ὁ κρίνων δικαιοσύνην, ᾧ σύμφωνόν ἐστι καὶ ἀκόλουθον τὸ ἐνταῦθα εἰρημένον·
5 θρόνου γὰρ μνημονεύσας, ὅπερ ἐστὶ τὸ δικαστικὸν ἀξίωμα, εὐθὺ καὶ ῥάβδον εὐθύτητος ἐπήγαγεν, ὅπερ σημαίνει τὸ ἐν ταῖς ἐξετάσεσιν ἀκριβὲς καὶ δίκαιον. Ἀνθρώπῳ δὲ οὐχ ἁρμόττουσα ἡ τοιαύτη φωνὴ — οὐδαμοῦ γοῦν τι τοιοῦτον εἰρημένον ἐπὶ ἀνθρώπου — φαίνεται, ἁρμόττουσα δὲ τῷ Θεῷ, περὶ οὗ καὶ ἑτέρωθί φησιν Καὶ αὐτὸς κρινεῖ τὴν οἰκουμένην ἐν δικαιοσύνῃ,
10 κρινεῖ λαοὺς ἐν εὐθύτητι, καὶ ἀλλαχοῦ Χρηστὸς καὶ εὐθὴς ὁ Κύριος, καὶ Ὅτι εὐθὴς ὁ λόγος τοῦ Κυρίου· ὅλως δὲ ἀρχὴ εὐθύτητος ἀνθρώπου οὐδαμοῦ λέγεται, ἐπειδὴ τούτῳ μόνῳ πρέπει τῷ Θεῷ τῷ μετὰ τῆς προσηκούσης ἀκριβείας καὶ ἀληθείας διέποντι τὴν οἰκείαν βασιλείαν τε καὶ ἀρχήν. Εἶτα ἀκολούθως ἐπάγει·

15 8ᵃ. Ἠγάπησας δικαιοσύνην καὶ ἐμίσησας ἀνομίαν. Οὕτω γὰρ εὐθὴς ἡ βασιλεία εὑρίσκεται τῇ τε περὶ τὸ καλὸν ἀγάπῃ καὶ τῷ μίσει τῶν περὶ τὸ ἐναντίον, ἐπαίνου μὲν ἀξιουμένων παρὰ τοῦ κριτοῦ τῶν τὸ δέον διαπραττομένων, κόλασιν δὲ ὑπομενόντων ἐξ ἀνάγκης τῶν τοῦ ψεύδους ἐργατῶν.

8ᵇ. Διὰ τοῦτο ἔχρισέ σε ὁ Θεός, ὁ Θεός σου. Ὅτι μὲν οὖν ἐφ᾽ ἑνὸς ταῦτα
20 λέγει πρόδηλον. Ἀλλὰ καὶ ὅτι μὴ δυνατὸν ἁρμόττειν ἐπὶ τοῦ Θεοῦ καὶ Πατρὸς τὸ Διὰ τοῦτο ἔχρισέ σε ὁ Θεὸς ὁ Θεός σου, φανερὸν ὑπόλοιπον ἄρα περὶ τοῦ Χριστοῦ ταῦτα
25 λέγεσθαι, ἐφ᾽ οὗ θαυμαστῶς ἡμῖν καὶ τὰς φύσεις διεῖλε καὶ τοῦ προσώπου τὴν ἕνωσιν ὑπέδειξε. Καὶ τὰς μὲν φύσεις διεῖλε τῷ διαφόρῳ τῶν νοημάτων ἐμφαντικὰς ἀφεῖναι φωνάς, —
30 πολλὴ γὰρ διαφορὰ πρὸς τὸ Ὁ θρόνος σου, ὁ Θεός, εἰς τὸν αἰῶνα τοῦ αἰῶνος τὸ Διὰ τοῦτο ἔχρισέ ὁ Θεὸς

Sed quia haec Deo Patri non conueniant, *Propterea unxit te Deus Deus tuus*, claret de reliquo quod haec de Christo dicantur, in quo mirabiliter et naturas diuisit, et personae unitatem demonstrauit. Et naturas quidem diuisit in eo quod diuersarum intelligentiarum declaratiuas uoces emisit, — multum enim differt ab inuicem *Sedes tua, Deus, in saeculum saeculi*, et *Propterea unxit te Deus,*

3-4 Ps. IX, 5ᵇ   9-10 ps. IX, 9   10 ps. XXIV, 8   10-11 ps. XXXII, 4.

2-5 L (p. 835, 30-32): Ὥσπερ δὲ ὁ θρόνος βασιλέως σύμβολον, οὕτω καὶ ἡ ῥάβδος καὶ τῆς βασιλικῆς καὶ τῆς δικαστικῆς ἐξουσίας.

Aᵉ 15-17 (p. 256, 5-7): Sic quippe derectum probatur imperium laudanda delegere et odisse damnanda.

say *The rod of your kingship a rod of equity:* for reigning and judging he used the term "throne," as when he says elsewhere, "Seated on your throne as the righteous judge,"[19] and the present expression is in keeping and consistent with this. After mentioning *throne,* in fact, which is the judicial rank, immediately he proceeded to say also *a rod of equity,* which suggests correctness and justice in prosecution. Such an expression, however, seems not applicable to a human being—at least such an expression occurs nowhere in reference to a human being—whereas it is applicable to God, of whom he says also in another place, "He will judge the world in righteousness; he will judge peoples in rectitude," and elsewhere, "Good and upright is the Lord," and "Because the word of the Lord is upright,"[20] whereas a rule of uprightness by a human being is nowhere mentioned, since it befits God alone, who manages his own kingship and rule with due correctness and truth.

He then proceeds logically to say *You loved righteousness and hated lawlessness* (v. 7): the kingship thus is shown immediately to be one of love for the good and hatred for what is opposed to it, since those doing their duty earn praise from the judge, and the doers of falsehood necessarily undergo punishment. *Hence, God your God anointed you.* So it is clear that he says this of one person; but because, however, it is also not possible to apply the clause *Hence, God your God anointed you* to the God and Father, it is clear from the remainder that it refers to Christ, in whose case for us he both separated the natures and gave a glimpse of the unity of the person. On the one hand, he separated the natures by uttering definite statements of different ideas (there being a great difference between *Your throne, O God, is forever and ever* and *Hence, God your God anointed | you*), and on the other hand,

19. Ps 9:4.
20. Pss 9:8; 25:8; 33:4.

ὁ Θεός σου, — τὴν δὲ ἕνωσιν ὑπέδειξε
τῷ περὶ ἑνὸς προσώπου ταῦτα εἰπεῖν.
Εἶτα εἰπὼν ὅτι ἔχρισέ σε, ἐπάγει·

Deus tuus, — unitatem uero ostendit personae, ea quae diuersa sunt
colligens in unitatem personae.

8ᶜ. Ἔλαιον ἀγαλλιάσεως παρὰ τοὺς μετόχους σου. Ἐλαίου γὰρ ἐμνημό- 5
νευσεν ἀκολούθως τῷ ἔχρισεν, ἐπειδήπερ οὕτως ἐχρίοντο τὸ παλαιόν· ὅτι
δὲ ἔλαιον οὐ τοῦτο λέγει, παρεσήμανεν εἰπὼν παρὰ τοὺς μετόχους σου·
ὅτι οἱ μὲν ἐν νόμῳ χριστοὶ ἐχρίοντο ἐλαίῳ, αὐτὸς δὲ Πνεύματι ἁγίῳ. Καλῶς
οὖν παρὰ τοὺς μετόχους σου — πολλὴ γὰρ ἡ διαφορὰ τοῦ χρίσματος. Δῆλον
δὲ κἀκεῖθεν ὅτι περὶ τοῦ Χριστοῦ τοῦτό φησιν, ἐπείπερ οὐδεὶς τῶν ἐν 10
νόμῳ ἔλαιον ἕτερον ἐχρίσθη παρὰ τοὺς μετόχους· ἓν γὰρ ἦν τὸ ἔλαιον
ὅπερ ἐχρίοντο οἱ ἐφ' οἵᾳ δήποτε προφάσει ἐν τῷ νόμῳ χριόμενοι.

9ᵃ. Σμύρνα καὶ στακτὴ καὶ κασία ἀπὸ τῶν ἱματίων σου. Ἱμάτιον αὐτοῦ
καλῶς ἐκάλεσε τὸ σῶμα, ὅπερ ἔξωθεν ἦν περικείμενον, ἔνδον οὔσης τῆς
θεότητος | κατὰ τὸν τῆς ἐνοικήσεως λόγον. Οὕτω γὰρ ὁ ἀπόστολος κατα- 15
πέτασμα αὐτὸ καλεῖ λέγων Ἔχοντες οὖν. ἀδελφοί, παρρησίαν εἰς τὴν
εἴσοδον τῶν ἁγίων, ἣν ἐνεκαίνισεν ἡμῖν ὁδὸν πρόσφατον καὶ ζῶσαν διὰ τοῦ
καταπετάσματος, τουτέστι τῆς σαρκὸς αὐτοῦ. Ἐπειδὴ οὖν τῇ σμύρνῃ ἐπὶ
τῶν τεθνηκότων κεχρῆσθαι εἰώθασι, βουλόμενος καὶ τὸ πάθος παρασημᾶ-
ναι καὶ τοῦ πάθους τὴν δόξαν, σμύρναν φησὶ καὶ στακτὴν καὶ κασίαν ἀπὸ 20
τῶν ἱματίων σου, — διὰ μὲν τῆς σμύρνης ὑποδείξας τὸ πάθος, διὰ δὲ τοῦ
εἰπεῖν στακτὴν καὶ κασίαν τοῦ πάθους τὸ εὐῶδες καὶ ἐπίδοξον παρασημ-
μαίνων, ἵνα εἴπῃ ὅτι καὶ αὐτὸ τὸ πάθος τὸ περὶ τὸν ναόν σου μετὰ πολλῆς εὐωδίας ἔσται καὶ δόξης, ὥστε τὴν ἐξ αὐτοῦ εὐωδίαν εἰς πᾶσαν διαδοθῆναι τὴν οἰκουμένην, καθὼς καὶ ὁ ἀπόστολός φησι ὅτι Χριστοῦ εὐωδία 25

---

8 Act. X, 33   16-18 Hebr. X, 19-20   25-291,1 II Cor. II, 15.

6-8 *Paraphrasis* (p. 827, 19-21): Ὅτι οἱ μὲν ἄλλοι οἱ χριόμενοι ἐλαίῳ ἐχρίοντο ..
αὐτὸς δὲ Πνεύματι ἁγίῳ ἐχρίσθη. *Eadem fere praebet* Cosmas Indicopleustes (253 C).
15-24 L (p. 836, 12-17): Συνῆψε δὲ τῇ κασίᾳ καὶ τὴν στακτήν, σημαίνων ὡς εὐωδίας τὸ
πάθος... Ἀπὸ ἱματίων δὲ εἶπεν, ἱμάτιον τὸ σῶμα τοῦ Χριστοῦ καλῶν, ὃ καὶ Παῦλος καλεῖ
καταπέτασμα.

Aᵉ 6-9 (p. 256, 8-12): *Exultationis* cum dicit *oleum*, significat se non de commoni ueroque oleo dicere... sed de Spiritu sancto, quo nemo praeter istum ita
unctus est.   9ᵃ (p. 256, 13-22): *Vestimentum* hic corpus appellat secundum illud
apostoli *Per uelamen, id est per carnem suam*, quo quasi uestimentum amicia-
batur diuinitas. *Murra* autem amica funiribus indicat passionem, *casia et gutta*
fragrantiam ipsius et gloriam passionis; commemorans sane *murram*, bene intulit *a uestimentis tuis*, ut intelligeremus quae fuerat in eo natura passibilis.

he gave a glimpse of the union by saying this of one person.

Then, after saying *He anointed you,* he goes on to say *with the oil of gladness beyond your partners.* He mentioned *oil* in keeping with the verb *anointed,* since in olden times they anointed this way; but the fact that he is not referring to this oil he implied by saying *beyond your partners,* because while those anointed under the law were anointed with oil, he was anointed by the Holy Spirit.[21] So *beyond your partners* was well put, there being a great difference in the anointing. Now, it is clear also from here that he says this of Christ, since none of those under the law were anointed with a different oil *beyond their partners:* it was one single oil with which those people were anointed who were anointed under the law by a kind of foreshadowing.

Myrrh, resin, and cassia from your garments (v. 8). By his *garments* he nicely referred to the body, in being something put on from outside, while inside there was the divinity on the basis of indwelling. The apostle, remember, likewise refers to it as a veil when he says, "Since we have confidence, brethren, to enter the sanctuary by the new and living way he opened for us through the veil, that is, through his flesh."[22] So since they are in the habit of using myrrh on the dead, in his wish to imply both the passion and the glory of the passion he says *myrrh, resin, and cassia from your garments,* suggesting by *myrrh* the passion, and by mention of *resin and cassia* implying the fragrance and splendor of the passion, as if to say, Even the passion itself, which affects your temple, will be accompanied by great fragrance and glory, with the result that the fragrance from it will spread to the whole world—as the apostle also says, | "We are the fragrance of Christ among those who

---

21. Cf. Acts 10:38.
22. Cf. Heb 10:19–20.

ἐσμὲν ἐν τοῖς σωζομένοις καὶ ἐν τοῖς ἀπολλυμένοις. Καλῶς δὲ εἰπὼν σμύρναν ἐπισυνῆψε τὸ ἀπὸ τῶν ἱματίων σου, ἵνα ἐλευθέραν τοῦ πάθους νοῶμεν
τὴν θεότητα. Πόθεν δὲ τοῦτο, ὅτι πολλὴ ἔσται δόξα περὶ τὸ πάθος, καὶ
οὐ τὸ ἐναντίον;

5   9ᵇ. Ἀπὸ βάρεων ἐλεφαντίνων, ἐξ ὧν ηὔφρανάι σε. Βάρεων εἰπεῖν βούλεται τῶν οἴκων· μετὰ γὰρ ταῦτά φησιν οἴκους ἐλεφαντίνους εἰς ἀρέσκειαν,
καὶ εἰς εὐφροσύνην, καὶ εἰς τιμὴν σὴν κατασκευάσουσι πάντες οἱ ἐπίδοξοι.
Ἐλεφαντίνους δὲ εἶπεν, οὐχ ὅτι πάντας ἀπὸ ἐλέφαντος πάντως εἶχον
κατασκευάσαι, ἀλλ᾽ ἐπειδὴ τιμία ἡ τοῦ ἐλέφαντος ὕλη τὸ ἐπίδοξον καὶ
10 κεκαλλωπισμένον τῶν οἴκων ἐντεῦθεν ἐβουλήθη παρασημάναι.

    10ᵃ⁻ᵇ. Θυγατέρες βασιλέων ἐν τῇ τιμῇ σου, παρέστη ἡ βασίλισσα ἐκ
δεξιῶν σου. Εἰ περὶ βασιλίσσης ἐνταῦθα κατὰ Ἰουδαίους — λεγέσθω γὰρ
συνεχῶς τὸ μυθικὸν εἰς αἰσχύνην τῶν μυθευόντων — γυναικὸς λέγει τινός,
ὡς ἐκεῖνοί φασι τῆς τοῦ Σολομῶντος, καὶ βασιλέα δὲ δηλονότι τὸν Σολο-
15 μῶντα | λέγει, ποίους οἴκους βασιλέων θυγατέρες κατεσκευασμέναι τῷ Σολο-
μῶντι φαίνονται; Ἐπὶ γὰρ τοῦ Χριστοῦ πρόδηλον, ὅτι κατὰ πᾶσαν τὴν
οἰκουμένην πλεῖστοι καὶ βασιλεῖς καὶ ἄρχοντες, καὶ τούτων γυναῖκές τε
καὶ υἱοὶ καὶ θυγατέρες ἔθεντο σπουδὴν ὥστε καὶ κατὰ πόλεις ἐγεῖραι καὶ
κατὰ κώμας οἴκους αὐτῷ καλλίστους καὶ διαπρεπεῖς, πολλοὺς μὲν εἰς αὐτοῦ
20 τιμήν, πλείους δὲ καὶ εἰς τιμὴν τῶν μαρτύρων τῶν δι᾽ αὐτὸν πεπονθότων·
καὶ ὅλως τὰ κάλλη καὶ τὰ μεγέθη τῶν κυριακῶν ἐστιν ἰδεῖν προφανῶς δι᾽
αὐτῶν τῶν ἔργων κατὰ πάσης τῆς οἰκουμένης.

    Οὐκοῦν καὶ περὶ βασιλέως λέγει Χριστοῦ καὶ βασιλίσσης τῆς Ἐκκλη-
σίας, ἣν αὐτὸς ὑπεστήσατο ἀπὸ τῶν ἐθνῶν καὶ ἀπὸ τῶν Ἰουδαίων. Ἐπειδὴ
25 τοίνυν ἐν ταῖς εἰκόσιν ἀεὶ τῶν βασιλέων γυναῖκάς τινας γράφουσι παρι-
στώσας οἳ ἐπὶ ἀνδρείαν ἢ ἀρετὴν ἢ εἴ τι τοιοῦτον ἐμφαίνοντες ὅτι ἀνδρεία

---

15 κατεσκευασμέναι conieci, κατεσκευα(ν?)|κοτες ms.
5-10 (p. 827): Βάρεις τοὺς οἴκους λέγει, ἐλεφαντίνους δὲ τὴν λαμπρότητα τῶν
οἴκων· διὰ τούτων δὲ τὰς ἐκκλησίας ὑπαινίττεται.   25-29₂, 3 Paraphrasis (p. 828):
Ἐπὶ τῶν εἰκόνων εἰώθασι ποιεῖν βασιλεῖς καθημένους, καὶ παριστῶσιν αὐτοῖς τινας γυναῖκας,
καὶ ἐπιγράφουσιν ἢ βασιλείαν, ἢ δικαιοσύνην, ἤ τι τοιοῦτον. Ἐκ μεταφορᾶς οὖν τῶν εἰκόνων
βούλεται εἰπεῖν ὅτι... παρεστήκει δὲ αὐτῷ ἡ ἐκκλησία βασιλίδος ἐπέχουσα τόπον.

Aᵉ 5-7. 17-22 (p. 256, 26-31): .. sed etiam a domibus praetiosis, quae ad eius
honorem et complacentiam construentur deuotione regum ac filiarum ... eclesiae
aedes ornatissimas fabricantur. 25-29₂, 3 (p. 257, 1-8): Quoniam figuris profetiam ornare desposuit... sic, inquit, tibi a dexteris adhesit regina tamquam
adherens atque unita, ut solent imaginibus regum uirtutes habitu feminarum
pingui, quae quasi stipent et ambiant imperantem.

are being saved and among those who are perishing."[23] Now, he did well to mention *myrrh* and associate it with the phrase *from your garments* for us to understand the divinity to be free of suffering.

Now, how does it come about that there will be great glory in connection with the passion, and not the opposite? *From ivory buildings, from which they delighted you.* By "buildings" he means "houses": After this, he is saying, all the famous people will build ivory houses for your pleasure, your joy and your honor. He mentioned *ivory,* not that they could make them all completely of ivory, but because the value of ivory was intended to imply here the splendid and adorned houses.

Daughters of kings in your honor, at your right hand stands the queen (v. 9). If at this point in connection with *the queen,* as Jews hold (let the fairy tale be repeatedly cited to the shame of its creators), he is referring to some wife, such as Solomon's (so they claim), and consequently he is referring to Solomon as king, which houses do *daughters of kings* prove to have built for Solomon? I mean, in the case of Christ it is obvious that throughout the world great numbers of kings and rulers and their wives and sons and daughters took pains to erect to him in cities and in towns beautiful and fitting houses, some to his honor and more also to the honor of the martyrs who suffered on his account. And overall the beauty and the magnitude of the churches[24] are perfectly obvious to see in the works themselves throughout the whole world. It is therefore to Christ he is referring by *king,* and by *queen* to the church, which he established from the nations and from the Jews.

So since people depicting kings' valor or virtue or something of that kind that shows manly virtue characterizing the king always represent in their images some women standing in attendance, | he did well after mentioning

---

23. 2 Cor 2:15.

24. The term for "churches" here is τὰ κυριακά. Theodore speaks of οἶκοι above for local churches, ἐκκλησία for the universal church.

ἡ ἀρετὴ πρόσεστι τῷ βασιλεῖ, καλῶς μνημονεύσας ὡς βασιλέως αὐτοῦ
ἐπήγαγε τὸ Παρέστη ἡ βασίλισσα ἐκ δεξιῶν σου, — παρέστη σοί φησιν ἡ
Ἐκκλησία ἐκ τοῦ δεξιοῦ μέρους, τουτέστι συνέσται σοι ἀεί. Καὶ γὰρ
σύνεστιν αὐτῷ ἡ Ἐκκλησία ἡνωμένη καὶ τῷ φρονήματι καὶ τῇ χάριτι τῆς
ἀναγεννήσεως, ὥσπερ μέλη καὶ σῶμα κεφαλῇ, καθὼς καὶ ὁ ἀπόστολος νῦν 5
μέν φησιν ὑμεῖς δέ ἐστε σῶμα Χριστοῦ καὶ μέλη ἐκ μέρους. νῦν δὲ περὶ
τῶν ἀφηνιαζόντων καὶ οὐ κρατούντων τὴν κεφαλήν, ἐξ οὗ πᾶν τὸ σῶμα
συναρμολογούμενον αὔξει τὴν αὔξησιν τοῦ Θεοῦ. Διὸ καλῶς εἶπεν ἐξ
δεξιῶν, ἵνα εἴπῃ ὅτι Παρέστη σοι πλείστης ἀπολαύουσα τῆς παρά σου
τιμῆς, ἀπὸ τοῦ κρείττονος μέρους τὴν τιμὴν ὑπεμφαίνων. Τί γὰρ τῆς συνα- 10
φείας ταύτης τιμιώτερον;

10ᶜ. Ἐν ἱματισμῷ διαχρύσῳ περιβεβλημένη πεποικιλμένη. Καὶ πολὺν
περικειμένη τὸν κόσμον· τιμῆς μὲν οὖν ἠξιώθη τῆς | υἱοθεσίας, σῶμά τε
κληθεῖσα καὶ γενομένη Χριστοῦ, κόσμον δὲ περιέθετο μέγιστον, τῶν πνευματικῶν χαρισμάτων τὸ κάλλος. Τὰ γὰρ ἐπιτελούμενα θαύματα διὰ τῶν 15
ἁγίων ὥσπερ τις κόσμος ἦν διάχρυσος καὶ θαυμαστός, ἐπιδόξους ἐργα-
ζόμενα τοὺς πιστεύοντας Χριστῷ καὶ εἰς τὴν Ἐκκλησίαν συντελοῦντας.
Σφόδρα μέντοι δι᾽ ὅλων τὴν τῶν πραγμάτων ἀκολουθίαν φυλάξας φαίνεται, πρῶτον τὴν χρῖσιν εἰπών, εἶτα τὸν θάνατον καὶ μετὰ τοῦτον τὴν
παρὰ πάντων τιμήν· ἀκολούθως μνημονεύσας τῆς προσλήψεως τῆς ἐκκλησίας, 20
καὶ τοῦ κόσμου, καὶ τῆς τιμῆς ἧς ἠξίωσε τοὺς πιστεύοντας εἰς αὐτὸν ὁ
Χριστός, τρέπει δὴ λοιπὸν τὸν λόγον πρὸς τὴν Ἐκκλησίαν, ἑξῆς παραινῶν
ἃ ποιεῖν δεῖ τοὺς πιστούς, — ἀκόλουθον γὰρ ἦν τοὺς πολλοὺς ἀξιωθέντας
τῆς τιμῆς ἐπιδείκνυσθαί τι καὶ παρ᾽ ἑαυτῶν εἰς διάθεσιν τοῦ τιμήσαντος
οὕτω δεσπότου, — καί φησιν· 25

11ᵃ. Ἄκουσον, θύγατερ, καὶ ἴδε καὶ κλῖνον τὸ οὖς σου. Ἄγε δὴ καὶ σύ
φησιν, ὦ θύγατερ, ὅπως ἂν μὴ ἀγνώμων φανείης περὶ τὸν εὐεργέτην,
ἐφάμιλλον δὲ τῇ τιμῇ τοῦ δεδωκότος τὴν οἰκείαν ἐπιδείξασθαι σπεῦσον διά-
θεσιν· οὕτω γὰρ ἕξεις προσηνῆ τὸν βασιλέα καὶ μειζόνων ἀπολαύσεις τῶν
ἀγαθῶν. Τὸ οὖν ἄκουσον, θύγατερ, καὶ ἴδε καὶ κλῖνον τὸ οὖς σου τουτέσ- 30
τιν Ἀπόβλεπε πρὸς τὸν βασιλέα, τούτῳ ὑπακούειν σπούδαζε, μηδένα ἕτερον περισκόπει, πρὸς τοῦτον ἔστω σοι τεταμένον τὸ ὄμμα τῆς ψυχῆς.

6 I Cor. XII, 27   7-8 Coloss. II, 19.

19 χρῆσιν ms.
13-15 Paraphrasis (p. 828, 13-15): Τὸ δὲ ἐν ἱματισμῷ διαχρύσῳ περιβεβλημένη
πεποικιλμένη, τὰ ποικίλα λέγει χαρίσματα τῆς ἐκκλησίας.

Aᵉ 11ᵃ (p. 257, 14-20): Respice, inquit, ad regem, huic festina obedire qui
te coabtauit et tam indulgenter ornauit, nihilque aliud praeter illum quasi con-
sideranter aspicias, sed in hunc totis oculis intende mentis.

the king himself to go on to say *At your right hand stands the queen.* The church is in attendance on you, he is saying, on your right—that is, it will always be assembled for you: the church is always assembled in union with him both in purpose and in the grace of rebirth, just as members and body are with the head, as the apostle says in one place, "You are the body of Christ and individually members of it," and in another place in reference to those out of control, "and not holding fast to the head, from which the whole body when attached grows with a growth that is from God."[25] For this reason, *at your right hand* was well put, as if to say by way of underlining the honor stemming from the more important member, She is in attendance on you, enjoying the greatest honor from you. After all, what could be more honorable than this association? *Clad in garments of gold, of a rich variety:* clothed in much adornment. So while she was vouchsafed the dignity of sonship, and called and made body of Christ, she was clothed in the greatest adornment, the beauty of the spiritual graces: the marvels performed through the saints were like a kind of golden and marvelous adornment, bringing splendor to the believers in Christ, who composed the church.

He seems, of course, very anxious throughout to preserve the sequence of detail, mentioning first the anointing, then the death, and after it the respect paid by all; proceeding in order, he mentions the growth of the church, the adornment, and the honor that Christ accorded those believing in him. He then directs attention to the church and goes on to recommend what the faithful ought to do. After all, it followed that the great numbers who were accorded honor would show something for it on their own account by way of affection for a Lord who honored them in such a way. He says *Listen, daughter, and incline your ear* (v. 10): Come now, daughter, be sure not to be ungrateful on your part for the favors; take pains to give evidence of your affection matching the honor of the donor, this being the way to have the king benevolent to you and to enjoy greater goods. The phrase *Listen, daughter, and incline your ear* means, Look to the king, be zealous in hearkening to him, have eyes for no one else, let your soul's gaze be fixed on him. |

---

25. 1 Cor 12:27; cf. Col 2:19.

11^b. Καὶ ἐπιλάθου τοῦ λαοῦ σου καὶ τοῦ οἴκου τοῦ πατρός σου. Καὶ
ἀπόστηθι μὲν τῶν πατρῴων ἐθῶν, ἀπόστηθι δὲ καὶ τῆς εἰδωλολατρείας, ἀπόστηθι δὲ καὶ πάντων ἐκείνων καὶ ἁπαξαπλῶς ὅσαπερ ἀδεῶς ἐπετέλεις τὸ
πρότερον παρὰ τοῖς πατράσιν οὖσα καὶ τοῖς τῆς ἀσεβείας διδασκάλοις.

5 12^a. Καὶ ἐπιθυμήσει ὁ βασιλεὺς τοῦ κάλλους σου. Αἰσχυνέσθωσαν | κάν-
ταῦθα Ἰουδαῖοι. Ἐπιθυμία μὲν γὰρ κάλλους σωματικοῦ ἀπὸ τῆς ἔξωθεν
εὐπρεπείας ἐγγίνεται, λήθη δὲ τῶν οἰκείων ἀπὸ τῆς διανοίας εὑρίσκεται.
Ποίαν τοίνυν ἀκολουθίαν ἔχει λήθην συμβουλεύειν ποιεῖσθαι τῶν πατρῴων,
ἵν᾽ οὕτως ἐπιθυμήσῃ τοῦ κάλλους αὐτῆς ὁ βασιλεύς; Εἰ γὰρ ὅλως ἐπέρασ-
10 τός ἐστι τῷ κάλλει τοῦ σώματος καὶ ταύτης ἐρασθῆναι ἀνάγκη τὸν Σολομῶντα, οὐχ ἡ λήθη τοῦτο ἐργάζεται τῆς ψυχῆς, ἀλλ᾽ αὐτὴ ἡ εὐμορφία καὶ
ἄκοντα πρὸς τὴν διάθεσιν ἑλκύσει τὸν Σολομῶντα. Ὥστε ἁρμόττον ἐπὶ
τοῦ Χριστοῦ καὶ τῆς ἐκκλησίας, ᾗ παραινεῖ τῶν παλαιῶν ἀποστῆναι κακῶν·
οὕτω γὰρ πάντων ἀποστᾶσα καὶ παντὸς καθαρεύουσα λογισμοῦ εὐπρεπὴς
15 μὲν ἀπετελεῖτο τῇ τῆς ἀρετῆς κατορθώσει. Ἐράσμιον δὲ αὐτῆς τοῦτο τὸ
κάλλος καθίστατο τῷ Χριστῷ προσιεμένῳ μετὰ πολλῆς τῆς διαθέσεως τὴν
Ἐκκλησίαν· τοῦτο γὰρ ἐν πᾶσι διαπράττεται. Ἐπὶ δὲ τοῦ Σολομῶντος καὶ
τῆς τούτου γυναικὸς οὐδαμῶς ἁρμόττειν δύναται· τοσοῦτον γὰρ ἀπέχει τοῦ
τῶν πατρῴων ἐθῶν εἰς λήθην ἢ διάθεσιν ἀγαγεῖν τὸν Σολομῶντα τὴν
20 οἰκείαν γυναῖκα, ὡς οὐκ ἂν δυνάμενον αὐτὴν ἀγαπῆσαι κατὰ τὴν τοῦ Δαυὶδ
φωνὴν εἰ μὴ πρότερον ἐκείνων ἐπιλάθοιτο, ὅτι τοὐναντίον ἐκεῖναι μὲν τῶν
οἰκείων ἐθῶν οὐκ ἀπέστησαν, τουτονὶ δὲ μετέβαλον τῆς εἰς τὸν Θεὸν
εὐσεβείας, ἐπὶ τὰ οἰκεῖα ἔθη μεταγαγοῦσαι καὶ τοῖς νενομισμένοις παρ᾽
αὐταῖς θεοῖς προσκυνεῖν αὐτὸν παρασκευάσασαι.

25 12^b. Ὅτι αὐτός ἐστιν κύριός σου. Καὶ μὴν οὐκ ἦν τῶν ἰδίων γαμετῶν
κύριος ὁ Σολομών, ἐπὶ δὲ τοῦ Κυρίου ἁρμόττον· καὶ γὰρ αὐτός ἐστι καὶ
ποιητὴς καὶ δεσπότης, ᾧ καὶ δικαίως πείθεσθαι παραινεῖ ὡς δεσπότῃ καὶ
ποιητῇ. Καλῶς δὲ ἐπήγαγε τὸ

13^a. Καὶ προσκυνήσουσιν αὐτῷ θυγατέρες Τύρου ἐν δώροις. Πείθου γὰρ
30 αὐτῷ φησιν ὡς σῷ δεσπότῃ, μὴ διὰ τὴν νομιζομένην τοῦ πάθους ἀτιμίαν
ἔλαττον φροντίσασα. Τί γὰρ Καὶ προσκυνήσουσιν αὐτῷ θυγατέρες Τύρου ἐν

A^e 2-4 (p. 257, 21-22): Cum profanitatibus, moribus et superstitione gen-
tili. 10-15 (p. 257, 23-28): Non ergo pulchritudine corporali quaelibet mulierum
reginarum, sed ob renuntiationem impietatis ueteris, Eclesia Christo amabilis
his uerbis effici iubetur. 18-25 (p. 257, 28-258, 2): Tantum autem abest ut Solomon regi nam quamlibet per officium pietatis habuerit cariorem, ut in illis et
per illas superstitiones amauerit. 26-27 (p. 258, 2-3): Quia ipse est Dominus
Deus tuus. 30-31. 294, 7-8 (p. 258, 8-9. 6-10): Non ergo uilescat tibi (ubi *1^a m.*)
ob contumiliam passionis... multo honore apud potentes quosque et ibi ipsa
uicinitate compertos habebitur.

Forget your people and your father's house: forsake the ancestral ways, forsake also idolatry, forsake also, in a nutshell, all those things that you had no qualms in performing in former times when you were with your ancestors and the teachers of impiety. *And the king will long for your beauty* (v. 11). Let Jews be ashamed at this as well: while desire for bodily beauty arises from exterior charm, forgetfulness of one's own emerges from the mind. So what connection is there in advising her to have forgetfulness of her ancestors so that the king may thus desire her beauty? After all, if she were completely appealing in bodily beauty and Solomon could not but be in love with her, far from forgetfulness of soul having this effect, her very charm would win Solomon to affection willy-nilly. And so it refers to Christ and the church, whom he urges to forsake the ancestral vices, for by forsaking them and being cleansed in all her thinking she was rendered seemly by the practice of virtue. This beauty of hers rendered the church desirable to Christ when he approached her with deep affection, as happens in the case of everyone. It cannot, on the contrary, be in any way applied to Solomon and his wife: Solomon was so far from bringing his own wife from her ancestral ways to forgetfulness or affection—incapable as he was of loving her on the condition that she first forgot them, in terms of David's statement—that those women, on the contrary, did not forsake their own ways and adopt instead true worship of God. Rather, they kept their own ways and caused him to adore what were thought gods by them.[26]

Because he is your Lord. Solomon was not, in fact, lord of his spouses, whereas it is applicable in the case of the Lord: it is he who is both maker and master, and it is obedience to him as master and maker that he recommends. He did well to go on to say *And daughters of Tyre will bow down to him with gifts* (v. 12): obey him as your master, having no less an opinion of him for the alleged dishonor of the passion.[27] Why is it that *daughters of Tyre will bow down to him with | gifts?* His lordship over all will be so obvi-

---

26. Cf. 1 Kgs 11:1–8.

27. *Pace* Devreesse, the text here seems to read, "You will bow down to him," before mentioning the daughter(s) of Tyre, to judge from Theodore's comment, as the three alternative versions also read (Theodoret tells us). Chrysostom knows both readings.

δώροις; Οὕτω γὰρ αὐτοῦ κατάδηλος ἔσται ἡ κατὰ πάντων δεσποτία, ὡς
τὰς ἀπανταχοῦ περιβλέπτους τιμῇ τε καὶ πλούτῳ τὴν προσκύνησιν αὐτῷ
μετὰ δώρων ἀναπέμπειν, ὁμολογούσας τὴν δεσποτίαν. Τοῦτο δὲ εἶπεν ἐκ
μεταφορᾶς τῶν ἐν ταῖς εἰκόσι γυναικῶν, αἳ γράφονται πολλάκις δῶρα
προσφέρουσαι τοῖς βασιλεῦσιν, ὡς τούτῳ τὴν ὑποταγὴν ὑπεμφαίνουσαι.   5
Θυγατέρας μὲν Τύρου τὰς πλουσίας καὶ τὰς ἐπιδόξους εἰπεῖν ἠβουλήθη ἀπὸ
τοῦ γνωρίμου τοῖς ἀκούουσιν· ἐπίσημος γὰρ ἦν ἡ πόλις καὶ πολλὴν
ἔχουσα τὴν ἐμπορείαν, καὶ τοῖς τότε ἀκούουσι διὰ τὴν ἐγγύτητα γνωρίμη.
Καὶ τίς τούτου ἡ ἀπόδειξις; Ὅτι τοσαύτη τις ἡ περὶ αὐτὸν ἔσται τιμή,
ὥστε μὴ δεῖν αὐτοῦ καταφρονεῖν διὰ τὴν νῦν προσεῖναι δοκοῦσαν εὐτέλειαν. 10

13ᵇ. Τὸ πρόσωπόν σου λιτανεύσουσιν οἱ πλούσιοι τοῦ λαοῦ τῆς γῆς. Ὅτι
δι' αὐτὸν καὶ τὰ παρ' αὐτοῦ σοι προσεσόμενα καλὰ τὸ ἐπίδοξόν σου
καὶ τὸ ἐπιφανές σου καὶ τὸ γνώριμον πάντες οἱ ἐπίδοξοι θαυμάσονται·
καὶ γὰρ γνώριμοι πᾶσίν εἰσιν οἱ ἐξ αὐτῆς ἅγιοι ἀπόστολοί τε καὶ μάρτυρες, ἤδη δὲ καὶ ἐν προστασίαις ἐκκλησιῶν διαπρεπεῖς γεγονότες, ὡς μεγί- 15
στην εἶναι αὐτῶν παρὰ πᾶσι τὴν μνήμην ἄχρι τῆς δεῦρο, μετὰ πολλῆς
τῆς σπουδῆς πάντων τιμᾶν αὐτοὺς ἐσπουδακότων καὶ οἰκείαν τὸ πρᾶγμα
κρινόντων εὐεργεσίαν. Καὶ θαυμάζομέν γε ἅπαντες τὴν παρασχεθεῖσαν τιμὴν ὑπὸ τοῦ Θεοῦ τῇ Ἐκκλησίᾳ, καὶ ὅσοι γε εὖ φρονοῦσι μακαριστ-
τόν τε τὸ συντελεῖν εἰς αὐτὴν τιθέμεθα καὶ πᾶν ὁτιοῦν ὑπὲρ αὐτῆς εὐχό- 20
μεθα παθεῖν, καθὼς ὁ ἀπόστολός φησιν Ἵνα γνωρισθῇ νῦν ταῖς ἀρχαῖς καὶ
ταῖς ἐξουσίαις ἐν τοῖς | ἐπουρανίοις διὰ τῆς ἐκκλησίας ἡ πολυποίκιλος σοφία
τοῦ Θεοῦ, κατὰ πρόθεσιν τῶν αἰώνων ἣν ἐποίησεν ἐν Χριστῷ Ἰησοῦ τῷ
κυρίῳ ἡμῶν, — ὥστε φησὶν εἰ οὕτω σὺ ἐπίδοξος καὶ οἱ σοί, ἦ πού γε ἐκεῖνος οὗ τούτων ἁπάντων αἴτιος ὑμῖν γεγονώς; Τὴν δὲ Ἐκκλησίαν δηλονότι 25
τοὺς πιστοὺς λέγει· τούτων γὰρ τὸν σύλλογον Ἐκκλησίαν καλεῖ, ὥστε
ὅταν τὰ περὶ τὴν Ἐκκλησίαν λέγῃ τὰ κοινῶς περὶ τοὺς ἁγίους γεγονότα
λέγει διὰ τὴν ἐπ' αὐτὸν πίστιν, — καὶ ὅταν τι πρὸς τὴν Ἐκκλησίαν λέγῃ
δῆλον ὅτι πρὸς τοὺς πιστοὺς λέγει, παραινῶν ἐκείνοις ἃ πράττειν αὐτοὺς
προσήκει.   30

14ᵃ. Πᾶσα ἡ δόξα τῆς θυγατρὸς βασιλέως ἔσωθεν. Ἐπειδὴ τὸν κόσμον
αὐτῆς ἐξηγησάμενος ἀπὸ τοῦ ἱματισμοῦ καὶ τῶν ἐκτός, τουτέστιν ἀπὸ τῶν

21-24 Ephes. III, 10-11.

Aᵉ 14-17 (p. 258, 13-17): ... Quod quidem rebus uidemus inpletum, cum apostolos eius et martires ac fideles quosque, in quibus est Eclesia, in gratiam
Christi a regibus conspicimus honorari.   31-295, 1 (p. 258, 18-22): Post enumerationem donorum spiritalium, quibus per largitoris sui indulgentiam fuerat
facta conspicua, bene et ordinate commendatur illi cura uirtutum.

ous that everywhere women conspicuous for rank and wealth will offer him adoration with gifts, confessing his lordship. Now, here he used a metaphor from the pictures of women who are often depicted offering gifts to kings to highlight subjection to him. He referred to rich and famous women by mention of *daughters of Tyre* on the basis of their being familiar to the listeners; the city was celebrated and did much trade, and it was familiar to listeners of the time because of its proximity. And what is the force of this? That esteem for him will be so great that there will be no call to despise him for the apparent dishonor now accruing to him.

The wealthy members of the people of the earth will entreat your countenance: because as a result of him and the good things accruing to you from him, all the famous people will admire your fame, your splendor, and your notoriety. In other words, its holy apostles and martyrs, already conspicuous for leadership of churches, will be familiar to everyone, so that to this day their memory is alive with everyone, since all are extremely zealous in honoring them and judging the affair as a favor to themselves. At any rate, we all admire the honor provided to the church by God, and all right-minded people among us consider it a blessing to be included in it, and we pray to suffer anything at all for it, as the apostle says, "so that there might be brought home now to the rulers and authorities in the heavenly places through the church God's wisdom in its rich variety, according to the eternal purpose that he has carried out in Christ Jesus our Lord."[28] And so, he asks, if you and yours are so famous, is it not he who is the cause of all this for you? Clearly, by the "church" he means the faithful: by the "church" he means their assembly, so that when he mentions the situation of the church, he is referring to what happened in general to the saints through their faith in him; and when he refers to anything affecting the church, it is clear that he is referring to the faithful, urging them to do as they are obliged.

All the glory of the king's daughter is within (v. 13). Since he had commented on her adornment in terms of clothing and externals—that is, in terms of | spiritual gifts—later he urged her to give evidence also of things

---

28. Eph 3:10–11.

πνευματικῶν χαρισμάτων, ὕστερον αὐτῇ παρήνεσεν ὥστε καὶ αὐτὴν ἀνάλογα τοῖς παρ᾽ αὐτοῦ δοθεῖσιν ἐπιδείκνυσθαι, βλέπουσάν τε πρὸς αὐτὸν
καὶ ἐν πᾶσιν ὑπακούουσαν αὐτῷ καὶ μεταθέσθαι μὲν πάντη τῶν παλαιῶν
ἐκείνων καὶ πατρῴων ἐθῶν, ὅλην δὲ εἶναι πρὸς αὐτὸν τεταμένην, μὴ κατα-
5 φρονοῦσαν διὰ τὴν νομιζομένην τοῦ πάθους ἀτιμίαν, ἀλλὰ μετὰ φόβου παντὸς ὡς δεσπότῃ δουλεύουσαν αὐτῷ. Ἐπεὶ καὶ πολλή τις ἔσται παρὰ πάντων, οὐ περὶ αὐτὸν μόνον ἀλλὰ γὰρ καὶ περὶ τοὺς τῆς Ἐκκλησίας ἐπισήμους
διὰ τὴν περὶ αὐτὸν διάθεσιν, καλῶς ἐπήγαγε τὸ Πᾶσα ἡ δόξα τῇ; θυγατρὸς τοῦ βασιλέως ἔσωθεν, τουτέστι Τούτων σοι ἐπιμελεῖσθαι συμβουλεύω
10 καὶ περὶ ταῦτα ἔχειν ὑπακούουσαν αὐτῷ μετὰ πάσης τῆς σπουδῆς, ἐπεὶ
αὕτη ἐστὶν ἡ ἀληθής σου δόξα ἡ ἔνδοθεν καὶ ἀπὸ τῆς κατὰ τὴν ψυχὴν
διαθέσεως δεικνυμένη· ἐκεῖνα μὲν γὰρ τὴν δωρεὰν γνωρίζει τοῦ δεσπότου,
ταῦτα δὲ τιμῆς ἀξίους ἀποφαίνει τοὺς κατωρθωκότας ἀπὸ τῆς οἰκείας προ-
θέσεώς τε καὶ ἀρετῆς.

15 Εἰ δὲ ἦν περὶ γυναικὸς τὸ λεγόμενον ὡς | πᾶσα ἡ δόξα ἔσωθεν, εἰ γὰρ
τοιαῦτα τὰ ἱμάτια οἷά φησιν, ἀνάγκη ἦν ἔξωθεν εἶναι τὴν δόξαν καὶ οὐκ
ἔσωθεν. Εἰ δὲ λέγοιεν κατὰ τὸ κάλλος λέγειν τὸ σωματικόν, ὡς ἔσωθεν
ὄντος καὶ κρυπτομένου ὑπὸ τῶν ἱματίων, εὔηθες καὶ ἰουδαϊκὸν τὸ εἰρημένον.
Πρῶτον μὲν γὰρ οὐκ εἶπεν « ἅπαν τὸ κάλλος », ἀλλὰ πᾶσα ἡ δόξα. Εἰ δὲ
20 δοίη τις καὶ οὕτω νοεῖσθαι, οὐδὲ τὸ σωματικὸν κάλλος ἔσωθεν, — τὸ γὰρ
σωματικὸν κάλλος ἀπὸ τοῦ προσώπου χαρακτηρίζεται, τὸ δὲ πρόσωπον
οὐκ ἔσωθέν ἐστιν ὑπὸ τῶν ἱματίων καλυπτόμενον, ἀλλ᾽ ἔξωθεν· εὐπρέπειαν δὲ καὶ δυσειδίαν οὐδέποτέ τις γυμνώσας ἀπὸ τῶν λοιπῶν σωμάτων
ἐδοκίμασεν, ἀλλ᾽ ἀπὸ τοῦ προσώπου καὶ τῶν λοιπῶν φαινομένων τοῦ
25 σώματος. Ὥστε δῆλον ὅτι τὸ ἔσωθεν κατὰ τὴν διάνοιαν λέγει καὶ οὐκ ἔνι
περὶ τοῦ σωματικοῦ κάλλους ὁ λόγος αὐτῷ, ἀλλὰ περὶ τῆς κατὰ ψυχὴν
ἀρετῆς· αὕτη γὰρ ἡ τῶν σπουδαίων ἀληθὴς δόξα, τῆς συνειδήσεως ἡ
καθαρότης, ἀφ᾽ ἧς ἐπίδοξοι παρὰ τῷ κριτῇ πάντως ἔσονται.

14b. Ἐν κροσσωτοῖς χρυσοῖς περιβεβλημένη πεποικιλμένη Διὰ τί οὖν τῆς
30 δόξης μνημονεύσας, ἐπήγαγε τὸ Ἐν κροσσωτοῖς χρυσοῖς περιβεβλημένη πεποι-

6 πολλή τις ἔσται, supple δόξα.   15-28 L (p. 839, 4-12): Ἐντεῦθεν δῆλον ὡς
οὐ περί τινος θνητοῦ ὁ λόγος. Ἡ γὰρ θνητὴ δόξα οὐκ ἀπὸ τῶν ἔνδοθεν καὶ λανθανόντων,
ἀλλ᾽ ἀπὸ τῶν ἔξω ὁρᾶται. Καὶ μὴν τὰ ἱμάτια μάλιστα πάντων ἔξωθεν. Ἀλλ᾽ ὅταν ᾖ σω-
ματικά, ὅταν δὲ πνευματικά, ἔνδον στρέφει τὸ τῆς διανοίας ὄμμα, πρὸς τὴν διάνοιαν εἰσῆλθε
τὸ κάλλος, ὅτι περὶ τῆς ἀρετῆς τὰ λεγόμενα.

Aᶜ 15-28 (p. 258, 30-259, 5): ...ab intus, non ergo de pulchritudine corporali, quae exterior (exterterior ms) est, laudat reginam, sed de habitu mentis
praedicat; et hortatur aeclisiam, cui est intus apud cogitationes conscientia pro-
uisa munditiae.

commensurate with what was given by him, by gazing at him, hearkening to him in everything and transforming completely those old ancestral ways, and to be completely focused on him by not scorning him for the alleged dishonor of the passion, instead serving him as her master with deep fear. Since there will be some considerable glory in the sight of everyone, in regard not only to him but also to the illustrious members of the church on account of affection for him, it was well that he went on to say *All the glory of the king's daughter is within*—in other words, I advise you to attend to these things and hearken to him in these matters with great zeal, since your true glory is revealed from within and in terms of the affection in your soul: while the former make known the Lord's gift, the latter reveal as worthy of honor those distinguished for their own resolve and virtue.

If, on the contrary, the statement *all glory is within* referred to a woman— if, for example, her garments were of that kind—it would follow that her glory is exterior and not interior. And if they were to claim that he refers to bodily beauty, as though of something within and concealed by garments, the claim is the silly one that the Jews make. After all, he did not begin by saying "all beauty," but *all glory*. If, on the other hand, you were to concede that it is to be taken this way, even so, bodily beauty is not within: bodily beauty is assessed from the face, and the face is not something within concealed by garments, but is on the outside. No one ever determined beauty and ugliness by stripping bare the entire body, but from the face and the body's other features. And so it is clear that by *within* he refers to the mind, and the words can refer only to, not bodily beauty, but virtue of soul. This, in fact, is the true glory of the devout, purity of conscience, for which they will be utterly conspicuous in the judge's sight.

In golden tassels, clad in many colors. Why, then, after mentioning *glory,* does he proceed to say *In golden tassels, clad in many colors?* | Because

κιλμένη; Ἐπειδὴ τῇ καθαρότητι τῆς ψυχῆς δεῖ συνεργεῖν καὶ τὴν τοῦ
Πνεύματος χάριν. Ἵνα τοίνυν μὴ οἰηθῇς οἰκεῖον πάντη κατόρθωμα τὴν ἀρετὴν τῶν πιστῶν τυγχάνειν καὶ μηδενὸς αὐτοὺς ἑτέρου πρὸς τοῦτο δεῖσθαι, καλῶς ἐπήγαγε τοῦ πνευματικοῦ κόσμου τὴν μνήμην, δεικνὺς ὅτι καὶ
τούτου χρεία τοῖς ἀρετῇ συζῆν προελομένοις, τῇ πνευματικῇ συνεργείᾳ 5
ῥᾳδίως ἁπάντων πληροῦσθαι δυναμένων τῶν πρὸς ἀρετὴν συντελούντων. Ἐπὶ
μέντοι γυναικὸς οὐδὲ τοῦτό ἐστιν ἔχον λόγον· τὸ γάρ τοι κάλλος τὸ σωματικὸν οὐκ ἀπὸ τοῦ κόσμου τοσοῦτον δείκνυται θαυμαστὸν ὅσον ἀπὸ τῆς
οἰκείας φύσεως, — ὁ γὰρ ἔξωθεν κόσμος ταῖς δυσειδέσι μᾶλλον συμβάλλε-
ται ἢ ταῖς ἔμφυτον κεκτημέναις τὸ κάλλος. | Μνημονεύσας τοίνυν τοῦ κατ' 10
ἀρετὴν κάλλους ⟨καὶ⟩ τὴν προσήκουσαν περὶ τούτου παραίνεσιν τοῖς πισ-
τοῖς προσαγαγών, εἰκότως λοιπὸν ἐπάγει τοῦ μείζονος ἐν τοῖς κατορθώμασι τῆς Ἐκκλησίας τὴν μνήμην ποιούμενος, δεικνὺς ὅτι οὐκ ἄχρηστον οὐδ
ἀνόνητον αὐτῷ τὸ τῆς παραινέσεως ἔσται, ἀλλὰ γὰρ καὶ μάλα πολλὴν
παρὰ τοῖς τῆς Ἐκκλησίας ἡ ἀρετὴ λήψεται τὴν ἐπίδοσιν, καί φησιν· 15

15ᵃ. Ἀπενεχθήσονται τῷ βασιλεῖ παρθένοι ὀπίσω αὐτῆς. Τὸ γὰρ μέγιστον καὶ ἐξαίρετον ἐν τῇ Ἐκκλησίᾳ κατόρθωμα, τοῦτο δὴ τὸ τῆς παρθενείας
ἐστίν, ὃ πρότερον μὲν οὕτως ἀδύνατον ἦν φυλάττειν ἀνθρώπους, ὡς καὶ
τοὺς δικαίους αὐτοὺς μόλις ἀρκεῖσθαι μιᾷ δύνασθαι γυναικί, ὕστερον δὲ καὶ
μετὰ τὴν Χριστοῦ παρουσίαν πολλοῖς καὶ τῶν ῥαθυμοτέρων εὐκατόρθωτον 20
ὑπὸ τῆς θείας ἐγένετο χάριτος. Τοῦτο οὖν λέγει ὅτι τότε πλεῖσται προσ-
κομισθήσονται παρθένοι τῷ βασιλεῖ εἰς τιμήν, τουτέστιν αὐτῷ τὴν παρθενείαν φυλάττουσαι. Πῶς οὖν ἀπενεχθήσονται τῷ βασιλεῖ παρθένοι ὀπίσω
αὐτῆς; Ὅτι ὅσοι τοῦτο μεταδιώκουσιν ἕπονται τῇ βασιλίσσῃ, τουτέστι τῇ
Ἐκκλησίᾳ, γνησίαν αὐτῇ καὶ τῆς ἀρετῆς τὴν ὑπηρεσίαν ἐκτελοῦσαι, ἐπείπερ 25
οἱ τοιοῦτοι μάλιστα φύλακές εἰσιν ἀκριβεῖς τῶν τῆς Ἐκκλησίας ἐντολῶν.

15ᵇ. Αἱ πλησίον αὐτῆς ἀπενεχθήσονταί σοι. Αὗταί σοί φησιν ἀπενεχθήσονται, αὗται μεταδιώξουσι τὴν ἐπαγγελίαν, αὗται ἀναθήσονταί σοι τὴν
ἑαυτῶν παρθενείαν αἱ πλησίον τῆς βασιλίσσης, τουτέστιν αἱ μάλιστα ἡνω-
μέναι αὐτῆς τῇ διαθέσει, αἱ συμφερόμεναι αὐτῆς τῷ φρονήματι· οἱ γὰρ 30

11 καὶ supplevi.

Aᵉ 1-6 (p. 259, 6-15): Oportet nimirum (ne mirum ms) ad obtinendam animi,
quam superiori uorsu laudauerat, puritatem gratia Spiritus sancti adi⟨u⟩uari...
sic ipse mentis decor et puritas per auxilium demum Spiritus sancti obtinent
firmitatem.   17-19 (p. 256, 16-20): Ipsi uidilicet uirginitatem suam sacrantes,
cuius apud ueteres adeo inpossibilis custodia uidebatur (uiatur ms), ut sancti
quique singulis mulieribus non possent esse contenti.   27-30 (p. 259, 21-25):
Quaecumque adfinitate uirtutum riginae... proximae esse curauerint, illae pro-
misiones tuas... uirginitatis studio persequentur.

even the grace of the Spirit has to operate in association with purity of soul. Lest you believe, then, that the virtue of the faithful is completely their own achievement and they require nothing else for it, it was well that he proceeded to make mention of spiritual adornment to bring out that those choosing to live a life of virtue need it, since all those practicing virtue are easily able to be imbued with the cooperation of the Spirit. This, too, of course, involves no reference to a woman, since bodily beauty appears admirable not so much on account of adornment as on account of the natural gift, external adornment contributing to ugly women rather than to those in possession of natural beauty.

Having mentioned the beauty of virtue, therefore, and offered to the faithful the due exhortation on it, he then was right to proceed by making mention of the more significant of the achievements of the church so as to bring out that, far from exhortation being without use or value, virtue will even experience very great increase in the churches. *Maidens will be brought to the king after her* (v. 14). That is to say, the greatest and most special achievement in the church is that of virginity, which formerly was so far beyond the power of human beings to preserve that even good men were scarcely able to be content with a single wife, whereas later, after the coming of Christ, it proved achievable with divine grace to many even of the less ardent.[29] So it means that great numbers of virgins will be presented to the king in his honor—that is, preserving their virginity for him. Why is it, then, that *Maidens will be brought to the king after her*? Because all who put it into practice follow the queen—that is, the church—also performing for her the true service of virtue, since people of this kind are particularly scrupulous in observing the church's commands.

Her neighbors will be brought to you: they are the ones who will be brought to you, they are the ones who will closely pursue the promise, they are the ones who will dedicate to you their virginity—namely, the queen's neighbors, that is, those joined to her in affection, those of one mind with her, since | people with deep desire for virtue in their soul are the ones who

---

29. Chrysostom, too, takes this to be a reference to virginity and embarks on a discourse on the deficiencies of the married state (as had Diodore), Theodoret thinking more broadly in terms of unadulterated faith.

πολὺν τῆς ἀρετῆς ἐπὶ τῆς ψυχῆς τὸν πόθον δεξάμενοι, οὗτοι νεύειν καὶ
βλέπειν πρὸς τὸν τῆς παρθενείας ἐπείγονται σκοπόν. Εἰ δὲ ἦν ἐπὶ ἀνδρὸς
λεγόμενον καὶ γυναικός, τὸ ἐναντίον ἂν εἶπεν· οὐ γὰρ αἱ τῇ βασιλίσσῃ
πάν|τ⟨　　⟩όμεναι ὑπηρετεῖν αὗται ἤμελλον προσάγεσθαι τῷ βασιλεῖ,
5　ἀλλὰ τοὐναντίον αἱ ἐκείνῳ προσαγόμεναι ἤμελλον ἐξ ἀνάγκης εἰς ὑπηρεσίαν
ἀπονέμεσθαι ταύτης.

16ᵃ. Ἀπενεχθήσονται ἐν εὐφροσύνῃ καὶ ἀγαλλιάσει. Τοῦτο μάλιστα
ἐναντίον τῇ ἰουδαϊκῇ διανοίᾳ. Οὐ γὰρ πάντως ὅσαι ἢ τῷ βασιλεῖ προσάγεσθαι ἔμελλον ἢ εἰς τὴν ὑπηρεσίαν ἀφορίζεσθαι τῆς βασιλίσσης μετὰ
10　εὐφροσύνης τοῦτο διεπράττοντο, μᾶλλον δ' ἂν ἠθύμουν καὶ ἔκλαιον τῶν
γονέων χωριζόμεναι. Ἐπὶ δὲ τῆς Ἐκκλησίας σφόδρα ἀληθὲς τὸ εἰρημένον·
μεταδιώκουσι γὰρ τὴν παρθενείαν, οὐ μόνον οὐκ ἀθυμοῦσαι ἐπὶ τῷ πράγματι, ἀλλ' αὐτοπροαιρέτως αὐτὸ μετιοῦσαι, μετὰ τοσαύτης χαρᾶς καὶ
εὐφροσύνης ὡς πολλοὺς πολλάκις καὶ ὑφίστασθαι κινδύνους ὑπὸ τῶν
15　κωλύειν ἐθελόντων.

16ᵇ. Ἀχθήσονται εἰς ναὸν βασιλέως. Φανερώτερον ἐνταῦθα εἴρηται,
βασιλέως οὐκ ἀνθρώπου λέγει· ναὸν γὰρ οὐδαμοῦ ἡ θεία γραφὴ ἀνθρώπου
καλεῖ τὸν οἶκον ἐν ᾧ καταμένει, ἀλλὰ πάντως τὸν ναὸν τοῦ Θεοῦ καλεῖ
ναὸν τὸν τοῦ ἀληθῶς Θεοῦ ἢ κατὰ τὴν προσηγορίαν τῶν ψευδονύμων
20　θεῶν, — ὅπως δ' ἂν ὁ βασιλεὺς νοεῖται, οὕτω δηλονότι καὶ ἡ βασίλισσα
νοηθήσεται. Τί οὖν λέγει ἐνταῦθα τὸ Ἀχθήσονται εἰς ναὸν βασιλέως; Ὅτι
ἀνατεθήσονταί φησιν αὐτῷ αὗται αἱ παρθένοι εἰς τὸ εἶναι ⟨ναός⟩· ναὸς
γὰρ ἀποτελοῦνται Θεοῦ διὰ τοῦ τῆς παρθενείας ἁγιασμοῦ, οἰκητήριον
ἑαυτὰς ἀποτελοῦσαι τοῦ ἁγίου Πνεύματος, καθὼς ὁ ἀπόστολός φησιν
25　Οὐκ οἴδατε ὅτι ναὸς τοῦ Θεοῦ ἐστε καὶ τὸ πνεῦμα τοῦ Θεοῦ οἰκεῖ ἐν ὑμῖν;
Δῆλον δὲ ὅτι ὅταν λέγῃ παρθένους οὐ πάντως ὅτι τὰς γυναῖκας λέγει
μόνον, ἀλλὰ καὶ ἄνδρας καὶ γυναῖκας καὶ ἅπαντας ὁμοῦ τοὺς τὴν αὐτὴν
ἐπαγγελίαν μετιόντας. Παρθένους δὲ εἶπεν ἐπειδὴ ὅλως βασιλίσσης ἐμνημόνευσεν, ἢ καὶ ὅτι πλείους αἱ γυναῖκες αἱ τὴν ἐπαγγελίαν μετιοῦσαι καὶ
30　διὰ τοῦτο ἀπὸ τοῦ πλείστου ὀνομάσαι ἠβουλήθη.

25 I Cor. III, 16.

4 *scriptura deleta evanuerunt litterae quattuor aut quinque; lege e. g.* πάντ⟨η
ἐναγ⟩όμεναι, πάν⟨τως ἀγ⟩όμεναι *uel* πάντ⟨ως προσαγ⟩όμεναι *ut in ll. 8-9*　22 ναός *supplevi*　22. 26-27 *cf. Paraphrasis* (p. 830, 4-7): ...ὥστε καὶ αὐτὰς γενέσθαι ναὸν βασιλέως. Ἀπὸ γὰρ τῶν παρθένων γυναικῶν δῆλον ὅτι καὶ τοὺς παρθένους ἄνδρας ὑπαινίττεται.

Aᵉ 14-15 (p. 259, 28-30): ...adeo ut pro studio boni operis pericula plerumque
adeant　17-18. 22 (p. 259, 31-26.), 1): Ipsae uirgines se consecrabunt, ut templa
ipsius regis existant: nusquam (nuscam *ms*) sane domum hominis templum
scriptum esse reperies.　27 (p. 260, 1-2): Virgines uero utriusque sexus dicit.

vigorously strive and have regard for the purpose of virginity. If, on the other hand, there were reference here to husband and wife, he would have said the opposite: those in service to the queen would not at all be likely to be presented to the king; instead, it would be those presented to him who would consequently be due to be assigned to her service. *They will be brought in joy and gladness.* This in particular contradicts the Jewish interpretation: it is not at all the case that all who were due to be presented to the king or assigned to the service of the queen acted with joy, being depressed instead and weeping over the separation from their parents. The saying is very properly applied to the church, by contrast: they practice virginity, not depressed by it, but voluntarily adopting it with such joy and gladness that many of them not infrequently even incur perils at the hands of those attempting to stop them.

They will be led to the king's temple. The statement is clearer here. He is not referring to a human king: the divine Scripture nowhere refers by *temple* to a human being's house in which he resides; rather, by God's temple it refers in every case to a temple of the true God or that named after the false gods. And obviously, the queen will be understood in the same way that the king is understood. So what is the meaning here of *They will be led to the king's temple*? That the virgins themselves will be dedicated to him so as to be a temple: they will be made God's temple through the consecration of virginity, making themselves a dwelling of the Holy Spirit, as the apostle says, "Do you not know that you are a temple of God, and the Spirit of God dwells in you?"[30] Now, it is clear that when he mentions virgins, he definitely does not mean women only, but men and women and all who partake of the same promise. He said *maidens* because he had in fact mentioned a queen, or also because more women partake of the same promise, and so he wished to name them on the score of their majority. |

---

30. 1 Cor 3:16.

Καὶ ἐπειδὴ λοιπὸν ἐν τοῖς κατορθώμασι τῆς ἀρετῆς ἐμνήσθη τοῦ πάντων
μείζονος, τῆς παρθενίας λέγω, μνημονεύει καὶ τοῦ πάντων μείζονος ἐν τοῖς
χαρίσμασι τοῖς πνευματικοῖς, λέγω δὴ τοῦ τῆς ἱερατείας (τοῦτο γὰρ καὶ τῆς
ἀναγεννήσεως ἀξιοῖ καὶ Πνεύματος μετουσίαν χαρίζεται τοῖς βαπτιζομένοις,
καὶ τὸ μυστήριον τελεσιουργεῖ καὶ ὅλως ἅπαντα πληροῖ τὰ ἐν τῇ Ἐκκλησίᾳ   5
γινόμενα) τοῦτο λέγων ὅτι ἀναδειχθήσονται μὲν ἐξ αὐτῆς ἐνάρετοι πολλοὶ
τὴν τελείαν μετιόντες ἀγνείαν, ἀναδειχθήσονται δὲ καὶ ἄνδρες ἄξιοι τοῦ ἱερα-
τεύειν ἕνεκεν, ἀξιωθήσονται τῆς τιμῆς ὡς κατὰ πάσης ἄρχειν αὐτοὺς τῆς οἰκου-
μένης· βούλεται γὰρ ἀπὸ τῆς ἱερατείας τὸ τοῦ δόγματος ἐπίσημον εἰπεῖν.
Οὐ χαλεπὸν γοῦν συνιδεῖν τὸν βουλόμενον ὅση περὶ τοὺς τῶν ἐκκλησιῶν   10
προεστῶτας ἡ τιμή, οὐ γὰρ τῶν οἰκείων μόνον ἀλλὰ καὶ παρὰ τῶν ἐναντίων τοῦ τῆς εὐσεβείας φρονήματος ἁπάντων μικροῦ πάσης ἀξίους αἰδοῦς
εἶναι νομιζόντων. Διὸ ἐπάγει·

17ᵃ. Ἀντὶ τῶν πατέρων σου ἐγεννήθησάν σοι υἱοί. Ἐπειδὴ γὰρ ἡ Ἐκκλησία συνέστη ἀπό τε ἐθνῶν καὶ Ἰουδαίων, τῶν μὲν ἐντεῦθεν τῶν δὲ ἐκεῖθεν   15
πιστευσάντων Χριστῷ, πατέρας αὐτῆς καλεῖ τοὺς παρ᾽ Ἕλλησι καὶ Ἰουδαίοις ἱερέας καὶ διδασκάλους, οὓς ἐπεγράφοντο τότε κατὰ τὴν οἰκείαν
θρησκείαν ἕκαστος πατέρας πρὸ τῆς πίστεως τῆς ἐπὶ τὸν δεσπότην Χριστόν. Τοῦτο οὖν λέγει ὅτι ἀντ᾽ ἐκείνων ἕξεις υἱούς, τουτέστιν ἐκείνους μὲν
οὐκέτι πατέρας ἐπιγράψῃ, ἀπό σου δὲ αὐτῆς τεχθήσονται ἱερεῖς καὶ διδάσ-   20
καλοι, οὓς ἐν τάξει πατέρων ἕξεις ἀντ᾽ ἐκείνων. Καὶ γὰρ ἡ Ἐκκλησία ἰδίαν
τε ἔσχεν ἱερατείαν καὶ ἀεὶ ἀπογεννᾷ ἱερέας τε καὶ διδασκάλους, καθ᾽ ἑκάστην γενεὰν ἐξ αὐτῆς ἐκδιδοῦσα τοὺς ἄρχειν τῶν κατὰ τόπον λαῶν δοκιμα-
ζομένους, οὓς καὶ πατέρας ἅπαντες οἱ τῆς | Ἐκκλησίας πνευματικοὺς καλεῖν
οὐκ αἰσχύνονται. Διὸ καλῶς ἐπάγει·   25

17ᵇ. Καταστήσεις αὐτοὺς ἄρχοντας ἐπὶ πᾶσαν τὴν γῆν. Οὗτοι δέ φησιν,
οἱ παρά σου καθ᾽ ἕκαστον ἐκδιδόμενοι πρὸς τοῦτο καιρόν, κατὰ πάσης
ἄρξουσι τῆς οἰκουμένης, τῶν κατὰ τόπον λαῶν τὴν προστασίαν ἀναδεχό-
μενοι. Τοῖς δὲ τοῦ Σολομῶντος υἱοῖς τοῦτο οὐχ ἁρμόττον, — ἵνα γὰρ τὸ
ἐπὶ πᾶσαν τὴν γῆν περὶ τῆς γῆς τῆς ἐπαγγελίας νοήσωμεν, οὐδ᾽ οὕτως   30
ἀληθὲς ἔσται τὸ λεγόμενον· ὁ γὰρ πρῶτος τὴν βασιλείαν δεξάμενος παρ᾽
αὐτοῦ τὸ πλεῖστον μέρος εὐθὺς ἀφηρέθη τῆς βασιλείας, δύο μόνων φυλῶν
ὑπολειφθεὶς βασιλεύς. Τί οὖν ἀντὶ τούτων;

22 ἱερεῖς ms.

Aᵉ 1-6 (p. 260, 3-9): Post uirginitatis inter uirtutes caeteras eminentiam,
rite sacerdotale locauit officium, per quod et regenerationis ipsius donum et
participatio Spiritus sancti datur et totius eclisiae gubernantur instituta et
misteria celebrantur.   26-28 (p. 260, 10-14): Singuli in singulis ciuitatibus
plebium curam gerentes... uniuersae terrae primatum tenebunt.

Since he had thus made mention among the works of virtue of the greatest of all—I mean virginity—he also makes mention of the greatest of all among the spiritual gifts, that of priesthood. It in fact confers regeneration and grants a share in the Spirit to the baptized, it celebrates the Eucharist, and in general it performs everything happening in the church. He means that many virtuous people of its number performing a pure role will emerge as those practicing perfect chastity, and will emerge also as men worthy of priestly service, and will be vouchsafed the honor of ruling throughout the whole world (referring to the distinguished role of teaching on the basis of priesthood). At any rate, for the one willing there is no difficulty in grasping the respect shown to the leaders of the churches, not only by their own, but also by those opposed to the teaching of the true religion, who think them worthy of well-nigh complete reverence.

He therefore proceeds to say *In place of your fathers your sons were born* (v. 16). Since the church is composed both of Gentiles and of Jews, some of the former and some of the latter coming to faith in Christ, by her *fathers* he refers to the priests and teachers among pagans and Jews, whom they each considered their fathers in their own religion at that time before faith in Christ as their master. So it means, In place of them you will have *sons*—that is, Instead of having them as fathers, priests and teachers will be born of you yourself, and them you will have as fathers in their place. The church, you see, had its own priesthood and always gives birth to both priests and teachers, in each generation producing from her ranks those thought fit to rule the peoples in each place, whom all members of the church are not ashamed to call spiritual fathers. Hence, he does well to continue by saying *You will set them as princes over the whole earth:* those emerging from you on each occasion as the time requires will rule throughout the world, succeeding to the leadership of the peoples in each place. Now, this is not applicable to the sons of Solomon, as if we should take *over the whole earth* to refer to the land of promise, which is not the true meaning: his immediate successor straightway lost the greater part of the kingdom, being left as king of only two tribes.

What, then, instead of them? | *I shall remember your name in every*

18ª. Μνησθήσομαι τοῦ ὀνόματος σου ἐν πάσῃ γενεᾷ καὶ γενεᾷ. Καλὴ καὶ ἀναγκαία μετὰ τὴν παραίνεσιν ἡ ἐπαγωγή. Τοῦτό φησιν ὑπὲρ τούτων εἶπεν, ὅτι διατελέσω ἀεί σου μεμνημένος καὶ τῆς περί σε οὐκ ἐξιστάμενος διαθέσεως. Ἐπειδὴ γὰρ εἶπεν ἄνω Ἐπιλάθου τοῦ λαοῦ σου καὶ τοῦ
5 οἴκου τοῦ πατρός σου, εἶτα ἐμνήσθη τῶν περὶ τὴν Ἐκκλησίαν ἐσομένων παρὰ τοῦ Θεοῦ καλῶν, καλῶς ἐνταῦθα ἐπήγαγε Μνησθήσομαί σου, ἀντὶ τοῦ Ἐκείνων μὲν ἐπιλάθου, πρὸς δὲ τὸν Θεὸν τοῦ μνημονεύειν αὐτοῦ διηνεκῶς κατάθου τὴν ὁμολογίαν. Τὸ γὰρ «εἶπεν» ἐνταῦθα ἐπὶ τῆς κατὰ ψυχὴν ἔλαβε δοκιμασίας ὡς τὸ Εἶπα Φυλάξω τὰς ὁδούς μου, ἀντὶ τοῦ Οὕτω ἐδοκίμασα
10 φρονεῖν τε καὶ πράττειν, — καὶ τὸ μὴ εἰπεῖν δὲ ὅτι «εἶπεν», ἀλλὰ κατὰ ἀποσιώπησιν ἀπὸ τῆς ἀκολουθίας αὐτὸ σημάναι, σύνηθες τῷ μακαρίῳ Δαυίδ, ὡς ἐν τοῖς προοιμίοις τοῦ ψαλμοῦ ἀκριβέστερον τὸ ἰδίωμα ἐπεσημηνάμεθα.

18ᵇ·ᶜ. Διὰ τοῦτο λαοὶ ἐξομολογήσονταί σοι εἰς τὸν αἰῶνα καὶ εἰς τὸν αἰῶνα τοῦ αἰῶνος. Καλῶς συμπληρώσας πρὸς τὴν Ἐκκλησίαν τὸν λόγον καὶ
15 τὴν παραίνεσιν, ἀπέστρεψε τὸν λόγον πρὸς τὸν Θεόν, τοῦτο λέγων ὅτι Οὐδὲν θαυμαστὸν εἰ ταῦτα εἴποιεν καὶ ταῦτα περί σε πληροῖεν. Εἰκότως γὰρ καὶ μάλα ὀφει\λομένως ὑπὲρ τῶν τοσούτων καὶ τηλικούτων ἀγαθῶν διατελέσουσιν ἅπαντες οἱ κατὰ τὴν οἰκουμένην ἄνθρωποι, διηνεκῶς σοι τὰς ὑπὲρ τῶν δοθέντων εὐχαριστίας ἀναπέμποντες, — ὅπερ δὴ καὶ γίνεται,
20 πάντων ἡμῶν εὐχαριστούντων ἀεὶ τῷ Χριστῷ ὑπὲρ τῆς εἰς ἡμᾶς εὐεργεσίας.

Ὑπὲρ μέντοι τοῦ κάλλους τῆς βασιλίσσης καὶ περὶ τῆς τοῦ Σολομῶντος γυναικός, καὶ ὑπὲρ τοῦ κόσμου τοῦ ἔξωθεν αὐτῇ περικειμένου, καὶ ὑπὲρ τῶν προσφερομένων αὐτῇ παρθένων τίς οὕτως εὐήθης ὥστ᾽ ἂν οἴεσθαι τὸν προφήτην εἰπεῖν πρὸς τὸν Θεὸν ὅτι ὑπὲρ τούτων εὐχαριστήσουσι
25 αὐτῷ λαοί; Τίς γὰρ δὴ καὶ ὑπὲρ τούτων εὐχαριστήσει ποτὲ τῷ Θεῷ, οὐ λέγω τῶν λοιπῶν ἀνθρώπων, ἀλλ᾽ αὐτῶν γοῦν Ἰουδαίων τῶν οὕτω ταῦτα ἑρμηνεύειν ἐπιχειρούντων; Ὥστε πανταχόθεν, καὶ πολλῷ μᾶλλον ἀπὸ τῆς ἀκολουθίας τῆς κατὰ τὴν ἑρμηνείαν, συναχθήσεται τὸ περὶ μηδενὸς ἑτέρου δύνασθαι λαμβάνεσθαι τὸν ψαλμὸν ἀλλ᾽ ἢ περὶ μόνου τοῦ Κυρίου καὶ τῆς
30 Ἐκκλησίας.

4-5 v. 11ᵇ   9 Ps. XXXVIII, 2   12 cf. supra, p. 280-281.

2-4 *Paraphrasis* (p. 830, 36-37): Ἐγὼ δέ φησιν ὁ Δαυὶδ ἔσομαι διὰ παντὸς μνημονευόμενος διά σου τοῦ Κυρίου.

Aᵉ 2-5 (p. 260, 15-19): Subauditur Sic profetere, quia, si oblita populi mei solius Dei ero memor, tantorum uidilicet ante me diuinorum munerum obliuisci non potero.   14-20 (p. 260, 20-28): Conpleto in aeclesia sermone atque praeceptis, conuertitur ad Dominum dicens Consequenter prursus et debete pro tantis ac talibus bonis tibi a cunctis populis, quanti sunt in orbe, gratiae refferentur; quod nimirum (ne mirum *ms*) cotidie in singulis uidemus ecclesi⟨i⟩s.   25-27 (p. 260, 28-29): Quod neque Iudei quidem ipsi pro Salamonis uxore fecerunt.

single generation (v. 17). This is a nice and necessary sequel to the exhortation. Speaking on their behalf he says, I shall always continue to remember you and never fail in my affection for you. You see, since he had said above *Forget your people and your father's house* and then mentioned developments in the church, referring to it as God's, he did well here to say further *I shall remember you,* in the sense of *Forget* them and constantly make a confession to God by way of recalling him. In fact, he used the words "He said" here in reference to a heartfelt decision, as in the verse "I said, 'I shall guard my ways,' "[31] meaning, "I decided to think and behave in this way," not meaning that he said something, but silently implied it from the flow of thought, as usual with blessed David—an idiom we indicated more precisely in the introduction to the psalm.

Hence, peoples will confess you for ages of ages. As a nice conclusion of his address and exhortation to the church, he directed his attention to God, meaning, No surprise if they were to say this and perform this in your regard: it would be right and very obligatory for all the people throughout the world to continue doing this in return for so many wonderful good things, constantly offering you thanks for what has been given. This actually happens, all of us thanking Christ always for his kindness to us.

Who would be so silly as to think that the author was saying to God that peoples would thank him for the queen's beauty (in reference to Solomon's wife), for the external adornment enveloping her, and for the maidens presented to her? I mean, who—not of the rest of humankind, but even of Jews themselves in their attempts at interpreting it this way—would ever thank God even for these things? And so on all scores, and much more on the basis of the movement of thought in the commentary, we are forced to the conclusion that it is impossible to take the psalm as referring to any other person than the Lord and the church alone. |

---

31. Ps 39:1. Theodore seems to be implying that the words "He said" occurs in his text, although this is not acknowledged by the other Antiochenes or other forms of the LXX or the Hebrew.

PSALMVS XLV

Μετὰ τὴν τοῦ Σολομῶντος τελευτὴν διηρέθησαν μὲν αἱ δώδεκα φυλαὶ
τοῦ Ἰσραήλ. Ἦν δὲ καθ᾽ ἑαυτὴν μὲν ἡ τοῦ Ἰούδα μετὰ μόνης τῆς Βενια-
μίτιδος τῶν ἐκ τοῦ σπέρματος Δαυὶδ κατὰ διαδοχὴν βασιλευόντων, αἱ δὲ
λοιπαὶ δέκα φυλαὶ διακεκριμένως ἐβασιλεύοντο διαφόρως καὶ ἄλλοτε ἄλλως, 5
νῦν μὲν τούτων αὖθις δὲ ἑτέρων βασιλευόντων· ἦν δὲ ἐν αὐταῖς προτιμοτέρα μὲν ἡ τοῦ Ἐφραίμ, μητρόπολις δὲ ἡ Σαμάρεια, ἐν ᾗ κατοικεῖν τὸν
βασιλεύοντα συνέβαινεν, ὥσπερ οὖν καὶ τῶν δύο φυλῶν μητρόπολις Ἱερουσαλὴμ καθειστήκει. Καί ποτε βασιλεύοντος τοῦ Ἄχαζ τῆς Ἰουδαίας, τουτέστι τῶν δύο φυλῶν, Φακεὲ ὁ τῆς Σαμαρείας βασιλεύς τε καὶ τῶν δέκα 10
φυλῶν, μετὰ παντὸς τοῦ ἰδίου λαοῦ συνεργὸν τοῦ ἐπιχειρήματος λαβὼν καὶ
τὸν Ῥαασὴν τὸν | τῆς Συρίας τῆς κατὰ Δάμασκον βασιλέα, ἔπεισι πολιορκῆ-
σαι τὴν Ἱερουσαλὴμ προαιρούμενος καὶ καθελεῖν τῶν δύο φυλῶν τὴν βασιλείαν ἐσπουδακώς. Ἀλλ᾽ ἐπηγγείλατο μὲν διὰ τοῦ προφήτου Ἡσαΐου βοηθήσειν αὐτοῖς ὁ Θεός, οὐ τοῦ Ἄχαζ ὄντος δικαίου, — τοῦτο γὰρ ἡμᾶς ἡ τῶν 15
Βασιλειῶν βίβλος παιδεύει λέγουσα Υἱὸς εἴκοσι ἐτῶν ἦν Ἄχαζ ἐν τῷ βασι-

9-15 cf. Is. VII, 1 ss.   9 ss. cf. IV Reg. XVI, 11 Paral. XXVIII   16-301, 2 IV Reg. XVI, 2.

Idem argumentum legitur in versione latina (Barbaro, p. 467-8), *paullo bre-*
vius exstat in codd. Paris. 139, fol. 119; Vat. 1682, fol. 173ᵛ-174; Vat. 1422, fol. 90ᵛ :
Μετὰ τὴν τοῦ Σολομῶντος — ἐβασιλεύοντό που αἱ μὲν ὑπὸ τούτων που αἱ δὲ ὑπὸ ἑτέρων.
Ἦν δὴ αὐτοῖς προτιμοτέρα — Σαμάρεια ἡ Ἱερουσαλήμ (προτιμοτέρα μὲν ἡ τοῦ Ἐφραὶμ
φυλή, — ἐκ ταύτης γὰρ καὶ Ἱεροβοὰμ ὁ πρῶτος ἀποστάτης ἐφύη, — μητρόπολις δὲ ἡ Σαμάρεια τοῦ ἀποστατήσαντος Ἰσραήλ, ὥσπερ καὶ Ἱερουσαλὴμ τοῦ Ἰούδα 1422). Καί ποτε βασιλεύοντος τοῦ Ἄχαζ τῶν δύο φυλῶν — πολιορκῆσαι τὴν Ἱερουσαλὴμ καὶ μεταστῆσαι τῶν δύο
φυλῶν τὴν ἀρχὴν εἰς ἑαυτόν. Ἀλλ᾽ ὁ Θεὸς ἐβοήθησε ταῖς δύο φυλαῖς, τὸν τῶν Ἀσσυρίων
βασιλέως ἐπισείσας τοῖς Συρίοις καὶ θορυβήσας αὐτοὺς καὶ παρασκευάσας τούτους ὑποστρέ-
ψαι ἀναχωρήσαντος τοῦ πολέμου, οὐ διὰ τοῦ Ἄχαζ — οὐδὲ γὰρ ἦν δίκαιος — ἀλλὰ διὰ τὸ μὴ
ἐκλείπειν τοὺς ἐκ σπέρματος τοῦ Δαυΐδ· τοῦτο γὰρ ἦν ἐπαγγελλάμενος διὰ τοῦ προφήτου
Ἡσαΐου, ὡς καὶ ἡ βίβλος αὐτοῦ δηλοῖ. Ὁ τοίνυν κ. τ. λ.

11 συνεργὸν scripsi, συνεργοὺς C συνεργῶν alii   12 τῆς κατὰ Δάμασκον om. C.

Aᵉ *Argumentum psalmi* (p. 260, 32-261, 13): Praecinuntur hoc carmine ea
tempora, quibus Face filius Rumuliae et Rasin rex Siriae aduersus Hierusalem
et Achaz regem duarum tribuum arma commouerant; contra quos, secundum
praeceptum Essaiae, qui dixerat *Cognoscite gentes et uincemini quia nobiscum
Deus,* inruit Assiriorum rex et turbatis eorum regionibus Hirusolimarum obse-
ditionem soluit, non Achaz merito, sed loci reuerentia in quo templum erat. Ex
persona ergo duarum tribuum, pro liberatione tantae uastationis gratias agentium, formatur hic psalmus.   Ps. BEDA (724): Ex persona canitur duarum tribuum, pro liberatione sua gratias agentium, quando Phaceas filius Rumeliae
et Rasin rex Syriae Achas regem et Ierosolyma uolentes expugnare, non ualue-
runt, sed ipsi potius sunt ab Assyriorum rege conquassati.

PSALM 46

After the death of Solomon, the twelve tribes of Israel split up. The tribe of
Judah was on its own except only for the tribe of Benjamin, with kings ruling
in succession from the line of David, whereas the ten tribes were ruled separately in different ways at different times, at one time some, and at another
time others, occupying the throne. The tribe of Ephraim was principal among
them, its being capital Samaria, where the king was, just as Jerusalem was
the capital of the two tribes. At the time when Ahaz was on the throne of
Judah—that is, of the two tribes—Pekah, king of Samaria and of the ten
tribes, along with all his people took as his ally in the endeavor Rezin, king
of Syria in Damascus, and advanced on Jerusalem, choosing to besiege it in
his anxiety to destroy the kingdom of the two tribes. But through the prophet
Isaiah God promised to help them, not that Ahaz was a good man (the book
of Kings teaching us this in the words "Ahaz was twenty years old when he
began | to reign in Jerusalem, and he did not do what was upright in the eyes

λεύειν αὐτὸν ἐν Ἱερουσαλήμ, καὶ οὐκ ἐποίησε τὸ εὐθὲς ἐν ὀφθαλμοῖς Κυρίου
τοῦ Θεοῦ αὐτοῦ, — διὰ δὲ τὸ ἐν τῇ μητροπόλει τῇ Ἱερουσαλὴμ εἶναι τὸν
ναόν, τήν τε ἐπαγγελίαν τοῦ Θεοῦ γεγενῆσθαι πρὸς τὸν Δαυὶδ ὥστε μὴ ἐκλι-
πεῖν τοὺς κατὰ διαδοχὴν ἐξ αὐτοῦ βασιλεύοντας, εὐσεβεστέρους τε εἶναι
5 πολλῷ τοὺς δύο φυλῶν τῶν λοιπῶν Ἰουδαίων. Ἐπαγαγὼν δὲ ὁ Θεὸς τὸν
τῶν Ἀσσυρίων βασιλέα τοῖς Σύροις, οὕτω τε θόρυβον ἐμβαλὼν ἅπασι μετὰ
πολλῆς τῆς σπουδῆς ἀποστρέψαι παρεσκεύασεν ἀποστάντας τῆς κατὰ τῶν
ὁμοφύλων ἐπιχειρήσεως, — καὶ δὴ ταύτην ἔσεσθαι τὴν βοήθειαν κατὰ τὸν τοῦ
πολέμου καιρὸν ὁ μακάριος Ἡσαΐας ὑποσχόμενος τῷ Ἄχατζ φησίν· Μεθ᾽
10 ἡμῶν ὁ Θεός, γνῶτέ τε ἔθνη καὶ ἡττᾶσθε.

Ὁ τοίνυν μακάριος Δαυὶδ ταῦτα πόρρωθεν ἐσόμενα προειδώς, ἐκ προσώπου τῶν δύο φυλῶν τὴν εὐχαριστίαν ποιούμενος ἐφ᾽ οἷς ἠξιώθησάν τε
τῆς τοῦ Θεοῦ εὐεργεσίας καὶ τῆς τῶν ἐναντίων ἐπιβουλῆς ἀπηλλάγησαν
παραδόξως, προλέγει τὸ πολλοῖς ὕστερον ἐσόμενον τοῖς χρόνοις.

15 2ᵃ. Ὁ Θεὸς ἡμῶν καταφυγὴ καὶ δύναμις. Καλῶς τὸ ὁ Θεὸς ἡμῶν.
Ἐπειδὴ γὰρ ὑμεῖς φησιν οἱ ἡμέτεροι συγγενεῖς ἐπιβουλεύετε ἀνάξια καὶ
ἀλλότρια τῆς συγγενείας φρονοῦντες, ὁ Θεὸς ἡμῶν, ὃς οὐκ ἀπαρνεῖται τὴν
ἡμετέραν οἰκειότητα, οὗτος καὶ καταφυγὴ καὶ δύναμις — καταφυγὴ μὲν ὡς
πολεμουμένους δεχόμενος καὶ σῴζων, δύναμις δὲ ὡς ἀσθενέσι τὴν οἰκείαν
20 ἐπαρκῶν βοήθειαν.

2ᵇ. Βοηθὸς ἐν θλίψεσιν ταῖς εὑρούσαις ἡμᾶς σφόδρα. Οὐ νῦν πρώταις,
ἀλλ᾽ ἐν πάσαις | θλίψεσιν ἐν αἷς ἂν ἐξεταζώμεθα, βοηθὸς ἡμῶν γενόμενος,
ὃς εἰκότως πάντοτε βοηθῶν καὶ νῦν ἐπαμύνει κἂν ὑμεῖς τὴν συγγένειαν
ἀρνεῖσθε τὰ τῶν πολεμίων διαπραττόμενοι.

25 3. Διὰ τοῦτο οὐ φοβηθησόμεθα ἐν τῷ ταράσσεσθαι τὴν γῆν καὶ μετατίθεσθαι ὄρη ἐν καρδίαις θαλασσῶν. Τούτου τοίνυν ἕνεκεν καὶ μεγάλην ὑμῶν
φησιν οὖσαν τὴν ἔφοδον οὐ δεδοίκαμεν. Μεγάλη μὲν γὰρ ὅτι καὶ οἰκεῖοι
πολεμισταὶ καὶ ἀλλότριοι συμμαχοῦσιν, ἀλλὰ καὶ πολλοί· ὑμεῖς τε γὰρ
δέκα φυλαὶ καὶ τὸ τῶν Σύρων πλῆθος οὐκ εὐκαταφρόνητον, ἡμεῖς δὲ ὀλί-
30 γοι τε καὶ συμμαχίας ἀνθρώπων ἔρημοι. Ἀλλ᾽ οὐδὲν ἡμᾶς τοῦτο φοβεῖ,
πάντα νικώσης τῆς τοῦ Θεοῦ βοηθείας. Ταράσσεσθαι δὲ τὴν γῆν εἶπεν, ὡς
ἀπὸ τοῦ πλήθους τῶν ἐπιόντων καὶ τῆς γῆς αὐτῆς ταρασσομένης.

9-10 Is. VIII, 8ᵇ-9ᵃ.

28-31 cf. Paraphrasis (p. 868): Δεδόσθω γάρ φησιν καὶ τὰς δέκα φυλὰς ἐπὶ τὸ
αὐτὸ συνεληλυθέναι, καὶ τοὺς Σύρους ἅμα τούτοις συμπεφωνηκέναι, ἀλλὰ κρεῖττόν ἐστιν ἡ
ἡμετέρα βοήθεια.

Aᵉ 2ᵃ (p. 261, 14-16): Consanguineis hostili abalienatis animo bene et oportune Deum tantum suum dicit. Deus, inquit, noster: in eo est subfragium inpul-
sorum et inbelicosorum corrobratio.

of the Lord his God").[1] Rather, it was because the temple was in the capital, Jerusalem, since God had promised David that there would not fail to be kings succeeding him, and since the two tribes were much more religious than the rest of the Jews. God brought the king of the Assyrians down upon the Syrians, and he thus instilled panic into them all, and with great zeal he caused them to desist from their endeavors against their fellows and take to their heels. In fact, blessed Isaiah promised Ahaz that this assistance would be forthcoming in time of war, saying, "God is with us: be aware, nations, and be defeated."[2]

Blessed David, therefore, foreseeing well in advance that this would happen, and speaking on the part of the two tribes to give thanks for being accorded God's kindness and for being freed unexpectedly from the plan of the adversaries, foretells what would happen a long time later. *Our God is a refuge and power* (v. 1). *Our God* was well put: Since you who are our kith and kin hatch unseemly plots and harbor thoughts unworthy of kinship, he is saying, *our God,* who does not deny our relationship, is the one who is both *refuge and power*—*refuge* in taking the side of those attacked and rescuing them, *power* in supplying his characteristic help to the weak. *Help in the tribulations coming upon us in great number:* in becoming our helper not now for the first time but in all the tribulations in which we find ourselves; he naturally helps us always and now assists us even if you deny your kinship in playing the part of foes.

Hence, we shall not fear at the shaking of the earth and the shifting of mountains in the hearts of the seas (v. 2): for this reason, then, we do not fear even your assault, great though it is—great because warriors of our own race and foreigners have joined forces, and are numerous as well. You ten tribes and the vast numbers of the Syrians are not to be despised, whereas we are few in number and bereft of human allies. But this does not disquiet us, since God's help overcomes everything. Now, he said *the shaking of the earth* in reference to the vast number of the attackers and the earth itself being shaken. | The expression *the shifting of mountains in the hearts of the*

1. Cf. 2 Kgs 16:1–2.
2. Isa 8:8–9 LXX.

Τὸ δὲ μετατίθεσθαι ὅρη ἐν καρδίαις θαλασσῶν οὕτω λέγει. Ὄρη καλεῖ
τοὺς βασιλεῖς διὰ τὸ ὅλως ὑπερφέρειν τῇ ἀξίᾳ· ὥσπερ καὶ ταύρους, τοὺς
δυνατοὺς καὶ πόλλα ἕτερα ἀπὸ τῶν ὁμοιωμάτων τιθεὶς τὰ ὀνόματα, οὕτω
κἀνταῦθα ὅρη λέγει τόν τε τῆς Συρίας βασιλέα καὶ τὸν τοῦ Ἰσραήλ,
θάλασσαν δὲ τὸ πλῆθος. Καὶ καλῶς οὐκ εἶπεν ἑνικῶς θαλάσσης   5
ἀλλὰ θαλασσῶν, ὡς πολλῶν ὄντων καὶ τῶν Ἰσραηλιτῶν, πολλῶν δὲ καὶ
τῶν Σύρων.

Τὸ δὲ ἐν καρδίαις θαλασσῶν τῇ τροπολογίᾳ ἑπόμενος λέγει· ἐπειδὴ καρδίαν πράγματος καλοῦμεν τὸ κυριώτερον, καὶ καρδίαν θαλάσσης εἴποι ἄν
τις τὸν βυθὸν αὐτόν, καρδίαν εἶπε θαλασσῶν τοῦ πολλοῦ πλήθους τὴν   10
συνδρομήν. Τὸ οὖν ἐν καρδίαις, ἀντὶ τοῦ σὺν καρδίαις, οὕτως ἀλλαχοῦ
Εἰσελεύσομαι εἰς τὸν οἶκόν σου ἐν ὁλοκαυτώμασιν, ἀντὶ τοῦ σὺν ὁλοκαυτώ-
μασι· συνεχῶς γὰρ τῇ τοῦ « ἐν » ἀντὶ τοῦ « σὺν » φωνῇ κέχρηται. Τῷ δὲ
πλήθει τῶν πολεμούντων — καὶ οἱ βασιλεῖς αὐτοὶ μετὰ παντὸς τοῦ πλήθους
μετατίθενται ἐφ᾽ ἡμᾶς — οὐ φοβούμεθα. Καλῶς δὲ τὸ με|τατίθεσθαι, φοβερώ- 15
τερον αὐτὸ δεικνύς, ἵνα τὸ αἰφνήδιον σημάνῃ τῆς ἐφόδου· μετατίθεσθαι
γὰρ λέγει τὸ μὴ κατὰ μέρος ἑλκόμενον ἢ βαδίζον, ἀλλ᾽ αἰφνήδιον τὴν ἀπὸ
τόπου εἰς τόπον μεταγωγὴν ὑπομένον. Καὶ ὅτι φησὶ δικαίως οὐ φοβούμεθα,
αὐτὰ δείκνυσι τὰ πράγματα. Πῶς;

4ᵃ. Ἤχησε καὶ ἐταράχθη τὰ ὕδατα αὐτῶν. Ἐπειδὴ θάλασσαν ὠνόμασε 20
τὸ πλῆθος, ἡ δὲ θάλασσα πνέοντος τοῦ ἀνέμου κινουμένη ὁμοῦ τε ταράτ-
τεται καὶ φοβερὸν τὸν ἦχον ἀποτελεῖ διὰ τῶν κυμάτων, τοῦτο λέγει ὅτι
συνεκινήθησάν φησι καὶ ἐπῆλθον ἡμῖν μετὰ πολλῆς τῆς ἀπειλῆς.

4ᵇ. Ἐταράχθησαν τὰ ὅρη ἐν τῇ κραταιότητι αὐτοῦ. Συνεκινήθη γάρ φησι
τὰ ὅρη, τουτέστιν οἱ βασιλεῖς μετὰ τῆς οἰκείας ἰσχύος, ὅμως οὐδὲν εἰς   25
πέρας ἀγαγεῖν ἠδυνήθησαν τῶν ἀπειληθέντων.

5ᵃ. Τοῦ ποταμοῦ τὰ ὁρμήματα εὐφραίνουσι τὴν πόλιν τοῦ Θεοῦ. Τινές
φασι περὶ τοῦ Ἄχαζ λέγειν τὸν προφήτην. Τὸν δὲ Ἄχαζ ὁ προφήτης Ἠσαΐας οὐ καλεῖ ποταμόν, — φησὶ γὰρ περὶ αὐτοῦ Διὰ τὸ μὴ βούλεσθαι τὸν λαὸν τοῦτον τὸ ὕδωρ τοῦ Σιλωὰμ τὸ πορευόμενον ἡσυχῇ, — ὁ δὲ   30

12 Ps. LXV, 13   29-30 Is. VIII, 6.

1-5 L (p. 871, 28·30): Δοκεῖ δὲ μᾶλλον ἐπιμένων τῇ τροπῇ ὕδατα καλεῖν τὰ πλήθη
τῶν πολεμίων, τοὺς ἀνδρείους, τοὺς ὑψηλούς.   20-23 cf. Paraphrasis (p. 868): Ὕδατα
νῦν καλεῖ τὰ πλήθη τῶν τε δέκα φυλῶν... ὅτι ὡς θάλασσα κυμαινομένη ὥρμησαν ἐφ᾽ ἡμᾶς.

Aᵉ 15-16 (p. 262, 10-11): ... ut repentina inruptione ambitum terroris expraemeret.   21-23 (p. 262, 12-14): Tamquam uento fluctus, sic Deo inminente
agmina turbabuntur hostilia.   24-25 (p. 262, 14-15): Conturbati sunt ipsi reges

seas is to be taken this way: by *mountains* he refers to the kings on account of their completely overbearing manner; as he gives names such as "bulls" to the high and mighty and many other things on the basis of similarity, so here as well he uses *mountains* of the king of Syria and the king of Israel, and the word "sea" of the vast numbers. He did well to speak not of "sea" in the singular, but rather *seas,* since the Israelites were numerous, and the Syrians also were numerous. And he continues the figurative style in saying *in the hearts of the seas:* since we refer to a thing's peculiar qualities as its heart, and you would speak of the very depths of the sea as its heart, he referred by "heart of the seas" to the combined surge of the vast numbers. Hence, the phrase *in the hearts*—that is, with the hearts—occurs elsewhere: "I shall come into your house in burnt offerings,"[3] meaning "with burnt offerings," as he constantly uses "in" to mean "with." We do not fear the vast numbers of those attacking, the kings themselves along with the whole horde being *shifted* against us; the verb *shift* was well put, giving a more fearsome impression to suggest the suddenness of the attack, since *shift* implies not a gradual movement or advance, but a sudden shifting from place to place.

That we are right not to fear, he says, the facts themselves demonstrate. How so? *Their waters roared and were disturbed* (v. 3). Since he had given the name "sea" to the vast numbers, and with the blowing of the wind the sea at the one time is disturbed and produces a fearsome sound with the waves, he means, They advanced together and attacked us very threateningly. *The mountains were shaken by his strength: the mountains* were moved together—that is, the kings with their might were unable to put into effect any of their threats. *The currents of the river gladden the city of God* (v. 4). Some commentators claim that the author is referring to Ahaz. The prophet Isaiah, however, does not refer to Ahaz as a river, saying of him, "Because this people has refused the waters of Shiloah that flow gently."[4] | Shiloah, however, is not a river

---

3. Ps 66:13.

4. Isa 8:6. John 9:7 does, in fact, refer to it as a pool, κολυμβήθρα (of Siloam), where a blind man washed and was cured.

Σιλωὰμ οὐ ποταμός, ἀλλὰ πηγὴ ἤτοι κολυμβήθρα κατὰ τὸν εὐαγγελιστήν. Οὔτε οὖν ἁρμόσει ἡ τοῦ ποταμοῦ φωνὴ τῷ Ἀχατζ, οὔτε τὰ ὁρμήματα — ἐναντίον γὰρ τὸ πορευόμενον ἡσυχῇ· ἀλλ' ἐπειδὴ ἐπικειμένων τοῖς περὶ τὴν Ἰερουσαλὴμ τῶν τε Σύρων καὶ τῶν περὶ τὸν Ἐφραὶμ Ἰσραηλιτῶν τοὺς
5 Ἀσσυρίους αὐτοῖς ἐπαγαγὼν ὁ Θεὸς ἀπέστρεψέ τε τοῦ ἐπιχειρήματος, καὶ τοὺς Σύρους αὐτάρκως ἐτιμωρήσατο, καθαιρεθῆναι μὲν τὴν μητρόπολιν αὐτῶν τὴν Δαμασκόν, ἀναιρεθῆναι δὲ καὶ τὸν βασιλέα παρασκευάσας, ποταμὸν δὲ τὸν Ἀσσύριον καὶ ὁ προφήτης Ἡσαΐας ἐκάλεσε λέγων· Διὰ τὸ μὴ βούλεσθαι τὸν λαὸν τοῦτον τὸ ὕδωρ τοῦ Σιλωάμ. τὸ πορευόμενον ἡσυχῇ, ἀλλὰ
10 βούλεσθαι ἔχειν τὸν Ῥασσὴν καὶ τὸν υἱὸν τοῦ Ῥωμελίου βασιλέα | ἐφ' ὑμῶν, διὰ τοῦτο ἀνάγει Κύριος ἐφ' ὑμᾶς τὸ ὕδωρ τοῦ ποταμοῦ τὸ ἰσχυρὸν καὶ τὸ πολύ, τὸν βασιλέα τῶν Ἀσσυρίων. Διὰ τοῦτο καὶ ὁ μακάριος Δαυὶδ φησι Τοῦ ποταμοῦ τὰ ὁρμήματα εὐφραίνουσι τὴν πόλιν τοῦ Θεοῦ, ποταμὸν καὶ αὐτὸς τὸν Ἀσσύριον καλῶν, ὁρμήματα δὲ αὐτοῦ τὴν κίνησιν καὶ τὴν ἔφοδον
15 τὴν κατὰ τῶν Σύρων. Ἐκείνου τοίνυν φησὶν ἡ κίνησις ἡ κατὰ τῶν Σύρων εὐφροσύνην τῇ πόλει τοῦ Θεοῦ παρέξει, τουτέστι τῇ Ἰερουσαλήμ· καὶ γὰρ καὶ ἀναιρεθέντων τῶν πολεμούντων αὐτοῖς καὶ πάσης ἀπαλλαγέντες ἐπιβουλῆς, εἰκότως ἐν εὐφροσύνῃ καθίσταντο.

5ᵇ. Ἡγίασεν τὸ σκήνωμα αὐτοῦ ὁ ὕψιστος. Ἡγίασεν, ἀντὶ τοῦ ἅγιον
20 ἀπέφηνε. Σκήνωμα δὲ αὐτοῦ τὴν πόλιν καλεῖ, ὡς ἐν αὐτῇ τυγχάνοντος ἐν ᾗπερ οἰκεῖν τὸν Θεὸν ἅπαντες ἐδόξαζον Ἰουδαῖοι· ἅγιον δὲ ἀπέφηνε διὰ τῆς κατὰ τῶν πολεμούντων τιμωρίας.

6ᵃ. Ὁ Θεὸς ἐν μέσῳ αὐτῆς, οὐ σαλευθήσεται. Τουτέστι τῆς πόλεως. Ἐπειδὴ γὰρ τὸ αὐτὸ λέγει τὴν πόλιν καὶ τὸ σκήνωμα, ἀκολούθως ἐπήγαγε
25 τὸ ἐν μέσῳ αὐτῆς. Τὸ δὲ ἐν μέσῳ λέγει διὰ τὸ τῆς βοηθείας ἰσχυρόν,

1 cf. Ioh. V, 2   4-7 cf. IV Reg. XVI, 9 ss.   8-12 Is. VIII, 6-7.

16 *Paraphrasis* (p. 869): Πόλιν τοῦ Θεοῦ καλεῖ τὴν Ἰερουσαλήμ.   16-18 L (p. 872, 34-35): …λύσιν δὲ τῆς πολιορκίας, ὃ καὶ εἰς εὐφροσύνην αὐτῇ γέγονε.   20-21 *Paraphrasis* (p. 869): Πάλιν σκήνωμα τοῦ Θεοῦ καλεῖ τὴν Ἰερουσαλήμ, ὡς τοῦ Θεοῦ ἐκεῖ κατοικοῦντος.

Aᵉ 4-12 (p. 262, 16-20): Excursus Assirius uastauit Siriam, rege pariter extincto, de quo Essaias: *Propter hoc inducat Dominus super uos aquam fluminis ualidam, regem Assiriorum.*   16-17 (p. 262, 20-22): Hic ergo Hirusolimas laetificauit uastandis hostibus et obseditione soluenda eius.   20 (p. 262, 26-27): Tabernaculum autem Dei ipsam ciuitatem dicit.   6ᵃ (p. 262, 28-263, 6): Id est ciuitatis eius... pro eo ut diceret: Non quasi in aliqua ciuitatis parte consistens ab alia recessit, sed in medio ipsius habitans et totam eam circa se habens, uniuersas eius partes de hostium opugnationibus liberauit; corporali autem appellatione uoluit indicare auxilii largitatem.

but a spring, or even a pool, according to the evangelist. So the terms *river* and *currents* are not applicable to Ahaz, who, on the contrary, was "flowing gently."

Since at that time, however, both the Syrians and the Israelites from Ephraim were pressing those from Jerusalem, and God brought the Assyrians upon them and both upset their plans and punished the Syrians adequately, causing their capital, Damascus, to be destroyed and their king to be slain, the prophet Isaiah referred to the Assyrian as a river in the words "Because this people has refused the waters of Shiloah that flow gently, and preferred to have Rezin and the son of Remaliah as king over them, hence the Lord brings upon you the mighty and abundant water of the River, the king of the Assyrians." Hence, blessed David also says *The currents of the river gladden the city of God,* he too referring to the Assyrian as *river,* and his advance and assault on the Syrians as *currents.* His advance on the Syrians, then, will provide gladness to the city of God—that is, Jerusalem: with the destruction of their attackers they were rid of every plot and rightly brought to a state of gladness. *The Most High sanctified his dwelling*—that is, made it holy. By *his dwelling* he refers to the city insofar as he was in it, the place where all Jews imagined God dwelt; he made it holy by punishment of the attackers.

God is in its midst, and he will not be moved (v. 5)—that is, in the midst of the city; since he calls the same thing *city* and *dwelling,* he logically went on to say *in its midst.* Now, by *in its midst* he means through the force of the assistance, | presenting the generosity of the assistance in a bodily expres-

σωματικῇ φωνῇ παραστήσας τῆς βοηθείας τὸ δαψιλές, — ἀντὶ τοῦ Οὐ κατά
τινος μέρους ὢν τῆς πόλεως ἑτέρου κεχώρισται, ἀλλ᾽ ἐν μέσῳ αὐτῆς τυγχάνων καὶ πᾶσαν ἔχων ἐν κύκλῳ, πᾶσαν ὁμοίως περισῴζει τῶν ἐχθρῶν· διὸ
καὶ ἀπαράτρεπτος διαμένει.

6ᵇ. Βοηθήσει αὐτῇ ὁ Θεός· τῷ πρωΐ πρωΐ. Ἐντεῦθέν φησι καὶ ὀξεῖαν 5
αὐτῇ ὁ Θεὸς παρέξει τὴν βοήθειαν. Πρωΐ γὰρ λέγει τὸ ταχέως, ἐπειδὴ καὶ
τῆς ἡμέρας τὸν πρῶτον καιρὸν καὶ ταχύτερον πρωϊνὸν καλοῦμεν, τῷ δὲ
διπλασιασμῷ τὴν ἐπίτασιν ἐσήμανε τῆς ὀξύτητος. Τί οὖν γέγονεν;

7ᵃ. Ἐταράχθησαν ἔθνη, ἔκλιναν βασιλεῖαι. Ὑπὸ γὰρ τῶν παρὰ πᾶσαν
ἐλπίδα ἐπελθόντων αὐτοῖς, τουτέστι τῶν Ἀσσυρίων, οἱ πρότερον ἡμᾶς 10
πολεμοῦντες ταραχῇ κατεσχέθησαν — ἀντὶ τοῦ ἐτράπησαν, κατέπεσον.

7ᵇ. Ἔδωκε φωνὴν αὐτοῦ, ἐσαλεύθη ἡ γῆ. Ὡς ἐπὶ στρατηγοῦ μόνῃ τῇ
φωνῇ καταπλήττοντες· μόνον τέ φησιν ἐβόησε καὶ ταραχὴ κατέσχεν ἅπαντας.

8. Κύριος τῶν δυνάμεων μεθ᾽ ἡμῶν, ἀντιλήμπτωρ ἡμῶν ὁ Θεὸς Ἰακώβ.
Ταῦτα δὲ ἡμῖν προσγέγονεν, ἐπειδὴ μεθ᾽ ἡμῶν ὁ πάσης ἰσχύος ἀνώτερος 15
δεσπότης, — τὸ δὲ μεθ᾽ ἡμῶν, ἀντὶ τοῦ ἐπεὶ παρ᾽ ἡμῖν ὁ Θεός, ὁ ἐν τῷ ναῷ
κατοικῶν· διὰ τοῦτό φησι πλεονεκτοῦμεν ἅπαντας ἀνθρώπους, καὶ ἀντιλαμ-
βάνεται ἡμῶν ὁ τοῦ Ἰακὼβ Θεός.

9. Δεῦτε καὶ ἴδετε τὰ ἔργα τοῦ Θεοῦ, ἃ ἔθετο τέρατα ἐπὶ τῆς γῆς.
Χρῆται λοιπὸν καὶ τῇ παραινέσει μετὰ τὴν τῶν γεγονότων ἐξήγησιν. 20
Ἔλθετέ φησιν καὶ θεάσασθε οἷα πεποίηκε θαυμάσια ὁ δεσπότης. Ὁ μὲν
οὖν μακάριος Ἡσαΐας μετὰ τὴν πρόρρησιν τοῖς ἔθνεσί φησιν ὀνειδίζων
Μεθ᾽ ἡμῶν ὁ Θεός, γνῶτε ἔθνη καὶ ἡττᾶσθε· ὁ δὲ μακάριος Δαυὶδ τῇ παραι-
νέσει τοὺς οἰκείους ποιῶν, τίνα οὖν ἃ πεποίηκεν.

23 Is. VIII, 8ᵇ-9ᵃ.

5-7 *Paraphrasis* (p. 869) : Τὸ τάχος λέγει καὶ τὴν ὀξυτάτην ἀντίληψιν.   7-8 L (p. 872,
24 25) : ...διὰ τοῦ ἀναδιπλασιασμοῦ σημαίνει.   12-13 *Paraphrasis* (869) : Ὡς γὰρ στρα-
τηγός φησιν ἄριστος ἐκ τῆς πόλεως ἐμβοήσας (*eadem apud* L, p. 872, 45-47).

Aᵉ 6ᵇ (p. 263, 7-12) : Celeritatem ipsam indulti adiutorii uocat; geminatione
autem nominum cumulum uoluit ipsius uelocitatis expraemere; « in die »
quippe primum tempus et citum matutinum uocamus.   7ᵇ (p. 263, 14-18) :
Tamquam de aliquo duce bellicoso hic locutus est, qui sola uoce exterrere
possit inimicos et uociferatione praeliari.   16-17 (p. 263, 18-20) : Propugnator,
quasi sic diceret Apud nos erit templum et ipse Dominus habitans in eo.
22-24 (p. 263, 22-27) : Beatus Essaias post huius operis praedicationem conuersus ad gentes exprobranter loquitur : *Scitote, gentes, et uincemini, quia nobiscum Deus.* Hic uero monitus erudit suos et meliores facere contendit.

sion, as if to say, He was not in one part of the city and cut off from another, but *in its midst,* surrounding it all, protecting it all equally from the foe. Hence, he also abides there unceasingly. *God will help it early in the morning.* Here he is saying that God will provide it with rapid assistance, by *early* referring to the rapidity, since we call the first and more rapid moments of the day "early." By the repetition[5] he suggested the degree of speed. So what happened? *Nations were in uproar, kingdoms tottered* (v. 6) as a result of those attacking them unexpectedly; that is, the Assyrians, who previously warred on us, were reduced to panic—that is, they were routed, they were overwhelmed. *He gave forth his voice; the earth moved:* terrifying them as if by the mere cry of a general; he merely shouted, and panic gripped them all. *The Lord God of hosts is with us; the God of Jacob is our support* (v. 7): this has been our good fortune because the Lord of all might above is with us (*with us* meaning, Since God, who dwells in the temple, is on our side); hence, we are better off than all people, and *the God of Jacob* assists us.

Come now, see the works of the Lord, portents he performed on earth (v. 8). He now adopts exhortation as well after the outline of what happened. Come and behold, he says, what marvels the Lord performed. While blessed Isaiah, after the prophecy to the nations, says in mockery, "God is with us: be aware, nations, and be defeated," blessed David exhorts his own people by telling them the things he had done. | *Bringing wars to an end as*

---

5. That is, "early" and "in the morning" (represented by a double adverb in some forms of the LXX).

10ᵃ. Ἀνταναιρῶν πολέμους μέχρι τῶν περάτων τῆς γῆς. Ἀντὶ τοῦ ἀφελῶν λέγει, ὡς καὶ ἀλλαχοῦ Ἀντανελεῖς τὸ πνεῦμα αὐτῶν καὶ ἐκλείψουσιν ἀντὶ τοῦ ἀφελεῖς, καὶ ἑτέρωθι Ὡσεὶ κηρὸς τακεὶς ἀντανειρεθήσονται. Ἀφεῖλεν οὖν φησιν ἀφ' ἡμῶν τὸν πόλεμον, ἀντὶ τοῦ ἀπήλλαξεν ἡμᾶς τοῦ πολέ-
5 μου. Τὸ δὲ μέχρι τῶν περάτων τῆς γῆς, ἀντὶ τοῦ Πᾶσαν ἡμῶν τὴν γῆν ἀπήλλαξεν τοῦ πολέμου ἀφελὼν αὐτοὺς ἀφ' ἡμῶν καὶ μεταστήσας τῷ φόβῳ τῶν Ἀσσυρίων.

10ᵇ. Τόξον συντρίψει καὶ συνκλάσει ὅπλον. Ταῦτα λέγει ἅπερ ἔπαθον οἱ Σύροι παρὰ τῶν Ἀσσυρίων· συνετρίβη φησὶ τὰ ὅπλα, τὰ τόξα, ἅπασα
10 αὐτῶν ἡ ἰσχύς.

10ᶜ. Καὶ θυρεοὺς κατακαύσει ἐν πυρί. Θυρεοὺς λέγει τὰς ἀσπίδας διὰ τὸ τετραγώνους ἔτι τότε τὰς ἀσπίδας εἶναι καὶ ταῖς θύραις ἐοικέναι, οἷασπερ νῦν τὰς τῶν μονομαχούντων ἐν ταῖς γυμνασίαις εἶναι συμβαίνει. Τὸ οὖν κατακαύσει θυρεοὺς ἐν πυρί, ὅτι τοσαύτη ἔσται φησὶν ἡ σφαγὴ καὶ
15 τοσοῦτος ὁ θάνατος ὡς μηδὲ περιποιηθῆναι αὐτῶν τοὺς θυρεούς, ἀλ|λὰ πυρὶ κατακαυθῆναι διὰ τὸ πλῆθος.

11ᵃ. Σχολάσατε, καὶ γνῶτε ὅτι ἐγώ εἰμι ὁ Θεός. Ὁ μὲν οὖν μακάριος Ἡσαΐας φησὶ Γνῶτε ἔθνη καὶ ἡττᾶσθε καλῶς τὴν γνῶσιν αὐτοῖς ἐπὶ ἥττᾳ σημαίνων ὡς ἐναντίοις, ὁ δὲ μακάριος Δαυὶδ πρέποντα οἰκείοις παραινεῖ·
20 ἀπαλλαγέντες φησὶ τοῦ πολέμου καὶ σχολὴν ἄγοντες τῇ γνώσει τῇ ἐμῇ, σχολάσατε ταῦτα λογιζόμενοι ὧνπερ ἀπηλαύσατε.

11ᵇ. Ὑψωθήσομαι ἐν τοῖς ἔθνεσιν, ὑψωθήσομαι ἐν τῇ γῇ. Ἐγὼ γάρ φησιν ὁ καὶ ἐν τοῖς ἔθνεσι μέγας δεικνύμενος καὶ ἐν τῇ γῇ, τουτέστι παρ' ὑμῖν. Διὰ τί δὲ καὶ ἐν ἐκείνοις μὲν διὰ τῆς παραινέσεως, ἐν ὑμῖν δὲ διὰ τῆς
25 σωτηρίας, καὶ πάλιν διὰ τὴν παραίνεσιν καὶ τὴν τῶν θαυμάτων ἐξήγησιν ἐπισφραγίζει τὸν ψαλμόν;

2 Ps. CIII, 29ᵇ   3 ps. LVII, 9   11-13 cf. p. 176, 6   18 ls. VIII, 9ᵃ; cf. supra p. 301, 9-10; 30ᵇ, 23.

Aᵉ 5-6 (p. 263, 28-29): Ac si diceret Omnem regionem nostram soluit a periculo.   8-9.15-16 (p. 263, 30-264, 2): Tanto dispectui sunt ab Assiriis (asriis *ms*) uastati, ⟨ut⟩ nemo interficientium in usum suum eorum arma dignaretur adsumere.   11ᵃ (p. 264, 3-10): Essaias dixerat *Scitote, gentes, et uincemini*, illam utique scientiam quam erat calamitas eis datura consignans; Dauid uero, ut domisticis competebat, hortatur. Omnibus, ait, discendendo (discendo *1ᵃ m.*) periculis desoluti ac totius perturbationis securi, huic cognitori soli uos dedi, ut eorum memores sitis semper quae uos laetamini consaecutos.   25-30ᵇ, 4 (p. 264, 13-18): Abtissime post monitus et miraculorum replicationem psalmus laude ipsius liberatoris (liberatioris *ms*) obsignat, per hoc adserens nimirum (ne mirum *ms*) eos uoti conpotes (conptotes *ms*) factos, quia apud eos esset templum et quod Deo institutis ritibus seruiebant.

far as the ends of the earth (v. 9), which means removing them, as he also says elsewhere, "You will bring their breath to an end, and they will be no more"—that is, you will remove; and elsewhere, "They will be carried away like melting wax."[6] So he is saying, He removed war—that is, He freed us from war. The phrase *as far as the ends of the earth* means, He freed all our land from war by removing them from us and striking them with fear of the Assyrians. *He will break the bow and smash weapons.* He mentions what the Syrians suffered from the Assyrians, saying that their weapons, their bows, all their might was smashed. *And he will burn square shields in fire.* By *square shields* he refers to shields on account of the square shape then in use that resembled doors,[7] of the kind that these days you find in use in the schools by those practicing hand-to-hand combat. So the clause *He will burn square shields in fire* means, Such will be the slaughter and so many the dead that not even their shields were kept, instead being burned because of the great number.

Be at rest, and know that I am God (v. 10). While blessed Isaiah says, "Be aware, nations, and be defeated," to give a good indication of defeat to them as adversaries, blessed David gives an exhortation befitting his own people. Freed from the enemy and being at peace in knowledge of me, he is saying, *be at rest* and ponder the things you have enjoyed. *I shall be exalted among the nations; I shall be exalted on the earth:* I am seen to be great both among the nations and on the earth—that is, by you. Why does he deal with them by exhortation and with you in terms of salvation, and again why does he conclude the psalm with an exhortation and with an account of the marvels? | *The Lord of hosts is with us; the God of Jacob is our supporter* (v. 11),

---

6. Pss 104:29; 58:8.

7. The oblong shield, θυρεός, as distinct from the smaller shield, ἀσπίς, was so called because of its resemblance to a door, θύρα (Theodore explains).

12. Κύριος τῶν δυνάμεων μεθ' ἡμῶν, ἀντιλήμπτωρ ἡμῶν ὁ Θεὸς Ἰακώβ. Διὰ τοῦ προγεγενῆσθαι πᾶσαν αὐτοῖς βοήθειαν σημαίνων καὶ σωτηρίαν, διὰ τὸ τῆς τοῦ Θεοῦ κατηξιῶσθαι ῥοπῆς καὶ παρ' αὐτοῖς εἶναι τε τὸν ναὸν καὶ θεραπεύεσθαι τὸν δεσπότην.

PSALMVS XLVI

Μετὰ τὴν ἀπὸ Βαβυλῶνος ἐπάνοδον ἐπὶ τῆς οἰκείας οἱ Ἰσραηλῖται γεγονότες πολλῷ τῷ χρόνῳ, καὶ βαθείας ἀπολαύσαντες εἰρήνης, πάλιν ἐπὶ τὸ χεῖρον ἐξώκειλαν. Ἐπὶ γὰρ Ἀντιόχου τοῦ βασιλέως τινὲς τῶν παρ' αὐτοῖς ἐπὶ τοσοῦτον τῶν νομίμων ἀποστῆναι παρήχθησαν, ὡς ἀπελθεῖν μὲν ἐπὶ τὸν Ἀντίοχον, αἰτῆσαι δὲ ταῦτα γενέσθαι παρ' αὐτοῖς ἃ καὶ παρὰ 10 τοῖς ἄλλοις ἔθνεσιν ἐναντίως τῇ τοῦ νόμου ⟨παρα⟩δόσει κρατεῖν συνέβαινε. Καὶ τοῦτο ἀκριβέστερόν ἐστι μαθεῖν ἀπὸ τῆς τῶν Μακκαβαίων ἱστορίας — λέγει γὰρ οὕτως Ἐν ταῖς ἡμέραις ἐκείναις ἐξῆλθον ἐξ Ἰσραὴλ υἱοὶ παράνο-μοι, καὶ ἀνέπεισαν πολλοὺς λέγοντες Πορευθῶμεν καὶ διαθώμεθα διαθήκην μετὰ τῶν ἐθνῶν τῶν κύκλῳ ἡμῶν, ὅτι ἀφ' ἧς ἡμέρας ἐχωρίσθημεν ἀπ' 15 αὐτῶν εὗρεν ἡμᾶς κακὰ πολλά. Καὶ ἠγαθύνθη ὁ λόγος ἐν ὀφθαλμοῖς αὐτῶν, καὶ προεθυμή|θησάν τινες τοῦ λαοῦ καὶ ἐπορεύθησαν πρὸς τὸν βασιλέα, καὶ ἔδωκεν αὐτοῖς ὁ βασιλεὺς ἐξουσίαν ποιῆσαι κατὰ τὸ δικαίωμα τῶν ἐθνῶν. Καὶ ἐποίησαν ἑαυτοῖς ἀκροβυστίαν καὶ ἀπέστησαν ἀπὸ διαθήκης ἁγίας Κυρίου, καὶ ἐζεύχθησαν ἐν τοῖς ἔθνεσι καὶ ἐπράθησαν τοῦ ποιῆσαι τὸ πονηρόν. 20

13-20 I Macch. I, 11-15.

11 δόσει ms.

Commentarium psalmi vulgavit H. LIETZMANN (*op. cit.*, p. 342-346). *Argumentum paullo breuius exhibent catenae* Paris. 139, fol. 122; Vat. 1682, fol. 178; Vat. gr. 1422, fol. 92 (anon.); Barbaro, p. 478: Ὥσπερ ἐπινίκιον ὕμνον ἀναπέμπων τῷ Θεῷ τοῦτον τὸν ψαλμὸν ὑπὲρ τῶν Μακκαβαίων ἀπεφθέγξατο ὁ μακάριος Δαυίδ. Μετὰ γὰρ τὴν ἐπάνοδον τὴν ἀπὸ τῆς αἰχμαλωσίας, πολλῆς ἀπολαύσαντες τῆς εἰρήνης, οὕτως ἐξώκειλάν τινες ἐπὶ τὸ χεῖρον ὡς προσελθεῖν τῷ Ἀντιόχῳ αὐθαιρέτως καὶ αἰτῆσαι ἀποστῆναι μὲν τοῦ πατρῴου νόμου, τοῖς δὲ Ἑλληνικοῖς ἔθεσιν διάγειν, ὡς καὶ ἐπιτρέψαι αὐτοῖς τὸν Ἀντίοχον καὶ γυμνάσιον αὐτοῖς ποιῆσαι καὶ τὰ ἄλλα θεάματα οἷς ἐχρῆτο τὰ ἔθνη· εἰς οὓς Ματταθίας μόνος ζηλωτὴς φανεὶς καὶ αὐτὸς ἐπολέμησεν κατὰ κράτος καὶ τοῖς υἱοῖς παρέπεμψεν τὸν ὑπὲρ τοῦ νόμου πόλεμον καὶ μάλιστα Ἰούδᾳ τῷ καὶ Μακκαβαίῳ, ὃς καὶ τοὺς Ἀντιόχου στρατιώτας ἐνίκησεν καὶ τοὺς ἐπαναστάντας μετὰ τὸ ἐγκαινισθῆναι τὸν ναὸν καὶ τὸ θυσιαστήριον ἐθνικούς, ἤδη δὲ καὶ τοὺς οἰκείους τοὺς συναραμένους ἐκείνοις.

Aᵉ *Argumentum ps. XLVI* (p. 268, 19-25): In tempora Machabeorum carmen ipsud tamquam triumphale praecinitur. Deuictis quippe gentibus uel Iudaeis praeuaricatoribus, qui instauranti ritus sacros aduersabantur (aduerserbantur *ms*) Iudae Machabeo, ex persona exultantium (exultultantium *ms*) oratio formatur. Cf. PSEUDO-BEDA (727).

indicating all the help and salvation coming to them through what happened before on account of the gift of God's favor and the attention shown by them to the temple and to the Lord.

PSALM 47

After the return from Babylon the Israelites were for a long time in their own land enjoying deep peace, and once again they took a turn for the worse. That is to say, in the time of King Antiochus some of their number were induced to forsake lawful practices to such an extent as to go to Antiochus and ask that the practices current among the other nations at variance with the tradition of the law be observed by them. You can gain a more precise account of this from the story of the Maccabees, where it says, "In those days lawless members came out of Israel and misled many with the words 'Let us go and make a covenant with the nations round about us, since from the time we separated from them we have encountered many troubles.' This proposal struck them as satisfactory, and some of the people eagerly went to the king, and the king authorized them to observe the ordinances of the nations. They removed their marks of circumcision, forsook the Lord's holy covenant, joined with the nations, and sold themselves to do evil."[1] |

---

1. Again Theodore accepts from Diodore without question an interpretation of the psalm based on ἱστορία, going to the trouble of filling it out for his readers by reference to 1 Macc 1:11–15, though omitting mention of the building of a gymnasium. He has, of course, told the story of the Maccabees (at length) before in introducing Ps 44.

Τούτων δὴ γεγονότων, ὡς ἐξ αὐτῆς μανθάνομεν τῆς ἱστορίας, ζηλωτὴς τοῦ νόμου πρῶτος ἦν καταστὰς Ματταθίας· ἤρατο μὲν πόλεμον πρὸς τοὺς Ἀντιόχου στρατηγούς, ἀνδραγαθήσας δὲ οὐ μικρῶς τελευτῶν παρέδωκε τοῖς υἱοῖς αὐτοῦ τὸν ὑπὲρ τοῦ νόμου πόλεμον. Καὶ δὴ πρῶτος ἐστρατήγει
5 Ἰούδας ὁ καὶ Μακκαβαῖος τοῦ πολέμου, — ὃς καὶ νικήσας τοὺς Ἀντιόχου στρατηγούς, ἡττήσας δὲ καὶ τῶν οἰκείων τοὺς βουλομένους συμπράττειν τοῖς ἐναντίοις ἐπεμελήσατο καὶ τῆς τοῦ ναοῦ διορθώσεως, πολλὴν ὑπὸ τῶν ἐναντίων τὴν ἐρήμωσιν ὑπομείναντος. Ταῦτα μαθόντες οἱ περίοικοι ἔχθρᾳ τε καὶ βασκανίᾳ συνελθόντες ἐμηχανῶντο πάντας ἄρδην ἀπολέσαι. Καὶ
10 τοῦτο δὲ ἡμᾶς ἡ τῶν Μακκαβαϊκῶν ἱστορία διδάσκει λέγουσα· Καὶ ἐγένετο ὅτε ἤκουσαν τὰ ἔθνη τὰ κυκλόθεν, ὅτι ᾠκοδομήθη τὸ θυσιαστήριον καὶ ἀνεκαινίσθη τὸ ἁγίασμα ὡς τὸ πρότερον, καὶ ὠργίσθησαν σφόδρα καὶ ἐβουλεύσαντο τοῦ ἆραι τὸ γένος Ἰακώβ. Ἀλλὰ ταῦτα μὲν ἐβουλεύοντο κατ' αὐτῶν ἐκεῖνοι, στρατηγούντων δὲ αὐτοῖς τῶν Μακκαβαίων τοῦ τε Ἰούδα, ὃς καὶ
15 μάλιστα κατῆρχε τοῦ πολέμου, καὶ τῶν ἀδελφῶν, περιεγένοντο καὶ τούτων. Καὶ οὕτω πάντας ἡττήσαντες τούς τε περιοίκους καὶ τοὺς Ἀντιόχοι, ἤδη δὲ καὶ τοὺς οἰκείους οὕσπερ αὐτοῖς ἀνθεστάναι συνέβαινεν, ἐπεμελήθησαν τοῦ τε ναοῦ καὶ τῶν νομίμων. Ταῦτα τοίνυν πόρρωθεν ὁ μακάριος προφητεύων Δαυὶδ ὥσπερ τινὰ ἐπινίκιον ὕμνον ἐπὶ τοῖς γεγονόσι τὸν ψαλ-
20 μὸν ἐξεφώνησεν.

2ᵃ. Πάντα τὰ ἔθνη κροτήσατε χεῖρας. Κροτήσατε, τουτέστιν ἐπευφημήσατε, ἐπειδὴ ἔθος ἐν ταῖς εὐφημίαις κροτεῖν τὰς χεῖρας. Τὸ δὲ πάντα τὰ ἔθνη οὐχ ἁπλῶς λέγει, ἀλλ' ἐπειδὴ καὶ περιοίκους ἥττησαν καὶ τοὺς Ἀντιόχου στρατηγούς, καὶ ὅλως πολλοὶ οἱ ἡττηθέντες, καὶ πολλοῖς ἡ τοῦ Θεοῦ
25 δύναμις ἐγεγόνει καταφανής.

2ᵇ. Ἀλαλάξατε τῷ Θεῷ ἐν φωνῇ ἀγαλλιάσεως. Καλῶς τὸ ἀλαλάξατε ὡς ἐπὶ νίκης· τοῦτο γὰρ ἀλαλαγμὸς λέγεται κυρίως ἡ ἐν ταῖς νίκαις φωνὴ παρὰ τοῦ στρατοῦ γιγνομένη. Μετὰ οὖν εὐφροσύνης φησὶν ἀλαλά-ξατε, εὐφροσύνης ἄξια ἐπιφθεγγόμενοι, ἐπειδὴ καὶ τοιαῦτα τὰ γενόμενα.

10-13 I Macch. V, 1-2.

25 γεγόνει ms   26-28 ἀλαλάξατε ... ἀλαλαγμὸς ms.
23-24 Paraphrasis (p. 886, 3-4): Τοὺς κατὰ Ἀντίοχον λέγει στρατηγοὺς καὶ τοὺς ἅμα αὐτοῖς πολεμίους.   2ᵇ (p. 885): Ἀλαλαγμός ἐστι κυρίως φωνὴ ἐπινίκιος... φωνὴν ἐπινίκιον μετ' εὐφροσύνης ἀναπέμψατε τῷ Θεῷ. Theodoretus (1208 A 9-10, 13-15): Νίκης δὲ ἴδιος ὁ κρότος καὶ ὁ ἀλαλαγμὸς νικώντων φωνή... καὶ οὗτος ὡσαύτως τοῖς τετυχηκόσι τῆς νίκης παρεγγυᾷ τῷ χορηγῷ τῆς νίκης τὸν ὕμνον προσενεγκεῖν.

Aᵉ 21-22 (p. 265, 1-2): Consuetudo est in laudatoriis clamationibus etiam manu plaudere.   24-25 (p. 265, 5-6): Diectis potestatibus solus excelsus apparuit.   27-28 (p. 265, 3-4): Iubilationem dicit uictoris exercitus conclamationem.

When this happened, as we learn from the story itself, a devotee of the law, Mattathias, was the first to take action: he declared war on Antiochus's generals, and shortly before dying after a life of bravery, he transmitted to his sons conduct of the war for the sake of the law. Judas, known also as Maccabeus, was the first to take charge of the war; he defeated Antiochus's generals, won over also those of his own people preferring to go along with the adversaries, and attended also to the renovation of the temple, which had suffered great devastation at the hands of the adversaries. When the neighboring peoples heard this, they conspired in hostility and envy and plotted to destroy them completely. The story of the Maccabees informs us of this in the words "When the nations round about heard that the temple had been rebuilt and the sanctuary restored to its former state, they became very angry and resolved to wipe out the race of Jacob."[2] But whereas they made this resolution against them, the Maccabees were in charge of their campaign, including Judas, who was in particular control of the war, and his brothers, and they prevailed over them as well. After thus defeating the neighboring peoples and Antiochus, and also any of their own people who chanced to resist them, they gave their attention to the temple and lawful observances.

These events, then, blessed David prophesied well in advance, giving voice to the psalm as a kind of triumphal hymn of praise for what had occurred. *All the nations, clap your hands* (v. 1). *Clap your hands* means, Sing praise, since people normally clap their hands in praise. The phrase *All the nations* he does not use without purpose: since they had conquered neighboring peoples and Antiochus's generals, and the conquered were very numerous, God's power had also become obvious to many people. *Shout to God with a cry of gladness. Shout* was well put in the case of victory: the cry raised by the army on conquering is appropriately referred to as shouting. So he says, *Shout* with joy, giving voice to what prompts joy, since the deeds are also of that kind. | *Because the Lord Most High is fearsome* (v. 2): since God

---

2. 1 Macc 5:1–2.

3ᵃ. Ὅτι Κύριος ὕψιστος φοβερός. Ἐπειδὴ δέδεικται ὁ Θεὸς ὕψιστος ὡς τοὺς ἰσχυροὺς καθελών, καὶ φοβερὸς ὡς τοὺς πολεμίους καταπλήξας.

3ᵇ. Βασιλεὺς μέγας ἐπὶ πᾶσαν τὴν γῆν. Ὡς πάντων κρατήσας καὶ πάντων περιγενόμενος.

4. Ὑπέταξε λαοὺς ἡμῖν, καὶ ἔθνη ὑπὸ τοὺς πόδας ἡμῶν. Πάντων γὰρ 5 ἡμᾶς ἀνωτέρους ἐποίησε. Καλῶς δὲ καὶ λαοὺς καὶ ἔθνη· πρὸ γὰρ τῶν Μακκαβαίων ἐκακουργοῦντο καὶ ὑπὸ τῶν ἰδίων, οἳ καὶ μάλιστα αἴτιοι γεγόνασιν αὐτοῖς τῶν κακῶν. Κἀκείνους οὖν ὑπέταξε καὶ τούτους· οὐδὲ γὰρ ἐκεῖνοι τολμῶσί τι, δεδιότες ἡμᾶς διὰ τὴν κατὰ τῶν ἐχθρῶν νίκην. Τὸ δὲ ὑπὸ τοὺς πόδας ἐπὶ τῶν ἐθνῶν ὡς ἐχθρῶν καλῶς εἶπεν, ἐπὶ δὲ τῶν ἰδίων 10 μόνον ὑπέταξεν.

5ᵃ. Ἐξελέξατο ἡμῖν τὴν κληρονομίαν αὐτοῦ. Ἅπαν, ὅπερ ἄν τις ἀπὸ πολλῶν ἐκλέξηται, ὡς κρεῖττον καὶ ἐξαίρετον ἀφορίζει τῶν λοιπῶν αὐτὸ δηλονότι. Τὸ οὖν ἐξελέξατο ἡμῖν ἀντὶ τοῦ ἀφώρισεν ἡμῖν. Τὴν κληρονομίαν αὐτοῦ, ἵνα εἴπῃ τὴν γῆν τῆς ἐπαγγελίας· ἐπειδὴ γὰρ πρότερον 15 ὑπ᾽ αὐτῶν κατείχετο, καλῶς εἶπεν ὅτι ἀφώρισεν ἡμῖν αὐτήν, τουτέστιν ἀφελόμενος αὐτὴν ἐκείνων πάλιν ἡμῖν ἀποδέδωκε. Καὶ οὐκ αὐτήν φησι μόνον, ἀλλὰ καὶ ἡμᾶς ἀφώρισέ τε καὶ ἀπήλλαξεν ἐκείνων, οὐκ ἐάσας ἡμᾶς ἐπὶ πλεῖστον ὑπὸ τοῖς πολεμίοις.

5ᵇ. Τὴν | δὲ καλλονὴν Ἰακὼβ ἣν ἠγάπησεν. Ἵνα εἴπῃ τὸν κάλλιστον 20 Ἰακώβ, κοσμῆσαι τὸ ἔθνος βουλόμενος, ὥσπερ ἡμῖν ἔθος λέγειν « τὴν καλοκαγαθίαν σου », « τὴν τιμιότητά σου », τιμῆς ἕνεκεν ταῦτα ἀποφθεγγομένοις.

6ᵃ. Ἀνέβη ὁ Θεὸς ἐν ἀλαλαγμῷ. Σχηματοποιεῖ λοιπὸν τὴν νίκην. Περιγεγονώς φησι τῶν ἐθνῶν μετὰ μεγάλης φωνῆς, ἣν ἐπὶ τῇ νίκῃ πεποίηται, ἀνέβη τε καὶ ἐφ᾽ ὑψηλοῦ δείκνυσιν ἑαυτόν· τὸ γὰρ ἀνέβη ὡς ἀπὸ τῆς νίκης 25 πάντων ἀνωτέρου δειχθέντος φησίν.

11 μόνων ms.   22 ἀποφθεγγόμενος ms.
14-15 Paraphrasis (p. 886): Ἐξελέξατο γὰρ ἡμᾶς φησι κτῆμα αὐτοῦ ὄντας καὶ κληρονομίαν.   21 (ib.) ... κόσμος ἐγενόμεθα τοῦ Ἰακώβ.

Aᵉ 7 (p. 265, 12) ... praeuaricatores Iudeos.   15-19 (p. 265, 15-19): Terram nostram, quam dudum ad possisionem gentium postea in ius nostrum dominiumque segregauit, etiam nunc pro uagationibus hostium, uindicabit. 6ᵃ (p. 265, 24-266, 5): Ascendit quoque, exaltatus et magnificatus est, dicit, cum uictoriam hostium indicat et ultionem secundum humanam utique exaestimationem .. quoniam triumpho de hostibus acto cunctis sublimis apparuit.

has been shown to be *Most High* in bringing down the mighty, and *fearsome* in striking the enemy with terror. *Great king over all the earth:* in gaining control over all and prevailing over all.

He subjected peoples to us, and nations under our feet (v. 3): he put us over all of them. *Peoples* and *nations* were well put: before the Maccabees they were abused even by their own, who in a particular way were responsible for their troubles. So he subjected both former and latter: The former dare to do nothing, he is saying, fearful of us on account of the victory against the foe. The phrase *under our feet* was well put in reference to the nations as a hostile force, whereas in the case only of their own race he used *subjected.* *He chose for us his inheritance* (v. 4): everything that anyone would choose from a great number he clearly he sets aside from the rest as better and special; so *He chose for us* in the sense of set it aside for us. *His inheritance* refers to the land of promise: since formerly it was occupied by them, he was right to say, He set it aside for us—that is, removed it from them and in turn gave it to us—and not only it, but also ourselves he set aside and liberated from them, not allowing us any longer to be subject to the enemy. *The beauty of Jacob, which he loved:* as if to say, Jacob in all his beauty, wishing to compliment the nation, just as we normally say, Your Honor, Your Excellency, expressing it this way out of respect.

God went up with a shout (v. 5). He now depicts the victory under certain aspects. After prevailing over the nations with a loud cry, which is raised in the case of victory, he is saying, *he went up* and shows himself on high (using *went up* in the case of one shown to be superior to all as a result of victory). | *The Lord with the sound of a trumpet*—that is, He went up with

6ᵇ. Κύριος ἐν φωνῇ σάλπιγγος. Τουτέστι μετὰ φωνῆς σάλπιγγος ἀνῆλ-
θεν, ἐπειδὴ ἐν τοῖς πολέμοις ἀρχόμενοί τε σαλπίζουσι καὶ τῇ τῆς σάλπιγγος πάλιν σημασίᾳ τῷ πολέμῳ τὸ πέρας ἐπάγουσιν.

7. Ψάλατε τῷ Θεῷ ἡμῶν, ψάλατε, ψάλατε τῷ βασιλεῖ ἡμῶν, ψάλατε.
5 Ἄιδετέ φησι διηνεκῶς ταύτην αὐτοῦ τὴν νίκην.

8. Ὅτι βασιλεὺς πάσης τῆς γῆς ὁ Θεός. Πάντων αὐτὸν ὁμολογοῦντες
βασιλέα· τοῦτο γὰρ δέδεικται διὰ τῆς νίκης.

9ᵃ. Ψάλατε συνετῶς. Τουτέστι μὴ τῷ ᾄδειν μόνῳ προσέχοντες μηδὲ
τῇ τέρψει τοῦ ᾄσματος, ἀλλὰ καὶ ἀναλογιζόμενοι τῆς χάριτος τὸ μέγεθος.

10 9ᵇ. Ἐβασίλευσεν ὁ Θεὸς ἐπὶ τὰ ἔθνη. Τουτέστιν ἐκράτησεν αὐτῶν,
ἐπειδὴ οἱ βασιλεύοντες κρατοῦσι τῶν βασιλευομένων.

9ᶜ. Ὁ Θεὸς κάθηται ἐπὶ θρόνου ἁγίου αὐτοῦ. Καλῶς ὡς ἐπικρατήσαντος
καὶ βασιλεύσαντος διὰ τῆς νίκης, τουτέστιν Ἐκάθισεν ἐπὶ τοῦ οἰκείου θρόνου
ἐν εἰρήνῃ, λοιπὸν ἀναπαυσόμενος τῶν πολέμων, ἐν ἀμεριμνίᾳ τῆς βασιλείας
15 ἀπολαύων — τῇ σωματοποιήσει τὸ γενόμενον διηγούμενος.

10ᵃ. Ἄρχοντες λαῶν συνήχθησαν μετὰ τοῦ Θεοῦ Ἀβραάμ. Οὕτω τε
πᾶσι σαφὴς καὶ ὡμολογημένη γέγονεν ἡ ἰσχὺς αὐτοῦ καὶ ἡ βασιλεία, ὡς
πολλοὺς ἄρχοντας τῶν ποτε μαχομένων συναχθῆναι πρὸς αὐτὸν ἐπὶ τῷ
κοινωνῆσαι τῆς εὐφροσύνης. Τοῦτο δὲ λέγει σημαίνων ὅτι πολλοὶ μετὰ τὴν
20 νίκην καταπλαγέντες τοῦ Θεοῦ τὴν δύναμιν προσεκοίνησαν τῷ Θεῷ. Καλῶς
οὖν τὸ μετ' αὐτοῦ συνήχθησαν, τουτέστι | πρὸς αὐτόν, κοινωνοῦντες αὐτῷ
τῆς εὐφροσύνης, θαυμάζοντες τὸ γενόμενον. Πόθεν οὖν ποιῆσαι τοῦτο
προήχθησαν;

10ᵇ. Ὅτι τοῦ Θεοῦ οἱ κραταιοὶ τῆς γῆς σφόδρα ἐπήρθησαν. Τὸ τοῦ Θεοῦ
25 προσυπακούεται· οὐδαμοῦ γὰρ τῆς γῆς κραταιούς λέγει τοὺς ἁγίους καὶ

8-9 Theodoretus (1209 B 7-10): Καλῶς δὲ καὶ τὸ Ψάλατε συνετῶς τέθεικε διδάσκων μὴ μόνῃ τῇ γλώττῃ προφέρειν τὴν ὑμνῳδίαν, ἀλλὰ καὶ τὴν διάνοιαν εἰς κατανόησιν
τῶν λεγομένων ἐγείρειν. 20-23 Paraphrasis (p. 887, 10-12): Ἀπὸ γὰρ γεγονότων
φησὶν οἱ πάντων τῶν ἐθνῶν ἄρχοντες ἅμα ἡμῖν συναχθέντες τὸν ἕνα ὑμνήσομεν Θεόν.

Aᵉ 7 (p. 266, 6-7): Iugiter hanc eius uictoriam cantate. 8-9 (p. 266, 9-10):
Non tantum modalationibus delectati sed materi⟨i⟩s canticorum. 9ᶜ (p. 266,
11-14): Pro Obtenuit eas et secura dominatione possedet ... tamquam uictor solidi et quieti demum potitus imperii. 19-20 (p. 265, 14-16): Indicat multos
post experimentum tantae potentiae ad cultum Dei Abrachae conuolasse.

the sound of a trumpet, since they begin by sounding the trumpet in time of battle and likewise bring the battle to a close with a signal from the trumpet. *Sing to our God, sing; sing to our king, sing* (v. 6): constantly hail this victory of his. *Because God is king of all the earth* (v. 7): confessing him king over all, this being shown through the victory. *Sing with understanding*—that is, not only giving attention to the singing or to the charm of the song, but also pondering the greatness of the favor.

God reigned over the nations (v. 8)—that is, he controlled them, since those who reign control those over whom they reign. *God sits on his holy throne.* The clause was well expressed of the one who had gained control of the throne through victory, namely, He was seated on his own throne in peace, now having brought war to an end, enjoying kingship free of worry (describing the event in a figurative manner). *Rulers of peoples are gathered with the God of Abraham* (v. 9): his power and kingship have become so clear to everyone and confessed by them that many rulers in battles once fought have been gathered to him in a sharing of joy. He says this to suggest that many who were struck by God's power after the victory have entered into communion with God. So *gathered with* was well put, meaning toward God, sharing joy with him, marveling at what had happened.

Why, then, were they brought to do this? *Because the mighty ones of God were raised to great heights over the earth.* The phrase *of God* is supplied: nowhere does he use *mighty ones of the earth* to describe those who are holy and | shown to be mighty with God's help. So it should be read this

τῇ τοῦ Θεοῦ βοηθείᾳ μεγάλους δεικνυμένους. Οὕτως οὖν ἀναγνωστέον· ὅτι τοῦ Θεοῦ οἱ κραταιοί, εἶτα διαστείλαντα εἰπεῖν χρὴ τῆς γῆς σφόδρα ἐπήρθησαν. Οἱ γάρ τοι τοῦ Θεοῦ κραταιοί φησι, τουτέστιν ἡμεῖς οἱ τῇ αὐτοῦ βοηθείᾳ μεγάλοι τυγχάνοντες, σφόδρα τῆς γῆς ἐπήρθημεν, ἀντὶ τοῦ ὑπεράνω πάντων τῶν τῆς γῆς ἐδείχθημεν· ἐπειδὴ οὖν ἡμεῖς φησι τῇ κατ᾽ αὐτῶν νίκῃ 5 πάντων ἐδείχθημεν μείζους, διὰ τοῦτο καὶ ἕτεροι πολλοὶ ἔσπευσαν κοινωνῆσαι τῆς εὐφροσύνης, τῶν μετ᾽ αὐτῶν τε ὄντων καὶ τὰ αὐτὰ φρονούντων ἑαυτοὺς δεῖξαι σπεύδοντες.

PSALMVS XLVII

Τὴν κατὰ τῶν Ἀσσυρίων νίκην γεγενημένην ἐπὶ τοῦ βασιλέως Ἐζεκίου 10 προφητεύων ὁ μακάριος Δαυὶδ ἐν τούτῳ τῷ ψαλμῷ ἐκπλήττεται μὲν τοῦ Θεοῦ τὴν βοήθειαν ὡς μεγάλην, πόρρωθεν δὲ πάντας ὑπὲρ τῶν γεγονότων ἐπὶ τὴν εὐχαριστίαν προτρέπεται, ὡς ἐκ προσώπου τῶν τότε κατὰ τὸ σύνηθες αὐτῷ λέγων ἅπαντα τὸν ψαλμόν.

2. Μέγας Κύριος καὶ αἰνετὸς σφόδρα ἐν πόλει τοῦ Θεοῦ ἡμῶν, ὄρει ἁγίῳ 15 αὐτοῦ. Προσυπακούεται τὸ «ἐδείχθη», ἀντὶ τοῦ Μέγας καὶ αἰνετὸς ἐκ τῶν περὶ τὴν πόλιν τὴν ἡμετέραν ἐδείχθη τοῖς ἀγνοοῦσιν αὐτὸν πρότερον ὁποῖός τις ἦν, — οὕτω καὶ ὅταν λέγῃ τὸ Ἐμεγαλύνθη, οὐχ ὡς αὔξησιν ἐπιδεχομένου, ἀλλ᾽ ὡς ἐκ τῶν γινομένων ἐν ταῖς τῶν ἀνθρώπων ὑπονοίαις μεγάλου ἐπιδεικνυμένου. Μέγας μὲν οὖν ἐδείχθη τῷ μεγέθει τῆς κατὰ τῶν 20 ἐχθρῶν τιμωρίας, αἰνετὸς δὲ ὡς ὕμνου παντὸς καὶ εὐχαριστίας ἄξιος | ἐφ᾽ οἷς οὕτω παραδόξως τοσούτων ἐχθρῶν ἐρρύσατο τὴν πόλιν. Τὸ δὲ ἐν πόλει καὶ ἐν ὄρει τὸ αὐτὸ λέγει· ἐπὶ γὰρ τοῦ ὄρους ἡ πόλις αὐτῶν ἔκειτο.

18 Ps. LVI, 11.

3-7 *Paraphrasis* (p. 887, 20-24): Ἡμεῖς οἱ παρὰ τοῦ Θεοῦ κρατούμενοι σφόδρα ὑπὲρ τὴν γῆν ἐπήρθημεν, ἀντὶ τοῦ ὑψώθημεν· τὰ γὰρ ὑπὲρ ἡμῶν γεγενημένα ἐνδόξως ἡμᾶς ὑπὲρ πᾶσαν τὴν γῆν ἐποίει.
10-14 Τὴν κατὰ — ἅπαντα τὸν ψαλμόν: Paris. 139, fol. 123ᵛ; Vat. gr. 1682, fol. 180ᵛ; Barbaro, p. 285.   20-22 *Paraphrasis* (p. 898): Πρὸς τὸ μέγεθος τῶν γεγενημένων λέγει τὸ Μέγας Κύριος. Ἀμέλει καὶ αἰνετὸς εἰπὼν ἐπήγαγε σφόδρα, ἵνα δείξῃ μεγάλα τὰ παρ᾽ αὐτοῦ γεγονότα... Πόλιν τοῦ Θεοῦ ἡμῶν καλεῖ τὴν Ἱερουσαλὴμ ὡς τοῦ Θεοῦ... σῴζοντος παραδόξως.

Aᵉ 3-5 (p. 265, 17-21): Ac si diceret: Hii, qui erant *dii potentes*, id est nos, qui ipsius adiutorio magni agimur, *super terram uechimenter* eleuati sumus atque emenentiores omnibus degentibus in terra apparemus.   16-17 (p. 266, 26. 23-25): Subauditur « ostensus est » ... estimatione hominum ignora⟨n⟩tium Deum, ex his quae in ciuitate operatus est *magnus* apparuit. (cf. PSEUDO-BEDA 729).

way: *Because the mighty ones of God;* then one should make a distinction and say *they were raised to great heights over the earth.* In other words, *the mighty ones of God*—that is, we who are great because of his help—*were raised to great heights over the earth*—that is, we were shown to be superior to all on earth. Since, then, he is saying, we were shown to be greater than everyone by the victory against them, for this reason many others also were anxious to share in the joy, anxious to show themselves of one heart and mind with them.

PSALM 48

In prophesying the victory won against the Assyrians in the time of King Hezekiah, blessed David in this psalm is struck by God's great assistance, and well in advance he urges everyone to thanksgiving for what has occurred, in his usual way reciting the whole psalm from the viewpoint of the people of the time.

Great is the Lord, and much to be praised in the city of our God, on his holy mountain (v. 1). The phrase "was shown to be" is understood, meaning, He was shown by the situation of our city to be *great* and *to be praised* to those previously unaware of who he was—likewise also when it says, "He was magnified,"[1] not in the sense that he underwent increase, but that he was shown to be great in people's perception. So he was shown to be great by the magnitude of the punishment of the enemy, and *to be praised* as worthy of all singing and thanksgiving for rescuing the city against the odds from so many foes. He means the same by *city* and *mountain:* their city was situated on the mountain. |

---

1. Cf. Ps 57:11.

3ᵃ·ᵇ. Εὐριζῶν ἀγαλλιάματι πάσης τῆς γῆς ὄρη Σιών, τὰ πλευρὰ τοῦ
βορρᾶ. Οὐ χρὴ διαιροῦντας, ὥς τινες, ἀναγινώσκειν λέγοντας εὖ, εἶτα ῥιζῶν,
ἀλλὰ συνάπτοντας εὐριζῶν, ἀντὶ τοῦ πλατύνων· εὐρὺ γὰρ λέγεται τὸ πλατύ.
Τὰ οὖν ὄρη φησὶ τὰ Σιὼν τῷ ἀγαλλιάματι πλατύνει, τουτέστι πλατείαν
5 αὐτοῖς τὴν εὐφροσύνην παρέχεται, πάντας ἀποδιώκων τοὺς ἐχθρούς. Τὸ δὲ
πάσης τῆς γῆς, ἀντὶ τοῦ Τῇ εὐφροσύνῃ, ἧς πάσῃ τῇ γῇ μετέδωκε τῇ ἡμετέρᾳ πᾶσαν αὐτὴν ἀπαλλάξας τῶν πολεμίων, ταύτῃ καὶ τὰ Σιὼν ὄρη
πλατύνει, — ἵνα εἴπῃ ὅτι πλατείαν καὶ τῇ γῇ πάσῃ καὶ τοῖς ὄρεσι τῆς
Σιών, ἀντὶ τοῦ τῇ μητροπόλει, τὴν εὐφροσύνην παρέχεται.
10 Πλευρὰ δὲ τοῦ βορρᾶ καλεῖ τὰ Σιὼν ὄρη, ὡς ὑπὸ τοῦ βορρᾶ σφόδρα
τῶν τόπων καταπνεομένων καὶ συνεχομένων, ἐπειδὴ καὶ ἐν τῷ σώματι τῇ
τῶν πλευρῶν ἰσχύϊ τὸ πᾶν ἔνδοθεν συνέχεται.

3ᶜ. Ἡ πόλις τοῦ βασιλέως τοῦ μεγάλου. Τοιούτων φησὶν ἡ τοῦ μεγάλου
βασιλέως ἀπολαύει πόλις. Πόθεν γὰρ ὅτι αὐτοῦ πόλις;

15 4. Ὁ Θεὸς ἐν ταῖς βάρεσιν αὐτῆς γινώσκεται, ὅταν ἀντιλαμβάνηται
αὐτῆς. Τουτέστι τοῖς οἰκήμασι· τὴν γὰρ γνῶσίν φησι τὴν οἰκείαν ἐν τοῖς
τῆς πόλεως οἰκήμασι παρέχεται βοηθῶν καὶ καταπίπτειν αὐτὰ οὐκ ἐῶν,
οὐδὲ συγχωρῶν ἀηδές τι πάσχειν αὐτοὺς ὑπὸ τῶν πολεμίων.

5. Ὅτι ἰδοὺ οἱ βασιλεῖς συνήχθησαν, ἦλθοσαν ἐπὶ τὸ αὐτό. Καὶ τούτου
20 φησὶν ἀπόδειξις τὰ γεγονότα. Ἰδοὺ γὰρ ἐπὶ τὸ αὐτὸ βασιλεῖς πολλοὶ
συνελθόντες ὥρμησαν αἱρήσοντες τὴν πόλιν. Βασιλεῖς δὲ λέγει τοὺς μετὰ τοῦ
βασιλέως τῶν Ἀσσυρίων σατράπας εἰς βοήθειαν ἐλθόντας. Καὶ τί γέγονεν
ὁρμησάντων αὐτῶν;

6. Αὐτοὶ ἰδόντες οὕτως ἐθαύμασαν. Αὐτοί φησιν ἐκεῖνοι οὕτως ἰδόντες
25 καὶ οὕτω θεασάμενοι ὅτι μετὰ πολλῆς τῆς βοηθείας | ἀντιλαμβάνῃ τῆς

17 αὐτὰς ms   19 βασιλεῖς τῆς γῆς ms.
3-5 Paraphrasis (p. 898): Τὸ εὐριζῶν ἀντὶ τοῦ « πλατύνων » λέγει· βούλεται γὰρ
εἰπεῖν ὅτι πλατύνει αὐτῆς τὸ ἀγαλλίαμα καὶ τὴν εὐφροσύνην ὁ πάσης τῆς γῆς Θεός.

Aᵉ 4-12 (p. 266, 28-267, 7): Pro eo ut diceret Latissimam et solidam exsul-
tationem et terrae nostrae et Sion montibus, metrapoli uidilicet ipsius regionis,
indulsit. **Montis Sion latera aquilonis.** Vocat montem Sion, quod huic uento
ciuitatem ipsam ambifariam constet obiectam, et quod eadem loca aquilonis
flatu assiduo uideantur quodammodo conteneri; siquidem et in corporibus
nostris tale aliquid aduerti licet, cum lateribus nostris omnia quae sunt intus
uiscera contenentur.   3ᶜ (p. 267, 7-8): Vere *ciuitas regis*, quae talibus gestis
honoratur.   17 (p. 267, 10): Cum eam adiuuat uetatque conruere.   22 (p. 267,
11-12): Assiriorum satrapae.   6 (p. 267, 13-17): Frustatio tantae inpugnationis
terrorque hostium et te magnum Deum conprobari fecit et tuam esse ciuitatem,
quae defenditur.

Rooting firmly in gladness of all the earth, mountains of Sion, ribs of the north (v. 2). In reading this, it is not necessary, as some commentators do, to make a division and say *firmly* and then *rooting,* but *rooting firmly* together in the sense of expanding, "broad" meaning "expanded."[2] So he is saying, He expands *the mountains of Sion in gladness*—that is, he provides them with an expanded joy, chasing off all their foes. The phrase *of all the earth*—that is, by its joy—which he communicated in all our land by freeing all of it from the enemy: by this he expands *the mountains of Sion,* as if to say, He provides expanded joy to all the land and to the mountains of Sion, meaning, to the capital. By *ribs of the north* he refers to the mountains of Sion, places that feel the effects of the winds from the north, since in the body as well everything within is held together by the strength of the ribs. *The city of the great king:* the city of the great king enjoys such benefits. How, in fact, does it come to be his city? *God is known in its buildings whenever he supports it* (v. 3)—that is, its dwellings. He provides his own knowledge, he is saying, in the city's dwellings by helping them and not allowing them to collapse or permitting them to experience anything unpleasant from the enemy.

Because, lo, the kings were assembled; they came together (v. 4). What happened is proof of this: *Lo,* many *kings* came together; they massed together and advanced to do away with the city. By *kings* he refers to the satraps accompanying the king of the Assyrians to help him. What was the result of their advance? *On seeing it they were amazed* (v. 5): they personally witnessed it, and on observing it they were astonished that he supported the city with abundant assistance. | So he is saying, He is the one who would

---

2. Although Dahood (*Psalms,* 1:289) concedes that the opening phrase is "much contested" in the Hebrew, Theodore makes heavy weather of the compound verb in the LXX (Chrysostom getting some capital from the intensive in the way Theodore criticizes), choosing to see the compound εὐ-ρίζειν related rather to εὐρύς, "broad."

πόλεως ἐξεπλάγησαν. Οὕτως οὖν φησιν αὐτός τε ἐν τῇ περὶ τὴν πόλιν βοηθείᾳ γνωρίζῃ καὶ ἡ πόλις ἡ τυγχάνουσα δείκνυται.

7ᵃ. Ἐταράχθησαν, ἐσαλεύθησαν· τρόμος ἐπελάβετο αὐτῶν. Ταραχῇ φησι καὶ φόβῳ κατεσχέθησαν διὰ τὴν ἐπαχθεῖσαν αὐτοῖς παρά σου τιμωρίαν.

7ᵇ. Ἐκεῖ ὠδῖνες ὡς τικτούσης. Τὸ ὀξὺ βούλεται καὶ φοβερὸν τῆς πληγῆς 5 παρασημάναι· οὕτω γάρ φησιν ἐπώδυνος ἦν ἡ ἐπαχθεῖσα αὐτοῖς παρά σου τιμωρία, ὡς ὁμοίας ταῖς τικτούσαις ἀφιέναι φωνάς.

8. Ἐν πνεύματι βιαίῳ συντρίψεις πλοῖα Θαρσίς. Θαρσὶς πόλις ἦν παραθαλασσία ἐμπορείας ἔχουσα πολλάς· ὅθεν καὶ τὰ τοῦ Σολομῶντος πλοῖα τῆς ἐμπορείας ἕνεκα εἰς Θαρσὶς ἀπέπλει. Πολλάκις οὖν τὸ παραθαλάσσιον 10 σημάναι βουλομένη ἡ γραφὴ « Θαρσὶς » λέγει· οὕτω καὶ ὅταν λέγῃ Βασιλεῖς Θαρσὶς καὶ νῆσοι δῶρα προσοίσουσι, τοῦτο βούλεται εἰπεῖν Καὶ αἱ νῆσοι δῶρά σοι προσκομιοῦσι. Τοῦτο οὖν κἀνταῦθά φησιν ὅτι ὥσπερ πνεύματος βιαιοτάτου ἐμπεσόντος συντρίβεται τῶν παραθαλασσίων πόλεων τὰ πλοῖα ὑπὸ τῆς τοῦ ἀνέμου σφοδρότητος, οὕτω φησὶ καὶ τὰ πλήθη τῶν Ἀσσυ- 15 ρίων ὥσπερ τινὶ ἀνέμῳ τῇ οἰκείᾳ τιμωρίᾳ συντρίψει.

9ᵃ⁻ᶜ. Καθάπερ ἠκούσαμεν, οὕτως εἴδομεν ἐν πόλει Κυρίου τῶν δυνάμεων, ἐν πόλει τοῦ Θεοῦ ἡμῶν. Καλῶς ὡς ἐκ προσώπου τῶν τότε φησὶν ὅτι Ὅσα ἠκούσαμεν παρὰ τῶν πατέρων ὡς ἐτιμωρήθησαν μὲν Αἰγύπτιοι, ἀπηλλάγησαν δὲ τῆς καταδυναστείας ἢ καὶ ὅσα ἕτερα γεγενῆσθαι ἠκούσαμεν, 20 τοιαῦτα καὶ τοῖς ὀφθαλμοῖς ἐθεασάμεθα τοῖς ἡμετέροις· οὐδενὸς γὰρ ἐκείνων ἔλαττον τὸ νῦν γεγονὸς περὶ τὴν ἀνακειμένην σοι πόλιν.

8-9 cf. in Ionam I, 3 (329 CD)   9-10 cf. III Reg. X, 22   11-12 Ps. LXXI, 10.

5-6 L (p. 903, 34-35): Τὸ γὰρ ὀξὺ καὶ ἐπώδυνον τῆς τιμωρίας διὰ τῆς ὠδῖνος ἐδήλωσε, cf. Paraphrasis (p. 899).   10-16 Paraphrasis (p. 899): Θάρσιν τοὺς παραθαλασσίους λέγει τόπους. Βούλεται οὖν εἰπεῖν, ὅτι ὥσπερ εἰ πλοῖα συνέβη ἑστάναι ἐν τοῖς παραθαλασσίοις τόποις, καὶ ἐξαίφνης πνεῦμα βίαιον ἀπελθόν, συντρίψει ἅπαντα καὶ ἀπωλέσει, οὕτω φησὶν ἐγένετο καὶ ἐπὶ τῶν Βαβυλωνίων.   19-21 cf. L (p. 904, 10-11): ... ἃ γὰρ ἠκούσαμέν φησι ἐπὶ τῶν ἔργων ἑωράκαμεν.

Aᵉ 7ᵇ (p. 267, 18-19): Vindictae celeritas et magnitudo doloris his uerbis ostenditur.   8-13 (p. 267, 23-27): Litoria ciuitas erat Tarsis, potens nauium; et generaliter omnia loca litoria « Tarsis » appellare Scriptura consueuit, sicut alibi dicit Reges Tarsis, id est litorum uel insolarum.   13-16 (p. 267, 20-22): Est sensus: Tamquam naues litorum uento ualido difficile conteruntur, ita Assiriorum deletus est exercitus.   18-19 (p. 277, 28-268, 5): Bene ex persona eorum qui tunc... quae patrum nostrorum memoria inpletae referentur.

thus make himself known by his help for the city, and the city is revealed as the recipient. *They were panic stricken, they staggered; trembling took hold of them* (v. 6): they were gripped with panic and fear as a result of the punishment inflicted on them by you. *Pains there as of a woman in labor:* he means to suggest the rapidity and fearsome character of the blow, saying, The punishment inflicted on them was so painful that they uttered cries like women in labor.

With a violent wind you will smash ships of Tarshish (v. 7). Tarshish was a coastal city involved in much trade; hence, Solomon's ships sailed for Tarshish for trading purposes.[3] So he often uses the term *Tarshish* to indicate the coast, as when he says, "Kings of Tarshish and islands will bring gifts,"[4] meaning, The islands will provide you with gifts. So he means here, too, Just as the ships of the coastal cities will be smashed by a violent wind buffeting them from a severe gale, so too he will smash the hordes of the Assyrians with his characteristic retribution like some wind. *As we have heard, so we have seen, in the city of the Lord of hosts, in the city of our God* (v. 8). He did well to express it from their point of view at the time: All we heard from our fathers about the Egyptians being punished and their being freed from their control, or whatever else we heard happening, this we have observed also with our own eyes, since what has happened in our day to the city dedicated to you is no less than those things. | *God established it forever:* you

---

3. Cf. 1 Kgs 10:22.
4. Ps 72:10.

9ᵈ. Ὁ Θεὸς ἐθεμελίωσεν αὐτὴν εἰς τὸν αἰῶνα. Ἔδειξας γὰρ ὅπως ἀσφαλὲς καὶ ἑδραῖον τὸ κατοικητήριον αὐτῆς κατεσκεύασας, οὐ δυνάμενον ἐχθροῖς ἡττᾶσθαι.

10. Ὑπελάβομεν, ὁ Θεός, τὸ ἔλεός σου ἐν μέσῳ τοῦ λαοῦ σου. Τὸ ὑπε-
5 λάβομεν ἀντὶ τοῦ προσεδοκήσαμεν, ἐπειδὴ τοῖς ὑπολαμβάνουσιν ἔσεσθαί τι ἔθος καὶ προσδοκᾶν τὸ ὑποπτευό|μενον, — οὕτω καὶ ὅταν λέγῃ Ὑπέλαβόν με ὡσεὶ λέων ἕτοιμος εἰς θήραν, ἀντὶ τοῦ οὕτω με προσεδόκησαν αἱρήσειν. Τοῦτο οὖν φησιν ὅτι προσεδοκῶμεν, περιεμένομεν ἔσεσθαί σου τὴν βοήθειαν ἐν μέσῳ τοῦ λαοῦ σου, ἀντὶ τοῦ εἰς τὸν λαόν σου, τουτέστιν εἰς
10 ἡμᾶς. Ἔλεον δὲ τὴν βοήθειαν ἐκάλεσεν ὡς φιλανθρωπίᾳ γεγενημένην καὶ οὐκ ὀφειλῇ τῶν δεξαμένων. Καλῶς δὲ εἶπε τὸ « προσεδοκήσαμεν » · ἐπαγγειλαμένου γὰρ τοῦ Θεοῦ διὰ τοῦ προφήτου Ἡσαΐου παρέχειν τὴν βοήθειαν, εἰκὸς ἦν αὐτοὺς καὶ περιμένειν τοῦτο — ὃ δὴ καὶ γέγονε. Τὸ δὲ ὑπελάβομεν· ὁ Θεός, Σύμμαχος λέγει Εἰκάσαμεν, ὁ Θεός, οὐδὲν ἀπᾷδον τοῦ « προσεδο-
15 κήσαμεν » εἰπών.

11ᵃ. Κατὰ τὸ ὄνομά σου, ὁ Θεός, οὕτως καὶ ἡ αἴνεσίς σου ἐπὶ τὰ πέρατα τῆς γῆς. Τὸ ὄνομα πολλάκις ἀντὶ τοῦ πράγματος ἡ γραφὴ λαμβάνουσα λέγει, μάλιστα ἐπὶ τοῦ Θεοῦ, ὡς ὅταν λέγῃ Ἐγώ εἰμι ὁ ὤν, τοῦτό μού ἐστι τὸ ὄνομα, — ὄνομα καλέσας τὸ ὑπάρχον αὐτῷ καὶ προσόν, — οὕτω
20 καὶ τὸ Ἐγώ εἰμι Κύριος, τοῦτό μού ἐστιν ὄνομα. Κἀνταῦθα κατὰ τὸ ὄνομά σου, ὁ Θεός, τοῦτό φησι· ἀνάλογός φησι τῷ μεγέθει τῷ σῷ ὕμνος κατὰ πᾶσαν ἀποδίδοταί σοι τὴν γῆν, πάντων ἐκπληττομένων τὸ γεγονὸς καὶ τῆς σῆς δυνάμεως ἐκ τοῦ γεγονότος στοχαζομένων. Τὸ δὲ ἐπὶ τὰ πέρατα τῆς γῆς, ἢ ἐν τῇ Ἰουδαίᾳ ὡς εὐχαριστούντων, ἢ καὶ πανταχοῦ· πανταχοῦ γὰρ

6-7 Ps. XVI, 12   12 cf. Is. VII, 7 ss.   18-19 Ex. III, 14, 15   20 Ex. VI, 2-3.

1-3 cf. Paraphrasis (p. 900, 11-12): Καὶ ὅτι αὐτὸς ἀσάλευτον αὐτὴν εἰργάσατο καὶ ἀπαράτρεπτον.   5-6 L (p. 904, 14-15): Ἀντὶ τοῦ ἠλπίσαμεν, προσεδοκήσαμεν, ἔγνωμεν τὴν φιλανθρωπίαν τὴν ἐπὶ τὸν λαόν σου, cf. Paraphrasis (p. 900).   23-314, 2 L (p. 904, 24-28) ... καὶ ἡ αἴνεσις, ἤτοι ἡ ἀπὸ τῶν ἔργων εὐφημία, εἰ καὶ ταῦτα ἐν Παλαιστίνῃ γέγονεν, ἀλλ' ἡ ἀπὸ τούτων δόξα διὰ τὸ μέγεθος καὶ τὸν ὄγκον καὶ αὐτὰς τῆς οἰκουμένης κατέλαβε τὰς ἐσχατίας.

Aᵉ 9ᵈ (p. 268, 6-8): Quam non passus est hostili inpugnatione cassari, sed praestitit alta pace et solida gaudere.   4-13 (p. 268, 9-14): Hoc uerbo indicat se etiam exspectasse et sperasse, quo laetatur, auxilium; non enim fere dicimur suscipisse quippiam nisi expectatum, sicut hanc liberationem post praedictum Issaiae iam iamque operiebantur inplendam.   17-23 (p. 268, 15-20): Pro maiestate nomen possuit, sicut alibi Ego sum Dominus, et hoc nomen meum est; concinniens magnitudini tuae in omnes terras laudatio difertur, uniuersis stupentibus tuae uirtutis effectum.

showed how you made its abode secure and stable, incapable of falling to the enemy.

We took up, O God, your mercy in the midst of your people (v. 9). *Took up* means expected, since those taking up something that will happen normally expect their guess to be true, as when he says, "They took me up like a lion ready for the prey"[5]—that is, they expected to capture me this way. So he is saying, We expected, we waited for your help to come *in the midst of your people*—that is, to your people—in other words, to us. By *mercy* he referred to help, since it is given out of lovingkindness and is not due to the recipients. "We expected" was well put: since God had promised through the prophet Isaiah to provide help, they probably were waiting for it, as actually happened. For *We took up* Symmachus says, "We inferred, O God," saying nothing at variance with "We expected."

As is your name, O God, so is your praise, to the ends of the earth (v. 10). Scripture often cites the name in place of the deed, especially in the case of God, as when it says, "I am the one who is, this is my name," by "name" referring to his existence and presence; likewise also the verse "I am the Lord, this is my name."[6] Here, too, by *As is your name, O God* he means the same thing: A hymn of praise commensurate with your greatness is rendered to you throughout the whole earth, with everyone astonished at what has happened and gaining an impression of your might from the deed. The phrase *to the ends of the earth* refers to those giving thanks either in Judea or even in every place: | the event was naturally bruited abroad everywhere,

---

5. Ps 17:12. Like the other Antiochenes, Theodore has not noticed that a scribe has evidently written λαοῦ, "people," for ναοῦ, "temple," in the local form of the LXX.

6. Exod 3:14; cf. Exod 6:2–3.

ἦν ἀνάγκη διαδοθῆναι τὸ γεγονός, Ἀσσυρίων τότε πάσης κρατούντων τῆς γῆς τῶν τὴν πληγὴν δεξαμένων.

11ᵇ. Δικαιοσύνης πλήρης ἡ δεξιά σου. Τουτέστιν ἡ εἰς ἡμᾶς βοήθεια· καὶ γὰρ δικαιοτάτην φησὶ παρέσχες τὴν βοήθειαν, ἐκείνους τε διὰ τὴν ἀσέβειαν εἰκότως τιμωρησάμενος καὶ ἡμᾶς διὰ τὴν γνῶσιν τὴν σὴν εἰκότως 5 ἀπαλλάξας τῶν κινδύνων.

12. Εὐφρανθήτω ὄρος Σιών, ἀγαλλιάσθωσαν αἱ θυγατέρες τῆς Ἰουδαίας ἕνεκα τῶν κριμάτων σου, Κύριε. Οὐκοῦν φησι καὶ οἱ τὰ ὄρη καὶ τὴν Ἰου- δαίαν οἰκοῦντες — τοῦτο γὰρ βούλεται εἰπεῖν τὸ αἱ θυγατέρες τῆς Ἰου- δαίας — πάντες μετ' εὐφροσύνης τὸ γεγονὸς δι|ηγείσθωσαν καὶ χαιρέτωσαν 10 διὰ τοῦτο μᾶλλον, ὅτι μετὰ πολλῆς τῆς κρίσεως καὶ τοῦ δικαίου ἅπαντα πράττων καὶ ἐπαμύνεις οἷς δεῖ καὶ τιμωρῇ οὓς προσήκει. Τὸ δὲ αἱ θυγα- τέρες τῆς Ἰουδαίας εἶπεν ἀντὶ τοῦ οἱ Ἰουδαῖοι, διὰ τὸ ἐπαγόμενον. Λέγει γάρ·

13ᵃ. Κυκλώσατε Σιὼν καὶ περιλάβετε αὐτήν. Ὡς γὰρ πρὸς τὰς θυγα- τέρας καλῶς τὸ κυκλώσατε, τουτέστι Κύκλους καὶ χοροὺς ἐν τῇ Σιὼν ποιή- 15 σατε, ἐπείπερ ἴδιον τοῦτο μάλιστα τῶν γυναικῶν. Τὸ δὲ καὶ περιλάβετε αὐτήν, ἀντὶ τοῦ Πᾶσαι κατὰ πάσης τῆς Σιὼν τοῦτο ποιεῖτε, ὥστε περιει- λῆφθαι αὐτὴν καὶ κυκλῶσθαι αὐτὴν ὑφ' ὑμῶν πασῶν καὶ πανταχοῦ καὶ καθ' ὅλης τοῦτο ποιουσῶν τῆς πόλεως.

13ᵇ. Διηγήσασθε ἐν τοῖς πύργοις αὐτῆς. Πύργοις, τουτέστι τοῖς οἴκοις. 20 Κατὰ πάσης οὖν φησι τῆς Σιὼν κύκλους ποιησάμεναι καὶ χορούς, ᾄδετε τοῦ Θεοῦ τὴν βοήθειαν.

14ᵃ. Θέσθε τὰς καρδίας ὑμῶν εἰς τὴν δύναμιν αὐτῆς. Σύνετε ὅπως ἐστὶν ἰσχυρά τε καὶ δυνατή, τῆς τοῦ Θεοῦ βοηθείας τοιαύτην αὐτὴν ἀποφαινούσης.

14ᵇ. Καὶ καταδιέλεσθε τὰς βάρεις αὐτῆς. Ἐπειδὴ τοῖς πόλιν καταλαμ- 25 βανομένοις ἴδιόν ἐστι τὰς οἰκήσεις διαιρεῖσθαι, παρὰ πᾶσαν δὲ προσδοκίαν

8-10 L (p. 904, 43-46): Ἐν εὐφροσύνῃ φησὶ κατάστητε οἱ τὸ ὄρος οἰκοῦντες καὶ πᾶσαι αἱ τῆς Ἰουδαίας γυναῖκες· ἀπὸ γὰρ μέρους τὸν πάντα δῆμον ὀνομάζει.

Aᵉ 11ᵇ (p. 268, 21-23): Dextera, quae Assirios puniuit, nos de manu eorum ob cultum religionis eripuit.   17-19 (p. 268, 25-29): Ac si diceret Vniuersi per omnes partes ciuitatis hoc agite, cunctis laudantibus, ut tota a uobis exsulta- tione occupata ciuitas uideatur.   14ᵃ (p. 268, 30-269, 2): Studete et deligenter curate, quatinus firmum sit quod collatum est adiutorium.   14ᵇ (p. 269, 3-8): Sic domus praeter opinionem urbis liberatae possedebitis quasi occupaueritis magis ciuitatem quam retinueritis; mos quippe est urbes capientibus habita- cula sibi sub quadam diuissionis sorte partiri.

since the Assyrians, who controlled the whole earth, had sustained the defeat. *Your right hand is filled with righteousness*—that is, your help for us: It was right of you to provide help, duly punishing them for their godlessness and duly freeing us from danger on account of your knowledge.

Let Mount Sion be glad, and the daughters of Judah rejoice because of your judgments, Lord (v. 11): those dwelling on the mountains and in Judea, therefore (the meaning of *the daughters of Judah*), all recounted the event with joy and rejoiced for this reason in particular, that you did everything with great judgment and righteousness, and you assist those requiring it and punish those who ought be punished. Now, the phrase *the daughters of Judah* means "the Jews," in the light of what follows. *Go around Sion and encircle it* (v. 12). To the daughters the direction is well given *Go around*—that is, go circling and dancing in Sion, since this is particularly characteristic of women. The phrase *and encircle it* means, Do so, everyone throughout Sion, so as to encircle and surround it by doing this at all points of the whole city. *Give an account in its towers:* by *towers* meaning "houses." So he is saying, Go circling and dancing throughout Sion; sing songs about God's help.

Set your hearts on its might (v. 13): realize how strong and mighty it is, since God's help makes it so. *Take its buildings one by one.* Since those taking possession of a city normally count the buildings, but against all expectation | they stayed and occupied the city, so now (he is saying to those

οὗτοι ἔμειναν τε καὶ κατέσχον τὴν πόλιν, ὡς νῦν αὐτῆς ἐπιλαβομένοις φησὶ
τὸ ⟨κατα⟩διέλεσθε · ἐξέσται γὰρ ὑμῖν φησιν ἐν διῃρημέναις ταῖς οἰκήσεσιν
ἕκαστον τῶν οἰκείων ἄνευ πάσης ἀπολαύειν τῆς ὀχλήσεως.

14ᶜ. Ὅπως ἂν διηγήσησθε εἰς γενεὰν ἑτέραν. Ταῦτα δὲ αὐτά φησι δι-
5 δάσκετε καὶ τοὺς ἐξ ὑμῶν, ἵνα εἰδῶσι τὰ γεγονότα.

15. Ὅτι οὗτός ἐστιν ὁ Θεὸς ἡμῶν εἰς τὸν αἰῶνα καὶ εἰς τὸν αἰῶνα τοῦ
αἰῶνος. Ἵνα μάθωσιν ὅτι οὗτος ἡμῶν ἀεὶ Θεὸς — τουτέστι βοηθὸς καὶ προστάτης — αὐτὸς ποιμανεῖ, καὶ πιστεύσωσιν ἐκ τῶν πάλαι τε καὶ πρὸ πολλοῦ
γεγενημένων καὶ τῶν νῦν ἐφ' ἡμῶν ὅτι καὶ εἰς τὸ ἐξῆς τῆς αὐτῆς ἡμᾶς ἀξιώ-
10 σει βοηθείας, ὥσπερ τις ἀγαθὸς ποιμὴν παντὸς ἀπαλλάττων κακοῦ καὶ
πάσης ἐφόδου πολεμίων, ἄνπερ καὶ ἡμεῖς ἀξίους ἑαυτοὺς τοῦ μετέχειν τῆς
αὐτοῦ χάρι|⟨τος⟩ δεικνύωμεν.

PSALMVS XLVIII

Παραίνεσιν κοινὴν πρὸς ἅπαντας ἀνθρώπους ποιεῖται, διδάσκων μὴ περὶ
15 πλοῦτον πτοεῖσθαι καὶ δόξαν, μηδὲ μέγα τι νομίζειν τὴν περὶ τὸν βίον
δυναστείαν, σπουδάζειν δὲ μᾶλλον ὅπως ἂν ἁμαρτίας τέως ἐλεύθεροι ὦσι,
καὶ ὅπως ἂν ὑπὲρ τῶν προσόντων ἀγαθῶν τὴν προσήκουσαν τῷ Θεῷ χάριν
ἀποδιδόναι δύνωνται, ὡς ἐντεῦθεν αὐτοῖς καὶ τῆς ἀπολαύσεως τῶν ὄντων
βεβαίας ἐσομένης.

20   **2ᵃ.** Ἀκούσατε ταῦτα, πάντα τὰ ἔθνη. Πρέπει τῷ προφήτῃ πᾶσιν ὁμοίως
παραινεῖν ἀνθρώποις. Εἰ γὰρ καὶ Ἰουδαῖοι διὰ τὸ τῆς γνώμης εὔκολον

2 διέλεσθε ms   12 χάρι ms   15 πτοεῖσθαι scripsi, ἐπτοῆσθαι ms.
14-15 THEODORETUS (1217 B 9-12)... προσφέρει παραίνεσιν, προσθεῖναι τῇ πίστει
τοῦ βίου τὴν ἀρετήν, καὶ διδάσκει τοῦ πλούτου τὸ μάταιον καὶ τῆς τοῦ κόσμου σοφίας τὸ
ἀκερδές.   20-316, 3 THEODORETUS (1217 C 3-6. 10-13): Ὅτι μόνοις Ἰουδαίοις οἱ
προφῆται διδασκαλίαν προσέφερον, παντί που δῆλον · ἀλλ' ἐνταῦθα ὁ προφητικὸς λόγος
τὴν οἰκουμένην πᾶσαν εἰς ἀκρόασιν συνεγείρει ... Δῆλον τοίνυν ὡς ἐξ αὐτῶν οἱ λόγοι προσ-
φέρονται οὐκ Ἰουδαίοις μόνοις, οὐδὲ τοῖσδε ἢ τοῖσδε τοῖς ἔθνεσιν, ἀλλὰ πάσῃ τῇ τῶν
ἀνθρώπων φύσει.

Aᵉ 14ᶜ (p. 269, 9): Hoc inquit, narrate quoniam sit.   7-10 (p. 269, 11-12):
Non solum tamquam dominus, sed etiam tamquam pastor quidam sollicitus ac
be⟨nig⟩nus.   *Argumentum ps. XLVIII* (p. 269, 13-22): Commones monitus ad
omnes homines hoc carmine beatus Dauid instituit, docens ut non magno
stupore capiantur earum rerum quae in hac uita gloriossae (-ssa *ms*) creduntur,
sed putius studeant quemadmodum pro adfluentibus commoditatibus gratias
Deo agant, ut ipsarum rerum possit illis manere certa perfussio uel functio.
Cf. PSEUDO-BEDA (733).

in occupation), *Take it one by one:* you will be able in counting the buildings to enjoy them without any trouble. *So that you may tell the next generation:* teach your offspring as well the same things so that they may know what happened. *That this is our God forever and ever* (v. 15): so that they may learn *that this is our God* always—that is, our helper and leader—and *he will shepherd us,* and that they may believe from what happened of old and in former times and now from us that he will continue to vouchsafe us the same help, like a good shepherd freeing us from every harm and every attack of the enemy, provided we show ourselves worthy of a share in his grace.

PSALM 49

He delivers a general exhortation to all people, teaching them not to get excited about riches and glory or to set much store by influence in life. Rather, they should be concerned about being free from sin in the time they have, and about giving due thanks to God for the good things that have come their way, this being a means of ensuring that the enjoyment of what they have will be lasting.

Hear this, all nations (v. 1). It is appropriate for the author to exhort everyone alike: even if Jews were bidden not to have much to do with the nations at the risk of familiarity, | it was still necessary for the biblical authors,

ἀκοινωνήτως ἔχειν πρὸς τὰ ἔθνη ἐκελεύοντο, ἀλλ' οὖν γε τοὺς προφήτας τῇ πνευματικῇ χάριτι φθεγγομένους ἀναγκαῖον ἦν ἅπασι μεταδιδόναι τῆς ὠφελείας. Καλῶς δὲ οὐκ ἀπὸ παρακλήσεως ἄρχεται, ἀλλὰ πρῶτον ἀκοῦσαι προστάττει καὶ περὶ τούτου διαλέγεται, δεικνὺς τῶν λεχθησομένων τὸ μέγεθος. Εἶτα προοιμιασάμενος ὅσα πρὸς τὴν ὑπόθεσιν ἐχρῆν, τότε λέγει τὴν 5
συμβουλήν.

2ᵇ. Ἐνωτίσασθε, πάντες οἱ κατοικοῦντες τὴν οἰκουμένην. Ἐνωτίσασθε, τουτέστι σπουδαίως ἀκούσατε· δι' ὅλων γὰρ τὸ ἀναγκαῖον τῶν λεχθησομένων δεῖξαι βουλόμενος, σπουδαίως αὐτοῖς ἀκούειν ἐγκελεύεται.

3ᵃ. Οἵ τε γηγενεῖς καὶ οἱ υἱοὶ τῶν ἀνθρώπων. Τὸ πάντα τὰ ἔθνη, καὶ 10
πάντες οἱ κατοικοῦντες τὴν οἰκουμένην, καὶ οἱ γηγενεῖς, καὶ οἱ υἱοὶ τῶν ἀνθρώπων τὸ αὐτὸ λέγει. Καλῶς δὲ τὸ οἱ γηγενεῖς· ἐπειδὴ γὰρ ἔμελλε διδάσκειν αὐτοὺς μὴ μέγα φρονεῖν ἐπὶ τῷ πλούτῳ καὶ τοῖς κατὰ τὸν παρόντα βίον ἀγαθοῖς γηγενεῖς ἐκάλεσεν, ὡς ἀπὸ τῆς γῆς γεννηθέντας τῷ εὐτελεῖ τῆς φύσεως. Ἐντεῦθεν ἤδη καταστέλλων αὐτοῖς τὸ φρόνημα καὶ εἰπὼν υἱοὶ 15
τῶν ἀνθρώπων ἐπάγει·

3ᵇ. Ἐπὶ τὸ αὐτὸ πλούσιος καὶ πένης. Τουτέστιν ἀπὸ τοῦ κοινοῦ τῆς φύσεως ὁμοίως ἅπαντας ἐπὶ τὴν ἀκρόασιν καλῶν, οὐ διακρίνων πλούσιον ἀπὸ πένητος διὰ τὴν τῆς κτήσεως | διαφοράν. Διὰ τί οὖν πλούσιον καὶ πένητα; Ἵνα μήτε οὗτος ἐφ' οἷς ἔχει μεγαλοφρονῇ, μήτε ἐκεῖνος ὡς μεγάλων ἐστε- 20
ρημένος ἀθυμῇ. Τούτοις τοῖς ῥήμασι συγκαλέσας πάντας εἰς τὴν ἀκρόασίν φησι·

4ᵃ. Τὸ στόμα μου λαλήσει σοφίαν. Καλῶ δὲ ὑμᾶς ἐπὶ τὸ ἀκούειν, ἐπειδὴ σοφίας ἁπάσης καὶ συνέσεως μεστὰ φθέγγεσθαι μέλλω.

14-15 *Paraphrasis* (p. 914, 5-6): Τὸ αὐτὸ λέγει· γηγενεῖς γὰρ καλεῖ τοὺς ἀπὸ γῆς γεγονότας.   23-24 THEODORETUS (1220 B 10-11): Σοφίας φησὶ μεστὰ τὰ παρ' ἐμοῦ προσφερόμενα ῥήματα.

Aᵉ 3-4 (p. 269, 23-270, 2): Ordinate primum auditum praeparat, ut consequenter subieciat audienda.   2ᵇ (p. 270, 3-5): Pro Intendite et diligenter audite; quibus uerbis quam sint magna et utilia quae dicuntur ostendit. 10-15 (p. 270, 6-12): Omnes gentes, qui uniuersum habitant orbem et terregenas filiosque hominum unum genus atque idem dicit; bene autem aduersus inflationem mentis, quae prosperorum successu uenit, et terregenae mentionem fecit originis.   19-21 (p. 270, 15-18): *Diues* ne deuitiarum possitione turgescat, *pauper* nequaquam magnis bonis se esse doleat priuatum ad audiendum uocatur. 4ᵃ (p. 270, 19-22): Scite prursus praedicat quae docturus est, ut ipsa doctrinae laudatio studium suscitet auditoris.

who spoke with the grace of the Spirit, to let everyone benefit from it. Now, it is good that he does not begin with an exhortation: he first instructs them to listen and speaks about this, bringing out the significance of what would be said. Then, after an introduction required by the theme, he gives the advice at that stage. *Give ear, all inhabitants of the world,* by *Give ear* meaning "listen carefully." In his wish to bring out the completely binding character of what would be said, he urges them to listen carefully.

Both earthborn people and human beings. The phrases *all nations, all inhabitants of the world,* and *earthborn people and human beings* mean the same thing. *Earthborn people* was well put: since he intended to teach them not to glory in wealth and the good things of this life, he called them *earthborn,* as being born from the earth by the insignificance of nature. At this point, after first depressing their self-importance and speaking of *human beings,* he goes on to say *Rich and poor alike*—that is, summoning everyone alike to attention on the basis of their common humanity, not separating rich from poor on the difference in possessions. Why, then, *rich and poor?* Lest the former take pride in what they have, and the latter be disheartened by being bereft of many things.

After summoning everyone to attention in these words, he says *My mouth will speak wisdom* (v. 3): I call on you to listen, since I am about to utter things full of all wisdom and understanding. | *And the pondering of my*

4ᵇ. Καὶ ἡ μελέτη τῆς καρδίας μου σύνεσιν. Τὸ αὐτὸ λέγει, τουτέστιν ὅτι σοφίας καὶ συνέσεως γέμει τὰ λέγεσθαι μέλλοντα. Τὸ δὲ ἡ μελέτη τῆς καρδίας μου, ἵνα εἴπῃ ὅτι οὐκ ἀδοκιμάστως φθέγγομαι ἀλλὰ σὺν πολλῇ μελέτῃ καὶ δοκιμασίᾳ τῇ κατὰ τὴν καρδίαν, τὸ ὠφέλιμον αὐτῶν γνωρίσας
5 ὧν καὶ αὐτὸς ἐπεμελήθην, ὧν μέλλω λέγειν δοκιμάσας καλῶς ἔχειν καὶ ἑτέροις συμβουλεῦσαι. Καὶ ἐπειδὴ εἶπε τὸ στόμα μου λαλήσει, καὶ ἡ μελέτη τῆς καρδίας μου, ἵνα μὴ νομισθῇ οἰκεῖα φθέγγεσθαι, καλῶς ἐπάγει·

5ª. Κλινῶ εἰς παραβολὴν τὸ οὖς μου. Τουτέστιν εἰς διήγησιν, — πρότερον γάρ φησιν ὑπέθηκα τὸ οὖς καὶ ἤκουσα, — ἵνα εἴπῃ ὅτι Ταῦτα ἐδι-
10 δάχθην παρὰ τοῦ Θεοῦ. Καὶ τότε τί;

5ᵇ. Ἀνοίξω ἐν ψαλτηρίῳ τὸ πρόβλημά μου. Πρῶτον ἤκουσα καὶ τότε λέγω· διδαχθεὶς γὰρ ἑτέρους παιδεύω ἅπερ ἐδιδάχθην — πρόβλημα οὖν, τουτέστι τὸ διήγημα, τὴν διδασκαλίαν. Ἐν ψαλτηρίῳ δὲ ἀνοίξω λέγει, τουτέστι μετ᾽ ᾠδῆς τὴν παραίνεσιν ποιήσομαι, ἐπειδὴ καὶ τοῦτο ἔργον ἦν τοῦ μα-
15 καρίου Δαυὶδ τὸ μετ᾽ ᾠδῆς τάς τε νουθεσίας ποιεῖσθαι καὶ τὰς προφητείας ἐργάζεσθαι. Καλῶς δὲ τὴν διδασκαλίαν πρόβλημα ἐκάλεσεν, ἐπειδὴ ὥσπερ ἀπὸ συζητήσεως ἄρχεται τῆς παραινέσεως, καί φησιν·

6ª. Ἵνα τί φοβοῦμαι ἐν ἡμέρᾳ πονηρᾷ. Ὡς συσκοπούμενος τοῖς διδασκομένοις λέγει Ἴδωμέν φησι καὶ συνεξετάσωμεν τί ποτε ἄρα φόβου νομισ-
20 τέον ἄξιον καὶ τί προσῆκον ἐν ἡμέρᾳ φοβεῖσθαι πονηρᾷ, ἵνα εἴπῃ ἐν

8-9 cf. in Abdiam I, 1 (309 A).

1-4 *Paraphrasis* (p. 914, 22-28): Καὶ διὰ τοῦτο μελέτην αὐτὸ ἐκάλεσεν, ὡς ἂν ἕκαστος μάθοι ὅτι οὐκ αὐτοσχεδιάζει πρὸς τὴν διδασκαλίαν (*cf.* L, p. 922. 8-9), ἀλλ᾽ ἐκ πολλῆς τῆς μελέτης, καὶ ἐκ πολλῆς τῆς τῶν πραγμάτων πείρας ἐπὶ τὸ διδάσκειν προάγεται.
8-10 L (p. 922, 11-13): ... ἀντὶ τοῦ ἔκλινα κἀγὼ τὸ οὖς εἰς διήγημα, καὶ ἐδιδάχθην κἀγώ (δῆλον δὲ ὡς παρὰ τοῦ Πνεύματος); *eadem fere praebet Paraphrasis* (p. 914).
12-13 *Paraphrasis* (p. 914, 35-36): Παραβολὴν γὰρ ἐνταῦθα τὸ διήγημα λέγει.
13-14 L (p. 922, 24-26): Ἐν ψαλτηρίῳ δὲ τὸ πνευματικὸν ἐμφαίνων τῆς διδασκαλίας, καὶ ἐν ᾄσματος τάξει ποιεῖται τὴν συμβούλην ἡδύνων τὸν λόγον.   16 *Paraphrasis* (p. 914, 42-43): Πρόβλημα πάλιν αὐτὴν τὴν διδασκαλίαν καλεῖ.

Aᵉ 3-4 (p. 270, 23-25): Ac si diceret Non explorata loquar, sed quae multa meditatione collegerim.   5ª (p. 270, 26-30): Ne putaretur quasi pro aliquo commentatus ingenio, rite intulit haec quae doceret, Deo se narrante et consuetis modis inbuente, dedicisse.   13-14 (p. 270, 31-271, 3): Vt doctrinam meam carmenum suauitate permisceam, pro Loquar eam ad erudiendum alios quae primo ipse sedulus ac deuotus accipi.   6ª (p. 271, 4-9): Quasi cum ipsis, qui erudiendi sunt, diliberans proponit, ac dicit Videamus quid sit illud quod in die malo timeri debeat. Malum autem diem tempus angorum appellat, quod experituri sunt omnes nocentes.

heart understanding. He means the same thing, namely, that what is about to be said is full of wisdom and understanding. The phrase *the pondering of my heart* means, I am not speaking lightly, but after meditation and testing in my heart, conveying what is of value in those things that I personally have pondered, and that I am about to mention after deciding to keep them and offer them as advice to others. And since he had said *My mouth will speak, and the pondering of my heart,* he went on in case it was thought that he was uttering his own ideas: *I shall incline my ear to a parable*—that is, to an exposition; in other words, I first gave ear and listened, as if to say, These things were taught by God. Then what? *I shall solve my riddle with a harp:* first I listened and then I speak; after being taught, I instruct others in what I was taught (*riddle* thus meaning "exposition, teaching"). He says *I shall solve it with a harp*—that is, I shall deliver my exhortation in song, since it was also blessed David's role to deliver admonitions and produce inspired utterances in song.

Now, teaching was well expressed as a *riddle,* since he begins the exhortation with a question, asking *What shall I fear on an evil day?* (v. 5). As though examining the issue jointly with the learners, he says, Let us see and investigate what on occasion is to be thought worth fearing and what should be feared *on an evil day,* as if to say | "at a time of tribulation" (by *evil day*

καιρῷ | θλίψεως — ἡμέραν πονηρὰν καλῶν τὸν θλίψεων καιρόν, ὡς κακῶν αἴτιον τοῖς πειρωμένοις.

6ᵇ. Ἡ ἀνομία τῆς πτέρνης μου κυκλώσει με. Τῆς πτέρνης, τουτέστι τῆς ὁδοῦ, ἐπειδὴ πτέρνη τρίβομεν τὰς ὁδούς — ἵνα εἴπῃ τῆς πράξεως· ὁδὸν γὰρ πανταχοῦ καλεῖ τὴν πρᾶξιν. Ἐγὼ τοίνυν φησὶν ἐν καιρῷ κινδύνων τότε λογίζομαι φοβεῖσθαι δεῖν, ἐπειδὰν ἀνόμοις τισὶ καὶ ἀτόποις πράξε- σιν ᾧ κεκλυκωμένος. Ἔρημος μὲν γὰρ ὁ τοιοῦτος τῆς τοῦ Θεοῦ βοηθείας, ἐν κινδύνῳ δὲ ὢν καὶ διὰ τὴν προσοῦσαν ἁμαρτίαν οὐκ ἀπολαύων τῆς τοῦ Θεοῦ βοηθείας, παντὶ λόγῳ τὸν κίνδυνον ἐκδέχεται. Τοῦτο δὲ εἶπεν ὁ μα- κάριος Δαυὶδ δεικνὺς ὡς πάντων χεῖρον ἁμαρτία, καὶ τοῦτο φοβεῖσθαι χρὴ — 10 οὐκ ἐὰν χρημάτων ἡμᾶς ἐνδεεῖς εἶναι συμβαίῃ — ἐπειδὴ πλούσιος μέν τις ὢν καὶ πλήθει κατεχόμενος ἁμαρτιῶν ἐν συμφοραῖς ἐξετασθεὶς ἀπαλλαγὴν οὐχ εὑρίσκει τῶν κακῶν, ὁ δὲ πένης καὶ διὰ τῆς οἰκείας ἀρετῆς προστάτην ἑαυτοῦ τὸν Θεὸν κατασκευάσας, καὶ ἐν μέσῳ κινδύνων παραδόξως τῆς τοῦ Θεοῦ βοηθείας δέχεται τὴν ἀπόλαυσιν. Τί οὖν φησιν ἐν καιρῷ κινδύνων τοῦτο 15 μόνον φοβεῖσθαι δεῖ τῆς ἁμαρτίας τὴν πρᾶξιν;

7-9. Οἱ πεποιθότες ἐπὶ τῇ δυνάμει αὐτῶν καὶ ἐπὶ τῷ πλήθει τοῦ πλού- του αὐτῶν καυχώμενοι. Ἀδελφὸς οὐ λυτροῦται· λυτρώσεται ἄνθρωπος; οὐ δώσει τῷ Θεῷ ἐξίλασμα αὐτοῦ καὶ τὴν τιμὴν τῆς λυτρώσεως τῆς ψυχῆς αὐτοῦ. Ἐπειδὴ κἂν πάνυ τις πλούσιός τε καὶ δυνατὸς ᾖ καὶ σφόδρα μὲν 20 τῇ οἰκείᾳ πεποιθὼς δυνάμει, μεγάλα δὲ καὶ ἐπὶ τῷ πλούτῳ φρονῶν, ἐν κιν- δύνοις ἐξετασθεὶς καὶ πλήθει βαρούμενος ἁμαρτιῶν οὐδεμίαν εὑρίσκει τῶν κακῶν ἀπαλλαγήν· οὔτε γὰρ φίλους εὑρίσκει τοὺς λύτρα διδόντας ὑπὲρ αὐτοῦ καὶ ῥυομένους τῶν κατεχόντων κακῶν, οὔτε αὐτὸς χρήματα δοὺς τότε τῷ Θεῷ δυσωπήσας ἀφιστᾷ τῆς τιμωρίας, οὐδὲ γὰρ ἀργυρίῳ ἐξωνήσασθαι 25 τὴν ἑαυτοῦ ψυχὴν ὑπὸ ἁμαρτίας βεβαρημένην δύναται. Ὥστε πάντων | ἁμαρ- τία χείρων, ἐπειδὴ μηδένα ἀπαλλάττειν κινδύνων δύναται τὸν ὑπὸ ταύτης

1-2 Paraphrasis (p. 915, 5-6): Ἡμέραν πονηρὰν καλεῖ ἐν ᾗ πόνος ἡμῖν ἢ συμφορά τις ἐπισυναθροίζεται. 3-4 Paraphrasis (p. 915, 11-12): Πτέρναν τὴν ὁδὸν καλεῖ, ἀπὸ τοῦ τῇ πτέρνῃ τρίβειν τὴν ὁδόν. 15-16 L (p. 922, 37-41): Δείκνυσιν οὖν καὶ τίνα δεῖ φοβεῖσ- θαι, οὐ τὰ πολλοῖς φοβερά ... ἀλλ' ἁμαρτίαν μόνην.

Aᵉ 5-16 (p. 271, 10-19): Ac si diceret Nihil aliud periculorum tempore per- pendo esse metuendum nisi iniqua hominem et indecora gesta circumdent, quibus solis ad liberationem (diliber- *ms*) impeditur (inpenditur *ms*.) adflictorum diui- num auxilium, cum ditissimis et ob peccata corruptis opes suae subuenire non possunt; prae caeteris ergo calamitatibus non indigentia pecuniae metuenda est, sed erumna peccati. 23-26 (p. 271, 23-27): Nemo amicorum neque pecu- niae suae oblatione redemi poterit in pericula diues ob peccata deductus, qui moribus propriis, non muneribus, absoluendus est.

referring to a time of tribulation as the cause of troubles for those experiencing them). *The iniquity of my heel will encircle me. Heel* means "way,"
since we tread ways with our heel—in other words, behavior, because he
everywhere refers by "way" to behavior. So he is saying, At a time of danger
I then consider what I must fear, whenever I am caught up in lawless and
wrong actions. Such a person is in fact bereft of God's help, and being at risk
and in view of the presence of sin not enjoying God's help, on every score
incurs the risk. Blessed David said this to bring out that sin is worse than
everything; it is this that must be feared, not the possibility of being in need
of money, since a person who is rich and in the grip of a multitude of sins is
in real difficulty and does not find release from the troubles, whereas a poor
person even through his own virtue acquires God as his patron, and in the
midst of dangers wins the enjoyment of God's help, to his surprise.

So why is it that in time of danger committing sin is the only thing we
must fear? *Those who trust in their power and boast of the abundance of
their wealth. If a brother is not redeemed, will anyone be redeemed? He will
not pay God a ransom for himself, or the price of redemption of his own soul*
(vv. 6–8): even if someone is wealthy and powerful, and if he trusts fully in
his own power and even boasts of his wealth, he is in danger and weighed
down with a load of sins and finds no relief from his troubles. In fact, he
finds no friends willing to pay a ransom for him and rescuing him from the
troubles besetting him; nor can he then himself by paying money to God prevail on him to desist from punishment; nor does he succeed in redeeming his
soul, weighed down as it is with sin. And so sin is worse than anything, since
no one who is weighed down by it and is consequently the object of punish-
ment by God can be freed from danger. |

βαρούμενον καὶ τὴν παρὰ τοῦ Θεοῦ τιμωρίαν ἀναγκαίως ἐκδεχόμενον. Καὶ
ὁ μὲν ὑπὸ τῆς ἀνομίας φησὶ κεκυκλωμένος, οὕτως ὁ δὲ ἁμαρτίας καθα-
ρός. Πῶς;

10. Καὶ ἐκοπίασεν εἰς τὸν αἰῶνα, καὶ ζήσεται εἰς τέλος. Ὁ τοιοῦτος
5 κἂν πεῖραν λαμβάνῃ ποτὲ συμφορῶν, κόπου μὲν αἰσθάνεται καὶ καμάτων,
εὑρίσκει δὲ πάντων τῶν κατεχόντων ἀπαλλαγήν, καὶ πρὸς ὀλίγον καμὼν
διηνεκῶς ἀπολαύει τῶν καλῶν τῇ τοῦ Θεοῦ βοηθείᾳ ῥαδίαν εὑρίσκων τὴν
λύσιν. Τὸ οὖν εἰς τὸν αἰῶνα τοῦτο εἶπεν ἀντὶ τοῦ πρὸς καιρόν, τουτέστι
κἂν εἰς ὀλίγον αἰῶνα κοπιάσῃ καὶ πρὸς καιρὸν βραχύν, ἀλλ᾽ εἰς τέλος ζή-
10 σεται, ἀντὶ τοῦ διηνεκῶς. Σαφέστερον δὲ αὐτὸ Ἀκύλας λέγει Παυσάμενος
τῷ αἰῶνι τούτῳ, ζῶν εἰς τὸν αἰῶνα διατελέσει, τοιοῦτό τι σημάναι βουλόμενος ὅτι κἂν ἐνταῦθα κἂν ἐν τῷ παρόντι αἰῶνι δόξῃ λυπηρῶν πεῖραν λαμβάνειν, ἀλλὰ διηνεκῆ μετὰ τὴν ἐντεῦθεν ἔξοδον δέξεται τὴν εὐφροσύνην.

11ᵃ. Οὐκ ὄψεται καταφθοράν, ὅταν ἴδῃ σοφοὺς ἀποθνήσκοντας. Ἐπειδὴ
15 ὅλως περὶ τοῦ μὴ μέγα τι νομίζειν τὰ παρόντα καλὰ διαλέγεται, ἐμνημόνευσε καὶ σοφῶν, σοφοὺς ἐνταῦθα καλῶν οὐκ ἐκείνους τοὺς τὴν κατὰ Θεὸν
σύνεσιν κεκτημένους, ἀλλὰ τοὺς οἰομένους διὰ τῶν οἰκείων λογισμῶν ἅπαντα
δύνασθαι, οἷς καὶ μάλιστα συμβούλοις οἱ πλούσιοι κέχρηνται. Τοῦτο οὖν
λέγει ὅτι ὁ δίκαιος καὶ ἁμαρτίας ἀπηλλαγμένος ἐκείνους μὲν θεωρεῖ πολ-
20 λάκις ἀποθνήσκοντας, — τοὺς οἰομένους καὶ τῷ πλήθει τῶν χρημάτων καὶ τῇ
συνέσει τῶν συμβούλων ἅπαντας ὑπερφέρειν ἀνθρώπους καὶ πάντων κρατήσειν, — αὐτὸς δὲ πείσεται τῶν ἀνηκέστων οὐδέν. Καλῶς εἶπεν Οὐκ ὄψεται
καταφθοράν, ἐπειδὴ καταφθορὰ λέγεται ἡ παντελὴς διάλυσις· εἰ γὰρ καὶ
πεῖραν δέχεται πολλάκις τῶν | λυπηρῶν, ἀφ᾽ ὧν καὶ κοπιᾷ, ἀλλ᾽ οὐ παντελῆ
25 τὴν διαφθορὰν ὑπομένει καίτοι τοὺς ἄλλους ὑπομένοντας ὁρῶν. Οὕτω καὶ
Ἀκύλας φησὶν Οὐκ ὄψεται διαφθορὰν ὅταν ὄψεται σοφοὺς ἀποθνήσκοντας,
τουτέστιν Οὐδὲν οὗτος ὑπομενεῖ χαλεπόν· τοὐναντίον γὰρ τοὺς ἄλλους
ταῦτα πάσχοντας θεάσεται.

11ᵇ. Ἐπὶ τὸ αὐτὸ ἄφρων καὶ ἄνους ἀπολοῦνται. Ἔδειξεν ὅτι σοφοὺς
30 ἀποθνήσκοντας ἐκάλεσεν οὐ τοὺς ἀληθῶς συνετούς, ἀλλὰ τοὺς εἶναι οἰομένους καὶ θαρροῦντας τοῖς οἰκείοις λογισμοῖς· εἰπὼν γὰρ σοφοὺς ἐπήγαγεν
ἄφρων καὶ ἄνους, τουτέστι Πάντες οἱ ἄφρονες καὶ ἀσύνετοι κατ᾽ αὐτὸ ἀπολοῦνται, — τὸ γὰρ ἄφρων καὶ ἄνους τὸ αὐτὸ λέγει.

Aᵉ 4-10 (p. 272, 3-9) ...etiam si omnibus diebus uitae suae in praesenti cala-
mitatum experimenta persentiat, habebit quidem sensum laboris, sed liberationis
securitatem atque, ad breue tempus adflictus, uita deinceps dilectabili iugiter
perfruetur. 23-25 (p. 272, 9-12): Etsi ad tempus uexetur iustus, plenam tamen
correptionem — id est, ut penitus intereat — sentire non potaerit.

While one person, he is saying, is caught up in iniquity, the other is thus guiltless of sin. How so? *He labored forever, and will live to the end* (v. 9): even if such a person ever has experience of disasters, and feels the effect of hardship and distress, he finds relief from all that oppresses him, and though laboring for a while, he has constant enjoyment of good things by finding a simple solution with God's help. So *forever* means "at the appropriate time"—that is, even if he struggles for a brief period and a short time, yet *he will live to the end,* meaning "unceasingly." Aquila said this more clearly, "Coming to an end in this age, he will continue to live forever," meaning something like this: Even if here in the present age he seems to experience distress, yet after departure from here he will gain endless joy.

He will not see ruin when he witnesses the death of wise people (v. 10). Since he was speaking generally about not glorying in the good things of this life, he mentioned also wise people, by *wise people* here referring not to those endowed with understanding in God's terms, but to those of the opinion that they were capable of everything through their own powers of thought, to which cast of mind the rich in particular had recourse. So his meaning here is that the righteous person who is also free from sin observes the death of those others in many cases—those believing that, thanks to the abundance of their assets and their grasp of issues, they were superior to everyone and had control of everyone—but will not personally incur any such fatal weakness. *He will not see ruin* was well put, since *ruin* means "utter undoing": even if he has frequent experience of distress as a cause of suffering, he will not undergo complete annihilation, though witnessing the others being subjected to it. Aquila also says in similar terms, "He will not see annihilation when he will witness the death of the wise"—that is, He will meet with no harsh fate; he will, by contrast, observe the others suffering it. *Fool and dolt will perish together.* He made clear that by *the death of wise people* he referred not to those with true understanding, but those with belief and confidence in their own powers of thought. Having said *wise,* note, he went on to mention *fool and dolt;* in other words, All fools and idiots *will perish at the same time*—by *fool and dolt* meaning the same thing. | *They will leave behind their*

11ᶜ. Καὶ καταλείψουσιν ἀλλοτρίοις τὸν πλοῦτον αὐτῶν. Καὶ τὰ μὲν χρήματα, ἐφ᾽ οἷς μεγάλα ἐφρόνουν, κληρονομήσουσιν ἕτεροι.

12ᵃ⁻ᵇ. Καὶ οἱ τάφοι αὐτῶν οἰκίαι αὐτῶν εἰς τὸν αἰῶνα, σκηνώματα αὐτῶν εἰς γενεὰν καὶ γενεάν. Αὐτοὶ δὲ οἰκητήριον τοὺς τάφους λαχόντες διηνεκὲς ἕξουσιν αὐτὸ καταγώγιον, οὔτε ἐξιέναι οὔτε κατέχειν ἐκείνων δυνάμενοι. 5

12ᶜ. Ἐπεκαλέσαντο τὰ ὀνόματα αὐτῶν ἐπὶ τῶν γαιῶν αὐτῶν. Σύμμαχος· Ἐπονομάσαντες τὰ ὀνόματα αὐτῶν ἐπὶ τῶν γαιῶν. Ἐπειδὴ τοῖς πλουσίοις πολλάκις ἔθος τοὺς ἀγροὺς ἀπὸ τῆς οἰκείας ὀνομάζειν προσηγορίας, πολλάκις δὲ καὶ λουτρά, οὕτω δὲ καὶ τὰς οἰκίας ἀπὸ τῶν κεκτημένων καλεῖν εἰώθασιν, τοῦτο λέγει ὅτι τοσοῦτον ἀπώναντο τοῦ πλούτου ὡς τήν τε γῆν 10 καὶ τὰ ἐπ᾽ αὐτῆς ὑπὸ τοῦ Θεοῦ γεγονότα ἀπὸ τῆς οἰκείας καλεῖν προσηγορίας· οὕτω καὶ πόλεις ἀπὸ τῶν οἰκησάντων λέγονται καὶ κῶμαι καὶ πολλὰ ἕτερα ἀπὸ τῶν κεκτημένων.

13. Καὶ ἄνθρωπος ἐν τιμῇ ὢν οὐ συνῆκε, παρασυνεβλήθη τοῖς κτήνεσι τοῖς ἀνοήτοις· καὶ ὡμοιώθη αὐτοῖς. Καὶ ὅμως φησὶ τοσαύτην ἔχοντες ἐν τῷ 15 παρόντι βίῳ τὴν ἀπόλαυσιν καὶ πολλὰ μὲν ἐν τῇ φύσει παρὰ τὰ λοιπὰ ζῷα κεκτημένοι τὰ πλεονεκτήματα, πλείστων δὲ καὶ ἀπολαύοντες, οὐ συνῆκαν τῆς παρὰ τοῦ Θεοῦ τιμῆς τὸ μέγεθος, ἀλλὰ τῇ ἀ|ναισθησίᾳ τῆς τῶν προσόντων κτήσεως διαλλάττουσιν οὐδὲν τῶν κτηνῶν τῶν ἐν τῇ φύσει τὸ ἀνοηταίνειν κεκτημένων. Ὥσπερ γὰρ ἐκεῖνα συνίησιν οὐδὲν τῶν προσόντων 20 αὐτοῖς καλῶν, ἀλλ᾽ ἀδιακρίτως ἔχει τὰ προσόντα, οὕτω καὶ οὗτοι πολλῶν καὶ μεγάλων δεξάμενοι παρὰ τοῦ Θεοῦ τὴν ἀπόλαυσιν, τοῦ μὲν εὐχαριστεῖν τῷ δεδωκότι φροντίζουσιν ἔλαττον, ἀνοησίᾳ δὲ συζῶντες ἐν ἁμαρτίαις καταγηράσκουσι· διὸ καὶ δικαίαν ἐκδέχονται παρὰ τοῦ Θεοῦ τὴν ἀπόφασιν.

7-9 L (p. 925, 42 45): Ἐπεκαλέσαντο λέγων τὰ ὀνόματα αὐτῶν ἐπὶ τῶν γαιῶν, τὸ περιτιθέναι τὰς ἐπωνυμίας τοῖς οἰκοδομήσασιν, ἀγροῖς καὶ λουτροῖς. Cf. Theodoretus (1225 A 4-8) atque Paraphrasis (p. 917).   17-18 cf. Theodoretus (1225 B 3-6): Ταύτης δέ φησιν αἴτιον τῆς ἀνοίας, τὸ μὴ θελῆσαι συνιέναι ἡμᾶς τὴν οἰκείαν τιμὴν καὶ τὴν παρὰ τοῦ Θεοῦ δοθεῖσαν ἡμῖν ἀξίαν.

Aᵉ 12ᵃ⁻ᵇ (p. 272, 23-27): Hic est finis inmodica cupientium, ut pro apetitu caducorum aeternitatem perferant sepulchrorum, et has solum domus sine fine possedeant.   12ᶜ (p. 273, 2-9): Ipsorum denominantes (dominantes ms.) de nominibus suis terras ad propagationem memoriae potientiaeque suae; opulentis quibusque mos est nomina sua conditis a se ciuitatibus, uicis, domibus, agris adfigere et res a Deo creatas propriis arroganter insignare uocabulis.   17-21 (p.273, 10-17): Tam rationis ussu quam totius mundi concesso dominatu, ut Deo subditus, neque prosperitatibus elatus, referet gratias largitori ... ut obuiis (obis ms) quibusque sicut illa indeferenter utatur, et apetitu, rerum impetu, non iudicio, moueatur.

wealth to strangers: their wealth, in which they gloried, others will inherit.

Their graves are their homes forever, their dwelling places from genera-tion to generation (v. 11): with graves assigned as their dwelling, they will have the same lodgings forever, capable neither of leaving nor of holding on to them. *They bestowed their names on their lands.* Symmachus: "They gave their names to the lands." Since in many cases the rich adopt the practice of naming their country estates, and often even their baths, after themselves, and so even the houses are commonly named after the owners, he means here that they owned so much wealth as to give their own name to the land and to what was produced on it by God. In this way cities and towns are called after the residents and many other things from their owners. *Though enjoying a state of honor, the human being did not understand; he was comparable with brute beasts, and likened to them* (v. 12): despite having so much enjoy-ment in the present life, possessing many natural advantages by comparison with other living creatures and enjoying a great number of gifts, they did not understand the greatness of the honor conferred on them by God; instead, by their insensitivity to the possession of their attributes they are no different from cattle, which possess no intelligence. That is to say, just as the latter have no realization of the good things given them, and instead enjoy indis-criminately what comes their way, so too the former are given the enjoyment of many wonderful things from God, and while giving little heed to thanking the giver, they live a heedless life and grow old in their sins. Hence, they also are the objects of a rigorous verdict from God. |

14ª. Αὕτη ἡ ὁδὸς αὐτῶν σκάνδαλον αὐτοῖς. Ἀκύλας· Τοῦτο ὁδὸς ἀνοησίας αὐτοῖς, τῶν κακῶν καὶ τῆς ἀπωλείας. Τὸ γὰρ αὕτη δεικτικῶς λέγει, τουτέστιν Ἡ τοιαύτη πρᾶξις αἰτία τῶν κακῶν αὐτοῖς καθίσταται, καὶ τὸ ἀναισθήτως ἀπολαύειν τῶν τοῦ Θεοῦ καλῶν ἀναγκαίως ἐφέλκεται τοῦ Θεοῦ
5 τὴν κατ᾽ αὐτῶν τιμωρίαν. Καὶ τί φησι; Τὸ πάντων χεῖρον.

14ᵇ. Καὶ μετὰ ταῦτα ἐν τῷ στόματι αὐτῶν εὐδοκήσουσι. Σύμμαχος ἀντὶ τοῦ Καὶ μετὰ ταῦτα, Οἱ δὲ μετ᾽ αὐτοὺς λέγει σαφέστερον εἰπών· λέγει γὰρ ὅτι καὶ οἱ μετ᾽ αὐτοὺς μιμοῦνται τοὺς προτέρους, — τὸ γὰρ ἐν τῷ στόματι αὐτῶν ἀντὶ τοῦ «οἷς λέγουσι», τὸ δὲ εὐδοκήσουσιν ἀντὶ τοῦ «ἀρέσκονται».
10 Ὁ δὲ βούλεται εἰπεῖν ὅτι καὶ τῶν προτέρων πλουσίων δεχομένων τὴν παρὰ τοῦ Θεοῦ τιμωρίαν καὶ δικαίαν τὴν κόλασιν ὑπομενόντων, οὐδὲ οὕτως οἱ καθεξῆς ἄνθρωποι σωφρονίζονται· τοὐναντίον δὲ ἀρέσκονται τοῖς ὑπ᾽ αὐτῶν λεγομένοις τε καὶ πραττομένοις καὶ ζηλοῦν τὰ ἐκείνων ἐσπουδάκασιν, ὁμοίως περὶ χρήματα ἔχοντες καὶ περὶ τὰ τοῦ βίου καλά, ἔλαττον τῆς ἀρετῆς φρον-
15 τίζοντες σωφρονίζεσθαι τῇ τῶν προλαβόντων τιμωρίᾳ.

15ª. Ὡς πρόβατα ἐν ᾅδῃ ἔθεντο, θάνατος ποιμαινεῖ αὐτούς. Καίτοι φησὶν ὁρῶντες ὅτι δίκην προβάτων πολλάκις αἰφνήδιον τὸν θάνατον ὑπομένουσιν, οὐκέτι τὴν ἐκ τοῦ θανάτου προσδοκῶντες ἀπαλλαγήν· τοῦτο γὰρ λέγει θάνατος ποιμανεῖ αὐτούς, ἀντὶ τοῦ καθέξει λοιπὸν καὶ κρατήσει.

20 **15ᵇ.** Καὶ κατακυριεύσουσιν αὐτῶν οἱ εὐθεῖς τὸ πρωΐ. Πολλάκις δέ φησι καὶ δίκαιοι τῇ τοῦ Θεοῦ βοηθείᾳ πολλῶν ἐκράτησαν ἰσχυρῶν τε καὶ πλουσίων, ὀξυτάτην καὶ παρὰ πᾶσαν προσδοκίαν τὴν κατ᾽ αὐτῶν νίκην δεξάμενοι, ὥσπερ πολλάκις οἱ Ἰσραηλῖται καὶ φαίνονται κεκρατηκότες ἀλλοφύλων· ἀπὸ γὰρ τῶν γεγενημένων παιδεύει.

25 **15ᶜ.** Καὶ ἡ βοήθεια αὐτῶν παλαιωθήσεται ἐν τῷ ᾅδῃ. Καὶ πᾶσά φησιν αὐτῶν ἡ ἰσχύς, ἀφ᾽ ἧς βοηθεῖσθαι προσδοκῶσιν, ἐν τῷ ᾅδῃ παλαιοῦται, ἵνα εἴπῃ ἐν τῷ θανάτῳ, τουτέστιν ἀφανίζεται θανάτῳ παραδιδομένων ἐκείνων.

10-13 *Paraphrasis* (p. 918, 7-9): Ἀντὶ τοῦ καὶ οἱ μετὰ ταῦτα οὐδὲν ἐκ τῶν προλαβόντων ὠφελήθησαν, ἀλλ᾽ ἡδόκησαν καὶ αὐτοὶ τὰ στόματα τῶν ἀπελθόντων.　　12-13 L (p. 925, 4-5): Μακαρίζουσι γὰρ ἑαυτοὺς καὶ ἀρέσκονται τοῖς πραττομένοις.

Aᵉ **14ª** (p. 273, 17-21): Haec, inquit, omnium malorum causa est et perditionis materia, quod sine discritione aliqua bonis, quae Deus contulit, perfruuntur; et hic stupor, qui in iumentis (iuuentis *ms*) utilis est, in diuitibus elatis reus est.　　**15ª** (p. 274, 2-6): Et quidem, inquit, uidentes quoniam instar ouium … subito plerumque subdantur exitio, nec ulterius audeant sperare mortis egresum.　　**15ᶜ** (p. 274, 11-13): Omnis potentia diuitum corrumpitur, cum illi traduntur exitio.

This way of theirs was a scandal for them (v. 13). Aquila: "This was a way of foolishness for them," of troubles and ruin. He uses *This* as a demonstrative, meaning, Such behavior is responsible for their troubles, and their heedless enjoyment of God's good things inevitably brings down on them God's punishment. What is he saying? The worst possible. *And afterwards they will take delight in their mouth.* For *And afterwards* Symmachus put more clearly, "But those coming after them," meaning, Those coming after them will imitate their forebears, *in their mouth* meaning "in what they say," and *will take delight* meaning "are pleased." He means, Even when those forebears who were in receipt of riches suffer retribution and just punishment from God, people after them do not come to their senses; on the contrary, they are pleased with the words and actions of the others and hasten to imitate them, acting in similar fashion regarding wealth and the good things of this life, giving too little heed to virtue to be brought around by the punishment of their predecessors.

Like sheep they were placed in Hades; death will shepherd them (v. 14): despite seeing that in many cases they meet a sudden death like sheep, they no longer expected release from death (the meaning of *death will shepherd them*—that is, it will finally lay hold of them and control them). *The upright will dominate them in the morning:* frequently also with God's help righteous people prevailed over many powerful and rich people, winning rapid and unexpected victory over them, just as on many occasions the Israelites also proved superior to foreigners. In fact, from these events he instructs them. *And their help will deteriorate in Hades:* all their strength, on which they rely for help, *deteriorates in Hades,* as if to say "in death"—that is, it disappears when they are handed over to death. | *They were rejected from their glory:*

15ᵈ. Ἐκ τῆς δόξης αὐτῶν ἐξώσθησαν. Καὶ πάσης τῆς περικειμένης δόξης αὐτοῖς ἔξω καθίστανται· ὥστε φησὶν ἔδει τούτοις τοὺς καθεξῆς ἀνθρώπους σωφρονίζεσθαι καὶ ὁρῶντας τῶν παρόντων τὸ πρόσκαιρον, καὶ μὴ σπουδάζειν περὶ ταῦτα ὧν ἀβέβαιος ἡ κτῆσις, οὐχὶ δὲ τοὐναντίον τοὺς προλαβόντας ἐπὶ τῷ τῆς τιμωρίας αὐτοῖς κοινωνῆσαι.   5

16. Πλὴν ὁ Θεὸς λυτρώσεται τὴν ψυχήν μου ἐκ χειρὸς ᾅδου ὅταν λαμβάνῃ μου. Τὸ πλὴν πανταχοῦ ἐν τοῖς ψαλμοῖς οὐ κατά τινα κεῖται διάνοιαν, ἀλλὰ προσερριμμένως ἀπὸ ἑβραϊκοῦ ἰδιώματος, ὡς καὶ τὸ « σὺν » καὶ τὸ « ἰδοὺ » πολλαχοῦ. Τοῦτο οὖν λέγει. Οὗτοι μὲν οὖν φησι τῷ θανάτῳ παραδίδονται πάντες, — οἱ μεγάλα μὲν ἐπὶ τοῖς ἐνταῦθα φρονοῦντες, ἀρε- 10 τῆς δὲ οὐκ ἐπιμελόμενοι, — Θεὸς δὲ δυνατὸς ἕλκειν ἐκ μέσου τοῦ θανάτου κἂν ἤδη κατέχειν δοκῇ· τὸ γὰρ ἐκ χειρὸς ᾅδου τοῦτο λέγει ὅτι κἂν ἤδη κρατῇ δυνατὸν καὶ μάλα ῥᾴδιον ἐκσπάσαι τῷ Θεῷ. Ἐπειδὴ γὰρ εἶπεν ἄνω ὅτι οὐδὲν ἄξιον φοβοῦμαι ἐν μέσῳ κινδύνων ἢ τὸ ὑπὸ ἁμαρτίας κεκυκλῶσθαι, — ἐπειδὴ κἂν μυριάκις τις πλούσιος εἶναι νομίζηται, ἁμαρτίας δὲ μὴ 15 καθαρεύῃ, ἐν κινδύνοις τῶν κινδύνων οὐχ εὑρήσει τὴν ἀπαλλαγήν, εἶτα πλατύτερον εἶπεν ὅσα καὶ οἷα πάσχουσιν, — καλῶς ἐνταῦθα ἐπήγαγεν ὅτι ὁ Θεὸς δυνατὸς ῥύεσθαι τῶν κακῶν καὶ διὰ τοῦτο προσῆκεν ἀρετῆς ἐπιμελεῖσθαι καὶ σπουδάζειν ἁμαρτίας καθαρεύειν· | οὕτω γάρ ἐστιν ἐν μέσοις τοῖς κινδύνοις εὑρίσκειν τῶν κακῶν τὴν ἀπαλλαγήν.   20

17-18. Μὴ φοβοῦ ὅταν πλουτήσῃ ἄνθρωπος, καὶ ὅταν πληθυνθῇ ἡ δόξα τοῦ οἴκου αὐτοῦ, ὅτι οὐκ ἐν τῷ ἀποθνήσκειν αὐτὸν λήμψεται τὰ πάντα, οὐδὲ συγκαταβήσεται αὐτῷ ἡ δόξα αὐτοῦ. Ἐπειδὴ εἶπεν ἄνω ὅτι τοῦτο δεῖ φοβεῖσθαι τῆς ἁμαρτίας τὴν πρᾶξιν, καλῶς ἐνταῦθα ἐπήγαγε τὸ Μὴ φοβοῦ, τουτέστιν ἐκεῖνο μὲν νόμιζε φοβερόν, τοῦτο δὲ μή. Καὶ μὴ τοῦτο νόμιζε 25 θαυμαστὸν τὸ πλουτεῖν μηδὲ οἷον μέγα τι προσεῖναι τῷ πλουτοῦντι· κἂν γὰρ δόξῃ πλουτεῖν, ἀλλὰ τελευτῶν ἀφίησιν ἅπαντα καὶ τὰ χρήματα καὶ τὴν δόξαν, μηδὲν μεθ' αὑτοῦ λαμβάνειν δυνάμενος.

7 cf. p. 239, 10; 240, 12   8 cf. p. 239, 15   13-14. 23-24 cf. supra in v. 6ᵇ (p. 318).

Aᵉ 9-10 (p. 274, 13-15): Atque a gloria, quam circumpossitam habere uidebantur ... exuti sunt.   13-20 (p. 274, 16-23): Oportet ergo studium nos habere uirtutis et id tantum periculorum tempore timere (temere *ms*) debere, ne iniquitatis uinculis circumdemur, quando diuersos in adflictionibus et penitus ab inferno retentos Deus solus extrachire possit, non conpensatione diuitiarum sed consideratione uirtutum.   17-18 (p. 274, 24-33): Quod dixerat superius, peccati tantum ui⟨n⟩cula formidanda, nunc ordinate non time⟨n⟩da; id est, spernendas esse diuitias praecipit, quae sperantibus in se prodisse non poterint, protenus relinquendae, utpute alieni iuris cum dies perditionis euenerit... quia non, cum moritur (commoritur *ms*), *accipiet omnia.*

they are stripped of all the glory surrounding them, and so there is need for people after them to come to their senses on seeing the impermanence of present realities, and not be anxious about these things whose possession is insecure, and by contrast with their predecessors not share in their punishment.

But God will ransom my soul from the hand of Hades when he receives me (v. 15). Everywhere in the psalms the word *but* occurs not to convey a particular meaning, but is inserted because of the Hebrew idiom, as is also the case with the words "with" and "lo" in many places; so too here.[1] So he is saying, They are all given over to death, all who glory in the things of this life while neglecting virtue, whereas God is able to pluck one from the midst of death even if it seems already to have taken hold (the phrase *from the hand of Hades* meaning, Even if it has one in its grasp, it is possible and very easy for God to snatch one away). You see, he had said above,[2] There was no reason for me to fear in the midst of dangers or from being surrounded by sin. At the same time, even if one is thought to be rich many times over but is not free from sin, one would not find relief from danger when in danger—and then he went on to elaborate on what they suffer. So he did well here to add that God is able to rescue from troubles—hence the need to attend to virtue and take pains to be rid of sin, this being the way to find relief from troubles in the midst of dangers.

Do not be afraid when someone becomes rich, or when the glory of his house is magnified, because when he dies he will not take it all, nor will his glory go down with him (vv. 16–17). Since he had said above that one should be afraid of committing sin, he did well to proceed to say *Do not be afraid*—that is, Consider that case fearsome, not this; and do not be surprised at someone's becoming rich, or set much store by the rich person's prospering; even if they seem to be rich, at their death they will leave all the money and the glory, unable to take anything with them. | *Because his soul will be*

---

1. Cf. Theodore's comment on Ps 39:5.
2. Ps 49:5.

19ᵃ. Ὅτι ἡ ψυχὴ αὐτοῦ ἐν τῇ ζωῇ αὐτοῦ εὐλογηθήσεται. Ἀντὶ τοῦ θαυμασθήσεται, ἐπαινεθήσεται ἡ ψυχὴ αὐτοῦ — ἀντὶ τοῦ αὐτός· ἐν γὰρ τῇ παρούσῃ φησὶ ζωῇ μόνον θαυμαστὸς νενόμισται καὶ μέχρι τοσούτου τοὺς ἐκπληττομένους καὶ θαυμάζοντας καὶ θεραπεύοντας ἔχει μέχρις ἂν ζῇ.

5 19ᵇ. Ἐξομολογήσεταί σοι ὅταν ἀγαθύνῃς αὐτῷ. Ἀλλὰ μηδὲ τὴν φιλίαν μέγα τι νόμιζε τοῦ τοιούτου, μέχρι γὰρ τοσούτου τὴν πρός σε φιλίαν ἀσπάζεται καὶ χάριτας ἕξει σοι· τὸ γὰρ ἐξομολογήσεται τοῦτο λέγει ἀντὶ τοῦ εὐχαριστήσει, φίλον λογιεῖται μέχρις ἂν δώροις αὐτὸν ἐκμειλίττῃ, — τὸ γὰρ ἀγαθύνεις τοῦτο λέγει ἀντὶ τοῦ τιμᾶς καὶ δῶρα προσφέρεις, καὶ 10 ἔσται τῶν δώρων οὐχὶ σὸς φίλος, — ἐπειδὰν δὲ παύσῃ τοῦ τιμᾶν, κακεῖνος ἀφίσταται τῆς φιλίας. Τοιοῦτοι γάρ εἰσιν οἱ πολλοὶ τῶν πλουσίων, κέρδους ἕνεκεν προεστῶτες τῶν πολλῶν, ἀφ' ὧν ἂν μὴ κερδαίνωσι μεταβαλλόμενοι μισοῦσι. Καὶ καλῶς τοῦτο ἔθηκεν, ἐπειδήπερ οἱ πολλοὶ περὶ τοὺς πλουσίους ἐπτοημένοι μέγα τι καὶ τὸ ᾠκειῶσθαι τοῖς τοιούτοις νομίζουσι. 15 Μήτε οὖν τὸν πλουτοῦντα φοβερόν φησι νόμιζε, μήτε τὴν φιλίαν αὐτοῦ ἀγαθὸν κρῖνε. Εἶτα λέγει καὶ ἑτέραν αἰτίαν, δι' ἣν οὐ προσῆκε τὴν τῶν πλουσίων προστασίαν ἡγεῖσθαι μεγάλην. Τί γάρ φησι;

20. Εἰσελεύσεται ἕως γενεᾶς πατέρων αὐτοῦ, ἕως αἰῶνος οὐκ ὄψεται φῶς. Ἀνάγκη γὰρ αὐτὸν πρὸς | τοὺς ἰδίους χωρῆσαι πατέρας, ἀντὶ τοῦ ἀποθα- 20 νεῖν, ὅθεν οὐκέτι δυνατὸν ὑποστρέψαι οὔτε μὴν πάλιν ἀπολαῦσαι τῆς παρούσης ζωῆς καὶ τοῦ ἐνθάδε φωτὸς — ὥστε καὶ διὰ τοῦτο καὶ διὰ τὸ ἄπιστον τῆς φιλίας καταφρονεῖν αὐτῶν προσῆκε μᾶλλον. Εἰρηκὼς δὲ περὶ τῶν πλουσίων ἃ πάσχουσι, καλῶς ἐπήγαγε πάλιν·

21. Καὶ ἄνθρωπος ἐν τιμῇ ὢν οὐ συνῆκεν, παρασυνεβλήθη τοῖς κτήνεσιν 25 τοῖς ἀνοήτοις καὶ ὡμοιώθη αὐτοῖς. Τουτέστιν ἅπαντα μὲν τοιαῦτα πάσχουσι

8 ἐκμιλίττη ms 14 οἰκειῶσθαι ms.

5-10 L (p. 929, 43-50): Σὺ μὲν κολακεύεις καὶ θεραπεύεις ὑποκρινόμενος, ἐκεῖνος δὲ χάριτά σοι ὁμολογήσει ὠνούμενος παρά σου τὸ τὰ ἀρέσκοντα αὐτῷ ποιεῖν· τότε γὰρ εὐχαριστήσει σοί φησι (τοῦτο γὰρ τὸ ἐξομολογήσεται) οὐχ ὅταν τι χρήσιμον ἐργάσῃ, ἀλλ' ὅταν τὰ ἀρεστὰ αὐτῷ καὶ κατὰ γνώμην ὑπηρετήσῃς.

Aᵉ 19ᵃ (p. 274, 34-275, 2): In praesenti enim tantummodo admirationi erit, et eius uitae homo tamdiu laudantium sedulis blanditur officiis donec in fragili prosperitate consisterit. 5-10 (p. 275, 9-16) ...(commonuit) neque eius amicitiam magnopere consectentur, qui non officia spectet sed munera, donorum magis amicus quam hominum; tamdiu quippe *confitebitur tibi*, id est gratus existet, quandiu benefeceris, id est monusculis cum delenueris animum cupientis et auaritiam disederantis expleueris. 19-22 (p. 275, 17-22): Id est morte morietur ... in hanc demum uitam diues redire non poterit; perque hoc nec emittendus est nec expectendus est cuius est incerta potentia et fragillis amicitia.

blessed in his lifetime (v. 18): admiration and commendation will come to *his soul*—that is, to him; only in the present life is he thought admirable, and only while he is alive does he have such people to be impressed and admiring and willing to attend on him.

He will bless you when you do him favors: do not set much store by such a person's friendship, for only up to a point does he show you friendship and accept favors from you (*He will bless you* meaning, He will thank you, he will consider you a friend as long as you ply him with gifts). *You do him favors* means, You flatter him and offer him gifts, and he will be friendly to the gifts, not to you: when you stop flattering, he too brings the friendship to an end. Many rich persons are like that, you see, patronizing the general run of people for the sake of gain, and changing to hatred if there is no profit in them. He did well to cite this behavior, since the general run of people flutter about the rich and consider it a great boon to be on good terms with them. So have no fear of the rich, he is saying, nor judge their friendship worthwhile.

He then mentions a further reason why one should not set much store by the patronage of the rich. What is it? *He will go to his ancestor's generation; he will not see light forever* (v. 19): he inevitably will join his ancestors—that is, die—whence there is no returning or enjoying again the present life and the light found here. Hence, all the more reason to despise them, considering also their fickle friendship. After mentioning what the rich suffer, he did well to proceed further: *Though enjoying a state of honor, man did not understand; he was comparable to brute beasts, and likened to them* (v. 20)—in other words, they rightly suffer all such things | because they receive good

δικαίως, ἐπειδὴ τῶν παρὰ τοῦ Θεοῦ καλῶν ἀναισθήτως ἀπολαύουσιν· ἐπήγαγε γὰρ αὐτὸ πάλιν καὶ τέλος ἐποιήσατο τῶν λόγων, οὐχ ἁπλῶς ἀλλὰ τῷ συνεχῶς ὀνειδίζειν τὴν ἐπὶ τοῖς παροῦσιν ἀγαθοῖς ἀναισθησίαν, ἐντρέπων τοὺς κεκτημένους μὴ μέγα φρονεῖν ἐπὶ τοῖς παροῦσιν, εὐχαριστεῖν δὲ μᾶλλον ἐσπουδακέναι Θεῷ καὶ πάσης ἀρετῆς ἐπιμελεῖσθαι. 5

PSALMVS XLIX

Ἐνταῦθα πρὸς τοὺς Ἰουδαίους σαφέστατα φαίνεται ποιούμενος τὸν λόγον ὁ μακάριος Δαυίδ, ἐλέγχων αὐτοὺς ὡς ἀμελοῦντας μὲν τῶν νομίμων, τῆς τε ἀρετῆς τοῦ βίου καὶ τῶν λοιπῶν τοῦ Θεοῦ προσταγμάτων, μόνων δὲ τῶν θυσιῶν ἐπιμελουμένους καὶ τὸ πᾶν ἐν ταύταις τιθεμένους, ὡς ἀρκοῦν- 10 τος αὐτοῖς τοῦ ταῦτα πληροῦν κἂν τῶν λοιπῶν ἀμελήσωσιν. Ἐλέγχει δὲ ὡς καὶ τῇ τοῦ νόμου προσέχοντας ἀναγνώσει μόνῃ, ἀκροωμένους τε τῶν λόγων καὶ φέροντας αὐτὰ διὰ τοῦ στόματος, πράττοντας δὲ τῶν γεγραμμένων οὐδέν, ἀλλ' ἐναντίον τῶν τοῦ νόμου προσταγμάτων τὸν βίον ἐπιδεικνυμένους. Οὗτος μὲν οὖν αὐτῷ σκοπὸς ἐν τῷ παρόντι ψαλμῷ. Φοβερώ- 15 τερον δὲ αὐτὸ κατασκευάσαι βουλόμενος σχηματοποιεῖ τὸ πᾶν, κριτήριόν τε καθίζων καὶ δικαιολογίαν εἰσάγων τοῦ Θεοῦ ἐλεγκτικὴν τῶν πραγμάτων καὶ τὸ πᾶν συντιθεὶς ὡς ἐνῆν φοβερώτερον | ἐργάσασθαι τὸν λόγον. Ἐν μὲν γὰρ τῷ πρὸ τούτου ψαλμῷ πρὸς πάντας ἀνθρώπους λογοποιούμενος ἐκ τῶν κοινῶν λογισμῶν μᾶλλον ἐποιεῖτο τῆς ἀτοπίας τὸν ἔλεγχον, ἐνταῦθα 20 δὲ πρὸς Ἰουδαίους διαλεγόμενος εἰκότως τὸ πᾶν ἀπὸ τῶν τοῦ Θεοῦ ῥημάτων σωφρονίζειν αὐτοὺς καὶ καταπλήττειν πειρᾶται.

Argumentum brevius praebent Cord. I, 963 (P. G., LXVI. 672) atque Barbaro (sub nomine THEODORETI): Καὶ οὗτος ἠθικὸς ὁ ψαλμός, ἀλλ' οὐκέτι πρὸς ἅπαντας ἀνθρώπους, πρὸς Ἰουδαίους δὲ μόνον, ὡσανεὶ ἀμελοῦντας μὲν ἀρετῆς, τὸ δὲ πᾶν τιθεμένους ἐν ταῖς θυσίαις τοῦ νόμου, ἕως τοῦ εἰδέναι τὰ ῥήματα μόνον ἐπιμελουμένους, οὐκέτι δὲ καὶ τὰ προστάγματα φυλάττειν. Καὶ φοβερότερον αὐτοῖς κατασκευάζων τὸν λόγον, σχηματοποιεῖ κριτὴν δικάζοντα καὶ τοὺς ἐλεγχομένους. Cf. L (p. 947-948).

Aᵉ 1-5 (p. 275, 22-26): Iterauit enim hanc sententiam et non de nihilo finem fecit, ut sepe insensibilitatem istam ingratae mentis agitaret. *Argumentum ps. XLIX* (p. 275, 27-276, 7): In priore psalmo ad homines omnes sermonem direxit, sed de his cogitationibus, quae quasi commones uiderentur, openionem quae esset inprobanda conuincit. In praesenti psalmo uero ad Iudeos loquens consequenter nimirum quasi ex Dei uerbis omnem orationem texuit, consternare uolens et emendare peccantes, qui uirtutem neglegentes solas curant hostias legalium, iusionum dicta tenus aure suscipeant et e rigione sanctionibus ligis contraria quaeque sectentur, hoc totum sequetur terrebiliore sugestu, uidilicet quasi tribunale iudicium discriptione confirmans, ut sit tota conpellatio Dei terroribus plena.

things from God without appreciating them. It was not without purpose, you see, that he went on to say the same thing and put an end to his treatment: it was to level his usual taunts at the lack of appreciation of the good things of this life, urging those possessing them not to glory in the present life, but rather to take pains to thank God and be concerned for every virtue.

PSALM 50

Here blessed David emerges as directing his words in the clearest manner to the Jews, charging them, on the one hand, with neglecting lawful observances, a virtuous life, and the other commands of God, and on the other hand with attending to sacrifices and devoting themselves entirely to them, as though it were sufficient for them to discharge these while neglecting the rest. He charges them also with giving heed only to the reading of the law, giving ear to the words and repeating them on their lips but doing nothing of what is written, instead giving evidence of a life at variance with the commandments of the law. While this, then, is his purpose in the present psalm, in his wish to make it more frightening he dramatizes it all, setting up a courtroom and introducing God's prosecution with accusations of the crimes, and arranging it all to make his words as intimidating as possible. In the psalm before this, remember, he had addressed all people in delivering an accusation of wrongdoing in rather general terms, whereas here he rightly speaks exclusively to Jews, and in God's words he tries to bring them to their senses and make an impression on them. |

1ᵃ. Θεὸς θεῶν Κύριος ἐλάλησε καὶ ἐκάλεσεν τὴν γῆν. Ὡς ἐπὶ βασιλέως μέλλοντος δικάζειν καὶ πολλοὺς συγκαλοῦντος εἰς τὴν τῆς δίκης ἀκρόασιν ἐφθέγξατό φησιν ὁ Θεός, πᾶσαν συγκαλῶν τὴν γῆν. Τὸ γὰρ ἐλάλησε
καὶ ἐκάλεσεν οὐχ ἕτερον καὶ ἕτερον λέγει, ἀλλ᾽ ἀντὶ τοῦ Ἐλάλησε καλῶν
5 τὴν γῆν. Θεοὺς δὲ καλεῖ τοὺς Ἰουδαίους ἐνταῦθα οὐχ ἁπλῶς, ἀλλ᾽ ἁμαρτάνοντας μέλλων ἐλέγχειν ἑξῆς, εἰκότως ἐπαίρει τῇ προσηγορίᾳ τὴν δοθεῖσαν αὐτοῖς παρὰ τοῦ Θεοῦ τιμήν, δεικνὺς ὥστε μειζόνως ἀγνωμονοῦντας
ἐλέγξαι.

1ᵇ. Ἀπὸ ἀνατολῶν ἡλίου καὶ μέχρι δυσμῶν. Ἵνα εἴπῃ τὴν σύμπασαν,
10 βαρύτερον Ἰουδαίοις κατασκευάζων τὸν ἔλεγχον, ὡς τοῦ Θεοῦ κρίνοντος
αὐτοὺς ἐπὶ πάντων τῶν ἐθνῶν· τοῦτο γὰρ ἦν βαρύτερον τὸ τῶν ἐναντίων
παρόντων ἁμαρτάνοντας καὶ ἀγνωμονοῦντας περὶ τὸν εὐεργέτην ἐλέγχεσθαι.

2. Ἐκ Σιὼν ἡ εὐπρέπεια τῆς ὡραιότητος αὐτοῦ. Τὸ ἐκ Σιών, τουτέστι
15 πρὸς τὸ ἐλάλησεν, ἐκεῖθεν ἐφθέγξατο, ὅπου ἡ εὐπρέπεια τῆς ὡραιότητος
αὐτοῦ, καλῶς — ἐπειδὴ πρὸς Ἰουδαίους διελέγετο, παρ᾽ οἷς ὑπελαμβάνετο
ὁ Θεὸς ἐν τῷ Σιὼν ὄρει οἰκεῖν τε καὶ διάγειν — εὐπρέπειαν ὡραιότητος
λέγων τὸ ὑπερβάλλον κάλλος, τὴν ὑπερβάλλουσαν δόξαν, τὴν ὑπερβάλλουσαν τιμήν, τουτέστιν Ἐκεῖθεν ἐφθέγξατο καὶ νῦν ἔνθα περίβλεπτος
20 ἀεὶ διὰ τῶν θαυμάτων γνωρίζεται. Οὕτω καὶ Ἀκύλας Ἐκ Σιὼν τετελεσ-
μένης κάλλει ὁ Θεὸς ἐπέφανη, τουτέστιν ἐκεῖθεν ἐφάνη, ἐκεῖθεν ἐφθέγξατο.

3ᵃ. Ὁ Θεὸς ἡμῶν ἐμφανῶς ἥξει, ὁ Θεὸς ἡμῶν, καὶ οὐ παρασιωπήσεται.
Ἐμφανῶς, ἵνα εἴπῃ Οὐχ ἁπλῶς | τὴν οἰκείαν παρουσίαν ποιήσεται, ἀλλὰ
μετὰ πολλῆς τῆς περιβολῆς καὶ τοῦ φόβου, ὥστε μηδὲ λαθεῖν τινα τὰ
25 λεγόμενα. Τὸ δὲ καὶ οὐ παρασιωπήσεται, ἀντὶ τοῦ Οὐ γὰρ ἀνέξεται τῶν
γινομένων ἐπὶ πολύ.

15 v. 1ᵃ.

Aᵉ 1-3 (p. 276, 8-11): Quasi regis ad iudicium procedentis (procid — *ms*) plu-
rimosque ad audientiam sui examinis conuocantis, Dei persona terram euocan-
tis inducitur (cf. PSEUDO-BEDA 739). 1ᵇ (p. 276, 12-18): Vt indicaret uniuersam
terram... ut grauiorem faceret occassionem Iudeorum, si coram inimicis ingratorum peccata puniret. 15-20 (p. 276, 19-25): Inde pronuntiauit... ubi erat
decor pulchritudinis, id est Sion; et hoc propter Iudeos, qui opinabantur ibi
tantum habitare Deum, quia illic erat miraculorum adsiduitate sepe conspicus.
23-24 (p. 276, 26-27): Cum magno ambitu magnoque terrore, ita ut quae geruntur nullus ignoret.

The Lord God of gods spoke and summoned the earth (v. 1). Like a king about to give judgment and summoning a great number to a hearing of the ruling, God spoke, he says, summoning the whole earth (*spoke* and *summoned* not implying different things, but meaning, He spoke to summon the earth). Now, in this place he calls the Jews *gods* not without purpose: intending to go on and charge them with sinning, he is right to highlight with this title the dignity given them by God so as to charge them with greater ingratitude. *From the rising of the sun to its setting,* as if to say, the totality, leveling a heavier accusation against Jews, as though God were judging them before all the nations: charging them as sinful and ungrateful to their benefactor was more serious when done in the presence of the adversaries. *Out of Sion the comeliness of his charm* (v. 2). The phrase *Out of Sion* goes with *He spoke,* meaning, He gave voice from there where *the comeliness of his charm is visible*—a nice touch, since he was speaking to Jews, by whom God was thought to dwell and live on Mount Sion. So by *comeliness of his charm* he refers to his surpassing beauty, his surpassing glory, his surpassing dignity—in short, He spoke from there where even today he is known as ever famous for his marvels. Aquila also in similar terms: "From Sion perfect in beauty God appeared"—that is, he appeared there, he spoke there.

God will come in an obvious manner, our God, and he will not keep silence (v. 3). In an obvious manner, as if to say, He will make himself present not casually, but with much pomp and fear, his words not failing to escape comment. The phrase *and he will not keep silence* means, He will not contain himself for long regarding what has happened. | *A fire will burn*

3^{b.c}. Πῦρ ἐνώπιον αὐτοῦ καυθήσεται, καὶ κυκλῷ αὐτοῦ καταιγὶς σφόδρα. Ἐπειδὴ τῶν βασιλέων ἔθος προηγεῖσθαι τοὺς ὁπλομάχους δόρατά τε ἐπιφερομένους καὶ τόξα, δι᾽ ὧν γνωρίζουσι τὸν βασιλέα τοῖς κατὰ τῶν ἐναντίων πολέμοις ἐναβρυνόμενον, διὰ τοῦτο καὶ ὁ μακάριος Δαυὶδ φησιν ἐπὶ τοῦ Θεοῦ ὅτι προηγούμενον ἔχει πῦρ καὶ περὶ αὐτὸν καταιγίδα σφοδροτάτην, ἵνα εἴπῃ Τὴν κόλασιν καὶ τὴν τιμωρίαν ἐπάγεται, ᾗ τοὺς ἁμαρτάνοντας παιδεύει. 5

4. Προσκαλέσεται τὸν οὐρανὸν ἄνω καὶ τὴν γῆν, διακρῖναι τὸν λαὸν αὐτοῦ. Ἐπειδὴ εἶπεν ὅτι ἐκ Σιὼν φανήσεται, ἵνα μηδὲν μικροπρεπὲς περὶ τοῦ Θεοῦ νοῶσιν, ἄνω φησὶ καλεῖ τὸν οὐρανόν, ὥστε δεῖξαι τὸν Θεὸν 10 πολὺ καὶ τοῦ οὐρανοῦ ἀνώτερον ὄντα. Καλεῖ δέ φησι τὸν οὐρανὸν καὶ τὴν γῆν, ἀντὶ τοῦ τὰς οὐρανίους δυνάμεις καὶ τοὺς ἐπὶ τῆς γῆς οἰκοῦντας ἀνθρώπους — ἵνα εἴπῃ τὰ σύμπαντα καλεῖ ἐπὶ τὴν τοῦ κριτηρίου ἀκρόασιν — ὥστε ἐπὶ πάντων ἐλέγξαι σφαλλομένους· τὸ γὰρ ὅλον, ὡς ἔφην, σχηματοποιεῖ τὴν ἐξέτασιν καὶ τὸν ἔλεγχον. 15

5^a. Συναγάγετε αὐτῷ τοὺς ὁσίους αὐτοῦ. Ὡς καθεσθέντος λοιπὸν τοῦ Θεοῦ καὶ παραγενομένων μὲν τῶν ὀφειλόντων παρεῖναι τῇ ἐξετάσει, ἑτοίμων δὲ ὄντων καὶ τῶν κολαστηρίων, καλῶς εἶπε τὸ Συναγάγετε, τουτέστιν Ἀγάγετε λοιπὸν τοὺς κρινομένους, ἕτοιμος γὰρ ὁ δικαστὴς ἐξετάζειν καὶ τὸ κριτήριον εὐτρεπές. Τοὺς δὲ ὁσίους εἶπεν ἐκ τῆς γνώσεως ἐπαίρων 20 αὐτοὺς πρὸ τῶν ἐλέγχων, ὥστε βαρύτερον δεῖξαι τὸ πταῖσμα, διδάσκων δὲ ἐπὶ τίνι καὶ συνάγονται οἱ κρίνεσθαι μέλλοντες. Καὶ ὥσπερ ὁριζόμενος τὸ ἔγκλημά φησί·

9-15 cf. supra p. 113-114, in ps. XVII, 9-12   20 cf. supra p. 142, 15-17; 166, 15-16.

5-6 *Paraphrasis* (p. 949, 19-20) : ...πῦρ ἔχει προηγούμενον καὶ καταιγίδα σφοδρὰν εἰς φόβον τῶν μελλόντων κρίνεσθαι.   12-13 L (p. 957, 3-4) ...ἐσήμανε τοὺς ἐν αὐτῇ οἰκοῦντας ἀνθρώπους.

A^e 3^{b.c} (p. 276, 30-277, 1): Quoniam regum mos est, ut eos praecedent armigeri stipentque armati procedentes (procid — ms) ad bella, beatus Dauid ignem et tempestatem diuino adscribit comitatui, ut praecedat ignis, terror, et circa eum sonet effecax ultio.   4 (p. 277, 2-8): Tamquam superior eminentiorque caelum ad se uocat, ne esset humile si tantum de Sion crederetur locutus Deus. *Caelum* autem *et terram* ponit pro his qui habitant in eis; tota plane discriptio pompam examinis et condemnationis extollit.   5^a (p. 227, 8-16): Praeparato sugestu, aduocatis iudicii testibus iam quasi adstantibus, imperatur ut audiendi praestentur (praestententur ms) rei. *Iustos* autem pro honore religionis sic appellat Iudeos, quomodo in principio hos eosdem d e o s, ne ante creminum manifestationem iniuriosa damnatione praeiudicasse uideatur, ut sit postea quo grauior peccatorum conuictio.

in his presence, with a severe storm around him. Since it is the custom of kings to be preceded by warriors bearing spears and bows, whose role it is to present the king as proud of the wars against the adversaries, for this reason blessed David also says in God's case that he has fire preceding him and *a very severe storm around him,* as if to say, He inflicts punishment and retribution, by which he chastises sinners.

He will summon heaven above and the earth to judge his people (v. 4). Since he had said that he will appear from Sion, to avoid their forming any unseemly notion of God, he says *He will summon heaven above* so as to present God as far above even heaven. *He will summon heaven and earth,* he says—that is, the heavenly powers and human beings dwelling on earth, as if to call all things to a hearing of his verdict, so as to accuse them of their failings in the presence of all. The whole scene, in fact, depicts in figurative fashion the examination and the accusation.

Assemble for him his holy ones (v. 5). As God has taken his seat and those due to attend the examination have arrived, and the prison is ready, he was right to say *Assemble*—that is, Bring in the accused at this point, for the judge is ready to examine, and the court is prepared. He said *holy ones* because of the inquiry, lifting them up before the charges so as to bring out the greater seriousness of the fall, conveying the purpose for which those due to be judged are assembling. And as if to detail the charge, he says | *Who*

5ᵇ. Τοὺς διατιθεμένους τὴν διαθήκην αὐτοῦ ἐπὶ θυσίαις. Τοὺς οὕτω διακειμένους ὡς ὅτι τὸ πᾶν τοῦ Θεοῦ τῆς νομοθεσίας ἐν ταῖς θυσίαις περιώρισται, — ὅπερ ἐστὶν ὕβρις οὐ μικρὰ τοῦ Θεοῦ, εἴπερ καταλιπὼν | τὸ τῆς ἀρετῆς ἐπιμελεῖσθαι, μόνον ταῖς θυσίαις αὐτοὺς προσέχειν κατηνάγκαζεν.

5   6ᵃ. Καὶ ἀναγγελοῦσιν οἱ οὐρανοὶ τὴν δικαιοσύνην αὐτοῦ. Ὅτι γὰρ ταῦτά φησιν οὐ δικαίως νομίζουσιν, οὔτε μὴν δίκαια πράττουσι γνώσονται οἱ οὐρανοί, τουτέστιν οἱ παρόντες, οἳ ἀπὸ τῶν κρινομένων παρὰ τῷ Θεῷ τὸ δίκαιον εὑρήσουσιν, ὥστε μετὰ τὴν ἐξέτασιν καὶ θαυμάζειν τοῦ Θεοῦ τὸ δίκαιον.

10   6ᵇ. Ὅτι ὁ Θεὸς κριτής ἐστιν. Ἀντὶ τοῦ Καὶ τοῦτο ἐροῦσιν ὅτι ἀληθὴς καὶ δίκαιος κριτής ἐστιν ὁ Θεός. Τὸ γὰρ κριτὴς ἀντὶ τοῦ δίκαιος κριτὴς λέγει, ὥσπερ καὶ ἡμεῖς πολλάκις εἰώθαμεν λέγειν « Ἰδοὺ δικαστὴς » περὶ τῶν ἀκριβῶς καὶ ὀρθῶς δικαζόντων.

7ᵃ. Ἄκουσον, λαός μου, καὶ λαλήσω σοι. Ὡς τοῦ κριτηρίου λοιπὸν
15 συγκεκροτημένου καὶ παρόντων τῶν ἀκουόντων, παρόντων δὲ καὶ τῶν κρινομένων, ἀρχόμενον τῆς πρὸς αὐτοὺς δικαιολογίας εἰσάγει τὸν Θεόν. Ἄκουσόν μού φησι καὶ φθέγξομαι, καλῶς τὸ Ἄκουσον πρῶτον ὡς πρὸς ἀπειθοῦντας ἤτοι καὶ ὡς πρὸς ἀπόδειξιν τοῦ φιλανθρώπως κρίνειν τὸν Θεόν, οὐκ ἀπὸ καταπλήξεως ἀρχόμενον ἀλλ᾽ ἀπὸ παραινέσεως.

20   7ᵇ. Ἰσραήλ, καὶ διαμαρτυροῦμαί σου. Πρός σε γάρ μοί φησιν ὁ λόγος. Καλῶς δὲ τὸ διαμαρτυροῦμαι, ὡς παρόντων τῶν ἀκουόντων καὶ μαρτυρεῖν τῇ ἀπειθείᾳ δυναμένων.

1-3 L (p. 957, 33-34): ... τοὺς διατιθεμένους, ἀντὶ τοῦ τοὺς νομίζοντας τὸ πᾶν τῆς διαθήκης τοῦ Θεοῦ εἶναι ἐν ταῖς θυσίαις. Eadem praefert Paraphrasis (p. 949, lin. 3-1 ab imo).

Aᵉ 5ᵇ (p. 277, 17-23): Qui opinantur omnem obseruantiam legis in hostiarum oblatione consistere; prima causa qua congregari debent iudicandi, quia putauerunt in contumiliam Dei quod neglectu uirtutis et honestatis sacrificiis eos tantum seruire conpullerit.   6ᵃ (p. 227, 25-31): Caeli... Iudeorum openionem iniustissimam cognoscent et in tales Dei sententiam equissimam mirabuntur; *iustitiam eius*, qui ... neque talem openionem relinquerit impunitam. 11 (p. 277, 24-25): Pro iusto iudice.   7ᵃ (p. 277, 32-278, 7): Quasi auditorio iam per cuncta dispossito et adstantibus qui ad audiendum uocati sunt, praesentibusque iudicandis (iudicandicandis *ms*), consequenter iam descutiens inducitur Deus; et bene *Audi* primum possuit ad eos qui inobidentes fuerint; uel certe, ad ostendendum quanta sit in iudicio Dei tranquilitas, inducit eum non a terrore sed a monitis inchoantem.   7ᵇ (p. 278, 8-12): Ad te mihi, inquit, sermo est... Bene autem possuit *testificabor*, quasi praesentibus auditoribus, qui testimonium possent ferre contra infidilitatem reorum.

made covenant with him by sacrifice: the covenant they made was to the effect that all God's legislation was confined to sacrifices, which would be no slight insult to God if he were to make no mention of attention to virtue and oblige them only to attend to sacrifices. *The heavens will announce his righteousness* (v. 6): the heavens—that is, those present—will know that their views on this are not right and their actions are not right, and they will find righteousness done in the case of those judged by God, thus admiring God's righteousness after the examination. *Because God is judge*—that is, This is what they will say, God is a true and just judge (by *judge* meaning "a just judge," as we also are often in the habit of saying, "See, a judge," of those who judge properly and uprightly).

Listen, my people, and I shall speak to you (v. 7). With the court assembled, the audience present, and the accused also in attendance, he presents God beginning his verdict on them. Listen and I shall speak, he says (nicely putting *Listen* first as though to disobedient people or by way of proof of God's judging lovingly, opening not with intimidation but with exhortation). *Israel, and I shall testify against you:* my speech is directed at you. The phrase *I shall testify* was well put, as though the listeners were present and in a position to testify to their disobedience. | *I am God your God:* your

7ᶜ. Ὁ Θεὸς ὁ Θεός σού εἰμι ἐγώ. Ὁ ποιήσας, ὁ πολλάκις εὐεργετήσας, ὁ τὸν νόμον δεδωκὼς ἐγὼ καὶ οὐχ ἕτερος. Τί τοίνυν ὃ λέγω;

8ᵃ. Οὐκ ἐπὶ ταῖς θυσίαις σου ἐλέγξω σε. Ὅτι μηδείς μοι λόγος πρός σε περὶ τῶν θυσιῶν· ἔλαττον γάρ μοι μέλει τούτου, κἂν μὴ πληροῦται, ὥστε μηδὲ παραλιμπάνοντας ἐλέγχειν.   5

8ᵇ. Τὰ δὲ ὁλοκαυτώμ.κτά σου ἐνώπιόν μού ἐστι διὰ παντός. Καὶ γὰρ ὁρῶ σε αὐτάρκως μοι θυσίας προσάγοντα, ὥστε τούτου γε ἕνεκεν οὐδ᾽ ἂν ἐδεήθην λόγου. Τί οὖν ἐστιν ὃ φημι;

9. Οὐ δέξομαι ἐκ τοῦ οἴκου σου μόσχους, οὐδὲ ἐκ τῶν ποιμνίων σου τράγους. Ὅτι οὐδὲ προσίεμαι ταῦτα διδόμενα, εἴτε καὶ μόσχον, εἴτε κα   10 τράγον προσφέροις. | Ἔν τισι δὲ τῶν ἀντιγράφων ἀντὶ τοῦ τράγους χιμά-ρους κεῖται, ἵνα εἴπῃ τοὺς χειμερίους, τοὺς ἐνιαυσιαίους, ἃ χειμῶνος ἑνὸς ἐν πείρᾳ γέγονε. Καὶ διὰ τί ταῦτα οὐ δέχομαι;

10-11. Ἐμὰ γάρ ἐστι παντὰ τὰ θηρία τοῦ δρυμοῦ, κτήνη ἐν τοῖς ὄρεσι καὶ βόες· ἔγνωκα πάντα τὰ πετεινὰ τοῦ οὐρανοῦ, καὶ ὡραιότης ἀγροῦ μετ᾽   15 ἐμοῦ ἐστιν. Σὺ μὲν γὰρ ὀλίγα μοι προσάγεις, ἅπαντα δέ ἐστιν ἐμά, εἴτε τὰ ἐν τοῖς ὄρεσι θηρία εἴτε τὰ κτήνη, τά τε ἄγρια καὶ τὰ ἥμερα, ἀλλὰ καὶ τὰ πετεινὰ τοῦ οὐρανοῦ, — τὸ γὰρ ἔγνωκα ἀντὶ τοῦ ὑπ᾽ ἐμέ ἐστιν, ὑπὸ τὴν γνῶσιν τὴν ἐμήν, — εἰ δὲ καί τι οἱ ἀγροὶ καλὸν ἔχουσι ταῦτα μετ᾽ ἐμοῦ ἐστιν, ἀντὶ τοῦ ἐμά, οὐδέν ἐστιν ἀλλότριον ἐμοῦ οὐδὲ κεχωρισμένον τῶν ἐν   20 τῇ κτίσει. Τί οὖν μοι προσάγεις τὰ ἐμά; Καὶ ἐπειδὴ παρὰ τοῖς ἀνθρώποις οἱ μὲν προσάγουσιν ὡς χαριζόμενοι, οἱ δὲ θύουσι χρείας ἕνεκεν τὰ αὐτῶν ἐκείνων ὥσπερ οἱ μάγειροι καταθύουσι τῶν δεσποτῶν ἕνεκεν, ἀνεῖλε δὲ τὸ πρῶτον ὅτι οὐ χρεία ταῦτα προσάγεσθαι, πάντα γὰρ ἐμὰ ἀναιρῶν, τὸ δεύ-τερόν φησιν.   25

4 μέλλει ms   21 κτήσει ms.
4-5 Paraphrasis (p. 950, 33-34): Τοῦτό φησιν γίνωσκε ὅτι οὐ πολὺν ποιοῦμαι λόγον τῶν θυσιῶν, οὐδὲ ἀμελουμένων τούτων.   17-21 Paraphrasis (p. 951, 13-16, 24-26): Ἄνω εἰπὼν τὰ θηρία, ἐνταῦθα εἶπεν κτήν. · βούλεται γὰρ εἰπεῖν ὅτι πάντα τὰ ἄγρια καὶ τὰ ἥμερα τῆς ἐμῆς ἐστι δεσποτείας καὶ ἐργασίας... Τὸ γὰρ ἔγνωκα κέκτημαι λέγει, ἀπὸ τοῦ τοὺς κεκτημένους γνῶσιν ἔχειν ὧν κέκτηνται.

Aᵉ 7ᶜ (p. 278, 12-14): Creator, adiutor, legislator ego sum, inquam, non alius.   8ᵃ (p. 278, 15-17): Non intermisione hostiarum offerendarum reus es: parua mihi quippe harum cura est, etiam si minime conplentur.   8ᵇ (p. 278, 18-21): Redundant in hac parte tuae deuotionis obsequia, tantum abest ut pro neglecto huiusmodi officio argueris (arguris ms).   16-17 (p. 278, 24-25): Tu enim mihi modica quaeque offerens, uniuersa autem iumenta mea sunt. 18-19 (p. 278, 26-28): Pro eo ut diceret Sub meo iure notitiaque consistunt.

maker, your frequent benefactor; I it was who gave you the law, no one else. So what have I to say? *It is not on the score of your sacrifices that I shall censure you* (v. 8): because there was no word of mine against you about sacrifices, it being my least concern to charge you with their neglect, even if not performed. *Your holocausts are ever before me:* I see you offering enough sacrifices to me, so that no word would be needed on that score.

So what is it I am saying? I shall not accept young bulls from your house, or goats from your flock (v. 9): I do not accept these gifts, whether it is a calf or a goat that you offer. Now, in some manuscripts "he-goats" appears in place of *goats,* in the sense of winter ones, yearlings that have experienced a single winter.[1] Why do I not accept them? *Because all the wild beasts of the wood are mine, cattle on mountains and oxen. I know all the birds in the sky, and the charm in the countryside is with me* (vv. 10–11): while you offer me little, everything is mine, wild beasts on the mountains or cattle wild and tame, birds in the sky, for I know them—that is, they are subject to me, subject to my knowledge. If the fields contain good things, they are from me—that is, they are mine: there is nothing outside my ken or removed from my creative power. So why offer me things that are mine?

Since with human beings, some offer things as though conferring a favor, and others sacrifice their own things to meet a need, like cooks killing for their masters, he abolished the first because there was no need for them to be offered, abolishing *all that is mine,* and refers to the second, | *If I were*

---

1. In place of the form τράγους, for "goats," which Theodore finds in his text, he is aware of an alternative form χιμάρους (occurring, in fact, in Diodore's and Chrysostom's text), which he ventures to relate to χεῖμα, by way of accounting for the variant. See further in the volume introduction.

12ᵃ. Ἐὰν πεινάσω, οὐ μή σοι εἴπω.ʳ Καλῶς τὸ ἐὰν πεινάσω, ἐπεὶ δῆλον ὡς οὐ πεινῇ Θεός. Κατὰ εἰρωνείαν γὰρ διδοὺς τὸ μὴ ἐγχωροῦν, ἐντρέπει μειζόνως· οὐδὲ γὰρ ἐὰν πεινάσω φησί σου χρήζω.

12ᵇ. Ἐμὴ γάρ ἐστιν ἡ οἰκουμένη καὶ τὸ πλήρωμα αὐτῆς. Τί γὰρ σμικρο-
5 λόγως τοῦδε καὶ τοῦδε μέμνημαι; Ἅπαντα ἁπλῶς ἐμά, ἐπειδὴ καὶ ὑπ᾽
ἐμοῦ γεγένηται. Καὶ ὥστε μὴ δόξαι τὴν εἰρωνείαν ἀληθῆ, — ἀσθενεστέροις
γὰρ οὖσιν Ἰουδαίοις ἐν τῇ περὶ τὸν Θεὸν γνώσει διελέγετο ὁ προφήτης, —
ἐπάγει·

13. Μὴ φάγομαι κρέα ταύρων, ἢ αἷμα τράγων πίομαι; Ἀλλὰ μὴν ταῦτα
10 ἐσθίω, καὶ ἐκ τούτων συνέστηκα, καὶ χαρίζῃ μοι προσκομίζων τροφήν;
Οὐ δῆτα. Ὥστε τούτων ἀπόστηθι· οὔτε γὰρ ὑπὸ ἐνδείας, οὔτε ὑπὸ χρείας
συνελαυνόμενος ζητῶ ἵνα ἢ πεινῶν παραμυθήσωμαι τὸ πάθος, ἢ οὐκ ἔχων
κτήσωμαι τὰ μὴ προσόντα. Τί δὲ ἃ ἐπιζητῶ;

14ᵃ. Θῦσον τῷ Θεῷ θυσίαν αἰνέσεως. Ἀκύλας· Θῦσον τῷ Θεῷ θυσίαν
15 εὐχαριστίας. Ταύτην μοι προσάγαγε τὴν θυσίαν τὴν τοῦ ὕμνου, | ἀντὶ τοῦ
Σαυτόν μοι θῦμα προσάγαγε, εὐχαρίστως μοι ζῆν ἐσπουδακὼς καὶ ὅλον
μοι σαυτὸν ἀνατιθείς.

14ᵇ. Καὶ ἀπόδος τῷ ὑψίστῳ τὰς εὐχάς σου. Ἀντὶ τοῦ Ἐμοὶ εὔχου πάντοτε περὶ πάντων, τοῦτό μοι ἀποδίδου καὶ ταῦτα πλήρου. Τὸ δὲ εὔχου
20 μοι περὶ πάντων, ἵνα εἴπῃ Ἐμὲ ἡγοῦ πάντων σοι τῶν ἀγαθῶν αἴτιον, καὶ
παρ᾽ ἐμοῦ πᾶν ὅτι ποτὲ καλὸν ἐκδέχου. Οὐδὲ γάρ ἐστιν εὔχεσθαι μὴ τοῦτο
πεπεισμένον.

15. Καὶ ἐπικάλεσαί με ἐν ἡμέρᾳ θλίψεως, καὶ ἐξελοῦμαί σε, καὶ δοξάσεις με. Οὐδὲ γὰρ εἰς κενόν σοι τὸ τῆς ὑπονοίας ἀποβήσεται, ἐπείπερ
25 οὕτως οἰόμενος κἂν ἐν μέσαις καλῆς ταῖς θλίψεσιν εἰσακουσθήσῃ καὶ τεύξῃ

12. 13 παραμυθήσομαι... κτήσομαι ms.
2 *Paraphrasis* (p. 951, 34): Τὸ μὴ ἐγχωροῦν εἶπεν.

Aᵉ 2-3 (p. 278, 33-35): ...Etiam si, inquit, esuriero — quod fieri non potest —
tuis tamen muneribus non egeo.   13 (p. 279, 1-9): Numquid istis utor ut do
uobis, uel tali condicione consisto, et propterea mihi de tuis oblationibus cibum
conaris inferre? Non utique. Igitur ab ista sedulitate cessato: neque enim uel
indigentia uel utilitate commoueor ut talia dona perquiram, ex quibus quasi
possim uel essuriem mitigare uel emendare pauperiem. Quae sunt autem quae
reuersione requiro?   15 (p. 279, 10-11): Immula Deo gratiarum actiones.
18-19 (p. 279, 11-13): Mihi, non aliis, amplica (uel subplica *add. in marg.*) quem
credere tuorum omnium causa bonorum.

hungry, I would not tell you (v. 12). The phrase *If I were hungry* was well put, since it is clear that God does not get hungry; after ironically conceding what is impossible, he goes even further, saying, Even if I were hungry, I would not need you. *The world is mine, and all its fullness:* why mention such trifling matters? The truth of it is that everything is mine, since it was actually made by me. And lest the irony be taken seriously (it was to Jews, whose knowledge of God was very imperfect, that the author was speaking), he goes on to say *Surely I do not eat the flesh of bulls or drink goats' blood?* (v. 13). Do I really eat such things? Am I nourished by them? Are you doing me a favor in bringing me food? Hardly. And so give them up: I am not driven by want or by need in looking for them to allay the feelings of hunger or to acquire things I do not have.

What is it that I do look for? *Sacrifice to God a sacrifice of praise* (v. 14). Aquila: "Sacrifice to God a sacrifice of thanksgiving." Offer me this sacrifice of praise—that is, Offer yourself as a victim to me, taking pains to live in thanksgiving to me and devoting yourself totally to me. *And pay your vows to the Most High*—that is, Pray always to me about everything; render me this and perform it. The phrase, Pray to me about everything, means, Consider me responsible for all your good things, and receive from me all that is at any time good, no one being able to pray unless persuaded of this. *Call upon me in the day of your tribulation, and I shall rescue you, and you will glorify me* (v. 15): it will be no idle conjecture for you, since with this attitude you will, even if calling in the midst of afflictions, be heard and will attain | what you aspire to, and so will take occasion from the beneficence to

τοῦ σπουδαζομένου, ὥστε καὶ μείζονα τοῦ πάλιν δοξάσαι λαβεῖν ἐκ τῆς εὐεργεσίας τὴν ἀφορμήν. Οὕτω τὸ ταῖς θυσίαις προσέχειν τῆς ἀρετῆς καταμελοῦντας ἐκβαλών, ἐντεῦθεν λοιπὸν περὶ τῆς τοῦ νόμου διαλέγεται ἀναγνώσεως, δεικνὺς καὶ ταύτην αὐτοῖς ἀνωφελῆ παραβαινομένων τῶν προσταγμάτων, ὥστε μηδὲ ἐπὶ τούτῳ μάτην μεγαλοφρονεῖν. Ἐντεῦθεν καὶ ὁ 5 ἀπόστολος λαβὼν εἰκότως ἐπὶ τοῖς ὁμοίοις, ὀνειδίζων αὐτοῖς φησιν Ὁ οὖν διδάσκων ἕτερον σεαυτὸν οὐ διδάσκεις; καὶ ὅσα κατ᾽ ἐκεῖνο τὸ μέρος τῆς αὐτῆς ἐχόμενα διανοίας φησί.

16. Τῷ δὲ ἁμαρτωλῷ εἶπεν ὁ Θεὸς Ἵνα τί σὺ διηγῇ τὰ δικαιώματά μου, καὶ ἀναλαμβάνεις τὴν διαθήκην μου διὰ στόματός σου; Ἀλλὰ τοῦτό φησιν 10 ὅτι πολλὴν ποιῇ τῆς ἀναγνώσεως τοῦ νόμου τὴν σπουδήν, καὶ φέρεις ἐπὶ τοῦ στόματος τὰ νόμιμα, καὶ ἀναγινωσκομένου ἀκούεις προθύμως, ἀλλὰ τοῦτο οὐκ ἀπολογία. Τοῦτο γὰρ αὐτὸ καὶ μᾶλλον ἐξάπτει με καθ᾽ ὑμῶν, ὅτι τὸν νόμον εἰδότες καὶ τῶν προσταγμάτων ἀκροώμενοι καὶ διὰ στόματος φέροντες, ἐν τῇ πράξει τὸ ἐναντίον ἐπιτηδεύετε· ὥστε περιττή σοι καὶ 15 ἡ ἀνάγνωσις, μᾶλλον δὲ ὕβρις ἐμὴ καὶ αὕτη τὸ λέγοντος μὲν ἀκούειν καὶ προστάττοντος ἐν τῷ νόμῳ, τῆς δὲ πράξεως πάντη καταρρᾳθυμεῖν.

17. Σὺ δὲ ἐμίσησας παιδίαν, καὶ ἐξέβαλες τοὺς λόγους μου εἰς τὰ ὀπίσω. Ἐν γὰρ ταῖς πράξεσι ζητῶν τὴν περὶ τὸν νόμον διάθεσιν, τὸ ἐναντίον εὑρίσκω ὅτι καὶ ἀποστρέφῃ, καὶ διαπτύεις, καὶ μακράν που βαλὼν ἐν οὐδε- 20 νὸς μέρει τίθεσαι τὰ νόμιμα. Καὶ πόθεν τοῦτο;

18ᵃ. Εἰ ἐθεώρεις κλέπτην συνέτρεχες αὐτῷ. Συμπράττεις τοῖς κλέπταις, ἀντὶ τοῦ κλέπτεις· οὐδὲ γὰρ ἑτέρως ἐστὶ συμπρᾶξαι.

18ᵇ. Καὶ μετὰ μοιχῶν τὴν μερίδα σου ἐτίθεις. Κοινωνὸς φαίνῃ καὶ τῶν μοιχῶν· τὰ γὰρ αὐτὰ καὶ τοῖς τοιούτοις ἐπιτηδεύεις. Οὕτω καὶ ὁ ἀπό- 25 στολος Ὁ κηρύσσων μὴ κλέπτειν κλέπτεις, ὁ λέγων μὴ μοιχεύειν μοιχεύεις· τὸ γὰρ ἐπὶ τοῖς ὁμοίοις ὀνειδίσαι, τούτων εἰς ὑπόμνησιν αὐτοὺς ἀγαγεῖν ἠβουλήθη.

6-7 Rom. II, 21   26 Rom. II, 22.

Aᵉ 1-5 (p. 279, 14-19): Vt obtanda per me adepisceris et per me formidanda effugies, ut tibi me glorificandi praebeatur digna materia; uerum hoc nec fructuose facies si praecepta mea temerans... 19-20 (p. 279, 29-31): Post te agendo distrues quod honoraueras praedicando. 22 (p. 279, 31-32): Cooperaris furibus iniquiter (inquiter ms). 25-26 (p. 279, 33-280, 2): Sic Apostolus *Qui praedicas non furandum furaris, qui dicis non mechandum mecharis.*

give even greater glory.

Having thus spurned the attention given to sacrifices on the part of those neglecting virtue, at this point he then goes on to speak about the reading aloud of the law, bringing out its futility for those transgressing the commandments lest they take an idle conceit in it. The apostle also rightly took occasion from this in connection with similar matters, reproaching them in the words "You who teach others, will you not teach yourself?" and addressing all the practices covered by that part of the theme.[2] *But to the sinner God said, Why do you outline my right judgments and take up my covenant in your mouth?* (v. 16). The fact, he is saying, that you take pains to read the law, mouth the words of its stipulations, and listen carefully to its being read is no excuse: it only sets me more against you, your knowing the law, listening to the commandments and putting them on your lips while in practice pursuing the opposite, the result being that the reading is useless for you. Instead, listening to me when I speak and give commands in the law is an insult to me when there is utter neglect of me in practice.

You hated discipline and cast my words behind you (v. 17): looking for a right attitude toward the law in your actions, I find on the contrary that you turn away from the law and loathe it, keeping it at a distance and setting no store by it. How does this come about? *If you saw a thief, you consorted with him* (v. 18): you are an accomplice of robbers—that is, you rob, complicity leaving you no choice. *You threw in your lot with adulterers:* you appear to keep the company of adulterers as well, involved in the same practices as they. The apostle likewise said, "While preaching against stealing, you steal; while forbidding adultery, you commit adultery," taunting them with similar crimes in his wish to bring these matters to their attention. | *Your mouth was*

---

2. Rom 2:21–24.

19ᵃ. Τὸ στόμα σου ἐπλεόνασε κακίας. *Φθέγγεται πᾶν ὅτι κακόν.*

19ᵇ. Καὶ ἡ γλῶσσά σου περιέπλεκε δολιότητα. *Οἱ γὰρ λόγοι σου παντὸς δόλου μεστοί· ὑποκρίνῃ γὰρ φιλίαν διὰ τῶν λόγων, ἐναντία φρονῶν ἐπὶ τῆς ψυχῆς. Τί γάρ;*

5   20. Καθήμενος κατὰ τοῦ ἀδελφοῦ σου κατελάλεις, καὶ κατὰ τοῦ υἱοῦ τῆς μητρός σου ἐτίθεις σκάνδαλον. *Τὸ αὐτὸ λέγει τῷ τοῦ ἀδελφοῦ, τῇ δὲ ἐπεξηγήσει ἐμφαντικώτερον αὐτὸ κατασκευάζει· ὅταν συλλαλῇς φιλίαν ὑπισχνῇ τοῖς ῥήμασι, χωρὶς δὲ γενόμενος ἐπιβουλεύεις φθεγγόμενος ἃ μὴ χρὴ περὶ αὐτούς, ἐπιβουλὰς ἀρτύων κατ' αὐτοῦ.*

10   21ᵃ. Ταῦτα ἐποίησας καὶ ἐσίγησα. *Ταῦτα πράττοντος ἠνειχόμην ἀεί, νῦν δὲ φθέγγομαι. Διὰ τί;*

21ᵇ. Ὑπέλαβες ἀνομίαν ὅτι ἔσομαί σοι ὅμοιος. *Ἁμαρτίας ὑπόθεσιν ἐποιήσω τὴν μακροθυμίαν τὴν ἐμήν, ὡς ἀρεσκομένῳ μοι προσεσχηκὼς οἷς ἔπραττες, καὶ τοῦτο στοχαζόμενος ἀφ' ὧν ἐσιώπουν. Ἵνα τοίνυν μὴ τοῦτο*
15   *νομίζῃς*

21ᶜ. Ἐλέγξω σε καὶ πκραστήσω κατὰ πρόσωπόν σου. *Σαφῆ ποιοῦμαι τῶν πταισμάτων τὸν ἔλεγχον τῶν σῶν, ἄγων εἰς μέσον τὰ πταίσματα, τιμωρούμενος ἐφ' οἷς ἔπραξας, ὥστε σὺ καὶ τούτου αἴτιος, ὃς πολλάκις μακροθυμήσαντος οὐκ ἀπέστης τοῦ πταίειν, ἀλλ' ὡς χαίροντος τοῖς γιγνο-*
20   *μένοις ἐπέμενες τῷ πράττειν. Δείκνυσι δὲ διὰ τούτων ὅτι κἂν κολάζῃ Θεὸς οὐ πάθος οἰκεῖον πληρῶν καὶ ἰδίαν ὀργὴν ἐπάγει τὴν τιμωρίαν, ἀλλὰ περιστέλλειν βουλόμενος τὸ κακὸν καὶ ἀφιστᾶν τοῦ πταίειν ἐσπουδακώς.*

2-3 cf. *Paraphrasis* (p. 953, 45-46): ...ὅτι ἐν προσποιήσει φιλίας πάντα αὐτοῖς κατεσκεύαζες τὰ δεινά.   13-14 cf. Theodoretus (1236 D 2-1237 A 2) atque L (p. 961, 48-50): Σὺ δὲ τὴν ἀνοχὴν εἰς ἀφορμὴν ἔλαβες δυσσεβείας, καὶ ἐτόπασας ἐφηδόμενός με τοιούτοις μὴ ἐπαγαγεῖν τὴν τιμωρίαν.

Aᵉ 19ᵃ (p. 280, 3-4): Loqueris, inquit, omne quod iniquum est.   19ᵇ (p. 280, 5-8): Sermones tui omni fallacia pleni sunt et dolo simulas quippe uerbis amicitiam, cum malitiam in corde custodias.   20 (p. 280, 9-14): *Filium matris* idem dicit quod et *fratrem*, ut per repetitionem clarescat; cum enim conloqueris, amicitiam sermonibus conloqueris (uel polliceris *in marg.*), at ubi direptus fueris, ea comminisceris quibus possis nocere.   21ᵃ (p. 280, 15-16): Te, inquit, talia agente diu patiens fui.   21ᵇ (p. 280, 17-21): Iuncsisti creminibus tuis profanitatem, patientiam meam creminando de dilatione uindictae, tamquam tuis faueret admisis.   16-17 (p. 280, 22-24): Conuictionem punitionemque creminum tuorum faciam esse manifestam.

awash with wickedness (v. 19): he utters everything that was evil. *And your tongue wrapped itself around deception:* your words are redolent of utter guile; you pretend friendship, but at heart you have thoughts of the opposite. Why? *You sat down to malign your brother, and put a stumbling block in the way of your mother's son* (v. 20). By the phrase *your brother* he means the same thing, with this comment making the point more emphatically: When you converse, you promise friendship with words, but when apart, you scheme and say what should not be said about them, hatching plots against him.

These things you did, and I kept silence (v. 21): when you did this, I always restrained myself, but now I have my say. Why so? *You suspected I would be like you where iniquity is concerned:* you made my long-suffering grounds for sin, intending in what you did to keep me happy and capitalizing on my silence. Lest you form this opinion, therefore, *I shall censure you and confront you face to face:* I level a clear accusation at your failings, bringing your failings to the fore, imposing punishment for what you have done, and so you are the guilty party also in this, not desisting from your crimes despite benefiting often from my long-suffering, and instead persisting in your behavior as though you had my approval for your deeds. Now, in this he brings out that even if God punishes and imposes retribution, he is not giving vent to his own feelings or personal rage, but wishes to contain the evil and is anxious to bring sinning to an end. |

Ἄρχεται λοιπὸν καὶ παραινέσεως· τοῦτο γὰρ πρέπον τῷ προφήτῃ, ἐπειδὴ τούτων ἕνεκεν καὶ τοῖς προλαβοῦσιν ἐχρήσατο καὶ τῇ προσωποποιήσει τὸ ἔγκλημα κατασκευάζων φοβερόν.

22ᵃ. Σύνετε δὴ ταῦτα, οἱ ἐπιλανθανόμενοι τοῦ Θεοῦ. Μὴ ἁπλῶς φησι τούτων ἀκούσητε, ἀλλὰ φοβηθέντες τῶν λεχθέντων τὴν ἀπειλὴν ἀπόστητε 5 τοῦ πταίειν, ἵνα μὴ κερδάνητε τὴν κόλασιν.

22ᵇ. Μή ποτε ἁρπάσῃ καὶ μὴ ἦ ὁ ῥυόμενος. Ὡς ἂν μὴ ἐπιμενόντων ὑμῶν τῷ πταίειν δίκην λέοντος ἁρπάζοντος σφοδρὰν ὑμῖν ἐπαγάγῃ τὴν τιμωρίαν ὁ Θεός· οὔτε γάρ ἐστιν ὁ ἀπαλλάξαι τῆς παρ᾽ αὐτοῦ τιμωρίας ἰσχύων. Τί δέ ἐστιν ὃ ζητεῖς καὶ πρᾶξαι προσήκει, ὥστε καὶ ἀπαλλαγῆναι 10 τῆς τιμωρίας;

23ᵃ. Θυσία κινέσεως δοξάσει με. Τοῦτο ἀπαιτεῖ καὶ τοῦτο λέγει, ὅτι Δόξαν οἰκείαν καὶ εὐφροσύνην λογίζομαι τὴν δι᾽ εὐχαριστίας θυσίαν, καὶ τοῦτο ὡς ἐκλεκτὸν προσίεμαι θῦμα.

23ᵇ. Καὶ ἐκεῖ ὁδός, ἣν δείξω αὐτῷ τὸ σωτήριόν μου. Τὸ ἐκεῖ πολλα- 15 χοῦ οὐκ ἐπὶ τόπου λέγει, ἀλλ᾽ ἐπὶ πράγματος. Οὕτως ἐν τῷ λε΄ ψαλμῷ Μὴ ἐλθέτω μοι πούς ὑπερηφανίας καὶ χεὶρ ἁμαρτωλοῦ μὴ σαλεύσῃ με. ἐκεῖ ἔπεσον πάντες οἱ ἐργαζόμενοι τὴν ἀνομίαν, ἀντὶ τοῦ Μὴ κρατήσαιέν μου οἱ ἁμαρτωλοί· ὑπὸ γὰρ τὴν τοιαύτην τιμωρίαν ἴδιον τῶν ἁμαρτωλῶν πίπτειν. Οὕτω καὶ ἐν τῷ ρλβ΄ Ὅτι ἐκεῖ ἐνετείλατο Κύριος τὴν εὐλογίαν ζωὴν ἕως 20 τοῦ αἰῶνος, ἀντὶ τοῦ Τοῖς ἐπὶ τὸ αὐτὸ κατοικοῦσιν ἀδελφοῖς, ἵνα εἴπῃ τοῖς ὁμονοοῦσιν. Καὶ ἐνταῦθα οὖν τὸ ἐκεῖ λέγει, ἀντὶ τοῦ Τῷ τοι τοιούτῳ ταύτην μοι θυσίαν προσάγοντι καὶ εὐχαρίστως ζῆν ἐσπουδακότι, τούτῳ δείκνυμι ὁδὸν τῆς παρ᾽ ἐμοῦ σωτηρίας, ἵνα εἴπῃ τοὺς τοιούτους σῴζω, τοὺς

17-18 Ps. XXXV, 12-13ᵃ (cf. p. 204)   20-21 ps. CXXXII, 3.

15-16 *Paraphrasis* (p. 955, 6-7): Τὸ γὰρ ἐκεῖ τόπον ἔλαβεν ἀντὶ πράγματος.

Aᵉ 1-3 (p. 280, 25-29): Hinc iam inchoatur monitus profetae, cuius gratia omnem illum in superioribus figurarum uariarum fecerat apparatum. 22ᵃ (p. 280, 29-31): Non remisse audite nec signiter, sed penitus in mentem utilem comminationem admittite. 23ᵃ (p. 280, 33-37): Ecce, inquit, quid a nobis reposcit; ecce, inquit, praecipit gloriam esse propriam, laetitiamque pronuntiat ut hostiam pro gratiarum actione studieris offerre. 22-25 (p. 281, 1-5): Pro eo ut diceret Huiusmodi homines *salutare* donabo, qui mihi *sacrificium laudis* offerre curauerant; hoc ergo munere, id est hoc genere, salutarem consequentur deuoti.

He now begins exhortation as well, this befitting the author, since for their sake he had presented the foregoing and delivered the fearsome accusation by dramatizing it. *Understand this, you who forget God* (v. 22): do not simply listen to this; be in fear of the threat in the words and desist from falling lest you incur retribution. *Lest at some time he snatch you away instead of being the one to rescue you:* lest God like a ravaging lion impose a severe penalty on you for persisting in your sin, there being no one else able to free you from his punishment. What is it that you seek and that must be done for you to be freed from the punishment? *A sacrifice of praise will glorify me* (v. 23): he requires this and stipulates this, I take the sacrifice of thanksgiving for my glory and joy, and this I accept as a chosen offering. *And there is the path by which I shall show him my salvation.* The word *there* refers often not to place but to deed: for example, in Psalm 36, "May the foot of arrogance not come my way, and a sinner's hand not move me; all evildoers fell there," meaning, May sinners not gain control of me, since falling victim to such punishment is the fate of sinners; likewise in Psalm 133, "Because there it was that the Lord ordained his blessing, life forever"[3]—that is, for the brethren inhabiting that same place, as if to say, for likeminded people. This, then, is the meaning of *there* in this case as well, namely, To such a person who offers me this sacrifice and is zealous in living thankfully I show the way of my salvation—as if to say, I save such people; | I confer blessings on such

---

3. Pss 36:11–12; 133:3.

τοιούτους εὐεργετῶ· αὐτῷ δὲ λέγει τῷ ἀνωτέρῳ τὸ Θῦσον τῷ Θεῷ θυσίαν αἰνέσεως, καὶ ἐπικάλεσαί με ἐν ἡμέρᾳ θλίψεώς σου, καὶ ἐξελοῦμαί σε, καὶ δοξάσεις με.

PSALMVS L

5 Οὐκ ἔστιν ἡ ἐ|πιγραφὴ τοῦ Δαυίδ, ἀλλὰ δηλονότι ὁ ψαλμός· ὁ ψαλμὸς δὲ πρόρρησίς ἐστιν, οὐκ ἐξαγόρευσις, καὶ τοῦτο δηλοῖ τὰ τελευταῖα, — Ἀγάθυνον γάρ φησιν ἐν τῇ εὐδοκίᾳ σου τὴν Σιών, καὶ οἰκοδομηθήτω τὰ τείχη Ἱερουσαλήμ. καὶ ἑξῆς. Ἐπὶ δὲ τοῦ Δαυίδ οὐδὲ κατελέλυτο ἡ Σιών, οὐδὲ τὰ τείχη περιῄρητο τῆς Ἱερουσαλήμ, οὐδ' ἡ τοῦ ⟨ναοῦ⟩ ἐπέπαυτο 10 λειτουργία, οὐδὲ καθῄρητο τὰ θυσιαστήρια, — οὐδὲ δεῖσθαι τοίνυν περὶ τοιούτων ὁ μακάριος Δαυὶδ ἠναγκάζετο, οὐδὲ γὰρ οὐδ' ἡ τούτου ἁμαρτία κοινὸν ἤνεγκεν τῷ ἔθνει κακόν· γελοῖον γὰρ εἰ οὗτος μὲν κατὰ προφήτην ἠφίετο τῆς ἁμαρτίας, ἀντ' αὐτοῦ δὲ τὸ ἔθνος ἅπαν μηδὲν κοινωνῆσαν τῆς παρανομίας ἐκολάζετο. Περὶ τίνος οὖν ταῦτα λέγει ἢ δηλονότι περὶ τοῦ 15 λαοῦ παντός, ὃς διὰ ὑπερβολὴν οἰκείων ἀσεβημάτων καὶ ἁμαρτημάτων αἰχμάλωτος γέγονε, τῆς πόλεως εἰς ἔδαφος πεσούσης, καὶ τοῦ ναοῦ πυρποληθέντος, καὶ τοῦ θυσιαστηρίου κατασκαφέντος;

Προφητεύων τοίνυν ὁ Δαυὶδ ἐκ προσώπου τοῦ λαοῦ ταῦτά φησιν ἐν τῇ προρρήσει, διδάσκων αὐτοὺς ὅπως ὀφείλουσι προσπίπτειν τῷ Θεῷ καὶ τὰς 20 ἑαυτῶν ἐξαγορεύειν πλημμελείας, μὴ ἀπογινώσκειν τε τῆς σωτηρίας διὰ τὸ μέγεθος τῆς κατεχούσης συμφορᾶς, ἀλλὰ ἀναμένειν τοῦ Θεοῦ τὴν βοήθειαν, ἣν φιλάνθρωπος ὢν καὶ ἐλεήμων μεταμελομένοις ἐφ' οἷς ἥμαρτον παρέξει, ἀφιείς τε τὰ ἁμαρτήματα καὶ ἐν τῇ τούτων συγχωρήσει λύων αὐτοῖς τὴν τιμωρίαν. Διὰ τοῦτο, πρῶτον τῶν ἁμαρτημάτων διδάξας αἰτεῖν τὴν συγχώρη- 25 σιν, ἐπάγει Ἀγάθυνον, Κύριε, ἐν τῇ εὐδοκίᾳ σου τὴν Σιὼν καὶ ἑξῆς, τοῦτο προλέγων ὅτι Εἰ ἀληθῶς μετανοήσαντες ἐπι|μένοιτε τεύξεσθε μὲν τῆς συγχωρήσεως καὶ ποιηθήσεται δὲ ὑμῖν ἅπαντα ἐπὶ τοῦ προτέρου σχήματος καὶ τῆς θαυμαζομένης εὐκοσμίας, ἣν ἐπὶ μὲν τῆς ἀλλοτρίας χώρας πληροῦν οὐκ ἠδύνασθε, ἐπανεληλυθότες δὲ πληροῦν ἐν ἐξουσίᾳ καταστήσεσθε. Ὑπὲρ τού- 30 των τοίνυν λέγει καὶ τὸ Σοὶ μόνῳ ἥμαρτον καὶ ἑξῆς, ἀντὶ τοῦ πολλῶν ἀνομημάτων ἐργάτης γέγονα ἐπ' ὄψεσι ταῖς σαῖς. Ἔστι δὲ καὶ ταῦτα ἀπόδειξις μὲν τῆς ἐμῆς κακίας, σύστασις δὲ τῆς σῆς ἀγαθότητός φησιν· εἰ γὰρ εἰς λόγους ἔλθοιμεν καὶ κριθείημεν πρὸς ἀλλήλους καὶ προφέροιτο δὲ τὰ σά, ἐγὼ μὲν ἡμαρτηκὼς πάντοτε φανοῦμαι, αὐτὸς δὲ πάντοτε εὐεργετῶν, — εἶτα 35 ἐγὼ μὲν ἀγνώμων κριθήσομαι διὰ πάντων καὶ τῆς νῦν με συνεχούσης τιμω-

2-3 vv. 14-15   7-8. 25 v. 20   12-13 II Reg. XII, 13   30 v. 6.

9 ναοῦ supplevi   11 ἀναγκάζετο ms   22 μετὰ μελλομένοις ms.

people. The meaning was the same in the verses above: *Sacrifice to God a sacrifice of praise; Call upon me in the day of your tribulation, and I shall rescue you, and you will glorify me.*[4]

PSALM 51

The title is not David's, but the psalm clearly is. The psalm is prophecy, not confession, as the final verses indicate: *Be good to Sion in your good pleasure, and let the walls of Jerusalem be built* and so on. Now, in David's time Sion had not been destroyed, nor the walls of Jerusalem razed, nor the temple worship brought to an end, nor the altars demolished. So blessed David therefore was not forced to pray for such things, either, nor had his sin brought the nation corporate troubles; after all, it would have been ridiculous if according to the author he had been forgiven while the whole nation was punished for the sin instead of him when it had not been involved. So is he saying this of some person, or obviously of the whole people, who were taken captive on account of the excess of their own godless and sinful actions, and the city was razed to the ground, the temple set on fire, and the altar brought down?

Under inspiration, then, David is saying this from the viewpoint of the people by way of prophecy, teaching them how they ought to prostrate themselves before God and confess their own sins, not despairing of salvation as a result of the magnitude of the calamity affecting them, but awaiting God's help, which in his love and mercy he will provide to those repenting of the sins they committed, both absolving the sins and in pardoning them canceling their punishment. Hence, after first instructing them to beg forgiveness for their sins, he goes on to say *Be good to Sion in your good pleasure, Lord* and so on, predicting that, If you truly confess and persevere, you will gain forgiveness, and everything will be restored to you with its former appearance and admirable beauty that you were unable to achieve in a foreign country, but are in a position to achieve now that you have returned. It is on their behalf, then, that he also says *Against you alone have I sinned* and so on[1]—that is, I was the agent of many crimes in your sight. Now, this is also a proof of my wickedness as well as a confirmation of your goodness, he is saying; if we were called to account and judged with one another, and if your doings were to be displayed, I would always emerge as the offender and you always as the benefactor; I would next be condemned as an ingrate in everything and liable to the punishment now befalling me, | whereas you would

---

4. Ps 50:14–15.
1. Ps 51:4.

ρίας ἔνοχος, αὐτὸς δὲ φανήσῃ δικαίως μοι ταῦτα ἐπαγαγών, ὥστε οὐδὲ
λόγος μοί τις δίκαιος ὑπολήψεται πρός σε εἰ μὴ τῇ συνήθει σου φιλανθρωπίᾳ παριδεῖν ἐθελήσῃς τὰ πλημμελήματα.

Καὶ μαρτυρεῖ ταῦτα περὶ Ἰουδαίων εἰρῆσθαι τῷ Δαυὶδ καὶ ὁ θεῖος
Παῦλος περὶ τῶν αὐτῶν ταῦτα διαλεγόμενος· εἰπὼν γὰρ Τί οὖν τὸ περισ- 5
σὸν τοῦ Ἰουδαίου; καὶ δείξας τί ποτε ἦν, καὶ λύσας τὴν ἀντίθεσιν τὴν λέγου-
σαν ὅτι πολλοὶ ἠπίστησαν Ἰουδαῖοι — καὶ ἐπειπὼν Γινέσθω ὁ Θεὸς ἀληθής,
πᾶς δὲ ἄνθρωπος ψεύστης — λοιπὸν ἐπάγει Καθὼς γέγραπται Ὅπως ἂν δικαιωθῇς ἐν τοῖς λόγοις σου καὶ νικήσεις ἐν τῷ κρίνεσθαι. Τοῦτο γὰρ σαφῶς λέγει
ὅτι τὰ περὶ τοὺς Ἰουδαίους γεγονότα μεγάλα· καὶ πρό γε πάντων ὅτι τῶν 10
ἐθνῶν διεκρίθησαν, ὅτι περιτομῇ κατεσημάνθησαν, ὅτι νόμους ὑπεδέξαντο
θείους, ὅτι παρὰ πάντας ἀνθρώπους μεγίστης ἐπιμελείας ἠξιώθησαν. Εἰ δὲ
τοιούτων τετυχηκότες αὐτοὶ πρὸς τὸ χεῖρον | εἶδον τοῦτο ⟨   ⟩ του-
τέστιν, ἀλλ᾽ οὐχὶ τοῦ Θεοῦ κατηγ⟨   ⟩αν· εἰ πάντες γὰρ εἵλοντο τὰ
χείρω, οὐδὲ τοῦτο τὸν Θεὸν διαβάλλει, ἔσται δὲ μᾶλλον ἀληθὲς ἐκεῖνο τὸ 15
περὶ αὐτῶν εἰρημένον παρὰ τοῦ προφήτου Δαυὶδ Ὅπως ἂν δικαιωθῇς ἐν τοῖς
λόγοις σου καὶ ἑξῆς· ὥστε δῆλον, καθὼς καὶ τῷ μακαρίῳ ἐξείληπται Παύλῳ,
ὅτι περὶ Ἰουδαίων ταῦτα προὔλεγεν ὁ Δαυίδ, ἀλλ᾽ οὐχὶ περὶ ἑαυτοῦ, περὶ
ὧν καὶ ἐπάγει Ἰδοὺ γὰρ ἐν ἀνομίαις. Οὗτοι γὰρ οὐ μόνον ἠσέβουν, ἀλλὰ καὶ
πρὸς πᾶσαν ἀκολασίαν ἐσύροντο, — ἕκαστος γάρ φησιν ἐπὶ τὴν γυναῖκα 20
τοῦ πλησίον αὐτοῦ ἐχρεμέτιζον, τὴν ὑπερβολὴν αὐτῶν τῆς ἀκολασίας διὰ
τοῦ προφήτου κατονειδίζων ὁ Θεός, — διὸ καὶ εἰκότως ἂν οἱ ἐκ τοιούτων
φύντες γάμων λέγοιεν Ἰδοὺ γὰρ ἐν ἀνομίαις συνελήμφθην.

Προφητεύει τὰ κατὰ τὸν ἐν Βαβυλῶνι λαόν, - καὶ τὸ ἐκείνων πρόσωπον
ἀναλαβὼν ὡς ἐξομολογουμένων μὲν ὑπὲρ ἁμαρτίας, αἰτούντων δὲ συγχώ- 25
ρησιν μὲν πταισμάτων, λύσιν δὲ τῶν κακῶν, οὕτω τὸν ψαλμὸν ἐξεφώνησεν.
Εἰ δὲ ἄλλην τὴν ἐπιγραφὴν εἶναι συμβαίνει, ξενιζέσθω μηδείς· οὐδαμοῦ
γὰρ ταῖς ἐπιγραφαῖς δουλεύοντες ἐφάνημεν, δεξάμενοι δὲ ταύτας μόνας
ὅσας εὕρομεν ἀληθεῖς εἰρήκαμεν· εἰρήκαμεν δὲ καὶ περὶ τούτου ὅσαπερ
ἐχρῆν ἐν τῷ προοιμίῳ, πρὸ τῆς κατὰ λέξιν ἐξηγήσεως. 30

3. Ἐλέησόν με, ὁ Θεός, κατὰ τὸ μέγα ἔλεός σου, καὶ κατὰ τὸ πλῆθος
τῶν οἰκτιρμῶν σου ἐξάλειψον τὸ ἀνόμημά μου. Ἐκ προσώπου τοῦ λαοῦ

5-9 Rom. III, 1. 3-4   19. 24 v. 7   20-21 Ierem. V. 8.

13-14 *litterae plures effluxerunt, scriptura humore deleta*.   15 ἀληθεῖς ms.
29 ἀληθεῖς εἰρρήκαμεν ms.
24-26 cf. Theodoretus (1240 B 10-C 3).

A^e 24-26 (p. 281, 9-15): ... Profetat hoc carmine captiuo populo in Babilone
quae supplicationis uerba et liberationis uerba facienda sint, atque suo exemplo
orationem format, qua uti debeat in adflictione captiuos (cf. Pseudo-Beda 747).

emerge as justly imposing it on me, so that no claim of mine would be justly directed against you if you were not prepared to overlook my sins in your habitual lovingkindness.

The divine Paul also confirms that this was said by David of Jews when he says this of the same people: after remarking, "So what advantage has the Jew?" and showing what it was, disposing of the objection that many Jews were unfaithful, and saying further, "Although every human being is a liar, let God be proved true," he then goes on to say, "As it is written, 'So that you may be justified in your words and prevail in your judging.' "[2] This means, in fact, that great things were done for the Jews, and principally that they were separated from the nations, they were sealed with circumcision, they received divine laws, and they were vouchsafed greater care than all other people. But if after receiving such benefits they took a turn for the worse…,[3] they could not accuse God: if all made a choice for the worse, and this is not God's fault, it would rather establish the truth of what was said of them by the inspired David, *So that you were justified in your words* and so on.[4] So it is clear that, as was understood also by blessed Paul, David foretold this of Jews, not of himself; and it is of them he also proceeds to say *For, lo, I was conceived in iniquities*[5]—that is, they not only were guilty of impiety, but also were swept away to every form of licentious behavior, "each neighing for his neighbor's wife,"[6] remember, where in the words of the prophet God reproaches the enormity of their licentiousness. Hence, it followed that those sprung from such unions would say *For, lo, I was conceived in iniquities.*

He prophesies the situation of the people in Babylon; adopting their viewpoint as making confession of sin, and begging forgiveness for failings and relief from their troubles, he thus gave voice to the psalm. If it happens that the title is to a different effect, let no one be surprised: at no stage have we given the impression of being dictated to by the titles, accepting only those we found to be true; and we said as much about this as was necessary in the preface before commentary on the text.[7]

Have mercy on me, O God, according to the greatness of your mercy, and according to the abundance of your compassion blot out my lawlessness (v. 1). He speaks on the part of the people. | The phrase *the greatness of your*

---

2. Rom 3:1, 3–4, citing Ps 51:4, and thus reinforcing Theodore's interpretation.

3. The codex is defective in places at this point.

4. Ps 51:44.

5. Ps 51:5.

6. Jer 5:8.

7. Unlike Chrysostom and Theodoret, Theodore takes the position of Diodore on the authenticity of the psalm titles.

λέγει. Τὸ δὲ μέγα ἔλεός σου καὶ τὸ πλῆθος τῶν οἰκτιρμῶν, ὥστε δεῖξαι ὅτι διὰ | πλῆθος καὶ μέγεθος τῶν ἀνομῶν τὴν αἰχμαλωσίαν ὑπέμειναν, ἃς οὐ δυνατὸν λυθῆναι μὴ πολλῆς τῆς τοῦ Θεοῦ φιλανθρωπίας περὶ αὐτοὺς δειχθείσης.

5 4ᵇ. Καὶ ἀπὸ τῆς ἁμαρτίας μου καθάρισόν με. Τὸ αὐτὸ σημαίνει καὶ διὰ τοῦ ἐπὶ πλεῖον πλῦνόν με, τουτέστι τελείως καθάρισόν με τῆς ἁμαρτίας τελείαν ποιησάμενος τὴν συγχώρησιν.

5. Ὅτι τὴν ἀνομίαν μου ἐγὼ γινώσκω, καὶ ἡ ἁμαρτία μου ἐνώπιόν μού ἐστιν διὰ παντός. Ἔδειξεν ὅτι δικαίως αἰτεῖ τῶν ἁμαρτημάτων τὴν συγ-
10 χώρησιν, ἐπιγινώσκων ὅτι ἥμαρτεν· οὔτε γὰρ μικρὰν ἀφορμὴν εἰς σωτη-
ρίαν τίθεται τοῦ πταίσματος τὴν ἐπίγνωσιν, ἐπίγνωσιν δὲ λέγει οὐκ αὐτὸ τοῦτο τὸ εἰδέναι ὡς ἁμαρτία τὸ πραχθέν, — κοινὸν γὰρ τοῦτο μικροῦ πάντων ἀνθρώπων, — ἀλλὰ τὸ ὡς ἐπὶ ἡμαρτημένοις ἐπιδείξασθαι τὴν μετα-
μέλειαν, ὅπερ ἐστὶ τῶν ἀληθῶς ἐγνωκότων ὅτι ἥμαρτον. Διὸ ἐπάγει Καὶ ἡ
15 ἁμαρτία μου ἐνώπιόν μού ἐστιν, διὰ παντός· ἀεὶ γοῦν πρὸ τῶν ὀφθαλμῶν ἔχω αὐτήν, τῷ συνεχεῖ τῆς μνήμης μονονουχὶ προσωποποιῶν καὶ πρὸ τῶν ὀφθαλμῶν αὐτὴν ἱστῶν.

6ᵃ. Σοὶ μόνῳ ἥμαρτον, καὶ τὸ πονηρὸν ἐνώπιόν σου ἐποίησα. Τὸ Σοὶ μόνῳ ὡς πρὸς τοὺς κατενέχοντας ἐν τῇ αἰχμαλωσίᾳ λέγει. Οἶδα μὲν οὖν
20 φησιν ὅτι ἥμαρτον, καὶ τούτου γε λήθην οὐκ ἄν ποτε ποιήσασθαι δυναίμην, ἀλλ᾿ ἥμαρτον εἴς σε, εἰς ὃν εὐεργετηθεὶς ἀγνώμων ἐφάνην, οὐκ εἰς τούτους· οὔτε γὰρ ἔπαθόν τι παρ᾿ ἐμοῦ, καὶ ποιοῦσιν ἀνήκεστα.

6ᵇ. Ὅπως ἂν δικαιωθῇς ἐν τοῖς λόγοις σου, καὶ νικήσεις ἐν τῷ κρίνεσθαί σε. Τὸ ὅπως κατὰ ἰδίωμα λέγει τὸ γραφικόν, οὐκ ἐπὶ αἰτίας, τὸ δὲ ἀναγκαίως
25 ἐκβὰν ὡς αἰτίαν τεθεικώς· τίθησι γὰρ ἀεὶ τὸ αἰτιατὸν ἀντὶ τοῦ αἰτίου ὅταν ἐξ ἀνάγκης ἑπόμενον ᾖ τῷ αἰτίῳ, — ἐπειδὴ γὰρ ἀπὸ τῶν αἰτίων ὡς ὁμο-

16 τὸ ms 21 ἐφάνη ms.
19-22 cf. Theodoretus (1241 C 12-D 2): Περὶ τὰς σάς φησι δωρεὰς ἐγενόμην ἀχά-
ριστος... καὶ παντοδαπῶν ἀγαθῶν ἀπολαύσας, ἀγνώμων περὶ ταῦτα γεγένημαι· τοὺς δὲ Βαβυλωνίους οὐδὲ ἀδικήσας μεγάλα παρ᾿ ἐκείνων ἠδίκημαι; cf. L (p. 987, 30-33) atque Paraphrasis (p. 982, 6-8).   24-26 Paraphrasis (p. 982, 33-36): Τὸ οὖν ὅπως· οὐ κεῖται ἐνταῦθα ἐπὶ αἰτίας (εἰ καὶ ἐμφαίνει τοῦτο) ἀλλ᾿ αὐτὴν ἀκολουθίαν ἐξηγεῖται.

Aᵉ 9-14 (p. 281, 28-31): Merito ueniam postulat qui iniquitatem prius agno-
scit sponte commisam, et ideo intenta penetentia et grandi misericordia delen-
dam (deluendam ms).   15-17 (p. 281, 32-34): Observatur semper oculis meis admissi qualitas.   21-22 (p. 282, 3-5): ...Tibi, inquit, soli peccaui, non in his a quibus tam crudiliter trachtor.

mercy and the abundance of compassion occurs to bring out that they underwent captivity on account of the abundance and magnitude of crimes, which
it was impossible to annul without a demonstration of God's great lovingkindness for them. *And purify me of my sin* (v. 2). He conveys the same idea
also through *Cleanse me yet further*—that is, Completely purify me from
sin by granting me complete forgiveness. *Because I know my iniquity, and
my sin is always before me* (v. 3). He brought out that it was right for him
to beg forgiveness of sins, acknowledging the fact of his sinning; he cites
acknowledgement of falling as no slight grounds for salvation. But he does
not use acknowledgment in the same sense as knowing sin as a fact (it being
common to almost all human beings), but as giving evidence of repentance
in the case of sinners (this being a mark of those who truly acknowledge that
they have sinned). Hence his adding *And my sin is always before me:* at least
I always have it before my eyes (dramatizing its frequent recall, as it were,
by having it before his eyes).

   Against you alone have I sinned, and done evil in your sight (v. 4). The
phrase *Against you alone* refers to those held in captivity. So he is saying, I
know that I have sinned, and may I never be able to forget this. No, I have
sinned against you and have appeared ungrateful for your favors. I did not
sin against them: they suffered nothing from me, and yet they do unbearable
things. *So that you were justified in your words and prevailed in your judging.* He uses *So that* as a literary idiom, not to do with cause, but expressing
as cause what is an inevitable outcome: he always mentions the effect in
place of the cause when it inevitably follows what causes it, since | we are

λογούμενα τὰ αἰτιατὰ κατασκευάζομεν ὅταν ἕπεσθαι αὐτὰ ἀναγκαίως συμβαίνῃ, οἷον εἴ τις λέγῃ ὅτι Εἰ τὸ πῦρ ἐνέπεσεν τῷ στυππείῳ ἐξ ἀνάγκης
αὐτὸ ἀνάλωσε, καὶ ὡς ὁμολογούμενον ἀπὸ τοῦ πρώτου τὸ δεύτερον λαβὼν
τὸ ἕπεσθαι τῇ τοῦ πυρὸς ἐπινεμήσει τοῦ στυππείου τὴν ἀνάλωσιν. Διὰ τοῦτο
ἔθος τῇ θείᾳ γραφῇ λέγειν ἀεὶ τὸ αἰτιατὸν ἀντὶ τοῦ αἰτίου, ἂν ἐπόμενον ἐξ   5
ἀνάγκης ᾖ. Ὥσπερ γὰρ τὰ αἴτια ἀπὸ δόξης ἐστὶ τῶν ὁμολογουμένων αἰτια-
τῶν, οὕτω καὶ τὸ αἰτιατὸν ἀπὸ δόξης εἶναι δύναται τοῦ αἰτίου, ἂν πάντως
ἐπόμενον εἶναι συμβαίνῃ, — οἷον ἕπεται τῷ ἡλίῳ φαίνοντι τὸ πάντως ἡμέραν εἶναι, τὸ τὸν ἥλιον φαίνειν λέγοι γὰρ ἄν τις ἡμέραν εἶναι, ἥλιος γὰρ
φαίνει καὶ τοῦ τὸν ἥλιον φαίνειν τὸ ἡμέραν εἶναι· δύναιτο γὰρ ἄν τις λέγειν,   10
ἀντιστρέψας εἰ βούλοιτο, ἀνάγκη τὸν ἥλιον φαίνειν, ἡμέρα γάρ ἐστιν. | Ἀπὸ
γὰρ τοῦ ἐπομένου τῷ αἰτίῳ ἀνάγκη ὁμοίως τὸ αἰτιατὸν ἀπὸ δόξης εἶναι δύναται τὸν αἴτιον, ὥσπερ οὖν καὶ τὸν αἴτιον τοῦ αἰτιατοῦ πάντως ἐπομένου.

Διὰ τοῦτο τοίνυν ἡ θεία γραφή, ὅταν τι ἀναγκαίως ἕπηται πάντως τῷ
γεγενημένῳ, ὡς αἰτίαν αὐτὸ τίθησιν, τὸ ἀναγκαῖον δηλοῦσα τοῦ πράγ-   15
ματος. Οὕτω γὰρ κἀνταῦθα, ἐπειδὴ τοῦ Θεοῦ τὸ μέγιστα αὐτοὺς εὐεργετη-
κότος ἀγνώμονες περὶ αὐτὸν οἱ τοῦ λαοῦ ἐγεγόνεισαν, ἀνάγκη ἦν, δικαστη-
ρίου καὶ κρίσεως γεγενημένης, φανῆναι τὸν Θεὸν δικαιότατα αὐτοὺς καὶ νῦν
ὑπὲρ τῆς ἀγνωμοσύνης τιμωρούμενον. Τέθεικε τοίνυν αὐτὸ ὡς αἰτίαν, δεικνὺς
ὅτι πάντως ἕπεται τοῖς γεγενημένοις τὸ δικαίως φανῆναι τὸν Θεὸν ἅπαντα   20
πεποιηκότα περὶ αὐτούς. Λέγει γὰρ ὅτι Εἴς σέ φησιν μόνον ἥμαρτον, οὐχὶ
τοὺς κατέχοντας. Διὰ τί; Ὅτι τοσαῦτα εὐεργετηθεὶς παρά σου οὕτως
ἀγνώμων ἐγενόμην, ὡς, εἰ κριτήριον γένοιτο καὶ λέγοις μὲν αὐτὸς διηγούμενος τὰς εἰς ἐμὲ χάριτας, τὰ ἐν Αἰγύπτῳ, τὰ κατὰ τὴν ἔρημον, τὰ μετὰ
ταῦτα, λέγοιτο δὲ καὶ τὰ παρ᾽ ἐμοῦ πάντοτε γενόμενα κακά — τοιαῦτα   25
γὰρ τὰ ἐμὰ — νικήσεις ἐν τῇ κρίσει καὶ φανήσῃ δικαιότατα τιμωρησάμενος,
οὕτως ἀγνώμονας εἰκότως κολάζων· ὥστε κατὰ ταύτην τὴν διάνοιαν καὶ
πολλὴν ἔχει τὴν ἀκολουθίαν πρὸς τῷ Σοὶ μόνῳ ἥμαρτον, ἐκείνοις δὲ ***
οὔτε γὰρ ἐναντίον φησὶν ἀδικοῦσιν ἐκεῖνοι παθόντες οὐδέν, ὥστε καὶ
δικαίους εἶναι δέξασθαι τὴν κόλασιν. Καλῶς δὲ καὶ ὁ ἀπόστολος πρὸς   30

2-4 στιππύῳ... στιπποίου ms   17 γεγόνεισαν ms   28 τὸ 1ᵃ m.   *** lacunam
statui.
21-26 L (p. 987, 18-20, 33-37): Πολλῶν γὰρ ἀπολαύσας παρά σου τοῖς ἐναντίοις
ἠμειψάμην... Εἰ γένοιτο οὖν φησι κρίσις τῶν εἰς ἐμὲ δωρεῶν καὶ τῆς ἐμῆς ἁμαρτίας, σὺ
μὲν δίκαιος φανήσει καὶ φιλάνθρωπος, ἐγὼ δὲ παράνομος καὶ ἀχάριτος προξενήσας ἐμαυτῷ
τὰ κακά.

Aᵉ 21-27 (p. 282, 10-19): Non quia peccaui, tu iustus appares, sed quia tam
beneficus totiesque contemptus aduersus ingratos iustus demum ultor adsurgis;
unde, si res quasi ad tribunal iudiciumque perueniat, necesse est te et uincere
potestate post enumerationem tantorum beneficiorum taliter uindicantem, cui
non sit non solum disputatio sed etiam ultio ista iustissima.

responsible for what are conceded to be effects on the basis of their causes when it happens that they inevitably follow. For example, if you say, "If fire falls on flax, it inevitably burns it," you take the burning of the flax as following on the spreading of the fire, as the second thing is conceded to result from the first. For this reason it is customary with the divine Scripture always to state the effect in place of the cause if it necessarily follows. In other words, just as causes are related to what are conceded to be effects on the basis of appearance, so too the effect can on the basis of appearance be the result of the cause provided it follows. For example, daytime follows on the appearance of the sun, and you would say that the appearance of the sun is daytime, for the sun appears, and the appearance of the sun is daytime; in fact, you would be able to claim conversely that the sun must have appeared since it is daytime. In other words, the effect necessarily follows on the cause, just as the cause is definitely related to the effect.

For this reason, then, when something inevitably follows what happened, the divine Scripture presents it as a cause to indicate its inevitability. This, in fact, is what happens here, too: since the people had proved ungrateful for God's wonderful favors, it was inevitable that once the trial was held and judgment delivered, God should be shown to punish them even now most justly for their ingratitude. So he expressed it as a cause to bring out that God's being shown to have justly imposed everything on them follows completely on what was done; he says, in fact, Against you only have I sinned, not against the captors. Why? Because despite your wonderful benefactions I was so ungrateful to you that, if a court were held and you were to give an account of the favors to me—in Egypt, in the wilderness, afterwards—and if all the evils I had ever done were told (such being my behavior), you would prevail in your judging and would seem most righteous in meting out punishment, thus rightly chastising the ingrate. And so in this sense the verse follows closely on *Against you only have I sinned* ... neither on the contrary, he is saying, are they guilty of wrongdoing without suffering anything, and so they deserve to be the object of punishment. The apostle also, in his words to | Jews aimed at pointing out that their dis-

Ἰουδαίους διαλεγόμενος, δεικνὺς ὡς ἡ ἐκείνων ἀπείθεια οὐδαμῶς τοῦ Θεοῦ διαβάλλει τὴν οἰκονομίαν, ἐ|χρήσατο τῇ μαρτυρίᾳ περὶ αὐτῶν εἰρημένῃ κατὰ πρόρρησιν τοῦ μακαρίου Δαυίδ. Πῶς δέ; Εἰ εἰσέλθοιμεν εἰς κρίσιν, νικήσεις.

7. Ἰδοὺ γὰρ ἐν ἀνομίαις συνελήφθην, καὶ ἐν ἁμαρτίαις ἐκίσσησέ με ἡ
5 μήτηρ μου. Οὐ τὴν τῶν τεχθέντων φύσιν αἰτιᾶται, ἄπαγε, οὐδὲ γὰρ περὶ ἐκείνων φύσιν ὅλως εἴρηται, ἀλλὰ τὴν τῶν τεκόντων γνώμην ἐξαγγέλλει, — τὸ γὰρ ἐν ἀνομίαις συλληφθῆναι καὶ ἐν ἀνομίαις κισσηθῆναι ὑπὸ τῆς μητρός, δῆλον ὅτι τῶν γεννώντων ἀλλ᾿ οὐ τῶν γεννωμένων μηνύει τὸ ἔγκλημα, — κἀκείνων γνώμην διαβάλλει, ἀλλ᾿ οὐ φύσιν τῶν τικτομένων, ὡς οἱ
10 ἀνόητοι βούλονται. Οὐ γὰρ περὶ αὐτοῦ ταῦτα λέγει ὁ Δαυίδ. Πῶς γὰρ ἂν ἐκεῖνος περὶ τῆς οἰκείας ταῦτα εἴποι φύσεως, περὶ οὗ φησιν ὁ Θεὸς Εὗρον ἄνδρα κατὰ τὴν καρδίαν μου, οὗ γε οὐ μόνον τὴν φύσιν οὐκ αἰτιᾶται, ἀλλὰ καὶ τὴν προαίρεσιν θαυμάζει; Οὐ περὶ αὐτοῦ τοίνυν ταῦτά φησιν ὁ Δαυίδ, οὐδ᾿ εἴ τις ἐκ πλάνης τὸν ψαλμὸν ἐπιγέγραφεν οὕτως, ἤδη τοῦτο τοῦ ψαλ-
15 μοῦ τὴν δύναμιν ἐλέγχει.

Ἐγὼ μὲν γὰρ ἐν ἁμαρτίαις φαίνομαι συνειλημμένος καὶ μηδέποτε τοῦ κακοῦ γενόμενος ἐκτός. Καλῶς δὲ ὡς πρὸς τὸν λαὸν τὸ Ἐν ἀνομίαις συνελήφθην, καὶ ἐν ἁμαρτίαις ἐκίσσησέν με ἡ μήτηρ μου, ἐπειδὴ ἐκ πολλοῦ πταίοντες καὶ παρὰ τῶν πατέρων οἱ καθεξῆς τὰς ἁμαρτίας διαδεχόμενοι
20 ἀπὸ τῶν τοιούτων καὶ τῆς γεννήσεως τὰς ἀφορμὰς πολλάκις ἐδέχοντο, οὐδέποτε ἐν μέσῳ τοῦ κακοῦ διαλείποντος ἐν αὐτοῖς. Οὕτω γοῦν φαίνεται καὶ ὁ Θεὸς πολλάκις ὀνειδίσας αὐτοῖς ὡς ἀδεῶς μοιχωμένοις, ποτὲ μὲν διὰ τοῦ Ἰερεμίου λέγων Ἕκαστος ἐπὶ τὴν γυναῖκα τοῦ πλησίον αὐτοῦ ἐχρεμέ-τιζον, ποτὲ δὲ διὰ τοῦ Ἰεζεκιὴλ Ἕκαστος φησι | τὴν γυναῖκα τοῦ πλησίον
25 αὐτοῦ ἠνόμουν. Εἰκότως οὖν ἐκ προσώπου τῶν τοιούτων εἶπεν Ἰδοὺ γὰρ ἐν ἀνομίαις συνελήφθην, ὡς ἐκ τοιούτων γάμων καὶ παρανόμων μίξεων τὴν σύλληψιν καὶ τὴν ἀφορμὴν τῆς γεννήσεως ἐσχηκότων. Τὸ δὲ Ἰδοὺ ἀπὸ τοῦ ἑβραϊκοῦ ἰδιώματος πρόσκειται, ἐπεὶ μηδὲ πρόκειται αὐτῷ εἰπεῖν τι δεικτικῶς. Τοιαῦτα μὲν οὖν φησι τὰ παρ᾿ ἐμοῦ, τὰ δὲ παρά σου ὁποῖα;

3 cf. Rom. III, 3-4   11-12 cf. Act. XIII, 22   23-24 Ierem. V, 8   24-25 Ezech. XXII, 11.

6 φύσιν] φη(σιν) ms   24 φησι φησι τὴν γυναῖ ms.

A᷄ 18-28 (p. 282, 24-283, 10): Quoniam non a breui tempore, sed ollim a patrum atque auorum aetate peccauimus, patrum uidilicet qui in peccatis suc-cessores fuerunt, et ipsam natiuitatem de huiusmodi plerumque occasionibus collegerunt. Sic enim sepe Deus per Heremiam et Iezechelum lequentiam (licen-tiam?) professionemque in illis exprobrat mechandi : hoc est ergo quod ex ini-quorum conuentu materiam conceptus inierit et eorundem exemplis sit in peiora infirmatus. Ecce enim hic redundat (ret — ms) : neque enim erat quod demonstra-tiue uellet affari ; seruiuit ergo ebreco idiomati.

obedience in no way discredited God's plan, was justified in using the text dealing with them in the prophecy of blessed David.[8] Why so? If we entered into judgment, *you would prevail.*

For, lo, I was conceived in iniquities, and in sins my mother carried me (v. 5). He finds no fault with offspring on the basis of nature—perish the thought—nor is there any reference to nature in their case; rather, he comments adversely on the mind-set of the parents. That is to say, it is clear from *conceived in iniquities* and *carried in sin* by the mother that he refers to the fault of the parents, not the offspring, criticizing the mind-set of the former, not the nature of the children, as some foolish people would like to hold.[9] David, in fact, is not referring to himself: how could he say this of his own nature, when God had said of him, "I found a man after my own heart,"[10] far from finding fault with his nature but even admiring his use of free will? So David is not saying this of himself; and even if someone mistakenly put a title on the psalm to this effect, it does not bring the drift of the psalm into question.

In other words, I appear to have been conceived in sin and never to have been free from wickedness. Now, *I was conceived in iniquities, and in sins my mother carried me* was well put in reference to the people, since later generations failed seriously and followed their parents in sinning, and on the basis of such people and their birth they often had occasion to do likewise, since wickedness was never absent from them. This is the way, at any rate, that God often seems to reproach them for having no qualms about adultery, at one time saying through Jeremiah, "Each man neighing after his neighbor's wife," at another through Ezekiel, "Each one sinned with his neighbor's wife."[11] Rightly, therefore, on the part of such people he said *Lo, I was conceived in iniquities,* receiving conception and the occasion of my birth in such marriages and unlawful unions. Now, the term *Lo* is inserted by way of a Hebrew idiom, there being no reason for him to use any demonstrative particle.

So he says, While this is true of me, what of you? | *For, lo, you loved*

---

8. Cf. Rom 3:3–4.

9. Like Theodoret after him, Theodore is quick to refute any conclusion drawn from this verse implying the impairment of human nature; punishable faults can be attributed to the individual's' mind-set, γνώμη. He thus would be opposed to his modern counterpart Dahood's paraphrase, "All men have a congenital tendency towards evil," (*Psalms,* 2:4), citing a range of Old Testament texts, whereas Theodore declines even to hint at such Old Testament texts or the fall pericope in Gen 3.

10. Paul's words in Acts 13:22, citing 1 Sam 13:14; David's free will, προαίρεσις, is above reproach.

11. Jer 5:8; Ezek 22:11.

8ᵃ. Ἰδοὺ γὰρ ἀλήθειαν ἠγάπησας. Παρ᾽ ἐμοῦ τὸ ἀληθές, τὸ δίκαιον, τὸν ὀρθὸν βίον καὶ οὐχ᾽ ἁπλῶς ἀπήτησας, ἀλλὰ πρότερον αὐτὸς ὑπέδειξας τὸ καλόν. Τί γάρ;

8ᵇ. Τὰ ἄδηλα καὶ τὰ κρύφια τῆς σοφίας μου ἐδήλωσάς μοι. Ἄδηλα καὶ κρύφια σοφίας λέγει αὐτὸν τὸν νόμον, τὰς εἰς αὐτοὺς οἰκονομίας, τὸ μέγεθος 5 τῶν θαυμάτων, τὸ πάντων μεῖζον τὰ πνευματικὰ χαρίσματα. Ἀντὶ τούτων φησὶν ἐξήτησας παρ᾽ ἐμοῦ ὥστε τὸ ἀληθὲς ἀγαπᾶν, ὅπερ ἦν κέρδος πάλιν ἐμόν· ἐγὼ δὲ τὸ ἐναντίον ἁμαρτίαις ἠμειψάμην τὴν χάριν. Οὐκοῦν ἐπειδὴ τούτων οὕτως ἐχόντων, εἰ κριτήριον γένοιτο, τὰ μὲν παρά σου ἐπαίνων μεστά, τὰ δὲ παρ᾽ ἐμοῦ ἄξια τιμωρίας. Διὰ τοῦτο τί; 10

9ᵃ. Ῥαντιεῖς με ὑσσώπῳ καὶ καθαρισθήσομαι. Αἰτῶ παρά σου τὴν συγχώρησιν παρασχεθῆναι· δυνήσῃ γὰρ βουληθεὶς καθαρόν με πάντων ἀποφῆναι τῶν κακῶν. Ὑσσώπῳ δὲ εἶπεν, ἐπειδὴ ἔθος ἦν τοῖς ἐν νόμῳ καθαίρουσιν τούτῳ κεχρῆσθαι.

9ᵇ. Πλυνεῖς με καὶ ὑπὲρ χιόνα λευκανθήσομαι. Ζοφώδη με ὄντα ταῖς 15 ἁμαρτίαις, ἂν βουληθῇς χιόνος ποιήσεις λευκότερον. Καὶ τί τὸ ἐκ τούτου κέρδος;

10ᵃ. Ἀκουτιεῖς με ἀγαλλίασιν καὶ εὐφροσύνην. Τότε ποιήσεις ῥημάτων ἀκοῦσαι εὐφροσύνης μεστῶν, — λέγει δὲ τῆς ἐπανόδου καὶ τῶν κατὰ τὴν ἐπάνοδον καλῶν· τὸ γὰρ ἀκουτιεῖς, ἀντὶ | τοῦ ἀκοῦσαι ποιήσεις. 20

10ᵇ. Ἀγαλλιάσονται ὀστέα τεταπεινωμένα. Τότε, ἐπειδὰν ἀφῇς τὰς ἁμαρτίας, οἱ ἰσχυρῶς συντετριμμένοι νῦν εὐφροσύνης ἐσόμεθα μεστοί· τὸ γὰρ ἰσχυρῶς συντετρῖφθαι διὰ τῆς τῶν ὀστέων σημαίνει φωνῆς, ἐπειδὴ ἰσχυρᾶς συντριβῆς σημεῖον τὸ τὰ ὀστᾶ παθεῖν.

11ᵃ. Ἀπόστρεψον τὸ πρόσωπόν σου ἀπὸ τῶν ἁμαρτιῶν μου. Καὶ μηδὲ 25 ἀποβλέψῃς ταῖς ἁμαρτίαις μου, ἵνα μὴ μυσαχθῇς μὲ διὰ τὸ πλῆθος.

11ᵇ. Καὶ πάσας τὰς ἀνομίας μου ἐξάλειψον. Ἀλλὰ μᾶλλον αὐτὰς ἀφάνισον τῇ οἰκείᾳ φιλανθρωπίᾳ.

Aᵉ 10ᵃ (p. 284, 7-9): ... Audiam quae sint plenissima gaudiorum, cum te adnuente tempus libertatis aduenerit. 10ᵇ (p. 284, 11-15): Remissionis tempore grauius attritio, quae nomine semper comminutorum ossuum indicatur, reliuabitur, et nos dulcidine exultationis impleuimur.

truth: far from simply requiring of me what is true and righteous and an upright life, you first gave evidence on your part of what is good. In what way? *You revealed to me the uncertain and hidden things of my wisdom.* By *uncertain and hidden things of wisdom* he refers to the law itself, the plans for them, the greatness of the marvels, and—greatest of all—the spiritual gifts. In return for these, he is saying, you sought from me a love of what is true, which in turn would have been to my advantage, whereas I, on the contrary, repaid gift with sin. So since this is the case, if a trial were held, what is from you would be deserving of commendation, whereas what is from me would call for punishment. What is the result of this?

You will purify me with hyssop, and I shall be cleansed (v. 7): I beg of you for forgiveness to be given, for if you wish, you can purify me of all evil. He mentioned hyssop because it was the custom for it to be used by those cleansing according to the law.[12] *You will wash me, and I shall be whiter than snow:* though I am grimy with sin, you can, if you wish, make me whiter than snow. And what advantage is there in this? *You will let me hear joy and gladness* (v. 8): then you will make me hear words full of gladness (referring to the return and the events of the return, and by *You will let me hear* meaning, You will make me hear). *Bones that are humbled will rejoice:* at that time when you forgive sins, we who were severely crushed will now be full of joy (indicating through the word bones severe crushing, since pain in the bones suggests severe crushing). *Turn away your face from my sins* (v. 9): and do not have regard to my sins lest you be disgusted with me because of their great number. *And wipe out all my iniquities:* instead do away with them in your lovingkindness. |

---

12. Cf. Exod 12:22–23.

12ª. Καρδίαν καθαρὰν κτίσον ἐν ἐμοί, ὁ Θεός. Ἀκύλας Ἀνάκτισον. Δός μοί φησι λογισμὸν καθαρόν, διάνοιαν ὀρθήν.

12ᵇ. Καὶ πνεῦμα εὐθὲς ἐγκαίνισον ἐν τοῖς ἐγκάτοις μου. Προαιρέσεώς φησιν ἀγαθῆς πλήρωσόν μου τὰ ἔνδον, ἀντὶ τοῦ Ὅλον με πλήρωσον καλῶν 5 λογισμῶν, ὀρθῆς διανοίας, ἀγαθῆς προαιρέσεως. Τὸ γὰρ πνεῦμα τὴν προαίρεσιν λέγει, οὐκ ἐνταῦθα μόνον ἀλλὰ καὶ ἑτέρωθι, — οὕτω καὶ ἐν τοῖς Ἀριθμοῖς περὶ τοῦ Χάλεβ ἐπὶ τῶν κατασκόπων, ὅτι μὴ εὑρέθη φησὶ πνεῦμα ἕτερον ἐν αὐτῷ, ἵνα εἴπῃ προαίρεσις ἄλλη καὶ ἐναντία.

13ª. Μὴ ἀπορρίψῃς με ἀπὸ τοῦ πρωσώπου σου. Καὶ μηκέτι εἰς αἰχμα- 10 λωσίαν ἀπελθεῖν με παρασκευάσῃς, ἀλλ᾽ εἶναι ἀεὶ ἐν τῷ ναῷ, καὶ πρὸ τοῦ προσώπου ἑστάναι τοῦ σοῦ καταξίωσον.

13ᵇ. Καὶ τὸ πνεῦμά σου τὸ ἅγιον μὴ ἀντανέλῃς ἀπ᾽ ἐμοῦ. Ἐπειδὴ τούτῳ τὰ κατὰ τὸν ναὸν ἡγιάζετο καὶ σύμβολον μὲν ἦν τοῦ Θεοῦ παρουσίας ἡ τοῦ ἁγίου Πνεύματος ἐπιφοίτησις, τεκμήριον δὲ τῆς ἀπουσίας ἡ ἀπόληψις, 15 μὴ λάβῃς φησὶν ἀφ᾽ ἡμῶν τὸ Πνεῦμά σου τὸ ἅγιον, ἀλλ᾽ οὕτω ποίησον ἵνα καὶ αὐτὸς ᾖς ἐν τῷ ναῷ καὶ τὸ Πνεῦμά σου παρῇ τὸ ἅγιον, καὶ ἡμεῖς ἁμαρτίας ἐλεύθεροι ἐκεῖ χορεύοντες παρά σοι πληρῶμεν τὰ νόμιμα, μὴ πάλιν μακρὰν εἰς αἰχμαλωσίαν πεμπόμενοι.

14ª. Ἀπόδος μοι τὴν ἀγαλλίασιν τοῦ σωτηρίου σου. Χάρισαί μοι τὴν 20 σωτηρίαν σου καὶ τὴν ἐπὶ σωτηρίαν εὐφροσύνην. Καλῶς δὲ εἶπεν τὸ Ἀπόδος, ἐπειδὴ πρὸ τούτου ἀπέλαυσεν.

14ᵇ. Καὶ πνεύματι ἡγεμονικῷ στήριξόν με. Καὶ οὕτω μέν φησιν κατάστησον ἰσχυρόν, ὥστε μὴ μόνον ἀπηλλάχθαι τῆς αἰχμαλωσίας καὶ ἔξω καθεστάναι τῆς παρούσης δουλείας, ἀλλὰ γὰρ καὶ ἡγεῖσθαι καὶ κρατεῖν ἑτέρων. 25 Πνεύματι δὲ εἶπεν ἡγεμονικῷ, ὡς ἐξ αὐτοῦ τοῦ κρατεῖν τὴν δύναμιν | λαμ-

7-8 Num. XIV, 24.

2 *Paraphrasis* (p. 984, 28-29): Καρδίαν δὲ τοὺς λογισμοὺς καλεῖ.

Aᵉ 2 (p. 284, 17-18): Pro rectis cogitationibus. · 5-8 (p. 284, 19-23): Spiritum pro intensione animi poni usitatum in Scripturis est, ut in libro Numerorum de Caleb: *Non enim*, inquit, *in eo inuentus est Spiritus alter.* 10-11 (p. 284, 24-25): Absolutum (obsol — *ms*) me facito semper in templo sub tuo stare conspectu. 13-16 (p. 284, 27-29): Ne captiuus deutius caream eo spiritu, quo sanctificabatur in templo populus in documentum praesentiae Dei. 23-25 (p. 285, 32-35): Vt non solum absoluar (obsol — *ms*), uerum etiam uicinarum gentium per gratiam spiritus obteneam principatum.

Create a pure heart in me, O God (v. 10). Aquila: "Re-create." Give me thinking that is pure, he is saying, an upright mind. *And renew a right spirit in my innards:* fill my interior with a good will—that is, Fill me completely with good thoughts, an upright mind, a good will. By *spirit* he refers to free will, not only here but also elsewhere, as in Numbers in reference to Caleb and the spies to the effect that "he did not have a different spirit"[13]—that is, a contrary use of free will. *Do not thrust me from your presence* (v. 11): no longer cause me to go off into slavery, but to be ever in your temple, and grant me the grace to stand in your presence. *And do not remove your Holy Spirit from me.* Since the coming of the Holy Spirit was a symbol of God's presence and the precincts of the temple were sanctified by it, and its removal was a sign of his absence, he is saying, Do not take from us your Holy Spirit, but guarantee that you are in the temple and your Holy Spirit is present, and we may be free from sin, and by assembling there in your presence we may discharge our obligations, not being sent off again into captivity.

Restore to me the joy of your salvation (v. 12): grant me your salvation and joy in salvation. Restore was well put, since he enjoyed it before this. *And strengthen me with a guiding spirit:* make me so strong as not only to be freed from captivity and removed from the present servitude, but also to lead and control others. He spoke of *a guiding spirit* in the sense of receiving from him the power to control: | since all the gifts are from the Holy Spirit,

---

13. Theodore's point is valid, even if he finds, or mistakenly reads, a negative in his text of Num 14:24.

βανόντων · ἐπειδὴ γὰρ τοῦ Πνεύματος πάντα τὰ χαρίσματα, τὰ χαρίσματα
δὲ ἦν τὸ καὶ τῶν ἀλλοφύλων κρατεῖν, αὐτῷ λογίζεται τὸ κατόρθωμα.

15. Διδάξω ἀνόμους τὰς ὁδούς σου, καὶ ἀσεβεῖς ἐπί σε ἐπιστρέψουσιν.
Τούτων γὰρ οὕτω γενομένων, δυνήσομαι πολλοὺς καὶ ἑτέρους ἐπιστρέψαι
εἰς τὸ δέον · κρατήσας γὰρ τῶν ἀλλοφύλων πιστοὺς ἐπὶ τὴν γνῶσιν μετάξω   5
τὴν σήν.

16. Ῥῦσαί με ἐξ αἱμάτων, ὁ Θεὸς τῆς σωτηρίας μου. Οὐκοῦν ἀπάλλαξόν με τούτων τῶν φονικῶν, τῶν περὶ αἵματα ἐσχολακότων. Βούλεται
δὲ καὶ ἀπὸ τοῦ ἐκείνων τρόπου δεῖξαι ἑαυτὸν ἄξιον ὄντα τοῦ τυχεῖν τῆς
εὐεργεσίας. Ἂν γὰρ τοῦτο ποιήσῃς, τί;   10

17ᵃ. Ἀγαλλιάσεται ἡ γλῶσσά μου τὴν δικαιοσύνην σου. Μετὰ πολλῆς
τῆς εὐφροσύνης διηγήσομαι ὡς ἐπεμελήθης τοῦ δικαίου, τῶν ἀσεβῶν καὶ
μοχθηρῶν ἀπαλλάξας ἡμᾶς τοὺς τὴν σὴν ἔχοντας γνῶσιν.

17ᵇ. Κύριε, τὰ χείλη μου ἀνοίξεις, καὶ τὸ στόμα μου ἀναγγελεῖ τὴν
αἴνεσίν σου. Σὺ γάρ, εἰ τὸ στόμα ἡμῶν ἀνοίγοις, ὁ τῇ εἰς ἡμᾶς εὐεργεσίᾳ   15
παρέχων ἡμῖν ἀφορμάς, ὑποθέσεις τοῦ πολλὰ μὲν εἰπεῖν, πολλαῖς δὲ
χρήσασθαι ταῖς εἴς σε ὑμνῳδίαις, εὐχαριστῆσαι δὲ ὅσον εἰκὸς διηγουμένους
τὰ γεγονότα.

18ᵃ. Ὅτι εἰ ἠθέλησας θυσίαν, ἔδωκα ἄν. Ἱκανὸν γάρ με καὶ τοῦτο
κινῆσαι πρὸς εὐχαριστίαν, ὅτι ἐγὼ μὲν κἂν εἰ θυσίας ἀπῄτης μετὰ πάσης   20
ἂν ἔδωκα τῆς προθυμίας, ὥστε δυνηθῆναι τῶν κατεχόντων ἀπαλλαγῆναι
κακῶν. Σὺ δὲ τί;

18ᵇ. Ὁλοκαυτώματα οὐκ εὐδοκήσεις. Τουτέστιν, οὐκ ᾔτησας τοιοῦτο
παρ' ἐμοῦ οὐδέν.

8 cf. Paraphrasis (p. 985, 21-22): Ἀπάλλαξον οὖν φησί με τῶν φονίων τούτων
ἀνδρῶν.   20-21 (p. 985, 38-40): ...εἰ κατεδέχου θυσίαν, καὶ ἐβούλου ἐν ἄλλῳ τόπῳ, καὶ
ἐν τῇ αἰχμαλωσίᾳ θυσίαν λαβεῖν, ἐποίησα ἄν.

Aᵉ 5-6 (p. 284, 37-39): Subditarum gentium ad agnitionem tuam corda
conuertam.   16 (p. 284, 40-285, 6): De potestate homicidarum, quibus est
familiaris crudilitas, quibus studium est inquinare (inchiare ms) sanguini. Vult
autem tali colore, per comparitionem scilicet pessimorum, se dignum liberatione
monstrare.   17ᵃ (p. 285, 7-10): Grate nimis et gratulenter tua facta narrabo,
qui me ob notitiam tui iuste dominationi subtraxeris impiorum.   15-16 (p. 285,
12-13): Materiam laudum tuarum beneficia tribuens.

and the gifts include controlling the foreigners, the achievement of this is attributed to him. *I shall teach lawless people your ways, and impious people will turn to you* (v. 13): when it happens this way, I shall be able to turn many others as well to their duty, for by controlling the foreigners I shall bring them to faith and knowledge of you. *Deliver me from bloodshed, O God of my salvation* (v. 14): so free me from all these murderous people involved in bloodshed.

Now, he wishes to show himself worthy of winning his favor, even in contrast to their behavior. If you do this, he is saying, what will result? *My tongue will rejoice in your righteousness:* with great joy I shall recount your attention to righteousness and your freeing us, who have knowledge of you, from the godless and depraved. *You will open my lips, O Lord, and my mouth will declare your praise* (v. 15): if you open our mouth—you who by your kindness to us provide us with the grounds and the basis for saying much and employing many hymns of praise to you and thanking you to the extent required by duly recounting what has happened. *Because if you had wanted sacrifice, I would have given it* (v. 16): this also is sufficient to prompt me to thanksgiving, that I would have given sacrifice with complete enthusiasm if you had wanted it so that I would be in a position to be freed from the troubles besetting me. But what of you? *You will not be pleased with holo-causts*—that is, you did not require anything of the sort from me. |

19. Θυσία τῷ Θεῷ πνεῦμα συντετριμμένον· καρδίαν συντετριμμένην καὶ τεταπεινωμένην ὁ Θεὸς οὐκ ἐξουθενώσει. Ἀλλὰ θεασάμενος ἡμᾶς καταπεπτω- κότας τοῖς λογισμοῖς καὶ ὑπὸ τῆς ἀθυμίας κεκακωμένους καὶ οὐδὲ λογίσασθαί τι ἢ συνιέναι δυναμένους ὑγιὲς διὰ τὸ πλῆθος τῶν κατεχόντων κακῶν, οὐδὲν
5 θεὶς θυσιῶν οὐδὲ ἀπαιτήσας ταῦτα παρ᾽ ἡμῶν, ἀπήλλαξας τῆς συμφορᾶς. Ἔδειξε δὲ τοῦ Θεοῦ τὸ εὐεργετικόν, ἄνω μὲν δι᾽ ὧν παρέσχεν αὐτοῖς ἄρξας οἰκείᾳ φιλανθρωπίᾳ τῆς εἰς αὐτοὺς εὐεργεσίας, ἐνταῦθα δὲ δι᾽ ὧν ἀπήλλαξε τῆς αἰχμαλωσίας οὐδὲν ἄξιον ἐπιδειξαμένους. Οὕτω καὶ τὸν λαὸν δείκνυσιν ἄξιον τοῦ τυχεῖν φιλανθρωπίας, ὅτι τε ἐπέγνω τὸ ἁμάρτημα, καὶ ὅτι χεί-
10 ρους οἱ κατέχοντες, καὶ ὅτι ἐπιγνώσεται τὴν χάριν τυχόν, καὶ σχολάσει τοῖς ὑπὲρ τῶν γεγονότων ὕμνοις, ἀλλὰ καὶ ὅτι τὰς θυσίας ἀδιαλείπτως πληρώσει τοῦ λοιποῦ· τοῦτο γὰρ ἐν τοῖς ἑξῆς λέγει. Τούτοις δὲ χρῆται τοῖς λόγοις, ὥστε καὶ τοῦ Θεοῦ τὸ ἀγαθὸν ἐμφῆναι καὶ τούτους παιδεῦσαι μὴ ἁπλῶς αἰτεῖν τὴν χρηστότητα, σπουδάζειν δὲ ὥστε καὶ τὰ παρ᾽ αὐτῶν
15 μὴ ἐλλείπειν.

20ᵃ. Ἀγάθυνον, Κύριε, ἐν τῇ εὐδοκίᾳ σου τὴν Σιών. Ἀρεσάσθω σοι ἀγαθόν τι περὶ αὐτῆς βουλεύσασθαι, θέλησον αὐτὴν τῶν οἰκείων ἀγαθῶν πληρῶσαι.

20ᵇ. Καὶ οἰκοδομηθήτω τὰ τείχη Ἱερουσαλήμ. Ἀπόδος αὐτῇ πάλιν τὸν
20 πρότερον κόσμον, ἀνακαινίσας καὶ ποιήσας περίβλεπτον. Εἰ δὲ κατὰ τὴν ἐπιγραφὴν ὑπὲρ τῆς οἰκείας ἁμαρτίας ταῦτα ὁ μακάριος Δαυὶδ ἔλεγεν, τί τὸ κατεπεῖγον ἦν μεμνῆσθαι τῆς Ἱερουσαλήμ; Ποίαν γὰρ ἦν ὑπομείνασα τότε καθαίρεσιν;

21ᵃ·ᵇ. Τότε εὐδοκήσεις θυσίαν δικαιοσύνης, ἀναφορὰν καὶ ὁλοκαυτώματα.
25 Τῆς γὰρ πόλεως οἰκοδομηθείσης πάλιν καὶ τοῦ ναοῦ κατασκευασθέντος, ἡδεῖά σοι καὶ τῶν θυσιῶν ἡ προσαγωγὴ φανήσεται ἐν τῷ καθήκοντι τόπῳ κατὰ τὸ τοῦ νόμου βούλημα γενομένη.

21ᶜ. Τότε ἀνοίσουσιν ἐπὶ τὸ θυσιαστήριόν σου μόσχους. Τὸ τηνικαῦτα γὰρ καὶ ἡμεῖς πληρώσομεν τὰ δέοντα, προσάγοντες τὰς θυσίας καὶ τοὺς
30 μόσχους ἀνάγοντες.

16 ἀρεσάσθω conieci, Ἀ.εσ...ω ms. ceteris madore effluxis   19-30 cf. THEO-
DORETUS (1252 B 9-C 6).

Aᵉ 16-17 (p. 285, 22-24): Complaciat tibi id quod ad Sionis prosperitatem respicit.   19-20 (p. 285, 24-25): ...ut restituas ei ueteris felicitatis ornatum. 25-27 (p. 285, 28-30): Quae in terra aliena neglexeras, instaurato templo grate suscipe.

A contrite spirit is a sacrifice to God; a contrite and humbled heart God will not despise (v. 17): instead you saw us depressed in thought, suffering from discouragement, and incapable of coming to any logical or healthy thinking on account of the great number of the troubles besetting us; so you stipulated no sacrifices nor required them of us when you freed us from the misfortune. He brought out God's beneficence, above through mention of the favors he had conferred on them in the beginning in his lovingkindness, and here by mentioning his freeing them from captivity when they gave no evidence of deserving it. Thus, he also shows the people as worthy of gaining lovingkindness because they acknowledged their sin, because their captors were worse, and because they perhaps would acknowledge the grace and occupy themselves in hymn-singing for what happened, but also because they would discharge the sacrifices unceasingly in the future, as he goes on to say. He uses these words so as to highlight God's goodness and to instruct them not simply to appeal to his kindness, but to take pains not to fall short in their own efforts, either.

Be good, O Lord, to Sion in your good pleasure (v. 18): let it please you to plan some good for it; decide to fill it with your good things. *And let the walls of Jerusalem be built:* return to it once more its former adornment, renewing it and making it famous. If, on the contrary, according to the title blessed David had said this in respect of his own sin, what was the obligation to make mention of Jerusalem? What destruction had it undergone by that time? *Then you will take pleasure in a sacrifice of righteousness, offering and holocausts* (v. 21): with the city once again rebuilt and the temple repaired, the presentation of sacrifices will also be attractive to you when made in the proper place according to the intention of the law. *Then they will offer up young bulls on your altar:* at that time we shall also perform the due rites, offering sacrifices and bringing calves. |

PSALMVS LI

Ἐπιστρατευσάντων ποτὲ Ἀσσυρίων ταῖς δέκα φυλαῖς, ἅπαντες μὲν οἱ
περὶ τὸν Ἐφραὶμ ἀπῆλθον αἰχμάλωτοι. Πολλοὶ δὲ καὶ τὴν τοῦ νόμου θρησκείαν προδεδωκότες καὶ ὅλους ἑαυτοὺς τοῖς Ἀσσυρίοις πιστοποιήσαντες
μετέβαλον τὸν τρόπον, τῆς ἐκείνων ἐχόμενοι γνώμης καὶ θεοὺς ἐπιγραφό-   5
μενοι τοὺς παρ᾽ ἐκείνων νομιζομένους. Τοιοῦτος ἦν καὶ ὁ Ῥαψάκης, Ἰουδαῖος μὲν τὸ γένος, μεταβαλλόμενος δὲ τὴν εὐσέβειαν. Ὅτε τοίνυν αἰχμαλώτους λαβόντες οἱ Ἀσσύριοι τοὺς τῶν δέκα φυλῶν ἐπῆλθον καὶ τὴν
Ἱερουσαλήμ, ὡς καὶ ταύτην ἐρημώσοντες εὐκόλως, σταθεὶς ἔξωθεν τοῦ τείχους ὁ Ῥαψάκης διελέγετο τοῖς ἐν τῇ πόλει ὥστε ἀνοῖξαι μὲν τὰς πύλας,   10
δέξασθαι δὲ τὸν Ἀσσύριον, ποτὲ μὲν ἀπειλῶν, ποτὲ δὲ ὀνειδίζων ὡς
οὐδὲν | αὐτοὺς ὠφελεῖν τοῦ Θεοῦ δυναμένου, ποτὲ δὲ καὶ ὑπισχνούμενος
εἰς κρείττονα γῆν αὐτοὺς ἀπελεύσεσθαι καὶ κρείττονα καρπώσασθαι χώραν
εἰ παραδοῖεν τὴν πόλιν, — ταῦτα πόρρωθεν ὁ μακάριος Δαυὶδ ἐν τῷδε προλέγει τῷ ψαλμῷ.   15

3ᵃ. Τί ἐγκαυχᾷ ἐν κακίᾳ, ὁ δυνατός; Ἐπειδὴ τῇ ἀσεβείᾳ τῶν ῥημάτων,
καὶ τῇ μοχθηρίᾳ τῆς γνώμης, καὶ τῇ ὠμότητι τοῦ τρόπου μετὰ πολλῆς
ἐκέχρητο τῆς παρρησίας ὁ Ῥαψάκης, ὡς πρὸς αὐτόν φησι Τί κέχρησαι
τῇ κακίᾳ μετὰ πολλῆς τῆς ἀναιδείας καὶ ὥσπερ καυχώμενος ἐπ᾽ αὐτῇ, δέον
αἰσχύνεσθαι μᾶλλον; Τὸ δὲ ὁ δυνατός κατ᾽ εἰρωνείαν εἶπεν, ἐπειδὴ μεγάλα   20
φρονῶν τοῦτο ἄνω καὶ κάτω φθεγγόμενος ἐφαίνετο.

7-14 cf. Is. XXXVI, 1-20 et argumentum ps. XIII (supra, p. 78-79).

Ἐπιστρατευσάντων — ψαλμῷ: P (= Paris. gr. 139), fol. 141ᵛ; V (= Vat. gr. 1682),
fol. 203ᵛ.   6-11 cf. L (Cord. II, p. 1, ll. 7-11 ab imo): Κυριώτερον δὲ εἰς Ῥαψάκην
ἀναφέρεσθαι δύναται, ὡς ἐξ Ἑβραίων ὢν καὶ ὑπ᾽ Ἀσσυρίων ἀνδραποδισθείς, τὴν ἐκείνων ἐκμα-
θών, βλασφήμοις ἐχρήσατο λόγοις κατὰ Θεοῦ.   6-14 Cord (p. 8, 5-10, sub nomine
Victoris): Τινὲς καὶ τὰ περὶ Ῥαψάκου φασὶ προφητεύειν τὸν Δαυίδ, ὡς Ἰουδαῖος μὲν
ὑπάρχων μετεβάλετο τοῖς τρόποις καὶ συνεβούλευεν αὐτοῖς προδοῦναι τοῖς Ἀσσυρίοις τὴν
Ἱερουσαλήμ, ὡς οὐδὲν αὐτοὺς ὠφελεῖν δυναμένου τοῦ Θεοῦ.   18-20 cf. Cord (p. 8, 10-13,
Victoris): Τί οὖν φησὶ κέχρησαι κακίᾳ μετὰ τοσαύτης ἀναιδείας; Τὸ δὲ ὁ δυνατὸς κατ᾽
εἰρωνείαν διὰ τὸ μεγαλοφρονεῖν αὐτόν.
3ᵃ. Ἐπειδὴ — ἐφαίνετο: P, fol. 142; V, fol. 204; Cord, p. 7.

Aᵉ 6-14 (p. 285, 35-286, 3): Aduersus uerba Rapsacis praeuaricatoris et
Iudeos non solum Assiriorum armis, uerum etiam religioni dedere persuaden-
tis, hoc carmen profeta longe ante conpossuit.   17-20 (p. 286, 9-14): Cum eru-
bescere pro proditione et consilii prauitate deberet; potest et per hironiam
dictum uideri pro inpotente *potens*, — siquidem arrogantiae sursum et deorsum
uerba promebat.

PSALM 52

When in the past the Assyrians made war on the ten tribes, all the people of Ephraim went off into captivity. Many abandoned the observance of the law, entrusted themselves completely to the Assyrians, and changed their ways, taking up their attitudes and adopting what were considered gods by them. Such a person was the Rabshakeh, Jewish by race but a convert by religion. When the Assyrians took people of the ten tribes captive and even advanced on Jerusalem with the intention of devastating it as well without difficulty, the Rabshakeh stood outside the wall and told those in the city to open the gates and admit the Assyrians, sometimes threatening, sometimes making the taunt that God was unable to offer them help, sometimes also promising that they would go to a better country and benefit from a better place if they handed the city over.[1] It is this that blessed David foretells in advance in this psalm.

Why do you boast of wickedness, mighty one? (v. 1). Since the Rab-shakeh employed godlessness in expression, a depraved attitude, and severity of manner along with extreme boldness, he says as if to him, Why do you use villainy with deep shamelessness as though glorying in it, whereas instead you ought to be ashamed? He said *mighty one* ironically, since he gave the impression of taking pride in the above behavior and in his speech below. |

---

1. Theodore sees reference in the psalm to the Assyrian assault on Jerusalem under Sennacherib, which is the subject of 2 Kgs 18.

3ᵇ⁻4ᵃ. Ἀνομίαν ὅλην τὴν ἡμέραν, ἀδικίαν ἐλογίσατο ἡ γλῶσσά σου. Ὅλην τὴν ἡμέραν ἐκείνην λέγει καθ᾽ ἣν κυκλώσαντες ἐφύλαττον τὰ Ἱεροσόλυμα. Διὰ πάσης φησι τῆς ἡμέρας φθέγγεται ἄδικα ἀκορέστως, οὐ διαλιμπάνων ἐν τοῖς κακοῖς. Τὸ δὲ ἐλογίσατο ἡ γλῶσσά σου, ἀντὶ τοῦ Ἄδι-
5 κους λογισμοὺς ἐφθέγξατο ἡ γλῶσσά σου· οὐ γὰρ αὐτὴ ἡ λογιζομένη, ἀλλ ἡ τοῖς λογισμοῖς ἐξυπηρετουμένη.

4ᵇ. Ὡσεὶ ξυρὸν ἠκονημένον ἐποίησας δόλον. Δόλον καλεῖ ἐκεῖνα τὰ ῥήματα, οἷς ἀπατᾶν αὐτοὺς ἐπειρᾶτο ὥστε προδοῦναι τὴν πόλιν, λέγων ἀπελεύσεσθαι καὶ πολὺ τῆς ἡμετέρας βελτίονα· ἐπενόησας γάρ φησι
10 πανουργίαν, δι᾽ ἧς ᾠήθης ἀπατῆσαι αὐτοὺς καὶ προδοῦναι τὴν πόλιν, παρασκευάσας ἄρδην ἀφανίσαι πάντας μετὰ πολλῆς τῆς εὐκολίας. Τοῦτο γὰρ εἶπεν τὸ ὡσεὶ ξυρὸν ἐκ μεταφορᾶς τοῦ ξυροῦ ῥᾳδίως τε καὶ ἀθρόως τὰς τρίχας ὑποτεμνομένου.

5ᵃ. Ἠγάπησας κακίαν ὑπὲρ ἀγαθωσύνην. Προετίμησας τῶν ἀγαθῶν τὰ
15 κακά, μᾶλλον τοῖς Ἀσσυρίοις προσθέμενος ἢ τὰ ἡμέτερα καὶ τὰ τοῦ Θεοῦ φρονῶν.

5ᵇ. Ἀδικίαν ὑπὲρ τὸ λαλῆσαι δικαιοσύνην. Κατὰ κοινοῦ τὸ ἠγάπησας. Εἵλω δέ φησι μᾶλλον ἄδικα λαλεῖν ἢ δίκαια· ἄδικον γὰρ ἦν τὸ πείθειν αὐτοὺς προδοῦναι τὴν πόλιν τοῖς ἐχθροῖς.

20 6. Ἠγάπησας πάντα τὰ ῥήματα καταποντισμοῦ, γλῶσσαν δολίαν. Ῥήματα καταποντισμοῦ καλεῖ ἅπερ ἐφθέγγετο ὡς ἱκανὰ ἀνελεῖν καὶ ἀφανίσαι τοὺς Ἰουδαίους, ἐκ μεταφορᾶς τῶν καταποντουμένων. Μᾶλλον δέ φησιν ἐσπού-

3ᵇ⁻4ᵃ. Ὅλην τὴν ἡμέραν — ἐξυπηρετουμένη: P, fol. 142; V, fol. 204ᵛ; Ambros. C 98 sup., fol. 103ᵛ; Cord, p. 8.   5-6 οὐ γὰρ — ἐξυπηρετουμένη affert L (p. 5, 20-22).
4ᵇ. Δόλον — ὑποτεμνομένου: P, fol. 142; V, fol. 204ᵛ; Cord, p. 9.   9 ἀπελεύσεσθε CV   ἀπελεύσασθαι Cord   ὑμετέρας CV   12 ξυρὸν des. Cord; eadem fere praebet Vat. gr. 2057, fol. 93ᵛ: Θεοδ゛ Ἀντιοχ   12-13 L (p. 5, 23-26): Ὡσεὶ ξυρὸν δὲ οἷον ἐπεπόνησάς φησι πανουργίαν, δι᾽ ἧς μετ᾽ εὐδοκίας τὴν πόλιν ἐξύρησας· ῥᾳδίως γὰρ τὸ ξυρὸν τὰς τρίχας ὑποτέμνεται.
5ᵃ. Προετίμησας — φρονῶν: P, fol. 142ᵛ; V, fol. 205.
5ᵇ. Κατὰ κοινοῦ — ἐχθροῖς: P, fol. 142ᵛ; V, fol. 205.   18-19 Εἵλω — ἐχθροῖς Cord, p. 10.
6. Ῥήματα — ἁμαρτίας: P, fol. 142ᵛ; V, fol. 205; Cord, p. 10 sub nomine THEODORETI.   21 δὲ] οὖν PV Cord.

Aᵉ 4ᵇ (p. 286, 15-21): Effectus doli, quo Iudeos meliorum terrarum oblatione ad ditionem uocabas, ut penitus interrirent funditus euertando, nouaculae conparantur, quae acuta praesertim nihil pilorum, quos radit, reliqui facit. 15 (p. 286, 22): Assiriis rem gessisse nobis.   6 (p. 286, 23-287, 2): Dilectionis nomine duxit profanitatem callidi, qui tantam malitiam non necessitate seruitii sed nocendi affectione sequebatur deditionis nostrae consilia, quibus conrueremus profunditus.

Your tongue gave thought to lawlessness all day long, to iniquity (vv. 1–2). By *all day long* he refers to the time they spent encircling Jerusalem and keeping an eye on it. For the whole day, he is saying, he makes unjust statements insatiably, giving no respite to the troubles. The phrase *Your tongue gave thought* means, Your tongue gave voice to unjust thoughts, not that it has the power of thought but that it ministered to the thoughts. *Like a sharp razor you perpetrated deceit.* By *deceit* he refers to the words he used to beguile them into giving up the city, telling them, Come out to a better place than ours. You plotted villainy, he is saying, and by it you thought to beguile them even into giving up the city, causing them all to disappear utterly with great ease (in the phrase *like a razor* using a metaphor from a razor, which easily and quickly cuts hair).

You loved evil more than goodness (v. 3): you preferred evil to good, giving preference to the Assyrians ahead of thoughts of us and of God. *Iniquity in preference to speaking righteousness.* The phrase *You loved* has a general reference. You chose unjust words, he is saying, rather than just ones, it being an unjust act to persuade them to give up the city to the foe. *You loved all the words involving drowning, a deceitful tongue* (v. 4). By *words involving drowning* he refers to the words he spoke that were calculated to bring down and destroy the Jews, by analogy with people drowning. You were anxious rather | to utter such things, he is saying, by which you hoped

δάξες τοιαῦτα φθέγγεσθαι, δι᾿ ὧν πάντως ἡμᾶς ἀφανίζειν ἤλπισας, καὶ ῥήμασιν ἐκέχρησο δόλου καὶ ὑποκρίσεως μεστοῖς. Τὸ δὲ ἠγάπησας λέγει δεικνὺς ὡς διαθέσει τὸ κακὸν ἔπραττεν, ὅπερ ἐστὶν ἐπίτασις τῆς ἁμαρτίας.

7ᵃ. Διὰ τοῦτο ὁ Θεὸς καθελεῖ σε εἰς τέλος. Διὰ τοῦτο παντελῆ τὴν καθαίρεσιν ὑπομενεῖς καὶ τελείαν ἐπάξει σοι τὴν τιμωρίαν ὁ δεσπότης. 5 Τὸ δὲ εἰς τέλος εἶπεν ὡς ἤδη μὲν καθαιρεθέντος δι᾿ ὧν αἰχμάλωτος ἐλήφθη, τελείαν δὲ ὑποστησομένου τὴν καθαίρεσιν παρὰ τοῦ Θεοῦ. Πῶς;

7ᵇ·ᶜ. Ἐκτίλαι σε, καὶ μεταναστεύσαι σε ἀπὸ σκηνώματος σου καὶ τὸ ῥίζωμά σου ἐκ γῆς ζώντων. Ἀπὸ σκηνώματος, ἵνα εἴπῃ ἀπὸ κατοικήσεως, τουτέστιν ἀπὸ τοῦ κατοικεῖν ἐν ἀνθρώποις. Ἀνασπάσει σέ φησιν ὁ Θεὸς ἀπὸ τῆς τῶν 10 ἀνθρώπων κατοικίας, — ἀντὶ τοῦ ἀναιρήσει· οὕτως γὰρ ἦν τῆς τῶν ἀνθρώπων κατοικίας ἐκσπασθῆναι διὰ τοῦ θανάτου. Διὸ ἐπήγαγεν Καὶ τὸ ῥίζωμά σου ἐκ γῆς ζώντων, ῥίζωμα λέγων τὸ γένος, ἐπειδὴ πᾶσιν ἀνθρώποις ἐν τάξει ῥίζης ἐστὶ τὸ γένος. Σὲ τοίνυν φησὶ μετὰ παντός σου τοῦ γένους ἀφανίσει καὶ ἀνασπάσει ὁ Θεὸς ἀπὸ κατοικήσεως ἀνθρώπων καὶ ἀπὸ τῶν ζώντων. 15

8ᵃ. Ὄψονται δίκαιοι καὶ φοβηθήσονται. Καὶ σὺ μέν φησι ταῦτα ὑπομενεῖς, οἱ δὲ δίκαιοι, τουτέστιν οἵ σου λαοί, θεασάμενοι τὴν σὴν ἀπώλειαν φόβῳ κατασχεθήσονται· ἱκανὴ γὰρ ἡ εἰς σε τιμωρία κἀκείνους φοβῆσαι, καίτοι διὰ τὴν εἰς ἐκείνους εὐεργεσίαν τοιαῦτά σου πάσχειν μέλλοντος.

8ᵇ. Καὶ ἐπ᾿ αὐτὸν γελάσονται καὶ ἐροῦσιν. Πῶς οὖν καὶ φοβηθήσονται 20 καὶ γελάσονται; Φοβηθήσονται διὰ τὸ μέγεθος τῆς πληγῆς, γελάσονται διὰ τὴν τοῦ πάσχοντος ἀλαζονείαν. Τί γὰρ ἐροῦσι καὶ γελάσονται;

2 τότε δὲ Cord.
7ᵃ. Διὰ τοῦτο — πῶς: P, fol. 142ᵛ; V, fol. 205; Cord, p. 10.   7 τὴν] τοῦ C   πῶς om. Cord.
7ᵇ·ᶜ. Ἀπὸ σκηνώματος — ἀπὸ τῶν ζώντων: P, fol. 142ᵛ; V, fol. 205ʳ·ᵛ; Cord, p. 11 sub nomine THEODORETI.   9-10 ἵνα εἴπῃ — ἀνθρώποις affert L (p. 5, 34-36) 13-14 ἐπεὶ — γένος affert L (p. 5, 38-39).
8ᵃ. Καὶ σὺ μέν — μέλλοντος: P, fol. 143; V, fol. 205ᵛ; Cord, p. 11 sub nomine ATHANASII (P. G., XXVII, 246 D 8-248 A 1).   16-17 ὑπομένεις codd. Cord   17 σου] τοῦ CV.
8ᵇ. Πῶς οὖν — γελάσονται: P, fol. 143; V, fol. 205ᵛ; Cord, p. 12.   21 φοβηθήσονται — γελάσονται om. Cord   γελάσονται] γελάσουσι CV.

Aᶜ 7ᵃ (p. 287, 3-6): Perfecte delebit quem iam ex parte distruxit, ut captiuus (captibus ms) sub hostium degeret potestate.   9-11 (p. 287, 7-8): Ac si diceret de habitatione et uita mortalium.   13-14 (p. 287, 9-10): Radicem dicit sobolem, cuius uim et uicem uidetur praebere successio.   18-19 (p. 287, 11-16): Habundet quippe in te prolata uindicta ad terrendos alios et quidem latiore (laetiore ms) iam effectu praeditos, cum pro ipsorum commodo in te uis exitii motata doceatur.

to destroy us totally, and you employed expressions full of deceit and pretense. He used the term *You loved* to bring out the attitude with which he perpetrated the evil, this being the enormity of his sin.

For this reason God will do away with you forever (v. 5). *For this reason you will suffer utter destruction, and the Lord will impose on you overwhelming punishment.* He used *forever* to imply his already being destroyed by those by whom he was taken captive and his enduring final destruction at God's hands. *To pluck you up and move you from your tent, and your root from the land of the living. From your tent* means from your dwelling—that is, from living among human beings. God will root you up, he is saying, from habitation with human beings—that is, he will destroy you (this being the way to be plucked up from human habitation by death). Hence he went on to say *and your root from the land of the living,* by *root* meaning "race," since for all human beings their race acts as a root. So he is saying, God will destroy you along with all your race, and will pluck you up from human habitation and from living things.

The righteous will see and be afraid (v. 6): while you will suffer this fate, the righteous—that is, your people—will observe your ruin and will be gripped with fear; your punishment will be sufficient to terrify them, even though it is by way of a favor to them that you are about to meet such a fate. *They will laugh at him and say.* So how is it that they will both fear and laugh? They will fear on account of the magnitude of the slaughter; they will laugh at the arrogance of the sufferer. What is it, in fact, that *they will say and laugh at?* | *Behold, the person who did not make God his helper, but trusted*

9ᵃ·ᵇ. Ἰδοὺ ἄνθρωπος ὃς οὐκ ἔθετο τὸν Θεὸν βοηθὸν αὐτοῦ, ἀλλ᾽ ἐπήλ
πισεν ἐπὶ τὸ πλῆθος τοῦ πλούτου αὐτοῦ. Ὅτι τὸν Θεὸν οὐ θέμενος | πρὸ
τῶν ὀφθαλμῶν, — ὠνείδιζε μὲν ἐπὶ τῇ εἰς αὐτὸν εὐσεβείᾳ, ὡς οὐδὲν ὠφελου-
μένους ἐκ τούτου, μεγάλα δὲ ἐφρόνει ἐπὶ τῇ οἰκείᾳ περιουσίᾳ, τῷ τε πλήθει τοῦ
5 στρατοπέδου καὶ τῶν ἵππων, — ταῦτα λέγοντος γελάσονται ὁρῶντες αὐτοῦ
τῶν ῥημάτων τὴν ἀλαζονείαν, ὅτι μεγάλα ἐπαγγελλόμενος τοιαύτην ἔδωκε δίκην.

9ᶜ. Καὶ ἐνεδυναμώθη ἐπὶ τῇ ματαιότητι αὐτοῦ. Καὶ τοῦ μὲν Θεοῦ τὸ
μέγεθός φησιν οὐ λογιζόμενος, ἐπὶ δὲ τῇ οἰκείᾳ περιουσίᾳ μεγάλα φρονῶν,
μετὰ μείζονος τῆς δυνάμεως κέχρηται τῇ οἰκείᾳ κακίᾳ· ματαιότητα γὰρ
10 καλεῖ τὴν μοχθηρίαν ὡς εἰκαίαν καὶ οὐδὲν αὐτὸν ὠφελῆσαι δυνηθεῖσαν.

10ᵃ. Ἐγὼ δὲ ὡσεὶ ἐλαία κατάκαρπος ἐν τῷ οἴκῳ τοῦ Θεοῦ. Κἀκεῖνος
μὲν πείσεται τοιαῦτα, ἐγὼ δὲ ἐν τῷ οἴκῳ τοῦ Θεοῦ διαφυλαχθήσομαι δίκην
ἐλαίας κατακάρπου, ἀεὶ φυλαττόμενος τῇ τοῦ Θεοῦ βοηθείᾳ καὶ ἀκμάζων
ἐν αὐτῇ, καὶ οὐδέποτε μεθιστάμενος ἐντεῦθεν ἀπὸ πολεμίων ἐφόδου, ἐπειδὴ
15 καὶ ἡ ἐλαία διηνεκὲς ἐν τῇ φύσει τὸ θάλλειν ἔχει.

10ᵇ. Ἤλπισα ἐπὶ τὸ ἔλεος τοῦ Θεοῦ εἰς τὸν αἰῶνα καὶ εἰς τὸν αἰῶνα
τοῦ αἰῶνος. Ταῦτα δέ μοι ὑπῆρξεν, ἐπειδὴ διηνεκῶς ἐλπίζων τῆς αὐτοῦ
φιλανθρωπίας τεύξεσθαι, εἰκότως καὶ ἀπολαύω τῶν προσδοκωμένων.

11ᵃ. Ἐξομολογήσομαί σοι εἰς τὸν αἰῶνα, ὅτι ἐποίησας. Καὶ οὐ μόνον ἐλπί-
20 ζων διατελέσω, | ἀλλὰ γὰρ καὶ ὑπὲρ ὧν ἐποίησας ἤδη διηνεκῶς εὐχαριστήσω.

11ᵇ. Καὶ ὑπομενῶ τὸ ὄνομά σου, ὅτι χρηστὸν ἐναντίον τῶν ὁσίων σου.
Καὶ διαμενῶ φησι τῆς σῆς ἐπικλήσεως οὐκ ἀφιστάμενος, ὑπομένων δὲ κἂν
ἐν θλίψεσιν ἐξετασθήσομαι, ἐκ τῶν προλαβόντων ἔχων τὴν πεῖραν ὅτι
ἄγαν ὠφελιμώτατον ἡ ἐπίκλησις ἡ σὴ γίνεται τοῖς κεκτημένοις αὐτήν.

9ᵃ·ᵇ. Ὅτι τὸν Θεὸν – ἔδωκε δίκην: P, fol. 143; V, fol. 205; Cord, p. 12.
9ᶜ. Καὶ τοῦ μὲν Θεοῦ — δυνηθεῖσαν: P, fol. 143; V, fol. 205ᵛ. 8 τὴν οἰκείαν
περιουσίαν C.
10ᵃ. Κἀκεῖνος — θάλλειν ἔχει: P, fol. 143; V, fol. 205ᵛ; Cord, p. 12. 15 θάλλεν C.
10ᵇ-11ᵃ. Ταῦτα — εὐχαριστήσω: P, fol. 143; V, fol. 206; Cord, p. 13.
11ᵇ. Καὶ διαμενῶ — αὐτήν: P, fol. 143; V, fol. 206ᵛ.

Aᵉ 9ᵃ·ᵇ (p. 287, 17. 18-20): Cuius cultum exprobrat in Iudeos... aequilatus
Assirii pompam exercitumque fidelium populo iactanter ostentans. 9-10 (p. 287,
21-23): Vanis inflatus nihil solidi in moribus, quo iuuaretur, inuenit. 13-15 (p. 287,
23-25): Fecundus uirtutibus et semper uiriens felicitate continua. 11ᵃ (p. 287,
29-31): Gratus semper existam, de praestitis sperare praestanda non cessans.
11ᵇ (p. 287, 32-288, 1): Manibit in me inuocandi te cura perpetua, etiam si cir-
cumder (circumdeder ms) aduersis, quando experimentis priorum dedici quid
commodi talis habeat intenta supplicatio.

in the abundance of his wealth (v. 7): because he did not set God before his eyes. He found fault with them for their reverence to God, claiming that they gained no benefit from him, and instead he gloried in his own resources, the great size of the army and the cavalry. Hence, the use of the phrase *they will laugh* on seeing the arrogance of his words, because, after lofty promises, he paid such a penalty. *And he was confirmed in his own futility:* taking no account of God's greatness, and instead glorying in his own resources, he exercised his own malice with greater force (by *futility* referring to his depravity as useless and incapable of helping him).

I, on the other hand, am like a fruitful olive tree in the house of God (v. 8): while he will meet such a fate, I shall be carefully protected *in the house of God like a fruitful olive tree,* always guarded by God's help and flourishing with it, never moved from there at the enemy's approach, since the olive can by nature flourish without interruption. *I hoped in the mercy of God forever and ever:* this was my lot, since I constantly hoped to be granted his lovingkindness, and I rightly receive what I expected. *I shall confess to you forever for what you have done* (v. 9): not only shall I continue hoping, but also I shall constantly give thanks for what you have already done. *And I shall wait on your name because it is good in the sight of your holy ones:* I shall persevere in invoking you without desisting, waiting upon you even if I am caught up in tribulations, knowing from previous experience that invocation of you is very beneficial for those having recourse to it. |

PSALMVS LII

Τὴν αὐτὴν καὶ ὅδε ὁ ψαλμὸς ὑπόθεσιν ἔχει· βραχὺ γοῦν τι καὶ ὑπήλλακται τῷ ιγ'. Εἰς τὸν Ῥαψάκην γὰρ καὶ τὰ τότε γενόμενα εἴρηται τῷ μακαρίῳ Δαυὶδ ὁ ψαλμὸς ὥσπερ οὖν κἀκεῖνος.

2ᵃ·ᵇ. Εἶπεν ἄφρων ἐν καρδίᾳ αὐτοῦ Οὐκ ἔστι Θεός. Τοῦτο γὰρ ἔλεγε. 5
Τίς ὁ Θεὸς ὃς ῥύσεται ὑμᾶς ἐκ χειρὸς τῶν Ἀσσυρίων παρεξοδικώτερον ἑρμηνεύομεν ἐπειδήπερ ἐν τῷ ιγ' ἑρμηνεύεται.

2ᶜ·ᵈ. Διεφθάρησαν καὶ ἐβδελύχθησαν ἐν ἀνομίαις, οὐκ ἔστι ποιῶν ἀγαθόν. Ἐδείχθη καθόλου περὶ τῶν Ἀσσυρίων λέγων | Οὐκ ἔστι ποιῶν ἀγαθόν, τουτέστι πάντες κακοί.
10

3-4. Ὁ Θεὸς ἐκ τοῦ οὐρανοῦ διέκυψεν ἐπὶ τοὺς υἱοὺς τῶν ἀνθρώπων τοῦ ἰδεῖν εἰ ἔστιν συνιὼν ἢ ἐκζητῶν τὸν Θεόν. Πάντες ἐξέκλιναν, ἅμα ἠχρειώθησαν, οὐκ ἔστι ποιῶν ἀγαθόν, οὐκ ἔστιν ἕως ἑνός. Τοῦτο οὖν αὐτό φησιν· καὶ ἐξετάσαι βουλόμενος ὁ Θεὸς εἶδεν ἐκ τῶν οὐρανῶν, καὶ ἐξετάσας εὗρεν ὅτι μηδεὶς ἐν αὐτοῖς συνιεὶς τὸ χρήσιμον, ἀλλὰ πάντες μὲν μοχθηροί, ἀγα- 15
θοποιῶν δὲ οὐδείς.

5-6ᵇ. Οὐχὶ γνώσονται πάντες οἱ ἐργαζόμενοι τὴν ἀνομίαν, οἱ κατεσθίοντες τὸν λαόν μου ἐν βρώσει ἄρτου; Τὸν Θεὸν οὐκ ἐπεκαλέσαντο. Ἐκεῖ φοβηθήσονται φόβον οὗ οὐκ ἦν φόβος, ὅτι ὁ Θεὸς διεσκόρπισεν ὀστᾶ ἀνθρωπαρέσκων. Μεθ' ὑπερβάτου ἐστίν· οὕτω γὰρ ἐπεσημηνάμεθα κἀκεῖ. Ἡ γὰρ ἀκολουθία 20
αὕτη· Οὐχὶ γνώσονται πάντες οἱ ἐργαζόμενοι τὴν ἀνομίαν, οἱ κατεσθίοντες τὸν λαὸν ἐν βρώσει ἄρτου, ὅτι ὁ Θεὸς διεσκόρπισεν ὀστᾶ ἀνθρωπαρέσκων; Τὰ

2-5 cf. supra (p. 78 ss.) exegesis ps. XIII   6 cf. Is. XXXVI, 15. 18   20 cf. p. 82, 2.

Τὴν αὐτὴν — ἑρμηνεύεται: P, fol. 144; V, fol. 206ᵛ.   1-5 cf. L (p. 17, ll. 5-3
ab imo atque p. 18, 5-10)   6 ἡμᾶς ms   7 αὐτὸ ἑρμηνεύομεν V.
2ᶜ·ᵈ. Ἐδείχθη — κακοί: P, fol. 144ᵛ; V, fol. 207; Cord, p. 22.
3-4. Τοῦτο οὖν — οὐδείς: P, fol. 144ᵛ; V, fol. 207ᶠ ᵛ; Cord, p. 23.   14 καὶ
ἐξετάσαι — Θεὸς om. C.
5-6ᵇ. Μεθ' ὑπερβάτου — ἐδέξαντο: P, fol. 145; V, fol. 207ᵛ-208; Cord, p. 25
(= P. G. LXVI, 672 AB).   20 μετ' ὑπέρβατον CPV   L (p. 21, 18): Καθ' ὑπέρβατόν ἐστιν ἡ φράσις.

Aᵉ 1-3 (p. 288, 4-8): Eadem materia est psalmi praesentis quae tertii decimi,
parua parte uorsum commotata; in Rapsacem enim et ea quae illis sunt gesta
temporibus a sancto Dauid longe ante formatus est. Cf. Pseudo-Beda (761).

PSALM 53

This psalm also has the same theme, being brief and an alternative form of Psalm 14. This psalm, like the former one, in fact, is composed by blessed David in reference to the Rabshakeh and the events of that time.

The fool has said in his heart, There is no God (v. 1). He had, in fact, said as much, "Who is this God who will rescue you from the hand of the Assyrians?"[1] and we make a passing comment, especially since it was commented on in Psalm 14. They became corrupt and loathsome in their transgressions. There is no one who does good. The clause *There is no one who does good* evidently referred to the Assyrians in general, meaning, All were evil. *God looked down from heaven on human beings to see if there are any who are intelligent or seek after God. All went astray and at the same time proved useless; there no one who does good, not even one* (vv. 2–3). So he is saying the same thing: in his wish to make an examination God looked from heaven, and on examining he found that no one among them had an understanding of goodness; rather, all were depraved, and no one was doing good.

Have they no knowledge, all those who commit lawlessness, those who eat up my people like a meal of bread? They did not invoke God. There they will be possessed by fear where there was no fear, because God scattered bones of those who pleased human beings (vv. 4–5). Hyperbaton is involved, as we remarked also in comment on Psalm 14, the sequence being as follows: *Have they no knowledge, all those who commit lawlessness, those who eat up my people, because God scattered bones of those who pleased human beings?* | The rest is placed in the middle to give the sense, Would the very

---

1. Cf. 2 Kgs 18:30.

δὲ λοιπὰ διὰ μέσου — τουτέστιν Οὐκ ἂν μάθοιεν αὐτοὶ οἱ τῆς ἀνομίας
ἐργάται, οἱ τὸν λαὸν κατεσθίειν καὶ καταναλίσκειν ὥσπερ τινὰ τροφὴν ἀναγκαίαν αὐτοῖς πειρώμενοι, ὅτι πάντας ἀναλίσκεις καὶ ἀφανίζεις τοὺς ἀνθρω-
παρέσκους; — ὡς ἀπὸ τοῦ Ῥαψάκου, ἐπειδὴ πρὸς χάριν ἀνθρώπων ἀσε-
5 βείας ἐφθέγγετο μεστά. Τὸ δὲ τὸν Θεὸν οὐκ ἐπεκαλέσαντο, ἐκεῖ φοβηθήσονται
φόβον οὗ οὐκ ἦν φόβος διὰ μέσου κεῖται, ἀντὶ τοῦ Θεοῦ μνήμην μὴ ποιησά-
μενοι, ἐφοβήθησαν ἃ μὴ προσεδόκησαν· καταφρονήσαντες γὰρ τῶν ἐν τῇ
Ἱερουσαλήμ, ὡς εὐτελῶν καὶ ὀλίγων, παρὰ πᾶσαν ἐλπίδα τὴν παρὰ τοῦ
Θεοῦ τιμωρίαν ἐδέξαντο.

10 6ᶜ. Κατησχύνθησαν ὅτι ὁ Θεὸς ἐξουδένωσεν αὐτούς. Ἅπαντες γάρ φησιν
οἵ τε τοῦ λαοῦ καὶ ὁ Ῥαψάκης αὐτὸς αἰσχύνης ἐπληρώθησαν, τοῦ Θεοῦ τὸ
μηδὲν πᾶσαν αὐτῶν ἀποφήναντος τὴν δύναμιν καὶ οὕτως ἐν μίᾳ ῥοπῇ πάντας
ἀνελόντος.

7ᵃ. Τίς δώσει ἐκ Σιὼν τὸ σωτήριον τοῦ Ἰσραήλ; Ἐπειδὴ ἐν τῇ Σιὼν
15 κατοικεῖν παρ' αὐτοῖς ὑπείληπτο ὁ Θεός, τίς ἡμῖν φησιν ἀπὸ τοῦ Σιὼν
ὄρους | παρέξει τὴν σωτηρίαν; — ἀντὶ τοῦ ὁ Θεός, ὡς ὁμολογούμενον
ἀποσιωπήσας, ἐπεὶ μηδὲ ἐνῆν παρ' ἑτέρου τινὸς ἐκδέξασθαι βοήθειαν ἐκ
τοῦ Σιὼν ὄρους ἢ τοῦ Θεοῦ τοῦ καὶ διάγειν ἐκεῖ πιστευομένου.

7ᵇ⁻ᶜ. Ἐν τῷ ἐπιστρέψαι τὸν Θεὸν τὴν αἰχμαλωσίαν τοῦ λαοῦ αὐτοῦ ἀγαλ-
20 λιάσεται Ἰακὼβ καὶ εὐφρανθήσεται Ἰσραήλ. Ἐπειδάν φησι κἀκείνων ἀνακα-
λέσηται τὴν αἰχμαλωσίαν, περὶ τῶν δέκα λέγων φυλῶν, τῷ τηνικαῦτα ἀληθῆ
δεξόμεθα τὴν εὐφροσύνην. Ἐμνημόνευσεν δὲ αὐτῶν, εἰκότως ὡς πρόσφατον
εἰς αἰχμαλωσίαν ἀπαχθέντων, δεικνὺς ὅτι συναλγεῖν αὐτοῖς δίκαιον.

2 κατεσθίοντες Cord   5 ἐθέγγετο C   6 φόβῳ CPV.
6ᶜ. Ἅπαντες — ἀνελόντος: P, fol. 145ᵛ; V, fol. 208ᵛ.
7ᵃ. Ἐπειδὴ — πιστευομένου: P, fol. 145ᵛ; V, fol. 208ᵛ; Cord, p. 27 (= P. G.,
672 C).
7ᵇ⁻ᶜ. Ἐπειδάν — δίκαιον; P, fol. 145ᵛ; V, fol. 209

Aᵉ 4-5 (p. 288, 20-23): Hominum sibi placentium, Rapsacis scilicet, qui in
gratiam hominum plena inquitatis uerba depromsit.   16-18 (p. 288, 23-26):
Subauditur « Quis nisi Deus? ». Quis, inquit, uobis de monte Sion, in quo Deus
habitare credebatur, dabit salutem?   7ᵇ⁻ᶜ (p. 288, 27-280, 2): Et perfecta laetitia in uniuerso populo tribuetur, cum x tribuum, quae hoc impitu adductae
sunt, fuerit laxata captiuitas; hoc autem ideo ut se calamitati fratrum germano
affectu condolere monstraret.

evildoers not realize, those who eat up and consume my people as though using them as some nourishment required by them, that you consume and destroy those who please human beings? This is on the part of the Rabshakeh, since he uttered words full of impiety to please human beings. The section *They did not invoke God. There they will be possessed by fear where there was no fear* is placed in the middle, meaning, By not recalling God they feared what they had not expected, scorning those in Jerusalem as vile and insignificant, and yet receiving punishment from God against all expectation. *They were put to shame because God scorned them:* all the members of the people and the Rabshakeh himself were filled with shame when God reduced to nothing all their might and thus did away with them all in one fell swoop.

Who will give from Sion the salvation of Israel? (v. 6). Since God was thought by them to dwell in Sion, he asks, Who will provide us with salvation from Mount Sion? He refers to God, but keeps it to himself as though a secret confession, since there was no chance of receiving help from any one other than God, who was believed to be actually living there. *When God averts the captivity of his people, Jacob will rejoice and Israel will be glad:* since he will recall even them from captivity (the ten tribes, that is), we shall feel true joy at that time. Now, he made mention of them, rightly so as people recently taken off into captivity, to bring out that it was proper to grieve along with them. |

PSALMVS LIII

Ἔστι μὲν καὶ ὅδε περὶ τῆς αὐτῆς ὑποθέσεως ὁ ψαλμός. Λέγει δὲ αὐτὸν ὡς ἀπὸ προσώπου τοῦ Ἐζεκίου· κἂν γὰρ μίαν πολλῶν ψαλμῶν ὑπόθεσιν εἶναι συμβαίνει, ἀλλὰ ποικίλως καὶ διαφόρως χρῆται τοῖς λόγοις.

3ᵃ. Ὁ Θεός, ἐν τῷ ὀνόματί σου σῶσόν με. Ἐπειδὴ τοῦτο μάλιστα ἐκεῖ- 5 νοι ὠνείδιζον, κεκυκλωκότες τὴν πόλιν, ὡς οὐδὲν αὐτοὺς ὀνῆσαι δύναται τὰ παρὰ τοῦ Ἐζεκίου λεγόμενα, — ταῦτα δὲ ἦν, ὡς προσῆκεν ἐπὶ τὸν Θεὸν πεποιθέναι, ὃς ἀπαλλάξει πάντως αὐτοὺς τοῦ κινδύνου, — καλῶς εἶπεν τὸ ἐν τῷ ὀνόματί σου σῶσόν με, τουτέστιν Ἐπειδὴ τὸ σὸν ὄνομα ἐπικαλού- μενος χλευάζομαι παρ' ἐκείνων, ἐν αὐτῷ τούτῳ τὴν σωτηρίαν μοι παρά- 10 σχου, ὥστε μὴ πολέμου, μὴ παρατάξεως δεηθῆναι, ἀλλὰ μόνῃ τῇ σῇ προσευχῇ τυχεῖν τῶν σπουδαζομένων, ἵνα μάθωσιν οὗτοι πόση τῶν τὴν σὴν βοήθειαν ἐπικαλουμένων ἡ ἰσχύς.

3ᵇ. Καὶ ἐν τῇ δυνάμει σου κρινεῖς μοι. Τινὲς κρινεῖς με διὰ τοῦ μ̄ καὶ ε̄ ἀναγινώσκουσι ἐπὶ τῆς αἰτιατικῆς πτώσεως· ἀναγνωστέον δὲ κρινεῖς μοι διὰ 15 τοῦ μ̄ καὶ ο̄ καὶ ῑ ἐπὶ τῆς δοτικῆς, ἀντὶ τοῦ Ἐμοὶ κρινεῖς. Ὅταν μὲν γὰρ λέγῃ Κρῖνον αὐτοὺς ἢ αὐτόν, κατάκρινον λέγει· ὅταν δὲ αὐτοῖς ἢ αὐτῷ, μέ, μοί, ἀντὶ τοῦ δίκασον. Ἐνταῦθα | δὲ οὐ κατα- κριθῆναι αἰτεῖ, ἀλλ' ἀντὶ τοῦ Τῇ σῇ δυνάμει χρησάμενος κρῖνον ἐμοί τε καὶ τούτοις, καὶ οὕτως ἀδικουμένῳ βοήθησον. 20

6-7 cf. Is. XXXVI, 18-20   13 ss. cf. supra p. 55 (in IX, 20).

Ἔστι — λόγοις: P, fol. 146; V, fol. 209.
3ᵃ. Ἐπειδὴ — ἡ ἰσχύς: P, fol. 146ᵛ; V, fol. 209ᵛ; Cord, p. 35 (= P. G., 672 CD); cf. Paraphrasis (p. 31) atque L (p. 33, 32-37).
3ᵇ. Τινὲς — βοήθησον: P, fol. 146ᵛ; V, fol. 209ᵛ; Vat, gr. 2057, fol. 95ᵛ-96 (Θεοδώ(ρ)ου Ἀντ(ι)οχ(είας) nonnullis mutatis; Ambros. C 98 sup., fol. 105ᵛ-106 (ed. Ioh. MERCATI, Varia Sacra, p. 112); cf. L (p. 33, 38-44): Ἔνιοι δὲ κρινεῖς μοι γράφουσι· βούλονται γὰρ τὴν αἰτιατικήν, οἷον κρῖνόν με, ἐπὶ κατακρίσεως τίθεσθαι· τὴν δὲ δοτικήν, οἷον κρινεῖς μοι, ἐπὶ βοηθείας καὶ ἀντιλήψεως. Ἐπεὶ οὖν κἀνταῦθα οὐ κατα- κριθῆναι αἰτεῖ, ἀλλ' ἀντιλήψεως τυχεῖν, κρινεῖς μοι ἀξιοῦσι γράφειν, οὐχὶ κρινεῖς με. 15 αἰτικῆς C.

Aᵉ 2-3 (p. 289, 6-7): Ex persona Ezechiae hoc canticum format profeta. 3ᵃ (p. 289, 12-17): In eo, inquit, nomine salutem tribue, quod profuturum nobis negant Assiri et quod me frustra subditis praedicare blasfemant.   3ᵇ (p. 289, 18-21): Ac si diceret Pro me; quotiesque enim legitur Iudica illos, ut condem- nentur petit. Me enim cum dicit iudica, defensionem rogat.

PSALM 54

While this psalm also has the same theme, he recites it in the person of Hezekiah. You see, even if many psalms happen to have the one theme, nevertheless he uses the words in a range of different ways. *Save me, God, in your name* (v. 1). Since it was their particular taunt, as they encircled the city, that the words of Hezekiah—to the effect that they should trust in God to free them completely from the danger[1]—*could not help them, Save me in your name* was well put. In other words, Since I am mocked by them for calling on your name, provide me with salvation by that very thing so that I may have no need of fighting or battle array, but simply with a prayer to you I may attain the object of my desire, so that they may learn how great is the power of people who call upon your help. *And in your might you will judge in my favor.* Some commentators read *you will judge me,* with "me" in the accusative case; but it should be read *you will judge in favor of me,* with "me" in the dative—that is, you will judge in my favor. You see, when it says, Judge them or him, it means, Condemn; whereas when it says, In their or his or my favor, it means, Give a ruling. Now, here he does not ask to be condemned, but says, By using your power, judge between me and them, and thus help the wronged. |

---

1. Cf. 2 Kgs 18:30, 32.

4ᵃ. Ὁ Θεός εἰσάκουσον τῆς προσευχῆς μου. Μὴ ἀποπέμψῃ μου τὴν δέησιν.

4ᵇ. Ἐνώτισαι τὰ ῥήματα τοῦ στόματός μου. Φρόντισον, καὶ μετὰ διαθέσεως ἄκουσον τῶν τῆς προσευχῆς μου ῥημάτων.

5ᵃ. Ὅτι ἀλλότριοι ἐπανέστησαν ἐπ᾽ ἐμέ. Οὐδὲ γὰρ πρὸς οἰκείους μοι ὁ
5 πόλεμος, ἀλλ᾽ ἐχθροὶ καὶ ἀλλόφυλοι οἱ πολεμοῦντες, ὥστε μηδὲ ἄξιον εἶναι
φείσασθαι αὐτῶν.

5ᵇ. Καὶ κραταιοὶ ἐζήτησαν τὴν ψυχήν μου. Ἀλλὰ καὶ ἰσχυροὶ οἱ τὴν
πρὸς ἐμὲ ἐνιστάμενοι μάχην.

5ᶜ. Καὶ οὐ προέθεντο τὸν Θεὸν ἐνώπιον αὐτῶν. Καὶ οὐδὲ εἰς ἔννοιαν
10 λαμβάνοντες τὸ παρά σου κριτήριον, ὥστε κἂν διὰ τοῦτο σύμμετρον ἢ
πεφεισμένην τὴν καθ᾽ ἡμῶν ὀργὴν ἐπιδείξασθαι. Οὐκοῦν φησιν ὅσῳ καὶ
ἀλλότριοι καὶ ἰσχυροὶ καὶ ἀσεβεῖς, τοσούτῳ δίκαιος τῆς παρά σου βοηθείας ἐγώ.

6. Ἰδοὺ γὰρ ὁ Θεὸς βοηθεῖ μοι, καὶ ὁ Κύριος ἀντιλήμπτωρ τῆς ψυχῆς
15 μου. Ἀλλὰ κἂν πρὸ τῶν πραγμάτων οὐκ ἠβουλήθησαν συνιέναι τὴν παρά
σου δύναμίν τε καὶ βοήθειαν, ἀλλ᾽ ἐξ αὐτῆς γνώσονται τῆς πείρας, ὅτι τε
βοηθεῖς καὶ κινδυνεύοντος ἀντιλαμβάνῃ, καὶ αἰσθήσονται μάτην ἡμᾶς ὀνειδίζοντες πρὸ τούτου. Κἀνταῦθα δὲ πρόσκειται τὸ Ἰδοὺ ἀπὸ τοῦ ἰδιώματος.

7ᵃ. Ἀποστρέψει τὰ κακὰ τοῖς ἐχθροῖς μου. Τὰ γὰρ κακὰ ἐπ᾽ ἐκείνους
20 μετοίσει, καλῶς τὸ Ἀποστρέψει εἰπών, | ἐπειδὴ προσεδόκων μὲν οἱ Ἀσσύριοι
τούτους ἀναιρήσειν· τοὐναντίον δὲ ἀπώλοντο μὲν ἐκεῖνοι, ἐρρύσθησαν δὲ
οὗτοι τῶν κακῶν.

4ᵃ. Μὴ — δέησιν: P. fol. 146ᵛ; V, fol. 210.   1 μοι C.
4ᵇ. Φρόντισον — ῥημάτων: P, fol. 146ᵛ; V, fol. 210; C 98 sup., fol. 106; Cord,
p. 36 (P. G., 672 D).
5ᵃ. Οὐδὲ γάρ — αὐτῶν: P, fol. 147; V, fol. 210; Cord, p. 37.   5 ὑπολεμοῦντες C.
5ᵇ. Ἀλλὰ καὶ — μάχην: P, fol. 147; V, fol. 210; C 98 sup., fol. 106.
5ᶜ. Καὶ οὐδὲ — ἐγώ: P, fol. 147; V, fol. 210ʳ·ᵛ; C 98 sup., fol. 106.
6. Ἀλλὰ κἂν — ἰδιώματος: P, f. 147; V, fol. 210ᵛ; Cord, p. 37.   15 συνεῖναι
CPV   16 τε om. Cord   17 ἡμῶν Cord.
7ᵃ. Τὰ γὰρ — κακῶν: P, fol. 147ᵛ; V, fol. 210ᵛ; C 98 sup., fol. 106.

Aᵉ 2-3 (p. 289, 22-25): Cura, inquit, de me et cum affectu auxiliandi uerba
meae supplicationis audito.   5-6 (p. 289, 26-28): Quorum non est deferenda
punitio impietatis.   11-13 (p. 289, 29-290, 1): Quanto igitur impugnatores mei
et externi sunt et uiribus insolentes et tui inimici, hoc ego dignor tuo praesidio.   15-16 (p. 290, 5-7): Experientur ipsi exitium, quod inferre molliti sunt.

O God, hearken to my prayer (v. 2): do not dismiss my petition. *Give ear to the words of my mouth:* pay attention, and listen to the words of my prayer with benevolence. *Because strangers have risen up against me* (v. 3): my fighting is not against my own; those fighting me are foes and foreigners, and so they do not deserve to be spared. *Powerful men have sought my life:* those doing battle with me are strong. *They do not set God before them:* they give no thought to judgment from you so as to exert their wrath against us with consequent restraint and mercy. Inasmuch as that they are foreign, strong, and godless, therefore, I deserve help from you on that account.

Lo, God in fact assists me, and the Lord is the support of my life (v. 4): even if before the event they were not prepared to grasp the might and assistance that comes from you, they nevertheless will recognize from experience itself that you help and support those in danger, and they will come to appreciate that it was pointless to taunt us before this. Here, too, *Lo* occurs by way of an idiom. *You will turn back the troubles on my foes* (v. 5): transfer the troubles onto them. *You will turn back* was well put, since the Assyrians expected to destroy them, but on the contrary they themselves perished while the others were rescued from the troubles. | *And in your truth destroy them*

7ᵇ. Ἐν τῇ ἀληθείᾳ σου ἐξολόθρευσον αὐτούς. Εἴρηται ὡς πολλάκις τοῦ Θεοῦ τῆς ἀληθείας μέμνηται εἰς παράστασιν τοῦ βεβαίου τῶν γιγνομένων· ἀληθῆ οὖν καὶ βεβαίαν καὶ ἰσχυρὰν τὴν ἐξολόθρευσιν αὐτῶν ἐργάσεται, τουτέστι σφόδρα αὐτοὺς ἀφανίσει.

8ᵃ. Ἑκουσίως θύσω σοι. Τούτων δὲ γενομένων, μετὰ πολλῆς τῆς σπου- 5
δῆς καὶ τῆς προθυμίας τὰς εὐχαριστηρίους προσάξω σοι θυσίας, — καλῶς
τὸ προθύμως ἑκουσίως εἰπών, ἐπειδὴ ταῦτα μάλιστα προθύμως ποιοῦμεν
ἅπερ ἂν ἑκοντὶ διαπραττώμεθα.

8ᵇ. Ἐξομολογήσομαι τῷ ὀνόματί σου, ὅτι ἀγαθόν. Εὐχαριστήσω δέ
φησιν ὑπὲρ τῶν γεγονότων, ἐπειδὴ καὶ κάλλιστον τὸ εὐχαριστεῖν· βεβαιοῖ 10
γὰρ τὰ δοθέντα ἀγαθά.

9. Ὅτι ἐκ πάσης θλίψεως ἐρρύσω με, καὶ ἐν τοῖς ἐχθροῖς μου ἐπεῖδεν ὁ
ὀφθαλμός μου. Ὑπὲρ ἀμφοτέρων δὲ εὐχαριστήσω· ἀμφότερα γὰρ ἅπερ
ἐχαρίσω μεγάλα, ὅτι τῶν κινδύνων ἐρρύσω καὶ ὅτι τῶν ἐχθρῶν ἰδεῖν με τὴν
ἀπώλειαν παρεσκεύασας. 15

7ᵇ. Εἴρηται — ἀφανίσει: P, fol. 147ᵛ; V, fol. 210ᵛ; C 98 sup., fol. 106; Cord,
p. 37 (l. ultima) — 38 pluribus praemissis quae ad nostrum non pertinent.
8ᵃ. Τούτων — διαπραττώμεθα: P, fol. 147; V, fol. 211; Cord, p. 38-39. 5 δὲ
om. Cord 7 ἑκουσίως — προθύμως om. ex homoiot. C.
8ᵇ. Εὐχαριστήσω — ἀγαθά: P, fol. 148; V, fol. 211; Cord, p. 39 sub nomine
Eusebii.
9. Ὑπὲρ ἀμφοτέρων — παρεσκεύασας: P, fol. 148; V, fol. 211; C 98 sup., fol. 106;
Cord, p. 39; cf. L (p. 34, 31-33): Εὐχαριστήσω σοί φησι καὶ ὑπὲρ ὧν ἀπήλλαξάς με
συμφορῶν καὶ ὑπὲρ ὧν τοὺς ἐχθροὺς εἶδον τιμωρηθέντας.

Aᵉ 7ʰ (p. 290, 7-11): Veritatem ubique ponit ut negotiorum, de quibus
loquitur, expraemat firmitatem; solida ergo et firmissima precor internicione
deperiant inimici.   5-6 (p. 290, 12-13): Prumpte libenterque gratificatorias tibi
hostias immolabo.   8ʰ (p. 290, 16-17): Gratum tibi esse officium est optimum.
9 (p. 290, 18-21): Pro utrisque donis agam gratias, quod et mea me liberatione
gauderem, et inimicorum interitum uidere ficisti.

utterly. It has been remarked that he often makes mention of God's truth to highlight the certainty of what is done. So he will render their destruction true, certain, and forceful—that is, he will firmly wipe them out.

I shall voluntarily sacrifice to you (v. 6): once this happens, I shall offer thanksgiving sacrifices to you with great zeal and enthusiasm (*voluntarily* well expressing "enthusiastically," since we do with particular enthusiasm whatever we perform willingly). *I shall confess to your name, Lord, because it is good:* I shall give thanks for what happens, since it is very good to give thanks, confirming as it does the good things given. *Because you have rescued me from every tribulation, and my eye has looked down on my foes* (v. 7): I shall thank you for both; both your gifts to me were great, your rescuing me from danger and your causing me to see the downfall of the foe. |

PSALMVS LIV

Τῆς αἰχμαλωσίας ἀπαλλαγέντες τῆς ἐν Βαβυλῶνι παραδόξως τῇ τοῦ
Θεοῦ δυνάμει, κατεσκεύασαν μὲν τὸν ναὸν καὶ οἰκείαν πάλιν ᾤκησαν γῆν,
ἀπειλήφει δὲ καὶ ἡ πόλις τὸν οἰκεῖον ἅπαντα κόσμον, ἀλλὰ καὶ βαθείας ἀπή-
5 λαυον τῆς εἰρήνης. Καὶ δὴ τοῦ χρόνου προβαίνοντος, ἀρχιερεὺς τοῦ ἔθνους
γεγένηται Ὀνίας ἀνὴρ δικαιότατος καὶ εὐσεβέστατος, — τότε δὲ τοὺς
ἀρχιερεῖς καὶ τὴν ἀρχὴν τοῦ ἔθνους ἐμπεπιστεῦθαι συνέβαινεν. Τῇ τοίνυν
ἐπιστασίᾳ τοῦ Ὀνίου, μετὰ πάσης ἀκριβείας τῶν νομίμων φυλαττομένων
καὶ τῆς εἰς τὸν Θεὸν εὐσεβείας ἄριστα πληρουμένης, Σίμων τις ἐκ τῆς
10 φυλῆς Βενιαμίν — Σελεύκου τότε βασιλεύοντος τῆς Ἀσίας ἀπάσης, Συρίας
τε καὶ Φοινίκης — προστασίαν τινὰ πεπιστευμένος τοῦ ἱεροῦ, διηνέχθη μὲν
οὐκ εὐλόγως πρὸς τὸν Ὀνίαν, ἐν δὲ τῇ πρὸς αὐτὸν ἡττηθεὶς διαφορᾷ κοι-
νοῦται Ἀπολλωνίῳ τῷ στρατηγῷ, φήσας ἀποκεῖσθαι πάμπολλα χρήματα
ἐν τῷ ναῷ, ἃ δυνατὸν ληφθέντα χρήσιμα τῷ βασιλεῖ γενέσθαι πρὸς στρα-
15 τολογίαν. Γίνεται δὲ τοῦτο καὶ τῷ βασιλεῖ γνώριμον διὰ τοῦ στρατηγοῦ,
καὶ δεξάμενος τὰ παρὰ τοῦ στρατηγοῦ μηνυθέντα, Ἡλιόδωρόν τινα τῶν
οἰκείων ἀποστέλλει ληψόμενον τὰ χρήματα. Καὶ δὴ παραγεγονὼς ὁ Ἡλιό-

2 ss. cf. II Macch. III-IV.

Τῆς αἰχμαλωσίας — βουλευόμενον: P, fol. 148ᵛ-149; V, fol. 211ᵛ-212 (ed. A. Maius
in N.P.B. III, 453-455; P. G., 673-676). 14 ἀδύνατον V.

Aᵉ *Argumentum psalmi LIV* (p. 290, 22-291, 22): Hoc carmen Oniae pontifici
profeta conponit, talem aptans orationem quae temporibus eius, meritis (metri-
tis *ms*) et uirtutibus eius et adflictionibus conpetat, qui pertullit primo Simonis inpugnationem. Is namque Beniaminitica tribu ortus sacerdotium ambit
proditione eius et pecuniae, quam in templo conditam Seleuco detulit; ex quo
in exsecutione rei ad expulsionem Oniae substitutionemque Simonis misus
Eliodorus signis a templo excluditur et ob honorem Oniae uissionibus uerbe-
ratur; huius postea intercessione seruatur in uitam. Post quas demum erumnas
pertulit sub Anteocho filio Seleuci. Iason quidam propinquus Oniae, honoris
eius et uitae emulus, ab Anteocho pontificatum redemit ea pactione, ut omnes
Iudeos in gentilium scita traduceret; quo honere percitus et adflictus sponte
Onias migrat in Egiptum atque ibi, altare constructo, ritus sacros, quos Hirusolimis Iason profanauerat, cum Iudeis, qui inueniri potuerunt, antestes deuotus instaurat. Horum ergo temporum mala deplorantem Oniam (Ioniam *ms*)
profeta praeuidet ac praedicat. PSEUDO-BEDA (764): Ex persona Oniae sacer-
dotis sponte Aegyptum petentis psalmus iste depromitur, quando Iason propinquus eius, sed honoris et uitae illius aemulus, ab Antiocho, Seleuci filio, pontificatum redemit, ea conditione, ut omnes Iudaeos in gentilnm scita traduceret.
Ipse uero Onias, constructo in Aegypto altari, ritus sacros, quos Ierosolymis Iason
profanauerat, cum Iudaeis, qui inueniri potuerant, antistes deuotus instaurauit.

PSALM 55

Freed unexpectedly from captivity in Babylon by God's power, they rebuilt the temple and again occupied their own land, the city recovered all its peculiar glory, and they enjoyed deep peace. With the passage of time Onias became high priest of the nation, a man of the greatest righteousness and piety;[1] and at that time it happened that the high priests were entrusted also with the government of the nation. During the term of Onias, then, when the laws were observed with great care, and reverence for God was excellently honored, Simon, of the tribe of Benjamin, was entrusted with supervision of the sanctuary when Seleucus reigned over all Asia, Syria, and Phoenicia. Being at odds with Onias for no good reason, he failed in his quarrel with him and entered into an association with Apollonius the general, claiming that huge amounts of money were stored in the temple that could be put to good use by the king in levying soldiers. This was made known also to the king through the general, and upon gaining the information from the general, he sent a certain Heliodorus, of his own retinue, to get hold of the money.

Heliodorus arrived | to find that there was not as much money in the

---

1. Theodore summarizes, and at times reproduces verbatim, the text of 2 Macc 3–4, accommodating this psalm of lament for hostility and betrayal to the situation of the high priest Onias (III) in the time of the Seleucids.

δωρος, ἔγνω χρημάτων μὲν οὐκ εἶναι τοσοῦτον πλῆθος ἐν τῷ ἱερῷ ὅσον ἡ
τοῦ Σίμωνος ἐβούλετο διαβολή, εἶναι δὲ ὀλίγα καὶ ταῦτα παρακαταθήκας
ἑτέρων, οἳ πρὸς τὴν ἀξιοπιστίαν τοῦ τόπου καὶ τὴν τοῦ Θεοῦ δύναμιν
ἀποβλέψαντες τὰς παρακαταθήκας ἀπέθεντο. Συνεβούλευεν δὲ ὁ Ὀνίας
μηδὲν ἐπιχειρῆσαι λαβεῖν τῶν ἀποκειμένων· ὕβρις γάρ φησιν εἰς τὸ θεῖον 5
τὸ γινόμενον, καὶ λυπήσεις ἐκεῖνον οὗ τὴν παρακαταθήκην ἀποσυλήσεις.
Ἔμελε τούτων οὐδὲν τῷ Ἡλιοδώρῳ μείζονα πάντων κρίναντι τὸ τοῦ βασιλέως εἰς πέρας ἀγαγεῖν πρόσταγμα· εὐχαὶ μὲν οὖν καὶ θρῆνοι κατὰ τὴν
πόλιν ἐγίγνοντο ἐπὶ τούτοις, ἱκετευόντων τὸν Θεὸν μὴ καταλιπεῖν ἀνεκ-
δίκητον τὴν τόλμαν, εἰσῄει δὲ τῇ ἑτέρᾳ ὡς τὰ χρήματα ληψόμενος. Καὶ ὁ 10
Θεὸς ταῖς ἱκεσίαις τοῦ πλήθους ἐπινεύσας, καὶ τοῦ ἀρχιερέως τὴν εὐσέβειαν ἀποδεξάμενος, φοβερωτάτῃ τινὶ ἐπιφανείᾳ τοῦ τολμήματος ἀπεσ-
κεύασεν. Ὤφθη γὰρ εἰσιέναι μέλλοντι ἵππος διὰ τοῦ ἀέρος φοβερὸς μὲν
ὄψιν, φαιδρὸς δὲ τὸ σχῆμα, ἐποχούμενόν τε ἔχων μετὰ χρυσῆς τῆς πανο-
πλίας, ὃς καὶ μετὰ πολλοῦ τοῦ ῥυξήματος ταῖς ἐμπροσθίαις ὁπλαῖς τὸν 15
Ἡλιόδωρον ἔπληξεν· δύο τε νεανίαι, φοβεροὶ καὶ οὗτοι τὴν θέαν, ἐπίδοξοι
τε τὸ σχῆμα, περιστάντες ἐντεῦθεν κἀκεῖθεν ἐμαστίγουν. Καὶ οὕτως ἀπὸ
τῆς ὀπτασίας καὶ τῶν πληγῶν καταπεσὼν ἤρθη μικροῦ νεκρὸς ὑπάρχων.
Δεήσεις ὑπὲρ τούτων πρὸς τὸν Ὀνίαν ἐγίγνοντο παρὰ τῶν συνόντων τῷ
Ἡλιοδώρῳ ἱκετεῦσαι τὸν Θεὸν χαρίσασθαι αὐτῷ τοῦ προσδοκωμένου θανά- 20
του τὴν ἀπαλλαγήν· ὃ καὶ ποιήσας ὁ Ὀνίας εὐθύς, καὶ θυσίας προσα-
γαγὼν ὑπὲρ αὐτοῦ, ἀπήλλαξε τῆς κατεχούσης νόσου, ἐπιφα|νέντος τε
αὐτῷ τοῦ Θεοῦ καὶ πολλὰς ἔχειν χάριτας τῷ ἀρχιερεῖ παρακελευσαμένου.
Οὕτω διασωθεὶς καὶ θυσίας τῷ Θεῷ προσκομίσας ἐπανῆλθεν πρὸς τὸν βασιλέα διηγησάμενος τὰ γεγονότα. Ἀλλ᾽ οὐκ ἀφίστατο τῆς οἰκείας μοχθηρίας 25
ὁ Σίμων, παρέμενεν δὲ πολλαῖς κατ᾽ αὐτοῦ κεχρημένος ταῖς διαβολαῖς. Καὶ
διὰ τοῦτο μέχρι τοῦ βασιλέως Ὀνίας γενόμενος, ἔγνω τὰς κατ᾽ αὐτοῦ
παῦσαι διαβολάς, ὥστε καὶ τῷ ἔθνει περιποιῆσαι τὴν προσήκουσαν εἰρήνην.
    Ἀλλ᾽ ἐν τούτοις ὄντος τοῦ Ὀνίου τελευτᾷ μὲν ὁ Σέλευκος, παραλαμ-
βάνει δὲ τὴν βασιλείαν ὁ Ἐπιφανὴς Ἀντίοχος, ἐφ᾽ οὗ Ἰάσων τις ἀδελφὸς 30
τοῦ Ὀνίου ἔφησε πολλῶν χρημάτων πρόσοδον τῷ βασιλεῖ προσάξαι εἰ
λάβοιτο τῆς ἀρχιερωσύνης αὐτός, δώσειν δὲ καὶ ἕτερα πλείονα εἰ καὶ γυμνάσιον κατασκευάσειεν ἐν τῇ πόλει καὶ τὴν περιτομὴν αὐτῶν λύσειεν, καὶ
ὅλως ἐξαλλάξαι τὰ νόμιμα συγχωρηθῇ. Ἐπείσθη τούτοις τοῖς ῥήμασι,
παραδίδωσί τε αὐτῷ τὴν ἀρχήν, καὶ ὁ μὲν Ὀνίας εὐσεβέστατός τε καὶ 35
δικαιότατος ὢν ἀνὴρ ἔξω τῆς ἀρχιερωσύνης κατέστη. Ὁ δὲ Ἰάσων τῆς τε
ἀρχιερωσύνης καὶ τῆς ἐξουσίας ἐπιλαβόμενος, εὐθὺς ἐπὶ τὸν ἑλληνικὸν

---

7 ἔμελλεν V   22 ⟨ἐπιφα⟩νέντος] sic prosequitur C, duobus ni fallor foliis perditis post f. 287ᵛ   23 αὐτοῦ Θεοῦ C   29-35 L (p. 41, 13-17): "Ἕτερος δὲ Μακ-
καβαϊκόν φησι τὸν ψαλμὸν ὡς ἐκ τοῦ ἀρχιερέως Ὀνίου, ὃν δωροδοκηθεὶς Ἀντίοχος τῆς
ἀρχιερωσύνης ἐξέβαλεν, ἕτερον δὲ ἀντεισήγαγεν   37 ἱερωσύνης V.

sanctuary as Simon's report would have it, but only a small amount, and this the deposits of other people who had made the deposits in view of the trustworthiness of the place and the power of God. Onias urged him to take nothing of the deposits, saying, "It is an insult to the divinity, and you are offending him by robbing his treasury." None of this made any difference to Heliodorus, who judged it more important than anything to implement the king's command. So despite prayers and lamentations breaking out across the city on all sides, with people imploring God not to allow the intolerable deed, he entered by a different route to seize the money. God acceded to the supplication of the multitude and deferred to the piety of the high priest, halting the attempt with a most fearsome apparition: to the man, bent on entering, a horse of fearsome aspect appeared in the sky, splendidly caparisoned, carrying a rider in golden armor. The horse, loudly neighing, struck Heliodorus with its front hooves. Two young men, themselves also fearsome to behold in glorious apparel, stood either side of it flogging him. And so he fell to the ground under the vision and the blows, and was carried off half dead.

On the part of the company of Heliodorus prayers were made on their behalf to Onias to grant him relief from his expected death; Onias immediately acceded, offered sacrifices for him, and freed him from the ailment possessing him. God appeared to him and bade him be very grateful to the high priest. Thus restored to good health, he brought sacrifices to God and returned to the king with an account of what happened.

Simon, however, did not desist from his depravity: he kept hatching many plots against him. For this reason Onias went to the king and was determined to bring the plots against him to an end so as to secure proper peace also for the nation. While Onias was still occupied with this, however, Seleucus died, and Antiochus Epiphanes came to the throne. Under him Jason, a brother of Onias, claimed that he would bring a contribution of much money if he secured the high priesthood, and that he would give much more if he built a gymnasium in the city, canceled circumcision, and allowed the laws to be relaxed. Convinced by these words, he put him in charge, while Onias, a man of the greatest piety and righteousness, was divested of the high priesthood. Once Jason got hold of the high priesthood and authority, he converted the Jews to Greek ways, | built a gymnasium in defiance of

χαρακτῆρα μετήγαγεν τοὺς Ἰουδαίους, γυμνάσιόν τε κατεσκεύασεν παρὰ
τὸ ἰουδαϊκὸν ἔθος, καὶ τὰ νόμιμα δὲ ἐξαλλάξαι παρασκευάσας ἅπαντας μὲν
ἀνελεῖν τῆς εἰς Θεὸν θεραπείας καὶ τῶν τοῦ νόμου προσταγμάτων ἔπεισεν,
προσέχειν δὲ τοῖς ἔθεσι τοῖς ἑλληνικοῖς, γυμνασίοις καὶ παλαίστραις καὶ
5 τοῖς τοιούτοις· ἠμελεῖτο δὴ λοιπὸν καὶ τὰ τῆς περιτομῆς, κατεφρονεῖτο
καὶ τῶν σαββάτων ἡ τήρησις, καὶ ὅλως εἰς ἑλληνικὸν σχῆμα τὰ κατὰ τὴν
πόλιν μετέ|πεσεν. Ταῦτα ὁρῶν ὁ μακάριος Ὀνίας ἐπὶ πολὺ γινόμενα ἠθύ-
μει καὶ ἠγανάκτει καὶ ἐστέναζεν· ὡς δὲ καὶ προβαῖνον ἑώρα τὸ κακὸν
καταλιπὼν ἀνεχώρησεν, καὶ εἰς τὴν Αἴγυπτον βαλὼν θυσιαστήριόν τε ἐπή-
10 ξατο καὶ ναὸν κατεσκεύασεν, καὶ τῆς εἰς τὸν Θεὸν εὐσεβείας ἐπεμελήσατο,
τοῖς ἐκεῖ Ἰουδαίοις τὰ δέοντα περὶ τὴν τοῦ Θεοῦ θεραπείαν ὑποτιθέμενος.

Ταῦτα ὁ μακάριος προφητεύει Δαυὶδ ἐν τῷ παρόντι ψαλμῷ· καὶ τὸ
τοῦ Ὀνίου πρόσωπον ἀναλαβὼν ταῦτα ἐφθέγγετο, ὅσα εἰκὸς ἦν λέγειν
ἐκεῖνον ἐπιβουλευόμενον ὑπὸ τῶν οἰκείων, ἐκβαλλόμενον τῆς ἱερωσύνης ὑπὸ
15 τῶν Ἀντιόχου, ὁρῶντα τὴν μοχθηρίαν τῶν τότε τὴν πόλιν οἰκούντων, διά
τε τὰς ἐν αὐτῇ πλεονεξίας καὶ τὴν τῶν νομίμων ἐναλλαγήν, καὶ τὴν ἑκάστοτε γιγνομένην τῶν κακῶν ἐπίτασιν, ἤδη καὶ περὶ φυγῆς βουλευόμενον.

2ᵃ. Ἐνώτισαι, ὁ Θεός, τὴν προσευχήν μου. Φρόντισον ἀκοῦσαι· οὐδὲ
γὰρ περὶ μικρῶν ποιοῦμαι τὴν δέησιν.

20 2ᵇ. Καὶ μὴ ὑπερίδῃς τὴν δέησίν μου. Μὴ διαπτύσῃς μηδὲ καταφρονήσῃς
μικρὰν αὐτὴν καὶ εὐτελῆ λογισάμενος· ὑπεριδεῖν γὰρ λέγεται τὸ κατα-
φρονῆσαι ὡς μικροῦ καὶ οὐδενός.

3ᵃ. Πρόσχες μοι καὶ εἰσάκουσόν μου. Διαφόρως ἐπὶ τὴν προσευχὴν
καλεῖ τὸν Θεόν, μετὰ σπουδῆς αἰτῶν γενέσθαι τὴν ἀκρόασιν, ὥστε τῶν
25 κακῶν ὑπὲρ ὧν αἰτεῖ τὸ μέγεθος ἐμφῆναι.

3ᵇ. Ἐλυπήθην ἐν τῇ ἀδολεσχίᾳ μου καὶ ἐταράχθην. Ἀδολεσχίαν καλεῖ
παντὸς πράγματος συνέχειαν. Τὸ οὖν ἐλυπήθην ἐν τῇ ἀδολεσχίᾳ μου καὶ
ἐταράχθην, τουτέστι Συνεχῆ τὴν λύπην ἔσχον καὶ τὴν ταραχὴν ἀπὸ τοῦ
πλήθους τῶν κακῶν, ἄλλων ἐπ᾽ ἄλλοις ἀεὶ συμβαινόντων.

2ᵃ. Φρόντισον — δέησιν: P, fol. 149; V. fol. 212ᵛ; C 98 sup., fol. 106ᵛ.
2ᵇ. Μὴ διαπτύσῃς — οὐδενός: P, fol. 149; V. fol. 212ᵛ; Cord, p. 53 (P. G.,
677 B).
3ᵃ. Διαφόρως - ἐμφῆναι: P, fol. 149; V, fol. 212ᵛ.
3ᵇ. Ἀδολεσχίαν — συμβαινόντων: P, fol. 149ᵛ; V. fol. 212ᵛ; Cord, p. 54 (P. G.,
677 BC). 26-27 Paraphrasis (p. 42, 6-7): ...ἀδολεσχίαν γὰρ ἐνταῦθα λέγει τὴν συνέχειαν τῶν κακῶν.

Aᵉ 28-29 (p. 292, 1-2): Quasi exercuerunt me mala continuatione sui.

Jewish custom, had the laws relaxed, and persuaded everyone to do away with the worship of God and the commandments of the law, and to attend rather to Greek customs, gymnasiums, wrestling schools, and the like. The practice of circumcision was then neglected, observance of the Sabbath was despised, and the affairs of the city took on a Greek character. On seeing this, blessed Onias lapsed into deep depression at what had happened, was vexed, and fell to groaning; when he saw the wickedness on the increase, he gave up and left, and in Egypt he built an altar, erected a temple, and devoted himself to the worship of God, urging the Jews there to their duty in the worship of God.[2]

This is what blessed David composes under inspiration in the present psalm. Adopting the point of view of Onias, he utters everything that he probably said when the object of scheming by his own people, divested of the priesthood by Antiochus, and observing the depravity of the city's inhabitants at the time due to their greed and the change in the laws as well as the intensifying of the troubles happening on each occasion, and also when he had already resolved on flight.

Give ear to my prayer, O God (v. 1): take care to listen; it is no slight matter I am making the object of my request. *And do not despise my petition:* do not scorn or belittle it in the belief that it is insignificant and lowly (despise meaning "belittling it as of little or no value"). *Heed me and hearken to me* (v. 2). He calls on God in prayer in different ways, zealously begging for a hearing, so as to highlight the magnitude of the troubles on which he is praying. *I am annoyed by my idle talk and troubled.* By *idle talk* he refers to the persistence of everything; so the clause *I am annoyed by my idle talk and troubled* means, I kept suffering constant distress and alarm from the magnitude of the misfortunes, different ones forever happening at different times. | *By the words of a foe and tribulation from a sinner* (v. 3):

---

2. 2 Macc 4:33 speaks rather of Onias withdrawing to Daphne near Antioch, Theodore probably confusing it with the Daphne (the Tahpanhes of Jer 2:16) in Egypt, now Tell Defneh.

4ᵃ. Ἀπὸ φωνῆς ἐχθροῦ καὶ ἀπὸ θλίψεως ἁμαρτωλοῦ. Λυπεῖ γάρ με οὐ μικρῶς τά τε παρὰ τῶν ἰδίων καὶ τὰ παρὰ τῶν ἐναντίων. Ἐχθροὺς δὲ λέγει καὶ ἁμαρτωλούς, τὸ μὲν ἀπὸ τῆς γνώμης, τὸ δὲ ἀπὸ τοῦ εἴδους τῆς πράξεως ἤτοι τῆς προθέσεως. Βούλεται γὰρ ἑαυτὸν οὐ μισούμενον δεῖξαι μόνον, ἀλλὰ καὶ ἀδίκως μισούμενον. 5

4ᵇ. Ὅτι ἐξέκλιναν ἐπ᾽ ἐμὲ ἀνομίαν. Ἐξέκλιναν, τουτέστιν ἐξήνεγκαν, ἐπειδὴ τὸ ἑστὸς καὶ κλινόμενόν που μεταφέρεται πάντως ἐφ᾽ ὅπερ ἂν κλιθῇ. Πᾶσαν οὖν φησιν ἐπ᾽ ἐμὲ μετήνεγκαν τὴν ἀνομίαν, πᾶν ὅτι κακὸν κατ᾽ ἐμοῦ μηχανησάμενοι. Τὸ δὲ ἐξέκλιναν εἶπεν καλῶς, δεικνὺς ὅτι οὐκ εἰς αὐτὸν μόνον ἡμάρτανον, ἀλλὰ γὰρ ἔργον ἔχοντες τὸ κάκιστα ζῆν καὶ πᾶν 10 ὅτι διαπράττεσθαι κακόν, νῦν τῆς οἰκείας μοχθηρίας εἰς αὐτὸν ἐπλήρουν τὸν σκοπόν, — καὶ ἄνω δὲ ἁμαρτωλοὺς ἐκάλεσεν καὶ ἐνταῦθα ἀνομίαν τὴν κατ᾽ αὐτοῦ πρᾶξιν τῶν τρόπων καὶ τῶν πράξεων τὸ εἶδος διαβάλλων.

4ᶜ. Καὶ ἐν ὀργῇ ἐνεχότουν μοι. Κότος λέγεται ὀργή, μῖσος· τὸ οὖν ἐνεχότουν μοι, ἀντὶ τοῦ ἐμνησικάκουν. Καλῶς δὲ εἶπεν ἐν ὀργῇ, ἀντὶ τοῦ 15 μετὰ ὀργῆς, ὥστε δεῖξαι τῆς μνησικακίας τὴν ἐπίτασιν. Διὰ τί δὲ τὸ «ἐμνησικάκουν» εἶπεν; Ἐπειδὴ διηνέχθη πρότερον πρὸς αὐτόν, εἶτα ἡττηθεὶς ὁ Σίμων ἐπὶ τοῦτο ἐτράπη.

5. Ἡ καρδία μου ἐταράχθη ἐν ἐμοί, καὶ δειλία θανάτου ἐπέπεσεν ἐπ᾽ ἐμέ. Ἐπὶ τούτοις πολλῆς τῆς ταραχῆς ἐπληρώθην τὴν ψυχήν, δεδιὼς λοι- 20 πὸν καὶ προσδοκῶν οὐδὲν ἕτερον ἢ θάνατον.

6ᵃ. Φόβος καὶ τρόμος ἦλθεν ἐπ᾽ ἐμέ. Οἶδεν γὰρ ὁ φόβος καὶ ἡ προσδοκία τοῦ θανάτου τρόμον ἐμποιεῖν.

6ᵇ. Καὶ ἐκάλυψέν με σκότος. Τοῦτο τῆς ἀθυμίας ἴδιον. Ὅταν γάρ τις διὰ μέγεθος τῶν κινδύνων ἀπελπίσῃ τὴν σωτηρίαν, ἀθυμίᾳ κρατηθεὶς ὥσπερ 25 σκότῳ τινὶ περιβάλλεται, μηδὲ διακρίνειν τὰ παρόντα προσηκόντως δυνάμενος.

4ᵃ. Λυπεῖ — μισούμενον: P, fol. 149ᵛ; V, fol. 213.
4ᵇ. Ἐξέκλιναν — διαβάλλων: P, fol. 150; V, fol. 213ʳ·ᵛ; C 98 sup., fol. 106ᵛ-107.
7 ἑστὼς codd.   ἐκκλιν. C 98   8 μετήνεγκαν ἄν C 98   9 μηχανώμενοι CPV des. C 98.
4ᶜ. Κότος — ἐτράπη: P, fol. 150; V, fol. 213ᵛ; C 98 sup., fol. 107.   18 τούτῳ C.
5. Ἐπὶ τούτοις — θάνατον: P, fol. 150ᵛ; V, fol. 213ᵛ.
6ᵃ. Οἶδεν — ἐμποιεῖν: P, fol. 150ᵛ; V, fol. 214; C 98 sup., fol. 107.
6ᵇ. Τοῦτο — δυνάμενος: P, fol. 150ᵛ; V, fol. 214; C 98 sup., fol. 107; Cord, p. 56.

Aᵉ 17-18 (p. 292, 9-11): Quia primo molestias certando Simon fecerat aequitate superatus, iam nunc furendo persequitur.   6ᵃ (p. 292, 12-13): Inminente scilicet morte, id est grandi periculo.   6ᵇ (p. 292, 14-16): Hoc proprium docetur angoris; defectu quippe solaciorum uiriumque aer etiam obtenebrari uidetur adflictis.

the doings of my fellows and of my adversaries both distress me to no slight degree (by *foes and sinners* referring to what comes from the mind-set, on the one hand, and what comes from a kind of behavior or disposition, on the other hand). He wishes to present himself, in other words, not only as hated, but also as unjustly hated.

Because they directed an unlawful attack on me: directed—that is, discharged, since what is standing and bending inevitably moves in the direction it is bending. So he is saying, They transferred their lawlessness onto me, devising every possible trouble for me. *Directed* was well put, bringing out that they did not merely sin against him; rather, making it their object to live the worst possible life and do all possible evil, they now discharged the thrust of their depravity against him. Above he had referred to them as sinners, and here he refers to the action against him as an *unlawful attack,* to criticize the form taken by their behavior and their actions. *And in wrath they were indignant with me.* Indignation indicates wrath, hatred; so *they were indignant with me* means that they had a grudge. *In wrath* was well put, meaning "with wrath," so as to bring out the intensity of the grudge. Why did he say that they had a grudge? Because Simon first quarreled with him, and then when he lost, he turned against him.

My heart was disturbed within me, and dread of death fell upon me (v. 4): at this my soul was filled with deep alarm, by now in dread and expectation of nothing other than death. *Fear and trembling came upon me* (v. 5): fear and expectation of death usually cause trembling. *And darkness overwhelmed me.* This is typical of depression: when anyone despairs of salvation on account of the enormity of the dangers, one is overcome by depression as though enveloped in a kind of darkness, unable to discern present realities in due fashion. |

7. Καὶ εἶπα Τίς δώσει μοι πτέρυγας ὡσεὶ περιστερᾶς, καὶ πετασθήσομαι καὶ καταπαύσω; Ὁρῶν οὖν τὸ πλῆθος τῶν κακῶν καὶ οὐδεμίαν ὑπολιμπανομένην ἐλπίδα τῶν κρειττόνων, ἐκεῖνο λοιπὸν ἐδοκίμαζον — κἀνταῦθα γὰρ τὸ εἶπα ἀντὶ τοῦ « ἐδοκίμασα » — εἴ πως οἷόν τε ἦν πτερωθέντα δίκην
5 περιστερᾶς ἀποπτῆναι, καὶ μακρὰν γενόμενον οὕτως εὑρεῖν | ἀνάπαυσιν τῶν κακῶν.

8. Ἰδοὺ ἐμάκρυνα φυγαδεύων, καὶ ηὐλίσθην ἐν τῇ ἐρήμῳ. Κἀνταῦθα τὸ Ἰδοὺ πρόσκειται κατὰ τὸ ἑβραϊκὸν ἰδίωμα. Λέγει γὰρ ὅτι εἰ προσέλαβον πτήσεως δύναμιν, φυγών τε καὶ μακρὰν γενόμενος τῶν οἰκείων εἱλόμην γενέσ-
10 θαι κατὰ τὴν ἔρημον κἀκεῖ διάγειν ἢ τῶν τῆς πόλεως ἀνέχεσθαι κακῶν. Σύμμαχος Πόρρω ἂν ἐποίησα τὴν ἀναχώρησίν μου· τὸ γὰρ ηὐλίσθην. ἀντὶ τοῦ ᾤκησα.

9. Προσεδεχόμην τὸν σῴζοντά με ἀπὸ ὀλιγοψυχίας καὶ καταιγίδος. Καὶ τοιούτων δέ φησι γενομένων, ἐγὼ τὴν παρά σου βοήθειαν ἀνέμενον, ὡς
15 ἱκανοῦ σῴζειν τε καὶ ἀπαλλάττειν τῆς ὀλιγοψυχίας, — ἣν ἀπὸ τοῦ πλήθους τῶν κακῶν ὑπέμενον πολλάκις, μικροῦ καὶ πρὸς αὐτὸν ἐγγίσας τὸν θάνατον, — εἴτε καὶ τῆς ἐφόδου τῶν ἐχθρῶν· καταιγίδα γὰρ ἐκάλεσεν τὴν ἔφοδον καὶ τὴν κατ᾽ αὐτοῦ τῶν ἐχθραινόντων ὁρμὴν ὡς θανάτου γέμουσαν καὶ κινδύνων, ἀπὸ τοῦ τὴν καταιγίδα ἀθρόως ἐπάγειν τοὺς θανάτους.

20 10ᵃ. Καταπόντισον, Κύριε, καὶ καταδίελε τὰς γλώσσας αὐτῶν. Σύμμαχος τὸ καταδίελε τὰς γλώσσας αὐτῶν οὕτω λέγει Ἀσυμφώνους ποίησον τὰς γλώσσας αὐτῶν. Ἀφάνισον αὐτοὺς καὶ ἀσυμφώνους ποίησον ἀλλήλοις, ἵνα εἰς αἱρέσεις ἐμπεσόντες ἀλλήλους ἀνέλωσί τε καὶ τιμωρήσωνται. Τὰς γλώσσας δὲ εἶπεν ἐπὶ τοῦ ἀσυμφώνου, ἐκ μεταφορᾶς τῶν ἀλλογλώσσων καὶ
25 οὔτε συμφωνεῖν οὔτε συμπράττειν ἀλλήλοις δυναμένων, οἷον δὴ καὶ ἐπὶ τῆς πυργοποιίας γεγένηται τῇ διαιρέσει τῶν γλωσσῶν παυθέντος | αὐτοῖς τοῦ σπουδαζομένου.

7. Ὁρῶν — κακῶν: P, fol. 151; V, fol. 214; Cord, p. 56-57.   4 ὀιόντες ην C.
8. Κἀνταῦθα — 10 κακῶν: P, fol. 151; V, fol. 214; C 98 sup., fol. 107.
9. Καὶ τοιούτων — θανάτους: P, fol. 151ᵛ; V, fol. 214ᵛ-215; Cord, p. 57-58; cf. Vat. gr. 2057, fol. 97ᵛ-98 (Θεοδ⁰ Ἀντιχ).   14 δὲ om. Cord   16 ἐγγίξας Cord   17 εἴτε καὶ] ἀπὸ Cord.
10ᵃ. Σύμμαχος — σπουδαζομένου: P, fol. 151ᵛ; V, fol. 215.

Aᵉ 9-10 (p. 292, 23-26): Et quam longissime discendens in solitudine commorarer, tantum ne mala urbis huius perpeterer.   15-16 (p. 292, 29-30): Pro persequutione ualida, quam multitudo infert angorum.   22-24 (p. 292, 31-293, 4): Vt nec consiliis nec sermonibus concinant atque per omnia inter se discordiis in exitium adiuuare non possint, sed intestinis et mutuis iurgiis (motuis iurgis ms) consummantur.

And I said, Who will give me wings like a dove's, and I shall fly and rest? (v. 6) Seeing the multitude of troubles, then, and no vestige of hope for better things, I then decided (here using *I said* for "I decided") if it was possible to take wings and fly away like a dove and thus find relief from the troubles at a distance. *Lo, I went a great distance in fleeing, and lodged in the wilderness* (v. 7). Here, too, *Lo* occurs as a result of Hebrew idiom. He is saying, If I had the power of flying, I would have chosen to flee, distance myself from my own people, and live in a desert there or put up with the troubles of the city. Symmachus: "I would have made my departure for distant regions" (*I lodged* meaning "I dwelt"). *I waited for him to save me from lack of spirit and a tempest* (v. 8): when such things happened, I waited for help from you, able as you were to save and free me from lack of spirit, which I frequently suffered as a result of the multitude of troubles, coming close to death itself. Or he could mean being freed from the foes' attack, by tempest referring to the attack and the advance of the enemy against him, threatening death and danger, on the basis of a tempest suddenly inflicting death.

Drown them, Lord, and divide their tongues (v. 9). For *divide their tongues* Symmachus says, "Make their tongues discordant." Do away with them and make them discordant to one another, so that they may be at odds with one another, commit murder, and be punished. He mentioned *tongues* to suggest discord, by analogy with people of different languages unable to understand or work with one another, as happened in the case of the building of the tower, when their zeal was halted by the difference in tongues.[3] |

---

3. Cf. Gen 11:1–9.

10ᵇ. Ὅτι εἶδον ἀνομίαν καὶ ἀντιλογίαν ἐν τῇ πόλει. Ἀναγκάζομαι δὲ ταῦτα αἰτεῖν, οὐ τιμωρηθῆναι τοὺς οἰκείους ἐπιθυμῶν, ἀλλ ὁρῶν πλεονάζοντα τὰ κακὰ καὶ τὴν πόλιν γέμουσαν ἀτοπίας τε καὶ πάσης ἔριδος, ἵν οὕτω τιμωρηθέντων ἐκείνων λάβῃ λύσιν τὰ κατὰ τὴν πόλιν κακά.

11. Ἡμέρας καὶ νυκτὸς κυκλώσει αὐτὴν ἐπὶ τὰ τείχη αὐτῆς. Κυκλώσει, 5 ἀντὶ τοῦ κυκλοῖ · ἐναλλαγὴ γάρ ἐστι χρόνου κἀνταῦθα.

12ᵃ. Καὶ ἀνομία καὶ κόπος. Κόπον λέγει τὰς ἀδικίας, αἷς καμάτων καὶ ὀδυνῶν ἐπλήρουν τοὺς πάσχοντας.

12ᵇ. Καὶ ἀδικία ἐν μέσῳ αὐτῆς. Βούλεται εἰπεῖν ὅτι πολὺ τὸ κακὸν ἐπλεόνασεν ἐν τῇ πόλει, τούτῳ κεκύκλωται ἡ πόλις. Τοῦτο ἐν μέσῳ στρε- 10 φόμενον καὶ εἰς ὁποῖον ἂν γένῃ μέρος τῆς πόλεως, ἐκεῖ τὰ κακὰ εὑρήσεις, τὴν ἀδικίαν καὶ τὴν ἁμαρτίαν.

12ᶜ. Καὶ οὐκ ἐξέλιπεν ἐκ τῶν πλατειῶν αὐτῆς τόκος καὶ δόλος. Τόκον καλεῖ τὴν πλεονεξίαν, δόλον τὴν πανουργίαν · πλεονεξίαν δὲ καλεῖ τὸν τόκον, ἐπειδὴ ἀπηγόρευτο ἐπὶ τῶν οἰκείων ἐν τῷ νόμῳ. Ἀδιάληπτον οὖν 15 φησιν ἐν αὐτῇ στρέφεται τὸ κακόν, πανουργία τὸ πᾶν καὶ πλεονεξία. Εἰκότως δὲ ταῦτα ὁ μακάριος Ὀνίας δυσφορῶν λέγει, πρότερον μὲν αὐτοὺς ἄγων μετὰ πολλῆς τῆς εὐσεβείας καὶ τῶν νομίμων σφόδρα παρασκευάζων ἐπιμελεῖσθαι καὶ τὴν πόλιν ἐν εὐκοσμίᾳ φυλάττων, ὁρῶν δὲ ἐπὶ τὸ ἐναντίον πάντα μεταβεβλημένα, πάντων τῶν κακῶν χαιρόντων καὶ τὴν ἀδικίαν μετὰ 20 πολλῆς ἐργαζομένων τῆς παρρησίας.

13. Ὅτι εἰ ἐχθρὸς ὠνείδισέν με, ὑπήνεγκα ἄν, καὶ εἰ ὁ μισῶν ἐπ ἐμὲ ἐμεγαλορρημόνησεν, ἐκρύβην ἂν ἀπ αὐτοῦ. Δείκνυσιν ὅτι δικαίως εἴλετο τὴν

10ᵇ. Ἀναγκάζομαι — κακά: P, fol. 152; V, fol. 215ʳ·ᵛ; C 98 sup., fol. 107; Cord, p. 59.
11. Κυκλώσει — κἀνταῦθα: P, fol. 152; V, fol. 215ᵛ.
12ᵃ. Κόπον — πάσχοντας: P, fol. 152ᵛ; V, fol. 216.
12ᵇ. Βούλεται — ἁμαρτίαν: P, fol. 152ᵛ; V, 216; C 98 sup., fol. 107.   10 τούτῳ κεκύκλωται ἡ πόλις om. C 98   ib. τούτω V.
12ᶜ. Τόκον — παρρησίας: P, fol. 152ᵛ; V, fol. 216; C 98 sup., fol. 107.   15 νόμῳ des. C 98   17 αὐτοῖς C.
13. Δείκνυσιν — ἐξανύσας: P, fol. 152ᵛ; V, fol. 216.

Aᵉ 10ᵇ (p. 293, 5-7): Haec autem ideo quia mala urbis exorreo, ut saltim inpeditis auctoribus cepta soluatur impietas.   10-11 (p. 293, 10-12): In medio eius posuit pro «palam», ac si diceret Quaquam uersus respexeris, profanitas occurret uidenti.

Because I have seen lawlessness and discord in the city: I am forced to make this request not wanting my own people to be punished, but seeing the troubles multiplying and the city awash with wrongdoing and utter strife, so that when they are punished in this way, the troubles affecting the city may be relieved.

Day and night he will encircle it on its walls (v. 10). *He will encircle* means "he encircles," a change in tense occurring here. *Lawlessness and trouble* (by *trouble* referring to the injustices with which they filled those who suffered with hardship and pain) *and injustice in its midst.* He means that great misfortune multiplied in the city; the city was encircled by it. Going around in its midst, he is saying, and to whatever part of the city, you will find trouble, iniquity, and sin. *Usury and deceit were not absent from its streets.* By *usury* he refers to greed, and by *deceit* to villainy: he calls greed *usury* because by the law it was forbidden to his people.[4] Evil was rife and out of control in it, he is saying, along with utter villainy and greed. Now, blessed Onias probably says this in some vexation, since formerly he had led them with great piety, caused them earnestly to observe the laws, and kept the city in good order, whereas now he sees everything changed to the opposite condition, all wicked people rejoicing and committing injustice with complete shamelessness.

Because if a foe reproached me, I would bear it; and if one who hated me used intemperate language to me, I would avoid his company (v. 12). He brings out that he made the right decision | in leaving the city and going

---

4. Cf. Exod 22:25–27; Lev 25:36–38; Deut 23:20.

πόλιν καλιπὼν ἀναχωρῆσαι, καὶ ὅτι δικαίως αὐτοὺς ἀξιοῖ τιμωρηθῆναι,
μάλιστα μὲν διὰ τὸ πλεονάζειν τὰ κακὰ τῇ πόλει καὶ διὰ τὸ λελύσθαι
πᾶσαν εὐκοσμίαν, οὐκ ἔλαττον καὶ δι' ἐκεῖνο ὅτι οὐ παρ' ἐχθρῶν τὰ εἰς
αὐτὸν γιγνόμενα ἀλλὰ παρὰ τῶν δοκούντων οἰκείων καὶ φίλων. Εἴτε γὰρ
5 ἐχθρὸς ἦν ὀνειδίζων, ἔφερον, εἴτε ὁ μεγαλορρημονῶν, τουτέστιν ὁ κατακαυ-
χώμενος, ὑπεχώρουν οὐδὲν ἀντιλέγων ἀλλὰ λογιζόμενος ὅτι πολέμιος ὢν
ἀκόλουθα τῷ οἰκείῳ τρόπῳ διαπράττεται. Τὸ μὲν οὖν ὠνείδισεν εἶπεν ὡς
ὄντων πολλῶν οἰκείων τῶν ἐπὶ δυσπραγίᾳ ὀνειδιζόντων, οἳ λυπηθέντες παρ'
αὐτοῦ καθ' ὃν καιρὸν τῆς ἀρχιερατείας ἐπιμελόμενος ἤλεγχεν αὐτοὺς ἀδικεῖν
10 πειρωμένους, οἳ ἐν ταῖς συμφοραῖς ὁρῶντες αὐτὸν ὠνείδιζον ἐφ' οἷς ἔπασχεν. Τὸ δὲ ἐμεγαλορρημόνουν διὰ τοὺς ἐπαναστάντας καὶ μάλιστα
διὰ τὸν Σίμωνα κυρίως, ὃς πρότερον διενεχθεὶς πρὸς αὐτὸν οὐ δικαίως
ἡττήθη, εἶτα μηχαναῖς ἑτέραις ἐπαγαγὼν αὐτῷ τὰς συμφορὰς κατεκαυχᾶτο
ὡς τὸ σπουδαζόμενον αὐτῷ ἐξανύσας.

15 **14.** Σὺ δέ, ἄνθρωπε ἰσόψυχε, ἡγεμών μου καὶ γνωστέ μου. Σύμμαχος
Ἀλλὰ σὺ ἄνθρωπος ὁμότροπος καὶ συνήθης καὶ γνώριμος. Τὸ δὲ ἡγεμὼν
μου καλῶς ὡς πρὸς τὸν Σίμωνα, ἐπειδὴ τοῦ μακαρίου Ὀνίου ἀρχιερα-
τεύοντος προστασίαν τινὰ ἐγκεχείριστο· οὕτως ἡγεμόνας καὶ ἄρχοντας
βασιλέων καλοῦμεν τοὺς ὑπ' αὐτῶν πράττοντας, | εἴτε παρ' αὐτῶν τὴν
20 ἀρχὴν ἐγκεχειρισμένους.

15ᵃ. Ὃς ἐπὶ τὸ αὐτὸ ἐγλύκανας ἐδέσματα. Ἐγλύκανας ἐδέσματα, τουτέστιν συνέφαγες μετὰ πολλῆς τῆς ἡδονῆς, οὐχ ὡς ξένος παρ' ἐμοὶ φαγὼν
ἀλλ' ὡς γνήσιος φίλος μετὰ πολλῆς τῆς ἡδονῆς καὶ τῆς τέρψεως καὶ τοῦ
θάρσους συμφαγών.

25 **15ᵇ.** Ἐν τῷ οἴκῳ τοῦ Θεοῦ ἐπορεύθημεν ἐν ὁμονοίᾳ. Τούτων ἐμνημόνευσεν ἁπάντων, ὅτι ἄνθρωπος, ὅτι ἰσόψυχος, ὅτι ἡγεμών, ὅτι γνωστός,
ὅτι ἐγλύκανεν ἐδέσματα, ὅτι συνεπορεύθη ἐν τῷ οἴκῳ τοῦ Θεοῦ, δεικνὺς ὡς
ἐν πολλοῖς τὴν πρὸς αὐτὸν ἔχοντες κοινωνίαν.

11-14 cf. II Macch. III, 4-5 et IV, 1-6.

14. Σύμμαχος — ἐγκεχειρισμένους: P, fol. 153; V, fol. 216ᵛ; Cord, p. 61 (P. G.,
677 C). 16 τὸ δὲ ἡγεμών μου ss. affert C 98 sup., fol. 107ᵛ; cf. P. G., LXXX,
1273 n. 30 18-19 cf. L (p. 50, 14-15): ...ἄρχοντάς φαμεν βασιλέων τοὺς ὑπ' αὐτοῖς.
15ᵇ. Τούτων — κοινωνίαν: P, fol. 153; V, fol. 216ᵛ-217.

Aᵉ 5 (p. 293, 14): Subportassem utique. 12 (p. 297, 17-19): His omnibus
indicat Simonem, quod familiaritatem quondam professus sit.

away, and that he was within his rights to ask for them to be punished, especially on account of the multiplication of evils in the city and the complete loss of good order—no less because what was done to him came not from enemies, but from those who were thought to be family and friends. *If it had been an enemy who reproached me,* he is saying, *I could have put up with it, and if it had been a loudmouth (that is, a boaster), I would have withdrawn without responding,* reasoning that as an enemy he does things in keeping with his attitudes. So he used the word *reproached* for the reason that they were many of his own who taunted him with his misfortune, feeling resentment for him for the time he had responsibility as high priest and accused them of attempting injustice, and taunting him for his sufferings on seeing him in his troubles. In speaking of those who used *intemperate language* he refers to the rebels, and most of all to Simon specifically for originally differing with him without reason and getting the worst of it, and then by other wiles bringing troubles on him and exulting as though achieving what he intended for him.

But it is you, soul mate, my leader and my friend (v. 13). Symmachus: "But you, someone of like mind, a familiar, a friend." *My leader* was well said of Simon, since he had been appointed to a supervisory role by blessed Onias the high priest; we likewise name as kings' leaders and rulers those acting under them or entrusted with government by them. *Who took sweetmeats together with me* (v. 14)—that is, was very pleased to eat with me; not eating as my guest, but dining with me as a close friend with great pleasure, satisfaction, and familiarity. *In the house of God we walked with harmony.* He mentioned all these details—someone who was a soul mate, a leader, a friend, who took sweetmeats with him, who walked together with him in the house of God—to bring out that in many respects they had a relationship with him.[5] |

---

5. Commentary on vv. 15–19a is missing from Devreesse's text.

20^b. Οὐ γάρ ἐστιν αὐτοῖς ἀντάλλαγμα. Δι᾽ ὅλων μέντοι τοὺς οἰκείους αἰτιώμενος φαίνεται μᾶλλον· ἐκεῖνοι γὰρ ἦσαν οἱ πάντων αἴτιοι γενόμενοι τῶν κακῶν. Δέξονται γοῦν φησι τὴν τιμωρίαν εἰκότως· οὐδὲ γάρ ἐστι χρήματα δόντας ἀνταλλάξασθαι τὴν τιμωρίαν καὶ ἐξιλεώσασθαι τὸν Θεόν, ὃν οὔτε ἐφοβήθησαν οὔτε εἰς διάνοιαν ἔθεντο, τοιαῦτα διαπραττόμενοι κακὰ 5 καὶ τὴν τῶν νομίμων λύοντες εὐταξίαν. Οἷα γὰρ ἐποίησαν;

21^a. Ἐξέτεινεν τὴν χεῖρα αὐτοῦ ἐν τῷ ἀποδιδόναι. Ὥρμησάν φησιν ἐπὶ τὸ τιμωρήσασθαι ἡμᾶς. Ἐκ μεταφορᾶς δὲ τῶν ἀποδιδόντων ἅπερ ὀφείλουσιν ἐκ παντὸς λόγου ἐπὶ τῇ ἀποδόσει τὴν χεῖρα ἐκτεινόντων, ἠβουλήθη δεῖξαι ὅτι μετὰ πολλῆς τῆς σπουδῆς καὶ τῆς ἐπείξεως ἐκέχρηντο τὴν κατ᾽ 10 αὐτοῦ ὕβριν τε καὶ ἀδικίαν. Τὸ οὖν ἐν τῷ ἀποδιδόναι ὥσπερ ἐν ἀποδόσει χρέους· πολλαχοῦ γὰρ δέδεικται ἡμῖν ἄνευ τοῦ « ὡς » λέγων τὴν παραβολὴν καὶ ἐν τάξει τιθεὶς τοῦ πράγματος τὸ ὁμοίωμα.

21^b. Ἐβεβήλωσαν τὴν διαθήκην αὐτοῦ. Ἐμίαναν καὶ ὕβρισαν τοῦ Θεοῦ τὰ νόμιμα. Οὕτω λέγει Σύμμαχος Παρεβίβασαν συνθήκην· παρέβησαν γὰρ 15 πολλαχοῦ, εἴτε τοῦ ἱεροῦ τὰ χρήματα προδοῦναι βουληθέντες τοῖς ἀλλοφύλοις, εἴτε ἀλλοφύλους ἐπαγαγόντες τῷ ἔθνει, καὶ τῆς λοιπῆς τῶν νομίμων φυλακῆς πάντη καταμελήσαντες.

22^a. Διεμερίσθησαν ἀπὸ ὀργῆς τοῦ προσώπου αὐτοῦ. Διὰ ταύτην γοῦν τὴν αἰτίαν καὶ τὴν τῶν νομίμων παράβασιν διεῖλον καὶ ἀφώρισαν αὐτοὺς 20 ἀπ᾽ ἐμοῦ, αὐτῷ τῷ προσώπῳ καὶ τῷ βλέμματι αὐτῶν τὴν ὀργὴν καὶ τὸ μῖσος ἐμφαίνοντες τὸ κατ᾽ ἐμοῦ· ὀργῆς γὰρ πρόσωπον λέγει τὸ πεπληρωμένον ὀργῆς, καὶ διὰ τῆς οἰκείας θέας τὴν ἐπὶ τῆς ψυχῆς ὀργὴν ἐμφανίζων. Τῷ οὖν διεμερίσθησαν προσυπακούεται τὸ « ἀπ᾽ ἐμοῦ ».

12 cf. supra p. 149, 16.

20^b. Δι᾽ ὅλων — εὐταξίαν: P, fol. 155; V, fol. 218^v; C 98 sup., fol. 108^{r·v}; Cord, p. 67.   3 γοῦν] γὰρ V   6 νόμων Cord   οἷα γὰρ ἐποίησαν om. Cord.
21^a. Ὥρμησαν — ὁμοίωμα: P, fol. 155; V. fol. 219; Cord, p. 68.
21^b. Ἐμίαναν — καταμελήσαντες: P, fol. 155^v; V, fol. 219; Cord, p. 69.   15 Σύμμαχος] καὶ add. Cord.
22^a. Διὰ ταύτην — ἐμοῦ: P, fol. 155^v; V, fol. 219^v.

A^e 3-6 (p. 294, 11-14): Nulla argenti oblationumque permotatione destinato eximentur exitio, quia Deum non timendo inmaniter dilinquerunt.   10-11 (p. 294, 15-17): Sic quippe studiosse in meas grasabantur iniurias, quasi non inferrent mala sed redderent (reterent ms).

There is no change in them, in fact (v. 19b). In general, of course, he seems to be blaming rather his own people: they were the ones responsible for all the troubles. So he is saying, They will rightly undergo punishment: there is no possibility of their escaping punishment and placating God by paying money, for they did not fear him or call him to mind, instead committing such awful evils and disturbing the good order of lawful observance. What, in fact, did they do? *He stretched out his hand in making retribution* (v. 20): they were bent on punishing us. By the analogy with those paying back what they owe on every score and stretching out their hand in repayment, he wanted to bring out that with great relish and haste they treated him with insult and injustice. So the phrase *in making retribution* means, as it were, "in repayment of a debt"; in many cases, in fact, we are shown the expression without the "as," using the figure and the likeness in the role of a fact.

They profaned his covenant: they besmirched and insulted God's laws. Symmachus says in similar terms, "They did violence to the agreement." In other words, They transgressed it at every turn, either by wanting to hand over the money in the sanctuary to foreigners, or by inflicting foreigners on the nation and completely neglecting the remaining observance of the laws. *They were divided in anger of their countenance* (v. 21): for that fault and the transgression of the laws they cut themselves off and parted from me, accentuating their anger and hatred for me by their very visage and gaze. By *countenance of anger* he means "one filled with anger," and he explains their heartfelt anger by its outward appearance. So "from me" is to be supplied after *They were divided.* | *And their hearts pressed hard:* those who previously

22ᵇ. Καὶ ἤγγισεν ἡ καρδία αὐτῶν. Καὶ τοσαύτην ἐπεδείκνυντο κατ᾽ ἐμοῦ τὴν ὀργὴν οἱ πρὸ τούτου τὸ ἐμοὶ πλησιάζειν καὶ ἐγγίζειν μεθ᾽ ὅλης καρδίας καὶ διαθέσεως προσποιούμενοι· ἠλέγχθη γὰρ ἐκ τῶν μετὰ ταῦτα προσποίησις ὄν. Τὸ γὰρ ἤγγισεν ἡ καρδία αὐτῶν, τουτέστιν ἤγγιζον ὡς ἀπὸ
5 καρδίας, ὡς ἀφ᾽ ὅλης ψυχῆς καὶ διανοίας.

22ᶜ. Ἡπαλύνθησαν οἱ λόγοι αὐτῶν ὑπὲρ ἔλαιον, καὶ αὐτοί εἰσι βολίδες. Σύμμαχος Λειότερα βουτύρου τὰ στόματα αὐτῶν, πολεμεῖ δὲ ἡ καρδία αὐτῶν. Τοῖς μὲν γὰρ ῥήμασιν ἐκέχρηντο οὕτω γλυκέσι καὶ ἡδέσιν ὥσπερ ἔλαιον τὴν τῶν λόγων ἀλείφοντες χρηστότητα τὸν ἀκούοντα. Ἦσαν δὲ οἱ λόγοι
10 αὐτῶν βολίδες, — βολίδας δὲ καλεῖ ὄργανόν τι πολεμικόν· ὑπόκρισις γὰρ ἦν ὁ λόγος ὁ δοκῶν χρηστότητος πεπληρῶσθαι, μώλωπας ἐξεργαζόμενος τοῖς ἀπατωμένοις.

23ᵃ. Ἐπίρριψον ἐπὶ Κύριον τὴν μέριμνάν σου, καὶ αὐτός σε διαθρέψει. Ὡς ἀφ᾽ ἑαυτοῦ λοιπὸν ὁ προφήτης πρὸς αὐτόν· Παῦσαί φησι φροντίζων
15 διὰ τὸ πλῆθος τῶν κακῶν, καὶ τὸ πᾶν ἀνάθου τῷ Θεῷ· αὐτὸς γάρ σοι βοηθήσει καὶ πάντων σε πληρώσει τῶν καλῶν, πάσης ῥυσάμενος στενοχωρίας.

23ᵇ. Οὐ δώσει εἰ; τὸν αἰῶνα σάλον τῷ δικαίῳ. Εἰ γὰρ καὶ ἔδοξας λυπεῖσθαι πρὸς βραχύ, ἀλλ᾽ οὐκ ἐάσει σε διηνεκῶς ἐν μέσῳ τῶν κακῶν
20 περιαντλεῖσθαι καὶ περιάγεσθαι.

24ᵃ. Σὺ δέ, ὁ Θεός, κατάξεις αὐτοὺς εἰς φρέαρ διαφθορᾶς. Αὐτὸς γὰρ ὁ Θεὸς κατασπάσει καὶ καταβαλεῖ τοιούτοις αὐτοὺς κακοῖς, ἐν οἷς πάντως διαφθαρήσονται, ὥσπερ ἐν φρέατι κατεχόμενοι καὶ ἀνάδυσιν ἐξ αὐτῶν τινα καὶ ἀπαλλαγὴν εὑρεῖν οὐ δυνάμενοι.

22ᵇ. Καὶ τοσαύτην — διανοίας: P, fol. 155ᵛ; V, fol. 219ᵛ.   2 καὶ ἐγγίζειν om. C   3 ἠλέχθη C.
22ᶜ. Σύμμαχος — ἀπατωμένοις: P, fol. 156; V, fol. 220; Vat. 1422, fol. 105; C 98 sup., fol. 108ᵛ.   9 χρηστότητα abrumpitur C, foliis pluribus perditis.
23ᵃ. Ὡς ἀφ᾽ ἑαυτοῦ — στενοχωρίας: P, fol. 156; V, fol. 220; Cord, p. 71.
23ᵇ. Εἰ γὰρ καὶ — περιάγεσθαι: P, fol. 156; V, f. 220ᵛ.
24ᵃ. Αὐτὸς γὰρ — δυνάμενοι: P, fol. 156ᵛ; V, fol. 220ᵛ-221.

Aᵉ 22ᵃ (p. 294, 21-25): Sacrilego furore sunt mea societate diuisi, ipso uultu iram, quam aduersum me conceperant, puplicantes; ideo et irae uultum gerebant.   4-5 (p. 294, 26-28): Hi sunt autem inimici, qui mihi prius toto se corde iunctos simulabant.   10-12 (p. 294, 29-31): Dulcibus uerbis tegebantur uenina et mollitudine sermonum iaculis locum parabant.   14 (p. 295, 2-3): Quasi ipse profeta iam doctus adloquitur.   23ᵇ (p. 295, 4-6): Licet ad tempus, ut probaretur, adflictus sit, in aeternum tamen fluctuare non sinitur. 23-24 (p. 295, 7-8): Vnde praecipitatorum facilis non fuit euersio.

pretended to be close to me and on my side with all their heart and affection gave evidence of such anger for me, the fact of pretense being proven by what happened later. *Their hearts pressed hard* means, in fact, They pressed hard as though from the heart, as from their whole soul and mind. *Their words became softer than oil, and in fact were javelins.* Symmachus: "Their mouths were smoother than butter, but their hearts were hostile." In other words, they employed sweet and pleasing words as though anointing the listener with the excellent oil of their words. But their words were *javelins* (by *javelins* referring to an instrument of war, since the word that seemed full of kindness was a pretense, inflicting wounds on those taken in).

Cast your care on the Lord, and he will sustain you (v. 22). As if on his own account the author now says to him, Cease worrying about the great number of troubles, and rely completely on God: he personally will help you and fill you will every good, rescuing you from all hardship. *He will not allow the righteous to be tossed about forever:* even if you seemed to be distressed for a while, he will not let you be worn out and perplexed in the midst of ceaseless troubles.

But you, O God, will cast them down into a pit of destruction (v. 23): God himself will pull them down and overwhelm them with such awful disasters, in which they will utterly perish, as though trapped in a pit without any means of finding escape and release from them. | *Bloodthirsty and*

24ᵇ. Ἄνδρες αἱμάτων καὶ δολιότητος οὐ μὴ ἡμισεύσωσιν τὰς ἡμέρας
αὐτῶν. Οὗτοι οὖν φησιν οἱ μοχθηροί, καὶ πανοῦργοι, καὶ τῶν αἱμάτων
ἐρῶντες τῶν σῶν τῇ τοῦ Θεοῦ περιβληθήσονται τιμωρίᾳ, καὶ οὐ φθάσουσι
τὸ ἥμισυ τῆς οἰκείας ζωῆς, ἀντὶ τοῦ οὐκ ἐκτενοῦσιν ἐπὶ μήκιστον τὴν
ζωήν, — οὐδὲ γὰρ ὡς ὡρισμένης αὐτοῖς ἡμέρας τοῦ θανάτου λέγει, ἀλλ᾿   5
ἀντὶ τοῦ Δυνάμενοι ὅσον ἐκ τῆς οἰκείας συστάσεως ἐπὶ πλεῖον βιῶναι,
ὀξύτερον τὴν τοῦ Θεοῦ τιμωρίαν τὸν θάνατον δέξονται.

24ᶜ. Ἐγὼ δὲ ἐλπιῶ ἐπὶ σε, Κύριε. Ὥστε φησὶ τοιαῦτα πείσας ἑαυτὸν
φρονεῖν περὶ τοῦ Θεοῦ, ταῦτα δὲ μὴ μᾶλλον λέγε πρὸς αὐτόν, ὅτι Τούτων ἕνεκεν τῆς εἴς σε ἐλπίδος οὐκ ἐκστήσομαι, πεπεισμένος ὡς ἐμὲ μὲν   10
ἀπαλλάξεις ποτὲ τῶν κακῶν, τουτουσὶ δὲ πάντως ὑπὲρ ὧν ποιοῦσι διαφόροις ταῖς τιμωρίαις περιβαλεῖς· τὸ γὰρ « εἶπεν » κατὰ τὸ σύνηθες ἑαυτῷ
κἀνταῦθα ἀπεσιώπησεν.

PSALMVS LV

Ὀνίου τοῦ ἀρχιερέως τὴν πόλιν καταλελοιπότος καὶ τῶν κατὰ τὴν   15
πόλιν κακῶν εἰς ἐπίδοσιν χωρούντων, βωμός τε προστάγματι τοῦ βασιλέως
ἐπὶ τῷ τοῦ Διὸς ὀνόματι κατὰ τὴν πόλιν ἀνέστη. Καὶ πολλῶν θύειν ἀναγ-
καζομένων, οἱ μὲν γνώμῃ πρὸς τὸ πρᾶγμα ἐχώρουν, οἱ δὲ καὶ ὑπὸ τῆς
ἀνάγκης συνωθούμενοι, Ματταθίας δή τις ἐκ τῶν Ἰουδαίων ἀνὴρ δικαιότατος, ζηλώσας τὸν νόμον ἀνεῖλε μὲν τὸν ἀναγκάζοντα θύειν, ἀνεῖλε δὲ καὶ   20

15 ss. cf. argumentum ps. XLIII (p.268-269).

24ᵇ. Οὗτοι — δέξονται: P, fol. 156ᵛ; V, fol. 221; Vat. 1422, fol. 105; C 98 sup.,
fol. 109; Cord, p. 72.   4-6 ἐπὶ μήκιστον -- ἀντὶ τοῦ] τὸ ἥμισυ τῆς οἰκείας ζωῆς οὐδὲ
γὰρ C 98   7 τῇ... τιμωρίᾳ C 98.
24ᶜ. Ὥστε — ἀπεσιώπησεν: P, fol. 156ᵛ; V, fol. 221.
Ὀνίου — συμφοραῖς: P, fol. 157ᵛ; V, fol. 221ᵛ; Cord, p. 88.

Aᵉ 24ᵇ (p. 295, 8-13): Crudiles effundendi sanguinis auidi... nec ad mediam,
qua uiuire poterant conpossitione corporis, aetatem, Deo puniente peruenient.
24ᶜ (p. 295, 14-15): Cousilium profetae est, ac si diceret: O tu, confitenter Deo
dicito quia speres in eum in aeternum.   Argumentum ps. LV (p. 295, 18-296, 4):
Praedicit in hoc psalmo profeta quae Machabeorum sunt acta temporibus; qui,
Onia Hirusolimas deserente, in ultionem legis suae patris Mathathiae exemplo
iurauerunt, bellum inferentes tam praeuaricatoribus ciuibus quam in id ipsum
cogentibus hostibus; formatur autem talis eius carminis oratio qualis possitis
in calamitatibus congruerat. Cf. PSEUDO-BEDA (776): Machabeorum supplicatio,
quando in ultionem legis coniurantes tam praeuaricatores ciues quam etiam
hostes expugnare tentabant.

deceitful men will not live out half their days: these depraved evildoers thirsting for your blood will be enveloped in God's punishment and will not reach half their due age—that is, they will not live to old age. He does not mean, in fact, that the day of their death is determined; rather, though capable of living longer by their own resources, they will meet death sooner as punishment from God. *But I for my part shall hope in you, Lord.* And so, he says, Being persuaded to set your mind on God, say this instead to him: In view of this I shall not abandon hope in you, convinced that you will free me at some time from the troubles and surely envelop those people in different punishments for what they do (the word "said" being understood here, too, in his customary manner).

PSALM 56

After the departure of Onias from the city and the increase in troubles affecting the city, an altar in the name of Zeus was erected in the city by order of the king. Many people were forced to offer sacrifice, some taking to the rite voluntarily, others forced to do so under pressure.[1] Mattathias, a most righteous man of the Jews, in his zeal for the law slew the person exercising pressure to sacrifice, and slew also | the one willingly coming

---

1. Theodore summarizes the story of 1 Macc 1–3, as he had done in introducing Ps 44.

τὸν ἐπὶ τὴν θυσίαν ὁρμήσαντα ἑκοντί. Οὕτω τε συστρατεύσας τῶν Ἰουδαίων τοὺς εὐσεβεστέρους εἴχετο τῆς κατὰ τῶν ἐναντίων μάχης. Ἀλλὰ τελευτᾷ
μὲν οὗτος εὐθύς, παραδίδωσι δὲ τοῖς υἱοῖς τὴν ἀρχήν, Ἰούδαν τὸν ἐπικα-
λούμενον Μακκαβαῖον στρατηγεῖν τε καὶ ἐξάρχειν τῶν πολεμίων παρακε-
5 λευσάμενος ὡς μείζονα καὶ τὴν προθυμίαν καὶ τὴν ἰσχὺν κεκτημένον παρὰ
τοὺς ἀδελφούς, καὶ ὅλως τοῦ ἄρχειν ἱκανόν. Ἀναδεξάμενοι δὴ τοὺς ὑπὲρ τοῦ
ἔθνους κινδύνους πολλοὺς καὶ συνεχεῖς, τοῦτο μὲν πρὸς τοὺς Ἀντιόχου στρατηγούς, τοῦτο δὲ πρὸς τοὺς περιοίκους ἔσχον τὰς μάχας, ἐκείνων ἀνελεῖν
αὐτοὺς παντὶ τρόπῳ βουλομένων. Ἦν δὲ καὶ τοῦτο πάντων χεῖρον ἡ τῶν
10 οἰκείων προδοσία· οὐδὲ γὰρ ὀλίγοι τινὲς πρὸς τὰ τῶν ἐναντίων ἔβλεπον, οἱ
καὶ τῆς ἀρχῆς τῶν κακῶν αἴτιοι γεγόνασιν. Τούτων τοίνυν προαγόρευσιν
ποιεῖται τόνδε ψαλμὸν ὁ μακάριος Δαυίδ, ἐκ τούτων Μακκαβαίων προσώπου
λέγων ὅσα ἐκείνοις εἰπεῖν ἥρμοττεν οὖσιν ἐν ταῖς συμφοραῖς.

2ª. Ἐλέησόν με, ὁ Θεός, ὅτι κατεπάτησέν με ἄνθρωπος. Κατεπάτησεν,
15 ἀντὶ τοῦ συνέθλιψε τῷ πλήθει τῶν κακῶν καὶ κατηνάλωσεν.

2ᵇ. Ὅλην τὴν ἡμέραν πολεμῶν ἔθλιψέ με. Ἀδιαλείπτως πολεμοῦντες
ἡμᾶς ἔθλιψον· δέδεικται γὰρ πολλαχοῦ τὸ « διηνεκῶς » καὶ « ἀδιαλείπτως »,
ὅλην τὴν ἡμέραν λέγων ἢ πᾶσαν ἡμέραν.

3ª. Κατεπάτησάν με οἱ ἐχθροί μου ὅλην τὴν ἡμέραν. Διαφόρως ποικίλ-
20 λει τὸν λόγον, τὸ αὐτὸ λέγων ὅτι ἔπαθον ἀνήκεστα. Ἴδιον δὲ τοῦτο τοῦ
μακαρίου Δαυὶδ ὅταν βούληται λέγειν τοῦ κακοῦ τὴν ἐπίτασιν.

3ᵇ-4ª. Ὅτι πολλοὶ οἱ πολεμοῦντές με ἀπὸ ὕψους ἡμερῶν. Ἔνια τῶν
ἀντιγράφων τὸ ὅτι πολλοὶ οἱ πολεμοῦντές με ἀπὸ ὕψους ἡμερῶν οὐκ ἔχει,
ἴσως τινῶν δευτερολογίαν περιττὴν νομισάντων καὶ διὰ τοῦτο τῆς βίβλου

18 cf. Ps. XXIV, 5ᶜ; XXXI, 3ᵇ et ps. XXXIV, 28ᵇ (p. 193).

2 εἶχε Cord   7. 8 τοῦτο μὲν... τοῦτο δὲ om. Cord   πρός τε τοὺς Cord   8 ἐκεῖνον PV   9 χείρω PV   11 τῆς ἀρχῆς τῶν] πολλῶν Cord   11-12 τούτων — ψαλ-
μὸν] τόνδε τοίνυν ποιεῖται ψ. Cord   13 οὖσιν om. Cord.
2ª. Κατεπάτησεν — κατηνάλωσεν: P, fol. 158; V, fol. 222; C 98 sup., fol. 109ʳ·ᵛ;
Cord, p. 89.
2ᵇ. Ἀδιαλείπτως — ἡμέραν: P, fol. 158; V, fol. 222ᵛ.
3ª. Διαφόρως — ἐπίτασιν: P, fol. 158ᵛ; V, fol. 222ᵛ; Cord, p. 90.
3ᵇ-4ª. Ἔνια — καταπλαγέντα: P, fol. 158ª; V, fol. 222ᵛ-223; Cord, p. 91.

Aᵉ 2ᵇ (p. 296, 12-13): Pro continuatione temporis negotiique.   3ᵇ (p. 296,
14-16): Diuersis modis id ipsum dicit suo more, cum uult magnitudinem calamitatis expraemere.

forward to sacrifice. He thus joined the most devoted Jews in waging war and was involved in fighting the adversaries. Upon his death he passed control to his sons, urging Judas surnamed Maccabeus to lead the forces and conduct the war against the enemy since he had more enthusiasm and strength than his brothers and was quite capable of ruling. They involved themselves in many unremitting dangers on behalf of their nation, some against the generals of Antiochus, some against neighboring peoples, and conducted campaigns, with the enemy anxious to destroy them in one way or another. Betrayal by their own, however, was worse than anything: not a few saw their future with the adversaries, and they proved responsible for the beginning of the troubles.

Blessed David, therefore, composes this psalm as a prediction of these events, saying from the viewpoint of these Maccabees everything applicable to them in their calamitous situations. *Have mercy on me, O God, for people have trampled on me* (v. 1). By *trampled* he means, They have afflicted me with the multitude of troubles and consumed me. *In hostile manner they have distressed me all day long:* warring against us unceasingly they have distressed us (often bringing out the meaning "constantly" or "unceasingly" by saying *all day long* or "the whole day"). *My foes trampled on me all day long* (v. 2). He varies the expression to the same effect, meaning, I suffered intolerably. It is typical of blessed David to mention the extremity of the misfortune whenever he wishes.

Because many are those warring against me from the height of the days. Some of the manuscripts do not have *Because many of those warring against me from the height of the days,* some scribes perhaps thinking the repetition superfluous and hence removing the phrase—and | they deserve our pity

περιελόντων, — οὓς ἐλεεῖν ἄξιον ὡς περιττόν τι τῆς γραφῆς νομίσαντας, — ἀμφότερα δὲ κεῖται παρὰ τῷ προφήτῃ καὶ μᾶλλον ἀναγκαίως. Τὸ γὰρ ἀπὸ ὕψους ἡμερῶν λέγει, ἀντὶ τοῦ ἄνωθεν, καὶ ἐξ ἀρχῆς, ἀπὸ τῶν ἄνω ἡμερῶν. Ἐπειδὴ γὰρ τὸ ἀνώτερον ἡμῶν πάντως καὶ ὑψηλότερον, ὕψους ἡμερῶν εἶπεν ἀντὶ τοῦ τ ῶν ἄνω· βούλεται δὲ εἰπεῖν ὅτι ἐξ ἀρχῆς καὶ 5 ἄνωθεν κατεφρόνησα τῶν | πολεμούντων μοι καὶ θλιβόντων με, οὐδέποτε δείσας αὐτοὺς καὶ καταπλαγείς, καίτοι γε ἄνωθεν ἔχων τοὺς ἐχθροὺς οὐδέποτε διαλείποντας τῆς πρὸς ἐμὲ φιλονεικίας. Λέγει δὲ τοῦτο ἀπὸ προσώπου τῶν Μακκαβαίων, οὐχ ὡς περὶ ἑαυτῶν λεγόντων, ἀλλ' ὡς ἀπὸ κοινοῦ τοῦ λαοῦ· ὑπὲρ πάντων γὰρ καὶ τὸν λόγον ἐποιοῦντο. Ἄνωθέν 10 φησιν ἔσχον τοὺς πολεμοῦντας, — μέμνημαι γὰρ τῶν κατ' Αἴγυπτον, μετὰ ταῦτα ἀλλοφύλων, ὅσων καὶ οἵων καθ' ἕκαστον ἐπειράθην καιρόν, — ἀλλὰ κατεπλάγην οὐδένα· τὸ μηδὲν γὰρ τοὺς πάντας ἐλογισάμην τῇ σῇ βοηθείᾳ πάντων περιγιγνόμενος. Ἀναγκαίως οὖν κεῖται καὶ τὸ δεύτερον· τοῦτο γὰρ ἦν τὸ μέγα, τὸ ἄνωθεν καὶ τοὺς πολεμοῦντας ἔχοντα ἀεὶ καταφρονῆσαι τῶν 15 ἐχθρῶν μηδέποτε καταπλαγέντα.

4ᵇ. Ἡμέρας οὐ φοβηθήσομαι, ἐγὼ δὲ ἐλπιῶ ἐπί σε. Ἀντὶ τοῦ οὐδέποτε, ἀλλ' οὐδεμίαν φησὶν ἡμέραν οὐκ ἂν φοβηθείην αὐτούς· πέποιθα γὰρ τῇ εἴς σε βοηθείᾳ.

5ᵃ. Ἐν τῷ Θεῷ ἐπαινέσω τοὺς λόγους μου. Ἐπειδὴ τὸ ἐπαίνων ἄξιον 20 πάντως καὶ θαυμαστόν φησι τῇ σῇ βοηθείᾳ, θαυμαστοὶ οἱ λόγοι μου καὶ πάσης γέμοντες ἀληθείας δειχθήσονται. Τοῦτο γὰρ αὐτὸ τὸ λέγειν με ὅτι μηδένα δέδοικα τῶν πολεμίων διὰ τὴν παρὰ τοῦ Θεοῦ βοήθειαν, δειχθήσεταὶ μεγάλως, ἀληθῶς καὶ εἰκότως λεγόμενον.

5ᵇ. Ἐπὶ τῷ Θεῷ ἤλπισα, οὐ φοβηθήσομαι τί ποιήσει μοι σάρξ. Διὰ γὰρ 25 τῆς εἴς σε ἐλπίδα παρ' οὐδενός τι παθεῖν προσδοκῶ. Καλῶς δὲ εἶπεν σάρξ, ἀπὸ τοῦ εὐτελεστέρου μᾶλλον σμικρύνων τοὺς πολεμοῦντας ὡς ἀσθενεῖς καὶ δυναμένους οὐδέν.

---

1 ἢ περιττὸν τὸ PV   10 γὰρ om. CV.
4ᵇ. Ἀντὶ τοῦ οὐδέποτε — βοηθείᾳ: P. fol. 158ᵛ; V, fol. 223; Cord, p. 91.
5ᵃ. Ἐπειδὴ — λεγόμενον: P. fol. 159; V, fol. 223; Cord, p. 92.   20 τὸ] δὲ Cord.
5ᵇ. Διὰ γὰρ τῆς — οὐδέν: P, fol. 159; V, fol. 223ᵛ; C 98 sup., fol. 109ᵛ.

Aᵉ 4ᵇ (p. 296, 17-19): Quacumque die territus fuero, ego in te confidam. 5ᵃ (p. 296, 19-22): Tuo, inquit adiutorio mei sermones mirabiles apparebunt atque laudabiles, quod neminem me timere alium profiteor.   27-29 (p. 296, 22-24: Bene carnem dicit, ut hostes suos ab inferiore hominis parte ostenderet non timere decipere.

for thinking anything of the Scripture is superfluous. Both phrases, however, occur in the inspired author of particular necessity: he is saying *from the height of the days* to mean from the beginning, from the outset, from earlier days—that is, since it was beyond us and above us, he used height of our days to mean those in the past. He means, From the beginning and from long ago I scorned those attacking me and afflicting me, in no way fearing them or being in shock, even though from the outset I had enemies who would not desist from their hostility to me. Now, he says this from the viewpoint of the Maccabees, not that they are speaking of themselves but of the whole people, as it were, for they made the statement on behalf of everyone. They had assailants from of old, he says; I refer to those in Egypt, foreigners later, all those of every kind whom I experienced on each occasion. But I was not deterred, treating them as of no significance and prevailing over them all, thanks to your help.

So the second phrase has to appear as well: It was significant that even from the outset I could ever despise the attackers without at any time being dismayed by the foe. *By day I shall not fear; instead, I shall hope in you* (v. 3): never—that is, not for a day—would I have feared them, for I trusted in your help. *In God I shall praise my words* (v. 4): since the fact of your help is completely worthy of praise and admiration, my words will be seen to be full of admiration and all truth. This statement of mine has, in fact, the same meaning as, I feared none of the enemy on account of help from God, and it will be seen to be rightly stated in grand and true fashion. *In God I hoped: I shall not fear what flesh will do to me:* on account of hope in you I expect to suffer nothing from anybody. *Flesh* was well put, from mention of the least significant element belittling the attackers as weak and incapable of anything. |

6ª. Ὅλην τὴν ἡμέραν τοὺς λόγους μου ἐβδελύσσοντο. Καλῶς εἶπε τὸ ἐβδελύσσοντο, — Θεοδοτίων ἐζήτησαν. Τοῦτο γὰρ λέγει ὅτι ἀεὶ παρετήρουν μου τοὺς λόγους, βουλόμενοι λαβὰς εὑρεῖν κατ᾽ ἐμοῦ. Ἔοικε δὲ τοῦτο περὶ τῶν οἰκείων λέγειν, οἳ πάντα ἐπιτηροῦντες τὰ παρ᾽ αὐτῶν λεγόμενα διαβάλ-
5 λειν ἐπειρῶντο πρὸς τοὺς πολεμίους, ὥστε μειζόνως αὐτοὺς παροξύνειν κατ᾽ αὐτῶν. Οὐκ ἀπεικότως δὲ εἶπεν τὸ ἐβδελύσσοντο, ἀντὶ τοῦ ἐζήτησαν· ἐπειδὴ γὰρ μισητὸν τὸ βδελυκτόν, ἐπετήρουν δὲ αὐτοὶ τοὺς λόγους ἐπὶ τὸ διαβάλλοντες αὐξῆσαι τὸ κατ᾽ αὐτοῦ μῖσος παρὰ τοῖς πολεμίοις, καλῶς ἀπὸ τοῦ σκοποῦ καὶ τοῦ ἀποβαίνοντος τὴν πρᾶξιν ἐκάλεσεν τὸ ἐπιτηρεῖν
10 τε καὶ βλάβας κατ᾽ αὐτοῦ ζητεῖν, βδελύσσεσθαι εἰπών, ἐπειδὴ τοῦτο εἰργάζοντο κατ᾽ αὐτοῦ.

6ᵇ. Κατ᾽ ἐμοῦ πάντες οἱ διαλογισμοὶ αὐτῶν εἰς κακόν. Πάντας φησὶ τοὺς διαλογισμοὺς αὐτῶν ἠσχόλουν κατ᾽ ἐμοῦ εἰς τό τι κακὸν εὑρεῖν τε καὶ μηχανήσασθαι, ἢ τὰ λεγόμενα τηροῦντες καὶ διαβάλλοντες, ἢ παροξύνοντες
15 καθ᾽ ἡμῶν τοὺς ἐχθρούς, ἢ ὅλως τι καθ᾽ ἡμῶν εὑρίσκοντες.

7. Παροικοῦσι καὶ κατακρύψουσιν, αὐτοὶ τὴν πτέρναν μου φυλάξουσι, καθάπερ ὑπέμειναν τὴν ψυχήν μου. Κατὰ τὴν ἀκολουθίαν οὕτως εἶχε· Παροικοῦσι κατακρύπτοντες καὶ τὴν πτέρναν μου φυλάττοντες, καθάπερ ὑπέμειναν τὴν ψυχήν μου. Ἴδιον δὲ τοῦτο τῷ μακαρίῳ Δαυὶδ καὶ πολλαχοῦ τῶν
20 ψαλμῶν εὑρισκόμενον, εἴτε ἀπὸ τοῦ ἑβραϊκοῦ ἰδιώματος, εἴτε ἀπὸ τῆς ἑρμηνείας οὕτω φαινόμενον τὸν πολλάκις ἀντιλέγοντα, ὥσπερ διαιροῦντα δύο λέγειν δοκεῖν — οἷον ὡς ὅταν λέγῃ Φθέγξονται καὶ λαλήσουσιν ἀδικίαν, ἀντὶ τοῦ «φθέγγονται» καὶ λαλήσουσιν ἀδικίαν· δοκεῖ γὰρ δύο λέγειν, κα μάλιστα τοῦ καὶ συνδέσμου μεσιτεύοντος, — ὅτι φθέγγονται καὶ λαλή-
25 σουσιν, — ἓν δέ ἐστιν ὅ φησιν, ὅτι φθέγγονται ἀδικίαν λαλοῦντες. Οὕτω

23 Ps. XCIII, 4ª.

6ª. Καλῶς — κατ᾽ αὐτοῦ: P, fol. 159ᵛ et V, fol. 223ᵛ sub nomine THEODORETI; Cord, p. 93.   2-6 L (p. 84, 48-85, 5): Ὁ δὲ Θεοδοτίων τὸ ἐβδελύσσοντο ἐζήτησαν εἶπε, τουτέστιν Ἀεὶ παρετήρουν τοὺς λόγους μου, βουλόμενοι — οἰκείων λαλεῖν, οἱ πάντα ἐπιτηροῦντες διαβάλλειν — πολεμίους, μείζονα βουλόμενοι παροξύνειν αὐτοὺς κατ᾽ αὐτοῦ 3 κατ᾽ ἐμοῦ des. Cord.
6ᵇ. Πάντας — εὑρίσκοντες: P, fol. 159ᵛ; V, fol. 223ᵛ-224.
7. Κατὰ τὴν ἀκολουθίαν — ἐπιτηρῶν: P, fol. 160ʳ·ᵛ et V, fol. 224ʳ·ᵛ sub nomine THEODORETI; Cord, p. 94-97.   18-19 παροικήσουσιν Cord   20 ἴδιον] οἶδα Cord 24 λαλοῦσιν Cord   25-26 ὅτι — λαλήσουσιν om. Cord.

Aᵉ 5-8 (p. 297, 5-7): …per quae autem hodia eorum iurgiaque inter hostes augerent et inpugnationes accenderent.   13-15 (p. 297, 8-9): Hostium in nos animum aspernabant.

All day long they loathed my words (v. 5). He did well to say *loathed* (Theodotion: "sought"). In fact, he means, They kept observing my words closely, wanting to find grounds against me. Now, they probably say this about their own people, who scrutinized everything said by them in an attempt to traduce them to the enemy so as to provoke them further against them. It is not unlikely that he said *loathed* in the sense of "sought": since loathing is hateful and they scrutinized his words to misrepresent him and heighten the enemy's hatred against him, he was right to use "loathe" of their aim of deterring him from his purpose by scrutiny and seeking grounds against him, since this was the aim of their efforts against him. *All their calculations of evil are against me:* all their thoughts are directed against me to find and devise something harmful, either by observing and misrepresenting what is said, or by provoking the foe against us, or in general by coming up with something against us.

They stay on my heels and will remain in hiding; they will watch for my weak point as though expecting to have my life (v. 6). The thought proceeds in the following sequence: They will stay on my heels, remaining in hiding and watching for my weak point as though expecting to have my life. Now, we found this idiom used by blessed David in many other places in the psalms as well, either arising from a Hebrew idiom or occurring this way in the translation, namely, the frequent contradiction where it seems that he is saying two different things, as when it says, "They will utter and they will speak injustice," meaning, They utter and will speak injustice. It seems that he is saying two things, especially with "and" coming in between, "They will utter and they will speak," whereas what he is saying is one thing, They give voice to injustice when they speak. Similarly, | in Psalm 50, "The Lord God

καὶ ἐν τῷ μθ' τὸ Θεὸς θεῶν Κύριος ἐλάλησε καὶ ἐκάλεσε τὴν γῆν ἑρμη-
νεύοντες, ἐπεσημηνάμεθα ὅτι ἕν ἐστιν ὃ βούλεται εἰπεῖν, δύο εἶναι δοκοῦντα.

Λέγει δὲ αὐτὸ Σύμμαχος οὕτω· Συνήγοντο λάθρα, καὶ τὰ ἴχνη μου
παρετηροῦντο προσδοκῶντες τὴν ψυχήν μου. Ἐνέδρας φησὶν εἰργάζοντο καὶ
ἐπετήρουν ἃ ἔπραττον, ὅπως ἄν με ἢ συλλαβόμενοι ἀνέλωσιν, ἢ προδόντες 5
τοῖς πολεμίοις. Τὸ μὲν οὖν κατακρύπτεσθαι εἶπεν ἀντὶ τοῦ «λα-
θραίως», — ἴδιον γὰρ | τῶν λανθάνειν βουλομένων τὸ κρύπτεσθαι, — πτέρ-
ναν δὲ τὴν ὁδόν, ἀντὶ τοῦ τὴν πρᾶξιν, ὡς καὶ ἐν τῷ μη' τὸ Ἡ ἀνομία τῆς
πτέρνης μου κυκλώσει με· εἴρηται δὲ ἐκεῖ καὶ ὅθεν λαβὼν τὴν πρᾶξιν οὕτω
καλεῖ. Τὸ δὲ «παρατηρεῖν» φυλάττειν ἐκάλεσεν, ἐπειδὴ τῶν φυλατ- 10
τόντων τὸ τηρεῖν ἴδιον, ὡς καὶ συμπίπτειν ἄμφω πολλάκις κατὰ τὴν σημασίαν καὶ τὴν χρῆσιν· πολλάκις γοῦν ἀντὶ τοῦ «φυλάττειν» τὸ «τηρεῖν»
φαμέν. Τὸ δὲ «προσδοκᾶν» ὑπομένειν, ἐπειδὴ ὁ ὑπομένων πάντως
ἔσεσθαί τι προσδοκῶν ὑπομένει μέχρις ἂν γένηται. Τὸ μέντοι «συνάγεσθαι»
παροικεῖν, ἐπειδὴ τῶν παροικούντων που ἴδιον τὸ ἐκεῖ συνεῖναι καὶ διά- 15
γειν καὶ ἅπαντα πράττειν οὗπερ ἂν παροικῶσιν· διὰ τοῦτο τὸ «συνάγονται» καὶ παροικοῦσιν ἐκάλεσεν, ἵνα δείξῃ τῆς πρὸς τοῦτο συνόδου τὸ
σπουδαῖον, ὅτι ὡς παροικοῦντες τῷ τόπῳ καὶ ἀναγκαίας ἐκ τῆς οἰκήσεως καὶ
τῆς ἐκεῖ διαγωγῆς τὰς συνόδους ποιούμενοι οὕτω διεμελέτων τὰ κατ' ἐμοῦ.
Συνήεσαν οὖν φησι κρύπτοντες, ἀντὶ τοῦ λάθρα, καὶ τὰ παρ' ἐμοῦ πρατ- 20
τόμενα ἐπιτηροῦντες· σπουδάζοντες γὰρ καὶ προσδοκῶντες μονονουχὶ τὴν
ἔξοδον ἰδεῖν τῆς ψυχῆς τῆς ἐμῆς, ἅπαντα ἔπραττον. Πρὸς τοῦτο τήν τε
ἐναλλαγὴν ταύτην εἰρήκαμεν γεγενῆσθαι τῶν ῥητῶν, καὶ τόδε μὲν ἀντὶ τοῦδε
εἰρῆσθαι, τόδε δὲ ἀντὶ τοῦδε.

Ἀλλὰ καὶ τὴν Συμμάχου ἔκδοσιν ἀντιπαραθέντες ἐδείξαμεν ἑκάστην 25
τῶν λέξεων ὅπως κειμένην ἐν τῇ θείᾳ γραφῇ κατὰ τὴν τῶν Ἑβδομήκοντα
ἔκδοσιν, ὅπως Σύμμαχος ἐν τῇ οἰκείᾳ ἐκδόσει φαίνεται εἰρηκώς. Ἡρμηνεύ-
σαμεν δὲ διὰ τί τόδε, ὥστε καὶ τὴν διάνοιαν σαφηνίσαι καὶ δεῖξαι ὅτι οὐκ
ἀπᾴδοντα εἰρήκασιν, ἀλλὰ καὶ πολλὴν ἔχοντα τὴν ἐγγύτητα ἀπὸ τῶν
σημαινομένων. Ἡ δὲ διαφορὰ ἐν τῷ τὸν μὲν σαφέστερον εἰπεῖν ἀπὸ τῆς 30
διανοίας φροντίσαντα, τοῦ δὲ ἀμαυρότερον ἐμφαντικωτέραις ταῖς λέξεσιν
καὶ κατὰ τὴν ἐν τῷ ἑβραϊκῷ διάνοιαν ἐκδοῦναι βουληθέντος — ὃ καὶ πολλαχοῦ καὶ μικροῦ ἐν τοῖς πλείοσίν ἐστιν εὑρεῖν. Ὅθεν οἱ Ἑβδομήκοντα μὲν

---

1 Ps. XLIX, 1 (cf. p. 325)   8-9 ps. XLVIII, 6ᵇ (cf. p. 318, 3-5).

5 ἑτήρουν Cord   11 ἄφνω Cord   13 πάντων Cord   14 ὑπομένειν C   15 συνιέναι Cord   19 τὰς om. Cord   διεμελέτων τὰ κατ' ἐμοῦ om. CPV   24 τόδε δὲ ἀντὶ
τοῦδε om. Cord   26 τῶν λέξεων ὅπως] λέξιν Cord   29 καὶ om. Cord   30 ἀπὸ
om. CPV   34 οἱ om. Cord   ἑβδομήκοντα om. CPV.

of gods spoke and summoned the earth";[2] in our commentary we indicated that he means one thing, but there seem to be two.

Symmachus, on the other hand, put it this way, "They assembled secretly and scrutinized my tracks, expecting to have my life": They laid ambushes and studied what I did so as to seize me and kill me or to hand me over to the enemy. So by *remain in hiding* he means "secretly," it being typical of those wishing to escape notice to lie low; and by *weak point* he means "path" in the sense of "my doings," as also in the Psalm 49, "The iniquity of my doings will encircle me,"[3] where he uses the word to mean "doings." By *watch for* he means "observe," since it is typical of those watching to observe, as both words often coincide in both meaning and use; at any rate, we often use "observe" for "watch." By *expecting* he means "waiting for," since the one expecting something to happen keeps waiting for it until it happens. By *stay on my heels* he means "gather together," since it is typical of those staying somewhere to assemble there, to live and do everything where they stay—hence his referring to their gathering as "staying," to bring out their enthusiasm in assembling for that purpose, because from staying in that place they formed assemblies as a necessary result of dwelling and living there, and so they plotted against me. So he is saying, They came together in hiding—that is, furtively—observing what was done by me; they did everything anxiously and expectantly as if to see my soul take its leave.

For this reason we mentioned that the change in words had occurred—this one in place of that, that one in place of this. But we also used Symmachus's version for comparison, and showed how each verse occurs in the divine Scripture according to the version of the Seventy, and how Symmachus seems to have expressed it in his version. We commented on it for this purpose, to clarify the meaning and to demonstrate that they were not speaking in discord, but actually have a close resemblance in meaning. Now, the difference is between one speaking more clearly by attending to the meaning, on the one hand, and the other in a less verbatim manner wanting to bring out the sense of the Hebrew by more striking expressions, on the other hand, as you can also find in many and almost the majority of places elsewhere as well. Hence, while the Seventy for their part | were more anx-

---

2. Pss 94:4; 50:1.
3. Ps 49:5.

ἐσπούδασαν μᾶλλον τὴν ἐν τῷ ἑβραϊκῷ ἔμφασιν ἀδιάφορον φυλάξαι, ὁ δὲ
Σύμμαχος τῆς σαφηνείας ἐπιμελεῖσθαι ἔδειξεν, ἐπιτυγχάνειν δὲ οὐ πανταχοῦ τῆς οἰκείας ἀξίως ἐπιχειρήσεως· πολλαχοῦ γὰρ παρὰ τὴν σαφήνειαν
ἀσχολῶν, ἑαυτὸν δῆθεν πολὺ ἀπᾴδοντα τῆς διανοίας τίθησιν.

5 Ὅθεν τινές, οὐ πρὸς τὴν ἀκολουθίαν ἰδόντες, ᾠήθησαν ἀπὸ τῆς κατὰ τὸ
πρόχειρον σαφηνείας κρείττονα εἶναι τὴν Συμμάχου ἔκδοσιν. Εἰ δέ τις
πρὸς τὴν ἀκολουθίαν ἴδοι καὶ τὴν ὑφὴν τῆς γραφικῆς διανοίας, οὐκ ἄν ποτε
ἑτέραν ἔκδοσιν τῆς τῶν Ἑβδομήκοντα προτιμήσειεν, οὐχ ὅτι καιρίως ἅπαντα
τούτοις ἡρμήνευται μᾶλλον, — ἔστι γὰρ ἐν οἷς ἀσθενέστερον τὴν ἑρμηνείαν
10 ἐξήνεγκαν, ἐνίοτε δὲ καὶ ἀπέτυχον τῶν ἄλλων σαφέστερον καὶ ἀκολουθότερον εἰπόντων, — ἀλλ᾿ ὅτι καθόλου τοῖς ἄλλοις συγκρινόμενοι κρείττους
εὑρίσκονται πολλῷ κἂν ἀσυνηθέστερον εἰπόντες τὰ πλείονα. Τοῦ δὲ τοὺς
μὲν Ἑβδομήκοντα τῆς ἐμφάσεως φροντίσαι μᾶλλον, τὸν δὲ Σύμμαχον τοῦ
σαφεστέρου ἐπιμεληθῆναι, πολλὰ μὲν τῷ ζητοῦντι τὰ γνωρίσματα.

15 Κείσθω δὲ ἐν ᾗ δύο πρὸς πᾶσαν σύστασιν τοῦ λεγομένου, οἷον ἐν τῷ
ξζ΄ Ἡ συναγωγὴ τῶν ταύρων ἐν ταῖς δαμάλεσιν· Σύμμαχος λέγει συνόδῳ παμμεγεθῶν, καὶ ἄλλοι μὲν συνηκολούθησαν τῇ τοῦ ἑβραϊκοῦ διανοίᾳ, ὁ δὲ
μᾶλλον ἐσαφήνισεν. Οὕ|τω καὶ ἐπὶ τῷ Ἐπιβεβηκότι ἐπὶ τὸν οὐρανὸν τοῦ
οὐρανοῦ κατὰ ἀνατολάς Σύμμαχος ἐκ πρώτης λέγει· οὗτος γὰρ μᾶλλον
20 σαφῶς εἶπε τὸ κείμενον. Ἡ δὲ αἰτία τούτων ἐστὶν αὕτη, ὅτι ὁ Ἑβραῖος
τὰ πολλὰ ὥσπερ ἐμφαντικῶς λέγει βουλόμενος, καὶ τοῦτο ἔχων ἰδίωμα δι᾿
ὁμοιωμάτων λέγειν καὶ παραβολῶν. Ταῦτα δὲ μόλις πρὸς παράστασιν
ἱκανά· λέγει γὰρ αὐτὰ οὐχ ὡς ὁμοιώματα, ἀλλ᾿ ἀντὶ πραγμάτων τιθείς, οἷον
τὸ νῦν ῥηθέν ταύρων εἶπεν ἀντὶ τοῦ « παμμεγεθῶν », οὐκ εἰπὼν ὡς τ α ύ ρ ω ν
25 ἀλλὰ ταύρων ἁπλῶς· ἀπὸ γὰρ τοῦ ἐν ταῖς ἀγέλαις τῶν βοῶν τοὺς ταύρους μάλιστα μεγάλους φαίνεσθαι, τὸ παμμέγεθος λαβὼν εἶπε ταύρων,
αὐτὸ τεθεικὼς ἀντὶ τῆς σημασίας, — οὕτω καὶ τὸ κατὰ ἀνατολάς, ἐπειδὴ
ἀρχὴ ἡμέρας ἡ πρώτη ἀνατολὴ τοῦ ἡλίου, τὸ ἐκ πρώτης φαύσεως ἀνατολὴν καλέσας, καὶ οὐκ εἰπὼν ὡς κατὰ ἀνατολάς. Ὁμοίως οὖν κἀνταῦθα καὶ
30 ἐν τοῖς τοιούτοις οἱ μὲν Ἑβδομήκοντα τὴν ἔμφασιν τοῦ ἐμφαντικοῦ μὴ παρα-
φθεῖραι ἔσπευσαν, Σύμμαχος δὲ τὴν διάνοιαν εἰπεῖν ἐν πολλοῖς προείλετο

16-17 Ps. LXVII, 31ᵇ   18-19 ps. LXVII, 34.

6-8 ἔκδοσιν — ποτε ἑτέραν *om.* Cord   8 προτιμήσειεν *om.* Cord   οὐχ ὅτι] ὅτι
οὐ Cord   9 μᾶλλον *om.* Cord   11 ἀλλ᾿ ὅτι] ἀλλὰ μὴν Cord   καθόλου] οὔτε *add.*
CPV   12 κἂν] καὶ CPV   τοῦ δὲ] οὐδὲ CPV   18 ἐπὶ *om.* CPV   19 μᾶλλον *om.*
Cord   20 προκείμενον Cord   ὅτι *om.* CPV   21 τὰ πολλὰ] πολλὰ Cord   καὶ
om. Cord   22 καὶ παρ. λέγειν Cord   λέγει V   δὲ] γὰρ CPV   μόλις τὰ CPV
23 γὰρ] δὲ CPV   28 ἡ πρώτη ἀνατολὴ τοῦ] καὶ πρῶτον ἀνατολὴν CPV   φαύσεως *om.* CPV   29 καὶ οὐκ εἰπὼν] οὐκ εἶπεν Cord   ὁμοίως οὖν κἀνταῦθα] ἐνταῦθα
CPV   31 προείλετο *om.* CPV.

ious to preserve the expression in the Hebrew unchanged, Symmachus for his part showed particular care for clarity. Not in every place, however, did he read the text in a manner worthy of his own aspirations, since in many places, being found at variance with clarity, he put himself in direct opposition to the meaning.

Hence, some commentators, lacking an eye to sequence, believed Symmachus's version superior on the basis of the clarity in what was before them. But if you have an eye to sequence and composition of the sense of the text, you would never prefer another version to that of the Seventy. Not that everything is translated better by them: there are places, in fact, where they offer the weaker interpretation, and sometimes they fall short of the others, who said things more clearly and logically. But in general, by comparison with the others, they are found far superior, even if they say a good many things in a rather unfamiliar way. For the student there are many signs of the greater attention to effect by the Seventy and the care for greater clarity by Symmachus.

Let one or two cases be cited by way of support of this claim. In Psalm 68, "The assembly of the bulls in the calves": Symmachus says, "In a gathering of immense things," and while others went along with the Hebrew meaning, he put it more clearly.[4] Likewise also in the verse "To the one who rides on the heaven of heavens like dawn," Symmachus saying "at first light," expressing the content more clearly.[5] Now, the reason for this is that the Hebrew, in its wish to say many things with greater effect, has this practice of speaking in similes and comparisons. But this hardly suffices for clarity of presentation: it mentions them by citing them not as similes but as facts, as in the above verse it said "bulls" for "immense things," not saying "like bulls" but simply "bulls." This is based on the fact that in herds of cattle the bulls appear as especially large, and so it said "bulls" to express immensity, using it for the meaning. It is likewise the case with the phrase "like dawn": since the first light of the sun is the beginning of the day, he referred to dawn in the phrase "at first light" instead of saying "like dawn."

Likewise, therefore, in the present cases and in ones like it, the Seventy were anxious that the effect of the emphasis not be lost, whereas Symmachus preferred in many cases to express the sense | while giving less attention to

---

4. Ps 68:30, a verse that has modern commentators at a loss as to the references.
5. Ps 68:33, the final phrase being in question.

τοῦ ἀκρώδους τῆς ἐμφάσεως φροντίσας, πολλαχοῦ μέντοι καὶ ὡς ἑρμηνείαν τὴν αὐτὴν ἐξηλλαγμέναις ταῖς λέξεσιν εἰπὼν διάνοιαν, οἷον δὴ καὶ ἐπὶ τῷ νῦν ἐπὶ τὸ πλεῖστον εὑρίσκεται. Τούτων δέ τις τῶν νῦν εἰρημένων ἔχων τὴν μνήμην ἐν πολλοῖς ἀκριβέστατον αὐτὰ καὶ σαφέστατον ἕξει κανόνα, τὴν ἑρμηνείαν ἐπιτηρῶν. 5

8ᵃ. Ὑπὲρ τοῦ μηθενὸς ὥσεις αὐτούς. Τινὲς « σώσεις » ἀναγινώσκουσιν, ἀντὶ τοῦ σωτηρίαν αὐτοῖς παρέξεις. Οὐ τοῦτο δὲ λέγει ὁ ψαλμῳδός, ἀλλ᾽ ὥσεις, ἀντὶ τοῦ ἀπώσεις· βούλεται γὰρ εἰπεῖν ὅτι ὡς τὰ μηδὲν ὄντα ἀπωθήσεις αὐτοὺς καὶ ἀποστήσεις, | εἰς ἔργον ἐκβαλεῖν ἐάσας ὧν ἐπιχειροῦσιν καθ᾽ ἡμῶν διαπράττεσθαι οὐδέν. Καλῶς δὲ τὸ ὥσεις εἶπεν, ὥστε δεῖξαι 10 ὅτι καὶ τούτων ἀφίστανται, καὶ αὐτοὶ τιμωρίᾳ περιβάλλονται. Ὁ γὰρ ὠθούμενος μακράν τε ἀποπέμπεται καὶ κατάπτωσιν ἀναγκαίως ὑπομένει ὅταν ἰσχυρὸν τὸν ὠθισμὸν εἶναι συμβαίνει.

8ᵇ. Ἐν ὀργῇ λαοὺς κατάξεις. Καὶ τῇ οἰκείᾳ φησὶν ὀργῇ σφοδρότερον κατ᾽ αὐτῶν κινηθείς, ταπεινώσεις αὐτοὺς καὶ καθελεῖς ἀπὸ τῆς προσούσης 15 αὐτοῖς δυναστείας· ὀργὴν γὰρ καλεῖ τὴν τιμωρίαν ἐπὶ τοῦ Θεοῦ.

9ᵃ. Ὁ Θεός, τὴν ζωήν μου ἐξήγγειλά σοι. Πᾶσάν μου τὴν ζωήν φησι καὶ πάντα σοι τὰ κατ᾽ ἐμαυτὸν ἐγνώρισα καί σοι ἀνεθέμην, ἀντὶ τοῦ ἐμαυτόν σοι ἐπέρριψα. Τὸ δὲ ἐξήγγειλα λέγει ἀπὸ τῶν τὰ καθ᾽ ἑαυτοὺς ἀπαγγελλόντων τε καὶ γνωριζόντων φίλοις, ὥστε εἰς βοήθειαν αὐτοὺς ἐπισπάσασθαι. 20

9ᵇ. Ἔθου τὰ δάκρυά μου ἐνώπιόν σου, ὡς καὶ ἐν τῇ ἐπαγγελίᾳ σου. Ἐπειδὴ πόρρωθεν διὰ τῶν προφητῶν προεμήνυσεν ὁ Θεὸς τὸ ἐσόμενον, τοῦτό φησι κατέστησάς με ἐν δάκρυσιν, ἐν συμφοραῖς, ἀκολούθως τῇ παρά σου ἐπαγγελίᾳ.

1 τοῦ ἀκρώδους om. Cord   2 εἰπὼν] εἶπε Cord   2-3 ἐπὶ — πλεῖστον] νῦν ποιήσας Cord   4 σαφέστερον Cord.
8ᵃ. Τινὲς — συμβαίνει: P, fol. 160ᵛ; V, fol. 225.   8-10 Paraphrasis (p. 82): Τὸ ὑπὲρ τοῦ μηθενός, ἀντὶ τοῦ ὡς οὐδέν. Βούλεται οὖν εἰπεῖν Ἀπώσῃ αὐτοὺς ὡς μηδὲν ὄντας.
8ᵇ. Καὶ τῇ οἰκείᾳ — Θεοῦ: P, fol. 160ᵛ; V, fol. 225.
9ᵃ. Πᾶσαν — ἐπισπάσασθαι: P. fol. 161; V, fol. 225; Cord, p. 97.   17-18 cf. Paraphrasis (p. 83, 7-8): Ἰδοὺ γάρ φησι πᾶσάν μου τὴν ζωήν σοι ἀνεθέμην   19-20 τὸ δὲ ἐξήγγειλα — ἐπισπάσασθαι affert Vat. 2057, fol. 101ᵛ; eadem iam in P, fol. 160ᵛ et V, fol. 224ᵛ.
9ᵇ. Ἐπειδὴ — ἐπαγγελίᾳ: P, fol. 161; V, fol. 225ᵛ.   22 διὰ τῶν om. C; cf. Paraphrasis (p. 83, 14-15): καὶ διὰ τῶν προφητῶν ἐπηγγείλω.

Aᵉ 23 (p. 297, 23-24): Distinasti me lacrimis et calamitatibus.

the effect, in many cases expressing the same sense in translation by changing the words, as is found, for example, also in the present case for the most part. If you keep in mind what has thus been said, in many cases you will find an extremely precise and clear norm for following the commentary.

You will have no trouble in banishing them (v. 7). Some commentators read "saving," which gives the meaning, You will provide them with salvation. The psalmist says not that, however, but rather *banishing*—that is, rejecting—meaning to say, You will reject and repel them as of no value, allowing nothing that they do against us to take effect.[6] Now, *banishing* was well put, to bring out that they keep their distance from them, and the others are beset with punishment; someone who is banished is sent off to a distance and consequently experiences a reversal when the one who banishes happens to be strong. *In wrath you will bring peoples down, O God:* severely moved to wrath against them, you will humble them and topple them from the position of influence they have attained (by *wrath* referring to God's retribution). *O God, I reported my life to you* (v. 8): I made known my whole life and all my affairs to you and dedicated them to you—that is, I cast myself upon you. He says *I reported* from the practice of those telling and informing their friends of their affairs so as to win help from them. *You laid out my tears before you, as in your promise.* Since God predicted the future from afar through the prophets, he says, You reduced me to tears, to misfortune, following on your promise. |

---

6. The verb in the Antiochene text (the result of scribal haplography) reads ὥσεις, "you will banish," whereas the reading in the other forms of the LXX, σώσεις, "you will save," corresponds to our Hebrew. Like Theodoret, Theodore can rationalize the inferior reading.

10ᵃ. Τότε ἐπιστρέψουσιν οἱ ἐχθροί μου εἰς τὰ ὀπίσω. Τότε ἐπιστρέψουσιν · τότε ὡς πρὸς τὰ ἄνω. Ἐπειδὴ τοίνυν φησὶ καὶ τὴν ζωὴν ἀνεθέμην ἐγώ σοι τὴν ἐμήν, καὶ τὰ λυπηρὰ τῆς καθ᾽ ἡμῶν ἐπαγγελίας πεπλήρωταί σοι, δίκαιον λοιπὸν καὶ τοὺς ἐχθροὺς δοῦναι τιμωρίαν. Τὸ οὖν ἐπιστρέψουσιν εἰς τὰ
5 ὀπίσω, ἀντὶ τοῦ Ἐπιστραφήτωσαν δὲ εἰς τὰ ὀπίσω, ἵνα εἴπῃ Ἀποσταῖεν λοιπὸν ἀφ᾽ ἡμῶν καὶ ἐντραπεῖεν εἰς φυγήν. Τὸ οὖν τότε ὡς πρὸς τὰ ἄνω, ἀντὶ τοῦ Τότε πείσονται ταῦτα οἱ ἐχθροὶ καὶ ὑποστήσονται δικαίως, ἐπειδὰν ἐγώ τέ σοι ἐμαυτὸν ἀναθῶμαι καὶ τὰ τῆς ἐπαγγελίας πέρας λάβῃ τῆς σῆς, ἵνα εἴπῃ ὅτι Τούτων γενομένων ἐκεῖνοι δώσουσι δίκας.

10 **10ᵇ·ᶜ.** Ἐν ᾗ ἂν ἡμέρᾳ ἐπικαλέσωμαί σε, ἰδοὺ ἔγνων ὅτι Θεός μου εἶ σύ · Ἐντεῦθεν λοιπὸν οὐκέτι καλοῦντά σε καὶ τὴν παρά σου βοήθειαν ὑπέρθεσιν εὑρεῖν, ἀλλ᾽ ὁμοῦ τε καλῶ καὶ ἕπεται ἡ παρά σου βοήθεια. Τὸ γὰρ Ἰδοὺ ἔγνων ὅτι Θεός μου εἶ σύ, ἀντὶ τοῦ Καὶ γνωριῶ ὅτι σύ μου εἶ ὁ προστάτης, ἵνα εἴπῃ ὅτι Ἀπολαύω τῆς προστασίας τῆς σῆς, — ἀντὶ τοῦ
15 πράγματος τὴν γνῶσιν κατὰ τὸ σύνηθες τεθεικώς, — ἐπειδ᾽ οὗπερ ἂν ἀπήλαυσε, τοῦτο πάντως καὶ οὕτως ἔχειν ἐγνώρισεν.

11ᵃ. Ἐπὶ τῷ Θεῷ αἰνέσω ῥῆμα. Αὐτός μου δείξει τοὺς λόγους θαυμαστούς, εἰς ἔργον ἐκφέρων ἅπερ αἰτῶ.

11ᵇ. Ἐπὶ τῷ Θεῷ αἰνέσω λόγον. Τὸ αὐτὸ λέγει ἐπὶ τῷ πλατυσμῷ καὶ
20 τῇ δευτερώσει, κοσμιώτερον δεικνὺς τὸ παρὰ τοῦ Θεοῦ γιγνόμενον.

12. Ἐπὶ τῷ Θεῷ ἤλπισα, οὐ φοβηθήσομαι τί ποιήσει μοι ἄνθρωπος. Αὐτῷ γὰρ πεποιθὼς οὐ δέδοικά φησι μή τι πάθω.

10ᵃ. Τότε ἐπιστρέψουσι — δίκας : P, fol. 161; V, fol. 225ᵛ; Cord, p. 98.　　5 δὲ εἰς τὰ ὀπίσω om. Cord　　6 τραπεῖεν] ἐντραπεῖεν Cord　　τότε οὖν C　　4-6 sequentia praebent P et V (ib.); Vat. 2057, fol. 101ᵛ (Θεοδ? Μοᵘ): 'Ἐναλλαγή ἐστι χρόνου · τὸ ἐπιστρέψουσιν, ἀντὶ τοῦ ἐπιστραφήτωσαν. Δίκαιον γὰρ λοιπὸν καὶ τοὺς ἐχθροὺς δοῦναί φησι τιμωρίαν (des. 2057), καὶ ἀποσταῖεν ἀφ᾽ ἡμῶν καὶ τραπεῖεν εἰς φυγήν.
10ᵇ·ᶜ. Ἐντεῦθεν — ἐγνώρισεν : P, fol. 161ᵛ; V, fol. 225ᵛ; Cord, p. 98.　　11 καλῶ Cord　　11-12 ὑπέρθεσιν] ὑστερῶ Cord　　14 προστάτης] ὁπλοστράτηγος Cord.
11ᵃ. Αὐτὸς — αἰτῶ : P, fol. 161ᵛ et V, fol. 225ᵛ (anon.).
11ᵇ. Τὸ αὐτὸ — γιγνόμενον : P, fol. 161ᵛ; V, fol. 226.
12. Αὐτῷ — πάθω : P, fol. 161ᵛ; V, fol. 226.

Aᵉ **10ᵃ** (p. 297, 25-298, 7): Quoniam igitur uitam meam tota tibi commisi deuotione et aduersa nostra secundum tuam promisionem constant inpleta, iustum est iam ut et inimici nostri subeant ultionem; uel sic poterit habere ad superiora contextum: *Tunc* uidilicet *dispertientur inimici mei retrorsum,* cum ego me tibi tota mente commissero et ea, quae praedixisti circa nos futura, finem iam sua aduersitatis acciperint.　　**11ᵃ** (p. 298, 13-16): Ipse mihi, inquit, mirabiles ostendit sermones, cum petitionibus meis largitur effectum laudumque suarum praebebit uberem materiam.

Then my foes will turn backwards (v. 9): then they will turn about; then they will go back. So he is saying, Since I dedicated my life to you, and the distress of your promise affecting us has been fulfilled, it is now time for the enemy also to pay the penalty. The phrase *they will turn backwards* means, therefore, Let them be turned backwards, as if to say, Now let them retreat and be put to flight. So the word *Then* means "in view of the past"[7]—that is, Then the foe will meet this fate and rightly suffer it, since I dedicate myself to you and your promise takes effect, as if to say, They will be accountable for what has been done. *On the day I call upon you, lo, I know you are my God:* from now on there is no possibility of delay when I call upon you and seek help from you; instead, at once I call upon you, and help from you follows. In fact, the clause *lo, I know you are my God* means, I shall discover that you are my protector, as if to say, I enjoy your protection (as usual, citing the knowledge in place of the fact, since from his enjoying it he knew that there was no doubt he had it in that fashion).

In God, whose word I shall praise (v. 10): he is the one who will let me see that the promises are marvelous, by putting into effect what I ask. *In God, whose promise I shall praise.* He says the same thing by way of extension and repetition to bring out the greater charm of what is done by God. *In God I hoped; I shall not fear what a mortal will do to me* (v. 11): trusting in him, I have no dread of suffering anything. |

---

7. Theodore finds in his text the particle "then," which appears in the Hebrew but not in Theodoret's text or in other forms of the LXX, and he feels obliged to make sense of it.

13. Ἐν ἐμοί, ὁ Θεός, αἱ εὐχαὶ ἃς ἀποδώσω αἰνέσεώς σοι. Ὅσα ἐπηγγειλάμην ἀποδοῦναι τυχὼν τῆς παρά σου βοηθείας, ταῦτα καὶ ἀποδώσω.
Ἐν ἐμοὶ γάρ εἰσιν, ἀντὶ τοῦ Οὐκ ἀπέβαλον τὴν μνήμην, οὐκ ἀπέβαλον τὴν
περὶ τὸ πρᾶγμα διάθεσιν, ἀλλ᾽ ἔχω αὐτὰς ἐν ἐμαυτῷ καὶ μέμνημαι, ὥστε
σοι ἐν καιρῷ μετὰ τὴν τῶν κακῶν ἀπαλλαγὴν ἀποδοῦναι ἅπερ ἐπηγγει-   5
λάμην.

14ᵃ·ᵇ. Ὅτι ἐρρύσω τὴν ψυχήν μου ἐκ θανάτου, καὶ τοὺς πόδας μου ἐξ
ὀλισθήματος. Τὰς ὑπὲρ τούτων φησὶν εὐχὰς ἐπηγγειλάμην τε καὶ ἀποδίδωμι, ὅτι τε ἀπήλλαξάς με κινδύνων καὶ θανάτων, καὶ ὅτι μικροῦ παρα-
τραπέντα καὶ καταπεσόντα καὶ ἀπωλόμενον ἤγειρας καὶ ἔστησας, οὐδὲ   10
περιτραπῆναι ὑπὸ τῶν πολεμίων ἐάσας. Τίνες μέντοι αἱ ὑπὲρ τούτων
εὐχαί;

14ᶜ. Εὐχρεστήσω ἐνώπιον τοῦ Θεοῦ ἐν φωτὶ ζώντων. Τοῦτο γὰρ ἀκό-
λουθόν ἐστι τῷ Ἐν ἐμοί, ὁ Θεός, εὐχαὶ ἃς ἀποδώσω αἰνέσεώς σοι, — τὰ
δὲ λοιπὰ διὰ μέσου. Παρενθεὶς γὰρ τὰς εὐεργεσίας, ὑπὲρ ὧν τὰς εὐχὰς   15
ἐποιήσατο, τότε ἐπήγαγε καὶ τὰς εὐχὰς αὐτάς, αἵτινές εἰσι λέγων. Ταύτας
γὰρ λέγει τὰς εὐχάς, ὧν καὶ | μεμνῆσθαί φησι καὶ ἀποδώσειν ἐπαγγέλλε-
ται, τὸ εὐαρεστεῖν Θεῷ. Τοῦτο οὖν φησιν ἐπηγγειλάμην καὶ τοῦτο πληρώσω, μεγάλων τῶν παρά σου τυχὼν καλῶν. Τὸ δὲ ἐν φωτὶ ζώντων, ἀντὶ
τοῦ Μέχρις ἂν ᾧ κατὰ τόνδε τὸν βίον καὶ ἀπολαύω τοῦδε τοῦ φωτὸς οὗπερ   20
πάντες ἀπολαύουσιν οἱ ζῶντες, μέχρι τότε καὶ τῆς εὐαρεστήσεως ἐπιμελή-
σομαι τῆς σῆς, μεμνημένος ὧν ἔτυχον. Καλῶς δὲ τοῦτο καὶ εὔχεσθαι
εἶπε καὶ ἀποδώσειν ἐπηγγείλατο, εἰ ῥυσθείη τῶν πολεμίων, ὡς δι᾽ ἁμαρτίας πασχόντων καὶ εἰκότως τῇ τῆς διορθώσεως ἐπαγγελίᾳ τὴν λύσιν λαμβανόντων.   25

---

13. Ὅσα ἐπηγγειλάμην — ἐπηγγειλάμην : P, fol. 161ᵛ; V, fol. 226; Cord, p. 99.
3 τὴν μνήμην οὐκ ἀπέβαλον om. Cord   4 ἑαυτῷ CPV.
14ᵃ·ᵇ. Τὰς ὑπὲρ τούτων — εὐχαί: P, fol. 162; fol. 226.
14ᶜ. Τοῦτο γὰρ ἀκόλουθον — λαμβανόντων: P, fol. 162; V, fol. 226ᵛ; Cord, p. 100.
13 τοῦτο γάρ] τούτῳ Cord   14 τῷ] τοῦ CV τὸ Cord   σοι] σου C   18 τὸ εὐαρεστεῖν Θεῷ] τῷ εὐαρεστεῖν τῷ Θεῷ Cord   18-19 πληρώσω] ἐπλήρωσα Cord   19-20 ἀντὶ
τοῦ] τουτέστι Cord.

Aᵉ 3-5 (p. 258, 20-25): Non abieci eorum me⟨m⟩oriam quae promisi, neque
succidente securitate studium tibi decatae deuotionis omisi, ut scilicet libertatis debita gratulatione (debitae gratulatiouis 1ᵃ m.) conlaudem.   15-18 (p. 298,
28-30): Interiectis caeteris quae spectabant ad beneficia praestita, ista sunt,
inquit, uota conplacere Deo.   22-25 (p. 299, 3-7): ...quasi qui sciret se propter
peccata hostibus traditum et in nulla re magis quam correptionis promisione
indignationem Dei posse molliri.

In me, O God, are vows of praise that I shall pay to you (v. 12): what I promised to render in response to attaining help from you I shall render, since it is *In me*—that is, I did not cancel the memory; I did not cancel the intention of doing the deed. Instead, I keep it within me and remember it so as in due course to render to you what I promised in return for the relief from the troubles. *Because you rescued my soul from death and my feet from stumbling* (v. 13): for this I made vows and I keep them, because you freed me from the danger of death, and you raised me up and restored me when I was on the verge of being confounded, dejected, and lost, not allowing me to be overwhelmed by the enemy. So what were the vows for this? *I shall be pleasing in God's sight in the light of the living.* This follows on from *In me, O God, are vows of praise that I shall pay to you,* the rest occurring in the middle: having included the blessings for which he made the vows, he then added also the vows themselves, saying what they were. He mentions the vows, which he promises to remember and repay by being *pleasing* to God. So he is saying, I promised this and shall fulfill it, being in receipt of wonderful goods from you. By the phrase *in the light of the living* he means, As long as I am in this life and enjoy this light that all the living enjoy, so long I shall attend to your pleasure, mindful of what I have received. He was right to mention vows and promise to repay upon being rescued from the enemy, since they were suffering for their sins and duly receiving relief by the promise of reform. |

PSALMVS LVI

Περὶ τῶν αὐτῶν κἀνταῦθα προλέγει, ἀλλ᾽ ἐν μὲν τῷ προτέρῳ ὡς ἐν συμφοραῖς ὄντων καὶ πασχόντων μεγάλα φησὶ καὶ διὰ τοῦτο τὴν παρὰ τοῦ Θεοῦ βοήθειαν αἰτούντων, ἐνταῦθα δὲ ὡς ἐπὶ γεγενημέναις νίκαις καὶ
5 κατὰ τῶν ἐχθρῶν εὐχαριστούντων, ἢ ὡς ὀλίγου τινὸς ὄντος ἔτι τοῦ περιλιμπανομένου κακοῦ.

2ᵃ. Ἐλέησόν με, ὁ Θεός, ἐλέησόν με. Δαψιλῆ μοί φησι παράσχου τὴν παρά σου φιλανθρωπίαν· τοῦ|το γὰρ τῷ διπλασιασμῷ σημαίνειν βούλεται.

10 2ᵇ·ᶜ. Ὅτι ἐπί σοι πέποιθεν ἡ ψυχή μου, καὶ ἐν τῇ σκιᾷ τῶν πτερύγων σου ἐλπιῶ. Τὸ ἐπί σοι καὶ τὸ ἐν σκιᾷ τῶν πτερύγων τὸ αὐτὸ λέγει. Καὶ γὰρ ἐπί σοί φησιν ἔχω πᾶσαν τὴν πεποίθησιν σκεπασθῆναι ταῖς σαῖς πτέρυξιν ἐλπίζων, — ἵνα εἴπῃ Τὴν ἀπόλαυσιν τῆς σῆς περιμένω βοηθείας, ἐκ μεταφορᾶς τῶν ὀρνίθων, αἳ τοὺς νεοττοὺς ὑπὸ τὰς πτέρυγας φυλάττουσιν.

15 2ᵈ. Ἕως οὗ παρέλθῃ ἡ ἀνομία. Τὸ ἕως; οὗ οὐχ ὁριστικῶς λέγει, — οὐδὲ γὰρ ἂν εἶπεν Μέχρι τότε ἐλπίζω, ὕστερον δὲ οὐκέτι, — ἀλλὰ κατὰ ἀναίρεσιν λέγει τοῦ ἐναντίου. Καὶ συνήθως δὲ οὕτω λέγει, οἷον τῷ τοῦ Θεοῦ πρώτῳ λαῷ τὸ Ἕως ἂν καταγηράσητε ἐγώ εἰμι· οὐχ ὅτι μετὰ τοῦτο οὐκ ἔσται, — ἀσεβὲς γὰρ καὶ νοῆσαι, — ἀλλ᾽ ἀντὶ τοῦ οὐχ οἷόν τέ με ἐν μέσῳ
20 ἔξω γενέσθαι τοῦ εἶναι, οὕτω καὶ τοῦ ἀποστόλου τὸ Δεῖ γὰρ αὐτὸν βασι-

---

18 Is. XLVI, 4   20-370, 1 I Cor. XV, 25.

Περὶ τῶν αὐτῶν — κακοῦ: P, fol. 162ᵛ; V, fol. 226ᵛ; Cord, p. 110.   2 *προλέγει*] *φησιν* Cord   4 *καὶ om.* Cord   5 *ἦ*] *εἰ καὶ* Cord.
2ᵃ. *Δαψιλῆ — βούλεται*: P, fol. 163; V, fol. 227; C 93 sup., fol. 111; Cord. p. 112.
2ᵇ·ᶜ. *Τὸ ἐπί σοι — φυλάττουσιν*: P, fol. 163; V, fol. 227ʳ·ᵛ; C 98 sup., fol. 111.
11 *αὐτὸ*] *ἐν σκιᾷ τῶν πτερύγων add.* C   14 cf. *Paraphrasis* (p. 104, 21-24): ἐκ μεταφορᾶς τῶν ὀρνίθων τῶν καλυπτούντων τοὺς νεοττοὺς ταῖς πτέρυξι καὶ φυλαττόντων αὐτοὺς ἀβλαβεῖς.
2ᵈ. *Τὸ ἕως οὗ — γιγνομένας*: P, fol. 163; V, fol. 227ᵛ.

Aᵉ *Argumentum ps. LVI* (p. 299, 13-19): De hisdem negotiationibus et in praesenti carmine profetat, uerum in superiore adhuc in calamitate degentium persona formata est; hoc uero quasi iam emergentium aut emersorum laetabunda aptatur oratio. Cf. PSEUDO-BEDA (778): Et hic Machabeorum. Verum incipiente iam uictoria laetabunda formatur oratio.   2ᵃ (p. 299, 22-24): Copiosum et citum auxilium geminata misericordiae inuocatione deposcit.   14 (p. 300, 2-4): A similitudine auium, quae pullos alarum in umbratione commoniunt.

PSALM 57

Here, too, he makes a prediction about those same people. But while in the former case it had to do with their being in difficult circumstances, suffering severely and hence asking help of God, in this case he speaks of them giving thanks for victories won against the foe or the limited extent of the troubles that still remained.

Have mercy on me, O God, have mercy on me (v. 1): extend to me lovingkindness on your behalf in generous measure (meaning to convey this by the repetition). *Because my soul trusted in you; in the shadow of your wings I shall hope.* The phrases *in you* and *in the shadow of your wings* mean the same thing: *in you* I have complete trust by hoping to be sheltered by *your wings, as* if to say, I await receipt of your help (using a metaphor from birds that protect their chicks under their wings). *Until iniquity passes.* The term *until* is not spoken definitively: he did not mean, I hope to that point but no longer; instead, he intends the denial of the opposite. Scripture habitually speaks this way, as, for example, to the first people of God, "Even to your old age I am he,"[1] not that he will not be afterwards—it would be blasphemous even to think that way—but that there is no possibility for him to be deprived of existence in the meantime, as emerges also from the apostle's statement "For he must reign | until he has put all his foes under his feet,"[2] meaning, It

---

1. Isa 46:4.
2. 1 Cor 15:25.

λεύειν ἄχρις οὗ θῇ πάντας τοὺς ἐχθροὺς ὑπὸ τοὺς πόδας αὐτοῦ, ἀντὶ τοῦ
Οὐκ ἔνεστιν αὐτοῦ ἐν τῷ μέσῳ παρασαλευθῆναι τὴν βασιλείαν. Οὕτω καὶ
ἐνταῦθα τὸ Ἕως οὗ παρέλθῃ ἡ ἀνομία ἀκολούθως τοῖς ἄνω ἐπαγαγών, τουτέστιν ὅτι μένω ἐλπίζων ἐπί σε ἄχρις ἂν τέλος λάβῃ τὰ ἐπικείμενα κακὰ
καὶ ὁ πόλεμος, καὶ οὐχ οἷόν τε ἐκστῆναί με τῆς ἐπί σε | ἐλπίδος μέχρις ἂν   5
τύχω τοῦ προσδοκουμένου. Ἀνομίαν δὲ ἐκάλεσεν τὰς εἰς αὐτόν, ὡς ἀνόμως
καὶ ἀδίκως παρὰ τῶν ἐχθρῶν καὶ ἄνευ παντὸς δικαίου λόγου γιγνομένας.

3. Κεκράξομαι πρὸς τὸν Θεὸν τὸν ὕψιστον, τὸν Θεὸν τὸν εὐεργετήσαντά
με. Καὶ γὰρ μέχρις ἂν τούτων ἀπολαύσω, διαμενῶ σε καλῶν τὸν καὶ ἤδη
τὴν εὐεργεσίαν χαρισάμενον καὶ τῶν μεγάλων ἀπαλλάξαντα κακῶν· ἀφ' ὧν   10
γὰρ ἔτυχον ἤδη πέπεισμαι καὶ πάλιν τυχεῖν. Καὶ λοιπὸν διηγεῖται τὴν
παρὰ τοῦ Θεοῦ εὐεργεσίαν ὁμοῦ καὶ τὴν χάριν σημαίνων καὶ πείθων ὅτι
δικαίως καὶ ὑπὲρ τῶν λειπομένων πιστεύει.

4ᵃ. Ἐξαπέστειλεν ἐξ οὐρανοῦ καὶ ἔσωσέ με. Τοιαῦτα γάρ φησιν ἃ
πεποίηκεν. Καλῶς δὲ τὸ ἐξαπέστειλεν, ὡς ἐπὶ βασιλέως δυνατοῦ βοήθειαν   15
καὶ συμμαχίαν ἀποστείλαντος. Ἐξ οὐρανοῦ δὲ εἰπὼν ἔδειξε τῆς βοηθείας τὸ
ἰσχυρόν· αὐτὸς γάρ φησι συμμαχήσας ἔσωσεν.

4ᵇ. Ἔδωκεν εἰς ὄνειδος τοὺς καταπατοῦντάς με. Ἐν τῷ πρὸ τούτου
λέγει κατεπάτησέν με ἄνθρωπος. Καλῶς οὖν ὧδε τοὺς κακαπατοῦντάς με, —
ἐκείνους φησὶ τοὺς παντὶ τρόπῳ διαπατεῖν καὶ διαλύειν βουλομένους, — τοσού-   20
τοις περιέβαλε κακοῖς, ὥστε ὀνειδίζεσθαι παρὰ πάντων ἐπὶ ταῖς συμφοραῖς.

4ᶜ. Ἐξαπέστειλεν ὁ Θεὸς τὸ ἔλεος αὐτοῦ καὶ τὴν ἀλήθειαν αὐτοῦ. Εἶπέν
τίς ἡ ἀποσταλεῖσα παρὰ τοῦ Θεοῦ συμμαχία, ἡ φιλανθρωπία καὶ ἡ ἀλήθεια, συνήθως αὐτὰ συνάψας ἀλλήλοις, ἵνα τῷ μὲν ἐλέῳ τὴν φιλανθρωπίαν
σημάνῃ καὶ τὴν χάριν, τῇ δὲ ἀληθείᾳ τὸ ἰσχυρὸν καὶ βέβαιον τῆς χάριτος.   25

19 Ps. LV, 2.

3. Καὶ γὰρ μέχρις — πιστεύει: P, fol. 163; V, fol. 227ᵛ; C 98 sup., fol. 111.
10 χαρισάμενον] δωρησάμενον C 98   12 Θεοῦ] om. C 98.
4ᵃ. Τοιαῦτα — ἔσωσεν: P, fol. 163ᵛ; V. fol. 227ᵛ; C 98 sup., fol. 111; Cord,
p. 113.   14 φησιν om. Cord   15 καλῶς δὲ καὶ C 98.
4ᵇ. Ἐν τῷ πρὸ τούτου — συμφοραῖς: P. fol. 163ᵛ; V, fol. 228; Cord, p. 113.
4ᶜ. Εἶπεν — χάριτος: P. fol. 163ᵛ; V, fol. 228; C 98 sup., fol. 111; Cord, p. 114.
23 τοῦ om. Cord.

Aᵉ 10-13 (p. 300, 8-11): Intentio deprecandi ad merendum noua praeteritis
beneficiorum tuorum adiuuatur exemplis.   16-17 (p. 300, 16-17): Pro dignitate
beneficii caelo misa liberatio dicitur.   4ᶜ (p. 300, 21-24): Misericordiae et ueritatis nomine firmitas indulgentiae et constantia subuenientis ostenditur.

is not possible for his kingdom to totter in the meantime. Likewise, here too he adds the clause *Until iniquity passes* to connect with what went before— that is, I keep hoping in you until the impending evils of war come to an end, and it is not possible for me to stop hoping in you until I attain what is expected. By *iniquity* he referred to what was done to him lawlessly and unjustly by the foe without any justification.

I shall cry to God the Most High, the God who did me favors (v. 2): until I enjoy these things, I shall continue calling on you who already granted me favors and freed me from awful troubles, believing I shall once again attain what I already attained. He goes on to outline God's beneficence, at the same time suggesting the grace and believing that this trust is justified also in regard to what remains. *He sent from heaven and saved me* (v. 3). He is referring to the kinds of things he has done. *He sent* was well put, as though of a king capable of sending help and support. He said *from heaven* to bring out the force of the help, meaning, He it was who saved by being an ally. *He put to shame those trampling on me.* In the psalm before this he said "people have trampled on me";[3] so *those trampling on me* was well put, referring to those wishing in every way to crush and destroy him, whom God enveloped in such awful troubles as to make them in their calamities an object of reproach to everyone. *God sent his mercy and his truth.* He referred to the support, lovingkindness, and truth sent by God, linking them with one another as usual, so as to suggest by *mercy* lovingkindness and grace, and by *truth* the force and stability of the grace. |

---

3. Ps 56:1.

5ᵃ. Καὶ ἐρρύσατο τὴν ψυχήν μου ἐκ μέσου σκύμνων. Καὶ ταύτῃ τῇ βοηθείᾳ ἀφειλετό με καὶ ἀπήλλαξεν τῶν πολεμίων, καίτοι ὥσπερ ἐπὶ λεόντων
κεκυκλωμένων· σκύμνους γὰρ ἐνταῦθα τὰ τῶν λεόντων ἔκγονα λέγει, ἵνα
δείξῃ τὸ δεινὸν καὶ θρασὺ τῶν πολεμίων.

5 5ᵇ. Ἐκοιμήθην τεταραγμένος. Ἐγὼ οὖν φησὶν ὑπὸ τοῦ πλήθους τῶν
κακῶν μέσου ληφθεὶς τῶν τοσούτων καὶ τηλικούτων πολεμίων, ὑπὸ ταραχῆς
τε καὶ ἀπορίας ἐταπεινώθην, — ἐπειδὴ ὥσπερ ὁ ὕπνος ἄπρακτον ἀποφαίνει
τὸν καθεύδοντα, οὕτω καὶ ταπείνωσις παρὰ πολεμίων ἐγγινομένη καὶ ταραχὴ
περιβαλοῦσα τὸν κατεχόμενον ἀργὸν πάντη ποιεῖ καὶ τῷ πάσχειν πρό-
10 χειρον.

5ᶜ. Υἱοὶ ἀνθρώπων, οἱ ὀδόντες αὐτῶν ὅπλα καὶ βέλη. Υἱοὺς ἀνθρώπων
λέγει, ἀντὶ τοῦ ἀνθρώπους· ὡς καὶ ἐν τῷ πρὸ τούτου τὸ Κατεπάτησέν με
ἄνθρωπος καὶ τὸ Οὐ φοβηθήσομαί τι ποιήσει μοι ἄνθρωπος, οὕτω κἀνταῦθα.
Ἀλλ' εἰ καὶ τῶν ἀνθρώπων τούτων φησὶν οἱ ὀδόντες ὅπλα τε καὶ βέλη, ἵνα
15 εἴπῃ ὅτι ὥσπερ ὀδοῦσί τισι κατεσθίον|τες, οὕτω τοῖς ὅπλοις καὶ τοῖς βέλε-
σιν ἅπαντας ἀναλίσκειν δυνατοὶ διὰ τὴν προσοῦσαν αὐτοῖς ἰσχύν.

5ᵈ. Καὶ ἡ γλῶσσα αὐτῶν μάχαιρα   Σφάττουσί φησι τῇ γλώττῃ εὐκό-
ὀξεῖα. Εἰ δὲ καὶ τῇ μαχαίρᾳ σφάτ-   λως ἐνδιαβάλλοντες, ὡς μαχαίραν
τουσιν, εὐκόλως ὡσεὶ γλῶτταν αὐτὴν αὐτὴν ῥαδίως κινοῦντες. Ἐπειδὴ γὰρ
20 ῥαδίως κινοῦντες κατὰ τῶν ἐναντίων, λέοντας ἐκάλεσε τοὺς πρὸς τὸ δια-
— ἐπειδὴ γὰρ λέοντας ἐκάλεσεν,   βάλλειν ἑτοίμους, εἰκότως ὀδόντων

12-13 Ps. LV, 2 et 5ᵇ.

5ᵃ. Καὶ ταύτῃ — πολεμίων: P, fol. 163ᵛ; V, fol. 228; C 98 sup., fol. 111ʳ·ᵛ.
3 καὶ κεκλωμένων C.
5ᵇ. Ἐγὼ οὖν — πρόχειρον: P, fol. 164; V, fol. 228; Cord, p. 115.   6 μέσον Cord
8 οὕτω καὶ] καὶ om. C   ἐνγενομένη C.
5ᶜ. Υἱοὺς ἀνθρώπων — ἰσχύν: P, fol. 164; V, fol. 228ʳ·ᵛ; Cord, p. 115.   12 τὸ
om. Cord   14 ἀλλ' εἰ καὶ om. Cord.
5ᵈ. Εἰ δὲ — ἀλλὰ τί: C; P, fol. 164; V, fol. 228ᵛ.   Σφάττουσι — χρωμένους:
Vat. 1422, fol. 107 (Θεοδ); Cord, p. 116.

Aᵉ 1-3 (p. 300, 26-29): Tamquam iam circumdantium aut tamquam leonum,
cum a seuis hostibus occupatus tenerer de (di ms) stupore quem experiuntur
adflicti.   7-8 (p. 301, 1-3): Difectum mentis torporemque, quo depraemuntur
humiliati, dormitationem uocat.   15-16 (p. 301, 4-6): Id est homines concul-
cantes me; tamquam molaribus, sic iaculis uidebantur obpraésos posse confi-
gere.   5ᵈ (p. 301, 10-13): Qui ussu bellandi tanta agilitate (aquilitate ms)
conferunt gladios, qua uelocitate lingua uibratur leonum in appetitum et con-
fectionem praedae.

He rescued my soul from the midst of lion cubs (v. 4): with this help he extricated me and freed me from the enemy, as though lions were encircling me (by *cubs* here referring to the lions' offspring so as to highlight the terrifying audacity of the enemy). *I lay down all alarmed:* caught up in the vast number of troubles from so many powerful enemies, I was brought low with alarm and bewilderment, since just as sleep renders the sleeper helpless, so too humbling by the enemy and alarm besetting the one affected make him completely useless and vulnerable to suffering. *Sons of human beings, their teeth are weapons and arrows.* By *sons of human beings* he means "human beings": as in the previous psalm he said "people have trampled on me" and "I shall not fear what a human being will do to me,"[4] so too here. But granting that these people's *teeth are weapons and arrows,* the meaning is, Just as they eat with their teeth, so they are capable of consuming everyone with weapons and arrows on account of the force belonging to them. *And their tongue is a sharp sword:* granting that they slay with a sword, they easily wield it against the enemy like a tongue.[5] You see, since he had referred to them as lions, | he was right to make mention of *teeth* and here speak of a

---

4. Ps 56:1, 4, though the text of the latter verse speaks rather of "flesh."

5. Is the tongue of the psalmist's enemies like a sword (as Theodore is represented as saying in some MSS), or is their sword used like a lion's tongue (as in the Codex Coislinianus)? In fact, he seems to take it both ways.

καλῶς εἶπεν τὸ ὀδόντας, καὶ γλῶσσα τοῦτό φησι, — τοῖς πολεμικοῖς ὀργάνοις οὕτω ῥαδίως κέχρηνται κατὰ τῶν ἐναντίων ὥσπερ λέων ὀδοῦσί τε καὶ γλώττῃ. Ἀλλὰ τί;

καὶ γλώσσης ἐμνημόνευσε, τροπικώτερον τὰ τῆς ὑποθέσεως παρῳδῶν, καὶ δεικνὺς μηδὲν ἀπῳδεῖν λεόντων τῇ ἀγριότητι τοὺς κατηγορίαις καὶ διαβολαῖς κατὰ τῶν πλησίον χρωμένους. 5

6. Ὑψώθητι ἐπὶ τοὺς οὐρανούς, ὁ Θεός, καὶ ἐπὶ πᾶσαν τὴν γῆν ἡ δόξα σου. Ἀλλ' αὐτὸς τῇ οἰκείᾳ βοηθείᾳ δεῖξον σεαυτόν τε μέγαν καὶ ὑψηλόν, καὶ ἐν αὐτοῖς ὄντα τοῖς οὐρανοῖς τῷ παραδόξῳ τῆς εἰς τούτους τιμωρίας. Οὕτω γὰρ κατὰ πᾶσαν ἐπίδοξος ἔσῃ τὴν γῆν, πάντων θαυμαζόντων καὶ ἐκπληττομένων τὸ γεγονός. 10

7ᵃ. Παγίδα ἡτοίμασαν τοῖς ποσί μου.⁷Πάλιν τὰς παρ' ἐκείνων ἐπιβουλὰς διηγεῖται· συνεχῶς γὰρ στέφει τὸν λόγον, ποτὲ μὲν τὴν τῶν ἐναντίων λέγων ἐπιβουλήν, ποτὲ δὲ τὴν παρὰ τοῦ Θεοῦ βοήθειαν ἐξαγγέλλων. Ἐνέδρας μοί φησι κατεσκεύασαν πολλάκις, ὥστε με συλλαβεῖν.

7ᵇ. Καὶ κατέκαμψαν τὴν ψυχήν μου. Ἀλλὰ καὶ εἰς ἀγῶνά με πολλάκις 15 κατέστησαν, ταπεινώ|σαντες τῷ πλήθει τῶν κακῶν καὶ περὶ τῆς σωτηρίας αὐτῆς ἀγωνιάσαι πολλάκις παρασκευάσαντες.

7ᶜ·ᵈ. Ὤρυξαν πρὸ προσώπου μου βόθρον, καὶ ἐνέπεσον εἰς αὐτόν. Πόσα δὲ ἐμηχανήσαντο κατ' ἐμοῦ οὕτω βαρέα τε καὶ χαλεπά, ὥστε ἐμπεσόντα μηδὲ ἔκδυσιν εὑρίσκειν τινὰ καὶ ἀπαλλαγὴν προσδοκᾶν· τοῦτο γὰρ λέγει βόθρον, 20 τὸ δυσαπάλλακτον καὶ ἀδιεξόδευτον κακόν. Καὶ τοιαῦτα μηχανησάμενοι κατ' ἐμοῦ, αὐτοὶ τοῖς κακοῖς περιεβλήθησαν· ὤφθην μὲν γὰρ ἐγὼ τῆς παρά σου τυχὼν βοηθείας, τιμωρίαν δὲ ἔδοσαν ἐκεῖνοι τοῦ καθ' ἡμῶν τολμήματος.

---

6. Ἀλλ' αὐτὸς — γεγονός : P, fol. 164ᵛ ; V, fol. 228ᵛ ; Cord, p. 116.   7 cf. Paraphrasis (p. 105, 27-28): Ἀλλ' αὐτός φησι, δέσποτα, δεῖξον σαυτὸν ὑψηλότερον   ἑαυτὸν CPV Cord   τε om. Cord   μέγα CPV   8 εἰς ex σῆς C   9 θαυμαζόντων om. Cord.
7ᵃ. Πάλιν — συλλαβεῖν : P, fol. 164ᵛ ; V, fol. 228ᵛ-229 ; Cord, p. 116.   12-13 ποτὲ μὲν — ἐξαγγέλλων] τῶν τὰς ἐναντίων λόγων Cord.
7ᵇ. Ἀλλὰ — παρασκευάσαντες : P, fol. 164ᵛ ; V, fol. 229.
7ᶜ·ᵈ. Πόσα δὲ ἐμηχανήσαντο — τολμήματος : P, fol. 164ᵛ ; V, fol. 229 ; Cord, p. 117.   18 πόσα] ὅσα Cord.

Aᵉ 7ᵇ (p. 301, 21-24): Onustam (honestam ms) meroribus et laboribus inclinatam, perque hoc humilem atque defectam fecerunt.   20-21 (p. 301, 25-27): Profunditatem malorum appellat foveam, de qua desperaretur (dispereretur ms) emersio.

tongue, since they have no difficulty in using warlike instruments against the enemy like lions using teeth and tongue. But why?

Be exalted on the heavens, O God, and let your glory be on all the earth (v. 5): with your characteristic help show yourself mighty and exalted and present in the very heavens with the unexpected nature of the punishment against them. Thus you will be glorious on all the earth, with everyone amazed and astonished at the event.

They set a snare for my feet (v. 6). Again he recounts the schemes on their part. He constantly alters his words, sometimes mentioning the adversaries' scheming, sometimes reporting on help from God. Frequently, he is saying, they hatched plots so as to catch me out. *And bowed my soul down:* and they often reduced me to anguish, bringing me down with the multitude of the troubles and often causing me to be exercised about salvation itself. *They dug a pit before me and fell in it:* they devised such dire and troublesome things against me that anyone falling in would not find a way to escape or expect deliverance (the meaning of *a pit,* a trouble from which deliverance and escape would be difficult). Though devising such things against me, they themselves were caught up in the troubles: whereas I was seen to receive help from you, they paid the penalty for their exploits against us. |

8. Ἑτοίμη ἡ καρδία μου, ὁ Θεός, ἑτοίμη ἡ καρδία μου, ᾄσομαι καὶ ψαλῶ. Ὅτι τὸ ἕτοιμον ἑδραῖον λέγει, καὶ διὰ τί, εἴρηται ἡμῖν ἑτέρωθι. Φησὶ τοίνυν ὅτι βέβαιον ἔχω τὸν λογισμὸν καὶ ἀπαρασάλευτον, — καρδίαν γὰρ τὸν λογισμὸν καλεῖ, ἀπαρασάλευτον δέ· διὰ τοῦτο ᾄσομαι καὶ ψαλῶ, του-
5 τέστι τελείας τυχὼν τῆς παρά σου βοηθείας καὶ εὐεργεσίας ὕμνοις καὶ ᾠδαῖς χρήσομαι πρεπούσαις ὑπὲρ τῶν γεγενημένων. Ὅμοιον δέ ἐστι τοῦτο τῷ κειμένῳ ἐν τῷ πρὸ τούτου ψαλμῷ. Καὶ γὰρ ἐκεῖ φησιν Ἐν ἐμοί, ὁ Θεός, εὐχαὶ ἃς ἀποδώσω αἰνέσεώς σοι, ἀντὶ τοῦ Ἐν ἐμαυτῷ κατέχω καὶ μέμνημαι τῶν ἐπαγγελμάτων, ἑτοίμως ἔχων ἀποδοῦναι ἐν καιρῷ· οὕτω κἀνταῦθα
10 Ἥδρασταί μοί φησιν ὁ λογισμὸς εἰς τὴν ἀπόδοσιν τῆς χάριτος. Χρῆται δὲ αὐτοῖς οὐχ ἁπλῶς, ἀλλ᾽ ἐπειδὴ τῆς ἐπανόδου τυχόντες τῆς ἀπὸ Βαβυλῶνος οὐ πρὸ πολλοῦ ἀγνώμονες ἐδείχθησαν τῇ ἐπὶ τὸ χεῖρον μεταβολῇ, ὥσπερ ἀσφαλίζεται | διὰ τῶν λόγων ὁ προφήτης, ὥστε κἂν νῦν γοῦν μὴ ἀγνώμονας φανῆναι.

15 9ᵃ. Ἐξεγέρθητι ἡ δόξα μου. Λοιπὸν ὥσπερ ἐγκελευόμενος περὶ τοῦ τὴν εὐχαριστίαν πληροῦν, ἐξεγέρθητί φησιν ἡ δόξα μου, ἀντὶ τοῦ Κινοῦ μοι πρὸς ψαλμῳδίαν καὶ ὑμνῳδίαν Θεοῦ. Δόξαν γὰρ ἰδίαν καλεῖ τὴν εἰς τὸν Θεὸν ὑμνῳδίαν, ἐπειδήπερ ἐκόσμει τε αὐτὸν καὶ ἐπίδοξον καθέστη ἡ περὶ τὸν Θεὸν συνείδησις.

20 9ᵇ. Ἐξεγέρθητι, ψαλτήριον καὶ κιθάρα. Ὡσπερεὶ τοῖς ὀργάνοις ἐγκελευόμενός φησι κινηθήτω κιθάρα, κινηθήτω ψαλτήριον, ἀντὶ τοῦ Ἄγε δὴ πληρούσθω ὕμνος, φθεγγέσθω ψαλτήριον, κινείσθω κιθάρα, πάντα ὅσα προσήκει πρὸς ὕμνον Θεοῦ γενέσθω.

2 cf. in Ps. XXXII, 14 (p. 152, 25-28)   7-8 ps. LV, 13.

8 Ὅτι τὸ ἕτοιμον — φανῆναι: P, fol. 165; V, fol. 229; Cord, p. 117.   2-4 cf. Paraphrasis (p. 106, 10-12): Πάλιν τὸ ἕτοιμ. ἀντὶ τοῦ ἑδραῖα· ἐμοῦ γάρ φησιν ἡ καρδία ἑδραῖά ἐστιν εἰς τὸ ὑμνεῖν σε καὶ δοξάζειν   3 ἔχων CPV   4 διὰ τοῦτο] πρὸς τὸ CPV   4-5 τουτέστι] πρὸς τὸ CPV   6 χρήσασθαι CPV   8 ἑαυτῷ CPV Cord   10 ὁ om. CPV.
9ᵃ. Λοιπὸν — συνείδησις: P, fol. 165; V, fol. 229ᵛ; Cord, p. 117-118.
9ᵇ. Ὡσπερεὶ — γενέσθω: P, fol. 165; V, fol. 229ᵛ; Cord, p. 118.

Aᵉ 2-3 (p. 301, 29-31): Firmas constantesque cogitationes ad laudandum Deum se habere demo⟨n⟩strat.   11-12 (p. 302, 1-3): ...nouerat quippe suos post Babiloniam liberationem ingratos beneficiorum Dei.   17-18 (p. 302, 11-12): ...gloriam suam uocat ipsam laudationem Dei, qua gloriosus fiebat.

My heart is ready, O God, my heart is ready; I shall praise and sing (v. 7). The fact that *ready* means "steadfast," and why it does, is mentioned by us elsewhere.[6] So he is saying, I have a firm and immovable resolve (by heart referring to resolve that is immovable). Hence, *I shall praise and sing*—that is, Having received perfect help and kindness from you, I shall employ fitting songs and hymns of praise for what has been done. Now, this resembles what was written in the previous psalm: there he said, "In me, O God, are vows of praise I shall pay to you"[7]—that is, I keep within myself and remember the promises, ready and able to fulfill them at the appropriate time. Likewise, here too he is saying, My purpose is in readiness to make a response to the gift. It is not without purpose that he employs them; rather, since they were granted return from Babylon not long before and were shown to be ungrateful by taking a turn for the worse, the inspired author is careful in his words not to have them appear ungrateful even now.

Awake, my glory! (v. 8). At this point, as though encouraged to give thanks, he says *Awake, my glory*—that is, Stir me up to sing hymns of praise to God (by his *glory* referring to the hymn-singing to God, since it was his consciousness of God that was his adornment and rendered him famous). *Awake, harp and lute!* As if instructing the instruments, he says, Let a lute be played, let a harp be played—that is to say, Come now, let a hymn be sung, a harp give voice, a lute be played; let everything that should do so celebrate with hymns to God. | *I shall awake at dawn:* I shall stir myself to morning

---

6. Cf. commentary on Ps 33:14.
7. Ps 56:12.

9ᶜ. Ἐξεγερθήσομαι ὄρθρου. Ὄρθριόν φησιν ἐμαυτὸν διεγείρω πρὸς τὴν ὑμνῳδίαν, ἀπὸ τοῦ καιροῦ τὸ σπουδαῖον εἰπεῖν βουληθείς.

10. Ἐξομολογήσομαί σοι ἐν λαοῖς, Κύριε, ψαλῶ σοι ἐν ἔθνεσιν. Εὐχαριστήσω σοι περὶ πάντων τῶν οἰκείων, ὑπὲρ τῶν γεγονότων, ψαλῶ σοι ἐν ἔθνεσιν, ἀνοίσω δέ σοι ὕμνους καὶ ἀλλοτρίων παρόντων, οἳ ἀπὸ τῆς τῶν 5 γεγονότων ἐκπλήξεως παρέσονται θεαταὶ τῶν εἰς τὸν ναὸν πληρουμένων.

11ᵃ. Ὅτι ἐμεγαλύνθη ἕως τῶν οὐρανῶν τὸ ἔλεός σου. Ἐδείχθη γὰρ ἡ φιλανθρωπία σού φησι δίκην οὐρανῶν ὑψηλή, τοσοῦτον ἡμῶν νικήσασα τὰς κακίας ὅσον ἡμῶν οὐρανὸς ὑπέρκειται.

11ᵇ. Καὶ ἕως τῶν νεφελῶν ἡ ἀλήθειά σου. Ἐπισυνῆπται τῷ ἀνωτέρῳ 10 τὴν ἀλήθειαν, τὸ ἔλεος συνήθως ἐπισυνάπτων. Βούλεται γὰρ εἰπεῖν ὅτι ἡ φιλανθρωπία σου ἡ περὶ ἡμᾶς, ἣν ἰσχυρὰν καὶ βεβαίαν ἡμῖν παρέσχες, ὑπὲρ τὰς νεφέλας καὶ τοὺς οὐρανοὺς ἐδείχθη· ἀμφότερα γὰρ τότε τῶν νεφελῶν καὶ τῶν οὐρανῶν ἀμφοτέροις περιτίθησιν. Ἐπείπερ οὐχὶ σκοπὸς ἦν αὐτῷ τὸ μὲν εἰπεῖν μεῖζον, τὸ δὲ ἔλαττον (πῶς γὰρ οἷόν τε συμπεπλεγ- 15 μένα;) ἀλλ᾽ ἡ διαίρεσις ἀπὸ τῆς τοῦ λόγου τάξεως γεγένηται.

12. Ὑψώθητι ἐπὶ τοὺς οὐρανούς, ὁ Θεός, καὶ ἐπὶ πᾶσαν τὴν γῆν ἡ δόξα σου. Καλῶς τῇ εὐχαριστίᾳ καὶ αἴτησιν προστίθησιν, ἀντὶ τοῦ Ἐπίμεινον νῦν δεικνύμενός φησι καὶ γνωριζόμενος ὅστις εἶ τὸ μέγεθος, καὶ ὅτι τῶν οὐρανῶν ὑπέρκεισαι. Τοῦτο γάρ σε θαυμαστὸν καὶ ἐπίδοξον παρὰ πᾶσι 20 ποιήσει τοῖς ἐπὶ τῆς γῆς, ἱκανῶν ὄντων τῶν παρά σου γιγνομένων πάντας παιδεύειν ἀνθρώπους ὅστις εἶ.

9ᶜ. Ὄρθριον — βουληθείς: P, fol. 165ᵛ; V. fol. 229ᵛ-230; Cord, p. 118.
10. Εὐχαριστήσω — πληρουμένων: P, fol. 165ᵛ; V, fol. 230.
11ᵃ. Ἐδείχθη — ὑπέρκειται: P, fol. 165ᵛ; V, fol. 230; Cord, p. 119.
11ᵇ. Ἐπισύνηπται — γεγένηται: P, fol. 165ᵛ; V, fol. 230.
12. Καλῶς — ὅστις εἶ: P. fol. 165ᵛ; V, fol. 230.

Aᵉ 9ᶜ (p. 302, 14-17): Huic operi matutinus cantator ancingar; ut solicitudinem deuoti cantatoris expraemeret, tempus signauit officii. 5 (p. 302, 18-19): Testibus multis populis gratus existam. 10 (p. 302, 20-23): Non solum autem nostris plebibus circumdatus canam laudes tuas, sed etiam sub externarum nationum auribus tua dona cantabo. 11ᵃ (p. 302, 24-31): *Misericordia tua et ueritas tua* caelum nubesque magnitudine et caelsitudine superant... eadem mensura elongans iniquitates nostras, qua caelum terraque secernitur. 12 (p. 301, 33-302, 1): Bene gratiarum actione subdidit precem, ut diceret Persiste proinde grandis et excealsus nostris apparere subsidiis, ut qui sis gloriosse omnibus innotescat et magnitudo tua quod caelo sit excelsior cunctorum lingua fatetur.

hymn-singing (indicating the enthusiasm by mention of the time of day). *I shall confess to you among peoples, Lord; I shall sing to you among nations* (v. 9): I shall give thanks to you for all that is yours, for your deeds; *I shall sing to you among nations;* I shall offer hymns to you even when foreigners are present, who in astonishment at the deeds will be come to witnesses what is performed in the temple.

Because your mercy has been magnified to the heavens (v. 10): your lovingkindness has been shown to be as high as the heavens, surpassing our evil deeds to the extent that heaven is above us. *And your truth to the clouds.* He relates *truth* to the preceding, as usual relating it to *mercy,* meaning, Your lovingkindness for us, which was your firm and steadfast gift to us, has been shown to surpass the clouds and the heavens (comparing both to both, the clouds and the heavens). It was, in fact, not his intention to say that one was greater and one less (how could they be compared?); rather, the difference emerges from the order of the expression.

Be exalted on the heavens, O God, and let your glory be on all the earth (v. 11). He did well to add the request to the thanksgiving, meaning, Continue in our time to emerge and be known for who you are in your greatness along with the fact that you surpass the heavens. You will, in fact, make this attract the admiration and glory of everyone on earth, since your deeds are sufficient to teach all people who you are. |

PSALMVS LVII

Πολλῆς καὶ παραδόξου τοῖς Μακκαβαίοις παρασχεθείσης τῆς παρὰ τοῦ
Θεοῦ βοηθείας, ἐχώρει μὲν ἐπὶ τὸ κρεῖττον ὁσημέραι τὰ κατ᾿ αὐτούς, πολ-
λὴν δὲ τὴν ἐπὶ τὸ χεῖρον ἐπίδοσιν | ἐλάμβανε τὸ τῶν ἐναντίων. Καὶ δὴ
5 τούτων οὕτω γιγνομένων, πολλοῖς οἱ ἐναντίοι τοῖς δόλοις ἐχρῶντο, ὡς ἂν
ἡττώμενοι ταῖς μάχαις πανουργίᾳ καὶ τῇ τῆς φιλίας ὑποκρίσει κατορθῶσαι
τὸ σπουδαζόμενον δυνηθῶσιν. Καὶ πρῶτον μὲν Δημήτριος ὁ βασιλεὺς Βακχίδην τὸν ἑαυτοῦ στρατηγὸν ἀπέστειλεν Ἀλκίμῳ τινὶ τῶν Ἰουδαίων τὴν
ἱερωσύνην καὶ τὴν ἡγεμονίαν ἐγχειρίσαι τοῦ ἔθνους. Οἳ καὶ παραγεγονότες
10 ἐπὶ τῆς Ἰουδαίας ἐπειρῶντο λόγοις ὑποκρίσεως μεστοῖς τόν τε Ἰούδαν συλ-
λαβέσθαι καὶ τοὺς ἀδελφούς. Ὡς δὲ τοῦτο ποιῆσαι οὐκ ἴσχυσαν, συνιέν-
των ἐκείνων τὴν ἐπιβουλήν, ἑτέρους τινὰς τῶν Ἰουδαίων ἀπατήσαντες καὶ
λαβεῖν δυνηθέντες, ἀνεῖλον ἅπαντας. Μετὰ δὲ τοῦτο τελευτήσαντος μὲν τοῦ
Ἰούδα, Ἰωνάθαν δὲ τοῦ ἀδελφοῦ διαδεξαμένου τὴν ἀρχήν, Τρύφων τις πολλῇ
15 τῇ πανουργίᾳ χρησάμενος, συνελάβετό τε αὐτὸν καὶ συγκλείσας ἀνεῖλεν,
καὶ ὅλως πολλοῖς ἐχρήσαντο τοῖς δόλοις κατ᾿ αὐτοῦ, τοῦτο μὲν οἱ ἀδελφοί, τοῦτο δὲ καὶ οἱ ἀπεχθῶς ἔχοντες πρὸς αὐτόν. Ταῦτα δὴ πόρρωθεν
σημαίνων ὁ μακάριος Δαυὶδ ἐν τῷδε προαγορεύει τῷ ψαλμῷ.

2ᵃ. Εἰ ἀληθῶς ἄρα δικαιοσύνην λαλεῖτε. Καθ᾿ ὑπόκρισιν ἀναγνωστέον.
20 Εἴπερ ἀληθῶς φησιν ὑμῖν μέλει τοῦ δικαίου, καὶ τὴν χρηστότητα ταύτην
οὐ ματαίως ἐπιδείκνυσθε.

2ᵇ. Εὐθείας κρίνατε, οἱ υἱοὶ τῶν ἀνθρώπων. Τοῦ δικαίου γενέσθαι κριταὶ
σπουδάσατε· οὕτως γὰρ ἀπ᾿ αὐτῶν δυνήσεσθε δεῖξαι τῶν πραγμάτων τὴν

2 ss. I Macch. VII-IX; XII, 48 ss.

Πολλῆς — ψαλμῷ: P, fol. 166; V, fol. 230-230ᵛ; Cord, p. 128-129.   4 τὸ] τὰ V
5 δούλοις C 1ᵃ m.   11 ποιῆσαι om. Cord   15 τῇ om. Cord   συνέλαβε Cord
18 σημαίνει Cord.
2ᵃ. Καθ᾿ ὑπόκρισιν — ἐπιδείκνυσθε: P, fol. 166ᵛ; V, fol. 230ᵛ; Cord, p. 130.
2ᵇ. Τοῦ δικαίου — ἄδικα: P, fol. 166ᵛ; V, fol. 231.

Aᵉ Argumentum ps. LVII (p. 303, 3-17): Cum multum auxilium et admirabile Machabei a Deo essent consecuti, eorumque in dies prosperitas augeretur,
nocere eis inimici fraudibus laborabant; et simulabant blanditias quoniam
ledere terram in aperto certamine non poterant. Haec ergo tempora beatus
Dauid praeuidet ac praedicit; uel quae sub Demetrio rege, duce Bachide, Seodo
pontifice Alchimo aduersus Iudam molliti sunt, uel quae defuncto eo aduersus
Ionathan fratrem omnemque Machabaeorum familiam duce Trifone gesta sunt
hoc carmine profetantur.

PSALM 58

After great assistance had against expectations been provided to the Maccabees from God, their situation daily improved, while that of the adversaries
suffered a notable depreciation. When this happened, the adversaries adopted
many stratagems so as to be in a position, though defeated in battle, to
achieve their goals even by villainy and a pretense of friendship. First, King
Demetrius sent his general Bacchides to appoint Alcimus, one of the Jews,
as high priest in control of the nation. Those who arrived in Judea tried with
words full of pretense to get the better of Judas and his brothers; failing to do
so, since Judas and his brothers recognized the scheming, they deceived some
other Jews, succeeded in capturing them, and slew them all. Later, upon the
death of Judas, Jonathan succeeded his brother in control; by adopting great
villainy, a certain Trypho apprehended him, and imprisoned and killed him.
People in general adopted many stratagems against him, the brothers in one
case, and in another those who were hostile to him.[1]

   Blessed David conveyed this from a distance and foretold it in this
psalm. *Are you really delivering righteous words?* (v. 1). It is to be read as a
pretense. Are you really interested in righteousness, he is asking, and is this
not an idle demonstration you give of goodness? *Give upright judgments,
sons of human beings:* take pains to be just judges, this being the way you
will be able to bring out from the facts themselves | the intention and the atti-

---

1. Cf. 1 Macc 7–9; 12.

τε | γνώμην καὶ τὸν σκοπὸν τῶν πραττομένων ἂν τοῦ δικαίου φροντίσαντες καὶ τὸ ἀληθὲς ἐξετάσαντες ἡμῖν μὲν ὡς ἀδικουμένοις κατὰ τὸ δυνατὸν ἐπαμύνειν ἐθελήσητε, τοὺς δὲ πολεμοῦντας ἡμῖν ἀποστήσετε ὡς πράττοντας ἄδικα.

3ᵃ. Καὶ γὰρ ἐν καρδίᾳ ἀνομίας ἐργάζεσθε ἐν τῇ γῇ. Τὸ γὰρ ἐναντίον 5
φησὶν ἐκ τῶν πραγμάτων γνωρίζω, ὅτι ἀνομίαν ἐπὶ τῆς καρδίας ἐργάζεσθε, —
τουτέστιν ὅτι ταῦτα βουλεύεσθε καὶ λογίζεσθε κατὰ διάνοιαν, τὸ ὅπως ἂν
ἡμᾶς ἀνέλητε. Τὸ δὲ ἐν τῇ γῇ ἀπὸ τοῦ ἰδιώματος τοῦ ἐν τοῖς ψαλμοῖς
εὑρισκομένου φησίν, ὡς τὸ Πονηρία ἐν ταῖς παροικίαις αὐτῶν, ἀντὶ τοῦ Πονηρίας ἐν τῷδε πράττουσι τῷ βίῳ, καὶ τὸ Ἐπ' ὀργὴν γῆς ἐλάλουν. Οὕτω κἀν- 10
ταῦθα· πολλά φησιν ἐν τῇ γῇ τυγχάνοντες ἐργάζεσθε κατὰ καρδίαν κακά, —
τοῦτο δὲ καὶ ἡμῖν σύνηθες τὸ λέγειν πολλάκις περὶ τῶν ἀνθρώπων ὅσα
ποιοῦσιν ἐν τῷδε τῷ βίῳ κακά.

3ᵇ. Ἀδικίαν αἱ χεῖρες ὑμῶν συμπλέκουσιν. Δοκιμάζω δέ φησιν ἃ κατὰ
τὴν καρδίαν λογίζεσθε, ἀφ' ὧν πράττετε κατὰ τὸ προφανές· τοῦτο γὰρ 15
λέγει τὸ αἱ χεῖρες, ἐπειδήπερ σαφῆ τὰ τῆς χειρὸς ἔργα. Καλῶς δὲ τὸ συμπλέκουσιν, ἀντὶ τοῦ Τοιαῦτα ἐπινοεῖτε καὶ πράττετε ἀφ' ὧν οὐδὲ διαφυγεῖν
ἐστιν ἐλπίσαι, ἐκ μεταφορᾶς τῶν συμπεπλεγμένων ἃ μάλιστα δυσδιάλυτα
εἶναι συμβαίνει.

4ᵃ. Ἀπηλλοτριώθησαν οἱ ἁμαρτωλοὶ ἀπὸ μήτρας. Τῷ ἀπηλλοτριώθησαν 20
προσυπακούεται τὸ «τοῦ Θεοῦ» κατὰ ἀποσιώπησιν εἰρημένον τῷ προφήτῃ.
Καὶ | οὐ θαυμάζομέν φησιν ἐφ' οἷς πράττετε, ἐπείπερ ἔργον ὑμῖν καὶ βίος
τὸ ἀπηλλοτριῶσθαι τοῦ Θεοῦ· ἀεὶ γὰρ τῷ κακῷ χαίροντες καὶ τὰ ἄδικα
μετὰ πολλῆς πράττοντες τῆς σπουδῆς, ἀλλότριοι τοῦ Θεοῦ διὰ τῶν πράξεων ἐδείχθητε. Τὸ δὲ ἀπὸ μήτρας, ἀντὶ τοῦ ἀφ' οὗ διεπλάσθησαν ἀπηλ- 25
λοτριώθησαν, εἴτε ὑπερβολικῶς, ἵνα εἴπῃ τὸ ἀεί, εἴτε καὶ ὡς τοῦ Θεοῦ κατὰ
πρόγνωσιν ἀλλοτρίους αὐτοὺς ἔκτοτε ἡγησαμένου, — ὥσπερ οὖν καὶ τὸν

9 Ps. LIV, 16ᵇ   10 Ps. XXXIV, 20 (cf. supra p. 189-190).

3ᵃ. Τὸ γὰρ — κακά: P, fol. 167; V, fol. 231.
3ᵇ. Δοκιμάζω — συμβαίνει: P, fol. 167; V, fol. 231ᵛ.
4ᵃ. Τῷ ἀπηλλοτριώθησαν — Θεός: P, fol. 167ᵛ; V, fol. 231ᵛ; Cord, 132.   20 τὸ
Cord   22 ὑμῖν] ἡμῖν CPV   25 διεπλάσθησαν] δὲ ἐπλάσθησαν CPV   25-377, 2 cf. L
(p. 126, 10-13) ... ἢ ἀπὸ μήτρας λέγει καθ' ὑπερβολήν, ἢ τῇ προγνωστικῇ τοῦ Θεοῦ προνοίᾳ
ἀπηλλοτριώθησαν τοῦ δικαίου, ὡς καὶ περὶ τοῦ Ἱερεμίου ἐκ μήτρας ἡγίακά σε.

Aᵉ 14-15 (p. 303, 34-304, 2): Quanta sint quae corde uoluatis conicio, cum
sint tam grandia ista quae operibus puplicatis.   25-377, 2 (p. 304, 4-7): ...iam
ab utero abhominabiles, sicut e regione Heremias praescientia uirtutum suarum
acceptabilis.

tude of what is done, if by attending to righteousness and examining the truth you mean as far as possible to assist us as the injured party, on the one hand, and to relieve us of those attacking us on account of their unjust behavior, on the other hand. *In your heart, in fact, you wreak crimes on the earth* (v. 2): on the contrary, I know from the facts that in your heart you are workers of iniquity—that is, you intend and plot in your mind how to destroy us. The phrase *on the earth* he uses as an idiom found in the psalms, as, for example, "Wickedness is in their lodgings" (that is, They are guilty of wickedness in this life), and "They spoke in anger of the earth."[2] Likewise, here too: You who live *on the earth* commit many crimes in your heart (it being our custom as well to make this remark about human beings in reference to all the evil they do in this life). *Your hands weave iniquity:* from what you do openly (the meaning of *hands,* since the works of one's hands are obvious) I form a judgment on what you plan in your heart. *Weave* was well put, meaning, You ponder such things and put them into practice, and it is not possible even to hope to escape them (using a metaphor from woven materials that are particularly difficult to unravel).

Sinners were estranged from the womb (v. 3). "From God" is to be understood with *were estranged* in the author's elliptical phrase. We are not surprised at what you do, he is saying, since your behavior and life represent an estrangement from God: by always rejoicing in evil and committing injustice with great relish you are shown by your actions to be at odds with God. The phrase *from the womb* means, From the time you were formed you *were estranged*—either speaking by way of hyperbole to mean "always," or saying that God knew by his foreknowledge that they were estranged from that time, just as also | God says that, in his foreknowledge of those who are

---

2. Ps 55:16; 35:20. There is nothing particularly idiomatic in the occurrence of the phrase "on the earth" here (though, admittedly, Dahood [*Psalms,* 2:58] prefers to read a different Hebrew form). Theodore is led to the contrary impression by his commentary on the obscure v. 20b of Ps 35 (q.v.), which involves a *hapax legomenon* in the Hebrew.

προφήτην Ἰερεμίαν πρὸ τῆς διαπλάσεως ἐν τοῖς ἁγίοις καταλελογισμένον
ἔχειν ἀπὸ τῆς προγνώσεως τῶν κατ' αὐτόν φησιν ὁ Θεός.

4ᵇ. Ἐπλανήθησαν ἀπὸ γαστρός, καὶ ἐλάλουν ψευδῆ. Τὸ αὐτὸ πάλιν
ἑτέρως λέγει. Ἐξότε φησὶν ἐτέχθησαν, πλανώμενοι διατελοῦσιν ἀπὸ τοῦ
5 Θεοῦ, οὐδέποτε τοῖς αὐτοῦ δόγμασιν ἐμμένοντες. Τοῦτο δὲ μᾶλλον ἁρμόσει τοῖς οἰκείοις· τῶν γὰρ ἐχόντων οἰκειότητά τινα καὶ γνῶσιν τὸ πλα-
νᾶσθαι ἴδιον. Τὸ καὶ ἐλάλουν ψευδῆ, Σύμμαχος λαλοῦντες ψευδῆ. Δῆλον
οὖν φησιν ὅτι οἱ τῷ ψεύδει χαίροντες καὶ τοῦτο διὰ στόματος ἔχοντες,
πόρρωθεν πλανῶνται τοῦ δεσπότου.

10 5ᵃ. Θυμὸς αὐτοῖς κατὰ τὴν ὁμοίωσιν τοῦ ὄφεως. Τοιαύτην ἔχουσι τὴν
ὀργὴν θανάτου γέμουσαν· ἴδιον γὰρ τοῦτο ὀργιζομένου τοῦ ὄφεως ποιεῖν.

5ᵇ-6ᵇ. Ὡσεὶ ἀσπίδος κωφῆς καὶ βυούσης τὰ ὦτα αὐτῆς, ἥτις οὐκ εἰσακούσεται φωνῆς ἐπᾳδόντων, φαρμάκου τε φαρμακευομένου παρὰ σοφοῦ. Ἐπίτασιν εἶπεν τῆς ὀργῆς, ἐπιφέρων ὡσεὶ ἀσπίδος. Χεῖρον γὰρ ἡ τῆς ἀσπί-
15 δος πληγή· οὕτω γὰρ ὀργίλοι καὶ μονιμώτατοι τὸ μῖσος καὶ περὶ τὸ
φονεύειν σπουδαῖοι, ὡς μηδὲν ἀπεοικέναι τῆς ἀσπίδος, ἢ καὶ θάνατον ἐργάζεται πλήττουσα καὶ τοὺς ἐπᾴδοντας οὐκ ἐπιστρέφεται, πάντων καὶ τῶν
γοητεύειν δυναμένων καταφρονοῦσα. Οὕτω γάρ φησι καὶ τούτους οὐδέν
ἐστιν ὃ μετατίθησι τῆς ὀργῆς. Λέγεται δὲ καὶ ἴδιον εἶναι τοῦτο τῆς ἀσπί-
20 δος πολλάκις οὐκ ἐπιστρέφεσθαι τὰς τῶν ἐπᾳδόντων φωνάς. Πλὴν ὅπως
ποτ' ἂν ἔχῃ, δῆλον ὅ φησιν. Τινὲς δὲ τὸ φαρμάκου τε συνῆψαν, οὕτως
ἀναγνόντες Φαρμακοῦται φαρμακευομένη παρὰ σοφοῦ· ἐναλλάξαντες γὰρ τὸ
φαρμακευομένου, τεθείκασι « φαρμακευομένη ». Τοῦτο δὲ ἀπὸ ἀπειρίας
πεπόνθασιν. Ἔστι γὰρ δύο μέρη λόγου, φαρμάκου, εἶτα τε. Λέγει γὰρ
25 οὕτως· ἐοίκασί φησι τῇ ἀσπίδι, ἢ μήτε ἐπακούει τῆς τῶν ἐπᾳδόντων
φωνῆς, μήτε τοῦ φαρμάκου τοῦ παρ' ἐκείνων φαρμακευομένου, — φάρμακον

1-2 cf. Ierem. I, 5.

4ᵇ. Τὸ αὐτὸ — δεσπότου: P, fol. 167ᵛ; V, fol. 232. 8 τὸ C.
5ᵃ. Τοιαύτην — ποιεῖν: P, fol. 168; V, fol. 232; Cord, p. 134. 10 τοιαύτην
ἔχουσι] ἔχουσι φησιν Cord.
5ᵇ-6ᵇ. Ἐπίτασιν — ἐπᾳδόντων: P, fol. 168; V, fol. 232ᵛ; Cord, p. 134. 13 ἐπί-
τασιν] καὶ ἐπ. Cord   14 ἐπιφέρων ὡσεὶ ἀσπίδος om. CPV   20 τῆς... φωνῆς Cord
21 ὃ] ὅτι Cord   φαρμάκου] φάρκω 1ᵃ m. C   25 οὕτως om. CPV   ὑπακούει Cord.

Aᵉ 3-5 (p. 304, 23-305, 2): Idem repetiuit, et bene aduersus eos qui sub lege
fuerunt possuit *Errauerunt.*   5ᵃ (p. 305, 2-3): Quorum est iratorum laetifer
mursus.   13-18 (p. 305, 7-13): Incrementum uoluit irae illius, quam accusabat,
expraemere. Ita, inquit, isti inmedicabilem aduersus nos habentes furorem tamquam aspides, quae et mortem inferunt uulnerantes et contemnant aduersum
uenina incantare colentes.

his, he has the prophet Jeremiah reckoned among the saints before his formation.[3] *They went astray from birth; they spoke falsehood.* He says the same
thing in a different way: From the time they were born they persisted in straying from God, never adhering to his teachings. This he will apply particularly
to his own people, since straying is proper to those having a relationship and
acquaintance. For *they spoke falsehood* Symmachus has "by speaking falsehood"; so it is clear that those rejoicing in falsehood and having it in their
mouths stray far from the Lord.

 They have anger in a way similar to the serpent (v. 4): they have such
awful wrath that communicates death (it being typical of an enraged serpent
to do this). *Like an asp that is deaf and stops its ears, that will not hearken
to the command of the charmers, and of a drug administered by a sage.* He
brought out the extent of the rage by introducing *like an asp,* the strike of
an asp being worse; similarly, wrathful people quite set in their hatred and
bent on taking life are no different from the asp, which brings death by striking and is not put off by the snake charmers, scorning everyone, including
those skilled in sorcery. In similar fashion there is nothing that can make
these people desist from their anger. Now, it is said to be characteristic of
the asp that it is often not put off by the music of the snake charmers; be this
as it may, what he means is clear. Some commentators combine *drug* with
and, and thus read, "It is drugged by being drugged by a sage," changing
being drugged [Gk.: masc. participle] to "being drugged" [Gk.: fem. parti-
ciple]. This is a result of their ignorance: there are two words involved, *drug*
and then *and.* His meaning, you see, goes this way: They are like the asp,
which heeds neither the snake charmers' music nor the drug administered by
them (by *drug* referring to the charm itself). Symmachus | suggests this more

3. Jer 1:5.

αὐτὴν τὴν ἐπῳδὴν καλέσας. Καὶ τοῦτο δηλοῖ Σύμμαχος σαφέστερον οὕτω λέγων ᾠδὴν ἐπαδόντων.

7ᵇ. Ὁ Θεὸς συντρίψει τοὺς ὀδόντας αὐτῶν ἐν τῷ στόματι αὐτῶν. Εἰρηκὼς τὸν δόλον αὐτῶν καὶ τὴν κακίαν, ἐνταῦθα λοιπὸν τὴν καταληψομένην αὐτοὺς σημαίνει τιμωρίαν, — ἀεὶ δὲ τοὺς ὀδόντας ἐπὶ τῆς πολλῆς λαμβάνει 5 συν|τριβῆς. Τοῦτο κἀνταῦθά φησιν, ὅτι οὕτως αὐτῶν τὴν δύναμιν συντρίψει καὶ πάντας αὐτοὺς ἀναλώσει, ὡς μηδὲ τοὺς ὀδόντας αὐτῶν σώους ἐν αὐτοῖς καταλιπεῖν.

7ᵇ. Τὰς μύλας τῶν λεόντων συνέθλασεν Κύριος. Ἀντὶ τοῦ συνθλάσει, κατ' ἐναλλαγὴν χρόνου. Τοὺς δὲ ὀδόντας εἰπὼν καλῶς ἐπήγαγε τὰς μύλας, 10 μύλας καλῶν τοὺς ἐνδοτέρους τῶν ὀδόντων οἷς τὸ μύλου δίκην ἀλήθειν πρόσεστι τὴν τροφήν, — τοῦτο λέγων ὅτι καὶ τοὺς ἐνδοτέρους τῶν ὀδόντων συντρίψει, ἐπιτατικώτερον τὴν παρὰ τοῦ Θεοῦ τιμωρίαν σημᾶναι βουλόμενος. Λέοντας δὲ αὐτοὺς καλεῖ διὰ τὸ θρασὺ τοῦ τρόπου.

8ᵃ. Ἐξουδενωθήσονται ὡς ὕδωρ διαπορευόμενον. Οὕτω φησὶν ὑπὸ τῆς 15 τιμωρίας ἀναλωθήσονται καὶ εἰς οὐδὲν περιστήσονται, ὥσπερ τὸ ὕδωρ τὸ ἐπὶ τῆς γῆς ἐκχυθὲν συμποθὲν ἀναλίσκεταί τε καὶ ἀφανίζεται. Σύμμαχος δὲ οὕτω λέγει· Διαλυθήσονται ὡς ὕδωρ παρερχόμενον ἑαυτῷ· σαφέστερον γὰρ ἐδήλωσε τὸ λεγόμενον τῷ εἰπεῖν παρερχόμενον ἑαυτῷ. Ἔστι γὰρ ὕδωρ κατὰ γνώμην ἀνθρώπων πορευόμενον κατασκευάσμασί τισιν, ὅπερ οὐ πάν- 20 τως ἀναλίσκεται, φυλάττεται δὲ διὰ τῶν κατασκευαζομένων ὀχετῶν ἀγόμενον· τὸ δὲ οὕτω καὶ ἁπλῶς καὶ ὡς ἔτυχεν ἐπὶ τῆς γῆς ἐκχυθέν, τοῦτο καὶ συμποθὲν ἀναλίσκεται πάντως.

8ᵇ. Ἐντενεῖ τὸ τόξον αὐτοῦ ἕως οὗ ἀσθενήσουσιν. Ἐσχημάτισε τὴν τοῦ Θεοῦ τιμωρίαν ὡς ἐπὶ τόξου συνεχῶς πέμποντος τὰ βέλη καὶ πάντας ἀναι- 25

7ᵃ. Εἰρηκὼς — καταλιπεῖν: P, fol. 169; V, fol. 233; Cord, p. 136.   6 συντριβεῖς C 1ᵃ m.
7ᵇ. Ἀντὶ — τρόπου: P, fol. 169; V, fol. 233; Cord, p. 136.   9-10 ἀντὶ τοῦ — χρόνου om. Cord   11 μύλας] οὕτως Cord.
8ᵃ. Οὕτω φησιν — πάντως: P, fol. 169; V, fol. 233; Cord, p. 137.   17 ἐκχεθὲν C   18 δὲ om. Cord   18.19 ἐν ἑαυτῷ Cord   22 καὶ om. Cord · ἐκχεθὲν CV Cord.
8ᵇ. Ἐσχημάτισε — ἐργάσηται: P, fol. 169ᵛ; V, fol. 233ᵛ; Cord, p. 137 sub nomine ORIGENIS.

Aᵉ 5-6 (p. 305, 19-21): Moris est autem eius, ut quoties grauissimam significet ultionem etiam dentes adserat conterendos.   9-10 (p. 305, 22-24): Confringet possuit, more suo permotans tempora.   19-23 (p. 355, 26-29): Cuius natura est ut non consistat, nisi ab aliquo contineatur loco; quae, cum effunditur, illico exauritur consummaturque prursus.

clearly by reading "charm of the charmers."[4]

God will smash their teeth in their mouths (v. 6). Having mentioned their duplicity and wickedness, at this point he goes on to indicate the punishment overtaking them, always using *teeth* in the case of violent smashing. This is the meaning here too: He will thus *smash* their might and consume them all, so that not even their teeth will be left untouched in their mouths. *The Lord broke the lions' molars*—that is, will break (with a change of tense). It was right for him, after mentioning *teeth,* to go on to say *molars,* by *molars* referring to the interior teeth, which we have like a mill for grinding food. The meaning is, He will even smash the interior teeth (his intention being to suggest God's punishment more extensively). He refers to them as *lions* for the boldness of their behavior.

They will be reduced to nothing, like water running away (v. 7): they will be consumed by the punishment and will leave no trace, in the same manner as water poured out on the earth, which, when absorbed, is destroyed and disappears. In similar terms Symmachus says, "They will be dissolved like water running away by itself," indicating the meaning more clearly by saying "running away by itself." You see, water can travel in accord with people's intentions, thanks to certain preparations. Then it is not completely destroyed, but is preserved because it is conducted by specially prepared channels, whereas when it is simply poured out on the earth by chance, it is completely lost by being absorbed. *He will bend his bow, and they will languish.* He presented God's retribution as the bow constantly dispatching arrows and wiping everyone out; | God will employ the dispatch of arrows,

---

4. Theodore is dealing with "some of the most difficult phrases in the Psalter," in the words of Dahood (*Psalms,* 2:57), who has to have recourse to Ugaritic to find a way through (Symmachus and "some commentators" being the only recourse for Theodore). Some commentators wanted to combine "drug" with the enclitic τε and read it as a verb form, "it is drugged," and apply it to the asp by making the original participle feminine; unlike Theodoret, Theodore will not accept that reading.

ρούντος· μέχρι γὰρ τοσούτου φησὶ ταῖς ἀφέσεσι χρήσεται τῶν βελῶν, μέχρις ἂν πάντας κατατοξεύων ἐκδαπανήσῃ καὶ | ἀσθενεῖς ἐργάσηται.

9ᵃ. Ὡσεὶ κηρὸς τακεὶς ἀνταναιρεθήσονται. Ἀντὶ τοῦ ἀπωλοῦνται, ἀφανισθήσονται ὡς κηρὸς ὑπὸ πυρὸς τηκόμενος καὶ εἰς τὸ μηδὲν περιϊστάμενος.

·5 Ταῖς δὲ ὁμοιώσεσι κέχρηται διαφόραις εἰς παράστασιν αὐτῶν τῆς ἀπωλείας, ἄνω μὲν ὡς ὕδωρ εἰπών, ἐνταῦθα δὲ ὡσεὶ κηρός, δι' ἀμφοτέρων δὲ τὸν ἀφανισμὸν αὐτῶν σημαίνων.

9ᵇ. Ἔπεσεν πῦρ ἐπ' αὐτούς, καὶ οὐκ εἶδον τὸν ἥλιον. Καλῶς πῦρ ἐνταῦθα τοῦ Θεοῦ τὴν ὀργὴν ἐκάλεσεν· ἐπειδὴ γὰρ εἶπεν ὡς κηρός (κηροῦ δὲ ἴδιον 10 τὸ πυρὶ τήκεσθαι) καλῶς ἐπήγαγε τὸ ἔπεσεν πῦρ ἐπ' αὐτούς. Ὥσπερ πῦρ ἐπ' αὐτοὺς ἐπενεχθὲν τήκει καὶ μειοῖ τὸν κηρόν, οὕτως ἡ τοῦ Θεοῦ ὀργὴ ἐπενεχθεῖσα ἅπαντας ἀφανίσει. Τὸ δὲ οὐκ εἶδον τὸν ἥλιον, ἀντὶ τοῦ ἀπώλοντο, ἀνῃρέθησαν· τῶν γὰρ τελευτώντων ἴδιον τὸ μηκέτι τοῦ ἡλιακοῦ φωτὸς ἀπολαύειν.

15 **10.** Πρὸ τοῦ συνιέναι τὰς ἀκάνθας ὑμῶν τὴν ῥάμνον, ὡσεὶ ζῶντας ὡσεὶ ἐν ὀργῇ καταπίεται ὑμᾶς. Σύμμαχος σαφέστερόν φησι Πρὶν ἢ αὐξήσουσιν αἱ ἄκανθαι ὑμῶν, ὥστε γενέσθαι ῥάμνον, ἔτι ζῶντας ὡς ὁλόξηρον λαίλαψ ἀρεῖ. Ῥάμνον ἡ θεία γραφὴ καλεῖ τὴν μεγάλην ἄκανθαν καὶ λευκήν, ἣ καὶ δένδρῳ παραπλησία διὰ τὸ μέγεθος· ἔστι δὲ καὶ ξηρὰ κατὰ φύσιν, καὶ 20 βραχύ τι πυρὸς ὀσφρανθεῖσα εὐθὺς καταναλίσκεται. Τοῦτο οὖν βούλεται εἰπεῖν ὅτι αἱ ἄκανθαι ὑμῶν — ἄκανθαν γὰρ καλεῖ τὴν πονηρίαν διὰ τὸ πληκτικὸν καὶ ἐπιβουλευτικόν ✱✱✱ Πρὶν ἢ οὖν φησι τὴν πο|νηρίαν ὑμῶν εἰς ἔργον ἐκβῆναι, αὐξηθεῖσαν ταῖς ἐπινοίαις καὶ μείζονα γενομένην, ὑμᾶς ἔτι στρεφομένους ἐν τοῖς κακοῖς καὶ δοκοῦντας ζῆν τε καὶ κινεῖσθαι ἐν αὐτοῖς,

---

1 γὰρ om. C   χρῆται Cord   2 ἐκδαπανήσῃ καὶ om. Cord.

9ᵃ. Ἀντὶ τοῦ — σημαίνων: P, fol. 169ʳ·ᵛ; V, fol. 233ᵛ; ταῖς ὁμοιώσεσι κ. τ. λ. affert Cord, p. 137 (anon.).   5 διαφόρως CPV   τῆς αὐτῶν Cord   6 ἄνωθεν Cord ὡσεὶ] ὡς CPV   δὲ om. Cord.

9ᵇ. Καλῶς — ἀπολαύειν: P, fol. 169ᵛ; V, fol. 233ᵛ; Cord, p. 138.   10 τὸ πῦρ Cord 11 ἐπ' αὐτοὺς om. Cord   12-14 L (p. 127, 46-48): Τὸ δὲ Οὐκ εἶδον τὸν ἥλιον ἀπὸ μεταφορᾶς τῶν θνησκόντων εἶπεν, ἐπεὶ κἀκεῖνοι ἀποθανόντες οὐχ ὁρῶσι τὸν ἥλιον.

10. Σύμμαχος — καταναλώσασα: P, fol. 170; V, fol. 234ᵛ; Σύμμαχος — 18 ἀρεῖ affert Cord, p. 138; sequentia (Ῥάμνον — καταναλώσασα) in pp. 138-139 sub lemmate Ἀνωνύμου.   20-21 τοῦτο οὖν — ὑμῶν om. Cord   21 γὰρ] δὲ Cord   22 ἐπιβουλευτικὸν lacunam statui   23 ὑμᾶς om. CPV.

Aᵉ 5 (p. 306, 1-2): Variis conparationibus iniquorum significat interitum. 8-9 (p. 306, 3-4): Pro ultione ignem.   21-22 (p. 306, 9-12): Vulnificamque spinam, id est perfectam malitiam *ramnum* dicit, quod non solum ui sed etiam quantitate potior est.

he is saying, until by shooting them all down he will waste them and render them weak.

They will be dissolved like melting wax (v. 8): they will perish; they will disappear like wax melted by fire, with nothing left. He uses these different comparisons to present their destruction, speaking of them above as water and here as wax, indicating in both their disappearance. *Fire fell on them, and they did not see the sun.* By *fire* here he did well to refer to God's wrath: since he had said *like wax* (it being typical of wax to be melted by fire), he did well to add the clause *Fire fell on them.* Just as fire directed at them melts and reduces the wax, so God's wrath directed at them makes them all disappear. The phrase *they did not see the sun* means that they perished, they were destroyed, since it is the fate of the dead no longer to enjoy the sun's light.

Before your thorns feel the bramble, as living, as in anger he will swallow you (v. 9). Symmachus says more clearly, "Before your thorns grow up to become a bramble, still living, as a cyclone snatches away a dry thing."[5] By *bramble* the divine Scripture refers to the large white thorn, even resembling a tree in size; it is naturally dry, and with the slightest suspicion of fire it is burnt up. So he means, Your thorns (by *thorn* referring to their wickedness because scratching and malicious ...). So before your wickedness takes effect, increasing with its schemes and growing larger, while you are still involved in the evils and give the appearance of living and being active in them, | God's retribution will fall on you like fire, wipe you all out, and con-

5. It is a verse that, in the Hebrew, Dahood (*Psalms,* 2:62) declares to be "unintelligible."

δίκην πυρὸς ἐπιπεσοῦσα τοῦ Θεοῦ ἡ τιμωρία πάντας ἀφανίσει καὶ κατα-
ναλώσει. Τὸ οὖν πρὶν ⟨ἢ⟩ αὐξήσουσιν εἶπεν πρὸ τοῦ συνιέναι, ἀντὶ τοῦ
Πρὸ τοῦ κἂν εἰς ἔννοιαν λαβεῖν ὑμᾶς τὴν πονηρίαν καὶ τὴν καθ᾽ ἡμῶν ἐπιβουλὴν εἰς αὔξηκτιν ἀγαγεῖν, φθάσει ὑμᾶς ἡ τοῦ Θεοῦ τιμωρία καταναλώσασα. 5

11ᵃ. Εὐφρανθήσεται δίκαιος ὅταν ἴδῃ ἐκδίκησιν. Ἡ δὲ εἰς ὑμᾶς φησι τιμωρία εὐφροσύνην παρέξει τοῖς δικαίοις, τοῖς νῦν ὑφ᾽ ὑμῶν ἐπιβουλευομένοις.

11ᵇ. Τὰς χεῖρας αὐτοῦ νίψεται ἐν τῷ αἵματι τοῦ ἁμαρτωλοῦ. Τὸ νίπτεσθαι ἡ θεία γραφὴ συνεχῶς λαμβάνει ἐπὶ τοῦ ἢ κοινωνεῖν τινι ἢ μὴ
κοινωνεῖν· τοῦτο γὰρ ἔθος τοῖς παλαιοῖς διὰ τοῦ νίπτεσθαι τὰς χεῖ- 10
ρας σημαίνειν ὁπότερον ἂν ἐβούλοντο. Οὕτω καὶ Πιλᾶτος ἐν τοῖς εὐαγγελίοις φαίνεται τῷ νίψασθαι τὰς χεῖρας σημαίνων ὅτι μὴ κοινωνῇ τῷ φόνῳ
τῷ κατὰ τοῦ Χριστοῦ. Οὕτω καὶ ἑτέρωθί φησιν ὁ μακάριος Δαυὶδ Νίψομαι
ἐν ἀθῴοις τὰς χεῖράς μου, τουτέστι τὴν πρὸς αὐτοὺς ἀσπάσομαι κοινωνίαν.
Ἐνταῦθα οὖν τοῦτο λέγει, ὅτι ὁ δίκαιος ἐν τῇ σφαγῇ καὶ τῷ θανάτῳ τοῦ 15
ἁμαρτωλοῦ διειχθήσεται μηδεμίαν ἔχων πρὸς αὐτοὺς κοινωνίαν, τουτέστιν
ἀποφανθήσεται δίκαιος. Ὅταν γὰρ ἐκεῖνοι διὰ τούτων κολάζωνται, οὗτοι
δὲ μένωσι μηδὲν πάσχοντες, δείκνυται τούτων ἡ ἀρετή.

12ᵃ. Καὶ ἐρεῖ ἄνθρωπος εἰ ἄρα ἐστὶν καρπὸς τῷ δικαίῳ. Τινὲς τὸ ἄρα
ἐστὶν καρπὸς τῷ δικαίῳ κατ᾽ ἐρώτησιν ἀνέγνωσαν, ὡσανεὶ πυνθανομένων ὅτι 20

11 Matth. XXVII, 24   13 Ps. XXV, 6.

1-2 καταλώσει C   2 ἢ supplevi.
11ᵃ. Ἡ δὲ εἰς ὑμᾶς — ἐπιβουλευομένοις : P, fol. 170ᵛ; V, fol. 234ᵛ; Cord, p. 139
(P. G., 677 D 1-3).
11ᵇ. Τὸ νίπτεσθαι – ἀρετή: P, fol. 170ᵛ; V, fol. 235; Cord, p. 140 (P. G., 677 D
4-680 A 4).   11 σημαίνει CPV   10-13 cf. L (p. 128, 19-23) : ...ἔθος τοῖς παλαιοῖς·
ἐφ᾽ ὧν πράξεων ἀκοινωνήτους ἑαυτοὺς παρῆν ποιεῖν, ὕδατι ἀπονίπτεσθαι, ὡς Πιλᾶτος ἐπὶ
τοῦ Κυρίου, δι᾽ οὗ ἐδείκνυ ἑαυτὸν μὴ κοινωνεῖν ἐθέλοντα τῇ τοῦ δικαίου ἀναιρέσει   13 τῷ
om. Cord   15 ὁ om. C Cord   16 ἔχειν Cord.
12ᵃ. Τινὲς τὸ ἄρα — αὐτοῖς: P, fol. 170ᵛ; V, fol. 235ᵛ; Cord, p. 140 (P. G.,
680 A 6-13).   20 ἀνέγνωσεν Cord.

Aᵉ 3-5 (p. 306, 15-16): ...priusquam in opus erumpat intentio, praeueniens
indignatio eius depopulabitur.   11ᵃ (p. 306, 18-20): Impiorum prolata autem
in eos ultio, inquit, gaudium iustis praebebit, quibus uidilicet tendebatis insidias.   8-14 (p. 306, 27-32): Ablutio manuum quippe in Scripturis consensum
indicat respuere impiorum et in commonem uenire innocentium, quod et Pilatus fecit; et Dauid pullicens gratulatur: *Lauabo inter innocentes manus meas.*
12ᵃ (p. 306, 34-307, 5): Determinatorie legendum, dubitatione exclusa; est prursus: Deus, qui agit curam piorum et omne quod erga eos est iusta lance dispo-
nit, ulciscaturque illos qui uexare cupiunt innocentes.

sume you. Hence his saying "Before they grow up" for *Before they feel*—that is, Before you take account of the wickedness and bring the plot against us to fruition, God's retribution will anticipate you and consume you.

The righteous will rejoice on seeing vindication (v. 10): your punishment will bring joy to the righteous, those up till now the object of your schemes. *He will wash his hands in the blood of the sinner.* The divine Scripture usually applies *wash* in the case of sharing or not sharing, it being the custom of the ancients to indicate whichever they intended by *washing hands.* Thus Pilate in the Gospels is also seen to wash his hands to suggest that he has no share in the killing of Christ.[6] Thus also elsewhere blessed David says, "I shall wash my hands among innocent people"[7]—that is, I shall enter into sharing with them. So here he means, The righteous person will be shown to have no share with them in the slaughter and death of the sinner—that is, he will be revealed as just; in other words, when those people are punished in this way while these will continue to suffer nothing, their virtue will be proven.

Someone will say, Surely there is some benefit for the righteous (v. 11). Some commentators have read *Surely there is some benefit for the righteous* as a question, as if there were an inquiry. | Is there? It is our custom in argu-

---

6. Cf. Matt 27:24.
7. Ps 26:6.

Εἰ ἔστιν ἄρα; ὅπερ ἔθος ἡμῖν ἐν τοῖς συλλογισμοῖς λέγειν, — εἰ μὴ τόδε, ἄρα τόδε, ἀντὶ τοῦ οὐκοῦν τόδε. Οὕτω κἀνταῦθα λέγει ὅτι Τούτων γενομένων, πάντες ἐροῦσιν ὅτι ἀληθῶς ἐστι τῷ δικαίῳ καρπὸς καὶ οὐκ ἀμισθὶ τὴν δικαιοσύνην ἐργάζεται· ἰδοὺ γὰρ ὑπὸ τούτων ἐτιμωρήθησαν οἱ ἐπιβου-
5 λεύοντες αὐτοῖς.

12ᵇ. Ἄρα ἐστὶν ὁ Θεὸς κρίνων αὐτοῖς ἐν τῇ γῇ. Κατ᾽ ἀπόφασιν καὶ τοῦτο, ἀντὶ τοῦ Ἀληθῶς ἐστιν ὁ ἐπιμελόμενος αὐτῶν Θεὸς καὶ δικάζων μὲν αὐτοῖς ἀδικουμένοις ἐπὶ τῆς γῆς, τιμωρούμενος δὲ τοὺς τολμῶντας αὐτοὺς ἀδικεῖν. Τινὲς δὲ κρίνων αὐτοὺς ἀνέγνωσαν· οὐκ ἔστιν δέ, ἀλλὰ κρίνων
10 αὐτοῖς. Ἐκείνως μὲν γὰρ εἰ λέγοιτο κατακρίνων σημαίνει, οὑτωσὶ δὲ δικάζων αὐτούς, ἀντὶ τοῦ ἐπαμύνων αὐτοῖς ἀδικουμένοις. Ἐπεσημηνάμεθα δὲ πολλαχοῦ ὅτι ὅταν ἐπὶ τῆς ἐκδικήσεως λέγῃ ἐπὶ τῆς δοτικῆς ἐκφωνεῖ πτώσεως Αὐτοῖς κρῖνον, ἐμοὶ κρῖνον, αὐτῷ κρῖνον καὶ ὅσα τοιαῦτα· ὅταν δὲ τὸ ἐναντίον λέγῃ τὸ κρίνειν καὶ καταδικάζειν, τότε λέγει ἐπὶ τῆς
15 αἰτιατικῆς πτώσεως ἢ αὐτούς, ἢ εἴ τι τοιοῦτον, — ὡς ὅταν λέγῃ Κρῖνον αὐτούς, ὁ Θεός, ἀντὶ τοῦ Κατάκρινον καὶ τιμώρησον.

PSALMVS LVIII

Τὰ κατὰ τοὺς Μακκαβαίους καὶ ἐν τῷ μετὰ χεῖρας προαγορεύει ψαλμῷ, ὡς ἐκ τοῦ ἐκείνων προσώπου λέγων ἅπερ εἰπεῖν αὐτοῖς ἥρμοττεν ἐν θλί-
20 ψεσί τε πολλαῖς ἐξεταζομένοις καὶ τῆς τοῦ Θεοῦ δεομένοις βοηθείας.

2ᵃ. Ἐξελοῦ με ἐκ τῶν ἐχθρῶν μου, ὁ Θεός. Ἀπάλλαξόν με αὐτῶν τῆς ἐπιβουλῆς.

2ᵇ. Καὶ ἐκ τῶν ἐπανισταμένων ἐπ᾽ ἐμὲ λύτρωσαί με. Ἤτοι τὸ αὐτὸ λέγει, συνηθῶς ἑαυτῷ πλατύνων τὸ λεγόμενον τῇ δευτερώσει, ἢ ἐπανιστα-
25 μένους τοὺς ἰδίους καλῶν.

11-16 cf. p. 55, 11-17   15-16 Ps. V, 11.

1 εἰ om. CPV   2 ἄρα τόδε om. Cord   4 ἐργάζονται CPV.
12ᵇ. Κατ᾽ ἀπόφασιν — τιμώρησον: P, fol. 171; V, fol. 235ᵛ.   7-9 affert L
(p. 141, 33-36): Ἔστιν οὖν ἀληθῶς ὁ ἐπιμελόμενος τῶν δικαίων Θεὸς — ἀδικεῖν.
Τὰ κατὰ — βοηθείας: P, fol. 171ᵛ; V, fol. 235ᵛ; Cord, p. 152.
2ᵃ. Ἀπάλλαξον — ἐπιβουλῆς: P, fol. 172; V, fol. 236.
2ᵇ. Ἤτοι — καλῶν: P, fol. 172; V, fol. 236ᵛ.

Aᵉ Argumentum ps. LVIII (p. 307, 8-11): Hic etiam psalmus in personam Machabeorum formatur (cf. Pseudo-Beda 786) per oportunitatem eius precis, quam in sua erumna conpossuit.   2ᵃ (p. 307, 12-13): Libera me, inquit, ab eorum fraudibus.   2ᵇ (p. 307, 13-15): ... uel geminauit suo more dictionem, uel insurgentes in se ciues appellat.

mentation to say, If not this, then this—that is, therefore this. Likewise, here too the meaning is, When this happens, everyone will say, There really is a benefit for the righteous, and he does not practice righteousness without reward, for, behold, those scheming against them were punished by them. *Surely it is God who judges in their favor on the earth.* This too is a statement, meaning, God really does care for them and judge in favor of those wronged on the earth while punishing those guilty of wronging them. Some commentators have read "judging them"; that is not the reading, however, but *judging in their favor:* if it were expressed that way, it would mean "condemning," just as "giving them the verdict" means "assisting those wronged." We often have indicated that when the text refers to justification, it uses the dative case: Judge in their favor, in my favor, in his favor, and so on; but when "judge" and "condemn" mean the opposite, then it uses the accusative case: Judge them, or the like, as when it says, "Judge them, O God,"[8] meaning, Condemn and punish.

PSALM 59

The fortunes of the Maccabees he prophesies also in the present psalm, telling from their viewpoint what suited them to say when experiencing great tribulations and needing God's help. *Deliver me from my foes, O God* (v. 1): free me from their scheming. *And redeem me from those rising up against me.* He obviously says the same thing, as usual amplifying the sentiment by repetition, or referring to his own people as *those rising up.* | *Rescue me*

---

8. Ps 5:10. Theodore made this point in comment also on Ps 54:1.

3ª. Ῥῦσαί με ἐκ τῶν ἐργαζομένων τὴν ἀνομίαν. Ὁπόταν ἐχθρῶν ὁ μακάριος μέμνηται Δαυίδ, εἴτε ὑπὲρ ἑαυτοῦ λέγων εἴτε καὶ ὑπὲρ ἑτέρων, μέμνηται καὶ ὡς ἁμαρτωλῶν ἢ ὡς ἁμαρτίαν ἐργαζομένων, δεικνὺς τῶν ἐχθρῶν τὸν τρόπον — ὡς ἂν ἐντεῦθεν αὐτὸς δὲ δικαίως αἰτεῖν νομίζοιτο τοῦ Θεοῦ τὴν βοήθειαν, κἀκεῖνοι διὰ τὸν τρόπον τῆς τιμωρίας ἄξιοι φαίνοιντο. Οὐκοῦν 5 ἀπάλλαξόν μέ φησι τούτων ἢ τῶν ὅτι κάκιστον πραττόντων.

3ᵇ. Καὶ ἐξ ἀνδρῶν αἱμάτων σῶσόν με. Καὶ ἀπάλλαξόν με τούτων τῶν φονικωτάτων τῆς ἐπιβουλῆς, — ἄνδρας αἱμάτων τοὺς φονεῖς λέγων.

4ª. Ὅτι ἰδοὺ ἐθήρευσαν τὴν ψυχήν μου. Σπουδὴν ἔθεντο ὥστε με συλλαβόμενοι ἀνελεῖν τε καὶ ἀφελέσθαι τὴν ψυχήν· ἴδιον γὰρ τῶν θηρευτῶν 10 τὸ μετὰ πολλῆς συλλαμβάνειν τὰ ἀγρευόμενα τῆς σπουδῆς.

4ᵇ. Ἐπέθεντο ἐπ᾽ ἐμὲ κραταιοί. Οὐκ ἐκ᾽ παρέργου φησὶ τὴν πρὸς ἐμὲ μάχην ἐνίστανται, ἀλλ᾽ ἐπίκεινται μὴ βραχὺν ἐνδιδόντες καιρόν, παντὶ δὲ τρόπῳ πολεμοῦντες ἡμᾶς. Κραταιοὺς δὲ εἶπεν, ὥστε καὶ ἀπὸ τῆς προσούσης αὐτοῖς ἰσχύος μείζονα δεῖξαι τὴν κατ᾽ αὐτοῦ ἐπιβουλήν. 15

4ᶜ. Οὔτε ἡ ἀνομία μου, οὔτε ἡ ἁμαρτία μου. Καίτοι φησὶν οὐδὲν ἐμαυτῷ συνῄδειν πλημμέλημα, ὃ τούτων αἴτιόν ἐστιν καὶ ὑπὲρ οὗ δικαίως ἐγκαλοῦντες, τοσαῦτα ποιοῦσιν. Τοῦτο δὲ οὐχ ὡς πρὸς τὸν Θεὸν λέγει, ἀλλ᾽ ὡς πρὸς ἐκείνους, ὅτι μηδὲν ἠδικημένοι τοιαῦτα διέθηκαν ἡμᾶς. Σύμμαχος δὲ σαφέστερόν φησιν ἀναιτίους καὶ ἀναμαρτήτους. 20

5ª. Κύριε, ἄνευ ἀνομίας ἔδραμον καὶ κατεύθυνα. Καὶ τοῦτο Σύμμαχος σαφέστερόν φησι Μὴ οὔσης ἁμαρτίας, ἐπιτρέχουσιν ἵνα πατάξωσί με. Οὐκ ἔχοντες περὶ τίνος ἐγκαλεῖν, σὺν πολλῇ τῇ προθυμίᾳ καταδιώκουσιν καὶ τῷ πλείστῳ δὲ μέρει κατορθοῦσι τὸ σπουδαζόμενον. Βούλεται δὲ δεῖξαι διὰ πολλῶν ὀξυτάτην ὀφείλοντα λαβεῖν ἑαυτῷ παρὰ τοῦ Θεοῦ τὴν βοή- 25 θειαν, ὅτι ἄδικοι οἱ πολεμοῦντες, ὅτι φονικοὶ τὸν τρόπον οὐ φείσασθαι

3ª. Ὁπόταν — πραττόντων: P, fol. 172; V, fol. 236ᵛ.
3ᵇ. Καὶ ἀπάλλαξον — λέγων: P, fol. 172; V, fol. 236ᵛ. 8 λέγω C.
4ª. Σπουδὴν — σπουδῆς: P, fol. 172ᵛ; V, fol. 236ᵛ; Cord, p. 154.
4ᵇ. Οὐκ ἐκ παρέργου — ἐπιβουλήν: P, fol. 172ᵛ; V, fol. 236ᵛ; Cord, p. 154 sub nomine ORIGENIS. 14 πολεμοῦντας C.
4ᶜ. Καίτοι — ἀναμαρτήτους: P, fol. 172ᵛ; V, fol. 236ᵛ.
5ª. Καὶ τοῦτό — φησι: P, fol. 173; V, fol. 237; Cord, p. 155. 26 οὐδὲ Cord.

Aᵉ **3ᵇ** (p. 307, 20-21): Cruoris auidis, in quibus studium interfectionis arderet. **4ª** (p. 307, 22-24): Insidiati sunt ut caperent necarentque captum. 19 (p. 307, 30-31): Sine iniquitate, quibus nihil peccauerit.

from those who commit iniquity (v. 2). Whenever blessed David mentions foes, speaking of them in connection with himself or with others, he mentions them as sinners or as committing sin, thus highlighting the foes' behavior so that as a result he personally may be thought to be within his rights in appealing for God's help and they may appear to deserve punishment on account of their behavior—hence his saying, Free me from them or from those acting as badly as possible. *And save me from men of blood:* and free me from the scheming of these murderers (calling the murderers *men of blood*).

Because, lo, they hunted down my soul (v. 3): they took pains to apprehend me, do away with me, and destroy my soul (it being typical of hunters to apprehend the quarry painstakingly). *Strong men beset me:* far from engaging me in battle idly, they spent no little time in harassing us, waging war against us in every manner. He called them *strong men* so as to depict more boldly the plot against him by mention also of the might they possessed. *There was no iniquity of mine, no sin of mine:* they do such things despite my being aware of no fault as a cause of this for which they could accuse me. Now, he addresses this not to God but to them, namely, It was not that they had been wronged when they took this attitude to us. Symmachus says more clearly "guiltless and sinless." *Lord, free of iniquity I proceeded and directed my steps* (v. 4). Symmachus says this more clearly as well: "Though there was no sin, they run after me to strike me." Though they have no grounds for censure, he is saying, they pursue me with great enthusiasm and to a great extent achieve their goal. He intends to bring out in many ways that he needs to receive help from God very rapidly because the assailants are unjust, because in their bloodthirsty ways they are incapable of pity, | because their strength is so great that it is impossible for them to fail,

δυνάμενοι, ὅτι μεγάλοι τὴν ῥώμην ὥστε μηδὲ ἐνδέχεσθαι διαμαρτεῖν, ὅτι ἀναιτίως τὴν πρὸς αὐτὸν ἐνίστανται μάχην, τὸ μεῖζον ὅτι τῷ πλείστῳ μέρει καὶ περιγεγόνασι | κατορθώσαντες τὸ σπουδαζόμενον. Τί οὖν λοιπόν φησι;

5   5ᵇ. Ἐξεγέρθητι εἰς συνάντησίν μοι καὶ ἴδε. Τινὲς εἰς συνάντησίν μου ἀνέγνωσαν· ἔχει δὲ οὐχ οὕτως. Οὐδὲ γὰρ εἰς ἀπάντησιν ἑαυτοῦ τὸν Θεὸν βοηθεῖν καλεῖ, λέγει δὲ εἰς συνάντησίν μοι· ὥσπερ γὰρ τὸ κρῖνόν μοι ὅταν λέγῃ, ἀντὶ τοῦ ἐμοὶ κρῖνον καὶ ὑπὲρ ἐμοῦ, οὕτω καὶ εἰς συνάντησίν μοι ὑπὲρ ἐμοῦ φησι καὶ ὑπὲρ τῆς εἰς ἐμὲ βοηθείας ἀπάντησον αὐτοῖς ἐρχομέ-
10 νοις εἰς τὸν κατ᾽ ἐμοῦ πόλεμον, καὶ θεασάμενος αὐτῶν τὴν ἀτοπίαν διακώλυσον αὐτοὺς τὸ σπουδαζόμενον εἰς πέρας ἀγαγεῖν. Σύμμαχος δὲ αὐτὸ σαφέστερον εἶπεν Ἐξ ἐναντίας ὑπὲρ ἐμοῦ, ἀντὶ τοῦ ἐξ ἐναντίας τῶν ἐχθρῶν ἔπελθε ὑπὲρ ἐμοῦ, σωματικώτερον αὐτὸ εἰπὼν ἐκ μεταφορᾶς τῶν τοῖς πολέμοις ἀπαντώντων πολλάκις καὶ ἐκκοπτόντων αὐτοῖς τὴν ὁρμήν.

15 6ᵃ·ᵇ. Καὶ σύ, Κύριε ὁ Θεὸς τῶν δυνάμεων, ὁ Θεὸς τοῦ Ἰσραήλ, πρόσχες τοῦ ἐπισκέψασθαι πάντα τὰ ἔθνη. Σὺ γάρ τοί φησιν, ὁ τῶν ἁπάντων δεσπότης καὶ ἡμῶν Θεός, ποιῆσαι δὴ ἐπίσκεψιν ἁπάντων τῶν ἐθνῶν καὶ ἐξέτασιν, καὶ τοῦ δικαίου γενόμενος κριτὴς τιμώρησαι τοὺς τὸν τρόπον μοχθηρούς.

6ᶜ. Μὴ οἰκτειρήσῃς πάντας τοὺς ἐργαζομένους τὴν ἀνομίαν. Ἐπισκεψά-
20 μενος δέ φησι καὶ ἐξετάσας τὰ κατὰ τοὺς ἀνθρώπους, οὓς ἂν εὕρης ἀδικοῦντας καὶ ἁμαρτάνοντας κόλασον μηδενὸς φεισάμενος, μηδενὶ χαρισάμενος.

7. Ἐπιστρέψουσιν εἰς ἑσπέραν καὶ λιμώξουσιν ὡς κύων, καὶ κυκλώσουσι πόλιν. Ἐναλλαγὴ κἀνταῦθα χρόνου, ἀντὶ τοῦ Ἐπιστρεψάτωσαν, καὶ λιμωξάτωσαν, καὶ κυκλωσάτωσαν. Ὃ δὲ λέγει τοιοῦτόν ἐστιν. Ἐπειδὴ τῶν κυνῶν

---

7 cf. supra in Ps. IX, 20 (p. 55, 13).

1 ὥστε — διαμαρτεῖν om. Cord   4 Cord add. (p. 155-156): Τῶν προειρημένων ἐχθρῶν ἐμμενόντων τῇ κατ᾽ ἐμοῦ σπουδῇ, ἐξεγερθεὶς συνάντησον εἰς τὸ βοηθῆσαί μοι, μηκέτι μακροθυμῶν ἐπ᾽ αὐτοῖς.
5ᵇ. Τινὲς — ὁρμήν: P, fol. 173; V, fol. 237.   12 εἰπεῖν C.
6ᵃ·ᵇ. Σὺ γάρ τοί φησιν — μοχθηρούς: P, fol. 173; V, fol. 237.
6ᶜ. Ἐπισκεψάμενος — χαρισάμενος: P, fol. 173ᵛ; fol. 237ᵛ.
7. Ἐναλλαγὴ — ἑσπέραν: P, fol. 173ᵛ; V, fol. 238; Cord, p. 157 (P. G., 680 AB).

Aᵉ 11-12 (p. 307, 35-308, 1): Vel, ut Symmachus dicit, *Exsurge et e contrario pro me occurre insurgentibus*.   6ᶜ (p. 308, 2-3): Vt iniqua sectantes subiecias ultioni.

because they have no grounds for rising to battle, and most of all because to a large extent they even manage to achieve their goal.

What now, then? *Arise to a meeting for me and see.* Some commentators have read "to my meeting," but it is not so: instead of calling God to help with an encounter of his own, he says *to a meeting for me.* In other words, just as when he says, Judge in my favor, in the sense of "judging for me and on behalf of me," so too by *to a meeting for me* he means, For me and with a view to helping me encounter those advancing to make war on me, and on perceiving their mischief prevent them from putting their purpose into effect. Symmachus said the same thing more clearly: "In opposition on my behalf"—that is, In opposition to the foe advance on my behalf (using a rather corporeal analogy from those who frequently encounter the enemy and check their advance). *Lord God of hosts, God of Israel, take the trouble to survey all the nations* (v. 5): you who are Lord of all and our God, conduct a survey and examination of all the nations, prove to be a judge of righteousness and punish those of depraved habits. *Have pity on none of the workers of iniquity:* survey and examine people's affairs, and punish those you find guilty of injustice and sin, sparing none, favoring none.

In the evening they will return; they will be as hungry as dogs, and will go around the city (v. 6). There is a change of mood here, too, for "let them return," "let them go hungry," and "let them go around." What he means is something like this: Since it is characteristic of dogs | to roam the entire

ἴδιον κατὰ τὸν τῆς νυκτὸς καιρὸν περιϊέναι τε τὴν πόλιν ἄπασαν καὶ μεί-
ζοσι κεχρῆσθαι ταῖς φωναῖς, — ποιοῦσι δὲ αὐτὸ μάλιστα ἐπειδὰν συμβαίνῃ
καὶ πεινῆν δεηθέντας τροφῆς, — τοιοῦτό τι περὶ τῶν ἐχθρῶν φησι. Μετα-
στραφήτωσαν ἀπὸ τῆς νῦν εὐπραγίας εἰς τὸ χεῖρον τῇ παρά σου τιμωρίᾳ·
καὶ ὥσπερ κύνες κατὰ τὸν καιρὸν τῆς νυκτὸς ὑπὸ λιμοῦ συνεχόμενοι κύκλῳ 5
βοῶντες τὴν πόλιν ἐκπεριϊάσιν, οὕτω καὶ οὗτοι τῇ παρά σου τιμωρίᾳ πλη-
γέντες ὀλολυζέτωσαν ὅμοια τοῖς κυσίν, ὥστε καὶ τὴν φωνὴν τῶν ὀλολυγῶν
φαίνεσθαι τῆς τιμωρίας σου τῆς εἰς αὐτοὺς τὸ μέγεθος. Τὴν δὲ ἐναλλαγὴν
τοῦ χρόνου δείκνυσι Σύμμαχος εἰπὼν Ἐπιστρεψάτωσαν εἰς ἑσπέραν.

8. Ἰδοὺ αὐτοὶ ἀποφθέγξονται ἐν τῷ στόματι αὐτῶν, καὶ ῥομφαία ἐν τοῖς 10
χείλεσιν αὐτῶν. Κἀνταῦθα τὸ Ἰδοὺ προσέρριπται ἀπὸ τοῦ ἑβραϊκοῦ ἰδιώματος. Σύμμαχος δέ φησιν Αὐτοὶ μὲν ἀποβλύζουσιν τοῖς στόμασιν ἑαυτῶν, καὶ
ὡς μαχαίρας | τοῖς χείλεσιν αὐτῶν. Κἀνταῦθα γὰρ ἐνήλλαξε τὸν χρόνον, μέλ-
λοντα εἰρηκὼς ἀντὶ τοῦ ἐνεστῶτος· αὐτοὶ γάρ φησι φθέγγονται ῥήματα διὰ
τοῦ στόματος αὐτῶν καὶ τῶν χειλέων πάσης χείρονα μαχαίρας καὶ παντὸς 15
ξίφους εὐτονώτερον πλήττειν δυνάμενα. Ποῖα δὲ ταῦτα;

9ᵃ. Ὅτι τίς ἤκουσεν; Ἀντὶ τοῦ Οὐδείς. Ἔστι δὲ κἀνταῦθα τὸ «λέγοντες» ἀπὸ κοινοῦ νοούμενον ὡς κατὰ ἀποσιώπησιν εἰρημένον τῷ προφήτῃ,
οἷον καὶ ἐν τῷ δευτέρῳ ψαλμῷ τὸ Παρέστησαν οἱ βασιλεῖς τῆς γῆς καὶ οἱ
ἄρχοντες συνήχθησαν ἐπὶ τὸ αὐτὸ κατὰ τοῦ κυρίου καὶ κατὰ τοῦ χριστοῦ 20
αὐτοῦ, διαρρήξωμεν τοὺς δεσμοὺς αὐτῶν, καὶ ἀπορρίψωμεν ἀφ' ἡμῶν τὸν
ζυγὸν αὐτῶν· ἀπὸ κοινοῦ γὰρ κἀκεῖ κατὰ ἀποσιώπησιν νοεῖται τὸ «λέγοντες», ἵνα ᾖ Λέγοντες Διαρρήξωμεν τοὺς δεσμοὺς αὐτῶν. Οὕτως οὖν κἀνταῦθά φησιν Ἰδοὺ αὐτοὶ ἀποφθέγξονται ἐν τῷ στόματι αὐτῶν, καὶ ῥομφαία
ἐν τοῖς χείλεσι αὐτῶν, ὅτι τίς ἤκουσεν; 25

Ἀκριβέστερον δὲ ἐν τῷ μδ´ ψαλμῷ ἐπεσημηνάμεθα ὡς ἔθος τῷ προφήτῃ
τὸ «εἶπεν» καὶ «λέγων» καὶ εἴ τι τοιοῦτον κατὰ ἀποσιώπησιν τιθέναι.
Βούλεται γὰρ περὶ αὐτῶν εἰπεῖν ὅτι φασὶν Οὐ προσῆκε δεδιέναι τινὰ τιμω-

19-21 Ps. II, 2-3   26 cf. supra p. 280-281; 299, 10.

3 πινᾶν δεχθέντας Cord   7 τῇ φωνῇ τῶν ὀλολυγμῶν Cord.
8. Κἀνταῦθα — ταῦτα: P, fol. 174; V, fol. 238ᵛ; Cord, p. 158-159 (P. G., 680 B
15-C 8).   17 ποῖα δὲ ταῦτα om. Cord.
9ᵃ. Ἀντὶ τοῦ — ἐπιζητεῖν: P, fol. 174; V, fol. 238ᵛ; Cord, p. 159 (P. G., 680 C
8-681 A 15).   24 φησιν om. Cord   28 τινὰ om. Cord.

Aᵉ 1-3 (p. 308, 9-13): Vt canibus mos est in ciuitate, aut famem aut ipsas
peruagationes ululatus exerceant... aut negatos quaerent cibos.   13-16 (p. 308,
15-18): Hic quoque cum admotatione temporum futurum pro praesenti, ut diceret Locuntur uerba peiora gladiis, quibus aut ipsi aut audientes ceteri uulne-
rentur.

city at night and utter louder cries, doing so particularly when short of food, he implies something similar of the foe. Let them take a turn for the worse from their present prosperity as a result of punishment from you; and like dogs at night in the grip of hunger roaming around the city howling, in like manner let those struck by your punishment wail like dogs so that the sound of the wailing may also betray the magnitude of your punishment of them. The change in mood Symmachus suggests by saying "Let them return in the evening."

Lo, with their own mouth they will speak out, and a sword on their lips (v. 7). Here, too, *Lo* has been inserted by Hebrew idiom. Symmachus says, "They blurt out from their mouths, and like a blade on their lips." Here, too, it changed the tense, using the future instead of the present: From their own mouth and lips, he is saying, they utter words worse than any sword and blade, capable of delivering a more vigorous blow. Of what kind are they? *Saying, Who has heard?* No one, he means. Here, too, *Saying* is generally understood to be spoken implicitly by the author, as also in Psalm 2, "The kings of the earth took their stand, and the rulers assembled together in concert against the Lord and against his Christ. Let us break their bonds and thrust away from us their yoke."[1] Thus generally, as here, "Saying" is understood to be said in the sense, "Saying, Let us break their bonds." Likewise, he says here too, then, *Lo, with their own mouth they will speak out, and a sword on their lips, saying, Who has heard?*

Now, we indicated more precisely in Psalm 45 that it is the author's custom to imply "he said" or "saying" or something similar. He means to say of them, in fact, They claim, There was no need to dread punishment; | instead,

---

1. Ps 2:2–3.

ρίαν, ἀλλ᾽ ἐπιβῶμεν αὐτοῖς ὅση δύναμις, ἀναιροῦντες καὶ κατασφάττοντες·
πολλὰ γὰρ καὶ ἕτερα πεποιηκότων ἡμῶν, τίς ἤκουσεν αὐτῶν στεναζόντων,
ἢ τίς προσέσχεν αὐτοῖς ἀδικουμένοις, ἢ τίς ἐπήμυνεν ἀναιρουμένοις; — οὐχ
ὅτι τοῦτο ἔλεγον πάντως οἱ ἐχθροί, ἀλλ᾽ ἀπὸ τοῦ πράγματος κατὰ τὸ
5 οἰκεῖον ἔθος τὸ « εἶπεν » τεθεικώς, — ὅμοιον γάρ ἐστι τῷ Εἶπε γὰρ ἐν καρδίᾳ αὐτοῦ Οὐκ ἐκζητήσει καὶ τῷ Εἶπον Τίς ὄψεται αὐτούς. Τὸ αὐτὸ γὰρ
κἀνταῦθα εἰπεῖν βούλεται, ὅτι οὕτως ἅπαντα πράττουσιν ὡς οὐκ ἀκούοντος
οὐδενός, οὐδὲ φρον|τίζοντος τῶν γιγνομένων. Ἴδιον δὲ τοῦ μακαρίου Δαυὶδ
τὸ διὰ τοῦτο μάλιστα αἰτεῖν τοῦ Θεοῦ τὴν κατὰ τῶν ἁμαρτανόντων τιμω-
10 ρίαν, διὰ τὸ τῶν πολλῶν ἐν ταῖς ἀδικίαις αἰτιωμένων τὸν Θεὸν ὡς οὐ προνοοῦντα τῶν ἀνθρωπίνων πραγμάτων, δίκαιον εἶναι τῇ ἐκδικίᾳ τῶν γιγνομένων δείκνυσθαι προνοοῦντα τὸν δεσπότην. Ὥσπερ γὰρ ἀδικοῦντες καὶ
πάσχοντες οὐδὲν τοιαύτην τοῖς πολλοῖς τὴν ὑπόνοιαν ἐνεργάζονται, οὕτω
τιμωρούμενοι τὸ ἐναντίον πάντας ὑποπτεύειν παρασκευάζουσιν· δείκνυσι γὰρ
15 ἑαυτὸν οὐ διὰ τὸ τί παθεῖν τὴν κατὰ τῶν ἀδικούντων αἰτοῦντα τιμωρίαν,
ἀλλ᾽ ὥστε κρείττονα περὶ τοῦ Θεοῦ τοῖς ἀνθρώποις ἐντεῦθεν ἐγγενέσθαι
τὴν ὑπόληψιν, ἡμᾶς παιδεύων διὰ πάντων τὸ πρὸς δόξαν τοῦ Θεοῦ συντελοῦν ἐπιζητεῖν.

9ᵇ. Καὶ σύ, Κύριε, ἐκγελάσῃς αὐτούς. Σύμμαχος Σὺ δέ, Κύριε, καταγε-
20 λάσεις αὐτῶν. Τοιαῦτα δέ φησιν ἐκείνων λεγόντων, γέλωτος καὶ χλεύης ἄξια
τὰ ῥήματα αὐτῶν ἀποφανεῖς· οἰομένων γὰρ ἐκείνων οὐδένα εἶναι τὸν ἐπαμύνοντα ἡμῖν, ἐπειδὰν αὐτοὺς τιμωρήσῃ τῇ φοβερᾷ σου δυνάμει ἀκριβῶς, κατα-
γελάστους αὐτῶν τοὺς λόγους ἀποφανεῖς.

9ᶜ. Ἐξουδενώσεις πάντα τὰ ἔθνη. Ἄνω εἶπεν Πρόσχες τοῦ ἐπισκέψασθαι
25 πάντα τὰ ἔθνη, ἐνταῦθα Ἐξουδενώσεις πάντα τὰ ἔθνη, πολλῇ διόλου τῇ τάξει
τοῦ λόγου καὶ διὰ τῶν ἐν μέσῳ χρησάμενος. Δεικνὺς γὰρ ὅτι μὴ ἁπλῶς αἰτεῖ
τὴν κατ᾽ αὐτῶν τιμωρίαν, πρότερον ἤτησεν ἐπιδεῖν τε τὸν Θεὸν καὶ ἐξε-
τάσαι τὰ γιγνόμενα | , — εἶτα διηγήσατο οἷα πράττουσιν, οὐδὲ εἶναί τινα

5-6 Ps. IX, 34ᵇ   6 ps. LXIII, 6c   24-25 v. 6ᵇ.

11-12 τῶν ἀνθρωπίνων — προνοοῦντα ex homoiot. om. Cord   11-12 Paraphrasis
(p. 146, 7-8): ἵν᾽ εἴπῃ, μὴ ἔχειν τὸ προνοοῦντα θεὸν τὸ ἔθνος τὸ ἡμέτερον   13 ἐργάζονται Cord   14 γάρ]. οὖν Cord.
9ᵇ. Σύμμαχος — ἀποφανεῖς: P, fol. 174ᵛ; fol. 239.   20-21 Paraphrasis (p. 146,
12-13): γέλωτος ἀξίαν τὴν ὑπόνοιαν αὐτῶν ἀποδείξας.
9ᶜ. Ἄνω εἶπεν — ἀποφανεῖς. Sub nomine ATHANASII: P, fol. 174ᵛ; V, fol. 239;
Cord, p. 160, 6-17 (P. G., XXVII, 265 B 8-C 2).

Aᵉ 9ᶜ (p. 308, 22-27): Quarum supra inspectionem poposcit dicendo Intende
ad uisitandas omnes gentes, enumeratis ut demum quae ab illis geruntur dice-
returque rite nunc ordinateque, ultionem his congruam imprecatur.

let us cry out to them at full strength, overwhelming and slaying them. After all, we have done many other things as well: who heard their groaning, or gave attention to their abuse, or came to assist them when overwhelmed? Not that the foe actually said this: on the basis of the facts in his peculiar idiom he implied "said," as, for example, "He said in his heart, 'He will not require an account,' " and, "They said, 'Who will see them?' "[2] The meaning is the same here, in fact: They do everything just as if there were no one listening or caring about what happens. Now, it is typical of blessed David to ask God for the punishment of sinners for this reason in particular, that the general run of people in their unjust actions blame God for not exercising providence in human affairs, and so it is right for the Lord to be seen exercising providence in avenging what happens. You see, just as people who do wrong and suffer no consequences encourage such a suspicion in the general run of people, so also their punishment causes everyone to have the opposite impression. In fact, he shows himself asking punishment of wrongdoers not with a view to their suffering something, but to the end that a better notion of God may arise in people from it, and thus he teaches us in everything to continue seeking the glory of God.

May you, Lord, mock them (v. 8). Symmachus: "But you, Lord, will mock them." When they say such things, he means, you will show their words worthy of laughter and mockery, since they believe that there is no one helping us, since you will punish them strictly with your fearsome power, showing their words to be ridiculous. *You will set all the nations at naught.* Above he said *Take the trouble to survey all the nations,* and here *You will set all the nations at naught,* generally preserving the order of thought even with what comes in between. I mean, after bringing out that it is not without purpose that he asks punishment for them, he first asked God to observe and examine what happens, then he outlined what they do in believing that there is no one | exercising providence, and finally he went on to mention the

---

2. Pss 10:13; 64:5.

τὸν προνοοῦντα νομίζοντες, καὶ τότε τὴν τιμωρίαν ἐπήγαγεν τοῦτο λέγων ὅτι Ἐπὶ τούτοις ἀξίως αὐτοὺς κολάσεις καὶ τῇ παρά σου τιμωρίᾳ τὸ μηδὲν ἀποφανεῖς.

10ᵃ. Τὸ κράτος μου πρός σε φυλάξω. Τὴν ψυχήν μού φησι καὶ τὴν δύναμίν μου πᾶσαν πρός σε βλέπουσαν ἔχω παρά σου φυλαττομένην.   5

10ᵇ. Ὅτι σύ, ὁ Θεὸς ἀντιλήπτωρ μου. Σὺ γὰρ εἶ βοηθός μου.

11ᵃ. Ὁ Θεός μου, τὸ ἔλεος αὐτοῦ προφθάσει με. Προκαταλήψεται γάρ μέ φησιν ἡ σὴ φιλανθρωπία, ὥστε πρὶν ἤ τι παρὰ τῶν πολεμίων παθεῖν τῆς εὐεργεσίας τῆς παρά σου τυχεῖν.

11ᵇ. Ὁ Θεός μου δείξει μοι ἐν τοῖς ἐχθροῖς μου. Ταῦτα δέ φησι, του- 10 τέστι τὸ ἔλεος αὐτοῦ καὶ τὴν φιλανθρωπίαν αὐτοῦ, ὄψομαι ἐν τοῖς ἐχθροῖς, τουτέστι διὰ τῆς ἐκείνων τιμωρίας γνώσομαι τὴν εἰς ἡμᾶς σου φιλανθρωπίαν.

12ᵃ. Μὴ ἀποκτείνῃς αὐτούς, μή ποτε ἐπιλάθωνται τοῦ νόμου σου. Κατ᾿ ἐρώτησιν ἀναγνωστέον, ἀντὶ τοῦ Ἀλλ᾿ οὐ μὴ αὐτοὺς ἀποκτείνῃς, ὥστε μὴ ἐπιλαθέσθαι τοῦ ὀνόματός σου; ὥστε φησὶν οὔτε διὰ τοῦτο οἷόν τε αὐτοὺς 15 κερδάναι | τὴν τιμωρίαν. Ὁ δὲ λέγει τοιοῦτόν ἐστιν. Πρὸ τῆς τοῦ δεσπότου Χριστοῦ παρουσίας τὴν προσήκουσαν καὶ τελείαν πίστιν περὶ τῆς ἀναστάσεως οὐκ ἔχοντες, ἡγοῦντο τοὺς τελευτῶντας παντελῶς τοῦ εἶναι ἐκτὸς γίνεσθαι καὶ μὴ δύνασθαι λόγον τινὰ ἢ μνήμην Θεοῦ ἔχειν. Διὰ τοῦτό φησί που Ὅτι οὐκ ἔστιν ἐν τῷ θανάτῳ ὁ μνημονεύων σου, καὶ ἀλλαχοῦ Οὐχ οἱ 20

15 cf. Ps. XLIII, 21   16-19 cf. supra p. 182, 25 ss.   20 ps. VI, 6   ps. CXIII, 25.

1 τοῦτο] οὕτω Cord.
10ᵃ. Τὴν ψυχήν — φυλαττομένην: P, fol. 175; V, fol. 239.
10ᵇ. Σὺ γὰρ εἶ βοηθός μου: P, fol. 175; V, fol. 239ᵛ.
11ᵃ. Προκαταλήψεται — τυχεῖν: P, fol. 175ᵛ; fol. 239ᵛ.
11ᵇ. Ταῦτα — φιλανθρωπίαν: P, fol. 175ᵛ; V, fol. 239ᵛ.
12ᵃ. Κατ᾿ ἐρώτησιν — τυχεῖν τινος: P, fol. 175ᵛ; V, fol. 239ᵛ-240; Cord, p. 162
(P. G., 681 BD).   15 ὀνόματος] νόμου Cord   19 ἔχειν om. CPV.

Aᵉ 10ᵃ (p. 308, 27-80). Quicquid in me uirium uitaeque est, ad te habeo semper intentum, ut a te custodiatur atque seruetur.   11-12 (p. 309, 1-2): Per illorum condemnationem quanta sit erga me largitas tuae benignitatis aspiciam. 12ᵃ (p. 309, 4-11): Id est, legis tuae; uel certe, non semplici et una plaga depereant, ne per uelocitatem consummationis memoria ultionis intereat (interteat ms). Per interrogationem legendum: an forte defessis debetam ultionem accipere? quia per mortem nullus confitebitur tibi, ut scilicet iusti in hac uita seruati memores esse possint legis tuae.

punishment, saying, For this you will punish them appropriately and by your retribution show them to be nothing. *My power, I shall keep watching for you* (v. 9): I have my soul with all my strength focused on you, protected as it is by you. *Because you, O God, are my support:* you are my help. *My God, his mercy will anticipate me* (v. 10): your lovingkindness anticipates me, with the result that before suffering anything from the enemy, I receive favors from you. *My God will show it to me among my foes:* in the midst of the foe I shall see it, namely, his *mercy* and lovingkindness—that is to say, Through their being punished I shall know your lovingkindness for us.

Do not kill them, lest they forget your law (v. 11). It is to be read as a question, thus: But surely you will not kill them, lest they forget your name? He is saying, And so for this reason they will not be able to profit from the punishment. What he means is something like this: Before the coming of Christ the Lord they lacked proper and perfect faith in the res-urrection, and they believed that the dead were completely deprived of existence and could retain no notion or memory of God. Hence he says in one place, "There is no one to remember you in death," and in another place, "The dead will not | praise you, Lord,"[3] and you can find this usage

---

3. Pss 6:5; 115:17.

νεκροὶ αἰνέσουσίν σε, Κύριε, — καὶ ὅλως πολλήν ἐστιν εὑρεῖν ταύτην τὴν χρῆσιν ἐν τῇ παλαιᾷ διαθήκῃ. Ἐπειδὴ τοίνυν ὡς τῶν μὲν ἐνταῦθα ὑμνούντων τὸν Θεόν, τῶν δὲ ἐκ τῶν τοῦ βίου γιγνομένων οὐδὲ μεμνῆσθαι ἔτι τοῦ Θεοῦ οἷόν τε ὄντων, τοῦτό φησιν Ἀλλ᾽ οὐκ ἀποκτενεῖς αὐτούς φησιν,
5 ἀλλ᾽ ὑπερθήσῃ τὴν κατ᾽ αὐτῶν τιμωρίαν ὡς ἂν μήποτε ἀποθανόντες εἰς λήθην τῆς σῆς ἔλθοιεν δυνάμεως — ἀντὶ τοῦ Οὐχ οἷόν τε οὐδὲ διὰ τοῦτο ἀναβάλλεσθαι τὴν τιμωρίαν. Εἰ μὲν γὰρ ἐμέμνηντό σου τῆς δυνάμεως καὶ τὴν γνῶσιν εἶχον τὴν σὴν καὶ ᾔδεσαν ἃ προσῆκον ἦν, εἰκὸς ἦν διὰ τοῦτο φείσασθαι, ὥστε μὴ ἀποθανόντων τὴν σὴν περιαιρεθῆναι μνήμην ἐξ αὐτῶν.
10 Ἐπειδὴ δὲ τοσοῦτον ἀπέχουσιν τοῦ ἐνταῦθά σου μνημονεύειν, ὡς τὸ ἐναντίον ἅπαντα μὲν πράττειν καὶ ἀδικεῖν ὡς οὐκ ὄντος τοῦ ἐφεστῶτος τῷ βίῳ καὶ διακρίνοντος τὰ πραττόμενα, τοιαῦτα δὲ καὶ λέγειν ὡς οὐδεὶς ὁ ἀκούων ἢ ὁ φροντίζων τῶν γιγνομένων καὶ οὐκ ἔνεστί σε ἐκεῖνα λογίσασθαι ἃ τῆς βελτίστης εἰσὶ μοίρας καὶ τῆς κρείττονος περί σου ὑπολήψεως,
15 μή ποτε νῦν μεμνημένοι λήθῃ παραδοῖεν τὰ κατὰ σε θανάτῳ τε ἅμα τιμώρησαι καὶ ποικίλαις κακώσεσι, καὶ ταύταις μᾶλλον ἢ τῷ θανάτῳ αὐτοὺς ὑπόβαλε· ὁ γὰρ παρελκυσμὸς τῶν δεινῶν ὑπόμνησιν ἐμποιεῖ τῶν ἁμαρτιῶν. Τοῦτο γὰρ βούλεται διὰ πάντων εἰπεῖν ὅτι οὐδὲν αὐτοῖς πρόσεστιν ἄξιον τοῦ φειδοῦς τυχεῖν τινος.

20 **12ᵇ.** Διασκόρπισον αὐτοὺς ἐν τῇ δυνάμει σου. Οὐκοῦν φησι διὰ πάντα κατὰ τὴν δύναμιν τὴν σὴν διασκόρπισον αὐτούς, | τουτέστιν εἰς φυγὴν τρέψον, ἐπειδὴ τῶν ἡττωμένων καὶ εἰς φυγὴν τρεπομένων ἐν τοῖς πολέμοις ἴδιον λοιπὸν τὸ ἀτάκτως διασκορπίζεσθαι.

12ᶜ-13ᵃ. Καὶ κατάγαγε αὐτούς, ὁ ὑπερασπιστής μου, Κύριε, τῇ ἁμαρτίᾳ
25 τοῦ στόματος αὐτῶν, λόγῳ χειλέων αὐτῶν. Ἐπειδὴ γὰρ εἶπεν Μὴ διὰ τοῦτο ἄρα ὑπερθῇ τὴν τιμωρίαν, μή ποτε νῦν σου μεμνημένοι ὑπὸ τοῦ θανάτου εἰς λήθην ἔλθωσι, καλῶς ἐπήγαγεν τὸ Διασκόρπισον αὐτούς, καὶ κατάγαγε αὐτοὺς τῇ ἁμαρτίᾳ τοῦ στόματος αὐτῶν. Τοὐναντίον γάρ φησι διὰ τοῦτο τιμωρηθῆναι δίκαιοι μᾶλλον ἢ ἀφεθῆναι, ὅτι οὐδεμίαν σου μνήμην ἔχουσιν,

4 ἀλλ᾽ οὐκ — φησιν om. C   5 μήποτε] μήτε Cord   8 ἦν διὰ] ἦν om. Cord
10 ὡς τὸ] ὥστε εἰς Cord   11 μὲν om. Cord   13 ὁ om. Cord   σε om. Cord
13-17 λογίσασθαι — ὑπόβαλε sic restituere dubitanter conieci   14 ἃ τῆς βελτίστης —
ὑπολήψεως om. CPV   15 μή ποτε νῦν μεμνημένοι] ὡς μὴ Cord   15-16 θανάτῳ —
θανάτῳ] ὑπὸ τοῦ θανάτου καὶ τῆς τιμωρίας πανταχόθεν δικαίαν αὐτοὺς τιμωρηθῆναι CPV
16-17 αὐτοὺς ὑπόβαλε conieci, ὑποβαλεῖν Cord   17 ὁ γὰρ — ἁμαρτιῶν om. CPV
18 τοῦτο γάρ] καὶ τοῦτο δὲ Cord.
12ᵇ. Οὐκοῦν — διασκορπίζεσθαι: P, fol. 176; V, fol. 240ᵛ
12ᶜ-13ᵃ. Ἐπειδὴ — τρόπῳ: P, fol. 176; V, fol. 240ᵛ.

Aᵉ 20-22 (p. 309, 12-13): A similitudine fusorum interfectorumque hostium.
Disperge possuit.   27-29 (p. 309, 14-15): Bene aduersus arrogantes possuit Distrue.

throughout the Old Testament. Since, then, those alive sing God's praises, while the departed cannot even remember God any longer, he says, Instead of killing them, you will heighten their punishment lest by dying they ever come to forget your power—in other words, It is not possible even for this reason for their punishment to be postponed. After all, if they remembered your power, possessed knowledge of you, and knew their duty, it would be proper for them to be spared so that memory of you would not be taken from them at death. But they were so far from remembering you in this life that, on the contrary, they committed every crime as if there were no one present in this life to make judgments on acts committed, on the one hand, and on the other hand they said such things as if there were no one to hear them or care what happens and it were impossible for you to calculate what springs from a better and superior way of understanding you. So lest they now remember you and consign to oblivion opposition to you, punish them with death[4] and all kinds of maltreatment, and submit them to this rather than to death, since postponement of dire events instills remembrance of sin. In all this, in fact, his meaning is, They have no claim on pity.

Scatter them in your power: for all that, then, *scatter them* in accord with your power—that is, put them to flight, since it is normal for those vanquished and put to flight in war to be scattered in disorderly fashion. *And bring them down, Lord, my protector, in a sin of their mouth, a word of their lips* (vv. 11–12). Since he had said, Do not on this account delay the punishment, lest on now remembering you they pass into oblivion at death, he did well to go on to say *Scatter them* and *Bring them down in a sin of their mouth:* On the contrary, he is saying, for this reason they deserve to be punished rather than done away with, because they have no memory of you |

---

4. In a verse that as a whole evokes divergent modern translations, the MSS represent this particular section in a variety of ways. Theodore's overall thought seems to be that the death of the miscreants (whoever they are) will not achieve the right purpose.

οὐδὲ εἶναί τινα κριτὴν τῶν γιγνομένων φασίν, τοσοῦτον ἀφιστᾶσιν τοῦ διὰ τοῦτο κερδάναι τὴν παρά σου τιμωρίαν. Κατάγαγε οὖν αὐτούς φησιν εἰς τὸν ᾅδην, σὺ ὁ ἐμὸς βοηθός, διὰ τοῦτο μᾶλλον, διὰ τὴν ἁμαρτίαν τοῦ στό- ματος αὐτῶν, διὰ τὸν λόγον τῶν χειλέων αὐτῶν. Ποῖα δὲ ταῦτα; Του- τέστι διὰ τὸ μηδεμίαν ἔχειν σου μνήμην, τοὐναντίον δὲ λέγειν τε καὶ 5 οἴεσθαι μὴ εἶναι ἀκούοντα τὰ λεγόμενα, — διὰ τοῦτο πολλῷ μᾶλλον δικαίως αὐτοὺς τιμωρησάμενος, ἔργῳ πεῖσον αὐτοὺς ὅτι κρινεῖς τε ἅπαντα καὶ βοηθήσεις ἡμῖν ἀδικουμένοις παντὶ τρόπῳ.

13ᵇ. Καὶ συλληφθήτωσαν ἐν τῇ ὑπερηφανίᾳ αὐτῶν. Ἀντὶ τοῦ Μὴ διαφυ- γέτωσαν τὴν τιμωρίαν· ἐπειδὴ τοῖς φεύγουσιν καὶ συλληφθεῖσιν ἀναγκαίως 10 ἡ τιμωρία ἔπεται, τιμωρηθήτωσαν ἐν αὐτῇ οὖν τῇ ὑπερηφανίᾳ αὐτῶν, — ὑπερηφανίαν δικαίως καλέσας τὸ μὴ ἐννοεῖν περὶ τοῦ πάντων δεσπότου τε καὶ κριτοῦ, ἀλλὰ πάντα πράττειν τε ἀδεῶς καὶ φθέγγεσθαι ἃ μὴ δεῖ.

14ᵃ. Καὶ ἐξ ἀρᾶς καὶ ψεύδους διαγγελήσονται ἐν συντελείᾳ. Ἐπειδὴ τὰ γιγνόμενα πάντως καὶ ἀπαγγέλλονται, πολλάκις ἀντὶ τοῦ γιγνομένου τὴν 15 ἀπαγγελίαν λέγει, ὡς τὸ Ἀκουτιεῖς με ἀγαλλίασιν καὶ εὐφροσύνην, ἀντὶ τοῦ παρέξεις μοι πάντως· τὸ γὰρ γιγνόμενον, τοῦτο καὶ ἀκουτιεῖν ἔμελλεν. Κἀνταῦθα οὖν τὸ διαγγελήσονται ἐν συντελείᾳ, ἀντὶ τοῦ ἔσονται. Ἀρὰν δὲ καὶ ψεῦδος καλεῖ τὰ παρ' ἐκείνων γιγνόμενα, ὡς ψεύδους μεστὰ καὶ κατά- ρας ἄξια· ἀπὸ τοίνυν τούτων φησίν, ὧν πράττουσιν, ἀπὸ τούτων συντε- 20 λεσθήσονται καὶ ἀποθανοῦνται, — ταῦτα γὰρ αὐτοῖς τῆς συντελείας ἔσται καὶ τοῦ θανάτου τὰ αἴτια. Διόλου δὲ ἑαυτῷ ἠκολούθησεν, ἀπὸ τοῦ τρόπου μείζονος αὐτοὺς τιμωρίας ἀξίους δεῖξαι βουληθείς. Οὕτω γάρ φησιν Οὐκ ἔνεστιν αὐτοὺς κερδάναι τὴν παρά σου τιμωρίαν ὡς μεμνημένους σου ἢ εἰδό- τας σε, ὅτι δι' αὐτὸ τοῦτο μᾶλλον ἄξιοι φαίνονται τιμωρίας, ἀφ' ὧν λέγουσί 25 τε καὶ ποιοῦσιν· ταῦτα γὰρ μάλιστα ἀναγκαίαν αὐτοῖς τὴν τιμωρίαν ἐπά- γεται, ἔτι δὲ καὶ τὴν συντέλειαν.

4 v. 9ª   16 Ps. L, 10.

1 γινομένων C   ἀφεστᾶσιν CPV   4 ποῖα δὲ ταῦτα] excerptum des. in codd. Verba Τουτέστι κ. τ. λ. praecedunt nomen Θεοδώρου, addito in C versiculo 9ª Ὅτι τίς ἤκουσεν.
13ᵇ. Ἀντὶ τοῦ — ἃ μὴ δεῖν: P, fol. 176; V. fol. 240ᵛ.
14ᵃ. Ἐπειδὴ — συντέλειαν: P, fol. 176ᵛ; V, fol. 241; Cord, p. 165 (P. G., 681-684). 16 ἐπαγγελίαν Cord   23 βουλόμενος Cord   26-27 ἐπάγει τὴν τιμωρίαν Cord   27 ἔτι δὲ καὶ τὴν om. CPV.

Aᵉ 21-22 (p. 309, 22-24): Id est Haec eorum cremina consummationis sunt eis mortisque causa.

and claim that there is no judge of what happens, and hence are unlikely to profit from punishment by you. So he says *Bring them down to Hades,* you my helper, for this reason in particular: the *sin of their mouth,* the word of *their lips.* Namely? Having no memory of you, but on the contrary saying and thinking that you are not hearing what is said. Hence, with much greater justice should you punish them and convince them in practice that you judge everything and in every way help us when wronged. *Let them be caught up in their own arrogance*—that is, Let them not escape punishment: since punishment necessarily follows those who flee and are apprehended, let them therefore be punished precisely *in their own arrogance* (by *arrogance* rightly referring to giving no thought to the Lord and judge of all, and instead doing everything without a qualm and giving voice to improper sentiments).

In cursing and falsehood they will be reported in consummation (v. 13). Since what happens is actually bruited abroad as well, he often mentions the report in place of the event, as, for example, "Let me hear joy and gladness"[5]—that is, you will ensure it completely: since it happened, he meant it to be heard of as well. So here, too, *they will be reported in consummation* means that they will be. By *cursing and falsehood* he refers to what was done by them, which was likely to attract falsehood and execration: On the basis of what they do, then, he is saying, they will be brought to an end and die, for it will be responsible for their end and their death. Now, he was quite consistent in his thinking, intending to show them deserving of death on this more compelling basis—hence his saying, It is impossible for them to profit from punishment at your hands by remembering you and acknowledging you, because they prove more deserving of punishment for the very reason of what they say and do (imposing the punishment on them as particularly necessary, including their extinction). |

---

5. Ps 51:8.

14ᵇ. Ἐν ὀργῇ συντελείας, καὶ οὐ μὴ ὑπάρξωσιν. Ἐν ὀργῇ τῇ τοῦ Θεοῦ λέγει · ἐπισυνῆπται δὲ καὶ τῷ ἄνω, ἵνα ᾖ τὸ διαγγελήσεται κατὰ κοινοῦ, τουτέστιν ἐν τῇ ὀργῇ τῇ τοῦ Θεοῦ, συντέλεια ἀπὸ συντελείας διαγγελήσεται. Οἱ θάνατοι αὐτῶν φησιν ἀλλήλους διαδέξονται, ὡς ὁμοῦ τε τῶν πρώτων
5 ἀκούεσθαι θανάτων καὶ πάλιν ἑτέρων ἀπαγγέλλεσθαι, καὶ μετ᾽ ἐκείνους ἑτέραν ἀγγελίαν ἐπιφθάνειν. Οὕτως ἡ τοῦ Θεοῦ ὀργὴ συνεχῇ κατ᾽ αὐτῶν ἐργάσεται τιμωρίαν τε καὶ κόλασιν μέχρις ἂν αὐτοὺς ἀνέλῃ πάντη καὶ ἀφανίσῃ, ὥστε μὴ ὑπάρχειν μήτε εἶναι.

14ᶜ. Καὶ γνώσονται ὅτι ὁ Θεὸς δεσπόζει τοῦ Ἰακὼβ καὶ τῶν περάτων τῆς
10 γῆς. Καὶ ἐπειδὴ πολλάκις ἡμῖν ὠνείδισαν, ὡς τῆς παρά σου προστασίας οὐκ ἀξιωθεῖσιν, καὶ διὰ τοῦτο μάλιστα ἀδεέστερον ταῖς καθ᾽ ἡμῶν ἐπιβουλαῖς ἐχρῶντο, διὰ τῆς τιμωρίας γνώσονται ὅτι δεσπότης τε εἶ καὶ κύριος οὐχ ἡμῶν μόνων, ἀλλὰ γὰρ καὶ πάσης τῆς γῆς. Διὰ τοῦτο ἡμῖν ἐπάμυνον ὅ τε βούλῃ καὶ τοὺς ἀδικοῦντας τιμωρούμενος ὅσα ἐθέλεις. Ἀπέδωκεν δὲ τὸ
15 πᾶν κατὰ ἀκολουθίαν τῷ Μὴ ἀποκτείνῃς αὐτούς, εἶτα ἀναλαμβάνει ἄνωθεν τὴν κατ᾽ αὐτῶν κατάραν καί φησιν.

15. Ἐπιστρέψουσιν εἰς ἑσπέραν καὶ λιμώξουσιν ὡς κύων, καὶ κυκλώσουσι πόλιν. Ὅπερ ἄνω εἶπεν ἐπαρώμενος αὐτοῖς, τοῦτο κἀνταῦθα ἀναλαμβάνων λέγει, μετὰ τὸ δεῖξαι αὐτοὺς ἀξίους ὄντας τῆς τιμωρίας. Οὐκοῦν φησιν
20 ἐπειδὴ καὶ φείσασθαι αὐτῶν οὐχ οἷόν τε, ὡς νῦν μέν σου φροντιζόντων, ἐπιλησομένων δὲ εἰ ἀποθάνοιεν, — τοὐναντίον γὰρ ἀγνώμονες ὄντες, ἀπὸ τῆς τιμωρίας τὸ δέον ἐπιγνώσονται, — δικαιωτάτην οὖν τιμωρίαν ὑπομεινάτωσαν, καὶ τῇ παρά σου τιμωρίᾳ βληθέντες ὀλολυζέτωσαν δίκην τῶν κατὰ τὴν πόλιν ἐκπεριϊόντων κυνῶν ἐν τῷ τῆς νυκτὸς καιρῷ.

25 16. Αὐτοὶ διασκορπισθήσονται τοῦ φαγεῖν · ἐὰν δὲ μὴ χορτασθῶσι, καὶ γογγύσωσιν. Ἠκολούθησεν ἑαυτῷ ἐχόμενος τοῦ ὑποδείγματος τοῦ ἐπὶ τῶν κυνῶν, καὶ τὸ ἐπ᾽ ἐ|κείνων συμβαῖνον ἀρασάμενος αὐτοῖς γενέσθαι. Ὥσπερ

18 supra p. 387.

14ᵇ. Ἐν ὀργῇ — εἶναι: P, fol. 176ᵛ; V, fol. 241.
14ᶜ. Καὶ ἐπειδὴ — καί φησιν: P, fol. 177; V, fol. 241ᵛ; Cord, p. 166 (P. G., 684 B).
10 ὀνειδίζουσιν Cord   12 εἶ om. Cord   14 ὅ τε βούλῃ καὶ om. Cord   15 τὸ CP Cord.
15. Ὅπερ ἄνω — καιρῷ: P, fol. 177; V, fol. 241ᵛ; Cord, p. 166 (P. G., 684).
21 γὰρ] δὴ Cord   22 οὖν om. CV   24 ἐκπεριόντων CV.
16. Ἠκολούθησεν — διατελείτωσαν: P, fol. 177; V, fol. 242; Cord, p. 167.
25 κυνῶν] κοινῶν C   ἀράμενος C.

Aᵉ 7-8 (p. 310, 1-2): Consume in furore, ut non subsistant.   16 (p. 310, 9-16): Adsecutus est adsumtae conparationis colorem, et quod canibus uidemus accedere — ut esurientes totam peruagentur urbem, cumque quo expleantur cibum inuenire nequierint, ad latratus se ululatusque conuertunt — hoc istis eueniet, ut mira calamitatis specie intabescant.

In wrath of consummation, and they are not to survive. He means *in the wrath* of God, relating this to the above, so that *will be reported* has general application—that is, *by the wrath* of God consummation will be reported from consummation. He means, Their dead will succeed one another, so that there is a report of the first to die and in turn an announcement of others, and after them a further message arrives. In this way God's wrath will bring unremitting retribution and punishment on them until it utterly destroys and annihilates them, so that they neither survive nor exist. *They will know that God is Lord of Jacob and of the ends of the earth:* since they often taunted us for not being granted your protection, and for this reason in particular they had no qualms about hatching plots against us, they will discover through retribution that you are Lord and master not only of us, but also of all the earth. For this reason assist us as you wish, and punish the wrongdoers as much as you please.

He brought everything back logically to *Do not kill them,* and then he resumes the curse against them from above, saying *In the evening they will return; they will be as hungry as dogs, and will prowl around the city.* What he had said above in cursing them, this he resumes here as well after showing them to be deserving of punishment. Since it is therefore not possible to spare them, he is saying, though they now pay you heed but would forget you if they died—on the contrary, they are ungrateful and will recognize their duty only through punishment—let them therefore suffer just punishment, and by being struck with punishment from you let them howl like dogs roaming the city at night time. *They are scattered for feeding; if they are not satisfied, they will growl* (v. 15). He was consistent in use of the example of the dogs and in praying for the curse to befall them: Just as | when they are

γὰρ ἐκεῖνοί φησιν, ὅταν ὑπὸ τοῦ λιμοῦ κατέχονται διασκίδνανται κατὰ τὴν
πόλιν διερευνώμενοι εἴ πού τις αὐτοῖς εὑρεθείη τροφή, εἶτα ἐπειδὰν μήτε
εὑρεῖν δυνηθῶσιν μήτε ἀπολαύσωσιν εἰς κόρον τῆς τροφῆς, γογγυσμοῖς
χρῶνται καὶ ὀλολυγαῖς ὠρυόμενοι τὴν κατέχουσαν αὐτοὺς ἔνδειαν, οὕτω φησι
καὶ αὐτοὶ διασκορπισθήτωσαν ἐν τῇ σῇ ἀπειλῇ καὶ ὥσπερ ὑπὸ λιμοῦ τῆς   5
συμφορᾶς πιεσθέντες καὶ μηδενὸς μετασχεῖν καλοῦ δυνηθέντες ὀλολυγαῖς
καὶ ταῖς φωναῖς τὴν κατέχουσαν αὐτοὺς τιμωρίαν δεικνύντες διατελείτωσαν.

17ᵃ. Ἐγὼ δὲ ἄσομαι τὴν δύναμίν σου Ὥσπερ ἀπὸ τοῦ ἐκείνων τρόπου
δείκνυσιν ἀξίους ὄντας τιμωρίας, οὕτω καὶ ἑαυτὸν ἄξιον ὄντα τυχεῖν τῆς
παρά σου φιλανθρωπίας καὶ συμμαχίας ἀπὸ τῶν πραττομένων δείκνυσιν.   10
Τὴν δὲ μετὰ πάσης ἰσχύος φησὶ παρά σου γιγνομένην εἰς ἡμᾶς βοήθειαν,
ταύτην ὑμνῶν διατελέσω.

17ᵇ. Καὶ ἀγαλλιάσομαι τὸ πρωῒ τὸ ἔλεός σου. Καὶ ὄρθρου διανιστάμενός
φησιν, ἀεὶ τὴν μνήμην τῆς εἰς ἡμᾶς σου φιλανθρωπίας μετὰ πολλῆς μεθέξω
τῆς εὐφροσύνης, ἀντὶ τοῦ μετ᾽ εὐφροσύνης ὑμνήσω σου τὴν εἰς ἡμᾶς χάριν.   15

17ᶜ·ᵈ. Ὅτι ἐγενήθης ἀντιλήπτωρ μου καὶ καταφυγή μου ἐν ἡμέρᾳ θλί-
ψεως. Ἐπειδὴ ἐβοήθησέν μοι ἐν τῷ καιρῷ τῶν | κακῶν.

18ᵃ. Βοηθός μου, σοὶ ψαλῶ. Ἐπειδὴ γὰρ αὐτὸς εἶ ὁ περισῴζων με ἀπὸ
τῶν κακῶν, σοὶ τοὺς ὑπὲρ τῆς χάριτος ὕμνους δικαίως ἀποδώσω.

18ᵇ. Ὁ Θεὸς ἀντιλήπτωρ μου εἶ, ὁ Θεός μου, τὸ ἔλεός μου. Σὺ γάρ   20
μου βοηθός, σύ μου καὶ φιλανθρωπία, παρ᾽ οὗ παντὸς ἀγαθοῦ τὴν ἀπόλαυσιν δέχομαι.

1 ὑπὸ] ἐπὶ CV   τοῦ om. Cord   2 εἶτα] εἴ C   4 ὀλολυγμοῖς Cord   6 καὶ]
κἂν CV.
17ᵃ. Ὥσπερ — διατελέσω: P, fol. 177ᵛ; V, fol. 242; Cord, p. 167.   9 αὐτὸν C
10 ὑμνωδίαν τελέσω CV.
17ᵇ. Καὶ ὄρθρου — χάριν: P, fol. 177ᵛ; V, fol. 242.
17ᶜ·ᵈ. Ἐπειδὴ — κακῶν: P, fol. 177ᵛ; V, fol. 242.
18ᵃ. Ἐπειδὴ — ἀποδώσω: P, fol. 177ᵛ; V, fol. 242.
18ᵇ. Σὺ γάρ — δέχομαι: P, fol. 177ᵛ; V, fol. 242.

Aᵉ 17ᵃ (p. 310, 16-23): Iteratur autem sententia, ut et illorum meritum
meretur (uel expraematur add. in marg.) et postulantis disiderium, per quem
hoc adceleratur ulciscentis effectio. Ostenderat illos dignos esse suplicio, mon-
strat se nunc dignum esse praesidio.   17ᵇ (p. 310, 24-27): Pro celebranda memoria bonorum tuorum, matutinus gratificator misericordiam praeparabo tuam.
17ᶜ·ᵈ (p. 310, 28-29): Adiuuasti quippe me in tempore malorum.

scattered through the city when in the grip of hunger searching for any food for themselves, and when they fail to find it and to have enough food, they fall to growling and howl for the need they feel, so too let these people be scattered by your threat and feel the pressure of the catastrophe like hunger, unable to share in any good thing, constantly betraying by wailing and crying the punishment gripping them.

But I shall sing the praises of your power (v. 16). Just as he shows them to be deserving of punishment on the basis of their behavior, so too he shows himself worthy of receiving from you lovingkindness and aid against the villains. With all my strength I shall continue to sing on this theme, the assistance coming to us from you. *And I shall rejoice at daybreak in your mercy:* rising at dawn, I shall ever with great happiness share in lovingkindness from you—that is, With happiness I shall sing the praises of your favor to us. *Because you have proved to be my support and my refuge in the day of my tribulation:* since you helped me in the time of trouble. *You are my help; I shall sing to you* (v. 18): since it is you who saves me from trouble, to you I shall in justice render songs of praise for the favor. *Because you are my support, O God, my mercy, O my God:* you are my help, you are my lovingkindness too; it is from you I receive enjoyment of every good. |

PSALMVS LIX

Περὶ τῶν αὐτῶν διαλέγεται κἀνταῦθα ὁ μακάριος Δαυὶδ ὡς ἐκ προσώπου τῶν Μακκαβαίων διηγουμένων μὲν τὰς ἰδίας θλίψεις, αἰτούντων δὲ καὶ
τὴν παρὰ τοῦ Θεοῦ φιλανθρωπίαν, ἀλλὰ καὶ ὡς ὅτι τεύξωνται πιστευόν-
5 των. Τοῖς δὲ σχήμασι τῆς διηγήσεως τούτοις κεχρημένος ὁ μακάριος Δαυὶδ
ἐπὶ τῶν τοιούτων δηλονότι τὰ ἐσόμενα προφητεύων λέγει.

3ᵃ. Ὁ Θεός, ἀπώσω ἡμᾶς καὶ καθεῖλες ἡμᾶς. Μακρὰν σεαυτοῦ πεποίηκας
ἡμᾶς, χωρίσας ἡμᾶς καὶ ἀποστήσας τῆς παρά σου προνοίας, κατέσπασάς
τε ἡμᾶς ἀπὸ πολλῆς τῆς δόξης, εἰς ἀτιμίαν ἐλθεῖν παρεσκεύασας καὶ ἀπὸ
10 πολλῆς εὐπραγίας εἰς μεγίστας συμφοράς. Τοῦτο δὲ περὶ τοῦ Θεοῦ, οὐχ
ὡς ποιήσαντος λέγει, ἀλλὰ τὴν συγχώρησιν συνηθῶς ἀντὶ πράξεως τεθεικώς.

3ᵇ. Ὠργίσθης καὶ ᾠκτείρησας ἡμᾶς. Ἀλλ᾽ εἰ καὶ ταῦτα παθεῖν συνεχώρησας, οὐ μὴν ἐναφῆκας τοῖς κακοῖς, ὀξυτάτην τὴν παρά σου φιλανθρωπίαν ἡμῖν παρεχόμενος.

15 **4ᵃ.** Συνέσεισας τὴν γῆν καὶ συνετάραξας αὐτήν. Γῆν ἐνταῦθα λέγει τὴν
τῆς ἐπαγγελίας, ἀντὶ τοῦ Εἰς ταραχὴν καὶ θόρυβον ἡμᾶς κατέστησας τῷ
πλήθει τῶν κακῶν, — τὴν γῆν δὲ εἶπεν ὥστε δεῖξαι τῆς ταραχῆς τὴν ἐπίτασιν, ὡσανεὶ πάσης αὐτῆς συγκινηθείσης.

4ᵇ. Ἴασαι τὰ συντρίμματα αὐτῆς, ὅτι ἐσαλεύθη. Ἐπειδὴ τὰ αὐτῶν πάθη
20 ἀνέλαβεν ἐπὶ τῆς γῆς, τῇ οἰκείᾳ ἐχρήσατο ἀκολουθίᾳ, καὶ διὰ τοῦτο, ὡσανεὶ

Περὶ τῶν αὐτῶν — λέγει: P, fol. 178ᵛ; V, fol. 243.
3ᵃ. Μακρὰν — τεθεικώς: P, fol. 179; V, fol. 243ᵛ; Cord, p. 178.   7 ἑαυτοῦ
codd. Cord.
3ᵇ. Ἀλλ᾽ εἰ καὶ — παρεχόμενος: P, fol. 179; V, fol. 243ᵛ-244; Cord, p. 179 (P. G.,
684).   14 παρασχόμενος CPV.
4ᵃ. Γῆν — συγκινηθείσης: P, fol. 179; V, fol. 244; Cord, p. 179 (anon.).
4ᵇ. Ἐπειδὴ — συμφοράς: P, fol. 179ᵛ; V, fol. 244; Cord, p. 180 (P. G., 684-685).

Aᵉ *Argumentum ps. LIX* (p. 311, 7-10): In Machabeorum tempora etiam
istam diregit profetiam per occasionem eius negotii triumphique, quem proue-
nisse et praesens titulus loquitur. Cf. PSEUDO-BEDA (792).   10-11 (p. 311, 14-15):
Hoc autem permisione, non intentione tua factum est.   3ᵇ (p. 311, 18-22):
Verum etsi indignatus, talia nos sustenere permiseris, non tamen in ipsis calamitatibus nos relinquisti, humanitatis tuae uidilicet opem nobis celeriter conferendo.   4ⁱ (p. 311, 23-24. 26-28): Repromisionis scilicet... possuit, tamquam
irascente Deo regio tota fuisse concussa.   4ᵇ (p. 311, 29-31): Ordinate et figu-
rate eius nomine medicinam postulat, quam dixerat fuisse commotam.

PSALM 60

Blessed David speaks here, too, about the same things from the viewpoint of the Maccabees, recounting their tribulations and also begging God's lovingkindness, believing as well that they will attain it. Using these forms of composition, blessed David clearly prophesies what will happen in the case of such people.

O God, you repulsed us and destroyed us (v. 1): you set us far from you, cut us off and removed us from your providence, depriving us of great glory and causing us to come into disrepute, into deep misfortune after high prosperity. Now, he does not say this of God as the cause; rather, as usual he cites the permission in place of the action. *You have been angry and had pity on us:* even if you also allowed us to suffer this, you did not actually surrender us to the troubles, providing us instead with lovingkindness from you without delay. *You have shaken the land and disturbed it* (v. 2). By land here he refers to the land of promise: You have reduced us to panic and alarm with the multitude of the troubles (mentioning *the land* to bring out the extremity of the panic, as if the whole of it were moved). *Heal its rents, for it has been shaken.* Since he applied their sufferings to the land, he followed this line of thinking, and consequently, as if | on the basis of the extraordinary degree of

ἀπὸ τῆς ὑπερβολῆς τοῦ συσσεισμοῦ τῆς γῆς συντριβείσης καὶ διαλυθείσης, οὕτω φησί Θεράπευσον αὐτῆς τὰ συντρίμματα — ἵνα εἴπῃ Ἴασαι ἡμῶν τὰ κακά, καὶ θεράπευσον τὰ πάθη, καὶ διάλυσον τὰς συμφοράς.

5ᵃ. Ἔδειξας τῷ λαῷ σου σκληρά. Πολλῶν ἡμᾶς χαλεπῶν πεῖραν λαβεῖν ἐποίησας.

5ᵇ. Ἐπότισας ἡμᾶς οἶνον κατανύξεως. Κατάνυξιν λέγει τὸ ἐφ᾿ ὁτῳδήποτε πράγματι παθεῖν | τὴν ψυχήν, οὕτως ὅταν λέγῃ τὸ Διεσχίσθησαν καὶ οὐ κατενύγησαν, τουτέστιν ἀποτυχόντες πολλάκις οὐδὲ οὕτως ἔπαθον τὴν ψυχήν, οὐδὲ κατέγνωσαν ἑαυτῶν. Τοιοῦτόν ἐστιν καὶ τὸ ᵃΑ λέγετε ἐν ταῖς καρδίαις ὑμῶν, ἐπὶ ταῖς κοίταις ὑμῶν κατανύγητε, τουτέστιν ᵃΑ βουλεύεσθε 10 κατὰ διάνοιαν, ἐφ᾿ ἡσυχίας ὄντες ἐν τῇ κλίνῃ λογισάμενοι κατάγνωτε ἑαυτῶν καὶ μεταμελήθητε ἐφ᾿ οἷς διεπράξασθε. Οὕτω καὶ ἐπὶ τῆς Σουσάννας περὶ τῶν πρεσβυτέρων φησὶν ὅτι κατενύγησαν τῇ καρδίᾳ, τουτέστιν ἔπαθον ἐπ᾿ αὐτῇ ὑπὸ τῆς ἐπιθυμίας συνεχόμενοι. Κἀνταῦθα οὖν κατάνυξιν καλεῖ τὴν ἐπιθυμίαν, ὡς πάθος ἀρκοῦν ἐνεργαζόμενον τῇ ψυχῇ· ὡς γὰρ μεταμέλεια καὶ 15 κατάνυξις πράγματος πάθος ἐμποιεῖ, καὶ ὡς ἐπιθυμία καὶ ἔρως χαλεπός, οὕτως καὶ ἀθυμία πάθος ἐνεργάζεται. Τὸν δὲ οἶνον ἐπὶ τῆς συμφορᾶς ἀεὶ λέγει καὶ τῆς τιμωρίας, ἀπὸ τοῦ τὸν οἶνον πλείονα δοθέντα παράγειν τοὺς λογισμοὺς καὶ παραφέρειν καὶ τὴν παρὰ τοῦ Θεοῦ τιμωρίαν ἐκτὸς τοῦ καθεστῶτος ἐργάζεσθαι. Τοῦτο οὖν φησιν ὅτι τιμωρίαν ἡμῖν ἐπενεχθῆναι συνε- 20 χώρησας, οὕτω μὲν δαψιλῶς ὥστε δοκεῖν εἰς ἀπόγνωσιν τῆς τιμωρίας μετέχειν, οὕτω δὲ χαλεπὴν ὡς πάθους καὶ ἀθυμίας αὐτάρκως πληροῦν τὴν ψυχήν.

6. Ἔδωκας τοῖς φοβουμένοις σε σημείωσιν τοῦ φυγεῖν ἀπὸ προσώπου τόξου. Ἀλλ᾿ ἐν μέσῳ τοσούτων ὄντας κακῶν | οὐκ ἀφῆκας παθεῖν, ὥσπερ 25 δὲ σημείῳ τινὶ διακρίνας ἡμᾶς, οὕτως ἐν μέσῳ τῶν κακῶν στρεφομένους ἀνεπιβουλεύτους φυλαχθῆναι ἐποίησας τῆς τῶν ἐναντίων ἐπιβουλῆς. Τοῦτο δὲ

7-8 Ps. XXXIV, 15ᶜ (cf. supra p. 186, 15-18)   9-10 ps. IV, 5ᵇ   13 Sus. 10.

1 σεισμοῦ Cord   2-3 αὐτῆς -- θεράπευσον om. Cord.
5ᵃ. Πολλῶν — ἐποίησας: P, fol. 179ᵛ; V, fol. 244.
5ᵇ. Κατάνυξιν — ψυχήν: P, fol. 179ᵛ; V, fol. 244ᵛ; Cord, p. 181 (P. G., 685 A 4-B 13).   9 οὐδὲ] καὶ CV   καὶ om. CV   10 βούλεσθε C   11 διάνοιαν] διάν C
15 ἀρκοῦν om. Cord   16 χαλεπὸν Cord   17 καὶ om. Cord   22 πληροῦντα CV.
6. Ἀλλ᾿ ἐν μέσῳ — ἐτιμωρήσατο: P, fol. 180; V, fol. 244ᵛ-245; Cord, p. 182 (P. G., 685ʹCD).   26 σημεῖον τί C.

Aᵉ 5ᵃ (p. 311, 31-32): Vt malorum magnorum conperemus experimentum. 17-19 (p. 312, 3-8): Vinum Scriptura pro plaga perturbationis sepe ponit et malorum consternatione (— nem ms); scilicet simili effectu, id est afflictione, nos ita nimia obrui permisisti, ut id in nobis, quod etiam ebrietas, uideretur operari.

the quake striking and destroying the earth, he speaks in these terms—*Cure its rents,* as if to say, *Heal* our troubles, cure our sufferings, and undo the misfortunes.

You let the people see your harsh side (v. 3): you made us experience many hardships. *You gave us wine of compunction to drink.* By *compunction* he refers to the soul's suffering from any cause, as when he says, "They were rent asunder, and felt no compunction"—that is, Though often failing in their purpose, they did not take it to heart, nor did they condemn themselves. Similarly, "Have compunction in bed for what you say in your hearts"—that is, When you are at peace in bed and are reflecting, condemn yourselves for what you have in mind, and repent of your actions. Likewise also in the case of Susanna in regard to the elders it says, "They felt compunction at heart"[1]—that is, they suffered in it for being affected by lust. So here, too, by *compunction* he refers to lust as productive of emotion in the soul: just as repentance and compunction for the offense give rise to emotion, as do lust and ill-tempered desire, so too despondency produces emotion. Now, he always speaks of *wine* in the case of misfortune and punishment, punishment from God causing one to be beside oneself, by analogy with the excess of wine causing the mind to be deranged. So he is saying, You allowed punishment to be inflicted on us, in one sense so liberally that we seemed to share in punishment to the point of despair, in another sense so harshly as to fill our soul sufficiently with emotion and despondency.

You gave to those who fear you a signal to flee before the bow (v. 4): though we were in the midst of such awful troubles, however, you did not allow us to suffer; instead, as though distinguishing us by some sign, you caused us to be protected from the scheming of the adversaries when we were caught up in the troubles and without a plan to follow. Now, he says this | by analogy with one side often mingling with the enemy in times of

---

1. Pss 35:15 LXX; 4:5; cf. Sus 1:10.

ἐκ μεταφορᾶς λέγει τῶν ἐναντίων ἐν τοῖς πολέμοις πολλάκις ἀναμιγνυμένων
τοῖς πολεμίοις, οἵτινες ἀλλήλοις διδόασι σημεῖα καὶ σύμβολα οἰκειότητος
καὶ γινώσκουσιν ἀλλήλους ἐν ἀπομιμήσει τοῦ ἐκείνων σχήματος, ὡς μὴ
ἀθρόαν καὶ ἀπροσδόκητον ὑποστῶσι τὴν τιμωρίαν. Οἱ γὰρ τοῦτο ποιοῦν-
5 τες ἀεὶ σημεῖόν τι πάντως ἀλλήλοις καὶ σύνθημα διδόασιν, ὡς ἂν μὴ ἀπὸ
τῆς κατὰ τὸ σχῆμα κοινότητος ἀλλήλους ἀντὶ τῶν πολεμίων ἀνέλωσιν·
σημείῳ δέ τινι γνωρίμῳ διακρίνοντες ἀλλήλους, φυλάττονται μὲν τῆς κατ'
ἀλλήλων σφαγῆς, πράττουσι δὲ μετὰ πάσης ἀδείας τὰ δοκοῦντα εἰς τοὺς
πολεμίους, — ὃ δὴ ποιῆσαί τε καὶ φυλάξασθαι ἐκείνους οὐχ οἷόν τε τῷ
10 σχήματι μὲν ἀπατωμένους, τὸ σύνθημα δὲ οὐκ εἰδότας. Τοῦτο οὖν φησιν
ὅτι ὥσπερ σημείῳ τινὶ διακρίνας πάσης ἡμᾶς ἐρρύσω τῆς παρ' ἐκείνων
ἐπιβουλῆς, ὡς ἂν μήτε ὑπὸ τόξων φερομένων μήτε ὑπό τινος ἑτέρου πάθοι-
μέν τι δεινόν. Τοῦτο δὲ καὶ ἀπὸ τῶν κατ' Αἴγυπτον λαβὼν εἶπεν, ὅτι
ὥσπερ σημείῳ τινὶ τῷ ἐπὶ τῶν φλιῶν αἵματι διακρίνας τούτους ἀπὸ τῶν
15 Αἰγυπτίων, τούτους μὲν ἀβλαβεῖς διετήρησεν, ἐκείνους δὲ ἐτιμωρήσατο.

7ᵃ. Ὅπως ἂν ῥυσθῶσιν οἱ ἀγαπητοί σου. Ταῦτα δέ φησιν ἐποίησας ὑπὲρ
ἡμῶν τῶν ἠγαπημένων ὑπό σου, ἵνα ἡμεῖς ἀπαλλαγῶμεν τῆς ἐκείνων ἐπιβουλῆς. Εἶτα καὶ εὐχόμενος,

7ᵇ. Σῶσον τῇ δεξιᾷ σου καὶ ἐπάκουσόν μου. Ἐπάκουσον καὶ βοηθήσας
20 περίσωσον. Καὶ προφητεύων λοιπὸν τὸ ἐσόμενα.

8ᵃ. Ὁ Θεὸς ἐλάλησεν ἐν τῷ ἁγίῳ αὐτοῦ. Ἐλάλησεν, ἀντὶ τοῦ ἐφθέγξατο
καὶ ἀπεφήνατο. Πολλαχοῦ γὰρ ὅταν τι λέγῃ περὶ τοῦ Θεοῦ ὡς ποιεῖν
μέλλοντος, τίθησι τὸ «ἐλάλησεν» ἢ «λαλήσει», ὡσανεὶ τοῦ Θεοῦ δίκην

---

14 cf. Ex. XII, 22.

1 ἐναντίων om. PV Cord   2-3 οἵτινες — ἀλλήλους om. CPV   3 ἐκείνων om.
Cord   ὡς μὴ] δεξάμενοι CPV   7-8 τὰς... σφαγὰς Cord   6-15 cf. Paraphrasis
(p. 172, 35-40).
7ᵃ. Ταῦτα — εὐχόμενος: P, fol. 180; V, fol. 245; Cord, p. 182-183, 3 (P. G.,
685 D 11-13).
7ᵇ. Ἐπάκουσον — ἐσόμενα: P, fol. 180; V, fol. 245.
8ᵃ. Ἐλάλησεν — ὤμοσεν: P, fol. 180ᵛ; V, fol. 245ᵛ; Cord, p. 184.   23 τοῦ θεοῦ
om. Cord.

Aᵉ 13-15 (p. 312, 15-18): ...hoc etiam de Aegiptia liberatione constat insertum (insertum ms), cum postes conseruandorum insignati sunt sanguine.
16-17 (p. 312, 20-22): Haec autem, inquit, uniuersa fecisti pro nobis, quos delegi
a te... 8¹ (p. 312, 24-313, 2): Sepe hoc uerbum ussurpat, ut dicat Locutus est
pro Statuit atque firmauit; sic in sexagissimo psalmo primo: Semel locutus est
Deus, Sanctitatem maiestatemque suam, quae inuiolata est, iurando.

war, giving one another signs and clues to their true colors and recognizing one another from the similarity of their appearance to prevent their incurring a sudden and unexpected retribution. Those doing this always give one another a sign or password to prevent by their shared appearance their slaying one another instead of the enemy; they distinguish one another by a sign, protecting one another from slaughter and with complete security achieving their purpose against the enemy, which it would be impossible for them to do and to avoid if they were misled by appearances and did not know the password. So he is saying, You rescued us from their scheming by distinguishing us with a sign, as it were, lest we suffer any ill effects from bows that are drawn or anything else. In this he referred also to the events in Egypt, the fact that God distinguished them from the Egyptians by the blood on the doorposts as a kind of sign,[2] keeping them unharmed and punishing the others. *So that your loved ones might be rescued* (v. 5): you did this for us in your love for us so that we might be freed from their scheming. Then he says, as a prayer, *Save with your right hand, and listen to me:* hearken and save by coming to our aid.

Then he says, by way of prophesying the future, *God spoke in his holy one* (v. 6). By *God spoke* he means, He uttered and pronounced. In many places, in fact, when he refers to God being about to act, he uses "he spoke" or "he will speak" as if God, like | a king, is pronouncing, and things hap-

---

2. Cf. Exod 12:22.

βασιλέως ἀποφαινομένου καὶ οὕτω πάντως γιγνομένων ὡς προσέταξεν· οἷόν ἐστι τὸ Ἀκούσομαι τί λαλήσει Κύριος ὁ Θεὸς ἐν τῷ πδ΄ ψαλμῷ κείμενον, — μαθήσομαι τί ποτε περὶ ἡμῶν ἀποφαίνεται γενέσθαι, — οὕτω καὶ ἐν τῷ ξα΄ τὸ Ἅπαξ ἐλάλησεν ὁ Θεός, ἀντὶ τοῦ ἀπεφήνατο, καὶ οἶδα ὅτι γενέσθαι πάντως ἀνάγκη. Τὸ δὲ ἐν τῷ ἁγίῳ αὐτοῦ, ἀντὶ τοῦ ἁγιάσματος αὐτοῦ λέγει, 5 ἀντὶ τοῦ κατὰ τῆς ἁγιωσύνης αὐτοῦ ἐλάλησεν, — τουτέστιν Ὤμοσε καθ᾽ ἑαυτοῦ, ἵνα δείξῃ τῆς ἀποφάσεως τὸ ἀμετάθετον, ὡς καὶ ἐν τῷ πη τὸ Ἅπαξ ὤμοσα ἐν τῷ ἁγίῳ μου, εἰ τῷ Δαυὶδ ψεύσομαι. Τί δὲ ποιήσειν ὤμοσεν;

8ᵇ. Ἀγαλλιάσομαι καὶ διαμεριῶ Σίκιμα. Τὸ ἀγαλλιάσομαι οὐχ ὡς περὶ 10 ἑαυτοῦ λέγει, ἀλλ᾽ ἀντὶ τοῦ ἀγαλλιασθῆναι ποιήσω· καὶ εἴρηται μὲν οὕτως ἐν τῷ ἑβραϊκῷ κατά τι οἰκεῖον ἰδίωμα τῆς γλώττης, ἀσαφέστερον δὲ γέγονεν ἐν τῷ ἑλληνικῷ διὰ μιᾶς λέξεως φρασθέν. Βούλεται δὲ εἰπεῖν ὅτι πολλῆς αὐτοῖς μεταδώσω τῆς εὐφροσύνης, ἀποδιδοὺς αὐτοῖς τὴν οἰκείαν γῆν, καὶ πάλιν αὐτὴν διαμερίζων αὐτοῖς, — ἀπὸ γὰρ τοῦ μέρους ἠβουλήθη τὸ 15 πᾶν σημᾶναι· ὡς οὖν ὑπὸ τῶν ἀλλοφύλων τότε κατεχομένης, ἤτοι τῶν περιοίκων ἢ τῶν Ἀντιόχου στρατηγῶν, ἀποδιώξας φησὶ τοὺς πολεμίους καὶ ἀφελόμενος ἀπ᾽ αὐτῶν πάλιν τὴν γῆν ἀποδώσω ὑμῖν καταμερίσας αὐτήν.

8ᶜ. Καὶ τὴν κοιλάδα τῶν σκηνῶν διαμετρήσω. Ἕτερον λέγει τόπον οὕτω καλούμενον. Ἐπειδὴ γὰρ ἴδιόν ἐστιν τῶν τὴν γῆν λαμβανόντων μέτρῳ ταύ- 20 την διαμερίζεσθαι καὶ διαλαγχάνειν, — οἷον δὴ τὸ γεγονὸς ἐπὶ Ἰησοῦ τοῦ Ναυῆ, ὅτε μετρήσας διεῖλεν αὐτοῖς τὴν γῆν, — τοῦτό φησιν ὅτι πάλιν αὐτὴν λαβὼν αὐτοῖς ἀποδώσω καὶ πάλιν αὐτὴν διέλω κατὰ μέτρον ὥστε νέμεσθαι τὴν ἰδίαν ἕκαστον χώραν.

9ᵃ. Ἐμός ἐστι Γαλαάδ, καὶ ἐμός ἐστι Μανασσή. Ὁ Γαλαὰδ τόπος ἐστὶ 25 τῆς Γαλιλαίας πλησιάζων μᾶλλον τῷ Λιβάνῳ, Μανασσῆς δὲ ἡ φυλή. Ὡς οὖν

2 Ps. LXXXIV, 9   4 ps. LXI, 12   8 ps. LXXXVIII, 36   21-22 Ios. XVIII, 5.

2 πδ΄] πα΄ CV   5-6 cf. Paraphrasis (p. 173, 9-11): Τὸ γὰρ ἐν τῷ ἁγίῳ αὐτοῦ, ἀντὶ τοῦ Ὡς ἥρμοσε τῇ ἁγιώτητι αὐτοῦ λέγει. 8ᵇ. Τὸ ἀγαλλιάσομαι — αὐτήν: P, fol. 180ᵛ; V, fol. 245ᵛ; Cord, p. 184-185. 13 ἐν τῷ ἑλληνικῷ] τὸ ἑλληνικὸν CPV   18 ἀπ᾽ om. CV   ὑμῖν] τούτοις CPV. 8ᶜ. Ἕτερον λέγει — χώραν: P, fol. 180ᵛ; V, fol. 245ᵛ.   22 μετρίσας C   μερίδας V. 9ᵃ. Ὁ Γαλαὰδ — σχῆμα: P, fol. 181; V, fol. 246; Vat. 1422, fol. 111ᵛ (anon.); Cord, p. 185 (anon.).   25 ὁ Γαλαὰδ om. CV.

Aᵉ 8ᶜ (p. 313, 8-13): Alium locum regionis ipsius nominauit, quem ereptum gentibus restituam iuri meorum, ea condicione possedendum qua dudum ab Iessu Naue fuerat distributus.   25-26 (p. 313, 14-16): Galath mons est in Galilia, uicinus est Libano.

pened in the way he ordered, as, for example, in Psalm 85, "I shall listen to
what the Lord God will say"—that is, I shall learn what he pronounces will
happen in our case; likewise in Psalm 62, "Once God has spoken"[3]—that
is, He has pronounced, and I know that it in consequence it definitely will
happen. He says *in his holy one,* meaning "in his holiness"—that is, *God
spoke* in his sanctity, meaning, He swore in his own name, the purpose being
to bring out the permanence of his pronouncement, as also Psalm 89, "Once
and for all I swore by my holiness not to be false to David."[4] What did he
swear to do? *I shall rejoice and divide up Shechem.* He uses the phrase *I shall
rejoice* not of himself, but to mean, I shall cause them to rejoice. While it was
stated this way in the Hebrew by a linguistic idiom, it proved to be expressed
with less clarity in the Greek in one word.[5] His meaning is, I shall communicate great happiness to them, restoring their own land to them and in turn
dividing it up among them (intending to suggest the whole by mention of the
part). So with the land occupied by foreigners, either by neighboring peoples
or by the generals of Antiochus, I shall drive off the enemy, remove the land
from them in turn, and restore it to you, dividing it up. *And I shall portion
out the valley of the tents.* He refers to a different place bearing this name:
since those occupying land portion it out and give lots by use of a measure,
as in the case of Joshua son of Nun when he measured and distributed the
land among them,[6] he means here, I shall take it again and restore it to them,
and divide it by measurement so as to allot everyone their place.

    Gilead is mine, and Manasseh is mine (v. 7). Gilead is a place closer to
Galilee than to Lebanon, while Manasseh is a tribe. So | with these places

---

3. Pss 85:8; 62:11.
4. Ps 89:35.
5. The Greek, in fact, reproduces the Hebrew exactly, except for the addition of the copu-
lative.
6. Cf. Josh 18.

τούτων τὸ πρότερον ὑπὸ τοὺς ἀλλοφύλους ὄντων τῶν τε τόπων καὶ τῶν
ἀνθρώπων, — οἱ μὲν γὰρ ἐδούλευον, οἱ δὲ κατείχοντο ὑπ' ἐκείνων, — τοῦτό
φησιν ὅτι οὐκέτι ἔσται ἑτέρων ὁ Γαλαάδ· ἀφελὼν γὰρ αὐτὸν τῶν πολεμίων καὶ πάλιν ἐμὸν ποιήσομαι. Ἀλλ' οὐδὲ ὁ Μανασσῆς ἑτέρῳ δουλεύσει·
5 ἀπαλλάξω γὰρ αὐτοὺς τῆς δουλείας. Βούλεται δὲ εἰπεῖν ὅτι Καὶ ὑμᾶς ἀπαλλάξω τοῦ δουλεύειν τοῖς ἐχθροῖς καὶ τοὺς προσήκοντας ὑμῖν ἀποδώσω
τόπους, καὶ εἰς τὸ ἀρχαῖον ὑμᾶς ἀποκαταστήσω σχῆμα.

9ᶜ. Ἰούδας βασιλεύς μου. Σύμμαχος τὸ βασιλεύς μου « Προτάσσων ἐμὸς »
λέγει, ὥστε δῆλον εἶναι ὅτι τὸ Μου τῷ Ἰούδᾳ ἐπισυνῆπται κατὰ διάνοιαν·
10 ἐν μέσῳ τοῦ Βασιλεὺς παρεγκειμένου, ἵνα ᾖ Ἰούδας μου βασιλεύς. Ἰούδας δὲ
φησιν ὁ ἐμὸς βασιλεύς, ἵνα εἴπῃ Ἡ τοῦ Ἰούδα φυλὴ πάλιν ἀναδώσει τοὺς
ἐξ αὐτῆς βασιλεῖς. Δι' ὅλων δὲ λέγει ὅτι τὰ ἀρχαῖα ὑμῖν πάλιν ἀποδοθήσεται.

10ᵃ. Μωὰβ λέβης τῆς ἐλπίδος μου. Οἱ μὲν οἰκεῖοί φησιν ἐν τούτοις, ὁ
15 δὲ Μωὰβ τί; Τὸ ἐναντίον ἐν τάξει μοι λέβητός ἐστιν. Ὁ γὰρ Σύρος τὸ
λέβης τῆς ἐλπίδος μου οὕτω φησὶν Λεκάνη τῆς καταπατήσεώς μου, τοιοῦτό
τι εἰπεῖν βουλόμενος ὅτι ὥσπερ ἐν λεκάνῃ ἱμάτια βαλλόμενα ὑπὸ τῶν πλυνόντων πατεῖται, οὕτω φησὶν καταπατήσω τὸν Μωάβ. Τοῦτο δὲ καὶ ἡ ἀκολουθία δείκνυσιν βουλόμενον εἰπεῖν τὸν προφήτην.

20 Τὸ δὲ λέβης εἴρηται ἴσως ἢ τῶν Ἑβραίων μιᾷ τῇ φωνῇ καλούντων ἀμφότερα τῶν παλαιῶν ἐν μικροτέροις τοῖς λέβησι πλυνόντων τε καὶ καταπα-
τούντων τὰ ἱμάτια. Τὸ δὲ ἐλπίδος μου καὶ καταπατήσεώς μου οὐδὲν δια-
φέρει· τοῦτο γὰρ λέγει τὸ ἐλπίδος μου. ἀντὶ τοῦ Ὥσπερ ἐλπίζω εἰς πέρας
ἄχθει. Τί γὰρ ἂν ἕτερον εἴη ἢ τὸ τιμωρηθῆναι τοὺς ἐχθρούς; ὃ καλῶς σαφέ-
25 στερον ὁ Σύρος ἑρμηνεύων κατάπατησιν ἐκάλεσεν, τῇ πρὸς τὴν ἑβραΐδα
ἐγγύτητι μᾶλλον συνεῖναί τε καὶ σαφηνίσαι τὸ λεχθὲν δυνηθείς.

1 τε] τότε C   3 ἔσται om. CV   ἀφέλωμαι Cord.
9ᶜ. Σύμμαχος — ἀποδοθήσεται: P, fol. 181ᵛ; V, fol. 247; Vat. 1422, fol. 112
(anon.); desideratur C.   10 ᾖ] καὶ add. 1422   12-13 ἀναδοθήσεται 1422.
10¹. Οἱ μὲν οἰκεῖοι — δυνηθείς: P, f. 181ᵛ; V, fol. 247; Οἱ μὲν — 19 προφήτην
affert Vat. 1422, fol. 112 (anon.); desideratur C.   16-18 cf. L (p. 176, 42-43): Μωὰβ
καταπάτημα ἔσται ὡς λέβης, ἐν ᾧ πλύνουσι τὰ ἱμάτια et Ps.-THEODORUS HERACLEENSIS
(Vat. 627, fol. 90ᵛ): λέβητα γὰρ ἐνταῦθα τὴν λεκάνην λέγει, ἐν ᾗ τὰ ἱμάτια πατεῖται.

Aᵉ 2-3 (p. 313, 16-19): Hunc quoque non sinam sub aliorum diutius potestate
consistere, neque Mannasse externis dominis seruire cogetur.   10-12 (p. 313,
35-314, 2): Ac si diceret Iudas autem rex meus regnauit; ex se (uel eo add. supra) semper principes profert; prior status ei ex toto reddetur.   15-18 (p. 314,
4-8): Ebreus Moab olla lauacri mei, Sirus Moab albeus conculcationis meae, ac
si diceret: Sicut in alueo (albeo ms) uestimenta a lauantibus conculcantur, ita
ego subieciam pedibus conculcandum Moab.

being formerly subject to the foreigners, both the places and the people (some being in slavery, others held by them), he is saying, No longer will Gilead belong to others, for I shall take it from the enemy and once again make it mine; Manasseh will not serve others, either: I shall free them from slavery. He means, I shall also free you from serving the foe and restore to you your proper places, and return you to your former condition. *Judah my king.* For *my king* Symmachus has "my commander," so it is clear that *my* has been attached to *Judah* in keeping with the thought, and placed between it and *king,* giving *Judah my king.*[7] He is saying, Judah is my king, in the sense, The tribe of Judah once again will provide the kings from its members. Overall, he is saying that the ancient regime once again will be restored to you.

Moab basin of my hope (v. 8): while the others will have their own place, what of Moab? On the contrary, it is in the role of my basin. The Syriac, in fact, for *basin of my hope* says "dish for my treading," meaning something like this: Just as garments thrown into a dish are trodden on by the washers, so I shall tread on Moab. The movement of thought also shows that the author intended this meaning. Each of the Hebrew words speaking of the ancients washing and treading the garments in rather small basins refers equally to the word *basin* in a single term. There is no difference between *of my hope* and "for my treading": this is what of my hope means—that is, It will come into effect just as I hope; after all, what else would it be than the foe being punished? The Syriac did well to bring out the meaning more clearly by referring to it as "treading," and by the closeness to the Hebrew it is capable of helping the reading to be understood and clarified. | *I shall*

---

7. The argument deals with the form and position of the pronoun in the Greek text. We have no comment from Theodore on the next phrase, "Ephraim the strength of my head," where the LXX "head" does call for (and from Theodoret receive) some comment.

10ᵇ. Ἐπὶ τὴν Ἰδουμαίαν ἐκτενῶ τὸ ὑπόδημά μου. Τοῦτο μάλιστα βεβαίω-
σίς ἐστι τῆς ἑρμηνείας τοῦ ἀνωτέρου· τοῦτο γὰρ λέγει ὅτι καὶ ἐπὶ Ἰδουμαίους τὸ ὑπόδημά μου ἐκτενῶ, ἀντὶ τοῦ κἀκείνους ὑποτάξω καὶ ὑποχειρίους
ποιησάμενος καὶ ὥσπερ ὑπὸ τοὺς πόδας βαλὼν καταπατήσω. Μωαβίτας δὲ
λέγει καὶ Ἰδουμαίους, ἐπειδὴ οὗτοι μάλιστα τῶν περιοικούντων ἐχθραίνοντες   5
αὐτοῖς ἀεὶ καὶ τότε πλεῖστα διέθηκαν αὐτοῖς κακά, οὓς καὶ κρατήσαντες
ὕστερον αὐτάρκως ἐτιμωρήσαντο. Ταῦτα εἰρηκὼς ὡς ἐκ τοῦ Θεοῦ, ὅτι ἐλά-
λησέ τε καὶ ποιήσειν ὑπέσχετο καὶ θαυμασιώτατα, χρησάμενος τῷ σχήματι
ὡς ἂν τοῦ Θεοῦ εἰπόντος ὅτι Πάλιν ἀποδίδωμι τὴν γῆν, πάλιν αὐτὴν εἰς
κατοίκησιν μερίζων, τῇ βασιλείᾳ τὸ σχῆμα ἀποδίδωμι, τῷ στρατῷ | τὴν   10
παλαιὰν ἰσχὺν τοὺς ἐναντίους τιμωρούμενος, ἀκολούθως ἑαυτῷ ὡς ἐκ προσώπου τῶν Μακκαβαίων φησίν·

10ᶜ. Ἐμοὶ ἀλλόφυλοι ὑπετάγησαν. Τουτέστιν, ἐπειδὴ ταῦτα ὁ Θεὸς ἀπεφήνατο καὶ ἐπηγγείλατο ἐκράτησα τῶν ἀλλοφύλων.

11ᵃ. Τίς ἀπάξει με εἰς πόλιν περιοχῆς; Πόλιν περιοχῆς φησι τὴν σφόδρα   15
περιεχομένην ὑπὸ τείχους ἀσφαλοῦς, καὶ ἀνεπιβούλευτον οὖσαν διὰ τοῦτο
τοῖς πολεμίοις. Τίς γάρ φησιν ἕτερος στρατηγήσει μου τοῖς πολεμίοις καὶ
προσάξει με πόλεσιν ὀχυραῖς;

11ᵇ. Τίς ὁδηγήσει με ἕως τῆς Ἰδουμαίας; Τίς δέ μοι καὶ μέχρι τῶν Ἰδου-
μαίων στρατηγήσει; Ὁ τὴν ὁδὸν ὑποδεικνὺς καὶ προθυμότερον εἰς τὸ πολε-   20
μεῖν ἐργαζόμενος.

12ᵃ. Οὐχὶ σύ, ὁ Θεός, ὁ ἀπωσάμενος ἡμᾶς; Καθ' ὑπόκρισιν ἀναγνωστέον, ἀντὶ τοῦ Μὴ ἕτερός μοι ταῦτα παρέξει; Οὐχὶ διά σοῦ φησι τούτων
ἀπολαύσω καὶ κρατήσω τῶν ἐναντίων; Τὸ δὲ ἀπάξει καὶ ὁδηγήσει σωματικῶς ἐπὶ τοῦ Θεοῦ ὡς προηγουμένου καὶ στρατηγοῦντος καὶ πάντα συμ-   25
πονοῦντος εἶπεν καλῶς.

10ᵇ. Τοῦτο μάλιστα — Μακκαβαίων φησίν: P, fol. 181ᵛ; V, fol. 247; Vat. 1422,
fol. 112 (anon.).   2 ἀνωτέρω 1422   3 ὑποτάξαι V   5 ἐχθραίνοντες] ἐχθρῶν 1422
6 διέθ. αὐτοῖς] αὐτοὺς V   7 ἐτιμωρήσατο 1422   9 πάλιν om. 1422.
10ᶜ. Τουτέστιν — ἀλλοφύλων: P, fol. 181ᵛ; V, fol. 247.
11ᵃ. Πόλιν — ὀχυραῖς: P, fol. 182; V, fol. 247ᵛ.
12ᵃ. Καθ' ὑπόκρισιν — καλῶς: P, fol. 182ᵛ; V, fol. 247ᵛ-248; Cord, p. 190.

Aᵉ 1-6 (p. 314, 9-14): Hic uorsus superiorem expossitione inlustrat. Cum
Moabditas contritos insultantibus plantis conculcauero, etiam in finibus Idu-
meorum progrediar; hae enim duae gentes potissimum in Iudeos ex professo
inimicitias exercebant.   20-21 (p. 314, 20-21): ...tamquam iteneris dux et labo-
rum particeps.   23-24 (p. 314, 21-23): Interroganter legendum est Numquid
alius quispiam haec mihi uniuersa contribuet?

stretch out my shoe upon Idumea. This is a particular confirmation of the above interpretation, his meaning being, Upon the Idumeans I shall stretch out my shoe—that is, I shall subject them as well, making them subservient, and I shall tread them down by casting them under my feet, as it were. Now, he speaks of Moabites and Idumeans since it was they in particular of all the neighboring peoples who were always hostile to them and at that time devised most troubles for them, though later they got the better of them and punished them sufficiently.

He said this on God's part, as it were, that he spoke and promised to perform even miraculous things, and adopted the point of view of God saying, Once again I shall restore the land; once again I shall divide it up for occupation; I shall restore the trappings of kingship, punishing the adversaries with the military force of old. He now proceeds to speak on the part of the Maccabees in keeping with his own line of thought: *Foreigners were made subject to me*—that is, Since God made these pronouncements and promises, I gained control of the foreigners. *Who will bring me to the fortified city?* (v. 9). By fortified city he means the one encircled by a secure wall, and hence impregnable to the enemy. Who else, he asks, will be my leader against the enemy and direct me against walled cities? *Who will lead me to Idumea?* Who will be my leader even as far as the Idumeans? It is the one showing the way and making me more enthusiastic about fighting.

Is it not you, O God, who repulsed us? (v. 10). It is to be read as if taking a part, with the meaning, Surely no one else will provide me with this? Is it not through you that I will enjoy this and gain control of the adversaries? The verbs *will bring* and *will lead* were well put in describing God in corporeal manner leading and directing and struggling with them. | *Will you not go out*

12ᵇ. Καὶ οὐκ ἐξελεύσῃ, ὁ Θεός, ἐν ταῖς δυνάμεσιν ἡμῶν; Καὶ τοῦτο καθ᾽ ὑπόκρισιν ἀναγνωστέον, τὸ δὲ Σὺ κατὰ κοινοῦ νοητέον — ἀντὶ τοῦ Οὐχὶ σὺ ὁ ἀπωσάμενος ἡμᾶς, σὺ καὶ ἐξελεύσῃ ἐν ταῖς δυνάμεσιν ἡμῶν; ἵνα εἴπῃ ὅτι Σὺ καὶ παθεῖν συνεχώρησας, σὺ καὶ ἐπαμυνεῖς καὶ συμμαχήσεις· τὸ γὰρ
5 ἐν ταῖς δυνάμεσιν λέγει ἀντὶ τοῦ σὺν ταῖς δυνάμεσι, τῷ ἐν ἀντὶ τοῦ « σὺν » συνηθῶς κεχρημένος κἀνταῦθα. Δυνάμεις δὲ λέγει τὰς στρατιάς, ἐπειδὴ τῶν πολεμούντων ἡ δύναμις ἐν τῷ στρατῷ· οὕτω δέ πως καὶ μέχρι τοῦ νῦν λέγεται παρὰ τοῖς πολλοῖς. Τοῦτο οὖν φησιν ὅτι Οὐ συνεξελεύσῃ ἡμῖν πολεμοῦσι καὶ συμμαχήσεις ἡμῖν;

10 13. Δὸς ἡμῖν βοήθειαν ἐκ θλίψεως, καὶ ματαία σωτηρία ἀνθρώπου. Οὐκοῦν φησιν ἐπειδὴ οὐχ ἕτερος ὁ βοηθεῖν δυνάμενος ἀλλ᾽ ἢ | μόνος αὐτός, χαρισάμενος τὴν παρά σου βοήθειαν ἀπάλλαξον τῆς κατεχούσης θλίψεως· οὐδὲ γὰρ οἷόν τε παρ᾽ ἀνθρώπου βοήθειαν ἐκδέξασθαι, ἐπειδὴ μάταιον καὶ κενὸν τὸ παρὰ ἀνθρώπου σῴζεσθαι προσδοκᾶν, πάντων ἀνθρώπων ἀσθενῶν τε
15 ὄντων καὶ βοηθείας τῆς παρά σου δεομένων.

14ᵃ. Ἐν τῷ Θεῷ ποιήσομεν δύναμιν. Ἐν γὰρ τῇ σῇ βοηθείᾳ φησὶ καὶ συμμαχίᾳ διαπράξομαί τι δυνατὸν καὶ ἰσχυρὸν κατὰ τῶν πολεμίων.

14ᵇ. Καὶ αὐτὸς ἐξουδενώσει τοὺς θλίβοντας ἡμᾶς. Αὐτὸς δὲ καὶ τιμωρησάμενος, τὸ μηδὲν ἀποφανεῖς τοὺς νῦν ἡμῖν πολεμεῖν πειρωμένους.

20 PSALMVS LX

Τὰ κατὰ Βαβυλῶνα προαγορεύει νῦν οὕτω τὸν ψαλμὸν ἐκφωνῶν, ὡσανεὶ αἰτούντων ἐκείνων τυχεῖν τῆς τοῦ Θεοῦ βοηθείας, ὁμοῦ καὶ τὴν ἐπάνοδον προϋπισχνούμενος.

12ᵇ. Καὶ τοῦτο — συμμαχήσεις ἡμῖν: P, fol. 182ᵛ; V, fol. 248.   3 Σὺ καὶ κ. τ. λ. Cord, p. 190 (anon.).   4 σὺ καὶ 1° l.] σὺ ὁ Cord   τὸ] ὁ CV   7 πως om. CV τοῦ om. CV·
13. Οὐκοῦν — δεομένων: P, fol. 182ᵛ; V, fol. 248; Cord, p. 190.
14ᵃ. Ἐν γὰρ — πολεμίων: P, fol. 182ᵛ et V, fol. 248 (anon.).
14ᵇ. Αὐτὸς — πειρωμένους: P, fol. 182ᵛ; V, fol. 248.   Paraphrasis (p. 175, 25-27): Τὰ δὲ τῶν δυναστευόντων ἐξουδένωσις διαδέχεται καὶ τὸ μηδὲν εἶναι.
Τὰ κατὰ — προϋπισχνούμενος: P, fol. 183; V, fol. 248ᵛ; Cord, p. 198-199.

Aᵉ 13 (p. 314, 27-315, 3): Proinde quia nullus est praeter te qui ferre possit auxilium, tuum (uel tu add. supra) confer adiutorium, cui nos confidere praestitisti, quando uanum et inane est opinari quod homo possit dare salutem.   14ᵃ (p. 315, 4-5): Tuo auxilio potens ero et magnum aliquid aversus hostes efficiam.   Argumentum ps. LX (p. 315, 7-11): Ex persona populi in Babilone possiti et pro libertate sua deprecantis psalmus iste conponitur; qui tamen spem nutrierat reuersionis in patriam. Cf. Pseudo-Beda (798).

in our forces, O God? This, too, is to be read as if taking a part, and the *you* is to be understood generally in the sense, Are you not the one who rejected us, and is it not you who also will go out with our armies? In other words, You who allowed us to suffer, you are also the one who will assist us and be our ally. By *in our forces,* in fact, he means "with our forces," here using *in* as usual for "with," and by *forces* he means "armies," since the force of the attackers is in the army, as is the usage with the general run of people to this day. So what he means is, Will you not go out in battle and fight with us? *Help us out of tribulation, where human solutions are worthless* (v. 11): so since there is no one else capable of helping but you alone, bestow on us your help and free us from the tribulation besetting us. It is, in fact, impossible for help to come from human beings, since it is futile and idle to expect to be saved by human beings, all human beings proving weak and needing help from you.

With God we shall exercise power (v. 12): with your help and assistance we shall do doughty deeds against the enemy. *And he himself will reduce our oppressors to naught:* you are the one who will wreak retribution, and will render useless those who now try to war against us.

PSALM 61

In uttering the psalm in these terms he now foretells the situation in Babylon, as though they were begging to receive God's help, and at the same time promises in advance the return as well. | *Hearken, O God, to my peti-*

2. Εἰσάκουσον, ὁ Θεός, τῆς δεήσεώς σου, πρόσχες τῇ προσευχῇ μου. Καὶ πρόσχες καὶ ἄκουσον, τουτέστιν ἀκοῦσαί | σοι μελησάτω.

3ᵃ. Ἀπὸ τῶν περάτων τῆς γῆς πρός σε ἐκέκραξα. Πέρατα τῆς γῆς πολλαχοῦ ἐκεῖνα λέγει τὰ μέρη τὰ Βαβυλῶνος καὶ Περσίδος, ὡσανεὶ πρὸς τὴν γῆν τῆς ἐπαγγελίας πόρρω τε ὄντων καὶ μικροῦ δεῖν πρὸς αὐτοῖς τοῖς 5 πέρασι τῆς γῆς· ἔτι τοίνυν φησὶν ἐν τῇ αἰχμαλωσίᾳ τυγχάνων καὶ ἐν ταῖς συμφοραῖς ἐξεταζόμενος, ἐβόησα πρός σε.

3ᵇ. Ἐν τῷ ἀκηδιάσαι τὴν καρδίαν μου. Σύμμαχος Ἐν τῷ ἀδημονεῖν φησιν· ἀλλὰ σαφέστερον μὲν Σύμμαχος, ἐνεργέστερον δὲ οἱ Ο΄ καὶ ἐμφαντικώτερον. Ἀδημονεῖν μὲν γὰρ καὶ ἐπὶ τοῖς μικροῖς λέγεται, ἀκηδιᾶν 10 δὲ ἐπὶ τοῖς μεγάλοις πάντως, ὅταν διὰ τὸ πλῆθος τῶν κακῶν λοιπὸν ὧν ἐν μέσῳ τις περιλαμβάνεται ἀπαγορεύει πρὸς αὐτά. Ἐν μέσοις τοίνυν φησὶν ὢν τοῖς κακοῖς καὶ οὐκέτι φέρειν αὐτὰ οἷός τε ὤν, ἀλλ᾽ ὥσπερ ἀκηδιάσας πρὸς αὐτά, ἐβόησα τὴν σὴν αἰτούμενος βοήθειαν.

3ᶜ. Ἐν πέτρᾳ ὕψωσάς με. Τὴν πέτραν ἐπὶ τῆς ἀσφαλείας λέγει πολ- 15 λαχοῦ. Ὑψηλόν με τοίνυν φησι καὶ ἐπίδοξον ἐποίησας, ὁμοῦ καὶ ἀσφάλειάν μοι χαρισάμενος τῇ παρά σου βοηθείᾳ, ὥστε μηδὲ ἐπισφαλῆ δοκεῖν εἶναι τὴν χάριν.

4ᵃ. Ὡδήγησάς με, ὅτι ἐγενήθης ἐλπίς μου. Καὶ μονονουχὶ ἐν ὁδηγοῦ τάξει καταστὰς ἐπανήγαγες εἰς τὴν γῆν τῆς ἐπαγγελίας, δικαιότατά γε 20 χρη|σάμενος, ἐπειδὴ καὶ παρά σου τοῦτο ἤλπιζον, οὐκ ἔχων ἄλλην προσδοκίαν τῆς χάριτος.

4ᵇ. Πύργος ἰσχύος ἀπὸ προσώπου ἐχθροῦ. Πύργον λέγει τὴν ἀσφάλειαν, ἀπὸ τοῦ πολλὴν ἀσφάλειαν ἀπὸ τῶν πύργων προσεῖναι τοῖς τε τείχεσι

2. Καὶ πρόσχες — μελησάτω: P, fol. 183; V, fol. 248ᵛ.
3ᵃ. Πέρατα — πρός σε: P, fol. 183ᵛ; V, fol. 248ᵛ.
3ᵇ. Σύμμαχος — βοήθειαν: P, fol. 183ᵛ; V, fol. 249; Cord, p. 200.　9-10 ἐνεργέστερον — ἐμφ.] ἐμφαντικώτερον δὲ οἱ Ο΄ Cord　10 μὲν om. Cord　12 ἐν μέσῳ τις περιλαμβάνεται om. CV　ἀπαγορεύει τις CV
3ᶜ. Τὴν πέτραν — χάριν: P, fol. 184; V, fol. 249ᵛ; Cord, p. 201.
4ⁱ. Καὶ μονονουχὶ -- χάριτος: P, fol. 184; V, fol. 249ᵛ.
4ᵇ. Πύργον — ἐπιβουλῆς: P, fol. 184; V, fol. 249ᵛ.

Aᵉ 2 (p. 315, 13-15): Intende et exaudi unum est; id est, supplicationem meam dignanter adnuito.　4-5 (p. 315, 16-17): Babilonis uel Persis prope in ultimo terrae sitae.　16-17 (p. 315, 19-20): Celsum me tuo numine praestitisti.
4ᵃ (p. 315, 20-24): Iuste mihi uicem ducis ac praeceptoris inplere dignatus es, cuius reuersionis spem ex tua solus sciebas expectatione pendere.　24 (p. 325, 25): Pro firmitate praesidii.

tion; heed my prayer (v. 1): give heed and listen—that is, take pains to listen. *From the ends of the earth I cried to you* (v. 2). In many places he refers to the parts of Babylon and Persia as *ends of the earth* as though at a distance from the land of promise and little short of the very ends of the earth. So he is saying, Being in captivity and finding myself in misfortune, I cried aloud to you. *When my heart sank.* Symmachus says, "When I was sorely troubled"; but while Symmachus says it more clearly, the Seventy said it more forcefully and emphatically: being sorely troubled is true of lesser matters, a sinking feeling true of greater ones, when on account of the multitude of the troubles in which one is enveloped one then despairs. So he is saying, Being in the midst of the troubles and no longer able to bear them, as though sinking before them I cried aloud in requesting your help.

You lifted me on a rock. In many places he refers to the rock with respect to security. So he is saying, You made me lofty and the cynosure of all eyes, at the same time granting me security with help from you, with the result that your grace did not even appear to be at risk. *You guided me because you became my hope* (v. 3): acting in the role of guide, as it were, you led me into the land of promise, acting most justly, since this was also my hope from you, having no other expectation of grace. *A tower of strength in the face of the foe.* By *tower* he refers to security, from the advantage of great security that comes to walls and cities from towers; | so by *tower of strength* he refers

καὶ ταῖς πόλεσιν· πύργον οὖν ἰσχύος τὴν ἰσχυρὰν ἀσφάλειαν λέγει. Τοῦτο δὲ ὡς πρὸς τὸν Θεόν φησι· Σύ μού φησι καὶ ἰσχὺς καὶ ἀσφάλεια, — ὁπηνίκα γὰρ ὑπὸ τῶν ἐχθρῶν διώκομαι, ὥσπερ ἐπὶ πύργον ἀσφαλῆ καταφυγὼν ἐπί σε, ἀπαλλάττομαι τῆς ἐκείνων ἐπιβουλῆς.

5ᵃ. Παροικήσω ἐν τῷ σκηνώματί σου εἰς τοὺς αἰῶνας. Διὰ τοῦτο γοῦν τοῦτο παρέξεις μοι καὶ τὸ διηνεκῶς κατοικεῖν ἐν τῷ σκηνώματί σου, ἵνα εἴπῃ πλησίον τοῦ ναοῦ, τουτέστιν ἐν τῇ γῇ τῆς ἐπαγγελίας.

5ᵇ. Σκεπασθήσομαι ἐν τῇ σκέπῃ τῶν πτερύγων σου. Παρέξεις δέ μοι καὶ τὴν σκέπην καὶ τὴν ἀσφάλειαν, τὴν παρά σου βοήθειαν.

6ᵃ. Ὅτι σύ, ὁ Θεός, εἰσήκουσας τῶν εὐχῶν μου. Τούτων ἀπολαύσω φησὶν ἐπείπερ εἰσήκουσας ὧν ᾔτησα.

6ᵇ. Ἔδωκας κληρονομίαν τοῖς φοβουμένοις τὸ ὄνομά σου. Ἐπειδὴ ἡ κληρονομία κτῆσίν τινα καὶ δεσποτείαν παρέχει τοῖς κληρονομοῦσιν, τοῦτό φησιν ὅτι Αἰχμα|λώτους ὄντας ἡμᾶς καὶ δουλεύοντας ἐν ἀλλοτρίοις, δέδωκας ἡμῖν τοῦ κατοικεῖν ἐν ἰδίοις, καὶ ὥσπερ κληρονομίαν τινὰ κατέχειν τε πάλιν καὶ νέμεσθαι καὶ δεσπόζειν τῆς γῆς τῆς ἐπαγγελίας.

7ᵃ. Ἡμέρας ἐφ᾽ ἡμέρας τοῦ βασιλέως προσθήσεις τὰ ἔτη αὐτοῦ. Ποιήσεις ἡμῶν φησι πολυετῆ καὶ τὸν βασιλέα· ἣν μὲν οὖν τὸ τοῦ Ζοροβάβελ βασίλειον αὐτῶν. Ὁ δὲ προφήτης τοῦτο βούλεται εἰπεῖν ὅτι Ἅπαντα ἡμῖν χαριεῖ, καὶ πάλιν ἡμῖν βασιλέα δώσεις ἥμερον, ὃν καὶ πολυετῆ ποιήσεις, — οὐ κατὰ πρόσωπον λέγων, ἀλλὰ περὶ τοῦ ἀξιώματος, — τουτέστιν Ἐπὶ πλεῖστον ποιήσεις ἡμᾶς ὑπὸ τοῖς ἰδίοις εἶναι βασιλεῦσιν, οὐκέτι πάλιν δεδιότας αἰχμαλωσίαν καὶ τὸ ὑφ᾽ ἑτέρους ὄντας δουλεύειν.

5ᵃ. Διὰ τοῦτο — ἐπαγγελίας: P, fol. 184; V, fol. 249ᵛ.   6-7 Paraphrasis (p. 196, 20-21): Σκήνωμα γὰρ αὐτοῦ καλεῖ τὸν ναὸν τὸν ἐν Ἱερουσαλήμ.
5ᵇ. Παρέξεις — βοήθειαν: P, fol. 184ᵛ; V, fol. 250.   9 τῇ... βοηθείᾳ V.
6ᵃ. Τούτων — ᾔτησα: P, fol. 184ᵛ; V, fol. 250.
6ᵇ. Ἐπειδὴ — ἐπαγγελίας: P, fol. 185; V, fol. 250; Cord, p. 202.   15 τε om. Cord.
7ᵃ. Ποιήσεις — δουλεύειν: P, fol. 185; V, fol. 250ᵛ.

Aᵉ 5ᵃ (p. 315, 29-31): ...iugiter templi tui uiciniam incolam, terram inhabitans repromisionis.   5ᵇ (p. 315, 32-33): Tutus protectione tua.   6ᵃ (p. 315, 34-35): Voti me conpotem reddidisti adnuendo suplici.   15-16 (p. 316, 1-3): Eam firmitatem possesionis restituens, quam dudum benigne tradideras. 21, 400-2 (p. 316, 4-7): Per longam aetatem nos a nostris et propriis regibus faciens gubernari, reges nostros continua succesione seruabis in aeternum.

to strong security. Now, he says this to God, You are my strength and security: when I am pursued by the foe, by taking refuge in you as though in a secure tower I am freed from their scheming.

I shall dwell in your tent forever (v. 4): for this reason, at any rate, you will provide me with this, to live constantly *in your tent,* as if to say, close to the temple—that is, in the land of promise. *I shall find shelter in the shadow of your wings:* you will provide me also with shelter and security, with help from you. *Because you, O God, hearkened to my prayers* (v. 5): I shall enjoy this, especially since you hearkened to what I asked. *You gave an inheritance to those who fear your name.* Since inheritance provides a kind of possession and ownership to the heirs, he says, When we were captives and slaves in foreign parts, you allowed us to dwell in our own country, gain possession of it like an inheritance, and once more inhabit and own the land of promise.

Days upon days you will apportion the king his years (v. 6): You will also make our king long-lived. While theirs was the reign of Zerubbabel, then, the inspired author means, You will grant us everything, and once more you will give us a gentle king, whom you will also make long-lived (a reference not to the person but to the position)—in other words, For a long time you will bring us under our own kings, no longer in dread once more of captivity and of being in service to others. | *His years as many as the days of generation*

7ᵇ. Ἕως ἡμέρας γενεᾶς καὶ γενεᾶς. Ἐκτενεῖς αὐτόν φησιν ἐπὶ πολὺ διαμένειν εἰς τὸν αἰῶνα.

8ᵃ. Διαμενεῖ εἰς τὸν αἰῶνα ἐνώπιον τοῦ Θεοῦ. Καὶ φυλαχθήσεται ἐπὶ
πλεῖστον ἐνώπιον τοῦ Θεοῦ, τουτέστιν ἐν τῇ Ἰερουσαλὴμ πλησίον τοῦ ναοῦ,
ἔνθα ὁ Κύριος κατοικεῖν ἐδοξάζετο, — ἔφην δὲ προλαβὼν ὅτι ταῦτα οὐ περὶ 5
προσώπου λέγει, — ἀντὶ τοῦ Ἐπὶ μήκιστον ἡμῖν χάρισαι τῶν ἡμετέρων βασιλέων τὴν διαδοχήν· ἐπεὶ πῶς ἐπὶ προσώπῳ ἁρμόσει τὸ ἕως ἡμέρας γενεᾶς
καὶ γενεᾶς; Πόσον γὰρ ἔμελλεν ἡ τοῦ ἑνὸς βασιλέως ἐκτείνεσθαι ζωὴ ὥστε
διαμένειν ἐπὶ πλείσταις γενεῶν διαδοχαῖς;

8ᵇ. Ἔλεον καὶ ἀλήθειαν αὐτοῦ τίς ἐκζητήσει; Ἀλλὰ ταῦτα μὲν παρέ- 10
ξεις οἰκείᾳ τῇ ἀγαθότητι. Μακαριστὸν δ᾽ ἂν εἴη τὸ καὶ αὐτόν τινα τὴν
οἰκείαν ἐπιδείκνυσθαι διάθεσιν πρός σέ τε βλέποντα, καὶ τῆς εἰς σε μὴ ἐξιστάμενον ἐλπίδος, καὶ παρά σου ταῦτα ζητοῦντα. Ἔλεον γὰρ καὶ ἀλήθειαν
συνηθῶς λέγει, τὴν βεβαίαν καὶ ἀληθῆ τοῦ Θεοῦ φιλανθρωπίαν οὕτω καλῶν
ἵνα εἴπῃ τὴν ἐπάνοδον. Καὶ καλῶς τοῦτο ἐπήγαγεν, δεικνὺς ὡς ὅτι καὶ αὐτοὺς 15
προσήκει τὰ παρ᾽ ἑαυτῶν ἐν ταῖς τοῦ Θεοῦ συνεισφέρειν δωρεαῖς διὰ τῆς
περὶ αὐτὸν διαθέσεώς τε καὶ ἐλπίδος καὶ τοῦ παρ᾽ αὐτοῦ τῶν καλῶν ἀνα-
μένειν τὴν δόσιν.

9ᵃ. Οὕτως ψαλῶ τῷ ὀνόματί σου εἰς τὸν αἰῶνα. Οὕτω γάρ μοι προσέσται τυχόντι τῶν παρά σου καλῶν διηνεκεῖς σοι τοὺς ὑπὲρ τούτων
ὕμνους ἀποδιδόναι. Τὸ γὰρ οὕτως ψαλῶ τοῦτο λέγει, ὅτι Τότε τεύξομαι
καὶ ἔξω τοῦ ὑμνεῖν σε τὰς ἀφορμάς, ὡς ἂν ἀπὸ τῆς ἐπανόδου καὶ τῆς
αἰνέσεως ἀφορμῆς αὐτῷ πάντως ἐσομένης εἰς τὸ τοῖς ὕμνοις σχολάζειν. Προ- 20
σέσται μοι οὖν τοῦτό φησιν εἰ ἔχοιμι περί σε, εἴς σέ τε ἐλπίζων, καὶ παρά
σου ζητῶν τὴν ἀπαλλαγὴν τῶν παρόντων κακῶν. Ὅμοιον δέ ἐστι τῷ λθ΄

5-6 cf. supra p. 339, 21.

7ᵇ. Ἐκτενεῖς — αἰῶνα: P, fol. 185; V, fol. 250ᵛ.
8ᵃ. Καὶ φυλαχθήσεται — διαδοχαῖς: P, fol. 185ᵛ; V, fol. 251ʳ·ᵛ.   5-8 cf. Paraphrasis (p. 198, 17-21): Οὐ περὶ ἑνὸς τοῦτο τοῦ προσώπου λέγει (γέλοιον γὰρ ἂν ἕνα
ἄνθρωπον δι᾽ αἰῶνος εὔχεσθαι διαμένειν) ἀλλὰ περὶ τοῦ βασιλικοῦ ἀξιώματος δηλονότι.
8ᵇ. Ἀλλὰ — δόσιν: P, fol. 185ᵛ; V, fol. 251ᵛ; Cord, p. 205.   15 ἵνα εἴπῃ om.
Cord   17 αὐτῶν C   τοῦ] οὕτω Cord.
9ᵃ. Οὕτω — ἀφορμάς: P, fol. 186; V, fol. 251ᵛ; Cord, p. 205.   18 τότε om. CV
19 τοῦ om. C   ὑμνεῖν σαι C   20 ἀφορμᾶς C.

Aᵉ 4-5 (p. 316, 8-9): Id est in Hirusalem, ubi habitare Dominus credebatur.

upon generation: you will give him length of life to abide forever. *He will remain forever before God* (v. 7): he will be preserved for a long time before God—that is, in Jerusalem close to the temple, where the Lord was believed to dwell (I previously remarked that he is not referring to a person). In other words, To grant us the succession of our kings for the longest possible time; for how would *as many as the days of generation upon generation* apply to a person? I mean, for how long was the life of one king likely to be extended so as to abide for a great number of successions of generations? *Who will seek out his mercy and truth?* While you will provide this in your characteristic goodness, he is saying, it would be a blessed thing for him also to give evidence of some disposition of his own in his regard for you, not losing hope in you, and seeking this from you (by *mercy* and *truth* as usual referring to the firm and true lovingkindness of God—that is, the return). He did well to add this, bringing out that they ought contribute what they had to offer to God's gifts by their disposition toward him, by hope and by awaiting the gift of good things from him.

In this way I shall sing to your name forever (v. 8): in this way it will be my good fortune to receive good things from you unceasingly and to respond with hymns of praise in return for them. This, in fact, is the meaning of *I shall sing:* Then I shall receive and have occasion to sing your praise, so as to devote myself to hymn-singing on the basis of the return and the grounds for praise of him that will undoubtedly follow. It will be my good fortune, then, if my attitude toward you is one of hoping in you and begging you for relief from the present troubles. This resembles | Psalm 40, composed on the

ψαλμῷ περὶ τῆς αὐτῆς ὑποθέσεως εἰρημένῳ, τῷ Καὶ ἐνέβαλεν εἰς τὸ στόμα
μου ᾆσμα καινόν, ἀντὶ τοῦ Ἐπαναγαγών με ἔδωκέν μοι τοῦ ὑμνεῖν αὐτὸν τὴν
ἀφορμήν· τὸ αὐτὸ γὰρ λέγει κἀνταῦθα. Διὰ τοῦτο οὕτως ψαλῶ, τουτέστιν
οὕτω μοι προσγενήσεται τὸ τούτων ἀπολαῦσαι, ἀφ' ὧν ἔξω τοῦ ὑμνεῖν
5 αὐτὸν πλείστας ἀφορμάς.

9ᵇ. Τοῦ ἀποδοῦναί με τὰς εὐχάς μου ἡμέραν ἐξ ἡμέρας. Καὶ τοῦ διηνεκῶς αὐτῷ ἀποδιδόναι τὰς ὀφειλομένας παρ' ἐμοῦ προσευχάς, — ἵνα εἴπῃ
τὴν ὀφειλο|μένην αὐτῷ κατὰ νόμον θρησκείαν παρ' ἐμοῦ, — ὡς ἂν τοῦτο
ἐν τῷ καιρῷ τῆς αἰχμαλωσίας εὐξάμενος τῷ Θεῷ καὶ ἐπαγγειλάμενος μετὰ
10 τὴν ἐπάνοδον πολλὴν ποιήσεσθαι τοῦ νόμου τὴν ἐπιμέλειαν, διὰ τὸ πρότερον ῥαθυμοῦντα τῆς τοῦ νόμου φυλακῆς τὴν αἰχμαλωσίαν ὑπομεῖναι καὶ
τὰς ἐκεῖ συμφοράς. Ἐπισυνῆπται δὲ τῷ ἀνωτέρῳ, ὡς πρὸς τὸ ἔλεον καὶ
ἀλήθειαν αὐτοῦ τίς ἐκζητήσει ἀποδεδομένον, ἵνα εἴπῃ ὅτι Εἰ καὶ ἐλπίζοιμεν
ἐπί σε καὶ παρά σου ταῦτα ζητοῖμεν, πάντως καὶ τευξόμεθα τῆς ἐπανό-
15 δου, ὥστε διηνεκῶς σοι λοιπὸν καὶ τοὺς ὑπὲρ αὐτῶν ὕμνους ἀποδιδόναι καὶ
πᾶσαν τὴν κατὰ νόμον ὀφειλομένην θρησκείαν παρ' ἐμοί.

PSALMVS LXI

2ᵃ. Οὐχὶ τῷ Θεῷ ὑποταγήσεται ἡ ψυχή μου; Κατ' ἐρώτησιν ἀναγνωστέον. Ἐπειδὴ γὰρ ἠνάγκαζον αὐτὸν ἐκεῖνοι ἀποστῆναι τῆς γνώσεως τοῦ
20 Θεοῦ καὶ θῦσαι τοῖς εἰδώλοις, Τί φησιν ὑμῖν βούλεται τὰ τῆς σπουδῆς;
Κἂν γὰρ μύρια ποιῆτε, οὐχ οἷόν τέ με ἑτέρῳ Θεῷ ὑποταγῆναι καὶ δουλεῦσαι ἀλλ' ἢ τῷ ἀληθῶς Θεῷ, ᾧ καὶ συνηθῶς δουλεύειν ἔμαθον. Τὸ οὖν

1-2 Ps. XXXIX, 4.

9ᵇ. Καὶ τοῦ διηνεκῶς — παρ' ἐμοί: P, fol. 186; V, fol. 251ᵛ-252.

C paucissima in sequentibus exhibet; omnia fere ex P et V eruta sunt; quae
praebent alii codices loco proprio signabuntur.

Argumentum ps. LXI periit, sed eius forma ex L (p. 207) et Aᵉ conieci potest.
2ᵃ. Κατ' ἐρώτησιν — γίνεται: P, fol. 187; V, fol. 252ᵛ; Vat. 1422, fol. 113ᵛ
(anon.). 20 τί] ὅτι PV 21 κἂν] καὶ PV ποιεῖται PV ἐμὲ PV 22-402, 1 ᾧ
καὶ — θεῷ om. 1422.

Aᵉ 2-3 (p. 316, 17-19): Reditum de captiuitate nostrum laudantibus celebrabo te carminibus.

Argumentum ps. LXI (p. 316, 25-30): Praedicit in praesenti psalmo ea quae
Machabeorum tempore acta memorantur; loquiturque ex persona eorum quae
illos audire conuenit id temporis, cum uel sacrificare uel ad notitiam deuiare
ab Antiocho rege cogerentur. Cf. Pseudo-Beda (801).   2ᵃ (p. 316, 32-317, 3):
Inquit Quid abducere nos a cultu Dei nostri tanto studio nitemini? Et si malis
nos ateratis innumeris, impossibile est nos alteri uel seruire Deo, uel esse subiec-
tos nisi illi tantum qui uerus Deus, quem dedicimus longua seruitute uenerari.

same theme, "He put into my mouth a new song"[1]—that is, By bringing me back he gave me the occasion to sing his praises, which is the meaning here, too. Hence, *In this way I shall sing* means, In this way it will be my good fortune to enjoy these things, and from them to have abundant grounds for singing his praises.

So as to render my vows day after day: to render to him constantly the prayers due from me, as if to say, The worship according to the law due to him from me, so that after making vows to God in time of captivity and promising to pay much attention to the law after the return on account of being formerly remiss about the observance of the law and thus suffering captivity and the misfortunes there. This is associated with the earlier part of the psalm, corresponding to the verse *Who will seek out his mercy and truth?* as if to say, If we were to hope in you and seek this from you, we would definitely also be granted the return, and so constantly in the future render to you hymns of praise for them and all the worship according to the law due from me.

PSALM 62

Will not my soul be subject to God? (v. 1). It is to be read as a question: since they forced him to forsake knowledge of God and to sacrifice to the idols, he says, Why the haste on your part? No matter what you do, it is impossible for me to be subject and in thrall to a god other than the true God, whom I have come to serve unswervingly. So | *Will not my soul be subject to God?* means,

---

1. Ps 40:3.

οὐχὶ τῷ Θεῷ, τουτέστι Μὴ οἷόν τέ με ἑτέρῳ τινὶ δουλεῦσαι; οὐχὶ τῷ Θεῷ με δουλεύειν ἀνάγκη; ὥστε μάτην ὑμῖν ὁ κάματος γίνεται.

2ᵇ. Παρ' αὐτοῦ γὰρ τὸ σωτήριόν μου. Καὶ γὰρ αὐτός μοι παρέξει τὴν σωτηρίαν ἀδικουμένῳ παρ' ὑμῶν, καὶ ἀπαλλάξει πάντως ὑμῶν τῆς μοχθηρίας. 5

3. Καὶ γὰρ αὐτὸς ὁ Θεός μου καὶ σωτήρ μου, ἀντιλήπτωρ μου· οὐ μὴ σαλευθῶ ἐπὶ πλεῖον. Οὐδὲ γὰρ τοῦτο παρέξει πρώτως, ἀεὶ δεσπότης τέ μου καὶ σωτὴρ φανεὶς καὶ βοηθός· ὅθεν πέπεισμαι καὶ νῦν ἀπαλλαγήσεσθαι τῆς ὑμετέρας κακίας καὶ μὴ ἐπὶ πλεῖστον περιάγεσθαι τῇδε κἀκεῖσε ταῖς ὑμετέραις ἐπιβουλαῖς. 10

4ᵃ. Ἕως πότε ἐπιτίθεσθε ἐπ' ἄνθρωπον; Ἀντὶ τοῦ ἐφ' ἡμᾶς μέχρις οὖν πότε τοσοῦτον ἐπιτίθεσθε, μάτην ἡμᾶς ἀδικεῖν προειρημένοι;

4ᵇ. Φονεύετε πάντες. Ταύτην ἔχοντες μόνην σπουδήν, τὸ φονεύειν ἡμᾶς καὶ ἀναιρεῖν ἡμᾶς.

4ᶜ. Ὡς τοίχῳ κεκλιμένῳ καὶ φραγμῷ ὠσμένῳ. Πρὸς τὸ Ἕως πότε ἐπι- 15 τίθεσθε ἐπ' ἄνθρωπον τοῦτο ἀπέδωκεν, ἐπειδὴ γὰρ ὁ κεκλιμένος τοῖχος εὔκολος περὶ τὸ καταπίπτειν ἐστίν, καὶ φραγμὸς ὁ ῥιζόθεν ἐξεσπασμένος καὶ περιτετραμμένος· τοῦτον γὰρ λέγει ὠσμένον τὸν ἤδη ὠθισθέντα καὶ κεκλιμένον. Ἐπειδὴ οὖν εὔκολα ταῦτα περὶ τὸ πεσεῖν, ταῦτά φησι Μέχρι πότε ἡμῖν ἐπίκεισθε πάντες κατ' αὐτὸν γενόμενοι, ὡς ἀσθενέσι τε καὶ εὐκό- 20 λοις περὶ τὸ καταπίπτειν καὶ πάσχειν ὅτι ἂν ὑμῖν δοκῇ; Εἰ γὰρ καὶ ἡμεῖς ἀσθενεῖς, ἀλλ' ἐπειδὴ μέγας ἡμῶν ὁ βοηθός, ἐκεῖνον ἔδει δεδιότας ἀποστῆναι τῆς καθ' ἡμῶν ἐπιβουλῆς.

2ᵇ. Καὶ γὰρ — μοχθηρίας: P, fol. 187; V, fol. 252ᵛ; Vat. 1422, fol. 113ᵛ (anon.); inter ATHANASIANA (P. G., XXVII, 276 A 10-12).

3. Οὐδὲ γὰρ — ἐπιβουλαῖς: P, fol. 187; V, fol. 252ᵛ.

4ᵃ. Ἀντὶ τοῦ — προειρημένοι: C, fol. 321ᵛ; P, fol. 187ᵛ; V, fol. 253; Cord, p. 216 sub nomine ATHANASII.

4ᵇ. Ταύτην — ἡμᾶς: C, fol. 321ᵛ; P, fol. 187ᵛ; V, fol. 253.

4ᶜ. Πρὸς τὸ — ἐπιβουλῆς: C, fol. 321ᵛ; P, fol. 187ᵛ; V, fol. 253ʳ·ᵛ; Vat. 1422, fol. 113ᵛ (anon.).   17 πίπτειν 1422   18 τοῦτο ... ὡς μένω CPV   18-19 καὶ κλιμένον C   20 κατ' αὐτὸ 1422   κατὰ ταυτὸν PV.

Aᵉ 3 (p. 317, 4-6): Consequenter subdendum se iugiter Deo esse professus est, cuius ope saluatus est atque saluandus.   4ᵇ (p. 317, 14-16):... omnes effundendi sanguinis furore raptamini.   19-21 (p. 317, 18-21): Sic in nos inruitis tamquam per inbicilitatem pronos iniuriae, et quasi infirmis ad ruinam pronis incumbitis.

It is impossible for me to serve any other; am I not obliged to serve God? So your effort is in vain. From him comes my salvation: he is the one who will provide me with salvation when wronged by you, and he will completely free me from your malice. *For he is also my God and my savior, my support; I shall no longer be moved* (v. 2): this will not be the first time he provides me with it, having always proved to be my lord, savior, and helper. Hence, I am convinced that this time also I shall be freed from your wickedness and no longer be tossed this way and that by your scheming.

How long will you beset a person? (v. 3). To what point do you beset us so much, making a futile choice to wrong us? *You are all murderers:* you have this single goal, to take our lives and do away with us. *As though a tottering wall or a toppled fence.* This responds to the verse *How long will you beset a person?* since the *tottering wall* is disposed to collapse, as also is a *fence* rooted up and overturned (*toppled* meaning "already pushed over and tottering"). So since these are ready to fall, he says, How long will you all together be hostile to us, weak as we are and ready to collapse and suffer anything you please? Even if we are weak, yet since our ally is strong, you ought to be in dread of him and desist from your scheming against us. |

5ᵃ. Πλὴν τὴν τιμήν μου ἐβουλεύσαντο ἀπώσασθαι. Τὸ πλὴν προσερρῖφθαι εἰρήκαμεν πολλαχοῦ. Πολλήν φησιν ἔθεντο σπουδὴν ἀφέλεσθαί μου τὴν τιμήν. Τιμὴν δὲ αὐτοῦ καλεῖ τὴν εἰς τὸν Θεὸν θεραπείαν· καὶ γάρ ἐστιν ἀληθὴς τιμὴ τῷ μετιόντι ἅπερ εὖ φρονεῖ, πάντων ἕνεκεν τίμιον αὐτὸν
5 παρ᾽ αὐτοῖς ἐργαζομένη.

5ᵇ. Ἔδραμον ἐν ψεύδει. Ἐπειδὴ ἀλήθειαν μὲν καλοῦμεν ὅταν τις τὸ ὂν εἴπῃ, ψεῦδος δὲ τὸ μὴ ὄν, ψεῦδος καλεῖ πολλάκις τὸ μάταιον καὶ οὐδέν· τὸ οὖν ἐν ψεύδει, ἀντὶ τοῦ ματαίως. Πολλῇ φησι περὶ τοῦτο ἐχρήσαντο τῇ σπουδῇ ματαίως καὶ ἀνωφελῶς· οὐδὲν γὰρ αὐτοῖς περιΐσταται, ἐπεὶ
10 μηδὲ ἰσχύσουσιν ἡμᾶς ἀποστῆναι τῆς τοῦ Θεοῦ θεραπείας.

5ᶜ. Τῷ στόματι αὐτῶν εὐλόγουν, καὶ τῇ καρδίᾳ αὐτῶν κατηρῶντο. Καὶ λόγοις μὲν γάρ φησι κολακευτικοῖς ἐχρῶντο πρὸς ἡμᾶς πολλάκις, ἵν᾽ οὕτω δελεάσωσι πεισθῆναί τε αὐτοῖς καὶ ἀποστῆναι τῆς τοῦ Θεοῦ θεραπείας, ἡ δὲ καρδία αὐτῶν πάσης ἔγεμεν κατάρας· κακὸν γὰρ ἦν τὸ βούλευμα τὸ
15 πάντα πράττειν αὐτούς, κολακίαις τε καὶ εὐφημίαις κεχρημένους εἰς τὸ μεταβάλλειν ἡμᾶς τῆς περὶ τὸν Θεὸν γνώσεως.

6ᵃ. Πλὴν τῷ Θεῷ ὑποτάγηθι, ψυχή μου. Ἀλλὰ τούτων φησὶ πρόσεχε μηδενί, μὴ τῇ τῶν ῥημάτων κολακείᾳ, μὴ τῇ καθ᾽ ἡμῶν σπουδῇ· ἔστω δέ σοι πάντων προτιμότερον τὸ τῷ Θεῷ ὑποτετάχθαι καὶ τούτῳ δουλεύειν
20 καὶ τοῦτον μόνον λέγειν δεσπότην.

6ᵇ. Ὅτι παρ᾽ αὐτοῦ ἡ ὑπομονή μου. Καὶ γὰρ πολλὰ τὰ παρὰ τούτων ἐπαγόμενα κακά, ἀλλὰ πρὸς αὐτὸν βλέπω, αὐτὸν ἔχων προσδοκίαν καὶ ἐλπίδα· διὸ καὶ ὑπομένω τὰ γενόμενα.

2 cf. supra, p. 239, 10 et 240, 11.

5ᵃ. Τὸ πλὴν — ἐργαζομένη: C, fol. 321ᵛ; P, fol. 188; V, fol. 253ᵛ.   2 ἔθεντο] abrumpitur C.

5ᵇ. Ἐπειδὴ — θεραπείας: P. fol. 188; V, fol. 253ᵛ.   8 τὸν μάταιον V.

5ᶜ. Καὶ λόγοις – γνώσεως: P, fol. 188; V, fol. 253ᵛ; Vat. 1422, fol. 113ᵛ (anon.). 12 γὰρ om. 1422   13 τε om. 1422   14 βούλευμα τῷ PV.

6ᵃ. Ἀλλὰ τούτων — δεσπότην: P, fol. 188ᵛ; V, fol. 254.

6ᵇ. Καὶ γὰρ — γενόμενα: P, fol. 188ᵛ; V, fol. 254; Vat. 1422, fol. 114 (anon.).

Aᵉ 3-5 (p. 317, 22-25): Honorem suum uocat cultum quem Deo exhibebant, quoniam per ipsum maximo inter homines honore gaudebant.   11-12 (p. 317, 29-31): Austum profani cordis in diceptionem nostram mollium uerborum arte uelabant.   17-18 (p. 317, 32.34): Vt nec minis impiorum terrearis, nec dolosis capiaris blanditiis.   6ᵇ (p. 317, 35-318, 2): Qui causa patentiae est, ad illius pendo uoluntatem; et ideo susteneo, licet ab illis ad me omnia aspera congregantur.

Yet they plotted to spurn my dignity (v. 4). We often have remarked on the insertion of *Yet*. They displayed great zeal in removing *my dignity,* he is saying (by *dignity* referring to the service of God, true dignity consisting in devotion to what appeals to right-minded people, and brings them everyone's respect). *They pursued their course falsely.* Since we speak of truth when someone says what is right, and falsehood when it is not, Scripture often refers to futility and nonsense as falsehood—hence, *falsely* means "in futile manner." The great trouble they went to in this, he is saying, was futile and pointless: it gained them nothing, since they were incapable of diverting us from God's service. *They blessed with their mouth but cursed in their heart:* they often used flattering words to beguile us into believing them and forsaking God's service, but their heart was full of cursing. Their evil purpose, in fact, was to commit every crime, employing flattery and fine words to turn us aside from the knowledge of God.

But be subject to God, my soul (v. 5): but pay no heed to any of this, neither their flattering words nor their frenzy; let subjection to God, service to him, and calling him alone lord be preferred by you to anything. *Because my endurance is from him:* though many troubles are brought upon us by them, yet my eyes are on him, having him as my expectation and hope. Hence, I also endure what happens. | *Because he is my God, my savior, my support; I*

7. Ὅτι αὐτὸς Θεός μου καὶ σωτήρ μου, ἀντιλήπτωρ μου· οὐ μὴ μετανασ-τεύσω. Εἰωθὼς γάρ μοι βοηθεῖν βοηθήσει καὶ νῦν, καὶ οὐ συγχωρήσει τού-τοις τὸν οἰκεῖον ἐξανύσαι σκοπὸν ὥστε περιγενέσθαι μὲν ἡμῶν, ἀναστῆσαι δὲ καὶ ἀποδιῶξαι τῶν ἡμετέρων καὶ ἐν φυγῇ καταστῆσαι.

8ᵃ. Ἐπὶ τῷ Θεῷ τὸ σωτήριόν μου καὶ ἡ δόξα μου. Ἐπ᾽ αὐτῷ τῆς 5 σωτηρίας καὶ τῆς δόξης ἔχω τὴν ἐλπίδα, τουτέστιν Αὐτός με καὶ περισώ-σει καὶ ἐπίδοξον ποιήσειν νικητὴν τούτων ἐργασάμενος.

8ᵇ. Ὁ Θεὸς τῆς βοηθείας μου, καὶ ἡ ἐλπίς μου ἐπὶ τῷ Θεῷ. Αὐτὸς ὁ τὴν βοήθειάν μοι παρέχων, ἐπ᾽ αὐτῷ καὶ ἐλπίζω.

9ᵃ. Ἐλπίσατε ἐπ᾽ αὐτόν, πᾶσα συναγωγὴ λαοῦ. Καλῶς ὡς ἀπὸ τῶν Μακ- 10 καβαίων πρὸς τὸν λαὸν προτρεπόντων αὐτοὺς μὴ δειλιᾶν μηδὲ καταπτήσ-σειν, ἀλλ᾽ ἔχεσθαι τῆς εἰς τὸν Θεὸν εὐσεβείας. Μὴ δείδιτέ φησι τούτους, ἀλλ᾽ ἔχετε ἐπὶ τὸν Θεὸν τὴν ἐλπίδα τῶν καλῶν.

9ᵇ. Ἐκχέατε ἐνώπιον αὐτοῦ τὰς καρδίας ὑμῶν. Πᾶσαν ὑμῶν αὐτῷ τὴν διάνοιαν ἀνάθεσθε. Καλῶς δὲ τὸ Ἐκχέατε, ὡς πρὸς τούτους τέως ἀμφιβό- 15 λους ὄντας τὴν γνώμην, τουτέστι Μὴ διστάζετε εἰς τὴν περὶ τὸν Θεὸν εὐσέβειαν, ἀλλ᾽ ὅλους ὑμῶν ἐπ᾽ αὐτὸν ῥίψατε τοὺς λογισμούς.

9ᶜ. Ὁ Θεὸς βοηθὸς ἡμῶν. Αὐτὸς γὰρ ἡμῖν πάντοτε ἐπαμύνει ἐὰν γνη-σίαν ἡμῶν ἴδῃ τὴν περὶ αὐτὸν διάθεσιν.

10ᵃ. Πλὴν μάταιοι οἱ υἱοὶ τῶν ἀνθρώπων. Οὔτε γὰρ προσῆκεν ὑμᾶς 20 φοβεῖσθαι τῶν πολεμούντων τὴν ἰσχύν, ἐπείπερ εἰκῇ καὶ ἀσθενεῖς πάντες ἄνθρωποι ἔρημοι τῆς τοῦ Θεοῦ βοηθείας τυγχάνονται.

7. Εἰωθὼς — καταστῆσαι: P, fol. 188ᵛ; V, fol. 254.   3 ἐξανοίσαι V.
8ᵃ. Ἐπ᾽ αὐτῷ — ἐργασάμενος: P, fol. 188ᵛ; V, fol. 254; Vat. 1422, fol. 114 (anon.); Cord, p. 219 sub nomine ATHANASII (P. G., XXVII, 276 C 6-8).
8ᵇ. Αὐτὸς — ἐλπίζω: P, fol. 188ᵛ; V, fol. 254ᵛ; Vat. 1422, fol. 114 (anon.).
9ᵃ. Καλῶς — καλῶν: P, fol. 189; V, fol. 254ᵛ; Vat. 1422, fol. 114 (anon.); Cord, p. 219-220.   12 μὴ δὲ δίετε V μὴ δεδίετε 1422.
9ᵇ. Πᾶσαν — λογισμούς: P, fol. 189; V, fol. 254ᵛ; Cord, p. 220, 15-20 (ἑτέρου). 14 αὐτῶν PV.
9ᶜ. Αὐτὸς — διάθεσιν: P, fol. 189; V, fol. 254ᵛ.
10ᵃ. Οὔτε — τυγχάνονται: P, fol. 189; V, fol. 255; Cord, p. 220, 20-23 (ἑτέρου). 20 ἡμᾶς Cord   21 εἴκεν V   καὶ ἀσθενεῖς] ἀσθενεῖς γὰρ Cord   22 τυγχάνοντες Cord.

Aᵉ 2-3 (p. 318, 3-5): Cuius protectionem sum semper expertus, eius tuebor auxilio.   8ᵃ (p. 318, 7-9): Ipse saluum faciet atque gloriossum, cum praesti-terit uictorem esse.   11-12 (p. 318, 12-13):... ne quis a populo cultum Dei ter-rore motaret.   10ᵃ (p. 318, 22-24): Pro hoc etiam non timendi, quia caduci et insolidi qui Dei adminiculis non utuntur.

shall not become a fugitive (v. 6): he is in the habit of helping and will come to my aid at this time, too, and not allow them to achieve their purpose of prevailing over us, rooting us up and driving us from our lands and putting us to flight. *In God is my salvation and my glory* (v. 7): in him I have hope of salvation and glory—that is, He will save me and render me glorious by making me their vanquisher. *God is my help, and my hope is in God:* he is the one who provides me with help, and in him I hope.

Hope in him, every assembly of peoples (v. 8). A fine sentiment from the Maccabees addressed to the people urging them not to fear or be distraught but to maintain reverence for God. Have no dread of them, he is saying; instead, have hope in God for good things. *Pour out your hearts before him:* devote all your mind to him. *Pour out* was well put in being addressed to them when wavering in their purpose at the time—in other words, Do not waver in reverence for God; rather, direct all your thoughts to him. *Because God is our help:* he is the one who always assists us if he sees our affection for him to be genuine.

But humankind is frivolous (v. 9): you should not fear the force of those attacking, especially since all human beings are ineffectual and weak when deprived of God's help. | *Humankind is deceptive, tilting the balance toward*

10ᵇ. Ψευδεῖς οἱ υἱοὶ τῶν ἀνθρώπων ἐν ζυγοῖς τοῦ ἀδικῆσαι. Ψευδεῖς, ἀντὶ τοῦ μάταιοι καὶ οὐδέν. Ἐπειδὴ δὲ ζυγοῖς ἀεὶ σταθμώμεθα ἅπερ βουλόμεθα καὶ τῇ ῥοπῇ τῶν βαρυτέρων δεχόμεθα τὴν διάκρισιν, τοῦτό φησιν ὅτι οἱ ἄνθρωποι, ἐπειδὰν ὡς ἐν ζυγῷ ῥίψωσιν πρὸς τὸ ἀδικεῖν, πολλῷ μᾶλ-
5 λον αὐτοὺς οὐ προσήκει φοβεῖσθαι· οὐδαμινοὶ γάρ εἰσι καὶ οὐδὲν ἰσχύοντες, ἔτι καὶ τὸν Θεὸν διὰ τὴν ἀδικίαν ἐναντιούμενον ἔχοντες.

10ᶜ. Αὐτοὶ ἐκ ματαιότητος ἐπὶ τὸ αὐτό. Σύμμαχος Ματαιοῦνται ὁμοῦ· ματαιωθήσονται γάρ φησι καὶ ἀποφανθήσονται πάντες ὁμοῦ τὸ μηδέν, τοῦ Θεοῦ διὰ τὴν ἀδικίαν αὐτοὺς τιμωρουμένου.

10 11ᵃ·ᵇ. Μὴ ἐλπίζετε ἐπὶ ἀδικίαν, καὶ ἐπὶ ἁρπάγματα μὴ ἐπιποθεῖτε. Ὥστε φησὶν μηδὲν νομίζετε τούτους διὰ τὴν νῦν προσοῦσαν αὐτοῖς τυραννίδα, ἢ κεχρημένοι οὕτως ἡμᾶς ἀδεῶς ἀδικεῖν τε καὶ ἁρπάζειν ἐσπουδάκασιν· οὐδὲν γάρ εἰσι διὰ τὴν παρὰ τοῦ Θεοῦ τιμωρίαν. Τὸ γὰρ Μὴ ἐλπίζετε, μηδὲ πεποίθετε, ἀντὶ τοῦ Μὴ μεγάλους αὐτοὺς νομίζετε, ἐπειδὴ ἴδιόν
15 ἐστι τῶν ἀνθρώπων ἐπὶ τοῖς μεγάλοις πεποιθέναι καὶ ἰσχυροῖς.

11ᶜ. Πλοῦτος ἐὰν ῥέῃ, μὴ προστίθεσθε καρδίαν. Ἀλλὰ κἂν ὁρᾶτε ἀπὸ τῆς ἀδικίας σφόδρα πλουτοῦντας καὶ οὕτως εὐκόλως, ὥστε δοκεῖν ῥέοντα ἐπ᾽ αὐτοὺς τὸν πλοῦτον φέρεσθαι, μηδὲ οὕτω ῥέψαι ποτὲ πρὸς αὐτοὺς ἀνάσχησθε καὶ τῆς ἐκείνων γενέσθαι μοίρας. Διὰ τί;

20 12. Ἅπαξ ἐλάλησεν ὁ Θεός, δύο ταῦτα ἤκουσα. Τὸ ἅπαξ ἀντὶ τοῦ βεβαίως· οὐκ ἀνακαλεῖταί φησι τὴν φωνήν, οὐ δευτεροῖ τὴν ἀπόφασιν, ἀλλ᾽ ἅπαξ ἀπεφήνατο καὶ γενέσθαι ἀνάγκη, — οὕτως καὶ ἐν τῷ πη´ τὸ Ἅπαξ

22 Ps. LXXXVIII, 36.

10ᵇ. Ψευδεῖς — ἔχοντες: P, fol. 189ᵛ; V, fol. 255.
10ᶜ. Σύμμαχος — τιμωρουμένου: P, fol. 189ᵛ; V, fol. 255; Vat. 1422, fol. 114 (anon.).
11ᵃ·ᵇ. Ὥστε — ἰσχυροῖς: P, fol. 190; V, fol. 255ᵛ.
11ᶜ. Ἀλλὰ — διὰ τί: P, fol. 190; V, fol. 255ᵛ; Vat. 1422, fol. 114 (anon.); Cord, p. 222 (anon.).
12. Τὸ ἅπαξ — ταῦτα: P. fol. 190; V, fol. 256; Vat. 1422, fol. 114ᵛ (anon.).

Aᵉ 10ᵇ (p. 318, 25-31): Quoniam homines, cum in deteriorem partem sicut in stateram declinauerint propensioresque fuerint ad nocendum, multo magis sunt condemnandi quoniam nihil sunt neque aliquid possunt; nam et Deo propter iniquitatem suam utuntur aduerso. 7-8 (p. 318, 32-319, 1): Simmachus dicit *Vani erunt et euanescent.* 11ᶜ (p. 319, 7-13): Si uideatis illos a praeda ac rapinis ad epulentiam peruenire et ita facile ditari, ut ultro in sinus eorum bona credatis influere, neque ita ad emulandum uos conuenit intrari neque illorum fieri uelle participes. 21-22 (p. 319, 14-17): Non necesse est iterari sententiam, quoniam primam iterationem comitatur effectus (affectus *ms*); sic in alio psalmo *Semel iuraui in sancto meo.*

wrongdoing. By *deceptive* he means "useless, worth nothing." Since we use balances to measure what we want and get a verdict from the weight of the heavier items, this means, Since human beings incline the balance toward wrongdoing, much more is there no need to fear them, since they are of no value and are powerless, since on account of their wrongdoing they have even God against them. *They themselves are likewise the fruit of frivolity.* Symmachus: "They are all frivolous together." They will come to nothing, he is saying, and all alike will be shown to be of no value when God punishes them for their wrongdoing.

Place no hope in wrongdoing, and hanker not after robbery (v. 10): so do not give them any importance for the tyranny they now exercise, on which they capitalize in their zeal to abuse and pillage us in this way without a qualm; they count for nothing before the punishment of God. *Place no hope* or trust means, Do not consider them important, because it is a human characteristic to trust in the high and mighty. *If wealth comes your way, do not set your heart on it:* even if you see them profiting from their wrongdoing so easily that wealth comes their way, never incline that way and surrender to them and become one of them. Why?

God said this once; twice I heard it (v. 11). *Once* means "firmly": He does not revoke his statement, he is saying, and he does not repeat his pronouncement; instead, he made one pronouncement, and of necessity it took effect. Similarly in Psalm 89, | "I swore by my holy one once."[1] He means,

---

1. Ps 89:35.

ὤμοσα ἐν τῷ ἁγίῳ μου. Βούλεται δὲ εἰπεῖν ὅτι δεῖ ταῦτα τὰ δύο γενέσθαι — ἀπεφήνατο ὁ Θεός, καὶ ἤκουσα, καὶ οἶδα αὐτὸν ἀποφηνάμενον, καὶ
ἔσεσθαι πεπίστευκα. Ποῖα οὖν ταῦτα;

13. Ὅτι τὸ κράτος τοῦ Θεοῦ. Καί σου, Κύριε, τὸ ἔλεος, ὅτι σὺ ἀποδώ-
σεις ἑκάστῳ κατὰ τὰ ἔργα αὐτοῦ. Ὅτι ἐν αὐτῷ τὸ βοηθεῖν καὶ ἐλεεῖν οὓς 5
βούλεται, ἐν αὐτῷ καὶ τὸ τιμωρεῖσθαι τοὺς πταίοντας· ὥστε οὐ δεῖ πτοεῖσθαι ἐπὶ τῇ τούτων ἰσχύϊ ἀδικεῖν προειρημένων, ἐπειδὴ ὁ Θεὸς κατ᾽ οἰκείαν
ἐπαγγελίαν ἐλεεῖ τε τοὺς ἀδικουμένους, βοηθῶν αὐτοῖς, καὶ τοῖς ἀδικοῦσι
κατὰ τὰς πράξεις ἀποδίδωσι. Ποῦ δὲ τοῦτο εἶπεν ὁ Θεός; Πρὸς τὸν Μωϋσέα, ἔνθα φησὶν Ἐγὼ Κύριος ἀποδοὺς ἁμαρτίας πατέρων ἐπὶ τέκνα ἐπὶ τρί- 10
την καὶ τετάρτην γενεάν, καὶ ποιῶν ἔλεος εἰς χιλιάδας τοῖς ἀγαπῶσίν με,
τοῦτο λέγων ὅτι κἀκείνους τιμωροῦμαι διὰ τὸ ἁμαρτάνειν καὶ τούτοις πολλὴν παρέχω τῶν ἀγαθῶν τὴν ἀπόλαυσιν διὰ τὴν εὐσέβειαν.

PSALMVS LXII

Τὰ κατὰ τὸν ἐν Βαβυλῶνι λαὸν προαγορεύει, ὡς ἐκ τῶν παρ᾽ αὐτοῖς 15
θαυμαστῶν λέγων τὰ ἐκείνοις ἁρμόζοντα.

2ᵃ. Ὁ Θεός, ὁ Θεός μου, πρός σε ὀρθρίζω. Πρός σε διανίσταμαι ὄρθρου,
εἰς τό σοι τούς τε ὕμνους καὶ τὰς εὐχαριστίας ἀναπέμψαι.

2ᵇ. Ἐδίψησέν σοι ἡ ψυχή μου. Οὐδὲ γὰρ ὀλίγον τινὰ πόθον ἔχω πρός
σε· ἔδειξε δὲ τοῦ πόθου τὴν ἐπίτασιν τῇ τοῦ δίψους παραβολῇ. 20

-11 Ex. XX, 5-6.

13. Ὅτι ἐν αὐτῷ — εὐσέβειαν: P, fol. 190ᵛ; V, fol. 256.
Argumentum Τὰ κατὰ — ἁρμόζοντα: P, fol. 191; V, fol. 256ᵛ; Vat. 1422,
ol. 114ᵛ (anon.); L (p. 227, ll. 2-1 ab imo): Ἄλλος δὲ τοῖς ἐν Βαβυλῶνι μᾶλλον
ἁρμόζειν φησὶν ὠφεληθεῖσι.
2ᵃ. Πρός σε — ἀναπέμψαι: P, fol. 191; V, fol. 256ᵛ; Cord, p. 235, 18-20 *sub*
nomine ATHANASII (P. G., XXVII, 277 C 2-3). 17 πρός σέ φησι Cord 18 εὐχάς
Cord.
2ᵇ. Οὐδὲ — παραβολῇ: P, fol. 191; V, fol. 256ᵛ; Vat. 1422, fol. 114ᵛ (anon.).
20 ἐπίτασιν τὴν ἐπὶ τοῦ 1422.

Aᵉ *Argumentum ps. LXII* (p. 319, 24-26): De populo in Babilone possito
prophetans, quia ex persona eorum loquitur. 2ᵃ (p. 419, 27-30): Consurgo,
inquit, antematutinus, ut gratiarum tibi actionem offeram. 2ᵇ (p. 219, 31-34):
Magno, inquit, tuo desiderio, magno ardore sollicitor; per conparationem sitis
expraesit desiderii quantitatem.

These two things must happen: God made a pronouncement, and *I heard it*, I knew he had pronounced, and I believe it will happen. What is it, then? *That power belongs to God, and mercy to you, Lord, because you repay everyone according to their works* (v. 12): that in him is help and mercy for those whom he wishes, and in him also punishment of the guilty, so that there is no need to be alarmed at the might of those who opt to do wrong, since God by his promise shows mercy to the wronged by helping them and repays the wrongdoers according to their crimes. Now, where did God say this? To Moses, where he says, "I am the Lord, taking recompense for parents' sins on children to the third and fourth generation, and having mercy on countless numbers of those who love me,"[2] meaning by this, I shall punish the former for their sin and provide the latter with great enjoyment of good things in reward for their piety.

PSALM 63

He foretells the people's situation in Babylon, mentioning what is applicable to them from the marvels in their midst. *O God, my God, I watch for you at break of day* (v. 1): I rise early to pray to you so as to offer hymns of praise and thanksgiving to you. *My soul has thirsted for you:* the desire that I have for you is not slight (bringing out the extent of the desire by the comparison with thirst). | *How often my flesh longs for you, in a wilderness, inaccessible*

---

2. Cf. Exod 20:5–6.

2ᶜ⁻3ᵃ. Ποσαπλῶς σοι ἡ σάρξ μου, ἐν γῇ ἐρήμῳ καὶ ἀβάτῳ καὶ ἀνύδρῳ, οὕτως ἐν τῷ ἁγίῳ ὤφθην σοι. Ἐπειδὴ ἀριθμοῦντες λέγομεν διπλάσιον καὶ τριπλάσιον καὶ πολλαπλάσιον, ποσαπλῶς λέγει, — τουτέστιν ἀντὶ τοῦ ποσάκις, ἀναριθμήτως· τὸ δὲ ἡ σάρξ μου ὁμοίως. Ποσάκις σοι οὖν φησιν ἐν 5 ἐρήμοις καὶ ἀβάτοις τόποις γενόμενος οὕτως ὤφθην καὶ παρέστην ὡς ἂν ἐν τῷ ἁγίῳ, ἵνα εἴπῃ ἐν τῷ ναῷ. Βούλεται δὲ εἰπεῖν ὅτι πολλάκις κατ᾽ ἐμαυτὸν εἰς ἐρήμους τόπους γενόμενος, οὕτως σοι παρέστην καὶ ὕμνησά σε ὡσανεὶ ἐν τῷ ναῷ καθεστώς, οὐδὲν τῶν δεόντων διὰ τὴν τῶν τόπων παραλιπὼν διαφοράν.

10 3ᵇ. Τοῦ ἰδεῖν τὴν δύναμίν σου καὶ τὴν δόξαν σου. Ταῦτα δὲ ἔπραττον ὥστε ἀπολαῦσαί σου τῆς δυνάμεως καὶ τῆς δόξης, τουτέστιν ὥστε βοηθῆναι τῇ δυνάμει τῇ σῇ καὶ τυχεῖν τῆς παρά σου δόξης, ἧς πάντας ἀπολαῦσαι ἔδει τῶν κατεχόντων ἀπαλλαγέντα κακῶν.

4ᵃ. Ὅτι κρεῖσσον τὸ ἔλεός σου ὑπὲρ ζωάς. Ἀντὶ τοῦ «ὑπὲρ ζωὴν» 15 εἶπεν ὑπὲρ ζωάς, πληθυντικῶς ὑπὲρ πολλὰς ζωάς. Κρεῖττον γάρ φησι καὶ τοῦ πολλάκις ζῆσαι ἡ παρά σου φιλανθρωπία· τὸ μὲν γὰρ καὶ διαλύεται πολλάκις, ἡ δὲ μέχρις ἂν ᾖ κἀκεῖνο συγκρατεῖ.

4ᵇ. Τὰ χείλη μου ἐπαινέσουσί σε. Τοῖς διὰ χειλέων ὕμνοις καὶ ἐπαίνοις τιμήσω.

20 5ᵃ. Οὕτως εὐλογήσω σε ἐν τῇ ζωῇ μου. Καὶ διαμενῶ φησι διὰ πάσης τῆς ζωῆς οὕτως ὑμνῶν, — ἀντὶ τοῦ ὁμοίως, ὡσαύτως.

2ᶜ⁻3ᵃ. Ἐπειδὴ — διαφοράν: P, fol. 191; V, fol. 257; Vat. 1422, fol. 114ᵛ (anon.). 3 τουτέστιν om. 1422   4 σοι] σὺ 1422   6 τῷ] ᾧ 1422   7 γιγνόμενος PV.
3ᵇ. Ταῦτα — κακῶν: P, fol. 191ᵛ; V, fol. 257ᵛ.
4ᵃ. Ἀντὶ — συγκρατεῖ: P, fol. 192; V, fol. 257ᵛ; Vat. 1422, fol. 115 (anon.); Cord, p. 237.   15 κρείττων Cord   16 τοῦ] τὸ V τοῦτο 1422   τὸ] ἡ PV   καὶ om. 1422 Cord   17 ἡ δὲ] τὸ δὲ PV   ᾖ] εἴη 1422   κἀκείνην PV.
4ᵇ. Τοῖς — τιμήσω: P, fol. 192; V, fol. 257ᵛ.
5ᵃ. Καὶ διαμενῶ — ὡσαύτως: P, fol. 192; V, fol. 257ᵛ.   20 διαμείνω V.

Aᵉ 6-9 (p. 320, 4-7): Tamquam in templo possitus, sic in auiis locis continuaui frequentauique laudationis ac deuotionis officia.   3ᵇ (p. 320, 8-12): Vt promererer defensionem frequenter expertam, qua aut ipse clarus es (est 1ᵃ m.) aut tuos efficis gloriosos, quos liberatione dignaris.   15-17 (p. 320, 13-19): Melior est ut misericordiam tuam consequatur quam frequenter in uitam redire; nam uita, etsi contingat gloriosior, desoluitur; misericordia uero tua, si adfuerit, potest breuis uitae spatia delatare.   4ᵇ (p. 320, 20-22): Oris, inquit, te officio praeconiis et laudibus celebrare curabo.   5ᵃ (p. 320, 23-24): Vsque ad finem uitae perseuerabo (perserabo 1ᵃ m.) deuotus.

and waterless. Thus I was seen by you in the holy place (vv. 1–2). Since in counting we say twice, thrice, many times, he says *How often*—that is, how many times, a countless number of times; and *my flesh* similarly. So he is saying, How many times in deserts and inaccessible places was I seen by you and was present as if in the holy place—that is, in the temple. He means, Frequently I was by myself in lonely places and thus became present to you and sang your praises as if standing in the temple, neglecting nothing of my duty on account of the difference in the places. *To see your power and your glory:* I did this so as to enjoy your power and glory—that is, to be helped by your power and receive glory from you, which are to be enjoyed upon release from the besetting troubles.

Because your mercy is better than lives (v. 3). He said *lives* to mean "life," using the plural to mean "better than many lives." Your lovingkindness, he is saying, is better than living many times: the latter also involves dissolution, whereas the former surpasses it also in duration. *My lips will praise you:* I shall honor you with hymns and praises on my lips. *Thus I shall praise you in my life* (v. 4): I shall continue singing your praises throughout my life in this fashion—that is, similarly, likewise. | *In your*

5ᵇ. Ἐν τῷ ὀνόματί σου ἀρῶ τὰς χεῖράς μου. Καὶ ἐκτενῶ τὰς χεῖρας ἐπικαλούμενός σε βοηθόν.

6ᵃ. Ὡς ἐκ στέατος καὶ πιότητος ἐμπλησθείη ἡ ψυχή μου. Τὴν εὐπραγίαν καὶ τὸν πλοῦτον πιότητα καὶ στέαρ πολλάκις καλεῖ, ἐπειδὴ αἱ μὲν συμφοραὶ τήκειν οἴδασιν τὸ σῶμα, ἡ δὲ εὐπραγία πιαίνειν μᾶλλον· οὕτω 5 λέγεται Τὸ στέαρ αὐτῶν συνέκλ.ισαν, ἀντὶ τοῦ τὴν εὐπραγίαν. Τοῦτο οὖν φησιν ὅτι Τοῦτο πράττων τῆς παρά σου εὐπραγίας πληρωθήσομαι, ὥστε εἶναί με τῷ πλήθει τῶν παρά σου ἀγαθῶν ὥσπερ στεατώδη καὶ πιμελῆ.

6ᵇ. Καὶ χείλη ἀγαλλιάσεως αἰνέσει τὸ στόμα μου. Καὶ ἀπολαύσω τῶν παρά σου ἀγαθῶν, φθέγξομαι διὰ χειλέων λόγους εὐφροσύνης μεστοὺς καὶ 10 ὕμνων γέμοντας τῶν εἴς σε.

7. Εἰ ἐμνημόνευόν σου ἐπὶ τῆς στρωμνῆς μου, ἐν τοῖς ὄρθροις ἐμελέτων εἴς σε. Ἐν τοῖς ὄρθροις, τουτέστι καὶ ἐν τοῖς ὄρθροις. Εἰ γάρ ποτέ φησιν διαναστὰς ἐννύκτιον ἔλαβόν σου μνήμην, ἐπὶ τῆς κοίτης ὢν πάντως μελέτην ἐποιούμην τοὺς εἴς σε ὕμνους ἄχρι τῶν ὄρθρων, ἵνα εἴπῃ Καὶ ἐπὶ τῆς κοίτης 15 σου μνήμην ἐποιούμην καὶ διετέλουν ἄχρι τῶν ὄρθρων ὕμνῶν σε. Σύμμαχος δὲ αὐτὸ σαφέστερον εἶπεν Ἀναμιμνησκόμενός σου ἐπὶ τῆς στρωμνῆς, καθ᾽ ἑκάστην φυλακὴν ἐμελέτων· καθ᾽ ἑκάστην δὲ φυλακὴν λέγει τὴν γ᾽ ὥραν τῆς νυκτὸς καὶ τὴν ϛ᾽ καὶ τὴν θ᾽ καὶ τελευταῖον, — ταύτας γὰρ ἐκάλουν φυλακάς, δι᾽ ὧν σημαίνει τὸ διηνεκὲς τῶν ὕμνων. 20

9ᵃ. Ἐκολλήθη ἡ ψυχή μου ὀπίσω σου. Προσεδέθησαν τῷ πόθῳ.

9ᵇ. Ἐμοῦ δὲ ἀντελάβετο ἡ δεξιά σου. Καὶ τῇ βοηθείᾳ τῇ σῇ ὥσπερ δεξιᾷ κατεσχηκὼς ἀνέσπασας τῶν κακῶν, πεσεῖν οὐκ ἐάσας· δεξιὰν γὰρ τὴν βοήθειαν λέγει.

6 Ps. XVI, 10ᵃ.

5ᵇ. Καὶ ἐκτενῶ — βοηθόν: P, fol. 192ᵛ; V, fol. 257ᵛ.
6ᵃ. Τὴν εὐπραγίαν — πιμελῆ: P, fol. 192ᵛ; V, fol. 258; Vat. 1422, fol. 115 (anon.); Cord, p. 238. 5 οἴδασι πολλάκις 1422.
6ᵇ. Καὶ ἀπολαύσω — εἴς σε: P, fol. 192ᵛ; V, f. 258.
7. Ἐν τοῖς ὄρθροις — ὕμνων: P, fol. 192ᵛ; V, fol. 258ʳ·ᵛ; Vat. 1422, fol. 115 (anon.). 16 ὕμνῶν σε des. 1422. Desideratur interpretatio v. 8.
9ᵃ. Προσεδέθησαν τῷ πόθῳ: P, fol. 193; V, fol. 258ᵛ; Vat. 1422, fol. 115 (anon.).
9ᵇ. Καὶ τῇ βοηθείᾳ — λέγει: P, fol. 193; V, fol. 258ᵛ-259.

Aᵉ 6-8 (p. 320, 30-33): Vt ita prosperitate replear et bonorum a te multitudine conlatorum, ut uidiam mihi quasi quodam adipe saginari. 6ᵇ (p. 320, 34-36): Repleatus muneribus tuis, uerba laudum tibi debitarum et meae laetitiae personabo. 13-15 (p. 321, 1-3): Si nocte mihi laudum tuarum celebratio occupauit, quanto id facilius tempore matutino perficiam. 9ᵇ (p. 321, 8-10): Adiutorio tuo uelut manu adpraehensus, malis hominibus sum liber effectus.

name I shall lift up my hands: and I shall extend my hands in invoking you as my helper.

Let my soul be filled as with suet and fatness (v. 5). By *suet and fatness* he often refers to prosperity and wealth, since calamity generally wastes the body and prosperity fattens it; hence the similar expression "They hemmed in their fatness"[1]—that is, their prosperity. So he is saying, In doing this I shall be filled with prosperity from you, with the result that I shall enjoy a multitude of good things from you like suet and soft fat. *My mouth will praise with lips of gladness:* and I shall enjoy good things from you; I shall have on my lips words full of happiness and brimming with hymns in praise of you. *If I remembered you on my bed, I meditated on you at daybreak* (v. 6), by *at daybreak* meaning "even at daybreak." In other words, he is saying, If ever I awoke at night and remembered you, on my bed I gave attention to hymns of praise to you up till dawn; as if to say, Even in bed I remembered you and continued singing your praises till dawn. Symmachus said it more clearly, "Remembering you on my bed, I meditated at each watch," by "each watch" meaning the third, sixth, ninth, and last hours of the night, referring to them as "watches," thus indicating the constancy of the hymn-singing.

My soul clung to you (v. 8):[2] they were held fast by desire. *Your right hand took hold of me:* grasping me with your help as though with your right hand, you plucked me from the troubles, not allowing me to fall (by *right hand* meaning "help"). |

---

1. Ps 16:10 LXX.
2. Commentary on v. 7 is missing.

10ª. Αὐτοὶ δὲ εἰς μάτην ἐζήτησαν τὴν ψυχήν μου. Καίτοι γε τῶν πολεμίων πᾶσαν σπουδὴν ἀνελεῖν με θεμένων εἰκῇ καὶ ἄνευ αἰτίας τινός· οὐ γὰρ
εἶχον ἀφορμὴν τῆς κατ᾽ ἐμοῦ ἔχθρας.

10ᵇ. Εἰσελεύσονται εἰς τὰ κατώτατα τῆς γῆς. Διὰ τοῦτο τῷ ᾅδη παρα-
5 δοθήσονται καὶ τῷ θανάτῳ.

11ª. Παραδοθήσονται εἰς χεῖρας ρομφαίας. Καὶ ἐν πολέμοις πεσοῦνται
τὸν διὰ ξίφους ὑπομείναντες θάνατον· ρομφαίαν γὰρ καλεῖ τὸ ξίφος.

11ᵇ. Μερίδες ἀλωπέκων ἔσονται. Λέγονται οἱ λέοντες, ἐπειδάν τινος ἐπι-
λάβωνται ζῴου, ῥοφεῖν τὸ αἷμα καὶ ἁρπακτικῶς ἐσθίειν τὸ προσπεσὸν καὶ
10 μάλιστα τὰ κυριώτερα τῶν μελῶν, τὰ δὲ περιττὰ καταλιμπάνειν καὶ μὴ
ἀξιοῦν ὥσπερ τὰ λοιπὰ τῶν θηρίων πάντα ἐπινέμεσθαι, τὰ δὲ αἱ ἀλώπεκες
εὑροῦσαι ἐσθίειν λέγονται. Ἐπεὶ τοίνυν ἐσθίουσιν ἐκεῖναι τὰ παρ᾽ ἐκείνων
ἤδη ἀναιρεθέντα καὶ καταβρωθέντα, τοῦτό φησιν ὅτι τιμωρίαι αὐτοὺς διάφοροι διαδέξονται, καὶ ἀπὸ τούτων εἰς ἑτέρους ἐμπεσόντες διαφόρῳ τῇ
15 τιμωρίᾳ περιβληθήσονται.

12ª. Ὁ δὲ βασιλεὺς εὐφρανθήσεται ἐπὶ τῷ Θεῷ. Ὁ μέντοι φησὶ βασιλεὺς
ἡμῶν, τῶν ἐχθρῶν ταύτην ὑφισταμένων τὴν τιμωρίαν, εὐφρανθήσεται ἐπί
σοι τῷ ταῦτα πράττοντι. Ἐβασίλευσεν δὲ τότε ὁ Ζοροβάβελ, ὃν εἰκὸς ἦν
εὐφραίνεσθαι διὰ τῆς κατὰ τῶν ἐχθρῶν τιμωρίας.

20   12ᵇ. Ἐπαινεθήσεται πᾶς ὁ ὀμνύων ἐν αὐτῷ. Ἐπειδὴ ἕκαστος ὅρκον
ποιεῖται ὃ σέβει, τοῦτό φησιν ὅτι ἐπαινετοὶ καὶ θαυμαστοὶ δειχθήσονται
πάντες οἱ σέβοντες αὐτόν, τουτέστι τὸν Θεόν, καὶ καταφρονοῦντες μὲν τῶν
εἰδώλων, ὅρκον δὲ αὐτὸν ποιούμενοι.

10ª. Καίτοι — ἔχθρας: P, fol. 193; V, fol. 259; Vat. 1422, fol. 115 (anon.).
10ᵇ. Διὰ τοῦτο — θανάτῳ: P, fol. 193; V, fol. 259.
11ª. Καὶ ἐν πολέμοις — ξίφος: P, fol. 193ᵛ; V, fol. 259.
11ᵇ. Λέγονται — περιβληθήσονται: P, fol. 193ᵛ; V, fol. 259; Vat. 1422, fol. 115ᵛ
(anon.).   12 τοίνυν] οὖν 1422   13 αὐτοῖς 1422.
12ª. Ο μέντοι — τιμωρίας: P, fol. 193ᵛ; V, fol. 259ᵛ; Vat. 1422, fol. 115ᵛ (anon.).
16 βασιλεύων PV.
12ᵇ. Ἐπειδὴ — ποιούμενοι: P, fol. 193ᵛ; V, fol. 259ᵛ; Vat. 1422, fol. 115ᵛ (anon.);
Cord, p. 241 (anon.).   21 καὶ θαυμαστοὶ om. 1422.

Aᵉ 2-3 (p. 321, 11-13): Aut sine fructu extinctionis, aut absque ulla causa
lesionis.   4-7 (p. 321, 14-15): Ad inferna migrabunt consumpti gladio (gaudio
1ᵃ m.).   8-13 (p. 321, 16-20): Leonum de cadaueribus reliquias minuta animalia
depasci dicuntur, unde etiam in partionem uictus sui quaedam inde ulpis usur-
pant.   16-17 (p. 321, 25-26): Inimici talia sustenendo rex noster laetabitur.

They, on the contrary, were after my life, but in vain (v. 9): yet the enemy took great pains to dispose of me for no good cause or reason; they had no grounds for their hostility against me. *They shall go into the depths of the earth:* hence, they will be dispatched to Hades and to death. *They shall be given into the hands of the sword* (v. 10): and they will fall in war, suffering death by the sword (by *sword* referring to the straight sword). *They will be foxes' portions.* It is said that when lions take any animal, they drain its blood, tear apart and eat the victim, especially the choice parts of the limbs, and leave the remnants, not thinking it worthwhile to scavenge like all the other beasts, whereas foxes are said to eat by foraging. Since, then, the latter eat what has already been killed and fed on by the others, he is saying that a range of punishments will overtake them, and overcome by one kind after another they will be enveloped in different punishments.

But the king will rejoice in God (v. 11): our king, on the contrary, once the enemy undergoes this punishment, will rejoice in you for doing it. At that time the reigning king was Zerubbabel, who probably rejoiced at the punishment of the enemy. *All who swear by him will be praised.* Since each person swears by what he reverences, he is saying that everyone reverencing him—namely, God—will be shown to be commendable and admirable for despising the idols and swearing oaths by him. | *Because the mouth of*

12ᶜ. Ὅτι ἐνεφράγη στόμα λαλούντων ἄδικα. Πάντων γὰρ τῶν ἐχθρῶν καὶ ὀνειδισάντων ἡμᾶς πολλάκις ὡς οὐδὲν ὠφεληθέντας παρὰ τοῦ Θεοῦ τὴν προσήκουσαν δεδωκότων τιμωρίαν, καὶ ὥσπερ ἐμφραχθέντων αὐτοῖς τῶν στομάτων τῷ μηδὲν ἔχειν εἰπεῖν διὰ τὴν εἰς ἡμᾶς βοήθειαν, ἀνάγκη πᾶσα τὸ θαῦμα ἡμῖν περιγίνεσθαι. 5

PSALMVS LXIII

Τοῦ μακαρίου Δαυὶδ ὁ ψαλμὸς δι᾿ ἑαυτὸν λέγοντος ὁπηνίκα ὑπὸ τοῦ Σαοὺλ ἐδιώκετο. Ἔοικε δὲ τῷ ι΄ ἐν πολλοῖς τῶν ῥητῶν ὥσπερ οὖν καὶ τῇ ὑποθέσει· ἐκεῖ μὲν γὰρ φησιν Ὅτι ἰδοὺ οἱ ἁμαρτωλοὶ ἐνέτειναν τόξον τῷ κατατοξεῦσαι ἐν σκοτομήνῃ τοὺς εὐθεῖς τῇ καρδίᾳ, ἐνταῦθα δὲ Ἐνέτειναν 10 τόξον αὐτῶν πρᾶγμα πικρόν.

2ᵃ. Εἰσάκουσον, ὁ Θεός, φωνῆς μου ἐν τῷ δέεσθαί με πρός σε. Εὐχομένου φησὶν ἄκουσον.

2ᵇ. Ἀπὸ φόβου ἐχθροῦ ἐξελοῦ τὴν ψυχήν μου. Ἀπάλλαξόν με τοῦ φόβου τῶν ἐναντίων, ἵνα εἴπῃ τῆς ἐπιβουλῆς αὐτῶν καὶ τοῦ θανάτου· 15 ταῦτα γὰρ ἐδεδίει μὴ πάθῃ παρ᾿ αὐτῶν.

3ᵃ. Σκέπασόν με ἀπὸ συστροφῆς πονηρευομένων. Συνηθῶς κἀνταῦθα ἄνω ἐχθροὺς εἰπὼν ἐνταῦθα πονηρευομένους ἐκάλεσεν, καὶ ἔτι κατωτέρω.

3ᵇ. Ἀπὸ πλήθους ἐργαζομένων ἀδικίαν. Δεικνὺς τῆς ἐπιβουλῆς καὶ τῆς ἔχθρας τὸ ἄδικον. Ἐπειδὴ τοίνυν φησὶν οὗτοι πάσης ὄντες μεστοὶ πονη- 20 ρίας τῷ οἰκείῳ πλήθει θαρροῦντες συνεστράφησαν κατ᾿ ἐμοῦ, αὐτός με τῇ σῇ βοηθείᾳ σκέπασον, τουτέστι φύλαξον τῆς ἐπιβουλῆς αὐτῶν· σκέπην γὰρ πανταχοῦ τὴν φυλακὴν λέγει.

9-10 Ps. X. 2 (cf. supra, p. 65).

12ᶜ. Πάντων — περιγίνεσθαι: P, fol. 194; V, fol. 259ᵛ.
Argumentum Τοῦ μακαρίου — πικρόν: P, fol. 194; V, fol. 259ᵛ.
2ᵃ. Εὐχομένου φησὶν ἄκουσον: P, fol. 194; V. fol. 259ᵛ.
2ᵇ. Ἀπάλλαξον — αὐτῶν: P, fol. 194; V, fol. 259ᵛ-260.
3ᵃ. Συνηθῶς — κατωτέρω: P, fol. 194ᵛ; V, fol. 260.
3ᵇ. Δεικνύς — λέγει: P, fol. 194ᵛ; V, fol. 260.

Aᵉ Argumentum ps. LXIII (p. 321, 32-36): De se ipso beatus Dauid hunc psalmum cicinit eo tempore, cum Saulis persequtionibus laborabat; est autem tam argumento quam uerbis decimo psalmo similis. 2ᵇ (p. 322, 2-4): Libera me, inquit, a timore aduersari⟨i⟩ et absidiis grauibus mortisque formidine.

those uttering iniquity has been stopped: since all the foe often mocked us for having been in no way helped by God through their paying the fitting penalty, and since their mouths were stopped, as it were, by their having nothing to say at the help given us, it was quite inevitable that the miracle should happen to us.

PSALM 64

The psalm is by blessed David describing on his own account his pursuit by Saul. In its theme it resembles Psalm 11 in many of its verses, saying there, "Because, lo, the sinners have bent the bow to shoot in the dark at the upright of heart,"[1] whereas here, *They bent their bow, a bitter thing.*

Hearken, O God, to my voice when I pray to you (v. 1): hear me when I pray. *Rescue my soul from fear of the foe:* rid me of fear of the adversaries, as if to say, from their scheming and from death. He was, in fact, afraid of suffering at their hands. *Shelter me from the massing of evildoers* (v. 2). Here, as usual, he called *evildoers* those whom above and also below he refers to as *foes. From the multitude of workers of iniquity* (bringing out the injustice of the scheming and hostility). So he is saying, Since they were full of utter wickedness and massed against me with confidence in their own numbers, *shelter me* with your help—that is, protect me from their scheming (by *shelter* everywhere meaning "protection"). |

---

1. Ps 11:2.

4ª. Οἵτινες ἠκόνησαν ὡς ῥομφαίαν τὰς γλώσσας αὐτῶν. Οἳ καὶ τῇ γλώττῃ
κέχρηνται οὐδὲν ἀπ᾽ ἔλαττον οὔσῃ μαχαίρας· παρεσκευασμένοι γάρ εἰσιν
εἰς τὸ φθέγγεσθαι κατ᾽ ἐμοῦ πᾶν ὅτι θάνατον καὶ ἐπιβουλὴν ἐργάσασθαι
δυνάμενον. Τοῦτο δὲ καλῶς εἶπεν πρὸς τοὺς διαβάλλοντας αὐτὸν καὶ ἐρε-
5 θίζοντας κατ᾽ αὐτοῦ τὸν Σαούλ· καὶ γὰρ αἰτιᾶται αὐτῷ πολλαχοῦ.

4ᵇ. Ἐνέτειναν τόξον αὐτῶν, πρᾶγμα πικρόν. Ἀντὶ τοῦ, ὥσπερ τόξον·
ἐπισημηνάμεθα γὰρ ὅτι πολλαχοῦ τὰς ὁμοιώσεις ἄνευ τοῦ «ὡς» λέγει. Καὶ
πράγματα δέ φησι πάσης πικρίας μεστὰ παρεσκευάσαντο κατ᾽ ἐμοῦ, ἐπιβουλὰς ἐπινοοῦντες οὕτως ὀξὺν καὶ αἰφνίδιον τὸν θάνατον ἐπαγαγεῖν δυνά-
10 μενα ὥσπερ τόξα ταθέντα.

5ª. Τοῦ κατατοξεῦσαι ἐν ἀποκρύφοις ἄμωμον. Ὥστε ἡμᾶς λάθρα ἀνελεῖν οὐδὲν ἄξιον θανάτου πεπραχότας, — τοῦτο γὰρ λέγει ἄμωμον, — τουτέστι μέμψεως αὐτοῖς ἀφορμὴν οὐ δεδωκότας. Ὅμοιον δέ ἐστι τὸ ἐν ἀποκρύφοις ἄμωμον τῷ ἐν σκοτομήνῃ τοὺς εὐθεῖς τῇ καρδίᾳ, ὅπερ ἐν τῷ ι΄ λέγει
15 ψαλμῷ. Βούλεται γὰρ εἰπεῖν ὅτι ὥσπερ ἐν σκότῳ καὶ οὐδενὸς βλέποντος
λαθραίως ἀναιρήσονται, οὕτως ἀδεῶς πάντα μηχανῶνται καθ᾽ ἡμῶν.

5ᵇ. Ἐξάπινα κατατοξεύσουσιν αὐτόν, καὶ οὐ φοβηθήσονται. Αἰφνιδίως
φησὶ πολλάκις, οὐ προσδοκώντων ἡμῶν, τοῖς οἰκείοις δόλοις κεχρημένοι
ἐπιτίθενται, οὐδένα φόβον ἔχοντες τῆς σῆς προνοίας. Βούλεται δὲ εἰπεῖν
20 δι᾽ ὅλων ὅτι καὶ θανάτου φθέγγονται μεστά, διαβάλλοντες καὶ ἐρεθίζοντες
κατ᾽ ἐμοῦ, καὶ δόλους καὶ ἐπιβουλὰς παρασκευάζοντες καθ᾽ ἡμῶν αἰφνιδίως,
καὶ πάντα πράττουσιν ἀνελεῖν ἡμᾶς μηχανώμενοι καὶ φοβούμενοι οὐδένα.

7 cf. supra p. 149, 16; 358, 12   14 Ps. X, 2ᶜ.

4ª. Οἳ καὶ — πολλαχοῦ: P, fol. 194ᵛ; V, fol. 260; Vat. 1422, fol. 116 (anon.).
2 ἀπ᾽ ἔλαττον] ἐλάττονι 1422   μαχαίρας] εἰς τὸ μὴν τὴν ἀπὸ κακίας καὶ δολιότητα add.
1422   3 πᾶν τὸ 1422   4 δυνάμενον des. 1422.
4ᵇ. Ἀντὶ τοῦ — ταθέντα: P, fol. 194ᵛ; V, fol. 260; Vat. 1422, fol. 116 (anon.).
8 παρασκευάσαντες 1422   9-10 δυνάμενον 1422.
5ª. Ὥστε ἡμᾶς — καθ᾽ ἡμῶν: P, fol. 194ᵛ; V, fol. 260; Cord, p. 250.   13 δεδωκότα Cord.
5ᵇ. Αἰφνιδίως — οὐδένα: P, fol. 195; V, fol. 260ᵛ.

Aᶜ 4-5 (p. 322, 13-14): Obtrachtatores gentis suae dicit, quorum malalo-
quis aduersus eum inritabatur Saul.   8-10 (p. 322, 15-18): Vt arcus inprouisa
pene iaculatione interimit, sic isti clandistinis in me insidiis et insperatis dolis
molliuntur adficere.   5ª (p. 322, 20-24): Ad opinionem eorum retulit, non ad
exitum rei; neque enim latere poterat tam inmane facinus, sed illi tam textis
insidiis instruebant dolos, quasi nullo uidente cuncta facturi.   17-19 (p. 322,
25-28): Frequenter, non praeuidentibus nobis, ita in nos dolis subitis inruerunt,
quasi nullum tuae prouidentiae haberent amorem.

They all sharpened their tongue like a sword (v. 3): they used their tongue as something no less harmful than a sword, ready to utter against me anything capable of producing death and plotting. This was well said in regard to his traducers setting Saul against him; he was denounced to him on many grounds. *They bent their bow, a bitter thing*—that is, like a bow; we have made the comment that in many places he implies similarity without the word "like." They devised schemes full of bitterness against me, he is saying, hatching plots in this way to bring sudden and unexpected death like drawn bows. *To strike down the innocent from ambush* (v. 4): so as to do away with us furtively, though guilty of nothing deserving of death (the meaning of *innocent*)—that is, though giving them no grounds for blame. The phrase *the innocent from ambush* resembles the phrase "in the dark at the upright of heart" in Psalm 11, his meaning being, Just as they will kill furtively in the dark with no one looking, so they have no qualms about devising everything against us. *They will strike him down without warning, and will not be afraid:* often suddenly, when we do not expect it, they will use their wiles to set upon us, having no fear of your providence. His overall meaning is, They utter words of death, traducing and arousing enmity against me, hatching plots and schemes suddenly against me, and so do everything to destroy us by skullduggery without fearing anything. |

6ᵃ. Ἐκραταίωσαν ἑαυτοῖς λόγον πονηρόν. Συνόντες καὶ συμβουλευόμενοι τὰς κατ' ἐμοῦ γνώμας ἐκύρουν· λόγον γὰρ πονηρὸν τὴν κατ' αὐτοῦ λέγει γνώμην κακίας γέμουσαν, ἣν ὡς εἰκὸς συνόντες ἐβεβαίουν ὥστε καὶ πρᾶξαι. Τίνες δὲ αἱ γνῶμαι;

6ᵇ. Διηγήσαντο τοῦ κρύψαι παγίδας. Διελέγοντο καὶ συνεβουλεύοντό 5 φησι πρὸς ἀλλήλους τίνας ἂν ἐφεύροιεν καθ' ἡμῶν μηχανάς.

6ᶜ. Εἶπαν Τίς ὄψεται αὐτούς; Οὐχ ὡς πάντων εἰρηκότων αὐτῶν ὅτι Πράξωμεν, οὐ γάρ ἐστιν ὁ θεωρῶν, ἀλλ' ὃ πολλάκις ἐπισημηνάμην ἀντὶ πράξεως τὸν λόγον εἰπών, ὅτι οὕτως ἔπραττον οὐχ ὡς ὄντος τοῦ θεωροῦντος καὶ κρίνοντος. 10

7ᵃ. Ἐξηρεύνησαν ἀνομίαν. Διετέλεσάν φησιν ἐν τοῖς πρὸς ἀλλήλους λόγοις, διερευνώμενοι καὶ ζητοῦντες τίνα τρόπον εὕροιεν πάντας ἡμᾶς ἀνελεῖν διὰ τούτου. Ἀνομίαν δὲ ἐκάλεσε τὸ βούλευμα, ἐπειδὴ ἄδικος ἡ μελέτη.

7ᵇ. Ἐξέλιπον ἐξερευνῶντες ἐξερευνήσεις. Ἐξερευνῶντες ἐξέλιπον, τουτέστιν ἐπέλιπον αὐτοὺς αἱ καθ' ἡμῶν ἐφευρέσεις· πλεῖστα γὰρ ἐπινοήσαντες 15 καὶ μηδὲν ἰσχύσαντες, οὐκέτι οὐδὲν ὅτι ἐφευρεῖν εἶχον, οὕτως αὐτοῖς καὶ τὰς μηχανὰς ἐπιλιπεῖν συνέβη.

7ᶜ. Προσελεύσεται ἄνθρωπος, καὶ καρδία βαθεῖα. Ἀλλὰ καὶ πολλάκις προσέρχονται ἡμῖν ἐνσχηματιζόμενοι μὲν δῆθεν φιλίας, οὐ ταῦτα δὲ ἃ σχη-

6ᵃ. Συνόντες — γνῶμαι: P, fol. 195; V, fol. 260ᵛ; Cord, p. 250.   3 εἰκὸς καὶ Cord.
6ᵇ. Διελέγοντο — μηχανάς: P, fol. 195; V, fol. 260ᵛ.
6ᶜ. Οὐχ ὡς – κρίνοντος: P, fol. 195; V, fol. 260ᵛ.
7ᵃ. Διετέλεσαν — μελέτη: P, fol. 195; V, fol. 260ᵛ; Vat. 1422, fol. 116 (anon.); Cord, p. 251.   11 τοῖς] τούτοις 1422   12 λόγους 1422   13 ἄδικος ἦν Cord.
7ᵇ. Ἐξερευνῶντες — συνέβη: P, fol. 195; V, fol. 261; Vat. 1422, fol. 116 (anon.); Cord, p. 251 (ἄλλου).   16 οὐκέτι om. 1422.
7ᶜ. Ἀλλὰ — πεποιηκώς: P, fol. 195ᵛ; V, fol. 261; Cord, p. 252 sub nomine Eusebii.

Aᵉ 6ᵃ (p. 322, 29-323, 4): Congregati in unum et contra me capientes consilia, uerbum malum, id est sententiam plenam iniquitatis, et consilia noxia concaeperunt. Quae est ista sententia?   6ᶜ (p. 323, 9-13): Non quod uere hoc dixerunt, sed res uertit in uerba, quod ita omnia facerent securi quasi nullum speculatorem malignorum operum formidarent, non uerbis sed rebus.   7ᵃ (p. 323, 13-17): Perseueranter et non transitorie quesserunt quomodo quaue oportunitate possent ad nostrum interitum peruenire; iniquitatem uocat iniustam oprisionem suam.   15-16 (p. 323, 18-21): Id est, ita sollicite occassiones excogitauerunt nocendi, ut putaretur inquisitio ista difectum; sic alibi ut inique agerent laborauerunt.   7ᶜ (p. 323, 23-27): Sub specie amicorum ad me accidunt frequenter, cum in oculto cordis nutrierierant uirus odiorum; quod sepe Saulem fecisse manifestum est.

They confirmed their wicked plan (v. 5): joining together and conspiring, they confirmed their intentions against me (by *wicked plan* referring to the intention full of malice against him that they probably came together to ratify for implementation). What kind of intentions? *They talked of laying snares secretly:* they discussed and pondered as a group what stratagems they could come up with against him. *They said, Who will see them?* It was not that they all said, Let us do it since no one is looking; rather, as I often have indicated, he uses the word for the action, meaning, They acted as though there were no one watching and condemning. *They sought out iniquity* (v. 6): they kept talking to one another, investigating and searching to find a means of doing away with us all (by *iniquity* meaning "plan," since their pondering was iniquitous). *They wore themselves out searching searchings.* By *They wore themselves out searching* he means that the investigations against us wore them out, since they gave great thought to it and came up with nothing, no longer able to investigate further, with the result that even their scheming came to an end.

Human beings will approach, their heart deep: they even approach us frequently with the pretense of friendship, not meaning what they pretend, | but

ματίζονται φρονοῦντες, ἀλλ᾽ ἐν τῷ βάθει τῆς καρδίας τὴν καθ᾽ ἡμῶν ἔχοντες ἔχθραν. Τοῦτο δὲ μάλιστα ὁ Σαοὺλ πολλαχοῦ φαίνεται πεποιηκώς.

᾽ 8ᵃ. Καὶ ὑψωθήσεται ὁ Θεός. Ἅμα διὰ τούτων πάντων μέγας ὀφθήσεται ὁ Θεός, ὡς καὶ ἐπιβουλευόντων καὶ διαβαλλόντων καὶ ὑποκρινομένων ἀπαλ-
5 λάττων.

8ᵇ. Βέλος νηπίων ἐγενήθησαν αἱ πληγαὶ αὐτῶν. Οὕτως γάρ φησι τὰς μηχανὰς αὐτῶν τὰς καθ᾽ ἡμῶν ἀσθενεῖς ἐργάζεται καὶ οὐδαμινάς, ὡς τὰ τῶν νηπίων ἀσθενῆ καὶ πλήττειν οὐ δυνάμενα βέλη.

9ᵃ. Καὶ ἐξησθένησαν ἐπ᾽ αὐτοὺς αἱ γλῶσσαι αὐτῶν. Καὶ πάντα ὅσαπερ
10 ἢ ἐφθέγξαντο ἢ εἶπον κατ᾽ ἐμοῦ, ἢ διαβάλλοντες ἢ ὀνειδίζοντες, ἐδείχθη πάντα ἀσθενῆ. Τὸ δὲ ἐπ᾽ αὐτοὺς ἐξησθένησαν, ἀντὶ τοῦ Μέχρι αὐτῶν ἔστη οὐδὲν δυνηθέντα, οὐδὲν ἰσχύοντα, οὐδὲν διαπραξάμενον.

9ᵇ. Ἐταράχθησαν πάντες οἱ θεωροῦντες αὐτούς. Πάντες γοῦν οἱ βλέποντες αὐτοὺς τοσαῦτα μὲν μηχανωμένους, ὠφελοῦντας δὲ οὐδέν, ταραχῇ τὴν
15 διάνοιαν κατεσχέθησαν.

10ᵃ. Καὶ ἐφοβήθη πᾶς ἄνθρωπος. Καὶ φόβῳ πάντες ἐλήφθησαν ἐκπληττόμενοι μεθ᾽ ὅσης τῆς σπουδῆς ἤνυον οὐδέν, τοὐναντίον δὲ καὶ δίκας ἔδοσαν.

10ᵇ. Καὶ ἀνήγγειλαν τὰ ἔργα τοῦ Θεοῦ. Καὶ πάντες ἀπήγγελον ὅτι σὸν ἔργον τοῦτο, καί σοι τὰ γιγνόμενα ἐπέγραψαν, γνωρίσαντες ὡς οὐκ ἦν
20 ἄλλου οὕτως αὐτοῖς πᾶσαν τὴν σπουδὴν εἰς τὸ μηδὲν περιτρέψαι, τοὐναντίον δὲ καὶ τιμωρήσασθαι.

8ᵃ. Ἅμα — ἀπαλλάττων: P, fol. 195ᵛ; V, fol. 261; Vat. 1422, fol. 116 (anon.).
8ᵇ. Οὕτως — βέλη: P, fol. 195ᵛ; V, fol. 261.
9ᵛ. Καὶ πάντα — διαπραξάμενον: P, fol. 195ᵛ; V, fol. 261.   12 διαπράξαμεν V.
9ᵇ. Πάντες — κατεσχέθησαν: P, fol. 196; V, fol. 261ᵛ; Cord, p. 252 sub nomine ATHANASII.
10ᵃ. Καὶ φόβῳ — ἔδοσαν: P, fol. 196; V, fol. 261ᵛ.
10ᵇ. Καὶ πάντες — τιμωρήσασθαι: P, fol. 196; V, fol. 261ᵛ; Vat. 1422, fol. 116 (anon.); Cord, p. 252 sub nomine ORIGENIS (P. G., XII, 1492 CD).   18 ἀπηγέλλοντο 1422   19 γενόμενα ἐπέτρεψαν 1422   20-21 περιτρέψαι ὁ θεῖος ἐθέλησεν ὀφθαλμός, τοὐναντίον — τιμωρήσασθαι ᾑρετίσατο 1422 Cord.

Aᵉ 8ᵃ (p. 323, 27-29): Mirabiliter Deus magnus ostenditur, emulorum quassatis (casatis ms) insidiis.   8ᵇ (p. 323, 31-34): Tam inefficaces ad perimendum sunt eorum insidiae quam sunt infirma ad uulnerandum tela paruulorum.
9ᵃ (p. 324, 1-4): Omnia quaecumque locuti fuerunt aduersum nos, exprobrantes atque detrachentes, effectu non sequente casata sunt.

with hostility against us in the depths of their heart. Saul in particular seems often to have been guilty of this. *God will be exalted* (v. 7): at the same time, in all this God will be seen to be great for freeing us from the schemers and traducers and pretenders. *Their blows were reduced to a children's dart:* God thus renders their wiles against us weak and insignificant, like children's darts, weak and incapable of harming. *Their tongues lost their force against them* (v. 8): everything they uttered or said against me, or used to traduce and taunt me, has all been shown to be powerless. They lost their force against them means, Nothing proved capable of reaching them, nothing worthwhile, nothing effective. *All who observed them were alarmed:* all who saw them, at any rate, when they were hatching such plots but achieving nothing, were reduced to alarm in their mind. *Every person was afraid* (v. 9): they were all struck by fear, astonished at their achieving nothing despite so much zeal, but on the contrary paying the penalty. *They reported the works of God:* everyone reported this deeds of yours and attributed to you what happened, admitting that it was due to no one else that all their efforts came to nothing, and that, on the contrary, they actually were punished. | *And they understood*

10ᶜ. Καὶ τὰ ποιήματα αὐτοῦ συνῆκαν. Ὅτι τὰ σὰ ποιήματα, ἀντὶ τοῦ Τῇ σῇ ἐγίγνετο δυνάμει τε καὶ σοφίᾳ.

11ᵃ. Εὐφρανθήσεται δίκαιος ἐπὶ τῷ Κυρίῳ, καὶ ἐλπιεῖ ἐπ᾽ αὐτόν. Ἡμῖν δέ φησιν ἔσται ἐπί σοι ἡ εὐφροσύνη, ἐφ᾽ ᾧ καὶ ἐλπίζομεν, παρ᾽ οὗ καὶ τὴν ἀπαλλαγὴν τῶν κακῶν δεχόμεθα. 5

11ᵇ. Καὶ ἐπαινεθήσονται πάντες οἱ εὐθεῖς τῇ καρδίᾳ. Καὶ θαυμασθησόμεθα παρὰ πάντων οἱ τοῦ δικαίου ἐπιμελώμενοι, ὅτι ἀναγκαίως καὶ ὠφελίμως ἅπαντα πράττοντες τοσούτων ἀγαθῶν καταξιούμεθα.

PSALMVS LXIV

Τὴν ἐπάνοδον τοῦ λαοῦ προαγορεύων ἐν τῷδε τῷ ψαλμῷ, ἐκ τοῦ ἐκεί- 10 νων προσώπου ταῦτά φησιν ἅπερ εἰπεῖν αὐτοῖς ἥρμοττεν τῆς ἐπανόδου μέλλουσιν ἀπολαύειν. Ἀπάσας μέντοι τὰς προφητείας ποιούμενος, ἐκ τοῦ προσώπου τὰ πλεῖστα ἢ καὶ πάντα σχεδὸν φθέγγεται τοῦ περὶ ὧν ποιεῖται τὴν προφητείαν, οὐχ ἁπλῶς, ἀλλ᾽ ἐκείνους παιδεύων εἴτε ἐπὶ τοῖς ἀγαθοῖς, ὥστε τοιούτοις ῥήμασι κεχρημένους τὴν εὐχαριστίαν ἀποδιδόναι τῷ 15 Θεῷ, εἴτε ἐν ταῖς συμφοραῖς μετὰ τοιούτων λόγων καὶ τὰ πταίσματα ἐξομολογεῖσθαι, καὶ τὰ ἀγαθὰ παρὰ τοῦ διδόντος αἰτεῖν Θεοῦ.

2ᵃ. Σοὶ πρέπει ὕμνος, ὁ Θεός, ἐν Σιών. Ἑτέρωθι λέγει ἐκ προσώπου τῶν αὐτῶν Πῶς ᾄσωμεν τὴν ᾠδὴν Κυρίου ἐπὶ γῆς ἀλλοτρίας; ἐπειδὴ καὶ ἀφορίσας ἦν ὁ Θεὸς τὸν ἐπὶ τοῦ Σιὼν τόπον εἰς τὴν ἑαυτοῦ θεραπείαν, 20

19 Ps. CXXXVI, 4.

10ᶜ. Ὅτι τὰ σὰ — σοφίᾳ: C, fol. 323 pluribus perditis; P, fol. 196; V, fol. 261ᵛ.
11ᵃ. Ἡμῖν — δεχόμεθα: C, fol. 323; P, fol. 196; V, fol. 261ᵛ; Cord, p. 253 sub nomine ATHANASII.
11ᵇ. Καὶ θαυμασθησόμεθα — καταξιούμεθα: C, fol. 323; P, fol. 196; V, fol. 261ᵛ; Cord, p. 253 (anon.).
Argumentum Τὴν ἐπάνοδον — Θεοῦ: C, fol. 323; P, fol. 196ᵛ; V, fol. 262; Cord, p. 265. 10-11 cf. L (p. 260, 13-16) Τοῖς ἐν Βαβυλῶνι τὰ ῥήματα πρόσφορα, οἳ τῆς ἐπανόδου γλιχόμενοι ταύτην τῷ Θεῷ τὴν ὑμνῳδίαν προσέφερον 12 ἀπολαβεῖν CPV.
2¹. Ἑτέρωθι — ἐκπληρούμενον: C, fol. 323ᵛ; P, fol. 196ᵛ; V, fol. 262; Cord, p. 265-266.

Aᵉ 6-7 (p. 324, 16-18): Taliter liberati erunt, apud omnes admiratione dignissimi. 10-12 (p. 324. 22-24): De Babilone reditum populi in praesente psalmo praedicit, ex persona reuertentium loquens. 19 (p. 324, 28-30): Quia canticum Domini in terra aliena cantare non poterant.

his doings: that the doings are yours—that is, they happened by your power and wisdom.

The just will rejoice in the Lord, and will hope in him (v. 10): we, on the contrary, will feel joy in you, in whom we also hope, for from you we also receive deliverance from the troubles. *All the upright in heart will be praised:* we who have attended to righteousness will be admired by all for doing everything that was necessary and beneficial, and for being vouchsafed such wonderful goods.

PSALM 65

In foretelling in this psalm the people's return, he speaks on their part in mentioning what applied to them when on the point of being granted the return. In composing all the inspired works, of course, he utters most things, or in fact nearly all, from the viewpoint of those about whom he is composing the work, not without purpose but to instruct them either in the case of good times to use such words in giving thanks to God, or in time of misfortune to confess their failings in such words and ask for good things from God the giver.

A hymn becomes you, O God, in Sion (v. 1). Elsewhere he says on behalf of the same people, "How shall we sing the song of the Lord in a foreign land?"[1] since God had determined Sion as the place for his worship, | and

---

1. Ps 137:4.

καὶ προστάξας ἑτέρωθι μήτε θυσίας αὐτῷ προσάγειν, μήτε τὴν λοιπὴν ἐκπληροῦν κατὰ νόμον λατρείαν. Διὰ τοῦτο ἐνταῦθά φησιν ὅτι πρέπον σοι καὶ καθηκόντως ἐκπληρούμενον.

2ᵇ. Καὶ σοὶ ἀποδοθήσεται εὐχὴ ἐν Ἱερουσαλήμ. Καλῶς τὸ ἀποδοθήσεται, 5 καὶ διὰ τὴν ἀγνωμοσύνην τοῦ πρὸ τῆς αἰχμαλωσίας καιροῦ καὶ διὰ τὴν ἀνάγκην τῶν ἀλλοτρίων τόπων, ἐν οἷς καθεστῶτες παρέλιπον τὰς προσευ- χάς. Πάντα οὖν φησι κατὰ ταὐτὸν ἀποδίδοται ἐκεῖ μετὰ τὴν ἐπάνοδον.

3ᵃ. Εἰσάκουσον προσευχῆς μου. Οὐκοῦν ὑπὲρ τούτων φησὶν ἀκούσας μου τῆς προσευχῆς ἐπανάγαγέ με.

10 3ᵇ. Πρός σε πᾶσα σὰρξ ἥξει. Τότε γὰρ οὐχ ἡμεῖς ἐλευσόμεθα μόνον, ἀλλὰ καὶ τῶν ἀλλοτρίων πολλοὶ ἐκ τοῦ περὶ ἡμᾶς θαύματος εἰς θεραπείαν τὴν σὴν ἐν τῷ τόπῳ παρέσονται.

4ᵃ. Λόγοι ἀνόμων ὑπερεδυνάμωσαν ἡμᾶς. Ἑτέρωθί φησιν Ἐγενήθη τὰ δάκρυά μου ἐμοὶ ἄρτος ἡμέρας καὶ νυκτὸς ἐν τῷ λέγεσθαί μοι καθ' ἑκάστην 15 ἡμέραν Ποῦ ἐστιν ὁ Θεός σου; Οὗτοι οὖν φησιν οἱ λόγοι, οὓς ἐποιοῦντο καθ' ἡμῶν ὀνειδίζοντες, τὴν συμφορὰν εἰς λύπην καθιστῶντες πολλὴν καὶ εἰς ἀπόγνωσιν ἄγοντες, σφόδρα ἡμᾶς ἀσθενῆσαι πεποιήκασιν. Τὸ γὰρ ὑπερεδυνάμωσαν, ἀντὶ τοῦ ἀδυναμῶσαι ἐποίησαν.

4ᵇ. Καὶ ταῖς ἀσεβείαις ἡμῶν σὺ ἱλάσῃ. Ἀλλ' ἐκεῖνοι μὲν τοιαῦτα ἔλεγον, 20 ἡμεῖς δὲ ἅπερ ἐπάσχομεν ὑπὲρ ὧν ἠσεβήσαμεν εἰς σε πολλάκις ἅπαντα

13-15 Ps. XLI, 4.

2ᵇ. Καλῶς — ἐπάνοδον: C, fol. 323ᵛ; P, fol. 196ᵛ; V, fol. 262; Vat. 1422, fol. 116ᵛ (anon.); Cord, p. 266 (anon.).   6 καθεστῶσι 1422.
3ᵃ. Οὐκοῦν — ἐπανάγαγέ με: C, fol. 323ᵛ; P, fol. 197; V, fol. 262ᵛ.
3ᵇ. Τότε — παρέσονται: C, fol. 323ᵛ; P, fol. 197; V, fol. 262ᵛ.
4ᵃ. Ἑτέρωθι — ἐποίησαν: P, fol. 197; V, fol. 262ᵛ; Cord, p. 267; ἑτέρωθί φησιν Ἐγενήθη τὰ δάκ(ρυα) affert C, fol. 323ᵛ et abrumpitur.   13-15 ἐγενήθη — φησιν om. Cord   18 ὑπερεδυνάμωσαν] ἠδυνάμωσαν PV.
4ᵇ. Ἀλλ' ἐκεῖνοι — ῥήματα: P, fol. 197 et V, fol. 262ᵛ (Θεοδωρήτου); Vat. 1422, fol. 116ᵛ (anon.); Cord, p. 267 (anon.).

Aᵉ 2ᵇ (p. 324, 31-34): Quod, aut in solo proprio ante negleximus aut in captiuitate offerre nequiuimus, reducti in Hirusalem deuoti iam et eruditi (? eruti ms) reddemus.   8-9 (p. 324, 35-325, 1): Pro reuersione poscentem.   3ᵇ (p. 325, 1-4): Nostro comitatui iu⟨n⟩gentur externi, qui in tuum cultum liberationis nostrae admiratione migrabunt.   14-18 (p. 325, 5-8): Dum dicerent nobis per singulos dies exprobrantes Vbi est Deus tuus, inbicellos nos infirmosque ficerunt. 4ᵇ (p. 325, 15-19): Nos uero ista, quae patimur, pro eo quod impietatem egimus, iuste omnia sustenemus, sed reatum nostrum ueniae impetratione desolue.

ordered them not to offer sacrifice to him or to discharge the rest of the cult anywhere else. Hence, he says here, It becomes you and is duly performed. *And a vow will be paid to you in Jerusalem. Paid* was well put both on account of the ingratitude at the time before the captivity and on account of the pressing need in foreign places where they found themselves, and where they neglected the prayers. So he is saying, Every duty is paid there at the same time after the return. *Hearken to my prayer* (v. 2): so hear my prayer for these things and lead me back. *All flesh will come to you:* at that time it will not be only ourselves who will come: many of the foreigners also will be present in that place to worship you out of admiration for us.

Lawless people's words overwhelmed us (v. 3). Elsewhere he says, "My tears have become my bread day and night as they say to me each day, 'Where is your God?' "[2] So he means, These words that they direct against us in their taunts, leading on from disaster to deep grief and bringing us to the point of despair, have made us very weak (*overwhelmed* meaning "rendered us helpless"). *You will have mercy on our impious deeds:* while they said such things, we suffered justly all the sufferings for our frequent impiety to you. | So he is saying, Having allowed the impious deeds, you will

---

2. Ps 42:3.

ἐπάσχομεν δικαίως. Συγχωρήσας οὖν φησι τὰς ἀσεβείας βοηθήσεις καὶ ἐπανάξεις εἰς τὰ οἰκεῖα, μάταια τῶν ὀνειδιζόντων ἀποφαίνων τὰ ῥήματα.

5ᵃ. Μάκαριος ὃν ἐξελέξω καὶ προσελάβου. Τότε τοίνυν μακάριοι ἡμεῖς ἐσόμεθα, οὓς ἐκλεξάμενος καὶ ἀφορίσας τῶν κατεχόντων προσλαμβάνεις καὶ πρὸς σεαυτὸν ἕλκεις. Ταῦτα λέγει ὡς τοῦ Θεοῦ κατὰ τὴν ἰουδαϊκὴν 5 ὑπόληψιν ἐν τῷ ὄρει ὄντος τῷ Σιών, κἀκεῖ πρὸς ἑαυτὸν αὐτοὺς ἕλκειν μέλλοντος.

5ᵇ. Κατασκηνώσει ἐν ταῖς αὐλαῖς σου. Ἵνα εἴπῃ ἐν τοῖς προσήκουσί σοι τόποις, ὡς τῷ Θεῷ πάσης ἐκείνης ἰδίως προσηκούσης τῆς γῆς, τῆς τῶν Ἰουδαίων. 10

5ᶜ⁻⁶ᵃ. Πλησθησόμεθα ἐν τοῖς ἀγαθοῖς τοῦ οἴκου σου· ἅγιος ὁ ναός σου. Ἀπολαύσομεν δέ φησι καὶ τῶν τοῦ οἴκου σου καλῶν, τουτέστι τῆς ἐν αὐτῷ λατρείας, τῶν θυσιῶν καὶ τῶν λοιπῶν, ὅσα ἔθος ἦν αὐτοῖς ἐπιτελεῖν ἐν τῷ ναῷ.

6ᵇ. Θαυμαστὸς ἐν δικαιοσύνῃ. Οὐ θαυμαστὸν γὰρ ἐὰν ἡμᾶς εὐεργετεῖς, 15 ὅπου γε καὶ πάσης τῆς οἰκουμένης αὐτὸς ἐλπὶς εἶ· κἂν γὰρ ἀγνωμονῶσιν ἐκεῖνοι, ἀλλὰ χρεία αὐτοῖς τῆς παρά σου φιλανθρωπίας καὶ τῶν παρά σου ὑετῶν, ἀφ᾽ ὧν ἀπολαύουσι τῆς τροφῆς.

6ᶜ. Ἐπάκουσον ἡμῶν, ὁ Θεὸς ὁ σωτὴρ ἡμῶν, ἡ ἐλπὶς πάντων τῶν περάτων τῆς γῆς. Οὐχὶ τούτους μόνον εὐεργετεῖς, ἀλλὰ καὶ τοὺς ἐν θαλάσσῃ 20 περισώζεις πολλάκις ἀπὸ κινδύνων. Βούλεται δὲ εἰπεῖν ὅτι πᾶσιν ἀπάντων αὐτοῖς εἶ τῶν καλῶν αἴτιος.

5¹. Τότε — μέλλοντος: P, fol. 197ᵛ; V, fol. 263; Vat. 1422, fol. 116ᵛ (anon.); Cord, p. 267.   4 κατεχόντων] πονηρευόντων Cord   5 ἑαυτὸν PV 1422 Cord   ταῦτα λέγει om. PV 1422.
5ᵇ. Ἵνα εἴπῃ — Ἰουδαίων: P, fol. 197ᵛ; V, fol. 263.
5ᶜ⁻⁶ᵃ. Ἀπολαύσομεν — ναῷ: P, fol. 197ᵛ; V, fol. 263; Cord, p. 268.   12 σου om. Cord.
6ᵇ. Οὐ θαυμαστὸν — τροφῆς: P. fol. 198; V, fol. 263ᵛ; Vat. 1422, fol. 117 (anon.). 18 ἐτῶν... ἀπολαύουσι 1422.
6ᶜ. Οὐχὶ — αἴτιος: P, fol. 198; V, fol. 263ᵛ.

Aᵉ 8-9 (p. 325, 23-24): Id est in locis tuae dominationis et iuris.   13 (p. 325, 25-27): Sacrificiorum apparitionibus et copiis perfruemur.   15-21 (p. 325, 34-326, 6): Non est ergo tibi difficile nos eripere, cum beneficiis tuis omnis terra foueatur, tam habitantes terram quem pererrantes mare prouidentiae tuae cura sustentat, foetandis scilicet terris, naufragiis mitigandis.

help us and bring us to our own land, rendering the words of the taunters ineffectual.

Blessed is the one you chose and adopted (v. 4): at that time we shall be blessed, since having chosen us and removed us from what beset us, you adopt us and draw us to yourself. He says this in the Jewish belief that God was on Mount Sion, ready to draw them to himself there. *He will dwell in your courts,* as if to say, in your special places, since all that land, the land of the Jews, was special to God. *We shall be filled with the good things of your house. Holy is your temple* (vv. 4–5): we shall enjoy the good things of your house—that is, worship in it, sacrifices and the rest, it being their custom to perform them in the temple. *Wondrous in righteousness:* it is no surprise if you are favorable to us, since you are the hope of the whole world. Even if they are ungrateful, they still have need of lovingkindness from you and rains from you, since from these they gain food.

Give ear to us, O God, our savior, hope of all the ends of the earth and of those far distant at sea: you not only help these people, but you also often save those at sea from danger.[3] He means, You are the cause of all the good things they enjoy. | *Preparing mountains in your strength* (v. 6). *Prepar-*

---

3. Although the final phrase of v. 5 is missing from some forms of the LXX, and Devreesse omits it from his text, Theodore (like his fellow Antiochene Theodoret) is reading something about seafarers, as the ancient Latin version also attests.

7ᵃ. Ἑτοιμάζων ὄρη ἐν τῇ ἰσχύϊ σου. Τὸ ἑτοιμάζων ἑδράζων εἴρηται πολλαχοῦ. Αὐτός φησι καὶ τὰ ὄρη τῇ σῇ δυνάμει ἑδραῖα ποιεῖς καὶ ἰσχυρά. Βούλεται δὲ εἰπεῖν ὅτι οὐδὲν οἰκείᾳ φύσει ἰσχυρόν, ἀλλὰ τῇ σῇ δυνάμει γενόμενον.

5 7ᵇ. Περιεζωσμένος ἐν δυναστείᾳ. Τὴν ζῶσιν ἐπὶ τοῦ ἑτοίμου καὶ εὐκόλου λαμβάνει, ἐκ μεταφορᾶς τῶν ἀνθρώπων, οἳ περὶ τὰς εὐεργεσίας ἔχοντες τὸ ζώννυσθαι καὶ τὴν ἑτοιμότητα ἐπιδείκνυνται, καὶ τὴν εὐκολίαν τοῦ ἔργου προσκτῶνται. Τοῦτο οὖν φησιν ὅτι ἑτοιμοτάτην ἔχεις προσοῦσάν σοι τὴν δύναμιν, καὶ μετὰ πολλῆς δύνῃ τῆς εὐκολίας ποιεῖν ὅσαπερ ἂν θέλῃς ὑπὸ 10 μηδενὸς κωλυόμενος.

8ᵃ. Ὁ συνταράσσων τὸ κύτος τῆς θαλάσσης. Ἐκεῖνο λέγει ὅπερ ἀλλαχοῦ καλεῖ περιβόλαιον αὐτῆς, οἷον τὸ Ἄβυσσος ὡς ἱμάτιον τὸ περιβόλαιον αὐτοῦ· τὴν γὰρ περιβολὴν αὐτῆς φησι καὶ τὴν ἔκτασιν, τουτέστι τὴν οὕτω μεγάλην, ὅτε θέλεις συγκινεῖς.

15 8ᵇ. Ἤχους κυμάτων αὐτῆς τίς ὑποστήσεται; Καὶ ἐπειδὰν τῷ σῷ προστάγματι ἡ θάλασσα ταραχὴν ὑπομείνῃ, οὐδὲ ὑποστῆναί τινα δυνατὸν ὑπὸ τοῦ φόβου. Βούλεται δὲ διὰ τούτων εἰπεῖν ὅτι αὐτὸς καὶ χορηγὸς τῶν ἀγαθῶν, αὐτὸς καὶ ἐνισχύων τὰ ἰσχυρά, αὐτὸς καὶ ταράττων τὰ μεγάλα, ἵνα ἀπὸ τοῦ κοινοῦ δείξῃ ὅτι εἰκότως καὶ αὐτῷ ταῦτα παρέξει. Ἐπάγει γοῦν 20 εὐθύς·

9ᵃ. Ταραχθήσονται τὰ ἔθνη. Οὕτω φησὶ καὶ τούτους ταράξεις ὡς τὴν θάλασσαν.

1 cf. p. 373, 2   13-14 ps. CIII, 6ᵃ.

7ᵃ. Τὸ ἑτοιμάζων - γενόμενον: P, fol. 198; V, fol. 263ᵛ; Cord, p. 269.   1 ἑτοιμάζων ἀντὶ Cord   1-2 *Paraphrasis* (p. 257, 34): Τὸ ἑτοιμάζων πανταχοῦ ἑδράζων λέγει 2 αὐτὸς γὰρ Cord.

7ᵇ. Τὴν ζῶσιν — κωλυόμενος: P, fol. 198; V, fol. 263ᵛ; Vat. 1422, fol. 117 (anon.); cf. THEODORETUS (1352 B et n. 48).   5 ἕτοιμον καὶ εὔκολον 1422   9 θέλῃς des. 1422.

8ᵃ. Ἐκεῖνο — συγκινεῖς: P, fol. 198; V, fol. 263ᵛ.

8ᵇ. Καὶ ἐπειδὰν — εὐθύς: P, fol. 198; V, fol. 264.

9ᵃ. Οὕτω — θάλασσαν: P, fol. 198ᵛ; V, fol. 264; Cord, p. 269 sub nomine ATHANASII.

Aᵉ 7ᵃ (p. 326, 7-9): Id est, stabilitate sua et mole confirmans; nihil per se aut ex aliquo, sed tua operatione et uirtute subsistunt.   5-8 (p. 326, 10-12): Oportuno uerbo ad praesentem liberationem ussus est, paratum siquidem et expeditum, quod nomine semper accinctionis ostenditur.

ing occurs for "establishing" in many places. You are the one, he is saying, who with your power make firm and strong even the *mountains*. He means, While nothing is naturally strong, it becomes so with your power. *Girt with his might.* He uses girding in the sense of readiness and ease, by analogy with people who have recourse to girding themselves up for good works and give evidence of readiness, thus gaining ease in action. So he is saying, The power you have is at the ready, and with great ease you can do whatever you wish without hindrance from anybody.

You who stir up the depths of the sea (v. 7). He refers to what he elsewhere calls its "garment," as, for example, "The depths his covering like a garment."[4] In other words, he is saying, When you wish, you stir up its surface and its mass, great as it is. *Who will bear the roar of its waves?* Since even the sea suffers disturbance at your command, he is saying, no one can withstand fear of you. In this he means, You are the one who supplies good things; you are the one who imparts strength to what is strong; you are the one who imparts disturbance to what is mighty, the purpose being to bring out from the general rule that he will provide this also for them. In fact, he goes on at once to say *The nations will be disturbed:* he will disturb them like the sea. | *Those who dwell at the extremities will be in fear as a result*

---

4. Ps 104:6.

9ᵇ. Καὶ φοβηθήσονται οἱ κατοικοῦντες τὰ πέρατα ἀπὸ τῶν σημείων σου. Καὶ τοσαῦτα περὶ ἡμᾶς σημεῖα καὶ τέρατα ἐργάσῃ, ὥστε πάντας τοὺς κατὰ τὴν οἰκουμένην καὶ ἀπὸ τῆς ἀκοῆς μόνης φρίττειν. Τινὲς δὲ ἀπὸ ἀμαθίας τὸ φοβηθήσονται τῷ ἄνω ἀποδεδώκασιν, ἔστι δὲ λοιπὸν οὐδὲν τὸ μένον· ἕωλον γάρ ἐστι τὸ περιληφθέν, τὸ Οἱ κατοικοῦντες τὰ πέρατα ἀπὸ τῶν σημείων 5 σου, οὐδενὸς προσκειμένου.

9ᶜ. Ἐξόδους πρωΐας καὶ ἑσπέρας τέρψεις. Εἰπὼν τῶν ἐναντίων τὴν ταραχὴν καὶ τὸν φόβον, λέγει καὶ τὴν αὐτῶν εὐφροσύνην. Ἐξόδους δὲ πρωΐας καλεῖ τὴν ἀνατολὴν τοῦ ἡλίου, ὡς τὸ Ἀπ᾿ ἄκρου τοῦ οὐρανοῦ ἡ ἔξοδος αὐτοῦ. Ἀπὸ τοίνυν τῆς ἀνατολῆς τοῦ ἡλίου καὶ μέχρι τῆς δύσεως ἡμεῖς ἐν 10 τῷ τέρπεσθαι καὶ εὐφραίνεσθαι ἐσόμεθα, ἀντὶ τοῦ διηνεκῆ τὰ τῆς εὐφροσύνης ἡμῖν ἔσται.

10ᵃ. Ἐπεσκέψω τὴν γῆν καὶ ἐμέθυσας αὐτήν. Ἐπίσκεψιν δὲ γῆς καλεῖ τοῦ ὑετοῦ τὴν χορηγίαν· παρέξεις γὰρ ἡμῖν φησι καὶ ὑετοὺς δαψιλεῖς.

10ᵇ. Ἐπλήθυνας τοῦ πλουτίσαι αὐτήν. Καὶ παρέξεις αὐτῇ πολλὴν καὶ 15 πλουσίαν τῶν καρπῶν τὴν χορηγίαν. Βούλεται δὲ διὰ πάντων εἰπεῖν ὅτι μετὰ τὴν ἐπάνοδον καὶ εὐημερίας πολλῆς ἡμᾶς ἀξιώσεις.

10ᶜ. Ὁ ποταμὸς τοῦ Θεοῦ ἐπληρώθη ὑδάτων. Τὸ ἀκολουθοῦν τοῖς ὑετοῖς εἶπεν· ἀπὸ γὰρ τοῦ πλήθους τῶν ὑετῶν φησιν αὔξεται ὁ ποταμός. Λέγει δὲ τὸν Ἰορδάνην, τοῦ Θεοῦ καλῶν αὐτόν, ὡς ἐν τῇ γῇ τῆς ἐπαγγελίας ὄντα. 20

10ᵈ. Ἡτοίμασας τὴν τροφὴν αὐτῶν, ὅτι οὕτως ἡ ἑτοιμασία σου. Καὶ τῇ παρά σου προνοίᾳ ἑτοίμην αὐτοῖς παρέξεις τὴν τροφήν, ὥστε μηδενὸς

9-10 Ps. XVIII, 7ᵃ.

9ᵇ. Καὶ τοσαῦτα — προσκειμένου: P, fol. 198ᵛ; V, fol. 264.
9ᶜ. Εἰπὼν — ἔσται: P, fol. 198ᵛ; V, fol. 264; Vat. 1422, fol. 117 (anon.); eadem, paucis mutatis, affert GARNERIUS sub nomine THEODORETI (1353, n. 63).
10ᵃ. Ἐπίσκεψιν — δαψιλεῖς: P, fol. 198ᵛ; V, fol. 264ᵛ; Vat. 1422, fol. 117 (anon.).
10ᵇ. Καὶ παρέξεις — ἀξιώσεις: P, fol. 198ᵛ; V, fol. 264ᵛ; cf. supplementum GARNERII (1353, n. 72).   17 ἡμᾶς ex Garn. supplevi.
10ᶜ. Τὸ ἀκολουθοῦν — ὄντα: P, fol. 199; V, fol. 264ᵛ; Cord, p. 270; cf. supplementum GARNERII (1353, n. 75).
10ᵈ. Καὶ τῇ — τὴν χρείαν: P, fol. 199; V, fol. 264ᵛ; Cord, p. 270, 47-271, 8 sub nomine ORIGENIS (P. G., XII, 1496 C 4-D 1); cf. supplementum GARNERII (ib.).

Aᵉ 2-3 (p. 326, 14-17): Tanta in nostri liberatione praesigna facies, ut ad omnes terrae habitatores nuntius operum tuorum terror perueniet.   14 (p. 326, 19-20): Imbrium infussione foetasti.   10ᶜ (p. 326, 22-27): Adsiduetate, inquit, pluiarum etiam fluius aquarum incrementa suscipiet. Fluium autem Dei Iordanen ideo uero eum uocat, quod lapsu suo terram repromisionis interluit.

of your signs (v. 8): you will work such marvelous signs and portents in our regard as to terrify everyone throughout the world at the mere report of it. Some commentators, for the reason of the uncertain reference, attribute *will be in fear* to the above, but there is nothing to be supplied: the subject follows, *those who dwell at the extremities as a result of your signs,* nothing further attached. *You bring gladness to departures by morning and evening.* After mentioning the disturbance and fear of the adversaries, he mentions also their happiness. By *departures by morning* he refers to the rising of the sun, as in the phrase "his emergence is from heaven's zenith."[5] So he means, From the rising of the sun to its setting we shall experience gladness and happiness—that is, we shall have lasting happiness.

You examined the earth and bedewed it (v. 9). By "examination" he refers to the provision of rain, meaning, You will provide us also with abundant rain. *You spared nothing to enrich it:* you will also provide it with an abundant and rich supply of crops. In this he means, After the return you will regale us also with great prosperity. *The river of God was filled with waters.* He mentions also the consequence of the rain: From the abundance of the rain *the river* will swell (referring to the Jordan, calling it *God's* because it is in the land of promise). *You prepared their nourishment, because this was your preparation:* you will provide us with food made ready by your providence so that we lack for nothing. | *This was your preparation* means, Since

---

5. Ps 19:6.

ἐνδεῖσθαι. Τὸ δὲ οὕτως ἡ ἑτοιμασία σου, τουτέστιν ἐπειδὴ ἔργον σοι τὰ τοιαῦτα εὐτρεπίζειν καὶ ἑτοιμάζειν τοῖς ἀνθρώποις, ἀφ᾽ ὧν ἁπάντων αὐτοῖς χορηγεῖς τὴν ἀφθονίαν. Ὥσπερ γὰρ τὸ ἑτοιμάζειν τὸ ἑδράζειν λέγει, ἀπὸ τοῦ τὰ παρεσκευασμένα ἕτοιμα εἶναι καὶ βέβαια πρὸς τὴν χρείαν,
5 οὕτω καὶ ἑτοιμασίαν αὐτὴν καλεῖ τὴν παρασκευήν, ὡς ἐνταῦθα, — ἵνα εἴπῃ ὅτι οὐδενὸς ἐνδεηθήσονται. Ἕτοιμα γὰρ αὐτοῖς πάντα καὶ παρεσκευασμένα ὡς μηδὲν δεῖν αὐτοῖς φροντίδος· τὸ δὲ τοιοῦτον καὶ βέβαιον, μέχρι γὰρ ἂν ᾖ παρεσκευασμένον βέβαιόν ἐστι πάντως πρὸς τὴν χρείαν.

11ᵃ. Τοὺς αὔλακας αὐτῆς μέθυσον. Ἔδειξεν ὅτι τὸ Ἐπεσκέψω καὶ Ἐπλή-
10 θυνας κατὰ ἐναλλαγὴν εἶπεν χρόνου, ἀντὶ τοῦ «ἐπίσκεψαι» καὶ «πλή-θυνον», ἐπεὶ τί χρεία τοῦ Μέθυσον εἰ περὶ παρεληλυθότος ἔλεγεν; Λέγει δὲ ὅτι καὶ οἱ αὔλακες τῆς γῆς πληρωθήσονται ὑδάτων· ἀκολουθεῖ γὰρ καὶ τοῦτο τοῖς ὑετοῖς.

11ᵇ. Πλήθυνον τὰ γενήματα αὐτῆς. Παρέξεις τὴν τῶν καρπῶν δαψιλίαν.

15 11ᶜ. Ἐν ταῖς σταγόσιν αὐτῆς εὐφρανθήσεται ἀνατέλλουσα. Ὁ Σύρος τὰς σταγόνας δρόσους λέγει εἰκότως, — τοιαύτη γὰρ ἡ δρόσος σταγόνας ἐκπέμπουσα σποράδην, — σταλαγμοὺς δὲ τῆς γῆς καλεῖ τὴν δρόσον, ἐπειδὴ διὰ τὴν χρείαν τῆς γῆς καὶ τῶν ἐξ αὐτῆς καρπῶν αἱ δρόσοι πέμπονται.

12ᵃ. Εὐλογήσεις τὸν στέφανον τοῦ ἐνιαυτοῦ τῆς χρηστότητός σου. Καὶ
20 πάντα τοῦ ἐνιαυτοῦ τὸν κύκλον εὐλογήσας, πληρώσεις πάντων τῶν καρπῶν, δαψιλῶς τὴν ἀνάδοσιν παρεχόμενος· ἐνιαυτὸν δὲ τῆς αὐτοῦ χρησ-τότητος εἶπεν τὸν τῆς εὐθηνίας, ὡς τῇ αὐτοῦ χρηστότητι τὴν εὐετηρίαν δεχόμενον.

1 ἐνδεεῖσθαι PV δεῖσθαι Cord   7 βέβαιον des. Cord.
11ᵃ. Ἔδειξεν — ὑετοῖς: P, fol. 199; V, fol. 264ᵛ; 9-11 cf. supplementum GAR-NERII (1356, n. 7).
11ᵇ. Παρέξεις — δαψιλίαν: P, fol. 199; V, fol. 264ᵛ.
11ᶜ. Ὁ Σύρος — πέμπονται: P, fol. 199ᵛ; V, fol. 265; Cord, p. 271; cf. supple-mentum GARNERII (1356, n. 7).
12ᵃ. Καὶ πάντα — δεχόμενον: P, fol. 199ᵛ; V, fol. 265; Cord, p. 272.   22 εὐθυ-νίας Cord.

Aᵉ 1-2 (p. 326, 28-30): Tui operis est et prouidentiae talia hominibus tan-taque largiri.   9-10 (p. 326, 33-327, 1): ... Multiplicasti per inmotationem temporis dictum.   12-13 (p. 326, 30-31: Quod praecidentibus pluiis ex more consequi-tur.   11ᶜ (p. 327, 3-7): Id est, plurimi roris sparsas super faciem terrae gutas stillicidia appellans, quoniam utilitati terrae proficit frequens et densa roris sparsio.   21-420, 2 (p. 327, 8-11): Benignitatis diuinae annus dicitur, quoniam liberalitate eius in nutrimenta frugum caeli temperies ministratur.

it is your role to prepare and furnish such things to human beings, from them all you will provide them with an abundant supply. You see, just as he used *prepared* for "secured," since what is prepared is made ready and reliable for use, so he calls the readiness itself *preparation,* as in this case, as if to say, They will lack for nothing. In fact, everything was prepared and ready so that they had no worry about anything, being of such a reliable nature as to be fit and ready for any need at all.

Bedew its furrows (v. 10). He brought out that *You examined* and *You spared nothing* involve a change of mood for *Examine* and *Spare nothing,* for what use would there be in saying *Bedew* if he were speaking about the past? He says also that the furrows of the earth will be filled with water, following on the rain. *Multiply its produce:* you will provide an abundance of crops. *In its drops it will enjoy growing up.* The Syriac logically calls *drops* "dews," dew having this habit of producing drops all over the place; he refers to the dew as the earth's *drops* because it is with a view to the needs of the earth and its crops that dew falls. *You will bless the crown of the year of your bounty* (v. 11): by blessing the whole cycle of the year, you will fill it with every crop, liberally providing the increase (by *year of your bounty* referring to prosperity, as it is by his bounty that it experiences prosperity). | *And*

12ᵇ. Καὶ τὰ πεδία σου πλησθήσονται πιότητος. Καὶ ἔσται μὲν εὐθηνοῦντα τὰ πεδία καὶ αἱ ἄρουραι.

13ᵃ. Πιανθήσονται τὰ ὡραῖα τῆς ἐρήμου. Ὡραῖα τῆς ἐρήμου λέγει τὰ ὀροπέδια τὰ λεγόμενα. Καὶ ὅσα φησὶν ἐν τῇ ἐρήμῳ καὶ ἐν τοῖς ὄρεσι πεδινώτερα, καὶ ταῦτα εὐκαρπίας πληρωθήσεται.   5

13ᵇ. Καὶ ἀγαλλίασιν οἱ βουνοὶ περιζώσονται. Καὶ ταῦτα πολλῆς εὐφροσύνης πληροῦται, τοὺς οἰκείους ἀναδιδόντα καρπούς.

14ᵃ. Ἐνεδύσαντο οἱ κριοὶ τῶν προβάτων. Πληροῦται δὴ καὶ τῆς ἐρέας τὰ πρόβατα· ὅσῳ γὰρ νέμεται δαψιλῶς τὴν βοτάνην, τοσούτῳ τῆς ἐρέας ἑτοιμοτάτην ποιεῖται τὴν ἀνάδοσιν.   10

14ᵇ. Καὶ αἱ κοιλάδες πληθυνοῦσι σῖτον. Τὰ βαθύτερα τῶν πεδίων· βούλεται δὲ εἰπεῖν ὅτι τὰ πάντα πληροῦται εὐθηνίας.

14ᶜ. Κεκράξονται· καὶ γὰρ ὑμνήσουσιν. Τὸ κεκράξονται πρὸς τὸ Ἐνεδύσαντο οἱ κριοὶ τῶν προβάτων· τὸ γὰρ αἱ κοιλάδες πληθυνοῦσι σῖτον διὰ μέσου παρέγκειται ἅτε πρὸς τὰ ἀνώτερα τὴν ἀκολουθίαν ἔχον. Τὰ τοίνυν 15 πρόβατα καὶ δώσει τὴν ἐρέαν καὶ ἀπὸ τῆς πλησμονῆς τῆς ἐν τῇ νομῇ μυκώμενα ὥσπερ τινὰς ὕμνους τὴν οἰκείαν φωνὴν ἀναπέμψει, δεικνύντα τὴν εὐετηρίαν τὴν σήν· ἴδιον γὰρ τῶν προβάτων τὸ μυκᾶσθαι πλησθέντα τῆς νομῆς.

12ᵇ. Καὶ ἔσται — ἄρουραι: P, fol. 199ᵛ; V, fol. 265; Cord, p. 273, 3-4.   1 εὐθυνοῦντα Cord.

13ᵃ. Ὡραῖα — πληρωθήσεται: P, fol. 200; V, fol. 265ᵛ; Cord, p. 273 sub nomine DIDYMI.   4 τὰ λεγόμενα om. Cord   4-5 καὶ ὅσα — πληρωθήσεται affert GARNERIUS (1358, n. 32).

13ᵇ. Καὶ ταῦτα — καρπούς: P, fol 200; V, fol. 265ᵛ; cf. supplementum GARNERII (1358, n. 32).

14ᵃ. Πληροῦται — ἀνάδοσιν: P, fol. 200; V, fol. 265ᵛ.

14ᵇ. Τὰ βαθύτερα — εὐθηνίας: P, fol. 200; V, fol. 265ᵛ.

14ᶜ. Τὸ κεκράξονται — νομῆς: P, fol. 200; V, fol. 265ᵛ; Cord, p. 273 (anon.); cf. supplementum GARNERII (1360, n. 49).   15 ἅτε om. PV   16 δώσει] δίδωσι Cord   17 ἀναπέμψειεν PV

Aᵉ 4-5 (p. 327, 15-16): Incultae quaeque magnopere ullatenus solitudines frugum fertilitate gaudebunt.

your fields will be filled with richness: and the fields and the furrows will be fertile.

The beauty spots of the wilderness will be enriched (v. 12). By *beauty spots of the wilderness* he refers to mountainous tracts: all the level parts even of the wilderness and the mountains will be filled with fertility. *And the hills will be encircled with joy:* and they will be filled with happiness, yielding their own particular crops. *The rams of the flocks were clad* (v. 13): the flocks will also bear much wool; the more generous the fodder they graze on, the more abundant the supply of wool they produce.[6] *The valleys will abound with grain:* the lowest parts of the fields (implying that everything abounds in prosperity). *They will shout and sing hymns.* The verb *They will shout* refers to *The rams of the flocks were clad,* the clause *The valleys will abound with grain* coming in between in having a connection with what is above. So he is saying, The flocks will give wool, and in bleating as a result of the abundance of fodder, they will utter their particular sound as a kind of hymn to demonstrate their satisfaction, bleating when full of fodder being characteristic of flocks. |

---

6. The LXX reads the Hebrew form as "rams" (cf. Deut 32:14) instead of "hollows, valleys." Quite unaware, Theodore proceeds to give a detailed interpretation of the verse under that misapprehension, unable to suggest a different sense.

PSALMVS LXV

Κἀνταῦθα μὲν προαγορεύει τὴν ἐπάνοδον. Οὐκέτι δὲ ὡς ἐκ προσώπου πάντων τὸν ψαλμόν φησιν, ἀλλ᾽ ἐκ μόνων τῶν παρ᾽ αὐτοῖς θαυμαστῶν τε καὶ ἐναρέτων ἀνδρῶν.

5   1. Ἀλαλάξατε τῷ Θεῷ, πᾶσα ἡ γῆ. Ὑμνήσατε τὸν Θεὸν πάντες. Καλῶς δὲ εἶπεν πάντες, ἐπειδὴ πάντας ἐξέπληξε τὰ κατὰ τὴν ἐπάνοδον.

2ᵃ. Ψάλατε δὴ τῷ ὀνόματι αὐτοῦ. Μεθ᾽ ὕμνων αὐτὸν ὀνομάζετε.

2ᵇ. Δότε δόξαν αἰνέσει αὐτοῦ. Ἡ δὲ εἰς αὐτὸν αἴνεσις ἐχέτω δόξαν, τουτέστιν Ἐπιδόξως αὐτὸν ὑμνήσατε.

10   3ᵃ. Εἴπατε τῷ Θεῷ Ὡς φοβερὰ τὰ ἔργα σου. Τοῦτο πρὸ πάντων ἐν τοῖς ὕμνοις λέγοντες καὶ ὁμολογοῦντες, ὅτι φόβου μεστὰ τὰ παρά σου γεγενημένα. Καὶ τίς τούτου ἡ ἀπόδειξις;

3ᵇ. Ἐν τῷ πλήθει τῆς δυνάμεώς σου ψεύσονταί σε οἱ ἐχθροί σου. Οὕτω γὰρ τῷ μεγέθει τῶν παρά σου γινομένων περιβλέπτους ἀποφανεῖς τούς σοι
15   προσήκοντας, ὡς πολλοὺς καὶ τῶν ἐναντίων ὑποκρίνεσθαι ψευδομένους τὴν σὴν δουλείαν. Τοῦτο δὲ γέγονεν ὅτε καὶ περιτμηθῆναι πολλοὶ τῶν ἐναντίων

Argumentum ps. LXV Κἀνταῦθα — ἀνδρῶν: P, fol. 200ᵛ; V, fol. 266; Cord, p. 287.
1. Ὑμνήσατε — ἐπάνοδον: P, fol. 200ᵛ; V, fol. 266; Cord, p. 288 *sub nomine* ATHANASII.
2ᵃ. Μεθ᾽ ὕμνων αὐτὸν ὀνομάζετε: P, fol. 200ᵛ; V, fol. 266.
2ᵇ. Ἡ δὲ — ὑμνήσατε: P, fol. 200ᵛ; V, fol. 265; Cord, p. 288 *sub nomine* ATHANASII.   7-9 Μεθ᾽ ὕμνων — ὑμνήσατε *praebet supplementum* GARNERII (1362, n. 74).
3ᵃ. Τοῦτο — ἀπόδειξις: P, fol. 201; V, fol. 266ᵛ; Cord, p. 289.   11 ὑμνολογοῦντες Cord   τὰ *om.* Cord.
3ᵇ. Οὕτω — πραγματεύσασθαι: P, fol. 201; V, fol. 266ᵛ; Cord, p. 290 *sub nomine* HESYCHII; *cf. supplementum* GARNERII (1364, n. 83).   14 παρά] περὶ Cord
15 ὑποκρίνασθαι PV.

Aᵉ 2-4 (p. 327, 26-30):... Vt in superiore reditur populi de Babilone praedicit, sed in hoc tantum defert quod hic ex persona eorum tantum loquitur qui erant inter eos meritis cels⟨i⟩oris.   1 (p. 328, 1-4): Pro ymnos dicite, quia nullam partem uicinae terrae latere poterit tantis signis soluta captiuitas.
2ᵇ (p. 328, 6-7): Gloriosse illum magnificeque laudate.   13-422, 2 (p. 348, 8-15): Ita magnitudine operum atque omnium signorum in seruos tuos ora conuertes, ut plurimi alienig⟨e⟩nae, circumcisione suscepta, in tuum simulent se uelle intrare seruitium; quod in libro Antiquitatum Iosepus temporibus Mordochei scripsit inpletum.

PSALM 66

While here, too, he foretells the return, he no longer recites the psalm on behalf of everyone, but only of the distinguished men admired by them. *Shout aloud to God, all the earth* (v. 1): sing hymns of praise to God, everyone. "Everyone" was well put, since the events of the return astonished everyone. *Sing to his name* (v. 2): recite his name in hymns. *Give glory in praise of him:* let praise give glory to him—that is, sing his praises in glorious fashion.

Say to God, How awesome are your deeds! (v. 3). That is, saying this before all in the hymns and confessing, What was done by you is fearsome. What is proof of this? *In the might of your power your foes will speak falsely of you:* you thus will render those dedicated to you conspicuous by the magnitude of what is done by you so as to respond to many of the adversaries falsely professing your service. Now, this happened when many of the adversaries were prepared even to be circumcised | in pretending to adopt Jewish

ἠνέσχοντο, ὑποκρινόμενοι τὸν ἰουδαϊσμόν. Καὶ τούτου μάρτυς Ἰώσηππος ἐν τῇ ια΄ τῆς Ἀρχαιολογίας, τὰ κατὰ τὸν Μαρδοχαῖον διηγούμενος καὶ λέγων οὕτως· «Οἱ μὲν οὖν ἱππεῖς οἱ τὰς ἐπιστολὰς διακομίζοντες, εὐθὺς ἐξορμήσαντες τὴν προκειμένην ὁδὸν ἤνυον. Ὁ δὲ Μαρδοχαῖος ἀναλαβὼν τὴν βασιλικὴν στολὴν καὶ τὸν στέφανον τὸν χρυσοῦν καὶ τὸν στρεπτὸν περιθέμενος 5 προῆλθεν· ἰδόντες δὲ αὐτὸν οὕτω τετιμημένον ὑπὸ τοῦ βασιλέως οἱ ἐν Σούσοις ὄντες Ἰουδαῖοι, κοινὴν ὑπέλαβον τὴν εὐπραγίαν. Χαρὰ δὲ καὶ σωτήριον φέγγος, ἐκτιθεμένων τῶν τοῦ βασιλέως γραμμάτων, καὶ τοὺς κατὰ πόλιν τῶν Ἰουδαίων καὶ τοὺς κατὰ χώραν κατέσχεν, ὡς πολλὰ καὶ τῶν ἄλλων ἐθνῶν διὰ τὸν τῶν Ἰουδαίων φόβον περιτεμνόμενα τὴν αἰδῶ, τὸ ἀκίνδυνον 10 αὐτοῖς ἐκ τούτου πραγματεύσασθαι».

4ᵃ. Πᾶσα ἡ γῆ προσκυνησάτωσάν σοι καὶ ψαλάτωσαν. Ἀπέδωκε τὸ πᾶν τῷ Ἀλαλάξατε τῷ Θεῷ, πᾶσα ἡ γῆ. Δίκαιον τοίνυν φησὶ διὰ ταῦτα πάντας σοι κατὰ πόλιν καὶ προσκυνεῖν καὶ ψάλλειν.

4ᵇ. Ψαλάτωσαν δὲ τῷ ὀνόματί σου, ὕψιστε. Ὑμνήσατε, ὡς ὑψηλοῦ μὲν 15 μνημονεύοντες.

5ᵃ. Δεῦτε, καὶ ἴδετε τὰ ἔργα τοῦ Θεοῦ. Ἥκετε δὴ πάντες, θεώμενοι τοῦ Θεοῦ τὰς οἰκονομίας.

5ᵇ. Ὡς φοβερὸς ἐν βουλαῖς ὑπὲρ τοὺς υἱοὺς τῶν ἀνθρώπων. Καὶ γνώτωσαν ὅπως τὰ τοῦ Θεοῦ ἐνθυμήματα φοβερώτερα πάσης ἐστὶν ἀνθρωπίνης 20 ἐννοίας.

6ᵃ. Ὁ μεταστρέφων τὴν θάλασσαν εἰς ξηράν. Καὶ τούτου ἀπόδειξις καὶ τὰ ἤδη γενόμενα, ὅπως τὴν θάλασσαν μετέβαλεν εἰς ξηράν. Σύμμαχος οὕτως λέγει· Μετέβαλεν θάλασσαν εἰς ξηράν.

3-11 Iosephus, Antiquit. XI, vi, 13.

5 τὸ στρεπτὸν PV   7 χαρὰν PV Cord   9 κατέσχον Cord   10 τὸν om. Cord
11 πραγματευομένων PV — ὅμενα Cord; cf. supplementum Garnerii (1364, n. 83).
4ᵃ. Ἀπέδωκε — ψάλλειν: P, fol. 201; V, fol. 266ᵛ.
4ᵇ. Ὑμνήσατε — μνημονεύοντες: P, fol. 201; V, fol. 267; Cord, p. 290 sub nomine Origenis.
5ᵃ. Ἥκετε — οἰκονομίας: P, fol. 201ᵛ; V, fol. 267; Cord, p. 290 sub nomine Athanasii.
5ᵇ. Καὶ γνώτωσαν — ἐννοίας: P, fol. 201ᵛ; V, fol. 267.
6ᵃ. Καὶ τούτου — ξηράν: P, fol. 201ᵛ; V, fol. 267; Cord, p. 291 sub nomine Athanasii (P. G., XXVII, 288 C).

Aᶜ 22-23 (p. 328, 27-28): Documento sunt ea quae ollim gesta memorantur.

ways. Josephus is witness to this in the eleventh book of the *Antiquities* in his account of the events of the time of Mordecai as follows: "The horsemen bearing the letters set out at speed and completed the journey before them. Mordecai put on the royal stole and golden crown, clad himself in the chain armor and issued forth. On seeing him so honored by the king, the Jews in the city of Susa gave way to general rejoicing. With the publication of the king's letters, exhilaration and a light of salvation gripped the Jews, both those in the cities and those in the provinces, with the result that many even of the other races circumcised themselves out of fear of the Jews and thus guaranteed for themselves freedom from danger."[1]

Let all the earth adore and sing to you (v. 4). All this corresponds to the verse *Shout aloud to God, all the earth.* So he is saying, For this it is right for everyone in the city to adore and sing to you. *Let them sing to your name, O Most High!* Sing his praises, mindful that he is most high. *Come and see the works of God* (v. 5): come, everyone, observe God's designs. *How fearsome in plans beyond the human race:* and recognize how his desires are too terrifying for human understanding. *He turns the sea into dry land* (v. 6): what has happened already is also proof of this, how he transformed the sea into dry land. Symmachus puts it this way, "He transformed the sea into dry land." | *They will cross the river on foot.* Symmachus: "They passed over

---

1. Theodore cites a passage from Josephus (see vol. 6 of Josephus, *Jewish Antiquities* [trans. Ralph Marcus; LCL; London: Heinemann, 1937], 450–51) that reproduces almost verbatim the LXX text of Esth 8:14–17 and not the biblical book itself. Esther probably did not appear in his canon, as it was not in the canon of Athanasius, Gregory Nazianzen, and other church fathers—nor, of course, does it occur in the Qumran materials for liturgical reasons, nor is it cited in the New Testament. Diodore, Chrysostom, and Theodoret seem not to cite Esther, either, while being content to cite books that we class as deuterocanonical.

6^b. Ἐν ποταμῷ διελεύσονται ποδί. Σύμμαχος διέβησαν ποδί. Ἐκείνων γὰρ μέμνηται τῶν τότε γενομένων, ὁπηνίκα ἐξήγαγεν αὐτοὺς ἐκ γῆς Αἰγύπτου.

6^c. Ἐκεῖ εὐφρανθησόμεθα ἐπ' αὐτῷ. Πολλὴν γοῦν τότε καὶ τὴν εὐφρο-σύνην ἐσχήκαμεν διὰ θαυμάτων οὕτω μεγάλων, παραδόξως τῶν ἐχθρῶν κρα-
5 τοῦντες.

7^a. Τῷ δεσπόζοντι ἐν τῇ δυναστείᾳ αὐτοῦ τοῦ αἰῶνος. Ηὔφρανεν γὰρ ἡμᾶς ταῖς οἰκείαις εὐεργεσίαις ὁ τοῦ παντὸς αἰῶνος δεσπότης.

7^b. Οἱ ὀφθαλμοὶ αὐτοῦ ἐπὶ τὰ ἔθνη ἐπιβλέπουσιν. Πᾶσι προσέχει καὶ πάντα ἐξετάζει τὰ γιγνόμενα.

10 7^c. Οἱ παραπικραίνοντες μὴ ὑψούσθωσαν ἐν ἑαυτοῖς. Ὥστε οἱ τὰ ἄτοπα πράττοντες καὶ παροργίζοντες τὸν Θεὸν μὴ μεγαλοφρονεῖτε, ὄντος τοῦ ἐφορῶντός τε καὶ ἐξετάζοντος· δώσεται γὰρ δίκας ὑπὲρ ὧν πλημμελεῖτε.

8^a. Εὐλογεῖτε, ἔθνη, τὸν Θεὸν ἡμῶν. Πάντες δὴ κατὰ ταὐτὸν γενόμενοι, μᾶλλον αὐτὸν ἐπαινεῖτε καὶ θαυμάζετε.

15 8^b. Καὶ ἀκουτίσατε τὴν φωνὴν τῆς αἰνέσεως αὐτοῦ. Ἀκουτίσατε, ἀντὶ τοῦ Ἀκουστὴν ποιήσατε, καὶ τὰς φωνάς φησι τῶν ὑμνούντων εἰς αὐτὸν ἀκουστὰς ποιεῖτε· ἀκόλουθον γὰρ ἦν αὐτοὺς ὑμνοῦντας καὶ ἀκούεσθαι.

9^a. Τοῦ θεμένου τὴν ψυχήν μου εἰς ζωήν. Ὁρᾶτε γὰρ οἷα τὰ γινόμενα, ὅτι θαύματος ἄξια καὶ ἐπαίνου, ὅπως ἀπήλλαξέν με κινδύνων καὶ θανάτων.

6^b. Σύμμαχος — Αἰγύπτου: P, fol. 201^v; V, fol. 267^v.
6^c. Πολλὴν — κρατοῦντες: P, fol. 202; V, fol. 267^v.
7^a. Ηὔφρανεν — δεσπότης: P, fol. 202; V, fol. 267^v.
7^b. Πᾶσι — γιγνόμενα: P, fol. 202; V, fol. 267^v; Cord, p. 292 sub nomine ATHA-NASII (P. G., XXVII, 288 D 10).
7^c. Ὥστε — πλημμελεῖτε: P, fol. 202; V, fol. 267^v; Cord, p. 293, 19-22.
8^a. Πάντες — θαυμάζετε: P, fol. 202^v; V, fol. 267^v; Cord, p. 293 sub nomine ATHANASII (= P. G., 289 A).
8^a. Ἀκουτίσατε — ἀκούεσθαι: P, fol. 202^v; V, fol. 268.
9^a. Ὁρᾶτε — θανάτων: P, fol. 202^v; V, fol. 268.

A^e 6^b (p. 328, 31-33): ...recordatur eorum quae gesta sunt, cum de Egipto populus fuisset egresus. 6^c (p. 348, 34-36):... cum hostes nostros numero et robore superiores tua uirtute occidisse conspeximus. 7^a (p. 329, 1-4): Haec uobis gaudia praestitit... cuius est proprium dominationis et regni sui initia et fines non habere. 7^c (p. 329, 10-14):... et operibus uestris Deum ad iracon-diam prouocare nolite uel inpunitate insolescere; est qui inspiciat atque deiu-dicet; ausus uestri non erunt inpuniti. 17 (p. 329, 20-23):... de midio me peri-culorum et a uicinia mortis eripuit et non dedit commoueri.

on foot." He makes mention of what happened at the time when he led them out of Egypt. *We shall rejoice in him there:* at that time, at any rate, we had great joy as well through such great marvels, surprisingly prevailing over the foe. *The one ruling by his might forever* (v. 7): the Lord of all ages gladdened us with his characteristic blessings. *His eyes gaze on the nations:* he heeds everyone and examines all their doings. *Let the rebellious not be exalted in their own estimation:* so that they may not glory in doing wrong and provoking God, since he is the one who scrutinizes and examines; for he will take vengeance for your wrongdoing.

Bless our God, O nations (v. 8): instead, since you are all in the same place, praise and admire him all the more. *And make the sound of his praise be heard*—that is, Let it be heard, and let the voices of those singing his praises be heard (it being logical for those singing praise to be heard). *The one who has brought my soul to life* (v. 9): observe how all that has happened is worthy of admiration and praise, his freeing me from danger and death. |

848 THEODORVS MOPSVESTENVS

9ᵇ. Καὶ μὴ δόντος εἰς σάλον τοὺς πόδας μου. Οὐκ ἔασέν με περιτραπῆναι ὑπὸ τῶν ἐπιβουλευόντων. Τίνος δὲ ἕνεκεν καὶ παθεῖν ἡμᾶς συνεχώρησεν;

10ᵃ. Ὅτι ἐδοκίμασας ἡμᾶς, ὁ Θεός. Ἵνα ταῖς θλίψεσι δοκίμους ποιήσῃ.

10ᵇ. Ἐπύρωσας ἡμᾶς ὡς πυροῦται τὸ ἀργύριον. Ἐπειδὴ τῷ πυρὶ καὶ τῇ χωνείᾳ καθαίρεται τὸ χρυσίον, ὡς πυρί φησι ταῖς θλίψεσιν ἀφελὼν ἡμῶν τὰ κακὰ δοκίμους εἰργάσω. 5

11ᵃ. Εἰσήγαγες ἡμᾶς εἰς τὴν παγίδα. Διὰ τοῦτο πεῖραν λαβεῖν τῶν κακῶν πεποίηκας· παγίδα δὲ καλεῖ τὰς συμφορὰς τῆς αἰχμαλωσίας, ὡς θάνατον ἐπαγούσας.

11ᵇ. Ἔθου θλίψεις ἐπὶ τὸν νῶτον ἡμῶν. Συντριβῆναι ταῖς θλίψεσι συνε- 10 χώρησας, ἐκ μεταφορᾶς τῶν πιπτόντων τὸν νῶτον καὶ συντριβόντων.

12ᵃ. Ἐπεβίβασας ἀνθρώπους ἐπὶ τὰς κεφαλὰς ἡμῶν. Μονονουχὶ πεποίηκας αὐτοὺς ἐπιβῆναι ταῖς κεφαλαῖς ἡμῶν.

12ᵇ. Διήλθομεν διὰ πυρὸς καὶ ὕδατος. Διὰ πολλῶν καὶ διαφόρων κακῶν ἀναλίσκειν καὶ συμπνίγειν δυναμένων. 15

12ᶜ. Καὶ ἐξήγαγες ἡμᾶς εἰς ἀναψυχήν. Ἀλλὰ διὰ πάντων ἐκείνων τῶν κακῶν ἐξέβαλες, οὐδὲν παθεῖν ἐάσας μέχρις ὅτε πάλιν ἡμᾶς εἰς ἄνεσιν κατέστησας.

9ᵇ. Οὐκ ἔασεν — συνεχώρησεν: P. fol. 202ᵛ; V, fol, 268.
10ᵃ. Ἵνα — ποιήσῃ: P, fol. 202ᵛ; V, fol. 268.
10ᵇ. Ἐπειδὴ — εἰργάσω: P. fol. 202ᵛ; V, fol. 268; Cord, p. 294 sub nomine
Eusebii.
11ᵃ. Διὰ τοῦτο — ἐπαγούσας: P, fol. 203; V, fol. 268ʳ·ᵛ; 8 παγίδα κτλ. affert Cord,
p. 295 sub nomine Athanasii.
11ᵇ. Συντριβῆναι — συντριβόντων: P. fol. 203; V, fol. 268ᵛ.
12ᵃ. Μονονουχὶ — ἡμῶν: P, fol. 203; V, fol. 268ᵛ; Cord, p. 295 sub nomine
Theodoreti.
12ᵇ. Διὰ πολλῶν — δυναμένων: P, fol. 203; V, fol. 268ᵛ.
12ᶜ. Ἀλλὰ — κατέστησας: P, fol. 203; V, fol. 268ᵛ: Vat. 1422, fol. 118ᵛ (anon.).

Aᵉ 1-2 (p. 329, 24):... non permisit moueri.   10ᵃ (p. 329, 25-28): Vt tribulationibus, inquit, miliores faceret et castigationibus erudiret.   4-5 (p. 329.
30-32):... uitia nostra sunt decocta ut metallorum sordes purgutorio igne pur-
gantur.   8-9 (p. 329, 33-34): Captiuitatis uinculis inretiti uicinia mortis acces-
simus.   11ᵇ (p. 329, 35-330, 1): Ita erumnis conflictati sumus, ut uerberibus
solent dorsa uexari.   12ᵃ (p. 330, 3-4): Conculcari nos superbo pede hostium
fastuque uoluisti.   12ᵇ (p. 330, 5-6): Per multa ac uaria periculorum genera
circumacti.

And has not let my feet slip: he did not allow me to come to grief at the hands of the schemers. But why did he also allow me to suffer? *Because you have tried us, O God* (v. 10): so as to try us in tribulation. *You tested us in fire as silver is tested:* since gold is purified in fire and furnace, you will remove our vices in tribulation as in fire and will make us true. *You led us into the trap* (v. 11): hence, you caused us to experience troubles (by *trap* referring to the hardships of captivity, bringing on death as they do). *You laid troubles on our back:* you allowed us to be crushed by tribulations (by analogy with people falling on their back and being crushed). *You put people over our heads* (v. 12): all but making them tread on our heads. *We passed through fire and water:* through many and varied troubles capable of burning us up and drowning us. *And you brought us out into refreshment:* yet you retrieved us from all those troubles, not allowing us to suffer any harm until once again you established us in repose. |

13-14. Εἰσελεύσομαι εἰς τὸν οἶκόν σου ἐν ὁλοκαυτώμασιν, ἀποδώσω σοι τὰς εὐχάς μου, ἃς διέστειλε τὰ χείλη μου καὶ ἐλάλησε τὸ στόμα μου ἐν τῇ θλίψει μου. Λοιπόν φησι μετὰ τὴν ἐπάνοδον τὰς συνήθεις θυσίας πάσας σοι ἀποδώσω, ὅσας ὥρισα καὶ ἐπηγγειλάμην ἀποδώσειν τῷ καιρῷ τῆς αἰχ-
5 μαλωσίας· τὸ γὰρ διέστειλεν ἀντὶ τοῦ ὥρισεν λέγει. Ποῖα δὲ ταῦτα;

15. Ὁλοκαυτώματα μεμυαλωμένα ἀνοίσω σοι μετὰ θυμιάματος καὶ κριῶν, ἀνοίσω σοι βόας μετὰ χιμάρων. Τουτέστιν ἁπάσας τὰς συνήθεις θυσίας ἀποδίδωμι, συμπλέξας καὶ θυμίαμα. Τὸ δὲ μεμυαλωμένα, ἀντὶ τοῦ πιμελώδη καὶ δόκιμα.

10 16. Δεῦτε, ἀκούσατε, καὶ διηγήσομαι ὑμῖν, πάντες οἱ φοβούμενοι τὸν Θεόν, ὅσα ἐποίησε τῇ ψυχῇ μου. Ἐρῶ ὑμῖν ὅσων ἀπήλαυσα.

17. Πρὸς αὐτὸν τῷ στόματί μου ἐκέκραξα, καὶ ὕψωσα ὑπὸ τὴν γλῶσσάν μου. Αἰτήσεις αὐτῷ προσήγαγον καὶ ηὐξάμην ἀπολυθῆναι.

18. Ἀδικίαν εἰ ἐθεώρουν ἐν καρδίᾳ μου, μὴ εἰσακουσάτω Κύριος. Ἀκύ-
15 λας Ἀνωφελὲς ἰδὼν ἐν καρδίᾳ μου, οὐκ εἰσακούσεται Κύριος. Βούλεται δὲ εἰπεῖν ὅτι Τὰς αἰτήσεις τῷ Θεῷ προσάγων, ἐπεμελούμην τοῦ πρέποντος, εἰδὼς ὡς οὐδέν μοι τῆς αἰτήσεως ὄφελος μὴ ποιοῦντι τὰ δέοντα.

19. Διὰ τοῦτο εἰσήκουσέν μου ὁ Θεός, προσέσχεν τῇ φωνῇ τῆς δεήσεώς μου. Ἐπειδὴ τοίνυν ἐπεμελούμην τῶν δεόντων, εἰκότως καὶ τὴν αἴτησιν
20 δεξάμενος, ἀπήλλαξέ με τῶν κατεχόντων κακῶν.

13-14. Λοιπὸν — ταῦτα; P, fol. 203 et V, fol. 268ᵛ in duas partes distributa; Cord, p. 296. 3-4 πάντα σοι ἀποδίδωμι ὅσα PV.
15. Τουτέστιν — δόκιμα; P, fol. 203ᵛ; V, fol. 269; Cord, p. 296 sub nomine ATHANASII.
16. Ἐρῶ — ἀπήλαυσα: P, fol. 203ᵛ; V, fol. 269.
17. Αἰτήσεις — ἀπολυθῆναι: P, fol. 203ᵛ; V, fol. 269.
18. Ἀκύλας — δέοντα: P, fol. 204 et V, fol. 269 (anon.); inter ATHANASIANA (P. G., XXVII, 289 D 6-10).
19. Ἐπειδὴ — κακῶν: P, fol. 204; V, fol. 269ᵛ; Cord, p. 298. 20 με om. PV.

Aᵉ 13-14 (p. 330, 15-19): Probabilia quaeque uota distincta uocat... quae uoui in captiuitate locatus, et de libera (de liberitate ms) promisione firmaui atque constitui. 16 (p. 330, 28-30): Dicam uobis qualia mihi bona quantaque contulerit. 17 (p. 330, 31): Obtuli, ait, preces et liberationem poposci. 18 (p. 330, 33-35): Suplicationis tempore fuit mihi cura iustitiae, quia sciebam iniquos impetrare nihil posse. 19 (p. 331, 1-4): Quoniam fuit mihi probitatis atque emendationis studium, ideo ea quae poposci libenter audiuit, et a malis, quae urgebant me, liberauit.

I shall enter your house with holocausts; I shall pay my vows to you, *which my lips uttered and my mouth spoke in my tribulation* (vv. 13–14): from now on after the return I shall render to you all the customary sacrifices that I determined and promised to render in time of captivity (by *uttered* meaning "determined"). What are they? *I shall offer you in sacrifice holocausts of fatlings with incense and rams; I shall offer oxen along with goats* (v. 15)—that is, I shall render all the customary offerings, combining them with incense (*fatlings* meaning "fat and acceptable").

Come, listen, and I shall recount to you, all you who fear God, everything he did for my soul (v. 16): I shall tell you all that I have received. *With my mouth I cried to him, and by my tongue I exalted him* (v. 17): I placed requests before him and prayed to be given relief. *If I saw iniquity in my heart, let the Lord not hearken to me* (v. 18). Aquila: "On seeing harm in my heart the Lord will not hearken." He means, In presenting requests to God I paid attention to what is proper, aware that no good will come of my request if I do not do my duty. *This is the reason the Lord hearkened to me, attended to the sound of my petition* (v. 19): since I did my duty, then, it followed that he also accepted my request and freed me from the troubles besetting me. | *Blessed be God, who did not reject my prayer or turn his mercy away*

20. Εὐλογητὸς ὁ Θεός, ὃς οὐκ ἀπέστησε τὴν προσευχήν μου καὶ τὸ ἔλεος
αὐτοῦ ἀπ᾽ ἐμοῦ. Ἀκόλουθος τῷ εἰσακουσθέντι ἡ φωνή. Βούλεται γὰρ εἰπεῖν
ὅτι Καὶ τυχὼν ἀναπέμψω αὐτῷ τὴν εὐχαριστίαν ὑπὲρ ὧν ἂν εὐεργετήσειέ
τε καὶ φιλανθρωπεύσαιτο, οὐκ αἰτῶν μὲν ἐν ταῖς συμφοραῖς, ἀγνωμονῶν δὲ
μετὰ τὸ λαβεῖν.   5

PSALMVS LXVI

Νόμος ἦν παρὰ τοῦ Θεοῦ δεδομένος τοῖς ἱερεῦσιν, ὥστε εὐλογεῖν τὸν
Ἰσραήλ. Ταύταις δὲ ταῖς φωναῖς ἐν τοῖς Ἀριθμοῖς ἡ θεία γραφὴ κέχρηται
λέγουσα οὕτως· Καὶ ἐλάλησεν Κύριος πρὸς Μωϋσὴν λέγων Λάλησον Ἀαρὼν
καὶ τοῖς υἱοῖς αὐτοῦ λέγων Οὕτως εὐλογήσετε τοὺς υἱοὺς Ἰσραὴλ λέγοντες 10
αὐτοῖς. Καὶ ἐπιθήσουσι τὸ ὄνομά μου ἐπ᾽ αὐτοὺς τοὺς υἱοὺς Ἰσραήλ, καὶ ἐγὼ
Κύριος εὐλογήσω αὐτούς. Εὐλογήσαι σε Κύριος καὶ φυλάξαι σε, ἐπιφάναι
Κύριος τὸ πρόσωπον αὐτοῦ ἐπί σε καὶ ἐλεήσαι σε, ἐπάραι Κύριος τὸ πρόσωπον αὐτοῦ ἐπί σε καὶ δῴη σοι εἰρήνην. Τὴν οὖν ἐπάνοδον τοῦ λαοῦ καὶ
ἐν τούτῳ προαγορεύων τῷ ψαλμῷ ὁ μακάριος Δαυίδ, ταῦτά φησιν οἷς   15
συμπέπλεκται τὰ τῆς εὐλογίας παρὰ τῶν ἱερέων εἰς τὸν λαὸν γιγνομένης
κατὰ πρόσταγμα τοῦ Θεοῦ, ὡς τότε ἁρμοζούσης τῆς εὐλογίας ταύτης
λέγεσθαι παρὰ τῶν ἱερέων, ὅτε ἐν τοῖς οἰκείοις ὄντες χώραν εἶχον τοῦ
λέγειν, ὁμοῦ καὶ τῶν πραγμάτων ἀληθευόντων.

2. Ὁ Θεός, οἰκτειρήσαι ἡμᾶς, καὶ εὐλογήσαι ἡμᾶς· ἐπιφάναι τὸ πρόσωπον 20
αὐτοῦ ἐφ᾽ ἡμᾶς, καὶ ἐλεήσαι ἡμᾶς. Ἐλεήσαι, τῆς οἰκείας εὐλογίας πληρῶσαι.

9-14 Num. VI, 22-26.

20. Ἀκόλουθος — λαβεῖν: P, fol. 204; V, fol. 269ᵛ; Cord, p. 299 (anon.).
Argumentum Νόμος — ἀληθευόντων: P, fol. 204ᵛ; V, fol. 270; Cord, p. 306 *sub*
nomine EUSEBII.   16 εἰς τὸν λαὸν] τῷ λαῷ Cord   19 προσταγμάτων Cord.
2. Ἐλέησαι — πλήρωσαι: P, fol. 204ᵛ; V, fol. 270.

Aᵉ 20 (p. 331, 5-8): Et inpetratis quae obtauerat, negat se per signi-
tiem securi oris familiarem tanti beneficii gratiam obliuione subpraemere.
14-19 (p. 331, 10-16): Hoc quoque carmine reditus populi ex Babilone praedicitur; his sane uerbis reuersorum alacritas indicatur, quibus, ut sacerdotes
populo benedicerent, lege praescriptum est. PSEUDO-BEDA (825). Oportune uero
hisdem benedictionis formulis populus reuersus instruitur, quibus fuerat, cum
ingrederetur, inbutus.   2 (p. 331, 18-20): In tribulationibus positis opem miser-
rationis inpertiat.

from me (v. 20). The verse is in keeping with the successful petitioner, the meaning being, On receiving it I shall offer thanksgiving to him for whatever kindness and love he showed me, not being one to ask in misfortune and be ungrateful upon receipt.

PSALM 67

A law was given by God to the priests to bless Israel. The divine Scripture used these words in the book of Numbers in these terms: "The Lord spoke to Moses thus, 'Speak to Aaron and his sons as follows, "You will bless the sons of Israel in these terms. And they will put my name on the sons of Israel themselves, and I shall bless them. 'The Lord bless you and keep you; the Lord make his face shine on you and have mercy on you; the Lord lift up his countenance upon you and give you peace.' " ' "[1] To foretell the people's return in this psalm as well, then, blessed David says this and combines it with the words of blessing bestowed upon the people by the priests according to God's command, so that in accord with this blessing it would be recited by the priests at the time when they were in their own land and had the opportunity to say it, as the events also confirm.

God have pity upon us and bless us, make his face shine on us and have mercy on us (v. 1). *Have mercy on us* means, Fill us with your characteristic blessing. | *So as to know your way on earth* (v. 2): to make it known—that is,

---

1. The Aaronic blessing at Num 6:22–27 in the order of the LXX, which Theodore (with a rare show of interest in genre and cultic context) sees recited in later times, such as the return from exile.

3ª. Τοῦ γνῶναι ἐν τῇ γῇ τὴν ὁδόν σου. Τοῦ ποιῆσαι γνῶναι, ἀντὶ τοῦ ὥστε πᾶσιν ἀνθρώποις καταφανῆ γενέσθαι τὴν εὐεργεσίαν σου καὶ τὴν φιλανθρωπίαν τὴν εἰς ἡμᾶς· ὁδὸν γὰρ αὐτοῦ τὴν πρᾶξιν λέγει τὴν εἰς αὐτούς, καὶ σωτήριον τὰ θαύματα.

3ᵇ. Ἐν πᾶσι ἔθνεσι τὸ σωτήριόν σου. Καὶ ὥστε πᾶσι τὴν εἰς ἡμᾶς σου σωτηρίαν σαφῆ γενέσθαι.

4. Ἐξομολογησάσθωσάν σοι λαοί. ὁ Θεός, ἐξομολογησάσθωσάν σοι λαοὶ πάντες. Δίκαιον δὲ ἐπὶ τούτοις πάντας εὐχαριστεῖν σοι κατὰ ταὐτό.

5ª. Εὐφρανθήτωσαν καὶ ἀγαλλιάσθωσαν ἔθνη. Ἔθνη ἐνταῦθα τοὺς Ἰουδαίους λέγει.

5ᵇ·ᶜ. Ὅτι κρινεῖς λαοὺς ἐν εὐθύτητι, καὶ ἔθνη ἐν τῇ γῇ ὁδηγήσεις. Πάλιν ἔθνη τοὺς αὐτοὺς λέγει. Δίκαιον αὐτούς φησιν εὐφραίνεσθαι, ἐπείπερ μετὰ πάσης ὀρθότητος δικάσας αὐτοῖς ἀδικουμένοις. Ἐπανάγεις τε αὐτοὺς καὶ ἄγεις εἰς τὴν οἰκείαν γῆν, ὥσπερ ὁδηγὸς αὐτοῖς γιγνόμενος διὰ τὸ ἐπανάγειν τῇ οἰκείᾳ δυνάμει.

6. Ἐξομολογησάσθωσάν σοι λαοί, ὁ Θεός, ἐξομολογησάσθωσάν σοι λαοὶ πάντες. Ἐπανέλαβεν τὰ αὐτά· καὶ γάρ ἐστιν ὅλος ὁ ψαλμὸς εὐλογίας καὶ εὐχαριστίας περιεκτικός.

7. Γῆ ἔδωκε τὸν καρπὸν αὐτῆς. Ἀπολαύσομέν φησι καὶ τῶν ἐκ τῆς γῆς καρπῶν, τὸ αὐτὸ λέγων ἐν τῷ ξδ' ὅτι εὐετηρίαν ἡμῖν χαριεῖται.

20 cf. Ps. LXIV, 10 ss.

3ª. Τοῦ ποιῆσαι — θαύματα: P, fol. 205; V, fol. 270ᵛ; Vat. 1422, fol. 119ᵛ (anon.); Cord, p. 307. 4 σωτηρίαν Cord.
3ᵇ. Καὶ ὥστε — γενέσθαι: P, fol. 205; V, fol. 270ᵛ.
4. Δίκαιον — ταὐτό: P, fol. 205; V, fol. 270ᵛ; Cord. p. 308 sub nomine ATHANASII.
5ª. Ἔθνη — λέγει: P, fol. 205; V, fol. 270ᵛ.
5ᵇ·ᶜ. Πάλιν — δυνάμει: P, fol. 205; V, fol. 270ᵛ.
6. Ἐπανέλαβεν — περιεκτικός: P, fol. 205ᵛ; V, fol. 270ᵛ-271; Vat. 1422, fol. 119ᵛ (Διˢ); Cord, p. 308.
7. Ἀπολαύσομεν — χαριεῖται: P, fol. 205ᵛ; V. fol. 271.

Aᵉ 3ª (p. 331, 21-23): Pro operatione (operaratione ms), nota fiat omni terrae uirtus absolutionis nostrae. 3ᵇ (p. 331, 23-24): Salus per te collecta. 4 (p. 331, 25-28): Iustum est pro operum tuorum et beneficiorum magnitudine omnes tibi in unum congregatos gratias agere. 5ª (p. 331, 28-29): Tribus familiaeque iudaicae. 14-15 (p. 331, 30-31): Tamquam iteneris ductor.

for your blessing and lovingkindness to us to become obvious to all people (by *way* referring to his action for them and by *saving power* to the marvels). *Your saving power in all the nations:* so that your saving us may be clear to everyone. *Let peoples confess to you, O God; let all peoples confess to you* (v. 3): it is right for all people to thank you together for these things.

Let nations be glad and rejoice (v. 4): *nations* here referring to the Jews. *Because you judge peoples with uprightness, and you guide nations on the earth:* again by *nations* referring to the same ones. It is right for them to rejoice, he is saying, especially since with complete integrity you judge in their favor when wronged. You will lead them back and bring them into their own land, becoming a guide for them in returning them with your characteristic power. *Let peoples confess to you, O God; let all peoples confess to you* (v. 5). He developed the same theme, the whole psalm being devoted to praising and thanksgiving.

Earth gave up its fruit (v. 6): we shall enjoy also the fruits of the earth (saying the same thing in Psalm 65, that he will accord us fertility).[2] | Bless

---

2. Cf. Ps 65:9–13.

8ᵃ. Εὐλογήσαι ἡμᾶς, ὁ Θεὸς ὁ Θεὸς ἡμῶν, εὐλογήσαι ἡμᾶς. Ἐπανέλαβεν καὶ τὴν εὐλογίαν.

8ᵇ. Καὶ φοβηθήτωσαν αὐτὸν πάντα τὰ πέρατα τῆς γῆς. Διὰ τὸ μέγεθος τῶν γεγονότων.

PSALMVS LXVII

Ἐπὶ Ἡλὶ τοῦ ἱερέως ἐπιστρατεύσαντες οἱ ἀλλόφυλοι πολλοὺς μὲν ἀπέκτειναν τῶν Ἰσραηλιτῶν, καὶ τὴν κιβωτὸν λαβόντες ἀπῆλθον, καὶ ὥσπερ τι λάφυρον εἰσάγοντες ἔθηκαν ἐν τῷ ναῷ τοῦ θεραπευομένου παρ' αὐτοῖς εἰδώλου. Ὡς δὲ πληγαῖς περιέβαλεν ἅπαντας, τὴν οἰκείαν αὐτοῦ δύναμιν ἐπιδεικνύμενος ὁ Θεός, ἀπέπεμψαν μὲν οἱ ἀλλόφυλοι τὴν κιβωτόν. Δεξά- 10 μενοι δὲ οἱ Ἰσραηλῖται ταύτην, τὸ μὲν πρότερον εἰς τὸν οἶκον ἀπέθεντο τοῦ Ἀμιναδάβ· μετὰ δὲ ταῦτα ὁ μάκαριος Δαυὶδ ἐβουλήθη πρὸς ἑαυτὸν αὐτὴν ἀναγαγεῖν, καὶ συναγαγὼν τοῦ Ἰσραὴλ ἅπαν τὸ πλῆθος μετὰ πολλῆς τιμῆς καὶ τῆς δόξης ἀναγαγεῖν αὐτὴν ἐπειρᾶτο. Ὡς δὲ συνέβη τοὺς τοῦ Ἀμιναδάβ υἱοὺς ὑπὸ προπετείας πληγῆναι ὑπὸ τοῦ Θεοῦ, δείσας ὁ Δαυὶδ 15 εἰσήγαγεν αὐτὴν εἰς τὸν τοῦ Ἀβεδδαρᾶ οἶκον. Καὶ μαθὼν πολλῆς εὐλογίας τετυχηκότα διὰ τὴν τῆς κιβωτοῦ παρουσίαν τὸν τοῦ Ἀβεδδαρᾶ οἶκον, πάλιν ἀπελθὼν μετὰ παντὸς τοῦ πλήθους ἐκόμισεν αὐτὴν πρὸς ἑαυτόν, φαιδρὰν τὴν πανήγυριν ἐπὶ τῇ ἀνόδῳ τῆς κιβωτοῦ ποιησάμενος, θύματά τε κατασφάξας πολλά, καὶ αὐτὸς ἔμπροσθεν σκιρτῶν τε καὶ ἀλλόμενος ὑπὸ τῆς 20

6-9 I Reg. IV   9-10 I Reg. V   10-11 I Reg. VII, 1   11-22 II Reg. VI.

8ᵃ. Ἐπανέλαβεν καὶ τὴν εὐλογίαν: P, fol. 205ᵛ; V, fol. 271; Cord, p. 308.
8ᵇ. Διὰ τὸ μέγεθος τῶν γεγονότων: P, fol. 205ᵛ; V, fol. 271.
Argumentum Ἐπὶ Ἡλὶ — καλεῖν: P, fol. 206; V, fol. 271ʳ·ᵛ; Vat. gr. 1422. fol. 119ᵛ-120; Cord, p. 335-336.   9 ἅπαντες Cord   14 καὶ συνέβη 1422   τοῦ om. Cord   16 τὸν τοῦ] τοῦ om. 1422 Cord   20 ἔμπροσθεν om. 1422   τε om. 1422 Cord.

Aᵉ 8ᵇ (p. 332, 5): Hoc debeatur magnitudini operum atque factorum.
Argumentum ps. LXVII (p. 332, 6-25): Cum arcam testamenti post frequentes migrationes, ex illo iam tempore quo sub Heli ab allophilis capta est, tandem rex profeta ad se grandi ambitu exsultationis transferret, carmen hoc cicinit; et quoniam de loco ad locum fuerat (fruerat ms) transducta sepe, ut quondam in herimo praeberet iter populo ac regeret ignaros Ebreorum, ob rerum similitudine⟨m⟩ talis psalmi istius formatur oratio atque narratio, quae ex persona illius temporis principum diceretur, signoque in solitudine decurrens ipso sui principio Moysi uocibus conueniret: ille namque, cum in signum profectionis arca moueretur, aiebat Exsurge, Domine, et disipentur inimici tui, et fugient omnes qui oderunt te. Cf. Pseudo-Beda (828).

us, God, our God; bless us (vv. 6–7). He developed the blessing as well. *And let all the ends of the earth fear him:* on account of the magnitude of what happened.

PSALM 68

In the time of Eli the priest the Philistines made an incursion and killed many of the Israelites; they seized the ark and made off, bringing it home like a kind of booty and putting it in the temple of the idol worshiped by them. As a demonstration of his peculiar power, God invested them all with afflictions, and the Philistines sent the ark away. The Israelites accepted it, and first of all deposited it in the house of Abinadab.[1] Later David wanted to bring it to his own place; summoning all the population of Israel, he tried with great respect and splendor to bring it back. Since it happened that the sons of Abinadab were afflicted by God for their rashness, David, out of respect, brought it into the house of Obed-edom. On learning that the house of Obed-edom was accorded great blessing on account of the ark's presence, he went off in turn, and in the company of all the population he brought it to his place, holding a splendid festival for the entry of the ark, slaughtering many victims and himself dancing before it and leaping for | joy, using the customary instruments

---

1. Cf. 1 Sam 4–7.

εὐφροσύνης, καὶ δὴ καὶ ὀργάνοις κεχρημένος τοῖς συνήθεσι, μεθ᾿ ὧν καὶ ᾠδὰς ἀπεφθέγγετο.

Ταύτην δὲ τὴν κιβωτόν, τοῦ μακαρίου Μωϋσέως κατασκευάσαντος προστάγματι τοῦ Θεοῦ, εἶχον ἐν τῇ ἐρήμῳ οἱ Ἰσραηλῖται· καὶ ἦν αὐτοῖς ἅπαντα 5 ἡ κιβωτὸς σύμβολον τοῦ ὅπου καταμεῖναι προσήκει καὶ τοῦ πότε μετελθεῖν ἀπὸ τοῦ τόπου ἔδει. Κινουμένης μὲν γὰρ τῆς κιβωτοῦ ἐκινοῦντο, ἱσταμένης δὲ ἵσταντο. Ἦν δὲ αὐτοῖς καὶ ὥσπερ στρατηγοῦσα τοὺς πολέμους· αὕτη γὰρ παρέσχεν αὐτοῖς καὶ τὴν εἴσοδον τὴν εἰς τὴν γῆν τῆς ἐπαγγελίας. Ὅτε μὲν γὰρ ἔδει τὸν Ἰορδάνην διελθεῖν, τῶν φερόντων αὐτὴν ἱερέων 10 ἁψαμένων τοῦ ὕδατος, διῃρέθη τοῦ ποταμοῦ τὸ ῥεῦμα, οὕτω τε διῆλθον ἅπαντες. Πολεμούντων δὲ τὴν Ἰεριχὼ περιῆγον αὐτὴν ἔξωθεν κύκλῳ, καὶ οὕτως ἡ τῶν τειχῶν κατάπτωσις ἐγίνετο. Ἐπεὶ τοίνυν τότε ἡ κιβωτὸς τόπον ἐκ τόπου μεθίστατο, ἐδόκει δέ τι καὶ παρόμοιον γίγνεσθαι ἐπὶ τοῦ μακαρίου Δαυΐδ. Τῆς κιβωτοῦ πρότερον μὲν ἀπὸ τῶν ἀλλοφύλων εἰς τὸν τοῦ 15 Ἀμιναδὰβ μετελθούσης οἶκον, ὕστερον δὲ παρὰ τῷ Ἀβεδδαρὰ γενομένης, μεταγομένης τε πάλιν ἐκεῖθεν πρὸς τὸν Δαυΐδ, ὡς ἀπὸ τῆς τοῦ πράγματος ὁμοιότητος τὸ τοῦ μακαρίου Μωϋσέως καὶ Ἰησοῦ πρόσωπον ἀναλαβών, εἴτε καὶ τῶν τότε ἁπάντων, ἐκεῖνά φησιν ἅπερ ἂν ἥρμοσεν εἰπεῖν ἐκείνοις κατ᾿ ἐκεῖνον τὸν καιρὸν διηγουμένοις τὰ κατὰ τὴν ἔρημον, τὴν εἴσοδον τὴν εἰς 20 τὴν γῆν τῆς ἐπαγγελίας, τῶν κατ᾿ ἐκεῖνο καιροῦ θαυμάτων τὸ μέγεθος, ὧν τὴν αἰτίαν ἐπιγράφων τῇ κιβωτῷ ὡς ἐπ᾿ αὐτῆς ὄντος τοῦ Θεοῦ, καὶ δι᾿ αὐτῆς πράττοντος ὅσα καὶ βούλεται. Ὅθεν καὶ προοίμιον ποιεῖται τῷ ψαλμῷ τοῦτο, ᾧπερ ἐκέχρητο ὁ μακάριος Μωϋσῆς κινουμένης τῆς κιβωτοῦ εἰς τὸ μεταστῆναι ἅπαντας. Τίνα δὲ ἅπερ ἐφθέγγετο ἐξ αὐτῆς μανθάνομεν 25 τῆς θείας γραφῆς· Καὶ ἐγένετο ἐν τῷ ἐξαίρειν τὴν κιβωτὸν καὶ εἶπεν Μωϋσῆς Ἐξεγέρθητι, Κύριε, καὶ διασκορπισθήτωσαν οἱ ἐχθροί σου, φυγέτωσαν ἅπαντες οἱ μισοῦντές σε. Τοῦτο δὴ καὶ ὁ μακάριος Δαυΐδ, ὥσπερ κινουμένης τότε τῆς κιβωτοῦ εἰς μετάστασιν κατὰ τὴν ἐπὶ τῆς ἐρήμου ὁμοιότητα, ποιεῖται προοίμιον ἀπὸ τῶν τοῦ μακαρίου Μωϋσέως φωνῶν ἀρχόμενος, καὶ 30 ὡς ἐκ τοῦ ἐκείνων προσώπου διηγούμενος τὰ τότε θαύματα εἰς ἔκπληξιν τῆς τοῦ Θεοῦ δυνάμεως. Τοῦτο δὲ καὶ παρὰ τοῖς ἐκτὸς ἄχρι τῆς δεῦρο γίνεται τὸ ἐκ προσώπου τινῶν πρὸ πολλοῦ γεγενημένων τοῦ χρόνου λέγειν ἅπερ ἂν ἐκείνοις εἰπεῖν ἥρμοττεν, ἃ καὶ ἠθοποιΐαν ἔθος αὐτοῖς καλεῖν.

4-6 cf. Num. X, 33   9-11 Ios. III, 14-17   11-12 Ios. VI, 8 ss.   25-27 Num. X, 35.

6 μὲν om. 1422 Cord   7 πολεμίους 1422   13 εἰς τόπον 1422 Cord   γίνεσθαι 1422   20 ⟨κατ᾿ ἐκ⟩εῖνον κ. τ. λ. affert C, fol. 324ᵛ   ἐκείνου Cord   21 ἐπιγράφει 1422 Cord   ὡς om. 1422   22 καὶ om. 1422   23 τούτῳ ὅπερ CPV   τούτῳ ᾧπερ Cord   29 τῶν om. P   τοῦ om. Cord   ἀρχόμενος des. Cord   31 ἄχρι] μέχρι 1422.

to give voice to songs.[2]

Blessed Moses had made this ark at God's command, and the Israelites had it in the wilderness. For them it was altogether a pointer to where they should abide and when they had a need of a change of location: when the ark moved, they moved, and when it stopped, they stopped. For them it acted like a general in war, providing them also with entry into the land of promise: when they had to cross the Jordan, the priests carrying it stopped at the water's edge, the river's flood was parted, and everyone thus crossed over.[3] When they were assaulting Jericho, they took it around on the outside in a circle, and in this way the fall of the walls occurred.[4] So since at that time the ark moved from place to place, it seemed that something similar happened also in the time of blessed David: the ark first moved from the Philistines into the house of Abinadab, later it was in the home of Obed-edom, and in turn moved from there to David's place.

As though adopting the viewpoint of blessed Moses and Joshua or even all the people of the time on the basis of the similarity of events, he says what was appropriate to them when recounting at that time the events of the wilderness, the entry into the land of promise, the magnitude of the marvels at that time, attributing responsibility for them to the ark, since God was within it and did through it whatever he wanted. Hence, he also composes this introduction to the psalm that blessed Moses used when the ark was prompted to set them all moving. Now, some things he uttered we learn from the divine Scripture itself: "It would happen when the ark set out that Moses would say, 'Arise, Lord, let your enemies be scattered, let all who hate you be put to flight.' "[5] As though the ark were at that time prompting them to move on in a fashion similar to the time in the wilderness, blessed David composes this introduction beginning with the words of blessed Moses, and from his point of view narrating the marvels of that time in astonishment at God's power. Now, even among profane writers to this day the practice occurs of speaking in the person of people living long ago and mentioning what would have been appropriate for them to say—something they usually call "speech-in-character." |

---

2. Cf. 2 Sam 6.
3. Cf. Josh 3:14–17.
4. Cf. Josh 6.
5. Num 10:35.

2ª. Ἀναστήτω ὁ Θεὸς καὶ διασκορπισθήτωσαν οἱ ἐχθροὶ αὐτοῦ. Εἴρηται
καὶ ἑτέρωθι ὅτι ἀνάστασιν Θεοῦ καλεῖ τὴν ἐπὶ βοηθείᾳ τῶν οἰκείων καὶ
τιμωρίᾳ τῶν ἐναντίων κίνησιν, ἐκ τοῦ παρ᾽ ἡμῖν ἔθους, καθὰ τοιοῦτό τι
πράττειν βουλόμενοι, καθεζόμενοι πρότερον καὶ ἀναπαυόμενοι διανιστάμεθα
πρὸς τὸ ἔργον. Ἔδειξε δὲ αὐτὸ τῷ σχηματισμῷ φοβερώτερον· καὶ γὰρ 5
ὅλος οὕτως σύγκειται ὁ ψαλμὸς προσωποποιίας γέμων καὶ σχηματισμῶν,
καὶ ὅλως πρέπων τῇ ὑποθέσει καὶ τῇ τοῦ μακαρίου διαθέσει Δαυίδ, μεθ᾽
ἧς τότε ὀρχούμενος πρὸ τῆς κιβωτοῦ καὶ ὥσπερ μεθύων τῇ τοῦ Πνεύματος
χάριτι μείζονα ἢ κατὰ τὸν οἰκεῖον ἐφθέγγετο λογισμόν. Ὡς γὰρ ἐπὶ φοβε-
ροῦ στρατηγοῦ καὶ ἄγαν ἰσχυροῦ, ἐὰν ἀναστῇ φησιν ἅπαντας διασκορπίζει 10
τοὺς ἐχθρούς, οὕτως ἀρκεῖ καὶ διαναστὰς μόνον ἅπαντας καταπλῆξαι.

2ᵇ. Καὶ φυγέτωσαν ἀπὸ προσώπου αὐτοῦ οἱ μισοῦντες αὐτόν. Οὐδὲ γὰρ
ἰδεῖν αὐτὸν ἀνέξονται, ἀλλὰ μόνον ὀφθεὶς εἰς φυγὴν ἅπαντας τρέπει τῷ
φόβῳ.

3ª. Ὡς ἐκλείπει καπνὸς ἐκλειπέτωσαν. Οὕτω γὰρ αὐτοὺς τιμωρήσει ὥστε 15
ἀφανισθῆναι πάντας δίκην καπνοῦ, ὃς διαλύεσθαι πέφυκεν εἰς τὸ μηκέτι
εἶναι περιιστάμενος.

3ᵇ·ᶜ. Ὡς τήκεται κηρὸς ἀπὸ προσώπου πυρός, οὕτως ἀπολοῦνται οἱ ἁμαρτωλοὶ ἀπὸ προσώπου τοῦ Θεοῦ. Ταῖς παραβολαῖς ἐμφαντικωτέραν τῶν ἐναντίων τὴν ἀπώλειαν ἐργάσασθαι βουλόμενος, ἐμνημόνευσε καὶ καπνοῦ καὶ 20

2 cf. in ps. VII, 7 (p. 38), in ps. IX, 20 (p. 55).

2ª. Εἴρηται — καταπλῆξαι: C, fol. 324ᵛ-324ʳ; P, fol. 206ᵛ; V, fol. 271ᵛ; Vat. 1422,
fol. 120; Cord, p. 336-337.   2 θεοῦ om. 1422   4 πρότερον καὶ ἀναπαυόμενοι om. 1422
6 ὅλος om. 1422 Cord   9-10 ὥσπερ φοβερὸς στρατηγὸς καὶ ἄγαν ἰσχυρὸς 1422 Cord
11 καταπλῆξαι] τοὺς ἐναντίους ὁ τῶν ἀοράτων δυνάμεων κύριος add. 1422 Cord.
2ᵇ. Οὐδὲ γὰρ — φόβῳ: C, fol. 324; P, fol. 206ᵛ; V, fol. 272; Vat. 1422, fol. 120
(anon.); Cord, p. 347; cf. Paraphrasis (p. 311): Μηδὲ ἀντιστῆναί φησι τολμάτωσαν,
μηδὲ ἀντοφθαλμεῖν τῷ Θεῷ οἱ ἐναντιούμενοι ἡμῖν.
3ª. Οὕτω γὰρ — περιιστάμενος: C, fol. 324; P, fol. 206ᵛ; V, fol. 272; Vat. 1422,
fol. 120; Cord, p. 337.   16 εἰς τὸ om. 1422   17 περιιστάμενοι C.
3ᵇ·ᶜ. Ταῖς παραβολαῖς — κηρός: C, fol. 324; P, fol. 206ᵛ; V, fol. 272; Cord.
p. 338 sub nomine ORIGENIS.

Aᵉ 1-5 (p. 332, 27-333, 3: Hoc uero scemate utitur quoties sibi auxilium,
inimicis poscit interitum; qua ui sermonis fortior impetus post requiem indicatur.   9-14 (p. 333, 6-11): Vim potentiae expraesit, cuius occursus terrore solo
semper egerint; a similitudine tractum est uiri fortis, cuius ipsum aspectum
rebelles ferre nequeunt et fugiant citius quam ad resistendum parantur.
3ª (p. 333, 12-15): Augenter totum, quorum scisionem fugamque poposcerat,
horum attritionem obliuionemque instar fumi uanescentis inplorat.

Let God arise, and let his enemies be scattered (v. 1). There is evidence elsewhere as well that by "God's rising" he refers to his taking steps to help his own and punish the adversaries, from the custom prevalent among us by which, when we intend to do something of this kind, we first sit down and pause and then rise to take action. By this figure he made it appear more fearsome; the whole psalm, in fact, is thus composed, brimful of imaginary speakers and figures of speech, and is completely in keeping with the theme and intention of blessed David, who under its influence danced before the ark, and as though inebriated with the grace of the Spirit expressed more than he intended. In other words, as in the case of a fearsome and very powerful general rising up and scattering all the foe, he is capable of scattering them all merely by rising. *Let those who hate him flee from his presence:* they are unable to bring themselves even to look on him; instead, he has only to be seen to put them all to flight in fear.

As smoke disappears, let them disappear (v. 2): he will impose on them such awful punishment that all will disappear like smoke, which is naturally dissipated so as to linger no further. *As wax melts before fire, let the sinners perish before God.* Wishing to represent the destruction of the adversaries more effectively by comparisons, he mentioned both smoke and | wax, since

κηροῦ· αὕτη γὰρ ἡ κηροῦ φύσις πυρὶ πλησιάζοντος τήκεσθαι καὶ ἀπόλλυσθαι. Οὕτως οὖν ἅπαντας αὐτοὺς ἀναλώσεις ὥσπερ τὸ πῦρ τὸν κηρόν.

4ᵃ. Καὶ οἱ δίκαιοι εὐφρανθήτωσαν. Ἡμῖν μέντοι τοῖς τὴν σὴν γνῶσιν
κεκτημένοις εὐφροσύνη πάντως ἐκ τῆς ἐκείνων περιέσται τιμωρίας.

5 4ᵇ·ᶜ. Ἀγαλλιάσθωσαν ἐνώπιον τοῦ Θεοῦ, τερφθήτωσαν ἐν εὐφροσύνῃ.
Ἐξέσται μέντοι φησὶ καὶ ὑμῖν τοῖς ἐκτὸς βουλομένοις μετασχεῖν τῆς
εὐφροσύνης ἐὰν μὴ τὴν ἡμετέραν εὐπραγίαν βαρέως φέρητε, ἀλλ᾽ ὑπαντᾶν
αὐτῷ σπουδάσητε ἐφηδόμενοι τοῖς κατορθώμασιν· τὸ γὰρ ἐνώπιον αὐτοῦ
τοῦτο λέγει, ἀντὶ τοῦ Ἀπαντήσατε αὐτῷ μετὰ χαρᾶς.

10 5ᵃ. Ἄσατε τῷ θεῷ, ψάλατε τῷ ὀνόματι αὐτοῦ. Καὶ μᾶλλον ἐκπλαγέντες
αὐτοῦ τὸ μέγεθος καὶ τῶν κατορθωμάτων τὴν ἰσχύν, ὕμνοις χρήσασθε καὶ
ψαλμοῖς τοῖς εἰς αὐτόν. Τοῦτο δὲ εἰκότως, ἐπεὶ καὶ ὁ μακάριος Μωϋσῆς
ὁπηνίκα ἐποιεῖτο τὴν εἴσοδον εἰς τὴν γῆν τῆς ἐπαγγελίας, ἔδει δὲ διὰ τῶν
ἐν μέσῳ ἐθνῶν παριέναι τὸν λαόν, ἀπέστειλε καὶ πρὸς τὸν Ἐδὼμ βασιλέα
15 καὶ πρὸς τὸν Ἀμορραῖον· οὕτω δὲ καὶ καθεξῆς ἐποίει ἀξιῶν τὴν πάροδον
αὐτοῖς συγχωρηθῆναι ἀκωλύτως, οἳ δὲ οὐκ ἐπέτρεπον. Ἐντεῦθέν τε αὐτοῖς
τοῦ πολέμου συγκροτουμένου, συνέβαινε μὲν κρατεῖν τὸν Ἰσραὴλ τῇ τοῦ
Θεοῦ ῥοπῇ, τιμωρίαν δὲ ἀξίαν ἐκείνους διδόναι οὐκ ἐπιτρέποντας αὐτοὺς
διελθεῖν. Τοῦτο οὖν ὡς πρὸς ἐκείνους καλῶς φησιν ὅτι Κοινωνήσατε καὶ
20 ὑμεῖς ἡμῖν μᾶλλον τῆς εὐφροσύνης καὶ προϋπαντήσατε τῷ Θεῷ, ἑτοίμως
ὑπακούοντες οἷς βούλεται. Οὐδὲ γὰρ μεγάλα αἰτεῖ, ἀλλὰ ποῖα ταῦτα;

5ᵇ. Ὁδοποιήσατε τῷ ἐπιβεβηκότι ἐπὶ δυσμῶν· Κύριος ὄνομα αὐτῷ. Καλῶς
τὸ Ὁδοποιήσατε, πάροδον γὰρ ἐξῄτει μόνον· ἐκ μεταφορᾶς οὖν τῶν εὐτρε-
πιζόντων τὰς ὁδοὺς ἐν ταῖς τῶν βασιλέων παρόδοις, μὴ ἀντιπέσητέ φησι,
25 μὴ κωλύσατε, ἀλλὰ μᾶλλον καὶ συνεργήσατε πρὸς τὴν πάροδον. Τὸ δὲ τῷ

14-19 cf. Num. XXI, 21 ss.; Deut. II.

4ᵃ. Ἡμῖν — τιμωρίας: C, fol. 324; P, fol. 207; V, fol. 272ᵛ; Vat. 1422, fol. 120;
Cord, p. 339.
4ᵇ·ᶜ. Ἐξέσται — χαρᾶς: C, fol. 324; P, fol. 207; V, fol. 272ᵛ.
5ᵃ. Καὶ μᾶλλον — ταῦτα: C, fol. 324; P, fol. 207ᵛ; V, fol. 272ᵛ; Cord, p. 339.
13 εἰς abrumpitur C   14 λαὸν διότι Cord.
5ᵇ. Καλῶς — ὁδεύοντας: P, fol. 207ᵛ; V, fol. 272ᵛ-273; Cord, p. 340.   23 ἐξή-
τει] ἔξητε PV   24 ἀντιπέρητε Cord   25 κωλύσητε PV.

Aᵉ 19-22 (p. 333, 25-28): ...gentes ergo hortatur, ut inuicti populi Dei laetitiam deuotione magis capiant quam experiantur eius de rebellione potentiam.
24-25 (p. 334, 2-4): Nolite resistere transeunti populo, sed laborem transitus
adminiculis quoque uestris praestate leuiorem.

wax naturally melts and is destroyed when fire comes near. So he is saying, In like manner you will consume them all as fire does wax. *Let the righteous be glad* (v. 3): by contrast, joy at their punishment will envelop us, possessing as we do knowledge of you. *Let them rejoice before God; let them be exultant with joy:* it will be possible also for you who do not belong to share the joy if you are not depressed by our prosperity, and instead take pleasure in virtuous behavior and take pains to come to terms with him (the meaning of *before* him—that is, You will meet him with joy).

Sing praise to God; sing to his name (v. 4): all the more struck by his greatness and the force of his deeds, take up songs of praise and psalms to him. Now, this makes sense, since blessed Moses also on making his entrance into the land of promise, when the people had to pass through the nations in between, sent messengers to the king of Edom and the king of the Amorites; and this he proceeded to do, asking for unobstructed passage to be granted them, but they were unwilling. Hence, war was declared on them, and it turned out that Israel prevailed by God's influence, and fitting punishment befell those who did not allow them to pass.[6] In reference to these peoples, then, he did well to say, Choose to share our joy and come to terms with God, readily responding to what he wishes. In fact, he does not ask great favors: what are they? *Make a way for him who ascends above the setting sun. Lord is his name. Make a way* is well put, for he was looking only for a way through, by analogy with those preparing the way when kings pass. He is saying, Instead of resisting or getting in the way, cooperate in providing passage. The phrase *who | ascends above the setting sun* refers to

---

6. Cf. Num 21.

ἐπιβεβηκότι ἐπὶ δυσμῶν ὡς ἐπὶ βασιλέως ἐφ' ἅρματος ὀχουμένου καὶ οὕτως
κατὰ τῶν πολεμίων ἐλαύνοντος· τὸ μέντοι δυσμῶν ὡς πρὸς τὴν θέσιν εἶπεν
τῶν τόπων, ἐπειδὴ γὰρ οὐκ εὐθεῖαν ἀπὸ τῆς Αἰγύπτου ἐπὶ τὴν Παλαιστίνην
ἦλθον, ἀλλὰ κυκλεύσαντες τὴν ἔρημον, οὕτω τοῦ Θεοῦ ἐντειλαμένου, ἡ οὖν
διὰ τῶν ἐθνῶν ἐκείνων ἐπὶ τὴν γῆν τῆς ἐπαγγελίας εἴσοδος ὡς πρὸς δυσ-   5
μὰς βλέπειν ποιεῖ τοὺς οὕτως ὀδεύοντας.

5ᶜ. Καὶ ἀγαλλιᾶσθε ἐνώπιον αὐτοῦ. Τὸ αὐτὸ πάλιν λέγει, καὶ μᾶλλον
οὕτω μετὰ χαρᾶς ὑπαντήσατε. Εἶτα, ἐπειδὴ οὐκ ἠνέσχοντο, διὰ τῶν ἐπαγομένων φοβεῖ.

6ᵃ. Ταραχθήτωσαν ἀπὸ προσώπου αὐτοῦ. Ἐπειδὴ συμπρᾶξαι αὐτῷ καὶ   10
μετασχεῖν τῆς χαρᾶς οὐκ ἠβουλήθησαν, μόνον αὐτοῖς φανεὶς μετὰ ὀργῆς
ἅπαντας ταράξει.

6ᵇ. Τοῦ πατρὸς τῶν ὀρφανῶν καὶ κριτοῦ τῶν χηρῶν. Προστάτης γάρ
ἐστι τῶν ἀσθενῶν καὶ τῶν τὴν ἀνθρωπίνην οὐκ ἐχόντων βοήθειαν, οἷον
ἡμεῖς. Τίς δὲ οὗτος καὶ οἷος;   15

6ᶜ. Ὁ Θεὸς ἐν τόπῳ ἁγίῳ αὐτοῦ. Μέγας φησὶν ὁ Θεὸς καὶ φοβερὸς καὶ
ὀφθεὶς ἡμῖν ἐν τῷ ἰδίῳ αὐτοῦ τόπῳ τῷ ἁγίῳ, — βούλεται δὲ εἰπεῖν ἐπὶ
τοῦ ὄρους τοῦ Σινᾶ, — ὅπερ λέγει σαφέστερον ἐξῆς Κύριος ἐν αὐτοῖς ἐν
Σινᾶ, ἐν τῷ ἁγίῳ. Ἐπ' αὐτοῦ γὰρ ὤφθη πᾶσιν ὁ Θεὸς τοῖς τοῦ λαοῦ ἐν
στύλῳ γνοφώδους νεφέλης, καὶ ἐν πυρὶ ἐκαπνίζετό τε ἅπαν τὸ ὄρος, καὶ   20
ἀστραπαὶ συνεχεῖς ἐγίγνοντο, καὶ φωναὶ σάλπιγγος, καὶ ὅλως ἅπαντα
φόβου γέμοντα καὶ ἐκπλήξεως εἰς τὸ δέος ἐγγίνεσθαι τοῖς Ἰουδαίοις· οὕτω

18-19 v. 18ᶜ   22-433, 3 cf. Ex. XIX, 16 ss.

2-3 *Paraphrasis* (p. 312, 3-4): Τοῦτο δὲ ὡς πρὸς τὴν θέσιν τῶν τόπων λέγει   4 οὖν
om. PV.

5ᶜ. Τὸ αὐτὸ — φοβεῖ: P, fol. 208; V, fol. 273ᵛ; Cord, p. 341.   8-9 διὰ τῶν ἐπαγομένων φοβεῖ om. PV.

6ᵃ. Ἐπειδὴ — ταράξει: P, fol. 208; V, fol. 273ᵛ; Cord, p. 342.

6ᵇ. Προστάτης — οἷος: P, fol. 208; V, fol. 273ᵛ; Cord, p. 342.   14 καὶ τῶν]
καὶ PV.

6ᶜ. Μέγας — λαοῦ: P, fol. 208; V, fol. 273ᵛ; Cord, p. 342.   17-19 cf. *Paraphrasis* (p. 312): Τόπον αὐτοῦ ἅγιον καλεῖ νῦν τὸ Σίναιον ὄρος, ὅπου ὤφθη αὐτοῖς ὁ
Θεός   20 τε] τότε Cord.

Aᵉ 5ᶜ (p. 334, 6-7): Eadem repetit, ut non aucrsis animis sed laetis studeant
obedire.   6ᵃ (p. 334, 8-11): Si quae gentes transitum praebere neglexerunt,
omnis eorum securitas solius aspectus terrore soluetur.   6ᵇ (p. 334, 15-17)
...quia infirmorum atque inbicillorum defensor est, quales nos esse manifestum
est.   18-19 (p. 334, 20): scilicet ille qui apparuit in Sina...

a king mounted on a chariot and thus charging the enemy, while *the setting sun* refers to the lie of the land, since it was not by a direct route they came from Egypt to Palestine; rather, they went around in circles in the wilderness. Under God's direction the entry through those nations into the land of promise made those traveling that way keep their eyes on the setting sun, as it were. *And exult before him.* He is saying the same thing again: Rather, come to terms with him joyfully. Then, since they could not bring themselves to do so, he makes them fearful by what follows. *They will be panic-stricken before him:* since they refused to cooperate with him and share the joy, he has but to appear to them in his wrath and he will strike them with panic.

Father of orphans and judge of widows (v. 5): he is protector of the weak and of people without help, like us. Who is he, and what is he like? *God is in his holy place:* God is mighty and fearsome, and has appeared to us in his own holy place (meaning Mount Sinai), as he says more clearly later, *The Lord among them, on Sinai, in the holy place* (v. 18). On it, remember, God appeared to all the people in a pillar of dark cloud; all the mountain was wreathed in smoke and fire, lightning flashes kept occurring and the sound of a trumpet, and in short everything instilled fear and alarm so as to provoke reverence in the Jews.[7] Likewise, | God spoke from the middle of the

---

7. Cf. Exod 19:16–20.

τε καὶ ἐκ μέσου τοῦ πυρὸς καὶ τῆς νεφέλης φθεγξάμενος ὁ Θεὸς πρὸς
αὐτοὺς ἐχρημάτισεν ὅσα εἰκὸς ἦν, τὴν οἰκείαν γνῶσιν αὐτοῖς παρεχόμενος
καὶ περὶ τῶν πρακτέων διατάττων. Τοῦτο οὖν βούλεται εἰπεῖν, ὅτι μέγας
οὗτος, ὃς καὶ ὤφθη ἡμῖν ἐπὶ τοῦ ἰδίου τόπου πάσης γέμοντος ἁγιωσύνης,
5 ὅθεν οὐδὲ προσεγγίσαι τις ἐτόλμα τῶν τοῦ λαοῦ.

7ᵃ. Ὁ Θεὸς κατοικίζει μονοτρόπους ἐν οἴκῳ. Οὗτός φησιν ὁ μέγας καὶ
φοβερὸς δίδωσι καὶ ἡμῖν κατοικίας τόπον τοῖς μάλιστα πάντων ἀνθρώπων
δεομένοις, ἐπειδὴ μονότροποί τε ὄντες καὶ τὸν βίον ἀκοινώνητον πρὸς τοὺς
ἄλλους ἔχοντες ἀνθρώπους, τοῦτο ἡμῖν ἐντειλαμένου τοῦ Θεοῦ, οἰκεῖν τε
10 καὶ διάγειν σὺν ἑτέροις οὐ δυνάμεθα. Καλῶς δὲ ὡς πρὸς τὸ ἄνω τὴν ἀκολουθίαν ἀπέδωκεν· ὥστε φησὶ μὴ ἀντιπίπτετε, — οὐ γὰρ δύνασθε, τοῦτο
τοῦ Θεοῦ προειρημένου.

7ᵇ. Ἐξάγων πεπεδημένους ἐν ἀνδρείᾳ. Παιδευέτω γὰρ ὑμᾶς φησι τὰ ἤδη
γεγενημένα, ὅπως ἐν δουλείᾳ ὄντας καὶ ὥσπερ ἔν τισι πέδαις ἐν τῇ Αἰγύπτῳ
15 κατεχομένους καίτοι γε οὐχ ὑπομένοντας τῶν δεινῶν, ἐξήγαγεν καὶ ἐξέ-
σπασεν βουληθεὶς μετὰ πολλῆς τῆς ἰσχύος.

7ᶜ. Ὁμοίως τοὺς παραπικραίνοντας, τοὺς κατοικοῦντας ἐν τάφοις. Καίτοι
οὐ πεπεδημένους μόνον, ἀλλ' ἔτι καὶ παραπικραίνοντας· τοῦτο γὰρ τὸ μεῖζον, ὅτι μήτε ἐπιμελουμένους τῆς προσηκούσης ἀκριβείας, ἀλλὰ καὶ μᾶλλον
20 παροργίζοντας αὐτὸν τῷ συνεχεῖ τῆς παραβάσεως ὅμως ἐξήγαγεν, δι' αὐτὸ
τοῦτο μόνον τὸ ἐν μέσῳ ἀνδρῶν εἶναι φονικῶν καὶ ὥσπερ ἐν τάφοις καὶ
μνήμασιν οἰκεῖν, νεκροὺς σχεδὸν ὄντας τῇ ἐπιτάσει τῶν ἐπαγομένων ἡμῖν
συμφορῶν. Πρὸς τοῦτο δὴ μόνον ἀποβλέψας, ἠλέησεν πάσχοντας δεινὰ
καίτοι οὐκ ἀξίους ἐκ τοῦ τρόπου· οὕτω γὰρ λέγει ἡ θεία γραφὴ Καὶ κατε-
25 στέναξαν οἱ υἱοὶ Ἰσραὴλ ἀπὸ τῶν ἔργων καὶ ἀνεβόησαν, καὶ ἀνέβη ἡ βοὴ

24-434, 2 Ex. II, 23-25.

1 καὶ om. PV.
7ᵃ. Οὗτος — προειρημένου: P, fol. 208; V, fol. 273ᵛ; Cord, p. 343.   10 οὐ δυνάμεθα om. Cord.
7ᵇ. Παιδευέτω — ἰσχύος: P, fol. 208ᵛ; V, fol. 274; Vat. 1422, fol. 120ᵛ.   12 ἡμᾶς
1422   15 καίτοι γε] καὶ τί γὰρ PV 1422.
7ᶜ. Καίτοι — αὐτῶν: P, fol. 208ᵛ; V, fol. 274; Cord, p. 343.   18 τὸ om. Cord
22 ἡμῖν om. Cord   23 ἐλέησας Cord.

Aᵉ 7ᵇ (p. 334, 30-335, 3): De Aegiptia seruitute praerogatiua praecidentium
signorum Aegiptiarumque cladium uult terrere aduersarios.   17-24 (p. 335,
4-8, 13-18): Non solum nos, inquit, uinctos conpedibus sed indignos moribus,
et qui prauitate mentis sepe eum in iracondiam mouimus, liberauit, ... qui ita in
medio hominum multa cede cedentium uersarentur, ut uicinia inpedientis semper exitii non in domibus, sed in sepulchris quodammodo habitare crederentur.

fire and cloud, pronouncing on everything required so as to provide them with knowledge of himself and detailing their duties. So his meaning here is, Great is the one who has also appeared to us in his own place characterized by complete holiness, which none of the people dared to approach.

God makes hermits live in a house (v. 6): mighty and fearsome as he is, he even gives us a place to live when we of all people most need it, since we are hermits and have no life in common like other people. God gave us this direction, and we are unable to dwell and live with others. Now, he did well to preserve the sequence with the above, and so he is saying, Do not resist: you cannot, since God has foretold it. *Leading out the fettered in boldness:* let what has already occurred teach you how, though we were in servitude and held in Egypt in shackles, as it were, yet did not suffer a harsh fate, he led us out and snatched us with great force merely by willing it. *Like the embittered, those living in tombs:* although not only *fettered* but also actually *embittered*—a worse condition because we were not committed to due diligence and instead provoked him with constant transgressions—nevertheless, he led us out simply because we were in the midst of murderous men and, as it were, dwelling in graves and tombs, reduced almost to corpses by the extremity of the hardships inflicted on us. With his eyes solely on this, he had mercy on us when suffering a dire fate, unworthy though we were for our behavior (the divine Scripture likewise saying, "The Israelites groaned under their hardship and cried aloud, and their cry | ascended to God from

αὐτῶν πρὸς τὸν Θεὸν ἀπὸ τῶν ἔργων, καὶ εἰσήκουσεν ὁ Θεὸς τῶν στεναγμῶν αὐτῶν.

8ᵃ. Ὁ Θεός, ἐν τῷ ἐκπορεύεσθαί σε ἐνώπιον τοῦ λαοῦ σου. Διὰ τῶν ἄνω τὴν ἐν τῇ γῇ τῆς ἐπαγγελίας εἴσοδον σχηματίσας, καὶ τὰ μὲν πρὸς τοὺς ἀντιπεσόντας εἰπών, τὰ δὲ λαμπρότερον ἐξηγησάμενος εἰς μήνυσιν τῆς τε 5 περὶ αὐτοὺς εὐεργεσίας τοῦ Θεοῦ καὶ τῆς κατὰ τῶν ἐναντίων τιμωρίας, διηγεῖται λοιπὸν λαμπρότερον τῶν τοῦ Θεοῦ θαυμάτων τὸ μέγεθος. Τότε τοίνυν ὁπηνίκα ἡμῶν προηγοῦ. Πότε δὲ τοῦτο ἐποίει;

8ᵇ. Ἐν τῷ διαβαίνειν σε ἐν τῇ ἐρήμῳ. Ὁπηνίκα κατὰ τὴν ἔρημον ἐβάδιζες προηγούμενος ἡμῶν. Καὶ γὰρ καὶ οὕτως ἐγίγνετο· ἀγνοούντων γὰρ ἁπάν- 10 των τὴν ὁδόν, πρότερον διὰ τῆς νεφέλης, ὕστερον δὲ διὰ τῆς κιβωτοῦ τὴν ὁδὸν αὐτοῖς ἐπεδείκνυ, καὶ ταύτῃ ἑπόμενοι τὴν ὅθεν ἐχρῆν βαδίζειν ἐγνώριζον.

9. Γῆ ἐσείσθη, καὶ γὰρ οἱ οὐρανοὶ ἔσταξαν ἀπὸ προσώπου τοῦ Θεοῦ τοῦ Σινᾶ, ἀπὸ προσώπου τοῦ Θεοῦ Ἰσραήλ. Σύμμαχος Γῆ ἐσείετο, οὐρανὸς δὲ ἔσταξεν ἀπὸ προσώπου τοῦ Θεοῦ τούτου τοῦ εἰς τὸ Σινά. Ἔδειξεν ὅτι καὶ 15 τὸ ἐν τόπῳ ἁγίῳ αὐτοῦ περὶ τοῦ ὄρους Σινᾶ λέγει. Τότε τοίνυν φησὶν ὁπηνίκα κατὰ τὴν ἔρημον προηγούμενος ἡμῶν ἐβάδιζες, πάντα ἦν μεστὰ θαύματος καὶ φόβου, — γῆ τε γὰρ ἐσείετο, καὶ οὐρανοὶ διὰ νεφελῶν ἔσταζον· λέγει δὲ τὴν τοῦ μάννα τροφὴν καθ᾿ ἑκάστην ἡμέραν βαλλομένην, ἣν συνέλεγον. Ταῦτα γάρ φησιν ἐγίγνετο διὰ τό σε φαίνεσθαι ἐν τῇ ἐρήμῳ ἀπὸ 20 προσώπου τοῦ Θεοῦ Ἰσραήλ· φαινόμενός φησιν ἐν τῷ Σινᾶ, φαινόμενος καὶ ἐν ἡμῖν διὰ τῆς περὶ ἡμᾶς κηδεμονίας, τὰ πάντα ἐφόβεις καὶ ἐτάραττες καὶ θαυμάτων ἐπλήρους.

10. Βροχὴν ἑκούσιον ἀφοριεῖς, ὁ Θεός, τῇ κληρονομίᾳ σου· καὶ ἠσθένησεν, σὺ δὲ κατηρτίσω αὐτήν. Ἅπερ εἶπεν, ὅτι οἱ οὐρανοὶ διὰ νεφελῶν ἔσταξαν, 25 τὸ αὐτὸ καὶ βροχὴν ἑκούσιον λέγει, τὴν τοῦ μάννα τροφὴν οὕτω καλέσας·

15 v. 6ᶜ.

8ᵃ. Διὰ τῶν ἄνω — ἐποίει: P, fol. 209; V, fol. 274ᵛ; Cord, p. 345.
8ᵇ. Ὁπηνίκα — ἐγνώριζον: P, fol. 209; V, fol. 274ᵛ.
9. Σύμμαχος — ἐπλήρους: P, fol. 209; V, fol. 274ᵛ; Cord, p. 345-346. 13-14 Σύμμαχος — Σινά om. Cord 16 τὸ om. Cord 17 ἐβάδιζε Cord μεστὰ] μετὰ Cord.
10. Ἅπερ εἶπεν — γιγνομένη: P, fol. 209ᵛ; V. fol. 275; Vat. 1422, fol. 121 (anon.); Cord, p. 347. 25 ἅπερ] ὅπερ 1422.

Aᵉ 8ᵃ (p. 335, 19-25): Superioris sermonis scemate ingresum in terram repromisionis explicuit; reliqua quoque, quae ad magnitudinem mirabilium pertinent, eadem relatione persequitur. Tunc, inquit, cum nos praecederis. Quo autem tempore? 9-10 (p. 335, 27-28): Praeuius ac ductor populi. 21-22 (p. 335, 29-31): Pro apparante Deo in Sina... apparante etiam nobis.

their hardship, and God hearkened to their groaning").[8]

When you went forth in the sight of your people, O God (v. 7). Having in the foregoing presented the entry into the land of promise and mentioned the fate of those who resisted and, as well, the events more clearly related to God's favor for them and punishment of the adversaries, he then describes in a more fulsome manner the magnitude of God's marvels. So he is saying, At the time when you led us. When did he do so? *When you passed through the wilderness:* when you moved through the wilderness, guiding us. That was the way it happened, in fact: with no one knowing the way, he showed them the way, first by the cloud, later by the ark, and by following it they found out where they had to travel. *Earth shook and the heavens sent down drops at the presence of the God of Sinai, at the presence of the God of Israel* (v. 8). Symmachus: "Earth shook and heavens sent down drops in the presence of this God who is on Sinai." He brought out that the phrase *in his holy place* means Mount Sinai. So he means, At the time when you moved through the wilderness, leading us, everything was full of wonder and fear: *earth shook and the heavens sent down drops in clouds* (a reference to food from the manna dropping down every day, which they gathered). He is saying, in fact, This happened on account of your appearing in the wilderness, *at the presence of the God of Israel:* by appearing on Sinai and appearing also among us through your care for us, you brought fear and panic to everything and filled it with marvels.

You will allot rain without stint for your inheritance, O God. It was failing, but you restored it (v. 9). What he had said in *the heavens sent down drops* in clouds he says again in *You will allot rain,* thus referring to food from the manna: | it fell on them like rain, as is said also in Psalm 78, "He

8. Exod 2:23–24.

ὑετοῦ γὰρ δίκην ἐπ᾽ αὐτοὺς ἐφέρετο, οὕτω καὶ ἐν τῷ οζ᾽ Καὶ ἐνετείλατο
νεφέλαις ὑπεράνωθεν, καὶ θύρας οὐρανοῦ ἠνέῳξεν, καὶ ἔβρεξεν ἐπ᾽ αὐτοὺς
μάννα φαγεῖν, — βροχήν τε καλέσας τὴν τοῦ μάννα καταφοράν, καὶ διὰ
νεφελῶν αὐτὸ πέμπεσθαι φήσας εἰς αὐτούς. Καὶ καλῶς εἶπεν ἑκούσιον, —
5 τουτέστιν οὐ τὴν συνήθη καὶ φυσικῶς ὑπὸ τῆς τοῦ ἀέρος συστροφῆς ἐκπεμ-
πομένην, ἀλλ᾽ ἰδίαν τινὰ καὶ θελητὴν τῇ σῇ γνώμῃ συστᾶσαν. Καλῶς δὲ
καὶ τὸ ἀφορμεῖς· οἱ μὲν γὰρ λοιποὶ ὑετοὶ κοινοὶ πάντων, ἡ δὲ τοῦ μάννα
καταφορὰ ἰδίως αὐτοῖς ἀφορισμένη καὶ δι᾽ αὐτοὺς γιγνομένη.

11ᵃ. Τὰ ζῷά σου κατοικοῦσιν ἐν αὐτῇ. Ἐν αὐτῇ τῇ γῇ λέγει τῆς ἐπαγ-
10 γελίας. Τοῦτο δὲ βούλεται εἰπεῖν ὅτι οὕτω πλατεῖαν ἕξομεν τὴν κατοίκη-
σιν, ὡς καὶ ζῴων ἡμᾶς ἔχειν ἀφθονίαν, οὐ στενοχωρουμένους ὑπὸ τῆς τῶν
τόπων βραχύτητος.

11ᵇ. Ἡτοίμασας ἐν τῇ χρηστότητί σου τῷ πτωχῷ, ὁ Θεός. Οἰκείᾳ γὰρ
χρηστότητι τοσαῦτα ἡμῖν ηὐτρέπισας ἀγαθά, πτωχοῖς οὖσι καὶ ταλαι-
15 πώροις.

12-13. Κύριος δώσει ῥῆμα τοῖς εὐαγγελιζομένοις δυνάμει πολλῇ, ὁ βασιλεὺς τῶν δυνάμεων τοῦ ἀγαπητοῦ, τοῦ ἀγαπητοῦ τῇ ὡραιότητι τοῦ οἴκου διελέσθαι σκῦλα. Ἀγαπητὸν λέγει τὸν λαὸν ὡς ἠγαπημένον ὑπὸ τοῦ Θεοῦ,
συνηθῶς τῷ διπλασιασμῷ τὴν ἐπίτασιν τῆς ἀγάπης δεικνύς. Οὗτος οὖν φησιν
20 ὁ Θεὸς παρέχει τοῖς εὐαγγελιζομένοις ἀφορμὰς ὁ τῶν δυνάμεων ἡμῶν βασιλεύς, τουτέστιν ὁ τῆς ἰσχύος ἡμῶν βασιλεὺς ὁ παρέχων ἡμῖν τὴν ἰσχύν, ὃς
καὶ διὰ τὴν τοῦ οἴκου ὡραιότητα διέληται σκῦλα. Βούλεται δὲ εἰπεῖν ὅτι
τροπὴν ἐργάσασθαι τῶν ἐναντίων καὶ πάντας ἀναιρεθῆναι ποιήσει, ὥστε ἡμᾶς
διελέσθαι τὰ σκῦλα· σκῦλα γὰρ λέγει τῶν ἐν πολέμῳ φονευομένων τὰ ὅπλα
25 καὶ ὑπὸ τῶν ἀναιρούντων λαμβανόμενα. Ταῦτα δὲ ποιήσεις, ὥστε ἡμᾶς

1-3 Ps. LXXVII, 23-24ᵃ.

1 οὕτω] ὅτω PV   3 τε om. 1422 Cord   4-6 cf. L (p. 325, 19-22): διὰ τὸ μὴ
κατὰ φυσικὸν γίνεσθαι τρόπον ὡς τὸν ὑετόν, ἀλλὰ ἰδιάζοντι καὶ παρηλλαγμένῳ τρόπῳ, κατὰ
θεῖον θέλημα· ὃ καὶ εἶπεν ἑκούσιον.
11ᵃ. Ἐν αὐτῇ — βραχύτητος: P, fol. 209ᵛ; V, fol. 275; Cord, p. 347.
11ᵇ. Οἰκείᾳ -- ταλαιπώροις: P, fol. 209ᵛ; V, fol. 275; Cord, p. 348.
12-13. Ἀγαπητὸν — ἐργάσεται: P, fol. 210; V, fol. 275ᵛ-276; Cord, p. 349.
18 τοῦ om. PV   21 τουτέστιν — βασιλεὺς om. Cord   23 ἐργάσεται Cord   24 πεφο-
νευμένων Cord.

Aᵉ 4-6 (p. 335, 33-336, 1): Non naturae legibus debetam, sed uoluntate
tua causae nouae seruientem.   11ᵃ (p. 336, 6-8): Id est in terra non minus
lata quam laeta, ut opima glebis, sic conferta peccoribus.   18 (p. 336, 16-17):
Populi delecti rex Deus est.   21-22 (p. 336, 18-20): Qui in pulchritudine domus
suae, triumphatis hostibus, partietur spolia.

gave directions to clouds from above and opened heaven's doors, and rained on them manna to eat,"[9] by *rain* referring to the fall of the manna, and saying that it was sent on them in clouds. *Without stint* was well put—that is, not falling normally and naturally from the makeup of the air, but some special substance willed by your knowledge. *You will allot* was also well put: while other showers are common to all, the fall of the manna was specially allotted to them and made for them. *Your animals dwell in it* (v. 10). He means in the very land of promise. His meaning is, We shall have such a broad place for dwelling as even to have an abundance of animals, and are not confined by limitations of space. *You provided in your goodness for the poor, O God:* in your characteristic goodness you prepared so many good things for us, poor and downtrodden though we were.

The Lord will give a word to those bringing good news with great power. King of the hosts of the beloved, the beloved, with the charm of the house divide the spoils (vv. 11–12). *Beloved* is the term he applies to the people as loved by God, as usual by the repetition bringing out the intensity of the love.[10] So he is saying, God, the king of our hosts, provides occasions for those bringing good news—that is, the king of our strength, who provides us with strength, and who also divided spoils on account of the charm of the house. He means, He will cause a rout of the adversaries and their total disappearance, with the result that we can divide the spoils (by *spoils* referring to the weapons of those slain in war and taken by those who slew them). You will do this so that we | shall enter and take possession of the land given

9. Ps 78:23–24.

10. It is not so much the repetition of the term (ignored by some forms of the LXX) but its meaning that clearly puzzles ancient and modern translators and commentators, the NRSV opting for "flee, flee," and Dahood (*Psalms,* 2:141), with help from Ugaritic, rendering it "bend low, bend low."

εἰσελθόντας καὶ κατεσχηκότας τῆς παρά σου διδομένης ἡμῖν γῆς, κατασκευάσαι σοι οἶκον εὐπρεπέστατον, ἐν ᾧπερ εἶναι μέλλεις, ἐν μέσῳ πάντων ἡμῶν διάγειν δοκιμάσας. Ἀκύλας Καὶ ὡραιότητος οἴκου μερίζεται λάφυρα, Σύμμαχος Καὶ ἡ δίαιτα τοῦ οἴκου διανεμεῖ λάφυρα, — σαφέστερον δηλώσαντες ὅτι ἡ αἰτία τῆς τοῦ οἴκου κατασκευῆς, ἐν ᾧπερ θεραπεύεσθαι μέλλει 5
τὸ θεῖον, τῶν ἐναντίων τὸν φόνον ἐργάσεται.

14ᵃ. Ἐὰν κοιμηθῆτε ἀνὰ μέσον τῶν κλήρων. Τὸ ἄνω ἀποδέδοται. Ταῦτα δέ φησιν γενήσεται καὶ ἔσται ἡ κατασκευὴ τοῦ οἴκου καὶ ἡ ὡραιότης, ἐπειδὰν εἰσελθόντες ἀναπαύσησθε ἐν τῇ γῇ. Κλήρους δὲ αὐτὴν εἶπεν, ἐπειδὴ κατὰ κλήρους αὐτὴν διείλοντο. 10

14ᵇ. Ἐκεῖ πτέρυγες περιστερᾶς περιηργυρωμέναι, καὶ τὰ μετάφρενα αὐτῆς ἐν χλωρότητι χρυσίου. Τὸ ἐκεῖ ἀντὶ τοῦ τότε, ἐπειδὴ γὰρ ἔθος ἐστὶν ἐν τοῖς εὐκτηρίοις οἴκοις, ἐνίοτε δὲ καὶ τοῖς τῶν ἄγαν εὐπόρων, ἕτερά τινα μιμουμένους ζῷα καὶ δὴ καὶ περιστερὰς ἀπὸ γύψου κατασκευάζειν καὶ ἀργύρου μὲν αὐτῶν τὰς πτέρυγας, χρυσίῳ δὲ κατακοσμεῖν τὰ μέσα τῶν ὤμων 15
ἢ ὅλως τὰ περὶ τὸν τράχηλον ἢ καὶ ἕτερα τῶν μελῶν· οὕτω γὰρ Σύμμαχος τὰ μετάφρενα τὰ μέλη λέγει. Ταῦτα δὲ πολλῆς τῶν ποιούντων εὐπορίας ἀπόδειξιν ἔχει τὸ μέχρι καὶ τῶν τοιούτων ἀργύρῳ τε καὶ χρυσίῳ κεχρῆσθαι· τὸ παράδειγμα ἐντεῦθεν λαβὼν ἠβουλήθη εἰπεῖν ὅτι Οὕτως ἔσεσθε παρὰ πᾶσιν ἐπὶ πλούτῳ τότε καὶ εὐθηνίᾳ περίβλεπτοι καὶ τοῖς 20
παρὰ τοῦ Θεοῦ διδομένοις ὑμῖν ἀγαθοῖς. Ὥσπερ οὖν τὸ τοιοῦτον εἶδος τῆς κατασκευῆς πολὺν ἐμφαίνει τῶν τοιούτων τὸν πλοῦτον, ὅτι δὲ τὰ ὁμοιώματα ἄνευ τοῦ «ὡς» λέγει πολλαχοῦ ἐσημηνάμεθα, οὕτω γὰρ κἀνταῦθα τὸ Ἐκεῖ πτέρυγες περιστερᾶς κατὰ ὁμοίωσιν λέγει, ἀκολούθως ἐνταῦθα τούτῳ χρησάμενος εἰς ἀπόδειξιν εὐπορίας τῷ παραδείγματι, ἐπειδὴ οἴκου ἐν τοῖς 25
ἀνωτέροις ἐποιήσατο μνήμην.

15ᵃ. Ἐν τῷ διαστέλλειν τὸν ἐπουράνιον βασιλεῖς ἐπ᾿ αὐτῆς. Ἐπειδὴ πρότερον ἦσαν ὑπὸ τῷ βασιλεῖ τῶν Αἰγυπτίων, ἤμελλον δὲ τὸν ἴδιον κατέ-

---

23 cf. p. 358, 12; 411, 17.

1 τὴν παρά σου δεδομένην ἡμῖν γῆν Cord.
14ᵃ. Τὸ ἄνω — διείλοντο: P, fol. 210ᵛ; V, fol. 276ᵛ.
14ᵇ. Τὸ ἐκεῖ — μνήμην: P, fol. 210ᵛ; V, fol. 276ᵛ.
15ᵃ. Ἐπειδὴ — ἔσται: P, fol. 211; V, fol. 277; Cord. p. 352-353.

Aᵉ 14ᵇ (p. 336, 22-337, 1): Moris est in locis orationibus dedicatis columbas giro factas ponere eorumque extrimas argento operire pennas, auro quoque uel alarum media uel colla depingere. Haec autem cum fiunt illos, a quibus fiunt, diuitiis testantur adfluere; quo exemplo uult dicere quod ita erunt prae omnibus gentibus diuites ac rerum omnium habundantia conspicui, sicut sunt hi quorum multas opes talis ornatuum species et pecuniarum testatur effussio.

us by you, and prepare for you a well-furnished house in which you intend to be, now that you have seen fit to dwell amidst us all. Aquila, "And booty of a house's charm will be divided," and Symmachus, "And the dwelling of the house will divide the booty," both indicate with greater clarity that it is because of the adornment of the house in which the divinity is due to be worshiped that he will bring about the slaughter of the adversaries.

If you lie down among the lots (v. 13). This corresponds to the foregoing: This will happen, he is saying, and the house will have adornment and charm, since on entering you will enjoy repose in the land (referring to it as *lots* because they divided it by lots). *There a dove's wings covered in silver, and its back in the pallor of gold. There* means "at that time," since it is normal in oratories, and sometimes also in the homes of the very affluent, for people to make representations of animals, including doves in plaster with their wings in silver, and to adorn the middle of their shoulders with gold, or even their neck and others of their limbs—hence Symmachus's speaking of the *back* as "limbs." The use even of such things in silver and gold gives proof of the great affluence of those who made them; by citing the example he means, Thus you will, at that time in the sight of everyone, be conspicuous for wealth and prosperity and the good things given you by God. So just as such display of ornamentation betrays the great wealth of such people (we often imply similarity without using the word "like"), so here too he implies similarity in the phrase *There a dove's wings,* in this case logically using it as an example to prove wealth, since he referred to a house in the foregoing.

When heaven divides king from king on it (v. 14). Since formerly they were under the king of the Egyptians, and were destined to occupy their own | land in future under their own kings, at that time, he says, when we are

χοντες τόπον ὑπὸ τοῖς ἰδίοις εἶναι λοιπὸν καὶ τοῖς βασιλεῦσι, τότε φησὶν ὅταν γενομένων ἡμῶν ἐπὶ τῆς γῆς τῆς ἐπαγγελίας, ὁρίζῃς καὶ τοὺς μέλλοντας ἡμῶν βασιλεύειν, — ὅπερ ἴδιον τῶν ἐν εἰρήνῃ καθ' ἑαυτοὺς ὄντων καὶ οὐχ ἑτέροις δουλευόντων, — οὕτω καὶ τὸ Ἀποδώσω σοι τὰς εὐχάς μου, ἅς
5 διέστειλεν τὰ χείλη μου, ἀντὶ τοῦ ὥρισεν καὶ ἔταξεν. Τότε οὖν τί ἔσται;

15ᵇ. Χιονωθήσονται ἐν Σελμών. Τότε λαμπροὶ φανούμεθα, καλῶς τὸ λαμπρυνθῆναι χιονωθῆναι εἰπὼν ἀπὸ τοῦ τοιαύτην εἶναι φύσει τὴν χιόνα· ἐν εἰρήνῃ γὰρ καὶ εὐθηνίᾳ διαιτωμένους, εἰκὸς ἦν καὶ ἐπιδόξους εἶναι τοῖς περιοίκοις. Ἐν Σελμὼν δὲ λέγει, ἀντὶ τοῦ τῆς Σαλήμ, ἔνθα καὶ ὁ ναὸς ᾠκο-
10 δόμητο, ὅθεν καὶ Ἱερουσαλὴμ ἡ πόλις ἐκαλεῖτο.

16ᵃ. Ὄρος τοῦ Θεοῦ ὄρος πῖον. Τοῦτο δή φησι τὸ ὄρος εὐθηνίας μεστόν, ἀντὶ τοῦ ἀγαθῶν παρεκτικὸν πολλῶν, ὡς τοῦ Θεοῦ ἐνοικοῦντος ἐν αὐτῷ τούτων ἀγαθῶν χορηγοῦ.

16ᵇ. Ὄρος τετυρωμένον, ὄρος πῖον. Πεπυκνωμένον καὶ συνεστώς, οὐκ
15 ἐπιδεχόμενον λύσιν καὶ ἧτταν, — ἐκ μεταφορᾶς τοῦ τυροῦ, ὃς μὴ πέφυκεν αὖθις ἀναλύειν εἰς γάλα.

17ᵃ. Ἱνα τί ὑπολαμβάνετε, ὄρη τετυρωμένα; Ἐπειδὴ προσέταξεν ὁ Θεὸς τοῦτον μόνον αὐτῷ τόπον εἰς προσκύνησιν ἀφορισθῆναι τὸν τοῦ ὄρους ἐν ᾧπερ ὁ ναὸς ᾠκοδόμητο, πολλοὶ δὲ καὶ ἐν ἑτέροις ὄρεσι προσεκύνουν τοῖς
20 εἰδώλοις — οὐ τῶν ἐναντίων μόνον, ἀλλὰ γὰρ καὶ τῶν ἰδίων πολλάκις — ἀπατηθέντες καὶ ἐκτραπέντες εἰς ἀσέβειαν, ὡς πρὸς ἐκείνους, Διὰ τί φησιν οὕτως ὑπολαμβάνετε, ὡς καὶ τῶν ἄλλων ὀρέων τὴν αὐτὴν ἰσχὺν ἐχόντων καὶ ὁμοίως ὑμᾶς ὠφελεῖν δυναμένων;

15ᵇ. Τότε λαμπροὶ — ἐκαλεῖτο: P, fol. 211; V, fol. 277; Cord, p. 353; *Paraphrasis* (p. 314): Τὸ Σελμὼν ἀντὶ τοῦ Σαλήμ, τουτέστι τῇ Ἱερουσαλήμ. Τὸ δὲ χιονωθήσονται, ἀντὶ τοῦ ἐν ᾗ λαμπροὶ ἀναδειχθήσονται.   9-10 Ἐν Σελμὼν — ἐκαλεῖτο affert Vat. 1422, fol. 121ᵛ (anon.).
16ᵃ. Τοῦτο — χορηγοῦ: P, fol. 211ᵛ; V, fol. 277ᵛ; Vat. 1422, fol. 121ᵛ; Cord, p. 354.   12 ἐν om. PV.
16ᵇ. Πεπυκνωμένον — γάλα: P, fol. 211ᵛ et V, fol. 277ᵛ (anon.); Vat. 1422, fol. 121ᵛ; Cord, p. 355 (2ᵃ pars excerpti, sub nomine THEODORETI).   15 ὃ codd.
17ᵃ. Ἐπειδὴ — δυναμένων: P, fol. 212; V, fol. 278; Vat. 1422, fol. 121ᵛ; Cord, p. 355.   19 καὶ om. 1422   20 ἰδιωτῶν 1422.

Aᵉ 2-3 (p. 337, 4-6): Reges nobis proprios, id est nostri generis, qui ullatenus iuris et dicionis eramus extraniae.   9-10 (p. 337, 12-14); *Silmon* pro Salem. in qua templum constructum est fuitque ciuitas regia.   16ᵇ (p. 337, 14-16): Sicut inpossibile est casseum in originem suam, id est liquorem lactis, resolui... concreatus atque duratus.   19-20 (p. 337, 20-21): Aduersus eos qui, relicto templo, sectabantur excelsa.

in the land of promise, you will determine also those due to reign over us—a state typical of those living in peace on their own and not in thrall to others—like the verse "I shall pay my vows to you, which my lips uttered"[11]—that is, determined and directed. So what will it then be? *They will be covered in snow on Zalmon:* we shall then emerge as famous (nicely referring to achieving fame as *covered in snow,* from the natural qualities of snow), living in peace and prosperity, and hence they probably also attracted the notice of the neighboring peoples. He says on *Zalmon*—that is, Salem—where the temple was built, hence the city's being called Jerusalem.

God's mountain, fat mountain (v. 15): this mountain is altogether prosperous—that is, the source of many goods—since there dwells in it God, the source of many good things. *Curdled mountain, fat mountain:* thickly covered and solidly constituted, invulnerable to destruction and conquest (by analogy with cheese, which by nature does not revert to milk). *Why are you suspicious, O curdled mountains?* (v. 16) Since God gave directions for this place alone to be chosen for his worship on the mountain where the temple was built, whereas many people worshiped the idols on other mountains, not only from the adversaries, but also even at many times from their own people, deceived and led astray into impiety, so to them he says Why do you suspect that other mountains have the same force and are capable of helping you in similar fashion? | *The mountain on which God was pleased to dwell:*

---

11. Ps 66:13.

17ᵇ. Τὸ ὄρος ὃ εὐδόκησεν ὁ Θεὸς κατοικεῖν ἐν αὐτῷ. Οὐκ ἔστι τοιαῦτα τὰ λοιπά, τοῦτο μόνον τοιοῦτον, ἐπειδήπερ καὶ ἐν αὐτῷ μόνῳ κατοικεῖν ᾑρέτισε τῷ Θεῷ, καὶ διὰ τοῦτο ταύτην ἔχει τὴν ἰσχύν.

17ᶜ. Καὶ γὰρ ὁ Κύριος κατασκηνώσει εἰς τέλος. Οὔτε γὰρ μετελθεῖν αὐτὸν ἐντεῦθεν οἷόν τε, ἀλλὰ διαμένει ἐνταῦθα διηνεκὲς ἑαυτῷ κατοικητή-   5
ριον ἐκλεξάμενος, ὥστε μάταιον ὑμῖν τὸ περὶ τὰ ἄλλα σπουδάζειν.

18ᵃ·ᵇ. Τὸ ἅρμα τοῦ Θεοῦ μυριοπλάσιον, χιλιάδες εὐθηνούντων. Ἐπειδὴ εἶπεν ἄνω Τῷ ἐπιβεβηκότι ἐπὶ δυσμῶν, ὡσανεὶ ἐφ᾽ ἅρματος ὀχουμένου καὶ ἐλαύνοντος, καλῶς ἅρμα ἐκάλεσε τὸν λαόν· ἐπ᾽ αὐτοῦ γὰρ ὥσπερ ὀχού-
μενος τὴν οἰκείαν ἐπεδείκνυτο δύναμιν, τιμωρούμενος μὲν δι᾽ αὐτῶν τοὺς ἐναν-   10
τίους, συγκρατῶν δὲ αὐτοὺς ὡς ἠβούλετο. Ἡμεῖς οὖν φησι τὸ ἅρμα αὐτοῦ,
ὧν ἐπιβέβηκεν καὶ ἐν οἷς γνωρίζεται, τούτῳ προσέχομεν τῷ ὄρει καὶ περὶ
αὐτὸ ἐσμὲν οἱ εἰς μυριάδας καὶ χιλιάδας εὐθηνοῦντες καὶ πληθυνόμενοι τῇ
αὐτοῦ δυνάμει.

18ᶜ. Κύριος ἐν αὐτοῖς ἐν Σινᾶ, ἐν τῷ ἁγίῳ. Ὁ γὰρ ἐνταῦθα νῦν Θεὸς   15
καὶ ἐν ἡμῖν ὤν, αὐτὸς ἦν ὁ καὶ τότε ἐν τῷ Σιναῖν ὄρει τῷ ἁγίῳ, ἐν μέσῳ
τῶν παρόντων γνωρισθείς τε καὶ φανείς· καλῶς δὲ ἅγιον ἐκάλεσεν τὸ ὄρος
ἐφ᾽ οὗπερ ὤφθη ὁ Θεός.

19ᵃ·ᵇ. Ἀνέβης εἰς ὕψος ᾐχμαλώτευσας αἰχμαλωσίαν, ἔλαβες δόματα ἐν ἀνθρώποις. Ἐπειδὴ γὰρ ἦν ὁ λαὸς ὥσπερ αἰχμάλωτος ἐν τῇ Αἰγύπτῳ   20

17ᵇ. Οὐκ ἔστιν — ἰσχύν: P, fol. 212; V, fol. 278; Vat. 1422, fol. 121ᵛ; Cord,
p. 355.   3 τῷ θεῷ des. 1422.
17ᶜ. Οὔτε γὰρ — σπουδάζειν: P. fol. 212 et V, fol. 278 (anon.); Cord. p. 356.
5-6 cf. Paraphrasis (p. 315): Καὶ οὐχ ἁπλῶς κατοικεῖν, ἀλλὰ καὶ χρονίζειν   5 ἑαυτῷ]
αὐτῷ PV.
18ᵃ·ᵇ. Ἐπειδὴ — δυνάμει: P, fol. 212ᵛ; V, fol. 278ᵛ; Cord, p. 356-357; cf. Paraphrasis (p. 315).
18ᶜ. Ὁ γὰρ — Θεός: P, fol. 212ᵛ; V, fol. 278ᵛ; Vat. 1422, fol. 122 sub nomine
Theodoreti; Cord, p. 357 sub eodem nomine.   15 ἐνταῦθα] om. Cord.
19ᵃ·ᵇ. Ἐπειδὴ — χαρίσματα: P. fol. 213; V, fol. 278ᵛ-279; Vat. 1422, fol. 122
(anon.); Cord, p. 357-358 (= P. G., 688).   20 γὰρ ἦν] οὖν Cord   ὥσπερ] ὡς 1422
Cord.

Aᵉ 17ᵇ (p. 337, 22-24): Auxit dignitatem loco habitatoris dignatione perpetua.   8-10 (p. 337, 25-27): Populum dicit, eo quod habenis (auenis ms) talis
aurigae et quod regatur, inuecta diuinitas proterat aduersarios.   18ᶜ (p. 337,
28-31): Ac si diceret Is Dominus in eis inuechitur ac triumphat, qui in Sina
monte sancto conspectus est; a dignitate apparentis mons quoque sanctus est.
20-439, 6 (p. 337, 34-3⁴8, 5):... ut uictor gentis Aegiptiae dominatricis iure belli
seruos tuae dicioni uendicas, quos tanquam armis coepissent, sic callida obpraesione habuere captiuos.

the others are not like this, only this one, since God was even pleased to dwell on it alone, and hence it possesses this force. *And the Lord will dwell there forever:* far from his being able to move away from there, he remains there forever, having chosen it for his own dwelling place, so that it is idle for you to be interested in the others.

God's chariotry, ten-thousandfold thousands of stalwarts (v. 17). Since he had said above *he who ascends above the setting sun,* as though mounted on a chariot and charging, he did well to call the people *chariotry:* mounted on them, as it were, he gave evidence of his peculiar power, punishing the adversaries through them and dominating them as he wished. So he is saying, We are his *chariotry,* and on us he is mounted, and through us he comes to be known; we pay heed to this mountain and are round about it in our thousands and tens of thousands, prospering and multiplying, thanks to his power. *The Lord among them on Sinai, in his holy place:* God, who here and now is also among us, is the one who even at that time was on the holy Mount Sion, made known and revealed in the midst of those present (nicely referring to the mountain on which God appeared as holy).

You ascended to the heights, taking captivity captive; you received gifts from among human beings (v. 18). The people were enslaved as though held captive in Egypt, | and God snatched them from slavery and freed them by

δουλεύων, ἐξέσπασε δὲ αὐτοὺς τῆς δουλείας ὁ Θεὸς καὶ ἀπήλλαξεν πολέμου
νόμῳ, — τιμωρησάμενος γὰρ τοὺς ἐναντίους, οὕτω τούτους ἀφεῖλεν, αἰχμα-
λωσία δὲ λέγεται ἅπαν τὸ ἐν πολέμου νόμῳ λαμβανόμενον, — τοῦτό φησιν
ὅτι Τὴν αἰχμαλωσίαν, δηλονότι ἡμᾶς τοὺς ὡς ἐν αἰχμαλωσίᾳ δουλεύοντας,
5 αἰχμαλωτεύσας, ὡς ἰσχυρὸς στρατιώτης πολέμου νόμῳ νικήσας, ἀφεῖλες καὶ
ἀπέσπασας. Τὸ δὲ ἀνέβης εἰς ὕψος, ἐδείχθης δὲ μέγας καὶ ὑψηλός· διὰ
τοῦτο ἔλαβες δόματα ἐν ἀνθρώποις. Προσέταξε γὰρ αὐτοῖς τότε ὁ Θεὸς
αἰτῆσαι σκεύη ἀργυρᾶ καὶ χρυσᾶ, καὶ ταῦτα αἰτήσαντες ἔλαβον. Εἶτα κατα-
λαβόντος τοῦ θανάτου τῶν πρωτοτόκων, ἐξώρμησαν τῆς Αἰγύπτου τῷ προσ-
10 τάγματι τοῦ Θεοῦ ἔχοντες καὶ τὰ σκεύη. Οὐχ ἡμᾶς οὖν φησι μόνον ἀφείλω
καὶ τῆς δουλείας ἀπήλλαξας, ἀλλὰ καὶ δόματα ἔλαβες παρὰ τῶν ἀνθρώπων,
ὡσανεὶ μετὰ δώρων πάντων αὐτοὺς ἐκπεμψάντων.

Ἐχρήσατο δὲ ὁ ἀπόστολος ταύτῃ τῇ μαρτυρίᾳ, οὐχ ὡς περὶ τοῦ Χριστοῦ προηγορευμένην, ἀλλ᾿ ὡς ἁρμόζουσαν λέγεσθαι περὶ τοῦ Χριστοῦ, ὅτι
15 καὶ αὐτὸς αἰχμαλώτους ἡμᾶς ὄντας ὑπὸ τοῦ διαβόλου μάχῃ τῇ πρὸς αὐτὸν
νικήσας ἀφείλετο. Διὰ τοῦτο ἐπειδὴ τὸ ἔλαβες δόματα οὐχ ἥρμοττεν κατὰ
τὸ παρ᾿ ἡμῖν ἔθος, ὥσπερ ἐν ταῖς διαλέξεσι ταῖς ἐκκλησιαστικαῖς κεχρήμεθα, ὑπαλλάξας τὸ ἔλαβες εἶπεν τὸ «ἔδωκας». Τοῦτο γὰρ ἁρμοδιώτερον
ἐπὶ τοῦ Χριστοῦ, οὐ λαβόντος ἀλλὰ μετὰ τὴν ἄνοδον τὴν ἐν τοῖς οὐρανοῖς
20 δεδωκότος τοῦ Πνεύματος τὰ χαρίσματα.

19ᶜ. Καὶ γὰρ ἀπειθοῦντες τοῦ κατασκηνῶσαι. Ὥσπερ ἄνω εἶπεν ὁμοίως
τοὺς παραπικραίνοντας, οὕτω κἀνταῦθα. Καὶ ταῦτά φησιν ἐποίεις ἀπειθούν-
των ἡμῶν, οἰκείᾳ φιλανθρωπίᾳ ἀπαλλάττων, καὶ οἰκητήριον ἡμῖν ὁρίζων εἰς
τὸ ἔχειν τε τόπον ἴδιον καὶ οἰκεῖν ἐν αὐτῷ.

25 20ᵃ. Κύριος ὁ Θεὸς εὐλογητός. Ἐπὶ τούτοις γὰρ ὕμνων ἄξιος.

20ᵇ. Εὐλογητὸς Κύριος ἡμέραν καθ᾿ ἡμέραν. Διηνεκῶς ὑμνεῖσθαι ἄξιος
κατὰ πᾶσαν ἡμέραν.

8 Ex. XI, 2; XII, 35   9-10 cf. Ex. XII, 29   16-18 Eph. IV, 8 (cf. ed. SWETE, I,
p. 166-167)   21-22 v. 7ᶜ.

1 δὲ om. Cord   2-3 ἀφεῖλεν αἰχμαλωσία] αἰχμαλώτους 1422   4 ὅτι] ὡς ἂν εἴπῃ
Cord   δηλονότι om. PV 1422   6 ἐδείχθης δὲ] ἐδείχθη φησὶν 1422   ὑψηλός des. 1422
13 οὐχ om. Cord   14 προηγορευμένην — Χριστοῦ om. Cord   19 τοῦ om. Cord.
19ᶜ. Ὥσπερ — ἐν αὐτῷ: P, fol. 213; V, fol. 279.
20ᵃ. Ἐπὶ — ἄξιος: P, fol. 213ᵛ; V, fol. 279ᵛ; Cord, p. 359.   25 γὰρ om. PV.
20ᵇ. Διηνεκῶς — ἡμέραν: P, fol. 213ᵛ; V, fol. 279ᵛ; Vat. 1422, fol. 122 (anon.).

Aᶜ 21-22 (p. 338, 10): Sic superius *Similiter qui exasperant*.   20ᵇ (p. 338,
13-14): Omnium laude celebrandus tantorum opernm testimonio.

the norms of war, punishing the adversaries, and thus took the people for himself. So the complete capture by norms of war is referred to as *captivity,* namely, ourselves serving as though in captivity, whom you captured like a strong general conquering by norms of war, reclaiming and rescuing. *You ascended to the heights* means, You were shown to be great and elevated; hence *you received gifts from among human beings:* God gave them orders to ask for "silver and gold vessels,"[12] and upon asking they were given them. Then when the death of the firstborn occurred, they abandoned Egypt at God's command with the vessels in their possession. So he is saying, It was not only that you removed us and freed us from slavery: *you also received gifts from human beings,* as if everyone dispatched them with gifts. Now, the apostle cited this text, not as a prophecy about Christ, but as one applicable to Christ in that while we were captives of the devil, he was victorious in battle with him and carried us off for himself. Hence, since the phrase *you received gifts* did not apply, in our normal practice in using it in ecclesiastical usage he replaced *you received* with "he gave," this being more applicable to Christ, who did not receive but gave the gifts of the Spirit after the ascension into heaven.[13] *Even those resisting your dwelling.* As he had spoken in similar terms above of *the embittered,* so too here: You did this, he is saying, though we resisted, freeing us by your lovingkindness, and allotting us a habitation to have as our own place and reside in it.

Blessed be the Lord God (v. 19), worthy of hymns of praise for these things. *Blessed be the Lord day after day,* constantly worthy of being praised every day. | *The God of our salvation will make our path plain:* he is the one

12. Exod 11:2; 12:35.
13. Cf. Eph 4:7–11.

20c. Κατευοδώσει ἡμῖν ὁ Θεὸς τῶν σωτηρίων ἡμῶν. Αὐτὸς γὰρ ἡμῖν καὶ τὴν ὁδὸν εὐτρεπίσει, τουτέστι Παρέξει ἡμῖν τὴν εἴσοδον τὴν εἰς τὴν γῆν τῆς ἐπαγγελίας ὁ περισῴζων ἡμᾶς καὶ ἀπαλλάττων τῶν κινδύνων, — ἐνταῦθα μάλιστα εὐκαίρως τὸ Ὁ Θεὸς τῶν σωτηριῶν ἡμῶν εἰπών· μὴ περισωζομένους γὰρ τῆς τῶν πολεμίων ἐπιβουλῆς οὐκ ἐνῆν δυνηθῆναι τῆς γῆς ἐπιλαβέσθαι.

21a. Ὁ Θεὸς ἡμῶν ὁ θεὸς τοῦ σῴζειν. Ὥσπερ Θεὸν ἐλέους λέγει ἀπὸ τοῦ « ἐλεεῖν », οὕτω καὶ Θεὸν τοῦ σῴζειν, τουτέστιν Αὐτὸς ὁ περισῴζειν ἀπὸ κινδύνων δυνάμενος.

21b. Καὶ τοῦ κυρίου κυρίου αἱ διέξοδοι τοῦ θανάτου. Διέξοδον δὲ λέγει τὴν ἀπαλλαγήν. Αὐτὸς ὁ καὶ διὰ μέσου πολλάκις τοῦ θανάτου ἐξάγων καὶ ἀπαλλάττων.

22a. Πλὴν ὁ Θεὸς συνθλάσει κεφαλὰς ἐχθρῶν αὐτοῦ. Ἡμᾶς δὲ ἀπαλλάξει, τοὺς ἐναντίους καὶ πολεμοῦντας ἡμῖν τιμωρούμενος.

22b. Κορυφὴν τριχὸς διαπορευομένων ἐν πλημμελείαις αὐτῶν. Οὕτω φησὶν αὐτοὺς τιμωρήσεται ὡς ὑπὲρ πάντων ὧν ἁμαρτάνουσι δοῦναι δίκην, καὶ μηδὲ τὴν ὑπὲρ τοῦ σμικροτάτου τιμωρίαν αὐτοὺς διαφυγεῖν. Τρίχας δὲ ὠνόμασεν τὸ σμικρότατον, κυρίως μὲν ἐπειδὴ τοῦτο ἐν ἡμῖν τὸ πάντων βραχύτατον, ἀκολούθως δὲ ἐπειδὴ κεφαλὰς εἶπεν ὅτι συνθλάσει.

23a. Εἶπεν Κύριος Ἐκ Βασὰν ἐπιστρέψω. Σύμμαχος Ἐπιστρέψαι ποιήσω. Ἔδειξεν ἐνταῦθα μάλιστα τὴν ὑπόθεσιν ἥτις ἐστίν, καὶ οὐχ, ὥς τινες ἐνό-

20c. Αὐτὸς — ἐπιλαβέσθαι: P, fol. 213v; V, fol. 279v; Cord, p. 359. 2 παρέξεις Cord.
21a. Ὥσπερ — δυνάμενος: P, fol. 213v; V, fol. 279v; Vat. 1422, fol. 122 (anon.); Cord, p. 359-360.
21b. Διέξοδον — ἀπαλλάττων: P, fol. 213v; V, fol. 279v; Cord, p. 360. 10 δὲ *om.* PV 11 ὁ *om.* Cord.
22a. Ἡμᾶς — τιμωρούμενος: P, fol. 213v; V, fol. 279v; Cord, p. 360.
22b. Οὕτω — συνθλάσει: P, fol. 214; V, fol. 279v.
23a. Σύμμαχος — ἀγαγεῖν: P, fol. 214v; V, fol. 279v; Cord, p. 361-362.

Ae 4-5 (p. 338, 18-21): Oportune inlatum est ***Deus salutaris noster***; nisi enim saluaret ex hostibus, quos introduceret non haberet. **21a** (p. 338, 22-24): Sic ***Deus saluos faciendi*** a saluando, sicut a miserendo ***misericordiarum Deus*** dicitur. **21b** (p. 338, 24-25): Exitum uocat liberationem, id est egressum. **22a** (p. 338, 27-339, 1): Saluationem nostram hostium atritione perficit. **22b** (p. 339, 2-6): Pulcre, quia caput dixerat, capillum subtexuit, quo nihil est in corpore nostro exilius; hoc autem idcirco, ut ne exigua quidem eorum peccata ostenderet inpunita.

who also will prepare the way for us—that is, he will provide us with entry into the land of promise, saving us and freeing us from danger (here saying with particular appropriateness *The God of our salvation*), as it was impossible for us to be rescued from the snare of the enemy and take possession of the land. *Our God is a God who saves* (v. 20). Just as he speaks of a God of mercy from the verb "to have mercy," so too *a God who saves*—that is, He is the one who is capable of saving from danger. *And from the Lord, the Lord, comes escape from death.* By *escape* he refers to deliverance: He is the one who leads out and delivers even from the midst of death on many occasions.

But God will shatter heads of his foes (v. 21): he will deliver us, also punishing the adversaries warring against us. *The hairy crown of those who cavort in their sins:* he will punish them in such a way that they will pay the penalty for all their sins and will not escape retribution in the slightest degree. He appropriately implied the slightest degree by "hair," since it is the smallest part of us, and it followed on his mentioning the shattering of their heads. *The Lord said, I shall bring them back from Bashan* (v. 22). Symmachus: "I shall cause them to turn back." Here in particular he showed what is his theme: he does not, as some commentators | believed, refer to the

μισαν, τὴν ἐπάνοδον λέγει τοῦ λαοῦ. Τί γὰρ βούλεται πρὸς τὴν Βαβυλῶνα ἡ Βασάν; Βασὰν δέ ἐστιν ἧς ἐβασίλευσεν ὁ Ὢγ, δι᾽ ἧς καὶ παρῆλθον τότε, ὡς αὐτὸς ἑτέρωθι μνημονεύων τῶν ἐξ Αἰγύπτου φησὶ Καὶ τὸν Ὢγ βασιλέα τῆς Βασάν. Ἐπηγγείλατο οὖν φησιν ὁ Θεὸς ἐκεῖθεν αὐτοὺς ἀγαγεῖν.

5   23ᵇ. Ἐπιστρέψω ἐν βυθοῖς θαλάσσης. Σύμμαχος Ἀναστρέψαι ποιήσω ἀπὸ βυθῶν θαλάσσης καὶ διὰ μέσου· τῶν τε Ἐδομιτῶν λέγων καὶ τῶν Μοαβιτῶν καὶ τῶν λοιπῶν ἁπάντων, δι᾽ ὧν παρῆλθον, ὡς ἂν καὶ διὰ μέσου τοῦ βυθοῦ τῆς θαλάσσης ἄξω, οὐδὲν παθεῖν ὑπὸ τοῦ πλήθους τῶν πολεμούντων ποιήσας.

10   24ᵃ. Ὅπως ἂν βαφῇ ὁ ποῦς σου ἐν αἵματι. Πάντας γὰρ αὐτοὺς τιμωρήσομαι. Καλῶς δὲ τὸ Ὅπως ἂν βαφῇ ὁ ποῦς σου ἐν αἵματι ἐσχημάτισεν, ὡς ἐπὶ στρατηγοῦ διώκοντος καὶ πολὺν ἐργαζομένου φόνον, καὶ τῷ αἵματι φύροντος τὸν οἰκεῖον πόδα. Τὸ δὲ ὅπως κατὰ τὸ ἰδίωμα εἶπεν τὸ γραφικόν, τὸ αἰτιατὸν ἀντὶ αἰτίας τεθεικώς. Οὐ γὰρ ἵνα τούτους ἀνέλη ἐκεί-
15   νους ἀπαλλάττει, τοὐναντίον δὲ ὑπὲρ τῆς ἐκείνων ἀπαλλαγῆς καὶ τούτους ἀνθισταμένους ἀναιρεῖ.

24ᵇ. Ἡ γλῶσσα τῶν κυνῶν σου ἐξ ἐχθρῶν παρ᾽ αὐτοῦ. Σαφέστερον Σύμμαχος Καὶ λάψει ἡ γλῶσσα τῶν κυνῶν σου ἀπὸ ἑκάστου τῶν ἐχθρῶν σου. Ὡς πολέμου νόμῳ πάντων ἀναιρουμένων, σχηματίσας τὸ πᾶν ἀπέδωκε τῷ
20   λόγῳ· καὶ ἀνελὼν αὐτούς φησι παραδώσει εἰς βορὰν τοῖς κυσίν.

25. Ἐθεωρήθησαν αἱ πορεῖαί σου, ὁ Θεός, αἱ πορεῖαι τοῦ Θεοῦ μου τοῦ βασιλέως τοῦ ἐν τῷ ἁγίῳ. Ὁπηνίκα ὤφθη ὁ Θεὸς τοῖς Ἰσραηλίταις ἐπὶ τοῦ ὄρους τοῦ Σινᾶ, μετὰ τὴν πρὸς αὐτοὺς διάλεξιν καὶ τὴν δοκοῦσαν ἀναχώρησιν, παρεσκεύασεν τὸν τόπον ἐφ᾽ οὗπερ ἑστάναι καὶ ὁμιλεῖν αὐτοῖς ἐδό-
25   κει φέρειν μὲν ὥσπερ ἴχνη τῶν ποδῶν· μεταβαλὼν δὲ τὸν περὶ τοὺς πόδας

3-4 Ps. CXXXIV, 11.

24ᵇ. Σύμμαχος — ποιήσας: P, fol. 214ᵛ; V. fol. 279ᵛ.
24ᵃ. Πάντας — ἀναιρεῖ: P, fol. 214ᵛ; V, fol. 280; Cord, p. 362.   10 πάντως Cord.
24ᵇ. Σαφέστερον — κυσίν: P, fol. 214ᵛ; V, fol. 280ᵛ.
25. Ὁπηνίκα — φιλανθρωπίας: P, fol. 215; V, fol. 280ᵛ; Cord, p. 362-363;
cf. Paraphrasis (p. 317-318).   24 αὐτοὺς PV.

Aᵉ 2-4 (p. 339, 8-10): Sub denuntiationis scemate per Basan promiserit Deus quod inde esset populus transiturus.   23ᵇ (p. 339, 11-16): Per medium, inquit, gentium ita eos transire faciam, ut uidear eos quasi de profundo maris, id est de midio liberare naufragii, nihil eos permitens ab hostium multitudine sustinere.   11-13 (p. 339, 18-22): Oportune ait Vt ⟨int⟩inguatur pes tuus in san-g⟨u⟩ine. Nam ducis strenui per hoc scema seruauit, qui occisorum sanguine pedes haberet aspersos.

people's return. I mean, what connection has Bashan with Babylon? Bashan is the country that Og ruled, and at that time they passed through it, as he himself mentions in another place of those coming from Egypt, "And Og, king of Bashan."[14] So he is saying, God promised to bring them out of there. *I shall bring them back in the depths of the sea.* Symmachus: "I shall cause them to turn back from the depths of the sea and through its midst," referring to the Edomites, the Moabites, and all the others they passed through, as if to say, I shall lead them through the midst of the depths of the sea, ensuring that they suffer nothing from the vast number of those attacking.

So that your foot may be dipped in blood (v. 23): I shall punish them all. *So that your foot may be dipped in blood* is an excellent image, presenting a general in pursuit committing much slaughter, and staining his own foot with blood. He used the term *so that* idiomatically to express result in place of cause: it is not that he frees them so as to slay the others; on the contrary, for the sake of their freedom he even slays the others when they resist. *Your dogs' tongues may have some of it from your foes.* Symmachus: "Your dogs' tongue will lick the blood of each of your enemies." With the slaughter of everyone by the norm of war, he represented it all figuratively in words, saying, He will do away with them and hand them over as food for dogs.

Your entries, O God, have been observed, the entries of my God the king, who is in his holy place (v. 24). When God appeared to the Israelites on Mount Sinai, after his address to them and his apparent withdrawal he caused the place on which he seemed to stand and converse with them to bear his footprints, as it were; but he changed the place under his feet | and

---

14. Cf. Pss 135:11; 136:20.

τόπον, τῷ τοῦ σαπφείρου τόπῳ πεποίηκεν ὅμοιον καὶ τῇ τοῦ οὐρανοῦ καθαρότητι παραπλήσιον. Οὕτω γὰρ γέγραπται Καὶ ἀνέβη Μωϋσῆς καὶ Ἀαρὼν καὶ Ναδὰβ καὶ Ἀβιοὺδ καὶ οἱ τῆς γερουσίας Ἰσραήλ, καὶ εἶδον τὸν τόπον οὗ εἱστήκει ὁ Θεὸς τοῦ Ἰσραήλ, καὶ τὸ ὑπὸ τοὺς πόδας αὐτοῦ ὡς ἔργον πλίνθου σαπφείρου καὶ ὥσπερ εἶδος στερεώματος τοῦ οὐρανοῦ τῇ καθαρότητι. 5
Τοῦτο οὖν φησιν Οὕτως κατηξίωσας κατελθεῖν ἐπὶ τοῦ ὄρους τοῦ Σινᾶ καὶ διαλεχθῆναι ἅπασιν ἡμῖν τοῖς παροῦσιν, ὡς καὶ τὴν πορείαν σου αὐτὴν καὶ τῶν ποδῶν τὰ ἴχνη ὠφθῆναί τε καὶ δῆλα γενέσθαι τοῖς ὁρῶσιν· ἀπόδειξιν δὲ εἶχεν τὸ λεγόμενον τῆς τοῦ Θεοῦ φιλανθρωπίας.

26ᵃ. Προέφθασαν ἄρχοντες ἐχόμενα ψαλλόντων. Σύμμαχος τὸ ἐχόμενα 10 ψαλλόντων ὀπίσω ψαλλόντων εἶπεν. Τοῦτο δή φησιν ὅτι προηγοῦντο μὲν οἱ ἄρχοντες, ἐπηκολούθουν δὲ οἱ ψάλλοντες.

26ᵇ·27. Ἐν μέσῳ νεανίδων τυμπανιστριῶν. Ἐν ἐκκλησίαις εὐλογεῖτε τὸν Θεὸν Κύριον ἐκ πηγῶν Ἰσραήλ. Περὶ τοὺς ψάλλοντας ἦσαν καὶ νεάνιδες τυμπανίζουσαι· τοῦτο δὲ γεγενῆσθαι σαφῶς ἡμᾶς ἡ θεία παιδεύει γραφή, 15 ὁπηνίκα διῆλθον μὲν οὗτοι τὴν θάλασσαν, κατεποντίσθησαν δὲ ἐπ' ὄψεσι ταῖς ἐκείνων οἱ Αἰγύπτιοι. Φησὶ γὰρ Καὶ ἔλαβεν Μαρία ἡ προφῆτις ἡ ἀδελφὴ Ἀαρὼν τὸ τύμπανον ἐν τῇ χειρὶ αὐτῆς, καὶ ἐξῆλθον πᾶσαι αἱ γυναῖκες ὀπίσω αὐτῆς μετὰ τυμπάνων καὶ χορῶν. Ἐξῆρχεν δὲ αὐτῶν Μαρία λέγουσα Ἄισωμεν τῷ Κυρίῳ, ἐνδόξως γὰρ δεδόξασται· ἵππον καὶ ἀναβάτην ἔρριψεν. Ἥιδεν 20 δὲ τὸ αὐτὸ καὶ ὁ λαός· φησὶ γὰρ Τότε ᾖσαν Μωϋσῆς καὶ υἱοὶ Ἰσραὴλ τὴν ᾠδὴν ταύτην τῷ Κυρίῳ, καὶ εἶπον λέγοντες Ἄισωμεν τῷ Κυρίῳ ἐνδόξως. Ὥστε σύμφωνον καὶ τὸ παρὰ τῷ μακαρίῳ Δαυὶδ κείμενον Ἐν ἐκκλησίαις εὐλογεῖτε τὸν Θεὸν Κύριον ἐκ πηγῶν Ἰσραήλ· ὑπὲρ τοίνυν τῶν τοσούτων καὶ τηλικούτων θαυμάτων, ὁσάκις ἂν ἐκκλησιάζητε καὶ κατ' αὐτὸ συνίητε, ὑμνεῖν 25 τὸν Θεὸν σπουδάζετε. Τὸ δὲ ἐκ πηγῶν Ἰσραήλ, ἵνα εἴπῃ Οἱ ἀπὸ τῶν

2-5 Ex. XXIV, 9-10   17-20 Ex. XV, 20-21   21-22 Ex. XV, 1.

26ᵃ. Σύμμαχος — ψάλλοντες: P, fol. 215ᵛ; V, fol. 281; Cord, p. 363.   11 ἐπίσω P
δὲ Cord   ὅτι om. PV.

26ᵇ-27. Περὶ τοὺς ψάλλοντας — ἀεί: P, fol. 215ᵛ; V, fol. 281; Cord, p. 363-364; cf.
Paraphrasis (p 318).   19 λέγουσα om. PV   25 ἐκκλησιάζεται PV   26 τῷ Θεῷ Cord.

Aᵉ 1-9 (p. 339, 26-32): Ita ut dignatus es discendere in monte Sina et omnibus nobis sermone misceri, ut ingressus tui a nobis et pedum uestigia cernerentur; qui locus secundum lectionis fidem lapidis saphiri erat similitudine et colore uestitus.   11-12 (p. 339, 33-35): Praecedebant principes et sequebatur corus sallentium.   14-19 (p. 340, 1-7): Cum sallentibus uiris erant etiam adoliscentulae timpanis personantes. *Accipit*, inquit, *Maria prophetiza soror Aaaron timpanum in manus suas, et exierunt omnes mulieres post eam cum timpanis et choris.* 24-26 (p. 340, 8-11): Pro tantorum et talium factorum beneficiis studete in honore Dei ac laudum eius uerba resonare.

made it resemble the place of sapphire, similar also to the clarity of heaven. The text, in fact, reads, "Moses and Aaron, Nadab and Abihu, and the elders of Israel went up and saw the place where the God of Israel stood. Under his feet there was a thing like a sapphire pavement and in appearance like the firmament of heaven for clarity."[15] So he is saying, You deigned to come down on Mount Sinai and speak with all of us present in such a fashion that your actual arrival and your footprints were seen and became visible to the onlookers. The description contained proof of God's lovingkindness.

At the head came rulers in the wake of singers (v. 25). Symmachus said "behind singers" for *in the wake of singers*. He means, The rulers led, and the singers followed. *In the midst of young girls playing drums. In assemblies bless the Lord God from fountains of Israel* (vv. 25–26). In the company of singers there were also young girls playing drums; the divine Scripture clearly teaches us that this happened when they passed through the sea, while the Egyptians drowned in sight of them, the text saying, "The prophet Miriam, Aaron's sister, took a drum in her hand, and all the women went out behind her with drums and with dancing. Miriam went ahead, singing, 'Let us sing to the Lord, for he has triumphed gloriously: horse and rider he has cast down.' " The people sang the same song, the text saying, "Then Moses and the children of Israel sang this song to the Lord as follows, 'Let us sing to the Lord, giving glory.' "[16] So what occurs in blessed David, *In assemblies bless the Lord God from fountains of Israel,* is consistent with that, meaning, For so many wonderful marvels, therefore, be careful to sing God's praises whenever you assemble and come together. The phrase *from fountains of Israel* means, Those of the | tribes of Israel—that is, the whole of Israel,

---

15. Exod 24:9–10.
16. Cf. Exod 15:20–21; 15:1.

φυλῶν τοῦ Ἰσραήλ, τουτέστι πᾶς ὁ Ἰσραήλ, καλῶς πηγὰς τοῦ Ἰσραήλ καλέσας τὰς ιβ΄ φυλάς, ὥσπερ τι ῥεῦμα πολὺ τῇ τοῦ Θεοῦ εὐλογίᾳ ἐκδιδόμενόν τε καὶ πληθυνόμενον καὶ διαμένον ἐν ταῖς διαδοχαῖς ἀεί.

28ᵃ. Ἐκεῖ Βενιαμεὶν νεώτερος ἐν ἐκστάσει. Καλῶς παρακελευσάμενος τὸ
5 ὑμνεῖν, ταῦτα ἐπήγαγεν ὅτι κοινὴ πάντων ἦν καὶ ἡ τότε γεγενημένη χάρις.

28ᵇ⁻ᵈ. Ἄρχοντες Ἰούδα ἡγεμόνες αὐτῶν, ἄρχοντες Ζαβουλών, ἄρχοντες Νεφθαλείμ. Ἵνα εἴπῃ πάντες ἀπὸ τοῦ κατὰ μέρος.

29ᵃ. Ἔντειλαι, ὁ Θεός, τῇ δυνάμει σου. Διηγησάμενος τοῦ Θεοῦ τὴν εὐεργεσίαν, τρέπει λοιπὸν εἰς εὐχὴν τὸν λόγον. Πρόσταξόν φησι τῇ δυνά-
10 μει σου, ὦ δέσποτα, ὡς ἐπὶ βασιλέως τῇ αὐτοῦ στρατιᾷ πρὸς τὸ ἀμύνειν κελεύοντος. Ἐπειδὴ γὰρ εἶπεν Ὁ βασιλεὺς τῶν δυνάμεων τοῦ ἀγαπητοῦ, καλῶς ἐνταῦθα τὸ Ἔντειλαι τῇ δυνάμει σου. Καὶ ἐπάγει·

29ᵇ. Δυνάμωσον, ὁ Θεός, τοῦτο ὃ κατειργάσω ἐν ἡμῖν. Τουτέστι Πρόσ-ταξον τὴν ἰσχύν σου ἐν ἡμῖν διαμεῖναι, εἰς τὸ ἰσχυρὸν καὶ βέβαιον ἡμῖν
15 παραμεῖναι τοῦτο ὅπερ ἡμῖν παρέσχες, — ἵνα εἴπῃ τὴν ἐν τοῖς τόποις κατοικίαν, — ὥστε μὴ μεταχθῆναι ἔνθεν.

30ᵃ. Ἀπὸ τοῦ ναοῦ σου καὶ ἐπὶ Ἱερουσαλήμ. Σύμμαχος Διὰ τὸν ναόν σου τὸν ἐπάνω τῆς Ἱερουσαλήμ. Παράσχου δέ φησι τοῦτο, εἰ καὶ μὴ δι᾽ ἡμᾶς οὐκ ὄντας ἀξίους, ἀλλ᾽ οὖν γε διὰ τὸ εἶναί σου τὸν ναὸν ἐν τούτῳ
20 τῷ τόπῳ καὶ ἐνταῦθα σπουδάζεσθαι τὴν σὴν θεραπείαν. Ναὸς γὰρ ἐλέγετο τότε καὶ ἡ σκηνὴ ἐν ᾗπερ ἡ κιβωτὸς τοῦ Θεοῦ κατέκειτο· δέδεικται δὲ τοῦτο παρ᾽ ἡμῶν ἐν τῷ ι΄ ψαλμῷ.

11 v. 13ᵃ 22 in ps. X, 4; supra p. 67.

2-3 cf. *Paraphrasis* (p. 318): ἵνα δείξῃ ὅτι ἑκάστη φυλὴ πηγὴν ἐμιμεῖτο βρύουσαν τὸ γένος.
• 28ᵃ. Καλῶς — χάρις: P, fol. 216; V, fol. 281ᵛ.
28ᵇ⁻ᵈ. Ἵνα — μέρος: P. fol. 216; V, fol. 281ᵛ; Cord, p. 365.
29ᵃ. Διηγησάμενος — ἐπάγει: P, fol. 216; V, fol. 282; Cord, p. 366. 12 καὶ ἐπάγει om. Cord.
29ᵇ. Τουτέστι — ἔνθεν: P, fol. 216; V, fol. 282.
30ᵃ. Σύμμαχος — ι΄ ψαλμῷ: P. fol. 216ᵛ; V, fol. 282; Cord, p. 366.

Aᵉ 1-3 (p. 340, 12-14): Fontes pro tribubus possuit, propter larga et continua inde manantis sobolis incrementa. 28ᵃ (p. 340, 24-26): Aperte omnes aut laudare Deum dicuntur, aut iubentur ut laudent. 8-11 (p. 340, 27-31): Post narrationem benefactorum Dei ad dipraecationem profetae sermo conuertitur, ut uirtutibus quarum rex dicitur percipit in suorum defensione constantiam. 18-20 (p. 340, 37-341, 3): Saltim propter templum tuum, praesta ut si nostris id est meritis non debetur, tamen quia templum tuum in hoc loco aedificatum est et cultus tui hic studia celebrantur.

nicely referring to twelve tribes as fountains of Israel, like some great flood issuing from God's blessing, expanding and ever continuing on its course. *There Benjamin, despite his youth, is in a trance* (v. 27). Having given a nice exhortation to hymn-singing, he proceeded to say that the grace that was given at that time was also meant for all in common. *Rulers of Judah, their governors, rulers of Zebulun, rulers of Naphthali*—that is, everyone individually.

Command, O God, in your might (v. 28). After recounting God's beneficence, he then directs his attention to prayer: Give orders in your power, O Lord, as in the case of a king directing his army to lend assistance. Since he had said *King of the hosts of the beloved,* he did well to say here *Command in your might.*[17] He goes on to say *Confirm, O God, what you worked among us*—that is, Give orders for your strength to abide with us, for what you gave us to continue strong and abiding among us (namely, habitation in these places) lest we be shifted from here. *From your temple in Jerusalem* (v. 29). Symmachus: "On account of your temple, which is above Jerusalem." Grant this, he is saying, even if not for our sake, unworthy as we are, but because your temple is in this place and is the site of your worship (by *temple* referring to the tabernacle in which at that time the ark of God dwelt, as was pointed out by us in Psalm 11).[18] | *Kings will offer you gifts:* while we

---

17. Theodore's point arises from reference to δυνάμεις, "hosts," in v. 12 compared with δυνάμει, "might," here.

18. Cf. comment on Ps 11:3.

30^b. Σοὶ οἴσουσι βασιλεῖς δῶρα. Ἡμῶν γάρ φησι μηδὲν χαλεπὸν ὑπομενόντων καὶ τοῦ ναοῦ ἐν τῇ συνήθει δόξῃ διαμένοντος, πολλοὶ καὶ τῶν ἐναντίων ἐκπληττόμενοί σου τὸ μέγεθος δῶρά σοι κομίσουσιν. Τοῦτο δὲ ἐπὶ πολλῶν γενόμενον φαίνεται τῶν χρόνων, καὶ πολλάκις ὁ Τύρου βασιλεὺς εἰς τὴν τοῦ ναοῦ κατασκευὴν ἐπὶ τοῦ Σολομῶντος δῆλός ἐστιν οὐκ 5 ὀλίγα δεδωκώς.

31^a. Ἐπιτίμησον τοῖς θηρίοις τοῦ δρυμοῦ. Διὰ ταῦτα ἡμῖν τε βεβαίαν παράσχου τὴν ἐνταῦθα κατοικίαν, καὶ τοὺς βουλομένους πολεμεῖν ἄπωσαι. Θηρία δὲ δρυμοῦ τοὺς πολεμοῦντας ἐκάλεσεν, εἰς παράστασιν τῆς ὠμότητος τοῦ τρόπου.

31^{b-c}. Ἡ συναγωγὴ τῶν ταύρων ἐν ταῖς δαμάλεσι τῶν λαῶν, τοῦ ἐγκλεισθῆναι τοὺς δεδοκιμασμένους τῷ ἀργυρίῳ. Σαφῶς αὐτὸ εἶπεν Σύμμαχος Συνόδῳ παμμεγεθῶν μετὰ συστροφῶν λαῶν τοῖς διαλακτίζουσι τοὺς εὐδοκήτους ὡς ἀδόκιμον ἀργύριον. Ἀποδέδοται τῷ Ἐπιτίμησον. Ἐπιτίμησον γάρ φησι τούτοις καὶ ταῖς συνόδοις τούτων τῶν ἰσχυρῶν καὶ ταῖς συστροφαῖς τῶν 15 ἄλλων, ἵνα εἴπῃ ὅτι Ἄπωσαι ἀφ᾽ ἡμῶν τοὺς ἐχθροὺς ἡμῶν καὶ ὠμοὺς ὄντας καὶ ἰσχυροὺς καὶ πολλούς, οἳ τοσοῦτον ἔχουσι καθ᾽ ἡμῶν τὸ μῖσος ὥστε ἡμᾶς σπουδάζειν ἀναιρεῖν καὶ ἀφανίζειν ὡς ἀργύριον ἀδόκιμον, — ἵνα εἴπῃ Οὐδεμίαν ἡμῶν φειδὼ ποιούμενοι, ὡς οὐδενὸς ἀξίους λόγου τιμωρεῖσθαι σπουδάζουσιν. 20

31^d. Διασκόρπισον ἔθνη τὰ τοὺς πολέμους θέλοντα. Τρόπωσαι αὐτοὺς καὶ τιμώρησαι φιλοπολέμους ὄντας. Ἔδειξε δὲ διὰ πολλῶν ἀξίους αὐτοὺς ὄντας τιμωρίας, ὅτι ὠμοὶ τὸν τρόπον, ὅτι ἰσχυροί, ὅτι πολλοί, ὅτι ἀφειδῶς κεχρημένοι, ὅτι χαίροντες τοῖς κακοῖς.

4-6 cf. II Paral. II, II Paral. IX.

30^b. Ἡμῶν — δεδωκώς: P, fol. 216^v; V, fol. 282^v. 3-5 cf. Paraphrasis (p. 319).
31^a. Διὰ ταῦτα — τρόπου: P, fol. 217; V, fol. 282^v; Vat. 1422, fol. 122^v-123 (anon.).
31^{b-c}. Σαφῶς — σπουδάζουσιν: P, fol. 217; V; fol. 282^v; Cord, p. 368.
31^d. Τρόπωσαι — κακοῖς: P, fol. 217^v; V, fol. 283; Cord, p. 368.

A^e 4-5 (p. 341, 7-8)... templi tui subibit reuerentia praecipue regem Tiri.
31^{b-c} (p. 341, 11-18): Simmachus manifestius Collectio praepotentium cum conuersatione populorum, qui proterunt bonos quasi reprobum argentum; ac si diceret Repelle a nobis inimicos nostros, crudeles multos ac fortes, ut non exclaudentur hi qui probati sunt argento.

suffer no harsh fate and the temple continues in its customary glory, many even of the adversaries will be struck by your magnificence and will bring you *gifts*. This proved to be the case many times, the king of Tyre frequently coming on the scene to make no little contribution to the building of the temple.[19]

Rebuke the wild animals of the grove (v. 30): for this reason provide us with a secure habitation here, and repel those intent on making war (by *wild animals of the grove* referring to those making war, stressing the ferocity of their behavior). *The assembly of the bulls in the calves of the peoples so as to confine those tested with silver.* Symmachus said the same thing clearly: "In an assembly of behemoths with masses of peoples for those spurning the famous like untried silver." It corresponds to *Rebuke:* Rebuke these people and their assemblies of potentates and the masses of others; as if to say, Repel from us our foes, savage and strong and numerous as they are, who have such hatred for us as to be striving to do away with us and eliminate us like untried silver; as if to say, Showing us no pity, they strive to punish us as of no account. *Scatter nations intent on war:* rout them and punish them for their love of warfare. In many ways he showed them to be worthy of punishment for being savage in manner, strong, numerous, showing no pity, rejoicing in misfortunes. |

---

19. Cf. 2 Chr 2; 9.

32ᵃ. Ἥξουσιν πρέσβεις ἐξ Αἰγύπτου. Ταῦτά σού φησι περὶ ἡμᾶς ποιοῦντος, ἀσπάζονται τὴν περὶ ἡμᾶς εἰρήνην οἱ Αἰγύπτιοι · εἰρήνης γὰρ οἱ πρέσβεις διάκονοι.

32ᵇ. Αἰθιοπία προφθάσει χεῖρα αὐτῆς τῷ Θεῷ. Βασιλέα σε ὁμολογήσει
5 καὶ δεσπότην. Τοῦτο δὲ προσωποποιήσας εἶπεν ἐκ μεταφορᾶς τῶν ἐν ταῖς εἰκόσι γραφόντων τὰς πόλεις ἤτοι τὰ ἔθνη, οἷον Περσίδα ἢ Γοτθίαν ἤ τι τοιοῦτον, ὅπως δοκοῦσι μὲν ὑποτιθέναι τὴν χεῖρα τοῖς τῶν βασιλέων ποσίν, ἐμφαίνουσι δὲ τῆς δεσποτείας τὴν ὁμολογίαν. Ταῦτα δὲ γέγονε καὶ ἐπὶ τοῦ Σολομῶντος, ὅτε πολλὰ μὲν πολλαχόθεν αὐτῷ ἀπεστέλλετο δῶρα, ἐλήλυθε
10 δὲ πρὸς αὐτὸν ἡ τῆς Αἰθιοπίας βασίλισσα πόθῳ τῆς προσούσης αὐτῷ σοφίας.

33. Αἱ βασιλεῖαι τῆς γῆς, ᾄσατε τῷ Θεῷ. Πάντες τοίνυν οἱ πανταχόθεν ὕμνους αὐτῷ ἀναπέμπετε.

34ᵃ. Ψάλατε τῷ Κυρίῳ τῷ ἐπιβεβηκότι ἐπὶ τὸν οὐρανὸν τοῦ οὐρανοῦ κατὰ
15 ἀνατολάς. Οὐρανὸν οὐρανοῦ καλεῖ τὸν ἀνώτερον, — ἐπειδὴ ὅπερ ἡμῖν οὗτος, τοῦτο ὁ ἀνώτερος. Σύμμαχος τὸ κατ' ἀνατολὰς « ἐκ πρώτης » λέγει ἀκολούθως. Εἰ γὰρ ἐπάνω τῶν οὐρανῶν, οὐκ ἂν εἶπεν ταύτην τὴν τοῦ ἡλίου ἀνατολήν · ἔνθα γὰρ τοῦτον εἶναι τὸν ἥλιον οὐ συμβαίνει, δῆλον ὡς οὐδέ ἐστι τὸ μὲν ἀνατολικόν, τὸ δὲ δυτικὸν μέρος. Ὑμνεῖτε οὖν τὸν ἐξ ἀρχῆς
20 καὶ ἀεὶ ἐπάνω ὄντα τῶν οὐρανῶν, — κατ' ἀνατολὰς εἰπὼν τὸ ἐξ ἀρχῆς καὶ τὸ ἐκ πρώτης, ἀπὸ τοῦ τῆς ἡμέρας ἀρχὴν εἶναι τοῦ ἡλίου τὴν ἀνατολὴν καὶ μὴ δύνασθαι πρὸ τῆς ἐκείνου ἀνατολῆς ἡμέραν φαίνεσθαι, ὥστε καθ' ὁμοιότητα

9-11 cf. III Reg. X   16 ss. cf. supra, p. 365, 19 ss.

32ᵃ. Ταῦτα — διάκονοι: C, fol. 322ᵛ; P, fol. 217ᵛ; V, fol. 283; Vat. 1422, fol. 123; Cord, p. 368.
32ᵇ. Βασιλέα — σοφίας: C, fol. 322ᵛ; P, fol. 217ᵛ; V, fol. 283.
33. Πάντες — ἀναπέμπετε: C, fol. 322ᵛ; P, fol. 317ᵛ; V, fol. 283.
34ᵃ. Οὐρανὸν — σημάναι: C, fol. 322ᵛ-322ʳ; P, fol. 218; V, fol. 283ᵛ.   20-22 Paraphrasis (p. 320, ult. lin. — 321, 2): τὸ δὲ κατὰ ἀνατολὰς, ἀντὶ τοῦ « ἐξ ἀρχῆς » καὶ ἐξ ἀϊδίου · τόπον γὰρ εἶπεν ἀντὶ χρόνου. Καὶ ἐπειδὴ ἀνατολή ἐστιν ἀρχὴ τῆς ἡμέρας, οὐχ εὑρίσκεται   21 τοῦ ἡλίου] τοῦ om. C.

Aᵉ 32ᵃ (p. 341, 21-23): Cum nos, inquit, cessis hostibus uindicaueris, obtabunt Egiptii nobis pace sociari.   32ᵇ (p. 341, 25-27): Regem quoque et dominum suum Ethiopia prophitebitur protentione manuum, summisione capitis, inclinatione totius corporis.   33 (p. 341, 28-30): Omnes itaque undique, laudes eius debitas personate.   20-22 (p. 342, 1-6): Ac si diceret Ab initio siue principio, et quomodo nobis oriens sol inchoat diem omnia molientem, Deum omnia praecidentem orientem uocauit; unde per similitudinem istam ostendit quod nihil sit ante Deum, sed Deus ante omnia.

Ambassadors will come from Egypt (v. 31): when he does this, the Egyptians will embrace peace with us (*ambassadors* being instruments of peace). *Ethiopia will take the lead in offering its hand to God:* it will confess you to be king and lord (speaking figuratively by analogy with those who represent in images cities and nations, like Persians, Goths, and the like, where they seem to be putting their hands under the feet of kings and declaring their confession of lordship). Now, this happened also in the time of Solomon, when many gifts were dispatched to him from many quarters, and the queen of Ethiopia came to him in search of the wisdom he possessed.[20]

Kingdoms of the earth, sing praise to God (v. 32): all of you from every quarter, then, offer him hymns of praise. *Sing to the Lord, who rides on the heaven of heaven like dawn* (v. 33). By *heaven of heaven* he refers to the higher one, since the higher one is whatever the word means to us. For *like dawn* Symmachus logically puts "at first light"; if he were above the heavens, he would not have mentioned this dawning of the sun, since where there is no sun, there is clearly no dawning or sunset, either. Sing the praises, then, of the one who from the beginning and always is above the heavens; by *like dawn* he refers to what is from the beginning and at first, since the day begins with the dawning of the sun and no day can appear before its dawning, the implication being | that is it impossible to imagine anything prior to

---

20. Cf. 1 Kgs 10.

μηδὲν δύνασθαι πρὸ τοῦ Θεοῦ νοεῖν. Σύμμαχος μὲν οὖν αὐτὸ σαφέστερον ἐδήλωσεν — οἱ δὲ Ο΄ ἐμφαντικώτερον καὶ μᾶλλον τῆς ἑβραϊκῆς καθικνούμενοι διανοίας — βουληθεὶς ἐκ παραδείγματος τὸ ἀρχαῖον τοῦ Θεοῦ σημάναι.

34ᵇ. Ἰδοὺ δώσει τῇ φωνῇ αὐτοῦ φωνὴν αἰνέσεως. Καὶ γάρ ἐστι μέγας καὶ φοβερὸς καὶ μόνῃ τῇ φωνῇ δυνάμενος τοὺς πολεμίους καταπλήττειν. 5 Φωνὴν δὲ αἰνέσεως εἶπεν τὴν φωνὴν αὐτοῦ, ὡς ὕμνων ἀξίαν διὰ τὸ μέγεθος. Ἐσχημάτισεν δὲ κἀνταῦθα ὡς ἐπὶ στρατηγοῦ φωνῇ μόνῃ καταπλήττοντος.

35ᵃ. Δότε δόξαν τῷ Θεῷ. Ἐπειδὴ τοίνυν τοιοῦτος, μὴ ἀνθίστασθε μηδὲ πολεμεῖτε, ἀλλὰ μᾶλλον αὐτὸν θαυμάσατε ὡς μέγαν καὶ παύσασθε τῆς 10 ἀκαίρου μάχης.

35ᵇ. Ἐπὶ τὸν Ἰσραὴλ ἡ μεγαλοπρέπεια αὐτοῦ. Ἐν ἡμῖν γὰρ τὸ μέγεθος αὐτοῦ δείκνυσι, τιμωρούμενος τοὺς πολεμεῖν ἡμῖν βουλομένους.

35ᶜ. Καὶ ἡ δύναμις αὐτοῦ ἐν ταῖς νεφέλαις. Ἔχει δὲ δύναμιν οὐ τῇ ἡμετέρᾳ μόνον βοηθείᾳ μετρουμένην, ἀλλὰ καὶ ὑπὲρ ἡμᾶς ἐν τῇ κτίσει φαινο- 15 μένην, — ἀπὸ γὰρ τοῦ μέρους τὸ πᾶν εἰπεῖν ἠβουλήθη, — ἢ καὶ ὅτι αὐτάρκη φόβον παρέχεται τοῦ ἀέρος ἡ πύκνωσις βροντῶν ἦχον ἀποτελοῦσα, ἀστραπῶν κατάπληξιν, ὑετοῦ φοράν, χιόνος καὶ χαλάζης βολήν.

36ᵃ. Θαυμαστὸς ὁ Θεὸς ἐν τοῖς ἁγίοις αὐτοῦ. Ἀλλ᾽ ὅμως καὶ οὕτως ὢν μέγας, αὐτάρκως ἑαυτὸν δείκνυσι φοβερὸν δι᾽ ἡμῶν. 20

34ᵇ. Καὶ γὰρ — καταπλήττοντος: C, fol. 322; P, fol. 218ᵛ; V, fol. 283ᵛ; Cord, p. 369.
35ᵃ. Ἐπειδὴ — μάχης: C, fol. 322; P, fol. 218ᵛ; V, fol. 284; Cord, p. 370.
35ᵇ. Ἐν ἡμῖν — βουλομένους: P, fol. 218ᵛ; V, fol. 284; Vat. 14e2, fol. 123 (anon.); Cord, p. 370.
35ᶜ. Ἔχει — βολήν: P, fol. 218ᵛ; V, fol. 284; Vat. 1422, fol. 123 (anon.); Cord, p. 370.   15-16 ἀλλὰ — φαινομένην om. Cord   16 ἠβουλήθη des. 1422.
36ᵃ. Ἀλλ᾽ ὅμως — ἡμῶν: P, fol. 219; V, fol. 284.

Aᵉ **34ᵇ** (p. 342, 9-15):... continuatione potentis defensionis, quo ait uocem uirtutis, ab strennua duce sumpta translatio; potentia uocis eius ac uirtutis debet multa laude celebrari, qui ita est terribilis ut audita tantum uoce multum possit hostibus timoris incutire. **35ᵇ** (p. 342, 17-18):... cum hostes nostros mirabili ultione detriuerit. 1℃-18 (p. 342, 19-25): Pro elimentis, partem pro toto, licet nūbes ferant edoneum timoris diuini testimonium uel congregatione aeris, sonitu tonitrui, coruscationis micatu, inruptione fulgorum, aspersione pluiarum, iectu niuis et grandinis. **36ᵃ** (p 342, 26-28): Non tantum per elimenta mirabilis, sed suorum etiam difensione terribilis.

God. While Symmachus indicated it more clearly, then, in his wish to imply by a comparison the antiquity of God, the Seventy did so more graphically and closer to the sense of the Hebrew. *Lo, he will give his voice a sound of praise:* he is great, fearsome, and capable of dismaying the enemy with his voice alone. By *sound of praise* he referred to his voice in being worthy of hymn-singing on account of his greatness. In this, too, he presented him as a general causing dismay by his voice alone.

Give glory to God (v. 34): since this is what he is like, then, do not resist or oppose him; rather, marvel at him in his greatness and desist from inappropriate conflict. *His magnificence is over Israel:* through us he shows his greatness, punishing those wanting to wage war on us. *And his power is on the clouds:* the power he has, far from being measured only by the help he gives us, appears also on our behalf in creation (implying the whole from the part) or also in the fact that the density of the air provokes considerable fear by producing the sound of thunder, lightning bolts, pouring rain, and falls of snow and hail. *Awesome is God in his holy ones* (v. 35): though thus great in himself, he shows himself to be quite fearsome through us. | *The God*

36ᵇ. Ὁ Θεὸς Ἰσραὴλ αὐτὸς δώσει δύναμιν καὶ κραταίωσιν τῷ λαῷ αὐτοῦ. Αὐτὸς γὰρ δεσπότης ἡμέτερος καὶ προστάτης, αὐτὸς ἡμῖν καὶ τὴν ἰσχὺν καὶ τὴν βεβαίωσιν παρέχει, καὶ διὰ τούτων αὐτάρκως ὧν ἡμῖν παρέχεται τὴν οἰκείαν ἐνδείκνυται δύναμιν.

5   36ᶜ. Εὐλογητὸς ὁ Θεός. Καὶ ἐπὶ τούτοις ἅπασιν ὕμνων καὶ εὐχαριστίας ἄξιος.

PSALMVS LXVIII

Προαγορεύων τὰ κατὰ τοὺς Μακκαβαίους διηγεῖται τῶν συμφορῶν τὸ μέγεθος, λέγων μὲν τοὺς παρὰ τῶν ἀλλοτρίων ἐπενεχθέντας αὐτοῖς πολέ-
10 μους, λέγων δὲ καὶ τὴν παρὰ τῶν ἰδίων ἐπιβουλήν, συνηθῶς μέντοι ὡς ἐξ ἐκείνων ἅπαντα λέγει τὰ κατ' αὐτούς.

2. Σῶσόν με, ὁ Θεός, ὅτι εἰσήλθοσαν ὕδατα ἕως ψυχῆς μου. Ὕδατα λέγει τὰς τῶν πολεμίων ἐφόδους, ὡς συμπνίγειν καὶ ἀναιρεῖν δυναμένας, ὡς τὸ Διήλθομεν διὰ πυρὸς καὶ ὕδατος. Τὰ κακά φησι τὰ παρὰ τῶν ἐθνῶν αὐτῆς
15 μου καθίκετο τῆς ψυχῆς.

3ᵃ. Ἐνεπάγην εἰς ὕλην βυθοῦ, καὶ οὐκ ἔστιν ὑπόστασις. Ὥσπερ ὕλην πράγματος λέγομεν τὸ πλῆθος αὐτοῦ καὶ τὰς περιστάσεις, οὕτω λέγει

14 Ps. LXV, 12ᵇ

36ᵇ. Αὐτὸς — δύναμιν: P, fol. 219; V, fol. 284; Vat. 1422, fol. 123ᵛ; Cord. p. 370-371.   2 γὰρ om. Cord   ἡμέτερος] ἡμῶν Cord.
36ᶜ. Καὶ ἐπὶ τούτοις — ἄξιος: P, fol. 219; V, fol. 284ᵛ; Vat. 1422, fol. 123ᵛ; (anon.); Cord, p. 371 (anon).
Argumentum Προαγορεύων — κατ' αὐτούς: P, fol. 219ᵛ; V, fol. 284ᵛ; Cord, p. 395-396.   8-9 L (p. 382, 4-7): Δύναται δέ, ὡς ἕτερος, καὶ Μακκαβαϊκὸς εἶναι, ὡς δείκνυσιν ἡ τῶν λεγομένων συμπάθεια καὶ τῶν συμφορῶν τὸ μέγεθος.
2. Ὕδατα — ψυχῆς: P, fol. 220; V, fol. 285; Vat. 1422, fol. 123ᵛ; Cord, p. 396.
3ᵃ. Ὥσπερ — σωτηρίας: P, fol. 220; V, fol. 285.

Aᶜ 36ᵇ (p. 342, 29-31): Non solum uindicauit, sed etiam fortes efficiet ac robustos, quos sua protectione dignabitur.   36ᶜ (p. 342, 31-343, 1): Pro his tantis ac talibus bonis amplius est celebrandus praeconis.
Argumentum ps. LXVIII (p. 343, 3-4): In tempore Machabeorum prophetali spiritu hoc carmen scribitur. Pseudo-Beda (842): Machabaeorum personis causisque conueniens optatur oratio.   12-13 (p. 343, 7-9): Familiare scripturis effusos in praedationem gentium populos aquas uocare.   16-17 (p. 343, 11-14): Augenter ad signandam emergendi dificultatem limum et quem profundum adflictiones hostium nominauit.

of Israel will give power and might to his people: he is the one who is our Lord and protector; he is the one who guarantees strength and permanence; and through what he supplies us he gives sufficient evidence of his peculiar might. *Blessed be God:* for all this he deserves praise and thanksgiving.

PSALM 69

Foretelling the situation of the Maccabees, he recounts the magnitude of the misfortunes, mentioning in one case the wars waged against them by the foreigners, and mentioning in another case also the plotting by their own people, as usual telling everything affecting them from their point of view. *Save me, O God, because waters have impinged on my soul* (v. 1). By *waters* he refers to the enemies' assaults as capable of choking and destroying him, like the expression "We passed through fire and water."[1] He is saying, The troubles from the nations reach my very soul. *I am caught in the deep mass, and there is no firm footing* (v. 2). As we refer to a thing's size and features as *mass,* so | by *deep mass* he refers to the great depths—that is, the extrem-

---

1. Ps 66:12.

ὕλην βυθοῦ τὸν μέγαν βυθόν, ἵνα εἴπῃ τῆς συμφορᾶς τὴν ἐπίτασιν. Σύμμαχος Ἐβαπτίσθην εἰς ἀπεράντους καταδύσεις · ἐμπέπτωκά φησι μεγίστοις κακοῖς, ὡς μηδὲ ὑφεστάναι δύνασθαι περὶ αὐτῆς κινδυνεύοντα τῆς σωτηρίας.

3ᵇ. Ἦλθον εἰς τὰ βάθη τῆς θαλάσσης, καὶ καταιγὶς κατεπόντισέν με. 5 Διαφόρως ταῖς τροπολογίαις χρῆται, τῶν κακῶν τὴν ἐπίτασιν σημάναι βουλόμενος, ὕδατα καὶ βυθὸν καὶ θάλασσαν καλῶν τῶν ἐναντίων τὰς ἐφόδους ὡς ἱκανὰς ἀνελεῖν. Ἐγενόμην οὖν φησιν ἐν μέσῳ τῶν κακῶν, καὶ συμφορά τις καταιγίδος δίκην κατενεχθεῖσα ἐκάλυψεν, ὡς μηδὲ ἐλπίσαι σωτηρίαν.

4ᵃ. Ἐκοπίασα κράζων, ἐβράγχιασεν ὁ λάρυξ μου. Ἀλλ᾿ ἐν μέσῳ τῶν 10 τηλικούτων κακῶν ἀνενδότως σοι προσηυχόμην.

4ᵇ. Ἐξέλιπον οἱ ὀφθαλμοί μου ἀπὸ τοῦ ἐλπίζειν με ἐπὶ τὸν Θεόν μου. Ὅλος ἤμην τεταμένος καὶ περιμένων τὴν παρά σου βοήθειαν. Καλῶς δὲ τὸ ἐξέλιπον. ἐκ μεταφορᾶς τῶν μετὰ πολλοῦ πόθου τι προσδοκώντων καὶ συντεταμένως ἀποβλεπόντων πρὸς τὰ ἐλπιζόμενα. 15

5ᵃ. Ἐπληθύνθησαν ὑπὲρ τὰς τρίχας τῆς κεφαλῆς μου οἱ μισοῦντές με δωρεάν. Ἀναριθμήτους ἔσχον τοὺς ἐχθρούς, καὶ ταῦτα ἄνευ εὐλόγου τινὸς προφάσεως τὸ κατ᾿ ἐμοῦ μῖσος ἔχοντας.

5ᵇ. Ἐκραταιώθησαν οἱ ἐχθροί μου οἱ ἐκδιώκοντές με ἀδίκως. Οἱ ἀδίκως ἐχθροί μου καὶ διώκοντές με · λέγει δὲ ὅτι μάτην καὶ ὑπὸ πολλῆς ἀδικίας 20 ἀράμενοι τὸν πρὸς ἡμᾶς πόλεμον ἔτι καὶ κατισχύουσι κρατοῦντες ἡμῶν.

3ᵇ. Διαφόρως — σωτηρίαν: P, fol. 220ᵛ; V, fol. 285ᵛ.
4ᵃ. Ἀλλ᾿ ἐν μέσῳ — προσυχόμην: P, fol. 220ᵛ; V, fol. 285ᵛ.
4ᵇ. Ὅλος — ἐλπιζόμενα: P, fol. 220ᵛ; V. fol. 285ᵛ; Cord, p. 398.   13 τεταμένος] τεταπεινωμένος Cord.
5ᵃ. Ἀναριθμήτους — ἔχοντας: P, fol. 221; V, fol. 285ᵛ; V, fol. 280ᵛ; Cord, p. 398. 18 τὸ] τοῦ Cord.
5ᵇ. Οἱ ἀδίκως — ἡμῶν: P, fol. 221; V, fol. 285.

Aᵉ 6 (p. 343, 15-16): In eundem sensum rem augentia uerba uariantur. 14-15 (p. 343, 19-21): Labore continuae expectationis, non motatione praepossiti. 5ᵃ (p. 342, 22-26): Inimicorum meorum multitudo conpraehendi numero non potest... eo magis seuientes, quo iustas in me odiorum suorum causas inuenere non possunt.

ity of the misfortune. Symmachus: "I was drowned in bottomless descents." He is saying, I fell foul of awful troubles so as to be unable to stand firm, my very survival being in danger. *I reached the depths of the sea, and a tempest overwhelmed me.* He employs a range of figures in his wish to convey the extent of the troubles, by *waters, depths,* and *sea* referring to the adversaries' assaults as sufficient to do away with him. I found myself in the midst of the troubles, he is saying, and disaster fell like some tempest and covered me so as to leave me with no hope of survival.

I was wearied with my crying; my throat was hoarse (v. 3): in the midst of such awful troubles I prayed to you unceasingly. *My eyes failed from my hoping in my God:* I was stretched to the limit, waiting for your help. *Failed* was well put, by analogy with those looking forward to something with great longing and with eyes anxiously fixed on the object of hope. *More numerous than the hairs of my head were those who hated me without cause* (v. 4): I had enemies beyond number, despite their having no reasonable grounds for hatred of me. *My foes grew strong, those who pursued me unjustly.* They were *my foes* unjustly and they were pursuing me. He means, Having no reason and motivated by deep injustice, they declared war on me and were strong enough to prevail over me. | *What I did not steal I then repaid:* He

5ᶜ. Ἃ οὐχ ἥρπαζον τότε ἀπετίννυον. Πλατύτερον εἶπεν τὸ Ἀδίκως ἐπολέμουν με καὶ ἐτιμωροῦντό με, οὐδεμίαν αἰτίαν |ἐγκλήματος ἔχοντες κατ᾽ ἐμοῦ, ἐκ μεταφορᾶς τῶν ἀδίκως ἀπαιτούντων ἃ μὴ δεδώκασιν.

6ᵃ. Ὁ Θεός, σὺ ἔγνως τὴν ἀφροσύνην μου. Εἰ γάρ τι ἥμαρτόν φησιν εἰς
5 αὐτούς, αὐτὸς ἐπίστασαι, ἀντὶ τοῦ Σύ μοι μάρτυς ὅτι μηδὲν ἔπραξα. Καλῶς
δὲ ἀφροσύνην ἐκάλεσεν τὴν ἀδικίαν, ὡς οὐκ ἂν συνετοῦ ποτε ἀδικεῖν ἑλομένου.

6ᵇ. Καὶ αἱ πλημμέλειαί μου ἀπό σου οὐκ ἀπεκρύβησαν. Εἰ δέ τι καὶ
ἥμαρτον εἰς αὐτοὺς οὐ λέληθέν᾽σε.

10 7. Μὴ αἰσχυνθείησαν ἐπ᾽ ἐμὲ οἱ ὑπομένοντές σε, Κύριε, Κύριε τῶν δυνάμεων. Μηδὲ ἐντραπείησαν ἐπ᾽ ἐμὲ οἱ ζητοῦντές σε, ὁ Θεὸς τοῦ Ἰσραήλ.
Ἐπειδὴ πολλοὺς οἱ Μακκαβαῖοι προτρεψάμενοι τῶν Ἰουδαίων μᾶλλον ἔχεσθαι τῆς εἰς Θεὸν εὐσεβείας, ὡς τευξομένους τῆς παρ᾽ αὐτοῦ βοηθείας ἀπέστησαν τοῦ συμπράττειν τοῖς λοιποῖς, ὑπομένοντας τὸν Θεὸν αὐτοὺς οὖν
15 ἐκάλεσεν ὡς τῇ ἐλπίδι τῆς παρ᾽ αὐτοῦ βοηθείας ἑλομένους μὲν αὐτοῖς συμ-
μαχεῖν, ἀποστάντας δὲ τῶν λοιπῶν, οὐκοῦν φησιν ἐπειδήπερ αὐτὸς ἐπίστασαι ὡς οὐδὲν ἥμαρτον εἰς αὐτούς, ἄνευ δὲ προφάσεως ἐγκαλοῦσι καὶ
ἀδικεῖν πειρῶνται, μὴ ποιήσῃς ἡμᾶς αἰσχυνθῆναι τοὺς τὴν σὴν ἐλπίζοντας
βοήθειαν.

20 8ᵃ. Ὅτι ἕνεκά σου ὑπήνεγκα ὀνειδισμόν. Διά σε γὰρ ὀνειδίζομαι καὶ τὸν
ζῆλον τοῦ σου νόμου.

5ᶜ. Πλατύτερον — δεδώκασιν: P, fol. 221; V, fol. 286; Cord, p. 399, sub nomine
THEODORETI.
6ᵃ. Εἰ γὰρ — ἑλομένου: P, fol. 221ᵛ; V, fol. 286; Vat. 1422, fol. 124: Cord, p. 399.
6 συνετοῦ] ἐπαινετοῦ 1422.
6ᵇ. Εἰ δέ τι — λέληθέν σε: P, fol. 221ᵛ; V, fol. 286ᵛ.
7. Ἐπειδὴ — βοήθειαν: P, fol. 222; V, fol. 286ᵛ-287: Cord, p. 401. 13-14 ἀπέστησεν τὸ PV   14 οὖν om. PV   15 ἐν τῇ Cord   16 φησιν om. PV.
8ᵃ. Διά σε — νόμου: P, fol. 222ᵛ; V, fol. 287.

Aᵉ 5ᶜ (p. 342, 30-33): Exsoluebam, per similitudinem eorum qui exigunt quod
motuo non dederunt, iniqua bella atque odia iniusta significat.   6ᵃ (p. 344,
2-6): Non effugit tuam notitiam, si quid in illis tale egi quod possit in culpam
uocari; grandis securitas bonae conscientiae Deum actuum suorum testem
facere.   7 (p. 344, 8-11): Ne subditorum fides nutaret suffundereturque, principibus obpraesis quorum ductu simulacra respuerant.   8ᵃ (p. 344, 17-18)... nomen
tuae legis emolatioque in contumiliam pudoris inpingitur.

labored the point that it was unjustly that they waged war and punished me, since they had no grounds for accusation against me (by analogy with those wrongly demanding what they did not give).

O God, you know my thoughtlessness (v. 5): you know if I committed anything against them—that is, you are my witness that I did nothing. *Thoughtlessness* was well put for injustice, since he was not aware of ever having chosen to do wrong. *And my failings are not hidden from you:* it would not have escaped your notice if I had committed any sin against them. *Do not let those who wait on you, O Lord, Lord of hosts, be put to shame on my account. Do not let those who seek you, O God of Israel, be confounded on my account* (v. 6). Since the Maccabees urged many of the Jews to show more piety toward God so that they would receive help from God and refuse to cooperate with the others, he therefore referred to them as "waiting on" God in the sense that by hope in help from him they chose to be allied with them and desert the others. So he is saying, Since you yourself are aware that I did no wrong to them, and yet without good grounds they accuse me and try to wrong me, do not cause us to be ashamed, hoping in your help as we do.

Because it is for your sake that I have borne reproach (v. 7): on your account and as a result of zeal for your law I am reproached. | *Shame has*

8ᵇ. Ἐκάλυψεν ἐντροπὴ τὸ πρόσωπόν μου. Καὶ ἀπὸ τῶν περιεχόντων κακῶν μονονουχὶ περιεκαλυψάμην τὴν ἐντροπήν, ὡς μηδὲ ἀνανεύειν τολμᾶν καὶ προσβλέπειν ἑτέροις.

9. Ἀπηλλοτριωμένος ἐγενήθην τοῖς ἀδελφοῖς μου, καὶ ξένος τοῖς υἱοῖς τῆς μητρός μου. Ἐγενόμην δὲ καὶ τῶν ἀδελφῶν μου πάντων ξένος καὶ ἀλλό- 5 τριος, — λέγει δὲ τῶν λοιπῶν Ἰουδαίων, ὧν ἀπέστη τοῖς χείροσι προθε- μένων, — ἀδελφοῖς δὲ καὶ υἱοῖς μητρὸς τὸ αὐτὸ λέγει, ὡς τὸ Καθήμενος· κατὰ τοῦ ἀδελφοῦ σου κατελάλεις, καὶ κατὰ τοῦ υἱοῦ τῆς μητρός σου ἐτί- θεις σκάνδαλον. Διὰ τί δὲ τῶν συγγενῶν καὶ τῶν ἀδελφῶν ἀλλοτριωθῆναι ἠνέσχου; 10

10ᵃ. Ὅτι ὁ ζῆλος τοῦ οἴκου σου κατέφαγέν με. Θεωρῶν γάρ σου τὸν οἶκον οὕτως ἐνυβριζόμενον καὶ βωμὸν μὲν ἐν αὐτῷ στάντα ἐπὶ τῷ τοῦ Διὸς ὀνόματι, θυσίας δὲ ἐπιτελουμένας εἰς θεραπείαν τῶν εἰδώλων, ζήλῳ καὶ ὀργῇ ληφθεὶς καὶ οὐδὲ ὁρᾶν ἐνεγκὼν ἀνεχώρησα. Μάλιστα δὲ ἁρμόττον τοῦτο τῷ Ματταθίᾳ, ὃς καὶ ἀνεῖλεν τὸν ἐπιτάττοντα σὺν τῷ θύοντι. 15

10ᵇ. Καὶ οἱ ὀνειδισμοὶ τῶν ὀνειδιζόντων σε ἐπέπεσον ἐπ᾽ ἐμέ. Τῶν μὲν καὶ χλευαζόντων τὴν εἴς σε θεραπείαν, λεγόντων δὲ προτιμοτέραν εἶναι τὴν τῶν εἰδώλων ἀκούων, οἰκεῖον ὄνειδος τὸ πρᾶγμα λογισάμενος ἠγανάκτουν· ἐμφαντικώτερον οὖν τὸ ἐπέπεσον, τῆς ἀκοῆς ὥσπερ ἐπενεχθείσης καὶ συν- τριψάσης τῇ ἀσθενείᾳ. 20

7-9 Ps. XLIX, 20   14 cf. supra p. 360-361.

8ᵇ. Καὶ ἀπὸ — ἑτέροις: P, fol. 222ᵛ; V, fol. 287; Cord. p. 402 (anon.).
9. Ἐγενόμην — ἠνέσχου: P, fol. 222ᵛ; V, fol. 287; Cord, p. 402 sub nomine ATHANASII.
10ᵃ. Θεωρῶν — θύοντι: P, fol. 222ᵛ; V, fol. 287; Vat. 1422, fol. 124 (anon.); Cord, p. 402-403, sub nomine ATHANASII.
10ᵇ. Τῶν μὲν — ἀσθενείᾳ: P, fol. 222ᵛ; V, fol. 287; Cord, p. 403 (anon.). 19 ἐνηχηθείσης Cord.

Aᵉ 8ᵇ (p. 344, 19-22): Ita coaceruata sunt in me mala, ut operient me atque contegerent adtollendaeque mihi frontis nulla libertas remaneret.   6-7 (p. 344, 27-28):... de his ludeis dicit qui a legis obseruatione discesserant.   10ᵃ (p. 344, 29-345, 4): Iniuriam, inquit, domus tuae ferre non poteram, in qua Iouis imago possita Iudei hostias immolabant. Mathathiae specialiter ista uox conuenit, qui et Iudeum sacrificantem et ministrum regis in id ipsum cogentem uno mocrone confodit.   16-18 (p. 345, 5-9): Cultus Dei oppropria et inrisiones eorum, qui dicebant praeferenda tibi idola, in proprium meum dolorem iniuriamque repotaui.

covered my face: from the troubles besetting me I was almost enveloped in shame so as not even to dare to raise my head and look others in the face. *I have become alienated from my brothers, and a stranger to my mother's sons:* I even became a stranger and a foreigner to all my brothers (referring to the other Jews, whose pernicious purposes he avoided). *Brothers* and *my mother's sons* have the same meaning, like the verse "You sat down to malign your brother, and put a stumbling block in the way of your mother's son."[2]

Why do you put up with being alienated from kith and kin? *Because zeal for your house consumed me* (v. 9): observing your house so violated and an altar in the name of Zeus standing in it, with sacrifices being performed in worship of the idols, I was seized with zeal and wrath, and I withdrew, unable to witness it. Now, this is particularly applicable to Mattathias, who even slew the man giving directions along with the one sacrificing.[3] *The reproaches of those reproaching you fell upon me:* upon hearing some people mocking the worship of you, and others claiming that the worship of the idols was to be preferred, I was distressed, taking the affair to be a personal reproach. The term *fell upon* is thus more effective, as though the report came upon him and reduced him to weakness. | *I enveloped my soul in fasting* (v. 10): I turned to

---

2. Ps 50:20.
3. Cf. 1 Macc 2:24–25. John (John 2:17) and Paul (Rom 15:3) might see both parts of this verse applicable to Jesus, but Theodore finds their application only within the Old Testament.

11ᵃ. Καὶ συνεκάλυψα ἐν νηστείᾳ τὴν ψυχήν μου. Ἐτράπην περὶ τὸ νησ-
τεύειν ὑπὲρ τῶν γιγνομένων κακῶν. Τὸ γοῦν συνεκάλυψα, ἀντὶ τοῦ ἐταπείνωσα, συνέσφιγξα — ἐκ μεταφορᾶς τῶν συγκαλυπτομένων καὶ συγκρυπτομένων.

5   11ᵇ. Καὶ ἐγενήθη εἰς ὀνειδισμοὺς ἐμοί. Καὶ ἐχλευαζόμην παρὰ τῶν ἐναντίων ἐπὶ τούτοις, ὡς εὔηθές τι καὶ ἀνωφελὲς διαπραττόμενος.

12ᵃ. Καὶ ἐθέμην τὸ ἔνδυμά μου σάκκον. Καὶ ἐπένθουν ἐπὶ τοῖς γιγνομένοις κακοῖς · ἐπὶ πένθους γὰρ ἀεὶ λαμβάνει τὸν σάκκον.

12ᵇ. Καὶ ἐγενόμην αὐτοῖς εἰς παραβολήν. Καὶ ἐπὶ τούτοις ἐχλεύαζον οἱ
10   δοκοῦντες οἰκεῖοι διηγούμενοι μὲν τὰς ἐμὰς συμφοράς, χλευάζοντες δὲ ὡς
οὐδὲν ὠφεληθέντα, οὔτε ἀπὸ τῆς νηστείας οὔτε ἀπὸ τῶν λοιπῶν.

13ᵃ. Κατ' ἐμοῦ ἠδολέσχουν οἱ καθήμενοι ἐν πύλῃ. Περὶ τὰς πύλας καὶ
τὰ ἔσω μέρη τῆς πόλεως ἔθος ἦν τὸ παλαιὸν ποιεῖσθαι τὰς συνόδους τοῖς
ἐν ταῖς πόλεσιν, — τοῦτο δὲ καὶ ἄχρι τῆς δεῦρο γίνεται ὡς ἐπὶ τὸ πολύ ·
15   περὶ γὰρ ἐκείνους τοὺς τόπους ἐξῄεσαν οἱ ταῖς κακηγορίαις μάλιστα χαίροντες. Συνιόντες οὖν φησιν ἀεί, τὰ ἐμὰ διηγοῦντο · τὸ γὰρ ἠδολέσχουν,
ἀντὶ τοῦ συνεχῶς καὶ ἀεὶ διηγοῦντο, — ἀδολεσχίαν γὰρ τὴν συνέχειαν λέγει.

13ᵇ. Καὶ εἰς ἐμὲ ἔψαλλον οἱ πίνοντες οἶνον. Τὸ γιγνόμενον εἶπεν · πίνον-
τές τε καὶ ᾄδοντές φησιν ὡς εἰκὸς ἐμὲ τῶν ᾀσμάτων εἶχον ἀφορμήν.

8 cf. supra, p. 184, 6-11   12-15 cf. in Amos V, 10 (P. G., 273 CD).

11ᵃ. Ἐτράπην — συγκρυπτομένων: P, fol. 223; V, fol. 287ᵛ; Cord, p. 404.
11ᵇ. Καὶ ἐχλευαζόμην — διαπραττόμενος: P, fol. 223; V, fol. 287ᵛ; Cord, p. 404.
6 ἀνωφελὲς] οὐκ ἐπωφελές Cord.
12ᵃ. Καὶ ἐπένθουν — σάκκον: P, fol. 223; V, fol. 287ᵛ; Cord, p. 404.
12ᵇ. Καὶ ἐπὶ τούτοις — λοιπῶν: P, fol. 223; V, fol. 287ᵛ; Cord, p. 404.
13ᵃ. Περὶ τὰς πύλας — λέγει: P, fol. 223; V, fol. 287ᵛ-288; Vat. 1422, fol. 124ᵛ;
Cord, p. 404-405.   13 ἔσω] ἐσώτερα 1422   15 κακηγορίαις] ἐωρήσεσι PV.
13ᵇ. Τὸ γιγνόμενον — ἀφορμήν: P, fol. 223; V, fol. 288; Vat. 1422, fol. 124ᵛ
(anon.); Cord, p. 405.   19 φησὶν om. PV.

Aᵉ 2-4 (p. 345, 12-13): Operui inpossuit, ut continuata indicaret et extin-
uata ieiunia.   11ᵇ (p. 343, 14-16): Cum deuotio mea profanis esset derisui
quasi res stulta et minime profutura.   12ᵇ (p. 345, 19-21): Hoc ipso uilior, quo
in me et suplicandi intensio et dilatio auxilii inridebatur.   13ᵃ (p. 345, 22-26):
Mos erat ueteribus circa portas et ciuitatis extrimas partes agitare conuenticula.
Omnis fabula de me illis nascebatur. Exercebantur autem possuit, id est continue
de me loquebantur et iugiter.   19 (p. 345, 27-28): Vt plerumque ussu euenit.

fasting over the troubles that had befallen. The term *enveloped,* at any rate, means "humbled, constrained," by analogy with what completely covers and conceals. *And it brought me reproaches:* I was mocked by the adversaries for it, as though guilty of something stupid and useless. *I took sackcloth for my clothing* (v. 11): I mourned for the troubles that had befallen (sackcloth always being worn for mourning).

And I became a byword to them: those seeming to be my friends mocked me for it, recounting my misfortunes and mocking my useless endeavors, fasting and the rest. *Those sitting at the gates gossiped about me* (v. 12). In ancient times it was the custom for those in the cities to hold meetings around the gates and the inner parts of the city, as happens even today for the most part, those enjoying gossip in particular going out to those places. So he is saying, They were forever getting together and discussing my affairs (*gossiped* meaning "discussed over and over," gossip implying repetition). *And in their cups they sang songs against me.* He reports what happened: When drinking and singing, they made me the theme of their songs. |

14ª. Ἐγὼ δὲ τῇ προσευχῇ μου πρός σε, Κύριε. Ἀλλ' οὐδέν μοι μέλει τῶν ὀνειδιζόντων, οὐδὲ ἀποστήσομαι τοῦ πρός σε βλέπειν καί σοι προσεύχεσθαι· οἶδα γὰρ ὅτι κἂν ὑπερθῇ πρὸς τὸ βραχύ, βοηθήσεις πάντως ὅτε χρησίμως αὐτὸ ποιεῖν ἐπίστασαι.

14ᵇ. Καιρὸς εὐδοκίας, ὁ Θεός. Ἀλλὰ καὶ ἐνέστησεν ὁ καιρός — αὐτάρκως 5 γὰρ πεπαιδεύμεθα — ἀπαιτῶν λοιπὸν παρά σου τὴν εἰς ἡμᾶς βοήθειαν.

14ᶜ·ᵈ. Ἐν τῷ πλήθει τοῦ ἐλέους σου ἐπάκουσόν μου, ἐν ἀληθείᾳ τῆς σωτηρίας σου. Πάλιν τῷ ἐλέῳ τὴν ἀλήθειαν ἐπισυνῆψεν. Ἐπάκουσόν μού φησι κατὰ τὴν σὴν φιλανθρωπίαν, τὴν ἀληθινὴν καὶ βεβαίαν μοι σωτηρίαν χαριζόμενος. 10

15ª. Σῶσόν με ἀπὸ πηλοῦ, ἵνα μὴ ἐνπαγῶ. Τροπικῶς δὲ πάλιν λέγει τῶν συμφορῶν τὴν ἐπίτασιν. Ἀπόσπασόν με τουτωνὶ τῶν δυσεκσπάστων κακῶν, ὥστε μὴ παντελῶς αὐτοῖς ἐναπομεῖναι.

15ᵇ. Ῥυσθείην ἐκ τῶν μισούντων με καὶ ἐκ τῶν βαθέων τῶν ὑδάτων. Προλαβὼν εἶπεν ἄνω ὕδατα, καὶ βάθος τῆς θαλάσσης, καὶ καταιγίδα, καὶ ὕλην 15 βυθοῦ. Τῶν οὖν κατεσχηκότων μέ φησι κακῶν, ἀπάλλαξον τῆς φοβερᾶς αὐτῶν ἐφόδου, τῆς ἀγρίας ἐπιβουλῆς, τοῦ χαλεποῦ πλήθους.

16. Μή με καταποντισάτω καταιγὶς ὕδατος, μηδὲ καταπιέτω με βυθός, μηδὲ συσχέτω ἐπ' ἐμὲ φρέαρ τὸ στόμα αὐτοῦ. Φρέαρ καλεῖ τὰς τῶν ἐναν-

8 cf. in ps. XXXIX, 11ᵈ (p. 251) et in ps. LVI, 4ᶜ (p. 370)   15-16 vv. 2 et 3.

14ª. Ἀλλ' οὐδέν — ἐπίστασαι: P, fol. 223ᵛ; V, fol. 288; Vat. 1422, fol. 124ᵛ (anon.).
14ᵇ. Ἀλλά — βοήθειαν: P, fol. 223ᵛ; V, fol. 288.
14ᶜ·ᵈ. Πάλιν — χαριζόμενος: P, fol. 223ᵛ; V, fol. 288; Cord, p. 406.
15ª. Τροπικῶς — ἐναπομεῖναι: P, fol. 223ᵛ; V, fol. 288; Cord, p. 406.   13 δὲ om. PV.
15ᵇ. Προλαβὼν — πλήθους: P, fol. 224; V, fol. 228ᵛ; Vat. 1422, fol. 124ᵛ.
16. Φρέαρ — ἀπαλλαγήν: P, fol. 224; V, fol. 288ᵛ; Cord, p. 407.

Aᵉ 14ª (p. 345, 29-33): Ac si diciret Mea autem oratio nulla inpeditur auxilii tarditate; nosti enim quae sit subueniendi oportunitas.   14ᶜ·ᵈ (p. 345, 34-346, 4): Iterum ueritatem misericordiae copulauit, ac si diceret Secundum tuam ueram certamque misericordiam exaudi me, ut mihi conferas ac praestes salutem.   15ª (p. 346, 5-9): Per translationem uerborum indicat mala quae patiuntur. Abstrache me, inquit, ab erumnis grauibus, a quibus sine tuo adiutorio propriis uiribus euelli non potero.   16 (p. 346, 10-15): Concludat, coartat ne fiat inposibilis euasio; puteum inimicorum insidias ac dolos uocat, ita ut uitari non possint; cui si obstruatur os, ei qui intra puteum conclusus fuerit, nullus euadendi exitus datur.

But as for me, my prayer is to you, O Lord (v. 13): but I took no notice of the mockers, nor did I stop looking to you and praying to you, aware that even if you delay somewhat, you definitely will help at the time you consider useful to do so. *An acceptable moment, O God:* the time has come, as we have been chastised sufficiently, and now I ask from you help for us. *In the abundance of your mercy hearken to me, in the truth of your salvation.* Once again he joined *truth* with *mercy.* Hearken to me, he is saying, in your lovingkindness, granting me true and abiding salvation. *Save me from the mire lest I be stuck fast* (v. 14). Again he refers in figurative fashion to the extremity of the misfortunes: Snatch me from these inescapable troubles lest I altogether remain in them. *Let me be rescued from those who hate me and from the deep waters.* He had spoken previously of *waters, depths of the sea, tempest,* and *deep mass,* so he is saying, With troubles gripping me, free me from their fearsome attack, their savage plot, the harsh mob. *Do not let the watery tempest drown me, nor the depths swallow me, nor the pit close its mouth over me* (v. 15). By *pit* he refers to the | schemes of the adversaries

τίων ἐπιβουλὰς ὅταν ὦσιν χαλεπαί, ὡς τῶν πολεμουμένων καὶ ἐπιβουλευομένων οὐδὲ διεξιέναι καὶ ἀπαλλάττεσθαι τῆς ἐπιβουλῆς δυναμένων ῥαδίως. Ἐπειδὴ τοίνυν εἰ ἐμφραγείη φρέατος στόμα, πάντη ἡ ἄνοδος τῷ κατεχομένῳ καθίσταται ἀδύνατος, μὴ ἐναπολ ηφθείην αὐτῶν φησι τοῖς κακοῖς, ὥστε
5 πάντη ἀδύνατόν μοι γενέσθαι τὴν ἐκεῖθεν ἀπαλλαγήν.

17ᵃ. Εἰσάκουσόν μου, Κύριε, ὅτι χρηστὸν τὸ ἔλεός σου. Ἄκουσον ἐν τοιούτοις ὄντος κακοῖς· καλλίστη γάρ σου ἡ φιλανθρωπία.

17ᵇ-18ᵃ. Κατὰ τὸ πλῆθος τῶν οἰκτιρμῶν σου ἐπίβλεψον ἐπ' ἐμέ. Μὴ ἀποστρέψῃς τὸ πρόσωπόν σου ἀπὸ τοῦ παιδός σου. Μόνον μὴ ἐπιμείνῃς ὀργι-
10 ζόμενος, — ἐκ μεταφορᾶς τῶν ἐν ταῖς ὀργαῖς ἀποστρεφόντων τὰ πρόσωπα.

18ᵇ. Ὅτι θλίβομαι, ταχὺ ἐπάκουσόν μου. Ὀξεῖαν παράσχου τὴν βοήθειαν διὰ τὴν κατέχουσαν θλίψιν· οὐ γὰρ ἐπιτρέπει τὰ κατέχοντα κακὰ γενέσθαι τινὰ ὑπέρθεσιν.

19ᵃ. Πρόσχες τῇ ψυχῇ μου καὶ λύτρωσαι αὐτήν. Ἄφελε τῶν κακῶν καὶ
15 ἀπάλλαξον.

19ᵇ. Ἕνεκα τῶν ἐχθρῶν μου ῥῦσαί με. Εἰ δὲ καὶ ὑπερτίθεσαι ὡς οὐκ ἀξίου ὄντος ἐμοῦ, ἀλλὰ διὰ τοὺς ἐναντίους ἀπάλλαξον.

20ᵃ·ᵇ. Σὺ γὰρ γινώσκεις τὸν ὀνειδισμόν μου, καὶ τὴν αἰσχύνην μου, καὶ τὴν ἐντροπήν μου. Οἶδας γὰρ ὅπως μοι ὀνειδίζουσιν ἀεὶ ὡς μάτην διά σε
20 τοιαῦτα πάσχοντι, ἀλλὰ καὶ ὅπως ἐπὶ τούτοις αἰσχύνομαι, οὐδὲ ἀντιβλέπειν αὐτοῖς ὀνειδίζουσι διὰ τὸ πλῆθος τῶν συμφορῶν δυναμένῳ.

1 ἐναντίων μᾶλλον Cord.
17ᵃ. Ἄκουσον — φιλανθρωπία: P, fol. 224ᵛ; V, fol. 289.
17ᵇ-18ᵃ. Μόνον — πρόσωπα: P, fol. 224ᵛ; V, fol. 289.
18ᵇ. Ὀξεῖαν — ὑπέρθεσιν: P, fol. 224ᵛ; V, fol. 289; Cord, p. 407-408.
19ᵃ. Ἄφελε — ἀπάλλαξον: P, fol. 224ᵛ; V, fol. 289.
19ᵇ. Εἰ δὲ — ἀπάλλαξον: P, fol. 224ᵛ; V, fol. 289; Cord, p. 408.
20ᵃ·ᵇ. Οἶδας — δυναμένῳ: P, fol. 225; V, fol. 289; Cord, p. 408.

Aᵉ 17ᵃ (p. 346, 16-20): Inclina aurem tuam inter aduersa possito, quoniam ut non mouearis misericordia, habes causas propriam consuetudinem atque bonitatem.   19ᵃ (p. 346, 27-28): Considera mala quae patior et malis meis terminum pone.   19ʰ (p. 346, 29-32): Etsi propriis meritis officientibus ut liberer obtinere non possim, saltim aduersariorum ad miserationem nequam te conatus inpellat.   20ᵃ (p. 346, 33-347, 8): Nosti qualiter mihi exprobret legis tuae custodia, ac dicant infructuose me sustinere quae patior, et quantum mihi tribulationes quas iugiter ferre pudoris incuttiant, ita ut deiecta in terram facie insolentias exprobrantium ferre non possum.

when they prove harsh, there being no easy way to escape and be freed from the schemes of those warring and scheming. If, then, the mouth of the pit is closed, exit for the prisoner is rendered completely impossible, and I would not be delivered from their malice, and as a result it would be altogether impossible for release from there to come to me.

Hearken to me, O Lord, because your mercy is good (v. 16): listen to me now that I am in such trouble; your lovingkindness is excellent. *In the abundance of your compassion keep your eye upon me; do not turn your face away from your servant* (vv. 16–17): only do not continue in your anger (by analogy with those who in anger turn their face away). *Because I am in distress, heed me promptly:* provide rapid assistance in view of the distress gripping me; the troubles gripping me do not brook any delay. *Give heed to my soul and redeem it* (v. 18): deliver and free me from the troubles. *On account of my enemies rescue me:* even if you delay for the reason that I am not worthy, yet on account of my enemies deliver me.

You in fact know my reproach, my shame, and my disgrace (v. 19): you know how they always taunt me for suffering such things on your account to no purpose, and also how I am ashamed at this, unable even to look them in the face when they taunt me for the great number of the misfortunes. |

20ᶜ. Ἐναντίον σου πάντες οἱ θλίβοντές με. Ὁρᾶς αὐτοὺς ἃ ποιοῦσιν.

21ᵃ. Ὀνειδισμὸν προσεδόκησεν ἡ ψυχή μου καὶ ταλαιπωρίαν. Καὶ τὰ παρ
ἐκείνων βλέπεις καὶ τὰ κατ' ἐμέ, οὐκ ἀγνοεῖς ἐν ὅσοις κακοῖς γέγονά τε καὶ
εἰμί, ὡς μηδὲ προσδοκίαν ἔχειν ἑτέραν ἢ ὀνειδισμοῦ καὶ ταλαιπωρίας· ταῦτα
γὰρ βλέπω πρὸ τῶν ὀφθαλμῶν καὶ ταῦτα φαντάζομαι.   5

21ᵇ. Καὶ ὑπέμεινα συλλυπούμενον καὶ οὐχ ὑπῆρξεν, καὶ παρακαλοῦντας
καὶ οὐχ εὗρον. Ἐζήτησα δέ τινα εὑρεῖν κοινωνοῦντά μοι τῆς λύπης καὶ παρα-
μυθούμενον τῇ κοινωνίᾳ· ἦν δὲ οὐδείς, χείρονα περὶ ἐμὲ τῶν οἰκείων τὴν
γνώμην ἐχόντων.

22. Καὶ ἔδωκαν εἰς τὸ βρῶμά μου   χολήν, καὶ εἰς τὴν δίψαν μου ἐπότι-   10
σάν με ὄξος. Ἐπειδὴ τὰ βρώματα καὶ   Quoniam cibi et po-
τὰ πόματα ἡδέα μὲν γίνεται ἐν εὐ-   tus suaues quidem fiunt in tem-
φροσύνῃ, σκληρώδη δὲ καὶ πικρὰ ἐν   pore gaudii, insuauia autem et
ταῖς λύπαις, — τοιαῦτα ἦν φησι τὰ   amara in tristitia, — talia erant,
παρ' ἐκείνων, ὡς ὑπὸ τῆς ἀθυμίας καὶ   inquit, quae ab illis fiebant, ut   15
τῆς ὀργῆς εἶναι μέν μοι ἐν τάξει τρο-   ex tristitia et ira esset quidem
φῆς τὴν χολήν, εἶναι δὲ καὶ τὸ ποτὸν   mihi in locum fellis cibus, esset
ὄξους οὐδὲν διαλλάττον, — μάλιστα   autem et potio aceto nihil diffe-
δὲ τοῦτο γίνεται ἐν ταῖς μετὰ ἀθυμίας rens, — maxime autem hoc fit in
ὀργαῖς, ὅπερ εἰκὸς ἦν πάσχειν αὐ-   iracundiis, quae cum tribulatione   20
τοὺς κατὰ τῶν οἰκείων. Ἐχρήσατο δὲ   fiunt, quod uerisimile erat pati

20ᶜ. Ὁρᾶς αὐτοὺς ἃ ποιοῦσιν: P, fol. 225; V, fol. 289.
21ᵃ. Καὶ τὰ — φαντάζομαι: P, fol. 225; V, fol. 289; Vat. 1422, fol. 125; Cord,
p. 408.
21ᵇ. Ἐζήτησα — ἐχόντων: P, fol. 225ᵛ; V, fol. 289ᵛ; Cord, p. 409.
22. Ἐπειδὴ — κηρυττομένης: P, fol. 225ᵛ; V, fol. 289ᵛ; Vat. 1422, fol. 125 (anon.).
21 οἰκείων des. 1422; cf. Paraphrasis in vv. 22 et 23 (p. 387).
Quoniam cibi — aceto praebent VIGILII Constitutum c. XXV (GUENTHER, p. 259)
et conc. Constantinopolitanum II (MANSI IX, 213; P. G., LXVI, 688-690).

Aᵉ 21ᵇ (p. 347, 19-24): Credebam ad malorum solacium leuandorum posse
proficere, si quispiam particeps tristitiae meae accederet, sed ita nullus inuentus est ut essent etiam illa quae fiebant mihi a domisticis tristiora et consulan-
tibus me.   22 (p. 347, 27-348, 8): Sicut in diebus letitiae cibus et potus de tempore quodam modo trachunt saporem, sic ad omnem amaritudinem conuertitur
quicquid animus tristis acciperit. Vssus est hoc euangelista testimonio, cum de
Domini passione loqueretur; quod quidem ad iudaicae profertur impietatis indicium, non in tempore passionis dominicae prodita, sed longue a diuina Scriptura ac multo ante praedicta; probatur ergo magis similibus aptata esse negotiis quam propria singulorum.

All those distressing you are before you: you see what they are doing. *My soul expected reproach and hardship* (v. 20): you have an eye both to their actions and to my situation, nor are you ignorant of all the troubles I suffered and now endure, with the result that I have no further expectation than of reproach and hardship; they are before my very eyes and in my imagination. *I looked for someone to grieve with, and there was none; for comforters, and I found none:* I searched for someone to share my grief with and console me with the sharing, but there was no one, my own friends having a worse attitude toward me.

They gave me bile for food, and offered me vinegar to drink for my thirst (v. 21). While food and drink prove palatable in happiness but tasteless and bitter in grief (that is what their behavior was like, he is saying, bile taking the place of nourishment for me under the influence of ill-feeling and anger, and drink being no different from vinegar), this happens in particular as a result of anger along with ill-feeling, as probably was their experience of their friends. Now, | the evangelist cited this text of the Lord; the Lord

ὁ εὐαγγελιστὴς ταύτῃ ἐπὶ τοῦ Κυρίου
τῇ μαρτυρίᾳ, καὶ αὐτὸς δὲ ὁ Κύριος
ὅτι Ὁ ζῆλος τοῦ οἴκου σου κατέφαγέν
με περὶ αὐτοῦ λέγων, καὶ ὁ μακά-
5 ριος Παῦλος περὶ τῶν Ἰουδαίων διαλεγόμενος τὸ Γενηθήτω ἡ τράπεζα
αὐτῶν καὶ τὰ ἑξῆς, καὶ πάλιν Γενηθήτω ἡ ἔπαυλις αὐτῶν ἔρημος, καίτοι
διαφόρων ὄντων τῶν πραγμάτων.
10 Οὐχ ὡς τοῦ ψαλμοῦ νῦν μὲν περὶ
τούτων εἰρημένου, αὖθις δὲ περὶ ἐκείνου καὶ πάλιν περὶ ἑτέρου, ἀλλ᾽ ἐπειδὴ
περὶ Ἰουδαίων εἴρηται τὰ πολλὰ
ἀποστάντων τοῦ Θεοῦ καὶ τοῦ νόμου
15 ἔλεγχον ἔχοντα τῆς ἐκείνων ἀγνωμοσύνης, ἀναγκαία τῶν μαρτυριῶν ἡ
χρῆσις, ὁμοῦ τε ἀπὸ τῶν πραγμάτων
λαμβανομένη — οἷον τὸ Ἔδωκαν εἰς
τὸ βρῶμά μου χολὴν καὶ εἰς τὴν δίψαν
20 μου ἐπότισάν με ὄξος — καὶ ἔλεγχον
ἔχουσα τῆς ἰουδαϊκῆς ἀγνωμοσύνης ὡς
τῇ θείᾳ γραφῇ κηρυττομένης.

eos contra suos. Vsus autem est
euangelista hoc testimonio in Domino, et ipse autem Dominus *Zelus domus tuae comedit me* de se
ipso dicens, et beatus Paulus de
Iudaeis loquens *Fiat mensa eorum* et cetera, et beatus Petrus de
Iuda *Fiat habitatio eius deserta.*
Et certe diuersis constitutis rebus, non quasi psalmo modo quidem pro his dicto, iterum autem
de illo et iterum de alio, sed quia
de Iudaeis dicta sunt plura, qui
se separauerunt de Deo et lege,
conuincentia illorum indeuotionem, necessarius est testimonio-
rum usus simul et ex rebus captus, quale est *Dederunt in esca
mea fel et in siti mea potauerunt
me aceto.*

οὐ νῦν ἀρξαμένης, ἀλλ᾽ ἄνωθεν ἐν

23ᵃ. Γενηθήτω ἡ τράπεζα αὐτῶν ἐνώπιον αὐτῶν εἰς παγίδα. *Τράπεζαν* λέγει τὴν εὐφροσύνην, *παγίδα* δὲ τὴν συμφοράν· τὴν οὖν τρυφὴν αὐτῶν
25 καὶ τὴν ἄνεσιν, ἧς ἀπολαύειν δοκοῦσιν νῦν, εἰς συμφορὰν μετάβαλε.

23ᵇ. Καὶ εἰς ἀνταπόδοσιν καὶ εἰς σκάνδαλον. Σύμμαχος Καὶ εἰς τιμωρίαν,
ὥστε συλληφθῆναι· καὶ ἀνταποδιδοὺς αὐτοῖς ὑπὲρ ὧν πράττουσιν, συμπτώ-
ματι κακῶν καὶ τιμωρίᾳ περίβαλε.

3-4 Ioh. II, 17   6-7 Rom. XI, 9 (cf. ed. K. Staab, *Pauluskommentare*, p. 155)
7-8 Act. I, 20.

23ᵃ. *Τράπεζαν — μετάβαλε*: P, fol. 226; V, fol. 290; Vat. 1422, fol. 125 (anon.)
pluribus mutatis; Cord, p. 410.
23ᵇ. *Σύμμαχος — περίβαλε*: P, fol. 226; V, fol. 290.

Aᵉ 23ᵃ (p. 348, 9-11): Iucunditatem ac requiem, quam habituros se crediderunt, in exitium illis luctumque conuerte.

personally applied to himself the verse *Zeal for your house consumed me;* blessed Paul in speaking of the Jews cited the verse *Let their table prove* and so on, and in turn *Let their fold be deserted,* though the circumstances were different. It is not as though the psalm was referring to these things, in one case to one and in another case to another; instead, since they generally refer to the Jews' abandonment of God and the law and involve an accusation of their ingratitude, the use of the citations was inevitable, arising from the circumstances, such as *They gave me bile for food, and offered me vinegar to drink,* and at the same time involving an accusation of Jewish ingratitude as not originating just now but announced by the divine Scripture from of old.[4]

Let their table prove to be a trap before them (v. 22). By *table* he refers to happiness, and by *trap* to misfortune. So he is saying, Change into misfortune the enjoyment and relief that they seem now to be enjoying. *And retribution and a stumbling block.* Symmachus: "And punishment," so that they may be caught up; wreaking retribution on them for their crimes, invest them in an incidence of misfortunes and in punishment. | *Let their eyes be*

---

4. Cf. Theodore's comment on v. 9, and also his reminder that the Pauline citation of Ps 68:18 was simply an instance of accommodation by the New Testament, not prophecy by the psalmist. Accordingly, in a similar vein here he denies such eschatological fulfillment also of vv. 21, 22, and 25 in, respectively, "the evangelist" (though no evangelist explicitly cites v. 21, implicit citation occurs in all four of them with mention of the offer of the ὄξος at the crucifixion: Matt 27:34 [some mss], 48; Mark 15:36; Luke 23:36; John 19:29), Paul in Rom 11:9, and Peter in Acts 1:20. Once again, his distinction is sound as far as it goes, convincing even Theodoret at this point, who, however, proceeds to point out that the New Testament composers recognized "the two levels of meaning of this inspired text"—an example of θεωρία, in fact, which Theodore (with his accent on Old Testament fulfillment of Old Testament texts) does not acknowledge.

24ᵃ. Σκοτισθήτωσαν οἱ ὀφθαλμοὶ αὐτῶν τοῦ μὴ βλέπειν. Τῷ πλήθει τῶν κακῶν οὕτω σκότισον αὐτούς, ὡς μηδὲ βλέπειν δύνασθαι.

24ᵇ. Καὶ τὸν νῶτον αὐτῶν διὰ παντὸς σύγκαμψον. Καὶ μὴ διαλίποις συντρίβων αὐτοὺς καὶ ἅπασαν αὐτῶν συνθλῶν τὴν ἰσχύν, — ἐκ μεταφορᾶς τῶν ταῖς κατὰ τοῦ νώτου πληγαῖς συγκαμπτόντων καὶ συντριβόντων. 5

25ᵃ. Ἔκχεον ἐπ᾽ αὐτοὺς τὴν ὀργήν σου. Πᾶν εἶδος τιμωρίας κένωσον ἐπ᾽ αὐτούς.

25ᵇ. Καὶ ὁ θυμὸς τῆς ὀργῆς σου καταλάβοι αὐτούς. Θυμὸν ὀργῆς λέγει τὴν σφοδρὰν ὀργήν, ἀπὸ τοῦ ὀξυτέρους ἡμᾶς εἶναι θυμουμένους. Μὴ διαφύγοιέν φησι τῆς τιμωρίας σου τὴν ὀξύτητα· ἐπειδὴ γὰρ ὀργὴν μᾶλλον 10 τὴν παραμονὴν λέγει τοῦ θυμοῦ, τὴν τιμωρίαν οὕτω καλεῖ ἀπὸ τοῦ παραμένοντας ταῖς ὀργαῖς ἐννοεῖν τὰς κατ᾽ ἐκείνων τιμωρίας καθ᾽ ὧν ἂν ὀργιζώμεθα.

26. Γενηθήτω ἡ ἔπαυλις αὐτῶν ἠρημωμένη, καὶ ἐν τοῖς σκηνώμασιν αὐτῶν μὴ ἔστω ὁ κατοικῶν. Τὰ οἰκητήρια αὐτῶν ἀφάνισον, ὡς μὴ εἶναι τὸν κατοι- 15 κοῦντα. Βούλεται δὲ εἰπεῖν ὅτι Πανωλέθριον τιμώρησαι ἅπαν αὐτῶν ἀφανίσας τὸ γένος, ὡς μηδὲ εἶναι τοὺς διαδεξομένους καὶ οἰκήσοντας ἐν ταῖς προσηκούσαις αὐτοῖς οἰκίαις.

27ᵃ. Ὅτι ὃν σὺ ἐπάταξας αὐτοὶ κατεδίωξαν. Οὐ γὰρ παθεῖν ἡμᾶς διὰ τὰς ἁμαρτίας ποιήσαντος εἰς ἐπιστρεφίαν πᾶσαν ἔθεντο σπουδήν, ὥστε 20

24ᵃ. Τῷ πλήθει — δύνασθαι: P, fol. 226; V, fol. 290; Cord, p. 410.   1 πλήθει δὲ Cord   2 αὐτοὺς om. PV.
24ᵇ. Καὶ μὴ — συντριβόντων: P, fol. 226; V, fol. 290; Cord, p. 410.
25ᵃ. Πᾶν εἶδος — αὐτούς: P, fol. 226 et V, fol. 290 (anon.).
25ᵇ. Θυμὸν — ὀργιζώμεθα: P, fol. 226; V, fol. 290; Cord, p. 410.   8 θυμὸν δὲ Cord.
26. Τὰ οἰκητήρια — οἰκίαις: P, fol. 226ᵛ; V, fol. 290ᵛ; Vat. 1422, fol. 125ᵛ; Cord, p. 410.   15 οἰκητήριά φησιν Cord   18 διαδεξαμένους PV.
27ᵃ. Οὐ γὰρ — εἰς ἡμᾶς: P, fol. 227; V, fol. 290ᵛ; Vat. 1422, fol. 125ᵛ (anon.).

Aᵉ 24ᵃ (p. 348, 12-13): Erumnis caecati monus lucis ignorent.   24ᵇ (p. 348, 14-18): Sic adsiduis adterantur miseris, ut omnis eorum fortitudo frangatur; a similitudine eorum dicit, qui curuantur multo honere uerberum uel labore. 25ᵃ (p. 348, 19-20): Omnis in eos uindictae species exacerbatur.   9-10 (p. 348, 21-23): Non effugiant, inquit, magnae ultionis celeritatem.   16-17 (p. 348, 24-25): Nullo successore generis relicto.   27ᵃ (p. 348, 26-349, 1): Vt erudieres, castigari pasus es delinquentes: oportunitatem offensae erga nos tuae in crudilitatem uertunt suam.

darkened so that they do not see (v. 23): bring darkness upon them with the multitude of troubles to such an extent that they will be unable even to see. *And continually bend their back:* do not stop oppressing them and crushing all their strength (by analogy with those who make people stoop and bend over with blows to the back). *Pour out your wrath upon them* (v. 24): discharge every form of punishment upon them. *And may the anger of your wrath take possession of them.* By *the anger of your wrath* he means "severe wrath," from our being so keenly angry. Let them not escape the edge of retribution, he is saying. Since he applies the term *wrath* to the persistence of anger, you see, he likewise refers to retribution on the basis of our thoughts of retribution, when we persist in wrath, against those with whom we are wrathful.

Let their fold be deserted, and let there be no inhabitant in their tents (v. 25): destroy their dwellings so that there will be no one in residence. He means, Inflict complete ruin by wiping out their whole race so that there will be no successors or residents in the houses belonging to them. *Because they personally harassed the one whom you struck* (v. 26): while you did not cause us to suffer for our sins with a view to conversion, they took great pains even to | destroy other things and treat us in a manner opposed to

καὶ ἀνελεῖν τῇ οἰκείᾳ ὠμότητι ἕτερα καὶ παρὰ τά σοι δοκοῦντα ποιοῦντες εἰς ἡμᾶς.

27ᵇ. Καὶ ἐπὶ τὸ ἄλγος τῶν τραυμάτων μου προσέθηκαν. Καὶ ἐπέκειντο πάντα δρῶντες καθ᾽ ἡμῶν, ἀεὶ ταῖς προλαμβανούσαις συμφοραῖς ἑτέρας
5 ἐπάγοντες, καὶ οὐδέποτε λήγοντες τοῦ πρὸς ἡμᾶς πολέμου.

28ᵃ. Πρόσθες ἀνομίαν ἐπὶ τὴν ἀνομίαν αὐτῶν. Ἀνομίαν καλεῖ πολλαχοῦ τὴν συμφοράν, καὶ τοῦτο ἐδείξαμεν, ὡς τὸ "Εως οὗ παρέλθῃ ἡ ἀνομία· ὥσπερ οὖν ἐπαλλήλους ἡμῖν αὐτοὶ τὰς συμφορὰς ἐπῆγον, οὕτω καὶ αὐτοῖς ἐπάλληλος ἡ παρά σου τιμωρία ἐπαχθήτω, ἀεὶ τῇ προτέρᾳ προστιθεμένης
10 ἑτέρας. Ἀνομίας δὲ αὐτὰς ἐκάλεσεν εἰκότως, ὡς ὑπὲρ ὧν ἥμαρτον εἰς αὐτοὺς μελλόντων πάσχειν δικαίως.

28ᵇ. Καὶ μὴ εἰσελθέτωσαν ἐν δικαιοσύνῃ σου. Καὶ μὴ ἀπολαύσαιεν τῶν παρά σου ἀγαθῶν, μηδὲ μετάσχοιεν ὧνπερ ἡμῖν μεταδοῦναι μέλλεις. Δικαιοσύνην δὲ αὐτὰ ἐκάλεσεν, ὡς δικαίως αὐτοῖς ὑπὲρ ὧν ἔπαθον δι᾽ αὐτὸν δίδοσ
15 θαι μέλλοντα.

29ᵃ. Ἐξαλειφθήτωσαν ἐκ βίβλου ζώντων. Ληφθεῖεν, τουτέστιν ἀποθάνοιεν. Βίβλον δὲ λέγει ζώντων, ὡς τοῦ Θεοῦ ὥσπερ ἐν βίβλῳ τινὶ τοὺς ζῶντας ἔχοντος καταλεγομένους, — ἐκ μεταφορᾶς τῶν βασιλέων τῶν ἐν ταῖς βίβλοις ἐχόντων ἐγγεγραμμένους τοὺς τῶν στρατιωτῶν καταλόγους.

20 29ᵇ. Καὶ μετὰ δικαίων μὴ γραφήτωσαν. Ἐπειδὴ τὸ παλαιὸν παρὰ τοῖς Ἰουδαίοις ἐγράφετο μάλιστα τῶν ἐναρέτων τελευτώντων τὰ ὀνόματα, — ὃ

7 Ps. LVI, 2ᵈ (p. 369-370).   20-458, 1 cf. in ps. XXXIV, 12ᵇ (p. 182-183).

27ᵇ. Καὶ ἐπέκειντο — πολέμου: P, fol. 227; V, fol. 291; Cord, p. 411 (P. G., 689).   3 ἀπέκειντο Cord   5 εἰσάγοντες Cord.
28ᵃ. Ἀνομίαν — δικαίως: P, fol. 227ᵛ; V, fol. 291; cf. Paraphrasis (p. 388).
28ᵇ. Καὶ μὴ ἀπολαύσαιεν — μέλλοντα: P, fol. 227ᵛ; V, fol. 291.
29ᵃ. Ληφθεῖεν — καταλόγους: P, fol. 227ᵛ; V, fol. 291ᵛ; Cord, p. 411 (P. G., 689).   16 ἐξαλειφθεῖεν Cord   17 εἰς τοὺς PV   18 κατηλεγμένους PV.
29ᵇ. Ἐπειδὴ — καλοῦ: P, fol. 227ᵛ; V, fol. 291ᵛ; Cord, p. 412, sub nomine Eusebii; cf. Paraphrasis, p. 388.

Aᵉ 27ᵇ (p. 349, 2-5): Non remise, sed instanter exercuerunt in nos odia, praecedentibus adflictionibus nouos cruciatus semper addentes.   6-7 (p. 349, 7-9): Iniquitatem uocat adflictionem, quam meretur iniquitas, ut est illud Donec transeat iniquitas.   12-13 (p. 349, 12-13): Non fruantur bonis quae nobis praeparas.   29ᵇ (p. 349, 14-21): Mos erat prisce consuitudinis apud Iudeos, ut scriberent nomina uirorum clarorum, non solum uiuentium sed etiam mortuorum; quod et nunc apud nos seruatur in eclesis. Cum mortui, inquit, fuerint, non sunt digni iustorum numero copulari; id est, sint ab hominibus bonis prursus alieni.

your wishes. *And added to the distress of my wounds:* by all they did they hounded us, forever adding further misfortunes to those originally besetting us, and never desisting from the war against us. *Add iniquity to their iniquity* (v. 27). By *iniquity* he refers in many places to misfortune, and we drew attention to it, as in the verse "until iniquity passes."[5] So he is saying, Just as they inflicted on us one misfortune after another, so let one punishment after another be inflicted also on them by you, constantly adding further ones to those that preceded. Now, he was right to refer to them as iniquities, for they were due to suffer justly for their sins against us. *And let them have no recourse to your righteousness:* let them not enjoy good things from you, nor share in what you intend to make available to us. These things he called *righteousness* as due to be given them justly for what they suffered on account of him.

Let them be blotted out of the book of the living (v. 28): let them be taken—that is, let them die. He speaks of a *book of the living* as though God has some living people listed in a book, by analogy with having lists of soldiers inscribed in books. *And let them not be enrolled with the righteous.* Since in olden times among the Jews the names of especially virtuous people were inscribed at their death | (a custom even now preserved with us in the

---

5. Ps 57:1.

καὶ νῦν παρ᾽ ἡμῖν ἐν ταῖς ἐκκλησίαις φυλάττεται, — καὶ τελευτήσαντές φησι μὴ ἀξιωθεῖεν τῆς τῶν δικαίων γραφῆς, τουτέστιν μηδενὸς ἡμῖν μετάσχοιεν καλοῦ.

30ᵃ. Πτωχὸς καὶ ἀλγῶν εἰμι ἐγώ. Εὐτελὴς καὶ θλιβόμενος.

30ᵇ. Ἡ σωτηρία τοῦ προσώπου σου, ὁ Θεός, ἀντελάβετό μου. Ἀλλ᾽ ἐπι- 5
φανεὶς καὶ περισώσας, ἐβοήθησας καὶ ἐρρύσω τῶν κακῶν · εἴρηται γὰρ πολλαχοῦ ὅτι πρόσωπον τὴν ἐπιφάνειαν καλεῖ.

31ᵃ. Αἰνέσω τὸ ὄνομα τοῦ Θεοῦ μου μετ᾽ ᾠδῆς. Ὑμνήσω τοίνυν αὐτὸν ὑπὲρ τούτων, μετ᾽ ᾠδῆς τὸν ὕμνον ποιούμενος.

31ᵇ. Μεγαλυνῶ αὐτὸν ἐν αἰνέσει. Καὶ καθ᾽ ὅσον οἷόν τε ἐν τοῖς ὕμνοις 10
σπουδὴν θήσομαι πᾶν ὅτι μέγα φθέγξασθαι περὶ αὐτοῦ.

32. Καὶ ἀρέσει τῷ Θεῷ ὑπὲρ μόσχον νέον κέρατα ἐκφέροντα καὶ ὁπλάς.
Ὁ δὲ ὕμνος οὗτος ὁ τῆς εὐχαριστίας ἡδύτερος αὐτῷ φανεῖται τῆς διὰ τῶν
ἀλόγων προσαγωγῆς καὶ κρείττων πάσης μόσχου προσφορᾶς, — κἂν νέος
εἶναι δοκῇ ἄρτι μέλλων ἐκφύειν τὰς ὁπλὰς καὶ τὰ κέρατα, ὡς τῶν τοιούτων 15
δοκιμωτέρων ὄντων εἰς προσαγωγήν · ἐπισημαντέον μέντοι ὅτι κἀνταῦθα προτιμᾷ τῶν θυσιῶν τὸν ὕμνον.

33ᵃ. Ἰδέτωσαν πτωχοὶ καὶ εὐφρανθήτωσαν. Πάντες οὗτοι, οἱ νῦν κοινωνοῦντές μοι τῆς πτωχείας καὶ τῆς συμφορᾶς, θεασάμενοι ταῦτα κοινωνησάτωσαν καὶ τῆς εὐφροσύνης. 20

2 ἡμῖν om. Cord.
30ᵃ. Εὐτελὴς καὶ θλιβόμενος: P, fol. 228; V, fol. 291ᵛ.
30ᵇ. Ἀλλ᾽ ἐπιφανεὶς — καλεῖ: P, fol. 228; V, fol. 291ᵛ.
31ᵃ. Ὑμνήσω — ποιούμενος: P, fol. 228; V, fol. 291ᵛ.
31ᵇ. Καὶ καθ᾽ ὅσον — περὶ αὐτοῦ: P, fol. 228; V, fol. 291ᵛ.
32. Ὁ δὲ ὕμνος — τὸν ὕμνον: P, fol. 228ᵛ; V, fol. 292; Cord, p. 413 (ἑτέρου).
14 προσφορᾶς] προσαγωγῆς PV.
33ᵃ. Πάντες — εὐφροσύνης: P, fol. 228ᵛ; V, fol. 292; Cord, p. 413.

Aᵉ 30ᵇ (p. 349, 25-26): Praesentia tua, inquit, me a malis liberauit, et adiutorio tuo contullit certam salutem. 31ᵃ (p. 349, 27-28): Laudes pro beneficiis eius debitas modolata uoce resonabo. 31ᵇ (p. 349, 29-31): Quantum mihi possibile est, dabo studium ut omnia in l⟨a⟩udes eius magna dicantur. 32 (p. 349, 32-350, 5): Quando et spiritales hostiae, id est psalmi et orationes, holochaustis praeferentur... et in meliorem uictimam, ut est uitulus, cuius primam aetatem et tenerae ungulae... pollicentur; talis enim aetatis uituli sacrificia rata faciebant. 33ᵃ (p. 350, 6): Socii merorum meorum, mutata rerum facie, gratulentur.

churches), he is saying, Let them not be thought worthy of the inscription of the righteous—that is, with none of them sharing good things with us. *I am poor and in pain* (v. 29), insignificant and oppressed. *The salvation from your person supported me, O God:* by appearing and saving me, you provided help and rescue from troubles (mention having often been made that by person he referred to appearance).

I shall praise the name of my God in song (v. 30): so I shall sing his praises for this, delivering my hymn in song. *I shall magnify him with praise:* I shall make every effort I can in the hymns that there be great exaltation of him. *It will please my God more than a young bull with horns and hooves* (v. 31): this hymn of thanksgiving will seem to him more satisfying than the offering of brute beasts and better than any sacrifice of a bull, even if it appears to be young and about to put forth *hooves and horns,* such creatures being more acceptable for sacrifice. It should be noted, of course, that here too he prefers the hymn to the sacrifices. *Let the poor see and be glad* (v. 32): let all those who are now sharing in poverty and misfortune see this and share also in happiness. | *Go in search of God, and your soul will live.* He

33^b. Ἐξζητήσατε τὸν Θεὸν καὶ ζήσεται ἡ ψυχὴ ὑμῶν. Καλῶς ἐπὶ παραίνεσιν τρέπεται, καὶ ἀπὸ παραινέσεως εἰς ὕμνον, ὡς σύνηθες αὐτῷ. Μελησάτω ὑμῖν φησι τῶν τοῦ Θεοῦ προσταγμάτων, καὶ ἔργον ὑμῖν γενέσθω ζητεῖν τὰ τῷ Θεῷ ἀρέσκοντα · οὕτω γὰρ ἀπολαύσετε τῆς παρ᾿ 5 αὐτοῦ σωτηρίας.

34. Ὅτι εἰσήκουσεν τῶν πενήτων ὁ Κύριος, καὶ τοὺς πεπεδημένους αὐτοῦ οὐκ ἐξουδένωσεν. Μέλει γὰρ αὐτῷ τῶν εὐτελῶν.

35. Αἰνεσάτωσαν αὐτὸν οἱ οὐρανοὶ καὶ ἡ γῆ, θάλασσα καὶ πάντα τὰ ἕρποντα ἐν αὐτῇ. Ἀντὶ τοῦ Τὰ πάντα αὐτὸν ὑμνείτω · ἀπὸ γὰρ τῶν κυριω-
10 τέρων τὰ κατὰ μέρος συμπεριέλαβεν.

36^{a·b}. Ὅτι ὁ Θεὸς σώσει τὴν Σιών, καὶ οἰκοδομηθήσονται αἱ πόλεις τῆς Ἰουδαίας. Οὗτος γὰρ ὁ περισώζων ἡμᾶς καὶ τὴν πόλιν ἀνιστῶν.

36^c. Καὶ κατοικήσουσιν ἐκεῖ, καὶ κληρονομήσουσιν αὐτήν. Καὶ διαμενοῦσιν οἰκοῦντες ὡς ἐν ἰδίαις κτήσεσιν, οὐκέτι ὑπὸ ἀλλοτρίοις ὄντες · τοῦτο γὰρ
15 λέγει τὸ κληρονομήσουσιν, ἐπειδὴ ἰδία τοῦ κληρονομοῦντος ἡ κτῆσις.

37^a. Καὶ τὸ σπέρμα τῶν δούλων σου καθέξουσιν αὐτήν. Καὶ οἱ ἐξ ἡμῶν διαδέξονται τὴν κτῆσιν.

37^b. Καὶ οἱ ἀγαπῶντες τὸ ὄνομά σου κατασκηνώσουσιν ἐν αὐτῇ. Καὶ διαμενοῦσιν οἰκοῦντες μάλιστα τῆς περί σε ἐλπίδος ἐπιμελόμενοι.

33^b. Καλῶς — σωτηρίας: P, fol. 228ᵛ; V, fol. 292; Cord, p. 414. 3 μελετη-
σάτω Cord.
34. Μέλει — εὐτελῶν: P, fol. 228ᵛ; V, fol. 292. 7 μέλλει PV.
35. Ἀντὶ τοῦ — συμπεριέλαβεν: P, fol. 229; V, fol. 292ᵛ.
36^{a·b}. Οὗτος — ἀνιστῶν: P, fol. 229; V, fol. 292ᵛ.
36^c. Καὶ διαμενοῦσιν — κτῆσις: P, fol. 229; V, fol. 292ᵛ.
37^a. Καὶ οἱ — κτῆσιν: P, fol. 229; V, fol. 292ᵛ.
37^b. Καὶ διαμενοῦσιν — ἐπιμελόμενοι: P, fol. 229; V, fol. 292ᵛ.

Aᵉ 1-2 (p. 350, 7-10): Oportune ad hortationem conuertitur, ad exemplum diuinae redemptionis adiutus, ac rursus ad laudem recurrit. 35 (p. 350, 14-15): Principalium rerum commemoratione uniuersa conplexus est, quibus et per quae laudari uult Deum. 36^c (p. 350, 21-22)... continua et propria eorum erit terra. 37^a (p. 350, 24-25): A posteris seruorum Dei habitabitur. 37^b (p. 350, 26-351, 1): Fruentur longua habitatione hi maxime qui eam ob studium tuae dilectionis acciperint.

does well to turn to exhortation, and from exhortation to hymn-singing, as usual with him. Let your attention be given to God's commands, he is saying, and your effort be directed to seeking what pleases God, this being the way you will enjoy salvation from him. *Because the Lord hearkened to the needy and did not scorn those of his that are in bonds* (v. 33): he is concerned for the lowly.

Let heaven and earth praise him, the sea and everything crawling in it (v. 34): that is, let everything sing his praises (including every individual item by mentioning the chief ones). *Because God will save Sion, and the cities of Judah will be built up* (v. 35): he is the one who saves us and raises up the city. *They will dwell there and receive it as an inheritance:* they will continue dwelling as though in property of their own, no longer being under foreigners (referring to it as an *inheritance,* since the property of heirs is their own). *The offspring of your servants will possess it* (v. 36): those following them will succeed to the property. *And those loving your name will dwell in it:* they will continue dwelling there, giving particular attention to hope in you. |

PSALMVS LXIX

Ἐν ταῖς παρὰ τοῦ Ἀβεσσαλὼμ συμφοραῖς ὁ μακάριος Δαυὶδ καθεστώς, προσευχόμενος ἐχρήσατο τῷ παρόντι ψαλμῷ.

2. Ὁ Θεός, εἰς τὴν βοήθειάν μου πρόσχες. Κύριε, εἰς τὸ βοηθῆσαί μοι σπεῦσον. Μελησάτω σοι τοῦ βοηθῆσαί μοι, καὶ ὀξυτάτην παράσχου τὴν 5 βοήθειαν.

3ᵃ. Αἰσχυνθήτωσαν καὶ ἐντραπήτωσαν οἱ ζητοῦντες τὴν ψυχήν μου. Οἱ ἐρῶντές μου τοῦ θανάτου μὴ ἐπιτύχοιεν τοῦ σκοποῦ.

3ᵇ. Ἀποστραφήτωσαν εἰς τὰ ὀπίσω καὶ καταισχυνθήτωσαν οἱ βουλόμενοί μοι κακά. Μὴ διανύσαιεν ἃ σπουδάζουσι κατ' ἐμοῦ. 10

4. Ἀποστραφήτωσαν παραυτίκα αἰσχυνόμενοι οἱ λέγοντές μοι Εὖγε Εὖγε. Οἱ εὐφραινόμενοί φησιν ἐπὶ ταῖς ἐμαῖς συμφοραῖς μὴ ἀπολαύσαιεν τῆς εὐφροσύνης· τὸ γὰρ εὖγε ἔθος ἐστὶ λέγειν τοῖς ἀνθρώποις, ὅταν τινὸς τύχωσι τῶν καθ' ἡδονήν. Πρέπων δὲ τῇ διαθέσει τοῦ μακαρίου Δαυὶδ ὁ ψαλμός· οὕτως γὰρ φαίνεται καὶ ἐν τῇ τῶν Βασιλειῶν ἱστορίᾳ ἑαυτοῦ ὑπε- 15 ρευξάμενος καὶ ὑπὲρ ἑαυτοῦ σπουδάσας, οὐ τοῦ Ἀβεσσαλὼμ κατευξάμενος.

13-14 cf. supra in⁻ps.⊰XXXIX, 16 (p. 252).

Ἐν ταῖς — ψαλμῷ: P, fol. 229ᵛ; V (= Vat. gr. 1683), fol. 1; Cord, p. 422. 2 παρὰ om. PV.

2. Μελησάτω — βοήθειαν: P, fol. 230; V, fol. 1; Vat. 1422, fol. 126ᵛ; Cord, p. 423 sub nomine ATHANASII.

3ᵃ. Οἱ ἐρῶντες — σκοποῦ: P, fol. 230; V. fol. 1; Cord, p. 423.

3ᵇ. Μὴ διανύσαιεν — ἐμοῦ: P, fol. 230; V, fol. 1; Cord, p. 423 sub nomine DIDYMI.

4. Οἱ εὐφραινόμενοι — κατευξάμενος: P, fol. 230; V, fol. 1; Vat. 1422, fol. 126ᵛ (anon.); Cord, p. 424. 15 γὰρ om. 1422 Cord 15-16 ὑπερευξάμενος des. 1422.

Aᵉ Argumentum ps. LXIX (p. 351, 3-6): In discrimen regni salutisque deductus, quod ei a filio Abisolon fuerat suscitatum, beatus Dauid psalmum possuit, qui uicem possit orationis inplere. 2 (p. 351, 8-9)... defensione facito, ut uelox mihi adiutorium festinus inpertias. 3ᵃ (p. 351, 10-12): Intensione frustrata, qua me molliuntur oprimere. 12-14 (p. 351, 14-18): Non potiantur fructu uoti sui qui meis dilectantur incommodis... Euge enim ad indicium laetitiae tunc consuerunt homines dicere, cum uoti sui fuerint conpotes facti.

PSALM 70

Finding himself in misfortune at the hands of Absalom, blessed David adopted the present psalm for praying. *O God, be prompt to help me; Lord, hasten to aid me* (v. 1): make it your concern to help me, and provide the quickest possible assistance. *Let those who seek my soul be put to shame and routed* (v. 2): let those longing for my death not attain their goal. *Let them be turned backwards, and let those bent on evil for me be confounded:* let them not achieve what they are intent on against me. *Let those saying to me, Aha, aha, immediately be put to flight in shame* (v. 3): let those rejoicing in my misfortunes not attain happiness (people being in the habit of saying "Aha" when they are pleased to achieve some goal). The psalm is suited to the feelings of blessed David: in the narrative of Kings he is presented this way, praying for his own welfare, not praying against Absalom's. |

5ᵃ. Ἀγαλλιάσθωσαν καὶ εὐφρανθήτωσαν ἐπί σοι πάντες οἱ ζητοῦντές σε, ὁ Θεός. Οἱ μέντοι φησὶ τῶν σῶν φροντίζοντες βουλευμάτων εὐφρανθεῖεν, θεασάμενοι τῶν ἐμῶν κακῶν τὴν λύσιν. Καλῶς δὲ ζητοῦντας εἶπεν τὸν Κύριον τοὺς τὰ αὐτοῦ φρονοῦντας, ἐπειδὴ ἅπαντες αὐτῷ συνέπραττον καὶ συνήλγουν
5 οἱ τοῦ ὀρθοῦ ἐπιμελόμενοι.

5ᵇ. Καὶ λεγέτωσαν διὰ παντὸς Μεγαλυνθήτω ὁ Θεός οἱ ἀγαπῶντες τὸ σωτήριόν σου. Καὶ οἱ τὴν παρά σού φησι στέργοντες σωτηρίαν καὶ ταύτην ζητοῦντες, ἵνα εἴπῃ οἱ πρός σε βλέποντες, θεασάμενοί σου τὴν εἰς ἡμᾶς βοήθειαν, εἰπάτωσάν τε καὶ ὁμολογησάτωσαν τὸ μέγεθος τῆς σῆς δυνάμεως.

10 6ᵃ. Ἐγὼ δὲ πτωχός εἰμι καὶ πένης· ὁ Θεός, βοήθησόν μοι. Εὐτελὴς καὶ μικρός, καὶ διὰ τοῦτο μάλιστα τῆς σῆς δεόμενος βοηθείας.

6ᵇ. Βοηθός μου καὶ ῥύστης μου εἶ σύ, Κύριε. μὴ χρονίσῃς. Σὲ δὲ καὶ βοηθὸν ἐπιγράφομαι, ὥστε δίκαιον μὴ βραδῦναι τὴν χάριν, καὶ διὰ τὰς συμφοράς, καὶ διὰ τὴν εἰς σε ἐλπίδα.

15   PSALMVS LXX

Τὰ κατὰ τὸν λαὸν προαγορεύει τὸν ἐν Βαβυλῶνι, ὅσα τε καὶ οἷα πείσονται λέγων, καὶ ὅτι εἰς διόρθωσιν αὐτοῖς ἔσται τοῦ βίου τὰ τῶν συμφορῶν. Ὑπαινίττεται δὲ ἅμα καὶ τὴν ἐπάνοδον· οὐδαμοῦ γὰρ ψιλὰς λέγει τὰς

5ᵃ. Οἱ μέντοι — ἐπιμελόμενοι: P, fol. 230ᵛ; V, fol. 1ᵛ; Vat. 1422, fol. 126ᵛ; Cord, p. 424.   2 φροντίζοντες] ἀπολαύοντες 1422 Cord   4 συνήργουν 1422 Cord.
5ᵇ. Καὶ οἱ — δυνάμεως: P, fol. 230ʳ; V, fol. 1ᵛ.
6ᵃ. Εὐτελὴς — βοηθείας: P, fol. 230ʳ; V, fol. 1ᵛ⁻²; Vat. 1422, fol. 126ᵛ (anon.); Cord, p. 425.   10 τουτέστιν εὐτ. Cord.
6ᵇ. Σὲ δὲ καὶ βοηθόν — ἐλπίδα: P, fol. 230ᵛ; V, fol. 2: Cord, p. 425.   12 δὲ καὶ] δὴ Cord.

Argumentum Τὸ κατὰ τὸν λαὸν — προσώπου: P, fol. 231; V, fol. 2ʳ⁻ᵛ; Vat. 1422, fol. 126ᵛ⁻127; Cord, p. 438-439.   16 κατά] κακὰ Cord.

Aᵉ 5ᵃ (p. 351, 19-22): In te uero exultatio eos teneat qui mea liberatione laetantur. Bene autem Deum quessise dicuntur qui... in Dauid parte consteterant.   5ᵇ (p. 351, 26-28): Qui non nisi ex te salutem expetunt, magnitudinem uirtutis tuae in nostra liberatione mirentur atque concelebrent.   6ᵇ (p. 351. 30-32): Quando et aduersis urgemur, et non nisi tuum praestulamur auxilium, equum est ut adiutor festinus occurras.   Argumentum ps LXX (p. 351, 36-352, 10): Praedicit ea quae erat populus in Babilone pasurus, et quod ad emendationem erant profutura ipsa captiuitatis aduersa. Reditum etiam populi pollicetur (= PSEUDO-BEDA 854); nec umquam ita mala uentura pronuntiat, ut non statim spem consolationis adiungat, propter infirmitatem populi, ne disperatione fractus studium emendationis abieciat. Omnia autem ex consuetudine sua personae eorum aptat, quos in huiusmodi uerba captiuitatis erat necessitas conectura.

Let all who seek you, O Lord, be glad and rejoice in you (v. 4): let those with a thought for your concerns rejoice on observing the solution to my problems. He did well to refer to those sharing his worries as "seeking the Lord,"[1] since those attentive to uprightness all cooperated with him and were distressed with him. *And let those who love your salvation say always, God be magnified!* May those groaning for salvation from you, he is saying, and seeking it—that is, those looking to you, observing your help for us—state and confess the greatness of your power. *But I am poor and needy, O God; help me* (v. 5): I am lowly and insignificant, and for this reason in particular need of your help. *You are my helper and my deliverer, Lord; do not delay:* I enlist you also as helper, so that it will not be fair to delay your grace, both because of the misfortunes and because of my hope in you.

PSALM 71

He foretells the situation of the people in Babylon, mentioning the number and kinds of things they suffered and the fact that their misfortunes would result in reform of their life. At the same time, he hints also at the return, nowhere mentioning the misfortunes as trifling | or predicting it, either, since

---

1. In fact, as Theodoret observes, other forms of the LXX have no vocative at all at this point in the text (*pace* Devreesse), unlike v. 16 in Ps 40.

συμφοράς, μὴ κἀκεῖνο προμηνύων, οὗ μάλιστα ἀναγκαία ἡ πρόρρησις Ἰουδαίοις οὖσιν ἀσθενεστέροις, ὥστε μὴ ἀπογνόντας ἀδιόρθωτον δέξασθαι τὸ κακόν, — ἅπαντα μέντοι συνηθῶς ἐκ τοῦ ἐκείνων λέγει προσώπου.

1. Ἐπί σοι, Κύριε, ἤλπισα, μὴ καταισχυνθείην εἰς τὸν αἰῶνα. Μὴ εἰς τὸ παντελὲς καταλίπῃς τοιαῦτα πάσχειν, ὥστε καὶ αἰσχύνεσθαι ἐπὶ τῇ τῶν 5 κατεχόντων θρασύτητι, ὡς οὐδὲν ἡμῶν ὠφεληθῆναι παρά σου δυνηθέντων· τοῦτο γὰρ σημαίνει τὸ Μὴ καταισχυνθείην.

2ª. Ἐν τῇ δικαιοσύνῃ σου ῥῦσαί με καὶ ἐξελοῦ με. Καλῶς πρὸς τὸ Μὴ καταισχυνθείην, Ἐν τῇ δικαιοσύνῃ σου. Εἰ γὰρ καὶ εἰς σε ἥμαρτον, ἀλλὰ τούτων με δικαίως ἀπαλλάξεις, ὅτι τε οὐδεμίαν ἔχουσι γνῶσιν τῆς σῆς θεότητος, 10 καὶ ὅτι μάτην ἡμᾶς ἀδικοῦσιν.

2ᵇ. Κλῖνον πρός με τὸ οὖς σου, καὶ σῶσόν με. Φρόντισον ἀκοῦσαί μου τῆς προσευχῆς καὶ σῶσαί με, — ἐκ μεταφορᾶς τῶν κλινόντων τὸ οὖς ὅταν τι σπουδαίως ἀκούειν βούλωνται.

3ª. Γενοῦ μοι εἰς Θεὸν ὑπερασπιστήν. Ὡς Θεὸς κατὰ τό σοι πρέπον βοή- 15 θησον, — ἐκ μεταφορᾶς τῶν ἐν τοῖς πολέμοις προτιθέντων τὰς ἀσπίδας, καὶ ταύταις σκεπόντων τοὺς κινδυνεύοντας.

3ᵇ. Καὶ εἰς τόπον ὀχυρὸν τοῦ σῶσαί με. Οὕτω φησὶ περίσωσον, μηδὲ ἐάσας παθεῖν, ὥσπερ οἱ ἐν τόποις ὀχυρωμένοις ἀσάλευτοι διαμένουσιν.

3ᶜ. Ὅτι στερέωμά μου καὶ καταφυγή μου εἶ σύ. Ἡ στερρότης, ἡ ἰσχύς, 20 ἡ ἀπὸ τῶν κακῶν καταφυγή, πάντα μου σύ.

1. Μὴ εἰς τὸ παντελὲς — μὴ καταισχυνθείην: P, fol. 231ᵛ; V, fol. 2ᵛ; Vat. 1422, fol. 127; Cord, p. 439; reliquiae mutilae apud C, fol. 325.
2ª. Καλῶς — ἀδικοῦσιν: C, fol. 325; P, fol. 231ᵛ; V, fol. 2ᵛ; Cord, p. 439 sub nomine HESYCHII. 10 θεότητος] ἰσχύος Cord.
2ᵇ. Φρόντισον — βούλωνται: C, fol. 325; P, fol. 231ᵛ et V, fol. 2ᵛ (anon.); Vat. 1422, fol. 127 (anon.); Paraphrasis, p. 428-429.
3ª. Ὡς Θεὸς — κινδυνεύοντας: C, fol. 325; P, fol. 232; V, fol. 3; Cord, p. 440. 15-16 Θεὸς — βοήθησον om. Cord.
3ᵇ. Οὕτω φησὶν — διαμένουσιν: C, fol. 325; P, fol. 232; V, fol. 3; Cord, p. 440.
3ᶜ. Ἡ στερρότης — παντά μου σύ: C, fol. 325; P, fol. 232; V, fol. 3; Paraphrasis (p. 429).

Aᵉ 1 (p. 352, 12-16): Ne longua adiutorii tui disimulatione patiaris nos tam grauia sustinere, quae nobis praeter malum tribulationis etiam monus pudoris inponant. 9-11 (p. 352, 18-20)... si ab his liberemur, qui et te nesciunt et nobis dominantur iniuste. 2ᵇ (p. 352, 22): Pro Audi dignanter atque sollicite.

the Jews in their weakness were in particular need of the prophecy, the danger being that they might despair and experience the troubles without reform. As usual, of course, he says everything from their viewpoint.

In you, O God, I hoped; let me not be put to shame forever (v. 1): do not abandon us to such a fate forever, with the result that we should be put to shame by the audacity of the captors so as to be unable to receive any benefit from you (the meaning of *let me not be put to shame*). *In your righteousness rescue me and deliver me* (v. 2). *In your righteousness* is a good reply to *let me not be put to shame:* Even if I sinned against you, he is saying, it is fair that you will free me from this, because they have no knowledge of your divinity, and because they wrong us without reason. *Incline your ear to me, and save me:* give a thought to hearing my prayer and saving me (by analogy with those inclining their ear when they are anxious to hear something). *As God, be for me a protector* (v. 3): as God, it becomes you to help me (by analogy with those brandishing their shields in time of war, and with them warding off danger). *And a secure place to save me:* save me this way without allowing me to suffer, as people in fortified places remain impregnable. *Because you are my foundation and my refuge:* stability, strength, refuge from the troubles—you are all these things for me. |

4. Ὁ Θεός μου, ῥῦσαί με ἐκ χειρὸς ἁμαρτωλοῦ, ἐκ χειρὸς παρανομοῦντος καὶ ἀδικοῦντος. Ἀπάλλαξόν με τούτων τῶν κρατούντων καὶ ὑπὸ τὴν δουλείαν ὥσπερ χειρί τινι κρατούντων, ἀνδρῶν ἁμαρτίαις πεπληρωμένων, ἀνόμων τε καὶ ἀδίκων.

5ᵃ. Ὅτι σὺ εἶ ἡ ὑπομονή μου, Κύριε. Σὲ γὰρ ἔχω προσδοκίαν καὶ ἐλπίδα τῆς βοηθείας.

5ᵇ. Κύριε, ἡ ἐλπίς μου ἐκ νεότητός μου. Οὐ νῦν πρώτως, ἀλλὰ καὶ ἄνωθεν καὶ ἐξ ἀρχῆς· δέδεικται γὰρ ἡμῖν ἐν τῷ κδ´ ψαλμῷ τὴν νεότητα ἐπὶ τοῦ λαοῦ ὅτι τὸν ἐν Αἰγύπτῳ καλεῖ καιρόν.

6ᵃ. Ἐπί σε ἐπεστηρίχθην ἀπὸ γαστρός. Πάντα στηριγμὸν καὶ βεβαίωσιν διά σου ἔσχον ἐξ οὗ καὶ γεγέννημαι, τουτέστιν ἐξότε τὸ γένος συνέστηκεν. Ὥσπερ γὰρ νεότητα λέγει τὸν καιρὸν ἐκεῖνον ἐν συγκρίσει τοῦ παρόντος, οὕτω γέννησιν τὴν ἀρχὴν τῆς συστάσεως, ἣν ἐκ τῶν πατέρων ἔσχον.

6ᵇ. Ἐκ κοιλίας μητρός μου σύ μου εἶ σκεπαστής. Ἐξότε ὅλως ἐκ τῶν πατέρων προήλθομεν. Σημαίνει δὲ διὰ τούτων ὅτι καὶ ἐν Αἰγύπτῳ ὄντων προενόει, μᾶλλον δὲ καὶ αὐτὴν τὴν εἴσοδον ἀπὸ προνοίας ἐποιήσατο· ἤδη γὰρ συνειστήκει τὸ γένος, εἰ καὶ ἐν ὀλίγοις τέως, — διέθρεψε γὰρ αὐτοὺς ἐν τοσαύτῃ λιμῷ, ἔτι καὶ τὴν κρείττονα τῆς Αἰγύπτου κατέχειν γῆν παρασκευάσας.

4. Ἀπάλλαξον — ἀδικῶν: C, fol. 325ᵛ; P, fol. 232; V, fol, 3; Cord, p. 440 sub nomine ATHANASII. 3 κρατούντων] ἀγόντων Cord.
5ᵃ. Σὲ γὰρ — βοηθείας: C, fol. 325ᵛ; P, fol. 232; V, fol. 3; Vat. 1422, fol. 127 (anon.); Cord, p. 441; Paraphrasis (p. 429).
5ᵇ. Οὐ νῦν — καιρόν: C, fol. 325ᵛ; P, fol. 232; V, fol. 3; Vat. 1422, fol. 127. 19 Paraphrasis (p. 429): Νεότητα τοῦ λαοῦ καλεῖ τὴν ἀπὸ τῶν Αἰγυπτίων ἐλευθερίαν cf. THEODORETUS (1421 B).
6ᵃ. Πάντα — ἔσχον: C, fol. 325ᵛ; P, fol. 232ᵛ; V, fol. 3ᵛ; Cord, p. 441.
6ᵇ. Ἐξότε — παρασκευάσας: C, fol. 325ᵛ; P, fol. 232ᵛ; V, fol. 3ᵛ. 15 σημαίνει des. abrupte C.

Aᶜ 5ᵃ (p. 353, 11-12): ... dum es mihi sola causa spei atque solacii. 5ᵇ (p. 353, 14-17): Non nunc primum in te sperare dedici, sed porro exordis gentis meae... in Aegipto. 11-13 (p. 353, 19-23): Sicut conparatione praesentis aeui adoliscentiam uocat Egiptiam seruitutem, sic natiuitatem illud tempus uocat quo coeperunt in patribus in Domini populum procreari. 17-19 (p. 353, 25-28)... uel eius congregationis, quae Egiptum ingressa est, appellat originem; quae ampliandae gentis seminarium fuit.

O my God, rescue me from the hand of a sinner, from the hand of a law-breaker and a wrongdoer (v. 4): free me from those with power over me, in whose thrall I am held as if by a hand, men full of sin, lawlessness, and wrongdoing. *Because you are my endurance, O Lord* (v. 5): in you I have expectation and hope of help. *O Lord, my hope from my youth:* not now for the first time, but beforehand and from the very beginning. We pointed out, in fact, that in Psalm 25 he refers by *youth* to the people at the time they were in Egypt.[1] *By you I have been supported from the womb* (v. 6): I had complete support and stability through you even from birth—that is, when the race was formed. As by *youth* he refers to the time back then by distinction from the present, so by birth he refers to the beginning of their formation, which they received from their ancestors. *From my mother's womb you have been my shelter:* from the time we issued from our ancestors. In this he suggests that God provided for them when they were in Egypt, and particularly that he also conducted their entry itself by his providence; the race was in fact already formed, even if of small numbers for the time being. He actually nourished them when they experienced such hunger, even causing them to occupy the land that was better than Egypt. |

---

1. Cf. Ps 25:7.

6ᶜ. Ἐν σοὶ ἡ ὕμνησίς μου διὰ παντός. Εἴ τίς μοι ὕμνος καὶ ἔπαινος προσγέγονέ ποτε παρὰ τῶν θαυμαζόντων με, διὰ τὰς παρά σου γέγονεν εὐεργεσίας· ταύταις γὰρ ἀεὶ περίβλεπτος ἐφάνην.

7ᵃ. Ὡσεὶ τέρας ἐγενήθην τοῖς πολλοῖς. Ἀλλ' ἰδοὺ νῦν, ὁ οὕτω πᾶσι περί- βλεπτος, ἐν τέρατός εἰμι τάξει τοῖς ἀνθρώποις, πάντων διὰ τὰς συμφορὰς 5 ὥσπερ τι σημεῖον καὶ τὸ ὁρᾶν ἀποτρεπομένων· διὰ γὰρ τὸ μέγεθος τῆς συμφορᾶς σύμβολον κακὸν ἡγοῦνταί μου τὴν θέαν.

7ᵇ. Καὶ σὺ βοηθός μου κραταιός. Καίτοι φησί σου τοῦ ἀεὶ βοηθοῦντός μου, ἰσχυροῦ τε ἄγαν ὄντος καὶ κραταιοῦ, ὥστε μὴ εἶναι ὑπονοεῖν μήποτε διὰ τὴν τοῦ βοηθοῦντός μοι ἀτονίαν, ταῦτα ὑπομένομεν. 10

8ᵃ. Πληρωθήτω τὸ στόμα μου κινέσεως. Οὐκοῦν ἐπειδὴ δύνῃ, ὕμνων πλή- ρωσόν μου τὸ στόμα. Βούλεται δὲ εἰπεῖν ὅτι Εὐεργέτησόν με· αἱ γὰρ εὐεργεσίαι εἰς ὕμνους ἐκκαλοῦνται.

8ᵇ·ᶜ. Ὅπως ὑμνήσω τὴν δόξαν σου, ὅλην τὴν ἡμέραν τὴν μεγαλοπρέπειάν σου. Ὥστε με διηνεκῶς ἐπαινεῖν καὶ θαυμάζειν ὅπως μὲν ἐπίδοξος εἶ, ὅπως 15 δὲ μεγαλοπρεπὴς καὶ θαυμάσιος.

9ᵃ. Μὴ ἀπορρίψῃς με εἰς καιρὸν γήρως. Νεότητα καλεῖ τὸν ἐν Αἰγύπτῳ καιρόν, ἐν παραθέσει τοῦ τότε καλῶς γῆρας ἐκεῖνον καλῶν τὸν χρόνον.

6ᶜ. Εἴ τίς μοι — ἐφάνην: P, fol. 233; V, fol. 4; Cord, p. 443.   1 καὶ ἔπαινος om. Cord.
7ᵃ. Ἀλλ' ἰδοὺ — θέαν: P, fol. 233; V, fol. 4; Cord, p. 444.   7 ἡγοῦντο PV.
7ᵇ. Καίτοι — ὑπομένομεν: P, fol. 233; V, fol. 4.
8ᵃ. Οὐκοῦν — ἐκκαλοῦνται: P, fol. 233·; V, fol. 4ᵛ; Cord, p. 444.
8ᵇ·ᶜ. Ὥστε — θαυμάσιος: P, fol. 233·; V, fol. 4ᵛ; Cord, p. 444, sub nomine ATHANASII.
9ᵃ. Νεότητα — προνοίας: P, fol. 233ᵛ; V, fol. 4ᵛ; Cord, p. 445.   18 τῶν τότε καλῶν Cord   17-18 Paraphrasis (p. 430, 12-14): Ὥσπερ νεότητα καλεῖ τοῦ λαοῦ τὴν ἔξοδον τὴν ἐξ Αἰγύπτου, οὕτω γῆρας καλεῖ τὴν αἰχμαλωσίαν τὴν εἰς Βαβυλῶνα atque THEODORETUS (1421 B); cf. supra in v. 5ᵇ.

Aᵉ 6ᶜ (p. 353, 29-354, 3): Quicquid umquam in laudem meam dictum est ab his qui me sunt sepe mirati, per te collocatum est, cuius effusis in me bene- ficiis factus sum omnibus ubique conspicuus.   7ᵃ (p. 354, 4-6): Multis ego, ille quondam clarus ac magnus et omnibus expetendus, nunc abhominabilis factus sum.   8-9 (p. 354, 11-14)... quorum adiutor uirtute multus et magnus est, uel certe cum singulari polleas fortitudine.   8ᵃ (p. 354, 18-21): Quia ergo plurimum potes, prosperitate concessa, in laudes tuas mea ora conuerte. 17-18 (p. 354, 24-26):... captiuitatem Babiloniam senectutis tempus appellat, qui iuuentutem dixerat Egiptiam seruitutem.

My hymn-singing was ever of you: if some praise or eulogy ever came my way from people admiring me, it was on account of kindness from you, since it was for this that I was always conspicuous. *I became like a portent to many* (v. 7): lo, now that I am thus conspicuous to everyone, I have the role of a portent to people, like a sign to all those declining to take notice on account of the misfortunes, since they consider sight of me an evil omen because of the magnitude of the calamity. *And you are my strong helper:* yet despite your always helping me in your great strength and power, lest they ever form the impression that this happens on account of the impotence of my helper, we submit to it. *Let my mouth be filled with praise* (v. 8): since you are able, fill my mouth with hymns of praise. He means, Show me your favors, for your favors prompt hymn-singing. *So that I may sing of your glory, all day long of your magnificence:* so that I shall constantly praise and admire how you are glorious, how you are magnificent and marvelous.

Do not cast me off in old age (v. 9). By *youth* he refers to the time in Egypt by comparison with the present, nicely referring to that time as *old age.* | *Do not cast me off* after such a long time and so much care, he is saying,

Μὴ νῦν μέ φησι μετὰ τοσοῦτον χρόνον καὶ τοσαύτην κηδεμονίαν ἀπορρίψῃς, καὶ ἔξω ποιήσῃς τῆς σῆς προνοίας.

9ᵇ. Ἐν τῷ ἐκλείπειν τὴν ἰσχύν μου, μὴ ἐγκαταλίπῃς με. Ἀσθενήσαντα λοιπὸν καὶ ἐνδόντα πρὸς τὰ κακὰ μὴ ἀφῇς.

5   10-11. Ὅτι εἶπαν οἱ ἐχθροί μου ἐμοί, καὶ οἱ φυλάσσοντες τὴν ψυχήν μου ἐβουλεύσαντο ἐπὶ τὸ αὐτό, λέγοντες Ὁ Θεὸς ἐγκατέλιπεν αὐτόν· καταδιώξατε καὶ καταλάβετε αὐτόν, ὅτι οὐκ ἔστιν ὁ ῥυόμενος. Ἰδοὺ γὰρ οἱ πολέμιοι καὶ πάντα ποιοῦντες καὶ παραφυλάττοντες ὅπως ἄν μου καὶ τὴν ψυχὴν ἀφέλωσιν τῷ πλήθει τῷ τῶν συμφορῶν, συνιόντες ἀεὶ κατὰ ταὐτὸ λέγουσιν
10   Οὐκέτι μέλει αὐτῶν τῷ Θεῷ, κρατήσατε, συνθλίψατε, ἀνέλετε· οὐ γάρ ἐστιν ὁ ἐπαμύνων αὐτοῖς. Βούλεται δὲ εἰπεῖν ὅτι ἀλλήλοις ἐγκελεύονται καὶ παρορμῶσιν ἀλλήλους κατ' ἐμοῦ.

12ᵃ. Ὁ Θεός μου, μὴ μακρύνῃς ἀπ' ἐμοῦ. Ἀλλ' εἰ καὶ ταῦτά φασιν ἐκεῖνοι καὶ ἔργῳ μοι ἐπιθῶνται, μὴ μακρύνῃς τοῦ πάλιν τὴν σὴν προσνεῖμαι βοήθειαν.

15   12ᵇ. Ὁ Θεός μου, εἰς τὴν βοήθειάν μου πρόσχες. Μελησάτω δέ σοι τοῦ βοηθῆσαί μου.

13ᵃ. Αἰσχυνθήτωσαν καὶ ἐκλιπέτωσαν οἱ ἐνδιαβάλλοντες τὴν ψυχήν μου. Σύμμαχος Οἱ ἀντικείμενοι τῇ ψυχῇ· ἴδιον γὰρ τῶν ἀντικειμένων τισὶ τὸ διαβάλλειν αὐτοὺς ἀεὶ πειρᾶσθαι. Ὡς οὖν πολλῶν ὄντων τῶν πολλὰ λεγόντων
20   τότε καὶ διαβαλλόντων εἰς τὸ μῖσος ἐγεῖραι κατ' αὐτῶν, τοῦτο ἔφησεν Αἰσχυνθήτωσαν οὖν οὗτοι, μηδενὸς αὐτοῖς εἰς πέρας ἀγομένου.

13ᵇ. Περιβαλέσθωσαν αἰσχύνην καὶ ἐντροπὴν οἱ ζητοῦντες τὰ κακά μοι. Οἱ πάντα πράττοντες εἰς τὸ κακοῖς με περιβαλεῖν.

9ᵇ. Ἀσθενήσαντα — ἀφῇς: P, fol. 233ᵛ; P, fol. 4ᵛ]; Cord, p. 445.
10-11. Ἰδοὺ — κατ' ἐμοῦ: P, fol. 234; V, fol. 5; Cord, p. 446.   9 πλήθει τῷ] πλήθει Cord.
12ᵃ. Ἀλλ' εἰ καὶ — βοήθειαν: P, fol. 234; V, fol. 5; Cord, p. 447.   14 μοι om Cord.
12ᵇ. Μελησάτω — βοηθῆσαί μου: P, fol. 234; V, fol. 5; Vat. 1422, fol. 127ᵛ (anon.).
13ᵃ. Σύμμαχος — ἀγομένου: P, fol. 234ᵛ; V, fol. 5ʳ·ᵛ; Cord, p. 447 sub nomine ΑΤΗΑΝΑSΙΙ.   18 Σύμμ. ἀντὶ οἱ ἐνδιαβάλλοντές φησιν Cord   τισι om. Cord.
13ᵇ. Οἱ πάντα — περιβαλεῖν: P, fol, 234ᵛ; V, fol. 5ᵛ.

Aᵉ 10-11 (p. 355, 2-3):... negantibus ergo prouidentiam tuam circa nos...
12ᵃ (p. 355, 3-5):... festinus occurre, ne sinas in longum uota nostra defferri.
18-19 (p. 355, 12-14): Proprium inimicorum signum est atque studium uiles facere quos oderunt.

nor deprive me of your providence. *When my strength fails, do not abandon me:* do not leave me to my troubles, now that I am weak and needy. *Because my foes said to me, and those protecting my soul arrived at the same decision together, saying, God has forsaken him, pursue and seize him, because there is no one to deliver him* (vv. 10–11): see the enemy doing everything and taking every precaution to do away with my soul by the vast number of the calamities; in their assemblies they are ever saying in unison, God is no longer concerned for them; lay hold of them, crush them, do away with them, for there is no one to help them. He means, They urge one another and drive one another against me.[2]

O my God, do not keep your distance from me (v. 12): even if they claim this and proceed to assault me, do not delay according me your help again. *O my God, have a thought for my help:* let it be your concern to help me. *Let those who calumniate my soul be affected with shame and want* (v. 13). Symmachus: "Those hostile to my soul," it being typical of those hostile to anyone to be ever trying to slander them. Since there were numerous people at that time making numerous statements and calumniating them so as to stir up hatred against them, he gave voice to the sentiment *Let them be affected with shame,* and none of their plans take effect. *Let those on the lookout for troubles for me be enveloped in shame and humiliation,* those doing everything to involve me in troubles. |

---

2. The inconsistency in the pronouns comes, of course, from Theodore's application to a predetermined historical situation of the people a psalm that is clearly, in Dahood's words, "a lament of an old man who prays for deliverance from personal enemies" (*Psalms,* 2:172). In his defense he could claim that he is only following the lead of his master Diodore.

932 THEODORVS MOPSVESTENVS

14ᵃ. Ἐγὼ δὲ διὰ παντὸς ἐλπιῶ ἐπί σε. Διαμένω γὰρ τῆς εἴς σε ἐλπίδος
ἐχόμενος. Καλῶς τοῦτο ὡς παρὰ τοῦ λαοῦ διὰ τὰς ἁμαρτίας ὄντος ἐν τῇ
συμφορᾷ καὶ ἐπαγγελλομένου τοῦ λοιποῦ τὴν διόρθωσιν.

14ᵇ. Καὶ προσθήσω ἐπὶ πᾶσαν τὴν αἴνεσίν σου. Καὶ οὐκ ἀποστήσομαι
τῶν εἴς σε ὕμνων ἀρκούμενος τῷ ἅπαξ ἢ δεύτερον τοῦτο ποιῆσαι, ἀλλὰ δια- 5
μένω προστιθεὶς τοῖς πρώτοις τὰ δεύτερα.

15ᵃ. Τὸ στόμα μου ἀναγγελεῖ τὴν δικαιοσύνην σου. Διατελέσω διηγούμενος ὅπως μετὰ πολλοῦ τοῦ δικαίου τοὺς ἐχθροὺς τιμωρησάμενος ἡμᾶς
περιέσωσας.

15ᵇ-16ᵃ. Ὅλην τὴν ἡμέραν τὴν σωτηρίαν σου, ὅτι οὐκ ἔγνων γραμματείας 10
εἰσελεύσομαι ἐν δυναστείᾳ Κυρίου. Σαφέστερον Σύμμαχος Οὐ γὰρ οἶδα ἐξα-
ριθμῆσαι. Κἂν γὰρ διηνεκῆ φησι τὴν εἴς σε εὐχαριστίαν ποιώμεθα, οὐδὲ
οὕτως ἀριθμῷ τὰς παρά σου χάριτας ὑποβαλεῖν δυνησόμεθα πᾶσαν ὑπερ-
βαινούσας διήγησιν. Γραμματείας δὲ εἶπεν, ἐπειδὴ τοῖς λεγομένοις τότε
γραμματεῦσιν ἔργον ἦν τὸ τοὺς ἀριθμοὺς ἔχειν καὶ τοὺς καταλόγους τῶν 15
στρατιωτῶν, καὶ ὅλως ἅπαντα πράττειν τὰ βασιλικά.

16ᵇ. Κύριε, μνησθήσομαι τῆς δικαιοσύνης σου μόνου. Καί σε ὡς δίκαιον
κριτὴν καὶ εὐεργέτην μόνον ἐπιγνώσομαι, οὐκέτι καὶ τοῖς εἰδώλοις προσκυ-
νῶν, — ὅπερ οἱ πατέρες φαίνονται πεποιηκότες μετὰ τὴν ἐξ Αἰγύπτου ἀναχώρησιν, τοῖς εἰδώλοις τὴν χάριν περιάψαντες · ἔδει γὰρ τῶν ἄνωθεν μνη- 20
μονεύσαντας ἐκ παραθέσεως ἐπαγγειλασθαι τὸ διάφορον.

14ᵃ. Διαμένω — διόρθωσιν: P, fol. 234ᵛ; V, fol. 5ᵛ.
14ᵇ. Καὶ οὐκ ἀποστήσομαι — δεύτερα: P, fol. 234ᵛ; V, fol. 5ᵛ.
15ᵃ. Διατελέσω — περιέσωσας: P, fol. 234ᵛ; V, fol. 5ᵛ.
15ᵇ-16ᵃ. Σαφέστερον — βασιλικά: P, fol. 234ᵛ; V, fol. 5ᵛ; Cord, p. 447-448.
12 ποιούμεθα PV.
16ᵇ. Καί σε — διάφορον: P, fol. 235; V, fol. 5ᵛ; Vat. 1422, fol. 128; Cord, p. 448.
21 ἐπαγγειλασθαι om. 1422.

Aᵉ 14ᵃ (p. 355, 18-23): Permanebit, inquit, haec sententia, ut de te iugiter
sperare non cessem; bene autem hoc ex persona populi possuit, qui propter peccata cladibus traditus, in reliquum promitat emendationem. 4-5 (p. 355,
26-28): ... sic ergo prima officia laudum tuarum deuota iteratione cumulabo.
15ᵃ (p. 355, 29-31): Pro a te collata laudabilis eademque iustitia, quae nos sal-
uauit et inimicos adflixit. 12-14 (p. 356, 1-7): Etiam si continua, inquit, te
gratiarum actione concelebrem, neque ita potero beneficia tua uelut in summa
redacta conprechendere ac laudibus exequare; neque enim beneficia tua possunt
numero contineri. 19-20 (p. 356, 11-13): Non ut patres mei, qui liberationis
suae ex Aegipto gratiam idolis deputabant.

I, on the contrary, shall hope in you continually (v. 14): I continue to have hope in you. This was well put on the part of the people suffering misfortune on account of sin and promising reform in the future. *And I shall add to all your praise:* far from ceasing hymn-singing to you, I shall not be content with doing it once or twice, but shall proceed to add one after another. *My mouth will announce your righteousness* (v. 15): I shall continue recounting how you saved us by punishing the foe with complete justice. *All day long your salvation. Because I am illiterate, I shall come under the power of the Lord* (vv. 15–16). Symmachus put it more clearly: "I do not know how to count." In other words, even if we offer constant thanksgiving to you, even so we shall be unable to number your favors, which beggar description. He mentioned literacy because it was the duty of those called scribes at that time to do the counting and listing of soldiers and to carry out all the royal commands.

Lord, I shall recall the righteousness of you alone: I shall acknowledge you as the only just judge and benefactor, and shall no longer bow down to the idols as well (something that the ancestors seem to have done after the departure from Egypt, attributing the favor to the idols). There was, in fact, need to recall the favors of old and to proclaim the difference by comparison. |

17. Ὁ Θεός μου, ἃ ἐδίδαξάς με ἐκ νεότητός μου, καὶ μέχρι τοῦ νῦν ἀπαγγελῶ τὰ θαυμάσιά σου. Τοὐναντίον γὰρ ἄνωθεν τὴν ἀρχὴν ποιησάμενος, ἅπαντα τὰ εἰς τὸ γένος γενόμενα διηγήσομαι.

18ᵃ. Καὶ ἕως γήρως καὶ πρεσβείου. Μόνον μή με ἀφεὶς νῦν ἐν αὐτοῖς
5 τοῖς ἐσχάτοις καὶ μετὰ τοσοῦτον χρόνον.

18ᵇ-19ᵃ. Ὁ Θεός μου, μὴ ἐγκαταλίπῃς με ἕως οὗ ἀναγγείλω τὸν βραχίονά σου τῇ γενεᾷ πάσῃ τῇ ἐρχομένῃ, τὴν δυναστείαν σου καὶ τὴν δικαιοσύνην σου. Τὸ ἕως οὐκ ἔστιν ὁριστικόν. Οὐ γὰρ τοῦτο λέγει, ὅτι μέχρι τότε μὴ ἐναφῇς, μετὰ δὲ ταῦτα ἄφες, — ἀτοπώτατον γάρ, — ἀλλ᾽ ἀντὶ τοῦ Βοή-
10 θησόν μοι καὶ νῦν συνηθῶς, ἵνα λαβὼν καιρὸν διηγήσωμαί σου τὴν ἰσχύν, εἴπω δὲ καὶ μεθ᾽ ὅσης δυνάμεως δικαιοτάτην ἡμῖν τῶν πολεμίων ἐχαρίσω τὴν ἀπαλλαγήν, ἐπὶ τῷ καὶ τῇ μεθ᾽ ἡμᾶς γενεᾷ μνήμῃ παραδοθῆναι τὰ γενόμενα διὰ τῆς ἡμετέρας διηγήσεως. Τὸ οὖν τὴν δυναστείαν σου καὶ τὴν δικαιοσύνην σου συνῆπται κατὰ τὴν διάνοιαν τῷ Ἕως οὗ ἀναγγείλω τὸν βραχίονά
15 σου, διὰ μέσου δὲ τὸ τῇ γενεᾷ πάσῃ τῇ ἐρχομένῃ, τρίτον ὂν τῇ δυνάμει τοῦ νοήματος, ἵνα ᾖ Ἕως οὗ ἀναγγείλω τὸν βραχίονά σου, τὴν δυναστείαν σου καὶ τὴν δικαιοσύνην σου τῇ γενεᾷ πάσῃ τῇ ἐρχομένῃ.

19ᵇ. Ὁ Θεός, ἕως τῶν ὑψίστων ἃ ἐποίησάς μοι μεγαλεῖα. Ἃ ἐποίησας θαυμάσιά σού φησι τοιαῦτα, ὡς μέχρι τῶν ὑψίστων εἶναι, — ἵνα εἴπῃ ὑψηλά.

20 19ᶜ. Ὁ Θεός, τίς ὅμοιός σοι; Οὐδεὶς γάρ σοι παραπλήσιος.

10 cf. Ps. LXXIV, 3.

17. Τοὐναντίον — διηγήσομαι: P, fol. 235ᵛ; V, fol. 6.
18ᵃ. Μόνον — χρόνον: P, fol. 235ᵛ; V, fol. 6.
18ᵇ-19ᵃ. Τὸ ἕως — ἐρχομένῃ: P, fol. 235ᵛ; V, fol. 6ᵛ; Cord, p. 449.   9-12 ἀντὶ τοῦ — ἀπαλλαγήν affert Paraphrasis (p. 432).   15-16 τρίτον — νοήματος om. Cord.
19ᵇ. Ἃ ἐποίησας — ὑψηλά: P, fol. 236; V, fol. 6ᵛ; Vat. 1422, fol. 128.
19ᶜ. Οὐδεὶς γάρ σοι παραπλήσιος: P, fol. 236; V, fol. 6ᵛ.

Aᵉ 17 (p. 356, 17-19)… omnia quae genti nostrae praestitisti, retro petens memoria laude celebrabo.   8-13 (p. 356, 21-32): Donec non est aduerbium finiti temporis, sed continui. Neque enim tamdiu se non relinqui rogabat donec adnuntiaret potentiam, ut uideretur uelle deseri postquam narrasset, sed donec pro « ut » possuit, ut sit sensus: Adiuua me etiam nunc ut, sicut beneficia iuuentutis, ita et senectute laetus enumerem; ut ego laudationem continuo, sic tu benefacta tua in senectam usque perpetua.   19ᵇ (p. 353, 35-357, 1): Tam magna sunt opera tua, ut laudibus in sublime tollantur.   19ᶜ (p. 357, 1-4): Ne longuo quidem interuallo est aliquis tuae gloriae conparandus.

O my God, your marvels you taught me from my youth, and to this day I shall announce them (v. 17): by contrast with the past, I have made a beginning and shall recount all the deeds performed for our race. *And to my mature years and old age* (v. 18): only do not neglect me now at the very end and after so long a time. *O my God, do not abandon me until I proclaim your strength to every generation to come, your power and your righteousness* (vv. 18–19). The word *until* is not definitive: he does not mean, Do not neglect me then, but afterwards ignore me, which would be absurd; instead, Help me now as always so that I may have the opportunity to recount your strength, and describe also how much power you showed in granting us a most just deliverance from the enemy, by transmitting the deeds to the memory of the generation after us as well through our narration. So the phrase *your power and your righteousness* is linked in meaning with the phrase *until I proclaim your strength,* while in the middle comes the phrase *to every generation to come,* being the third item in the force of the expression, so that it reads *Until I proclaim your strength, your power and your righteousness to every generation to come.*

O God, to the heights, which you made as mighty works for me: the marvels *you made* are so great as to reach *to the heights*—in other words, lofty. *O God, who is like you?* No one is comparable to you. | *How many*

20. Ὅσας ἔδειξάς μοι θλίψεις πολλὰς καὶ κακάς, καὶ ἐπιστρέψας ἐζωοποίησά; με. Ἀλλ᾽ οὐκ ἀφῆκας πάσχειν ἀεί· μεταβαλόμενος γὰρ ἐρρύσω τῶν θανάτων καὶ τῶν κινδύνων, — ἐκ μεταφορᾶς τῶν ὁδόν τινα ποιουμένων, εἶτα, ὅταν μεταμεληθῶσιν, ἐπιστρεφόντων.

21ᵃ. Καὶ ἐκ τῶν ἀβύσσων τῆς γῆς πάλιν ἀνήγαγές με. Καὶ μονονουχὶ 5 ἐν τῷ βαθυτέρῳ τῆς γῆς γενομένους καὶ καταποθέντας, ὅσον ἀπὸ τοῦ πλήθους τῶν κινδύνων ἐξέσπασας.

21ᵇ. Ἐπλεόνασας ἐπ᾽ ἐμὲ τὴν μεγαλωσύνην σου. Πολλήν σου τὴν δύναμιν ἐπεδείξω τῆς εἰς ἡμᾶς εὐεργεσίας.

21ᶜ. Καὶ ἐπιστρέψας παρεκάλεσάς με, καὶ ἐκ τῶν ἀβύσσων τῆς γῆς πάλιν 10 ἀνήγαγές με. Δευτεροῖ τὴν εὐεργεσίαν ὡς ἀξίαν τοῦ πολλάκις λέγεσθαι.

22ᵃ. Καὶ γὰρ ἐγὼ ἐξομολογήσομαί σοι ἐν λαοῖς. Κύριε. Τὸ γὰρ οὐ πάντως κατὰ ἀκολουθίαν κεῖται, ἀλλ᾽ ἀπὸ τοῦ ἰδιώματος πολλαχοῦ προσέρριπται, — ὡς τὸ Γῆ ἐσείσθη καὶ γὰρ οἱ οὐρανοί, ἀντὶ τοῦ Γῆ ἐσείετο καὶ οἱ οὐρανοί. Οὕτως κἀνταῦθα Καὶ γὰρ ἐγώ, ἀντὶ τοῦ καὶ ἐγώ. Οὕτως 15 λέγει Σύμμαχος Κἀγὼ οὖν ἐξομολογήσομαί σοι. — ὑπὸ τούτων φησὶ διαπράξομαι κἀγὼ τὸ προσῆκον ἐμοί. Τί δὲ τοῦτο; Ἡ εἰς σε εὐχαριστία.

22ᵇ. Ἐν σκεύεσι ψαλμοῦ τὴν ἀλήθειάν σου. ὁ Θεός. Σκεύη λέγει ψαλμοῦ τὰ ὄργανα δι᾽ ὧν ἔψαλλον, τύμπανον καὶ ὄργανον, ψαλτήριον καὶ κιθάραν, καὶ εἴ τι τοιοῦτον. Διὰ πάντων οὖν τούτων φησὶ τὴν ἀληθινήν σου καὶ 20 θαυμαστὴν βοήθειαν αἰτήσομαι.

14 Ps. LXVII, 9

20. Ἀλλ᾽ οὐκ ἀφῆκας — ἐπιστρεφόντων: P, fol. 236ᵛ; V, fol. 7; Vat. 1422, fol. 128ᵛ; Cord, p. 450.   3 ὁδόν] ὀδόντων 1422.
21ᵃ. Καὶ μονονουχὶ — ἐξέσπασας: P, fol. 236ᵛ; V, fol. 7.
21ᵇ. Πολλήν — εὐεργεσίας: P, fol. 237; V, fol. 7ᵛ.
21ᶜ. Δευτεροῖ — λέγεσθαι: P, fol. 237; V, fol. 7ᵛ.
22ᵃ. Τὸ γὰρ — εὐχαριστία: P, fol. 237; V, fol. 7ᵛ.
22ᵇ. Σκεύη — αἰτήσομαι: P, fol. 237ᵛ; V, fol. 7ᵛ; Vat. 1422, fol. 128ᵛ (anon.); Cord, p. 452.   19 ψαλτήριον] ψαλμόν PV.

Aᵉ 21ᵃ (p. 357, 12-16): Ita nos malorum opraeserat multitudo, ut putaremur ad terrarum ima deducti, sed tua tamen sumus potentia liberati.   22ᵇ (p. 357, 24-358, 1)... uassa psalmi organa quibus psallebatur enumerat, timpanum et chitharam atque alia huiusmodi quorum omnium concentu uerum et mirum opus tui adiutorii sonabo, quo certam, non ludifactoriam (laudif. ms) salutem confers.

tribulations you revealed to me, numerous and evil; relenting, you gave me life (v. 20): but you did not let me suffer forever; you changed and rescued me from death and disaster (by analogy with those setting out on a journey, then thinking better of it and relenting). *And from the depths of the earth you brought me up again:* as if we were sunken in the deepest parts of the earth, you snatched us out of the multitude of dangers. *You multiplied your magnanimity in my regard* (v. 21): you gave evidence of your great power in your favors to me. *And relenting, you consoled me, and from the depths of the earth you brought me up again.* He makes a second mention of the favor as one worthy of frequent mention.

And I, in fact, shall confess to you among peoples, Lord (v. 22). The particle *in fact* is not completely in place here, instead being inserted, as often, by idiom, as in the verse "Earth shook and in fact the heavens,"[3] meaning, The earth was shaken and the heavens; likewise *And I, in fact,* meaning "And I." Thus Symmachus says, "And so I shall confess to you," meaning, For this I, too, shall do everything required of me. What is it? Offering thanks to you. *With musical instruments I shall sing of your truth, O God.* By *musical instruments* he refers to the instruments with which he sang the psalm—drum and pipe, harp and lyre, and the like. So he is saying, By every means I shall beg true and remarkable help from you. | *I shall sing to you on the lyre, O*

---

3. Ps 68:8. See the volume introduction for Theodore's unfamiliarity with the Hebrew particle involved.

938 THEODORVS MOPSVESTENVS

22ᶜ. Ψαλῶ σοι ἐν κιθάρᾳ, ὁ ἅγιος τοῦ Ἰσραήλ. Τοὺς διὰ ταύτης ὕμνους ἀποδώσω σοι· ἡρμήνευσε δὲ τὸ ἐν σκεύεσι.

23ᵃ. Ἀγαλλιάσονται τὰ χείλη μου ὅταν ψαλῶ σοι. Καὶ αὐτὸ δέ φησι, τὸ ὑμνῆσαί σε, οὐ μικρὰν ἐμοὶ παρέξεται τὴν εὐφροσύνην.

5 23ᵇ. Καὶ ἡ ψυχή μου, ἣν ἐλυτρώσω. Πολλῆς φησι καὶ αὐτὴ μεθέξει τῆς χαρᾶς, ἥτις ἀπαλλαγεῖσα τῶν κακῶν διὰ τῆς σῆς βοηθείας ἀφ᾽ ὧν ἀπήλαυσεν οἶδεν τὴν χάριν.

24. Ἔτι δὲ καὶ ἡ γλῶσσά μου ὅλην τὴν ἡμέραν μελετήσει τὴν δικαιοσύνην σου, ὅταν αἰσχυνθῶσιν καὶ ἐντραπῶσιν οἱ ζητοῦντες τὰ κακά μοι. Ὅπερ 10 εἶπεν διὰ τοῦ Προσθήσω ἐπὶ πᾶσαν τὴν αἴνεσιν, τὸ αὐτὸ κἀνταῦθα λέγει. Καὶ οὐχ ἅπαξ αὐτὸ ποιήσας παύσομαι, ἀλλ᾽ ἔτι καὶ ἔτι προσθήσω, καὶ ποιήσομαι διηνεκῆ τῆς σῆς εὐεργεσίας τὴν διήγησιν, ἐπειδὰν ἀπαλλαγῶ μὲν ἐγὼ τῶν κακῶν, αἰσχυνθῶσιν δὲ οἱ νῦν ὀνειδίζοντες καὶ ὀχλοῦντες τῶν προσδοκωμένων εἰς πέρας ἐξελθεῖν δυνηθέντος.

15 PSALMVS LXXI

Τινὲς ἔφασαν τοῦ ψαλμοῦ τὰ μὲν εἶναι εἰς τὸν Σολομῶντα, τὰ δὲ εἰς τὸν Χριστόν, — ἔστι δὲ τὸ πᾶν γέλως· οὔτε γὰρ ἔπρεπεν ταῖς περὶ τοῦ Χριστοῦ προφητείαις τὰ περὶ ἀνθρώπων συναναμεμίχθαι. Τοῦτο γὰρ οὐδαμοῦ τῶν περὶ τοῦ ⟨Χριστοῦ⟩ ψαλμῶν ἐστιν εὑρεῖν· εἰσὶ δὲ οἱ αὐτοῦ ἴδιοι

10 v. 14ᵇ   16 cf. arg. Ps. XLIV (p. 277).

22ᶜ. Τοὺς διὰ ταύτης — σκεύεσι: P, fol. 237ᵛ; V, fol. 8.
23ᵃ. Καὶ αὐτὸ — εὐφροσύνην: P, fol. 237ᵛ; V, fol. 8.
23ᵇ. Πολλῆς — χάριν: P, fol. 237ᵛ; V, fol. 8.
24. Ὅπερ εἶπεν — δυνηθέντος: P, fol. 237ᵛ; V, fol. 8.
Argumentum Τινὲς — κατ᾽ αὐτόν: P, fol. 238; V, fol. 8ʳ·ᵛ.   19 Χριστοῦ supplevi.

Aᶜ 23ᵇ (p. 358, 3-6): Participauit anima mea gaudis, quae a malis tuo adiutorio liberata ipsis beneficis dedicit tibi gratias refferre.   24 (p. 358, 7-15): Hoc est, quod superius dixerat, Adieciam super omnem laudem tuam, cum non solum multis organis canticorum, sed pene omnibus membris praeconia Dei se celebratum ire pronuntiat... uere pronuntiat inimicis obtatorum frustratione suffusis. Argumentum ps. LXXI (p. 358, 16-359, 1): Praesens hic psalmus non sempliciter in Salamonem, sed propter commonem populi prosperitatem, quae erat cum regis felicitate coniuncta, et in Salamonem canitur (= Pseudo-Beda, 862). Cumque beatum Dauid regendi populi cura disting⟨u⟩eret et cognoscendi quis suorum post se regnaturus esset desiderio teneretur, indicatur ei quod filium multae gloriae ac profundae securitatis et pacis successorem esset habiturus; atque hac reuelatione factus laetior quaedam in hoc carmine futura praedicit, quaedam pro testimonio uaticinii, ut inplentur, rogat; neque sufficere credidit agnouisse futura, nisi ea quae ostensa sunt in praedicationis fidem poposcerat adinpleri.

Holy One of Israel: I shall render you its songs of praise (thus explaining the phrase *with musical instruments*). *My lips will rejoice when I sing to you* (v. 23): the very singing of your praises will bring me no little joy. *And my soul, which you redeemed:* it will partake of great joy in being freed from the troubles by your help, for enjoyment of which it is indebted to your grace. *My tongue, too, will continue to meditate all day long on your righteousness when those seeking troubles for me are ashamed and confounded* (v. 24). As he said in the verse *I shall add to all your praise* (v. 14), he says again here: Having done this once, he is saying, I shall not stop; I shall keep on adding, and I shall give a continuous account of your kindness when I am freed from the troubles, while they are put to shame who now taunt and mock me, since I have been able to emerge at last from what was expected.

PSALM 72

Some commentators claimed that some parts of the psalm refer to Solomon and some to Christ; but that is quite ridiculous: things to do with human beings should not be mixed with prophecies about Christ. In fact, you cannot find this anywhere in the psalms to do with Christ; rather, they are peculiar to him | and totally confined to him.[1] How would it also not be quite ridiculous

---

1. Solomon comes into focus as a result of the psalm's title.

καὶ διόλου προσκήκοντες αὐτῷ. Πῶς δὲ οὐχὶ κἀκεῖνο παγγέλοιον τὸ τὰ μὲν
ἑρμηνεύειν ἐπὶ τοῦ Σολομῶντος, τὰ δὲ ἐπὶ τοῦ Χριστοῦ, πάλιν τε ἐπ' ἐκεῖνον μεθίστασθαι καὶ πάλιν ἐπὶ τοῦτον χωρεῖν, καὶ μονονουχὶ ἐπὶ ἀδελφῶν
ἐξ ἴσου διελομένων τὴν δόξαν τὴν ἑρμηνείαν ποιεῖσθαι τοῦ ψαλμοῦ; Αἴτιον
δὲ τούτου γεγένηται τὸ τοὺς ἑρμηνεύοντας ἐπὶ τῶν ῥητῶν γιγνομένους τοῦ 5
ψαλμοῦ τῇ λέξει δουλεύειν καὶ μὴ τὴν διάνοιαν περισκοπεῖν, — ὃ δὴ μάλιστα
πολλάκις ἐν τοῖς ψαλμοῖς εὑρίσκεται, οἷον λέγει Τῷ ἐπιβεβηκότι ἐπὶ τὸν
οὐρανὸν τοῦ οὐρανοῦ κατὰ ἀνατολάς (καὶ ποῖαι ἀνατολαὶ ἐπάνω τῶν οὐρανῶν;
ἀλλ' ἀπὸ τῆς διανοίας ἡ λύσις εὑρίσκεται· Σύμμαχος γάρ φησιν ἐκ πρώτης,
ὡς δῆλον εἶναι ὅτι διὰ τὸ ἀρχὴν εἶναι τῆς ἡμέρας τὴν ἀνατολὴν τὸ ἐκ πρώ- 10
τ η s καὶ ἐ ξ ἀ ρ χ ῆ s ἀνατολὰς ἐκάλεσεν). Ἔστι δὲ ὁ ψαλμὸς οὐδὲ ἰδικῶς
ἁπλῶς εἰς τὸν Σολομῶντα· πάντες γὰρ οἱ ψαλμοὶ τοῦ μακαρίου Δαυὶδ πρὸς
τὴν ὠφέλειαν τοῦ κοινοῦ βλέπουσιν, ὥστε οὐδὲ μέγα τι ἔχων φανεῖται εἰ
μέλλοι περὶ ἑνὸς εἶναι προφητεία. Τί οὖν ἐστιν;

Βασιλεὺς ὢν ὁ μακάριος Δαυὶδ καὶ δίκαιος καὶ προφήτης πολλὴν εἶχεν 15
τοῦ λαοῦ φροντίδα, καὶ ἔμελεν αὐτῷ μετὰ τὴν αὐτοῦ τελευτὴν ὅπως ἂν τὰ
κατὰ τὸν λαὸν διοικεῖσθαι μέλλοι. Ἐπιθυμοῦντι δὴ περὶ τούτων καὶ εὐχο-
μένῳ ἐμήνυσεν ὁ Θεὸς ὡς ὁ διαδεξόμενος αὐτὸν υἱὸς τιμῆς τε καὶ δόξης
πολλῆς ἀξιωθήσεται καὶ ἐν εἰρήνῃ βαθυτάτῃ διατελέσει, καὶ τοῦ δικαίου
ἐπιμελήσεται, καὶ ἐν εὐθηνίᾳ πολλῇ ἔσται ὁ λαὸς καὶ δόξῃ καὶ τιμῇ δι' 20
αὐτόν. Ἐπὶ τούτοις ἡσθεὶς ὁ μακάριος Δαυὶδ τὰ μὲν προφητεύει, τὰ δὲ
εὔχεται, — τῇ μὲν προφητείᾳ ὅτι ἔσται σημαίνων, τῇ δὲ προσευχῇ ὥστε
διαμεῖναι αὐτῶν, — ὥσπερ οὖν καὶ ἕτερα πολλὰ προαγορεύων, ἐν προσευχῆς
εἴδει γενέσθαι αἰτῶν, ὅτι ἔσται σημαίνων, τοὺς τότε παιδεύων μὴ ἀρκεῖσθαι
τοῦ γνῶναι ὅτι ἔσται, αἰτεῖν δὲ ὡς ἂν καὶ γένοιτο, ἐπὶ τὸ καὶ σπουδάζειν 25
αὐτοὺς ἀξίους ἑαυτοὺς τῶν προρρηθέντων κατασκευάζειν τῇ τοῦ βίου
ὀρθότητι, τοιοῦτοι πολλοὶ μὲν τῶν περὶ τοῦ ἐν Βαβυλῶνι λαοῦ, πολλοὶ δὲ
καὶ τῶν περὶ τοῦ Ἐζεκίου. Ἔστιν οὖν καὶ οὗτος οὐχ ἁπλῶς εἰς τὸν Σολομῶντα ὁ ψαλμός, ἀλλ' ὑπὲρ τοῦ κοινοῦ εἰς τὰ κατ' αὐτόν.

1. Ὁ Θεός, τὸ κρίμα σου τῷ βασιλεῖ δός, καὶ τὴν δικαιοσύνην σου τῷ 30
υἱῷ τοῦ βασιλέως. Ἐπειδὴ πρὸ τούτων μάλιστα ἐπιτηδείαν σοφίαν ἐδέξατο
παρὰ τοῦ Θεοῦ, συνετῶς τε κρίνων καὶ δικαίως, — ἁπάντων δὲ ἦν τοῦτο
βασιλεῖ προτιμότερον καὶ πρὸς τὴν κοινὴν λυσιτέλειαν συμβαλλόμενον, —

7-8 ps. LXVII, 34.   17-21 cf. II Reg. VII   III Reg. I, 30   I Paral. XXVIII. XXIX.

1. Ἐπειδὴ — κρίνειν: P, fol. 238ᵛ; V, fol. 8ᵛ-9; Cord, p. 466-467.   32 συνεχῶς Cord.

Aᵉ 32-33 (p. 359, 2-4): Optime a principio inpraecatur quae et utilitati subditorum et regentium gloriae conuenirent.

to take some parts in reference to Solomon and some parts to Christ, at one time to switch back to the former and in turn to move to the latter, and to conduct the commentary on the psalm as if it dealt with brothers equally sharing the credit? Now, the cause of this is that some people comment on the words by slavishly keeping to the text of the psalm and by not having an overall view of the meaning. This is found with particular frequency in the psalms, as, for example, "He who rides on the heaven of heavens at sunrise": what kind of sunrise is there above the heavens? Instead, the solution is found in the sense. Symmachus, in fact, says "from the outset," from which it emerges that by "sunrise" he referred to the origin and beginning because sunrise is the beginning of the day.[2] Nor, however, does the psalm refer simply and solely to Solomon: all the psalms of blessed David have in view the benefit of everyone in common, and so it is of no great significance if a piece of inspired composition were likely to deal with one person.

So what is the meaning, then? Blessed David, being a king, a righteous man, and an inspired author, had deep concern for the people, and he was interested in how after his death the people's situation was likely to be managed. When he was anxious and prayerful about this, God informed him that the son succeeding him would be accorded great honor and glory, would live in complete peace, and would have a concern for justice, and the people would enjoy great prosperity, glory, and honor on his account. Pleased with this, blessed David both prophesies it and prays for it, indicating in the prophecy that it will happen and begging in the prayer for it to continue. Likewise he foretells other things as well, asks in the form of a prayer for them to happen, indicating that they will happen, teaching those of the time not to be content with knowing that they will happen but also to ask that they should happen, and to take pains to make themselves worthy of what is foretold by the uprightness of their life.

While many of the psalms about the people in Babylon are of this kind, so are many of those about Hezekiah as well. This psalm, therefore, is not simply directed to Solomon, but is of general relevance in what applies to him. *O God, give your judgment to the king, and your righteousness to the king's son* (v. 1). Since he received wisdom from God as particularly suitable for judging with understanding and righteousness (and this was more majestic than all else for a king and was given for the common good),[3] | he prays

---

2. Ps 68:33. Theodore's exegetical priorities and abilities emerge in this admission, that the overall meaning, not textual details (in the original), determines how individual verses are to be taken. His choice is inevitable, his access to the original being what it is, as emerges also in the example that he cites, where the Hebrew form allows for either meaning but where, as usual, he decides on the basis of logic, ἀκολουθία, rather than λέξις, the textual detail in question.

3. Cf. 1 Kgs 3:9–14.

τοῦτο μάλιστα καὶ πρὸ πάντων εὔχεται αὐτῷ προσεῖναι. Τῷ βασιλεῖ οὖν φησι καὶ τῷ τούτου βασιλεῖ υἱῷ, ἵνα εἴπῃ τῷ μέλλοντι διαδέχεσθαι, καὶ δύναμιν δὸς τοῦ κρίνειν καὶ γνώμην τοῦ δικαίως κρίνειν.

2. Κρίνειν τὸν λαόν σου ἐν δικαιοσύνῃ καὶ τοὺς πτωχοὺς ἐν κρίσει. Ἐὰν
5 γὰρ τούτων φησι τύχῃ παρά σου, μετὰ τοῦ δικαίου ποιήσεται τοῦ λαοῦ τὴν ἐξέτασιν, καὶ ἐπαμυνεῖ τοῖς πτωχοῖς ἀδικουμένοις ὑπὸ τῶν δυνατωτέρων.

3. Ἀναλαβέτω τὰ ὄρη εἰρήνην τῷ λαῷ, καὶ οἱ βουνοὶ δικαιοσύνην. Ἔδειξεν ἐντεῦθεν μάλιστα ὅτι ὑπὲρ τοῦ κοινοῦ προσεύχεται· πάντα φησὶ πληρωθήτω εἰρήνης.

10 4ᵃ. Κρινεῖ τοὺς πτωχοὺς τοῦ λαοῦ. Καὶ παρὰ πᾶσι κρατείτω τὸ δίκαιον.
Πῶς οὖν τοῦτο γένηται;

4ᵇ. Καὶ σώσει τοὺς υἱοὺς τῶν πενήτων. Δικαιώσει τε γὰρ αὐτοὺς ἀδικουμένους, καὶ σώσει κινδυνεύοντας διὰ τὴν πενίαν.

4ᶜ. Καὶ ταπεινώσει συκοφάντην. Συκοφάντην λέγει τὸν ἐπηρεάζοντα,
15 ἐπειδὴ ἴδιον τῶν συκοφαντούντων τὸ ἐπηρεάζειν. Τιμωρήσεταί φησι τοὺς
ἀδικοῦντας· οὕτως οὖν τὰ πάντα καθέξει εἰρήνη καὶ δικαιοσύνη, ὅτε τοιαῦτα
ποιεῖ τῇ χορηγίᾳ τῆς παρά σου σοφίας.

5ᵃ. Καὶ συμπαραμενεῖ τῷ ἡλίῳ. Οἱ περὶ τοῦ Σολομῶντος ψιλῶς οἰηθέντες εἰρῆσθαι τὸν ψαλμόν, τοῦτο ὡς οὐχ ἁρμόττον ἐκείνῳ τὸ ῥητὸν ἔλα-
20 βον περὶ τοῦ Χριστοῦ. Ἔστι δὲ οὐχ οὕτως· πρὸς γὰρ τὸ Ἀναλαβέτω τὰ
ὄρη εἰρήνην τῷ λαῷ καὶ οἱ βουνοὶ δικαιοσύνην καὶ τὰ ἑξῆς ἔχει τὴν ἀκολουθίαν. Ἐκείνου γάρ φησιν οὕτω πράττοντος καὶ τοῖς πένησιν ἐπαμύ-

2. Ἐὰν γὰρ — δυνατωτέρων; P, fol. 238ᵛ; V, fol. 9.
3. Ἔδειξεν — εἰρήνης: P, fol. 239; V, fol. 9.   8-9 πάντα πληρωθήτω εἰρήνης
affert Paraphrasis (p. 457).
4ᵃ. Καὶ παρὰ — γένηται: P, fol. 239; V, fol. 9.
4ᵇ. Δικαιώσει — πενίαν: P, fol. 239; V, fol. 9; Cord. p. 468.   12 γὰρ om. Cord.
4ᶜ. Συκοφάντην — σοφίας: P, fol. 239; V, fol. 9ᵛ; Cord. p. 468.
5ᵃ. Οἱ περὶ τοῦ Σολομῶντος — σοφίας: P, fol. 239ᵛ; V, fol. 9ᵛ; Vat. 1422, fol. 129ᵛ
(anon.).   18 περὶ] παρά 1422   19 τῷ ῥητῷ 1422   21 τῷ λαῷ om. PV.

Aᵉ 2 (p. 359, 11-17): Sic hoc... fuerit... consecutus, erit illi grandis adseruandae cura iustitiae, ut.. pauperes quosque a diuitum iniquitate defendat.
3 (p. 359, 18-20): Probauit uoto pacis profunde quod... commoni omnium utilitate praecaretur.   4ᵇ (p. 359, 20-22): Ausibus praedonum conpraesis uera et
multa pax redderetur adflictis.

to acquire this in particular, even ahead of everything else. So he says, *to the king* and to his son the king, as if to say, Give to the one who will follow in succession both the power to judge and the will to judge justly. *To judge your people in righteousness, and your poor in judgment* (v. 2): if he receives this from you, he will perform his examination of the people with justice and will defend the poor when they are wronged by the more powerful.

May the mountains restore peace to the people, and the hills, righteousness (v. 3). In this he showed particularly that he prays for the common good, meaning, Let everything be filled with peace. *He will judge the poor of the people* (v. 4): and let him administer justice to everyone. So how will this happen? *And he will save the children of the needy:* he will secure justice for those who are wronged, and save those who are at risk from their poverty. *And he will humble a calumniator.* By *calumniator* he refers to the insolent person, since it is typical of calumniators to be insolent. He will punish wrongdoers, he is saying; thus peace and righteousness will take control of everything when he brings everything to this condition through the gift of wisdom from you.

He will endure as long as the sun (v. 5). Those commentators who were of the view that the psalm refers simply to Solomon took this verse in reference to Christ as not suited to the former.[4] That is not so, however: it follows on from the verse *May the mountains restore peace to the people, and the hills, righteousness* and so on. He means, in fact, that if he behaves in this fashion, assisting the poor | and punishing the wrongdoers, deep peace will

---

4. That is, even the commentators who otherwise applied the psalm exclusively to Solomon had problems with this clause and so applied v. 5a to Christ.

νοντος καὶ τιμωρουμένου τοὺς ἀδικοῦντας, ἡ εἰρήνη βαθεῖα παραμενεῖ καὶ τὸ δίκαιον παραπλήσιον τῷ ἡλίῳ διαμονὴν ἔχοντα· ἀνάγκη γὰρ ἦν τοῦ βασιλέως ἐπιμελομένου τῶν πρεπόντων κρατεῖν τὸ καλόν. Ὡς οὖν οὐχ οἷόν τέ φησι παύσασθαι τὸν ἥλιον τοῦ τε ἀνατέλλειν καὶ φαίνειν, οὕτως οὐχ οἷόν τε τοῦ βασιλέως τῇ σῇ βοηθείᾳ τούτων ἐπιμελομένου παύσασθαι κρατοῦσαν 5 τὴν εἰρήνην. Τὸ οὖν συμπαραμενεῖ τῷ ἡλίῳ οὐ περὶ τοῦ Σολομῶντος λέγει, ἀλλὰ περὶ τῆς εἰρήνης καὶ τοῦ δικαίου, ὡς οὕτω κρατησάντων ὑπ' αὐτοῦ μέχρι ἂν ἄγηται ὑπὸ τῆς τοῦ Θεοῦ σοφίας.

5ᵇ. Καὶ πρὸ τῆς σελήνης γενεᾶς γενεῶν. Τὸ πρὸ οὐχ ὡς ἐπὶ χρόνου λέγει, ὥς τινες ᾠήθησαν, ἐπεὶ ποίαν ἕξει πρὸς τὸ «παραμένειν» ἀκολου- 10 θίαν; Συμπαραμενεῖ γάρ φησι τῷ ἡλίῳ, καὶ πρὸ τῆς σελήνης γενεᾶς γενεῶν. Τὸ μὲν γὰρ «συμπαραμένειν» εἰς τὸ ἑξῆς λέγεται, τὸ δὲ «πρὸ» ἐπὶ τῶν προλαβόντων· οὐδεὶς οὖν λέγει ὅτι «πρὸ τοῦδε συμπαραμενεῖ» ἀλλ' εἰ ἄρα «αὐτῷ συμπαραμενεῖ». Εἰ δέ τις τὸ συμπαραμενεῖ μὴ βούλοιτο κατὰ κοινοῦ νοεῖσθαι, τὸ Καὶ πρὸ τῆς σελήνης γενεᾶς γενεῶν οὐδὲν ποιήσει ἀλλ' ἢ 15 χωλὸν καὶ ἀπλήρωτον ἔχον τὴν διάνοιαν· οὐ γὰρ συνῆπται αὐτῷ ὅτι ἐστίν, ὅτι ὑπάρχει, ἢ ὅτι ἦν, ἤ τι τοιοῦτον. Τὸ μὲν οὖν συμπαραμενεῖ κατὰ κοινοῦ λέγει, τὸ δὲ πρὸ οὐκ ἐπὶ τῆς τοῦ χρόνου λέγει ὑπεροχῆς, ἀλλ' ἐπὶ τῆς κατ' αὐτὸ τὸ διαμένειν. Διαμενεῖ τοίνυν φησί, καὶ διαφυλαχθήσονται ἡ εἰρήνη καὶ τὸ δίκαιον ἴσα τῷ ἡλίῳ λάμποντα καὶ ὑπὲρ τὴν σελήνην, ὥστε καὶ προέ- 20 χειν τῆς σελήνης κατὰ τοῦτο. Διὰ τί δὲ καὶ προέχει τῆς σελήνης; Ὅτι ἡ μὲν ἔχει καὶ μειώσεως πολλοὺς καιρούς, αὕτη δὲ ἐν τῷ διαμένειν ἀεὶ καὶ αὔξειν φυλάττεται. Τὸ δὲ γενεᾶς γενεῶν κατὰ τὸ οἰκεῖον ἰδίωμα εἶπεν, ἀντὶ τοῦ ἐπὶ πολύ.

6. Καταβήσεται ὡς ὑετὸς ἐπὶ πόκον, καὶ ὡσεὶ σταγὼν ἡ στάζουσα ἐπὶ 25 τὴν γῆν. Ἔσται γὰρ καὶ ἡδὺς καὶ εὐπαράδεκτος παντὶ τῷ πλήθει, τοῦ ὀρθοῦ καὶ τοῦ δικαίου ἐπιμελούμενος οὐκ ἔλαττον σταγόνας ὑετῶν πόκῳ τε καὶ γῇ φερομένας προσίεται.

9-11 cf. in Zach. IX, 10-12 (P. G., 561 A).

3-4 οὐχ οἰόντων τε 1422   7 καὶ om. 1422.
5ᵇ. Τὸ πρὸ — ἐπὶ πολύ: P, fol. 239ᵛ; V, fol. 9ᵛ-10; Vat. 1422, fol. 129ᵛ (anon.); Cord, p. 469 (= P. G., 689).   11 πρὸ om. 1422   13-14 ἀλλ' εἰ — συμπαραμενεῖ om. 1422 Cord   15 τῷ καὶ PV   καὶ τὸ 1422 Cord   16 ἔχων PV   23 αὔξειν] αὔξει καὶ 1422 Cord.
6. Ἔσται — προσίεται: P, fol. 240; V, fol. 10; Vat. 1422, fol. 129ᵛ; Cord, p. 470.   26 γὰρ καὶ] γὰρ 1422 Cord   27-28 οὐκ ἔλαττον γὰρ τοὺς προσφερομένους προσίεται ἢ τὰς σταγόνας τῶν ὑετῶν πόκος καὶ γῆ 1422 Cord.

Aᵉ 19-23 (p. 359, 30-360, 1): Pax autem conparata aequitati solis antestabit lunae officiis, cuius claritas incrementis detrimentisque uariatur.

endure and righteousness like the sun will enjoy permanence, there being need for the king to show interest in what is required for good to prevail. Just as it is not possible for the sun to stop rising and shining, therefore, so it is not possible for the king to stop showing an interest in having peace prevail with your help for them. The verse *He will endure as long as the sun,* therefore, refers not to Solomon but to peace and righteousness as thus prevailing, thanks to him, as long as he is motivated by God's wisdom. *And generations of generations before the moon.* The word *before* does not refer to time, as some commentators believed: What relation would it have to "will last"? The text says, note, *He will endure as long as the sun, and generations of generations before the moon:* while *will endure* refers to the future, *before* refers to the past; so no one says "he will endure before this," though perhaps one might say "he will endure at this very time." If, on the other hand, you were unwilling that *he will endure* be taken in the customary way, the phrase *and generations of generations before the moon* would have no other effect than to leave the sense deficient and incomplete: it is not attached to him "because he is," "because he exists," or "because he was," or anything of the like. Therefore, he says *he will endure* as it is commonly used, but he does not say *before* of an earlier time but of the moon's continuance in itself. So it means, He will continue, and peace and righteousness will be kept equal in brightness to the sun and greater than the moon so as even to be superior to the moon in this respect. But why is it even superior to the moon? Because whereas the latter also has many phases of waning, the former is kept ever continuing and waxing. Now, the phrase *generations of generations* is an idiomatic expression meaning "for a long time."

He will come down like a shower on a fleece, and like a drop falling on the ground (v. 6): he will be both pleasant and welcome to all the populace, giving attention to uprightness and righteousness and bringing no less benefit than drops of rain falling on fleece and soil. | *Righteousness will arise in his*

7ᵃ. Ἀνατελεῖ ἐν ταῖς ἡμέραις αὐτοῦ δικαιοσύνην. Ἔδειξεν ὅτι τὸ Συμπαρμενεῖ τῷ ἡλίῳ ἐπὶ τῆς εἰρήνης εἶπεν καὶ τοῦ δικαίου. Ἐχρήσατο οὖν καὶ τῇ ὁμοιότητι, τὸ Ἀνατελεῖ ὡς ἐπὶ τοῦ ἡλίου εἰπὼν ἀντὶ τοῦ *φανήσεται·* οὕτως λάμψει φησὶν ὡς ὁ ἥλιος.

5   7ᵇ. Καὶ πλῆθος εἰρήνης ἕως οὗ ἀνταναιρεθῇ ἡ σελήνη. Νῦν οὖν αὐτὸ ἐδήλωσε σαφέστερον. Καὶ οὕτω φησὶ βαθεῖα τὰ πάντα καθέξει ἡ εἰρήνη διὰ τὴν παρά σου κηδεμονίαν, ὡς ὁμοίως ἀδύνατον εἶναι λυθῆναί τε τὴν ἐπ᾽ αὐτοῦ εἰρήνην καὶ τῆς σελήνης τὴν ὕπαρξιν. Ταῖς δὲ ὑπερβολαῖς ἐπὶ τῶν τοιούτων ἔθος κεχρῆσθαι τῇ θείᾳ γραφῇ, – ὡς καὶ ἐν τῷ πη᾽ ψαλμῷ τὸ
10 Θήσομαι εἰς τὸν αἰῶνα τοῦ αἰῶνος τὸ σπέρμα αὐτοῦ καὶ τὸν θρόνον αὐτοῦ ὡς τὰς ἡμέρας τοῦ οὐρανοῦ, ὑπερβολικώτερον εἰπὼν τὸ τὴν βασιλείαν ἐν τοῖς διαδόχοις τοῦ Δαυὶδ ἴσα τῷ οὐρανῷ ἀδιάλυτον παραμένειν, καὶ ἑξῆς δὲ πάλιν Καὶ ὁ θρόνος αὐτοῦ ὡς ὁ ἥλιος ἐναντίον μου, καὶ ὡς ἡ σελήνη κατηρτισμένη εἰς τὸν αἰῶνα, — ἅπερ κατὰ μὲν τὸ ἀκριβὲς οὐχ οὕτω γέγο-
15 νεν, ὑπερβολικώτερον δὲ εἴρηται τῇ θείᾳ γραφῇ.

8. Καὶ κατακυριεύσει ἀπὸ θαλάσσης ἕως θαλάσσης, καὶ ἀπὸ ποταμῶν ἕως περάτων τῆς οἰκουμένης. Οὐχ ὅτι κρατήσει πάντως καὶ βασιλεύσει, ἀλλ᾽ ὅτι τῇ φήμῃ καὶ τῇ δόξῃ πάντες ὡς κύριον ἑαυτῶν θαυμάσονται· ὃ καὶ ἀληθῶς γεγονὸς εὑρίσκεται. Σαφέστερον γοῦν αὐτὸ ἑξῆς λέγει.

20 9. Ἐνώπιον αὐτοῦ προσπεσοῦνται Αἰθίοπες, καὶ οἱ ἐχθροὶ αὐτοῦ χοῦν λείξουσιν. Τοῦτο δὲ γέγονεν ὅτε ἐλήλυθεν ἡ τῆς Αἰθιοπίας βασίλισσα ὑπὸ τῆς περὶ αὐτοῦ δόξης κινηθεῖσα.

10-11 Ps. LXXXVIII, 30   13-14 ps. LXXXVIII, 37ᵇ-38ᵃ   21-22 cf. supra p. 445, 10-11.

7ᵃ. Ἔδειξεν — ἥλιος: P, fol. 240ᵛ; V, fol. 10ᵛ; Vat. 1422, fol. 129ᵛ; Cord, p. 471. 7ᵇ. Νῦν οὖν αὐτὸ — γραφῇ: P, fol. 240ᵛ; V, fol. 10ᵛ; Cord, p. 471.   5 οὖν om. PV   6 φησὶ om. PV   τὰ om. Cord   ἡ om. PV   11 τὸ om. Cord. 8. Οὐχ ὅτι — λέγει: P, fol. 241; V, fol. 10ᵛ; Cord, p. 472 (= P. G., 692 B). 19 σαφέστερον — λέγει om. Cord. 9. Τοῦτο — κινηθεῖσα: P, fol. 241; V, fol. 11; Cord, p. 473.

Aᵉ 7ᵃ (p. 360, 9-15): Quia praemiserat de pace *Et permanebit cum sole*, bene nunc intulit *Orietur*, tamquam de sole loqueretur, ac si diceret: Ita clara erit sub eo iustitia, ita lucebit omnia conparata pax, ut splendorem solis uideantur emitari.   7ᵇ (p. 360, 16-25): Consuetudo profetae est emfasses addictorum suorum pondus commendationemque commouere, sicut est illud in LXXXVIII psalmo *Et ponam in saeculum saeculi semen eius et tronus eius* usque *caeli*, et paulo post *Et tronus eius sicut sol* usque *in aeternum erit*. Haec autem omnia exaggerenter, dum in successoribus Dauitici regni continuationem diuturnitati elimentorum uidetur equare.   18 (p. 361, 1): Fama, non iure, non imperiis, sed honore.   21 (p. 361, 2-3): Per reginam Sabam.

days (v. 7). He made clear that the verse *He will endure as long as the sun* referred to peace and righteousness—hence his employing also a metaphor, *will arise,* as if in reference to the sun, meaning "will shine." He is saying, He will be as bright as the sun. *And abundance of peace until the moon is no more.* At this point, then, he conveyed the same thing more clearly, giving this meaning: Deep peace will take possession of everything as a result of care on your part, so that it will be impossible equally for peace to be lost, as for the moon's existence. The divine Scripture is in the habit of using hyperbole in such cases, as, for example, in Psalm 89, "I shall establish his offspring forever and his throne like the days of heaven," referring by hyperbole to continuance of the kingship in David's successors without end like heaven; and further on likewise, "And his throne like the sun before me, and like the moon established forever."[5] In in actual fact it did not happen this way, but is expressed hyperbolically by the divine Scripture.

He will have dominion from sea to sea, and from rivers to the end of the world (v. 8): not that he will be totally in control in his exercise of kingship, but that because of his name and reputation all will admire him as their lord—which is found to have actually happened. What follows, at any rate, says the same thing more clearly. *Ethiopians will fall down before him, and his foes will lick the dust* (v. 9). This happened when the queen of Ethiopia came, attracted by his reputation.[6] | *Kings of Tarshish and the islands*

---

5. Ps 89:29, 36–37.
6. Cf. 1 Kgs 10.

10ᵃ. Βασιλεῖς Θαρσεῖς καὶ νῆσοι δῶρα προσοίσουσιν. Εἴρηται ὅτι Θαρσεῖς τὰς παραθαλασσίους λέγει πόλεις ὁ Δαυίδ. Πάντες οὖν φησι, καὶ οἱ ἀπὸ τῶν παραθαλασσίων πόλεων καὶ ἀπὸ τῶν νήσων ἀποτελοῦσιν αὐτῷ δῶρα· πολλὴ γὰρ αὐτῷ διὰ τῶν πλοίων ἡ ἐμπορία ἐκομίζετο. Οὕτως οὖν κατα-κυριεύσει ἀπὸ θαλάσσης ἕως θαλάσσης τῷ τὰ δῶρα αὐτῷ ἀποστέλλεσθαι, 5 τῷ τιμᾶσθαι παρὰ πάντων.

10ᵇ. Βασιλεῖς Ἀράβων καὶ Σαβὰ δῶρα προσάξουσιν. Ἦν γὰρ ὁ ἐναντιού-μενος οὐδείς, φίλοι δὲ ὄντες εἰκότως ἐπλήρουν.

11ᵃ. Καὶ προσκυνήσουσιν αὐτῷ πάντες οἱ βασιλεῖς τῆς γῆς. Τίμιον λογιοῦνται. 10

11ᵇ. Πάντα τὰ ἔθνη δουλεύσουσιν αὐτῷ. Αὐτῷ ὑποταγήσονται ἅπαντες, καὶ οὐ πολεμήσουσι.

12. Ὅτι ἐρρύσατο πτωχὸν ἐκ δυνάστου, καὶ πένητα ᾧ οὐχ ὑπῆρχε βοη-θός. Τούτων δὲ ἁπάντων φησὶ βασιλεύσει διὰ τὴν περιοῦσαν αὐτῷ σοφίαν, ἀφ᾽ ἧς καὶ τὸ τοῦ δικαίου ἐπιμελεῖσθαι κέκτηται. 15

13. Φείσεται πτωχοῦ καὶ πένητος, καὶ ψυχὰς πενήτων σώσει. Ἀδικου-μένους ἐλεήσει καὶ περισώσει τῶν ἀδικούντων· τὸ γὰρ φείσεται λέγει ἀντὶ τοῦ ἐλεήσει, — ἐλεοῦντες γὰρ τὴν φειδὼ ποιούμεθα.

14ᵃ. Ἐκ τόκου καὶ ἐξ ἀδικίας λυτρώσεται τὰς ψυχὰς αὐτῶν. Ἀπαλλάξει πάσης πλεονεξίας καὶ ἀδικίας· τόκον γὰρ τὴν πλεονεξίαν λέγει, ὡς τὸ 20 Οὐκ ἐξέλιπεν ἐκ τῶν πλατειῶν αὐτῆς τόκος.

1-5 cf. in ps. XLVII, 8 (p. 312)   21 Ps. LIV, 12c.

10ᵃ. Εἴρηται — πάντων: P, fol. 241ᵛ; V, fol. 11; Cord, p. 473 (anon.).
10ᵇ. Ἦν γὰρ — ἐπλήρουν: P, fol. 241ᵛ; V, fol. 11ᵛ; Paraphrasis (p. 458).
11ᵃ. Τίμιον λογιοῦνται: P, fol. 242; V, fol. 11ᵛ.
11ᵇ. Αὐτῷ — πολεμήσουσιν: P, fol. 242; V, fol. 11ᵛ; Vat. 1422, fol. 130 (anon.);
Paraphrasis (p. 458).
12. Τούτων — κέκτηται: P. fol. 242; V, fol. 11ᵛ; Cord, p. 475.
13 Ἀδικουμένους — ποιούμεθα: P, fol. 242; V, fol. 11ᵛ-12; Cord, p. 475.   17 ἀδικ.
δὲ Cord.
14ᵃ. Ἀπαλλάξει — τόκος: P, fol. 242ᵛ; V, fol. 12; Cord, p. 476.   20 cf. THEO-
DORETUS (1437 A 2).

Aᵉ 1-2 (p. 361, 7-8): Tharsis uocat litorias ciuitates.   12 (p. 361, 23-25):
Haec autem regni potentia adquiritur ei sufragio sapientiae atque iustitiae.
17-18 (p. 361, 29-362, 1) ...parcet autem inopi dixit pro Miserebitur.   20 (p. 362,
6-8): ...usurae autem nomine malum auaritiae et cupiditatis ostendit.

will bring gifts (v. 10). It is said that by *Tarshish* David refers to the coastal cities. So he is saying, All those from the coastal cities and from the islands will present him with gifts, since a lot of trade came his way by ship. So *he will have dominion from sea to sea* because gifts are sent to him, honor being paid him by everyone. *Kings from Arabia and Seba will bring gifts:* there was no one hostile, so being friends they did the right thing. *All the kings of the earth will bow down to him* (v. 11): they will reckon him deserving of respect. *All nations will serve him:* they will all be subject to him and not be hostile.

Because he rescued the poor from the powerful one, and the needy who had no helper (v. 12): he will rule over all these in the wisdom in his possession, by which he also exercised a commitment to righteousness. *He will spare the poor and needy, and save the souls of the needy* (v. 13): he will have mercy on the wronged and save them from the wrongdoers (by *spare* meaning "have mercy," for the merciful are sparing). *He will redeem their souls from usury and injustice* (v. 14): he will free them from all avarice and injustice (by *usury* referring to avarice, as in the verse "Usury was not absent from its streets").[7] | *His name will be honorable in their sight:* he will enjoy

---

7. Ps 55:11.

14ᵇ. Καὶ ἔντιμον τὸ ὄνομα αὐτοῦ ἐνώπιον αὐτῶν. Ὑπὲρ τούτων φησὶ πολλῇ ἔσται τῇ τιμῇ, πάντων αὐτὸν θαυμαζόντων.

15ᵃ. Καὶ ζήσεται καὶ δοθήσεται αὐτῷ ἐκ τοῦ χρυσίου τῆς Ἀραβίας. Ἀλλὰ καὶ μακροημερεύσει διὰ τὴν τοῦ δικαίου ἐπιμέλειαν, καὶ κύριος ἔσται τῶν
5 ἀλλοτρίων ἀγαθῶν.

15ᵇ. Καὶ προσεύξονται περὶ αὐτοῦ διὰ παντός. Καὶ διὰ τὴν περὶ αὐτὸν διάθεσιν εὔξονται αὐτὸν ἐπὶ πολὺ διαβιῶναι· οὕτω καὶ ἀνωτέρω εἶπεν τὸ καταβήσεται ὡς ὑετὸς ἐπὶ πόκον.

15ᶜ. Ὅλην τὴν ἡμέραν εὐλογήσουσιν αὐτόν. Διατελέσουσιν πάντοτε ἐπαι-
10 νοῦντες αὐτὸν καὶ θαυμάζοντες.

16ᵃ. Ἔσται στήριγμα ἐν τῇ γῇ ἐπ᾽ ἄκρων τῶν ὀρέων. Στήριγμα λέγεται πᾶν ὅ τι δι᾽ ἀσθένειαν ἐπιστηρίζεται καὶ βοηθεῖται, ὥσπερ καὶ βακτηρία πρεσ-βύτης διὰ τὸ γῆρας· στήριγμα οὖν ἐκάλεσεν ὡς βοηθὸν τῶν πενήτων. Θαυ-μάσονται τοίνυν αὐτὸν καὶ ἐπαινέσουσιν, ἐπειδὴ τοῖς ἀσθενέσι καὶ τοῖς ἀδι-
15 κουμένοις ἅπασιν ἐν τάξει στρατηγήματος ἔσται τῇ παρ᾽ αὐτοῦ βοηθείᾳ, τοσοῦτον ἀνωτέρους γίνεσθαι τῶν ἀδικούντων ὡς μηδὲν διαλλάττειν τῶν ἐπ᾽· ἄκρων τῶν ὀρέων ἑστώτων.

16ᵇ. Ὑπεραρθήσεται ὑπὲρ τὸν Λίβανον ὁ καρπὸς αὐτοῦ. Τεύξεται καὶ εὐπαιδίας οὐ μικρᾶς, ἀλλ᾽ ὥστε θαυμάζειν ἅπαντας τῶν τέκνων τό τε κάλ-
20 λος καὶ τὸ πλῆθος καὶ τὴν ἰσχὺν οὐκ ἔλαττον ἢ τὰς ἐν τῷ Λιβάνῳ κέδρους.

8 v. 6ᵃ.

14ᵇ. Ὑπὲρ τούτων — θαυμαζόντων: P, fol. 242ᵛ; V, fol. 12.
15ᵃ. Ἀλλὰ — ἀγαθῶν: P, fol. 242ᵛ: V, fol. 12ᵛ.
15ᵇ. Καὶ διὰ τὴν — πόκον: P, fol. 243; V, fol. 12ᵛ.
15ᶜ. Διατελέσουσιν — θαυμάζοντες: P, fol. 243; V, fol. 12ᵛ; Vat. 1422, fol. 130ᵛ (anon.).
16ᵃ. Στήριγμα — ἑστώτων: P, fol. 243; V, fol. 12ᵛ. 11-13 στήριγμα — γῆρας affert Vat. 1422, fol. 130ᵛ (anon.) 12 καὶ om. PV 13 θαυμάσονται κτλ. apud Cord (p. 477) sub nomine ATHANASII 14 ἐπαινέσονται Cord 16 ἀδικουμένων Cord.
16ᵇ. Τεύξεται — κέδρους: P, fol. 243ᵛ; V, fol. 13'; Cord, p. 477. 18 δὲ καὶ Cord.

Aᵉ 14ᵇ (p. 362, 9-11): Hac iusti rectique cura multusque ei honor multaque dignitas conferentur. 6-7 (p. 362, 14-16): In beneficiorum uicem uota pro eo suplicationesque facient. 14-17 (p. 362, 21-24) ... sustentabit egentes, ut exae-quati montibus firmitate praesedii infra se inimicos uideant nihilque eorum ab exaltatione distantes. 16ᵇ (p. 362, 25-27); Testabuntur, inquit, felicitatem eius filiorum examina; et cedris Libani numerus speciosae prolis aequatur.

great respect from them, everyone admiring him. *He will live, and to him will be given some of the gold of Arabia* (v. 15): he will enjoy length of days for his attention to righteousness, and will be owner of others' possessions. *They will ever pray for him:* in their affection for him they will pray for him to live long (as it likewise said above as well, *He will come down like a shower on a fleece*). *They will bless him all day long:* they will continue praising and admiring him without end.

There will be a support in the land on the summit of the mountains (v. 16). In *support* there is reference to everything that on account of weakness is supported and helped, like an old person also with a staff on account of age; so by *support* he referred to a helper of the needy. So they will admire and commend him, since he will act as a leader for all the weak and the wronged with help from him, so that they become so superior to the wrongdoers as to be no different from those standing *on the summit of the mountains. His fruit will be raised above Lebanon:* he will also be granted no insignificant number of children, so that everyone will admire the beauty, number, and strength of his children no less than the cedars of Lebanon. | *They will blossom from a*

16ᶜ. Καὶ ἐξανθήσουσιν ἐκ πόλεως· ὡσεὶ χόρτος τῆς γῆς. Ἀπὸ γὰρ τῆς ἄγαν εὐπαιδίας ἀθρῶον αὐτοῦ τὸ γένος ἀρθήσεται καὶ φανεῖται δίκην τοῦ χόρτου.

17ᵃ. Ἔσται τὸ ὄνομα αὐτοῦ εὐλογημένον εἰς τοὺς αἰῶνας. Ὑπὲρ τούτων ἐπὶ πολὺ διαμενεῖ θαυμαζόμενος. 5

17ᵇ. Πρὸ τοῦ ἡλίου διαμενεῖ τὸ ὄνομα αὐτοῦ. Ἔδειξε κἀνταῦθα ὅτι τὸ πρὸ οὐκ ἐπὶ χρόνου λέγει, ἵνα τῷ Χριστῷ ἁρμόττειν νομισθῇ — ὅ τινες ᾠήθησαν. Εἰ γὰρ τὸ πρὸ ἐπὶ χρόνου λέγει καὶ προϋπάρξεως, πῶς τὸ δια-μενεῖ, ὅπερ ἐπὶ τῶν ἑξῆς, λέγει; Οὕτω τοίνυν φησὶ τὸ ὄνομα αὐτοῦ δια-μενεῖ θαυμαζόμενον, οὐκ ἔλαττον ἢ ὁ ἥλιος καὶ ἡ σελήνη. Καὶ τούτου ἀπό- 10 δειξις τὸ ἄχρι τῆς δεῦρο, τοῦ τε ἡλίου καὶ τῆς σελήνης διαμενόντων, διαμένειν κἀκεῖνον παρὰ πᾶσιν ἀνθρώποις μνημονευόμενόν τε καὶ θαυμαζόμενον ἐπὶ τῇ σοφίᾳ, ἐπὶ τῇ δόξῃ, ἐπὶ τῇ τιμῇ, ἧς παρὰ πάντων ἔτυχεν

17ᶜ. Καὶ ἐνευλογηθήσονται ἐν αὐτῷ πᾶσαι αἱ φυλαὶ τῆς γῆς. Ἐνταῦθα μάλιστα συνήγαγε τῶν εἰς αὐτὸν λόγων τὴν αἰτίαν, ὅτι διὰ τὸ κοινὸν τοῦ 15 πλήθους τὰ περὶ αὐτὸν διηγεῖται καλά. Πᾶσα γὰρ τιμὴ βασιλέως, καὶ μάλιστα ἡ τοῦ δικαίου φροντίς, κοινὸν ὄφελος τῶν βασιλευομένων. Θαυ-μασθήσονται γάρ φησι δι' αὐτὸν πᾶσαι αἱ φυλαί, τουτέστι πᾶς ὁ Ἰσραήλ. Καὶ τούτου ἀπόδειξις τὸ τὴν τοῦ νότου βασίλισσαν παραγενομένην μακα-ρίσαι τοὺς ὑπηρετουμένους ὅτι διηνεκῶς ταύτης ἀπήλαυον τῆς σοφίας. 20

17ᵈ. Πάντα τὰ ἔθνη μακαριοῦσιν αὐτόν. Οὐδὲ τοῦτο λόγου δεῖται ὅτι ἀληθές, — ἐδείχθη γὰρ ἐκ τῶν πραγμάτων.

7 cf. supra p. 472, in v. 5ᵇ.   19 cf. III Reg. X, 1-9; cf. supra p. 455, p. 473.

16ᶜ. Ἀπὸ γὰρ – χόρτου: P, fol. 243ᵛ; V, fol. 13.
17ᵃ. Ὑπὲρ τούτων – θαυμαζόμενος: P, fol. 243ᵛ; V, fol. 13.
17ᵇ. Ἔδειξε – ἔτυχεν: P, fol. 244; V, fol. 13; Vat. 1422, fol. 130ᵛ (anon.); Cord, p. 478 (= P. G., 692). 9-10 διαμενεῖ] μένει Cord.
17ᶜ. Ἐνταῦθα – σοφίας: P, fol. 244; V, fol. 13ᵛ; Cord, p. 478 (= P. G., 692).
17ᵈ. Οὐδὲ – πραγμάτων: P, fol. 244; V, fol. 13ᵛ.

Aᵉ 16ᶜ (p. 362. 28-363, 2): Per feni pasim nascentis conparationem uoluit multitudinem succesionis expraemere. 9-10 (p. 363, 3-4): Ita continue clarum erit nomen eius, ut iugis est solis cursus et lunae. 17ᶜ (p. 333, 5-11): Ser-uauit causam laudatae in rege felicitatis, quoniam cum populi esset utilitate conseruata; in honorem quippe gentis gloria praedicabatur rectoris, quod ostendit regina Austri, quae beatos appellat regi sapientissimo seruientes.

city like grass of the soil: as a result of his very numerous children his race will become populous and emerge like grass.

His name will be blessed forever (v. 17): he will continue to be admired for these for a long time. *His name will endure before the sun.* He made clear here, too, that *before* does not refer to time so that a reference would be thought to be made to Christ, as some commentators believed. After all, if *before* refers to time and preexistence, what is the reference in *will endure,* which is about the future? So he is saying, *His name will endure* as an object of admiration no less than the sun and the moon. Proof of this is that to this very day, when the sun and the moon remain, that man also remains as an object of remark and admiration by everyone for wisdom, for reputation, for honor accorded by him by all. *All the tribes of the earth will be blessed in him.* At this point in particular he concentrated on the reason for the plaudits directed at him, that it was for the common good of the community that he recounts the good things about him: a king's entire status and especially his attention to righteousness are for the common benefit of his subjects. *All the tribes*—that is, all Israel—will be admired on his account, he is saying. Proof of this is the coming of the queen of the south to declare his servants blessed for having constant enjoyment of this wisdom.[8] *All the nations will declare him blessed.* No comment is required to prove the truth of this; it was demonstrated by the facts. |

---

8. Cf. 1 Kgs 10:8. Theodore takes advantage of the inadequate rendering of the Hebrew as "before" to disallow the reference to Christ that he finds in other commentators (although his own mention of "queen of the south" suggests that he has his eye also on the dominical saying in Matt 12:42 and Luke 11:31).

18ᵃ-19ᵃ. Εὐλογητὸς Κύριος ὁ θεὸς Ἰσραήλ, ὁ ποιῶν θαυμάσια μόνος, καὶ εὐλογημένον τὸ ὄνομα τῆς δόξης αὐτοῦ εἰς τὸν αἰῶνα καὶ εἰς τὸν αἰῶνα τοῦ αἰῶνος. Ὁ δὲ περὶ αὐτὸν μακαρισμὸς ὕμνον τῷ Θεῷ προξενεῖ ὡς μόνῳ δυναμένῳ θαυμαστὰ ποιεῖν· ἅπασα γὰρ ἡ γῆ ταῦτα θεασαμένη αὐτὸν θαυ-
5 μάσεται ὡς τούτων αἴτιον, ὃ δὴ καὶ γένοιτο, καλῶς ἐπαγαγὼν τῆς βεβαιώ-σεως τὴν προσευχήν.

19ᵇ. Καὶ πληρωθήσεται τῆς δόξης αὐτοῦ πᾶσα ἡ γῆ· γένοιτο, γένοιτο. Ὁ ἐπιδιπλασιασμὸς δὲ τοῦ γένοιτο παρίστησι ὡς ἀδιαστάτως καὶ συνεχῶς προσευκτέον. Τὸ δὲ ἑβραϊκὸν πανταχοῦ τὸ γένοιτο γένοιτο ἀμὴν ἀμὴν
10 λέγει· ταῦτα δὲ δείκνυσιν ὅλον τὸν ψαλμὸν εὐκτικῶς εἰρημένον.

PSALMVS LXXII

Ἅπαντα ὁ μακάριος Δαυὶδ πρὸς τὴν κοινὴν ἁπάντων ὠφέλειαν λέγων διατελεῖ, ποιούμενος μὲν τοὺς ψαλμοὺς ἀπὸ τῶν ὑποθέσεων, βλέπων δὲ πρὸς τὴν κοινὴν ἁπάντων ὠφέλειαν. Κἀνταῦθα τοίνυν ἐστὶν ὑπόθεσις αὐτῷ
15 τοῦ ψαλμοῦ ὁ ἐν Βαβυλῶνι λαός, ὡς ἐκ προσώπου τοῦ ἐκείνων λέγοντος οἷα εἰκὸς ἦν ἐν τῷ καιρῷ τῆς αἰχμαλωσίας καὶ τῶν συμφωρῶν αὐτοὺς λογι-

12-14 cf. supra, p 470, 12 17, 33.

18ᵃ-19ᵃ. Ὁ δὲ περὶ αὐτὸν — προσευχήν: P, fol. 244ᵛ; V, fol. 13ᵛ. 5-6 Para-phrasis (p. 460, 6-7): ὕμνων φησὶ πολλῶν ἄξιος ὁ Θεός, ὁ τούτων αὐτῶν τῶν ἀγαθῶν αἴτιος 5 τοῦτον PV.
19ᵇ. Ὁ ἐπιδιπλασιασμὸς — εἰρημένον: P, fol. 245 et V, fol. 14 (anon.); Cord, p. 480. 7-8 L (p. 466, 9-11): Διά τε τοῦ ἐπιδιαπλασιάζειν τὴν εὐχήν, δείκνυσιν ὡς ἀδιαστάτως καὶ συνεχῶς δεῖ τοῦτο ποιεῖν.
Argumentum Ἅπαντα — τοῖς πᾶσιν: P, fol. 245ᵛ; V, fol. 14ᵛ; Cord, p. 497. 14 ss. L (p. 484, ll. 12-7 ab imo): Εἴρηται δὲ οὗτος ὡς ἐκ τῶν Βαβυλωνίων, μᾶλλον δὲ τῶν ἐν αὐτοῖς φιλαρέτων, οἱ κατὰ τὸν καιρὸν τῶν θλίψεων ἀμελεῖσθαι παρὰ Θεοῦ ἐνόμι-ζον· ὁ δὲ ἔδειξεν αὐτοῖς μετὰ τὴν ἔκβασιν, ὅσην τῶν δικαίων ποιεῖται κἂν ταῖς συμφοραῖς πρόνοιαν 15 τοῦ ἐκείνων] τοῦ om. Cord.

Aᵉ 18-19 (p. 363, 13-17): ...eius quippe debetur gloriae, quod alios quoque efficit gloriosos; omnis proinde terra auctorem tanti muneris digna et debita laude celebrauit, unde bene adiunxit Fiat, fiat, inpleri optans quae ostensa lae-tatur. Argumentum ps. LXXII (p. 363, 21-264, 6): Qua expostulatione populus in Babilone constitutus aduersus prouidentiam ussus sit, hoc psalmo discribi-tur; quae querella familiaris est adflictis. Docetur etiam in utilitatem multorum, quod dispensationum diuinarum profunditas pro exploratione uirtutis in hac uita plerumque suos contra meritum patiatur adfligi, quorum tamen magnia-nimitatem praeter spem interdum remuneratur rerum obtatiore successu. Talis sane causatio non uulgaribus sed paucis uirtutis studio praeditis, ut ussitata est, sic aptata est. Cf. Pseudo-Beda (868).

Blessed be the Lord, the God of Israel, who alone works wonders, and blessed be the name of his glory forever, and forever and ever (vv. 18–19). The blessing accorded him produces a hymn of praise to God as the only one capable of performing marvels; on seeing them, all the land will admire him as responsible for them, which he nicely went on to say with Amen as a prayer of confirmation. *All the earth will be filled with his glory. Amen, Amen.* The duplication of *Amen* gives the impression of something to be prayed for without interruption or cessation. The Hebrew universally says "Amen, Amen," which shows that the whole of the psalm is recited as a prayer.

PSALM 73

Blessed David continues saying everything with a view to the common good of everyone, on the one hand developing the psalms from their themes, while on the other hand having an eye to the common good of everyone. Here too, therefore, the people in Babylon form his theme, as he tells from their point of view everything that probably was in their mind at the time of the captivity and the misfortunes, | but of which after the return they repented

σαμένους ἀτοπώτατά τε καὶ ἀπρεπῆ περὶ Θεοῦ μεταγινώσκειν ἐπὶ τούτοις μετὰ τὴν ἐπάνοδον. Λέγει δὲ καὶ ταῦτα οὐχ ἁπλῶς, ἀλλ᾽ ἐπειδήπερ ἔθος ἐστὶν τοῖς ἀνθρώποις ἐν ταῖς συμφοραῖς εἰς λογισμούς τε καταπίπτειν ἀτόπους καὶ ἐννοίας ἀπρεπεῖς, ἀπὸ τῶν κατὰ τὸν λαὸν παιδεύει πάντας μὴ τοῦτο ὑπομένειν, διὰ τούτων ὥσπερ πράγματι παιδεύων ἡμᾶς εἰδέναι ὡς ὁ 5 Θεὸς πολλάκις οἰκονομῶν τι καταλιμπάνει μὲν πρὸς ὀλίγον πάσχειν ὑπὸ ἀσεβῶν τε καὶ ἀδίκων ἀνθρώπων, παρέχει δὲ πάντως καὶ ἀπροσδόκητον τὴν ἀπαλλαγήν. Φαίνεται δὲ ἀπὸ τῶν ῥητῶν μᾶλλον τοῖς ἐναρέτοις ἁρμόττων ὁ ψαλμὸς ἢ τοῖς πᾶσιν.

1ᵃ. Ὡς ἀγαθὸς ὁ Θεὸς τῷ Ἰσραήλ. Ὁ Θεός, ὡς μετὰ τὴν ἐπάνοδον 10 ἐκείνων λεγόντων τοῦτό φησιν, ὦ πῶς ἀγαθὸς περὶ τὸν Ἰσραὴλ ὁ Θεός, δαψιλῶς αὐτὸν καὶ φιλοτίμως εὐεργετῶν· τοῦτο γάρ με λοιπὸν τὰ πράγματα πείθει.

1ᵇ. Τοῖς εὐθέσι τῇ καρδίᾳ. Καὶ μάλιστα ἂν τοῦ πρέποντος ἐπιμελώμεθα, καὶ περὶ τὸ ὀρθὸν καὶ δίκαιον ἔχωμεν. 15

2ᵃ. Ἐμοῦ δὲ παρὰ μικρὸν ἐσαλεύθησαν οἱ πόδες. Ἐγὼ μέντοι παρὰ μικρὸν παρατραπεὶς ἤμην τῆς εὐθείας ὁδοῦ καὶ παρολισθήσας· ἐν γὰρ τῷ καιρῷ τῶν συμφορῶν οὕτως ἦσαν οἱ λογισμοί μου χαῦνοι, δίκην ὕδατος στάσιν οὐκ ἔχοντος.

2ᵇ. Παρ᾽ ὀλίγον ἐξεχύθη τὰ διαβήματά μου. Ἐγγὺς ἐγενόμην τοῦ δια- 20 δεχθῆναι καὶ διαλυθῆναι τῶν ποδῶν τὰς βάσεις, ὡς μηδὲ ἑστάναι δύνασθαι τοῦ λοιποῦ. Βούλεται δὲ εἰπεῖν τῶν λογισμῶν τὴν παρατροπήν· ὥσπερ γὰρ ὁδὸν καλεῖ τὴν πρᾶξιν, οὕτω διαβήματα τοὺς λογισμοὺς οἷς πρὸς τὸ τὴν πρᾶξιν ἀνύειν κεχρήμεθα. Πόθεν δὲ τοῦτο ἔπαθον;

23-24 cf. p. 364, 7-10; THEODORETUS 1444 B 8-9.

1ᵃ. Ὁ Θεὸς — πείθει: P, fol. 246; V, fol. 15, Vat. 1422, fol. 131 (anon.).
1ᵇ. Καὶ μάλιστα — ἔχωμεν: P, fol. 246; V, fol. 15.
2ᵃ. Ἐγὼ — ἔχοντος: P, fol. 246; V, fol 15.
2ᵇ. Ἐγγὺς — ἔπαθον: P, fol. 246; V, fol. 15; Vat. 1422, fol. 131ᵛ (anon.);
Cord, p. 498-499. 20-21 τοῦ διαδεχθῆναι καὶ om. Cord 24 ἔπαθον] ἐκ τοῦ θεωρεῖν ἀνόμους ἐν εὐθηνίᾳ φησὶν add. 1422 Cord.

Aᵉ 10-15 (p. 364, 7-13): Post reditum de Babilone bonum Deum populus, soluta captiuitate, ipsis rebus instructus, libenter praedicat et decenter; quando sunt in remuneratione uirtutes apud illum, erit uobis studium recti et curet cura iustitiae. 2ᵃ (p. 364, 14-16): Dum me, inquit, mala captiuitatis urgerent, perturbato rationis itenere, lubricum cogitationis incurri. 20-22 (p. 364, 17-19): Iudicii claudicante uestigio, ita ruinae proximus fui, ut fixo sententiae meae pede stare non possim.

as very wrong and unseemly before God. Now, it was not without purpose that he says this: since people in misfortune normally are reduced to wrongful thoughts and improper ideas, he instructs everyone on the basis of the people's situation not to submit to this attitude, and thus he teaches us from experience, as it were, to be aware that, while God disposes that we be abandoned for a while to suffer at the hands of godless and unjust people, he definitely also provides unexpected relief.

Now, it emerges from the sentiments that the psalm applies more to the virtuous than to all and sundry. *How good is God to Israel* (v. 1). *God* is said by the people after the return, as it were, meaning, How good is God in regard to Israel, liberal and generous in his favors to them, something that the facts now persuade me of. *To the upright of heart:* and especially if we attend to our duty and are concerned for what is upright and just.

But my feet had come close to stumbling (v. 2): as for me, on the other hand, I had almost been diverted from the straight and narrow and lost my footing; in time of misfortune my thoughts were scattered, lacking stability, like water. *My steps had nearly slipped:* I was close to losing my footing so as no longer to be capable of standing firm. He refers to disarray in thought: as by "way" he refers to behavior, so by *steps* he refers to thoughts, which we use to achieve our goal. What was the cause of my suffering this? | *Because my zeal*

3. Ὅτι ἐζήλωσα ἐπὶ τοῖς ἀνόμοις, εἰρήνην τῶν ἁμαρτωλῶν θεωρῶν. Ζήλῳ καὶ ὀργῇ λαμβανόμενος ἐπὶ τοῖς κατέχουσιν ἡμᾶς, ὅτι πάσης πεπληρωμένους ἀσεβείας καὶ ἁμαρτίας ἐν εἰρήνῃ διατελοῦντας ἑώρων.

4ᵃ. Ὅτι οὐκ ἔστιν ἀνάνευσις ἐν τῷ θανάτῳ αὐτῶν. Ἐπειδὴ τῷ ἀνανεύειν
5 ἀπαγορεύομεν ὅτι ποτ' ἂν βουλώμεθα, ἠβουλήθη εἰπεῖν ὅτι Εἰ καί ποτε ἐν κινδύνοις ἔδοξαν ἐξετάζεσθαι, οὐκ ἐνῆν ἰδεῖν αὐτοὺς ἀπαγορευθέντας ἀπὸ τῶν ἐπικειμένων κινδύνων, ἀλλὰ πρὸς ὀλίγον πάσχειν δοκοῦντες πάλιν ἀπηλλάττοντο. Σαφέστερον δὲ Ἀκύλας εἶπεν τὸ ἀνάνευσις « δυσπάθεια », τουτέστιν Οὐκ ἐνῆν ἰδεῖν αὐτοὺς βαρὺ πάθος ὑπομένοντας ὥστε καὶ ἀπαγο-
10 ρευθῆναι.

4ᵇ. Καὶ στερέωμα ἐν τῇ μάστιγι αὐτῶν. Οὐδὲ στερράν τινα καὶ μεγάλην ἐδέχοντο τὴν μάστιγα, ἀλλὰ τοσαύτην ὅση μηδὲ λυπεῖν ῥαδίως δύναται.

5ᵃ. Ἐν κόποις ἀνθρώπων οὐκ εἰσίν. Οὐδὲ τὰ ἀνθρώπινα παθεῖν ὑπο-
15 μένουσιν.

5ᵇ. Καὶ μετὰ ἀνθρώπων οὐ μαστιγωθήσονται. Οὐδὲν ὅμοιον πάσχουσι τοῖς λοιποῖς.

6ᵃ. Διὰ τοῦτο ἐκράτησεν αὐτοὺς ἡ ὑπερηφανία εἰς τέλος. Ἐντεῦθεν γὰρ μάλιστα καὶ μεγάλα ἐφρόνουν, ὅλοι τῇ ὑπερηφανίᾳ κρατούμενοι.

3. Ζήλῳ — ἑώρων: P, fol. 246ᵛ; V, fol. 15ᵛ: Vat. 1422, fol. 131ᵛ (anon.); Cord, p. 499.
4ᵃ. Ἐπειδὴ — ἀπαγορευθῆναι: P, fol. 246ᵛ; V, fol. 15ᵛ; Vat. 1422. fol. 131ᵛ (anon.); Cord, p. 499.   5 ὅτι om. PV   6 αὐτοὺς ἰδεῖν 1422 Cord   8 Ἀκύλας κτλ. affert L (p. 490, 38-40)   9 ἐνῆν] ἦν Cord L   βαρὺ om. 1422 Cord   βαρυπαθές τι L.
4ᵇ. Οὐδὲ στερράν — δύναται: P, fol. 246ᵛ; V, fol. 15ᵛ; Vat. 1422, fol. 131ᵛ (anon.) et Cord, p. 499, usque ad μάστιγα.
5ᵃ. Οὐδὲ — ὑπομένουσιν: P, fol. 246ᵛ; V, fol. 15ᵛ; Vat. 1422, fol. 131ᵛ et Cord, p. 499 sub nomine HESYCHII.
5ᵇ. Οὐδὲν — λοιποῖς: P, fol. 246ᵛ; V, fol. 15ᵛ.
6ᵃ. Ἐντεῦθεν — κρατούμενοι: P, fol. 247; V, fol. 15ᵛ.

Aᵉ 3 (p. 364, 20-24): Dum intueor hostes meos, quibus nulla recti, nulla erat cura iustitiae, alta pace perfrui, oculum rationis meae ira ac zelus inpleuit. 8-10 (p. 365, 1-4): Aquila dicit Non est adflictio in morte eorum, ut sit sensus Numquam ita adflicti sunt, ut disperare cogerentur salutem.   11-12 (p. 365, 5-6): Numquam uehimenter castigati sunt.   14-17 (p. 365, 7-9): Sic illis omnia, inquit, cedunt prospere, ut uideantur extra condicionem agere uarietatis uel fragillitatis humanae.

was aroused at the lawless on observing sinners' peace (v. 3): seized with zeal and wrath at those oppressing us, because I saw that despite their being filled with all godlessness and sin, they continued to live in peace. *Because there is no denial in their death* (v. 4): since by denying we renounce anything we wanted, he means, Even if ever they were thought to be in danger, it was impossible to see them despairing in the face of the dangers besetting them; instead, though seeming to suffer for a while, they were in turn set free. Aquila expressed *denial* more clearly as "misfortune"—that is, It was impossible to see them undergoing such severe suffering that they would despair. *And strength in their scourge:* neither did they suffer a very severe scourging; instead, it was such as to be incapable of easily making them feel pain.

They are not affected by human troubles (v. 5): they do not undergo human suffering, either. *And they will not be scourged along with other people:* they suffer nothing like other people. *Hence, arrogance gained control of them in the end* (v. 6): this in particular made them conceited, being in the grip of arrogance. | *They were enveloped in their iniquity and impiety:*

6ᵇ. Περιεβάλοντο ἀδικίαν καὶ ἀσέβειαν ἑαυτῶν. Ἐκύκλωσαν ἑαυτοὺς τῇ τε ἀδικίᾳ καὶ τῇ ἀσεβείᾳ, ἐν τούτοις ὄντες ἀεί, ἐν τούτοις φαινόμενοι, — ἐκ μεταφορᾶς τῶν τὰ ἱμάτια περιβαλλομένων καὶ ἐν αὐτοῖς φαινομένων ἐν τοῖς ὄρεσιν.

7ᵃ. Ἐξελεύσεται ὡς ἐκ στέατος ἡ ἀδικία αὐτῶν. Εἴρηται ἡμῖν καὶ ἐν τῷ 5 ξβ´ ὅτι στέαρ καὶ πιότητα τὴν εὐθηνίαν λέγει· ὡς οὖν ἐν πολλῇ ὄντων τῇ εὐθηνίᾳ, οὕτω καὶ προσῄει ἡ ἀδικία, ἵνα εἴπῃ ὅτι σφόδρα ἠδίκουν. Ἔθος γάρ ἐστι τοῖς ἀνθρώποις ἀδικεῖν προειρημένοις ἐν εὐθηνίᾳ οὖσι καὶ πλούτῳ καὶ τιμῇ μειζόνως ἀδικεῖν.

7ᵇ. Διῆλθοσαν εἰς διάθεσιν καρδίας. Λέγεται διάθεσις κυρίως ἡ περί 10 τι σχέσις. Λέγομεν οὖν καὶ διάθεσιν τὴν περί τινα ἀγάπην, ἀπὸ τοῦ περὶ αὐτὸν ἔχειν τε καὶ διακεῖσθαι τὴν γνώμην· οὕτω καὶ περὶ πρᾶγμα διάθεσιν λέγομεν ψυχῆς, ἀπὸ τοῦ τοιῶσδε περὶ τὸ πρᾶγμα ἔχειν. Κἀνταῦθα οὖν διάθεσιν καρδίας λέγει τὴν σχέσιν, ἀκολουθῶν τῷ ἄνω. Ἠδίκουν γάρ φησι διὰ τὴν προσοῦσαν αὐτοῖς ἀσθένειαν οὕτως, ὡς καὶ εἰς πολλὴν ἐλθεῖν διάθεσιν 15 τοῦ πράγματος τὴν διάνοιαν. Βούλεται δὲ τῆς κακίας τοῦ τρόπου τὴν ἐπίτασιν εἰπεῖν ἀπὸ τοῦ στέργειν τε αὐτὸ καὶ σπουδαίως ἐπιτελεῖν.

8ᵃ. Διενοήθησαν καὶ ἐλάλησαν ἐν πονηρίᾳ. Λογιζόμενοι δὲ ἄτοπα καὶ ἐφθέγγοντο.

8ᵇ. Ἀδικίαν εἰς τὸ ὕψος ἐλάλησαν. Ῥήματα ἐφθέγγοντο καθ᾽ ἡμῶν εἰς 20 σε τὴν ὕβριν ἔχοντα τεταμένην. Ἔδειξε δὲ κατὰ αὔξησιν αὐτῶν τὴν κακίαν καὶ τὴν ἀσέβειαν· ἀπὸ γὰρ τῆς εὐθηνίας φησὶν ἠδίκουν, καὶ οὐ μόνον ἠδίκουν, ἀλλὰ καὶ τὴν περὶ τὸ πρᾶγμα διάθεσιν ἐκέκτηντο, εἶτα διακείμενοι καὶ λογιζόμενοι καὶ ἐφθέγγοντο βλάσφημα.

5-6 in ps. LXII, 6 (p. 408).

6ᵇ. Ἐκύκλωσαν — ὄρεσιν: P, fol. 247; V, fol. 15ᵛ; Vat. 1422, fol. 131ᵛ (anon.); Cord, p. 500.   2 τε... τῇ om. Cord   3 φαινομένων des. Cord   ἐν om. 1422.
7ᵃ. Εἴρηται — ἀδικεῖν: P, fol. 247; V, fol. 15ᵛ-16.   6 ξα´ PV.
7ᵇ. Λέγεται — ἐπιτελεῖν: P, fol. 247; V, fol. 16; Cord, p. 500-501.   10 λέγεται δὲ Cord   10-11 διάθεσις — σχέσις affert 1422, fol. 131ᵛ (anon.)   11 τινας PV.
8ᵃ. Λογιζόμενοι — ἐφθέγγοντο: C, fol. 325; P, fol. 247; V, fol. 16; Vat. 1422, fol. 131ᵛ (anon.); Cord, p. 501.
8ᵇ. Ῥήματα — βλάσφημα: C, fol. 325; P, fol. 247; V, fol. 16.

Aᵉ 6ᵇ (p. 365, 13-16): Scelera sceleribus operienda duxerunt, et adeo habundauere malefactis, ut tanquam uestimento sic amicarentur creminibus
8ᵇ (p. 363, 12-16): Licet in nos contumiliarum uerba iacerentur, tuam tamen iniuriam continebant; per hos autem gradus ad summum impietatis euecti sunt.

they wrapped themselves in iniquity and impiety, always guilty of it, always giving an impression of it (by analogy with people putting on clothes and appearing in them to bystanders). *Their iniquity developed as though from fatness* (v. 7). We remarked also in Psalm 63 that by *fatness* and richness he refers to prosperity.[1] So he is saying, As they enjoyed much prosperity, so also did iniquity accrue to them, as if to say, They committed much iniquity (it being customary with people in affluent circumstances to choose to do wrong, and when in wealth and distinction to do worse wrong). *They passed on to their heart's disposition.* The precise meaning of *disposition* is the "attitude toward something"; so we say that love for others is a disposition on the basis of having an attitude toward them and the mind-set being thus directed. Likewise, we also speak of the soul's disposition for something on the basis of the attitude toward it. So here, too, by *the heart's disposition* he refers to the attitude, in keeping with what went before. They kept doing wrong, he is saying, on account of the weakness they had to such an extent that the idea of criminal behavior became a deep-seated disposition. He conveys the extent of their evil behavior from their love and zealous performance of it.

They were disposed to wickedness and spoke of it (v. 8): pondering improper actions, they also gave voice to them. *They extolled iniquity:* they uttered words against us that contained a blatant insult to you. He brought out in increasing measure their malice and godlessness: As a result of prosperity, he is saying, they not only did wrong but also acquired a disposition for practicing it; then, when so disposed and so minded, they also gave voice to blasphemies. | *They lifted their mouth to heaven* (v. 9): they blasphemed

---

1. Cf. Ps 63:5.

9ª. Ἔθεντο εἰς οὐρανὸν τὸ στόμα αὐτῶν. Ἐβλασφήμουν εἴς σε. Ἐμφαντικώτερον δὲ αὐτὸ εἶπεν ὅτι ἐκεῖ ἔθηκαν αὐτῶν τὸ στόμα, περὶ τοῦτο ἠσχόλουν τὴν γλῶσσαν, τὸ ὅτι βλάσφημον φθέγξονται κατά σου.

9ᵇ. Καὶ ἡ γλῶσσα αὐτῶν διῆλθεν ἐπὶ τῆς γῆς. Διέτρεχε δέ φησι καὶ κατὰ
5 τὴν γῆν ἅπασαν· οὐδενὸς γὰρ ἐφείδοντο, — ἵνα εἴπῃ Ἐβλασφήμουν εἰς ἡμᾶς, εἰς τὸν ναόν, εἰς τὴν πόλιν, εἰς τὴν γῆν τῆς ἐπαγγελίας, δι᾽ ἡμῶν σε βλασφημοῦντες καὶ ἀφ᾽ ἡμῶν εἴς σε μεθιστάμενοι καὶ φειδόμενοι οὐδενός.

10ª. Διὰ τοῦτο ἐπιστρέψει ὁ λαός μου ἐνταῦθα. Ἀποφηναμένου καὶ λέγοντος Διὰ ταύτην αὐτῶν τὴν κακίαν, ὁποῖοι δήποτ᾽ ἂν ὦσιν, πάντως ἀφέλω
10 τοὺς ἐμοὺς ἐξ αὐτῶν καὶ ἐπαναγαγὼν ἀποδώσω τοὺς οἰκείους τόπους.

10ᵇ. Καὶ ἡμέραι πλήρεις εὑρεθήσονται ἐν αὐτοῖς. Καὶ ζήσονται μετὰ ἀδείας, συγκροτουμένης αὐτοῖς τῆς ζωῆς, ὡς μὴ παραιρεῖσθαι μηδεμίαν αὐτῶν ἡμέραν τοῦ βίου προλαμβανομένων ὑπὸ τοῦ θανάτου. Τοῦτο δὲ λέγει οὐχ ὡς πάντως ὡρισμένον καιρὸν παντὸς ἀνθρώπου ζῶντος, ἀλλ᾽ ὡς πολλάκις
15 ἡμῶν διὰ τὸ παθητοὺς εἶναι τὴν φύσιν ὑπὸ συμφορῶν καὶ θλίψεως ἢ καί τινων τοιούτων ὑπομενόντων θάνατον, ὃν εἰ δυνηθείημεν ἂν ἐκκλίναντες ἐπὶ μήκιστον βιῶναι. Ἕτεροι γὰρ οἱ ἀπὸ τῶν συμφορῶν ἐπιγιγνόμενοι θάνατοι καὶ ἕτεροι οἱ οὐκ ἐκ τῶν ἔξωθεν κακῶν, ἀλλ᾽ ἀπ᾽ αὐτῶν τῶν ἐν τῇ κατασκευῇ τῆς φύσεως συμβαίνοντες· κἂν γὰρ μηδὲν ἔξωθεν ἐπιγένηται, οἷον ὁ διὰ
20 ξίφους ἤ τινος τοιούτου θάνατος, ἀλλ᾽ αὐτὴ πάντως ἡ φύσις εἰς γῆρας ἐλάσασα, ἀναγκαίως ἐφέλκεται τὸν θάνατον. Ὡς οὖν πρότερον αὐτῶν πολλὰ τοιαῦτα ὑπομενόντων καὶ ὑπὸ τῶν κατεχόντων κακῶν πολλάκις προλαμβανομένων εἰς τὸν θάνατον, τοῦτό φησιν ὅτι οὐκέτι πείσονται τοιοῦτο οὐδέν, ἀλλ᾽ ἕξουσι τὰς ἡμέρας πλήρεις, τὸν ἀπὸ τῆς φύσεως θάνατον ἐκδεχόμε
25 νοι μόνον.

13-25 cf. in ps. XXXVIII, 6ª (p. 234-238).

9ª. Ἐβλασφήμουν — κατά σου: C, fol. 326; P, fol. 247ᵛ; V, fol. 16; Vat. 1422, fol. 131ᵛ (anon.).
9ᵇ. Διέτρεχε — οὐδενός: C, fol. 326; P, fol. 247ᵛ; V, fol. 16; Vat. 1422, fol. 131ᵛ-132 (anon.)   4 καὶ om. PV 1422.
10ª. Ἀποφηναμένου — τόπους: C, fol. 326ᵛ; P, fol. 248; V, fol. 16ᵛ.
10ᵇ. Καὶ ζήσονται — μόνον: C, fol. 326ᵛ; P, fol. 248; V, fol. 248; V, fol. 16ᵛ-17; Cord, p. 502-503 (P. G., 692-693).   17 γιγνόμενοι Cord   24 τὸν ἀπὸ abrumpitur C.

Aᵉ 9ᵇ (p. 366, 29-367, 3): In terram repromisionis, in templum sacrosque ritus, in ciuitatem dicatam ceremonis, in nosque quondam tui iuris et nominis maledictis conuicisque in tuam contumiliam uolabant.   10ª (p. 367, 4-8): Quasi ex persona Dei sermo formatur, quod etiam si merita deessent populo, reuersionem tamen eius sola hostium accelaret inmanitas.

against you. He expressed the same thing to greater effect: they set their mouth in that direction, they exercised their tongue in this—uttering blasphemies against you. *And their tongue went abroad on earth:* it went throughout the whole earth; they spared no one, as if to say, They blasphemed against us, against the temple, against the city, against the land of promise, through us blaspheming against you, moving from us to you and sparing no one.

For this reason my people will turn back here (v. 10). He declares and states, For reason of their wickedness, no matter who they are, I shall absolutely remove from them my people, lead them back, and restore their own land. *And full days will be found in them:* they will live in security, their life organized for them so that no day of their life will be snatched from them by an early death. Now, he means not that a time is definitely set for every person's life, but that death awaits us in our passible nature from disasters or tribulations or such like things, and if we were able to avoid them, we would live for a long time. Some deaths, in fact, occur as a result of disasters, and others not from external troubles but as a result of the very make-up of our nature: even if nothing befalls us from external circumstances, like death from a sword or something similar, nevertheless nature advances to old age and necessarily involves death. So he is saying, Although they formerly were subject to many such things and often went to an early death from troubles befalling them, they will no longer suffer anything like that, instead having *full days,* being subject only to natural death. |

11ᵃ. Καὶ εἶπον Πῶς ἔγνω ὁ Θεός. Τὸ προκείμενον διστίχιον — τὸ Διὰ τοῦτο ἐπιστρέψει ὁ λαός μου, καὶ ἡμέραι πλήρεις εὑρεθήσονται ἐν αὐτοῖς — ἐκ τοῦ Θεοῦ εἰρημένον παρέγκειται διὰ μέσου· τὸ γὰρ Καὶ εἶπον Πῶς ἔγνω ὁ Θεὸς πρὸς τὰ ἀνώτερα τὴν ἀκολουθίαν ἔχει. Ἐγὼ γάρ φησιν οὕτω μὲν εὐθηνουμένων ἐκείνων, τοιαῦτα δὲ καὶ πραττόντων καὶ λεγόντων, ἔλεγον κατ' 5 ἐμαυτὸν Οἶδεν ἆρα ταῦτα ὁ Θεός; τὸ δέ γε πῶς καὶ πρὸς τὰ κάτω βλέπει, ἐπισυνηγμένου αὐτοῖς κατὰ τὴν διάνοιαν. Ἐπάγει γάρ·

11ᵇ. Καὶ εἰ ἔστι γνῶσις ἐν τῷ ὑψίστῳ. Ἀντὶ τοῦ Εἰ οἶδεν ταῦτα καὶ φροντίζει τούτων;

12ᵃ. Ἰδοὺ οὗτοι ἁμαρτωλοὶ καὶ εὐθηνοῦντες. Τούτοις ἀποδίδοται τὸ 10 πῶς. Ἔλεγον γάρ φησιν Οἶδεν ἆρα ταῦτα; καὶ πῶς, εἴπερ οἶδεν καὶ ἔχει τούτων τὴν γνῶσιν, ἐν τοσαύταις ἁμαρτίαις οὗτοι στρεφόμενοι ἐν τοσαύτῃ καθεστήκασιν εὐθηνίᾳ;

12ᵇ. Εἰς τὸν αἰῶνα κατέσχον πλούτου. Καὶ διαμένουσι πλουτοῦντες, οὐδενὸς αὐτοῖς τὴν εὐπραγίαν διακόπτοντος. 15

13ᵃ. Καὶ εἶπον Ἄρα ματαίως ἐδικαίωσα τὴν καρδίαν μου. Ἐλογιζόμην οὖν φησιν ὅτι τάχα εἰκῇ καὶ οὐδενὸς κέρδους ἕνεκεν ἐφρόντιζον ἐπιμελεῖσθαι τοῦ δικαίου. Σύμμαχος Ἴσως οὖν ἔγνω, μάτην ἐκάθηρα τὴν καρδίαν μου. Πανταχοῦ δὲ ὥσπερ καὶ ἐνταῦθα τὸ εἶπον ἀντὶ τοῦ ἐλογιζόμην λέγει, ἐπειδὴ ὁ λογιζόμενος καθ' ἑαυτὸν ὥσπερ λέγων ἐστὶν ἑαυτῷ τὸ ἐνθύμημα. 20

13ᵇ. Καὶ ἐνιψάμην ἐν ἀθῴοις τὰς χεῖράς μου. Καὶ εἰκῇ ἐσπούδασα πρὸς τοὺς ἀθῴους ἔχειν τὴν κοινωνίαν καὶ πάντων καθαρεύειν τῶν πταισμάτων· εἴρηται γὰρ ὅτι διὰ τοῦ ἐνιψάμην τὴν κοινωνίαν ἐμφαίνει, καὶ ἐν τῷ κε΄ καὶ ἐν τῷ νξ΄. Διὰ τί δὲ ταῦτα ἐλογιζόμην;

24-25 cf. supra in ps. XXV, 6 (p. 129) et in LVII, 11ᵇ (p. 380).

11ᵃ. Τὸ προκείμενον — ἐπάγει γάρ: P, fol. 248; V, fol. 17; Vat. 1422, fol. 132.
11ᵇ. Ἀντὶ τοῦ — τούτων: P, fol. 248; V, fol. 17; Vat. 1422, fol. 132.
12ᵃ. Τούτοις — εὐθηνίᾳ: P, fol. 248; V, fol. 17.
12ᵇ. Καὶ διαμένουσι — διακόπτοντος: P, fol. 248; V, fol. 17; Vat. 1422, fol. 132 (anon.).
13ᵃ. Ἐλογιζόμην — ἐνθύμημα: P, fol. 248ᵛ; V, fol. 17; Cord, p. 503. 18 ἔγνω om. Cord 19 ὥσπερ καὶ om. PV.
13ᵇ. Καὶ εἰκῇ — ἐλογιζόμην: P, fol. 248ᵛ; V, fol. 17; Vat. 1422, fol. 132. 23 ἐφαίνει PV ἐμφαίνων 1422 et des.

Aᵉ 12ᵇ (p. 368, 1-3): Permanet apud eos bonorum fixa possesio, nec aliquo damnosso feriuntur incursu.   16-18 (p. 368, 5-7): Cogitationes mihi agitatio suggerebat, infructuosse forsitan me studium iustitiae suscipisse.   21-22 (p. 368, 8-10): Frustra studiui, dum ab omni maledicto absteneo, similis innocentibus inueniri.

They said, How does God know? (v. 11). The foregoing two clauses, *For this reason my people will turn back here, and full days will be found in them,* as spoken on God's part, come in the middle, the clause *They said, How does God know?* being connected with what is above. He is saying, Whereas they prospered in that fashion, doing and saying such things, I said to myself, Surely God knows this? The word *How* is prospective, associated in thought with what follows. He goes on, in fact, to say *Is there knowledge in the Most High?* Does he know this and care about it? *Look at these people, sinners and prospering* (v. 12). The *How* corresponds to this: I asked, he is saying, Does he know this? And how so, if he is aware and has knowledge of them, living in sin as they are and established in such prosperity? *For ages they possessed wealth:* they remained wealthy, no one robbing them of their prosperity.

And I said, Surely it is in vain that I kept my heart righteous (v. 13): I wondered if it was therefore perhaps in vain and to no point that I devoted my thinking to attending to righteousness. Symmachus: "I was perhaps aware, therefore, that it was in vain that I purified my heart." Everywhere, as here too, he uses *I said* for "I wondered," since the one who wonders within himself is like someone expressing his thoughts to himself. *I washed my hands among the innocent:* I wasted the effort of sharing with the innocent and being guiltless of all mistakes (there was mention, remember, in Psalms 26 and 58 that by "I washed" he brings out sharing).[2] Why did I wonder this? | *Scourg-*

---

2. Cf. Pss 26:6; 58:10, where in fact the washing of hands, plausibly, denotes rejection of sharing.

14ᵃ. Καὶ ἐγενόμην μεμαστιγωμένος ὅλην τὴν ἡμέραν. Ὅτι ἑώρων ἐμαυτὸν ἀεὶ ἐν μάστιξιν.

14ᵇ. Καὶ ὁ ἔλεγχός μου εἰς τὰς πρωΐας. Σύμμαχος Καὶ ἐλεγχόμενος καθ' ἕκαστον ὄρθρον, καὶ ὥσπερ εἰς τοῦτο ὀρθρίζων — εἰς τὸ ἐλέγχεσθαι ἐφ' 5 οἷς ἥμαρτον καὶ μαστίζεσθαι· οὕτω γὰρ ἀεὶ διετέλουν ταῦτα ὑπομένων.

15ᵃ. Εἰ ἔλεγον Διηγήσομαι οὕτως. Πολλάκις δέ φησιν ἐλογιζόμην ὅτι μᾶλλον ἐκεῖνο προσῆκεν ἐννοεῖν τε καὶ λέγειν· τὸ γὰρ Διηγήσομαι οὕτως, ἀντὶ τοῦ μᾶλλον τοῦτο λογίσασθαι καὶ εἰπεῖν τάχα προσήκει, — ὥσπερ γὰρ τὸ ἔλεγον, οὕτως καὶ τὸ διηγήσομαί φησιν ἐπὶ τοῦ ἐννοεῖν καὶ λέγειν. 10 Ποῖον οὖν ὡς ἀληθέστερον τάχα ὃ οὐ δεῖν λογίζεσθαι;

15ᵇ. Ἰδοὺ τῇ γενεᾷ τῶν υἱῶν σου ἠσυνθέτηκας. Ὅτι τάχα τὰς συνθήκας πρὸς τὸ γένος τὸ ἡμέτερον, τὰς πρὸς ἡμᾶς, οὓς τῇ διαθέσει ἐν υἱῶν τάξει ἔχειν ἠξίωσεν, ταύτας ἔλυσεν. Ἀπὸ γὰρ τῆς συνθήκης εἶπεν τὸ ἠσυνθέτηκας, τουτέστιν παρέλυσας τὰς πρὸς ἡμᾶς συνθήκας· οὐ γὰρ ὡς πολλοὶ τὸ 15 κείμενον οὐκ εἰδότες καὶ ἕτερόν τι νομίσαντες γραώδεις μύθους ἑρμηνειῶν μᾶλλον ἀνέπλασαν.

16ᵃ. Καὶ ὑπέλαβον τοῦ γνῶναι. Σύμμαχος Καὶ διελογιζόμην ἐπιγνῶναι, ἀντὶ τοῦ Ὑπέλαβον τόδε δεῖν εἰδέναι τε καὶ φρονεῖν περὶ τῶν παρόντων μᾶλλον. Ποίων;

14ᵃ. Ὅτι — μάστιξιν: P, fol. 248ᵛ: V, fol. 17. 1-2 ἐμαυτὸν] ἑαυτὸν PV.
14ᵇ. Σύμμαχος — ὑπομένων: P, fol. 249; V, fol. 17ᵛ; Vat. 1422, fol. 132; Paraphrasis (p. 487). 3 Σύμμαχος supplevi.
15ᵃ. Πολλάκις — λογίζεσθαι; P, fol. 249ᵛ; V, fol. 18; Cord, p. 504. 9 φησιν om. PV 10 ποῖον — λογίζεσθαι om. Cord.
15ᵇ. Ὅτι τάχα — ἀνέπλασαν: P, fol. 249ᵛ; V, fol. 18. 12-14 Paraphrasis (p. 487): Τουτέστι παρέλυσας τὰς πρὸς ἡμᾶς συνθήκας, τοῦ ἔχειν ἡμᾶς ἀεὶ ἐν τάξει τῶν υἱῶν σου.
16ᵃ. Σύμμαχος — ποίων: P, fol. 249ᵛ; V, fol. 18.

Aᵉ 14ᵃ (p. 369, 13-11): ...uidebam me sub adflictionis continuo uerbere constitutum. 14ᵇ (p. 368, 15-19): Simmachus dicit *Et castigatio mea per omnem matutinum*, quasi propter hoc matutinus adsurgerem ut peccata mea cotidie praesens ultio castigaret. 11-14 (p. 368, 22-27): Cui dispossuisti forte. Pacta, inquid, quae cum genere nostro ac nobiscum, quos in locum filiorum affectu patrio recipisti, desoluta sunt. Nam ex more placiti et conuentionis dixit *dispossuisti*, id est Pactum, quod statueras, dissoluisti. 16ᵃ (p. 368, 28-369, 2): Id est existimabam me inter haec diuersa et aduersa quid tenendum esset rationis iudicio praeuidere.

ing was my lot all day long (v. 14): because I saw myself suffering scourging unceasingly. *And in the morning my testing.* Symmachus: "And being tested every morning," as if I got up for this purpose, to be tested and scourged by those who sinned—hence my continuing unceasingly to suffer this.

If I had said, I shall give this version of things (v. 15): often I wondered if I should rather form this idea and speak it (by *I shall give this version of things* meaning, I should perhaps rather think and say this). In other words, just as *I had said,* so too *I shall give a version* refers to pondering and saying. So what is it, then, that is perhaps more truthful but should not be considered? *Lo, you would have been faithless to the generation of your children:* that perhaps the treaties with our race, with us whom he vouchsafed to hold affectionately as children, he abrogated. He said *been faithless* in reference to the treaty—that is, You abolished the treaties with us—not, as is the case with many, who were unaware of the contents and had a different idea, and came up rather with old wives' tales by way of interpretation.[3]

I came to the realization (v. 16). Symmachus: "I gave thought to the way to recognize"—that is, I formed this impression of what should be known and considered regarding the present situation. What sort of situation? | *This is*

---

3. The Antiochene text reads the verb in the second person, which makes this final remark particularly unclear.

968 THEODORVS MOPSVESTENVS

16ᵇ. Τοῦτο κόπος ἐστὶν ἐνώπιόν μου. Ὅτι τὰς μὲν συνθήκας οὐκ ἔλυσε τὰς πρὸς ἡμᾶς, ταῦτα δὲ νῦν ἃ πάσχω καὶ ἐν οἷς ἐξετάζομαι κόπον μοι καὶ θλίψιν ἐπήγαγεν.

17ᵃ. Ἕως οὗ εἰσέλθω εἰς τὸ ἁγιαστήριον τοῦ Θεοῦ. Ἀντὶ τοῦ Οὐ διηνεκῆ, οὐχ ὥστε ἐν θλίψεσιν ἐξετάζεσθαι καὶ συμφοραῖς ἀεί, — ὅπερ ἐστὶ 5 τοῦ τὰς συνθήκας λύσαντος, — ἀλλὰ Μέχρις ἂν εἰς τὸ ἁγιαστήριόν με πάλιν εἰσαγάγῃς, ἀντὶ τοῦ Μέχρις ἂν ἐπαναγάγῃς εἰς τὴν γῆν τῆς ἐπαγγελίας καὶ τὸν ἅγιον τόπον · ἵνα εἴπῃ ὅτι Εἰσάξεις με πάντως καὶ τὰ νῦν θλίψις ἐστὶ πρὸς καιρὸν ἐπενεχθεῖσα, ἣ πέρας ἕξει τὴν εἴσοδόν μου τὴν εἰς τὴν γῆν τῆς ἐπαγγελίας πάντως ἐσομένην. 10

17ᵇ. Καὶ συνῶ εἰς τὰ ἔσχατα αὐτῶν. Τότε ὄψομαι καὶ τούτων τὰ τέλη εἰς τί ποτε, ἆρα ποτὲ αὐτοῖς τὰ τῆς εὐθηνίας καὶ τὰ τῆς ἀδικίας ἀποβήσεται.

18ᵃ. Πλὴν διὰ τὰς δολιότητας αὐτῶν ἔθου αὐτοῖς κακά. Διὰ γὰρ τὴν κακίαν αὐτῶν καὶ τὴν πανουργίαν, μυρίοις αὐτοὺς περιβαλεῖς κακοῖς.

18ᵇ. Κατέβαλες αὐτοὺς ἐν τῷ ἐπαρθῆναι. Ἐπαρθέντας καὶ μεγάλα φρο- 15 νήσαντας ἀπὸ τῆς εὐπραγίας κατασπάσεις καὶ καθελεῖς.

19ᵃ. Πῶς ἐγένοντο εἰς ἐρήμωσιν ἐξάπινα; Ὥστε τὸ ἐναντίον με θαυμάζειν ὅπως αἰφνιδίως εἰς πολλὴν περιέστησαν τὴν ἐρήμωσιν, ἐν βραχείᾳ τῇ ῥοπῇ πολλὴν δεξάμενοι τὴν μεταβολήν.

16ᵇ. Ὅτι τὰς — ἐπήγαγεν: P, fol. 250; V, fol. 18; Vat. 1422, fol. 132 (anon.).
17ᵃ. Ἀντὶ τοῦ — ἐσομένην: P, fol. 250; V, fol. 18ᵛ.
17ᵇ. Τότε — ἀποβήσεται: P, fol. 250; V, fol. 18ᵛ; Vat. 1422, fol. 132ᵛ (anon.).
18ᵃ. Διὰ γὰρ — κακοῖς: P, fol. 250ᵛ; V, fol. 18ᵛ; Vat. 1422, fol. 132ᵛ (anon.):
Paraphrasis (p. 488).
18ᵇ. Ἐπαρθέντας — καθελεῖς: P, fol. 250ᵛ; V, fol. 18ᵛ; Vat. 1422, fol. 132ᵛ
(anon.); Paraphrasis (p. 488).   16 κατασπαρεῖς καὶ καθέλοις PV.
19ᵃ. Ὥστε τὸ ἐναντίον — μεταβολήν: P, fol. 250ᵛ; V, fol. 18ᵛ; Vat. 1422, fol. 132ᵛ
(anon.); Cord, p. 505-506.

Aᵉ 16ᵇ (p. 369, 4-7): ...discernere utrum ... pacta quae nobiscum desoluta fecerat; hoc itaque deiudicare et laboris et difficultatis est maxime.   7-9 (p. 369, 8-12): Id est Donec me in terram repromisionis et locum sanctum reducas; quod cum feceris, omnis tribulatio cum omni cogitationum uarietate cessabit.
17ᵇ (p. 369, 13-16): Tunc certissime peruidebo qui iniquitatis eorum ausus, qui affluentiam rerum omnium, quae insolentes eos fecerat, finis excipiat.
18ᵃ (p. 369, 17-19): Versutiam eorum atque nequitiam impunitam esse noluisti.
19ᵃ (p. 369, 24-370, 1): Stupor, inquit, meus, quo felicitatem eorum ante mirabar, subito est in contrarium motatus, ut desolutionem eorum ac miserias uelut attonitus aspiciam quae illis breuiter tempore contigerunt.

hardship for me: that while he did not annul the treaties with us, the things I now suffer and am exposed to he inflicted on me as *hardship* and tribulation. *Until I entered God's sanctuary* (v. 17): that is, not interminably, not so as to be ever exposed to tribulations and misfortunes (which is the effect of the one canceling the treaties), but, Until you lead me again into the sanctuary— that is, Until you bring me back to the land of promise and the holy place; as if to say, You will definitely bring me in, and the present situation is a trial imposed for a time, which will reach its end with my entry into the land of promise that is definitely coming. *May I understand their fate:* I shall then see also how their fortunes are concluded, whether their prosperity and their evildoing will ever disappear. *But you put troubles in their way on account of their deceitful acts* (v. 18): on account of their malice and evildoing you enveloped them in countless troubles. *You brought them down by lifting them up:* when they were conceited and carried away with their prosperity, you brought them down and humbled them.

How did they meet with desolation all of a sudden? (v. 19). The result by contrast was that I was amazed how they suddenly encountered great desolation, undergoing a great change in a flash. | *They failed; they were*

19ᵇ-20ᵃ. Ἐξέλιπον, ἀπώλοντο διὰ τὴν ἀνομίαν αὐτῶν ὡσεὶ ἐνύπνιον ἐξε-
γειρομένου. Κατὰ κοινοῦ τὸ Πῶς αἰφνίδιον ἠρημώθησαν; ἀπώλοντο, ὡς μηδὲν
ἐνυπνίου διαλλάττειν αὐτῶν τὴν εὐπραγίαν. Πάντα μὲν οὖν ἐναργῆ τῆς θείας
γραφῆς τὰ παραδείγματα, μάλιστα δὲ τοῦτο. Τοιοῦτο γὰρ τὸ ἐνύπνιον, φαν-
5 τάζον μὲν πρὸς βραχὺ τὴν ψυχήν, εἰ δέ τις αἰφνίδιον διαναστήσειε τὸν καθεύδοντα πάντα διαλέλυται καὶ οὐδὲν ὑφέστηκεν, μόνη δὲ μένει ἡ τοῦ δοκεῖν τι
ἑωρακέναι μνήμη. Οὕτω φησὶ καὶ ἡ τούτων εὐπραγία ἔσται, φαντασίαν ἔχουσα
μόνον, αἰφνιδίως δὲ ἀπολλυμένην ὡς μηδὲν ἔχειν λείψανον τοῦ πράγματος.

20ᵇ. Κύριε, ἐν τῇ πόλει σου τὴν εἰκόνα αὐτῶν ἐξουδενώσεις. Καὶ ἐν τῷ
10 λη΄ ψαλμῷ εὐπραγούντων μνημονεύων φησὶ Μέντοι γε ἐν εἰκόνι διαπορεύεται
ἄνθρωπος, — τουτέστιν ἐν εἰκόνι καὶ γραφῇ σχῆμα μόνον ἐστὶν ὁ ἄνθρωπος, δοκῶν μὲν πλουτεῖν καὶ θησαυρίζειν, μετὰ βραχὺ δὲ ἀπιὼν μέν, ἀπολαύων δὲ οὐδενός, — οὕτω κἀνταῦθα λέγει Ἐν τῇ πόλει σού φησι, τουτέστι
διὰ τὴν σὴν πόλιν, ὑπὲρ τοῦ ἐκείνην πάλιν οἰκοδομηθῆναι καὶ πάλιν ἡμᾶς
15 συστῆναι, εἰς οὐδὲν περιστήσεις τούτων τὴν δοκοῦσαν αὐτοῖς εἰκόνα προσεῖναι καὶ τὸ σχῆμα. Εἰκόνα δὲ ἐκάλεσεν εἰκότως, ὡς πρὸς ὀλίγον μὲν φαινομένων, ἀπολλυμένων δὲ ὕστερον.

21. Ὅτι ἐξεκαύθη ἡ καρδία μου, καὶ οἱ νεφροί μου ἠλλοιώθησαν. Ὅτι
νεφροὺς τοὺς λογισμοὺς καλεῖ ἐπεσημηνάμεθα πολλαχοῦ, καὶ τὴν αἰτίαν
20 εἰρήκαμεν. Ἐγὼ μέντοι φησὶν οὐδὲν ἐπιστάμενος τούτων, ὅτι ἔσται μόνον
ἐπὶ τοῖς παροῦσιν ἐνεθυμούμην καὶ ἐξεκαιόμην τὴν διάνοιαν, δυσφορῶν ἀεὶ
ἐπὶ τῇ ἐκείνων εὐπραγίᾳ ἠλλοιώμην τε καὶ μετεβαλόμην τοὺς λογισμούς,
νῦν μὲν ταῦτα, νῦν δὲ ἐκεῖνα λογιζόμενος.

10-11 Ps. XXXVIII, 7   19 cf. in ps. XXXVII, 8ᵃ (p, 225) et Theodoretus (1499 B 11-12).

19ᵇ-20ᵃ. Κατὰ κοινοῦ — πράγματος : P, fol. 250ʳ; V, fol. 19; Vat. 1422, fol. 132ᵛ
(anon.).   4 γραφῆς] ἀρχῆς 1422   5 πρὸς βραχὺ om. 1422
20ᵇ. Καὶ ἐν τῷ — ὕστερον: P, fol. 251; V, fol. 19; Cord, p. 506-507.   13-16 τουτέστι — σχῆμα affert Paraphrasis (p. 488).   14 καὶ om. PV.
21. Ὅτι νεφροὺς — λογιζόμενος: P, fol. 251; V, fol 19ᵛ; Vat. 1422, fol. 132ᵛ
(anon.); Cord, p. 507.   19 καλεῖν PV   23 ἠλλοιούμην PV ἠλλοιόμην Cord.

Aᶜ 19ᵇ-20ᵃ (p. 370, 2-11): Quomodo subito perierunt, ita ut nihil amplius
prosperitas eorum, — quam id quod somnio ostenditur habuisse uideatur, nihilque ex his quae uidet praeter inanem memoriam retinet, — ita, inquit, et ini⟨u⟩s-
torum omnis felicitas uice imaginis desoluta, nullas potuit praeteritae (praeteri-
tatae ms) iucunditatis reliquias obtinere.   13-15 (p. 370, 12-15): Id est, propter
ciuitatem tuam, ut illam reaedifices, ut nos de nouo habi⟨ta⟩tores efficias.
16-17 (p. 370, 18-20) ...imaginem uocauit, cuius est proprium, cum uissa paululum fuerit, deperire.   21 (p. 370, 21-29): Frequenter ostendimus renes a Scriptura cogitationes uocari. Ego, inquit, nihil horum sciens quae erant futura, et
tantum praesentia intuiens, inflammabar animo atque hostium prospiritate tor-
quebar, sententiamque meam uariis cogitationibus inmotabam.

lost on account of their lawlessness, like a dream when people awake (vv. 19–20). The general sense of *How* suddenly they were made desolate is, They perished, with the result that their prosperity was no different from a dream. While all the comparisons of the divine Scripture are clear, this one is particularly so: the effect of a dream is that it wraps the soul in fantasies for a time, but if anyone suddenly wakes the sleeper, all is dissolved and nothing remains, only the recollection persisting of seeming to have seen something. Such, he is saying, is their prosperity, which merely involves an impression, which is suddenly lost, with the result that no remnant of it is left. *Lord, in your city, you have brought their image to nothing.* In Psalm 39, in mentioning prosperous people, he says, "At any rate, man goes about in an image"[4]—that is, in an image and a painting a man is only an appearance that seems to be rich and to store up wealth, but after a while he departs, enjoying nothing. Likewise here, too, he says *in your city*—that is, on account of your city for the sake of rebuilding it and our once again being brought together, you will reduce to nothingness the image and phantasm that seems to belong to them. Now, he rightly called it an *image* as appearing for a while but later disappearing.

Because my heart was inflamed and my kidneys were moved (v. 21). The fact that by *kidneys* he refers to thoughts we have indicated in many places and explained the reason. I, on the other hand, he is saying, had no idea of these things being only a temporary thing, and so I was angered and inflamed in mind, I was constantly irritated at their prosperity, I took it amiss and had a change of heart, thinking one thing at one time, another at another. | *I*

---

3. Ps 39:6.

22ª. Κἀγὼ ἐξουδενωμένος καὶ οὐκ ἔγνων. Σύμμαχος Ἥμην δὲ ἀνεπι-στήμων καὶ μὴ εἰδώς, — τουτέστιν Ἥμην δὲ ὡς εἰς γνῶσιν οὐδὲν, ἀντὶ τοῦ οὐδὲν τῶν δεόντων ἐπιστάμενος.

22ᵇ. Κτηνώδης ἐγενήθην παρά σοι. Οὐδὲν δὲ κτήνους διήλλαττον πρός σε συγκρινόμενος, καὶ τὰς παρά σου οἰκονομίας οὕτως οὐδὲν εἰδώς, οὔτε 5 ὅπως βούλει, οὔτε ὅπως οἰκονομεῖς, ὥσπερ καὶ τὰ κτήνη τοὺς λογισμοὺς ἡμῶν καὶ τὰ βουλεύματα οὐκ ἐπίστανται.

23ª. Κἀγὼ διὰ παντὸς μετά σου. Τοῦ δὲ μηδὲν εἰδέναι τῶν παρά σου οἰκονομουμένων ἀπόδειξις τὰ πολλὰ καὶ διάφορα ἐμοῦ λογισαμένου καὶ πολ-λάκις ἀπευδοκήσαντος τὴν σωτηρίαν ἐπανελθεῖν τε καὶ εἶναι πάλιν μετά 10 σου, κατὰ τὴν ἰουδαϊκὴν ὑπόληψιν τοῦτο εἰπὼν ὡς τοῦ Θεοῦ ἐν τῷ Σιὼν ὄρει διατρίβοντος.

23ᵇ. Ἐκράτησας τῆς χειρὸς τῆς δεξιᾶς μου. Ἐκ μεταφορᾶς τῶν χειρὶ κατεχόντων αὐτοὺς καὶ ἑλκόντων ἐκ μέσου τῶν κατεχόντων, καὶ οὕτως ἀπο-σπώντων· ὥσπερ γάρ φησι λαβόμενός μου τῆς χειρός, οὕτως με εἵλκυσας. 15

24ª. Καὶ ἐν τῇ βουλῇ σου ὡδήγησάς με. Καὶ κατὰ τὴν σὴν βουλήν, του-τέστι κατὰ τὴν σὴν σύνεσιν, ἄχρι τῆς γῆς τῆς ἐπαγγελίας ὡδήγησας.

24ᵇ. Καὶ μετὰ δόξης προσελάβου με. Εἵλκυσας δὲ πρὸς σεαυτὸν καὶ ἐπ-ανήγαγές με μετὰ πολλῶν θαυμάτων, ὡς καὶ μεγάλην μοι περιποιησάμενος δόξαν ἐκ τοῦ πράγματος, πάντων ἐκπληττομένων τὰ περὶ ἐμὲ γιγνόμενα· 20

22ª. Σύμμαχος — ἐπιστάμενος: P, fol. 251; V, fol. 19ᵛ; Cord, p. 507.
22ᵇ. Οὐδὲν — ἐπίστανται: P, fol. 251; V, fol. 19ᵛ; Vat. 1422, fol. 132ᵛ sub nomine Eusebii; Cord, p. 508. 4 δὲ] τοῦ 1422 ὡς πρὸς 1422 5 παρά σου] σὰς 1422 εἰδὼς om. 1422 6 βουλεύει 1422 καὶ om. 1422 7 ἐπίστανται κτήνη 1422.
23ª. Τοῦ δὲ μηδὲν — διατρίβοντος: P, fol. 251ᵛ; V, fol. 19ᵛ.
23ᵇ. Ἐκ μεταφορᾶς — εἵλκυσας: P, fol, 251ᵛ; V, fol. 19ᵛ.
24ª. Καὶ κατὰ — ὡδήγησας: P, fol. 251ᵛ et V, fol. 19ᵛ (anon.).
24ᵇ. Εἵλκυσας — γιγνόμενα: P, fol. 251ᵛ; V, fol. 20; Vat. 1422, fol. 133; Cord, p. 509. 18 ἑαυτὸν mss Cord.

Aᵉ 22ᵇ (p. 370, 32-371, 1): In tantum mihi uera rerum cogitatio defuit atque ita dispensationes tuas üidere non potui, qualiter ista cogitares, qualiter dispo-neres, ut conparatus tibi nihil me defferre a pecode confiterer. 10-12 (p. 371, 2-5): ...habitabo tecum; hoc autem secundum opinionem iudaicam, quae Deum in templo habitare credebat. 23ᵇ-24ª (p. 371, 6-8): Prosequutor pariter ac praeuius, praeductor atque deductor, terram, quam disperaueram, me intrare fecisti. 24ᵇ (p. 371, 9-13): Id est, ut reditus meus stuporem uidentibus face-ret, stupor uero atque admiratio eorum qui me intuebantur, mihi proficeret ad honorem.

was brought to nothing and was ignorant (v. 22). Symmachus: "I was without understanding or knowledge"—that is, I arrived at no grasp of it, as if to say, Realizing nothing of what I should. *I was like a brute beast before you:* in comparison I was no different from cattle before you, grasping nothing of your plans or your wishes or the way your arrange things, just as cattle likewise do not understand your thoughts and intentions.

I am ever with you (v. 23): proof of my grasping nothing of the arrangements made by you is my having many and varied thoughts and often despairing of salvation and of returning, and of being with you once again (saying this according to the Jewish idea that God lived on Mount Sion). *You held my right hand* (by analogy with people holding them by the hand and leading them from the midst of those detaining them, and thus dragging them away). You drew me in this fashion, he is saying, as though clutching my hand. *In your counsel you guided me* (v. 24): by your counsel—that is, by your understanding—you guided me to the very land of promise. *And supported me with glory:* you drew me to yourself and led me back with great marvels, as though also winning me great glory from the affair, with everyone struck by what was done for me. |

25. Τί γάρ μοι ὑπάρχει ἐν τῷ οὐρανῷ, καὶ παρά σου τί ἠθέλησα ἐπὶ τῆς γῆς; Τί γὰρ ἕτερον ἔχων ἐζήτησα λαβεῖν ἢ ἐν τῷ οὐρανῷ ἢ ἐπὶ τῆς γῆς, ἢ τοῦτο; Οὐ γὰρ διεῖλεν, τῷ μὲν ἐν τῷ οὐρανῷ τὸ ὑπάρχει προσνεῖμαι βουληθείς, τῷ δὲ ἐπὶ τῆς γῆς τὸ ἠθέλησα, ἀλλὰ κατὰ κοινοῦ καὶ τὸ
5 ὑπάρχει καὶ τὸ ἠθέλησα, ἀντὶ τοῦ Οὔτε ἔχω τι ἄλλο τούτου παραπλήσιον, οὔτε ζητῶ οὐ μόνον ἐπὶ τῆς γῆς, ἀλλ᾽ οὐδὲ ἐν τῷ οὐρανῷ· οὕτω μοι καὶ τῶν ἐκεῖ κτημάτων τοῦτο τιμιώτερον τὸ σοὶ συνεῖναι. Ἑνὸς δὲ ὄντος, ἡ δοκοῦσα διαίρεσις συνηθῶς γεγένηται, καθὼς ἐν τῷ νβ´ ψαλμῷ ἀκριβέστερον περὶ τούτου ἐπεσημηνάμεθα.

10 26ᵃ. Ἐξέλιπεν ἡ καρδία μου καὶ ἡ σάρξ μου, ὁ Θεὸς τῆς καρδίας μου. Τούτου γοῦν καὶ ἐπεθύμησα, τοῦ σε ὁρᾶν καὶ μετά σου εἶναι πάντοτε τοῦ ἐμοῦ δεσπότου. Τὸ γὰρ ὁ Θεὸς τῆς καρδίας μου, ἀντὶ τοῦ ὁ Θεός μου λέγει, συνηθῶς ἀπὸ τοῦ μέρους τὸ ὅλον καλέσας.

26ᵇ. Καὶ ἡ μερίς μου ὁ Θεὸς εἰς τὸν αἰῶνα. Τὸ κέρδος μου τὸ ἐξαί-
15 ρετον καὶ ἀγαθὸν αὐτὸς εἶ· τούτου οὖν ἐπεθύμησα, οὐδὲν ἴσον τούτου κρίνων καλόν.

27ᵃ. Ὅτι ἰδοὺ οἱ μακρύνοντες ἑαυτοὺς ἀπό σου ἀπολοῦνται. Καὶ γὰρ ὅσοι ἀφίστανταί σου καὶ μακρὰν γίνονται τῇ διαθέσει, οὐδὲν ἕτερον ἢ τὴν ἀπώλειαν ἐκδέχονται.

---

8 locum ps. LII non inueni; cf. p. 363 (in ps. LV, 7).

---

25. Τί γάρ ἕτερον — ἐπεσημηνάμεθα: P, fol. 252; V, fol. 20; Cord, p. 509.
2-3 ἢ ἐπὶ τῆς γῆς — οὐρανῷ om. Cord   3-4 τὸ μὲν ... τὸ δὲ PV   3 ὑπάρχειν PV
7 δέοντος PV.
26ᵃ. Τούτου γοῦν   καλέσας: P, fol. 252; V, fol. 20ᵛ; Cord, p. 509.   11 τοῦτο PV.
26ᵇ. Τὸ κέρδος — καλόν: P, fol. 252; V, fol. 20ᵛ; Vat. 1422, fol. 133.   15 εἶ]
ἂν εἴη 1422.
27ᵃ. Καὶ γὰρ — ἐκδέχονται: P, fol. 252ᵛ; V, fol. 20ᵛ; Vat. 1422, fol. 133
(anon.).

Aᵉ 5-7 (p. 371, 15-19): Ac si diceret Neque habeo amplius neque peto, non solum super terram uerum neque in caelo, excepto hoc nisi ut tecum semper sim.   12-13 (p. 371, 20-21): Ac si diceret Deus meus, a parte totum indicans.
26ᵇ (p. 372, 1-4): ... ad quem omnis disiderii tendit intentio, cui nihil bonorum omnium ualeat exaequari.   27ᵃ (p. 372, 6-9): ... uideo enim eos qui a tuo (tua ms) amore discendunt... perditioni proximos fieri, ad uiciniam mortis accedere.

After all, what is there for me in heaven, and what have I wanted on earth beyond you? (v. 25). What else was there for me to seek to receive than this, either *in heaven* or *on earth*? He did not make a distinction, note, by intending to attribute *is* to one *in heaven,* and *wanted* to one *on earth;* instead, he speaks of *is* and *wanted* in general—in other words, Neither do I have anything else like this, nor do I seek it either on earth or in heaven. Understanding you is thus more precious to me than possessions there. When only one thing is involved, the apparent distinction often occurs, as we indicated more precisely on this matter in Psalm 53.[4] *My heart failed, and my flesh, God of my heart* (v. 26): this at least I also longed for, seeing you and being with you, my master, forever (*God of my heart* meaning "my God," from his habit of referring to the whole by the part). *God my portion forever:* you are the benefit and good that I desire; this I long for, judging no other good to be its equal.

Because, behold, those keeping their distance from you will perish (v. 27): all who withdraw from you and are distant in their affections incur nothing other than destruction. | *You destroyed everyone who was unfaithful to*

---

4. Devreesse thinks that Theodore may have in mind, rather, his comments on Ps 56:6.

27ᵇ. Ἐξωλόθρευσας πάντα τὸν πορνεύοντα ἀπὸ σου. Πάντα γὰρ ἀφιστάμενόν σου καὶ εἰδώλοις προσέχειν βουλόμενον σφοδροτάτῃ τιμωρίᾳ περιβάλλεις, πορνεύοντα εἰρηκὼς τὸν ἀπὸ τῆς περὶ αὐτὸν διαθέσεως ἐξιστάμενον καὶ εἰδώλοις ἑαυτὸν προσνέμοντα, ἐν τάξει μὲν γυναικὸς πολλαχοῦ τὴν τῶν πιστῶν καὶ οἰκείων συναγωγήν, πορνείαν δὲ καλῶν τὴν ἀπὸ τῆς περὶ 5 τὸν Θεὸν διαθέσεως διαίρεσιν. Καὶ τοῦτο εὕροι ἄν τις σαφέστερον παρὰ τῷ Ἰεζεκιήλ. Φησὶ γὰρ οὕτως Καὶ ἐγένετο λόγος Κυρίου πρός με λέγων Υἱὲ ἀνθρώπου, δύο γυναῖκες ἦσαν θυγατέρες μητρὸς μιᾶς, — μίαν καλῶν μητέρα τὴν συναγωγὴν τῶν Ἰουδαίων ἐπὶ τὸ αὐτὸ συνηθροισμένων τὸ πρότερον, δύο δὲ θυγατέρας αὐτῆς τὰς ι' φυλὰς καὶ τὰς δύο μετὰ τὴν διαίρε- 10 σιν, ὥσπερ ἀπὸ μητρὸς τῆς συναγωγῆς ἀποτεχθέντων τῶν ὕστερον, ἐφ' ὧν καὶ τὴν εἰς δύο διαίρεσιν τοῦ λαοῦ γενέσθαι συνέβη. Εἶτα ὀνειδίσας αὐτοῖς τὰ ἐν Αἰγύπτῳ, ὡς ἔκτοτε αὐτοὺς οἰκειωσάμενος καὶ τὴν συναγωγὴν αὐτῶν ὡσανεὶ πρὸς γάμου κοινωνίαν λαβών, τῇ παραβολῇ καὶ τὴν ἑαυτοῦ διάθεσιν μειζόνως ἐμφαίνων καὶ τὴν ἐκείνων ἀγνωμοσύνην, — ἐπειδὴ μεγάλη μὲν 15 ἀνδρὸς καὶ γνησία ἡ πρὸς γυναῖκα διάθεσις, μεγάλη δὲ παρανομία τὸ ἀνδρὸς ἀθετῆσαι γάμον, — Ὀλλὰ ἡ πρεσβυτέρα καὶ Ὀλλίβα ἡ νεωτέρα· καὶ ἐγένοντό μοι, καὶ ἔτεκον υἱοὺς καὶ θυγατέρας· καὶ τὰ ὀνόματα αὐτῶν, Σαμάρεια ἡ Ὀλλά, καὶ Ἱερουσαλήμ ἡ Ὀλλίβα. Καὶ εἰπὼν ὅτι καὶ ἐτεκνοποίησαν ἐξ ἐμοῦ, τουτέστιν ὅτι τῇ ἐμῇ οἰκειώσει εἰς πλῆθος ἐπέδωκαν, ἐπάγει Καὶ ἐξεπόρ- 20 νευσεν ἡ Ὀλλὰ ἀπ' ἐμοῦ, ὀνειδίσας τε διὰ πλειόνων τοῖς τῶν δέκα φυλῶν τὴν ἀσέβειαν, ἑξῆς φησι Καὶ εἶδεν ἡ ἀδελφὴ αὐτῆς ἡ Ὀλλίβα, καὶ διέφθειρεν τὴν ἐπίθεσιν αὐτῆς ὑπὲρ αὐτήν, καὶ τὴν πορνείαν αὐτῆς ὑπὲρ τὴν πορνείαν τῆς ἀδελφῆς αὐτῆς.

28ᵃ. Ἐμοὶ δὲ τὸ προσκολλᾶσθαι τῷ Θεῷ ἀγαθόν ἐστιν. Διὰ τοῦτο τοίνυν 25 ἐπειδὴ τὸ ἀφίστασθαί σου τοσούτων αἴτιον γίνεται κακῶν, προτιμότερον ἁπάντων εἶναι λογίζομαι τὸ συνῆφθαι καὶ συνεῖναί σοι.

7-8 Ezech. XXIII, 1   17-19 v. 4; cf. supra p. 287-288   20-21 v. 5   22-24 v. 11.

27ᵇ. Πάντα γὰρ — ἀδελφῆς αὐτῆς: P, fol. 252ᵛ; V, fol. 20ᵛ-21; Cord. p. 510. 3 περιβαλεῖς Cord   3-4 Paraphrasis (p. 489): Πορνεύοντα πάλιν τὸν ἀφιστάμενον αὐτοῦ καὶ τὸν εἰδώλοις προσέχοντα λέγει   6 διαίρεσιν des. Cord. 28ᵃ. Διὰ τοῦτο — συνεῖναι σοι: P, fol. 253: V, fol. 21; Cord, p. 510.   26 τοσοῦτον PV.

Aᵉ 3-4 (p. 372, 10-12): Fornicatorem autem dicit eum, qui affectum Deo debitum praeuaricationis uitio idulis mancipauit.   28ᵃ (p. 372, 13-16): Ob hoc itaque, quoniam discensionem a te factam mala omnia consequuntur, coniungi tibi ambio tecumque uotis expostulo.

you: you will invest with most severe retribution everyone who withdraws from you and is bent on attending to idols (calling *unfaithful* those who fail in affection for him and devote themselves to idols, in many places casting the assembly of his own faithful in the role of a wife, speaking of rupture in affection for God as infidelity). You would find this more clearly in Ezekiel, where it says, "The word of the Lord came to me in these terms: Mortal, there were two women, daughters of one mother," by "one mother" referring to the assembly of the Jews formerly assembled as one, and by "two daughters" to the ten tribes and the two after the division, as though born later from the assembly as mother, when the division of the people into two took place. He then reproached them with the events in Egypt, as though claiming them from that time as his own and admitting their assembly into a union like that of marriage, by the comparison emphasizing his affection and their ingratitude, since the husband had a deep and genuine affection for the wife, but grave lawlessness annulled the marriage with a husband. "The elder was Oholah, and the younger was Oholibah; they became mine, and they bore sons and daughters; as to their names, Oholah is Samaria, and Oholibah is Jerusalem." After saying, They had children by me—that is, through my relationship they grew into a vast number—he goes on, "Oholah was unfaithful to me." Having reproached in many ways the people of the ten tribes for their impiety, he proceeds to say, "Her sister Oholibah saw this and became more corrupt than she, her infidelity exceeding that of her sister."[5]

For me, on the contrary, it is good to cleave to God (v. 28): so since withdrawing from you proves to be the cause of such awful troubles, I believe that association with you and being in your company is preferable to everything. | *To put my hope in the Lord:* to have hope in you and receive

---

5. Ezek 23:1–5, 11.

28ᵇ. Τίθεσθαι ἐν τῷ Κυρίῳ τὴν ἐλπίδα μου. Τοῦ ἐπί σε τὴν ἐλπίδα ἔχειν καὶ παρά σου πᾶν ὅ τι καλὸν ἐκδέχεσθαι.

28ᶜ. Τοῦ ἐξαγγεῖλαί με πάσας τὰς αἰνέσεις σου ἐν ταῖς πύλαις τῆς θυγατρὸς Σιών. Καὶ τὸ διηνεκῶς τοὺς ὕμνους καὶ τὰς εὐχαριστίας ὑπὲρ ὧν
5 εὐεργετούμεθα ἀποδιδόναι σοι ἐν τῇ Ἰερουσαλὴμ γενομένους, ὡς ἐκεῖ καὶ ὄντος τοῦ Θεοῦ καὶ προσιεμένου τοὺς ἐκεῖ γιγνομένους. Εἴρηται δὲ καὶ ἐν τῷ θ΄ ὅτι θυγατέρα Σιὼν τὴν πόλιν καλεῖ.

PSALMVS LXXIII

Τῶν Μακκαβαίων ἐνταῦθα διηγεῖται τὰς συμφοράς, ὡς ἂν ἐκείνων λεγόν-
10 των τό τε μέγεθος τῶν τότε περιεχόντων αὐτοὺς κακῶν, καὶ ἀπαλλαγῆναι τὸν Θεὸν ἐπὶ τούτοις ἀξιούντων.

1ᵃ. Ἵνα τί, ὁ Θεός, ἀπώσω εἰς τέλος; Οὐκ ἐπὶ μέμψεως τὸ Ἵνα τί, ἀλλὰ διαπορούντος· καὶ γὰρ σύνηθες τοῦτο τῷ προφήτῃ τὸ Ἵνα τί. Κέχρηται μέντοι αὐτῷ συνεχῶς, οὐχ ἁπλῶς, ἀλλ᾽ ἢ ὥστε δεῖξαι ὅτι ἔστι τις αἰτία τῶν
15 χαλεπῶν ἁπάντων ἄδηλος τοῖς ἀνθρώποις, καὶ οὐχ ἁπλῶς τοῖς βαρυτέροις ἡμᾶς περιπίπτειν ἐᾷ κακοῖς ὁ Θεός. Τίς οὖν ἄρα φησὶν ἡ αἰτία, δι᾽ ἣν οὕτως ἡμᾶς ἀπέβαλες; — ἐκ μεταφορᾶς τῶν ἀπωθουμένων οὓς μισοῦσι, καὶ οὐ προσιεμένων οὐδὲ ἐγγίζειν συγχωρούντων.

---

3 in IX, 15 (p. 53, 30-31)

28ᵇ. Τοῦ ἐπί σε — ἐκδέχεσθαι: P, fol. 253; V, fol. 21.
28ᶜ. Καὶ τὸ διηνεκῶς — καλεῖ: P, fol. 253; V, fol. 21; Cord. p. 510-511.   4 διηνεκὲς PV   5 γενομένους] εὐδιακρίτου καὶ σπουδαίας δεῖγμα γνώμης ἐστίν add. Cord.
Argumentum Τῶν Μακκαβαίων — ἀξιούντων: P, fol. 253ᵛ; V, fol. 22; Vat. 1422,
fol. 133ᵛ; Ambros. C 98 sup., fol. 143ᵛ; Cord, p. 529; cf. L (p. 517): Ἐκ προσώπου τῶν Μακκαβαίων... δεομένων ἀπαλλαγῆς.
1ᵃ. Οὐκ ἐπὶ — συγχωρούντων: P, fol. 254; V, fol. 22; Vat. 1422, fol. 133ᵛ; Cord,
p. 529.   14 ἢ om. 1422 Cord   16 οὖν om. 1422.

Aᵉ 28ᵇ (p. 372, 17-19): De futura bonorum perceptione securus, praesentem statum rerum expectatione consolabor.   28ᶜ (p. 372, 21-24): Filiam Hierusalem dicit, in qua effica⟨c⟩ior laudationum oblatio credebatur et gratior pro praesentia Dei ibi semper habitantis.   Argumentum ps. LXXIII (p. 372, 25-28): Machabeorum in hoc psalmo pericula discribuntur, atque ex persona eorum tam aduersorum, quae passi sunt, narratur magnitudo, quam a Deo solutio postulatur.   12-13 (p. 372, 29-30): Non est uox querellae, sed inquisitionis (iniq — ms).

from you every good. *So as to sing all your praises in the gates of the daughter of Sion:* constantly rendering to you the hymns of praise and thanksgiving for benefits received when we are in Jerusalem, since God is there and makes his approach to those who are there. Now, there was mention in Psalm 9 that he refers to the city as "daughter of Sion."[6]

PSALM 74

Here he recounts the misfortunes of the Maccabees, as though it were they telling of the magnitude of the troubles besetting them at that time, and in that situation begging God for relief. *Why, O God, did you reject us forever?* (v. 1). The term *Why* is not of one of reproach but of bewilderment, the author being in the habit of using it. His frequent use of it, however, is not without point: it is to bring out that a cause of all the hardships is unclear to human beings, and God does not allow us to fall foul of very severe troubles without a purpose. So he is saying, What is the reason for your rejection of us this way (by analogy with people rejecting those they hate, and not approaching them or allowing them near)? | *Your anger was vented on sheep*

6. Cf. Ps 9:14.

1ᵇ. Ὠργίσθη ὁ θυμός σου ἐπὶ πρόβατα νομῆς σου; Ἐπισεσήμανται ἡμῖν
καὶ ἑτέρωθι ὅτι πολλαχοῦ τὴν ὀργὴν ἐπιτετηρημένως λέγει τὴν παράτασιν τοῦ θυμοῦ· λέγει μὲν οὖν καὶ ἀδιαφόρως τὸν θυμὸν ὀργὴν καὶ τὴν ὀργὴν
θυμόν. Ἔστι δὲ καὶ ὅπου τετηρημένως τὴν ὀργὴν αὐτὴν λέγει τὴν παράτασιν, ὡς θυμοῦ κυρίως ὄντος τῆς κινήσεως· τοῦτο γοῦν κἀνταῦθα δείκνυσι 5
διὰ τοῦ Ὠργίσθη ὁ θυμός σου. Λέγει γὰρ ὅτι Παρέτεινες τὸν καθ' ἡμῶν σου
θυμόν, καὶ ἐπέμεινας ἐπὶ πολὺ θυμούμενος ἡμῖν τοῖς προβάτοις τῆς σῆς
νομῆς, ἵνα εἴπῃ Οὓς αὐτὸς ἐποίμαινες ἀεί καὶ ἔμενες φροντίζων τε ἡμῶν
καὶ διοικῶν τὰ καθ' ἡμᾶς.

2ᵃ. Μνήσθητι τῆς συναγωγῆς σου, ἧς ἐκτήσω ἀπ' ἀρχῆς. Καὶ ἐν τῷ μγ' 10
ψαλμῷ τὰ κατὰ τοὺς Μακκαβαίους λέγων μέμνηται τῶν παλαιῶν τῶν κατ'
Αἴγυπτον, κἀνταῦθα ὁμοίως. Μνήσθητί φησιν ἡμῶν τῆς συναγωγῆς σου, ὅτι
αὐτὸς συνήγαγες διεσπαρμένους κατὰ χώραν τότε, ὡς εἰκός, καὶ δουλεύοντας. Καλῶς δὲ τὸ ἐκτήσω, ἐπειδήπερ οἱ κτώμενοί τι διὰ καμάτων ἀεὶ τὰς
κτήσεις ἑαυτοῖς περιποιοῦνται· οὕτω γὰρ καὶ ὁ Θεὸς πολλοῖς τοῖς θαύ- 15
μασιν ἀφελὼν αὐτοὺς τῆς τῶν Αἰγυπτίων καταδυναστείας ἰδίους ἀπέφηνεν.

2ᵇ. Ἐλυτρώσω ῥάβδῳ κληρονομίας σου. Τὸ ἐλυτρώσω τῷ ἄνω συνῆπται,
τουτέστι Μνήσθητι τῆς συναγωγῆς σου, ἧς ἐκτήσω ἀπ' ἀρχῆς, ἐλυτρώσω
ῥάβδῳ κληρονομίας σου, — οὕτω λέγει καὶ Σύμμαχος Οὓς ἐλυτρώσω σκήπτρῳ
κληρουχίας σου. Ὑπομνήσθητί φησιν ὅπως μὲν ἡμᾶς συνήγαγες καὶ ἐκτήσω, 20
ὅπως δὲ ἀπαλλάξας τῶν τότε κατεχόντων κακῶν ἰδίαν ἡμᾶς ἐποίησω βασιλείαν καὶ ἰδίαν κληρονομίαν, — ἀντὶ τοῦ ὥσπερ ἐξαίρετόν σου κτῆμα καὶ
ἐξαιρέτως τῇ σῇ βασιλείᾳ προσήκοντας διὰ τῆς περὶ ἡμᾶς σου προνοίας
σαφῶς ἀπέφηνας. Ὅτι γὰρ τὴν ῥάβδον ἐπὶ τῆς βασιλείας λέγει ἐπισεσήμανται ἡμῖν καὶ ἑτέρωθι καὶ μάλιστα ἐν τῷ μδ' ψαλμῷ, σαφῶς αὐτὸ λέ- 25

1-2 cf. in ps. XXIX, 6 (p. 136)   LXVIII, 25ᵇ (p. 456)   10-11 cf. p. 270   25-491, 3 cf. in
ps. XLIV, 7ᵇ (p. 288).

1ᵇ. Ἐπισεσήμανται — καθ' ἡμᾶς: P, fol. 254; V, fol. 22; Cord, p. 530.   2-3 Paraphrasis (p. 517): Σημαίνει τὴν παράτασιν τοῦ θυμοῦ   3 οὖν om. PV   7 καὶ om. PV
8 ἐποίμανες Cord.

2ᵃ. Καὶ ἐν τῷ μγ' — ἀπέφηνεν: P, fol. 254ᵛ; V, fol. 22; Vat. 1422, fol. 133ᵛ;
Cord, p. 530.   12 ὅτι om. PV 1422   13 χώρας Cord   16 τῶν om. 1422 Cord.

2ᵇ. Τὸ ἐλυτρώσω — παραινέσεως: P, fol. 254ᵛ; V, fol. 22ᵛ.   20-491, 3 ὑπομνήσ-
θητι — παραινέσεως affert Cord, p. 531 (anon.)   23 σῇ om. Cord.

Aᵉ 2-3 (p. 372, 31-33): Continuationem indignationis furorem appellat.
2ᵃ (p. 372, 31-373, 9): Et in xl tertio psalmo, cum de Machabeis loqueretur, gesto-
rum in Egipto mentionem fecit; et nunc idem faciens dicit Memor esto nostri,
quos errantes et dispersos in regione Egipti congregasti. Bene autem ait quam
possidisti, ut in nomine posessionis suscitaret maiorem affectum; solemus enim
ea plus dilegire quae proprio et studiosso labore quessiuimus.

of your pasture. It was indicated by us elsewhere as well that in many places he speaks more deliberately of wrath as the display of anger; sometimes he speaks indiscriminately of anger as wrath or of wrath as anger. But at other times he deliberately calls the visible display itself wrath when there is a real emotion of anger, as is exemplified here with *Your anger was vented,* his meaning being, You intensified your anger against us, and for a long time persisted in being angry with us sheep of your pasture; as if to say, Though you always shepherded us and kept showing us consideration and managing our affairs.

Remember your congregation, which you acquired from the beginning (v. 2). He made mention also in Psalm 44 on the Maccabees of olden times in Egypt,[1] and likewise here. *Remember your congregation,* he is saying, because at that time you personally assembled them when scattered throughout the land, in all probability, and enslaved. *You acquired* was well put, since owners get ownership of their possessions by means of hard work; God likewise with many marvels removed them from the power of the Egyptians and made them his own. *You redeemed with a rod your inheritance.* The term *You redeemed* goes with the above—that is, *Remember your congregation, which you acquired from the beginning, you redeemed with a rod your inheritance,* as Symmachus also says, "Whom you redeemed with a scepter of your allotment." Recall, he is saying, how you gathered and *acquired* us, how you freed us from the troubles besetting us and made us your own kingdom and your own inheritance; as if to say, You clearly made us, as it were, your own special possession and specially associated with your kingship through your providence for us. The fact that he speaks of a *rod* in connection with kingship, of course, has been mentioned by us in other places as well, and especially in Psalm 45,[2] a clear statement of the same thing | by

---

1. Cf. Ps 44:1.
2. Cf. Ps 45:6.

γοντος ἐκ μεταφορᾶς τῶν βασιλέων τῶν τὰ σκῆπτρα μετακεχειρισμένων·
πανταχοῦ γὰρ ἐπὶ τῶν τοιούτων τὸ σκῆπτρον καλεῖ τὴν ῥάβδον, ὡς καὶ
ἐνταῦθα δέδεικται ἐκ τῆς Συμμάχου παραινέσεως.

2ᶜ. Ὅρος Σιὼν τοῦτο, ὃ κατεσκήνωσας ἐν αὐτῷ. Καὶ ἤγαγες εἰς τοῦτο
5 τοῦ Σιὼν τὸ ὅρος, ἐν ᾧ καὶ αὐτὸς κατοικεῖν ἐδικαίωσας. Λέγει δὲ ὅτι Ἀπαλλάξας τῶν κατεχόντων, ἐκτήσω ἡμᾶς τοῖς οἰκείοις κατορθώμασιν καὶ ἰδίους
μάλιστα παρὰ πάντας ἡμᾶς ἀπέφηνας ἀνθρώπους ἐν τῷδε τῷ τόπῳ ἐν ᾧ
καὶ κατοικεῖς, ἔχων ἀεὶ μεθ᾽ ἑαυτοῦ· σωματικώτερον δὲ τὴν περὶ αὐτοὺς
πρόνοιαν μεγίστην οὖσαν ἐνέφηνεν.

10 3ᵃ. Ἔπαρον τὰς χεῖράς σου ἐπὶ τὰς ὑπερηφανίας αὐτῶν εἰς τέλος. Τιμώρησαι αὐτοὺς ὑπερηφανευομένους καθ᾽ ἡμῶν καὶ μεγαλοφρονοῦντας ἐφ᾽ οἷς
τοσαῦτα καὶ τηλικαῦτα ἡμᾶς διέθηκαν κακά, — ἐκ μεταφορᾶς τῶν ταῖς χερσὶ
παιόντων οὓς βούλονται· καὶ γὰρ ἀπανταχοῦ χεῖρα Θεοῦ τὴν ἐνέργειαν
αὐτοῦ καλεῖ εἴτε ἐπὶ καλῷ εἴτε ἐπὶ κακῷ γιγνομένην. Τὸ δὲ ὅπως ἡ ἀκο-
15 λουθία δείκνυσιν.

3ᵇ. Ὅσα ἐπονηρεύσατο ὁ ἐχθρὸς ἐν τῷ ἁγίῳ σου. Καὶ γὰρ οὐ μικρὰ τὰ
παρὰ τούτων εἰς ἡμᾶς γιγνόμενα.

4. Καὶ ἐνεκαυχήσαντο οἱ μισοῦντές σε ἐν μέσῳ τῆς ἑορτῆς σου. Σύμμαχος Ἐν μέσῳ τῆς συναγωγῆς σου. Καλῶς δὲ αὐτὴν ἑορτὴν ἐκάλεσεν ἀπὸ
20 τοῦ συνιόντας ἑορτάζειν Θεῷ. Πολλά φησιν ἃ κατεκαυχήσαντο ἡμῶν ἐφ᾽
οἷς ἠδίκησαν.

3 συμμάχου om. Cord.
2ᶜ. Καὶ ἤγαγες — ἐνέφηνεν: P, fol. 254ᵛ; V, fol. 22ᵛ.
3ᵃ. Τιμώρησαι — δείκνυσιν: P, fol. 255; V, fol. 22ᵛ; Vat. 1422, fol. 133ᵛ (anon.).
10-12 τιμώρησαι — κακὰ affert Paraphrasis (p. 517)   12-15 ἐκ μεταφορᾶς — δείκνυσιν
Cord. p. 531 sub nomine THEODORETI   12 μεταφορᾶς τέθεικε Cord   τῶν om.
1422   13 παιόντων — ἀπανταχοῦ] τοὺς ἁμαρτάνοντας μαστιγούντων· καὶ γὰρ ἀπανταχῇ
Cord   14 γιγνομένην des. 1422   τὸ δὲ ὅπως] τοῦτο δὲ καὶ Cord.
3ᵇ. Καὶ γὰρ — γιγνόμενα: P, fol. 255 et V, fol. 22ᵛ (anon.); Paraphrasis (p. 518).
4. Σύμμαχος — ἠδίκησαν: P, fol. 255; V, fol. 22ᵛ; Paraphrasis (p. 518).

Aᶜ   2ᶜ (p. 373, 10-19): Adduxisti nos in hunc montem Sion, in quo tibi habitationem esse uoluisti ... eo quod propria uirtute olìm eos a malis abduxerit et quod
pro omnibus hominibus uoluerit eos suos uocari atque unius eiusdemque loci sibi
eos habitatione coniunxerit; per quae omnia speciali fuisse eos prouidentia conprobatur.   11-12 (p. 373, 20-22): Elationem eorum tumoremque cordis, quo nos
dispiciunt et malis innumeris adterunt.   3ᵇ (p. 373, 24-25): Non sunt parua quae
ad nos admisserunt.   19-21 (p. 373, 28-374, 3): Sollemnitatem sinagogam uocauit, ab eo quod conuenientes in unum dies sollemnes Deo festosque celebra-
rent. Victoriae, inquit, successu, qua nos opraeserunt, in gloriam sunt elati.

analogy with kings holding scepters; in fact, everywhere in such cases he refers by *rod* to the scepter, as emerges here as well with encouragement from Symmachus.

This is Mount Sion, where you took up your dwelling: you led us to this mountain, Sion, where you thought fit to dwell in person. He means, After freeing us from our captors, you *acquired* us by your own actions, and of all people you made us your own in this place where you dwell, keeping us always to yourself (in bodily language presenting the providence in their regard as the greatest possible). *Lift your hands at their arrogance forever* (v. 3): punish them for being arrogant in our regard and glorying in all their awful hostility to us (by analogy with people who strike with their hands those they choose, and by "hand of God" referring everywhere to his action directed either to good or to bad). The manner emerges from the following. *All the malice that the foe practiced in your holy place:* what was done by them was not insignificant.

Those who hate you boasted in the middle of your festival (v. 4). Symmachus: "in the middle of your assembly." He did well to call it a festival, since they came together to celebrate in God's honor. What he means is, They made many boasts against us through the wrongs they had done. | *The emblems they*

5. Έθεντο τὰ σημεῖα αὐτῶν σημεῖα, καὶ οὐκ ἔγνωσαν ὡς εἰς τὴν ἔξοδον ὑπεράνω. Ἔχει μὲν πολλὴν ἀπὸ τῆς ἑρμηνείας τὴν δυσκολίαν τὸ ῥητόν. Λέγει δὲ αὐτὸ Σύμμαχος σαφῶς, Ἔθεντο τὰ σημεῖα αὐτῶν ἐπισήμως γνώρισμα κατὰ τὴν εἴσοδον ἐπάνω. Ἐπειδὴ γὰρ ἔθος ἦν τοῖς παλαιοῖς, εἴ πού τινα ἐκράτησαν πόλιν, ἐπὶ τῆς πύλης γράμματα διαχαράττειν τὴν ἑαυτῶν προσ-   5
ηγορίαν ἐμφαίνοντα ὡς ἐνίκησάν τε καὶ ἔλαβον τὴν πόλιν αἰχμάλωτον, πολλάκις δὲ καί τινα ὡς σημεῖα καὶ σύμβολα ἐγκαταπηγνύμενοι, - - οἷα δὴ πολλὰ καὶ ἄχρι τῆς δεῦρο διαμένοντα ἐν πύλαις πόλεών ἐστιν εὑρεῖν, — τοῦτο οὖν λέγει Ὡς κρατήσαντες ἡμῶν τὰ τρόπαια καὶ τὰ σύμβολα ἐπισήμως πρὸ τῆς πύλης ἔθηκαν ὡς κρατήσαντες, ὡς αἰχμάλωτον αὐτὴν λαβόντες.   10

6a. Ὡς ἐν δρυμῷ ξύλων ἀξίναις ἐξέκοψαν τὰς θύρας αὐτῆς. Οὕτω τε αὐτὴν ἀφειδῶς ἐπόρθησαν, ὡς καὶ τὰς τῶν οἰκημάτων θύρας ἀξίναις κατακόπτειν, ὡσανεὶ ξύλα τις ἐν ὕλαις τέμνοι ἀναγκαίως διὰ τὴν τῶν ἀνθρώπων τεμνόμενα χρείαν.

6b. Ἐπὶ τὸ αὐτὸ ἐν πελέκει καὶ λαξευτηρίῳ κατέρραξαν αὐτήν. Λαξευ-   15
τήριον λέγεται τὸ τῶν λιθοξόων ὄργανον, οἷς τοὺς λίθους διατέμνουσιν. Ἔχοντες οὖν φησιν ἐν χερσὶν καὶ πέλεκυν καὶ τὰ τοιαῦτα ὄργανα, πᾶσι καταχρησάμενοι κατέβαλον τὰ τείχη.

7a. Ἐνεπύρισαν ἐν πυρὶ τὸ ἁγιαστήριόν σου. Πυρὶ παρέδωκαν τὸν ναόν.

7b. Εἰς τὴν γῆν ἐβεβήλωσαν τὸ σκήνωμα τοῦ ὀνόματός σου. Βέβηλον οὐ   20
πάντως τὸ ἀκάθαρτον καλεῖ, ἀλλὰ πολλαχοῦ καὶ τὸ κοινόν, οὕτως ἐν ταῖς

---

5. Ἔχει μὲν πολλὴν — λαβόντες: P, fol. 255ᵛ; V. fol. 23; Vat. 1422, fol. 133ᵛ; Cord, p. 532 (= P. G., 693).   6 ὡς] ὧν 1422   8-9 καὶ ἄχρι — κρατήσαντες om. 1422 Cord   10 ὡς αἰχμ.] ὡς om. 1422.

6a. Οὕτω — χρείαν: P, fol. 255ᵛ; V, fol. 23; Vat. 1422, fol. 134 (anon.); Cord, p. 532 (= P. G., 693).   12 τὰς om. 1422   13 τέμενοι Cord.

6b. Λαξευτήριον — τείχη: P. fol. 255ᵛ; V, fol. 23ᵛ; Vat. 1422, fol. 134 (anon.); Cord, p. 533 sub nomine EVSEBII.

7a. Πυρὶ παρέδωκαν τὸν ναόν: P, fol. 255ᵛ; V, fol. 23ᵛ; Paraphrasis (p. 518).

7b. Βέβηλον — κατασπάσαντες: P, fol. 255ᵛ; V. fol. 23ᵛ; Vat. 1422, fol. 134 (anon); Cord, p. 533.   21-493, 1 οὕτως — τὸ] ὡς τὸ 1422.

Aᵉ 8-10 (p. 374, 3-9): Hoc est ergo quod dicit. Posteaquam nos ceperunt, manubeas suas ad documenta uictoriae ante portam in locis euidentibus conlocauerunt, ad indicium uel suae uictoriae uel nostrae captiuitatis.   6ª (p. 374, 11-16): Ita passim ac uiliter urbs excissa est, ita ciuitate capta uictorum iram nulla lenitas temperauit, ut domorum claustra ab eis in morem lignorum uilium truncarentur in id ipsum.   7b (p. 374, 26-375, 6): Pullutum non semper inmundum uocat, sed commone, ut est illud in Regum historia Non sunt polluti panes... Nulla ait discritio inter templum tuum et priuatas aedes habeta est, sed tanquam uile et uulgare aedificium, ita usque ad fundamentum muros tui sacri (vel sacrari .i. templi in marg.) diruerunt.

set up were their emblems. They were as ignorant as in the exodus previously (vv. 4–5). The verse involves great difficulty in the translation.[3] Symmachus, on the other hand, says it more clearly: "They placed their signs conspicuously as emblems above the entrance." You see, it was the custom of the ancients in taking control of a city to inscribe notices on the gate disclosing their name to the effect that they had conquered and taken the city captive, often affixing as well something as tokens and signs; even to this day you can find many of this kind on gates of cities. So the meaning is, Like men in control of us, they set up trophies and signs conspicuously before the gate, as if in control, as if having taken it captive. *They hacked its doors with axes, as though in a forest of trees* (vv. 5–6): they thus showed no pity in sacking it, chopping down dwellings' *doors with axes,* as though out of people's need someone cut down trees as firewood. *At the same time, they razed it with a two-edged axe and an adze.* The name *adze* is given to a tool for stonecutters. So he is saying, With a two-edged axe and such tools in hand they toppled the walls by using them all.

With fire they burned your sanctuary (v. 7): they consigned the temple to the flames. *To the ground they profaned the tabernacle of your name.* By "profane" he does not mean "unclean" in general, but often uses the word to mean "ordinary," as in | Kings, "They are not ordinary loaves."[4] He is saying,

---

3. Dahood classes vv. 5–6 as "among the most obscure and difficult of the entire Psalter," admitting that his own version of the Hebrew is "in the realm of conjecture" (*Psalms,* 2:202). Theodore blames the LXX for the difficulty.

4. 1 Sam 21:4.

Βασιλείαις τὸ Οὐκ εἰσὶ βέβηλοι ἄρτοι. Οὐκ αἰδεσθέντες φησὶν οὐδ' ὅτι ναὸς ἦν σός, ὡς τι κοινὸν οἰκοδόμημα καθεῖλον ἀδιαφόρως μέχρι τῆς γῆς κατασπάσαντες.

8. Εἶπαν ἐν τῇ καρδίᾳ αὐτῶν, αἱ συγγένειαι αὐτῶν ἐπὶ τὸ αὐτό, Δεῦτε 5 καὶ καταπαύσωμεν πάσας τὰς ἑορτὰς τοῦ Θεοῦ ἀπὸ τῆς γῆς. Συνελάλουν δέ φησιν ἀλλήλοις καὶ ἐκελεύοντο — ὅπερ ἴδιον μάλιστα τῶν μετὰ θυμοῦ τι πραττόντων — Ἐπέλθωμεν ἐπ' αὐτούς, καθέλωμεν αὐτῶν τὴν πόλιν καὶ τὸν ναόν, ὥστε μηδὲν αὐτοῖς ὑπολειφθῆναι τοιοῦτον ἐφ' οὗ δυνήσονται συνιόντες ἑορτάζειν Θεῷ καὶ τῆς θεραπείας ἐπιμελεῖσθαι ταύτης ἐφ' ᾗ μεγαλο10 φρονοῦσιν.

9ᵃ. Τὰ σημεῖα ἡμῶν οὐκ εἴδομεν. Οὔτε γάρ ἐστι φοβηθῆναι μήποτέ τι πάθωμεν. Διὰ τί; Ἐπεὶ μηδὲν ὁρῶμέν τι ἐν αὐτοῖς γιγνόμενον σημεῖον, οἷα πολλὰ γεγενῆσθαι παρ' αὐτοῖς ψευδόμενοι λέγουσιν, ἃ θεασάμενοι δικαίως ἂν πιστεύσαντες κατεπλάγημεν. Ἐπειδὴ γὰρ ἐπὶ τούτοις μεγάλα 15 ἐφρόνουν οἱ Ἰουδαῖοι, δικαίως τοῦτό φησιν ὅτι Πάντα ἡμᾶς διατιθέασι τὰ κακά, ὡς οὐδὲν πεισόμενοι, ἔτι καὶ χλευάζοντες ὡς οὐδενὸς οὐδέποτε γενομένου τοιούτου, οἷα πολλὰ περὶ ἡμᾶς γεγενῆσθαι καυχώμεθα, ἀλλὰ μάτην ἡμῶν αὐχούντων καὶ ψευδομένων.

9ᵇ. Οὐκ ἔστιν ἔτι προφήτης, καὶ ἡμᾶς οὐ γνώσεται ἔτι. Ἀλλ' οὐδὲ προ20 φήτης τίς ἐστιν παρ' αὐτοῖς, ὃς δυνήσεται τὰ ἐν κρυφῇ παρ' ἡμῶν ἢ λεγόμενα ἢ γιγνόμενα προλέγειν αὐτοῖς, καὶ φυλάττεσθαι τὴν ἡμετέραν ἔφοδον. Ἐγίγνετο γὰρ καὶ ταῦτα παρ' αὐτοῖς διὰ τῶν προφητῶν, — οἷον καὶ τὸ παρὰ Ἐλισσαίου τοῦ προφήτου, ὅπως τῶν τῆς Συρίας βασιλέων πολεμούντων προλαμβάνων ἔλεγεν αὐτοῖς ὅσαπερ ἐβουλεύοντο· καὶ τοῦτο ἡμᾶς 25 σαφέστερον ἡ τετάρτη τῶν Βασιλειῶν διδάσκει.

1 I Reg. XXI, 4   23-25 cf. IV Reg. VI, 12 ss.

1 ἄρτοι des. 1422   2-3 ὥς τι — κατασπάσαντες affert Paraphrasis (p. 518).
8. Συνελάλουν — μεγαλοφρονοῦσιν: P, fol. 256; V, fol. 23ᵛ; Vat. 1422, fol. 134; Paraphrasis (p. 518).   6-7 ὅπερ — πραττόντων om. Par.   6 τι om. 1422   7 καὶ om. PV 1422   8 συνιέντες 1422 Par.
9ᵃ. Οὔτε — ψευδομένων: P, fol. 256; V, fol. 23ᵛ-24.
9ᵇ. Ἀλλ' οὐδὲ — διδάσκει: P, fol. 256; V, fol. 24; Vat. 1422, fol. 134; Cord, p. 534.   21 καὶ] ἢ 1422.

Aᶜ 8 (p. 375, 9-14): Tota gens hostium his se consiliis in nostrum exitium ausibusque flammabat, ut nostra festa, deletis cultoribus, subuersis moenibus, facerent otiari.   19-23 (p. 375, 16-20): Vt Heleseus... Nulla deffendentis eos Dei signa conspicimus, nullus in eis est profetarum, qui consiliorum nostrorum illis secreta denudet.

They showed no respect for the temple being yours, destroying it like any ordinary building and razing it to the ground. *They said in their heart, their fellows with them, Come, let us abolish from the earth all God's festivals* (v. 8): they conspired and gave orders (typical particularly of people acting with anger), Let us attack them; let us destroy their city and temple so that they may have nothing left to them where they can assemble and celebrate festivals to God and perform this cult in which they glory.

We do not see our signs (v. 9): there is no need to be afraid of coming to any harm. Why? Because we see no sign happening in their midst of the kind they falsely claim happens frequently among them; if we should see such signs, we should rightly give them credence and be alarmed. You see, since the Jews took pride in those things, he rightly says, They are bent on causing every trouble to us, being not at all convinced and actually mocking us for nothing of the kind ever occurring that we boasted to have happened frequently among us, our boasts and claims being false. *There is no longer a prophet, and no one to know us any longer:* there is no prophet in their midst capable of telling our secrets or of foretelling what will happen to them and of safeguarding against our attack. This, in fact, was what happened to them through the prophets, as in the case of Elisha the prophet, who gave advance warning to them of all the plans of the kings of Syria when they were making war, as the fourth book of Kings reports more clearly.[5] |

---

5. Cf. 2 Kgs 6:12.

10ᵃ. Έως πότε, ὁ Θεός, ὀνειδιεῖ ὁ ἐχθρός; Μέχρις οὖν πότε δώσεις αὐτοῖς τοιαῦτα καυχᾶσθαι καθ᾽ ἡμῶν καὶ ὀνειδίζειν ἡμᾶς ἐπὶ τούτοις;

10ᵇ. Παροξυνεῖ ὁ ὑπεναντίος τὸ ὄνομά σου εἰς τέλος; Πρὸς τὸ ἕως πότε βλέπει καὶ τοῦτο τῷ ἄνω ἐπισυνημμένον, ἀντὶ τοῦ Έως πότε ὀνειδιεῖ καὶ παροξυνεῖ; Μέχρι πότε ἐνδώσεις αὐτοῖς ὀνειδίζειν τε ἡμᾶς ἐπὶ τούτοις καὶ 5 φθέγγεσθαι ῥήματα παροξυσμῶν καὶ χλεύης μεστά; Σύμμαχος δὲ τὸ παρο- ξυνεῖ σαφέστερον εἶπεν π ρ ο π η λ α κ ί ζ ε ι, ἀντὶ τοῦ χλευάσει, παίξει· ταῦτα γὰρ ἔλεγον ὡς οὐδὲ τῶν προτέρων γεγενημένων, ἀλλὰ μάτην αὐτῶν ὅτι γέγονεν εἰς αὐτοὺς τοιαῦτα καυχωμένων.

11ᵃ. Ἵνα τι ἀποστρέφεις τὴν χεῖρά σου; Ἐπειδὴ χεῖρα καλεῖ τὴν ἐνέρ- 10 γειαν, οὐκέτι φησὶν ὑπερτίθεσθαι δίκαιον, τοιούτων ὄντων τῶν παρὰ τῶν ἐχθρῶν, τὸ ἡμῖν τε βοηθῆσαι κἀκείνους τιμωρήσασθαι. Τοῦτο γὰρ οὐ γι- γνόμενον ἐπὶ πλεῖον αὐτοὺς ἐπιτρέψει τοῦ καὶ χρήσασθαι τοῖς λόγοις καὶ ὀνειδίζειν ἡμᾶς, ὡς οὐδενὸς μὲν οὐδέποτε τοιούτου περὶ ἡμᾶς γεγενημένου· μάτην δὲ ἡμῶν ψευδομένων δοκοῦνται ἐγγύθεν ἔχειν ὧν λέγουσιν τὴν ἀπό- 15 δειξιν. Ἐκ μεταφορᾶς δὲ αὐτὸ εἶπεν τῶν ἐπὶ τῆς χειρὸς ἐχόντων τι ἀγα- θόν, καὶ ἀποστρεφόντων εἰς τοὐπίσω ὅταν διδόναι μὴ βούλωνται.

11ᵇ. Καὶ τὴν δεξιάν σου ἐκ μέσου τοῦ κόλπου σου εἰς τέλος. Ὥσπερ χεῖρα καλεῖ τὴν ἐνέργειαν, οὕτω δεξιὰν τὴν βοήθειαν, ἀπὸ τοῦ κρείττονος τὴν ἐπωφελῆ αὐτῶν ἐνέργειαν σημαίνων. Ἐπειδὴ γὰρ χεῖρα εἰπὼν ἄδηλον 20 ἦν τὴν ὁποίαν λέγειν βούλεται, τῇ ἐπαγωγῇ τῆς δεξιᾶς ἐδήλωσεν σαφέστερον τὸ λεγόμενον. Ἵνα τί οὖν φησι τὸ βοηθῆσαι ἡμῖν ὑπερτίθεσαι; Τὸ δὲ ἐκ μέσου τοῦ κόλπου ἀκολούθως εἶπεν τῷ « ἀποστρέφειν »· κόλπος γὰρ τὸ ἔμπροσθεν μέρος λέγεται. Κατὰ οὖν τὴν σωματοποίησιν ἀκολούθως εἶπεν Διὰ τί τὴν χεῖρά σου ἀπέμπροσθεν λαβὼν εἰς τὰ ὀπίσω μετάγεις οὐδενὸς 25 ἡμῖν μεταδιδούς;

16-17 cf. THEODORETUS (1460 B 1-4).

10ᵃ. Μέχρις — τούτοις: P, fol. 256ᵛ; V, fol. 24; *Paraphrasis* (p 519). 10ᵇ. Πρὸ τὸ ·· καυχωμένων: P, fol. 256ᵛ; V, fol. 24; Cord, p. 534.   6-9 Σύμμα- χος κτλ. *affert* Vat. 1422, fol. 134ᵛ   7 προπηλακίσει Cord   8 οὐδὲ] οὕτως 1422. 11. Ἐπειδὴ — βούλωνται: P, fol. 256ᵛ; V, fol. 24; Cord, p. 534-535.   13 αὐτοῖς Cord   κεχρήσθασθαι PV   15 δοκοῦντας PV δοκοῦντα Cord   17 ἀγαθῶν Cord. 11ᵇ. Ὥσπερ — μεταδιδούς: P, fol. 256ᵛ; V, fol. 24ᵛ.

Aᵉ 10ᵃ (p. 375, 30-376, 1): Quandiu, inquit, deferentem te ultionem prospe- ritate hostis insolens ac securus insultat?   5-6 (p. 376, 2-6): Quam ad finem exprobrantes nobis et alia loquentes, qui te possint in uindictam iustissime commouere, securos esse patieris?   22-26 (p. 376, 7-15): Ne nobis defensionis opem familiarem tibi indulgentissimus largiaris. Pulchra translatio ad similitu- dinem eorum qui sinu prolatum gremioque aliquid largiuntur, quique mota sen- tentia largiendi auertunt a gremio ad dorsum manum.

How long, O God, will the foe taunt us? (v. 10). How long will you allow them to make such boasts against us and taunt us with these things? *Will the adversary challenge your name forever?* This has reference to *How long* and is related to the above, meaning, How long will he taunt and challenge? How long will you allow them to taunt us with this and to utter words full of provocation and mockery? Symmachus, on the other hand, for *challenge* says more clearly "insult"—that is, "mock, ridicule." They said this, note, not because of what had happened previously, but because they were idly boasting that such things had happened to them. *Why do you turn aside your hand?* (v. 11). Since by *hand* he refers to action, his meaning is, With the enemy guilty of such actions, it is not fair to delay any longer helping us and punishing them. If this does not take place, in fact it will permit them all the more to use such words to taunt us, claiming that nothing of that kind had ever been worked in our favor; while we are making false claims, they seem to have proof of what they say. Now, he says this by analogy with people holding something good in their hand and putting it behind their back when they are unwilling to give it. *And your right hand from the midst of your bosom forever.* Just as he refers to action by *hand,* so he refers to help by *right hand,* suggesting by the intensive the action in their favor: since it was not clear what he meant by *hand,* he clarified his statement by the addition of *right hand.* So he is saying, Why do you postpone helping us? The phrase *from the midst of your bosom* is in keeping with *turn aside,* the bosom being the part in front. It is therefore in a corporeal manner he is speaking in asking, Why do you move your hand from the front to the back and give nothing to us? |

12ᵃ. Ὁ δὲ Θεὸς βασιλεὺς ἡμῶν πρὸ αἰῶνος. Τὰ προκείμενα — τὸ Ἔως πότε ὀνειδιεῖ ὁ ἐχθρὸς — παρενθέσεως μᾶλλον ἔχει δύναμιν κἂν ἀκουλούθως ἐπῆχθαι δοκῶσιν. Οὐδὲ γὰρ αἱ παρενθέσεις περιτταί εἰσιν καὶ τῆς ὑποθέσεως ἀλλότριαι, ἀλλὰ βλέπουσαι μὲν πρὸς τὴν ὑπόθεσιν, ἐν μέσῳ δὲ νοή-
5 ματος ἢ διὰ τὸ μέτρον ἢ διὰ τὸ ἀναγκαῖον παρεγκείμεναι πολλάκις τῷ μέλλειν τὴν ἐπαγωγὴν μακροτέραν εἶναι, — ὥσπερ οὖν ἐνταῦθα ἡ τοῦ Ὁ δὲ Θεὸς βασιλεὺς ἡμῶν ἐπαγωγή, τῶν τε ἑξῆς μακροτέρα οὖσα, ἀπέκλειεν ἐν τούτοις τοῖς νῦν ἐν μέσῳ παρεντεθεῖσι ῥητοῖς ἀναγκαίοις οὖσι πρὸς τὰ παρ' ἐκείνων λεγόμενα καὶ κινητικοῖς καὶ πάθος ἐμποιῆσαι δυναμένοις. Εἰ
10 γὰρ καὶ μὴ ἔχρῃζεν τούτων ὁ Θεός, ἀλλὰ τῷ προλέγοντι προφήτῃ ἀναγ-καῖον ἦν ἐκ πάντων κοσμεῖν τὸν λόγον. Τοιοῦτο δὲ καὶ παρὰ τῷ ἀπο-στόλῳ εὑρίσκεται. Εἰπὼν γὰρ Οὐ θέλω δὲ ὑμᾶς ἀγνοεῖν, ἀδελφοί, ὅτι πολ-λάκις προεθέμην ἐλθεῖν πρὸς ὑμᾶς, δέον ἀκολούθως ἐπαγαγεῖν ἵνα τινὰ καρπὸν σχῶ καὶ ἐν ὑμῖν καὶ τὰ ἑξῆς, ἀλλὰ διὰ τὸ μακρότερα εἶναι πα-
15 ρενέθηκεν τὸ ἐκωλύθην ἄχρι τοῦ δεῦρο, ἵνα μὴ ἀναγκαῖον ὃν ἀπὸ τοῦ μήκους τῶν ἑξῆς ἐξωσθεὶς παρενθεῖναι ζημιώσῃ τὸν λόγον· ἀπολογίας γὰρ τόπον ἐπεῖχεν.

Τὸ οὖν Ὁ δὲ Θεὸς βασιλεὺς ἡμῶν πρὸς τὸ ἄνω βλέπει. Εἰπὼν γὰρ ὅτι ἐκεῖνοι οὕτω χλευάζουσιν ἡμᾶς — ποῖα γὰρ παρ' αὐτοῖς λέγοντες σημεῖα;
20 τίς δὲ προφήτης; οἷα γεγενῆσθαι πολλὰ παρ' αὐτοῖς φασιν; — ἐκπλήττειν μᾶλλον καὶ ἀπατᾶν βουλόμενοι τοὺς ἀκούοντας ὥστε οὐδὲν αὐτοὺς δεδιέναι προσήκει, ὁρμήσαντας δὲ πᾶν ὅ τι κακὸν αὐτοὺς διαθεῖναι, εἶτα ἐπαγαγὼν τὴν παρένθεσιν ὡς ἀναγκαίαν, — τὸ μέχρι πότε τοιαῦτα λέγειν αὐτοῖς ἐπι-τρέψῃς οὐ βοηθῶν ἡμῖν, ἀλλὰ διὰ τούτου παρέχων αὐτοῖς τοῦ τοιαῦτα
25 λέγειν τὰς ἀφορμάς; — ἐνταῦθα ἀπέδωκεν τὰς ἀφορμάς, Ὁ δὲ Θεὸς βασιλεὺς ἡμῶν πρὸ αἰώνων, τουτέστιν Σὺ γὰρ ἡμῶν ἀεὶ δεσπότης κἂν ἐκεῖνοι χλευ-άζουσι καὶ ἀρνῶνται, ὥστε δίκαιον καὶ νῦν τῇ εἰς ἡμᾶς σου βοηθείᾳ βεβαιω-θῆναι μὲν τῶν τότε τὴν ἀλήθειαν, φανῆναι δὲ τούτους βλασφήμως μᾶλλον ἀρνουμένους τὰ γινόμενα.

12ᵇ. Εἰργάσατο σωτηρίαν ἐν μέσῳ τῆς γῆς. Σὺ γὰρ ὁ τότε τὴν σωτη-ρίαν ἡμῖν παρασχόμενος. Τὸ ἐν μέσῳ τῆς γῆς, ἵνα εἴπῃ Οὕτως ἡμᾶς περιέ-

---

1-2 v. 10   12-15 Rom. I, 13   19-20 v. 9.

12ᵃ. Τὰ προκείμενα — γινόμενα: P, fol. 257; V, fol. 24ᵛ.   5 πολλάκις τὸ PV
9 δυναμέναις PV   16 ζημιώσει PV.
12ᵇ. Σὺ γὰρ — ὁρῶνται: P, fol. 257; V, fol. 24ᵛ-25.

Aᵉ 25 29 (p. 376, 16-20): Et si nos, inquit, inimici iuridiant et si negent tuo nos aliquando auxilio esse defensos, nostra tamen erit iugis ista confessio, quae te Deum regemque fateatur.

Yet God is our king from of old (v. 12). The phrase *How long will the foe taunt* that went before has the force of an insertion, even if seeming to be introduced in keeping with the sense. In fact, far from being pointless or foreign to the theme, insertions have relevance to the theme, occurring in the middle of the thought, either on account of the meter or often out of necessity through the sequel coming at a distance. In this case, therefore, the sequel of the phrase *Yet God is our king,* being far from what follows, would interrupt the words now inserted in the middle that are necessary as a response to what was said by them, and are moving and capable of arousing feeling. That is to say, even if God did not proclaim these words, yet they were required by the prophet in his forecast for complete ordering of his message. A similar usage also can be found in the apostle: he said, "I do not want you to be ignorant, brethren, that I have often intended to come to you," and there was need to proceed logically, "so as to reap some harvest among you" and so on; but because of the inserted phrase "but thus far I have been prevented" lying too far away, it was necessary, if he was not to lose the force of the thought (an apology being in order), to insert the phrase that was left out as a result of the length of the sentence.[6]

The phrase *Yet God is our king* refers to what precedes. He first said that they mock us by asking what kinds of *signs* occur in their midst, what *prophet,* what are the many things that they claim to have happened. They wished all the more to astonish and deceive the listeners so that they had no need to fear anything but were disposed to rush into every kind of abuse. He then proceeds to make a necessary insertion by asking how long you will allow them to say such things without helping us, instead providing them through this with grounds for saying such things. And at this point he supplied the grounds *Yet God is our king from of old*—that is, You are our Lord always, even if they mock and deny the claim, with the result that it is now right also to confirm with your help for us the truth of those past events and make clear that it was blasphemy rather for them to deny what happened.

He brought about salvation in the midst of the earth: you who at that time provided us with salvation. The phrase *in the midst of the earth* means, You so achieved our salvation | with great marvels that they escaped no one's

---

6. Rom 1:13.

σώσας μετὰ μεγάλων θαυμάτων, ὡς μηδένα διαλαθεῖν τὰ γιγνόμενα, – ἐκ μεταφορᾶς τῶν ἐν μέσῳ πλήθους ὄντων, οἳ τῷ κυκλῶσθαι μάλιστα παρὰ πάντων ὁρῶνται.

13ᵃ. Σὺ ἐκραταίωσας ἐν τῇ δυνάμει σου τὴν θάλασσαν. Σὺ τότε συνήγαγες τὴν θάλασσαν, καὶ ὀλισθηρὰν οὖσαν τὴν φύσιν ἔπηξας κατὰ τὴν 5 σὴν δύναμιν, ἐν τάξει τειχῶν ἐργασάμενος τὰ ὕδατα.

13ᵇ. Σὺ συνέτριψας τὰς κεφαλὰς τῶν δρακόντων ἐπὶ τοῦ ὕδατος. Καὶ ἡμᾶς μὲν οὕτω διαβῆναι πεποίηκας, τοὺς δὲ πολεμίους δίκην δρακόντων ἕρποντας καθ᾽ ἡμῶν ἐπ᾽ αὐτῷ συνέτριψας καὶ ἀπώλεσας τῷ ὕδατι· τοῦτο γὰρ δὴ τὸ θαυμαστόν, ὅτι τὸ ὑπὲρ ἡμῶν παγὲν ἐκείνους κατεπόντωσεν. 10

13ᶜ. Σὺ συνέθλασας τὴν κεφαλὴν τοῦ δράκοντος. Ἵνα εἴπῃ τοῦ Φαραώ· καὶ αὐτὸν δὲ τὸν ἔξαρχον ἀνεῖλες. Καλῶς τὸ Σὺ δι᾽ ὅλου ὡς πρὸς ἀντιδιαστολὴν τῶν ἀρνουμένων καὶ χλευαζόντων, δράκοντας δὲ μεταφορικῶς διὰ τὴν πονηρίαν αὐτοὺς καλέσας. Τὸ συνέτριψας τὰς κεφαλὰς αὐτῶν καὶ συνέθλασας ἐμφαντικωτέραν τὴν κατ᾽ αὐτῶν τιμωρίαν ἐποίησεν. Οὐχ ἁπλῶς δὲ 15 πάντας τοὺς πονηροὺς δράκοντας καλεῖ, ἀλλὰ τοὺς ἐξάρχοντας τῶν πονηρῶν, ἐπειδὴ τοιοῦτον ἐν τοῖς ἑρπετοῖς ὁ δράκων. Βούλεται οὖν εἰπεῖν Τοὺς παρ᾽ αὐτοῖς στρατηγοὺς καὶ σατράπας, διὰ τοῦτο εἰπὼν τῶν δρακόντων κεχωρισμένως, πάλιν εἶπεν τοῦ δράκοντος τὸν βασιλέα λέγων.

14. Ἔδωκας αὐτὸν βρῶμα λαοῖς τοῖς Αἰθίοψιν. Πόλεμος ἦν Αἰγυπτίοις 20 ἀεὶ πρὸς Αἰθίοπας πλησιοχωροῦντας αὐτοῖς. Τῆς οὖν πληγῆς γενομένης, καὶ ἀπολομένου τοῦ βασιλέως, ἀπολομένων δὲ τῶν ἀρχόντων, ἀπολομένου

13ᵃ. Σὺ τότε — ὕδατα: P, fol. 257ᵛ; V, fol. 25; *Paraphrasis* (p. 519).
13ᵇ. Καὶ ἡμᾶς — κατεπόντωσεν: P, fol. 257ᵛ; V, fol. 25; Vat. 1422, fol. 134ᵛ (anon.); *Paraphrasis* (p. 519).   8 διατριβῆναι 1422.
13ᶜ. Ἵνα εἴπῃ — λέγων: P, fol. 257ᵛ; V, fol. 25.
14. Πόλεμος — κατέφαγον: P, fol. 258; V, fol. 25ᵛ; Cord, p. 536.

Aᵉ 1 (p. 376, 22-24): ...ut neminem id quod in difensionem nostri contingerat possit latere.   13ᵃ (p. 376, 25-27): Tu aquas natura sui lubricas in ministerium transitus nostri stare iussisti firmiter ac durari.   13ᵇ (p. 376, 28-377, 2): Nos quidem per medium fluentis sicco pede transire fecisti, hostes uero nostros, qui uice nos sequebantur draconum, ad ma⟨io⟩rem operum tuorum admirationem in ipsis, quae propter nos duratae fuerant, aquis necasti.   14 (p. 377, 5-11): Erat Egiptiis aduersus Ethiopas per regionis uicinitatem frequens causa certaminis; sed post illam plagam... tam rex quam princepes et om⟨n⟩is est deletus (dilectus *ms*) exercitus; inruentes Ethiopes omnem terram Egiptiam uastauerunt.

notice (by analogy with people in the midst of a crowd, who are noticed particularly by being surrounded on all sides). *You dominated the sea with your might* (v. 13): at that time you massed the sea together and firmed it up in your might though it was naturally fluid, causing the water to act as walls. *You smashed the heads of the dragons on the water:* whereas you caused us to cross over, you smashed the enemy crawling against us like dragons and destroyed them in water, the marvel being that what was firmed up to our benefit drowned them. *You broke the head of the dragon* (v. 14), meaning Pharaoh: You destroyed him to start with. The pronoun *You* was well employed in clear contrast to those denying and mocking, while the term *the dragons* was used to refer to them metaphorically for their wickedness; by saying that he *smashed* and *broke* their heads he presented the punishment of them to greater effect. Now, he does not refer simply to all the wicked people as *dragons,* but to the leaders of the wicked ones, the dragon being like that among serpents. So he means the generals and satraps among them, hence referring to *the dragons* separately and then mentioning the king as the dragon.

You gave him as food to the Ethiopian people. The Egyptians were ever at war with their neighbors the Ethiopians; so when this blow struck and their king perished along with the leaders and | all the army, the Ethiopians

δὲ τοῦ στρατοῦ παντός, ἐπελθόντες οἱ Αἰθίοπες κάκιστα τὴν χώραν διέθηκαν. Ἔδωκας τοίνυν φησὶν αὐτόν, ἵνα εἴπῃ τὸν Αἰγύπτιον, κατάβρωμα τῶν Αἰθιόπων, οἳ τὴν χώραν ἐπελθόντες ἔρημον οὖσαν στρατοῦ τε καὶ βασιλέως ἐνεμήθησαν καὶ κατέφαγον.

5 **15ᵃ.** Σὺ διέρρηξας πηγὰς καὶ χειμάρρους. Ὕδατά φησιν ἡμῖν κατὰ τὴν ἔρημον οὖσιν ἀνέδωκας. Τὸ δὲ χειμάρρους, ἵνα εἴπῃ τὸ τῶν ὑδάτων αἰφνίδιον, ὅτι μὴ κατὰ συνήθειαν ῥέοντα ὕδατα διὰ μόνην τὴν αὐτῶν χρείαν ἐκδοθῆναι πεποίηκεν· τοιοῦτοι γὰρ οἱ χείμαρροι, οὐ κατὰ συνήθειαν φερόμενοι, ἀλλ᾽ αἰφνίδιον ἐπιρρέοντες.

10 **15ᵇ.** Σὺ ἐξήρανας ποταμοὺς Ἠθάμ. Τὰ μὲν δέδωκας ὕδατα παρὰ συνήθειαν, τὰ δὲ ἐπέσχες παρὰ τὴν φύσιν, οἷον δὴ τὸ τοῦ Ἰορδάνου. Ἡ μὲν οὖν δευτέρα τῶν Βασιλειῶν μέμνηται τοῦ βασιλέως Ἠθὰμ Ἰεδδοῦρον τὸν ἑαυτοῦ υἱὸν πρὸς τὸν Δαυὶδ μετὰ πολλῶν ἀποστείλαντος δώρων, ὑπὲρ ὧν τὸν Ἀδραζὰρ ἐτιμωρήσατο σφόδρα πρὸς αὐτὸν πολεμίως διακείμενον. Συμ-
15 βαίνει δέ που καὶ δι᾽ ἐκείνων ὡς εἰκὸς φέρεσθαι τὸ ὕδωρ τοῦ Ἰορδάνου· ὅθεν ἀπὸ τοῦ μερικοῦ ποταμοῦ Ἠθὰμ τὸν Ἰορδάνην ὠνόμασεν ὁ προφήτης. Οὐκ εὔδηλον μέντοι νῦν ἡμῖν, οὐδὲ σαφὲς τοῦτο καθέστηκεν ἀκριβῶς, τίς ἄρα ὁ Ἠθάμ, τόπος ἢ χώρα, ἀπὸ τῆς ἐγγενομένης ταῖς ὀνομασίαις τῶν τε τόπων καὶ τῶν πόλεων ἐναλλαγῆς, ἣν μάλιστα πολλὴν καὶ διάφορον προβαίνων ὁ
20 χρόνος εἰργάσατο.

16ᵃ. Σή ἐστιν ἡ ἡμέρα καὶ σή ἐστιν ἡ νύξ. Συνηθῶς ἀπὸ τοῦ μερικοῦ ἐπὶ τὸ καθολικώτερον ἐκβαίνει. Καὶ οὐδὲν θαυμαστὸν εἰ ταῦτα πεποίηκας, αὐτὸς ὢν ὁ τῶν πάντων δεσπότης, ὃς ἡμέραν τε καὶ νύκτα κατεσκεύασας.

12-14 II Reg. VIII, 9-11.

1 ἀπελθόντες Cord   2 ἔδωκας] ἔθηκας Cord.
15ᵃ. Ὕδατα — ἐπιρρέοντες: P, fol. 258; V, fol. 25ᵛ; Vat. 1422, fol. 135; Cord, p. 537.   6 ἀνέδωκας] δέδωκας 1422 ἔδωκας Cord   τὸ om. PV.
15ᵇ. Τὰ μὲν — εἰργάσατο: P, fol. 258ᵛ; V, fol. 25ᵛ-26; Cord, p. 537.   11 τὸ om. Cord   13 ἀποστείλαντες Cord.
16ᵃ. Συνηθῶς — κατεσκεύασας: P, fol. 258ᵛ; V, fol. 26.

Aᵉ **15ᵃ** (p. 377, 12-17): Aquarum in nobis in herimo copias prae⟨s⟩titisti. *Torrentes* autem dixit, ut subitos et praeter morem aquae cursus ostenderet, quod est proprie torrentum, qui non iugi meatu fluunt, sed aquis pluialibus intumescunt.   12-15 (p. 377, 21-24): Etham regio est per quam meat Iordanus; cuius prouinciae rex filium suum gratulatum cum muneribus ad Dauid missit, quia emulum eius rex extinxerit.   22-23 (p. 377, 25-28): Nihil mirum si haec in defensionem populi tui signa perfeceris, cuius potentia conditus, ordinatus inlustratusque hic mundus est.

attacked and devastated the country. So he is saying, *You gave him*—that is, the Egyptian—as food for the Ethiopians, who invaded the land that was devoid of army and king, and consumed and devoured it. *You cut openings for springs and torrents* (v. 15): you supplied us with water when we were in the desert. By *torrents* he refers to the sudden appearance of the water, since he caused water that normally did not flow to appear simply for their needs, torrents being like that, not flowing normally but gushing out suddenly. *You dried up rivers of Etham:* whereas you provided some water in unaccustomed fashion, you checked other water in opposition to nature, like that of the Jordan. So the second book of Kings records that the king of Etham sent his son Joram to David with many gifts in return for his severely punishing Hadadezer, who was hostile to him. Now, it happens that the water of the Jordan probably flows somewhere through their territory—hence, by *Etham* the prophet is referring to the Jordan as by part to whole. It is not, however, completely clear to us now, nor did he give a precise presentation of what Etham is, place or district, as a result of the change that has occurred in the names of places and cities, so many and varied changes being due to the lapse of time.[7]

Yours is the day, and yours is the night (v. 16). As usual he proceeds from part to whole. It is not surprising if you did this, he is saying, being Lord of all, who created both day and night. | *You brought light and sun to perfection:*

---

7. At a loss again, the LXX is content to transliterate the Hebrew *'eythan,* "constant," leading Theodore to recognize the place name Hamath, as referred to in 2 Sam 8:9–11, where its King Toi and his son Joram are mentioned.

16^b. Σὺ κατηρτίσω φαῦσιν καὶ ἥλιον. Αὐτὸς πεποίηκας τὸν ἥλιον εἰς τὸ φαίνοντα τὴν ἡμέραν ἐργάζεσθαι.

17^a. Σὺ ἐποίησας πάντα τὰ ὅρια τῆς γῆς. Καὶ κοινῶς τὰ πάντα κατεσκεύασας αὐτός.

17^b. Θέρος καὶ ἔαρ σὺ ἔπλασας αὐτά. Αὐτὸς καὶ τὰς τροπὰς εἰργάσω. 5

18. Μνήσθητι ταύτης· ἐχθρὸς ὠνείδισε τὸν Κύριον, καὶ λαὸς ἄφρων παρώξυνε τὸ ὄνομά σου. Ἐπειδὴ εἶπεν ἄνω Ἕως πότε ὁ Θεὸς ὀνειδιεῖ ὁ ἐχθρός; παροξυνεῖ ὁ ὑπεναντίος τὸ ὄνομά σου εἰς τέλος; καλῶς ἐνταῦθα Μνήσθητι ταύτης, τουτέστι τῆς συναγωγῆς, ὑπὲρ ἧς τοσαῦτα ἐποίησας, ὑπὲρ ἧς τοσαῦτα εἰργάσω· ἀπόβλεψον πρὸς τοὺς ἐχθροὺς ὀνειδίζοντας, καὶ ὀργῆς ἄξια φθεγ- 10 γομένους ὡς οὐ γενομένων ποτὲ τοιούτων, καὶ ἀπόδειξιν τούτου τιθεμένους τὰ νῦν κατέχοντα κακά, καὶ δεῖξον ὅτι γέγονεν δι' ὧν νῦν ἐπαμύνεις.

19^a. Μὴ παραδῷς τοῖς θηρίοις ψυχὴν ἐξομολογουμένην σοι. Καὶ μὴ τούτοις ἐναφῇς τοὺς εἰδότας εὐχαριστεῖν σοι ὑπὲρ ὧν ἂν λάβωμεν.

19^b. Τῶν ψυχῶν τῶν πενήτων σου μὴ ἐπιλάθῃ εἰς τέλος. Ἡμῶν τῶν σῶν 15 καὶ ἐν συμφοραῖς ἐξεταζομένων μὴ ποιήσῃς λήθην.

20^a. Ἐπίβλεψον εἰς τὴν διαθήκην σου. Πρόσχες ἡμῖν, πρὸς οὓς διέθου καὶ οἷς ἀεὶ βοηθήσειν συνέθου.

20^b. Ὅτι ἐπληρώθησαν οἱ ἐσκοτισμένοι τῆς γῆς οἰκῶν ἀνομιῶν. Πανοικεὶ λέγομεν ἀεὶ ἀντὶ τοῦ «πάντες». Ἡμεῖς οὖν φησιν οἱ ἐσκοτισμένοι τῆς γῆς, 20

7-8 v. 10.

16^b. Αὐτὸς — ἐργάζεσθαι: P, fol. 258^v; V, fol. 26.
17^a. Καὶ κοινῶς — αὐτός: P, fol. 259; V, fol. 26^v; Paraphrasis (p. 520).
17^b. Αὐτὸς — εἰργάσω: P, fol. 259; V, fol. 26^v; Paraphrasis (p. 520).
18. Ἐπειδὴ — ἐπαμύνεις: P, fol. 259; V, fol. 26^v; Cord, p. 539.   11 τιθέμενος Cord   12 δι' ὧν] διὸ Cord.
19^a. Καὶ μὴ τούτοις — λάβωμεν: P, fol. 259; V, fol. 26^v.
19^b. Ἡμῶν — λήθην: P, fol. 259; V, fol. 26^v.
20^a. Πρόσχες — συνέθου: P, fol. 259^v; V, fol. 26^v.
20^b. Πανοικεὶ — νήπια: P, fol. 259^v; V, fol. 26^v-27.

A^e 9 (p. 378, 3): Subauditur congregationis tuae.   20^a (p. 378, 17-20): ...conuerte in nos oculos tuos, cum quibus testamenta pactaque fecisti, et quibus es iugiter defensum ire pullicitus.   20^b (p. 378, 21-29): Omnes itaque nos sine alicuius exceptione, qui inter alios homines tenebris quibusdam uilitatis et calamitatis inuoluemur, habemus domus iniquitatibus plenas, id est sumus in adflictione et in miseris constituti et nemo nostrum expers mali est, non infans, non senex, non uilis quisque, non nobilis.

you caused the sun to make the day dawn. *You made all the ends of the earth* (v. 17): and in general it was you who created everything. *You shaped the very summer and spring:* it was you who also made the seasons.

Remember this: a foe taunted the Lord, and a witless people challenged your name (v. 18). Since he had said above *How long, O God, will the foe reproach us? Will the adversary challenge your name forever?* he did well here to say *Remember this*—that is, the congregation for which you worked such marvelous wonders, for which you did such wonderful things: have regard to the foe's taunts, claiming as they do in a way deserving of wrath that these things never happened, citing as proof of this the troubles now in force, and make clear through your now assisting us that they did happen. *Do not deliver to wild beasts a soul confessing to you* (v. 19): do not do away with those in the habit of thanking you for what we receive. *Do not forget the souls of your needy ones forever:* do not consign us to oblivion, especially now that your people find themselves in misfortune.

Have regard for your covenant (v. 20): pay heed to us, whom you are fond of and to whom you ever agree to lend assistance. *Because those in the land who have fallen into darkness were filled with iniquitous dealings.* By *without exception* we mean "always"—that is, "everyone."[8] So he is saying, We who have fallen into darkness; | as if to say, We who of all people are in

---

8. Is Theodore reading this term, πανοικεί, in his text?

ἵνα εἴπῃ οἱ παρὰ πάντας ἀνθρώπους ἐν σκότῳ καὶ συμφοραῖς ὄντες, τοὺς
οἴκους τῶν ἀνομιῶν ἔχομεν πεπληρωμένους, ἀντὶ τοῦ Πανοικεὶ τῶν κακῶν
ἀπηλαύσαμεν, καὶ οὐδεὶς ἡμῶν τῆς βλάβης ἀπείραστος, οὐ γυναῖκες οὐ
νήπια.

5   21ᵃ. Μὴ ἀποστραφήτω τεταπεινωμένος κατῃσχυμμένος. Ἡμεῖς τοίνυν οἱ
ἀπὸ τῶν συμφορῶν τεταπεινωμένοι, μὴ ἀποστραφείημεν κατῃσχυμμένοι καὶ
οὐδενὸς ἀπολαύσαντες καλοῦ.

21ᵇ. Πτωχὸς καὶ πένης αἰνέσουσι τὸ ὄνομά σου. Ἡμεῖς γὰρ οἱ μικροὶ καὶ
τοιαῦτα πάσχοντες, ἀπολαύσαντες τῆς παρά σου βοηθείας, ὕμνους σοι τοὺς
10 προσήκοντας ἀναπέμψομεν.

22ᵃ. Ἀνάστα, ὁ Θεός, δίκασον τὴν δίκην σου. Δίκασον· σὴ γὰρ ἡ δίκη,
ἐπειδὴ σὺ ὁ δι᾽ ἡμῶν ὑβριζόμενος παρ᾽ ἐκείνων, — σαφέστερον δὲ αὐτὸ
λέγων πῶς αὐτοῦ ἡ δίκη ἐπάγει.

22ᵇ. Μνήσθητι τοῦ ὀνειδισμοῦ σου, τοῦ ὑπὸ ἄφρονος ὅλην τὴν ἡμέραν.
15 Ὅτι σε διὰ παντὸς ὀνειδίζουσι καὶ εἰς σε βλασφημοῦσι δι᾽ ἡμῶν, ὡς οὐδενὸς πώποτε τοιούτου γενομένου παρά σου ἀλλ᾽ ἡμῶν ψευδομένων.

23. Μὴ ἐπιλάθῃ τῆς φωνῆς τῶν ἱκετῶν σου, ἡ ὑπερηφανία τῶν μισούντων
σε ἀνέβη διὰ παντός. Ἀμφοτέρων δὴ ἀκούσας, ἀμφοτέροις τὸ εἰκὸς φύλαξον, ὧν τε ἡμεῖς ἱκετεύομεν καὶ ὧν ἐκεῖνοι βλασφημοῦντες φθέγγονται.

21ᵃ. Ἡμεῖς — καλοῦ: P, fol. 259ᵛ; V, fol. 27; Paraphrasis (p. 521).
21ᵇ. Ἡμεῖς — ἀναπέμψομεν: P, fol. 259ᵛ; V, fol. 27; Paraphrasis (p. 521).
22ᵃ. Δίκασον — ἐπάγει: P, fol. 260; V, fol. 27; Vat. 1422, fol. 135ᵛ.   11-12 σὴ
γὰρ — ἐκείνων affert Paraphrasis (p. 521)   12 δι᾽ ἡμῶν] δι᾽ ἡμᾶς 1422 Par.
22ᵇ. Ὅτι σε — ψευδομένων: P, fol. 260; V, fol. 27ᵛ.
23. Ἀμφοτέρων — φθέγγονται: P, fol. 260; V, fol. 27ᵛ; Vat. 1422, fol. 135ᵛ
(anon.); Paraphrasis (p. 521).

Aᵉ 21ᵇ (p. 379, 2-8): Nostrae quoque uires calamitatibus adtenuatae sunt;
quos exiguos misseriae reddiderunt, opes tuae, quarum inpertione liberasti, continuo teste studemus honore et laude celebrare.   22ᵃ (p. 379, 9-12): Hoc igitur
magis uindicis adsume censuram, quo nos in tuam uides iniuriam hostibus
uiluisse.   22ᵇ (p. 379, 14-20): Hostes, inquit, per insolentiam obproprii in te
plasfemias et maladicta iaculantur, eo quod nihil aliquando in defensionem
populi tui feceris, sed nos relationis lecentia mendaciter ista iectemus. 23 (p. 379,
22-26): Auris tua utriusque partis uoce pulsetur, et iusto examine tam suplican-
tibus quam plasfemantibus pro meritis digna restitue.

darkness and misfortune have our houses filled with iniquitous dealings—that is, Without exception we are the butt of troubles, and none of us is without experience of harm, neither women nor children. *Let a lowly person not be turned away in shame* (v. 21): let us therefore, who have been humbled by the disasters, not be turned away in shame and deprived of every good. *Poor and needy will praise your name:* we who are insignificant and the butt of such awful treatment enjoy help from you and will offer you the hymns of praise that are due.

Rise up, O God, vindicate your cause (v. 22): it is your cause, since it is you who in us are insulted by them. To put the same thing more clearly he proceeds to explain how it is his cause. *Remember your reproach on the part of the foolish all day long:* because they constantly reproach you and blaspheme you through us, claiming that nothing of the like was ever done by you, and instead that we are lying. *Do not forget the voice of your suppliants; the arrogance of those who hate you rose up constantly* (v. 23): having heard both parties, render justice to both in response to our supplication and their words of blasphemy. |

PSALMVS LXXIV

Τὴν κατὰ τῶν Ἀσσυρίων ἐπὶ τοῦ Ἐζεκίου νίκην γενομένην ἐν τούτῳ προφητεύει τῷ ψαλμῷ, ὡς ἐκ προσώπου κοινοῦ πάντων τὴν εὐχαριστίαν ἐπὶ τοῖς γεγενημένοις ἀναφθεγγόμενος.

2ᵃ. Ἐξομολογησόμεθά σοι, ὁ Θεός, ἐξομολογησόμεθά σοι. Εὐχαριστήσο-   5
μέν σοι ὑπὲρ τῶν γεγενημένων · τῷ δὲ διπλασιασμῷ συνηθῶς τὴν ἐπίτασιν
τῆς εὐχαριστίας δείκνυσιν.

2ᵇ. Καὶ ἐπικαλεσόμεθα τὸ ὄνομά σου. Καὶ ἀπὸ τοῦ σοῦ ὀνόματος καλέ-
σομεν ἑαυτούς, ἀντὶ τοῦ Δεσπότην σε ὁμολογήσομεν, εὐεργέτην, προστάτην, εἰκότως ἀφ' ὧν ἀπηλαύσαμεν τὸ ὠφέλιμον παιδευόμενοι. Ἴδιον γὰρ τῶν   10
ἀνθρώπων τὸ ἀπ' ἐκείνων καλεῖσθαι τῶν δεσποζόντων ἢ εὐεργετούντων,
οἷον ὅταν λέγωμεν Ὁ τοῦδε εἴτε δοῦλος, εἴτε οἰκεῖος, εἴθ' ὁτιδήποτε
τοιοῦτον.

3. Διηγήσομαι πάντα τὰ θαυμάσιά σου, ὅταν λάβω καιρόν, ἐγὼ εὐθύτητας κρινῶ. Ἐνταῦθα ἑνικῶς εἶπεν οὐ Διηγησόμεθα πάντα τὰ θαυμάσιά   15
σου, ἀλλὰ Διηγήσομαι. οὐκ ἄλλο τι βουλόμενος εἰπεῖν, ἀλλ' ὡς ἑκάστου
τοῦτο λέγοντος ὅπερ ἐν τῇ κοινῇ πάντων γίγνεται φωνῇ. Λαβόμενος οὖν
νῦν σχολῆς καὶ εὐκαιρίας, καὶ ἀπαλλαγεὶς τῆς ἐφόδου τῶν πολεμούντων·
ἔργον θήσομαι τὸ μέγεθος τῶν γενομένων διηγεῖσθαι. Τοῦτο δὲ αὐτὸ τὴν

Τὴν κατὰ — ἀναφθεγγόμενος: P, fol. 260; V, fol. 27ᵛ; Cord, p. 550.
2ᵃ. Εὐχαριστήσομεν — δείκνυσιν: P, fol. 260ᵛ; V, fol. 27ᵛ; Cord, p. 550.   5 εὐ-
χαριστοῦμεν Cord   6-7 L (p. 548, ll. 11-8 ab imo): τῷ διπλασιασμῷ τῆς ἐξομολογήσεως τὴν ἐπίτασιν παρίστησι τῆς εὐχαριστίας.
2ᵇ. Καὶ ἀπὸ — τοιοῦτον: P, fol. 260ᵛ; V, fol. 28; Cord, p. 551 (= P. G., 693 C).
8 ὀνόματός φησι Cord   9 ἑαυτοῖς PV.
3. Ἐνταῦθα — ἐπισημασίας: P, fol. 261; V, fol. 28; Cord, p. 551-552 (= P. G.,
693 C-696 A).   17 τοῦτο] τοῦ Cord   18 νῦν om. Cord.

Aᵉ *Argumentum ps. LXXIV* (p. 379, 29-380, 5): Canticum post uictoriam,
quae de Asiris sub Ezechia rege facta est, in hoc psalmo praedicit, et quasi ex
totius populi persona canit officia uotaque gratiarum. Cf. Pseudo-Beda (881).
6-7 (p. 380, 10-12)... repetitione autem uerbi ex more suo facta, deuotum se fore
iugiter pollicetur.   8-10 (p. 380, 13-19): Certatim dicemus nos tuos esse ac tuo
uocari nomine gestemus, id est te habere nos Dominum gloriabimur, te defensorem atque beneficum continua nostra lingua resonabit, nec inmerito.
17-19 (p. 380, 22-28): Vacatione (vocatione *ms*), inquit, mihi et temporis oportunitate conlata, id est cum ab incursu hostium liber fuero, huic operi manci-
pabo ut factorum tuorum magnitudinem adsiduo sermone concelebrem.

PSALM 75

In this psalm he prophesies the victory worked against the Assyrians in the time of Hezekiah, speaking from the general viewpoint of everyone in offering thanksgiving for what was achieved. *We shall confess to you, O Lord; we shall confess to you* (v. 1): we shall give thanks to you for what was achieved (as usual, by the repetition bringing out the intensity of the thanksgiving). *And we shall call upon your name:* we shall call ourselves by your name—that is, We shall confess you to be Lord, benefactor, protector—and rightly so, since we learned the benefits we received. It is, of course, typical of people to call themselves after those whose control or beneficence they experience, such as when we speak of so-and-so's slave, or domestic, or the like.

I shall narrate all your wonders when I take the opportunity; I shall deliver upright judgments (v. 2). At this point he used the singular—not "We shall narrate," but *I shall narrate all your wonders,* his meaning being simply that it is as if each one states what is the general sentiment of everyone. So he is saying, Taking the time and opportunity, and freed from the assault of the attackers, I go to the trouble of describing the magnitude of the events. He uses the same statement | to express thanksgiving, thanks to God being

εὐχαριστίαν λέγει· εὐχαριστία γὰρ εἰς Θεὸν τὸ ὁμολογεῖν εὐεργετεῖσθαι διηγούμενον τὰς χάριτας, οἷον καὶ ἐν τῷ θ′ ψαλμῷ τὸ Ἐξομολογήσομαί σοι, Κύριε, ἐν ὅλῃ καρδίᾳ μου, διηγήσομαι πάντα τὰ θαυμάσιά σου. Ποῖα οὖν θαυμάσια διηγῇ; — ἐγὼ εὐθύτητας κρινῶ, — ταῦτα, ὅτι ἐπηγγείλω κρίνειν
5 εὐθύτητας, ὡς τοῦ Θεοῦ τοῦτο εἰπόντος καὶ ἐπαγγειλαμένου. Δέδεικται γὰρ πολλαχοῦ ἀντὶ τοῦ ἔργου τὸν λόγον καὶ τὴν ἐπαγγελίαν λαμβάνων. Οὐ δεῖ δὲ θαυμάζειν ὅτι μὴ εἶπεν Διηγήσομαι τὰ θαυμάσιά σου ὅταν λάβω και- ρὸν ὅτι εἶπας Ἐγὼ εὐθύτητας· κρινῶ. Ἴδιον γὰρ αὐτοῦ τὸ ἐκ τῆς ἀκολου- θίας λέγειν τὰ ἔκ τινων ῥηθέντα, καὶ μὴ προστιθέναι τὸ εἰπὼν ἢ λέγων
10 ἤ τι τοιοῦτον. Καὶ πολλαχοῦ τοῦτο ἄν τις εὕροι ζητήσας τῶν ψαλμῶν, οἷον τὸ ἐν τῷ ριθ′ Πρὸς Κύριον ἐν τῷ θλίβεσθαί με ἐκέκραξα, καὶ εἰσήκουσέν μου. Καὶ οὐ προστεθεικὼς τὸ εἰπὼν ἐπήγαγεν Κύριε, ῥῦσαι τὴν ψυχήν μου ἀπὸ χειλέων ἀδίκων· ἀκόλουθον γὰρ ἦν εἰπεῖν ὅτι Πρὸς Κύριον ἐν τῷ θλίβεσθαί με ἐκέκραξα εἰπὼν Κύριε ῥῦσαι τὴν ψυχήν μου, ἀλλ᾽ οὐκ εἶπεν, κατὰ ἀπο-
15 σιώπησιν σημάνας ἐκ τῆς ἀκολουθίας τὸ εἰπών. Καὶ σαφέστερον ἐν τῷ β′ ψαλμῷ· παρέστησαν γάρ φησιν οἱ βασιλεῖς τῆς γῆς καὶ οἱ ἄρχοντες συνήχθησαν ἐπὶ τὸ αὐτὸ κατὰ τοῦ Κυρίου καὶ κατὰ τοῦ Χριστοῦ αὐτοῦ, Διαρ- ρήξωμεν τοὺς δεσμοὺς αὐτῶν. Νῦν δὲ παραλιπὼν τὸ λέγοντες, ἐχρήσατο τῇ οἰκείᾳ δι᾽ ὅλων ἀκολουθίᾳ· καὶ ὅλως πολλαχοῦ τοῦτό ἐστιν εὑρεῖν.
20 Ἀρκεῖ γὰρ ταῦτα παραθεμένους εἰς μαρτυρίαν τοῦ παρ᾽ ἡμῶν λεγομένου ἐν αὐτῇ τῇ καθεξῆς ἑρμηνείᾳ δεῖξαι πολλαχοῦ φερόμενον τὸ ἰδίωμα, τῶν ἀναγινωσκόντων μέντοι εἴη ἂν μνημονεύειν ἁπανταχοῦ τῆς ἐπισημασίας.

4ᵃ. Ἐτάκη ἡ γῆ καὶ πάντες οἱ κατοικοῦντες ἐν αὐτῇ. Μόνον τε γὰρ τοῦτο ἐπηγγείλω, καὶ ἤρκεσεν ἡ ἀπειλὴ καταπλῆξαι τὴν γῆν καὶ τοὺς ἐν
25 αὐτῇ. Καλῶς δὲ τὸ ἐτάκη· ἴδιον γὰρ τῶν τιμωρίαν προσδοκώντων τὸ τήκεσ- θαι ὑπὸ τῆς ἀθυμίας.

4ᵇ. Ἐγὼ ἐστερέωσα τοὺς στύλους αὐτῆς. Τὸ ἐγὼ ἐστερέωσα τῷ ἐγὼ εὐθύτητας κρινῶ ἐπισυνῆπται. Ταῦτά φησιν εἶπας καὶ ἐπηγγείλω, Ἐγὼ κρινῶ καὶ τοῦ ὀρθοῦ δικαστὴς ἔσομαι· ἐγὼ γάρ εἰμι ὁ καὶ τὴν σύμπασαν

2-3 Ps. IX, 2   6 cf. p. 280, 23-24; 388, 15 (ἀπαγγελία).   7 cf. p. 281, 21-23
9 ss. cf. 280, 32-281, 3   11-13 ps. CXIX, 1-2   16-18 ps. II, 2-3.

2 ψαλμῷ om. PV   σοι om. PV   3 σου om. PV   4 διηγῇ] διηγεῖται Cord
8 ὅτι — κρινῶ om. Cord   10 τοῦτο om. Cord   11 τὸ om. Cord   12-14 ἀπὸ χειλέων — οὐκ εἶπεν om. Cord.
4ᵃ. Μόνον — ἀθυμίας: P, fol. 261ᵛ; V, fol. 28ᵛ; Cord, p. 553.
4ᵇ. Τὸ Ἐγὼ — τιμωρίαν: P, fol. 261ᵛ; V, fol. 28ᵛ.

Aᵉ 23-25 (p. 381, 3-5): Denuntiatio sola adseruandae iustitiae consternatio- nem terrae sufficit, quam proprie dixit sub exspectatione poenalis edicti lique- scere.   27-502, 2 (p. 381, 8-10): Haec quoque ex persona Dei. Ego, qui con- ditor operum meorum sum, arbiter eorumdem ero aequissimus.

given by the one describing the graces confessing their conferral, as in Psalm 9, "I shall confess to you, Lord, with all my heart, I shall recount all your wonders."[1] So what wonders are you recounting? *I shall deliver upright judgments:* the promise to deliver upright judgments (as though God is saying and promising this). It has been shown in many places, remember, that he uses word and promise in the place of deed.

Now, there is no need for surprise that he did not say *I shall narrate your wonders when I take the opportunity* because you said *I shall deliver upright judgments,* for it is typical of him to include things said by people in the flow of the thought and not to insert the word "stating" or "saying" or the like. You would often find this in the psalms if you looked for it, as in Psalm 120, "I cried to the Lord in my tribulation, and he hearkened to me," where he did not insert the word "saying" in proceeding, "Lord, rescue my soul from unjust lips";[2] it would have been logical for him to say, "I cried to the Lord in my tribulation, saying, 'Lord, rescue my soul,'" but he did not say it, by the silent omission implying the word "saying" from the flow of thought. This is seen more clearly in Psalm 2, "The kings of the earth took their stand, and the rulers came together in concert against the Lord and against his Christ. 'Let us break their bonds,'"[3] where in this case he omitted "saying," relying on the general flow of thought. And you can find this generally in many places; it is enough for us to cite these examples in confirmation of what we have said and to bring out in the rest of the commentary the idiom at work in many places, the readers noting the observations wherever they occur.

The earth was wasted, and all its inhabitants in it (v. 3): I merely made this promise, and the threat was sufficient to strike the earth and everyone in it. *It was wasted* was well put: it is typical of those expecting punishment to waste away with apprehension. *I strengthened its pillars.* The words *I strengthened* are connected to *I shall deliver upright judgments:* You made this statement and promise, he is saying, *I shall deliver judgments* and shall be a judge of uprightness, for I am the one who created and established the whole earth, | and so I am a trustworthy judge who is about to deliver a ver-

---

1. Ps 9:1. Theodore's difficulty with the interchange of viewpoints here is compounded by the poor rendition by the LXX.
2. Ps 120:1–2.
3. Ps 2:2–3.

γῆν ἐργασάμενός τε καὶ ἑδράσας, ὥστε ἀξιόπιστός εἰμι κριτὴς τοῖς οἰκείοις
μέλλων δικάζειν ἔργοις. Τὸ δὲ ἐτάκη ἡ γῆ διὰ μέσου παρέγκειται, διὰ τὸ
μέτρον τοῦ προφήτου παρεντεθεικότος· εἴρηται δὲ καὶ πρὸς κατάπληξιν,
ὡς μόνῃ τῇ ἀπειλῇ τοῦ Θεοῦ καταπλῆξαι ποιήσαντος. Ὅλον μέντοι ἐπισυνῆπται τῷ Διηγήσομαι τὰ θαυμάσιά σου, — ἀντὶ τοῦ Ταῦτα διηγήσομαι,   5
ὅπως ἐπηγγείλω κρίνειν ὡς ἰδίους, καὶ ἤρκεσεν ἡ ἀπειλὴ μόνη πρὸς τιμωρίαν.

5ᵃ. Εἶπα τοῖς παρανομοῦσι Μὴ παρανομεῖτε. Ταῦτα δέ φησιν εἰδὼς ἐγὼ
καὶ πρὸ τοῦ γενέσθαι, συνεβούλευον ἀποστῆναι τῆς κακίας.

5ᵇ. Καὶ τοῖς ἁμαρτάνουσι Μὴ ὑψοῦτε κέρας. Συνεβούλευον δὲ αὐτοῖς καὶ
μὴ μεγάλα φρονεῖν ἐπὶ τῇ οἰκείᾳ ἰσχύϊ· τὸ γὰρ κέρας ἐπὶ τῆς δυνάμεως   10
καὶ τῆς ἰσχύος λαμβάνει, ἐκ μεταφορᾶς τῶν τοῖς κέρασιν κεχρημένων ζῴων
εἰς ἄμυναν.

6. Μὴ ἐπαίρετε εἰς ὕψος τὸ κέρας ὑμῶν, καὶ μὴ λαλεῖτε κατὰ τοῦ Θεοῦ
ἀδικίαν. Μὴ μεγάλα φρονοῦντες ἐπὶ τῇ προσούσῃ ὑμῖν δυνάμει, τοσοῦτον
αὐτὴν μεγάλην νομίσητε ὡς ἀδεὲς οἴεσθαι καὶ τὸ κατὰ τοῦ Θεοῦ τι εἰπεῖν.   15
Καιρίως δὲ τοῦτο μάλιστα πρὸς Ἀσσυρίους πολλὰ τοὺς Ἰσραηλίτας ὀνει-
δίσαντας, ὡς μάτην περὶ τὴν τοῦ Θεοῦ θεραπείαν ἔχοντας.

7-8ᵃ. Ὅτι οὔτε ἐξ ἐξόδων, οὔτε ἀπὸ δυσμῶν, οὔτε ἀπὸ ἐρήμων ὀρέων,
ὅτι ὁ Θεὸς κριτής ἐστιν. Ἔξοδον πολλαχοῦ καλεῖ τὴν τοῦ ἡλίου ἀνατολήν, ὡς τὸ Ἐξόδους πρωΐας καὶ ἑσπέρας τέρψεις. Ἐπειδὴ καὶ ἔξοδον τοῦ   20
ἡλίου καλεῖ αὐτὴν τὴν ἀνατολήν, ὡς τὸ Ἀπ᾿ ἄκρου τοῦ οὐρανοῦ ἡ ἔξοδος
αὐτοῦ, ἔξοδον οὖν λέγει τῶν ἀνατολῶν, ἐρήμων δὲ ὀρέων ἄρκτου καὶ μεσημ-

5ᵃ. Ταῦτα — κακίας: P, fol. 262; V, fol. 28ᵛ; Cord: p. 554.
5ᵇ. Συνεβούλευον — ἄμυναν: P, fol. 262; V, fol. 29; Cord, p. 554.   10 οἰκείᾳ]
ἰδίᾳ Cord.
6. Μὴ μεγάλα — ἔχοντας: P, fol. 262; V, fol. 29.   15 νομίσετε PV.
7-8ᵃ. Ἔξοδον — παρόντα: P, fol. 262ᵛ; V, fol. 29ʳˑᵛ; Vat. 1422, fol. 136 (anon.);
Cord, p. 555 (= P. G., 696 B).   19 πολλαχοῦ om. 1422   20 ἐξόδους] ἐξόδου PV
20-22 τέρψεις — ἀνατολῶν om. 1422, qui sequentia hac ratione praebet: ἔρημον δὲ
ὄρη, ἄρκτον καὶ μεσημβρίαν, ἐπειδὴ τὰ μὲν ἀρκτῷα εἰσιν ἀοίκητα καὶ ἔρημα δι᾿ ὑπερβολὴν
κρύους, τὰ δὲ μεσημβρινὰ δι᾿ ὑπερβολὴν καύματος. Βούλεται δὲ εἰπεῖν ὅτι οὐδαμόθεν ἐστὶ
διαφυγεῖν τὸν Θεόν, οὐδ᾿ ἂν διὰ τῶν δ᾿ κλιμάτων ἐπέλθῃς κοινὸν ὄντα δικαστὴν καὶ πανταχοῦ παρόντα.

Aᵉ 5ᵃ (p. 381, 16-17): Postquam talem Deum dedici, iniquos monere non
destiti.   10-12 (p. 381, 18-20): Potentiam praecellentem a similitudine eorum
animalium, quae cornibus armantur in praelia.

dict by my characteristic works. Now, the phrase *The earth was wasted* is inserted in the middle, the prophet making the insertion with a view to the meter; it was said for the sake of making an impression, God causing the impression by his threat alone. It is all connected with the clause *I shall narrate your wonders*—that is, I shall narrate how you promised to judge them as your own, and your mere threat sufficed for punishment.

I said to the transgressors, Do not transgress (v. 4): aware of this even before it happened, I gave the recommendation to abstain from evildoing. *And to the sinners, Do not raise your horn:* I recommended to them also not to glory in their own strength (taking the word *horn* in the sense of power and might, by analogy with animals using their horns for defense). *Do not lift up your horn on high, and do not speak iniquity against God* (v. 5): do not boast of the power you have, and do not suppose it so great that you have no qualms about saying anything against God. This was appropriately directed against Assyrians for taunting the Israelites that their worship of God was in vain.

Because it is not from the departures or from the west or from desert mountains, because the Lord is judge (vv. 6–7). By "departure" he refers in many places to the rising of the sun, as in the verse "You bring gladness to departures by morning and evening." Since he also refers to the sun's rising itself as "departure," as in "His departure is from heaven's zenith,"[4] so by *departures* he refers to the east, and by *desert mountains* to the north and the south. | You see, since one of these latter two regions is uninhabited and des-

---

4. Pss 65:8; 19:6, ἔξοδος being the term in question.

βρίας. Ἐπειδὴ γὰρ τῶν δύο τούτων κλιμάτων τὰ μέν ἐστιν ἀοίκητα καὶ ἔρημα δι᾽ ὑπερβολὴν κρύους, — λέγω δὲ τὰ ἀρκτῷα, — τὰ δὲ δι᾽ ὑπερβολὴν θάλπους, — ὡς τὰ μεσημβρινά, — ἐμήμων ὀρέων ἐκάλεσεν ταῦτα τὰ δύο κλίματα. Βούλεται δὲ εἰπεῖν ὅτι οὐδαμόθεν ἐστὶν διαφυγεῖν τὸν Θεόν· ὅπου
5 ποτὲ γὰρ ἂν ἀπέλθῃς τῶν τεσσάρων κλιμάτων τῆς οἰκουμένης διαφυγεῖν οὐχ οἷόν τε τὸν Θεὸν κοινὸν ὄντα δικαστὴν καὶ πανταχοῦ παρόντα.

8ᵇ. Τοῦτον ταπεινοῖ καὶ τοῦτον ὑψοῖ. Ποιεῖ τοίνυν ὅσα βούλεται, τὸν μὲν κατασπῶν καὶ εἰς πολλὴν ἕλκων ταπείνωσιν, τὸν δὲ ἀνεγείρων παρ᾽ ἐλπίδα. Ἐκ τοῦδε τοῦ πράγματος αὐτὸ λαβὼν εἶπεν· παρ᾽ ἐλπίδας γὰρ
10 καὶ Ἀσσυρίους ἐταπείνωσεν καὶ Ἰσραηλίτας ἀνήγειρεν.

9ᵃ. Ὅτι ποτήριον ἐν χειρὶ Κυρίου, οἴνου ἀκράτου πλῆρες κεράσματος. Τὸν οἶνον ἐπὶ τῆς τιμωρίας λαμβάνει, ἀπὸ τοῦ περιάγεσθαι καὶ καταπίπτειν τῇ τοῦ Θεοῦ πληγῇ τοὺς τιμωρουμένους δίκην μεθυόντων· ἔχει γάρ φησιν ἐν τῇ ἑαυτοῦ χειρὶ ποτήριον πεπληρωμένον ἀκράτου οἴνου, — ἵνα εἴπῃ
15 φοβερωτέρας τιμωρίας, ἀπὸ τοῦ τὸν ἄκρατον οἶνον μειζόνως καθάπτεσθαι. Τὸ δὲ κεράσματο:, οὐ «κεκραμένου» λέγει (πῶς γὰρ οἷόν τε εἰπόντα ἀκράτου πάλιν εἰπεῖν «κεκραμένου»;) ἀλλ᾽ ἐπειδὴ κρᾶσιν πολλάκις καλοῦμεν τὸ μέτρον, ὃ πρὸς πόσιν ἀρκεῖ, τοῦτο ἠβουλήθη εἰπεῖν ὅτι τοιαύτην κρᾶσιν οὕτω μεγίστην ὥστε πληρῶσαι τὸ ποτήριον. Βού-
20 λεται δὲ εἰπεῖν ἐξ ἀμφοτέρων τῆς τιμωρίας τὴν ἐπίτασιν, καὶ ἐκ τοῦ ἄκρατον εἶναι τὸν οἶνον, καὶ ἐκ τοῦ πεπληρῶσθαι τὸ ποτήριον, τῷ μὲν ἀκράτῳ τὸ αὐστηρὸν καὶ εὔτονον δεικνύς, τῷ δὲ πλήρει τὸ διαρκὲς καὶ πάντων ἀπτόμενον.

---

1 τούτου Cord   ἄοικα Cord   3 ὀρέων] ὡραίων PV   5 τῆς οἰκουμένης] τοῦ οὐρανοῦ Cord.

8ᵇ. Ποιεῖ — ἀνήγειρεν: P, fol. 262ᵛ; V, fol. 29ᵛ; Cord, p. 556.

9ᵃ. Τὸν οἶνον — ἀπτόμενον: P, fol. 263; V, fol. 29ᵛ; Cord, p. 556 (= P. G., 696 CD).   21 πεπληρῶσαι Cord.

Aᶜ 2-6 (p. 382, 7-9; 381, 23-382, 6): Qui aut nimio frigore aut multo igne deserti sunt; significat autem septimtrionales aut australes plagas. Quatuor principalium climatum istius mundi enumerat, ut sit sensus: neque qui primi... neque illi... Dei praesentiam effugere possunt aut potentiam.   9ᵃ (p. 382, 15-383, 6): Vinum saepe a profetis pro seueritate et graui ponitur ultione, quando iuxta ebrietatem ut erumnis plagisque sensus hominum perturbati incertique sunt; augenter pro ultione districta neque infracta leuitatis admixtu, quae citius perturbat bibentem. Etiam mixtionem dicit pro mensura, quae ex more bibentibus datur, uel potionis plenitudine tam grandi ut poculum possit inplere. Per merum ergo poene seueritatem, per mixtionem plenae mensurae modum uoluit indicare.

olate on account excessive cold (I mean the far north), and one on account of excessive heat (I mean the south), he referred to these two regions as *desert mountains.* His meaning is, It is nowhere possible to escape God: wherever you go in the four regions of the world, you cannot escape God, who is judge of all and present everywhere. *He humbles one and elevates another:* he therefore does what he wishes, pulling one person down and dragging him to the depths while uplifting another against all hope. He took this from the same event: against hope he humbled Assyrians and raised up Israelites.

Because in the Lord's hand there is a cup full of pure wine of mixing (v. 8). He understands *wine* as punishment, from the staggering and falling in the manner of drunkards in the case of those punished by the intervention of God, who has in his hand, he is saying, a cup filled with *pure wine*—that is, with fearsome punishment, on the basis of the greater effect of pure wine. Now, he speaks of *mixing,* not "mixed": how could he speak of *pure wine* and then say that it was mixed? Rather, since we often refer to measuring what is sufficient for drinkers as mixing, he means that the mixing was so generous as to fill the cup. On both scores he refers to the severity of the punishment, both from the wine being pure and from the cup being filled, bringing out the harshness and intensity from the purity, and the continuity and universal effect from the fullness. | *And he moved from one to the other:* and it contains

9ᵇ. Καὶ ἔκλινεν ἐκ τούτου εἰς τοῦτο. *Καὶ ἐν αὐτῷ φησίν ἐστιν ὃν βούλεται ποτίζειν, ἵνα εἴπῃ ὃν θέλει τιμωρεῖσθαι. Ἡμῶν γὰρ προσδοκώντων κινδυνεύειν, ἔδοξεν αὐτῷ μετακλῖναι τοῦ ποτηρίου τὴν πόσιν ἐφ᾽ ὑμᾶς, καὶ ἰδοὺ ἡμεῖς μὲν ἐκτὸς κατέστημεν τῶν κινδύνων, ὑμεῖς δὲ τὴν τιμωρίαν ἐδέξασθε.* 5

9ᶜ. Πλὴν ὁ τρυγίας αὐτοῦ οὐκ ἐξεκενώθη. *Καὶ οὐκ ἐκένωσεν τὴν τιμωρίαν οὕτως, ὡς μὴ δύνασθαι πάλιν ἑτέρους κολάζειν, ἀλλ᾽ ἔχει παρ᾽ ἑαυτῷ ἔτι.*

9ᵈ. Πίονται πάντες οἱ ἁμαρτωλοὶ τῆς γῆς. *Ἔστι γὰρ λείψανον παρ᾽ αὐτῷ, ᾧ τοὺς λοιποὺς τιμωρήσεται. Βούλεται δὲ εἰπεῖν ὅτι κἂν ἄλλοι τοιαῦτα ἡμᾶς διαθεῖναι βουληθῶσιν, τοιαῦτα πείσονται.* 10

10. Ἐγὼ δὲ ἀγαλλιάσομαι εἰς τὸν αἰῶνα, ψαλῶ τῷ Θεῷ Ἰακώβ. *Ἐγὼ μέντοι διηνεκῶς ἐπὶ τοῖς δοθεῖσιν εὐφρανθήσομαι, καὶ ὑμνήσω τὸν ταῦτα παρέχοντα δεσπότην.*

11ᵃ. Καὶ πάντα τὰ κέρατα τῶν ἁμαρτωλῶν συνθλάσω. *Τῇ γὰρ αὐτοῦ δυνάμει πάντας τοὺς ἐπανισταμένους μοι ἐχθροὺς τιμωρήσομαι.* 15

11ᵇ. Καὶ ὑψωθήσεται τὸ κέρας τοῦ δικαίου. *Φανοῦμαι δὲ μέγας ἐγὼ καὶ πάντων μείζων ὁ τῆς σῆς γνώσεως ἐχόμενος λαός· δίκαιον γὰρ κατὰ τοῦτο λέγει.*

9ᵇ. *Καὶ ἐν αὐτῷ — ἐδέξασθε*: P, fol. 263; V, fol. 30.   1-2 *καὶ ἐν — τιμωρεῖσθαι affert Paraphrasis* (p. 546).

9ᶜ. *Καὶ οὐκ ἐκένωσεν — ἔτι*: P, fol. 263; V, fol. 30.

9ᵈ. *Ἔστι — πείσονται*: P, fol. 263ᵛ; V, fol. 30; Vat. 1422, fol. 136 (anon.). 8 *παρ᾽ om.* 1422.

10. *Ἐγὼ — δεσπότην*: P, fol. 263ᵛ; V, fol. 30ᵛ; *Paraphrasis* (p. 546).

11ᵃ. *Τῇ γὰρ — τιμωρήσομαι*: P, fol. 263ᵛ; V, fol. 30ᵛ; *Paraphrasis* (p. 546).

11ᵇ. *Φανοῦμαι — λέγει*: P, fol. 263ᵛ; V, fol. 30ᵛ.

Aᵉ 9ᵇ (p. 383, 7-10): Quoscumque mereri conspexirit, calicis eius ingestione potabit; nam a nobis auersum (aduersum *1ᵃ m.*) inclinauit in Assyrios, qui nos obsederant.   9ᶜ⁻ᵈ (p. 383, 11-17): Non sunt in Assiriorum excidio uires ulciscentis (ulcisciscentis *ms*) absumptae, superest adhuc in eius potentia unde puniantur quos propria merita subiecerint ultioni. Similia ergo patientur Assiriis, qui nos pari aussu obpugnari temptauerunt.   10 (p. 383, 19-23): Ego autem in saecula gaudebo, cessis hostibus meis; repletus gaudio augtorem tantorum operum Deum continuo laude praedicabo.   11ᵇ (p. 384, 2-6): Rerum gestarum testimonio, ut potentem me ac superiorem omnes aspiciant; iustum se ob Dei appellat scientiam.

what he wants to give them to drink—that is, what he wishes for their punishment. Though we were expecting to be in trouble, he is saying, he decided to transfer the drinking of the cup to you, and, lo, we were brought out of trouble while you underwent punishment. *But its dregs will not be emptied:* he did not exhaust the punishment to the extent of not being able to punish others at another time; he still has some left. *All the sinners of the earth will drink:* he still has something left for punishing the others, meaning, Even if others insist on this attitude toward us, they will meet a similar fate.

As for me, on the contrary, I shall rejoice forever; I shall sing to the God of Jacob (v. 9): I shall constantly rejoice in what is given, and sing the praises of the Lord, who provides it. *I shall break all the horns of sinners* (v. 10): with his power I shall punish all the enemies rising up against me. *And the horn of the righteous will be exalted:* I shall emerge as a person of might, and the people with knowledge of you will become greater than all (this being the meaning he gives to *righteous*). |

PSALMVS LXXV

Ἐπὶ τῇ αὐτῇ ὑποθέσει καὶ οὗτος εἴρηται ὁ ψαλμός.

2ᵃ. Γνωστὸς ἐν τῇ Ἰουδαίᾳ ὁ Θεός. Γνωρίζεται παρ' ἡμῖν ἀεὶ διὰ τῶν εἰς ἡμᾶς εὐεργεσιῶν.

5　**2ᵇ.** Ἐν τῷ Ἰσραὴλ μέγα τὸ ὄνομα αὐτοῦ. Πάντες γοῦν αὐτὸν ὡς μέγαν θαυμάζουσιν, ἐκ τῶν περὶ ἡμᾶς τὴν ἀπόδειξιν λαμβάνοντες.

3ᵃ. Καὶ ἐγενήθη ἐν εἰρήνῃ ὁ τόπος αὐτοῦ. Ὁ οὖν αὐτῷ προσήκων τόπος καὶ ἀφωρισμένος, ἵνα εἴπῃ τὰ Ἱεροσόλυμα, τηλικαύτης ἐφόδου πολεμίων παρὰ πᾶσαν ἀπαλλαγεὶς προσδοκίαν, εἰρήνης ἀπολαύει βαθείας. Ποῖος δὲ
10　αὐτοῦ τόπος, φανερώτερον ἐπάγει.

3ᵇ. Καὶ τὸ κατοικητήριον αὐτοῦ ἐν Σιών. Τουτέστιν ὁ ναὸς ὁ τοῦ Σιών, ἐν ᾧ κατοικεῖ.

4. Ἐκεῖ συνέτριψε τὰ κράτη τῶν τόξων, ὅπλον καὶ ῥομφαίαν καὶ πόλεμον. Πάντας γὰρ ἐκεῖ τοὺς τὴν πόλιν κυκλώσαντας κατηνάλωσεν, τὰ τόξα
15　συντρίψας, τοὺς θυρεούς, τὰ ξίφη, καὶ οὕτω διαλύσας τὸν πόλεμον.

Ἐπὶ τῇ αὐτῇ — ψαλμός: P, fol. 264; V, fol. 30.
2ᵃ. Γνωρίζεται — εὐεργεσιῶν: P, fol. 264ᵛ; V, fol. 31; Vat. 1422, fol. 136ᵛ (anon.).
2ᵇ. Πάντες — λαμβάνοντες: P, fol. 264ᵛ; V, fol. 231; Vat. 1422, fol. 136ᵛ (anon.); Paraphrasis (p. 561).
3ᵃ. Ὁ οὖν — ἐπάγει: P, fol. 265; V, fol. 31ᵛ; Paraphrasis (p. 561).　7 ὁ οὖν] οὗτος γὰρ Par　8 καὶ ἀφωρισμένος om. Par.
3ᵇ. Τουτέστιν — κατοικεῖ: P, fol. 265; V, fol. 31ᵛ; Paraphrasis (p. 561).　11 τοῦ] τῆς Par.
4. Πάντας — πόλεμον: P, fol. 265 et V, fol. 21ᵛ sub nomine THEODORETI; Paraphrasis (p. 561).

Argumentum ps. LXXV (p. 384, 9-11): Idem argumentum esse praesentis psalmi et superioris... **3ᵃ⁻ᵇ** (p. 384, 22-27) Locus Dei habitatioque eius, id est Sion templumque in ea, quod solum incolere credebatur, pacatum est ac securum, deletis Assiriis.

PSALM 76

This psalm is also recited on the same theme. *God is known in Judah* (v. 1): he is always known by us through his favors to us. *Great is his name in Israel:* everyone admires him for his greatness, finding proof in his treatment of us. *His place has been established in peace* (v. 2): the place that is proper to him and set aside for him—namely, Jerusalem[1]—freed from such an assault of the enemy against all expectation, enjoys deep peace. Now, what kind of place is his he goes on to explain more clearly. *And his dwelling in Sion*—that is, the temple on Sion, in which he dwells. *There he broke the force of the bows, shield and sword and war* (v. 3): there he consumed all who encircled the city, breaking bows, shields, and swords, and thus bringing the war to an end. |

---

1. The LXX has read *shalom,* "peace," where our Hebrew reads *Salem*—Jerusalem, to be sure, but not a conclusion to be reached via a solecism, as does Theodore.

5. Φωτίζεις σὺ θαυμαστῶς ἀπὸ ὀρέων αἰωνίων. Ὥσπερ σκότος καλεῖ τὰς θλίψεις, οὕτω φωτισμὸν καλεῖ τοῦ Θεοῦ τὴν ἀντίληψιν, ὡς λύουσαν τὰς θλίψεις· καὶ τοῦτο ἡμῖν ἐπισεσήμανται πολλαχοῦ. Ἀπὸ γὰρ ἐκείνων σού φησι τῶν ὀρέων — ἵνα εἴπῃ τοῦ Σιὼν — ἀεὶ ἐπιφαινόμενος μετὰ πολλοῦ τοῦ θαύματος, πάντα λύεις τὰ λυπηρά, καὶ πάντα φωτὸς πληροῖς καὶ 5 εὐφροσύνης. Αἰώνιον δὲ εἶπεν τὸ ὄρος ὡς διαμένον ἰσχυρόν, καὶ οὐδέποτε ὑπὸ πολέμοις γενόμενον μέχρις ἂν μὴ τῷ Θεῷ δοκῇ.

6ᵃ. Ἐταράχθησαν πάντες οἱ ἀσύνετοι τῇ καρδίᾳ. Οἱ γὰρ εὐηθέστατοι ἐκεῖνοι καὶ οἰηθέντες τὸν σὸν τόπον κρατήσειν ἀπροσδόκητον ὑπέστησαν ταραχήν, ὡς μήτε συνορᾶν τίς ἂν αὐτοῖς γένοιτο φυγὴ τῶν κατεχόντων 10 κακῶν.

6ᵇ. Ὕπνωσαν ὕπνον αὐτῶν καὶ οὐχ εὗρον οὐδέν. Ἐπειδὴ ἐκαθεύδησαν παρὰ τῷ τείχει, ὡς πρωῒ τὴν πόλιν κατασκάψοντες, εἶτα διὰ τῆς νυκτὸς αἰφνίδιον ἅπαντες ἀπώλοντο. Ἐκαθεύδησάν φησι καὶ ηὑρέθη οὐδέν, τουτέστιν εἰς τὸ μηδὲν περιέστησαν πάντες αἰφνίδιον ἀποθανόντες. 15

6ᶜ. Πάντες οἱ ἄνδρες τοῦ πλούτου ταῖς χερσὶν αὐτῶν. Ἅπαντες γὰρ οὗτοι οἱ δυνατοὶ καὶ εὔποροι ἀεὶ ταῖς ἰδίαις πεποίθασι χερσίν, ἵνα εἴπῃ τῇ οἰκείᾳ δυνάμει.

---

5. Ὥσπερ — δοκῇ: P, fol. 265ᵛ; V, fol. 31ᵛ; Vat. 1422, fol. 136ᵛ; Cord, p. 569. 2 λύουσαν] λύσαν 1422   3 θλίψεις des. 1422   4 τοῦ] τῆς Cord   4-5 μετὰ πολλοῦ τοῦ θαύματος om. Cord.

6ᵃ. Οἱ γὰρ — κακῶν: P, fol. 265ᵛ; V, fol. 32; Vat. 1422, fol. 137; Paraphrasis (p. 561).   9 κρατῆσαι 1422.

6ᵇ. Ἐπειδὴ — ἀποθανόντες: P, fol. 266; V, fol. 32; Vat. 1422, fol. 137 (anon.); Paraphrasis (p. 561).   14 εὑρέθησαν 1422.

6ᶜ. Ἅπαντες — δυνάμει: P, fol. 266; V, fol. 32.

Aᵉ 5 (p. 384, 34-385, 4): More suo, ut tribulationum pondus tenebras, ita laetitiam diuina protexione conlatam lumen appellat; aeternos autem montes appellat, quod pro sempeterna uirtute in se Dei habitantis numquam essent in ius hostium transituri.   6ᵃ (p. 385, 8-10): Vt nullum Assirii inuenirent effugium, quia in Deum contumiliosi uictoriam praesumebant.   6ᵇ (p. 385, 12-16): Cum se in somno dedisent, altero uelut die capturi urbem, poenali aeternoque sopore depresi sunt, ut uix aliquis superfuisset.   6ᶜ (p. 385, 20-22): Qui sucesum uictoriae in suis manibus, id est in uirtute propria, collocabant.

You shed light marvelously from everlasting mountains (v. 4). Just as by "darkness" he refers to the tribulations, so by *light* he refers to God's support because of the relief it brings to the tribulations, as has been indicated by us in many places. From those mountains of yours (namely, Sion's), he is saying, you ever shed light in marvelous fashion and relieve all the hardships, filling everything with light and joy. He called the mountain *everlasting* for remaining strong and at no time falling to the enemy as long as it was not God's will. *All the foolish of heart were confused* (v. 5): being simple-minded, those men thought that they had control of your place, and suffered such an unexpected shock as to espy no way of escaping the troubles besetting them. *They slept their sleep and found nothing:* after going to rest by the wall in readiness for demolishing the city in the morning, they then all perished in a flash in the night.[2] They went to sleep, he is saying, and came to nothing—that is, they all died suddenly and left no trace. *All the men of wealth in their hands:* all these powerful and well-equipped men trusted in their own hands—that is, their own strength. |

---

2. Even Theodoret, with his proclivity for an eschatological interpretation, sees the similarity here to the events of the angelic destruction of Sennacherib's forces in 701 B.C.E. as described in 2 Kgs 19:35.

7. Ἀπὸ ἐπιτιμήσεώς σου, ὁ Θεὸς Ἰακώβ, ἐνύσταξαν πάντες οἱ ἐπιβεβη-κότες τοῖς ἵπποις. Ἀλλὰ μόνον ὠργίσθης καὶ ἐπετίμησας, καὶ ὥσπερ τινὶ νυσταγμῷ κατασχεθέντες ἅπαντες τῶν ἵππων κατηνέχθησαν, οὐδὲ τοῦ τρόπου τῆς τιμωρίας ἐπαισθανόμενοι, — ἀπὸ τοῦ τοὺς νυστάζοντας ἄγαν
5 αἰφνιδίως καὶ ἀνεπαισθήτως καταπίπτειν, τὸ αἰφνίδιον παραστῆσαι βουλη-θεὶς τῆς πληγῆς.

8ᵃ. Σὺ φοβερὸς εἶ, καὶ τίς ἀντιστήσεταί σοι; Κατὰ πρόσωπόν σου · φόβου γὰρ γέμεις, καὶ οὐ δυνατὸν οὐδὲ ἀντιβλέψαι σοί τινα.

8ᵇ. Ἀπὸ τότε ἡ ὀργή σου. Καὶ οὐ νῦν ἤρξω τοῦ ὀργιζόμενος τιμωρεῖ-
10 σθαι οὓς ἐθέλεις, ἀλλ᾽ ἄνωθεν καὶ ἐκ μακροῦ τοῦ χρόνου δύνασαί τε ταῦτα καὶ ποιεῖς.

9ᵃ. Ἐκ τοῦ οὐρανοῦ ἠκούτισας κρίσιν. Συνηθῶς οὖν ἄνωθεν καὶ νῦν τῆς κρίσεως, ἧς ἀποφαίνῃ, πάντας ἀκοῦσαι ποιήσεις. Ἐσχημάτισεν δὲ αὐτὸ ὡς τοῦ Θεοῦ ἄνωθεν ἀποφαινομένου πάντας ἀπολέσθαι, καὶ οὕτως αὐτῶν
15 ἀπολομένων.

9ᵇ. Γῆ ἐφοβήθη καὶ ἡσύχασεν. Ὅμοιόν ἐστιν τῷ ἐν τῷ πρὸ τούτου ψαλμῷ. Μόνον φησὶν ἀπεφήνω καὶ ἔλαβεν πάντας φόβος καὶ ἡσυχία · ἀπώλοντο γὰρ πολεμοῦντες καὶ ταράττοντες.

10. Ἐν τῷ ἀναστῆναι εἰς κρίσιν τὸν Θεόν, τοῦ σῶσαι πάντας τοὺς πραεῖς
20 τῆς γῆς. Ἀναστάντος οὖν φησιν εἰς τὸ δικάσαι καὶ περισῶσαι ἡμᾶς τοὺς μάτην παρ᾽ ἐκείνων ἀδικουμένους, ἐκεῖνοι ταῦτα πείσονται.

16 Ps. LXXIV, 4.

7. Ἀλλὰ μόνον — πληγῆς: P. fol. 266; V, fol. 32ᵛ; *Paraphrasis* (p. 562).　2 καὶ μόνον Par　4 ἐπαισθανόμενοι des. Par.

8ᵃ. Κατὰ πρόσωπον — τινα: P, fol. 266ᵛ; V, fol. 32ᵛ; *Paraphrasis* (p. 562).

8ᵇ. Καὶ οὐ νῦν — ποιεῖς: P, fol. 266ᵛ; V, fol. 32ᵛ-33; *Paraphrasis* (p. 562, 10-11).

9ᵃ. Συνηθῶς – ἀπολομένων: P, fol. 266ᵛ; V. fol. 33; *Paraphrasis* (p. 562).　12 καὶ νῦν] τὰ Par　13 ἧς ἀποφαίνῃ] σόν Par.

9ᵇ. Ὅμοιον – ταράττοντες: P, fol. 266ᵛ; V. fol. 33; *Paraphrasis* (p. 562).

10. Ἀναστάντος — πείσονται: P, fol. 267; V. fol. 33; Vat. 1422, fol. 137.

Aᵉ 7 (p. 385, 23-29): Sola comminutione (communititione *ms*) tua deterriti sunt... Per similitudinem dormitantium nihilque prospicientium subitum exitium et inspiratum uoluit malum mortis expraemere.　8ᵇ (p. 385. 30-386, 1): Non nunc primum in aduersarios terrae motus incanduit, sed cunctis retro temporibus hanc censuram agitasti.　9ᵇ (p. 386, 7-10): Simile est illi uersui *Liquefacta est terra et omnes qui habitant in ea*, pro eo ut diceret Omnes hos terror metusque con-sumsit.　10 (p. 386, 11-12): Cum uno iudicio tuos saluares, hostes adfligeres

At your rebuke, O God of Jacob, those riding the horses fell into a sleep (v. 6): but you merely became angry and issued a rebuke, and as though gripped in a kind of slumber they were all thrown from their horses without perceiving the manner of punishment (wishing to present the suddenness of the strike by a comparison with people sleepwalking and quite suddenly and unconsciously collapsing). *You are fearsome, and who will withstand you,* (v. 7) to your face? You instill fear, and it is impossible for anyone even to look at you. *From then your wrath:* it is not at this time that you began in your wrath to punish those you wish; from the beginning and long beforehand you were able and have been doing it. *From heaven you made judgment heard* (v. 8): from above, as is usual, at this time as well you will make everyone hear the judgment you decree. He used the same figure, God decreeing from on high the destruction of all, and thus they would perish. *Earth feared and was still.* This resembles the verse in the preceding psalm:[3] You merely decreed, and fear and paralysis seized them all, those responsible for battle and panic perishing. *When God arose to judgment, to save all the gentle of the earth* (v. 9): when you arise to give judgment and save us who were wronged by them without cause, they will meet this fate. |

---

3. Cf. Ps 75:3.

11ᵃ. Ὅτι ἐνθύμιον ἀνθρώπου ἐξομολογήσεταί σοι. Ὑπὲρ τούτων φησὶ
τὰ ἐνθυμήματα ἡμῶν εὐχαριστήσει σοι, — ἵνα εἴπῃ Αἱ διάνοιαι ἡμῶν καὶ οἱ
λογισμοὶ ἡμῶν περὶ τοῦτο ἀσχοληθήσονται, ὡς μηδὲ βουλεύσασθαί τι
ἕτερον.

11ᵇ. Καὶ ἐγκατάλειμμα ἐνθυμίου ἑορτάσει σοι. Ἐπειδὴ ἔθος ἡμῖν ἐν ταῖς 5
συμφοραῖς λειποψυχεῖν, τοῦτό φησιν ὅτι Ἡ ψυχὴ ἡμῶν καὶ ὁ λογισμός, ὁ
περιληφθεὶς ἡμῖν διὰ τὴν παρά σου βοήθειαν, οὗτος ἐν ἑορτῆς μέρει θήσεται τῶν σῶν ἀγαθῶν τὴν μνήμην.

12ᵃ. Εὔξασθε καὶ ἀπόδοτε Κυρίῳ τῷ Θεῷ ἡμῶν. Τοῦτο λοιπὸν ὁ προφήτης ἐγκελεύεται ˙ ὑπὲρ ὧν τετυχήκατέ φησιν εὐχόμενοι τὰ ὀφειλόμενα αὐτῷ 10
ἀπόδοτε.

12ᵇ-13. Πάντες οἱ κύκλῳ αὐτοῦ οἴσουσι δῶρα τῷ φοβερῷ καὶ ἀφαιρου-
μένῳ πνεύματα ἀρχόντων, φοβερῷ παρὰ τοῖς βασιλεῦσι τῆς γῆς. Οὐδὲ γὰρ
θαυμαστόν φησιν ὑμᾶς τοῦτο διαπράττεσθαι ὁπότε τῶν γενομένων τὸ μέγεθος εἰς ἔκπληξιν πάντας καταστήσει τοὺς περιοικοῦντας, ὥστε δῶρα αὐτῷ 15
προσαγαγεῖν ὡς μεγάλῳ καὶ ποιοῦντι ὅσα βούλεται, καὶ ἀναιροῦντι ἄρχοντας, καὶ βασιλέας τιμωρουμένῳ. Εἰκὸς δὲ ἦν τοῦτο γενέσθαι παρὰ τῶν

11ᵃ. Ὑπὲρ τούτων — ἕτερον: P, fol. 267; V, fol. 33ᵛ; Vat. gr. 2057, fol. 153ᵛ
et Barb. gr. 340, fol. 225 (Θεοδώρου Ἀντιοχ'); Paraphrasis (p. 562). 3 περὶ τούτων 2057 Barb.
11ᵇ. Ἐπειδὴ — μνήμην: P, fol. 267; V, fol. 33'; Vat. gr. 2057, fol. 153' et Barb.
gr. 340, fol. 225 (Θεοδώρου Ἡρακλείας); Cord, p. 572.
12ᵃ. Τοῦτο λοιπὸν — ἀπόδοτε: P, fol. 267ᵛ; V, fol. 33ᵛ; Vat. 1422, fol. 137ᵛ;
Cord, p. 573. 10 ὑπὲρ] περὶ 1422 Cord φησιν om. 1422.
12ᵇ-13. Οὐδὲ — θάνατος: P, fol. 267ᵛ; V, fol. 34; Cord, p. 574 sub nomine
THEODORETI. 16-17 ἀναιροῦντι — τιμωρουμένῳ affert Paraphrasis (p. 563).

Aᶜ 1-2 (p. 386, 13-15): Grata erit iugiter liberatorum tota mentis intentio.
11ᵇ (p. 386, 18-24): Quoniam moris est inter aduersa possitis difectum animae
sustinere, hoc ait quoniam et anima nostra et quicquid cogitationis est reli-
qu⟨u⟩m, quod non extinxit tribulatio, memoriam benefactorum tuorum iugi
sollemnitate celebrabit. 12ᵃ (p. 386, 25-27): Exortatio profetae est, ut matu-
rent exsoluere quod promittunt. 12ᵇ-13 (p. 386, 28-387, 1): Non mirum nec
satis magnum est si a uobis promisa uotorum reddantur, quando quidem operum eius magnitudo finitimos quosque facere admirationem eius munerumque
oblationem conpulerit, qui Assiriorum dominationi subacti aut pro sua quoque
liberatione egerunt gratias aut rei tam magnae etiam apud illos gestae stupore
miraculoque.

Because human pondering will confess to you (v. 10): our thinking will
be to give thanks to you for this; as if to say, our ideas and purposes will be
directed toward this end, never to intend anything different. *And remnant of*
pondering will celebrate you. Since we normally lose heart in misfortune,
he is saying, Our spirits and thoughts rallied, thanks to your help, and will
be directed to recalling your good things in the manner of a festival. *Make*
vows and perform them to the Lord our God (v. 11). The author now gives
this recommendation: In return for what you have received, make vows that
are due to him and fulfill them. *All those in his circle will bring gifts for the*
fearsome one, who removes breaths from rulers, fearsome before the kings
of the earth (vv. 12–13): it is not surprising that you do this when the magnitude of the events will bring amazement to the neighboring peoples, with
the result that they will offer gifts to the one who is mighty and does all that
he wishes, destroys rulers and punishes kings. Now, this probably was done
by the | neighboring peoples, who not only were astonished at the event,

περιοικούντων, οὐ μόνον ἐκπληττομένων τὸ γενόμενον, ἀλλὰ καὶ εὐχαριστούντων. Κοινῶς γὰρ πάντας τοὺς Ἀσσυρίους ἀπονεμηθέντος καὶ μικροῦ ἀπολέσαντος, κοινὴ πάντων ἦν ἐλευθερία ὁ ἐκείνων θάνατος.

PSALMVS LXXVI

5 Λέγει μὲν κἀνταῦθα τὰ κατὰ τὸν ἐν Βαβυλῶνι λαὸν ἐξηγούμενος. Ἔχει δέ τινα ὁμοιότητα ἐν τῷ σχήματι πρὸς τὸν οβ΄. Ὥσπερ γὰρ ἐκεῖ φησιν ὅσα τε καὶ οἷα ὑπὸ τῶν συμβαινόντων πραγμάτων λογίζεσθαι προσήγοντο, οὕτως κἀνταῦθα λέγει ὅσα μὲν ἔπασχον καὶ οἷα, τίνα δὲ καὶ ἐννοεῖν ὑπὸ τῶν συμφορῶν ἠναγκάζοντο. Λέγει δὲ ταῦτα κατὰ τὸ σύνηθες ἀπὸ τοῦ 10 ἐκείνων προσώπου, ὡσανεὶ μετὰ τὴν ἐπάνοδον λεγόντων τὰ τότε συμβάντα καὶ τίνα ἐλογίσαντο.

2-3ª. Φωνῇ μου πρὸς Κύριον ἐκέκραξα, φωνῇ μου πρὸς τὸν Θεόν, καὶ προσέσχεν μοι· ἐν ἡμέρᾳ θλίψεώς μου τὸν Θεὸν ἐξεζήτησα. Ἐβόησά φησι πρὸς αὐτὸν καὶ ἐφρόντισέν μου.

15 3ᵇ. Ταῖς χερσί μου νυκτὸς ἐναντίον αὐτοῦ, καὶ οὐκ ἠπατήθην. Σύμμαχος τὸ ταῖς χερσί μου νυκτὸς ἐναντίον αὐτοῦ σαφέστερον εἶπεν Ἡ χείρ μου νυκτὸς ἐκτέταται διηνεκῶς. Ὁπηνίκα φησὶν ἐθλιβόμην ᾔτουν τὴν παρὰ τοῦ Θεοῦ βοήθειαν, διὰ πάσης τῆς νυκτὸς πρὸς τὸν Θεὸν ἐκτείνων τὰς χεῖρας· καὶ οὐ διεψεύσθην τῶν ἐλπίδων, ἔτυχον δὲ ὧν ἐχρῆν.

20 3ᶜ. Ἀπηνήνατο παρακληθῆναι ἡ ψυχή μου. Πολλάκις φησὶν ὑπὸ τοῦ μεγέθους τῶν κακῶν καὶ τῶν συμφορῶν ἀπηρνησάμην καὶ ἀπηγόρευσα πᾶσαν

2 κοινῶς] αὐτῇ Cord   μικροῦ δεῖν Cord   3 τὸ κοινῇ PV.
Argumentum Λέγει — ἐλογίσαντο: P, fol. 268; V, fol. 34; Cord, p. 588-589.
6 οβ΄ ψαλμόν Cord.
2-3ª. Ἐβόησα — ἐφρόντισέν μου: P, fol. 268; V, fol. 34ᵛ; Cord, p. 589.
3ᵇ. Σύμμαχος — ἐχρῆν: P, fol. 268; V, fol. 34ᵛ; Cord, p. 590.
3ᶜ. Πολλάκις — συγχωρεῖ: P, fol. 268ᵛ; V, fol. 34ᵛ; Cord, p. 590.

Aᵉ *Argumentum ps. LXXVI* (p. 387, 5-10): Praedicit in praesenti psalmo quae erat populus in Babilone passurus; omnisque contextus psalmi ʟxxɪɪ huic similitudine non parua coniungitur tam experiundi austera, quam ob ea ipsa libertatem (libere *ms*) conquirendi. Cf. Pseudo-Beda (888).   17-19 (p. 387, 16-20): Cum pondere, inquit, tribulationis urgerer, extensis tota nocte manibus, a Deo auxilium postulaui, nec me spes fefellit; praestitit enim bonitas Dei quae petebam.   3ᶜ (p. 387, 23-29): Ita frequenta me mala continuaque praeserunt, ut nihil libertatis (libere *ms*) et consulationis admitterem nec ullam sperarem tristium solutionem; in locum namque solacii proficit, si credas mala quae patiaris aliquando posse disolui.

but also gave thanks: since he had wasted and effectively destroyed all the Assyrians to the benefit of all, their death meant freedom for them all.

PSALM 77

While here, too, he comments on the situation of the people in Babylon, it bears some similarity in presentation to Psalm 73. That is to say, just as there he mentioned all the many and varied things that were adduced as being attributable to events that befell them, so here as well he tells of all their many and varied sufferings, and what they were led to ponder by force of circumstances. He tells it, as usual, from their viewpoint, as if after the return they were telling what then happened and what they thought.

I cried with my voice to the Lord, with my voice to God, and he heeded me; in a day of my tribulation I sought out God (vv. 1–2): I cried aloud to him, and he heeded me. *With my hands at night before him, and I was not disappointed.* The phrase *With my hands at night before him* Symmachus put more clearly: "My hand at night was stretched out constantly." When distressed, I begged help from God, stretching out my hands to God all night long, and I was not mistaken in my hope, receiving what was required. *My soul refused to be consoled:* often I was depressed by the magnitude of the troubles and despaired of all | consolation. In other words, I did not hope that

παράκλησιν, τουτέστιν Οὐκ ἤλπισα ἔσεσθαί τινα λύσιν καὶ παραμυθίαν τῶν λυπηρῶν· τὸ μὴ γὰρ ἐλπίζειν ὅτι λυθήσεται οὐδεμίαν ἔχειν παράκλησιν συγχωρεῖ.

4ᵃ. Ἐμνήσθην τοῦ Θεοῦ καὶ εὐφράνθην. Ἀλλ᾽ εἰ καί ποτε ὑπὸ τῶν συμφορῶν ἀπηγόρευσα τὰ κατ᾽ ἐμαυτόν, τῇ μνήμῃ τοῦ Θεοῦ ηὐφραινόμην, 5 λογιζόμενος ὅτι μέγας ὁ δεσπότης καὶ πάντων δυνατώτερος, ἀρκῶν πρὸς πᾶσαν λύσιν συμφορῶν. Ἐντεῦθεν λοιπὸν ἐξηγεῖται πλατύτερον ὅπως μὲν ἀπηγόρευεν τὰ καθ᾽ ἑαυτόν, οὐδὲ παρακαλεῖσθαι δυνάμενος, ὅπως δὲ ηὐφραίνετο τῇ μνήμῃ τοῦ Θεοῦ.

4ᵇ. Ἠδολέσχησα καὶ ὠλιγοψύχησε τὸ πνεῦμά μου. Εἰρήκαμεν πολλαχοῦ 10 ὅτι ἀδολεσχίαν τὴν συνέχειαν λέγει ὁτουδήποτε πράγματος· τὸ οὖν ἠδολέσχησα καὶ ὠλιγοψύχησε τὸ πνεῦμά μου, ἀντὶ τοῦ Συνεχῶς καὶ πλεονάκις ὑπὸ τῶν πολλῶν καὶ κακῶν λογισμῶν εἰς ὀλιγοψυχίαν κατέπεσον.

5. Προκατελάβοντο φυλακὰς οἱ ὀφθαλμοί μου, ἐταράχθην καὶ οὐκ ἐλάλησα. Ὥσπερ ἐπὶ τῆς ἡμέρας ἔθος ἡμῖν εἰς τέσσαρα διαιρεῖν τὰς ὥρας καὶ φαμὲν 15 γ ς θ καὶ ιβ τὴν ἑσπέραν, οὕτω καὶ ἐπὶ τῆς νυκτὸς ἡ διαίρεσις γίνεται. Καλεῖ μέντοι αὐτὰς φυλακὰς ἡ θεία γραφή, πρώτην φυλακὴν τὰς πρώτας τρεῖς, δευτέραν τὰς δευτέρας, τρίτην τὰς τρίτας, τετάρτην τὰς τελευταίας ἀπὸ τοῦ τοὺς ἀγρυπνοῦντας καὶ φυλάττοντας ἐκ διαδοχῆς τὰς νύκτας ἐν ταύταις ταῖς ὥραις παυομένους τῆς φυλακῆς ἑτέροις παραδιδόναι. Τοῦτο 20 οὖν βούλεται εἰπεῖν ὅτι ἀπὸ τῶν κακῶν ἀφίστατό μου καὶ ὁ ὕπνος, ὡς ἀεὶ ἐγρηγορότος μου ὑφ᾽ ἑκάστης φυλακῆς ἠνεωγμένους τοὺς ὀφθαλμούς μου καταλαμβάνεσθαι, — ἵνα εἴπῃ ὅτι Συνεχῶς ὑπὸ τῶν κακῶν οὐδὲ λαλεῖν πολλάκις ἠδυνάμην, ὥσπερ κημωμένος ὑπὸ τῶν συμφορῶν τὸ στόμα.

2 μὴ] μὲν PV.
4ᵃ. Ἀλλ᾽ εἰ καὶ — τοῦ Θεοῦ: P, fol. 268ᵛ; V, fol. 35.
4ᵇ. Εἰρήκαμεν — κατέπεσον: P, fol. 269; V, fol. 35; Cord, p. 591-592.   11 L (p. 583, 8-9): Ἀδολεσχίαν γὰρ τὴν συνέχειαν καλεῖ τὴν περί τι πρᾶγμα.
5. Ὥσπερ — τὸ στόμα: P, fol. 269; V, fol. 35ᵛ; Vat. 1422, fol. 138.   16 καὶ ιβ᾽] καὶ om. PV   17 πρώτην φυλ.] προφυλακὴν 1422   19 τοῦ om. 1422   23-24 ἵνα — στόμα affert Paraphrasis (p. 579)   24 ἠδυνήμην PV   κημωμένος] κινούμενος 1422

Aᵉ 4ᵃ (p. 387, 30-388, 1): Cum aduersorum facies in abruptum disperationis urgeret me et tamen iuuabat Domini recordatio; iam hinc latius explicat causas quibus aut disperare coactus sit, aut a quibus per memoriam Dei sit factus alacrior.   12-13 (p. 388, 2-4): Frequenter malis cogitationibus in difectum animae uenire conpulsus sum.   5 (p. 388, 6-13): Vigiliae dicuntur quatuor partes noctis in ternas horas diuisas. Cum soleant singulas noctium uigilias sortito uicissim uigiles obseruare custodes. ego angentibus malis aliorum uice uigelando praeueni, id est insomnis tota nocte fui.

there would be any relief from the hardships or any comfort, for the absence of hope that I would be relieved did not allow me to have any consolation. *I called God to mind, and was made glad* (v. 3): but even if I despaired of my plight under the influence of the misfortunes, I was made glad by remembrance of God, reckoning that the Lord is mighty and more powerful than anyone, sufficient for total relief from misfortune.

At this point he goes on to explain at greater length how, on the one hand, he despaired of his own situation and was unable to be consoled, and on the other hand how he was gladdened by remembrance of God. *I pondered, and my spirit fainted.* We have often remarked that pondering refers to constant attention to something or other; so the clause *I pondered, and my spirit fainted* means, Under the constant and repeated influence of many evil thoughts I became a victim of faintheartedness. *My eyes anticipated watches; I was disturbed and did not speak* (v. 4). Just as with the day we normally divide it into four periods and speak of the third, sixth, and ninth hours and of the twelfth as evening, likewise the division is made in the case of the night as well. The divine Scripture refers to the same watches, the first watch being the first three hours, the second the second three, the third the third three, and the fourth the last three, on the basis of men staying awake and watching during the night in succession, and concluding their watch at these times and handing on to others. So he means, On account of the troubles even sleep left me, ever on the alert at each watch with eyes open lest I be surprised—in other words, Without relief from the troubles I often could not even speak, as though muzzled by the misfortunes. |

6ᵃ. Διελογισάμην ἡμέρας ἀρχαίας. Ὑπεμιμνησκόμην ἐκείνων τῶν παλαιῶν ἡμερῶν.

6ᵇ⁻⁷ᵃ. Καὶ ἔτη αἰώνια ἐμνήσθην καὶ ἐμελέτησα. Σύμμαχος τὰ ἔτη τὰ ἀπὸ αἰῶνος λέγει. Καὶ τῶν παλαιῶν ἐκείνων ἐτῶν μνήμην ἐλάμβανον. Βού-
5 λεται δὲ εἰπεῖν ὅτι Ὑπεμιμνησκόμην τῶν ἐν τῇ ἡμετέρᾳ γῇ καὶ τῆς ἐκεῖ εὐετηρίας, ὅπως διήγομεν ἐκεῖ καὶ ἐν οἷς ἦμεν καὶ οἵων ἀπηλαύομεν.

7ᵇ. Νυκτὸς μετὰ τῆς καρδίας μου ἠδολέσχουν. Συνεχῶς δὲ ἐν ταῖς νυξὶν διανιστάμενος, ταῦτα ἐπὶ τῆς ἐμαυτοῦ διανοίας ἔστρεφον λογιζόμενος.

7ᶜ. Καὶ ἔσκαλλε τὸ πνεῦμά μου. Ἐπὶ τούτοις οὖν ἐταραττόμην τὴν ψυχὴν
10 λογιζόμενος οἷα μὲν τὰ παλαιά, οἷα δὲ τὰ παρόντα, καὶ εἶπα·

8ᵃ. Μὴ εἰς τοὺς αἰῶνας ἀπώσεται Κύριος; Λοιπὸν οὖν φησι τοῦτο ἐνεθυμούμην Ἄρα πάντως ἡμᾶς ἀπορρίψει;

8ᵇ. Καὶ οὐ προσθήσει τοῦ εὐδοκῆσαι ἔτι; Καὶ οὐ φροντίσει πάλιν χρηστόν τι περὶ ἡμᾶς διαπράξασθαι;

15 9ᵃ. Ἢ εἰς τέλος τὸ ἔλεος αὐτοῦ ἀποκόψει; Ἀλλὰ παντελῶς τὴν χρηστότητα αὐτοῦ καὶ τὴν εἰς ἡμᾶς φιλανθρωπίαν ἀποτεμών, οὐδενὸς ἡμῖν καλοῦ μεταδώσει;

9ᵇ. Συνετέλεσε ῥῆμα ἀπὸ γενεᾶς εἰς γενεάν. Σύμμαχος Συνετέλεσεν ῥῆσιν περὶ γενεᾶς ἑκάστης. Ἐλογιζόμην δέ φησι κἀκεῖνο, ὅτι μηδὲν ἁπλῶς καὶ ὡς

6ᵃ. Ὑπεμιμνησκόμην — ἡμερῶν: P, fol. 269; V, fol. 35ᵛ.
6ᵇ⁻⁷ᵃ. Σύμμαχος — ἀπηλαύομεν: P, fol. 269; V, fol. 35ᵛ.
7ᵇ. Συνεχῶς — λογιζόμενος: P, fol. 269ᵛ; *Paraphrasis* (p. 579).
7ᶜ. Ἐπὶ τούτοις — εἶπα: P, fol. 269ᵛ; *Paraphrasis* (p. 579).   9 ψυχήν μου Par.
8ᵃ. Λοιπὸν — ἀπορρίψει: P, fol. 269ᵛ; *Paraphrasis* (p. 579).
8ᵇ. Καὶ οὐ φροντίσει — διαπράξασθαι: P, fol. 269ᵛ; *Paraphrasis* (p. 579).
9ᵃ. Ἀλλὰ παντελῶς — μεταδώσει: P, fol. 269ᵛ; *Paraphrasis* (p. 579-580).
9ᵇ. Σύμμαχος — κακοῖς: P, fol. 269ᵛ.   19-512, 3 ἐλογιζόμην — γενέσθαι affert *Paraphrasis* (p. 580).

Aᵉ 6ᵃ (p. 388, 17-19): Praeteritorum mihi temporum ante oculos memoria recurrit.   6ᵇ⁻⁷ᵃ (p. 388, 20-25): Vult dicere quemadmodum in memoriam eius uel terra repromisionis uenerit, uel quali, cum ibi habitaret, sit rerum ubertate perfruitus, quantaque bona semper habuerit.   7ᵇ·ᶜ (p. 388, 26-389, 1): Frequenter cogitationes incurri etiam noctis tempore, quo curarum tormenta laxantur; haec cum animo ac mente tractaui inter praeteritorum memoriam et praesentium statum uistigia sententiae meae lubricabant.

I pondered days gone by (v. 5): I remembered the days of yore. *And recalled and meditated on eternal years.* Symmachus says "the years of eternity." I called to mind those past years. He means, I remembered the people in our country and the prosperity there, how we lived there, what we experienced and the things we enjoyed. *By night I communed with my heart* (v. 6): in the nighttime I constantly went away and spent time pondering these things in my mind. *And I stirred up my spirit:* with these things I was thus disturbed in spirit, pondering what the past was like and what the present was like, and I said, *Surely the Lord will not reject us forever?* (v. 7). Then I came to this conclusion: Surely he will not completely reject us? *And will he not proceed to be pleased?* Will he not in turn think of doing something good for us? *Will he terminate his mercy forever?* (v. 8). Will he instead completely cut short his goodness and his lovingkindness for us, imparting no good thing to us? *He has put an end to his word from generation to generation.* Symmachus: "He put an end to his talking about each generation." He is saying, I considered the fact that you do nothing idly or | by chance; rather, knowing

ἔτυχεν ποιεῖς, πόρρωθεν δὲ ἕκαστα εἰδὼς καὶ περὶ ἑκάστου τῶν μελλόντων
τίκτεσθαι ἀνθρώπων γινώσκων ἀκριβῶς ἅπαντα, οὕτω περὶ ἑκάστης γενεᾶς
προλαμβάνων ὁρίζεις ἕκαστόν τί τε παθεῖν καὶ ἐν οἷς προσήκει γενέσθαι·
καὶ τοῦτο αὐτὸ μάλιστα ἐδεδίειν μή τι ἄρα παντελῶς περὶ ἡμῶν προλαβὼν
ἐδοκίμασας τοιοῦτο, ὥστε παραδοῦναι πάντη καὶ ἐναφεῖναι τοῖς κακοῖς.   5

10ᵃ. Μὴ ἐπιλήσεται τοῦ οἰκτειρῆσαι ὁ Θεός; Ἐντεῦθέν φησιν ἐκεῖνο
μάλιστα κατ᾽ ἐμαυτὸν ἐλογιζόμην Μήποτε τί τοιοῦτον καὶ περὶ ἡμῶν ἀπο-
φηνάμενος οὐκέτι λογιεῖται, οὔτε ἀνέξεται τοῦτο φιλάνθρωπον ποιῆσαι
περὶ ἡμᾶς;

10ᵇ. Ἡ συνέξει ἐν τῇ ὀργῇ αὐτοῦ τοὺς οἰκτιρμοὺς αὐτοῦ; Ἀλλὰ συ-   10
σφίξει καὶ καθέξει παρ᾽ ἑαυτῷ πᾶσαν χρηστότητα διὰ τὴν καθ᾽ ἡμῶν ὀργήν,
καὶ οὐδὲν ἡμᾶς ἀγαθὸν διαθήσει; Καλῶς δὲ συνεχῶς ἔθηκεν ταῦτα — ἢ εἰς
τέλος τὸ ἔλεος αὐτοῦ ἀποκόψει, ἢ ἐπιλήσεται τοῦ οἰκτειρῆσαι ὁ Θεὸς καὶ
ὅσα τοιαῦτα. Ἴδιον γὰρ μάλιστα τῶν ἐν ταῖς συμφοραῖς συνεχῶς στρέ-
φειν τὸν λογισμόν (Ἄρα ἔσται τι χρηστόν, ἆρα οὐκ ἔσται;) καὶ μᾶλλον   15
ἀμφιβάλλειν ἢ προσδοκᾶν τι καλόν. Πάντα μέντοι πρὸς τὸ Ἀπηνήνατο
παρακληθῆναι ἡ ψυχή μου ἀπέδωκεν, ἐκεῖνο πλατύτερον εἰπών· τὸ γὰρ
λέγειν Ἄρα ποιήσει τόδε; ἆρα ἔσται τόδε; ἀμφιβάλλοντος ἦν καὶ μικροῦ
ἀπαγορεύοντος τὰ καθ᾽ ἑαυτόν.

11ᵃ. Καὶ εἶπα Νῦν ἠρξάμην. Συντόμως σφόδρα εἰρημένον ἐν τῷ ἑβραϊκῷ   20
οὐκ ἐπεδέξατο μετὰ τῆς αὐτῆς συντομίας ἐν τῷ ἑλληνικῷ τὴν σαφήνειαν·
οὐ δύναται γοῦν οὐδὲ φρασθῆναι συντόμως ἡ τοῦ ῥητοῦ διάνοια. Ὅμοιον
δέ ἐστι τῷ Ἐπεφέρετο ἐπάνω τοῦ ὕδατος κειμένῳ ἐν τῇ ἀρχῇ τῆς κτίσεως·
καὶ γὰρ κἀκεῖνο πλειόνων χρείαν ἔχει πρὸς παράστασιν τῆς διανοίας. Βούλεται δὲ εἰπεῖν ὅτι λογιζόμενος ἐκεῖνα τὰ παλαιὰ καὶ τὴν ἀρχαίαν εὐετη-   25
ρίαν, ὁρῶν δὲ μεγάλα τὰ παρόντα κακά, ἔλεγον ὅτι Τάχα ἀρχή μοι αὕτη
τῶν συμφορῶν· ἐννοῶν γὰρ ὅσων καὶ οἵων ἔτυχεν ἡμῶν τὸ γένος τὸ

16-17 v. 3ᵉ   23 Gen. I, 2

4 δεδίειν P.
10ᵃ. Ἐντεῦθεν — ἡμᾶς: P, fol. 270; Cord, p. 593.   8 οὔτε] οὐδὲ P.
10ᵇ. Ἀλλὰ συσφίξει: P, fol. 270; Cord, p. 593.
11ᵃ. Συντόμως — ἐπάγει: P, fol. 270; Cord, p. 594.   21 αὐτῆς om. Cord.

Aᵉ 14-16 (p. 389, 25-29)... familiares sunt sane adflictis hii luctus animorum,
ut repulsa consolatione spem suam alterutra suspicione suspendant et dubia
cogitatione consumant.   27-513, 5 (p. 390, 1-6): Cum apud patres beneficiorum
principia diuinorum nouis et sequentibus cumularentur augmentis, nunc in
peiorem sortem, motato statu nostro, credibile est haec esse initia dolorum,
quibus, motata erga nos diuina dispensatione, incrementum et perfectio debeatur.

everything from afar and having a precise knowledge of everything affecting every single human being yet to be born, you thus determine in advance about each generation everything they will suffer and what will be their situation. My particular concern was that you might make a judgment about us in advance to consign us completely to the troubles and expose us to them.

Surely God has not forgotten to have pity? (v. 9). At this point I gave particular thought to this question: Surely he is no longer making such a decision about us and pondering it, and will not be able to refrain from doing this kindly act for us? *Surely in his anger he will not withhold his pity?* Will he instead reduce and keep to himself all goodness on account of his anger with us, and not be well disposed toward us? Now, he did well to keep expressing this thought: *Will he terminate his mercy forever, or has God forgotten to have pity?* and the like. It is, in fact, normal in misfortune in particular to keep turning over the thought—Will there be anything good? Will there not be?—and so to be all the more uncertain or expect some good outcome. It is all, of course, a response to *My soul refused to be consoled* (v. 2), expressing it at greater length, since the questions Will he do this? and Will this happen? are typical of someone uncertain and close to despairing of his situation.

And I said, Now I have begun (v. 10). The extremely concise statement in the Hebrew does not admit clarity with the same conciseness in the Greek; at any rate, the sense of the verse cannot be articulated concisely. It is like the verse "It moved over the water" at the beginning of Genesis, which requires further detail for presentation of its meaning.[1] His meaning is, Pondering days of yore and the former prosperity, and seeing the current troubles in their magnitude, I said, Perhaps this is the beginning of disaster for me: thinking of all the kinds of things our race received | in olden times compared with what I now experience, I often thought that perhaps, just as at one time

---

1. Gen 1:2. Here in Ps 77:10, however, cryptic expression is not the issue: the LXX is simply confusing the Hebrew verb found in the text, which means "be sick," with a similar Hebrew verb meaning "begin."

παλαιόν, ἐν οἷς δὲ νῦν εἰμι, ἐνενόησα πολλάκις ὅτι τάχα ὥσπερ ποτὲ ἔδοξεν αὐτῷ εὐποιῆσαι ἡμᾶς καὶ εἰς τοῦτο προέβαινε τὰ καθ᾽ ἡμᾶς, οὕτω καὶ
νῦν τάχα τι ἕτερον περὶ ἡμῶν δοκιμάσας πάντη ἡμᾶς ἀπέβαλεν τοῖς κακοῖς
παραδούς, καὶ τάχα ταῦτα τὰ νῦν κατέχοντα κακὰ ἀρχὴ τῶν λοιπῶν ἐστιν
5 τῶν καθεξῆς μελλόντων συμβαίνειν. Καὶ ὥσπερ ἤρξατο μέν ποτε εὐεργετεῖν
ἡμᾶς, ὁσημέραι δὲ προεκόπτομεν ἐν τούτῳ, οὕτω καὶ νῦν ἤρξατο τῶν ἐναντίων, καὶ δεῖ τὴν ἐπὶ τὸ χεῖρον προκοπὴν προσδοκᾶν. Ὅμοιον δέ ἐστι τῷ
ἐν τῷ οβ´ Εἰ ἔλεγον διηγήσομαι, ἰδοὺ τῇ γενεᾷ τῶν υἱῶν σου ἠσυνθέτηκας.
Τοιοῦτο γάρ τι εἰπεῖν ἠβουλήθη κἀνταῦθα, ὅτι ὑπὸ τῶν κακῶν ἐνενόουν
10 ὅτι τάχα πάντη ἡμᾶς ἀπέρριψας, καὶ οὐδὲν δεῖ τοῦ λοιποῦ χρηστὸν προσδοκᾶν, ἀλλ᾽ ἀρχὴν ἡγεῖσθαι ταῦτα τῶν ἐσομένων κακῶν. Διὰ τοῦτο καλῶς
ἑξῆς ἐπάγει·

11ᵇ. Αὕτη ἡ ἀλλοίωσις τῆς δεξιᾶς τοῦ ὑψίστου. Ἀλλοιοῦσθαι λέγεται τὸ τρέπεσθαι καὶ μεταβάλλεσθαι. Δεξιὰν δὲ τοῦ Θεοῦ εἰρήκαμεν πολ-
15 λαχοῦ ὅτι τὴν βοήθειαν λέγει. Ἐνενόουν φησὶν ὅτι μετέβαλες καὶ μετέ-
στρεψας τὴν περὶ ἡμᾶς σου γνώμην, οὐκέτι βοηθεῖν ἡμῖν θέλων ἐν κακοῖς
οὖσι, παραδοῦναι δὲ ἡμᾶς ἅπαξ καὶ ἐναφεῖναι δοκιμάσας τοῖς κακοῖς· ὅθεν
δὴ καὶ συμβαίνειν ἐλογιζόμην τὸ ἐν τούτοις ἐξετάζεσθαι καὶ τοιαῦτα πάσχειν ἡμᾶς. Μέχρι τούτου πρὸς τὸ Ἀπηνήνατο πάντα ἀποδεδωκώς, καὶ πλα-
20 τύτερον αὐτὸ εἰπὼν τὸ ὅπως ἀπηγόρευον πολλάκις τὰ καθ᾽ ἑαυτόν, ὡς
μηδὲ παράκλησιν προσίεσθαί τινα, ἐντεῦθεν πάλιν ὅπως αὐτὸν ηὔφραινεν
ἡ τοῦ Θεοῦ μνήμη πλατύτερόν φησιν.

12ᵃ. Ἐμνήσθην τῶν ἔργων Κυρίου. Ἀλλὰ μετὰ πάντας φησὶ τοὺς λογισμοὺς τούτους αὐτάρκη παράκλησιν εἶχον τῶν ἔργων σου τὴν μνήμην. Ὃ
25 γὰρ εἶπεν διὰ συντόμου ἐν τοῖς προοιμίοις, τοῦτο πλατύτερον διὰ παντὸς
ἠβουλήθη εἰπεῖν τοῦ ψαλμοῦ· εἰπὼν γὰρ Ἀπηνήνατο παρακληθῆναι ἡ
ψυχή μου. ἐμνήσθην τοῦ Θεοῦ καὶ ηὐφράνθην, εἶπεν πλατύτερον ὅπως τὴν
παράκλησιν ἀπηγόρευσεν, οἵων μὲν ὄντων τῶν κακῶν, οἷα δὲ λογίζεσθαι
ἀναγκαζόμενος. Λέγει λοιπὸν ἐντεῦθεν καὶ πῶς ηὔφρανεν αὐτὸν ἡ τοῦ Θεοῦ
30 μνήμη, — ἐμνημόνευον οὖν φησιν ὧν ἐποίησας.

8 Ps. LXXII, 15   14-15 cf. supra p. 408, 23   19 v. 3ᶜ   26-27 vv. 3ᶜ-4ᵃ.

3 περὶ ἡμῶν] περὶ ἡμᾶς Cord   5 καθεξῆς] μετεξῆς Cord   ποτὲ μὲν Cord   7 τῷ
ἐν] τοῦ ἐν P   8 οβ´ ψαλμῷ Cord.

11ᵇ. Ἀλλοιοῦσθαι — πλατύτερόν φησιν: P, fol. 270ᵛ; V, fol. 36; Cord, p. 595.
20 τὸ ὅπως — ἑαυτὸν om. Cord   21 προίεσθαι PV.

12ᵃ. Ἀλλὰ μετὰ — ἐποίησας: P, fol. 270ᵛ; V, fol. 36; Cord, p. 595.

Aᵉ 19-21 (p. 390, 11-13): Hucusque metus animi aegrescentis malis praesentibus, hinc quibus sit rebus erectus exsequitur.

he decided to favor us and our situation improved, so too now perhaps he has made a different decision in our regard and has rejected us by consigning us to the troubles, and perhaps these current troubles are the beginning of others due to befall us in future. Just as he began at one time to be favorable to us, and we daily profited from it, so too now he began the opposite, and we must expect a reversal of fortunes. It resembles the verse in Psalm 73, "If I had said, 'I shall give this version of things,' behold, you would have been faithless to the generation of your children."[2] This, in fact, is his meaning here: Under pressure of the troubles I began to think that perhaps you have rejected us completely, and we must expect no good in future, and instead consider this the beginning of coming troubles. Hence, he does well to go on to say *This change of the right hand of the Most High.* By "changing" he refers to turning away or being transformed; and we have often remarked that God's *right hand* means his "assistance." He is saying, I came to the conclusion that you changed and altered your attitude toward us, no longer wishing to help us when in trouble, but seeing fit to consign us once and for all to the troubles and expose us to them. Hence, I presumed that this predicament and our suffering this fate were actually happening.

To this point he had been responding in everything to the phrase *My soul refused,* and explaining at greater length his often despairing of his situation, with the resulting lack of any consolation. At this point he goes on to explain at greater length how remembering God brought him joy. *I remembered the works of the Lord* (v. 11): despite all these thoughts, however, I gained sufficient consolation from memory of your works. What he said concisely in the introduction he meant to bring out at greater length in the psalm as a whole: after saying *My soul refused to be consoled; I called God to mind and was made glad,* he explained at greater length how he despaired of consolation, the troubles being what they were and the kinds of things he was forced to ponder. At this point he goes on to state also how recalling God made him glad, saying, I remembered what you had done. | *Because I shall remember your marvels from the beginning:* I recalled those initial ones, meaning those

---

2. Ps 73:15.

12ᵇ. Ὅτι μνησθήσομαι ἀπὸ τῆς ἀρχῆς τῶν θαυμασίων σου. Καὶ ὑπεμιμνησκόμην ἐκείνων τῶν πρώτων, ἵνα εἴπῃ τῶν κατ᾿ Αἴγυπτον.

13ᵃ. Καὶ μελετήσω ἐν πᾶσι τοῖς ἔργοις σου. Προβαίνων δὲ καθεξῆς ἁπάντων ἐμεμνήμην.

13ᵇ. Καὶ ἐν τοῖς ἐπιτηδεύμασίν σου ἀδολεσχήσω. Καὶ συνεχῶς ἔστρεφον 5
ἐπὶ τῆς διανοίας οἷα πεποίηκας ἡμῖν. Τούτων δὲ ἡ μνήμη οὐ τὴν τυχοῦσάν
μοι προσῆγε παράκλησιν, λογιζόμενος ὅτι τοσαῦτα ποιήσας ὑπὲρ ἡμῶν
οὐκ ἀνέξεται πάντῃ καταλιπεῖν ἡμᾶς. Εἶτα λοιπὸν ἐξηγεῖται τὴν παλαιὰν
εὐεργεσίαν εἰς μείζονα πίστωσιν.

14ᵃ. Ὁ Θεός, ἐν τῷ ἁγίῳ ἡ ὁδός σου. Ὅμοιόν ἐστι τοῦτο τῷ ἐν τῷ ξζ′ 10
ψαλμῷ τῷ Ἐθεωρήθησαν αἱ πορεῖαί σου ὁ Θεός, αἱ πορεῖαι τοῦ Θεοῦ τοῦ
βασιλέως τοῦ ἐν τῷ ἁγίῳ. Τοῦτο γὰρ βούλεται εἰπεῖν, ὅτι ἐπὶ τοῦ ὄρους
τοῦ Σινᾶ ἐφάνη σου ἡ ὁδὸς καὶ τὰ ἴχνη. Οὕτω φησὶν ἠξίωσας αὐτὸς
παραγενόμενος πρὸς τὸν λαὸν διαλεχθῆναι αὐτοῖς, ὡς καὶ τὴν ὁδόν σου
καὶ τὰ ἴχνη σου ἅπασι φανῆναι· ἀκριβέστερον δὲ εἴρηται ἐκεῖ, ἵνα μὴ τὰ αὐτὰ 15
ἑκάστοτε πλατύνειν δοκῶμεν.

14ᵇ. Τίς Θεὸς μέγας ὡς ὁ Θεὸς ἡμῶν; Καὶ ταῦτά φησιν ἠξίωσας ποιῆσαι, οὐ μικρός τις ὤν, ἀλλὰ καὶ ἄγαν μέγας, ὡς μηδὲ εἶναί τινα τὸν ἰσούμενόν σοι.

15ᵃ. Σὺ εἶ ὁ Θεὸς ὁ ποιῶν θαυμάσια. Αὐτὸς γὰρ εἶ ὁ τὰ μεγάλα καὶ 20
θαύματος ἄξια ποιεῖν δυνάμενος.

11-12 ps. LXVII, 25.

12ᵇ. Καὶ ὑπεμιμνησκόμην — Αἴγυπτον: P, fol. 270ᵛ; V, fol. 36.
13ᵃ. Προβαίνων — ἐμεμνήμην: P, fol. 270ᵛ; V, fol. 36.
13ᵇ. Καὶ συνεχῶς — πίστωσιν: P, fol. 270ᵛ; V, fol. 36ᵛ; Paraphrasis (p. 580-581).
7 λογιζομένῳ Par.　　8 ἀνέξῃ Par.
14ᵃ. Ὅμοιον — δοκῶμεν: P, fol. 271; V, fol. 36ᵛ; Cord, p. 596.　　10 τῷ om.
Cord　　13 καὶ om. PV　　ἴχνη σου Cord.
14ᵇ. Καὶ ταῦτα — ἰσούμενόν σοι: P, fol. 271; V, fol. 36ᵛ; Vat. 1422, fol, 138ᵛ;
Cord, p. 596-597; Paraphrasis (p. 581).
15ᵃ. Αὐτὸς — δυνάμενος: P, fol. 271; V, fol. 36ᵛ; Cord, p.597.　　21 θαύματος]
γεννήματος Cord.

Aᵉ 12ᵇ (p. 390, 17): Quae scilicet signa Aegiptia secula sunt.　　5-6 (p. 390,
18-19): In his reuoluendis exercebar.　　10-13 (p. 390, 20-22): Cum in monte
Sina uestigium eius apparuit; sic in LXVII psalmo Visi sunt ingressus tui, Deus.
14ᵇ (p. 390, 27-391, 1)... ut quod apparuit dignitatis, non mediocritatis eius fuisse
credatur.　　15ᵃ (p. 391, 2-3): Tibi soli proprium est talia et tam ingentia agere.

in Egypt. *I shall meditate on all your works* (v. 12): I proceeded to remember everything. *And I shall muse on your exploits:* and I constantly turned over in my mind all that you did for us. Memory of them brought me no slight consolation, as I reflected that having worked such things for us, you will not bring yourself to abandon us completely.

He then recounts the former beneficence to strengthen their faith. *O God, your way in the holy place* (v. 13). This resembles the verse in Psalm 68, "Your entries, O God, have been observed, the entries of God the king, who is in his holy place," meaning, On Mount Sion your way and your footprints were seen. Likewise, he is saying, You visited your people and vouchsafed to converse with them, with the result that your way and your footprints were seen by all. But it was commented on with greater precision there to prevent our seeming to give the same lengthy treatment in each case.[3] *What god is so great as our God?* You vouchsafed to do these things, since you are not someone insignificant but actually so very great that no one is your equal. *You are the God who works wonders* (v. 15): you are the one who is capable of doing mighty deeds that are worthy of *wonder.* | *You made your power known among the people:* from your deeds for us you made your power obvious to

---

3. Cf. Theodore's comment on Ps 68:24.

15ᵇ. Ἐγνώρισας ἐν τοῖς λαοῖς τὴν δύναμίν σου. Ἅπασιν ἀνθρώποις σαφῆ σου τὴν δύναμιν ἐκ τῶν περὶ ἡμᾶς κατεσκεύασας.

16ᵃ. Ἐλυτρώσω ἐν τῷ βραχίονί σου τὸν λαόν σου. Οὕτως μετὰ πολλῆς τῆς ἰσχύος ἀπήλλαξας ἡμᾶς τῶν ἐν Αἰγύπτῳ κακῶν.

5 16ᵇ. Τοὺς υἱοὺς Ἰακὼβ καὶ Ἰωσήφ. Ἵνα εἴπῃ ἡμᾶς.

17-18ᵃ. Εἴδοσάν σε ὕδατα, ὁ Θεός, εἴδοσάν σε ὕδατα καὶ ἐφοβήθησαν, ἐταράχθησαν ἄβυσσοι · πλῆθος ἤχους ὑδάτων. Σχηματίζει συνηθῶς ὡς τοῦ Θεοῦ προηγουμένου καὶ στρατηγοῦντος αὐτοῖς. Ἅμα τέ φησιν ἐθεάσατό σε τὰ ὕδατα, καὶ φόβῳ ληφθέντα ἐταράχθη καὶ πᾶσα ἐκείνη ἡ ἄβυσσος 10 μετὰ πολλοῦ τοῦ ἤχου ὑπεχώρει τῇδε κακεῖσε διαιρουμένων τῶν ὑδάτων καὶ μετὰ πολλῆς τῆς σπουδῆς ὑπαναχωρούντων μὲν παρὰ φύσιν, δίοδον δέ σοι κατασκευαζόντων.

18ᵇ. Φωνὴν ἔδωκαν αἱ νεφέλαι. Σύμμαχος Ἦχον ἔδωκεν αἰθήρ, σφόδρα ὧδε ἀκολούθως εἴρηται. Ἐπειδὴ γὰρ τοῦ Θεοῦ προστάξαντος ἄνεμος ἐπι-15 πνεύσας, ὡς ἐν τῇ Ἐξόδῳ γέγραπται, πεποίηκεν τῶν ὑδάτων τὴν διαίρεσιν, καλῶς εἶπεν ὅτι καὶ ὁ ἀὴρ ἐπήχει · σφοδροῦ γὰρ ὄντος τοῦ ἀνέμου, καὶ οὕτως σφοδροῦ ὡς διαίρεσιν ἐργάσασθαι τῶν ὑδάτων, ἀνάγκη πᾶσα ἦν καὶ τὸν ἀπὸ τοῦ ἀνέμου ἦχον μέγαν ἀποτελεῖσθαι. Καὶ τὸ αἱ νεφέλαι δὲ οὐδὲν διαλλάττει · ἴδιον γὰρ μάλιστα τοῦ ἀέρος εἰς νεφέλας συστρεφομένου σφο-20 δροτέρους ἀποτελεῖν τοὺς ἀνέμους.

15 cf. Ex. XIV, 21.

15ᵇ. Ἅπασιν — κατεσκεύασας: P, fol. 271; V, fol. 36ᵛ; *Paraphrasis* (p. 581).
16ᵃ. Οὕτως — κακῶν: P, fol. 271; V, fol. 36ᵛ; *Paraphrasis* (p. 581).
16ᵇ. Ἵνα εἴπῃ ἡμᾶς: P, fol. 271ᵛ; V, fol. 37.
17-18ᵃ. Σχηματίζει — κατασκευαζόντων: P, fol. 271ᵛ; V, fol. 37; Vat. 1422, fol. 138ᵛ. 7-8 *Paraphrasis* (p. 581): Καλῶς σχηματίζει ὡς τοῦ Θεοῦ προηγουμένου τοῦ λαοῦ.
18ᵇ. Σύμμαχος — ἀνέμους: P, fol. 271ᵛ; V, fol. 37ʳ·ᵛ.

Aᵉ 16ᵃ (p. 391, 5-7): Dum abducis nos Aegiptia seruitute, documenta tui roboris uirtutisque claruerunt.   7-8 (p. 391, 12-15): Scemate ex more facto, Deum uice principis adserit duxisse populum uel praecessisse totum. 18ᵇ (p. 391, 18-26): Consequenter dictum est quoniam, cum ad praeceptum Domini flante uento, ut in Exodo scriptum est, aquarum esset facta diuisio, aer uoces dederit. Incumbente (incumbentente *ms*) enim flatu nimio atque uechimenti, ita ut scindi aquas cogeret, necesse erat inmormurare caelum; proprium namque est, ut cum tenuitas aeris densetur in nubem inpulsi spiritus uiolentia ... resonent.

all people. *With your arm you redeemed your people* (v. 15): in this way with great strength you freed us from the troubles in Egypt. *The children of Jacob and Joseph*—in other words, us.

Waters saw you, O God, waters saw you and were afraid; depths were troubled, a mighty sound of waters (v. 16). As usual he presents it figuratively as though God were giving the orders and leading them. He is saying, As soon as the waters observed you, they were seized with fear and were panic-stricken, and all that great deep with a loud sound gave way in this direction and that, the waters dividing and parting in great haste in defiance of nature to provide a way for you. *The clouds uttered a sound* (v. 17). Symmachus: "The sky gave a roar," an expression in keeping with the subject: since at God's direction the wind blew, as recorded in Exodus,[4] and made a separation of the waters, he did well to say that the sky also made a sound, the wind being strong, so strong in fact as to cause a separation of the waters—consequently, the loud sound of the wind was produced. The term *the clouds* is no different: the sky, especially when heaped up into clouds, normally produces very strong winds. | *And your arrows pass through:* it was for us and against the foe that your punishments and your threats were directed.

---

4. Cf. Exod 14:21.

18ᶜ. Καὶ γὰρ τὰ βέλη σου διαπορεύονται. Καὶ ὑπὲρ ἡμῶν φησι ταῦτα, κατὰ δέ γε τῶν ἐχθρῶν αἱ τιμωρίαι σου καὶ αἱ ἀπειλαί σου διέτρεχον.

19ᵃ. Φωνὴ τῆς βροντῆς σου ἐν τῷ τροχῷ. Σύμμαχος ἐν τοῖς τροχοῖς. Βροντὴν γάρ φησιν ἐπαφεὶς μεγίστην, συνεπόδισας τοὺς τροχοὺς καὶ τὰ ἅρματα τῶν Αἰγυπτίων, ὥστε μηδὲ βραχὺ δυνηθῆναι προβῆναι, ἀλλ᾽ ὑπὸ 5 τῶν ὑδάτων ἅπαντας καταποντωθέντας ἀπολέσθαι.

19ᵇ. Ἔφαναν αἱ ἀστραπαί σου τῇ οἰκουμένῃ. Αὗται δέ σου αἱ ἀπειλαὶ καὶ αἱ καταπλήξεις, καὶ φόβοι οἱ κατὰ τῶν Αἰγυπτίων πᾶσιν ἐγένοντο καταφανεῖς· οὐδένα γὰρ ἔλαθεν ἡ ἐκείνων τιμωρία.

19ᵇ. Ἐσαλεύθη καὶ ἔντρομος ἐγενήθη ἡ γῆ. Πάντες γοῦν ἀκούσαντες 10 φόβῳ καὶ τρόμῳ συνεσχέθησαν ἐπὶ τῇ ἀκοῇ τῶν τοιούτων.

20ᵃ·ᵇ. Ἐν τῇ θαλάσσῃ ἡ ὁδός σου, καὶ αἱ τρίβοι σου ἐν ὕδασι πολλοῖς. Ἠκολούθησεν τῇ οἰκείᾳ σωματοποιήσει. Ὡς γὰρ στρατηγοῦντος αὐτοῖς τοῦ Θεοῦ καὶ προηγουμένου καὶ οὕτω διάγοντος αὐτοὺς τὴν θάλασσαν, ἐφάνης φησὶ προοδεύσας ἡμῶν ἐν τῇ θαλάσσῃ. 15

20ᶜ. Καὶ τὰ ἴχνη σου οὐ γνωσθήσονται. Οὐ μήν φησιν ἴχνη σου ἐθεάθη, ἵνα εἴπῃ ὅτι Οὐ σωματικῶς ὤφθη σου ἡ ὁδὸς, ἀλλὰ διὰ τῶν θαυμάτων.

18ᶜ. Καὶ ὑπὲρ — διέτρεχον: P, fol. 272; V, fol. 38; Vat. 1422, fol. 139 (anon.).
19ᵃ. Σύμμαχος — ἀπολέσθαι: P, fol. 272: V, fol. 38; Vat. 1422, fol. 139 (anon.).
19ᵇ. Αὗται — τιμωρία: P, fol. 272: V, fol. 38; Paraphrasis (p. 581).
19ᶜ. Πάντες — τοιούτων: P, fol. 272 et V, fol. 38 (anon.); Paraphrasis p. 582).
  10 γοῦν] γὰρ Par   11 καὶ τρόμῳ om. Par.
20ᵃ·ᵇ. Ἠκολούθησεν — θαλάσσῃ: P, fol. 272ᵛ; V, fol. 38; Paraphrasis (p. 582)·
20ᶜ. Οὐ μὴν — θαυμάτων: P, fol. 272ᵛ; V, fol. 38; Cord, p. 601; Paraphrasis
(p. 582).   17 ὅτι om. Cord Par.

Aᵉ 19ᵃ (p. 391, 29-32)... Conlissis in tonitruo nubibus, turbati sunt Aegiptiorum currus; rotae axibus adhiserunt, ut tamquam inmobiles aquis rediuntibus mergerentur.   19ᵇ (p. 391, 33-392, 2): Et ea quae Aegiptiis fuere terrore claritatis suae in orbis terrae notitiam peruenerunt.   19ᶜ (p. 392, 3-5): In magnitudine operum tuorum omnis auditor intremuit.   16-17 (p. 392, 9-10): Haec omnia potenter magis quam corporaliter facta sunt.

Sound of your thunder in the wheel (v. 18). Symmachus: "in the wheels."
You released a loud thunderclap, he is saying, and made the Egyptians'
wheels and chariots stick fast so that they could not in the slightest move
forward, and instead were overwhelmed by the waters and all perished. *Your
lightning flashed in the world:* Your very threats and blows and the fear gripping the Egyptians proved obvious to everyone, the punishment escaping no
one's notice. *The earth shook and was all of a tremble:* everyone who heard
it, at least, was gripped by fear and trembled at the report of such things. *Your
way was in the sea, and your paths in many waters* (v. 19). This is in keeping
with his characteristically corporeal imagery: with God giving orders and
directions and thus guiding them through the sea, he is saying, You traveled
before us in the sea. *And your footprints will not be found:* no footprint of
yours was seen, as if to say, Your way was not seen in bodily fashion, only in
the marvels.[5] |

---

5. We have no comment from Theodore on the final verse of the psalm.

PSALMVS LXXVII

Νόμος ἦν τοῦ Θεοῦ δοθεὶς πρὸς τὸν μακάριον Μωϋσέα, ὥστε τοὺς Ἰουδαίους τὰ γενόμενα θαύματα ἔν τε τῇ Αἰγύπτῳ καὶ τὰ κατὰ τὴν ἔρημον ἅπαντα διηγεῖσθαι συνεχῶς τοῖς ἰδίοις υἱοῖς, εἰς τὸ κἀκείνους μαθόντας τὰ
5 γενόμενα διηγεῖσθαι τοῖς ἐξ αὐτῶν. Προσέταξεν δὲ τοῦτο ὁ Θεὸς οὐχ ἁπλῶς, ἀλλ᾽ ἵνα γνόντες ὅσων μὲν καὶ οἵων ἠξιώθησαν παρὰ τοῦ δεσπότου καλῶν, καὶ ὅτι τῇ αὐτοῦ βοηθείᾳ τε καὶ δυνάμει κέκτηνται τὴν γῆν ἣν κατέχουσιν καὶ τῆς ἐλευθερίας ἀπολαύουσιν, σπουδάσωσι μὴ ἀγνώμονες εἶναι περὶ τὸν εὐεργέτην, ἀλλὰ τῇ φυλακῇ τοῦ νόμου καὶ τῇ περὶ τὸν βίον
10 σπουδῇ τιμῶσι τὸν δεδωκότα τὸν νόμον, ὃς εὐεργετήσας πρότερον καὶ πολλῶν ἀπαλλάξας κακῶν οὕτω δέδωκε τὸν νόμον ὑπὲρ τῆς ἐκείνων διορθώσεως, γνόντες δὲ τῶν πατέρων τὴν ἀγνωμοσύνην καὶ τὰς ὑπὲρ τούτων τιμωρίας φυλάξωνται μὴ εἰς τὴν ὁμοίαν αὐτοῖς ἀπιστίαν καταπεσεῖν. Τοῦτο τοίνυν ὅπερ πᾶσι ποιεῖν προσετέτακτο, μάλιστα πάντων ποιεῖν ἥρμοττε
15 τοῖς προφήταις κεκτημένοις ἐκ τῆς τοῦ Πνεύματος χάριτος τὸ διδασκαλικὸν ἀξίωμα. Διὸ καὶ ὁ μακάριος Δαυὶδ πάντας Ἰουδαίους προτρέπων ἐπ᾽ ἀρετὴν καὶ σπουδαιοτέρους περὶ τὴν τοῦ νόμου φυλακὴν ἐργάσασθαι βουλόμενος, κέχρηται τῷδε τῷ ψαλμῷ, διηγούμενος τὰ περὶ τὸ γένος ὑπὸ τοῦ Θεοῦ γεγονότα, ὅπως ἐξήγαγεν τῆς Αἰγύπτου, ὅπως διήγαγεν τὴν ἔρημον,
20 ὅπως τε εἰσήγαγεν εἰς τὴν γῆν τῆς ἐπαγγελίας, διὰ πάντων παιδεύων ἀνάλογον τῇ χάριτι τοῦ εὐεργέτου τὴν οἰκείαν ἐπιδείκνυσθαι προαίρεσιν, τελευταῖον μέντοι καὶ περὶ τῆς πρὸς ἀλλήλους αὐτῶν ὁμονοίας τε καὶ συμφωνίας τὰ εἰκότα διαλέγεται.

1ᵃ. Προσέχετε, λαός μου, εἰς τὸν νόμον μου. Ἐν ταῖς κοιναῖς καὶ σπου-
25 δαιοτέραις παραινέσεσιν ὁ μακάριος Δαυὶδ προτρέπει πρότερον σπουδαίως ἀκούειν τῶν λεγομένων, οὕτως ἐν τῷ μὴ ᾽ τὸ Ἀκούσατε ταῦτα, πάντα τὰ

26-518, 1 Ps. XLVIII, 1.

Argumentum Νόμος — διαλέγεται: P, fol. 273; V, fol. 38ᵛ-39; Vat. 1422, fol. 139ʳ·ᵛ (anon.); Ambros. C 9˙ sup., fol. 154ᵛ; Cord. p. 630-631.   3 καὶ τὰ] τὰ om. 1422 Amb Cord   6 γνόντες] γνῶντας PV   μὲν om. 1422 Amb Cord. 13 μὴ om. PV   14 προστέτακται Amb   18 τῷδε om. 1422 Amb Cord.

1ᵃ. Ἐν ταῖς κοιναῖς — προφήτη: P, fol. 2˙3ᵛ; V, fol. 39ʳ·ᵛ: Vat. 1422, fol. 139ᵛ; C 98 sup., fol. 155; Cord, p. 632.

Aᵉ 16-23 (p. 392, 25-393, 5): Virtutis studia legis custodiamque profeta commendans populo hunc psalmum conpossuit... docet quanta sit illis recordationis utilitas, ac monet ut eum reuerenter metuent qui sanctiones legis suae beneficiorum largitate praeuenerit, ut hi qui iam erant obnoxii facilius subderentur; postremo hortatur ut ferant intente mente concordiam. Cf. PSEVDO-BEDA (893).

Psalm 78

God's law was given to blessed Moses so that the Jews might constantly narrate to their children the wonders worked in Egypt and all the events in the desert, for them also to learn what had happened and narrate it to their successors. It was not without purpose that God gave this command: it was for them to know the many and varied benefits they were granted by the Lord and the fact that they obtained the land they occupied and enjoyed freedom thanks to his help and power, and thus might take care not to be ungrateful to the benefactor. Instead, they might by observing the law and being zealous for that way of life show respect for the giver of the law, who, after being their benefactor previously and freeing them from many troubles, gave the law for their correction, so that by acknowledging the ingratitude of their ancestors and the penalty they paid they might be on their guard not to fall into a disbelief like theirs.

Accordingly, it behooved in particular the biblical authors who received the privilege of teaching from the grace of the Spirit to do what he had commanded them all to do. Hence, blessed David also urged all Jews to virtuous behavior and wanted to make them more zealous for the observance of the law, and he used this psalm to that purpose, recounting the deeds worked by God for the race, how he had led them out of Egypt, how he had led them through the wilderness, and how he had led them into the land of promise, teaching them in everything to give evidence of their own good will similar to the gift of the benefactor. Finally, he speaks also of their obligations of harmony and accord with one another.

Attend, my people, to my law (v. 1). In his very zealous exhortations addressed to everyone, blessed David first urges them to listen zealously to what is said, as in Psalm 49, "Hear this, all | nations."[1] Similar in character is the verse *Attend, my people,* properly referring by his own *people* to Jews,

---

1. Ps 49:1.

ἔθνη. Τοιοῦτο γάρ ἐστιν καὶ τὸ Προσέχετε. λαός μου, λαὸν ἑαυτοῦ καλέσας εἰκότως Ἰουδαίους ἀρχομένους ὑπ᾽ αὐτοῦ. Τὸ δὲ εἰς τὸν νόμον μου, τουτέστιν εἰς ἃ μέλλω λέγειν, εἰκότως νόμον καλέσας τὴν τῶν χρησίμων διδασκαλίαν· διχόθεν γὰρ αὐτῷ νομοτεθεῖν ἐξῆν, καὶ ὡς βασιλεῖ καὶ ὡς προφήτῃ.   5

1ᵇ. Κλίνατε τὸ οὖς ὑμῶν εἰς τὰ ῥήματα τοῦ στόματός μου. Σπουδαίως ἀκούσατε ὧν λέγω.

2ᵃ. Ἀνοίξω ἐν παραβολαῖς τὸ στόμα μου. Τουτέστιν ἐν διηγήσεσι. Καλῶς δὲ αὐτὸ πληθυντικῶς εἶπεν· πολλῶν γὰρ ἤμελλεν μνημονεύειν θαυμάτων.

2ᵇ. Φθέγξομαι προβλήματα ἀπ᾽ ἀρχῆς. Διηγήματα ἀρχαῖα ἐρῶ. Πόθεν 10 εἰδὼς ἃ λέγεις, εἴπερ ἀρχαῖα καί σου πρεσβύτερα;

3ᵃ. Ὅσα ἠκούσαμεν καὶ ἔγνωμεν αὐτά. Ἃ ἀκούσαντες μεμαθήκαμέν τινων εἰπόντων.

3ᵇ. Καὶ οἱ πατέρες ἡμῶν διηγήσαντο ἡμῖν. Ἀξιόπιστα οὖν τὰ λεγόμενα, εἰ πατέρες οἱ διηγησάμενοι, οὐκ ἀνασχόμενοι ψεύσασθαι τοῖς ἰδίοις 15 υἱοῖς.

4. Οὐκ ἐκρύβη ἀπὸ τῶν τέκνων αὐτῶν εἰς γενεὰν ἑτέραν. ἀπαγγέλλοντες τὰς αἰνέσεις τοῦ Κυρίου καὶ τὰς δυναστείας αὐτοῦ καὶ τὰ θαυμάσια αὐτοῦ ἃ ἐποίησεν. Ἡ ἑρμηνεία τὸ κακοσύνθετον ἐποίησεν, οἷόν ἐστιν τὸ ἐν τῇ Ἐξόδῳ Ὁ γὰρ Μωϋσῆς οὗτος, ὃς ἐξήγαγεν ἡμᾶς ἐκ γῆς Αἰγύπτου, οὐκ 20

20-519, 1 Ex. XXXII, 1.

1ᵇ. Σπουδαίως — λέγω: P, fol. 273ᵛ; V, fol. 39ᵛ; Paraphrasis (p. 608).
2ᵃ. Τουτέστιν — θαυμάτων: P, fol. 273ᵛ; V, fol. 39ᵛ; Vat. 1422, fol. 139ᵛ (anon.); C 98 sup., fol. 155; Paraphrasis (p. 608).   9 πληθυντικῶς] πλη⁰ 1422.
2ᵇ. Διηγήματα — πρεσβύτερα: P, fol. 273ᵛ; V, fol. 39ᵛ; Vat. 1422, fol. 139ᵛ (anon.); C 98 sup., fol. 155; Cord. p. 632.   10 ἀρχαίων ἐρῶ 1422.
3ᵃ. Ἃ ἀκούσαντες — εἰπόντων: P, fol. 273ᵛ; V, fol. 39ᵛ; Vat. 1422, fol. 139ᵛ (anon.); C 98 sup., fol. 155; Paraphrasis (p. 608).   12 ἃ] τουτέστι 1422.
3ᵇ. Ἀξιόπιστα — υἱοῖς: P, fol. 273ᵛ; V, fol. 39ᵛ; Paraphrasis (p. 608).
4. Ἡ ἑρμηνεία — διηγεῖσθαι: P, fol. 273ᵛ; V, fol. 39ᵛ; Vat. 1422, fol. 140; C 98 sup., fol. 155; Cord, p. 633.

Aᵉ 2-5 (p. 393, 6-9): Bene exortationem suam legem uocat... profetalis et regalis personam eius, ex quo loquebatur, adsumens.   1ᵇ (p. 393, 13-14): Sollicitius omnia quae sum dicturus accipite.   2ᵃ (p. 393, 15-17): Pro narratione multiplici, siquidem multa erat mirabilia narraturus.

who were ruled by him. By *to my law*—that is, to what I am about to say—he rightly refers to the law as teaching useful things, it being possible for him to legislate on two grounds, as king and as inspired author. *Incline your ears to the words of my mouth:* listen zealously to what I am saying. *I shall open my mouth in parables* (v. 2): that is, in narratives. He did well to speak of them in the plural, intending to recall many marvels. *I shall utter riddles from the beginning:* I shall recount ancient narratives. Where do you get knowledge of what you tell, if they are ancient and older than you? *The very things that we have heard and known* (v. 3): we learned what we heard from people telling us. *And our ancestors recounted to us:* what is said is therefore trustworthy if those telling them were our fathers, who could not bring themselves to lie to their children. *They were not hidden from their children in another generation, announcing the praises of the Lord, his powers and his marvels that he worked* (v. 4). The translation resulted in poor syntax, as in the line in Exodus, "This Moses, who brought us out of the land of Egypt, we do not | know what happened to him."[2] The meaning is, in fact, The doings of their children did not escape our attention, who belong to another generation

---

2. See Exod 32:1.

οἴδαμεν τί γέγονεν αὐτῷ. Τοῦτο γὰρ βούλεται εἰπεῖν, ὅτι οὐκ ἔλαθεν ἡμᾶς τὰ ἐκείνων τῶν τέκνων τοὺς τῆς ἑτέρας γενεᾶς (ἑτέρα γὰρ γενεὰ οἱ υἱεῖς πρὸς τοὺς πατέρας) διὰ τὸ ἐκείνους μετὰ πάσης τῆς σπουδῆς ἀπαγγέλλειν ἀεὶ τὰ ὑπὸ τοῦ Θεοῦ γενόμενα, καὶ τοὺς προσήκοντας αὐτῷ ὕμνους ἐπὶ
5 τούτῳ ἀποδιδόναι. Τί δὲ ἦν τὸ κατεπεῖγον ἐκείνους διηγεῖσθαι;

5ᵃ. Καὶ ἀνέστησεν μαρτύριον ἐν Ἰακώβ. Σύμμαχος Καὶ ἐνέστησεν διαμαρτυρίαν τῷ Ἰακώβ. Ἐπειδὴ ὁ Θεός φησι τοῦτο ποιεῖν αὐτοὺς διεμαρτύρατο.

5ᵇ. Καὶ νόμον ἔθετο ἐν Ἰσραήλ. Νόμον καὶ πρόσταγμα τοῦτο θέμενος
10 αὐτοῖς.

5ᶜ. Ὅσα ἐνετείλατο τοῖς πατράσιν ἡμῶν τοῦ γνωρίσαι αὐτὰ τοῖς υἱοῖς αὐτῶν. Ὥστε ὅσα ἔμαθον οὗτοι παρὰ τοῦ Θεοῦ, ὅσα τε ἔγνωσαν καὶ εἶδον, ταῦτα δῆλα καὶ τοῖς ἐξ αὐτῶν τῇ διηγήσει καταστῆσαι. Διὰ τί;

6ᵃ. Ὅπως ἂν γνῶ γενεὰ ἑτέρα, υἱοὶ οἱ τεχθησόμενοι. Ὥστε μὴ λαθεῖν
15 αὐτοὺς τὰ γενόμενα, ἀλλὰ κἀκείνους μαθόντας παρὰ τῶν πατέρων εἰδέναι.

6ᵇ. Καὶ ἀναστήσονται καὶ ἀπαγγελοῦσιν αὐτὰ τοῖς υἱοῖς αὐτῶν. Ὥστε πάλιν κἀκείνους τοῖς ἐξ αὐτῶν διηγεῖσθαι. Διὰ πάντων δὲ τοῦτο δείκνυσιν, ὅτι τε ἀναγκαῖον ἅπαντας πάντοτε διηγεῖσθαι ἀλλήλοις καὶ διδάσκειν τοὺς ἐξ αὐτῶν, ὥστε μένειν κατὰ διαδοχὴν ἐν μνήμῃ τοῦ γένους τὰ παρασχε-
20 θέντα αὐτοῖς παρὰ τοῦ Θεοῦ, καὶ αὐτὸς δικαίως τοῦτο ποιεῖν κατὰ νόμον Θεοῦ ὁμοῦ τε ὑπομιμνήσκων καὶ παιδεύων. Τίς δὲ ἡ αἰτία φησὶ δι᾽ ἣν ἐκέλευσε τοῦτο τοὺς πατέρας διηγεῖσθαι τοῖς τέκνοις ἐπὶ τὸ παραμεῖναι τὴν μνήμην;

2 τῶν om. PV   τοὺς] τὰ Cord.
5ᵃ. Σύμμαχος – διεμαρτύρατο: P, fol. 274; V, fol. 40; Paraphrasis (p. 608).
5ᵇ. Νόμον – αὐτοῖς: P, fol. 274; V, fol. 40; Paraphrasis (p 608).
5ᶜ. Ὥστε — διὰ τί: P, fol. 274 et V, fol. 40 (anon.); Paraphrasis (p. 609).
13 δῆλα om. Par   διὰ τί om. Par.
6ᵃ. Ὥστε — εἰδέναι: P, fol. 274; V, fol. 40; Vat. 1422, fol. 140 (anon.); Paraphrasis (p. 609).
6ᵇ. Ὥστε πάλιν — μνήμην: P, fol. 274; V, fol. 40; Cord, p. 634.   18 πάντοτε] τότε Cord   19-20 παρασχέντα Cord.

Aᵉ 3-4 (p. 393, 27-30): Ita quippe Moyses praeciperat, ut tali genere nos, qui eramus longe post geniti, mirabilium Dei scientiam caperemus.   5ᵃ (p. 394, 1-3): ... ut hoc facerent patres Dei contestantis uoce praeceptum erat.   5ᵇ (p. 394, 4-5): Legis id praecipit sanctione seruari.   5ᶜ (p. 394, 6-9): Quaecumque scilicet oculis, quaecumque auribus acciperant sedula interpraetatione posteris traderent.   6ᵃ (p. 394, 12-14): Vt tradant uidilicet minoribus quod ipsi a maioribus acciperant.

(children being a different generation from their fathers, after all), on account of their always reporting with utter zeal what was done by God, and offering the hymns due to him for it.

Now, what was of urgency for them to recount? *He raised up testimony in Jacob* (v. 5). Symmachus: "And introduced solemn testimony for Jacob." He is saying, Since God adjured them to do it. *And set a law in Israel:* setting them this law and commandment. *What he commanded to our fathers for making known to their children:* so that all they learned from God and all they knew and acknowledged they would make clear also to their offspring by recounting it. Why? *So that another generation might be aware, children to be born to them* (v. 6): so that the events might not be hidden from them, but rather they too should come to know them by learning them from their parents. *And they also will rise up and announce them to their children:* so that they in turn might also recount them to their offspring. In all this he brings out that it was necessary for them all always to recount it to one another and teach their offspring so that what was provided by God would by succession stay in the memory of the race, the author himself also duly remembering and teaching to do this in accord with God's law.

Now, what was the reason, he asks, why he bade the parents recount this to the children for the memory to continue? | *That they might place their hope in God:* so that on the basis of what they had already received

7ª. Ἵνα θῶνται ἐπὶ τὸν Θεὸν τὴν ἐλπίδα αὐτῶν. Ἵν᾽ ἀφ᾽ ὧν ἔλαβον ἤδη, ἀπ᾽ αὐτῶν καὶ περὶ τῶν μελλόντων ἐλπίζωσι.

7ᵇ. Καὶ μὴ ἐπιλάθωνται τῶν ἔργων τοῦ Θεοῦ. Καὶ μὴ λήθῃ τὰ ἤδη γενόμενα παραδῶσιν.

7ᶜ. Καὶ τὰς ἐντολὰς αὐτοῦ ἐκζητήσουσιν. Μεμνημένοι δὲ ὧν ἐποίησεν, 5 φροντίζωσιν ὡς προσέταξεν.

8ª. Ἵνα μὴ γένωνται ὡς οἱ πατέρες αὐτῶν. Καὶ φυλάξωνται ταῦτα, οἷς οἱ πατέρες αὐτῶν περιέπεσον.

8ᵇ. Γενεὰ σκολιὰ καὶ παραπικραίνουσα. Ἵνα μὴ τοιοῦτοι γένωνται οὕτω σκολιοὶ καὶ διεστραμμένοι καὶ παροξύνοντες τὸν Θεόν. Λέγει δὲ περὶ τῶν 10 ἐξελθόντων ἐξ Αἰγύπτου, ὧν οὐδεὶς ἠξιώθη εἰς τὴν γῆν τῆς ἐπαγγελίας εἰσελθεῖν, πάντων κατὰ τὴν ἔρημον διὰ τὴν οἰκείαν ἀπολομένων κακίαν. Τοιοῦτο δὲ καὶ ὁ ἀπόστολός φησι Μὴ πορνεύωμεν ὡς ἐκεῖνοι ἐπόρνευσαν, μηδὲ πειράσωμεν ὡς ἐπείρασαν, εἶτα ἑξῆς ταῦτα δὲ πάντα ὡς τύποι ἡμῶν συνέβαινον ἐκείνοις. πρὸς νουθεσίαν δὲ ἐγράφη ἡμῶν. 15

8ᶜ. Γενεὰ ἥτις οὐ κατεύθυνε τὴν καρδίαν ἑαυτῆς. Πρὸς τὸ Ἵνα μὴ γένωνται ἀπέδωκεν καὶ τοῦτο, τουτέστιν Ὅπως μὴ τοιοῦτοι γενώμεθα οἷοίπερ ἦσαν ἐκεῖνοι, οὐδὲν εὐθὲς οὐδὲ ὀρθὸν ἐπὶ τῆς οἰκείας ἔχοντες καρδίας, ἀλλ᾽ ἀεὶ διαφόρως στρεβλούμενοι τὴν διάνοιαν.

13-15 1 Cor. X, 8-11 pluribus omissis.

7ª. Ἵν᾽ ἀφ᾽ ὧν — ἐλπίζωσι: P, fol. 274; V, fol. 40; Vat. 1422, fol. 140 (anon.); Paraphrasis (p. 609).   2 καὶ om. PV.
7ᵇ. Καὶ μὴ — παραδῶσιν: P, fol 274; V. fol. 40; Vat. 1422, fol. 140 (anon.); Paraphrasis (p. 609).
7ᶜ. Μεμνημένοι — προσέταξεν: P, fol. 274; V, fol. 40; Vat. 1422, fol. 140 (anon.); Paraphrasis (p. 609).   6 φροντίζουσιν PV.
8ª. Καὶ φυλάξωνται — περιέπεσον: P, fol. 274; V, fol. 40; Paraphrasis (p. 609). 7 καὶ] ἀλλὰ Par.
8ᵇ. Ἵνα μὴ — ἡμῶν: P, fol. 274; V, fol. 40; Vat. 1422, fol. 140 (anon.); Cord, p. 635.   14 ὡς om. PV.
8ᶜ. Πρὸς τὸ — διάνοιαν: P, fol. 274ᵛ; V, fol. 40ᵛ; Vat. 1422, fol. 140 (anon.). 17-19 τουτέστιν — διάνοιαν affert Paraphrasis (p. 609).

Aᵉ 7ª (p. 394, 13-15): Vt praeteritorum exempla fiant magisteria futurorum. 7ᶜ (p. 394, 17-18): Dum memores sunt quae fecit, solliciti sunt ad cognoscenda quae eius sunt.   10-12 (p. 394, 26-28): De his dicit qui egressi sunt ex Aegipto, quorum nullus terram repromisionis ingresus est.

from them they might hope also in future goods. *And not forget the works of God:* and not consign to oblivion what had previously been done. *And they will seek out his commandments:* that mindful of what he had done, they might bring their thinking into line with his commands. *Lest they become like their ancestors* (v. 8): and take precautions against the failings of their ancestors. *A generation twisted and embittered:* lest they become similarly twisted and depraved, provoking God. He is referring to those leaving Egypt, none of whom were thought fit to enter the land of promise, all of them perishing in the desert because of their own vicious ways. The apostle also says the same thing, "Let us not be sexually depraved like them, or put him to the test as they did," and in what follows, "All this happened to them to serve as examples for us, and was written down to instruct us."[3] *A generation that did not direct its heart.* This corresponds to the words *Lest they become*—that is, Lest they become like those others were, with nothing honest and upright in their heart, with their mind always twisted in various directions. | *And its spirit was not fixed on God,* with spirit meaning "free will," as we showed also in Psalm 51 that by *spirit* he refers in many

---

3. Cf. 1 Cor 10:8–11.

8ᵈ. Καὶ οὐκ ἐπιστώθη μετὰ τοῦ Θεοῦ τὸ πνεῦμα αὐτῆς. Τὸ πνεῦμα, τουτέστιν ἡ προαίρεσις, — ἐδείξαμεν γὰρ καὶ ἐν τῷ ν´ ψαλμῷ ὅτι πολλαχοῦ τὴν προαίρεσιν πνεῦμα καλεῖ. Ἀκύλας Καὶ ἀβέβαιος πρὸς τὸν Θεὸν τῷ πνεύματι τῷ ἑαυτῆς, τουτέστιν Οὐκ ἔσχεν πίστιν καὶ βεβαίαν πρὸς τὸν Θεὸν τὴν
5 προαίρεσιν. Πρῶτον μὲν γὰρ μόσχον ποιήσαντες εἶπον Οὗτοι οἱ θεοί σου, Ἰσραήλ· εἶτα, τῶν κατασκόπων ἀποσταλέντων, ἐφιλονείκουν μὴ εἰσελθεῖν εἰς τὴν γῆν τῆς ἐπαγγελίας ὡς τοὺς κατέχοντας τότε διὰ τὴν ἰσχὺν δεδιότες. Καὶ πολλὰ ἄν τις εὕροι τῆς ἀπιστίας αὐτῶν ἐν ταῖς ἱστορίαις σύμβολα, ὡς ἂν μὴ νῦν αὐτὰ διὰ μακρωτέρων λέγωμεν. Εἶθ´ οὕτω καθεξῆς διηγεῖται οἵων μὲν
10 ἔτυχον, ὅπως δὲ ἠπείθησαν, διδάσκων αὐτοὺς μαθόντας οἷα ἔπαθον ἀπὸ τῆς ἀπειθίας μιμήσασθαι τὸν τρόπον ὡς ἂν μὴ κοινωνήσαιεν τῆς τιμωρίας.

9ᵃ. Υἱοὶ Ἐφραΐμ ἐντείνοντες καὶ βάλλοντες τόξοις. Ἀπὸ μέρους τὸ πᾶν εἰπεῖν ἠβουλήθη, — πολεμικώτατοι γάρ φησι καὶ ἰσχυροὶ κατὰ τῶν πολεμίων πολλάκις φανέντες τῇ τοῦ Θεοῦ δυνάμει.

15 9ᵇ. Ἐστράφησαν ἐν τῇ ἡμέρᾳ πολέμου Πολέμου καταλαμβάνοντος, πάντων ἐπιλανθανόμενοι ἐπὶ τὴν οἰκείαν ἐχώρουν ἀπιστίαν· ἀπαλλαγέντες μὲν γὰρ τῆς Αἰγύπτου παρὰ τὴν Ἐρυθρὰν ἐγόγγυξον θάλασσαν, ἀναχωρήσαντες δὲ κἀκεῖθεν περὶ τοῦ πολέμου τοῦ πρὸς τοὺς κατέχοντας τὴν Παλαιστίνην ἐγόγγυζον καὶ ἐμηχάνοντο, ὡς οὐ δυνάμενοι πρὸς αὐτούς. Δείκνυσι δὲ
20 διὰ πάντων ὅπως ἀβέβαιοι περὶ τὸν Θεὸν ἦσαν.

10ᵃ. Οὐκ ἐφύλαξαν τὴν διαθήκην τοῦ Θεοῦ. Ἀπέστησαν τῆς διαθήκης, ἣν πρὸς αὐτοὺς ὁ Θεὸς ἔθετο — λέγει δὲ τῆς ἐπ´ αὐτὸν πίστεως. Ἐξαγαγὼν γὰρ αὐτοὺς τῆς Αἰγύπτου ταύτην ἔθετο πρὸς αὐτοὺς διαθήκην, ὥστε

---

2 cf. in ps. L, 12ᵇ (p. 339)   5-6 Ex. XXXII, 4   6-7 cf. Deut. I, 28-33.

8ᵈ. Τὸ πνεῦμα — τιμωρίας: P, fol. 274ᵛ; V, fol. 40ᵛ; Cord, p. 635.   2 ψαλμῷ om. PV   6-7 εἰς τὴν γῆν τῆς ἐπαγγελίας om. PV   7 ὡς om. Cord   δεδιότας PV 11 ἀπειθίας des. Cord.
9ᵃ. Ἀπὸ μέρους — δυνάμει: P, fol. 274ᵛ; V, fol. 40ᵛ; Paraphrasis (p. 609). 13 πολεμιώτατοι PV.
9ᵇ. Πολέμου — ἦσαν: P, fol. 274ᵛ; V, fol. 41; Cord, p. 636.   19 ἐμάχοντο PV.
10ᵃ. Ἀπέστησαν — προστάξας: P, fol. 274ᵛ; V, fol. 41; Cord, p. 637.

Aᵉ 7-8 (p. 394, 29): Multiplex eorum pertinacia sacra contenetur historia. 9ᵃ (p. 394, 30-34): A parte, id est ab una tribu, totum agmen uoluit indicare. Cum essent, inquit, strennui ac bellorum periti, Deique inter hostes suos uirtute superiores, quid fecerunt?   9ᵇ (p. 344, 35-395, 6): Instante praelii necessitate, uelut obliti successorum prosperorum, susciperunt de propria infidelitate tripitationem; nam, cum educti fuissent de Aegipto ac per rubris maris litora consedissent, timorem instantis belli degenere mormore prodiderunt.

places to free will. Aquila: "Not firmly directed to God in its spirit"—in other words, It did not have its faith and free will firmly set on God. Firstly, remember, they made a calf and said, "These are your gods, Israel"; and then, when the spies were dispatched, they argued against entering the land of promise out of fear of the inhabitants of the time for their strength.[4] You could find many examples of their disobedience in the histories, so we shall not mention them at greater length here.

He then proceeds to recount the sorts of things that happened and how they showed disobedience, instructing them to portray their behavior so that, having learned from what they suffered for their disobedience, they might not share in their punishment. *Children of Ephraim aiming and firing arrows* (v. 9), implying the whole by mention of a part: Though often appearing bellicose and strong against the enemy with God's power, he is saying, *they were turned back on the day of battle:* when war caught up with them, they forgot everything and had recourse to their characteristic disobedience. After being freed from Egypt, in fact, they kept murmuring by the Red Sea, and on leaving there they kept murmuring and scheming in regard to fighting the occupants of Palestine, claiming that they were powerless before them.[5] In all this he shows that they lacked commitment to God. *They did not keep God's covenant* (v. 10): they forsook the covenant that God made with them (meaning faith in him); having led them out of Egypt, he made this covenant with them so that | they should know him to be God, pay deference to him, and be accorded providence by him. In fact, he appeared to them and spoke in these

---

4. Cf. Exod 32:1–4; Deut 1:21–33.
5. Cf. Exod 16–17; Num 14.

γνωρίζειν αὐτὸν Θεόν, καὶ τῆς περὶ αὐτὸν ἔχεσθαι θεραπείας, καὶ ἀξιοῦσθαι τῆς παρ᾽ αὐτοῦ προνοίας. Ὀφθεὶς γὰρ αὐτοῖς οὕτω φησὶν Ἐγώ εἰμι ὁ θεός, ὃς ἐξήγαγον ὑμᾶς ἐκ γῆς Αἰγύπτου, οὐ ποιήσετε θεοὺς ἑτέρους, οὐδὲ λατρεύσετε θεοῖς ἑτέροις, — τοῦτο παρ᾽ αὐτῶν αἰτήσας καὶ τοῦτο φυλάττειν αὐτοῖς προστάξας.   5

10ᵇ. Καὶ ἐν τῷ νόμῳ αὐτοῦ οὐκ ἐβουλήθησαν πορεύεσθαι. Τὸ αὐτὸ λέγει· νόμος γὰρ ἦν τοῦ Θεοῦ καὶ πρόσταγμα τὸ ἔχεσθαι αὐτοὺς μετὰ πάσης ἐπιμελείας τῆς αὐτοῦ γνώσεως.

11. Καὶ ἐπελάθοντο τῶν εὐεργεσιῶν αὐτοῦ, καὶ τῶν θαυμασίων αὐτοῦ ὧν ἔδειξεν αὐτοῖς. Πάντων ἐκείνων ἡμνημόνησαν ὧν ἔτυχον εὐεργετηθέντες, οὕτω   10 μεγάλων τε ὄντων καὶ θαυμαστῶν.

12ᵃ. Ἐναντίον τῶν πατέρων αὐτῶν ἃ ἐποίησε θαυμάσια. Τῶν πατέρων αὐτῶν λέγει, ἀντὶ τοῦ αὐτῶν ἐκείνων. Ἠκολούθησε δὲ αὐτῷ. Ἐπειδὴ γὰρ εἶπεν ἄνω Καὶ ἀναστήσονται καὶ ἀπαγγελοῦσιν αὐτὰ τοῖς υἱοῖς αὐτῶν, τουτέστι τοῖς καθεξῆς, ἵνα μὴ γένωνται ὡς οἱ πατέρες αὐτῶν, — ἀντὶ τοῦ   15 μὴ αὐτοὶ ἐκείνοις ὅμοιοι γενώμεθα, ὁποῖοί τε ἦσαν ἐκεῖνοι εἰρηκὼς ἐν μέσῳ καὶ πλατύτερον αὐτῶν τὴν ἀγνωμοσύνην, ἐπήγαγεν λοιπὸν οἵων ἀξιωθέντες, οἷοι ἦσαν, — ἀκολούθως ἑαυτῷ νῦν ἐπήγαγεν τὸ Ἐναντίον τῶν πατέρων αὐτῶν ἃ ἐποίησεν θαυμάσια, ἀντὶ τοῦ Καίτοι ὑπ᾽ ὀφθαλμοῖς τοῖς αὐτῶν μεγάλα τοῦ Θεοῦ θαύματα πεποιηκότος. Τὸ οὖν τῶν πατέρων αὐτῶν, ἀντὶ τοῦ τῶν   20 πατέρων ἡμῶν, καθ᾽ ὁμοιότητα τοῦ ἵνα μὴ γένωνται ὡς οἱ πατέρες αὐτῶν, τουτέστιν ἵνα μὴ γενώμεθα ὅμοιοι τοῖς πατράσιν ἡμῶν, ὧν γέγονε μὲν ἐναντίον τὰ θαύματα, ἔμενον δὲ ἀπιστοῦντες ὁμοίως.

12ᵇ. Ἐν γῇ Αἰγύπτῳ, ἐν πεδίῳ Τάνεως. Τὸν τόπον εἶπεν ἐν ᾧ τὰ θαύματα ἐγένετο, ἔνθα καὶ τὸν Φαραὼ διάγειν συνέβαινεν.   25

2-3 Ex. XX, 2   14 v. 6ᵇ   15 v. 8ᵃ.

10ᵇ. Τὸ αὐτὸ — γνώσεως: P, fol. 275; V, fol. 41; Paraphrasis (p. 609).
11. Πάντων — θαυμαστῶν: P, fol. 275; V, fol. 41; Paraphrasis (p. 610).
12ᵃ. Τῶν πατέρων — ὁμοίως: P, fol. 275; V, fol 41; Cord, p. 637.   19 ἃ om.
PV   22 ὅμοιοι om. PV.
12ᵇ. Τὸν τόπον — συνέβαινεν: P, fol. 275; V, fol. 41ᵛ; Paraphrasis (p. 610).

Aᵉ 3-4 (p. 395, 7): Ne umquam alium deum crederent.   10ᵇ (p. 395, 11):
Vt permanerent in agnitione diuina.   11 (p. 395, 14-16): ... certauerunt, ut tantorum operum memoria ingratorum selentio deperiret.   20-23 (p. 395, 17-21):
Id est, coram patribus nostris, ut uel recentia nos ab emitatione exempla deducant, neque emulamur eos ante quorum oculos facta mirabilia nihil de infidilitatis uitio depullerunt.   12ᵇ (p. 395, 22-24): Id est urbis, quam habitabat Farao, in qua ea quae referuntur miraculo contigerunt.

terms: "I am God, who brought you out of the land of Egypt"; you will not have other gods or worship other gods[6]—making this request of them and commanding them to observe it. *And refused to walk in his law.* He says the same thing: God's law and commandment meant their giving total attention to knowing him.

They forgot his kindnesses and the marvels he had shown them (v. 11): they were unmindful of all they had received as favors from him, despite their being so great and marvelous. *Marvels that he worked in the sight of their ancestors* (v. 12). By *their ancestors* he means "those same people." This is in keeping with his thought. He had said above *They also will rise up and announce them to their children* (that is, to those coming after them), *lest they become like their ancestors* (that is, lest they themselves resemble them), and had described in the middle the kind of people they were, and at greater length their ingratitude. So he continued his train of thought, considering what they deserved and who they were, by proceeding here with *marvels that he worked in the sight of their ancestors,* meaning, despite his working great marvels under their very eyes. Hence *their ancestors* has the sense "our ancestors," in keeping with *lest they become like their ancestors*—that is, lest we become like our ancestors, in whose sight the marvels were worked but who likewise continued to be unbelieving.

In the land of Egypt, in the field of Tanis. He mentioned the place where the wonders were worked, where in fact Pharaoh lived as well. | *He parted the sea and led them through* (v. 13): not only this, but as well he divided

---

6. Cf. Exod 20:2–3.

13ᵃ. Διέρρηξε θάλασσαν καὶ διήγαγεν αὐτούς. Καὶ οὐ τοῦτο μόνον φησίν, ἀλλὰ καὶ θάλασσαν διελὼν ἅπαντας διεβίβασεν.

13ᵇ. Παρέστησεν ὕδατα ὡσεὶ ἀσκόν. Καιριώτατον τὸ ὑπόδειγμα· ἐπειδὴ γὰρ ὀλισθηρὰ τῶν ὑδάτων ἡ φύσις, ἐν ἀσκῷ δὲ συσχεθέντα ἐκ πάσης ἀνάγ-
5 κης κατέχεται, οὐδαμοῦ διαρρεῖν δυνάμενα, οὕτω φησὶν αὐτὰ συνεῖχες τῷ προστάγματι τῷ σῷ ὥστε εἶναι κατεχόμενα ὡς ἐν ἀσκῷ, μὴ διολισθαίνοντα μηδὲ διαρρέοντα μηδὲ ἐπιφερόμενα καὶ καλύπτοντα τὴν γῆν.

14. Καὶ ὡδήγησεν αὐτοὺς ἐν νεφέλῃ ἡμέρας, καὶ ὅλην τὴν νύκτα ἐν φωτισμῷ πυρός. Ἄγων τε αὐτοὺς κατὰ τὴν ἔρημον, ἐν μὲν τῷ τῆς ἡμέρας
10 καιρῷ ἐπισκιάζων αὐτοὺς τῇ νεφέλῃ ψυχραῖς ἀπὸ τοῦ καύσωνος παρεμυ-θεῖτο ταῖς αὔραις, οὐδὲ φέρεσθαι τὴν ἀκτῖνα συγχωρῶν ἐπ' αὐτούς, — ἐν δὲ τῇ νυκτὶ ἀδιαλείπτῳ τῷ πυρὶ φωτεινὸν αὐτοῖς τὸν καιρὸν τοῦ σκότους εἰργάζετο· οὕτως ἑκάστου καιροῦ τὸ βλαβερὸν ἀπεκώλυεν.

15. Διέρρηξε πέτραν ἐν ἐρήμῳ καὶ ἐπότισεν αὐτοὺς ὡς ἐν ἀβύσσῳ πολλῇ.
15 Ἐν ἐρήμῳ διελὼν πέτραν οὕτως αὐτοῖς δαψιλὲς παρέσχετο ποτὸν ὡσανεὶ ὅλης ἀβύσσου παρακειμένης. Βούλεται δὲ εἰπεῖν ὅτι δαψιλὲς ὑπὲρ τὴν χρείαν αὐτοῖς τὸ ποτὸν τοῦ ὕδατος παρέσχεν. Πῶς δὲ τοῦτο ἐγένετο;

16. Καὶ ἐξήγαγεν ὕδωρ ἐκ πέτρας, καὶ κατήγαγεν ὡς ποταμοὺς ὕδατα. Ὅτι μὴ ἁπλῶς προχυθῆναι ὕδωρ βραχύ τι παρεσκεύασας, ἀλλ' ἐκ πολλῶν
20 μερῶν ῥεῖθρά τε ἀνεδίδους καὶ ποταμοὺς ἀπετέλεις πολλούς, ἐξ ὧν οὐ μόνον αὐτοῖς ἡ χρεία περιεγίγνετο ἀλλὰ καὶ ὑπὲρ τὴν χρείαν ἦν ἡ δαψιλία.

3-7 cf. supra in ps. XXXII, 7 (p. 149-150) atque Theodoretus (1488 B).

13ᵃ. Καὶ οὐ τοῦτο — διεβίβασεν: P, fol. 275; V, fol. 41; Vat. 1422, fol. 140ᵛ sub lemmate Ἀθ(ανασίου?) [P. G., XXVII, 353 A 12-14]; Paraphrasis (p. 610).
13ᵇ. Καιριώτατον — τὴν γῆν: P, fol. 275; V, fol. 41ᵛ; Vat. 1422, fol. 140ᵛ-141 (anon.).
14. Ἄγων — ἀπεκώλυεν: P, fol. 275ᵛ; V, fol. 41ᵛ; Vat. 1422, fol. 141; Cord, p. 638.
15. Ἐν ἐρήμῳ — ἐγένετο: P, fol. 275ᵛ; V, fol. 41ᵛ. 16-17 βούλεται — αὐτοῖς affert Paraphrasis (p. 610) ὅτι ἐν ἐρήμῳ δαψιλὲς καὶ Par.
16. Ὅτι μὴ ἁπλῶς — δαψιλία: P, fol. 275ᵛ; V, fol. 42. 19 προχεθῆναι PV.

Aᵉ 13ᵃ (p. 395, 26-28):... accessit etiam hoc, quod transitum eis aquae maris diuisae ac seperatae longius praebuerunt. 13ᵇ (p. 395, 29-35): Diuisarum aqua-rum stationem atque inmobilitatem satis congrua conparatione signauit, quod ita natura fluentis elimenti standi necessitate passa sit, ut fluere nòn sinitur cum uteris inclusione retenetur. 14 (p. 395, 36-396, 1): Quae etiam inumbraret eos et regeret... qui lumine tenebrarum densa disrumperet. 16-17 (p. 396, 2-4): Gemina signi admiratio, quod et petra scinditur et copia fluentis abissi instar erumpit.

the sea and conducted them all through. *He pushed waters aside like a wine bottle.* The figure is most apposite: since water is naturally liquid, and is collected and held in a wine bottle without choice, quite incapable of escaping, so by your command you collected it so that it was held fast as if in a wine bottle, not moving or escaping or flowing and covering the earth. *He guided them with a cloud by day, and with a light of fire all through the night* (v. 14): leading them in the desert, he overshadowed them in the daytime with a cloud and thus gave them relief from the heat with cool breezes, not letting the sun's rays touch them, while by night he provided them with a light from unfailing fire in time of darkness. Thus he headed off any harm at either time. *He split rock in the wilderness, and gave them to drink as if from a great depth* (v. 15): but cutting open a rock in the wilderness, he provided them with such a generous drink as if from deep waters nearby. He means, He provided them with a generous drink of water beyond their needs. How did this happen? *He made water gush from rock, and brought down waters like rivers* (v. 16): because you did not simply cause water to flow to some extent; you supplied streams from many parts and produced many rivers, from which not only were our needs met, but also the supply exceeded our needs. |

17ᵃ. Καὶ προσέθεντο ἔτι τοῦ ἁμαρτάνειν αὐτῷ. Ἀλλ᾽ ὅμως τούτων γενομένων τοῦ πταίειν οὐκ ἀφίσταντο.

17ᵇ. Παρεπίκραναν τὸν ὕψιστον ἐν ἀνύδρῳ. Καὶ παρεπίκραναν τὸν ὕψιστον· βραχὺ γὰρ αὐτοῖς ἐλλείψαντος τοῦ ὕδατος ἐγόγγυζον κατὰ τοῦ Θεοῦ τὴν ἔνδειαν ὀνειδίζοντες.　　　　　　　　　　　　　　　　　　　　　5

18. Καὶ ἐξεπείρασαν τὸν Θεὸν ἐν ταῖς καρδίαις αὐτῶν, τοῦ αἰτῆσαι βρώματα ταῖς ψυχαῖς αὐτῶν. Ἔτι φησὶ καὶ πεῖραν προσῆγον τῷ Θεῷ τροφὴν τὴν οὐ δοθεῖσαν αἰτοῦντες· σαφέστερον δὲ αὐτὸ λέγει ἑξῆς.

19-20. Καὶ κατελάλησαν τοῦ Θεοῦ καὶ εἶπον Μὴ δυνήσεται ὁ Θεὸς ἑτοιμάσαι τράπεζαν ἐν ἐρήμῳ; Ἐπεὶ ἐπάταξεν πέτραν, καὶ ἐρρύησαν ὕδατα, καὶ 10
χείμαρροι κατεκλύσθησαν, μὴ καὶ ἄρτον δύναται δοῦναι, ἢ ἑτοιμάσαι τράπεζαν τῷ λαῷ αὐτοῦ; Ταῦτα αἰτοῦντες τὰ βρώματα, τὸν Θεὸν αὐτοὺς πειράσαι φησίν. Ἔλεγον γὰρ Ἰδοὺ πέτρα ἐρράγη, καὶ ὕδατα ἐδόθη, καὶ πλεῖστα ῥεύματα ἠνέχθη παρὰ πᾶσαν προσδοκίαν· ἄρτον εἴπερ δύναται, τίνος ἕνεκεν οὐ δίδωσιν; διὰ τί δὲ καὶ τράπεζαν ἡμῖν οὐκ εὐτρεπίζει, — 15
ἵνα εἴπῃ Πάντα ὅσα ἐσθίειν ἔθος ἀνθρώποις καὶ οἷς τράπεζα κοσμεῖται, — ἀλλὰ μόνον ἡμῖν τὸ μάννα δίδωσι; (τὸ γὰρ τράπεζαν Ἀκύλας καὶ Σύμμαχος κρέα ἡρμήνευσαν). Οὕτω γὰρ καὶ φαίνονται τοῦτο ὀνειδίσαντες τῷ Θεῷ, ὅτι μόνου τοῦ μάννα μετελάμβανον, ὅπερ ἦν τῶν καὶ τὰ λοιπὰ ζητούντων οἷς ἔθος ἀνθρώποις ἑστιᾶσθαι.　　　　　　　　　　　　　　　　20

17ⁱ. Ἀλλ᾽ ὅμως — ἀφίσταντο: P, fol. 275ᵛ; V, fol. 42; Paraphrasis (p. 610)
17ᵇ. Καὶ παρεπίκραναν — ὀνειδίζοντες: P, fol. 275ᵛ; V, fol. 42; Vat. 1422, fol. 141 (anon.).　　4-5 βραχὺ — ὀνειδίζοντες affert Paraphrasis (p. 610).　　4 αὐτοὺς ἐκλείψαντος 1422.
18. Ἔτι — ἑξῆς: P, fol. 275ᵛ; V, fol. 42; Paraphrasis (p. 610).　　8 αὐτὸ] ταῦτα Par.
19-20. Ταῦτα — ἑστιᾶσθαι: P, fol. 276; V, fol. 42ʳ·ᵛ.　　15-17 διὰ τί — δίδωσι affert Paraphrasis (p. 611)　　15 δὲ] φησι Par.　　16 ἵνα εἴπῃ — καὶ] καὶ ἄρτον καὶ κρέατα Par.

Aᵉ　17ᵃ (p. 396, 6-8): Et grande peccati studium, quod nec tantis miraculis impeditum (impet- ms) est.　17ᵇ (p. 396, 9-15): Ob perfunctoriam paruamque mormurantes sitim, paruum aquae sustinentes difectum deformi mormurationis querella inopiam suam ad Dei contumiliam contullerunt.　18 (p. 396, 16-21): In hoc capere uoluerunt experimentum uirtutis diuinae, si talem cibum ab eo, cuius prius ussum non habuerunt, postularent; quod quidem dicit manifestius in sequenti.　12-16 (p. 396, 23-25): Hoc enim uidentur exprobrare de Deo, cum de mannae cibo solitario conquiruntur.　18-20 (p. 396, 26-28):... mormurare de inopia, cum superesset manna.

They piled sin on sin against him (v. 17): nevertheless, despite these events they did not stop sinning. *They provoked the Most High in a waterless place;* and *they provoked the Most High:* when they were short of water for a time, they began to complain against God, taunting him with the shortage. *They tested God in their hearts to request food for their souls* (v. 18): they still put God to the test by asking for food that was not given. In what follows he says the same thing more clearly. *They spoke against God and said, Surely God will not be able to lay a table in the wilderness, will he? He struck rock there, and water flowed and torrents poured: surely he also will not be able to give bread or lay a table for his people, will he?* (vv. 19–20). He says that they put God to the test by asking for this food, saying, Lo, rock was split, water was given, and streams gushed forth in quantities exceeding all expectation; if he can supply bread, why does he not do so? Why does he not also lay a table for us (that is, with all that people normally eat and that normally furnishes a table)? Why does he give us only the manna instead? (Aquila and Symmachus rendered *table* as "meat.") That, in fact, is the way they gave the impression of taunting God with this, that he gave them only manna, which they had when they were looking also for other things that people normally eat. |

21ᵃ. Διὰ τοῦτο ἤκουσε Κύριος καὶ ἀνεβάλετο. Ταύτην αὐτῶν ὁρῶν τὴν ἀπιστίαν ὑπερέθετο τὰ κατ' αὐτούς· δυνατὸν γὰρ αὐτῷ συντόμως εἰσαγαγεῖν, τοῦτο μὲν οὐκ ἐποίησεν, ἐπὶ τοσοῦτον δὲ κατέσχεν τῷ χρόνῳ ἄχρις οὗ πάντες διαφόρως περιπεσόντες ταῖς τιμωρίαις ἀπώλοντο.

5 21ᵇ. Καὶ πῦρ ἀνήφθη ἐν Ἰακώβ. Εἶδος εἶπεν τιμωρίας ᾧ περιέπεσον· καὶ γὰρ· ἀνηλώθησαν πλεῖστοι πυρὶ διὰ τὸ γογγύσαι.

21ᶜ. Καὶ ὀργὴ ἀνέβη ἐπὶ τὸν Ἰσραήλ. Ὠργίσθη γὰρ κατ' αὐτῶν ὁ δεσπότης.

22ᵃ. Ὅτι οὐκ ἐπίστευσαν ἐν τῷ Θεῷ. Ἐπειδὴ ἑώρα αὐτοὺς οὐδέποτε 10 πιστὴν ἔχοντας περὶ αὐτὸν τὴν γνώμην, ἀλλ᾽ ἀεὶ ἐπὶ μὲν τοῖς δοθεῖσιν ἀχαριστοῦντας, περὶ δὲ τῶν μὴ δοθέντων ἀμφιβάλλοντας.

22ᵇ. Οὐδὲ ἤλπισαν ἐπὶ τὸ σωτήριον αὐτοῦ. Δέον ἀφ᾽ ὧν ἔλαβον ἐλπίζειν ὅτι πᾶν ὅ τι καλὸν καὶ σωτηριῶδες αὐτοῖς παρέξει.

23ᵃ. Καὶ ἐνετείλατο νεφέλαις ὑπεράνωθεν. Καὶ γὰρ οὐ μικρά φησιν ἦν 15 τὰ παρὰ τοῦ Θεοῦ γενόμενα, ἀφ᾽ ὧν αὐτάρκως ἠδύναντο πρὸς τὴν πίστιν χειραγωγεῖσθαι· διαφόρως γὰρ ποτὲ μὲν αὐτῶν τὴν ἀπιστίαν λέγει, ποτὲ δὲ τοῦ Θεοῦ τὰ θαύματα, δεικνὺς οἵων μὲν ἔτυχον, οἷοι δὲ περὶ τὸν Θεὸν γεγόνασιν, τοῦτον ἔχων ἄνωθεν σκοπὸν καὶ δι᾽ ὅλων τούτους παιδεύειν ἐσπουδακὼς μὴ τοιούτους εἶναι, ἀλλ᾽ εὐχαρίστους ὑπὲρ ὧν ἔλαβον.

21ᵃ. Ταύτην — ἀπώλοντο: P, fol. 276; V, fol. 42ᵛ; Vat. 1422, fol. 141ᵛ; Cord, p. 638-639. 2 γὰρ ἂν 1422 Cord 3 χρόνῳ] θρόνῳ 1422.

21ᵇ. Εἶδος — γογγύσαι: P, fol. 276; V, fol. 42ᵛ; Vat. 1422, fol. 141ᵛ (anon.); Paraphrasis (p. 611).

21ᶜ. Ὠργίσθη — δεσπότης: P, fol. 276; V, fol. 42ᵛ; Cord, p. 639 sub nomine Hesychii.

22ᵃ. Ἐπειδὴ — ἀμφιβάλλοντας: P, fol. 276; V, fol. 42ᵛ; Cord, p. 639 sub nomine Hesychii. 10 ἐπὶ om. Cord 11 τῶν om. Cord.

22ᵇ. Δέον — παρέξει: P, fol. 276; V, fol. 42ᵛ; Vat. 1422, fol. 141ᵛ (anon.); Paraphrasis (p. 611). 12 δέον δὲ Par 13 πᾶν ὅ τι] ὅ τι om. Par.

23ᵃ. Καὶ γὰρ — ἔλαβον: P, fol. 276; V, fol. 42ᵛ; Cord, p. 639. 16 χειραγωγηθῆναι Cord 17 τοῦ Θεοῦ om. Cord.

Aᵉ 21ᵇ (p. 397, 7-12): Vnam de multis speciem subplici, qua finiti sunt, indicauit; nam propter mormurationis offensam in multis est flammis atque incendio uindicatum. 22ᵃ (p. 397, 13-18): Malum incredulitatis eorum iustam in se Dei iracondiam concitauit... et praeteritis pristinis (uel pristitis add. in marg.) ingrati, et de futuris dubii.

Hence, the Lord heard and tarried (v. 21): on seeing this unbelief of theirs, he delayed the lot in store for them—that is to say, he could have brought them in promptly, but instead of doing so, he held them in check until they all fell foul of various punishments and perished. *Fire was kindled toward Jacob.* He mentioned one form of punishment that they encountered: a great number were consumed by fire for murmuring. *And anger arose against Israel:* the Lord became angry with them. *Because they did not believe in God* (v. 22): since he saw them never having an attitude of belief toward him, and instead being ever ungrateful for what was given and lacking confidence in what was not given. *Nor did they hope in his salvation:* on the basis of what they received they should have hoped that he would supply them with everything good and salutary.

He gave directions to clouds from above (v. 23): they were no slight marvels worked by God, and on that basis they had sufficient reason to be led to faith. In different ways, in fact, he mentions their unbelief at one time, and at another God's marvels, bringing out all they received and what their attitude was toward God, this being his purpose from the beginning in his anxiety to instruct them in general not to be like that, but to be grateful for what they received. | *And he opened heaven's doors.* He presented everything in figu-

23ᵇ. Καὶ θύρας οὐρανοῦ ἀνέῳξεν. Ἐσχημάτισεν τὸ πᾶν. Ἐπειδὴ παρ᾽ ἡμῖν ἔθος ἐστὶ τὰ ταμεῖα ἀνοιγνύναι, οὕτω τε προκομίζειν ὅτου ποτ᾽ ἂν ᾖ χρεία, ὥσπερ οὖν ταμείου φησὶ θύρας ἀνέῳξεν. Οὐρανοῦ δὲ λέγει, οὐκ αὐτοῦ τοῦ οὐρανοῦ, ἀλλὰ τοῦ ὑπὲρ ἡμᾶς τόπου, ὡς ὅταν λέγῃ καὶ τὰ πετεινὰ τοῦ οὐρανοῦ· ἐπειδὴ γὰρ ὑπὲρ ἡμᾶς ὁ οὐρανός, τὸν ὑπὲρ ἡμᾶς   5
τόπον πολλαχοῦ οὐρανὸν καλεῖ, ὡς αὐτῷ μᾶλλον προσήκοντα.

24ᵃ. Καὶ ἔβρεξεν αὐτοῖς μάννα φαγεῖν. Καὶ οὕτω φησὶ διὰ τῶν νεφελῶν οὐ κατὰ τὴν συνήθειαν ὕδατος ὑετόν, ἀλλὰ τοῦ μάννα τροφὴν παρὰ φύσιν ἄφθονον αὐτοῖς ἐχορήγει.

24ᵇ. Καὶ ἄρτον οὐρανοῦ ἔδωκεν αὐτοῖς. Ἄνωθεν αὐτοῖς καταπέμπων ἐδί- 10
δου τροφήν. Μέγα δὲ ἦν καὶ παράδοξον τὸ πάντων ἀνθρώπων ἀπὸ τῆς γῆς τοὺς καρποὺς καὶ τὴν τροφὴν δεχομένων, ἐκείνους ἄνωθεν αὐτόματον πεμπομένην δέχεσθαι τὴν τροφήν.

25ᵃ. Ἄρτον ἀγγέλων ἔφαγεν ἄνθρωπος. Οὐχ ὃν ἄγγελοι ἤσθιον, ἀλλ᾽ οὗ πρὸς τὴν καταγωγὴν ἄγγελοι διηκόνουν, — ὥσπερ καὶ τὸ ἄρτον οὐρανοῦ, 15
οὐχ ὃν ὁ οὐρανὸς ἤσθιεν, ἀλλ᾽ ὁ ἐκεῖθεν καταφερόμενος. Καλῶς δὲ ἀπὸ συγκρίσεως ἔδειξε τὴν διαφοράν, ἣν πρὸς τὸν ἄρτον εἶχεν τὸν συνήθη· ὁ μὲν γὰρ ἀπὸ γῆς δίδοται, ὁ δὲ ἀπ᾽ οὐρανῶν ἐφέρετο, καὶ ὁ μὲν ὑπηρεσίᾳ ἀνθρώπων πεττόμενος κατεσκευάζετο, ὁ δὲ διὰ τῶν ἀγγέλων ἐφέρετο.   20

4-5 Ps. XLIX, 11.

23ᵇ. Ἐσχημάτισεν — προσήκοντα : P, fol. 276; V, fol. 42ᵛ ; Cord, p. 639.
24ᵃ. Καὶ οὕτω — ἐχορήγει : P, fol. 276ᵛ ; V, fol. 43; *Paraphrasis* (p. 611).
24ᵇ. Ἄνωθεν — τροφήν : P, fol. 276ᵛ ; V, fol. 43; Cord, p. 640.
25ᵃ. Οὐχ ὃν — ἐφέρετο : P, fol. 276ᵛ ; V, fol. 43; Vat. 1422, fol. 142; Vat. 2057, fol. 159ᵛ-160 *et* Barb. 340, fol. 233 *sub nomine* THEODORI HERACLEENSIS ; Cord, p. 640.   15 οἱ ἄγγ. Cord   16 φερόμενος 1422   17 ἄρτον om. 1422.

Aᵉ 1-3 (p. 397, 20-26): A similitudine nostra scema petitum conpossuit ; siquidem nobis moris est, cum aliquid large in ussum proferre uolumus, resserrare horrea dicimur.   24ᵃ⁻ᵇ (p. 397, 27-33): Instar pluiae fluxit mannae copia ; miro nouoque more non terrae produxerunt fructus, quibus populus uesceretur, sed in apparatum aepulationum caeli ministeria festinauerunt.   25ᵃ (p. 397, 34-398, 4): Non quo uescerentur, sed quem angeli detulerunt, sicut et illud dicitur *Panem caeli dedit eis* non quem caelum manducaret, sed quo de caelo ministratus sit.

rative fashion: since it our custom to open up storehouses and thus to meet needs of any kind, so here he says that God *opened doors* of a storehouse. He says *heaven's* not of heaven itself but of the place above us, as when he says also "the birds of heaven";[7] since heaven is above us, by "heaven" he refers at many points to the place above us, as a more appropriate name for it. *He rained on them manna to eat* (v. 24): in this way he supplied through the clouds not the normal showers of rain but, in defiance of nature, manna as a food in abundance for them. *And he gave them bread of heaven:* he gave them food by sending it down from above. It was marvelous and unheard of that whereas all people receive crops and food from the earth, they received food sent from above without their effort. *A human being ate bread of angels* (v. 25): not what angels ate, but of what they were ministers in bringing it down, just as the *bread of heaven,* too, is not what heaven ate but what was brought down from there. He did well to bring out the difference from ordinary bread by a comparison: one comes from earth, the other was brought from heaven; one is prepared through the ministry of human beings by being cooked, the other was brought by means of angels. | *He sent them provisions*

---

7. Ps 50:11.

25ᵇ. Ἐπισιτισμὸν ἀπέστειλεν αὐτοὺς εἰς πλησμονήν. Ἐπισιτίσασθαι λέγεται τὸν μέλλοντα ὁδοιπορεῖν τὴν τροφὴν ἀποκομίσασθαι. Τοῦτο οὖν λέγει ὅτι μετὰ πολλῆς τῆς περιουσίας προευτρέπιζεν αὐτοῖς καὶ προαπετίθετο τὴν τροφήν.

5   26. Ἀπῆρεν νότον ἐξ οὐρανοῦ, καὶ ἐπήγαγεν ἐν τῇ δυνάμει αὐτοῦ λίβα. Τὸ αὐτὸ λέγει λίβα καὶ νότον· ὁ γὰρ αὐτός ἐστιν ἄνεμος βραχύ τι πλαγιάζων. Τινὲς δὲ λίβα τὸν ζέφυρον λέγουσιν, ἔστι δὲ σφόδρα ἀπᾷδον· ὑετοὺς μὲν γὰρ ὁ ζέφυρος οὐ ποιεῖ, ὁ δὲ λεγόμενος παρ᾽ αὐτοῖς λὶψ ποιεῖ ὅπερ ἴδιόν ἐστι τοῦ νότου.

10   27. Καὶ ἔβρεξεν ἐπ᾽ αὐτοὺς ὡσεὶ χνοῦν σάρκας, καὶ ὡσεὶ ἄμμον θαλασσῶν πετεινὰ πτερωτά. Ἐπήγαγέν τε αὐτοῖς πλῆθος πετεινῶν, δίκην ἄμμου σωρεύσας αὐτοῖς τὰ πετεινά, οὕτως ἦν παμπληθῆ.

28. Καὶ ἐπέπεσεν εἰς μέσον τῆς παρεμβολῆς αὐτῶν, κύκλῳ τῶν σκηνωμάτων αὐτῶν. Μονονουχὶ πρὸ τῶν θυρῶν αὐτοῖς ἠνέχθη τὰ ὄρνεα· τοῦτο
15 γὰρ θαυμαστὸν ὅτι μηδὲ καμάτου αὐτοῖς ἔδει πρὸς τὴν σύλληψιν.

29ᵃ. Καὶ ἔφαγον καὶ ἐνεπλήσθησαν σφόδρα Καὶ ἀπήλαυσαν ὑπὲρ ὃ ἔδει.

29ᵇ. Καὶ τὴν ἐπιθυμίαν αὐτῶν ἤνεγκεν αὐτοῖς. Καλῶς τὸ ἤνεγκεν αὐτοῖς· ἀπεκόμισέν φησιν ἃ ἐπεθύμησαν, μονονουχὶ καὶ τὰ ὑπὲρ τῆς αὐτῶν χρείας ἥδιστα ἐνδεικνύμενος.

25ᵇ. Ἐπισιτίσασθαι — τροφήν: P, fol. 276ᵛ; V, fol. 43; Vat. 1422, fol. 142 (anon.). 1-2 λέγεσθαι 1422   2 τὸ μέλλον τὰ PV   3 προαπετίθη 1422.
26. Τὸ αὐτὸ — νότου: P, fol. 276ᵛ; V, fol. 43;   6 τὸ αὐτὸ — ἄνεμος praebet Paraphrasis (p. 611).
27. Ἐπήγαγεν — παμπληθῆ: P, fol. 276ᵛ; V, fol. 43; Vat. 1422, fol. 142 (anon.); Paraphrasis (p. 611-612).
28. Μονονουχὶ — σύλληψιν: P, fol. 276ᵛ; V, fol. 43; Paraphrasis (p. 612).
29ᵃ. Καὶ ἀπήλαυσαν ὑπὲρ ὃ ἔδει: P, fol. 276ᵛ; V, fol. 43; Paraphrasis (p. 612).
29ᵇ. Καλῶς — ἐνδεικνύμενος: P, fol. 276ᵛ: V, fol. 43ᵛ; Paraphrasis (p. 612).

Aᵉ 2-4 (p. 398, 6-9): Hoc ita ait, quod tantas eis in herimo copias ministrauerit quae possint uictui eorum uoluntatique sufficere.   27 (p. 398, 15-17):… auium, id est cuturnicum, quae eis in escam datae sunt, multitu⟨di⟩nes indicauit.   14-15 (p. 398, 18-22): Ad quantitatem copiarum accessit etiam hoc, ut cadentibus ante tabernacula auibus, in capiendo nihil laboris, nihil molestiae sustinerent.   29ᵃ (p. 398, 24-25): … usque ad crapulam sunt repleti.   29ᵇ (p. 398, 26-28): Omnia ad quae eos concupiscentiae flamma rapiebat sunt eorum uoluntatibus repleta.

in abundance. By a supply of *provisions,* the person about to go on a journey is said to be provided with food. So this means, In great abundance he prepared them in advance and laid up food.

He took the south wind from heaven, and brought on the African in his power (v. 26). *African* and *south* mean the same thing: the same wind comes in at an angle. Now, some people call the west wind *African,* but that is quite wrong: the west wind does not bring rain, whereas what is called "African" by them brings what normally comes from the south.[8] *He rained flesh on them like dust, and winged birds like sand of the sea* (v. 27): he brought upon them a multitude of birds, heaping birds upon them like sand, so numerous were they. *They fell in the middle of their camp around their dwellings* (v. 28): the birds were brought for them as if at their doorstep, the marvel being that no effort was required on their part to catch them. *They ate and were completely satisfied* (v. 29): they had all they needed. *He met their desires. Met* was well put: he provided what they desired (as if to bring out that it was far more palatable than they needed). | *They were not disap-*

---

8. Theodore disputes the identification of the southwest wind, λίψ (from λείβειν, "to bring rain"; Latin: *Africus*), with the west wind, ζέφυρος, due south being the direction of rain-bearing winds.

30ᵃ. Οὐκ ἐστερήθησαν ἀπὸ τῆς ἐπιθυμίας αὐτῶν. Ὧν γοῦν ἐπεθύμουν οὐκ ἀπέτυχον.

30ᵇ-31ᵃ. Ἔτι τῆς βρώσεως οὔσης ἐν τῷ στόματι αὐτῶν, καὶ ὀργὴ τοῦ Θεοῦ ἀνέβη ἐπ' αὐτούς. Ἀπὸ τῆς τοῦ Θεοῦ ὀργῆς τὸ πταῖσμα τὸ ἐκείνων εἶπεν, ὡς οὐκ ἂν τοῦ Θεοῦ ὀργισθέντος εἰ μὴ παρέσχον τὴν αἰτίαν, ὁμοῦ 5 καὶ ὡς δῆλον ὂν ἐν τῇ ἱστορίᾳ παρασιωπήσας ἀδιαφόρως· ἐτιμωρήθησαν γὰρ διὰ τὸ ὑπὸ λαιμαργίας ὠμῶν αὐτοὺς μεταλαβεῖν τῶν σαρκῶν μηδὲ ἐθίσαντας. Ἐν αὐτῷ οὖν φησιν ὄντες τῷ ἐσθίειν μὴ δεόντως φαγόντες παρώργισαν τὸν Θεόν.

31ᵇ. Καὶ ἀπέκτεινεν ἐν τοῖς πλείοσιν αὐτῶν. Καὶ πλείστους ἐξ αὐτῶν 10 ἀνεῖλεν.

31ᶜ. Καὶ τοὺς ἐκλεκτοὺς τοῦ Ἰσραὴλ συνεπόδισεν. Τοὺς μάλιστα κρείττονας αὐτῶν ἀφελών. Σύμμαχος τὸ καὶ τοὺς ἐκλεκτοὺς τοὺς νεανίσκους λέγει.

32ᵃ. Ἐν πᾶσι τούτοις ἥμαρτον ἔτι. Οὐδὲ ταῦτα αὐτοὺς ἐσωφρόνιζεν. 15

32ᵇ. Καὶ οὐκ ἐπίστευσαν ἐν τοῖς θαυμασίοις αὐτοῦ. Οὔτε μὴν ἀπὸ τούτων προσήγοντο πρὸς τὸ πιστεύειν τοῖς ὑπ' αὐτοῦ γιγνομένοις.

30ᵃ. Ὧν — ἀπέτυχον: P, fol. 277; V, fol. 43ᵛ; Vat. 1422, fol. 142 (anon.). 2 ἔτυχον 1422 ἀπέτυχεν Par.
30ᵇ-31ᵃ. Ἀπὸ τῆς — Θεόν: P, fol. 277; V, fol. 43ᵛ; Vat. 1422, fol. 142 (anon.). 4 τὸ om. 1422   5 εἶπεν] λέγει 1422   6 ἀδιαφόρως om. 1422   7 αὐτοὺς om. 1422 σαρκῶν des. 1422   8-9 ἐν αὐτῷ — Θεοῦ affert Paraphrasis (p. 612).
31ᵇ. Καὶ — ἀνεῖλε: P, fol. 277; V, fol. 43ᵛ; Vat. 1422, fol. 142 (anon.); Paraphrasis (p. 612).
31ᶜ. Τοὺς μάλιστα — λέγει: P, fol. 277; V, fol. 43ᵛ; Paraphrasis (p. 612). 13 ἀνελῶν PV   τὸ καὶ τοὺς] ἀντὶ τοῦ Par.
32ᵃ. Οὐδὲ — ἐσωφρόνιζεν: P, fol. 277; V, fol. 43ᵛ; Paraphrasis (p. 612). 15 μετὰ ταῦτα Par.
32ᵇ. Οὔτε — γιγνομένοις: P, fol. 277; V, fol. 43ᵛ; Vat. 1422, fol. 142ᵛ (anon.); Paraphrasis (p. 612).

Aᵉ 6-8 (p. 398, 29-32): Ita namque eos rabies manducandi accenderat, ut moram cocendi non ferentes crudis carnibus uiscerentur. 31ᵇ·ᶜ (p. 399, 7-8): Non est paucorum morte conpraesa seueritas uindicantis. 32ᵃ·ᵇ (p. 399, 12-13): Nec signis ad emendationem sunt nec uerberibus eruditi.

pointed in their desires (v. 30): they were not short of anything, at least of what they desired.

Food was still in their mouths when God's anger came upon them (vv. 30–31). He made reference to their fault by mention of God's anger, since God would not have been angry if they had not given him cause, though he passed over it indiscriminately for the reason that it is quite evident in the historical narrative. They were in fact punished for partaking of raw meat out of gluttony when not used to it.[9] In the very act of eating, he is saying, they provoked God by not eating properly. *He slew some of their strongest:* he did away with most of them. *And he bound the elect of Israel hand and foot* by doing away with their stronger ones in particular. Symmachus says for *the elect* "their young men." *In all this they kept sinning* (v. 32): even this did not bring them to their senses. *And did not believe his marvels:* nor were they led by this to believe what had been done by him. | *Their days*

9. Cf. Num 11:33–34; Exod 12:9.

33ᵃ. Καὶ ἐξέλιπον ἐν ματαιότητι αἱ ἡμέραι αὐτῶν. Καὶ οὕτως εἰς οὐδὲν τὰς ἡμέρας αὐτῶν κατανάλωσαν, — ἵν᾽ εἴπῃ Ἀπώλοντο καὶ εἰς τὸ μηδὲν περιέστησαν.

33ᵇ. Καὶ τὰ ἔτη αὐτῶν μετὰ σπουδῆς. Καὶ μετὰ πολλῆς τῆς ὀξύτητος
5 ἀναλώθησαν· ἡμέρας γὰρ αὐτῶν καὶ ἔτη αὐτῶν τὸν βίον αὐτῶν λέγει, τουτέστιν αὐτούς. Καλῶς δὲ εἶπεν τὸ μετὰ σπουδῆς· τὸ γὰρ ὑπὸ τιμωρίᾳ τῇ τοῦ Θεοῦ χιλιάδας κατ᾽ αὐτῶν ἀπόλλυσθαι, τοῦτο ἦν ὀξύτητος, οὐ καθ᾽ ἕνα καὶ κατὰ μέρος ἀποθνησκόντων, ἀλλ᾽ ὑφ᾽ ἑνὶ καιρῷ πολλῶν ὁμοῦ τῇ τοῦ Θεοῦ τιμωρίᾳ περιβαλλομένων.

10 **34ᵃ.** Ὅταν ἀπέκτενεν αὐτοὺς τότε ἐξεζήτουν αὐτόν. Τιμωρούμενοι καὶ ἀναιρούμενοι ἐδόκουν μεταμελεῖσθαι καὶ καταφεύγειν ἐπ᾽ αὐτόν.

34ᵇ. Καὶ ἐπέστρεφον καὶ ὤρθριζον πρὸς τὸν Θεόν. Καὶ τότε δὴ μετὰ πολλῆς τῆς ταχύτητος ἐδόκουν ἐπὶ τὴν τοῦ Θεοῦ συνιέναι θεραπείαν.

35. Καὶ ἐμνήσθησαν ὅτι ὁ Θεὸς βοηθὸς αὐτῶν ἐστι, καὶ ὁ Θεὸς ὁ ὕψισ-
15 τος λυτρωτὴς αὐτῶν ἐστιν. Μνημονεύειν τε τότε ἐδόκουν ὧν ἔτυχον παρὰ τοῦ βοηθήσαντος καὶ ἀπαλλάξαντος τῆς ἐν Αἰγύπτῳ δουλείας.

36. Καὶ ἠγάπησαν αὐτὸν ἐν τῷ στόματι αὐτῶν, καὶ τῇ γλώσσῃ αὐτῶν ἐψεύσαντο αὐτῷ. Ἦν δὲ σχῆμα καὶ ὑπόκρισις τὰ λεγόμενα· ψευδόμενοι γὰρ τῷ στόματι τὴν ἀγάπην ἐπηγγέλλοντο.

33ᵃ. Καὶ οὕτως — περιέστησαν: P, fol. 277; V, fol. 43ᵛ; *Paraphrasis* (p. 612).
33ᵇ. Καὶ μετὰ — περιβαλλομένων: P, fol. 277; V, fol. 43ᵛ; Cord, p. 641.　8 ὑφ᾽]
ἐφ᾽ Cord.
34ᵃ. Τιμωρούμενοι — ἐπ᾽ αὐτόν: P, fol. 277; V, fol. 43ᵛ; *Paraphrasis* (p. 613).
34ᵇ. Καὶ τότε — θεραπείαν: P, fol. 277; V, fol. 43ᵛ; *Paraphrasis* (p. 613).
35. Μνημονεύειν — δουλείας: P, fol. 277ᵛ; V, fol. 44; Vat. 1422, fol. 142ᵛ (anon.);
Paraphrasis (p. 613).　15 τε om. 1422 Par.
36. Ἦν δὲ σχῆμα — ἐπηγγέλλοντο: P. fol. 277ᵛ; V, fol. 44; Vat. 1422, fol. 142ᵛ
(anon.); *Paraphrasis* (p. 613).

Aᵉ **33ᵃ** (p 399, 14-16): Nullo accidente uirtutis studio, omne uitae suae spatium in uitiis ac reatibus exigerunt.　4-5 (p. 399, 17-19): Adcelerata est ignauorum perfidorumque mors, multis pariter extinctis.　**34ᵃ** (p. 399, 20-22): Supplicium terrorque mortis admonebat eos ad studium emendationis redire. **34ᵇ** (p. 399, 25-27): Reuocato ab errore gradu, festinos se Dei curationibus offerebant.　**35** (p. 399, 28-31): Tunc, inquit, in memoriam reuersi sunt, quali quantoque Dei auxilio fuissent de seruitute Aegyptia liberati.　**36** (p. 399, 32-34): Per confessiones (consiones *1ᵃ m.*) beneficiorum Dei, quas metus extorserat, non cordis testimonium, sed oris officium praeferebant.

were wasted in futility (v. 33): thus they spent their days to no effect, as if to say, They perished without a trace. *And their years with haste:* they were consumed with great speed (by *their days* and *their years* meaning "their life"—that is, themselves). *With haste* was well put: their perishing in thousands as a result of God's punishment of them was speedy, since they died not singly or in part; instead, great numbers fell victim to God's punishment at one fell swoop.

When he slew them, then it was that they sought him out (v. 34): on being punished and destroyed they decided to repent and take refuge in him. *They were converted, and rose early [to pray] to God:* and at that time they decided with great promptness to assemble for the worship of God. *They remembered that God is their helper, and God the Most High is their redeemer* (v. 35): at that time they decided to recall what they had received from the one who had helped them and had freed them from slavery in Egypt. *They loved him with their mouth, and were false to him with their tongue* (v. 36): what was said was acting and pretense; in lying words they made a promise of love. |

37ᵃ. Ἡ δὲ καρδία αὐτῶν οὐκ εὐθεῖα μετ᾽ αὐτοῦ. Οὐ γὰρ εἶχον πρὸς αὐτὸν ὀρθὴν τὴν διάθεσιν.

37ᵇ. Οὐδὲ ἐπιστώθησαν ἐν τῇ διαθήκῃ αὐτοῦ. Οὔτε μὴν βέβαιοι ἦσαν περὶ τὸ πιστεύειν αὐτῷ καὶ ἔχεσθαι τῆς αὐτοῦ θεραπείας· εἰρήκαμεν γὰρ ἀνώτερον ὅτι διαθήκην αὐτοῦ ταύτην λέγει τὴν ἐπ᾽ αὐτὸν πίστιν.   5

38ᵃ. Αὐτὸς δέ ἐστιν οἰκτίρμων. Εἰ καὶ τὰ μάλιστα φιλάνθρωπος ὢν ἠνέσχετο αὐτῶν πολλάκις, οὐκ ἀφανίζων αὐτούς, ὥσπερ οὖν ἄξιοι διὰ τὸν τρόπον ὄντες ἐφαίνοντο.

38ᵇ⁻ᵈ. Καὶ ἱλάσεται ταῖς ἁμαρτίαις αὐτῶν, καὶ οὐ διαφθερεῖ, καὶ πληθυνεῖ τοῦ ἀποστρέψαι τὸν θυμὸν αὐτοῦ. Ἀλλὰ γὰρ καὶ πλεῖστον ὅσον   10
ἀπέσχετο τῆς κατ᾽ αὐτῶν ὀργῆς. Ἐνήλλακται δὲ διόλου ὁ χρόνος, — ἀντὶ τοῦ ἱλάσατο καὶ οὐ διέφθειρεν καὶ ἀπέστρεψεν, εἰπὼν τὸ ἱλάσεται, καὶ οὐ διαφθερεῖ, καὶ πληθυνεῖ τοῦ ἀποστρέψαι καὶ ἑξῆς οὕτως.

38ᶜ. Καὶ οὐχὶ ἐκκαύσει πᾶσαν τὴν ὀργὴν αὐτοῦ. Οὐδὲ γὰρ ὅλῃ ἐχρήσατο κατ᾽ αὐτῶν τῇ τιμωρίᾳ, — καλῶς δὲ εἶπεν τὸ πᾶσαν. Ἐτιμωρήσατο   15
μὲν γὰρ ἀξίους ὄντας, οὐ μὴν κατὰ τὴν ἐκείνων ἀξίαν· ὑφ᾽ ἑνὶ γὰρ τῷ καιρῷ πάντας κατ᾽ αὐτὸ ὀφείλοντας ἀπολέσθαι ἤνεγκεν ἐπὶ πολλοῖς τοῖς ἔτεσιν, ἄχρις οὗ τοῖς διαδόχοις ἡ γενεὰ ἀνεδόθη.

4-5 supra, p. 521-522 (in v. 10¹).

37ᵃ. Οὐ γὰρ — διάθεσιν: P, fol. 277ᵛ; V, fol. 44; *Paraphrasis* (p. 612).
37ᵇ. Οὔτε — πίστιν: P, fol. 277ᵛ; V, fol. 44; Vat. 1422, fol. 142ᵛ (anon.);
Paraphrasis (p. 613).
38ᵃ. Εἰ καὶ — ἐφαίνοντο: P, fol. 277ᵛ; V, fol. 44; *Paraphrasis* (p. 613).   7 ἠνή-
χετο PV.
38ᵇ⁻ᵈ. Ἀλλὰ γὰρ — οὕτως: P, fol. 277ᵛ; V, fol. 44.
38ᶜ. Οὐδὲ γὰρ — ἀνεδόθη: P, fol. 277ᵛ; fol. 44; Vat. 1422, fol. 142ᵛ (anon.).
17 κατὰ τὸ αὐτὸ ὀφείλων 1422   18 τῶν διαδόχων PV.

Aᵉ 3-4 (p. 400, 3-4): Non erat quippe apud eos de Deo fixa sententia.
38ᵃ (p. 400, 6-10): Quamuis conuersationis merito ultricem in se iram moue-
rent, tamen bonitas eius non passa est omnes pro modo peccatorum perire.
38ᶜ (p. 400, 16-22): Non omnis in uendictam seueritas uindicantis incanduit;
bene autem dicit *omnem*. Nam cum interire omnes uno tempore conuenis-
set, ultio dispensatione protracta est, ut supleret successio, quod mors inlata
rapiebat.

Their heart was not straight with him (v. 37): they did not have an honest disposition toward him. *Nor were they true to his covenant:* they were really not steadfast in believing in him and practicing his worship. We mentioned above, remember, that by *his covenant* he means "faith in him." *He, on the contrary, is full of pity* (v. 38): even if he often could not bear them, being loving, he does not do away with them, as though they appeared worthy in behavior. *And will forgive their sins and not destroy them, and will go to lengths to deflect his anger:* as far as possible he refrains from wrath against them. The tense generally has been changed, the meaning being "he forgave, did not destroy, deflected" instead of *will forgive, will not destroy, will go to lengths to deflect* and so on. *And will not enkindle his wrath altogether:* nor will he inflict complete punishment on them, *altogether* being well put: he punished those deserving it, but not to the extent deserved, refraining from destroying all the guilty ones together at any one time over a period of years until the generation should be increased by natural succession. | *He remembered that they are flesh, a breeze that passes and*

39. Καὶ ἐμνήσθη ὅτι σάρξ εἰσιν, πνεῦμα πορευόμενον καὶ οὐκ ἐπιστρέφον. Ἔδειξεν ἐνταῦθα ὅτι ὁ χρόνος ἐνήλλακται· οὐκέτι γὰρ εἶπεν καὶ μνησθήσεται, ἀλλ' ἐμνήσθη, — καὶ τὰ ἑξῆς δὲ σαφέστερον δείκνυσιν τὴν ἐναλλαγὴν τοῦ χρόνου. Ἐννοῶν γάρ φησιν ὅτι οὐδέν εἰσι, φθείρονται
5 δὲ μετὰ βραχύ, οὐκέτι ἐπαναδραμεῖν εἰς ταύτην δυνάμενοι τὴν ζωήν, ἠνέσχετο αὐτῶν, συγχωρῶν αὐτοῖς ἔτι ἐπιβιῶναι.

40. Ποσάκις παρεπίκραναν αὐτὸν ἐν τῇ ἐρήμῳ, παρώργισαν αὐτὸν ἐν γῇ ἀνύδρῳ. Τὸ ἐν τῇ ἐρήμῳ καὶ ἀνύδρῳ τὸ αὐτὸ λέγει. Πολλάκις γοῦν παροξυνάντων αὐτὸν κατὰ τὴν ἔρημον, ὅμως ἠνέσχετο ἐπὶ πολλῷ τῷ χρόνῳ. Καλῶς
10 δὲ εἶπεν ποσάκις· καὶ τοῦτο γὰρ τῆς τοῦ Θεοῦ χρηστότητος ἀπόδειξις.

41ᵃ. Καὶ ἐπέστρεψαν καὶ ἐπείρασαν τὸν Θεόν. Ἀξιούμενοι γὰρ ἐπὶ τοῖς προλαβοῦσιν τῆς τοῦ Θεοῦ φιλανθρωπίας, πάλιν μεταβαλλόμενοι τῆς οἰκείας εἴχοντο γνώμης, αὖθις αὐτὸν πειράζοντες.

41ᵇ. Καὶ τὸν ἅγιον τοῦ Ἰσραὴλ παρώξυναν Καὶ παρώργιζον τὸν οἰκεῖον
15 δεσπότην.

42ᵃ. Οὐκ ἐμνήσθησαν τῆς χειρὸς αὐτοῦ. Οὐχ ὑπομιμνησκόμενοι ὧν ἐποίησεν εἰς αὐτούς.

42ᵇ. Ἡμέρας ἧς ἐλυτρώσατο αὐτοὺς ἐκ χειρὸς θλίβοντος. Οὐδὲ τοῦ καιροῦ ἐμνήσθησαν καθ' ὃν ἀπήλλαξεν αὐτοὺς τῶν κατεχόντων, καὶ πᾶν ὅ τι
20 διατιθέντων ὠμόν.

39. Ἐννοῶν — ἐπιβιῶναι: P, fol. 277ᵛ; V, fol. 44.   4-6 ἐννοῶν — ἐπιβιῶναι affert Paraphrasis (p. 613).
40. Τὸ ἐν τῇ — ἀπόδειξις: P, fol. 277ᵛ; V, fol. 44ʳ·ᵛ; Paraphrasis (p. 613-614). 8-9 παροξύνοντες PV.
41ᵃ. Ἀξιούνενοι — πειράζοντες: P, fol. 278; V, fol. 44ᵛ.   13-17 αὖθις — αὐτούς affert Paraphrasis (p. 614).
41ᵇ. Καὶ παρώργιζον τὸν οἰκεῖον δεσπότην: P, fol. 278; V, fol. 44ᵛ; Vat. 1422, fol. 143 (anon.).
42ᵃ. Οὐχ — αὐτούς: P, fol. 278; V, fol. 44ᵛ; Vat. 1422, fol. 143 (anon.).
42ᵇ. Οὐδὲν — ὠμόν: P, fol. 278; V, fol. 44ᵛ; Paraphrasis (p. 614).   19 ἐμνήσθησαν om. PV.

Aᵉ 2-4 (p. 400, 22-25): Consequens hic temporis praeteriti conlatio ostendit superiora per commo⟨ta⟩tionem (temporis add. supra) dicta esse de futuro. Recordatus est, inquit, non recordabitur.   40 (p. 401, 5-10): Quod dicit in diserto et in aquosso unam rem diuersis nominibus appellat. Non semel, sed sepe in herimi uasta solitudine prauitate morum Dei in se iracondiam concitauerunt. 41ᵃ (p. 401, 12-15): Post ueniam peccatis semper indultam, ignoscentis clementia abussi sunt ad dilinquendi securitatem.   41ᵇ (p. 401, 17-18): ... obliuisci lenitatis suae Dominum conpellerunt.

does not return (v. 39). He gave a clear indication here that the tense has been changed, no longer saying "He will remember," but *He remembered,* and in what follows showing the change in tense. Realizing that they are nothing, he is saying, and will disappear in a short time, incapable of returning to this life, he had patience with them, allowing them to go on for a while.

How often they provoked him in the wilderness, enraged him in waterless land (v. 40). The phrases *in the wilderness* and *in waterless land* mean the same thing: Though they provoked him frequently in the desert, he yet put up with them for a long time. *How often* was well said, this being a proof of God's goodness. *They turned about and tested God* (v. 41): though deserving of God's lovingkindness for their previous behavior, they then changed and clung to their own way of looking at things, once again testing him. *And irritated the Holy One of Israel:* they provoked their own master. *They did not remember his hand* (v. 42), not being mindful of what he had done for them. *On the day when he redeemed them from the hand of the persecutor:* they did not even recall the time when he freed them from those holding them and showing them cruelty of all kinds. | *As he set his signs in Egypt and his*

43. Ὡς ἔθετο ἐν Αἰγύπτῳ τὰ σημεῖα αὐτοῦ, καὶ τὰ τέρατα αὐτοῦ ἐν πεδίῳ Τάνεως. Οὐχ ὡς θαυμαστοποιητὴν ἐμνημόνευσαν, οὐχ ὅπως τοὺς ἐναντίους ἐτιμωρήσατο · τέρας γὰρ κυρίως τὸ ἐπὶ τιμωρίᾳ τινῶν θαῦμα λέγεται.

44. Καὶ μετέστρεψεν εἰς αἷμα τοὺς ποταμοὺς αὐτῶν, καὶ τὰ ὀμβρήματα αὐτῶν ὅπως μὴ πίωσιν. Ὅπως μὲν ἅπαν ὕδωρ εἰς αἷμα μετεποίησεν, ὡς   5
μηδὲ ἐξεῖναι αὐτοῖς ποτοῦ μεταλαβεῖν.

45ᵃ. Ἐξαπέστειλεν εἰς αὐτοὺς κυνόμυιαν καὶ κατέφαγεν αὐτούς. Ὅπως δὲ αὐτοὺς κατηνάλωσεν, τὴν κυνόμυιαν ἐπ᾽ αὐτοὺς ἀποστείλας.

45ᵇ. Καὶ βάτραχον καὶ διέφθειρεν αὐτούς. Ὅπως ἀπώλεσεν αὐτοὺς μικροῦ τοῖς βατράχοις.   10

46. Καὶ ἔδωκεν τῇ ἐρυσίβῃ τοὺς καρποὺς αὐτῶν, καὶ τοὺς πόνους αὐτῶν τῇ ἀκρίδι. Ὅπως ἐρυσίβῃ καὶ ἀκρίσιν πάντας αὐτῶν ἠφάνισεν τοὺς καρπούς, ματαίους αὐτῶν ἀποφαίνων τοὺς πόνους.

47. Ἀπέκτεινεν ἐν χαλάζῃ τὴν ἄμπελον αὐτῶν, καὶ τὰς συκαμίνους αὐτῶν ἐν τῇ πάχνῃ. Ἀπέκτεινεν, ἀντὶ τοῦ ἐνέκρωσεν, ἀκάρπους εἰργάσατο. Τὴν   15
δὲ ἄμπελον καὶ τὰς συκαμίνους εἶπεν, ἀντὶ τοῦ πᾶν ξύλον κάρπιμον.

48ᵃ. Καὶ παρέδωκεν εἰς χάλαζαν τὰ κτήνη αὐτῶν. Ἀνάλωσεν αὐτὰ διὰ χαλάζης.

43. Οὐχ ὡs — λέγεται : P, fol. 278; V, fol. 44ᵛ; Vat. 1422, fol. 143; *Paraphrasis* (p. 614).   2 ἐμνημόνευσεν 1422.
44. Ὅπως — μεταλαβεῖν : P, fol. 278; V, fol. 44ᵛ; Vat. 1422, fol. 143 (anon.); *Paraphrasis* (p. 614).
45ᵃ. Ὅπως — ἀποστείλας : P, fol. 278; V, fol. 44ᵛ; *Paraphrasis* (p. 614).
45ᵇ. Ὅπως — βατράχοις : P, fol. 278; V, fol. 45; *Paraphrasis* (p. 614).   9 καὶ ὅπως Par.   10 τοῖς *om.* Par.
46. Ὅπως — πόνους : P, fol. 278; V, fol. 45; *Paraphrasis* (p. 614).
47. Ἀπέκτεινεν — κάρπιμον : P, fol. 278; V, fol. 45; Vat. 1422, fol. 143ᵛ (anon.); *Paraphrasis* (p. 614).   15 ἀπέκτεινεν] τὸ ἀπεκτ. τὴν ἄμπελον αὐτῶν 1422   15-16 τὴν δὲ] τὸ δὲ 1422   16 ξύλον] δένδρον 1422.
48ᵃ. Ἀνάλωσεν αὐτὰ διὰ χαλάζης : P, fol. 278ᵛ; V, fol. 45; *Paraphrasis* (p. 615) : τὰ κτήνη ἀνάλωσεν διὰ χαλάζης.

Aᵉ 42ᵃ (p. 401, 19-21): Nihil beneficiorum eius, nihil operum in memoriam reduxerunt.   42ᵇ (p. 401, 22-25): Neque tribulationis meminisse suae eos, quo duris et crudilibus seruierunt dominis.   43 (p. 401, 27-29): Neque sua eos beneficia in memoriam mirabiliter factorum, neque hostium poena reuocauit.
46 (p. 402, 4-8): Exigua paruaque animalia ita in exitium eorum fuerunt potentia, ut facile sumerent (sumurent *ms*) quod fuerat eorum uel labore quessitum.
47 (p. 402, 9-12): *Occidit*, id est omni uiuacitate contexuit, dum infructuosas ac steriles facit ablata uiriditate.

prodigies in the field of Tanis (v. 43): they did not call to mind his wonder-working, nor how he punished the adversaries (*prodigy* referring specifically to some people's amazement at the punishment). *He turned their rivers and their rain waters into blood so that that they could not drink* (v. 44): how he changed all the water into blood so that they could not get a drink from it. *He sent dogflies on them, and they devoured them* (v. 45): how he wasted them by sending dogflies on them. *And frogs, and they destroyed them:* how he almost ruined them with frogs.

    He delivered up their crops to the blight, and their labors to locusts (v. 46): how with blight and locusts he wiped out all their crops, rendering their labors futile. *He killed their vineyards with hail, and their mulberries with frost* (v. 47): he *killed*—that is, caused them to wither, made them fruitless. By *vineyards* and *mulberries* he refers to every fruit-bearing tree. *He gave their cattle over to the hail* (v. 48): he wasted them with hail. | *And their pos-*

48ᵇ. Καὶ τὴν ὕπαρξιν αὐτῶν τῷ πυρί. Καὶ πᾶν ὅ τί ποτε εἶχον πυρὶ κατανάλωσεν· λέγει δὲ ὁπηνίκα τὰς φλυκταίνας ἐξεδίδοσαν ἐν τοῖς σώμασιν, αὐτοί τε καὶ τὰ ὑπηρετούμενα ζῷα.

49ᵃ·ᵇ. Ἐξαπέστειλεν εἰς αὐτοὺς ὀργὴν θυμοῦ αὐτοῦ, θυμὸν καὶ ὀργὴν καὶ
5 θλῖψιν. Καὶ πᾶν ὅ τι κακὸν ἐπήνεγκεν αὐτοῖς.

49ᶜ. Ἀποστολὴν δι' ἀγγέλων πονηρῶν. Τὸν τῶν πρωτοτόκων λέγει θάνατον, ὡς δι' ἀγγέλων γενόμενον. Οὕτω γὰρ καὶ ὁ μακάριος Μωϋσῆς παραγγέλλων τοῖς Ἰσραηλίταις χρῖσαι τὸ αἷμα ἐπὶ τῶν φλιῶν φησιν ὅτι παρελεύσεται ὁ ἄγγελος ὁ ὀλοθρεύων, καὶ θεασάμενος τὸ αἷμα τῆς οἰκίας οὐχ
10 ἅψεται. Πονηροὺς δὲ αὐτοὺς εἶπεν, ὡς ἐκείνους πονηροὺς τοῖς δι' αὐτῶν ἀναιρουμένοις· τὸ γὰρ πονηρὸν οὐδαμοῦ ἀπὸ τῆς φύσεως λέγει — ἐπεὶ μηδὲν οἶδέν τι ἀπὸ φύσεως πονηρὸν — ἡ θεία γραφή, ἐνίοτε δὲ οὐδὲ ἀπὸ γνώμης, ἀλλ' ἀπὸ τοῦ πράγματος, ὡς ὅταν λέγῃ Ἐν ἡμέρᾳ πονηρᾷ — πονηρὰν λέγων ἡμέραν τῶν θλιβομένων. Σύμμαχος δὲ τὸ δι' ἀγγέλων πονη-
15 ρῶν ἀγγέλων εἶπεν κακούντων σαφέστερον αὐτὸ εἰπών.

50ᵃ. Ὡδοποίησεν τρίβον τῇ ὀργῇ αὐτοῦ. Ἐπειδὴ τῆς ὁδοῦ εὐτρεπισμένης ῥᾳδίως οἱ διοδεύοντες παρίασιν, τοῦτο ἠβουλήθη εἰπεῖν ὅτι ὀξύτατα καὶ εὐκόλως τὴν οἰκείαν αὐτοῖς ὀργὴν ἐπήνεγκεν, ἐν μιᾷ ῥοπῇ πάντας τιμωρησάμενος.

20 50ᵇ. Οὐκ ἐφείσατο ἀπὸ θανάτου τῶν ψυχῶν αὐτῶν, καὶ τὰ κτήνη αὐτῶν εἰς θάνατον συνέκλεισεν. Συντόμως κἀκείνους ἀνελὼν καὶ τὰ κτήνη· βούλεται δὲ εἰπεῖν τὸν τῶν πρωτοτόκων θάνατον, ὃ καὶ σαφέστερον ἑξῆς ἐπάγει.

1-3 cf. Ex. IX, 8-10   6-10 cf. Ex. XII, 22-23   13 Ps. XL, 2ᵗ.

48ᵇ. Καὶ πᾶν — ζῷα: P, fol. 278ᵛ; V, fol. 45; Paraphrasis (p. 615).
49ᵃ·ᵇ. Καὶ πᾶν — αὐτοῖς: P, fol. 278ᵛ; V, fol. 45; Paraphrasis (p. 615).
49ᶜ. Τὸν τῶν πρωτοτόκων — εἰπών: P, fol. 278ᵛ; V, fol. 45; Vat. 1422, fol. 143ᵛ
(anon.); Cord, p. 642.   6 τῶν om. 1422   10 ἐκείνοις 1422 et des.   δι' αὐτὸν PV.
50ᵃ. Ἐπειδὴ — τιμωρησάμενος: P, fol. 278ᵛ; V, fol. 45; Paraphrasis (p. 615).
17 ὁδεύοντες Par.
50ᵇ. Συντόμως — ἐπάγει: P, fol. 278ᵛ; V, fol. 45; Paraphrasis (p. 615).   22 θάνατον des. Par.

Aᵒ 48ᵇ (p. 402, 17-19): Pro uesicis candentibus, quae tam in hominum quam in peccorum corporibus erumpere.   49ᶜ (p. 402, 24-34): Mortem hic primogenitorum indicat, quae angelis exterminatoribus facta est... Malos autem angelos dicit illos illis qui erant utique perdituri, quoniam nihil dici potest malum naturaliter; interdum malum uocamus quod non est de essentia, sed rerum prouenit de qualitate, ut est In die mala; mala autem dies appellatur ab eo qui patitur tribulationem.   50ᵃ (p. 402, 35-403, 2): His itaque dispossitis nihil inpedimenti fuit quoniam celere disperirent quibus intendebatur exitium.
50ᵇ (p. 403, 3-6): Nullae, inquit, intercesserant morae temporum, ut tam homines quam omne peccoris genus mors inmisa consumeret.

sessions to the fire: all they possessed he consumed with fire. He is referring to the time they broke out in blisters on their bodies, they and the animals serving them.[10] *He sent against them the wrath of his anger—anger, wrath, tribulation* (v. 49), whatever trouble he inflicted on them. *A dispatch of evil angels.* He is referring to the death of the firstborn as the work of angels. In this case, remember, Moses bade the Israelites mark the doorposts with blood, saying, "The avenging angel will pass by, and upon seeing the blood on your house, he will not touch you."[11] Now, he called them *evil* in being evil to those destroyed by them; the divine Scripture, in fact, never calls anything naturally evil, since nothing can be evil of its nature, though sometimes not even from the mind-set but in behavior, as when it says, "On an evil day,"[12] calling the day evil for those in tribulation. Symmachus expressed the phrase *of evil angels* more clearly by saying "angels who do evil."

He made a path for his wrath (v. 50). Since travelers easily take a path with gentle bends, he meant that he swiftly and easily vented his wrath on them, punishing them all in one fell swoop. *He did not spare their souls from death; he confined their cattle to death:* briefly disposing of them and the cattle. He means the death of the firstborn, which he goes on to state more clearly. | *He struck every firstborn in Egypt, firstfruits of every labor of theirs,*

---

10. Cf. Exod 9:8–11.
11. Exod 12:22–23, loosely recalled.
12. Ps 41:1.

51. Καὶ ἐπάταξε πᾶν πρωτότοκον ἐν γῇ Αἰγύπτῳ, ἀπαρχὴν παντὸς πόνου αὐτῶν ἐν τοῖς σκηνώμασι Χάμ. Πάντα αὐτῶν ἀπώλεσεν τὰ πρωτότοκα, καλῶς ἀπαρχὴν καλέσας τὰ πρωτότοκα καὶ ὡς τιμιώτερα, καὶ ἐπειδὴ ἐν νόμῳ ἀπαρχῆς λόγῳ τῷ Θεῷ προσηγάγετο. Τὸ δὲ παντὸς πόνου, ἵνα εἴπῃ παντὸς καρποῦ αὐτῶν, ἀντὶ τοῦ πάντων τῶν προσόντων αὐτοῖς τὰ πρω- 5 τότοκα ἀνεῖλεν, οὐκ αὐτῶν μόνων, ἀλλὰ καὶ τῶν κτηνῶν ὅσαπερ ἦν αὐτοῖς. Καλῶς δὲ εἶπεν τὸ ἐν τοῖς σκηνώμασιν Χάμ· πάντες γὰρ οἱ ὑπὸ Αἰγυπ- τίοις τόποι τῶν ἀπογόνων ἦσαν τοῦ Χάμ.

52ᵃ. Καὶ ἀπῆρεν ὡς πρόβατα τὸν λαὸν αὐτοῦ. Κἀκείνους τιμωρησάμενος τούτους ἔλαβεν καὶ ἀπήγαγεν δίκην προβάτων, οὐδ᾽ εἰδότας ὅποι ἀπελ- 10 θεῖν δεῖ.

52ᵇ. Καὶ ἀνήγαγεν αὐτοὺς ὡσεὶ ποίμνιον ἐν ἐρήμῳ. Οὕτως ἄγων τε καὶ περιάγων ὅποιπερ ἴδῃ χρήσιμον εἶναι.

53ᵃ. Καὶ ὡδήγησεν αὐτοὺς ἐπ᾽ ἐλπίδι καὶ οὐκ ἐδειλίασαν. Καὶ τῇ ἐπ᾽ αὐτὸν ἐλπίδι, τουτέστιν τῇ οἰκείᾳ βοηθείᾳ, διήγαγεν αὐτούς, οὐδένα φοβη- 15 θῆναι συγχωρήσας. Τὸ δὲ οὐκ ἐδειλίασαν εἶπεν ὡς πρὸς τὴν τοῦ Θεοῦ βοή- θειαν. Εἰ γὰρ κἀκεῖνοι ἀπιστοῦντες συνεχῶς ἠγωνίων, ἀλλ᾽ αὐτῶν ἦν ὄνειδος τὸ πρᾶγμα· τὰ γὰρ ὑπὸ τοῦ Θεοῦ γιγνόμενα σαφῶς αὐτοὺς ἐδίδασκεν ὡς οὐδὲν φοβεῖσθαι προσῆκεν.

53ᵇ. Καὶ τοὺς ἐχθροὺς αὐτῶν ἐκάλυψε θάλασσα. Ἔδειξεν ὅτι τὸ οὐκ 20 ἐδειλίασαν ἀπὸ τοῦ πράγματος λέγει· τῇ γὰρ θαλάσσῃ τοὺς πολεμοῦντας καλύψας καὶ ἀνελών, ἀπήλλαξεν τοῦ ἐπικειμένου φόβου τούτου.

3 cf. Ex. XXIII, 19.

51. Πάντα — τοῦ Χάμ: P, fol. 278ᵛ; V, fol. 45ᵛ; Cord, p. 642-643.
52ᵃ. Κἀκείνους — δεῖ: P, fol. 278ᵛ; V, fol. 45ᵛ; Paraphrasis (p. 615).
52ᵇ. Οὕτως — εἶναι: P, fol. 278ᵛ; V, fol. 45ᵛ.
53ᵃ. Καὶ τῇ — προσῆκεν: P, fol. 279; V, fol. 45ᵛ; Vat. 1422, fol. 144 (anon.);
Paraphrasis (p. 615). 17 βοήθειαν des. Par ἐκεῖνοι 1422 19 οὐδένα 1422.
53ᵇ. Ἔδειξεν — τούτου: P, fol. 279; V, fol. 45ᵛ. 21-22 τῇ γὰρ θαλάσσῃ — τούτου affert Paraphrasis (p. 615). 22 τούτους Par.

Aᵉ 7-8 (p. 403, 16-17): Omnis regio Aegipti filiorum Cham fuerat prisca
atque auita possesio. 52ᵃ (p. 403, 19-21):... in morem pecoris quae loca pete-
ret ignorantem pastoris est officio prosecutus. 16-19 (p. 403, 24-30):... hoc
quantum ad Dei spectat adiutorium; nam etsi illorum infidelitas tripidauit in
aliquo, non hoc ad Dei protectionem, sed ad illorum spectat; ignauiam satis
enim eos opere docuerat quod se adiutore nullum possint nec deberent timere.
20-21 (p. 403, 31): Rebus probauit id, quod dixerat, non timuerunt.

in the tents of Ham (v. 51): he destroyed all their firstborn (nicely referring to the firstborn as *firstfruits* in being also first in importance and because by law they were offered to God on the basis of being firstfruits). The phrase *of every labor* means "of all their crops"—that is, he destroyed the firstborn of all they possessed, not of their own family alone, but also of all the cattle they owned. *The tents of Ham* was well put: all the places under the control of the Egyptians belonged to descendants of Ham.[13]

He took away his people like sheep (v. 52): after punishing the others, he took these and led them away like sheep without their knowing whither they had to go. *And led them up into the wilderness like a flock:* leading them hither and yon in whichever direction he saw was to their advantage. *He guided them in hope, and they were not afraid* (v. 53): he led them on by hope in him—that is, by his peculiar help, allowing them to fear no one. The phrase *they were not afraid* refers to God's help: if they too were constantly distrustful and uneasy, it was not a matter of disgrace for them; what was done by God clearly taught them that they had no need to fear. *And the sea covered their foes.* He made clear that the phrase *they were not afraid* refers to actual events: by covering the assailants with the sea and destroying them, he rid them of this fear besetting them. | *He brought them to his*

---

13. There is a cryptic reference here to Gen 10:6, where Egypt (Mizraim in Hebrew and LXX) is mentioned as one of Ham's descendants.

54ᵃ. Καὶ εἰσήγαγεν αὐτοὺς εἰς ὅρος ἁγιάσματος αὐτοῦ. Ἵνα εἴπῃ εἰς τὴν γῆν τῆς ἐπαγγελίας. Λέγει δὲ αὐτὸ ἀπὸ τοῦ κυριωτέρου, τουτέστιν εἰς τοῦτο τὸ σκήνωμα ἐν ᾧπερ αὐτὸς οἰκεῖν καὶ διάγειν ἐδοκίμασεν· τοῦτο γὰρ ἐποίει καὶ τὸν τόπον θαυμαστόν.

5 54ᵇ. Ὅρος τοῦτο, ὃ ἐκτήσατο ἡ δεξιὰ αὐτοῦ. Καὶ εἰσήγαγεν αὐτοὺς εἰς τοῦτο τὸ ὅρος, ὅπερ αὐτὸς ἐκτήσατο, — καλῶς εἰπὼν τὸ ἐκτήσατο, ὅτι ὥσπερ οἰκείοις πόνοις τοὺς κατέχοντας ἀνελὼν ἴδιον ἀπέφηνεν τὸ ὅρος.

55ᵃ. Καὶ ἐξέβαλεν ἀπὸ προσώπου αὐτῶν ἔθνη. Πάντας τοὺς κατέχοντάς φησιν ἀπώλεσεν.

10 55ᵇ. Καὶ ἐκληροδότησεν αὐτοὺς ἐν σχοινίῳ κληροδοσίας. Καὶ παρέδωκεν αὐτοῖς τὴν γῆν, ὥστε μέτρῳ καὶ κλήρῳ καταδιελέσθαι γῆν τὴν οὐ προσήκουσαν αὐτοῖς.

55ᶜ. Καὶ κατεσκήνωσεν ἐν τοῖς σκηνώμασιν αὐτῶν τὰς φυλὰς τοῦ Ἰσραήλ. Ἐν τοῖς σκηνώμασιν αὐτῶν — τῶν ἐθνῶν λέγει — ἀντὶ τοῦ Καὶ τοὺς ἀλλο-
15 τρίους τόπους αὐτοῖς παρέδωκεν.

56-57ᵃ. Καὶ ἐπείρασαν καὶ παρεπίκραναν τὸν Θεὸν τὸν ὕψιστον, καὶ τὰ μαρτύρια αὐτοῦ οὐκ ἐφυλάξαντο, καὶ ἀπέστρεψαν καὶ ἠθέτησαν καθὼς καὶ οἱ πατέρες αὐτῶν. Εἶτά φησι κατεσχηκότες τὴν γῆν τῆς ἐπαγγελίας, καὶ οὗτοι τοὺς ἰδίους ἐμιμήσαντο πατέρας ἀπιστοῦντες τῷ Θεῷ, παροργίζοντες
20 αὐτόν, ἀμελοῦντες τοῦ νόμου, ἀφιστάμενοι τοῦ Θεοῦ, ἐπὶ τὴν τῶν εἰδώλων προσκύνησιν μεταβαλλόμενοι.

54ᵃ. Ἵνα — εἴπῃ θαυμαστόν: P, fol. 279; V, fol. 45ᵛ.
54ᵇ. Καὶ εἰσήγαγεν — τὸ ὅρος: P, fol. 279; V, fol. 46.
55ᵃ. Πάντας — ἀπώλεσεν: P, fol. 279; V, fol. 46; Paraphrasis (p. 616).
55ᵇ. Καὶ παρέδωκεν — αὐτοῖς; P, fol. 279; V, fol. 46; Paraphrasis (p. 616).
11 τὴν γῆν l'ar.
55ᶜ. Ἐν τοῖς — παρέδωκεν: P, fol. 279; V, fol. 46; Paraphrasis (p. 616).
56-57ᵃ. Εἶτα — μεταβαλλόμενοι: P, fol. 279ᵛ; V, fol. 46; Cord, p. 643. 18-19 γῆν
καὶ οὗτοι τῆς ἐπ. τοὺς PV 19 θεῷ καὶ Cord 20 καὶ ἀμελοῦντες καὶ ἀφιστάμενοι Cord.

Aᵉ 1-3 (p. 403, 32-404, 2): Locum, in quo templum factum est, id est terra repromisionis, totum indicans a parte meliore. 54ᵇ (p. 404, 4-6):... in montem, quem ereptum de iure hostium, in possessionis suae locum propria uirtute quaesiuit. 55ᶜ (p. 404, 13-14): In tabernaculis eorum, id est populorum qui iecti sunt. 56-57ᵃ (p. 404, 16-23): Post dominationem terrae atque heriditatis sortionem exempla sunt infidelium parentum secuti, ut et fidem susceptam dese-⟨re⟩rent; et malo conuersationis suae Deum ad iracondiam concitauerunt, ⟨ut⟩ a lege discederent ac se idulorum seruitio manciparent.

mountain of holiness (v. 54): as if to say, the land of promise. His specific reference is to this abode where he saw fit to dwell and live in person; he made this place, too, an object of wonder. *This mountain that his right hand acquired:* he brought them to *this mountain,* which he personally *acquired* (nicely employing the term *acquired* because by destroying with his own effort those in possession, he made the mountain his own). *He drove out nations before them* (v. 55): he destroyed all those in possession. *He gave them a heritage with a cord of inheritance:* he handed the land over to them so that by measure and allotment they might divide up the land that was not theirs. *He settled the tribes of Israel in their tents.* By *their tents* he refers to those of the nations—in other words, He handed over to them also the foreign places.

They tested and provoked God the Most High, and did not observe his testimonies. They turned away and were rebellious, just as their ancestors were too (vv. 56–57): they next took possession of the land of promise, and in their own case imitated their ancestors in disobeying God, provoking him, ignoring the law, forsaking God, and turning to the worship of the idols. |

57ᵇ. Μετεστράφησαν εἰς τόξον στρεβλόν. Τὰ τόξα οὐ μόνον ἀπὸ τοῦ
εὐθέως περιαγόμενα κάμπτεται, ἀλλὰ καὶ αὐτὴν οὕτω τὴν κατασκευὴν καμ-
πυλοειδῆ καὶ διάφορον ἔχει· ἄλλο μὲν γὰρ αὐτοῦ τὸ περὶ τὴν νευρὰν
σχῆμα, ἄλλο δὲ τὸ ὅθεν κατέχεσθαι δεῖ, ἕτερον δὲ τὸ τῶν ἑκατέρωθεν
μερῶν. Οὕτως οὖν φησι καὶ οὗτοι ἀνώμαλοι πανταχόθεν τὸν τρόπον ὄντες   5
τοῦ ὀρθοῦ ἀποστάντες ἐπὶ τὸ χεῖρον συνώθησαν ἑαυτοὺς καὶ μετέβαλον.

58. Καὶ παρώργισαν αὐτὸν ἐν τοῖς βουνοῖς αὐτῶν, καὶ ἐν τοῖς γλυπτοῖς
αὐτῶν παρεζήλωσαν αὐτόν. Τὸ μὲν γὰρ εὐθὲς ἦν τὸ τῷ Θεῷ προσκυνεῖν·
ἀποστάντες δὲ τούτου καὶ περὶ τὴν τῶν εἰδώλων γενόμενοι θεραπείαν καὶ
ἐν τοῖς ἄλσεσι — τούτους γὰρ λέγει τοὺς βουνοὺς — περὶ τὴν τῶν εἰδώ-   10
λων ἔχοντες θεραπείαν, ἐκίνησαν κατ᾽ αὐτῶν τὸν Θεόν.

59. Ἤκουσεν ὁ Θεός, καὶ ὑπερεῖδεν, καὶ ἐξουδένωσε σφόδρα τὸν Ἰσραήλ.
Ταῦτα θεασάμενος κατεφρόνησεν αὐτῶν.

60ᵃ. Καὶ ἀπώσατο τὴν σκηνὴν Σηλώμ. Καὶ ἀπέβαλεν τοῦ Σηλὼμ τὴν
σκηνήν, ἵνα εἴπῃ αὐτὸ τὸ κατοικεῖν ἐν τῷ ὄρει· οὐ γὰρ μόνον αὐτοὺς ὑπὸ   15
ἀλλοφύλοις πολλάκις πεποίηκεν, ἀλλὰ καὶ τὸ ἔσχατον αὐτὴν αὐτοῖς τὴν
κιβωτὸν εἰς χεῖρας παρέδωκεν.

60ᵇ. Σκήνωμα ὃ κατεσκήνωσεν ἐν ἀνθρώποις. Τὸ «ὃ» δασύνοντας δεῖ
λέγειν, ἀντὶ τοῦ τοῦτο, — οὐ ψιλοῦντας κατὰ ἀπαγόρευσιν, ὥς τινες
ᾠήθησαν. Τοῦτό φησι τὸ σκήνωμα ἀπεποιήσατο, ἔνθα αὐτὸς κατοικεῖν ἐν   20
μέσῳ τῶν ἀνθρώπων ἐδοκίμασεν· ἀπόδειξις δὲ μεγίστη τῆς ὀργῆς τὸ ὅπερ
αὐτὸς οἰκείᾳ φιλανθρωπίᾳ ποιήσας, ἐδοκίμασε τούτου μεταβαλέσθαι, — καὶ
ὃν ἀφώρισεν ἑαυτῷ τόπον, τοῦτον δι᾽ ὀργὴν τοῖς ἐναντίοις παραδοῦναι.

57ᵇ. Τὰ τόξα — μετέβαλον: P, fol. 279ᵛ; V, fol. 46.
58. Τὸ μὲν γὰρ — Θεόν: P. fol. 279ᵛ; V, fol. 46.
59. Ταῦτα — αὐτῶν: P, fol. 279ᵛ; V, fol. 46ᵛ.
60¹. Καὶ ἀπέβαλεν — παρέδωκεν: P, fol. 279ᵛ; V, fol. 46ᵛ; Paraphrasis (p. 616).
17 εἰς χεῖρας om. PV.
60ᵇ. Τὸ ὃ — παραδοῦναι: P, fol. 280; V, fol. 46ᵛ.

Aᵉ 3-6 (p. 404, 24-26): Ita prauitate curui et intorti profanitate, ut arcuum
est flexuossa formatio.   58 (p. 404, 27-34): Exigerat recti norma, ut Deo soli
quicquid erat uenerationis inpenderent; a quo recidentes idulorum se cultui
mancipant, quae colebant in lucis, id est sub arborum densitate, — et ob hoc
Deum in offensam sui iusta indignatione mouerunt.   59 (p. 405, 1-5); Consi-
derans ... Deus et nullius estimationis ac praetii dignos eos... iudicauit.
60ᵃ (p. 405, 6-10): Non solum eos, sed etiam arcam alienigenarum tradidit potes-
tati inuidia eorum, sacrata quoque sibi loca deseruit.

They were bent into a crooked bow. Bows are not only twisted from a straight line by being bent, but also in this way acquire a distorted and inaccurate shape in actual fact: their shape in regard to the string is one thing, while the way they must be held is another, and still another is the effect of the two components. Similarly, then, he is saying, these people were also irregular in behavior on all scores and departed from the straight and narrow; they took a turn for the worse and underwent change. *They provoked him on their hills, and with their carvings aroused his jealousy* (v. 58): the straight and narrow meant worshiping God; but they left this to become involved in the cult of idols and conduct the cult of the idols in the groves (the meaning of *hills*), thus arousing God against them. *God heard, and was scornful, and he brought Israel down altogether* (v. 59): upon seeing this, he despised them.

He rejected the dwelling at Shiloh (v. 60): he forsook the dwelling at Shiloh—that is, his residing on the mountain; he not only made them often subject to the Philistines, but also even ultimately surrendered the ark itself into their hands.[14] *An abode in which he dwelt among human beings.* We must read *which* with a rough breathing [οὗ] so as to mean "this," and not, as some commentators thought, with a smooth breathing [οὐ] to mean negation. He abandoned this abode, he is saying, where he had seen fit to dwell personally in the midst of human beings; his deciding to change what he himself had made in his lovingkindness was the clearest indication of his anger, as was his consigning the place he had destined for himself to the adversaries in his anger. | *He handed over their power to captivity* (v. 61): that is, their

---

14. Cf. 1 Sam 4.

61ª. Καὶ παρέδωκεν εἰς αἰχμαλωσίαν τὴν ἰσχὺν αὐτῶν. Ἀντὶ τοῦ Τοὺς ἰσχυροὺς αὐτῶν καὶ τοὺς νεανίσκους.

61ᵇ. Καὶ τὴν καλλονὴν αὐτῶν εἰς χεῖρας ἐχθρῶν. Τὸ αὐτὸ λέγει, — καλλονὴ γὰρ ἡ πλήθους οἱ νεανίσκοι, — λέγει δὲ τὰ πρὸ αὐτοῦ γενόμενα, ὅτι
5 πολλάκις ὑπὸ ἀλλοφύλοις ἐγένοντο, καὶ πολλάκις αὐτῶν ἐκράτησαν ἐπὶ τῶν Κριτῶν οἱ ἀλλόφυλοι, ὡς καὶ αὐτοὺς καὶ τοὺς τόπους αὐτῶν ὑπ᾿ ἐκείνοις γενέσθαι.

62ª. Καὶ συνέκλεισεν εἰς ῥομφαίαν τὸν λαὸν αὐτοῦ. Παρέδωκεν αὐτοὺς τῷ διὰ ξίφους θανάτῳ.

10 **62ᵇ.** Καὶ τὴν κληρονομίαν αὐτοῦ ὑπερεῖδεν. Τὴν κτῆσιν αὐτοῦ, ἵνα εἴπῃ Κατεφρόνησεν τῶν ἰδίων, εἴτε τοῦ λαοῦ εἴτε τῶν τόπων.

63ª. Τοὺς νεανίσκους αὐτῶν κατέφαγε πῦρ. Διαφόρως ἅπερ ἔπαθον σημᾶναι βούλεται· οἱ ἱερεῖς μέν φησιν ἀπώλοντο ξίφει, ἀναλώθησαν δὲ πυρὶ οἱ νεανίσκοι, — τοῦτο γὰρ τὸ βαρύτερον, ὅτι νεώτεροι οὐκ ἀνδραγα-
15 θοῦντες ἐν πολέμοις ἀπώλοντο, ἀλλὰ πυρὶ καὶ τιμωρίαις.

63ᵇ. Καὶ αἱ παρθένοι αὐτῶν οὐκ ἐπενθήθησαν. Ἃς μάλιστα πενθεῖν ἔδει διὰ τὴν ἡλικίαν, οὐδὲ αὗται πένθους ἠξιώθησαν, πάντων περὶ τὰ οἰκεῖα ἀσχολουμένων κακά.

64ª. Οἱ ἱερεῖς αὐτῶν ἐν ῥομφαίᾳ ἔπεσαν. Τοῦτο βαρύτατον, ὅτι μηδὲ τῶν
20 ἱερέων γέγονέν τις φειδώ, — γέγονε δὲ ἐπὶ τῶν υἱῶν Ἠλεὶ σαφῶς.

20 cf. I Reg. IV, 11.

61ª. Ἀντὶ τοῦ — νεανίσκους: P, fol. 280; V, fol. 46ᵛ.
61ᵇ. Τὸ αὐτὸ — γενέσθαι: P, fol. 280; V, fol. 46ᵛ.
62ª. Παρέδωκεν — θανάτῳ: P, fol. 280; V, fol. 46ᵛ; *Paraphrasis* (p. 617).
62ᵇ. Τὴν κτῆσιν — τόπων: P, fol. 280; V, fol. 46ᵛ-47; *Paraphrasis* (p. 617).
63ª. Διαφόρως — τιμωρίαις: P, fol. 280; V, fol. 47; *Paraphrasis* (p. 617).   13 διὰ ξίφους Par.   14 τὸ *om.* Par.
63ᵇ. Ἃς μάλιστα — κακά: P, fol. 280; V, fol. 47; *Paraphrasis* (p. 617).
64ª. Τοῦτο — σαφῶς: P, fol. 280; V, fol. 47.

Aᵉ **61ª** (p. 405, 13-15): Quicquid illis praetiosius fuit uel aetate uel robore facta est praeda uictoris.   **62ª** (p. 405, 16-18): Passus est populum suum quondam hostium gladiis ac mocrone truncari.   **62ᵇ** (p. 405, 19-22): Dispexit populum siue loca, quae speciali affectu uidebantur et iure proprio possedere.
63ᵇ (p. 405, 26-28): Non est inuentus qui inmaturum misereatur interitum, cunctis propria infelicitate distructis.   **64ª** (p. 405, 30-406, 2): Grandis indignatio Dei, cum nec ministri eo exitio uindicantur; quod uel filiorum Heli internecione perductum est.

warriors and young men. *And their pride into the hands of foes.* It means the same thing, *pride* in numbers referring to the young men. He is referring to what had happened previously, that often they had been subject to the Philistines, and the Philistines often had gained control over them in the time of the judges, with the result that both they and their places fell under their power.

He hemmed in his people with the sword (v. 62): he handed them over to dying by the sword. *And ignored his inheritance,* his possession—that is, He scorned his own, both people and places. *Fire consumed their young men* (v. 63). He wanted to indicate in various ways what they suffered. The priests, he is saying, fell to the sword, while the young men were consumed by fire—a worse fate, since the younger men capable of brave deeds perished not in war but in fire and retribution. *There was no lamentation for their maidens:* those for whom there should have been particular lamentation on the score of age were not thought worthy of it, since all were occupied with their own plight. *Their priests were put to the sword* (v. 64): the worst fate, no pity being shown even to the priests—something that clearly happened in the case of Eli's sons.[15] | *And there was no grieving for their widows.*

---

15. Cf. 1 Sam 4:11.

64ᵇ. Καὶ αἱ χῆραι αὐτῶν οὐ κλαυσθήσονται. Βούλεται εἰπεῖν δι᾽ ὅλων ὅτι διαφόρως αὐτοὺς ἐπενεμήθη τὰ κακά, εἴτε νεανίσκους, εἴτε πρεσβύτας, εἴτε ἱερέας, οὐδενὸς αὐτῶν φεισαμένου τοῦ Θεοῦ διὰ τὴν τοῦ τρόπου κακίαν.

65ᵃ. Καὶ ἐξηγέρθη ὡς ὁ ὑπνῶν Κύριος. Ἀλλ᾽ εἴ ποτε παθεῖν αὐτοὺς συνεχώρησεν ὁ Θεὸς ταῦτα, δι᾽ ὧν ἔδει σωφρονεῖσθαι, αἰφνίδιον πολλάκις 5 ὥσπερ ἀπό τινος ὕπνου διανίστατο. Ἀεὶ δὲ ἐπὶ μὲν τῆς μακροθυμίας λέγει τὸν ὕπνον, ἐπὶ δὲ τοῦ βοηθοῦντα τοῖς ἰδίοις τιμωρεῖσθαι τοὺς ἐναντίους τὸ «ἐγείρεσθαι», ὡς καὶ ἀλλαχοῦ Ἐξεγέρθητι, ἵνα τί ὑπνοῖς, Κύριε. Ἐπειδὴ ἡμεῖς ἄπρακτοι μὲν ἐν τῷ καθεύδειν, ποιεῖν δέ τι τῶν ἀναγκαίων βουλό- μενοι, καὶ μάλιστα κατὰ τῶν πολεμίων, πρότερον διανιστάμεθα πάντως, διὰ 10 τοῦτο εἰς μείζονα παράστασιν τοῦ ὑποδείγματος τοῖς ῥηθεῖσιν ἐχρήσατο καὶ καλῶς ἐπήγαγεν·

65ᵇ. Ὡς δυνατὸς καὶ κεκραιπαληκὼς ἐξ οἴνου. Ἵνα εἴπῃ τῆς μακροθυμίας τὴν ἐπίτασιν, ἀπὸ τοῦ τοὺς ἀπὸ οἴνου κραιπαλῶντας ἐπὶ πλείονα καθεύ- δειν, καὶ μᾶλλον βαρυτέρῳ τῷ ὕπνῳ κεχρημένους μηδὲν τῶν ἐπειγόντων ἐπι- 15 τελεῖν. Τὸ γοῦν καὶ κεκραιπαληκὼς τῷ ὑπνῶν ἐπισυνῆπται, ἵνα ᾖ Ἐξηγέρθη Κύριος ὡς δυνατὸς ὑπνῶν καὶ κεκραιπαληκὼς ἐξ οἴνου, τουτέστιν Ἀλλὰ τοιαῦτα πασχόντων αὐτῶν ἀνεχόμενος καὶ μηδὲν ἀντιδιατιθεὶς τοῖς ἐχθροῖς, τοὐναν- τίον δὲ τῷ μεγέθει τῆς ἀνεξικακίας ὥσπερ ἐν ὕπνῳ τινὶ καθεστάναι δοκῶν ἀπὸ μέθης ἐπιγενομένῳ, αἰφνίδιον διανίστατο μετὰ πολλῆς τῆς ὀργῆς παρε- 20 χόμενος τῆς οἰκείας δυνάμεως τὴν ἀπόδειξιν ἐν τῇ κατὰ τῶν ἐχθρῶν τιμω- ρίᾳ. Τίνα δὲ ἃ ἐποίησεν;

8 Ps. XLIII, 24.

64ᵇ. Βούλεται — κακίαν: P, fol. 280; V, fol. 47; Cord, p. 644.
65ᵃ. Ἀλλ᾽ εἴ ποτε — ἐπήγαγεν: P, fol. 280ᵛ; V, fol. 47; Cord, p. 644-645.
11-12 τοῖς ῥηθεῖσιν ἐχρήσατο καὶ om. PV.
65ᵇ. Ἵνα εἴπῃ — ἐποίησεν: P, fol. 280ᵛ; V, fol. 47. 16. 17 κεκεκρεπαληκὼς PV
15 ὕπνω PV.

Aᵉ 64ᵇ (p. 406, 3-6): Probat nullam aetatem, nullum relegiosum officium inmonem posse esse uindictae, nisi merita subfragantur.   8-12 (p. 406, 7-13): Ad indicandam patientiam uel disimulationem, similitudinem dormientis indu- xit, eundemque surgere et excitari dicit, cum uel in exitium aduersariorum... accingitur.   65ᵇ (p. 406, 14-26): Vt pat⟨i⟩entiam ostenderet in longum protrac- tam, crapulatum dicit uino. Nobis, inquit, in tam uariis cladibus possitis, et cum nihil propter defensionem nostram miseriae hostibus reponeret, sed longua desimulatione, uino obpraesum imitaretur ac somno, subito cummulato furore surrexit poena atque exitio inimicorum documenta propriae uirtutis ostendens. Quae sunt autem quae fecit. uorsu sequente ostendit.

His overall meaning is that troubles were inflicted on them in various ways, whether young men or elders or priests, with none of them spared by God on account of their vicious behavior.

The Lord was awakened as if from sleep (v. 65). But if at one time God allowed them to suffer this, as was needed to bring them to their senses, he often would awake suddenly as if from some sleep. Now, by *sleep* he often refers to long-suffering, and by being *awakened* to his helping his own by punishing the adversaries, as also in another place, "Wake up! Why do you sleep, Lord?"[16] Since we are inactive when asleep, we first wake up when we want to do something necessary, especially against the enemy; hence, for a more effective presentation by way of a figure he employed these words, and went on in fine fashion to say *Like a warrior drunk with wine,* to bring out the extent of the long-suffering by a comparison with people drunk with excessive wine and in their deeper sleep showing no response to those stirring them. In any case, the phrase *drunk with wine* is introduced so that the Lord, like a *warrior* sleeping and *drunk with wine,* might be *awakened.* In other words, Instead of allowing them to suffer these things and taking no action against the foe, and by contrast giving the impression by the extent of his forbearance of someone reduced to slumber through a fit of inebriation, he suddenly arises in great anger and provides proof of his characteristic power by punishing the foe. What was it he did? | *He struck their foes in the*

---

16. Ps 44:23.

66ᵃ. Καὶ ἐπάταξεν τοὺς ἐχθροὺς αὐτῶν εἰς τὰ ὀπίσω. Ἀντὶ τοῦ Ἔτρε-
ψεν αὐτοὺς εἰς φυγήν· οἱ γὰρ φεύγοντες ἐν τοῖς πολέμοις ὄπισθεν τὰς
πληγὰς λαμβάνουσιν.

66ᵇ. Ὄνειδος αἰώνιον ἔδωκεν αὐτοῖς. Καὶ παρεσκεύασεν αὐτοὺς εἰς διη-
5 νεκὲς ὄνειδος εἶναι ὑπὸ τῶν κακῶν. Διὰ τούτων δὲ εἶπεν ὃ δὴ καὶ ἐπὶ τῶν
Κριτῶν ἐγένετο· πολλάκις μὲν γὰρ ὑπὸ ἀλλοφύλοις ἐγένοντο, πολλάκις δὲ
διὰ τῶν κατὰ καιρὸν Κριτῶν ἔξω τῶν κατεχόντων κατέστησαν.

67-68ᵃ. Καὶ ἀπώσατο τὸ σκήνωμα Ἰωσήφ, καὶ τὴν φυλὴν Ἐφραΐμ οὐκ ἐξελέξατο, καὶ ἐξελέξατο τὴν φυλὴν Ἰούδα. Φυλὴν Ἐφραΐμ καὶ σκήνωμα Ἰωσήφ
10 τὸ αὐτὸ λέγει· υἱὸς γὰρ ἦν τοῦ Ἰωσὴφ ὁ Ἐφραΐμ. Ἐπειδὴ δὲ πολλάκις
οἱ τῆς τοῦ Ἐφραΐμ φυλῆς τῇ τοῦ Ἰούδα κατεπανέστησαν, — ὡς καὶ ἐπ᾽
αὐτοῦ τοῦ Δαυὶδ ἀναστῆναι βασιλέα τὸν Σεβεέ, ὃν καὶ ἀποκεφαλίσαντες
ὕστερον οἱ τῆς πόλεως ἀνεῖλον ὑποθήκαις καὶ παρακλήσεσι τῆς σοφῆς
γυναικός, — ὑπέσμυχέν τε ἤδη τοῦτο τὸ γένος ὕστερον τῶν δέκα φυλῶν ἡ
15 διαίρεσις, ὧν ἐξῆρχεν ἡ τοῦ Ἐφραΐμ φυλὴ διὰ πλῆθος καὶ ἰσχύν, πόρρωθεν τοῦτο καταστεῖλαι ἠβούλετο διὰ τῆς παραινέσεως. Καὶ γὰρ ᾔδει κακοῦ
μεγίστου αἴτιον ἐσόμενον τὸ μὴ συμφωνεῖν αὐτοὺς ἅπαντας ἀλλήλοις καὶ
εἶναι ὑπὸ τὸν βασιλέα τὸν ἐκ τοῦ Ἰούδα καὶ ἐν τῇ μητροπόλει διάγοντα
ἔνθα καὶ τὸν ναὸν εἶναι συνέβαινεν. Τούτου μὲν γὰρ γιγνομένου ἐκ παντὸς
20 λόγου παρ᾽ αὐτῶν ἐθρησκεύετο τὸ θεῖον· ἴδιον δὲ βασιλέα ἐχόντων, καὶ
καθ᾽ ἑαυτοὺς ὄντων, τὸ ἐναντίον ἐγίγνετο, μήτε ἐπιβαίνειν τοῦ τόπου καὶ
τῆς τοῦ Θεοῦ θεραπείας καταμελεῖν, καὶ καταπίπτειν εἰς τὴν τῶν εἰδώλων
θρησκείαν. Ταῦτα γὰρ ἅπαντα ἀπὸ τῆς διαιρέσεως ἐγίγνετο. Πόρρωθεν τοίνυν, ὥσπερ διαμαρτυρούμενος καὶ διορθούμενος, ταῦτά φησιν ὅτι ὥσπερ
25 παρὰ πάντα ἡμᾶς ἐξελέξατο τὰ ἔθνη, οὕτω πάλιν παρὰ πάντας Ἰουδαίους
τὴν τοῦ Ἰούδα φυλὴν ἐξελέξατο εἰς τὸ βασιλεύειν, οὐχὶ δὲ τὰς λοιπάς. Διὰ

12-14 cf. II Reg. XX, 21-22.

66ᵃ. Ἀντὶ χτοῦ — λαμβάνουσιν: P, fol. 280ᵛ; V, fol. 47; Paraphrasis (p. 617).
66ᵇ. Καὶ παρεσκεύασεν — κατέστησαν: P, fol. 280ᵛ; V, fol. 47ᵛ.
67. Φυλὴν Ἐφραΐμ — προετιμήθη: P, fol. 280ᵛ; V, fol. 47ᵛ; Cord, p. 645-646.
9 φυλὴν δὲ Cord   24 διαμαρτυρώμενος PV.

Aᵉ **66ᵃ** (p. 406, 27-30): Significat quod hostes uertere dorsa conpulerit et
fugae praesidia postulare; fugientes autem e bello uulnera non aduerso corpore exciperunt, sed auerso.   9-10 (p. 407, 4-5); Vnus atque idem est; filius
siquidem Ioseph fuit Effraim.   14-16 (p. 406, 34-407, 2; 407, 6-7): Praeuidens
quantum mali x tribuum disensio... inlatura esset genti... Ob hoc solius fecit
mentionem, quia potentior caeteris erat.

rear (v. 66): that is, He put them to flight (those in flight being exposed to attacks by the enemy from the rear). *He gave them everlasting disgrace:* he brought them into unremitting disgrace by the troubles. Now, in this he mentions what actually happened in the time of the judges: they often fell subject to the Philistines, and often through the judges of the time they were rescued from their grasp.

He rejected the tent of Joseph, and did not choose the tribe of Ephraim; he chose the tribe of Judah (vv. 67–68). The terms *tribe of Ephraim* and *tent of Joseph* mean the same thing, Ephraim being Joseph's son. Those of the tribe of Ephraim often rebelled against that of Judah, as against David there arose as king Sheba, whom his fellow citizens later beheaded at the suggestion and advice of the wise woman.[17] And the separation of the ten tribes, which the tribe of Ephraim promoted on the basis of its numerical strength, fomented bad feeling in this race. So from a distance his intention was to suppress it with this exhortation, knowing that the lack of accord with one another and refusal to be under the king from Judah living in the capital, where in fact the temple was, would be a cause of awful trouble. In fact, as long as this was done, the divinity was honored by them in perfect order; but when they had their own king and lived by their own rules, the contrary occurred: they set no foot in the place, neglected the worship of God, and fell into the cult of the idols—all the result of the separation. From a distance, accordingly, as though adjuring and correcting them, he says that just as he chose us against all other nations, so likewise against all Jews he chose the tribe of Judah to reign, not the others. | This was the reason why he

---

17. Cf. 2 Sam 20.

τοῦτο οὐδὲ ἑτέρας ἐμνημόνευσεν, ἀλλὰ τῆς τοῦ Ἐφραΐμ, ⟨ἣν⟩ μάλιστα μεγα-
λοφρονοῦσαν κατ' ἀρχὴν τοῦ πράγματος συνέβαινεν. Διὰ τί δὲ ἡ τοῦ Ἰούδα
φυλὴ τῶν λοιπῶν προετιμήθη;

68. Τὸ ὄρος τὸ Σιὼν ὃ ἠγάπησεν. Τὴν φυλὴν ἐξελέξατο διὰ τὸ ὄρος.
Ἐπειδὴ γὰρ ταύτην περὶ τὸ ὄρος εἶναι τὴν φυλὴν συνέβαινεν, ἔδει διὰ τὸν 5
τόπον ταύτην προτιμᾶσθαι, ὥστε ἡ ταύτης προτίμησις εἰς τὸν τόπον ἔχει
τὴν ἀναφοράν.

69ᵃ. Καὶ ᾠκοδόμησεν ὡς μονοκέρωτος τὸ ἁγίασμα αὐτοῦ. Οὔπω τοῦ ναοῦ
κατεσκευασμένου τὴν νίκην λέγει· ὡς ὅτι πεποίηκεν αὐτήν φησιν οὕτως
περίβλεπτον καὶ μεγάλην ἅπασι καὶ φοβεράν. 10

69ᵇ. Ἐν τῇ γῇ ἐθεμελίωσεν αὐτὴν εἰς τὸν αἰῶνα. Ἔδειξεν ὅτι ἁγίασμα
τὴν σκηνὴν λέγει, εἰπὼν αὐτήν. Καὶ ταύτην φησὶ τὴν σκηνὴν ἐν τῇ γῇ τῆς
ἐπαγγελίας ἥδρασε διηνεκῶς, — τουτέστιν ἐν πάσῃ τῇ γῇ τῆς ἐπαγγελίας
τοῦτον ἐξελέξατο τὸν τόπον, ἐφ' οὗ τὴν σκηνὴν ἀμετάθετον εἶναι ἠβουλήθη, οὐχ ὥστε νῦν μὲν ἐνταῦθα εἶναι, ὕστερον δὲ μεταχθῆναι, ἀλλ' ὥστε 15
τοῦτον εἶναι τὸν τόπον ἀεὶ τῇ σκηνῇ ἀφωρισμένον. Ὅμοιον δέ ἐστι τούτῳ
τὸ ἐν τῷ ξζ' Τὸ ὄρος ὃ ηὐδόκησεν ὁ Θεὸς κατοικεῖν ἐν αὐτῷ, καὶ γὰρ ὁ
Κύριος κατασκηνώσει εἰς τέλος.

70ᵃ. Καὶ ἐξελέξατο Δαυὶδ τὸν δοῦλον αὐτοῦ. Διὰ τοῦτο κἀγώ φησιν
ἐξελέχθην. 20

70ᵇ. Καὶ ἀνέλαβεν αὐτὸν ἐκ τῶν ποιμνίων τῶν προβάτων. Ἔδειξε μείζονα τὴν χάριν, ὅτι ἀπὸ προβάτων εἰς βασιλέα μετέστησεν.

17-18 Ps. LXVII, 17ᵇ.

1 ἣν supplevi   1-2 μάλιστα γὰρ μεγαλοφρονεῖν Cord.
68. Τὴν φυλὴν — ἀναφοράν: P, fol. 281; V, fol. 47ᵛ-48; Cord, p. 646.
69ᵃ. Οὔπω — φοβεράν: P, fol. 281; V, fol. 48; Cord, p. 646; Paraphrasis (p. 618).
69ᵇ. Ἔδειξεν — εἰς τέλος: P, fol. 281; V, fol. 48.
70ᵃ. Διὰ τοῦτο — ἐξελέχθην: P, fol. 281; V, fol. 48.   20 ἐξελέχθην conieci, ἐξε-
λέγειν PV.
70ᵇ. Ἔδειξε — μετέστησεν: P, fol. 281; V, fol. 48ᵛ; Paraphrasis (p. 618).

Aᵉ 69ᵇ (p. 407, 14-17): Stabilitum ibi tabernaculum, nulla, ut prius, migra-
tione conuulsum est, sed in uno, in eodemque loco iugi habitatione consistere.
70ᵃ (p. 408, 17-19): In huius autem loci honorem placuit me anteferri omnibus.
70ᵇ (p. 407, 22-24): Auget dignitatem eligentis, cum se sub magisterio pecoris
egisse significat.

mentioned no others except Ephraim, who proved to be especially ambitious from the outset.

Why was the tribe of Judah preferred to the others? *Mount Sion, which he loved:* he chose the tribe for the sake of the mountain; since this tribe was in fact in the vicinity of the mountain, it gained preference in view of the place, with the result that its precedence has reference to the place. *He built his sanctuary like a unicorn* (v. 69). As the temple had not yet been built, he refers to the victory, meaning that he caused it to be great and fearsome and the cynosure of all eyes.[18] *He founded it in the land forever.* He made clear that by *sanctuary* he refers to the tabernacle. He established this tabernacle to last *in the land* of promise, he is saying—that is, in all the land of promise he chose this place, where he wanted the tabernacle to be without change, so that it would not be in one place at one time and later changed to another; instead, this place was to be set aside for the tabernacle forever. Resembling this is the verse in Psalm 68, "The mountain on which God was pleased to dwell, and the Lord will dwell there forever."[19]

He chose his servant David (v. 70): this is why I was chosen. *And brought him up from the flocks of sheep.* He made clear the greater grace, his promoting him from sheep to kingship. | *He took him from behind the young*

---

18. Theodore is wise not to expatiate on the unicorn, which appears in his text because of the LXX's reading *r'emim* for the Hebrew *ramim,* "high (places)." He is, of course, unable to correct the error.

19. Ps 68:16.

71ª. Ἐξόπισθεν τῶν λοχευομένων ἔλαβεν αὐτόν. Ἔθος ἐστὶ τοῖς ἄρτι τικτομένοις τῶν προβάτων τὰ παιδία μάλιστα ποιμαίνειν. Τοῦτο οὖν φησιν ὅτι Οὐδὲ ποιμὴν ἤμην ἀξιόλογος, ἀλλὰ παῖς ἔτι καὶ περὶ τὰ νῦν λοχευόμενα ἔχων, τουτέστι τὰ τικτόμενα. Καὶ ὅμως οὕτως με οὐδὲν ὄντα ἐξελέ-
5 ξατο, ὥστε τι ποιεῖν;

71ᵇ. Ποιμαίνειν Ἰακὼβ τὸν δοῦλον αὐτοῦ καὶ Ἰσραὴλ τὴν κληρονομίαν αὐτοῦ. Πεποίηκε τοῦ Ἰσραὴλ βασιλέα. Βούλεται δὲ διὰ τούτων αὐτοὺς παιδεῦσαι ὅτι οὐ προσῆκεν αὐτοὺς εἰς διαστάσεις ἐλθεῖν, ἀλλ᾿ ὑποτάσσεσθαι τοῖς ἀπὸ τοῦ Ἰούδα βασιλεῦσιν, ὡς τοῦ Θεοῦ τὴν φυλὴν ἐκλεξαμένου διὰ
10 τὸν τόπον περὶ ὃν ἡ φυλή, καὶ τὸν βασιλέα ἀπὸ τῆς φυλῆς.

72ª. Καὶ ἐποίμανεν αὐτοὺς ἐν τῇ ἀκακίᾳ τῆς καρδίας αὐτοῦ. Ἀλλὰ καὶ προχειρισθεὶς φησιν εἰς τοῦτο, ἴστε πῶς ὑμῶν ἦρξα, οὐδὲν χαλεπὸν καὶ ἐπίπονον καὶ κακίας γέμον περὶ ὑμᾶς ποτε βουλευσάμενος.

72ᵇ. Καὶ ἐν ταῖς συνέσεσι τῶν χειρῶν αὐτοῦ ὡδήγησεν αὐτούς. Ἀλλ᾿
15 οὐδὲ παρέλιπον ὁτιοῦν ἐχρῆν ποτε εἰς κυβέρνησιν ὑμετέραν διαπράξασθαι, ἀλλὰ μετὰ πάσης, ὡς οἶμαι, συνέσεως ἤγαγον ὑμᾶς καθὼς ἐχρῆν. Ἔστι δὲ οὐ καυχωμένου τὸ ῥῆμα, ἀλλὰ τὴν ἐπ᾿ αὐτὸ ψῆφον τοῦ Θεοῦ καὶ χάριν συστῆσαι καὶ μεγίστην δεῖξαι βουλομένου. Διὰ πάντων μέντοι τοῦτό φησιν ὅτι Ἀναγκαῖον ὑμᾶς μένειν ἐν ὁμονοίᾳ καὶ ἀνέχεσθαι βασιλέων τῶν ἐκ τῆς
20 φυλῆς ταύτης, ἵνα οὕτως ὑμῖν ἀδεὲς ᾖ καὶ τῷ τόπῳ ἐπιβαίνειν ἔνθα ὁ Θεὸς θρησκεύεται. Ἀμφότερα γὰρ πληροῦται, τούτων οὖν οὕτω γιγνομένων, ἥ τε ὑμετέρα συμφωνία καὶ ἡ περὶ τὸν Θεὸν εὐσέβεια· ἀμφότερα δὲ λύεται, ἕτερα ὑμῶν βουλευσαμένων.

71ª. Ἔθος — ποιεῖν: P, fol. 281ᵛ; V, fol. 48ᵛ; Vat. 1422, fol. 145; Cord, p. 647. 2 ποιμενομαίνων 1422.
71ᵇ. Πεποίηκε — φυλῆς: P, fol. 281ᵛ; V, fol. 48ᵛ; Cord, p. 647.
72ª. Ἀλλὰ — βουλευσάμενος: P, fol. 281ᵛ; V, fol. 48ᵛ; Cord, p. 647; Paraphrasis (p. 618). 13 ποτε om. Cord Par.
72ᵇ. Ἀλλ᾿ οὐδὲ — βουλευσαμένων: P, fol. 281ᵛ; V, fol. 48ᵛ; Cord, p. 648. 21 οὖν om. Cord.

Aᵉ 1-2 (p. 407, 24-26): Minorum quippe custodum est ista curatio, effoetas oues discretas a foetibus adseruare. 71ᵇ (p. 408, 2-6): .. uult autem per haec instruere eos ac docere quoniam non oporteat eos diuisione scindi atque separari, sed regibus de Iuda ortis subieci, — quae tribus propter locorum honorem ad imperandum Dei iudicio sit electa. 72ᵇ (p. 403, 7-16): Pro moderato reg⟨i⟩mine ac religioso auctoritate non solum rexit, sed potestate contenuit, sed magisterio erudiuit et diuina scientia inbuit. Cumque huius tranquillitatis et unionis commendat utilitatem, docet concordiae duplex commodum, dum et constantius hostes reppellunt unianimes et religionem tenacius amplexentur pacifici; latenter sane his laudandis carpit futura discidia utroque offectura diuissis.

(v. 71). Children normally have the particular task of looking after the new-born sheep. So he is saying, I was no famous shepherd, just a child concerned for the young—that is, the newborn. Yet he chose me in my insignificance. To do what? *To be shepherd to Jacob his servant and Israel his inheritance:* he made him king of Israel. In this he means to instruct them that instead of rebelling they should be subject to the kings from Judah, since God chose the tribe on account of the place in the midst of the tribe, and chose the king from the tribe. *He shepherded them in the innocence of his heart* (v. 72): you know how I ruled you, appointed as I was for this, never resolving on anything in your regard that was harsh or burdensome or malicious. *And guided them with the skills of his hands:* instead, I did not neglect anything that I ever should have done for your guidance; rather, in my view I led you with complete understanding as I ought. Now, far from this being a boast, it is actually the verdict on the matter from God in his wish to provide and demonstrate a wonderful grace. In everything, of course, he is saying, You must maintain good relations and put up with the kings from this tribe so that in this way you will have no qualms even about setting foot in this place where God is honored. Both things will in fact be fulfilled when this is done in that manner, both your good relations and reverence for God, whereas both will be lost if you decide upon on a different course. |

PSALMVS LXXVIII

Ἀντίοχος ὁ Ἐπιφανὴς μάλιστα πάντων πλεῖστα διέθηκεν κακὰ τὴν Ἰερουσαλήμ, πολλοὺς μὲν ἀνελὼν καὶ κατασφάξας τῶν Ἰουδαίων, μολύνας δὲ καὶ τοῦ Θεοῦ τὸν ναόν· ναὸν γὰρ αὐτὸν πεποιηκὼς τοῦ Διὸς καὶ βωμὸν ἀνέστησεν ἐπὶ τῷ Διὸς ὀνόματι καὶ θυσίας ἐπετέλει. Ἐντεῦθεν οἱ μὲν συνέ- 5
πραττον τῶν Ἰουδαίων, οἱ δὲ ἀναγκαζόμενοι θύειν καὶ μὴ βουλόμενοι ἀπώλ-
λυντο ἀδίκως καὶ παρανόμως σφαττόμενοι, ἀναιρούμενοι διαφόροις ἀπολλύ-
μενοι θανάτοις, ὡς πολὺ μὲν ἀνθρώπειον αἷμα περὶ τὸν ναὸν ἐκχεῖσθαι καὶ
τὴν πόλιν, μένειν δὲ ὡς ἐπὶ τὸ πλεῖστον καὶ ἄταφα τῶν τελευτώντων τὰ
σώματα, καὶ τὰ μὲν ὑπὸ θηρίων, τὰ δὲ καὶ ὑπὸ τῶν ὀρνέων ὡς εἰκὸς ἀνα- 10
λίσκεσθαι. Γέγονε δὲ παραπλήσιον τούτοις καὶ ἐπὶ Δημητρίου τοῦ βασιλέως,
καὶ τούτου μάρτυς ἀξιόπιστος ἡ Μακκαβαϊκὴ γραφή, μετὰ τὴν διήγησιν
τῶν γεγονότων αὐτῆς τοῦ ψαλμοῦ τῆς μαρτυρίας μεμνημένη ὡς τότε λαβού-
σης τὴν ἔκβασιν. Καὶ περὶ μὲν τοῦ Ἀντιόχου πολλὰ διηγησαμένη ἕτερά
φησιν οὕτως· Καὶ ἐξέχεαν αἷμα ἀθῷον κύκλῳ τοῦ ἁγιάσματός σου, καὶ ἐμό- 15
λυναν τὸ ἁγίασμα. Περὶ δὲ τῶν κατὰ Δημήτριον εἰπών, — ὅπως Βακχίδην
ἀπέστειλεν ὁ βασιλεὺς ἅμα Ἀλκίμῳ τινὶ τῶν Ἰουδαίων ἐπὶ τὸ παραδοῦναι
μὲν αὐτῷ τὴν ἀρχὴν τοῦ ἔθνους, κατασφάξαι δὲ τοὺς τοῦ Ματταθία υἱούς,
ὅπως δὲ μετὰ δόλου προσενεχθέντες τοὺς τοῦ λαοῦ πολλοὺς ἀνεῖλον, —
ὕστερόν φησι Καὶ συνέλαβεν ἐξ αὐτῶν ἑξήκοντα ἄνδρας, καὶ ἀπέκτεινεν αὐτοὺς 20
ἐν ἡμέρᾳ μιᾷ κατὰ τοὺς λόγους οὓς ἔγραψεν Τὰς σάρκας τῶν ὁσίων σου, καὶ
αἵματα αὐτῶν ἐξέχεαν κύκλῳ Ἰερουσαλήμ, καὶ οὐκ ἦν ὁ θάπτων.

Ταῦτα οὖν ὁ μακάριος Δαυὶδ ἐκ προσώπου τῶν Μακκαβαίων φησίν, οἳ
τὸν ὑπὲρ πάντων πόλεμον πρὸς τοὺς Ἀντιόχου στρατηγοὺς ἀνεδέξαντο,
Ματταθία μὲν ἀρξαμένου, διαδεξαμένου δὲ παρ' ἐκείνου τὸν πόλεμον τοῦ 25
υἱοῦ. Εἰκότως οὖν ἐκείνοις καὶ ἁρμόσει τὸ ἀθυμεῖν τε ἐπὶ τοῖς γεγενημένοις
καὶ λέγειν αὐτὰ πρὸς τὸν Θεὸν αἰτοῦντας τυχεῖν τῆς παρ' αὐτοῦ βοηθείας, οἳ ἐκ τῆς ὑπὲρ τοῦ νόμου προθυμίας καὶ τὸ δικαίως αἰτεῖν ἐκέκτηντο.

2 ss. cf. arg. Ps. LV (p. 360-361)   15-16 I Macch. I, 37   16 ss. cf. arg. ps. LVII
(p. 375)   20-22 I Macch. VII, 16-17.

Argumentum Ἀντίοχος — ἐκέκτηντο: P, fol. 281ᵛ; V, fol. 48ᵛ; Vat. 1422, fol. 145ᵛ;
Cord, p. 659-660.   3 μὲν *om.* 1422.   9 μέλειν δὲ ἐπὶ πλεῖστον 1422 μένειν δὲ
ἐπὶ πλ. Cord   18 μὲν αὐτῷ] αὐτὴν Cord   19 τούς] τοῖς PV   20 συνέλαβεν] συνέ-
λεξεν PV ἑξήκοντα] ἐξ PV ἔξω 1422   23-25 L (p. 653): Ἀντιόχου, τοῦ ἐπίκλην Ἐπιφά-
νους, τὴν κατὰ τοῦ λαοῦ τῶν Ἰουδαίων μανίαν ὁ προφητικὸς προθεσπίζει λόγος   25 ματθία
PV 1422   25-26 τὸν πόλεμον — υἱοῦ] τὸν υἱὸν PV   26 τε *om.* 1422   28 οἳ] ὁ Cord.

Aᵉ *Argumentum ps. LXXVIII* (p. 408, 18-23): In personam Machabeorum hoc
carmen inscribitur, qui sub Anti⟨o⟩cho Epifane patreas leges moeniaque patre
Mathathia auctore defendere, ultimis coacti malis adgressi sunt (PSEUDO-BEDA
910); unde conuenit eis ista narratio quos Dei zelus armauerat.

PSALM 79

Antiochus Epiphanes caused greatest harm to Jerusalem in particular, doing away with great numbers of the Jews and slaying them, and also defiling God's temple; he had in fact made an actual temple to Zeus, erected an altar in the name of Zeus, and performed sacrifice to him. At this stage some of the Jews cooperated; others under pressure to sacrifice refused and were unjustly killed by being slaughtered in lawless fashion, perishing in various forms of death, with the result that much human blood was shed in the temple and the city, the bodies of the deceased remaining unburied for a long time, probably being consumed in some cases by wild beasts, and in other cases by the birds.[1]

Something similar to this happened also under Demetrius the king, the Maccabean scriptures being a reliable record of it, and after the account of what happened citing the very text of the psalm as being fulfilled at that time. After recounting many other things about Antiochus, they go on in these terms: "They shed innocent blood around your sanctuary, and defiled the sanctuary."[2] After mentioning events concerning Demetrius, how the king sent Bacchides together with Alcimus, one of the Jews, to hand government of the nation over to him and to slay the sons of Mattathias, how they craftily assembled many of the people and slew them, the text later says, "He seized sixty men of their number and killed them in one day according to the words he wrote, *The flesh of your holy ones and their blood he poured out around Jerusalem, and there was no one to bury them*."[3]

These things, then, blessed David says from the viewpoint of the Maccabees, who waged war on everyone's behalf against the generals of Antiochus—Mattathias in the beginning, and his son succeeding him in conduct of the war. So he will be right to apply to them the distress at what happened and the expression of it to those making an appeal to God to receive help from him, since they had the right to make the appeal out of zeal for the law. | *O God, the nations entered your inheritance* (v. 1). Since

---

1. Details of Antiochus's assault on Jerusalem and the temple in 169 B.C.E. are taken from 1 and 2 Maccabees.

2. 1 Macc 1:37, a close reference to the opening verses of this psalm.

3. 1 Macc 7:16–17, which cites v. 3 of this psalm.

1ᵃ. Ὁ Θεός, ἦλθοσαν ἔθνη εἰς τὴν κληρονομίαν σου. Ἐπειδὴ κληρονομία καὶ κτῆσις ἰδία τοῦ Θεοῦ ἐλέγετο ἡ γῆ τῆς ἐπαγγελίας καὶ μάλιστα Ἱερουσαλήμ, — ὡς καὶ τὸν ναὸν ἐκλεξαμένου καὶ τὸν τόπον ἐκεῖνον εἰς τὸ ἐν αὐτῷ ὡς ἐν ἰδίῳ τοὺς αὐτῷ προσήκοντας οἰκεῖν, — ἰδού φησι τῶν σῶν 5 ἐκράτησαν ἄλλοι καὶ τὰ σὰ ὑπὸ ἀλλοφύλων κατέχεται.

1ᵇ. Ἐμίαναν τὸν ναὸν τὸν ἅγιόν σου. Καὶ οὐ κατέσχον ἁπλῶς, ἀλλὰ γὰρ καὶ ἐμόλυναν ἐκεῖνον τὸν ναὸν τὸν τῇ σῇ θρησκείᾳ ἀφωρισμένον.

1ᶜ. Ἔθεντο Ἱερουσαλὴμ εἰς ὀπωροφυλάκιον. Ἐν τοσαύτῃ κατέστησαν ἐρημίᾳ τὴν πόλιν, οὕτω τὰς οἰκήσεις πανταχόθεν καταρρίψαντες, ὡς μηδὲν 10 ἀφεστάναι ἐκείνης τῆς πρὸς βραχὺ γιγνομένης ἐπὶ τῇ τῶν ὀπωρῶν φυλακῇ.

2. Ἔθεντο τὰ θνησιμαῖα τῶν δούλων σου βρώματα τοῖς πετεινοῖς τοῦ οὐρανοῦ, τὰς σάρκας τῶν ὁσίων σου τοῖς θηρίοις τῆς γῆς. Ἔτι καὶ τὰ νεκρὰ σώματα ἄταφα καταλιμπάνοντες παρεσκεύαζον ὑπὸ ὀρνέων τε καὶ θηρίων καταναλίσκεσθαι. Ἐν γάρ ἐστι, κατὰ τὸ σύνηθες αὐτῷ δοκοῦν διαιρεῖσθαι, 15 ἀντὶ τοῦ δῆθεν τὸ τὰς θνησιμαίας σάρκας τῶν δούλων σου βρώματα τοῖς πετεινοῖς καὶ τοῖς θηρίοις τῆς γῆς. Ἐπεσημηνάμεθα δὲ καὶ ἐν τῷ νε΄, ὅτι ἰδίωμα τοῦτο παρὰ τῷ μακαρίῳ Δαυὶδ συνεχῶς εὑρισκόμενον.

3. Ἐξέχεαν τὸ αἷμα αὐτῶν ὡσεὶ ὕδωρ κύκλῳ Ἱερουσαλήμ, καὶ οὐκ ἦν ὁ θάπτων. Σφόδρα αὐτὸ ἐμφαντικῶς εἶπεν. Τοσοῦτος γὰρ ἦν ὁ φόνος, ὥστε 20 αἷμα δίκην ποταμίου ῥεύματος φέρεσθαι περὶ τὴν πόλιν κινούμενον, οὐδὲ

17 in ps. LV, 7 (p. 363, 20 ss.); cf. in ps. LVI, 11ᵇ (p. 374).

1ᵃ. Ἐπειδὴ — κατέχεται: P, fol. 282; V, fol. 49; Cord, p. 660.　　5 ἀλλοφύλων] ἄλλων Cord.

1ᵇ. Καὶ οὐ κατέσχον — ἀφωρισμένον: P, fol. 282; V, fol. 49; Cord, p. 660.　　7 σῇ om. Cord.

1ᶜ. Ἐν τοσαύτῃ — φυλακῇ: P, fol. 282; V, fol. 49; Cord, p. 660.

2. Ἔτι — εὑρισκόμενον: P, fol. 282; V, fol. 49; Cord, p. 660-661.　　14-15 διαιρεῖσθαι — τὸ] μὴ διαιρεῖσθαι τὰ ἐκλεκτὰ τῶν μεμολυσμένων καὶ Cord　　15 θνησιμαίους PV 16 προκεῖσθαι καὶ τοῖς Cord　　17 νε΄ corr., νς΄ PV Cord.

3. Σφόδρα — ἠξίουν: P, fol. 282; V, fol. 49; Cord, p. 661.　　20 ποταμίου ῥεύματος] ὕδατος Cord　　κινουμένον] κενούμενον PV κενουμένην Cord.

Aᵉ 1ᵃ (p. 408, 24-25): Pro possessione, quam tuam esse uolueras, in ius uenit externum.　　1ᵇ (p. 408, 26-27): Profanatis ritibus sacris, loca quoque impiata sunt.　　1ᶜ (p. 408, 29-409, 4): Tanta ciuitatis solitudo (in marg., sollicitudo in textu) facta est, inpulsis ubique aedibus in ruinam, ut nihil differat (deferat ms) umbraculo, quod in pomorum custodiam ad tempus exstructum, sublatis pomis a custode diseritur.　　12-14 (p. 490, 5-9): Nihil post cedem hostilis gladii humanitatis, nihil est misserationis secutum, ut mandarentur terrae cessorum corpora et inmundis auibus et bestiarum dentibus non paterent.

the land of promise and especially Jerusalem were called God's inheritance and special possession, insofar as he chose the temple and that place for those belonging to him to dwell in as their own, he says, Lo, others gained control of your possessions, and what is yours is in the hands of foreigners. *They defiled your holy temple:* they did not simply gain possession, but even defiled that temple dedicated to your worship. *They turned Jerusalem into a hut of a garden-watcher:* they reduced the city to such devastation, tearing down dwellings on all sides to such an extent that it shortly became no different from a hut for a garden-watcher.

They turned the corpses of your servants into food for the birds of heaven, the flesh of your holy ones for the beasts of the earth (v. 2): by continuing to leave even the dead bodies unburied, they caused them to be consumed by birds and wild beasts. In accord with his usual impression of differentiating, these two are in fact one, in the sense of the dead bodies *of your servants* being *food for birds and for the beasts of the earth;* we noted also in Psalm 56 that we find this idiom repeatedly in blessed David.[4] *They shed their blood like water around Jerusalem, and there was no one to bury them* (v. 3). He expressed it for particular effect: the slaughter was so great that blood flowed around the stricken city like river streams, | the dead not

---

4. In Ps 56:6 Theodore recognized hendiadys occurring.

ταφῆς ἀξιουμένων τῶν τελευτώντων. Καλῶς δὲ τὸ Οὐκ ἦν ὁ θάπτων ἐπήγαγεν. Καὶ οὕτω φησὶν ἀφειδῶς ἀναιροῦντες, οὐδὲν ἐκ τούτων κόρον ἔλαβον, ἀλλ᾽ ἔτι καὶ μετὰ τοσοῦτον φόνον καὶ τοσαύτην ὀργὴν καὶ τὸν θάνατον τῶν ἀπολλυμένων, περὶ τοὺς ἀποθανόντας τὴν ὀργὴν ἐπιδεικνύμενοι
ταφῆς αὐτοὺς οὐκ ἠξίουν. 5

4. Ἐγενήθημεν ὄνειδος τοῖς γείτοσιν ἡμῶν, μυκτηρισμὸς καὶ χλευασμὸς
τοῖς κύκλῳ ἡμῶν. Τότε οὖν ἡμᾶς οἱ περιοικοῦντες ἐφ᾽ οἷς πάσχομεν
ἐχλεύαζον, ὀνειδίζοντες ὡς οὐδὲν ὄφελος δεξαμένους ἀπὸ τῆς περί σε διαθέσεως. Πολλαχοῦ δὲ ἐν τοῖς ψαλμοῖς τῶν Μακκαβαίων μέμνηται τῶν γει-
τόνων ὡς ὀνειδιζόντων εἰκότως, ἐπειδὴ καὶ πολλοὺς παρ᾽ αὐτῶν ὑπέμειναν 10
πολέμους.

5ᵃ. Ἕως πότε, Κύριε, ὀργισθήσῃ εἰς τέλος; Ποῦ συστήσεται τὰ τῆς καθ᾽
ἡμῶν ὀργῆς;

5ᵇ. Ἐκκαυθήσεται ὡς πῦρ ὁ ζῆλός σου; Ἐκκαίεται ἀεὶ ἐπίδοσιν λαμ-
βάνων· οὕτω γὰρ ἀεὶ προσθήκην τὰ καθ᾽ ἡμᾶς ἐπιδέχεται κακά. Καλῶς δὲ 15
ἐνταῦθα ζῆλον ἐκάλεσεν τὴν ὀργὴν τοῦ Θεοῦ, ὡς ὑπὲρ ὧν ἠσέβουν καὶ
ἐξύβριζον εἰς τὸν νόμον περὶ τὰ ἑλληνικὰ ἔθη καὶ τῇ τῶν εἰδώλων θρησκείᾳ
ἑαυτοὺς ἀσχολήσαντες, παρακινηθέντος τοῦ Θεοῦ κατ᾽ αὐτῶν καὶ ζηλώσαντος.

6ᵃ. Ἔκχεον τὴν ὀργήν σου ἐπὶ τὰ ἔθνη τὰ μὴ γινώσκοντά σε. Εἰ γὰρ 20
τούτων ἕνεκέν φησι χαλεπαίνεις ὅτι ἔλαττον τῶν σῶν ἐφροντίσαμεν νομίμων, τιμώρησαι δικαίως ἐκείνους τοὺς οὐδὲ ἐγνωκότας σε τὴν ἀρχήν.

2 καὶ οὕτω] οὕτω γὰρ Cord   ἀφειδῶς] ἀναιδῶς Cord   3 τοσούτων φόνων PV
4 ἐπιδεικνύμενος PV   5 ἠξίουν] ἀξιοῦντες PV.
4. Τότε — πολέμους: P, fol. 282ᵛ; V, fol. 49ᵛ; Cord, p. 661-662.   7-9 τότε —
διαθέσεως affert Paraphrasis (p. 654)   7 οὖν om. Par   ἐφ᾽ οἷς πάσχομεν om.
Cord Par   8 περὶ εἰς σὲ PV   10 καὶ om. Cord.
5ᵃ. Ποῦ — ὀργῆς: P, fol. 282ᵛ; V, fol. 49ᵛ; Vat. 1422, fol. 146 sub nomine
ATHANASII; Paraphrasis (p. 654).   ποῦ φησί σοι στήσεται Par.
5ᵇ. Ἐκκαίεται — ζηλώσαντος: P, fol 282ᵛ; V, fol. 49ᵛ.
6ᵃ. Εἰ γὰρ — ἀρχήν: P, fol. 282ᵛ; V, fol. 49ᵛ; Paraphrasis (p. 654).

Aᵉ 2-3 (p. 409, 14-15): ...omnem effectum humanitatis exuerant.   4 (p. 409,
16-25): Sepe sane legitur in his psalmis, qui Mach⟨ab⟩eorum personae dicti
(dictae ms) sunt, quod finitimae gentes calamitatibus eorum laetatae sunt...
tamquam sine causa morientes insultauerunt finitimae, quod nihil nobis ad de-
pellendam calamitatem tua cultura profuerit.   6ᵃ (p. 409, 31-410, 4): Si relictae
legis tuae hac poena luimus, rectius in eos tua ira deseueat poenis, apud quos
nominis quoque tui nulla commemoratio est.

even being accorded burial. *There was no one to bury them* was an effective addition: They were so pitiless in destroying them, he is saying, as not to be sated by it; instead, despite so much slaughter and so much wrath and the death of the deceased, they took their wrath out on the dead by not according them burial. *We have become a laughingstock to our neighbors, a mockery and taunt to those around us* (v. 4): at that time those nearby mocked us for our sufferings, taunting us for experiencing no benefit from our commitment to you. At many places in the psalms he mentions the neighbors of the Maccabees rightly taunting them for being the butt of many wars on their part.

How long, Lord? Will you be angry forever? (v. 5) To what point will the effects of your anger reach? *Will your jealousy burn like fire?* It is forever burning and on the increase; the troubles affecting us are always gaining additional force. He did well here to refer to God's anger as *jealousy,* since God was provoked by them and made jealous by their acts of impiety and insult for the law concerning Greek customs in devoting themselves to the worship of the idols. *Pour out your anger on the nations that do not know you* (v. 6): if for this reason you are irked by our giving less thought to your laws, inflict just punishment on those who do not even know you to begin with. | *And on kingdoms that do not call on your name:* those who have never

6ᵇ. Καὶ ἐπὶ βασιλείας αἳ τὸ ὄνομά σου οὐκ ἐπεκαλέσαντο. Ἐκείνους τοὺς οὐδέποτέ σε Θεὸν καλέσαντας ἢ λογισαμένους.

7. Ὅτι κατέφαγον τὸν Ἰακὼβ καὶ τὸν τόπον αὐτοῦ ἠρήμωσαν. Καὶ γὰρ οὐ μικρὰ διέθηκαν ἡμᾶς κακά, ἡμᾶς γε μικροῦ καταναλώσαντες καὶ τὸ οἰκη-
5 τήριον ἡμῶν ἅπαν ἀφανίσαντες.

8ᵃ. Μὴ μνησθῇς ἡμῶν ἀνομιῶν ἀρχαίων. Ἄνωθέν φησι καὶ ἐξ ἀρχῆς πολλὰ παρ᾽ ἡμῶν ἔπταισται καὶ ἠγνωμόνηται εἴς σε. Μὴ δὴ πάντων ἐκεί-νων νῦν λάβῃς μνήμην· πρὸς γὰρ σύγκρισιν ἐκείνων καὶ μικρὰ ἅπερ ἐπά-θομεν.

10 8ᵇ. Ταχὺ προκαταλαβέτωσαν ἡμᾶς οἱ οἰκτιρμοί σου, Κύριε, ὅτι ἐπτωχεύ-σαμεν σφόδρα. Ὀξεῖαν δὲ μᾶλλον χάρισαι τὴν σὴν φιλανθρωπίαν, καὶ προ-καταλαβοῦ ἡμᾶς ἐν πολλῇ πτωχείᾳ καταστάντας καὶ ὀλίγους γενομένους καὶ μικροῦ πάντη καταναλωθῆναι κινδυνεύοντας. Καλῶς δὲ τὸ προκαταλα-βέτωσαν, ὡς ἐγγὺς ὄντων τοῦ παντελῶς ἀπολέσθαι, καὶ οὐδὲ δυναμένων
15 λοιπὸν ἀνακληθῆναι τῶν κατ᾽ αὐτῶν εἰ νῦν ὑπέρθεσιν λάβοιεν.

9ᵃ. Βοήθησον ἡμῖν, ὁ Θεὸς ὁ σωτὴρ ἡμῶν. Οὕτως οὖν χάρισαι τὴν σὴν βοήθειαν.

9ᵇ. Ἕνεκεν τῆς δόξης τοῦ ὀνόματός σου, Κύριε, ῥῦσαι ἡμᾶς. Καὶ εἰ μὴ δι᾽ ἡμᾶς, οὐκ ἄξιοι γάρ, – διὰ σαυτὸν γοῦν ἀπάλλαξον, καὶ ὅτι πάντες ἐπὶ
20 τῷ παραδόξῳ θαυμάζοντες μετὰ πολλῆς σου τῆς δόξης μνημονεύσουσιν.

___

6ᵇ. Ἐκείνους — λογισαμένους: P, fol. 282ᵛ; V, fol. 49ᵛ; Vat. 1422, fol. 146; *Paraphrasis* (p. 654). 1 ἐκείνους *om.* Par.
7. Καὶ γὰρ — ἀφανίσαντες: P, fol. 282ᵛ; V, fol. 49; *Paraphrasis* (p. 654).
8ⁱ. Ἄνωθεν — ἐπάθομεν: P, fol. 282ᵛ; V, fol. 50; Cord, p. 662.
8ᵇ. Ὀξεῖαν — λάβοιεν: P, fol. 282ᵛ; V, fol. 50; Cord, p. 662-663. 13 κινδυνεύ-οντα PV 15 τῶν *om.* Cord.
9ᵃ. Οὕτως — βοήθειαν: P, fol. 283 *et* V, fol. 50 (anon.); Cord, p. 663 *sub* *nomine* HESYCHII.
9ᵇ. Καὶ εἰ μὴ — μνημόνεύσουσιν: P, fol. 283; V, fol. 50; Cord, p. 663.

___

Aᵉ 8ᵃ (p. 410, 9-11):... sufficiat poena praesentium; ceterum praeteritarum ultionem ferre quis poterit? 8ᵇ (p. 410, 14-17):... auxilium nobis festinus impertiri benignus praeueni, quia si paululum adiutorium tuum deferas, necesse est nos omnes perire. 9ᵇ (p. 410, 20-21): Et si nulla nostrorum intercedat meritorum contemplatio, tamen uel ob hoc nos libera, ut stupore ac magnitu-dine operis tui... honor tui nominis augeatur.

called or considered you God. *Because they devoured Jacob and laid waste to his place* (v. 7): they caused us no little harm, almost wiping us out and destroying all our habitation.

Do not remember our ancient iniquities (v. 8): of old, from the very outset, failings and ingratitude on our part toward you were numerous. Do not now call them all to mind; what we have suffered is slight in comparison with them. *Let your pity quickly take the initiative in our regard, Lord, because we have been reduced to severe poverty:* grant us instead your prompt lovingkindness, and take the initiative in our regard, reduced as we are to acute poverty, made few in number and at risk of being almost completely wasted. *Let your pity take the initiative* was well put: they were close to perishing altogether, unable any longer to recover from their fate if they were now to meet with delay. *Help us, O God our savior* (v. 9): so grant us your help as we ask. *For the sake of the glory of your name, O Lord, rescue us:* even if not for our sake, unworthy as we are, at least for your own sake free us, and for the reason that everyone will marvel at the remarkable event and remember you with great glory. | *Forgive our sins for your name's sake:*

9ᶜ. Καὶ ἱλάσθητι ταῖς ἁμαρτίαις ἡμῶν ἕνεκεν τοῦ ὀνόματός σου. Καὶ ὑπὲρ τοῦ σε παρὰ πᾶσιν ὀνομάζεσθαι θαυμαζόμενον, μᾶλλον ἑλοῦ παριδεῖν ἡμῶν τὰ πταίσματα.

10ᵃ. Μή ποτε εἴπωσι τὰ ἔθνη. Εἰ γὰρ ἡμᾶς πάντη παραδοίης τοῖς κακοῖς, πολὺς ἔσται μᾶλλον παρὰ τοῖς ἐχθροῖς ὁ λόγος στρεφόμενος.   5

10ᵇ. Ποῦ ἐστιν ὁ Θεὸς αὐτῶν; Τί τὸ κέρδος τῆς ἐπ᾽ αὐτὸν πίστεως; Διὰ πολλῶν δὲ ἔδειξεν ὅτι δικαίως τῆς παρ᾽ αὐτοῦ τυχεῖν βοηθείας ὀφείλουσιν. Πρῶτον ὅτι ἡ αὐτοῦ κτῆσις παρὰ τῶν ἐχθρῶν κατέχεται, εἶτα ὅτι ὁ ναὸς μεμόλυνται, πρὸς τούτοις ὅτι πολὺς φόνος αὐτῶν ἐγένετο, ὅτι ὀνειδίζουσιν οἱ ἐχθροί, ὅτι δικαιότερον ἂν εἴη εἰ οἱ ἐχθροὶ τιμωρηθεῖεν μάλιστα   10 οὐ γνωρίζοντες τὸν Θεόν, ὅτι καὶ πρὸς δόξαν αὐτοῦ συμβάλλεται τὸ πρᾶγμα, ὅτι εἰ μὴ βοηθήσειε πολλὴ παρὰ τῶν ἐχθρῶν παρακολουθήσει ἡ χλεύη.

10ᶜ·ᵈ. Καὶ γνωσθήτω ἐν τοῖς ἔθνεσιν ἐνώπιον τῶν ὀφθαλμῶν ἡμῶν ἡ ἐκδίκησις τοῦ αἵματος τῶν δούλων σου τοῦ ἐκκεχυμένου. Καὶ ποίησον ἡμᾶς   15 φησιν αὐτοῖς θεάσασθαι τοῖς ὀφθαλμοῖς τὴν ἐκδίκησιν τοῦ φόνου τῶν δούλων σου, τουτέστιν Ἴδοιμεν τοὺς ἐχθροὺς ὑπὲρ τούτων τιμωρουμένους.

11ᵃ. Εἰσελθέτω ἐνώπιόν σου ὁ στεναγμὸς τῶν πεπεδημένων. Μελησάτω δέ σοι τοῦ στεναγμοῦ ἡμῶν, ὃν ἀπὸ μεγάλων ἀφίεμεν τῶν συμφορῶν.

9ᶜ. Καὶ — πταίσματα: P, fol. 283; V, fol. 50; Cord, p. 663.   2 περιϊδεῖν Cord.
10ᵃ. Εἰ γὰρ — στρεφόμενος: P, fol. 283; V, fol. 50; Vat. 1422, fol. 146 (anon.); Paraphrasis (p. 655).
10ᵇ. Τί τὸ κέρδος — χλεύη: P, fol. 283; V, fol. 50ʳ·ᵛ; Cord, p. 663.   6 τί τὸ — πίστεως om. Cord.
10ᶜ·ᵈ. Καὶ ποίησον — τιμωρουμένους: P, fol. 283; V, fol. 50ᵛ; Vat. 1422, fol. 146 (anon.); Paraphrasis (p. 655).
11ᵃ. Μελησάτω — συμφορῶν: P, fol. 283; V, fol. 50ᵛ; Paraphrasis (p. 655).

Aᵉ 9ᶜ (p. 410, 22-28): Maiore indulgentia nostra peccata disimulato, ut omnium te admirantium sermo concelebret.   10ᵇ (p. 410, 29-411, 8): Variae alligat quam ob rem uindicari mereatur. Primum, quod ab inimicis gentibus sit peruersa possesio; deinde, quod uiluerit templi reu⟨er⟩entia, pullutionis iniuria; quod multam cedem suorum uiderint; quod mala hostilia finimitorum obprobriis (obpropribriis ms) creuerint; quod iustius ignorantes penitus Deum puniri mirantur; quod ad multam gloriam eius spectet suorum difensio; quod haec nisi subuenerit multa inrisione hostis insultet.   10ᶜ·ᵈ (p. 411, 9-13): Seueritas ultionis... ita adceleretur, ut nostris quoque oculis possit uideri. 11ᵃ (p. 411, 15-17): Intenta et potenti aure gemitus nostros accipito, in quos uaria discriminum genera conpullerunt.

choose to overlook our failings—something more remarkable than your name being invoked by everyone. *In case the nations ever say* (v. 10): if you consign us completely to misfortune, word of it circulating among the foe will be much greater. *Where is their God?* What benefit is faith in him?

Now, in all this he brought out that they ought fairly to receive help from him—firstly because his possession was in the hands of the foe, next because the temple was defiled, and in addition to this because their blood had been shed in vast quantities, because the enemy taunts them, because it would be fairer if the foe were punished for the particular reason of their not knowing God, because the affair even redounds to his glory, and because considerable mockery by the foe would ensue if he were not to help. *Let the avenging of the shedding of the blood of your servants be known to the nations in our sight:* make us see with our very eyes the avenging of the blood of your servants—in other words, let us see the foe punished for them.

Let the groaning of those in bondage come in before you (v. 11): give heed to our groaning, which we utter out of deep distress. | *In keeping with*

11ᵇ. Κατὰ τὴν μεγαλωσύνην τοῦ βραχίονός σου περιποίησαι τοὺς υἱοὺς τῶν τεθανατωμένων. Περιποίησαι, τουτέστι περίσωσον· ἀνάλογόν φησι τῇ ἰσχύϊ σου τὴν περὶ ἡμᾶς βοήθειαν ἐπιδειξάμενος, οὕτως ἡμᾶς περίσωσον, — ἀντὶ τοῦ πάντη τῶν κακῶν ἀπάλλαξον.

5　12. Ἀπόδος τοῖς γείτοσιν ἡμῶν ἑπταπλασίονα εἰς τὸν κόλπον αὐτῶν τὸν ὀνειδισμὸν αὐτῶν, ὃν ὠνείδισάν σε, Κύριε. Ἐν τῷ λδ΄ σαφέστερον ἐπεσημηνάμεθα ὅπως τὸν κόλπον τὸ συνημμένον λέγει καὶ ἀχώριστον ἡ θεία γραφή, ὅταν μὴ αὐτὸν λέγῃ τὸν παρ᾽ ἡμῖν ὀνομαζόμενον κόλπον. Ὑπὲρ ὧν οὖν φησιν ὠ ιείδισάν σε οἱ περίοικοι ἡμῶν, ὡς οὐδὲν οὔτε δυνάμενον οὔτε
10　βοηθήσοντα ἡμῖν, ἀπόδος αὐτοῖς πολλαπλασίως, ἀντὶ τοῦ μετ᾽ ἐπιτάσεως. Τί δέ ἐστιν τὸ πολυπλάσιον ὃ λέγει; Ἔξεστιν εἰς τὸν κόλπον αὐτῶν, ἀντὶ τοῦ ὥστε τὴν τιμωρίαν τὴν παρά σου καὶ τὸν ὀνειδισμὸν τὸν ἐπαγόμενον αὐτοῖς ὑπὲρ ὧν ὠνείδισάν σε, ἀδιάλυτον καὶ ἀχώριστον αὐτοῖς παραμεῖναι, καὶ μὴ ὥσπερ τὰ καθ᾽ ἡμᾶς τῇ σῇ βοηθείᾳ λύσιν λαμβάνῃ οὕτω καὶ τὰ
15　κατ᾽ ἐκείνους λάβοι, ἀλλὰ τοιαύτην δέξαιντό φησι τιμωρίαν ὥστε διηνεκὲς ἔχειν τὸ ὄνειδος.

13. Ἡμεῖς δὲ λαός σου καὶ πρόβατα νομῆς σου ἀνθομολογησόμεθά σοι, ὁ Θεός, εἰς τὸν αἰῶνα· εἰς γενεὰν καὶ γενεὰν ἐξαγγελοῦμεν τὴν αἴνεσίν σου. Ἡμεῖς μέντοι φησὶν οἱ σοὶ καὶ ὑπὸ τῆς σῆς ποιμαινόμενοι βοηθείας, τούτων
20　γενομένων, διατελέσομεν εὐχαριστοῦντές σοι καὶ διηνεκῆ σοι τὴν ὑπὲρ τούτων εὐχαριστίαν ἀποδιδόντες.

6 in ps. XXXIV, 13ᶜ (supra, p. 184-185).

11ᵇ. Περιποίησαι — ἀπάλλαξον: P, fol. 283; V, fol. 50ᵛ; Vat. 1422, fol. 146 (anon.); Paraphrasis (p. 655).　3 ἐπιδειξάμενος des. Par.
12. Ἐν τῷ λδ΄ — ὄνειδος: P, fol. 283ᵛ; V, fol. 50ᵛ.　7 κόλπον τὸν PV　8-10 ὑπὲρ ὧν — ἐπιτάσεως affert Paraphrasis (p. 656).
13. Ἡμεῖς — ἀποδιδόντες: P, fol. 283ᵛ; V, fol. 50ᵛ-51; Paraphrasis (p. 656). 19 ποιμαινόμενοι] νεμόμενοι Par.

Aᵉ 11ᵇ (p. 411, 19-21): Tam gloriosa claraque sit nostra redemptio, quam est magna potentia tua.　6-10 (p. 411, 22-29): Sinum sepe pro re indiuisa profeta ponit atque coniuncta. Ordo est: mala, quae inpraecor inimicis, aeterno sinu illis et obprobrio choherescant. Pro his ergo omnibus, quod exprobrauerunt tibi inimici nostri, tuae inbicilitati nostras clades et miserias inputando, obprobriis quibus nos molliebantur aspergere meritissimis obruantur.　13 (p. 411, 33-412, 1):... nos, qui in morem pecodis tua prouidentia gubernamur, gratiarum tibi actiones iugiter offeremus.

the greatness of your arm, preserve the children of those put to death. By *preserve* he means "save": Give evidence of help to us in keeping with your strength, he is saying, and thus save us—in other words, free us completely from the troubles. *Repay our neighbors sevenfold into their bosom for the taunts they leveled at you, Lord* (v. 12). In Psalm 35 we indicated more clearly that by *bosom* the divine Scripture means "something attached and inseparable," not referring to the bosom as such in our terms.[5] So he is saying, For our neighbors taunting you as someone impotent and unhelpful to us, *repay* them many times over—that is, to the fullest extent. Now, what does he mean by "many times over"? Even *into their bosom*—that is, so that the punishment from you and the taunting leveled against them for their taunting you will continue to affect them without let or hindrance, and that just as our situation is relieved by help from you, so theirs will not be, and instead they will experience such punishment as to be subject to unceasing reproach. *We for our part, your people, sheep of your pasture, shall freely confess to you, O God, forever, and proclaim your praise for generation after generation* (v. 13): we, on the contrary, who are yours and are shepherded by your help, will continue giving thanks to you when this happens, and will render you unceasing thanks for it. |

---

5. Cf. Theodore's comment on Ps 35:13.

PSALMVS LXXIX

Διήγησις εἴτε καὶ προαγόρευσις τῶν κατὰ τοὺς Μακκαβαίους καὶ ὅδε ὁ ψαλμὸς ἀπὸ τῶν τότε εἰρημένος, παραδεικνύντων μὲν τὰ οἰκεῖα κακά, μνημονευόντων δὲ καὶ τῆς παλαιᾶς τοῦ Θεοῦ περὶ αὐτοὺς εὐεργεσίας, καὶ ἀξιούντων ὁμοίως καὶ νῦν τυχεῖν τῆς προνοίας παραπλησίως.   5

2ᵃ. Ὁ ποιμαίνων τὸν Ἰσραὴλ πρόσχες. Ὁ ἀεὶ προστάτης ἡμῶν καὶ προνοητὴς φανείς, καὶ δίκην ποιμένος καλοῦ ἐπιμεληθεὶς ἡμῶν, πρόσχες ἡμῖν καὶ νῦν.

2ᵇ. Ὁ ὁδηγῶν ὡσεὶ πρόβατον τὸν Ἰωσήφ. Τὸ αὐτὸ λέγει ἀπὸ ἑνὸς τὸ ἔθνος συνήθως καλῶν. Σύ φησιν, ὃς δίκην ποιμένος ἐξήγαγές τε ἡμᾶς τῆς Αἰγύπτου καὶ ἤγαγες διὰ τῆς ἐρήμου τῇ οἰκείᾳ ἐπιμελείᾳ, πάντων ἀξιώσας τῶν καλῶν, ὅμοια δὴ περὶ ἡμᾶς καὶ νῦν διάπραξον.	Ἰσραὴλ καὶ Ἰωσὴφ τὸν αὐτὸν λέγει, παρ' ἑνὸς καὶ αὐτοῦ κατὰ τὸ 10 εἰωθὸς τὸ ἔθνος καλῶν. Σύ φησιν, ὁ καθάπερ ποιμὴν ἡμᾶς ἐξήγαγες ἐξ Αἰγύπτου, καὶ δι' ἐρήμου τῇ σῇ κηδεμονίᾳ ἤγαγες, παντοδαπῶν αὐτοὺς ἀγαθῶν ἀξιώμενος, τὰ ὅμοια καὶ νῦν 15 ποίησον περὶ ἡμῖν.

Argumentum Διήγησις — παραπλησίως: P, fol. 283ᵛ; V, fol. 51; Vat. 1422, fol. 146ᵛ; Cord, p. 675.   2 ὅδε ὁ] ὅδε Cord   3 ἀπὸ] ὑπὸ 1422 Cord.
2ᵃ. Ὁ ἀεὶ — νῦν: P, fol. 284; V, fol. 51; Paraphrasis (p. 667).   7 πρόσχες ἡμῶν PV.
2ᵇ. Τὸ αὐτὸ — διάπραξον: P, fol. 284; V, fol. 51ᵛ.   Ἰσραὴλ — περὶ ἡμῖν: Cord, p. 676.   11 ὅς] ὡς PV.

Aᵉ Argumentum ps. LXXIX (p. 412, 3-12): Narratio siue praedicatio est earum rerum quae Machabeorum tempore contigerunt. Nam et praesens psalmus ex persona canitur eorum, quos constat illis interfuisse temporibus, qui nunc tam propria mala deflent quam Dei beneficia praeterita recordantur, et postulant ut dignetur eos pari ope etiam nunc et prouidentia confouere. Pseudo-Beda (914): Et hic Machabaeorum preces resonant, ut Dominus consueta beneficia non subtrahat.   2ᵃ (p. 312, 13-18): Qui officium effectumque pastoris semper gregis custodiae nostrae salutique praebuisti, etiam nunc gregem tuum laborantem conuersis oculis intuere.   2ᵇ (p. 412, 19-24): Pro Deduxisti per herimum saluatos ex Aegypto; ad opus simile etiam nunc pari studio curaque praecingere; eadem repetiuit quae dixerat, per tribus Ioseph totum populum uolens intellegi.

PSALM 80

This psalm, too, in the form of narration or prophecy, is a recital of events affecting the Maccabees from the viewpoint of people of that time, on the one hand representing their particular problems, and on the other hand recalling as well the former kindness of God in their regard, and appealing in similar fashion also to be granted his providence now in like manner. *You who shepherd Israel, give heed* (v. 1): you who have always proved to be our protector and provider, and have been concerned for us like a good shepherd, heed us now, too. *Who guide Joseph like a flock.* He means the same thing by referring to the race, as usual, by mention of one member: You who led us out of Egypt like a shepherd and led us through the wilderness by your characteristic care, granting us all good things, do likewise for us now, too. | *Seated*

2ᶜ. Ὁ καθήμενος ἐπὶ τῶν χερουβὶμ ἐμφάνηθι. Ἐπὶ τοῦ δυνατοῦ τὰ
Χερουβὶμ λέγει ἀεί. Ὁ ἐπὶ πάντων φησὶν ὢν τῶν δυνατῶν, καὶ πάντας
ἔχων ὑφ' ἑαυτὸν εἴτε ἀοράτους δυνάμεις εἴτε καὶ ὁρατάς, δεῖξον σεαυτὸν
διὰ τῆς εἰς ἡμᾶς βοηθείας.

5　3ᵃ. Ἐναντίον Ἐφραὶμ καὶ Βενιαμεὶν καὶ Μανασσή. Ἵνα εἴπῃ παντὸς
τοῦ ἔθνους περιληπτικῶς. Ἐμφάνηθι
οὖν φησὶν ἐναντίον ἡμῶν, τουτέστιν
Ἔμπροσθεν ἡμῶν δείχθητι, στρατη-
10　γῶν ἡμῶν ἐν τοῖς πολέμοις καὶ τρο-
πούμενος τοὺς ἐναντίους· καὶ γὰρ
ἔθος τοῖς γενναίοις τῶν στρατηγῶν
προηγεῖσθαι καὶ προκινδυνεύειν.

Ὡς ἂν εἴπῃ συλλήβδην τοῦ παντὸς γένους. Ἐμφάνηθι γοῦν φησιν
ἐναντίον ἡμῶν, τουτέστι πρὸ ἡμῶν
σὺ καθηγοῦ ἐν πολέμοις, καὶ εἰς φυγὴν τρέπε τοὺς ἐναντίους· καὶ γὰρ
εἰώθασιν οἱ εὐδόκιμοι τῶν στρατηγῶν
προηγεῖσθαι καὶ προκινδυνεύειν τῶν
ἄλλων.

3ᵇ. Ἐξέγειρον τὴν δυναστείαν σου, καὶ ἐλθὲ εἰς τὸ σῶσαι ἡμᾶς. Καλῶς
15　τὸ ἐξέγειρον, ὡς νῦν ἡσυχάζοντος καὶ οὐ κεχρημένου τῇ δυνάμει· κίνησον
αὐτήν φησι καὶ παραγενοῦ πρὸς ἡμᾶς ἐπὶ τὸ σῶσαι ἡμᾶς.

4ᵃ. Ὁ Θεός, ἐπίστρεψον ἡμᾶς. Ἀντὶ τοῦ Μετάβαλε τὰς καθ' ἡμῶν συμφοράς, ταύτας εἰς εὐπραγίαν μεταποιήσας.

4ᵇ. Καὶ ἐπίφανον τὸ πρόσωπόν σου, καὶ σωθησόμεθα. Μόνον φάνηθι καὶ
20　σεσώσμεθα· ἀρκεῖς γὰρ καὶ δείξας σεαυτὸν τοὺς ἐναντίους καταπλῆξαι.

2ᶜ. Ἐπὶ τοῦ δυνατοῦ — βοηθείας: P, fol. 284; V, fol. 51ᵛ; Vat. 142?, fol. 147
(anon.); Ὁ ἐπὶ Χερουβὶμ, τουτέστιν ἐπὶ πάντων — βοηθείας affert Paraphrasis (p. 667).
2 πάσας Par.
3ᵃ. Ἵνα εἴπῃ — προκινδυνεύειν; P, fol. 284; V, fol. 51ᵛ.　　Ὡς ἂν εἴπῃ — τῶν
ἄλλων: Cord, p. 676.
3ᵇ. Καλῶς — ἡμᾶς: P, fol. 284; V, fol. 51ᵛ; Vat. 1422, fol. 147 (anon.); Paraphrasis (p. 667).
4ᵃ. Ἀντὶ τοῦ — μεταποιήσας: P, fol. 284; V, fol. 51ᵛ; Paraphrasis (p. 667).
4ᵇ. Μόνον — καταπλῆξαι: P, fol. 284; V, fol. 51ᵛ; Vat. 1422, fol. 147 (anon.);
Paraphrasis (p. 667).　　19 καὶ μόνον Par.　　20 σεαυτὸν] ἑαυτὸν PV.

Aᵉ　2ᶜ (p. 412, 25-413, 6): Ad indicium potentiae diuinae Chirubin semper
subiecta dicuntur. Tu, inquit, cui magna quaeque famulantur, in cuius obsequium
uirtutum inuisibilium dignitas inclinatur, praesentiam tuam adiutorii effectu uelut
testimonio conprobato.　　3ᵃ (p. 413, 6-10):... totius gentis populos paucis nominibus inclusit. Ostende, inquit, nobis praesentiam tuam, et more ducis strennui ac
uindicis agmina nostra praecede.　　3ᵇ (p. 413, 12-15):... commoue in opus potentiam tuam, atque aduentum tuum conlatione nobis salutis ostende.　　4ᵃ (p. 413,
16-17): Faciem tristium rerum prosperitate commota.　　4ᵇ (p. 413, 19-23) ...in-
pertire aliqua tuae documenta praestantiae; quae, cum apparuerit, statim nos
quidem salus, hostes uero nostros sequetur interitus.

above the cherubim, shine forth. It is always in reference to power that he mentions the cherubim: You who are above all the powers and have under you forces both invisible and visible, reveal yourself in your help for us. *Before Ephraim, Benjamin, and Manasseh* (v. 2): as if to mention the entire nation as a whole. So he is saying, Make yourself visible before us—that is, Become visible in our sight, leading us in war and putting the adversaries to flight (brave generals normally lead from the front and expose themselves to risk). *Stir up your might, and come to save us. Stir up* was well put, implying someone now resting and not activating his power. Put it into effect, he is saying, and come to our side to save us.

O God, turn us back (v. 3): that is, Reverse our misfortunes; change them into prosperity. *Let your face shine forth, and we shall be saved: only appear, and we shall be saved;* it is sufficient for you to show yourself to dismay the adversaries. | *Lord God of hosts, how long will you be angry with the prayer*

5. Κύριε, ὁ Θεὸς τῶν δυνάμεων, ἕως πότε ὀργίζῃ ἐπὶ τὴν προσευχὴν τοῦ δούλου σου; Ὦ δέσποτά φησι, δυνατέ, ἀρκῶν μὲν ἅπαντα ποιεῖν, ὑπερτιθέμενος δὲ ὡς ἔοικεν ἀφ᾽ ὧν πάσχομεν, μέχρι πού τὰ τῆς καθ᾽ ἡμῶν ὀργῆς ἐπεκτείνεις; οὐδὲ τὰς προσευχὰς ἡμῶν πολλάκις προσιέμενος, οὕτως ἄρα πάντῃ ἀπεγένου ἡμῶν; Τὸ δὲ τοῦ δούλου σου τοῦ λαοῦ σοῦ λέγει, ἑνικῇ 5 φωνῇ τοὺς πάντας ἡμᾶς — [6ᵃ] Ψωμιεῖς ἡμᾶς ἄρτον δακρύων — ἔδειξεν τῇ ἐπαγωγῇ· εἰπὼν γὰρ δοῦλον ἐπήγαγεν ἡμᾶς, δεικνὺς ὅτι δοῦλον αὐτοῦ τὸν λαὸν εἶπεν, τουτέστιν αὐτούς. Τοσούτοις ἡμᾶς φησι περιέβαλες κακοῖς, ὥστε μηδὲ τῆς τροφῆς ἄνευ δακρύων μεταλαβεῖν δύνασθαι.

6ᵇ. Καὶ ποτιεῖς ἡμᾶς ἐν δάκρυσιν ἐν μέτρῳ. Καὶ τὸ ποτὸν δὲ πολλάκις 10 τοῖς δάκρυσι πληροῦμεν, οὕτως οὐδένα καιρὸν ἑαυτοὺς ἀνεῖναι δυνάμεθα. Τὸ οὖν ἐν μέτρῳ, τουτέστι πλῆρες. Οὕτω φησὶ πληροῦμεν δακρύων τὸ ποτόν, ὥσπερ οἱ μέτρῳ τι διδόντες καὶ πληροῦντες αὐτὸ πάντως διὰ τὴν τοῦ μέτρου συμπλήρωσιν. Τί δὲ τούτων τὸ αἴτιον;

7. Ἔθου ἡμᾶς εἰς ἀντιλογίαν τοῖς γείτοσιν ἡμῶν, καὶ οἱ ἐχθροὶ ἡμῶν 15 ἐμυκτήρισαν ἡμᾶς. Καλῶς τὸ εἰς ἀντιλογίαν Σύμμαχος διὰ μάχης εἶπεν. Οἱ γὰρ περιοικοῦντές φησιν ἅπαντες ἐπανέστησαν ἡμῖν εἰς ἀντίστασιν συμμάχων, καὶ τὸ χεῖρον· περιγενόμενοι γὰρ καὶ χλευάζουσιν ἐπὶ ταῖς συμφοραῖς.

8. Κύριε, ὁ Θεὸς τῶν δυνάμεων, ἐπίστρεψον ἡμᾶς· καὶ ἐπίφανον τὸ πρό- 20 σωπόν σου, καὶ σωθησόμεθα. Τοιούτων ὄντων φησὶν ὧν πάσχομεν, αὐτὸς ὁ μόνος δυνατὸς μετάβαλε τὰ καθ᾽ ἡμᾶς, καὶ δείξας σεαυτὸν παράσχου τὴν σωτηρίαν.

5. Ὦ δέσποτα — πάντας ἡμᾶς: P, fol. 284ᵛ; V, fol. 51ᵛ-52; Paraphrasis (p. 667). 2 ὑποτιθέμενος PV ὑπερτεθέμενος Par   4 ἐκτείνεις Par   οὕτως] ὄντως Par. 6ᵃ. Ἔδειξεν — δύνασθαι: P, fol. 284ᵛ; V, fol. 52; Paraphrasis (p. 668).   6 ἔδειξεν] ὡς ἐδ. Par.   7 γὰρ om. Par.   8-9 τοσούτοις — μεταλαβεῖν affert Vat. 1422, fol. 147 (anon.)   9 ὥστε] ὡς 1422   τῆς om. 1422   μεταλαβεῖν] μεταλαγχάνειν 1422. 6ᵇ. Καὶ τὸ ποτὸν — αἴτιον: P, fol. 284ᵛ; V, fol. 52; Vat. 1422, fol. 147 (anon.); Cord, p. 677.   10 τοῦ ποτοῦ 1422   12-13 πληροῦμεν — μέτρῳ] πληρουμένου· τὸ γὰρ ἐν μέτρῳ 1422   14 συμπλήρωσιν des. 1422. 7. Καλῶς — συμφοραῖς: P, fol. 284ᵛ; V, fol. 52; Vat. 1422, fol. 147; Paraphrasis (p. 668).   17 ἀντίστασιν] ἀνάστασιν 1422. 8. Τοιούτων — σωτηρίαν: P, fol. 284ᵛ; V, fol. 52; Paraphrasis (p. 668).

Aᵉ 8-9 (p. 413, 26-29): Tantis, inquit, inplicuisti nos miseriis, ut nec uescendi tempore possimus a lacrimis temperare.   10-11 (p. 413, 30-414, 1): Pocula... impleuimus multis fletibus riuisque lacrimarum, ita ut nullo tempore a continuis angoribus relaxemur.   17-19 (p. 414, 2-4) ...rebelli in nos animo ac mente consurgunt, miseriisque nostris insultant.

of your servant? (v. 4). O Lord, powerful one, capable of doing everything, on the one hand, and on the other hand evidently protracting our sufferings, how far will you extend your anger against us? Surely in often dismissing our prayers you have not thus completely abandoned us? Now, by *your servant* he means "your people," referring to us all in the singular, as he showed in the following verse, *You will feed us bread of tears* (v. 5): after saying *servant* he went on to say *us,* proving that the people is his servant—that is, they themselves. You invested us in so many troubles, he is saying, that we are unable even to eat food without tears. *And you will give us tears to drink in full measure:* we often fill our drink with tears, and so are incapable of enjoying any respite (the phrase *in full measure* thus meaning "full"). You fill our drink with tears to such an extent, he is saying, like those measuring something out and filling it up to the very brim. Now, what is responsible for this? *You made us a sign of contradiction to our neighbors, and our foes sneered at us* (v. 6). Symmachus did well to render *a sign of contradiction* as "in battle": the neighboring peoples all rebelled against us in joint revolt, intending no good; they prevailed over us and mocked us for our misfortunes.

Lord, God of hosts, turn us back; let your face shine, and we shall be saved (v. 7): our sufferings being what they are, you, the sole powerful one, personally reverse our fortunes, and by showing yourself, provide salvation. | *You moved a vine out of Egypt* (v. 8): we are the ones you uprooted

9ᵃ. Ἄμπελον ἐξ Αἰγύπτου μετῆρας. Ἡμεῖς φησιν ἐσμὲν ἐκεῖνοι, οὓς δίκην ἀμπέλου ἐν τῇ Αἰγύπτῳ διάγοντας ἐξήσπασάς τε καὶ μετήγαγες.

9ᵇ. Ἐξέβαλες ἔθνη καὶ κατεφύτευσας αὐτήν. Καὶ περιελὼν τοὺς κατοικοῦντας τότε ἐπὶ τῆς γῆς, ἡμῖν ἀπεκλήρωσας τὸν τόπον, ὥσπερ φυτείᾳ
5 τινὶ τῆς οἰκήσεως τὸ βέβαιον ἐπαγγειλάμενος.

10ᵃ. Ὡδοποίησας ἔμπροσθεν αὐτῆς. Οὐδὲν κώλυμα ἀφῆκας γενέσθαι, οὐδὲ συνεχώρησάς τινι τῇ παρόδῳ ἡμῶν ἐναντιωθῆναι, ἀνελὼν ἅπαντας καὶ ὥσπερ ὁδόν τινα ἐξομαλίσας καὶ ἐξευμαρίσας ἡμῖν τὰ πράγματα.

10ᵇ. Καὶ κατεφύτευσας τὰς ῥίζας αὐτῆς, καὶ ἐπλήρωσε τὴν γῆν. Οὕτως
10 ἡμᾶς κατὰ πάσης τῆς γῆς κατῴκισας, — λέγει δὲ τῆς γῆς τῆς ἐπαγγελίας.

11ᵃ. Ἐκάλυψεν ὄρη ἡ σκιὰ αὐτῆς. Κατῴκησαν καὶ ἐπὶ τῶν ὀρέων.

11ᵇ. Καὶ αἱ ἀναδενδράδες αὐτῆς τὰς κέδρους τοῦ Θεοῦ. Καὶ ἐξετάθησαν μέχρι τοσούτου, καὶ εἰς πλῆθος ἐπέδωκαν, ὡς καὶ μέχρι τῶν ὑψηλοτέρων τόπων, ἐν οἷς τὰς κέδρους συμβαίνει εἶναι, τὴν κατοικίαν ποιήσασθαι.

15 12ᵃ. Ἐξέτεινε τὰ κλήματα αὐτῆς ἕως θαλάσσης. Ἐξετάθησαν δὲ καὶ μέχρι τῆς θαλάσσης· ἦσαν γὰρ οἱ καὶ τὴν παραθαλασσίαν οἰκοῦντες.

9ᵃ. Ἡμεῖς — μετήγαγες: P, fol. 284ᵛ; V, fol. 52; Vat. 1422, fol. 147ᵛ; Cord, p. 677; Paraphrasis (p. 668).
9ᵇ. Καὶ περιελὼν — ἐπαγγειλάμενος: P, fol. 284ᵛ; V, fol. 52; Vat. 1422, fol. 147ᵛ (anon.); Paraphrasis (p. 668).
10ᵃ. Οὐδὲν — τὰ πράγματα: P, fol. 284ᵛ; V, fol. 52; Cord, p. 677.　6 οὐδὲν] ἀλλὰ καὶ οὐδὲν Cord.
10ᵇ. Οὕτως — ἐπαγγελίας: P, fol. 284ᵛ; V, fol. 52; Cord, p. 677.　9 καὶ οὕτως Cord.
11ᵃ. Κατῴκησαν καὶ ἐπὶ τῶν ὀρέων: P, fol. 285; V, fol. 52.
11ᵇ. Καὶ ἐξετάθησαν — ποιήσασθαι: P, fol. 285; V, fol. 52ᵛ; Paraphrasis (p. 668). 13 πλῆθος] ὕψος Par　ὡς καὶ] ὡς Par.
12ᵃ. Ἐξετάθησαν — οἰκοῦντες: P, fol. 285; V, fol. 52ᵛ; Cord, p. 678; Paraphrasis (p. 669).　15 δὲ] γὰρ Cord Par.　16 θαλάσσης des. Par.

Aᵉ　9ᵃ (p. 414, 7-10)... nos, inquit, sumus illi, quos in morem uiniae uulsos, de terra Aegipti transtulisti.　9ᵇ (p. 414, 11-13): Iectis atque interfectis locorum habitatoribus, nos terram eorum possedere fecisti.　11ᵃ (p. 414, 21-22): ... sed etiam montium uertices occupauit.　11ᵇ (p. 414, 23-27): Ita... adoleuimus et in altum ascendimus, ut excelsa quaeque in quibus cedri nascuntur... caperemus.　12ᵃ (p. 414, 29-31):... sed usque ad maris uicina peruenit; multi namque filiorum Israhel loca mari proxima possederunt.

like a vine when we were living in Egypt, and you changed our abode. *You drove out nations and planted it:* having done away with the land's inhabitants of the time, you assigned us the place, guaranteeing stability of tenure by a kind of planting. *You went as a guide before it* (v. 9): you allowed nothing to be an obstacle, nor permitted anything to stand in our way as a sort of diversion, destroying everything and smoothing things out for us as though clearing a path of some kind. *You sank its roots, and filled the land:* thus you settled us throughout the land (referring to the land of promise). *Its shadow covered mountains* (v. 10): they even dwelt on the mountains. *Its branches, the cedars of God:* they spread so far and grew so much in number as to make their dwelling even on the highest places, where, in fact, the cedars are. *It extended its tendrils to the sea* (v. 11): they spread even as far as the sea, being occupants also of the coast. | *And its offshoots as far as rivers:* as far as

12ᵇ. Καὶ ἕως ποταμῶν τὰς παραφυάδας αὐτῆς. Μέχρι τοῦ ποταμοῦ τοῦ
Ἰορδάνου φησίν· ἠβουλήθη γὰρ εἰπεῖν ὅτι εἰς πλῆθος ἐπέδωκαν καὶ κατέσχον πᾶσαν τὴν γῆν, τὰ ὄρη, τὰ παραθαλάσσια, τοὺς ποταμούς, ὥστε
ἁπάντων ἔχειν τὴν ἀπόλαυσιν, εἴτε τι ἀπὸ θαλάσσης καλόν, εἴτε τι ἀπὸ
ὀρέων, εἴτε καὶ ἑτέρωθεν. Τῷ δὲ ὁμοιώματι μᾶλλον ἐλάμπρυνε τὸν λόγον ἐν 5
ἀμπέλου τάξει τὸν λαὸν εἰσαγαγών, καὶ ἐκσπασθέντα ἐκ τῆς Αἰγύπτου,
καὶ μετενεχθέντα εἰς τὴν Παλαιστίνην ἐκεῖ τε φυτευθέντα καὶ ἐκτείναντα
ὥσπερ κλήματα τὸ πλῆθος, ἁψάμενον τῶν ὀρέων, ἁψάμενον τῆς θαλάσσης,
κυκλώσαντα τὸν ποταμόν, — διὰ πάντων μέντοι τὴν παλαιὰν εὐπραγίαν
αὐτῶν ἐσήμανεν. 10

13. Ἵνα τι καθεῖλες τὸν φραγμὸν αὐτῆς καὶ τρυγῶσιν αὐτὴν πάντες οἱ
παραπορευόμενοι τὴν ὁδόν; Ἤρκεσεν αὐτῷ ἡ τῆς ἀμπέλου παραβολὴ καὶ
εἰς ἀπόδειξιν τῆς παλαιᾶς εὐπραγίας καὶ εἰς παράστασιν τῆς νῦν συμφορᾶς. Ἄμπελος γὰρ οὐδεμᾶς ἀσφαλείας ἠξιωμένη πρόκειται πᾶσιν τοῖς
παρερχομένοις εἰς λύμην, ἑκάστου καὶ διὰ τὸ ὥριμος εἶναι καὶ διὰ τὸ ἐκ 15
τοῦ καρποῦ ὀρέγεσθαι εὐκόλως ἐπεισιόντος ὅταν μηδὲν τὸ κωλῦον ᾖ. Περιελὼν οὖν τὸν φραγμόν φησι τὸν ἡμέτερον, δηλαδὴ τὴν ἀσφάλειαν ἡμῶν καὶ
τὴν παρά σου φυλακήν, ἔδωκας ἡμᾶς τοῖς ἐναντίοις, ὥστε εὐχειρώτους εἶναι
παντὶ τῷ βουλομένῳ, οὕτω πᾶσιν εὐάλωτοι καθεστήκαμεν.

14. Ἐλυμήνατο αὐτὴν ὗς ἐκ δρυμοῦ, καὶ μονιὸς ἄγριος κατενεμήσατο 20
αὐτήν. Τὸν Ἀντίοχον λέγει μάλιστα πάντων κακῶς αὐτοῖς χρησάμενον καὶ
πολλὰ διαθέντα κατὰ τὴν πόλιν, τὴν χώραν, τὸ ἔθνος, τὸν ναόν, οὐδὲν
εἶδος ἐλλελοιπότα πονηρίας, ὅπως δὲ κατὰ αὔξησιν παρέστησεν τῶν κακῶν
τὴν ἐπίτασιν. Σφόδρα γὰρ ἄμπελον λυμαίνεται κἂν κοινὸν εἶναι κἂν ἥμερον
τὸν χοῖρον συμβαίνῃ, πλέον δὲ ὅταν εἰ καὶ ἄγριος εἴη καὶ τῶν ἐν ὄρεσι 25

12ᵇ. Μέχρι τοῦ ποταμοῦ — ἐσήμανεν: P, fol. 285; V, fol. 52ᵛ; Cord, p. 678;
Paraphrasis (p. 669).   1 τοῦ om. Cord καὶ μέχρι ποτ. Par   2 γὰρ] δὲ Cord
4 ἀπόλαυσιν des. Par   τι ἀπὸ ὀρέων] ἀπὸ ὀρ. PV   7 τε om. PV   καὶ om. PV.
13. Ἤρκεσεν — καθεστήκαμεν: P, fol. 285; V, fol. 52ᵛ; Vat. 1422, fol. 147ᵛ;
Cord, p. 678.   14 πρόκειται] ὑπόκειται 1422   παρερχομένοις] ἐρχομένοις 1422   15 καὶ
— εἶναι καὶ om. Cord   16 ὀρέγεσθαι om. PV   ἐπισείοντος PV   17 δηλαδὴ om. PV.
14. Τὸν Ἀντίοχον — λυμαίνεται: P, fol. 285ʳ; V, fol. 52ᵛ-53; Cord, p. 679.
21 χρησαμένῳ PV   23 ὅπως δὲ] ὅρα δὲ ὅπως Cord   25 συμβαίνει PV   ὅταν εἰ
καὶ] ὄντα καὶ εἰ καὶ PV.

Aᵉ   1-2 (p. 414, 32-33): Id est, Iordanen possesum.   12-14 (p. 415, 1-4): Seruauit conpararationis tenorem, ut solutis quibus cludiebantur praesidiis, expos-
sitam diripientibus uiniam diceret.   21-24 (p. 415, 10-13): ...hoc uoluit ostendere quod talem Antiochum passi fuerint, qualem singularem aprum uiniarum
uastitas experitur.

the river Jordan, his meaning being that they grew in numbers and took possession of all the land, the mountains, the coast, the rivers, with the result that they had enjoyment of everything, whether good things from the sea or from mountains or also from other sources. Now, he considerably embellished the account with figurative language, introducing the people in the role of a vine: uprooted from Egypt, transferred to Palestine, planted there, growing in number like branches, reaching the mountains, reaching the sea, encircling the river (in everything, of course, implying their former prosperity).

Why have you done away with its wall, and so all who pass that way pick its grapes? (v. 12). The figure of the vine sufficed to provide him both with a proof of the former prosperity and with a presentation of the current disaster: a vine not accorded any security is exposed to harm from all those who pass by, everyone making inroads on account of its ripeness and by easily picking fruit when there is no obstacle. By destroying our wall—that is, our security and the protection from you—he is saying, you exposed us to the adversaries so as to be vulnerable to anyone interested, and thus made us easy pickings for anyone. *A forest boar ravaged it, and a solitary animal fed off it* (v. 13). He is referring to Antiochus, who most of all treated them badly and made many incursions against the city, the country, the nation, and the temple, neglecting no form of vicious behavior in his endeavors to take the extent of their troubles to extremes. A pig, in fact, causes considerable damage to a vine, even if it is ordinary and tame, but worse damage if it is actually wild and one of those living in the mountains; | if it is a solitary beast and keeps

διαιτωμένων· ἂν δὲ καὶ τῶν ἀγρίων μεμονωμένος καὶ πρὸς τοὺς ἄλλους
ἀγρίους τῶν χοίρων ἀκοινώνητος, ἔτι χαλεπότερον τὸ κακόν, — οἱ γὰρ
τοιοῦτοι ἰσχυροὶ καὶ μάλιστα ἄγριοι, οἷοίπερ καὶ ἐπὶ τῶν λύκων, — οἱ γὰρ
μεμονωμένοι καὶ καθ᾿ ἑαυτοὺς διάγοντες μείζονα ἔτι τοῦ κακοῦ τὴν ἐπίτασιν
5 φέρουσι. Τὸ γὰρ μονιὸς ἄγριος τοῦτο λέγει, — τουτέστι ὥσπερ ὗς ἄγριος
μεμονωμένος καὶ πρὸς πάντας ἀκοινώνητος, οὕτως ἡμᾶς κατενεμήσατο· καὶ
γὰρ ἐκεῖνος οὐ τοῦ καρποῦ μόνον ἅπτεται, ἀλλὰ καὶ αὐτοῖς πολλάκις τοῖς
φυτοῖς λυμαίνεται.

15ᵃ. Ὁ Θεὸς τῶν δυνάμεων, ἐπίστρεψον δή. Ὅταν μνημονεύσῃ τῶν ἐπα-
10 γομένων κακῶν, καὶ ἀναγκαίως τῇ ἐπαγωγῇ ταύτῃ χρῆται. Οὐκοῦν φησιν,
ὁ δυνατός, μετάβαλε τὰ καθ᾿ ἡμᾶς.

15ᵇ. Καὶ ἐπίβλεψον ἐξ οὐρανοῦ, καὶ ἴδε. Πρόσχες δὴ τοῖς καθ᾿ ἡμᾶς ἐκ
τῶν οὐρανῶν.

15ᶜ. Καὶ ἐπίσκεψαι τὴν ἄμπελον ταύτην. Σφόδρα ἐμπαθῶς αὐτὸ εἶπεν
15 καὶ ἐλεεινῶς· αὐτάρκως ἐν τοῖς ἄνω ἀποδειξάμενος αὐτῆς τὴν ἐρήμωσιν καὶ
τῆς ἐρημώσεως τὴν ἐπίτασιν, ἐπήγαγεν καιρίως τὸ Ἐπίσκεψαι τὴν ἄμπελον
ταύτην, δεικτικῶς ὁμοῦ καὶ ἐμπαθῶς. Σὺ τοίνυν φησίν, ὁ τῆς ἀμπέλου ταύτης γεωργός, βλέπε αὐτῆς τὴν ἐρήμωσιν καὶ τὴν διαφθοράν, — ὡς οὐκ
ἀρκοῦντος λόγου δεῖξαι τὴν ἐρήμωσιν εἰ μὴ καὶ ὠφθείη.

20 **16ᵃ.** Καὶ κατάρτισαι αὐτήν, ἣν ἐφύτευσεν ἡ δεξιά σου. Καὶ τῇ σῇ ἐπι-
μελείᾳ πάλιν αὐτὴν σύσφιγξον καὶ συνάγαγε καὶ συγκρότησον, ἐπειδὴ σόν
ἐστι γεώργιον, - διὰ τὸ κάλλος τὸ ἣν ἐφύτευσεν κινητικῶς εἰπών.

16ᵇ. Καὶ ἐπὶ υἱὸν ἀνθρώπου, ὃν ἐκραταίωσας σεαυτῷ. Ἀπὸ τοῦ παραδείγματος ἐπὶ τὸ πρόσωπον μετέβη· ἃ γὰρ αὐτῷ προσήκοντα ὡς ἐπὶ

---

2 ἔτι — κακὸν om. PV   4-5 μείζονα — φέρουσι] μείζων ἔτι τοῦ κακοῦ ἡ ἐπίτασις PV.
15ᵃ. Ὅταν — καθ᾿ ἡμᾶς: P, fol. 285ᵛ; V, fol. 53; Paraphrasis (p. 669).   10 καὶ
om. Par.
15ᵇ. Πρόσχες – οὐρανῶν: P, fol. 285ᵛ; V, fol. 53.
15ᶜ. Σφόδρα — ὠφθείη: P, fol. 285ᵛ; V, fol. 53; Cord, p. 680.   17-18 Σὺ —
διαφθορὰν affert Paraphrasis (p. 669).
16ᵃ. Καὶ τῇ σῇ — εἰπών: P, fol. 285ᵛ; V, fol. 53; Paraphrasis (p. 669).   22 γεώργιον des. Par.
16ᵇ. Ἀπὸ τοῦ παραδείγματος — θαύμασιν: P, fol. 285ᵛ; V, fol. 53ʳ·ᵛ; Cord, p. 680.
23-24 ἀπὸ — μετέβη affert Paraphrasis (p. 669).

Aᵉ 18-19 (p. 415, 19-22): ...quando eas uerbis nequeat explicare, ut aspectae
miseriae facilius moueant misserantis affectum.

apart from the other wild pigs, it causes even more severe damage, such beasts being strong and particularly wild, resembling even wolves, since by being isolated and living on their own they go to even further limits of harm. Hence his reference to *a solitary animal:* just like a wild pig on its own that keeps apart from other ones, so he ravaged us, not only taking fruit, but often damaging the crops themselves as well.

O God of hosts, turn back (v. 14). When mentioning the troubles inflicted, he also inevitably supplies this refrain: Accordingly, powerful one, reverse our fortunes. *Look down from heaven and see:* take notice of our situation from heaven. *And have regard for this vine.* He said this with particular feeling and pity. Having given sufficient indication above to its devastation and the extent of its devastation, he proceeded to say appropriately as well *Have regard for this vine,* positively and with feeling. So he is saying, You, the dresser of this vine, consider its devastation and destruction—as though words were not sufficient without sight of it as well. *Mature that which your right hand planted* (v. 15): with your attention bind up, support, and sustain it, since dressing it is your duty (effectively saying *planted* for effect). *And on a son of man, whom you confirmed for yourself.* He moved from the example to the person: what was true of him | he said by employing the vine as an

παραδείγματος ἔλεγεν περὶ τῆς ἀμπέλου, ταῦτα εἰς αὐτὸν πάλιν ἐπάγει καλῶς. Ὥσπερ οὖν καὶ ἄνω εἰπὼν ἐπὶ τὴν προσευχὴν τοῦ δούλου σου καὶ ψωμιεῖς ἡμᾶς μετῆλθεν ἐπὶ τὸ παράδειγμα, ὡς περὶ ἀμπέλου λέγων καὶ τὰ ἀκόλουθα, οὕτως πάλιν ἀπὸ τοῦ παραδείγματος ἀνατρέχει υἱὸν ἀνθρώ- που, ἵνα εἴπῃ ἡμᾶς, ἀπὸ τοῦ ἑνικοῦ τὸν λαὸν λέγων, — ὡς ὅταν λέγῃ τὸ 5 Κατεπάτησέν με ἄνθρωπος οὐ περὶ ἑνὸς λέγει, ἀλλὰ περὶ πολλῶν. Ἀπο- δέδωκεν μέντοι αὐτῷ τὸ ἐπίβλεψον, ἵνα ᾖ Καὶ ἐπίβλεψον ἐξ οὐρανοῦ ἐπὶ τὴν ἄμπελον ταύτην. Ποίαν, σαφὲς αὐτὸ ποιῶν ἐπάγει· καὶ ἐπὶ τὸν υἱὸν τοῦ ἀνθρώπου, ὃν ἐκραταίωσας σεαυτῷ, τουτέστιν ἡμᾶς. Πρόσχες ἡμῖν φησιν, οὓς αὐτὸς συνεστήσω, καὶ ἰσχυροὺς τοὺς οἰκείους πολλάκις ἀπέφηνας θαύ- 10 μασιν.

17ᵃ. Ἐμπεπυρισμένη πυρὶ καὶ ἀνεσκαμμένη. Τὸ ἐμπεπυρισμένη ὡς πρὸς τὸ καταρτίσαι αὐτὴν ἔχει τὴν ἀκολουθίαν, ἵνα ᾖ Καὶ κατάρτισαι αὐτὴν ἣν ἐφύτευσεν ἡ δεξιά σου ἐμπεπυρισμένην ἐν πυρὶ καὶ ἀνεσκαμμένην, — του- τέστι Πρόσχες τῇ ἀμπέλῳ, ὅπως πυρί τε διέφθαρται καὶ κατέσκαπται· 15 ταῦτα γὰρ ὑπέμεινεν ἡ πόλις παρὰ τοῦ Ἀντιόχου. Τὸ δὲ ἐπὶ υἱὸν ἀνθρώ- που, ὃν ἐκραταίωσας σεαυτῷ διὰ μέσου, ὥσπερ οὖν καὶ ἕτερα πολλὰ διὰ τὸ μέτρον, ὁμοῦ καὶ σαφὲς ποιῶν ὅτι ποτὲ λέγει τὴν ἄμπελον.

17ᵇ. Ἀπὸ ἐπιτιμήσεως τοῦ προσώπου σου ἀπολοῦνται. Ἀλλ᾿ εἰ μόνον ἐπιτιμήσῃς, ἅπαντες οἱ τοσαῦτα ἡμᾶς διαθέντες ἀπολοῦνται. 20

18-19ᵃ. Γενηθήτω ἡ χείρ σου ἐπ᾿ ἄνδρα δεξιᾶς σου καὶ ἐπὶ υἱὸν ἀνθρώ- που ὃν ἐκραταίωσας σεαυτῷ, καὶ οὐ μὴ ἀποστῶμεν ἀπό σου. Τὸ σκολιὸν ἐν

2-3 v. 5ᵇ-6ᵃ   6 ps. LV, 2   7-8 v. 15ᵇ.c.

2 ὥσπερ οὖν καὶ ἄνω] ὥσπερ οὐκ ἄνω PV.   8 ποιῶν om. Cord   ἐπὶ om. Cord
9-11 πρόσχες — θαύμασιν affert Paraphrasis (p. 670).
17ᵃ. Τὸ ἐμπεπυρισμένη — ἄμπελον: P, fol. 286; V, fol. 53ᵛ; cf. Paraphrasis (p. 670): Τοῦτο τὴν ἀκολουθίαν ἔχει πρὸς τὸ καταρτίσαι αὐτήν, τουτέστι Πρόσχες τῇ ἀμπέλῳ. Τὸ δὲ ἐπὶ τὸν υἱὸν τοῦ ἀνθρώπου διὰ μέσου κεῖται.
17ᵇ. Ἀλλ᾿ εἰ μόνον — ἀπολοῦνται: V, fol. 286; P, fol. 53ᵛ; Paraphrasis (p. 670)·
18-19ᵃ. Τὸ σκολιὸν — ἡγούμενοι: P, fol. 286; V, fol. 53ᵛ.

Aᵉ 3-5 (p. 415, 27-416, 1): Populum adoptatum; quam uiniam supra dixis- set aperuit.   9-11 (p. 416, 2-3): Populum scilicet eundemque filium diuinis mi- raculis sepe firmatum.   14-17 (p. 416, 4-8): Quae hostili arete non solum con- ruit, sed etiam igni est emisa flammisque consumpta; haec autem utraque ciuitati sub rege Antiocho peruenerunt.   17ᵇ (p. 416, 10-12): ...tamen subfi- cere illis ad perditionem uel hoc solum potest, si eos tantum uultu indignantis aspicias.

example. He nicely goes on to apply the same things to him again. Thus, just as he also above had said *with your servant's prayer* and *you will feed us,* and then turned to the example by speaking of the vine and so on, so in turn he leaves the example and retraces his steps to *a son of man*—that is, us, referring to the people in the singular. Thus, when he says, "People have trampled on me,"[1] he is referring not to one person but to many individuals. Moreover, it was to him he directed the words *Look down,* as if to say, Look down from heaven on this vine. To make clear what it is like, he proceeds to say *And on a son of man, whom you confirmed for yourself*—that is, us. Attend to us, he is saying, whom you personally formed, and often by marvels you made your own strong.

Put to the torch and dug up (v. 16). The phrase *put to the torch* has a logical connection with *mature it,* as if to say, And mature what your right hand planted, put to the torch as it was and dug up—that is, Take note of the vine, how it has been destroyed by fire and razed to the ground (a fate that the city met at the hands of Antiochus). The phrase *on a son of man, whom you confirmed for yourself* comes in the middle on account of the meter, as in many other cases, also making clear that he is referring to the vine. *They will perish at the rebuke of your countenance:* if you simply rebuke them, everyone bearing this attitude toward us will perish. *Let your hand be on the man at your right, and on a son of man, whom you confirmed for yourself. May we not depart from you* (vv. 17–18). The confusion in | the structure comes

---

1. Ps 56:1.

τῇ φράσει ἀπὸ τῆς ἑρμηνείας γεγένηται. Ἐπειδὴ γὰρ χεῖρα καλεῖ τὴν
ἐνέργειαν, δεξιὰν δὲ τὴν βοήθειαν, τοῦτο λέγει Ἡ ἐνέργειά σου φησιν, ἡ
εἰς βοήθειαν — ἀντὶ τοῦ αὐτή σου ἡ βοήθεια — γενέσθω εἰς ἡμᾶς τοὺς σοὺς
καὶ ὑπό σου δειχθέντας ἀεὶ μεγάλους, ἵνα ᾖ ἡ ἀκολουθία Γενηθήτω ἡ χείρ
5 τῆς δεξιᾶς σου ἐπὶ ἄνδρα καὶ ἐπὶ υἱὸν ἀνθρώπου, ὃν ἐκραταίωσας σεαυτῷ,
καὶ οὐ μὴ ἀποστῶμεν ἀπό σου καὶ ἀπὸ τῆς δεξιᾶς τοῦ ἐλέους σου. Τυχόντες γὰρ τούτων, οὐκ ἀφεξόμεθά σου τῆς γνώσεως, ἀλλὰ μενοῦμεν ἀεὶ τὴν
παρά σου δεξιάν τε καὶ φιλανθρωπίαν ζητοῦντες, ἀντὶ τοῦ Σὲ Θεὸν καὶ
βοηθὸν ἡγούμενοι.

10 19ᵇ. Ζωώσεις ἡμᾶς, καὶ τὸ ὄνομά σου ἐπικαλεσόμεθα. Ἀπὸ γὰρ νεκρό-
τητος καὶ κινδύνων εἰς ζωὴν καὶ τὴν παρά σου σωτηρίαν καταστάντες, εἰκότως σε Θεὸν γνωρίσομεν.

20. Κύριε, ὁ Θεὸς τῶν δυνάμεων, ἐπίστρεψον ἡμᾶς καὶ ἐπίφανον τὸ πρόσωπόν σου, καὶ σωθησόμεθα. Καλῶς τὸ αὐτὸ καὶ τέλος ἐποιήσατο τοῦ ψαλ-
15 μοῦ. Αὐτὸς οὖν φησι τῇ σαυτοῦ βοηθείᾳ καὶ ἐπιφανείᾳ περίσωσαι ἡμᾶς.

2 cf. supra p. 513, 14-15.

3-8 ἀντὶ τοῦ — ζητοῦντες affert Paraphrasis (p. 670).
19ᵇ. Ἀπὸ γὰρ — γνωρίσομεν: P, fol. 286; V, fol. 53ᵛ; Paraphrasis (p. 670).
20. Καλῶς — ἡμᾶς: P, fol. 286; V, fol. 54; Vat. 1422, fol. 148ᵛ (anon.); Paraphrasis (p. 670).   15 περίσωσον PV.

Aᵉ 1-6 (p. 416, 13-20): Pro Contingat adiutorium operis tui; manum siquidem pro opere, dexteram pro auxilio ponit. Hoc ait: Operatio adiutori tui,
id est auxilium tuum, adsit etiam nunc nobis, qui tui sumus, quos magnos
uideri semper tuo fauore fecisti.   14-15 (p. 416, 29-30): ...et titulo carminis
quoque fine respondet.

from the translation: since by *hand* he refers to activity, and by *right* to help, it means, Let your activity aimed at giving help—that is, your help itself—be directed to us, who are your own and who thanks to you are ever shown to be great. This results in the following order: *Let your hand on your right be on the man and on a son of man, whom you confirmed for yourself, and may we not depart from you* and from the right hand of your mercy. If, in fact, we attain this, we shall not part from your knowledge, abiding instead ever at your right hand and seeking lovingkindness—in other words, believing you to be God and helper.

You will make us live, and we shall call on your name: being restored from a state of death and danger to one of life and salvation from you, we shall duly acknowledge you to be God. *Lord, God of hosts, turn us back; let your face shine, and we shall be saved* (v. 19). He did well to make the same verse the ending of the psalm. So he is saying, Save us yourself by your help and your appearing. |

PSALMVS LXXX

Τὴν ἀπὸ Βαβυλῶνος ἐπάνοδον τοῦ λαοῦ προαγορεύων, ἐπὶ εὐχαριστίαν ἅπαντας ὁ μακάριος Δαυὶδ διὰ τοῦδε προτρέπεται τοῦ ψαλμοῦ.

2ᵃ. Ἀγαλλιᾶσθε τῷ Θεῷ τῷ βοηθῷ ἡμῶν. Εὐφραίνεσθέ φησιν ἐπὶ τῇ
παρ᾽ αὐτοῦ βοηθείᾳ, τῶν παρ᾽ αὐτοῦ μνημονεύοντες ἀεὶ καλῶν.   5

2ᵇ. Ἀλαλάξατε τῷ Θεῷ Ἰακώβ. Καὶ μετὰ τῆς οἰκείας εὐφροσύνης αὐτῷ
τοὺς προσήκοντας ὕμνους ἐπινικίους ἀποδίδοτε. Τὸ δὲ Ἀλαλάξατε συνηθῶς ἐπὶ νίκης.

3ᵃ. Λάβετε ψαλμὸν καὶ δότε τύμπανον. Ὅπερ ἔθος ἐστὶν ἄχρι τῆς
δεῦρο τὸ τὰς μὲν ᾠδὰς γίνεσθαι παρ᾽ ἑτέρων, ἑτέρους δὲ ἢ ἐν ὀργάνοις ἢ   10
ἐν αὐλοῖς ἢ ἔν τισιν ἑτέροις τὰς ᾠδὰς λέγειν, τοῦτο ἦν καὶ τότε. Ὁ γὰρ
μακάριος Δαυὶδ τῇ τοῦ Πνεύματος χάριτι τοὺς ψαλμοὺς εἰργάζετό τε καὶ
ἔλεγεν· ἕτεροι δὲ ἦσαν οἱ περὶ ταῦτα ἐπιτήδειοι καὶ διαφόροις τοῖς ὀργάνοις, κιθάρᾳ τε καὶ αὐλῷ, κυμβάλοις τε καὶ τυμπάνοις καὶ τοῖς τοιούτοις
τὰς ᾠδὰς ἀνακρουόμενοι. Ὡς οὖν πρὸς ἐκείνους φησὶ Λάβετε τὸν ψαλμόν, 15
τουτέστιν τὴν ᾠδήν, καὶ δότε παρ᾽ ἑαυτῶν τὰ ὄργανα· ὃ μὴ ἔχετε λαβόντες, τὰ παρ᾽ ἑαυτῶν δότε τῶν ὀργάνων τὴν χρῆσιν.

3ᵇ. Ψαλτήριον τερπνὸν μετὰ κιθάρας. Καλὴ γάρ φησιν ἡ ᾠδὴ καὶ τερπνή,
ὅταν διὰ τῶν ὀργάνων καὶ τῆς ποικιλίας καὶ τῶν διαφόρων ῥυθμῶν μείζονα
τοῖς ἀκούουσι τὴν ἡδονὴν παρέχεται. Σύμμαχος τὸ ψαλτήριον τερπνὸν αὖραν   20
ἡδεῖαν λέγει, ἀντὶ τοῦ Καλὴ ἡ πνοὴ καὶ ἡδεῖα ἡ τοιαύτη.

Argumentum Τὴν ἀπὸ Βαβυλῶνος — ψαλμοῦ: P, fol. 286ᵛ; V, fol. 54; Cord,
p. 691; cf. L (p. 685, 8-11).
2ᵃ. Εὐφραίνεσθε — καλῶν: P, fol. 286ᵛ; V, fol. 54; Vat. 1422, fol. 148ᵛ sub
nomine HESYCHII; Paraphrasis (p. 685).
2ᵇ. Καὶ μετὰ — νίκης: P, fol. 286ᵛ; V, fol. 54.
3ᵃ. Ὅπερ ἔθος — χρῆσιν: P, fol. 286ᵛ; V, fol. 54; Cord, p. 692.   14 τε 2°loco
om. PV.
3ᵇ. Καλὴ — τοιαύτη: P, fol. 286ᵛ; V, fol. 53; Cord, p. 692.

Aᵉ Argumentum ps. LXXX (p. 416, 32-417, 2): Reditum populi de Babilone
praedicens beatus Dauid in hoc psalmo, omnes ad gratiarum actiones prouocat.
Cf. PSEUDO-BEDA (919).   2ᵃ (p. 417, 6-8): Laetis animis agite beneficiorum
memores.   13. 16-17 (p. 417, 14-17): Carmen hoc meo labore conpossitum,
diuersis musicorum organis personate.

PSALM 81

In foretelling the people's return from Babylon, blessed David in this psalm urges everyone to thanksgiving. *Rejoice in God our help* (v. 1): be glad of help from him, ever mindful of the good things from him. *Shout aloud to the God of Jacob:* and with joy of your own render to him the due triumphal hymns (to *shout aloud* being customary in the case of victory). *Take up a psalm, and beat a drum* (v. 2). As is the custom to this day, songs were sung by some people; others sang songs to the accompaniment of instruments such as flutes and other kinds. This happened at that time also: blessed David, remember, under the influence of the Spirit's grace, composed and recited psalms,[1] and there were other people occupied with this, also striking up songs on a range of instruments, including lyre and flute, cymbals and drums, and the like. So it is to those he says *Take up a psalm*—that is, a song—and play the instruments yourselves; take up what is not your own work, and contribute on your part the playing of the instruments. *A pleasing harp with a lyre:* a song is lovely and pleasing when it provides greater pleasure to the listeners to the accompaniment of instruments and a variety and range of beats. For *a pleasing harp* Symmachus says "a sweet air"—in other words, a lovely tune of such sweetness. |

---

1. Cf. 1 Sam 16:18–23.

4. Σαλπίσατε ἐν νεομηνίᾳ σάλπιγγι, ἐν εὐσήμῳ ἡμέρᾳ ἑορτῆς ὑμῶν. Ἐκβοᾶτέ φησι καὶ ταῖς σάλπιγξιν ἐν ταῖς νεομηνίαις, — ἑορτὴν γὰρ ἦγον τὴν νεομηνίαν, — ἀλλὰ καὶ ἐν πάσῃ φησὶν ἐπισήμῳ ἑορτῇ. Βούλεται δὲ εἰπεῖν Ὁσάκις συνίητε, διὰ πάντων ψάλατε τῷ Θεῷ τῶν ὀργάνων.

5   5. Ὅτι πρόσταγμα τῷ Ἰσραήλ ἐστιν, καὶ κρίμα τῷ Θεῷ Ἰακώβ. Μετὰ γὰρ πολλῆς κρίσεως καὶ δοκιμασίας τοῦτο ὁ Θεὸς τῷ λαῷ τῷ ἡμετέρῳ ποιεῖν προσέταξεν, ὥστε μηδὲν παραλιμπάνειν δεῖ.

6ᵃ·ᵇ. Μαρτύριον ἐν τῷ Ἰωσὴφ ἔθετο αὐτόν, ἐν τῷ ἐξελθεῖν αὐτὸν ἐκ γῆς Αἰγύπτου. Διεμαρτύρατο αὐτῷ φησιν ὁπηνίκα τῆς Αἰγύπτου αὐτὸν ἐξήγα-
10 γεν, τοῦτο ποιεῖν ὑπὲρ ἐκείνης τῆς ἐλευθερίας ἐντειλάμενος. Τὸ οὖν ἔθετο αὐτόν, ἀντὶ τοῦ τὸν λόγον, — ἵνα εἴπῃ Τοῦτον ἐν διαμαρτυρίας αὐτῷ τάξει τὸν λόγον ἔθετο.

6ᶜ. Γλῶσσαν ἣν οὐκ ἔγνω ἤκουσεν. Τότε γὰρ καὶ μεγάλων ἠξιώθη, ὅτε τὸ πρόσταγμα τοῦτο ἐδέξατο, θείας ἀκούων φωνῆς, ἧς οὐδέποτε πρὸ τού-
15 του ἀκούσας ἦν, – ὥστε καὶ ὑπὲρ αὐτοῦ τούτου δεῖν μετὰ σπουδῆς πράτ-τειν τὸ προσταχθέν, ὅτιπερ ἠξίωσεν αὐτὸς ὁ Θεὸς οἰκείᾳ φωνῇ δοῦναι τὸ πρόσταγμα.

7ᵃ. Ἀπέστησεν ἀπὸ ἄρσεων τὸν νῶτον αὐτοῦ. Ἄρσεων λέγει τῶν βασ-ταγμάτων, ἀπὸ τοῦ αἴρειν, — ἵνα εἴπῃ Τοῦ πηλοῦ καὶ τῆς πλινθείας

---

4. Ἐκβοᾶτε — ὀργάνων: P, fol. 286ᵛ; V, fol. 54ᵛ; Paraphrasis (p. 685).   4 ψάλ-λετε Par.
5. Μετὰ — δεῖ: P, fol. 286ᵛ; V, fol. 54ᵛ; Paraphrasis (p. 685).   7 μηδὲν]
οὐδαμῶς 1422 οὐδὲν Par.
6ᵃ·ᵇ. Διεμαρτύρατο — ἔθετο: P, fol. 287 et V, fol. 54ᵛ (anon.); Vat. 1422, fol. 149
(anon.); Paraphrasis (p. 686).   10 ἐντειλαμένου PV   11 αὐτῷ] αὐτὸν 1422 Par.
6ᶜ. Τότε — πρόσταγμα: P, fol. 287; V, fol. 54ᵛ; Cord, p. 693-694.   15 ὑπὲρ]
ὑπὸ PV   17 αὐτοὺς Cord.
7ᵃ. Ἄρσεων — ἠλευθέρωσεν: P, fol. 287; V, fol. 54ᵛ. Eadem fere praebet CYRIL-
LUS ALEX. (P. G., LXIX, 1204 B); cf. Paraphrasis (p. 686).

Aᵉ 4 (p. 417, 18-21); Canite initio mensis tubae; tubis quoque, quibus initia mensium et omnia festa celebratis, in hac gratiarum actione utemini.   5-6 (p. 417, 24-25):... Deo non leuiter imperatum est.   6ᵃ·ᵇ (p. 417, 25-31): Cum educeren-tur patres ex Aegipto, in memoriam liberationis suae illis sub quadam contes-tatione inpraesa est... ut redemtionis suae memores esse.it adtestatione constrin-xit.   6ᶜ (p. 418, 3-7): Tunc, inquit, eis haec praecepta data sunt, quando diuinae uocis auditores, quae numquam ante eis insonauerat, facti sunt, ut dignitate conloqui quod praecipiebatur memoriae eorum tenacius inhereret.   7ᵃ (p. 418, 8-11): Honera appellata sunt ea quae in fingendis lateribus conuechebant; libe-rauit ergo eos a labore grauium operum uel Aegiptia seruitute.

Blow a trumpet on a new moon, on your special festival day (v. 3): give vent also on the trumpets on the new moons—for they considered the new moon a festival—and also on every special festival. He means, As often as you assemble, sing praise to God on every instrument. *Because it is a command for Israel, a judgment for the God of Jacob* (v. 4): with careful judgment and discretion God ordered our people to do this so that nothing should be left undone. *He made it a testimony in Joseph when he went out from the land of Egypt* (v. 5): he adjured him when he led him out of Egypt, bidding him do this in return for their liberation—hence, *He made it*—that is, the direction; as if to say, He gave this direction by way of adjuring him.

He heard a tongue that he did not know: at that time he was accorded great favors on receiving this command, hearing a divine voice, which he previously had never heard,[2] the result being that in response to this also he had to carry out the command with zeal, since God personally had vouchsafed to give the command in his own voice. *He relieved his back of burdens* (v. 6). He means "loads" by *burdens,* from the verb "to carry burdens," as if to say, | He freed him from the slavery of making bricks, and saved his back

2. Cf. Exod 4.

ἀπήλλαξεν αὐτόν φησιν ἐκείνης τῆς δουλείας, καὶ τοῦ φέρειν βαρέα βασ-
τάγματα τὸν νῶτον ἠλευθέρωσεν.

7ᵇ. Αἱ χεῖρες αὐτοῦ ἐν τῷ κοφίνῳ ἐδούλευσαν. Κατετρίβη γὰρ μικροῦ,
καὶ κατεδαπανήθη τὰς χεῖρας ἐν τῇ τοῦ κοφίνου δουλείᾳ, τὸ αὐτὸ λέγων.
Τότε οὖν φησιν, ὁπηνίκα τούτων αὐτοὺς ἀπαλλάξας ἐξήγαγε τῆς Αἰγύπ- 5
του, τότε αὐτῷ τοῦτο τὸ πρόσταγμα δέδωκεν. Τί εἰπὼν πρὸς αὐτόν;

8ᵃ·ᵇ. Ἐν θλίψει ἐπεκαλέσω με καὶ ἐρρυσάμην σε, ἐπήκουσά σου ἐν ἀποκρύφῳ καταιγίδος. Τοῦ Θεοῦ λέγει τοὺς λόγους, οὓς τότε πρὸς αὐτοὺς
εἶπεν ἐν τῷ ὄρει τῷ Σινᾶ ὀφθεὶς αὐτοῖς, καὶ εἰπὼν δι᾽ ἑαυτοῦ ὅτι Ἀνήγαγόν
σε ἐξ Αἰγύπτου, διήγαγον τὴν θάλασσαν, ἐμὲ γνώριζε τὸν δεσπότην καὶ 10
ποιητήν, τῆς τῶν εἰδώλων θεραπείας ἀφίστασο. Τοῦτο οὖν αὐτοὺς ὑπομι-
μνήσκει. Εἶπεν οὖν ὁ Θεὸς τότε πρὸς τὸν λαὸν Ἐν τῇ θλίψει τῆς δουλείας
σου ὄντος σου ἤκουσα, καὶ ἀπήλλαξά σε πρὸς τῇ Ἐρυθρᾷ θαλάσσῃ γενόμενον καὶ περὶ τῆς σωτηρίας κινδυνεύοντα. Ἐν νεφέλῃ ὀφθεὶς ἤκουσά σου
καὶ διελὼν τὴν θάλασσαν ἀπήλλαξα τῶν ἐπικειμένων θανάτων. Ἐν ἀποκρύφῳ 15
οὖν καταιγίδος εἶπεν τὴν νεφέλην, ἐν ᾗ ὥσπερ ἀποκεκρυμμένος αὐτοῖς διελέγετο, ὡς τῆς νεφέλης καὶ ἀνέμους πέμπειν σφοδροτάτους φύσιν ἐχούσης
καὶ οὕτω τὰς καταιγίδας ἀποτελούσης.

8ᶜ. Ἐδοκίμασά σε ἐπὶ ὕδατος ἀντιλογίας. Τοῦ πικροῦ λέγει τοῦ ἐν
Μέρρα, ὅτε ἐλοιδορήθησαν τῷ Μωϋσῇ. Ἀλλὰ καὶ μετὰ τοῦτό φησί σου 20
τὴν δοκιμὴν τῆς ἀπιστίας παρασχομένου, ἐγὼ καὶ οὕτω τὸ ὕδωρ μεταβαλὼν
χρήσιμον ὑμῖν ἐποίησα τὸ ποτόν. Τί οὖν ὑπὲρ τούτων;

8 ss. cf. Ex. XX   15-16 cf. Ex. XIX, 16   19-20 cf. Ex. XV, 23-26.

7ᵇ. Κατετρίβη — πρὸς αὐτόν: P, fol. 287; V, fol. 54ᵛ.
8ᵃ·ᵇ. Τοῦ Θεοῦ — ἀποτελούσης: P, fol. 287; V, fol. 54ᵛ-55; Cord, p. 694.   9 δι᾽
αὐτοῦ PV   17 καὶ om. Cord.
8ᶜ. Τοῦ πικροῦ — τούτων: P, fol. 287; V, fol. 55.   20-22 Ἀλλὰ — ποτόν affert
Paraphrasis (p. 686).   20 ἀλλὰ μὴν καὶ Par.

Aᵉ 3-4 (p. 418, 12-15): In collectione palearum ac luti subiectione, non solum
dorsa terebantur portantium, sed et manus iugi opere fatiscebant.   8ᵃ·ᵇ (p. 418,
16-31): Eductis ex Aegipto quid mandatum sit replicat, et ex persona Dei formatur oratio, qua enumerantur praestita et beneficiorum commendatur memoria, in eum sensum quod apud Sinam usum esse redemtorem Moyses refert.
Aliter, cum et tribulatio seruitutis urgeret, clamori tuo aurem meam festinus
admoui... Cum inter Aegyptios in terra persequentes et mare robrum conclusus
formidares exitium, in nubibus, quarum conpraesu tempestas gignitur, tectus
ergo nube et absconditus loquebar tecum et pugnabam pro te.   19-20 (p. 419,
1-4): Aquam contradictionis dicit aquam Mirrae, cuius amaritudine offensi male
dixerunt Moysi in iniuriam Dei.

from carrying heavy loads. *His hands served in the basket:* he was almost crushed and his hands worn out from the slavery of the baskets (the meaning being the same). So he is saying, At the time when he freed them from that and led them out of Egypt, then it was that he gave him this command.

What did he say to him?[3] *In tribulation you called upon me, and I rescued you; I hearkened to you in a tempest's secret place* (v. 7). He refers to God's words that he spoke to them on Mount Sinai at the time when he appeared to them, saying of himself, I led you up from Egypt; I led you through the sea; I made myself known as master and creator; I removed you from the worship of the idols. He is reminding them of this, therefore. So God at that time said to the people, When you were in *tribulation* I heard you, and I rescued you when you were near the Red Sea with your life in danger. Appearing in a cloud, I heard you, and by parting the sea I freed you from impending death (by *a tempest's secret place* thus referring to the cloud, in which as though concealed he spoke to them, as though the cloud was able also to dispatch strong winds and thus cause tempests). *I tested you at the water of contradiction.* He refers to the bitter water at Marah, when they abused Moses. Even despite this, he is saying, when you gave proof of unbelief, I thus changed the water and made it good for drinking.[4]

So what is the response to this? | *Listen, my people, and I shall take you*

---

3. This question is prompted by a difference in pronouns between Greek and Hebrew in vv. 5b–6, resulting in God only now speaking in the LXX version.
4. Cf. Exod 15:23–25.

1118 THEODORVS MOPSVESTENVS

9ᵃ. Ἄκουσον, λαός μου, καὶ διαμαρτυροῦμαί σοι. Οὐκοῦν ἄκουε τοῦ λοιποῦ, καὶ μέμνησο ὧν λέγω.

9ᵇ-10. Ἰσραήλ, ἐὰν ἀκούσῃς μου, οὐκ ἔσται ἔν σοι θεὸς πρόσφατος, οὐδὲ προσκυνήσεις θεῷ ἀλλοτρίῳ. Ἐάνπερ ἔχειν ἐθέλῃς περὶ ἐμέ, καὶ τῆς ἐμῆς
5 ἐπιμελεῖσθαι θεραπείας καὶ τῶν παρ' ἐμοῦ ἀπολαύειν ἀγαθῶν, — ἔλαβες γὰρ ὧν παρέχειν δύναμαι τὴν πεῖραν, — μή μοι καινοὺς καὶ ἐπεισάκτους θεούς, τοὺς ἀνθρωπίναις ἐπινοίαις ποθὲν χθὲς καὶ σήμερον ἐπεισαχθέντας, ἐπεισάξῃς.

11ᵃ·ᵇ. Ἐγὼ γάρ εἰμι Κύριος ὁ Θεός σου, ὁ ἀναγαγών σε ἐκ γῆς Αἰγύπ-
10 του. Δεῖ γάρ σε δεσπότην ἡγεῖσθαι ἐμὲ τὸν ἀπαλλάξαντά σε τῆς δουλείας, ἀφ' ὧν ἔλαβες ἔχοντα τὴν πεῖραν.

11ᶜ. Πλάτυνον τὸ στόμα σου καὶ πληρώσω αὐτό. Οὐ γὰρ μόνον ὅτι δέδωκα λέγω, ἀλλὰ καὶ δώσειν ὑπισχνοῦμαι· κἂν γὰρ ἀνοίξῃς σου τὸ στόμα, τοσούτων αὐτὸ πληρώσω ἀγαθῶν, ὅσων ἂν δέχεσθαι δύνῃ, — ἀντὶ τοῦ Δαψιλῆ
15 σοι παρέξω τῶν ἀγαθῶν τὴν περιουσίαν ἄνπερ αὐτὸς μὴ ἐμποδὼν γίγνῃ.

12ᵃ. Καὶ οὐκ ἤκουσεν ὁ λαός μου τῆς φωνῆς μου. Ἀλλὰ τούτων οὐκ ἐφρόντισεν τῶν ῥημάτων.

12ᵇ. Καὶ Ἰσραὴλ οὐ προσέσχεν μοι. Ἔλαττον δέ μου τῆς γνώσεως ἐφρόντισεν.

9ᵃ. Οὐκοῦν — λέγω: P, fol. 287ᵛ; V, fol. 55.
9ᵇ-10. Ἐάνπερ – ἐπεισάξῃς: P, fol. 287ᵛ; V, fol. 55; Cord, p. 694-695.   4 ἐάνπερ φησὶν Cord   6 κενοὺς PV   7 τοὺς] καὶ ταῖς Cord   8 ἐπεισάξῃς Cord.
11ᵃ·ᵇ. Δεῖ γὰρ — πεῖραν: P, fol. 287ᵛ; V, fol. 55ᵛ; Vat. 1422, fol. 149 (anon.);
Paraphrasis (p. 687).   11 δουλείας des. Par.
11ᶜ. Οὐ γὰρ μόνον — γίγνῃ: P, fol. 287ᵛ; V, fol. 55ᵛ; Vat. 1422, fol. 149 (anon.);
Paraphrasis (p. 687).   12 δέδωκεν 1422   15 γίνῃ Par.
12ᵃ. Ἀλλὰ — ῥημάτων: P, fol. 287ᵛ; V, fol. 55ᵛ.
12ᵇ. Ἔλαττον — ἐφρόντισεν: P, fol. 287ᵛ; V, fol. 55ᵛ.

Aᵉ 9ᵇ-10 (p. 419, 5-13): Pro his omnibus nihil reposco praeter notitiam mei detestationemque idulorum... si dedigneris caput tuum diis alienis ac recentibus inclinare, quibus formam et aetatem artes et manus hominum contullerunt.
11ᵃ·ᵇ (p. 419, 14-17): Rerum testimonio te oportet illum uere Deum credere, quia te seruitutis iniuria uindicauit.   11ᶜ (p. 419, 18-25): Non solum te agnitione mei prae caeteris beneficiis, sed etiam futurorum promissione conuenit obligari; tantis enim bonis os tuum inpleam, quantum potest capacitas eius expleri, — id est usum tibi omnium rerum, si tamen ipse tuis meritis non resistas, ad omnem copiam ministrabo.   12ᵇ (p. 419, 27-29): Non grandem curam adhibuit, ut perfecte ad meam notitiam peruiniret.

to task (v. 8): so now listen, and take note of what I say. *Israel, if you listen to me, there will be no novel god among you, nor will you adore a foreign god* (vv. 8–9): If you are prepared to adopt this attitude toward me, to devote yourselves to worship of me and to receive good things from me, having experience of what I can provide, do not introduce any new and exotic gods, thought up by human beings on one day or another. *I am the Lord your God, who brought you up from the land of Egypt* (v. 10): you must believe me to be the Lord who freed you from slavery, from the things you experienced. *Open wide your mouth, and I shall fill it:* I am not only saying that I have given you things, but I also promise to give you them in the future; if you open your mouth, I shall fill it with as many good things as you can receive—in other words, I shall provide you with a generous supply of good things if you for your part prove to be no obstacle.

My people did not listen to my voice (v. 11): but they did not heed my words. *Israel did not heed me:* they cared less for knowledge of me. | *He*

13. Καὶ ἐξαπέστειλα αὐτοὺς κατὰ τὰ ἐπιτηδεύματα τῶν καρδιῶν αὐτῶν, πορεύσονται ἐν τοῖς ἐπιτηδεύμασιν αὐτῶν. Σύμμαχος σαφέστερον Ἀφῆκα οὖν αὐτοὺς τῇ ἀρεσκείᾳ τῆς καρδίας αὐτῶν ὁδεύειν ταῖς βουλαῖς αὐτῶν. Ταύτην αὐτοῖς τὴν τιμωρίαν ἐπήγαγον βουλομένοις οὐκ ὀρθῶς ζῆν· ἀφῆκα, οὐδεμίαν αὐτῶν ἐπιμέλειαν ποιησάμενος τοῦ λοιποῦ, ὥστε κατὰ τὴν οἰκείαν 5 γνώμην ἅπαντα πράττειν· τὴν ζημίαν, ὅση τίς ἐστιν, ἔγνωσαν εὐκόλως. Καὶ γὰρ καὶ πρὸς τὸ χεῖρον εἶδον, καὶ τὸν βίον ἔσχον διεφθαρμένον, καὶ τοὺς καρποὺς τούτων ἔλαβον τήν τε αἰχμαλωσίαν καὶ τὰ ἐκεῖθεν κακά. Δέδεικται μέντοι κἀνταῦθα, ὡς πολλάκις ἡμῖν εἴρηται, ὅτι ἡ γραφὴ τὴν συγχώρησιν ἀντὶ πράγματος λέγει. Τὸ γὰρ ἀφῆκα ἐξαπέστειλεν εἶπεν, ἅπερ συνε- 10 χώρησεν αὐτοὺς παθεῖν τε καὶ κατὰ τὴν οἰκείαν γνώμην αὐτοὺς ἁμαρτάνειν, ταῦτα ὡς τοῦ Θεοῦ ἀποστείλαντος ἐπ᾽ αὐτοὺς καὶ ποιήσαντος εἰπών.

14-15. Εἰ ὁ λαός μου ἤκουσέν μου, Ἰσραὴλ ταῖς ὁδοῖς μου εἰ ἐπορεύθη, ἐν τῷ μηδενὶ ἂν τοὺς ἐχθροὺς αὐτῶν ἐταπείνωσα, καὶ ἐπὶ τοὺς θλίβοντας αὐτοὺς ἐπέβαλον ἂν τὴν χεῖρά μου. Εἰ δέ φησιν ἐμέμνηντο τῶν ἐμῶν ῥημά- 15 των ἐπιμεληθέντες ὧν προσέταξα, οὐδ᾽ ἂν ἔπαθον ταῦτα· καὶ γὰρ σφόδρα ῥαδίως τοὺς ἐχθροὺς αὐτῶν ἐτιμωρησάμην, καὶ περιέβαλον ἂν αὐτοὺς εὐκό- λως μεγίστοις κακοῖς ὥστε οὐδ᾽ ἂν ἔπαθόν τι δεινόν. Ταῦτα δὲ λαβὼν ὁ προφήτης ἀπὸ τῆς τότε φωνῆς τοῦ Θεοῦ καὶ τὰ ἀκόλουθα εἶπεν, ὡσανεὶ βουληθείη καὶ νῦν χρήσασθαι φωνῇ, ἁρμοσόντων αὐτῷ τῶν ἑξῆς, — διὰ 20 πάντων τούτους παιδεύων ὅτι εὐεργετηθέντες καὶ νόμον δεξάμενοι παρὰ τοῦ Θεοῦ, εἰ μὲν ὑπήκουσαν, ἔπαθον ἂν οὐδέν· ἐπειδὴ δὲ ἔλαττον ἐφρόν- τισαν τῶν προσταγμάτων, ἀνηκέστοις περιέπεσον κακοῖς, — παιδεύων αὐτοὺς φυλάξασθαι τὸ τοῖς αὐτοῖς περιπεσεῖν ἑξῆς, μὴ τὰ αὐτὰ πάλιν παθεῖν. Τὸ δὲ κατὰ τὴν ἀκολουθίαν ἀπὸ τῶν εἰρημένων παρὰ τοῦ Θεοῦ 25 καὶ τὰ ἑξῆς εἰπεῖν ἀπ᾽ αὐτοῦ ὡς ἂν ἁρμόζειν αὐτῷ δυνάμενα, μειζόνως ἐντρέποντος ἦν τοὺς ἀκούοντας, ὅσῳ καὶ ἐκ τοῦ Θεοῦ λέγεσθαι δοκῇ τὰ λεγόμενα.

9 cf. p. 391, 10-11.

13. Σύμμαχος — εἰπών: P, fol. 287ᵛ; V, fol. 55ᵛ; Cord, p. 695-696.   11 τε καὶ] τι PV   12 ταῦτα] τοῦτο PV.

14-15. Εἰ δὲ ἐμέμνηντο — τὰ λεγόμενα: P, fol. 288; V, fol. 55ᵛ-56; Cord, p. 696. 15 φησιν om. PV   16 οὐδ᾽ ἄν] οὐδὲ PV   21 τούτων παιδεύει Cord   22 ἐπεὶ δὲ PV 23 παιδεύει Cord   24 καὶ μὴ Cord   25 παθεῖν des. Cord.

Aᵉ 4-6 (p. 419, 30-32): Neglegentes me ipse quoque deserui; hanc iniqui- tatis pro peccatis poenam intuli, ut uolentes praue uiuere desererem (disse- rerem ms).   22-28 (p. 419, 34-420, 5): Si uel paruisset praeceptis uel credi⟨di⟩s- set promisis, inlaborata fuisset aduersus omnes hostes mea pro plebe difensio; quod ergo diserti sunt, meritis suis, non meis debebunt inputare iudiciis. Tenor iste docendi consequentissime ad causam psalmi et ad praesentes auditores ref- ferri potest.

dismissed them in keeping with the concerns of their hearts; they will travel in the way of their concerns (v. 12). Symmachus says more clearly, "So I sent them off in the desire of their heart to journey by their own plans." I imposed this punishment on them when they preferred not to live uprightly; "I dismissed them," taking no further care of them, leaving them to do everything by their own choice. They soon found out the extent of their loss: they went from bad to worse; they led a corrupt life, and as fruit of this they suffered captivity and the troubles stemming from it. It emerges here, too, of course, as we have often said, that Scripture mentions the permission in place of the event: *He dismissed*[5] means "I sent," the sense being that what I allowed them to suffer and to sin by their own choice, this was what God sent on them and caused.

If my people had listened to me, if Israel had traveled in my ways, I would have brought their foes down to nothing, and laid my hands on those afflicting them (vv. 13–14): if they had attentively recalled the commands I gave them, they would not have suffered this; I would easily have severely punished their foes, and without difficulty invested them with the worst troubles, the result being that they would not have suffered any dire plight. Now, the author took this from God's utterance at that time and spoke in keeping with it, as if wanting to apply it to the present, since the sequel fitted it. His purpose was in everything to teach them that as beneficiaries and recipients of the law from God, they would have suffered nothing if they had obeyed; but since they had little interest in the commands, they fell foul of intolerable troubles, the purpose being to teach them to avoid falling foul of the same ones in future lest they have the same experience again.

Now, in keeping with the thought of what was said by God, the expression of the following verses can also be attributed to him, more earnestly urging the listeners the more the words seem to come from God. | *The Lord's*

---

5. As does Aquila, the Antiochene text seems to read the verb in the third person (*pace* Devreesse).

16ᵃ. Οἱ ἐχθροὶ Κυρίου ἐψεύσαντο αὐτῷ. Λέγει λοιπὸν καὶ τῆς ἐπανόδου τὸ μέγεθος, πρὸς τὴν ἀρχὴν καὶ τὸ προοίμιον ✶✶ κεχρημένος, ἵνα εἴπῃ ✶✶ ὥσπερ ἐν μέσῳ ἡ παραίνεσις. Ὅμοιον δέ ἐστι τὸ ἐνταῦθα λεγόμενον τῷ ἐν τῷ ξε΄ ψαλμῷ, τῷ Ἐν τῷ πλήθει τῆς δυνάμεώς σου ψεύσονταί σε οἱ ἐχθροί
5 σου. Ὑπὲρ τούτων οὖν φησιν εὐχαριστεῖν ὑμῖν παρακελεύομαι, ὅτι μετὰ τοσαύτην ἀγνωμοσύνην οὕτω μεγάλης τετυχήκατε τῆς παρὰ τοῦ Θεοῦ χάριτος, ὡς καὶ πολλοὺς τῶν ἐναντίων καταπλαγέντας τὴν περὶ ἡμᾶς τιμὴν ὑποκρίνασθαι, ψευδομένους τοῦ δόγματος τὴν κοινωνίαν. Ἐν αὐτῷ δὲ τῷ προειρημένῳ ψαλμῷ καὶ ἡ ἀπόδειξις ἡμῖν παράκειται.

10 **16ᵇ.** Καὶ ἔσται ὁ καιρὸς αὐτῶν εἰς τὸν αἰῶνα. Ἀλλ᾽ οὐδὲν αὐτοῖς ὄφελος ἐκ τῆς ὑποκρίσεως ἔσται· μένει γὰρ αὐτοὺς ὁ τῆς τιμωρίας καιρός, ὃν οὐ πρὸς βραχὺ ἀλλ᾽ εἰς τὸ διηνεκὲς δέξονται.

17ᵃ. Καὶ ἐψώμισεν αὐτοὺς ἐκ στέατος πυροῦ. Ἀλλ᾽ ἐκεῖνα μὲν εἰς τοὺς ἐναντίους ἔσται, τοὺς δὲ οἰκείους πληρώσει πολλῆς τῆς ἀπὸ τῶν γεννημάτων
15 εὐθηνίας· πυροῦ γὰρ λέγει τοῦ σίτου, στέας δὲ πυροῦ τὴν εὐθηνίαν αὐτοῦ καλεῖ.

17ᵇ. Καὶ ἐκ πέτρας μέλι ἐχόρτασεν αὐτούς. Καὶ ἀπὸ χαλεπῶν καὶ σκληρῶν πραγμάτων εἰς πολλὴν αὐτοὺς ἄνεσιν καὶ ἡδονὴν καταστήσει.

4. 9 Ps. LXV, 3ᵇ (cf. p. 421-422).

16ᵃ. Λέγει — παράκειται: P, fol. 288; V, fol. 56.　　2 lacunas statui　　2-9 ὅμοιον — παράκειται affert Cord, p. 696.　　4 ξζ΄ PV　　ψαλμῷ τῷ] ψαλμῷ Cord　　8 τῷ om. Cord.
16ᵇ. Ἀλλ᾽ οὐδὲν — δέξονται: P, fol. 288; V, fol. 56.
17ᵃ. Ἀλλ᾽ ἐκεῖνα — καλεῖ: P, fol. 288; V, fol. 56; Vat. 1422, fol. 149ᵛ; Paraphrasis (p. 688).　　13 ἀλλ᾽ om. 1422　　14 τῆς om. Par.　　15 εὐθηνίας des. Par.
17ᵇ. Καὶ ἀπὸ — καταστήσει: P, fol. 288; V, fol. 56; Paraphrasis (p. 688).

Aᵉ 5-12 (p. 420, 7-12): Nihil, inquam, hostibus uestris proderit simulatio; qui stupore felicitatis uestrae, non fidei puritate ad consortium uestri cultus accedunt; manet illos poena debita, quam non breui sed longuo tempore sustinebunt.　　14-16 (p. 420, 14-15): laetissima frugum ubertate satiabit.

foes were false to him (v. 15). He now mentions also the greatness of the return, using … words similar to the beginning and the introduction, as if to say, … the exhortation in the middle. What is said here resembles the verse in Psalm 66, "In the might of your power your foes will speak falsely of you."[6] So he is saying, I bid you give thanks for this, that despite your awful ingratitude you have received such gifts from God that even large numbers of the adversaries are astonished and pretend to have respect for you, falsely claiming to share your beliefs. In that aforementioned psalm also the proof is available to us. *Their time will be forever:* they will gain nothing from their pretense; the moment of retribution awaits them, and they will endure it not for a short time but forever. *He fed them with the pick of the crop* (v. 16): while this will be the fate of the adversaries, he will fill his own with a prosperous yield (referring by *crop* to grain, and calling its abundance *pick of the crop*). *And satisfied them with honey from the rock:* he will bring them from harsh and difficult events to deep relief and satisfaction.[7]

---

6. Ps 66:3.

7. Unfortunately, beyond this point Devreesse has to admit, "I found nothing preserved that could be, with complete certainty, attributed to Theodore of Mopsuestia" (*Le commentaire,* xxx). His coverage of this half of the Psalter, however, has allowed us to become well acquainted with The Interpreter's style of commentary.

SELECT BIBLIOGRAPHY

Bardy, Gustave. "Interprétation chez les pères." *DBSup* 4:569–91.

Barthélemy, Dominic. *Les devanciers d'Aquila.* VTSup 10. Leiden: Brill, 1963.

Bouyer, Louis. *The Spirituality of the New Testament and the Fathers.* Translated by Mary Perkins Ryan. London: Burns & Oates, 1963.

Brock, Sebastian P. "Bibelübersetzungen I,2." *TRE* 6:166–67.

Bruns, Peter. "Theodor von Mopsuestia." *TRE* 33:240–46.

Crouzel, Henri. *Origen.* Translated by A. S. Worrall. San Francisco: Harper & Row, 1989.

Dahood, Mitchell. *Psalms.* 3 vols. AB 16–17a. Garden City, N.Y.: Doubleday, 1965–1970.

Devreesse, Robert. *Essai sur Théodore de Mopsueste.* ST 141. Vatican City: Biblioteca Apostolica Vaticana, 1948.

———, ed. *Le commentaire de Théodore de Mopsueste sur les Psaumes (I–LXXX).* ST 93. Vatican City: Biblioteca Apostolica Vaticana, 1939.

Dibelius, Martin. "Zur Formgeschichte des Neuen Testaments (außerhalb der Evangelien)." *TRu* NS 3 (1931): 209–42.

Drewery, Benjamin, "Antiochien." *TRE* 3:103–13.

Ebedjesus. *Catalogue des livres ecclésiastiques syriens.* Pages 30–35 in vol. 3 of *Bibliotheca orientalis Clementino-Vaticana.* Edited by G. S. Assemani. Rome: Sacrae Congregationis de Propaganda Fide, 1926.

Fernández Marcos, Natalio. *The Septuagint in Context: Introduction to the Greek Version of the Bible.* Translated by Wilfred G. E. Watson. Leiden: Brill, 2000.

———. "Some Reflections on the Antiochian Text of the Septuagint." Pages 219–29 in *Studien zur Septuaginta: Robert Hanhart zu Ehren aus Anlaß seines 65. Geburtstages.* Edited by Detlef Fraenkel, Udo Quast, and John William Wevers. MSU 20. Göttingen: Vandenhoeck & Ruprecht, 1990.

Fitzmyer, Joseph A. "The Letter to the Romans." *NJBC,* 830–68.

Greer, Rowan A. *Theodore of Mopsuestia, Exegete and Theologian*. London: Faith Press, 1961.

Henry, René, ed. and trans. *Photius: Bibliothéque*. 9 vols. Paris: Belles Lettres, 1959–91.

Hill, Robert C. "Chrysostom's Terminology for the Inspired Word." *EstBib* 41 (1983): 367–73.

———. "His Master's Voice: Theodore of Mopsuestia on the Psalms." *HeyJ* 44 (2004): 40–53.

———. "Orientale Lumen: Western Biblical Scholarship's Unacknowledged Debt." Pages 157–72 in *Orientale Lumen Australasia—Oceania 2000: Proceedings*. Edited by Lawrence Cross. Melbourne: Australian Catholic University, 2000.

———. "A Pelagian Commentator on the Psalms?" *ITQ* 63 (1998): 263–71.

———. "Psalm 41(42): A Classic Text for Antiochene Spirituality." *ITQ* 68 (2003): 25–33.

———. "Psalm 45: A *locus classicus* for Patristic Thinking on Biblical Inspiration." *StPatr* 25 (1993): 95–100.

———. *Reading the Old Testament in Antioch*. Bible in Ancient Christianity 5. Leiden: Brill, 2005.

———. "*Sartor resartus:* Theodore under Review by Theodoret." *Aug* 41 (2001): 465–76.

———. "The Spirituality of Chrysostom's Commentary on the Psalms." *JECS* 5 (1997): 569–79.

———. "Theodore of Mopsuestia, Interpreter of the Prophets." *Sacris erudiri* 40 (2001): 107–29.

———. "Two Antiochene Commentators on the Psalms." *StPatr* 34 (2001): 353–69.

———, trans. *Diodore of Tarsus: Commentary on Psalms 1–51*. SBLWGRW 9. Atlanta: Society of Biblical Literature; Leiden: Brill, 2005.

———. *St. John Chrysostom: Commentary on the Psalms*. 2 vols. Brookline, Mass.: Holy Cross Orthodox Press, 1998.

———. *St. John Chrysostom: Old Testament Homilies*. 3 vols. Brookline, Mass.: Holy Cross Orthodox Press, 2003.

———. *Theodore of Mopsuestia: Commentary on the Twelve Prophets*. FC 108. Washington, D.C.: Catholic University of America Press, 2004.

———. *Theodoret of Cyrus: Commentary on the Psalms*. 2 vols. FC 101–102. Washington, D.C.: Catholic University of America Press, 2000–2001.

Jellicoe, Sidney. *The Septuagint and Modern Study*. Oxford: Clarendon, 1968.

Kahle, Paul E. *The Cairo Genizah*. 2nd ed. Oxford: Blackwell, 1959.

Kalantzis, George. "*Duo Filii* and the *Homo Assumptus* in the Christology of Theodore of Mopsuestia." *ETL* 78 (2002): 473–93.

――――. "Theodore of Mopsuestia's *Commentarius in evangelium Iohannis apostoli:* Text and Transmission." *Aug* 43 (2003): 473-93.

――――, trans. *Theodore of Mopsuestia: Commentary on the Gospel of John.* Early Christian Studies. Strathfield NSW: St Pauls, 2004.

Kelly, John N. D. *Early Christian Doctrines.* 5th ed. New York: Harper & Row, 1978.

――――. *Golden Mouth: The Story of John Chrysostom—Ascetic, Preacher, Bishop.* Ithaca, N.Y.: Cornell University Press, 1995.

――――. *Jerome: His Life, Writings, and Controversies.* London: Duckworth, 1975.

Klostermann, E., ed. *Origenes, Eustathius von Antiochen, und Gregor von Nyssa über die Hexe von Endor.* KlT 83. Bonn: Marcus & Weber, 1912.

Kugel, James L., and Rowan A. Greer. *Early Biblical Interpretation.* LEC 3. Philadelphia: Westminster, 1986.

Leonhard, Clemens. *Ishodad of Merw's Exegesis of the Psalms 119 and 139–147: A Study of His Interpretation in the Light of the Syriac Translation of Theodore of Mopsuestia's Commentary.* CSCO 585. Louvain: Peeters, 2001.

Mingana, Alphonse, ed. and trans. *Commentary of Theodore of Mopsuestia on the Lord's Prayer and on the Sacraments of Baptism and the Eucharist.* Woodbrooke Studies 6. Heffer & Sons, 1933.

――――. *Commentary of Theodore of Mopsuestia on the Nicene Creed.* Woodbrooke Studies 5. Cambridge: Heffer & Sons, 1932.

Nassif, Bradley. " 'Spiritual Exegesis' in the School of Antioch." Pages 342–77 in *New Perspectives in Historical Theology.* Edited by Bradley Nassif. Grand Rapids: Eeerdmans, 1996.

Norris, Richard A. *Manhood and Christ: A Study in the Christology of Theodore of Mopsuestia.* Oxford: Clarendon, 1963.

Olivier, Jean-Marie, ed. *Diodori Tarsensis commentarii in Psalmos.* CCSG 6. Turnhout: Brepols, 1980.

Pirot, Louis. L'oeuvre exégétique de Théodore de Mopsueste, 350–428 après J.-C. Rome: Sumptibus Pontificii Instituti Biblici, 1913.

Quasten, Johannes. *Patrology.* 3 vols. Westminster, Md.: Newman, 1950–1960.

Rahlfs, Alfred, ed. *Psalmi cum Odis.* Vol. 10 of *Septuaginta: Vetus Testamentum graecum.* 2nd ed. Göttingen: Vandenhoeck & Ruprecht, 1967.

Rondeau, Marie-Josèphe. *Les commentaires patristiques du Psautier (IIIe–Ve siècles).* 2 vols. OrChrAn 219–220. Rome: Pontificium Institutum Orientalium Studium, 1982–1985.

Schäublin, Christoph. "Diodor von Tarsus." *TRE* 8:763–67.

———. *Untersuchungen zu Methode und Herkunft der antiochenischen Exegese.* TBRKA 23. Cologne: Hanstein, 1974.

Simonetti, Manlio. *Biblical Interpretation in the Early Church: An Historical Introduction to Patristic Exegesis.* Translated by John A. Hughes. Edinburgh: Clark, 1994.

Sprenger, Hans N., ed. *Theodori Mopsuesteni commentarius in XII Prophetas.* GO, Biblica et patristica 1. Wiesbaden: Harrassowitz, 1977.

Stirnemann, Alfred, and Gerhard Wilflinger, eds. *Third Non-official Consultation of Dialogue within the Syriac Tradition.* Syriac Dialogue 3. Vienna: Pro Oriente, 1998.

Sullivan, Francis A. *The Christology of Theodore of Mopsuestia.* AG 82. Rome: Universitas Gregoriana, 1956.

Swete, Henry B., ed. *Theodori episcopi Mopsuesteni in Epistolas B. Pauli commentarii.* 2 vols. Cambridge: Cambridge University Press, 1880–1882.

Ternant, Paul. "La θεωρία d'Antioche dans le cadre de sens de l'Ecriture." *Bib* 34 (1953): 135–58, 354–83, 456–86.

Thiselton, Anthony C. *New Horizons in Hermeneutics: The Theory and Practice of Transforming Biblical Reading.* London: HarperCollins, 1992.

Vaccari, Alberto. "Il testo dei salmi nel commento di Teodoro Mopsuesteno." *Bib* 23 (1942): 1–17.

———. "La θεωρία nella scuola esegetica di Antiochia." *Bib* 1 (1920): 3–36.

Vosté, Jacques M. "La chronologie de l'activité littéraire de Théodore de Mopsueste." *RB* 34 (1925): 54–81.

———. "Le commentaire de Théodore de Mopsueste sur S. Jean d'après la version syriaque." *RB* 32 (1923): 522–51.

Vosté, Jacques M., ed. and trans. *Theodori Mopsuesteni commentarius in Evangelium Iohannis apostoli.* 2 vols. CSCO 115–116, Scriptores syri 4.3. Louvain: Peeters, 1940.

Wallace-Hadrill, David S. *Christian Antioch: A Study of Early Christian Thought in the East.* Cambridge: Cambridge University Press, 1982.

Weiser, Artur, *The Psalms.* Translated by Herbert Hartwell. OTL. London: SCM, 1962.

Weitzman, Michael P. *The Syriac Version of the Old Testament.* Cambridge: Cambridge University Press, 1999.

Young, Frances M. *Biblical Exegesis and the Formation of Christian Culture.* Cambridge: Cambridge University Press, 1997.

Zaharopoulos, Dimitri Z. *Theodore of Mopsuestia on the Bible: A Study of His Old Testament Exegesis.* New York: Paulist, 1989.

General Index

accommodation, xxxii, xxxviii, 275, 277, 911
Akiba, 479
akolouthia, xxii, xxvi, xxvii, 185, 941
akribeia, xxv–xxvi, xxviii
Alexandria, xx, xxxii, xxxiv
allegorical, xxx–xxxi, xxxii
anthropomorphism, xxix, 295
Antioch, *passim*
Antiochus, 539, 613, 705, 1085, 1105
Apamea, xv
Aquila, *passim*
Apollinaris, xvi, xxxiv
Aramaic xv
Arius, xvi, xxxiv
Aristarchus, xxx
ark, 857,
ascetical, xv, xxv
asketerion, xvii, xviii, xix
Athanasius, 845
authenticity, xix–xxvi, 1123
authorship, xx

canon, 845
catenae, xix
Christology, xv, xviii, xxxi, xxxiii–xxxv, xxxvii, 23, 25, 85, 87, 93, 95, 199, 275, 555–99
Chrysostom, *passim*
conciseness, xxviii, 1025
Constantinople, xvi, xxxiv, 93
council, xvi, xxxiii, xxxiv, xxxv
Cyril of Alexandria, xvi

David, *passim*

deuterocanonical, 845
dianoia, xxvii, xxx, 85
Diodore, passim
dyophysite, xxxiv, xxxv

Ebedjesus, xvi, 1125
eschatology, xxvi
Esther, 845
Eunomius, xvi
Eusebius of Caesarea, xx, xxii
Eustathius, xxxi
exegesis, xv, xx, xxii–xxix, xxxviii, 941

Facundus of Hermianae, xvii
fall, xxxv, xxxvi, 675

genre, xxiii–xxiv, 411, 853
grace, xxxv
Gregory of Nazianzen, 845

Hebrew, *passim*
hermeneutics, xx, xxix–xxviii, 72
heretic, 27
Hexapla, xxi, xxii, 259, 429
historical, xxiv, xxx–xxxi, xxxiii, 7, 613, 931
homiletics, xix
homoousion, xxxiv
hypostatic union, xxxiv

imagery, xxix
Incarnation, xxxv
individualism, xxxv
inspiration, xxiii, 557, 559, 565

INDEX OF BIBLICAL CITATIONS

Index of Modern Authors